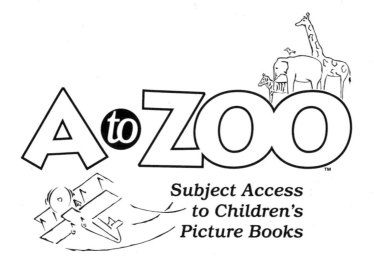

A to ZOO™

*Subject Access
to Children's
Picture Books*

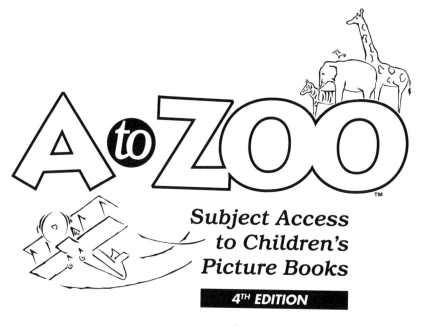

A to ZOO™

Subject Access to Children's Picture Books

4TH EDITION

Carolyn W. Lima
John A. Lima

R.R. BOWKER®
A Reed Reference Publishing Company
New Providence, New Jersey

Published by R. R. Bowker,
a Reed Reference Publishing Company
Copyright © 1993 by Reed Publishing (USA) Inc.
Printed and bound in the United States of America

Interior illustrations by Jean Catherine Lima

Library of Congress Cataloging-in-Publication Data

Lima, Carolyn W.
   A to Zoo: subject access to children's picture books/
Carolyn W. Lima, John A. Lima. -- 4th ed.

   p. cm.
   Includes bibliographical references (p.   ) and indexes.
ISBN 0-8352-3201-8 (hardcover)
1. Picture books for children--Indexes. 2. Children's
literature, English--Indexes. I. Lima, John A. II. Title.
Z1037.L715 1993
[PR990]
011.62--dc20
                      93-6224
                      CIP
                      AC

ISBN 0-8352-3201-8

9 780835 232012

To Courtney Elizabeth Keyte who dearly loves
her picture books
and
To the loving memory of her
great-grandmother Merle Elizabeth Lima

Contents

Preface

The picture book, long a source of delight and learning for young readers, has gained even more importance during the past few years with the increasing emphasis on early childhood education and the growing need for supervised child care for working mothers. Teachers, librarians, and parents are finding the picture book to be an important learning and entertainment tool. Choosing the right book for a particular situation is time-consuming and frustrating without some guidance. Many responsible professionals and parents do not have the time nor the materials to develop an intimate familiarity with the field. Rather than simply choosing the first title that appears to treat a specific subject from among the many thousands of books available, the user can now identify a book confident that it will cover the desired subject. This fourth edition of *A to Zoo: Subject Access to Children's Picture Books,* the only comprehensive guide of its kind, provides the necessary help making the task easier for the user. It contains more than 14,000 titles cataloged under nearly 800 subjects.

Originally, the titles in *A to Zoo* (first edition) were based on the San Diego (California) Public Library's collection of picture books for children. This large and versatile collection remains typical of the best and most carefully chosen children's works acquired over a period of time exceeding 100 years. In the effort to ensure that the most up-to-date information is included in this fourth edition, the authors consulted many sources. Other public and university library collections, review copies from various publishers, published reviews, and the authors' personal searches of titles and literature provided an information base. Nearly every book was read by the authors to determine subject information and suitability. Out-of-print titles were included because school and public library collections contain many out-of-print materials.

The picture book, as broadly defined within the scope of this book, is a fiction or nonfiction title with illustrations occupying as much or more space than the text and with text vocabulary or concepts suitable for preschool to grade two.

The "Introduction: Genesis of the English-Language Picture Book" has been updated, and recent sources and reference works were added to the list of suggested titles for further reading. Developments of historical proportions have not been discerned in the years since 1989, the year the third edition was published. Some trends, however, still seem evident: mechanical and "pop-up" books continue to be prolific; attention to the very young reader is reflected in a large number of "board books"—books with cardboard pages designed for tiny tots; and, there is a continued trend toward picture books of a serious nature, bearing a message or a lesson, designed to accomplish some social purpose other than mere entertainment for the young reader. Indeed, one issue of *Publishers Weekly* (Nov. 23, 1992, p. 38) makes note of the "crossover" book—one book with two markets—such as picture books that also appeal to adults. Graeme Base's books *Animalia* and *The Sign of the Seahorse* are prominent examples. A large number of classics continue to be reissued, some with new illustrations. A significant trend is the improved quality of artwork in picture books. Such artists as Barry Moser, William Joyce, Chris Van Allsburg, and Thomas Locker have contributed to the improvement of picture books and to the acceptance of picture books as quality literature.

HOW TO USE THIS BOOK

A to Zoo can be used to obtain information about children's picture books in two ways: to learn the titles, authors, and illustrators of books on a particular subject, such as "farms" or "magic"; or to ascertain the subject (or subjects) when only the title, author and title, or illustrator and title are known. For example, if the title *Northern Lullaby* is known, this volume will enable the user to discover that *Northern Lullaby* is written by Nancy White Carlstrom, illustrated by Leo and Diane Dillon, and published by Putnam in 1992, and that it also concerns the subjects "Bedtime," "Eskimos," "Lullabies," "Nature," and "Poetry, rhyme."

For ease and convenience of reference use, *A to Zoo* is divided into five sections:

> Subject Headings
> Subject Guide
> Bibliographic Guide
> Title Index
> Illustrator Index

SUBJECT HEADINGS: This section contains an alphabetical list of the subjects cataloged in this book. The subject headings reflect the established terms used commonly in public libraries, originally based on questions asked by parents and teachers and then modified and adapted by librarians. To facilitate reference use, and because subjects are requested in a variety of terms, the list of subject headings contains numerous cross-references. Subheadings are arranged alphabetically under each general topic, for example:

> Animals (general topic)
> Animals—anteaters (subheading)
> Animals—antelopes (subheading)
> Animals—apes *see* Animals—gorillas; Animals—monkeys (cross-reference)

SUBJECT GUIDE: This subject-arranged guide to more than 14,000 picture books for pre-school children through second graders is cataloged under nearly 800 subjects. The guide reflects the arrangement in the Subject Headings, alphabetically arranged by main subject heading and subheading. Many books, of course, relate to more than one subject, and this comprehensive list provides a means of identifying all those books that may contain any information or material on a particular subject.

If, for example, the user wants books on crabs (crustacea), the Subject Headings section will show that Crustacea is a subject classification. A look in the Subject Guide reveals that under Crustacea there are 14 titles listed alphabetically by author.

BIBLIOGRAPHIC GUIDE: Each book is listed with full bibliographic information. This section is arranged alphabetically by author, or by title when the author is unknown, or by uniform (classic) title. Each entry contains bibliographic information in this order: author, title, illustrator, publisher and date of publication, miscellaneous notes when given, International Standard Book Number (ISBN), and subjects, listed according to the alphabetical classification in the Subject Headings section. Where ISBNs appear they indicate entries new to the third and fourth editions and are the library binding edition or the next best quality edition available.

The user can consult the Bibliographic Guide to find complete data on each of the 14 titles listed in the Subject Guide under the subject of Crustacea, as for example:

> **Knutson, Barbara.** *Why the crab has no head: an African tale* ill. by author. Carolrhoda Books, 1987. ISBN 0-87614-322-2. Subj: Behavior—boasting. Crustacea. Folk and fairy tales. Foreign lands—Africa. Foreign lands—Zaire.

In the case of joint authors, the second author is listed in alphabetical order, followed by the book title and the name of the primary author or main entry. The user can then locate the first-named author for complete bibliographic information. For example:

> **Stoker, Wayne.** *I can be a welder* (Lillegard, Dee)

Bibliographic information for this title will be found in the Bibliographic Guide section under "Lillegard, Dee."

Titles for an author who is both a single author and a joint author are interfiled alphabetically.

Where the author is not known, the entry is listed alphabetically by title with complete bibliographic information following the same format as given above.

Library of Congress conventions regarding the cataloged name of the author(s) have been followed in this edition. Thus, books published under the name "Aliki" are listed in alphabetical order under Aliki; a cross-reference from the name "Brandenberg, Aliki" refers the user to the name preferred.

TITLE INDEX: This section contains an alphabetical list of all titles in the book with authors in parentheses, followed by the page number of the full listing in the Bibliographic Guide, such as:

> *Albert's story* (Long, Claudia), 699

If a title has no known author, the name of the illustrator is given if available.

When multiple versions of the same title are listed, the illustrator's name is given with the author's name (when known) in parentheses:

The night before Christmas, ill. by Michael Foreman (Moore, Clement C.), 699
The night before Christmas, ill. by Scott Gustafson (Moore, Clement C.), 700

ILLUSTRATOR INDEX: This section contains an alphabetical list of illustrators with titles and authors, followed by the page number of the full listing in the Bibliographic Guide, for example:

Glasser, Judy. *Albert's story* (Long, Claudia), 669

Titles listed under an illustrator's name appear in alphabetical sequence. When the author is the same as the illustrator then the author's name is not repeated.

Acknowledgments

The authors wish to express their thanks for the assistance provided by many people in bringing this book together. Special thanks to our publisher at R. R. Bowker, Marion Sader, Publisher of Professional and Reference Books, for her patience, confidence, and assistance in guiding this fourth edition of *A to Zoo* through the production process. We also wish to thank many book publishers for providing review copies of their picture books, especially HarperCollins; Harcourt Brace; Firefly Books; Little, Brown; Crowell; Lothrop; Lippincott; Holiday House, Greenwillow and Morrow; and Hyperion Books.

Introduction
Genesis of the English-Language Picture Book

Each year increasing numbers of children's books are published, with nearly twice as many titles appearing in 1986 as in 1984, and each one touched in some way by those that preceded it.[1] But how or by what path did the unique genre known as children's picture books arrive at this present and prolific state? Certainly, to imagine a time when children's books did not exist takes more than a little effort. Probably the roots of what we know as children's literature lie in the stories and folktales told and retold through the centuries in every civilization since human beings first learned to speak. These stories were narrated over and over as a sort of oral history, literature, and education.[2] But they were not intended, either primarily or exclusively, for children. It was only through the passing years, as the children who were at least part of any audience responded with interest and delight to these tales, and as adults found less leisure time to be entertained in an increasingly busy world, that the stories and folktales came to be regarded as belonging to the world of the child. These were repeated or retold often by traveling storytellers. Some tales were written down, printed, and spread throughout England and Europe. In the nineteenth century, the brothers Grimm, Jacob and Wilhelm, invited storytellers to their home to narrate the tales and folk stories of Germany, and to collect them and refine them. They altered stories to make them more acceptable for children, or for adults who were concerned about what children read and heard. Nevertheless, they created a stylistic ideal for the fairy tale, making them "more proper and prudent for bourgeois audiences."[3]

Book art or book illustration began with manuscripts—handwritten on parchment or other materials, rolled or scrolled, and later loosely bound into books—that were illuminated or "decorated in lively, vigorous and versatile styles."[4] In time, these decorations, some realistic, some intricate, some imaginative, took on the technological advances of other art forms, notably stained glass, and color was introduced to these illustrated texts.[5]

The children's books that existed in the Middle Ages, before the invention of movable type, were rarely intended to amuse the reader. They were, instead, mostly instructional and moralizing. Monastic teachers, writing essentially for the children of wealthy families, usually wrote in Latin and "began the tradition of didacticism that was to dominate children's books for hundreds of years."[6]

Children's books of that day frequently followed either the rhymed format or the question-and-answer form, both attributed to Aldhelm, abbot of Malmesbury.[7] An early encyclopedia, thought to be the work of Anselm (1033–1109), archbishop of Canterbury, addressed such subjects as "manners and customs, natural science, children's duties, morals, and religious precepts."[8] The books were intended for instruction and indoctrination in the principles of moral and religious belief and behavior,[9] an intent that persisted even after the invention of movable type. Indeed, "children were not born to live happy but to die holy, and true education lay in preparing the soul to meet its maker."[10]

Perhaps the first printed book that was truly intended for children, other than elementary Latin grammar texts, was the French *Les Contenances de la Table,* on the courtesies and manners of dining.[11] Printed and illustrated children's books in Europe followed the invention of printing in the fifteenth century. Those first books were printed in lowercase letters, and "blank spaces were left on the page for initials and marginal decorations to be added in color by hand. In general, the effect was the same as in manuscript.[12] Some well-known and important artists of the time did the illustrations, using woodcuts, engravings, and lithographic processes.[13]

This combination of pictures and printed text, still with the intent of teaching and incorporating the earlier, but persistent dedication to moral and religious education, finally resulted in what is often assumed to be the first real children's picture book in 1657—the *Orbis Pictus of John Amos Comenius.*[14] The simple idea by this Czechoslovakian author was that a child would learn most quickly by naming and showing the object at the same time, a seventeenth-century ABC! Noted for its many illustrations, the book contained the seeds of future children's publications, softening somewhat the earlier "harshness with which, in the unsympathetic age, the first steps of learning were always associated."[15]

In the English language, children's books followed a parallel pattern. William Caxton, England's first printer, was responsible for printing many books, which although intended for adults, were often adopted by children as their own. One, *Æsop's Fables* (about 1484), featured woodcut illustrations, and is an early "milestone" in the history of children's literature.[16] His stories, the first for English children in their own language, gave the lessons of "The Fox and the Grapes" and "The Tortoise and the Hare" to children of the fifteenth century and all who followed thereafter.

Nearly 200 years later, American authors and books for American children, in English, began to appear. Like English publications before them, these books reflected a basic profile of moral and religious education. American John Cotton's *Spiritual Milk for Boston Babes* (1646) was not an especially easy text for the young minds that had to master its Puritan lessons. Later came similar books such as *Pilgrim's Progress* by John Bunyan (1678), *The New England Primer* with its rhyming alphabet (1691), and *Divine and Moral Songs for Children* by Isaac Watts (1715).

In the early eighteenth century, a significant movement began in English children's books with the publication of *Robinson Crusoe* by Daniel

Defoe (1715), a narrative that delighted children as well as adults. This innovation, utilizing children's books to carry more intricate messages, perhaps aimed at adults as well as older children, reflected a growing sophistication of society, and perhaps some shifting of purely religious or moral bases toward political morality. An all-time favorite with young readers, *Gulliver's Travels* by Jonathan Swift, published in 1726, illustrates this dual thrust. This work, embellished with a wit and rather pointed sarcasm that is sure to escape the young, nonetheless delighted children with the inhabitants of mythical lands and has managed to survive through the years. Perhaps the ultimate development of this trend is found in Lewis Carroll's *Alice's Adventures in Wonderland* (1865), which manages to be perfectly palatable and interesting to children, yet contains subtle lessons for adult society. Although based on earlier plays and vignettes that had been written only for the purpose of entertainment and use of imagination, *Alice,* and other books of the time, began to reflect a change in society's view of children and of reading materials suitable for children.

The English translation of *Tales of Mother Goose* by Charles Perrault in 1729 made moral lessons for young readers less didactic, but it was in 1744 that "saw the real foundation of something today everywhere taken for granted—the production of books for children's enjoyment."[17] This book from a small bookstall in London was *A Little Pretty Pocket-Book,* "now famous as the first book for children published by John Newbery"[18] and may indeed be the first book recognizing children as people with intelligence and other human needs, notably the need for humor and entertainment.[19]

For the next 20 years or so, Newbery published well-illustrated and inexpensive little books for young readers. Soon other books designed especially for children followed this trend. Pictures became an essential and integral part of the book, somewhat downplaying the soul-saving educational harshness of earlier books and promoting amusement and enlightened education. Thomas Bewick's first book specifically intended for children, *A Pretty Book of Pictures for Little Masters and Misses, or Tommy Trip's History of Beasts and Birds,* was published in 1779; and its particular effort represented major strides in the refinements of woodcuts used for book illustration. Bewick "developed better tools for this work, made effective use of the white line, and carried the woodcut to a new level of beauty."[20] His efforts and those of his brother John not only achieved a high level of artistic achievement for woodcuts, but had a more lasting effect on illustrators and illustrations for children's books."[21] Some talented artists lovingly produced children's books with special artistic achievement, although their principal skills may have been directed toward adults. For example, William Blake, an artist and poet of considerable renown, published *Songs-of-Innocence* in 1789.[22] An engraver, he produced this "first great original picture book" using etched plates in which the garlands and scrolls were lovingly engraved, of his own original designs, and hand-colored after printing.[23]

Some efforts were also great commercial successes. When John Harris published, in 1805, *The Comic Adventures of Old Mother Hubbard and Her*

Dog, by "S.C.M." [Sarah Catherine Martin], he sold some 10,000 copies in a few months. Within a year, twenty editions had been issued. Adults as well as children enjoyed the humor of Old Mother Hubbard.[24] The serious business of writing and illustrating children's books was now respectable and worthwhile, and those books had a feeling of class. But such loving dedication as that of William Blake and others, did not long enjoy a singular place in publishing history. Before long commercialism entered the scene and, although some very dedicated people in America and England alike continued to develop books for children, some hackwork also appeared. "Publishers, realizing that children formed a new and somewhat undiscriminating market, were quick to take advantage of the fact. Having chosen a suitable title, and having available some spare woodcut blocks that might be sufficiently relevant for a juvenile book, a publisher would commission a story or series of tales to be woven around the illustrations. One of the results of this was that illustrations of different proportions might be used in the same story, while on other occasions it was clear that the pictures were by different hands. Sometimes the inclusion of a picture was obviously forced. A good example occurs in one of the editions of *Goody Two-Shoes,*" attributed to Oliver Goldsmith.[25]

Fortunately, the "hacks" did not totally invade the field of children's picture books. Carefully designed works, crafted with an eye toward the complete and final unit, with special consideration for the means of reproduction, appeared under the guidance of innovative and bold publishers. Beautiful printing became the mark of publishers such as Edmund Evans, printer and artist in his own right, who with his special skill in color engraving published the works of Walter Crane, Randolph Caldecott, and Kate Greenaway. "The work of the three great English picture-book artists of the nineteenth century represents the best to be found in picture books for children in any era; the strength of design and richness of color and detail of Walter Crane's pictures; the eloquence, humor, vitality, and movement of Randolph Caldecott's art; and the tenderness, dignity, and grace of the very personal interpretation of Kate Greenaway's enchanted land of childhood."[26]

These three were indeed great names of the century in the history of children's picture books. The first nursery picture books of Walter Crane, an apprentice wood engraver, were *Sing a Song for Sixpence, The House That Jack Built, Dame Trot and Her Comical Cat,* and *The History of Cock Robin and Jenny Wren,* published by the firm of Warne in 1865 and 1866. Crane was one of the first modern illustrators who believed that text and illustrations should be in harmony, forming a complete unit.

Randolph Caldecott, who began drawing at age six, could make animals seemingly come alive on a page. During his short life (1846–1886), he illustrated numerous books for children with fine examples of fun and good humor such as *The Diverting History of John Gilpin, The Babes in the Wood,* and many others from about 1877 until near his death. His preeminence in the art of the children's picture book has been acknowledged by many more recent artists, and is certainly a seminal factor in the establishment of the English style as a standard from which to measure picture book art.[27]

Kate Greenaway's simple verses made an appropriate accompaniment to her lovely drawings. *Under the Window* was her first picture book published by Routledge in 1878. Everywhere in her books are the flowers she so loved. She is probably best known for her *Almanacs,* published between 1883 and 1897.

Like Crane, Caldecott, and Greenaway, the works of Beatrix Potter became as well known to American children as to English. Potter, a self-taught artist addicted to pets with charming characteristics, produced a number of tales for young children, the best known being *The Tale of Peter Rabbit* (1901), which presented the illustrations as an integral part of the story and marked a pivotal point in the development of the modern picture book in Europe.

The very excellence of the growing children's book field in England eclipsed the technologically inferior American product, virtually driving the American efforts from the marketplace until nearly 15 years after World War I.[28] Meanwhile, the books of English artists such as L. Leslie Brooke, Arthur Rackham, Edmund Dulac, Charles Folkard, and others continued the tradition of excellence through the first three decades of the twentieth century.

Despite the superior English publications, "a self-conscious and systematic concern for children and the books they read had been growing in the United States."[29] Children's libraries and children's librarians appeared around the turn of the century. In 1916, the Bookshop for Boys and Girls was founded in Boston.[30] In 1924 the Bookshop published *The Horn Book Magazine,* "the first journal in the world to be devoted to the critical appraisal of children's books."[31] Another publication, *Junior Libraries,* made its appearance in 1954; this periodical later became *School Library Journal,* published by R. R. Bowker. In this area, the Americans were ten years ahead of the Europeans.

Publishers and editors were becoming more and more oriented toward children's literature. In 1919, Macmillan established a Children's Book Department to be separate from its adult publishing line; other publishing houses began to do the same. Children's Book Week was instituted, an idea that started with Franklin K. Mathiews and was later supported by Frederic G. Melcher. A landmark in children's book publishing was established in the United States in 1922 when Melcher, then chief editor of *Publishers Weekly,* proposed at the 1921 American Library Association meeting that a medal be awarded each year for the year's most distinguished contribution to American literature for children written by an American citizen or resident and published in the United States. Named for John Newbery, the medal was first awarded to Hendrick Willem van Loon for his book *The Story of Mankind.*

Melcher, who was always aware of the significance of books in the lives of children, later proposed the establishment of a similar award for picture books, named in honor of Randolph Caldecott whose pictures still delight today's children. Since 1938, the Caldecott Medal has been awarded annually by the Association for Library Service to Children, a division of the American Library Association, to the illustrator of the most distinguished American picture book for children published in the United States during the preceding year. Again, the recipient must reside in or be a citizen of the United States.

The end of the 1920s marked the newly emerging prominence of the modern children's picture book in America. Mainly imported from Europe until that time, children's picture books now began to be published in America. William Nicholson's *Clever Bill* (1927) was followed the next year by one of the most successful picture books of all time, *Millions of Cats* by Wanda Gág. The near perfect marriage of the rhythmic prose and flowing movement of her dramatic black-and-white illustrations tell a simple, direct story with a folk flavor. This title is still included in the repertoire of today's storytellers and continues to be taken from the shelves by young readers; it ushered in the "Golden Thirties" of children's book publishing.[32]

By 1930, many publishers had set up separate editing departments expressly for the purpose of publishing children's materials. The White House Conference on Child Health and Protection was held that year to study the plight of the child.[33] Improved technologies accelerated and economized book production. The stage was set for the modern picture book with its profuse illustration. Until this time there were only a few great children's books, illustrated with pictures that were largely an extension of the text. "Yet in a very few years, in respect to the books for the younger children, the artist has attained a place of equal importance with the writer."[34]

The period between World War I and World War II brought many foreign authors and illustrators to America to join and collaborate with American authors and artists. Their talents and varied backgrounds have contributed immensely to the changes in the picture book in America, which truly came into its own in this period of lower production costs. The years of the 1930s, known as the "Golden Thirties," and the years of the 1940s produced a spectacular number and variety of profusely illustrated books for young children.[35] The many new authors and illustrators then beginning their careers in this developing field of children's picture books have continued to keep their places in the hearts of children: such familiar names as Marjorie Flack, Maud and Miska Petersham, Ingri and Edgar d'Aulaire, Ludwig Bemelmans, Theodor Geisel (Dr. Seuss), Marcia Brown, Feodor Rojankovsky, James Daugherty, Robert Lawson, Marguerite de Angeli, Virginia Lee Burton, Robert McCloskey, and many, many more.

The war years of the mid-1940s affected the progress of children's picture books with shortages of materials, priorities, poor quality paper, narrow margins, inferior bindings, and less color and illustration. However, the postwar years began to boom in children's publishing, adding to the list of talented authors and illustrators such names as Maurice Sendak, Brian Wildsmith, Trina Schart Hyman, Paul Galdone, Leo Politi, Ezra Jack Keats, Gyo Fujikawa, Arnold Lobel, and so many more.

Through the years many factors have contributed to the growth, even explosion, of children's picture books—society's changing attitudes toward the child; the development of children's libraries, awards, councils, and studies; increasing interest in children's reading on the part of publishers, educators, and literary critics; changing technologies; and the development of American artists and authors. More recently, new directions in publishing, challenging the library as the principal outlet for children's books, seeking consumer markets and applying modern marketing strategies have affected the nature of the children's picture book.[36] Today the picture book is a part of growing up, a teaching tool, an entertainment medium, a memory to treasure. Perhaps only imagination and the talent of the artist and author can define its limits.

Emphasizing the need for quality materials, some proclaim the 1980s and 1990s as the "day of the artist" in children's books.[37] Significantly, others decry the lack of quality in children's materials and are critical of the abundance of "commercial fluff" published today.[38] Certainly, some of the modern trends give one pause. Spectacular color, shading, and texture are all very evident today, along with broader subject perspectives, picture books that are aimed more at older children (and adults?) than at the traditional audience, and a general sophistication of the product. More mechanical books (pop-ups) reminiscent of the Victorian age are reappearing, as are gimmicks and the trading on the familiarity of prior themes.[39] Many old favorites are being reissued, often showcasing a new illustrator's talents. Many collections or compendiums of an author's or illustrator's works are being published, often in large formats with 60 to 120 or more pages, straining the definition and concept of "picture book." At times, these appear in what can only be called a "coffee-table" format; impressive but hardly "child-friendly." Other trends include the large number of "board" books and other unusual formats, and the development of themes that emphasize reality, such as everyday situations, misbehavior or mischievous behavior, and multicultural or multiethnic experiences.

Professionalism, curiosity on all subjects, and freedom of expression have brought the children's picture book into the late twentieth century with a bewildering array of materials from which to choose. Imaginary animals of the past and future line the shelves with the cats, dogs, horses, and dolphins of the modern day. Fantasy lands complete with tales of spaceships and astronauts; dreams of the future can be found with the realities of the past; picture books of all kinds for all kinds of children—and adults—to enjoy!

For the teacher, librarian, or parent who wishes to open this fantastic world of color and imagination for the child, some tool is necessary to put oneself in touch with the great number of possibilities for enjoyment in the picture book field today. *A to Zoo: Subject Access to Children's Picture Books* is designed with just this purpose in mind.

For those interested in exploring more deeply the world of children's publishing and the children's picture book, a list of suggested titles for further reading begins on page xxiii.

Notes

1. Jill Rachlin, "Timeless Tales = Big Sales," *U.S. News & World Report,* 105:5 (Aug. 1, 1988): 50.

2. Caroline M. Hewins, "The History of Children's Books (1988)," in *Children and Literature: Views and Reviews.* comp. Virginia Haviland (New York: Lothrop, 1974), p. 30.

3. Jack Zipes, tr. "Once There Were Two Brothers Named Grimm," in *The Complete Fairy Tales of the Brothers Grimm* (New York: Bantam, 1987), pp. xvii–xxxi.

4. Donnarae MacCann and Olga Richard, *The Child's First Books: A Critical Study of Pictures and Texts* (New York: Wilson, 1973), p. 11.

5. Ibid.

6. Zena Sutherland and May Hill Arbuthnot, *Children and Books,* 8th ed. (New York: HarperCollins College, 1991), p. 54.

7. Ibid.

8. Ibid.

9. Ibid.

10. Bettina Hürlimann, *Three Centuries of Children's Books in Europe,* tr. and ed. by Brian Alderson (London: Oxford Univ. Pr., 1967), p. xii.

11. Sutherland and Arbuthnot, *Children and Books,* p. 54.

12. MacCann and Richard, *The Child's First Books,* p. 11.

13. Ibid.

14. Hürlimann, *Three Centuries of Children's Books in Europe,* pp. 127–129.

15. Ruth Sunderlin Freeman, *Children's Picture Books, Yesterday and Today* (Watkins Glen, N.Y.: Century House, 1967), p. 12.

16. Sutherland and Arbuthnot, *Children and Books,* pp. 54, 71, 136–137.

17. John Newbery, *A Little Pretty Pocket-Book: A Facsimile* (London: Oxford Univ. Pr., 1966), p. 2.

18. Ibid., p. 3.

19. Ibid., p. 2.

20. Sutherland and Arbuthnot, *Children and Books,* pp. 63, 138.

21. Ibid.

22. Ibid., p. 138.

23. Brian Alderson, *Sing a Song for Sixpence: The English Picture Book Tradition and Randolph Caldecott* (Cambridge, England: Cambridge Univ. Pr., 1986), p. 46.

24. Ibid., pp. 49–51.

25. Joyce Irene Whalley, *Cobwebs to Catch Flies: Illustrated Books for the Nursery and Schoolroom 1700–1900* (Berkeley: Univ. of California Pr., 1975), p. 14.

26. Alderson, *Sing a Song for Sixpence,* p. 8.

27. Ruth Hill Viguers, "Introduction," in Kate Greenaway, *The Kate Greenaway Treasury* (Cleveland: World, 1967), p. 13.

28. Barbara Bader, *American Picturebooks from Noah's Ark to the Beast Within* (New York: Macmillan, 1976), p. 7.

29. Viguers, "Introduction," p. 39.

30. Ibid.

31. Ibid.

32. Sutherland and Arbuthnot, *Children and Books,* p. 142.

33. Binnie Tate Wilkin, *Survival Themes in Fiction for Children and Young People* (Metuchen, N.J.: Scarecrow, 1978), p. 21.

34. Cornelia Meigs et al., *A Critical History of Children's Literature* (New York: Macmillan, 1953), p. 587.

35. Ibid., p. 438.

36. Barbara Elleman, "Current Trends in Literature for Children," *Library Trends* 35: 3 (Winter 1987): 421.

37. Sutherland and Arbuthnot, *Children and Books,* p. 161.

38. Rachlin, "Timeless Tales = Big Sales," p. 51.

39. Elleman, "Current Trends in Literature for Children," pp. 415, 421.

Further Reading

Alderson, Brian. *The Brothers Grimm: Popular Folk Tales.* London: Victor Gollancz Ltd., 1978.

_____. *Looking at Picture Books 1973.* Chicago: Children's Book Council, 1974.

*_____. *Sing a Song for Sixpence: The English Picture Book Tradition and Randolph Caldecott.* Cambridge, England: Cambridge Univ. Pr., 1986. 0-521-33179-X.

Andersson, Theodore. *A Guide to Family Reading in Two Languages: The Preschool Years.* Wheaton, Md.: National Clearinghouse for Bilingual Education, 1981. 0-89755-055-2.

Arbuthnot, May Hill et al. *The Arbuthnot Anthology of Children's Literature,* 4th ed. Glenview, Ill.: Scott, Foresman, 1976. 0-673-15000-1.

*Bader, Barbara. *American Picturebooks from Noah's Ark to the Beast Within.* New York: Macmillan, 1976. 0-02-708080-3.

Barchilon, Jacques, and Petit, Henry. *The Authentic Mother Goose Fairy Tales and Nursery Rhymes.* Athens, Ohio: Swallow Pr., 1960.

Barry, Florence V. *A Century of Children's Books.* London: Methuen, 1922. 0-87968-828-9.

Bauer, Caroline Feller. *Read for the Fun of It: Active Programming with Books for Children.* New York: Wilson, 1992. 0-8242-0824-2.

Bingham, Jane, ed. *Writers for Children.* New York: Scribner's, 1988. 0-684-18165-7.

*_____, and Scholt, Grayce, eds. *Fifteen Centuries of Children's Literature: An Annotated Chronology of British and American Works in Historical Context.* Westport, Conn.: Greenwood Pr., 1980. 0-313-22164-2.

Bland, David. *A History of Book Illustration,* 2nd ed. London: Faber & Faber, 1969.

_____. *The Illustration of Books.* London: Faber & Faber, 1962.

Bodger, Joan. *How the Heather Looks.* New York: Viking, 1965.

Bottigheimer, Ruth B. *Grimms' Bad Girls and Bold Boys.* New Haven, Conn.: Yale Univ. Pr., 1987. 0-300-03908-5.

_____. *Fairy Tales and Society: Illusion, Allusion, and Paradigm.* Philadelphia: Univ. of Pennsylvania Pr., 1986. 0-8122-8021-0.

Braun, Saul. "Sendak Raises the Shade on Childhood." *New York Times Magazine* (June 7, 1970): 34 +.

Bush, Margaret A. *Children's Literature: A Guide to Reference Services and Monographs.* Englewood, Colo.: Libraries Unlimited, 1988. 0-87287-531-8.

Butler, Dorothy. *Babies Need Books.* New York: Atheneum, 1980. 0-689-11112-6.

_____, and Clay, Marie. *Reading Begins at Home,* 2nd ed. Exeter, N.H.: Heinemann, 1987. 0-435-08443-7.

Butler, Francelia, and Robert, Richard W., eds. *Reflections on Literature for Children.* Hamden, Conn.: Shoe String Pr., 1984. 0-208-02054-3.

_____. *Triumphs of the Spirit in Children's Literature.* Hamden, Conn.: Library Professional Publications, 1986. 0-208-02111-6.

Carroll, Frances Laverne, and Meacham, Mary, eds. *Exciting, Funny, Scary, Short, Different, and Sad Books Kids Like about Animals, Science, Sports, Families, Songs, and Other Things.* Chicago: ALA, 1984. 0-8389-0423-8.

_____. *More Exciting, Funny, Scary, Short, Different, and Sad Books Kids Like about Animals, Science, Sports, Families, Songs, and Other Things.* Chicago: ALA, 1992. 0-8389-0585-4.

Cianciola, Patricia. *Illustrations in Children's Books,* 2nd ed. Dubuque, Iowa: William C. Brown, 1976. 0-697-06208-2.

Clay, Marie. "Introduction." In *Cushla and Her Books,* by Dorothy Butler. Boston: Horn Book, 1980. 0-87675-283-0.

*Indicates especially recommended titles in this reading list.

_____, and Butler, Dorothy. *Reading Begins at Home,* 2nd ed. Exeter, N.H.: Heinemann, 1987.

Comenius, John Amos. *The Orbis Pictus of John Amos Comenius,* repr. of 1887 ed. Detroit: Gale, 1968. 0-8103-3476-3.

Crouch, Marcus. *Treasure Seekers and Borrowers: Children's Books in Britain 1900–1960.* London: Library Association. 1962.

Daniel, Eloise. *A Treasury of Books for Family Enjoyment: Books for Children from Infancy to Grade 2.* Pontiac, Mich.: Blue Engine Pr., 1983. 0-9611370-0-2.

Darling, Richard L. *The Rise of Children's Book Reviewing in America, 1865–1881.* New York: R. R. Bowker, 1968.

Darrell, Margery, ed. *Once Upon a Time: The Fairy-Tale World of Arthur Rackham.* New York: Viking, 1972.

*Darton, F. J. H. *Children's Books in England: Five Centuries of Social Life,* 3rd ed. Ed. by Brian Alderson. New York: Cambridge Univ. Pr., 1982. 0-521-24020-4.

*Delamar, Gloria T. *Mother Goose: From Nursery to Literature.* Jefferson, N.C.: McFarland, 1987. 0-89950-280-6.

Demers, Patricia, ed. *A Garland from the Golden Age: Children's Literature from 1850–1900.* New York: Oxford Univ. Pr., 1984. 0-19-540414-9.

Demers, R. A., and Moyles, R. Gordon, eds. *From Instruction to Delight: An Anthology of Children's Literature to 1850.* New York: Oxford Univ. Pr., 1982. 0-19-540384-3.

Duvoisin, Roger. "Children's Book Illustration: The Pleasure and Problems." *Top of the News* 22: (Nov. 1965) p. 30.

Earle, Alice Morse. *Child Life in Colonial Days,* New York: Macmillan, 1899; Detroit: Omnigraphics, 1989. 1-55888-822-5.

Eckenstein, Lina. *Comparative Studies in Nursery Rhymes.* London: Duckworth, 1906; New York: Gordon Pr., 1973. 0-87968-912-9.

Egoff, Sheila A.; Stubbs, G. T.; and Ashley, L. F., eds. *Only Connect: Readings on Children's Literature,* 2nd ed. New York: Oxford Univ. Pr., 1980. 0-19-540309-6.

_____. *Worlds Within: Children's Fantasy from the Middle Ages to Today.* Chicago: ALA, 1988. 0-8389-0494-7.

Ellis, Alec. *A History of Children's Reading and Literature.* Elmsford, N.Y.: Pergamon Pr., 1968. 0-08-012586-7.

Estes, Glen, ed. *American Writers for Children Since 1960.* Detroit: Gale, 1987. 0-810-31739-7.

Ettlinger, John R. T., and Spirt, Diana L. *Choosing Books for Young People,* Vol. 2. Phoenix: Oryx, 1987. 0-89774-247-8.

Eyre, Frank. *British Children's Books in the Twentieth Century.* New York: Dutton, 1973. 0-525-27230-5.

_____. *Twentieth Century Children's Books.* Cambridge, Mass.: Robert Bentley, 1953.

Fiction, Folklore, Fantasy and Poetry for Children, 1876–1985, 2 vols. New York: R. R. Bowker, 1986. 0-8352-1831-7.

Field, Louise F. *The Child and His Book: Some Account of the History and Progress of Children's Literature in England.* New York: Gordon Pr., 1972. 0-87968-848-3.

Fisher, Margery Turner. *Intent upon Reading: A Critical Appraisal of Modern Fiction for Children.* Leicester, England: Brockhampton Pr., 1961.

_____. *Who's Who in Children's Books: A Treasury of the Familiar Characters of Childhood.* New York: Holt, 1975. 0-03-015091-4.

Fox, Geoffrey Percival et al., eds. *Writers, Critics, and Children: Articles from Children's Literature in Education.* New York: Agathon Pr., 1976. 0-87586-054-0.

*Freeman, Ruth Sunderlin. *Children's Picture Books, Yesterday and Today.* Watkins Glen, N.Y.: Century House, 1967. 0-87282-063-7.

Galinsky, Ellen, and David, Judy. *The Preschool Years: Family Strategies That Work—From Experts and Parents.* New York: Times Books, 1988. 0-345-36597-6.

*Gillespie, John T., and Naden, Corinne J., eds. *Best Books for Children: Preschool Through Grade Six,* 4th ed. New Providence, N.J.: R. R. Bowker, 1990. 0-8352-2668-9.

Gillespie, Margaret C., and Connor, John W. *Creative Growth Through Literature for Children and Adolescents.* Columbus, Ohio: Merrill, 1975. 0-675-08751-1.

Gottlieb, Gerald. *Early Children's Books and Their Illustration.* Boston: Godine, 1975. 0-87923-158-0.

Green, Percy B. *A History of Nursery Rhymes.* New York: Gordon Pr., 1972. 0-8490-0340-7.

Green, Roger Lancelyn. *Tellers of Tales: British Authors of Children's Books from 1800 to 1964.* New York: Watts, 1965.

*Greenaway, Kate. *The Kate Greenaway Treasury.* Cleveland: Collins, 1978. 0-529-00313-9.

Halsey, Rosalie V. *Forgotten Books of the American Nursery.* New York: Gordon Pr., 1972. 0-8490-0182-X.

Harrison, Barbara G., and Maguire, Gregory. *Innocence and Experience: Essays and Conversations on Children's Literature.* New York: Lothrop, 1987. 0-688-06123-0.

*Haviland, Virginia, comp. *Children and Literature: Views and Reviews.* New York: Lothrop, 1974. 0-673-07676-8.

_____. *Children's Literature: A Guide to Reference Sources.* Washington, D.C.: Library of Congress, 1966; first supplement, 1972; second supplement, 1977.

Hendrickson, Linnea. *Children's Literature: A Guide to the Criticism.* Boston: G. K. Hall, 1987. 0-8161-8670-7.

Huber, Miriam Blanton. *Story and Verse for Children,* 3rd ed. New York: Macmillan, 1965. 0-02-357500-X.

*Hürlimann, Bettina. *Three Centuries of Children's Books in Europe.* Ed. and tr. by Brian Alderson. London: Oxford Univ. Pr., 1967; Cleveland: World, 1968.

Inglis, Fred. *The Promise of Happiness.* New York: Cambridge Univ. Pr., 1981. 0-521-23142-6.

James, Philip. *Children's Books of Yesterday.* Ed. by C. Geoffrey Holme. London and New York: Studio, 1933; Detroit: Gale, 1976. 0-8103-4135-2.

Jan, Isabelle. *On Children's Literature.* Ed. by Catherine Storr. New York: Schocken Books, 1974. 0-8052-3564-7.

Katz, Lillian G., ed. *Current Topics in Early Childhood Education,* Vol. 7. Norwood, N.J.: Ablex, 1987. 0-89391-407-X.

Kiefer, Monica. *American Children Through Their Books, 1700–1835.* Philadelphia: Univ. of Pennsylvania Pr., 1948, 1970. 0-8122-7007-X.

Klemin, Diana. *The Art of Art for Children's Books.* Greenwich, Conn.: Murton Pr., 1966, 1982. 0-9608042-0-X.

_____. *The Illustrated Book.* Greenwich, Conn.: Murton Pr., 1970, 1983. 0-9608042-1-8.

Lanes, Selma G. "The Art of Maurice Sendak: A Diversity of Influences Inform an Art for Children," *Artforum* IX (May 1971): 70–73.

_____. *The Art of Maurice Sendak.* New York: Abradale Pr., 1984. 0-8109-8063-0.

Leif, Irving P. *Children's Literature: A Historical and Contemporary Bibliography.* Troy, N.Y.: Whitston, 1977. 0-685-88021-4.

Lewis, John. *The Twentieth Century Book: Its Illustration and Design.* New York: Van Nostrand Reinhold, 1967.

Linder, Leslie L. *The Art of Beatrix Potter,* 6th rev. ed. London: Warne, 1972. 0-7232-1457-3.

*Lipson, Eden Ross. *The New York Times Parent's Guide to the Best Books for Children,* 2nd ed. New York: Times Books, 1991. 0-8129-1889-4.

Lukens, Rebecca J. *A Critical Handbook of Children's Literature,* 4th ed. Glenview, Ill.: Scott, Foresman, 1989. 0-673-38773-9.

Lynn, Ruth Nadelman. *Fantasy Literature for Children and Young Adults: An Annotated Bibliography,* 3rd ed. New York: R. R. Bowker, 1989. 0-8352-2347-7.

Lystad, Mary. *From Dr. Mather to Dr. Seuss: Two Hundred Years of American Books for Children.* Cambridge, Mass.: Schenkman, 1980. 0-87073-210-2.

*MacCann, Donnarae, and Richard, Olga. *The Child's First Books.* New York: Wilson, 1973. 0-8242-0501-4.

_____, and Woodard, Gloria, eds. *The Black American in Books for Children: Readings in Racism,* 2nd ed. Metuchen, N.J.: Scarecrow, 1985. 0-8108-1826-4.

MacDonald, Margaret Read. *The Storyteller's Sourcebook: A Subject, Title, and Motif Index to Folklore Collections for Children.* Detroit: Neal-Schuman Publishers, Inc., in association with Gale Research Co., 1982. 0-8103-0471-6.

MacDonald, Ruth K. *Dr. Seuss.* Boston: Twayne, 1988. 0-8057-7524-2.

*McTigue, Bernard, ed. *A Child's Garden of Delights: Pictures, Poems, and Stories for Children from the Collection of the New York Public Library.* New York: Abrams, 1987. 0-8109-0791-7.

Mahoney, Ellen, and Wilcox, Leah. *Ready, Set, Read: Best Books to Prepare Preschoolers.* Metuchen, N.J.: Scarecrow, 1985. 0-8108-1684-9.

Mahony, Bertha E.; Latimer, Louise P.; and Folmsbee, Beulah, comps. *Illustrators of Children's Books, 1744–1945.* Boston: Horn Book, 1947. 0-87675-015-3.

Meacham, Mary. *Information Sources in Children's Literature.* New York: Macmillan, 1953; rev. ed., 1969. 0-313-20045-9.

*Meigs, Cornelia et al. *A Critical History of Children's Literature.* New York: Macmillan, 1953; rev. ed. 1969. 0-02-583900-4.

Monson, Diane L., ed. *Adventuring with Books: A Booklist for Pre-K–Grade 6.* Urbana, Ill.: NCTE, 1985. 0-8141-0076-7.

Moore, Anne Carroll. *My Roads to Childhood.* Boston: Horn Book, 1961.

Moransee, Jesse R., ed. *Children's Prize Books.* Ridgewood, N.J.: K. G. Saur, 1983. 3-598-03250-1.

Muir, Percey. *English Children's Books, 1600–1900.* New York: Praeger, 1969.

*Newbery, John. *A Little Pretty Pocket-Book: A Facsimile.* London: Oxford Univ. Pr., 1966.

*Nodelman, Perry. *Words about Pictures: The Narrative Art of Children's Picture Books.* Athens, Ga.: Univ. of Georgia Pr., 1989. 0-8203-1036-0.

Opie, Iona, and Opie, Peter. *A Family of Nursery Rhymes.* New York: Oxford Univ. Pr., 1964.

_____, eds. *I Saw Esau.* Cambridge, Mass.: Candlewick Pr., 1992. 1-56402-046-0.

_____. *A Nursery Companion.* New York: Oxford Univ. Pr., 1964. 0-19-212213-4.

_____. *The Oxford Dictionary of Nursery Rhymes.* New York: Oxford Univ. Pr., 1951. 0-19-869111-4.

_____, Opie, Robert, and Alderson, Brian. *The Treasures of Childhood: Books, Toys, and Games from the Opie Collection.* New York: Arcade, 1989. 1-55970-047-5.

Oppenheim, Joanne F. et al. *Choosing Books for Kids.* New York: Ballantine, 1986. 0-345-32683-0.

The Original Mother Goose's Melody, As First Issued by John Newbery, of London, about A.D. 1760. Reproduced in facsimile from the edition as reprinted by Isaiah Thomas of Worcester, Mass., about A.D. 1785, with introductory notes by William H. Whitmore. Detroit: Gale, 1969. 0-8103-3485-2.

Paterson, Katherine. *The Spying Heart: More Thoughts on Reading and Writing Books for Children.* New York: Lodestar, 1990. 0-525-67267-2.

*Pellowski, Anne. *The Family Storytelling Handbook.* New York: Watson-Guptill, 1963. 0-20-770610-9.

Potter, Beatrix. *Beatrix Potter: The V and A Collection.* London: Warne, 1986. 0-7232-3260-1.

Prentice, Jeffrey, and Bird, Bettina. *Dromkeen: A Journey into Children's Literature.* New York: Henry Holt, 1988.

Preschool Services and Parent Education Committee, Association for Library Service to Children. *Opening Doors for Preschool Children and Their Parents,* 2nd ed. Chicago: ALA, 1981. 0-8389-3260-6.

Richard, Olga. "The Visual Language of the Picture Book." *Wilson Library Bulletin* (Dec. 1969).

Roback, Diane, ed. "Arnold Lobel's Three Years with Mother Goose." *Publishers Weekly* 230: (Aug. 22, 1986) p. 8.

Roberts, Ellen E. M. *The Children's Picture Book.* Cincinnati, Ohio: Writer's Digest, 1981, 1987. 0-89879-254-1.

Rosenbach, Abraham S. W. *Early American Children's Books with Bibliographical Descriptions of the Books in His Private Collection.* Foreword by A. Edward Newton. Reprint of 1933 ed. New York: Dover, 1971. 0-486-22467-8.

Sadker, Myra, and Sadker, David Miller. *Now Upon a Time: A Contemporary View of Children's Literature.* New York: Harper, 1977. 0-06-045693-0.

Salway, Lance, ed. *A Peculiar Gift.* New York: Penguin, 1976.

San Diego Museum of Art Staff, eds. *Dr. Seuss from Then to Now.* New York: Random House, 1987. 0-9371-0805-7.

Sendak, Maurice. *Caldecott & Co.: Notes on Books and Pictures.* New York: Farrar, Straus & Giroux, 1988. 0-374-22598-2.

_____. "Mother Goose's Garnishings." *Book Week.* Fall Children's Issue (Oct. 31, 1965): 5, 38–40; also printed in Haviland, *Children and Literature,* pp. 188–195.

Senick, Gerald J., ed. *Children's Literature Review,* Vols. 12, 13. Detroit: Gale, 1987. 0-8103-0344-2; 0-8103-0348-5.

Smith, Dora V. *Fifty Years of Children's Books, 1910–1960.* Urbana, Ill.: NCTE, 1963.

*Smith, Elva S. *The History of Children's Literature: A Syllabus with Selected Bibliographies,* rev. and enlarged by Margaret Hodges and Susan Steinfirst. Chicago: ALA, 1980. 0-8389-0286-3.

Stott, Jon. *Children's Literature from A to Z: A Guide for Parents and Teachers.* New York: McGraw-Hill, 1984. 0-07-061791-0.

Sutherland, Zena, ed. *The Best in Children's Books: The University of Chicago Guide to Children's Literature, 1985–1990*. Chicago: Univ. of Chicago Pr., 1991. 0-226-78064-3.

*_____, and Arbuthnot, May Hill. *Children and Books*, 8th ed. New York: HarperCollins College, 1991. 0-673-46357-5.

Targ, William, ed. *Bibliophile in the Nursery*. Metuchen, N.J.: Scarecrow, 1969.

*Taylor, Judy. *Beatrix Potter: Artist, Storyteller and Countrywoman*. London: Warne, 1986. 0-7232-3314-4.

_____ et al. *Beatrix Potter, 1866–1943: The Artist and Her World*. London: Warne, 1988. 0-7232-3521-X.

Thomas, James L. *Play, Learn, and Grow: An Annotated Guide to the Best Books and Materials for Very Young Children*. New Providence, N.J.: R. R. Bowker, 1992. 0-8352-3019-8.

Thomas, Katherine Elwes. *The Real Personages of Mother Goose*. New York: Lothrop, 1930.

Thomson, Susan Ruth, ed. *Kate Greenaway: A Catalogue of the Kate Greenaway Collection, Rare Book Room, Detroit Public Library*. Detroit: Wayne State Univ. Pr., 1977. 0-8143-1581-X.

Thwaite, Mary. *From Primer to Pleasure in Reading*, Boston: Horn Book, 1972. 0-87675-275-X.

Townsend, John Rowe. *Written for Children: An Outline of English-Language Children's Literature*, 3rd rev. ed. New York: Harper, 1992. 0-06-446125-4.

Welch, D'Alte A. *A Bibliography of American Children's Books Printed Prior to 1821*. Worcester, Mass.: American Antiquarian Society, 1972. 0-8271-7133-1.

*Whalley, Joyce, Irene. *Cobwebs to Catch Flies: Illustrated Books for the Nursery and Schoolroom 1700–1900*. Berkeley: Univ. of California Pr., 1975. 0-520-02931-3.

White, Burton L. *Educating the Infant and Toddler*. New York: Free Pr., 1987. 0-669-13136-9.

White, Dorothy M. Neal. *Books Before Five*. Portsmouth, N.H.: Heinemann, 1984. 0-435-08215-9.

White, Mary Lou. *Adventuring with Books: A Booklist for Pre-K–Grade 6*. Chicago: ALA, 1981. 0-8141-0075-9.

_____. *Children's Literature: Criticism and Response*. Columbus, Ohio: Merrill, 1976. 0-675-08621-3.

*Wilkin, Binnie Tate. *Survival Themes in Fiction for Children and Young People*. Metuchen, N.J.: Scarecrow, 1978. 0-8108-1048-4.

Wilson, Elizabeth L. *Books Children Love*. Westchester, Ill.: Crossway Books, 1987. 0-89107-441-4.

Winkel, Lois, and Kimmel, Sue. *Mother Goose Comes First: An Annotated Guide to the Best Books and Recordings for Your Preschool Child*. New York: Henry Holt, 1990. 0-8050-1001-7.

*Zipes, Jack, tr. *The Complete Fairy Tales of the Brothers Grimm*. New York: Bantam, 1987. 0-553-05184-9.

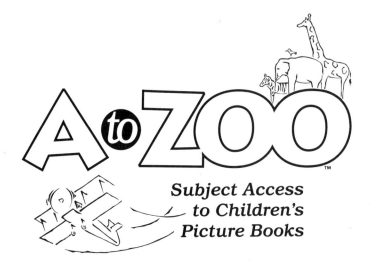

A to ZOO

Subject Access
to Children's
Picture Books

Subject Headings

Main headings, subheadings, and cross-references are arranged alphabetically and provide a quick reference to the subjects used in the Subject Guide section where author and title names appear under appropriate headings.

Aardvarks *see* Animals – aardvarks
ABC books
Accordion books *see* Format, unusual
Activities
Activities – baby-sitting
Activities – ballooning
Activities – bathing
Activities – cooking
Activities – dancing
Activities – digging
Activities – drawing
Activities – flying
Activities – gardening *see* Gardens, gardening
Activities – jumping
Activities – knitting
Activities – making things
Activities – painting
Activities – photographing
Activities – picnicking
Activities – playing
Activities – reading
Activities – sewing
Activities – shopping *see* Shopping
Activities – singing
Activities – swinging
Activities – trading
Activities – traveling
Activities – vacationing
Activities – walking
Activities – weaving
Activities – whistling
Activities – working
Activities – writing
Actors *see* Careers – actors
Adoption
Africa *see* Foreign lands – Africa
Afro-Americans *see* Ethnic groups in the U.S. – Afro-Americans
Aged *see* Old age
Airplane pilots *see* Careers – airplane pilots
Airplanes, airports
Airports *see* Airplanes, airports
Alaska
Albatrosses *see* Birds – albatrosses
Alligators *see* Reptiles – alligators, crocodiles

Ambition *see* Character traits – ambition
American Indians *see* Indians of North America; Indians of South America
Amphibians *see* Frogs and toads; Reptiles
Anatomy
Anatomy – ears
Anatomy – eyes
Anatomy – faces
Anatomy – feet
Anatomy – hands
Anatomy – heads
Anatomy – mouths
Anatomy – noses
Anatomy – skeletons
Anatomy – toes
Angels
Anger *see* Emotions – anger
Animals
Animals – aardvarks
Animals – anteaters
Animals – apes *see* Animals – gorillas; Animals – monkeys; Animals – chimpanzees
Animals – armadillos
Animals – baboons
Animals – badgers
Animals – bandicoots
Animals – bats
Animals – bears
Animals – beavers
Animals – bobcats
Animals – buffaloes
Animals – bulls, cows
Animals – bushbabies
Animals – camels
Animals – cats
Animals – cheetahs
Animals – chimpanzees
Animals – chipmunks
Animals – cougars
Animals – coyotes
Animals – deer
Animals, dislike of *see* Behavior – animals, dislike of
Animals – dogs
Animals – dolphins
Animals – donkeys
Animals – elephants
Animals – elephant seals

Animals – endangered animals
Animals – foxes
Animals – gerbils
Animals – giraffes
Animals – goats
Animals – gorillas
Animals – groundhogs
Animals – guinea pigs
Animals – hamsters
Animals – hedgehogs
Animals – hippopotami
Animals – horses
Animals – hyenas
Animals – kangaroos
Animals – kindness to animals
Animals – koala bears
Animals – lemmings
Animals – lemurs
Animals – leopards
Animals – lions
Animals – llamas
Animals – mice
Animals – minks
Animals – moles
Animals – mongooses
Animals – monkeys
Animals – moose
Animals – mules
Animals – muskrats
Animals – octopuses *see* Octopuses
Animals – otters
Animals – oxen
Animals – pack rats
Animals – pandas
Animals – pigs
Animals – polar bears
Animals – porcupines
Animals – possums
Animals – prairie dogs
Animals – rabbits
Animals – raccoons
Animals – rats
Animals – reindeer
Animals – rhinoceros
Animals – salamanders
Animals – sea lions
Animals – seals
Animals – sheep
Animals – shrews
Animals – skunks
Animals – sloths
Animals – snails
Animals – squirrels

Animals – tapirs
Animals – tigers
Animals – walruses
Animals – warthogs
Animals – water buffaloes
Animals – weasels
Animals – whales
Animals – wildebeests
Animals – wolves
Animals – wombats
Animals – worms
Animals – yaks
Animals – zebras
Antarctic see Foreign lands –
    Antarctic
Anteaters see Animals –
    anteaters
Anti-violence see Violence,
    anti-violence
Ants see Insects – ants
Apes see Animals – gorillas;
    Animals – monkeys
Appearance see Character
    traits – appearance
April Fools' Day see Holidays
    – April Fools' Day
Aquariums
Arabia see Foreign lands –
    Arabia
Architects see Careers –
    architects
Arctic see Foreign lands –
    Arctic
Arguing see Behavior –
    fighting, arguing
Arithmetic see Counting,
    numbers
Armadillos see Animals –
    armadillos
Armenia see Foreign lands –
    Armenia
Art
Artists see Careers – artists
Asian-Americans see Ethnic
    groups in the U.S. –
    Asian-Americans
Assertive see Character traits –
    assertiveness
Astrology see Zodiac
Astronauts see Space and
    space ships
Astronomy
Aunts see Family life – aunts,
    uncles
Australia see Foreign lands –
    Australia
Austria see Foreign lands –
    Austria
Authors, children see Children
    as authors
Automobiles
Autumn see Seasons – fall

Babies
Baby-sitting see Activities –
    baby-sitting
Bad day see Behavior – bad
    day
Badgers see Animals –
    badgers
Bakers see Careers – bakers

Bali see Foreign lands – Bali
Ballooning see Activities –
    ballooning
Balloons see Toys – balloons
Balls see Toys – balls
Barbers see Careers – barbers
Barns
Barons see Royalty
Baseball see Sports – baseball
Basketball see Sports –
    basketball
Bathing see Activities –
    bathing
Bats see Animals – bats
Bavaria see Foreign lands –
    Austria; Foreign lands –
    Germany
Beaches see Sea and seashore
Bears see Animals – bears
Beasts see Monsters
Beavers see Animals – beavers
Beds see Furniture – beds
Bedtime
Bees see Insects – bees
Beetles see Insects – beetles
Behavior
Behavior – animals, dislike of
Behavior – bad day
Behavior – boasting
Behavior – boredom
Behavior – bullying
Behavior – carelessness
Behavior – collecting things
Behavior – disbelief
Behavior – dissatisfaction
Behavior – fighting, arguing
Behavior – forgetfulness
Behavior – gossip
Behavior – greed
Behavior – growing up
Behavior – hiding
Behavior – hiding things
Behavior – hurrying
Behavior – imitation
Behavior – indifference
Behavior – laziness
Behavior – losing things
Behavior – lost
Behavior – lying
Behavior – messy
Behavior – misbehavior
Behavior – mistakes
Behavior – misunderstanding
Behavior – nagging
Behavior – name calling
Behavior – needing someone
Behavior – running away
Behavior – saving things
Behavior – secrets
Behavior – seeking better
    things
Behavior – sharing
Behavior – shyness
Behavior – solitude
Behavior – stealing
Behavior – talking to
    strangers
Behavior – tardiness
Behavior – toilet training see
    Toilet training
Behavior – trickery

Behavior – unnoticed, unseen
Behavior – wishing
Behavior – worrying
Being different see Character
    traits – being different
Bicycling see Sports –
    bicycling
Bigotry see Prejudice
Birds
Birds – albatrosses
Birds – blackbirds
Birds – bluejays
Birds – buzzards
Birds – canaries
Birds – cardinals
Birds – chickens
Birds – cockatoos
Birds – cormorants
Birds – cranes
Birds – crows
Birds – cuckoos
Birds – dodos
Birds – doves
Birds – ducks
Birds – eagles
Birds – egrets
Birds – flamingos
Birds – geese
Birds – guinea fowl
Birds – hawks
Birds – hornbills
Birds – humming birds
Birds – loons
Birds – mockingbirds
Birds – nightingales
Birds – ostriches
Birds – owls
Birds – parakeets, parrots
Birds – peacocks, peahens
Birds – pelicans
Birds – penguins
Birds – pigeons
Birds – puffins
Birds – ravens
Birds – robins
Birds – sandpipers
Birds – sea gulls
Birds – sparrows
Birds – spoonbills
Birds – storks
Birds – swallows
Birds – swans
Birds – toucans
Birds – turkeys
Birds – vultures
Birds – woodpeckers
Birds – wrens
Birth
Birthdays
Black Americans see Ethnic
    groups in the U.S. –
    Afro-Americans
Blackbirds see Birds –
    blackbirds
Blackouts see Power failure
Blindness see Handicaps –
    blindness
Blocks see Toys – blocks
Bluejays see Birds – bluejays
Board books see Format,
    unusual – board books

Boasting *see* Behavior – boasting

Boat builders *see* Careers – boat builders

Boats, ships

Bobcats *see* Animals – bobcats

Boogy man *see* Monsters

Books *see* Activities – reading; Libraries

Boots *see* Clothing – shoes

Boredom *see* Behavior – boredom

Borneo *see* Foreign lands – Borneo

Bravery *see* Character traits – bravery

Bridges

Brothers *see* Family life; Family life – brothers; Sibling rivalry

Brownies *see* Elves and little people

Buffaloes *see* Animals – buffaloes

Bugs *see* Insects

Buildings

Bulls *see* Animals – bulls, cows

Bullying *see* Behavior – bullying

Bumble bees *see* Insects – bees

Burglars *see* Crime

Burma *see* Foreign lands – Burma

Burros *see* Animals – donkeys

Bus drivers *see* Careers – bus drivers

Bus drivers *see* Careers – bus drivers

Buses

Bushbabies *see* Animals – bushbabies

Butchers *see* Careers – butchers

Butterflies *see* Insects – butterflies, caterpillars

Buzzards *see* Birds – buzzards

Cab drivers *see* Careers – taxi drivers

Cable cars, trolleys

Cabs *see* Taxis

Caldecott award book

Caldecott award honor book

Cambodia *see* Foreign lands – Cambodia

Camels *see* Animals – camels

Camps, camping

Canada *see* Foreign lands – Canada

Canaries *see* Birds – canaries

Caps *see* Clothing – hats

Cardboard page books *see* Format, unusual – board books

Cardinals *see* Birds – cardinals

Careers

Careers – actors

Careers – airplane pilots

Careers – architects

Careers – artists

Careers – astronauts

Careers – bakers

Careers – barbers

Careers – boat builders

Careers – bus drivers

Careers – butchers

Careers – cab drivers *see* Careers – taxi drivers

Careers – carpenters

Careers – chefs

Careers – clockmakers

Careers – composers

Careers – dentists

Careers – detectives

Careers – doctors

Careers – electricians

Careers – farmers

Careers – firefighters

Careers – fishermen

Careers – forest rangers *see* Careers – park rangers

Careers – fortune tellers

Careers – garbage collectors

Careers – geologists

Careers – handyman

Careers – hatters

Careers – housekeepers

Careers – journalists

Careers – judges

Careers – librarians

Careers – mail carriers

Careers – mechanics

Careers – military

Careers – miners

Careers – models

Careers – musicians

Careers – nuns

Careers – nurses

Careers – park rangers

Careers – peddlers

Careers – physicians *see* Careers – doctors

Careers – police officers

Careers – printers

Careers – race car drivers

Careers – railroad engineers

Careers – rangers *see* Careers – park rangers

Careers – sailors *see* Careers – military

Careers – seamstresses

Careers – shepherds

Careers – shoemakers

Careers – soldiers *see* Careers – military

Careers – storekeepers

Careers – tailors

Careers – taxi drivers

Careers – teachers

Careers – telephone operators

Careers – train engineers *see* Careers – railroad engineers

Careers – truck drivers

Careers – veterinarians

Careers – waiters, waitresses

Careers – waitresses *see* Careers – waiters, waitresses

Careers – welders

Careers – window cleaners

Careers – writers

Careers – zookeepers

Carelessness *see* Behavior – carelessness

Caribbean Islands *see* Foreign lands – Caribbean Islands

Carnivals *see* Fairs

Carousels *see* Merry-go-rounds

Carpenters *see* Careers – carpenters

Cars *see* Automobiles

Caterpillars *see* Insects – butterflies, caterpillars

Cats *see* Animals – cats

Cavemen

Caves

Central America *see* Foreign lands – Central America

Chairs *see* Furniture – chairs

Chanukah *see* Holidays – Hanukkah

Character traits

Character traits – ambition

Character traits – appearance

Character traits – assertiveness

Character traits – being different

Character traits – bravery

Character traits – cleanliness

Character traits – cleverness

Character traits – completing things

Character traits – compromising

Character traits – conceit

Character traits – confidence

Character traits – cruelty to animals *see* Character traits – kindness to animals

Character traits – curiosity

Character traits – flattery

Character traits – foolishness

Character traits – fortune *see* Character traits – luck

Character traits – freedom

Character traits – generosity

Character traits – helpfulness

Character traits – honesty

Character traits – incentive *see* Character traits – ambition

Character traits – individuality

Character traits – kindness

Character traits – kindness to animals

Character traits – laziness

Character traits – littleness *see* Character traits – smallness

Character traits – loyalty

Character traits – luck

Character traits – meanness

Character traits – optimism

Character traits – ostracism *see* Character traits – being different

Character traits – patience

Character traits – perseverance

Character traits – persistence

Character traits – practicality

Character traits – pride

Character traits – questioning

Character traits – selfishness
Character traits – shyness
Character traits – smallness
Character traits – solitude
Character traits – stubbornness
Character traits – vanity
Character traits – willfulness
Cheetahs *see* Animals – cheetahs
Chefs *see* Careers – chefs
Chickens *see* Birds – chickens
Child abuse
Children as authors
Children as illustrators
Chimpanzees *see* Animals – chimpanzees
China *see* Foreign lands – China
Chinese-Americans *see* Ethnic groups in the U.S. – Asian-Americans; Ethnic groups in the U.S. – Chinese-Americans
Chinese New Year *see* Holidays – Chinese New Year
Chipmunks *see* Animals – chipmunks
Christmas *see* Holidays – Christmas
Cinco de Mayo *see* Holidays – Cinco de Mayo
Circular tales
Circus
City
Cleanliness *see* Character traits – cleanliness
Cleverness *see* Character traits – cleverness
Clockmakers *see* Careers – clockmakers
Clocks, watches
Clothing
Clothing – coats
Clothing – gloves
Clothing – hats
Clothing – pants
Clothing – shirts
Clothing – shoes
Clothing – socks
Clothing – sweaters
Clouds *see* Weather – clouds
Clowns, jesters
Clubs, gangs
Coats *see* Clothing – coats
Cockatoos *see* Birds – cockatoos
Codes *see* Secret codes
Cold *see* Weather – cold
Collecting things *see* Behavior – collecting things
Color *see* Concepts – color
Color *see* Concepts – color
Columbus Day *see* Holidays – Columbus Day
Communication
Communities, neighborhoods
Competition *see* Sibling rivalry
Completing things *see* Character traits – completing things

Composers *see* Careers – composers
Compromising *see* Character traits – compromising
Computers
Conceit *see* Character traits – conceit
Concepts
Concepts – color
Concepts – counting *see* Counting, numbers
Concepts – distance
Concepts – in and out
Concepts – left and right
Concepts – measurement
Concepts – opposites
Concepts – perspective
Concepts – self *see* Self-concept
Concepts – shape
Concepts – size
Concepts – speed
Concepts – up and down
Concepts – weight
Confidence *see* Character traits – confidence
Conservation *see* Ecology
Contests
Cooking *see* Activities – cooking
Cooks *see* Careers – bakers
Copying *see* Behavior – copying
Coral Islands *see* Foreign lands – South Sea Islands
Cormorants *see* Birds – cormorants
Costa Rica *see* Foreign lands – Costa Rica
Couches, sofas *see* Furniture – couches, sofas
Cougars *see* Animals – cougars
Counting, numbers
Countries, foreign *see* Foreign lands
Country
Cousins *see* Family life – cousins
Cowboys
Cows *see* Animals – bulls, cows
Coyotes *see* Animals – coyotes
Crabs *see* Crustacea
Cranes *see* Birds – cranes
Creatures *see* Goblins; Monsters
Creeks *see* Rivers
Crickets *see* Insects – crickets
Crime
Criminals *see* Crime; Prisons
Crippled *see* Handicaps
Crocodiles *see* Reptiles – alligators, crocodiles
Crows *see* Birds – crows
Cruelty to animals *see* Character traits – kindness to animals
Crustacea
Cuckoos *see* Animals – cuckoos
Cumulative tales

Curiosity *see* Character traits – curiosity
Currency *see* Money
Cycles *see* Motorcycles; Sports – bicycling
Czechoslovakia *see* Foreign lands – Czechoslovakia

Dancing *see* Activities – dancing
Dark *see* Night
Darkness – fear *see* Emotions – fear
Dawn *see* Morning
Days of the week, months of the year
Deafness *see* Handicaps – deafness; Senses – hearing
Death
Deer *see* Animals – deer
Demons *see* Devil; Monsters
Denmark *see* Foreign lands – Denmark
Dentists *see* Careers – dentists
Department stores *see* Stores
Desert
Detectives *see* Careers – detectives
Detective stories *see* Problem solving
Devil
Dictionaries
Digging *see* Activities – digging
Dinosaurs
Disbelief *see* Behavior – disbelief
Dissatisfaction *see* Behavior – dissatisfaction
Distance *see* Concepts – distance
Diving *see* Sports – skin diving
Divorce
Doctors *see* Careers – doctors
Dodos *see* Birds – dodos
Dogs *see* Animals – dogs
Dolls *see* Toys – dolls
Dolphins *see* Animals – dolphins
Donkeys *see* Animals – donkeys
Doves *see* Birds – doves
Down and up *see* Concepts – up and down
Dragonflies *see* Insects – dragonflies
Dragons
Drawing *see* Activities – drawing
Drawing games *see* Games
Dreams
Dressers *see* Furniture – dressers
Droughts *see* Weather – droughts
Ducks *see* Birds – ducks
Dwarfs *see* Elves and little people
Dying *see* Death

Eagles *see* Birds – eagles
Ears *see* Anatomy – ears;
  Handicaps – deafness;
  Senses – hearing
Earth
Easter *see* Holidays – Easter
Eating *see* Food
Ecology
Ecuador *see* Foreign lands –
  Ecuador
Education *see* School
Eggs
Egrets *see* Birds – egrets
Egypt *see* Foreign lands –
  Egypt
Egyptian language *see*
  Hieroglyphics
Elderly *see* Old age
Electricians *see* Careers –
  electricians
Elephants *see* Animals –
  elephants
Elephant seals *see* Animals –
  elephant seals
Elevators, escalators
El Salvador *see* Foreign lands
  – El Salvador
Elves and little people
Embarrassment *see* Emotions
  – embarrassment
Emergencies *see* Hospitals
Emotions
Emotions – anger
Emotions – embarrassment
Emotions – envy, jealousy
Emotions – fear
Emotions – happiness
Emotions – hate
Emotions – jealousy *see*
  Emotions – envy, jealousy
Emotions – loneliness
Emotions – love
Emotions – sadness
Emotions – unhappiness *see*
  Emotions – happiness;
  Emotions – sadness
Emperors *see* Royalty –
  emperors
Endangered animals *see*
  Animals – endangered
  animals
Engineered books *see* Format,
  unusual – toy and movable
  books
England *see* Foreign lands –
  England
Entertainment *see* Theater
Envy *see* Emotions – envy,
  jealousy
Eskimos
Ethnic groups in the U.S
Ethnic groups in the U.S. –
  Afro-Americans
Ethnic groups in the U.S. –
  Asian-Americans
Ethnic groups in the U.S. –
  Black Americans *see* Ethnic
  groups in the U.S. –
  Afro-Americans
Ethnic groups in the U.S. –
  Chinese-Americans
Ethnic groups in the U.S. –

Hispanic-Americans
Ethnic groups in the U.S. –
  Irish-Americans
Ethnic groups in the U.S. –
  Italian-Americans
Ethnic groups in the U.S. –
  Japanese-Americans
Ethnic groups in the U.S. –
  Korean-American
Ethnic groups in the U.S. –
  Mexican-Americans
Ethnic groups in the U.S. –
  Puerto Rican-Americans
Ethnic groups in the U.S. –
  Vietnamese-Americans
Etiquette
Europe *see* Foreign lands –
  Europe
Evening *see* Twilight
Experiments *see* Science
Eye glasses *see* Glasses
Eyes *see* Anatomy – eyes;
  Handicaps – blindness;
  Senses – seeing

Fables *see* Folk and fairy tales
Faces *see* Anatomy – faces
Fairies
Fairs
Fairy tales *see* Folk and fairy
  tales
Fall *see* Seasons – fall
Families *see* Family life
Family life
Family life – aunts, uncles
Family life – brothers
Family life – cousins
Family life – fathers
Family life – grandfathers
Family life – grandmothers
Family life – grandparents
Family life –
  great-grandparents
Family life – mothers
Family life – only child
Family life – sisters
Family life – stepchildren *see*
  Divorce; Family life – step
  families
Family life – step families
Family life – stepparents *see*
  Divorce; Family life – step
  families
Farmers *see* Careers – farmers
Farms
Fathers *see* Family life –
  fathers
Father's Day *see* Holidays –
  Father's Day
Fear *see* Emotions – fear
Feeling *see* Senses – touching
Feelings *see* Emotions
Feet *see* Anatomy – feet
Fighting *see* Behavior –
  fighting, arguing
Fingers *see* Anatomy – hands
Finishing things *see* Character
  traits – completing things
Finland *see* Foreign lands –
  Finland
Fire

Fire engines *see* Careers –
  firefighters; Trucks
Firefighters *see* Careers –
  firefighters
Fireflies *see* Insects – fireflies
Fish
Fishermen *see* Careers –
  fishermen
Fishing *see* Sports – fishing
Fish – sharks
Flamingos *see* Birds –
  flamingos
Flattery *see* Character traits –
  flattery
Fleas *see* Insects – fleas
Flies *see* Insects – flies
Floods *see* Weather – floods
Flowers
Flying *see* Activities – flying
Fog *see* Weather – fog
Fold out books *see* Format,
  unusual
Folk and fairy tales
Food
Foolishness *see* Character
  traits – foolishness
Football *see* Sports – football
Foreign lands
Foreign lands – Africa
Foreign lands – Antarctic
Foreign lands – Arabia
Foreign lands – Arctic
Foreign lands – Armenia
Foreign lands – Australia
Foreign lands – Austria
Foreign lands – Bali
Foreign lands – Bavaria *see*
  Foreign lands – Austria;
  Foreign lands – Germany
Foreign lands – Borneo
Foreign lands – Burma
Foreign lands – Cambodia
Foreign lands – Canada
Foreign lands – Caribbean
  Islands
Foreign lands – Central
  America
Foreign lands – China
Foreign lands – Costa Rica
Foreign lands –
  Czechoslovakia
Foreign lands – Denmark
Foreign lands – Ecuador
Foreign lands – Egypt
Foreign lands – El Salvador
Foreign lands – England
Foreign lands – Europe
Foreign lands – Finland
Foreign lands – France
Foreign lands – Germany
Foreign lands – Ghana
Foreign lands – Greece
Foreign lands – Greenland
Foreign lands – Guatemala
Foreign lands – Guyana
Foreign lands – Holland
Foreign lands – Hungary
Foreign lands – Iceland
Foreign lands – India
Foreign lands – Ireland
Foreign lands – Israel

Foreign lands – Italy
Foreign lands – Japan
Foreign lands – Kenya
Foreign lands – Korea
Foreign lands – Laos
Foreign lands – Lapland
Foreign lands – Latvia
Foreign lands – Malaysia
Foreign lands – Mexico
Foreign lands – Nepal
Foreign lands – New Guinea
Foreign lands – Nicaragua
Foreign lands – Nigeria
Foreign lands – Norway
Foreign lands – Pakistan
Foreign lands – Panama
Foreign lands – Persia
Foreign lands – Peru
Foreign lands – Philippines
Foreign lands – Poland
Foreign lands – Portugal
Foreign lands – Puerto Rico
Foreign lands – Romania
Foreign lands – Russia
Foreign lands – Sahara Desert
Foreign lands – Scotland
Foreign lands – Siam *see*
   Foreign lands – Thailand
Foreign lands – South Africa
Foreign lands – South
   America
Foreign lands – South Sea
   Islands
Foreign lands – Spain
Foreign lands – Sweden
Foreign lands – Switzerland
Foreign lands – Taiwan
Foreign lands – Thailand
Foreign lands – Tibet
Foreign lands – Trinidad
Foreign lands – Turkey
Foreign lands – Tyrol
Foreign lands – Ukraine
Foreign lands – Vatican City
Foreign lands – Venezuela
Foreign lands – Vietnam
Foreign lands – Zaire
Foreign lands – Zanzibar
Foreign languages
Forest rangers *see* Careers –
   park rangers
Forest, woods
Forgetfulness *see* Behavior –
   forgetfulness
Format, unusual
Format, unusual – board
   books
Format, unusual – toy and
   movable books
Fortune *see* Character traits –
   luck
Fortune tellers *see* Careers –
   fortune tellers
Fourth of July *see* Holidays –
   Fourth of July
Foxes *see* Animals – foxes
France *see* Foreign lands –
   France
Freedom *see* Character traits –
   freedom
Friendship
Frogs and toads

Furniture
Furniture – beds
Furniture – chairs
Furniture – couches, sofas
Furniture – dressers
Furniture – tables

Games
Gangs *see* Clubs, gangs
Garage sales
Garbage collectors *see* Careers
   – garbage collectors
Gardening *see* Gardens,
   gardening
Gardens, gardening
Geese *see* Birds – geese
Generosity *see* Character traits
   – generosity
Geologists *see* Careers –
   geologists
Gerbils *see* Animals – gerbils
Germany *see* Foreign lands –
   Germany
Ghana *see* Foreign lands –
   Ghana
Ghosts
Giants
Gilbert Islands *see* Foreign
   lands – South Sea Islands
Giraffes *see* Animals – giraffes
Glasses
Gloves *see* Clothing – gloves
Gnats *see* Insects – gnats
Gnomes *see* Elves and little
   people
Goats *see* Animals – goats
Goblins
Gorillas *see* Animals – gorillas
Gossip *see* Behavior – gossip
Grammar *see* Language
Grandfathers *see* Family life –
   grandfathers; family life –
   grandparents
Grandmothers *see* Family life
   – grandmothers; family life
   – grandparents
Grandparents *see* Family life –
   grandfathers; Family life –
   grandmothers; Family life –
   grandparents
Grasshoppers *see* Insects –
   grasshoppers
Great-grandparents *see* Family
   life – great-grandparents
Greece *see* Foreign lands –
   Greece
Greed *see* Behavior – greed
Greenland *see* Foreign lands –
   Greenland
Griffins *see* Mythical creatures
Grocery stores *see* Shopping;
   Stores
Groundhog Day *see* Holidays
   – Groundhog Day
Groundhogs *see* Animals –
   groundhogs
Growing up *see* Behavior –
   growing up
Guatemala *see* Foreign lands –
   Guatemala

Guinea fowl *see* Birds –
   guinea fowl
Guinea pigs *see* Animals –
   guinea pigs
Guns *see* Weapons
Guyana *see* Foreign lands –
   Guyana
Guy Fawkes Day *see* Holidays
   – Guy Fawkes Day
Gymnastics *see* Sports –
   gymnastics
Gypsies

Hair
Halloween *see* Holidays –
   Halloween
Hamsters *see* Animals –
   hamsters
Handicaps
Handicaps – blindness
Handicaps – deafness
Handicaps – physical
Hands *see* Anatomy – hands
Handyman *see* Careers –
   handyman
Hanukkah *see* Holidays –
   Hanukkah
Happiness *see* Emotions –
   happiness
Hares *see* Animals – rabbits
Hate *see* Emotions – hate
Hats *see* Clothing – hats
Hatters *see* Careers – hatters
Hawaii
Hawks *see* Birds – hawks
Heads *see* Anatomy – heads
Health
Hearing *see* Handicaps –
   deafness; Senses – hearing
Heavy equipment *see*
   Machines
Hedgehogs *see* Animals –
   hedgehogs
Helicopters
Helpfulness *see* Character
   traits – helpfulness
Hens *see* Birds – chickens
Hibernation
Hiding *see* Behavior – hiding
Hiding things *see* Behavior –
   hiding things
Hieroglyphics
Hiking *see* Sports – hiking
Hippopotami *see* Animals –
   Hippopotami
Hispanic-Americans *see* Ethnic
   groups in the U.S. –
   Hispanic-Americans
Hobby horses *see* Toys –
   rocking horses
Hockey *see* Sports – hockey
Holidays
Holidays – April Fools' Day
Holidays – Chanukah *see*
   Holidays – Hanukkah
Holidays – Chinese New Year
Holidays – Christmas
Holidays – Cinco de Mayo
Holidays – Columbus Day
Holidays – Easter
Holidays – Father's Day

Holidays – Fourth of July
Holidays – Groundhog Day
Holidays – Guy Fawkes Day
Holidays – Halloween
Holidays – Hanukkah
Holidays – Independence Day
see Holidays – Fourth of
July
Holidays – Kwanzaa
Holidays – Mardi Gras *see*
Mardi Gras
Holidays – Memorial Day
Holidays – Mother's Day
Holidays – New Year's
Holidays – Passover
Holidays – Purim
Holidays – Rosh Hashanah
Holidays – St. Patrick's Day
Holidays – Sukkot
Holidays – Thanksgiving
Holidays – Valentine's Day
Holidays – Washington's
Birthday
Holidays – Yom Kippur
Holland *see* Foreign lands –
Holland
Homeless
Homes *see* Houses
Homosexuality
Honesty *see* Character traits –
honesty
Honey bees *see* Insects – bees
Hope
Hornbills *see* Birds – hornbills
Hornets *see* Insects – hornets
Horses *see* Animals – horses
Horses, rocking *see* Toys –
rocking horses
Hospitals
Hotels
Housekeepers *see* Careers –
housekeepers
Houses
Humming birds *see* Birds –
humming birds
Humor
Hungary *see* Foreign lands –
Hungary
Hunting *see* Sports – hunting
Hurrying *see* Behavior –
hurrying
Hyenas *see* Animals – hyenas

Iceland *see* Foreign lands –
Iceland
Ice skating *see* Sports – ice
skating
Iguanas *see* Reptiles – iguanas
Illness
Illness – Alzheimer's
Illusions, optical *see* Optical
illusions
Illustrators, children *see*
Children as illustrators
Imaginary friends *see*
Imagination – imaginary
friends
Imagination
Imagination – imaginary
friends

Imitation *see* Behavior –
imitation
In and out *see* Concepts – in
and out
Incentive *see* Character traits
– ambition
Independence Day *see*
Holidays – Fourth of July
India *see* Foreign lands –
India
Indians, American *see* Indians
of North America; Indians
of South America
Indians of North America
Indians of South America
Indifference *see* Behavior –
indifference
Indifference *see* Behavior –
indifference
Individuality *see* Character
traits – individuality
Indonesian Archipelago *see*
Foreign lands – South Sea
Islands
Insects
Insects – ants
Insects – bees
Insects – beetles
Insects – butterflies,
caterpillars
Insects – caterpillars *see*
Insects – butterflies,
caterpillars
Insects – crickets
Insects – dragonflies
Insects – fireflies
Insects – fleas
Insects – flies
Insects – gnats
Insects – grasshoppers
Insects – hornets
Insects – lady birds *see* Insects
– ladybugs
Insects – ladybugs
Insects – lightning bugs *see*
Insects – fireflies
Insects – mosquitoes
Insects – moths
Insects – praying mantis
Insects – wasps
Interracial marriage *see*
Marriage, interracial
Ireland *see* Foreign lands –
Ireland
Irish-Americans *see* Ethnic
groups in the U.S. –
Irish-Americans
Islands
Israel *see* Foreign lands –
Israel
Italian-Americans *see* Ethnic
groups in the U.S. –
Italian-Americans
Italy *see* Foreign lands – Italy

Jackets *see* Clothing – coats
Jail *see* Prisons
Japan *see* Foreign lands –
Japan
Japanese-Americans *see* Ethnic
groups in the U.S. –

Asian-Americans; Ethnic
groups in the U.S. –
Japanese-Americans
Jealousy *see* Emotions – envy,
jealousy
Jesters *see* Clowns, jesters
Jewish culture
Jobs *see* Careers
Jokes *see* Riddles
Journalists *see* Careers –
journalists
Judges *see* Careers – judges
Jumping *see* Activities –
jumping
Jungle

Kangaroos *see* Animals –
kangaroos
Kenya *see* Foreign lands –
Kenya
Kindness *see* Character traits
– kindness
Kindness to animals *see*
Character traits – kindness
to animals
Kings *see* Royalty – kings
Kinkajous *see* Animals –
kinkajous
Kites
Knights
Knitting *see* Activities –
knitting
Koala bears *see* Animals –
koala bears
Korea *see* Foreign lands –
Korea
Korean-Americans *see* Ethnic
groups in the U.S. –
Asian-Americans; Ethnic
groups in the U.S. –
Korean-Americans
Kwanzaa *see* Holidays –
Kwanzaa

Lady birds *see* Insects –
ladybugs
Ladybugs *see* Insects –
ladybugs
Language
Language, foreign *see* Foreign
languages
Laos *see* Foreign lands – Laos
Lapland *see* Foreign lands –
Lapland
Latvia *see* Foreign lands –
Latvia
Laundry
Law *see* Careers – judges;
Crime
Laziness *see* Character traits –
laziness
Left and right *see* Concepts –
left and right
Left-handedness
Legends *see* Folk and fairy
tales
Lemmings *see* Animals –
lemmings
Lemurs *see* Animals – lemurs

Leopards *see* Animals –
 leopards
Leprechauns *see* Elves and
 little people
Letters
Librarians *see* Careers –
 librarians
Libraries
Lightening bugs *see* Insects –
 fireflies
Lighthouses
Lights
Lions *see* Animals – lions
Littleness *see* Character traits
 – smallness
Little people *see* Elves and
 little people
Lizards *see* Reptiles – lizards
Llamas *see* Animals – llamas
Lobsters *see* Crustacea
Loneliness *see* Emotions –
 loneliness
Loons *see* Birds – loons
Losing things *see* Behavior –
 losing things
Lost *see* Behavior – lost
Love *see* Emotions – love
Loyalty *see* Character traits –
 loyalty
Luck *see* Character traits –
 luck
Lullabies
Lying *see* Behavior – lying

Machines
Magic
Mail *see* Letters
Mail carriers *see* Careers –
 mail carriers
Making things *see* Activities –
 making things
Malaysia *see* Foreign lands –
 Malaysia
Manners *see* Etiquette
Maps
Mardi Gras
Marionettes *see* Puppets
Markets *see* Stores
Marriage, interracial
Marriages *see* Weddings
Math *see* Counting, numbers
Meanness *see* Character traits
 – meanness
Measurement *see* Concepts –
 measurement
Mechanical men *see* Robots
Mechanics *see* Careers –
 mechanics
Memorial Day *see* Holidays –
 Memorial Day
Mermaids *see* Mythical
 creatures – mermaids
Merry-go-rounds
Messy *see* Behavior – messy
Mexican-Americans *see* Ethnic
 groups in the U.S. –
 Hispanic-Americans; Ethnic
 groups in the U.S. –
 Mexican-Americans
Mexico *see* Foreign lands –
 Mexico

Mice *see* Animals – mice
Middle ages
Military *see* Careers – military
Mimes *see* Clowns, jesters
Miners *see* Careers – miners
Minks *see* Animals – minks
Minorities *see* Ethnic groups
 in the U.S
Mirages *see* Optical illusions
Misbehavior *see* Behavior –
 misbehavior
Missions
Mist *see* Weather – fog
Mistakes *see* Behavior –
 mistakes
Misunderstanding *see*
 Behavior –
 misunderstanding
Mittens *see* Clothing – gloves
Mockingbirds *see* Birds –
 mockingbirds
Models *see* Careers – models
Moles *see* Animals – moles
Money
Mongooses *see* Animals –
 mongooses
Monitor lizards *see* Reptiles –
 monitor lizards
Monkeys *see* Animals –
 monkeys
Monsters
Months of the year *see* Days
 of the week, months of the
 year
Moon
Moose *see* Animals – moose
Mopeds *see* Motorcycles
Morning
Mosquitoes *see* Insects –
 mosquitoes
Mother Goose *see* Nursery
 rhymes
Mothers *see* Family life –
 mothers
Mother's Day *see* Holidays –
 Mother's Day
Moths *see* Insects – moths
Motorcycles
Mountain climbing *see* Sports
 – mountain climbing
Mouths *see* Anatomy –
 mouths
Moving
Mules *see* Animals – mules
Multi-ethnic *see* Ethnic groups
 in the U.S
Multiple birth children *see*
 Triplets; Twins
Muppets *see* Puppets
Museums
Music
Musical instruments *see* Music
Musicians *see* Careers –
 musicians
Muskrats *see* Animals –
 muskrats
Mysteries *see* Problem solving
Mythical creatures
Mythical creatures –
 mermaids
Mythical creatures – unicorns

Nagging *see* Behavior –
 nagging
Name calling *see* Behavior –
 name calling
Names
Napping *see* Sleep
Native Americans *see* Eskimos;
 Indians of North America;
 Indians of South America
Nature
Needing someone *see*
 Behavior – needing
 someone
Neighborhoods *see*
 Communities,
 neighborhoods
Nepal *see* Foreign lands –
 Nepal
New Guinea *see* Foreign lands
 – New Guinea
New Year's *see* Holidays –
 New Year's
Nicaragua *see* Foreign lands –
 Nicaragua
Nigeria *see* Foreign lands –
 Nigeria
Night
Nightingales *see* Birds –
 nightingales
Nightmares *see* Bedtime;
 Goblins; Monsters; Night;
 Sleep
Noah *see* Religion – Noah
Noise, sounds
Norway *see* Foreign lands –
 Norway
Noses *see* Anatomy – noses;
 Senses – smelling
No text *see* Wordless
Numbers *see* Counting,
 numbers
Nuns *see* Careers – nuns
Nursery rhymes
Nursery school *see* School
Nurses *see* Careers – nurses

Oceans *see* Sea and seashore
Octopuses
Oil
Old age
Olympics *see* Sports –
 Olympics
Only child *see* Family life –
 only child
Opossums *see* Animals –
 possums
Opposites *see* Concepts –
 opposites
Optical illusions
Optimism *see* Character traits
 – optimism
Orphans
Ostracism *see* Character traits
 – being different
Ostriches *see* Birds – ostriches
Otters *see* Animals – otters
Out and in *see* Concepts – in
 and out
Owls *see* Birds – owls
Oxen *see* Animals – oxen

Pack rats *see* Animals – pack rats
Painters *see* Activities – painting; Careers – artists
Painting *see* Activities – painting
Pakistan *see* Foreign lands – Pakistan
Panama *see* Foreign lands – Panama
Pandas *see* Animals – pandas
Panthers *see* Animals – leopards
Pants *see* Clothing – pants
Paper
Parades
Parakeets *see* Birds – parakeets, parrots
Park rangers *see* Careers – park rangers
Parrots *see* Birds – parakeets, parrots
Participation
Parties
Passover *see* Holidays – Passover
Patience *see* Character traits – patience
Peacocks, peahens *see* Birds – peacocks, peahens
Peddlers *see* Careers – peddlers
Pelicans *see* Birds – pelicans
Penguins *see* Birds – penguins
Pen pals
Perseverance *see* Character traits – perseverance
Persia *see* Foreign lands – Persia
Persistence *see* Character traits – persistence
Perspective *see* Concepts – perspective
Peru *see* Foreign lands – Peru
Petroleum *see* Oil
Pets
Philippines *see* Foreign lands – Philippines
Phoenix *see* Mythical creatures
Photography *see* Activities – photographing
Physical handicaps *see* Handicaps – physical
Physicians *see* Careers – doctors
Picnics *see* Activities – picnicking
Pigeons *see* Birds – pigeons
Pigs *see* Animals – pigs
Pilots *see* Careers – airplane pilots
Pirates
Pixies *see* Elves and little people; Fairies
Planes *see* Airplanes, airports
Plants
Playing *see* Activities – playing
Plays *see* Theater
Poetry, rhyme
Poland *see* Foreign lands – Poland

Polar bears *see* Animals – polar bears
Police officers *see* Careers – police officers
Poltergeists *see* Ghosts
Poor *see* Homeless; Poverty
Pop-up books *see* Format, unusual – toy and removable books
Porcupines *see* Animals – porcupines
Porpoise *see* Animals – dolphins
Portugal *see* Foreign lands – Portugal
Possums *see* Animals – possums
Potty training *see* Toilet training
Poverty
Power failure
Practicality *see* Character traits – practicality
Prairie dogs *see* Animals – prairie dogs
Praying mantis *see* Insects – praying mantis
Prejudice
Pride *see* Character traits – pride
Princes *see* Royalty – princes
Princesses *see* Royalty – princesses
Printers *see* Careers – printers
Prisons
Problem solving
Progress
Puerto Rican-Americans *see* Ethnic groups in the U.S. – Hispanic-Americans; Ethnic groups in the U.S. – Puerto Rican-Americans
Puerto Rico *see* Foreign lands – Puerto Rico
Puffins *see* Birds – puffins
Pumas *see* Animals – cougars
Puppets
Purim *see* Holidays – Purim
Puzzles *see* Rebuses; Riddles

Queens *see* Royalty – queens
Questioning *see* Character traits – questioning
Quicksand *see* Sand
Quilts

Rabbits *see* Animals – rabbits
Raccoons *see* Animals – raccoons
Race car drivers *see* Careers – race car drivers
Racing *see* Sports – racing
Railroad engineers *see* Careers – railroad engineers
Railroads *see* Trains
Rain *see* Weather – rain
Rainbows *see* Weather – rainbows
Rangers *see* Careers – park rangers

Rats *see* Animals – rats
Ravens *see* Birds – ravens
Reading *see* Activities – reading
Rebuses
Reindeer *see* Animals – reindeer
Religion
Religion – Noah
Repetitive stories *see* Cumulative tales
Reptiles
Reptiles – alligators, crocodiles
Reptiles – crocodiles *see* Reptiles – alligators, crocodiles
Reptiles – iguanas
Reptiles – lizards
Reptiles – monitor lizards
Reptiles – snakes
Reptiles – turtles, tortoises
Rest *see* Sleep
Rhinoceros *see* Animals – rhinoceros
Rhyming text *see* Poetry, rhyme
Riddles
Right and left *see* Concepts – left and right
Rivers
Roads
Robbers *see* Crime
Robins *see* Birds – robins
Robots
Rockets *see* Space and space ships
Rocking chairs *see* Furniture – chairs
Rocking horses *see* Toys – rocking horses
Rocks
Roller skating *see* Sports – roller skating
Romania *see* Foreign lands – Romania
Roosters *see* Chickens – hens
Rosh Hashanah *see* Holidays – Rosh Hashanah
Royalty
Royalty – emperors
Royalty – kings
Royalty – princes
Royalty – princesses
Royalty – queens
Royalty – sultans
Running *see* Sports – racing
Running away *see* Behavior – running away
Russia *see* Foreign lands – Russia

Sadness *see* Emotions – sadness
Safety
Sahara Desert *see* Foreign lands – Sahara Desert
Sailors *see* Careers – military
Saint Patrick's Day *see* Holidays – St. Patrick's Day

St. Patrick's Day *see* Holidays
– St. Patrick's Day
Salamanders *see* Animals –
salamanders
Sand
Sandcastles *see* Sand
Sandman
Sandpipers *see* Birds –
sandpipers
Saving things *see* Behavior –
saving things
Scarecrows
School
Science
Scotland *see* Foreign lands –
Scotland
Scuba diving *see* Sports – skin
diving
Sea and seashore
Sea gulls *see* Birds – sea gulls
Seahorses *see* Crustacea
Sea lions *see* Animals – sea
lions
Seals *see* Animals – seals
Seamstresses *see* Careers –
seamstresses
Sea serpents *see* Monsters;
Mythical creatures
Seashore *see* Sea and seashore
Seasons
Seasons – autumn *see* Seasons
– fall
Seasons – fall
Seasons – spring
Seasons – summer
Seasons – winter
Secret codes
Secrets *see* Behavior – secrets
Seeds
Seeing *see* Anatomy – eyes;
Handicaps – blindness;
Senses – seeing
Seeking better things *see*
Behavior – seeking better
things
Self-concept
Self-esteem *see* Self-concept
Self-image *see* Self-concept
Selfishness *see* Character traits
– selfishness
Senses
Senses – hearing
Senses – seeing
Senses – smelling
Senses – tasting
Senses – touching
Sewing *see* Activities – sewing
Shadows
Shakespeare
Shape *see* Concepts – shape
Shaped books *see* Format,
unusual
Sharing *see* Behavior –
sharing
Sheep *see* Animals – sheep
Shepherds *see* Careers –
shepherds
Ships *see* Boats, ships
Shirts *see* Clothing – shirts
Shoemakers *see* Careers –
shoemakers
Shopping

Shops *see* Stores
Shows *see* Theater
Shrews *see* Animals – shrews
Shyness *see* Character traits –
shyness
Siam *see* Foreign lands –
Thailand
Sibling rivalry
Sickness *see* Health; Illness
Sight *see* Anatomy – eyes;
Handicaps – blindness;
Senses – seeing
Singing *see* Activities – singing
Sisters *see* Family life; Family
life – sisters; Sibling rivalry
Size *see* Concepts – size
Skating *see* Sports – ice
skating
Skeletons *see* Anatomy –
skeletons
Skiing *see* Sports – skiing
Skin diving *see* Sports – skin
diving
Skunks *see* Animals – skunks
Sky
Sledding *see* Sports – sledding
Sleep
Slight-of-hand *see* Magic
Sloths *see* Animals – sloths
Smallness *see* Character traits
– smallness
Smelling *see* Anatomy – noses;
Senses – smelling
Snails *see* Animals – snails
Snakes *see* Reptiles – snakes
Snow *see* Weather – snow
Snowmen
Snowplows *see* Machines
Soccer *see* Sports – soccer
Society Islands *see* Foreign
lands – South Sea Islands
Socks *see* Clothing – socks
Sofas *see* Furniture – couches,
sofas
Soldiers *see* Careers – military
Soldiers, toy *see* Toys –
soldiers
Solitude *see* Behavior –
solitude
Songs
Sounds *see* Noise, sounds
South Africa *see* Foreign lands
– South Africa
South America *see* Foreign
lands – South America
South Sea Islands *see* Foreign
lands – South Sea Islands
Space and space ships
Spain *see* Foreign lands –
Spain
Sparrows *see* Birds – sparrows
Spectacles *see* Glasses
Speech *see* Language
Speed *see* Concepts – speed
Spelunking *see* Caves
Spiders
Split page books *see* Format,
unusual
Spooks *see* Ghosts; Goblins
Spoonbills *see* Birds –
spoonbills
Sports

Sports – baseball
Sports – basketball
Sports – bicycling
Sports – camping *see* Camps,
camping
Sports – fishing
Sports – football
Sports – gymnastics
Sports – hiking
Sports – hockey
Sports – hunting
Sports – ice skating
Sports – mountain climbing
Sports – Olympics
Sports – racing
Sports – roller skating
Sports – skiing
Sports – skin diving
Sports – sledding
Sports – soccer
Sports – surfing
Sports – swimming
Sports – T-ball
Sports – wrestling
Spring *see* Seasons – spring
Squirrels *see* Animals –
squirrels
Stage *see* Theater
Stars
Stealing *see* Behavior –
stealing
Steamrollers *see* Machines
Steam shovels *see* Machines
Stepchildren *see* Divorce;
Family life – Step families
Step families *see* Divorce;
Family life – step families
Stepparents *see* Divorce;
Family life – step families
Stones *see* Rocks
Storekeepers *see* Careers –
storekeepers
Stores
Storks *see* Birds – storks
Storms *see* Weather – storms
Streams *see* Rivers
Streets *see* Roads
String
Stubbornness *see* Character
traits – stubbornness
Sukkot *see* Holidays – Sukkot
Sullivan Islands *see* Foreign
lands – South Sea Islands
Sultans *see* Royalty – sultans
Summer *see* Seasons –
summer
Sun
Surfing *see* Sports – surfing
Swallows *see* Birds – swallows
Swans *see* Birds – swans
Sweaters *see* Clothing –
sweaters
Sweden *see* Foreign lands –
Sweden
Swimming *see* Sports –
swimming
Swinging *see* Activities –
swinging
Switzerland *see* Foreign lands
– Switzerland

Tables *see* Furniture – tables
Tailors *see* Careers – tailors
Taiwain *see* Foreign lands – Taiwain
Talking to strangers *see* Behavior – talking to strangers
Tapirs *see* Animals – tapirs
Tardiness *see* Behavior – tardiness
Tasting *see* Senses – tasting
Taxi drivers *see* Careers – taxi drivers
Taxis
T-ball *see* Sports – T-ball
Teachers *see* Careers – teachers
Teddy bears *see* Toys – teddy bears
Teeth
Telephone
Telephone operators *see* Careers – telephone operators
Television
Telling time *see* Clocks, watches; Time
Temper tantrums *see* Emotions – anger
Textless *see* Wordless
Thailand *see* Foreign lands – Thailand
Thanksgiving *see* Holidays – Thanksgiving
Theater
Thumbsucking
Thunder *see* Weather – storms; Weather – thunder
Tibet *see* Foreign lands – Tibet
Tigers *see* Animals – tigers
Time
Tin soldiers *see* Toys – soldiers
Toads *see* Frogs and toads
Toes *see* Anatomy – toes
Toilet training
Tongue twisters
Tools
Tortoises *see* Reptiles – turtles, tortoises
Toucans *see* Birds – toucans
Touching *see* Senses – touching
Towns *see* City
Toy and movable books *see* Format, unusual – toy and movable books
Toys
Toys – balloons
Toys – balls
Toys – bears *see* Toys – teddy bears
Toys – blocks
Toys – dolls
Toys – hobby horses *see* Toys – rocking horses
Toys – pandas *see* Toys – teddy bears
Toys – rocking horses
Toys – soldiers
Toys – teddy bears

Toys – tin soldiers *see* Toys – soldiers
Toys – trains
Tractors
Trading *see* Activities – trading
Traffic, traffic signs
Train engineers *see* Careers – railroad engineers
Trains
Trains, toy *see* Toys – trains
Transportation
Traveling *see* Activities – traveling
Trees
Trickery *see* Behavior – trickery
Tricks *see* Magic
Trinidad *see* Foreign lands – Trinidad
Triplets
Trolleys *see* Cable cars, trolleys
Trolls
Truck drivers *see* Careers – truck drivers
Trucks
Turkey *see* Foreign lands – Turkey
Turkeys *see* Birds – turkeys
Turtles *see* Reptiles – turtles, tortoises
TV *see* Television
Twilight
Twins
Tyrol *see* Foreign lands – Tyrol

Ukraine *see* Foreign lands – Ukraine
Umbrellas
Uncles *see* Family life – aunts, uncles
Unhappiness *see* Emotions – happiness; Emotions – sadness
UNICEF
Unicorns *see* Mythical creatures – unicorns
Unnoticed *see* Behavior – unnoticed, unseen
Unseen *see* Behavior – unnoticed, unseen
Unusual format *see* Format, unusual
Up and down *see* Concepts – up and down
U.S. history

Vacationing *see* Activities – vacationing
Vacuum cleaners *see* Machines
Valentine's Day *see* Holidays – Valentine's Day
Values
Vampires *see* Monsters
Vanity *see* Character traits – vanity
Vatican City *see* Foreign lands – Vatican City

Venezuela *see* Foreign lands – Venezuela
Veterinarians *see* Careers – veterinarians
Vietnam *see* Foreign lands – Vietnam
Vietnamese-Americans *see* Ethnic groups in the U.S. – Asian-Americans; Ethnic groups in the U.S. – Vietnamese-Americans
Violence, anti-violence
Volcanoes
Vultures *see* Birds – vultures

Waiters *see* Careers – waiters, waitresses
Waitresses *see* Careers – waiters, waitresses
Walking *see* Activities – walking
Walruses *see* Animals – walruses
War
Warthogs *see* Animals – warthogs
Washington's Birthday *see* Holidays – Washington's Birthday
Wasps *see* Insects – wasps
Watches *see* Clocks, watches
Water
Water buffaloes *see* Animals – water buffaloes
Weapons
Weasels *see* Animals – weasels
Weather
Weather – clouds
Weather – cold
Weather – droughts
Weather – floods
Weather – fog
Weather – mist *see* Weather – fog
Weather – rain
Weather – rainbows
Weather – snow
Weather – storms
Weather – thunder
Weather – wind
Weaving *see* Activities – weaving
Weddings
Weekdays *see* Days of the week, months of the year
Weight *see* Concepts – weight
Welders *see* Careers – welders
Werewolves *see* Monsters
Whales *see* Animals – whales
Wheels
Whistling *see* Activities – whistling
Wildebeests *see* Animals – wildebeests
Willfulness *see* Character traits – willfulness
Wind *see* Weather – wind
Windmills
Window cleaners *see* Careers – window cleaners
Winter *see* Seasons – winter

Wishing *see* Behavior – wishing
Witches
Wizards
Wolves *see* Animals – wolves
Wombats *see* Animals – wombats
Woodchucks *see* Animals – groundhogs
Woodpeckers *see* Birds – woodpeckers
Woods *see* Forest, woods
Word games *see* Language
Wordless
Words *see* Language

Working *see* Activities – working
World
Worms *see* Animals – worms
Worrying *see* Behavior – worrying
Wrecking machines *see* Machines
Wrens *see* Birds – wrens
Wrestling *see* Sports – wrestling
Writers *see* Careers – writers
Writing *see* Activities – writing
Writing letters *see* Letters

Yaks *see* Animals – yaks
Yom Kippur *see* Holidays – Yom Kippur

Zaire *see* Foreign lands – Zaire
Zanzibar *see* Foreign lands – Zanzibar
Zebras *see* Animals – zebras
Zodiac
Zookeepers *see* Careers – zookeepers
Zoos

Subject Guide

This is a subject-arranged guide to picture books. Under appropriate subject headings and subheadings, titles appear alphabetically by author name, or by title when author is unknown. Complete bibliographic information for each title cited will be found in the Bibliographic Guide.

Aardvarks *see* Animals – aardvarks

ABC books

A is for alphabet, ill. by George Suyeoka
ABCDEF..., ill. by Robert Tallon
Abrons, Mary. *For Alice a palace*
Ackerman, Karen. *Flannery Row*
Alda, Arlene. *Arlene Alda's ABC*
Alexander, Anne (Anna Barbara Cooke).
   ABC of cars and trucks
Allington, Richard L. *Letters*
Anglund, Joan Walsh. *A is for always*
Anno, Mitsumasa. *Anno's alphabet*
   Anno's magical ABC
Argent, Kerry. *Animal capers*
Arnosky, Jim. *Mouse numbers and letters*
   Mouse writing
Asch, Frank. *Little Devil's ABC*
Ashton, Elizabeth Allen. *An old-fashioned ABC book*
Aylesworth, Jim. *The folks in the valley*
   Old Black Fly
Azarian, Mary. *A farmer's alphabet*
Babson, Jane F. *Babson's bestiary*
Balian, Lorna. *Humbug potion*
Barry, Katharina. *A is for anything*
Barry, Robert E. *Animals around the world*
Base, Graeme. *Animalia*
Baskin, Leonard. *Hosie's alphabet*
Bayer, Jane. *A my name is Alice*
Beller, Janet. *A-B-C-ing*
Berenstain, Stan. *The Berenstains' B book*
Berger, Terry. *Ben's ABC day*
Bishop, Ann. *Riddle-iculous rid-alphabet book*
Black, Floyd. *Alphabet cat*
Blake, Quentin. *Quentin Blake's ABC*
Bond, Jean Carey. *A is for Africa*

Bond, Michael. *Paddington's ABC*
Bove, Linda. *Sign language ABC with Linda Bove*
Bowen, Betsy. *Antler, bear, canoe*
Boxer, Deborah. *26 ways to be somebody else*
Boynton, Sandra. *A is for angry*
Bridwell, Norman. *Clifford's ABC*
Brown, Judith Gwyn. *Alphabet dreams*
Brown, Marcia. *All butterflies*
   Peter Piper's alphabet
Brown, Margaret Wise. *Sleepy ABC*
Brown, Ruth. *Alphabet times four*
Bruna, Dick. *B is for bear*
Brunhoff, Laurent de. *Babar's ABC*
Budd, Lillian. *The pie wagon*
Budney, Blossom. *N is for nursery school*
Burningham, John. *John Burningham's ABC*
Burton, Marilee Robin. *Aaron awoke*
Chaplin, Susan Gibbons. *I can sign my ABCs*
Chardiet, Bernice. *C is for circus*
Charles, Donald. *Shaggy dog's animal alphabet*
Charlip, Remy. *Handtalk*
Chase, Catherine. *An alphabet book*
   Baby mouse learns his ABC's
Chess, Victoria. *Alfred's alphabet walk*
A child's picture English-Hebrew dictionary
Chouinard, Roger. *The amazing animal alphabet book*
Chwast, Seymour. *Alphabet parade*
   Still another alphabet book
Cleary, Beverly. *The hullabaloo ABC*
Cleaver, Elizabeth. *ABC*
Cohen, Peter Zachary. *Authorized autumn charts of the Upper Red Canoe River country*
Coletta, Irene. *From A to Z*
Conran, Sebastian. *My first ABC book*
Cooney, Barbara. *A garland of games and other diversions*
Cox, Lynn. *Crazy alphabet*
Cremins, Robert. *My animal ABC*
Crews, Donald. *We read: A to Z*
Crowther, Robert. *The most amazing hide-and-seek alphabet book*

Dauphin, Francine Legrand. *A French A. B. C.*

DeLage, Ida. *ABC Easter bunny*
ABC triplets at the zoo

Delaunay, Sonia. *Sonia Delaunay's alphabet*

De Mejo, Oscar. *Oscar de Mejo's ABC*

Demi. *Demi's find the animals A B C*

Domanska, Janina. *A was an angler*

Doolittle, Eileen. *The ark in the attic*

Doubilet, Anne. *Under the sea from A to Z*

Downie, Jill. *Alphabet puzzle*

Dragonwagon, Crescent. *Alligator arrived with apples*

Dreamer, Sue. *Circus ABC*

Drucker, Malka. *A Jewish holiday ABC*

Duke, Kate. *The guinea pig ABC*

Duvoisin, Roger Antoine. *A for the ark*

Edwards, Michelle. *Alef-bet*

Eichenberg, Fritz. *Ape in cape*

Elliot, David. *An alphabet of rotten kids!*

Elting, Mary. *Q is for duck*

Emberley, Ed (Edward Randolph). *Ed Emberley's ABC*

Falls, C. B. (Charles Buckles). *ABC book*

Farber, Norma. *As I was crossing Boston Common*

Feelings, Muriel. *Jambo means hello*

Feldman, Judy. *The alphabet in nature*

Fife, Dale. *Adam's ABC*

Floyd, Lucy. *Agatha's alphabet, with her very own dictionary*

Freeman, Don. *Add-a-line alphabet*

Fujikawa, Gyo. *Gyo Fujikawa's A to Z picture book*

Gág, Wanda. *ABC bunny*

Gantz, David. *The genie bear with the light brown hair word book*

Gardner, Beau. *Have you ever seen...?*

Garten, Jan. *The alphabet tale*

Geraghty, Paul. *The cow is mooing anyhow*

Greenaway, Kate. *A apple pie*

Gretz, Susanna. *Teddy bears ABC*

Groening, Matt. *Maggie Simpson's alphabet book*

Grossbart, Francine. *A big city*

Gundersheimer, Karen. *A B C say with me*

Gunning, Monica. *The two Georges*

Hague, Kathleen. *Alphabears*

Harada, Joyce. *It's the ABC book*

Harrison, Ted. *A northern alphabet*

Hawkins, Colin. *Busy ABC*

Hepworth, Cathi. *ANTicks! an alphabetical anthology*

Hillman, Priscilla. *A Merry-Mouse Christmas A B C*

Hoban, Tana. *A B See!*
26 letters and 99 cents

Hoberman, Mary Ann. *Nuts to you and nuts to me*

Hoguet, Susan Ramsay. *I unpacked my grandmother's trunk*

Holabird, Katharine. *The little mouse ABC*

Holl, Adelaide. *The ABC of cars, trucks and machines*

Hooper, Patricia. *A bundle of beasts*

Howard-Gibbon, Amelia Frances. *An illustrated comic alphabet*

Hughes, Shirley. *Lucy and Tom's A.B.C.*

Hyman, Trina Schart. *A little alphabet*

Ilsley, Velma. *A busy day for Chris*
M is for moving

Ipcar, Dahlov. *I love my anteater with an A*

Isadora, Rachel. *City seen from A to Z*

Jefferds, Vincent. *Disney's elegant ABC book*

Jewell, Nancy. *ABC cat*

Johnson, Crockett. *Harold's ABC*

Johnson, Jean. *Teachers A to Z*

Johnson, Odette. *Apples, alligators, and also alphabets*

Jonas, Ann. *Aardvarks, disembark!*

Kellogg, Steven (Stephen). *Aster Aardvark's alphabet adventures*

Kightley, Rosalinda. *ABC*

Kitamura, Satoshi. *From acorn to zoo and everything in between in alphabetical order What's inside?*

Kitchen, Bert. *Animal alphabet*

Kuskin, Karla. *ABCDEFGHIJKLMNOPQRSTUVWXYZ*

Lalicki, Barbara. *If there were dreams to sell*

Lalli, Judy. *Feelings alphabet*

Leander, Ed. *Q is for crazy*

Lear, Edward. *A was once an apple pie*, ill. by Julie Lacome
ABC
An Edward Lear alphabet, ill. by Carol Newsom
Edward Lear's ABC, ill. by Carol Pike
Nonsense alphabets, ill. by Richard Scarry

Lecourt, Nancy. *Abracadabra to zigzag*

Lillie, Patricia. *One very, very quiet afternoon*

Linscott, Jody. *Once upon A to Z*

Lionni, Leo. *Letters to talk about*

A little ABC book

Little, Mary E. *ABC for the library*

Lobel, Anita. *Alison's zinnia*

Lobel, Arnold. *On Market Street*

Low, Joseph. *Adam's book of odd creatures*

Lyon, George-Ella. *A B Cedar*

MacDonald, Suse. *Alphabatics*

McGinley, Phyllis. *All around the town*

McKissack, Patricia C. *Big bug book of the alphabet*
My Bible ABC book

McMillan, Bruce. *The alphabet symphony*

McPhail, David. *Animals A to Z*

Magee, Doug. *All aboard ABC*

Manson, Beverlie. *The fairies' alphabet book*

Margalit, Avishai. *The Hebrew alphabet book*

Mayer, Marianna. *The Brambleberrys animal alphabet*

Mayer, Mercer. *Little Monster's alphabet book*

Mayers, Florence Cassen. *Egyptian art from the Brooklyn Museum: ABC*
The Museum of Fine Arts, Boston: ABC
The Museum of Modern Art, New York: ABC
The National Air and Space Museum: ABC
Mendoza, George. *The alphabet boat*
Alphabet sheep
Norman Rockwell's American ABC
Merriam, Eve. *Good night to Annie*
Goodnight to Annie
Halloween ABC
Where is everybody?
Miles, Miska. *Apricot ABC*
Miller, Edna. *Mousekin's ABC*
Miller, Jane. *Farm alphabet book*
Milne, A. A. (Alan Alexander). *Pooh's alphabet book*
Moak, Allan. *A big city ABC*
Montresor, Beni. *A for angel*
Morice, Dave. *A visit from St. Alphabet*
Morse, Samuel French. *All in a suitcase*
Moss, Jeffrey. *The Sesame Street ABC storybook*
Mother Goose. *ABC rhymes*, ill. by Lulu Delarce
In a pumpkin shell, ill. by Joan Walsh Anglund
Munari, Bruno. *ABC*
Musgrove, Margaret. *Ashanti to Zulu*
Neumeier, Marty. *Action alphabet*
Newberry, Clare Turlay. *The kittens' ABC*
Niland, Deborah. *ABC of monsters*
Obligado, Lilian. *Faint frogs feeling feverish and other terrifically tantalizing tongue twisters*
Ogle, Lucille. *A B See*
Oliver, Dexter. *I want to be...*
O'Shell, Marcia. *Alphabet Annie announces an all-American album*
Owens, Mary Beth. *A caribou alphabet*
Oxenbury, Helen. *Helen Oxenbury's ABC of things*
Peaceable kingdom, ill. by Alice and Martin Provensen
Pearson, Tracey Campbell. *A apple pie*
Pelham, David. *A is for animals*
Peppé, Rodney. *The alphabet book*
Petersham, Maud. *An American ABC*
Phillips, Tamara. *Day care ABC*
Piatti, Celestino. *Celestino Piatti's animal ABC*
Piers, Helen. *Puppy's ABC*
Pittman, Helena Clare. *Miss Hindy's cats*
Potter, Beatrix. *Peter Rabbit's ABC*
Reeves, James. *Ragged Robin: poems from A to Z*
Rey, H. A. (Hans Augusto). *Curious George learns the alphabet*
Look for the letters

Rice, James. *Cajun alphabet*
Roe, Richard. *Animal ABC*
Rojankovsky, Feodor. *ABC, an alphabet of many things*
Animals in the zoo
Rosario, Idalia. *Idalia's project ABC*
Ruben, Patricia. *Apples to zippers*
Rubin, Cynthia Elyce. *ABC Americana from the National Gallery of Art*
Ryden, Hope. *Wild animals of Africa ABC*
Samton, Sheila White. *Amazing Aunt Agatha*
Scarry, Richard. *Richard Scarry's ABC word book*
The Sea World alphabet book
Sendak, Maurice. *Alligators all around*
The Sesame Street book of letters
Seuss, Dr. *Dr. Seuss's ABC*
Hooper Humperdink...? Not him!
Shelby, Anne. *Potluck*
Shuttlesworth, Dorothy E. *ABC of buses*
Silverman, Maida. *Bunny's ABC*
Simpson, Gretchen Dow. *Gretchen's ABC*
Sloat, Teri. *From letter to letter*
Smith, William Jay. *Puptents and pebbles*
Snow, Alan. *The monster book of ABC sounds*
Steiner, Charlotte. *Charlotte Steiner's ABC*
Stevenson, James. *Grandpa's great city tour*
Stock, Catherine. *Alexander's midnight snack*
Thornhill, Jan. *Wildlife ABC*
Tryon, Leslie. *Albert's alphabet*
Van Allsburg, Chris. *The Z was zapped*
Waber, Bernard. *An anteater named Arthur*
Walters, Marguerite. *The city-country ABC*
Watson, Clyde. *Applebet*
Watson, Nancy Dingman. *What does A begin with?*
Wild, Robin. *The bears' ABC book*
Williams, Garth. *The big golden animal ABC*
Wilner, Isabel. *A garden alphabet*
Wilson, Barbara Ker. *ABC et/and 123*
Wolf, Janet. *Adelaide to Zeke*
Yolen, Jane. *All in the woodland early*
Elfabet

Accordion books *see* Format, unusual

Activities

Accorsi, William. *Short short short stories*
Alderson, Sue Ann. *Bonnie McSmithers is at it again!*
Aliki. *Overnight at Mary Bloom's*
Allington, Richard L. *Feelings*
Hearing
Looking
Smelling
Tasting
Touching
Andre, Evelyn M. *Places I like to be*
Anno, Mitsumasa. *All in a day*
Arnold, Caroline. *How do we have fun?*

Azarian, Mary. *A farmer's alphabet*
Baird, Anne. *The guppies of Hilly Dale House*
Behrens, June. *Can you walk the plank?*
Beller, Janet. *A-B-C-ing*
Beni, Ruth. *Sir Baldergog the great*
Benjamin, Alan. *Busy bunnies*
Bennett, Jill. *Days are where we live and other poems*
Boyd, Lizi. *The not-so-wicked stepmother*
Brandenberg, Franz. *Otto is different*
Brann, Esther. *A book for baby*
Brown, Elinor. *The little story book*
Brown, Margaret Wise. *The little fur family*
Brown, Ruth. *Our cat Flossie*
Bryant, Dean. *Here am I*
Bulla, Clyde Robert. *Daniel's duck*
Burdekin, Harold. *A child's grace*
Burningham, John. *Skip trip*
  Sniff shout
  Wobble pop
Calmenson, Stephanie. *The kindergarten book*
Carlson, Nancy. *Bunnies and their hobbies*
Cartlidge, Michelle. *The bear's bazaar*
  A mouse's diary
Carton, Lonnie Caming. *Mommies*
Cauley, Lorinda Bryan. *Clap your hands*
Chernoff, Goldie Taub. *Clay-dough, play-dough*
  Just a box?
  Pebbles and pods
  Puppet party
Creighton, Jill. *One day there was nothing to do*
Crume, Marion W. *Let me see you try*
  Listen!
  What do you say?
Dahl, Tessa. *The same but different*
Davies, Kay. *My balloon*
  My mirror
Delton, Judy. *I'm telling you now*
Denslow, Sharon Phillips. *Night owls*
Dinosaurs and monsters, ill. by Louise Nevett
Dodds, Siobhan. *Words and pictures*
Dunn, Phoebe. *Busy, busy toddlers*
Ehrlich, Amy. *Bunnies all day long*
Ernst, Lisa Campbell. *Sam Johnson and the blue ribbon quilt*
Erskine, Jim. *Bert and Susie's messy tale*
Facklam, Margery. *So can I*
Fair, Sylvia. *The bedspread*
Faunce-Brown, Daphne. *Snuffles' house*
Flournoy, Valerie. *The best time of day*
Foord, Jo. *The book of babies*
Freeman, Don. *The day is waiting*
Fujikawa, Gyo. *My favorite thing*
  Surprise! Surprise!
Gibbons, Gail. *The missing maple syrup sap mystery*

Gipson, Morrell. *Hello, Peter*
Goennel, Heidi. *My day*
  Sometimes I like to be alone
Gomi, Taro. *My friends*
  Seeing, saying, doing, playing
Goor, Ron. *In the driver's seat*
Gore, Sheila. *My shadow*
Hallinan, P. K. (Patrick K.). *I'm glad to be me*
  Just being alone
Hawkins, Colin. *Busy ABC*
Henley, Claire. *At the zoo*
Holzenthaler, Jean. *My feet do*
  My hands can
Hughes, Shirley. *Bouncing*
Hynard, Julia. *Percival's party*
Hynard, Stephen. *Snowy the rabbit*
Isadora, Rachel. *Babies*
  Friends
Jabar, Cynthia. *Bored blue? Think what you can do!*
Jennings, Sharon. *When Jeremiah found Mrs. Ming*
Jensen, Helen Zane. *When Panda came to our house*
Jonas, Ann. *When you were a baby*
Kaufman, Curt. *Hotel boy*
Kelley, True. *Look, baby! Listen, baby! Do, baby!*
Kilroy, Sally. *Busy babies*
Krementz, Jill. *Katherine goes to nursery school*
Kunhardt, Edith. *Which one would you choose?*
  Which pig would you choose?
Kunnas, Mauri. *The nighttime book*
Lawson, Carol. *Teddy bear, teddy bear*
Leedy, Loreen. *A dragon Christmas*
Lester, Alison. *Clive eats alligators*
  Tessa snaps snakes
Le-Tan, Pierre. *The afternoon cat*
Lilly, Kenneth. *Animal builders*
  Animal climbers
  Animal jumpers
  Animal runners
  Animal swimmers
Lionni, Leo. *Let's make rabbits*
McDonald, Amy. *Let's do it*
  Let's try
McKié, Roy. *Snow*
McMillan, Bruce. *Step by step*
McNaughton, Colin. *Autumn*
  Winter
Maestro, Betsy. *Busy day*
Mainwaring, Jane. *My feather*
Mangin, Marie-France. *Suzette and Nicholas and the seasons clock*
  Masks and puppets
Mazer, Anne. *Watch me*
Milios, Rita. *Yo soy - I am*
Miller, Margaret. *Every day*

Moncure, Jane Belk. *Now I am five!*
Now I am four!
Now I am three!
Motyka, Sally Mitchell. *An ordinary day*
Myers, Arthur. *Kids do amazing things*
Nelson, Brenda. *Mud fore sale*
Neumeier, Marty. *Action alphabet*
Noble, Trinka Hakes. *The day Jimmy's boa
ate the wash*
Noll, Sally. *Jiggle wiggle prance*
O'Brien, Anne Sibley. *Come play with us*
Oxenbury, Helen. *I can*
Tom and Pippo's day
Parish, Peggy. *I can - can you?*
Pelham, David. *Worms wiggle*
Peyo. *What do smurfs do all day?*
Pirotta, Saviour. *Little bird*
Pitcher, Caroline. *Animals*
Cars and boats
Pizer, Abigail. *Harry's night out*
Pluckrose, Henry Arthur. *Join it!*
Pomerantz, Charlotte. *Serena Katz*
Rice, Eve. *Aren't you coming too?*
Rockwell, Anne F. *In our house*
Rockwell, Harlow. *I did it*
Look at this
Ross, H. L. *Not counting monsters*
Ross, Tony. *Treasure of Cozy Cove*
Rubel, Nicole. *Me and my kitty*
Rukeyser, Muriel. *More night*
Sage, Chris. *That's mine, that's yours*
Samuels, Barbara. *Duncan and Dolores*
Simon, Norma. *I'm busy, too*
What do I do?
Stevenson, James. *Rolling Rose*
Stickland, Paul. *A child's book of things*
Stock, Catherine. *Halloween monster*
Tafuri, Nancy. *Do not disturb*
Takeshita, Fumiko. *The park bench*
Thompson, Carol. *Baby days*
Thomson, Ruth. *My bear: I can...can you?*
Thorne, Jenny. *My uncle*
Türk, Hanne. *The rope skips Max*
Van Laan, Nancy. *People, people, everywhere*
Vasiliu, Mircea. *What's happening?*
Voake, Charlotte. *First things first*
Weiss, Nicki. *On a hot, hot day*
Wellington, Monica. *All my little ducklings*
What we do, ill. by Roser Capdevila
Winn, Chris. *Archie's acrobats*
Helping
Winteringham, Victoria. *Penguin day*
Wood, Audrey. *King Bidgood's in the bathtub*
Yolen, Jane. *Elfabet*
Zalben, Jane Breskin. *Oliver and Alison's
week*
Ziefert, Harriet. *Baby Ben's busy book*
Baby Ben's noisy book
Bear's busy morning
Piggety Pig from morn 'til night

Activities – baby-sitting

Abel, Ruth. *The new sitter*
Anderson, Peggy Perry. *Time for bed, the
babysitter said*
Berenstain, Stan. *The Berenstain bears and
the sitter*
Berman, Linda. *The goodbye painting*
Blaustein, Muriel. *Baby Mabu and Auntie
Moose*
Brown, Marc Tolon. *Arthur babysits*
Carlson, Natalie Savage. *Marie Louise's
heyday*
Carrick, Carol. *The climb*
Cazet, Denys. *Big shoe, little shoe*
Chalmers, Mary. *Be good, Harry*
Christelow, Eileen. *Jerome the babysitter*
Cole, William. *What's good for a three-year-
old?*
Crowley, Arthur. *Bonzo Beaver*
Finfer, Celentha. *Grandmother dear*
Gordon, Margaret. *Frogs' holiday*
Greenberg, Barbara. *The bravest babysitter*
Gretz, Susanna. *Roger takes charge!*
Harris, Robie H. *Don't forget to come back*
Hellard, Susan. *Eleanor and the babysitter*
Hindley, Judy. *Mrs. Mary Malarky's seven
cats*
Hines, Anna Grossnickle. *Grandma gets
grumpy*
Hughes, Shirley. *An evening at Alfie's*
George the babysitter
Hurd, Edith Thacher. *Hurry, hurry!*
Stop, stop
Impey, Rose. *Joe's café*
Johnson, Dolores. *What kind of baby-sitter is
this?*
Joyce, William. *George shrinks*
Keller, Holly. *What Alvin wanted*
Lawson, Annetta. *The lucky yak*
Loomis, Christine. *My new baby-sitter*
McCully, Emily Arnold. *The grandma mix-
up*
Martin, C. L. G. *The dragon nanny*
Miranda, Anne. *Baby-sit*
Moore, Lilian. *Little Raccoon and no trouble
at all*
Mueller, Virginia. *Monster and the baby*
Newberry, Clare Turlay. *T-Bone, the baby-
sitter*
Nilsson, Ulf. *Little sister rabbit*
Paterson, Bettina. *Bun and Mrs. Tubby*
Puner, Helen Walker. *The sitter who didn't
sit*
Quackenbush, Robert M. *Henry babysits*
Rayner, Mary. *Mr. and Mrs. Pig's evening
out*
Richardson, Jean. *Thomas's sitter*
Rubel, Nicole. *Uncle Henry and Aunt
Henrietta's honeymoon*
Schick, Eleanor. *Peter and Mr. Brandon*
Sendak, Maurice. *Outside over there*

Steel, Danielle. *Max and the baby sitter*
Tsutsui, Yoriko. *Anna in charge*
Van den Honert, Dorry. *Demi the baby sitter*
Viorst, Judith. *The good-bye book*
Waggoner, Karen. *The lemonade babysitter*
Wahl, Jan. *Peter and the troll baby*
Watson, Jane Werner. *My friend the babysitter*
Watson, Pauline. *Curley Cat baby-sits*
Wells, Rosemary. *Max's dragon shirt*
 Shy Charles
 Stanley and Rhoda
Williams, Barbara. *Jeremy isn't hungry*
Winthrop, Elizabeth. *Bear and Mrs. Duck*
 Bear's Christmas surprise
Yolen, Jane. *Baby Bear's bedtime book*
Young, Ruth. *My baby-sitter*
Zweifel, Frances. *Animal baby-sitters*

Activities – ballooning

Adams, Adrienne. *The great Valentine's Day balloon race*
Calhoun, Mary. *Hot-air Henry*
Coerr, Eleanor. *The big balloon race*
Delacre, Lulu. *Nathan's balloon adventure*
Gibbons, Gail. *Flying*
Goffe, Toni. *Toby's animal rescue service*
Hayes, Sarah. *The grumpalump*
Johnson, Neil. *Fire and silk*
Peppé, Rodney. *The mice and the flying basket*
Quin-Harkin, Janet. *Benjamin's balloon*
Wade, Alan. *I'm flying!*
Wegen, Ron. *The balloon trip*
Wildsmith, Brian. *Bear's adventure*

Activities – bathing

Alborough, Jez. *Bare bear*
Allen, Pamela. *Mr. Archimedes' bath*
Ambrus, Victor G. *The Sultan's bath*
Anderson, Lena Castell. *Bunny bath*
Aulaire, Ingri Mortenson d'. *Children of the northlights*
Bethell, Jean. *Bathtime*
Blocksma, Mary. *Rub-a-dub-dub*
Burningham, John. *Time to get out of the bath, Shirley*
Buxbaum, Susan Kovacs. *Splash!*
Conrad, Pam. *The tub people*
Dickens, Lucy. *Dirty Henry*
Edwards, Frank B. *Mortimer Mooner stopped taking a bath*
Faulkner, Matt. *The amazing voyage of Jackie Grace*
Hall, Derek. *Elephant bathes*
Hazen, Barbara Shook. *The me I see*
Hedderwick, Mairi. *Katie Morag and the two grandmothers*
Henkes, Kevin. *Clean enough*
Hughes, Shirley. *Bathwater's hot*

Jackson, Ellen B. *The bear in the bathtub*
Kudrna, C. Imbior. *To bathe a boa*
Lindbloom, Steven. *Let's give kitty a bath!*
Lindgren, Barbro. *Sam's bath*
McLeod, Emilie Warren. *One snail and me*
McPhail, David. *Andrew's bath*
Manushkin, Fran. *Bubblebath!*
Paterson, Diane. *The bathtub ocean*
Pryor, Ainslie. *The baby blue cat and the dirty dog brothers*
Reavin, Sam. *Hurray for Captain Jane!*
Roffey, Maureen. *Bathtime*
Shott, Stephen. *Bathtime*
Slate, Joseph. *The mean, clean, giant canoe machine*
Stevens, Kathleen. *The beast in the bathtub*
Sutherland, Harry A. *Dad's car wash*
Thompson, Richard. *Effie's bath*
Varekamp, Marjolein. *Little Sam takes a bath*
Wabbes, Marie. *Rose's bath*
Watanabe, Shigeo. *I can take a bath!*
Wells, Rosemary. *Max's bath*
Willis, Jeanne. *The tale of Georgie Grub*
Wilson, Sarah. *Uncle Albert's flying birthday*
Wood, Audrey. *King Bidgood's in the bathtub*
Woodruff, Elvira. *Tubtime*
Yolen, Jane. *No bath tonight*
Ziefert, Harriet. *Harry takes a bath*
Zion, Gene. *Harry, the dirty dog*

Activities – cooking

Abolafia, Yossi. *A fish for Mrs. Gardenia*
Bastin, Marjolein. *Vera in the kitchen*
Blundell, Tony. *Beware of boys*
Brown, Marcia. *Skipper John's cook*
Brunhoff, Laurent de. *Babar learns to cook*
Cauley, Lorinda Bryan. *The bake-off*
 Pease porridge hot
Cunliffe, John. *The king's birthday cake*
Da Rif, Andrea. *The blueberry cake that little fox baked*
Darling, Abigail. *Teddy bears' picnic cookbook*
De Paola, Tomie (Thomas Anthony). *Pancakes for breakfast*
 The popcorn book
 Things to make and do for Valentine's Day
De Regniers, Beatrice Schenk. *Sam and the impossible thing*
Devlin, Wende. *Old Black Witch*
 Old Witch and the polka-dot ribbon
 Old Witch rescues Halloween
Douglass, Barbara. *The chocolate chip cookie contest*
Dragonwagon, Crescent. *This is the bread I baked for Ned*
Feder, Harriet K. *What can you do with a bagel?*
Gibbons, Gail. *The too-great bread bake book*
Goldin, Barbara Diamond. *Cakes and miracles*

Greenberg, Melanie Hope. *My father's luncheonette*
Gretz, Susanna. *Teddybears cookbook*
Heath, Amy. *Sofie's role*
Hoban, Lillian. *Arthur's Christmas cookies*
Kahl, Virginia. *The Duchess bakes a cake*
Krasilovsky, Phyllis. *The man who entered a contest*
Lasker, Joe. *Lentil soup*
Latimer, Jim. *James Bear's pie*
Lemerise, Bruce. *Sheldon's lunch*
Levitin, Sonia. *Nobody stole the pie*
Lindman, Maj. *Flicka, Ricka, Dicka bake a cake*
Lindsey, Treska. *When Batistine made bread*
Long, Earlene. *Johnny's egg*
MacDonald, Elizabeth. *Miss Poppy and the honey cake*
Mr. Badger's birthday pie
Mayer, Marianna. *Marcel the pastry chef*
Miller, Alice P. *The mouse family's blueberry pie*
Nixon, Joan Lowery. *Beats me, Claude*
Parker, Nancy Winslow. *Love from Aunt Betty*
Patron, Susan. *Burgoo stew*
Petie, Haris. *The seed the squirrel dropped*
Rice, Eve. *Benny bakes a cake*
Rockwell, Anne F. *The Mother Goose cookie-candy book*
Schwalje, Marjory. *Mr. Angelo*
Shecter, Ben. *The big stew*
Spohn, Kate. *Ruth's bake shop*
Swendson, Patsy. *The potluck adventures of Mrs. Marmalade*
Tomchek, Ann Heinrichs. *I can be a chef*
Tornborg, Pat. *The Sesame Street cookbook*
Ungerer, Tomi. *Zeralda's ogre*
Wagner, Karen. *Chocolate chip cookies*
Wallis, Diz. *Pip's adventure*
Willard, Nancy. *The high rise glorious skittle skat roarious sky pie angel food cake*
Wilson-Kelly, Becky. *Mother Grumpy's dog biscuits*
Yee, Paul. *Roses sing on new snow*
Young, Miriam Burt. *The sugar mouse cake*

Activities – dancing

Ackerman, Karen. *Song and dance man*
Allen, Pamela. *Bertie and the bear*
Ambrus, Victor G. *The seven skinny goats*
Ancona, George. *Dancing is*
Andersen, H. C. (Hans Christian). *The red shoes*, ill. by Chihiro Iwasaki
Asch, Frank. *Moongame*
Babbitt, Natalie. *Nellie, a cat on her own*
Bell, Anthea. *Swan Lake*
Bianco, Margery Williams. *The hurdy-gurdy man*
Blocksma, Mary. *The best dressed bear*
Bornstein, Ruth Lercher. *The dancing man*

Bottner, Barbara. *Messy Myra*
Brighton, Catherine. *Nijinsky*
Charlot, Martin. *Felisa and the magic tikling bird*
Chevance, Audrey. *Tutu*
Childress, Mark. *Joshua and Bigtooth*
Cox, David. *Ayu and the perfect moon*
Craig, Janet. *Ballet dancer*
De Paola, Tomie (Thomas Anthony). *Oliver Button is a sissy*
Edelman, Elaine. *Boom-de-boom*
Eversole, Robyn Harbert. *The magic house*
Fern, Eugene. *Pepito's story*
French, Vivian. *One ballerina two*
Gauch, Patricia Lee. *Bravo, Tanya*
Dance, Tanya
Geringer, Laura. *Molly's new washing machine*
Getz, Arthur. *Humphrey, the dancing pig*
Goble, Paul. *Star boy*
Grimm, Jacob. *The twelve dancing princesses*, ill. by Kinuko Y. Craft
The twelve dancing princesses, ill. by Anne Dalton
The twelve dancing princesses, ill. by Dennis Hockerman
The twelve dancing princesses, ill. by Errol Le Cain
The twelve dancing princesses, ill. by Gerald McDermott
The twelve dancing princesses, ill. by Uri Shulevitz
Hoban, Russell. *Charlie Meadows*
The dancing tigers
Hoffmann, E. T. A. *The nutcracker*, ill. by Francesca Crespi
The nutcracker, ill. by Rachel Isadora
The nutcracker, ill. by Maurice Sendak
Holabird, Katharine. *Angelina and the princess*
Angelina ballerina
Angelina on stage
Hurd, Edith Thacher. *I dance in my red pajamas*
Isadora, Rachel. *Max*
My ballet class
Opening night
Jabar, Cynthia. *Shimmy shake earthquake*
Jennings, Linda M. *Coppelia*
Crispin and the dancing piglet
The sleeping beauty: the story of the ballet
Kingsland, Robin. *Bus stop bop*
Kuklin, Susan. *Going to my ballet class*
Lee, Jeanne M. *Silent lotus*
McKissack, Patricia C. *Mirandy and brother wind*
Maiorano, Robert. *A little interlude*
Marshall, James. *The Cut-Ups carry on*
George and Martha encore

Martin, Bill (William Ivan). *Barn dance!*
Mathers, Petra. *Sophie and Lou*
Mayer, Mercer. *The queen always wanted to dance*
Medearis, Angela Shelf. *Dancing with the Indians*
Medina, Nina. *Have you ever noticed that rabbits don't sing?*
Nelson, Esther L. *Holiday singing and dancing games*
Oxenbury, Helen. *The dancing class*
Paxton, Tom. *Engelbert the elephant*
Quin-Harkin, Janet. *Peter Penny's dance*
Richardson, Jean. *Clara's dancing feet*
   The sleeping beauty: the story of Tchaikovsky's ballet
Riddell, Chris. *The bear dance*
Scheffrin-Falk, Gladys. *Another celebrated dancing bear*
Schertle, Alice. *Bill and the google-eyed goblins*
Schick, Eleanor. *I have another language: the language is dance*
Schroeder, Alan. *Ragtime Tumpie*
Shannon, George. *Dancing the breeze*
Simon, Carly. *Amy the dancing bear*
Sorine, Stephanie Riva. *Our ballet class*
Stapler, Sarah. *Cordellia, dance!*
Sutton, Jane. *What should a hippo wear?*
Tompert, Ann. *Savina, the gypsy dancer*
Waters, Kate. *Lion dancer: Ernie Wan's Chinese new year*
Westman, Barbara. *Dancing dogs: Charlotte and Emilio at the circus*
Whittington, Mary K. *Carmina, come dance!*
Wilkes, Larry. *The king's egg dance*
Wood, Audrey. *Little Penguin's tale*
Wright, Jill. *The old woman and the Willy Nilly Man*
Ziefert, Harriet. *Dancing*

Activities – digging

Aliki. *Digging up dinosaurs*
Ayres, Pam. *When dad fills in the garden pond*
Baynton, Martin. *Fifty gets the picture*
Cleary, Beverly. *The real hole*
Gibbons, Gail. *Tunnels*
Kumin, Maxine. *Speedy digs downside up*
Perkins, Al. *The digging-est dog*
Rawlins, Donna. *Digging to China*

Activities – drawing

Moss, Marissa. *Regina's big mistake*

Activities – flying

Abolafia, Yossi. *Yanosh's Island*
Adoff, Arnold. *Flamboyan*
Allard, Harry. *The Stupids take off*
Allen, Laura Jean. *Where is Freddy?*

Anderson, Joan. *Harry's helicopter*
Anderson, Lonzo. *Mr. Biddle and the birds*
Arabian Nights. *The flying carpet*, ill. by Marcia Brown
Arvetis, Chris. *Why does it fly?*
Aulaire, Ingri Mortenson d'. *Wings for Per*
Ayal, Ora. *The adventures of Chester the chest*
Ayres, Becky Hickox. *Victoria flies high*
Balian, Lorna. *Wilbur's space machine*
Benchley, Nathaniel. *The flying lessons of Gerald Pelican*
Blathwayt, Benedict. *Tangle and the silver bird*
Bradfield, Roger (Jolly Roger). *The flying hockey stick*
Breathed, Berkeley. *A wish for wings that work*
Brenner, Barbara A. *The flying patchwork quilt*
Brock, Emma Lillian. *Surprise balloon*
Brown, Marc Tolon. *Wings on things*
Brown, Margaret Wise. *Streamlined pig*
Buchanan, Heather S. *George Mouse learns to fly*
Buckingham, Simon. *Alec and his flying bed*
Collins, Pat Lowery. *Tomorrow, up and away!*
Corbalis, Judy. *Porcellus, the flying pig*
Crews, Donald. *Flying*
Dorros, Arthur. *Abuela*
Duvoisin, Roger Antoine. *Petunia takes a trip*
Florian, Douglas. *Airplane ride*
Fort, Patrick. *Redbird*
Gay, Michel. *Bibi takes flight*
Gibbons, Gail. *Flying*
Gramatky, Hardie. *Loopy*
Hays, Hoffman Reynolds. *Charley sang a song*
Hill, Eric. *Up there*
Hoban, Russell. *Ace Dragon Ltd.*
Hughes, Shirley. *Up and up*
Jenny, Anne. *The fantastic story of King Brioche the First*
Jeschke, Susan. *Perfect the pig*
Johnson, Neil. *Fire and silk*
Kaufmann, John. *Flying giants of long ago*
King, Christopher. *The boy who ate the moon*
Kojima, Naomi. *The flying grandmother*
Kuskin, Karla. *Just like everyone else*
Lindgren, Barbro. *Shorty takes off*
McConnachie, Brian. *Flying boy*
McPhail, David. *First flight*
Munsch, Robert N. *Angela's airplane*
Myers, Bernice. *The flying shoes*
Osborne, Mary Pope. *Moonhorse*
Peet, Bill (William Bartlett). *The kweeks of Kookatumdee*
   Merle the high flying squirrel
Pirotta, Saviour. *Little bird*

Pomerantz, Charlotte. *Flap your wings and try*
Provensen, Alice. *The glorious flight*
Ransome, Arthur. *The fool of the world and the flying ship*
Rigby, Rodney. *Hello, this is your penguin speaking*
Ringgold, Faith. *Tar Beach*
Ross, Pat. *Your first airplane trip*
Schumacher, Claire. *Nutty's birthday*
Scruton, Clive. *Pig in the air*
Smith, Lane. *Flying Jake*
Spurr, Elizabeth. *Mrs. Minetta's car pool*
Stadler, John. *Three cheers for hippo!*
Stevenson, James. *Grandpa's great city tour*
Taylor, Judy. *Dudley goes flying*
Testa, Fulvio. *The paper airplane*
Titus, Eve. *Anatole over Paris*
Trez, Denise. *Maila and the flying carpet*
Ungerer, Tomi. *The Mellops go flying*
Valens, Evans G. *Wingfin and Topple*
Walter, Mildred Pitts. *Brother to the wind*
Waterton, Betty. *Orff, 27 dragons (and a snarkel)*
Watson, Clyde. *Midnight moon*
Weisner, David. *Tuesday*
Wende, Philip. *Bird boy*
West, Ian. *Silas, the first pig to fly*
Wheeling, Lynn. *When you fly*
Wolkstein, Diane. *The cool ride in the sky*
The magic wings
Woodruff, Elvira. *The wing shop*
Yolen, Jane. *Wings*
Young, Miriam Burt. *If I flew a plane*

Activities - gardening *see* Gardens, gardening

Activities – jumping

Bright, Robert. *My hopping bunny*
Cole, Joanna. *Norma Jean, jumping bean*
Easton, Violet. *Elephants never jump*
Stephens, Karen. *Jumping*

Activities – knitting

Anholt, Catherine. *Tom's rainbow walk*
Blackwood, Mary. *Derek the knitting dinosaur*
Hilton, Nette. *The long red scarf*
Hissey, Jane. *Jolly Tall*
Holl, Adelaide. *Mrs. McGarrity's peppermint sweater*
Laurin, Anne. *Little things*
Martinez, Ruth. *Mrs. McDockerty's knitting*
Storr, Catherine (Cole). *Hugo and his grandma*
Wild, Margaret. *Mr. Nick's knitting*
Ziefert, Harriet. *With love from Grandma*

Activities – making things

Arnold, Tedd. *The simple people*
Balterman, Lee. *Girders and cranes*
The big Peter Rabbit book
Blocksma, Mary. *Easy-to-make spaceships that really fly*
Blos, Joan W. *The grandpa days*
Calder, Lyn. *Walt Disney's Alice's tea party*
Crowley, Michael. *The new kid on Spurwick Ave.*
De Paola, Tomie (Thomas Anthony). *Things to make and do for Valentine's Day*
Engel, Diana. *The little lump of clay*
Fallwell, Cathryn. *Nicky and Alex*
Flint, Russ. *Let's build a house*
Florian, Douglas. *A potter*
Gibbons, Gail. *How a house is built*
Gliori, Debi. *New big house*
Graham, Thomas. *Mr. Bear's chair*
Himmelman, John. *The day-off machine*
The great leaf blast-off
Hindley, Judy. *The little train*
Huff, Vivian. *Let's make paper dolls*
Hughes, Shirley. *The big concrete lorry*
Kiser, SuAnn. *The birthday thing*
Kreye, Walter. *The giant from the little island*
Kunhardt, Edith. *Danny's Christmas star*
Leedy, Loreen. *A dragon Christmas*
Lohf, Sabine. *Things I can make with buttons*
Things I can make with cloth
Things I can make with cork
Things I can make with paper
Lopshire, Robert. *How to make snop snappers and other fine things*
Martin, Jacqueline Briggs. *Good times on Grandfather Mountain*
Moss, Marissa. *Knick knack paddywack*
Pfanner, Louise. *Louise builds a boat*
Louise builds a house
Radford, Derek. *Harry builds a house*
Rosenberg, Liz. *The scrap doll*
Thelen, Gerda. *The toy maker*
Tryon, Leslie. *Albert's alphabet*
Ziefert, Harriet. *Before I was born*

Activities – painting

Adams, Adrienne. *The Easter egg artists*
Agee, Jon. *The incredible painting of Felix Clousseau*
Asch, Frank. *Bread and honey*
Baker, Alan. *Benjamin's portrait*
Bang, Molly. *Tye May and the magic brush*
Becker, Edna. *Nine hundred buckets of paint*
Beim, Jerrold. *Jay's big job*
Bond, Michael. *Paddington's art exhibit*
Bromhall, Winifred. *Mary Ann's first picture*
Carrick, Donald. *Morgan and the artist*

Coats, Laura Jane. *Marcella and the moon*
Craven, Carolyn. *What the mailman brought*
Decker, Dorothy W. *Stripe visits New York*
Demi. *Liang and the magic paintbrush*
De Paola, Tomie (Thomas Anthony). *The legend of the Indian paintbrush*
Duvoisin, Roger Antoine. *The house of four seasons*
Ernst, Lisa Campbell. *Hamilton's art show*
Freeman, Don. *The chalk box story*
Himmelman, John. *Ellen and the goldfish*
Johnston, Tony. *Pages of music*
Kessler, Leonard P. *Mr. Pine's purple house*
Leaf, Margaret. *Eyes of the dragon*
Lindsay, Elizabeth. *A letter for Maria*
McPhail, David. *Lorenzo*
  Something special
Martin, Charles E. *For rent*
Menter, Ian. *The Albany Road mural*
Miller, Warren. *Pablo paints a picture*
Morris, Jill. *The boy who painted the sun*
Nerlove, Miriam. *If all the world were paper*
Pinkwater, Daniel Manus. *The big orange splot*
Rogers, Paul (Patrick). *Don't blame me!*
Rylant, Cynthia. *All I see*
Silsbe, Brenda. *Just one more color*
Spier, Peter. *Oh, were they ever happy!*
Wabbes, Marie. *Rose's picture*
Walsh, Ellen Stoll. *Mouse paint*
Weisgard, Leonard. *Mr. Peaceable paints*

Activities – photographing

Levinson, Riki. *I go with my family to Grandma's*
McPhail, David. *Pig Pig and the magic photo album*
Manushkin, Fran. *The perfect Christmas picture*
Marshall, Janet Perry. *My camera: at the zoo*
Morrow, Barbara. *Edward's portrait*
Seguin-Fontes, Marthe. *A wedding book*
Tison, Annette. *Animal hide-and-seek*
Türk, Hanne. *Snapshot Max*
Villarejo, Mary. *The tiger hunt*
Vincent, Gabrielle. *Smile, Ernest and Celestine*
Watts, Mabel (Pizzey). *Weeks and weeks*
Willard, Nancy. *Simple pictures are best*
Wyllie, Stephen. *Snappity snap*

Activities – picnicking

Asch, Frank. *Sand cake*
Benjamin, Alan. *A change of plans*
Berger, Terry. *The turtles' picnic and other nonsense stories*
Binnamin, Vivian. *The case of the anteater's missing lunch*
Bishop, Bonnie. *Ralph rides away*

Bowden, Joan Chase. *The Ginghams and the backward picnic*
Bratton, John. *The teddy bears' picnic*, ill. by Renate Kozikowski
Browne, Eileen. *Where's that bus?*
Brunhoff, Laurent de. *Babar's picnic*
Butler, Dorothy. *Higgledy, piggledy, hobbledy hoy*
Chalmers, Mary. *Here comes the trolley*
  Mr. Cat's wonderful surprise
Christelow, Eileen. *Five little monkeys sitting in a tree*
Christian, Mary Blount. *Go west, swamp monsters*
Claverie, Jean. *The picnic*
Darling, Abigail. *Teddy bears' picnic cookbook*
Daugherty, James Henry. *The picnic*
Delton, Judy. *On a picnic*
Denton, Kady MacDonald. *The picnic*
Dickinson, Mary. *Alex's outing*
Dubanevich, Arlene. *Pig William*
Dunham, Meredith. *Picnic: how do you say it?*
Du Quette, Keith. *Rippening day for a picnic*
Ernst, Lisa Campbell. *Up to ten and down again*
Ets, Marie Hall. *In the forest*
Freschet, Berniece. *The ants go marching*
Garland, Sarah. *Having a picnic*
Goodall, John S. *The surprise picnic*
Gordon, Margaret. *Wilberforce goes on a picnic*
Graham, Bob. *Libby, Oscar and me*
Graham, Thomas. *Mr. Bear's boat*
Hayes, Sarah. *This is the bear and the picnic lunch*
Higham, Jon Atlas. *Aardvark's picnic*
Hill, Eric. *Spot's first picnic*
Hines, Anna Grossnickle. *Come to the meadow*
Hurd, Edith Thacher. *No funny business*
Iwamura, Kazuo. *The fourteen forest mice and the spring meadow picnic*
Kasza, Keiko. *The pigs' picnic*
Keller, Holly. *Henry's Fourth of July*
Kennedy, Jimmy. *The teddy bears' picnic*, ill. by Alexandra Day
  The teddy bears' picnic, ill. by Michael Hague
  The teddy bears' picnic, ill. by Prue Theobalds
Killingback, Julia. *Busy Bears' picnic*
King, Bob. *Sitting on the farm*
Knox-Wagner, Elaine. *The oldest kid*
Kroll, Steven. *It's Groundhog Day!*
Lathrop, Dorothy Pulis. *Who goes there?*
Little, Jean. *Once upon a golden apple*
McCully, Emily Arnold. *Picnic*
MacGregor, Marilyn. *Helen the hungry bear*
Maestro, Betsy. *The perfect picnic*

Maris, Ron. *In my garden*
Marshall, Edward. *Three by the sea*
Radlauer, Ruth Shaw. *Molly*
  Molly goes hiking
Rappus, Gerhard. *When the sun was shining*
Robertson, Lilian. *Picnic woods*
Rodgers, Richard. *A real nice clambake*
Roffey, Maureen. *Meatime*
Rogers, Paul (Patrick). *Lily's picnic*
Saunders, Susan. *Charles Rat's picnic*
  Fish fry
Scarry, Richard. *My first word book*
Schroeder, Binette. *Tuffa and the picnic*
Shapiro, Arnold L. *Square*
Szekeres, Cyndy. *Ladybug, ladybug, where are you?*
Taylor, Judy. *Sophie and Jack*
Tether, Graham. *Skunk and possum*
Tsutsui, Yoriko. *Before the picnic*
Vaës, Alain. *The porcelain pepper pot*
Van Stockum, Hilda. *A day on skates*
Vincent, Gabrielle. *Ernest and Celestine's picnic*
Wasmuth, Eleanor. *The picnic basket*
Watson, Clyde. *Hickory stick rag*
The weekend, ill. by Roser Capdevila
Westcott, Nadine Bernard. *The giant vegetable garden*
Weston, Martha. *Bea's four bears*
Wheeler, Cindy. *Marmalade's picnic*
Wood, Joyce. *Grandmother Lucy goes on a picnic*
Yeoman, John. *The bear's water picnic*
Yolen, Jane. *Picnic with Piggins*

Activities – playing

Adam, Barbara. *The big big box*
Adorjan, Carol. *I can! Can you?*
Agee, Jon. *Ellsworth*
Ahlberg, Janet. *Funnybones*
Alexander, Martha G. *I'll be the horse if you'll play with me*
Aliki. *Overnight at Mary Bloom's*
Allen, Pamela. *I wish I had a pirate suit*
Allen, Robert. *Ten little babies play*
Arnold, Caroline. *How do we have fun?*
Arnosky, Jim. *Watching foxes*
Artis, Vicki Kimmel. *Pajama walking*
Asch, Frank. *Rebecka*
Aulaire, Ingri Mortenson d'. *Children of the northlights*
Ayal, Ora. *Ugbu*
Baillie, Allan. *Drac and the gremlin*
Bang, Molly. *Yellow ball*
Bauer, Helen. *Good times in the park*
Baugh, Dolores M. *Slides*
  Swings
Benét, William Rose. *Angels*
Bethell, Jean. *Playmates*
Blegvad, Lenore. *Rainy day Kate*

Bonsall, Crosby Newell. *And I mean it, Stanley*
Boyd, Lizi. *Willy and the cardboard boxes*
Bram, Elizabeth. *Saturday morning lasts forever*
Breinburg, Petronella. *Doctor Shawn*
Brinckloe, Julie. *Playing marbles*
Brown, Myra Berry. *First night away from home*
Brown, Ruth. *Our puppy's vacation*
Browne, Anthony. *Things I like*
Bruna, Dick. *Miffy at the playground*
  Miffy's dream
Buckley, Helen Elizabeth. *"Take care of things," Edward said*
Burningham, John. *Where's Julius?*
Burns, Maurice. *Go ducks, go!*
Burstein, Fred. *Whispering in the park*
Carlstrom, Nancy White. *Heather hiding*
Carrier, Lark. *Scout and Cody*
Carroll, Ruth. *Where's the bunny?*
Cartlidge, Michelle. *Pippin and Pod*
Cauley, Lorinda Bryan. *Clap your hands*
Christian, Mary Blount. *The sand lot*
Coffelt, Nancy. *Good night, Sigmund*
Cole, William. *What's good for a four-year-old?*
  What's good for a six-year-old?
Creighton, Jill. *Maybe a monster*
Crowley, Michael. *New kid on Spurwick Ave.*
Dickens, Lucy. *At the beach*
  Our day
  Outside
  Playtime
Duke, Kate. *The playground*
Emecheta, Buchi. *Nowhere to play*
Ets, Marie Hall. *Play with me*
Fallwell, Cathryn. *Nicky and Alex*
  Nicky and grandpa
  Where's Nicky?
Fitzhugh, Louise. *Bang, bang, you're dead*
Fujikawa, Gyo. *That's not fair!*
Gebert, Warren. *The old ball and the sea*
Gibbons, Gail. *Playgrounds*
Goffstein, M. B. (Marilyn Brooke). *Our snowman*
Greenfield, Eloise. *Big friend, little friend*
  My doll, Keshia
Gretz, Susanna. *Duck takes off*
Hann, Jacquie. *Follow the leader*
Haus, Felice. *Beep! Beep! I'm a jeep*
Havill, Juanita. *Jamaica Tag-Along*
Hawkins, Colin. *Dip, dip, dip*
  One finger, one thumb
  Oops-a-Daisy
  Where's bear?
Hendrickson, Karen. *Baby and I can play*
  Fun with toddlers
Henkes, Kevin. *A weekend with Wendell*
Hill, Eric. *Spot at play*
  Spot goes to the beach

Spot sleeps over
Hillert, Margaret. *Play ball*
  What is it?
Hines, Anna Grossnickle. *Bethany for real*
  It's just me, Emily
  Keep your old hat
  They really like me!
Hissey, Jane. *Jolly snow*
Hoffman, Phyllis. *We play*
Houghton, Eric. *The backwards watch*
Hughes, Shirley. *Alfie's feet*
Hutchins, Hazel J. *Norman's snowball*
Ichikawa, Satomi. *Let's play*
  Suzanne and Nicholas in the garden, St.
    Martin's 1978
Impey, Rose. *Joe's café*
Jensen, Patricia. *The mess*
Jewell, Nancy. *Try and catch me*
Johnson, Mildred D. *Wait, skates!*
Keats, Ezra Jack. *Skates*
  The snowy day
Keeping, Charles. *Willie's fire-engine*
Kent, Jack. *Joey*
Kline, Suzy. *Don't touch!*
Knutson, Kimberley. *Muddigush*
Kobayashi, Yuji. *Miss Josephine's secret walk*
Krahn, Fernando. *Robot-bot-bot*
Kraus, Robert. *Come out and play, little*
  mouse
Krementz, Jill. *Lily goes to the playground*
Krupp, Robin Rector. *Get set to wreck!*
Landa, Norbert. *Rabbit and chicken play*
  hide and seek
Lenski, Lois. *Let's play house*
Lewis, Kim. *Floss*
Lindgren, Barbro. *The wild baby goes to sea*
Lipkind, William. *Sleepyhead*
McCarthy, Ruth. *Katie and the smallest bear*
McCord, David. *Every time I climb a tree*
McCully, Emily Arnold. *First snow*
McLerran, Alice. *Roxaboxen*
McMillan, Bruce. *Play day*
McNulty, Faith. *When a boy wakes up in the*
  morning
McPhail, David. *Pig Pig rides*
Maestro, Betsy. *Harriet at play*
Major, Beverly. *Playing sardines*
Manushkin, Fran. *The best toy of all*
  Swinging and swinging
Marino, Dorothy. *Edward and the boxes*
Marshall, James. *Three up a tree*
Mayers, Patrick. *Just one more block*
Mayper, Monica. *Oh snow*
Meeks, Esther K. *The hill that grew*
Merriam, Eve. *Boys and girls, girls and boys*
Meryl, Debra. *Baby's peek-a-boo album*
Miller, Margaret. *Playtime*
Miranda, Anne. *Baby walk*
Mitchell, Cynthia. *Halloweena Hecatee*
  Playtime
Moss, Elaine. *Polar*
Moss, Marissa. *Want to play?*

Mueller, Virginia. *A playhouse for Monster*
Naylor, Phyllis Reynolds. *King of the*
  playground
Oppenheim, Joanne. *James will never die*
Oram, Hiawyn. *In the attic*
Ormerod, Jan. *The saucepan game*
Oxenbury, Helen. *All fall down*
  Clap hands
  Grandma and Grandpa
  Playing
  Say goodnight
  Tickle, tickle
  Tom and Pippo and the dog
Packard, Mary. *Where is Jake?*
Paré, Roger. *Summer days*
Pearson, Susan. *That's enough for one day!*
Pirani, Felix. *Abigail at the beach*
Pocock, Rita. *Annabelle and the big slide*
Pollock, Penny. *Water is wet*
Quinlan, Patricia. *Emma's sea journey*
Raebeck, Lois. *Who am I?*
Raney, Ken. *Stick horse*
Rockwell, Anne F. *At the beach*
  I play in my room
  My back yard
Rogers, Fred. *Making friends*
Rosner, Ruth. *Arabba gah zee, Marissa and*
  me!
Russ, Lavinia. *Alec's sand castle*
Russo, Marisabina. *The line up book*
  Where is Ben?
Sato, Satoru. *I wish I had a big, big tree*
Sendak, Maurice. *Maurice Sendak's Really*
  Rosie
  The sign on Rosie's door
Shearer, Marilyn J. *I like to play*
Shott, Stephen. *Playtime*
Snyder, Zilpha Keatley. *Come on, Patsy*
Standon, Anna. *Three little cats*
Steiner, Charlotte. *Kiki's play house*
  Look what Tracy found
Steptoe, John. *Baby says*
Stevenson, Suçie. *Do I have to take Violet?*
Stine, Jovial Bob. *Pork and beans: play date*
Stinson, Kathy. *The dressed up book*
Thompson, Richard. *Jenny's Neighbours*
Thwaites, Lyndsay. *Super Adam and Rosie*
  Wonder
Todd, Kathleen. *Snow*
Townson, Hazel. *What on earth...?*
Turkle, Brinton. *Obadiah the Bold*
Turner, Charles. *The turtle and the moon*
Udry, Janice May. *Mary Ann's mud day*
Vasiliu, Mircea. *A day at the beach*
Vigna, Judith. *Boot weather*
Viorst, Judith. *Sunday morning*
Waber, Bernard. *Ira sleeps over*
Waddell, Martin. *Squeak-a-lot*
Wahl, Jan. *Push Kitty*
Wasmuth, Eleanor. *An alligator day*
Watanabe, Shigeo. *Daddy, play with me!*

I can build a house!
I can ride it!
I'm the king of the castle!
Wells, Rosemary. *A lion for Lewis*
Winn, Chris. *Playing*
Winthrop, Elizabeth. *Bunk beds*
 That's mine
Wood, Jakki. *Dads are such fun*
Young, Miriam Burt. *Jellybeans for breakfast*
Ziefert, Harriet. *Baby Ben's go-go book*
 Come out, Jessie!
 Lewis the fire fighter
 Strike four!
Zimelman, Nathan. *Walls are to be walked*
Ziner, Feenie. *Counting carnival*
Zinnemann-Hope, Pam. *Let's play ball, Ned*
Zolotow, Charlotte (Shapiro). *The park book*
 The white marble

Activities – reading

Aliki. *How a book is made*
Allington, Richard L. *Reading*
Baker, Betty. *Worthington Botts and the steam machine*
Bank Street College of Education. *People read*
Barasch, Lynne. *Rodney's inside story*
Bauer, Caroline Feller. *Too many books!*
Baumgart, Klaus. *The little green dragon steps out*
Black, Irma Simonton. *The little old man who could not read*
Brillhart, Julie. *Story hour—starring Megan!*
Browne, Anthony. *I like books*
Bruna, Dick. *I can read difficult words*
Bunting, Eve (Anne Evelyn). *The Wednesday surprise*
Cohen, Miriam. *When will I read?*
DiFiori, Lawrence. *My first book*
Duvoisin, Roger Antoine. *Petunia*
Friskey, Margaret (Margaret Richards). *Mystery of the gate sign*
Funk, Tom (Thompson). *I read signs*
Furtado, Jo. *Sorry, Miss Folio!*
Giff, Patricia Reilly. *The beast in Ms. Rooney's room*
Gillham, Bill. *The early words picture book*
Goor, Ron. *Signs*
Hallinan, P. K. (Patrick K.). *Just open a book*
Hoban, Lillian. *Arthur's prize reader*
Hoban, Tana. *I read signs*
 I read symbols
 I walk and read
Holl, Adelaide. *Most-of-the-time Maxie*
Holleyman, Sonia. *Mona the vampire*
Hopkins, Lee Bennett. *Good books, good times*
Huff, Barbara A. *Once inside the library*
Hurd, Edith Thacher. *Johnny Lion's book*

Hutchins, H. J. (Hazel J.). *Nicholas at the library*
Hutchins, Pat. *The tale of Thomas Mead*
Kuskin, Karla. *Watson, the smartest dog in the U.S.A.*
Lattimore, Deborah Nourse. *The sailor who captured the sea*
Levinson, Nancy Smiler. *Clara and the bookwagon*
Lexau, Joan M. *Olaf reads*
Lillegard, Dee. *Sitting in my box*
Little, Jean. *Once upon a golden apple*
McLenighan, Valjean. *One whole doughnut, one doughnut hole*
McPhail, David. *Fix-it*
Maestro, Betsy. *Harriet reads signs and more signs*
Marshall, James. *Wings: a tale of two chickens*
Minsberg, David. *The book monster*
Most, Bernard. *There's an ant in Anthony*
O'Neill, Catharine. *Mrs. Dunphy's dog*
Ormerod, Jan. *Reading*
Ormondroyd, Edward. *Broderick*
Pearson, Susan. *That's enough for one day!*
Porazińska, Janina. *The enchanted book*
Purdy, Carol. *Least of all*
Radlauer, Ruth Shaw. *Molly at the library*
Seuss, Dr. *I can read with my eyes shut*
Sharmat, Marjorie Weinman. *My mother never listens to me*
Viorst, Judith. *The good-bye book*
Wiesner, David. *Free fall*

Activities – sewing

Brown, Craig McFarland. *Patchwork farmer*
Woolf, Virginia. *Nurse Lugton's curtain*

Activities – shopping *see* Shopping

Activities – singing

Saul, Carol P. *Peter's song*
Sundgaard, Arnold. *The bear who loved Puccini*

Activities – swinging

Anderson, Robin. *Sinabouda Lily*
Baugh, Dolores M. *Swings*
Manushkin, Fran. *Swinging and swinging*
Marks, Marcia Bliss. *Swing me, swing tree*

Activities – trading

Andersen, H. C. (Hans Christian). *The old man is always right*, ill. by Feodor Rojankovsky
Burdick, Margaret. *Bobby Otter and the blue boat*
Bushey, Jerry. *The barge book*
Chorao, Kay. *The cherry pie baby*

Davidson, Jill A. *And that's what happened to little Lucy*

De Regniers, Beatrice Schenk. *Was it a good trade?*

Dick Whittington and his cat. *Dick Whittington*, ill. by Edward Ardizzone
Dick Whittington and his cat, ill. by Marcia Brown
Dick Whittington, ill. by Antony Maitland
Dick Whittington and his cat, ill. by Kurt Werth

Gill, Bob. *A balloon for a blunderbuss*

Hale, Irina. *The lost toys*

Hirsh, Marilyn. *The pink suit*

Hughes, Shirley. *David and dog*
Dogger

Langstaff, John M. *The swapping boy*

McAllister, Angela. *Matepo*

Shannon, George. *The Piney Woods peddler*

Stroyer, Poul. *It's a deal*

Watts, Mabel (Pizzey). *Something for you, something for me*

Activities – traveling

Aardema, Verna. *Traveling to Tondo*

Aksakov, Sergei. *The scarlet flower*

Arnold, Caroline. *How do we travel?*

Ball, Duncan. *Jeremy's tail*

Barklem, Jill. *The high hills*

Bate, Lucy. *How Georgina drove the car very carefully from Boston to New York*

Baum, Louis. *JuJu and the pirate*

Beatty, Hetty Burlingame. *Moorland pony*

Bemelmans, Ludwig. *Quito express*

Billout, Guy. *By camel or by car*

Biro, Val. *The wind in the willows: the open road*

Blech, Dietlind. *Hello Irina*

Bolognese, Don. *A new day*

Borchers, Elisabeth. *Dear Sarah*

Brandenberg, Franz. *Everyone ready?*

Brann, Esther. *'Round the world*

Bridgman, Elizabeth. *How to travel with grownups*
Nanny bear's cruise

Brisson, Pat. *Magic carpet*
Your best friend, Kate

Bröger, Achim. *Bruno takes a trip*

Bromhall, Winifred. *Johanna arrives*

Brown, Laurie Krasny. *Dinosaurs travel*

Brown, Marc Tolon. *Arthur meets the president*

Brown, Margaret Wise. *Three little animals*

Bruna, Dick. *The sailor*

Brunhoff, Jean de. *The travels of Babar*

Buchanan, Heather S. *George Mouse's covered wagon*

Buffett, Jimmy. *The jolly mon*

Bunting, Eve (Anne Evelyn). *The traveling men of Ballycoo*

Bursik, Rose. *Amelia's fantastic flight*

Butler, Dorothy. *A happy tale*

Caines, Jeannette. *Just us women*

Calmenson, Stephanie. *Zip, whiz, zoom!*

Carle, Eric. *The rooster who set out to see the world*
Rooster's off to see the world

Carmi, Giora. *And Shira imagined*

Cech, John. *My grandmother's journey*

Chalmers, Mary. *Here comes the trolley*

Chwast, Seymour. *Tall city, wide country*

Coerr, Eleanor. *The Josefina story quilt*

Cooney, Barbara. *Miss Rumphius*

Davis, Maggie S. *The best way to Ripton*

Day, Edward C. *John Tabor's ride*

Demi. *The adventures of Marco Polo*

Denslow, Sharon Phillips. *Riding with Aunt Lucy*

Denton, Terry. *Home is the sailor*

Ekker, Ernest A. *What is beyond the hill?*

Fairclough, Chris. *Take a trip to China*
Take a trip to England
Take a trip to Holland
Take a trip to Israel
Take a trip to Italy
Take a trip to West Germany

Feldman, Barbara. *Going, going*

Field, Rachel Lyman. *A road might lead to anywhere*

Fox, Mem. *Possum magic*

Gackenbach, Dick. *With love from Gran*

Gantschev, Ivan. *The train to Grandma's*

Gay, Michel. *Night ride*

Gikow, Louise. *Follow that Fraggle!*

Gomi, Taro. *Bus stop*

Goodall, John S. *Paddy goes traveling*

Grahame, Kenneth. *The open road*

Gray, Genevieve. *How far, Felipe?*

Greene, Carla. *A motor holiday*

Gretz, Susanna. *Teddy bears take the train*

Haley, Patrick. *The little person*

Handford, Martin. *Find Waldo now*
The great Waldo search
Where's Waldo?

Hannan, Peter. *Sillyville or bust*

Hayashi, Akiko. *Aki and the fox*

Heckman, Philip. *The moon is following me*

Heuck, Sigrid. *Who stole the apples?*

Holabird, Katharine. *Alexander and the magic boat*

Howard, Elizabeth Fitzgerald. *The train to Lulu's*

Hurd, Thacher. *Hobo dog*

Isadora, Rachel. *No, Agatha!*
Over the green hills

Isele, Elizabeth. *Pooks*

Janosch. *The trip to Panama*

Jonas, Ann. *Round trip*

Kalman, Maira. *Sayonara, Mrs. Kackleman*

Kellogg, Steven (Stephen). *Johnny Appleseed*

Kesselman, Wendy. *There's a train going by my window*

Kessler, Leonard P. *Mrs. Pine takes a trip*
Kilroy, Sally. *On the road*
Krementz, Jill. *Jamie goes on an airplane*
  A visit to Washington, D.C.
Lenski, Lois. *Davy goes places*
Lester, Alison. *The journey home*
Lewin, Hugh. *Jafta—the journey*
Lewis, Thomas P. *Clipper ship*
Lindbergh, Reeve. *Johnny Appleseed*
Locker, Thomas. *Sailing with the wind*
Loof, Jan. *Uncle Louie's fantastic sea voyage*
Lyndon, Kerry Raines. *A birthday for Blue*
Lyon, George-Ella. *A regular rolling Noah*
McCormack, John E. *Rabbit travels*
McKissack, Patricia C. *Big bug book of places to go*
McToots, Rudi. *The kid's book of games for cars, trains and planes*
Maestro, Betsy. *Ferryboat*
Manson, Christopher. *Two travelers*
Marshak, Samuel. *The pup grew up!*
Martin, Charles E. *Sam saves the day*
May, Charles Paul. *High-noon rocket*
Meddaugh, Susan. *Maude and Claude go abroad*
Miller, Edna. *Mouskin takes a trip*
Milton, Nancy. *The giraffe that walked to Paris*
Munro, Roxie. *The inside-outside book of Washington, D.C.*
Nixon, Joan Lowery. *If you say so, Claude*
Nordqvist, Sven. *Willie in the big world*
Oechsli, Helen. *Fly away!*
O'Kelley, Mattie Lou. *Moving to town*
Owen, Annie. *Bumper to bumper*
Patz, Nancy. *Gina Farina and the Prince of Mintz*
Petty, Kate. *On a plane*
Poulin, Stéphane. *Travels for two*
Rabe, Berniece. *A smooth move*
Raney, Ken. *Stick horse*
Robbins, Ken. *City/country*
Rogers, Fred. *Going on an airplane*
Rose, Gerald. *PB takes a holiday*
Rylant, Cynthia. *The relatives came*
Salter, Mary Jo. *The moon comes home*
Schories, Pat. *Mouse around*
Schulz, Charles M. *Bon voyage, Charlie Brown (and don't come back!!)*
Seuss, Dr. *I had trouble getting to Solla Sollew*
Slater, Teddy. *The fabulous fish from Lake Wiggawalla*
Smith, Barry. *The first voyage of Christopher Columbus*
Smyth, Gwenda. *A pet for Mrs. Arbuckle*
Steger, Hans-Ulrich. *Traveling to Tripiti*
Stevenson, James. *Are we almost there?*
Suben, Eric. *Pigeon takes a trip*
Tapio, Pat Decker. *The lady who saw the good side of everything*

Türk, Hanne. *Max packs*
Turner, Ann Warren. *Nettie's trip south*
Vevers, Gwynne. *Animals that travel*
Willard, Nancy. *The voyage of the Ludgate Hill*
Willis, Jeanne. *Earth mobiles as explained by Professor Xargle*
Wood, Audrey. *Silly Sally*
Ziefert, Harriet. *A car trip for mole and mouse*
  Keeping daddy awake on the way home from the beach

Activities – vacationing

Adams, Adrienne. *The Easter egg artists*
Bemelmans, Ludwig. *Hansi*
Berenstain, Stan. *The Berenstain bears and too much vacation*
Bond, Michael. *Paddington at the seaside*
Bornstein, Ruth Lercher. *I'll draw a meadow*
Brandenberg, Franz. *A fun weekend*
Briggs, Raymond. *Father Christmas goes on holiday*
Bright, Robert. *Georgie and the noisy ghost*
Brisson, Pat. *Your best friend, Kate*
Brown, Ruth. *Our puppy's vacation*
Brunhoff, Laurent de. *Babar's cousin, that rascal Arthur*
  Babar's mystery
Buchanan, Heather S. *George Mouse's covered wagon*
Carlstrom, Nancy White. *The moon came too*
Carrick, Carol. *The washout*
Chall, Marsha Wilson. *Up north at the cabin*
Cole, Joanna. *The Clown-Arounds go on vacation*
Du Bois, William Pène. *Otto and the magic potatoes*
Duvoisin, Roger Antoine. *Petunia takes a trip*
Everton, Macduff. *El circo magico modelo: Finding the magic circus*
Fatio, Louise. *The happy lion's vacation*
Florian, Douglas. *A summer day*
Gili, Phillida. *Fanny and Charles*
Goodall, John S. *Paddy Pork's holiday*
Goyder, Alice. *Holiday in Catland*
Graham, Bob. *Greetings from Sandy Beach*
Hale, Kathleen. *Orlando and the water cats*
Kellogg, Steven (Stephen). *Ralph's secret weapon*
Kessler, Leonard P. *Are we lost, daddy?*
Khalsa, Dayal Kaur. *My family vacation*
Lazard, Naomi. *What Amanda saw*
Lindman, Maj. *Snipp, Snapp, Snurr and the red shoes*
Lippman, Peter. *The Know-It-Alls take a winter vacation*
McPhail, David. *Emma's pet*

Emma's vacation

Maestro, Betsy. *The pandas take a vacation*

Marshall, James. *George and Martha round and round*

Martin, Charles E. *Sam saves the day*

Newton, Patricia Montgomery. *Vacation surprise*

Rockwell, Anne F. *On our vacation*

Roffey, Maureen. *I spy on vacation*

Shea, Pegi Deitz. *Bungalow fungalow*

Stevenson, James. *The Sea View Hotel*

Thomson, Ruth. *Peabody all at sea*

Tobias, Tobi. *At the beach*

Weiss, Nicki. *Weekend at Muskrat Lake*

Williams, Jay. *The city witch and the country witch*

Activities – walking

Alexander, Martha G. *Where does the sky end, Grandpa?*

Arnosky, Jim. *Crinkleroot's guide to walking in wild places*
Outdoors on foot

Aylesworth, Jim. *Siren in the night*

Bax, Martin. *Edmond went far away*

Berry, Christine. *Mama went walking*

Bodsworth, Nan. *A nice walk in the jungle*

Brown, Margaret Wise. *Four fur feet*

Buchanan, Joan. *It's a good thing*

Buckley, Helen Elizabeth. *Grandfather and I*

Bullock, Kathleen. *It chanced to rain*

Davidson, Jill A. *And that's what happened to little Lucy*

De Regniers, Beatrice Schenk. *Going for a walk*

Fallwell, Cathryn. *Nicky loves daddy*
Nicky's walk

Florian, Douglas. *Nature walk*

Hill, Eric. *The park*
Spot's first walk

Hoban, Tana. *I walk and read*

Jonas, Ann. *The trek*

Kingman, Lee. *Peter's long walk*

Klein, Leonore. *Henri's walk to Paris*

Lenski, Lois. *I went for a walk*

Lobe, Mira. *The snowman who went for a walk*

McNaughton, Colin. *Walk rabbit walk*

Oxenbury, Helen. *Our dog*

Radlauer, Ruth Shaw. *Molly*
Molly goes hiking

Ray, Deborah Kogan. *The cloud*

Rockwell, Anne F. *Willy can count*

Sarton, May. *A walk through the woods*

Sharmat, Marjorie Weinman. *Burton and Dudley*

Showers, Paul. *The listening walk*

Smalls-Hector, Irene. *Jonathan and his mommy*

Stevenson, James. *Rolling Rose*

Thomas, Ianthe. *Walk home tired, Billy Jenkins*

Thompson, Richard. *I have to see this*

Tobias, Tobi. *The dawdlewalk*

Türk, Hanne. *Rainy day Max*

Turner, Ethel. *Walking to school*

Tworkov, Jack. *The camel who took a walk*

Viorst, Judith. *Try it again, Sam*

Watanabe, Shigeo. *I can take a walk!*

Williams, David. *Walking to the creek*

Williams, Sue. *I went walking*

Wood, Joyce. *Grandmother Lucy goes on a picnic*

Zolotow, Charlotte (Shapiro). *One step, two...*
Say it!
The summer night

Activities – weaving

Bang, Molly. *Dawn*

Blood, Charles L. *The goat in the rug*

Coombs, Patricia. *Tilabel*

Ernst, Lisa Campbell. *Nattie Parsons' good-luck lamb*

Lattimore, Deborah Nourse. *The dragon's robe*

Le Tord, Bijou. *Picking and weaving*

San Souci, Robert D. *The enchanted tapestry*

Trân-Khánh-Tuyêt. *The little weaver of Thái-Yên Village*

Yagawa, Sumiko. *The crane wife*

Activities – whistling

Alexander, Anne (Anna Barbara Cooke). *I want to whistle*

Ambrus, Victor G. *The three poor tailors*

Bason, Lillian. *Pick a raincoat, pick a whistle*

Blackwood, Gladys Rourke. *Whistle for Cindy*

Keats, Ezra Jack. *Whistle for Willie*

Activities – working

Ackerman, Karen. *When mama retires*

Alda, Arlene. *Sonya's mommy works*

Allen, Jeffrey. *Mary Alice, operator number 9*

Ardizzone, Edward. *Paul, the hero of the fire*

Arkin, Alan. *Tony's hard work day*

Asch, Frank. *Good lemonade*

Aylesworth, Jim. *Shenandoah Noah*

Bach, Othello. *Lilly, Willy and the mail-order witch*

Barton, Byron. *Machines at work*

Basso, Bill. *The top of the pizzas*

Beim, Jerrold. *Jay's big job*

Bethell, Jean. *Three cheers for Mother Jones!*

Blance, Ellen. *Monster gets a job*

Bond, Michael. *Paddington cleans up*

Brooks, Ben. *Lemonade parade*

Burton, Virginia Lee. *Mike Mulligan and his steam shovel*
Caple, Kathy. *The purse*
Carle, Eric. *Walter the baker*
Civardi, Anne. *Things people do*
Clark, Ann Nolan. *The little Indian basket maker*
  The little Indian pottery maker
Claverie, Jean. *Working*
Cole, Babette. *The trouble with dad*
Dahl, Roald. *The giraffe and the pelly and me*
Delaney, Ned. *Terrible things could happen*
Delton, Judy. *My mother lost her job today*
Duke, Kate. *Clean-up day*
Dumbleton, Mike. *Dial-a-croc*
Eisenberg, Phyllis Rose. *You're my Nikki*
Euvremer, Teryl. *Sun's up*
Fleischman, Paul. *The animal hedge*
Florian, Douglas. *People working*
  A potter
Gág, Wanda. *Gone is gone*
Gallo, Giovanni. *The lazy beaver*
Gibbons, Gail. *Deadline!*
  Zoo
Goffstein, M. B. (Marilyn Brooke). *An actor*
  A writer
Goodall, John S. *Paddy Pork: odd jobs*
Grossman, Patricia. *The night ones*
Hall, Donald. *The ox-cart man*
Harper, Anita. *How we work*
Harvey, Brett. *My prairie year*
Hautzig, Deborah. *It's not fair!*
Hazen, Barbara Shook. *Mommy's office*
Heide, Florence Parry. *The day of Ahmed's secret*
Heine, Helme. *Merry-go-round*
Henderson, Kathy. *In the middle of the night*
Hoban, Russell. *Charlie the tramp*
Horvath, Betty F. *Jasper makes music*
Killingback, Julia. *Monday is washing day*
Krahn, Fernando. *Robot-bot-bot*
Kroll, Steven. *Howard and Gracie's luncheonette*
Lasker, Joe. *Mothers can do anything*
Leiner, Katherine. *Both my parents work*
Lewis, Kim. *Floss*
Lindsey, Treska. *When Batistine made bread*
Lockwood, Primrose. *Cissy Lavender*
Lyon, David. *The biggest truck*
McCunn, Ruthanne L. *Pie-Biter*
McGowen, Tom (Thomas). *The only glupmaker in the U.S. Navy*
McPhail, David. *Annie and Co.*
  Pig Pig gets a job
Maestro, Betsy. *Harriet at work*
Marshall, James. *Fox on the job*
Maynard, Joyce. *New house*
Merriam, Eve. *Mommies at work*

Mitchell, Joyce Slayton. *My mommy makes money*
100 words about working, ill. by Richard Eric Brown
Paterson, Diane. *Soap and suds*
Petrides, Heidrun. *Hans and Peter*
Puner, Helen Walker. *Daddys, what they do all day*
Purdy, Carol. *Least of all*
Quinlan, Patricia. *My dad takes care of me*
Rose, Deborah Lee. *Meredith's mother takes the train*
Ross, Jessica. *Ms. Klondike*
Rylant, Cynthia. *Mr. Griggs' work*
Sandberg, Inger. *Come on out, Daddy!*
Shipton, Jonathan. *Busy! Busy! Busy!*
Simon, Norma. *I'm busy, too*
Skurzynski, Gloria. *Martin by himself*
Stolz, Mary Slattery. *Zekmet, the stone carver*
Türk, Hanne. *Raking leaves with Max*
Valens, Amy. *Jesse's day care*
Williams, Sherley Anne. *Working cotton*
Yeoman, John. *The wild washerwomen*

Activities – writing

Allington, Richard L. *Writing*
Arnosky, Jim. *Mouse writing*
Caseley, Judith. *Dear Annie*
Cobb, Vicki. *Writing it down*
Felt, Sue. *Rosa-too-little*
Heide, Florence Parry. *The day of Ahmed's secret*
Hoban, Lillian. *Arthur's pen pal*
Joslin, Sesyle. *Dear dragon*
Krauss, Ruth. *I write it*
Lattimore, Deborah Nourse. *The sailor who captured the sea*
Leedy, Loreen. *The Furry News*
  Messages in the mailbox
Lockwood, Primrose. *Cissy Lavender*
Miles, Miska. *The pointed brush...*
Nixon, Joan Lowery. *If you were a writer*
Oakley, Graham. *The diary of a church mouse*
Seuss, Dr. *I can write!*

Actors *see* Careers – actors

Adoption

Banish, Roslyn. *A forever family*
Bawden, Nina. *Princess Alice*
Bloom, Suzanne. *A family for Jamie*
Bunin, Catherine. *Is that your sister?*
Caines, Jeannette. *Abby*
Chapman, Noralee. *The story of Barbara*
Fisher, Iris L. *Katie-Bo*
Freudberg, Judy. *Susan and Gordon adopt a baby*
Gabel, Susan L. *Where the sun kisses the sea*

Girard, Linda Walvoord. *Adoption is for always*
Greenberg, Judith E. *Adopted*
Hess, Edith. *Peter and Susie find a family*
Keller, Holly. *Horace*
Koehler, Phoebe. *The day we met you*
Lapsley, Susan. *I am adopted*
Livingston, Carole. *"Why was I adopted?"*
MacKay, Jed. *The big secret*
Milgram, Mary. *Brothers are all the same*
Nixon, Joan Lowery. *You bet your britches, Claude*
Pellegrini, Nina. *Families are different*
Rondell, Florence. *The family that grew*
Rosenberg, Maxine B. *Being adopted*
Schnitter, Jane. *William is my brother*
Sobol, Harriet Langsam. *We don't look like our mom and dad*
Stanek, Muriel. *My little foster sister*
Stein, Sara Bonnett. *The adopted one*
Turner, Ann Warren. *Through moon and stars and night skies*
Udry, Janice May. *Theodore's parents*
Voake, Charlotte. *Mrs. Goose's baby*
Wasson, Valentina Pavlovna. *The chosen baby*

Africa *see* Foreign lands – Africa

Afro-Americans *see* Ethnic groups in the U.S. – Afro-Americans

Aged *see* Old age

Airplane pilots *see* Careers – airplane pilots

Airplanes, airports

Bagwell, Richard. *This is an airport*
Baker, Donna. *I want to be a pilot*
Barton, Byron. *Airplanes*
Airport
Baumann, Kurt. *The paper airplane*
Brenner, Anita. *I want to fly*
Brown, Margaret Wise. *Streamlined pig*
Buchanan, Heather S. *George Mouse learns to fly*
Bunting, Eve (Anne Evelyn). *Fly away home*
Bursik, Rose. *Amelia's fantastic flight*
Butler, Dorothy. *A happy tale*
Cave, Ron. *Airplanes*
Cotler, Joanna. *Sky above earth below*
Crews, Donald. *Flying*
Duchess of York. *Budgie at Bendick's Point*
Budgie the little helicopter
Emberley, Ed (Edward Randolph). *Cars, boats, and planes*
Florian, Douglas. *Airplane ride*
Fort, Patrick. *Redbird*
Gay, Michel. *Bibi takes flight*

Little plane
Gibbons, Gail. *Flying*
Gramatky, Hardie. *Loopy*
Ingoglia, Gina. *The big book of real airplanes*
Krementz, Jill. *Jamie goes on an airplane*
Lenski, Lois. *The little airplane*
McPhail, David. *First flight*
Munsch, Robert N. *Angela's airplane*
Nolan, Dennis. *Wizard McBean and his flying machine*
Oechsli, Helen. *Fly away!*
Olschewski, Alfred. *We fly*
Petty, Kate. *On a plane*
Planes
Potter, Tony. *See how it works: planes*
Provensen, Alice. *The glorious flight*
Rand, Gloria. *Salty takes off*
Rockwell, Anne F. *Planes*
Rogers, Fred. *Going on an airplane*
Ross, Pat. *Your first airplane trip*
Schulz, Charles M. *Snoopy's facts and fun book about planes*
Spier, Peter. *Bored—nothing to do!*
Testa, Fulvio. *The paper airplane*
Thompson, Brenda. *Famous planes*
Ungerer, Tomi. *The Mellops go flying*
Wheeling, Lynn. *When you fly*
Young, Miriam Burt. *If I flew a plane*
Zaffo, George J. *The big book of real airplanes*
The giant nursery book of things that go

Airports *see* Airplanes, airports

Alaska

Rand, Gloria. *Salty takes off*
Schoenherr, John. *Bear*

Albatrosses *see* Birds – albatrosses

Alligators *see* Reptiles – alligators, crocodiles

Ambition *see* Character traits – ambition

American Indians *see* Indians of North America; Indians of South America

Amphibians *see* Frogs and toads; Reptiles

Anatomy

Boynton, Sandra. *Horns to toes and in between*
Campbell, Rod. *It's mine*
Caputo, Robert. *More than just pets*
Carle, Eric. *My very first book of heads and tails*
Castle, Sue. *Face talk, hand talk, body talk*
Cole, Brock. *The giant's toe*

Cummings, Phil. *Goodness gracious!*
Elkin, Benjamin. *Gillespie and the guards*
Facklam, Margery. *But not like mine*
Hazen, Barbara Shook. *The me I see*
Hirschmann, Linda. *In a lick of a flick of a tongue*
Jeram, Anita. *Bill's belly button*
Kilroy, Sally. *Babies' bodies*
Krauss, Ruth. *Eyes, nose, fingers, toes*
Markle, Sandra. *Outside and inside you*
Martin, Bill (William Ivan). *Here are my hands*
My body, ill. by Sue Porter
Pluckrose, Henry Arthur. *Fur and feathers*
Paws and claws
Skin, shell and scale
Rothman, Joel. *This can lick a lollipop*
Royston, Angela. *My body*
Schoen, Mark. *Bellybuttons are navels*
Sharmat, Marjorie Weinman. *Helga high-up*
Shott, Stephen. *Look at me*
Showers, Paul. *A drop of blood*
How you talk
You can't make a move without your muscles
Your skin and mine
Smallman, Clare. *Outside in*
Stinson, Kathy. *The bare naked book*
Waxman, Stephanie. *What is a girl? What is a boy?*

Anatomy – ears

Bolliger, Max. *The rabbit with the sky blue ears*
Perkins, Al. *The ear book*
Showers, Paul. *Ears are for hearing*

Anatomy – eyes

Bailey, Jill. *Eyes*
Seuss, Dr. *The eye book*
Showers, Paul. *Look at your eyes*
Thomson, Ruth. *Eyes*
Worthy, Judith. *Eyes*

Anatomy – faces

Anno, Mitsumasa. *Anno's faces*
Brenner, Barbara A. *Faces, faces, faces*
Emberley, Ed (Edward Randolph). *Ed Emberley's crazy mixed-up face game*
Pieńkowski, Jan. *Faces*
Yudell, Lynn Deena. *Make a face*

Anatomy – feet

Aliki. *My feet*
Bailey, Jill. *Feet*
Blanchard, Arlene. *Sounds my feet make*
Chase, Catherine. *Feet*
Goor, Ron. *All kinds of feet*

Hamm, Diane Johnston. *How many feet in the bed?*
Holzenthaler, Jean. *My feet do*
Machotka, Hana. *What neat feet!*
Morgenstern, Constance. *Good night, feet*
Schertle, Alice. *My two feet*
Schubert, Ingrid. *Little big feet*
Seuss, Dr. *The foot book*
Weiss, Leatie. *Funny feet!*

Anatomy – hands

Aliki. *My hands*
Holzenthaler, Jean. *My hands can*
Perkins, Al. *Hand, hand, fingers, thumb*

Anatomy – heads

Bishop, Claire Huchet. *The man who lost his head*

Anatomy – mouths

Bailey, Jill. *Mouths*

Anatomy – noses

Noses
Bentley, Nancy. *I've got your nose!*
Boujon, Claude. *The fairy with the long nose*
Caple, Kathy. *The biggest nose*
Dubov, Christine Salac. *Aleksandra, where is your nose?*
Hutton, Warwick. *The nose tree*
Johnston, Tony. *The badger and the magic fan*
Krüss, James. *Johnny Longnose*
Machotka, Hana. *Breathtaking noses*
Moncure, Jane Belk. *What your nose knows!*
Ormerod, Jan. *This little nose*
Perkins, Al. *The nose book*

Anatomy – skeletons

Ahlberg, Allan. *The black cat*
Dinosaur dreams
Mystery tour
The pet shop
Balestrino, Philip. *The skeleton inside you*
Gross, Ruth Belov. *A book about your skeleton*
Hall, Katy. *Skeletons! Skeletons! All about bones*
Johnston, Tony. *Soup bone*
Spohn, David. *Nate's treasure*

Anatomy – toes

Dubov, Christine Salac. *Aleksandra, where are your toes?*
Hawkins, Colin. *This little pig*

Angels

Andersen, H. C. (Hans Christian). *The red shoes*, ill. by Chihiro Iwasaki

Benét, William Rose. *Angels*
Brown, Abbie Farwell. *The Christmas angel*
Collington, Peter. *The angel and the soldier boy*
Greeson, Janet. *The stingy baker*
Kavanaugh, James J. *The crooked angel*
Knight, Hilary. *Angels and berries and candy canes*
Krahn, Fernando. *A funny friend from heaven*
Lathrop, Dorothy Pulis. *An angel in the woods*
Martin, Judith. *The tree angel*
Sawyer, Ruth. *The Christmas Anna angel*
Tazewell, Charles. *The littlest angel*, ill. by Paul Micich
Thomas, Kathy. *The angel's quest*
Wallace, Ian. *Morgan the magnificent*
Willard, Nancy. *The high rise glorious skittle skat roarious sky pie angel food cake*
Zimelman, Nathan. *The star of Melvin*

Anger see Emotions – anger

Animals

Aardema, Verna. *Princess Gorilla and a new kind of water*
Rabbit makes a monkey of lion
Traveling to Tondo
The vingananee and the tree toad
What's so funny, Ketu?
Who's in Rabbit's house?
Why mosquitoes buzz in people's ears
Abisch, Roz. *The clever turtle*
Abolafia, Yossi. *Fox tale*
Adler, David A. *The carsick zebra and other riddles*
Æsop. *Seven fables from Æsop*, ill. by Robert W. Alley
Aitken, Amy. *Kate and Mona in the jungle*
Wanda's circus
Alborough, Jez. *Beaky*
Aldridge, Josephine Haskell. *The best of friends*
Alexander, Martha G. *Pigs say oink*
Aliki. *Wild and woolly mammoths*
Allamand, Pascale. *The animals who changed their colors*
Allard, Harry. *Bumps in the night*
Allen, Gertrude E. *Everyday animals*
Allen, Jeffrey. *Mary Alice, operator number 9*
Nosey Mrs. Rat
Allen, Jonathan. *A bad case of animal nonsense*
Allen, Linda. *Mrs. Simkin's bed*
Allen, Marjorie N. *One, two, three - ah-choo!*
Allen, Martha Dickson. *Real life monsters*
Allen, Pamela. *Mr. Archimedes' bath*
Who sank the boat?

Allen, Robert. *The zoo book*
Amery, H. *At the zoo*
The farm picture book
The zoo picture book
Ancona, George. *Handtalk zoo*
Andersen, H. C. (Hans Christian). *The emperor's new clothes*, ill. by Robert Byrd
Anderson, Lena Castell. *Bunny story*
Anholt, Catherine. *Chaos at Cold Custard Farm*
Twins, two by two
Anno, Mitsumasa. *Anno's animals*
Apple, Margot. *Blanket*
Applebaum, Stan. *Going my way?*
Archambault, John. *Counting sheep*
Argent, Kerry. *Animal capers*
Ariane. *Animal stories*
Armour, Richard Willard. *Animals on the ceiling*
Have you ever wished you were something else?
Arnold, Caroline. *Five nests*
Aruego, José. *Look what I can do*
We hide, you seek
Arvetis, Chris. *Why does it fly?*
Why is it dark?
Asbjørnsen, P. C. (Peter Christian). *The man who kept house*
Asch, Frank. *Bread and honey*
Ashabranner, Brent. *I'm in the zoo, too*
Asimov, Isaac. *Animals of the Bible*
Atwood, Margaret. *Anna's pet*
Aulaire, Ingri Mortenson d'. *Animals everywhere*
Children of the northlights
Aylesworth, Jim. *One crow*
B. B. *Blacksheep and Company*
Babson, Jane F. *Babson's bestiary*
Bahr, Robert. *Blizzard at the zoo*
Bailey, Jill. *Eyes*
Feet
Mouths
Noses
Baker, Alan. *Two tiny mice*
Baker, Betty. *Sonny-Boy Sim*
Baker, Eugene. *Bicycles*
Fire
Home
Outdoors
School
Water
Baker, Jeffrey J. W. *Patterns of nature*
Baker, Laura Nelson. *The friendly beasts*
Bang, Betsy. *The old woman and the red pumpkin*
The old woman and the rice thief
Bang, Molly. *Delphine*
Banks, Merry. *Animals of the night*
Bannon, Laura. *The best house in the world*
Little people of the night
Red mittens

The scary thing
Barasch, Marc Ian. *No plain pets!*
Barbot, Daniel. *A bicycle for Rosaura*
Bare, Colleen Stanley. *Who comes to the water hole?*
Barrett, Judi. *Animals should definitely not act like people*
Animals should definitely not wear clothing
Snake is totally tail
Barry, Robert E. *Animals around the world*
Baruch, Dorothy. *Kappa's tug-of-war with the big brown horse*
Base, Graeme. *Animalia*
My grandma lived in Gooligulch
Baskin, Leonard. *Hosie's zoo*
Bason, Lillian. *Castles and mirrors and cities of sand*
Bassett, Lisa. *A clock for Beany*
Batherman, Muriel. *Animals live here*
Battles, Edith. *What does the rooster say, Yoshio?*
Baugh, Dolores M. *Let's see the animals*
Baumann, Hans. *Chip has many brothers*
Bax, Martin. *Edmond went far away*
Bayer, Jane. *A my name is Alice*
Bayley, Nicola. *One old Oxford ox*
Baylor, Byrd. *Desert voices*
We walk in sandy places
Beach, Stewart. *Good morning, sun's up!*
Beim, Jerrold. *Eric on the desert*
Belling the cat and other stories, ill. by Harold Berson
Belloc, Hilaire. *The bad child's book of beasts*
The bad child's book of beasts, and more beasts for worse children
The bad child's pop-up book of beasts
More beasts for worse children
Bellville, Rod. *Large animal veterinarians*
Belpré, Pura. *Dance of the animals*
Bemelmans, Ludwig. *Rosebud*
Bendick, Jeanne. *Why can't I?*
Bennett, David. *One cow moo moo*
Bennett, Jill. *Animal fair*
Berger, Melvin. *Prehistoric mammals*
Berger, Terry. *The turtles' picnic and other nonsense stories*
Bernstein, Joanne E. *Creepy crawly critter riddles*
Bernstein, Margery. *Coyote goes hunting for fire*
The first morning
Berson, Harold. *Why the jackal won't speak to the hedgehog*
Bester, Roger. *Guess what?*
Bethell, Jean. *Bathtime*
Playmates
Bible, Charles. *Hamdaani*
Bierhorst, John. *Doctor Coyote*
The big Peter Rabbit book
Binzen, Bill. *Alfred goes house hunting*

Biro, Val. *The wind in the willows: home sweet home*
The wind in the willows: the open road
The wind in the willows: the river bank
The wind in the willows: the wild wood
Bishop, Roma. *Animals*
Blathwayt, Benedict. *Tangle and the silver bird*
Blough, Glenn O. *Who lives in this meadow?*
Bodsworth, Nan. *Monkey business*
Bograd, Larry. *Egon*
Bohdal, Susi. *Tom cat*
Bonino, Louise. *The cozy little farm*
Boon, Emilie. *1 2 3 how many animals can you see?*
Peterkin's very own garden
Peterkin's wet walk
Borden, Beatrice Brown. *Wild animals of Africa*
Borg, Inga. *Plupp builds a house*
Bottner, Barbara. *Zoo song*
Bourgeois, Paulette. *Too many chickens*
Boyd, Selma. *I met a polar bear*
Boynton, Sandra. *A is for angry*
The going to bed book
Good night, good night
Moo, baa, lalala
Bradman, Tony. *See you later, alligator*
Brandenberg, Franz. *Aunt Nina and her nephews and nieces*
Cock-a-doodle-doo
Brasch, Kate. *Prehistoric monsters*
Brennan, John. *Zoo day*
Brenner, Barbara A. *Ostrich feathers*
Brett, Jan. *Annie and the wild animals*
Brice, Tony. *Baby animals*
Brierley, Louise. *King Lion and his cooks*
Brister, Hope. *The cunning fox and other tales*
Bro, Marguerite H. *The animal friends of Peng-u*
Brock, Emma Lillian. *Nobody's mouse*
Surprise balloon
Brooke, L. Leslie (Leonard Leslie). *Johnny Crow's garden*
Johnny Crow's new garden
Johnny Crow's party
Brown, Craig McFarland. *My barn*
Brown, Marc Tolon. *Arthur goes to camp*
Arthur's April fool
Arthur's Christmas
Arthur's eyes
Arthur's Halloween
Arthur's teacher trouble
Arthur's Thanksgiving
Arthur's tooth
Arthur's Valentine
The bionic bunny show
D. W. flips!
The silly tail book

The true Francine
Brown, Marcia. *The blue jackal*
The bun
Once a mouse...
Brown, Margaret Wise. *Baby animals*, ill.
   by Mary Cameron
Baby animals, ill. by Susan Jeffers
The big fur secret
Big red barn, ill. by Felicia Bond
Big red barn, ill. by Rosella Hartman
Don't frighten the lion
The duck
Fox eyes
The golden birthday book
The little fur family
Once upon a time in pigpen and three
   other stories
Streamlined pig
They all saw it
Three little animals
Wait till the moon is full
Where have you been?
Brown, Richard Eric. *One hundred words*
   about animals
Browne, Anthony. *Bear goes to town*
The little bear book
Browner, Richard. *Everyone has a name*
Brunhoff, Laurent de. *Babar's counting*
   book
Babar's little circus star
Buck, Frank. *Jungle animals*
Buff, Mary. *Forest folk*
Buller, Jon. *Toad on the road*
Bullock, Kathleen. *It chanced to rain*
Bunting, Eve (Anne Evelyn). *Happy*
   birthday, dear duck
Night tree
Terrible things
Burdick, Margaret. *Bobby Otter and the blue*
   boat
Sara Raccoon and the secret place
Burgess, Thornton. *Old Mother West Wind*
Burningham, John. *Cluck baa*
Hey! Get off our train
Mr. Gumpy's outing
Burton, Jane. *Animals at home*
Animals at night
Animals at rest
Animals at work
Animals eating
Animals fighting
Animals keeping clean
Animals keeping cool
Animals keeping safe
Animals keeping warm
Animals learning
Animals talking
Burton, Marilee Robin. *The elephant's nest*
Tail toes eyes ears nose
Butler, Dorothy. *Higgledy, piggledy, hobbledy*
   hoy

Butterworth, Nick. *One blowy night*
One snowy night
Byars, Betsy Cromer. *The groober*
Calhoun, Mary. *Euphonia and the flood*
Calmenson, Stephanie. *All aboard the*
   goodnight train
Dinner at the Panda Palace
The kindergarten book
Where will the animals stay?
Campbell, Rod. *Dear zoo*
It's mine
Carle, Eric. *1, 2, 3 to the zoo*
The very busy spider
Carlson, Nancy. *Arnie and the new kid*
Arnie and the stolen markers
Louanne Pig in making the team
The talent show
Carlson, Natalie Savage. *Surprise in the*
   mountains
Carrick, Carol. *In the moonlight, waiting*
Patrick's dinosaurs
Carrick, Malcolm. *I can squash elephants!*
Carrier, Lark. *A Christmas promise*
Carroll, Kathleen Sullivan. *One red rooster*
Carter, Noelle. *I'm a little mouse*
My house
My pet
Cartwright, Ann. *Norah's ark*
Cassedy, Sylvia. *Red dragonfly on my*
   shoulder
Cassidy, Dianne. *Circus animals*
Castle, Caroline. *Herbert Binns and the*
   flying tricycle
Catalanotto, Peter. *Mr. Mumble*
Catchpole, Clive. *Deserts*
Grasslands
Jungles
Mountains
Cathon, Laura E. *Tot Botot and his little*
   flute
Cauley, Lorinda Bryan. *The animal kids*
The bake-off
The cock, the mouse and the little red hen
Causley, Charles. *"Quack!" said the billy-goat*
Cave, Kathryn. *Out for the count*
Cazet, Denys. *Are there any questions?*
The duck with squeaky feet
Frosted glass
Lucky me
Mother night
Never spit on your shoes
Sunday
Chalmers, Audrey. *Hundreds and hundreds*
   of pancakes
Chalmers, Mary. *A Christmas story*
Easter parade
Charles, Donald. *Calico Cat at the zoo*
Shaggy dog's animal alphabet
Chen, Tony. *Animals showing off*
Cherry, Lynne. *Who's sick today?*

Chicken Little. *Chicken Licken*, ill. by Jutta Ash

Chicken Licken, ill. by Gavin Bishop

Henny Penny, ill. by Stephen Butler

Henny Penny, ill. by Paul Galdone

Henny Penny, ill. by William Stobbs

The story of Chicken Licken, adapt. and ill. by Jan Ormerod

Chorao, Kay. *Lemon moon*

Chouinard, Roger. *The amazing animal alphabet book*

One magic box

Christelow, Eileen. *Glenda Feathers casts a spell*

Olive and the magic hat

The robbery at the diamond dog diner

Christensen, Gardell Dano. *Mrs. Mouse needs a house*

Christiana, David. *White nineteens*

Christmas in the stable, ill. by Beverly K. Duncan

Clewes, Dorothy. *Henry Hare's boxing match*

The wild wood

Climo, Shirley. *The cobweb Christmas*

Clymer, Ted. *The horse and the bad morning*

Coats, Laura Jane. *Ten little animals*

Coatsworth, Elizabeth. *A peaceable kingdom, and other poems*

Cober, Alan E. *Cober's choice*

Cock Robin. *The courtship, merry marriage, and feast of Cock Robin and Jenny Wren*, ill. by Barbara Cooney

Who killed Cock Robin? ill. by William Stobbs

Cohen, Caron Lee. *Pigeon, pigeon*

Colby, C. B. (Carroll Burleigh). *Who lives there?*

Who went there?

Cole, Joanna. *Animal sleepyheads*

Evolution

It's too noisy

Large as life daytime animals

Large as life nighttime animals

Cole, Michael. *Head in the sand*

Cole, Sheila. *When the tide is low*

Cole, William. *I went to the animal fair*

Collins, Pat Lowery. *Tomorrow, up and away!*

Colman, Hila. *Watch that watch*

Conklin, Gladys. *I caught a lizard*

Cooper, Susan. *Matthew's dragon*

Corey, Dorothy. *A shot for baby bear*

Will it ever be my birthday?

Cormack, M. Grant. *Animal tales from Ireland*

Cortesi, Wendy W. *Explore a spooky swamp*

Cosgrove, Margaret. *Wintertime for animals*

Cousins, Lucy. *Country animals*

Farm animals

Garden animals

Pet animals

What can rabbit hear?

What can rabbit see?

Coville, Bruce. *Sarah's unicorn*

Cowcher, Helen. *Rain forest*

Coxe, Molly. *Whose footprints?*

Craig, M. Jean. *Spring is like the morning*

Craver, Mike. *Beaver ball at the bug club*

Creighton, Jill. *One day there was nothing to do*

Cremins, Robert. *My animal ABC*

My animal Mother Goose

Cristini, Ermanno. *In the pond*

In the woods

Cross, Genevieve. *A trip to the yard*

Crowe, Robert L. *Tyler Toad and the thunder*

Croxford, Vera. *All kinds of animals*

Crump, Donald J. *Creatures small and furry*

Curle, Jock J. *The four good friends*

Curry, Peter. *Animals*

Cutler, Ivor. *The animal house*

Herbert

Cuyler, Margery. *That's good! That's bad!*

Dahl, Roald. *The enormous crocodile*

The giraffe and the pelly and me

Daly, Kathleen N. *Today's biggest animals*

Unusual animals

Davidson, Jill A. *And that's what happened to little Lucy*

Davis, Douglas F. *There's an elephant in the garage*

Day, Marie. *Dragon in the rocks*

DeLage, Ida. *ABC triplets at the zoo*

Delamare, David. *The Christmas secret*

Demarest, Chris L. *Kitman and Willy at sea*

Demi. *A Chinese zoo*

Demi's count the animals 1-2-3

Demi's find the animals A B C

Demi's opposites

Demuth, Patricia Brennan. *Ornery morning*

Dennis, Suzanne E. *Answer me that*

Dennis, Wesley. *Flip*

Denton, Terry. *Home is the sailor*

De Paola, Tomie (Thomas Anthony). *Country farm*

The hunter and the animals

De Posadas Mane, Carmen. *Mister North Wind*

De Regniers, Beatrice Schenk. *It does not say meow!*

May I bring a friend?

DiFiori, Lawrence. *Baby animals*

Dijs, Carla. *Are you my daddy?*

Are you my mommy?

Dionetti, Michelle. *The day Eli went looking for bear*

Dodd, Lynley. *Wake up, bear*

Dodds, Dayle Ann. *Do bunnies talk?*

Dodds, Siobhan. *Charles Tiger*

Elizabeth Hen

Domanska, Janina. *What do you see?*

Domestic animals
Dowling, Paul. *Happy birthday, Owl*
Dragonwagon, Crescent. *Alligator arrived with apples*
Dryden, Emma. *Good morning—good night*
Du Bois, William Pène. *Bear circus*
  Bear party
Dubov, Christine Salac. *Oink! and other sounds*
Duff, Maggie (Margaret K.). *Dancing turtle*
Duffy, Dee Dee (Deborah). *Barnyard tracks*
Duke, Kate. *Aunt Isabel tells a good one*
Duncan, Riana. *A nutcracker in a tree*
  When Emily woke up angry
Dunn, Judy. *The animals of Buttercup Farm*
Dunn, Phoebe. *Baby's animal friends*
Dunrea, Olivier. *Deep down underground*
Du Quette, Keith. *Rippening day for a picnic*
Durrell, Julie. *Mouse tails*
Duvoisin, Roger Antoine. *A for the ark*
  The crocodile in the tree
  Jasmine
  Our Veronica goes to Petunia's farm
  Petunia
  Petunia and the song
  Petunia, beware!
  Petunia takes a trip
  Petunia, the silly goose
  Petunia's treasure
Easton, Violet. *Elephants never jump*
Ehrlich, Amy. *Lucy's winter tale*
Eichenberg, Fritz. *Dancing in the moon*
Elborn, Andrew. *Noah and the ark and the animals*
Elkin, Benjamin. *Why the sun was late*
Elting, Mary. *Q is for duck*
Emberley, Barbara. *One wide river to cross*
Emberley, Ed (Edward Randolph). *Animals*
Erickson, Russell E. *Warton's Christmas eve adventure*
Ernst, Lisa Campbell. *Hamilton's art show*
Ets, Marie Hall. *Another day*
  Beasts and nonsense
  Elephant in a well
  In the forest
  Just me
  Mister Penny
  Mister Penny's circus
  Play with me
Euvremer, Teryl. *The thieves of Peck's pocket*
Evans, Eva Knox. *Sleepy time*
  Where do you live?
Facklam, Margery. *But not like mine*
  So can I
Farber, Norma. *As I was crossing Boston Common*
  How the hibernators came to Bethlehem
  How the left-behind beasts built Ararat
  How to ride a tiger
Farm animals, photos. sel. by Debby Slier

Farm animals [Macmillan, 1991]
Farm house, ill. by Kate Klimo
Fay, Hermann. *My zoo*
Feczko, Kathy. *Umbrella parade*
Feldman, Eve B. *Animals don't wear pajamas*
Fiddle-i-fee, ill. by Diane Stanley
Fife, Dale. *The little park*
Finzel, Julia. *Large as life*
Fischer, Hans. *The birthday*
Fischetto, Laura. *Inside Noah's ark*
  The jungle is my home
Fisher, Aileen Lucia. *Do bears have mothers too?*
  We went looking
  Where does everyone go?
Flack, Marjorie. *Ask Mr. Bear*
Flanders, Michael. *Creatures great and small*
Fleming, Denise. *Count!*
Fletcher, Elizabeth. *What am I?*
Flora, James. *The day the cow sneezed*
Florian, Douglas. *At the zoo*
  A bird can fly
Foreman, Michael. *Panda and the bushfire*
Fournier, Catharine. *The coconut thieves*
Fowler, Allan. *Cubs and colts and calves and kittens*
Fowler, Richard. *Mr. Little's noisy car*
  Mr. Little's noisy truck
Fox, Charles Philip. *Mr. Stripes the gopher*
Fox, Mem. *Hattie and the fox*
Francis, Frank. *The magic wallpaper*
Frascino, Edward. *My cousin the king*
Freedman, Russell. *Farm babies*
  Hanging on
  Tooth and claw
  When winter comes
Freeman, Don. *Add-a-line alphabet*
French, Fiona. *Anancy and Mr. Dry-Bone*
Freschet, Berniece. *Owl in the garden*
  Where's Henrietta's hen?
Friedrich, Priscilla. *The wishing well in the woods*
The friendly beasts, ill. by Sarah Chamberlain
Frith, Michael K. *Some of us walk, some fly, some swim*
A frog he would a-wooing go (folk-song).
  Froggie went a-courting, ill. by Chris Conover
  Wendy Watson's frog went a-courting
From King Boggen's hall to nothing-at-all, ill. by Blair Lent
Fromm, Lilo. *Muffel and Plums*
Fussenegger, Gertrud. *Noah's ark*
Futamata, Eigorō. *How not to catch a mouse*
Gackenbach, Dick. *Supposes*
Galdone, Paul. *Cat goes fiddle-i-fee*
Gammell, Stephen. *Once upon MacDonald's farm*
Gantos, Jack (John, Jr.). *The perfect pal*

Gardam, Catharine. *The animals' Christmas*
Gardner, Beau. *Can you imagine...?*
Guess what?
Garelick, May. *Look at the moon*
Garland, Sarah. *Billy and Belle*
Garten, Jan. *The alphabet tale*
Gay, Michel. *Bibi's birthday surprise*
Night ride
Gay, Zhenya. *Look!*
George, William T. *Fishing at Long Pond*
Geraghty, Paul. *The cow is mooing anyhow*
Over the steamy swamp
Gerrard, Roy. *Mik's mammoth*
Gerstein, Mordicai. *William, where are you?*
Gibbons, Gail. *Prehistoric animals*
Zoo
Ginsburg, Mirra. *Four brave sailors*
The fox and the hare
Mushroom in the rain
Goble, Paul. *The great race: of the birds and animals*
Goennel, Heidi. *If I were a penguin...*
Goffe, Toni. *Toby's animal rescue service*
Goffstein, M. B. (Marilyn Brooke). *Natural history*
Gomi, Taro. *Guess who?*
My friends
Goodspeed, Peter. *A rhinoceros wakes me up in the morning*
Goor, Ron. *All kinds of feet*
Gordon, Shirley. *Grandma zoo*
Grabianski, Janusz. *Grabianski's wild animals*
Graham, Bob. *First there was Frances*
Graham, John. *A crowd of cows*
I love you, mouse
Grahame, Kenneth. *The open road*
Greeley, Valerie. *Farm animals*
Field animals
Pets
Where's my share?
White is the moon
Zoo animals
Greenaway, Shirley. *Burrows*
Forests
Jungles
Greenfield, Karen R. *Sister Yessa's story*
Gretz, Susanna. *Duck takes off*
Frog, duck and rabbit
Frog in the middle
Rabbit rambles on
Greydanus, Rose. *Animals at the zoo*
Griffith, Helen V. *Grandaddy's place*
Grimm, Jacob. *The Bremen town musicians*, ill. by Donna Diamond
The Bremen town musicians, ill. by Janina Domanska
The Bremen town musicians, ill. by Paul Galdone
Bremen town musicians, ill. by Josef Paleček

The Bremen town musicians, ill. by Ilse Plume
The Bremen town musicians, ill. by Bernadette Watts
Little Red Riding Hood, ill. by John S. Goodall
The musicians of Bremen, ill. by Svend Otto S.
The musicians of Bremen, ill. by Martin Ursell
The traveling musicians of Bremen, ill. by Kady MacDonald Denton
Groening, Maggie. *Maggie Simpson's book of animals*
Grosvenor, Donna. *Zoo babies*
Guarino, Deborah. *Is your mama a llama?*
Gullikson, Sandy. *Trouble for breakfast*
Gundersheimer, Karen. *Colors to know*
Hadithi, Mwenye. *Crafty chameleon*
Lazy lion
Tricky tortoise
Haley, Gail E. *Noah's ark*
Hall, Malcolm. *CariCATures*
Hamberger, John. *The day the sun disappeared*
Hands, Hargrave. *Duckling sees*
Little lamb sees
Hanna, Jack. *The petting zoo*
Harris, Joel Chandler. *Jump!*
Jump again!
Harris, Susan. *Creatures that look alike*
Harrison, David Lee. *Wake up, sun!*
Harrison, Sarah. *In granny's garden*
Hartman, Gail. *As the crow flies*
Haseley, Dennis. *The cave of snores*
Hawkins, Colin. *Max and the magic word*
Where's my mommy?
Hawkinson, John. *Robins and rabbits*
Hayes, Ann. *Meet the orchestra*
Hayes, Sarah. *The grumpalump*
Haywood, Carolyn. *Hello, star*
Hazen, Barbara Shook. *Where do bears sleep?*
Heine, Helme. *Friends*
Mollywoop
Three little friends: the alarm clock
Three little friends: the racing cart
Three little friends: the visitor
Hellen, Nancy. *Animals of the jungle*
A visit to the farm
A visit to the zoo
Heller, Nicholas. *Mathilda the dream bear*
Heller, Ruth. *Animals born alive and well*
How to hide a polar bear
How to hide an octopus
Helweg, Hans. *Farm animals*
Henkes, Kevin. *Chrysanthemum*
Henley, Claire. *At the zoo*
Farm day
In the ocean
Jungle day

Henley, Karyn. *Hatch!*
Herriot, James. *Only one woof*
Herson, Kathleen. *The copycat*
Heuck, Sigrid. *Who stole the apples?*
Hewitt, Kathryn. *The three sillies*
Higham, Jon Atlas. *Aardvark's picnic*
Hill, Eric. *Spot at play*
  Spot at the fair
  Spot counts from 1 to 10
  Spot goes to the farm
  Spot on the farm
Himmelman, John. *Amanda and the magic garden*
  A guest is a guest
  Montigue on the high seas
Hines, Anna Grossnickle. *I'll tell you what they say*
Hirschi, Ron. *Fall*
  Forest
  Loon lake
  Ocean
  Spring
  Summer
  Who lives in... Alligator Swamp?
  Who lives in... the forest?
  Winter
Hirschmann, Linda. *In a lick of a flick of a tongue*
Hoban, Julia. *Quick chick*
Hoban, Lillian. *The case of the two masked robbers*
Hoban, Tana. *Big ones, little ones*
  A children's zoo
Hoberman, Mary Ann. *A fine fat pig other animal poems*
Hoff, Carol. *The four friends*
Holder, Heidi. *Carmine the crow*
Holl, Adelaide. *The rain puddle*
  Small Bear builds a playhouse
Holm, Mayling Mack. *A forest Christmas*
Hood, Thomas. *Before I go to sleep*
Hooper, Patricia. *A bundle of beasts*
Hoopes, Lyn Littlefield. *My own home*
Hopkins, Lee Bennett. *Animals from Mother Goose*
  To the zoo
Hoppe, Matthias. *Mouse and elephant*
Houston, John A. *A room full of animals*
Howe, James. *Hot fudge*
Hubbard, Woodleigh. *Two is for dancing*
Hurd, Edith Thacher. *Christmas eve*
Hurd, Thacher. *A night in the swamp*
Hurford, John. *The dormouse*
Hutchins, Pat. *1 hunter*
  The silver Christmas tree
  The surprise party
  What game shall we play?
Ichikawa, Satomi. *Nora's castle*
  Nora's duck
Inkpen, Mick. *Billy's beetle*
  One bear at bedtime

Ipcar, Dahlov. *Animal hide and seek*
  Bright barnyard
  Brown cow farm
  The calico jungle
  A flood of creatures
  I like animals
  I love my anteater with an A
  Lost and found
  Wild and tame animals
Irvine, Georgeanne. *The nursery babies*
  Tully the tree kangaroo
Isenbart, Hans-Heinrich. *Baby animals on the farm*
Jacobs, Joseph. *Hereafterthis*
Janosch. *Tonight at nine*
Jaynes, Ruth M. *Tell me please! What's that?*
Jenkin-Pearce, Susie. *Bad Boris goes to school*
Joerns, Consuelo. *Oliver's escape*
Johnson, Crockett. *We wonder what will Walter be? When he grows up*
Johnson, Russell. *Trouble at Christmas*
Johnston, Deborah. *Mathew Michael's beastly day*
Jonas, Ann. *Aardvarks, disembark!*
  The trek
Jorgensen, Gail. *Crocodile Beat*
Kamen, Gloria. *"Paddle," said the swan*
  The ringdoves
Kane, Henry B. *Wings, legs, or fins*
Kasza, Keiko. *A mother for Choco*
  When the elephant walks
Katz, Bobbi. *The creepy crawly book*
Kaufmann, John. *Flying giants of long ago*
Keats, Ezra Jack. *Pet show!*
Keller, Holly. *Too big*
  Will it rain?
Kellogg, Steven (Stephen). *Aster Aardvark's alphabet adventures*
  Chicken Little
Kemp, Anthea. *Mr. Percy's magic greenhouse*
Kennaway, Adrienne. *Little elephant's walk*
Kent, Jack. *Joey runs away*
  Little Peep
Kepes, Juliet. *Five little monkeys*
Kessler, Ethel. *Are there hippos on the farm?*
  Do baby bears sit in chairs?
  Is there an elephant in your kitchen?
Kessler, Leonard P. *The big mile race*
  Do you have any carrots?
Kherdian, David. *The animal*
  The cat's midsummer jamboree
Kilroy, Sally. *Animal noises*
  Babies' zoo
Kimmel, Eric A. *Anansi and the moss-covered rock*
  I took my frog to the library
King, Bob. *Sitting on the farm*
Kingman, Lee. *Peter's long walk*
Kipling, Rudyard. *The elephant's child*, ill. by Louise Brierley

The elephant's child, ill. by Lorinda Bryan Cauley
The elephant's child, ill. by Tim Raglin
How the camel got his hump, ill. by Quentin Blake
How the camel got his hump, ill. by Tim Raglin
The miracle of the mountain, ill. by Willi Baum
Kirn, Ann. *Beeswax catches a thief*
Kitchen, Bert. *Animal alphabet*
Animal numbers
Pig in a barrow
Tenrec's twigs
Knuppel, Helga. *The adventures of Christabel Crocodile*
Knutson, Barbara. *How the guinea fowl got her spots*
Kobayashi, Robert. *Maria Mazaretti loves spaghetti*
Kobayashi, Yuji. *Miss Josephine's secret walk*
Koch, Michelle. *Hoot, howl, hiss*
Koelling, Caryl. *Animal mix and match*
Koide, Tan. *May we sleep here tonight?*
Koller, Jackie French. *Fish fry tonight*
Komori, Atsushi. *Animal mothers*
Koopmans, Loek. *The woodcutter's mitten*
Koralek, Jenny. *The friendly fox*
Koscielniak, Bruce. *Euclid Bunny delivers the mail*
Krahn, Fernando. *The biggest Christmas tree on earth*
Kramer, Anthony Penta. *Numbers on parade*
Krauze, Andrzej. *What's so special about today?*
Kroll, Steven. *It's Groundhog Day!*
Krüss, James. *3 X 3*
Kubler, Susanne. *The three friends*
Kuchalla, Susan. *Baby animals*
Kuklin, Susan. *Taking my dog to the vet*
Kuskin, Karla. *The animals and the ark*
James and the rain
Roar and more
Something sleeping in the hall
Kwitz, Mary DeBall. *When it rains*
Lady Eden's School. *Just how stories*
Laird, Elizabeth. *The day the ducks went skating*
The day Veronica was nosy
Langstaff, John M. *Over in the meadow*
Lapp, Eleanor. *The mice came in early this year*
Lathrop, Dorothy Pulis. *Who goes there?*
Laurencin, Geneviève. *I wish I were*
Lavies, Bianca. *Lily pad pond*
Tree trunk traffic
Lazard, Naomi. *What Amanda saw*
Lee, Jeanne M. *Toad is the uncle of heaven*
Leedy, Loreen. *The Furry News*
The great trash bash

Leigh, Oretta. *The merry-go-round*
Lenski, Lois. *Animals for me*
Big little Davy
Leonard, Marcia. *Noisy neighbors*
Lesser, Carolyn. *The goodnight circle*
Lester, Alison. *Imagine*
Lester, Helen. *It wasn't my fault*
Lewin, Betsy. *Animal snackers*
Lewis, J. Patrick. *A hippopotamusn't*
Two-legged, four-legged, no-legged rhymes
Lewis, Naomi. *Hare and badger go to town*
Lewis, Sheri. *Baby Lamb Chop loves animals*
Lewis, Stephen. *Zoo city*
Lewison, Wendy C. *Going to sleep on the farm*
Lillegard, Dee. *Sitting in my box*
Lillie, Patricia. *When the rooster crowed*
Lilly, Kenneth. *Animal builders*
Animal climbers
Animal jumpers
Animal runners
Animal swimmers
Animals at the zoo
Animals in the country
Animals in the jungle
Animals on the farm
Lindberg, Reeve. *Midnight farm*
Lindbergh, Reeve. *Benjamin's barn*
The day the goose got loose
Lionni, Leo. *The biggest house in the world*
Frederick's fables
Lipkind, William. *The boy and the forest*
Lippman, Peter. *New at the zoo*
The little red hen. *The cock, the mouse and the little red hen*, ill. by Graham Percy
The little red hen, ill. by Janina Domanska
The little red hen, ill. by Paul Galdone
The little red hen, ill. by Mel Pekarsky
The little red hen, ill. by William Stobbs
The little red hen, ill. by Margot Zemach
Livingston, Myra Cohn. *Valentine poems*
Lloyd, David. *Duck*
Hello, goodbye
Lobel, Anita. *King Rooster, Queen Hen*
Lobel, Arnold. *Fables*
A holiday for Mister Muster
A zoo for Mister Muster
Löfgren, Ulf. *Alvin the zookeeper*
One-two-three
Loomans, Diane. *The lovables in the kingdom of self-esteem*
Lorenz, Lee. *Hugo and the spacedog*
A weekend in the city
Lorian, Nicole. *A birthday present for Mama*
Low, Joseph. *Adam's book of odd creatures*
Lüton, Mildred. *Little chicks' mothers and all the others*
Luttrell, Ida. *Mattie and the chicken thief*
Three good blankets
Lyfick, Warren. *Animal tales*

Lynn, Sara. *Big animals*
 Farm animals
 Garden animals
 1 2 3
 Small animals
Lyon, George-Ella. *A regular rolling Noah*
McAllister, Angela. *Matepo*
McCauley, Jane. *The way animals sleep*
McClung, Robert. *How animals hide*
McConnachie, Brian. *Lily of the forest*
McCrea, Lilian. *Mother hen*
MacDonald, Elizabeth. *My aunt and the animals*
McGee, Marni. *The quiet farmer*
Machotka, Hana. *Breathtaking noses*
 What do you do at a petting zoo?
 What neat feet!
McKee, David. *The sad story of Veronica who played the violin*
MacKeen, Leslie Ann. *Who can fix it?*
McKissack, Patricia C. *The little red hen*
McLeod, Emilie Warren. *One snail and me*
McNally, Darcie. *In a cabin in a wood*
McNaught, Harry. *Baby animals*
McNeer, May Yonge. *Little Baptiste*
McPhail, David. *Andrew's bath*
 Animals A to Z
 Farm morning
 Lorenzo
 The party
 Where can an elephant hide?
Mado, Michio. *The animals*
Maestro, Giulio. *Leopard is sick*
 One more and one less
Mahy, Margaret. *17 kings and 42 elephants*
Mann, Peggy. *King Laurence, the alarm clock*
Manning, Linda. *Animal hours*
Mari, Iela. *Eat and be eaten*
Maris, Ron. *I wish I could fly*
 In my garden
Marks, Burton. *Animals*
Marshall, Edward. *Fox all week*
Marshall, James. *Four little troubles*
 Willis
Marshall, Janet Perry. *My camera: at the zoo*
Martin, Bill (William Ivan). *Polar bear, polar bear, what do you hear?*
Martin, Rafe. *Will's mammoth*
Marzollo, Jean. *Pretend you're a cat*
Massie, Diane Redfield. *The baby beebee bird*
Maxner, Joyce. *Nicholas Cricket*
Mayer, Marianna. *Beauty and the beast*
 The Brambleberrys animal alphabet
 The Brambleberrys animal book of big and small shapes
 The Brambleberrys animal book of counting
 The little jewel box
Mayer, Mercer. *Appelard and Liverwurst*
 What do you do with a kangaroo?

Mayne, William. *Come, come to my corner*
Meeks, Esther K. *Friendly farm animals*
 Something new at the zoo
Mendoza, George. *Need a house? Call Ms. Mouse*
Merriam, Eve. *The birthday cow*
 Goodnight to Annie
 Where is everybody?
Miklowitz, Gloria D. *The zoo that moved*
Miles, Miska. *Noisy gander*
 Sylvester Jones and the voice in the forest
Miller, Edna. *Mouskin's Thanksgiving*
Miller, J. P. (John Parr). *Farmer John's animals*
Miller, Jane. *Farm noises*
 Seasons on the farm
Millhouse, Nicholas. *Blue-footed booby*
Minarik, Else Holmelund. *The little girl and the dragon*
Mitchell, Adrian. *Our mammoth*
Mizumura, Kazue. *If I were a cricket...*
Modesitt, Jeanne. *The night call*
Mollel, Tolowa M. *Rhinos for lunch and elephants for supper*
Moncure, Jane Belk. *Riddle me a riddle*
Monsell, Mary Elise. *Underwear!*
Moore, Elaine. *Grandma's house*
Moore, John. *Granny Stickleback*
Mora, Emma. *Animals of the forest*
Morgan, Michaela. *Edward gets a pet*
Morozumi, Atsuko. *One gorilla*
Morris, Linda Lowe. *Morning milking*
Morrison, Sean. *Is that a happy hippopotamus?*
Morse, Samuel French. *All in a suitcase*
Moser, Erwin. *The crow in the snow and other bedtime stories*
Most, Bernard. *The cow that went oink*
 Dinosaur cousins?
 Zoodles
Mother Goose. *Hey diddle diddle*, ill. by Marilyn Janovitz
 Pat-a-cake, ill. by Marilyn Janovitz
Mullins, Edward S. *Animal limericks*
Munari, Bruno. *Animals for sale*
 Bruno Munari's zoo
 The elephant's wish
 Who's there? Open the door
Musicant, Elke. *The night vegetable eater*
My first book of baby animals, ill. by Karen Lee Schmidt
Myers, Bernice. *The flying shoes*
Nakabayashi, Ei. *The rainy day puddle*
Nakano, Hirotaka. *Elephant blue*
Nakatani, Chiyoko. *The zoo in my garden*
Nash, Ogden. *Custard the dragon*, ill. by Linell Nash
Nerlove, Miriam. *I made a mistake*
Newton, Patricia Montgomery. *The frog who drank the waters of the world*
Nichol, B. P. *Once: a lullaby*

Noll, Sally. *Jiggle wiggle prance*
Norman, Charles. *The hornbean tree and other poems*
Novak, Matt. *Mr. Floop's lunch*
Obligado, Lilian. *Faint frogs feeling feverish and other terrifically tantalizing tongue twisters*
O'Donnell, Peter. *Moonlit journey*
Old MacDonald had a farm. *Old MacDonald had a farm*, ill. by Lorinda Bryan Cauley
Old MacDonald had a farm, ill. by Mel Crawford
Old MacDonald had a farm, ill. by David Frankland
Old MacDonald had a farm, ill. by Abner Graboff
Old MacDonald had a farm, ill. by Nancy Hellen
Old MacDonald had a farm, ill. by Carol Jones
Old MacDonald had a farm, ill. by Tracey Campbell Pearson
Old MacDonald had a farm, ill. by Robert M. Quackenbush
Old MacDonald had a farm, ill. by Glen Rounds
Old MacDonald had a farm, ill. by William Stobbs
Old MacDonald had a farm, ill. by Prue Theobalds
Oppenheim, Joanne. *"Not now!" said the cow*
You can't catch me!
Ormerod, Jan. *When we went to the zoo*
Over in the meadow, ill. by Paul Galdone
Over in the meadow, ill. by Ezra Jack Keats
Oxenbury, Helen. *Friends*
Monkey see, monkey do
Pippo gets lost
729 curious creatures
729 merry mix-ups
Pack, Robert. *Then what did you do?*
Palazzo, Tony (Anthony D.). *Animal babies*
Animals 'round the mulberry bush
Palmer, Mary Babcock. *No-sort-of-animal*
Paré, Roger. *Animal capers*
Circus days
Play time
Summer days
Park, W. B. *Bakery business*
The costume party
Parker, Nancy Winslow. *Working frog*
Parnall, Peter. *Alfalfa Hill*
Winter barn
Parsons, Alexandra. *Amazing mammals*
Partridge, Jenny. *Colonel Grunt*
Grandma Snuffles
Hopfellow
Mr. Squint
Peterkin Pollensnuff

Paterson, Bettina. *My first wild animals*
Paterson, Diane. *If I were a toad*
Patterson, Geoffrey. *The lion and the gypsy*
Paul, Jan S. *Hortense*
Paxton, Tom. *Belling the cat and other Æsop fables*
Payne, Joan Balfour. *The stable that stayed*
Peaceable kingdom, ill. by Alice and Martin Provensen
Pearce, Q. L. *In the African grasslands*
In the desert
Peek, Merle. *The balancing act*
Mary wore her red dress and Henry wore his green sneakers
Peet, Bill (William Bartlett). *The ant and the elephant*
Cock-a-doodle Dudley
Farewell to Shady Glade
The gnats of knotty pine
No such things
Pelham, David. *A is for animals*
Worms wiggle
Peppé, Rodney. *Little circus*
Peters, Sharon. *Animals at night*
Peterson, Esther Allen. *Frederick's alligator*
Pevear, Richard. *Mister Cat-and-a-Half*
Peyo. *The Smurfs and their woodland friends*
Piatti, Celestino. *Celestino Piatti's animal ABC*
Pieńkowski, Jan. *Farm*
Homes
Zoo
Pirotta, Saviour. *Little bird*
Pitcher, Caroline. *Animals*
Pittman, Helena Clare. *Once when I was scared*
Pizer, Abigail. *It's a perfect day*
Plante, Patricia. *The turtle and the two ducks*
Pluckrose, Henry Arthur. *Fur and feathers*
Paws and claws
Skin, shell and scale
Poole, Valerie. *Obadiah Coffee and the music contest*
Porter, Sue. *One potato*
Porter-Gaylord, Laurel. *I love my daddy because...*
I love my mommy because...
Potter, Beatrix. *Appley Dapply's nursery rhymes*
Beatrix Potter's nursery rhyme book
Cecily Parsley's nursery rhymes
Ginger and Pickles
More tales from Beatrix Potter
Peter Rabbit's ABC
The tale of Jemima Puddle-Duck and other farmyard tales
The tale of Peter Rabbit and other stories
A treasury of Peter Rabbit and other stories
Yours affectionately, Peter Rabbit
Pouyanne, Rési. *What I see hidden by the pond*

Powzyk, Joyce. *Tasmania*
Prelutsky, Jack. *Beneath a blue umbrella*
  The pack rat's day and other poems
Price, Mathew. *Do you see what I see?*
Price-Thomas, Brian. *The magic ark*
Provensen, Alice. *Our animal friends*
  The year at Maple Hill Farm
Pryor, Bonnie. *Greenbrook farm*
The pudgy book of farm animals, ill. by Julie
  Durrell
Purcell, John Wallace. *African animals*
Quackenbush, Robert M. *Pete Pack Rat*
Raskin, Ellen. *And it rained*
  Who, said Sue, said whoo?
Rayner, Shoo. *My first picture joke book*
Reddix, Valerie. *Millie and the mud hole*
Reeves, Mona Rabun. *I had a cat*
Reiser, Lynn. *Any kind of dog*
Rey, H. A. (Hans Augusto). *Tit for tat*
  Where's my baby?
Rey, Margret (Margret Elisabeth
  Waldstein). *Billy's picture*
Rice, Eve. *Sam who never forgets*
Richter, Mischa. *Quack?*
Riddell, Chris. *Bird's new shoes*
Robinson, Irene Bowen. *Picture book of
  animal babies*
Robinson, W. W. (William Wilcox). *On the
  farm*
Rockwell, Anne F. *Big bad goat*
  The good llama
  Honk honk!
  Poor Goose
  Root-a-toot-toot
Roddie, Shen. *Animal stew*
Roe, Richard. *Animal ABC*
Roffey, Maureen. *I spy at the zoo*
Rojankovsky, Feodor. *Animals in the zoo*
  Animals on the farm
  The great big animal book
  The great big wild animal book
Root, Phyllis. *Moon tiger*
Roscoe, William. *The butterfly's ball*
Rose, Anne. *Spider in the sky*
Rose, Gerald. *Trouble in the ark*
Rosen, Michael J. *How the animals got their
  colors*
  Little rabbit Foo Foo
Roughsey, Dick. *The giant devil-dingo*
Rounds, Glen. *Washday on Noah's ark*
Rowan, James P. *I can be a zoo keeper*
Royston, Angela. *Jungle animals*
  Small animals
Runcie, Jill. *Cock-a-doodle-doo*
Rupprecht, Siegfried P. *The tale of the
  vanishing rainbow*
Rusling, Albert. *The mouse and Mrs.
  Proudfoot*
Russell, Solveig Paulson. *What good is a
  tail?*
Ryder, Joanne. *Fog in the meadow*

  The night flight
Rylant, Cynthia. *Night in the country*
Sage, Angie. *Monkeys in the jungle*
Saleh, Harold J. *Even tiny ants must sleep*
San Diego Zoological Society. *Families*
  A visit to the zoo
Sandberg, Inger. *Nicholas' favorite pet*
Saunders, Dave. *Snowtime*
Savage, Stephen. *Making tracks*
Scarry, Richard. *Is this the house of Mistress
  Mouse?*
  Richard Scarry's animal nursery tales
  Richard Scarry's great big mystery book
  Richard Scarry's mix or match storybook
  *Richard Scarry's Postman Pig and his busy
    neighbors*
Scharer, Niko. *Emily's house*
Schatz, Letta. *The extraordinary tug-of-war*
Scheidl, Gerda Marie. *Can we help you,
  Saint Nicholas?*
Schick, Eleanor. *A surprise in the forest*
Schindler, Regina. *The bear's cave*
Schmid, Eleonore. *Farm animals*
Schongut, Emanuel. *Look kitten*
Schumacher, Claire. *King of the zoo*
  Nutty's birthday
  Tim and Jim
Schweitzer, Iris. *Hilda's restful chair*
Scruton, Clive. *Mary's pets*
Seignobosc, Françoise. *The big rain*
  The story of Colette
Selberg, Ingrid. *Nature's hidden world*
Selkowe, Valrie M. *Spring green*
Selsam, Millicent E. *All kinds of babies*
  *A first look at kangaroos, koalas and other
    animals with pouches*
  A first look at seashells
  Hidden animals
  Keep looking!
  Night animals
Sendak, Maurice. *Very far away*
Seuss, Dr. *Mr. Brown can moo! Can you?*
  Would you rather be a bullfrog?
Severn, Jeffrey. *George and his giant shadow*
Sewall, Marcia. *Animal song*
Seymour, Peter. *Animals in disguise*
Shapiro, Arnold L. *Who says that?*
Sharmat, Marjorie Weinman. *Bartholomew
  the bossy*
  Taking care of Melvin
  The 329th friend
  Walter the wolf
Short, Mayo. *Andy and the wild ducks*
Simon, Mina Lewiton. *If you were an eel,
  how would you feel?*
Simon, Paul. *At the zoo*
Simon, Seymour. *Animal fact—animal fable*
Singer, Isaac Bashevis. *Why Noah chose the
  dove*
Singer, Marilyn. *Turtle in July*
Siracusa, Catherine. *No mail for Mitchell*

Skaar, Grace Marion. *What do the animals say?*
Skofield, James. *Crow moon, worm moon*
Skorpen, Liesel Moak. *All the Lassies*
Slate, Joseph. *Who is coming to our house?*
Slobodkin, Louis. *Friendly animals*
  Melvin, the moose child
  Our friendly friends
Slobodkina, Esphyr. *The wonderful feast*
Small, David. *Imogene's antlers*
Smith, Donald. *Who's wearing my baseball cap?*
  Who's wearing my bow tie?
  Who's wearing my sneakers?
  Who's wearing my sunglasses?
Smith, Jim. *The frog band and the onion seller*
  The frog band and the owlnapper
  Nimbus the explorer
Smith, Lane. *The big pets*
Smith, Mavis. *Fred, is that you?*
Smith, Roger. *How the animals saved the ark and put two and two together*
Smith, William Jay. *Birds and beasts*
Sneed, Brad. *Lucky Russell*
Snyder, Dick. *One day at the zoo*
  Talk to me tiger
Solotareff, Grégoire. *Never trust an ogre*
Spier, Peter. *Gobble, growl, grunt*
  The pet store
Spilka, Arnold. *Little birds don't cry*
Spohn, David. *Nate's treasure*
Stadler, John. *Animal cafe*
  Cat is back at bat
  Gorman and the treasure chest
Stafford, William. *The animal that drank up sound*
Staines, Bill. *All God's critters got a place in the choir*
Stamper, Judith. *What's it like to be a veterinarian*
Stehr, Frédéric. *Quack-quack*
Steig, William. *Sylvester and the magic pebble*
Steinmetz, Leon. *Clocks in the woods*
Stevens, Carla. *Hooray for pig!*
  Pig and the blue flag
  Stories from a snowy meadow
Stevens, Harry. *Fat mouse*
  Parrot told snake
Stevens, Janet. *Animal fair*
Stevenson, James. *Clams can't sing*
  Happy Valentine's Day, Emma!
  Mr. Hacker
  National worm day
  No need for Monty
  We can't sleep
  Which one is Whitney?
Stevenson, Suçie. *I forgot*
Stobbs, William. *Animal pictures*
Stoddard, Sandol. *Bedtime mouse*
Stratemeyer, Clara Georgeanna. *Pepper*

Struppi
Sutton, Jane. *What should a hippo wear?*
Sweet, Melissa. *Fiddle-i-fee*
Swendson, Patsy. *The potluck adventures of Mrs. Marmalade*
Szekeres, Cyndy. *Long ago*
Tafuri, Nancy. *Do not disturb*
  Junglewalk
  My friends
  Rabbit's morning
  Where we sleep
  Who's counting?
Tanaka, Beatrice. *The chase*
Taylor, Mark. *"Lamb," said the lion, "I am here."*
Tensen, Ruth M. *Come to the zoo!*
Testa, Fulvio. *Wolf's favor*
Tester, Sylvia Root. *Chase!*
  A visit to the zoo
Thaler, Mike. *Hippo lemonade*
  It's me, hippo!
  Pack 109
Thayer, Jane. *Andy and his fine friends*
Thomas, Patricia. *"Stand back," said the elephant, "I'm going to sneeze!"*
Thornhill, Jan. *Wildlife ABC*
  The wildlife 1-2-3
Tison, Annette. *Animal hide-and-seek*
  Animals in color magic
Titus, Eve. *The kitten who couldn't purr*
Tomkins, Jasper. *The catalog*
Tresselt, Alvin R. *The mitten*
  Wake up, farm! ill. by author
  Wake up, farm! ill. by Carolyn Ewing
Trinca, Rod. *One woolly wombat*
Tripp, Valerie. *Happy, happy Mother's Day*
Troughton, Joanna. *Make-believe tales*
  Mouse-Deer's market
Tryon, Leslie. *Albert's play*
Tworkov, Jack. *The camel who took a walk*
Udry, Janice May. *Is Susan here?*
Ueno, Noriko. *Elephant buttons*
Unwin, Pippa. *The great zoo hunt!*
Upton, Pat. *Who lives in the woods?*
Van Caster, Nancy. *An alligator lives in Benjamin's house*
Van Laan, Nancy. *The big fat worm*
  A mouse in my house
  This is the hat
Van Vorst, M. L. *A Norse lullaby*
Van Woerkom, Dorothy. *The rat, the ox and the zodiac*
Varga, Judy. *The monster behind Black Rock*
Vaughan, Marcia K. *Wombat stew*
Velthuijs, Max. *Frog and the birdsong*
Venino, Suzanne. *Animals helping people*
Ver Dorn, Bethea. *Moon glows*
Vevers, Gwynne. *Animal homes*
  Animal parents
  Animals of the dark
  Animals that store food

Animals that travel
Vigna, Judith. *Couldn't we have a turtle instead?*
Villarejo, Mary. *The tiger hunt*
A visit to a pond
Waber, Bernard. *"You look ridiculous," said the rhinoceros to the hippopotamus*
Waddell, Martin. *Farmer Duck*
The happy hedgehog band
Wagner, Karen. *Silly Fred*
Wahl, Jan. *Pleasant Fieldmouse*
Pleasant Fieldmouse's Halloween party
The sleepytime book
Wallner, John. *Old MacDonald had a farm*
Ward, Lynd. *Nic of the woods*
Ward, Nanda Weedon. *The black sombrero*
The elephant that ga-lumphed
Watts, Barrie. *Bird's nest*
Wegen, Ron. *Where can the animals go?*
Weil, Ann. *Animal families*
Weiss, Nicki. *Dog boy cap skate*
Where does the brown bear go?
Welber, Robert. *Goodbye, hello*
Wells, Rosemary. *Hazel's amazing mother*
West, Colin. *Go tell it to the toucan*
I brought my love a tabby cat
"Pardon?" said the giraffe
Westcott, Nadine Bernard. *There's a hole in the bucket*
Whitney, Dorothy B. *Creatures of an exceptional kind*
Whybrow, Ian. *Quacky quack-quack!*
Wildsmith, Brian. *Animal games*
Animal homes
Animal shapes
Animal tricks
Brian Wildsmith's wild animals
Goat's trail
Python's party
What the moon saw
Willard, Nancy. *The voyage of the Ludgate Hill*
Williams, Garth. *The big golden animal ABC*
Williams, Jenny. *Ride a cockhorse*
Williams, Sue. *I went walking*
Wilner, Isabel. *A garden alphabet*
Winch, Madeleine. *Come by chance*
Windham, Sophie. *Noah's ark*
Winter, Jeanette. *The girl and the moon man*
Wiseman, Bernard. *Doctor Duck and Nurse Swan*
Little new kangaroo
Tails are not for painting
Wolcott, Patty. *Eeeeeek!*
Wolff, Ashley. *A year of beasts*
Wolkstein, Diane. *Little Mouse's painting*
Wood, A. J. *Amazing animals*
Wood, Audrey. *Little Penguin's tale*
The napping house
Silly Sally
Wood, Douglas. *Old Turtle*

Wood, Jakki. *Dads are such fun*
Moo moo, brown cow
Wood, Jenny. *The animal kingdom*
Wood, John Norris. *Jungles*
Woolf, Virginia. *Nurse Lugton's curtain*
Worthington, Phoebe. *Teddy bear farmer*
Worthy, Judith. *Eyes*
Wyler, Rose. *Puddles and ponds*
Wyllie, Stephen. *The great race*
Snappity snap
Yabuuchi, Masayuki. *Animals sleeping*
Whose baby?
Whose footprints?
Yen, Clara. *Why rat comes first*
Ylla. *Animal babies*
Yolen, Jane. *Dragon night and other lullabies*
An invitation to the butterfly ball
Picnic with Piggins
Piggins
Yoshi. *Who's hiding here?*
Yoshida, Toshi. *Elephant crossing*
Rhinoceros mother
Young animals in the zoo
Young domestic animals
Youngs, Betty. *One panda*
Pink pigs in mud
Zalben, Jane Breskin. *Basil and Hillary*
Norton's nighttime
Ziefert, Harriet. *All clean!*
All gone!
Baby Ben's bow-wow book
Cock-a-doodle-doo!
Happy birthday, Grandpa!
Listen! Piggety Pig
On our way to the barn
On our way to the zoo
Run! Run!
Zoll, Max Alfred. *Animal babies*
Zolotow, Charlotte (Shapiro). *Sleepy book*
Zoo animals, Macmillan 1991
Zoo animals, Imported Pubs, 1983
Zweifel, Frances. *Animal baby-sitters*

Animals — aardvarks

Brown, Marc Tolon. *Arthur babysits*
Arthur meets the president
Arthur's baby
Arthur's birthday
Arthur's pet business
Caple, Kathy. *Inspector Aardvark and the perfect cake*
Higham, Jon Atlas. *Aardvark's picnic*
Kellogg, Steven (Stephen). *Aster Aardvark's alphabet adventures*
Mwalimu. *Awful aardvark*
Schaffer, Libor. *Arthur sets sail*

Animals — anteaters

Binnamin, Vivian. *The case of the anteater's missing lunch*

Brown, Marc Tolon. *D. W. all wet*
Hall, Malcolm. *The friends of Charlie Ant Bear*
Hellard, Susan. *Eleanor and the babysitter*
Waber, Bernard. *An anteater named Arthur*

Animals - apes *see* Animals – gorillas; Animals – monkeys

Animals – armadillos

Allard, Harry. *The cactus flower bakery*
Kipling, Rudyard. *The beginning of the armadilloes*, ill. by Charles Keeping
The beginning of the armadillos, ill. by Lorinda Bryan Cauley
Lewis, Robin Baird. *Aunt Armadillo*
Monsell, Mary Elise. *Armadillo*
Saunders, Susan. *Charles Rat's picnic*
Simon, Sidney B. *The armadillo who had no shell*
Singer, Marilyn. *Archer Armadillo's secret room*

Animals – baboons

Ching. *The baboon's umbrella*

Animals – badgers

Baker, Betty. *Partners*
Carlstrom, Nancy White. *No nap for Benjamin Badger*
Hoban, Russell. *A baby sister for Frances*
A bargain for Frances
Bedtime for Frances
Best friends for Frances
A birthday for Frances
Bread and jam for Frances
Johnston, Tony. *The badger and the magic fan*
MacDonald, Elizabeth. *Mr. Badger's birthday pie*
Potter, Beatrix. *The tale of Mr. Tod*
Silverman, Erica. *Warm in winter*
Tompert, Ann. *Badger on his own*
Varley, Susan. *Badger's parting gifts*
Wells, Rosemary. *Hazel's amazing mother*

Animals – bandicoots

Argent, Kerry. *Wombat and Bandicoot: best friends*

Animals – bats

Carlson, Natalie Savage. *Spooky and the wizard's bats*
Freeman, Don. *Hattie the backstage bat*
Hoban, Russell. *Lavina bat*
Horowitz, Ruth. *Bat time*
Jarrell, Randall. *A bat is born*
Mollel, Tolowa M. *A promise to the sun*
Ungerer, Tomi. *Rufus*

Animals – bears

Alborough, Jez. *Where's my teddy?*
Alexander, Martha G. *And my mean old mother will be sorry, Blackboard Bear*
Blackboard Bear
I sure am glad to see you, Blackboard Bear
We're in big trouble, Blackboard Bear
Alexander, Sally Hobart. *Maggie's whopper*
Allen, Pamela. *Bertie and the bear*
Amoit, Pierre. *Bijou the little bear*
Anglund, Joan Walsh. *Cowboy and his friend*
The cowboy's Christmas
Asch, Frank. *Bear shadow*
Bear's bargain
Bread and honey
Goodbye house
Happy birthday, moon!
Just like daddy
Moon bear
Mooncake
Moongame
Popcorn
Sand cake
Skyfire
Bach, Alice. *Millicent the magnificent*
The smartest bear and his brother Oliver
Warren Weasel's worse than measles
Baker, Jill. *Basil of Bywater Hollow*
Barrett, John M. *The bear who slept through Christmas*
The Easter bear
Barto, Emily N. *Chubby bear*
Bartoli, Jennifer. *Snow on bear's nose*
Bassett, Lisa. *Beany and Scamp*
Beany wakes up for Christmas
A clock for Beany
Beck, Martine. *Rescue of Brown Bear and White Bear*
The wedding of Brown Bear and White Bear
Bellows, Cathy. *The Grizzly sisters*
Benton, Robert. *Don't ever wish for a 7-foot bear*
Berenstain, Stan. *After the dinosaurs*
The bear detectives: the case of the missing pumpkin
Bears in the night
Bears on wheels
The Berenstain bears and mama's new job
The Berenstain bears and the bad dream
The Berenstain bears and the bad habit.
The Berenstain bears and the big road race
The Berenstain bears and the double dare
The Berenstain bears and the ghost of the forest
The Berenstain bears and the messy room
The Berenstain bears and the missing dinosaur bone
The Berenstain bears and the missing honey

The Berenstain bears and the prize pumpkin
The Berenstain bears and the sitter
The Berenstain bears and the slumber party
The Berenstain bears and the spooky old tree
The Berenstain bears and the trouble with friends
The Berenstain bears and the truth
The Berenstain bears and the week at grandma's
The Berenstain bears and the wild, wild honey
The Berenstain bears and too much birthday
The Berenstain bears and too much junk food
The Berenstain bears and too much TV
The Berenstain bears and too much vacation
The Berenstain bears blaze a trail
The Berenstain bears' Christmas tree
The Berenstain bears' counting book
The Berenstain bears don't pollute anymore
The Berenstain bears forget their manners
The Berenstain bears get in a fight
The Berenstain bears get stage fright
The Berenstain bears get the gimmies
The Berenstain bears go out for the team
The Berenstain bears go to camp
The Berenstain bears go to school
The Berenstain bears go to the doctor
The Berenstain bears in the dark
The Berenstain bears learn about strangers
The Berenstain bears meet Santa Bear
The Berenstain bears' moving day
The Berenstain bears: No girls allowed
The Berenstain bears on the moon
The Berenstain bears ready, set, go!
The Berenstain bears' science fair
The Berenstain bears trick or treat
The Berenstain bears' trouble at school
The Berenstain bears' trouble with money
The Berenstain bears' trouble with pets
The Berenstain bears visit the dentist
The Berenstains' B book
He bear, she bear
Inside outside upside down
Old hat, new hat
Bird, E. J. *How do bears sleep?*
Bishop, Claire Huchet. *Twenty-two bears*
Blathwayt, Benedict. *Bear's adventure*
Blocksma, Mary. *The best dressed bear*
Boegehold, Betty. *Bear underground*
Bond, Michael. *Paddington and the knickerbocker rainbow*
Paddington at the circus
Paddington at the fair
Paddington at the palace
Paddington at the seaside

Paddington at the tower
Paddington at the zoo
Paddington bear
Paddington cleans up
Paddington's ABC
Paddington's art exhibit
Paddington's colors
Paddington's garden
Paddington's lucky day
Paddington's 1 2 3
Boon, Emilie. *Belinda's balloon*
Bowden, Joan Chase. *The bear's surprise party*
Brandenberg, Franz. *A fun weekend*
Brenner, Barbara A. *Two orphan cubs*
Bridgman, Elizabeth. *Nanny bear's cruise*
Bright, Robert. *Me and the bears*
Brimner, Larry Dane. *Country Bear's good neighbor*
Country bear's surprise
Brinckloe, Julie. *Gordon's house*
Browne, Anthony. *Bear goes to town*
Bear hunt
The little bear book
Bunting, Eve (Anne Evelyn). *The Valentine bears*
Cahill, Chris. *Bear magic*
Caple, Kathy. *Fox and bear*
Carleton, Barbee Oliver. *Benny and the bear*
Carlstrom, Nancy White. *Better not get wet, Jesse Bear*
It's about time, Jesse Bear
Jesse Bear, what will you wear?
Cartlidge, Michelle. *The bear's bazaar*
Teddy trucks
Chambless, Jane. *Tucker and the bear*
Chevalier, Christa. *The little bear who forgot*
Crespi, Francesca. *Little Bear and the oompah-pah*
Dabcovich, Lydia. *Sleepy bear*
Day, Alexandra. *Frank and Ernest*
Degen, Bruce. *Jamberry*
Delton, Judy. *Bear and Duck on the run*
Brimhall comes to stay
Brimhall turns detective
Brimhall turns to magic
The elephant in Duck's garden
A pet for Duck and Bear
Dennis, Morgan. *Burlap*
De Regniers, Beatrice Schenk. *How Joe the bear and Sam the mouse got together*
Dodd, Lynley. *Wake up, bear*
Dorian, Marguerite. *When the snow is blue*
Dubois, Claude K. *He's my jumbo!*
Looking for Ginny
Dunbar, Joyce. *A cake for Barney*
Duvoisin, Roger Antoine. *Snowy and Woody*
Edwards, Roberta. *Anna Bear's first winter*
Fatio, Louise. *The happy lion and the bear*
Flack, Marjorie. *Ask Mr. Bear*

Turkle, Brinton. *Deep in the forest*
Upham, Elizabeth. *Little brown bear loses his clothes*
Van Pallandt, Nicholas. *The butterfly night of Old Brown Bear*
Van Woerkom, Dorothy. *Becky and the bear*
Venable, Alan. *The checker players*
Vincent, Gabrielle. *Bravo, Ernest and Celestine!*
Breakfast time, Ernest and Celestine
Ernest and Celestine
Ernest and Celestine at the circus
Ernest and Celestine's patchwork quilt
Ernest and Celestine's picnic
Merry Christmas, Ernest and Celestine
Smile, Ernest and Celestine
Where are you, Ernest and Celestine?
Waddell, Martin. *Can't you sleep, Little Bear?*
Let's go home, Little Bear
Wahl, Jan. *Sylvester Bear overslept*
Ward, Andrew. *Baby bear and the long sleep*
Ward, Lynd. *The biggest bear*
Warren, Cathy. *Springtime bears*
Watanabe, Shigeo. *Daddy, play with me!*
How do I put it on?
I can build a house!
I can ride it!
I can take a bath!
I can take a walk!
Ice cream is falling!
I'm the king of the castle!
It's my birthday
Let's go swimming
What a good lunch!
Where's my daddy?
Weinberg, Lawrence. *The Forgetful Bears*
The Forgetful Bears meet Mr. Memory
Wijngaard, Juan. *Bear*
Wild, Robin. *The bears' ABC book*
The bears' counting book
Wildsmith, Brian. *Bear's adventure*
The lazy bear
Williams, Leslie. *A bear in the air*
Winter, Paula. *The bear and the fly*
Winthrop, Elizabeth. *Bear and Mrs. Duck*
Bear's Christmas surprise
Wiseman, Bernard. *Christmas with Morris and Borris*
Morris and Boris at the circus
Morris has a birthday party!
Wood, Audrey. *Oh my baby bear!*
Wood, Jakki. *One bear with bees in his hair*
Yektai, Niki. *Bears in pairs*
Yeoman, John. *The bear's water picnic*
Ylla. *Two little bears*
Yolen, Jane. *Baby Bear's bedtime book*
The three bears rhyme book
Yulya. *Bears are sleeping*
Zalben, Jane Breskin. *Beni's first Chanukah*
Happy Passover, Rosie
Leo and Blossom's Sukkah
Ziefert, Harriet. *Bear all year*
Bear gets dressed
Bear goes shopping
Bear's busy morning
Zimnik, Reiner. *The bear on the motorcycle*
Zirbes, Laura. *How many bears?*

Animals – beavers

Barr, Cathrine. *Little Ben*
Bowen, Vernon. *The lazy beaver*
Carlson, Nancy. *Take time to relax*
Crowley, Arthur. *Bonzo Beaver*
Dabcovich, Lydia. *Busy beavers*
Gallo, Giovanni. *The lazy beaver*
George, William T. *Beaver at Long Pond*
Hamsa, Bobbie. *Your pet beaver*
Himmelman, John. *The day-off machine*
The great leaf blast-off
Hoban, Russell. *Charlie the tramp*
Kalas, Sybille. *The beaver family book*
Minarik, Else Holmelund. *Percy and the five houses*
Pryor, Bonnie. *The beaver boys*
Sheehan, Angela. *The beaver*
Tresselt, Alvin R. *The beaver pond*

Animals – bobcats

Rockwell, Anne F. *A bear, a bobcat and three ghosts*

Animals – buffaloes

Baker, Olaf. *Where the buffaloes begin*
Goble, Paul. *Her seven brothers*
McCarthy, Bobette. *Buffalo girls*

Animals – bulls, cows

Asch, Frank. *Oats and wild apples*
Barker, Melvern J. *Country fair*
Bulla, Clyde Robert. *Dandelion Hill*
Carlson, Natalie Savage. *Time for the white egret*
Carrick, Donald. *The deer in the pasture*
Milk
Cole, Joanna. *A calf is born*
Cushman, Jerome. *Marvella's hobby*
Dennis, Wesley. *Flip and the cows*
Drescher, Henrik. *Looking for Santa Claus*
Du Bois, William Pène. *Elisabeth the cow ghost*
Ernst, Lisa Campbell. *When Bluebell sang*
Ets, Marie Hall. *The cow's party*
Forrester, Victoria. *The magnificent moo*
Glass, Andrew. *Chickpea and the talking cow*
Gomi, Taro. *Spring is here*
Greenstein, Elaine. *Emily and the crows*
Hader, Berta Hoerner. *The story of Pancho and the bull with the crooked tail*
Hancock, Sibyl. *Old Blue*

Herriot, James. *Blossom comes home*
Kaizuki, Kiyonori. *A calf is born*
Kirby, David. *Cows are going to Paris*
Koch, Dorothy Clarke. *When the cows got out*
Krasilovsky, Phyllis. *The cow who fell in the canal*
Leaf, Munro. *The story of Ferdinand the bull*
Lent, Blair. *Pistachio*
Le Tord, Bijou. *A brown cow*
Lindgren, Astrid. *A calf for Christmas*
MacFarland, Cynthia. *Cows in the parlor*
Martin, Bill (William Ivan). *White Dynamite and Curly Kidd*
Meeks, Esther K. *The curious cow*
Merrill, Jean. *Tell about the cowbarn, Daddy*
Moers, Hermann. *Camomile heads for home*
Morris, Linda Lowe. *Morning milking*
Pellowski, Michael. *Clara joins the circus*
Royston, Angela. *Cow*
Scruton, Clive. *Circus cow*
Sewall, Marcia. *The wee, wee mannie and the big, big coo*
Thomas, Patricia. *"There are rocks in my socks!" said the ox to the fox*
Wiseman, Bernard. *Morris the moose*
Oscar is a mama
Wright, Dare. *Look at a calf*

Animals – bushbabies

Kennaway, Adrienne. *Bushbaby*

Animals – camels

Goodenow, Earle. *The last camel*
Hamsa, Bobbie. *Your pet camel*
Kipling, Rudyard. *How the camel got his hump*, ill. by Quentin Blake
How the camel got his hump, ill. by Tim Raglin
McKee, David. *The day the tide went out and out and out*
Parker, Nancy Winslow. *The Christmas camel*
Peet, Bill (William Bartlett). *Pamela Camel*
Tworkov, Jack. *The camel who took a walk*
Wells, Rosemary. *Abdul*

Animals – cats

Abercrombie, Barbara. *Charlie Anderson*
Adam, Barbara. *The big big box*
Ahlberg, Allan. *The black cat*
Allen, Jonathan. *My cat*
Allen, Pamela. *My cat Maisie*
Althea. *Jeremy Mouse and cat*
Ambrus, Victor G. *Grandma, Felix, and Mustapha Biscuit*
Anderson, Douglas. *Let's draw a story*
Arbeit, Eleanor Werner. *Mrs. Cat hides something*

Armitage, Ronda. *The lighthouse keeper's catastrophe*
Asare, Meshack. *Cat... in search of a friend*
Astley, Judy. *When one cat woke up*
Aulaire, Ingri Mortenson d'. *Foxie, the singing dog*
Averill, Esther. *The fire cat*
Aylesworth, Jim. *Mother Halverson's new cat*
Baba, Noboru. *Eleven cats and a pig*
Eleven cats and albatrosses
Eleven cats in a bag
Eleven hungry cats
Babbitt, Natalie. *Nellie, a cat on her own*
Baker, Barbara. *Digby and Kate*
Digby and Kate again
Baker, Leslie A. *The antique store cat*
The third-story cat
Balian, Lorna. *Amelia's nine lives*
Leprechauns never lie
Ballard, Robin. *Cat and Alex and the magic flying carpet*
Barbaresi, Nina. *Firemouse*
Barber, Antonia. *The mousehole cat*
Bare, Colleen Stanley. *Critter, the class cat*
To love a cat
Barrows, Marjorie Wescott. *Fraidy cat*
Bascom, Joe. *Malcolm Softpaws*
Malcolm's job
Bayley, Nicola. *Crab cat*
Elephant cat
Parrot cat
Polar bear cat
Spider cat
Beecroft, John. *What? Another cat!*
Beisner, Monika. *Catch that cat!*
Berg, Jean Horton. *The O'Learys and friends*
The wee little man
Bernhard, Josephine Butkowska. *Lullaby*
Berson, Harold. *Raminagrobis and the mice*
Bible. Old Testament. Jonah. *Jonah*, ill. by Kurt Mitchell
Bingham, Mindy. *Minou*
Black, Floyd. *Alphabet cat*
Blegvad, Lenore. *Mr. Jensen and cat*
Mittens for kittens and other rhymes about cats
Boegehold, Betty. *In the castle of cats*
Pawpaw's run
Three to get ready
Bohdal, Susi. *Tom cat*
Bonsall, Crosby Newell. *The amazing the incredible super dog*
Listen, listen!
Boynton, Sandra. *Chloë and Maude*
Brandenberg, Franz. *Aunt Nina and her nephews and nieces*
Aunt Nina's visit
No school today!
A robber! A robber!
What's wrong with a van?

Brent, Isabelle. *Cameo cats*
Brett, Jan. *Annie and the wild animals*
Brewster, Patience. *Ellsworth and the cats from Mars*
Bright, Robert. *Miss Pattie*
Brown, Marc Tolon. *The cloud over Clarence*
Brown, Marcia. *Felice*
Brown, Margaret Wise. *House of a hundred windows*
 Night and day
 Pussycat's Christmas
 Sneakers
 When the wind blew
Brown, Myra Berry. *Benjy's blanket*
Brown, Ruth. *Our cat Flossie*
Bruna, Dick. *Kitten Nell*
Bryan, Ashley. *The cat's purr*
Buck, Pearl S. (Pearl Sydenstricker). *The Chinese story teller*
Buckmaster, Henrietta. *Lucy and Loki*
Bulla, Clyde Robert. *Valentine cat*
Burch, Robert. *Joey's cat*
Burns, Theresa. *You're not my cat*
Burton, Jane. *Kitten*
Butterworth, Nick. *Just like Jasper*
Byrd, Robert. *Marcella was bored*
Calder, S. J. *If you were a cat*
Calhoun, Mary. *Audubon cat*
 Cross-country cat
 High-wire Henry
 Hot-air Henry
 The nine lives of Homer C. Cat
 The witch of Hissing Hill
 The witch who lost her shadow
 Wobble the witch cat
Cameron, John. *If mice could fly*
Cameron, Polly. *The cat who thought he was a tiger*
Campbell, Rod. *Misty's mischief*
Carle, Eric. *Have you seen my cat?*
Carlson, Natalie Savage. *Spooky and the bad luck raven*
 Spooky and the ghost cat
 Spooky and the witch's goat
 Spooky and the wizard's bats
 Spooky night
Carroll, Ruth. *Old Mrs. Billups and the black cats*
Carter, Anne. *Bella's secret garden*
Cass, Joan E. *The cat thief*
 The cats go to market
Cassedy, Sylvia. *The best cat suit of all*
Cate, Rikki. *A cat's tale*
Cazet, Denys. *Are there any questions?*
 Good morning, Maxine!
 Never spit on your shoes
Cecil, Mirabel. *Lottie's cats*
Chalmers, Audrey. *Fancy be good*
Chalmers, Mary. *Be good, Harry*
 Boots finds a house

The cat who liked to pretend
Come to the doctor, Harry
George Appleton
Merry Christmas, Harry
Mr. Cat's wonderful surprise
Take a nap, Harry
Throw a kiss, Harry
Chapman, Jean. *Moon-Eyes*
Charles, Donald. *Calico Cat at school*
 Calico Cat at the zoo
 Calico Cat meets bookworm
 Calico Cat's exercise book
 Calico cat's year
 Time to rhyme with Calico Cat
Chenery, Janet. *Pickles and Jake*
Cherry, Lynne. *Archie, follow me*
Chittum, Ida. *The cat's pajamas*
Chorao, Kay. *Ida and Betty and the secret eggs*
Cleary, Beverly. *Two dog biscuits*
Coats, Laura Jane. *City cat*
Coatsworth, Elizabeth. *The giant golden book of cat stories*
Coffelt, Nancy. *Good night, Sigmund*
Cohen, Caron Lee. *Whiffle Squeek*
Cohn, Norma. *Brother and sister*
Collington, Peter. *My darling kitten*
Cook, Bernadine. *Looking for Susie*
Coombs, Patricia. *The magician and McTree*
Cooper, Jacqueline. *Angus and the Mona Lisa*
Corrin, Ruth. *Mister cat*
Costa, Nicoletta. *The birthday party*
 Dressing up
 A friend comes to play
 The missing cat
Craft, Ruth. *Carrie Hepple's garden*
Crawford, Phyllis. *The blot: little city cat*
Cretan, Gladys Yessayan. *Lobo and Brewster*
Damjan, Mischa. *The little prince and the tiger cat*
Dauer, Rosamond. *The 300 pound cat*
Daugherty, Charles Michael. *Wisher*
Davis, Douglas F. *There's an elephant in the garage*
Degen, Bruce. *Aunt Possum and the pumpkin man*
DeJong, David Cornel. *Looking for Alexander*
Demarest, Chris L. *Kitman and Willy at sea*
Dennis, Morgan. *Skit and Skat*
De Paola, Tomie (Thomas Anthony). *Bonjour, Mister Satie*
De Regniers, Beatrice Schenk. *Cats cats cats*
 Everyone is good for something
 Picture book theater
 So many cats!
Desimini, Lisa. *I am running away today*
Dick Whittington and his cat. *Dick Whittington*, ill. by Edward Ardizzone

Jack Sprat. *The life of Jack Sprat, his wife and his cat*, ill. by Paul Galdone
James, Betsy. *He wakes me*
Janice. *Minette*
Jenkin-Pearce, Susie. *Bad Boris and the new kitten*
Jeschke, Susan. *Lucky's choice*
Jessell, Camilla. *The kitten book*
Jewell, Nancy. *ABC cat*
Kahl, Virginia. *Whose cat is that?*
Kamen, Gloria. *Second-hand cat*
Kanao, Keiko. *Kitten up a tree*
Kangas, Juli. *Ginger Kitten's surprise*
Kay, Helen. *A stocking for a kitten*
Keats, Ezra Jack. *Hi, cat!*
Kitten for a day
Psst, doggie
Kellogg, Steven (Stephen). *A rose for Pinkerton*
Tallyho, Pinkerton!
Kent, Lorna. *No, no, Charlie Rascal!*
Kerr, Judith. *Mog and bunny*
Mog's Christmas
Kettner, Christine. *An ordinary cat*
Kherdian, David. *The cat's midsummer jamboree*
Country cat, city cat
King, Deborah. *Cloudy*
Kitamura, Satoshi. *Captain Toby*
Knotts, Howard. *The summer cat*
The winter cat
Koči, Marta. *Katie's kitten*
Koenig, Marion. *The tale of fancy Nancy*
The wonderful world of night
Komoda, Beverly. *Simon's soup*
Koontz, Robin Michal. *Pussycat ate the dumplings*
Krahn, Fernando. *Catch that cat!*
Krasilovsky, Phyllis. *Scaredy cat*
Kraus, Robert. *Come out and play, little mouse*
Kroll, Steven. *Branigan's cat and the Halloween ghost*
It's April Fools' Day!
Kunhardt, Dorothy. *Kitty's new doll*
Kunhardt, Edith. *Pat the cat*
Kyte, Dennis. *Mattie and Cataragus*
Landshoff, Ursula. *Cats are good company*
Lansdown, Brenda. *Galumpf*
Larrick, Nancy. *Cats are cats*
Laskowski, Jerzy. *Master of the royal cats*
Lasson, Robert. *Orange Oliver*
Lawrence, John. *Rabbit and pork*
Lear, Edward. *The owl and the pussycat*, ill. by Jan Brett
The owl and the pussycat, ill. by Lorinda Bryan Cauley
The owl and the pussy-cat, ill. by Barbara Cooney
The owl and the pussycat, ill. by Emma Crosby

The owl and the pussy-cat, ill. by William Pène Du Bois
The owl and the pussycat, ill. by Lori Farbanish
The owl and the pussy-cat, ill. by Gwen Fulton
The owl and the pussycat, ill. by Paul Galdone
The owl and the pussy-cat, ill. by Elaine Muis
The owl and the pussycat, ill. by Erica Rutherford
The owl and the pussycat, ill. by Janet Stevens
The owl and the pussycat, ill. by Louise Voce
The owl and the pussycat, ill. by Colin West
The owl and the pussy-cat, ill. by Owen Wood
Le Guin, Ursula K. *A visit from Dr. Katz*
Leonard, Marcia. *The kitten twins*
Le-Tan, Pierre. *The afternoon cat*
Levitin, Sonia. *All the cats in the world*
Lewin, Betsy. *Cat count*
Lewis, Naomi. *The stepsister*
Lexau, Joan M. *Come here, cat*
Lillie, Patricia. *Jake and Rosie*
Lindbloom, Steven. *Let's give kitty a bath!*
Lindgren, Barbro. *Sam's ball*
Lindman, Maj. *Flicka, Ricka, Dicka and the three kittens*
Lipkind, William. *Russet and the two reds*
The two reds
Livermore, Elaine. *Find the cat*
Three little kittens lost their mittens
Livingston, Myra Cohn. *Cat poems*
Lloyd, David. *Cat and dog*
Lobel, Arnold. *The rose in my garden*
Whiskers and rhymes
Lockwood, Primrose. *Cat boy!*
MacArthur-Onslow, Annette Rosemary. *Minnie*
McGurn, Patty. *Me and Marie*
McLerran, Alice. *I want to go home*
McMillan, Bruce. *Kitten can...*
McPhail, David. *Great cat*
Macsolis. *Baile de luna: Dance moon*
Mandry, Kathy. *The cat and the mouse and the mouse and the cat*
Mantegazza, Giovanna. *The cat*
Maris, Ron. *My book*
Martinez, Ruth. *Mrs. McDockerty's knitting*
Marzollo, Jean. *Uproar on Hollercat Hill*
Maschler, Fay. *T. G. and Moonie go shopping*
T. G. and Moonie have a baby
T. G. and Moonie move out of town
Matthias, Catherine. *I love cats*
Mayer, Mercer. *The great cat chase*
Mayne, William. *The patchwork cat*

Tibber
Meddaugh, Susan. *Too short Fred*
Merriam, Eve. *The birthday door*
Micucci, Charles. *A little night music*
Miller, Edna. *Patches finds a new home*
Minarik, Else Holmelund. *Cat and dog*
  It's spring!
Modell, Frank. *Seen any cats?*
Moncure, Jane Belk. *The talking tabby cat*
Moore, Inga. *Six dinner Sid*
Moore, Lilian. *See my lovely poison ivy, and other verses about witches, ghosts and things*
Mooser, Stephen. *The fat cat*
Moskin, Marietta D. *Lysbet and the fire kittens*
Mother Goose. *Cats by Mother Goose*, ill. by Carol Newsom
  Kitten rhymes, ill. by Lulu Delarce
  The three little kittens, ill. by Lorinda Bryan Cauley
  The three little kittens, ill. by Paul Galdone
  The three little kittens, ill. by Dorothy Stott
  The three little kittens, ill. by Shelley Thornton
The moving adventures of Old Dame Trot and her comical cat, ill. by Paul Galdone
Murphey, Sara. *The animal hat shop*
Newberry, Clare Turlay. *April's kittens*
  The kittens' ABC
  Marshmallow
  Pandora
  Percy, Polly and Pete
  Smudge
  T-Bone, the baby-sitter
  Widget
Nicoll, Helen. *Meg and Mog*
  Meg at sea
  Meg on the moon
  Meg's eggs
  Mog's box
Nones, Eric Jon. *Wendell*
Nordqvist, Sven. *Festus and Mercury: ruckus in the garden*
  The fox hunt
  Pancake pie
Northrup, Mili. *The watch cat*
Oakley, Graham. *The church cat abroad*
  The church mice and the moon
  The church mice at bay
  The church mice spread their wings
  The church mouse
  The diary of a church mouse
Oana, Kay D. *Shasta and the shebang machine*
Obrist, Jürg. *Fluffy*
Okimoto, Jean Davies. *Blumpoe the grumpoe meets Arnold the cat*
Olson, Arielle North. *Noah's cats and the devil's fire*

Ormerod, Jan. *Come back, kittens*
  Kitten day
  The saucepan game
Otto, Margaret Glover. *The little brown horse*
Panek, Dennis. *Catastrophe Cat*
  Catastrophe Cat at the zoo
Paré, Roger. *A friend like you*
Parish, Peggy. *The cat's burglar*
  Scruffy
Parker, Nancy Winslow. *Puddums, the Cathcarts' orange cat*
Passen, Lisa. *Grammy and Sammy*
Pearson, Tracey Campbell. *The storekeeper*
Peet, Bill (William Bartlett). *Jennifer and Josephine*
Peppé, Rodney. *Cat and mouse*
Perrault, Charles. *Puss in boots*, ill. by Marcia Brown
  Puss in boots, ill. by Lorinda Bryan Cauley
  Puss in boots, ill. by Jean Claverie
  Puss in boots, ill. by Hans Fischer
  Puss in boots, ill. by Paul Galdone
  Puss in boots, retold and ill. by John S. Goodall
  Puss in boots, retold and ill. by Gail E. Haley
  Puss in boots, ill. by Julia Noonan
  Puss in boots, ill. by Tony Ross
  Puss in boots, ill. by William Stobbs
  Puss in boots, ill. by Alain Vaes
  Puss in boots, ill. by Barry Wilkinson
Pevear, Richard. *Mister Cat-and-a-Half*
Pfloog, Jan. *Kittens*
Pilkey, Dav. *When cats dream*
Pinkwater, Daniel Manus. *Roger's umbrella*
Pittman, Helena Clare. *Miss Hindy's cats*
Pizer, Abigail. *Harry's night out*
  Nosey Gilbert
Polette, Nancy. *The little old woman and the hungry cat*
Politi, Leo. *Lito and the clown*
Polushkin, Maria. *Here's that kitten*
  Kitten in trouble
  Who said meow? ill. by Giulio Maestro
  Who said meow? ill. by Ellen Weiss
Pomerantz, Charlotte. *The ballad of the long-tailed rat*
  Buffy and Albert
Potter, Beatrix. *The pie and the patty-pan*
  Rolly-polly pudding
  The sly old cat
  The story of Miss Moppet
  The tale of Tom Kitten
Poulin, Stéphane. *Can you catch Josephine?*
  Have you seen Josephine?
Pryor, Ainslie. *The baby blue cat and the dirty dog brothers*
  The baby blue cat and the smiley worm doll
  The baby blue cat who said no

Puppies and kittens
Redies, Rainer. *The cats' party*
Reiser, Lynn. *Bedtime cat*
  Dog and cat
Ridlon, Marcia. *Kittens and more kittens*
Robertus, Polly M. *The dog who had kittens*
Robinson, Thomas P. *Buttons*
Roffey, Maureen. *Here, kitty kitty!*
Rose, Agatha. *Hide-and-seek in the yellow house*
Ross, George Maxim. *When Lucy went away*
Ross, Tony. *I want a cat*
  Treasure of Cozy Cove
Rubel, Nicole. *Me and my kitty*
  Sam and Violet are twins
  Sam and Violet go camping
Rylant, Cynthia. *Henry and Mudge in puddle trouble*
Samuels, Barbara. *Duncan and Dolores*
San Souci, Robert D. *The white cat*
Sara. *Across town*
Scamell, Ragnhild. *Solo plus one*
Schaffer, Marion. *I love my cat!*
Schatz, Letta. *Whiskers, my cat*
Schertle, Alice. *That Olive!*
Schilling, Betty. *Two kittens are born*
Scruton, Clive. *Scaredy cat*
Seguin-Fontes, Marthe. *The cat's surprise*
Seidler, Rosalie. *Grumpus and the Venetian cat*
Seignobosc, Françoise. *Minou*
Selsam, Millicent E. *A first look at cats*
  How kittens grow
Seuss, Dr. *The cat in the hat*
  The cat in the hat comes back!
Shaw, Richard. *The kitten in the pumpkin patch*
Siekkinen, Raija. *Mister King*
Simmonds, Posy. *Fred*
Simon, Norma. *Cats do, dogs don't*
  Mama cat's year
  Oh, that cat!
  Where does my cat sleep?
Skaar, Grace Marion. *Nothing but (cats) and all about (dogs)*
  The very little dog
Slate, Joseph. *Lonely Lula cat*
Sloan, Carolyn. *Carter is a painter's cat*
Slobodkin, Louis. *Colette and the princess*
Slobodkina, Esphyr. *Billy, the condominium cat*
  Pinky and the petunias
Smart, Christopher. *For I will consider my cat Jeoffry*
Smyth, Gwenda. *A pet for Mrs. Arbuckle*
Sneed, Brad. *Lucky Russell*
Spanner, Helmut. *I am a little cat*
Spier, Peter. *Little cats*
Spohn, Kate. *Clementine's winter wardrobe*
Standon, Anna. *Three little cats*
Stanley, Diane. *Captain Whiz-Bang*

A country tale
Siegfried
Steel, Danielle. *Max and the baby sitter*
Steig, William. *Solomon the rusty nail*
Stein, Sara Bonnett. *Cat*
Steiner, Charlotte. *Kiki and Muffy*
Stern, Peter. *Floyd, a cat's story*
Stevens, Cat. *Teaser and the firecat*
Stock, Catherine. *Sampson the Christmas cat*
Stoddard, Sandol. *My very own special particular private and personal cat*
Stone, Bernard. *The charge of the mouse brigade*
Stratemeyer, Clara Georgeanna. *Pepper*
Sturgis, Matthew. *Tosca's surprise*
Sumiko. *Kittymouse*
Sutton, Eve. *My cat likes to hide in boxes*
Szekeres, Cyndy. *Suppertime for Frieda Fuzzypaws*
Taber, Anthony. *Cats' eyes*
Tapio, Pat Decker. *The lady who saw the good side of everything*
Taylor, Mark. *The case of the missing kittens*
Teague, Mark. *The trouble with the Johnsons*
Thayer, Jane. *The cat that joined the club*
Thompson, Harwood. *The witch's cat*
Titus, Eve. *Anatole and the cat*
  The kitten who couldn't purr
Turkle, Brinton. *Do not open*
Turnbull, Ann. *The tapestry cats*
Uchida, Yoshiko. *The two foolish cats*
Udry, Janice May. *"Oh no, cat!"*
Ungerer, Tomi. *No kiss for mother*
Untermeyer, Louis. *The kitten who barked*
Vagin, Vladimir. *Here comes the cat!*
Van Haeringen, Annemarie. *The cats' tale*
Van Horn, William. *Harry Hoyle's giant jumping bean*
Vesey, A. *Merry Christmas, Thomas!*
Viorst, Judith. *The tenth good thing about Barney*
Voake, Charlotte. *Tom's cat*
Waber, Bernard. *Mice on my mind*
  Rich cat, poor cat
Wagner, Jenny. *John Brown, Rose and the midnight cat*
Wahl, Jan. *Dracula's cat*
  Dracula's cat and Frankenstein's dog
  Push Kitty
Wallis, Diz. *Pip's adventure*
Ward, Cindy. *Cookie's week*
Watson, Pauline. *Curley Cat baby-sits*
Watts, Barrie. *Kitten*
Weihs, Erika. *Count the cats*
Welch, Martha McKeen. *Will that wake mother?*
Westell, Kerry. *Amanda's book*
Wezel, Peter. *The naughty bird*
Wheeler, Cindy. *Marmalade's Christmas present*
  Marmalade's nap

Marmalade's picnic
Marmalade's snowy day
Marmalade's yellow leaf
Whitmore, Adam. *Max in America*
Max in Australia
Max in India
Max leaves home
Whitney, Alma Marshak. *Leave Herbert alone*
Wijngaard, Juan. *Cat*
Wild, Margaret. *The very best of friends*
Wild, Robin. *Spot's dogs and the alley cats*
Wilkoń, Piotr. *The brave little kittens*
Wilkoń, Piotr. *Rosie the cool cat*
Willis, Jeanne. *Earth tigerlets as explained by Professor Xargle*
Wilson, Joyce Lancaster. *Tobi*
Withers, Carl. *The tale of a black cat*
Wolff, Ashley. *Only the cat saw*
Wood, Jakki. *Moo moo, brown cow*
Wright, Betty Ren. *The cat next door*
Wright, Dare. *The doll and the kitten*
The lonely doll learns a lesson
Look at a kitten
Wright, Josephine Lord. *Cotton Cat and Martha Mouse*
Yashima, Mitsu. *Momo's kitten*
Yeoman, John. *Mouse trouble*
Ylla. *I'll show you cats*
Young, Ed (Edward). *Up a tree*
Young, James. *Penelope and the pirates*
Ziefert, Harriet. *Nicky upstairs and down*
Nicky's Christmas surprise
Nicky's friends
No, no, Nicky!
Where's the cat?
Zimelman, Nathan. *The great adventure of Wo Ti*
Mean Murgatroyd and the ten cats

Animals – cheetahs

Adamson, Joy. *Pippa the cheetah and her cubs*
Conklin, Gladys. *Cheetahs, the swift hunters*
Irvine, Georgeanne. *Sasha the cheetah*

Animals – chimpanzees

Browne, Anthony. *I like books*
Things I like
Willy and Hugh
Willy the champ
Willy the wimp
Hurd, Edith Thacher. *The mother chimpanzee*

Animals – chipmunks

Angelo, Valenti. *The acorn tree*
Berenstain, Michael. *Peat Moss and Ivy and the birthday present*
Peat Moss and Ivy's backyard adventure

Conger, Marion. *The chipmunk that went to church*
Moore, Lilian. *Little Raccoon and no trouble at all*
Price, Dorothy E. *Speedy gets around*
Ryder, Joanne. *Chipmunk song*
Stevenson, James. *Wilfred the rat*
Williams, Barbara. *Chester Chipmunk's Thanksgiving*

Animals – cougars

Anderson, C. W. (Clarence Williams). *Blaze and the mountain lion*

Animals – coyotes

Aardema, Verna. *Borreguita and the coyote*
Baker, Betty. *And me, coyote!*
Partners
Baylor, Byrd. *Coyote cry*
Moon song
Bernstein, Margery. *Coyote goes hunting for fire*
Bierhorst, John. *Doctor Coyote*
Carrick, Carol. *Two coyotes*

Animals – deer

Aragon, Jane Chelsea. *Salt hands*
Winter harvest
Arnosky, Jim. *Deer at the brook*
Asch, Frank. *Oats and wild apples*
Bemelmans, Ludwig. *Parsley*
Boegehold, Betty. *Small Deer's magic tricks*
Buff, Mary. *Dash and Dart*
Forest folk
Carrick, Donald. *The deer in the pasture*
Harold and the great stag
Eberle, Irmengarde. *Fawn in the woods*
Frankel, Bernice. *Half-As-Big and the tiger*
Lindman, Maj. *Snipp, Snapp, Snurr and the reindeer*
Prusski, Jeffrey. *Bring back the deer*
Schlein, Miriam. *Deer in the snow*
Troughton, Joanna. *Mouse-Deer's market*

Animals – dogs

Agee, Jon. *Ellsworth*
Alexander, Martha G. *Bobo's dream*
Maggie's moon
The magic picture
Allen, Jeffrey. *The secret life of Mr. Weird*
Allen, Jonathan. *My dog*
Allen, Pamela. *Bertie and the bear*
Ambler, Christopher Gifford. *Ten little foxhounds*
Anderson, Douglas. *Let's draw a story*
Annett, Cora. *The dog who thought he was a boy*
Ardizzone, Edward. *Tim's friend Towser*

Argueta, Manlio. *The magic dogs of the volcanoes*
Asch, Frank. *The last puppy*
Rebecka
Aulaire, Ingri Mortenson d'. *Foxie, the singing dog*
Aylesworth, Jim. *The bad dream*
Baker, Barbara. *Digby and Kate*
Digby and Kate again
Baker, Charlotte. *Little brother*
Baker, Jeannie. *Home in the sky*
Baker, Margaret. *A puppy called Spinach*
Bare, Colleen Stanley. *To love a dog*
Barner, Bob. *Elevator escalator book*
Barr, Cathrine. *Hound dog's bone*
Barracca, Debra. *Maxi, the hero*
Barracca, Sal. *The adventures of taxi dog*
Barton, Byron. *Jack and Fred*
Where's Al?
Bastin, Marjolein. *A little dog for Vera*
Batherman, Muriel. *Some things you should know about my dog*
Battles, Edith. *The terrible terrier*
Baumann, Kurt. *Piro and the fire brigade*
Baylor, Byrd. *Coyote cry*
Baynes, Pauline. *How dog began*
Beim, Lorraine. *The little igloo*
Belting, Natalia Maree. *Verity Mullens and the Indian*
Bemelmans, Ludwig. *Madeline's rescue*
Benchley, Peter. *Jonathan visits the White House*
Berends, Polly Berrien. *Ladybug and dog and the night walk*
Berenstain, Stan. *The Berenstain bears on the moon*
Beresford, Elisabeth. *Snuffle to the rescue*
Bettina (Bettina Ehrlich). *Pantaloni*
Bingham, Mindy. *My way Sally*
Black, Irma Simonton. *Big puppy and little puppy*
Blackwood, Gladys Rourke. *Whistle for Cindy*
Blegvad, Lenore. *Hark! Hark! The dogs do bark, and other poems about dogs*
Bliss, Corinne Demas. *That dog Melly!*
Blocksma, Mary. *The pup went up*
Rub-a-dub-dub
Bolognese, Elaine. *The sleepy watchdog*
Bonsall, Crosby Newell. *The amazing the incredible super dog*
And I mean it, Stanley
Listen, listen!
Who's afraid of the dark?
Bontemps, Arna Wendell. *The fast sooner hound*
Bornstein, Ruth Lercher. *I'll draw a meadow*
Jim
Bottner, Barbara. *Horrible Hannah*

Bowden, Joan Chase. *Boo and the flying flews*
Boynton, Sandra. *Doggies*
Bradford, Ann. *The mystery of the blind writer*
The mystery of the missing dogs
Brenner, Barbara A. *A dog I know*
Brett, Jan. *The first dog*
Bridgman, Elizabeth. *A new dog next door*
Bridwell, Norman. *Clifford goes to Hollywood*
Clifford's ABC
Clifford's good deeds
Clifford's Halloween
Bright, Robert. *Georgie and the little dog*
Bröger, Achim. *Francie's paper puppy*
Brown, Marc Tolon. *Arthur's pet business*
Brown, Margaret Wise. *Big dog, little dog*
The country noisy book
Don't frighten the lion
The indoor noisy book
The quiet noisy book
The winter noisy book
Brown, Ruth. *I don't like it!*
Our puppy's vacation
Bryan, Dorothy. *Friendly little Jonathan*
Just Tammie!
Buck, Pearl S. (Pearl Sydenstricker). *The Chinese story teller*
Buckley, Helen Elizabeth. *Josie's Buttercup*
Buckmaster, Henrietta. *Lucy and Loki*
Bunting, Eve (Anne Evelyn). *Ghost's hour, spook's hour*
Jane Martin, dog detective
Burningham, John. *Cannonball Simp*
The dog
Burton, Jane. *Puppy*
Calhoun, Mary. *High-wire Henry*
Houn' dog
Mrs. Dog's own house
Campbell, Rod. *Henry's busy day*
Carlson, Nancy. *Harriet and the garden*
Harriet and the roller coaster
Harriet and Walt
Harriet's Halloween candy
Harriet's recital
Poor Carl
Carrick, Carol. *The accident*
Ben and the porcupine
The foundling
Carrier, Lark. *Scout and Cody*
Carroll, Ruth. *What Whiskers did*
Carter, Debby L. *Clipper*
Catalanotto, Peter. *Dylan's day out*
Cazet, Denys. *Frosted glass*
Saturday
Chalmers, Audrey. *Hector and Mr. Murfit*
Charles, Donald. *Shaggy dog's birthday*
Shaggy dog's Halloween
Shaggy dog's tall tale
Time to rhyme with Calico Cat

Chase, Catherine. *Pete, the wet pet*
Chenery, Janet. *Pickles and Jake*
Chorao, Kay. *The cherry pie baby*
Christelow, Eileen. *Gertrude, the bulldog detective*
Christian, Mary Blount. *No dogs allowed, Jonathan!*
Ciardi, John. *Scrappy the pup*
Cleary, Beverly. *Two dog biscuits*
Cohen, Caron Lee. *Bronco dogs*
 Three yellow dogs
Cohen, Miriam. *Jim's dog Muffins*
Cole, Joanna. *My puppy is born*
Cook, Marion B. *Waggles and the dog catcher*
Coontz, Otto. *The quiet house*
Costa, Nicoletta. *The naughty puppy*
 The new puppy
Cretan, Gladys Yessayan. *Lobo and Brewster*
Cuyler, Margery. *Freckles and Jane*
 Freckles and Willie
 Shadow's baby
Dale, Ruth Bluestone. *Benjamin — and Sylvester also*
Daly, Kathleen N. *The Giant little Golden Book of dogs*
Daly, Maureen. *Patrick visits the library*
Damjan, Mischa. *Atuk*
Day, Alexandra. *Paddy's pay-day*
Delaney, Ned. *Bad dog!*
Delton, Judy. *I'll never love anything ever again*
Denison, Carol. *A part-time dog for Nick*
Dennis, Morgan. *Burlap*
 The pup himself
 The sea dog
 Skit and Skat
Dickens, Lucy. *Dirty Henry*
Dodd, Lynley. *Hairy Maclary from Donaldson's dairy*
 Hairy Maclary Scattercat
 Hairy Maclary's bone
Doughtie, Charles. *Gabriel Wrinkles, the bloodhound who couldn't smell*
Du Bois, William Pène. *Giant Otto*
 Otto and the magic potatoes
 Otto at sea
 Otto in Africa
 Otto in Texas
Dumas, Philippe. *Laura, Alice's new puppy*
 Laura and the bandits
 Laura loses her head
 Laura on the road
Dunn, Judy. *The little puppy*
Dunrea, Olivier. *Fergus and Bridey*
Dupré, Ramona Dorrel. *Too many dogs*
Duvoisin, Roger Antoine. *Day and night*
Eagle, Ellen. *Gypsy's cleaning day*
Eastman, P. D. (Philip D.). *Go, dog, go!*
Erickson, Phoebe. *Just follow me*
Ernst, Lisa Campbell. *Ginger jumps*

Walter's tail
Ets, Marie Hall. *Mr. T. W. Anthony Woo*
Evans, Katie. *Hunky Dory ate it*
Fechner, Amrei. *I am a little dog*
Fehlner, Paul. *Dog and cat*
Ferns, Ronald. *Osbert and Lucy*
Fischer-Nagel, Heiderose. *A puppy is born*
Fisher, Aileen Lucia. *I like weather*
Flack, Marjorie. *Angus and the cat*
 Angus and the ducks
 Angus lost
Foster, Sally. *A pup grows up*
Fox, Mem. *Night noises*
Freeman, Don. *Ski pup*
Frith, Michael K. *I'll teach my dog 100 words*
Fujikawa, Gyo. *Millie's secret*
 Shags finds a kitten
Furchgott, Terry. *Phoebe and the hot water bottles*
Gackenbach, Dick. *A bag full of pups*
 Claude and Pepper
 Claude the dog
 The dog and the deep dark woods
 Dog for a day
 Pepper and all the legs
 What's Claude doing?
Gág, Wanda. *Nothing at all*
Gannett, Ruth S. *Katie and the sad noise*
Gerson, Corinne. *Good dog, bad dog*
Gerstein, Mordicai. *The new creatures*
Ghigna, Charles. *Good dogs / Bad dogs*
Gikow, Louise. *Follow that Fraggle!*
Goennel, Heidi. *My dog*
Goldsmith, Howard. *Little lost dog*
Goodspeed, Peter. *Hugh and Fitzhugh*
Gordon, Sharon. *What a dog!*
Graham, Amanda. *Who wants Arthur?*
Graham, Bob. *Libby, Oscar and me*
Graham, Margaret Bloy. *Benjy and his friend Fifi*
 Benjy and the barking bird
 Benjy's boat trip
 Benjy's dog house
Green, Phyllis. *Bagdad ate it*
Gregory, Valiska. *Sunny side up*
 Terribly wonderful
Griffith, Helen V. *Alex and the cat*
 Alex remembers
 Mine will, said John
 More Alex and the cat
 Pluck's dreams
Grimm, Jacob. *The horse, the fox, and the lion*, ill. by Paul Galdone
Grindley, Sally. *Four black puppies*
Hains, Harriet. *My new puppy*
Hamberger, John. *Hazel was an only pet*
 The lazy dog
Harriott, Ted. *Coming home*
Harsh, Fred. *Alfie*
Hausherr, Rosmarie. *My first puppy*

Hawkins, Colin. *Tog the dog*
Hayes, Sarah. *This is the bear and the picnic lunch*
Hazen, Barbara Shook. *Fang*
  Stay, Fang
Heine, Helme. *Mr. Miller the dog*
Heller, Nicholas. *Happy birthday, Moe dog*
Herriot, James. *Only one woof*
Hewett, Joan. *Rosalie*
Hill, Eric. *Spot at home*
  Spot at play
  Spot at the fair
  Spot counts from 1 to 10
  Spot goes to school
  Spot goes to the beach
  Spot goes to the circus
  Spot goes to the farm
  Spot in the garden
  Spot looks at colors
  Spot looks at opposites
  Spot looks at shapes
  Spot looks at the weather
  Spot on the farm
  Spot sleeps over
  Spot visits the hospital
  Spot's baby sister
  Spot's big book of words; El libro grande de las palabras de Spot
  Spot's first Christmas
  Spot's first Easter
  Spot's first picnic
  Spot's first walk
  Spot's first words
  Spot's toy box
Hillert, Margaret. *What is it?*
Himmelman, John. *The talking tree*
Hines, Anna Grossnickle. *I'll tell you what they say*
Hoban, Lillian. *The laziest robot in zone one*
Hoban, Russell. *The stone doll of Sister Brute*
Hoff, Syd. *Barkley*
  Lengthy
Holmes, Efner Tudor. *Carrie's gift*
Hooks, William H. *Where's Lulu?*
Hopkins, Lee Bennett. *A dog's life*
Howe, James. *Creepy-crawly birthday*
  Scared silly
Hurd, Edith Thacher. *The black dog who went into the woods*
  Little dog, dreaming
Hurd, Thacher. *Hobo dog*
Hürlimann, Bettina. *Barry: the story of a brave St. Bernard*
Inkiow, Dimiter. *Me and Clara and Snuffy the dog*
Inkpen, Mick. *Kipper*
  Kipper's toybox
Ipcar, Dahlov. *Black and white*
Isele, Elizabeth. *Pooks*

Iwamura, Kazuo. *Ton and Pon: big and little*
  Ton and Pon: two good friends
Iwasaki, Chihiro. *What's fun without a friend?*
Jacka, Martin. *Waiting for Billy*
Janice. *Angélique*
  Mr. and Mrs. Button's wonderful watchdogs
Jeram, Anita. *It was Jake*
Jessell, Camilla. *The puppy book*
Joerns, Consuelo. *Oliver's escape*
Johnson, Crockett. *The blue ribbon puppies*
  Terrible terrifying Toby
Jones, Rebecca C. *The biggest, meanest, ugliest dog in the whole wide world*
Joosse, Barbara M. *Better with two*
Jordan, June. *Kimako's story*
Kahl, Virginia. *Away went Wolfgang*
  Maxie
Keats, Ezra Jack. *Kitten for a day*
  My dog is lost!
  Psst, doggie
  Skates
  Whistle for Willie
Keller, Holly. *Goodbye, Max*
Kelley, Anne. *Daisy's discovery*
Kellogg, Steven (Stephen). *Best friends*
  Pinkerton, behave!
  Prehistoric Pinkerton
  A rose for Pinkerton
  Tallyho, Pinkerton!
Keyser, Marcia. *Roger on his own*
Khalsa, Dayal Kaur. *I want a dog*
Kimmelman, Leslie. *Frannie's fruits*
Kimura, Yasuko. *Fergus and the sea monster*
King, Deborah. *Sirius and Saba*
Kitamura, Satoshi. *Lily takes a walk*
Kočí, Marta. *Blackie and Marie*
Kopczynski, Anna. *Jerry and Ami*
Kraus, Robert. *The detective of London*
Kroll, Steven. *Don't get me in trouble*
  The magic rocket
  Woof, woof!
Kumin, Maxine. *What color is Caesar?*
Kuskin, Karla. *Watson, the smartest dog in the U.S.A.*
Lacome, Julie. *Funny business*
Laird, Elizabeth. *The day Patch stood guard*
Lamm, C. Drew. *Anniranni and Mollymishi, the wild-haired doll*
Laskowski, Jerzy. *Master of the royal cats*
Lathrop, Dorothy Pulis. *Puppies for keeps*
Lawlor, Laurie. *Second-grade dog*
Leaf, Munro. *Noodle*
Leichman, Seymour. *Shaggy dogs and spotty dogs and shaggy and spotty dogs*
Lenski, Lois. *Davy and his dog*
  Debbie and her dolls
  A dog came to school

Leonard, Marcia. *Laura Jean the yard sale queen*

Lewis, Kim. *Floss*

Lewis, Thomas P. *Call for Mr. Sniff*
Mr. Sniff and the motel mystery

Lexau, Joan M. *The dog food caper*
Go away, dog
I'll tell on you

Lindenbaum, Pija. *Boodil, my dog*

Lindgren, Barbro. *Sam's bath*
Sam's wagon

Lindman, Maj. *Flicka, Ricka, Dicka and a little dog*
Snipp, Snapp, Snurr and the seven dogs
Snipp, Snapp, Snurr and the yellow sled

Lipkind, William. *Even Steven*
Finders keepers

Livingston, Myra Cohn. *Dog poems*

Lloyd, David. *Cat and dog*

Lockwood, Primrose. *One winter's night*

Lopshire, Robert. *Put me in the zoo*

Lorenz, Lee. *Hugo and the spacedog*

Low, Joseph. *My dog, your dog*

Ludwig, Warren. *Good morning, Granny Rose*

Machetanz, Sara. *A puppy named Gia*

MacLachlan, Patricia. *Three names*

Mahy, Margaret. *Making friends*

Manushkin, Fran. *Walt Disney's one hundred one dalmations*

Marie, Geraldine. *The magic box*

Marshak, Samuel. *In the van*
The pup grew up!

Marshall, James. *Miss Dog's Christmas*
Speedboat

Martin, Charles E. *Dunkel takes a walk*

Martin, Sarah Catherine. *The comic adventures of Old Mother Hubbard and her dog*, ill. by Arnold Lobel
Old Mother Hubbard, ill. by Colin Hawkins
Old Mother Hubbard and her dog, ill. by Lisa Amoroso
Old Mother Hubbard and her dog, ill. by Paul Galdone
Old Mother Hubbard and her dog, ill. by Evaline Ness
Old Mother Hubbard and her wonderful dog, ill. by James Marshall

Martinez, Ruth. *Mrs. McDockerty's knitting*

Mathers, Petra. *Theodor and Mr. Balbini*

Meddaugh, Susan. *The witches' supermarket*

Miles, Miska. *Show and tell...*
Somebody's dog

Minarik, Else Holmelund. *Cat and dog*

Modell, Frank. *Skeeter and the computer*
Tooley! Tooley!

Moore, Inga. *Little dog lost*

Morris, Terry Nell. *Lucky puppy! Lucky boy!*

Moss, Marissa. *Knick knack paddywack*

Myller, Rolf. *A very noisy day*

Nakatani, Chiyoko. *The day Chiro was lost*

Newberry, Clare Turlay. *Barkis*

O'Neill, Catharine. *Mrs. Dunphy's dog*

Ormerod, Jan. *Come back, puppies*

Otto, Svend. *Taxi dog*

Overbeck, Cynthia. *Rusty the Irish setter*

Oxenbury, Helen. *Our dog*
Tom and Pippo and the dog

Pape, D. L. (Donna Lugg). *Doghouse for sale*

Parker, Nancy Winslow. *Cooper, the McNallys' big black dog*
Poofy loves company

Patent, Dorothy Hinshaw. *Maggie, a sheep dog*

Pearson, Tracey Campbell. *The howling dog*

Peet, Bill (William Bartlett). *The Whingdingdilly*

Perkins, Al. *The digging-est dog*

Pfloog, Jan. *Puppies*

Phillips, Joan. *My new boy*

Piers, Helen. *Puppy's ABC*

Pinkwater, Daniel Manus. *Aunt Lulu*

Pizer, Abigail. *Charlie the puppy*
Nosey Gilbert

Politi, Leo. *Emmet*
The nicest gift

Polushkin, Maria. *Who said meow?* ill. by Giulio Maestro
Who said meow? ill. by Ellen Weiss

Porte, Barbara Ann. *Harry's dog*

Potter, Beatrix. *The pie and the patty-pan*

Prather, Ray. *Double dog dare*

Pryor, Ainslie. *The baby blue cat and the dirty dog brothers*

Puppies and kittens

Rand, Gloria. *Salty dog*
Salty takes off

Rayner, Mary. *Marathon and Steve*

Reiser, Lynn. *Any kind of dog*
Dog and cat

Rey, Margret (Margret Elisabeth Waldstein). *Pretzel*
Pretzel and the puppies

Rice, Eve. *Benny bakes a cake*
Papa's lemonade and other stories

Robertus, Polly M. *The dog who had kittens*

Robins, Joan. *Addie meets Max*

Rockwell, Anne F. *Fire engines*
Hugo at the park
Hugo at the window
When Hugo went to school
Willy runs away

Roffey, Maureen. *Quick, catch Dan!*

Rose, Gerald. *Scruff*

Rose, Mitchell. *Norman*

Ross, Tony. *This old man*
Towser and the terrible thing

Round, Graham. *Hangdog*

Rowand, Phyllis. *George*
George goes to town

Ruby-Spears Enterprises. *The puppy's new adventures*
Rylant, Cynthia. *Henry and Mudge*
  Henry and Mudge in puddle trouble
  Henry and Mudge in the green time
  Henry and Mudge in the sparkle days
  Henry and Mudge under the yellow moon
Saltzberg, Barney. *Cromwell*
Sandberg, Inger. *Nicholas' favorite pet*
Sarrazin, Johan. *Tootle*
Saunders, Susan. *Wales' tale*
Saxon, Charles D. *Don't worry about Poopsie*
Schneider, Elisa. *The merry-go-round dog*
Schroeder, Binette. *Tuffa and her friends*
  Tuffa and the bone
  Tuffa and the ducks
  Tuffa and the picnic
  Tuffa and the snow
Schulman, Janet. *The great big dummy*
Schulz, Charles M. *Snoopy's facts and fun book about boats*
  Snoopy's facts and fun book about farms
  Snoopy's facts and fun book about houses
  Snoopy's facts and fun book about nature
  Snoopy's facts and fun book about planes
  Snoopy's facts and fun book about seasons
  Snoopy's facts and fun book about seashores
  Snoopy's facts and fun book about trucks
Schwartz, Amy. *Oma and Bobo*
Schweninger, Ann. *Autumn days*
  Wintertime
Scott, Sally. *Little Wiener*
  There was Timmy!
Seligson, Susan. *The amazing Amos and the greatest couch on earth*
  Amos ahoy: a couch adventure on land and sea
  Amos camps out: a couch adventure in the woods
  Amos: the story of an old dog and his couch
Selsam, Millicent E. *A first look at dogs*
  How puppies grow
Sendak, Maurice. *Some swell pup*
Sewall, Marcia. *The little wee tyke*
Sewell, Helen Moore. *Birthdays for Robin*
  Ming and Mehitable
Sharmat, Andrew. *Smedge*
Sharmat, Marjorie Weinman. *I'm the best*
  Nate the Great and the fishy prize
  Sasha the silly
Shibano, Tamizo. *The old man who made the trees bloom*
Shortall, Leonard W. *Andy, the dog walker*
Shyer, Marlene Fanta. *Stepdog*
Simon, Norma. *Cats do, dogs don't*
Singer, Marilyn. *The dog who insisted he wasn't*
Skaar, Grace Marion. *Nothing but (cats) and all about (dogs)*
  The very little dog

Skorpen, Liesel Moak. *All the Lassies*
  His mother's dog
  Old Arthur
Snoopy on wheels
Spier, Peter. *Little dogs*
Stadler, John. *Hector, the accordion-nosed dog*
Steig, William. *Caleb and Kate*
  Tiffky Doofky
Steiner, Charlotte. *Lulu*
  Pete and Peter
Stern, Mark. *It's a dog's life*
Stevenson, James. *Are we almost there?*
Stevenson, Suçie. *Jessica the blue streak*
Stratemeyer, Clara Georgeanna. *Tuggy*
Sugita, Yutaka. *My friend Little John and me*
Surany, Anico. *Kati and Kormos*
Szekeres, Cyndy. *Nothing-to-do puppy*
Tabler, Judith. *The new puppy*
Tafuri, Nancy. *Who's counting?*
Tallon, Robert. *Latouse my moose*
Tanaka, Hideyuki. *The happy dog*
Taylor, Mark. *The case of the missing kittens*
  Old Blue, you good dog you
Taylor, Sydney. *The dog who came to dinner*
Thaler, Mike. *My puppy*
Thayer, Jane. *The puppy who wanted a boy*, ill. by Seymour Fleishman
  The puppy who wanted a boy, ill. by Lisa McCue
Thomson, Ruth. *Peabody all at sea*
  Peabody's first case
Titus, Eve. *Anatole and the poodle*
Turkle, Brinton. *The sky dog*
Turnbull, Ann. *Rob goes a-hunting*
Udry, Janice May. *Alfred*
  What Mary Jo wanted
Untermeyer, Louis. *The kitten who barked*
Updike, David. *A winter's journey*
Van Allsburg, Chris. *The garden of Abdul Gasazi*
Van den Honert, Dorry. *Demi the baby sitter*
Waber, Bernard. *Bernard*
Waddell, Martin. *We love them*
Wagner, Jenny. *John Brown, Rose and the midnight cat*
Wahl, Jan. *The adventures of Underwater Dog*
  Dracula's cat and Frankenstein's dog
  Frankenstein's dog
Wahl, Mats. *Grandfather's laika*
Walt Disney Productions. *Tod and Copper*
  Tod and Vixey
Ward, Lynd. *Nic of the woods*
Weiss, Harvey. *The sooner hound*
Weller, Frances Ward. *Riptide*
Wellington, Monica. *The sheep follow*
Westman, Barbara. *Dancing dogs: Charlotte and Emilio at the circus*
  The day before Christmas: A story of Charlotte and Emilio
Widerberg, Siv. *The boy and the dog*

Wiese, Kurt. *The dog, the fox and the fleas*
Wijngaard, Juan. *Dog*
Wild, Robin. *Spot's dogs and the alley cats*
Wildsmith, Brian. *Give a dog a bone*
  Hunter and his dog
Wilhelm, Hans. *I'll always love you*
  A new home, a new friend
  Schnitzel's first Christmas
Williamson, Stan. *The no-bark dog*
Willoughby, Elaine Macmann. *Boris and the monsters*
Wilson-Kelly, Becky. *Mother Grumpy's dog biscuits*
Wirth, Beverly. *Margie and me*
Wold, Jo Anne. *Well! Why didn't you say so?*
Wood, Leslie. *A dog called Mischief*
Yeoman, John. *Old Mother Hubbard's dog dresses up*
  Old Mother Hubbard's dog learns to play
  Old Mother Hubbard's dog needs a doctor
  Old Mother Hubbard's dog takes up sport
Yorinks, Arthur. *Hey, Al*
Ziefert, Harriet. *A dozen dogs*
  Sam and Lucy
  Sleepy dog
  Where's the dog?
Zimelman, Nathan. *Mean Murgatroyd and the ten cats*
Zion, Gene. *Harry, the dirty dog*
  No roses for Harry
Zolotow, Charlotte (Shapiro). *The poodle who barked at the wind*

Animals – dolphins

Anderson, Lonzo. *Arion and the dolphins*
DeSaix, Frank. *The girl who danced with dolphins*
Gordon, Sharon. *Dolphins and porpoises*
Jacka, Martin. *Waiting for Billy*
Lilly, Kenneth. *Animals of the ocean*
Nakatani, Chiyoko. *Fumio and the dolphins*
Orstadius, Brita. *The dolphin journey*

Animals – donkeys

Æsop. *The miller, his son and their donkey*, ill. by Roger Antoine Duvoisin
  The miller, his son and their donkey, ill. by Eugen Sopko
Bates, H. E. (Herbert Ernest). *Achilles and Diana*
  Achilles the donkey
Berger, Barbara Helen. *The donkey's dream*
Bettina (Bettina Ehrlich). *Cocolo comes to America*
  Cocolo's home
  Piccolo
Brown, Marcia. *Tamarindo!*
Calhoun, Mary. *Old man Whickutt's donkey*
Cohen, Barbara. *The donkey's story*
Daugherty, Sonia. *Vanka's donkey*

Devlin, Wende. *Cranberry summer*
Dumas, Philippe. *Lucy, a tale of a donkey*
  The story of Edward
Duvoisin, Roger Antoine. *Donkey-donkey*
Evans, Katherine. *The man, the boy and the donkey*
Gramatky, Hardie. *Bolivar*
Gray, Genevieve. *How far, Felipe?*
Grimm, Jacob. *The donkey prince*, ill. by Barbara Cooney
Hale, Irina. *Donkey's dreadful day*
Hurd, Edith Thacher. *Under the lemon tree*
La Fontaine, Jean de. *The miller, the boy and the donkey*, adapt. and ill. by Brian Wildsmith
McCrea, James. *The king's procession*
Maris, Ron. *Hold tight, bear!*
Morpurgo, Michael. *Jo-Jo the melon donkey*
Ness, Evaline. *Josefina February*
Oppenheim, Joanne. *Donkey's tale*
Raphael, Elaine. *Donkey and Carlo*
  Donkey, it's snowing
Seignobosc, Françoise. *Chouchou*
Showalter, Jean B. *The donkey ride*
Silver, Jody. *Isadora*
Steig, William. *Farmer Palmer's wagon ride*
  Sylvester and the magic pebble
Van Woerkom, Dorothy. *Donkey Ysabel*
Winter, Paula. *Sir Andrew*

Animals – elephant seals

Bare, Colleen Stanley. *Elephants on the beach*

Animals – elephants

Allinson, Beverley. *Effie*
Ambrus, Victor G. *Mishka*
Barner, Bob. *Elephant facts*
Bishop, Ann. *The Ella Fannie elephant riddle book*
Blumberg, Rhoda. *Jumbo*
Bohman, Nils. *Jim, Jock and Jumbo*
Bos, Burny. *Ollie the elephant*
Boynton, Sandra. *If at first...*
Brunhoff, Jean de. *Babar and Father Christmas*
  Babar and his children
  Babar and Zephir
  Babar the king
  Babar the king, facsimile ed
  The story of Babar, the little elephant
  The travels of Babar
Brunhoff, Laurent de. *Babar and the ghost*
  Babar and the ghost
  Babar and the Wully-Wully
  Babar comes to America
  Babar learns to cook
  Babar the magician
  Babar visits another planet
  Babar's ABC

Babar's battle
Babar's birthday surprise
Babar's book of color
Babar's castle
Babar's counting book
Babar's cousin, that rascal Arthur
Babar's fair will be opened next Sunday
Babar's little circus star
Babar's little girl
Babar's mystery
Babar's picnic
Babar's visit to Bird Island
Burns, Diane L. *Elephants never forget!*
Cantieni, Benita. *Little Elephant and Big Mouse*
Caple, Kathy. *The biggest nose*
Chorao, Kay. *George told Kate*
Kate's box
Kate's car
Kate's quilt
Kate's snowman
Cole, Babette. *Nungu and the elephant*
Cole, Joanna. *Aren't you forgetting something, Fiona?*
Day, Alexandra. *Frank and Ernest*
Delacre, Lulu. *Nathan and Nicholas Alexander*
Nathan's balloon adventure
Nathan's fishing trip
Delton, Judy. *The elephant in Duck's garden*
Penny wise, fun foolish
DiVito, Anna. *Elephants on ice*
Domanska, Janina. *Why so much noise?*
DuBois, Ivy. *Baby Jumbo*
Easton, Violet. *Elephants never jump*
Ets, Marie Hall. *Elephant in a well*
Fechner, Amrei. *I am a little elephant*
Fern, Eugene. *What's he been up to now?*
Foulds, Elfrida Vipont. *The elephant and the bad baby*
Freschet, Berniece. *Elephant and friends*
Greene, Carol. *The insignificant elephant*
Hall, Derek. *Elephant bathes*
Hamsa, Bobbie. *Your pet elephant*
Hawkins, Colin. *The elephant*
Hewett, Joan. *The mouse and the elephant*
Hoff, Syd. *Oliver*
Hoffman, Mary. *Animals in the wild: elephant*
Hogan, Inez. *About Nono, the baby elephant*
Hoppe, Matthias. *Mouse and elephant*
Irvine, Georgeanne. *Elmer the elephant*
Jenkin-Pearce, Susie. *Bad Boris and the new kitten*
Boris's big ache
Jeram, Anita. *Bill's belly button*
Joslin, Sesyle. *Baby elephant and the secret wishes*
Baby elephant goes to China
Baby elephant's trunk
Brave Baby Elephant

Señor Baby Elephant, the pirate
Kennaway, Adrienne. *Little elephant's walk*
Kipling, Rudyard. *The elephant's child*, ill. by Louise Brierley
The elephant's child, ill. by Lorinda Bryan Cauley
The elephant's child, ill. by Tim Raglin
Klein, Suzanne. *An elephant in my bed*
Kraus, Robert. *Boris bad enough*
Lawrence, John. *Pope Leo's elephant*
Lewin, Hugh. *An elephant came to swim*
Lipkind, William. *Chaga*
Lobel, Arnold. *Uncle Elephant*
Löfgren, Ulf. *The traffic stopper that became a grandmother visitor*
Ludwig, Warren. *Old Noah's elephants*
McKee, David. *Tusk tusk*
McPhail, David. *Where can an elephant hide?*
Maestro, Betsy. *Around the clock with Harriet*
Harriet at home
Harriet at play
Harriet at school
Harriet at work
Harriet goes to the circus
Harriet reads signs and more signs
On the go
On the town
Through the year with Harriet
Where is my friend?
Manson, Christopher. *Two travelers*
Martin, Bill (William Ivan). *Smoky Poky*
Mayer, Mercer. *Ah-choo*
Mitra, Annie. *Tusk! Tusk!*
Mogensen, Jan. *The tiger's breakfast*
Moser, Erwin. *Wilma the elephant*
Murphy, Jill. *All in one piece*
Five minutes' peace
A piece of cake
Nakano, Hirotaka. *Elephant blue*
Paterson, Bettina. *Bun and Mrs. Tubby*
Bun's birthday
Patz, Nancy. *No thumpin' no bumpin' no rumpus tonight!*
Pumpernickel tickle and mean green cheese
Paxton, Tom. *Engelbert the elephant*
Pearce, Philippa. *Emily's own elephant*
Peek, Merle. *The balancing act*
Peet, Bill (William Bartlett). *The ant and the elephant*
Ella
Encore for Eleanor
Perkins, Al. *Tubby and the lantern*
Tubby and the Poo-Bah
Petersham, Maud. *The circus baby*
Pluckrose, Henry Arthur. *Elephants*
Propp, James. *Tuscanini*
Quigley, Lillian Fox. *The blind men and the elephant*
Richardson, Judith Benet. *The way home*

Riddell, Chris. *The trouble with elephants*
Rogers, Edmund. *Elephants*
Sadler, Marilyn. *Alistair's elephant*
Saxe, John Godfrey. *The blind men and the elephant*
Schlein, Miriam. *Elephant herd*
Schwartz, Roslyn. *Rose and Dorothy*
Seuss, Dr. *Horton hatches the egg*
 Horton hears a Who!
Sheppard, Jeff. *The right number of elephants*
Simont, Marc. *How come elephants?*
Slobodkina, Esphyr. *Pezzo the peddler and the circus elephant*
Smath, Jerry. *But no elephants*
 Elephant goes to school
Steig, William. *Doctor De Soto goes to Africa*
 An eye for elephants
Stock, Catherine. *Alexander's midnight snack*
Talbot, John. *Pins and needles*
Tresselt, Alvin R. *Smallest elephant in the world*
Velthuijs, Max. *Crocodile's masterpiece*
Wahl, Jan. *Hello, elephant*
Ward, Nanda Weedon. *The elephant that ga-lumphed*
Weinberg, Lawrence. *The Forgetful Bears meet Mr. Memory*
Weisgard, Leonard. *Silly Willy Nilly*
Weiss, Leatie. *My teacher sleeps in school*
Wells, H. G. (Herbert George). *The adventures of Tommy*
Westcott, Nadine Bernard. *Peanut butter and jelly*
Williamson, Hamilton. *Little elephant*
Ylla. *The little elephant*
Yoshida, Toshi. *Elephant crossing*
Young, Ed (Edward). *Seven blind mice*
Young, Miriam Burt. *If I rode an elephant*

Animals – endangered animals

Cowcher, Helen. *Tigress*
Cromie, William J. *Steven and the green turtle*
Jonas, Ann. *Aardvarks, disembark!*
Kalman, Benjamin. *Animals in danger*
Paladino, Catherine. *Our vanishing farm animals*
Raffi. *Baby beluga*
Sackett, Elisabeth. *Danger on the African grassland*
 Danger on the Arctic ice

Animals – foxes

Abolafia, Yossi. *Fox tale*
Æsop. *The raven and the fox*, ill. by Gerald Rose
 Three fox fables, ill. by Paul Galdone
Ambrus, Victor G. *Country wedding*

Anderson, Paul S. *Red fox and the hungry tiger*
Anno, Mitsumasa. *Anno's Æsop*
Arnosky, Jim. *Watching foxes*
Barr, Cathrine. *Hound dog's bone*
Baynton, Martin. *Fifty and the fox*
Bemelmans, Ludwig. *Welcome home*
Bergman, Donna. *City fox*
Berson, Harold. *Henry Possum*
 Joseph and the snake
Bingham, Mindy. *My way Sally*
Blyler, Allison. *Finding foxes*
Brown, Marcia. *The neighbors*
Brown, Margaret Wise. *Fox eyes*
Buck, Pearl S. (Pearl Sydenstricker). *The little fox in the middle*
Burningham, John. *Harquin: the fox who went down to the valley*
Burton, Jane. *Trill the fox cub*
Calhoun, Mary. *Houn' dog*
Caple, Kathy. *Fox and bear*
Carroll, Ruth. *What Whiskers did*
Carter, Anne. *Ruff leaves home*
Chaucer, Geoffrey. *Chanticleer and the fox*, ill. by Barbara Cooney
Christelow, Eileen. *Henry and the red stripes*
Conover, Chris. *Mother Goose and the sly fox*
Cunningham, Julia. *The vision of Francois the fox*
Davis, Lavinia (Riker). *Roger and the fox*
Delton, Judy. *Duck goes fishing*
Domanska, Janina. *The best of the bargain*
DuBois, Ivy. *Mother fox*
Ehlert, Lois. *Moon rope: Un lazo a la luna*
Fatio, Louise. *The red bantam*
Firmin, Peter. *Basil Brush and the windmills*
Fox, Charles Philip. *A fox in the house*
The fox went out on a chilly night, ill. by Peter Spier
Giffard, Hannah. *Red Fox*
 Red Fox on the move
Ginsburg, Mirra. *Across the stream*
 The fox and the hare
 Mushroom in the rain
 Two greedy bears
Grimm, Jacob. *The horse, the fox, and the lion*, ill. by Paul Galdone
 Mrs. Fox's wedding, ill. by Errol Le Cain
Guzzo, Sandra E. *Fox and Heggie*
Hartley, Deborah. *Up north in the winter*
Hayes, Sarah. *Nine ducks nine*
Hayward, Linda. *All stuck up*
Hogrogian, Nonny. *One fine day*
Hurd, Edith Thacher. *Under the lemon tree*
Hutchins, Pat. *Rosie's walk*
Isami, Ikuyo. *The fox's egg*
Kent, Jack. *Silly goose*
Koralek, Jenny. *The friendly fox*
Leverich, Kathleen. *The hungry fox and the foxy duck*

Lifton, Betty Jean. *The many lives of Chio and Goro*
Lindgren, Astrid. *The tomten and the fox*
Lionni, Leo. *In the rabbitgarden*
Lipkind, William. *The Christmas bunny*
The little tiny rooster
Livermore, Elaine. *Follow the fox*
McKissack, Patricia C. *Flossie and the fox*
Marshall, Edward. *Fox all week*
Fox and his friends
Fox at school
Fox in love
Fox on wheels
Marshall, James. *Fox on the job*
Rapscallion Jones
Wings: a tale of two chickens
Mayne, William. *A house in town*
Meddaugh, Susan. *Maude and Claude go abroad*
Miles, Miska. *The fox and the fire*
Miller, Edward. *Frederick Ferdinand Fox*
Nordqvist, Sven. *The fox hunt*
Pevear, Richard. *Mister Cat-and-a-Half*
Potter, Beatrix. *The tale of Mr. Tod*
Preston, Edna Mitchell. *Squawk to the moon, little goose*
Roach, Marilynne K. *Dune fox*
Rockwell, Anne F. *Big boss*
Sara. *The rabbit, the fox, and the wolf*
Schlein, Miriam. *The four little foxes*
Selsam, Millicent E. *A first look at dogs*
Sharmat, Marjorie Weinman. *The best Valentine in the world*
Small, David. *Eulalie and the hopping head*
Steig, William. *Doctor De Soto*
Roland, the minstrel pig
Szekeres, Cyndy. *Good night, Sammy*
Tejima, Keizaburo. *Fox's dream*
Thomas, Patricia. *"There are rocks in my socks!" said the ox to the fox*
Threadgall, Colin. *Proud rooster and the fox*
The three little pigs. *The three little pigs and the fox*, ill. by S. D. Schindler
Tompert, Ann. *Grandfather Tang's story*
Little Fox goes to the end of the world
Turner, Ann Warren. *Hedgehog for breakfast*
Varga, Judy. *The mare's egg*
Walsh, Ellen Stoll. *You silly goose*
Walt Disney Productions. *Tod and Copper*
Tod and Vixey
Watson, Clyde. *Father Fox's feast of songs*
Tom Fox and the apple pie
Valentine foxes
Watson, Wendy. *Tales for a winter's eve*
Weil, Lisl. *Gillie and the flattering fox*
Wells, Rosemary. *Don't spill it again, James*
Westwood, Jennifer. *Going to Squintum's*
Wiese, Kurt. *The dog, the fox and the fleas*
Wilhelm, Hans. *More bunny trouble*
Wyllie, Stephen. *Dinner with fox*

Animals – gerbils

Petty, Kate. *Gerbils*

Animals – giraffes

Brenner, Barbara A. *Mr. Tall and Mr. Small*
Brunhoff, Laurent de. *Serafina the giraffe*
Cooke, Ann. *Giraffes at home*
Doughtie, Charles. *High Henry...the cowboy who was too tall to ride a horse*
Duvoisin, Roger Antoine. *Periwinkle*
Hamsa, Bobbie. *Your pet giraffe*
Irvine, Georgeanne. *Georgie the giraffe*
Le Guin, Ursula K. *Solomon Leviathan's nine hundred and thirty-first trip around the world*
Milton, Nancy. *The giraffe that walked to Paris*
Rey, H. A. (Hans Augusto). *Cecily G and the nine monkeys*
Riches, Judith. *Giraffes have more fun*
Sharmat, Marjorie Weinman. *Helga high-up*

Animals – goats

Allamand, Pascale. *The little goat in the mountains*
Ambrus, Victor G. *The seven skinny goats*
The three poor tailors
Asbjørnsen, P. C. (Peter Christen). *The three billy goats Gruff*, ill. by Marcia Brown
Three billy goats Gruff, ill. by Tom Dunnington
The three billy goats Gruff, ill. by Paul Galdone
The three billy goats Gruff, ill. by Janet Stevens
The three billy goats Gruff, ill. by William Stobbs
Berson, Harold. *Balarin's goat*
Blood, Charles L. *The goat in the rug*
Bornstein, Ruth Lercher. *Of course a goat*
Carigiet, Alois. *Anton the goatherd*
Carlson, Natalie Savage. *Spooky and the witch's goat*
Chandoha, Walter. *A baby goat for you*
Chiefari, Janet. *Kids are baby goats*
Damjan, Mischa. *The wolf and the kid*
Daudet, Alphonse. *The brave little goat of Monsieur Séguin*
Dunn, Judy. *The little goat*
Fletcher, Elizabeth. *The little goat*
Gage, Wilson. *Mrs. Gaddy and the fast-growing vine*
Grimm, Jacob. *Nanny goat and the seven little kids*, ill. by Janet Stevens
The wolf and the seven kids, ill. by Kinuko Y. Craft

The wolf and the seven little kids, ill. by
Svend Otto S.
The wolf and the seven little kids, ill. by
Martin Ursell
Hillert, Margaret. *The three goats*
Hoff, Syd. *Happy birthday, Henrietta!*
Kroll, Steven. *The goat parade*
Leaf, Munro. *Gordon, the goat*
Lipkind, William. *Billy the kid*
Mahy, Margaret. *The queen's goat*
Mills, Alan. *The hungry goat*
Pizer, Abigail. *Hattie the goat*
Rappus, Gerhard. *When the sun was shining*
Royston, Angela. *The goat*
Sattler, Helen Roney. *No place for a goat*
Seignobosc, Françoise. *Biquette, the white
goat*
Springtime for Jeanne-Marie
Sharmat, Mitchell. *Gregory, the terrible eater*
Siddiqui, Ashraf. *Bhombal Dass, the uncle of
lion*
Slobodkin, Louis. *The polka-dot goat*
Up high and down low
Suhl, Yuri. *The Purim goat*
Tudor, Tasha. *Corgiville fair*
Watson, Nancy Dingman. *The birthday goat*
Wildsmith, Brian. *Goat's trail*
Wolkstein, Diane. *The banza*

Animals – gorillas

Aardema, Verna. *Princess Gorilla and a new
kind of water*
Browne, Anthony. *Gorilla*
Willy and Hugh
Willy the champ
Willy the wimp
Conklin, Gladys. *Little apes*
Delton, Judy. *On a picnic*
Hall, Derek. *Gorilla builds*
Harrison, David Lee. *Detective Bob and the
great ape escape*
Hazen, Barbara Shook. *The gorilla did it!*
Gorilla wants to be the baby
Hoff, Syd. *Julius*
Howe, James. *The day the teacher went
bananas*
Krahn, Fernando. *The great ape*
Meyers, Susan. *The truth about gorillas*
Morozumi, Atsuko. *One gorilla*
Most, Bernard. *There's an ape behind the
drape*
Schertle, Alice. *The gorilla in the hall*
Selsam, Millicent E. *A first look at monkeys*
Weller, Frances Ward. *The closet gorilla*
Zimelman, Nathan. *Positively no pets allowed*

Animals – groundhogs

Balian, Lorna. *A garden for a groundhog*
Bond, Felicia. *Wake up, Vladimir*
Cohen, Carol L. *Wake up, groundhog!*

Coombs, Patricia. *Tilabel*
Delton, Judy. *Groundhog's Day at the doctor*
Glass, Marvin. *What happened today, Freddy
Groundhog?*
Hamberger, John. *This is the day*
Johnson, Crockett. *Will spring be early?*
Kesselman, Wendy. *Time for Jody*
McNulty, Faith. *Woodchuck*
Palazzo, Tony (Anthony D.). *Waldo the
woodchuck*
Stanovich, Betty Jo. *Hedgehog adventures*
Tompert, Ann. *Nothing sticks like a shadow*
Watson, Wendy. *Has winter come?*

Animals – guinea pigs

Bare, Colleen Stanley. *Guinea pigs don't
read books*
Brooks, Andrea. *The guinea pigs' adventure*
Burton, Jane. *Dazy the guinea pig*
Duke, Kate. *Bedtime*
Clean-up day
The guinea pig ABC
Guinea pigs far and near
The playground
What bounces?
Mayne, William. *Barnabas walks*
Meshover, Leonard. *The guinea pigs that
went to school*
Potter, Beatrix. *The tale of Tuppeny*
Pursell, Margaret Sanford. *Polly the guinea
pig*
Ziefert, Harriet. *Where's the guinea pig?*

Animals – hamsters

Ambrus, Victor G. *Grandma, Felix, and
Mustapha Biscuit*
Baker, Alan. *Benjamin and the box*
Benjamin bounces back
Benjamin's balloon
Benjamin's book
Benjamin's dreadful dream
Benjamin's portrait
Blacker, Terence. *Herbie Hamster, where are
you?*
Blegvad, Lenore. *The great hamster hunt*
Brandenberg, Franz. *The hit of the party*
Brook, Judy. *Hector and Harriet the night
hamsters*
Claude-Lafontaine, Pascale. *Monsieur Bussy,
the celebrated hamster*
Leonard, Marcia. *Hannah the hamster
hunter*
Petty, Kate. *Hamsters*
Vaës, Alain. *The wild hamster*
Watts, Barrie. *Hamster*

Animals – hedgehogs

Berson, Harold. *Why the jackal won't speak
to the hedgehog*

Brook, Judy. *Tim mouse goes down the stream*
Tim mouse visits the farm
Cartwright, Ann. *The winter hedgehog*
Domanska, Janina. *The best of the bargain*
Flot, Jeannette B. *Princess Kalina and the hedgehog*
Guzzo, Sandra E. *Fox and Heggie*
Holden, Edith. *The hedgehog feast*
McClure, Gillian. *Prickly pig*
MacDonald, Maryann. *Rabbit's birthday kite*
Myller, Lois. *No! No!*
Potter, Beatrix. *The tale of Mrs. Tiggy-Winkle*
Ruck-Pauquèt, Gina. *Little hedgehog*
Stanovich, Betty Jo. *Hedgehog adventures*
Stott, Rowena. *The hedgehog feast*
Turner, Ann Warren. *Hedgehog for breakfast*
Waddell, Martin. *The happy hedgehog band*
Yeoman, John. *The bear's water picnic*

Animals – hippopotami

Allen, Frances Charlotte. *Little hippo*
Bennett, Rainey. *The secret hiding place*
Bohman, Nils. *Jim, Jock and Jumbo*
Boynton, Sandra. *But not the hippopotamus*
Hester in the wild
Hippos go berserk
Brown, Marcia. *How, hippo!*
Calmenson, Stephanie. *The birthday hat*
Where is Grandma Potamus?
Caple, Kathy. *The coolest place in town*
Cole, Babette. *Nungu and the hippopotamus*
Croswell, Volney. *How to hide a hippopotamus*
Duvoisin, Roger Antoine. *Lonely Veronica*
Our Veronica goes to Petunia's farm
Veronica
Veronica and the birthday present
Veronica's smile
Flanders, Michael. *The hippopotamus song*
Hadithi, Mwenye. *Hot hippo*
Hill, Eric. *Spot's baby sister*
The hippo, ill. by Caroline Binch
Jenkin-Pearce, Susie. *Percy Short and Cuthbert*
Kishida, Eriko. *The hippo boat*
Lasher, Faith B. *Hubert Hippo's world*
Leemis, Ralph. *Mister Momboo's hat*
Leonard, Marcia. *Swimming in the sand*
Lewin, Betsy. *Hip, hippo, hooray!*
McCarthy, Bobette. *Ten little hippos*
MacDonald, Maryann. *Little Hippo gets glasses*
Little Hippo starts school
Mahy, Margaret. *The boy who was followed home*
Mantegazza, Giovanna. *The hippopotamus*
Marshall, James. *George and Martha*
George and Martha back in town

George and Martha encore
George and Martha one fine day
George and Martha rise and shine
George and Martha round and round
George and Martha, tons of fun
Martin, Bill (William Ivan). *The happy hippopotami*
Mayer, Marianna. *Marcel the pastry chef*
Mayer, Mercer. *Hiccup*
Oops
Panek, Dennis. *Matilda Hippo has a big mouth*
Parker, Nancy Winslow. *Love from Uncle Clyde*
Patz, Nancy. *To Annabella Pelican from Thomas Hippopotamus*
Slobodkin, Louis. *Hustle and bustle*
Stadler, John. *Three cheers for hippo!*
Sugita, Yutaka. *Helena the unhappy hippopotamus*
Sutton, Jane. *What should a hippo wear?*
Taylor, Judy. *Sophie and Jack*
Sophie and Jack help out
Thaler, Mike. *Hippo lemonade*
It's me, hippo!
There's a hippopotamus under my bed
What could a hippopotamus be?
Tyler, Linda Wagner. *Waiting for mom*
When daddy comes home
Waber, Bernard. *"You look ridiculous," said the rhinoceros to the hippopotamus*
Wahl, Jan. *Old Hippo's Easter egg*
Wharton, Thomas. *Hildegard sings*
Woychuk, Denis. *The other side of the wall*
Pirates
Young, Miriam Burt. *Please don't feed Horace*
Ziefert, Harriet. *Harry takes a bath*

Animals – horses

Aarle, Thomas Van. *Don't put your cart before the horse race*
Anderson, C. W. (Clarence Williams). *Billy and Blaze*
Blaze and the forest fire
Blaze and the gray spotted pony
Blaze and the gypsies
Blaze and the Indian cave
Blaze and the lost quarry
Blaze and the mountain lion
Blaze and Thunderbolt
Blaze finds forgotten roads
Blaze finds the trail
Blaze shows the way
The crooked colt
Linda and the Indians
Lonesome little colt
A pony for Linda
A pony for three
The rumble seat pony
Arundel, Jocelyn. *Shoes for Punch*

Asch, Frank. *Goodnight horsey*
Baker, Betty. *Three fools and a horse*
Balet, Jan B. *Five Rollatinis*
Barr, Cathrine. *A horse for Sherry*
Barrett, Lawrence Louis. *Twinkle, the baby colt*
Beatty, Hetty Burlingame. *Bucking horse*
 Little Owl Indian
 Moorland pony
Bemelmans, Ludwig. *Madeline in London*
Blech, Dietlind. *Hello Irina*
Bowden, Joan Chase. *A new home for Snow Ball*
Brett, Jan. *Fritz and the beautiful horses*
Burningham, John. *Humbert, Mister Firkin and the Lord Mayor of London*
Callan, Elizabeth Koda. *Good luck pony*
Chan, Chin-Yi. *Good luck horse*
Chandler, Edna Walker. *Pony rider*
Charmatz, Bill. *The Troy St. bus*
Climo, Lindee. *Clyde*
Coerr, Eleanor. *Chang's paper pony*
Cohen, Carol L. *The mud pony*
Cox, David. *Tin Lizzie and Little Nell*
Cretien, Paul D. *Sir Henry and the dragon*
Cummings, W. T. (Walter Thies). *The kid*
Damrell, Liz. *With the wind*
Demi. *The hallowed horse*
Dennis, Wesley. *Flip and the cows*
 Flip and the morning
 Tumble, the story of a mustang
Duncan, Lois. *Horses of dreamland*
Elborn, Andrew. *Noah and the ark and the animals*
Ets, Marie Hall. *Mr. Penny's race horse*
Fain, James W. *Rodeos*
Farley, Walter. *Black stallion*
Fatio, Louise. *Anna, the horse*
Felton, Harold W. *Pecos Bill and the mustang*
Fregosi, Claudia. *The happy horse*
Friskey, Margaret (Margaret Richards). *Indian Two Feet and his horse*
Garbutt, Bernard. *Roger, the rosin back*
Gaston, Susan. *New boots for Salvador*
Goble, Paul. *The gift of the sacred dog*
 The girl who loved wild horses
Grabianski, Janusz. *Horses*
Greydanus, Rose. *Horses*
Grimm, Jacob. *The horse, the fox, and the lion*, ill. by Paul Galdone
Gross, Ruth Belov. *The girl who wouldn't get married*
Hasler, Eveline. *Martin is our friend*
Hawkinson, John. *Where the wild apples grow*
Heilbroner, Joan. *Robert the rose horse*
Herriot, James. *Bonny's big day*
Heuck, Sigrid. *Pony and Bear are friends*
Hirschi, Ron. *What is a horse?*
 Where do horses live?

Hoban, Russell. *The rain door*
Hoberman, Mary Ann. *Mr. and Mrs. Muddle*
Hoff, Syd. *Chester*
 The horse in Harry's room
Hol, Coby. *Henrietta saves the show*
Inkiow, Dimiter. *Me and Clara and Baldwin the pony*
Ipcar, Dahlov. *One horse farm*
 World full of horses
Jacka, Martin. *Waiting for Billy*
James, Shirley Kerby. *Going to a horse farm*
Jeffers, Susan. *All the pretty horses*
Keeping, Charles. *Molly o' the moors*
King, Deborah. *Custer: the true story of a horse*
Kinsey-Warnock, Natalie. *The wild horses of Sweetbriar*
Kraus, Robert. *Springfellow*
Krauss, Ruth. *Charlotte and the white horse*
Krum, Charlotte. *The four riders*
La Farge, Phyllis. *Joanna runs away*
Lasell, Fen. *Michael grows a wish*
Le Guin, Ursula K. *A ride on the red mare's back*
Lobel, Arnold. *Lucille*
Locker, Thomas. *The mare on the hill*
Low, Alice. *David's windows*
McGinley, Phyllis. *The horse who lived upstairs*
Martin, Claire. *The finest horse in town*
Martin, Patricia Miles. *Friend of Miguel*
Mayer, Marianna. *The black horse*
Medearis, Angela Shelf. *The zebra-riding cowboy*
Meeks, Esther K. *Playland pony*
Osborne, Mary Pope. *Moonhorse*
Otsuka, Yuzo. *Suho and the white horse*
Otto, Margaret Glover. *The little brown horse*
Paterson, A. B. (Andrew Barton). *Mulga Bill's bicycle*
Peet, Bill (William Bartlett). *Cowardly Clyde*
Pender, Lydia. *Barnaby and the horses*
Peterson, Jeanne Whitehouse. *Sometimes I dream horses*
Pluckrose, Henry Arthur. *Horses*
Primavera, Elise. *Basil and Maggie*
Rabinowitz, Sandy. *A colt named mischief*
 What's happening to Daisy?
Richard, Jane. *A horse grows up*
Rounds, Glen. *Once we had a horse*
 The strawberry roan
Royston, Angela. *The pony*
Saville, Lynn. *Horses in the circus ring*
Scott, Ann Herbert. *Someday rider*
Sewall, Marcia. *Ridin' that strawberry roan*
Sewall, Helen Moore. *Peggy and the pony*
Slobodkina, Esphyr. *The wonderful feast*
Sonberg, Lynn. *A horse named Paris*

Sutton, Elizabeth Henning. *A pony for keeps*
Thayer, Jane. *Andy and the runaway horse*
The horse with the Easter bonnet
Thompson, Vivian Laubach. *The horse that liked sandwiches*
Tinkelman, Murray. *Cowgirl*
Ward, Lynd. *The silver pony*
Wells, Rosemary. *Abdul*
Wondriska, William. *The stop*
Wright, Dare. *Look at a colt*
Yeoman, John. *The young performing horse*
Yolen, Jane. *Sky dogs*
Young, Miriam Burt. *If I rode a horse*
Zimnik, Reiner. *The proud circus horse*
Zolotow, Charlotte (Shapiro). *I have a horse of my own*

Animals – hyenas

Prelutsky, Jack. *The mean old mean hyena*

Animals – kangaroos

Braun, Kathy. *Kangaroo and kangaroo*
Brown, Margaret Wise. *Young kangaroo*
Cole, Joanna. *Norma Jean, jumping bean*
Hamsa, Bobbie. *Your pet kangaroo*
Harper, Anita. *It's not fair!*
Hurd, Edith Thacher. *The mother kangaroo*
Johnson, Crockett. *Upside down*
Kent, Jack. *Joey*
Joey runs away
Kipling, Rudyard. *The sing-song of old man kangaroo*, ill. by Michael C. Taylor
Pape, D. L. (Donna Lugg). *Where is my little Joey?*
Payne, Emmy. *Katy no-pocket*
Sanchez, Jose Louis Garcia. *Kangaroo*
Schlein, Miriam. *Big talk*, ill. by Joan Auclair
Big talk, ill. by Laura Lydecker
Selig, Sylvie. *Kangaroo*
Stonehouse, Bernard. *Kangaroos*
Townsend, Anita. *The kangaroo*
Wiseman, Bernard. *Little new kangaroo*

Animals – kindness to animals

Devlin, Wende. *Cranberry summer*
Sheldon, Dyan. *The whales' song*

Animals – koala bears

Bassett, Lisa. *Koala Christmas*
Broome, Errol. *The smallest koala*
Du Bois, William Pène. *Bear circus*
Bear party
Fox, Mem. *Koala Lou*
Gelman, Rita Golden. *A koala grows up*
Hellard, Susan. *Eleanor and the babysitter*
Irvine, Georgeanne. *Sydney the koala*
Krings, Antoon. *Oliver's bicycle*

Oliver's pool
Oliver's strawberry patch
Levens, George. *Kippy the koala*
Quackenbush, Robert M. *I don't want to go, I don't know how to act*
Ruck-Pauquèt, Gina. *Oh, that koala!*
Snyder, Dick. *One day at the zoo*
Walsh, Grahame L. *Didane the koala*

Animals – lemmings

Steig, Jeanne. *Consider the lemming*

Animals – lemurs

Clark, Emma Chichester. *Lunch with Aunt Augusta*

Animals – leopards

Aardema, Verna. *Half-a-ball-of-kenki*
Ipcar, Dahlov. *Stripes and spots*
Irvine, Georgeanne. *Lindi the leopard*
Keller, Holly. *Horace*
Kepes, Juliet. *Run little monkeys, run, run, run*
Kipling, Rudyard. *How the leopard got his spots*, ill. by Caroline Ebborn
How the leopard got his spots, ill. by Lori Loestoeter
Livermore, Elaine. *Looking for Henry*
Maestro, Giulio. *Leopard is sick*

Animals – lions

Adamson, Joy. *Elsa*
Elsa and her cubs
Æsop. *Androcles and the lion*, ill. by Janet Stevens
Androcles and the lion, ill. by Janusz Grabianski
The lion and the mouse, ill. by Gerald Rose
The lion and the mouse, ill. by Ed Young
Allen, Pamela. *A lion in the night*
Balet, Jan B. *Ned and Ed and the lion*
Bannerman, Helen. *The story of the teasing monkey*
Belloc, Hilaire. *Jim, who ran away from his nurse, and was eaten by a lion*
Bible. Old Testament. Daniel. *Daniel in the lions' den*, ill. by Leon Baxter
Bohman, Nils. *Jim, Jock and Jumbo*
Bridges, William. *Lion Island*
Brown, Margaret Wise. *The sleepy little lion*
Clark, Emma Chichester. *The story of Horrible Hilda and Henry*
Daugherty, James Henry. *Andy and the lion*
The picnic
Davies, Andrew. *Poonam's pets*
Davis, Douglas F. *The lion's tail*
Delton, Judy. *On a picnic*
Demarest, Chris L. *Clemens' kingdom*

Devlin, Wende. *Aunt Agatha, there's a lion under the couch!*
Du Bois, William Pène. *Lion*
Fatio, Louise. *The happy lion*
  The happy lion and the bear
  The happy lion in Africa
  The happy lion roars
  The happy lion's quest
  The happy lion's rabbits
  The happy lion's treasure
  The happy lion's vacation
  The three happy lions
Fechner, Amrei. *I am a little lion*
Freeman, Don. *Dandelion*
Galdone, Paul. *Androcles and the lion*
Gay, Zhenya. *I'm tired of lions*
Grimm, Jacob. *The horse, the fox, and the lion*, ill. by Paul Galdone
Hadithi, Mwenye. *Lazy lion*
Hancock, Joy Elizabeth. *The loudest little lion*
Hawkins, Mark. *A lion under her bed*
Hoban, Russell. *The rain door*
Hodges, Margaret. *St. Jerome and the lion*
Hooks, William H. *Lion and lamb*
Hurd, Edith Thacher. *Johnny Lion's bad day*
  Johnny Lion's book
  Johnny Lion's rubber boots
Kishida, Eriko. *The lion and the bird's nest*
Kleven, Elisa. *The lion and the little red bird*
La Fontaine, Jean de. *The lion and the rat*
Mahy, Margaret. *A lion in the meadow*
Makower, Sylvia. *Samson's breakfast*
Mann, Peggy. *King Laurence, the alarm clock*
Michael, Emory H. *Androcles and the lion*
Michel, Anna. *Little wild lion cub*
Moers, Hermann. *Hugo's baby brother*
Ness, Evaline. *Fierce: the lion*
Newberry, Clare Turlay. *Herbert the lion*
Peet, Bill (William Bartlett). *Eli*
  Hubert's hair-raising adventures
  Randy's dandy lions
Pluckrose, Henry Arthur. *Lions and tigers*
Presencer, Alain. *Roaring lion tales*
Siddiqui, Ashraf. *Bhombal Dass, the uncle of lion*
Siepmann, Jane. *The lion on Scott Street*
Skorpen, Liesel Moak. *If I had a lion*
Stephenson, Dorothy. *How to scare a lion*
Stewart, Elizabeth Laing. *The lion twins*
Townsend, Kenneth. *Felix, the bald-headed lion*
Varga, Judy. *Miss Lollipop's lion*
Wagener, Gerda. *Leo the lion*
Yoshida, Toshi. *Young lions*
Zelinsky, Paul O. *The lion and the stoat*
Zimelman, Nathan. *Treed by a pride of irate lions*

Animals – llamas

Alexander, Ellen. *Llama and the great flood*
Guarino, Deborah. *Is your mama a llama?*
Rockwell, Anne F. *The good llama*

Animals – mice

Æsop. *The country mouse and the city mouse*, ill. by Laura Lydecker
  The lion and the mouse, ill. by Gerald Rose
  The lion and the mouse, ill. by Ed Young
  The town mouse and the country mouse, ill. by Janet Stevens
  The town mouse and the country mouse, ill. by Lorinda Bryan Cauley
  The town mouse and the country mouse, ill. by Paul Galdone
  The town mouse and the country mouse, ill. by Tom Garcia
Alexander, Sue. *Dear Phoebe*
Aliki. *At Mary Bloom's*
Allen, Laura Jean. *Rollo and Tweedy and the case of the missing cheese*
Allen, Linda. *The mouse bride*
Althea. *Jeremy Mouse and cat*
Angelo, Nancy Carolyn Harrison. *Camembert*
Angelo, Valenti. *The candy basket*
Arnosky, Jim. *Mouse numbers and letters*
  Mouse writing
Asch, Frank. *Pearl's promise*
Augarde, Steve (Stephen). *Barnaby Shrew, Black Dan and...the mighty wedgwood*
Aylesworth, Jim. *The completed hickory dickory dock*
  Two terrible frights
Baker, Alan. *Two tiny mice*
Balzano, Jeanne. *The wee moose*
Barbaresi, Nina. *Firemouse*
Barkan, Joanne. *Whiskerville bake shop*
  Whiskerville firehouse
  Whiskerville post office
  Whiskerville school
Barklem, Jill. *Autumn story*
  The big book of Brambly Hedge
  The high hills
  The secret staircase
  Spring story
  Summer story
  Winter story
Barrows, Marjorie Wescott. *The book of favorite Muggins Mouse stories*
  Muggins' big balloon
  Muggins Mouse
  Muggins takes off
Bastin, Marjolein. *A little dog for Vera*
  My name is Vera
  Vera and her friends
  Vera dresses up
  Vera in the kitchen

Vera the mouse
Vera's special hobbies
Belpré, Pura. *Perez and Martina*
Berson, Harold. *A moose is not a mouse*
Raminagrobis and the mice
Bible. Old Testament. Jonah. *Jonah*, ill. by
  Kurt Mitchell
Boegehold, Betty. *Here's Pippa again!*
Pippa Mouse
Pippa pops out!
Bond, Felicia. *The Halloween performance*
Boynton, Sandra. *If at first...*
Brady, Irene. *Wild mouse*
Brady, Susan. *Find my blanket*
Brandenberg, Franz. *Everyone ready?*
Six new students
Brenner, Barbara A. *Mr. Tall and Mr.
  Small*
Bright, Robert. *Georgie and the runaway
  balloon*
Brook, Judy. *Tim mouse goes down the
  stream*
Tim mouse visits the farm
Brown, Palmer. *Something for Christmas*
Buchanan, Heather S. *Emily Mouse saves
  the day*
Emily Mouse's beach house
Emily Mouse's first adventure
Emily Mouse's garden
*George and Matilda Mouse and the
  floating school*
*George and Matilda Mouse and the moon
  rocket*
George Mouse learns to fly
George Mouse's covered wagon
George Mouse's first summer
George Mouse's riverboat band
Bullock, Kathleen. *A surprise for Mitzi
  Mouse*
Bunting, Eve (Anne Evelyn). *The Mother's
  Day mice*
Burningham, John. *Trubloff*
Cameron, John. *If mice could fly*
Cantieni, Benita. *Little Elephant and Big
  Mouse*
Carle, Eric. *Do you want to be my friend?*
Carlstrom, Nancy White. *I'm not moving,
  mama!*
Carter, Noelle. *I'm a little mouse*
Cartlidge, Michelle. *A mouse's diary*
Pippin and Pod
Castle, Caroline. *Herbert Binns and the
  flying tricycle*
Charles, Donald. *Calico Cat's exercise book*
Chase, Catherine. *Baby mouse goes shopping*
Baby mouse learns his ABC's
The mouse in my house
Chorao, Kay. *Cathedral mouse*
Christensen, Gardell Dano. *Mrs. Mouse
  needs a house*
Claret, Maria. *Melissa Mouse*

Coombs, Patricia. *Mouse Café*
Cressey, James. *Max the mouse*
Cunningham, Julia. *A mouse called Junction*
Dauer, Rosamond. *Bullfrog grows up*
Daugherty, James Henry. *The picnic*
Delacre, Lulu. *Nathan and Nicholas
  Alexander*
Nathan's balloon adventure
Nathan's fishing trip
Delessert, Etienne. *How the mouse was hit
  on the head by a stone and so discovered the
  world*
Demarest, Chris L. *Kitman and Willy at sea*
De Paola, Tomie (Thomas Anthony).
  Charlie needs a cloak
De Regniers, Beatrice Schenk. *How Joe the
  bear and Sam the mouse got together*
Picture book theater
Dominguez, Angel. *Diary of a Victorian
  mouse*
Doty, Roy. *Old-one-eye meets his match*
Dubanevich, Arlene. *Tom's tail*
Duke, Kate. *Aunt Isabel tells a good one*
Durrell, Julie. *Mouse tails*
Elzbieta. *Brave Babette and sly Tom*
Emberley, Michael. *Ruby*
Engel, Diana. *Gino Badino*
Ernst, Lisa Campbell. *The rescue of Aunt
  Pansy*
Ets, Marie Hall. *Mr. T. W. Anthony Woo*
Felix, Monique. *The further adventures of
  the little mouse trapped in a book*
*The story of a little mouse trapped in a
  book*
Field, Rachel Lyman. *A road might lead to
  anywhere*
Fisher, Aileen Lucia. *The house of a mouse*
Sing, little mouse
Freeman, Don. *The guard mouse*
Norman the doorman
Freeman, Lydia. *Pet of the Met*
Freschet, Berniece. *Bear mouse*
Bernard of Scotland Yard
Fuchshuber, Annegert. *Giant story – Mouse
  tale*
Futamata, Eigorō. *How not to catch a mouse*
Gackenbach, Dick. *The perfect mouse*
Gág, Wanda. *Snippy and Snappy*
Gantz, David. *The genie bear with the light
  brown hair word book*
Gay, Marie-Louise. *Moonbeam on a cat's ear*
Geraghty, Paul. *Look out, Patrick!*
Gili, Phillida. *Fanny and Charles*
Ginsburg, Mirra. *Four brave sailors*
Goodall, John S. *Creepy castle*
Gordon, Margaret. *The supermarket mice*
Goundaud, Karen Jo. *A very mice joke book*
Graham, John. *I love you, mouse*
Greaves, Margaret. *The mice of Nibbling
  Village*
Greene, Carol. *A computer went a-courting*

Grimm, Jacob. *Godfather Cat and Mousie*,
  ill. by Ann Schweninger
Little Red Riding Hood, ill. by John S.
  Goodall
Gundersheimer, Karen. *1 2 3 play with me*
Shapes to show
Hale, Irina. *Chocolate mouse and sugar pig*
Hale, Linda. *The glorious Christmas soup
  party*
Hall, Malcolm. *And then the mouse...*
Harris, Leon A. *The great diamond robbery*
The great picture robbery
Hawkinson, John. *The old stump*
Hazen, Barbara Shook. *The Fat Cats,
  Cousin Scraggs and the monster mice*
Henkes, Kevin. *Chester's way*
Sheila Rae, the brave
A weekend with Wendell
Henrietta. *A mouse in the house*
Hewett, Joan. *The mouse and the elephant*
Hillman, Priscilla. *A Merry-Mouse book of
  favorite poems*
A Merry-Mouse book of months
A Merry-Mouse Christmas A B C
The Merry-Mouse schoolhouse
Himmelman, John. *Montigue on the high
  seas*
Hoban, Lillian. *It's really Christmas*
The sugar snow spring
Hoban, Russell. *Charlie Meadows*
Flat cat
Hoff, Carol. *The four friends*
Hoff, Syd. *Mrs. Brice's mice*
Hoffmann, E. T. A. *The nutcracker*, ill. by
  Francesca Crespi
The nutcracker, ill. by Rachel Isadora
The nutcracker, ill. by Maurice Sendak
The nutcracker, ill. by Lisbeth Zwerger
Holabird, Katharine. *Angelina and Alice*
Angelina and the princess
Angelina at the fair
Angelina ballerina
Angelina on stage
Angelina's baby sister
Angelina's birthday surprise
The little mouse ABC
Holl, Adelaide. *A mouse story*
Hopkins, Margaret. *Sleepytime for baby
  mouse*
Hoppe, Matthias. *Mouse and elephant*
House mouse, ill. by David Thompson
Houston, John A. *A mouse in my house*
Howard, Jean G. *Of mice and mice*
Hurd, Edith Thacher. *Come and have fun*
Hurd, Thacher. *Blackberry ramble*
Little Mouse's big Valentine
Little Mouse's birthday cake
The pea patch jig
Tomato soup
Hurford, John. *The dormouse*

Hürlimann, Ruth. *The mouse with the daisy
  hat*
Inkpen, Mick. *Kipper's toybox*
Ivimey, John William. *The complete story of
  the three blind mice*, ill. by Paul Galdone
The complete version of ye three blind mice,
  ill. by Walton Corbould
Three blind mice, ill. by Lorinda Bryan
  Cauley
Three blind mice, ill. by Victoria Chess
Iwamura, Kazuo. *The fourteen forest mice
  and the harvest moon watch*
*The fourteen forest mice and the spring
  meadow picnic*
*The fourteen forest mice and the summer
  laundry day*
*The fourteen forest mice and the winter
  sledding day*
Joerns, Consuelo. *The foggy rescue*
The lost and found house
Johnson, Pamela. *A mouse's tale*
Joly-Berbesson, Fanny. *Marceau Bonappetit*
Karlin, Nurit. *Little big moose*
Keenan, Martha. *The mannerly adventures of
  Little Mouse*
Keller, Holly. *The new boy*
Kellogg, Steven (Stephen). *The island of the
  skog*
Kerr, Phyllis Forbes. *I tricked you*
Kimmel, Eric A. *The greatest of all*
Koenig, Marion. *The tale of fancy Nancy*
Koller, Jackie French. *Fish fry tonight*
Kraus, Robert. *Another mouse to feed*
Come out and play, little mouse
I, Mouse
Where are you going, little mouse?
Whose mouse are you?
Kumin, Maxine. *Joey and the birthday
  present*
Kuskin, Karla. *What did you bring me?*
Kwitz, Mary DeBall. *Mouse at home*
Layton, Aviva. *The squeakers*
Lexau, Joan M. *The dog food caper*
Linch, Elizabeth Johanna. *Samson*
Lionni, Leo. *Alexander and the wind-up
  mouse*
A busy year
Colors to talk about
Frederick
Geraldine, the music mouse
The greentail mouse
In the rabbitgarden
Letters to talk about
Matthew's dream
Mouse days
Nicholas, where have you been?
Numbers to talk about
Theodore and the talking mushroom
Tillie and the wall
What?
When?

Where?
Who?
Words to talk about
Little, Mary E. *Ricardo and the puppets*
Lobel, Arnold. *Martha, the movie mouse*
  Mouse soup
  Mouse tales
  The rose in my garden
Low, Joseph. *The Christmas grump*
  Mice twice
Lubin, Leonard B. *Christmas gift-bringers*
McCully, Emily Arnold. *The Christmas gift*
  First snow
  New baby
  Picnic
  School
McKissack, Patricia C. *Country mouse and
  city mouse*
McNulty, Faith. *Mouse and Tim*
Majewski, Joe. *A friend for Oscar Mouse*
Mandry, Kathy. *The cat and the mouse and
  the mouse and the cat*
Mantinband, Gerda. *Three clever mice*
Manushkin, Fran. *Moon dragon*
Martin, Jacqueline Briggs. *Bizzy Bones and
  Moosemouse*
  Bizzy Bones and the lost quilt
  Bizzy Bones and Uncle Ezra
Mason, Christopher. *The marvellous blue
  mouse*
Mathers, Petra. *Sophie and Lou*
Mayer, Marianna. *Alley oop!*
Mayne, William. *Mousewing*
Mendoza, George. *Henri Mouse*
  Henri Mouse, the juggler
  Need a house? Call Ms. Mouse
Miles, Miska. *Mouse six and the happy
  birthday*
Miller, Alice P. *The mouse family's blueberry
  pie*
Miller, Edna. *Mousekin finds a friend*
  Mousekin's ABC
  Mousekin's Christmas eve
  Mousekin's close call
  Mousekin's fables
  Mousekin's family
  Mousekin's golden house
  Mousekin's lost woodland
  Mousekin's mystery
  Mouskin takes a trip
  Mouskin's Easter basket
  Mouskin's frosty friend
  Mouskin's Thanksgiving
Miller, Moira. *Oscar Mouse finds a home*
  The proverbial mouse
Mogensen, Jan. *The tiger's breakfast*
Moore, Inga. *The vegetable thieves*
Morimoto, Junko. *Mouse's marriage*
Morris, Ann. *Eleanora Mousie catches a cold*
  Eleanora Mousie in the dark
  Eleanora Mousie makes a mess

Eleanora Mousie's gray day
Moss, Marissa. *But not Kate*
Mouse house, ill. by Zokeisha
Noll, Sally. *Watch where you go*
Numeroff, Laura Joffe. *If you give a mouse
  a cookie*
Oakley, Graham. *The church cat abroad*
  The church mice adrift
  The church mice and the moon
  The church mice at bay
  The church mice at Christmas
  The church mice in action
  The church mice spread their wings
  The church mouse
  The diary of a church mouse
Olson, Arielle North. *Noah's cats and the
  devil's fire*
Ormondroyd, Edward. *Broderick*
Ostheeren, Ingrid. *Jonathan Mouse*
  Jonathan Mouse and the baby bird
  Jonathan Mouse and the magic box
Peppé, Rodney. *Cat and mouse*
  The kettleship pirates
  The mice and the clockwork bus
  The mice and the flying basket
  The mice who lived in a shoe
Piers, Helen. *The mouse book*
Polushkin, Maria. *Mother, Mother, I want
  another*
Potter, Beatrix. *The tailor of Gloucester*
  The tale of Johnny Town-Mouse
  The tale of Mrs. Tittlemouse
  *The tale of Mrs. Tittlemouse and other
    mouse stories*
  The tale of two bad mice
  The two bad mice: pop-up book
Pryor, Bonnie. *The porcupine mouse*
Quackenbush, Robert M. *Chuck lends a
  paw*
Ravilious, Robin. *Two in a pocket*
Roach, Marilynne K. *Two Roman mice*
Roche, P. K. (Patrick K.). *Good-bye, Arnold!*
  Webster and Arnold go camping
Ross, Tony. *Hugo and Oddsock*
  Hugo and the bureau of holidays
  Hugo and the man who stole colors
Schermer, Judith. *Mouse in house*
Schlein, Miriam. *Home, the tale of a mouse*
Schoenherr, John. *The barn*
Schories, Pat. *Mouse around*
Schumacher, Claire. *Tommy the winner*
Schwartz, Roslyn. *Rose and Dorothy*
Scruton, Clive. *Bubble and squeak*
Seidler, Rosalie. *Grumpus and the Venetian
  cat*
Seignobosc, Françoise. *Small-Trot*
Selden, George. *The mice, the monks and the
  Christmas tree*
Silverman, Maida. *Mouse's shape book*
Simon, Sidney B. *Henry, the uncatchable
  mouse*

Slate, Joseph. *Who is coming to our house?*
Smith, Jim. *The frog band and Durrington Dormouse*
Smith, Wendy. *The lonely, only mouse*
Twice mice
Standiford, Natalie. *Dollhouse mouse*
Stanley, Diane. *The conversation club*
Steig, William. *Abel's Island*
Doctor De Soto
Doctor De Soto goes to Africa
Stein, Sara Bonnett. *Mouse*
Steptoe, John. *The story of jumping mouse*
Stern, Peter. *Max the dragon*
Stevens, Harry. *Fat mouse*
Stevenson, James. *The Sea View Hotel*
The stowaway
Stoddard, Sandol. *Bedtime mouse*
Stone, Bernard. *The charge of the mouse brigade*
Emergency mouse
Sumiko. *Kittymouse*
Szekeres, Cyndy. *Cyndy Szekeres' counting book, 1 to 10*
Ladybug, ladybug, where are you?
Talbot, John. *Pins and needles*
Taylor, Judy. *Dudley and the monster*
Dudley and the strawberry shake
Dudley goes flying
Dudley in a jam
Titus, Eve. *Anatole*
Anatole and the cat
Anatole and the piano
Anatole and the Pied Piper
Anatole and the poodle
Anatole and the robot
Anatole and the thirty thieves
Anatole and the toyshop
Anatole in Italy
Anatole over Paris
Tsultim, Yeshe. *The mouse king*
Türk, Hanne. *Goodnight Max*
Happy birthday Max
Max packs
Max the artlover
Max versus the cube
Merry Christmas Max
Rainy day Max
Raking leaves with Max
The rope skips Max
Snapshot Max
A surprise for Max
Udry, Janice May. *Thump and Plunk*
Vagin, Vladimir. *Here comes the cat!*
Vincent, Gabrielle. *Bravo, Ernest and Celestine!*
Breakfast time, Ernest and Celestine
Ernest and Celestine
Ernest and Celestine at the circus
Ernest and Celestine's patchwork quilt
Ernest and Celestine's picnic
Merry Christmas, Ernest and Celestine

Smile, Ernest and Celestine
Where are you, Ernest and Celestine?
Vinson, Pauline. *Willie goes to the seashore*
Vreeken, Elizabeth. *Henry*
Waber, Bernard. *Mice on my mind*
Waddell, Martin. *Squeak-a-lot*
Wahl, Jan. *Old Hippo's Easter egg*
Pleasant Fieldmouse
Pleasant Fieldmouse's Halloween party
Wallis, Diz. *Pip's adventure*
Walsh, Ellen Stoll. *Mouse count*
Mouse paint
You silly goose
Waters, Tony. *Sailor's bride*
Watson, Clyde. *How Brown Mouse kept Christmas*
Wells, Rosemary. *Noisy Nora*
Shy Charles
Stanley and Rhoda
Wenning, Elisabeth. *The Christmas mouse*
Wilson, Ron. *Mice*
Wolkstein, Diane. *Little Mouse's painting*
Wood, David. *Happy birthday, Mouse!*
Wooding, Sharon L. *Arthur's Christmas wish*
Woychuk, Denis. *The other side of the wall*
Pirates
Wright, Josephine Lord. *Cotton Cat and Martha Mouse*
Yamashita, Haruo. *Mice at the beach*
Yeoman, John. *Mouse trouble*
Young, Ed (Edward). *Seven blind mice*
Young, Miriam Burt. *The sugar mouse cake*
Zelinsky, Paul O. *The maid and the mouse and the odd-shaped house*
Ziefert, Harriet. *A car trip for mole and mouse*
A clean house for Mole and Mouse
Let's go! Piggety Pig
A new house for Mole and Mouse
No more! Piggety Pig
Zimmermann, H. Werner (Heinz Werner). *Alphonse knows...twelve months make a year*

Animals – minks

Holder, Heidi. *Crows*

Animals – moles

Browne, Eileen. *Where's that bus?*
Carter, Anne. *Molly in danger*
Ehlert, Lois. *Moon rope: Un lazo a la luna*
Firmin, Peter. *Basil Brush and the windmills*
Gantschev, Ivan. *Where is Mr. Mole?*
Himmelman, John. *Montigue on the high seas*
Hoban, Lillian. *Silly Tilly and the Easter bunny*
Hoban, Russell. *The mole family's Christmas*
Johnston, Tony. *Mole and Troll trim the tree*
Koller, Jackie French. *Mole and shrew*
Murschetz, Luis. *Mister Mole*

Obrist, Jürg. *They do things right in Albern*
Takihara, Koji. *Rolli*
Walt Disney Productions. *Walt Disney's The adventures of Mr. Toad*
Wouters, Anne. *This book is for us*
This book is too small
Yolen, Jane. *Eeny, meeny, miney mole*
Ziefert, Harriet. *A car trip for mole and mouse*
A clean house for Mole and Mouse
A new house for Mole and Mouse

Animals – mongooses

Carlson, Natalie Savage. *Marie Louise and Christophe at the carnival*
Marie Louise's heyday
Runaway Marie Louise
Mwalimu. *Awful aardvark*

Animals – monkeys

Bannerman, Helen. *The story of the teasing monkey*
Brunhoff, Jean de. *Babar and Zephir*
Brunhoff, Laurent de. *Babar the magician*
Bulette, Sara. *The splendid belt of Mr. Big*
Bunting, Eve (Anne Evelyn). *Monkey in the middle*
Christelow, Eileen. *Five little monkeys jumping on the bed*
Five little monkeys sitting in a tree
Curious George and the dinosaur
Curious George and the dump truck
Curious George and the pizza
Curious George at the fire station
Curious George goes hiking
Curious George goes sledding
Curious George goes to an ice cream shop
Curious George goes to school
Curious George goes to the aquarium
Curious George goes to the circus
Curious George goes to the dentist
Curious George visits the zoo
DeLuise, Dom. *Charlie the caterpillar*
Dodds, Dayle Ann. *The color box*
Drescher, Henrik. *The yellow umbrella*
Elkin, Benjamin. *Such is the way of the world*
Galdone, Paul. *The monkey and the crocodile*
Goodall, John S. *Jacko*
Guy, Rosa. *Mother crocodile*
Hoban, Lillian. *Arthur's Christmas cookies*
Arthur's funny money
Arthur's honey bear
Arthur's pen pal
Arthur's prize reader
Hoffman, Mary. *Animals in the wild: monkey*
Horio, Seishi. *The monkey and the crab*
Hurd, Edith Thacher. *Last one home is a green pig*
Irvine, Georgeanne. *Bo the orangutan*

Iwamura, Kazuo. *Tan Tan's hat*
Tan Tan's suspenders
Kaye, Geraldine. *The sea monkey*
Kepes, Juliet. *Five little monkeys*
Run little monkeys, run, run, run
Knight, Hilary. *Where's Wallace?*
Komoda, Beverly. *Simon's soup*
McAllister, Angela. *Matepo*
McKissack, Patricia C. *Who is coming?*
Mathiesen, Egon. *Oswald, the monkey*
Meshover, Leonard. *The monkey that went to school*
Moore, Inga. *Fifty red night-caps*
Olds, Helen Diehl. *Miss Hattie and the monkey*
Oxenbury, Helen. *Tom and Pippo and the dog*
Tom and Pippo go shopping
Tom and Pippo in the garden
Tom and Pippo on the beach
Tom and Pippo see the moon
Tom and Pippo's day
Parish, Peggy. *Jumper goes to school*
Pen Cai Ying. *Monkey creates havoc in heaven*
Preston, Edna Mitchell. *Monkey in the jungle*
Reitveld, Jane Klatt. *Monkey island*
Rey, H. A. (Hans Augusto). *Cecily G and the nine monkeys*
Curious George
Curious George gets a medal
Curious George learns the alphabet
Curious George rides a bike
Curious George takes a job
Rey, Margret (Margret Elisabeth Waldstein). *Curious George flies a kite*
Curious George goes to the hospital
Rockwell, Anne F. *The stolen necklace*
Schubert, Dieter. *Where's my monkey?*
Selsam, Millicent E. *A first look at monkeys*
Shi, Zhang Xiu. *Monkey and the white bone demon*
Slobodkina, Esphyr. *Caps for sale*
Suba, Susanne. *The monkeys and the pedlar*
Teleki, Geza. *Aerial apes*
Thaler, Mike. *Moonkey*
Williamson, Hamilton. *Monkey tale*
Wolkstein, Diane. *The cool ride in the sky*
Woodruff, Elvira. *Mrs. McCloskey's monkeys*

Animals – moose

Alexander, Martha G. *Even that moose won't listen to me*
Allen, Jonathan. *Mucky moose*
Brown, Marc Tolon. *Moose and goose*
Bunting, Eve (Anne Evelyn). *A turkey for Thanksgiving*
Carlstrom, Nancy White. *Moose in the garden*
Foreman, Michael. *Moose*

Freschet, Berniece. *Moose baby*
Hoff, Syd. *Santa's moose*
Latimer, Jim. *Going the moose way home*
McNeer, May Yonge. *My friend Mac*
Marshall, James. *The guest*
Numeroff, Laura Joffe. *If you gave a moose a muffin*
Prøysen, Alf. *Mrs. Pepperpot and the moose*
Seuss, Dr. *Thidwick, the big-hearted moose*
Slobodkin, Louis. *Melvin, the moose child*
Stadler, John. *The ballad of Wilbur and the moose*
Stapler, Sarah. *Spruce the moose cuts loose*
Wiseman, Bernard. *Christmas with Morris and Borris*
   Morris and Boris at the circus
   Morris has a birthday party!
   Morris the moose

Animals – mules

Beatty, Hetty Burlingame. *Droopy*
Brown, Kathryn. *Muledred*
Sharmat, Marjorie Weinman. *Hooray for Father's Day!*
Snyder, Anne. *The old man and the mule*
Zemach, Margot. *Jake and Honeybunch go to heaven*

Animals – muskrats

Arnosky, Jim. *Come out, muskrats*
Hoban, Russell. *Harvey's hideout*
Wilson, Sarah. *Muskrat, muskrat, eat your peas!*

Animals - octopuses *see* Octopuses

Animals – otters

Allen, Laura Jean. *Ottie and the star*
Burdick, Margaret. *Bobby Otter and the blue boat*
Hall, Derek. *Otter swims*
Harshman, Terry Webb. *Porcupine's pajama party*
Hoban, Russell. *Emmet Otter's jug-band Christmas*
Shaw, Evelyn S. *Sea otters*
Sheehan, Angela. *The otter*
Tompert, Ann. *Little Otter remembers and other stories*
Wisbeski, Dorothy Gross. *Pícaro, a pet otter*

Animals – oxen

Hong, Lily Toy. *How the ox star fell from heaven*

Animals – pack rats

Miller, Edna. *Pebbles, a pack rat*
Quackenbush, Robert M. *Pete Pack Rat*

Van Horn, William. *Harry Hoyle's giant jumping bean*

Animals – pandas

Calmenson, Stephanie. *Dinner at the Panda Palace*
Foreman, Michael. *Panda and the bushfire*
Greaves, Margaret. *Once there were no pandas*
Grosvenor, Donna. *Pandas*
Hall, Derek. *Panda climbs*
Hoban, Tana. *Panda, panda*
Hoffman, Mary. *Animals in the wild: panda*
Jensen, Helen Zane. *When Panda came to our house*
Leedy, Loreen. *Pingo the plaid panda*
Maestro, Betsy. *The pandas take a vacation*
Pluckrose, Henry Arthur. *Bears*
Rigby, Shirley Lincoln. *Smaller than most*

Animals – pigs

Allard, Harry. *There's a party at Mona's tonight*
Anholt, Catherine. *Truffles in trouble*
   Truffles is sick
Augarde, Steve (Stephen). *Pig*
Aylesworth, Jim. *Hanna's hog*
Ayres, Becky Hickox. *Victoria flies high*
Ayres, Pam. *Piggo and the nosebag*
   Piggo has a train ride
Baldner, Gaby. *Joba and the wild boar*
Berson, Harold. *Truffles for lunch*
Bianchi, John. *Swine snafu*
Bishop, Claire Huchet. *The truffle pig*
Blake, Jon. *Wriggly Pig*
Blegvad, Lenore. *This little pig-a-wig and other rhymes about pigs*
Bloom, Suzanne. *We keep a pig in the parlor*
Bond, Felicia. *Mary Betty Lizzie McNutt's birthday*
   Poinsettia and her family
   Poinsettia and the firefighters
Boynton, Sandra. *Hester in the wild*
Brand, Millen. *This little pig named Curly*
Brock, Emma Lillian. *Pig with a front porch*
Brown, Judith Gwyn. *Max and the truffle pig*
Brown, Marc Tolon. *Perfect pigs*
Browne, Anthony. *Piggybook*
Bruna, Dick. *Poppy Pig goes to market*
Calhoun, Mary. *The witch's pig*
Calmenson, Stephanie. *Never take a pig to lunch and other funny poems about animals*
Carlson, Nancy. *The mysterious Valentine*
   The perfect family
   Witch lady
Cole, Brock. *Nothing but a pig*
Coontz, Otto. *Starring Rosa*
Corbalis, Judy. *Porcellus, the flying pig*

Craig, Helen. *The night of the paper bag monsters*
 Susie and Alfred in the knight, the princess and the dragon
 A welcome for Annie
Cushman, Doug. *Once upon a pig*
Denslow, Sharon Phillips. *Riding with Aunt Lucy*
Dubanevich, Arlene. *Pig William*
 The piggest show on earth
 Pigs at Christmas
 Pigs in hiding
Dunrea, Olivier. *Eddy B, pigboy*
Dyke, John. *Pigwig*
 Pigwig and the pirates
Edwards, Frank B. *Melody Mooner stayed up all night*
 Mortimer Mooner stopped taking a bath
Eriksson, Ake. *Joel, Jasper, and Julia*
Ernst, Lisa Campbell. *The prize pig surprise*
Erskine, Jim. *Bert and Susie's messy tale*
Fischetto, Laura. *All pigs on deck*
Gackenbach, Dick. *Harvey, the foolish pig*
 Hurray for Hattie Rabbit!
 The pig who saw everything
Galdone, Paul. *The amazing pig*
Getz, Arthur. *Humphrey, the dancing pig*
Goodall, John S. *The adventures of Paddy Pork*
 The ballooning adventures of Paddy Pork
 Paddy goes traveling
 Paddy Pork: odd jobs
 Paddy Pork's holiday
 Paddy to the rescue
 Paddy under water
 Paddy's evening out
 Paddy's new hat
Gray, Nigel. *Little pig's tale*
Gretz, Susanna. *It's your turn, Roger*
 Roger loses his marbles!
 Roger takes charge!
Grossman, Bill. *Tommy at the grocery store*
Hale, Irina. *Chocolate mouse and sugar pig*
Haswell, Peter. *Pog*
 Pog climbs Mount Everest
Hauptmann, Tatjana. *A day in the life of Petronella Pig*
Hawkins, Colin. *Mig the pig*
 This little pig
Heine, Helme. *The pigs' wedding*
Hellard, Susan. *This little piggy*
Hewitt, Kathryn. *The three sillies*
Hoban, Lillian. *Mr. Pig and family*
 Mr. Pig and Sonny too
Hoff, Syd. *Happy birthday, Henrietta!*
Hofstrand, Mary. *Albion pig*
 By the sea
Inkpen, Mick. *If I had a pig*
Jennings, Linda M. *Crispin and the dancing piglet*
Jeschke, Susan. *Perfect the pig*

Johnston, Tony. *Farmer Mack measures his pig*
Kasza, Keiko. *The pigs' picnic*
Keller, Holly. *Geraldine's big snow*
 Geraldine's blanket
Kent, Jack. *Piggy Bank Gonzalez*
King-Smith, Dick. *All pigs are beautiful*
Korth-Sander, Irmtraut. *Will you be my friend?*
Koscielniak, Bruce. *Hector and Prudence*
 Hector and Prudence—all aboard!
Krause, Ute. *Pig surprise*
Kroll, Steven. *Pigs in the house*
Laird, Donivee Martin. *The three little Hawaiian pigs and the magic shark*
Laird, Elizabeth. *The day Sidney ran off*
Lawrence, John. *Rabbit and pork*
Leonard, Marcia. *Birthday in a bathtub*
Levine, Abby. *You push, I ride*
Lewis, Bobby. *Home before midnight*
Lobel, Arnold. *Small pig*
 A treeful of pigs
Lorenz, Lee. *A weekend in the country*
McClenathan, Louise. *The Easter pig*
MacDonald, Elizabeth. *Miss Poppy and the honey cake*
McPhail, David. *Pig Pig and the magic photo album*
 Pig Pig gets a job
 Pig Pig goes to camp
 Pig Pig grows up
 Pig Pig rides
McQueen, Lucinda. *Tidy pig*
Maestro, Betsy. *The guessing game*
Marshall, James. *Portly McSwine*
 Yummers!
 Yummers too: the second course
Martinez, Ruth. *Mrs. McDockerty's knitting*
Mathews, Louise. *The great take-away*
Miles, Miska. *This little pig*
Moon, Cliff. *Pigs on the farm*
Moore, Inga. *The truffle hunter*
Mother Goose. *This little pig*, ill. by Leonard Lubin
 This little pig went to market, ill. by L. Leslie Brooke
Munsch, Robert N. *Pigs*
Newton, Patricia Montgomery. *Vacation surprise*
Nightingale, Sandy. *Pink pigs aplenty*
Offen, Hilda. *Nice work, little wolf!*
Oxenbury, Helen. *Pig tale*
Patterson, Geoffrey. *A pig's tale*
Peck, Robert Newton. *Hamilton*
Peet, Bill (William Bartlett). *Chester the worldly pig*
Pizer, Abigail. *Penelope pig*
Pomerantz, Charlotte. *The piggy in the puddle*
Potter, Beatrix. *The tale of Little Pig Robinson*

The tale of Pigling Bland
Pryor, Bonnie. *Amanda and April*
  Merry Christmas, Amanda and April
Rayner, Mary. *Garth Pig and the ice cream
  lady*
  Mr. and Mrs. Pig's evening out
  Mrs. Pig gets cross and other stories
  Mrs. Pig's bulk buy
Reddix, Valerie. *Millie and the mud hole*
Ross, Tony. *The enchanted pig*
Royston, Angela. *The pig*
Saul, Carol P. *Peter's song*
Scarry, Richard. *Mr. Frumble's worst day
  ever*
  Pig Will and Pig Won't
  Pig Will/Pig Won't
  *Richard Scarry's Peasant Pig and the
  terrible dragon*
Schaffer, Libor. *Arthur sets sail*
Schwartz, Mary. *Spiffen*
Scieszka, Jon. *The true story of the three little
  pigs by A. Wolf, as told to John*
Scruton, Clive. *Pig in the air*
Sharmat, Mitchell. *The seven sloppy days of
  Phineas Pig*
Shecter, Ben. *Partouche plants a seed*
Slate, Joseph. *The mean, clean, giant canoe
  machine*
Stadler, John. *The ballad of Wilbur and the
  moose*
Steig, William. *The amazing bone*
  Farmer Palmer's wagon ride
  Roland, the minstrel pig
Stepto, Michele. *Snuggle Piggy and the
  magic blanket*
Stevens, Carla. *Hooray for pig!*
  Pig and the blue flag
Stine, Jovial Bob. *Pork and beans: play date*
Stobbs, William. *This little piggy*
Tharlet, Eve. *Little pig, big trouble*
The three little pigs. *The original three little
  pigs re-told*, ill. by Jonathan Smith
  The story of the three little pigs, ill. by L.
  Leslie Brooke
  The story of the three little pigs, ill. by
  William Stobbs
  Three little pigs [Facsimile ed]
  The three little pigs, retold and ill. by Val
  Biro
  The three little pigs, retold and ill. by
  Gavin Bishop
  The three little pigs, ill. by Erik Blegvad
  The three little pigs, ill. by Caroline
  Bucknall
  The three little pigs, ill. by Stephen
  Cartwright
  The three little pigs, ill. by Lorinda Bryan
  Cauley
  The three little pigs, ill. by Jean Claverie
  The three little pigs, ill. by William Pène
  Du Bois

The three little pigs, ill. by Paul Galdone
The three little pigs, retold and ill. by
  James Marshall
The three little pigs, ill. by Rodney Peppé
The three little pigs, ill. by Edda Reinl
The three little pigs, ill. by John Wallner
The three little pigs, ill. by Irma Wilde
The three little pigs, ill. by Margot
  Zemach
The three little pigs and the big bad wolf,
  retold and ill. by Glen Rounds
The three little pigs and the fox, ill. by S.
  D. Schindler
The three pigs, ill. by Tony Ross
Tripp, Wallace. *The tale of a pig*
Tyler, Linda Wagner. *The sick-in-bed
  birthday book*
Ungerer, Tomi. *Christmas eve at the Mellops*
  The Mellops go diving for treasure
  The Mellops go flying
  The Mellops go spelunking
  The Mellops strike oil
Uttley, Alison. *The Christmas box*
  Sam Pig and the dragon
  Sam Pig and the hurdy-gurdy man
  Sam Pig and the wind
Van der Meer, Ron. *Pigs at home*
Van Leeuwen, Jean. *More tales of Oliver
  Pig*
Varekamp, Marjolein. *Little Sam takes a
  bath*
Vernon, Tannis. *Little Pig and the blue-
  green sea*
Wabbes, Marie. *Rose is hungry*
  Rose is muddy
  Rose's bath
  Rose's picture
Waechter, Friedrich Karl. *Three is company*
Wagner, Karen. *Silly Fred*
Wahl, Jan. *Mrs. Owl and Mr. Pig*
Walker, Barbara K. (Barbara Kerlin). *Pigs
  and pirates*
Watson, Pauline. *Wriggles, the little wishing
  pig*
Weiss, Ellen. *Pigs in space*
Wells, Rosemary. *The little lame prince*
West, Ian. *Silas, the first pig to fly*
West, Keith. *Little Pig's special day*
Weston, Martha. *Peony's rainbow*
Wheeler, Cindy. *Rose*
Wild, Robin. *Little Pig and the big bad wolf*
Wilhelm, Hans. *Oh, what a mess*
Winthrop, Elizabeth. *Sloppy kisses*
Wiseman, Bernard. *Don't make fun!*
Wondriska, William. *Mr. Brown and Mr.
  Gray*
Wood, David. *Piggies*
Yeoman, John. *The bear's water picnic*
Yolen, Jane. *Picnic with Piggins*
  Piggins

Zakhoder, Boris Vladimirovich. *How a piglet crashed the Christmas party*
Zalben, Jane Breskin. *Basil and Hillary*
Ziefert, Harriet. *Let's go! Piggety Pig*
No more! Piggety Pig
Piggety Pig from morn 'til night

Animals – polar bears

Alborough, Jez. *Bare bear*
Running Bear
Bishop, Adela. *The Christmas polar bear*
Dasent, George W. *East o' the sun, west o' the moon*
De Beer, Hans. *Ahoy there, little polar bear*
Little polar bear
Little polar bear finds a friend
Dickens, Lucy. *Go fish*
Duvoisin, Roger Antoine. *Snowy and Woody*
Hall, Derek. *Polar bear leaps*
Harlow, Joan Hiatt. *Shadow bear*
Heller, Ruth. *How to hide a polar bear*
Lilly, Kenneth. *Animals of the ocean*
Pluckrose, Henry Arthur. *Bears*
Rose, Gerald. *PB takes a holiday*
Ryder, Joanne. *White bear, ice bear*
Wouters, Anne. *This book is for us*
This book is too small
Ylla. *Polar bear brothers*

Animals – porcupines

Annett, Cora. *When the porcupine moved in*
Carrick, Carol. *Ben and the porcupine*
Harshman, Terry Webb. *Porcupine's pajama party*
Lester, Helen. *A porcupine named Fluffy*
Massie, Diane Redfield. *Tiny pin*
Pfister, Marcus. *Where is my friend?*
The porcupine, ill. by Patrick Oxenham
Schlein, Miriam. *Lucky porcupine!*
Stren, Patti. *Hug me*
Thomas, Patricia. *The one and only, super-duper, golly-whopper, jim-dandy, really-handy clock-tock-stopper*
Weiner, Beth Lee. *Benjamin's perfect solution*

Animals – possums

Berson, Harold. *Henry Possum*
Burch, Robert. *Joey's cat*
Carlson, Natalie Savage. *Marie Louise's heyday*
Conford, Ellen. *Eugene the brave*
Impossible, possum
Just the thing for Geraldine
Cushman, Doug. *Possum stew*
Degen, Bruce. *Aunt Possum and the pumpkin man*
Fox, Mem. *Possum magic*
Freschet, Berniece. *Possum baby*
Glaser, Linda. *Keep your socks on, Albert!*
Hoban, Russell. *Nothing to do*

Hurd, Thacher. *Mama don't allow*
Keller, Holly. *Henry's Fourth of July*
Swendson, Patsy. *The potluck adventures of Mrs. Marmalade*
Taylor, Mark. *Old Blue, you good dog you*
Tether, Graham. *Skunk and possum*
Van Laan, Nancy. *Possum come a-knocking*
Weiner, Beth Lee. *Benjamin's perfect solution*
Winthrop, Elizabeth. *Potbellied possums*
Young, James. *Everyone loves the moon*

Animals – prairie dogs

Baylor, Byrd. *Amigo*
Casey, Denise. *The friendly prairie dog*
Luttrell, Ida. *Lonesome Lester*

Animals – rabbits

Adams, Adrienne. *The Christmas party*
The Easter egg artists
The great Valentine's Day balloon race
Adler, David A. *Bunny rabbit rebus*
Æsop. *The hare and the frogs*, ill. by William Stobbs
The hare and the tortoise, ill. by Paul Galdone
The hare and the tortoise, ill. by Gerald Rose
The hare and the tortoise, ill. by Peter Weevers
The tortoise and the hare, ill. by Janet Stevens
Alexander, Martha G. *The magic hat*
Anderson, Lena Castell. *Bunny bath*
Bunny box
Bunny fun
Bunny party
Bunny story
Bunny surprise
Anderson, Lonzo. *Two hundred rabbits*
Annett, Cora. *When the porcupine moved in*
Baby's first book of colors, ill. by Nina Barbaresi
Balian, Lorna. *Humbug rabbit*
Barasch, Lynne. *Rodney's inside story*
Barrett, John M. *The Easter bear*
Bartoli, Jennifer. *In a meadow, two hares hide*
Barton, Byron. *Jack and Fred*
Bate, Lucy. *Little rabbit's loose tooth*
Baumann, Hans. *The hare's race*
Becker, John Leonard. *Seven little rabbits*
Benjamin, Alan. *Busy bunnies*
Bergström, Gunilla. *Is that a monster, Alfie Atkins?*
Berson, Harold. *Pop! goes the turnip*
Bianco, Margery Williams. *The velveteen rabbit*, ill. by Allen Atkinson
The velveteen rabbit, ill. by Michael Green

The velveteen rabbit, ill. by Michael Hague
The velveteen rabbit, ill. by David Jorgensen
The velveteen rabbit, ill. by William Nicholson
The velveteen rabbit, ill. by Ilse Plume
The velveteen rabbit, ill. by S. D. Schindler
The velveteen rabbit, ill. by Tien
Bishop, Adela. *The Easter wolf*
Blau, Judith. *Bunny Mitten's book*
Bolliger, Max. *The rabbit with the sky blue ears*
Bornstein, Ruth Lercher. *Indian bunny*
Bowden, Joan Chase. *Bouncy baby bunny finds his bed*
 Little grey rabbit
Brewster, Patience. *Rabbit Inn*
Bright, Robert. *My hopping bunny*
Brown, Marc Tolon. *The bionic bunny show*
 One, two buckle my shoe
 What do you call a dumb bunny? and other rabbit riddles, games, jokes and cartoons
Brown, Marcia. *The neighbors*
Brown, Margaret Wise. *The golden egg book*
 Goodnight moon
 Little chicken
 The runaway bunny
Browne, Eileen. *Where's that bus?*
Bruna, Dick. *Miffy*
 Miffy at the beach
 Miffy at the playground
 Miffy at the seaside
 Miffy at the zoo
 Miffy goes to school
 Miffy in the hospital
 Miffy in the snow
 Miffy's bicycle
 Miffy's dream
Bryant, Donna. *My rabbit Roberta*
Bullock, Kathleen. *Rabbits are coming*
Burton, Jane. *Freckles the rabbit*
Cahill, Chris. *Bunny magic*
Caldwell, Mary. *Morning, rabbit, morning*
Calmenson, Stephanie. *Wanted: warm, furry friend*
Campbell, Alison. *Are you asleep, rabbit?*
Carlson, Nancy. *Bunnies and their hobbies*
 Bunnies and their sports
 Loudmouth George and the big race
 Loudmouth George and the cornet
 Loudmouth George and the fishing trip
 Loudmouth George and the new neighbors
 Loudmouth George and the sixth-grade bully
Carlstrom, Nancy White. *Kiss your sister, Rose Marie*
 Who gets the sun out of bed?
Carrick, Carol. *A rabbit for Easter*

Carroll, Ruth. *What Whiskers did*
 Where's the bunny?
Carter, Anne. *Bella's secret garden*
Cazet, Denys. *Big shoe, little shoe*
 Christmas moon
 December 24th
 You make the angels cry
Chalmers, Mary. *Come for a walk with me Kevin*
Chandoha, Walter. *A baby bunny for you*
Christelow, Eileen. *Henry and the dragon*
 Henry and the red stripes
Claret, Maria. *The chocolate rabbit*
Cleveland, David. *The April rabbits*
Coatsworth, Elizabeth. *Pika and the roses*
Coldrey, Jennifer. *The world of rabbits*
Compton, Joanne. *Little Rabbit's Easter surprise*
Cosgrove, Stephen (Edward). *Sleepy time bunny*
Cousins, Lucy. *What can rabbit hear?*
 What can rabbit see?
Cross, Genevieve. *My bunny book*
Darling, Kathy (Mary Kathleen). *The Easter bunny's secret*
Delacre, Lulu. *Peter Cottontail's Easter book*
DeLage, Ida. *ABC Easter bunny*
 Am I a bunny?
Delton, Judy. *Brimhall turns detective*
 Brimhall turns to magic
 Rabbit goes to night school
 Three friends find spring
Demi. *Fleecy bunny*
Dennis, Lynne. *Raymond Rabbit's early morning*
De Paola, Tomie (Thomas Anthony). *Too many Hopkins*
Dodds, Dayle Ann. *Do bunnies talk?*
Dorsky, Blanche. *Harry, a true story*
Dowling, Paul. *You can do it, Rabbit*
Du Bois, William Pène. *The hare and the tortoise and the tortoise and the hare*
Dunbar, Joyce. *Lollopy*
Dunn, Judy. *The little rabbit*
Dutton, Sandra. *The cinnamon hen's autumn day*
Ehrlich, Amy. *Bunnies all day long*
 Bunnies and their grandma
 Bunnies at Christmastime
 Bunnies on their own
Ernst, Lisa Campbell. *Miss Penny and Mr. Grubbs*
Fatio, Louise. *The happy lion's rabbits*
Ferns, Ronald. *Osbert and Lucy*
Fisher, Aileen Lucia. *Listen, rabbit*
 Rabbits, rabbits
Flory, Jane. *The bear on the doorstep*
Friskey, Margaret (Margaret Richards). *Mystery of the gate sign*
Gackenbach, Dick. *Hattie be quiet, Hattie be good*

Hattie rabbit
  Hurray for Hattie Rabbit!
  Mother Rabbit's son Tom
Gág, Wanda. *ABC bunny*
Galdone, Paul. *A strange servant*
Gay, Michel. *Rabbit express*
Gay, Zhenya. *Small one*
Geringer, Laura. *Molly's new washing
  machine*
Ginsburg, Mirra. *The fox and the hare*
Gordon, Sharon. *Easter Bunny's lost egg*
Greene, Carol. *The insignificant elephant*
Gretz, Susanna. *Rabbit rambles on*
Grossman, Virginia. *Ten little rabbits*
Hands, Hargrave. *Bunny sees*
Hayward, Linda. *All stuck up*
Heine, Helme. *Superhare*
Henkes, Kevin. *Bailey goes camping*
Herford, Oliver. *The most timid in the land*
Heyward, Du Bose. *The country bunny and
  the little gold shoes*
Hoban, Lillian. *Harry's song*
Hoban, Tana. *Where is it?*
Hogrogian, Nonny. *Carrot cake*
Hooks, William H. *Three rounds with rabbit*
Howe, James. *Scared silly*
Huriet, Genevieve. *Dandelion's vanishing
  vegetable garden*
Hynard, Stephen. *Snowy the rabbit*
Jabar, Cynthia. *Party day!*
Jaquith, Priscilla. *Bo Rabbit smart for true*
Jewell, Nancy. *The snuggle bunny*
Johnston, Mary Anne. *Sing me a song*
Kangas, Juli. *Fluffy Bunny's friend*
Keller, Holly. *Cromwell's glasses*
Keller, Irene. *Benjamin Rabbit and the
  stranger danger*
Kelley, True. *A Valentine for Fuzzboom*
Kirn, Ann. *The tale of a crocodile*
Komoda, Beerly. *The winter day*
Komoda, Beverly. *The too hot day*
Koscielniak, Bruce. *Euclid Bunny delivers
  the mail*
Kraus, Robert. *Big brother*
  Daddy Long Ears
  Good night Richard Rabbit
  The littlest rabbit
  Phil the ventriloquist
Kroll, Steven. *The big bunny and the Easter
  eggs*
  The big bunny and the magic show
Kuratomi, Chizuko. *Mr. Bear and the
  robbers*
Kwitz, Mary DeBall. *Rabbits' search for a
  little house*
Lacome, Julie. *Hocus pocus*
La Fontaine, Jean de. *The hare and the
  tortoise*
Landa, Norbert. *Rabbit and chicken find a
  box*
  Rabbit and chicken play hide and seek

Lawrence, John. *Rabbit and pork*
Leach, Michael. *Rabbits*
Leedy, Loreen. *The bunny play*
Leonard, Alain. *Barnaby and the big gorilla*
Leonard, Marcia. *Shopping for snowflakes*
Le Tord, Bijou. *Rabbit seeds*
Lifton, Betty Jean. *The rice-cake rabbit*
Lionni, Leo. *Let's make rabbits*
Lipkind, William. *The Christmas bunny*
Littlefield, William. *The whiskers of Ho Ho*
Lorian, Nicole. *A birthday present for Mama*
McCormack, John E. *Rabbit tales*
  Rabbit travels
McDermott, Gerald. *Zomo the rabbit*
MacDonald, Maryann. *Rabbit's birthday kite*
  Rosie runs away
  Rosie's baby tooth
McLenighan, Valjean. *Turtle and rabbit*
McNaughton, Colin. *Walk rabbit walk*
Mangas, Brian. *A nice surprise for Father
  Rabbit*
Manushkin, Fran. *Little rabbit's baby brother*
Maril, Lee. *Mr. Bunny paints the eggs*
Martin, Rafe. *Foolish rabbit's big mistake*
Mathews, Louise. *Bunches and bunches of
  bunnies*
Mayne, William. *Come, come to my corner*
Medina, Nina. *Have you ever noticed that
  rabbits don't sing?*
Mendelson, S. T. *Stupid Emilien*
Meroux, Felix. *The prince of the rabbits*
Michels, Tilde. *Rabbit spring*
Miles, Miska. *Rabbit garden*
  Small rabbit
Miller, J. P. (John Parr). *Good night, Little
  Rabbit*
  Learn to count with Little Rabbit
Milne, A. A. (Alan Alexander). *Prince
  Rabbit*
Moore, Inga. *Oh, little Jack*
Moremen, Grace E. *No, no, Natalie*
Newberry, Clare Turlay. *Marshmallow*
Nilsson, Ulf. *Little sister rabbit*
Norman, Philip Ross. *The carrot war*
Parish, Peggy. *Too many rabbits*
Parry, Marian. *King of the fish*
Peet, Bill (William Bartlett). *Huge Harold*
Peters, Sharon. *Ready, get set, go!*
  Stop that rabbit
Petty, Kate. *Rabbits*
Pfister, Marcus. *Hopper*
Pizer, Abigail. *Loppylugs*
Poole, Valerie. *Obadiah Coffee and the music
  contest*
Potter, Beatrix. *The complete adventures of
  Peter Rabbit*
  Peter Rabbit's one two three
  The story of fierce bad rabbit
  The tale of Benjamin Bunny
  The tale of Mr. Tod

The tale of Peter Rabbit, ill. by Margot
  Apple
The tale of Peter Rabbit, ill. by Beatrix
  Potter
The tale of the Flopsy Bunnies
Where's Peter Rabbit?
The pudgy bunny book, ill. by Ruth
  Sanderson
Quackenbush, Robert M. *First grade jitters*
  Funny bunnies
Ratnett, Michael. *Marmaduke and the scary
  story*
Ratz de Tagyos, Paul. *A coney tale*
Rey, Margret (Margret Elisabeth
  Waldstein). *Spotty*
Roberts, Bethany. *Waiting-for-Papa stories*
  Waiting for spring stories
Rosen, Michael J. *Little rabbit Foo Foo*
Sadler, Marilyn. *It's not easy being a bunny*
Sara. *The rabbit, the fox, and the wolf*
Schlein, Miriam. *Little Rabbit, the high
  jumper*
Schotter, Roni. *Bunny's night out*
Schweninger, Ann. *Birthday wishes*
  Christmas secrets
  Halloween surprises
  The hunt for rabbit's galosh
  Off to school!
  Valentine friends
Seuss, Dr. *The eye book*
Sharmat, Marjorie Weinman. *Thornton, the
  worrier*
Silverman, Erica. *Warm in winter*
Silverman, Maida. *Bunny's ABC*
Smith, Cara Lockhart. *Twenty-six rabbits
  run riot*
Solotareff, Grégoire. *Don't call me little
  bunny*
Sonnenschein, Harriet. *Harold's runaway
  nose*
Spier, Peter. *Little rabbits*
Steig, William. *Solomon the rusty nail*
Steiner, Charlotte. *My bunny feels soft*
Steiner, Jörg. *Rabbit Island*
Stevenson, James. *Monty*
Stevenson, Suçie. *Christmas eve*
  Do I have to take Violet?
Szekeres, Cyndy. *Hide-and-seek duck*
Tafuri, Nancy. *Rabbit's morning*
Tarrant, Graham. *Rabbits*
Tejima, Keizaburo. *Ho-limlim*
Thomas, Patricia. *The one and only, super-
  duper, golly-whopper, jim-dandy, really-
  handy clock-tock-stopper*
Tompert, Ann. *Nothing sticks like a shadow*
Tresselt, Alvin R. *The rabbit story,* ill. by
  Carolyn Ewing
  Rabbit story, ill. by Leonard Weisgard
Trez, Denise. *Rabbit country*
Tripp, Wallace. *My Uncle Podger*
Troughton, Joanna. *How rabbit stole the fire*

Van Emst, Charlotte. *Little Rabbit's big day*
Van Woerkom, Dorothy. *Harry and
  Shelburt*
Velthuijs, Max. *Little Man to the rescue*
Wabbes, Marie. *Good night, Little Rabbit*
  Happy birthday, Little Rabbit
  It's snowing, Little Rabbit
  Little Rabbit's garden
Waddell, Martin. *We love them*
Wahl, Jan. *Carrot nose*
  Doctor Rabbit's foundling
  The five in the forest
  Rabbits on roller skates!
Watson, Wendy. *The bunnies' Christmas eve*
  Lollipop
Watts, Barrie. *Rabbit*
Wayland, April Halprin. *To Rabbittown*
Weil, Lisl. *The candy egg bunny*
Weisgard, Leonard. *The funny bunny factory*
Wells, Rosemary. *Hooray for Max*
  Max's bath
  Max's bedtime
  Max's birthday
  Max's breakfast
  Max's chocolate chicken
  Max's Christmas
  Max's dragon shirt
  Max's first word
  Max's new suit
  Max's ride
  Max's toys
Wiese, Kurt. *Happy Easter*
Wilhelm, Hans. *Bunny trouble*
  More bunny trouble
Williams, Garth. *The rabbits' wedding*
Wolf, Ann. *The rabbit and the turtle*
Wolf, Winfried. *The Easter bunny*
Worth, Bonnie. *Peter Cottontail's surprise*
Wyllie, Stephen. *White Rabbit builds a
  dream house*
  White Rabbit builds a dream house
Zakhoder, Boris Vladimirovich. *Rosachok*
Ziefert, Harriet. *Breakfast time!*
  Bye-bye, daddy!
  Good morning, sun!
  Happy birthday, Grandpa!
  Happy Easter, Grandma!
  Let's get dressed!
Zolotow, Charlotte (Shapiro). *The bunny
  who found Easter*
  Mr. Rabbit and the lovely present

Animals – raccoons

Arnosky, Jim. *Raccoons and ripe corn*
Bellows, Cathy. *The royal raccoon*
Bradford, Ann. *The mystery at Misty Falls*
  The mystery of the missing raccoon
Brown, Margaret Wise. *Wait till the moon is
  full*
Burdick, Margaret. *Sara Raccoon and the
  secret place*

Duvoisin, Roger Antoine. *Petunia, I love you*

Freschet, Berniece. *Five fat raccoons*

Hoban, Lillian. *The case of the two masked robbers*
Here come raccoons

Johnson, Donna Kay. *Brighteyes*

Lewison, Wendy C. *Where is Sammy's smile?*

McPhail, David. *Something special*
Stanley: Henry Bear's friend

Miklowitz, Gloria D. *Save that raccoon!*

Miles, Miska. *The raccoon and Mrs. McGinnis*

Moore, Lilian. *Little Raccoon and no trouble at all*
Little Raccoon and the outside world
Little Raccoon and the thing in the pool

Morgan, Allen. *Molly and Mr. Maloney*

Noguere, Suzanne. *Little raccoon*

St. George, Judith. *The Halloween pumpkin smasher*

Sharmat, Marjorie Weinman. *The 329th friend*

Steiner, Barbara (Annette). *But not Stanleigh*

Thayer, Jane. *The clever raccoon*

Wells, Rosemary. *Timothy goes to school*

Whelan, Gloria. *A week of raccoons*

Young, James. *Everyone loves the moon*

Animals – rats

Annixter, Jane. *Brown rats, black rats*

Augarde, Steve (Stephen). *Barnaby Shrew, Black Dan and...the mighty wedgwood*
Barnaby Shrew goes to sea

Bartos-Hoppner, Barbara. *The Pied Piper of Hamelin*

Baynton, Martin. *Fifty saves his friend*

Bellows, Cathy. *Four fat rats*

Berson, Harold. *The rats who lived in the delicatessen*

Biro, Val. *The pied piper of Hamelin*

Black, Floyd. *Alphabet cat*

Browning, Robert. *The pied piper of Hamelin*, ill. by Patricia and Robin DeWitt
The pied piper of Hamelin, ill. by Kate Greenaway
The pied piper of Hamelin, ill. by Anatoly Ivanov
The pied piper of Hamelin, ill. by Errol Le Cain

Bryan, Ashley. *The cat's purr*

Cole, Babette. *Hurray for Ethelyn*

Cressey, James. *Fourteen rats and a rat-catcher*

Cunningham, Julia. *A mouse called Junction*

Doty, Roy. *Old-one-eye meets his match*

Erickson, Russell E. *Warton and the traders*

Hearn, Michael Patrick. *The porcelain cat*

Hoban, Russell. *Flat cat*

Hurd, Thacher. *Mystery on the docks*

Kouts, Anne. *Kenny's rat*

La Fontaine, Jean de. *The lion and the rat*

Lager, Claude. *A tale of two rats*

McNaughton, Colin. *The rat race*

Mayer, Mercer. *The Pied Piper of Hamelin*

Miles, Miska. *Wharf rat*

Moore, Inga. *Aktil's big swim*

Oakley, Graham. *The church mice adrift*

Peppé, Rodney. *The mice and the clockwork bus*
The mice and the flying basket

Pomerantz, Charlotte. *The ballad of the long-tailed rat*

Potter, Beatrix. *The sly old cat*

Ross, Tony. *The pied piper of Hamelin*

Saunders, Susan. *Charles Rat's picnic*

Schiller, Barbara. *The white rat's tale*

Sharmat, Marjorie Weinman. *Mooch the messy*

Snow, Alan. *The monster book of ABC sounds*

Stevenson, James. *Wilfred the rat*

Van Woerkom, Dorothy. *The rat, the ox and the zodiac*

Walt Disney Productions. *Walt Disney's The adventures of Mr. Toad*

Zemach, Kaethe. *The beautiful rat*

Animals – reindeer

Brett, Jan. *The wild Christmas reindeer*

Cleaver, Elizabeth. *The enchanted caribou*

Haywood, Carolyn. *How the reindeer saved Santa*

Hoff, Syd. *Where's Prancer?*

May, Robert Lewis. *Rudolph the red-nosed reindeer*

Owens, Mary Beth. *A caribou alphabet*

Animals – rhinoceros

Ardizzone, Edward. *Diana and her rhinoceros*

Brunhoff, Laurent de. *Babar's battle*

Bush, John. *The cross-with-us rhinoceros*

Cazet, Denys. *Great-Uncle Felix*

Johnson, Louise. *Malunda*

Kipling, Rudyard. *How the rhinoceros got his skin*, ill. by Leonard Weisgard

Maestro, Giulio. *Just enough Rosie*

Sackett, Elisabeth. *Danger on the African grassland*

Sis, Peter. *Rainbow Rhino*

Standon, Anna. *The singing rhinoceros*

Yoshida, Toshi. *Rhinoceros mother*

Animals – salamanders

Mazer, Anne. *The salamander room*

Animals – sea lions

Hamsa, Bobbie. *Your pet sea lion*

Olds, Elizabeth. *Plop plop ploppie*
Schreiber, Georges. *Bambino the clown*

Animals – seals

Barr, Cathrine. *Sammy seal ov the sircus*
Cooper, Susan. *The Selkie girl*
Duran, Bonté. *The adventures of Arthur and Edmund*
Freeman, Don. *The seal and the slick*
Gerstein, Mordicai. *The seal mother*
Hoff, Syd. *Sammy the seal*
Lilly, Kenneth. *Animals of the ocean*
Sackett, Elisabeth. *Danger on the Arctic ice*
The seal, ill. by Charlotte Knox
Yolen, Jane. *Greyling*

Animals – sheep

Aardema, Verna. *Borreguita and the coyote*
Alborough, Jez. *The grass is always greener*
Baird, Anne. *The Christmas lamb*
Beskow, Elsa Maartman. *Pelle's new suit*
Blanchard, Arlene. *The naughty lamb*
Brown, Margaret Wise. *Little lost lamb*
Cazzola, Gus. *The bells of Santa Lucia*
Coe, Lloyd. *Charcoal*
Demi. *Fleecy lamb*
  Little baby lamb
De Paola, Tomie (Thomas Anthony).
  Charlie needs a cloak
  Haircuts for the Woolseys
Dunn, Judy. *The little lamb*
Ernst, Lisa Campbell. *Nattie Parsons' good-luck lamb*
Galdone, Paul. *Little Bo-Peep*
Ginsburg, Mirra. *The strongest one of all*
Gordon, Jeffie Ross. *Six sleepy sheep*
Grejniec, Michael. *When I open my eyes*
Hale, Sarah Josepha. *Mary had a little lamb*, ill. by Tomie de Paola
  Mary had a little lamb, photos. by Bruce Millan
Heck, Elisabeth. *The black sheep*
Hedderwick, Mairi. *Katie Morag and the two grandmothers*
Helldorfer, M. C. (Mary Claire). *Daniel's gift*
Hooks, William H. *Lion and lamb*
Inkpen, Mick. *If I had a sheep*
Ipcar, Dahlov. *The land of flowers*
Kitamura, Satoshi. *When sheep cannot sleep*
Lewis, Kim. *Emma's lamb*
  The shepherd boy
Lewis, Robin Baird. *Friska, the sheep that was too small*
Lunn, Janet. *Amos's sweater*
McCully, Emily Arnold. *Speak up, Blanche!*
McGee, Barbara. *Counting sheep*
MacGregor, Marilyn. *On top*
Mendoza, George. *Alphabet sheep*
  Silly sheep and other sheepish rhymes

Novak, Matt. *While the shepherd slept*
O'Brien, Mary. *Counting sheep to sleep*
Patent, Dorothy Hinshaw. *Maggie, a sheep dog*
Peet, Bill (William Bartlett). *Buford the little bighorn*
Rogers, Paul (Patrick). *Sheepchase*
Royston, Angela. *The sheep*
Russell, Betty. *Run sheep run*
Ryder, Joanne. *Beach party*
Shaw, Nancy. *Sheep in a jeep*
  Sheep in a shop
  Sheep on a ship
Slobodkin, Louis. *Up high and down low*
Snyder, Zilpha Keatley. *The changing maze*
Steiner, Charlotte. *Red Ridinghood's little lamb*
Strete, Craig Kee. *Big thunder magic*
Sundgaard, Arnold. *The lamb and the butterfly*
Wallace, Barbara Brooks. *Argyle*
Weiss, Ellen. *Clara the fortune-telling chicken*
Wellington, Monica. *The sheep follow*
Widman, Christine. *The star grazers*
Wild, Jocelyn. *Florence and Eric take the cake*

Animals – shrews

Augarde, Steve (Stephen). *Barnaby Shrew, Black Dan and...the mighty wedgwood*
  Barnaby Shrew goes to sea
Goodall, John S. *Shrewbettina's birthday*
Koller, Jackie French. *Mole and shrew*

Animals – skunks

De Regniers, Beatrice Schenk. *A special birthday party for someone very special*
Hoban, Brom. *Skunk Lane*
Jones, Chuck. *William the backwards skunk*
Latimer, Jim. *James Bear's pie*
Reeves, Mona Rabun. *The spooky eerie night noise*
Schlein, Miriam. *What's wrong with being a skunk?*
Schoenherr, John. *The barn*
Tether, Graham. *Skunk and possum*
Wells, Rosemary. *Fritz and the mess fairy*

Animals – sloths

Knight, Hilary. *Sylvia the sloth*
Sharmat, Mitchell. *Sherman is a slowpoke*

Animals – snails

Lord, John Vernon. *Mr. Mead and his garden*
McAllister, Angela. *Snail's birthday problem*
Marshall, James. *The guest*
O'Hagan, Caroline. *It's easy to have a snail visit you*

Oleson, Jens. *Snail*
Rockwell, Anne F. *The story snail*
Ryder, Joanne. *Snail in the woods*
  The snail's spell
Stadler, John. *Hooray for snail!*
  Snail saves the day
Ungerer, Tomi. *Snail, where are you?*

Animals – squirrels

Alexander, Sue. *There's more...much more*
Angelo, Valenti. *The acorn tree*
Ashabranner, Brent. *I'm in the zoo, too*
Bare, Colleen Stanley. *Busy, busy squirrels*
  Tree squirrels
Bassett, Lisa. *Beany and Scamp*
  Beany wakes up for Christmas
Browne, Eileen. *Where's that bus?*
Buff, Mary. *Hurry, Skurry and Flurry*
Carey, Valerie Scho. *Harriet and William and the terrible creature*
Carter, Anne. *Scurry's treasure*
Coldrey, Jennifer. *The world of squirrels*
Collins, Pat Lowery. *Tomorrow, up and away!*
Crane, Donn. *Flippy and Skippy*
DeLage, Ida. *The squirrel's tree party*
Drummond, Violet H. *Phewtus the squirrel*
Earle, Olive L. *Squirrels in the garden*
Jones, Penelope. *I didn't want to be nice*
Kroll, Steven. *The squirrels' Thanksgiving*
Lane, Margaret. *The squirrel*
Miller, Edna. *Scamper: a gray tree squirrel*
Oxford Scientific Films. *Grey squirrel*
Peet, Bill (William Bartlett). *Merle the high flying squirrel*
Peterson, Hans. *Erik has a squirrel*
Potter, Beatrix. *The tale of Squirrel Nutkin*
  The tale of Timmy Tiptoes
Schumacher, Claire. *Nutty's birthday*
  Nutty's Christmas
Shannon, George. *The surprise*
Sharmat, Marjorie Weinman. *Attila the angry*
  Sophie and Gussie
  The trip
Stage, Mads. *The lonely squirrel*
Stevenson, James. *Wilfred the rat*
Yeoman, John. *The bear's water picnic*
Young, Miriam Burt. *Miss Suzy's Easter surprise*
Zion, Gene. *The meanest squirrel I ever met*
Zweifel, Frances. *Bony*

Animals – tapirs

Maestro, Giulio. *The tortoise's tug of war*

Animals – tigers

Adams, Richard (Richard Newbold). *The tyger voyage*

Anderson, Paul S. *Red fox and the hungry tiger*
Baker, Keith. *Who is the beast?*
Bannerman, Helen. *The story of little black Sambo*
Barrows, Marjorie Wescott. *Timothy Tiger*
Blaustein, Muriel. *Bedtime, Zachary!*
  Make friends, Zachary!
Canning, Kate. *A painted tale*
Cowcher, Helen. *Tigress*
Dines, Glen. *A tiger in the cherry tree*
Dodds, Siobhan. *Charles Tiger*
Domanska, Janina. *Why so much noise?*
Farber, Norma. *How to ride a tiger*
Fenner, Carol. *Tigers in the cellar*
Frankel, Bernice. *Half-As-Big and the tiger*
Hall, Derek. *Tiger runs*
Hoban, Russell. *The dancing tigers*
Hoffman, Mary. *Animals in the wild: tiger*
Ipcar, Dahlov. *Stripes and spots*
Justice, Jennifer. *The tiger*
Kepes, Juliet. *Cock-a-doodle-doo*
Kraus, Robert. *Leo the late bloomer*
Lewis, Sharon. *Tiger!*
Paul, Anthony. *The tiger who lost his stripes*
Pluckrose, Henry Arthur. *Lions and tigers*
Prelutsky, Jack. *The terrible tiger*
Rockwell, Anne F. *Big boss*
Root, Phyllis. *Moon tiger*
Rose, Gerald. *The tiger-skin rug*
Round, Graham. *Hangdog*
Taylor, Mark. *Henry explores the jungle*
Tworkov, Jack. *The camel who took a walk*
Villarejo, Mary. *The tiger hunt*
Wahl, Jan. *Tiger watch*
Wersba, Barbara. *Do tigers ever bite kings?*
Whitney, Alex. *Once a bright red tiger*
Wolkstein, Diane. *The banza*
Wolski, Slawomir. *Tiger cat*
Xiong, Blia. *Nine-in-one Grr! Grr!*

Animals – walruses

Bridges, William. *Ookie, the walrus who likes people*
Hoff, Syd. *Walpole*
Stevenson, James. *Winston, Newton, Elton, and Ed*

Animals – warthogs

Hazen, Barbara Shook. *Wally the worry-warthog*

Animals – water buffaloes

Gobhai, Mehlli. *Lakshmi, the water buffalo who wouldn't*

Animals – weasels

Bach, Alice. *Warren Weasel's worse than measles*

Ernst, Lisa Campbell. *Zinnia and Dot*
Holder, Heidi. *Crows*
Lobel, Arnold. *Mouse soup*
Mathews, Louise. *Cluck one*
Zelinsky, Paul O. *The lion and the stoat*

Animals – whales

Appelbaum, Neil. *Is there a hole in your head?*
Armitage, Ronda. *The lighthouse keeper's rescue*
Armour, Richard Willard. *Sea full of whales*
Baumann, Kurt. *The story of Jonah*
Behrens, June. *Whales of the world Whalewatch!*
Bellamy, David. *How green are you?*
Benchley, Nathaniel. *The deep dives of Stanley Whale*
Bible. Old Testament. Jonah. *The Book of Jonah*, ill. by Peter Spier
Jonah, ill. by Kurt Mitchell
Jonah and the great fish, ill. by Leon Baxter
Bulla, Clyde Robert. *Jonah and the great fish*
Clark, Harry. *The first story of the whale*
Climo, Shirley. *The adventure of Walter*
Conklin, Gladys. *Journey of the gray whales*
Day, Edward C. *John Tabor's ride*
Duvoisin, Roger Antoine. *The Christmas whale*
Engle, Joanna. *Cap'n kid goes to the South Pole*
Gibbons, Gail. *Whales*
Haiz, Danah. *Jonah's journey*
Hudson, Eleanor. *A whale of a rescue*
Hurd, Edith Thacher. *What whale? Where?*
Hutton, Warwick. *Jonah and the great fish*
James, Simon. *Dear Mr. Blueberry*
My friend whale
Johnston, Johanna. *Whale's way*
Johnston, Tony. *Whale song*
King, Patricia. *Mable the whale*
Le Guin, Ursula K. *Solomon Leviathan's nine hundred and thirty-first trip around the world*
Lent, Blair. *John Tabor's ride*
Lewis, Sharon. *Orca! the killer whale*
Lilly, Kenneth. *Animals of the ocean*
Lobato, Arcadio. *The greatest treasure*
McCloskey, Robert. *Bert Dow, deep-water man*
Maestro, Giulio. *The tortoise's tug of war*
Patterson, Geoffrey. *Jonah and the whale*
Pluckrose, Henry Arthur. *Whales*
Postgate, Oliver. *Noggin and the whale*
Raffi. *Baby beluga*
Roy, Ronald. *A thousand pails of water*
Ryder, Joanne. *Winter whale*
Selsam, Millicent E. *A first look at whales*

Sheldon, Dyan. *The whales' song*
Siberell, Anne. *Whale in the sky*
Stansfield, Ian. *The legend of the whale*
Steiner, Barbara (Annette). *The whale brother*
Strange, Florence. *Rock-a-bye whale*
Thorne, Jenny. *Jonah and the whale*
Tokuda, Wendy. *Humphrey the lost whale*
Watanabe, Yuichi. *Wally the whale who loved balloons*
Williams, Marcia. *Jonah and the whale*
Wilson, Bob. *Stanley Bagshaw and the twenty-two ton whale*
Wilson, Lynn. *Baby whale*
Wood, Audrey. *Little Penguin's tale*

Animals – wildebeests

Berliner, Franz. *Wildebeest*

Animals – wolves

Allen, Jonathan. *Mucky moose*
Ambrus, Victor G. *Country wedding*
Baynes, Pauline. *How dog began*
Bishop, Adela. *The Easter wolf*
Blades, Ann. *Mary of mile 18*
Blundell, Tony. *Beware of boys*
Bradman, Tony. *Look out, he's behind you*
Brett, Jan. *The first dog*
Curti, Anna. *Seasons*
Damjan, Mischa. *Atuk*
The wolf and the kid
Daudet, Alphonse. *The brave little goat of Monsieur Séguin*
Delaney, A. *The gunnywolf*
De Marolles, Chantal. *The lonely wolf*
De Regniers, Beatrice Schenk. *Red Riding Hood*
Dinardo, Jeffrey. *The wolf who cried boy*
Evans, Katherine. *The boy who cried wolf*
Firmin, Peter. *Chicken stew*
Friskey, Margaret (Margaret Richards). *Indian Two Feet and the wolf cubs*
Gackenbach, Dick. *Harvey, the foolish pig*
Gay, Michel. *The Christmas wolf*
Goble, Paul. *The friendly wolf*
Grimm, Jacob. *Little red cap*, ill. by Lisbeth Zwerger
Little Red Riding Hood, ill. by Frank Aloise
Little Red Riding Hood, ill. by Gwen Connelly
Little Red Riding Hood, ill. by Paul Galdone
Little Red Riding Hood, ill. by John S. Goodall
Little Red Riding Hood, ill. by Trina Schart Hyman
Little Red Riding Hood, ill. by Bernadette Watts

Nanny goat and the seven little kids, ill. by
  Janet Stevens
The wolf and the seven kids, ill. by
  Kinuko Y. Craft
The wolf and the seven little kids, ill. by
  Svend Otto S.
The wolf and the seven little kids, ill. by
  Martin Ursell
Gunthrop, Karen. *Adam and the wolf*
Harper, Wilhelmina. *The gunniwolf*
Hawkins, Colin. *What time is it, Mr. Wolf?*
Kasza, Keiko. *The wolf's chicken stew*
Lester, Helen. *Tacky the penguin*
Lewis, Robin Baird. *Friska, the sheep that
  was too small*
McClure, Gillian. *What's the time, Rory
  Wolf?*
McPhail, David. *A wolf story*
Marshall, James. *Red Riding Hood*
Morris, Ann. *The Little Red Riding Hood
  rebus book*
Murphy, Jim. *The call of the wolves*
Offen, Hilda. *Nice work, little wolf!*
Parish, Peggy. *Granny, the baby and the big
  gray thing*
Peck, Robert Newton. *Hamilton*
Porter, Sue. *Little Wolf and the giant*
Prokofiev, Sergei Sergeievitch. *Peter and
  the wolf*, ill. by Reg Cartwright
Peter and the wolf, ill. by Warren
  Chappell
Peter and the wolf, ill. by Barbara
  Cooney
Peter and the wolf, ill. by Frans Haacken
Peter and the wolf, ill. by Alan Howard
Peter and the wolf, ill. by Charles
  Mikolaycak
Peter and the wolf, ill. by Jörg Müller
Peter and the wolf, ill. by Josef Paleček
Peter and the wolf, ill. by Kozo Shimizu
Peter and the wolf, ill. by Erna Voigt
Prusski, Jeffrey. *Bring back the deer*
Rayner, Mary. *Garth Pig and the ice cream
  lady*
Mr. and Mrs. Pig's evening out
Rockwell, Anne F. *The wolf who had a
  wonderful dream*
Ross, Tony. *The boy who cried wolf*
Stone soup
Roth, Susan L. *Kanahena*
Sara. *The rabbit, the fox, and the wolf*
Schick, Alice. *Just this once*
Scieszka, Jon. *The true story of the three little
  pigs by A. Wolf, as told to John*
Selsam, Millicent E. *A first look at dogs*
Sharmat, Marjorie Weinman. *Walter the
  wolf*
Storr, Catherine (Cole). *Clever Polly and the
  stupid wolf*
The three little pigs. *The original three little
  pigs re-told*, ill. by Jonathan Smith

The story of the three little pigs, ill. by L.
  Leslie Brooke
The story of the three little pigs, ill. by
  William Stobbs
Three little pigs [Facsimile ed]
The three little pigs, retold and ill. by Val
  Biro
The three little pigs, retold and ill. by
  Gavin Bishop
The three little pigs, ill. by Erik Blegvad
The three little pigs, ill. by Caroline
  Bucknall
The three little pigs, ill. by Stephen
  Cartwright
The three little pigs, ill. by Lorinda Bryan
  Cauley
The three little pigs, ill. by Jean Claverie
The three little pigs, ill. by William Pène
  Du Bois
The three little pigs, ill. by Paul Galdone
The three little pigs, retold and ill. by
  James Marshall
The three little pigs, ill. by Rodney Peppé
The three little pigs, ill. by Edda Reinl
The three little pigs, ill. by John Wallner
The three little pigs, ill. by Irma Wilde
The three little pigs, ill. by Margot
  Zemach
The three little pigs and the big bad wolf,
  retold and ill. by Glen Rounds
The three pigs, ill. by Tony Ross
Wild, Robin. *Little Pig and the big bad wolf*
Wyllie, Stephen. *Dinner with fox*
Young, Ed (Edward). *Lon Po Po*

Animals – wombats

Argent, Kerry. *Happy birthday, Wombat!*
  Wombat and Bandicoot: best friends
Elks, Wendy. *Charles B. Wombat and the
  very strange thing*

Animals – worms

Ahlberg, Janet. *The little worm book*
Lindgren, Barbro. *A worm's tale*
O'Hagan, Caroline. *It's easy to have a worm
  visit you*
Scarry, Richard. *Richard Scarry's busy houses*
Thayer, Jane. *Andy and the wild worm*
Wong, Herbert H. *Our earthworms*

Animals – yaks

Lawson, Annetta. *The lucky yak*

Animals – zebras

Goodall, Daphne Machin. *Zebras*
Hadithi, Mwenye. *Greedy zebra*
Peet, Bill (William Bartlett). *Zella, Zack,
  and Zodiac*

Animals, dislike of *see* Behavior – animals, dislike of

Antarctic *see* Foreign lands – Antarctic

Anteaters *see* Animals – anteaters

Anti-violence *see* Violence, anti-violence

Ants *see* Insects – ants

Apes *see* Animals – chimpanzees; Animals – gorillas; Animals – monkeys

Appearance *see* Character traits – appearance

April Fools' Day *see* Holidays – April Fools' Day

Aquariums
Binnamin, Vivian. *The case of the mysterious mermaid*
Calder, S. J. *If you were a fish*
Curious George goes to the aquarium

Arabia *see* Foreign lands – Arabia

Architects *see* Careers – architects

Arctic *see* Foreign lands – Arctic

Arguing *see* Behavior – fighting, arguing

Arithmetic *see* Counting, numbers

Armadillos *see* Animals – armadillos

Armenia *see* Foreign lands – Armenia

Art
Agee, Jon. *The incredible painting of Felix Clousseau*
Anderson, Douglas. *Let's draw a story*
Angelo, Nancy Carolyn Harrison. *Camembert*
Baker, Jeannie. *Grandmother*
Baylor, Byrd. *When clay sings*
Blizzard, Gladys S. *Come look with me*
Bond, Michael. *Paddington's art exhibit*
Borten, Helen. *Do you see what I see?*
A picture has a special look
Brent, Isabelle. *Cameo cats*
Brett, Jan. *The first dog*
Bröger, Achim. *Francie's paper puppy*
Bromhall, Winifred. *Mary Ann's first picture*
Brown, Laurie Krasny. *Visiting the art museum*
Browne, Anthony. *Bear goes to town*

Bear hunt
The little bear book
Bulla, Clyde Robert. *Daniel's duck*
Canning, Kate. *A painted tale*
Carrick, Donald. *Morgan and the artist*
Cazet, Denys. *Frosted glass*
The Christmas story
Cober, Alan E. *Cober's choice*
Cohen, Miriam. *No good in art*
Craig, Helen. *Susie and Alfred in the knight, the princess and the dragon*
Decker, Dorothy W. *Stripe visits New York*
De Mejo, Oscar. *Oscar de Mejo's ABC*
De Paola, Tomie (Thomas Anthony). *The art lesson*
Bonjour, Mister Satie
Dionetti, Michelle. *Thalia Brown and the blue bug*
Elliott, Dan. *Ernie's little lie*
Emberley, Ed (Edward Randolph). *Ed Emberley's big green drawing book*
Ed Emberley's big orange drawing book
Ed Emberley's big purple drawing book
Ed Emberley's crazy mixed-up face game
Ed Emberley's drawing book: make a world
Emberley, Michael. *More dinosaurs!*
Emberley, Rebecca. *Drawing with numbers and letters*
Ernst, Lisa Campbell. *Hamilton's art show*
Everett, Gwen. *Li'l Sis and Uncle Willie*
Fifield, Flora. *Pictures for the palace*
Florian, Douglas. *A potter*
Freeman, Don. *Norman the doorman*
Goffstein, M. B. (Marilyn Brooke). *Artists' helpers enjoy the evening*
Green, Marion. *The magician who lived on the mountain*
Harris, Leon A. *The great picture robbery*
Haskins, Jim. *The Statue of Liberty: America's proud lady*
Hurd, Edith Thacher. *Wilson's world*
Ingoglia, Gina. *The art class*
Johnson, Crockett. *Harold and the purple crayon*
A picture for Harold's room
Kesselman, Wendy. *Emma*
Kilroy, Sally. *Copycat drawing book*
Lehan, Daniel. *This is not a book about dodos*
Lessac, Frané. *Caribbean canvas*
Lionni, Leo. *Let's make rabbits*
MacDonald, Elizabeth. *John's picture*
MacGill-Callahan, Sheila. *And still the turtle watched*
McPhail, David. *The magical drawings of Moony B. Finch*
Maestro, Betsy. *The story of the Statue of Liberty*
Mayers, Florence Cassen. *Egyptian art from the Brooklyn Museum: ABC*
The Museum of Fine Arts, Boston: ABC

*The Museum of Modern Art, New York:
ABC*
Mendoza, George. *Henri Mouse*
Menter, Ian. *The Albany Road mural*
Peet, Bill (William Bartlett). *Encore for
Eleanor*
Pilkey, Dav. *When cats dream*
Pinkwater, Daniel Manus. *The bear's picture*
Rauch, Hans-Georg. *The lines are coming*
Rey, Margřet (Margřet Elisabeth
Waldstein). *Billy's picture*
Rubin, Cynthia Elyce. *ABC Americana from
the National Gallery of Art*
Rylant, Cynthia. *All I see*
Schick, Eleanor. *Art lessons*
Seuss, Dr. *I can draw it myself*
Sharon, Mary Bruce. *Scenes from childhood*
Simpson, Gretchen Dow. *Gretchen's ABC*
Steiner, Barbara (Annette). *The whale
brother*
Türk, Hanne. *Max the artlover*
Tusa, Tricia. *Stay away from the junkyard!*
Villarejo, Mary. *The art fair*
Wabbes, Marie. *Rose's picture*
Waddell, Martin. *Alice the artist*
Williams, Vera B. *Cherries and cherry pits*
Winter, Jonah. *Diego*
Wolf, Janet. *The best present is me*
Zelinsky, Paul O. *The lion and the stoat*

Artists *see* Careers – artists

Asian-Americans *see* Ethnic groups in
the U.S. – Asian-Americans

Assertive *see* Character traits –
assertiveness

Astrology *see* Zodiac

Astronauts *see* Space and space ships

Astronomy
Hirst, Robin. *My place in space*
Jones, Brian. *Space*

Aunts *see* Family life – aunts, uncles

Australia *see* Foreign lands – Australia

Austria *see* Foreign lands – Austria

Authors, children *see* Children as
authors

Automobiles
Aldag, Kurt. *Some things never change*
Alexander, Anne (Anna Barbara Cooke).
ABC of cars and trucks
Aulaire, Ingri Mortenson d'. *The two cars*

Baugh, Dolores M. *Trucks and cars to ride*
Biro, Val. *Gumdrop, the adventures of a
vintage car*
Brandenberg, Franz. *What's wrong with a
van?*
Bridwell, Norman. *Clifford's good deeds*
Broekel, Ray. *I can be an auto mechanic*
Buller, Jon. *Toad on the road*
Burningham, John. *Mr. Gumpy's motor car
Slam bang*
Caines, Jeannette. *Just us women*
Cars and trucks, ill. by Daisuke Yokoi
Cave, Ron. *Automobiles*
Cummings, W. T. (Walter Thies). *Miss
Esta Maude's secret*
DiFiori, Lawrence. *If I had a little car*
Emberley, Ed (Edward Randolph). *Cars,
boats, and planes*
Ets, Marie Hall. *Little old automobile*
Feldman, Barbara. *Going, going*
Florian, Douglas. *An auto mechanic*
Fowler, Richard. *Mr. Little's noisy car*
Gay, Michel. *Little auto*
Gibbons, Gail. *Fill it up!*
Greenblat, Rodney A. *Uncle Wizzmo's new
used car*
Greve, Andreas. *Christopher's dream car*
Hannan, Peter. *Sillyville or bust*
Holl, Adelaide. *The ABC of cars, trucks and
machines*
Janosch. *The magic auto*
Lenski, Lois. *The little auto*
Löfgren, Ulf. *The traffic stopper that became
a grandmother visitor*
MacKeen, Leslie Ann. *Who can fix it?*
Marshall, James. *The Cut-Ups crack up*
Mitgutsch, Ali. *From rubber tree to tire*
Newton, Laura P. *William the vehicle king*
Osborne, Victor. *Rex, the most special car in
the world*
Owen, Annie. *Bumper to bumper*
Oxenbury, Helen. *The car trip*
Peet, Bill (William Bartlett). *Jennifer and
Josephine*
Peppé, Rodney. *Little wheels*
Petrie, Catherine. *Hot Rod Harry*
Pinkwater, Daniel Manus. *Tooth-gnasher
superflash*
Pitcher, Caroline. *Cars and boats*
Potter, Tony. *See how it works: cars*
Robbins, Ken. *City/country*
Rockwell, Anne F. *Cars*
Royston, Angela. *Cars*
Scarry, Huck. *On the road*
Scarry, Richard. *The great big car and truck
book*
Spier, Peter. *Bill's service station*
Spurr, Elizabeth. *Mrs. Minetta's car pool*
Stobbs, William. *A car called beetle*
Wilkinson, Sylvia. *Automobiles
I can be a race car driver*

Wood, Tim. *Motor racing*
Young, Miriam Burt. *If I drove a car*
Ziefert, Harriet. *A car trip for mole and mouse*
  Where's daddy's car?

Autumn *see* Seasons – fall

Babies

Ahlberg, Janet. *The baby's catalogue*
  Peek-a-boo!
Alexander, Martha G. *Nobody asked me if I wanted a baby sister*
  When the new baby comes, I'm moving out
Aliki. *At Mary Bloom's*
  Welcome, little baby
Allen, Pamela. *A lion in the night*
Allen, Robert. *Ten little babies count*
  Ten little babies dress
  Ten little babies eat
  Ten little babies play
Ancona, George. *It's a baby!*
Andry, Andrew C. *Hi, new baby*
  How babies are made
Anglund, Joan Walsh. *Love is a baby*
Anholt, Catherine. *Aren't you lucky!*
  When I was a baby
Arbeit, Eleanor Werner. *Mrs. Cat hides something*
Arnstein, Helene S. *Billy and our new baby*
Asch, Frank. *Baby in the box*
  Starbaby
Baby's words, ill. by Debby Slier
Baird, Anne. *Baby socks*
  Kiss, kiss
Baker, Charlotte. *Little brother*
Baker, Gayle. *Special delivery*
Banish, Roslyn. *I want to tell you about my baby*
  Let me tell you about my baby
Bendick, Jeanne. *What made you you?*
Birdseye, Tom. *Waiting for baby*
Bogart, Jo Ellen. *Daniel's dog*
Bolognese, Don. *A new day*
Boyd, Lizi. *Sam is my half brother*
Bradman, Tony. *This little baby*
Brandenberg, Franz. *Aunt Nina and her nephews and nieces*
Brann, Esther. *A book for baby*
Brice, Tony. *Baby animals*
Brooks, Robert B. *So that's how I was born*
Brown, Marc Tolon. *Arthur's baby*
Browne, Anthony. *Changes*
Burningham, John. *Avocado baby*

Busy baby, ill. by Debby Slier
Byars, Betsy Cromer. *Go and hush the baby*
Byers, Rinda M. *Mycca's baby*
Byrne, David. *Stay up late*
Carlstrom, Nancy White. *Kiss your sister, Rose Marie*
Caseley, Judith. *Silly baby*
Chaffin, Lillie D. *Tommy's big problem*
Chess, Victoria. *Poor Esmé*
Chorao, Kay. *Baby's Christmas treasury*
  The baby's good morning book
  The cherry pie baby
Christenson, Larry. *The wonderful way that babies are made*
Clarke, Gus. *Along came Eric*
Clifton, Lucille. *Everett Anderson's nine months long*
Cole, Joanna. *A calf is born*
  How you were born
  The new baby at your house
Collins, Pat Lowery. *Waiting for baby Joe*
Corey, Dorothy. *Will there be a lap for me?*
Cuyler, Margery. *Shadow's baby*
Dahl, Tessa. *Babies, babies, babies*
De Paola, Tomie (Thomas Anthony). *Baby's first Christmas*
Dragonwagon, Crescent. *Wind Rose*
Dunn, Phoebe. *Baby's animal friends*
  Busy, busy toddlers
  I'm a baby!
Fallwell, Cathryn. *Nicky and Alex*
  Nicky and grandpa
  Nicky loves daddy
  Nicky, 1-2-3
  Nicky's walk
  Where's Nicky?
Ferguson, Alane. *That new pet!*
Fisher, Iris L. *Katie-Bo*
Foord, Jo. *The book of babies*
Foreman, Michael. *Ben's baby*
Foulds, Elfrida Vipont. *The elephant and the bad baby*
Franklin, Jonathan. *Don't wake the baby*
Frasier, Debra. *On the day you were born*
Galbraith, Kathryn Osebold. *Roommates*
  Waiting for Jennifer
Garland, Sarah. *All gone!*
  Billy and Belle
  Polly's puffin
Gelbard, Jane. *My bye-bye bottle book*
  My dressing book
  My eating book
  My sharing book
Gerstein, Mordicai. *The gigantic baby*
Gewing, Lisa. *Mama, daddy, baby and me*
Gill, Joan. *Hush, Jon!*
Girard, Linda Walvoord. *You were born on your very first birthday*
Gliori, Debi. *New big sister*
Graham, Bob. *Crusher is coming!*
Graham, Richard. *Jack and the monster*

Greenberg, Barbara. *The bravest babysitter*
Greenberg, Judith E. *Adopted*
Greenfield, Eloise. *She come bringing me that little baby girl*
Hains, Harriet. *My baby brother*
Hamilton-Merritt, Jane. *Our new baby*
Hanson, Joan. *I don't like Timmy*
Harper, Anita. *It's not fair!*
Hayes, Sarah. *Eat up, Gemma*
Hayward, Linda. *Baby Moses*
Hazen, Barbara Shook. *Why couldn't I be an only kid like you, Wigger?*
Hedderwick, Mairi. *Katie Morag and the tiresome Ted*
Hello, baby, ill. by Debby Slier
Helmering, Doris Wild. *We're going to have a baby*
Henderson, Kathy. *The baby's book of babies*
Hendrickson, Karen. *Baby and I can play*
Fun with toddlers
Herter, Jonina. *Eighty-eight kisses*
Hines, Anna Grossnickle. *Big like me*
Hirsh, Marilyn. *Leela and the watermelon*
Where is Yonkela?
Hobson, Laura Z. *"I'm going to have a baby!"*
Hoffman, Phyllis. *Baby's first year*
Hoffman, Rosekrans. *Sister Sweet Ella*
Hol, Coby. *Tippy Bear and little Sam*
Holabird, Katharine. *Angelina's baby sister*
Holland, Viki. *We are having a baby*
Horton, Barbara Savadge. *What comes in spring?*
Hudson, Cheryl Willis. *Good morning baby*
Good night baby
Hughes, Shirley. *Angel Mae*
Hush little baby. *Hush little baby*, ill. by Aliki
Hush little baby, ill. by Jeanette Winter
Hush little baby, ill. by Margot Zemach
Hutchins, Pat. *Where's the baby?*
Hutton, Warwick. *Moses in the bulrushes*
Isadora, Rachel. *Babies*
I hear
I see
Jam, Teddy. *Night cars*
Jarrell, Mary. *The knee baby*
Keats, Ezra Jack. *Peter's chair*
Keller, Holly. *What Alvin wanted*
Kelley, True. *Look, baby! Listen, baby! Do, baby!*
Kilroy, Sally. *Babies' bodies*
Baby colors
Busy babies
Koehler, Phoebe. *The day we met you*
Kopper, Lisa. *Ten little babies*
Krasilovsky, Phyllis. *The very little boy*
The very little girl
Kraus, Robert. *Big brother*
Kunhardt, Edith. *Where's Peter?*
Lagerlöf, Selma. *The changeling*

Lakin, Patricia. *Don't touch my room*
Langstaff, Nancy. *A tiny baby for you*
Lasky, Kathryn. *A baby for Max*
Levine, Abby. *What did mommy do before you?*
Levinson, Riki. *Me baby!*
Lexau, Joan M. *Finders keepers, losers weepers*
Lindgren, Astrid. *I want a brother or sister*
MacGregor, Marilyn. *Baby takes a trip*
McMillan, Bruce. *Step by step*
Malecki, Maryann. *Mom and dad and I are having a baby!*
Manushkin, Fran. *Baby*
Baby, come out!
Little rabbit's baby brother
Miller, Margaret. *At my house*
In my room
Me and my clothes
Time to eat
Miranda, Anne. *Baby talk*
Baby walk
Monfried, Lucia. *Baby's world*
Mueller, Virginia. *Monster and the baby*
Naylor, Phyllis Reynolds. *The baby, the bed, and the rose*
Newberry, Clare Turlay. *Cousin Toby*
T-Bone, the baby-sitter
Ormerod, Jan. *Bend and stretch*
Dad's back
Just like me
Making friends
Messy baby
Mom's home
101 things to do with a baby
Our Ollie
The saucepan game
Silly goose
Sleeping
This little nose
Young Joe
Oxenbury, Helen. *All fall down*
Clap hands
I can
I hear
I see
I touch
Playing
Say goodnight
Tickle, tickle
Parish, Peggy. *Granny, the baby and the big gray thing*
Patent, Dorothy Hinshaw. *Babies!*
Pearson, Susan. *When baby went to bed*
Politi, Leo. *Rosa*
Polushkin, Maria. *Baby brother blues*
Pryor, Bonnie. *Greenbrook farm*
The pudgy book of babies, ill. by Kathy Wilburn
Pursell, Margaret Sanford. *A look at birth*
Reader, Dennis. *Butterfingers*

Rice, Eve. *What Sadie sang*
Rigby, Shirley Lincoln. *Smaller than most*
Rippon, Penelope. *My day*
Robins, Joan. *My brother, Will*
Roddie, Shen. *Hatch, egg, hatch!*
Rogers, Fred. *The new baby*
Rosenberg, Liz. *Window, mirror, moon*
Ross, Katharine. *When you were a baby*
Russo, Marisabina. *Waiting for Hannah*
Sage, Chris. *Happy baby*
  Sleepy baby
  The trouble with babies
Schick, Eleanor. *Peggy's new brother*
Schlein, Miriam. *Laurie's new brother*
Sendak, Maurice. *Outside over there*
Shapp, Martha. *Let's find out about babies*
Sheffield, Margaret. *Before you were born*
  Where do babies come from?
Showers, Paul. *Before you were a baby*
Smith, Peter. *Jenny's baby brother*
Steel, Danielle. *Max's new baby*
Stein, Sara Bonnett. *That new baby*
Steptoe, John. *Baby says*
Stevenson, James. *Rolling Rose*
  Worse than Willy!
Tafuri, Nancy. *The ball bounced*
  My friends
Thayer, Jane. *Gus and the baby ghost*
Thomas, Iolette. *Janine and the new baby*
Thompson, Carol. *Baby days*
Titherington, Jeanne. *Baby's boat*
  A place for Ben
Tucker, Sian. *At home*
  Going out
  My clothes
  My toys
Van der Beek, Deborah. *Superbabe!*
Vigna, Judith. *Couldn't we have a turtle instead?*
Von Königslöw, Andrea Wayne. *That's my baby?*
Wahl, Jan. *The sleepytime book*
Wattenberg, Jane. *Mrs. Mustard's baby faces*
Watts, Bernadette. *David's waiting day*
West, Keith. *Little Pig's special day*
What do babies do?
What do toddlers do?
Williams, Barbara. *Jeremy isn't hungry*
Williams, Susan. *Poppy's first year*
Williams, Vera B. *"More more more," said the baby*
Willis, Jeanne. *Earthlets as explained by Professor Xargle*
Wishinsky, Frieda. *Oonga boonga*
Young, Ruth. *My blanket*
  The new baby
Ziefert, Harriet. *Baby Ben's bow-wow book*
  Baby Ben's busy book
  Baby Ben's go-go book
  Baby Ben's noisy book
  Before I was born

Breakfast time!
Bye-bye, daddy!
Getting ready for new baby
Good morning, sun!
Let's get dressed!
Zolotow, Charlotte (Shapiro). *But not Billy*
  Do you know what I'll do?

Baby-sitting *see* Activities – baby-sitting

Bad day *see* Behavior – bad day

Badgers *see* Animals – badgers

Bakers *see* Careers – bakers

Bali *see* Foreign lands – Bali

Ballooning *see* Activities – ballooning

Balloons *see* Toys – balloons

Balls *see* Toys – balls

Barbers *see* Careers – barbers

Barns

Brown, Craig McFarland. *My barn*
Brown, Margaret Wise. *Big red barn*, ill. by Felicia Bond
  Big red barn, ill. by Rosella Hartman
Carrick, Carol. *The old barn*
Climo, Lindee. *Chester's barn*
Lindbergh, Reeve. *Benjamin's barn*
Martin, Bill (William Ivan). *Barn dance!*
Merrill, Jean. *Tell about the cowbarn, Daddy*
Miles, Miska. *The raccoon and Mrs. McGinnis*
Parnall, Peter. *Winter barn*
Schoenherr, John. *The barn*
Sewell, Helen Moore. *Blue barns*

Barons *see* Royalty

Baseball *see* Sports – baseball

Basketball *see* Sports – basketball

Bathing *see* Activities – bathing

Bats *see* Animals – bats

Bavaria *see* Foreign lands – Austria; Foreign lands – Germany

Beaches *see* Sea and seashore

Bears *see* Animals – bears

Beasts *see* Monsters

Beavers *see* Animals – beavers

Beds *see* Furniture – beds

Bedtime

Allison, Diane Worfolk. *In window eight, the moon is late*
Anderson, Lena Castell. *Bunny box*
 Bunny story
Anderson, Peggy Perry. *Time for bed, the babysitter said*
Anholt, Catherine. *Twins, two by two*
Apple, Margot. *Blanket*
Archambault, John. *Counting sheep*
Arnold, Tedd. *No jumping on the bed!*
Asch, Frank. *Goodnight horsey*
Asher, Sandy. *Princess Bee and the royal good-night story*
Aylesworth, Jim. *Tonight's the night*
Baird, Anne. *No sheep*
Bang, Molly. *Ten, nine, eight*
 Wiley and the hairy man
Barasch, Lynne. *Rodney's inside story*
Barrett, Judi. *I hate to go to bed*
Baum, Louis. *I want to see the moon*
Beckman, Kaj. *Lisa cannot sleep*
Berenstain, Stan. *Bears in the night*
 The Berenstain bears and the slumber party
Berridge, Celia. *Grandmother's tales*
Blaustein, Muriel. *Bedtime, Zachary!*
Blocksma, Mary. *Did you hear that?*
Bond, Felicia. *Poinsettia and the firefighters*
Bottner, Barbara. *There was nobody there*
Bowden, Joan Chase. *Bouncy baby bunny finds his bed*
Bowers, Kathleen Rice. *At this very minute*
Boyd, Lizi. *Sweet dreams, Willy*
Boynton, Sandra. *The going to bed book*
 Good night, good night
Brandenberg, Franz. *Aunt Nina, good night*
Brown, Margaret Wise. *A child's good night book*
 Goodnight moon
Bunting, Eve (Anne Evelyn). *No nap*
Calhoun, Mary. *While I sleep*
Callen, Larry. *Dashiel and the night*
Calmenson, Stephanie. *All aboard the goodnight train*
Cameron, Ann. *Harry (the monster)*
Campbell, Alison. *Are you asleep, rabbit?*
Carlstrom, Nancy White. *Northern lullaby*
Catalanotto, Peter. *Christmas always*
Cave, Kathryn. *Out for the count*
Cazet, Denys. *I'm not sleepy*
 Mother night
Chevalier, Christa. *Spence and the sleepytime monster*
Chislett, Gail. *Whump*
Chorao, Kay. *Lemon moon*

Christelow, Eileen. *Five little monkeys jumping on the bed*
 Henry and the dragon
Coatsworth, Elizabeth. *Good night*
Cole, William. *Frances face-maker*
Corddry, Thomas I. *Kibby's big feat*
Cosgrove, Stephen (Edward). *Sleepy time bunny*
Cousins, Lucy. *Maisy goes to bed*
Dahl, Roald. *Dirty beasts*
Denton, Kady MacDonald. *Granny is a darling*
De Paola, Tomie (Thomas Anthony). *Fight the night*
 Pajamas for Kit
Dowling, Paul. *Splodger*
Duke, Kate. *Aunt Isabel tells a good one*
 Bedtime
Edwards, Frank B. *Melody Mooner stayed up all night*
Engvick, William. *Lullabies and night songs*
Eriksson, Eva. *Hocus-pocus*
Erskine, Jim. *Bedtime story*
Feldman, Eve B. *Animals don't wear pajamas*
Fox, Siv Cedering. *The blue horse and other night poems*
Freedman, Sally. *Devin's new bed*
Gackenbach, Dick. *Poppy the panda*
Gay, Marie-Louise. *Moonbeam on a cat's ear*
Gerstein, Mordicai. *William, where are you?*
Ginsburg, Mirra. *Asleep, asleep*
 Which is the best place?
Goffstein, M. B. (Marilyn Brooke). *Sleepy people*
Goode, Diane. *I hear a noise*
Goodspeed, Peter. *A rhinoceros wakes me up in the morning*
Gordon, Jeffie Ross. *Two badd babies*
Greenleaf, Ann. *No room for Sarah*
Gretz, Susanna. *Hide-and-seek*
 I'm not sleepy
 Ready for bed
 Too dark!
Grindley, Sally. *Knock, knock! Who's there?*
Hamm, Diane Johnston. *How many feet in the bed?*
Hancock, Joy Elizabeth. *The loudest little lion*
Harris, Dorothy Joan. *Goodnight Jeffrey*
Harshman, Terry Webb. *Porcupine's pajama party*
Hawkins, Colin. *Dip, dip, dip*
 I'm not sleepy!
 One finger, one thumb
 Oops-a-Daisy
 Where's bear?
Hawkins, Mark. *A lion under her bed*
Heiligman, Deborah. *Into the night*
Hill, Eric. *Baby Bear's bedtime*
Hindley, Judy. *Maybe it's a pirate*

The sleepy book
Hoban, Russell. *Bedtime for Frances*
Goodnight
Holabird, Katharine. *Alexander and the dragon*
Hood, Thomas. *Before I go to sleep*
Hopkins, Lee Bennett. *Go to bed!*
Hopkins, Margaret. *Sleepytime for baby mouse*
Horowitz, Ruth. *Bat time*
Impey, Rose. *The flat man*
Scare yourself to sleep
Inkpen, Mick. *One bear at bedtime*
Ipcar, Dahlov. *The calico jungle*
Jeffers, Susan. *All the pretty horses*
Johnson, Jane. *Today I thought I'd run away*
Jonas, Ann. *The quilt*
Joslin, Sesyle. *Brave Baby Elephant*
Kalman, Maira. *Hey Willy, see the pyramids!*
Keller, Holly. *Ten sleepy sheep*
Kent, Jack. *The once-upon-a-time dragon*
Khalsa, Dayal Kaur. *Sleepers*
Kitamura, Satoshi. *When sheep cannot sleep*
Koide, Tan. *May we sleep here tonight?*
Kotzwinkle, William. *The nap master*
Krahn, Fernando. *Sleep tight, Alex Pumpernickel*
Kraus, Robert. *Good night little one*
Good night Richard Rabbit
Krauss, Ruth. *The bundle book*
Kuskin, Karla. *The Dallas Titans get ready for bed*
Night again
A space story
Larrick, Nancy. *When the dark comes dancing*
Leaf, Munro. *Boo, who used to be scared of the dark*
Lesser, Carolyn. *The goodnight circle*
Lester, Alison. *Ruby*
Levine, Joan. *A bedtime story*
Lifton, Betty Jean. *Goodnight orange monster*
Lipniacka, Ewa. *To bed...or else!*
Lippman, Peter. *New at the zoo*
Lloyd, Errol. *Nandy's bedtime*
Lobe, Mira. *Valerie and the good-night swing*
McGuire, Leslie. *Baby night owl*
Mack, Stanley (Stan). *Ten bears in my bed*
McPhail, David. *The dream child*
Mählqvist, Stefan. *I'll take care of the crocodiles*
Marcin, Marietta. *A zoo in her bed*
Maris, Ron. *My book*
Marshall, James. *What's the matter with Carruthers?*
Marshall, Margaret. *Mike*
Marzollo, Jean. *Close your eyes*
Matura, Mustapha. *Moon jump*
Mayer, Mercer. *Little Monster's bedtime book*
There's a nightmare in my closet

There's an alligator under my bed
Mayper, Monica. *After good-night*
Merriam, Eve. *Good night to Annie*
Goodnight to Annie
Miles, Sally. *Alfi and the dark*
Miller, J. P. (John Parr). *Good night, Little Rabbit*
Montgomery, Michael. *'Night, America*
Montresor, Beni. *Bedtime!*
The moon's the north wind's cooky, ill. by Susan Russo
Morgan, Allen. *Nicole's boat*
Morgenstern, Constance. *Good night, feet*
Morris, Ann. *Cuddle up*
Kiss time
Night counting
Sleepy, sleepy
Morris, Terry Nell. *Good night, dear monster!*
Morris, Winifred. *What if the shark wears tennis shoes?*
Mother Goose. *Hush-a-bye baby*, ill. by Nicola Bayley
Mueller, Virginia. *Monster can't sleep*
Munsch, Robert N. *Mortimer*
Murphy, Jill. *What next, baby bear!*
Nichol, B. P. *Once: a lullaby*
O'Brien, Mary. *Counting sheep to sleep*
Oppenheim, Joanne. *The story book prince*
Orgel, Doris. *Little John*
Ormerod, Jan. *Moonlight*
Otto, Carolyn. *Dinosaur chase*
Oxenbury, Helen. *Good night, good morning*
Pearson, Susan. *When baby went to bed*
Petersham, Maud. *Off to bed*
Plath, Sylvia. *The bed book*
Plotz, Helen. *A week of lullabies*
Pomerantz, Charlotte. *All asleep*
Posy
Preston, Edna Mitchell. *Monkey in the jungle*
Pryor, Ainslie. *The baby blue cat who said no*
Rees, Mary. *Ten in a bed*
Reiser, Lynn. *Bedtime cat*
Rice, Eve. *Goodnight, goodnight*
Richter, Mischa. *To bed, to bed!*
Robison, Deborah. *No elephants allowed*
Rockwell, Anne F. *Buster and the bogeyman*
Rogers, Paul (Patrick). *Somebody's sleepy*
Rosen, Michael J. *Under the bed*
Rosenberg, Liz. *Adelaide and the night train*
Russo, Marisabina. *Why do grownups have all the fun?*
Sage, James. *To sleep*
Saltzberg, Barney. *It must have been the wind*
Schertle, Alice. *Goodnight, Hattie, my dearie, my dove*
Schindel, John. *Who are you?*
Schneider, Nina. *While Susie sleeps*
Schotter, Roni. *Bunny's night out*

Schreier, Joshua. *Luigi's all-night parking lot*
Schubert, Ingrid. *There's a crocodile under my bed!*
Sharmat, Marjorie Weinman. *Go to sleep, Nicholas Joe*
Goodnight, Andrew. Goodnight, Craig
Shepperson, Rob. *The sandman*
Shipton, Jonathan. *In the night*
Simms, Laura. *The squeaky door*
Skorpen, Liesel Moak. *Outside my window*
Smee, Nicola. *Finish the story, dad*
Smith, Robert Paul. *Nothingatall, nothingatall, nothingatall*
Steiner, Charlotte. *The sleepy quilt*
Stevens, Kathleen. *The beast in the bathtub*
Stevenson, James. *We can't sleep*
What's under my bed?
Stock, Catherine. *Alexander's midnight snack*
Stoddard, Sandol. *Bedtime for bear*
Bedtime mouse
Stone, Kazuko G. *Goodnight Twinklegator*
Strahl, Rudi. *Sandman in the lighthouse*
Strand, Mark. *The planet of lost things*
Sugita, Yutaka. *Good night 1, 2, 3*
Sussman, Susan. *Hippo thunder*
Sutherland, Harry A. *Dad's car wash*
Swados, Elizabeth. *Lullaby*
Taylor, Livingston. *Pajamas*
Titherington, Jeanne. *Baby's boat*
A child's prayer
Tobias, Tobi. *Chasing the goblins away*
Trez, Denise. *Good night, Veronica*
Türk, Hanne. *Goodnight Max*
Twining, Edith. *Sandman*
Viorst, Judith. *My mama says there aren't any zombies, ghosts, vampires, creatures, demons, monsters, fiends, goblins, or things*
Wabbes, Marie. *Good night, Little Rabbit*
Waber, Bernard. *Ira sleeps over*
Wahl, Jan. *Humphrey's bear*
The sleepytime book
Watson, Clyde. *Fisherman lullabies*
Midnight moon
Weir, Alison. *Peter, good night*
Weiss, Nicki. *Where does the brown bear go?*
Wells, Rosemary. *Max's bedtime*
Westcott, Nadine Bernard. *Going to bed*
Whiteside, Karen. *Lullaby of the wind*
Wiesner, David. *Free fall*
Willis, Jeanne. *The monster bed*
Winthrop, Elizabeth. *Bunk beds*
Maggie and the monster
Wood, Audrey. *Moonflute*
Oh my baby bear!
Yolen, Jane. *Baby Bear's bedtime book*
Dragon night and other lullabies
The lullaby songbook
Zalben, Jane Breskin. *Norton's nighttime*
Ziefert, Harriet. *Good night everyone!*
I want to sleep in your bed!
I won't go to bed!

Say good night!
Zinnemann-Hope, Pam. *Time for bed, Ned*
Zolotow, Charlotte (Shapiro). *Flocks of birds*
Sleepy book
The sleepy book
The summer night
Wake up and good night
When the wind stops

Bees *see* Insects – bees

Beetles *see* Insects – beetles

Behavior

Arnold, Tedd. *Mother Goose's words of wit and wisdom: a book of months*
Babbitt, Lorraine. *Pink like the geranium*
Beim, Jerrold. *The swimming hole*
Belloc, Hilaire. *The bad child's book of beasts*
Berenstain, Stan. *The Berenstain bears' trouble at school*
Bertrand, Cecile. *Mr. and Mrs. Smith have only one child, but what a child!*
Blake, Jon. *Wriggly Pig*
Blundell, Tony. *Joe on Sunday*
Boegehold, Betty. *Three to get ready*
Bond, Felicia. *Poinsettia and her family*
Carle, Eric. *The grouchy ladybug*
Caudill, Rebecca. *Contrary Jenkins*
Cole, Joanna. *Don't tell the whole world*
Delton, Judy. *I'm telling you now*
Elliot, David. *An alphabet of rotten kids!*
Erickson, Karen. *Do I have to go home?*
Ets, Marie Hall. *Bad boy, good boy*
Play with me
Gackenbach, Dick. *Hattie be quiet, Hattie be good*
Gaeddert, Lou Ann Bigge. *Noisy Nancy Nora*
Gambill, Henrietta. *Self-control*
Grindley, Sally. *I don't want to!*
Harris, Robie H. *Don't forget to come back*
Haugaard, Erik Christian. *Princess Horrid*
Hoban, Russell. *Dinner at Alberta's*
Hogrogian, Nonny. *Carrot cake*
Horvath, Betty F. *Be nice to Josephine*
Hutchins, Pat. *Tidy Titch*
Keller, Holly. *The new boy*
Kerr, Phyllis Forbes. *I tricked you*
Kettner, Christine. *An ordinary cat*
Livingston, Myra Cohn. *Higgledy-Piggledy*
Low, Joseph. *Don't drag your feet...*
My dog, your dog
Luttrell, Ida. *Ottie Slockett*
Myller, Lois. *No! No!*
Panek, Dennis. *Matilda Hippo has a big mouth*
Parker, Nancy Winslow. *Puddums, the Cathcarts' orange cat*
Paterson, Diane. *Wretched Rachel*

Quackenbush, Robert M. *I don't want to go, I don't know how to act*
Remkiewicz, Frank. *Greedyanna*
Ringi, Kjell (Arne Sorensen). *The winner*
Scarry, Richard. *Pig Will and Pig Won't Pig Will/Pig Won't*
Sharmat, Marjorie Weinman. *Scarlet Monster lives here*
Stover, Jo Ann. *If everybody did*
Supraner, Robyn. *Would you rather be a tiger?*
Svendsen, Carol. *Hulda*
Swope, Sam. *The Araboolies of Liberty Street*
Thomas, Karen. *The good thing...the bad thing*
Van Laan, Nancy. *A mouse in my house*
Waggoner, Karen. *The lemonade babysitter*
Wahl, Robert. *Pyxx*
Walker, Alice. *Finding the green stone*
Wittels, Harriet. *Things I hate!*

Behavior – animals, dislike of

Bemelmans, Ludwig. *Madeline and the bad hat*
Kay, Helen. *An egg is for wishing*
Udry, Janice May. *Alfred*

Behavior – bad day

Alborough, Jez. *Running Bear*
Andrews, F. Emerson (Frank Emerson). *Nobody comes to dinner*
Baker, Alan. *Benjamin's portrait*
Balzola, Asun. *Munia and the day things went wrong*
Berenstain, Stan. *The Berenstain bears get in a fight*
Demuth, Patricia Brennan. *Ornery morning*
Duncan, Jane. *Janet Reachfar and Chickabird*
Fujikawa, Gyo. *Sam's all-wrong day*
Giff, Patricia Reilly. *Today was a terrible day*
Griffith, Helen V. *Nata*
Haywood, Carolyn. *Santa Claus forever!*
Hoban, Russell. *The sorely trying day*
Hurd, Thacher. *Mystery on the docks*
Johnston, Deborah. *Mathew Michael's beastly day*
Keith, Eros. *Bedita's bad day*
Kline, Suzy. *Ooops!*
Krahn, Fernando. *Here comes Alex Pumpernickel!*
Lexau, Joan M. *I should have stayed in bed*
Morris, Ann. *Eleanora Mousie's gray day*
Oxenbury, Helen. *The car trip*
Prater, John. *The perfect day*
Scarry, Richard. *Mr. Frumble's worst day ever*
Smath, Jerry. *Mr. Digby's bad day*
Sondheimer, Ilse. *The boy who could make his mother stop yelling*

Van Leeuwen, Jean. *Too hot for ice cream*
Viorst, Judith. *Alexander and the terrible, horrible, no good, very bad day*
Vreeken, Elizabeth. *One day everything went wrong*
Wells, Rosemary. *Unfortunately Harriet*

Behavior – boasting

Augarde, Steve (Stephen). *Barnaby Shrew, Black Dan and...the mighty wedgwood*
Bonsall, Crosby Newell. *The amazing the incredible super dog*
Mine's the best
Browne, Anthony. *Look what I've got!*
Butterworth, Nick. *My dad is awesome*
Carlson, Nancy. *Loudmouth George and the big race*
Loudmouth George and the cornet
Loudmouth George and the fishing trip
Loudmouth George and the new neighbors
Loudmouth George and the sixth-grade bully
Collins, Pat Lowery. *My friend Andrew*
Diot, Alain. *Better, best, bestest*
Duvoisin, Roger Antoine. *See what I am*
Ellentuck, Shan. *A sunflower as big as the sun*
Gretz, Susanna. *Rabbit rambles on*
Johnston, Tony. *Farmer Mack measures his pig*
Kepes, Juliet. *The story of a bragging duck*
Knutson, Barbara. *Why the crab has no head*
Lopshire, Robert. *I am better than you*
Lund, Doris Herold. *You ought to see Herbert's house*
Miller, Moira. *The moon dragon*
Miller, Warren. *The goings on at Little Wishful*
Oppenheim, Joanne. *You can't catch me!*
Parker, Kristy. *My dad the magnificent*
Pavey, Peter. *I'm Taggarty Toad*
Peterson, Esther Allen. *Frederick's alligator*
Raphael, Elaine. *Turnabout*
Schindler, Regina. *The bear's cave*
Schlein, Miriam. *Big talk*, ill. by Joan Auclair
Big talk, ill. by Laura Lydecker
Schwartz, Amy. *Her Majesty, Aunt Essie*
Simmonds, Posy. *The chocolate wedding*
Slater, Teddy. *The cow that could tap dance The fabulous fish from Lake Wiggawalla*

Behavior – boredom

Alexander, Martha G. *We never get to do anything*
Ayal, Ora. *The adventures of Chester the chest*
Creighton, Jill. *One day there was nothing to do*
Delton, Judy. *My mom hates me in January*
Duvoisin, Roger Antoine. *Veronica's smile*

Eriksson, Eva. *One short week*
Hannan, Peter. *Sillyville or bust*
Henkes, Kevin. *Once around the block*
Hoban, Russell. *Nothing to do*
Jennings, Sharon. *When Jeremiah found Mrs. Ming*
Krauss, Ruth. *A good man and his good wife*
Lawlor, Laurie. *Second-grade dog*
McConnachie, Brian. *Lily of the forest*
McGovern, Ann. *Nicholas Bentley Stoningpot III*
McLaughlin, Lissa. *Why won't winter go?*
Meroux, Felix. *The prince of the rabbits*
Noble, Trinka Hakes. *Meanwhile back at the ranch*
Oram, Hiawyn. *In the attic*
Raskin, Ellen. *Nothing ever happens on my block*
Reit, Seymour. *The king who learned to smile*
Spier, Peter. *Bored—nothing to do!*
Stevenson, James. *There's nothing to do!*
Thayer, Jane. *Mr. Turtle's magic glasses*
Watts, Marjorie-Ann. *Crocodile medicine*

Behavior – bullying

Alexander, Martha G. *I sure am glad to see you, Blackboard Bear*
Move over, Twerp
Berquist, Grace. *The boy who couldn't roar*
Boyd, Lizi. *Bailey the big bully*
Browne, Anthony. *Willy the champ*
Bryant, Bernice. *Follow the leader*
Carlson, Nancy. *Loudmouth George and the sixth-grade bully*
Cauley, Lorinda Bryan. *The trouble with Tyrannosaurus Rex*
Chapman, Carol. *Herbie's troubles*
Charlton, Elizabeth. *Terrible tyrannosaurus*
Cohen, Miriam. *Tough Jim*
Cole, Babette. *Hurray for Ethelyn*
Cole, Joanna. *Don't call me names!*
De Paola, Tomie (Thomas Anthony). *Katie, Kit and cousin Tom*
Dodd, Lynley. *Hairy Maclary Scattercat*
Freschet, Berniece. *Furlie Cat*
Gretz, Susanna. *Roger takes charge!*
Hadithi, Mwenye. *Crafty chameleon*
Tricky tortoise
Henkes, Kevin. *Chester's way*
Isenberg, Barbara. *Albert the running bear gets the jitters*
Janice. *Angélique*
Keats, Ezra Jack. *Goggles*
Kroll, Steven. *It's April Fools' Day!*
Lagercrantz, Rose. *Brave little Pete of Geranium Street*
Laurencin, Geneviève. *I wish I were*
Little, Emily. *David and the giant*
Little, Jean. *Jess was the brave one*
Marton, Jirina. *Flowers for mom*

Minarik, Else Holmelund. *The little girl and the dragon*
Naylor, Phyllis Reynolds. *King of the playground*
Passen, Lisa. *Fat, fat Rose Marie*
Peet, Bill (William Bartlett). *Big bad Bruce*
Rayner, Mary. *Crocodarling*
Roche, P. K. (Patrick K.). *Plaid bear and the rude rabbit gang*
Staunton, Ted. *Taking care of Crumley*
Taylor, Scott. *Dinosaur James*
Wagner, Jenny. *Amy's monster*
Wilhelm, Hans. *Tyrone the horrible*

Behavior – carelessness

Aliki. *Keep your mouth closed, dear*
Bottner, Barbara. *Messy*
Brown, Marc Tolon. *The cloud over Clarence*
Brunhoff, Laurent de. *Babar's little girl*
Buchanan, Joan. *It's a good thing*
Carrick, Carol. *A rabbit for Easter*
Chislett, Gail. *The rude visitors*
Claret, Maria. *The chocolate rabbit*
Cleary, Beverly. *Lucky Chuck*
De Paola, Tomie (Thomas Anthony). *The quicksand book*
Strega Nona's magic lessons
Gackenbach, Dick. *Binky gets a car*
Gantos, Jack (John, Jr.). *Aunt Bernice*
Harris, Robie H. *Messy Jessie*
Ilsley, Velma. *The pink hat*
Kline, Suzy. *Ooops!*
Koscielniak, Bruce. *Euclid Bunny delivers the mail*
Mayer, Mercer. *Oops*
Moskin, Marietta D. *Lysbet and the fire kittens*
Oram, Hiawyn. *Reckless Ruby*
Panek, Dennis. *Catastrophe Cat*
Pender, Lydia. *Barnaby and the horses*
Reader, Dennis. *Butterfingers*
Roberts, Sarah. *Ernie's big mess*
Serfozo, Mary. *Dirty Kurt*
Sommers, Tish. *Bert and the broken teapot*

Behavior – collecting things

Bauer, Caroline Feller. *Too many books!*
Beim, Lorraine. *Lucky Pierre*
Bram, Elizabeth. *Woodruff and the clocks*
Braun, Kathy. *Kangaroo and kangaroo*
Carlstrom, Nancy White. *The moon came too*
Cleary, Beverly. *Janet's thingamajigs*
Couture, Susan Arkin. *The block book*
Enderle, Judith A. *Good junk*
Engel, Diana. *Josephina, the great collector*
Evans, Eva Knox. *That lucky Mrs. Plucky*
Gans, Roma. *Rock collecting*
Geringer, Laura. *A three hat day*

Greenblat, Rodney A. *Aunt Ippy's museum of junk*
Heyduck-Huth, Hilde. *The starfish*
  The strawflower
Johnson, Pamela. *A mouse's tale*
Lewis, Naomi. *The butterfly collector*
Tusa, Tricia. *Stay away from the junkyard!*
Van Horn, William. *Harry Hoyle's giant jumping bean*
Weil, Lisl. *To sail a ship of treasures*
Westell, Kerry. *Amanda's book*

Behavior – disbelief

Alexander, Martha G. *Even that moose won't listen to me*
Cole, Brock. *The king at the door*
Gunthrop, Karen. *Adam and the wolf*
Jackson, Ellen B. *Ants can't dance*
Norman, Howard. *The owl-scatterer*
Turner, Ann Warren. *Nettie's trip south*

Behavior – dissatisfaction

Aliki. *The twelve months*
  The wish workers
Allen, Jeffrey. *The secret life of Mr. Weird*
Balet, Jan B. *The king and the broom maker*
Bentley, Nancy. *I've got your nose!*
Brewster, Patience. *Nobody*
Brock, Emma Lillian. *Pig with a front porch*
Brothers, Aileen. *Sad Mrs. Sam Sack*
Byars, Betsy Cromer. *The groober*
Chapman, Carol. *The tale of Meshka the Kvetch*
Clymer, Ted. *The horse and the bad morning*
Cole, Babette. *King Change-A-Lot*
Crowley, Arthur. *The boogey man*
Cushman, Doug. *Nasty Kyle the crocodile*
Dale, Ruth Bluestone. *Benjamin — and Sylvester also*
Day, Shirley. *Waldo's back yard*
Duvoisin, Roger Antoine. *Petunia, beware!*
Elborn, Andrew. *Bird Adalbert*
Ets, Marie Hall. *The cow's party*
Fish, Hans. *Pitschi, the kitten who always wanted to do something else*
Gackenbach, Dick. *Mother Rabbit's son Tom*
Gay, Zhenya. *I'm tired of lions*
Getz, Arthur. *Humphrey, the dancing pig*
Hautzig, Deborah. *It's not fair!*
Hazen, Barbara Shook. *The Fat Cats, Cousin Scraggs and the monster mice*
Hest, Amy. *The mommy exchange*
Hille-Brandts, Lene. *The little black hen*
Hoban, Lillian. *Stick-in-the-mud turtle*
Jenkin-Pearce, Susie. *Percy Short and Cuthbert*
Johnson, Evelyne. *The cow in the kitchen*
Keats, Ezra Jack. *Jennie's hat*
McDermott, Gerald. *The stonecutter*

McGinley, Phyllis. *The horse who lived upstairs*
Massie, Diane Redfield. *Walter was a frog*
O'Donnell, Elizabeth Lee. *Maggie doesn't want to move*
Olujic, Grozdana. *Rose of Mother-of-Pearl*
Oram, Hiawyn. *Jenna and the troublemaker*
Palmer, Mary Babcock. *No-sort-of-animal*
Peet, Bill (William Bartlett). *The caboose who got loose*
  The luckiest one of all
  The Whingdingdilly
Price, Roger. *The last little dragon*
Russo, Marisabina. *Why do grownups have all the fun?*
Sadler, Marilyn. *It's not easy being a bunny*
Sarnoff, Jane. *That's not fair*
Sharmat, Marjorie Weinman. *Grumley the grouch*
Testa, Fulvio. *Never satisfied*
Turnage, Sheila. *Trout the magnificent*
Wiesner, William. *Turnabout*
Yaffe, Alan. *The magic meatballs*
Zakhoder, Boris Vladimirovich. *Rosachok*
Zolotow, Charlotte (Shapiro). *It's not fair*

Behavior – fighting, arguing

Alexander, Martha G. *I'll be the horse if you'll play with me*
Beim, Lorraine. *Two is a team*
Berry, Joy Wilt. *Fighting*
Burningham, John. *Mr. Gumpy's outing*
Burton, Jane. *Animals fighting*
Christian, Mary Blount. *The sand lot*
Dayton, Mona. *Earth and sky*
Ernst, Lisa Campbell. *Zinnia and Dot*
Gekiere, Madeleine. *The frilly lily and the princess*
Gilchrist, Theo E. *Halfway up the mountain*
Goffin, Josse. *Who is the boss?*
Hoban, Russell. *Harvey's hideout*
  The sorely trying day
  Tom and the two handles
Hodges, Margaret. *The kitchen knight*
Holabird, Katharine. *Alexander and the dragon*
Hooks, William H. *Peach boy*
Lasker, Joe. *A tournament of knights*
Levitin, Sonia. *Who owns the moon?*
Lionni, Leo. *It's mine!*
McKee, David. *Tusk tusk*
  Two monsters
Merriam, Eve. *Fighting words*
Minarik, Else Holmelund. *No fighting, no biting!*
Rose, Gerald. *Trouble in the ark*
St. Germain, Sharon. *The terrible fight*
Sharmat, Marjorie Weinman. *I'm not Oscar's friend any more*
  Rollo and Juliet...forever!
  Sometimes mama and papa fight

Shute, Linda. *Momotaro, the peach boy*
Slobodkin, Louis. *Hustle and bustle*
Steadman, Ralph. *The bridge*
Stevenson, James. *Are we almost there?*
Udry, Janice May. *Let's be enemies*
Venable, Alan. *The checker players*
Waggoner, Karen. *Dad Gummit and Ma Foot*
Widman, Christine. *Housekeeper of the wind*
Winthrop, Elizabeth. *That's mine*
Yorinks, Arthur. *Oh, brother*
Zolotow, Charlotte (Shapiro). *The quarreling book*
The unfriendly book

Behavior – forgetfulness

Alexander, Sue. *Witch, Goblin and sometimes Ghost*
Aliki. *Use your head, dear*
Arnold, Tedd. *Ollie forgot*
Cole, Joanna. *Aren't you forgetting something, Fiona?*
Copp, James (Andrew James). *Martha Matilda O'Toole*
De Paola, Tomie (Thomas Anthony). *Strega Nona*
Dines, Glen. *A tiger in the cherry tree*
Domanska, Janina. *Palmiero and the ogre*
Fox, Mem. *Wilfrid Gordon McDonald Partridge*
Galdone, Joanna. *Gertrude, the goose who forgot*
Galdone, Paul. *The magic porridge pot*
Guthrie, Donna. *Grandpa doesn't know it's me*
Hale, Irina. *The lost toys*
Hutchins, Pat. *Don't forget the bacon!*
King-Smith, Dick. *Farmer Bungle forgets*
MacGregor, Ellen. *Theodor Turtle*
Miles, Miska. *Chicken forgets*
Parish, Peggy. *Be ready at eight*
Patz, Nancy. *Pumpernickel tickle and mean green cheese*
Rogers, Paul (Patrick). *Forget-me-not*
Schatell, Brian. *The McGoonys have a party*
Schweninger, Ann. *The hunt for rabbit's galosh*
Stevenson, Suçie. *I forgot*
Van Allsburg, Chris. *The stranger*
Weinberg, Lawrence. *The Forgetful Bears*
The Forgetful Bears meet Mr. Memory
Weisgard, Leonard. *Silly Willy Nilly*

Behavior – gossip

Allen, Jeffrey. *Nosey Mrs. Rat*
Andersen, H. C. (Hans Christian). *It's perfectly true!* ill. by Janet Stevens
Berson, Harold. *The thief who hugged a moonbeam*
Brenner, Barbara A. *Good news*

Chicken Little. *Chicken Licken*, ill. by Jutta Ash
Chicken Licken, ill. by Gavin Bishop
Henny Penny, ill. by Stephen Butler
Henny Penny, ill. by Paul Galdone
Henny Penny, ill. by William Stobbs
The story of Chicken Licken, adapt. and ill. by Jan Ormerod
Holl, Adelaide. *The runaway giant*
Hutchins, Pat. *The surprise party*
Kraus, Robert. *Mert the blurt*
Mantinband, Gerda. *Blabbermouths*
Stevens, Harry. *Parrot told snake*
Varga, Judy. *The monster behind Black Rock*
Zolotow, Charlotte (Shapiro). *The hating book*

Behavior – greed

Afanas'ev, Aleksandr N. *Salt*
Aliki. *The eggs*
Allen, Pamela. *Hidden treasure*
Andersen, H. C. (Hans Christian). *The woman with the eggs*, ill. by Ray Cruz
Angelo, Valenti. *The candy basket*
Arnold, Caroline. *The terrible Hodag*
Aulaire, Ingri Mortenson d'. *Don't count your chicks*
Aylesworth, Jim. *Mary's mirror*
Barker, Inga-Lil. *Why teddy bears are brown*
Bascom, Joe. *Malcolm Softpaws*
Battles, Edith. *The terrible terrier*
The terrible trick or treat
Bellows, Cathy. *Four fat rats*
Berenstain, Stan. *The Berenstain bears get the gimmies*
Berson, Harold. *The rats who lived in the delicatessen*
Bohdal, Susi. *The magic honey jar*
Bolliger, Max. *The golden apple*
Bonsall, Crosby Newell. *It's mine! A greedy book*
Brenner, Barbara A. *Ostrich feathers*
Brown, Marcia. *The bun*
Buckley, Richard. *The greedy python*
Bunting, Eve (Anne Evelyn). *The man who could call down owls*
Carlson, Nancy. *Harriet's Halloween candy*
Carter, Anne. *Bella's secret garden*
Christian, Mary Blount. *The devil take you, Barnabas Beane!*
Coco, Eugene Bradley. *The wishing well*
Cooper, Susan. *The silver cow*
Corbalis, Judy. *The cuckoo bird*
Dauer, Rosamond. *The 300 pound cat*
De Paola, Tomie (Thomas Anthony). *Andy (that's my name)*
Ernst, Lisa Campbell. *The prize pig surprise*
Evans, Katherine. *The maid and her pail of milk*
Gerson, Mary-Joan. *Why the sky is far away*
Ginsburg, Mirra. *Two greedy bears*

Green, Phyllis. *Bagdad ate it*
Grimm, Jacob. *The fisherman and his wife*, ill. by Monika Laimgruber
The fisherman and his wife, ill. by Alan Marks
The fisherman and his wife, ill. by Margot Tomes
The fisherman and his wife, ill. by Margot Zemach
Mother Holly, ill. by Bernadette Watts
Hadithi, Mwenye. *Greedy zebra*
Hewitt, Kathryn. *King Midas and the golden touch*
Ishii, Momoko. *The tongue-cut sparrow*
Jacobs, Joseph. *Hudden and Dudden and Donald O'Neary*
Kennedy, Richard. *The lost kingdom of Karnica*
Kismaric, Carole. *The rumor of Pavel and Paali*
Kuskin, Karla. *What did you bring me?*
Lewis, J. Patrick. *The Tsar and the amazing cow*
Lionni, Leo. *The biggest house in the world*
Lorenz, Lee. *Pinchpenny John*
Lussert, Anneliese. *The farmer and the moon*
McClenathan, Louise. *My mother sends her wisdom*
McKissack, Patricia C. *King Midas and his gold*
McLenighan, Valjean. *Three strikes and you're out*
Mahy, Margaret. *Rooms for rent*
Marshall, James. *Yummers too: the second course*
Matsutani, Miyoko. *How the withered trees blossomed*
Obrist, Jürg. *The miser who wanted the sun*
Peet, Bill (William Bartlett). *Kermit the hermit*
The kweeks of Kookatumdee
Peppé, Rodney. *The mice and the flying basket*
Perkins, Al. *King Midas and the golden touch*
Porter, David Lord. *Mine!*
Roffey, Maureen. *Look, there's my hat!*
Rohmer, Harriet. *The invisible hunters*
Ross, Tony. *The greedy little cobbler*
San Souci, Robert D. *The enchanted tapestry*
Selway, Martina. *Greedyguts*
Shibano, Tamizo. *The old man who made the trees bloom*
Solotareff, Grégoire. *Never trust an ogre*
Stadler, John. *Animal cafe*
Stage, Mads. *The greedy blackbird*
Storr, Catherine (Cole). *King Midas*
Wells, Rosemary. *The little lame prince*
Winthrop, Elizabeth. *That's mine*

Behavior – growing up

Alexander, Sue. *Dear Phoebe*
Aliki. *I'm growing!*
Allison, Alida. *The toddler's potty book*
Anholt, Catherine. *When I was a baby*
Appell, Clara. *Now I have a daddy haircut*
Ardizzone, Edward. *Paul, the hero of the fire*
Aseltine, Lorraine. *First grade can wait*
Aulaire, Ingri Mortenson d'. *Too big*
Balzola, Asun. *Munia and the red shoes*
Barrett, Judi. *I hate to take a bath*
I'm too small, you're too big
Bogot, Howard. *I'm growing*
Bolliger, Max. *The magic bird*
Bonnici, Peter. *The festival*
Bourgeois, Paulette. *Big Sarah's little boots*
Brentano, Clemens. *Schoolmaster Whackwell's wonderful sons*
Brinckloe, Julie. *Fireflies!*
Bromhall, Winifred. *Bridget's growing day*
Brown, Myra Berry. *Benjy's blanket*
Bruna, Dick. *I can dress myself*
Bryant, Bernice. *Follow the leader*
Buckley, Kate. *Love notes*
Bulla, Clyde Robert. *Dandelion Hill*
Carle, Eric. *My very first book of growth*
Carrier, Lark. *Scout and Cody*
Caseley, Judith. *Annie's potty*
Chaffin, Lillie D. *Tommy's big problem*
Ciardi, John. *Scrappy the pup*
Civardi, Anne. *Potty time*
Cleary, Beverly. *The growing-up feet*
Janet's thingamajigs
Coats, Laura Jane. *Mr. Jordan in the park*
Cobb, Vicki. *Feeding yourself*
Getting dressed
Cohen, Miriam. *Jim meets the thing*
Cole, Joanna. *Your new potty*
Cooney, Nancy Evans. *The blanket that had to go*
Donald says thumbs down
Corey, Dorothy. *Tomorrow you can*
Dauer, Rosamond. *Bullfrog grows up*
Delton, Judy. *The best mom in the world*
DeLuise, Dom. *Charlie the caterpillar*
De Paola, Tomie (Thomas Anthony). *Katie's good idea*
Drescher, Joan. *I'm in charge!*
Esbensen, Barbara Juster. *Who shrank my grandmother's house?*
Faison, Eleanora. *Becoming*
Fassler, Joan. *Don't worry dear*
The man of the house
Felt, Sue. *Rosa-too-little*
Fox, Mem. *Shoes from grandpa*
Freedman, Sally. *Devin's new bed*
Fribourg, Marjorie G. *Ching-Ting and the ducks*
Galbraith, Kathryn Osebold. *Roommates*
Garelick, May. *Just my size*

Gelbard, Jane. *My bye-bye bottle book*
  My dressing book
  My eating book
  My sharing book
Goennel, Heidi. *When I grow up...*
Gould, Deborah. *Aaron's shirt*
Graham, Bob. *The red woolen blanket*
Grifalconi, Ann. *Flyaway girl*
Hale, Irina. *Small big bad boy*
Hall, Derek. *Elephant bathes*
  Gorilla builds
  Polar bear leaps
Hanson, Joan. *I won't be afraid*
Harris, Robie H. *I hate kisses*
Hayes, Geoffrey. *Patrick and Ted*
Heitler, Susan M. *David decides about*
  thumbsucking
Hines, Anna Grossnickle. *All by myself*
  Big like me
Hoban, Brom. *Skunk Lane*
Hoffman, Phyllis. *Baby's first year*
Horner, Althea J. *Little big girl*
Iverson, Genie. *I want to be big*
Jenkin-Pearce, Susie. *Boris's big ache*
Johnson, Crockett. *We wonder what will*
  Walter be? When he grows up
Jonas, Ann. *When you were a baby*
Joosse, Barbara M. *Fourth of July*
Kandoian, Ellen. *Maybe she forgot*
Khalsa, Dayal Kaur. *I want a dog*
Klinting, Lars. *Regal the golden eagle*
Krasilovsky, Phyllis. *The very little boy*
  The very little girl
Kraus, Robert. *Leo the late bloomer*
Levine, Abby. *What did mommy do before*
  you?
Lexau, Joan M. *I hate red rover*
Lindgren, Barbro. *Sam's potty*
McPhail, David. *Pig Pig grows up*
Marshak, Samuel. *The pup grew up!*
Massie, Diane Redfield. *Tiny pin*
Miller, Virginia. *On your potty!*
Moers, Hermann. *Camomile heads for home*
Moncure, Jane Belk. *Now I am five!*
  Now I am four!
  Now I am three!
Mordvinoff, Nicolas. *Coral Island*
Munsch, Robert N. *I have to go!*
Newberry, Clare Turlay. *Percy, Polly and*
  Pete
Noll, Sally. *That bothered Kate*
Nordlicht, Lillian. *I love to laugh*
Otto, Svend. *The giant fish and other stories*
Parish, Peggy. *I can—can you?*
Pellowski, Anne. *Stairstep farm*
Poulin, Stéphane. *My mother's loves: stories*
  and lies from my childhood
Power, Barbara. *I wish Laura's mommy was*
  my mommy
Reichmeier, Betty. *Potty time!*
Rogers, Fred. *Going to the potty*

Ross, Anna. *I did it!*
  I have to go
Ross, Katharine. *When you were a baby*
Ross, Tony. *I want my potty*
Schlein, Miriam. *Billy, the littlest one*
  Herman McGregor's world
  When will the world be mine?
Schwartz, Amy. *Begin at the beginning*
Scott, Ann Herbert. *Someday rider*
Sharmat, Marjorie Weinman. *Bartholomew*
  the bossy
Smith, Robert Paul. *When I am big*
Snyder, Zilpha Keatley. *Come on, Patsy*
Solomon, Chuck. *Moving up*
Stanley, Diane. *Captain Whiz-Bang*
Stevenson, James. *Higher on the door*
Strub, Susanne. *Lulu goes swimming*
  Lulu on her bike
Turkle, Brinton. *Obadiah the Bold*
Waber, Bernard. *You're a little kid with a*
  big heart
Waddell, Martin. *Once there were giants*
Waxman, Stephanie. *What is a girl? What*
  is a boy?
Weiss, Nicki. *Barney is big*
Welber, Robert. *Goodbye, hello*
Wells, Rosemary. *Timothy goes to school*
Willis, Val. *Silly little chick*
Wittman, Sally. *A special trade*
Wood, Audrey. *Oh my baby bear!*
Yoshida, Toshi. *Young lions*
Young, Helen. *A throne for Sesame*
Young, Ruth. *My potty chair*
Zagone, Theresa. *No nap for me*
Zagwyn, Deborah Turney. *Pumpkin blanket*
Zimelman, Nathan. *If I were strong*
  enough...
Zolotow, Charlotte (Shapiro). *But not Billy*
  I like to be little
  May I visit?
  Someone new
  When I have a son

Behavior – hiding

Aruego, José. *We hide, you seek*
Asch, Frank. *Moongame*
Blacker, Terence. *Herbie Hamster, where are*
  you?
Blanchard, Arlene. *The naughty lamb*
Chorao, Kay. *Kate's box*
Cole, Michael. *Head in the sand*
Dubanevich, Arlene. *Pigs in hiding*
Gerstein, Mordicai. *William, where are you?*
Gomi, Taro. *Where's the fish?*
Gretz, Susanna. *Hide-and-seek*
Greydanus, Rose. *My secret hiding place*
Heller, Ruth. *How to hide a butterfly*
  How to hide a polar bear
Hulse, Gillian. *Morris, where are you?*
Kudrna, C. Imbior. *To bathe a boa*
Livermore, Elaine. *Looking for Henry*

McClung, Robert. *How animals hide*
McPhail, David. *Where can an elephant hide?*
Major, Beverly. *Playing sardines*
Matus, Greta. *Where are you, Jason?*
Milios, Rita. *Sneaky Pete*
Mintzberg, Yvette. *Sally, where are you?*
Oppenheim, Shulamith Levey. *The lily cupboard*
Oxford Scientific Films. *Danger colors*
Hide and seek
Schertle, Alice. *Jeremy Bean's St. Patrick's Day*
That Olive!
Szekeres, Cyndy. *Hide-and-seek duck*
Tulloch, Richard. *Danny in the toybox*
Unwin, Pippa. *The great zoo hunt!*
Vigna, Judith. *The hiding house*
Walsh, Ellen Stoll. *Mouse paint*
Warren, Cathy. *Springtime bears*
Wood, John Norris. *Jungles*
Oceans
Ziefert, Harriet. *Where's the cat?*
Where's the dog?
Where's the guinea pig?
Where's the turtle?
Zion, Gene. *Hide and seek day*

Behavior – hiding things

Allen, Pamela. *Hidden treasure*
Bason, Lillian. *Those foolish Molboes!*
Baylor, Byrd. *Your own best secret place*
Brady, Susan. *Find my blanket*
Croswell, Volney. *How to hide a hippopotamus*
Demi. *Demi's find the animals A B C*
Wood, Leslie. *A dog called Mischief*

Behavior – hurrying

Gomi, Taro. *First comes Harry*
Greydanus, Rose. *Willie the slowpoke*
Hurd, Edith Thacher. *Hurry, hurry!*
Myers, Bernice. *It happens to everyone*
Steiner, Charlotte. *What's the hurry, Harry?*
Thoreau, Henry D. *What befell at Mrs. Brooks's*

Behavior – imitation

Allamand, Pascale. *The animals who changed their colors*
Aruego, José. *Look what I can do*
Asch, Frank. *Just like daddy*
Barrett, Judi. *Animals should definitely not act like people*
Animals should definitely not wear clothing
Bendick, Jeanne. *Why can't I?*
Blakeley, Peggy. *What shall I be tomorrow?*
Buckmaster, Henrietta. *Lucy and Loki*
Calhoun, Mary. *The nine lives of Homer C. Cat*

Canning, Kate. *A painted tale*
Cauley, Lorinda Bryan. *The animal kids*
Charlton, Elizabeth. *Terrible tyrannosaurus*
Clewes, Dorothy. *Henry Hare's boxing match*
Cole, Brock. *Nothing but a pig*
Farber, Norma. *There goes feathertop!*
Gauch, Patricia Lee. *Dance, Tanya*
Graham, Amanda. *Who wants Arthur?*
Hallinan, P. K. (Patrick K.). *Where's Michael?*
Heine, Helme. *Mr. Miller the dog*
Herson, Kathleen. *The copycat*
Inkpen, Mick. *Kipper*
Jones, Chuck. *William the backwards skunk*
Kellogg, Steven (Stephen). *A rose for Pinkerton*
Kent, Jack. *The once-upon-a-time dragon*
Marzollo, Jean. *Pretend you're a cat*
Moore, Inga. *Fifty red night-caps*
Noll, Sally. *That bothered Kate*
Numeroff, Laura Joffe. *If you give a mouse a cookie*
Riddell, Chris. *Bird's new shoes*
Ross, Christine. *Lily and the bears*
Saltzberg, Barney. *The yawn*
Schwartz, Amy. *Bea and Mr. Jones*
Van Caster, Nancy. *An alligator lives in Benjamin's house*

Behavior – indifference

Blos, Joan W. *Old Henry*
Dubanevich, Arlene. *Pig William*
Hogrogian, Nonny. *The hermit and Harry and me*
Roy, Ronald. *Three ducks went wandering*
Sendak, Maurice. *Pierre*
Sharmat, Marjorie Weinman. *I don't care*
Watts, Mabel (Pizzey). *The day it rained watermelons*

Behavior – laziness

De Paola, Tomie (Thomas Anthony). *Jamie O'Rourke and the big potato*

Behavior – losing things

Abolafia, Yossi. *A fish for Mrs. Gardenia*
Ackerman, Karen. *Araminta's paint box*
Ahlberg, Allan. *Mystery tour*
Amoss, Berthe. *What did you lose, Santa?*
Ardizzone, Edward. *The little girl and the tiny doll*
Armitage, Ronda. *The lighthouse keeper's catastrophe*
Ayer, Jacqueline. *Nu Dang and his kite*
Bannon, Laura. *Red mittens*
Barrows, Marjorie Wescott. *The funny hat*
Bassett, Lisa. *Beany and Scamp*
Birdseye, Tom. *Airmail to the moon*
Bond, Michael. *Paddington at the zoo*
Bottner, Barbara. *Big boss! Little boss!*

Bowden, Joan Chase. *Who took the top hat trick?*
Boyle, Constance. *The story of little owl*
Brett, Jan. *The mitten*
Bromhall, Winifred. *Middle Matilda*
Burningham, John. *The blanket*
Chorao, Kay. *Molly's lies*
  Molly's Moe
Coman, Carolyn. *Losing things at Mr. Mudd's*
Coombs, Patricia. *The lost playground*
Craft, Ruth. *The day of the rainbow*
Davidson, Amanda. *Teddy in the garden*
Denton, Terry. *The school for laughter*
Dodds, Siobhan. *Charles Tiger*
Eagle, Ellen. *Gypsy's cleaning day*
Eriksson, Eva. *The tooth trip*
Garland, Sarah. *Polly's puffin*
Gay, Michel. *Little shoe*
Guthrie, Donna. *Grandpa doesn't know it's me*
Haddon, Mark. *Gilbert's gobstopper*
Handford, Martin. *Where's Waldo?*
Havill, Juanita. *Jamaica's find*
Hissey, Jane. *Little Bear lost*
Hutchins, H. J. (Hazel J.). *Leanna builds a genie trap*
Hutchins, Hazel J. *Norman's snowball*
Inkpen, Mick. *Billy's beetle*
Jeram, Anita. *Bill's belly button*
Johnson, B. J. *My blanket Burt*
Jonas, Ann. *Where can it be?*
Kay, Helen. *One mitten Lewis*
Keenen, George. *The preposterous week*
Kelley, Anne. *Daisy's discovery*
Kellogg, Steven (Stephen). *The mystery of the magic green ball*
  The mystery of the missing red mitten
Lexau, Joan M. *Finders keepers, losers weepers*
Livermore, Elaine. *Lost and found*
  Three little kittens lost their mittens
Lyon, George-Ella. *Basket*
McGinley, Phyllis. *Lucy McLockett*
McNeely, Jeannette. *Where's Izzy?*
Marcus, Susan. *The missing button adventure*
Marks, Alan. *Nowhere to be found*
Marshak, Samuel. *The pup grew up!*
Martin, Jacqueline Briggs. *Bizzy Bones and the lost quilt*
Morgan, Allen. *Matthew and the midnight money van*
Mother Goose. *The three little kittens*, ill. by Lorinda Bryan Cauley
  The three little kittens, ill. by Paul Galdone
  The three little kittens, ill. by Dorothy Stott
  The three little kittens, ill. by Shelley Thornton
Munari, Bruno. *Jimmy has lost his cap*

Murrow, Liza Ketchum. *Good-bye, Sammy*
O'Brien, Anne Sibley. *Where's my truck?*
Oxenbury, Helen. *Pippo gets lost*
Parr, Letitia. *A man and his hat*
Precek, Katharine Wilson. *Penny in the road*
Price, Mathew. *Do you see what I see?*
Pryor, Ainslie. *The baby blue cat and the smiley worm doll*
  The baby blue cat and the whole batch of cookies
Rabe, Berniece. *Where's Chimpy?*
Rogers, Jean. *Runaway mittens*
Rogers, Paul (Patrick). *Forget-me-not*
Ryder, Eileen. *Winston's new cap*
Schubert, Dieter. *Where's my monkey?*
Sharmat, Marjorie Weinman. *The trip*
Smith, Barry. *Cumberland Road*
Sonnenschein, Harriet. *Harold's runaway nose*
Upham, Elizabeth. *Little brown bear loses his clothes*
Walsh, Jill Paton. *Lost and found*
White, Florence Meiman. *How to lose your lunch money*
Yorinks, Arthur. *Christmas in July*
Zander, Hans. *My blue chair*
Ziefert, Harriet. *Good night, Jessie!*
Zinnemann-Hope, Pam. *Find your coat, Ned*

Behavior – lost

Alexander, Liza. *Ernie gets lost*
Allen, Laura Jean. *Where is Freddy?*
Anderson, C. W. (Clarence Williams). *Blaze finds forgotten roads*
  Blaze finds the trail
Ayer, Jacqueline. *Little Silk*
Bacheller, Irving. *Lost in the fog*
Balian, Lorna. *Amelia's nine lives*
Barklem, Jill. *Autumn story*
Bartoli, Jennifer. *Snow on bear's nose*
Barton, Byron. *Where's Al?*
Bassett, Lisa. *Beany and Scamp*
Belting, Natalia Maree. *Verity Mullens and the Indian*
Bemelmans, Ludwig. *Madeline and the gypsies*
Beni, Ruth. *Sir Baldergog the great*
Benjamin, Alan. *Ribtickle Town*
Berson, Harold. *Henry Possum*
Boegehold, Betty. *Pawpaw's run*
Bograd, Larry. *Lost in the store*
Bolliger, Max. *Sandy at the children's zoo*
Bornstein, Ruth Lercher. *Annabelle Jim*
Bothwell, Jean. *Paddy and Sam*
Brewster, Patience. *Ellsworth and the cats from Mars*
Brown, Jane Clark. *Whonk, and whonk again*

Brown, Judith Gwyn. *Max and the truffle pig*

Brown, Marcia. *Tamarindo!*

Brown, Margaret Wise. *Little lost lamb*
Three little animals

Brunhoff, Laurent de. *Babar's little girl*

Buffett, Jimmy. *Trouble dolls*

Bunting, Eve (Anne Evelyn). *Jane Martin, dog detective*

Calmenson, Stephanie. *Where is Grandma Potamus?*

Carigiet, Alois. *Anton the goatherd*

Carle, Eric. *Have you seen my cat?*

Carrick, Carol. *The highest balloon on the common*
Left behind

Carter, Anne. *Ruff leaves home*

Carter, Noelle. *I'm a little mouse*

Cartlidge, Michelle. *Pippin and Pod*

Cohen, Miriam. *Lost in the museum*

Cole, Joanna. *The Clown-Arounds go on vacation*

Corddry, Thomas I. *Kibby's big feat*

Cummings, Betty Sue. *Turtle*

De Beer, Hans. *Little polar bear*

Delaney, Ned. *Bad dog!*

Drummond, Violet H. *Phewtus the squirrel*

Erickson, Phoebe. *Just follow me*

Farber, Norma. *Where's Gomer?*

Flack, Marjorie. *Angus lost*

Fletcher, Elizabeth. *The little goat*

Francis, Frank. *The magic wallpaper*

Gay, Michel. *Take me for a ride*

Gay, Zhenya. *Small one*

Goble, Paul. *The friendly wolf*

Goldsmith, Howard. *Little lost dog*

Goode, Diane. *Where's our mama?*

Grimm, Jacob. *Hansel and Gretel*, ill. by Winslow P. Pels

Grossman, Bill. *Tommy at the grocery store*

Guilfoile, Elizabeth. *Have you seen my brother?*

Guthrie, Donna. *Grandpa doesn't know it's me*

Hader, Berta Hoerner. *Lost in the zoo*

Hamm, Diane Johnston. *Laney's lost momma*

Hawkins, Colin. *Tog the dog*

Hayes, Sarah. *This is the bear*

Henkes, Kevin. *Sheila Rae, the brave*

Hill, Eric. *Where's Spot?*

Hines, Anna Grossnickle. *Don't worry, I'll find you*

Hirsh, Marilyn. *Where is Yonkela?*

Hoban, Lillian. *The laziest robot in zone one*

Hutchins, Pat. *Where's the baby?*

Irving, Washington. *Rip Van Winkle*, ill. by John Howe
Rip Van Winkle, ill. by Thomas Locker
Rip Van Winkle, ill. by Peter Wingham

Jaques, Faith. *Tilly's rescue*

Joerns, Consuelo. *The foggy rescue*

The forgotten bear

Jonas, Ann. *Two bear cubs*

Keats, Ezra Jack. *My dog is lost!*

Kessler, Leonard P. *Are we lost, daddy?*

Knuppel, Helga. *The adventures of Christabel Crocodile*

Koči, Marta. *Katie's kitten*

Krause, Ute. *Nora and the great bear*

Lisker, Sonia O. *Lost*

Livermore, Elaine. *Follow the fox*

Lobel, Arnold. *Uncle Elephant*

Lubell, Winifred. *Rosalie, the bird market turtle*

McCloskey, Robert. *Blueberries for Sal*

McCully, Emily Arnold. *Picnic*

McPhail, David. *Lost*

Maris, Ron. *Are you there, bear?*

Marks, Alan. *Nowhere to be found*

Martin, Jacqueline Briggs. *Bizzy Bones and Moosemouse*

Mendoza, George. *Alphabet sheep*

Miles, Miska. *This little pig*

Modell, Frank. *Tooley! Tooley!*

Mogensen, Jan. *When Teddy woke early*

Moser, Erwin. *Wilma the elephant*

Nakatani, Chiyoko. *The day Chiro was lost*

Nims, Bonnie Larkin. *Where is the bear?*

Olsen, Ib Spang. *Cat alley*

Parenteau, Shirley. *I'll bet you thought I was lost*

Paul, Jan S. *Hortense*

Peet, Bill (William Bartlett). *Ella*

Politi, Leo. *The nicest gift*

Remkiewicz, Frank. *The last time I saw Harris*

Rey, Margret (Margret Elisabeth Waldstein). *Curious George goes to the hospital*

Rubel, Nicole. *It came from the swamp*

Rylant, Cynthia. *Henry and Mudge*

Sauer, Julia Lina. *Mike's house*

Saxon, Charles D. *Don't worry about Poopsie*

Schertle, Alice. *Little Frog's song*

Schumacher, Claire. *Tim and Jim*

Seignobosc, Françoise. *Minou*
Springtime for Jeanne-Marie

Shortall, Leonard W. *Andy, the dog walker*

Slobodkin, Louis. *Yasu and the strangers*

Smith, Cara Lockhart. *Twenty-six rabbits run riot*

Standon, Anna. *Little duck lost*

Stevenson, James. *Howard*

Tan, Amy. *The moon lady*

Taylor, Mark. *The case of the missing kittens*
Henry the castaway
Henry the explorer

Titherington, Jeanne. *Where are you going, Emma?*

Tokuda, Wendy. *Humphrey the lost whale*

Tsutsui, Yoriko. *Anna in charge*

Turnbull, Ann. *Rob goes a-hunting*

Vincent, Gabrielle. *Where are you, Ernest and Celestine?*
Vreeken, Elizabeth. *The boy who would not say his name*
Waddell, Martin. *Sailor Bear*
Watanabe, Shigeo. *Where's my daddy?*
Waters, Tony. *Sailor's bride*
Wells, Rosemary. *Max's dragon shirt*
Wold, Jo Anne. *Well! Why didn't you say so?*
Ylla. *Two little bears*
Young, Evelyn. *The tale of Tai*

Behavior – lying

Æsop. *Wolf! Wolf!* ill. by Gerald Rose
Belloc, Hilaire. *Matilda who told lies and was burned to death*
Berenstain, Stan. *The Berenstain bears and the truth*
Brown, Marc Tolon. *The true Francine*
Chorao, Kay. *Molly's lies*
Cohen, Miriam. *Liar, liar, pants on fire!*
Collodi, Carlo. *The adventures of Pinocchio,* ill. by Diane Goode
Dinardo, Jeffrey. *The wolf who cried boy*
Elliott, Dan. *Ernie's little lie*
Elzbieta. *Dikou the little troon who walks at night*
Evans, Katherine. *The boy who cried wolf*
Gackenbach, Dick. *Crackle, Gluck and the sleeping toad*
Helena, Ann. *The lie*
Jeram, Anita. *It was Jake*
Lexau, Joan M. *Finders keepers, losers weepers*
Lloyd, David. *The ridiculous story of Gammer Gurton's needle*
Pearson, Kit. *The singing basket*
Ross, Tony. *The boy who cried wolf*
Sharmat, Marjorie Weinman. *A big fat enormous lie*
Turkle, Brinton. *The adventures of Obadiah*

Behavior – messy

Jensen, Patricia. *The mess*
McKissack, Patricia C. *Ada, la desordenada: Messy Bessy*
Messy Bessey's closet

Behavior – misbehavior

Agard, John. *Dig away two-hole Tim*
Alexander, Martha G. *We're in big trouble, Blackboard Bear*
Allard, Harry. *Miss Nelson is back*
Miss Nelson is missing!
Arnold, Tedd. *No jumping on the bed!*
The signmaker's assistant
Ashley, Bernard. *Dinner ladies don't count*
Auer, Martin. *Now, now Markus*
Baba, Noboru. *Eleven cats and a pig*
Eleven cats and albatrosses
Eleven cats in a bag
Eleven hungry cats
Baker, Alan. *Benjamin's book*
Benjamin's dreadful dream
Baker, Margaret. *A puppy called Spinach*
Baumann, Kurt. *The story of Jonah*
Baumgart, Klaus. *Anna and the little green dragon*
Beech, Caroline. *Peas again for lunch*
Beim, Jerrold. *The taming of Toby*
Belloc, Hilaire. *Jim, who ran away from his nurse, and was eaten by a lion*
Matilda who told lies and was burned to death
Bellows, Cathy. *The Grizzly sisters*
Bemelmans, Ludwig. *Madeline and the bad hat*
Berenstain, Stan. *The Berenstain bears and the truth*
Berry, Joy Wilt. *Being destructive*
Being selfish
Disobeying
Fighting
Throwing tantrums
Whining
Blaustein, Muriel. *Baby Mabu and Auntie Moose*
Bedtime, Zachary!
Boyd, Lizi. *Half wild and half child*
Bradman, Tony. *The bad babies' book of colors*
The bad babies' counting book
Michael
Brown, Margaret Wise. *Sneakers*
Brunhoff, Laurent de. *Babar's cousin, that rascal Arthur*
Calhoun, Mary. *The goblin under the stairs*
Campbell, Rod. *Henry's busy day*
Misty's mischief
Cartlidge, Michelle. *Pippin and Pod*
Chalmers, Audrey. *Fancy be good*
Chapman, Carol. *Herbie's troubles*
Chess, Victoria. *Alfred's alphabet walk*
Christelow, Eileen. *Five little monkeys jumping on the bed*
Five little monkeys sitting in a tree
Christian, Mary Blount. *Go west, swamp monsters*
Clark, Emma Chichester. *The story of Horrible Hilda and Henry*
Claverie, Jean. *The party*
Cohen, Miriam. *Starring first grade*
Cole, William. *That pest Jonathan*
Colette. *The boy and the magic*
Collington, Peter. *Little pickle*
Collins, Pat Lowery. *Taking care of Tucker*
Collodi, Carlo. *The adventures of Pinocchio,* ill. by Diane Goode
Costa, Nicoletta. *The naughty puppy*
The new puppy
Craig, Helen. *A welcome for Annie*

Crowley, Arthur. *The boogey man*
Dauer, Rosamond. *My friend, Jasper Jones*
Delaney, A. *The gunnywolf*
Delaney, Ned. *Bad dog!*
  Rufus the doofus
Douglass, Barbara. *Good as new*
Dowling, Paul. *Splodger*
Eastman, P. D. (Philip D.). *Are you my mother?*
Flack, Marjorie. *The story about Ping*
Froment, Eugène. *The story of a round loaf*
Gackenbach, Dick. *Pepper and all the legs*
Gág, Wanda. *The sorcerer's apprentice*
Galbraith, Kathryn Osebold. *Katie did!*
Gantos, Jack (John, Jr.). *Happy birthday, Rotten Ralph*
  Rotten Ralph
  Worse than Rotten Ralph
Gerson, Corinne. *Good dog, bad dog*
Ghigna, Charles. *Good cats / Bad cats*
  Good dogs / Bad dogs
Goodall, John S. *Naughty Nancy*
  Naughty Nancy goes to school
Gordon, Margaret. *Wilberforce goes to a party*
Graham, Bob. *Has anyone here seen William?*
Grindley, Sally. *Four black puppies*
Gullikson, Sandy. *Trouble for breakfast*
Harper, Wilhelmina. *The gunniwolf*
Havill, Juanita. *Magic fort*
Hawkes, Kevin. *Then the troll heard the squeak*
Hayes, Sarah. *Bad egg*
Hedderwick, Mairi. *Katie Morag and the big boy cousins*
  Katie Morag and the tiresome Ted
  Katie Morag delivers the mail
Henkes, Kevin. *A weekend with Wendell*
Hill, Eric. *Spot visits the hospital*
  Spot's first picnic
Hiller, Catherine. *Argentaybee and the boonie*
Hilton, Nette. *Prince Lachlan*
Himmelman, John. *Amanda and the witch switch*
Hirsh, Marilyn. *Deborah the dybbuk*
Hoban, Russell. *How Tom beat Captain Najork and his hired sportsmen*
Hodeir, André. *Warwick's three bottles*
Hogan, Inez. *About Nono, the baby elephant*
Hort, Lenny. *The boy who held back the sea*
Hughes, Shirley. *The snow lady*
Hutchins, Pat. *Where's the baby?*
Inkiow, Dimiter. *Me and Clara and Baldwin the pony*
  Me and Clara and Snuffy the dog
  Me and my sister Clara
Jeffers, Susan. *Wild Robin*
Jeram, Anita. *It was Jake*
Johnston, Tony. *Lorenzo the naughty parrot*
Joosse, Barbara M. *The thinking place*

Keller, Beverly. *When mother got the flu*
Keller, Holly. *A bear for Christmas*
Kellogg, Steven (Stephen). *Prehistoric Pinkerton*
Kent, Jack. *The scribble monster*
Kent, Lorna. *No, no, Charlie Rascal!*
Kline, Suzy. *Don't touch!*
Koenig, Marion. *The wonderful world of night*
Krasilovsky, Phyllis. *The man who entered a contest*
Krause, Ute. *Pig surprise*
Kroll, Steven. *Otto*
  Pigs in the house
Leaf, Munro. *A flock of watchbirds*
Levinson, Riki. *Touch! Touch!*
Lexau, Joan M. *I'll tell on you*
Lillie, Patricia. *One very, very quiet afternoon*
Lindbergh, Reeve. *The day the goose got loose*
Lindgren, Barbro. *The wild baby*
Lipkind, William. *Nubber bear*
Lippman, Peter. *The Know-It-Alls go to sea*
  The Know-It-Alls help out
  The Know-It-Alls mind the store
  The Know-It-Alls take a winter vacation
Littlewood, Valerie. *The season clock*
Lobel, Arnold. *Prince Bertram the bad*
Lorimer, Janet. *The biggest bubble in the world*
Luttrell, Ida. *Mattie and the chicken thief*
McPhail, David. *Andrew's bath*
Mahiri, Jabari. *The day they stole the letter J*
Mahy, Margaret. *The boy with two shadows*
Malloy, Judy. *Bad Thad*
Marshall, Edward. *Fox and his friends*
  Fox on wheels
Marshall, James. *The Cut-Ups*
  The Cut-Ups at Camp Custer
  The Cut-Ups crack up
  The Cut-Ups cut loose
  Fox on the job
  George and Martha back in town
Marzollo, Jean. *Uproar on Hollercat Hill*
Mayer, Mercer. *Appelard and Liverwurst*
Moremen, Grace E. *No, no, Natalie*
Morgan, Allen. *Molly and Mr. Maloney*
Moss, Marissa. *Who was it?*
Munsch, Robert N. *Angela's airplane*
  Moira's birthday
Murphy, Jill. *All in one piece*
Myller, Lois. *No! No!*
Nones, Eric Jon. *Wendell*
Oana, Kay D. *Shasta and the shebang machine*
Obrist, Jürg. *Bear business*
O'Kelley, Mattie Lou. *Circus!*
Oldfield, Pamela. *Melanie Brown climbs a tree*
Olson, Helen Kronberg. *The strange thing that happened to Oliver Wendell Iscovitch*

Oram, Hiawyn. *Ned and the Joybaloo*
Oxenbury, Helen. *The car trip*
  The important visitor
Parker, Nancy Winslow. *Cooper, the*
  McNallys' big black dog
  Poofy loves company
Paterson, Diane. *Soap and suds*
Pearson, Tracey Campbell. *The howling dog*
  Sing a song of sixpence
Polushkin, Maria. *Kitten in trouble*
Potter, Beatrix. *The complete adventures of*
  Peter Rabbit
  The tale of Benjamin Bunny
  The tale of Peter Rabbit, ill. by Margot
    Apple
  The tale of Peter Rabbit
  The tale of two bad mice
  The two bad mice: pop-up book
  Where's Peter Rabbit?
Poulin, Stéphane. *Can you catch Josephine?*
Prater, John. *"No!" said Joe*
  On Friday something funny happened
  You can't catch me!
Preston, Edna Mitchell. *Horrible Hepzibah*
  Squawk to the moon, little goose
Provensen, Alice. *Punch in New York*
Quackenbush, Robert M. *Mouse feathers*
Rabinowitz, Sandy. *A colt named mischief*
Rappus, Gerhard. *When the sun was shining*
Rice, Eve. *Benny bakes a cake*
Richardson, Jean. *Thomas's sitter*
Robison, Deborah. *Your turn, doctor*
Rockwell, Anne F. *Honk honk!*
Ross, Tony. *Oscar got the blame*
Rovetch, Lissa. *Trigwater did it*
Rubel, Nicole. *Goldie's nap*
Ruck-Pauquèt, Gina. *Oh, that koala!*
Sadler, Marilyn. *Alistair's elephant*
Sandberg, Inger. *Dusty wants to help*
  Nicholas' red day
Sarrazin, Johan. *Tootle*
Schatell, Brian. *Farmer Goff and his turkey*
  Sam
Schroeder, Binette. *Tuffa and the picnic*
Schumacher, Claire. *King of the zoo*
Schwartz, Amy. *Camper of the week*
Sendak, Maurice. *Where the wild things are*
Sherrow, Victoria. *There goes the ghost*
Simmonds, Posy. *The chocolate wedding*
Small, David. *Paper John*
Smith, Barry. *A child's guide to bad behavior*
Smith, Cara Lockhart. *Twenty-six rabbits*
  run riot
Smith, Janice Lee. *The monster in the third*
  dresser drawer and other stories about Adam
  Joshua
Solotareff, Grégoire. *Don't call me little*
  bunny
Standon, Anna. *Three little cats*
Stevenson, Suçie. *Jessica the blue streak*

Tharlet, Eve. *Little pig, big trouble*
Tierney, Hanne. *Where's your baby brother,*
  Becky Bunting?
Van Allsburg, Chris. *The garden of Abdul*
  Gasazi
Vigna, Judith. *Anyhow, I'm glad I tried*
  She's not my real mother
Vincent, Gabrielle. *Breakfast time, Ernest*
  and Celestine
Waddell, Martin. *Amy said*
Wade, Barrie. *Little monster*
Wahl, Jan. *Little Eight John*
Wallace, Ian. *Morgan the magnificent*
  The sparrow's song
Ward, Cindy. *Cookie's week*
Ward, Nick. *Giant*
Ward, Sally G. *Charlie and Grandma*
Watanabe, Yuichi. *Wally the whale who loved*
  balloons
Watson, Wendy. *Lollipop*
We wish you a merry Christmas, ill. by
  Tracey Campbell Pearson
Wells, Rosemary. *Fritz and the mess fairy*
  Good night, Fred
  Hazel's amazing mother
White, Florence Meiman. *How to lose your*
  lunch money
Willard, Nancy. *The well-mannered balloon*
Williams, Barbara. *Whatever happened to*
  Beverly Bigler's birthday?
Wiseman, Bernard. *Don't make fun!*
Wood, Audrey. *Elbert's bad word*
Woodruff, Elvira. *Mrs. McCloskey's monkeys*
Wright, Jill. *The old woman and the jar of*
  ums
Yeoman, John. *The wild washerwomen*
Zemach, Margot. *Jake and Honeybunch go to*
  heaven
Zemke, Deborah. *The shadow of Matilda*
  Hunt
Ziefert, Harriet. *Strike four!*

Behavior – mistakes

Aliki. *Jack and Jake*
Boyd, Selma. *The how: making the best of a*
  mistake
Brandenberg, Franz. *No school today!*
Bridwell, Norman. *Clifford's good deeds*
Chevalier, Christa. *Spence makes circles*
Cohen, Peter Zachary. *Olson's meat pies*
Cresswell, Helen. *Two hoots and the king*
  Two hoots in the snow
Erickson, Karen. *No one is perfect*
Gág, Wanda. *Gone is gone*
Galdone, Paul. *Obedient Jack*
Geringer, Laura. *Molly's new washing*
  machine
Hoff, Syd. *Henrietta, the early bird*
Jacobs, Joseph. *Hereafterthis*
Lexau, Joan M. *It all began with a drip,*
  drip, drip

Martin, Rafe. *Foolish rabbit's big mistake*
Springstubb, Tricia. *The magic guinea pig*
Waber, Bernard. *Nobody is perfick*
Walker, Barbara K. (Barbara Kerlin). *New patches for old*
Weiner, Beth Lee. *Benjamin's perfect solution*
Wiseman, Bernard. *Tails are not for painting*

Behavior – misunderstanding

Allard, Harry. *The Stupids die*
Berg, Jean Horton. *The O'Learys and friends*
Berson, Harold. *Kassim's shoes*
Boyd, Lizi. *The not-so-wicked stepmother*
Bryant, Sara Cone. *Epaminondas and his auntie*
Bush, John. *The cross-with-us rhinoceros*
Carrick, Carol. *Old Mother Witch*
Catalanotto, Peter. *Mr. Mumble*
Demuth, Patricia Brennan. *Max, the bad-talking parrot*
Dickinson, Mike. *My dad doesn't even notice*
Gackenbach, Dick. *Arabella and Mr. Crack King Wacky*
Hopkins, Lee Bennett. *I loved Rose Ann*
Komaiko, Leah. *Earl's too cool for me*
Kraus, Robert. *Ladybug, ladybug!*
Krause, Ute. *Pig surprise*
Lionni, Leo. *Fish is fish*
McClintock, Marshall. *A fly went by*
Nixon, Joan Lowery. *Bigfoot makes a movie*
Nordqvist, Sven. *Porker finds a chair*
Polushkin, Maria. *Mother, Mother, I want another*
Roberts, Sarah. *Bert and the missing mop mix-up*
Schatell, Brian. *The McGoonys have a party*
Sharmat, Marjorie Weinman. *Gila monsters meet you at the airport*
Stoeke, Janet Morgan. *Minerva Louise*
Turner, Ann Warren. *Hedgehog for breakfast*
Tusa, Tricia. *Chicken*
Waber, Bernard. *Funny, funny Lyle*
Wild, Jocelyn. *Florence and Eric take the cake*
Wiseman, Bernard. *Morris has a birthday party!*
Morris the moose
Wold, Jo Anne. *Well! Why didn't you say so?*
Yorinks, Arthur. *Company's coming*
Zemke, Deborah. *The way it happened*

Behavior – nagging

Dickinson, Mary. *Alex's outing*
Mahy, Margaret. *Mrs. Discombobulous*
Stalder, Valerie. *Even the devil is afraid of a shrew*

Behavior – name calling

Merriam, Eve. *Fighting words*
Waber, Bernard. *But names will never hurt me*

Behavior – needing someone

Asare, Meshack. *Cat... in search of a friend*
Asher, Sandy. *Princess Bee and the royal good-night story*
Billam, Rosemary. *Fuzzy rabbit*
Bingham, Mindy. *Minou*
Bulla, Clyde Robert. *The stubborn old woman*
Collins, Pat Lowery. *Taking care of Tucker*
Corey, Dorothy. *Will there be a lap for me?*
Fine, Anne. *Poor Monty*
Gauch, Patricia Lee. *Christina Katerina and the time she quit the family*
Guilfoile, Elizabeth. *Nobody listens to Andrew*
Hawkins, Colin. *Where's my mommy?*
Hayes, Sarah. *Mary Mary*
Herriot, James. *Blossom comes home*
Hughes, Richard. *Gertrude's child*
Hughes, Shirley. *Alfie gives a hand*
Jeschke, Susan. *Lucky's choice*
Keats, Ezra Jack. *Louie's search*
Kent, Jack. *There's no such thing as a dragon*
Lewis, Kim. *Emma's lamb*
Livermore, Elaine. *Follow the fox*
Lobel, Anita. *A birthday for the princess*
McLerran, Alice. *The mountain that loved a bird*
McPhail, David. *Emma's pet*
Great cat
Mayer, Mercer. *Whinnie the lovesick dragon*
Morris, Terry Nell. *Lucky puppy! Lucky boy!*
Moser, Erwin. *Wilma the elephant*
Munsch, Robert N. *Millicent and the wind*
Olsen, Ib Spang. *The grown-up trap*
Oppenheim, Joanne. *On the other side of the river*
Peet, Bill (William Bartlett). *Zella, Zack, and Zodiac*
Rayner, Mary. *Crocodarling*
Roberts, Sarah. *I want to go home!*
Schubert, Dieter. *Where's my monkey?*
Scott, Ann Herbert. *On mother's lap*
Sam
Sendak, Maurice. *Very far away*
Singer, Marilyn. *Pickle plan*
Skorpen, Liesel Moak. *Charles*
Spinelli, Eileen. *Somebody loves you, Mr. Hatch*
Stehr, Frédéric. *Quack-quack*
Strauss, Gwen. *The night shimmy*
Sugita, Yutaka. *Helena the unhappy hippopotamus*
Tennyson, Noel. *The lady's chair and the ottoman*

Tokuda, Wendy. *Humphrey the lost whale*
Tompert, Ann. *Will you come back for me?*
Vigna, Judith. *Mommy and me by ourselves again*
Wells, Rosemary. *Noisy Nora*
Wilhelm, Hans. *Schnitzel's first Christmas*
Wolde, Gunilla. *Betsy and the chicken pox*

Behavior – running away

Adoff, Arnold. *Where wild Willie?*
Alexander, Martha G. *And my mean old mother will be sorry, Blackboard Bear*
Baker, Leslie A. *The antique store cat*
The third-story cat
Barrett, Lawrence Louis. *Twinkle, the baby colt*
Bates, H. E. (Herbert Ernest). *Achilles the donkey*
Belloc, Hilaire. *Jim, who ran away from his nurse, and was eaten by a lion*
Bond, Felicia. *Wake up, Vladimir*
Brown, Margaret Wise. *The runaway bunny*
Brunhoff, Jean de. *The story of Babar, the little elephant*
Burton, Virginia Lee. *Choo choo*
Byrd, Robert. *Marcella was bored*
Carlson, Natalie Savage. *Runaway Marie Louise*
Carroll, Ruth. *What Whiskers did*
Christian, Mary Blount. *Go west, swamp monsters*
Clifton, Lucille. *My brother fine with me*
Coombs, Patricia. *Lisa and the grompet*
Desimini, Lisa. *I am running away today*
Dumas, Philippe. *Lucy, a tale of a donkey*
DuPasquier, Philippe. *The great escape*
Duvoisin, Roger Antoine. *The missing milkman*
Elzbieta. *Dikou and the mysterious moon sheep*
Ferns, Ronald. *Osbert and Lucy*
Freeman, Don. *Beady Bear*
Gackenbach, Dick. *Claude and Pepper*
Galbraith, Richard. *Reuben runs away*
Gianni, Peg. *Alex, the amazing juggler*
The gingerbread boy. *The gingerbread boy, ill. by Scott Cook*
The gingerbread boy, ill. by Paul Galdone
The gingerbread boy, ill. by Joan Elizabeth Goodman
The gingerbread boy, ill. by William Curtis Holdsworth
The gingerbread man, ill. by Gerald Rose
The pancake boy, ill. by Lorinda Bryan Cauley
Whiff, sniff, nibble and chew, ill. by Monica Incisa
Goodall, John S. *The adventures of Paddy Pork*
Gray, Nigel. *I'll take you to Mrs. Cole!*
Greenberg, Dan. *The bed who ran away from home*

Greene, Graham. *The little train*
Hale, Irina. *Chocolate mouse and sugar pig*
Hamilton, Morse. *My name is Emily*
Hanson, Joan. *I'm going to run away*
Heck, Elisabeth. *The black sheep*
Heller, Wendy. *Clementine and the cage*
Hillert, Margaret. *The little runaway*
Hoban, Russell. *A baby sister for Frances*
Hughes, Richard. *Gertrude's child*
Hyman, Robin. *Casper and the rainbow bird*
Isenberg, Barbara. *The adventures of Albert, the running bear*
Jeschke, Susan. *Lucky's choice*
Joerns, Consuelo. *Oliver's escape*
Johnson, Jane. *Today I thought I'd run away*
Kent, Jack. *Joey runs away*
Knight, Hilary. *Where's Wallace?*
Kraus, Robert. *Where are you going, little mouse?*
La Farge, Phyllis. *Joanna runs away*
Langner, Nola. *By the light of the silvery moon*
Lasker, Joe. *The do-something day*
Lisowski, Gabriel. *Roncalli's magnificent circus*
Lobel, Arnold. *The man who took the indoors out*
Small pig
McClure, Gillian. *Fly home McDoo*
McConnachie, Brian. *Lily of the forest*
MacDonald, Maryann. *Rosie runs away*
McKissack, Patricia C. *Who is coming?*
McPhail, David. *Stanley: Henry Bear's friend*
Marol, Jean-Claude. *Vagabul escapes*
Miles, Miska. *This little pig*
Moore, Inga. *Little dog lost*
Oakley, Graham. *Hetty and Harriet*
O'Donnell, Elizabeth Lee. *Maggie doesn't want to move*
Otto, Svend. *Taxi dog*
Parker, Nancy Winslow. *The crocodile under Louis Finneberg's bed*
Patterson, Geoffrey. *A pig's tale*
Paxton, Tom. *Jennifer's rabbit*
Pearson, Susan. *Saturday, I ran away*
Peet, Bill (William Bartlett). *Pamela Camel*
Pittaway, Margaret. *The rainforest children*
Pizer, Abigail. *Loppylugs*
Poulin, Stéphane. *Have you seen Josephine?*
Prater, John. *You can't catch me!*
Ravilious, Robin. *The runaway chick*
Robins, Joan. *Addie runs away*
Rockwell, Anne F. *Willy runs away*
Rogers, Paul (Patrick). *Sheepchase*
Seligman, Dorothy Halle. *Run away home*
Sendak, Maurice. *Very far away*
Sharmat, Marjorie Weinman. *Rex*
Singer, Marilyn. *Archer Armadillo's secret room*
Vernon, Tannis. *Little Pig and the blue-green sea*

Waber, Bernard. *Bernard*
Whitmore, Adam. *Max leaves home*
Wilkoń, Piotr. *Rosie the cool cat*
Woolaver, Lance. *From Ben Loman to the sea*
Wright, Dare. *Edith and Mr. Bear*
Yolen, Jane. *The girl who loved the wind*
Yorinks, Arthur. *Hey, Al*
Ziefert, Harriet. *Sam and Lucy*
Zimnik, Reiner. *The bear on the motorcycle*
The proud circus horse
Zion, Gene. *Harry, the dirty dog*
Zolotow, Charlotte (Shapiro). *Big sister and little sister*

Behavior – saving things

Calhoun, Mary. *The traveling ball of string*
Ciardi, John. *John J. Plenty and Fiddler Dan*
Delton, Judy. *Penny wise, fun foolish*
Foster, Doris Van Liew. *A pocketful of seasons*
Mayne, William. *The patchwork cat*

Behavior – secrets

Aardema, Verna. *What's so funny, Ketu?*
Allard, Harry. *Miss Nelson has a field day*
Auerbach, Marjorie. *King Lavra and the barber*
Bahr, Amy C. *Sometimes it's ok to tell secrets*
Bang, Molly. *Dawn*
Barklem, Jill. *The secret staircase*
Baylor, Byrd. *Your own best secret place*
Beisner, Monika. *Secret spells and curious charms*
Brandenberg, Franz. *A secret for grandmother's birthday*
Brighton, Catherine. *Five secrets in a box*
Christelow, Eileen. *The robbery at the diamond dog diner*
Cole, Joanna. *Don't tell the whole world*
Compton, Kenn. *Happy Christmas to all!*
Coombs, Patricia. *The magician and McTree*
Cummings, W. T. (Walter Thies). *Miss Esta Maude's secret*
Davis, Maggie S. *Grandma's secret letter*
Galbraith, Kathryn Osebold. *Waiting for Jennifer*
Gretz, Susanna. *Frog in the middle*
Hayes, Sarah. *This is the bear*
Heide, Florence Parry. *The day of Ahmed's secret*
Hines, Anna Grossnickle. *The secret keeper*
Hughes, Shirley. *Sally's secret*
Krahn, Fernando. *The secret in the dungeon*
Lifton, Betty Jean. *The secret seller*
Pevear, Richard. *Our king has horns!*
Russell, Pamela. *Do you have a secret?*
Thomson, Peggy. *The king has horse's ears*
Willis, Val. *The secret in the matchbox*
Zemke, Deborah. *The way it happened*

Behavior – seeking better things

Abolafia, Yossi. *Yanosh's Island*
Alborough, Jez. *The grass is always greener*
Allen, Jeffrey. *The secret life of Mr. Weird*
Brandenberg, Franz. *What's wrong with a van?*
Buckley, Richard. *The foolish tortoise*
Carter, Anne. *The fisherwoman*
Climo, Lindee. *Clyde*
Cole, Brock. *Nothing but a pig*
Cummings, W. T. (Walter Thies). *The kid*
Demarest, Chris L. *Benedict finds a home*
Gackenbach, Dick. *Little bug*
Gage, Wilson. *Mrs. Gaddy and the fast-growing vine*
Gantschev, Ivan. *Where is Mr. Mole?*
Ganz, Yaffa. *The story of Mimmy and Simmy*
Giff, Patricia Reilly. *Next year I'll be special*
Heilbroner, Joan. *Tom the TV cat*
Ivanov, Anatoly. *Ol' Jake's lucky day*
Jennings, Linda M. *Crispin and the dancing piglet*
Joly-Berbesson, Fanny. *Marceau Bonappetit*
Kent, Jack. *Joey runs away*
Kraus, Robert. *Where are you going, little mouse?*
Lasky, Kathryn. *Sea swan*
Le Guin, Ursula K. *Solomon Leviathan's nine hundred and thirty-first trip around the world*
Lindgren, Astrid. *My nightingale is singing*
Lionni, Leo. *Tillie and the wall*
Lopshire, Robert. *I want to be somebody new!*
McCunn, Ruthanne L. *Pie-Biter*
McKee, David. *The hill and the rock*
Mahy, Margaret. *The man whose mother was a pirate*
Marshall, James. *Rapscallion Jones*
Miller, Moira. *Oscar Mouse finds a home*
Moore, Inga. *The truffle hunter*
Nixon, Joan Lowery. *If you say so, Claude*
Pittaway, Margaret. *The rainforest children*
Rose, Anne. *As right as right can be*
Stanley, Diane. *A country tale*
Watts, Bernadette. *St. Francis and the proud crow*
Williams, Vera B. *A chair for my mother*
Yorinks, Arthur. *Bravo, Minski*

Behavior – sharing

Albert, Burton. *Mine, yours, ours*
Azaad, Meyer. *Half for you*
Beim, Jerrold. *The smallest boy in the class*
Berliner, Franz. *Wildebeest*
Caudill, Rebecca. *A pocketful of cricket*
Cohen, Miriam. *Don't eat too much turkey!*
Corey, Dorothy. *Everybody takes turns*
We all share
Croll, Carolyn. *Too many babas*

Davis, Gibbs. *The other Emily*
Delacre, Lulu. *Nathan and Nicholas Alexander*
DeLage, Ida. *Beware! Beware! A witch won't share*
De Lynam, Alicia Garcia. *It's mine!*
Demarest, Chris L. *Morton and Sidney*
Devlin, Wende. *Cranberry Christmas*
Dowling, Paul. *Meg and Jack's new friends*
Dubois, Claude K. *He's my jumbo!*
Ets, Marie Hall. *The cow's party*
Flory, Jane. *The unexpected grandchild*
Gackenbach, Dick. *Claude the dog*
Galdone, Paul. *The magic porridge pot*
Gelbard, Jane. *My sharing book*
Goldin, Barbara Diamond. *Just enough is plenty*
Gould, Deborah. *Brendan's best-timed birthday*
Gretz, Susanna. *It's your turn, Roger*
Heuck, Sigrid. *Who stole the apples?*
Holder, Heidi. *Carmine the crow*
Hooker, Ruth. *Sara loves her big brother*
Houston, John A. *The bright yellow rope*
Hutchins, Pat. *The doorbell rang*
Johnston, Tony. *Mole and Troll trim the tree*
Keats, Ezra Jack. *Peter's chair*
Klein, Norma. *Visiting Pamela*
Lakin, Patricia. *Don't touch my room*
Lesikin, Joan. *Down the road*
Lester, Helen. *The wizard, the fairy and the magic chicken*
Lindgren, Barbro. *Sam's car*
    Sam's cookie
Littledale, Freya. *The farmer in the soup*
Luttrell, Ida. *Three good blankets*
McAllister, Angela. *The battle of Sir Cob and Sir Filbert*
Maiorano, Robert. *A little interlude*
Miles, Lauren. *The rag coat*
Noble, June. *Two homes for Lynn*
Novak, Matt. *Mr. Floop's lunch*
O'Brien, Anne Sibley. *I want that!*
Oram, Hiawyn. *Mine!*
Ormerod, Jan. *101 things to do with a baby*
Parkinson, Kathy. *The enormous turnip*
Paterson, Bettina. *Bun's birthday*
Pinkwater, Daniel Manus. *Doodle flute*
Porte, Barbara Ann. *Harry's visit*
Riddell, Chris. *Ben and the bear*
Rylant, Cynthia. *Birthday presents*
Sage, Chris. *That's mine, that's yours*
Sharmat, Marjorie Weinman. *The trip*
Sherman, Ivan. *I do not like it when my friend comes to visit*
Smith, Wendy. *The lonely, only mouse*
Spinelli, Eileen. *Thanksgiving at Tappletons'*
Spurr, Elizabeth. *The biggest birthday cake in the world*
Stadler, John. *Gorman and the treasure chest*
Stage, Mads. *The greedy blackbird*

Stanek, Muriel. *My little foster sister*
Turkle, Brinton. *Rachel and Obadiah*
Vigna, Judith. *The hiding house*
Vincent, Gabrielle. *Bravo, Ernest and Celestine!*
    Ernest and Celestine's patchwork quilt
Waber, Bernard. *Bernard*
Wahl, Jan. *Mrs. Owl and Mr. Pig*
Watson, Clyde. *Tom Fox and the apple pie*
Watts, Mabel (Pizzey). *Something for you, something for me*
Weston, Martha. *Bea's four bears*
Wezel, Peter. *The good bird*
Wilson, Christopher Bernard. *Hobnob*
Winthrop, Elizabeth. *That's mine*
Wright, Josephine Lord. *Cotton Cat and Martha Mouse*
Yolen, Jane. *Spider Jane*
Ziefert, Harriet. *Me, too! Me, too!*
Zolotow, Charlotte (Shapiro). *The new friend*

Behavior – shyness

Smith, Wendy. *Say hello, Tilly*

Behavior – solitude

Bennett, Rainey. *The secret hiding place*
Bulla, Clyde Robert. *Keep running, Allen!*
Burdick, Margaret. *Sara Raccoon and the secret place*
Carrick, Carol. *Sleep out*
Dragonwagon, Crescent. *Katie in the morning*
    When light turns into night
Ehrlich, Amy. *The everyday train*
Hall, Donald. *The man who lived alone*
Hallinan, P. K. (Patrick K.). *Just being alone*
Hayes, Geoffrey. *Bear by himself*
Henkes, Kevin. *All alone*
Keller, Beverly. *Pimm's place*
Keyser, Marcia. *Roger on his own*
Luttrell, Ida. *Lonesome Lester*
Morris, Jill. *The boy who painted the sun*
Reesink, Marijke. *The princess who always ran away*
Schertle, Alice. *In my treehouse*
Stubbs, Joanna. *Happy Bear's day*
Tresselt, Alvin R. *I saw the sea come in*
Yezback, Steven A. *Pumpkinseeds*

Behavior – stealing

Ada, Alma F. *The gold coin*
Ahlberg, Janet. *Jeremiah in the dark wood*
Aylesworth, Jim. *Hanna's hog*
Barr, Cathrine. *Hound dog's bone*
Brennan, Patricia D. *Hitchety hatchety up I go!*
Carlson, Nancy. *Arnie and the stolen markers*

Loudmouth George and the sixth-grade bully
Cass, Joan E. *The cat thief*
Cate, Rikki. *A cat's tale*
Christian, Mary Blount. *The doggone mystery*
Cole, Joanna. *The secret box*
Collington, Peter. *The angel and the soldier boy*
Cooper, Jacqueline. *Angus and the Mona Lisa*
De Gerez, Toni. *Louhi, witch of North Farm*
De Paola, Tomie (Thomas Anthony). *Bill and Pete go down the Nile*
Devlin, Wende. *Cranberry Halloween*
Dyke, John. *Pigwig*
Euvremer, Teryl. *The thieves of Peck's pocket*
The firebird, ill. by Moira Kemp
The firebird, ill. by Kris Waldherr
The firebird, ill. by Boris Zvorykin
Foulds, Elfrida Vipont. *The elephant and the bad baby*
Freschet, Berniece. *Owl in the garden*
Ginsburg, Mirra. *Striding slippers*
Goodall, John S. *Paddy to the rescue*
Hare, Norma Q. *Mystery at mouse house*
Hennessy, B. G. *The missing tarts*
Hogrogian, Nonny. *Rooster brother*
Kroll, Steven. *Amanda and the giggling ghost*
Moore, Inga. *Fifty red night-caps*
Ross, Tony. *Hugo and the man who stole colors*
Yolen, Jane. *Piggins*

Behavior – talking to strangers

Bahr, Amy C. *It's ok to say no*
Berenstain, Stan. *The Berenstain bears learn about strangers*
Boegehold, Betty. *Hurray for Pippa!*
Bradman, Tony. *Look out, he's behind you*
Chlad, Dorothy. *Strangers*
Conover, Chris. *Mother Goose and the sly fox*
De Regniers, Beatrice Schenk. *Red Riding Hood*
Emberley, Michael. *Ruby*
Grimm, Jacob. *Little red cap*, ill. by Lisbeth Zwerger
Little Red Riding Hood, ill. by Frank Aloise
Little Red Riding Hood, ill. by Gwen Connelly
Little Red Riding Hood, ill. by Paul Galdone
Little Red Riding Hood, ill. by John S. Goodall
Little Red Riding Hood, ill. by Trina Schart Hyman
Little Red Riding Hood, ill. by Bernadette Watts
Joyce, Irma. *Never talk to strangers*

Keller, Irene. *Benjamin Rabbit and the stranger danger*
Marshall, James. *Red Riding Hood*
Meyer, Linda D. *Safety zone*
Morris, Ann. *The Little Red Riding Hood rebus book*
Petty, Kate. *Being careful with strangers*
Potter, Beatrix. *The tale of Little Pig Robinson*
Vogel, Carole Garbuny. *The dangers of strangers*
Wood, Audrey. *Heckedy Peg*

Behavior – tardiness

Boyd, Selma. *I met a polar bear*
Burningham, John. *John Patrick Norman McHennessy—the boy who was always late*
Grossman, Bill. *The guy who was five minutes late*

Behavior - toilet training *see* Toilet training

Behavior – trickery

Aardema, Verna. *Borreguita and the coyote Rabbit makes a monkey of lion*
Abolafia, Yossi. *Fox tale*
Æsop. *Three fox fables*, ill. by Paul Galdone
Wolf! Wolf! ill. by Gerald Rose
Allard, Harry. *There's a party at Mona's tonight*
Althea. *Jeremy Mouse and cat*
Annett, Cora. *When the porcupine moved in*
Aylesworth, Jim. *Hanna's hog*
Bartos-Hoppner, Barbara. *The Pied Piper of Hamelin*
Bingham, Mindy. *My way Sally*
Biro, Val. *The pied piper of Hamelin*
Blundell, Tony. *Beware of boys*
Boegehold, Betty. *Small Deer's magic tricks*
Bowden, Joan Chase. *Strong John*
Brown, Marcia. *The blue jackal*
Browning, Robert. *The pied piper of Hamelin*, ill. by Patricia and Robin DeWitt
The pied piper of Hamelin, ill. by Kate Greenaway
The pied piper of Hamelin, ill. by Anatoly Ivanov
The pied piper of Hamelin, ill. by Errol Le Cain
Calhoun, Mary. *The pixy and the lazy housewife*
Carey, Valerie Scho. *The devil and mother Crump*
Chicken Little. *Chicken Licken*, ill. by Jutta Ash
Chicken Licken, ill. by Gavin Bishop
Henny Penny, ill. by Stephen Butler
Henny Penny, ill. by Paul Galdone

Henny Penny, ill. by William Stobbs
The story of Chicken Licken, adapt. and ill. by Jan Ormerod
Christelow, Eileen. *Jerome the babysitter*
Olive and the magic hat
The robbery at the diamond dog diner
Cohen, Caron Lee. *Sally Ann Thunder Ann Whirlwind Crockett*
Craig, Helen. *A welcome for Annie*
Cushman, Doug. *Possum stew*
Dinardo, Jeffrey. *The wolf who cried boy*
Dines, Glen. *Gilly and the wicharoo*
Domanska, Janina. *The best of the bargain*
Duff, Maggie (Margaret K.). *Dancing turtle*
Duvoisin, Roger Antoine. *Petunia, I love you*
Elkin, Benjamin. *Gillespie and the guards*
Evans, Katherine. *The boy who cried wolf*
Gage, Wilson. *The crow and Mrs. Gaddy*
Galdone, Paul. *A strange servant*
Goble, Paul. *Iktomi and the buffalo skull*
Iktomi and the ducks
Goldman, Dara. *There's no such thing!*
Grimm, Jacob. *The horse, the fox, and the lion*, ill. by Paul Galdone
Hayward, Linda. *All stuck up*
Isenberg, Barbara. *Albert the running bear gets the jitters*
Jennings, Michael. *Robin Goodfellow and the giant dwarf*
Johnston, Tony. *The badger and the magic fan*
Joyce, James. *The cat and the devil*
Kellogg, Steven (Stephen). *Chicken Little*
Kimmel, Eric A. *Anansi and the moss-covered rock*
Anansi goes fishing
Baba Yaga
Kraus, Robert. *Come out and play, little mouse*
The king's trousers
McAfee, Annalena. *The visitors who came to stay*
McDermott, Gerald. *Tim O'Toole and the wee folk*
Zomo the rabbit
Magnus, Erica. *The boy and the devil*
Mahy, Margaret. *The great white man-eating shark*
Mason, Christopher. *The marvellous blue mouse*
Mayer, Marianna. *The black horse*
Mayer, Mercer. *The Pied Piper of Hamelin*
Mirkovic, Irene. *The greedy shopkeeper*
Mogensen, Jan. *The tiger's breakfast*
Nordqvist, Sven. *The fox hunt*
O'Callahan, Jay. *Tulips*
Oppenheim, Joanne. *Mrs. Peloki's substitute*
Parker, Nancy Winslow. *The crocodile under Louis Finneberg's bed*
Potter, Beatrix. *The pie and the patty-pan*

The story of Miss Moppet
Rockwell, Anne F. *The gollywhopper egg*
Ross, Tony. *The boy who cried wolf*
Smith, Mavis. *A snake mistake*
Snyder, Dianne. *The boy of the three-year nap*
Steig, William. *Solomon the rusty nail*
Stevenson, James. *Emma*
Fried feathers for Thanksgiving
Szekeres, Cyndy. *Suppertime for Frieda Fuzzypaws*
Thayer, Jane. *The clever raccoon*
Turkle, Brinton. *Do not open*
Ungerer, Tomi. *The beast of Monsieur Racine*
Varga, Judy. *The mare's egg*
Wegen, Ron. *Billy Gorilla*
Wild, Robin. *Spot's dogs and the alley cats*
Wildsmith, Brian. *Python's party*
Wright, Jill. *The old woman and the Willy Nilly Man*
Zemach, Harve. *The tricks of Master Dabble*
Zimelman, Nathan. *The great adventure of Wo Ti*

Behavior – unnoticed, unseen

Bishop, Bonnie. *No one noticed Ralph*
Hadithi, Mwenye. *Crafty chameleon*
Kroll, Steven. *The candy witch*
Levinson, Riki. *Me baby!*
Udry, Janice May. *How I faded away*

Behavior – wishing

Aliki. *I wish I was sick, too!*
The wish workers
Allen, Pamela. *I wish I had a pirate suit*
A lion in the night
Ayer, Jacqueline. *A wish for little sister*
Baker, Betty. *My sister says*
Baruch, Dorothy. *I would like to be a pony and other wishes*
Bentley, Nancy. *I've got your nose!*
Benton, Robert. *Don't ever wish for a 7-foot bear*
Beresford, Elisabeth. *Jack and the magic stove*
Berson, Harold. *Truffles for lunch*
Bodsworth, Nan. *Monkey business*
Bos, Burny. *Ollie the elephant*
Breathed, Berkeley. *A wish for wings that work*
Brett, Jan. *Fritz and the beautiful horses*
Bright, Robert. *Me and the bears*
Bush, John. *The fish who could wish*
Butcher, Julia. *The sheep and the rowan tree*
Chapman, Carol. *Barney Bipple's magic dandelions*
Chess, Victoria. *Poor Esmé*
Christensen, Jack. *The forgotten rainbow*
Clifton, Lucille. *Three wishes*

Three wishes, ill. by Michael Hays
Coco, Eugene Bradley. *The wishing well*
Coopersmith, Jerome. *A Chanukah fable for Christmas*
Daugherty, Charles Michael. *Wisher*
Dragonwagon, Crescent. *Coconut Diana, maybe*
Fox, Mem. *Possum magic*
Friedrich, Priscilla. *The wishing well in the woods*
Fuchshuber, Annegert. *The wishing hat*
Gackenbach, Dick. *Hattie rabbit*
Greenberg, Polly. *Oh, Lord, I wish I was a buzzard*
Haas, Irene. *The Maggie B*
Haddon, Mark. *Toni and the tomato soup*
Hale, Irina. *Small big bad boy*
Himmelman, John. *Amanda and the witch switch*
Hines, Anna Grossnickle. *Moon's wish*
Hoban, Lillian. *It's really Christmas*
Howe, James. *I wish I were a butterfly*
Iwasaki, Chihiro. *The birthday wish*
Jaffe, Rona. *Last of the wizards*
Janosch. *Just one apple*
Kay, Helen. *An egg is for wishing*
Kent, Jack. *Knee-high Nina*
Kojima, Naomi. *The flying grandmother*
Kovalski, Maryann. *Pizza for breakfast*
Krauss, Ruth. *Mama, I wish I was snow. Child, you'd be very cold*
Kreye, Walter. *The giant from the little island*
Lasell, Fen. *Michael grows a wish*
Laurencin, Geneviève. *I wish I were*
Littledale, Freya. *The snow child*
McKissack, Patricia C. *King Midas and his gold*
Maris, Ron. *I wish I could fly*
Mayer, Marianna. *The spirit of the blue light*
Mitra, Annie. *Penguin moon*
Munari, Bruno. *The elephant's wish*
Munsch, Robert N. *Millicent and the wind*
Myers, Bernice. *Sidney Rella and the glass sneaker*
Orbach, Ruth. *Please send a panda*
Osborne, Mary Pope. *Moonhorse*
Paterson, Diane. *If I were a toad*
Perkins, Al. *King Midas and the golden touch*
Power, Barbara. *I wish Laura's mommy was my mommy*
Prater, John. *The gift*
Ratnett, Michael. *Jenny's bear*
Reed, Kit. *When we dream*
Riddell, Chris. *The wish factory*
Rosen, Winifred. *Henrietta and the day of the iguana*
Sachs, Marilyn. *Fleet-footed Florence*
Schweninger, Ann. *Birthday wishes*

Seignobosc, Françoise. *Jeanne-Marie counts her sheep*
Seuss, Dr. *I wish that I had duck feet*
Please try to remember the first of Octember!
Sewell, Helen Moore. *Peggy and the pony*
Shecter, Ben. *The discontented mother*
Shimin, Symeon. *I wish there were two of me*
Simon, Norma. *I wish I had my father*
Stevenson, James. *The wish card ran out!*
Storr, Catherine (Cole). *King Midas*
Thaler, Mike. *Hippo lemonade*
Tobias, Tobi. *Jane wishing*
Tornqvist, Rita. *The Christmas carp*
Turkle, Brinton. *Do not open*
Turnbull, Ann. *The tapestry cats*
Varga, Judy. *Janko's wish*
Vigna, Judith. *I wish my daddy didn't drink so much*
Waber, Bernard. *You're a little kid with a big heart*
Watson, Pauline. *Wriggles, the little wishing pig*
Weisgard, Leonard. *Who dreams of cheese?*
Willard, Nancy. *The marzipan moon*
Williams, Barbara. *Someday, said Mitchell*
Wolkstein, Diane. *The magic wings*
Wooding, Sharon L. *Arthur's Christmas wish*
Zemach, Margot. *The three wishes*
Zimelman, Nathan. *To sing a song as big as Ireland*
Zolotow, Charlotte (Shapiro). *Someday*

Behavior – worrying

Benedek, Elissa P. *The secret worry*
Carlson, Nancy. *What if it never stops raining?*
Delton, Judy. *The elephant in Duck's garden*
On a picnic
Devlin, Wende. *Cranberry Easter*
Greene, Carol. *The golden locket*
Gross, Alan. *Sometimes I worry... What if the teacher calls on me?*
Hazen, Barbara Shook. *Wally the worry-warthog*
Herman, Charlotte. *My mother didn't kiss me good-night*
Levitin, Sonia. *A single speckled egg*
Lindenbaum, Pija. *Else-Marie and her seven little daddies*
MacDonald, Maryann. *Sam's worries*
Magorian, Michelle. *Who's going to take care of me?*
Marshall, James. *Portly McSwine*
Segal, Lore. *The story of old Mrs. Brubeck and how she looked for trouble and where she found him*
Sewall, Marcia. *The cobbler's song*
Sharmat, Marjorie Weinman. *Lucretia the unbearable*
Thornton, the worrier

Tyler, Linda Wagner. *Waiting for mom*
Williams, Marcia. *Not a worry in the world*

Being different *see* Character traits –
being different

Bicycling *see* Sports – bicycling

Bigotry *see* Prejudice

Birds

Adoff, Arnold. *Birds*
Alborough, Jez. *Beaky*
Alexander, Martha G. *Out! Out! Out!*
Aliki. *The wish workers*
Allred, Mary. *Grandmother Poppy and the
funny-looking bird*
Anderson, Lonzo. *Mr. Biddle and the birds*
Arnold, Caroline. *Five nests*
Arnosky, Jim. *Mouse writing*
Asch, Frank. *Bear's bargain*
Moon bear
Mooncake
Ash, Jutta. *Wedding birds*
Ayer, Jacqueline. *A wish for little sister*
Azaad, Meyer. *Half for you*
Bailey, Jill. *Eyes*
Feet
Mouths
Baker, Jeffrey J. W. *Patterns of nature*
Bang, Betsy. *Tuntuni the tailor bird*
Barber, Antonia. *The enchanter's daughter*
Bash, Barbara. *Urban roosts*
Baskin, Leonard. *Hosie's aviary*
Baum, Willi. *Birds of a feather*
Beisert, Heide Helene. *Poor fish*
Berliner, Franz. *Miserable Marabou*
Borden, Beatrice Brown. *Wild animals of
Africa*
Boyle, Constance. *Little Owl and the weed*
Bright, Robert. *Georgie and the baby birds*
Brock, Emma Lillian. *The birds' Christmas
tree*
Bruna, Dick. *Little bird tweet*
Brunhoff, Laurent de. *Babar's visit to Bird
Island*
Burstein, Fred. *Anna's rain*
Chönz, Selina. *Florina and the wild bird*
Christelow, Eileen. *The robbery at the
diamond dog diner*
Climo, Shirley. *King of the birds*
Coatsworth, Elizabeth. *Under the green
willow*
Colby, C. B. (Carroll Burleigh). *Who lives
there?*
Who went there?
Cole, Michael. *Head in the sand*
Conklin, Gladys. *If I were a bird*
Cortesi, Wendy W. *Explore a spooky swamp*
Cousins, Lucy. *Portly's hat*
Cristini, Ermanno. *In the woods*

Cross, Diana Harding. *Some birds have
funny names*
Cross, Genevieve. *A trip to the yard*
Cutler, Ivor. *Doris*
Dalmais, Anne-Marie. *The butterfly book of
birds*
Damjan, Mischa. *Goodbye little bird*
Darby, Gene. *What is a bird?*
Demarest, Chris L. *Benedict finds a home*
De Paola, Tomie (Thomas Anthony). *Bill
and Pete go down the Nile*
Dobson, Clive. *Fred's TV*
Eastman, P. D. (Philip D.). *Are you my
mother?*
Flap your wings
Elborn, Andrew. *Bird Adalbert*
Elzbieta. *Brave Babette and sly Tom*
Fender, Kay. *Odette!*
Fisher, Aileen Lucia. *We went looking*
Fitzsimons, Cecilia. *My first birds*
Flanders, Michael. *Creatures great and small*
Flora. *Feathers like a rainbow*
Fowler, Allan. *It could still be a bird*
Freeman, Don. *Fly high, fly low*
French, Fiona. *The blue bird*
Freschet, Berniece. *The little woodcock*
Owl in the garden
Friskey, Margaret (Margaret Richards).
Birds we know
Fujita, Tamao. *The boy and the bird*
Gans, Roma. *Hummingbirds in the garden*
When birds change their feathers
Givens, Janet Eaton. *Just two wings*
Goble, Paul. *The great race: of the birds and
animals*
Greeley, Valerie. *Where's my share?*
Grimm, Jacob. *The bear and the kingbird*,
ill. by Chris Conover
Hader, Berta Hoerner. *Mister Billy's gun*
Hautzig, Deborah. *Get well, Granny Bird*
Hawkinson, Lucy. *Birds in the sky*
Helweg, Hans. *Farm animals*
Hirschi, Ron. *What is a bird?*
Where do birds live?
Who lives in... the forest?
Hoban, Tana. *A children's zoo*
Hubbard, Woodleigh. *Two is for dancing*
Hurd, Edith Thacher. *Look for a bird*
Ipcar, Dahlov. *Bright barnyard*
*"The song of the day birds" and "The song
of the night birds"*
John, Naomi. *Roadrunner*
Kamal, Aleph. *The bird who was an elephant*
Kantrowitz, Mildred. *When Violet died*
Kasza, Keiko. *A mother for Choco*
Kaufmann, John. *Birds are flying*
Flying giants of long ago
Kellogg, Steven (Stephen). *Aster Aardvark's
alphabet adventures*
Kishida, Eriko. *The lion and the bird's nest*
Kleven, Elisa. *The lion and the little red bird*

Krauss, Ruth. *The happy egg*
Kuchalla, Susan. *Birds*
Kumin, Maxine. *Mittens in May*
Lifton, Betty Jean. *Joji and the Amanojaku*
 Joji and the dragon
 Joji and the fog
Lionni, Leo. *Inch by inch*
 Tico and the golden wings
Lubell, Winifred. *Rosalie, the bird market turtle*
Lyfick, Warren. *The little book of fowl jokes*
McCauley, Jane. *Baby birds and how they grow*
McLerran, Alice. *The mountain that loved a bird*
McPhail, David. *Farm morning*
Marshak, Samuel. *The merry starlings*
Martchenko, Michael. *Bird feeder banquet*
Massie, Diane Redfield. *The baby beebee bird*
Mayer, Marianna. *The little jewel box*
Mayer, Mercer. *Two moral tales*
Meddaugh, Susan. *Tree of birds*
Millhouse, Nicholas. *Blue-footed booby*
Mollel, Tolowa M. *A promise to the sun*
Most, Bernard. *Zoodles*
Munari, Bruno. *Bruno Munari's zoo*
 Tic, Tac and Toc
Nesbit, Edith. *Cockatoucan*
Ness, Evaline. *Pavo and the princess*
Norman, Charles. *The hornbean tree and other poems*
Oana, Kay D. *Robbie and the raggedy scarecrow*
O Huigin, Sean. *King of the birds*
Olds, Elizabeth. *Feather mountain*
Oppenheim, Joanne. *Have you seen birds?*
Parnall, Peter. *Alfalfa Hill*
Parsons, Alexandra. *Amazing birds*
Pearson, Susan. *Lenore's big break*
Pedersen, Judy. *The tiny patient*
Peet, Bill (William Bartlett). *The kweeks of Kookatumdee*
 The pinkish, purplish, bluish egg
Pirotta, Saviour. *Little bird*
Pomerantz, Charlotte. *Flap your wings and try*
Postgate, Oliver. *Noggin the king*
Potter, Beatrix. *The tale of Jemima Puddle-Duck and other farmyard tales*
Rockwell, Anne F. *Honk honk!*
 Our yard is full of birds
Rose, Gerald. *The bird garden*
Rossetti, Christina Georgina. *Fly away, fly away over the sea*, ill. by Bernadette Watts
Schumacher, Claire. *Alto and Tango*
Seidler, Rosalie. *Grumpus and the Venetian cat*
Selsam, Millicent E. *A first look at bird nests*

 A first look at owls, eagles and other hunters of the sky
Seuss, Dr. *Horton hatches the egg*
 Thidwick, the big-hearted moose
Sis, Peter. *Rainbow Rhino*
Smith, Lane. *Flying Jake*
Smith, William Jay. *Birds and beasts*
Snoopy on wheels
Stage, Mads. *The greedy blackbird*
Stanley, Diane. *Birdsong lullaby*
Stone, A. Harris. *The last free bird*
Taylor, Sydney. *Mr. Barney's beard*
Troughton, Joanna. *How the birds changed their feathers*
 The quail's egg
Tusa, Tricia. *Maebelle's suitcase*
Van Laan, Nancy. *The big fat worm*
Varley, Dimitry. *The whirly bird*
Velthuijs, Max. *The painter and the bird*
Vyner, Sue. *The stolen egg*
Waechter, Friedrich Karl. *Three is company*
Walsh, Grahame L. *The goori goori bird*
Watts, Barrie. *Bird's nest*
Weatherill, Stephen. *The very first Lucy Goose book*
West, Colin. *Have you seen the crocodile?*
Wezel, Peter. *The good bird*
 The naughty bird
Wildsmith, Brian. *Brian Wildsmith's birds*
Williams, Julie Stewart. *And the birds appeared*
Wolff, Ashley. *A year of birds*
Wood, A. J. *Beautiful birds*
Wood, Audrey. *Little Penguin's tale*
Yolen, Jane. *Spider Jane*
Yoshida, Toshi. *Rhinoceros mother*
Ziefert, Harriet. *Happy Easter, Grandma!*
Zirkel, Lynn. *The shell dragon*
Zolotow, Charlotte (Shapiro). *Flocks of birds*

Birds – albatrosses

Hoff, Syd. *Albert the albatross*

Birds – blackbirds

Duff, Maggie (Margaret K.). *Rum pum pum*

Birds – bluejays

Angelo, Valenti. *The acorn tree*
Margolis, Richard J. *Big bear, spare that tree*
Newton, Patricia Montgomery. *The frog who drank the waters of the world*

Birds – buzzards

Sandburg, Helga. *Anna and the baby buzzard*
Wolkstein, Diane. *The cool ride in the sky*

Birds – canaries

Foreman, Michael. *Cat and canary*
Freeman, Don. *Quiet! There's a canary in the library*
Heller, Wendy. *Clementine and the cage*
Nones, Eric Jon. *Canary prince*

Birds – cardinals

Galinsky, Ellen. *The baby cardinal*

Birds – chickens

Allard, Harry. *I will not go to market today*
Allen, Pamela. *Fancy that!*
Ambrus, Victor G. *The little cockerel*
Auch, Mary Jane. *The Easter egg farm*
Aulaire, Ingri Mortenson d'. *Don't count your chicks*
  Foxie, the singing dog
Back, Christine. *Chicken and egg*
Barbot, Daniel. *A bicycle for Rosaura*
Belpré, Pura. *Santiago*
Berquist, Grace. *Speckles goes to school*
Bishop, Adela. *The Easter wolf*
Bishop, Ann. *Chicken riddle*
Bond, Felicia. *Christmas in the chicken coop*
Boreman, Jean. *Bantie and her chicks*
Bourgeois, Paulette. *Too many chickens*
Bourke, Linda. *Ethel's exceptional egg*
Boutwell, Edna. *Red rooster*
Brothers, Aileen. *Jiffy, Miss Boo and Mr. Roo*
Brown, Margaret Wise. *Little chicken*
Burton, Jane. *Chester the chick*
  Chick
Carle, Eric. *The rooster who set out to see the world*
  Rooster's off to see the world
Casey, Patricia. *Quack quack*
Cazet, Denys. *Lucky me*
Chaucer, Geoffrey. *Chanticleer and the fox*, ill. by Barbara Cooney
Chicken Little. *Chicken Licken*, ill. by Jutta Ash
  Chicken Licken, ill. by Gavin Bishop
  Henny Penny, ill. by Stephen Butler
  Henny Penny, ill. by Paul Galdone
  Henny Penny, ill. by William Stobbs
  The story of Chicken Licken, adapt. and ill. by Jan Ormerod
Chukovsky, Korney. *Good morning, chick*
Coerr, Eleanor. *The Josefina story quilt*
Coldrey, Jennifer. *The world of chickens*
Cole, Joanna. *A chick hatches*
Cousins, Lucy. *Hen on the farm*
Dabcovich, Lydia. *Mrs. Huggins and her hen Hannah*
Delaney, Ned. *Cosmic chickens*
Denslow, Sharon Phillips. *Hazel's circle*
Dodds, Siobhan. *Elizabeth Hen*
Dumas, Philippe. *Caesar, cock of the village*

Dutton, Sandra. *The cinnamon hen's autumn day*
Edwards, Dorothy. *A wet Monday*
Edwards, Michelle. *Chicken man*
Ehrhardt, Reinhold. *Kikeri: or, The proud red rooster*
Ernst, Lisa Campbell. *Zinnia and Dot*
Fatio, Louise. *The red bantam*
Firmin, Peter. *Chicken stew*
Fox, Mem. *Hattie and the fox*
Freschet, Berniece. *Where's Henrietta's hen?*
Froissart, Bénédicte. *Uncle Henry's dinner guests*
Ginsburg, Mirra. *Across the stream*
  The chick and the duckling
The golden goose, ill. by William Stobbs
Hader, Berta Hoerner. *Cock-a-doodle doo*
Hariton, Anca. *Egg story*
Hartelius, Margaret A. *The chicken's child*
Heine, Helme. *Mollywoop*
  The most wonderful egg in the world
  Three little friends: the alarm clock
  Three little friends: the racing cart
  Three little friends: the visitor
Hille-Brandts, Lene. *The little black hen*
Hoban, Julia. *Quick chick*
Hoff, Syd. *Happy birthday, Henrietta!*
  Henrietta, circus star
  Henrietta goes to the fair
  Henrietta, the early bird
  Henrietta's Halloween
  Merry Christmas, Henrietta!
Houselander, Caryll. *Petook*
Hutchins, Pat. *Rosie's walk*
Isami, Ikuyo. *The fox's egg*
Jackson, Jacqueline. *Chicken ten thousand*
Jaynes, Ruth M. *Three baby chicks*
Kasza, Keiko. *The wolf's chicken stew*
Kellogg, Steven (Stephen). *Chicken Little*
Kent, Jack. *Little Peep*
Kepes, Juliet. *Cock-a-doodle-doo*
Kwitz, Mary DeBall. *Little chick's breakfast*
  Little chick's story
Landa, Norbert. *Rabbit and chicken find a box*
  Rabbit and chicken play hide and seek
Lane, Megan Halsey. *Something to crow about*
Lester, Helen. *The revenge of the magic chicken*
  The wizard, the fairy and the magic chicken
Lexau, Joan M. *Crocodile and hen*
Lifton, Betty Jean. *The many lives of Chio and Goro*
Lindman, Maj. *Flicka, Ricka, Dicka and the big red hen*
Lipkind, William. *The little tiny rooster*
The little red hen. The cock, the mouse and the little red hen, ill. by Graham Percy

The little red hen, ill. by Janina
  Domanska
The little red hen, ill. by Paul Galdone
The little red hen, ill. by Mel Pekarsky
The little red hen, ill. by William Stobbs
The little red hen, ill. by Margot Zemach
Little Tuppen, ill. by Paul Galdone
Littlefield, William. *The whiskers of Ho Ho*
Lloyd, Megan. *Chicken tricks*
Lobel, Anita. *King Rooster, Queen Hen*
Lobel, Arnold. *How the rooster saved the day*
Luttrell, Ida. *Mattie and the chicken thief*
McConnachie, Brian. *Elmer and the chickens
  vs. the big league*
McCrea, Lilian. *Mother hen*
McCue, Lisa. *The little chick*
McKelvey, David. *Bobby the mostly silky*
McKissack, Patricia C. *The little red hen*
Marshall, James. *Wings: a tale of two
  chickens*
Mathers, Petra. *Maria Theresa*
Mathews, Louise. *Cluck one*
Miles, Miska. *Chicken forgets*
Murphey, Sara. *The animal hat shop*
Myers, Bernice. *The millionth egg*
Oakley, Graham. *Hetty and Harriet*
O'Neill, Mary. *Big red hen*
Otto, Margaret Glover. *The little brown
  horse*
Peet, Bill (William Bartlett). *Cock-a-doodle
  Dudley*
Polushkin, Maria. *The little hen and the
  giant*
Provensen, Alice. *My little hen*
Pursell, Margaret Sanford. *Jessie the chicken*
Ravilious, Robin. *The runaway chick*
Rockwell, Anne F. *The wonderful eggs of
  Furicchia*
Roddie, Shen. *Hatch, egg, hatch!*
Ross, Tony. *Stone soup*
Royston, Angela. *The hen*
Rubel, Nicole. *Goldie*
  Goldie's nap
Scarry, Richard. *Egg in the hole*
Scheffler, Ursel. *Stop your crowing, Kasimir!*
Selsam, Millicent E. *Egg to chick*
Sharmat, Marjorie Weinman. *Hooray for
  Mother's Day!*
Sherman, Nancy. *Gwendolyn and the
  weathercock*
  Gwendolyn the miracle hen
Sondergaard, Arensa. *Biddy and the ducks*
Stoeke, Janet Morgan. *Minerva Louise*
Threadgall, Colin. *Proud rooster and the fox*
*The three little pigs. The three little pigs
  and the fox*, ill. by S. D. Schindler
Tripp, Valerie. *Sillyhen's big surprise*
Tusa, Tricia. *Chicken*
Van Horn, Grace. *Little red rooster*
Van Woerkom, Dorothy. *Something to crow
  about*

Voake, Charlotte. *Mrs. Goose's baby*
Waber, Bernard. *How to go about laying an
  egg*
Walton, Rick. *Dumb clucks!*
Weil, Lisl. *Gillie and the flattering fox*
Weiss, Ellen. *Clara the fortune-telling chicken*
Williams, Garth. *The chicken book*
Willis, Val. *Silly little chick*

Birds – cockatoos

Cummings, W. T. (Walter Thies). *Wickford
  of Beacon Hill*
Pershall, Mary K. *Hello, Barney!*

Birds – cormorants

Bunting, Eve (Anne Evelyn). *Magic and
  the night river*

Birds – cranes

Bang, Molly. *Dawn*
  The paper crane
Laurin, Anne. *Perfect crane*
The peasant's pea patch, ill. by Robert M.
  Quackenbush
Yagawa, Sumiko. *The crane wife*

Birds – crows

DeLage, Ida. *The old witch and the crows*
Frascino, Edward. *Nanny Noony and the
  magic spell*
Freeman, Don. *Cyrano the crow*
Gage, Wilson. *The crow and Mrs. Gaddy*
Goble, Paul. *Crow chief*
Greenstein, Elaine. *Emily and the crows*
Guy, Ginger Foglesong. *Black crow, black
  crow*
Harsh, Fred. *Alfie*
Hazelton, Elizabeth Baldwin. *Sammy, the
  crow who remembered*
Holder, Heidi. *Carmine the crow*
  Crows
Hyman, Robin. *Casper and the rainbow bird*
Latimer, Jim. *James Bear's pie*
Lionni, Leo. *Six crows*
Oppenheim, Joanne. *"Not now!" said the
  cow*
Van Laan, Nancy. *Rainbow crow*

Birds – cuckoos

Corbalis, Judy. *The cuckoo bird*

Birds – dodos

Lehan, Daniel. *This is not a book about
  dodos*

Birds – doves

Æsop. *The ant and the dove*, ill. by Ching
Agostinelli, Maria Enrica. *On wings of love*

Alexander, Martha G. *The magic hat*
Baker, Keith. *The dove's letter*
Freeman, Don. *The turtle and the dove*
Peet, Bill (William Bartlett). *The pinkish, purplish, bluish egg*
Potter, Beatrix. *The tale of the faithful dove*
Sage, James. *The boy and the dove*
Singer, Isaac Bashevis. *Why Noah chose the dove*
Wolff, Ashley. *The bells of London*

Birds – ducks

Allen, Jeffrey. *Mary Alice, operator number 9*
Mary Alice returns
Andersen, H. C. (Hans Christian). *The ugly duckling*, ill. by Adrienne Adams
The ugly duckling, ill. by Lorinda Bryan Cauley
The ugly duckling, ill. by Troy Howell
The ugly duckling, ill. by Tadasu Izawa and Shigemi Hijikata
The ugly duckling, ill. by Monika Laimgruber
The ugly duckling, ill. by Johannes Larsen
The ugly duckling, ill. by Thomas Locker
The ugly duckling, ill. by Alan Marks
The ugly duckling, ill. by Josef Paleček
The ugly duckling, ill. by Daniel San Souci
The ugly duckling, ill. by Robert Van Nutt
The ugly little duck, ill. by Peggy Perry Anderson
Barnhart, Peter. *The wounded duck*
Blocksma, Mary. *Where's that duck?*
Bothwell, Jean. *Paddy and Sam*
Boyd, Lizi. *The not-so-wicked stepmother*
Brown, Margaret Wise. *The duck*
The golden egg book
Bunting, Eve (Anne Evelyn). *Happy birthday, dear duck*
Burton, Jane. *Dabble the duckling*
Casey, Patricia. *Quack quack*
Cazet, Denys. *The duck with squeaky feet*
Coats, Laura Jane. *Marcella and the moon*
Conover, Chris. *Six little ducks*
Delton, Judy. *Bear and Duck on the run*
Duck goes fishing
The elephant in Duck's garden
A pet for Duck and Bear
Three friends find spring
Demi. *Little lucky ducky*
Dunn, Judy. *The little duck*
Duvoisin, Roger Antoine. *Two lonely ducks*
Ellis, Anne Leo. *Dabble Duck*
Flack, Marjorie. *Angus and the ducks*
The story about Ping
Freschet, Berniece. *Wood duck baby*

Fribourg, Marjorie G. *Ching-Ting and the ducks*
Friskey, Margaret (Margaret Richards). *Seven diving ducks*
Garland, Sarah. *Having a picnic*
Georgiady, Nicholas P. *Gertie the duck*
Gerstein, Mordicai. *Follow me!*
Gibson, Betty. *The story of Little Quack*
Ginsburg, Mirra. *Across the stream*
The chick and the duckling
Goldin, Augusta. *Ducks don't get wet*
Gordon, Gaelyn. *Duckat*
Gretz, Susanna. *Duck takes off*
Grimm, Jacob. *The ugly duckling*, ill. by Maria Ruis
Hader, Berta Hoerner. *Cock-a-doodle doo*
Hayes, Sarah. *Nine ducks nine*
Hillert, Margaret. *The funny baby*
Hurd, Edith Thacher. *Last one home is a green pig*
Ichikawa, Satomi. *Nora's duck*
Isenbart, Hans-Heinrich. *A duckling is born*
Janice. *Angélique*
Joyce, William. *Bently and egg*
Kepes, Juliet. *The story of a bragging duck*
Laird, Elizabeth. *The day the ducks went skating*
Leverich, Kathleen. *The hungry fox and the foxy duck*
Lloyd, David. *Duck*
Lorenz, Lee. *A weekend in the country*
Lunn, Janet. *Duck cakes for sale*
McCloskey, Robert. *Make way for ducklings*
Mamin-Sibiryak, D. N. *Grey Neck*
Miles, Miska. *Noisy gander*
Moore, Sheila. *Samson Svenson's baby*
Otto, Carolyn. *Ducks, ducks, ducks*
Paterson, Katherine. *The tale of the Mandarin ducks*
Pizer, Abigail. *Percy the duck*
Pomerantz, Charlotte. *One duck, another duck*
Potter, Beatrix. *The tale of Jemima Puddle-Duck*
Quackenbush, Robert M. *Henry babysits*
Richter, Mischa. *Eric and Matilda*
Quack?
Roy, Ronald. *Three ducks went wandering*
Saunders, Dave. *Snowtime*
Scamell, Ragnhild. *Solo plus one*
Schroeder, Binette. *Tuffa and the ducks*
Scruton, Clive. *Bubble and squeak*
Seignobosc, Françoise. *Springtime for Jeanne-Marie*
Sewell, Helen Moore. *Blue barns*
Shaw, Evelyn S. *Nest of wood ducks*
Sheehan, Angela. *The duck*
Smith, Mavis. *Fred, is that you?*
Sondergaard, Arensa. *Biddy and the ducks*
Spier, Peter. *Little ducks*
Standon, Anna. *Little duck lost*

Stehr, Frédéric. *Quack-quack*
Stevenson, James. *Howard*
 Monty
Stott, Dorothy. *Little Duck's bicycle ride*
 Too much
Szekeres, Cyndy. *Hide-and-seek duck*
Tafuri, Nancy. *Have you seen my duckling?*
Thiele, Colin. *Farmer Schulz's ducks*
Tryon, Leslie. *Albert's alphabet*
Tudor, Bethany. *Samuel's tree house*
 Skiddycock Pond
Turska, Krystyna. *The woodcutter's duck*
Velthuijs, Max. *Frog in love*
Waddell, Martin. *Farmer Duck*
Wahl, Jan. *Old Hippo's Easter egg*
Watts, Barrie. *Duck*
Wellington, Monica. *All my little ducklings*
Wijngaard, Juan. *Duck*
Wildsmith, Brian. *The little wood duck*
Winthrop, Elizabeth. *Bear and Mrs. Duck*
 Bear's Christmas surprise
Withers, Carl. *The wild ducks and the goose*
Wright, Dare. *Edith and the duckling*

Birds – eagles

Foreman, Michael. *Moose*
Klinting, Lars. *Regal the golden eagle*
Melville, Herman. *Catskill eagle*

Birds – egrets

Carlson, Natalie Savage. *Time for the white egret*

Birds – flamingos

McCloskey, Kevin. *Mrs. Fitz's flamingos*
Rossetti, Christina Georgina. *What is pink?*
Zoll, Max Alfred. *A flamingo is born*

Birds – geese

Asch, Frank. *MacGooses's grocery*
Bacheller, Irving. *Lost in the fog*
Brenner, Barbara A. *Good news*
Brown, Marc Tolon. *Moose and goose*
Bunting, Eve (Anne Evelyn). *Goose dinner*
Burningham, John. *Borka*
Cauley, Lorinda Bryan. *The goose and the golden coins*
Chandoha, Walter. *A baby goose for you*
Conover, Chris. *Mother Goose and the sly fox*
Day, Betsy. *Stefan and Olga*
Deedy, Carmen Agra. *Agatha's feather bed*
Delton, Judy. *On a picnic*
Duvoisin, Roger Antoine. *Petunia*
 Petunia and the song
 Petunia, beware!
 Petunia, I love you
 Petunia takes a trip
 Petunia, the silly goose
 Petunia's Christmas
 Petunia's treasure
Freeman, Don. *Will's quill*
Galdone, Joanna. *Gertrude, the goose who forgot*
George, Lindsay Barrett. *William and Boomer*
Holmes, Efner Tudor. *Amy's goose*
Houston, James. *Kiviok's magic journey*
Illyés, Gyula. *Matt the gooseherd*
Kalas, Sybille. *The goose family book*
Kent, Jack. *Silly goose*
Koch, Dorothy Clarke. *Gone is my goose*
Lasell, Fen. *Fly away goose*
Le Tord, Bijou. *Good wood bear*
Lindbergh, Reeve. *The day the goose got loose*
Low, Joseph. *Benny rabbit and the owl*
 Boo to a goose
Mother Goose. *The golden goose book*, ill. by L. Leslie Brooke
Pizer, Abigail. *Nosey Gilbert*
Polacco, Patricia. *Rechenka's eggs*
Preston, Edna Mitchell. *Squawk to the moon, little goose*
Rockwell, Anne F. *Poor Goose*
Ryder, Joanne. *Catching the wind*
Saunders, Dave. *Snowtime*
Sewell, Helen Moore. *Blue barns*
Voake, Charlotte. *Mrs. Goose's baby*
Walsh, Ellen Stoll. *You silly goose*
Weatherill, Stephen. *The very first Lucy Goose book*
Zijlstra, Tjerk. *Benny and his geese*

Birds – guinea fowl

Knutson, Barbara. *How the guinea fowl got her spots*

Birds – hawks

Baylor, Byrd. *Hawk, I'm your brother*
Bliss, Corinne Demas. *Matthew's meadow*

Birds – hornbills

Shepard, Steve. *Elvis Hornbill, international business bird*

Birds – humming birds

Ryder, Joanne. *Dancers in the garden*

Birds – loons

Hirschi, Ron. *Loon lake*

Birds – mockingbirds

Ryder, Joanne. *Mockingbird morning*

Birds – nightingales

Andersen, H. C. (Hans Christian). *The*

emperor and the nightingale, ill. by James Watling
The emperor's nightingale, ill. from the Disney arcives
The emperor's nightingale, ill. by Georges Lemoine
The nightingale, ill. by Harold Berson
The nightingale, ill. by Nancy Ekholm Burkert
The nightingale, ill. by Demi
The nightingale, ill. by Alison Claire Darke
The nightingale, ill. by Beni Montresor
The nightingale, ill. by Josef Paleček
The nightingale, ill. by Regolo Ricci
The nightingale, ill. by Lisbeth Zwerger
Chase, Catherine. *The nightingale and the fool*

Birds – ostriches

Burton, Marilee Robin. *Oliver's birthday*
Delton, Judy. *Penny wise, fun foolish*
Peet, Bill (William Bartlett). *Zella, Zack, and Zodiac*
Ylla. *Look who's talking*

Birds – owls

Bennett, Rainey. *After the sun goes down*
Boyle, Constance. *The story of little owl*
Bunting, Eve (Anne Evelyn). *The man who could call down owls*
Burton, Jane. *Buffy the barn owl*
Carey, Mary. *The owl who loved sunshine*
Cresswell, Helen. *Two hoots and the king*
Two hoots in the snow
DeLage, Ida. *The old witch and the crows*
Delton, Judy. *Duck goes fishing*
Dowling, Paul. *Happy birthday, Owl*
Duvoisin, Roger Antoine. *Day and night*
Eastman, P. D. (Philip D.). *Sam and the firefly*
Flower, Phyllis. *Barn owl*
Foster, Doris Van Liew. *Tell me, Mr. Owl*
Freschet, Berniece. *Owl in the garden*
Funazaki, Yasuko. *Baby owl*
Gantschev, Ivan. *Where is Mr. Mole?*
Goodenow, Earle. *The owl who hated the dark*
Harshman, Terry Webb. *Porcupine's pajama party*
Hoban, Russell. *Charlie Meadows*
Hoopes, Lyn Littlefield. *My own home*
Hutchins, Pat. *Good night owl*
Kirn, Ann. *I spy*
Kraus, Robert. *Owliver*
Lear, Edward. *The owl and the pussycat*, ill. by Jan Brett
The owl and the pussycat, ill. by Lorinda Bryan Cauley

The owl and the pussy-cat, ill. by Barbara Cooney
The owl and the pussycat, ill. by Emma Crosby
The owl and the pussy-cat, ill. by William Pène Du Bois
The owl and the pussycat, ill. by Lori Farbanish
The owl and the pussy-cat, ill. by Gwen Fulton
The owl and the pussycat, ill. by Paul Galdone
The owl and the pussy-cat, ill. by Elaine Muis
The owl and the pussycat, ill. by Erica Rutherford
The owl and the pussycat, ill. by Janet Stevens
The owl and the pussycat, ill. by Louise Voce
The owl and the pussycat, ill. by Colin West
The owl and the pussy-cat, ill. by Owen Wood
Leonard, Marcia. *Little owl leaves the nest*
Lionni, Leo. *Six crows*
Lobel, Arnold. *Owl at home*
McDonald, Megan. *Whoo-oo is it?*
McGuire, Leslie. *Baby night owl*
McKeever, Katherine. *A family for Minerva*
Maschler, Fay. *T. G. and Moonie go shopping*
T. G. and Moonie have a baby
T. G. and Moonie move out of town
Nicoll, Helen. *Meg at sea*
Meg's eggs
Norman, Howard. *The owl-scatterer*
Panek, Dennis. *Detective Whoo*
Pfister, Marcus. *The sleepy owl*
Piatti, Celestino. *The happy owls*
Potter, Beatrix. *The tale of Squirrel Nutkin*
Schären, Beatrix. *Tillo*
Schoenherr, John. *The barn*
Shles, Larry. *Moths and mothers, feathers and fathers*
Slobodkin, Louis. *Wide-awake owl*
Smith, Jim. *The frog band and the owlnapper*
Tejima, Keizaburo. *Owl lake*
Thaler, Mike. *Owley*
Tompert, Ann. *Badger on his own*
Wahl, Jan. *Mrs. Owl and Mr. Pig*
Wildsmith, Brian. *The owl and the woodpecker*
Yolen, Jane. *Owl moon*

Birds – parakeets, parrots

Augarde, Steve (Stephen). *Barnaby Shrew, Black Dan and...the mighty wedgwood*
Banchek, Linda. *Snake in, snake out*
Baum, Louis. *JuJu and the pirate*
Bishop, Bonnie. *No one noticed Ralph*

Ralph rides away
Blegvad, Lenore. *The parrot in the garret and other rhymes about dwellings*
Bradford, Ann. *The mystery of the tree house*
Cressey, James. *Pet parrot*
Demuth, Patricia Brennan. *Max, the bad-talking parrot*
Dragonwagon, Crescent. *Coconut*
Gordon, Sharon. *Pete the parakeet*
Graham, Bob. *Pete and Roland*
Graham, Margaret Bloy. *Benjy and the barking bird*
Hamsa, Bobbie. *Polly wants a cracker*
Holman, Felice. *Victoria's castle*
Hyman, Robin. *Casper and the rainbow bird*
Johnston, Tony. *Lorenzo the naughty parrot*
McDermott, Gerald. *Papagayo, the mischief maker*
Mahy, Margaret. *The horrendous hullabaloo*
Potter, Stephen. *Squawky, the adventures of a clasperchoice*
Remkiewicz, Frank. *The last time I saw Harris*
Zacharias, Thomas. *But where is the green parrot?*
Zusman, Evelyn. *The Passover parrot*

Birds – peacocks, peahens

Alan, Sandy. *The plaid peacock*
Daniel, Doris Temple. *Pauline and the peacock*
Hamberger, John. *The peacock who lost his tail*
Kepes, Juliet. *The seed that peacock planted*
Peet, Bill (William Bartlett). *The spooky tail of Prewitt Peacock*
Polacco, Patricia. *Just plain Fancy*
Wittman, Sally. *Pelly and Peak*
Plenty of Pelly and Peak

Birds – pelicans

Benchley, Nathaniel. *The flying lessons of Gerald Pelican*
Crane, Alan. *Pepita bonita*
Freeman, Don. *Come again, pelican*
Hewett, Joan. *Fly away free*
Jenkin-Pearce, Susie. *Percy Short and Cuthbert*
Lear, Edward. *The pelican chorus*, ill. by Harold Berson
The pelican chorus and the quangle wangle's hat, ill. by Kevin W. Maddison
O'Reilly, Edward. *Brown pelican at the pond*
Patz, Nancy. *To Annabella Pelican from Thomas Hippopotamus*
Wildsmith, Brian. *Pelican*
Wittman, Sally. *Pelly and Peak*
Plenty of Pelly and Peak

Birds – penguins

Benson, Patrick. *Little penguin*
Breathed, Berkeley. *A wish for wings that work*
Bright, Robert. *Which is Willy?*
Coldrey, Jennifer. *Penguins*
Cousins, Lucy. *Portly's hat*
Fatio, Louise. *Hector and Christina Hector penguin*
Gay, Michel. *Bibi takes flight Bibi's birthday surprise*
Hamsa, Bobbie. *Your pet penguin*
Hogan, Paula Z. *The penguin*
Howe, Caroline Walton. *Counting penguins*
Johnston, Johanna. *Penguin's way*
Lester, Helen. *Tacky the penguin*
Lilly, Kenneth. *Animals of the ocean*
Mitra, Annie. *Penguin moon*
Nichols, Cathy. *Tuxedo Sam*
The penguin, ill. by Norman Weaver
Rigby, Rodney. *Hello, this is your penguin speaking*
Sheehan, Angela. *The penguin*
Somme, Lauritz. *The penguin family book*
Stevenson, James. *Winston, Newton, Elton, and Ed*
Weiss, Leatie. *Funny feet!*
Winteringham, Victoria. *Penguin day*
Wood, Audrey. *Little Penguin's tale*

Birds – pigeons

Baker, Jeannie. *Home in the sky Millicent*
Benchley, Nathaniel. *Walter the homing pigeon*
Kingman, Lee. *Pierre Pigeon*
McClure, Gillian. *Fly home McDoo*
Peet, Bill (William Bartlett). *Fly, Homer, fly*
Shulman, Milton. *Prep, the little pigeon of Trafalgar Square*
Suben, Eric. *Pigeon takes a trip*

Birds – puffins

Drew, Patricia. *Spotter Puff*
Hall, Pam. *On the edge of the eastern ocean*
Lawson, Annetta. *The lucky yak*
Lewis, Naomi. *Puffin*

Birds – ravens

Æsop. *The raven and the fox*, ill. by Gerald Rose
Aiken, Joan. *Arabel and Mortimer*
Dixon, Ann. *How raven brought light to people*
Grimm, Jacob. *The seven ravens*, ill. by Felix Hoffmann
The seven ravens, ill. by Lisbeth Zwerger

Birds – robins

Calder, S. J. *If you were a bird*
Cock Robin. *The courtship, merry marriage, and feast of Cock Robin and Jenny Wren*, ill. by Barbara Cooney
Who killed Cock Robin? ill. by William Stobbs
Flack, Marjorie. *The restless robin*
Hawkinson, John. *Robins and rabbits*
Kent, Jack. *Round Robin*
Kraus, Robert. *The first robin*
Rockwell, Anne F. *My spring robin*
Stern, Elsie-Jean. *Wee Robin's Christmas song*
Tresselt, Alvin R. *Hi, Mister Robin*

Birds – sandpipers

Hurd, Edith Thacher. *Sandpipers*
Mendoza, George. *The scribbler*

Birds – sea gulls

Armitage, Ronda. *The lighthouse keeper's lunch*
Carrick, Carol. *Beach bird*
Duvoisin, Roger Antoine. *Snowy and Woody*
Ness, Evaline. *Do you have the time, Lydia?*
Pursell, Margaret Sanford. *Shelley the sea gull*
Turkle, Brinton. *Thy friend, Obadiah*

Birds – sparrows

Crabtree, Judith. *The sparrow's story at the king's command*
Fregosi, Claudia. *The pumpkin sparrow*
Gerstein, Mordicai. *Prince Sparrow*
Ishii, Momoko. *The tongue-cut sparrow*
Ostheeren, Ingrid. *Jonathan Mouse and the baby bird*
Selden, George. *Sparrow socks*
Wallace, Ian. *The sparrow's song*

Birds – spoonbills

Guiberson, Brenda Z. *Spoonbill swamp*

Birds – storks

Berliner, Franz. *Miserable Marabou*
Bos, Burny. *Prince Valentino*
Brown, Margaret Wise. *Wheel on the chimney*
Gantschev, Ivan. *Journey of the storks*

Birds – swallows

Politi, Leo. *Song of the swallows*

Birds – swans

Andersen, H. C. (Hans Christian). *The ugly duckling*, ill. by Adrienne Adams
The ugly duckling, ill. by Lorinda Bryan Cauley
The ugly duckling, ill. by Troy Howell
The ugly duckling, ill. by Tadasu Izawa and Shigemi Hijikata
The ugly duckling, ill. by Monika Laimgruber
The ugly duckling, ill. by Johannes Larsen
The ugly duckling, ill. by Thomas Locker
The ugly duckling, ill. by Alan Marks
The ugly duckling, ill. by Josef Paleček
The ugly duckling, ill. by Daniel San Souci
The ugly duckling, ill. by Robert Van Nutt
The ugly little duck, ill. by Peggy Perry Anderson
The wild swans, ill. by Angela Barrett
The wild swans, ill. by Susan Jeffers
Auer, Martin. *Now, now Markus*
Bell, Anthea. *Swan Lake*
Canfield, Jane White. *Swan cove*
Clement, Claude. *The painter and the wild swans*
Day, David. *The swan children*
DeChristopher, Marlowe. *Greencoat and the swanboy*
Grimm, Jacob. *The six swans*, ill. by Daniel San Souci
The six swans, ill. by Margot Tomes
The ugly duckling, ill. by Maria Ruis
Hillert, Margaret. *The funny baby*
Hogan, Paula Z. *The black swan*
Lewis, Naomi. *Swan*
Tejima, Keizaburo. *Swan sky*
Willington, Monica. *Seasons of swans*

Birds – toucans

McKee, David. *Two can toucan*

Birds – turkeys

Balian, Lorna. *Sometimes it's turkey*
Bunting, Eve (Anne Evelyn). *A turkey for Thanksgiving*
Kroll, Steven. *One tough turkey*
Pilkey, Dav. *'Twas the night before Thanksgiving*
Schatell, Brian. *Farmer Goff and his turkey Sam*
Sam's no dummy, Farmer Goff
Wickstrom, Sylvie (Sylvie Kantrovitz). *Turkey on the loose!*

Birds – vultures

Duvoisin, Roger Antoine. *Petunia, I love you*
Peet, Bill (William Bartlett). *Eli*
Ungerer, Tomi. *Orlando, the brave vulture*
Wolkstein, Diane. *The cool ride in the sky*

Birds – woodpeckers

Tejima, Keizaburo. *Woodpecker forest*
Wildsmith, Brian. *The owl and the woodpecker*

Birds – wrens

Brock, Emma Lillian. *Mr. Wren's house*
Cock Robin. *The courtship, merry marriage, and feast of Cock Robin and Jenny Wren*, ill. by Barbara Cooney
Who killed Cock Robin? ill. by William Stobbs
Ravilious, Robin. *Two in a pocket*

Birth

Andry, Andrew C. *Hi, new baby*
 How babies are made
Baker, Gayle. *Special delivery*
Brooks, Robert B. *So that's how I was born*
Burton, Jane. *Chick*
 Kitten
 Puppy
Carrick, Carol. *In the moonlight, waiting*
Christenson, Larry. *The wonderful way that babies are made*
Cole, Joanna. *A calf is born*
 How you were born
 My puppy is born
Corrin, Ruth. *Mister cat*
Dahl, Tessa. *Babies, babies, babies*
Fischer-Nagel, Heiderose. *A kitten is born*
 A puppy is born
Frasier, Debra. *On the day you were born*
Girard, Linda Walvoord. *You were born on your very first birthday*
Gliori, Debi. *New big sister*
Hariton, Anca. *Egg story*
Hobson, Laura Z. *"I'm going to have a baby!"*
Horton, Barbara Savadge. *What comes in spring?*
Isenbart, Hans-Heinrich. *A duckling is born*
Jarrell, Randall. *A bat is born*
Jessell, Camilla. *The kitten book*
 The puppy book
Kaizuki, Kiyonori. *A calf is born*
Manushkin, Fran. *Baby, come out!*
Oppenheim, Joanne. *Waiting for Noah*
Pursell, Margaret Sanford. *A look at birth*
Rabinowitz, Sandy. *What's happening to Daisy?*
Roddie, Shen. *Hatch, egg, hatch!*
Russo, Marisabina. *Waiting for Hannah*
Schilling, Betty. *Two kittens are born*
Selsam, Millicent E. *Egg to chick*
Sheffield, Margaret. *Before you were born*
 Where do babies come from?
Showers, Paul. *Before you were a baby*
Taylor, Kim. *Frog*
Watts, Barrie. *Duck*

 Kitten
 Rabbit
Willington, Monica. *Seasons of swans*

Birthdays

Abrons, Mary. *For Alice a palace*
Alexander, Sue. *World famous Muriel*
Aliki. *June 7!*
 Use your head, dear
Amoss, Berthe. *It's not your birthday*
Anderson, C. W. (Clarence Williams). *Billy and Blaze*
Anderson, Lena Castell. *Stina's visit*
Anholt, Catherine. *Snow fairy and the spaceman*
Annett, Cora. *The dog who thought he was a boy*
Argent, Kerry. *Happy birthday, Wombat!*
Armitage, Ronda. *The bossing of Josie*
Arnold, Caroline. *Everybody has a birthday*
Arthur, Catherine. *My sister's silent world*
Asch, Frank. *Happy birthday, moon!*
Ashley, Bernard. *Dinner ladies don't count*
Ayer, Jacqueline. *A wish for little sister*
Bannon, Laura. *Manuela's birthday*
Barbot, Daniel. *A bicycle for Rosaura*
Barklem, Jill. *Spring story*
Barrett, Judi. *Benjamin's 365 birthdays*
Bassett, Lisa. *A clock for Beany*
Bauer, Helen. *Good times in the park*
Baum, Arline. *Opt*
Bell, Norman. *Linda's airmail letter*
Bemelmans, Ludwig. *Madeline in London*
Benchley, Peter. *Jonathan visits the White House*
Berenstain, Michael. *Peat Moss and Ivy and the birthday present*
Berenstain, Stan. *The Berenstain bears and too much birthday*
Beskow, Elsa Maartman. *Peter in Blueberry Land*
 Peter's adventures in Blueberry land
Bible, Charles. *Jennifer's new chair*
Billam, Rosemary. *Fuzzy rabbit*
Blocksma, Mary. *Grandma Dragon's birthday*
Bond, Felicia. *Mary Betty Lizzie McNutt's birthday*
Bradman, Tony. *The bad babies' book of colors*
Brandenberg, Franz. *Aunt Nina and her nephews and nieces*
 A secret for grandmother's birthday
Brimner, Larry Dane. *Country bear's surprise*
Bromhall, Winifred. *Mary Ann's first picture*
Brown, Marc Tolon. *Arthur's birthday*
Brown, Margaret Wise. *The golden birthday book*
Brown, Tricia. *Hello, amigos!*
Browne, Anthony. *Gorilla*

Bruna, Dick. *Tilly and Tess*
Brunhoff, Laurent de. *Babar's birthday surprise*
Serafina the giraffe
Buntain, Ruth Jaeger. *The birthday story*
Bunting, Eve (Anne Evelyn). *Happy birthday, dear duck*
The robot birthday
The Wednesday surprise
Burton, Marilee Robin. *Oliver's birthday*
Calmenson, Stephanie. *The birthday hat*
Zip, whiz, zoom!
Carle, Eric. *The secret birthday message*
Caseley, Judith. *Three happy birthdays*
Cazet, Denys. *December 24th*
A fish in his pocket
Chalmers, Mary. *A hat for Amy Jean*
Charles, Donald. *Shaggy dog's birthday*
Charlip, Remy. *Handtalk birthday*
Clifton, Lucille. *Don't you remember?*
Cole, William. *What's good for a three-year-old?*
Corey, Dorothy. *Will it ever be my birthday?*
Costa, Nicoletta. *The birthday party*
Cunliffe, John. *The king's birthday cake*
Daly, Maureen. *Patrick visits the library*
Da Rif, Andrea. *The blueberry cake that little fox baked*
Davidson, Amanda. *Teddy's birthday*
Davis, Lavinia (Riker). *The wild birthday cake*
Dayton, Laura. *LeRoy's birthday circus*
De Paola, Paula. *Rosie and the yellow ribbon*
De Regniers, Beatrice Schenk. *A special birthday party for someone very special*
Dowling, Paul. *Happy birthday, Owl*
Duncan, Lois. *Birthday moon*
Duvoisin, Roger Antoine. *Veronica and the birthday present*
Eberstadt, Isabel. *What is for my birthday?*
Emberley, Michael. *The present*
Eriksson, Eva. *One short week*
Fern, Eugene. *Birthday presents*
Fischer, Hans. *The birthday*
Flack, Marjorie. *Ask Mr. Bear*
Fleischman, Paul. *The birthday tree*
Fowler, Richard. *Inspector Smart gets the message!*
Fox, Mem. *Night noises*
Freedman, Sally. *Monster birthday party*
Freeman, Don. *Corduroy's party*
The guard mouse
Mop Top
Gackenbach, Dick. *Binky gets a car*
Gantos, Jack (John, Jr.). *Happy birthday, Rotten Ralph*
Swampy alligator
Gibbons, Gail. *Happy birthday!*
Giff, Patricia Reilly. *Happy birthday, Ronald Morgan!*
Goble, Paul. *Iktomi and the boulder*

Goldin, Barbara Diamond. *World's birthday*
Goodall, John S. *Shrewbettina's birthday*
Gordon, Margaret. *Wilberforce goes to a party*
Gould, Deborah. *Brendan's best-timed birthday*
Gray, Nigel. *Little pig's tale*
Greene, Carol. *The world's biggest birthday cake*
Gretz, Susanna. *Frog in the middle*
Roger loses his marbles!
Hawkins, Colin. *Jen the hen*
Heller, Nicholas. *Happy birthday, Moe dog*
Henrietta. *A mouse in the house*
Hertz, Ole. *Tobias has a birthday*
Hill, Eric. *Spot's birthday party*
Hillert, Margaret. *The birthday car*
Happy birthday, dear dragon
Hoban, Russell. *A birthday for Frances*
Hoff, Syd. *Happy birthday, Henrietta!*
Holabird, Katharine. *Angelina's birthday surprise*
Homme, Bob. *The friendly giant's birthday*
Howe, James. *Creepy-crawly birthday*
Hughes, Shirley. *Alfie gives a hand*
Wheels
Hurd, Thacher. *Little Mouse's birthday cake*
Hutchins, Pat. *Happy birthday, Sam*
King Henry's palace
Iwasaki, Chihiro. *The birthday wish*
Jabar, Cynthia. *Party day!*
Jaynes, Ruth M. *What is a birthday child?*
Johnson, Odette. *One prickly porcupine*
Jones, Penelope. *I didn't want to be nice*
Keller, Holly. *Henry's happy birthday*
Lizzie's invitation
Kelley, Anne. *Daisy's discovery*
Ketteman, Helen. *Not yet, Yvette*
Kiser, SuAnn. *The birthday thing*
Krauze, Andrzej. *What's so special about today?*
Kumin, Maxine. *Joey and the birthday present*
Lasell, Fen. *Michael grows a wish*
Laurence, Margaret. *The Christmas birthday story*
Lenski, Lois. *A surprise for Davy*
Leonard, Marcia. *Birthday in a bathtub*
Lewis, Thomas P. *Call for Mr. Sniff*
Lexau, Joan M. *Go away, dog*
Me day
Lindman, Maj. *Flicka, Ricka, Dicka bake a cake*
Snipp, Snapp, Snurr and the red shoes
Little, Lessie Jones. *I can do it by myself*
Livingston, Myra Cohn. *Birthday poems*
Lobel, Anita. *A birthday for the princess*
Lorian, Nicole. *A birthday present for Mama*
Lowrey, Janette Sebring. *Six silver spoons*
Lundell, Margo. *Teddy bear's birthday*
Lyndon, Kerry Raines. *A birthday for Blue*

McAllister, Angela. *The enchanted flute*
  Snail's birthday problem
McCue, Lisa. *Corduroy's party*
MacDonald, Elizabeth. *Mr. Badger's birthday
  pie*
MacDonald, Maryann. *Rabbit's birthday kite*
McKee, David. *King Rollo and the birthday*
McNeill, Janet. *The giant's birthday*
Marie, Geraldine. *The magic box*
Merriam, Eve. *The birthday door*
Miklowitz, Gloria D. *Bearfoot boy*
Miles, Miska. *Mouse six and the happy
  birthday*
Miller, Margaret. *My birthday*
Minarik, Else Holmelund. *Little Bear*
Modell, Frank. *Ice cream soup*
Moon, Grace Purdie. *One little Indian*
Morice, Dave. *The happy birthday handbook*
Mother Goose. *Pat-a-cake*, ill. by Marilyn
  Janovitz
Mueller, Virginia. *Monster's birthday hiccups*
Munari, Bruno. *The birthday present*
Munsch, Robert N. *Moira's birthday*
Myers, Bernice. *Charlie's birthday present*
Myller, Rolf. *How big is a foot?*
Myrick, Jean Lockwood. *Ninety-nine pockets*
Ness, Evaline. *Josefina February*
Noble, Trinka Hakes. *Jimmy's boa and the
  big splash birthday bash*
Owen, Annie. *Bumper to bumper*
Oxenbury, Helen. *The birthday party*
Parish, Peggy. *Be ready at eight*
  Scruffy
  Snapping turtle's all wrong day
Park, W. B. *Bakery business*
Parker, Nancy Winslow. *Love from Uncle
  Clyde*
Paterson, Bettina. *Bun's birthday*
Patz, Nancy. *No thumpin' no bumpin' no
  rumpus tonight!*
Pearson, Susan. *Happy birthday, Grampie*
Peek, Merle. *Mary wore her red dress and
  Henry wore his green sneakers*
Peppé, Rodney. *The kettleship pirates*
Perkins, Al. *Tubby and the lantern*
Peters, Sharon. *Happy birthday*
Peterson, Esther Allen. *Penelope gets wheels*
Pittman, Helena Clare. *A dinosaur for
  Gerald*
Polacco, Patricia. *Some birthday!*
Pomerantz, Charlotte. *The half-birthday
  party*
Prager, Annabelle. *The surprise party*
Quin-Harkin, Janet. *Helpful Hattie*
Radlauer, Ruth Shaw. *Breakfast by Molly*
Rice, Eve. *Benny bakes a cake*
Rockwell, Anne F. *Happy birthday to me*
  Hugo at the window
Roffey, Maureen. *Meatime*
Root, Phyllis. *Gretchen's grandma*
Russo, Marisabina. *Only six more days*

Rylant, Cynthia. *Birthday presents*
Samuels, Barbara. *Happy birthday, Dolores*
Sandberg, Inger. *Nicholas' favorite pet*
Sawicki, Norma Jean. *Something for mom*
Schumacher, Claire. *Nutty's birthday*
Schweninger, Ann. *Birthday wishes*
Seuss, Dr. *Happy birthday to you!*
  Hooper Humperdink...? Not him!
Sewell, Helen Moore. *Birthdays for Robin*
Shannon, George. *The surprise*
Sherrow, Victoria. *Wilbur waits*
Shimin, Symeon. *A special birthday*
Singer, Marilyn. *Minnie's Yom Kippur
  birthday*
Sis, Peter. *Going up!*
Smith, Wendy. *Say hello, Tilly*
Spurr, Elizabeth. *The biggest birthday cake
  in the world*
Stapler, Sarah. *Spruce the moose cuts loose*
Steiner, Charlotte. *Birthdays are for everyone*
Steptoe, John. *Birthday*
Stevenson, Suçie. *I forgot*
Stock, Catherine. *The birthday present*
Sutton, Elizabeth Henning. *A pony for
  keeps*
Türk, Hanne. *Happy birthday Max*
Turnbull, Ann. *The tapestry cats*
Tyler, Linda Wagner. *The sick-in-bed
  birthday book*
Uchida, Yoshiko. *Sumi's special happening*
Van der Beek, Deborah. *Alice's blue cloth*
Vigna, Judith. *Mommy and me by ourselves
  again*
Wabbes, Marie. *Happy birthday, Little Rabbit*
Waber, Bernard. *Lyle and the birthday party*
Watanabe, Shigeo. *It's my birthday*
Watson, Nancy Dingman. *The birthday goat
  Tommy's mommy's fish*
Weiss, Ellen. *Mokey's birthday present*
Wells, Rosemary. *Max's birthday*
West, Colin. *Go tell it to the toucan*
Whittington, Mary K. *The patchwork lady*
Wickstrom, Sylvie (Sylvie Kantrovitz).
  Mothers can't get sick
Willard, Nancy. *The high rise glorious skittle
  skat roarious sky pie angel food cake*
  The marzipan moon
Williams, Barbara. *Whatever happened to
  Beverly Bigler's birthday?*
Williams, Vera B. *Something special for me*
Wilson, Sarah. *Uncle Albert's flying birthday*
Wood, David. *Happy birthday, Mouse!*
Worth, Bonnie. *Peter Cottontail's surprise*
Yashima, Tarō. *Umbrella*
Yolen, Jane. *Picnic with Piggins*
Ziefert, Harriet. *Happy birthday, Grandpa!*
  Surprise!
Zimelman, Nathan. *Once when I was five*
Zolotow, Charlotte (Shapiro). *Mr. Rabbit
  and the lovely present*

Black Americans *see* Ethnic groups in the U.S. – Afro-Americans

Blackbirds *see* Birds – blackbirds

Blackouts *see* Power failure

Blindness *see* Handicaps – blindness

Blocks *see* Toys – blocks

Bluejays *see* Birds – bluejays

Board books *see* Format, unusual – board books

Boasting *see* Behavior – boasting

Boat builders *see* Careers – boat builders

Boats, ships
Agell, Charlotte. *The sailor's book*
Alexander, Anne (Anna Barbara Cooke). *Boats and ships from A to Z*
Allen, Pamela. *Who sank the boat?*
Amoss, Berthe. *Old Hannibal and the hurricane*
Anderson, Lonzo. *Arion and the dolphins*
Ardizzone, Edward. *Little Tim and the brave sea captain*
Ship's cook Ginger
Tim all alone
Tim and Charlotte
Tim and Ginger
Tim and Lucy go to sea
Tim in danger
Tim to the rescue
Tim's friend Towser
Tim's last voyage
Augarde, Steve (Stephen). *Barnaby Shrew goes to sea*
Baker, Betty. *My sister says*
Barton, Byron. *Boats*
Bate, Norman. *What a wonderful machine is a submarine*
Baynes, Pauline. *Noah and the ark*
Benjamin, Alan. *A change of plans*
Berenstain, Michael. *The ship book*
Brent, Isabelle. *Noah's ark*
Bridgman, Elizabeth. *Nanny bear's cruise*
Brown, Jane Clark. *Whonk, and whonk again*
Brown, Judith Gwyn. *The happy voyage*
Brown, Marcia. *Skipper John's cook*
Bruna, Dick. *The sailor*
Buchanan, Heather S. *George Mouse's riverboat band*
Burchard, Peter. *The Carol Moran*
Burningham, John. *Mr. Gumpy's outing*
Bushey, Jerry. *The barge book*
Calhoun, Mary. *Euphonia and the flood*

Campbell, Ann. *Let's find out about boats*
Carrick, Carol. *The washout*
Carryl, Charles Edward. *A capital ship: or, The walloping window-blind*, ill. by Paul Galdone
The walloping window blind, ill. by Ted Rand
Carter, Katharine. *Ships and seaports*
Chalmers, Mary. *Boats finds a house*
Cohen, Peter Zachary. *Authorized autumn charts of the Upper Red Canoe River country*
Crews, Donald. *Harbor*
Day, Alexandra. *River parade*
DeLage, Ida. *Pilgrim children on the Mayflower*
Demi. *The magic boat*
Dennis, Morgan. *The sea dog*
Denton, Terry. *Home is the sailor*
De Paola, Tomie (Thomas Anthony). *Four stories for four seasons*
Devlin, Harry. *The walloping window blind*
Domanska, Janina. *I saw a ship a-sailing*
Dorros, Arthur. *Pretzels*
Du Bois, William Pène. *Otto at sea*
Dunrea, Olivier. *Fergus and Bridey*
Dupasquier, Philippe. *Dear Daddy...*
Jack at sea
Elting, Mary. *The big book of real boats and ships*
Emberley, Ed (Edward Randolph). *Cars, boats, and planes*
Faulkner, Matt. *The amazing voyage of Jackie Grace*
Fischetto, Laura. *All pigs on deck*
Flack, Marjorie. *The boats on the river*
Flora, James. *Fishing with dad*
Foreman, Michael. *Jack's fantastic voyage*
French, Fiona. *Rise and shine*
Fry, Christopher. *The boat that mooed*
Fussenegger, Gertrud. *Noah's ark*
Gay, Michel. *Little boat*
Gedin, Birgitta. *The little house from the sea*
Gerrard, Roy. *Sir Francis Drake*
Gibbons, Gail. *Boat book*
Ginsburg, Mirra. *Four brave sailors*
Goodall, John S. *Jacko*
Graham, Margaret Bloy. *Benjy's boat trip*
Graham, Thomas. *Mr. Bear's boat*
Gramatky, Hardie. *Little Toot*
Little Toot and the Loch Ness monster
Little Toot on the Mississippi
Little Toot on the Thames
Little Toot through the Golden Gate
Haas, Irene. *The Maggie B*
Hansen, Carla. *Barnaby Bear builds a boat*
Helldorfer, M. C. (Mary Claire). *Sailing to the sea*
Hest, Amy. *A sort-of sailor*
Hillert, Margaret. *The yellow boat*
Hogrogian, Nonny. *Noah's ark*

Holabird, Katharine. *Alexander and the magic boat*
Hurd, Edith Thacher. *What whale? Where?*
Isadora, Rachel. *No, Agatha!*
Joerns, Consuelo. *The foggy rescue*
Johnson, Pamela. *A mouse's tale*
Kellogg, Steven (Stephen). *The island of the skog*
Kuskin, Karla. *The animals and the ark*
Lenski, Lois. *Mr. and Mrs. Noah*
Lewis, Thomas P. *Clipper ship*
Lindman, Maj. *Sailboat time*
Lippman, Peter. *The Know-It-Alls go to sea*
Locker, Thomas. *Sailing with the wind*
Loof, Jan. *Uncle Louie's fantastic sea voyage*
Ludwig, Warren. *Old Noah's elephants*
McCaughrean, Geraldine. *The story of Noah and the ark*
McCloskey, Robert. *Bert Dow, deep-water man*
McGovern, Ann. *Nicholas Bentley Stoningpot III*
McGowan, Alan. *Sailing ships*
Maestro, Betsy. *Big city port Ferryboat*
Mahy, Margaret. *Sailor Jack and the twenty orphans*
Marshall, James. *Speedboat*
Meddaugh, Susan. *Maude and Claude go abroad*
Mendoza, George. *The alphabet boat*
Miles, Miska. *No, no, Rosina*
Morgan, Allen. *Nicole's boat*
Nakawatari, Harutaka. *The sea and I*
Olson, Arielle North. *Noah's cats and the devil's fire*
Partridge, Jenny. *Hopfellow*
Patrick, Denice. *Look inside a ship*
Peppé, Rodney. *The kettleship pirates*
Perkins, Al. *Tubby and the Poo-Bah*
Pfanner, Louise. *Louise builds a boat*
Pitcher, Caroline. *Cars and boats*
Potter, Beatrix. *The tale of Little Pig Robinson*
Rand, Gloria. *Salty dog*
Ransome, Arthur. *The fool of the world and the flying ship*
Reavin, Sam. *Hurray for Captain Jane!*
Reesink, Marijke. *The golden treasure*
Rettich, Margret. *The voyage of the jolly boat*
Rockwell, Anne F. *Boats*
Round, Graham. *Hangdog*
Rubel, Nicole. *Uncle Henry and Aunt Henrietta's honeymoon*
Samton, Sheila White. *Jenny's journey*
Schaffer, Libor. *Arthur sets sail*
Schulz, Charles M. *Snoopy's facts and fun book about boats*
Shaw, Nancy. *Sheep on a ship*
Shecter, Ben. *If I had a ship*
Shortall, Leonard W. *Tod on the tugboat*

Smith, Barry. *The first voyage of Christopher Columbus*
Spier, Peter. *Noah's ark*
Stevenson, James. *The stowaway*
Stevenson, Jocelyn. *Jim Henson's Muppets at sea*
Surany, Anico. *Ride the cold wind*
Swift, Hildegarde Hoyt. *The little red lighthouse and the great gray bridge*
Tagore, Rabindranath. *Paper boats*
Taylor, Mark. *Henry the castaway*
Thomson, Ruth. *Peabody all at sea*
Thorne, Jenny. *Noah's ark*
Titherington, Jeanne. *Baby's boat*
Tudor, Bethany. *Skiddycock Pond*
Twining, Edith. *Sandman*
Van Allsburg, Chris. *The wreck of the Zephyr*
Venable, Alan. *The checker players*
Vernon, Tannis. *Little Pig and the blue-green sea*
Waddell, Martin. *Sailor Bear*
Waters, Tony. *Sailor's bride*
Willard, Nancy. *The voyage of the Ludgate Hill*
Williams, Vera B. *Three days on a river in a red canoe*
Young, James. *Penelope and the pirates*
Young, Miriam Burt. *If I sailed a boat*
Young, Ruth. *Daisy's taxi*
Zaffo, George J. *The giant nursery book of things that go*
Ziefert, Harriet. *My sister says nothing ever happens when we go sailing*

Bobcats *see* Animals – bobcats

Boogy man *see* Monsters

Books *see* Activities – reading; Libraries

Boots *see* Clothing – shoes

Boredom *see* Behavior – boredom

Borneo *see* Foreign lands – Borneo

Bravery *see* Character traits – bravery

Bridges

Carlisle, Norman. *Bridges*
Lobel, Anita. *Sven's bridge*
Neville, Emily Cheney. *The bridge*
Oppenheim, Joanne. *On the other side of the river*
Steadman, Ralph. *The bridge*
Swift, Hildegarde Hoyt. *The little red lighthouse and the great gray bridge*
Yagelski, Robert. *The day the lifting bridge stuck*

Brothers *see* Family life; Family life –
brothers; Sibling rivalry

Brownies *see* Elves and little people

Buffaloes *see* Animals – buffaloes

Bugs *see* Insects

Buildings

Balterman, Lee. *Girders and cranes*
Barkan, Joanne. *Whiskerville bake shop*
  Whiskerville firehouse
  Whiskerville post office
  Whiskerville school
Gibbons, Gail. *Up goes the skyscraper!*
Henri, Adrian. *The postman's palace*

Bulls *see* Animals – bulls, cows

Bullying *see* Behavior – bullying

Bumble bees *see* Insects – bees

Burglars *see* Crime

Burma *see* Foreign lands – Burma

Burros *see* Animals – donkeys

Bus drivers *see* Careers – bus drivers

Bus drivers *see* Careers – bus drivers

Buses

Blance, Ellen. *Monster on the bus*
Browne, Eileen. *Where's that bus?*
Cossi, Olga. *Gus the bus*
Crews, Donald. *School bus*
Fuller, Ted. *Barney the bus*
Gomi, Taro. *Bus stop*
Hellen, Nancy. *Bus stop*
Hirst, Robin. *My place in space*
Jewell, Nancy. *Bus ride*
Kilroy, Sally. *On the road*
Kingsland, Robin. *Bus stop bop*
Kovalski, Maryann. *The wheels on the bus*
Matthias, Catherine. *Out the door*
Nichols, Paul. *Big Paul's school bus*
Peppé, Rodney. *The mice and the clockwork
  bus*
Shuttlesworth, Dorothy E. *ABC of buses*
Wolcott, Patty. *Double-decker, double-decker,
  double-decker bus*
Young, Miriam Burt. *If I drove a bus*
Zelinsky, Paul O. *The wheels on the bus*
Ziefert, Harriet. *Jason's bus ride*

Bushbabies *see* Animals – bushbabies

Butchers *see* Careers – butchers

Butterflies *see* Insects – butterflies,
caterpillars

Buzzards *see* Birds – buzzards

Cab drivers *see* Careers – taxi drivers

Cable cars, trolleys

Burton, Virginia Lee. *Maybelle, the cable
  car*
Chalmers, Mary. *Here comes the trolley*
Gramatky, Hardie. *Sparky*
Taniuchi, Kota. *Trolley*

Cabs *see* Taxis

Caldecott award book

Aardema, Verna. *Why mosquitoes buzz in
  people's ears*
Ackerman, Karen. *Song and dance man*
Alger, Leclaire Gowans. *Always room for
  one more*
Aulaire, Ingri Mortenson d'. *Abraham
  Lincoln*
Bemelmans, Ludwig. *Madeline's rescue*
Brown, Marcia. *Once a mouse...*
Brown, Margaret Wise. *The little island*
Burton, Virginia Lee. *The little house*
Cendrars, Blaise. *Shadow*
Chaucer, Geoffrey. *Chanticleer and the fox*,
  ill. by Barbara Cooney
De Regniers, Beatrice Schenk. *May I bring
  a friend?*
Emberley, Barbara. *Drummer Hoff*
Ets, Marie Hall. *Nine days to Christmas*
Field, Rachel Lyman. *Prayer for a child*
A frog he would a-wooing go (folk-song).
  Frog went a-courtin', ill. by Feodor
  Rojankovsky
Goble, Paul. *The girl who loved wild horses*
Hader, Berta Hoerner. *The big snow*
Haley, Gail E. *A story, a story*
Hall, Donald. *The ox-cart man*
Handforth, Thomas. *Mei Li*
Hodges, Margaret. *Saint George and the
  dragon*
Hogrogian, Nonny. *One fine day*
Keats, Ezra Jack. *The snowy day*
Lawson, Robert. *They were strong and good*
Lipkind, William. *Finders keepers*
Lobel, Arnold. *Fables*

McCloskey, Robert. *Make way for ducklings*
  Time of wonder
McDermott, Gerald. *Arrow to the sun*
Milhous, Katherine. *The egg tree*
Mosel, Arlene. *The funny little woman*
Musgrove, Margaret. *Ashanti to Zulu*
Ness, Evaline. *Sam, Bangs, and moonshine*
Perrault, Charles. *Cinderella*, ill. by Marcia
  Brown
Petersham, Maud. *The rooster crows*
Politi, Leo. *Song of the swallows*
Provensen, Alice. *The glorious flight*
Ransome, Arthur. *The fool of the world and
  the flying ship*
Robbins, Ruth. *Baboushka and the three
  kings*
Sendak, Maurice. *Where the wild things are*
Spier, Peter. *Noah's ark*
Steig, William. *Sylvester and the magic pebble*
Thurber, James. *Many moons*, ill. by Louis
  Slobodkin
Tresselt, Alvin R. *White snow, bright snow*
Udry, Janice May. *A tree is nice*
Van Allsburg, Chris. *Jumanji*
  The polar express
Ward, Lynd. *The biggest bear*
Weisner, David. *Tuesday*
Yolen, Jane. *Owl moon*
Yorinks, Arthur. *Hey, Al*
Young, Ed (Edward). *Lon Po Po*
Zemach, Harve. *Duffy and the devil*

Caldecott award honor book

Alger, Leclaire Gowans. *All in the morning
  early*
Armer, Laura Adams. *The forest pool*
Artzybasheff, Boris. *Seven Simeons*
Baker, Olaf. *Where the buffaloes begin*
Bang, Molly. *The grey lady and the
  strawberry snatcher*
  Ten, nine, eight
Baskin, Leonard. *Hosie's alphabet*
Baylor, Byrd. *The desert is theirs*
  Hawk, I'm your brother
  The way to start a day
  When clay sings
Belting, Natalia Maree. *The sun is a golden
  earring*
Bemelmans, Ludwig. *Madeline*
Birnbaum, Abe. *Green eyes*
Brown, Marcia. *Henry fisherman*
  Skipper John's cook
  Stone soup
Brown, Margaret Wise. *A child's good night
  book*
  Little lost lamb
  Wheel on the chimney
Buff, Mary. *Dash and Dart*
Cathon, Laura E. *Tot Botot and his little
  flute*
Caudill, Rebecca. *A pocketful of cricket*

Chan, Chin-Yi. *Good luck horse*
Clark, Ann Nolan. *In my mother's house*
Crews, Donald. *Freight train*
  Truck
Dalgliesh, Alice. *The Thanksgiving story*
Daugherty, James Henry. *Andy and the lion*
Davis, Lavinia (Riker). *Roger and the fox*
  The wild birthday cake
Dayrell, Elphinstone. *Why the sun and the
  moon live in the sky*
De Angeli, Marguerite. *The book of nursery
  and Mother Goose rhymes*
  Yonie Wondernose
De Paola, Tomie (Thomas Anthony).
  Strega Nona
Dick Whittington and his cat. *Dick
  Whittington and his cat*, ill. by Marcia
  Brown
Domanska, Janina. *If all the seas were one
  sea*
Du Bois, William Pène. *Bear party*
  Lion
Ehlert, Lois. *Color zoo*
Eichenberg, Fritz. *Ape in cape*
Elkin, Benjamin. *Gillespie and the guards*
Emberley, Barbara. *One wide river to cross*
Ets, Marie Hall. *In the forest*
  Just me
  Mister Penny
  Mr. Penny's race horse
  Mr. T. W. Anthony Woo
  Play with me
Feelings, Muriel. *Jambo means hello*
  Menjo means one
Fish, Helen Dean. *Four and twenty
  blackbirds*
Flack, Marjorie. *The boats on the river*
Ford, Lauren. *The ageless story*
The fox went out on a chilly night, ill. by
  Peter Spier
Freeman, Don. *Fly high, fly low*
Gág, Wanda. *Nothing at all*
Goffstein, M. B. (Marilyn Brooke). *Fish for
  supper*
Goudey, Alice E. *The day we saw the sun
  come up*
  Houses from the sea
Graham, Al. *Timothy Turtle*
Grifalconi, Ann. *The village of round and
  square houses*
Grimm, Jacob. *The Bremen town musicians*,
  ill. by Ilse Plume
  Hansel and Gretel, ill. by Paul O.
  Zelinsky
  Little Red Riding Hood, ill. by Trina
  Schart Hyman
  Snow White and the seven dwarfs, ill. by
  Wanda Gág
Hader, Berta Hoerner. *Cock-a-doodle doo*
  The mighty hunter
Hodges, Margaret. *The wave*

Hogrogian, Nonny. *The contest*
Holbrook, Stewart. *America's Ethan Allen*
Holling, Holling C. (Holling Clancy). *Paddle-to-the-sea*
The house that Jack built. *The house that Jack built*, ill. by Antonio Frasconi
Isadora, Rachel. *Ben's trumpet*
Jonas, Ann. *Holes and peeks*
Jones, Jessie Mae Orton. *Small rain*
Joslin, Sesyle. *What do you say, dear?*
Keats, Ezra Jack. *Goggles*
Kepes, Juliet. *Five little monkeys*
Kimmel, Eric A. *Hershel and the Hanukkah goblins*
Kingman, Lee. *Pierre Pigeon*
Krauss, Ruth. *The happy day*
A very special house
Leaf, Munro. *Wee Gillis*
Lionni, Leo. *Alexander and the wind-up mouse*
Frederick
Inch by inch
Swimmy
Lipkind, William. *The two reds*
Lobel, Arnold. *Frog and Toad are friends*
On Market Street
Low, Joseph. *Mice twice*
Macaulay, David. *Castle*
Cathedral
McCloskey, Robert. *Blueberries for Sal*
One morning in Maine
McDermott, Beverly Brodsky. *The Golem*
McDermott, Gerald. *Anansi the spider*
MacDonald, Suse. *Alphabatics*
McGinley, Phyllis. *All around the town*
The most wonderful doll in the world
McKissack, Patricia C. *Mirandy and brother wind*
Malcolmson, Anne. *The song of Robin Hood*
Minarik, Else Holmelund. *Little Bear's visit*
Mother Goose. *Mother Goose*, ill. by Tasha Tudor
Mother Goose and nursery rhymes, ill. by Philip Reed
The three jovial huntsmen, ill. by Susan Jeffers
Newberry, Clare Turlay. *April's kittens*
Barkis
Marshmallow
T-Bone, the baby-sitter
Olds, Elizabeth. *Feather mountain*
Peet, Bill (William Bartlett). *Bill Peet*
Perrault, Charles. *Puss in boots*, ill. by Marcia Brown
Petersham, Maud. *An American ABC*
Politi, Leo. *Juanita*
Pedro, the angel of Olvera Street
Preston, Edna Mitchell. *Pop Corn and Ma Goodness*
Reyher, Becky. *My mother is the most beautiful woman in the world*

Ringgold, Faith. *Tar Beach*
Ryan, Cheli Durán. *Hildilid's night*
Rylant, Cynthia. *The relatives came*
When I was young in the mountains
San Souci, Robert D. *The talking eggs*
Sawyer, Ruth. *The Christmas Anna angel*
Journey cake, ho!
Scheer, Julian. *Rain makes applesauce*
Schick, Eleanor. *The little school at Cottonwood Corners*
Schlein, Miriam. *When will the world be mine?*
Schreiber, Georges. *Bambino the clown*
Sendak, Maurice. *In the night kitchen*
Outside over there
Seuss, Dr. *Bartholomew and the Oobleck*
If I ran the zoo
McElligot's pool
Shulevitz, Uri. *The treasure*
Sleator, William. *The angry moon*
Snyder, Dianne. *The boy of the three-year nap*
Steig, William. *The amazing bone*
Steptoe, John. *Mufaro's beautiful daughters*
The story of jumping mouse
Tafuri, Nancy. *Have you seen my duckling?*
The three bears. *Goldilocks and the three bears*, ill. by James Marshall
Titus, Eve. *Anatole*
Anatole and the cat
Tom Tit Tot. *Tom Tit Tot*, ill. by Evaline Ness
Tresselt, Alvin R. *Hide and seek fog*
Rain drop splash
Tudor, Tasha. *1 is one*
Turkle, Brinton. *Thy friend, Obadiah*
Udry, Janice May. *The moon jumpers*
Van Allsburg, Chris. *The garden of Abdul Gasazi*
Wheeler, Opal. *Sing in praise*
Sing Mother Goose
Wiese, Kurt. *Fish in the air*
You can write Chinese
Wiesner, David. *Free fall*
Willard, Nancy. *A visit to William Blake's inn*
Williams, Vera B. *A chair for my mother*
"More more more," said the baby
Wood, Audrey. *King Bidgood's in the bathtub*
Yashima, Tarō. *Crow boy*
Seashore story
Umbrella
Yolen, Jane. *The emperor and the kite*
Zemach, Harve. *The judge*
Zemach, Margot. *It could always be worse*
Zion, Gene. *All falling down*
Zolotow, Charlotte (Shapiro). *Mr. Rabbit and the lovely present*
The storm book

Cambodia *see* Foreign lands – Cambodia

Camels *see* Animals – camels

Camps, camping

Armitage, Ronda. *One moonlit night*
Berenstain, Stan. *The Berenstain bears go to camp*
Blaustein, Muriel. *Make friends, Zachary!*
Boynton, Sandra. *Hester in the wild*
Brown, Marc Tolon. *Arthur goes to camp*
Brown, Myra Berry. *Pip camps out*
Carrick, Carol. *Sleep out*
Gould, Deborah. *Camping in the Temple of the Sun*
Graham, Bob. *Greetings from Sandy Beach*
Henkes, Kevin. *Bailey goes camping*
McPhail, David. *Pig Pig goes to camp*
Maestro, Betsy. *Camping out*
Marino, Dorothy. *Buzzy Bear goes camping*
Marshall, James. *The Cut-Ups at Camp Custer*
Mayer, Mercer. *Just me and my dad*
You're the scaredy cat
Maynard, Joyce. *Camp-out*
Peters, Sharon. *Fun at camp*
Price, Dorothy E. *Speedy gets around*
Robins, Joan. *Addie runs away*
Roche, P. K. (Patrick K.). *Webster and Arnold go camping*
Rockwell, Anne F. *The night we slept outside*
On our vacation
Rubel, Nicole. *Sam and Violet go camping*
Schulman, Janet. *Camp Kee Wee's secret weapon*
Schwartz, Amy. *Camper of the week*
Schwartz, Henry. *How I captured a dinosaur*
Seligson, Susan. *Amos camps out: a couch adventure in the woods*
Shulevitz, Uri. *Dawn*
Stock, Catherine. *Sophie's knapsack*
Tafuri, Nancy. *Do not disturb*
Thompson, Vivian Laubach. *Camp-in-the-yard*
Warren, Cathy. *The ten-alarm camp-out*
Weiss, Nicki. *Battle day at Camp Delmont*
Williams, Vera B. *Three days on a river in a red canoe*
Yolen, Jane. *The giants go camping*

Canada *see* Foreign lands – Canada

Canaries *see* Birds – canaries

Caps *see* Clothing – hats

Cardboard page books *see* Format, unusual – board books

Cardinals *see* Birds – cardinals

Careers

Aitken, Amy. *Ruby!*
Arnold, Caroline. *What is a community?*
Who keeps us safe?
Who works here?
Azaad, Meyer. *Half for you*
Baker, Eugene. *I want to be a computer operator*
Bank Street College of Education. *People read*
Bauer, Caroline Feller. *My mom travels a lot*
Berenstain, Stan. *The Berenstain bears and mama's new job*
Boxer, Deborah. *26 ways to be somebody else*
Brentano, Clemens. *Schoolmaster Whackwell's wonderful sons*
Brott, Ardyth. *Jeremy's decision*
Civardi, Anne. *Things people do*
Dupasquier, Philippe. *Dear Daddy...*
Florian, Douglas. *People working*
Freeman, Don. *The night the lights went out*
Gibbons, Gail. *Farming*
Fill it up!
The pottery place
Goffstein, M. B. (Marilyn Brooke). *An actor*
Greenberg, Melanie Hope. *My father's luncheonette*
Greene, Carol. *I can be a baseball player*
Grossman, Patricia. *The night ones*
Harper, Anita. *How we work*
Harris, Steven Michael. *This is my trunk*
Hazen, Barbara Shook. *Mommy's office*
Klein, Norma. *Girls can be anything*
Kraus, Robert. *Owliver*
Kroll, Steven. *Howard and Gracie's luncheonette*
Lasker, Joe. *Mothers can do anything*
Lenski, Lois. *Lois Lenski's big book of Mr. Small*
Le-Tan, Pierre. *Timothy's dream book*
McPhail, David. *Pig Pig gets a job*
Matthias, Catherine. *I can be a computer operator*
Mayer, Mercer. *Little Monster at work*
Merriam, Eve. *Mommies at work*
Miller, Margaret. *Who uses this?*
Whose hat?
Mitchell, Joyce Slayton. *My mommy makes money*
Morrison, Bill. *Louis James hates school*
Myers, Bernice. *The gold watch*
Nichols, Paul. *Big Paul's school bus*
Oliver, Dexter. *I want to be...*
100 words about working, ill. by Richard Eric Brown
Oppenheim, Joanne. *On the other side of the river*
Portnoy, Mindy Avra. *Ima on the Bima: my mommy is a Rabbi*

Puner, Helen Walker. *Daddys, what they do all day*
Rowan, James P. *I can be a zoo keeper*
Rowe, Jeanne A. *City workers*
Sandberg, Inger. *Come on out, Daddy!*
Scarry, Richard. *Richard Scarry's busiest people ever*
  Richard Scarry's Postman Pig and his busy neighbors
Seignobosc, Françoise. *What do you want to be?*
The Sesame Street book of people and things
Sharmat, Marjorie Weinman. *I'm Santa Claus and I'm famous*
Shepard, Steve. *Elvis Hornbill, international business bird*
Stewart, Robert S. *The daddy book*
Thaler, Mike. *What could a hippopotamus be?*
Upton, Pat. *Who does this job?*
Williams, Barbara. *I know a salesperson*

Careers – actors

McCully, Emily Arnold. *Zaza's big break*

Careers – airplane pilots

Baker, Donna. *I want to be a pilot*
Barton, Byron. *Airport*
Behrens, June. *I can be a pilot*
Krementz, Jill. *Jamie goes on an airplane*
Young, Miriam Burt. *If I flew a plane*

Careers – architects

Clinton, Susan. *I can be an architect*
Demi. *The artist and the architect*

Careers – artists

Adams, Adrienne. *The great Valentine's Day balloon race*
Angelo, Nancy Carolyn Harrison. *Camembert*
Baker, Alan. *Benjamin's portrait*
Baynton, Martin. *Fifty gets the picture*
Carrick, Donald. *Morgan and the artist*
Demi. *The artist and the architect*
Edwards, Michelle. *A baker's portrait*
Everett, Gwen. *Li'l Sis and Uncle Willie*
Kleven, Elisa. *The lion and the little red bird*
Lager, Claude. *A tale of two rats*
Leaf, Margaret. *Eyes of the dragon*
Lehan, Daniel. *This is not a book about dodos*
Lionni, Leo. *Matthew's dream*
Locker, Thomas. *The young artist*
Miller, Warren. *Pablo paints a picture*
Moss, Marissa. *Regina's big mistake*
Payne, Joan Balfour. *The stable that stayed*
Pinkwater, Daniel Manus. *The bear's picture*
Sharon, Mary Bruce. *Scenes from childhood*

Sloan, Carolyn. *Carter is a painter's cat*
Turnbull, Ann. *The sand horse*
Velthuijs, Max. *Crocodile's masterpiece*
  The painter and the bird
Ventura, Piero. *The painter's trick*
Waddell, Martin. *Alice the artist*
Weisgard, Leonard. *Mr. Peaceable paints*
Willard, Nancy. *Pish posh, said Hieronymous Bosch*
Winter, Jonah. *Diego*
Wolkstein, Diane. *Little Mouse's painting*
Yacowitz, Caryn. *The jade stone*

Careers – astronauts

Barton, Byron. *I want to be an astronaut*
Behrens, June. *I can be an astronaut*
Eco, Umberto. *The three astronauts*

Careers – bakers

Allard, Harry. *The cactus flower bakery*
Barkan, Joanne. *Whiskerville bake shop*
Caple, Kathy. *Inspector Aardvark and the perfect cake*
Carle, Eric. *Walter the baker*
Craig, M. Jean. *The man whose name was not Thomas*
De Paola, Tomie (Thomas Anthony). *Tony's bread*
Edwards, Michelle. *A baker's portrait*
Forest, Heather. *The baker's dozen*
Green, Melinda. *Bembelman's bakery*
Greeson, Janet. *The stingy baker*
Heath, Amy. *Sofie's role*
Kessler, Leonard P. *Soup for the king*
Lillegard, Dee. *I can be a baker*
Mayer, Marianna. *Marcel the pastry chef*
Pinkwater, Daniel Manus. *The Frankenbagel monster*
Sundvall, Viveca. *Mimi and the biscuit factory*
Westcott, Nadine Bernard. *Peanut butter and jelly*
Worthington, Phoebe. *Teddy bear baker*
Young, Miriam Burt. *The sugar mouse cake*
Ziegler, Sandra. *A visit to the bakery*

Careers – barbers

Appell, Clara. *Now I have a daddy haircut*
Auerbach, Marjorie. *King Lavra and the barber*
Barry, Robert E. *Next please*
Freeman, Don. *Mop Top*
Kunhardt, Dorothy. *Billy the barber*
Mahiri, Jabari. *The day they stole the letter J*
Peet, Bill (William Bartlett). *Hubert's hair-raising adventures*
Rockwell, Anne F. *My barber*

Careers – boat builders

Rand, Gloria. *Salty dog*

Careers – bus drivers

Young, Miriam Burt. *If I drove a bus*

Careers – butchers

Kobayashi, Robert. *Maria Mazaretti loves spaghetti*
Yorinks, Arthur. *Louis the fish*

Careers - cab drivers *see* Careers – taxi drivers

Careers – carpenters

Baker, Keith. *The magic fan*
Denslow, Sharon Phillips. *At Taylor's place*
Florian, Douglas. *A carpenter*
Greene, Carla. *I want to be a carpenter*
Hest, Amy. *The ring and the window seat*
Lillegard, Dee. *I can be a carpenter*

Careers – chefs

Pillar, Marjorie. *Pizza man*
Tomchek, Ann Heinrichs. *I can be a chef*

Careers – clockmakers

Ardizzone, Edward. *Johnny the clockmaker*

Careers – composers

Brighton, Catherine. *Mozart*

Careers – dentists

Barnett, Naomi. *I know a dentist*
Berenstain, Stan. *The Berenstain bears visit the dentist*
Curious George goes to the dentist
Duvoisin, Roger Antoine. *Crocus*
Krementz, Jill. *Taryn goes to the dentist*
Kuklin, Susan. *When I see my dentist*
Lapp, Carolyn. *The dentists' tools*
Linn, Margot. *A trip to the dentist*
Mitra, Annie. *Tusk! Tusk!*
Richter, Alice Numeroff. *You can't put braces on spaces*
Rockwell, Harlow. *My dentist*
Stamper, Judith. *What's it like to be a dentist?*
Steig, William. *Doctor De Soto goes to Africa*
Watson, Jane Werner. *My friend the dentist*
Wolf, Bernard. *Michael and the dentist*
Zalben, Jane Breskin. *Buster gets braces*

Careers – detectives

Allen, Laura Jean. *Where is Freddy?*
Berenstain, Stan. *The bear detectives: the case of the missing pumpkin*
Bunting, Eve (Anne Evelyn). *Jane Martin, dog detective*
Christelow, Eileen. *Gertrude, the bulldog detective*
Lawrence, James. *Binky Brothers and the fearless four*
Binky Brothers, detectives
Panek, Dennis. *Detective Whoo*
Sharmat, Marjorie Weinman. *Nate the Great*
Nate the Great and the lost list
Nate the Great and the phony clue
Nate the Great goes undercover
Thomson, Ruth. *Peabody all at sea*
Peabody's first case

Careers – doctors

Arnold, Caroline. *Who keeps us healthy?*
Berenstain, Stan. *The Berenstain bears go to the doctor*
Bertrand, Lynne. *One day, two dragons*
Breinburg, Petronella. *Doctor Shawn*
Charlip, Remy. *"Mother, mother I feel sick"*
Chislett, Gail. *Melinda's no's cold*
Cobb, Vicki. *How the doctor knows you're fine*
Corey, Dorothy. *A shot for baby bear*
DeSantis, Kenny. *A doctor's tools*
Fine, Anne. *Poor Monty*
Freeman, Don. *Corduroy's busy street and Corduroy goes to the doctor*
Gilbert, Helen Earle. *Dr. Trotter and his big gold watch*
Goodsell, Jane. *Katie's magic glasses*
Greene, Carla. *Doctors and nurses: what do they do?*
Hanklin, Rebecca. *I can be a doctor*
Kuklin, Susan. *When I see my doctor*
Lerner, Marguerite Rush. *Doctors' tools*
Linn, Margot. *A trip to the doctor*
Marcus, Susan. *Casey visits the doctor*
Oxenbury, Helen. *The checkup*
Robison, Deborah. *Your turn, doctor*
Rockwell, Harlow. *My doctor*
Rogers, Fred. *Going to the doctor*
Roop, Peter. *Stick out your tongue!*
Stein, Sara Bonnett. *A hospital story*
Viorst, Judith. *The tenth good thing about Barney*
Wahl, Jan. *Doctor Rabbit's foundling*
Watson, Jane Werner. *My friend the doctor*
Wolde, Gunilla. *Betsy and the doctor*

Careers – electricians

Lillegard, Dee. *I can be an electrician*

Careers – farmers

Brown, Craig McFarland. *Patchwork farmer*
Demuth, Patricia Brennan. *Ornery morning*
Henderson, Kathy. *I can be a farmer*

Henley, Claire. *Farm day*
Kightley, Rosalinda. *The farmer*
Kunhardt, Edith. *I want to be a farmer*
Laird, Elizabeth. *The day the ducks went
    skating*
    The day Veronica was nosy
Nordqvist, Sven. *The fox hunt*
Waddell, Martin. *Farmer Duck*

Careers – firefighters

Averill, Esther. *The fire cat*
Barbaresi, Nina. *Firemouse*
Barkan, Joanne. *Whiskerville firehouse*
Barr, Jene. *Fire snorkel number 7*
Baumann, Kurt. *Piro and the fire brigade*
Bester, Roger. *Fireman Jim*
Bridwell, Norman. *Clifford's good deeds*
Brown, Margaret Wise. *Five little firemen*
    The little fireman
Bundt, Nancy. *The fire station book*
Bushey, Jerry. *Building a fire truck*
Chalmers, Mary. *Throw a kiss, Harry*
Curious George at the fire station
Elliott, Dan. *A visit to the Sesame Street
    firehouse*
Fast rolling fire trucks, ill. by Carolyn
    Bracken
Firehouse, ill. by Zokeisha
Fisher, Leonard Everett. *Pumpers, boilers,
    hooks and ladders*
Gibbons, Gail. *Fire! Fire!*
Gramatky, Hardie. *Hercules*
Greydanus, Rose. *Big red fire engine*
Hanklin, Rebecca. *I can be a fire fighter*
Hansen, Jeff. *Being a fire fighter isn't just
    squirtin' water*
Hill, Mary Lou. *My dad's a smokejumper*
Homme, Bob. *The friendly giant's book of
    fire engines*
Keeping, Charles. *Willie's fire-engine*
Killingback, Julia. *Busy Bears at the fire
    station*
Kunhardt, Edith. *I want to be a fire fighter*
Lenski, Lois. *The little fire engine*
Leonard, Marcia. *Jeffrey Lee, future fireman*
Marston, Hope Irvin. *Fire trucks*
Mayer, Mercer. *Fireman critter*
Munsch, Robert N. *The fire station*
Rey, H. A. (Hans Augusto). *Curious George*
Robinson, Nancy K. *Firefighters!*
Rockwell, Anne F. *Fire engines*
Spiegel, Doris. *Danny and Company 92*
Spier, Peter. *Firehouse*
Steel, Danielle. *Max's daddy goes to the
    hospital*
Weiss, Harvey. *The sooner hound*
Zaffo, George J. *Big book of real fire
    engines*

Careers – fishermen

Aldridge, Josephine Haskell. *Fisherman's
    luck*
Beim, Lorraine. *Lucky Pierre*
Brown, Marcia. *Henry fisherman*
Brown, Margaret Wise. *The little fisherman*
Bunting, Eve (Anne Evelyn). *Magic and
    the night river*
Edwards, Roberta. *Five silly fishermen*
Flora, James. *Fishing with dad*
Gibbons, Gail. *Surrounded by sea*
Gramatky, Hardie. *Nikos and the sea god*
Le Tord, Bijou. *Joseph and Nellie*
Matsutani, Miyoko. *The fisherman under the
    sea*
Miles, Miska. *No, no, Rosina*
Moxley, Susan. *Abdul's treasure*
Nakawatari, Harutaka. *The sea and I*
Napoli, Guillier. *Adventure at Mont-Saint-
    Michel*
Pallotta, Jerry. *Going lobstering*
Parker, Dorothy D. *Liam's catch*
Rettich, Margret. *The voyage of the jolly boat*
Weil, Lisl. *Gertie and Gus*
Yolen, Jane. *Greyling*

Careers - forest rangers *see* Careers –
park rangers

Careers – fortune tellers

Alexander, Lloyd. *Fortune tellers*
Jeschke, Susan. *Firerose*
Weiss, Ellen. *Clara the fortune-telling chicken*

Careers – garbage collectors

Steig, William. *Tiffky Doofky*
Zion, Gene. *Dear garbage man*

Careers – geologists

Sipiera, Paul P. *I can be a geologist*

Careers – handyman

Rockwell, Anne F. *Handy Hank will fix it*

Careers – hatters

Chetwin, Grace. *Box and Cox*

Careers – housekeepers

Widman, Christine. *Housekeeper of the wind*

Careers – journalists

Leedy, Loreen. *The Furry News*

Careers – judges

Mirkovic, Irene. *The greedy shopkeeper*
Zemach, Harve. *The judge*

Careers – librarians

Baker, Donna. *I want to be a librarian*
Brillhart, Julie. *Story hour—starring Megan!*
Pinkwater, Daniel Manus. *Aunt Lulu*
Porte, Barbara Ann. *Harry in trouble*

Careers – mail carriers

Ahlberg, Janet. *The jolly Christmas postman
The jolly postman*
Barkan, Joanne. *Whiskerville post office*
Beim, Jerrold. *Country mailman*
Brandt, Betty. *Special delivery*
Buchheimer, Naomi. *Let's go to a post office*
Drummond, Violet H. *The flying postman*
Gibbons, Gail. *The post office book*
Haley, Gail E. *The post office cat*
Hedderwick, Mairi. *Katie Morag delivers the
mail*
Henri, Adrian. *The postman's palace*
Kightley, Rosalinda. *The postman*
Koscielniak, Bruce. *Euclid Bunny delivers
the mail*
Marshak, Samuel. *Hail to mail*
Maury, Inez. *My mother the mail carrier: Mi
mama la cartera*
Pryor, Bonnie. *Mr. Munday and the space
creatures*
Rylant, Cynthia. *Mr. Griggs' work*
Scarry, Richard. *Richard Scarry's Postman
Pig and his busy neighbors*
Siracusa, Catherine. *No mail for Mitchell*
Spinelli, Eileen. *Somebody loves you, Mr.
Hatch*

Careers – mechanics

Aldag, Kurt. *Some things never change*
Broekel, Ray. *I can be an auto mechanic*
Florian, Douglas. *An auto mechanic*

Careers – military

Ambrus, Victor G. *Brave soldier Janosch*
Brown, Marcia. *Stone soup*
Emberley, Barbara. *Drummer Hoff*
Langstaff, John M. *Soldier, soldier, won't you
marry me?*
McGowen, Tom (Thomas). *The only
glupmaker in the U.S. Navy*
McKinley, Robin. *My father is in the Navy*
Mahy, Margaret. *Sailor Jack and the twenty
orphans*
VanRynbach, Iris. *The soup stone*

Careers – miners

Brown, Margaret Wise. *Two little miners*
Nixon, Joan Lowery. *Fat chance, Claude*

Careers – models

Greene, Carol. *I can be a model*

Careers – musicians

Brighton, Catherine. *Mozart*
Linscott, Jody. *Once upon A to Z*
McKee, David. *The sad story of Veronica who
played the violin*
Poole, Valerie. *Obadiah Coffee and the music
contest*
Raschka, Chris. *Charlie Parker played be bop*

Careers – nuns

Routh, Jonathan. *The Nuns go to Africa*

Careers – nurses

Arnold, Caroline. *Who keeps us healthy?*
Behrens, June. *I can be a nurse*
Greene, Carla. *Doctors and nurses: what do
they do?*
Kraus, Robert. *Rebecca Hatpin*
Stein, Sara Bonnett. *A hospital story*
Whitney, Alma Marshak. *Just awful*
Woolf, Virginia. *Nurse Lugton's curtain*

Careers – park rangers

Greene, Carol. *I can be a forest ranger*
Hill, Mary Lou. *My dad's a park ranger*

Careers – peddlers

Crossley-Holland, Kevin. *The pedlar of
Swaffham*
Jacobs, Joseph. *The crock of gold*
Lewis, J. Patrick. *The moonbow of Mr. B.
Bones*
McDonald, Megan. *The potato man*
Rockwell, Anne F. *A bear, a bobcat and
three ghosts*
Slobodkina, Esphyr. *Caps for sale
Pezzo the peddler and the circus elephant
Pezzo the peddler and the thirteen silly
thieves*
Suba, Susanne. *The monkeys and the pedlar*

Careers – physicians *see* Careers –
doctors

Careers – police officers

Adelson, Leone. *Who blew that whistle?*
Ahlberg, Allan. *Cops and robbers*
Baker, Donna. *I want to be a police officer*
Brown, David. *Someone always needs a
policeman*
Chapin, Cynthia. *Squad car 55*
Erdoes, Richard. *Policemen around the world*
Goodall, John S. *Paddy's new hat*
Guilfoile, Elizabeth. *Have you seen my
brother?*
Keats, Ezra Jack. *My dog is lost!*
Lattin, Anne. *Peter's policeman*
Lenski, Lois. *Policeman Small*
McCloskey, Robert. *Make way for ducklings*

Mayer, Mercer. *Policeman critter*
Schlein, Miriam. *The amazing Mr. Pelgrew*
Vreeken, Elizabeth. *The boy who would not say his name*

Careers – printers

Chetwin, Grace. *Box and Cox*

Careers – race car drivers

Wilkinson, Sylvia. *I can be a race car driver*

Careers – railroad engineers

Lenski, Lois. *The little train*

Careers - rangers *see* Careers – park rangers

Careers - sailors *see* Careers – military

Careers – seamstresses

Chevance, Audrey. *Tutu*
Olds, Helen Diehl. *Miss Hattie and the monkey*

Careers – shepherds

Garaway, Margaret Kahn. *Ashkii and his grandfather*
Lewis, Kim. *The shepherd boy*
Wellington, Monica. *The sheep follow*

Careers – shoemakers

Gilbert, Helen Earle. *Mr. Plum and the little green tree*
Grimm, Jacob. *The elves and the shoemaker*, ill. by Paul Galdone
The elves and the shoemaker, ill. by Bernadette Watts
The shoemaker and the elves, ill. by Adrienne Adams
The shoemaker and the elves, ill. by Cynthia and William Birrer
The shoemaker and the elves, ill. by Ilse Plume
Oppenheim, Joanne. *Left and right*
Ross, Tony. *The greedy little cobbler*
Sheldon, Aure. *Of cobblers and kings*

Careers - soldiers *see* Careers – military

Careers – storekeepers

Kimmelman, Leslie. *Frannie's fruits*
Pearson, Tracey Campbell. *The storekeeper*
Shelby, Anne. *We keep a store*

Careers – tailors

Ackerman, Karen. *Just like Max*
Ambrus, Victor G. *The three poor tailors*
Galdone, Paul. *The monster and the tailor*

Grimm, Jacob. *The brave little tailor*, ill. by Mark Corcoran
The brave little tailor, ill. by Svend Otto S.
The brave little tailor, ill. by Daniel San Souci
The brave little tailor, ill. by Eve Tharlet
The brave little tailor, ill. by James Warhola
The valiant little tailor, ill. by Victor G. Ambrus
Hest, Amy. *The purple coat*
Hilton, Nette. *Dirty Dave*
Potter, Beatrix. *The tailor of Gloucester*
West, Colin. *I brought my love a tabby cat*
Yorinks, Arthur. *Oh, brother*

Careers – taxi drivers

Moore, Lilian. *Papa Albert*
Otto, Svend. *Taxi dog*
Ross, Jessica. *Ms. Klondike*

Careers – teachers

Allard, Harry. *Miss Nelson is back*
Miss Nelson is missing!
Arnold, Caroline. *Where do you go to school?*
Barkan, Joanne. *Whiskerville school*
Beckman, Beatrice. *I can be a teacher*
Brillhart, Julie. *Anna's goodbye apron*
Cummings, W. T. (Walter Thies). *Miss Esta Maude's secret*
Feder, Paula Kurzband. *Where does the teacher live?*
Glennon, Karen M. *Miss Eva and the red balloon*
Houston, Gloria. *My Great-Aunt Arizona*
James, Simon. *Dear Mr. Blueberry*
Johnson, Jean. *Teachers A to Z*
Myers, Bernice. *It happens to everyone*
Powers, Mary E. *Our teacher's in a wheelchair*
Weiss, Leatie. *My teacher sleeps in school*

Careers – telephone operators

Allen, Jeffrey. *Mary Alice, operator number 9*
Mary Alice returns

Careers - train engineers *see* Careers – railroad engineers

Careers – truck drivers

Behrens, June. *I can be a truck driver*
Cartlidge, Michelle. *Teddy trucks*
Horenstein, Henry. *Sam goes trucking*
Young, Miriam Burt. *If I drove a truck*

Careers – veterinarians

Bellville, Rod. *Large animal veterinarians*
Herriot, James. *Moses the kitten*
  Only one woof
Hewett, Joan. *Fly away free*
Kuklin, Susan. *Taking my dog to the vet*
Lumley, Katheryn Wentzel. *I can be an animal doctor*
Polhamus, Jean Burt. *Doctor Dinosaur*
Stamper, Judith. *What's it like to be a veterinarian*

Careers – waiters, waitresses

Krementz, Jill. *Benjy goes to a restaurant*
Mooser, Stephen. *Funnyman's first case*
Peters, Sharon. *Happy Jack*

Careers - waitresses *see* Careers – waiters, waitresses

Careers – welders

Lillegard, Dee. *I can be a welder*

Careers – window cleaners

Dahl, Roald. *The giraffe and the pelly and me*
Rey, H. A. (Hans Augusto). *Curious George takes a job*

Careers – writers

Broekel, Ray. *I can be an author*
Goffstein, M. B. (Marilyn Brooke). *A writer*

Careers – zookeepers

Löfgren, Ulf. *Alvin the zookeeper*

Carelessness *see* Behavior – carelessness

Caribbean Islands *see* Foreign lands – Caribbean Islands

Carnivals *see* Fairs

Carousels *see* Merry-go-rounds

Carousels *see* Merry-go-rounds

Carpenters *see* Careers – carpenters

Cars *see* Automobiles

Caterpillars *see* Insects – butterflies, caterpillars

Cats *see* Animals – cats

Cavemen

Hoff, Syd. *Stanley*
Seyton, Marion. *The hole in the hill*
Slobodkin, Louis. *Dinny and Danny*

Caves

Baynes, Pauline. *How dog began*
Brett, Jan. *The first dog*
Tettelbaum, Michael. *The cave of the lost Fraggle*
Ungerer, Tomi. *The Mellops go spelunking*

Central America *see* Foreign lands – Central America

Chairs *see* Furniture – chairs

Chanukah *see* Holidays – Hanukkah

Character traits

Johnson, Crockett. *The emperor's gift*
Seignobosc, Françoise. *Jeanne-Marie in gay Paris*
Wahl, Jan. *Mrs. Owl and Mr. Pig*
Walker, Alice. *Finding the green stone*
Wilde, Oscar. *Fairy tales of Oscar Wilde: The selfish giant, and The star child*, adapt. and ill. by P. Craig Russell
Wilson-Kelly, Becky. *Mother Grumpy's dog biscuits*

Character traits – ambition

Balet, Jan B. *Joanjo*
Barton, Byron. *I want to be an astronaut*
Claude-Lafontaine, Pascale. *Monsieur Bussy, the celebrated hamster*
Graham, Al. *Timothy Turtle*
Gramatky, Hardie. *Little Toot*
Greaves, Margaret. *Henry's wild morning*
Horwitz, Elinor Lander. *Sometimes it happens*
Kumin, Maxine. *Speedy digs downside up*
Ringi, Kjell (Arne Sorensen). *My father and I*
Seignobosc, Françoise. *What do you want to be?*
Shecter, Ben. *Hester the jester*
Turska, Krystyna. *The magician of Cracow*
Uchida, Yoshiko. *Sumi's prize*

Character traits – appearance

Andersen, H. C. (Hans Christian). *The ugly duckling*, ill. by Adrienne Adams
  The ugly duckling, ill. by Lorinda Bryan Cauley
  The ugly duckling, ill. by Troy Howell
  The ugly duckling, ill. by Tadasu Izawa and Shigemi Hijikata

The ugly duckling, ill. by Monika
  Laimgruber
The ugly duckling, ill. by Johannes
  Larsen
The ugly duckling, ill. by Thomas Locker
The ugly duckling, ill. by Alan Marks
The ugly duckling, ill. by Josef Paleček
The ugly duckling, ill. by Daniel San
  Souci
The ugly duckling, ill. by Robert Van
  Nutt
The ugly little duck, ill. by Peggy Perry
  Anderson
Balestrino, Philip. *Fat and skinny*
Beim, Jerrold. *Freckle face*
Bonsall, Crosby Newell. *Listen, listen!*
Caseley, Judith. *Molly Pink goes hiking*
Charles, Donald. *Shaggy dog's Halloween*
Chevalier, Christa. *Spence isn't Spence
  anymore*
Cohen, Burton. *Nelson makes a face*
Collins, Judith Graham. *Josh's scary dad*
Crowley, Arthur. *The ugly book*
Dellinger, Annetta. *You are special to Jesus*
De Paola, Tomie (Thomas Anthony). *Big
  Anthony and the magic ring*
Eco, Umberto. *The three astronauts*
Elborn, Andrew. *Bird Adalbert*
Fatio, Louise. *The happy lion and the bear*
Freeman, Don. *Dandelion*
Ginsburg, Mirra. *The Chinese mirror*
Girion, Barbara. *The boy with the special
  face*
Goble, Paul. *Star boy*
Greenfield, Eloise. *Grandpa's face*
Grimm, Jacob. *The ugly duckling*, ill. by
  Maria Ruis
Hale, Irina. *Brown bear in a brown chair*
Heine, Helme. *The most wonderful egg in
  the world*
Hillert, Margaret. *The funny baby*
Iké, Jane Hori. *A Japanese fairy tale*
Kasza, Keiko. *The pigs' picnic*
Keller, Irene. *The Thingumajig book of
  manners*
Lindenbaum, Pija. *Boodil, my dog*
McDermott, Gerald. *The magic tree*
Maestro, Betsy. *On the town*
Mayer, Marianna. *Beauty and the beast*
Mayer, Mercer. *How the trollusk got his hat*
Moore, Sheila. *Samson Svenson's baby*
Munsch, Robert N. *The paper bag princess*
Myers, Amy. *I know a monster*
Nesbit, Edith. *Beauty and the beast*
Ness, Evaline. *The girl and the goatherd*
Numeroff, Laura Joffe. *Amy for short*
Ormerod, Jan. *Just like me*
  Our Ollie
  Silly goose
Ormondroyd, Edward. *Theodore*
Park, Ruth. *When the wind changed*

Primavera, Elise. *Basil and Maggie*
Quinsey, Mary Beth. *Why does that man
  have such a big nose?*
Ring, Elizabeth. *Tiger lilies and other beastly
  plants*
Salus, Naomi Panush. *My daddy's mustache*
Schaffer, Libor. *Arthur sets sail*
Scott, Natalie (Anderson). *Firebrand, push
  your hair out of your eyes*
Small, David. *Imogene's antlers*
Stren, Patti. *Mountain Rose*
Thomson, Peggy. *The king has horse's ears*

Character traits – assertiveness

Dunbar, Joyce. *A cake for Barney*
Ingoglia, Gina. *The art class*
Martchenko, Michael. *Bird feeder banquet*
Moss, Marissa. *After-school monster*

Character traits – being different

Allinson, Beverley. *Effie*
Andersen, H. C. (Hans Christian). *The
  ugly duckling*, ill. by Adrienne Adams
The ugly duckling, ill. by Lorinda Bryan
  Cauley
The ugly duckling, ill. by Troy Howell
The ugly duckling, ill. by Tadasu Izawa
  and Shigemi Hijikata
The ugly duckling, ill. by Monika
  Laimgruber
The ugly duckling, ill. by Johannes
  Larsen
The ugly duckling, ill. by Thomas Locker
The ugly duckling, ill. by Alan Marks
The ugly duckling, ill. by Josef Paleček
The ugly duckling, ill. by Daniel San
  Souci
The ugly duckling, ill. by Robert Van
  Nutt
The ugly little duck, ill. by Peggy Perry
  Anderson
Aulaire, Ingri Mortenson d'. *Nils*
Baumann, Hans. *Mischa and his brothers*
Beim, Jerrold. *Freckle face*
Blos, Joan W. *Old Henry*
Blue, Rose. *I am here: Yo estoy aqui*
Brandenberg, Franz. *Otto is different*
Brightman, Alan. *Like me*
Burningham, John. *Borka*
Caple, Kathy. *The biggest nose*
Carle, Eric. *The mixed-up chameleon*
Chapman, Elizabeth. *Suzy*
Cohen, Miriam. *It's George!*
Coombs, Patricia. *The lost playground*
Corbalis, Judy. *Porcellus, the flying pig*
Counsel, June. *But Martin!*
Crossley-Holland, Kevin. *The green children*
De Veaux, Alexis. *An enchanted hair tale*
Dinan, Carolyn. *Say cheese!*
Dubanevich, Arlene. *Pigs at Christmas*

Duvoisin, Roger Antoine. *Our Veronica goes to Petunia's farm*
Veronica
Emberley, Ed (Edward Randolph). *Rosebud*
Escudie, René. *Paul and Sebastian*
Fern, Eugene. *Pepito's story*
Grimm, Jacob. *The ugly duckling*, ill. by Maria Ruis
Hayes, Sarah. *Mary Mary*
Heine, Helme. *Superhare*
Hillert, Margaret. *The funny baby*
Hoff, Syd. *Mrs. Brice's mice*
Karlin, Nurit. *The blue frog*
Keller, Holly. *Horace*
Krasilovsky, Phyllis. *The very tall little girl*
Kuklin, Susan. *Thinking big*
Leedy, Loreen. *Pingo the plaid panda*
Lerner, Marguerite Rush. *Lefty, the story of left-handedness*
Levine, Rhoda. *Harrison loved his umbrella*
Lionni, Leo. *Cornelius*
McGovern, Ann. *Mr. Skinner's skinny house*
McKelvey, David. *Bobby the mostly silky*
Nordlicht, Lillian. *I love to laugh*
Paek, Min. *Aekyung's dream*
Passen, Lisa. *Fat, fat Rose Marie*
Payne, Sherry Neuwirth. *A contest*
Peet, Bill (William Bartlett). *The spooky tail of Prewitt Peacock*
Polisar, Barry Louis. *The trouble with Ben*
Quinsey, Mary Beth. *Why does that man have such a big nose?*
Reesink, Marijke. *The princess who always ran away*
Rey, Margřet (Margřet Elisabeth Waldstein). *Spotty*
Riddell, Chris. *Bird's new shoes*
Schertle, Alice. *Jeremy Bean's St. Patrick's Day*
Schotter, Roni. *Captain Snap and the children of Vinegar Lane*
Sharmat, Marjorie Weinman. *Helga high-up*
Shles, Larry. *Moths and mothers, feathers and fathers*
Shub, Elizabeth. *Dragon Franz*
Simon, Norma. *Why am I different?*
Simon, Sidney B. *The armadillo who had no shell*
Stapler, Sarah. *Cordellia, dance!*
Voake, Charlotte. *Mrs. Goose's baby*
Wadhams, Margaret. *Anna*
Wallace, Barbara Brooks. *Argyle*
Wells, Rosemary. *Abdul*
Whitmore, Adam. *Max in America*
Max in Australia
Max in India
Max leaves home
Wilkoń, Piotr. *Rosie the cool cat*
Willis, Jeanne. *The long blue blazer*
Wood, Audrey. *Weird parents*

Character traits – bravery

Aitken, Amy. *Ruby, the red knight*
Aliki. *George and the cherry tree*
Andersen, H. C. (Hans Christian). *The snow queen*, ill. by Angela Barrett
The snow queen, ill. by Toma Bogdanovic
The snow queen, ill. by June Atkin Corwin
The snow queen, ill. by Sally Holmes
The snow queen, ill. by Susan Jeffers
The snow queen, ill. by Errol Le Cain
The snow queen, ill. by Bernadette Watts
The snow queen, ill. by Arieh Zeldich
Anglund, Joan Walsh. *The brave cowboy*
Ardizzone, Edward. *Little Tim and the brave sea captain*
Paul, the hero of the fire
Peter the wanderer
Tim and Charlotte
Tim to the rescue
Aulaire, Ingri Mortenson d'. *Wings for Per*
Baldner, Gaby. *Joba and the wild boar*
Bannon, Laura. *Hat for a hero*
Barr, Cathrine. *Little Ben*
Barrows, Marjorie Wescott. *Fraidy cat*
Baumann, Kurt. *Piro and the fire brigade*
Bawden, Nina. *William Tell*
Beim, Jerrold. *Eric on the desert*
Benchley, Nathaniel. *The deep dives of Stanley Whale*
Blegvad, Lenore. *Anna Banana and me*
Bornstein, Ruth Lercher. *Jim*
Brook, Judy. *Tim mouse goes down the stream*
Brown, Margaret Wise. *Streamlined pig*
Burgert, Hans-Joachim. *Samulo and the giant*
Cameron, Ann. *Harry (the monster)*
Carleton, Barbee Oliver. *Benny and the bear*
Carlson, Nancy. *Harriet and the roller coaster*
Chaffin, Lillie D. *We be warm till springtime comes*
Chapouton, Anne-Marie. *Billy the brave*
Charlton, Elizabeth. *Jeremy and the ghost*
Church, Kristine. *My brother John*
Conford, Ellen. *Eugene the brave*
Coombs, Patricia. *Molly Mullett*
Coville, Bruce. *The foolish giant*
Craft, Ruth. *Carrie Hepple's garden*
De La Mare, Walter (Walter John). *Molly Whuppie*
De Posadas Mane, Carmen. *Mister North Wind*
Douglas, Richard Keens. *The nutmeg princess*
Dreifus, Miriam W. *Brave Betsy*
Dyke, John. *Pigwig*
Fatio, Louise. *The red bantam*
Fern, Eugene. *The most frightened hero*

Fuchshuber, Annegert. *Giant story - Mouse tale*

Furchgott, Terry. *Phoebe and the hot water bottles*

Gantschev, Ivan. *The Christmas train*

Ginsburg, Mirra. *The strongest one of all*

Goodall, John S. *Paddy to the rescue*

Grant, Joan. *The monster that grew small*

Grasshopper to the rescue, ill. by Tasha Tudor

Greaves, Margaret. *Once there were no pandas*

Grimm, Jacob. *The brave little tailor*, ill. by Mark Corcoran

The brave little tailor, ill. by Svend Otto S.

The brave little tailor, ill. by Daniel San Souci

The brave little tailor, ill. by Eve Tharlet

The brave little tailor, ill. by James Warhola

The valiant little tailor, ill. by Victor G. Ambrus

Haley, Gail E. *Jack and the fire dragon*

Harris, Leon A. *The great diamond robbery*

Hayes, Sarah. *This is the bear and the scary night*

Hazen, Barbara Shook. *Fang*

Helldorfer, M. C. (Mary Claire). *The mapmaker's daughter*

Henkes, Kevin. *Sheila Rae, the brave*

Hiser, Berniece T. *The adventure of Charlie and his wheat-straw hat*

Holl, Adelaide. *Sir Kevin of Devon*

Hooks, William H. *Peach boy*

Hort, Lenny. *The boy who held back the sea*

Horvath, Betty F. *Jasper and the hero business*

Hürlimann, Bettina. *Barry: the story of a brave St. Bernard*

Jakes, John. *Susanna of the Alamo*

Jaques, Faith. *Tilly's rescue*

Keller, Beverly. *Pimm's place*

Lagercrantz, Rose. *Brave little Pete of Geranium Street*

Le Guin, Ursula K. *A ride on the red mare's back*

Leonard, Alain. *Barnaby and the big gorilla*

Lewis, Robin Baird. *Friska, the sheep that was too small*

Lexau, Joan M. *It all began with a drip, drip, drip*

Little, Jean. *Jess was the brave one*

Little, Lessie Jones. *I can do it by myself*

Littlewood, Valerie. *The season clock*

Low, Joseph. *Benny rabbit and the owl*
Boo to a goose

Marshak, Samuel. *The tale of a hero nobody knows*

Martin, Bill (William Ivan). *Knots on a counting rope*

Matsutani, Miyoko. *The witch's magic cloth*

Mayer, Marianna. *The unicorn and the lake*

Mayer, Mercer. *Liverwurst is missing*
Liza Lou and the Yeller Belly Swamp

Milne, A. A. (Alan Alexander). *Winnie-the-Pooh*

Moss, Marissa. *After-school monster*

Nash, Ogden. *The adventures of Isabel*, ill. by Walter Lorraine

The adventures of Isabel, ill. by James Marshall

Custard the dragon, ill. by Linell Nash

Nishikawa, Osamu. *Alexander and the blue ghost*

Olson, Arielle North. *The lighthouse keeper's daughter*

Oppenheim, Shulamith Levey. *The lily cupboard*

Peet, Bill (William Bartlett). *Cowardly Clyde*

Polushkin, Maria. *The little hen and the giant*

Pryor, Bonnie. *The porcupine mouse*

San Souci, Robert D. *The enchanted tapestry*

Scarry, Richard. *Richard Scarry's Peasant Pig and the terrible dragon*

Schertle, Alice. *The gorilla in the hall*

Schumacher, Claire. *Brave Lily*

Sewell, Helen Moore. *Jimmy and Jemima*

Shire, Ellen. *The mystery at number seven, Rue Petite*

Shute, Linda. *Momotaro, the peach boy*

Small, Terry. *The legend of William Tell*

Stanek, Muriel. *All alone after school*

Steig, William. *Brave Irene*

Stevenson, Drew. *The ballad of Penelope Lou...and me*

Taylor, Mark. *Henry explores the jungle*
Henry explores the mountains
Henry the explorer

Titus, Eve. *Anatole and the cat*

Va, Leong. *A letter to the king*

Van Woerkom, Dorothy. *Becky and the bear*

Wells, H. G. (Herbert George). *The adventures of Tommy*

Wetterer, Margaret. *Kate Shelley and the midnight express*

Wilkoń, Piotr. *The brave little kittens*

Wolkstein, Diane. *The banza*

Character traits – cleanliness

Adelborg, Ottilia. *Clean Peter and the children of Grubbylea*

Allen, Jonathan. *Mucky moose*

Bowling, David Louis. *Dirty Dingy Daryl*

Bucknall, Caroline. *One bear in the picture*

Burch, Robert. *The jolly witch*

Cobb, Vicki. *Keeping clean*

Cummings, Pat. *Clean your room, Harvey Moon!*

De Paola, Tomie (Thomas Anthony). *Marianna May and Nursey*

Dickinson, Mary. *Alex's bed*
Eagle, Ellen. *Gypsy's cleaning day*
Edwards, Frank B. *Mortimer Mooner stopped taking a bath*
Flot, Jeannette B. *Princess Kalina and the hedgehog*
Gantos, Jack (John, Jr.). *Swampy alligator*
Groves-Raines, Antony. *The tidy hen*
Hamsa, Bobbie. *Dirty Larry*
Hare, Lorraine. *Who needs her?*
Haseley, Dennis. *The soap bandit*
Hickman, Martha Whitmore. *Eeps creeps, it's my room!*
Howells, Mildred. *The woman who lived in Holland*
Hurd, Edith Thacher. *Stop, stop*
Hutchins, Pat. *Where's the baby?*
Jackson, Ellen B. *The bear in the bathtub*
Krasilovsky, Phyllis. *The man who did not wash his dishes*
Lindbergh, Anne. *Tidy lady*
McKissack, Patricia C. *Ada, la desordenada: Messy Bessy*
McQueen, Lucinda. *Tidy pig*
Madden, Don. *The Wartville wizard*
Mahy, Margaret. *Keeping house*
Miller, Edward. *The curse of Claudia*
Morris, Ann. *Eleanora Mousie makes a mess*
Nerlove, Miriam. *I meant to clean my room today*
Peters, Sharon. *Messy Mark*
Polushkin, Maria. *Bubba and Babba*
Potter, Beatrix. *The tale of Mrs. Tittlemouse*
Rockwell, Anne F. *Nice and clean*
Rounds, Glen. *Washday on Noah's ark*
Schwartz, Mary. *Spiffen*
Serfozo, Mary. *Dirty Kurt*
Sharmat, Marjorie Weinman. *Mooch the messy*
Sharmat, Mitchell. *The seven sloppy days of Phineas Pig*
Stanton, Elizabeth. *The very messy room*
Wabbes, Marie. *Rose is muddy*
Wells, Rosemary. *Fritz and the mess fairy*
Wilhelm, Hans. *Oh, what a mess*
Willis, Jeanne. *The tale of Georgie Grub*
Wilson, Sarah. *The day that Henry cleaned his room*
Ziefert, Harriet. *A clean house for Mole and Mouse*
Hurry up, Jessie!

Character traits – cleverness

Alderson, Sue Ann. *Ida and the wool smugglers*
Aliki. *The eggs*
Andersen, H. C. (Hans Christian). *The swineherd*, ill. by Erik Blegvad
The swineherd, ill. by Dorothée Duntze
The swineherd, ill. by Deborah Hahn
The swineherd, ill. by Lisbeth Zwerger

Anderson, Paul S. *Red fox and the hungry tiger*
Ardizzone, Edward. *Peter the wanderer*
Asbjørnsen, P. C. (Peter Christen). *The three billy goats Gruff*, ill. by Marcia Brown
Three billy goats Gruff, ill. by Tom Dunnington
The three billy goats Gruff, ill. by Paul Galdone
The three billy goats Gruff, ill. by Janet Stevens
The three billy goats Gruff, ill. by William Stobbs
Baker, Betty. *And me, coyote!*
Partners
Bang, Betsy. *The old woman and the red pumpkin*
The old woman and the rice thief
Bang, Molly. *Wiley and the hairy man*
Bannerman, Helen. *The story of little black Sambo*
Bason, Lillian. *Those foolish Molboes!*
Bell, Anthea. *The wise queen*
Bemelmans, Ludwig. *Welcome home*
Berson, Harold. *How the devil got his due*
Joseph and the snake
Why the jackal won't speak to the hedgehog
Bishop, Claire Huchet. *The five Chinese brothers*
Boegehold, Betty. *Pawpaw's run*
Brett, Jan. *Fritz and the beautiful horses*
Brown, Marcia. *The bun*
Stone soup
Brown, Margaret Wise. *Don't frighten the lion*
Buchanan, Heather S. *George Mouse's first summer*
Burningham, John. *Harquin: the fox who went down to the valley*
The shopping basket
Byfield, Barbara Ninde. *The haunted churchbell*
Calhoun, Mary. *Cross-country cat*
Jack and the whoopee wind
Cameron, John. *If mice could fly*
Caseley, Judith. *Ada potato*
Castle, Caroline. *Herbert Binns and the flying tricycle*
Cauley, Lorinda Bryan. *The cock, the mouse and the little red hen*
The trouble with Tyrannosaurus Rex
Christelow, Eileen. *Jerome the babysitter*
Climo, Shirley. *King of the birds*
Coatsworth, Elizabeth. *Pika and the roses*
Cohen, Caron Lee. *Renata, Whizbrain and the ghost*
Cole, Joanna. *Doctor Change*
Crompton, Anne Eliot. *The lifting stone*
Damjan, Mischa. *The wolf and the kid*
Daniels, Guy. *The Tsar's riddles*

Dee, Ruby. *Two ways to count to ten*
De La Mare, Walter (Walter John). *Molly Whuppie*
Demi. *Under the shade of the mulberry tree*
De Regniers, Beatrice Schenk. *Catch a little fox*
Dickens, Frank. *Boffo*
Dines, Glen. *Gilly and the wicharoo*
Dodd, Lynley. *Hairy Maclary's bone*
Domanska, Janina. *The best of the bargain*
King Krakus and the dragon
Why so much noise?
Dos Santos, Joyce Audy. *The diviner*
Elkin, Benjamin. *Gillespie and the guards*
Lucky and the giant
Erickson, Russell E. *Warton and the traders*
Ernst, Lisa Campbell. *The prize pig surprise*
Frankel, Bernice. *Half-As-Big and the tiger*
Frascino, Edward. *My cousin the king*
Freschet, Berniece. *Elephant and friends*
Galdone, Paul. *The monkey and the crocodile*
What's in fox's sack?
Ginsburg, Mirra. *The fisherman's son*
Goldman, Dara. *There's no such thing!*
Grimm, Jacob. *The four clever brothers*, ill. by Felix Hoffmann
Harrison, David Lee. *Little boy soup*
Hayes, Sarah. *Nine ducks nine*
Hazen, Barbara Shook. *The Fat Cats, Cousin Scraggs and the monster mice*
Hillert, Margaret. *The three goats*
Hirsh, Marilyn. *The Rabbi and the twenty-nine witches*
Hogrogian, Nonny. *Rooster brother*
Hooks, William H. *Three rounds with rabbit*
Huck, Charlotte. *Princess Furball*
Hutton, Warwick. *The nose tree*
Jaffe, Rona. *Last of the wizards*
Jameson, Cynthia. *The house of five bears*
Kennedy, Richard. *The contests at Cowlick*
Laroche, Michel. *The snow rose*
Leverich, Kathleen. *The hungry fox and the foxy duck*
Lobel, Anita. *The straw maid*
Lobel, Arnold. *How the rooster saved the day*
Mouse soup
Logue, Christopher. *The magic circus*
Lorenz, Lee. *The feathered ogre*
McClenathan, Louise. *My mother sends her wisdom*
McCormack, John E. *Rabbit tales*
McCurdy, Michael. *The devils who learned to be good*
Mahy, Margaret. *The seven Chinese brothers*
Mantinband, Gerda. *Three clever mice*
Martin, Charles E. *Dunkel takes a walk*
Mogensen, Jan. *The tiger's breakfast*
Obrist, Jürg. *The miser who wanted the sun*
Parish, Peggy. *Zed and the monsters*
Parry, Marian. *King of the fish*

Paterson, A. B. (Andrew Barton). *The man from Ironbark*
Patron, Susan. *Burgoo stew*
Paul, Anthony. *The tiger who lost his stripes*
Perrault, Charles. *Puss in boots*, ill. by Marcia Brown
Puss in boots, ill. by Lorinda Bryan Cauley
Puss in boots, ill. by Jean Claverie
Puss in boots, ill. by Hans Fischer
Puss in boots, ill. by Paul Galdone
Puss in boots, retold and ill. by John S. Goodall
Puss in boots, retold and ill. by Gail E. Haley
Puss in boots, ill. by Julia Noonan
Puss in boots, ill. by Tony Ross
Puss in boots, ill. by William Stobbs
Puss in boots, ill. by Alain Vaes
Puss in boots, ill. by Barry Wilkinson
Pittman, Helena Clare. *A grain of rice*
Potter, Beatrix. *The sly old cat*
The tale of the Flopsy Bunnies
Prokofiev, Sergei Sergeievitch. *Peter and the wolf*, ill. by Reg Cartwright
Peter and the wolf, ill. by Warren Chappell
Peter and the wolf, ill. by Barbara Cooney
Peter and the wolf, ill. by Frans Haacken
Peter and the wolf, ill. by Alan Howard
Peter and the wolf, ill. by Charles Mikolaycak
Peter and the wolf, ill. by Jörg Müller
Peter and the wolf, ill. by Josef Paleček
Peter and the wolf, ill. by Kozo Shimizu
Peter and the wolf, ill. by Erna Voigt
Ransome, Arthur. *The fool of the world and the flying ship*
Rockwell, Anne F. *Big boss*
The bump in the night
The stolen necklace
Ross, Tony. *Stone soup*
Schatell, Brian. *Sam's no dummy, Farmer Goff*
Schatz, Letta. *The extraordinary tug-of-war*
Sheldon, Aure. *Of cobblers and kings*
Siddiqui, Ashraf. *Bhombal Dass, the uncle of lion*
Simon, Sidney B. *Henry, the uncatchable mouse*
Singh, Jacquelin. *Fat Gopal*
Small, David. *Paper John*
Steig, William. *Doctor De Soto*
Stewig, John Warren. *Stone soup*
Storr, Catherine (Cole). *Clever Polly and the stupid wolf*
Threadgall, Colin. *Proud rooster and the fox*
The three little pigs. *The original three little pigs re-told*, ill. by Jonathan Smith

The story of the three little pigs, ill. by L. Leslie Brooke

The story of the three little pigs, ill. by William Stobbs

Three little pigs [Facsimile ed]

The three little pigs, retold and ill. by Val Biro

The three little pigs, retold and ill. by Gavin Bishop

The three little pigs, ill. by Erik Blegvad

The three little pigs, ill. by Caroline Bucknall

The three little pigs, ill. by Stephen Cartwright

The three little pigs, ill. by Lorinda Bryan Cauley

The three little pigs, ill. by Jean Claverie

The three little pigs, ill. by William Pène Du Bois

The three little pigs, ill. by Paul Galdone

The three little pigs, retold and ill. by James Marshall

The three little pigs, ill. by Rodney Peppé

The three little pigs, ill. by Edda Reinl

The three little pigs, ill. by John Wallner

The three little pigs, ill. by Irma Wilde

The three little pigs, ill. by Margot Zemach

The three little pigs and the big bad wolf, retold and ill. by Glen Rounds

The three little pigs and the fox, ill. by S. D. Schindler

The three pigs, ill. by Tony Ross

Troughton, Joanna. *Mouse-Deer's market*

VanRynbach, Iris. *The soup stone*

Van Woerkom, Dorothy. *The rat, the ox and the zodiac*

Walker, Barbara K. (Barbara Kerlin). *Teeny-Tiny and the witch-woman*

Westwood, Jennifer. *Going to Squintum's*

Wetterer, Margaret. *Patrick and the fairy thief*

Wild, Robin. *Little Pig and the big bad wolf*

Williams, Jay. *School for sillies*

Wolkstein, Diane. *The cool ride in the sky*

Wood, Audrey. *Heckedy Peg*

Young, Ed (Edward). *The terrible Nung Gwama*

Zakhoder, Boris Vladimirovich. *The good stepmother*

Zemach, Harve. *Nail soup*

Character traits – completing things

Flack, Marjorie. *Angus and the cat*

Ness, Evaline. *Do you have the time, Lydia?*

Petrides, Heidrun. *Hans and Peter*

Character traits – compromising

Hogrogian, Nonny. *Carrot cake*

Wildsmith, Brian. *The owl and the woodpecker*

Character traits – conceit

Bellows, Cathy. *The royal raccoon*

Brenner, Barbara A. *Mr. Tall and Mr. Small*

Flack, Marjorie. *Angus and the ducks*

Goble, Paul. *Iktomi and the boulder*
Iktomi and the buffalo skull

Grimm, Jacob. *King Grisly-Beard*, ill. by Maurice Sendak

Peet, Bill (William Bartlett). *Ella*

Sharmat, Marjorie Weinman. *I'm terrific*

Williams, Barbara. *So what if I'm a sore loser?*

Character traits – confidence

Alexander, Martha G. *My outrageous friend Charlie*

Barrett, Joyce Durham. *Willie's not the hugging kind*

Callan, Elizabeth Koda. *Good luck pony*

Caseley, Judith. *Harry and Willy and Carrothead*

Pocock, Rita. *Annabelle and the big slide*

Seed, Jenny. *Ntombi's song*

Wilhelm, Hans. *A cool kid—like me!*

Character traits - cruelty to animals *see* Character traits – kindness to animals

Character traits – curiosity

Adamson, Gareth. *Old man up a tree*

Alden, Laura. *When?*

Allen, Jeffrey. *Nosey Mrs. Rat*

Ames, Mildred. *The wonderful box*

Bang, Molly. *Dawn*

Bird, E. J. *How do bears sleep?*

Bograd, Larry. *Egon*

Broome, Errol. *The smallest koala*

Campbell, Rod. *Buster's afternoon*
Buster's morning

Clark, Roberta. *Why?*

Climo, Shirley. *The adventure of Walter*

Curious George and the dump truck

Curious George and the pizza

Curious George at the fire station

Curious George goes hiking

Curious George goes sledding

Curious George goes to the aquarium

Curious George goes to the circus

Curious George visits the zoo

Demarest, Chris L. *Clemens' kingdom*

Fisher, Aileen Lucia. *Anybody home?*

Flack, Marjorie. *Angus and the cat*
Angus and the ducks

Gackenbach, Dick. *The pig who saw everything*

Kanao, Keiko. *Kitten up a tree*

Kipling, Rudyard. *The elephant's child*, ill. by Louise Brierley
The elephant's child, ill. by Lorinda Bryan Cauley
The elephant's child, ill. by Tim Raglin
MacGregor, Marilyn. *Baby takes a trip*
Meeks, Esther K. *The curious cow*
Moncure, Jane Belk. *Where?*
Napoli, Guillier. *Adventure at Mont-Saint-Michel*
Pinkwater, Daniel Manus. *Devil in the drain*
Ravilious, Robin. *The runaway chick*
Reece, Colleen L. *What?*
Rey, H. A. (Hans Augusto). *Curious George*
Curious George gets a medal
Curious George learns the alphabet
Curious George rides a bike
Curious George takes a job
Rey, Margret (Margret Elisabeth Waldstein). *Curious George flies a kite*
Curious George goes to the hospital
Rylant, Cynthia. *Miss Maggie*
Sandberg, Inger. *Dusty wants to borrow everything*
Waber, Bernard. *Lorenzo*
Weil, Lisl. *Pandora's box*
Yolen, Jane. *Eeny, meeny, miney mole*

Character traits – flattery

Æsop. *Three fox fables*, ill. by Paul Galdone
Chaucer, Geoffrey. *Chanticleer and the fox*, ill. by Barbara Cooney

Character traits – foolishness

Bason, Lillian. *Those foolish Molboes!*
Bradman, Tony. *Not like this, like that*
Gackenbach, Dick. *Harvey, the foolish pig*
Gammell, Stephen. *The story of Mr. and Mrs. Vinegar*
Grimm, Jacob. *Hans in luck*, ill. by Paul Galdone
Hans in luck, ill. by Felix Hoffmann
Lucky Hans, ill. by Eugen Sopko
Hewitt, Kathryn. *The three sillies*
Jacobs, Joseph. *Lazy Jack*, ill. by Barry Wilkinson
Johnson, Evelyne. *The cow in the kitchen*
Keenen, George. *The preposterous week*
Maitland, Antony. *Idle Jack*
Phillips, Louis. *The brothers Wrong and Wrong Again*
Schwartz, Amy. *Yossel Zissel and the wisdom of Chelm*
Scruton, Clive. *Circus cow*
Zemach, Margot. *The three wishes*

Character traits - fortune *see* Character traits – luck

Character traits – freedom

Andersen, H. C. (Hans Christian). *The emperor and the nightingale*, ill. by James Watling
The emperor's nightingale, ill. from the Disney arcives
The emperor's nightingale, ill. by Georges Lemoine
The nightingale, ill. by Harold Berson
The nightingale, ill. by Nancy Ekholm Burkert
The nightingale, ill. by Demi
The nightingale, ill. by Alison Claire Darke
The nightingale, ill. by Beni Montresor
The nightingale, ill. by Josef Paleček
The nightingale, ill. by Regolo Ricci
The nightingale, ill. by Lisbeth Zwerger
Babbitt, Natalie. *Nellie, a cat on her own*
Bayar, Steven. *Rachel and Mischa*
Baylor, Byrd. *Hawk, I'm your brother*
Blaustein, Muriel. *Baby Mabu and Auntie Moose*
Bradford, Ann. *The mystery of the missing raccoon*
Bunting, Eve (Anne Evelyn). *How many days to America?*
De Beer, Hans. *Little polar bear finds a friend*
Dennis, Wesley. *Tumble, the story of a mustang*
Fatio, Louise. *Hector and Christina*
Fujita, Tamao. *The boy and the bird*
Hawkinson, John. *Where the wild apples grow*
McPhail, David. *A wolf story*
Steiner, Jörg. *Rabbit Island*
Stern, Mark. *It's a dog's life*
Sundgaard, Arnold. *The lamb and the butterfly*

Character traits – generosity

Ainsworth, Ruth. *The mysterious Baba and her magic caravan*
Aliki. *The story of Johnny Appleseed*
Anglund, Joan Walsh. *Christmas is a time of giving*
Bawden, Nina. *St. Francis of Assisi*
Bohanon, Paul. *Golden Kate*
Brown, Palmer. *Something for Christmas*
Chalmers, Mary. *A hat for Amy Jean*
Christian, Mary Blount. *The devil take you, Barnabas Beane!*
Chute, Beatrice Joy. *Joy to Christmas*
Cohen, Barbara. *Even higher*
Cohen, Miriam. *Liar, liar, pants on fire!*
Emberley, Michael. *The present*
Erickson, Russell E. *Warton and the traders*
Farjeon, Eleanor. *Mrs. Malone*

Fontane, Theodor. *Nick Ribbeck of Ribbeck of Havelland*
Sir Ribbeck of Ribbeck of Havelland
Fox, Mem. *With love, at Christmas*
Grimm, Jacob. *The falling stars*, ill. by Eugen Sopko
Henry, O. *The gift of the Magi*
Hoban, Russell. *Emmet Otter's jug-band Christmas*
The mole family's Christmas
Houston, John A. *The bright yellow rope*
Hush little baby. *Hush little baby*, ill. by Aliki
Hush little baby, ill. by Jeanette Winter
Hush little baby, ill. by Margot Zemach
Janice. *Little Bear's Christmas*
Johnson, Crockett. *The emperor's gift*
Kasza, Keiko. *The wolf's chicken stew*
Kunnas, Mauri. *Twelve gifts for Santa Claus*
Lattimore, Deborah Nourse. *The dragon's robe*
Lexau, Joan M. *A house so big*
Lindman, Maj. *Snipp, Snapp, Snurr and the red shoes*
Lionni, Leo. *Tico and the golden wings*
McClenathan, Louise. *The Easter pig*
Marton, Jirina. *Flowers for mom*
Muntean, Michaela. *Mokey and the festival of the bells*
Ness, Evaline. *Josefina February*
Rockwell, Anne F. *Gogo's pay day*
Rodanas, Kristina. *The story of Wali Dâd*
Schotter, Roni. *Captain Snap and the children of Vinegar Lane*
Shecter, Ben. *If I had a ship*
Silverstein, Shel. *The giving tree*
Testa, Fulvio. *Wolf's favor*
Timmermans, Felix. *A gift from Saint Nicholas*
Tolstoĭ, Alekseĭ Nikolaevich. *Shoemaker Martin*
Wang, Rosalind C. *The fourth question*
Ward, Sally G. *What goes around comes around*

Character traits – helpfulness

Adelson, Leone. *Who blew that whistle?*
Adshead, Gladys L. *Brownies—hush!*
Brownies - they're moving
Æsop. *Androcles and the lion*, ill. by Janet Stevens
Androcles and the lion, ill. by Janusz Grabianski
The ant and the dove, ill. by Ching
The lion and the mouse, ill. by Gerald Rose
The lion and the mouse, ill. by Ed Young
Aliki. *The two of them*
Ancona, George. *Helping out*
Aylesworth, Jim. *Mr. McGill goes to town*
Baker, Betty. *Partners*

Bakken, Harold. *The special string*
Beim, Jerrold. *Country mailman*
Bridwell, Norman. *Clifford's good deeds*
Bright, Robert. *Georgie and the baby birds*
Georgie and the ball of yarn
Georgie and the little dog
Georgie and the runaway balloon
Brown, Myra Berry. *Company's coming for dinner*
Buchanan, Heather S. *Emily Mouse saves the day*
Calhoun, Mary. *Euphonia and the flood*
Jack the wise and the Cornish cuckoos
Carey, Valerie Scho. *Harriet and William and the terrible creature*
Chevalier, Christa. *Spence is small*
Clements, Andrew. *Santa's secret helper*
Clifton, Lucille. *My friend Jacob*
Cole, William. *Aunt Bella's umbrella*
Collier, Ethel. *Who goes there in my garden?*
Curle, Jock J. *The four good friends*
Cuyler, Margery. *Fat Santa*
Daly, Niki. *Thank you Henrietta*
Davis, Alice Vaught. *Timothy Turtle*
Day, Alexandra. *Frank and Ernest*
Day, Shirley. *Waldo's back yard*
Devlin, Wende. *Cranberry Christmas*
Dowling, Paul. *You can do it, Rabbit*
Du Bois, William Pène. *Bear circus*
Erickson, Karen. *I like to help*
Ets, Marie Hall. *Elephant in a well*
Graham, Al. *Timothy Turtle*
Graham, Margaret Bloy. *Benjy and his friend Fifi*
Gray, Genevieve. *Send Wendell*
Green, Norma B. *The hole in the dike*
Greene, Laura. *Help*
Grimm, Jacob. *The elves and the shoemaker*, ill. by Paul Galdone
The elves and the shoemaker, ill. by Bernadette Watts
Mother Holly, ill. by Bernadette Watts
The shoemaker and the elves, ill. by Adrienne Adams
The shoemaker and the elves, ill. by Cynthia and William Birrer
The shoemaker and the elves, ill. by Ilse Plume
Herold, Ann Bixby. *The helping day*
Hill, Elizabeth Starr. *Evan's corner*
Hol, Coby. *Tippy Bear hunts for honey*
Holmes, Efner Tudor. *Amy's goose*
Houston, John A. *The bright yellow rope*
Hürlimann, Bettina. *Barry: the story of a brave St. Bernard*
Joyce, William. *Bently and egg*
Kishida, Eriko. *The lion and the bird's nest*
Kraus, Robert. *Herman the helper*
Rebecca Hatpin
La Fontaine, Jean de. *The lion and the rat*

Landa, Norbert. *Rabbit and chicken find a box*
Lewis, Eils Moorhouse. *The snug little house*
Lindman, Maj. *Flicka, Ricka, Dicka and the new dotted dress*
 Snipp, Snapp, Snurr and the red shoes
Lloyd, Errol. *Nini at carnival*
McConnachie, Brian. *Flying boy*
Marcus, Susan. *The missing button adventure*
Marshall, James. *What's the matter with Carruthers?*
Mayer, Mercer. *Just for you*
Mayne, William. *The blue book of hob stories*
 The green book of Hob stories
 The red book of Hob stories
 The yellow book of Hob stories
Michael, Emory H. *Androcles and the lion*
Nakano, Hirotaka. *Elephant blue*
Ness, Evaline. *Pavo and the princess*
Oxenbury, Helen. *Mother's helper*
Parker, Nancy Winslow. *Cooper, the McNallys' big black dog*
Partridge, Jenny. *Peterkin Pollensnuff*
Paul, Sherry. *2-B and the rock 'n roll band*
Peet, Bill (William Bartlett). *The ant and the elephant*
 Cyrus the unsinkable sea serpent
Porte, Barbara Ann. *Harry in trouble*
Potter, Beatrix. *The tailor of Gloucester*
Quackenbush, Robert M. *Chuck lends a paw*
Rayner, Mary. *The rain cloud*
Rockwell, Anne F. *Big bad goat*
 The bump in the night
 Can I help?
 Handy Hank will fix it
Seuss, Dr. *Horton hatches the egg*
Simon, Norma. *What do I do?*
Slobodkin, Louis. *Dinny and Danny*
Snow, Pegeen. *Mrs. Periwinkle's groceries*
Stevenson, James. *Will you please feed our cat?*
Suhl, Yuri. *The Purim goat*
Udry, Janice May. *Is Susan here?*
Venino, Suzanne. *Animals helping people*
Waber, Bernard. *Lyle, Lyle Crocodile*
Waddell, Martin. *Farmer Duck*
Williams, Barbara. *Someday, said Mitchell*
Wolde, Gunilla. *Betsy's fixing day*
Zemach, Margot. *To Hilda for helping*

Character traits – honesty

Aardema, Verna. *Pedro and the padre*
Alexander, Lloyd. *The truthful harp*
Aliki. *Diogenes*
Ardizzone, Edward. *Peter the wanderer*
Demi. *Chen Ping and his magic axe*
Gallant, Kathryn. *The flute player of Beppu*
Goldsmith, Howard. *Little lost dog*
Gretz, Susanna. *Rabbit rambles on*
Havill, Juanita. *Jamaica's find*

Langton, Jane. *The hedgehog boy*
McLenighan, Valjean. *I know you cheated*
Matsuno, Masako. *A pair of red clogs*
 Taro and the Tofu
Mayer, Mercer. *How the trollusk got his hat*
Moss, Marissa. *Who was it?*
Torre, Betty L. *The luminous pearl*
Turkle, Brinton. *The adventures of Obadiah*
Wilson, Julia. *Becky*

Character traits - incentive *see*
 Character traits – ambition

Character traits – individuality

Abolafia, Yossi. *My three uncles*
Alderson, Sue Ann. *Bonnie McSmithers is at it again!*
Aliki. *Jack and Jake*
Allamand, Pascale. *The animals who changed their colors*
Anglund, Joan Walsh. *Look out the window*
Anholt, Catherine. *What I like*
Baker, Jeannie. *Millicent*
Beim, Jerrold. *Country train*
 Freckle face
Berliner, Franz. *Wildebeest*
Bradman, Tony. *Michael*
Bright, Robert. *Which is Willy?*
Carey, Mary. *The owl who loved sunshine*
Carlson, Nancy. *I like me*
Caseley, Judith. *Cousins*
Charlip, Remy. *Hooray for me!*
Conford, Ellen. *Impossible, possum*
Delaney, Ned. *One dragon to another*
Dellinger, Annetta. *You are special to Jesus*
Delton, Judy. *I'm telling you now*
De Paola, Tomie (Thomas Anthony). *Oliver Button is a sissy*
Duvoisin, Roger Antoine. *Jasmine*
Fatio, Louise. *Hector penguin*
Gerrard, Roy. *Mik's mammoth*
Gramatky, Hardie. *Little Toot through the Golden Gate*
Horvath, Betty F. *Will the real Tommy Wilson please stand up?*
Jaynes, Ruth M. *What is a birthday child?*
Jeffery, Graham. *Thomas the tortoise*
Kraus, Robert. *Owliver*
Kuskin, Karla. *Which horse is William?*
Lampert, Emily. *A little touch of monster*
Leaf, Munro. *The story of Ferdinand the bull*
Lester, Alison. *Clive eats alligators*
 Tessa snaps snakes
Lester, Helen. *Tacky the penguin*
Levine, Rhoda. *Harrison loved his umbrella*
Lionni, Leo. *A color of his own*
 Pezzettino
 Tico and the golden wings
Littledale, Freya. *The magic plum tree*
Lopshire, Robert. *I want to be somebody new!*

Lystad, Mary H. *That new boy*
McConnachie, Brian. *Flying boy*
McCormack, John E. *Rabbit tales*
MacGregor, Marilyn. *On top*
Manushkin, Fran. *Shirleybird*
Moss, Marissa. *But not Kate*
Oram, Hiawyn. *Ned and the Joybaloo*
Peet, Bill (William Bartlett). *Buford the little bighorn*
The spooky tail of Prewitt Peacock
Pinkwater, Daniel Manus. *The big orange splot*
Rand, Gloria. *Salty dog*
Redies, Rainer. *The cats' party*
Rogers, Fred. *If we were all the same*
Rubel, Nicole. *Sam and Violet are twins*
Sam and Violet go camping
Ruck-Pauquèt, Gina. *Mumble bear*
Sendak, Maurice. *Pierre*
Seuling, Barbara. *The triplets*
Seuss, Dr. *I can draw it myself*
Sharmat, Marjorie Weinman. *What are we going to do about Andrew?*
Sharmat, Mitchell. *Sherman is a slowpoke*
Silverstein, Shel. *The missing piece*
Simon, Norma. *I know what I like*
Why am I different?
Singer, Marilyn. *The dog who insisted he wasn't*
Pickle plan
Slobodkin, Louis. *Millions and millions and millions*
Tafuri, Nancy. *Have you seen my duckling?*
Thomson, Pat. *Beware of the aunts!*
Tusa, Tricia. *Camilla's new hairdo*
Tyrrell, Anne. *Mary Ann always can*
Viorst, Judith. *Try it again, Sam*
Waber, Bernard. *"You look ridiculous," said the rhinoceros to the hippopotamus*
Waxman, Stephanie. *What is a girl? What is a boy?*
Wells, Rosemary. *Shy Charles*
Whitney, Dorothy B. *Creatures of an exceptional kind*

Character traits – kindness

Aliki. *The story of William Penn*
Bang, Molly. *The paper crane*
Barber, Antonia. *Satchelmouse and the doll's house*
Barbour, Karen. *Mr. Bow Tie*
Baumann, Kurt. *The prince and the lute*
Bishop, Adela. *The Easter wolf*
Brown, Margaret Wise. *Dr. Squash the doll doctor*
Butterworth, Nick. *Amanda's butterfly*
Calhoun, Mary. *The thieving dwarfs*
Caswell, Helen. *Parable of the good Samaritan*
Cazet, Denys. *A fish in his pocket*
Cole, Brock. *The king at the door*

Coville, Bruce. *The foolish giant*
Sarah and the dragon
Davis, Maggie S. *Grandma's secret letter*
DeArmond, Dale. *The seal oil lamp*
Elzbieta. *Dikou and the baby star*
Dikou the little troon who walks at night
Fatio, Louise. *The happy lion's rabbits*
Fleischman, Sid. *The scarebird*
Fyleman, Rose. *A fairy went a-marketing*
Gannett, Ruth S. *Katie and the sad noise*
Goodsell, Jane. *Toby's toe*
Grimm, Jacob. *The golden goose*, ill. by Dorothée Duntze
The golden goose, ill. by Isadore Seltzer
The golden goose, ill. by Martin Ursell
Hasler, Eveline. *Martin is our friend*
Hastings, Selina. *The singing ringing tree*
Heyward, Du Bose. *The country bunny and the little gold shoes*
Karlin, Nurit. *The tooth witch*
Kent, Jack. *Clotilda*
Kraus, Robert. *The first robin*
La Rochelle, David. *A Christmas guest*
Lee, Jeanne M. *Ba-Nam*
Lipkind, William. *The magic feather duster*
Mayer, Marianna. *The little jewel box*
Meddaugh, Susan. *Beast*
Mizumura, Kazue. *If I built a village*
Munsch, Robert N. *David's father*
Nesbit, Edith. *The last of the dragons*
Newton, Patricia Montgomery. *The five sparrows*
Noble, Trinka Hakes. *Hansy's mermaid*
Ormondroyd, Edward. *Theodore*
Peterson, Hans. *Erik and the Christmas horse*
Postgate, Oliver. *Noggin the king*
Rohmer, Harriet. *Atariba and Niguayona*
San Souci, Robert D. *The talking eggs*
Schotter, Roni. *Captain Snap and the children of Vinegar Lane*
Seuss, Dr. *Horton hears a Who!*
Shibano, Tamizo. *The old man who made the trees bloom*
Small, David. *Eulalie and the hopping head*
Steptoe, John. *Mufaro's beautiful daughters*
Stevens, Carla. *Stories from a snowy meadow*
Stock, Catherine. *Secret Valentine*
Tolstoï, Alekseï Nikolaevich. *Shoemaker Martin*
Torre, Betty L. *The luminous pearl*
Ungerer, Tomi. *Zeralda's ogre*
Vigna, Judith. *Anyhow, I'm glad I tried*
Warren, Cathy. *Saturday belongs to Sara*
Wells, H. G. (Herbert George). *The adventures of Tommy*
Wilde, Oscar. *The selfish giant*, ill. by Dom Mansell
The selfish giant, ill. by Lisbeth Zwerger
Wittman, Sally. *The boy who hated Valentine's Day*
Zolotow, Charlotte (Shapiro). *I know a lady*

Character traits – kindness to animals

Æsop. *Androcles and the lion*, ill. by Janet Stevens
Androcles and the lion, ill. by Janusz Grabianski
Allred, Mary. *Grandmother Poppy and the funny-looking bird*
Anderson, C. W. (Clarence Williams). *Lonesome little colt*
The rumble seat pony
Aragon, Jane Chelsea. *Winter harvest*
Baker, Jeannie. *Home in the sky*
Barnhart, Peter. *The wounded duck*
Baumann, Hans. *Chip has many brothers*
Beatty, Hetty Burlingame. *Moorland pony*
Bergman, Donna. *City fox*
Berson, Harold. *Joseph and the snake*
Birrer, Cynthia. *The lady and the unicorn*
Bolliger, Max. *The magic bird*
Boon, Emilie. *It's spring, Peterkin*
Brenner, Barbara A. *Two orphan cubs*
Brighton, Catherine. *Hope's gift*
Brock, Emma Lillian. *The birds' Christmas tree*
Brunhoff, Laurent de. *Babar's little girl*
Bryan, Ashley. *Sh-ko and his eight wicked brothers*
Buchanan, Heather S. *Emily Mouse's first adventure*
Bunting, Eve (Anne Evelyn). *Night tree*
Burch, Robert. *The hunting trip*
Butterworth, Nick. *One blowy night*
One snowy night
Carey, Mary. *The owl who loved sunshine*
Carter, Anne. *Bella's secret garden*
Clewes, Dorothy. *The wild wood*
Cowcher, Helen. *Tigress*
Curle, Jock J. *The four good friends*
Daugherty, James Henry. *Andy and the lion*
De Marolles, Chantal. *The lonely wolf*
Dobson, Clive. *Fred's TV*
Drew, Patricia. *Spotter Puff*
Dunn, Judy. *The little lamb*
Duvoisin, Roger Antoine. *The happy hunter*
Freeman, Don. *The seal and the slick*
Galdone, Paul. *Androcles and the lion*
Gantschev, Ivan. *Otto the bear*
Georgiady, Nicholas P. *Gertie the duck*
Goffstein, M. B. (Marilyn Brooke). *Natural history*
The good-hearted youngest brother, ill. by Diane Goode
Graham, Bob. *Pete and Roland*
Grant, Joan. *The monster that grew small*
Hader, Berta Hoerner. *Mister Billy's gun*
Harriott, Ted. *Coming home*
Harrison, David Lee. *Little turtle's big adventure*
Herriot, James. *Christmas Day kitten*
Hewett, Joan. *Rosalie*
Hirsh, Marilyn. *Deborah the dybbuk*

Hodges, Margaret. *St. Jerome and the lion*
Holmes, Efner Tudor. *Amy's goose*
Carrie's gift
Ichikawa, Satomi. *Nora's duck*
Ikeda, Daisaku. *The snow country prince*
Ishii, Momoko. *The tongue-cut sparrow*
Jeffery, Graham. *Thomas the tortoise*
Keats, Ezra Jack. *Jennie's hat*
Kumin, Maxine. *Mittens in May*
Laird, Elizabeth. *The day the ducks went skating*
Lathrop, Dorothy Pulis. *Who goes there?*
Levitin, Sonia. *All the cats in the world*
Lipkind, William. *The boy and the forest*
McNally, Darcie. *In a cabin in a wood*
McNulty, Faith. *The lady and the spider*
Mouse and Tim
McPhail, David. *The bear's toothache*
A wolf story
Mamin-Sibiryak, D. N. *Grey Neck*
Martchenko, Michael. *Bird feeder banquet*
Meddaugh, Susan. *Tree of birds*
Michael, Emory H. *Androcles and the lion*
Miklowitz, Gloria D. *Save that raccoon!*
Miller, Edna. *Mouskin's frosty friend*
Mogensen, Jan. *Teddy's Christmas gift*
Moore, Sheila. *Samson Svenson's baby*
Nakatani, Chiyoko. *Fumio and the dolphins*
Newberry, Clare Turlay. *Percy, Polly and Pete*
Novak, Matt. *Mr. Floop's lunch*
Numeroff, Laura Joffe. *If you gave a moose a muffin*
If you give a mouse a cookie
Orstadius, Brita. *The dolphin journey*
Pedersen, Judy. *The tiny patient*
Peet, Bill (William Bartlett). *Huge Harold*
Roy, Ronald. *A thousand pails of water*
Rylant, Cynthia. *Henry and Mudge in puddle trouble*
Sandburg, Helga. *Anna and the baby buzzard*
Turkle, Brinton. *Thy friend, Obadiah*
Turska, Krystyna. *The woodcutter's duck*
Tyler, Linda Wagner. *After Christmas tree*
Varley, Dimitry. *The whirly bird*
Velthuijs, Max. *Little Man to the rescue*
Wallace, Ian. *The sparrow's song*
Ward, Lynd. *The biggest bear*
Waterton, Betty. *A salmon for Simon*
Wersba, Barbara. *Do tigers ever bite kings?*
Whitney, Alma Marshak. *Leave Herbert alone*
Wildsmith, Brian. *Hunter and his dog*
Wondriska, William. *The stop*
Yagawa, Sumiko. *The crane wife*

Character traits – laziness

Aylesworth, Jim. *Hush up!*
Baker, Betty. *Partners*
Bolognese, Elaine. *The sleepy watchdog*

Bowen, Vernon. *The lazy beaver*
Bright, Robert. *Gregory, the noisiest and strongest boy in Grangers Grove*
Du Bois, William Pène. *Lazy Tommy pumpkinhead*
Geraghty, Paul. *Slobcat*
Grimm, Jacob. *Mother Holly*, ill. by Bernadette Watts
Hadithi, Mwenye. *Lazy lion*
Holding, James. *The lazy little Zulu*
Jacobs, Joseph. *Lazy Jack*, ill. by Barry Wilkinson
Krasilovsky, Phyllis. *The man who did not wash his dishes*
The man who tried to save time
The man who was too lazy to fix things
Lazy Jack. *Lazy Jack*, ill. by Bert Dodson
Lazy Jack, ill. by Tony Ross
Lazy Jack, ill. by Kurt Werth
The little red hen. *The cock, the mouse and the little red hen*, ill. by Graham Percy
The little red hen, ill. by Janina Domanska
The little red hen, ill. by Paul Galdone
The little red hen, ill. by Mel Pekarsky
The little red hen, ill. by William Stobbs
The little red hen, ill. by Margot Zemach
Lobel, Arnold. *A treeful of pigs*
Lorenz, Lee. *Big Gus and Little Gus*
McKissack, Patricia C. *The little red hen*
Mathews, Louise. *The great take-away*
Oppenheim, Joanne. *"Not now!" said the cow*
Pack, Robert. *How to catch a crocodile*
Papas, William. *Taresh the tea planter*
Schmidt, Eric von. *The young man who wouldn't hoe corn*
Sharmat, Marjorie Weinman. *Burton and Dudley*
Snyder, Dianne. *The boy of the three-year nap*
Taylor, Sydney. *Mr. Barney's beard*
Wildsmith, Brian. *The lazy bear*

Character traits - littleness *see* Character traits – smallness

Character traits – loyalty

Aliki. *The two of them*
Ardizzone, Edward. *Tim to the rescue*
Boyle, Vere. *Beauty and the beast*
Bridwell, Norman. *Clifford goes to Hollywood*
Calhoun, Mary. *The witch who lost her shadow*
Collodi, Carlo. *The adventures of Pinocchio*, ill. by Diane Goode
Cooney, Barbara. *Little brother and little sister*
Crompton, Anne Eliot. *The winter wife*

Haywood, Carolyn. *How the reindeer saved Santa*
Hurd, Edith Thacher. *Under the lemon tree*
Hutton, Warwick. *Beauty and the beast*
Lasker, Joe. *He's my brother*
McCrea, James. *The king's procession*
McLerran, Alice. *The mountain that loved a bird*
Nesbit, Edith. *Beauty and the beast*
Potter, Beatrix. *The tale of the faithful dove*
Stanovich, Betty Jo. *Hedgehog adventures*
Va, Leong. *A letter to the king*
Whittier, John Greenleaf. *Barbara Frietchie*
Wright, Freire. *Beauty and the beast*

Character traits – luck

Aldridge, Josephine Haskell. *Fisherman's luck*
Aliki. *Three gold pieces*
Beim, Lorraine. *Lucky Pierre*
Bond, Michael. *Paddington's lucky day*
Breckler, Rosemary K. *Hoang breaks the lucky teapot*
Brown, Margaret Wise. *Wheel on the chimney*
Butler, Dorothy. *Another happy tale*
A happy tale
Callan, Elizabeth Koda. *Good luck pony*
Cazet, Denys. *Lucky me*
Delton, Judy. *I never win!*
It happened on Thursday
Elkin, Benjamin. *Lucky and the giant*
Gackenbach, Dick. *Harvey, the foolish pig*
Geraghty, Paul. *Look out, Patrick!*
Grimm, Jacob. *Hans in luck*, ill. by Paul Galdone
Hans in luck, ill. by Felix Hoffmann
Lucky Hans, ill. by Eugen Sopko
Hann, Jacquie. *Up day, down day*
Holland, Janice. *You never can tell*
Ivanov, Anatoly. *Ol' Jake's lucky day*
Mayer, Marianna. *The little jewel box*
Moeri, Louise. *The unicorn and the plow*
Russell, Betty. *Big store, funny door*
Seuss, Dr. *Did I ever tell you how lucky you are?*
Stafford, Kay. *Ling Tang and the lucky cricket*
Stanley, Diane. *The good-luck pencil*
Velthuijs, Max. *Little Man's lucky day*
Walsh, Jill Paton. *Lost and found*
Ziefert, Harriet. *Good luck, bad luck*

Character traits – meanness

Bellows, Cathy. *Four fat rats*
Bottner, Barbara. *Mean Maxine*
Burningham, John. *Borka*
Carey, Valerie Scho. *The devil and mother Crump*
Carrick, Carol. *Old Mother Witch*

Coville, Bruce. *Sarah's unicorn*
Freeman, Don. *Tilly Witch*
Gantos, Jack (John, Jr.). *Rotten Ralph's rotten Christmas*
 Rotten Ralph's show and tell
 Rotten Ralph's trick or treat
 Worse than Rotten Ralph
Glazer, Lee. *Cookie Becker casts a spell*
Goodsell, Jane. *Toby's toe*
Himmelman, John. *Amanda and the witch switch*
Hoban, Russell. *Big John Turkle*
 The little Brute family
Jones, Rebecca C. *The biggest, meanest, ugliest dog in the whole wide world*
Kidd, Bruce. *Hockey showdown*
Kismaric, Carole. *The rumor of Pavel and Paali*
McCrea, James. *The magic tree*
Mahy, Margaret. *The boy with two shadows*
Manushkin, Fran. *Hocus and Pocus at the circus*
Nickl, Peter. *Ra ta ta tam*
Patz, Nancy. *Gina Farina and the Prince of Mintz*
Prelutsky, Jack. *The mean old mean hyena*
Price, Michelle. *Mean Melissa*
Seuss, Dr. *How the Grinch stole Christmas*
Shibano, Tamizo. *The old man who made the trees bloom*
Snyder, Anne. *The old man and the mule*
Steptoe, John. *Mufaro's beautiful daughters*
Stevenson, James. *Fried feathers for Thanksgiving*
 Happy Valentine's Day, Emma!
 The worst person's Christmas
Udry, Janice May. *The mean mouse and other mean stories*
Zimelman, Nathan. *Mean Murgatroyd and the ten cats*
Zion, Gene. *The meanest squirrel I ever met*

Character traits – optimism

Alexander, Sue. *Marc the Magnificent*
Aliki. *The twelve months*
Atwood, Margaret. *Anna's pet*
Ayer, Jacqueline. *The paper-flower tree*
Butterworth, Nick. *One blowy night*
Carey, Valerie Scho. *Maggie Mab and the bogey beast*
Delton, Judy. *My mother lost her job today*
Dionetti, Michelle. *Coal mine peaches*
Gregory, Valiska. *Sunny side up*
 Terribly wonderful
Hall, Malcolm. *The friends of Charlie Ant Bear*
Hoff, Syd. *Oliver*
Krauss, Ruth. *The carrot seed*
Lindgren, Astrid. *Of course Polly can do almost everything*

Lionni, Leo. *Theodore and the talking mushroom*
Martin, Jacqueline Briggs. *Good times on Grandfather Mountain*
Peet, Bill (William Bartlett). *The Whingdingdilly*
Piatti, Celestino. *The happy owls*
Rice, Inez. *A long long time*
Seuss, Dr. *Would you rather be a bullfrog?*
Tapio, Pat Decker. *The lady who saw the good side of everything*
Wiesner, William. *Happy-Go-Lucky*
Zakhoder, Boris Vladimirovich. *Rosachok*

Character traits - ostracism *see* Character traits – being different

Character traits – patience

Erickson, Karen. *Waiting my turn*
Hellen, Nancy. *Bus stop*
Ketteman, Helen. *Not yet, Yvette*
Kibbey, Marsha. *My grammy*
Laurin, Anne. *Little things*
Steiner, Charlotte. *What's the hurry, Harry?*
Weiss, Nicki. *Waiting*
Wells, Rosemary. *Max's breakfast*

Character traits – perseverance

Abisch, Roz. *Sweet Betsy from Pike*
Æsop. *The miller, his son and their donkey*, ill. by Roger Antoine Duvoisin
 The miller, his son and their donkey, ill. by Eugen Sopko
Alexander, Martha G. *Move over, Twerp*
 We never get to do anything
Aliki. *A weed is a flower*
Ambrus, Victor G. *The little cockerel*
 Mishka
Bethell, Jean. *Hooray for Henry*
Blades, Ann. *Mary of mile 18*
Boynton, Sandra. *If at first...*
Brennan, Joseph Killorin. *Gobo and the river*
Calhoun, Mary. *Old man Whickutt's donkey*
Conford, Ellen. *Just the thing for Geraldine*
Day, Shirley. *Ruthie's big tree*
Erickson, Karen. *I'll try*
Gray, Genevieve. *How far, Felipe?*
Hoff, Syd. *Slugger Sal's slump*
Jensen, Virginia Allen. *Sara and the door*
Kahl, Virginia. *Maxie*
Keats, Ezra Jack. *John Henry*
Lindgren, Astrid. *Of course Polly can do almost everything*
Piper, Watty. *The little engine that could*
Riordan, James. *The three magic gifts*
Shearer, Marilyn J. *The crown of fools*
Shine, Deborah. *The little engine that could pudgy word book*
Skorpen, Liesel Moak. *All the Lassies*

Steig, William. *Brave Irene*
Thomas, Kathy. *The angel's quest*
Ungerer, Tomi. *The Mellops go spelunking*
Watanabe, Shigeo. *I can build a house!*
I can ride it!
Where's my daddy?
Waterton, Betty. *Orff, 27 dragons (and a snarkel)*

Character traits – persistence

Adler, David A. *A picture book of Helen Keller*
Birdseye, Tom. *Airmail to the moon*
Bulla, Clyde Robert. *The stubborn old woman*
Day, Marie. *Dragon in the rocks*
Lattimore, Deborah Nourse. *The sailor who captured the sea*
Patz, Nancy. *Gina Farina and the Prince of Mintz*
Rigby, Rodney. *Hello, this is your penguin speaking*
Ross, Tony. *I want a cat*
Ward, Sally G. *Molly and Grandpa*
West, Colin. *"Pardon?" said the giraffe*

Character traits – practicality

Aylesworth, Jim. *Mother Halverson's new cat*
Evans, Katherine. *The man, the boy and the donkey*
Gág, Wanda. *Millions of cats*
Gretz, Susanna. *Roger loses his marbles!*
La Fontaine, Jean de. *The miller, the boy and the donkey*, adapt. and ill. by Brian Wildsmith
Modell, Frank. *One zillion Valentines*
Oppenheim, Joanne. *Donkey's tale*
Schlein, Miriam. *The pile of junk*

Character traits – pride

Andersen, H. C. (Hans Christian). *The emperor's new clothes*, ill. by Erik Blegvad
The emperor's new clothes, ill. by Virginia Lee Burton
The emperor's new clothes, ill. by Robert Byrd
The emperor's new clothes, ill. by Jack and Irene Delano
The emperor's new clothes, ill. by Hélène Desputeaux
The emperor's new clothes, ill. by Birte Dietz
The emperor's new clothes, ill. by Dorothée Duntze
The emperor's new clothes, ill. by Pamela Baldwin Ford
The emperor's new clothes, ill. by Jack Kent
The emperor's new clothes, ill. by Monika Laimgruber

The emperor's new clothes, ill. by Anne F. Rockwell
The emperor's new clothes, ill. by Janet Stevens
The emperor's new clothes, ill. by Nadine Bernard Westcott
The red shoes, ill. by Chihiro Iwasaki
Bemelmans, Ludwig. *Rosebud*
Birch, David. *The king's chessboard*
Burningham, John. *Humbert, Mister Firkin and the Lord Mayor of London*
Calhoun, Mary. *The runaway brownie*
Clifton, Lucille. *All us come cross the water*
Crary, Elizabeth. *I'm proud*
Dionetti, Michelle. *Thalia Brown and the blue bug*
Duvoisin, Roger Antoine. *Crocus Petunia*
Edwards, Dorothy. *A wet Monday*
Ehrhardt, Reinhold. *Kikeri: or, The proud red rooster*
Friskey, Margaret (Margaret Richards). *Indian Two Feet rides alone*
Gackenbach, Dick. *The dog and the deep dark woods*
Hamberger, John. *The peacock who lost his tail*
Hürlimann, Ruth. *The proud white cat*
Keats, Ezra Jack. *John Henry*
McKissack, Patricia C. *The king's new clothes*
McLenighan, Valjean. *What you see is what you get*
Pomerantz, Charlotte. *The ballad of the long-tailed rat*
Rogasky, Barbara. *The water of life*
Ross, Anna. *I did it!*
Rylant, Cynthia. *Mr. Griggs' work*
Schwartz, Amy. *Annabelle Swift, kindergartner*
Sharmat, Marjorie Weinman. *I'm terrific*
Tettelbaum, Michael. *The cave of the lost Fraggle*
Whitney, Alex. *Once a bright red tiger*
Winthrop, Elizabeth. *Tough Eddie*
Zimnik, Reiner. *The proud circus horse*

Character traits – questioning

Adler, David A. *A little at a time*
Alden, Laura. *When?*
Alexander, Martha G. *Where does the sky end, Grandpa?*
Allard, Harry. *May I stay?*
Anholt, Catherine. *All about you*
Baynton, Martin. *Why do you love me?*
Bird, E. J. *How do bears sleep?*
Brown, Margaret Wise. *Wait till the moon is full*
Carlstrom, Nancy White. *Goodbye geese*
Clark, Roberta. *Why?*
Deveaux, Alexis. *Na-ni*
Dunbar, Joyce. *Why is the sky up?*

Haswell, Peter. *Pog*
Hopkins, Lee Bennett. *Animals from
    Mother Goose*
    People from Mother Goose
Hulbert, Jay. *Armando asked "Why?"*
Jacobs, Leland B. *Is somewhere always far
    away?*
Keven, Elisa. *Ernest*
Krauze, Andrzej. *What's so special about
    today?*
Lionni, Leo. *Tico and the golden wings*
Lyon, George-Ella. *Who came down that
    road?*
Mahood, Kenneth. *Why are there more
    questions than answers, Grandad?*
Miller, M. L. *Dizzy from fools*
Moncure, Jane Belk. *Where?*
Reece, Colleen L. *What?*
Schertle, Alice. *That's what I thought*
Simont, Marc. *How come elephants?*
Slater, Teddy. *The cow that could tap dance*
Stover, Jo Ann. *Why? Because*
Thaler, Mike. *Owley*
Vance, Eleanor Graham. *Jonathan*
Williams, Barbara. *If he's my brother*
Ziefert, Harriet. *Sarah's questions*

Character traits – selfishness

Andersen, H. C. (Hans Christian). *The
    swineherd*, ill. by Erik Blegvad
    The swineherd, ill. by Dorothée Duntze
    The swineherd, ill. by Deborah Hahn
    The swineherd, ill. by Lisbeth Zwerger
Angelo, Valenti. *The acorn tree*
Baba, Noboru. *Eleven cats and a pig*
    Eleven cats and albatrosses
    Eleven cats in a bag
    Eleven hungry cats
Barrett, John M. *Oscar the selfish octopus*
Bascom, Joe. *Malcolm Softpaws*
Berquist, Grace. *The boy who couldn't roar*
Berry, Joy Wilt. *Being selfish*
Bryant, Bernice. *Follow the leader*
Christian, Mary Blount. *The devil take you,
    Barnabas Beane!*
Coombs, Patricia. *Mouse Café*
Douglas, Richard Keens. *The nutmeg
    princess*
Elkin, Benjamin. *Lucky and the giant*
Garrett, Jennifer. *The queen who stole the
    sky*
Henkes, Kevin. *A weekend with Wendell*
Kahl, Virginia. *The perfect pancake*
Kraus, Robert. *Rebecca Hatpin*
Lattimore, Deborah Nourse. *The dragon's
    robe*
Lipkind, William. *Even Steven*
    Finders keepers
Peet, Bill (William Bartlett). *The ant and
    the elephant*
Reader, Dennis. *I want one!*

Reesink, Marijke. *The golden treasure*
Remkiewicz, Frank. *Greedyanna*
Warburton, Nick. *Mr. Tite's belongings*
Ward, Helen. *The moonrat and the white
    turtle*
Wilde, Oscar. *The selfish giant*, ill. by Dom
    Mansell
    The selfish giant, ill. by Lisbeth Zwerger
Winthrop, Elizabeth. *The Best Friends Club*

Character traits – shyness

Brice, Tony. *The bashful goldfish*
Devlin, Wende. *Cranberry Valentine*
Dines, Glen. *A tiger in the cherry tree*
Goffstein, M. B. (Marilyn Brooke).
    Neighbors
Hamilton, Morse. *How do you do, Mr.
    Birdsteps?*
Hogrogian, Nonny. *Carrot cake*
Keats, Ezra Jack. *Louie*
Keller, Beverly. *Fiona's bee*
Krasilovsky, Phyllis. *The shy little girl*
Lexau, Joan M. *Benjie*
McCully, Emily Arnold. *Speak up, Blanche!*
Mathers, Petra. *Sophie and Lou*
Richardson, Jean. *Clara's dancing feet*
Udry, Janice May. *What Mary Jo shared*
Wold, Jo Anne. *Tell them my name is
    Amanda*
Yashima, Tarō. *Crow boy*
    The youngest one
Zolotow, Charlotte (Shapiro). *A tiger called
    Thomas*, ill. by Catherine Stock
    A tiger called Thomas, ill. by Kurt Werth

Character traits – smallness

Andersen, H. C. (Hans Christian).
    Thumbelina, ill. by Adrienne Adams
    Thumbelina, ill. by Wayne Anderson
    Thumbelina, ill. by Alison Claire Darke
    Thumbelina, ill. by Demi
    Thumbelina, ill. by Susan Jeffers
    Thumbelina, ill. by Kaarina Kaila
    Thumbelina, ill. by Christine Willis
    Nigognossian
    Thumbelina, ill. by Gustaf Tenggren
    Thumbelina, ill. by Lisbeth Zwerger, tr.
    by Richard and Clara Winston
    Thumbeline, ill. by Lisbeth Zwerger; tr.
    by Anthea Bell
Bang, Betsy. *The cucumber stem*
Beim, Jerrold. *The smallest boy in the class*
Bromhall, Winifred. *Bridget's growing day*
Burgess, Gelett. *The little father*
Chevalier, Christa. *Spence is small*
Cooper, Susan. *The silver cow*
Cuneo, Mary Louise. *Inside a sandcastle
    and other secrets*
Curry, Jane Louise. *Little, little sister*

De Paola, Tomie (Thomas Anthony). *Andy (that's my name)*
Gay, Michel. *Little helicopter*
Glass, Andrew. *Chickpea and the talking cow*
Hoff, Syd. *The littlest leaguer*
Horvath, Betty F. *Hooray for Jasper*
Johnston, Johanna. *Sugarplum*
Kraus, Robert. *The littlest rabbit*
Kumin, Maxine. *Sebastian and the dragon*
Kuskin, Karla. *Herbert hated being small*
Lindgren, Barbro. *Shorty takes off*
Lipkind, William. *The little tiny rooster*
Lurie, Morris. *The story of Imelda, who was small*
Meddaugh, Susan. *Too short Fred*
Miles, Miska. *No, no, Rosina*
Moore, Inga. *Oh, little Jack*
Orgel, Doris. *On the sand dune*
Prøysen, Alf. *Mrs. Pepperpot and the moose*
Rigby, Shirley Lincoln. *Smaller than most*
Schlein, Miriam. *Billy, the littlest one*
Stanley, John. *It's nice to be little*
Tresselt, Alvin R. *Smallest elephant in the world*
Williams, Barbara. *Someday, said Mitchell*
Yolen, Jane. *The emperor and the kite*
  The emperor and the kite [Rev. ed.]

Character traits – solitude

Goennel, Heidi. *Sometimes I like to be alone*

Character traits – stubbornness

Beatty, Hetty Burlingame. *Droopy*
Bulla, Clyde Robert. *The stubborn old woman*
Garrett, Jennifer. *The queen who stole the sky*
Leaf, Margaret. *Eyes of the dragon*
Minarik, Else Holmelund. *The little girl and the dragon*
O'Brien, Anne Sibley. *I'm not tired*
Steig, William. *Spinky sulks*
Tusa, Tricia. *Miranda*

Character traits – vanity

Andersen, H. C. (Hans Christian). *It's perfectly true!* ill. by Janet Stevens
Brown, Marcia. *Once a mouse...*
Brown, Margaret Wise. *The duck*
Frascino, Edward. *My cousin the king*
Kepes, Juliet. *The story of a bragging duck*
McCormack, John E. *Rabbit tales*
Marshall, James. *George and Martha, tons of fun*
Sharmat, Marjorie Weinman. *Sasha the silly*
Wall, Lina Mao. *Judge Rabbit and the tree spirit*
Winter, Paula. *Sir Andrew*

Character traits – willfulness

Alexander, Sue. *Nadia the willful*
Boyd, Lizi. *Half wild and half child*
Cox, David. *Bossyboots*
Grimm, Jacob. *The princess and the frog*, retold and ill. by Rachel Isadora
Lattimore, Deborah Nourse. *The prince and the golden ax*
Lester, Helen. *Pookins gets her way*
Quin-Harkin, Janet. *Benjamin's balloon*
Vesey, A. *The princess and the frog*

Cheetahs *see* Animals – cheetahs

Chefs *see* Careers – chefs

Chickens *see* Birds – chickens

Child abuse

Caines, Jeannette. *Chilly stomach*

Children as authors

Baskin, Leonard. *Hosie's alphabet*
  Hosie's aviary
Children's prayers from around the world
Haidle, Elizabeth. *Elmer the grump*
Krauss, Ruth. *Somebody else's nut tree, and other tales from children*
Lady Eden's School. *Just how stories*
MacKeen, Leslie Ann. *Who can fix it?*
O'Reilly, Edward. *Brown pelican at the pond*
Phumla. *Nomi and the magic fish*
St. Pierre, Wendy. *Henry finds a home*
Salter, Heidi. *Taddy McFinley and the great grey grimly*

Children as illustrators

De Paola, Tomie (Thomas Anthony). *Criss-cross applesauce*
Haidle, Elizabeth. *Elmer the grump*
MacKeen, Leslie Ann. *Who can fix it?*
Salter, Heidi. *Taddy McFinley and the great grey grimly*

Chimpanzees *see* Animals – chimpanzees

China *see* Foreign lands – China

Chinese New Year *see* Holidays – Chinese New Year

Chinese-Americans *see* Ethnic groups in the U.S. – Asian-Americans; Ethnic groups in the U.S. – Chinese-Americans

Chipmunks *see* Animals – chipmunks

Christmas *see* Holidays – Christmas

Cinco de Mayo *see* Holidays – Cinco de Mayo

Circular tales

Ada, Alma F. *The gold coin*
Arnold, Tedd. *Ollie forgot*
Bonners, Susan. *Just in passing*
Coco, Eugene Bradley. *The wishing well*
Dodds, Dayle Ann. *Wheel away!*
Greeley, Valerie. *Where's my share?*
Leemis, Ralph. *Mister Momboo's hat*
McAllister, Angela. *Matepo*
MacDonald, Elizabeth. *The very windy day*
Numeroff, Laura Joffe. *If you gave a moose a muffin*
  If you give a mouse a cookie
Rogers, Paul (Patrick). *Don't blame me!*
Root, Phyllis. *The old red rocking chair*
Rosenberg, Liz. *Window, mirror, moon*
Runcie, Jill. *Cock-a-doodle-doo*
Schories, Pat. *Mouse around*
Stevens, Harry. *Fat mouse*
Ueno, Noriko. *Elephant buttons*
Van Laan, Nancy. *The big fat worm*
  This is the hat
Vyner, Sue. *The stolen egg*
Whybrow, Ian. *Quacky quack-quack!*
Wolf, Sallie. *Peter's trucks*
Wolff, Ferida. *The woodcutter's coat*

Circus

Adler, David A. *You think it's fun to be a clown!*
Aitken, Amy. *Wanda's circus*
Allen, Jeffrey. *Bonzini! the tattooed man*
Ambrus, Victor G. *Mishka*
Amoit, Pierre. *Bijou the little bear*
Anno, Mitsumasa. *Dr. Anno's magical midnight circus*
Austin, Margot. *Barney's adventure*
Bach, Alice. *Millicent the magnificent*
Balet, Jan B. *Five Rollatinis*
Baningan, Sharon Stearns. *Circus magic*
Barr, Cathrine. *Sammy seal ov the sircus*
Barton, Byron. *Harry is a scaredy-cat*
Blance, Ellen. *Monster goes to the circus*
Blumberg, Rhoda. *Jumbo*
Bond, Michael. *Paddington at the circus*
Booth, Eugene. *At the circus*
Bowden, Joan Chase. *Boo and the flying flews*
Brown, Marc Tolon. *Lenny and Lola*
Brunhoff, Laurent de. *Babar's little circus star*
Burningham, John. *Cannonball Simp*
Cameron, Polly. *The cat who thought he was a tiger*
Cassidy, Dianne. *Circus animals*
  Circus people
Chardiet, Bernice. *C is for circus*

Come to the circus
Coontz, Otto. *A real class clown*
Coxe, Molly. *Louella and the yellow balloon*
Curious George goes to the circus
Day, Alexandra. *Paddy's pay-day*
Dayton, Laura. *LeRoy's birthday circus*
De Regniers, Beatrice Schenk. *Circus*
Dreamer, Sue. *Circus ABC*
  Circus 1, 2, 3
Dubanevich, Arlene. *The piggest show on earth*
Du Bois, William Pène. *Bear circus*
Ehlert, Lois. *Circus*
Ehrlich, Amy. *Lucy's winter tale*
Elks, Wendy. *Charles B. Wombat and the very strange thing*
Ernst, Lisa Campbell. *Ginger jumps*
Ets, Marie Hall. *Mister Penny's circus*
Everton, Macduff. *El circo magico modelo: Finding the magic circus*
Fallwell, Cathryn. *Clowning around*
Flack, Marjorie. *Wait for William*
Fox, Charles Philip. *Come to the circus*
Freeman, Don. *Bearymore*
Garbutt, Bernard. *Roger, the rosin back*
Gascoigne, Bamber. *Why the rope went tight*
Gay, Michel. *Night ride*
Goennel, Heidi. *The circus*
Goodall, John S. *The adventures of Paddy Pork*
Gramatky, Hardie. *Homer and the circus train*
Greaves, Margaret. *Little Bear and the Papagini circus*
Hale, Irina. *Donkey's dreadful day*
Harris, Steven Michael. *This is my trunk*
Herrmann, Frank. *The giant Alexander and the circus*
Hill, Eric. *Spot goes to the circus*
Hoff, Syd. *Barkley*
  Henrietta, circus star
  Oliver
Hol, Coby. *Henrietta saves the show*
Holl, Adelaide. *Mrs. McGarrity's peppermint sweater*
Hopkins, Lee Bennett. *Circus! Circus!*
The house that Jack built. The house that Jack built, ill. by Janet Stevens
Johnson, Crockett. *Harold's circus*
Johnson, Jane. *Bertie on the beach*
Karn, George. *Circus big and small*
  Circus colors
Lacome, Julie. *Funny business*
Lent, Blair. *Pistachio*
Lipkind, William. *Circus rucus*
Lisowski, Gabriel. *Roncalli's magnificent circus*
Logue, Christopher. *The magic circus*
Lopshire, Robert. *Put me in the zoo*
Maestro, Betsy. *Busy day*
  Harriet goes to the circus

Maley, Anne. *Have you seen my mother?*
Marokvia, Merelle. *A French school for Paul*
Mayer, Mercer. *Liverwurst is missing*
Modell, Frank. *Seen any cats?*
Munari, Bruno. *The circus in the mist*
Myers, Bernice. *Herman and the bears and the giants*
Ness, Evaline. *Fierce: the lion*
Nightingale, Sandy. *Pink pigs aplenty*
O'Kelley, Mattie Lou. *Circus!*
Panek, Dennis. *Detective Whoo*
Paré, Roger. *Circus days*
Peet, Bill (William Bartlett). *Chester the worldly pig*
Ella
Randy's dandy lions
Pellowski, Michael. *Clara joins the circus*
Peppé, Rodney. *Circus numbers*
Little circus
Thumbprint circus
Petersham, Maud. *The circus baby*
Piumini, Roberto. *The saint and the circus*
Prelutsky, Jack. *Circus*
Price, Mathew. *Do you see what I see?*
Quackenbush, Robert M. *The man on the flying trapeze*
Rey, H. A. (Hans Augusto). *Curious George rides a bike*
See the circus
Rounds, Glen. *The day the circus came to Lone Tree*
Saville, Lynn. *Horses in the circus ring*
Scheffrin-Falk, Gladys. *Another celebrated dancing bear*
Schulz, Charles M. *Life is a circus, Charlie Brown*
Seignobosc, Françoise. *Small-Trot*
Seligson, Susan. *The amazing Amos and the greatest couch on earth*
Seuss, Dr. *If I ran the circus*
Slobodkina, Esphyr. *Pezzo the peddler and the circus elephant*
Slocum, Rosalie. *Breakfast with the clowns*
Taylor, Mark. *Henry explores the jungle*
Tester, Sylvia Root. *Parade!*
Tresselt, Alvin R. *Smallest elephant in the world*
Varga, Judy. *Circus cannonball*
Miss Lollipop's lion
Vincent, Gabrielle. *Ernest and Celestine at the circus*
Wahl, Jan. *Sylvester Bear overslept*
The toy circus
Wallace, Ian. *Morgan the magnificent*
Weil, Lisl. *Let's go to the circus*
Westman, Barbara. *Dancing dogs: Charlotte and Emilio at the circus*
Wildsmith, Brian. *Brian Wildsmith's circus*
Winn, Chris. *Archie's acrobats*
Wiseman, Bernard. *Morris and Boris at the circus*

Zimnik, Reiner. *The bear on the motorcycle*
The proud circus horse

City

Adoff, Arnold. *Where wild Willie?*
Asch, Frank. *City sandwich*
Asch, George. *Linda*
Baker, Jeannie. *Home in the sky*
Millicent
Bank Street College of Education. *Around the city*
Green light, go
In the city
My city
Uptown, downtown
Barracca, Debra. *Maxi, the hero*
Barracca, Sal. *The adventures of taxi dog*
Barrett, Judi. *Old MacDonald had an apartment house*
Bash, Barbara. *Urban roosts*
Baylor, Byrd. *The best town in the world*
Bemelmans, Ludwig. *Sunshine*
Bergere, Thea. *Paris in the rain with Jean and Jacqueline*
Bergman, Donna. *City fox*
Binzen, Bill. *Carmen*
Blance, Ellen. *Monster comes to the city*
Blue, Rose. *How many blocks is the world?*
Bowden, Joan Chase. *Emilio's summer day*
Bozzo, Maxine Zohn. *Toby in the country, Toby in the city*
Bright, Robert. *Georgie to the rescue*
Brock, Emma Lillian. *Nobody's mouse*
Brown, Jane Clark. *Whonk, and whonk again*
Brown, Marcia. *The little carousel*
Brown, Margaret Wise. *Three little animals*
Burton, Virginia Lee. *Katy and the big snow*
The little house
Maybelle, the cable car
Busch, Phyllis S. *City lots*
Carrick, Carol. *Left behind*
Chalmers, Mary. *Kevin*
Chapouton, Anne-Marie. *Ben finds a friend*
Chwast, Seymour. *Tall city, wide country*
City, ill. by Roser Capdevila
Clifton, Lucille. *The boy who didn't believe in spring*
Everett Anderson's Christmas coming
Coats, Laura Jane. *City cat*
Colman, Hila. *Peter's brownstone house*
Come out to play, ill. by Jeanette Winter
Corcos, Lucille. *The city book*
Craft, Ruth. *The day of the rainbow*
Crews, Donald. *Parade*
Crowell, Maryalicia. *A horse in the house*
Daly, Niki. *Not so fast Songololo*
Decker, Dorothy W. *Stripe visits New York*
De Paola, Paula. *Rosie and the yellow ribbon*
Deveaux, Alexis. *Na-ni*
Donnelly, Liza. *Dinosaur beach*

Roach, Marilynne K. *Two Roman mice*
Rockwell, Anne F. *Come to town*
  Hugo at the window
Rogers, Paul (Patrick). *Tumbledown*
Rosario, Idalia. *Idalia's project ABC*
Rosenblum, Richard. *The old synagogue*
Roth, Harold. *Let's look all around the town*
Rowe, Jeanne A. *City workers*
Ryder, Joanne. *The night flight*
Sara. *Across town*
Sauer, Julia Lina. *Mike's house*
Scarry, Richard. *Richard Scarry's Postman Pig and his busy neighbors*
Schick, Eleanor. *City green*
  City in the winter
  One summer night
  Peter and Mr. Brandon
Scott, Ann Herbert. *Let's catch a monster*
Shannon, George. *Beanboy*
Shecter, Ben. *Emily, girl witch of New York*
Silverman, Erica. *On Grandma's roof*
Simon, Norma. *What do I do?*
Smalls-Hector, Irene. *Irene and the big, fine nickel*
  Jonathan and his mommy
Smucker, Anna Egan. *No star nights*
Sonneborn, Ruth A. *Friday night is papa night*
  I love Gram
  Lollipop's party
Sopko, Eugen. *Townsfolk and countryfolk*
Stanley, Diane. *A country tale*
Steel, Barry. *Greek cities*
Steptoe, John. *Uptown*
Stevenson, James. *Grandpa's great city tour*
Thomas, Ianthe. *Walk home tired, Billy Jenkins*
Tresselt, Alvin R. *It's time now!*
  Wake up, city!
Trimby, Elisa. *Mr. Plum's paradise*
Van Laan, Nancy. *People, people, everywhere*
Vasiliu, Mircea. *What's happening?*
Walters, Marguerite. *The city-country ABC*
Williams, Jay. *The city witch and the country witch*
Williamson, Mel. *Walk on!*
Wold, Jo Anne. *Well! Why didn't you say so?*
Yashima, Tarō. *Umbrella*
Yezback, Steven A. *Pumpkinseeds*
Ziefert, Harriet. *City shapes*
Zion, Gene. *Dear garbage man*
  Hide and seek day
Zolotow, Charlotte (Shapiro). *One step, two...*
  The park book

Cleanliness *see* Character traits – cleanliness

Cleverness *see* Character traits – cleverness

Clockmakers *see* Careers – clockmakers

Clocks, watches

Aiken, Conrad Potter. *Tom, Sue and the clock*
Ardizzone, Edward. *Johnny the clockmaker*
Aylesworth, Jim. *The completed hickory dickory dock*
Bassett, Lisa. *A clock for Beany*
Berg, Jean Horton. *The noisy clock shop*
Bragdon, Lillian J. *Tell me the time, please*
Bram, Elizabeth. *Woodruff and the clocks*
Brown, Kathryn. *Muledred*
Cohen, Carol L. *Wake up, groundhog!*
Colman, Hila. *Watch that watch*
Gibbons, Gail. *Clocks and how they go*
Gilbert, Helen Earle. *Dr. Trotter and his big gold watch*
Gordon, Sharon. *Tick tock clock*
Gould, Deborah. *Brendan's best-timed birthday*
Hutchins, Pat. *Clocks and more clocks*
Katz, Bobbi. *Tick-tock, let's read the clock*
Llewelyn, Claire. *My first book of time*
Lloyd, David. *The stopwatch*
McGinley, Phyllis. *Wonderful time*
McMillan, Bruce. *Time to...*
Maestro, Betsy. *Around the clock with Harriet*
Mother Goose. *The real Mother Goose clock book*, ill. by Jane Chambless
Mueller, Virginia. *Monster goes to school*
Myers, Bernice. *The gold watch*
Pieńkowski, Jan. *Time*
Slobodkin, Louis. *The late cuckoo*
Stanley, Diane. *Siegfried*
Steinmetz, Leon. *Clocks in the woods*
Thomas, Patricia. *The one and only, super-duper, golly-whopper, jim-dandy, really-handy clock-tock-stopper*
Thompson, Carol. *Time*

Clothing

Alda, Arlene. *Matthew and his dad*
Allen, Robert. *Ten little babies count*
  Ten little babies dress
Andersen, H. C. (Hans Christian). *The emperor's new clothes*, ill. by Erik Blegvad
  The emperor's new clothes, ill. by Virginia Lee Burton
  The emperor's new clothes, ill. by Robert Byrd
  The emperor's new clothes, ill. by Jack and Irene Delano
  The emperor's new clothes, ill. by Hélène Desputeaux
  The emperor's new clothes, ill. by Birte Dietz
  The emperor's new clothes, ill. by Dorothée Duntze

Let's get dressed!
Zion, Gene. *No roses for Harry*

Clothing – coats

De Paola, Tomie (Thomas Anthony). *Charlie needs a cloak*
Garelick, May. *Just my size*
Hest, Amy. *The purple coat*
Pulver, Robin. *Mrs. Toggle's zipper*
Taback, Simms. *Joseph had a little overcoat*
Tafuri, Nancy. *One wet jacket*
Watson, Pauline. *The walking coat*
Williams, Marcia. *Joseph and his magnificent coat of many colors*
Wolff, Ferida. *The woodcutter's coat*
Ziefert, Harriet. *A new coat for Anna*
Zinnemann-Hope, Pam. *Find your coat, Ned*

Clothing – gloves

Bannon, Laura. *Red mittens*
Kay, Helen. *One mitten Lewis*
Kumin, Maxine. *Mittens in May*
Rogers, Jean. *Runaway mittens*

Clothing – hats

Bailey, Debbie. *Hats*
Bannon, Laura. *Hat for a hero*
Barrows, Marjorie Wescott. *The funny hat*
Blos, Joan W. *Martin's hats*
Bowden, Joan Chase. *A hat for the queen*
Carrick, Malcolm. *The extraordinary hatmaker*
Chalmers, Mary. *A hat for Amy Jean*
Christelow, Eileen. *Olive and the magic hat*
Cousins, Lucy. *Portly's hat*
Fisher, Leonard Everett. *A head full of hats*
Geringer, Laura. *A three hat day*
Hindley, Judy. *Uncle Harold and the green hat*
Hiser, Berniece T. *The adventure of Charlie and his wheat-straw hat*
Holland, Isabelle. *Kevin's hat*
Howard, Elizabeth Fitzgerald. *Aunt Flossie's hats (and crab cakes later)*
Hürlimann, Ruth. *The mouse with the daisy hat*
Iwamura, Kazuo. *Tan Tan's hat*
Jaynes, Ruth M. *Benny's four hats*
Johnson, B. J. *A hat like that*
Johnston, Tony. *The witch's hat*
Kahn, Rosemary. *Grandma's hat*
Keats, Ezra Jack. *Jennie's hat*
Kroll, Steven. *Princess Abigail and the wonderful hat*
Lear, Edward. *The quangle wangle's hat*, ill. by Emma Crosby
The quangle wangle's hat, ill. by Helen Oxenbury
The quangle wangle's hat, ill. by Janet Stevens
Two laughable lyrics, ill. by Paul Galdone
Leemis, Ralph. *Mister Momboo's hat*
Lexau, Joan M. *Who took the farmer's hat?*
Mayer, Mercer. *Two moral tales*
Miller, Margaret. *Whose hat?*
Moore, Inga. *Fifty red night-caps*
Morris, Ann. *Hats, hats, hats*
Morris, Neil. *Where's my hat?*
Murphey, Sara. *The animal hat shop*
Parr, Letitia. *A man and his hat*
Roy, Ronald. *Whose hat is that?*
Ryder, Eileen. *Winston's new cap*
Scheller, Melanie. *My grandfather's hat*
Slobodkina, Esphyr. *Caps for sale*
Smith, Donald. *Who's wearing my baseball cap?*
Thayer, Jane. *The horse with the Easter bonnet*
Ungerer, Tomi. *The hat*
Van Laan, Nancy. *This is the hat*
Walbrecker, Dirk. *Benny's hat*
Ward, Nanda Weedon. *The black sombrero*
Weiss, Harvey. *My closet full of hats*
Westerberg, Christine. *The cap that mother made*

Clothing – pants

Hissey, Jane. *Little Bear's trousers*
Kraus, Robert. *The king's trousers*
Rice, Eve. *Peter's pockets*
Uttley, Alison. *Sam Pig and the wind*

Clothing – shirts

Anderson, Leone Castell. *The wonderful shrinking shirt*
Gould, Deborah. *Aaron's shirt*
Rudolph, Marguerita. *How a shirt grew in the field*

Clothing – shoes

Andersen, H. C. (Hans Christian). *The red shoes*, ill. by Chihiro Iwasaki
Bailey, Debbie. *Shoes*
Balzola, Asun. *Munia and the red shoes*
Bourgeois, Paulette. *Big Sarah's little boots*
Brenner, Barbara A. *Somebody's slippers, somebody's shoes*
Denton, Kady MacDonald. *Christmas boot*
Gay, Michel. *Little shoe*
Hughes, Shirley. *Two shoes, new shoes*
LeRoy, Gen. *Billy's shoes*
McKee, David. *King Rollo and the new shoes*
Matsuno, Masako. *A pair of red clogs*
Miller, Margaret. *Whose shoe?*
Myers, Bernice. *The flying shoes*
Rice, Eve. *New blue shoes*
Riddell, Chris. *Bird's new shoes*
Roy, Ronald. *Whose shoes are these?*

Smith, Donald. *Who's wearing my sneakers?*
Tafuri, Nancy. *Two new sneakers*
Vigna, Judith. *Boot weather*
Weiss, Leatie. *Funny feet!*
Winthrop, Elizabeth. *Shoes*

Clothing – socks

Baird, Anne. *Baby socks*
Daly, Niki. *Joseph's other red sock*
Glaser, Linda. *Keep your socks on, Albert!*
Selden, George. *Sparrow socks*

Clothing – sweaters

Lunn, Janet. *Amos's sweater*

Clouds see Weather – clouds

Clowns, jesters

Adler, David A. *You think it's fun to be a clown!*
Allen, Jeffrey. *Bonzini! the tattooed man*
Amoit, Pierre. *Bijou the little bear*
Anno, Mitsumasa. *Dr. Anno's magical midnight circus*
Austin, Margot. *Barney's adventure*
Barr, Cathrine. *Sammy seal ov the sircus*
Bradford, Ann. *The mystery of the midget clown*
Burningham, John. *Cannonball Simp*
Cole, Joanna. *The Clown-Arounds go on vacation*
  Get well, Clown-Arounds!
Coontz, Otto. *A real class clown*
De Paola, Tomie (Thomas Anthony). *Sing, Pierrot, sing*
Douglass, Barbara. *The chocolate chip cookie contest*
Faulkner, Nancy. *Small clown*
Freeman, Don. *Forever laughter*
Harris, Steven Michael. *This is my trunk*
Krahn, Fernando. *A funny friend from heaven*
Lacome, Julie. *Funny business*
Lent, Blair. *Pistachio*
Lynn, Sara. *Colors*
Marceau, Marcel. *The story of Bip*
Mendoza, George. *The Marcel Marceau counting book*
Miller, M. L. *Dizzy from fools*
Olds, Elizabeth. *Plop plop ploppie*
Pellowski, Michael. *Clara joins the circus*
Petersham, Maud. *The circus baby*
Politi, Leo. *Lito and the clown*
Quackenbush, Robert M. *The man on the flying trapeze*
Richardson, Jean. *Tall inside*
Rockwell, Anne F. *Gogo's pay day*
Schreiber, Georges. *Bambino goes home*
  Bambino the clown
Shecter, Ben. *Hester the jester*

Slocum, Rosalie. *Breakfast with the clowns*
Sobol, Harriet Langsam. *Clowns*
Thurber, James. *Many moons*, ill. by Marc Simont
Many moons, ill. by Louis Slobodkin

Clubs, gangs

Alexander, Sue. *Seymour the prince*
Berenstain, Stan. *The Berenstain bears: No girls allowed*
Bradford, Ann. *The mystery at Misty Falls*
  The mystery in the secret club house
  The mystery of the blind writer
  The mystery of the midget clown
  The mystery of the missing dogs
  The mystery of the square footsteps
  The mystery of the tree house
Crowley, Michael. *The new kid on Spurwick Ave.*
Kotzwinkle, William. *The day the gang got rich*
Stanley, Diane. *The conversation club*
Thaler, Mike. *Pack 109*
Winthrop, Elizabeth. *The Best Friends Club*

Coats see Clothing – coats

Cockatoos see Birds – cockatoos

Codes see Secret codes

Cold see Weather – cold

Collecting things see Behavior – collecting things

Color see Concepts – color

Color see Concepts – color

Columbus Day see Holidays – Columbus Day

Communication

Allington, Richard L. *Talking Words*
Ancona, George. *Handtalk zoo*
Arnold, Caroline. *How do we communicate?*
Bohdal, Susi. *Tom cat*
Borchers, Elisabeth. *Dear Sarah*
Brown, Margaret Wise. *The big fur secret*
Buchheimer, Naomi. *Let's go to a post office*
Charlip, Remy. *Handtalk*
Chukovsky, Korney. *The telephone*
Clifford, Eth. *A bear before breakfast*
Emberley, Ed (Edward Randolph). *Green says go*
Engdahl, Sylvia. *Our world is earth*
Gibbons, Gail. *The post office book*
Goor, Ron. *Signs*

Hoban, Tana. *I read signs*
  I read symbols
Joslin, Sesyle. *Dear dragon*
Leedy, Loreen. *The Furry News*
Potter, Beatrix. *Yours affectionately, Peter Rabbit*
Showers, Paul. *How you talk*
Stanley, Diane. *The conversation club*
Telephones
Tolkien, J. R. R. (John Ronald Reuel). *The Father Christmas letters*
Van Woerkom, Dorothy. *Hidden messages*

Communities, neighborhoods

Arnold, Caroline. *What is a community?*
  Where do you go to school?
  Who works here?
Arnold, Tedd. *The simple people*
Berridge, Celia. *On my street*
Blakeley, Peggy. *Two little ducks*
Crowley, Michael. *The new kid on Spurwick Ave.*
Denslow, Sharon Phillips. *Hazel's circle*
Edwards, Michelle. *Chicken man*
Freeman, Don. *Corduroy's busy street and Corduroy goes to the doctor*
Greenfield, Eloise. *Night on Neighborhood Street*
Groner, Judyth. *My very own Jewish community*
Haskins, Francine. *I remember "one hundred twenty-one"*
Henkes, Kevin. *Once around the block*
Henwood, Simon. *The troubled village*
Isadora, Rachel. *Over the green hills*
Komaiko, Leah. *My perfect neighborhood*
Leedy, Loreen. *The Furry News*
Miller, Margaret. *On my street*
Ratz de Tagyos, Paul. *A coney tale*
Rogers, Fred. *Moving*
Scheffler, Ursel. *Stop your crowing, Kasimir!*
Smalls-Hector, Irene. *Irene and the big, fine nickel*
  Jonathan and his mommy
Smith, Barry. *Cumberland Road*
Spinelli, Eileen. *Somebody loves you, Mr. Hatch*
Swope, Sam. *The Araboolies of Liberty Street*
Ward, Sally G. *What goes around comes around*
Yeoman, John. *Our village*
Yoaker, Harry. *The view*

Competition *see* Sibling rivalry

Completing things *see* Character traits – completing things

Composers *see* Careers – composers

Compromising *see* Character traits – compromising

Computers

Baker, Eugene. *I want to be a computer operator*
D'Ignazio, Fred. *Katie and the computer*
Greene, Carol. *A computer went a-courting*
Lyon, David. *The brave little computer*
Matthias, Catherine. *I can be a computer operator*
Modell, Frank. *Skeeter and the computer*
Ross, David. *Space Monster Gorp and the runaway computer*
Skulavik, Mary Alys. *Bert*
Steadman, Ralph. *The little red computer*

Conceit *see* Character traits – conceit

Concepts

Albert, Burton. *Mine, yours, ours*
Anno, Mitsumasa. *Anno's math games*
  Anno's math games II
  Anno's math games III
Arvetis, Chris. *Why is it dark?*
Balestrino, Philip. *Hot as an ice cube*
Bauman, A. F. *Guess where you're going, guess what you'll do*
Beisner, Monika. *Topsy turvy*
Berenstain, Stan. *Inside outside upside down*
Berkley, Ethel S. *Ups and down*
Bodger, Joan. *Belinda's ball*
Booth, Eugene. *At the circus*
  At the fair
  In the air
  In the garden
  In the jungle
  Under the ocean
Borten, Helen. *Do you see what I see?*
Brown, Marcia. *Touch will tell*
  Walk with your eyes
Browner, Richard. *Look again!*
Carle, Eric. *My very first book of motion*
Charosh, Mannis. *Number ideas through pictures*
Chase, Catherine. *Hot and cold*
Crews, Donald. *Light*
  We read: A to Z
Cushman, Doug. *Nasty Kyle the crocodile*
Dantzer-Rosenthal, Marya. *Some things are different, some things are the same*
Duke, Kate. *Guinea pigs far and near*
  What bounces?
Emberley, Ed (Edward Randolph). *Ed Emberley's amazing look through book*
Fisher, Leonard Everett. *Boxes! Boxes!*
Freudberg, Judy. *Some, more, most*
Froman, Robert. *Angles are easy as pie*
  A game of functions
Garland, Sarah. *All gone!*

Gillham, Bill. *Where does it go?*
Green, Mary McBurney. *Is it hard? Is it easy?*
Greene, Laura. *Change*
Griest, Virginia. *In between*
Hartman, Gail. *For strawberry jam or fireflies*
Hennessy, B. G. *A, B, C, D, tummy, toes, hands, knee*
Hoban, Tana. *All about where*
Dots, spots, speckles, and stripes
Is it rough? Is it smooth? Is it shiny?
Look! Look! Look!
Take another look
Hughes, Shirley. *Lucy and Tom's 1, 2, 3*
Jensen, Virginia Allen. *What's that?*
Johnson, Ryerson. *Upstairs and downstairs*
Jonas, Ann. *Reflections*
Kuskin, Karla. *All sizes of noises*
Lopshire, Robert. *The biggest, smallest, fastest, tallest things you've ever heard of*
McMillan, Bruce. *Becca backward, Becca forward*
Dry or wet?
One, two, one pair!
Maestro, Betsy. *Temperature and you*
Where is my friend?
Magnus, Erica. *Around me*
Matthias, Catherine. *Arriba y abajo: Over and under*
Matthiesen, Thomas. *Things to see*
Mayer, Mercer. *Mine!*
Mazer, Anne. *The yellow button*
Peppé, Rodney. *Odd one out*
Rodney Peppé's puzzle book
Pragoff, Fiona. *Odd one out*
Rahn, Joan Elma. *Holes*
Ruben, Patricia. *True or false?*
Scarry, Richard. *Richard Scarry's best first book ever!*
The Sesame Street book of people and things
Sis, Peter. *Beach ball*
Supraner, Robyn. *Giggly-wiggly, snickety-snick*
Wallner, John. *Look and find*
Webb, Angela. *Light*
Reflections
Sound
Wood, A. J. *Look! The ultimate spot-the-difference book*
Yektai, Niki. *Bears in pairs*
Zaslavsky, Claudia. *Zero! Is it something? Is it nothing?*
Ziefert, Harriet. *My getting-ready-for-school book*

Concepts – color

Abisch, Roz. *Open your eyes*
Adoff, Arnold. *Greens*
Allamand, Pascale. *The animals who changed their colors*

Allen, Robert. *Ten little babies play*
Allington, Richard L. *Colors*
Anholt, Catherine. *Tom's rainbow walk*
Asch, Frank. *Yellow, yellow*
Baby's first book of colors, ill. by Nina Barbaresi
Baker, Alan. *Benjamin's portrait*
Berger, Judith. *Butterflies and rainbows*
Bond, Michael. *Paddington's colors*
Bradman, Tony. *The bad babies' book of colors*
Brenner, Barbara A. *The color wizard*
Bright, Robert. *I like red*
Brown, Margaret Wise. *Afro-bets: book of colors*
Red light, green light
Brunhoff, Laurent de. *Babar's book of color*
Burningham, John. *John Burningham's colors*
Campbell, Ann. *Let's find out about color*
Carle, Eric. *The mixed-up chameleon*
My very first book of colors
Carroll, Kathleen Sullivan. *One red rooster*
Charlip, Remy. *Harlequin and the gift of many colors*
Chermayeff, Ivan. *Tomato and other colors*
Clifford, Eth. *Red is never a mouse*
De Paola, Paula. *Rosie and the yellow ribbon*
Dines, Glen. *Pitadoe, the color maker*
Dodds, Dayle Ann. *The color box*
Dunham, Meredith. *Colors: how do you say it?*
Duvoisin, Roger Antoine. *The house of four seasons*
See what I am
Ehlert, Lois. *Color farm*
Color zoo
Emberley, Ed (Edward Randolph). *Green says go*
Ernst, Lisa Campbell. *A colorful adventure of the bee who left home one Monday morning and what he found along the way*
Fallwell, Cathryn. *Nicky's walk*
Feeney, Stephanie. *Hawaii is a rainbow*
Fisher, Leonard Everett. *Boxes! Boxes!*
Flora. *Feathers like a rainbow*
Freeman, Don. *The chalk box story*
A rainbow of my own
Gillham, Bill. *Let's look for colors*
Goennel, Heidi. *Colors*
Goffstein, M. B. (Marilyn Brooke). *Artists' helpers enjoy the evening*
Graham, Amanda. *Picasso, the green tree frog*
Graham, Bob. *The red woolen blanket*
Greeley, Valerie. *White is the moon*
Groening, Maggie. *Maggie Simpson's book of colors and shapes*
Gundersheimer, Karen. *Colors to know*
Haskins, Ilma. *Color seems*
Hest, Amy. *The purple coat*

Hill, Eric. *Spot looks at colors*
Hoban, Tana. *Dots, spots, speckles, and stripes*
Is it red? Is it yellow? Is it blue?
Of colors and things
Red, blue, yellow shoe
Hughes, Shirley. *Colors*
Imershein, Betsy. *Finding red, finding yellow*
Jenkins, Jessica. *Thinking about colors*
Karn, George. *Circus colors*
Kessler, Leonard P. *Mr. Pine's purple house*
Kilroy, Sally. *Baby colors*
Kirkpatrick, Rena K. *Look at rainbow colors*
Kleven, Elisa. *The lion and the little red bird*
Konigsburg, E. L. (Elaine Lobl). *Samuel Todd's book of great colors*
Kumin, Maxine. *What color is Caesar?*
Kunhardt, Edith. *Red day, green day*
Lacome, Julie. *Funny business*
Lewis, Naomi. *Once upon a rainbow*
Lionni, Leo. *A color of his own*
Colors to talk about
Little blue and little yellow
A little book of colors
Lobel, Arnold. *The great blueness and other predicaments*
Löfgren, Ulf. *The color trumpet*
Lopshire, Robert. *Put me in the zoo*
Lynn, Sara. *Colors*
McMillan, Bruce. *Growing colors*
Maril, Lee. *Mr. Bunny paints the eggs*
Marks, Burton. *Colors and numbers*
Martin, Bill (William Ivan). *Brown bear, brown bear, what do you see?*
Miller, J. P. (John Parr). *Do you know color?*
Learn about colors with Little Rabbit
Oliver, Stephen. *My first look at colors*
Ostheeren, Ingrid. *Jonathan Mouse*
Oxford Scientific Films. *Danger colors*
Hide and seek
Peek, Merle. *Mary wore her red dress and Henry wore his green sneakers*
Pieńkowski, Jan. *Colors*
Pinkwater, Daniel Manus. *The bear's picture*
The big orange splot
Podendorf, Illa. *Color*
Reiss, John J. *Colors*
Rikys, Bodel. *Red bear*
Rogers, Margaret. *Green is beautiful*
Rosen, Michael J. *How the animals got their colors*
Ross, Tony. *Hugo and the man who stole colors*
Rossetti, Christina Georgina. *Color*
What is pink?
Sandberg, Inger. *Nicholas' red day*
Sawicki, Norma Jean. *The little red house*
Scott, Rochelle. *Colors, colors all around*
Selkowe, Valrie M. *Spring green*

Serfozo, Mary. *Who said red?*
Shub, Elizabeth. *Dragon Franz*
Sieveking, Anthea. *What color?*
Silsbe, Brenda. *Just one more color*
Silverman, Maida. *Ladybug's color book*
Sis, Peter. *Going up!*
Spier, Peter. *Oh, were they ever happy!*
Steiner, Charlotte. *My slippers are red*
Stinson, Kathy. *Red is best*
Tafuri, Nancy. *In a red house*
Testa, Fulvio. *If you take a paintbrush*
Tison, Annette. *The adventures of the three colors*
Troughton, Joanna. *How the birds changed their feathers*
Turner, Gwenda. *Colors*
Van Laan, Nancy. *Rainbow crow*
Wells, Tony. *Allsorts*
Puzzle doubles
Williams, Sue. *I went walking*
Wolff, Robert Jay. *Feeling blue*
Hello, yellow!
Seeing red
Wood, Jakki. *Moo moo, brown cow*
Youldon, Gillian. *Colors*
Young, James. *A million chameleons*
Youngs, Betty. *Pink pigs in mud*
Zacharias, Thomas. *But where is the green parrot?*
Ziefert, Harriet. *No more! Piggety Pig*
Zolotow, Charlotte (Shapiro). *Mr. Rabbit and the lovely present*

Concepts - counting see Counting, numbers

Concepts – distance

Tresselt, Alvin R. *How far is far?*

Concepts – in and out

Banchek, Linda. *Snake in, snake out*
Daughtry, Duanne. *What's inside?*
Matthias, Catherine. *Sal y entra: Out the door*
Ueno, Noriko. *Elephant buttons*

Concepts – left and right

Chase, Catherine. *Feet*
McMillan, Bruce. *Beach ball—left, right*
Oppenheim, Joanne. *Left and right*
Rehm, Karl. *Left or right?*
Stanek, Muriel. *Left, right, left, right!*

Concepts – measurement

Adler, David A. *3D, 2D, 1D*
Allington, Richard L. *Measuring*
Branley, Franklyn M. *How little and how much*
Lionni, Leo. *Inch by inch*

Myller, Rolf. *How big is a foot?*
Thompson, Brenda. *The winds that blow*

Concepts – opposites

Allington, Richard L. *Opposites*
Anholt, Catherine. *Good days, bad days*
Banchek, Linda. *Snake in, snake out*
Barrett, Judi. *I'm too small, you're too big*
Boynton, Sandra. *Opposites*
Butterworth, Nick. *Nice or nasty*
Crowther, Robert. *The most amazing hide-and-seek opposites book*
Demi. *Demi's opposites*
Dijs, Carla. *Big and small*
Gillham, Bill. *Let's look for opposites*
  What's the difference?
Green, Suzanne. *The little choo-choo*
Hill, Eric. *Spot looks at opposites*
Hoban, Tana. *Push-pull, empty-full*
Hughes, Shirley. *Bathwater's hot*
Karn, George. *Circus big and small*
Kightley, Rosalinda. *Opposites*
Koch, Michelle. *By the sea*
Lankford, Mary D. *Is it dark? Is it light?*
Leonard, Marcia. *The kitten twins*
Lippman, Peter. *Peter Lippman's opposites*
McKissack, Patricia C. *Big bug book of opposites*
McLenighan, Valjean. *Stop-go, fast-slow*
McMillan, Bruce. *Becca backward, Becca forward*
  Here a chick, there a chick
McNaughton, Colin. *At home*
  At playschool
  At the park
  At the party
  At the stores
Maestro, Betsy. *Traffic*
Matthias, Catherine. *Over-under*
Mendoza, George. *The Sesame Street book of opposites with Zero Mostel*
Milios, Rita. *Yo soy—I am*
Miller, Margaret. *Playtime*
Oliver, Stephen. *Opposites*
Pragoff, Fiona. *Opposites*
Provensen, Alice. *Karen's opposites*
Spier, Peter. *Fast-slow, high-low*
Watson, Carol. *Opposites*
Wildsmith, Brian. *What the moon saw*
Young, Ruth. *Daisy's taxi*
Ziefert, Harriet. *Let's go! Piggety Pig*

Concepts – perspective

Adler, David A. *3D, 2D, 1D*
Cohen, Caron Lee. *Pigeon, pigeon*
Davies, Kay. *My balloon*
  My mirror
Gore, Sheila. *My shadow*
Mainwaring, Jane. *My feather*

Titherington, Jeanne. *Big world, small world*
Wakefield, Joyce. *From where you are*
Yolen, Jane. *All those secrets of the world*

Concepts - self *see* Self-concept

Concepts – shape

Adler, David A. *3D, 2D, 1D*
Allen, Robert. *Round and square*
Allington, Richard L. *Shapes*
Anno, Mitsumasa. *Anno's faces*
Atwood, Ann. *The little circle*
Berenstain, Stan. *Old hat, new hat*
Bishop, Roma. *Shapes*
Brown, Marcia. *Listen to a shape*
Brown, Margaret Wise. *Afro-bets: book of shapes*
Budney, Blossom. *A kiss is round*
Carle, Eric. *My very first book of shapes*
Charosh, Mannis. *The ellipse*
Craig, M. Jean. *Boxes*
Crews, Donald. *Ten black dots*
De Mejo, Oscar. *La Bella Magellona and the little cavalier*
Dunbar, Fiona. *You'll never guess!*
Dunham, Meredith. *Shapes: how do you say it?*
Ehlert, Lois. *Color farm*
  Color zoo
Fallwell, Cathryn. *Clowning around*
Feldman, Judy. *Shapes in nature*
Fisher, Leonard Everett. *Look around!*
Friskey, Margaret (Margaret Richards). *Three sides and the round one*
Gardner, Beau. *Guess what?*
  What is it?
Gerstein, Mordicai. *The gigantic baby*
Gillham, Bill. *Let's look for shapes*
Goldblatt, Eli. *Leo loves round*
Gomi, Taro. *The big book of boxes*
Groening, Maggie. *Maggie Simpson's book of colors and shapes*
Gundersheimer, Karen. *Shapes to show*
Hatcher, Charles. *What shape is it?*
Hefter, Richard. *The strawberry book of shapes*
Heinst, Marie. *My first number book*
Hill, Eric. *Spot looks at shapes*
Hoban, Tana. *Circles, triangles, and squares*
  Dots, spots, speckles, and stripes
  Is it red? Is it yellow? Is it blue?
  Round and round and round
  Shapes and things
  Shapes, shapes, shapes
Hughes, Peter. *The emperor's oblong pancake*
Hughes, Shirley. *All shapes and sizes*
Jensen, Virginia Allen. *Catching*
Kightley, Rosalinda. *Shapes*
Lacome, Julie. *Funny business*
Lionni, Leo. *Pezzettino*

MacKinnon, Debbie. *What shape?*
McMillan, Bruce. *Fire engine shapes*
Mayer, Marianna. *The Brambleberrys animal book of big and small shapes*
Newth, Philip. *Roly goes exploring*
Oliver, Stephen. *My first look at shapes*
Pieńkowski, Jan. *Shapes*
Pluckrose, Henry Arthur. *Shape*
Podendorf, Illa. *Shapes, sides, curves and corners*
Pragoff, Fiona. *Shapes*
Reiss, John J. *Shapes*
Reit, Seymour. *Round things everywhere*
Roberts, Cliff. *The dot*
  Start with a dot
Rogers, Paul (Patrick). *The shapes game*
Salazar, Violet. *Squares are not bad*
Santoro, Christopher. *Book of shapes*
Schlein, Miriam. *Shapes*
The Sesame Street book of shapes
Seuss, Dr. *The shape of me and other stuff*
Shapiro, Arnold L. *Circle*
  Square
  Triangles
Shaw, Charles Green. *It looked like spilt milk*
Silverman, Maida. *Mouse's shape book*
Silverstein, Shel. *The missing piece*
Smith, Mavis. *Circles*
Smith-Moore, J. J. *Sally Small*
Stoddard, Sandol. *Curl up small*
Testa, Fulvio. *If you look around*
Turner, Gwenda. *Shapes*
Watson, Carol. *Shapes*
Wells, Tony. *Allsorts*
Wildsmith, Brian. *Animal shapes*
Youldon, Gillian. *Shapes*
Ziefert, Harriet. *City shapes*
Zimmermann, H. Werner (Heinz Werner). *Alphonse knows...a circle is not a Valentine*

Concepts – size

Allington, Richard L. *Shapes*
Anno, Mitsumasa. *The king's flower*
Aulaire, Ingri Mortenson d'. *Too big*
Balian, Lorna. *Where in the world is Henry?*
Barrett, Judi. *I hate to take a bath*
Benson, Patrick. *Little penguin*
Berenstain, Stan. *Old hat, new hat*
Black, Irma Simonton. *Big puppy and little puppy*
Blue, Rose. *How many blocks is the world?*
Brown, Marcia. *Once a mouse...*
Brown, Margaret Wise. *Big dog, little dog*
  Bumble bugs and elephants
Bulette, Sara. *The splendid belt of Mr. Big*
Cantieni, Benita. *Little Elephant and Big Mouse*
Chalmers, Audrey. *Hector and Mr. Murfit*
Craig, M. Jean. *Boxes*

Croswell, Volney. *How to hide a hippopotamus*
De Mejo, Oscar. *La Bella Magellona and the little cavalier*
Finzel, Julia. *Large as life*
Gerstein, Mordicai. *The gigantic baby*
Hoban, Tana. *Big ones, little ones*
  Is it larger? Is it smaller?
  Is it red? Is it yellow? Is it blue?
Hughes, Shirley. *All shapes and sizes*
Hutchins, Pat. *Titch*
Ipcar, Dahlov. *The biggest fish in the sea*
  The land of flowers
Iwamura, Kazuo. *Ton and Pon: big and little*
Joyce, William. *George shrinks*
Kalan, Robert. *Blue sea*
Karlin, Nurit. *Little big moose*
Kraus, Robert. *The little giant*
Krauss, Ruth. *Big and little*
  A bouquet of littles
Kuskin, Karla. *Herbert hated being small*
Lipkind, William. *Chaga*
Long, Earlene. *Gone fishing*
MacKinnon, Debbie. *What shape?*
Mayer, Marianna. *The Brambleberrys animal book of big and small shapes*
Nakabayashi, Ei. *The rainy day puddle*
Oliver, Stephen. *My first look at sizes*
Peet, Bill (William Bartlett). *Huge Harold*
Pieńkowski, Jan. *Sizes*
Pluckrose, Henry Arthur. *Big and little*
Pragoff, Fiona. *Shapes*
Prøysen, Alf. *Mrs. Pepperpot and the moose*
Schwartz, David M. *How much is a million?*
Shapp, Charles. *Let's find out what's big and what's small*
Smith, Mavis. *Circles*
Smith-Moore, J. J. *Sally Small*
Stickland, Paul. *Machines as big as monsters*
Stoddard, Sandol. *Curl up small*
Ueno, Noriko. *Elephant buttons*
Van Emst, Charlotte. *Little Rabbit's big day*
Watson, Carol. *Sizes*
Wells, Tony. *Puzzle doubles*
Youldon, Gillian. *Sizes*

Concepts – speed

Schlein, Miriam. *Fast is not a ladybug*
Spier, Peter. *Fast-slow, high-low*

Concepts – up and down

Berkley, Ethel S. *Ups and down*
Hoban, Tana. *Look up, look down*
Johnson, Crockett. *Upside down*
Knight, Hilary. *Sylvia the sloth*
Matthias, Catherine. *Sal y entra: Out the door*
Seuss, Dr. *A great day for up*
Slobodkin, Louis. *Up high and down low*

Zion, Gene. *All falling down*

Concepts – weight
Fischer, Vera Kistiakowsky. *One way is down*
MacDonald, George. *The light princess*, ill. by Katie Thamer Treherne
Pluckrose, Henry Arthur. *Weight*
Schlein, Miriam. *Heavy is a hippopotamus*

Confidence *see* Character traits – confidence

Conservation *see* Ecology

Contests
Marshall, James. *The Cut-Ups carry on*

Cooking *see* Activities – cooking

Cooks *see* Careers – bakers

Copying *see* Behavior – copying

Coral Islands *see* Foreign lands – South Sea Islands

Cormorants *see* Birds – cormorants

Costa Rica *see* Foreign lands – Costa Rica

Couches, sofas *see* Furniture – couches, sofas

Cougars *see* Animals – cougars

Counting, numbers
Adams, Pam. *This old man*
Adler, David A. *Base five*
Alexander, Anne (Anna Barbara Cooke). *My daddy and I*
Allbright, Viv. *Ten go hopping*
Allen, Robert. *Numbers: a first counting book*
Ten little babies count
Ten little babies dress
Ten little babies eat
Ten little babies play
Allington, Richard L. *Numbers*
Ambler, Christopher Gifford. *Ten little foxhounds*
Anno, Mitsumasa. *Anno's counting book*
Anno's counting house
Anno's hat tricks
Anno's math games
Anno's math games II
Anno's math games III
Archambault, John. *Counting sheep*
Arnosky, Jim. *Mouse numbers and letters*
Asch, Frank. *Little Devil's 123*

Ashton, Elizabeth Allen. *An old-fashioned one two three book*
Astley, Judy. *When one cat woke up*
Aylesworth, Jim. *The completed hickory dickory dock*
One crow
Baker, Bonnie Jeanne. *A pear by itself*
Baker, Jeannie. *One hungry spider*
Bang, Molly. *Ten, nine, eight*
Baum, Arline. *One bright Monday morning*
Bawden, Juliet. *One year old*
Bayley, Nicola. *One old Oxford ox*
Becker, John Leonard. *Seven little rabbits*
Bennett, David. *One cow moo moo*
Berenstain, Stan. *Bears on wheels*
The Berenstain bears' counting book
Bertrand, Lynne. *One day, two dragons*
Bishop, Claire Huchet. *Twenty-two bears*
Bishop, Roma. *Numbers*
Blegvad, Lenore. *One is for the sun*
Blumenthal, Nancy. *Count-a-saurus*
Bond, Michael. *Paddington's 1 2 3*
Boon, Emilie. *1 2 3 how many animals can you see?*
Boynton, Sandra. *Hippos go berserk*
Bradman, Tony. *The bad babies' counting book*
Not like this, like that
Brenner, Barbara A. *The snow parade*
Bridgman, Elizabeth. *All the little bunnies*
Bright, Robert. *My red umbrella*
Bruna, Dick. *I know more about numbers*
Poppy Pig goes to market
Brunhoff, Laurent de. *Babar's counting book*
Bucknall, Caroline. *One bear all alone*
Burningham, John. *Count up*
Five down
Just cats
Pigs plus
Read one
Ride off
The shopping basket
Calmenson, Stephanie. *Dinner at the Panda Palace*
Carle, Eric. *My very first book of numbers*
1, 2, 3 to the zoo
The rooster who set out to see the world
Rooster's off to see the world
Carlstrom, Nancy White. *Graham cracker animals 1-2-3*
Carroll, Kathleen Sullivan. *One red rooster*
Cave, Kathryn. *Out for the count*
Challoner, Jack. *The science book of numbers*
Charlip, Remy. *Thirteen*
Charosh, Mannis. *Number ideas through pictures*
Chouinard, Roger. *One magic box*
Christelow, Eileen. *Five little monkeys jumping on the bed*
Five little monkeys sitting in a tree

Chwast, Seymour. *Still another number book*
Cleveland, David. *The April rabbits*
Coats, Laura Jane. *Ten little animals*
Cole, Joanna. *Animal sleepyheads*
Conover, Chris. *Six little ducks*
Corbett, Grahame. *What number now?*
Count me in
Counting rhymes, ill. by Corinne Malvern
Cretan, Gladys Yessayan. *Ten brothers with camels*
Crews, Donald. *Ten black dots*
Crowther, Robert. *Hide and seek counting book*
Dalmais, Anne-Marie. *In my garden*
Dayton, Laura. *LeRoy's birthday circus*
DeCaprio, Annie. *One, two*
Demi. *Demi's count the animals 1-2-3*
De Regniers, Beatrice Schenk. *So many cats!*
Dijs, Carla. *How many?*
Dodd, Lynley. *The nickle nackle tree*
Dodds, Siobhan. *Elizabeth Hen*
Doolittle, Eileen. *World of wonders*
Dreamer, Sue. *Circus 1, 2, 3*
Dunham, Meredith. *Numbers: how do you say it?*
Dunrea, Olivier. *Deep down underground*
Duvoisin, Roger Antoine. *Two lonely ducks*
Edwards, Roberta. *Five silly fishermen*
Eichenberg, Fritz. *Dancing in the moon*
Elkin, Benjamin. *Six foolish fishermen*
Ernst, Lisa Campbell. *Up to ten and down again*
Fallwell, Cathryn. *Nicky, 1-2-3*
Farber, Norma. *Up the down elevator*
Feelings, Muriel. *Menjo means one*
Fisher, Leonard Everett. *Boxes! Boxes!*
Fleming, Denise. *Count!*
Florian, Douglas. *A summer day*
Freeman, Lydia. *Corduroy's day*
French, Vivian. *One ballerina two*
Freschet, Berniece. *The ants go marching*
Where's Henrietta's hen?
Friskey, Margaret (Margaret Richards).
Chicken Little, count-to-ten
Seven diving ducks
Gantz, David. *Captain Swifty counts to 50*
Gardner, Beau. *Can you imagine...?*
Gerstein, Mordicai. *Roll over!*
Giganti, Paul. *Each orange had eight slices*
How many snails?
Gillham, Bill. *Let's look for numbers*
Ginsburg, Mirra. *Kitten from one to ten*
Gregor, Arthur S. *One, two, three, four, five*
Gretz, Susanna. *Teddy bears ABC*
Teddy bears 1 - 10
Grimm, Jacob. *Mrs. Fox's wedding*, ill. by Errol Le Cain
Groening, Matt. *Maggie Simpson's counting book*
Grossman, Virginia. *Ten little rabbits*

Gundersheimer, Karen. *1 2 3 play with me*
Hague, Kathleen. *Numbears*
Hamm, Diane Johnston. *How many feet in the bed?*
Hamsa, Bobbie. *Polly wants a cracker*
Harada, Joyce. *It's the 0-1-2-3 book*
Haskins, Jim. *Count your way through China*
Count your way through Japan
Count your way through Russia
Count your way through the Arab world
Hawkins, Colin. *Take away monsters*
Hay, Dean. *Now I can count*
Heinst, Marie. *My first number book*
Hill, Eric. *Spot counts from 1 to 10*
Hoban, Russell. *Ten what?*
Hoban, Tana. *Count and see*
1, 2, 3
26 letters and 99 cents
Holder, Heidi. *Crows*
Holmes, Stephen. *Hidden numbers*
Hooper, Meredith. *Seven eggs*
Howard, Katherine. *I can count to 100... can you?*
Howe, Caroline Walton. *Counting penguins*
Hubbard, Woodleigh. *Two is for dancing*
Hughes, Shirley. *Lucy and Tom's 1, 2, 3*
When we went to the park
Hulme, Joy. *Sea squares*
Hutchins, Pat. *1 hunter*
Inkpen, Mick. *Kipper's toybox*
One bear at bedtime
Ipcar, Dahlov. *Brown cow farm*
Ten big farms
Jabar, Cynthia. *Party day!*
Johnson, Odette. *One prickly porcupine*
Johnston, Tony. *Whale song*
Jones, Carol. *This old man*
Katz, Michael Jay. *Ten potatoes in a pot and other counting rhymes*
Kessler, Ethel. *Two, four, six, eight*
Kitamura, Satoshi. *When sheep cannot sleep*
Kitchen, Bert. *Animal numbers*
Koch, Michelle. *Just one more*
Koontz, Robin Michal. *This old man*
Kopper, Lisa. *Ten little babies*
Kramer, Anthony Penta. *Numbers on parade*
Kraus, Robert. *Good night little one*
Good night Richard Rabbit
Krüss, James. *3 X 3*
Langstaff, John M. *Over in the meadow*
Lasker, Joe. *Lentil soup*
Leedy, Loreen. *A number of dragons*
Let's count and count out, ill. by Deborah Derr McClintock
Lewin, Betsy. *Cat count*
Hip, hippo, hooray!
Lewis, Sheri. *Baby Lamb Chop loves numbers*
Lindberg, Reeve. *Midnight farm*
Linden, Ann Marie. *One smiling grandma*
Lionni, Leo. *Numbers to talk about*

Lippman, Peter. *Peter Lippman's numbers*
A little book of numbers
Livermore, Elaine. *One to ten, count again*
Löfgren, Ulf. *One-two-three*
Lynn, Sara. *1 2 3*
McCarthy, Bobette. *Ten little hippos*
McCrea, Lilian. *Mother hen*
MacDonald, Elizabeth. *Mike's kite*
My aunt and the animals
MacDonald, Suse. *Numblers*
McGee, Barbara. *Counting sheep*
McGough, Roger. *Counting by numbers*
McGuire, Richard. *The orange book*
Mack, Stanley (Stan). *Ten bears in my bed*
McKissack, Patricia C. *Big bug book of counting*
McLeod, Emilie Warren. *One snail and me*
McMillan, Bruce. *Counting wildflowers*
Eating fractions
One, two, one pair!
Maestro, Betsy. *Dollars and cents for Harriet*
Harriet goes to the circus
Maestro, Giulio. *One more and one less*
Magee, Doug. *Trucks you can count on*
Manushkin, Fran. *Walt Disney's one hundred one dalmations*
Maris, Ron. *In my garden*
Marks, Burton. *Colors and numbers*
Marshall, Ray. *Pop-up numbers #1*
Pop-up numbers #2
Pop-up numbers #3
Pop-up numbers #4
Martin, Bill (William Ivan). *Sounds I remember*
Sounds of numbers
Mathews, Louise. *Bunches and bunches of bunnies*
Cluck one
The great take-away
Matthias, Catherine. *Too many balloons*
Mayer, Marianna. *Alley oop!*
The Brambleberrys animal book of counting
Mayer, Mercer. *Little Monster's counting book*
Meeks, Esther K. *One is the engine*, ill. by Ernie King
One is the engine, ill. by Joe Rogers
Merriam, Eve. *Train leaves the station*
Merrill, Jean. *How many kids are hiding on my block?*
Miller, J. P. (John Parr). *Learn to count with Little Rabbit*
Miller, Jane. *Farm counting book*
Milne, A. A. (Alan Alexander). *Pooh's counting book*
Morozumi, Atsuko. *One gorilla*
Morris, Ann. *Night counting*
Morse, Samuel French. *Sea sums*
Moss, Marissa. *Knick knack paddywack*
Namm, Diane. *Monsters!*
Nightingale, Sandy. *Pink pigs aplenty*

Nikola-Lisa, W. *One, two, three Thanksgiving!*
Noll, Sally. *Off and counting*
Nordqvist, Sven. *Willie in the big world*
O'Brien, Mary. *Counting sheep to sleep*
O'Donnell, Elizabeth Lee. *I can't get my turtle to move*
The twelve days of summer
O'Keefe, Susan Heyboer. *One hungry monster*
Oliver, Stephen. *My first look at numbers*
One rubber duckie
One, two, buckle my shoe, ill. by Rowan Barnes-Murphy
One, two, buckle my shoe, ill. by Gail E. Haley
Ormerod, Jan. *Come back, kittens*
Come back, puppies
Young Joe
Over in the meadow, ill. by Paul Galdone
Over in the meadow, ill. by Ezra Jack Keats
Oxenbury, Helen. *Numbers of things*
Pacovska, Kveta. *One, five, many*
Pavey, Peter. *One dragon's dream*
Pearson, Susan. *When baby went to bed*
Peek, Merle. *The balancing act*
Peppé, Rodney. *Circus numbers*
Little numbers
Petie, Haris. *Billions of bugs*
Pieńkowski, Jan. *Numbers*
Pluckrose, Henry Arthur. *Counting*
Numbers
Pomerantz, Charlotte. *One duck, another duck*
Potter, Beatrix. *Peter Rabbit's one two three*
Price, Christine. *One is God*
The pudgy fingers counting book, ill. by Doug Cushman
Rand, Ann. *Little 1*
Rees, Mary. *Ten in a bed*
Reiss, John J. *Numbers*
Rockwell, Anne F. *Willy can count*
Rockwell, Norman. *Norman Rockwell's counting book*
Roll over! ill. by Merle Peek
Ross, H. L. *Not counting monsters*
Ross, Tony. *This old man*
Samton, Sheila White. *Moon to sun*
On the river
The world from my window
Sazer, Nina. *What do you think I saw?*
Scarry, Richard. *Richard Scarry's best counting book ever!*
Schertle, Alice. *Goodnight, Hattie, my dearie, my dove*
Schwartz, David M. *How much is a million?*
Scott, Ann Herbert. *One good horse*
Seignobosc, Françoise. *Jeanne-Marie counts her sheep*
Sendak, Maurice. *One was Johnny*
Seven little monsters

Serfozo, Mary. *Who wants one?*
The Sesame Street book of numbers
Seuss, Dr. *Ten apples up on top*
Sharmat, Marjorie Weinman. *The 329th friend*
Sheppard, Jeff. *The right number of elephants*
Shostak, Myra. *Rainbow candles*
Sis, Peter. *Going up!*
Waving
Sitomer, Mindel. *How did numbers begin?*
Smith, Donald. *Farm numbers 1, 2, 3*
Stanek, Muriel. *One, two, three for fun*
Steiner, Charlotte. *Five little finger playmates*
Stobbs, Joanna. *One sun, two eyes, and a million stars*
Stobbs, William. *This little piggy*
Sugita, Yutaka. *Good night 1, 2, 3*
Szekeres, Cyndy. *Cyndy Szekeres' counting book, 1 to 10*
Tafuri, Nancy. *Who's counting?*
Testa, Fulvio. *If you take a pencil*
Thompson, Susan L. *One more thing, dad*
Thornhill, Jan. *The wildlife 1-2-3*
Trinca, Rod. *One woolly wombat*
Tudor, Tasha. *1 is one*
Wadsworth, Olive A. *Over in the meadow*
Walsh, Ellen Stoll. *Mouse count*
Warren, Cathy. *The ten-alarm camp-out*
Watson, Nancy Dingman. *What is one?*
Weihs, Erika. *Count the cats*
Weiss, Monica. *Mmmm...cookies!*
Wells, Rosemary. *Max's toys*
Weston, Martha. *Bea's four bears*
Wild, Robin. *The bears' counting book*
Williams, Garth. *The chicken book*
Williams, Jenny. *One, two, buckle my shoe*
Wilson, Barbara Ker. *ABC et/and 123*
Wood, David. *Happy birthday, Mouse!*
Wood, Jakki. *Moo moo, brown cow*
One bear with bees in his hair
Wyllie, Stephen. *Snappity snap*
Yolen, Jane. *An invitation to the butterfly ball*
Street rhymes around the world
Yoshi. *One, two, three*
Youldon, Gillian. *Counting*
Numbers
Youngs, Betty. *One panda*
Zaslavsky, Claudia. *Count on your fingers African style*
Zero! Is it something? Is it nothing?
Ziefert, Harriet. *A dozen dogs*
Zimmermann, H. Werner (Heinz Werner). *Alphonse knows...zero is not enough*
Ziner, Feenie. *Counting carnival*
Zirbes, Laura. *How many bears?*
Zolotow, Charlotte (Shapiro). *One step, two...*

Countries, foreign *see* Foreign lands

Country

Asch, Frank. *Country pie*
Atwood, Margaret. *Anna's pet*
Barklem, Jill. *The big book of Brambly Hedge*
Barton, Pat. *A week is a long time*
Borden, Louise. *The watching game*
Bozzo, Maxine Zohn. *Toby in the country, Toby in the city*
Bröger, Achim. *Francie's paper puppy*
Brown, Margaret Wise. *The country noisy book*
Browne, Caroline. *Mrs. Christie's farmhouse*
Burns, Maurice. *Go ducks, go!*
Burton, Virginia Lee. *The little house*
Carlstrom, Nancy White. *The snow speaks*
Caudill, Rebecca. *Contrary Jenkins*
Chorao, Kay. *Ida and Betty and the secret eggs*
Chwast, Seymour. *Tall city, wide country*
Cole, Sheila. *When the rain stops*
Cousins, Lucy. *Country animals*
Dale, Ruth Bluestone. *Benjamin — and Sylvester also*
Day, Alexandra. *Paddy's pay-day*
DeFelice, Cynthia C. *When Grampa kissed his elbow*
Dickinson, Mary. *Alex's outing*
Florian, Douglas. *A year in the country*
Goffstein, M. B. (Marilyn Brooke). *Our prairie home*
Griffith, Helen V. *Grandaddy's place*
Hawkesworth, Jenny. *The lonely skyscraper*
Hodeir, André. *Warwick's three bottles*
Holl, Adelaide. *A mouse story*
Kingman, Lee. *Peter's long walk*
Lorenz, Lee. *A weekend in the city*
A weekend in the country
McKissack, Patricia C. *Country mouse and city mouse*
McPhail, David. *Ed and me*
Maestro, Betsy. *Delivery van*
Martin, Bill (William Ivan). *Barn dance!*
Merriam, Eve. *Fighting words*
Moore, Elaine. *Grandma's house*
Grandma's promise
Moore, Inga. *Little dog lost*
The truffle hunter
Nikola-Lisa, W. *Night is coming*
Payne, Joan Balfour. *The stable that stayed*
Pedersen, Judy. *Out in the country*
Pender, Lydia. *Barnaby and the horses*
Polacco, Patricia. *Meteor!*
Provensen, Alice. *Town and country*
Roach, Marilynne K. *Two Roman mice*
Rockwell, Anne F. *Willy can count*
Roe, Eileen. *Staying with Grandma*
Rylant, Cynthia. *Appalacia: the voices of sleeping birds*
Night in the country
Scheffler, Ursel. *Stop your crowing, Kasimir!*
Sopko, Eugen. *Townsfolk and countryfolk*

Stanley, Diane. *A country tale*
Van Allsburg, Chris. *The stranger*
Walters, Marguerite. *The city-country ABC*
The weekend, ill. by Roser Capdevila
Williams, David. *Walking to the creek*
Williams, Jay. *The city witch and the country witch*
Yolen, Jane. *Letting Swift River go*

Cousins *see* Family life – cousins

Cowboys

Anderson, C. W. (Clarence Williams).
 Blaze and the Indian cave
 Blaze and the lost quarry
 Blaze and the mountain lion
 Blaze and Thunderbolt
 Blaze finds forgotten roads
 Blaze finds the trail
Anglund, Joan Walsh. *The brave cowboy*
 Cowboy and his friend
 The cowboy's Christmas
 Cowboy's secret life
Aulaire, Ingri Mortenson d'. *Nils*
Beatty, Hetty Burlingame. *Bucking horse*
Bishop, Ann. *Wild Bill Hiccup's riddle book*
Bright, Robert. *Georgie goes west*
Chandler, Edna Walker. *Cattle drive*
 Cowboy Andy
 Pony rider
 Secret tunnel
Cohen, Caron Lee. *Bronco dogs*
Dewey, Ariane. *Pecos Bill*
Doughtie, Charles. *High Henry...the cowboy who was too tall to ride a horse*
Fain, James W. *Rodeos*
Felton, Harold W. *Pecos Bill and the mustang*
Fitzhugh, Louise. *Bang, bang, you're dead*
Gerrard, Roy. *Rosie and the rustlers*
Hancock, Sibyl. *Old Blue*
Hillert, Margaret. *The little cowboy and the big cowboy*
Hooker, Ruth. *Matthew the cowboy*
Kellogg, Steven (Stephen). *Pecos Bill*
Kennedy, Richard. *The contests at Cowlick*
Krasilovsky, Phyllis. *The girl who was a cowboy*
Lenski, Lois. *Cowboy Small*
Mayer, Mercer. *Cowboy critter*
Medearis, Angela Shelf. *The zebra-riding cowboy*
Moon, Dolly M. *My very first book of cowboy songs*
Quackenbush, Robert M. *Pete Pack Rat*
Rounds, Glen. *Cowboys*
Scott, Ann Herbert. *Big Cowboy Western*
 One good horse
 Someday rider
Sewall, Marcia. *Ridin' that strawberry roan*

Stadler, John. *The ballad of Wilbur and the moose*
Ward, Nanda Weedon. *The black sombrero*
Wood, Nancy C. *Little wrangler*

Cows *see* Animals – bulls, cows

Coyotes *see* Animals – coyotes

Crabs *see* Crustacea

Cranes *see* Birds – cranes

Creatures *see* Goblins; Monsters

Creeks *see* Rivers

Crickets *see* Insects – crickets

Crime

Ada, Alma F. *The gold coin*
Adamson, Gareth. *Old man up a tree*
Ahlberg, Allan. *Cops and robbers*
Ahlberg, Janet. *Burglar Bill*
Alderson, Sue Ann. *Ida and the wool smugglers*
Allard, Harry. *It's so nice to have a wolf around the house*
Anderson, C. W. (Clarence Williams).
 Blaze and the gypsies
Barracca, Debra. *Maxi, the hero*
Berson, Harold. *The thief who hugged a moonbeam*
Blake, Quentin. *Snuff*
Bradford, Ann. *The mystery in the secret club house*
 The mystery of the blind writer
 The mystery of the tree house
Brandenberg, Franz. *A robber! A robber!*
Bright, Robert. *Georgie and the robbers*
Brunhoff, Laurent de. *Babar's mystery*
Calders, Pere. *Brush*
Carlson, Nancy. *Arnie and the stolen markers*
Cass, Joan E. *The cat thief*
Christelow, Eileen. *The robbery at the diamond dog diner*
Christian, Mary Blount. *The doggone mystery*
Cohen, Caron Lee. *Bronco dogs*
Cox, David. *Bossyboots*
Cressey, James. *Max the mouse*
 Pet parrot
Dahl, Roald. *The giraffe and the pelly and me*
Daly, Niki. *Vim, the rag mouse*
Dumas, Philippe. *Laura and the bandits*
Duvoisin, Roger Antoine. *Petunia and the song*
Euvremer, Teryl. *The thieves of Peck's pocket*
French, Fiona. *Snow White in New York*
Gage, Wilson. *Down in the boondocks*

Gerrard, Roy. *Rosie and the rustlers*
Goodall, John S. *Paddy to the rescue*
Harris, Leon A. *The great diamond robbery*
  The great picture robbery
Haseley, Dennis. *The thieves' market*
Heller, George. *Hiroshi's wonderful kite*
Heymans, Margriet. *Pippin and Robber Grumblecroak's big baby*
Hickman, Martha Whitmore. *When can daddy come home?*
Hilton, Nette. *Dirty Dave*
Hogrogian, Nonny. *The contest*
  Rooster brother
Jacobs, Joseph. *Hereafterthis*
Janice. *Mr. and Mrs. Button's wonderful watchdogs*
Kirn, Ann. *I spy*
Krahn, Fernando. *Mr. Top*
Kraus, Robert. *The detective of London*
Kroll, Steven. *Looking for Daniela*
  Woof, woof!
Levitin, Sonia. *Nobody stole the pie*
Lobel, Anita. *The straw maid*
Lobel, Arnold. *How the rooster saved the day*
McKee, David. *123456789 Benn*
McPhail, David. *Stanley: Henry Bear's friend*
Marzollo, Jean. *Jed and the space bandits*
Mathews, Louise. *The great take-away*
Mayer, Mercer. *Liverwurst is missing*
Miles, Miska. *The raccoon and Mrs. McGinnis*
Moore, John. *Granny Stickleback*
Mooser, Stephen. *Funnyman and the penny dodo*
Myller, Rolf. *A very noisy day*
Noyes, Alfred. *The highwayman*, ill. by Neil Waldman
Parish, Peggy. *The cat's burglar*
  Granny and the desperadoes
Partch, Virgil Franklin. *The Christmas cookie sprinkle snitcher*
Politi, Leo. *Emmet*
Propp, James. *Tuscanini*
Pryor, Bonnie. *Mr. Munday and the rustlers*
Reidel, Marlene. *Jacob and the robbers*
Rose, Gerald. *The tiger-skin rug*
Rosenbloom, Joseph. *Deputy Dan and the bank robbers*
Ruby-Spears Enterprises. *The puppy's new adventures*
Scarry, Richard. *Richard Scarry's great big mystery book*
Seabrooke, Brenda. *The best burglar alarm*
Shire, Ellen. *The mystery at number seven, Rue Petite*
Slobodkina, Esphyr. *Pezzo the peddler and the thirteen silly thieves*
Solotareff, Grégoire. *Don't call me little bunny*
Thomson, Ruth. *Peabody all at sea*
  Peabody's first case

Titus, Eve. *Anatole and the thirty thieves*
Ungerer, Tomi. *The three robbers*
Wahl, Jan. *The adventures of Underwater Dog*
Watson, Nancy Dingman. *The birthday goat*
Wolff, Ferida. *The woodcutter's coat*

Criminals *see* Crime; Prisons

Crippled *see* Handicaps

Crocodiles *see* Reptiles – alligators, crocodiles

Crows *see* Birds – crows

Cruelty to animals *see* Character traits – kindness to animals

Crustacea

Carle, Eric. *A house for Hermit Crab*
Carrick, Carol. *The blue lobster*
Coldrey, Jennifer. *The world of crabs*
Heller, Ruth. *How to hide an octopus*
Heyduck-Huth, Hilde. *The starfish*
Horio, Seishi. *The monkey and the crab*
James, Simon. *Sally and the limpet*
Kipling, Rudyard. *The crab that played with the sea*, ill. by Michael Foreman
Knutson, Barbara. *Why the crab has no head*
McDonald, Megan. *Is this a house for Hermit Crab?*
Manson, Christopher. *The crab prince*
Mogensen, Jan. *Teddy in the undersea kingdom*
Peet, Bill (William Bartlett). *Kermit the hermit*
Yamaguchi, Tohr. *Two crabs and the moonlight*

Cuckoos *see* Animals – cuckoos

Cumulative tales

Aardema, Verna. *Bringing the rain to Kapiti Plain*
  The riddle of the drum
Ada, Alma F. *The gold coin*
Adams, Pam. *There was an old lady who swallowed a fly*
Adoff, Arnold. *The cabbages are chasing the rabbits*
Alexander, Lloyd. *Fortune tellers*
Alger, Leclaire Gowans. *Always room for one more*
Aliki. *June 7!*
Allbright, Viv. *Ten go hopping*
Asbjørnsen, P. C. (Peter Christen). *The three billy goats Gruff*, ill. by Marcia Brown

The house that Jack built, ill. by Nadine Bernard Westcott

This is the house that Jack built, ill. by Liz Underhill

Houston, John A. *A mouse in my house*

Hughes, Shirley. *Alfie gets in first*

Hush little baby. *Hush little baby*, ill. by Aliki

Hush little baby, ill. by Jeanette Winter

Hush little baby, ill. by Margot Zemach

Hutchins, Pat. *Don't forget the bacon!*

Good night owl

Titch

Inkpen, Mick. *Billy's beetle*

Jacobs, Joseph. *Johnny-cake*, ill. by Emma Lillian Brock

Johnny-cake, ill. by William Stobbs

Johnston, Tony. *Yonder*

Kahl, Virginia. *Whose cat is that?*

Kalan, Robert. *Jump, frog, jump!*

Kasza, Keiko. *When the elephant walks*

King, Bob. *Sitting on the farm*

Krahn, Fernando. *The mystery of the giant footprints*

Krasilovsky, Phyllis. *The cow who fell in the canal*

Kroll, Steven. *The tyrannosaurus game*

Kuskin, Karla. *A boy had a mother who bought him a hat*

Lazy Jack. *Lazy Jack*, ill. by Bert Dodson

Lazy Jack, ill. by Tony Ross

Lazy Jack, ill. by Kurt Werth

Lear, Edward. *Whizz!* ill. by Janina Domanska

Lenski, Lois. *Susie Mariar*

Lester, Helen. *It wasn't my fault*

Lewis, Bobby. *Home before midnight*

Lewison, Wendy C. *Going to sleep on the farm*

Lexau, Joan M. *Crocodile and hen*

Lillegard, Dee. *Sitting in my box*

Lillie, Patricia. *When the rooster crowed*

Lindbergh, Anne. *Tidy lady*

Lindman, Maj. *Snipp, Snapp, Snurr and the buttered bread*

The little red hen. *The cock, the mouse and the little red hen*, ill. by Graham Percy

The little red hen, ill. by Janina Domanska

The little red hen, ill. by Paul Galdone

The little red hen, ill. by Mel Pekarsky

The little red hen, ill. by William Stobbs

The little red hen, ill. by Margot Zemach

Little Tuppen, ill. by Paul Galdone

Lobel, Anita. *The pancake*

Lobel, Arnold. *The rose in my garden*

Lorenz, Lee. *Big Gus and Little Gus*

McClintock, Marshall. *A fly went by*

MacDonald, Elizabeth. *Mike's kite*

McKissack, Patricia C. *The little red hen*

Manning, Linda. *Animal hours*

Martin, Bill (William Ivan). *Brown bear, brown bear, what do you see?*

Martinez, Ruth. *Mrs. McDockerty's knitting*

Milhous, Katherine. *The turnip*

Mollel, Tolowa M. *Rhinos for lunch and elephants for supper*

Moss, Marissa. *Knick knack paddywack*

Murphey, Sara. *The roly poly cookie*

Neitzel, Shirley. *The jacket I wear in the snow*

Noble, Trinka Hakes. *The king's tea*

Nolan, Dennis. *Wizard McBean and his flying machine*

Old MacDonald had a farm. *Old MacDonald had a farm*, ill. by Lorinda Bryan Cauley

Old MacDonald had a farm, ill. by Mel Crawford

Old MacDonald had a farm, ill. by David Frankland

Old MacDonald had a farm, ill. by Abner Graboff

Old MacDonald had a farm, ill. by Nancy Hellen

Old MacDonald had a farm, ill. by Carol Jones

Old MacDonald had a farm, ill. by Tracey Campbell Pearson

Old MacDonald had a farm, ill. by Robert M. Quackenbush

Old MacDonald had a farm, ill. by Glen Rounds

Old MacDonald had a farm, ill. by William Stobbs

Old MacDonald had a farm, ill. by Prue Theobalds

The old woman and her pig. *The old woman and her pig*, ill. by Paul Galdone

The troublesome pig

Oppenheim, Joanne. *"Not now!" said the cow*

You can't catch me!

Pack, Robert. *Then what did you do?*

Parkinson, Kathy. *The enormous turnip*

Peet, Bill (William Bartlett). *The ant and the elephant*

Petie, Haris. *The seed the squirrel dropped*

Polette, Nancy. *The little old woman and the hungry cat*

Prelutsky, Jack. *The terrible tiger*

Preston, Edna Mitchell. *One dark night*

Quackenbush, Robert M. *No mouse for me*

Raskin, Ellen. *Ghost in a four-room apartment*

Riddell, Chris. *Bird's new shoes*

Robart, Rose. *The cake that Mack ate*

Rockwell, Anne F. *Honk honk!*

Poor Goose

Root-a-toot-toot

Roddie, Shen. *Animal stew*

Rose, Anne. *The talking turnip*

Sawyer, Ruth. *Journey cake, ho!*
Scott, William R. *This is the milk that Jack drank*
Seeger, Pete. *The foolish frog*
Segal, Lore. *All the way home*
Seuss, Dr. *Green eggs and ham*
Seymour, Dorothy Z. *The tent*
Shannon, George. *Beanboy*
   Oh, I love!
Silverstein, Shel. *A giraffe and a half*
Simms, Laura. *The squeaky door*
Skorpen, Liesel Moak. *All the Lassies*
Snow, Pegeen. *Mrs. Periwinkle's groceries*
Steger, Hans-Ulrich. *Traveling to Tripiti*
Stoddard, Sandol. *Bedtime mouse*
Stone, Rosetta. *Because a little bug went ka-choo!*
Suhl, Yuri. *Simon Boom gives a wedding*
Sutton, Eve. *My cat likes to hide in boxes*
Sweet, Melissa. *Fiddle-i-fee*
Tanaka, Beatrice. *The chase*
Tolstoĭ, Alekseĭ Nikolaevich. *The great big enormous turnip*
Tresselt, Alvin R. *Rain drop splash*
Troughton, Joanna. *The quail's egg*
The twelve days of Christmas. English folk song. *Brian Wildsmith's The twelve days of Christmas*
   Jack Kent's twelve days of Christmas
   The twelve days of Christmas, ill. by Jan Brett
   The twelve days of Christmas, ill. by Ilonka Karasz
   The twelve days of Christmas, ill. by Ilse Plume
   The twelve days of Christmas, ill. by Erika Schneider
   The twelve days of Christmas, ill. by Sophie Windham
Tworkov, Jack. *The camel who took a walk*
Van Laan, Nancy. *Possum come a-knocking*
Varga, Judy. *The monster behind Black Rock*
Wahl, Jan. *Follow me cried Bee*
Wallner, John. *Old MacDonald had a farm*
West, Colin. *Go tell it to the toucan*
   Have you seen the crocodile?
   The king of Kennelwick castle
   The king's toothache
Wiesner, William. *Happy-Go-Lucky*
Wildsmith, Brian. *Goat's trail*
Williams, Linda. *The little old lady who was not afraid of anything*
Wolkstein, Diane. *The magic wings*
Wood, Audrey. *The napping house*
   Silly Sally
Ziner, Feenie. *Counting carnival*
Zolotow, Charlotte (Shapiro). *The quarreling book*

Curiosity *see* Character traits – curiosity

Currency *see* Money

Cycles *see* Motorcycles; Sports – bicycling

Czechoslovakia *see* Foreign lands – Czechoslovakia

Dancing *see* Activities – dancing

Dark *see* Night

Darkness - fear *see* Emotions – fear

Dawn *see* Morning

Days of the week, months of the year

Arnold, Tedd. *Mother Goose's words of wit and wisdom: a book of months*
Baden, Robert. *And Sunday makes seven*
Borchers, Elisabeth. *There comes a time*
Carle, Eric. *The very hungry caterpillar*
Charles, Donald. *Calico cat's year*
Clifton, Lucille. *Some of the days of Everett Anderson*
Coleridge, Sara. *January brings the snow*
De Regniers, Beatrice Schenk. *Little Sister and the Month Brothers*
Gág, Flavia. *Chubby's first year*
Giff, Patricia Reilly. *I love Saturday*
Harmer, Juliet. *Prayers for children*
Hillman, Priscilla. *A Merry-Mouse book of months*
Hooper, Meredith. *Seven eggs*
Howell, Lynn. *Winifred's new bed*
Keenen, George. *The preposterous week*
Lasker, Joe. *Lentil soup*
Lewis, Robin Baird. *Hello, Mr. Scarecrow*
Llewelyn, Claire. *My first book of time*
Lord, Beman. *The days of the week*
MacDonald, Elizabeth. *My aunt and the animals*
Maestro, Betsy. *Through the year with Harriet*
Molnar, Dorothy E. *Who will pick me up when I fall?*
Plotz, Helen. *A week of lullabies*
Prater, John. *On Friday something funny happened*
Provensen, Alice. *The year at Maple Hill Farm*
Scarry, Richard. *Richard Scarry's best first book ever!*
Sendak, Maurice. *Chicken soup with rice*
Shulevitz, Uri. *One Monday morning*

Singer, Marilyn. *Turtle in July*
Tafuri, Nancy. *All year long*
Tudor, Tasha. *Around the year*
Tyrrell, Anne. *Elizabeth Jane gets dressed*
Ward, Cindy. *Cookie's week*
Wolff, Ashley. *A year of beasts*
  A year of birds
Wood, Audrey. *Heckedy Peg*
Yolen, Jane. *No bath tonight*
Young, Ed (Edward). *Seven blind mice*
Zimmermann, H. Werner (Heinz Werner).
  Alphonse knows...twelve months make a year

Deafness see Handicaps – deafness;
  Senses – hearing

Death

Aliki. *Mummies made in Egypt*
Anders, Rebecca. *A look at death*
Andersen, H. C. (Hans Christian). *It's
  perfectly true!* ill. by Janet Stevens
Arnold, Caroline. *What we do when someone
  dies*
Baker, Betty. *Rat is dead and ant is sad*
Barker, Peggy. *What happened when
  grandma died*
Barnhart, Peter. *The wounded duck*
Bartoli, Jennifer. *Nonna*
Beim, Jerrold. *With dad alone*
Bernstein, Joanne E. *When people die*
Brown, Margaret Wise. *The dead bird*
Bunting, Eve (Anne Evelyn). *The big red
  barn*
  The happy funeral
Burningham, John. *Grandpa*
Carlstrom, Nancy White. *Blow me a kiss,
  Miss Lilly*
Carrick, Carol. *The accident*
Carson, Jo. *You hold me and I'll hold you*
Caseley, Judith. *When Grandpa came to stay*
Cazet, Denys. *A fish in his pocket*
Cazzola, Gus. *The bells of Santa Lucia*
Clifton, Lucille. *Everett Anderson's goodbye*
Cock Robin. *The courtship, merry marriage,
  and feast of Cock Robin and Jenny Wren,*
  ill. by Barbara Cooney
  Who killed Cock Robin? ill. by William
  Stobbs
Cohen, Miriam. *Jim's dog Muffins*
Cohn, Janice. *I had a friend named Peter*
Cooney, Barbara. *Island boy*
Coutant, Helen. *First snow*
Dabcovich, Lydia. *Mrs. Huggins and her
  hen Hannah*
DeArmond, Dale. *The seal oil lamp*
De Paola, Tomie (Thomas Anthony).
  Nana upstairs and Nana downstairs
Fassler, Joan. *My grandpa died today*
Fox, Mem. *With love, at Christmas*
Gerstein, Mordicai. *The mountains of Tibet*
Goble, Paul. *Beyond the ridge*

Gould, Deborah. *Grandpa's slide show*
Gregory, Valiska. *Through the mickle woods*
Grimm, Wilhelm. *Dear Mili*, ill. by
  Maurice Sendak
Harranth, Wolf. *My old grandad*
Harriott, Ted. *Coming home*
Haseley, Dennis. *Ghost catcher*
Hastings, Selina. *The man who wanted to
  live forever*
Hazen, Barbara Shook. *Why did Grandpa
  die?*
Hines, Anna Grossnickle. *Remember the
  butterflies*
Hoffmann, E. T. A. *The strange child*
Hogan, Bernice. *My grandmother died but I
  won't forget her*
Hoopes, Lyn Littlefield. *Nana*
Horio, Seishi. *The monkey and the crab*
Hurd, Edith Thacher. *The black dog who
  went into the woods*
Jewell, Nancy. *Time for Uncle Joe*
Joosse, Barbara M. *Better with two*
Kaldhol, Marit. *Goodbye Rune*
Kantrowitz, Mildred. *When Violet died*
Keats, Ezra Jack. *Maggie and the pirate*
Keller, Holly. *Goodbye, Max*
Kroll, Virginia L. *Helen the fish*
Kübler-Ross, Elisabeth. *Remember the secret*
Lanton, Sandy. *Daddy's chair*
Le Tord, Bijou. *My Grandma Leonie*
Madenski, Melissa. *Some of the pieces*
Maguire, Gregory. *Lucas Fishbone*
Mattingley, Christobel. *The angel with a
  mouth-organ*
Mendoza, George. *The hunter I might have
  been*
Peavy, Linda. *Allison's grandfather*
Porte, Barbara Ann. *Harry's mom*
Rappaport, Doreen. *Journey of Meng*
Rogers, Fred. *When a pet dies*
Sanford, Doris. *David has AIDS*
Scheller, Melanie. *My grandfather's hat*
Simmonds, Posy. *Fred*
Simon, Norma. *The saddest time*
Spohn, David. *Nate's treasure*
Stein, Sara Bonnett. *About dying*
Stevens, Carla. *Stories from a snowy meadow*
Stevens, Margaret (Dean). *When grandpa
  died*
Stiles, Norman. *I'll miss you, Mr. Hooper*
Stilz, Carol Curtis. *Kirsty's kite*
Taha, Karen T. *A gift for Tia Rose*
Tejima, Keizaburo. *Swan sky*
Thomas, Jane Resh. *Saying good-bye to
  grandma*
Townsend, Maryann. *Pop's secret*
Varley, Susan. *Badger's parting gifts*
Velthuijs, Max. *Frog and the birdsong*
Vigna, Judith. *Saying goodbye to daddy*
Viorst, Judith. *The tenth good thing about
  Barney*

Wahl, Jan. *Tiger watch*
Wahl, Mats. *Grandfather's laika*
Walker, Alice. *To hell with dying*
Wallace, Ian. *The sparrow's song*
Wild, Margaret. *The very best of friends*
Wilhelm, Hans. *I'll always love you*
Wright, Betty Ren. *The cat next door*
Zolotow, Charlotte (Shapiro). *My grandson Lew*

Deer *see* Animals – deer

Demons *see* Devil; Monsters

Denmark *see* Foreign lands – Denmark

Dentists *see* Careers – dentists

Department stores *see* Stores

Desert

Bash, Barbara. *Desert giant*
Baylor, Byrd. *The desert is theirs*
  Desert voices
  I'm in charge of celebrations
  We walk in sandy places
Beim, Jerrold. *Eric on the desert*
Buchanan, Ken. *This house is made of mud*
Busch, Phyllis S. *Cactus in the desert*
Catchpole, Clive. *Deserts*
Caudill, Rebecca. *Wind, sand and sky*
Clark, Ann Nolan. *Tia Maria's garden*
Cretan, Gladys Yessayan. *Ten brothers with camels*
Guiberson, Brenda Z. *Cactus hotel*
Holmes, Anita. *The 100-year-old cactus*
John, Naomi. *Roadrunner*
Keats, Ezra Jack. *Clementina's cactus*
McKee, David. *The day the tide went out and out and out*
McLerran, Alice. *Roxaboxen*
Pearce, Q. L. *In the desert*
Reynolds, Jan. *Sahara*
Siebert, Diane. *Mojave*
Ungerer, Tomi. *Orlando, the brave vulture*
Wondriska, William. *The stop*

Detective stories *see* Problem solving

Detectives *see* Careers – detectives

Devil

Alger, Leclaire Gowans. *Kellyburn Braes*
Asch, Frank. *Little Devil's ABC*
  Little Devil's 123
Berson, Harold. *How the devil got his due*
Carey, Valerie Scho. *The devil and mother Crump*
Coombs, Patricia. *The magic pot*
Elwell, Peter. *The king of the pipers*

Galdone, Joanna. *Amber day*
Grimm, Jacob. *The bearskinner*, ill. by Felix Hoffmann
  The devil with the green hairs, ill. by Nonny Hogrogian
Joyce, James. *The cat and the devil*
McCurdy, Michael. *The devils who learned to be good*
Magnus, Erica. *The boy and the devil*
Olson, Arielle North. *Noah's cats and the devil's fire*
Pinkwater, Daniel Manus. *Devil in the drain*
Scribner, Charles. *The devil's bridge*
Shute, Linda. *Momotaro, the peach boy*
Stalder, Valerie. *Even the devil is afraid of a shrew*
Turska, Krystyna. *The magician of Cracow*
Zemach, Harve. *Duffy and the devil*

Dictionaries

A child's picture English-Hebrew dictionary
Daly, Kathleen N. *The Macmillan picture wordbook*
Dodds, Siobhan. *Words and pictures*
Floyd, Lucy. *Agatha's alphabet, with her very own dictionary*
Halsey, William D. *The magic world of words*
Howard, Katherine. *My first picture dictionary*
Krensky, Stephen. *My first dictionary*
MacBean, Dilla Wittemore. *Picture book dictionary*
McIntire, Alta. *Follett beginning to read picture dictionary*
Parke, Margaret B. *Young reader's color-picture dictionary*
Rand McNally picturebook dictionary
Scarry, Richard. *Richard Scarry's biggest word book ever!*
  Richard Scarry's storybook dictionary
Schulz, Charles M. *The Charlie Brown dictionary*
Seuss, Dr. *The cat in the hat beginner book dictionary*
Wilkes, Angela. *My first word book*

Digging *see* Activities – digging

Dinosaurs

Ahlberg, Allan. *Dinosaur dreams*
Aliki. *Digging up dinosaurs*
  Dinosaur bones
  Dinosaurs are different
  Fossils tell of long ago
  My visit to the dinosaurs
Barber, Antonia. *Satchelmouse and the dinosaurs*
Barton, Byron. *Bones, bones, dinosaur bones*
  Dinosaurs, dinosaurs

Berenstain, Stan. *After the dinosaurs*
  The day of the dinosaur
Binnamin, Vivian. *The case of the snoring stegosaurus*
Birchman, David F. *Brother Billy Bronto's bygone blues band*
Blackwood, Mary. *Derek the knitting dinosaur*
Blumenthal, Nancy. *Count-a-saurus*
Bradman, Tony. *Dilly speaks up*
Brasch, Kate. *Prehistoric monsters*
Brown, Laurie Krasny. *Dinosaurs alive and well*
  Dinosaurs to the rescue
  Dinosaurs travel
Brown, Marc Tolon. *Dinosaurs, beware!*
Carrick, Carol. *Big old bones*
  The crocodiles still wait
  Patrick's dinosaurs
  What happened to Patrick's dinosaurs?
Cauley, Lorinda Bryan. *The trouble with Tyrannosaurus Rex*
Charlton, Elizabeth. *Terrible tyrannosaurus*
Cohen, Daniel. *Dinosaurs*
Craig, M. Jean. *Dinosaurs and more dinosaurs*
Cremins, Robert. *Pop up baby brontosaurus*
  Pop up baby coelophysis
  Pop up baby pteranodon
  Pop up baby stegosaurus
  Pop up baby triceratops
  Pop up baby tyrannosaurus rex
Curious George and the dinosaur
Cutts, David. *More about dinosaurs*
Cuyler, Margery. *Baby Dot: a dinosaur story*
Daly, Kathleen N. *Dinosaurs*
De Paola, Tomie (Thomas Anthony). *Little Grunt and the big egg*
Dinosaurs and monsters, ill. by Louise Nevett
Donnelly, Liza. *Dinosaur beach*
  Dinosaur garden
  Dinosaurs' Halloween
Eastman, David. *The story of dinosaurs*
Emberley, Michael. *More dinosaurs!*
Fleischman, Paul. *Time train*
Gay, Tenner Ottley. *Dinosaurs and their relatives in action*
Gibbons, Gail. *Dinosaurs*
Gorbaty, Norman. *Get up and go, little dinosaur!*
Gordon, Sharon. *Dinosaurs in trouble*
Harrison, Sarah. *In granny's garden*
Haynes, Max. *Dinosaur island*
Hennessy, B. G. *The dinosaur who lived in my backyard*
Hodgetts, Blake Christopher. *Dream of the dinosaurs*
Hurd, Edith Thacher. *Dinosaur, my darling*
Joyce, William. *Dinosaur Bob*

Kellogg, Steven (Stephen). *Prehistoric Pinkerton*
Klein, Robin. *Thing*
Knight, David C. *Dinosaur days*
Koontz, Robin Michal. *Dinosaur dream*
Kroll, Steven. *The tyrannosaurus game*
Lorenz, Lee. *Dinah's egg*
McGuire, Leslie. *Who will play with Little Dinosaur?*
Mansell, Dom. *If dinosaurs came to town*
Mayhew, James. *Katie and the dinosaurs*
Milton, Joyce. *Dinosaur days*
Morgan, Michaela. *Dinostory*
Moseley, Keith. *Dinosaurs*
Mosley, Francis. *The dinosaur eggs*
Most, Bernard. *Dinosaur cousins?*
  A dinosaur named after me
  Happy holidaysaurus!
  If the dinosaurs came back
  The littlest dinosaurs
  Whatever happened to the dinosaurs?
Murphy, Jim. *Dinosaur for a day*
Nicoll, Helen. *Meg's eggs*
Nolan, Dennis. *Dinosaur dream*
Oram, Hiawyn. *A boy wants a dinosaur*
Otto, Carolyn. *Dinosaur chase*
Parish, Peggy. *Dinosaur time*
Penner, Lucille Recht. *Dinosaur babies*
Petty, Kate. *Dinosaurs*
Pittman, Helena Clare. *A dinosaur for Gerald*
Polhamus, Jean Burt. *Dinosaur do's and don'ts*
  Doctor Dinosaur
Prelutsky, Jack. *Tyrannosaurus was a beast*
Pulver, Robin. *Mrs. Toggle and the dinosaur*
Riehecky, Janet. *Apatosaurus*
Ripley, Catherine. *Two dozen dinosaurs*
Royston, Angela. *Dinosaurs*
Rubel, Nicole. *Bruno Brontosaurus*
Sant, Laurent Sauveur. *Dinosaurs*
Schwartz, Henry. *Albert goes Hollywood*
  How I captured a dinosaur
Selsam, Millicent E. *A first look at dinosaurs*
Sharmat, Marjorie Weinman. *Mitchell is moving*
Sibbick, John. *Creatures of long ago: dinosaurs*
Silverman, Maida. *Dinosaur babies*
Simon, Seymour. *The largest dinosaurs*
  The smallest dinosaurs
Sirois, Allen. *Dinosaur dress up*
Slobodkin, Louis. *Dinny and Danny*
Smith, Jim. *Nimbus the explorer*
Stewart, Frances Todd. *Dinosaurs and other creatures of long ago*
Sundgaard, Arnold. *Jethro's difficult dinosaur*
Talbott, Hudson. *Going Hollywood! A dinosaur's dream*
Taylor, Scott. *Dinosaur James*

Teague, Mark. *The trouble with the Johnsons*
Thayer, Jane. *Quiet on account of dinosaur*
Watson, Claire. *Big creatures from the past*
Wilhelm, Hans. *Tyrone the horrible*
Zalben, Jane Breskin. *Buster gets braces*
Zallinger, Peter. *Dinosaurs*

Disbelief *see* Behavior – disbelief

Dissatisfaction *see* Behavior – dissatisfaction

Distance *see* Concepts – distance

Diving *see* Sports – skin diving

Divorce

Baum, Louis. *One more time*
Berger, Terry. *How does it feel when your parents get divorced?*
Bienenfeld, Florence. *My mom and dad are getting a divorce*
Boegehold, Betty. *Daddy doesn't live here anymore*
Caines, Jeannette. *Daddy*
Christiansen, C. B. *My mother's house, my father's house*
Dragonwagon, Crescent. *Always, always*
Girard, Linda Walvoord. *At Daddy's on Saturdays*
Goff, Beth. *Where's daddy?*
Hazen, Barbara Shook. *Two homes to live in*
Lexau, Joan M. *Me day*
Lisker, Sonia O. *Two special cards*
Mayle, Peter. *Divorce can happen to the nicest people*
Why are we getting a divorce?
Noble, June. *Two homes for Lynn*
Norris, Lori P. *D is for divorce*
Paris, Lena. *Mom is single*
Perry, Patricia. *Mommy and daddy are divorced*
Peterson, Jeanne Whitehouse. *That is that*
Pursell, Margaret Sanford. *A look at divorce*
Rogers, Helen Spelman. *Morris and his brave lion*
Roy, Ronald. *Breakfast with my father*
Schuchman, Joan. *Two places to sleep*
Simon, Norma. *The daddy days*
Steel, Danielle. *Martha's new daddy*
Stein, Sara Bonnett. *On divorce*
Stinson, Kathy. *Mom and dad don't live together any more*
Tangvald, Christine. *Mom and dad don't live together anymore*
Vigna, Judith. *Daddy's new baby*
Grandma without me
She's not my real mother

Watson, Jane Werner. *Sometimes a family has to split up*
Willhoite, Michael. *Daddy's roomate*

Doctors *see* Careers – doctors

Dodos *see* Birds – dodos

Dogs *see* Animals – dogs

Dolls *see* Toys – dolls

Dolphins *see* Animals – dolphins

Donkeys *see* Animals – donkeys

Doves *see* Birds – doves

Down and up *see* Concepts – up and down

Dragonflies *see* Insects – dragonflies

Dragons

Agell, Charlotte. *The sailor's book*
Anderson, Wayne. *Dragon*
Aruego, José. *The king and his friends*
Baumgart, Klaus. *Anna and the little green dragon*
The little green dragon steps out
Bertrand, Lynne. *One day, two dragons*
Boswell, Stephen. *King Gorboduc's fabulous zoo*
Bradfield, Roger (Jolly Roger). *A good night for dragons*
Buckaway, C. M. *Alfred, the dragon who lost his flame*
Chalmers, Mary. *George Appleton*
Christelow, Eileen. *Henry and the dragon*
Company González, Mercè. *Killian and the dragons*
Cooper, Susan. *Matthew's dragon*
Coville, Bruce. *Sarah and the dragon*
Craig, M. Jean. *The dragon in the clock box*
Cressey, James. *The dragon and George*
Cretien, Paul D. *Sir Henry and the dragon*
Davis, Reda. *Martin's dinosaur*
Day, Marie. *Dragon in the rocks*
DeLage, Ida. *The old witch and the dragon*
Delaney, Ned. *One dragon to another*
Demi. *Dragon kites and dragonflies*
De Paola, Tomie (Thomas Anthony). *The knight and the dragon*
Dewey, Ariane. *Dorin and the dragon*
Domanska, Janina. *King Krakus and the dragon*
Emberley, Ed (Edward Randolph). *Klippity klop*
Fassler, Joan. *The man of the house*
Gág, Wanda. *The funny thing*
Garrison, Christian. *The dream eater*

Goode, Diane. *I hear a noise*
Grimm, Jacob. *The four clever brothers*, ill. by Felix Hoffmann
Haley, Gail E. *Jack and the fire dragon*
Hillert, Margaret. *Happy birthday, dear dragon*
Merry Christmas, dear dragon
Hillman, Elizabeth. *Min-Yo and the moon dragon*
Hoban, Russell. *Ace Dragon Ltd.*
Holabird, Katharine. *Alexander and the dragon*
Janosch. *Just one apple*
Jeschke, Susan. *Firerose*
Jones, Maurice. *I'm going on a dragon hunt*
Joslin, Sesyle. *Dear dragon*
Kent, Jack. *The once-upon-a-time dragon*
There's no such thing as a dragon
Kimmel, Margaret Mary. *Magic in the mist*
Krahn, Fernando. *The secret in the dungeon*
Kumin, Maxine. *Sebastian and the dragon*
Lattimore, Deborah Nourse. *The dragon's robe*
Leaf, Margaret. *Eyes of the dragon*
Leedy, Loreen. *A dragon Christmas*
The dragon Halloween party
The dragon Thanksgiving feast
A number of dragons
Lifton, Betty Jean. *Joji and the dragon*
Lindgren, Astrid. *The dragon with red eyes*
Lobel, Arnold. *Prince Bertram the bad*
Long, Claudia. *Albert's story*
McCaughrean, Geraldine. *Saint George and the dragon*
McCrea, James. *The story of Olaf*
McMullen, Eunice. *Dragon for breakfast*
Mahood, Kenneth. *The laughing dragon*
Mahy, Margaret. *The dragon of an ordinary family*
A lion in the meadow
Manushkin, Fran. *Moon dragon*
Martin, C. L. G. *The dragon nanny*
Mayer, Mercer. *Whinnie the lovesick dragon*
Minarik, Else Holmelund. *The little girl and the dragon*
Mogensen, Jan. *Teddy and the Chinese dragon*
Munsch, Robert N. *The paper bag princess*
Murphy, Shirley Rousseau. *Valentine for a dragon*
Nash, Ogden. *Custard and Company*
Custard the dragon, ill. by Linell Nash
Custard the dragon and the wicked knight
Nesbit, Edith. *The last of the dragons*
Nolan, Dennis. *The castle builder*
Oksner, Robert M. *The incompetent wizard*
Pattison, Darcy. *The river dragon*
Pavey, Peter. *One dragon's dream*
Peet, Bill (William Bartlett). *How Droofus the dragon lost his head*

Phillips, Louis. *The brothers Wrong and Wrong Again*
Price, Roger. *The last little dragon*
Reddix, Valerie. *Dragon kite of the autumn moon*
Rosen, Winifred. *Dragons hate to be discreet*
Scarry, Richard. *Richard Scarry's Peasant Pig and the terrible dragon*
Scullard, Sue. *Miss Fanshawe and the great dragon adventure*
Sherman, Nancy. *Gwendolyn the miracle hen*
Shub, Elizabeth. *Dragon Franz*
Slote, Elizabeth. *Nelly's garden*
Stern, Peter. *Max the dragon*
Stern, Simon. *Vasily and the dragon*
Stock, Catherine. *Emma's dragon hunt*
Thayer, Jane. *The popcorn dragon*, ill. by Jay Hyde Barnum
The popcorn dragon, ill. by Lisa McCue
Torre, Betty L. *The luminous pearl*
Trez, Denise. *The little knight's dragon*
Uttley, Alison. *Sam Pig and the dragon*
Van Woerkom, Dorothy. *Alexandra the rock-eater*
Waterton, Betty. *Orff, 27 dragons (and a snarkel)*
Wiesner, David. *Free fall*
The loathsome dragon
Williams, Jay. *Everyone knows what a dragon looks like*
Willis, Val. *The secret in the matchbox*
Wilson, Sarah. *Beware the dragons!*
Zirkel, Lynn. *The shell dragon*

Drawing *see* Activities – drawing

Drawing games *see* Games

Dreams

Adoff, Arnold. *Flamboyan*
Ahlberg, Allan. *Dinosaur dreams*
Alexander, Martha G. *Bobo's dream*
Allison, Diane Worfolk. *In window eight, the moon is late*
Anrooy, Frans van. *The sea horse*
Arnold, Tedd. *No jumping on the bed!*
Axworthy, Anni. *Ben's Wednesday*
Aylesworth, Jim. *The bad dream*
Tonight's the night
Balet, Jan B. *Joanjo*
Balzola, Asun. *Munia and the orange crocodile*
Baumgart, Klaus. *The little green dragon steps out*
Berenstain, Stan. *The Berenstain bears and the bad dream*
Berger, Barbara Helen. *The donkey's dream*
Bider, Djemma. *A drop of honey*
Bohdal, Susi. *The magic honey jar*
Bond, Felicia. *Wake up, Vladimir*
Boyd, Lizi. *Sweet dreams, Willy*

Brown, M. K. *Let's go swimming with Mr. Sillypants*

Brown, Margaret Wise. *Dream book*
The little farmer

Bruna, Dick. *Miffy's dream*

Buckley, Helen Elizabeth. *Someday with my father*

Burningham, John. *Hey! Get off our train*

Callen, Larry. *Dashiel and the night*

Carroll, Lewis. *The nursery "Alice"*, ill. by Sir John Tenniel

Cazet, Denys. *Daydreams*

Chesworth, Michael. *Rainy day dream*

Chorao, Kay. *Lemon moon*

Chwast, Seymour. *Still another children's book*

Collington, Peter. *Little pickle*

Cooper, Susan. *Matthew's dragon*

Craig, M. Jean. *What did you dream?*

Crossley-Holland, Kevin. *Sleeping Nanna*

Crowley, Arthur. *The wagon man*

Cuyler, Margery. *Fat Santa*

Dahl, Roald. *Dirty beasts*

Daugherty, Charles Michael. *Wisher*

Dennis, Wesley. *Flip*

DeSaix, Frank. *The girl who danced with dolphins*

Dewey, Ariane. *Dorin and the dragon*

Donaldson, Lois. *Karl's wooden horse*

Dragonwagon, Crescent. *Half a moon and one whole star*

Drescher, Henrik. *Simon's book*

Duncan, Lois. *Horses of dreamland*

Duvoisin, Roger Antoine. *The missing milkman*

Elzbieta. *Dikou and the mysterious moon sheep*

Erskine, Jim. *Bedtime story*

Field, Rachel Lyman. *A road might lead to anywhere*

Foreman, Michael. *Jack's fantastic voyage*
Land of dreams

Francis, Anna B. *Pleasant dreams*

Francis, Frank. *The magic wallpaper*

Gantos, Jack (John, Jr.). *Greedy Greeny*

Garrison, Christian. *The dream eater*

Gay, Marie-Louise. *Moonbeam on a cat's ear*

Giff, Patricia Reilly. *Next year I'll be special*

Ginsburg, Mirra. *Across the stream*
Four brave sailors

Gould, Deborah. *Grandpa's slide show*

Greenfield, Eloise. *Africa dream*

Greenwood, Ann. *A pack of dreams*

Griffith, Helen V. *Pluck's dreams*

Hague, Kathleen. *Out of the nursery, into the night*

Hale, Irina. *Donkey's dreadful day*

Hayes, Geoffrey. *The secret inside*

Heine, Helme. *The marvelous journey through the night*

Heller, Nicholas. *Mathilda the dream bear*

Henri, Adrian. *The postman's palace*

Hill, Susan. *Go away, bad dreams!*

Hodgetts, Blake Christopher. *Dream of the dinosaurs*

Hurd, Edith Thacher. *Little dog, dreaming*

Jacobs, Joseph. *The crock of gold*

James, Betsy. *The dream stair*

Jennings, Michael. *The bears who came to breakfix*

Johnson, Jane. *Bertie on the beach*

Jonas, Ann. *The quilt*

Karlin, Nurit. *The dream factory*

Keats, Ezra Jack. *Dreams*

Keith, Eros. *Nancy's backyard*

Knotts, Howard. *The lost Christmas*

Koontz, Robin Michal. *Dinosaur dream*

Kotzwinkle, William. *The nap master*

Krahn, Fernando. *Sebastian and the mushroom*

Lester, Alison. *Ruby*

Le-Tan, Pierre. *Visit to the North Pole*

Low, Joseph. *Don't drag your feet...*

McDermott, Gerald. *Daniel O'Rourke*

McLerran, Alice. *Dreamsong*

McMullan, Kate. *The noisy giant's tea party*

McPhail, David. *Adam's smile*
The dream child
Mistletoe
The train

Mählqvist, Stefan. *I'll take care of the crocodiles*

Martin, Bill (William Ivan). *Barn dance!*

Marton, Jirina. *I'll do it myself*
Midnight visit at Molly's house

Mayer, Mercer. *There's something in my attic*

Mayper, Monica. *After good-night*

Montresor, Beni. *Bedtime!*
The witches of Venice

Morgan, Allen. *Nicole's boat*

Nightingale, Sandy. *A giraffe on the moon*

Nobens, C. A. *Montgomery's time zone*

Nolan, Dennis. *Dinosaur dream*

Oram, Hiawyn. *A boy wants a dinosaur*

Orgel, Doris. *Little John*

Osofsky, Audrey. *Dreamcatcher*

Pavey, Peter. *One dragon's dream*

Paxton, Tom. *Jennifer's rabbit*

Pilkey, Dav. *When cats dream*

Polacco, Patricia. *Appelemando's dreams*

Reed, Kit. *When we dream*

Riddell, Chris. *The wish factory*

Ringgold, Faith. *Tar Beach*

Rockwell, Anne F. *Buster and the bogeyman*
The wolf who had a wonderful dream

Ross, Lillian Hammer. *The little old man and his dreams*

Ryder, Joanne. *The night flight*

Sage, James. *To sleep*

Say, Allen. *A river dream*

Sendak, Maurice. *In the night kitchen*

Shepperson, Rob. *The sandman*

Shimin, Symeon. *I wish there were two of me*

Shulevitz, Uri. *The treasure*
Simmonds, Posy. *The chocolate wedding*
Simons, Traute. *Paulino*
Smee, Nicola. *Finish the story, dad*
Smith, Lane. *The big pets*
Smith-Moore, J. J. *Sally Small*
Spier, Peter. *Dreams*
Steig, William. *The Zabajaba Jungle*
Stevens, Janet. *Animal fair*
Strand, Mark. *The planet of lost things*
Strauss, Gwen. *The night shimmy*
Strub, Susanne. *Lulu goes swimming*
  Lulu on her bike
Tafuri, Nancy. *Junglewalk*
Tejima, Keizaburo. *Fox's dream*
Thorne, Jenny. *My uncle*
Tompert, Ann. *Will you come back for me?*
Trez, Denise. *Good night, Veronica*
Troughton, Joanna. *Tortoise's dream*
Tudor, Tasha. *A tale for Easter*
Twining, Edith. *Sandman*
Updike, David. *A winter's journey*
Van Pallandt, Nicholas. *The butterfly night
  of Old Brown Bear*
Wahl, Jan. *Humphrey's bear*
  The toy circus
Ward, Lynd. *The silver pony*
Waterton, Betty. *Orff, 27 dragons (and a
  snarkel)*
Weisgard, Leonard. *Who dreams of cheese?*
Wende, Philip. *Bird boy*
Wersba, Barbara. *Amanda dreaming*
Wiesner, David. *Free fall*
Wildsmith, Brian. *Carousel*
Willard, Nancy. *The mountains of quilt
  Night story*
Yorinks, Arthur. *Hey, Al*
Zemach, Kaethe. *The funny dream*
Zolotow, Charlotte (Shapiro). *I have a horse
  of my own
  Someday*

Dressers *see* Furniture – dressers

Droughts *see* Weather – droughts

Ducks *see* Birds – ducks

Dwarfs *see* Elves and little people

Dying *see* Death

Eagles *see* Birds – eagles

Ears *see* Anatomy – ears; Handicaps –
  deafness; Senses – hearing

Earth

Asimov, Isaac. *The best new things*
Bernstein, Margery. *Earth namer*
Branley, Franklyn M. *Earthquakes
  What makes day and night*
Dayton, Mona. *Earth and sky*
Engdahl, Sylvia. *Our world is earth*
Lauber, Patricia. *How we learned the earth is
  round*
Leutscher, Alfred. *Earth*
Lewis, Claudia Louise. *When I go to the
  moon*
Luenn, Nancy. *Mother earth*
Simon, Seymour. *Beneath your feet*
Wyler, Rose. *The starry sky*

Easter *see* Holidays – Easter

Eating *see* Food

Ecology

Anholt, Laurence. *The forgotten forest*
Arneson, D. J. *Secret places*
Baker, Jeannie. *Where the forest meets the sea
  Window*
Balian, Lorna. *Wilbur's space machine*
Baylor, Byrd. *The desert is theirs*
Beisert, Heide Helene. *Poor fish*
Bellamy, David. *How green are you?
  The roadside
  The rock pool*
Berenstain, Stan. *The Berenstain bears don't
  pollute anymore*
Bloome, Enid. *The air we breathe!
  The water we drink!*
Brown, Laurie Krasny. *Dinosaurs to the
  rescue*
Brown, Ruth. *The world that Jack built*
Burton, Virginia Lee. *The little house*
Busch, Phyllis S. *Puddles and ponds*
Caputo, Robert. *More than just pets*
Carrick, Carol. *A clearing in the forest*
Cherry, Lynne. *A river ran wild*
De Paola, Tomie (Thomas Anthony).
  Michael Bird-Boy
Duvoisin, Roger Antoine. *The happy hunter*
Fife, Dale. *The little park*
Firmin, Peter. *Basil Brush and the windmills*
Fischetto, Laura. *The jungle is my home*
Freeman, Don. *The seal and the slick*
Gibbons, Gail. *Recycle!*
Greene, Carol. *The old ladies who liked cats*
Guiberson, Brenda Z. *Cactus hotel*
Hader, Berta Hoerner. *The mighty hunter*
Haley, Gail E. *Noah's ark*
Hamberger, John. *The day the sun
  disappeared*

Hamilton, Virginia. *Drylongso*
Hirschi, Ron. *Forest*
Hoff, Syd. *Grizzwold*
Hurd, Edith Thacher. *Wilson's world*
Ichikawa, Satomi. *Suzanne and Nicholas in the garden*, Watts 1976
James, Simon. *Sally and the limpet*
Jewell, Nancy. *Try and catch me*
Kalman, Benjamin. *Animals in danger*
Koch, Michelle. *World water watch*
Krull, Kathleen. *It's my earth too*
Leedy, Loreen. *The great trash bash*
Leutscher, Alfred. *Water*
Lewis, Naomi. *Hare and badger go to town*
Locker, Thomas. *The land of gray wolf*
Luenn, Nancy. *Mother earth*
Mabey, Richard. *Oak and company*
Margolis, Richard J. *Big bear, spare that tree*
Mazer, Anne. *The salamander room*
Meyer, Louis A. *The clean air and peaceful contentment dirigible airline*
Michels, Tilde. *At the frog pond*
Miles, Miska. *Rabbit garden*
Miller, Edna. *Mousekin's lost woodland*
Mizumura, Kazue. *If I built a village*
Murschetz, Luis. *Mister Mole*
Newton, James R. *Forest log*
Parnall, Peter. *The great fish*
    The rock
Peet, Bill (William Bartlett). *The caboose who got loose*
    Farewell to Shady Glade
    Fly, Homer, fly
    The gnats of knotty pine
    The wump world
Ray, Mary Lyn. *Pumpkins*
Roach, Marilynne K. *Dune fox*
Selzer, Meyer. *Here comes the recycling truck!*
Seuss, Dr. *The Lorax*
Short, Mayo. *Andy and the wild ducks*
Snape, Juliet. *Frog odyssey*
Stone, A. Harris. *The last free bird*
Tate, Suzanne. *Crabby's water wish*
Thornhill, Jan. *A tree in a forest*
Torgersen, Don Arthur. *The troll who lived in the lake*
Tresselt, Alvin R. *The beaver pond*
    The dead tree
    The gift of the tree
Wegen, Ron. *Where can the animals go?*
Williams, Terry Tempest. *Between cattails*
Wood, Douglas. *Old Turtle*

Ecuador *see* Foreign lands – Ecuador

Education *see* School

Eggs

Andersen, H. C. (Hans Christian). *The woman with the eggs*, ill. by Ray Cruz
Asch, Frank. *MacGooses's grocery*

Auch, Mary Jane. *The Easter egg farm*
Back, Christine. *Chicken and egg*
Bourke, Linda. *Ethel's exceptional egg*
Brown, Margaret Wise. *The golden egg book*
Campbell, Rod. *Oh dear!*
Casey, Patricia. *Quack quack*
Chorao, Kay. *Ida and Betty and the secret eggs*
Claret, Maria. *The chocolate rabbit*
Coontz, Otto. *The quiet house*
Dodds, Siobhan. *Elizabeth Hen*
Eastman, P. D. (Philip D.). *Flap your wings*
Eggs, ill. by Esmé Eve
Ernst, Lisa Campbell. *Zinnia and Dot*
Gordon, Sharon. *Easter Bunny's lost egg*
Hariton, Anca. *Egg story*
Heller, Ruth. *Chickens aren't the only ones*
Hill, Eric. *Spot's first Easter*
Hoban, Lillian. *The case of the two masked robbers*
Hooper, Meredith. *Seven eggs*
Isami, Ikuyo. *The fox's egg*
Joyce, William. *Bently and egg*
Kay, Helen. *An egg is for wishing*
Kent, Jack. *The egg book*
Krauss, Ruth. *The happy egg*
Kumin, Maxine. *Eggs of things*
Kwitz, Mary DeBall. *Little chick's story*
Lasell, Fen. *Fly away goose*
Lauber, Patricia. *What's hatching out of that egg?*
Levitin, Sonia. *A single speckled egg*
Lloyd, Megan. *Chicken tricks*
Long, Earlene. *Johnny's egg*
Lorenz, Lee. *Dinah's egg*
McCrea, Lilian. *Mother hen*
McGovern, Ann. *Eggs on your nose*
Mathews, Louise. *Cluck one*
Milgrom, Harry. *Egg-ventures*
Myers, Bernice. *The millionth egg*
Nicoll, Helen. *Meg's eggs*
O'Neill, Mary. *Big red hen*
Peet, Bill (William Bartlett). *The pinkish, purplish, bluish egg*
Polacco, Patricia. *Chicken Sunday*
    Just plain Fancy
    Rechenka's eggs
Potter, Beatrix. *The tale of Jemima Puddle-Duck*
Pursell, Margaret Sanford. *Jessie the chicken*
    Sprig the tree frog
Rockwell, Anne F. *The gollywhopper egg*
    The wonderful eggs of Furicchia
Roddie, Shen. *Hatch, egg, hatch!*
San Souci, Robert D. *The talking eggs*
Scamell, Ragnhild. *Solo plus one*
Scarry, Richard. *Egg in the hole*
Schick, Eleanor. *A surprise in the forest*
Selsam, Millicent E. *Egg to chick*
Seuss, Dr. *Horton hatches the egg*
Smith, Mavis. *A snake mistake*

Standon, Anna. *Little duck lost*
Stevenson, James. *The great big especially beautiful Easter egg*
Sundgaard, Arnold. *Jethro's difficult dinosaur*
Tresselt, Alvin R. *The world in the candy egg*
Troughton, Joanna. *The quail's egg*
Vyner, Sue. *The stolen egg*
Waber, Bernard. *How to go about laying an egg*
Wahl, Jan. *The five in the forest*
Wilhelm, Hans. *More bunny trouble*
Wilkes, Larry. *The king's egg dance*
Wright, Dare. *Edith and the duckling*
Ziefert, Harriet. *Happy Easter, Grandma!*

Egrets *see* Birds – egrets

Egypt *see* Foreign lands – Egypt

Egyptian language *see* Hieroglyphics

El Salvador *see* Foreign lands – El Salvador

Elderly *see* Old age

Electricians *see* Careers – electricians

Elephant seals *see* Animals – elephant seals

Elephants *see* Animals – elephants

Elevators, escalators

Barner, Bob. *Elevator escalator book*
Farber, Norma. *Up the down elevator*
Sis, Peter. *Going up!*

Elves and little people

Adams, Pam. *This old man*
Adshead, Gladys L. *Brownies—hush!*
Brownies—it's Christmas
Brownies—they're moving
Balian, Lorna. *Leprechauns never lie*
Barrie, J. M. (James M.). *Peter Pan*, ill. by Diane Goode
Baruch, Dorothy. *Kappa's tug-of-war with the big brown horse*
Berenstain, Michael. *The dwarks*
Berg, Jean Horton. *The wee little man*
Beskow, Elsa Maartman. *Peter in Blueberry Land*
Peter's adventures in Blueberry land
Bolliger, Max. *The magic bird*
Borg, Inga. *Plupp builds a house*
Brennan, Patricia D. *Hitchety hatchety up I go!*
Bulette, Sara. *The elf in the singing tree*

Calhoun, Mary. *The hungry leprechaun*
The pixy and the lazy housewife
The runaway brownie
The thieving dwarfs
Chenault, Nell. *Parsifal the Poddley*
Compton, Kenn. *Happy Christmas to all!*
Cooper, Susan. *Tam Lin*
Cox, Palmer. *Another Brownie book*
The Brownies: their book
Davis, Maggie S. *Grandma's secret letter*
De Paola, Tomie (Thomas Anthony).
Jamie O'Rourke and the big potato
The Prince of the Dolomites
Elves, fairies and gnomes, ill. by Rosekrans Hoffman
Fish, Helen Dean. *When the root children wake up*, published by Green Tiger Pr., 1988
When the root children wake up, published by Lippincott, 1930
Funai, Mamoru. *Moke and Poki in the rain forest*
Grimm, Jacob. *The earth gnome*, ill. by Margot Tomes
The elves and the shoemaker, ill. by Paul Galdone
The elves and the shoemaker, ill. by Bernadette Watts
The shoemaker and the elves, ill. by Adrienne Adams
The shoemaker and the elves, ill. by Cynthia and William Birrer
The shoemaker and the elves, ill. by Ilse Plume
Snow White, ill. by Trina Schart Hyman
Snow White, ill. by Bernadette Watts
Snow White and Rose Red, ill. by Adrienne Adams
Snow-White and Rose-Red, ill. by Barbara Cooney
Snow White and Rose Red, ill. by John Wallner
Snow White and Rose Red, ill. by Bernadette Watts
Snow White and the seven dwarves, ill. by Chihiro Iwasaki
Haidle, Elizabeth. *Elmer the grump*
Hastings, Selina. *The singing ringing tree*
Irving, Washington. *Rip Van Winkle*, ill. by John Howe
Rip Van Winkle, ill. by Thomas Locker
Rip Van Winkle, ill. by Peter Wingham
Jones, Carol. *This old man*
Kennedy, Richard. *The leprechaun's story*
Koontz, Robin Michal. *This old man*
Krauss, Ruth. *Everything under a mushroom*
Kunnas, Mauri. *Santa Claus and his elves*
Twelve gifts for Santa Claus
Lester, Helen. *Pookins gets her way*
Lobel, Anita. *The dwarf giant*

McDermott, Gerald. *Daniel O'Rourke*
McLenighan, Valjean. *You can go jump*
Madden, Don. *Lemonade serenade or the thing in the garden*
May, Robert Lewis. *Rudolph the red-nosed reindeer*
Mayer, Marianna. *The little jewel box*
Mayne, William. *The blue book of hob stories*
  The green book of Hob stories
  The red book of Hob stories
  The yellow book of Hob stories
Minarik, Else Holmelund. *The little giant girl and the elf boys*
Mogensen, Jan. *The forty-six little men*
Moncure, Jane Belk. *Happy healthkins*
  The healthkin food train
  Healthkins exercise!
  Healthkins help
Morimoto, Junko. *The inch boy*
Nones, Eric Jon. *Wendell*
Norby, Lisa. *The Herself the elf storybook*
Shub, Elizabeth. *Seeing is believing*
Shute, Linda. *Clever Tom and the leprechaun*
Smith, Mary. *Long ago elf*
Steiner, Charlotte. *Red Ridinghood's little lamb*
Tom Thumb. *Grimm Tom Thumb*, ill. by Svend Otto S.
  Tom Thumb, ill. by L. Leslie Brooke
  Tom Thumb, ill. by Dennis Hockerman
  Tom Thumb, ill. by Felix Hoffmann
  Tom Thumb, ill. by Lidia Postma
  Tom Thumb, ill. by Richard Jesse Watson
  Tom Thumb, ill. by William Wiesner
Velthuijs, Max. *Little Man finds a home*
  Little Man to the rescue
  Little Man's lucky day
Walt Disney Productions. *Walt Disney's Snow White and the seven dwarfs*
Yolen, Jane. *Elfabet*
Zimelman, Nathan. *To sing a song as big as Ireland*

Embarrassment *see* Emotions – embarrassment

Emergencies *see* Hospitals

Emotions

Aliki. *Feelings*
Allington, Richard L. *Feelings*
Andersen, H. C. (Hans Christian). *The snow queen*, ill. by Bernadette Watts
Andersen, Karen Born. *What's the matter, Sylvie, can't you ride?*
Anholt, Catherine. *What I like*
Bach, Alice. *The day after Christmas*
Berger, Terry. *How does it feel when your parents get divorced?*
  I have feelings
  I have feelings too

Bienenfeld, Florence. *My mom and dad are getting a divorce*
Borten, Helen. *Do you move as I do?*
Brenner, Barbara A. *Faces, faces, faces*
Brown, Tricia. *Someone special, just like you*
Calhoun, Mary. *The witch who lost her shadow*
Castle, Sue. *Face talk, hand talk, body talk*
Christiansen, C. B. *My mother's house, my father's house*
Clifford, Eth. *Your face is a picture*
Clifton, Lucille. *Everett Anderson's goodbye*
Cohen, Miriam. *Jim's dog Muffins*
Cole, William. *Frances face-maker*
Conta, Marcia Maher. *Feelings between brothers and sisters*
  Feelings between friends
  Feelings between kids and grownups
  Feelings between kids and parents
Crary, Elizabeth. *I'm frustrated*
Cunningham, Julia. *A mouse called Junction*
Curtis, Gavin. *Grandma's baseball*
Dabcovich, Lydia. *Mrs. Huggins and her hen Hannah*
Dragonwagon, Crescent. *Rainy day together*
Galdone, Paul. *The teeny-tiny woman*
Hann, Jacquie. *Crybaby*
Hazen, Barbara Shook. *Happy, sad, silly, mad*
  Two homes to live in
Helena, Ann. *The lie*
Hoban, Russell. *La corona and the tin frog*
  The stone doll of Sister Brute
Hopkins, Lee Bennett. *I loved Rose Ann*
Horvath, Betty F. *Will the real Tommy Wilson please stand up?*
Isadora, Rachel. *At the crossroads*
Jenkins, Jessica. *Thinking about colors*
Jewell, Nancy. *Time for Uncle Joe*
Johnson, Angela. *The leaving morning*
Keller, Holly. *Lizzie's invitation*
Kherdian, David. *Right now*
Knox-Wagner, Elaine. *My grandpa retired today*
Krauss, Ruth. *The bundle book*
Lalli, Judy. *Feelings alphabet*
Lanton, Sandy. *Daddy's chair*
Laskin, Pamela L. *Wish upon a star*
Lewin, Hugh. *Jafta*
  Jafta—the journey
  Jafta—the town
McCrea, James. *The magic tree*
McGovern, Ann. *Feeling mad, feeling sad, feeling bad, feeling glad*
Mayer, Mercer. *Mine!*
Mayers, Patrick. *Just one more block*
Mendoza, George. *The hunter I might have been*
Millward, David Wynn. *Jenny and Bob*
Mitchell, Cynthia. *Playtime*
Modesitt, Jeanne. *The story of Z*

Nave, Yolanda. *Goosebumps and butterflies*
Ness, Evaline. *Pavo and the princess*
O'Donnell, Elizabeth Lee. *Maggie doesn't want to move*
Pursell, Margaret Sanford. *A look at divorce*
Rogers, Fred. *Making friends*
  Moving
Ross, David. *More hugs!*
Selway, Martina. *Don't forget to write*
The Sesame Street book of people and things
Sharratt, Nick. *I look like this*
Simon, Norma. *How do I feel?*
  I am not a crybaby!
Smith, Wendy. *Twice mice*
Stanton, Elizabeth. *Sometimes I like to cry*
Sussman, Susan. *Hippo thunder*
Tobias, Tobi. *Moving day*
Tresselt, Alvin R. *What did you leave behind?*
Turner, Ethel. *Walking to school*
Vigna, Judith. *Saying goodbye to daddy*
Waber, Bernard. *Ira says goodbye*
Walsh, Ellen Stoll. *Two too much*
Wittels, Harriet. *Things I hate!*
Wolde, Gunilla. *This is Betsy*
Yudell, Lynn Deena. *Make a face*

Emotions – anger

Alexander, Martha G. *And my mean old mother will be sorry, Blackboard Bear*
Aliki. *We are best friends*
Andrews, F. Emerson (Frank Emerson). *Nobody comes to dinner*
Andrews, Jan. *The auction*
Aseltine, Lorraine. *I'm deaf and it's okay*
Boegehold, Betty. *Daddy doesn't live here anymore*
Craft, Ruth. *The day of the rainbow*
Crary, Elizabeth. *I'm mad*
Du Bois, William Pène. *Bear party*
Duncan, Riana. *When Emily woke up angry*
Erickson, Karen. *I was so mad*
Hapgood, Miranda. *Martha's mad day*
Hautzig, Deborah. *Why are you so mean to me?*
Hoban, Lillian. *Arthur's great big Valentine*
Joosse, Barbara M. *Dinah's mad, bad wishes*
Sharmat, Marjorie Weinman. *Attila the angry*
  I'm not Oscar's friend any more
  Rollo and Juliet...forever!
Simon, Norma. *I was so mad!*
Small, David. *Paper John*
Tulloch, Richard. *Danny in the toybox*
Watson, Jane Werner. *Sometimes I get angry*
Widman, Christine. *Housekeeper of the wind*
Wilhelm, Hans. *Let's be friends again!*
Zolotow, Charlotte (Shapiro). *The quarreling book*

Emotions – embarrassment

Alexander, Martha G. *Sabrina*
Aylesworth, Jim. *Shenandoah Noah*
Boyd, Selma. *The how: making the best of a mistake*
Bulla, Clyde Robert. *Daniel's duck*
Carlson, Nancy. *Loudmouth George and the big race*
Caseley, Judith. *Molly Pink*
Cazet, Denys. *Great-Uncle Felix*
Cooney, Nancy Evans. *Donald says thumbs down*
Corrigan, Kathy. *Emily Umily*
Davis, Gibbs. *Katy's first haircut*
Freeman, Don. *Quiet! There's a canary in the library*
Hirsh, Marilyn. *The pink suit*
Hoff, Syd. *A walk past Ellen's house*
Lexau, Joan M. *I should have stayed in bed*
Shalev, Meir. *My father always embarrasses me*
Stanek, Muriel. *Left, right, left, right!*
Townsend, Kenneth. *Felix, the bald-headed lion*
Udry, Janice May. *How I faded away*
Wood, Audrey. *Weird parents*

Emotions – envy, jealousy

Abisch, Roz. *Mai-Ling and the mirror*
Alexander, Martha G. *Nobody asked me if I wanted a baby sister*
  When the new baby comes, I'm moving out
Asch, Frank. *Bear's bargain*
Aylesworth, Jim. *Mary's mirror*
Bach, Alice. *Millicent the magnificent*
Baker, Charlotte. *Little brother*
Beim, Jerrold. *Country mailman*
Brown, Ruth. *I don't like it!*
Buck, Pearl S. (Pearl Sydenstricker). *The Chinese story teller*
Bullock, Kathleen. *A surprise for Mitzi Mouse*
Bunting, Eve (Anne Evelyn). *Monkey in the middle*
Burningham, John. *Humbert, Mister Firkin and the Lord Mayor of London*
Caines, Jeannette. *I need a lunch box*
Calhoun, Mary. *High-wire Henry*
Carlson, Nancy. *Poor Carl*
Castle, Caroline. *Herbert Binns and the flying tricycle*
Cole, Babette. *Hurray for Ethelyn*
Cole, Joanna. *The new baby at your house*
Conford, Ellen. *Why can't I be William?*
Corey, Dorothy. *Will it ever be my birthday?*
Cretan, Gladys Yessayan. *Lobo and Brewster*
Demi. *The artist and the architect*
Doherty, Berlie. *Paddiwak and cozy*
Drescher, Joan. *My mother's getting married*
Eriksson, Eva. *Jealousy*

Ernst, Lisa Campbell. *Miss Penny and Mr. Grubbs*

Ferguson, Alane. *That new pet!*

Gantos, Jack (John, Jr.). *Rotten Ralph's rotten Christmas*

Ganz, Yaffa. *The story of Mimmy and Simmy*

Gill, Joan. *Hush, Jon!*

Graham, Margaret Bloy. *Benjy and the barking bird*

Graham, Richard. *Jack and the monster*

Greenfield, Eloise. *She come bringing me that little baby girl*

Gretz, Susanna. *Frog in the middle*

Grimm, Jacob. *Snow White*, ill. by Trina Schart Hyman
Snow White, ill. by Bernadette Watts
Snow White and the seven dwarves, ill. by Chihiro Iwasaki

Hathorn, Libby. *Freya's fantastic surprise*

Hazen, Barbara Shook. *Why couldn't I be an only kid like you, Wigger?*

Hedderwick, Mairi. *Katie Morag and the tiresome Ted*

Hoban, Russell. *A baby sister for Frances*
A birthday for Frances

Howe, James. *I wish I were a butterfly*

Jenkin-Pearce, Susie. *Bad Boris and the new kitten*

Kellogg, Steven (Stephen). *Best friends*

Levine, Abby. *Sometimes I wish I were Mindy*

Lindgren, Astrid. *I want a brother or sister*

Lionni, Leo. *Alexander and the wind-up mouse*

McAllister, Angela. *The battle of Sir Cob and Sir Filbert*

McLenighan, Valjean. *You can go jump*

Manushkin, Fran. *Little rabbit's baby brother*

Mayer, Mercer. *One frog too many*

Miller, Warren. *The goings on at Little Wishful*

Mills, Claudia. *A visit to Amy-Claire*

Ormondroyd, Edward. *Theodore's rival*

Peet, Bill (William Bartlett). *The luckiest one of all*

Schick, Eleanor. *Peggy's new brother*

Shyer, Marlene Fanta. *Stepdog*

Skorpen, Liesel Moak. *His mother's dog*

Stanley, Diane. *Siegfried*

Velthuijs, Max. *Little Man to the rescue*

Vigna, Judith. *Couldn't we have a turtle instead?*

Waber, Bernard. *Lyle and the birthday party*

Walt Disney Productions. *Walt Disney's Snow White and the seven dwarfs*

Watson, Jane Werner. *Sometimes I'm jealous*

Zemach, Margot. *To Hilda for helping*

Ziefert, Harriet. *Getting ready for new baby*

Zolotow, Charlotte (Shapiro). *It's not fair*

Emotions – fear

Alexander, Anne (Anna Barbara Cooke). *Noise in the night*

Alexander, Martha G. *I'll protect you from the jungle beasts*
Maybe a monster

Alexander, Sally Hobart. *Sarah's surprise*

Alexander, Sue. *Witch, Goblin and sometimes Ghost*

Anrooy, Frans van. *The sea horse*

Aseltine, Lorraine. *I'm deaf and it's okay*

Aylesworth, Jim. *Siren in the night*
Two terrible frights

Babbitt, Natalie. *The something*

Bannon, Laura. *Little people of the night*
The scary thing

Barton, Byron. *Harry is a scaredy-cat*

Benedek, Elissa P. *The secret worry*

Berenstain, Stan. *The Berenstain bears get stage fright*
The Berenstain bears learn about strangers

Bergström, Gunilla. *Who's scaring Alfie Atkins?*

Berry, Christine. *Mama went walking*

Blegvad, Lenore. *Anna Banana and me*

Bonsall, Crosby Newell. *Who's afraid of the dark?*

Bourgeois, Paulette. *Franklin in the dark*

Brown, Margaret Wise. *Night and day*

Bunting, Eve (Anne Evelyn). *Ghost's hour, spook's hour*
Terrible things

Byfield, Barbara Ninde. *The haunted churchbell*

Caines, Jeannette. *Chilly stomach*

Callan, Elizabeth Koda. *Good luck pony*

Cameron, Ann. *Harry (the monster)*

Carlson, Nancy. *Harriet's recital*
Witch lady

Carrick, Carol. *Dark and full of secrets*

Chorao, Kay. *Lester's overnight*

Church, Kristine. *My brother John*

Clifton, Lucille. *Amifika*

Cohen, Miriam. *Jim meets the thing*
The real-skin rubber monster mask

Coles, Alison. *Michael and the sea*
Michael in the dark
Michael's first day

Company González, Mercè. *Killian and the dragons*

Conford, Ellen. *Eugene the brave*

Cooney, Nancy Evans. *Go away monsters, lickety split!*

Credle, Ellis. *Big fraid, little fraid*

Crowe, Robert L. *Clyde monster*

Cunningham, Julia. *A mouse called Junction*

Devlin, Wende. *Aunt Agatha, there's a lion under the couch!*

Dickens, Lucy. *Go fish*

Dinardo, Jeffrey. *Timothy and the night noises*

Dodd, Lynley. *Hairy Maclary from Donaldson's dairy*
Erickson, Karen. *It's dark*
Farber, Werner. *Night lion*
Freschet, Berniece. *Furlie Cat*
Gackenbach, Dick. *Harry and the terrible whatzit*
Gay, Zhenya. *Who's afraid?*
Gikow, Louise. *Boober Fraggle's ghosts*
Girard, Linda Walvoord. *Jeremy's first haircut*
Glaser, Linda. *Keep your socks on, Albert!*
Goode, Diane. *I hear a noise*
Goodenow, Earle. *The owl who hated the dark*
Graham, Margaret Bloy. *Benjy and his friend Fifi*
Grant, Joan. *The monster that grew small*
Greenberg, Barbara. *The bravest babysitter*
Gretz, Susanna. *Hide-and-seek*
Too dark!
Grifalconi, Ann. *Darkness and the butterfly*
Hall, Derek. *Otter swims*
Panda climbs
Tiger runs
Hamilton, Morse. *Who's afraid of the dark?*
Hanlon, Emily. *What if a lion eats me and I fall into a hippopotamus' mud hole?*
Hanson, Joan. *I won't be afraid*
Harlow, Joan Hiatt. *Shadow bear*
Hawkins, Colin. *Snap! Snap!*
Hazen, Barbara Shook. *Fang*
The knight who was afraid of the dark
Wally the worry-warthog
Hest, Amy. *A sort-of sailor*
Hill, Susan. *Go away, bad dreams!*
Hindley, Judy. *Maybe it's a pirate*
Hoban, Russell. *Goodnight*
Howe, James. *There's a monster under my bed*
Impey, Rose. *The flat man*
Scare yourself to sleep
Jonas, Ann. *Holes and peeks*
Jones, Rebecca C. *Down at the bottom of the deep dark sea*
Joosse, Barbara M. *Spiders in the fruit cellar*
Kasza, Keiko. *When the elephant walks*
Keller, Beverly. *Pimm's place*
Kelley, True. *Day-care teddy bear*
Kitamura, Satoshi. *Lily takes a walk*
Klinting, Lars. *Regal the golden eagle*
Kraus, Robert. *Noel the coward*
Lakin, Patricia. *Don't touch my room*
Leaf, Munro. *Boo, who used to be scared of the dark*
Lifton, Betty Jean. *Goodnight orange monster*
Lindgren, Astrid. *The ghost of Skinny Jack*
Little, Jean. *Jess was the brave one*
Low, Joseph. *Benny rabbit and the owl*
Boo to a goose

Lyon, George-Ella. *Cecil's story*
McCully, Emily Arnold. *The evil spell*
Martin, C. L. G. *Three brave women*
Martin, Jacqueline Briggs. *Bizzy Bones and Uncle Ezra*
Mayer, Mercer. *There's a nightmare in my closet*
There's an alligator under my bed
There's something in my attic
You're the scaredy cat
Mollel, Tolowa M. *Rhinos for lunch and elephants for supper*
Moore, Lilian. *Little Raccoon and the thing in the pool*
Morris, Winifred. *What if the shark wears tennis shoes?*
Moss, Marissa. *After-school monster*
Nash, Ogden. *The adventures of Isabel*, ill. by Walter Lorraine
The adventures of Isabel, ill. by James Marshall
O'Donnell, Peter. *Moonlit journey*
Oppenheim, Shulamith Levey. *The lily cupboard*
Pittman, Helena Clare. *Once when I was scared*
Pizer, Abigail. *Nosey Gilbert*
Polacco, Patricia. *Thunder cake*
Pryor, Bonnie. *The porcupine mouse*
Ratnett, Michael. *Marmaduke and the scary story*
Reed, Jonathan. *Do armadillos come in houses?*
Reeves, Mona Rabun. *The spooky eerie night noise*
Robison, Deborah. *No elephants allowed*
Rodgers, Frank. *Who's afraid of the ghost train?*
Ross, Pat. *Your first airplane trip*
Ross, Tony. *Happy blanket*
I'm coming to get you!
Sabraw, John. *I wouldn't be scared*
Schertle, Alice. *The gorilla in the hall*
Scruton, Clive. *Scaredy cat*
Seuss, Dr. *The Sneetches, and other stories*
Shortall, Leonard W. *Tony's first dive*
Simms, Laura. *The squeaky door*
Smith, Janice Lee. *The monster in the third dresser drawer and other stories about Adam Joshua*
Smith, Maggie (Margaret C.). *There's a witch under the stairs*
Steel, Danielle. *Max and the baby sitter*
Stevenson, Drew. *The ballad of Penelope Lou...and me*
Stevenson, James. *What's under my bed?*
Stock, Catherine. *Halloween monster*
Strand, Mark. *The night book*
Stubbs, Joanna. *With cat's eyes you'll never be scared of the dark*
Szilagyi, Mary. *Thunderstorm*

Taylor, Anelise. *Lights on, lights off*
Tompert, Ann. *The Tzar's bird*
 Will you come back for me?
Townson, Hazel. *Terrible Tuesday*
Trez, Denise. *The royal hiccups*
Tsutsui, Yoriko. *Anna in charge*
Udry, Janice May. *Alfred*
Vigna, Judith. *Nobody wants a nuclear war*
Viorst, Judith. *My mama says there aren't*
 any zombies, ghosts, vampires, creatures,
 demons, monsters, fiends, goblins, or things
Vogel, Ilse-Margaret. *The don't be scared*
 book
Waddell, Martin. *Can't you sleep, Little*
 Bear?
 The park in the dark
Wallace, Ian. *Chin Chiang and the dragon's*
 dance
Watson, Jane Werner. *Sometimes I'm afraid*
Wharton, Thomas. *Hildegard sings*
Widerberg, Siv. *The boy and the dog*
Williams, Gweneira Maureen. *Timid*
 Timothy, the kitten who learned to be brave
Williams, Linda. *The little old lady who was*
 not afraid of anything
Willis, Jeanne. *The monster bed*
Winthrop, Elizabeth. *Potbellied possums*
Wolf, Bernard. *Michael and the dentist*
Wondriska, William. *The stop*
Zolotow, Charlotte (Shapiro). *The storm*
 book

Emotions – happiness

Asch, George. *Linda*
Low, Joseph. *The Christmas grump*
McCrea, James. *The magic tree*
Miller, Edward. *The curse of Claudia*
Piatti, Celestino. *The happy owls*
Rice, Eve. *What Sadie sang*
Steig, William. *Spinky sulks*
Tapio, Pat Decker. *The lady who saw the*
 good side of everything
Tobias, Tobi. *Jane wishing*
Tripp, Paul. *The strawman who smiled by*
 mistake
Williams, Barbara. *Someday, said Mitchell*
Wondriska, William. *Mr. Brown and Mr.*
 Gray
Yabuki, Seiji. *I love the morning*

Emotions – hate

Udry, Janice May. *Let's be enemies*
Zolotow, Charlotte (Shapiro). *The hating*
 book

Emotions - jealousy *see* Emotions – envy, jealousy

Emotions – loneliness

Alexander, Sue. *Dear Phoebe*

Aliki. *We are best friends*
Ardizzone, Edward. *Lucy Brown and Mr.*
 Grimes
Battles, Edith. *One to teeter-totter*
Blegvad, Lenore. *Mr. Jensen and cat*
Bolliger, Max. *The lonely prince*
Brett, Jan. *Annie and the wild animals*
Bröger, Achim. *Francie's paper puppy*
Brown, Marcia. *The little carousel*
Buck, Pearl S. (Pearl Sydenstricker). *The*
 little fox in the middle
Buntain, Ruth Jaeger. *The birthday story*
Burningham, John. *Aldo*
Chenault, Nell. *Parsifal the Poddley*
Chess, Victoria. *Poor Esmé*
Clewes, Dorothy. *Happiest day*
Coatsworth, Elizabeth. *Lonely Maria*
Conaway, Judith. *I'll get even*
Conger, Marion. *The chipmunk that went to*
 church
Coontz, Otto. *The quiet house*
Craven, Carolyn. *What the mailman brought*
Cummings, W. T. (Walter Thies). *The kid*
Delton, Judy. *My grandma's in a nursing*
 home
Duvoisin, Roger Antoine. *Periwinkle*
Ellis, Anne Leo. *Dabble Duck*
Fatio, Louise. *The happy lion roars*
Fujikawa, Gyo. *Shags finds a kitten*
Funazaki, Yasuko. *Baby owl*
Gág, Wanda. *Nothing at all*
Goffstein, M. B. (Marilyn Brooke).
 Neighbors
Harranth, Wolf. *My old grandad*
Hofsepian, Sylvia A. *Why not?*
Hughes, Shirley. *Moving Molly*
Keats, Ezra Jack. *The trip*
Kesselman, Wendy. *Angelita*
 Emma
Khalsa, Dayal Kaur. *How pizza came to our*
 town
Knaff, Jean Christian. *Manhattan*
Lukešová, Milena. *The little girl and the*
 rain
Luttrell, Ida. *Lonesome Lester*
McClure, Gillian. *What's the time, Rory*
 Wolf?
McGovern, Ann. *Mr. Skinner's skinny house*
 Nicholas Bentley Stoningpot III
McNeer, May Yonge. *My friend Mac*
Munthe, Adam John. *I believe in unicorns*
Murphy, Shirley Rousseau. *Valentine for a*
 dragon
Norton, Natalie. *A little old man*
Olsen, Ib Spang. *The grown-up trap*
Park, W. B. *The costume party*
Sarton, May. *Punch's secret*
Seignobosc, Françoise. *The story of Colette*
Siekkinen, Raija. *Mister King*
Skurzynski, Gloria. *Martin by himself*
Slate, Joseph. *Lonely Lula cat*

Smith, Wendy. *The lonely, only mouse*
Sonneborn, Ruth A. *Lollipop's party*
Spang, Günter. *Clelia and the little mermaid*
Stage, Mads. *The lonely squirrel*
Stanek, Muriel. *All alone after school*
Stevenson, James. *Mr. Hacker*
Stren, Patti. *Hug me*
Sugita, Yutaka. *Helena the unhappy hippopotamus*
Surany, Anico. *Kati and Kormos*
Timlock, Jason. *Basil, the loneliest boy*
Titherington, Jeanne. *A place for Ben*
Waddell, Martin. *The hidden house*
Wagener, Gerda. *Leo the lion*
Walter, Mildred Pitts. *My mama needs me*
Yashima, Tarō. *Crow boy*
Zindel, Paul. *I love my mother*
Zolotow, Charlotte (Shapiro). *Janey*
  Three funny friends
  A tiger called Thomas, ill. by Catherine Stock
  A tiger called Thomas, ill. by Kurt Werth

Emotions – love

Agostinelli, Maria Enrica. *On wings of love*
Alexander, Sue. *Dear Phoebe*
  Nadia the willful
Andersen, H. C. (Hans Christian). *The snow queen*, ill. by Angela Barrett
  The snow queen, ill. by Toma Bogdanovic
  The snow queen, ill. by June Atkin Corwin
  The snow queen, ill. by Sally Holmes
  The snow queen, ill. by Susan Jeffers
  The snow queen, ill. by Errol Le Cain
  The snow queen, ill. by Arieh Zeldich
Anglund, Joan Walsh. *Love is a baby*
  Love is a special way of feeling
Baker, Keith. *The dove's letter*
Barrett, Joyce Durham. *Willie's not the hugging kind*
Baynton, Martin. *Why do you love me?*
Bergström, Gunilla. *You have a girlfriend, Alfie Atkins?*
Bianco, Margery Williams. *The velveteen rabbit*, ill. by Allen Atkinson
  The velveteen rabbit, ill. by Michael Green
  The velveteen rabbit, ill. by Michael Hague
  The velveteen rabbit, ill. by David Jorgensen
  The velveteen rabbit, ill. by William Nicholson
  The velveteen rabbit, ill. by Ilse Plume
  The velveteen rabbit, ill. by S. D. Schindler
  The velveteen rabbit, ill. by Tien
Billam, Rosemary. *Fuzzy rabbit*
Birdseye, Tom. *A song of stars*
Boegehold, Betty. *Pawpaw's run*

Boyle, Vere. *Beauty and the beast*
Brown, Palmer. *Something for Christmas*
Buckley, Helen Elizabeth. *Grandmother and I*
Carter, Anne. *Beauty and the beast*
Caseley, Judith. *Dear Annie*
Clifton, Lucille. *Everett Anderson's goodbye*
Cole, Babette. *Cupid*
De Mejo, Oscar. *La Bella Magellona and the little cavalier*
De Paola, Tomie (Thomas Anthony). *Helga's dowry*
Dragonwagon, Crescent. *Wind Rose*
Dyke, John. *Pigwig*
Eisenberg, Phyllis Rose. *You're my Nikki*
Fatio, Louise. *The happy lion's treasure*
Flack, Marjorie. *Ask Mr. Bear*
Flanders, Michael. *The hippopotamus song*
Fox, Mem. *Koala Lou*
Freedman, Florence B. *Brothers*
Freeman, Don. *Corduroy*
Gerstein, Mordicai. *Prince Sparrow*
Girard, Linda Walvoord. *At Daddy's on Saturdays*
Glass, Andrew. *Chickpea and the talking cow*
Greene, Carol. *The golden locket*
Haseley, Dennis. *Ghost catcher*
Hazen, Barbara Shook. *Even if I did something awful*
Hest, Amy. *The go-between*
Hodges, Margaret. *The kitchen knight*
Hoopes, Lyn Littlefield. *When I was little*
Jacobs, Joseph. *Tattercoats*, ill. by Margot Tomes
Jenkins, Jordan. *Learning about love*
Jewell, Nancy. *The snuggle bunny*
Joosse, Barbara M. *Mama, do you love me?*
Kasza, Keiko. *A mother for Choco*
Kočí, Marta. *Sarah's bear*
Krauss, Ruth. *Big and little*
Lagerlöf, Selma. *The changeling*
Lasky, Kathryn. *I have four names for my grandfather*
Levitin, Sonia. *The man who kept his heart in a bucket*
Lexau, Joan M. *A house so big*
McCloskey, Kevin. *Mrs. Fitz's flamingos*
McPhail, David. *Sisters*
Mangas, Brian. *A nice surprise for Father Rabbit*
Marshall, Edward. *Fox in love*
Martin, Bill (William Ivan). *Knots on a counting rope*
Mayer, Marianna. *Beauty and the beast*
Mayer, Mercer. *Just for you*
  Whinnie the lovesick dragon
Mayne, William. *The patchwork cat*
Miles, Betty. *Around and around... love*
Mizumura, Kazue. *If I were a cricket...*
Morris, Ann. *Loving*

Naylor, Phyllis Reynolds. *The baby, the bed, and the rose*
Nesbit, Edith. *Beauty and the beast*
Newton, Laura P. *Me and my aunts*
Noyes, Alfred. *The highwayman*, ill. by Neil Waldman
Otsuka, Yuzo. *Suho and the white horse*
Paterson, Diane. *Wretched Rachel*
Pochocki, Ethel. *Rosebud and red flannel*
Porter-Gaylord, Laurel. *I love my daddy because...*
I love my mommy because...
Price, Leontyne. *Aïda*
Reinl, Edda. *The little snake*
Rohmer, Harriet. *Mother scorpion country*
Rowand, Phyllis. *Every day in the year*
Samuels, Barbara. *Faye and Dolores*
Scott, Ann Herbert. *On mother's lap*
Shecter, Ben. *If I had a ship*
Shipton, Jonathan. *Busy! Busy! Busy!*
Silverman, Maida. *The magic well*
Steig, William. *Tiffky Doofky*
Thompson, Richard. *Foo*
Tudor, Tasha. *Miss Kiss and the nasty beast*
Vaës, Alain. *The porcelain pepper pot*
Velthuijs, Max. *Frog in love*
Wade, Barrie. *Little monster*
Wahl, Jan. *Old Hippo's Easter egg*
Watson, Wendy. *A Valentine for you*
Woychuk, Denis. *The other side of the wall*
Zalben, Jane Breskin. *A perfect nose for Ralph*
Ziefert, Harriet. *With love from Grandma*
Zindel, Paul. *I love my mother*
Zola, Meguido. *Only the best*
Zolotow, Charlotte (Shapiro). *Do you know what I'll do?*
May I visit?
A rose, a bridge, and a wild black horse
Say it!
The sky was blue

Emotions – sadness

Alexander, Sue. *Nadia the willful*
Allen, Frances Charlotte. *Little hippo*
Andrews, Jan. *The auction*
Baker, Betty. *Rat is dead and ant is sad*
Bartoli, Jennifer. *Nonna*
Carson, Jo. *You hold me and I'll hold you*
Delton, Judy. *I'll never love anything ever again*
De Paola, Tomie (Thomas Anthony). *Nana upstairs and Nana downstairs*
Deveaux, Alexis. *Na-ni*
Kaldhol, Marit. *Goodbye Rune*
Lindgren, Astrid. *My nightingale is singing*
Low, Joseph. *The Christmas grump*
McLerran, Alice. *The mountain that loved a bird*
Madenski, Melissa. *Some of the pieces*
Sharmat, Marjorie Weinman. *I don't care*

Sugita, Yutaka. *Helena the unhappy hippopotamus*
Wolff, Ashley. *The bells of London*

Emotions - unhappiness *see* Emotions – happiness; Emotions – sadness

Emperors *see* Royalty – emperors

Endangered animals *see* Animals – endangered animals

Engineered books *see* Format, unusual – toy and moveable books

England *see* Foreign lands – England

Entertainment *see* Theater

Envy *see* Emotions – envy, jealousy

Eskimos

Andrews, Jan. *Very last first time*
Beim, Lorraine. *The little igloo*
Carlstrom, Nancy White. *Northern lullaby*
Damjan, Mischa. *Atuk*
DeArmond, Dale. *The seal oil lamp*
Harlow, Joan Hiatt. *Shadow bear*
Hopkins, Marjorie. *Three visitors*
Houston, James. *Kiviok's magic journey*
Joosse, Barbara M. *Mama, do you love me?*
Loverseed, Amanda. *Tikkatoo's journey*
Luenn, Nancy. *Nessa's fish*
Machetanz, Sara. *A puppy named Gia*
Morrow, Suzanne Stark. *Inatuck's friend*
Munsch, Robert N. *A promise is a promise*
Parish, Peggy. *Ootah's lucky day*
San Souci, Robert D. *Song of Sedna*
Scott, Ann Herbert. *On mother's lap*
Steiner, Barbara (Annette). *The whale brother*

Ethnic groups in the U.S

Banish, Roslyn. *A forever family*
Barrett, Joyce Durham. *Willie's not the hugging kind*
Belpré, Pura. *Santiago*
Bettinger, Craig. *Follow me, everybody*
Blue, Rose. *I am here: Yo estoy aqui*
Brenner, Barbara A. *Faces, faces, faces*
Caseley, Judith. *Apple pie and onions*
Clifford, Eth. *Your face is a picture*
Cohen, Miriam. *Will I have a friend?*
Crume, Marion W. *Listen!*
Dooley, Norah. *Everybody cooks rice*
Dorros, Arthur. *Abuela*
Feldman, Eve B. *Animals don't wear pajamas*
Fisher, Iris L. *Katie-Bo*
Greene, Roberta. *Two and me makes three*

Heinst, Marie. *My first number book*
Hoffman, Phyllis. *Meatball*
Hogan, Paula Z. *The hospital scares me*
Hughes, Shirley. *The big concrete lorry*
James, Betsy. *The dream stair*
Jaynes, Ruth M. *Benny's four hats*
  Friends! friends! friends!
  Tell me please! What's that?
  That's what it is!
  What is a birthday child?
Jenkins, Jessica. *Thinking about colors*
Keats, Ezra Jack. *My dog is lost!*
Kesselman, Wendy. *Angelita*
Klein, Leonore. *Just like you*
Kuklin, Susan. *How my family lives in America*
Lansdown, Brenda. *Galumpf*
May, Julian. *Why people are different colors*
Medearis, Angela Shelf. *The zebra-riding cowboy*
Merriam, Eve. *Boys and girls, girls and boys*
Merrill, Jean. *How many kids are hiding on my block?*
Moss, Marissa. *After-school monster*
Paek, Min. *Aekyung's dream*
Pellegrini, Nina. *Families are different*
Reit, Seymour. *Round things everywhere*
Rosenberg, Maxine B. *Being adopted*
Sage, James. *The little band*
Shelby, Anne. *Potluck*
Simon, Norma. *I am not a crybaby!*
  What do I say?
Sobol, Harriet Langsam. *We don't look like our mom and dad*
Stanek, Muriel. *One, two, three for fun*
Udry, Janice May. *What Mary Jo shared*
Williams, Vera B. *"More more more," said the baby*

Ethnic groups in the U.S. – Afro-Americans

Adler, David A. *A picture book of Martin Luther King, Jr.*
Adoff, Arnold. *Big sister tells me that I'm black*
  In for winter, out for spring
  Where wild Willie?
Alexander, Martha G. *Bobo's dream*
  The story grandmother told
Aliki. *A weed is a flower*
Allison, Diane Worfolk. *This is the key to the kingdom*
Bang, Molly. *Ten, nine, eight*
  Wiley and the hairy man
Beim, Jerrold. *The swimming hole*
Beim, Lorraine. *Two is a team*
Blue, Rose. *Black, black, beautiful black*
  How many blocks is the world?
Bogart, Jo Ellen. *Daniel's dog*
Breinburg, Petronella. *Doctor Shawn*
  Shawn goes to school

Shawn's red bike
Bryan, Ashley. *All night, all day: a child's first book of African-American spirituals*
  I'm going to sing
Burch, Robert. *Joey's cat*
Caines, Jeannette. *Abby*
  Daddy
  Just us women
Calloway, Northern J. *Northern J. Calloway presents Super-vroomer!*
Carlstrom, Nancy White. *Wild wild sunflower child Anna*
Children go where I send thee
Chocolate, Deborah M. Newton. *Kwanzaa*
Clifton, Lucille. *All us come cross the water*
  Amifika
  The boy who didn't believe in spring
  Don't you remember?
  Everett Anderson's Christmas coming
  Everett Anderson's friend
  Everett Anderson's goodbye
  Everett Anderson's nine months long
  Everett Anderson's 1-2-3
  Everett Anderson's year
  My brother fine with me
  My friend Jacob
  Some of the days of Everett Anderson
  Three wishes
  Three wishes, ill. by Michael Hays
Cummings, Pat. *Clean your room, Harvey Moon!*
  Jimmy Lee did it
Curtis, Gavin. *Grandma's baseball*
Dale, Penny. *You can't*
De Veaux, Alexis. *An enchanted hair tale*
Dionetti, Michelle. *Thalia Brown and the blue bug*
Dragonwagon, Crescent. *Home place*
Evans, Mari. *Singing black*
Everett, Gwen. *Li'l Sis and Uncle Willie*
Fassler, Joan. *Don't worry dear*
Fife, Dale. *Adam's ABC*
Flournoy, Valerie. *The best time of day*
  The patchwork quilt
Fraser, Kathleen. *Adam's world, San Francisco*
Freeman, Don. *Corduroy*
  A pocket for Corduroy
Gambill, Henrietta. *Self-control*
George, Jean Craighead. *The wentletrap trap*
Gill, Joan. *Hush, Jon!*
Giovanni, Nikki. *Spin a soft black song*
Gray, Genevieve. *Send Wendell*
Gray, Nigel. *I'll take you to Mrs. Cole!*
Greenberg, Polly. *Oh, Lord, I wish I was a buzzard*
Greenfield, Eloise. *Big friend, little friend*
  Daddy and I
  Daydreamers
  First pink light

To hell with dying
Walsh, Ellen Stoll. *Two too much*
Walter, Mildred Pitts. *My mama needs me*
Williams, Sherley Anne. *Working cotton*
Williams, Vera B. *Cherries and cherry pits*
Williamson, Mel. *Walk on!*
Williamson, Stan. *The no-bark dog*
Wilson, Beth P. *Jenny*
Wilson, Julia. *Becky*
Winter, Jeanette. *Follow the drinking gourd*
Yezback, Steven A. *Pumpkinseeds*
Young, Ruth. *Golden Bear*
Zemach, Margot. *Jake and Honeybunch go to heaven*
Ziner, Feenie. *Counting carnival*

Ethnic groups in the U.S. – Asian-Americans

Gabel, Susan L. *Where the sun kisses the sea*

Ethnic groups in the U.S. - Black Americans *see* Ethnic groups in the U.S. – Afro-Americans

Ethnic groups in the U.S. – Chinese-Americans

Behrens, June. *Soo Ling finds a way*
Bunting, Eve (Anne Evelyn). *The happy funeral*
Coerr, Eleanor. *Chang's paper pony*
Levine, Ellen. *I hate English!*
McCunn, Ruthanne L. *Pie-Biter*
Politi, Leo. *Moy Moy*
Wallace, Ian. *Chin Chiang and the dragon's dance*
Waters, Kate. *Lion dancer: Ernie Wan's Chinese new year*
Yee, Paul. *Roses sing on new snow*

Ethnic groups in the U.S. – Hispanic-Americans

Weiss, Nicki. *On a hot, hot day*

Ethnic groups in the U.S. – Irish-Americans

Kroll, Steven. *Mary McLean and the St. Patrick's Day parade*

Ethnic groups in the U.S. – Italian-Americans

Dionetti, Michelle. *Coal mine peaches*

Ethnic groups in the U.S. – Japanese-Americans

Copeland, Helen. *Meet Miki Takino*
Hawkinson, Lucy. *Dance, dance, Amy-Chan!*
Sakai, Kimiko. *Sachiko means happiness*
Yashima, Mitsu. *Momo's kitten*
Yashima, Tarō. *Umbrella*

The youngest one

Ethnic groups in the U.S. – Korean-Americans

Pellegrini, Nina. *Families are different*

Ethnic groups in the U.S. – Mexican-Americans

Behrens, June. *Fiesta!*
Bolognese, Don. *A new day*
Brown, Tricia. *Hello, amigos!*
Ets, Marie Hall. *Bad boy, good boy*
  Gilberto and the wind
  Nine days to Christmas
Felt, Sue. *Rosa-too-little*
Fife, Dale. *Rosa's special garden*
Fraser, James Howard. *Los Posadas*
Havill, Juanita. *Treasure nap*
Jaynes, Ruth M. *Melinda's Christmas stocking*
  Tell me please! What's that?
  That's what it is!
  What is a birthday child?
Molnar, Joe. *Graciela*
Ormsby, Virginia H. *Twenty-one children plus ten*
Politi, Leo. *Juanita*
  Pedro, the angel of Olvera Street
  Song of the swallows
Roe, Eileen. *Con mi hermano—With my brother*
Serfozo, Mary. *Welcome Roberto! Bienvenido, Roberto!*
Taha, Karen T. *A gift for Tia Rose*

Ethnic groups in the U.S. – Puerto Rican-Americans

Belpré, Pura. *Santiago*
Blue, Rose. *I am here: Yo estoy aqui*
Bowden, Joan Chase. *Emilio's summer day*
Keats, Ezra Jack. *My dog is lost!*
Kesselman, Wendy. *Angelita*
Simon, Norma. *What do I do?*
  What do I say?
Sonneborn, Ruth A. *Friday night is papa night*
  Lollipop's party
  Seven in a bed

Ethnic groups in the U.S. – Vietnamese-Americans

Breckler, Rosemary K. *Hoang breaks the lucky teapot*
Surat, Michele Maria. *Angel child, dragon child*

Etiquette

Ackley, Edith Flack. *Please*
  Thank you
Alden, Laura. *Saying I'm sorry*

Aliki. *Manners*
Anastasio, Dina. *Pass the peas, please*
Behrens, June. *The manners book*
Berenstain, Stan. *The Berenstain bears forget their manners*
Betz, Betty. *Manners for moppets*
Brown, Marc Tolon. *Perfect pigs*
Brown, Myra Berry. *Company's coming for dinner*
Charles, Donald. *Shaggy dog's birthday*
Cole, Joanna. *Monster manners*
Demuth, Patricia Brennan. *Max, the bad-talking parrot*
Duvoisin, Roger Antoine. *Periwinkle*
Edwards, Lisa. *Disney's Beauty and the beast, a book of manners*
Gardner, Martin. *Never make fun of a turtle, my son*
Gordon, Margaret. *Wilberforce goes to a party*
Hawkins, Colin. *Max and the magic word*
Himmelman, John. *A guest is a guest*
Hoban, Russell. *Dinner at Alberta's*
  The little Brute family
Jefferds, Vincent. *Disney's elegant book of manners*
Joslin, Sesyle. *Dear dragon*
  What do you do, dear?
  What do you say, dear?
Kandoian, Ellen. *Is anybody up?*
Keenan, Martha. *The mannerly adventures of Little Mouse*
Keller, Irene. *The Thingumajig book of manners*
Keller, John G. *Krispin's fair*
Leaf, Munro. *A flock of watchbirds*
  How to behave and why
  Manners can be fun
Lexau, Joan M. *Cathy is company*
Miller, Virginia. *On your potty!*
Myller, Lois. *No! No!*
Parish, Peggy. *Mind your manners*
Paxton, Tom. *Engelbert the elephant*
Petersham, Maud. *The circus baby*
Polhamus, Jean Burt. *Dinosaur do's and don'ts*
Potter, Beatrix. *The sly old cat*
Quackenbush, Robert M. *I don't want to go, I don't know how to act*
Ross, Anna. *Say the magic word, please*
Scarry, Richard. *Richard Scarry's please and thank you book*
Seignobosc, Françoise. *The thank-you book*
Sherman, Ivan. *I do not like it when my friend comes to visit*
Slobodkin, Louis. *Thank you—you're welcome*
Smaridge, Norah. *You know better than that*
Smith, Barry. *A child's guide to bad behavior*
Stover, Jo Ann. *If everybody did*
Weiss, Ellen. *Telephone time*

Europe *see* Foreign lands – Europe

Evening *see* Twilight

Experiments *see* Science

Eye glasses *see* Glasses

Eyes *see* Anatomy – eyes; Handicaps – blindness; Senses – seeing

Fables *see* Folk and fairy tales

Faces *see* Anatomy – faces

Fairies

Anderson, Lonzo. *Two hundred rabbits*
Barker, Cicely Mary. *Berry flower fairies*
  Blossom flower fairies
  Flower fairies of the garden
  Flower fairies of the seasons
  Flower fairies of the spring
  Flower fairies of the summer
  Flower fairies of the trees
  Flower fairies postcard book
  Spring flower fairies
  Summer flower fairies
Bate, Lucy. *Little rabbit's loose tooth*
Beim, Lorraine. *Sasha and the samovar*
Boujon, Claude. *The fairy with the long nose*
Butterworth, Nick. *Amanda's butterfly*
Christiana, David. *White nineteens*
Coombs, Patricia. *Lisa and the grompet*
Elves, fairies and gnomes, ill. by Rosekrans Hoffman
Fairy poems for the very young, ill. by Beverlie Manson
Forest, Heather. *The woman who flummoxed the fairies*
Fyleman, Rose. *A fairy went a-marketing*
Gardner, Mercedes. *Scooter and the magic star*
Griffith, Helen V. *Nata*
Gunther, Louise. *A tooth for the tooth fairy*
Heller, Nicholas. *The tooth tree*
Hoffmann, E. T. A. *The nutcracker*, ill. by Rachel Isadora
  The nutcracker, ill. by Maurice Sendak
Hollyn, Lynn. *Lynn Hollyn's Christmas toyland*
Jeschke, Susan. *Mia, Grandma and the genie*
Karlin, Nurit. *The tooth witch*
Kaye, Marilyn. *The real tooth fairy*
Kent, Jack. *Clotilda*

Kroll, Steven. *Loose tooth*
Lagerlöf, Selma. *The changeling*
Lester, Helen. *The wizard, the fairy and the magic chicken*
MacDonald, George. *Little Daylight*
MacDonald, Maryann. *Rosie's baby tooth*
Mahy, Margaret. *Pillycock's shop*
Manson, Beverlie. *The fairies' alphabet book*
Mayne, William. *The green book of Hob stories*
The red book of Hob stories
The yellow book of Hob stories
Myers, Bernice. *Sidney Rella and the glass sneaker*
Nesbit, Edith. *Melisande*
Newbolt, Henry John, Sir. *Rilloby-rill*
Ross, Tony. *A fairy tale*
Silverman, Maida. *The magic well*
Turnbull, Ann. *The tapestry cats*
Waddell, Martin. *The tough princess*
Wallace, Daisy. *Fairy poems*
Wells, Rosemary. *Fritz and the mess fairy*
Wetterer, Margaret. *Patrick and the fairy thief*

Fairs

Amery, H. *Going to the fair*
Baker, Jill. *Basil of Bywater Hollow*
Barker, Melvern J. *Country fair*
Baynton, Martin. *Fifty and the great race*
Bond, Michael. *Paddington at the fair*
Booth, Eugene. *At the fair*
Bourke, Linda. *Ethel's exceptional egg*
Brunhoff, Laurent de. *Babar's fair will be opened next Sunday*
Carrick, Carol. *The highest balloon on the common*
Chiefari, Janet. *Kids are baby goats*
Delton, Judy. *Penny wise, fun foolish*
Devlin, Wende. *Old Witch and the polka-dot ribbon*
Dorros, Arthur. *Tonight is carnaval*
Ernst, Lisa Campbell. *Miss Penny and Mr. Grubbs*
Ets, Marie Hall. *Mr. Penny's race horse*
Gauch, Patricia Lee. *On to Widecombe Fair*
Hedderwick, Mairi. *Katie Morag and the two grandmothers*
Herriot, James. *Bonny's big day*
Hill, Eric. *Spot at the fair*
Hoff, Syd. *Henrietta goes to the fair*
Holabird, Katharine. *Angelina at the fair*
Leech, Jay. *Bright Fawn and me*
Miles, Miska. *Jump frog jump*
Schatell, Brian. *Farmer Goff and his turkey Sam*
Seignobosc, Françoise. *Jeanne-Marie at the fair*
Stevens, Janet. *Animal fair*
Tudor, Tasha. *Corgiville fair*
Watson, Clyde. *Tom Fox and the apple pie*

Watson, Nancy Dingman. *The birthday goat*
Widdecombe Fair, ill. by Christine Price
Wildsmith, Brian. *Carousel*

Fairy tales *see* Folk and fairy tales

Fall *see* Seasons – fall

Families *see* Family life

Family life

Abercrombie, Barbara. *Charlie Anderson*
Ackerman, Karen. *I know a place*
Just like Max
Adoff, Arnold. *Big sister tells me that I'm black*
Black is brown is tan
In for winter, out for spring
Ma nDa La
Make a circle, keep us in
Ahlberg, Janet. *The baby's catalogue*
Peek-a-boo!
Aitken, Amy. *Wanda's circus*
Alexander, Martha G. *Even that moose won't listen to me*
I'll be the horse if you'll play with me
Marty McGee's space lab, no girls allowed
Alexander, Sue. *Dear Phoebe*
Nadia the willful
Aliki. *Christmas tree memories*
Jack and Jake
June 7!
Keep your mouth closed, dear
Welcome, little baby
Allen, Laura Jean. *Ottie and the star*
Allen, Thomas B. *On grandaddy's farm*
Amoss, Berthe. *Tom in the middle*
Anderson, C. W. (Clarence Williams). *Billy and Blaze*
Anderson, Douglas. *Let's draw a story*
Anderson, Lonzo. *The day the hurricane happened*
Anholt, Catherine. *Good days, bad days*
When I was a baby
Arbeit, Eleanor Werner. *Mrs. Cat hides something*
Arkin, Alan. *Tony's hard work day*
Armitage, Ronda. *The bossing of Josie*
Don't forget, Matilda
One moonlit night
Arnstein, Helene S. *Billy and our new baby*
Arthur, Catherine. *My sister's silent world*
Asbjørnsen, P. C. (Peter Christian). *The man who kept house*
Asch, Frank. *Goodbye house*
Asher, Sandy. *Princess Bee and the royal good-night story*
Aulaire, Ingri Mortenson d'. *Children of the northlights*
Nils
Ayer, Jacqueline. *A wish for little sister*

Aylesworth, Jim. *The bad dream*
 Siren in the night
Babbitt, Lorraine. *Pink like the geranium*
Bach, Alice. *Millicent the magnificent*
 The smartest bear and his brother Oliver
Baird, Anne. *Kiss, kiss*
Baisch, Cris. *When the lights went out*
Baker, Betty. *Sonny-Boy Sim*
Baker, Charlotte. *Little brother*
Balet, Jan B. *The fence*
 Five Rollatinis
Ballard, Robin. *Granny and me*
Balzola, Asun. *Munia and the day things
 went wrong*
Banish, Roslyn. *A forever family*
 I want to tell you about my baby
 Let me tell you about my baby
Banks, Kate. *Alphabet soup*
Barbato, Juli. *From bed to bus*
Barbour, Karen. *Little Nino's pizzeria*
 Mr. Bow Tie
Barrett, Joyce Durham. *Willie's not the
 hugging kind*
Bartoli, Jennifer. *Nonna*
Bascom, Joe. *Malcolm's job*
Battles, Edith. *One to teeter-totter*
Bawden, Nina. *Princess Alice*
Beatty, Hetty Burlingame. *Moorland pony*
Beckman, Kaj. *Lisa cannot sleep*
Beim, Jerrold. *Jay's big job*
Beim, Lorraine. *Lucky Pierre*
Bemelmans, Ludwig. *Quito express*
 Sunshine
Benjamin, Alan. *A change of plans*
Bennett, Olivia. *A Turkish afternoon*
Benson, Ellen. *Philip's little sister*
Benton, Robert. *Little brother, no more*
Berenstain, Michael. *The dwarks*
Berenstain, Stan. *The Berenstain bears and
 the truth*
 The Berenstain bears and too much TV
 The Berenstain bears' Christmas tree
 The Berenstain bears forget their manners
 The Berenstain bears in the dark
 The Berenstain bears learn about strangers
 The Berenstain bears' moving day
Berger, Terry. *How does it feel when your
 parents get divorced?*
Bernheim, Marc. *In Africa*
Berridge, Celia. *At my house*
Bianchi, John. *Swine snafu*
Bible, Charles. *Jennifer's new chair*
Birdseye, Tom. *Waiting for baby*
Bishop, Claire Huchet. *The five Chinese
 brothers*
Blaine, Marge (Margery Kay). *The terrible
 thing that happened at our house*
Blake, Jon. *Wriggly Pig*
Blaustein, Muriel. *Bedtime, Zachary!*
Bloom, Suzanne. *A family for Jamie*
Blue, Rose. *How many blocks is the world?*

Blume, Judy. *The one in the middle is a
 green kangaroo*
 The Pain and The Great One
Boegehold, Betty. *Daddy doesn't live here
 anymore*
Bograd, Larry. *Felix in the attic*
Boholm-Olsson, Eva. *Tuan*
Bolliger, Max. *The fireflies*
 The golden apple
Bolognese, Don. *A new day*
Bond, Felicia. *Poinsettia and her family*
Bond, Michael. *Paddington bear*
 Paddington's garden
Bonsall, Crosby Newell. *The day I had to
 play with my sister*
Boon, Emilie. *Belinda's balloon*
Bornstein, Ruth Lercher. *Of course a goat*
Bos, Burny. *Ollie the elephant*
Bourgeois, Paulette. *Big Sarah's little boots*
Boyd, Lizi. *Sam is my half brother*
Bradman, Tony. *Through my window*
 Wait and see
Brady, Susan. *Find my blanket*
Brandenberg, Franz. *Everyone ready?*
 A fun weekend
 What's wrong with a van?
Brann, Esther. *A book for baby*
Breckler, Rosemary K. *Hoang breaks the
 lucky teapot*
Brennan, Jan. *Born two-gether*
Brenner, Barbara A. *The prince and the
 pink blanket*
Bright, Robert. *Georgie*
Brisson, Pat. *Your best friend, Kate*
Brock, Emma Lillian. *Mr. Wren's house*
 A pet for Barbie
Brooks, Robert B. *So that's how I was born*
Brothers, Aileen. *Sad Mrs. Sam Sack*
Brothers and sisters are like that!
Brown, Jeff. *Flat Stanley*
Brown, Marc Tolon. *Arthur's baby*
Brown, Myra Berry. *Pip camps out*
Brown, Tricia. *Hello, amigos!*
Browne, Anthony. *Changes*
Bruna, Dick. *Miffy*
Buchanan, Heather S. *Emily Mouse saves
 the day*
Buck, Pearl S. (Pearl Sydenstricker). *The
 little fox in the middle*
Bunin, Catherine. *Is that your sister?*
Bunting, Eve (Anne Evelyn). *The big red
 barn*
 Ghost's hour, spook's hour
 Night tree
 The Wednesday surprise
Burch, Robert. *The hunting trip*
 Joey's cat
Burningham, John. *Avocado baby*
 Where's Julius?
Burns, Maurice. *Go ducks, go!*
Burstein, Fred. *Rebecca's nap*

Butler, Dorothy. *Another happy tale*
Byars, Betsy Cromer. *Go and hush the baby*
Byers, Rinda M. *Mycca's baby*
Byrd, Robert. *Marcella was bored*
Byrne, David. *Stay up late*
Caines, Jeannette. *Abby*
  Chilly stomach
  I need a lunch box
Cairo, Shelley. *Our brother has Down's
  syndrome*
Calders, Pere. *Brush*
Cameron, Polly. *"I can't," said the ant*
Campbell, Wayne. *What a catastrophe!*
Caple, Kathy. *The purse*
Carlson, Nancy. *The perfect family*
  Take time to relax
Carlstrom, Nancy White. *Baby-O*
  Heather hiding
  Jesse Bear, what will you wear?
Carmi, Giora. *And Shira imagined*
Carson, Jo. *You hold me and I'll hold you*
Caseley, Judith. *Silly baby*
Castiglia, Julie. *Jill the pill*
Cazet, Denys. *Sunday*
Chaffin, Lillie D. *Tommy's big problem*
Chalmers, Mary. *Mr. Cat's wonderful
  surprise*
  Take a nap, Harry
Charlip, Remy. *Hooray for me!*
Chase, Catherine. *Pete, the wet pet*
Chevalier, Christa. *The little bear who forgot*
Chislett, Gail. *Whump*
Chocolate, Deborah M. Newton. *Kwanzaa*
Chorao, Kay. *Lester's overnight*
Christenson, Larry. *The wonderful way that
  babies are made*
Christiansen, C. B. *My mother's house, my
  father's house*
Clark, Ann Nolan. *In my mother's house*
Claverie, Jean. *Shopping*
Cleary, Beverly. *The growing-up feet*
  Janet's thingamajigs
Clifton, Lucille. *Amifika*
  Don't you remember?
  Everett Anderson's goodbye
  Everett Anderson's nine months long
  Everett Anderson's 1-2-3
  My brother fine with me
  Some of the days of Everett Anderson
Cole, Barbara Hancock. *Texas star*
Cole, Joanna. *How you were born*
  The new baby at your house
Cole, William. *Frances face-maker*
  That pest Jonathan
Collins, Pat Lowery. *Taking care of Tucker*
Conford, Ellen. *Why can't I be William?*
Conta, Marcia Maher. *Feelings between
  brothers and sisters*
  Feelings between kids and parents
Cook, Bernadine. *Looking for Susie*

Coombs, Patricia. *Lisa and the grompet*
Cooney, Barbara. *Hattie and the wild waves*
  Island boy
Corey, Dorothy. *Will there be a lap for me?*
Cornish, Sam. *Grandmother's pictures*
Coxe, Molly. *Whose footprints?*
Craig, M. Jean. *The dragon in the clock box*
Credle, Ellis. *Down, down the mountain*
Cressey, James. *Fourteen rats and a rat-
  catcher*
Crompton, Margaret. *The house where Jack
  lives*
Crowley, Arthur. *The boogey man*
Curry, Jane Louise. *Little, little sister*
Curry, Nancy. *The littlest house*
Curti, Anna. *At home*
Cuyler, Margery. *Shadow's baby*
Dahl, Tessa. *Babies, babies, babies*
  The same but different
Daniel, Doris Temple. *Pauline and the
  peacock*
Davis, Maggie S. *Something magic*
De Angeli, Marguerite. *Yonie Wondernose*
Delton, Judy. *Brimhall comes to stay*
  It happened on Thursday
Denison, Carol. *A part-time dog for Nick*
Dennis, Lynne. *Raymond Rabbit's early
  morning*
Denton, Kady MacDonald. *The picnic*
De Paola, Tomie (Thomas Anthony). *The
  art lesson*
  The family Christmas tree book
  Katie, Kit and cousin Tom
  Too many Hopkins
De Regniers, Beatrice Schenk. *The giant
  story*
  A little house of your own
Dickens, Lucy. *At the beach*
  Our day
  Outside
  Playtime
Dooley, Norah. *Everybody cooks rice*
Dowling, Paul. *Meg and Jack are moving*
Dragonwagon, Crescent. *Diana, maybe*
  Home place
  Rainy day together
Drescher, Joan. *I'm in charge!*
  The marvelous mess
  Your family, my family
Duke, Kate. *Bedtime*
  Clean-up day
  The playground
  What bounces?
Dunbar, Joyce. *Why is the sky up?*
Dupasquier, Philippe. *I can't sleep*
Edwards, Frank B. *Mortimer Mooner
  stopped taking a bath*
Edwards, Michelle. *Alef-bet*
Ehrlich, Amy. *Bunnies at Christmastime*
  Bunnies on their own
  Zeek Silver Moon

Elzbieta. *Brave Babette and sly Tom*
  Dikou and the mysterious moon sheep
Engel, Diana. *Gino Badino*
  Josephina hates her name
Escudie, René. *Paul and Sebastian*
Ets, Marie Hall. *Bad boy, good boy*
Factor, Jane. *Summer*
Fassler, Joan. *One little girl*
Felt, Sue. *Rosa-too-little*
Fenton, Edward. *Fierce John*
Fiday, Beverly. *Time to go*
Fisher, Aileen Lucia. *In one door and out
  the other*
Flack, Marjorie. *Wait for William*
Fleisher, Robbin. *Quilts in the attic*
Florian, Douglas. *A summer day*
Flournoy, Valerie. *The best time of day*
Foreman, Michael. *Ben's baby*
Fox, Charles Philip. *Mr. Stripes the gopher*
Fraser, Kathleen. *Adam's world, San
  Francisco*
Freudberg, Judy. *Susan and Gordon adopt a
  baby*
Friedman, Ina R. *How my parents learned to
  eat*
Galbraith, Kathryn Osebold. *Katie did!
  Waiting for Jennifer*
Galdone, Paul. *Obedient Jack*
Ganly, Helen. *Jyoti's journey*
Garland, Michael. *My cousin Katie*
Garland, Sarah. *Going shopping
  Having a picnic*
Gauch, Patricia Lee. *Christina Katerina and
  the time she quit the family*
Gay, Marie-Louise. *Rainy day magic*
Gewing, Lisa. *Mama, daddy, baby and me*
Giffard, Hannah. *Red Fox on the move*
Gill, Joan. *Hush, Jon!*
Girard, Linda Walvoord. *Adoption is for
  always
  At Daddy's on Saturdays*
Glass, Andrew. *Chickpea and the talking cow*
Gliori, Debi. *New big house
  New big sister*
Gobhai, Mehlli. *Usha, the mouse-maiden*
Goffstein, M. B. (Marilyn Brooke). *Family
  scrapbook
  Our prairie home
  Our snowman*
Goldman, Susan. *Cousins are special*
Goudey, Alice E. *The day we saw the sun
  come up*
Gould, Deborah. *Camping in the Temple of
  the Sun*
Graham, Bob. *First there was Frances
  Greetings from Sandy Beach
  The wild*
Graham, Richard. *Jack and the monster*
Graham, Thomas. *Mr. Bear's chair*

Gray, Catherine. *Tammy and the gigantic
  fish*
Gray, Genevieve. *Send Wendell*
Gray, Nigel. *A country far away
  It'll all come out in the wash
  Little pig's tale*
Greaves, Margaret. *Little Bear and the
  Papagini circus*
Greenfield, Eloise. *I make music
  Me and Nessie*
Griffith, Helen V. *Mine will, said John*
Hague, Kathleen. *The man who kept house*
Hale, Kathleen. *Orlando and the water cats*
Hale, Lucretia. *The lady who put salt in her
  coffee*
Hall, Derek. *Elephant bathes
  Gorilla builds
  Polar bear leaps*
Hamilton-Merritt, Jane. *Our new baby*
Hamm, Diane Johnston. *How many feet in
  the bed?*
Harper, Anita. *It's not fair!*
Harris, Robie H. *Don't forget to come back
  Hot Henry
  Messy Jessie*
Harvey, Brett. *Immigrant girl*
Haskins, Francine. *I remember "one hundred
  twenty-one"*
Hautzig, Esther (Rudomin). *At home*
Havill, Juanita. *Treasure nap*
Hayes, Sarah. *Happy Christmas, Gemma*
Hazelton, Elizabeth Baldwin. *Sammy, the
  crow who remembered*
Hazen, Barbara Shook. *Even if I did
  something awful
  Tight times*
Heath, Amy. *Sofie's role*
Hedderwick, Mairi. *Katie Morag and the big
  boy cousins
  P. D. Pebbles' summer or winter book*
Heller, Linda. *Lily at the table*
Heller, Nicholas. *The monster in the cave*
Helmering, Doris Wild. *We're going to have
  a baby*
Hendershot, Judith. *In coal country*
Hendrickson, Karen. *Baby and I can play
  Fun with toddlers*
Hendry, Diana. *Not anywhere house*
Henkes, Kevin. *Bailey goes camping
  Julius, the baby of the world
  Shhhh*
Hennessy, B. G. *A, B, C, D, tummy, toes,
  hands, knee*
Hess, Edith. *Peter and Susie find a family*
Hessell, Jenny. *Staying at Sam's*
Hest, Amy. *The purple coat
  The ring and the window seat*
Hickman, Martha Whitmore. *When can
  daddy come home?*
Hill, Elizabeth Starr. *Evan's corner*
Hill, Eric. *At home*

Spot goes to the beach
Hill, Susan. *Go away, bad dreams!*
Himmelman, John. *The great leaf blast-off*
Hines, Anna Grossnickle. *Big like me*
 Daddy makes the best spaghetti
 Moon's wish
 The secret keeper
 They really like me!
Hirsh, Marilyn. *The pink suit*
Hoban, Julia. *Amy loves the rain*
 Amy loves the snow
 Amy loves the sun
Hoban, Lillian. *Arthur's prize reader*
 Mr. Pig and family
Hoban, Russell. *A baby sister for Frances*
 Harvey's hideout
 They came from Aargh!
Hoberman, Mary Ann. *Fathers, mothers, sisters, brothers*
Hobson, Laura Z. *"I'm going to have a baby!"*
Hoffman, Phyllis. *Steffie and me*
Hoffman, Rosekrans. *Sister Sweet Ella*
Hoffmann, E. T. A. *The strange child*
Hofstrand, Mary. *By the sea*
Hoke, Helen L. *The biggest family in the town*
Hol, Coby. *Tippy Bear and little Sam*
Holabird, Katharine. *Alexander and the magic boat*
Holland, Viki. *We are having a baby*
Hooker, Ruth. *At Grandma and Grandpa's house*
 Sara loves her big brother
Hoopes, Lyn Littlefield. *Daddy's coming home*
 Mommy, daddy, me
Hopkins, Margaret. *Sleepytime for baby mouse*
Horton, Barbara Savadge. *What comes in spring?*
Horvath, Betty F. *Be nice to Josephine*
Houston, Gloria. *The year of the perfect Christmas tree*
Hughes, Shirley. *Angel Mae*
 Bathwater's hot
 David and dog
 Dogger
 An evening at Alfie's
 Lucy and Tom's A.B.C.
 Lucy and Tom's Christmas
 Lucy and Tom's 1, 2, 3
 Moving Molly
 Noisy
 Out and about
 When we went to the park
Hunt, Nan. *Families are funny*
Hurd, Edith Thacher. *The mother kangaroo*
Hutchins, H. J. (Hazel J.). *Katie's babbling brother*
Hutchins, Hazel J. *Norman's snowball*

Hutchins, Pat. *The doorbell rang*
 Tidy Titch
 Titch
 You'll soon grow into them, Titch
Ichikawa, Satomi. *Suzanne and Nicholas at the market*
 Suzanne and Nicholas in the garden, St. Martin's 1978
Imoto, Yoko. *Skipper at the beach*
 Skipper is the daddy
Isadora, Rachel. *At the crossroads*
 I hear
 I see
Iwasaki, Chihiro. *Staying home alone on a rainy day*
Jack Sprat. *The life of Jack Sprat, his wife and his cat,* ill. by Paul Galdone
Jarrell, Mary. *The knee baby*
Johnson, Angela. *The leaving morning*
Johnston, Deborah. *Mathew Michael's beastly day*
Johnston, Tony. *I'm gonna tell mama I want an iguana*
 The quilt story
Jones, Penelope. *I'm not moving!*
Joosse, Barbara M. *Jam day*
Jordan, June. *Kimako's story*
Joyce, William. *A day with Wilbur Robinson*
 George shrinks
Kaufman, Curt. *Hotel boy*
Keats, Ezra Jack. *Apartment 3*
 Louie's search
 Peter's chair
Keller, Holly. *A bear for Christmas*
 Cromwell's glasses
 Geraldine's blanket
Kelley, Anne. *Daisy's discovery*
Kellogg, Steven (Stephen). *Can I keep him?*
Kent, Jack. *Joey runs away*
Kerr, Judith. *Mog and bunny*
Kessler, Leonard P. *Are we lost, daddy?*
Khalsa, Dayal Kaur. *I want a dog*
 My family vacation
Killingback, Julia. *Monday is washing day*
 What time is it, Mrs. Bear?
Kilroy, Sally. *What a week!*
Kimmelman, Leslie. *Frannie's fruits*
Kingman, Lee. *Catch the baby!*
Kiser, SuAnn. *The birthday thing*
Koch, Dorothy Clarke. *I play at the beach*
Koehler, Phoebe. *The day we met you*
Komoda, Beverly. *The too hot day*
Konigsburg, E. L. (Elaine Lobl). *Samuel Todd's book of great inventions*
Koscielniak, Bruce. *Hector and Prudence*
Krasilovsky, Phyllis. *The very little boy*
 The very little girl
 The very tall little girl
Kraus, Robert. *Another mouse to feed*
 Big brother
 Phil the ventriloquist
Krauss, Ruth. *The backward day*

Mosley, Francis. *The dinosaur eggs*
Motyka, Sally Mitchell. *An ordinary day*
Munsch, Robert N. *I have to go!*
Murphy, Jill. *All in one piece*
  Five minutes' peace
Myller, Lois. *No! No!*
Naylor, Phyllis Reynolds. *The baby, the bed, and the rose*
Nelson, Vaunda Micheaux. *Always Gramma*
Ness, Evaline. *Exactly alike*
Neville, Emily Cheney. *The bridge*
Nikola-Lisa, W. *One, two, three Thanksgiving!*
Nilsson, Ulf. *Little sister rabbit*
Nixon, Joan Lowery. *You bet your britches, Claude*
Noble, June. *Two homes for Lynn*
Nolan, Madeena Spray. *My daddy don't go to work*
Nones, Eric Jon. *Wendell*
O'Donnell, Elizabeth Lee. *Maggie doesn't want to move*
O'Kelley, Mattie Lou. *Circus!*
Olsen, Ib Spang. *The grown-up trap*
Oppenheim, Joanne. *Rooter remembers*
Oram, Hiawyn. *Reckless Ruby*
Ormerod, Jan. *Moonlight*
Osofsky, Audrey. *Dreamcatcher*
Oxenbury, Helen. *Beach day*
  Family
  Our dog
Paterson, Diane. *Wretched Rachel*
Pearce, Philippa. *Emily's own elephant*
Pearson, Susan. *Karin's Christmas walk*
  Saturday, I ran away
Pedersen, Judy. *Out in the country*
Pellegrini, Nina. *Families are different*
Pellowski, Anne. *Stairstep farm*
Pinkney, Gloria Jean. *Back home*
Pinkwater, Daniel Manus. *Wempires*
Politi, Leo. *Little Leo*
Polushkin, Maria. *Baby brother blues*
Pomerantz, Charlotte. *The mango tooth*
  Posy
Porte, Barbara Ann. *Harry's mom*
Portnoy, Mindy Avra. *Mommy never went to Hebrew school*
Poulin, Stéphane. *My mother's loves: stories and lies from my childhood*
  Travels for two
Prater, John. *Along came Tom*
Price, Mathew. *Peekaboo!*
Provensen, Alice. *An owl and three pussycats*
Prusski, Jeffrey. *Bring back the deer*
Purdy, Carol. *Iva Dunnit and the big wind*
  Least of all
Quackenbush, Robert M. *I don't want to go, I don't know how to act*
  Mouse feathers
Quindlen, Anna. *The tree that came to stay*
Raffi. *One light, one sun*

Raphael, Elaine. *Turnabout*
Raskin, Ellen. *Ghost in a four-room apartment*
Ray, Deborah Kogan. *Sunday morning we went to the zoo*
Rayner, Mary. *Mrs. Pig gets cross and other stories*
Redies, Rainer. *The cats' party*
Rees, Mary. *Ten in a bed*
Reiser, Lynn. *Any kind of dog*
Remkiewicz, Frank. *Greedyanna*
Rice, Eve. *City night*
  Ebbie
  Papa's lemonade and other stories
Rider, Alex. *Chez nous. At our house*
Rigby, Shirley Lincoln. *Smaller than most*
Riggio, Anita. *Wake up, William!*
Rippon, Penelope. *My day*
Robb, Brian. *My grandmother's djinn*
Roche, P. K. (Patrick K.). *Good-bye, Arnold!*
Rockwell, Anne F. *Blackout*
  In our house
Roffey, Maureen. *Bathtime*
  Family scramble
  Here, kitty kitty!
  Meatime
  Quick, catch Dan!
Rogers, Fred. *Moving*
Rogers, Paul (Patrick). *Lily's picnic*
  Somebody's awake
  Somebody's sleepy
Rosenberg, Maxine B. *Being adopted*
Ross, Katharine. *When you were a baby*
Roy, Ronald. *Breakfast with my father*
Ruffins, Reynold. *My brother never feeds the cat*
Russo, Marisabina. *The line up book*
  Why do grownups have all the fun?
Ryder, Joanne. *Beach party*
Rylant, Cynthia. *Birthday presents*
  Henry and Mudge in the sparkle days
  The relatives came
  When I was young in the mountains
Samuels, Vyanne. *Carry go bring come*
Sarnoff, Jane. *That's not fair*
Say, Allen. *A river dream*
Schermbrucker, Reviva. *Charlie's house*
Schermer, Judith. *Mouse in house*
Schertle, Alice. *That's what I thought*
Schick, Eleanor. *Peggy's new brother*
  A piano for Julie
Schlein, Miriam. *Billy, the littlest one*
  Laurie's new brother
  My family
  My house
Schuchman, Joan. *Two places to sleep*
Schumacher, Claire. *Brave Lily*
Schweninger, Ann. *Valentine friends*
Scott, Ann Herbert. *On mother's lap*
  Sam
Segal, Lore. *Tell me a Mitzi*

Valentine foxes

Watson, Jane Werner. *Sometimes a family has to move*

Sometimes a family has to split up

Watson, Pauline. *Days with Daddy*

Watson, Wendy. *Hurray for the Fourth of July*

Thanksgiving at our house

Watts, Bernadette. *David's waiting day*

Wegen, Ron. *The balloon trip*

Weil, Lisl. *Gertie and Gus*

Weiss, Nicki. *Barney is big*

Sun sand sea sail

Weekend at Muskrat Lake

Wells, Rosemary. *Shy Charles*

West, Keith. *Little Pig's special day*

Westcott, Nadine Bernard. *Getting up*

Going to bed

Peanut butter and jelly

Wickstrom, Sylvie (Sylvie Kantrovitz). *Mothers can't get sick*

Wild, Jocelyn. *Florence and Eric take the cake*

Wilhelm, Hans. *A new home, a new friend*

Williams, Barbara. *Donna Jean's disaster*

If he's my brother

So what if I'm a sore loser?

Williams, Karen Lynn. *When Africa was home*

Williams, Marcia. *Not a worry in the world*

Williams, Sherley Anne. *Working cotton*

Williams, Vera B. *A chair for my mother*

"More more more," said the baby

Music, music for everyone

Something special for me

Wilson, Sarah. *Muskrat, muskrat, eat your peas!*

Winn, Chris. *My day*

Winthrop, Elizabeth. *Bunk beds*

I think he likes me

Wohl, Lauren L. *Matzoh mouse*

Wolde, Gunilla. *Betsy and Peter are different*

Betsy and the vacuum cleaner

Betsy's fixing day

This is Betsy

Wolff, Ashley. *Only the cat saw*

Wood, Audrey. *Elbert's bad word*

Weird parents

Yaffe, Alan. *The magic meatballs*

Yamashita, Haruo. *Mice at the beach*

Yardley, Joanna. *The red ball*

Young, Evelyn. *Wu and Lu and Li*

Zalben, Jane Breskin. *Beni's first Chanukah*

Happy Passover, Rosie

Leo and Blossom's Sukkah

Zemach, Kaethe. *The funny dream*

Zemach, Margot. *To Hilda for helping*

Ziefert, Harriet. *Before I was born*

Good night, Jessie!

I want to sleep in your bed!

Keeping daddy awake on the way home from the beach

My sister says nothing ever happens when we go sailing

A new coat for Anna

Strike four!

Zimelman, Nathan. *If I were strong enough...*

Zinnemann-Hope, Pam. *Let's play ball, Ned*

Zolotow, Charlotte (Shapiro). *Big sister and little sister*

Do you know what I'll do?

If it weren't for you

It's not fair

May I visit?

My grandson Lew

The quiet mother and the noisy little boy

A rose, a bridge, and a wild black horse

The sky was blue

Someone new

The summer night

When I have a son

William's doll

Zusman, Evelyn. *The Passover parrot*

Family life – aunts, uncles

Abolafia, Yossi. *My three uncles*

Alexander, Sally Hobart. *Maggie's whopper*

Allan, Nicholas. *The thing that ate Aunt Julia*

Bettina (Bettina Ehrlich). *Of uncles and aunts*

Blaustein, Muriel. *Baby Mabu and Auntie Moose*

Brandenberg, Franz. *Aunt Nina and her nephews and nieces*

Aunt Nina, good night

Aunt Nina's visit

Brecht, Bertolt. *Uncle Eddie's moustache*

Brisson, Pat. *Magic carpet*

Brock, Emma Lillian. *A present for Auntie*

Bryant, Sara Cone. *Epaminondas and his auntie*

Carson, Jo. *Pulling my leg*

Cazet, Denys. *Great-Uncle Felix*

Clark, Emma Chichester. *Lunch with Aunt Augusta*

Cole, Babette. *The trouble with Uncle*

Cole, William. *Aunt Bella's umbrella*

Degen, Bruce. *Aunt Possum and the pumpkin man*

Delton, Judy. *My Uncle Nikos*

Denslow, Sharon Phillips. *Riding with Aunt Lucy*

De Paola, Tomie (Thomas Anthony). *Bonjour, Mister Satie*

Devlin, Wende. *Aunt Agatha, there's a lion under the couch!*

Duke, Kate. *Aunt Isabel tells a good one*

Edwards, Michelle. *A baker's portrait*

Edwards, Patricia Kier. *Chester and Uncle Willoughby*

Ernst, Lisa Campbell. *The rescue of Aunt Pansy*

Everett, Gwen. *Li'l Sis and Uncle Willie*

Froissart, Bénédicte. *Uncle Henry's dinner guests*

Gantos, Jack (John, Jr.). *Aunt Bernice*

Go tell Aunt Rhody. *Go tell Aunt Rhody*, ill. by Aliki

Go tell Aunt Rhody, ill. by Robert M. Quackenbush

Green, Phyllis. *Uncle Roland, the perfect guest*

Greenblat, Rodney A. *Aunt Ippy's museum of junk*

Uncle Wizzmo's new used car

Helldorfer, M. C. (Mary Claire). *Sailing to the sea*

Hindley, Judy. *Uncle Harold and the green hat*

Hoff, Syd. *My Aunt Rosie*

Houston, Gloria. *My Great-Aunt Arizona*

Howard, Elizabeth Fitzgerald. *Aunt Flossie's hats (and crab cakes later)*

Jewell, Nancy. *Time for Uncle Joe*

Levoy, Myron. *The Hanukkah of Great-Uncle Otto*

Lewis, Robin Baird. *Aunt Armadillo*

Lobel, Arnold. *Uncle Elephant*

Loof, Jan. *Uncle Louie's fantastic sea voyage*

MacDonald, Elizabeth. *My aunt and the animals*

Mahy, Margaret. *The horrendous hullabaloo*

Martin, Jacqueline Briggs. *Bizzy Bones and Uncle Ezra*

Merriam, Eve. *Epaminondas*

Newton, Laura P. *Me and my aunts*

Parker, Nancy Winslow. *Love from Aunt Betty*

Love from Uncle Clyde

Paterson, Diane. *Smile for auntie*

Pinkwater, Daniel Manus. *Aunt Lulu*

Rubel, Nicole. *Uncle Henry and Aunt Henrietta's honeymoon*

Schwartz, Amy. *Her Majesty, Aunt Essie*

Selway, Martina. *Don't forget to write*

Thomas, Ianthe. *Lordy, Aunt Hattie*

Thomson, Pat. *Beware of the aunts!*

Thorne, Jenny. *My uncle*

Tripp, Wallace. *My Uncle Podger*

Weller, Frances Ward. *The closet gorilla*

Wyse, Lois. *Two guppies, a turtle and Aunt Edna*

Family life – brothers

Afanas'ev, Aleksandr N. *Salt*

Baumann, Hans. *Mischa and his brothers*

Berenstain, Stan. *The Berenstain bears: No girls allowed*

Bogart, Jo Ellen. *Daniel's dog*

Buckley, Helen Elizabeth. *"Take care of things," Edward said*

Caple, Kathy. *The coolest place in town*

Chall, Marsha Wilson. *Mattie*

Church, Kristine. *My brother John*

Clarke, Gus. *Along came Eric*

Collins, Pat Lowery. *Waiting for baby Joe*

Croll, Carolyn. *The three brothers*

Cummings, Pat. *Jimmy Lee did it*

Degen, Bruce. *Teddy bear towers*

Dubois, Claude K. *Looking for Ginny*

Fallwell, Cathryn. *Nicky and Alex*

Franklin, Jonathan. *Don't wake the baby*

Freedman, Florence B. *Brothers*

Gerstein, Mordicai. *The gigantic baby*

Hains, Harriet. *My baby brother*

Havill, Juanita. *Jamaica Tag-Along*

Magic fort

Holcomb, Nan. *Patrick and Emma Lou*

Impey, Rose. *Joe's café*

Johnson, Angela. *Do like Kyla*

Johnston, Tony. *Slither McCreep and his brother, Joe*

Keller, Holly. *What Alvin wanted*

Kroll, Virginia L. *Helen the fish*

Le Guin, Ursula K. *A ride on the red mare's back*

Lester, Alison. *The journey home*

Levine, Arthur. *All the lights in the night*

Livingston, Myra Cohn. *Poems for brothers, poems for sisters*

Magorian, Michelle. *Who's going to take care of me?*

Manushkin, Fran. *Be brave, baby rabbit*

Oppenheim, Joanne. *Left and right*

Pelham, David. *Sam's sandwich*

Reader, Dennis. *Butterfingers*

Robins, Joan. *My brother, Will*

Roche, P. K. (Patrick K.). *Webster and Arnold go camping*

Roe, Eileen. *Con mi hermano—With my brother*

Rosenberg, Maxine B. *Brothers and sisters*

San Souci, Robert D. *The enchanted tapestry*

Schertle, Alice. *Witch Hazel*

Schnitter, Jane. *William is my brother*

Stevenson, James. *That's exactly the way it wasn't*

Titherington, Jeanne. *A place for Ben*

Walsh, Ellen Stoll. *Two too much*

Weisner, David. *Hurricane*

Wells, Rosemary. *Max's dragon shirt*

Williams, Susan. *Poppy's first year*

Wishinsky, Frieda. *Oonga boonga*

Woodruff, Elvira. *Mrs. McCloskey's monkeys*

Tubtime

Yorinks, Arthur. *Oh, brother*

Ugh

Zalben, Jane Breskin. *Buster gets braces*

Family life – cousins

Caseley, Judith. *Cousins*
Wagner, Jenny. *Amy's monster*

Family life – fathers

Aksakov, Sergei. *The scarlet flower*
Alda, Arlene. *Matthew and his dad*
Alexander, Anne (Anna Barbara Cooke).
  My daddy and I
Asch, Frank. *Goodnight horsey*
  Just like daddy
Ayres, Pam. *When dad cuts down the
  chestnut tree*
  When dad fills in the garden pond
Bailey, Debbie. *My dad*
Baker, Betty. *My sister says*
Barbato, Juli. *Mom's night out*
Barrett, Judi. *I'm too small, you're too big*
Baum, Louis. *One more time*
Baynton, Martin. *Why do you love me?*
Beim, Jerrold. *With dad alone*
Bergström, Gunilla. *Who's scaring Alfie
  Atkins?*
Blake, Robert J. *The perfect spot*
Blaustein, Muriel. *Play ball, Zachary!*
Bradman, Tony. *Not like this, like that*
Brooks, Ben. *Lemonade parade*
Browne, Anthony. *Gorilla*
Buckley, Helen Elizabeth. *Someday with my
  father*
Bunting, Eve (Anne Evelyn). *Fly away
  home*
  A perfect Father's Day
Burgess, Gelett. *The little father*
Burstein, Fred. *Anna's rain*
Butterworth, Nick. *My dad is awesome*
Caines, Jeannette. *Daddy*
Carlstrom, Nancy White. *Goodbye geese*
Cazet, Denys. *I'm not sleepy*
Claverie, Jean. *Working*
Clifton, Lucille. *Amifika*
Cole, Babette. *The trouble with dad*
Cole, Sheila. *When the rain stops*
Croll, Carolyn. *The three brothers*
Day, Alexandra. *River parade*
Diot, Alain. *Better, best, bestest*
Dupasquier, Philippe. *Dear Daddy...*
Fallwell, Cathryn. *Nicky loves daddy*
Fassler, Joan. *All alone with daddy*
Gay, Michel. *Night ride*
Gray, Nigel. *A balloon for grandad*
Greenberg, Melanie Hope. *My father's
  luncheonette*
Greenfield, Eloise. *Daddy and I*
  First pink light
Grindley, Sally. *Knock, knock! Who's there?*
Haseley, Dennis. *Kite flier*
Hendershot, Judith. *In coal country*
Hillert, Margaret. *The little cowboy and the
  big cowboy*

Hines, Anna Grossnickle. *Daddy makes the
  best spaghetti*
Hooks, William H. *Moss gown*
Horenstein, Henry. *Sam goes trucking*
Horowitz, Ruth. *Bat time*
Hort, Lenny. *How many stars in the sky*
Impey, Rose. *My mom and our dad*
Jam, Teddy. *Night cars*
Kauffman, Lois. *What's that noise?*
Kessler, Leonard P. *Are we lost, daddy?*
Ketteman, Helen. *Not yet, Yvette*
Kidd, Nina. *June Mountain secret*
Kilroy, Sally. *Market day*
Kroll, Steven. *Happy Father's Day*
Lanton, Sandy. *Daddy's chair*
Lauture, Denize. *Father and son*
Lenski, Lois. *Papa Small*
Lewin, Hugh. *Jafta's father*
Lexau, Joan M. *Every day a dragon*
  Me day
Lindenbaum, Pija. *Else-Marie and her seven
  little daddies*
Livingston, Myra Cohn. *Poems for fathers*
Long, Earlene. *Gone fishing*
Lubell, Winifred. *Here comes daddy*
McAfee, Annalena. *The visitors who came to
  stay*
McKinley, Robin. *My father is in the Navy*
McPhail, David. *Ed and me*
  The party
Madenski, Melissa. *Some of the pieces*
Mangas, Brian. *A nice surprise for Father
  Rabbit*
Marzollo, Jean. *Amy goes fishing*
  Close your eyes
Mayer, Mercer. *Just me and my dad*
Minarik, Else Holmelund. *Father Bear
  comes home*
Monjo, F. N. *The one bad thing about father*
Morgan, Allen. *Nicole's boat*
Munsch, Robert N. *Something good*
Myers, Bernice. *The gold watch*
Nolan, Madeena Spray. *My daddy don't go
  to work*
Ormerod, Jan. *Dad's back*
  Messy baby
  Reading
  Sleeping
Otey, Mimi. *Daddy has a pair of striped
  shorts*
Paris, Lena. *Mom is single*
Parker, Kristy. *My dad the magnificent*
Pettigrew, Eileen. *Night-time*
Polacco, Patricia. *Some birthday!*
Porte, Barbara Ann. *Harry's dog*
  Harry's mom
Porter-Gaylord, Laurel. *I love my daddy
  because...*
Puner, Helen Walker. *Daddys, what they do
  all day*
Quinlan, Patricia. *My dad takes care of me*

Rabe, Berniece. *Where's Chimpy?*
Radlauer, Ruth Shaw. *Molly at the library*
Ringi, Kjell (Arne Sorensen). *My father and I*
Roberts, Bethany. *Waiting-for-Papa stories*
Sachar, Louis. *Monkey soup*
Sandberg, Inger. *Come on out, Daddy!*
Schwartz, Amy. *Bea and Mr. Jones*
Shalev, Meir. *My father always embarrasses me*
Shannon, George. *Dancing the breeze*
Shepard, Steve. *Elvis Hornbill, international business bird*
Simmonds, Posy. *Lulu and the flying babies*
Simon, Norma. *The daddy days*
  I wish I had my father
Slater, Teddy. *Jan and Dan and the super dads*
Smee, Nicola. *Finish the story, dad*
Sonneborn, Ruth A. *Friday night is papa night*
Spohn, David. *Winter wood*
Stecher, Miriam B. *Daddy and Ben together*
Steel, Danielle. *Max's daddy goes to the hospital*
Steiner, Charlotte. *Daddy comes home*
Steptoe, John. *Daddy is a monster...sometimes*
Stevens, Bryna. *Handel and the famous sword swallower of Halle*
Stevenson, Suçie. *Jessica the blue streak*
Stewart, Robert S. *The daddy book*
Stock, Catherine. *Christmas time*
Thomas, Ianthe. *Willie blows a mean horn*
Thompson, Richard. *I have to see this*
Townson, Hazel. *What on earth...?*
Tyler, Linda Wagner. *When daddy comes home*
Udry, Janice May. *What Mary Jo shared*
Van Woerkom, Dorothy. *Something to crow about*
Vigna, Judith. *Daddy's new baby*
  I wish my daddy didn't drink so much
  Saying goodbye to daddy
Waddell, Martin. *Can't you sleep, Little Bear?*
  Let's go home, Little Bear
Watanabe, Shigeo. *Daddy, play with me!*
  I can take a bath!
  Let's go swimming
  Where's my daddy?
Watson, Pauline. *Days with Daddy*
Willhoite, Michael. *Daddy's roomate*
Wood, Jakki. *Dads are such fun*
Worley, Daryl. *Billy and the attic adventure*
Yolen, Jane. *All those secrets of the world*
  The emperor and the kite
  The emperor and the kite [Rev. ed.]
  Owl moon
Zagwyn, Deborah Turney. *Pumpkin blanket*
Ziefert, Harriet. *When daddy had the chicken pox*

Zimelman, Nathan. *Treed by a pride of irate lions*
Zola, Meguido. *Only the best*
Zolotow, Charlotte (Shapiro). *The summer night*

Family life – grandfathers

Ackerman, Karen. *Song and dance man*
Adler, David A. *A little at a time*
Alexander, Martha G. *Where does the sky end, Grandpa?*
Aliki. *The two of them*
Anderson, Lena Castell. *Stina*
  Stina's visit
Andrews, Jan. *The auction*
Barrett, Judi. *Cloudy with a chance of meatballs*
Behrens, June. *Soo Ling finds a way*
Blos, Joan W. *The grandpa days*
Bond, Ruskin. *Cherry tree*
Borack, Barbara. *Grandpa*
Brooks, Ron. *Timothy and Gramps*
Brown, Kathryn. *Muledred*
Buckley, Helen Elizabeth. *Grandfather and I*
Bunting, Eve (Anne Evelyn). *The happy funeral*
  Magic and the night river
Burningham, John. *Grandpa*
Carlstrom, Nancy White. *Grandpappy*
Caseley, Judith. *Dear Annie*
  When Grandpa came to stay
Cazet, Denys. *December 24th*
Coatsworth, Elizabeth. *Lonely Maria*
DeFelice, Cynthia C. *When Grampa kissed his elbow*
De Paola, Tomie (Thomas Anthony). *Now one foot, now the other*
Dionetti, Michelle. *Coal mine peaches*
Douglas, Barbara. *Good as new!*
Douglass, Barbara. *Good as new*
Dumas, Philippe. *Laura loses her head*
Fallwell, Cathryn. *Nicky and grandpa*
Fassler, Joan. *My grandpa died today*
Flora, James. *Grandpa's farm*
  Grandpa's ghost stories
Foreman, Michael. *Jack's fantastic voyage*
Fox, Mem. *Shoes from grandpa*
Garaway, Margaret Kahn. *Ashkii and his grandfather*
George, William T. *Fishing at Long Pond*
Gerstein, Mordicai. *The new creatures*
Gray, Nigel. *A balloon for grandad*
Greenfield, Eloise. *Grandpa's face*
Griffith, Helen V. *Georgia music*
  Grandaddy's place
Guthrie, Donna. *Grandpa doesn't know it's me*
Harranth, Wolf. *My old grandad*
Hartley, Deborah. *Up north in the winter*
Hayes, Geoffrey. *Patrick and his grandpa*

Hazen, Barbara Shook. *Why did Grandpa die?*

Henkes, Kevin. *Grandpa and Bo*

Hest, Amy. *The crack-of-dawn walkers*
The purple coat

Hilton, Nette. *The long red scarf*

Hines, Anna Grossnickle. *Remember the butterflies*

Hines, Gary. *A ride in the crummy*

Houghton, Eric. *The backwards watch*

Hughes, Shirley. *When we went to the park*

Hutchins, Pat. *Happy birthday, Sam*

Isadora, Rachel. *Jesse and Abe*

Jacobs, Joseph. *Tattercoats*, ill. by Margot Tomes

Johnson, Angela. *When I am old with you*

Johnston, Tony. *Grandpa's song*

Kirk, Barbara. *Grandpa, me and our house in the tree*

Knox-Wagner, Elaine. *My grandpa retired today*

Langner, Nola. *Freddy my grandfather*

Lapp, Eleanor. *In the morning mist*

Lasky, Kathryn. *I have four names for my grandfather*

Locker, Thomas. *The mare on the hill*
Where the river begins

Lyon, George-Ella. *Basket*

McCully, Emily Arnold. *The Christmas gift*

McDonald, Megan. *The great pumpkin switch*
The potato man

Mahood, Kenneth. *Why are there more questions than answers, Grandad?*

Marron, Carol A. *No trouble for Grandpa*

Martin, Bill (William Ivan). *Knots on a counting rope*

Mayer, Mercer. *Little Monster at work*

Michaels, William. *Clare and her shadow*

Nikola-Lisa, W. *Night is coming*

Nomura, Takaaki. *Grandpa's town*

Oram, Hiawyn. *A boy wants a dinosaur*

Otto, Carolyn. *That sky, that rain*

Paterson, Diane. *Hey, cowboy!*

Pearson, Susan. *Happy birthday, Grampie*

Peavy, Linda. *Allison's grandfather*

Pomerantz, Charlotte. *Buffy and Albert Timothy Tall Feather*

Radin, Ruth Yaffe. *High in the mountains*

Reddix, Valerie. *Dragon kite of the autumn moon*

Rice, Eve. *Aren't you coming too?*

Rigby, Shirley Lincoln. *Smaller than most*

Rodgers, Frank. *Who's afraid of the ghost train?*

Roth, Susan L. *We'll ride elephants through Brooklyn*

Salter, Heidi. *Taddy McFinley and the great grey grimly*

Sandberg, Inger. *Dusty wants to help*

Scheller, Melanie. *My grandfather's hat*

Schlein, Miriam. *Go with the sun*

Schwartz, David M. *Sugargrandpa*

Selway, Martina. *Don't forget to write*

Shulevitz, Uri. *Dawn*

Stevens, Margaret (Dean). *When grandpa died*

Stevenson, James. *Brr!*
"Could be worse!"
Grandpa's great city tour
Grandpa's too-good garden
The great big especially beautiful Easter egg
No friends
That dreadful day
That terrible Halloween night
That's exactly the way it wasn't
There's nothing to do!
We can't sleep
What's under my bed?
Will you please feed our cat?
Worse than Willy!

Stilz, Carol Curtis. *Kirsty's kite*

Stock, Catherine. *Emma's dragon hunt*
Thanksgiving treat

Stolz, Mary Slattery. *Storm in the night*

Titherington, Jeanne. *Where are you going, Emma?*

Tompert, Ann. *Grandfather Tang's story*

Townsend, Maryann. *Pop's secret*

Wahl, Jan. *The fishermen*

Wahl, Mats. *Grandfather's laika*

Wallace, Ian. *Chin Chiang and the dragon's dance*

Walsh, Jill Paton. *Lost and found*

Ward, Sally G. *Molly and Grandpa*
Punky goes fishing

Ziefert, Harriet. *Happy birthday, Grandpa!*

Zolotow, Charlotte (Shapiro). *My grandson Lew*

Family life – grandmothers

Addy, Sharon Hart. *A visit with great-grandma*

Alexander, Martha G. *The story grandmother told*

Allen, Linda. *Mr. Simkin's grandma*

Allred, Mary. *Grandmother Poppy and the children's tea party*
Grandmother Poppy and the funny-looking bird

Ambrus, Victor G. *Grandma, Felix, and Mustapha Biscuit*

Anholt, Catherine. *Tom's rainbow walk*

Baker, Jeannie. *Grandmother*

Balian, Lorna. *Humbug rabbit*

Ballard, Robin. *Granny and me*

Barker, Peggy. *What happened when grandma died*

Bartoli, Jennifer. *Nonna*

Base, Graeme. *My grandma lived in Gooligulch*

Berenstain, Stan. *The Berenstain bears and the week at grandma's*

Berridge, Celia. *Grandmother's tales*

Bible, Charles. *Jennifer's new chair*

Borden, Louise. *The watching game*

Bowles, Brad. *Grandma's band*

Brandenberg, Franz. *A secret for grandmother's birthday*

Bryan, Ashley. *Turtle knows your name*

Buckley, Helen Elizabeth. *Grandmother and I*

Bunting, Eve (Anne Evelyn). *The Wednesday surprise*

Caines, Jeannette. *Window wishing*

Calmenson, Stephanie. *Zip, whiz, zoom!*

Carlstrom, Nancy White. *The moon came too*

Caseley, Judith. *Apple pie and onions*

Cazzola, Gus. *The bells of Santa Lucia*

Cech, John. *My grandmother's journey*

Chorao, Kay. *Lemon moon*

Cole, Babette. *The trouble with Gran*

Corbalis, Judy. *The cuckoo bird*

Cornish, Sam. *Grandmother's pictures*

Coutant, Helen. *First snow*

Daly, Niki. *Not so fast Songololo*

DeJong, David Cornel. *Looking for Alexander*

Delton, Judy. *My grandma's in a nursing home*

Denton, Kady MacDonald. *Granny is a darling*

De Paola, Tomie (Thomas Anthony). *Haircuts for the Woolseys*
Nana upstairs and Nana downstairs

Dorros, Arthur. *Abuela*

Drucker, Malka. *Grandma's latkes*

Ehrlich, Amy. *Bunnies and their grandma*

Eisenberg, Phyllis Rose. *A mitzvah is something special*

Fernandes, Kim. *Visiting granny*

Finfer, Celentha. *Grandmother dear*

Flournoy, Valerie. *The patchwork quilt*

Gackenbach, Dick. *With love from Gran*

Goffstein, M. B. (Marilyn Brooke). *Fish for supper*

Goldman, Susan. *Grandma is somebody special*

Gomi, Taro. *Coco can't wait!*

Goodman, Louise. *Ida's doll*

Gordon, Shirley. *Grandma zoo*

Hamm, Diane Johnston. *Grandma drives a motor bed*

Hautzig, Deborah. *Get well, Granny Bird*

Hayashi, Akiko. *Aki and the fox*

Hayes, Sarah. *Happy Christmas, Gemma*

Hedderwick, Mairi. *Katie Morag and the big boy cousins*
Katie Morag and the two grandmothers
Katie Morag delivers the mail

Hennessy, B. G. *When you were just a little girl*

Henriod, Lorraine. *Grandma's wheelchair*

Hest, Amy. *The midnight eaters*

Hines, Anna Grossnickle. *Come to the meadow*
Grandma gets grumpy

Hiser, Berniece T. *The adventure of Charlie and his wheat-straw hat*

Hogan, Bernice. *My grandmother died but I won't forget her*

Hoopes, Lyn Littlefield. *Nana*

Ichikawa, Satomi. *Nora's stars*

Isadora, Rachel. *Over the green hills*

James, Betsy. *The dream stair*

Jarrell, Mary. *The knee baby*

Jeschke, Susan. *Mia, Grandma and the genie*

Kahn, Rosemary. *Grandma's hat*

Karkowsky, Nancy. *Grandma's soup*

Kay, Helen. *A stocking for a kitten*

Keller, Holly. *The best present*

Ketner, Mary Grace. *Ganzy remembers*

Khalsa, Dayal Kaur. *Tales of a gambling grandma*

Kibbey, Marsha. *My grammy*

Kimmelman, Leslie. *Me and Nana*

Kojima, Naomi. *The flying grandmother*

Kovalski, Maryann. *The wheels on the bus*

Kraus, Robert. *Rebecca Hatpin*

Kroll, Steven. *If I could be my grandmother*

Kunhardt, Edith. *Danny's mystery Valentine*

Lasky, Kathryn. *My island grandma*

Lenski, Lois. *Debbie and her grandma*

Le Tord, Bijou. *My Grandma Leonie*

Levine, Evan. *Not the piano, Mrs. Medley!*

Levinson, Riki. *I go with my family to Grandma's*
Watch the stars come out

Lexau, Joan M. *Benjie*
Benjie on his own

Linden, Ann Marie. *One smiling grandma*

Lindgren, Astrid. *The ghost of Skinny Jack*

Lloyd, David. *Duck*
Grandma and the pirate
The stopwatch

Low, Alice. *David's windows*

Luenn, Nancy. *Nessa's fish*

McCully, Emily Arnold. *The grandma mix-up*

McQueen, John Troy. *A world full of monsters*

Maguire, Gregory. *Lucas Fishbone*

Martin, C. L. G. *Three brave women*

Mason, Ann Maree. *The weird things in Nanna's house*

Moore, Elaine. *Grandma's house*
Grandma's promise

Morris, Winifred. *Just listen*

Mower, Nancy. *I visit my Tūtū and Grandma*

Neasi, Barbara J. *Listen to me*

Nelson, Vaunda Micheaux. *Always Gramma*

O'Callahan, Jay. *Tulips*
Olson, Arielle North. *Hurry home, Grandma!*
Orbach, Ruth. *Please send a panda*
Palmisciano, Diane. *Garden partners*
Parish, Peggy. *Granny and the desperadoes*
Granny and the Indians
Granny, the baby and the big gray thing
Passen, Lisa. *Grammy and Sammy*
Peterson, Jeanne Whitehouse. *Sometimes I dream horses*
Polacco, Patricia. *Chicken Sunday*
Thunder cake
Roberts, Sarah. *I want to go home!*
Robertson, Joanne. *Sea witches*
Rockwell, Anne F. *When I go visiting*
Roe, Eileen. *Staying with Grandma*
Rogers, Paul (Patrick). *From me to you*
Root, Phyllis. *Gretchen's grandma*
Roth, Susan L. *Patchwork tales*
Sakai, Kimiko. *Sachiko means happiness*
Scheffler, Ursel. *A walk in the rain*
Schwartz, Amy. *Oma and Bobo*
Scott, Ann Herbert. *Grandmother's chair*
Shecter, Ben. *Grandma remembers*
Sheldon, Dyan. *The whales' song*
Silverman, Erica. *On Grandma's roof*
Smith, Maggie (Margaret C.). *My grandma's chair*
Sonneborn, Ruth A. *I love Gram*
Stanovich, Betty Jo. *Big boy, little boy*
Steiner, Charlotte. *Kiki and Muffy*
Storr, Catherine (Cole). *Hugo and his grandma*
Thomas, Jane Resh. *Saying good-bye to grandma*
Udry, Janice May. *Mary Jo's grandmother*
Vigna, Judith. *Everyone goes as a pumpkin*
Grandma without me
Waddell, Martin. *Amy said*
Ward, Sally G. *Charlie and Grandma*
What goes around comes around
Waterton, Betty. *Pettranella*
Whitlock, Susan Love. *Donovan scares the monsters*
Wilhelm, Hans. *A cool kid—like me!*
Willard, Nancy. *The mountains of quilt*
Williams, Barbara. *Kevin's grandma*
Williams, Vera B. *Music, music for everyone*
Wilson, Beth P. *Jenny*
Wolf, Janet. *The best present is me*
Wood, Audrey. *The napping house*
Wood, Joyce. *Grandmother Lucy goes on a picnic*
Grandmother Lucy in her garden
Wright, Betty Ren. *The cat next door*
Yolen, Jane. *No bath tonight*
Zelinsky, Paul O. *The wheels on the bus*
Ziefert, Harriet. *With love from Grandma*
Zolotow, Charlotte (Shapiro). *William's doll*

Family life – grandparents

Allen, Linda. *Mr. Simkin's grandma*
Bate, Lucy. *How Georgina drove the car very carefully from Boston to New York*
Bonners, Susan. *The wooden doll*
Bunting, Eve (Anne Evelyn). *Winter's coming*
Caseley, Judith. *Grandpa's garden lunch*
Cazet, Denys. *Big shoe, little shoe*
Saturday
Child, Lydia Maria. *Over the river and through the wood*
Copeland, Helen. *Meet Miki Takino*
Curtis, Gavin. *Grandma's baseball*
De Paola, Tomie (Thomas Anthony). *Pajamas for Kit*
Eisenberg, Phyllis Rose. *A mitzvah is something special*
Farber, Norma. *How does it feel to be old?*
Feldman, Barbara. *Stephens' frog*
Flory, Jane. *The unexpected grandchild*
Gantschev, Ivan. *The train to Grandma's*
Gould, Deborah. *Grandpa's slide show*
Greve, Andreas. *Christopher's dream car*
Hamm, Diane Johnston. *Grandma drives a motor bed*
Hawes, Judy. *Fireflies in the night*
Haywood, Carolyn. *Hello, star*
Heller, Linda. *The castle on Hester Street*
Hest, Amy. *The go-between*
Hooker, Ruth. *At Grandma and Grandpa's house*
Hurd, Edith Thacher. *I dance in my red pajamas*
Joosse, Barbara M. *Jam day*
Kilroy, Sally. *Grandpa's garden*
Kitamura, Satoshi. *Captain Toby*
Kroll, Steven. *Toot! Toot!*
Maris, Ron. *Is anyone home?*
Minarik, Else Holmelund. *Little Bear's visit*
Morgan, Michaela. *Visitors for Edward*
Newman, Shirlee. *Tell me, grandma; tell me, grandpa*
Oechsli, Helen. *Fly away!*
Oppenheim, Joanne. *Waiting for Noah*
Oxenbury, Helen. *Grandma and Grandpa*
Porte, Barbara Ann. *Harry's mom*
Raynor, Dorka. *Grandparents around the world*
Rice, Eve. *At Grammy's house*
Rockwell, Anne F. *When I go visiting*
Rosen, Winifred. *Henrietta and the gong from Hong Kong*
Sandberg, Inger. *Dusty wants to borrow everything*
Scheffler, Ursel. *A walk in the rain*
Skofield, James. *Snow country*
Stevenson, James. *Higher on the door*
July
Van Haeringen, Annemarie. *The cats' tale*
Waddell, Martin. *Grandma's Bill*

Watanabe, Shigeo. *It's my birthday*
Ziefert, Harriet. *Chocolate mud cake*

Family life – great-grandparents

Bornstein, Ruth Lercher. *A beautiful seashell*
Budd, Lillian. *The people on Long Ago Street*
Herter, Jonina. *Eighty-eight kisses*
Ketner, Mary Grace. *Ganzy remembers*
Knotts, Howard. *Great-grandfather, the baby and me*
MacLachlan, Patricia. *Three names*
Russo, Marisabina. *A visit to Oma*
Waddell, Martin. *My great grandpa*
Whittington, Mary K. *Carmina, come dance!*

Family life – mothers

Ackerman, Karen. *When mama retires*
Alda, Arlene. *Sonya's mommy works*
Anderson, Lena Castell. *Bunny box*
Asch, Frank. *Bread and honey*
Bailey, Debbie. *My mom*
Baker, Gayle. *Special delivery*
Bauer, Caroline Feller. *My mom travels a lot*
Baum, Louis. *After dark*
Berry, Christine. *Mama went walking*
Blaine, Marge (Margery Kay). *The terrible thing that happened at our house*
Brillhart, Julie. *Story hour—starring Megan!*
Browne, Anthony. *Piggybook*
Carton, Lonnie Caming. *Mommies*
Cole, Babette. *The trouble with mom*
Delton, Judy. *The best mom in the world*
My mom made me go to school
My mother lost her job today
Dionetti, Michelle. *The day Eli went looking for bear*
Drescher, Joan. *My mother's getting married*
Eastman, P. D. (Philip D.). *Are you my mother?*
Eisenberg, Phyllis Rose. *You're my Nikki*
Elizabeth Winthrop. *A very noisy girl*
English, Jennifer. *My mommy's special*
Fallwell, Cathryn. *Nicky's walk*
Fassler, Joan. *The man of the house*
Feldman, Barbara. *Going, going*
Fine, Anne. *Poor Monty*
Fisher, Aileen Lucia. *Do bears have mothers too?*
My mother and I
Flack, Marjorie. *Ask Mr. Bear*
Fox, Mem. *Koala Lou*
Gackenbach, Dick. *Alice's special room*
Hurray for Hattie Rabbit!
Galbraith, Kathryn Osebold. *Laura Charlotte*
Goode, Diane. *Where's our mama?*
Hamm, Diane Johnston. *Laney's lost momma*
Hawkins, Colin. *Where's my mommy?*
Hazen, Barbara Shook. *Mommy's office*

Hest, Amy. *The mommy exchange*
Hines, Anna Grossnickle. *It's just me, Emily*
Maybe a band-aid will help
Hurd, Edith Thacher. *The mother chimpanzee*
Impey, Rose. *My mom and our dad*
Jenkins, Jordan. *Learning about love*
Jennings, Michael. *The bears who came to breakfix*
Johnson, Angela. *Tell me a story, mama*
Johnson, Dolores. *What will mommy do when I'm at school?*
Jonas, Ann. *Two bear cubs*
Joosse, Barbara M. *Dinah's mad, bad wishes*
Mama, do you love me?
Kanao, Keiko. *Kitten up a tree*
Kandoian, Ellen. *Maybe she forgot*
Kasza, Keiko. *A mother for Choco*
Keller, Beverly. *When mother got the flu*
Keller, Holly. *When Francie was sick*
Kent, Jack. *Joey*
Ketteman, Helen. *Not yet, Yvette*
Kilroy, Sally. *On the road*
Krauss, Ruth. *The bundle book*
Lasker, Joe. *Mothers can do anything*
Levine, Abby. *What did mommy do before you?*
Lewin, Hugh. *Jafta's mother*
Lexau, Joan M. *A house so big*
Lindgren, Barbro. *The wild baby*
The wild baby goes to sea
MacLachlan, Patricia. *Mama one, Mama two*
Maley, Anne. *Have you seen my mother?*
Martin, C. L. G. *Three brave women*
Marton, Jirina. *I'll do it myself*
Mayer, Mercer. *Just for you*
Merriam, Eve. *Mommies at work*
Miles, Miska. *Mouse six and the happy birthday*
Miranda, Anne. *Baby-sit*
Mitchell, Joyce Slayton. *My mommy makes money*
Mizumura, Kazue. *If I were a mother*
Morris, Ann. *Cuddle up*
Moss, Marissa. *Who was it?*
Ormerod, Jan. *Bend and stretch*
Making friends
Mom's home
This little nose
Oxenbury, Helen. *Mother's helper*
Paris, Lena. *Mom is single*
Patz, Nancy. *No thumpin' no bumpin' no rumpus tonight!*
Polushkin, Maria. *Mother, Mother, I want another*
Pomerantz, Charlotte. *The chalk doll*
Porte, Barbara Ann. *Harry's mom*
Porter-Gaylord, Laurel. *I love my mommy because...*
Portnoy, Mindy Avra. *Ima on the Bima: my mommy is a Rabbi*

Power, Barbara. *I wish Laura's mommy was my mommy*

Pulver, Robin. *Nobody's mother is in second grade*

Quinlan, Patricia. *Anna's red sled*
My dad takes care of me

Radlauer, Ruth Shaw. *Breakfast by Molly*

Ray, Deborah Kogan. *Stargazing sky*

Reimold, Mary Gallagher. *My mom is a runner*

Reuter, Margaret. *My mother is blind*

Reyher, Becky. *My mother is the most beautiful woman in the world*

Rice, Eve. *New blue shoes*

Rockwell, Anne F. *Willy can count*

Rose, Deborah Lee. *Meredith's mother takes the train*

Russo, Marisabina. *Waiting for Hannah*

Sawicki, Norma Jean. *Something for mom*

Say, Allen. *Tree of cranes*

Scott, Ann Herbert. *On mother's lap*

Sharmat, Marjorie Weinman. *My mother never listens to me*

Shipton, Jonathan. *Busy! Busy! Busy!*

Silverman, Maida. *The magic well*

Skurzynski, Gloria. *Martin by himself*

Smalls-Hector, Irene. *Jonathan and his mommy*

Sondheimer, Ilse. *The boy who could make his mother stop yelling*

Standon, Anna. *Little duck lost*

Stanek, Muriel. *All alone after school*

Stehr, Frédéric. *Quack-quack*

Stilz, Carol Curtis. *Kirsty's kite*

Stock, Catherine. *Easter surprise*

Thaler, Mike. *Owley*

Titherington, Jeanne. *Big world, small world*

Tompert, Ann. *Little Otter remembers and other stories*

Turner, Ann Warren. *Stars for Sarah*

Tyler, Linda Wagner. *Waiting for mom*

Udry, Janice May. *Is Susan here?*
Thump and Plunk

Ungerer, Tomi. *No kiss for mother*

Valens, Amy. *Jesse's day care*

Vigna, Judith. *Couldn't we have a turtle instead?*
Mommy and me by ourselves again

Viorst, Judith. *My mama says there aren't any zombies, ghosts, vampires, creatures, demons, monsters, fiends, goblins, or things*

Waber, Bernard. *Lyle finds his mother*

Warren, Cathy. *Saturday belongs to Sara*

Watson, Nancy Dingman. *Tommy's mommy's fish*

Weiss, Nicki. *On a hot, hot day*

Wells, Rosemary. *Hazel's amazing mother*

Wetterer, Margaret. *Patrick and the fairy thief*

Wickstrom, Sylvie (Sylvie Kantrovitz). *Mothers can't get sick*

Willard, Nancy. *The high rise glorious skittle skat roarious sky pie angel food cake*

Williams, Suzannne. *Mommy doesn't know my name*

Wynot, Jillian. *The Mother's Day sandwich*

Ziefert, Harriet. *Sarah's questions*
Surprise!

Zindel, Paul. *I love my mother*

Zinnemann-Hope, Pam. *Time for bed, Ned*

Zolotow, Charlotte (Shapiro). *I like to be little*
Mr. Rabbit and the lovely present
Say it!
The seashore book
Some things go together
This quiet lady

Family life – only child

Bertrand, Cecile. *Mr. and Mrs. Smith have only one child, but what a child!*

Conford, Ellen. *Why can't I be William?*

Dragonwagon, Crescent. *Rainy day together*

Hallinan, P. K. (Patrick K.). *I'm glad to be me*
Just being alone

Hamberger, John. *Hazel was an only pet*

Hazen, Barbara Shook. *Tight times*
Why couldn't I be an only kid like you, Wigger?

Iwasaki, Chihiro. *Staying home alone on a rainy day*

Schick, Eleanor. *City in the winter*

Sharmat, Marjorie Weinman. *I want mama*

Shyer, Marlene Fanta. *Here I am, an only child*

Skorpen, Liesel Moak. *All the Lassies*

Smith, Wendy. *The lonely, only mouse*

Family life – sisters

Ackerman, Karen. *Moveable Mabeline*

Adoff, Arnold. *Hard to be six*

Adorjan, Carol. *I can! Can you?*

Anholt, Catherine. *Aren't you lucky!*

Berenstain, Stan. *The Berenstain bears: No girls allowed*

Bogart, Jo Ellen. *Daniel's dog*

Brown, Marc Tolon. *Arthur meets the president*

Bullock, Kathleen. *A surprise for Mitzi Mouse*

Caple, Kathy. *The coolest place in town*

Carlstrom, Nancy White. *Kiss your sister, Rose Marie*

Caseley, Judith. *My sister Celia*

Chall, Marsha Wilson. *Mattie*

Church, Kristine. *My brother John*

Collins, Pat Lowery. *Waiting for baby Joe*

Curry, Jane Louise. *Little, little sister*

Delaney, Molly. *My sister*
Dubois, Claude K. *Looking for Ginny*
Eversole, Robyn Harbert. *The magic house*
Franklin, Jonathan. *Don't wake the baby*
Galbraith, Kathryn Osebold. *Roommates*
Garland, Sarah. *Billy and Belle*
Gerstein, Mordicai. *The gigantic baby*
Glaser, Linda. *Keep your socks on, Albert!*
Goodman, Louise. *Ida's doll*
Hains, Harriet. *My baby brother*
Hamilton, Morse. *Little sister for sale*
Havill, Juanita. *Jamaica Tag-Along*
Henkes, Kevin. *Sheila Rae, the brave*
Hines, Anna Grossnickle. *Jackie's lunch box*
Holabird, Katharine. *Angelina's baby sister*
Holcomb, Nan. *Patrick and Emma Lou*
Howard, Elizabeth Fitzgerald. *The train to Lulu's*
Impey, Rose. *Joe's café*
Johnson, Angela. *Do like Kyla*
  One of three
Kalman, Maira. *Hey Willy, see the pyramids!*
Keller, Holly. *What Alvin wanted*
Le Guin, Ursula K. *A ride on the red mare's back*
Lester, Alison. *The journey home*
Little, Jean. *Jess was the brave one*
Livingston, Myra Cohn. *Poems for brothers, poems for sisters*
Magorian, Michelle. *Who's going to take care of me?*
Manushkin, Fran. *Be brave, baby rabbit*
Martin, Rafe. *The rough-face girl*
Mills, Claudia. *A visit to Amy-Claire*
Noll, Sally. *That bothered Kate*
Pelham, David. *Sam's sandwich*
Porazińska, Janina. *The enchanted book*
Prall, Jo. *My sister's special*
Price, Mathew. *Have you seen my sister?*
Pryor, Bonnie. *Amanda and April*
  Merry Christmas, Amanda and April
Reader, Dennis. *Butterfingers*
Rosenberg, Maxine B. *Brothers and sisters*
Sage, Chris. *That's mine, that's yours*
Samuels, Barbara. *Duncan and Dolores*
  What's so great about Cindy Snappleby?
Walsh, Ellen Stoll. *Two too much*
Weisner, David. *Hurricane*
Weiss, Nicki. *A family story*
  Princess Pearl
Wells, Rosemary. *Max's dragon shirt*
Wilhelm, Hans. *Let's be friends again!*
Williams, Susan. *Poppy's first year*
Wishinsky, Frieda. *Oonga boonga*
Woodruff, Elvira. *Tubtime*
Zalben, Jane Breskin. *Buster gets braces*

Family life – step families

Boyd, Lizi. *The not-so-wicked stepmother*
  Sam is my half brother
French, Fiona. *Snow White in New York*

Helmering, Doris Wild. *I have two families*
Lewis, Naomi. *The stepsister*
Seuling, Barbara. *What kind of family is this?*
Steel, Danielle. *Martha's new daddy*
Zakhoder, Boris Vladimirovich. *The good stepmother*

Family life - stepchildren *see* Divorce; Family life – step families

Family life - stepparents *see* Divorce; Family life – step families

Farmers *see* Careers – farmers

Farms

Adams, Pam. *This old man*
Alborough, Jez. *The grass is always greener*
Allen, Pamela. *Fancy that!*
Allen, Thomas B. *On grandaddy's farm*
Amery, H. *The farm picture book*
Andrews, Jan. *The auction*
Anholt, Catherine. *Chaos at Cold Custard Farm*
Arnosky, Jim. *Raccoons and ripe corn*
At the farm, ill. by Roser Capdevila
Augarde, Steve (Stephen). *Pig*
Aulaire, Ingri Mortenson d'. *Wings for Per*
Aylesworth, Jim. *One crow*
Azarian, Mary. *A farmer's alphabet*
Baker, Betty. *Partners*
Balian, Lorna. *A garden for a groundhog*
Balzano, Jeanne. *The wee moose*
Barr, Cathrine. *A horse for Sherry*
Barrett, Judi. *Old MacDonald had an apartment house*
Baruch, Dorothy. *Kappa's tug-of-war with the big brown horse*
Bax, Martin. *Edmond went far away*
Baynton, Martin. *Fifty and the fox*
  Fifty and the great race
  Fifty gets the picture
  Fifty saves his friend
Blades, Ann. *Mary of mile 18*
Blanchard, Arlene. *The naughty lamb*
Blocksma, Mary. *Where's that duck?*
Bloom, Suzanne. *We keep a pig in the parlor*
Bohanon, Paul. *Golden Kate*
Bonino, Louise. *The cozy little farm*
Brand, Millen. *This little pig named Curly*
Brandenberg, Franz. *Cock-a-doodle-doo*
Bright, Robert. *Georgie*
Brook, Judy. *Tim mouse visits the farm*
Brown, Craig McFarland. *My barn*
  Patchwork farmer
Brown, Margaret Wise. *Big red barn*, ill. by Felicia Bond
  Big red barn, ill. by Rosella Hartman
  The little farmer
  The summer noisy book

Brown, Ruth. *The big sneeze*
Browne, Caroline. *Mrs. Christie's farmhouse*
Bruna, Dick. *Farmer John*
  Little bird tweet
Budbill, David. *Christmas tree farm*
Bulla, Clyde Robert. *Dandelion Hill*
Bunting, Eve (Anne Evelyn). *Goose dinner*
  Winter's coming
Burton, Marilee Robin. *Aaron awoke*
Butler, Dorothy. *Another happy tale*
Campbell, Rod. *Oh dear!*
Carlson, Natalie Savage. *Time for the white
  egret*
Carrick, Carol. *In the moonlight, waiting*
Carrick, Donald. *The deer in the pasture*
  Harold and the giant knight
  Milk
Cartwright, Ann. *Norah's ark*
Caudill, Rebecca. *A pocketful of cricket*
Chaucer, Geoffrey. *Chanticleer and the fox*,
  ill. by Barbara Cooney
Child, Lydia Maria. *Over the river and
  through the wood*
Cleary, Beverly. *The hullabaloo ABC*
Clewes, Dorothy. *Hide and seek*
Climo, Lindee. *Chester's barn*
Collier, Ethel. *I know a farm*
Cook, Bernadine. *Looking for Susie*
Cousins, Lucy. *Farm animals*
  Hen on the farm
Coxe, Molly. *Whose footprints?*
Croll, Carolyn. *The three brothers*
Curry, Jane Louise. *Little, little sister*
Dalgliesh, Alice. *The little wooden farmer*
Daniel, Doris Temple. *Pauline and the
  peacock*
Day, Betsy. *Stefan and Olga*
De Angeli, Marguerite. *Yonie Wondernose*
Delaney, Ned. *Cosmic chickens*
Demuth, Patricia Brennan. *Ornery morning*
Dennis, Wesley. *Flip*
  Flip and the cows
Denslow, Sharon Phillips. *At Taylor's place*
De Paola, Tomie (Thomas Anthony).
  Country farm
Dewey, Ariane. *Febold Feboldson*
DeWitt, Jamie. *Jamie's turn*
DiFiori, Lawrence. *The farm*
Dodds, Siobhan. *Elizabeth Hen*
Domanska, Janina. *The turnip*
Dorros, Arthur. *Tonight is carnaval*
Dragonwagon, Crescent. *Jemima remembers*
Duncan, Jane. *Janet Reachfar and
  Chickabird*
Dunn, Judy. *The animals of Buttercup Farm*
  The little lamb
Dunrea, Olivier. *Eddy B, pigboy*
Duvoisin, Roger Antoine. *The crocodile in
  the tree*
  Crocus
  Jasmine

Our Veronica goes to Petunia's farm
Petunia
Petunia and the song
Petunia, beware!
Petunia, I love you
Petunia, the silly goose
Petunia's treasure
Two lonely ducks
Veronica
Veronica and the birthday present
Eriksson, Ake. *Joel, Jasper, and Julia*
Ets, Marie Hall. *Mister Penny*
  Mr. Penny's race horse
Euvremer, Teryl. *Sun's up*
Farm animals [Macmillan, 1991]
Farm house, ill. by Kate Klimo
Fatio, Louise. *The red bantam*
Feldman, Barbara. *Stephens' frog*
Fiday, Beverly. *Time to go*
Fleischman, Paul. *The animal hedge*
Fleischman, Sid. *The scarebird*
Flora, James. *Grandpa's farm*
Florian, Douglas. *A year in the country*
Fox, Mem. *Hattie and the fox*
Frascino, Edward. *Nanny Noony and the
  dust queen*
  Nanny Noony and the magic spell
Freedman, Russell. *Farm babies*
Freschet, Berniece. *Where's Henrietta's hen?*
Gackenbach, Dick. *Crackle, Gluck and the
  sleeping toad*
  The pig who saw everything
Gammell, Stephen. *Once upon MacDonald's
  farm*
Garland, Michael. *My cousin Katie*
Gibbons, Gail. *Farming*
  The milk makers
Gibson, Betty. *The story of Little Quack*
Glass, Andrew. *Chickpea and the talking cow*
Goodall, John S. *The story of a farm*
Greeley, Valerie. *Farm animals*
Green, Mary McBurney. *Everybody has a
  house and everybody eats*
Greenberg, Polly. *Oh, Lord, I wish I was a
  buzzard*
Gunthrop, Karen. *Rina at the farm*
Hader, Berta Hoerner. *Cock-a-doodle doo*
Hale, Kathleen. *Orlando buys a farm*
Hall, Donald. *The ox-cart man*
Hamilton, Virginia. *Drylongso*
Hansen, Carla. *Barnaby Bear visits the farm*
Harranth, Wolf. *My old grandad*
Harvey, Brett. *My prairie year*
Haseley, Dennis. *The old banjo*
Hawes, Judy. *Fireflies in the night*
Haywood, Carolyn. *Hello, star*
Hellen, Nancy. *A visit to the farm*
Helweg, Hans. *Farm animals*
Henderson, Kathy. *I can be a farmer*
Henley, Claire. *Farm day*
Herriot, James. *Blossom comes home*

Bonny's big day
Hill, Eric. *Spot goes to the farm*
Spot on the farm
Himmelman, John. *A guest is a guest*
Hines, Anna Grossnickle. *I'll tell you what they say*
Hoban, Julia. *Quick chick*
Hopkins, Lee Bennett. *On the farm*
Hurd, Edith Thacher. *Under the lemon tree*
Hurd, Thacher. *Blackberry ramble*
Tomato soup
Hutchins, Pat. *Rosie's walk*
Ipcar, Dahlov. *Bright barnyard*
Brown cow farm
Hard scrabble harvest
One horse farm
Ten big farms
Isenbart, Hans-Heinrich. *Baby animals on the farm*
Israel, Marion Louise. *The tractor on the farm*
Jacobs, Joseph. *Hereafterthis*
James, Shirley Kerby. *Going to a horse farm*
Johnston, Tony. *Farmer Mack measures his pig*
Jones, Carol. *This old man*
Kent, Jack. *Little Peep*
Kessler, Ethel. *Are there hippos on the farm?*
Kightley, Rosalinda. *The farmer*
King-Smith, Dick. *Cuckoobush farm*
Farmer Bungle forgets
Koch, Dorothy Clarke. *When the cows got out*
Koontz, Robin Michal. *This old man*
Koralek, Jenny. *The friendly fox*
Kunhardt, Edith. *I want to be a farmer*
Which pig would you choose?
Kwitz, Mary DeBall. *Little chick's breakfast*
Laird, Elizabeth. *The day Patch stood guard*
The day Sidney ran off
The day the ducks went skating
The day Veronica was nosy
Lapp, Eleanor. *The mice came in early this year*
Lasson, Robert. *Orange Oliver*
Lenski, Lois. *The little farm*
Levitin, Sonia. *A single speckled egg*
Lewis, Kim. *Emma's lamb*
Lewison, Wendy C. *Going to sleep on the farm*
Lexau, Joan M. *Who took the farmer's hat?*
Lillie, Patricia. *When the rooster crowed*
Lilly, Kenneth. *Animals on the farm*
Lindberg, Reeve. *Midnight farm*
Lindbergh, Reeve. *Benjamin's barn*
The day the goose got loose
Lindgren, Astrid. *The dragon with red eyes*
The tomten
Lindman, Maj. *Snipp, Snapp, Snurr and the buttered bread*
Lionni, Leo. *Six crows*

The little red hen. *The cock, the mouse and the little red hen*, ill. by Graham Percy
The little red hen, ill. by Janina Domanska
The little red hen, ill. by Paul Galdone
The little red hen, ill. by Mel Pekarsky
The little red hen, ill. by William Stobbs
The little red hen, ill. by Margot Zemach
Littledale, Freya. *The farmer in the soup*
Lobel, Arnold. *Small pig*
A treeful of pigs
Locker, Thomas. *Family farm*
The mare on the hill
Lorenz, Lee. *Hugo and the spacedog*
Low, Joseph. *Benny rabbit and the owl*
Boo to a goose
Lüton, Mildred. *Little chicks' mothers and all the others*
McConnachie, Brian. *Elmer and the chickens vs. the big league*
McCrea, Lilian. *Mother hen*
McCue, Lisa. *The little chick*
MacFarland, Cynthia. *Cows in the parlor*
McGee, Marni. *The quiet farmer*
McKissack, Patricia C. *The little red hen*
McNeer, May Yonge. *Little Baptiste*
McPhail, David. *Farm boy's year*
Farm morning
Maris, Ron. *Is anyone home?*
Mayer, Mercer. *Appelard and Liverwurst*
Mayne, William. *Tibber*
Meeks, Esther K. *Friendly farm animals*
Merrill, Jean. *Tell about the cowbarn, Daddy*
Miles, Miska. *Noisy gander*
This little pig
Milhous, Katherine. *The turnip*
Miller, J. P. (John Parr). *Farmer John's animals*
Miller, Jane. *Farm alphabet book*
Farm counting book
Farm noises
Seasons on the farm
Moeri, Louise. *The unicorn and the plow*
Moon, Cliff. *Pigs on the farm*
Morris, Linda Lowe. *Morning milking*
Nakatani, Chiyoko. *My day on the farm*
O'Brien, Mary. *Counting sheep to sleep*
O'Kelley, Mattie Lou. *Circus!*
Old MacDonald had a farm. *Old MacDonald had a farm*, ill. by Lorinda Bryan Cauley
Old MacDonald had a farm, ill. by Mel Crawford
Old MacDonald had a farm, ill. by David Frankland
Old MacDonald had a farm, ill. by Abner Graboff
Old MacDonald had a farm, ill. by Nancy Hellen
Old MacDonald had a farm, ill. by Carol Jones

Old MacDonald had a farm, ill. by Tracey Campbell Pearson

Old MacDonald had a farm, ill. by Robert M. Quackenbush

Old MacDonald had a farm, ill. by Glen Rounds

Old MacDonald had a farm, ill. by William Stobbs

Old MacDonald had a farm, ill. by Prue Theobalds

Olney, Ross R. *Farm giants*

Oppenheim, Joanne. *"Not now!" said the cow*

Ostheeren, Ingrid. *Jonathan Mouse and the baby bird*

Otto, Carolyn. *That sky, that rain*

Paladino, Catherine. *Our vanishing farm animals*

Patterson, Geoffrey. *A pig's tale*

Paul, Jan S. *Hortense*

Pearson, Susan. *Well, I never!*

Peck, Robert Newton. *Hamilton*

Peet, Bill (William Bartlett). *Cock-a-doodle Dudley*

Pellowski, Anne. *Stairstep farm*

Pieńkowski, Jan. *Farm*

Pinkney, Gloria Jean. *Back home*

Pizer, Abigail. *Charlie the puppy*
 Hattie the goat
 It's a perfect day
 Penelope pig
 Percy the duck

Polacco, Patricia. *Just plain Fancy*

Polushkin, Maria. *Morning*

Potter, Beatrix. *The tale of Peter Rabbit*

Provensen, Alice. *Our animal friends*
 An owl and three pussycats
 The year at Maple Hill Farm

Pryor, Bonnie. *Greenbrook farm*
 Mr. Munday and the rustlers

The pudgy book of farm animals, ill. by Julie Durrell

Raphael, Elaine. *Donkey and Carlo*
 Donkey, it's snowing

Reddix, Valerie. *Millie and the mud hole*

Rider, Alex. *A la ferme. At the farm*

Robart, Rose. *The cake that Mack ate*

Robinson, W. W. (William Wilcox). *On the farm*

Rockwell, Anne F. *The gollywhopper egg*

Rojankovsky, Feodor. *Animals on the farm*
 The great big animal book

Roth, Harold. *Let's look all around the farm*

Royston, Angela. *Cow*
 The goat
 The hen
 The pig
 The pony
 The sheep

Runcie, Jill. *Cock-a-doodle-doo*

Russell, Sandra Joanne. *A farmer's dozen*

Schlein, Miriam. *Something for now, something for later*

Schmid, Eleonore. *Farm animals*

Schmidt, Eric von. *The young man who wouldn't hoe corn*

Schoenherr, John. *The barn*

Schulz, Charles M. *Snoopy's facts and fun book about farms*

Seignobosc, Françoise. *The big rain*

Selsam, Millicent E. *Keep looking!*
 More potatoes!

Selway, Martina. *Don't forget to write*

Sewell, Helen Moore. *Blue barns*

Sherman, Nancy. *Gwendolyn and the weathercock*

Short, Mayo. *Andy and the wild ducks*

Skofield, James. *Snow country*

Slobodkina, Esphyr. *The wonderful feast*

Smith, Donald. *Farm numbers 1, 2, 3*

Smith, Mavis. *A snake mistake*

Sneed, Brad. *Lucky Russell*

Staines, Bill. *All God's critters got a place in the choir*

Stevenson, James. *"Could be worse!"*

Stott, Dorothy. *Little Duck's bicycle ride*

Sweet, Melissa. *Fiddle-i-fee*

Tafuri, Nancy. *Early morning in the barn*
 Who's counting?

Thiele, Colin. *Farmer Schulz's ducks*

Threadgall, Colin. *Proud rooster and the fox*

Tolstoĭ, Alekseĭ Nikolaevich. *The great big enormous turnip*

Torgersen, Don Arthur. *The girl who tricked the troll*

Tresselt, Alvin R. *Sun up*, ill. by author
 Sun up, ill. by Henri Sorensen
 Wake up, farm! ill. by author
 Wake up, farm! ill. by Carolyn Ewing

Tripp, Paul. *The strawman who smiled by mistake*

Turner, Ann Warren. *Dakota dugout*

Udry, Janice May. *Emily's autumn*

Vaës, Alain. *The porcelain pepper pot*

Van Horn, Grace. *Little red rooster*

Waddell, Martin. *Farmer Duck*

Wallner, John. *Old MacDonald had a farm*

Watson, Nancy Dingman. *What does A begin with?*
 What is one?

Wellington, Monica. *The sheep follow*

Westcott, Nadine Bernard. *Skip to my Lou*
 There's a hole in the bucket

Wheeler, Cindy. *Rose*

Wiesner, William. *Happy-Go-Lucky*

Wild, Margaret. *The very best of friends*

Willis, Val. *Silly little chick*

Wolff, Ashley. *A year of beasts*

Wood, Jakki. *Moo moo, brown cow*

Worthington, Phoebe. *Teddy bear farmer*

Wright, Dare. *Look at a calf*

Look at a colt
Yolen, Jane. *The giant's farm*
Zalben, Jane Breskin. *Basil and Hillary*
Ziefert, Harriet. *On our way to the barn*

Fathers *see* Family life – fathers

Father's Day *see* Holidays – Father's Day

Fear *see* Emotions – fear

Feeling *see* Senses – touching

Feelings *see* Emotions

Feet *see* Anatomy – feet

Fighting *see* Behavior – fighting, arguing

Fingers *see* Anatomy – hands

Finishing things *see* Character traits – completing things

Finland *see* Foreign lands – Finland

Fire

Anderson, C. W. (Clarence Williams). *Blaze and the forest fire*
Augarde, Steve (Stephen). *Pig*
Baker, Eugene. *Fire*
Barr, Jene. *Fire snorkel number 7*
Baumann, Kurt. *Piro and the fire brigade*
Beatty, Hetty Burlingame. *Little Owl Indian*
Belloc, Hilaire. *Matilda who told lies and was burned to death*
Bernstein, Margery. *Coyote goes hunting for fire*
Bester, Roger. *Fireman Jim*
Bible, Charles. *Jennifer's new chair*
Bond, Ruskin. *Flames in the forest*
Brenner, Barbara A. *Mr. Tall and Mr. Small*
Brown, Margaret Wise. *The little fireman*
Charles, Donald. *Chancay and the secret of fire*
De Regniers, Beatrice Schenk. *Willy O'Dwyer jumped in the fire*
Du Bois, William Pène. *Otto and the magic potatoes*
Elliott, Dan. *A visit to the Sesame Street firehouse*
Fire, ill. by Michael Ricketts
Firehouse, ill. by Zokeisha
Foreman, Michael. *Panda and the bushfire*
Gramatky, Hardie. *Hercules*
Greene, Graham. *The little fire engine*
Haines, Gail Kay. *Fire*
Kirn, Ann. *The tale of a crocodile*
Lawrence, John. *Pope Leo's elephant*
Mahood, Kenneth. *The laughing dragon*

Miklowitz, Gloria D. *Save that raccoon!*
Miles, Miska. *The fox and the fire*
Moskin, Marietta D. *Lysbet and the fire kittens*
Newton, James R. *A forest is reborn*
Quackenbush, Robert M. *There'll be a hot time in the old town tonight*
Roth, Susan L. *Fire came to the earth people*
Spiegel, Doris. *Danny and Company 92*
Taylor, Mark. *Henry explores the mountains*
Troughton, Joanna. *How rabbit stole the fire*
Ungerer, Tomi. *The Mellops strike oil*
Van Laan, Nancy. *Rainbow crow*
Ziefert, Harriet. *Lewis the fire fighter*

Fire engines *see* Careers – firefighters; Trucks

Firefighters *see* Careers – firefighters

Fireflies *see* Insects – fireflies

Fish

Aliki. *The long lost coelacanth and other living fossils*
Aruego, José. *Pilyo the piranha*
Balet, Jan B. *Joanjo*
Beisert, Heide Helene. *Poor fish*
Brice, Tony. *The bashful goldfish*
Broekel, Ray. *Dangerous fish*
Brown, Margaret Wise. *The little fisherman*
Bruna, Dick. *The fish*
Burstein, Fred. *Whispering in the park*
Bush, John. *The fish who could wish*
Calder, S. J. *If you were a fish*
Coatsworth, Elizabeth. *Under the green willow*
Cole, Joanna. *A fish hatches*
  Hungry, hungry sharks
Cook, Bernadine. *The little fish that got away*
Cooper, Elizabeth K. *The fish from Japan*
Curious George goes to the aquarium
Damjan, Mischa. *The little sea horse*
Darby, Gene. *What is a fish?*
Eastman, David. *What is a fish?*
Gibbons, Gail. *Sharks*
Gomi, Taro. *Where's the fish?*
Greenaway, Shirley. *Water*
Hall, Bill. *Fish tale*
Hawes, Judy. *Shrimps*
Henley, Claire. *In the ocean*
Himmelman, John. *Ellen and the goldfish*
Hirschi, Ron. *Ocean*
Hogan, Paula Z. *The salmon*
Ipcar, Dahlov. *The biggest fish in the sea*
Kalan, Robert. *Blue sea*
Kroll, Virginia L. *Helen the fish*
Laird, Donivee Martin. *The three little Hawaiian pigs and the magic shark*
Lionni, Leo. *Fish is fish*

Swimmy
Lubach, Peter. *Harry and the singing fish*
Maddern, Eric. *Curious clownfish*
Mendoza, George. *The gillygoofang*
Parnall, Peter. *The great fish*
Parry, Marian. *King of the fish*
Schatell, Brian. *Midge and Fred*
Schlein, Miriam. *That's not Goldie!*
Schumacher, Claire. *Alto and Tango*
Selsam, Millicent E. *A first look at sharks*
Seuss, Dr. *McElligot's pool*
  One fish, two fish, red fish, blue fish
Shaw, Evelyn S. *Fish out of school*
Stevenson, James. *Which one is Whitney?*
Turnage, Sheila. *Trout the magnificent*
Valens, Evans G. *Wingfin and Topple*
Waber, Bernard. *Lorenzo*
Waechter, Friedrich Karl. *Three is company*
Walton, Rick. *Something's fishy!*
Wezel, Peter. *The good bird*
Wildsmith, Brian. *Brian Wildsmith's fishes*
Wong, Herbert H. *My goldfish*
Wood, John Norris. *Oceans*
Wyse, Lois. *Two guppies, a turtle and Aunt Edna*
Yorinks, Arthur. *Louis the fish*
Zimelman, Nathan. *The great adventure of Wo Ti*

Fish – sharks

Gay, Tenner Ottley. *Sharks in action*
Mahy, Margaret. *The great white man-eating shark*

Fishermen *see* Careers – fishermen

Fishing *see* Sports – fishing

Flamingos *see* Birds – flamingos

Flattery *see* Character traits – flattery

Fleas *see* Insects – fleas

Flies *see* Insects – flies

Floods *see* Weather – floods

Flowers

Aksakov, Sergei. *The scarlet flower*
Allison, Diane Worfolk. *This is the key to the kingdom*
Andersen, H. C. (Hans Christian). *Little Ida's flowers*, ill. by Linda Allen
Anno, Mitsumasa. *The king's flower*
Baker, Jeffrey J. W. *Patterns of nature*
Barker, Cicely Mary. *Berry flower fairies*
  Blossom flower fairies
  Flower fairies of the garden
  Flower fairies of the seasons
  Flower fairies of the spring
  Flower fairies of the summer
  Flower fairies of the trees
  Flower fairies postcard book
  Spring flower fairies
  Summer flower fairies
Campbell, Rod. *Buster's afternoon*
Chapman, Carol. *Barney Bipple's magic dandelions*
Cooney, Barbara. *Miss Rumphius*
Cousins, Lucy. *Flower in the garden*
Delaney, A. *The gunnywolf*
Denver, John. *The children and the flowers*
De Paola, Tomie (Thomas Anthony). *The legend of the bluebonnet*
  The legend of the Indian paintbrush
Ehlert, Lois. *Planting a rainbow*
Ellentuck, Shan. *A sunflower as big as the sun*
Fisher, Aileen Lucia. *And a sunflower grew*
  Petals yellow and petals red
Givens, Janet Eaton. *Something wonderful happened*
Harper, Wilhelmina. *The gunniwolf*
Heilbroner, Joan. *Robert the rose horse*
Heller, Ruth. *The reason for a flower*
Heyduck-Huth, Hilde. *The strawflower*
Hidaka, Masako. *Girl from the snow country*
Hoban, Julia. *Amy loves the sun*
Ichikawa, Satomi. *Suzanne and Nicholas in the garden*, St. Martin's 1978
Ipcar, Dahlov. *The land of flowers*
Kirkpatrick, Rena K. *Look at flowers*
Lagerlöf, Selma. *The legend of the Christmas rose*
Lerner, Carol. *Flowers of a woodland spring*
Lobel, Anita. *Alison's zinnia*
Lobel, Arnold. *The rose in my garden*
McMillan, Bruce. *Counting wildflowers*
Maris, Ron. *In my garden*
Marton, Jirina. *Flowers for mom*
Montresor, Beni. *The witches of Venice*
O'Callahan, Jay. *Tulips*
Olson, Arielle North. *The lighthouse keeper's daughter*
Rockwell, Anne F. *My spring robin*
Selsam, Millicent E. *A first look at flowers*
Shannon, George. *Dancing the breeze*
Slobodkina, Esphyr. *Pinky and the petunias*
Slote, Elizabeth. *Nelly's garden*
Steig, William. *Rotten island*
Sugita, Yutaka. *The flower family*
Williams, Barbara. *Hello, dandelions!*

Flying *see* Activities – flying

Fog *see* Weather – fog

Fold out books *see* Format, unusual

Folk and fairy tales

Aardema, Verna. *Bimwili and the Zimwi*
Borreguita and the coyote
Bringing the rain to Kapiti Plain
Half-a-ball-of-kenki
Ji-nongo-nongo means riddles
Oh, Kojo! How could you!
Pedro and the padre
Princess Gorilla and a new kind of water
The riddle of the drum
Traveling to Tondo
The vingananee and the tree toad
Who's in Rabbit's house?
Why mosquitoes buzz in people's ears
Abisch, Roz. *The clever turtle*
Mai-Ling and the mirror
Sweet Betsy from Pike
Adams, Pam. *There was an old lady who swallowed a fly*
Adshead, Gladys L. *Brownies—hush!*
Æsop. *Æsop's fables*, ill. by Gaynor Chapman
Æsop's fables, ill. by Claire Littlejohn
Æsop's fables, ill. by Nick Price
Æsop's fables, ill. by Lisbeth Zwerger
Androcles and the lion, ill. by Janet Stevens
Androcles and the lion, ill. by Janusz Grabianski
Androcles and the lion, ill. by Robert Rayevsky
The ant and the dove, ill. by Ching
The best of Æsop's fables, ill. by Charlotte Voake
The country mouse and the city mouse, ill. by Laura Lydecker
The fables of Æsop, ill. by Frank Baber
The hare and the frogs, ill. by William Stobbs
The hare and the tortoise, ill. by Paul Galdone
The hare and the tortoise, ill. by Gerald Rose
The hare and the tortoise, ill. by Peter Weevers
The lion and the mouse, ill. by Gerald Rose
The lion and the mouse, ill. by Ed Young
The miller, his son and their donkey, ill. by Roger Antoine Duvoisin
The miller, his son and their donkey, ill. by Eugen Sopko
Once in a wood, ill. by Eve Rice
The raven and the fox, ill. by Gerald Rose
Seven fables from Æsop, ill. by Robert W. Alley
Tales from Æsop, ill. by Harold Jones
Three fox fables, ill. by Paul Galdone
The tortoise and the hare, ill. by Janet Stevens
The town mouse and the country mouse, ill. by Janet Stevens
The town mouse and the country mouse, ill. by Lorinda Bryan Cauley
The town mouse and the country mouse, ill. by Paul Galdone
The town mouse and the country mouse, ill. by Tom Garcia
Wolf! Wolf! ill. by Gerald Rose
Afanas'ev, Aleksandr N. *Russian folk tales*
Salt
Ahlberg, Allan. *The Cinderella show*
Aleichem, Sholem. *Hanukah money*
Alexander, Ellen. *Llama and the great flood*
Alexander, Lloyd. *The king's fountain*
The truthful harp
Alger, Leclaire Gowans. *All in the morning early*
Always room for one more
Aliki. *Diogenes*
The eggs
George and the cherry tree
The story of Johnny Appleseed
Three gold pieces
The twelve months
The all-amazing ha ha book
Allard, Harry. *May I stay?*
Allen, Linda. *The giant who had no heart*
The mouse bride
Ambrus, Victor G. *The little cockerel*
The seven skinny goats
The Sultan's bath
The three poor tailors
Andersen, H. C. (Hans Christian). *The emperor and the nightingale*, ill. by James Watling
The emperor's new clothes, ill. by Erik Blegvad
The emperor's new clothes, ill. by Virginia Lee Burton
The emperor's new clothes, ill. by Robert Byrd
The emperor's new clothes, ill. by Jack and Irene Delano
The emperor's new clothes, ill. by Hélène Desputeaux
The emperor's new clothes, ill. by Birte Dietz
The emperor's new clothes, ill. by Dorothée Duntze
The emperor's new clothes, ill. by Pamela Baldwin Ford
The emperor's new clothes, ill. by Jack Kent
The emperor's new clothes, ill. by Monika Laimgruber
The emperor's new clothes, ill. by Anne F. Rockwell
The emperor's new clothes, ill. by Janet Stevens

The emperor's new clothes, ill. by Nadine Bernard Westcott
The emperor's nightingale, ill. from the Disney arcives
The emperor's nightingale, ill. by Georges Lemoine
The fir tree, ill. by Stephanie Britt
The fir tree, ill. by Nancy Elkholm Burkert
The fir tree, ill. by Diane Goode
The fir tree, ill. by Rita Marshall
The fir tree, ill. by Bernadette Watts
It's perfectly true! ill. by Janet Stevens
Little Ida's flowers, ill. by Linda Allen
The little match girl, ill. by Rachel Isadora
The little match girl, ill. by Blair Lent
The little mermaid, ill. by Edward Frascino
The little mermaid, ill. by Chihiro Iwasaki
The little mermaid, ill. by Dorothy Pulis Lathrop
The little mermaid, ill. by Josef Paleček
The little mermaid, ill. by Daniel San Souci
The little mermaid, ill. by Katie Thamer Treherne
The nightingale, ill. by Harold Berson
The nightingale, ill. by Nancy Ekholm Burkert
The nightingale, ill. by Demi
The nightingale, ill. by Alison Claire Darke
The nightingale, ill. by Beni Montresor
The nightingale, ill. by Josef Paleček
The nightingale, ill. by Regolo Ricci
The nightingale, ill. by Lisbeth Zwerger
The old man is always right, ill. by Feodor Rojankovsky
The princess and the pea, ill. by Dorothée Duntze
The princess and the pea, ill. by Dick Gackenbach
The princess and the pea, ill. by Paul Galdone
The princess and the pea, ill. by Janet Stevens
The princess and the pea, ill. by Eve Tharlet
The snow queen, ill. by Angela Barrett
The snow queen, ill. by Toma Bogdanovic
The snow queen, ill. by June Atkin Corwin
The snow queen, ill. by Sally Holmes
The snow queen, ill. by Susan Jeffers
The snow queen, ill. by Errol Le Cain
The snow queen, ill. by Bernadette Watts
The snow queen, ill. by Arieh Zeldich
The snow queen and other stories from Hans Andersen, ill. by Edmund Dulac

The steadfast tin soldier, ill. by Thomas Di Grazia
The steadfast tin soldier, ill. by Paul Galdone
The steadfast tin soldier, ill. by David Jorgensen
The steadfast tin soldier, ill. by Monika Laimgruber
The steadfast tin soldier, ill. by P. J. Lynch
The steadfast tin soldier, ill. by Fred Marcellino
The steadfast tin soldier, ill. by Alain Vaës
The swineherd, ill. by Erik Blegvad
The swineherd, ill. by Dorothée Duntze
The swineherd, ill. by Deborah Hahn
The swineherd, ill. by Lisbeth Zwerger
Thumbelina, ill. by Adrienne Adams
Thumbelina, ill. by Wayne Anderson
Thumbelina, ill. by Alison Claire Darke
Thumbelina, ill. by Demi
Thumbelina, ill. by Susan Jeffers
Thumbelina, ill. by Kaarina Kaila
Thumbelina, ill. by Christine Willis Nigognossian
Thumbelina, ill. by Gustaf Tenggren
Thumbelina, ill. by Lisbeth Zwerger, tr. by Richard and Clara Winston
Thumbeline, ill. by Lisbeth Zwerger; tr. by Anthea Bell
The tinderbox, ill. by Warwick Hutton
The tinderbox, ill. by Barry Moser
The ugly duckling, ill. by Adrienne Adams
The ugly duckling, ill. by Lorinda Bryan Cauley
The ugly duckling, ill. by Troy Howell
The ugly duckling, ill. by Tadasu Izawa and Shigemi Hijikata
The ugly duckling, ill. by Monika Laimgruber
The ugly duckling, ill. by Johannes Larsen
The ugly duckling, ill. by Thomas Locker
The ugly duckling, ill. by Alan Marks
The ugly duckling, ill. by Josef Paleček
The ugly duckling, ill. by Daniel San Souci
The ugly duckling, ill. by Robert Van Nutt
The ugly little duck, ill. by Peggy Perry Anderson
The wild swans, ill. by Angela Barrett
The wild swans, ill. by Susan Jeffers
The woman with the eggs, ill. by Ray Cruz
Anderson, Lonzo. *Arion and the dolphins*
Anderson, Robin. *Sinabouda Lily*
Anglund, Joan Walsh. *Nibble nibble mousekin*
Anno, Mitsumasa. *Anno's Æsop*
In shadowland
Arabian Nights. *Arabian Nights*

entertainments, comp. by Charles Mozley
The flying carpet, ill. by Marcia Brown
The tale of Aladdin and the wonderful lamp, ill. by Ju-Hong Chen
Ariane. *Small Cloud*
Armitage, Marcia. *Lupatelli's favorite nursery tales*
Arnold, Caroline. *The terrible Hodag*
Arnott, Kathleen. *Spiders, crabs and creepy crawlers*
Aronin, Ben. *The secret of the Sabbath fish*
Aruego, José. *A crocodile's tale*
Look what I can do
Asbjørnsen, P. C. (Peter Christian). *The man who kept house*
The three billy goats Gruff, ill. by Marcia Brown
Three billy goats Gruff, ill. by Tom Dunnington
The three billy goats Gruff, ill. by Paul Galdone
The three billy goats Gruff, ill. by Janet Stevens
The three billy goats Gruff, ill. by William Stobbs
Ata, Te. *Baby rattlesnake*
Auerbach, Marjorie. *King Lavra and the barber*
Aulaire, Ingri Mortenson d'. *Children of the northlights*
Don't count your chicks
East of the sun and west of the moon
Ayres, Becky Hickox. *Matreshka*
Azarian, Mary. *The tale of John Barleycorn or, From barley to beer*
The babes in the woods. The old ballad of the babes in the woods, ill. by Edward Ardizzone
Baden, Robert. *And Sunday makes seven*
Baker, Betty. *And me, coyote!*
Rat is dead and ant is sad
Baker, Olaf. *Where the buffaloes begin*
Balet, Jan B. *The fence*
Balian, Lorna. *Leprechauns never lie*
Bang, Betsy. *The cucumber stem*
The old woman and the red pumpkin
The old woman and the rice thief
Tuntuni the tailor bird
Bang, Molly. *Dawn*
The paper crane
Wiley and the hairy man
Bannerman, Helen. *Sambo and the twins*
Baring, Maurice. *The blue rose*
Barrie, J. M. (James M.). *Peter Pan*, ill. by Diane Goode
Bartos-Hoppner, Barbara. *The Pied Piper of Hamelin*
Baruch, Dorothy. *Kappa's tug-of-war with the big brown horse*
Basile, Giambattista. *Petrosinella*
Bason, Lillian. *Those foolish Molboes!*

Baumann, Hans. *Chip has many brothers*
The hare's race
Baumann, Kurt. *The prince and the lute*
Bawden, Nina. *William Tell*
Baylor, Byrd. *The desert is theirs*
A God on every mountain top
Moon song
The way to start a day
Bechstein, Ludwig. *The rabbit catcher and other fairy tales*
The bedtime book, ill. by Daniel San Souci
Bell, Anthea. *Swan Lake*
The wise queen
Belling the cat and other stories, ill. by Harold Berson
Belpré, Pura. *Dance of the animals*
Perez and Martina
Belting, Natalia Maree. *The sun is a golden earring*
Bemelmans, Ludwig. *Rosebud*
Bennett, Jill. *Teeny tiny*
Berenstain, Michael. *The troll book*
Berenzy, Alix. *A frog prince*
Beresford, Elisabeth. *Jack and the magic stove*
Berg, Leila. *Folk tales for reading and telling*
Berger, Barbara Helen. *Grandfather Twilight*
Bernhard, Josephine Butkowska. *Lullaby*
Nine cry-baby dolls
Bernstein, Margery. *Coyote goes hunting for fire*
Earth namer
The first morning
How the sun made a promise and kept it
Berson, Harold. *Balarin's goat*
Barrels to the moon
The boy, the baker, the miller and more
Charles and Claudine
How the devil got his due
Joseph and the snake
Kassim's shoes
Raminagrobis and the mice
Why the jackal won't speak to the hedgehog
Bess, Clayton. *The truth about the moon*
Bianco, Margery Williams. *The velveteen rabbit*, ill. by Allen Atkinson
The velveteen rabbit, ill. by Michael Green
The velveteen rabbit, ill. by Michael Hague
The velveteen rabbit, ill. by David Jorgensen
The velveteen rabbit, ill. by William Nicholson
The velveteen rabbit, ill. by Ilse Plume
The velveteen rabbit, ill. by S. D. Schindler
The velveteen rabbit, ill. by Tien
Bible, Charles. *Hamdaani*
Bider, Djemma. *The buried treasure*

A drop of honey
Bierhorst, John. *Doctor Coyote*
  The ring in the prairie
Billy Boy, ill. by Glen Rounds
Birdseye, Tom. *A song of stars*
Biro, Val. *The pied piper of Hamelin*
Birrer, Cynthia. *The lady and the unicorn*
  Song to Demeter
Bishop, Claire Huchet. *The five Chinese
  brothers*
Black, Algernon D. *The woman of the wood*
Blackmore, Vivien. *Why corn is golden*
Blake, Quentin. *The story of the dancing
  frog*
Bolliger, Max. *The fireflies*
Bonne, Rose. *I know an old lady*, ill. by
  Abner Graboff
  I know an old lady who swallowed a fly,
    ill. by William Stobbs
Bouhuys, Mies. *The lady of Stavoren*
Boutwell, Edna. *Red rooster*
Bowden, Joan Chase. *Strong John*
Boyle, Vere. *Beauty and the beast*
Brand, Oscar. *When I first came to this land*
Brennan, Patricia D. *Hitchety hatchety up I
  go!*
Brentano, Clemens. *Schoolmaster
  Whackwell's wonderful sons*
Brett, Jan. *Fritz and the beautiful horses*
  The mitten
Briggs, Raymond. *Jim and the beanstalk*
Brister, Hope. *The cunning fox and other
  tales*
Bro, Marguerite H. *The animal friends of
  Peng-u*
Brodmann, Aliana. *Such a noise!*
Brown, Marcia. *The blue jackal*
  The bun
  Once a mouse...
  Stone soup
Browning, Robert. *The pied piper of
  Hamelin*, ill. by Patricia and Robin
  DeWitt
  The pied piper of Hamelin, ill. by Kate
    Greenaway
  The pied piper of Hamelin, ill. by Anatoly
    Ivanov
  The pied piper of Hamelin, ill. by Errol
    Le Cain
Bruchac, Joseph. *Thirteen moons on turtle's
  back*
Bryan, Ashley. *Beat the story-drum, pum-
  pum*
  The cat's purr
  Lion and the ostrich chicks
  Sh-ko and his eight wicked brothers
  Turtle knows your name
Bryant, Sara Cone. *Epaminondas and his
  auntie*
Bryson, Bernarda. *The twenty miracles of
  Saint Nicolas*

Buck, Pearl S. (Pearl Sydenstricker). *The
  Chinese story teller*
Buckley, Richard. *The foolish tortoise*
  The greedy python
Burland, Brian. *St. Nicholas and the tub*
Caldecott, Randolph. *The Randolph
  Caldecott treasury*
Calhoun, Mary. *The goblin under the stairs*
  Jack the wise and the Cornish cuckoos
  Old man Whickutt's donkey
  The pixy and the lazy housewife
  The runaway brownie
  The thieving dwarfs
  The witch's pig
Carey, Valerie Scho. *The devil and mother
  Crump*
  Maggie Mab and the bogey beast
Carle, Eric. *Twelve tales from Æsop*
Carrick, Malcolm. *I can squash elephants!*
Carter, Angela. *The sleeping beauty and
  other favourite fairy tales*
Carter, Anne. *Beauty and the beast*
Cauley, Lorinda Bryan. *The cock, the mouse
  and the little red hen*
  The goose and the golden coins
Cendrars, Blaise. *Shadow*
Chafetz, Henry. *The legend of Befana*
Chapman, Carol. *The tale of Meshka the
  Kvetch*
Chapman, Gaynor. *The luck child*
Chapman, Jean. *Moon-Eyes*
Charles, Donald. *Chancay and the secret of
  fire*
Charlip, Remy. *Harlequin and the gift of
  many colors*
Charlot, Martin. *Felisa and the magic tikling
  bird*
Chase, Catherine. *The nightingale and the
  fool*
Chase, Richard. *Jack and the three sillies*
Chaucer, Geoffrey. *Chanticleer and the fox*,
  ill. by Barbara Cooney
Chicken Little. *Chicken Licken*, ill. by Jutta
  Ash
  Chicken Licken, ill. by Gavin Bishop
  Henny Penny, ill. by Stephen Butler
  Henny Penny, ill. by Paul Galdone
  Henny Penny, ill. by William Stobbs
  The story of Chicken Licken, adapt. and
    ill. by Jan Ormerod
Ching. *The baboon's umbrella*
Chorao, Kay. *The child's story book*
Christensen, Jack. *The forgotten rainbow*
Christian, Mary Blount. *April fool*
Cleaver, Elizabeth. *The enchanted caribou*
Clement, Claude. *The painter and the wild
  swans*
Climo, Shirley. *The Egyptian Cinderella*
  The match between the winds

Coatsworth, Elizabeth. *The giant golden book of cat stories*

Cocagnac, A. M. (Augustin Maurice). *The three trees of the Samurai*

Cohen, Barbara. *The demon who would not die*

Here come the Purim players!

Cohen, Carol L. *The mud pony*

Cohen, Caron Lee. *Renata, Whizbrain and the ghost*

Sally Ann Thunder Ann Whirlwind Crockett

Cole, Babette. *Prince Cinders*

Cole, Brock. *The giant's toe*

Cole, Joanna. *Bony-legs*

Doctor Change

Don't tell the whole world

Golly Gump swallowed a fly

It's too noisy

Collodi, Carlo. *The adventures of Pinocchio*, ill. by Diane Goode

Conger, Lesley. *Tops and bottoms*

Conover, Chris. *Mother Goose and the sly fox*

Coombs, Patricia. *The magic pot*

Tilabel

Cooney, Barbara. *Little brother and little sister*

Cooper, Susan. *The Selkie girl*

The silver cow

Tam Lin

Cormack, M. Grant. *Animal tales from Ireland*

Costa, Nicoletta. *The mischievous princess*

Coville, Bruce. *Sarah and the dragon*

Credle, Ellis. *Big fraid, little fraid*

Croll, Carolyn. *The little snowgirl*

The three brothers

Crompton, Anne Eliot. *The lifting stone*

The winter wife

Crossley-Holland, Kevin. *The green children*

The pedlar of Swaffham

Cummings, E. E. (Edward Estlin). *Fairy tales*

Czernecki, Stefan. *The sleeping bread*

Daniels, Guy. *The Tsar's riddles*

Dasent, George W. *East o' the sun, west o' the moon*

Daugherty, Sonia. *Vanka's donkey*

Davis, Douglas F. *The lion's tail*

Day, David. *The swan children*

Day, Edward C. *John Tabor's ride*

Dayrell, Elphinstone. *Why the sun and the moon live in the sky*

DeArmond, Dale. *The seal oil lamp*

DeChristopher, Marlowe. *Greencoat and the swanboy*

Dee, Ruby. *Tower to heaven*

Two ways to count to ten

De Gerez, Toni. *Louhi, witch of North Farm*

De Mejo, Oscar. *La Bella Magellona and the little cavalier*

Demi. *The artist and the architect*

Chen Ping and his magic axe

A Chinese zoo

Demi's reflective fables

The hallowed horse

The magic boat

Under the shade of the mulberry tree

De Paola, Tomie (Thomas Anthony). *Favorite nursery tales*

Fin M'Coul

Jamie O'Rourke and the big potato

The legend of Old Befana

The legend of the bluebonnet

The legend of the Indian paintbrush

Little Grunt and the big egg

The mysterious giant of Barletta

The Prince of the Dolomites

Tony's bread

De Regniers, Beatrice Schenk. *Everyone is good for something*

Little Sister and the Month Brothers

Red Riding Hood

Dewey, Ariane. *Febold Feboldson*

The fish Peri

Laffite, the pirate

Pecos Bill

The thunder god's son

Dick Whittington and his cat. *Dick Whittington*, ill. by Edward Ardizzone

Dick Whittington and his cat, ill. by Marcia Brown

Dick Whittington, ill. by Antony Maitland

Dick Whittington and his cat, ill. by Kurt Werth

Dinardo, Jeffrey. *The wolf who cried boy*

Dixon, Ann. *How raven brought light to people*

Dobbs, Rose. *More once-upon-a-time stories*

Once-upon-a-time story book

Domanska, Janina. *The best of the bargain*

Busy Monday morning

King Krakus and the dragon

Look, there is a turtle flying

Marek, the little fool

Palmiero and the ogre

A scythe, a rooster and a cat

The tortoise and the tree

The turnip

What happens next?

Why so much noise?

Dos Santos, Joyce Audy. *The diviner*

Henri and the Loup-Garou

Du Bois, William Pène. *The hare and the tortoise and the tortoise and the hare*

Duff, Maggie (Margaret K.). *Dancing turtle*

The princess and the pumpkin

Rum pum pum

Dukas, P. (Paul Abraham). *The sorcerer's apprentice*, ill. by Ryohei Yanagihara

Durell, Ann. *The Diane Goode book of American folk tales and songs*

Edwards, Lisa. *Disney's Beauty and the beast, a book of manners*
Edwards, Roberta. *Five silly fishermen*
Ehlert, Lois. *Moon rope: Un lazo a la luna*
Ehrlich, Amy. *Pome and Peel*
Elkin, Benjamin. *The king's wish and other stories*
Six foolish fishermen
Such is the way of the world
The wisest man in the world
Elwell, Peter. *The king of the pipers*
Emberley, Barbara. *One wide river to cross*
Esbensen, Barbara Juster. *Ladder to the sky*
The star maiden
Esterl, Arnica. *The fine round cake*
Evans, Katherine. *The boy who cried wolf*
A bundle of sticks
The maid and her pail of milk
The man, the boy and the donkey
Felton, Harold W. *Pecos Bill and the mustang*
Fiddle-i-fee, ill. by Diane Stanley
The firebird, ill. by Moira Kemp
The firebird, ill. by Kris Waldherr
The firebird, ill. by Boris Zvorykin
Fisher, Leonard Everett. *Cyclops*
Star signs
Theseus and the minotaur
Fleischman, Paul. *The animal hedge*
Flora. *Feathers like a rainbow*
Flot, Jeannette B. *Princess Kalina and the hedgehog*
Foley, Bernice Williams. *The gazelle and the hunter*
A walk among clouds
Forest, Heather. *The baker's dozen*
The woman who flummoxed the fairies
Fournier, Catharine. *The coconut thieves*
The fox went out on a chilly night, ill. by Peter Spier
Francis, Frank. *Natasha's new doll*
Frasconi, Antonio. *The snow and the sun, la nieve y el sol*
Freedman, Florence B. *Brothers*
Fregosi, Claudia. *The pumpkin sparrow*
Snow maiden
French, Fiona. *Anancy and Mr. Dry-Bone*
Fritz, Jean. *The good giants and the bad Pukwudgies*
Gackenbach, Dick. *Arabella and Mr. Crack*
The perfect mouse
Gág, Wanda. *The sorcerer's apprentice*
Galdone, Joanna. *Amber day*
The little girl and the big bear
Galdone, Paul. *The amazing pig*
Androcles and the lion
The greedy old fat man
King of the cats
The magic porridge pot
The monkey and the crocodile
Obedient Jack

A strange servant
The teeny-tiny woman
What's in fox's sack?
Gammell, Stephen. *The story of Mr. and Mrs. Vinegar*
Gauch, Patricia Lee. *The little friar who flew*
On to Widecombe Fair
Gerson, Mary-Joan. *Why the sky is far away*
Gerstein, Mordicai. *The seal mother*
Giannini, Enzo. *Little Parsley*
Gilleo, Alma. *Learning about monsters*
The gingerbread boy. *The gingerbread boy*, ill. by Scott Cook
The gingerbread boy, ill. by Paul Galdone
The gingerbread boy, ill. by Joan Elizabeth Goodman
The gingerbread boy, ill. by William Curtis Holdsworth
The gingerbread man, ill. by Gerald Rose
The pancake boy, ill. by Lorinda Bryan Cauley
Whiff, sniff, nibble and chew, ill. by Monica Incisa
Ginsburg, Mirra. *The Chinese mirror*
The fisherman's son
The fox and the hare
How the sun was brought back to the sky
Pampalche of the silver teeth
Striding slippers
Go tell Aunt Rhody. *Go tell Aunt Rhody*, ill. by Aliki
Gobhai, Mehlli. *Usha, the mouse-maiden*
Goble, Paul. *Buffalo woman*
Crow chief
The dream wolf
The gift of the sacred dog
The great race: of the birds and animals
Her seven brothers
Iktomi and the berries
Iktomi and the boulder
Iktomi and the buffalo skull
Iktomi and the ducks
Star boy
The golden goose, ill. by William Stobbs
The good-hearted youngest brother, ill. by Diane Goode
Gramatky, Hardie. *Nikos and the sea god*
Grant, Joan. *The monster that grew small*
Greene, Jacqueline Dembar. *What his father did*
Greeson, Janet. *The stingy baker*
Gregory, Valiska. *Through the mickle woods*
Grieg, E. H. (Edvard Hagerup). *E. H. Grieg's Peer Gynt*
Grifalconi, Ann. *The village of round and square houses*
Grimm, Jacob. *The bear and the kingbird*, ill. by Chris Conover
The bearskinner, ill. by Felix Hoffmann
The brave little tailor, ill. by Mark Corcoran

The brave little tailor, ill. by Svend Otto S.

The brave little tailor, ill. by Daniel San Souci

The brave little tailor, ill. by Eve Tharlet

The brave little tailor, ill. by James Warhola

The Bremen town musicians, ill. by Donna Diamond

The Bremen town musicians, ill. by Janina Domanska

The Bremen town musicians, ill. by Paul Galdone

Bremen town musicians, ill. by Josef Paleček

The Bremen town musicians, ill. by Ilse Plume

The Bremen town musicians, ill. by Bernadette Watts

Cinderella, ill. by Nonny Hogrogian

Cinderella, ill. by Svend Otto S.

Clever Kate, ill. by Anita Lobel

The devil with the green hairs, ill. by Nonny Hogrogian

The donkey prince, ill. by Barbara Cooney

The earth gnome, ill. by Margot Tomes

The elves and the shoemaker, ill. by Paul Galdone

The elves and the shoemaker, ill. by Bernadette Watts

The falling stars, ill. by Eugen Sopko

The fisherman and his wife, ill. by Monika Laimgruber

The fisherman and his wife, ill. by Alan Marks

The fisherman and his wife, ill. by Margot Tomes

The fisherman and his wife, ill. by Margot Zemach

The four clever brothers, ill. by Felix Hoffmann

The frog prince, ill. by Binette Schroeder

The glass mountain, ill. by Nonny Hogrogian

Godfather Cat and Mousie, ill. by Ann Schweninger

The golden bird, ill. by Sandro Nardini

The golden goose, ill. by Dorothée Duntze

The golden goose, ill. by Isadore Seltzer

The golden goose, ill. by Martin Ursell

The goose girl, ill. by Sabine Bruntjen

Hans in luck, ill. by Paul Galdone

Hans in luck, ill. by Felix Hoffmann

Hansel and Gretel, ill. by Adrienne Adams

Hansel and Gretel, ill. by Anthony Browne

Hansel and Gretel, ill. by Susan Jeffers

Hansel and Gretel, ill. by Winslow P. Pels

Hansel and Gretel, ill. by Conxita Rodriguez

Hansel and Gretel, ill. by John Wallner

Hansel and Gretel, ill. by Paul O. Zelinsky

Hansel and Gretel, ill. by Lisbeth Zwerger

The horse, the fox, and the lion, ill. by Paul Galdone

Jorinda and Joringel, ill. by Adrienne Adams

Jorinda and Joringel, ill. by Jutta Ash

Jorinda and Joringel, ill. by Margot Tomes

King Grisly-Beard, ill. by Maurice Sendak

Little red cap, ill. by Lisbeth Zwerger

Little Red Riding Hood, ill. by Frank Aloise

Little Red Riding Hood, ill. by Gwen Connelly

Little Red Riding Hood, ill. by Paul Galdone

Little Red Riding Hood, ill. by John S. Goodall

Little Red Riding Hood, ill. by Trina Schart Hyman

Little Red Riding Hood, ill. by Bernadette Watts

Lucky Hans, ill. by Eugen Sopko

Mother Holly, ill. by Bernadette Watts

Mrs. Fox's wedding, ill. by Errol Le Cain

The musicians of Bremen, ill. by Svend Otto S.

The musicians of Bremen, ill. by Martin Ursell

Nanny goat and the seven little kids, ill. by Janet Stevens

The princess and the frog, retold and ill. by Rachel Isadora

Rapunzel, ill. by Jutta Ash

Rapunzel, ill. by Bert Dodson

Rapunzel, ill. by Trina Schart Hyman

Rapunzel, ill. by Kris Waldherr

Rapunzel, ill. by Bernadette Watts

Rumpelstiltskin, ill. by Jacqueline Ayer

Rumpelstiltskin, ill. by Donna Diamond

Rumpelstiltskin, ill. by Paul Galdone

Rumpelstiltskin, ill. by Jonathan Langley

Rumpelstiltskin, ill. by Gennady Spirin

Rumpelstiltskin, ill. by John Wallner

Rumpelstiltskin, ill. by Paul O. Zelinsky

The seven ravens, ill. by Felix Hoffmann

The seven ravens, ill. by Lisbeth Zwerger

The shoemaker and the elves, ill. by Adrienne Adams

The shoemaker and the elves, ill. by Cynthia and William Birrer

The shoemaker and the elves, ill. by Ilse Plume

The six swans, ill. by Daniel San Souci

The six swans, ill. by Margot Tomes

The sleeping beauty, ill. by Warwick Hutton

The sleeping beauty, ill. by Trina Schart Hyman
The sleeping beauty, ill. by Mercer Mayer
Sleeping Beauty, ill. by Fina Rifa
The sleeping beauty, ill. by Ruth Sanderson
Sleeping Beauty, ill. by John Wallner
Snow White, ill. by Trina Schart Hyman
Snow White, ill. by Bernadette Watts
Snow White and Rose Red, ill. by Adrienne Adams
Snow-White and Rose-Red, ill. by Barbara Cooney
Snow White and Rose Red, ill. by John Wallner
Snow White and Rose Red, ill. by Bernadette Watts
Snow White and the seven dwarfs, ill. by Wanda Gág
Snow White and the seven dwarves, ill. by Chihiro Iwasaki
The table, the donkey and the stick, ill. by Paul Galdone
Three Grimms' fairy tales, ill. by Bernadette Watts
The traveling musicians of Bremen, ill. by Kady MacDonald Denton
The twelve dancing princesses, ill. by Kinuko Y. Craft
The twelve dancing princesses, ill. by Anne Dalton
The twelve dancing princesses, ill. by Dennis Hockerman
The twelve dancing princesses, ill. by Errol Le Cain
The twelve dancing princesses, ill. by Gerald McDermott
The twelve dancing princesses, ill. by Uri Shulevitz
The ugly duckling, ill. by Maria Ruis
The valiant little tailor, ill. by Victor G. Ambrus
The wishing table, ill. by Eve Tharlet
The wolf and the seven kids, ill. by Kinuko Y. Craft
The wolf and the seven little kids, ill. by Svend Otto S.
The wolf and the seven little kids, ill. by Martin Ursell
Grimm, Wilhelm. *Dear Mili*, ill. by Maurice Sendak
Gross, Michael. *The fable of the fig tree*
Gross, Ruth Belov. *The girl who wouldn't get married*
Guy, Rosa. *Mother crocodile*
Hadithi, Mwenye. *Greedy zebra*
Hague, Kathleen. *The man who kept house*
Haley, Gail E. *Jack and the bean tree*
Jack and the fire dragon
A story, a story
Hall, Amanda. *The gossipy wife*

Hall, Malcolm. *And then the mouse...*
Hallinan, P. K. (Patrick K.). *I'm thankful each day!*
Harber, Frances. *My king has donkey ears*
Harris, Joel Chandler. *Jump!*
Jump again!
Harshman, Marc. *Rocks in my pocket*
Haseley, Dennis. *The cave of snores*
Hastings, Selina. *The man who wanted to live forever*
The singing ringing tree
Haugaard, Erik Christian. *Prince Boghole*
Princess Horrid
Haviland, Virginia. *The talking pot*
Hayward, Linda. *All stuck up*
Hazen, Barbara Shook. *The sorcerer's apprentice*
Hearn, Michael Patrick. *The porcelain cat*
Heller, Linda. *Alexis and the golden ring*
Hewitt, Kathryn. *King Midas and the golden touch*
The three sillies
Heyer, Marilee. *The weaving of a dream*
Hidaka, Masako. *Girl from the snow country*
High on a hill
Hill, Eric. *Spot's birthday party*
Where's Spot?
Hillert, Margaret. *The funny baby*
The magic beans
The three bears
The three goats
Hillman, Elizabeth. *Min-Yo and the moon dragon*
Hirsh, Marilyn. *Captain Jiri and Rabbi Jacob*
Joseph who loved the Sabbath
One little goat
Hobzek, Mildred. *We came a-marching...1, 2, 3*
Hodges, Margaret. *Buried moon*
The fire bringer
The kitchen knight
Saint George and the dragon
St. Jerome and the lion
Hoffmann, E. T. A. *The nutcracker*, ill. by Francesca Crespi
The nutcracker, ill. by Rachel Isadora
The nutcracker, ill. by Maurice Sendak
The nutcracker, ill. by Lisbeth Zwerger
The strange child
Hogrogian, Nonny. *The cat who loved to sing*
The contest
Rooster brother
Holland, Janice. *You never can tell*
Hong, Lily Toy. *How the ox star fell from heaven*
Hooks, William H. *Moss gown*
Peach boy
Hort, Lenny. *The boy who held back the sea*

Houston, James. *Kiviok's magic journey*
Huck, Charlotte. *Princess Furball*
Hunt Angela Elwell. *The tale of three trees*
Hunter, C. W. *The green gourd*
Hürlimann, Ruth. *The proud white cat*
Hush little baby. *Hush little baby*, ill. by Jeanette Winter
Hutton, Warwick. *Beauty and the beast*
The nose tree
Ichikawa, Satomi. *A child's book of seasons*
Sun through small leaves
Iké, Jane Hori. *A Japanese fairy tale*
Ikeda, Daisaku. *The snow country prince*
Illyés, Gyula. *Matt the gooseherd*
Irving, Washington. *The legend of Sleepy Hollow*, ill. by Daniel San Souci
Rip Van Winkle, ill. by John Howe
Rip Van Winkle, ill. by Thomas Locker
Rip Van Winkle, ill. by Peter Wingham
Isele, Elizabeth. *The frog princess*
Ishii, Momoko. *The tongue-cut sparrow*
Ivanov, Anatoly. *Ol' Jake's lucky day*
Jack and the beanstalk. *The history of Mother Twaddle and the marvelous achievements of her son Jack*, ill. by Paul Galdone
Jack and the beanstalk, ill. by Val Biro
Jack and the beanstalk, ill. by Lorinda Bryan Cauley
Jack and the beanstalk, ill. by Ed Parker
Jack and the beanstalk, ill. by Tony Ross
Jack and the beanstalk, ill. by William Stobbs
Jack and the beanstalk, ill. by James Warhola
Jack and the beanstalk, ill. by Anne Wilsdorf
Jack the giant killer, ill. by Anne Wilsdorf
Jack the giantkiller, ill. by Tony Ross
Jacobs, Joseph. *The crock of gold*
Hereafterthis
Hudden and Dudden and Donald O'Neary
Johnny-cake, ill. by Emma Lillian Brock
Johnny-cake, ill. by William Stobbs
Lazy Jack, ill. by Barry Wilkinson
Master of all masters, ill. by Anne F. Rockwell
Old Mother Wiggle-Waggle
Tattercoats, ill. by Margot Tomes
The three sillies, ill. by Paul Galdone
Jagendorf, Moritz A. *Kwi-na the eagle*
Jameson, Cynthia. *The house of five bears*
A January fog will freeze a hog
Jaquith, Priscilla. *Bo Rabbit smart for true*
Jennings, Linda M. *Coppelia*
The sleeping beauty: the story of the ballet
Johnson, Crockett. *Harold's fairy tale*
Johnston, Tony. *The badger and the magic fan*
Karlin, Barbara. *Cinderella*
Keats, Ezra Jack. *John Henry*

Kellogg, Steven (Stephen). *Chicken Little*
Johnny Appleseed
Pecos Bill
Kent, Jack. *Jack Kent's happy-ever-after book*
Jack Kent's hokus pokus bedtime book
Kimmel, Eric A. *Anansi and the moss-covered rock*
Anansi goes fishing
Baba Yaga
Bearhead
Boots and his brothers
The greatest of all
Kirn, Ann. *The tale of a crocodile*
Kismaric, Carole. *The rumor of Pavel and Paali*
Knight, Hilary. *Hilary Knight's Cinderella*
Knutson, Barbara. *How the guinea fowl got her spots*
Why the crab has no head
Koenig, Marion. *The tale of fancy Nancy*
Kroll, Steven. *Princess Abigail and the wonderful hat*
La Fontaine, Jean de. *The hare and the tortoise*
The lion and the rat
The miller, the boy and the donkey, adapt. and ill. by Brian Wildsmith
The north wind and the sun
Lagerlöf, Selma. *The legend of the Christmas rose*
Langstaff, John M. *Oh, a-hunting we will go*
Ol' Dan Tucker
On Christmas day in the morning
Over in the meadow
Soldier, soldier, won't you marry me?
The swapping boy
The two magicians
Langton, Jane. *The hedgehog boy*
Laroche, Michel. *The snow rose*
Lattimore, Deborah Nourse. *The dragon's robe*
The prince and the golden ax
Lazy Jack. *Lazy Jack*, ill. by Bert Dodson
Lazy Jack, ill. by Tony Ross
Lazy Jack, ill. by Kurt Werth
Le Guin, Ursula K. *A ride on the red mare's back*
Lee, Jeanne M. *Legend of the Li River*
The legend of the milky way
Toad is the uncle of heaven
Lenski, Lois. *Susie Mariar*
Lent, Blair. *John Tabor's ride*
Lester, Julius. *The knee-high man and other tales*
Levine, Abby. *Too much mush!*
Lewis, J. Patrick. *The Tsar and the amazing cow*
Lexau, Joan M. *Crocodile and hen*
It all began with a drip, drip, drip
Lindbergh, Reeve. *Johnny Appleseed*

Lindgren, Astrid. *The ghost of Skinny Jack*
Lipkind, William. *The magic feather duster*
Little, Jean. *Once upon a golden apple*
The little red hen. *The cock, the mouse and
   the little red hen*, ill. by Graham Percy
The little red hen, ill. by Janina
   Domanska
The little red hen, ill. by Paul Galdone
The little red hen, ill. by Mel Pekarsky
The little red hen, ill. by William Stobbs
The little red hen, ill. by Margot Zemach
Little Tuppen, ill. by Paul Galdone
Littledale, Freya. *The farmer in the soup*
Peter and the north wind
Littlefield, William. *The whiskers of Ho Ho*
Lloyd, David. *The ridiculous story of
   Gammer Gurton's needle*
Lobel, Anita. *The dwarf giant*
Löfgren, Ulf. *The boy who ate more than the
   giant and other Swedish folktales*
Lorenz, Lee. *Big Gus and Little Gus*
The feathered ogre
Pinchpenny John
Scornful Simkin
Louie, Al-Ling. *Yeh Shen*
Loverseed, Amanda. *The thunder king*
Tikkatoo's journey
Ludwig, Warren. *Good morning, Granny
   Rose*
Old Noah's elephants
Luenn, Nancy. *The dragon kite*
MacBeth, George. *Jonah and the Lord*
McCaughrean, Geraldine. *Saint George and
   the dragon*
McCurdy, Michael. *The devils who learned
   to be good*
McDermott, Beverly Brodsky. *The crystal
   apple*
The Golem
McDermott, Gerald. *Anansi the spider*
Arrow to the sun
Daniel O'Rourke
Daughter of earth
The stonecutter
Tim O'Toole and the wee folk
The voyage of Osiris
MacDonald, George. *The light princess*, ill.
   by Maurice Sendak
The light princess, ill. by Katie Thamer
   Treherne
Little Daylight
MacDonald, Suse. *Once upon another*
McFarland, John. *The exploding frog and
   other fables from Æsop*
MacGill-Callahan, Sheila. *And still the turtle
   watched*
McGuire-Turcotte, Casey A. *How Honu the
   turtle got his shell*
McHale, Ethel Kharasch. *Son of thunder*
McKee, David. *The man who was going to
   mind the house*

McKissack, Patricia C. *Cinderella*
A million fish...more or less
Mirandy and brother wind
McLenighan, Valjean. *Turtle and rabbit*
What you see is what you get
You are what you are
You can go jump
McNaughton, Colin. *Guess who's just moved
   in next door?*
Maestro, Giulio. *The tortoise's tug of war*
Magnus, Erica. *The boy and the devil*
Old Lars
Mahy, Margaret. *The seven Chinese brothers*
Maitland, Antony. *Idle Jack*
Malcolmson, Anne. *The song of Robin Hood*
Mamin-Sibiryak, D. N. *Grey Neck*
Manson, Christopher. *The crab prince*
A gift for the king
Mantinband, Gerda. *Blabbermouths*
Marshall, James. *Hansel and Gretel*
Red Riding Hood
Martin, Bill (William Ivan). *Sounds of
   laughter*
Martin, Claire. *Boots and the glass mountain*
The race of the golden apples
Martin, Rafe. *Foolish rabbit's big mistake*
The hungry tigress
The rough-face girl
Matsuno, Masako. *Taro and the bamboo
   shoot*
Matsutani, Miyoko. *The fisherman under the
   sea*
The witch's magic cloth
Mayer, Marianna. *Beauty and the beast*
The black horse
The little jewel box
My first book of nursery tales
The spirit of the blue light
Mayer, Mercer. *The Pied Piper of Hamelin*
Mendelson, S. T. *Stupid Emilien*
Merriam, Eve. *Epaminondas*
Michael, Emory H. *Androcles and the lion*
Milhous, Katherine. *The turnip*
Miller, Edna. *Mousekin's fables*
Miller, Moira. *The moon dragon*
Milne, A. A. (Alan Alexander). *Prince
   Rabbit*
Mirkovic, Irene. *The greedy shopkeeper*
Mobley, Jane. *The star husband*
Moeri, Louise. *Star Mother's youngest child*
Mollel, Tolowa M. *Orphan boy*
Moncure, Jane Belk. *The talking tabby cat*
Moon, Dolly M. *My very first book of cowboy
   songs*
Moore, Inga. *The sorcerer's apprentice*
Morel, Eve. *Fairy tales*
Fairy tales and fables
Morimoto, Junko. *The inch boy*
Mouse's marriage
Morris, Ann. *The Little Red Riding Hood
   rebus book*

Morris, Winifred. *The future of Yen-Tzu*
The magic leaf
Mosel, Arlene. *Tikki Tikki Tembo*
Mother Goose. *The golden goose book*, ill. by
L. Leslie Brooke
London Bridge is falling down, ill. by Ed
Emberley
London Bridge is falling down, ill. by
Peter Spier
Moxley, Susan. *Abdul's treasure*
Muller, Robin. *The lucky old woman*
The sorcerer's apprentice, ill. by Robin
Muller
Munsch, Robert N. *A promise is a promise*
Mwalimu. *Awful aardvark*
Myers, Walter Dean. *The golden serpent*
Neale, J. M. (John Mason). *Good King
Wenceslas*
Nesbit, Edith. *Beauty and the beast*
The last of the dragons
Melisande
Ness, Evaline. *The girl and the goatherd*
Newton, Pam. *The stonecutter*
Newton, Patricia Montgomery. *The five
sparrows*
Nikly, Michelle. *The princess on the nut*
Nister, Ernest. *Little tales from long ago*
Nixon, Joan Lowery. *Bigfoot makes a movie*
Nones, Eric Jon. *Canary prince*
Norman, Howard. *Who-Paddled-Backward-
With-Trout*
Nunes, Susan. *Tiddalick the frog*
O'Connor, Jane. *The teeny tiny woman*
Odoyevsky, Vladimir. *Old Father Fròst*
O Huigin, Sean. *King of the birds*
The old woman and her pig. *The old
woman and her pig*, ill. by Paul Galdone
The troublesome pig
The old-fashioned children's storybook
Olson, Arielle North. *Noah's cats and the
devil's fire*
Oppenheim, Joanne. *Donkey's tale*
Oram, Hiawyn. *Skittlewonder and the wizard*
Osofsky, Audrey. *Dreamcatcher*
Oughton, Jerrie. *How the stars fell into the
sky*
Over in the meadow, ill. by Ezra Jack Keats
A paper of pins, ill. by Margaret Gordon
Parkinson, Kathy. *The enormous turnip*
Parnall, Peter. *The great fish*
Parry, Marian. *King of the fish*
Parsons, Virginia. *Pinocchio and Gepetto*
Pinocchio and the money tree
Pinocchio goes on the stage
Pinocchio plays truant
Paterson, Katherine. *The tale of the
Mandarin ducks*
Patron, Susan. *Burgoo stew*
Pattison, Darcy. *The river dragon*
Paxton, Tom. *Belling the cat and other Æsop
fables*

Pearson, Kit. *The singing basket*
The peasant's pea patch, ill. by Robert M.
Quackenbush
Pellowski, Anne. *The nine crying dolls*
Pen Cai Ying. *Monkey creates havoc in
heaven*
Perrault, Charles. *Cinderella*, ill. by Sheilah
Beckett
Cinderella, ill. by Marcia Brown
Cinderella, ill. by Paul Galdone
Cinderella, ill. by Diane Goode
Cinderella, ill. by Susan Jeffers
Cinderella, ill. by Emanuele Luzzati
Cinderella, ill. by James Marshall
Cinderella, ill. by Phil Smith
Puss in boots, ill. by Marcia Brown
Puss in boots, ill. by Lorinda Bryan
Cauley
Puss in boots, ill. by Jean Claverie
Puss in boots, ill. by Hans Fischer
Puss in boots, ill. by Paul Galdone
Puss in boots, retold and ill. by John S.
Goodall
Puss in boots, retold and ill. by Gail E.
Haley
Puss in boots, ill. by Julia Noonan
Puss in boots, ill. by Tony Ross
Puss in boots, ill. by William Stobbs
Puss in boots, ill. by Alain Vaes
Puss in boots, ill. by Barry Wilkinson
The sleeping beauty, ill. by David Walker
Pevear, Richard. *Mister Cat-and-a-Half*
Our king has horns!
Phillips, Mildred. *The sign in Mendel's
window*
Phumla. *Nomi and the magic fish*
Pittman, Helena Clare. *The gift of the
willows*
A grain of rice
Plante, Patricia. *The turtle and the two ducks*
Plume, Ilse. *The story of Befana*
Polacco, Patricia. *Rechenka's eggs*
Polushkin, Maria. *Bubba and Babba*
The little hen and the giant
Porazińska, Janina. *The enchanted book*
Prather, Ray. *The ostrich girl*
Presencer, Alain. *Roaring lion tales*
Preussler, Otfried. *The tale of the unicorn*
The prince who knew his fate, ill. by Lise
Manniche
Prokofiev, Sergei Sergeievitch. *Peter and
the wolf*, ill. by Reg Cartwright
Peter and the wolf, ill. by Warren
Chappell
Peter and the wolf, ill. by Barbara
Cooney
Peter and the wolf, ill. by Frans Haacken
Peter and the wolf, ill. by Alan Howard
Peter and the wolf, ill. by Charles
Mikolaycak
Peter and the wolf, ill. by Jörg Müller

Peter and the wolf, ill. by Josef Paleček
Peter and the wolf, ill. by Kozo Shimizu
Peter and the wolf, ill. by Erna Voigt
Quackenbush, Robert M. *Clementine*
She'll be comin' 'round the mountain
Skip to my Lou
There'll be a hot time in the old town tonight
Quigley, Lillian Fox. *The blind men and the elephant*
Raphael, Elaine. *Turnabout*
Rappaport, Doreen. *Journey of Meng*
Rayevsky, Inna. *The talking tree*
Reesink, Marijke. *The golden treasure*
The princess who always ran away
Reit, Seymour. *Rebus bears*
Richardson, Jean. *The sleeping beauty: the story of Tchaikovsky's ballet*
Riordan, James. *The three magic gifts*
Robbins, Ruth. *Baboushka and the three kings*
How the first rainbow was made
Robertson, Joanne. *Sea witches*
Robinson, Adjai. *Femi and old grandaddie*
Rockwell, Anne F. *Bafana*
The old woman and her pig and 10 other stories
Poor Goose
The three bears and 15 other stories
Thump thump thump!
The wolf who had a wonderful dream
The wonderful eggs of Furicchia
Rodanas, Kristina. *The dragonfly's tale*
Rogasky, Barbara. *The water of life*
Rogers, Margaret. *Green is beautiful*
Rohmer, Harriet. *How we came to the fifth world*
The invisible hunters
Mother scorpion country
Ronay, Jadja. *Ginger*
Root, Phyllis. *Soup for supper*
Rose, Anne. *Akimba and the magic cow*
Pot full of luck
Spider in the sky
The talking turnip
The triumphs of Fuzzy Fogtop
Rosen, Michael J. *How the animals got their colors*
Ross, Tony. *The boy who cried wolf*
The enchanted pig
Hansel and Gretel
The pied piper of Hamelin
Stone soup
Roth, Susan L. *Fire came to the earth people*
Kanahena
The story of light
Roughsey, Dick. *The giant devil-dingo*
Rounds, Glen. *The boll weevil*
Casey Jones
Sweet Betsy from Pike
Sahagun, Bernardino de. *Spirit child*

Sanderson, Ruth. *The enchanted wood*
San Souci, Robert D. *The enchanted tapestry*
The legend of Scarface
Song of Sedna
Sukey and the mermaid
The talking eggs
The white cat
Sawyer, Ruth. *Journey cake, ho!*
Say, Allen. *Once under the cherry blossom tree*
Scarry, Richard. *Richard Scarry's animal nursery tales*
Schatz, Letta. *The extraordinary tug-of-war*
Schiller, Barbara. *The white rat's tale*
Schwartz, Alvin. *All of our noses are here and other stories*
Schwartz, Amy. *Yossel Zissel and the wisdom of Chelm*
Scieszka, Jon. *The frog prince, continued*
The true story of the three little pigs by A. Wolf, as told to John
Scott, Sally. *The magic horse*
The three wonderful beggars
Scribner, Charles. *The devil's bridge*
Seeger, Pete. *Abiyoyo*
The foolish frog
Service, Pamela F. *The wizard of wind and rock*
Seuling, Barbara. *The teeny tiny woman*
Sewall, Marcia. *Animal song*
The little wee tyke
The wee, wee mannie and the big, big coo
Shannon, George. *Oh, I love!*
The Piney Woods peddler
Shearer, Marilyn J. *The crown of fools*
Sherman, Josepha. *Vassilisa the wise*
Shi, Zhang Xiu. *Monkey and the white bone demon*
Showalter, Jean B. *The donkey ride*
Shub, Elizabeth. *Seeing is believing*
Shulevitz, Uri. *The treasure*
Shute, Linda. *Clever Tom and the leprechaun*
Momotaro, the peach boy
Siberell, Anne. *A journey to paradise*
Whale in the sky
Siddiqui, Ashraf. *Bhombal Dass, the uncle of lion*
Simms, Laura. *The squeaky door*
Sleator, William. *The angry moon*
Slobodkin, Louis. *Colette and the princess*
Small, Terry. *The legend of William Tell*
Snyder, Dianne. *The boy of the three-year nap*
Snyder, Zilpha Keatley. *The changing maze*
Spier, Peter. *The Erie Canal*
The legend of New Amsterdam
The squire's bride, ill. by Marcia Sewall
Stalder, Valerie. *Even the devil is afraid of a shrew*
Stan-Padilla, Viento. *Dream Feather*
Stansfield, Ian. *The legend of the whale*
Steptoe, John. *Mufaro's beautiful daughters*

The story of jumping mouse
Stern, Simon. *Vasily and the dragon*
Stevens, Bryna. *Borrowed feathers and other fables*
Stewig, John Warren. *Stone soup*
Still, James. *Jack and the wonder beans*
Tanaka, Beatrice. *The chase*
Tarrant, Margaret. *Fairy tales*
Taylor, Mark. *The bold fisherman*
Old Blue, you good dog you
Tempest, P. *How the cock wrecked the manor*
Thompson, Harwood. *The witch's cat*
The three bears. *Goldilocks and the three bears*, retold and ill. by H. Amery
Goldilocks and the three bears, ill. by Yvette Banek
Goldilocks and the three bears, ill. by Jan Brett
Goldilocks and the three bears, ill. by Lorinda Bryan Cauley
Goldilocks and the three bears, ill. by Jane Dyer
Goldilocks and the three bears, ill. by Lynn Bywaters Ferris
Goldilocks and the three bears, ill. by James Marshall
Goldilocks and the three bears, ill. by Janet Stevens
Goldilocks and the three bears, ill. by Bernadette Watts
The story of the three bears, ill. by L. Leslie Brooke
The story of the three bears, ill. by William Stobbs
The three bears, adapt. and ill. by Byron Barton
The three bears, ill. by Paul Galdone
The three bears, ill. by Feodor Rojankovsky
The three bears, ill. by Robin Spowart
The three little pigs. *The original three little pigs re-told*, ill. by Jonathan Smith
The story of the three little pigs, ill. by L. Leslie Brooke
The story of the three little pigs, ill. by William Stobbs
Three little pigs [Facsimile ed]
The three little pigs, retold and ill. by Val Biro
The three little pigs, retold and ill. by Gavin Bishop
The three little pigs, ill. by Caroline Bucknall
The three little pigs, ill. by Stephen Cartwright
The three little pigs, ill. by Lorinda Bryan Cauley
The three little pigs, ill. by Jean Claverie
The three little pigs, ill. by William Pène Du Bois
The three little pigs, ill. by Paul Galdone

The three little pigs, retold and ill. by James Marshall
The three little pigs, ill. by Rodney Peppé
The three little pigs, ill. by Edda Reinl
The three little pigs, ill. by John Wallner
The three little pigs, ill. by Irma Wilde
The three little pigs, ill. by Margot Zemach
The three little pigs and the big bad wolf, retold and ill. by Glen Rounds
The three little pigs and the fox, ill. by S. D. Schindler
The three pigs, ill. by Tony Ross
Tolhurst, Marilyn. *Somebody and the three Blairs*
Tolstoĭ, Alekseĭ Nikolaevich. *The great big enormous turnip*
Tom Thumb. *Grimm Tom Thumb*, ill. by Svend Otto S.
Tom Thumb, ill. by L. Leslie Brooke
Tom Thumb, ill. by Dennis Hockerman
Tom Thumb, ill. by Felix Hoffmann
Tom Thumb, ill. by Lidia Postma
Tom Thumb, ill. by Richard Jesse Watson
Tom Thumb, ill. by William Wiesner
Tom Tit Tot. *Tom Tit Tot*, ill. by Evaline Ness
Torre, Betty L. *The luminous pearl*
Towle, Faith M. *The magic cooking pot*
Toye, William. *Fire stealer*
How summer came to Canada
The loon's necklace
The mountain goats of Temlaham
Tresselt, Alvin R. *The mitten*
Tripp, Wallace. *The tale of a pig*
Troughton, Joanna. *How rabbit stole the fire*
How the birds changed their feathers
Make-believe tales
Tortoise's dream
What made Tiddalik laugh
Who will be the sun?
Tsultim, Yeshe. *The mouse king*
Tune, Suelyn Ching. *How Maui slowed the sun*
Turkle, Brinton. *Deep in the forest*
Turska, Krystyna. *The magician of Cracow*
The woodcutter's duck
Uchida, Yoshiko. *The two foolish cats*
Va, Leong. *A letter to the king*
Valentine, Johnny. *The duke who outlawed jelly beans and other stories*
Van Laan, Nancy. *The legend of El Dorado*
Rainbow crow
VanRynbach, Iris. *The soup stone*
Van Woerkom, Dorothy. *Alexandra the rock-eater*
The queen who couldn't bake gingerbread
The rat, the ox and the zodiac
Sea frog, city frog
Varga, Judy. *The mare's egg*
Vernon, Adele. *The riddle*

Vesey, A. *The princess and the frog*
Volkmer, Jane Anne. *Song of Chirimia: La Musica de la Chirimia*
Waddell, Martin. *The tough princess*
Wahl, Jan. *Little Eight John*
Walker, Barbara K. (Barbara Kerlin). *New patches for old*
Wall, Lina Mao. *Judge Rabbit and the tree spirit*
Walsh, Grahame L. *Didane the koala*
 The goori goori bird
Walt Disney Productions. *Walt Disney's Snow White and the seven dwarfs*
Walter, Mildred Pitts. *Ty's one-man band*
Wang, Rosalind C. *The fourth question*
Ward, Helen. *The golden pear*
Watts, Bernadette. *St. Francis and the proud crow*
Weil, Lisl. *Pandora's box*
Weiss, Harvey. *The sooner hound*
Weiss, Nicki. *If you're happy and you know it*
Wells, Rosemary. *The little lame prince*
Westcott, Nadine Bernard. *Skip to my Lou*
Westerberg, Christine. *The cap that mother made*
Westwood, Jennifer. *Going to Squintum's Widdecombe Fair*, ill. by Christine Price
Wiesner, David. *The loathsome dragon*
Wilde, Oscar. *Fairy tales of Oscar Wilde: The selfish giant, and The star child*, adapt. and ill. by P. Craig Russell
Wildsmith, Brian. *The true cross*
Williams, Jay. *The practical princess*
 The surprising things Maui did
Williams, Julie Stewart. *And the birds appeared*
Wilson, Barbara Ker. *The turtle and the island*
Wilson, Sarah. *Beware the dragons!*
Winter, Jeanette. *The girl and the moon man*
Winthrop, Elizabeth. *Vasilissa the beautiful*
Wisniewski, David. *Elfwyn's saga*
 The warrior and the wise man
Wolf, Ann. *The rabbit and the turtle*
Wolkstein, Diane. *The banza*
 The cool ride in the sky
 The legend of Sleepy Hollow
 The magic wings
 Oom razoom; or, Go I know not where, Bring back I know not what
 White wave
Wood, Audrey. *Heckedy Peg*
Wright, Freire. *Beauty and the beast*
Wright, Jill. *The old woman and the Willy Nilly Man*
Xiong, Blia. *Nine-in-one Grr! Grr!*
Yacowitz, Caryn. *The jade stone*
Yagawa, Sumiko. *The crane wife*
Yashima, Tarō. *Seashore story*
Yeoman, John. *The wild washerwomen*
Yolen, Jane. *Greyling*

Sky dogs
The three bears rhyme book
Young, Ed (Edward). *Lon Po Po*
 The rooster's horns
 The terrible Nung Gwama
Zelinsky, Paul O. *The maid and the mouse and the odd-shaped house*
Zemach, Harve. *Duffy and the devil*
 Nail soup
Zemach, Kaethe. *The beautiful rat*
Zemach, Margot. *It could always be worse*
 Jake and Honeybunch go to heaven
 The little tiny woman
 The three wishes
Zijlstra, Tjerk. *Benny and his geese*
Zola, Meguido. *The dream of promise*

Food

Adler, David A. *Bunny rabbit rebus*
Allamand, Pascale. *Cocoa beans and daisies*
Allard, Harry. *The cactus flower bakery*
Allen, Laura Jean. *Rollo and Tweedy and the case of the missing cheese*
Allen, Robert. *Ten little babies eat*
Ambrus, Victor G. *Country wedding*
Andrews, Jan. *Very last first time*
Armitage, Ronda. *Ice creams for Rosie*
 The lighthouse keeper's lunch
Arnosky, Jim. *Raccoons and ripe corn*
Aronin, Ben. *The secret of the Sabbath fish*
Asch, Frank. *Good lemonade*
 Moon bear
 Popcorn
Azarian, Mary. *The tale of John Barleycorn or, From barley to beer*
Bach, Alice. *The smartest bear and his brother Oliver*
Banks, Kate. *Alphabet soup*
Barasch, Lynne. *Rodney's inside story*
Barbato, Juli. *Mom's night out*
Barbour, Karen. *Little Nino's pizzeria*
Barklem, Jill. *The secret staircase*
Barrett, Judi. *An apple a day*
 Cloudy with a chance of meatballs
Basso, Bill. *The top of the pizzas*
Baugh, Dolores M. *Supermarket*
Benchley, Nathaniel. *Walter the homing pigeon*
Benedictus, Roger. *Fifty million sausages*
Benjamin, Alan. *Ribtickle Town*
Berenstain, Stan. *The Berenstain bears and too much junk food*
Berson, Harold. *Pop! goes the turnip*
 The rats who lived in the delicatessen
Beskow, Elsa Maartman. *Peter in Blueberry Land*
 Peter's adventures in Blueberry land
Bethell, Jean. *Hooray for Henry*
Black, Irma Simonton. *Is this my dinner?*
Bolliger, Max. *The giants' feast*
 The golden apple

Bond, Michael. *Paddington and the knickerbocker rainbow*
Boutell, Clarence Burley. *The fat baron*
Brandenberg, Franz. *Fresh cider and apple pie*
Brierley, Louise. *King Lion and his cooks*
Bright, Robert. *Gregory, the noisiest and strongest boy in Grangers Grove*
Brimner, Larry Dane. *Country Bear's good neighbor*
Broome, Errol. *The smallest koala*
Brown, Judith Gwyn. *Max and the truffle pig*
Brown, Marc Tolon. *Pickle things*
Brown, Marcia. *Stone soup*
Bruna, Dick. *The fish*
Budd, Lillian. *The pie wagon*
Burch, Robert. *The hunting trip*
Burningham, John. *Avocado baby*
  The cupboard
  Where's Julius?
Burt, Olive. *Let's find out about bread*
Burton, Jane. *Animals eating*
Calhoun, Mary. *Audubon cat*
  The hungry leprechaun
Carle, Eric. *My very first book of food*
  Pancakes, pancakes
  Walter the baker
Carlstrom, Nancy White. *Moose in the garden*
Carrick, Donald. *Milk*
Caseley, Judith. *Grandpa's garden lunch*
Cauley, Lorinda Bryan. *Pease porridge hot*
Cazet, Denys. *Lucky me*
Chalmers, Audrey. *Hundreds and hundreds of pancakes*
Clark, Emma Chichester. *Lunch with Aunt Augusta*
Coatsworth, Elizabeth. *Under the green willow*
Cohen, Peter Zachary. *Olson's meat pies*
Coontz, Otto. *Starring Rosa*
Croll, Carolyn. *Too many babas*
Curious George and the pizza
Curious George goes to an ice cream shop
Cushman, Doug. *Possum stew*
Czernecki, Stefan. *The sleeping bread*
Darling, Abigail. *Teddy bears' picnic cookbook*
Degen, Bruce. *Jamberry*
Demarest, Chris L. *No peas for Nellie*
De Paola, Tomie (Thomas Anthony).
  Pancakes for breakfast
  The popcorn book
  Tony's bread
De Regniers, Beatrice Schenk. *Sam and the impossible thing*
Devlin, Wende. *Old Witch and the polka-dot ribbon*
Dooley, Norah. *Everybody cooks rice*
Dragonwagon, Crescent. *This is the bread I baked for Ned*

Drucker, Malka. *Grandma's latkes*
Du Quette, Keith. *Rippening day for a picnic*
Ehlert, Lois. *Growing vegetable soup*
Engel, Diana. *Gino Badino*
Esterl, Arnica. *The fine round cake*
Evans, Katie. *Hunky Dory ate it*
Feder, Harriet K. *What can you do with a bagel?*
Fernandes, Kim. *Visiting granny*
Flory, Jane. *We'll have a friend for lunch*
Fontaine, Jan. *The spaghetti tree*
Forest, Heather. *The woman who flummoxed the fairies*
Fox, Mem. *Possum magic*
Gackenbach, Dick. *Mother Rabbit's son Tom*
Gág, Wanda. *The funny thing*
Galdone, Paul. *The magic porridge pot*
Gantschev, Ivan. *RumpRump*
Gelbard, Jane. *My eating book*
Gibbons, Gail. *The milk makers*
  The missing maple syrup sap mystery
  The seasons of Arnold's apple tree
Giffard, Hannah. *Red Fox*
The gingerbread boy. *The gingerbread boy*, ill. by Paul Galdone
  The gingerbread boy, ill. by Joan Elizabeth Goodman
  The gingerbread boy, ill. by William Curtis Holdsworth
  The gingerbread man, ill. by Gerald Rose
  The pancake boy, ill. by Lorinda Bryan Cauley
Goldin, Barbara Diamond. *Cakes and miracles*
Goldstein, Bobbye S. *What's on the menu?*
Goodall, John S. *The surprise picnic*
Greeley, Valerie. *Where's my share?*
Greene, Carol. *The world's biggest birthday cake*
Greene, Ellin. *The pumpkin giant*
Greene, Jacqueline Dembar. *What his father did*
Gretz, Susanna. *It's your turn, Roger*
Gross, Ruth Belov. *What's on my plate?*
Gullikson, Sandy. *Trouble for breakfast*
Gunthrop, Karen. *Adam and the wolf*
Haddon, Mark. *Toni and the tomato soup*
Hale, Irina. *Chocolate mouse and sugar pig*
Hale, Linda. *The glorious Christmas soup party*
Hayes, Sarah. *Eat up, Gemma*
Heller, Linda. *Lily at the table*
Hellsing, Lennart. *The wonderful pumpkin*
Hennessy, B. G. *Jake baked the cake*
Hirsh, Marilyn. *Leela and the watermelon*
  Potato pancakes all around
Hoban, Russell. *Bread and jam for Frances*
  Dinner at Alberta's
Holden, Edith. *The hedgehog feast*
Holl, Adelaide. *Small Bear solves a mystery*

Hong, Lily Toy. *How the ox star fell from heaven*

Howe, James. *Hot fudge*

Hughes, Peter. *The emperor's oblong pancake*
The king who loved candy

Hutchins, Pat. *Don't forget the bacon!*

Jack Sprat. *The life of Jack Sprat, his wife and his cat*, ill. by Paul Galdone

Jacobs, Joseph. *Johnny-cake*, ill. by Emma Lillian Brock
Johnny-cake, ill. by William Stobbs

Janice. *Little Bear's pancake party*
Little Bear's Sunday breakfast

Joly-Berbesson, Fanny. *Marceau Bonappetit*

Kahl, Virginia. *The Duchess bakes a cake*
The perfect pancake
Plum pudding for Christmas

Kandoian, Ellen. *Is anybody up?*

Kantor, MacKinlay. *The preposterous week*

Kasza, Keiko. *The wolf's chicken stew*

Kelley, True. *Let's eat*

Kennaway, Adrienne. *Bushbaby*

Kessler, Leonard P. *Do you have any carrots?*
Soup for the king

Khalsa, Dayal Kaur. *How pizza came to our town*

Kobayashi, Robert. *Maria Mazaretti loves spaghetti*

Koller, Jackie French. *Fish fry tonight*

Komoda, Beverly. *Simon's soup*

Kovalski, Maryann. *Pizza for breakfast*

Krings, Antoon. *Oliver's strawberry patch*

Kroll, Steven. *The Hokey-Pokey man*

Kwitz, Mary DeBall. *Little chick's breakfast*

Lapp, Eleanor. *The blueberry bears*

Lasker, Joe. *Lentil soup*

Leedy, Loreen. *The dragon Thanksgiving feast*

Lemerise, Bruce. *Sheldon's lunch*

Leonard, Marcia. *Rainboots for breakfast*

Levine, Abby. *Too much mush!*

Levitin, Sonia. *Nobody stole the pie*

Lewin, Betsy. *Animal snackers*

Lindsey, Treska. *When Batistine made bread*

Lobel, Anita. *The pancake*

Lurie, Morris. *The story of Imelda, who was small*

Lynn, Sara. *Food*

Lyon, George-Ella. *The outside inn*

McCloskey, Robert. *Blueberries for Sal*

McGovern, Ann. *Eggs on your nose*

MacGregor, Marilyn. *Helen the hungry bear*

McGuire, Richard. *The orange book*

McKee, David. *King Rollo and the bread*

Maestro, Betsy. *How do apples grow?*

Mahy, Margaret. *Jam*

Manushkin, Fran. *Moon dragon*

Marshall, James. *Miss Dog's Christmas*
Yummers!
Yummers too: the second course

Martchenko, Michael. *Bird feeder banquet*

Mayer, Mercer. *Frog goes to dinner*

Miller, Edna. *Mouskin's frosty friend*

Miller, Margaret. *Time to eat*

Mitgutsch, Ali. *From lemon to lemonade*

Morris, Ann. *Bread, bread, bread*

Murphey, Sara. *The roly poly cookie*

Murphy, Jill. *A piece of cake*

Nordqvist, Sven. *Pancake pie*

Norman, Philip Ross. *The carrot war*

O'Keefe, Susan Heyboer. *One hungry monster*

Orbach, Ruth. *Apple pigs*

Oxenbury, Helen. *Eating out*

Paterson, Diane. *Eat*

Patron, Susan. *Burgoo stew*

Patz, Nancy. *No thumpin' no bumpin' no rumpus tonight!*

Pelham, David. *Sam's sandwich*

Petie, Haris. *The seed the squirrel dropped*

Pieńkowski, Jan. *Food*

Pillar, Marjorie. *Pizza man*

Porter, Sue. *One potato*

Radlauer, Ruth Shaw. *Breakfast by Molly*

Rayner, Mary. *Mrs. Pig's bulk buy*

Retan, Walter. *The steam shovel that wouldn't eat dirt*

Rice, Eve. *Sam who never forgets*

Robart, Rose. *The cake that Mack ate*

Rockwell, Anne F. *Apples and pumpkins*
The Mother Goose cookie-candy book
The wolf who had a wonderful dream

Rockwell, Harlow. *My kitchen*

Roffey, Maureen. *Meatime*

Rogers, Paul (Patrick). *Somebody's awake*

Rogow, Zak. *Oranges*

Root, Phyllis. *Soup for supper*

Schwalje, Marjory. *Mr. Angelo*

Seuss, Dr. *Green eggs and ham*
Scrambled eggs super!

Sharmat, Marjorie Weinman. *Nate the Great*
Nate the Great and the lost list
Nate the Great and the phony clue
Nate the Great goes undercover

Sharmat, Mitchell. *Gregory, the terrible eater*

Shecter, Ben. *The big stew*

Shelby, Anne. *Potluck*

Shott, Stephen. *Mealtime*

Slepian, Jan. *The hungry thing returns*

Slobodkina, Esphyr. *The wonderful feast*

Slocum, Rosalie. *Breakfast with the clowns*

Sobol, Harriet Langsam. *A book of vegetables*

Sondheimer, Ilse. *The magic of Pomme*

Spier, Peter. *Food market*

Spohn, Kate. *Introducing Fanny.*

Springer, Sally. *Let's make latkes*

Spurr, Elizabeth. *The biggest birthday cake in the world*

Stadler, John. *Animal cafe*

Stamaty, Mark Alan. *Minnie Maloney and Macaroni*
Stevenson, Jocelyn. *Red and the pumpkins*
Stewig, John Warren. *Stone soup*
Stock, Catherine. *Alexander's midnight snack*
Szekeres, Cyndy. *Suppertime for Frieda Fuzzypaws*
Taylor, Judy. *Dudley and the strawberry shake*
Dudley in a jam
Testa, Fulvio. *The land where the ice cream grows*
Thayer, Jane. *The popcorn dragon*, ill. by Jay Hyde Barnum
The popcorn dragon, ill. by Lisa McCue
Thompson, Vivian Laubach. *The horse that liked sandwiches*
Towle, Faith M. *The magic cooking pot*
Uchida, Yoshiko. *The two foolish cats*
VanRynbach, Iris. *The soup stone*
Van Woerkom, Dorothy. *Alexandra the rock-eater*
Vevers, Gwynne. *Animals that store food*
Wabbes, Marie. *Rose is hungry*
Wallner, Alexandra. *Munch*
Ward, Sally G. *Molly and Grandpa*
Wasmuth, Eleanor. *The picnic basket*
Watanabe, Shigeo. *What a good lunch!*
Watson, Clyde. *Tom Fox and the apple pie*
Valentine foxes
Watson, Nancy Dingman. *Sugar on snow*
Weir, Bob. *Panther dream*
Weiss, Monica. *Mmmm...cookies!*
Westcott, Nadine Bernard. *Peanut butter and jelly*
Wikler, Madeline. *My first seder*
Willard, Nancy. *The marzipan moon*
Williams, Gweneira Maureen. *Timid Timothy, the kitten who learned to be brave*
Wilson, Sarah. *Muskrat, muskrat, eat your peas!*
Wilson-Kelly, Becky. *Mother Grumpy's dog biscuits*
Windham, Sophie. *Noah's ark*
Winthrop, Elizabeth. *Potbellied possums*
Wood, Audrey. *Heckedy Peg*
Wood, Leslie. *A dog called Mischief*
Wyllie, Stephen. *Dinner with fox*
Wynot, Jillian. *The Mother's Day sandwich*
Young, Miriam Burt. *The sugar mouse cake*
Ziefert, Harriet. *Breakfast time!*
Surprise!

Foolishness *see* Character traits – foolishness

Football *see* Sports – football

Foreign lands

Aleichem, Sholem. *Hanukah money*
Allen, Thomas B. *Where children live*

Anglund, Joan Walsh. *Love one another*
Anno, Mitsumasa. *All in a day*
Baylor, Byrd. *The way to start a day*
Berg, Leila. *Folk tales for reading and telling*
Borchers, Elisabeth. *Dear Sarah*
Brann, Esther. *'Round the world*
Bridgman, Elizabeth. *How to travel with grownups*
Bryson, Bernarda. *The twenty miracles of Saint Nicolas*
De Regniers, Beatrice Schenk. *Little Sister and the Month Brothers*
Domanska, Janina. *Marek, the little fool*
Douglas, Michael. *Round, round world*
Gerrard, Roy. *Sir Francis Drake*
Goffstein, M. B. (Marilyn Brooke). *Across the sea*
Gray, Nigel. *A country far away*
Handford, Martin. *Where's Waldo?*
Knight, Margy Burns. *Talking walls*
Mitchell, Cynthia. *Here a little child I stand*
Morris, Ann. *Loving*
On the go
Orstadius, Brita. *The dolphin journey*
Otto, Svend. *The giant fish and other stories*
Rehnman, Mats. *The clay flute*
Robb, Brian. *My grandmother's djinn*
Schulz, Charles M. *Bon voyage, Charlie Brown (and don't come back!!)*
Scott, Sally. *The magic horse*
Singer, Marilyn. *Nine o'clock lullaby*
Van Woerkom, Dorothy. *Alexandra the rock-eater*
Yolen, Jane. *Street rhymes around the world*

Foreign lands – Africa

Aardema, Verna. *Bimwili and the Zimwi*
Bringing the rain to Kapiti Plain
Half-a-ball-of-kenki
Ji-nongo-nongo means riddles
Oh, Kojo! How could you!
Princess Gorilla and a new kind of water
Rabbit makes a monkey of lion
The vingananee and the tree toad
Who's in Rabbit's house?
Why mosquitoes buzz in people's ears
Abisch, Roz. *The clever turtle*
Adamson, Joy. *Elsa*
Elsa and her cubs
Pippa the cheetah and her cubs
Adoff, Arnold. *Ma nDa La*
Alexander, Lloyd. *Fortune tellers*
Arkin, Alan. *Black and white*
Arnott, Kathleen. *Spiders, crabs and creepy crawlers*
Aruego, José. *We hide, you seek*
Bare, Colleen Stanley. *Who comes to the water hole?*
Bemelmans, Ludwig. *Rosebud*
Bernheim, Marc. *In Africa*
A week in Aya's world

Bernstein, Margery. *The first morning*
Berson, Harold. *Kassim's shoes*
  Why the jackal won't speak to the hedgehog
Bess, Clayton. *The truth about the moon*
Bible, Charles. *Hamdaani*
Bond, Jean Carey. *A is for Africa*
Borden, Beatrice Brown. *Wild animals of
  Africa*
Bryan, Ashley. *Beat the story-drum, pum-
  pum*
  Lion and the ostrich chicks
Carrick, Malcolm. *I can squash elephants!*
Cendrars, Blaise. *Shadow*
Ching. *The baboon's umbrella*
Cole, Babette. *Nungu and the elephant*
  Nungu and the hippopotamus
Daly, Niki. *Not so fast Songololo*
Davis, Douglas F. *The lion's tail*
Dayrell, Elphinstone. *Why the sun and the
  moon live in the sky*
Dee, Ruby. *Two ways to count to ten*
De Paola, Tomie (Thomas Anthony). *Bill
  and Pete*
Domanska, Janina. *The tortoise and the tree*
Du Bois, William Pène. *Otto in Africa*
Economakis, Olga. *Oasis of the stars*
Elkin, Benjamin. *Such is the way of the
  world*
Fatio, Louise. *The happy lion in Africa*
Feelings, Muriel. *Jambo means hello*
  Menjo means one
Fournier, Catharine. *The coconut thieves*
Graham, Lorenz B. *Song of the boat*
Greenfield, Eloise. *Africa dream*
Grifalconi, Ann. *Darkness and the butterfly*
  Flyaway girl
  The village of round and square houses
Guy, Rosa. *Mother crocodile*
Hadithi, Mwenye. *Greedy zebra*
  Hot hippo
Haley, Gail E. *A story, a story*
Holding, James. *The lazy little Zulu*
Kennaway, Adrienne. *Bushbaby*
  Little elephant's walk
Kimmel, Eric A. *Anansi goes fishing*
Kipling, Rudyard. *The elephant's child*, ill.
  by Louise Brierley
  The elephant's child, ill. by Lorinda Bryan
  Cauley
  The elephant's child, ill. by Tim Raglin
  How the camel got his hump, ill. by
  Quentin Blake
  How the camel got his hump, ill. by Tim
  Raglin
Kirn, Ann. *The tale of a crocodile*
Kitchen, Bert. *Tenrec's twigs*
Knutson, Barbara. *Why the crab has no head*
Laskowski, Jerzy. *Master of the royal cats*
Lewin, Hugh. *An elephant came to swim*
  Jafta
  Jafta and the wedding

Jafta—the journey
Jafta—the town
Jafta's father
Jafta's mother
Lexau, Joan M. *Crocodile and hen*
McDermott, Gerald. *Anansi the spider*
  Zomo the rabbit
McKissack, Patricia C. *Who is coming?*
Mantegazza, Giovanna. *The hippopotamus*
Musgrove, Margaret. *Ashanti to Zulu*
Mwalimu. *Awful aardvark*
Pearce, Q. L. *In the African grasslands*
Phumla. *Nomi and the magic fish*
Prather, Ray. *The ostrich girl*
Purcell, John Wallace. *African animals*
Robinson, Adjai. *Femi and old grandaddie*
Rose, Anne. *Akimba and the magic cow*
  Pot full of luck
Roth, Susan L. *Fire came to the earth people*
Routh, Jonathan. *The Nuns go to Africa*
Ryden, Hope. *Wild animals of Africa ABC*
Sackett, Elisabeth. *Danger on the African
  grassland*
Schatz, Letta. *The extraordinary tug-of-war*
Shepard, Steve. *Elvis Hornbill, international
  business bird*
Steig, William. *Doctor De Soto goes to Africa*
Steptoe, John. *Mufaro's beautiful daughters*
Troughton, Joanna. *Tortoise's dream*
Walter, Mildred Pitts. *Brother to the wind*
Ward, Leila. *I am eyes, ni macho*
Weir, Bob. *Panther dream*
Williams, Karen Lynn. *Galimoto*
  When Africa was home
Yoshida, Toshi. *Elephant crossing*
  Rhinoceros mother
  Young lions
Zaslavsky, Claudia. *Count on your fingers
  African style*
Zimelman, Nathan. *Treed by a pride of irate
  lions*

Foreign lands – Antarctic

Benson, Patrick. *Little penguin*
Wood, Audrey. *Little Penguin's tale*

Foreign lands – Arabia

Alexander, Sue. *Nadia the willful*
Arabian Nights. *Arabian Nights
  entertainments*, comp. by Charles Mozley
Haskins, Jim. *Count your way through the
  Arab world*

Foreign lands – Arctic

Damjan, Mischa. *Atuk*
De Beer, Hans. *Little polar bear finds a
  friend*
Raffi. *Baby beluga*
Reynolds, Jan. *Far north*
Ryder, Joanne. *White bear, ice bear*

Sackett, Elisabeth. *Danger on the Arctic ice*

Foreign lands – Armenia

Bider, Djemma. *A drop of honey*
Hogrogian, Nonny. *The contest*

Foreign lands – Australia

The all-amazing ha ha book
Argent, Kerry. *Animal capers*
  Wombat and Bandicoot: best friends
Baker, Jeannie. *Where the forest meets the sea*
  Window
Base, Graeme. *My grandma lived in Gooligulch*
Bassett, Lisa. *Koala Christmas*
Cox, David. *Bossyboots*
  Tin Lizzie and Little Nell
Dumbleton, Mike. *Dial-a-croc*
Factor, Jane. *Summer*
Foreman, Michael. *Panda and the bushfire*
Fox, Mem. *Possum magic*
Hilton, Nette. *Dirty Dave*
Jacka, Martin. *Waiting for Billy*
Kipling, Rudyard. *The sing-song of old man kangaroo*, ill. by Michael C. Taylor
Lester, Alison. *Rosie sips spiders*
Niland, Kilmeny. *A bellbird in a flame tree*
Nunes, Susan. *Tiddalick the frog*
Paterson, A. B. (Andrew Barton). *Mulga Bill's bicycle*
  Waltzing Matilda
Pershall, Mary K. *Hello, Barney!*
Pittaway, Margaret. *The rainforest children*
Powzyk, Joyce. *Tasmania*
Reynolds, Jan. *Down under*
Roughsey, Dick. *The giant devil-dingo*
Thiele, Colin. *Farmer Schulz's ducks*
Trinca, Rod. *One woolly wombat*
Troughton, Joanna. *What made Tiddalik laugh*
Turner, Ethel. *Walking to school*
Vaughan, Marcia K. *Wombat stew*
Wagner, Jenny. *The bunyip of Berkeley's Creek*
Walsh, Grahame L. *Didane the koala*
  The goori goori bird
Whitmore, Adam. *Max in Australia*

Foreign lands – Austria

Kahl, Virginia. *Away went Wolfgang*

Foreign lands – Bali

Cox, David. *Ayu and the perfect moon*

Foreign lands - Bavaria *see* Foreign lands – Austria; Foreign lands – Germany

Foreign lands – Borneo

Climo, Shirley. *The match between the winds*

Foreign lands – Burma

Troughton, Joanna. *Make-believe tales*

Foreign lands – Cambodia

Lee, Jeanne M. *Silent lotus*
Wall, Lina Mao. *Judge Rabbit and the tree spirit*

Foreign lands – Canada

Adams, Pam. *There was an old lady who swallowed a fly*
Andrews, Jan. *Very last first time*
Blades, Ann. *Mary of mile 18*
Bonne, Rose. *I know an old lady*, ill. by Abner Graboff
  I know an old lady who swallowed a fly, ill. by William Stobbs
Climo, Lindee. *Chester's barn*
Dos Santos, Joyce Audy. *The diviner*
  Henri and the Loup-Garou
Holling, Holling C. (Holling Clancy). *Paddle-to-the-sea*
Moak, Allan. *A big city ABC*
Munsch, Robert N. *A promise is a promise*
Norman, Howard. *The owl-scatterer*
Pearson, Kit. *The singing basket*
Poulin, Stéphane. *Can you catch Josephine?*
  Have you seen Josephine?
Speare, Jean. *A candle for Christmas*
Ward, Lynd. *The biggest bear*
  Nic of the woods
Waterton, Betty. *Pettranella*
Woolaver, Lance. *Christmas with the rural mail*

Foreign lands – Caribbean Islands

Anderson, Lonzo. *The day the hurricane happened*
  Izzard
Buffett, Jimmy. *The jolly mon*
Carlstrom, Nancy White. *Baby-O*
Dobrin, Arnold Jack. *Josephine's 'magination*
Douglas, Richardo Keens. *The nutmeg princess*
George, Jean Craighead. *The wentletrap trap*
Greenfield, Eloise. *Under the Sunday tree*
Lessac, Frané. *Caribbean canvas*
  My little island
Linden, Ann Marie. *One smiling grandma*
Ness, Evaline. *Josefina February*

Foreign lands – Central America

Ada, Alma F. *The gold coin*
Wisniewski, David. *Rain player*

Foreign lands – China

Abisch, Roz. *Mai-Ling and the mirror*
Andersen, H. C. (Hans Christian). *The emperor and the nightingale*, ill. by James Watling
The emperor's nightingale, ill. from the Disney arcives
The emperor's nightingale, ill. by Georges Lemoine
The nightingale, ill. by Harold Berson
The nightingale, ill. by Nancy Ekholm Burkert
The nightingale, ill. by Demi
The nightingale, ill. by Alison Claire Darke
The nightingale, ill. by Beni Montresor
The nightingale, ill. by Josef Paleček
The nightingale, ill. by Regolo Ricci
The nightingale, ill. by Lisbeth Zwerger
Behrens, June. *Soo Ling finds a way*
Birdseye, Tom. *A song of stars*
Bishop, Claire Huchet. *The five Chinese brothers*
Bright, Robert. *The travels of Ching*
Bro, Marguerite H. *The animal friends of Peng-u*
Buck, Pearl S. (Pearl Sydenstricker). *The Chinese story teller*
Cheng, Hou-Tien. *The Chinese New Year*
Demi. *The adventures of Marco Polo*
The artist and the architect
Chen Ping and his magic axe
A Chinese zoo
Demi's reflective fables
Dragon kites and dragonflies
The magic boat
Under the shade of the mulberry tree
Fairclough, Chris. *Take a trip to China*
Flack, Marjorie. *The story about Ping*
Foley, Bernice Williams. *A walk among clouds*
Fribourg, Marjorie G. *Ching-Ting and the ducks*
Handforth, Thomas. *Mei Li*
Haskins, Jim. *Count your way through China*
Heyer, Marilee. *The weaving of a dream*
High on a hill
Hillman, Elizabeth. *Min-Yo and the moon dragon*
Holland, Janice. *You never can tell*
Hong, Lily Toy. *How the ox star fell from heaven*
Jensen, Helen Zane. *When Panda came to our house*
Lattimore, Deborah Nourse. *The dragon's robe*
Leaf, Margaret. *Eyes of the dragon*
Lee, Jeanne M. *Legend of the Li River*
The legend of the milky way
Levinson, Riki. *Our home is the sea*
Littlefield, William. *The whiskers of Ho Ho*

Lobel, Arnold. *Ming Lo moves the mountain*
Louie, Al-Ling. *Yeh Shen*
Mahy, Margaret. *The seven Chinese brothers*
Miles, Miska. *The pointed brush...*
Miller, Moira. *The moon dragon*
Morris, Winifred. *The future of Yen-Tzu*
The magic leaf
Mosel, Arlene. *Tikki Tikki Tembo*
Pattison, Darcy. *The river dragon*
Pen Cai Ying. *Monkey creates havoc in heaven*
Perkins, Al. *Tubby and the lantern*
Pittman, Helena Clare. *A grain of rice*
Rappaport, Doreen. *Journey of Meng*
San Souci, Robert D. *The enchanted tapestry*
Shi, Zhang Xiu. *Monkey and the white bone demon*
Skipper, Mervyn. *The fooling of King Alexander*
Slobodkin, Louis. *Moon Blossom and the golden penny*
Stafford, Kay. *Ling Tang and the lucky cricket*
Stone, Jon. *Big Bird in China*
Tan, Amy. *The moon lady*
Tompert, Ann. *Grandfather Tang's story*
Torre, Betty L. *The luminous pearl*
Va, Leong. *A letter to the king*
Van Woerkom, Dorothy. *The rat, the ox and the zodiac*
Wang, Rosalind C. *The fourth question*
Wiese, Kurt. *Fish in the air*
Williams, Jay. *Everyone knows what a dragon looks like*
Wolkstein, Diane. *The magic wings*
White wave
Yacowitz, Caryn. *The jade stone*
Yen, Clara. *Why rat comes first*
Yolen, Jane. *The emperor and the kite*
The emperor and the kite [Rev. ed.]
The seeing stick
Young, Ed (Edward). *Lon Po Po*
The rooster's horns
The terrible Nung Gwama
Young, Evelyn. *The tale of Tai*
Wu and Lu and Li
Zimelman, Nathan. *The great adventure of Wo Ti*

Foreign lands – Costa Rica

Baden, Robert. *And Sunday makes seven*

Foreign lands – Czechoslovakia

Bolliger, Max. *The fireflies*
Ginsburg, Mirra. *How the sun was brought back to the sky*
Marshak, Samuel. *The Month-Brothers*

Foreign lands – Denmark

Andersen, H. C. (Hans Christian). *The*

snow queen, ill. by Toma Bogdanovic
Bason, Lillian. *Those foolish Molboes!*
Blegvad, Lenore. *Mr. Jensen and cat*
Bodecker, N. M. (Nils Mogens). *"It's raining," said John Twaining*
Brande, Marlie. *Sleepy Nicholas*
A Christmas book
Coombs, Patricia. *The magic pot*
Haviland, Virginia. *The talking pot*
Kent, Jack. *Hoddy doddy*
Lobel, Anita. *King Rooster, Queen Hen*

Foreign lands – Ecuador

Bemelmans, Ludwig. *Quito express*

Foreign lands – Egypt

Aliki. *Mummies made in Egypt*
Climo, Shirley. *The Egyptian Cinderella*
De Paola, Tomie (Thomas Anthony). *Bill and Pete go down the Nile*
Goodenow, Earle. *The last camel*
Grant, Joan. *The monster that grew small*
Hayward, Linda. *Baby Moses*
Heide, Florence Parry. *The day of Ahmed's secret*
Hutton, Warwick. *Moses in the bulrushes*
Laskowski, Jerzy. *Master of the royal cats*
McDermott, Gerald. *The voyage of Osiris*
Mayers, Florence Cassen. *Egyptian art from the Brooklyn Museum: ABC*
Price, Leontyne. *Aïda*
The prince who knew his fate, ill. by Lise Manniche
Stolz, Mary Slattery. *Zekmet, the stone carver*

Foreign lands – El Salvador

Argueta, Manlio. *The magic dogs of the volcanoes*

Foreign lands – England

Ahlberg, Allan. *Cops and robbers*
Ambler, Christopher Gifford. *Ten little foxhounds*
Anno, Mitsumasa. *Anno's Britain*
Ardizzone, Edward. *Lucy Brown and Mr. Grimes*
Armitage, Ronda. *Don't forget, Matilda*
Azarian, Mary. *The tale of John Barleycorn or, From barley to beer*
Barber, Antonia. *The mousehole cat*
Beatty, Hetty Burlingame. *Moorland pony*
Belting, Natalia Maree. *Christmas folk*
Summer's coming in
Bemelmans, Ludwig. *Madeline in London*
Bennett, Jill. *Teeny tiny*
Bennett, Olivia. *A Turkish afternoon*
Bentley, Anne. *The Groggs' day out*
The Groggs have a wonderful summer

Bond, Michael. *Paddington and the knickerbocker rainbow*
Paddington at the circus
Paddington at the fair
Paddington at the palace
Paddington at the seaside
Paddington at the tower
Paddington at the zoo
Paddington bear
Paddington cleans up
Paddington's art exhibit
Paddington's garden
Paddington's lucky day
Brown, Ruth. *A dark, dark tale*
Burningham, John. *Borka*
Calhoun, Mary. *The pixy and the lazy housewife*
The witch's pig
Carrick, Donald. *Harold and the great stag*
Christian, Mary Blount. *April fool*
Cole, Brock. *The king at the door*
Conger, Lesley. *Tops and bottoms*
Cooper, Susan. *The silver cow*
Cressey, James. *The dragon and George*
Crompton, Margaret. *The house where Jack lives*
Crossley-Holland, Kevin. *The green children*
Davidson, Amanda. *Teddy at the seashore*
Davis, Reda. *Martin's dinosaur*
Dick Whittington and his cat. *Dick Whittington*, ill. by Edward Ardizzone
Dick Whittington and his cat, ill. by Marcia Brown
Dick Whittington, ill. by Antony Maitland
Dick Whittington and his cat, ill. by Kurt Werth
Dines, Glen. *Gilly and the wicharoo*
Dominguez, Angel. *Diary of a Victorian mouse*
Drummond, Violet H. *The flying postman*
Emecheta, Buchi. *Nowhere to play*
Esterl, Arnica. *The fine round cake*
Fairclough, Chris. *Take a trip to England*
Freeman, Don. *The guard mouse*
Will's quill
Freschet, Berniece. *Bernard of Scotland Yard*
Ganly, Helen. *Jyoti's journey*
Gauch, Patricia Lee. *On to Widecombe Fair*
Gerrard, Jean. *Matilda Jane*
Goodall, John S. *An Edwardian Christmas*
An Edwardian summer
The story of a castle
The story of a farm
The story of an English village
Gramatky, Hardie. *Little Toot on the Thames*
Haley, Gail E. *The post office cat*
Herrmann, Frank. *The giant Alexander*
The giant Alexander and the circus
Hughes, Shirley. *Bathwater's hot*
Lucy and Tom's A.B.C.

Lucy and Tom's Christmas
Noisy
Out and about
The snow lady
When we went to the park
Ivory, Lesley Anne. *A day in London*
Jacobs, Joseph. *The crock of gold*
Tattercoats, ill. by Margot Tomes
Keeping, Charles. *Alfie finds the other side of the world*
Through the window
Laird, Elizabeth. *The day Patch stood guard*
The day Sidney ran off
Lawrence, John. *The giant of Grabbist*
Lodge, Bernard. *Door to door*
Menter, Ian. *Carnival*
Mother Goose. *London Bridge is falling down*, ill. by Ed Emberley
London Bridge is falling down, ill. by Peter Spier
Munro, Roxie. *The inside-outside book of London*
Oakley, Graham. *The church cat abroad*
The church mice and the moon
The church mice at bay
The church mice spread their wings
The church mouse
Oldfield, Pamela. *Melanie Brown climbs a tree*
Oxenbury, Helen. *The queen and Rosie Randall*
Petty, Kate. *On a plane*
Rogers, Paul (Patrick). *Don't blame me!*
Ross, Diana. *The story of the little red engine*
Service, Pamela F. *The wizard of wind and rock*
Seuling, Barbara. *The teeny tiny woman*
Sewall, Marcia. *The little wee tyke*
Shulman, Milton. *Prep, the little pigeon of Trafalgar Square*
Smith, Barry. *Minnie and Ginger*
Solomon, Joan. *A present for Mum*
Southey, Robert. *The cataract of Lodore*
Storr, Catherine (Cole). *Robin Hood*
Thompson, Harwood. *The witch's cat*
Widdecombe Fair, ill. by Christine Price
Willard, Barbara. *To London! To London!*
Wolff, Ashley. *The bells of London*
Wood, Joyce. *Grandmother Lucy in her garden*
Worthington, Phoebe. *Teddy bear baker*
Teddy bear coalman
Zemach, Harve. *Duffy and the devil*

Foreign lands – Europe

Bornstein, Ruth Lercher. *The dancing man*
Sopko, Eugen. *Townsfolk and countryfolk*

Foreign lands – Finland

Allen, Linda. *The mouse bride*

De Gerez, Toni. *Louhi, witch of North Farm*

Foreign lands – France

Aliki. *The king's day*
Allen, Laura Jean. *Rollo and Tweedy and the case of the missing cheese*
Angelo, Nancy Carolyn Harrison. *Camembert*
Bemelmans, Ludwig. *Madeline*
Madeline [pop-up book]
Madeline and the bad hat
Madeline and the gypsies
Madeline's Christmas
Madeline's rescue
Bergere, Thea. *Paris in the rain with Jean and Jacqueline*
Berson, Harold. *Barrels to the moon*
Charles and Claudine
How the devil got his due
Joseph and the snake
Bingham, Mindy. *Minou*
Bishop, Claire Huchet. *The truffle pig*
Bring a torch, Jeannette, Isabella, ill. by Adrienne Adams
Brown, Judith Gwyn. *Max and the truffle pig*
Brunhoff, Jean de. *The story of Babar, the little elephant*
Charlip, Remy. *Harlequin and the gift of many colors*
Daudet, Alphonse. *The brave little goat of Monsieur Séguin*
Dauphin, Francine Legrand. *A French A. B. C.*
De Paola, Tomie (Thomas Anthony). *Bonjour, Mister Satie*
Diska, Pat. *Andy says ... Bonjour!*
Dumas, Philippe. *Caesar, cock of the village*
Laura loses her head
The story of Edward
Fatio, Louise. *The happy lion*
The happy lion and the bear
The happy lion in Africa
The happy lion roars
The happy lion's quest
The happy lion's rabbits
The happy lion's treasure
The three happy lions
Fender, Kay. *Odette!*
Froment, Eugène. *The story of a round loaf*
Goffstein, M. B. (Marilyn Brooke). *Artists' helpers enjoy the evening*
Goode, Diane. *Where's our mama?*
Harris, Leon A. *The great picture robbery*
Hautzig, Esther (Rudomin). *At home*
In the park
Ichikawa, Satomi. *Suzanne and Nicholas at the market*
Suzanne and Nicholas in the garden, Watts 1976
Joslin, Sesyle. *Baby elephant's trunk*
Kirby, David. *Cows are going to Paris*

Klein, Leonore. *Henri's walk to Paris*
Lubell, Winifred. *Rosalie, the bird market turtle*
Marokvia, Merelle. *A French school for Paul*
Meddaugh, Susan. *Maude and Claude go abroad*
Mendoza, George. *Henri Mouse, the juggler*
Milton, Nancy. *The giraffe that walked to Paris*
Moore, Inga. *The truffle hunter*
Moore, Lilian. *Papa Albert*
Munro, Roxie. *The inside-outside book of Paris*
Napoli, Guillier. *Adventure at Mont-Saint-Michel*
O'Callahan, Jay. *Tulips*
Patron, Susan. *Burgoo stew*
Perrault, Charles. *Puss in boots*, ill. by Julia Noonan
Raffi. *Wheels on the bus*
Rider, Alex. *A la ferme. At the farm*
Chez nous. At our house
Rockwell, Anne F. *Poor Goose*
The wolf who had a wonderful dream
Schiller, Barbara. *The white rat's tale*
Scribner, Charles. *The devil's bridge*
Seignobosc, Françoise. *The big rain*
Biquette, the white goat
Chouchou
Jeanne-Marie at the fair
Jeanne-Marie counts her sheep
Jeanne-Marie in gay Paris
Minou
Noël for Jeanne-Marie
Springtime for Jeanne-Marie
Shecter, Ben. *Partouche plants a seed*
Slobodkin, Louis. *Colette and the princess*
Titus, Eve. *Anatole*
Anatole and the cat
Anatole and the piano
Anatole and the Pied Piper
Anatole and the poodle
Anatole and the robot
Anatole and the thirty thieves
Anatole and the toyshop
Anatole over Paris
Ungerer, Tomi. *The beast of Monsieur Racine*
Weelen, Guy. *The little red train*

Foreign lands – Germany

Allard, Harry. *May I stay?*
Attenberger, Walburga. *The little man in winter*
Who knows the little man?
Bartos-Hoppner, Barbara. *The Pied Piper of Hamelin*
Bechstein, Ludwig. *The rabbit catcher and other fairy tales*
Biro, Val. *The pied piper of Hamelin*

Browning, Robert. *The pied piper of Hamelin*, ill. by Patricia and Robin DeWitt
The pied piper of Hamelin, ill. by Kate Greenaway
The pied piper of Hamelin, ill. by Anatoly Ivanov
The pied piper of Hamelin, ill. by Errol Le Cain
Calhoun, Mary. *The thieving dwarfs*
Coombs, Patricia. *Tilabel*
Cooney, Barbara. *Little brother and little sister*
Croll, Carolyn. *The three brothers*
Delaney, A. *The gunnywolf*
Fairclough, Chris. *Take a trip to West Germany*
Grimm, Jacob. *The elves and the shoemaker*, ill. by Paul Galdone
The elves and the shoemaker, ill. by Bernadette Watts
The shoemaker and the elves, ill. by Adrienne Adams
The shoemaker and the elves, ill. by Cynthia and William Birrer
The shoemaker and the elves, ill. by Ilse Plume
Harper, Wilhelmina. *The gunniwolf*
Hürlimann, Ruth. *The proud white cat*
Kahl, Virginia. *Droopsi*
Maxie
Mayer, Marianna. *The spirit of the blue light*
Mayer, Mercer. *The Pied Piper of Hamelin*
Morgenstern, Elizabeth. *The little gardeners*
Ross, Tony. *The pied piper of Hamelin*
Spang, Günter. *Clelia and the little mermaid*
Van Woerkom, Dorothy. *The queen who couldn't bake gingerbread*

Foreign lands – Ghana

Appiah, Sonia. *Amoko and Efua Bear*
Dee, Ruby. *Tower to heaven*

Foreign lands – Greece

Aliki. *Diogenes*
The eggs
Three gold pieces
The twelve months
Anderson, Lonzo. *Arion and the dolphins*
Birrer, Cynthia. *Song to Demeter*
Brown, Marcia. *Tamarindo!*
Delton, Judy. *My Uncle Nikos*
Steel, Barry. *Greek cities*
Walker, Barbara K. (Barbara Kerlin). *Pigs and pirates*

Foreign lands – Greenland

Hertz, Ole. *Tobias catches trout*
Tobias goes ice fishing
Tobias goes seal hunting

Tobias has a birthday

Foreign lands – Guatemala

Czernecki, Stefan. *The sleeping bread*

Foreign lands – Guyana

Agard, John. *Dig away two-hole Tim*

Foreign lands – Holland

Bouhuys, Mies. *The lady of Stavoren*
Bromhall, Winifred. *Johanna arrives*
Chasek, Judith. *Have you seen Wilhelmina Krumpf?*
Fairclough, Chris. *Take a trip to Holland*
Green, Norma B. *The hole in the dike*
Howells, Mildred. *The woman who lived in Holland*
Krasilovsky, Phyllis. *The cow who fell in the canal*
Reesink, Marijke. *The golden treasure*
Van Stockum, Hilda. *A day on skates*

Foreign lands – Hungary

Ambrus, Victor G. *Brave soldier Janosch*
The three poor tailors
Brown, Margaret Wise. *Wheel on the chimney*
Ginsburg, Mirra. *Two greedy bears*
The good-hearted youngest brother, ill. by Diane Goode
Illyés, Gyula. *Matt the gooseherd*
Surany, Anico. *Kati and Kormos*
Varga, Judy. *Janko's wish*

Foreign lands – Iceland

Wisniewski, David. *Elfwyn's saga*

Foreign lands – India

Alan, Sandy. *The plaid peacock*
Ambrus, Victor G. *The Sultan's bath*
Bang, Betsy. *The cucumber stem*
The old woman and the red pumpkin
The old woman and the rice thief
Tuntuni the tailor bird
Bannerman, Helen. *Sambo and the twins*
The story of little black Sambo
Bond, Ruskin. *Cherry tree*
Flames in the forest
Bonnici, Peter. *The festival*
Brown, Marcia. *The blue jackal*
Once a mouse...
Cassedy, Sylvia. *Moon-uncle, moon-uncle*
Cathon, Laura E. *Tot Botot and his little flute*
Chase, Catherine. *The nightingale and the fool*
Demi. *The hallowed horse*
Domanska, Janina. *Why so much noise?*

Duff, Maggie (Margaret K.). *Rum pum pum*
Ganly, Helen. *Jyoti's journey*
Gobhai, Mehlli. *Lakshmi, the water buffalo who wouldn't*
Usha, the mouse-maiden
Hirsh, Marilyn. *Leela and the watermelon*
Kamal, Aleph. *The bird who was an elephant*
Kipling, Rudyard. *The miracle of the mountain*, ill. by Willi Baum
Lexau, Joan M. *It all began with a drip, drip, drip*
Myers, Walter Dean. *The golden serpent*
Newton, Pam. *The stonecutter*
Papas, William. *Taresh the tea planter*
Quigley, Lillian Fox. *The blind men and the elephant*
Rockwell, Anne F. *The stolen necklace*
Rodanas, Kristina. *The story of Wali Dâd*
Siberell, Anne. *A journey to paradise*
Singh, Jacquelin. *Fat Gopal*
Slobodkin, Louis. *The polka-dot goat*
Towle, Faith M. *The magic cooking pot*
Trez, Denise. *Maila and the flying carpet*
Villarejo, Mary. *The tiger hunt*
Wahl, Jan. *Tiger watch*
Ward, Nanda Weedon. *The elephant that ga-lumphed*
Whitmore, Adam. *Max in India*
Young, Ed (Edward). *Seven blind mice*

Foreign lands – Ireland

Balian, Lorna. *Leprechauns never lie*
Bromhall, Winifred. *Bridget's growing day*
Bunting, Eve (Anne Evelyn). *Clancy's coat*
Calhoun, Mary. *The hungry leprechaun*
Cooper, Susan. *The Selkie girl*
Cormack, M. Grant. *Animal tales from Ireland*
Day, David. *The swan children*
De Paola, Tomie (Thomas Anthony). *Fin M'Coul*
Jamie O'Rourke and the big potato
Patrick: patron saint of Ireland
Haugaard, Erik Christian. *Prince Boghole*
Jacobs, Joseph. *Hudden and Dudden and Donald O'Neary*
Kennedy, Richard. *The leprechaun's story*
Lattimore, Deborah Nourse. *The sailor who captured the sea*
McDermott, Gerald. *Daniel O'Rourke*
Parker, Dorothy D. *Liam's catch*
What do you feed your donkey on? ill. by Jenny Rodwell
Zimelman, Nathan. *To sing a song as big as Ireland*

Foreign lands – Israel

Adler, David A. *A picture book of Israel*
Brin, Ruth F. *David and Goliath*

The story of Esther
Carmi, Giora. *And Shira imagined*
Edwards, Michelle. *Chicken man*
Elkin, Benjamin. *The wisest man in the world*
Fairclough, Chris. *Take a trip to Israel*
Kuskin, Karla. *Jerusalem, shining still*
Segal, Sheila. *Joshua's dream*

Foreign lands – Italy

Æsop. *Androcles and the lion*, ill. by Janet Stevens
  Androcles and the lion, ill. by Janusz Grabianski
  Androcles and the lion, ill. by Robert Rayevsky
Anno, Mitsumasa. *Anno's Italy*
Atene, Ann (Anna). *The golden guitar*
Basile, Giambattista. *Petrosinella*
Bettina (Bettina Ehrlich). *Pantaloni*
Brighton, Catherine. *Five secrets in a box*
Brown, Marcia. *Felice*
Cauley, Lorinda Bryan. *The goose and the golden coins*
Cazzola, Gus. *The bells of Santa Lucia*
Chafetz, Henry. *The legend of Befana*
Chapman, Jean. *Moon-Eyes*
De Paola, Tomie (Thomas Anthony). *The clown of God*
  The legend of Old Befana
  Merry Christmas, Strega Nona
  The mysterious giant of Barletta
  The Prince of the Dolomites
  Tony's bread
Ehrlich, Amy. *Pome and Peel*
Fairclough, Chris. *Take a trip to Italy*
Galdone, Paul. *Androcles and the lion*
Giannini, Enzo. *Little Parsley*
Kroll, Steven. *Looking for Daniela*
Lager, Claude. *A tale of two rats*
Manson, Christopher. *The crab prince*
Michael, Emory H. *Androcles and the lion*
Morpurgo, Michael. *Jo-Jo the melon donkey*
Nones, Eric Jon. *Canary prince*
Plume, Ilse. *The story of Befana*
Politi, Leo. *Little Leo*
Rayevsky, Inna. *The talking tree*
Rockwell, Anne F. *The wonderful eggs of Furicchia*
Seidler, Rosalie. *Grumpus and the Venetian cat*
Titus, Eve. *Anatole in Italy*
Ungerer, Tomi. *The hat*

Foreign lands – Japan

Baker, Keith. *The magic fan*
Bang, Molly. *Dawn*
Bartoli, Jennifer. *Snow on bear's nose*
Baruch, Dorothy. *Kappa's tug-of-war with the big brown horse*

Battles, Edith. *What does the rooster say, Yoshio?*
Bryan, Ashley. *Sh-ko and his eight wicked brothers*
Bunting, Eve (Anne Evelyn). *Magic and the night river*
Cassedy, Sylvia. *Red dragonfly on my shoulder*
Cocagnac, A. M. (Augustin Maurice). *The three trees of the Samurai*
Damjan, Mischa. *The little prince and the tiger cat*
DeForest, Charlotte B. *The prancing pony*
Dines, Glen. *A tiger in the cherry tree*
Don't tell the scarecrow
Fifield, Flora. *Pictures for the palace*
Fujita, Tamao. *The boy and the bird*
Gackenbach, Dick. *The perfect mouse*
Garrison, Christian. *The dream eater*
Haskins, Jim. *Count your way through Japan*
Heller, George. *Hiroshi's wonderful kite*
Hidaka, Masako. *Girl from the snow country*
Hooks, William H. *Peach boy*
Iké, Jane Hori. *A Japanese fairy tale*
Ikeda, Daisaku. *The cherry tree*
  The snow country prince
Ishii, Momoko. *The tongue-cut sparrow*
Johnston, Tony. *The badger and the magic fan*
Kalman, Maira. *Sayonara, Mrs. Kackleman*
Kimmel, Eric A. *The greatest of all*
Laurin, Anne. *Perfect crane*
Lifton, Betty Jean. *Joji and the Amanojaku*
  Joji and the dragon
  The many lives of Chio and Goro
  The rice-cake rabbit
Luenn, Nancy. *The dragon kite*
McDermott, Gerald. *The stonecutter*
Matsuno, Masako. *A pair of red clogs*
  Taro and the bamboo shoot
  Taro and the Tofu
Matsutani, Miyoko. *The fisherman under the sea*
  How the withered trees blossomed
  The witch's magic cloth
Mosel, Arlene. *The funny little woman*
Nakatani, Chiyoko. *Fumio and the dolphins*
Newton, Patricia Montgomery. *The five sparrows*
Nomura, Takaaki. *Grandpa's town*
Paterson, Katherine. *The tale of the Mandarin ducks*
Pittman, Helena Clare. *The gift of the willows*
Roy, Ronald. *A thousand pails of water*
Say, Allen. *The bicycle man*
  Once under the cherry blossom tree
  Tree of cranes
Shute, Linda. *Momotaro, the peach boy*
Slobodkin, Louis. *Yasu and the strangers*
Takeshita, Fumiko. *The park bench*

Tejima, Keizaburo. *Ho-limlim*
Uchida, Yoshiko. *Sumi's prize*
 Sumi's special happening
Van Woerkom, Dorothy. *Sea frog, city frog*
Wisniewski, David. *The warrior and the wise man*
Yagawa, Sumiko. *The crane wife*
Yashima, Mitsu. *Plenty to watch*
Yashima, Tarō. *Crow boy*
 The village tree

Foreign lands – Kenya

McLean, Virginia O. *Kenya, jambo!*
Mollel, Tolowa M. *Orphan boy*
 A promise to the sun
 Rhinos for lunch and elephants for supper

Foreign lands – Korea

Fregosi, Claudia. *The pumpkin sparrow*
Ginsburg, Mirra. *The Chinese mirror*
Parry, Marian. *King of the fish*

Foreign lands – Laos

Xiong, Blia. *Nine-in-one Grr! Grr!*

Foreign lands – Lapland

Aulaire, Ingri Mortenson d'. *Children of the northlights*
Borg, Inga. *Plupp builds a house*
Lindman, Maj. *Snipp, Snapp, Snurr and the red shoes*
McHale, Ethel Kharasch. *Son of thunder*
Reynolds, Jan. *Far north*
Stalder, Valerie. *Even the devil is afraid of a shrew*

Foreign lands – Latvia

Langton, Jane. *The hedgehog boy*

Foreign lands – Malaysia

Kaye, Geraldine. *The sea monkey*

Foreign lands – Mexico

Aardema, Verna. *Borreguita and the coyote*
 Pedro and the padre
 The riddle of the drum
Balet, Jan B. *The fence*
Bannon, Laura. *Hat for a hero*
 Manuela's birthday
Blackmore, Vivien. *Why corn is golden*
Crane, Alan. *Pepita bonita*
Czernecki, Stefan. *Pancho's piñata*
De Gerez, Toni. *My song is a piece of jade*
De Paola, Tomie (Thomas Anthony). *The Lady of Guadalupe*
Ets, Marie Hall. *Nine days to Christmas*
Everton, Macduff. *El circo magico modelo: Finding the magic circus*

Fraser, James Howard. *Los Posadas*
Grifalconi, Ann. *The toy trumpet*
Hader, Berta Hoerner. *The story of Pancho and the bull with the crooked tail*
Johnston, Tony. *Lorenzo the naughty parrot*
Kent, Jack. *The Christmas piñata*
Lewis, Thomas P. *Hill of fire*
Martin, Bill (William Ivan). *My days are made of butterflies*
Martin, Patricia Miles. *Friend of Miguel*
Morrow, Elizabeth Cutter. *The painted pig*
Politi, Leo. *Lito and the clown*
 Rosa
Rohmer, Harriet. *How we came to the fifth world*
Sahagun, Bernardino de. *Spirit child*
Tompert, Ann. *The silver whistle*
Ungerer, Tomi. *Orlando, the brave vulture*
Volkmer, Jane Anne. *Song of Chirimia: La Musica de la Chirimia*
Wisniewski, David. *Rain player*

Foreign lands – Nepal

Reynolds, Jan. *Himalaya*

Foreign lands – New Guinea

Anderson, Robin. *Sinabouda Lily*
Wilson, Barbara Ker. *The turtle and the island*

Foreign lands – Nicaragua

Rohmer, Harriet. *The invisible hunters*
 Mother scorpion country

Foreign lands – Nigeria

Gerson, Mary-Joan. *Why the sky is far away*

Foreign lands – Norway

Allard, Harry. *May I stay?*
Allen, Linda. *The giant who had no heart*
Asbjørnsen, P. C. (Peter Christian). *The man who kept house*
Aulaire, Ingri Mortenson d'. *Ola*
 The terrible troll-bird
Dasent, George W. *East o' the sun, west o' the moon*
Grieg, E. H. (Edvard Hagerup). *E. H. Grieg's Peer Gynt*
Hague, Kathleen. *The man who kept house*
Kimmel, Eric A. *Boots and his brothers*
Magnus, Erica. *The boy and the devil*
 Old Lars
Martin, Claire. *Boots and the glass mountain*
Reynolds, Jan. *Far north*
The squire's bride, ill. by Marcia Sewall
Wiesner, William. *Happy-Go-Lucky*
 Turnabout

Foreign lands – Pakistan

Siddiqui, Ashraf. *Bhombal Dass, the uncle of lion*

Foreign lands – Panama

Janosch. *The trip to Panama*

Foreign lands – Persia

Chaikin, Miriam. *Esther*
Foley, Bernice Williams. *The gazelle and the hunter*
Manson, Christopher. *A gift for the king*

Foreign lands – Peru

Alexander, Ellen. *Llama and the great flood*
Charles, Donald. *Chancay and the secret of fire*
Dewey, Ariane. *The thunder god's son*
Dorros, Arthur. *Tonight is carnaval*
Ehlert, Lois. *Moon rope: Un lazo a la luna*
Loverseed, Amanda. *The thunder king*

Foreign lands – Philippines

Aruego, José. *A crocodile's tale*
Look what I can do
Charlot, Martin. *Felisa and the magic tikling bird*

Foreign lands – Poland

Adler, David A. *The children of Chelm*
Bernhard, Josephine Butkowska. *Lullaby*
Nine cry-baby dolls
Din dan don, it's Christmas
Domanska, Janina. *The best of the bargain*
Busy Monday morning
King Krakus and the dragon
Look, there is a turtle flying
Pellowski, Anne. *The nine crying dolls*
Porazińska, Janina. *The enchanted book*
Turska, Krystyna. *The magician of Cracow*
The woodcutter's duck

Foreign lands – Portugal

Balet, Jan B. *The gift*
Joanjo

Foreign lands – Puerto Rico

Belpré, Pura. *Dance of the animals*
Perez and Martina
Martel, Cruz. *Yagua days*
Rohmer, Harriet. *Atariba and Niguayona*

Foreign lands – Romania

Olson, Arielle North. *Noah's cats and the devil's fire*

Foreign lands – Russia

Afanas'ev, Aleksandr N. *Russian folk tales*
Salt
Aksakov, Sergei. *The scarlet flower*
Ayres, Becky Hickox. *Matreshka*
Beim, Lorraine. *Sasha and the samovar*
Bider, Djemma. *The buried treasure*
Black, Algernon D. *The woman of the wood*
Brighton, Catherine. *Nijinsky*
Brown, Marcia. *The neighbors*
Stone soup
Campbell, M. Rudolph. *The talking crocodile*
Cohen, Barbara. *The demon who would not die*
Cole, Joanna. *Bony-legs*
Croll, Carolyn. *The little snowgirl*
Daniels, Guy. *The Tsar's riddles*
Daugherty, Sonia. *Vanka's donkey*
De Marolles, Chantal. *The lonely wolf*
De Regniers, Beatrice Schenk. *Everyone is good for something*
Domanska, Janina. *A scythe, a rooster and a cat*
The turnip
The firebird, ill. by Moira Kemp
The firebird, ill. by Kris Waldherr
The firebird, ill. by Boris Zvorykin
Francis, Frank. *Natasha's new doll*
Fregosi, Claudia. *Snow maiden*
Galdone, Paul. *A strange servant*
Ginsburg, Mirra. *The fisherman's son*
The fox and the hare
Pampalche of the silver teeth
The strongest one of all
Which is the best place?
Hall, Amanda. *The gossipy wife*
Haskins, Jim. *Count your way through Russia*
Hautzig, Esther (Rudomin). *At home*
In the park
Heller, Linda. *Alexis and the golden ring*
Isele, Elizabeth. *The frog princess*
Ivanov, Anatoly. *Ol' Jake's lucky day*
Jameson, Cynthia. *The house of five bears*
Kimmel, Eric A. *Baba Yaga*
Bearhead
Levine, Arthur. *All the lights in the night*
McDermott, Beverly Brodsky. *The crystal apple*
Marshak, Samuel. *The tale of a hero nobody knows*
Mendelson, S. T. *Stupid Emilien*
Milhous, Katherine. *The turnip*
Odoyevsky, Vladimir. *Old Father Frost*
The peasant's pea patch, ill. by Robert M. Quackenbush
Pevear, Richard. *Our king has horns!*
Polushkin, Maria. *The little hen and the giant*
Prokofiev, Sergei Sergeievitch. *Peter and the wolf*, ill. by Reg Cartwright

Peter and the wolf, ill. by Warren
   Chappell
Peter and the wolf, ill. by Barbara
   Cooney
Peter and the wolf, ill. by Frans Haacken
Peter and the wolf, ill. by Alan Howard
Peter and the wolf, ill. by Charles
   Mikolaycak
Peter and the wolf, ill. by Jörg Müller
Peter and the wolf, ill. by Josef Paleček
Peter and the wolf, ill. by Kozo Shimizu
Peter and the wolf, ill. by Erna Voigt
Robbins, Ruth. *Baboushka and the three
   kings*
Sherman, Josepha. *Vassilisa the wise*
Slobodkina, Esphyr. *Boris and his balalaika*
Stern, Simon. *Vasily and the dragon*
Tolstoĭ, Alekseĭ Nikolaevich. *The great big
   enormous turnip*
Tompert, Ann. *The Tzar's bird*
Trivas, Irene. *Annie...Anya: a month in
   Moscow*
Varga, Judy. *The mare's egg*
Winter, Jeanette. *The girl and the moon man*
Winthrop, Elizabeth. *Vasilissa the beautiful*
Wiseman, Bernard. *Little new kangaroo*
Wolkstein, Diane. *Oom razoom; or, Go I
   know not where, Bring back I know not
   what*
Zakhoder, Boris Vladimirovich. *The good
   stepmother*
Zimmerman, Andrea Griffing. *Yetta, the
   trickster*

Foreign lands – Sahara Desert

Reynolds, Jan. *Sahara*

Foreign lands – Scotland

Alger, Leclaire Gowans. *All in the morning
   early*
   Always room for one more
   Kellyburn Braes
Blegvad, Erik. *Burnie's hill*
Calhoun, Mary. *The runaway brownie*
Cate, Rikki. *A cat's tale*
Cooper, Susan. *The Selkie girl*
   Tam Lin
Duncan, Jane. *Janet Reachfar and
   Chickabird*
Fern, Eugene. *The most frightened hero*
Forest, Heather. *The woman who flummoxed
   the fairies*
Gramatky, Hardie. *Little Toot and the Loch
   Ness monster*
Hedderwick, Mairi. *Katie Morag and the big
   boy cousins*
   Katie Morag and the tiresome Ted
   Katie Morag and the two grandmothers
   Katie Morag delivers the mail
Jeffers, Susan. *Wild Robin*

Leaf, Munro. *Wee Gillis*
Lewis, Naomi. *Puffin*
Robertson, Joanne. *Sea witches*
Sewall, Marcia. *The wee, wee mannie and the
   big, big coo*
Yolen, Jane. *Greyling*

Foreign lands - Siam *see* Foreign lands –
Thialand

Foreign lands – South Africa

Daly, Niki. *Not so fast Songololo*
Isadora, Rachel. *At the crossroads*
   Over the green hills
Kahn, Rosemary. *Grandma's hat*
Mennen, Ingrid. *Somewhere in Africa*
Schermbrucker, Reviva. *Charlie's house*
Seed, Jenny. *Ntombi's song*

Foreign lands – South America

Aruego, José. *Pilyo the piranha*
Cowcher, Helen. *Rain forest*
Fischetto, Laura. *The jungle is my home*
Flora. *Feathers like a rainbow*
Frasconi, Antonio. *The snow and the sun, la
   nieve y el sol*
Gramatky, Hardie. *Bolivar*
Maestro, Giulio. *The tortoise's tug of war*
Maiorano, Robert. *Francisco*
Reynolds, Jan. *Amazon*
Rockwell, Anne F. *The good llama*
Surany, Anico. *Ride the cold wind*
Troughton, Joanna. *How the birds changed
   their feathers*
Van Laan, Nancy. *The legend of El Dorado*

Foreign lands – South Sea Islands

Mordvinoff, Nicolas. *Coral Island*

Foreign lands – Spain

Duff, Maggie (Margaret K.). *The princess
   and the pumpkin*
García Lorca, Federico. *The Lieutenant
   Colonel and the gypsy*
Hautzig, Esther (Rudomin). *At home*
   In the park
Leaf, Munro. *The story of Ferdinand the bull*
Oleson, Claire. *For Pipita, an orange tree*
Vernon, Adele. *The riddle*

Foreign lands – Sweden

Beskow, Elsa Maartman. *Children of the
   forest*
   Pelle's new suit
   Peter in Blueberry Land
   Peter's adventures in Blueberry land
Lindgren, Astrid. *A calf for Christmas*
   Christmas in noisy village
   Christmas in the stable

Lotta's Christmas surprise
The tomten
The tomten and the fox
Lindman, Maj. *Flicka, Ricka, Dicka and a little dog*
Flicka, Ricka, Dicka and the new dotted dress
Flicka, Ricka, Dicka bake a cake
Sailboat time
Snipp, Snapp, Snurr and the buttered bread
Snipp, Snapp, Snurr and the magic horse
Snipp, Snapp, Snurr and the reindeer
Snipp, Snapp, Snurr and the seven dogs
Snipp, Snapp, Snurr and the yellow sled
Peterson, Hans. *Erik and the Christmas horse*
Schwartz, David M. *Sugargrandpa*
Sundvall, Viveca. *Mimi and the biscuit factory*
Westerberg, Christine. *The cap that mother made*
Zemach, Harve. *Nail soup*

Foreign lands – Switzerland

Allamand, Pascale. *Cocoa beans and daisies*
Baumann, Kurt. *Piro and the fire brigade*
Bawden, Nina. *William Tell*
Carigiet, Alois. *The pear tree, the birch tree and the barberry bush*
Chönz, Selina. *A bell for Ursli*
Florina and the wild bird
The snowstorm
Freeman, Don. *Ski pup*

Foreign lands – Taiwain

Reddix, Valerie. *Dragon kite of the autumn moon*

Foreign lands – Thailand

Ayer, Jacqueline. *Nu Dang and his kite*
The paper-flower tree
A wish for little sister
Northrup, Mili. *The watch cat*

Foreign lands – Tibet

Tsultim, Yeshe. *The mouse king*

Foreign lands – Trinidad

Joseph, Lynn. *Coconut kind of day*

Foreign lands – Turkey

Bennett, Olivia. *A Turkish afternoon*
Dewey, Ariane. *The fish Peri*
Walker, Barbara K. (Barbara Kerlin). *Teeny-Tiny and the witch-woman*

Foreign lands – Tyrol

Bemelmans, Ludwig. *Hansi*

Foreign lands – Ukraine

Brett, Jan. *The mitten*
Kay, Helen. *An egg is for wishing*
Lisowski, Gabriel. *How Tevye became a milkman*
Rudolph, Marguerita. *How a shirt grew in the field*
Tresselt, Alvin R. *The mitten*

Foreign lands – Vatican City

Lawrence, John. *Pope Leo's elephant*

Foreign lands – Venezuela

Barbot, Daniel. *A bicycle for Rosaura*

Foreign lands – Vietnam

Boholm-Olsson, Eva. *Tuan*
Lee, Jeanne M. *Ba-Nam*
Trân-Khánh-Tuyêt. *The little weaver of Thái-Yên Village*

Foreign lands – Zaire

Aardema, Verna. *Traveling to Tondo*
Knutson, Barbara. *Why the crab has no head*

Foreign lands – Zanzibar

Aardema, Verna. *Bimwili and the Zimwi*

Foreign languages

ABCDEF..., ill. by Robert Tallon
Alger, Leclaire Gowans. *Kellyburn Braes*
Anglund, Joan Walsh. *Love one another*
Baden, Robert. *And Sunday makes seven*
Baldner, Gaby. *Joba and the wild boar*
Blue, Rose. *I am here: Yo estoy aqui*
Breckler, Rosemary K. *Hoang breaks the lucky teapot*
Brown, Ruth. *Alphabet times four*
A child's picture English-Hebrew dictionary
Dabcovich, Lydia. *The keys to my kingdom*
Dauphin, Francine Legrand. *A French A. B. C.*
De Gerez, Toni. *My song is a piece of jade*
Delacre, Lulu. *Arroz con leche*
Las Navidades
Diska, Pat. *Andy says ... Bonjour!*
Dorros, Arthur. *Abuela*
Du Bois, William Pène. *The hare and the tortoise and the tortoise and the hare*
Dunham, Meredith. *Colors: how do you say it?*
Numbers: how do you say it?
Picnic: how do you say it?
Shapes: how do you say it?
Edwards, Michelle. *Alef-bet*
Ehlert, Lois. *Moon rope: Un lazo a la luna*
Everton, Macduff. *El circo magico modelo: Finding the magic circus*

Feelings, Muriel. *Jambo means hello*
  Menjo means one
Frasconi, Antonio. *See again, say again*
  See and say
  The snow and the sun, la nieve y el sol
Gunning, Monica. *The two Georges*
Hautzig, Esther (Rudomin). *At home*
  In the park
Hill, Eric. *Spot's big book of words; El libro*
  grande de las palabras de Spot
The house that Jack built. *The house that*
  Jack built, ill. by Antonio Frasconi
Jaynes, Ruth M. *Tell me please! What's that?*
Joslin, Sesyle. *Baby elephant goes to China*
  Baby elephant's trunk
  Señor Baby Elephant, the pirate
Kahn, Michèle. *My everyday Spanish word*
  book
Keats, Ezra Jack. *My dog is lost!*
Koplow, Lesley. *Tanya and the tobo man /*
  Tanya y el hombre tobo
McKissack, Patricia C. *Ada, la desordenada:*
  Messy Bessy
Macsolis. *Baile de luna: Dance moon*
Matsutani, Miyoko. *How the withered trees*
  blossomed
Matthias, Catherine. *Arriba y abajo: Over*
  and under
  Demasiados globos: Too many balloons
  Sal y entra: Out the door
Maury, Inez. *My mother the mail carrier: Mi*
  mama la cartera
Milios, Rita. *Yo soy—I am*
Moore, Lilian. *Papa Albert*
Mother Goose. *Mother Goose in French*, ill.
  by Barbara Cooney
  Mother Goose in Spanish, ill. by Barbara
  Cooney
  Rimes de la Mere Oie, ill. by Seymour
  Chwast, Milton Glaser, and Barry
  Zaid
Nomura, Takaaki. *Grandpa's town*
On the little hearth, ill. by Gabriel Lisowski
Pomerantz, Charlotte. *If I had a Paka*
  The tamarindo puppy and other poems
Rider, Alex. *A la ferme. At the farm*
  Chez nous. At our house
Roe, Eileen. *Con mi hermano—With my*
  brother
Rosario, Idalia. *Idalia's project ABC*
Rothman, Joel. *This can lick a lollipop*
Schaffer, Marion. *I love my cat!*
Serfozo, Mary. *Welcome Roberto! Bienvenido,*
  Roberto!
Shott, Stephen. *El mundo del bebe (Baby's*
  World)
Simon, Norma. *What do I say?*
Standon, Anna. *Three little cats*
Steiner, Charlotte. *A friend is "Amie"*
Stevens, Cat. *Teaser and the firecat*
Takeshita, Fumiko. *The park bench*

Va, Leong. *A letter to the king*
Vagin, Vladimir. *Here comes the cat!*
Volkmer, Jane Anne. *Song of Chirimia: La*
  Musica de la Chirimia
Wiese, Kurt. *You can write Chinese*
Wilson, Barbara Ker. *ABC et/and 123*
Winter, Jonah. *Diego*
Yolen, Jane. *Street rhymes around the world*
Zola, Meguido. *The dream of promise*

Forest rangers *see* Careers – park rangers

Forest, woods
Adler, David A. *Redwoods are the tallest*
  trees in the world
Ahlberg, Janet. *Jeremiah in the dark wood*
Alborough, Jez. *Where's my teddy?*
Allen, Gertrude E. *Everyday animals*
Anglund, Joan Walsh. *Nibble nibble*
  mousekin
Anholt, Laurence. *The forgotten forest*
Armer, Laura Adams. *The forest pool*
Arneson, D. J. *Secret places*
Arnold, Caroline. *The terrible Hodag*
Arnosky, Jim. *Crinkleroot's guide to knowing*
  the trees
Baker, Jeannie. *Where the forest meets the sea*
Baumann, Hans. *Mischa and his brothers*
Berenstain, Stan. *The Berenstain bears and*
  the ghost of the forest
Beskow, Elsa Maartman. *Children of the*
  forest
Biro, Val. *The wind in the willows: the wild*
  wood
Blake, Robert J. *The perfect spot*
Bond, Ruskin. *Flames in the forest*
Bowen, Betsy. *Antler, bear, canoe*
Bradman, Tony. *Look out, he's behind you*
Buff, Mary. *Dash and Dart*
  Forest folk
Carrick, Carol. *A clearing in the forest*
Carrick, Donald. *Harold and the great stag*
Chall, Marsha Wilson. *Up north at the cabin*
Cherry, Lynne. *Archie, follow me*
Christiana, David. *White nineteens*
Cowcher, Helen. *Rain forest*
Cristini, Ermanno. *In the woods*
Davidson, Jill A. *And that's what happened*
  to little Lucy
Ets, Marie Hall. *Another day*
  In the forest
Frost, Robert. *Stopping by woods on a snowy*
  evening
Greenaway, Shirley. *Forests*
Greene, Carol. *I can be a forest ranger*
Gregory, Valiska. *Through the mickle woods*
Grimm, Jacob. *Hansel and Gretel*, ill. by
  Adrienne Adams
  Hansel and Gretel, ill. by Anthony
  Browne
  Hansel and Gretel, ill. by Susan Jeffers

Hansel and Gretel, ill. by Winslow P. Pels
Hansel and Gretel, ill. by Conxita
 Rodriguez
Hansel and Gretel, ill. by John Wallner
Hansel and Gretel, ill. by Paul O.
 Zelinsky
Hansel and Gretel, ill. by Lisbeth Zwerger
Hill, Mary Lou. *My dad's a smokejumper*
Hirschi, Ron. *Forest*
 Who lives in... Alligator Swamp?
 Who lives in... the forest?
Hodges, Margaret. *Buried moon*
Holder, Heidi. *Carmine the crow*
Hyman, Trina Schart. *The enchanted forest*
Iwamura, Kazuo. *The fourteen forest mice
 and the harvest moon watch*
 *The fourteen forest mice and the spring
 meadow picnic*
 *The fourteen forest mice and the summer
 laundry day*
 *The fourteen forest mice and the winter
 sledding day*
Jones, Chuck. *William the backwards skunk*
Latimer, Jim. *Going the moose way home*
Leister, Mary. *The silent concert*
Lerner, Carol. *Flowers of a woodland spring*
Lipkind, William. *The boy and the forest*
Lukešová, Milena. *Julian in the autumn
 woods*
McConnachie, Brian. *Lily of the forest*
Maris, Ron. *Hold tight, bear!*
Marshall, Edward. *Troll country*
Marshall, James. *Hansel and Gretel*
Miklowitz, Gloria D. *Save that raccoon!*
Miles, Miska. *The fox and the fire*
 Sylvester Jones and the voice in the forest
Miller, Edna. *Mousekin's ABC*
 Mousekin's close call
 Mousekin's lost woodland
 Mouskin's Thanksgiving
Moore, Inga. *Fifty red night-caps*
Mora, Emma. *Animals of the forest*
 Gideon, the little bear cub
Newton, James R. *A forest is reborn*
 Forest log
O'Donnell, Peter. *Moonlit journey*
Parnall, Peter. *The rock*
Paul, Anthony. *The tiger who lost his stripes*
Peet, Bill (William Bartlett). *Big bad Bruce*
Peyo. *The Smurfs and their woodland friends*
Porter, Sue. *Little Wolf and the giant*
Prather, Ray. *The ostrich girl*
Prusski, Jeffrey. *Bring back the deer*
Ross, Tony. *Hansel and Gretel*
Scheidl, Gerda Marie. *Can we help you,
 Saint Nicholas?*
Schick, Eleanor. *A surprise in the forest*
Seligson, Susan. *Amos camps out: a couch
 adventure in the woods*
Seymour, Peter. *What's in the prehistoric
 forest?*

Slobodkin, Louis. *Melvin, the moose child*
Spohn, David. *Winter wood*
Storr, Catherine (Cole). *Robin Hood*
Tejima, Keizaburo. *Fox's dream*
 Woodpecker forest
Thornhill, Jan. *A tree in a forest*
Tresselt, Alvin R. *The gift of the tree*
Upton, Pat. *Who lives in the woods?*
Wahl, Jan. *The five in the forest*
Ward, Lynd. *Nic of the woods*
Weir, Bob. *Panther dream*
Yolen, Jane. *All in the woodland early*
 Owl moon
Zalben, Jane Breskin. *Norton's nighttime*
Ziefert, Harriet. *On our way to the forest*

Forgetfulness *see* Behavior –
 forgetfulness

Format, unusual
Adams, Pam. *There was an old lady who
 swallowed a fly*
 This old man
Ahlberg, Janet. *The jolly Christmas postman*
 Peek-a-boo!
Alexander, Martha G. *The magic box*
 The magic hat
 The magic picture
Amery, H. *The zoo picture book*
Anno, Mitsumasa. *Anno's faces*
 Anno's peekaboo
Barrows, Marjorie Wescott. *Fraidy cat*
 The funny hat
Bratton, John. *The teddy bears' picnic*, ill. by
 Renate Kozikowski
Brown, Margaret Wise. *The little fur family*
Burlson, Joe. *Space colony*
Burton, Jane. *Chick*
Cahill, Chris. *Spider magic*
 Turtle magic
Campbell, Rod. *Henry's busy day*
 Misty's mischief
Carle, Eric. *My very first book of colors*
 My very first book of growth
 My very first book of homes
 My very first book of motion
 My very first book of numbers
 My very first book of shapes
 My very first book of touch
 My very first book of words
 The very hungry caterpillar
 The very quiet cricket
Carrier, Lark. *There was a hill...*
Carter, Noelle. *I'm a little mouse*
Chwast, Seymour. *Tall city, wide country*
Cousins, Lucy. *Flower in the garden*
 Hen on the farm
 Kite in the park
 Teddy in the house
De Paola, Tomie (Thomas Anthony).
 Country farm

Dodds, Dayle Ann. *Wheel away!*
Dryden, Emma. *Good morning—good night*
Ehlert, Lois. *Color farm*
Color zoo
Emberley, Ed (Edward Randolph). *Ed Emberley's amazing look through book*
Ernst, Lisa Campbell. *The rescue of Aunt Pansy*
Fallwell, Cathryn. *Nicky and Alex*
Nicky and grandpa
Nicky loves daddy
Nicky, 1-2-3
Nicky's walk
Where's Nicky?
Fort, Patrick. *Redbird*
Fuchshuber, Annegert. *Giant story—Mouse tale*
Gantschev, Ivan. *The train to Grandma's*
Where is Mr. Mole?
Ghigna, Charles. *Good cats / Bad cats*
Good dogs / Bad dogs
Golden tales from long ago
Gomi, Taro. *Hi, butterfly!*
Goodall, John S. *The adventures of Paddy Pork*
The ballooning adventures of Paddy Pork
Creepy castle
An Edwardian Christmas
An Edwardian summer
Jacko
The midnight adventures of Kelly, Dot and Esmeralda
Naughty Nancy
Naughty Nancy goes to school
Paddy goes traveling
Paddy Pork: odd jobs
Paddy Pork's holiday
Paddy under water
Paddy's evening out
Paddy's new hat
Shrewbettina's birthday
The story of a castle
The story of a farm
The story of a main street
The story of an English village
The surprise picnic
Gorey, Edward (St. John). *The tunnel calamity*
Grimm, Jacob. *Little Red Riding Hood*, ill. by John S. Goodall
Grindley, Sally. *Shhh!*
Hague, Michael. *Michael Hague's world of unicorns*
Hannant, Judith Stuller. *Doorknob collection of nursery rhymes*
Hauptmann, Tatjana. *A day in the life of Petronella Pig*
Hawkins, Colin. *Jen the hen*
Tog the dog
Hayden, Lea. *Sunny day - rainy day*

Hedderwick, Mairi. *P. D. Pebbles' summer or winter book*
Hellard, Susan. *This little piggy*
Time to get up
Hellen, Nancy. *Bus stop*
Hoban, Tana. *Look! Look! Look!*
26 letters and 99 cents
Hooper, Meredith. *Seven eggs*
Howell, Lynn. *Winifred's new bed*
Hyman, Trina Schart. *The enchanted forest*
Imershein, Betsy. *Finding red, finding yellow*
Inkpen, Mick. *The blue balloon*
Threadbear
Jensen, Virginia Allen. *Catching*
Jonas, Ann. *Reflections*
The thirteenth clue
Jones, Carol. *This old man*
Kent, Lorna. *No, no, Charlie Rascal!*
Ladybug, ladybug, and other nursery rhymes, ill. by Eloise Wilkin
Lenski, Lois. *Sing a song of people*
Lewis, Stephen. *Zoo city*
Lewison, Wendy C. *Where is Sammy's smile?*
Lodge, Bernard. *Door to door*
Rhyming Nell
MacDonald, Suse. *Once upon another*
McNaughton, Colin. *Guess who's just moved in next door?*
Magnus, Erica. *Around me*
Mari, Iela. *Eat and be eaten*
Martin, Jerome. *Carrot—parrot*
Mitten—kitten
Miranda, Anne. *Baby walk*
Monfried, Lucia. *Baby's world*
Mother Goose. *Hickory dickory dock and other nursery rhymes*, ill. by Carol Jones
Munari, Bruno. *The circus in the mist*
Newell, Peter. *Topsys and turvys*
Newth, Philip. *Roly goes exploring*
Old MacDonald had a farm. *Old MacDonald had a farm*, ill. by Carol Jones
Ormerod, Jan. *Come back, kittens*
Come back, puppies
Pacovska, Kveta. *One, five, many*
Pearson, Tracey Campbell. *A apple pie*
Pelham, David. *Sam's sandwich*
Potter, Beatrix. *Where's Peter Rabbit?*
Potter, Tony. *See how it works: cars*
See how it works: earth movers
See how it works: planes
See how it works: trucks
Price, Mathew. *Do you see what I see?*
Have you seen my sister?
Rey, H. A. (Hans Augusto). *Anybody at home?*
How do you get there?
See the circus
Where's my baby?
Roddie, Shen. *Animal stew*

Roffey, Maureen. *Family scramble*
  Here, kitty kitty!
  Look, there's my hat!
  Quick, catch Dan!
Ross, Tony. *Happy blanket*
Royston, Angela. *Shells*
  Small animals
Russell, Naomi. *The tree*
Savage, Stephen. *Making tracks*
Scarry, Richard. *Egg in the hole*
  Pig Will/Pig Won't
  Richard Scarry's biggest word book ever!
Scruton, Clive. *Mary's pets*
Scullard, Sue. *Miss Fanshawe and the great
  dragon adventure*
Sharratt, Nick. *I look like this*
  Look what I found!
Steiner, Charlotte. *The climbing book*
Taback, Simms. *Joseph had a little overcoat*
Tarrant, Graham. *Rabbits*
Tison, Annette. *The adventures of the three
  colors*
  Animal hide-and-seek
  Animals in color magic
  Inside and outside
The twelve days of Christmas. English
  folk song. *The twelve days of Christmas,*
  ill. by Erika Schneider
Van der Meer, Ron. *Pigs at home*
Waber, Bernard. *The snake*
Wahl, Jan. *Dracula's cat and Frankenstein's
  dog*
Walters, Marguerite. *The city-country ABC*
Watson, Wendy. *The bunnies' Christmas eve*
Wattenberg, Jane. *Mrs. Mustard's baby faces*
Watts, Barrie. *Rabbit*
Wildsmith, Brian. *Give a dog a bone*
  Goat's trail
  Pelican
Windham, Sophie. *Noah's ark*
Wood, David. *Happy birthday, Mouse!*
Wood, John Norris. *Jungles*
  Oceans
Wyllie, Stephen. *The great race*
  White Rabbit builds a dream house
Youldon, Gillian. *Counting*
  Shapes
  Sizes
Ziefert, Harriet. *Where's the cat?*
  Where's the dog?
  Where's the guinea pig?
  Where's the turtle?

Format, unusual – board books

Allen, Robert. *Ten little babies count*
  Ten little babies dress
  Ten little babies eat
  Ten little babies play
Anderson, Lena Castell. *Bunny bath*
  Bunny box
  Bunny fun

Bunny party
Bunny story
Bunny surprise
Aronin, Ben. *The secret of the Sabbath fish*
At the farm, ill. by Roser Capdevila
Baby's first book of colors, ill. by Nina
  Barbaresi
Baby's words, ill. by Debby Slier
Bailey, Debbie. *Clothes*
  Hats
  My dad
  My mom
  Shoes
  Toys
Bailey, Jill. *Eyes*
  Feet
  Mouths
  Noses
Baird, Anne. *Baby socks*
  Kiss, kiss
  Little tree
  No sheep
Bambi, ill. by Christa Stephan
Barkan, Joanne. *Boxcar*
  Caboose
  Locomotive
  Passenger car
  Whiskerville bake shop
  Whiskerville firehouse
  Whiskerville post office
  Whiskerville school
Bishop, Roma. *Animals*
  Numbers
  Shapes
  Toys
Blades, Ann. *Fall*
  Spring
  Summer
  Winter
Bohdal, Susi. *Bobby the bear*
  Harry the hare
Boon, Emilie. *It's spring, Peterkin*
  Peterkin's very own garden
Boynton, Sandra. *But not the hippopotamus*
  Doggies
  The going to bed book
  Horns to toes and in between
  Moo, baa, lalala
  Opposites
Burningham, John. *Count up*
  The dog
  Five down
  Just cats
  Pigs plus
  Read one
  Ride off
Burton, Jane. *Kitten*
  Puppy
Busy baby, ill. by Debby Slier
Cahill, Chris. *Bear magic*
  Bunny magic

Spider magic
Turtle magic
Campbell, Rod. *Look inside! All kinds of places*
Look inside! Land, sea, air
Cars and trucks, ill. by Daisuke Yokoi
Cassidy, Dianne. *Circus animals*
Circus people
The caterpillar who turned into a butterfly
Children's Television Workshop. *Muppets in my neighborhood*
City, ill. by Roser Capdevila
Cock Robin. *Who killed Cock Robin?* ill. by William Stobbs
Come to the circus
Corbett, Grahame. *Guess who?*
What number now?
Who is hiding?
Who is inside?
Who is next?
Cosgrove, Stephen (Edward). *Sleepy time bunny*
Costa, Nicoletta. *The birthday party*
Dressing up
A friend comes to play
The missing cat
Cousins, Lucy. *Country animals*
Farm animals
Garden animals
Pet animals
Davidson, Amanda. *Teddy goes outside*
Demi. *Fleecy bunny*
Fleecy lamb
Little baby lamb
Little lucky ducky
De Paola, Tomie (Thomas Anthony). *Katie and Kit at the beach*
Katie, Kit and cousin Tom
Katie's good idea
My first Chanukah
Pajamas for Kit
Dickens, Lucy. *At the beach*
Our day
Outside
Playtime
DiFiori, Lawrence. *Baby animals*
The farm
If I had a little car
My first book
My toys
Domestic animals
Dreamer, Sue. *Circus ABC*
Circus 1, 2, 3
Dubov, Christine Salac. *Aleksandra, where are your toes?*
Aleksandra, where is your nose?
Ding dong! and other sounds
Knock! and other sounds
Oink! and other sounds
Duke, Kate. *Bedtime*
Clean-up day

The playground
What bounces?
Dunn, Phoebe. *Baby's animal friends*
Busy, busy toddlers
I'm a baby!
Edwards, Roberta. *Anna Bear's first winter*
Eisenberg, Ann. *I can celebrate*
Emberley, Ed (Edward Randolph). *Animals*
Cars, boats, and planes
Home
Sounds
Farm animals, photos. sel. by Debby Slier
Farm house, ill. by Kate Klimo
Fast rolling fire trucks, ill. by Carolyn Bracken
Fast rolling work trucks, ill. by Alan Singer
Fechner, Amrei. *I am a little dog*
I am a little elephant
I am a little lion
Firehouse, ill. by Zokeisha
Fitzsimons, Cecilia. *My first birds*
My first butterflies
Fowler, Richard. *Cat's story*
Freeman, Don. *Corduroy's busy street and Corduroy goes to the doctor*
Corduroy's party
Freeman, Lydia. *Corduroy's day*
Fujikawa, Gyo. *Let's grow a garden*
Millie's secret
My favorite thing
Surprise! Surprise!
Gelbard, Jane. *My bye-bye bottle book*
My dressing book
My eating book
My sharing book
Gellman, Ellie. *It's Chanukah!*
It's Rosh Hashanah!
Shai's Shabbat walk
Gomi, Taro. *Guess who?*
Gorbaty, Norman. *Get up and go, little dinosaur!*
Greeley, Valerie. *Farm animals*
Field animals
Pets
Zoo animals
Greenfield, Eloise. *Big friend, little friend*
Daddy and I
I make music
My doll, Keshia
Gretz, Susanna. *Hide-and-seek*
I'm not sleepy
Ready for bed
Too dark!
Groner, Judyth. *Where is the Afikomen?*
Hands, Hargrave. *Bunny sees*
Duckling sees
Little lamb sees
Hannant, Judith Stuller. *Doorknob collection of nursery rhymes*
Haus, Felice. *Beep! Beep! I'm a jeep*
Hawkins, Colin. *Hey diddle diddle*

Humpty Dumpty
Hayes, Geoffrey. *Patrick and his grandpa*
Hello, baby, ill. by Debby Slier
Hill, Eric. *Spot at home*
  Spot at the fair
  Spot counts from 1 to 10
  Spot goes to the circus
  Spot goes to the farm
  Spot in the garden
  Spot looks at colors
  Spot looks at opposites
  Spot looks at shapes
  Spot looks at the weather
  Spot on the farm
  Spot's first words
  Spot's toy box
Hoban, Tana. *1, 2, 3*
  Panda, panda
  Red, blue, yellow shoe
  What is it?
Hopkins, Margaret. *Sleepytime for baby mouse*
Hudson, Cheryl Willis. *Good morning baby*
  Good night baby
Johnson, John E. *My first book of things*
Kahn, Katherine Janus. *The Shofar calls to us*
Kangas, Juli. *Fluffy Bunny's friend*
  Ginger Kitten's surprise
  Hello, Honey Bear
Karn, George. *Circus big and small*
  Circus colors
Kessler, Ethel. *Are there hippos on the farm?*
  Is there an elephant in your kitchen?
Kilroy, Sally. *Animal noises*
  Babies' bodies
  Babies' homes
  Babies' outings
  Babies' zoo
  Baby colors
  Busy babies
  Noisy homes
Koelling, Caryl. *Animal mix and match*
  Mad monsters mix and match
  Silly stories mix and match
Koenner, Alfred. *Be quite quiet beside the lake*
  High flies the ball
Krementz, Jill. *Benjy goes to a restaurant*
  Jack goes to the beach
  Jamie goes on an airplane
  Katherine goes to nursery school
  Lily goes to the playground
  Taryn goes to the dentist
Landa, Norbert. *Rabbit and chicken find a box*
Lewis, Sheri. *Baby Lamb Chop loves animals*
  Baby Lamb Chop loves numbers
  Baby Lamb Chop loves nursery school
  Baby Lamb Chop loves the beach
  Baby Lamb Chop loves words

Lilly, Kenneth. *Animal builders*
  Animal climbers
  Animal jumpers
  Animal runners
  Animal swimmers
  Animals at the zoo
  Animals in the country
  Animals in the jungle
  Animals of the ocean
  Animals on the farm
Lionni, Leo. *Colors to talk about*
  Letters to talk about
  Numbers to talk about
  What?
  When?
  Where?
  Who?
  Words to talk about
  A little ABC book
  A little book of colors
  A little book of numbers
Lundell, Margo. *Teddy bear's birthday*
Lynn, Sara. *Big animals*
  Clothes
  Farm animals
  Food
  Garden animals
  Home
  Small animals
  Toys
McCue, Lisa. *Corduroy's party*
  Corduroy's toys
  The little chick
McDonald, Amy. *Let's do it*
  Let's make a noise
  Let's try
McNaught, Harry. *Baby animals*
McNaughton, Colin. *At home*
  At playschool
  At the park
  At the party
  At the stores
  Autumn
  Spring
  Summer
  Winter
Maestro, Betsy. *Harriet at home*
  Harriet at play
  Harriet at school
  Harriet at work
Mantegazza, Giovanna. *The cat*
  The hippopotamus
Mayer, Mercer. *Astronaut critter*
  Cowboy critter
  Fireman critter
  Policeman critter
Miller, J. P. (John Parr). *Good night, Little Rabbit*
Miller, Margaret. *At my house*
  Every day
  In my room

Me and my clothes
My birthday
On my street
Playtime
Time to eat
Mother Goose. *ABC rhymes*, ill. by Lulu
  Delarce
Baa, baa, black sheep, ill. by Moira Kemp
Baa baa black sheep, ill. by Sue Porter
Baa baa black sheep, ill. by Ferelith Eccles
  Williams
Hey diddle diddle, ill. by Moira Kemp
Hey diddle diddle, ill. by Nita Sowter
Hey diddle diddle, ill. by Eleanor
  Wasmuth
Hickory dickory dock, ill. by Moira Kemp
Humpty Dumpty, ill. by Colin and Jacqui
  Hawkins
Jack and Jill, ill. by Eleanor Wasmuth
Kate Greenaway's Mother Goose
Kitten rhymes, ill. by Lulu Delarce
Little boy blue, ill. by Nita Sowter
Mother Goose house, ill. by Kate Klimo
The old woman in a shoe, ill. by Eleanor
  Wasmuth
Pussy cat, pussy cat, ill. by Ferelith Eccles
  Williams
Sing a song of sixpence, ill. by Margaret
  Chamberlain
Sing a song of sixpence, ill. by Ferelith
  Eccles Williams
This little pig, ill. by Eleanor Wasmuth
This little pig went to market, ill. by
  Ferelith Eccles Williams
This little piggy, ill. by Moira Kemp
The three little kittens, ill. by Dorothy
  Stott
Mouse house, ill. by Zokeisha
My body, ill. by Sue Porter
My first book of baby animals, ill. by Karen
  Lee Schmidt
Nickl, Peter. *Ra ta ta tam*
O'Brien, Anne Sibley. *Come play with us*
I want that!
I'm not tired
Where's my truck?
Our house, ill. by Roser Capdevila
Oxenbury, Helen. *All fall down*
  Beach day
  Clap hands
  Dressing
  Family
  Friends
  I can
  I hear
  I see
  I touch
  Playing
  Say goodnight
  729 curious creatures
  729 merry mix-ups

729 puzzle people
The shopping trip
Tickle, tickle
Parish, Peggy. *I can—can you?*
Paterson, Bettina. *In my house*
  In my yard
  My clothes
  My toys
Patrick, Denice. *Look inside a house*
  Look inside a ship
Pearson, Susan. *Baby and the bear*
  When baby went to bed
Peppé, Rodney. *Little circus*
  Little dolls
  Little games
  Little numbers
  Little wheels
Pfister, Marcus. *Where is my friend?*
Pfloog, Jan. *Kittens*
  Puppies
Phillips, Joan. *Peek-a-boo! I see you!*
Pieńkowski, Jan. *Faces*
  Food
Pragoff, Fiona. *Odd one out*
  Opposites
  Shapes
The pudgy book of babies, ill. by Kathy
  Wilburn
The pudgy book of farm animals, ill. by Julie
  Durrell
The pudgy book of here we go, ill. by Beth
  Lee Weiner
The pudgy book of make-believe
The pudgy book of Mother Goose, ill. by
  Richard Walz
The pudgy book of toys, ill. by Julie Durrell
The pudgy bunny book, ill. by Ruth
  Sanderson
The pudgy fingers counting book, ill. by Doug
  Cushman
The pudgy pals, ill. by Kathy Wilburn
The pudgy pat-a-cake book, ill. by Teri Super
The pudgy peek-a-boo book, ill. by Amye
  Rosenberg
The pudgy rock-a-bye book, ill. by Kathy
  Wilburn
Puppies and kittens
Roosevelt, Michelle Chopin. *Zoo animals*
Roth, Harold. *Autumn days*
  A checkup
  Nursery school
  Winter days
Royston, Angela. *Cars*
Sage, Chris. *Happy baby*
  Sleepy baby
Scarry, Richard. *My first word book*
  Richard Scarry's busy houses
  Richard Scarry's Lowly Worm word book
Schanzer, Roz. *In the synagogue*
Schmid, Eleonore. *Farm animals*
Schroeder, Binette. *Tuffa and her friends*

Tuffa and the bone
Tuffa and the ducks
Tuffa and the picnic
Tuffa and the snow
Sesame Street. *Ernie and Bert can...can you?*
Shine, Deborah. *The little engine that could pudgy word book*
Shostak, Myra. *Rainbow candles*
Shott, Stephen. *Bathtime*
  Look at me
  Mealtime
  Playtime
Sieveking, Anthea. *Mary had a little lamb and other animal rhymes*
  Polly put the kettle on and other play rhymes
  Rub-a-dub-dub and other splashy rhymes
  Twinkle, twinkle, little star and other bedtime rhymes
Silverman, Maida. *Bunny's ABC*
  Ladybug's color book
  Mouse's shape book
Smith, Donald. *Who's wearing my baseball cap?*
  Who's wearing my bow tie?
  Who's wearing my sneakers?
  Who's wearing my sunglasses?
Spanner, Helmut. *I am a little cat*
Spier, Peter. *Bill's service station*
  Firehouse
  Food market
  Little cats
  Little dogs
  Little ducks
  Little rabbits
  My school
  The pet store
  The toy shop
Springer, Sally. *Let's make latkes*
Stevens, Harry. *Fat mouse*
  Parrot told snake
Struppi
Suben, Eric. *Pigeon takes a trip*
Szekeres, Cyndy. *Good night, Sammy*
  Hide-and-seek duck
  Nothing-to-do puppy
  Suppertime for Frieda Fuzzypaws
Tabler, Judith. *The new puppy*
Tafuri, Nancy. *In a red house*
  My friends
  One wet jacket
  Two new sneakers
  Where we sleep
Taylor, Kim. *Frog*
The three bears. *Goldilocks and the three bears*, ill. by Jane Dyer
The three little pigs. *The three little pigs*, retold and ill. by Val Biro
Tucker, Sian. *At home*
  Going out

My clothes
My toys
A visit to a pond
Watts, Barrie. *Duck*
  Kitten
Wells, Rosemary. *Hooray for Max*
  Max's bath
  Max's bedtime
  Max's birthday
  Max's breakfast
  Max's first word
  Max's new suit
  Max's ride
  Max's toys
What do babies do?
What do toddlers do?
Wijngaard, Juan. *Bear*
  Cat
  Dog
  Duck
Wikler, Madeline. *Let's build a Sukkah*
  My first seder
  The Purim parade
Willis, Val. *The mystery in the bottle*
Winn, Chris. *Helping*
  Holiday
  My day
  Playing
Young animals in the zoo
Young domestic animals
Ziefert, Harriet. *Baby Ben's bow-wow book*
  Baby Ben's busy book
  Baby Ben's go-go book
  Baby Ben's noisy book
  My getting-ready-for-school book
  Nicky's friends
  No, no, Nicky!
  On our way to the barn
  On our way to the forest
  On our way to the water
  On our way to the zoo
  Where's the cat?
  Where's the dog?
  Where's the guinea pig?
  Where's the turtle?
Zoo animals, Imported Pubs. 1983

Format, unusual – toy and movable books

Æsop. *Æsop's fables*, ill. by Claire Littlejohn
Alexander, Martha G. *3 magic flip books: The magic hat; The magic box; The magic picture*
Anno, Mitsumasa. *Anno's magical ABC*
Argent, Kerry. *Happy birthday, Wombat!*
Belloc, Hilaire. *The bad child's pop-up book of beasts*
Bemelmans, Ludwig. *Madeline [pop-up book]*
Benjamin, Alan. *1000 monsters*
Berger, Melvin. *Early humans*

Prehistoric mammals
Bishop, Roma. *Animals*
Numbers
Shapes
Toys
Bowman, Peter. *The Christmas songbook*
Bradman, Tony. *Look out, he's behind you*
See you later, alligator
Brown, Marc Tolon. *Can you jump like a frog?*
One, two buckle my shoe
What do you call a dumb bunny? and other rabbit riddles, games, jokes and cartoons
Campbell, Rod. *Buster's afternoon*
Buster's morning
Dear zoo
It's mine
Oh dear!
Carle, Eric. *My very first book of food*
My very first book of heads and tails
My very first book of sounds
My very first book of tools
Papa, please get the moon for me
The secret birthday message
Watch out! A giant!
Carter, David A. *How many bugs in a box?*
Carter, Noelle. *My house*
My pet
Cassidy, Dianne. *Circus animals*
Circus people
Chen, Tony. *Animals showing off*
Cousins, Lucy. *Maisy goes to bed*
Masy goes swimming
What can rabbit hear?
What can rabbit see?
Cremins, Robert. *My animal ABC*
My animal Mother Goose
Pop up baby brontosaurus
Pop up baby coelophysis
Pop up baby pteranodon
Pop up baby stegosaurus
Pop up baby triceratops
Pop up baby tyrannosaurus rex
Crespi, Francesca. *Santa Clause is coming!*
Silent Night
Crowther, Robert. *Hide and seek counting book*
The most amazing hide-and-seek alphabet book
The most amazing hide-and-seek opposites book
Pop goes the weasel!
Dijs, Carla. *Are you my daddy?*
Are you my mommy?
Big and small
How many?
Dodds, Dayle Ann. *The color box*
Facklam, Margery. *But not like mine*
So can I
Faulkner, Keith. *Sam at the seaside*

Sam helps out
Fowler, Richard. *Mr. Little's noisy car*
Mr. Little's noisy truck
Gardner, Beau. *What is it?*
Whooo's a fright on Halloween night?
Gay, Tenner Ottley. *Dinosaurs and their relatives in action*
Sharks in action
Gerstein, Mordicai. *William, where are you?*
Grimm, Jacob. *Sleeping Beauty*, ill. by John Wallner
Hanna, Jack. *The petting zoo*
Hawkins, Colin. *The elephant*
Incy wincy spider
Round the garden
Take away monsters
This little pig
What time is it, Mr. Wolf?
Hellen, Nancy. *A visit to the farm*
A visit to the zoo
Hill, Eric. *Spot goes to school*
Spot goes to the beach
Spot sleeps over
Spot's baby sister
Spot's birthday party
Spot's first Christmas
Spot's first Easter
Spot's first walk
Where's Spot?
Holmes, Stephen. *Hidden numbers*
The house that Jack built. *The house that Jack built*, ill. by Seymour Chwast
The house that Jack built, ill. by Nadine Bernard Westcott
Hurd, Thacher. *A night in the swamp*
Johnson, B. J. *A hat like that*
My blanket Burt
Jonas, Ann. *Where can it be?*
Kunhardt, Edith. *Pat the cat*
Lacome, Julie. *Funny business*
Hocus pocus
Lagerlöf, Selma. *The changeling*
Lippman, Peter. *Peter Lippman's numbers*
Peter Lippman's opposites
Llewelyn, Claire. *My first book of time*
Lobel, Arnold. *The frog and toad pop-up book*
McGowan, Alan. *Sailing ships*
Maris, Ron. *Is anyone home?*
Marshall, Ray. *Pop-up numbers #1*
Pop-up numbers #2
Pop-up numbers #3
Pop-up numbers #4
The train
Martin, Sarah Catherine. *Old Mother Hubbard*, ill. by Colin Hawkins
Mason, Lura. *A book of boxes*
Meggendorfer, Lothar. *The genius of Lothar Meggendorfer*
Meryl, Debra. *Baby's peek-a-boo album*

Milne, A. A. (Alan Alexander). *House at Pooh corner [a pop-up book]*
Pooh and some bees
Pooh goes visiting
Winnie-the-Pooh
Miranda, Anne. *Baby talk*
Baby-sit
Moseley, Keith. *Dinosaurs*
Mother Goose. *Sing a song of sixpence*, ill. by Ray Marshall and Korky Paul
Munari, Bruno. *The elephant's wish*
Jimmy has lost his cap
Tic, Tac and Toc
Who's there? Open the door
Oakley, Graham. *Graham Oakley's magical changes*
Pelham, David. *A is for animals*
Worms wiggle
Potter, Beatrix. *The two bad mice: pop-up book*
Presencer, Alain. *Roaring lion tales*
Price, Mathew. *Peekaboo!*
Prokofiev, Sergei Sergeievitch. *Peter and the wolf*, ill. by Barbara Cooney
Roddie, Shen. *Hatch, egg, hatch!*
Roffey, Maureen. *Home sweet home*
Ross, Tony. *This old man*
Roth, Harold. *Let's look all around the farm*
Let's look all around the house
Let's look all around the town
Let's look for surprises all around
Ruby-Spears Enterprises. *The puppy's new adventures*
Scarry, Huck. *Looking into the Middle Ages*
Scarry, Richard. *Richard Scarry's mix or match storybook*
Selberg, Ingrid. *Nature's hidden world*
Seymour, Peter. *Animals in disguise*
How the weather works
Insects
The pop-up book of big trucks
What lives in the sea?
What's in the deep blue sea?
What's in the prehistoric forest?
Shapiro, Arnold L. *Circle*
Square
Triangles
Shopping, ill. by Roser Capdevila
Sibbick, John. *Creatures of long ago: dinosaurs*
Smallman, Clare. *Outside in*
Smith, Mavis. *Fred, is that you?*
Stapler, Sarah. *Trilby's trumpet*
The Superman mix or match storybook
The three little pigs. *The three little pigs*, ill. by John Wallner
Varekamp, Marjolein. *Little Sam takes a bath*
Wallner, John. *Old MacDonald had a farm*
Watson, Claire. *Big creatures from the past*
Wyllie, Stephen. *Dinner with fox*

Snappity snap
Yoshi. *Who's hiding here?*
Youldon, Gillian. *Colors*
Numbers
Zelinsky, Paul O. *The wheels on the bus*
Ziefert, Harriet. *Bear all year*
Bear gets dressed
Bear goes shopping
Bear's busy morning
Where's daddy's car?
Where's mommy's truck?

Fortune *see* Character traits – luck

Fortune tellers *see* Careers – fortune tellers

Fourth of July *see* Holidays – Fourth of July

Foxes *see* Animals – foxes

France *see* Foreign lands – France

Freedom *see* Character traits – freedom

Friendship

Æsop. *The ant and the dove*, ill. by Ching
Aldridge, Josephine Haskell. *The best of friends*
Alexander, Martha G. *My outrageous friend Charlie*
Alexander, Sue. *Small plays for you and a friend*
Witch, Goblin and sometimes Ghost
Aliki. *Feelings*
Overnight at Mary Bloom's
We are best friends
Allard, Harry. *The cactus flower bakery*
Allen, Pamela. *My cat Maisie*
Allinson, Beverley. *Effie*
Anderson, Lena Castell. *Stina's visit*
Anderson, Paul S. *Red fox and the hungry tiger*
Anglund, Joan Walsh. *Cowboy and his friend*
A friend is someone who likes you
Anholt, Catherine. *Snow fairy and the spaceman*
Ardizzone, Edward. *Tim and Lucy go to sea*
Argent, Kerry. *Wombat and Bandicoot: best friends*
Artis, Vicki Kimmel. *Pajama walking*
Aruego, José. *The king and his friends*
Asare, Meshack. *Cat... in search of a friend*
Asch, Frank. *Oats and wild apples*
Aylesworth, Jim. *Mr. McGill goes to town*
Baker, Alan. *Benjamin and the box*
Baker, Barbara. *Digby and Kate*
Digby and Kate again
Baker, Betty. *Partners*

Balian, Lorna. *Wilbur's space machine*
Barbour, Karen. *Nancy*
Barrett, Joyce Durham. *Willie's not the hugging kind*
Bassett, Lisa. *Beany wakes up for Christmas*
Bastin, Marjolein. *My name is Vera*
Vera and her friends
Battles, Edith. *One to teeter-totter*
Baylor, Byrd. *Guess who my favorite person is*
Baynton, Martin. *Fifty saves his friend*
Beim, Jerrold. *The swimming hole*
Beim, Lorraine. *Two is a team*
Bell, Norman. *Linda's airmail letter*
Berends, Polly Berrien. *Ladybug and dog and the night walk*
Berenstain, Stan. *The Berenstain bears and the trouble with friends*
The Berenstain bears' moving day
Berger, Barbara Helen. *When the sun rose*
Berger, Terry. *Friends*
Bergman, Donna. *City fox*
Bergstrom, Corinne. *Losing your best friend*
Bianchi, John. *Swine snafu*
Binzen, Bill. *Carmen*
Blance, Ellen. *Monster looks for a friend*
Blaustein, Muriel. *Make friends, Zachary!*
Bliss, Corinne Demas. *That dog Melly!*
Bohdal, Susi. *Bobby the bear*
Bolliger, Max. *The lonely prince*
Bond, Felicia. *Four Valentines in a rainstorm*
Bonsall, Crosby Newell. *It's mine! A greedy book*
Bornstein, Ruth Lercher. *The seedling child*
Bos, Burny. *Prince Valentino*
Bottner, Barbara. *Horrible Hannah*
Mean Maxine
Boyd, Selma. *The how: making the best of a mistake*
Boynton, Sandra. *Chloë and Maude*
Breinburg, Petronella. *Shawn goes to school*
Briggs, Raymond. *The snowman*
Bright, Robert. *Me and the bears*
Brown, Marc Tolon. *Arthur's birthday*
The cloud over Clarence
Brown, Myra Berry. *Best friends*
First night away from home
Browne, Anthony. *Willy and Hugh*
Browne, Eileen. *Where's that bus?*
Bryan, Dorothy. *Friendly little Jonathan*
Buck, Pearl S. (Pearl Sydenstricker). *The little fox in the middle*
Buntain, Ruth Jaeger. *The birthday story*
Bunting, Eve (Anne Evelyn). *Clancy's coat*
Monkey in the middle
Summer wheels
Burdick, Margaret. *Sara Raccoon and the secret place*
Burningham, John. *Aldo*
The friend

Calhoun, Mary. *The witch who lost her shadow*
Calmenson, Stephanie. *Wanted: warm, furry friend*
Caple, Kathy. *Fox and bear*
Harry's smile
Carle, Eric. *Do you want to be my friend?*
Carlson, Nancy. *Arnie and the new kid*
Louanne Pig in making the team
Carlstrom, Nancy White. *Blow me a kiss, Miss Lilly*
Carrier, Lark. *A Christmas promise*
Caseley, Judith. *Harry and Willy and Carrothead*
Cassedy, Sylvia. *The best cat suit of all*
Cech, John. *My grandmother's journey*
Chambless, Jane. *Tucker and the bear*
Chapouton, Anne-Marie. *Ben finds a friend*
Chorao, Kay. *Ida and Betty and the secret eggs*
Molly's lies
Clarke, Gus. *Eddie and Teddy*
Clifton, Lucille. *Everett Anderson's friend*
My friend Jacob
Three wishes
Three wishes, ill. by Michael Hays
Cohen, Miriam. *Best friends*
First grade takes a test
Liar, liar, pants on fire!
See you in second grade!
Will I have a friend?
Cohn, Janice. *I had a friend named Peter*
Cole, Babette. *Silly book*
Cole, Brock. *Nothing but a pig*
Cole, Joanna. *Don't call me names!*
Collins, Pat Lowery. *Tumble, tumble, tumbleweed*
Conford, Ellen. *Why can't I be William?*
Conta, Marcia Maher. *Feelings between friends*
Coontz, Otto. *The quiet house*
Costa, Nicoletta. *A friend comes to play*
Coville, Bruce. *The foolish giant*
Craig, Helen. *The night of the paper bag monsters*
A welcome for Annie
Crowley, Michael. *New kid on Spurwick Ave.*
Cunningham, Julia. *A mouse called Junction*
Cuyler, Margery. *Freckles and Jane*
Freckles and Willie
Dabcovich, Lydia. *Mrs. Huggins and her hen Hannah*
Damjan, Mischa. *Goodbye little bird*
Dauer, Rosamond. *Bullfrog builds a house*
Day, Betsy. *Stefan and Olga*
De Beer, Hans. *Little polar bear*
Little polar bear finds a friend
De Bruyn, Monica. *Lauren's secret ring*
Degen, Bruce. *The little witch and the riddle*
Delacre, Lulu. *Nathan's fishing trip*
Delamare, David. *The Christmas secret*

Delaney, Ned. *Bert and Barney*
Delton, Judy. *Duck goes fishing*
  A pet for Duck and Bear
  Three friends find spring
De Paola, Paula. *Rosie and the yellow ribbon*
De Paola, Tomie (Thomas Anthony). *Andy (that's my name)*
De Regniers, Beatrice Schenk. *How Joe the bear and Sam the mouse got together*
  May I bring a friend?
Dickinson, Mary. *Alex and Roy*
Dowling, Paul. *Meg and Jack's new friends*
Drdek, Richard E. *Horace the friendly octopus*
Dugan, Barbara. *Loop the loop*
Dunrea, Olivier. *Fergus and Bridey*
Duvoisin, Roger Antoine. *The crocodile in the tree*
  Periwinkle
  Petunia
  Petunia and the song
  Petunia, I love you
  Petunia's treasure
  Snowy and Woody
Ehrlich, Amy. *Leo, Zack and Emmie*
  Leo, Zack, and Emmie together again
Ellis, Anne Leo. *Dabble Duck*
Eriksson, Eva. *Hocus-pocus*
  Jealousy
  One short week
  The tooth trip
Ernst, Lisa Campbell. *The rescue of Aunt Pansy*
Escudie, René. *Paul and Sebastian*
Fassler, Joan. *Boy with a problem*
Fatio, Louise. *The happy lion*
  Hector and Christina
Felt, Sue. *Hello-goodbye*
Fern, Eugene. *What's he been up to now?*
Ferns, Ronald. *Osbert and Lucy*
Fink, Dale Borman. *Mr. Silver and Mrs. Gold*
Fleischman, Sid. *The scarebird*
Flory, Jane. *We'll have a friend for lunch*
Frankel, Ben. *Tertius and Pliny*
Fuchshuber, Annegert. *Giant story—Mouse tale*
Gantschev, Ivan. *RumpRump*
Gay, Michel. *Rabbit express*
Giff, Patricia Reilly. *Happy birthday, Ronald Morgan!*
Ginsburg, Mirra. *The fox and the hare*
Goldsmith, Howard. *Little lost dog*
Graham, Al. *Timothy Turtle*
Graham, Bob. *Crusher is coming!*
  Rose meets Mr. Wintergarten
Greenfield, Eloise. *Big friend, little friend*
Gretz, Susanna. *Duck takes off*
  Frog, duck and rabbit
  Frog in the middle
  Rabbit rambles on

Haidle, Elizabeth. *Elmer the grump*
Hale, Irina. *How I found a friend*
Hallinan, P. K. (Patrick K.). *That's what a friend is*
Hanson, Joan. *I don't like Timmy*
Havill, Juanita. *Jamaica Tag-Along*
Heine, Helme. *Friends*
  Mollywoop
  Three little friends: the alarm clock
  Three little friends: the racing cart
  Three little friends: the visitor
Helena, Ann. *The lie*
Henkes, Kevin. *Jessica*
Hest, Amy. *Best-ever good-bye party*
  The go-between
Heuck, Sigrid. *Pony and Bear are friends*
Hickman, Martha Whitmore. *My friend William moved away*
Hill, Eric. *Spot sleeps over*
Himmelman, John. *Ellen and the goldfish*
Hissey, Jane. *Old Bear*
Hoban, Lillian. *Arthur's great big Valentine*
Hoban, Russell. *A bargain for Frances*
  Best friends for Frances
Hoff, Syd. *Who will be my friends?*
Hoffman, Phyllis. *Meatball*
  Steffie and me
Hogrogian, Nonny. *The hermit and Harry and me*
Holabird, Katharine. *Alexander and the dragon*
  Angelina and Alice
Hooks, William H. *Lion and lamb*
Hopkins, Lee Bennett. *Best friends*
Hoppe, Matthias. *Mouse and elephant*
Horvath, Betty F. *Will the real Tommy Wilson please stand up?*
Hughes, Shirley. *Moving Molly*
  Wheels
Hurd, Thacher. *Axle the freeway cat*
Hutchins, Pat. *The doorbell rang*
  My best friend
Hutton, Warwick. *The nose tree*
Inkpen, Mick. *If I had a pig*
  If I had a sheep
Isadora, Rachel. *Friends*
Iwamura, Kazuo. *Ton and Pon: big and little*
  Ton and Pon: two good friends
Iwasaki, Chihiro. *Will you be my friend?*
Jaques, Faith. *Tilly's rescue*
Jaynes, Ruth M. *Friends! friends! friends!*
Jenkin-Pearce, Susie. *Percy Short and Cuthbert*
Jeschke, Susan. *Lucky's choice*
Jewell, Nancy. *Try and catch me*
Joerns, Consuelo. *Oliver's escape*
Johnston, Tony. *Soup bone*
Jones, Rebecca C. *The biggest, meanest, ugliest dog in the whole wide world*
  Matthew and Tilly

Kaldhol, Marit. *Goodbye Rune*
Kamen, Gloria. *The ringdoves*
Kangas, Juli. *Fluffy Bunny's friend*
 Ginger Kitten's surprise
 Hello, Honey Bear
Kantrowitz, Mildred. *I wonder if Herbie's home yet*
Keats, Ezra Jack. *A letter to Amy*
 Peter's chair
Keller, Holly. *Lizzie's invitation*
Keller, John G. *Krispin's fair*
Kellogg, Steven (Stephen). *Best friends*
Kent, Jack. *Socks for supper*
Kimmelman, Leslie. *Me and Nana*
Kimura, Yasuko. *Fergus and the sea monster*
King, Deborah. *Custer: the true story of a horse*
King, Larry L. *Because of Lozo Brown*
Kingman, Lee. *Peter's long walk*
Kishida, Eriko. *The lion and the bird's nest*
Klein, Norma. *Visiting Pamela*
Knaff, Jean Christian. *Manhattan*
Knutson, Barbara. *How the guinea fowl got her spots*
Kočí, Marta. *Blackie and Marie*
Koller, Jackie French. *Fish fry tonight*
 Mole and shrew
Komaiko, Leah. *Annie Bananie*
 Earl's too cool for me
Kopczynski, Anna. *Jerry and Ami*
Koralek, Jenny. *The friendly fox*
Korth-Sander, Irmtraut. *Will you be my friend?*
Kotzwinkle, William. *The day the gang got rich*
 Up the alley with Jack and Joe
Krahn, Fernando. *The great ape*
Krasilovsky, Phyllis. *The shy little girl*
Kraus, Robert. *How spider saved Valentine's Day*
 Ladybug, ladybug!
 The three friends
 The trouble with spider
Krauss, Ruth. *A good man and his good wife*
 I'll be you and you be me
Kreye, Walter. *The giant from the little island*
Kroll, Steven. *Big Jeremy*
 Don't get me in trouble
Kubler, Susanne. *The three friends*
Kyte, Dennis. *Mattie and Cataragus*
Lager, Claude. *A tale of two rats*
Landa, Norbert. *Rabbit and chicken find a box*
 Rabbit and chicken play hide and seek
Lasky, Kathryn. *Fourth of July bear*
Latimer, Jim. *Going the moose way home*
Leedy, Loreen. *Pingo the plaid panda*
Lester, Helen. *The wizard, the fairy and the magic chicken*
Lexau, Joan M. *Cathy is company*

Lillie, Patricia. *Jake and Rosie*
Lindgren, Barbro. *A worm's tale*
Lionni, Leo. *Alexander and the wind-up mouse*
 Fish is fish
 Little blue and little yellow
 Nicholas, where have you been?
Lipkind, William. *The two reds*
Lipniacka, Ewa. *To bed...or else!*
Lobato, Arcadio. *The greatest treasure*
Lobel, Arnold. *Days with Frog and Toad*
 Frog and Toad all year
 Frog and Toad are friends
 Frog and Toad together
Lund, Doris Herold. *You ought to see Herbert's house*
Luttrell, Ida. *Ottie Slockett*
Lyon, George-Ella. *Together*
Lystad, Mary H. *That new boy*
McClure, Gillian. *What's the time, Rory Wolf?*
McCormack, John E. *Rabbit tales*
 Rabbit travels
MacGregor, Ellen. *Mr. Pingle and Mr. Buttonhouse*
McKay, Louise. *Marny's ride with the wind*
MacLachlan, Patricia. *Moon, stars, frogs and friends*
Maestro, Giulio. *Leopard is sick*
Mahy, Margaret. *Making friends*
Majewski, Joe. *A friend for Oscar Mouse*
Mallett, Anne. *Here comes Tagalong*
Malone, Nola Langner. *A home*
Mandry, Kathy. *The cat and the mouse and the mouse and the cat*
Manson, Christopher. *Two travelers*
Marshall, Edward. *Fox all week*
 Three by the sea
Marshall, James. *The Cut-Ups cut loose*
 George and Martha
 George and Martha back in town
 George and Martha encore
 George and Martha one fine day
 George and Martha rise and shine
 George and Martha round and round
 The guest
 Speedboat
 What's the matter with Carruthers?
 Willis
Martin, Jacqueline Briggs. *Bizzy Bones and Moosemouse*
 Bizzy Bones and the lost quilt
Mayer, Mercer. *A boy, a dog, a frog and a friend*
 A boy, a dog and a frog
 Frog, where are you?
Miles, Betty. *Having a friend*
Miles, Lauren. *The rag coat*
Miles, Sally. *Alfi and the dark*
Miller, Edna. *Mousekin finds a friend*

Moonkey
Tharlet, Eve. *Little pig, big trouble*
Thayer, Jane. *Gus was a friendly ghost*
The popcorn dragon, ill. by Jay Hyde
  Barnum
The popcorn dragon, ill. by Lisa McCue
Thompson, Richard. *Effie's bath*
Jenny's Neighbours
Tibo, Gilles. *Simon and the snowflakes*
Tripp, Paul. *The strawman who smiled by
  mistake*
Trivas, Irene. *Annie...Anya: a month in
  Moscow*
Tsutsui, Yoriko. *Anna's secret friend*
Tudor, Bethany. *Samuel's tree house*
Udry, Janice May. *Let's be enemies*
Van Woerkom, Dorothy. *Harry and
  Shelburt*
Varley, Susan. *Badger's parting gifts*
Venable, Alan. *The checker players*
Vigna, Judith. *The hiding house*
Vincent, Gabrielle. *Breakfast time, Ernest
  and Celestine*
Ernest and Celestine's patchwork quilt
Merry Christmas, Ernest and Celestine
Viorst, Judith. *Rosie and Michael*
Waber, Bernard. *Ira says goodbye*
Ira sleeps over
Lovable Lyle
Nobody is perfick
Waddell, Martin. *We love them*
Wade, Anne. *A promise is for keeping*
Waechter, Friedrich Karl. *Three is company*
Walker, Alice. *To hell with dying*
Ward, Helen. *The golden pear*
Warren, Cathy. *Fred's first day*
Weil, Lisl. *Gillie and the flattering fox*
Weiss, Ellen. *Mokey's birthday present*
Weiss, Nicki. *Battle day at Camp Delmont*
A family story
Maude and Sally
Wiesner, William. *Tops*
Wild, Margaret. *Mr. Nick's knitting*
The very best of friends
Wildsmith, Brian. *The lazy bear*
Wilhelm, Hans. *Let's be friends again!*
A new home, a new friend
Williams, Barbara. *Kevin's grandma*
Williams, Karen Lynn. *When Africa was
  home*
Winthrop, Elizabeth. *The Best Friends Club*
Katharine's doll
Lizzie and Harold
Sloppy kisses
Wittman, Sally. *The boy who hated Valentine's
  Day*
Pelly and Peak
Plenty of Pelly and Peak
A special trade
The wonderful Mrs. Trumbly

Wolcott, Patty. *Double-decker, double-decker,
  double-decker bus*
Wolde, Gunilla. *Betsy and Peter are different*
Wolkstein, Diane. *Little Mouse's painting*
Yashima, Tarō. *The youngest one*
Yeoman, John. *Mouse trouble*
Zalben, Jane Breskin. *Beni's first Chanukah*
Oliver and Alison's week
Zelinsky, Paul O. *The lion and the stoat*
Ziefert, Harriet. *Mike and Tony: best friends*
Nicky's friends
Zion, Gene. *The meanest squirrel I ever met*
Zolotow, Charlotte (Shapiro). *The hating
  book*
Hold my hand
Janey
My friend John
The new friend
Three funny friends
Timothy too!
The unfriendly book
The white marble

Frogs and toads

Æsop. *The hare and the frogs*, ill. by
  William Stobbs
Alexander, Martha G. *No ducks in our
  bathtub*
Anderson, Peggy Perry. *Time for bed, the
  babysitter said*
Back, Christine. *Tadpole and frog*
Berenzy, Alix. *A frog prince*
Berson, Harold. *Charles and Claudine*
Bos, Burny. *Prince Valentino*
Brown, Marc Tolon. *Can you jump like a
  frog?*
Buller, Jon. *Toad on the road*
Campbell, Wayne. *What a catastrophe!*
Canfield, Jane White. *The frog prince*
Charles, R. H. (Robert Henry). *The
  roundabout turn*
Chenery, Janet. *The toad hunt*
Coldrey, Jennifer. *The world of frogs*
Cole, Joanna. *Don't call me names!*
Cortesi, Wendy W. *Explore a spooky swamp*
Dauer, Rosamond. *Bullfrog builds a house*
Bullfrog grows up
Dinardo, Jeffrey. *Timothy and the night
  noises*
Duke, Kate. *Seven froggies went to school*
Duvoisin, Roger Antoine. *Periwinkle*
Erickson, Russell E. *Warton and the traders*
Warton's Christmas eve adventure
Feldman, Barbara. *Stephens' frog*
Flack, Marjorie. *Tim Tadpole and the great
  bullfrog*
Freschet, Berniece. *The old bullfrog*
A frog he would a-wooing go (folk-song).
  Frog went a-courtin', ill. by Feodor
  Rojankovsky

Froggie went a-courting, ill. by Chris Conover
Wendy Watson's frog went a-courting
Gackenbach, Dick. *Crackle, Gluck and the sleeping toad*
Gordon, Margaret. *Frogs' holiday*
Graham, Amanda. *Picasso, the green tree frog*
Gretz, Susanna. *Frog in the middle*
Greydanus, Rose. *Freddie the frog*
Grimm, Jacob. *The frog prince*, ill. by Binette Schroeder
The princess and the frog, retold and ill. by Rachel Isadora
Gwynne, Fred. *Pondlarker*
Harrison, David Lee. *The case of Og, the missing frog*
Hawes, Judy. *Spring peepers*
Why frogs are wet
Hellard, Susan. *Froggie goes a-courting*
Himmelman, John. *Amanda and the witch switch*
Hoban, Russell. *Jim Frog*
Hogan, Paula Z. *The frog*
Isele, Elizabeth. *The frog princess*
Kalan, Robert. *Jump, frog, jump!*
Karlin, Nurit. *The blue frog*
Keith, Eros. *Rrra-ah*
Kellogg, Steven (Stephen). *The mysterious tadpole*
Kent, Jack. *The caterpillar and the polliwog*
Kepes, Juliet. *Frogs, merry*
Kraus, Robert. *Mert the blurt*
Kumin, Maxine. *Eggs of things*
Lane, Margaret. *The frog*
Lee, Jeanne M. *Toad is the uncle of heaven*
Leonard, Marcia. *Rainboots for breakfast*
Lionni, Leo. *Fish is fish*
It's mine!
Lobel, Arnold. *Days with Frog and Toad*
Frog and Toad all year
Frog and Toad are friends
The frog and toad pop-up book
Frog and Toad together
Lucas, Barbara. *Sleeping over*
MacLachlan, Patricia. *Moon, stars, frogs and friends*
McLenighan, Valjean. *You are what you are*
McPhail, David. *Captain Toad and the motorbike*
Maris, Ron. *Better move on, frog!*
Massie, Diane Redfield. *Walter was a frog*
Mayer, Mercer. *A boy, a dog, a frog and a friend*
A boy, a dog and a frog
Frog goes to dinner
Frog on his own
Frog, where are you?
One frog too many
Michels, Tilde. *At the frog pond*
Miles, Miska. *Jump frog jump*

Newton, Patricia Montgomery. *The frog who drank the waters of the world*
Noll, Sally. *Off and counting*
Nunes, Susan. *Tiddalick the frog*
Parker, Nancy Winslow. *Working frog*
Partridge, Jenny. *Hopfellow*
Pavey, Peter. *I'm Taggarty Toad*
Pendery, Rosemary. *A home for Hopper*
Potter, Beatrix. *The tale of Mr. Jeremy Fisher*, ill. by David Jorgensen
The tale of Mr. Jeremy Fisher, ill. by author
Priceman, Marjorie. *Friend or frog*
Pursell, Margaret Sanford. *Sprig the tree frog*
Rockwell, Anne F. *Big boss Toad*
Samuels, Barbara. *What's so great about Cindy Snappleby?*
Saul, Carol P. *Peter's song*
Schertle, Alice. *Little Frog's song*
Schumacher, Claire. *Brave Lily*
Scieszka, Jon. *The frog prince, continued*
Seeger, Pete. *The foolish frog*
Seuss, Dr. *Would you rather be a bullfrog?*
Small, David. *Eulalie and the hopping head*
Smith, Jim. *The frog band and Durrington Dormouse*
The frog band and the onion seller
The frog band and the owlnapper
Snape, Juliet. *Frog odyssey*
Solotareff, Grégoire. *The ogre and the frog king*
Steig, William. *Gorky rises*
Steptoe, John. *The story of jumping mouse*
Stevenson, James. *Monty*
Stratemeyer, Clara Georgeanna. *Frog fun*
Tuggy
Taylor, Kim. *Frog*
Thayer, Mike. *In the middle of the puddle*
Tresselt, Alvin R. *Frog in the well*
Troughton, Joanna. *What made Tiddalik laugh*
Turska, Krystyna. *The woodcutter's duck*
Van Woerkom, Dorothy. *Sea frog, city frog*
Velthuijs, Max. *Frog and the birdsong*
Frog in love
Little Man to the rescue
Vesey, A. *The princess and the frog*
Wahl, Jan. *Doctor Rabbit's foundling*
Walt Disney Productions. *Walt Disney's The adventures of Mr. Toad*
Weisner, David. *Tuesday*
Weiss, Monica. *Mmmm...cookies!*
West, Colin. *"Pardon?" said the giraffe*
Wynne-Jones, Tim. *The hour of the frog*
Yeoman, John. *The bear's water picnic*
Zakhoder, Boris Vladimirovich. *Rosachok*

Furniture

Devlin, Wende. *Aunt Agatha, there's a lion under the couch!*

Hutchins, H. J. (Hazel J.). *Leanna builds a genie trap*

Furniture — beds

Allen, Linda. *Mrs. Simkin's bed*
Arnold, Tedd. *No jumping on the bed!*
Buckingham, Simon. *Alec and his flying bed*
Chislett, Gail. *Whump*
Deedy, Carmen Agra. *Agatha's feather bed*
Dickinson, Mary. *Alex's bed*
Dillon, Barbara. *The beast in the bed*
Freedman, Sally. *Devin's new bed*
Greenberg, Dan. *The bed who ran away from home*
Hamm, Diane Johnston. *Grandma drives a motor bed*
Hawkins, Mark. *A lion under her bed*
Howe, James. *There's a monster under my bed*
Howell, Lynn. *Winifred's new bed*
Klein, Suzanne. *An elephant in my bed*
Parker, Nancy Winslow. *The crocodile under Louis Finneberg's bed*
Rosen, Michael J. *Under the bed*
Schubert, Ingrid. *There's a crocodile under my bed!*
Stevenson, James. *What's under my bed?*
Thaler, Mike. *There's a hippopotamus under my bed*
Willis, Jeanne. *The monster bed*
Winthrop, Elizabeth. *Bunk beds*

Furniture — chairs

Bible, Charles. *Jennifer's new chair*
Graham, Thomas. *Mr. Bear's chair*
Hale, Irina. *Brown bear in a brown chair*
Keats, Ezra Jack. *Peter's chair*
Kessler, Ethel. *Do baby bears sit in chairs?*
Lanton, Sandy. *Daddy's chair*
Nordqvist, Sven. *Porker finds a chair*
Root, Phyllis. *The old red rocking chair*
Schweitzer, Iris. *Hilda's restful chair*
Scott, Ann Herbert. *Grandmother's chair*
Smith, Maggie (Margaret C.). *My grandma's chair*
Tennyson, Noel. *The lady's chair and the ottoman*
Williams, Vera B. *A chair for my mother*
Zander, Hans. *My blue chair*

Furniture — couches, sofas

Seligson, Susan. *The amazing Amos and the greatest couch on earth*
Amos ahoy: a couch adventure on land and sea
Amos camps out: a couch adventure in the woods
Amos: the story of an old dog and his couch

Furniture — dressers

Montenegro, Laura Nyman. *One stuck drawer*

Furniture — tables

Grimm, Jacob. *The table, the donkey and the stick*, ill. by Paul Galdone
The wishing table, ill. by Eve Tharlet
Heller, Linda. *Lily at the table*

Games

Agostinelli, Maria Enrica. *I know something you don't know*
Ahlberg, Janet. *Each peach pear plum*
Peek-a-boo!
Alexander, Martha G. *We never get to do anything*
Allen, Jeffrey. *The secret life of Mr. Weird*
Allington, Richard L. *Letters*
Anderson, Douglas. *Let's draw a story*
Anglund, Joan Walsh. *The brave cowboy*
Cowboy's secret life
Anno, Mitsumasa. *Anno's animals*
Anno's Britain
Anno's counting house
Anno's flea market
Anno's Italy
Anno's journey
Anno's magical ABC
Anno's U.S.A.
Topsy turvies: more pictures to stretch the imagination
Topsy turvies: pictures to stretch the imagination
Upside-downers
Appelbaum, Neil. *Is there a hole in your head?*
Aruego, José. *Look what I can do*
We hide, you seek
Asch, Frank. *Goodnight horsey*
Baillie, Allan. *Drac and the gremlin*
Baker, Keith. *Hide and snake*
Ball, Duncan. *Jeremy's tail*
Battles, Edith. *One to teeter-totter*
Bauman, A. F. *Guess where you're going, guess what you'll do*
Baylor, Byrd. *Guess who my favorite person is*

Beach, Stewart. *Good morning, sun's up!*
Behrens, June. *Can you walk the plank?*
The big Peter Rabbit book
Blacker, Terence. *Herbie Hamster, where are you?*
Blanchard, Arlene. *The naughty lamb*
Bonsall, Crosby Newell. *The day I had to play with my sister*
Booth, Eugene. *At the circus*
  At the fair
  In the air
  In the garden
  In the jungle
  Under the ocean
Brinckloe, Julie. *Playing marbles*
Brown, Marc Tolon. *Finger rhymes*
  Hand rhymes
  One, two buckle my shoe
  Play rhymes
  What do you call a dumb bunny? and other rabbit riddles, games, jokes and cartoons
Brown, Margaret Wise. *The indoor noisy book*
Byars, Betsy Cromer. *Go and hush the baby*
Carroll, Ruth. *Where's the bunny?*
Cauley, Lorinda Bryan. *Clap your hands*
Charlip, Remy. *Arm in arm*
  Where is everybody?
Civardi, Anne. *Things people do*
Clark, Harry. *The first story of the whale*
Cohen, Peter Zachary. *Authorized autumn charts of the Upper Red Canoe River country*
Craig, M. Jean. *Boxes*
Dale, Penny. *You can't*
Delacre, Lulu. *Arroz con leche*
Delaney, Ned. *One dragon to another*
Delton, Judy. *I never win!*
Demi. *Demi's opposites*
De Paola, Tomie (Thomas Anthony). *Andy (that's my name)*
  Things to make and do for Valentine's Day
De Regniers, Beatrice Schenk. *What can you do with a shoe?*
Dubanevich, Arlene. *Pigs in hiding*
Duffy, Dee Dee (Deborah). *Barnyard tracks*
Dunbar, Fiona. *You'll never guess!*
Elting, Mary. *Q is for duck*
Emberley, Ed (Edward Randolph). *Ed Emberley's crazy mixed-up face game*
  Klippity klop
Fallwell, Cathryn. *Where's Nicky?*
The farmer in the dell. The farmer in the dell, ill. by Kathy Parkinson
  The farmer in the dell, ill. by Mary Maki Rae
  The farmer in the dell, ill. by Diane Stanley
Finzel, Julia. *Large as life*
Fisher, Leonard Everett. *Look around!*

Fleisher, Robbin. *Quilts in the attic*
Fox, Dorothea Warren. *Follow me the leader*
French, Fiona. *Hunt the thimble*
Gardner, Beau. *Guess what?*
  What is it?
Gillham, Bill. *Can you see it?*
  What can you do?
  What's the difference?
  Where does it go?
Go tell Aunt Rhody. *Go tell Aunt Rhody*, ill. by Aliki
  Go tell Aunt Rhody, ill. by Robert M. Quackenbush
Gomi, Taro. *Guess who?*
  Who ate it?
  Who hid it?
Gretz, Susanna. *Hide-and-seek*
  I'm not sleepy
Grindley, Sally. *Knock, knock! Who's there?*
Hahn, Hannelore. *Take a giant step*
Handford, Martin. *Find Waldo now*
  The great Waldo search
  Where's Waldo?
Hann, Jacquie. *Follow the leader*
Hawkins, Colin. *Incy wincy spider*
  Round the garden
  This little pig
Hayes, Sarah. *Clap your hands*
Haynes, Max. *Sparky's rainbow repair*
Heinst, Marie. *My first number book*
Henrietta. *A mouse in the house*
Hillert, Margaret. *Play ball*
Hissey, Jane. *Little Bear lost*
Hoban, Russell. *How Tom beat Captain Najork and his hired sportsmen*
Hoff, Syd. *The littlest leaguer*
Hoguet, Susan Ramsay. *I unpacked my grandmother's trunk*
Holmes, Stephen. *Hidden numbers*
Hurd, Edith Thacher. *Last one home is a green pig*
Hutchins, Pat. *What game shall we play?*
  Which witch is which?
Johnson, Elizabeth. *All in free but Janey*
Jonas, Ann. *The trek*
Kahn, Joan. *Seesaw*
Keeshan, Robert. *She loves me, she loves me not*
Khalsa, Dayal Kaur. *Tales of a gambling grandma*
Knight, Joan. *Tickle-toe rhymes*
Koch, Dorothy Clarke. *I play at the beach*
Krauss, Ruth. *The bundle book*
  Mama, I wish I was snow. Child, you'd be very cold
Kroll, Steven. *The tyrannosaurus game*
Kunhardt, Edith. *Where's Peter?*
Landa, Norbert. *Rabbit and chicken play hide and seek*
Leslie, Amanda. *Hidden toys*

Let's count and count out, ill. by Deborah Derr McClintock
Lexau, Joan M. *Every day a dragon*
I hate red rover
Lipkind, William. *Sleepyhead*
Livermore, Elaine. *Find the cat*
Lost and found
One to ten, count again
Three little kittens lost their mittens
Lopshire, Robert. *How to make snop snappers and other fine things*
McDonald, Amy. *Let's do it*
Machotka, Hana. *Breathtaking noses*
What neat feet!
McToots, Rudi. *The kid's book of games for cars, trains and planes*
Maestro, Giulio. *The tortoise's tug of war*
Major, Beverly. *Playing sardines*
Marshall, Janet Perry. *My camera: at the zoo*
Merrill, Jean. *How many kids are hiding on my block?*
Meryl, Debra. *Baby's peek-a-boo album*
Miles, Miska. *Rolling the cheese*
Miller, Margaret. *Whose shoe?*
Milne, A. A. (Alan Alexander). *Pooh's quiz book*
Mitchell, Cynthia. *Halloweena Hecatee*
Montgomerie, Norah. *This little pig went to market*
Morris, Neil. *Find the canary*
Hide and seek
Search for Sam
Where's my hat?
Most, Bernard. *There's an ape behind the drape*
Mother Goose. *London Bridge is falling down*, ill. by Ed Emberley
London Bridge is falling down, ill. by Peter Spier
Mother Goose in hieroglyphics, ill. by George S. Appleton
This little pig went to market, ill. by Ferelith Eccles Williams
The three little kittens, ill. by Lorinda Bryan Cauley
The three little kittens, ill. by Shelley Thornton
Munari, Bruno. *The birthday present*
Myers, Amy. *I know a monster*
Nelson, Esther L. *Holiday singing and dancing games*
Nims, Bonnie Larkin. *Where is the bear at school?*
Oppenheim, Joanne. *The eency weency spider*
Oram, Hiawyn. *Skittlewonder and the wizard*
Oxenbury, Helen. *All fall down*
The queen and Rosie Randall
Packard, Mary. *Where is Jake?*
Patterson, Pat. *Hickory dickory duck*
Peppé, Rodney. *Little games*

Odd one out
Rodney Peppé's puzzle book
Pragoff, Fiona. *Odd one out*
The pudgy pat-a-cake book, ill. by Teri Super
The pudgy peek-a-boo book, ill. by Amye Rosenberg
Ra, Carol F. *Trot, trot to Boston*
Raebeck, Lois. *Who am I?*
Ripley, Catherine. *Two dozen dinosaurs*
Rockwell, Norman. *Norman Rockwell's counting book*
Rosales, Melodye. *Double Dutch and the voodoo shoes*
Rosen, Michael J. *We're going on a bear hunt*
Russo, Marisabina. *The line up book*
Where is Ben?
Sandberg, Inger. *Little Anna saved*
Scruton, Clive. *Mary's pets*
Selsam, Millicent E. *Is this a baby dinosaur?*
Sharratt, Nick. *I look like this*
Shaw, Charles Green. *The blue guess book*
The guess book
It looked like spilt milk
Siewert, Margaret. *Bear hunt*
Sivulich, Sandra Stroner. *I'm going on a bear hunt*
Steig, William. *The bad speller*
Steiner, Charlotte. *Five little finger playmates*
Red Ridinghood's little lamb
Stine, Jovial Bob. *Pork and beans: play date*
Taylor, Mark. *Old Blue, you good dog you*
Thwaite, Ann. *The day with the Duke*
Tison, Annette. *Animal hide-and-seek*
Ueno, Noriko. *Elephant buttons*
Ungerer, Tomi. *One, two, where's my shoe?*
Snail, where are you?
Van Allsburg, Chris. *Jumanji*
Venable, Alan. *The checker players*
Weil, Lisl. *Owl and other scrambles*
Wells, Tony. *Allsorts*
Puzzle doubles
Westcott, Nadine Bernard. *The lady with the alligator purse*
Wildsmith, Brian. *Animal games*
Brian Wildsmith's puzzles
Williams, Jenny. *Ring around a rosy*
Wisniewski, David. *Rain player*
Withers, Carl. *The tale of a black cat*
The wild ducks and the goose
Wittington, Mary K. *Troll games*
Wood, A. J. *Look! The ultimate spot-the-difference book*
Wood, David. *Piggies*
Yektai, Niki. *What's missing?*
Yolen, Jane. *The lap-time song and play book*
Street rhymes around the world
Yudell, Lynn Deena. *Make a face*
Zacharias, Thomas. *But where is the green parrot?*

Ziefert, Harriet. *Bear all year*
  Bear gets dressed
  Bear goes shopping
  Bear's busy morning
Zion, Gene. *Hide and seek day*
  Jeffie's party

Gangs see Clubs, gangs

Garage sales

Rockwell, Anne F. *Our garage sale*

Garbage collectors see Careers – garbage
  collectors

Gardening see Gardens, gardening

Gardens, gardening

Aliki. *Corn is maize*
  The story of Johnny Appleseed
Balian, Lorna. *A garden for a groundhog*
Barker, Cicely Mary. *Flower fairies of the
  garden*
Barrett, Judi. *Old MacDonald had an
  apartment house*
Berson, Harold. *Pop! goes the turnip*
Bishop, Gavin. *Mrs. McGinty and the bizarre
  plant*
Bond, Michael. *Paddington's garden*
Boon, Emilie. *Peterkin's very own garden*
Boyle, Constance. *Little Owl and the weed*
Brown, Marc Tolon. *Your first garden book*
Browne, Caroline. *Mrs. Christie's farmhouse*
Buchanan, Heather S. *Emily Mouse's garden*
Carlstrom, Nancy White. *Moose in the
  garden*
Caseley, Judith. *Grandpa's garden lunch*
Cavagnaro, David. *The pumpkin people*
Collier, Ethel. *Who goes there in my garden?*
Craft, Ruth. *Carrie Hepple's garden*
Cristini, Ermanno. *In my garden*
Davidson, Amanda. *Teddy in the garden*
De Paola, Tomie (Thomas Anthony). *Four
  stories for four seasons*
  Too many Hopkins
Domanska, Janina. *The best of the bargain*
Donnelly, Liza. *Dinosaur garden*
Douglas, Richard Keens. *The nutmeg
  princess*
Ehlert, Lois. *Growing vegetable soup*
  Planting a rainbow
Ernst, Lisa Campbell. *Hamilton's art show*
  Miss Penny and Mr. Grubbs
Farjeon, Eleanor. *Mr. Garden*
Fatio, Louise. *Marc and Pixie and the walls
  in Mrs. Jones's garden*
Fife, Dale. *Rosa's special garden*
Firmin, Peter. *Chicken stew*
Fisher, Aileen Lucia. *Mysteries in the garden*
Florian, Douglas. *Vegetable garden*

Fontaine, Jan. *The spaghetti tree*
Fujikawa, Gyo. *Let's grow a garden*
Gage, Wilson. *Anna's garden songs*
  Mrs. Gaddy and the fast-growing vine
Gans, Roma. *Hummingbirds in the garden*
Goldin, Augusta. *Where does your garden
  grow?*
Griffith, Helen V. *Georgia music*
Hader, Berta Hoerner. *Mister Billy's gun*
Hall, Fergus. *Groundsel*
Hawkins, Colin. *Round the garden*
Hill, Eric. *Spot in the garden*
Himmelman, John. *Amanda and the magic
  garden*
Hurd, Thacher. *The pea patch jig*
Huriet, Genevieve. *Dandelion's vanishing
  vegetable garden*
Ichikawa, Satomi. *Suzanne and Nicholas in
  the garden*, Watts 1976
  Suzanne and Nicholas in the garden,
    St. Martin's 1978
Ipcar, Dahlov. *The land of flowers*
Jenkin-Pearce, Susie. *The enchanted garden*
Jordan, Helene J. (Helene Jamieson). *How
  a seed grows*
Keeping, Charles. *Joseph's yard*
Kemp, Anthea. *Mr. Percy's magic greenhouse*
Kilroy, Sally. *Grandpa's garden*
King, Elizabeth. *Pumpkin patch*
Krauss, Ruth. *The carrot seed*
Krementz, Jill. *A very young gardener*
Krings, Antoon. *Oliver's strawberry patch*
Leonard, Marcia. *Gregory and Mr. Grump*
Le Tord, Bijou. *Rabbit seeds*
Lobel, Arnold. *The rose in my garden*
Lord, John Vernon. *Mr. Mead and his
  garden*
Lynn, Sara. *Garden animals*
Maguire, Gregory. *Lucas Fishbone*
Mahy, Margaret. *The pumpkin man and the
  crafty creeper*
Marino, Dorothy. *Buzzy Bear in the garden*
Maris, Ron. *In my garden*
Miles, Miska. *Rabbit garden*
Moore, Inga. *The vegetable thieves*
Morgenstern, Elizabeth. *The little gardeners*
Muller, Gerda. *The garden in the city*
Muntean, Michaela. *Alligator's garden*
Musicant, Elke. *The night vegetable eater*
Nordqvist, Sven. *Festus and Mercury: ruckus
  in the garden*
O'Callahan, Jay. *Tulips*
Oechsli, Helen. *In my garden*
Oxenbury, Helen. *Tom and Pippo in the
  garden*
Palmisciano, Diane. *Garden partners*
Pike, Norman. *The peach tree*
Ray, Mary Lyn. *Pumpkins*
Rockwell, Anne F. *How my garden grew*
Rockwell, Harlow. *The compost heap*
Russo, Marisabina. *Waiting for Hannah*
Ryder, Joanne. *Dancers in the garden*

Rylant, Cynthia. *This year's garden*
Sharpe, Sara. *Gardener George goes to town*
Shecter, Ben. *Partouche plants a seed*
Slote, Elizabeth. *Nelly's garden*
Sobol, Harriet Langsam. *A book of vegetables*
Stevenson, James. *Grandpa's too-good garden*
Taylor, Judy. *Sophie and Jack help out*
Titherington, Jeanne. *Pumpkin pumpkin*
Trimby, Elisa. *Mr. Plum's paradise*
Wabbes, Marie. *Little Rabbit's garden*
Watts, Barrie. *Tomato*
Watts, Bernadette. *Tattercoats*
Westcott, Nadine Bernard. *The giant vegetable garden*
Wilner, Isabel. *A garden alphabet*
Wolf, Janet. *The rosy fat magenta radish*
Zagwyn, Deborah Turney. *Pumpkin blanket*

Geese *see* Birds – geese

Generosity *see* Character traits – generosity

Geologists *see* Careers – geologists

Gerbils *see* Animals – gerbils

Germany *see* Foreign lands – Germany

Ghana *see* Foreign lands – Ghana

Ghosts

Ahlberg, Janet. *Funnybones*
Alexander, Sue. *More Witch, Goblin, and Ghost stories*
  Witch, Goblin and Ghost are back
  Witch, Goblin, and Ghost in the haunted woods
  Witch, Goblin and sometimes Ghost
Allard, Harry. *Bumps in the night*
Bennett, Jill. *Teeny tiny*
Berenstain, Stan. *The Berenstain bears and the ghost of the forest*
Bergström, Gunilla. *Who's scaring Alfie Atkins?*
Birchman, David F. *Brother Billy Bronto's bygone blues band*
Bright, Robert. *Georgie*
  Georgie and the baby birds
  Georgie and the ball of yarn
  Georgie and the buried treasure
  Georgie and the little dog
  Georgie and the magician
  Georgie and the noisy ghost
  Georgie and the robbers
  Georgie and the runaway balloon
  Georgie goes west
  Georgie to the rescue
  Georgie's Christmas carol
  Georgie's Halloween

Brown, Marc Tolon. *Spooky riddles*
Brunhoff, Laurent de. *Babar and the ghost*
  Babar and the ghost [Easy-to-read ed.]
Bunting, Eve (Anne Evelyn). *In the haunted house*
Charlton, Elizabeth. *Jeremy and the ghost*
Cohen, Caron Lee. *Bronco dogs*
  Renata, Whizbrain and the ghost
Cuyler, Margery. *Sir William and the pumpkin monster*
DeLage, Ida. *The old witch and the ghost parade*
Du Bois, William Pène. *Elisabeth the cow ghost*
Flora, James. *Grandpa's ghost stories*
Friedrich, Priscilla. *The marshmallow ghosts*
Gage, Wilson. *Mrs. Gaddy and the ghost*
Galdone, Joanna. *The tailypo*
Galdone, Paul. *King of the cats*
  The monster and the tailor
  The teeny-tiny woman
Gikow, Louise. *Boober Fraggle's ghosts*
Hancock, Sibyl. *Esteban and the ghost*
Haseley, Dennis. *Ghost catcher*
Hayes, Geoffrey. *The mystery of the pirate ghost*
Herman, Emily. *Hubknuckles*
Hirsh, Marilyn. *Deborah the dybbuk*
Johnston, Tony. *Four scary stories*
Khdir, Kate. *Little ghost*
Kroll, Steven. *Amanda and the giggling ghost*
  Branigan's cat and the Halloween ghost
Kunnas, Mauri. *One spooky night and other scary stories*
Lexau, Joan M. *Millicent's ghost*
Lindgren, Astrid. *The ghost of Skinny Jack*
McMillan, Bruce. *Ghost doll*
Mooser, Stephen. *The ghost with the Halloween hiccups*
Nishikawa, Osamu. *Alexander and the blue ghost*
Nixon, Joan Lowery. *The Thanksgiving mystery*
O'Connor, Jane. *The teeny tiny woman*
Olson, Helen Kronberg. *The strange thing that happened to Oliver Wendell Iscovitch*
Raskin, Ellen. *Ghost in a four-room apartment*
Rockwell, Anne F. *A bear, a bobcat and three ghosts*
Rodgers, Frank. *Who's afraid of the ghost train?*
Rubel, Nicole. *The ghost family meets its match*
Sandberg, Inger. *Little ghost Godfry*
San Souci, Robert D. *The boy and the ghost*
Seuling, Barbara. *The teeny tiny woman*
Sharmat, Marjorie Weinman. *Two ghosts on a bench*
Sherrow, Victoria. *There goes the ghost*

Thayer, Jane. *Gus and the baby ghost*
Gus loved his happy home
Gus was a friendly ghost
Gus was a gorgeous ghost
Gus was a real dumb ghost
What's a ghost going to do?
Wallace, Daisy. *Ghost poems*
Wolkstein, Diane. *The legend of Sleepy Hollow*
Zemach, Margot. *The little tiny woman*
Ziefert, Harriet. *Who can boo the loudest?*

Giants

Allen, Linda. *The giant who had no heart*
Auer, Martin. *Now, now Markus*
Balian, Lorna. *A sweetheart for Valentine*
Benjamin, Alan. *Ribtickle Town*
Biro, Val. *Miranda's umbrella*
Bodwell, Gaile. *The long day of the giants*
Bolliger, Max. *The giants' feast*
The magic bird
Bradfield, Roger (Jolly Roger). *Giants come in different sizes*
Briggs, Raymond. *Jim and the beanstalk*
Carle, Eric. *Watch out! A giant!*
Cole, Brock. *The giant's toe*
Coville, Bruce. *The foolish giant*
Cunliffe, John. *Sara's giant and the upside down house*
Cushman, Doug. *Giants*
De La Mare, Walter (Walter John). *Molly Whuppie*
De Paola, Tomie (Thomas Anthony). *Fin M'Coul*
The mysterious giant of Barletta
De Regniers, Beatrice Schenk. *The giant story*
Du Bois, William Pène. *Giant Otto*
Otto and the magic potatoes
Otto at sea
Otto in Africa
Otto in Texas
Elkin, Benjamin. *Lucky and the giant*
Foreman, Michael. *The two giants*
Fritz, Jean. *The good giants and the bad Pukwudgies*
Fuchshuber, Annegert. *Giant story—Mouse tale*
Greene, Ellin. *The pumpkin giant*
Grimm, Jacob. *The brave little tailor*, ill. by Mark Corcoran
The brave little tailor, ill. by Svend Otto S.
The brave little tailor, ill. by Daniel San Souci
The brave little tailor, ill. by Eve Tharlet
The brave little tailor, ill. by James Warhola
The glass mountain, ill. by Nonny Hogrogian

The valiant little tailor, ill. by Victor G. Ambrus
Grindley, Sally. *Shhh!*
Haley, Gail E. *Jack and the bean tree*
Hayes, Sarah. *Mary Mary*
Herrmann, Frank. *The giant Alexander*
The giant Alexander and the circus
Hillert, Margaret. *The magic beans*
Homme, Bob. *The friendly giant's birthday*
The friendly giant's book of fire engines
Jack and the beanstalk. *The history of Mother Twaddle and the marvelous achievements of her son Jack*, ill. by Paul Galdone
Jack and the beanstalk, ill. by Val Biro
Jack and the beanstalk, ill. by Lorinda Bryan Cauley
Jack and the beanstalk, ill. by Ed Parker
Jack and the beanstalk, ill. by Tony Ross
Jack and the beanstalk, ill. by William Stobbs
Jack and the beanstalk, ill. by James Warhola
Jack and the beanstalk, ill. by Anne Wilsdorf
Jack the giant killer, ill. by Anne Wilsdorf
Jack the giantkiller, ill. by Tony Ross
Jennings, Michael. *Robin Goodfellow and the giant dwarf*
Johnson, Odette. *One prickly porcupine*
Kahl, Virginia. *Giants, indeed!*
Kraus, Robert. *The little giant*
Kreye, Walter. *The giant from the little island*
Kroll, Steven. *Big Jeremy*
Lawrence, John. *The giant of Grabbist*
Little, Emily. *David and the giant*
Lobel, Anita. *The dwarf giant*
Lobel, Arnold. *Giant John*
Löfgren, Ulf. *The boy who ate more than the giant and other Swedish folktales*
McNeill, Janet. *The giant's birthday*
Minarik, Else Holmelund. *The little giant girl and the elf boys*
Munsch, Robert N. *David's father*
Nash, Ogden. *The adventures of Isabel*, ill. by Walter Lorraine
The adventures of Isabel, ill. by James Marshall
O Huigin, Sean. *King of the birds*
Polushkin, Maria. *The little hen and the giant*
Porter, Sue. *Little Wolf and the giant*
Roddie, Shen. *Animal stew*
Root, Phyllis. *Soup for supper*
Selway, Martina. *Greedyguts*
Sherman, Ivan. *I am a giant*
Still, James. *Jack and the wonder beans*
Tompert, Ann. *Charlotte and Charles*
Ungerer, Tomi. *Zeralda's ogre*
Van Haeringen, Annemarie. *The cats' tale*

Wallace, Daisy. *Giant poems*
Ward, Nick. *Giant*
Wiesner, William. *Tops*
Yolen, Jane. *The giant's farm*
  The giants go camping

Gilbert Islands *see* Foreign lands – South Sea Islands

Giraffes *see* Animals – giraffes

Glasses

Brown, Marc Tolon. *Arthur's eyes*
Cousins, Lucy. *What can rabbit see?*
Giff, Patricia Reilly. *Watch out, Ronald Morgan!*
Goodsell, Jane. *Katie's magic glasses*
Keller, Holly. *Cromwell's glasses*
Kessler, Leonard P. *Mr. Pine's mixed-up signs*
Lasson, Robert. *Orange Oliver*
MacDonald, Maryann. *Little Hippo gets glasses*
Motomora, Mitchell. *Specs*
Raskin, Ellen. *Spectacles*
Smith, Donald. *Who's wearing my sunglasses?*
Smith, Lane. *Glasses...who needs 'em?*
Thayer, Jane. *Mr. Turtle's magic glasses*
Tusa, Tricia. *Libby's new glasses*

Gloves *see* Clothing – gloves

Gnats *see* Insects – gnats

Gnomes *see* Elves and little people

Goats *see* Animals – goats

Goblins

Alexander, Sue. *More Witch, Goblin, and Ghost stories*
  Witch, Goblin and Ghost are back
  Witch, Goblin, and Ghost in the haunted woods
  Witch, Goblin and sometimes Ghost
Bang, Molly. *The goblins giggle and other stories*
Bunting, Eve (Anne Evelyn). *Scary, scary Halloween*
Calhoun, Mary. *The goblin under the stairs*
Haley, Gail E. *Go away, stay away*
Impey, Rose. *The flat man*
  Scare yourself to sleep
Johnston, Tony. *Four scary stories*
Kimmel, Eric A. *Hershel and the Hanukkah goblins*
Lifton, Betty Jean. *Joji and the Amanojaku*
Schertle, Alice. *Bill and the google-eyed goblins*

Sendak, Maurice. *Outside over there*
Tobias, Tobi. *Chasing the goblins away*

Gorillas *see* Animals – gorillas

Gossip *see* Behavior – gossip

Grammar *see* Language

Grandfathers *see* Family life – grandfathers; family life – grandparents

Grandmothers *see* Family life – grandmothers; family life – grandparents

Grandparents *see* Family life – grandfathers; Family life – grandmothers; Family life – grandparents

Grasshoppers *see* Insects – grasshoppers

Great-grandparents *see* Family life – great-grandparents

Greece *see* Foreign lands – Greece

Greed *see* Behavior – greed

Greenland *see* Foreign lands – Greenland

Griffins *see* Mythical creatures

Grocery stores *see* Shopping; Stores

Groundhog Day *see* Holidays – Groundhog Day

Groundhogs *see* Animals – groundhogs

Growing up *see* Behavior – growing up

Guatemala *see* Foreign lands – Guatemala

Guinea fowl *see* Birds – guinea fowl

Guinea pigs *see* Animals – guinea pigs

Guns *see* Weapons

Guy Fawkes Day *see* Holidays – Guy Fawkes Day

Guyana *see* Foreign lands – Guyana

Gymnastics *see* Sports – gymnastics

Gypsies

Anderson, C. W. (Clarence Williams). *Blaze and the gypsies*

Bemelmans, Ludwig. *Madeline and the gypsies*

García Lorca, Federico. *The Lieutenant Colonel and the gypsy*

Kellogg, Steven (Stephen). *The mystery of the magic green ball*

Mahy, Margaret. *Mrs. Discombobulous*

Oram, Hiawyn. *Skittlewonder and the wizard*

Patterson, Geoffrey. *The lion and the gypsy*

Tompert, Ann. *Savina, the gypsy dancer*

Hair

Abisch, Roz. *The Pumpkin Heads*

Appell, Clara. *Now I have a daddy haircut*

Bright, Robert. *I like red*

Davis, Gibbs. *Katy's first haircut*

De Veaux, Alexis. *An enchanted hair tale*

Freeman, Don. *Mop Top*

Girard, Linda Walvoord. *Jeremy's first haircut*

Goldin, Augusta. *Straight hair, curly hair*

Grimm, Jacob. *Rapunzel*, ill. by Jutta Ash
Rapunzel, ill. by Bert Dodson
Rapunzel, ill. by Trina Schart Hyman
Rapunzel, ill. by Kris Waldherr
Rapunzel, ill. by Bernadette Watts

Hair, ill. by Christine Sharr

Kunhardt, Dorothy. *Billy the barber*

Marton, Jirina. *I'll do it myself*

Nesbit, Edith. *Melisande*

Quin-Harkin, Janet. *Helpful Hattie*

Rockwell, Anne F. *My barber*

Scott, Natalie (Anderson). *Firebrand, push your hair out of your eyes*

Tether, Graham. *The hair book*

Townsend, Kenneth. *Felix, the bald-headed lion*

Tusa, Tricia. *Camilla's new hairdo*

Halloween *see* Holidays – Halloween

Hamsters *see* Animals – hamsters

Handicaps

Adler, David A. *A picture book of Helen Keller*

Arnold, Katrin. *Anna joins in*

Bradford, Ann. *The mystery of the missing dogs*

Brightman, Alan. *Like me*

Briscoe, Jill. *The innkeeper's daughter*

Brown, Tricia. *Someone special, just like you*

Cairo, Shelley. *Our brother has Down's syndrome*

Charlot, Martin. *Felisa and the magic tikling bird*

Clifton, Lucille. *My friend Jacob*

Corrigan, Kathy. *Emily Umily*

English, Jennifer. *My mommy's special*

Fanshawe, Elizabeth. *Rachel*

Fassler, Joan. *Howie helps himself*
One little girl

Hamm, Diane Johnston. *Grandma drives a motor bed*

Hasler, Eveline. *Martin is our friend*

Henriod, Lorraine. *Grandma's wheelchair*

Kaufman, Curt. *Rajesh*

Kuklin, Susan. *Thinking big*

Larsen, Hanne. *Don't forget Tom*

Lasker, Joe. *He's my brother*
Nick joins in

Marron, Carol A. *No trouble for Grandpa*

Payne, Sherry Neuwirth. *A contest*

Powers, Mary E. *Our teacher's in a wheelchair*

Prall, Jo. *My sister's special*

Rabe, Berniece. *The balancing girl*
Where's Chimpy?

Rosenberg, Maxine B. *My friend Leslie*

Schatell, Brian. *The McGoonys have a party*

Small, David. *Ruby Mae has something to say*

Smith, Lucia B. *A special kind of sister*

Stein, Sara Bonnett. *About handicaps*

Wahl, Jan. *Button eye's orange*

White, Paul. *Janet at school*

Whitney, Dorothy B. *Creatures of an exceptional kind*

Wolf, Bernard. *Don't feel sorry for Paul*

Handicaps – blindness

Bradford, Ann. *The mystery of the blind writer*

Brighton, Catherine. *My hands, my world*

Chapman, Elizabeth. *Suzy*

Cohen, Miriam. *See you tomorrow*

DeArmond, Dale. *The seal oil lamp*

Goldin, Barbara Diamond. *Cakes and miracles*

Herman, Bill. *Jenny's magic wand*

Jensen, Virginia Allen. *Catching*
Red thread riddles
What's that?

Johnson, Donna Kay. *Brighteyes*

Keats, Ezra Jack. *Apartment 3*

Litchfield, Ada B. *A cane in her hand*

Martin, Bill (William Ivan). *Knots on a counting rope*

Newth, Philip. *Roly goes exploring*

Quigley, Lillian Fox. *The blind men and the elephant*

Reuter, Margaret. *My mother is blind*
Sargent, Susan. *My favorite place*
Saxe, John Godfrey. *The blind men and the elephant*
Wisniewski, David. *Elfwyn's saga*
Yolen, Jane. *The seeing stick*
Young, Ed (Edward). *Seven blind mice*

Handicaps – deafness

Ancona, George. *Handtalk zoo*
Arthur, Catherine. *My sister's silent world*
Aseltine, Lorraine. *I'm deaf and it's okay*
Baker, Pamela J. *My first book of sign*
Bove, Linda. *Sign language ABC with Linda Bove*
Chaplin, Susan Gibbons. *I can sign my ABCs*
Charlip, Remy. *Handtalk Handtalk birthday*
Gage, Wilson. *Down in the boondocks*
Greenberg, Judith E. *What is the sign for friend?*
Lee, Jeanne M. *Silent lotus*
Litchfield, Ada B. *A button in her ear*
Mother Goose. *Nursery rhymes from Mother Goose in signed English*
Pace, Elizabeth. *Chris gets ear tubes*
Wahl, Jan. *Jamie's tiger*
Wolf, Bernard. *Anna's silent world*

Handicaps – physical

Carlson, Nancy. *Arnie and the new kid*
Caseley, Judith. *Harry and Willy and Carrothead*
Damrell, Liz. *With the wind*
Edwards, Michelle. *Alef-bet*
Holcomb, Nan. *Patrick and Emma Lou*
Lee, Jeanne M. *Silent lotus*
Waddell, Martin. *My great grandpa*
Wells, Rosemary. *The little lame prince*

Hands *see* Anatomy – hands

Handyman *see* Careers – handyman

Hanukkah *see* Holidays – Hanukkah

Happiness *see* Emotions – happiness

Hares *see* Animals – rabbits

Hate *see* Emotions – hate

Hats *see* Clothing – hats

Hatters *see* Careers – hatters

Hawaii

Funai, Mamoru. *Moke and Poki in the rain forest*

Laird, Donivee Martin. *The three little Hawaiian pigs and the magic shark*
Lewis, Richard. *In the night, still dark*
McGuire-Turcotte, Casey A. *How Honu the turtle got his shell*
Mower, Nancy. *I visit my Tūtū and Grandma*
Tune, Suelyn Ching. *How Maui slowed the sun*
Williams, Jay. *The surprising things Maui did*
Williams, Julie Stewart. *And the birds appeared*

Hawks *see* Birds – hawks

Heads *see* Anatomy – heads

Health

Berger, Melvin. *Ouch! a book about cuts, scratches and scrapes*
Why I cough, sneeze, shiver, hiccup and yawn
Borten, Helen. *Do you move as I do?*
Brown, Laurie Krasny. *Dinosaurs alive and well*
Burnstein, John. *Slim Goodbody*
Cobb, Vicki. *How the doctor knows you're fine*
Fassler, David. *What's a virus, anyway?*
Gross, Ruth Belov. *A book about your skeleton*
Isenberg, Barbara. *Albert the running bear's exercise book*
Kuklin, Susan. *When I see my dentist*
Leaf, Munro. *Health can be fun*
Marcus, Susan. *Casey visits the doctor*
Marshall, Lyn. *Yoga for your children*
Moncure, Jane Belk. *Happy healthkins*
The healthkin food train
Healthkins exercise!
Healthkins help
Oxenbury, Helen. *The checkup*
Radlauer, Ruth Shaw. *Of course, you're a horse!*
Rockwell, Harlow. *My doctor*
Roth, Harold. *A checkup*
Seuss, Dr. *The tooth book*
Sharmat, Marjorie Weinman. *Lucretia the unbearable*
Watson, Jane Werner. *My friend the dentist*
My friend the doctor

Hearing *see* Handicaps – deafness; Senses – hearing

Heavy equipment *see* Machines

Hedgehogs *see* Animals – hedgehogs

Helicopters

Anderson, Joan. *Harry's helicopter*

Cartwright, Ann. *The winter hedgehog*
Drummond, Violet H. *The flying postman*
Duchess of York. *Budgie at Bendick's Point*
Budgie the little helicopter
Gay, Michel. *Little helicopter*
Ingoglia, Gina. *The big book of real airplanes*
Taylor, Mark. *Henry explores the mountains*
Zaffo, George J. *The big book of real airplanes*

Helpfulness *see* Character traits – helpfulness

Hens *see* Birds – chickens

Hibernation

Barrett, John M. *The bear who slept through Christmas*
Bartoli, Jennifer. *Snow on bear's nose*
Bassett, Lisa. *Beany wakes up for Christmas*
Bird, E. J. *How do bears sleep?*
Cohen, Carol L. *Wake up, groundhog!*
De Paola, Tomie (Thomas Anthony). *Four stories for four seasons*
Evans, Eva Knox. *Sleepy time*
Fisher, Aileen Lucia. *Where does everyone go?*
Freeman, Don. *Bearymore*
Gammell, Stephen. *Wake up, bear ... It's Christmas!*
Janice. *Little Bear's Christmas*
Kepes, Juliet. *Frogs, merry*
Kesselman, Wendy. *Time for Jody*
Krauss, Ruth. *The happy day*
Ludwig, Warren. *Good morning, Granny Rose*
McClure, Gillian. *Prickly pig*
Marshall, James. *What's the matter with Carruthers?*
Miller, Edna. *Mousekin's golden house*
Patz, Nancy. *Sarah Bear and Sweet Sidney*
Piers, Helen. *Grasshopper and butterfly*
Stott, Rowena. *The hedgehog feast*
Ward, Andrew. *Baby bear and the long sleep*
Watson, Wendy. *Has winter come?*
Yulya. *Bears are sleeping*

Hiding *see* Behavior – hiding

Hiding things *see* Behavior – hiding things

Hieroglyphics

Mother Goose. *Mother Goose in hieroglyphics*, ill. by George S. Appleton
The prince who knew his fate, ill. by Lise Manniche

Hiking *see* Sports – hiking

Hippopotami *see* Animals – Hippopotami

Hispanic-Americans *see* Ethnic groups in the U.S. – Hispanic-Americans

Hobby horses *see* Toys – rocking horses

Hockey *see* Sports – hockey

Holidays

Adler, David A. *The children's book of Jewish holidays*
A picture book of Jewish holidays
Alexander, Sue. *Small plays for special days*
Belting, Natalia Maree. *Summer's coming in*
Bonnici, Peter. *The festival*
Cazet, Denys. *December 24th*
Chaikin, Miriam. *Esther*
Cohen, Barbara. *Even higher*
Conger, Marion. *The little golden holiday book*
Crespi, Francesca. *Little Bear and the oompah-pah*
Drucker, Malka. *A Jewish holiday ABC*
Eisenberg, Ann. *I can celebrate*
Fisher, Aileen Lucia. *Arbor day*
Skip around the year
Forrester, Victoria. *Oddward*
Gellman, Ellie. *Shai's Shabbat walk*
Groner, Judyth. *Where is the Afikomen?*
Hopkins, Lee Bennett. *Ring out, wild bells*
Kumin, Maxine. *Follow the fall*
Livingston, Myra Cohn. *Celebrations*
Mason, Lura. *A book of boxes*
Menter, Ian. *Carnival*
Meyer, Elizabeth C. *The blue china pitcher*
Most, Bernard. *Happy holidaysaurus!*
Roop, Peter. *Let's celebrate!*
Ross, Tony. *Hugo and the bureau of holidays*
Tan, Amy. *The moon lady*
Wikler, Madeline. *Let's build a Sukkah*
Winn, Chris. *Holiday*
Zolotow, Charlotte (Shapiro). *Over and over*

Holidays – April Fools' Day

Brown, Marc Tolon. *Arthur's April fool*
Christian, Mary Blount. *April fool*
Krahn, Fernando. *April fools*
Kroll, Steven. *It's April Fools' Day!*
Modell, Frank. *Look out, it's April Fools' Day*
Rockwell, Norman. *Norman Rockwell's counting book*
Wegen, Ron. *Billy Gorilla*

Holidays - Chanukah *see* Holidays – Hanukkah

Holidays – Chinese New Year

Cheng, Hou-Tien. *The Chinese New Year*
Handforth, Thomas. *Mei Li*
Politi, Leo. *Moy Moy*
Wallace, Ian. *Chin Chiang and the dragon's dance*
Waters, Kate. *Lion dancer: Ernie Wan's Chinese new year*
Young, Evelyn. *The tale of Tai*

Holidays – Christmas

Adams, Adrienne. *The Christmas party*
Adshead, Gladys L. *Brownies—it's Christmas*
Ahlberg, Allan. *The Cinderella show*
  Cops and robbers
Ahlberg, Janet. *The jolly Christmas postman*
Aichinger, Helga. *The shepherd*
Aliki. *Christmas tree memories*
Ambrus, Victor G. *Santa Claus takes off*
Amoss, Berthe. *What did you lose, Santa?*
Andersen, H. C. (Hans Christian). *The fir tree*, ill. by Stephanie Britt
  The fir tree, ill. by Nancy Elkholm Burkert
  The fir tree, ill. by Diane Goode
  The fir tree, ill. by Rita Marshall
  The fir tree, ill. by Bernadette Watts
Anglund, Joan Walsh. *Christmas is a time of giving*
  The cowboy's Christmas
Aoki, Hisako. *Santa's favorite story*
Ardizzone, Aingelda. *The night ride*
Armour, Richard Willard. *The year Santa went modern*
Ashley, Jill. *Riddles about Christmas*
Bach, Alice. *The day after Christmas*
Bach, Othello. *Hector McSnector and the mail-order Christmas witch*
Baird, Anne. *The Christmas lamb*
Baker, Laura Nelson. *The friendly beasts*
  O children of the wind and pines
Balet, Jan B. *The gift*
Balian, Lorna. *Bah! Humbug?*
Barrett, John M. *The bear who slept through Christmas*
Barry, Robert E. *Mr. Willowby's Christmas tree*
Bassett, Lisa. *Beany wakes up for Christmas*
  Koala Christmas
Behrens, June. *Christmas-magic wagon*
Belting, Natalia Maree. *Christmas folk*
Bemelmans, Ludwig. *Hansi*
  Madeline's Christmas
Berenstain, Stan. *The Berenstain bears' Christmas tree*
  The Berenstain bears meet Santa Bear
Berger, Barbara Helen. *The donkey's dream*
Bible. New Testament. Gospels. *Christmas*, ill. by Jan Pieńkowski
  The Nativity, ill. by Julie Vivas
  The story of Christmas, ill. by Jane Ray
Bishop, Adela. *The Christmas polar bear*
Blough, Glenn O. *Christmas trees and how they grow*
Bolognese, Don. *A new day*
Bond, Felicia. *Christmas in the chicken coop*
Bowman, Peter. *The Christmas songbook*
Breathed, Berkeley. *A wish for wings that work*
Brett, Jan. *The wild Christmas reindeer*
Briggs, Raymond. *Father Christmas*
  Father Christmas goes on holiday
Bright, Robert. *Georgie's Christmas carol*
Bring a torch, Jeannette, Isabella, ill. by Adrienne Adams
Brock, Emma Lillian. *The birds' Christmas tree*
Bröger, Achim. *The Santa Clauses*
Brown, Abbie Farwell. *The Christmas angel*
Brown, Marc Tolon. *Arthur's Christmas*
Brown, Margaret Wise. *Christmas in the barn*
  The little fir tree
  On Christmas eve
  Pussycat's Christmas
  The steamroller
Brown, Palmer. *Something for Christmas*
Bruna, Dick. *Christmas*
  The Christmas book
Brunhoff, Jean de. *Babar and Father Christmas*
Bryson, Bernarda. *The twenty miracles of Saint Nicolas*
Budbill, David. *Christmas tree farm*
Bunting, Eve (Anne Evelyn). *Night tree*
Burland, Brian. *St. Nicholas and the tub*
Butterworth, Nick. *The Nativity play*
Carlson, Natalie Savage. *Surprise in the mountains*
Carrier, Lark. *A Christmas promise*
Catalanotto, Peter. *Christmas always*
Cazet, Denys. *Christmas moon*
Chafetz, Henry. *The legend of Befana*
Chalmers, Mary. *A Christmas story*
  Merry Christmas, Harry
Chapman, Jean. *Moon-Eyes*
Chorao, Kay. *Baby's Christmas treasury*
A Christmas book
Christmas in the stable, ill. by Beverly K. Duncan
The Christmas story
Chute, Beatrice Joy. *Joy to Christmas*
Clements, Andrew. *Santa's secret helper*
Clifton, Lucille. *Everett Anderson's Christmas coming*
Climo, Shirley. *The cobweb Christmas*
Coatsworth, Elizabeth. *The children come running*
Compton, Kenn. *Happy Christmas to all!*
Cooney, Barbara. *The little juggler*
Crespi, Francesca. *Santa Clause is coming!*

Jones, Jessie Mae Orton. *A little child*
Joslin, Sesyle. *Baby elephant and the secret wishes*
Jüchen, Aurel von. *The Holy Night*
Kahl, Virginia. *Plum pudding for Christmas*
Keats, Ezra Jack. *The little drummer boy*
Keller, Holly. *A bear for Christmas*
Kellogg, Steven (Stephen). *The Christmas witch*
Kent, Jack. *The Christmas piñata*
Kerr, Judith. *Mog's Christmas*
King, B. A. *The very best Christmas tree*
Knight, Hilary. *Angels and berries and candy canes*
Knotts, Howard. *The lost Christmas*
Koscielniak, Bruce. *Hector and Prudence— all aboard!*
Kovalski, Maryann. *Jingle bells*
Krahn, Fernando. *The biggest Christmas tree on earth*
Kraus, Robert. *The tree that stayed up until next Christmas*
Kroll, Steven. *Santa's crash-bang Christmas*
Kunhardt, Edith. *Danny's Christmas star*
Kunnas, Mauri. *Santa Claus and his elves*
Twelve gifts for Santa Claus
Lagerlöf, Selma. *The legend of the Christmas rose*
Langstaff, John M. *On Christmas day in the morning*
La Rochelle, David. *A Christmas guest*
Lathrop, Dorothy Pulis. *An angel in the woods*
Laurence, Margaret. *The Christmas birthday story*
Leedy, Loreen. *A dragon Christmas*
Linch, Elizabeth Johanna. *Samson*
Lindgren, Astrid. *A calf for Christmas*
Christmas in noisy village
Christmas in the stable
Lotta's Christmas surprise
Of course Polly can do almost everything
Lines, Kathleen. *Once in royal David's city*
Lipkind, William. *The Christmas bunny*
Low, Joseph. *The Christmas grump*
Lubin, Leonard B. *Christmas gift-bringers*
McCully, Emily Arnold. *The Christmas gift*
McGinley, Phyllis. *How Mrs. Santa Claus saved Christmas*
McPhail, David. *Mistletoe*
Manushkin, Fran. *The perfect Christmas picture*
Mariana. *The journey of Bangwell Putt*
Marshall, James. *Merry Christmas, space case*
Miss Dog's Christmas
Martin, Judith. *The tree angel*
Mattingley, Christobel. *The angel with a mouth-organ*
Maxfield, Christine. *Christmas in Water Village*

May, Robert Lewis. *Rudolph the red-nosed reindeer*
Merriam, Eve. *The Christmas box*
Miller, Edna. *Mousekin's Christmas eve*
Moeri, Louise. *Star Mother's youngest child*
Mogensen, Jan. *Teddy's Christmas gift*
Mohr, Joseph. *Silent night*
Monsell, Helen Albee. *Paddy's Christmas*
Moore, Clement C. *The night before Christmas*, ill. by Tomie de Paola
The night before Christmas, ill. by Michael Foreman
The night before Christmas, ill. by Gyo Fujikawa
The night before Christmas, ill. by Scott Gustafson
The night before Christmas, ill. by Cheryl Harness
The night before Christmas, ill. by Anita Lobel
The night before Christmas, ill. by James Marshall
The night before Christmas, ill. by Jacqueline Rogers
The night before Christmas, ill. by Robin Spowart
The night before Christmas, ill. by Gustaf Tenggren
The night before Christmas, ill. by Tasha Tudor
The night before Christmas, ill. by Wendy Watson
The night before Christmas, ill. by Jody Wheeler
A visit from St. Nicholas, ill. by Paul Galdone
Munro, Roxie. *Christmastime in New York City*
Murdocca, Sal. *Christmas bear*
Naylor, Phyllis Reynolds. *Old Sadie and the Christmas bear*
Neale, J. M. (John Mason). *Good King Wenceslas*
Nerlove, Miriam. *Christmas*
Newland, Mary Reed. *Good King Wenceslas*
Niland, Kilmeny. *A bellbird in a flame tree*
Nixon, Joan Lowery. *That's the spirit, Claude*
Noble, Trinka Hakes. *Apple tree Christmas*
Nussbaumer, Mares. *Away in a manger*
Oakley, Graham. *The church mice at Christmas*
Olson, Arielle North. *Hurry home, Grandma!*
Parker, Nancy Winslow. *The Christmas camel*
Partch, Virgil Franklin. *The Christmas cookie sprinkle snitcher*
Pearson, Susan. *Karin's Christmas walk*
Peet, Bill (William Bartlett). *Countdown to Christmas*

Holidays – Cinco de Mayo

Behrens, June. *Fiesta!*

Holidays – Columbus Day

Showers, Paul. *Columbus Day*

Holidays – Easter

Adams, Adrienne. *The Easter egg artists*
Armour, Richard Willard. *The adventures of Egbert the Easter egg*
Auch, Mary Jane. *The Easter egg farm*
Balian, Lorna. *Humbug rabbit*
Barrett, John M. *The Easter bear*
Bishop, Adela. *The Easter wolf*
Brown, Margaret Wise. *The golden egg book*
The runaway bunny
Carrick, Carol. *A rabbit for Easter*
Chalmers, Mary. *Easter parade*
Claret, Maria. *The chocolate rabbit*
Compton, Joanne. *Little Rabbit's Easter surprise*
Cross, Genevieve. *My bunny book*
Darling, Kathy (Mary Kathleen). *The Easter bunny's secret*
Delacre, Lulu. *Peter Cottontail's Easter book*
DeLage, Ida. *ABC Easter bunny*
Devlin, Wende. *Cranberry Easter*
Dunn, Judy. *The little rabbit*
Duvoisin, Roger Antoine. *Easter treat*
Friedrich, Priscilla. *The Easter bunny that overslept*
Gibbons, Gail. *Easter*
Gordon, Sharon. *Easter Bunny's lost egg*
Heyward, Du Bose. *The country bunny and the little gold shoes*
Hill, Eric. *Spot's first Easter*
Hoban, Lillian. *Silly Tilly and the Easter bunny*
Hopkins, Lee Bennett. *Easter buds are springing*
Houselander, Caryll. *Petook*
Kay, Helen. *An egg is for wishing*
Kraus, Robert. *Daddy Long Ears*
Kroll, Steven. *The big bunny and the Easter eggs*
The big bunny and the magic show
Kunhardt, Edith. *Danny and the Easter egg*
Littlefield, William. *The whiskers of Ho Ho*
McClenathan, Louise. *The Easter pig*
Maril, Lee. *Mr. Bunny paints the eggs*
Milhous, Katherine. *The egg tree*
Miller, Edna. *Mouskin's Easter basket*
Pieńkowski, Jan. *Easter*
Polacco, Patricia. *Chicken Sunday*
Stock, Catherine. *Easter surprise*
Thayer, Jane. *The horse with the Easter bonnet*
Tresselt, Alvin R. *The world in the candy egg*
Tudor, Tasha. *A tale for Easter*

Wahl, Jan. *The five in the forest*
Weil, Lisl. *The candy egg bunny*
Weisgard, Leonard. *The funny bunny factory*
Wells, Rosemary. *Max's chocolate chicken*
Wiese, Kurt. *Happy Easter*
Wilhelm, Hans. *More bunny trouble*
Winthrop, Elizabeth. *He is risen*
Wolf, Winfried. *The Easter bunny*
Young, Miriam Burt. *Miss Suzy's Easter surprise*
Ziefert, Harriet. *Happy Easter, Grandma!*
Zolotow, Charlotte (Shapiro). *The bunny who found Easter*
Mr. Rabbit and the lovely present

Holidays – Father's Day

Bunting, Eve (Anne Evelyn). *A perfect Father's Day*
Kroll, Steven. *Happy Father's Day*
Livingston, Myra Cohn. *Poems for fathers*
Sharmat, Marjorie Weinman. *Hooray for Father's Day!*
Simon, Norma. *I wish I had my father*

Holidays – Fourth of July

Devlin, Wende. *Cranberry summer*
Joosse, Barbara M. *Fourth of July*
Keller, Holly. *Henry's Fourth of July*
Lasky, Kathryn. *Fourth of July bear*
Shortall, Leonard W. *One way*
Watson, Wendy. *Hurray for the Fourth of July*
Zion, Gene. *The summer snowman*

Holidays – Groundhog Day

Balian, Lorna. *A garden for a groundhog*
Cohen, Carol L. *Wake up, groundhog!*
Delton, Judy. *Groundhog's Day at the doctor*
Glass, Marvin. *What happened today, Freddy Groundhog?*
Hamberger, John. *This is the day*
Johnson, Crockett. *Will spring be early?*
Kesselman, Wendy. *Time for Jody*
Kroll, Steven. *It's Groundhog Day!*
Palazzo, Tony (Anthony D.). *Waldo the woodchuck*

Holidays – Guy Fawkes Day

Buchanan, Heather S. *George and Matilda Mouse and the moon rocket*

Holidays – Halloween

Adams, Adrienne. *A Halloween happening*
A woggle of witches
Anderson, Lonzo. *The Halloween party*
Asch, Frank. *Popcorn*
Balian, Lorna. *Humbug witch*
Battles, Edith. *The terrible trick or treat*
Beim, Jerrold. *Sir Halloween*

Benarde, Anita. *The pumpkin smasher*
Berenstain, Stan. *The Berenstain bears trick or treat*
Bond, Felicia. *The Halloween performance*
Borten, Helen. *Halloween*
Bradford, Ann. *The mystery of the live ghosts*
Bridwell, Norman. *Clifford's Halloween*
Bright, Robert. *Georgie's Halloween*
Brown, Marc Tolon. *Arthur's Halloween*
Bunting, Eve (Anne Evelyn). *In the haunted house*
Scary, scary Halloween
Calhoun, Mary. *The witch of Hissing Hill*
Wobble the witch cat
Carlson, Natalie Savage. *Spooky and the ghost cat*
Spooky and the wizard's bats
Spooky night
Carrick, Carol. *Old Mother Witch*
Cassedy, Sylvia. *The best cat suit of all*
Cavagnaro, David. *The pumpkin people*
Cecil, Mirabel. *Lottie's cats*
Charles, Donald. *Shaggy dog's Halloween*
Charlton, Elizabeth. *Jeremy and the ghost*
Cohen, Miriam. *The real-skin rubber monster mask*
Cooper, Paulette. *Let's find out about Halloween*
Corey, Dorothy. *Will it ever be my birthday?*
Cummings, E. E. (Edward Estlin). *Hist whist*
Cuyler, Margery. *Sir William and the pumpkin monster*
Davis, Maggie S. *Rickety witch*
Degen, Bruce. *Aunt Possum and the pumpkin man*
DeLage, Ida. *The old witch and her magic basket*
Devlin, Wende. *Cranberry Halloween*
Old Witch rescues Halloween
Donnelly, Liza. *Dinosaurs' Halloween*
Embry, Margaret. *The blue-nosed witch*
Feczko, Kathy. *Halloween party*
Foster, Doris Van Liew. *Tell me, Mr. Owl*
Freeman, Don. *Space witch*
Tilly Witch
Friedrich, Priscilla. *The marshmallow ghosts*
Gantos, Jack (John, Jr.). *Rotten Ralph's trick or treat*
Gardner, Beau. *Whooo's a fright on Halloween night?*
Gibbons, Gail. *Halloween*
Greene, Carol. *The thirteen days of Halloween*
Greene, Ellin. *The pumpkin giant*
Guthrie, Donna. *The witch who lives down the hall*
Hellsing, Lennart. *The wonderful pumpkin*
Herman, Emily. *Hubknuckles*
Hoff, Syd. *Henrietta's Halloween*

Howe, James. *Scared silly*
Hurd, Edith Thacher. *The so-so cat*
Hutchins, Pat. *Which witch is which?*
Irving, Washington. *The legend of Sleepy Hollow*, ill. by Daniel San Souci
Johnston, Tony. *Soup bone*
The vanishing pumpkin
Keats, Ezra Jack. *The trip*
Kellogg, Steven (Stephen). *The mystery of the flying orange pumpkin*
Khdir, Kate. *Little ghost*
King, Elizabeth. *Pumpkin patch*
Kroll, Steven. *Branigan's cat and the Halloween ghost*
The candy witch
Kunhardt, Edith. *Trick or treat, Danny!*
Kunnas, Mauri. *One spooky night and other scary stories*
Leedy, Loreen. *The dragon Halloween party*
Low, Alice. *The witch who was afraid of witches*
Witch's holiday
Maestro, Giulio. *Halloween howls*
Manushkin, Fran. *Be brave, baby rabbit*
Hocus and Pocus at the circus
Marshall, Edward. *Space case*
Martin, Bill (William Ivan). *The magic pumpkin*
Massey, Jeanne. *The littlest witch*
Meddaugh, Susan. *The witches' supermarket*
Merriam, Eve. *Halloween ABC*
Miller, Edna. *Mousekin's golden house*
Mooser, Stephen. *The ghost with the Halloween hiccups*
Mueller, Virginia. *A Halloween mask for Monster*
Nerlove, Miriam. *Halloween*
Nicoll, Helen. *Meg and Mog*
Nolan, Dennis. *Witch Bazooza*
Numeroff, Laura Joffe. *Emily's bunch*
Ott, John. *Peter Pumpkin*
Paul, Sherry. *2-B and the space visitor*
Peters, Sharon. *Trick or treat Halloween*
Prager, Annabelle. *The spooky Halloween party*
Preston, Edna Mitchell. *One dark night*
Racioppo, Larry. *Halloween*
Rockwell, Anne F. *Apples and pumpkins*
A bear, a bobcat and three ghosts
Rose, David S. *It hardly seems like Halloween*
Rylant, Cynthia. *Henry and Mudge under the yellow moon*
St. George, Judith. *The Halloween pumpkin smasher*
Schertle, Alice. *Bill and the google-eyed goblins*
Hob Goblin and the skeleton
Schweninger, Ann. *Halloween surprises*
Scott, Ann Herbert. *Let's catch a monster*
Shaw, Richard. *The kitten in the pumpkin patch*

Slobodkin, Louis. *Trick or treat*
Stevenson, James. *That terrible Halloween night*
Stock, Catherine. *Halloween monster*
Thayer, Jane. *Gus was a gorgeous ghost*
Titherington, Jeanne. *Pumpkin pumpkin*
Vigna, Judith. *Everyone goes as a pumpkin*
Von Hippel, Ursula. *The craziest Halloween*
Wahl, Jan. *Pleasant Fieldmouse's Halloween party*
Watson, Jane Werner. *Which is the witch?*
Wegen, Ron. *The Halloween costume party*
Weller, Frances Ward. *The closet gorilla*
Wolkstein, Diane. *The legend of Sleepy Hollow*
Zimmer, Dirk. *The trick-or-treat trap*
Zolotow, Charlotte (Shapiro). *A tiger called Thomas*, ill. by Catherine Stock
A tiger called Thomas, ill. by Kurt Werth

Holidays – Hanukkah

Adler, David A. *A picture book of Hanukkah*
A picture book of Jewish holidays
Aleichem, Sholem. *Hanukah money*
Behrens, June. *Hanukkah*
Chaikin, Miriam. *Hanukkah*
Chanover, Hyman. *Happy Hanukah everybody*
Coopersmith, Jerome. *A Chanukah fable for Christmas*
De Paola, Tomie (Thomas Anthony). *My first Chanukah*
Drucker, Malka. *Grandma's latkes*
Fisher, Aileen Lucia. *My first Hanukkah book*
Gellman, Ellie. *It's Chanukah!*
Goffstein, M. B. (Marilyn Brooke). *Laughing latkes*
Goldin, Barbara Diamond. *Just enough is plenty*
Groner, Judyth. *All about Hanukkah*
Hirsh, Marilyn. *I love Hanukkah*
Potato pancakes all around
Kimmel, Eric A. *The Chanukkah guest*
Hershel and the Hanukkah goblins
Koralek, Jenny. *Hanukkah: the festival of lights*
Levine, Arthur. *All the lights in the night*
Levoy, Myron. *The Hanukkah of Great-Uncle Otto*
Manushkin, Fran. *Latkes and applesause*
Modesitt, Jeanne. *Songs of Chanukah*
Nerlove, Miriam. *Hanukkah*
Poskanzer, Susan Cornell. *Riddles about Hannukah*
Rosen, Michael J. *Elijah's angel*
Schotter, Roni. *Hanukkah!*
Sherman, Eileen Bluestone. *The odd potato*
Shostak, Myra. *Rainbow candles*
Zalben, Jane Breskin. *Beni's first Chanukah*

Holidays - Independence Day *see* Holidays – Fourth of July

Holidays – Kwanzaa

Chocolate, Deborah M. Newton. *Kwanzaa*

Holidays - Mardi Gras *see* Mardi Gras

Holidays – Memorial Day

Scott, Geoffrey. *Memorial Day*

Holidays – Mother's Day

Bunting, Eve (Anne Evelyn). *The Mother's Day mice*
Howe, James. *The case of the missing mother*
Kroll, Steven. *Happy Mother's Day*
Livingston, Myra Cohn. *Poems for mothers*
Morgan, Allen. *Matthew and the midnight money van*
Sharmat, Marjorie Weinman. *Hooray for Mother's Day!*
Tripp, Valerie. *Happy, happy Mother's Day*
Wynot, Jillian. *The Mother's Day sandwich*

Holidays – New Year's

Andersen, H. C. (Hans Christian). *The little match girl*, ill. by Rachel Isadora
The little match girl, ill. by Blair Lent
Janice. *Little Bear's New Year's party*
Modell, Frank. *Goodbye old year, hello new year*

Holidays – Passover

Adler, David A. *A picture book of Jewish holidays*
A picture book of Passover
Auerbach, Julie Jaslow. *Everything's changing—It's pesach!*
Behrens, June. *Passover*
Feder, Harriet K. *Not yet, Elijah!*
Hirsh, Marilyn. *I love Passover*
One little goat
Rosen, Anne. *A family Passover*
Schwartz, Lynne Sharon. *The four questions*
Wikler, Madeline. *My first seder*
Wohl, Lauren L. *Matzoh mouse*
Zalben, Jane Breskin. *Happy Passover, Rosie*
Zusman, Evelyn. *The Passover parrot*

Holidays – Purim

Cohen, Barbara. *Here come the Purim players!*
Suhl, Yuri. *The Purim goat*
Wikler, Madeline. *The Purim parade*

Holidays – Rosh Hashanah

Gellman, Ellie. *It's Rosh Hashanah!*
Goldin, Barbara Diamond. *World's birthday*

Kahn, Katherine Janus. *The Shofar calls to us*

Holidays – St. Patrick's Day

Bunting, Eve (Anne Evelyn). *St. Patrick's Day in the morning*
Calhoun, Mary. *The hungry leprechaun*
Janice. *Little Bear marches in the St. Patrick's Day parade*
Kroll, Steven. *Mary McLean and the St. Patrick's Day parade*
Schertle, Alice. *Jeremy Bean's St. Patrick's Day*
Zimelman, Nathan. *To sing a song as big as Ireland*

Holidays – Sukkot

Zalben, Jane Breskin. *Leo and Blossom's Sukkah*

Holidays – Thanksgiving

Balian, Lorna. *Sometimes it's turkey*
Behrens, June. *The feast of Thanksgiving*
Berenstain, Stan. *The Berenstain bears and the prize pumpkin*
Brown, Marc Tolon. *Arthur's Thanksgiving*
Bunting, Eve (Anne Evelyn). *How many days to America?*
 A turkey for Thanksgiving
Child, Lydia Maria. *Over the river and through the wood*
Dalgliesh, Alice. *The Thanksgiving story*
Devlin, Wende. *Cranberry Thanksgiving*
Dragonwagon, Crescent. *Alligator arrived with apples*
Gibbons, Gail. *Thanksgiving Day*
Hopkins, Lee Bennett. *Merrily comes our harvest in*
Ipcar, Dahlov. *Hard scrabble harvest*
Janice. *Little Bear's Thanksgiving*
Kroll, Steven. *One tough turkey*
 The squirrels' Thanksgiving
Leedy, Loreen. *The dragon Thanksgiving feast*
Lowitz, Sadyebeth. *The pilgrims' party*
Miller, Edna. *Mouskin's Thanksgiving*
Nerlove, Miriam. *Thanksgiving*
Nikola-Lisa, W. *One, two, three Thanksgiving!*
Nixon, Joan Lowery. *The Thanksgiving mystery*
Ott, John. *Peter Pumpkin*
Pilkey, Dav. *'Twas the night before Thanksgiving*
Quackenbush, Robert M. *Sheriff Sally Gopher and the Thanksgiving caper*
Rylant, Cynthia. *Henry and Mudge under the yellow moon*
Spinelli, Eileen. *Thanksgiving at Tappletons'*
Stock, Catherine. *Thanksgiving treat*

Tresselt, Alvin R. *Autumn harvest*
Watson, Wendy. *Thanksgiving at our house*
Williams, Barbara. *Chester Chipmunk's Thanksgiving*
Zion, Gene. *The meanest squirrel I ever met*

Holidays – Valentine's Day

Adams, Adrienne. *The great Valentine's Day balloon race*
Balian, Lorna. *A sweetheart for Valentine*
Bond, Felicia. *Four Valentines in a rainstorm*
Brown, Marc Tolon. *Arthur's Valentine*
Buckley, Kate. *Love notes*
Bulla, Clyde Robert. *Valentine cat*
Bunting, Eve (Anne Evelyn). *The Valentine bears*
Carlson, Nancy. *The mysterious Valentine*
Cohen, Miriam. *Bee my Valentine!*
De Paola, Tomie (Thomas Anthony). *Things to make and do for Valentine's Day*
Devlin, Wende. *Cranberry Valentine*
Geringer, Laura. *Yours 'til the ice cracks*
Gibbons, Gail. *Valentine's Day*
Greene, Carol. *A computer went a-courting*
Guilfoile, Elizabeth. *Valentine's Day*
Hoban, Lillian. *Arthur's great big Valentine*
Hurd, Thacher. *Little Mouse's big Valentine*
Keeshan, Robert. *She loves me, she loves me not*
Kelley, True. *A Valentine for Fuzzboom*
Krahn, Fernando. *Little love story*
Kraus, Robert. *How spider saved Valentine's Day*
Kunhardt, Edith. *Danny's mystery Valentine*
Livingston, Myra Cohn. *Valentine poems*
Modell, Frank. *One zillion Valentines*
Murphy, Shirley Rousseau. *Valentine for a dragon*
Nixon, Joan Lowery. *The Valentine mystery*
Sabuda, Robert James. *St. Valentine*
Schweninger, Ann. *The hunt for rabbit's galosh*
 Valentine friends
Sharmat, Marjorie Weinman. *The best Valentine in the world*
Spinelli, Eileen. *Somebody loves you, Mr. Hatch*
Stevenson, James. *Happy Valentine's Day, Emma!*
Stock, Catherine. *Secret Valentine*
Watson, Clyde. *Valentine foxes*
Watson, Wendy. *A Valentine for you*
Wittman, Sally. *The boy who hated Valentine's Day*
Zimmermann, H. Werner (Heinz Werner). *Alphonse knows...a circle is not a Valentine*

Holidays – Washington's Birthday

Bulla, Clyde Robert. *Washington's birthday*

Holidays – Yom Kippur

Singer, Marilyn. *Minnie's Yom Kippur birthday*

Holland *see* Foreign lands – Holland

Homeless

Barbour, Karen. *Mr. Bow Tie*
Bunting, Eve (Anne Evelyn). *Fly away home*
Komaiko, Leah. *Lenora O'Grady*
Rosen, Michael J. *Home*

Homes *see* Houses

Homosexuality

Willhoite, Michael. *Daddy's roomate*

Honesty *see* Character traits – honesty

Honey bees *see* Insects – bees

Hope

Ikeda, Daisaku. *The cherry tree*

Hornbills *see* Birds – hornbills

Hornets *see* Insects – hornets

Horses *see* Animals – horses

Horses, rocking *see* Toys – rocking horses

Hospitals

Baker, Gayle. *Special delivery*
Bemelmans, Ludwig. *Madeline
  Madeline [pop-up book]*
Blance, Ellen. *Monster goes to the hospital*
Bruna, Dick. *Miffy in the hospital*
Bucknall, Caroline. *One bear in the hospital*
Ciliotta, Claire. *"Why am I going to the hospital?"*
Collier, James Lincoln. *Danny goes to the hospital*
Elliott, Ingrid Glatz. *Hospital roadmap*
Hautzig, Deborah. *A visit to the Sesame Street hospital*
Hill, Eric. *Spot visits the hospital*
Hogan, Paula Z. *The hospital scares me*
Keller, Holly. *The best present*
Ketner, Mary Grace. *Ganzy remembers*
Marino, Barbara Pavis. *Eric needs stitches*
Martin, Charles E. *Island rescue*
Pace, Elizabeth. *Chris gets ear tubes*
Pope, Billy N. *Your world: let's visit the hospital*

Rey, Margret (Margret Elisabeth Waldstein). *Curious George goes to the hospital*
Rockwell, Anne F. *The emergency room*
Rogers, Fred. *Going to the hospital*
Shay, Arthur. *What happens when you go to the hospital*
Sobol, Harriet Langsam. *Jeff's hospital book*
Sonneborn, Ruth A. *I love Gram*
Steel, Danielle. *Max's daddy goes to the hospital*
Stein, Sara Bonnett. *A hospital story*
Stone, Bernard. *Emergency mouse*
Tamburine, Jean. *I think I will go to the hospital*
Watts, Marjorie-Ann. *Crocodile medicine
  Crocodile plaster*
Weber, Alfons. *Elizabeth gets well*
Wild, Margaret. *Mr. Nick's knitting*
Wolde, Gunilla. *Betsy and the doctor*

Hotels

Brewster, Patience. *Rabbit Inn*
Mahy, Margaret. *Rooms for rent*
Parkin, Rex. *The red carpet*
Stevenson, James. *The Sea View Hotel*
Vaughan, Marcia K. *The Sea-Breeze Hotel*

Housekeepers *see* Careers – housekeepers

Houses

Ackerman, Karen. *I know a place*
Adler, David A. *The house on the roof*
Alger, Leclaire Gowans. *Always room for one more*
Arkin, Alan. *Tony's hard work day*
Ayars, James Sterling. *Caboose on the roof*
Bannon, Laura. *The best house in the world*
Barton, Byron. *Building a house*
Becker, Edna. *Nine hundred buckets of paint*
Bemelmans, Ludwig. *Sunshine*
Berridge, Celia. *At my house*
Binzen, Bill. *Alfred goes house hunting*
Biro, Val. *The wind in the willows: home sweet home*
Blegvad, Lenore. *The parrot in the garret and other rhymes about dwellings*
Blos, Joan W. *Old Henry*
Borg, Inga. *Plupp builds a house*
Bour, Danièle. *The house from morning to night*
Brown, Marc Tolon. *There's no place like home*
Brown, Marcia. *The neighbors*
Brown, Margaret Wise. *House of a hundred windows
  The wonderful house*
Buchanan, Ken. *This house is made of mud*

Sattler, Helen Roney. *No place for a goat*
Scarry, Richard. *Is this the house of Mistress Mouse?*
Richard Scarry's busy houses
Schaaf, Peter. *An apartment house close up*
Scharer, Niko. *Emily's house*
Schermbrucker, Reviva. *Charlie's house*
Schertle, Alice. *In my treehouse*
Schlein, Miriam. *My house*
Schulz, Charles M. *Snoopy's facts and fun book about houses*
Seuss, Dr. *Come over to my house*
In a people house
Shapp, Martha. *Let's find out about houses*
Sharr, Christine. *Homes*
Shecter, Ben. *Emily, girl witch of New York*
Shefelman, Janice. *Victoria House*
Sherrow, Victoria. *There goes the ghost*
Silsbe, Brenda. *Just one more color*
Silverman, Erica. *On Grandma's roof*
Stern, Simon. *Mrs. Vinegar*
Strathdee, Jean. *The house that grew*
Tallarico, Tony. *At home*
Testa, Fulvio. *The ideal home*
Thayer, Jane. *What's a ghost going to do?*
Tison, Annette. *Inside and outside*
Tudor, Bethany. *Samuel's tree house*
Van Allsburg, Chris. *Two bad ants*
Velthuijs, Max. *Little Man finds a home*
Vevers, Gwynne. *Animal homes*
Watanabe, Shigeo. *I can build a house!*
Wildsmith, Brian. *Animal homes*
Winch, Madeleine. *Come by chance*
Worley, Daryl. *Billy and the attic adventure*
Wyllie, Stephen. *White Rabbit builds a dream house*
Yoaker, Harry. *The view*
Zelinsky, Paul O. *The maid and the mouse and the odd-shaped house*
Ziefert, Harriet. *A new house for Mole and Mouse*

Humming birds *see* Birds – humming birds

Humor

Aardema, Verna. *Oh, Kojo! How could you!*
What's so funny, Ketu?
Who's in Rabbit's house?
Accorsi, William. *Short short short stories*
Adams, Pam. *There was an old lady who swallowed a fly*
Adams, Richard (Richard Newbold). *The tyger voyage*
Adamson, Gareth. *Old man up a tree*
Adler, David A. *The children of Chelm*
Æsop. *The miller, his son and their donkey*, ill. by Roger Antoine Duvoisin
Ahlberg, Allan. *Mystery tour*
Ahlberg, Janet. *The little worm book*
Alborough, Jez. *Bare bear*

Alexander, Martha G. *Move over, Twerp*
Alexander, Sue. *World famous Muriel*
Aliki. *Digging up dinosaurs*
The eggs
The all-amazing ha ha book
Allamand, Pascale. *The animals who changed their colors*
Allard, Harry. *Miss Nelson has a field day*
The Stupids die
The Stupids have a ball
The Stupids step out
The Stupids take off
There's a party at Mona's tonight
Allen, Jonathan. *A bad case of animal nonsense*
Allen, Linda. *Mr. Simkin's grandma*
Mrs. Simkin's bed
Allen, Marjorie N. *One, two, three - ah-choo!*
Allen, Pamela. *Mr. Archimedes' bath*
Ambrus, Victor G. *Grandma, Felix, and Mustapha Biscuit*
The seven skinny goats
Andersen, H. C. (Hans Christian). *The emperor's new clothes*, ill. by Erik Blegvad
The emperor's new clothes, ill. by Virginia Lee Burton
The emperor's new clothes, ill. by Robert Byrd
The emperor's new clothes, ill. by Jack and Irene Delano
The emperor's new clothes, ill. by Hélène Desputeaux
The emperor's new clothes, ill. by Birte Dietz
The emperor's new clothes, ill. by Dorothée Duntze
The emperor's new clothes, ill. by Pamela Baldwin Ford
The emperor's new clothes, ill. by Jack Kent
The emperor's new clothes, ill. by Monika Laimgruber
The emperor's new clothes, ill. by Anne F. Rockwell
The emperor's new clothes, ill. by Janet Stevens
The emperor's new clothes, ill. by Nadine Bernard Westcott
The old man is always right, ill. by Feodor Rojankovsky
Anderson, Leone Castell. *The wonderful shrinking shirt*
Anno, Mitsumasa. *Anno's Britain*
Anno's counting house
Anno's flea market
Anno's Italy
Anno's journey
Anno's U.S.A.
Topsy turvies: more pictures to stretch the imagination

Carroll, Ruth. *Old Mrs. Billups and the black cats*

Caudill, Rebecca. *Contrary Jenkins*

Causley, Charles. *"Quack!" said the billy-goat*

Cerf, Bennett Alfred. *Bennett Cerf's book of animal riddles*
Bennett Cerf's book of laughs
Bennett Cerf's book of riddles
More riddles

Chalmers, Audrey. *Hundreds and hundreds of pancakes*

Chalmers, Mary. *Six dogs, twenty-three cats, forty-five mice, and one hundred sixteen spiders*

Charlip, Remy. *Arm in arm*
Fortunately
"Mother, mother I feel sick"
Thirteen

Chetwin, Grace. *Box and Cox*

Chevalier, Christa. *Spence makes circles*

Christian, Mary Blount. *Nothing much happened today*

Chukovsky, Korney. *The telephone*

Cole, Joanna. *The Clown-Arounds go on vacation*
Get well, Clown-Arounds!
Golly Gump swallowed a fly
It's too noisy

Collins, Judith Graham. *Josh's scary dad*

Coontz, Otto. *Starring Rosa*

Copp, James (Andrew James). *Martha Matilda O'Toole*

Craig, M. Jean. *The man whose name was not Thomas*

Daugherty, James Henry. *Andy and the lion*

Davis, Maggie S. *The best way to Ripton*

Delaney, M. C. (Michael Clark). *The marigold monster*

Delaney, Ned. *Terrible things could happen*

Dennis, Suzanne E. *Answer me that*

De Paola, Tomie (Thomas Anthony). *Bill and Pete*
Flicks
Strega Nona
Strega Nona's magic lessons

De Regniers, Beatrice Schenk. *May I bring a friend?*

Dorros, Arthur. *Pretzels*

Duvoisin, Roger Antoine. *Petunia's Christmas*

Easton, Violet. *Elephants never jump*

Ellentuck, Shan. *Did you see what I said?*
A sunflower as big as the sun

Ets, Marie Hall. *Beasts and nonsense*
Mister Penny

Evans, Katherine. *The maid and her pail of milk*
The man, the boy and the donkey

Farber, Norma. *There once was a woman who married a man*

Fenton, Edward. *The big yellow balloon*

Flora, James. *The day the cow sneezed Grandpa's farm*
My friend Charlie

Folsom, Marcia. *Easy as pie*

Freeman, Don. *Forever laughter*

Frith, Michael K. *I'll teach my dog 100 words*

A frog he would a-wooing go (folk-song). *Frog went a-courtin'*, ill. by Feodor Rojankovsky

Fuchshuber, Annegert. *The wishing hat*

Gackenbach, Dick. *The pig who saw everything*

Gardner, Beau. *Have you ever seen...?*

Gelman, Rita Golden. *Hey, kid*

The golden goose, ill. by William Stobbs

Grimm, Jacob. *Clever Kate*, ill. by Anita Lobel
The golden goose, ill. by Dorothée Duntze
The golden goose, ill. by Isadore Seltzer
The golden goose, ill. by Martin Ursell

Hale, Lucretia. *The lady who put salt in her coffee*

Hall, Donald. *Andrew the lion farmer*

Hample, Stoo. *Stoo Hample's silly joke book*

Hannan, Peter. *Sillyville or bust*

Hart, Jeanne McGahey. *Scareboy*

Heilbroner, Joan. *Robert the rose horse*

Hellard, Susan. *Froggie goes a-courting*

Hirsh, Marilyn. *Could anything be worse?*

Hoban, Lillian. *Silly Tilly and the Easter bunny*

Hoban, Russell. *A near thing for Captain Najork*

Holman, Felice. *Victoria's castle*

Hunter, Norman. *Professor Branestawn's building bust-up*

Hutchins, Pat. *Clocks and more clocks*
Don't forget the bacon!
Rosie's walk

Jeschke, Susan. *Firerose*

Johnson, Crockett. *Harold and the purple crayon*
Harold's circus
Upside down

Joslin, Sesyle. *Dear dragon*
What do you do, dear?
What do you say, dear?

Joyce, Irma. *Never talk to strangers*

Kantor, MacKinlay. *The preposterous week*

Keats, Ezra Jack. *Skates*

Keenen, George. *The preposterous week*

Keller, Charles. *School daze*

Kennedy, Richard. *The contests at Cowlick*

Kent, Jack. *Hoddy doddy*

King-Smith, Dick. *Farmer Bungle forgets*

Koelling, Caryl. *Silly stories mix and match*

Krahn, Fernando. *April fools*

Krauss, Ruth. *I'll be you and you be me*
This thumbprint

Kumin, Maxine. *Eggs of things*

Speedy digs downside up
La Fontaine, Jean de. *The miller, the boy and the donkey*, adapt. and ill. by Brian Wildsmith
Laurin, Anne. *Little things*
Lear, Edward. *The dong with the luminous nose*, ill. by Edward Gorey
Edward Lear's nonsense book, ill. by Tony Palazzo
A Learical lexicon
Lear's nonsense verses, ill. by Tomi Ungerer
The nutcrackers and the sugar-tongs, ill. by Marcia Sewall
The pelican chorus, ill. by Harold Berson
The pelican chorus and the quangle wangle's hat, ill. by Kevin W. Maddison
The pobble who has no toes, ill. by Emma Crosby
The pobble who has no toes, ill. by Kevin W. Maddison
The quangle wangle's hat, ill. by Emma Crosby
The quangle wangle's hat, ill. by Helen Oxenbury
The quangle wangle's hat, ill. by Janet Stevens
Two laughable lyrics, ill. by Paul Galdone
Whizz! ill. by Janina Domanska
Lent, Blair. *John Tabor's ride*
LeRoy, Gen. *Lucky stiff!*
Lionni, Leo. *Where?*
Lloyd, David. *The ridiculous story of Gammer Gurton's needle*
Lloyd, Megan. *Chicken tricks*
Lobel, Arnold. *Lucille*
Mouse tales
A treeful of pigs
Löfgren, Ulf. *The boy who ate more than the giant and other Swedish folktales*
Macaulay, David. *Why the chicken crossed the road*
McGovern, Ann. *Too much noise*
McKié, Roy. *The riddle book*
McKissack, Patricia C. *The king's new clothes*
McLenighan, Valjean. *What you see is what you get*
McPhail, David. *Alligators are awful (and they have terrible manners, too)*
The cereal box
Maestro, Giulio. *Just enough Rosie*
A raft of riddles
The remarkable plant in apartment 4
Mahood, Kenneth. *The laughing dragon*
Mahy, Margaret. *The boy who was followed home*
Manes, Esther. *The bananas move to the ceiling*
Manes, Stephen. *Life is no fair!*
Marsh, Jeri. *Hurrah for Alexander*

Marshall, Edward. *Fox at school*
Marshall, James. *The Cut-Ups carry on*
Martin, Bill (William Ivan). *Sounds of laughter*
Mayer, Mercer. *The queen always wanted to dance*
What do you do with a kangaroo?
Merriam, Eve. *The birthday cow*
Meyer, Louis A. *The clean air and peaceful contentment dirigible airline*
Miles, Miska. *Chicken forgets*
Mills, Alan. *The hungry goat*
Milne, A. A. (Alan Alexander). *Pooh's quiz book*
Mitchell, Adrian. *Our mammoth*
Modell, Frank. *Tooley! Tooley!*
Moffett, Martha A. *A flower pot is not a hat*
Monsell, Mary Elise. *Underwear!*
Mooser, Stephen. *Funnyman and the penny dodo*
Morrison, Sean. *Is that a happy hippopotamus?*
Mother Goose. *The golden goose book*, ill. by L. Leslie Brooke
Myller, Rolf. *How big is a foot?*
Nash, Ogden. *The animal garden*, ill. by Hilary Knight
A boy is a boy
Custard and Company
Newell, Peter. *Topsys and turvys*
Nixon, Joan Lowery. *Beats me, Claude*
That's the spirit, Claude
You bet your britches, Claude
Noble, Trinka Hakes. *Jimmy's boa bounces back*
Meanwhile back at the ranch
Olson, Helen Kronberg. *The strange thing that happened to Oliver Wendell Iscovitch*
Oppenheim, Joanne. *Donkey's tale*
Pack, Robert. *Then what did you do?*
Parish, Peggy. *Granny and the desperadoes*
Granny and the Indians
Granny, the baby and the big gray thing
Parkin, Rex. *The red carpet*
Paterson, Diane. *Eat*
Smile for auntie
Patz, Nancy. *Pumpernickel tickle and mean green cheese*
Pearson, Tracey Campbell. *Sing a song of sixpence*
Peet, Bill (William Bartlett). *Big bad Bruce*
Buford the little bighorn
Chester the worldly pig
Countdown to Christmas
Cowardly Clyde
Eli
Hubert's hair-raising adventures
Huge Harold
Jennifer and Josephine
Jethro and Joel were a troll
Kermit the hermit

Merle the high flying squirrel
Randy's dandy lions
Postgate, Oliver. *Noggin and the whale*
Noggin the king
Potter, Beatrix. *The tale of Tom Kitten*
Prather, Ray. *Double dog dare*
Prelutsky, Jack. *The baby uggs are hatching*
The queen of Eene
The Random House book of poetry for children
The snopp on the sidewalk and other poems
Preston, Edna Mitchell. *Horrible Hepzibah*
Pop Corn and Ma Goodness
Pulver, Robin. *Mrs. Toggle's zipper*
Puner, Helen Walker. *The sitter who didn't sit*
Quackenbush, Robert M. *Funny bunnies*
Pete Pack Rat
Raskin, Ellen. *Franklin Stein*
Nothing ever happens on my block
Rayner, Shoo. *My first picture joke book*
Reid, Alastair. *Supposing*
Rey, H. A. (Hans Augusto). *Cecily G and the nine monkeys*
Curious George
Curious George gets a medal
Curious George rides a bike
Curious George takes a job
Elizabite, adventures of a carnivorous plant
Tit for tat
Rey, Margřet (Margřet Elisabeth Waldstein). *Billy's picture*
Curious George flies a kite
Curious George goes to the hospital
Rosen, Michael J. *Smelly jelly smelly fish*
You can't catch me!
Rossner, Judith. *What kind of feet does a bear have?*
Rounds, Glen. *The day the circus came to Lone Tree*
Roy, Ronald. *Three ducks went wandering*
Rubel, Nicole. *It came from the swamp*
Rusling, Albert. *The mouse and Mrs. Proudfoot*
Saddler, Allen. *The Archery contest*
The king gets fit
Sage, Michael. *Dippy dos and don'ts*
If you talked to a boar
Saltzberg, Barney. *Cromwell*
Samuels, Barbara. *Duncan and Dolores*
Sazer, Nina. *What do you think I saw?*
Schatell, Brian. *Midge and Fred*
Scheer, Julian. *Rain makes applesauce*
Schmidt, Eric von. *The young man who wouldn't hoe corn*
Schwalje, Marjory. *Mr. Angelo*
Schwartz, Alvin. *All of our noses are here and other stories*
Seligson, Susan. *The amazing Amos and the greatest couch on earth*

Amos: the story of an old dog and his couch
Sendak, Maurice. *Pierre*
Seuss, Dr. *And to think that I saw it on Mulberry Street*
Bartholomew and the Oobleck
The cat in the hat
The cat in the hat beginner book dictionary
The cat in the hat comes back!
The cat's quizzer
Did I ever tell you how lucky you are?
Dr. Seuss's ABC
Dr. Seuss's sleep book
The foot book
Fox in sox
A great day for up
Green eggs and ham
Happy birthday to you!
Hooper Humperdink...? Not him!
Hop on Pop
Horton hatches the egg
Horton hears a Who!
How the Grinch stole Christmas
I am not going to get up today!
I can lick 30 tigers today and other stories
I can read with my eyes shut
I can write!
I had trouble getting to Solla Sollew
If I ran the circus
If I ran the zoo
In a people house
The king's stilts
The Lorax
McElligot's pool
Marvin K. Mooney, will you please go now!
Mr. Brown can moo! Can you?
Oh say can you say?
Oh, the thinks you can think!
On beyond zebra
One fish, two fish, red fish, blue fish
Please try to remember the first of October!
Scrambled eggs super!
The shape of me and other stuff
The Sneetches, and other stories
There's a wocket in my pocket
Thidwick, the big-hearted moose
Wacky Wednesday
Shannon, George. *Beanboy*
Showalter, Jean B. *The donkey ride*
Silverstein, Shel. *A giraffe and a half*
Singer, Marilyn. *The dog who insisted he wasn't*
Slobodkina, Esphyr. *Caps for sale*
Pezzo the peddler and the circus elephant
Pezzo the peddler and the thirteen silly thieves
Smith, Jim. *The frog band and the onion seller*
The frog band and the owlnapper

Smith, Robert Paul. *Jack Mack*
Smith, William Jay. *Puptents and pebbles*
Spier, Peter. *Bored—nothing to do!*
 Oh, were they ever happy!
Spilka, Arnold. *A lion I can do without*
 A rumbudgin of nonsense
Spinelli, Eileen. *Thanksgiving at Tappletons'*
Stamaty, Mark Alan. *Minnie Maloney and Macaroni*
Steig, William. *Farmer Palmer's wagon ride*
Stevenson, James. *Happy Valentine's Day, Emma!*
 The worst person in the world at Crab Beach
Stinson, Kathy. *Those green things*
Stone, Rosetta. *Because a little bug went ka-choo!*
Stroyer, Poul. *It's a deal*
Suba, Susanne. *The monkeys and the pedlar*
Suhl, Yuri. *Simon Boom gives a wedding*
Sundgaard, Arnold. *Jethro's difficult dinosaur*
Tapio, Pat Decker. *The lady who saw the good side of everything*
Thaler, Mike. *Pack 109*
 The yellow brick toad
Thomas, Patricia. *"Stand back," said the elephant, "I'm going to sneeze!"*
Tobias, Tobi. *Jane wishing*
Tomkins, Jasper. *The catalog*
Tripp, Wallace. *My Uncle Podger*
Tulloch, Richard. *Stories from our house*
The twelve days of Christmas. English folk song. *Jack Kent's twelve days of Christmas*
Ueno, Noriko. *Elephant buttons*
Ungerer, Tomi. *The beast of Monsieur Racine*
 Crictor
 Emile
Van der Meer, Ron. *Oh Lord!*
Van Woerkom, Dorothy. *Donkey Ysabel*
 The queen who couldn't bake gingerbread
Viorst, Judith. *Sunday morning*
Waber, Bernard. *How to go about laying an egg*
 Nobody is perfick
Wahl, Jan. *Cabbage moon*
Watanabe, Shigeo. *What a good lunch!*
Watson, Clyde. *Hickory stick rag*
Weatherill, Stephen. *The very first Lucy Goose book*
Westcott, Nadine Bernard. *The lady with the alligator purse*
Wiese, Kurt. *Fish in the air*
Wiesner, William. *Happy-Go-Lucky*
 Turnabout
Willard, Nancy. *Simple pictures are best*
Williams, Barbara. *Jeremy isn't hungry*
Williams, Jay. *School for sillies*

Wiseman, Bernard. *Tails are not for painting*
Wolkstein, Diane. *The legend of Sleepy Hollow*
Wood, Audrey. *King Bidgood's in the bathtub*
Wright, Jill. *The old woman and the Willy Nilly Man*
Yorinks, Arthur. *Company's coming*
Zemach, Harve. *The tricks of Master Dabble*
Zemach, Margot. *It could always be worse*
Zimmerman, Andrea Griffing. *Yetta, the trickster*

Hungary *see* Foreign lands – Hungary

Hunting *see* Sports – hunting

Hurrying *see* Behavior – hurrying

Hyenas *see* Animals – hyenas

Ice skating *see* Sports – ice skating

Iceland *see* Foreign lands – Iceland

Iguanas *see* Reptiles – iguanas

Illness

Aliki. *I wish I was sick, too!*
Anholt, Catherine. *Truffles is sick*
Arnold, Katrin. *Anna joins in*
Bains, Rae. *Hiccups, hiccups*
Barrett, Judi. *An apple a day*
Bemelmans, Ludwig. *Madeline's Christmas*
Berger, Melvin. *Germs make me sick!*
 Ouch! a book about cuts, scratches and scrapes
 Why I cough, sneeze, shiver, hiccup and yawn
Bradman, Tony. *Through my window*
Brown, Margaret Wise. *When the wind blew*
Bruna, Dick. *Miffy in the hospital*
Buckley, Helen Elizabeth. *Someday with my father*
Bucknall, Caroline. *One bear in the hospital*
Carrick, Carol. *Old Mother Witch*
Cassedy, Sylvia. *The best cat suit of all*
Chalmers, Mary. *Come to the doctor, Harry*
Charlip, Remy. *"Mother, mother I feel sick"*
Cherry, Lynne. *Who's sick today?*
Chislett, Gail. *Melinda's no's cold*
Christelow, Eileen. *Henry and the red stripes*
Ciliotta, Claire. *"Why am I going to the hospital?"*

Cole, Joanna. *Get well, Clown-Arounds!*
Craven, Carolyn. *What the mailman brought*
De Groat, Diane. *Alligator's toothache*
Delton, Judy. *Groundhog's Day at the doctor*
 It happened on Thursday
De Paola, Tomie (Thomas Anthony). *Now one foot, now the other*
DeWitt, Jamie. *Jamie's turn*
Duff, Maggie (Margaret K.). *The princess and the pumpkin*
Dugan, Barbara. *Loop the loop*
Duvoisin, Roger Antoine. *The Christmas whale*
Eberstadt, Isabel. *What is for my birthday?*
Elliott, Ingrid Glatz. *Hospital roadmap*
Eriksson, Eva. *Jealousy*
Fassler, David. *What's a virus, anyway?*
Fern, Eugene. *Pepito's story*
Fine, Anne. *Poor Monty*
Fleischman, Sid. *Kate's secret riddle*
Gackenbach, Dick. *Hattie be quiet, Hattie be good*
 What's Claude doing?
Galbraith, Kathryn Osebold. *Spots are special*
Gay, Marie-Louise. *Rainy day magic*
Goldsmith, Howard. *Little lost dog*
Gomi, Taro. *Toot!*
Gretz, Susanna. *Teddy bears cure a cold*
Gullikson, Sandy. *Trouble for breakfast*
Hamm, Diane Johnston. *Grandma drives a motor bed*
Hautzig, Deborah. *Get well, Granny Bird*
Hewett, Joan. *Fly away free*
Hogan, Paula Z. *The hospital scares me*
Holl, Adelaide. *Small Bear solves a mystery*
Hurd, Edith Thacher. *Johnny Lion's bad day*
Hurd, Thacher. *Tomato soup*
Ives, Penny. *Mrs. Santa Claus*
Jenkins, Jordan. *Learning about love*
Johnson, Louise. *Malunda*
Keller, Beverly. *When mother got the flu*
Keller, Holly. *When Francie was sick*
Kibbey, Marsha. *My grammy*
Knotts, Howard. *The lost Christmas*
Komoda, Beerly. *The winter day*
Koplow, Lesley. *Tanya and the tobo man / Tanya y el hombre tobo*
Kraus, Robert. *The first robin*
Kroll, Steven. *The big bunny and the Easter eggs*
Kunhardt, Edith. *Trick or treat, Danny!*
Laskin, Pamela L. *Wish upon a star*
Le Guin, Ursula K. *A visit from Dr. Katz*
Lerner, Marguerite Rush. *Dear little mumps child*
 Michael gets the measles
 Peter gets the chickenpox
Lewin, Betsy. *Hip, hippo, hooray!*
Lexau, Joan M. *Benjie on his own*

Lobel, Arnold. *A holiday for Mister Muster*
London, Jonathan. *The lion who had asthma*
Lyon, George-Ella. *Cecil's story*
McDonald, Amy. *Rachel Fister's blister*
MacLachlan, Patricia. *Mama one, Mama two*
McPhail, David. *Adam's smile*
 The bear's toothache
Maestro, Giulio. *Leopard is sick*
Mann, Peggy. *King Laurence, the alarm clock*
Marshall, James. *Yummers!*
Mayer, Mercer. *Ah-choo*
 Hiccup
Morris, Ann. *Eleanora Mousie catches a cold*
Moss, Elaine. *Polar*
Mueller, Virginia. *Monster's birthday hiccups*
Nourse, Alan Edward. *Lumps, bumps and rashes*
Numeroff, Laura Joffe. *Phoebe Dexter has Harriet Peterson's sniffles*
Ormerod, Jan. *This little nose*
Ostrovsky, Vivian. *Mumps!*
Pace, Elizabeth. *Chris gets ear tubes*
Pedersen, Judy. *The tiny patient*
Polhamus, Jean Burt. *Doctor Dinosaur*
Porte, Barbara Ann. *Harry's dog*
Rockwell, Anne F. *The emergency room*
 Sick in bed
Rogers, Fred. *Going to the hospital*
Rohmer, Harriet. *Atariba and Niguayona*
Roth, Susan L. *We'll ride elephants through Brooklyn*
Sachar, Louis. *Monkey soup*
Sandberg, Inger. *Nicholas' red day*
Sanford, Doris. *David has AIDS*
Say, Allen. *A river dream*
Seignobosc, Françoise. *Biquette, the white goat*
Sharmat, Marjorie Weinman. *I want mama*
Shay, Arthur. *What happens when you go to the hospital*
Showers, Paul. *No measles, no mumps for me*
Siracusa, Catherine. *No mail for Mitchell*
Sonneborn, Ruth A. *I love Gram*
Sonnenschein, Harriet. *Harold's runaway nose*
Steel, Danielle. *Max's daddy goes to the hospital*
Stein, Sara Bonnett. *A hospital story*
Stephenson, Dorothy. *How to scare a lion*
Thurber, James. *Many moons*, ill. by Marc Simont
 Many moons, ill. by Louis Slobodkin
Tobias, Tobi. *A day off*
Trez, Denise. *The royal hiccups*
Tyler, Linda Wagner. *The sick-in-bed birthday book*
Udry, Janice May. *Mary Jo's grandmother*
Vigna, Judith. *I wish my daddy didn't drink so much*
Wadhams, Margaret. *Anna*
Wahl, Jan. *Jamie's tiger*

Watson, Wendy. *Tales for a winter's eve*
Watts, Marjorie-Ann. *Crocodile medicine*
 Crocodile plaster
Weber, Alfons. *Elizabeth gets well*
West, Colin. *The king's toothache*
Whitney, Alma Marshak. *Just awful*
Wickstrom, Sylvie (Sylvie Kantrovitz).
 Mothers can't get sick
Wild, Margaret. *Mr. Nick's knitting*
Wildsmith, Brian. *Carousel*
Williams, Barbara. *Albert's toothache*
Williams, Vera B. *Music, music for everyone*
Wolde, Gunilla. *Betsy and the chicken pox*
 Betsy and the doctor
Ziefert, Harriet. *When daddy had the chicken pox*

Illness – Alzheimer's

Guthrie, Donna. *Grandpa doesn't know it's me*
Karkowsky, Nancy. *Grandma's soup*
Nelson, Vaunda Micheaux. *Always Gramma*
Sakai, Kimiko. *Sachiko means happiness*

Illusions, optical *see* Optical illusions

Illustrators, children *see* Children as illustrators

Imaginary friends *see* Imagination – imaginary friends

Imagination

Abisch, Roz. *Open your eyes*
Adam, Barbara. *The big big box*
Adler, David A. *I know I'm a witch*
Agee, Jon. *Ellsworth*
 The incredible painting of Felix Clousseau
Aiken, Joan. *Arabel and Mortimer*
Aitken, Amy. *Kate and Mona in the jungle*
 Ruby!
 Ruby, the red knight
Alexander, Martha G. *Bobo's dream*
 Marty McGee's space lab, no girls allowed
Allan, Nicholas. *The thing that ate Aunt Julia*
Allen, Jeffrey. *The secret life of Mr. Weird*
Allen, Pamela. *I wish I had a pirate suit*
 A lion in the night
Andersen, H. C. (Hans Christian). *The emperor's new clothes*, ill. by Erik Blegvad
The emperor's new clothes, ill. by Virginia Lee Burton
The emperor's new clothes, ill. by Robert Byrd
The emperor's new clothes, ill. by Jack and Irene Delano
The emperor's new clothes, ill. by Hélène Desputeaux

The emperor's new clothes, ill. by Birte Dietz
The emperor's new clothes, ill. by Dorothée Duntze
The emperor's new clothes, ill. by Pamela Baldwin Ford
The emperor's new clothes, ill. by Jack Kent
The emperor's new clothes, ill. by Monika Laimgruber
The emperor's new clothes, ill. by Anne F. Rockwell
The emperor's new clothes, ill. by Janet Stevens
The emperor's new clothes, ill. by Nadine Bernard Westcott
Anderson, C. W. (Clarence Williams). *Linda and the Indians*
Anderson, Joan. *Harry's helicopter*
Anderson, Wayne. *Dragon*
Anglund, Joan Walsh. *Cowboy's secret life*
Anno, Mitsumasa. *Anno's alphabet*
 Anno's animals
 Anno's Britain
 Anno's counting book
 Anno's counting house
 Anno's flea market
 Anno's Italy
 Anno's journey
 Anno's magical ABC
 Anno's U.S.A.
 Dr. Anno's magical midnight circus
 The king's flower
 Topsy turvies: more pictures to stretch the imagination
 Topsy turvies: pictures to stretch the imagination
 Upside-downers
Armour, Richard Willard. *Animals on the ceiling*
Arnold, Tedd. *No jumping on the bed!*
Asch, Frank. *City sandwich*
 Goodnight horsey
 Rebecka
Ayal, Ora. *The adventures of Chester the chest*
 Ugbu
Bach, Othello. *Lilly, Willy and the mail-order witch*
Baillie, Allan. *Drac and the gremlin*
Baker, Alan. *Benjamin bounces back*
Baker, Betty. *My sister says*
Baker, Keith. *The magic fan*
Balet, Jan B. *Ned and Ed and the lion*
Bang, Molly. *The grey lady and the strawberry snatcher*
Banks, Kate. *Alphabet soup*
Bannon, Laura. *The best house in the world*
Barber, Antonia. *Satchelmouse and the dinosaurs*
Barrett, Judi. *Cloudy with a chance of meatballs*

I hate to go to bed
Barry, Katharina. *A bug to hug*
Barthelme, Donald. *The slightly irregular fire engine*
Bate, Lucy. *How Georgina drove the car very carefully from Boston to New York*
Baumann, Kurt. *The paper airplane*
Bayley, Nicola. *Crab cat*
　Elephant cat
　Parrot cat
　Polar bear cat
　Spider cat
Beech, Caroline. *Peas again for lunch*
Behrens, June. *Can you walk the plank?*
Beim, Jerrold. *The taming of Toby*
Benedictus, Roger. *Fifty million sausages*
Benjamin, Alan. *Ribtickle Town*
Bennett, Rowena. *The day is dancing and other poems*
　Songs from around a toadstool table
Berenstain, Stan. *The Berenstain bears in the dark*
Berry, Christine. *Mama went walking*
Blakeley, Peggy. *What shall I be tomorrow?*
Blegvad, Lenore. *Anna Banana and me*
　Rainy day Kate
Blocksma, Mary. *The pup went up*
Blos, Joan W. *Martin's hats*
Blundell, Tony. *Joe on Sunday*
Bodsworth, Nan. *Monkey business*
Boegehold, Betty. *Hurray for Pippa!*
　In the castle of cats
Boon, Emilie. *Peterkin meets a star*
　Peterkin's wet walk
Bottner, Barbara. *Mean Maxine*
　Myra
　There was nobody there
Boutell, Clarence Burley. *The fat baron*
Bowers, Kathleen Rice. *At this very minute*
Boyd, Lizi. *Sweet dreams, Willy*
　Willy and the cardboard boxes
Boyd, Selma. *I met a polar bear*
Brenner, Anita. *I want to fly*
Briggs, Raymond. *Walking in the air*
Brisson, Pat. *Magic carpet*
Bröger, Achim. *Francie's paper puppy*
　Little Harry
Brooks, Gregory. *Monroe's island*
Browne, Anthony. *Bear goes to town*
　Changes
　Gorilla
　The little bear book
　Look what I've got!
Bruce, Sheilah B. *The radish day jubilee*
Buckaway, C. M. *Alfred, the dragon who lost his flame*
Buckingham, Simon. *Alec and his flying bed*
Budd, Lillian. *The people on Long Ago Street*
Bulette, Sara. *The elf in the singing tree*
Burningham, John. *Come away from the water, Shirley*

John Patrick Norman McHennessy—the boy who was always late
Time to get out of the bath, Shirley
Where's Julius?
Would you rather...
Bursik, Rose. *Amelia's fantastic flight*
Calders, Pere. *Brush*
Callen, Larry. *Dashiel and the night*
Carmi, Giora. *And Shira imagined*
Carrick, Carol. *Patrick's dinosaurs*
　What happened to Patrick's dinosaurs?
Carrier, Lark. *Scout and Cody*
　There was a hill...
Carroll, Lewis. *The nursery "Alice"*, ill. by Sir John Tenniel
Cazet, Denys. *Daydreams*
Chalmers, Mary. *The cat who liked to pretend*
Chapouton, Anne-Marie. *Sebastian is always late*
Chevalier, Christa. *Spence and the sleepytime monster*
Chislett, Gail. *The rude visitors*
Chorao, Kay. *Lester's overnight*
Cole, Babette. *The trouble with Uncle*
Collins, Pat Lowery. *My friend Andrew*
Cooper, Elizabeth K. *The fish from Japan*
Craig, Helen. *Susie and Alfred in the knight, the princess and the dragon*
Craig, M. Jean. *The dragon in the clock box*
Craven, Carolyn. *What the mailman brought*
Creighton, Jill. *Maybe a monster*
　One day there was nothing to do
Crowley, Michael. *The new kid on Spurwick Ave.*
　New kid on Spurwick Ave.
Cummings, E. E. (Edward Estlin). *Fairy tales*
Cutler, Ivor. *Herbert*
Davis, Douglas F. *There's an elephant in the garage*
Degen, Bruce. *Teddy bear towers*
Delaney, A. *Monster tracks?*
Delessert, Etienne. *A long long song*
Demarest, Chris L. *No peas for Nellie*
　Orville's odyssey
De Regniers, Beatrice Schenk. *Laura's story*
　A little house of your own
　Waiting for mama
　What can you do with a shoe?
De Veaux, Alexis. *An enchanted hair tale*
Devlin, Wende. *Aunt Agatha, there's a lion under the couch!*
Dickinson, Mary. *Alex and Roy*
Dickinson, Mike. *My dad doesn't even notice*
DiFiori, Lawrence. *If I had a little car*
D'Ignazio, Fred. *Katie and the computer*
Dobrin, Arnold Jack. *Josephine's 'magination*
Doolittle, Eileen. *World of wonders*
Dorian, Marguerite. *When the snow is blue*
Dowling, Paul. *Splodger*

Drescher, Henrik. *Looking for Santa Claus*

Edwards, Patricia Kier. *Chester and Uncle Willoughby*

Ekker, Ernest A. *What is beyond the hill?*

Elizabeth Winthrop. *A very noisy girl*

Elzbieta. *Dikou and the mysterious moon sheep*

Etherington, Frank. *The spaghetti word race*

Ets, Marie Hall. *In the forest*

Eversole, Robyn Harbert. *The magic house*

Faulkner, Matt. *The amazing voyage of Jackie Grace*

Felix, Monique. *The further adventures of the little mouse trapped in a book*
The story of a little mouse trapped in a book

Fenner, Carol. *Tigers in the cellar*

Fenton, Edward. *Fierce John*

Fleischman, Paul. *Rondo in C*

Fontaine, Jan. *The spaghetti tree*

Francis, Frank. *The magic wallpaper*

Franklin, Jonathan. *Don't wake the baby*

Freeman, Don. *The paper party*
Quiet! There's a canary in the library

Furtado, Jo. *Sorry, Miss Folio!*

Gackenbach, Dick. *Harry and the terrible whatzit*
Mag the magnificent
Supposes

Gage, Wilson. *Mrs. Gaddy and the ghost*

Galbraith, Kathryn Osebold. *Spots are special*

Gay, Marie-Louise. *Rainy day magic*

Gillham, Bill. *What can you do?*

Glass, Andrew. *My brother tries to make me laugh*

Goennel, Heidi. *If I were a penguin ...*

Greenstein, Elaine. *Emily and the crows*

Grejniec, Michael. *When I open my eyes*

Greve, Andreas. *Christopher's dream car*

Guy, Ginger Foglesong. *Black crow, black crow*

Gwynne, Fred. *A little pigeon toad*

Hamsa, Bobbie. *Your pet bear*
Your pet beaver
Your pet camel
Your pet elephant
Your pet giraffe
Your pet kangaroo
Your pet penguin
Your pet sea lion

Hanlon, Emily. *What if a lion eats me and I fall into a hippopotamus' mud hole?*

Haseley, Dennis. *The thieves' market*

Haus, Felice. *Beep! Beep! I'm a jeep*

Heller, Nicholas. *An adventure at sea*
The front hall carpet
A troll story

Hennessy, B. G. *The dinosaur who lived in my backyard*

Hillert, Margaret. *What is it?*

Himler, Ronald. *The girl on the yellow giraffe*

Hindley, Judy. *Maybe it's a pirate*

Hines, Anna Grossnickle. *Bethany for real*

Hoban, Russell. *The flight of Bembel Rudzuk Goodnight*
The great gum drop robbery
The rain door

Hoffmann, E. T. A. *The nutcracker*, ill. by Francesca Crespi
The nutcracker, ill. by Rachel Isadora
The nutcracker, ill. by Maurice Sendak
The nutcracker, ill. by Lisbeth Zwerger

Holabird, Katharine. *Alexander and the magic boat*

Holl, Adelaide. *Most-of-the-time Maxie*

Holleyman, Sonia. *Mona the vampire*

Holman, Felice. *Victoria's castle*

Hood, Thomas. *Before I go to sleep*

Hooker, Ruth. *Matthew the cowboy*

Horwitz, Elinor Lander. *Sometimes it happens*

Howard, Jane R. *When I'm sleepy*

Hughes, Shirley. *Up and up*

Hurd, Edith Thacher. *The white horse*

Hutchins, H. J. (Hazel J.). *Nicholas at the library*

Inkpen, Mick. *The blue balloon*
If I had a pig
If I had a sheep
One bear at bedtime

Isadora, Rachel. *The pirates of Bedford Street*

Ivanov, Anatoly. *Ol' Jake's lucky day*

James, Simon. *Dear Mr. Blueberry*

Janosch. *Hey Presto! You're a bear!*

Jenkin-Pearce, Susie. *The enchanted garden*

Jeschke, Susan. *Tamar and the tiger*

Jewell, Nancy. *Try and catch me*

Johnson, Crockett. *The blue ribbon puppies*
Ellen's lion
Harold and the purple crayon
Harold at the North Pole
Harold's ABC
Harold's circus
Harold's fairy tale
Harold's trip to the sky
A picture for Harold's room

Johnson, Elizabeth. *All in free but Janey*

Johnson, Jane. *Sybil and the blue rabbit*

Johnston, Deborah. *Mathew Michael's beastly day*

Jonas, Ann. *The trek*

Kalman, Maira. *Hey Willy, see the pyramids!*

Keats, Ezra Jack. *Dreams*
Regards to the man in the moon
The trip

Keeping, Charles. *Willie's fire-engine*

Kellogg, Steven (Stephen). *Ralph's secret weapon*

King, Larry L. *Because of Lozo Brown*

Kitamura, Satoshi. *Lily takes a walk*
Knaff, Jean Christian. *Manhattan*
Knight, Hilary. *Hilary Knight's the owl and the pussy-cat*
Kojima, Naomi. *The flying grandmother*
Krahn, Fernando. *Amanda and the mysterious carpet*
Krauss, Ruth. *A moon or a button*
  Open house for butterflies
  Somebody else's nut tree, and other tales from children
  This thumbprint
  A very special house
Kroll, Steven. *Are you pirates?*
  The magic rocket
  Toot! Toot!
  The tyrannosaurus game
Krupp, Robin Rector. *Get set to wreck!*
Kumin, Maxine. *Follow the fall*
Kuskin, Karla. *Which horse is William?*
Lasell, Fen. *Fly away goose*
Lester, Alison. *Magic beach*
Le-Tan, Pierre. *Timothy's dream book*
  Visit to the North Pole
Lewis, Stephen. *Zoo city*
Lexau, Joan M. *A house so big*
Lifton, Betty Jean. *The secret seller*
Lindbergh, Reeve. *Benjamin's barn*
Lindgren, Barbro. *The wild baby goes to sea*
Lionni, Leo. *Let's make rabbits*
Lloyd, David. *Grandma and the pirate*
Löfgren, Ulf. *Alvin the pirate*
  The wonderful tree
London, Jonathan. *The lion who had asthma*
Long, Claudia. *Albert's story*
McClintock, Marshall. *What have I got?*
McConnachie, Brian. *Elmer and the chickens vs. the big league*
McCormack, John E. *Rabbit tales*
McDermott, Beverly Brodsky. *The crystal apple*
McHargue, Georgess. *Private zoo*
McKissack, Patricia C. *The king's new clothes*
McLenighan, Valjean. *What you see is what you get*
McLeod, Emilie Warren. *One snail and me*
McLerran, Alice. *Roxaboxen*
McMullan, Kate. *The noisy giant's tea party*
McPhail, David. *The cereal box*
  Mistletoe
  Pig Pig and the magic photo album
  Pig Pig rides
  The train
Mansell, Dom. *If dinosaurs came to town*
Marceau, Marcel. *The story of Bip*
Mariotti, Mario. *Hands off!*
  Hanimations
Marshall, James. *George and Martha round and round*
  Three up a tree
Martin, Rafe. *Will's mammoth*

Marzollo, Jean. *Pretend you're a cat*
  The silver bear
Matura, Mustapha. *Moon jump*
Matus, Greta. *Where are you, Jason?*
Mayer, Mercer. *Bubble bubble*
  I am a hunter
  Terrible troll
Mazer, Anne. *The salamander room*
Mogensen, Jan. *The forty-six little men*
Morgan, Michaela. *Edward gets a pet*
  Visitors for Edward
Morris, Winifred. *What if the shark wears tennis shoes?*
Moser, Erwin. *The crow in the snow and other bedtime stories*
Most, Bernard. *If the dinosaurs came back*
Murphy, Jill. *What next, baby bear!*
Nerlove, Miriam. *I meant to clean my room today*
  If all the world were paper
Nesbit, Edith. *Cockatoucan*
Ness, Evaline. *Sam, Bangs, and moonshine*
Newton, Laura P. *William the vehicle king*
Nolan, Dennis. *The castle builder*
Nygren, Tord. *The red thread*
Oakley, Graham. *Graham Oakley's magical changes*
Olsen, Ib Spang. *The grown-up trap*
Oram, Hiawyn. *In the attic*
Ormerod, Jan. *The saucepan game*
Oxenbury, Helen. *729 curious creatures*
  729 merry mix-ups
  729 puzzle people
Pack, Robert. *How to catch a crocodile*
Paterson, Diane. *The bathtub ocean*
Pavey, Peter. *I'm Taggarty Toad*
Peppé, Rodney. *The kettleship pirates*
Pfanner, Louise. *Louise builds a house*
Pinkwater, Daniel Manus. *I was a second grade werewolf*
  Tooth-gnasher superflash
  Wempires
Pirani, Felix. *Abigail at the beach*
Pittman, Helena Clare. *Once when I was scared*
Polacco, Patricia. *Appelemando's dreams*
Pomerantz, Charlotte. *Timothy Tall Feather*
Ponti, Claude. *Adele's album*
Postma, Lidia. *The stolen mirror*
Prelutsky, Jack. *The baby uggs are hatching*
  Ride a purple pelican
  The snopp on the sidewalk and other poems
Price, Mathew. *Have you seen my sister?*
Price-Thomas, Brian. *The magic ark*
Pringle, Laurence. *Jesse builds a road*
  The pudgy book of make-believe
Radlauer, Ruth Shaw. *Of course, you're a horse!*
Radley, Gail. *The night Stella hid the stars*
Raskin, Ellen. *Franklin Stein*
  Spectacles

Ratnett, Michael. *Jenny's bear*
Reavin, Sam. *Hurray for Captain Jane!*
Reid, Alastair. *Supposing*
Renberg, Dalia Hardof. *Hello, clouds!*
Ressner, Phil. *Dudley Pippin*
Rice, Inez. *A long long time*
  The March wind
Riches, Judith. *Giraffes have more fun*
Riddle, Tohby. *Careful with that ball,*
  Eugene!
Ringi, Kjell (Arne Sorensen). *My father*
  and I
Roberts, Thom. *Pirates in the park*
Rodgers, Frank. *Who's afraid of the ghost*
  train?
Root, Phyllis. *Moon tiger*
Rosen, Winifred. *Dragons hate to be discreet*
Rosner, Ruth. *Arabba gah zee, Marissa and*
  me!
Russ, Lavinia. *Alec's sand castle*
Russo, Marisabina. *Why do grownups have*
  all the fun?
Sabraw, John. *I wouldn't be scared*
Salter, Heidi. *Taddy McFinley and the great*
  grey grimly
Samton, Sheila White. *Jenny's journey*
Sato, Satoru. *I wish I had a big, big tree*
Schoberle, Ceile. *Beyond the Milky Way*
Schreier, Joshua. *Luigi's all-night parking lot*
Scott, Ann Herbert. *Big Cowboy Western*
Seligson, Susan. *The amazing Amos and the*
  greatest couch on earth
  Amos ahoy: a couch adventure on land
  and sea
  Amos: the story of an old dog and his
  couch
Sendak, Maurice. *In the night kitchen*
  The sign on Rosie's door
  Where the wild things are
Seuss, Dr. *And to think that I saw it on*
  Mulberry Street
  McElligot's pool
  Oh say can you say?
  Oh, the thinks you can think!
Sharmat, Marjorie Weinman. *My mother*
  never listens to me
Shaw, Charles Green. *It looked like spilt*
  milk
Shecter, Ben. *Conrad's castle*
  If I had a ship
Sherman, Ivan. *I am a giant*
Shimin, Symeon. *I wish there were two of me*
Shulevitz, Uri. *One Monday morning*
Sicotte, Virginia. *A riot of quiet*
Siepmann, Jane. *The lion on Scott Street*
Simmonds, Posy. *Lulu and the flying babies*
Skorpen, Liesel Moak. *If I had a lion*
Sleator, William. *That's silly*
Slobodkin, Louis. *Clear the track*
  Magic Michael
Smith, Jim. *Nimbus the explorer*

Smith, Maggie (Margaret C.). *My*
  grandma's chair
  There's a witch under the stairs
Stanley, Diane. *Birdsong lullaby*
Steiner, Charlotte. *Look what Tracy found*
Stemp, Robin. *Guy and the flowering plum*
  tree
Stevens, Cat. *Teaser and the firecat*
Stevenson, James. *Worse than Willy!*
Stevenson, Jocelyn. *Red and the pumpkins*
Stinson, Kathy. *The dressed up book*
  Those green things
Stoddard, Sandol. *Curl up small*
  The thinking book
Stone, Kazuko G. *Goodnight Twinklegator*
Sundgaard, Arnold. *Meet Jack Appleknocker*
Supraner, Robyn. *Would you rather be a*
  tiger?
Sutherland, Harry A. *Dad's car wash*
Tafuri, Nancy. *Junglewalk*
Taniuchi, Kota. *Trolley*
Testa, Fulvio. *The land where the ice cream*
  grows
Thayer, Jane. *Andy and the wild worm*
Thomas, Ianthe. *Walk home tired, Billy*
  Jenkins
Thompson, Richard. *Effie's bath*
  Gurgle, bubble, splash
  Jenny's Neighbours
  Jesse on the night train
  Sky full of babies
Tompert, Ann. *Little Fox goes to the end of*
  the world
Townson, Hazel. *Terrible Tuesday*
  What on earth...?
Turkle, Brinton. *The sky dog*
Tusa, Tricia. *Camilla's new hairdo*
Udry, Janice May. *Is Susan here?*
Updike, David. *An autumn tale*
Van Allsburg, Chris. *The garden of Abdul*
  Gasazi
  Jumanji
  The mysteries of Harris Burdick
  The polar express
Van Caster, Nancy. *An alligator lives in*
  Benjamin's house
Velthuijs, Max. *Crocodile's masterpiece*
  The painter and the bird
Vigna, Judith. *Boot weather*
Viorst, Judith. *The good-bye book*
  My mama says there aren't any zombies,
  ghosts, vampires, creatures, demons,
  monsters, fiends, goblins, or things
Vogel, Ilse-Margaret. *The don't be scared*
  book
Vreeken, Elizabeth. *The boy who would not*
  say his name
Wahl, Robert. *Pyxx*
Watson, Clyde. *Midnight moon*
Wayland, April Halprin. *To Rabbittown*
Weisner, David. *Hurricane*

Wells, Rosemary. *Good night, Fred*
  A lion for Lewis
Westell, Kerry. *Amanda's book*
Whittington, Mary K. *Carmina, come dance!*
Willard, Nancy. *A visit to William Blake's inn*
Williams, Vera B. *Cherries and cherry pits*
Winthrop, Elizabeth. *Bunk beds*
Woodruff, Elvira. *Tubtime*
Woolf, Virginia. *Nurse Lugton's curtain*
Yardley, Joanna. *The red ball*
Yorinks, Arthur. *Hey, Al*
  Louis the fish
Young, Miriam Burt. *Jellybeans for breakfast*
Young, Ruth. *A trip to Mars*
Ziefert, Harriet. *Lewis the fire fighter*
Zimelman, Nathan. *Once when I was five*
Zolotow, Charlotte (Shapiro). *The seashore book*
  When I have a son

Imagination – imaginary friends

Alexander, Martha G. *And my mean old mother will be sorry, Blackboard Bear*
  Blackboard Bear
  I sure am glad to see you, Blackboard Bear
  I'll protect you from the jungle beasts
  We're in big trouble, Blackboard Bear
Andrews, F. Emerson (Frank Emerson). *Nobody comes to dinner*
Anglund, Joan Walsh. *Cowboy and his friend*
  The cowboy's Christmas
Berger, Barbara Helen. *When the sun rose*
Bornstein, Ruth Lercher. *The seedling child*
Bram, Elizabeth. *There is someone standing on my head*
Brewster, Patience. *Nobody*
Brighton, Catherine. *My hands, my world*
Burningham, John. *Aldo*
Cummings, Pat. *Jimmy Lee did it*
Dauer, Rosamond. *My friend, Jasper Jones*
Dillon, Barbara. *The beast in the bed*
Dinan, Carolyn. *The lunch box monster*
Geringer, Laura. *Look out, look out, it's coming!*
Greenfield, Eloise. *Me and Nessie*
Hazen, Barbara Shook. *The gorilla did it!*
  Gorilla wants to be the baby
Henkes, Kevin. *Jessica*
Hiller, Catherine. *Argentaybee and the boonie*
Hoff, Syd. *The horse in Harry's room*
Jeschke, Susan. *Angela and Bear*
  The devil did it
Joosse, Barbara M. *The thinking place*
Krahn, Fernando. *The creepy thing*
Krensky, Stephen. *The lion upstairs*
Langner, Nola. *By the light of the silvery moon*

Morris, Terry Nell. *Good night, dear monster!*
Noble, June. *Two homes for Lynn*
Oram, Hiawyn. *Ned and the Joybaloo*
Patz, Nancy. *No thumpin' no bumpin' no rumpus tonight!*
Pinkwater, Daniel Manus. *Pickle creature*
Ross, Tony. *Hugo and Oddsock*
Rovetch, Lissa. *Trigwater did it*
St. George, Judith. *The Halloween pumpkin smasher*
Steiner, Charlotte. *Lulu*
Strauss, Gwen. *The night shimmy*
Thaler, Mike. *My puppy*
Thayer, Jane. *Andy and his fine friends*
Watts, Marjorie-Ann. *Zebra goes to school*
Zemke, Deborah. *The shadow of Matilda Hunt*
Zolotow, Charlotte (Shapiro). *Three funny friends*

Imitation *see* Behavior – imitation

In and out *see* Concepts – in and out

Incentive *see* Character traits – ambition

Independence Day *see* Holidays – Fourth of July

India *see* Foreign lands – India

Indians, American *see* Indians of North America; Indians of South America

Indians of North America

Abisch, Roz. *'Twas in the moon of wintertime*
Accorsi, William. *My name is Pocahontas*
Aliki. *Corn is maize*
Anderson, C. W. (Clarence Williams). *Linda and the Indians*
Ata, Te. *Baby rattlesnake*
Aulaire, Ingri Mortenson d'. *Pocahontas*
Baker, Betty. *And me, coyote!*
  Rat is dead and ant is sad
  Three fools and a horse
Baker, Laura Nelson. *O children of the wind and pines*
Baker, Olaf. *Where the buffaloes begin*
Baylor, Byrd. *The desert is theirs*
  A God on every mountain top
  Hawk, I'm your brother
  If you are a hunter of fossils
  Moon song
  When clay sings
Beatty, Hetty Burlingame. *Little Owl Indian*
Behrens, June. *Powwow*
Belting, Natalia Maree. *Verity Mullens and the Indian*
Bernstein, Margery. *Coyote goes hunting for fire*

Street rhymes around the world

Indians of South America

Flora. *Feathers like a rainbow*
Reynolds, Jan. *Amazon*
Van Laan, Nancy. *The legend of El Dorado*

Indifference *see* Behavior – indifference

Indifference *see* Behavior – indifference

Individuality *see* Character traits – individuality

Individuality *see* Character traits – individuality

Indonesian Archipelago *see* Foreign lands – South Sea Islands

Insects

Adelson, Leone. *Please pass the grass*
Aldis, Dorothy. *Quick as a wink*
Barrett, Judi. *Snake is totally tail*
Belpré, Pura. *Perez and Martina*
Bernstein, Joanne E. *Creepy crawly critter riddles*
Boegehold, Betty. *Bear underground*
Brouillette, Jeanne S. *Moths*
Carter, David A. *How many bugs in a box?*
Colby, C. B. (Carroll Burleigh). *Who lives there?*
Cole, Joanna. *Find the hidden insect*
Conklin, Gladys. *I caught a lizard*
  We like bugs
  When insects are babies
Cristini, Ermanno. *In the pond*
Farber, Norma. *Never say ugh to a bug*
Fisher, Aileen Lucia. *When it comes to bugs*
Gackenbach, Dick. *Little bug*
George, Jean Craighead. *All upon a stone*
Geraghty, Paul. *Over the steamy swamp*
Goudey, Alice E. *Red legs*
Griffen, Elizabeth. *A dog's book of bugs*
Heller, Ruth. *How to hide a butterfly*
Ipcar, Dahlov. *Bug city*
Jaynes, Ruth M. *That's what it is!*
Katz, Bobbi. *The creepy crawly book*
Kaufmann, John. *Flying giants of long ago*
Kraus, Robert. *How spider saved Valentine's Day*
Lavies, Bianca. *Tree trunk traffic*
Lionni, Leo. *Inch by inch*
Lobel, Arnold. *Grasshopper on the road*
McKissack, Patricia C. *Big bug book of counting*
  Big bug book of opposites
  Big bug book of places to go
  Big bug book of the alphabet
Maxner, Joyce. *Lady Bugatti*

Milne, A. A. (Alan Alexander). *Pooh and some bees*
Parker, Nancy Winslow. *Bugs*
Petie, Haris. *Billions of bugs*
Peyo. *The Smurfs and their woodland friends*
Roop, Peter. *Going buggy!*
Rounds, Glen. *The boll weevil*
Selsam, Millicent E. *Where do they go? Insects in winter*
Seymour, Peter. *Insects*
Soya, Kiyoshi. *A house of leaves*
Stone, Rosetta. *Because a little bug went ka-choo!*
Tison, Annette. *Animal hide-and-seek*
Van Woerkom, Dorothy. *Hidden messages*

Insects – ants

Æsop. *The ant and the dove*, ill. by Ching
Allinson, Beverley. *Effie*
Calder, S. J. *If you were an ant*
Cameron, Polly. *"I can't," said the ant*
Ciardi, John. *John J. Plenty and Fiddler Dan*
Clay, Pat. *Ants*
Dorros, Arthur. *Ant cities*
Freschet, Berniece. *The ants go marching*
Hepworth, Cathi. *ANTics! an alphabetical anthology*
Peet, Bill (William Bartlett). *The ant and the elephant*
Pluckrose, Henry Arthur. *Ants*
Van Allsburg, Chris. *Two bad ants*

Insects – bees

Baran, Tancy. *Bees*
Barton, Byron. *Buzz, buzz, buzz*
Ernst, Lisa Campbell. *A colorful adventure of the bee who left home one Monday morning and what he found along the way*
Galdone, Joanna. *Honeybee's party*
Hawes, Judy. *Watch honeybees with me*
Hogan, Paula Z. *The honeybee*
Keller, Beverly. *Fiona's bee*
Lobel, Arnold. *The rose in my garden*
Pizer, Abigail. *Nosey Gilbert*
Pluckrose, Henry Arthur. *Bees and wasps*
Rockwell, Anne F. *Big bad goat*
Wahl, Jan. *Follow me cried Bee*

Insects – beetles

Conklin, Gladys. *I like beetles*
Hoban, Russell. *Jim Frog*
Inkpen, Mick. *Billy's beetle*

Insects – butterflies, caterpillars

Aardema, Verna. *Who's in Rabbit's house?*
Abisch, Roz. *Let's find out about butterflies*
Carle, Eric. *The very hungry caterpillar*
Carrick, Malcolm. *I can squash elephants!*
  The caterpillar who turned into a butterfly

Conklin, Gladys. *I like butterflies*
I like caterpillars
Cutts, David. *Look...a butterfly*
Darby, Gene. *What is a butterfly?*
Delaney, A. *The butterfly*
Delaney, Ned. *One dragon to another*
DeLuise, Dom. *Charlie the caterpillar*
Fitzsimons, Cecilia. *My first butterflies*
Fleming, Denise. *In the tall, tall grass*
Garelick, May. *Where does the butterfly go when it rains?*
Gibbons, Gail. *Monarch butterfly*
Gomi, Taro. *Hi, butterfly!*
Grifalconi, Ann. *Darkness and the butterfly*
Heller, Ruth. *How to hide a butterfly*
Hines, Anna Grossnickle. *Remember the butterflies*
Hogan, Paula Z. *The butterfly*
Kent, Jack. *The caterpillar and the polliwog*
Lewis, Naomi. *The butterfly collector*
McClung, Robert. *Sphinx*
O'Hagan, Caroline. *It's easy to have a caterpillar visit you*
Piers, Helen. *Grasshopper and butterfly*
Pluckrose, Henry Arthur. *Butterflies and moths*
Roscoe, William. *The butterfly's ball*
Ryder, Joanne. *Where butterflies grow*
Selsam, Millicent E. *A first look at caterpillars*
Sundgaard, Arnold. *The lamb and the butterfly*
Thompson, Susan L. *Diary of a monarch butterfly*
Van Pallandt, Nicholas. *The butterfly night of Old Brown Bear*
Watts, Barrie. *Butterfly and caterpillar*
Wong, Herbert H. *Our caterpillars*

Insects - caterpillars *see* Insects – butterflies, caterpillars

Insects – crickets

Carle, Eric. *The very quiet cricket*
Caudill, Rebecca. *A pocketful of cricket*
Kimmel, Eric A. *Why worry?*
Maxner, Joyce. *Nicholas Cricket*
Mizumura, Kazue. *If I were a cricket...*
Stafford, William. *The animal that drank up sound*

Insects – dragonflies

Rodanas, Kristina. *The dragonfly's tale*

Insects – fireflies

Berends, Polly Berrien. *Ladybug and dog and the night walk*
Bolliger, Max. *The fireflies*
Brinckloe, Julie. *Fireflies!*
Buckley, Paul. *Amy Belligera and the fireflies*

Callen, Larry. *Dashiel and the night*
Eastman, P. D. (Philip D.). *Sam and the firefly*
Harris, Louise Dyer. *Flash, the life of a firefly*
Hawes, Judy. *Fireflies in the night*
Knight, Hilary. *A firefly in a fir tree*
Ryder, Joanne. *Fireflies*

Insects – fleas

Wiese, Kurt. *The dog, the fox and the fleas*

Insects – flies

Aardema, Verna. *Half-a-ball-of-kenki*
Aylesworth, Jim. *Old Black Fly*
Brandenberg, Franz. *Fresh cider and apple pie*
Conklin, Gladys. *I watch flies*
Elkin, Benjamin. *Why the sun was late*
Kraus, Robert. *The trouble with spider*
McClintock, Marshall. *A fly went by*
Oppenheim, Joanne. *You can't catch me!*
Winter, Paula. *The bear and the fly*
Yolen, Jane. *Spider Jane*

Insects – gnats

Peet, Bill (William Bartlett). *The gnats of knotty pine*

Insects – grasshoppers

Ciardi, John. *John J. Plenty and Fiddler Dan*
Du Bois, William Pène. *Bear circus*
Grasshopper to the rescue, ill. by Tasha Tudor
Kimmel, Eric A. *Why worry?*
Lobel, Arnold. *Grasshopper on the road*
Newbolt, Henry John, Sir. *Rilloby-rill*
Piers, Helen. *Grasshopper and butterfly*

Insects – hornets

Laird, Elizabeth. *The day Veronica was nosy*

Insects - lady birds *see* Insects – ladybugs

Insects – ladybugs

Berends, Polly Berrien. *Ladybug and dog and the night walk*
Brown, Ruth. *Ladybug, ladybug*
Carle, Eric. *The grouchy ladybug*
Conklin, Gladys. *Lucky ladybugs*
Finzel, Julia. *Large as life*
Fisher, Aileen Lucia. *We went looking*
Hawes, Judy. *Ladybug, ladybug, fly away home*
Kepes, Juliet. *Lady bird, quickly*
Kraus, Robert. *Ladybug, ladybug!*
Schlein, Miriam. *Fast is not a ladybug*
Silverman, Maida. *Ladybug's color book*

Sueyoshi, Akiko. *Ladybird on a bicycle*
Szekeres, Cyndy. *Ladybug, ladybug, where are you?*
Watts, Barrie. *Ladybug*
Wong, Herbert H. *My ladybug*

Insects – mosquitoes

Aardema, Verna. *Why mosquitoes buzz in people's ears*

Insects – moths

Pluckrose, Henry Arthur. *Butterflies and moths*

Insects – praying mantis

Conklin, Gladys. *Praying mantis*

Insects – wasps

Pluckrose, Henry Arthur. *Bees and wasps*

Insects – lightning bugs *see* Insects – fireflies

Interracial marriage *see* Marriage, interracial

Ireland *see* Foreign lands – Ireland

Irish-Americans *see* Ethnic groups in the U.S. – Irish-Americans

Islands

Abolafia, Yossi. *Yanosh's Island*
Adoff, Arnold. *Flamboyan*
Albert, Burton. *Where does the trail lead?*
Alderson, Sue Ann. *Ida and the wool smugglers*
Armitage, Ronda. *Ice creams for Rosie*
Beni, Ruth. *Sir Baldergog the great*
Brock, Emma Lillian. *Skipping Island*
Brown, Margaret Wise. *The little island*
Brunhoff, Laurent de. *Babar's visit to Bird Island*
Civardi, Anne. *Things people do*
Coatsworth, Elizabeth. *Lonely Maria*
Cooney, Barbara. *Island boy*
Crossley-Holland, Kevin. *Sleeping Nanna*
Farley, Walter. *Black stallion*
Gantschev, Ivan. *The train to Grandma's*
Gibbons, Gail. *Surrounded by sea*
Greene, Carol. *The old ladies who liked cats*
Greenfield, Eloise. *Under the Sunday tree*
Haynes, Max. *Dinosaur island*
Hedderwick, Mairi. *Katie Morag and the big boy cousins*
Katie Morag and the tiresome Ted
Katie Morag and the two grandmothers
Katie Morag delivers the mail
Hoopes, Lyn Littlefield. *Mommy, daddy, me*

Johnston, Tony. *Pages of music*
Joseph, Lynn. *Coconut kind of day*
Kellogg, Steven (Stephen). *The island of the skog*
Kessler, Leonard P. *The pirates' adventure on Spooky Island*
King, Deborah. *Sirius and Saba*
Kinsey-Warnock, Natalie. *The wild horses of Sweetbriar*
Krahn, Fernando. *The great ape*
Lasky, Kathryn. *My island grandma*
Lent, Blair. *Bayberry Bluff*
Lessac, Frané. *My little island*
McCloskey, Robert. *Time of wonder*
McGovern, Ann. *Nicholas Bentley Stoningpot III*
McPhail, David. *Great cat*
Martin, Charles E. *For rent*
Island rescue
Island winter
Millhouse, Nicholas. *Blue-footed booby*
Mordvinoff, Nicolas. *Coral Island*
Olson, Arielle North. *The lighthouse keeper's daughter*
Poulin, Stéphane. *Travels for two*
Rockwell, Anne F. *On our vacation*
Round, Graham. *Hangdog*
Smith, Roger. *The empty island*
Steig, William. *Abel's Island*
Rotten island
Wallis, Lisa. *Island child*
Wilson, Barbara Ker. *The turtle and the island*

Israel *see* Foreign lands – Israel

Italian-Americans *see* Ethnic groups in the U.S. – Italian-Americans

Italy *see* Foreign lands – Italy

Jackets *see* Clothing – coats

Jail *see* Prisons

Japan *see* Foreign lands – Japan

Japanese-Americans *see* Ethnic groups in the U.S. – Asian-Americans; Ethnic groups in the U.S. – Japanese-Americans

Jealousy *see* Emotions – envy, jealousy

Jesters *see* Clowns, jesters

Jewish culture

Adler, David A. *The children of Chelm*
  The children's book of Jewish holidays
  The house on the roof
  The number on my grandfather's arm
  A picture book of Hanukkah
  A picture book of Israel
  A picture book of Jewish holidays
  A picture book of Passover
Aleichem, Sholem. *Hanukah money*
Aronin, Ben. *The secret of the Sabbath fish*
Auerbach, Julie Jaslow. *Everything's changing—It's pesach!*
Bayar, Steven. *Rachel and Mischa*
Behrens, June. *Hanukkah*
  Passover
Bogot, Howard. *I'm growing*
Brodmann, Aliana. *Such a noise!*
Burstein, Chaya M. *Joseph and Anna's time capsule*
Caseley, Judith. *When Grandpa came to stay*
Chaikin, Miriam. *Esther*
  Exodus
  Hanukkah
Chanover, Hyman. *Happy Hanukah everybody*
Chapman, Carol. *The tale of Meshka the Kvetch*
A child's picture English-Hebrew dictionary
Cohen, Barbara. *Even higher*
  Gooseberries to oranges
  Here come the Purim players!
Cole, Joanna. *It's too noisy*
Coopersmith, Jerome. *A Chanukah fable for Christmas*
De Paola, Tomie (Thomas Anthony). *My first Chanukah*
Drucker, Malka. *Grandma's latkes*
  A Jewish holiday ABC
Edwards, Michelle. *Alef-bet*
  A baker's portrait
Ehrlich, Amy. *The story of Hannukkah*
Eisenberg, Ann. *I can celebrate*
Eisenberg, Phyllis Rose. *A mitzvah is something special*
Fass, David E. *The shofar that lost its voice*
Fassler, Joan. *My grandpa died today*
Feder, Harriet K. *Not yet, Elijah!*
  What can you do with a bagel?
Fisher, Aileen Lucia. *My first Hanukkah book*
Freedman, Florence B. *Brothers*
Ganz, Yaffa. *The story of Mimmy and Simmy*
Gellman, Ellie. *It's Chanukah!*
  It's Rosh Hashanah!
  Shai's Shabbat walk
Gershator, Phillis. *Honi and his magic circle*
Goffstein, M. B. (Marilyn Brooke).
  Laughing latkes

Goldin, Barbara Diamond. *Cakes and miracles*
  Just enough is plenty
  World's birthday
Greene, Jacqueline Dembar. *Butchers and bakers, rabbis and kings*
  What his father did
Groner, Judyth. *All about Hanukkah*
  My very own Jewish community
  Where is the Afikomen?
Gross, Michael. *The fable of the fig tree*
Harvey, Brett. *Immigrant girl*
Hirsh, Marilyn. *Captain Jiri and Rabbi Jacob*
  Could anything be worse?
  I love Hanukkah
  I love Passover
  Joseph who loved the Sabbath
  One little goat
  The pink suit
  Potato pancakes all around
  The Rabbi and the twenty-nine witches
  Where is Yonkela?
Hutton, Warwick. *Moses in the bulrushes*
Kahn, Katherine Janus. *The Shofar calls to us*
Karkowsky, Nancy. *Grandma's soup*
Karlinsky, Ruth Schild. *My first book of Mitzvos*
Kimmel, Eric A. *The Chanukkah guest*
  Hershel and the Hanukkah goblins
Koralek, Jenny. *Hanukkah: the festival of lights*
Levine, Arthur. *All the lights in the night*
Levoy, Myron. *The Hanukkah of Great-Uncle Otto*
Levy, Sara G. *Mother Goose rhymes for Jewish children*
Lisowski, Gabriel. *How Tevye became a milkman*
McDermott, Beverly Brodsky. *The Golem*
Manushkin, Fran. *Latkes and applesause*
Margalit, Avishai. *The Hebrew alphabet book*
Modesitt, Jeanne. *Songs of Chanukah*
Nerlove, Miriam. *Hanukkah*
  Passover
On the little hearth, ill. by Gabriel Lisowski
Patterson, José. *Mazal-Tov*
Phillips, Mildred. *The sign in Mendel's window*
Portnoy, Mindy Avra. *Ima on the Bima: my mommy is a Rabbi*
  Mommy never went to Hebrew school
Rosen, Anne. *A family Passover*
Rosen, Michael J. *Elijah's angel*
Rosenblum, Richard. *The old synagogue*
Ross, Lillian Hammer. *Buba Leah and her paper children*
  The little old man and his dreams
Schanzer, Roz. *In the synagogue*
Schotter, Roni. *Hanukkah!*

Schwartz, Amy. *Mrs. Moskowitz and the
Sabbath candlesticks*
Yossel Zissel and the wisdom of Chelm
Schwartz, Lynne Sharon. *The four questions*
Segal, Lore. *Tell me a Mitzi*
Tell me a Trudy
Segal, Sheila. *Joshua's dream*
Sherman, Eileen Bluestone. *The odd potato*
Shostak, Myra. *Rainbow candles*
Shulevitz, Uri. *The magician*
Singer, Marilyn. *Minnie's Yom Kippur
birthday*
Springer, Sally. *Let's make latkes*
Suhl, Yuri. *Simon Boom gives a wedding*
Weilerstein, Sadie Rose. *The best of K'tonton*
Wikler, Madeline. *Let's build a Sukkah*
My first seder
The Purim parade
Wohl, Lauren L. *Matzoh mouse*
Zalben, Jane Breskin. *Beni's first Chanukah*
Happy Passover, Rosie
Leo and Blossom's Sukkah
Zemach, Margot. *It could always be worse*
Zola, Meguido. *The dream of promise*
Zusman, Evelyn. *The Passover parrot*

Jobs *see* Careers

Jokes *see* Riddles

Journalists *see* Careers – journalists

Judges *see* Careers – judges

Jumping *see* Activities – jumping

Jungle

Aardema, Verna. *Rabbit makes a monkey of
lion*
Aitken, Amy. *Kate and Mona in the jungle*
Bare, Colleen Stanley. *Who comes to the
water hole?*
Bodsworth, Nan. *A nice walk in the jungle*
Booth, Eugene. *In the jungle*
Catchpole, Clive. *Jungles*
Clark, Emma Chichester. *Lunch with Aunt
Augusta*
Corddry, Thomas I. *Kibby's big feat*
Drescher, Henrik. *The yellow umbrella*
Emberley, Rebecca. *Jungle sounds*
Fischetto, Laura. *The jungle is my home*
Greenaway, Shirley. *Jungles*
Hadithi, Mwenye. *Tricky tortoise*
Hellen, Nancy. *Animals of the jungle*
Henley, Claire. *Jungle day*
Kemp, Anthea. *Mr. Percy's magic greenhouse*
Kitchen, Bert. *Tenrec's twigs*
Lilly, Kenneth. *Animals in the jungle*
McAllister, Angela. *Matepo*
Mahy, Margaret. *17 kings and 42 elephants*
Royston, Angela. *Jungle animals*

Sage, Angie. *Monkeys in the jungle*
Smith, Jim. *Nimbus the explorer*
Steig, William. *The Zabajaba Jungle*
Tafuri, Nancy. *Junglewalk*
Van Allsburg, Chris. *Jumanji*
Wood, John Norris. *Jungles*

Kangaroos *see* Animals – kangaroos

Kenya *see* Foreign lands – Kenya

Kindness *see* Character traits – kindness

Kindness to animals *see* Character traits
– kindness to animals

Kings *see* Royalty – kings

Kinkajous *see* Animals – kinkajous

Kites

Ayer, Jacqueline. *Nu Dang and his kite*
Brown, Marcia. *The little carousel*
Cooper, Elizabeth K. *The fish from Japan*
Cousins, Lucy. *Kite in the park*
Gerstein, Mordicai. *The mountains of Tibet*
Haseley, Dennis. *Kite flier*
Heller, George. *Hiroshi's wonderful kite*
Luenn, Nancy. *The dragon kite*
MacDonald, Elizabeth. *Mike's kite*
MacDonald, Maryann. *Rabbit's birthday kite*
Miller, Moira. *The moon dragon*
Packard, Mary. *The kite*
Peet, Bill (William Bartlett). *Merle the high
flying squirrel*
Reddix, Valerie. *Dragon kite of the autumn
moon*
Rey, Margret (Margret Elisabeth
Waldstein). *Curious George flies a kite*
Ruthstrom, Dorotha. *The big kite contest*
Stilz, Carol Curtis. *Kirsty's kite*
Strauss, Gwen. *The night shimmy*
Thayer, Jane. *Gus loved his happy home*
Titus, Eve. *Anatole over Paris*
Uchida, Yoshiko. *Sumi's prize*
Vaughan, Marcia K. *The Sea-Breeze Hotel*
Wiese, Kurt. *Fish in the air*
Yolen, Jane. *The emperor and the kite*
The emperor and the kite [Rev. ed.]

Knights

Blake, Quentin. *Snuff*
Boutell, Clarence Burley. *The fat baron*

Bradfield, Roger (Jolly Roger). *A good night for dragons*

Carrick, Donald. *Harold and the giant knight*

Cressey, James. *The dragon and George*

Cretien, Paul D. *Sir Henry and the dragon*

De Paola, Tomie (Thomas Anthony). *The knight and the dragon*

Emberley, Ed (Edward Randolph). *Klippity klop*

Fradon, Dana. *Sir Dana—a knight*

Gerrard, Roy. *Sir Cedric rides again*

Goodall, John S. *Creepy castle*

Haley, Gail E. *The green man*

Hazen, Barbara Shook. *The knight who was afraid of the dark*

Hodges, Margaret. *The kitchen knight*

Holl, Adelaide. *Sir Kevin of Devon*

Ipcar, Dahlov. *Sir Addlepate and the unicorn*

Lasker, Joe. *A tournament of knights*

McCrea, James. *The story of Olaf*

Mayer, Mercer. *Terrible troll*

Nolan, Dennis. *The castle builder*

Peet, Bill (William Bartlett). *Cowardly Clyde How Droofus the dragon lost his head*

Scarry, Huck. *Looking into the Middle Ages*

Trez, Denise. *The little knight's dragon*

Knitting *see* Activities – knitting

Koala bears *see* Animals – koala bears

Korea *see* Foreign lands – Korea

Korean-Americans *see* Ethnic groups in the U.S. – Asian-Americans; Ethnic groups in the U.S. – Korean-Americans

Kwanzaa *see* Holidays – Kwanzaa

Lady birds *see* Insects – ladybugs

Ladybugs *see* Insects – ladybugs

Language

The all-amazing ha ha book

Allington, Richard L. *Letters Talking Words*

Ancona, George. *Handtalk zoo*

Anholt, Catherine. *All about you*

Baby's words, ill. by Debby Slier

Baer, Edith. *Words are like faces*

Baker, Pamela J. *My first book of sign*

Battles, Edith. *What does the rooster say, Yoshio?*

Benjamin, Alan. *Rat-a-tat, pitter pat*

Berson, Harold. *A moose is not a mouse*

Bond, Michael. *Paddington and the knickerbocker rainbow*

Bossom, Naomi. *A scale full of fish and other turnabouts*

Bove, Linda. *Sign language ABC with Linda Bove*

Carle, Eric. *My very first book of words*

Chaplin, Susan Gibbons. *I can sign my ABCs*

Charlip, Remy. *Handtalk Handtalk birthday*

Chislett, Gail. *Melinda's no's cold*

Clifford, Eth. *A bear before breakfast*

Cohen, Caron Lee. *Three yellow dogs*

Day, Alexandra. *Frank and Ernest*

Dodds, Dayle Ann. *Do bunnies talk?*

Dunham, Meredith. *Colors: how do you say it? Numbers: how do you say it? Picnic: how do you say it? Shapes: how do you say it?*

Ellentuck, Shan. *Did you see what I said?*

Fallwell, Cathryn. *Clowning around*

Folsom, Marcia. *Easy as pie*

Gibbons, Gail. *Weather words and what they mean*

Gomi, Taro. *Seeing, saying, doing, playing*

Goodspeed, Peter. *Hugh and Fitzhugh*

Gordon, Jeffie Ross. *Six sleepy sheep*

Greenberg, Judith E. *What is the sign for friend?*

Gwynne, Fred. *A little pigeon toad*

Hartman, Gail. *For strawberry jam or fireflies*

Hawkins, Colin. *Tog the dog*

Heller, Ruth. *A cache of jewels and other collective nouns Kites sail high*

Hill, Eric. *Spot's big book of words; El libro grande de las palabras de Spot Spot's first words*

Hirschi, Ron. *Seya's song*

Hoban, Tana. *All about where More than one*

Hunt, Bernice Kohn. *Your ant is a which*

Koch, Michelle. *By the sea Just one more*

Krauss, Ruth. *A hole is to dig*

Krupp, Robin Rector. *Get set to wreck!*

Leaf, Munro. *Grammar can be fun*

Leeton, Will C. *The Tower of Babel*

Levine, Ellen. *I hate English!*

Lewis, Sheri. *Baby Lamb Chop loves words*

Lionni, Leo. *Words to talk about*

MacCarthy, Patricia. *Herds of words*

McMillan, Bruce. *One sun Play day*

Super, super, superwords
McNaught, Harry. *Words to grow on*
Maestro, Betsy. *All aboard overnight*
  Camping out
  Delivery van
  On the go
  Taxi
Marks, Alan. *Nowhere to be found*
Martin, Jerome. *Carrot—parrot*
  Mitten—kitten
Miller, Margaret. *Every day*
  My birthday
  On my street
  Playtime
Moncure, Jane Belk. *Word Bird's fall words*
  Word Bird's spring words
  Word Bird's summer words
  Word Bird's winter words
Monfried, Lucia. *Baby's world*
Most, Bernard. *Pets in trumpets and other word-play riddles*
  There's an ape behind the drape
100 words about transportation, ill. by Richard Eric Brown
100 words about working, ill. by Richard Eric Brown
Pluckrose, Henry Arthur. *Join it!*
Preiss, Byron. *The first crazy word book: verbs*
Rand, Ann. *Sparkle and spin*
Richardson, Jack E. *Six in a mix*
Riddell, Edwina. *One hundred first words*
Root, Phyllis. *Gretchen's grandma*
Rose, Gerald. *The bird garden*
Sage, Michael. *If you talked to a boar*
Salt, Jane. *See and say picture word book*
Sattler, Helen Roney. *Train whistles*
Scarry, Richard. *Richard Scarry's biggest word book ever!*
Sesame Street. *Sesame Street sign language fun*
  Sesame Street word book
Sherman, Ivan. *Walking talking words*
Showers, Paul. *How you talk*
Small, David. *Ruby Mae has something to say*
Snell, Nigel. *A bird in hand...*
Snow, Alan. *My first dictionary*
Steig, William. *The bad speller*
Steptoe, John. *My special best words*
Tester, Sylvia Root. *Never monkey with a monkey*
  What did you say?
Trân-Khánh-Tuyêt. *The little weaver of Thái-Yên Village*
Wall, Lina Mao. *Judge Rabbit and the tree spirit*
Wells, Rosemary. *Max's first word*
  Max's ride
Wiesner, William. *The Tower of Babel*
Wildsmith, Brian. *What the moon saw*
Wilkes, Angela. *My first word book*

Wood, Audrey. *Elbert's bad word*

Language, foreign *see* Foreign languages

Laos *see* Foreign lands – Laos

Lapland *see* Foreign lands – Lapland

Latvia *see* Foreign lands – Latvia

Laundry

Behrens, June. *Soo Ling finds a way*
Freeman, Don. *A pocket for Corduroy*
Iwamura, Kazuo. *The fourteen forest mice and the summer laundry day*
Ormondroyd, Edward. *Theodore*

Law *see* Careers – judges; Crime

Laziness *see* Character traits – laziness

Left and right *see* Concepts – left and right

Left-handedness

Lerner, Marguerite Rush. *Lefty, the story of left-handedness*

Legends *see* Folk and fairy tales

Lemmings *see* Animals – lemmings

Lemurs *see* Animals – lemurs

Leopards *see* Animals – leopards

Leprechauns *see* Elves and little people

Letters

Baker, Keith. *The dove's letter*
Bell, Norman. *Linda's airmail letter*
Brandt, Betty. *Special delivery*
Brisson, Pat. *Your best friend, Kate*
Caseley, Judith. *Dear Annie*
James, Simon. *Dear Mr. Blueberry*
Keats, Ezra Jack. *A letter to Amy*
Leedy, Loreen. *Messages in the mailbox*
Ross, Lillian Hammer. *Buba Leah and her paper children*
Schumacher, Claire. *Tommy the winner*
Selway, Martina. *Don't forget to write*
Seuss, Dr. *On beyond zebra*
Siracusa, Catherine. *No mail for Mitchell*

Librarians *see* Careers – librarians

Libraries

Alexander, Martha G. *How my library grew by Dinah*

Alexander, Sue. *World famous Muriel and the magic mystery*
Aliki. *How a book is made*
Baker, Donna. *I want to be a librarian*
Bartlett, Susan. *A book to begin on libraries*
Bauer, Caroline Feller. *Too many books!*
Baugh, Dolores M. *Let's take a trip*
Brillhart, Julie. *Story hour—starring Megan!*
Charles, Donald. *Calico Cat meets bookworm*
Daly, Maureen. *Patrick visits the library*
Daugherty, James Henry. *Andy and the lion*
Demarest, Chris L. *Clemens' kingdom*
De Paola, Tomie (Thomas Anthony). *The knight and the dragon*
Felt, Sue. *Rosa-too-little*
Freeman, Don. *Quiet! There's a canary in the library*
Furtado, Jo. *Sorry, Miss Folio!*
Gay, Zhenya. *Look!*
Gibbons, Gail. *Check it out!*
Houghton, Eric. *Walter's magic wand*
Huff, Barbara A. *Once inside the library*
Hulbert, Jay. *Armando asked "Why?"*
Hutchins, H. J. (Hazel J.). *Nicholas at the library*
Kimmel, Eric A. *I took my frog to the library*
Levinson, Nancy Smiler. *Clara and the bookwagon*
Lewis, Robin Baird. *Aunt Armadillo*
Little, Mary E. *ABC for the library*
   Ricardo and the puppets
Radlauer, Ruth Shaw. *Molly at the library*
Rockwell, Anne F. *I like the library*
Sadler, Marilyn. *Alistair in outer space*
Sauer, Julia Lina. *Mike's house*
Tudor, Tasha. *Mildred and the mummy*
Weil, Lisl. *Let's go to the library*

Lightening bugs see Insects – fireflies

Lighthouses

Armitage, Ronda. *The lighthouse keeper's catastrophe*
   The lighthouse keeper's lunch
   The lighthouse keeper's rescue
Barker, Melvern J. *Little island star*
Olson, Arielle North. *The lighthouse keeper's daughter*
Strahl, Rudi. *Sandman in the lighthouse*
Swift, Hildegarde Hoyt. *The little red lighthouse and the great gray bridge*

Lights

Baisch, Cris. *When the lights went out*
Berger, Melvin. *Switch on, switch off*
Crews, Donald. *Light*

Lions see Animals – lions

Little people see Elves and little people

Littleness see Character traits – smallness

Lizards see Reptiles – lizards

Llamas see Animals – llamas

Lobsters see Crustacea

Loneliness see Emotions – loneliness

Loons see Birds – loons

Losing things see Behavior – losing things

Lost see Behavior – lost

Love see Emotions – love

Loyalty see Character traits – loyalty

Luck see Character traits – luck

Lullabies

Aragon, Jane Chelsea. *Lullaby*
Bernhard, Josephine Butkowska. *Lullaby*
Calmenson, Stephanie. *All aboard the goodnight train*
Carlstrom, Nancy White. *Northern lullaby*
Duncan, Lois. *Songs from dreamland*
Engvick, William. *Lullabies and night songs*
Gilbert, Yvonne. *Baby's book of lullabies and cradle songs*
Ginsburg, Mirra. *Asleep, asleep*
Highwater, Jamake. *Moonsong lullaby*
Hopkins, Lee Bennett. *And God bless me*
Hush little baby. *Hush little baby*, ill. by Aliki
   Hush little baby, ill. by Jeanette Winter
   Hush little baby, ill. by Margot Zemach
Meigs, Mildred Plew. *Moon song*
Merriam, Eve. *Goodnight to Annie*
Messenger, Jannat. *Lullabies and baby songs*
Nichol, B. P. *Once: a lullaby*
Pfister, Marcus. *I see the moon*
Plotz, Helen. *A week of lullabies*
Pomerantz, Charlotte. *All asleep*
Sleep, baby, sleep, ill. by Trudi Oberhänsli
Stanley, Diane. *Birdsong lullaby*
Swados, Elizabeth. *Lullaby*
Taylor, Livingston. *Pajamas*
Titherington, Jeanne. *Baby's boat*
Van Vorst, M. L. *A Norse lullaby*
Watson, Clyde. *Fisherman lullabies*
Whiteside, Karen. *Lullaby of the wind*
Wilkoń, Józef. *Lullaby for a newborn king*
Yolen, Jane. *Dragon night and other lullabies*
   The lullaby songbook

Lying see Behavior – lying

Machines

Adkins, Jan. *Heavy equipment*
Baker, Betty. *Worthington Botts and the steam machine*
Balterman, Lee. *Girders and cranes*
Barton, Byron. *Machines at work*
Bate, Norman. *Vulcan*
Who built the bridge?
Who built the highway?
Baugh, Dolores M. *Let's take a trip*
Benedictus, Roger. *Fifty million sausages*
Bennett, Jill. *Machine poems*
Bradfield, Roger (Jolly Roger). *The flying hockey stick*
Brown, Margaret Wise. *The steamroller*
Burton, Virginia Lee. *Katy and the big snow*
Mike Mulligan and his steam shovel
Calhoun, Mary. *Jack and the whoopee wind*
Climo, Lindee. *Clyde*
Cowcher, Helen. *Rain forest*
Cox, David. *Tin Lizzie and Little Nell*
Du Bois, William Pène. *Lazy Tommy pumpkinhead*
Fleishman, Seymour. *Too hot in Potzburg*
Gackenbach, Dick. *Dog for a day*
Geringer, Laura. *Molly's new washing machine*
Goor, Ron. *In the driver's seat*
Henstra, Friso. *Wait and see*
Hill, Eric. *Spot goes to the farm*
Hoban, Tana. *Dig, drill, dump, fill*
Holl, Adelaide. *The ABC of cars, trucks and machines*
Hunter, Norman. *Professor Branestawn's building bust-up*
Hutchings, Tony. *Things that go word book*
Ipcar, Dahlov. *One horse farm*
Jacobs, Daniel. *What does it do?*
Löfgren, Ulf. *The traffic stopper that became a grandmother visitor*
Munsch, Robert N. *Jonathan cleaned up— then he heard a sound*
Neville, Emily Cheney. *The bridge*
Olney, Ross R. *Construction giants*
Farm giants
Potter, Tony. *See how it works: earth movers*
Pringle, Laurence. *Jesse builds a road*
Radford, Derek. *Building machines and what they do*
Cargo machines and what they do
Retan, Walter. *The snowplow that tried to go south*
The steam shovel that wouldn't eat dirt

Rockwell, Anne F. *Big wheels*
Machines
Royston, Angela. *Diggers and dump trucks*
Monster road builders
Sadler, Marilyn. *Alistair's time machine*
Small, David. *Ruby Mae has something to say*
Smucker, Anna Egan. *No star nights*
Stickland, Paul. *Machines as big as monsters*
Wolde, Gunilla. *Betsy and the vacuum cleaner*
Yagelski, Robert. *The day the lifting bridge stuck*
Zaffo, George J. *The giant nursery book of things that work*

Magic

Alexander, Martha G. *The magic box*
The magic hat
My outrageous friend Charlie
3 magic flip books: The magic hat; The magic box; The magic picture
Alexander, Sue. *Marc the Magnificent*
World famous Muriel and the magic mystery
Aliki. *The wish workers*
Andersen, H. C. (Hans Christian). *The tinderbox*, ill. by Warwick Hutton
The tinderbox, ill. by Barry Moser
The wild swans, ill. by Angela Barrett
The wild swans, ill. by Susan Jeffers
Anderson, Lonzo. *Two hundred rabbits*
Anderson, Robin. *Sinabouda Lily*
Anno, Mitsumasa. *Anno's hat tricks*
Arabian Nights. *The flying carpet*, ill. by Marcia Brown
The tale of Aladdin and the wonderful lamp, ill. by Ju-Hong Chen
Argueta, Manlio. *The magic dogs of the volcanoes*
Armitage, Ronda. *The bossing of Josie*
Ayres, Becky Hickox. *Victoria flies high*
Babbitt, Samuel F. *The forty-ninth magician*
Bach, Othello. *Hector McSnector and the mail-order Christmas witch*
Lilly, Willy and the mail-order witch
Balian, Lorna. *Humbug potion*
Ballard, Robin. *Cat and Alex and the magic flying carpet*
Baningan, Sharon Stearns. *Circus magic*
Barber, Antonia. *The enchanter's daughter*
Satchelmouse and the dinosaurs
Baumann, Hans. *Chip has many brothers*
Behrens, June. *Christmas-magic wagon*
Beisner, Monika. *Secret spells and curious charms*
Bell, Anthea. *Swan Lake*
Bemelmans, Ludwig. *Madeline's Christmas*
Bentley, Nancy. *I've got your nose!*
Berenstain, Stan. *The Berenstain bears and the sitter*
Berson, Harold. *Charles and Claudine*

The thief who hugged a moonbeam
Beskow, Elsa Maartman. *Peter in Blueberry Land*
Peter's adventures in Blueberry land
Bianco, Margery Williams. *The velveteen rabbit*, ill. by Allen Atkinson
The velveteen rabbit, ill. by Michael Green
The velveteen rabbit, ill. by Michael Hague
The velveteen rabbit, ill. by David Jorgensen
The velveteen rabbit, ill. by William Nicholson
The velveteen rabbit, ill. by Ilse Plume
The velveteen rabbit, ill. by S. D. Schindler
The velveteen rabbit, ill. by Tien
Birrer, Cynthia. *The lady and the unicorn*
Blance, Ellen. *Monster and the magic umbrella*
Boujon, Claude. *The fairy with the long nose*
Bowden, Joan Chase. *Who took the top hat trick?*
Boyle, Vere. *Beauty and the beast*
Brenner, Barbara A. *The flying patchwork quilt*
Bridwell, Norman. *The witch grows up*
Bright, Robert. *Georgie and the magician*
Brown, Marcia. *Once a mouse...*
Brunhoff, Laurent de. *Babar the magician*
Buckaway, C. M. *Alfred, the dragon who lost his flame*
Buckley, Paul. *Amy Belligera and the fireflies*
Buffett, Jimmy. *Trouble dolls*
Bunting, Eve (Anne Evelyn). *The man who could call down owls*
Carlson, Natalie Savage. *Spooky and the ghost cat*
Spooky and the witch's goat
Spooky and the wizard's bats
Carter, Anne. *Beauty and the beast*, ill. by Binette Schroeder
The fisherwoman
Chapman, Carol. *Barney Bipple's magic dandelions*
Chouinard, Roger. *One magic box*
Christelow, Eileen. *Olive and the magic hat*
Cleaver, Elizabeth. *The enchanted caribou*
Climo, Shirley. *The cobweb Christmas*
Coco, Eugene Bradley. *The wishing well*
Cole, Babette. *Nungu and the elephant*
Prince Cinders
Cole, Joanna. *Bony-legs*
Colette. *The boy and the magic*
Coombs, Patricia. *The magic pot*
The magician and McTree
Coville, Bruce. *The foolish giant*
Sarah and the dragon
Degen, Bruce. *The little witch and the riddle*
Delton, Judy. *Brimhall turns to magic*

Rabbit goes to night school
Demi. *Chen Ping and his magic axe*
Liang and the magic paintbrush
The magic boat
De Paola, Tomie (Thomas Anthony). *Big Anthony and the magic ring*
Merry Christmas, Strega Nona
Strega Nona
Strega Nona's magic lessons
Dewey, Ariane. *Dorin and the dragon*
The fish Peri
The thunder god's son
Dines, Glen. *A tiger in the cherry tree*
Domanska, Janina. *Palmiero and the ogre*
Dukas, P. (Paul Abraham). *The sorcerer's apprentice*, ill. by Ryohei Yanagihara
Ehrlich, Amy. *Pome and Peel*
The firebird, ill. by Moira Kemp
The firebird, ill. by Kris Waldherr
The firebird, ill. by Boris Zvorykin
Flot, Jeannette B. *Princess Kalina and the hedgehog*
Frascino, Edward. *Nanny Noony and the dust queen*
Nanny Noony and the magic spell
Fuchshuber, Annegert. *The wishing hat*
Gackenbach, Dick. *Ida Fanfanny*
Gág, Wanda. *Nothing at all*
The sorcerer's apprentice
Galdone, Paul. *The magic porridge pot*
Ginsburg, Mirra. *Striding slippers*
Glazer, Lee. *Cookie Becker casts a spell*
Glennon, Karen M. *Miss Eva and the red balloon*
The good-hearted youngest brother, ill. by Diane Goode
Green, Marion. *The magician who lived on the mountain*
Greeson, Janet. *The stingy baker*
Grimm, Jacob. *The donkey prince*, ill. by Barbara Cooney
The earth gnome, ill. by Margot Tomes
Rumpelstiltskin, ill. by Jacqueline Ayer
Rumpelstiltskin, ill. by Donna Diamond
Rumpelstiltskin, ill. by Paul Galdone
Rumpelstiltskin, ill. by Jonathan Langley
Rumpelstiltskin, ill. by Gennady Spirin
Rumpelstiltskin, ill. by John Wallner
Rumpelstiltskin, ill. by Paul O. Zelinsky
The seven ravens, ill. by Felix Hoffmann
The seven ravens, ill. by Lisbeth Zwerger
The six swans, ill. by Daniel San Souci
The six swans, ill. by Margot Tomes
Snow White, ill. by Trina Schart Hyman
Snow White, ill. by Bernadette Watts
Snow White and Rose Red, ill. by Adrienne Adams
Snow White and Rose Red, ill. by John Wallner
Snow White and Rose Red, ill. by Bernadette Watts

Snow White and the seven dwarves, ill. by Chihiro Iwasaki

Guthrie, Donna. *The witch who lives down the hall*

Haley, Gail E. *Jack and the bean tree*

Haller, Danita Ross. *Not just any ring*

Haseley, Dennis. *The cave of snores*

Hastings, Selina. *The singing ringing tree*

Hazen, Barbara Shook. *The sorcerer's apprentice*

Hearn, Michael Patrick. *The porcelain cat*

Helldorfer, M. C. (Mary Claire). *The mapmaker's daughter*

Heller, Linda. *Alexis and the golden ring*

Hiller, Catherine. *Abracatabby*

Himmelman, John. *Amanda and the magic garden*

Hindley, Judy. *Uncle Harold and the green hat*

Hoffman, Rosekrans. *Sister Sweet Ella*

Hoffmann, E. T. A. *The strange child*

Hooks, William H. *Moss gown*

Houghton, Eric. *Walter's magic wand*

Hutton, Warwick. *Beauty and the beast*

Isele, Elizabeth. *The frog princess*

Janosch. *Joshua and the magic fiddle*
The magic auto

Jeschke, Susan. *Angela and Bear*
Firerose
Mia, Grandma and the genie
Rima and Zeppo

Johnston, Tony. *The badger and the magic fan*
The witch's hat

Kemp, Anthea. *Mr. Percy's magic greenhouse*

Kennedy, Richard. *The porcelain man*

Kepes, Juliet. *The seed that peacock planted*

Kimmel, Eric A. *Boots and his brothers*

Kimmel, Margaret Mary. *Magic in the mist*

Knight, Hilary. *Hilary Knight's the owl and the pussy-cat*

Kobayashi, Robert. *Maria Mazaretti loves spaghetti*

Krahn, Fernando. *Amanda and the mysterious carpet*

Kroll, Steven. *The big bunny and the magic show*
The candy witch
Fat magic

Lacome, Julie. *Hocus pocus*

Langstaff, John M. *The two magicians*

Laurin, Anne. *Perfect crane*

Leichman, Seymour. *The wicked wizard and the wicked witch*

Lester, Helen. *The revenge of the magic chicken*

Levine, Abby. *Too much mush!*

Lewis, J. Patrick. *The moonbow of Mr. B. Bones*

Lindman, Maj. *Snipp, Snapp, Snurr and the magic horse*

Lipkind, William. *The boy and the forest*
The magic feather duster

Lobel, Anita. *The troll music*

Lopshire, Robert. *It's magic*

Lorenz, Lee. *The feathered ogre*

Lussert, Anneliese. *The farmer and the moon*

McAllister, Angela. *The enchanted flute*

McDermott, Gerald. *The magic tree*
Tim O'Toole and the wee folk

MacDonald, George. *Little Daylight*

McLenighan, Valjean. *Three strikes and you're out*
You can go jump

McPhail, David. *The magical drawings of Moony B. Finch*

Mahiri, Jabari. *The day they stole the letter J*

Marie, Geraldine. *The magic box*

Martin, Bill (William Ivan). *The magic pumpkin*

Mayer, Marianna. *The black horse*
The little jewel box
The spirit of the blue light

Mayer, Mercer. *Mrs. Beggs and the wizard*
A special trick
Whinnie the lovesick dragon

Mendoza, George. *Henri Mouse, the juggler*

Moncure, Jane Belk. *Riddle me a riddle*

Moore, Inga. *The sorcerer's apprentice*

Moss, Marissa. *But not Kate*

Muller, Robin. *The sorcerer's apprentice*, ill. by Robin Muller

Myers, Bernice. *The flying shoes*

Nesbit, Edith. *Melisande*

Nicoll, Helen. *Meg and Mog*
Meg at sea
Meg on the moon
Meg's eggs
Mog's box

Nolan, Dennis. *Wizard McBean and his flying machine*

Nones, Eric Jon. *Canary prince*

Norby, Lisa. *The Herself the elf storybook*

Oksner, Robert M. *The incompetent wizard*

Ostheeren, Ingrid. *Jonathan Mouse*
Jonathan Mouse and the magic box

Peet, Bill (William Bartlett). *Countdown to Christmas*
Jethro and Joel were a troll

Phumla. *Nomi and the magic fish*

Postma, Lidia. *The stolen mirror*

Poulin, Stéphane. *Benjamin and the pillow saga*
The prince who knew his fate, ill. by Lise Manniche

Rehnman, Mats. *The clay flute*

Rockwell, Anne F. *The story snail*
The wonderful eggs of Furicchia

Rogasky, Barbara. *The water of life*

Ronay, Jadja. *Ginger*
Rosales, Melodye. *Double Dutch and the voodoo shoes*
Rose, Anne. *Akimba and the magic cow*
Ross, Tony. *The enchanted pig*
Sachs, Marilyn. *Fleet-footed Florence*
Saddler, Allen. *The Archery contest*
San Souci, Robert D. *The talking eggs*
  The white cat
Saunders, Susan. *A sniff in time*
Scott, Sally. *The magic horse*
Seeger, Pete. *Abiyoyo*
Shecter, Ben. *Emily, girl witch of New York*
Shulevitz, Uri. *The magician*
Silverman, Maida. *The magic well*
Sleator, William. *That's silly*
Slobodkin, Louis. *Magic Michael*
Snyder, Zilpha Keatley. *The changing maze*
Sondheimer, Ilse. *The magic of Pomme*
Stanley, Diane. *The good-luck pencil*
Steig, William. *The amazing bone*
  Caleb and Kate
  Gorky rises
  Solomon the rusty nail
  Sylvester and the magic pebble
  Tiffky Doofky
Steptoe, John. *The story of jumping mouse*
Stevenson, James. *Yuck!*
Stubbs, Joanna. *With cat's eyes you'll never be scared of the dark*
Tempest, P. *How the cock wrecked the manor*
Thaler, Mike. *Madge's magic show*
Thayer, Jane. *Mr. Turtle's magic glasses*
Tom Tit Tot. *Tom Tit Tot*, ill. by Evaline Ness
Towle, Faith M. *The magic cooking pot*
Tresselt, Alvin R. *The world in the candy egg*
Trez, Denise. *Maila and the flying carpet*
Tune, Suelyn Ching. *How Maui slowed the sun*
Turkle, Brinton. *The magic of Millicent Musgrave*
Turska, Krystyna. *The magician of Cracow*
Ungerer, Tomi. *The hat*
Van Allsburg, Chris. *The garden of Abdul Gasazi*
Varga, Judy. *Janko's wish*
Waber, Bernard. *You're a little kid with a big heart*
Walt Disney Productions. *Walt Disney's Snow White and the seven dwarfs*
Weisner, David. *Tuesday*
Wiesner, David. *The loathsome dragon*
Willard, Nancy. *The marzipan moon*
  The mountains of quilt
Wisniewski, David. *Elfwyn's saga*
Wolkstein, Diane. *Oom razoom; or, Go I know not where, Bring back I know not what*
Woodruff, Elvira. *Show and tell*

Wright, Freire. *Beauty and the beast*
Wright, Jill. *The old woman and the jar of ums*
Yaffe, Alan. *The magic meatballs*

Mail *see* Letters

Mail carriers *see* Careers – mail carriers

Making things *see* Activities – making things

Malaysia *see* Foreign lands – Malaysia

Manners *see* Etiquette

Maps

Hartman, Gail. *As the crow flies*
Helldorfer, M. C. (Mary Claire). *The mapmaker's daughter*

Mardi Gras

Lionni, Leo. *The greentail mouse*

Marionettes *see* Puppets

Markets *see* Stores

Marriage, interracial

Adoff, Arnold. *Black is brown is tan*

Marriages *see* Weddings

Math *see* Counting, numbers

Meanness *see* Character traits – meanness

Measurement *see* Concepts – measurement

Mechanical men *see* Robots

Mechanics *see* Careers – mechanics

Memorial Day *see* Holidays – Memorial Day

Mermaids *see* Mythical creatures – mermaids

Merry-go-rounds

Ardizzone, Edward. *Paul, the hero of the fire*
Brown, Marcia. *The little carousel*
Charles, R. H. (Robert Henry). *The roundabout turn*
Crews, Donald. *Carousel*
Leigh, Oretta. *The merry-go-round*

Martin, Bill (William Ivan). *Up and down on the merry-go-round*
Perera, Lydia. *Frisky*
Schneider, Elisa. *The merry-go-round dog*
Thomas, Art. *Merry-go-rounds*
Wildsmith, Brian. *Carousel*

Messy *see* Behavior – messy

Mexican-Americans *see* Ethnic groups in the U.S. – Hispanic-Americans; Ethnic groups in the U.S. – Mexican-Americans

Mexico *see* Foreign lands – Mexico

Mice *see* Animals – mice

Middle ages
Althea. *Castle life*
Arnold, Tedd. *Ollie forgot*
Azarian, Mary. *The tale of John Barleycorn or, From barley to beer*
Biro, Val. *The pied piper of Hamelin*
Bishop, Ann. *The riddle ages*
Carrick, Donald. *Harold and the great stag*
Cohen, Barbara. *Here come the Purim players!*
Coombs, Patricia. *The magician and McTree*
Cressey, James. *The dragon and George*
Dick Whittington and his cat. *Dick Whittington*, ill. by Edward Ardizzone
Dick Whittington and his cat, ill. by Marcia Brown
Dick Whittington, ill. by Antony Maitland
Dick Whittington and his cat, ill. by Kurt Werth
Fradon, Dana. *Sir Dana—a knight*
Gerrard, Roy. *Sir Cedric rides again*
Hazen, Barbara Shook. *The knight who was afraid of the dark*
Herford, Oliver. *The most timid in the land*
Hodges, Margaret. *The kitchen knight*
Kahl, Virginia. *The Baron's booty*
The Duchess bakes a cake
McAllister, Angela. *The battle of Sir Cob and Sir Filbert*
Mason, Christopher. *The marvellous blue mouse*
Mayer, Mercer. *Whinnie the lovesick dragon*
Phillips, Louis. *The brothers Wrong and Wrong Again*
Richardson, Jean. *Stephen's feast*
Scarry, Huck. *Looking into the Middle Ages*
Scarry, Richard. *Richard Scarry's Peasant Pig and the terrible dragon*
Storr, Catherine (Cole). *Robin Hood*
Tompert, Ann. *Charlotte and Charles*
Woychuk, Denis. *The other side of the wall*

Military *see* Careers – military

Mimes *see* Clowns, jesters

Miners *see* Careers – miners

Minks *see* Animals – minks

Minorities *see* Ethnic groups in the U.S.

Mirages *see* Optical illusions

Misbehavior *see* Behavior – misbehavior

Missions
Politi, Leo. *Song of the swallows*

Mist *see* Weather – fog

Mistakes *see* Behavior – mistakes

Misunderstanding *see* Behavior – misunderstanding

Mittens *see* Clothing – gloves

Mockingbirds *see* Birds – mockingbirds

Models *see* Careers – models

Moles *see* Animals – moles

Money
Arnold, Caroline. *What will we buy?*
Berenstain, Stan. *The Berenstain bears' trouble with money*
Brenner, Barbara A. *The five pennies*
Brooks, Ben. *Lemonade parade*
Brown, Marcia. *The little carousel*
Caple, Kathy. *The purse*
Cole, Joanna. *Don't tell the whole world*
Day, Alexandra. *Paddy's pay-day*
Hoban, Lillian. *Arthur's funny money*
Kent, Jack. *Piggy Bank Gonzalez*
Maestro, Betsy. *Dollars and cents for Harriet*
Mantinband, Gerda. *Blabbermouths*
A paper of pins, ill. by Margaret Gordon
Rockwell, Anne F. *Gogo's pay day*
Rose, Anne. *As right as right can be*
Slobodkin, Louis. *Moon Blossom and the golden penny*
Stewart, Sarah. *The money tree*
Turkle, Brinton. *Rachel and Obadiah*
Vincent, Gabrielle. *Bravo, Ernest and Celestine!*
Viorst, Judith. *Alexander, who used to be rich last Sunday*
Wondriska, William. *Mr. Brown and Mr. Gray*

Mongooses *see* Animals – mongooses

Monitor lizards *see* Reptiles – monitor lizards

Monkeys *see* Animals – monkeys

Monsters

Alexander, Martha G. *The magic box*
  Maybe a monster
Allen, Martha Dickson. *Real life monsters*
Arnold, Caroline. *The terrible Hodag*
Axworthy, Anni. *Ben's Wednesday*
Babbitt, Natalie. *The something*
Bang, Molly. *Wiley and the hairy man*
Barden, Rosalind. *TV monster*
Basso, Bill. *The top of the pizzas*
Benjamin, Alan. *1000 monsters*
Bennett, Jill. *Spooky poems*
Bergström, Gunilla. *Is that a monster, Alfie Atkins?*
Blance, Ellen. *Lady Monster has a plan*
  Lady Monster helps out
  Monster and the magic umbrella
  Monster and the mural
  Monster and the surprise cookie
  Monster at school
  Monster buys a pet
  Monster cleans his house
  Monster comes to the city
  Monster gets a job
  Monster goes around the town
  Monster goes to school
  Monster goes to the beach
  Monster goes to the circus
  Monster goes to the hospital
  Monster goes to the museum
  Monster goes to the zoo
  Monster has a party
  Monster, Lady Monster and the bike ride
  Monster looks for a friend
  Monster looks for a house
  Monster meets Lady Monster
  Monster on the bus
Brown, Marc Tolon. *Marc Brown's full house*
  Spooky riddles
Bunting, Eve (Anne Evelyn). *Scary, scary Halloween*
Cameron, Ann. *Harry (the monster)*
Carey, Valerie Scho. *Harriet and William and the terrible creature*
Carrick, Malcolm. *I can squash elephants!*
Chapouton, Anne-Marie. *Billy the brave*
Chevalier, Christa. *Spence and the sleepytime monster*
Christian, Mary Blount. *Go west, swamp monsters*
Church, Kristine. *My brother John*
Ciardi, John. *The monster den: or, Look what happened at my house—and to it*
Cohen, Barbara. *The demon who would not die*
Cohen, Caron Lee. *Whiffle Squeek*
Cohen, Daniel. *America's very own monsters*
Cohen, Miriam. *Jim meets the thing*
Cole, Joanna. *Monster manners*
Conger, Lesley. *Tops and bottoms*
Coombs, Patricia. *Molly Mullett*
Cooney, Nancy Evans. *Go away monsters, lickety split!*
Craig, Helen. *The night of the paper bag monsters*
Crowe, Robert L. *Clyde monster*
Crowley, Arthur. *The boogey man*
Dahl, Roald. *Dirty beasts*
Delaney, M. C. (Michael Clark). *The marigold monster*
Demarest, Chris L. *Morton and Sidney*
Denton, Kady MacDonald. *Granny is a darling*
De Regniers, Beatrice Schenk. *Sam and the impossible thing*
Dillon, Barbara. *The beast in the bed*
Dinan, Carolyn. *The lunch box monster*
Dinosaurs and monsters, ill. by Louise Nevett
Dos Santos, Joyce Audy. *Henri and the Loup-Garou*
Drescher, Henrik. *Simon's book*
Fassler, Joan. *The man of the house*
Flora, James. *Leopold, the see-through crumbpicker*
Francis, Anna B. *Pleasant dreams*
Freedman, Sally. *Monster birthday party*
Gackenbach, Dick. *Harry and the terrible whatzit*
  Mag the magnificent
Gág, Wanda. *The funny thing*
Galdone, Paul. *The monster and the tailor*
Gantos, Jack (John, Jr.). *Greedy Greeny*
  The werewolf family
Geringer, Laura. *Look out, look out, it's coming!*
Gilleo, Alma. *Learning about monsters*
Ginsburg, Mirra. *Ookie-Spooky*
Goodall, John S. *Creepy castle*
Goode, Diane. *I hear a noise*
Gorey, Edward (St. John). *The tunnel calamity*
Gramatky, Hardie. *Little Toot and the Loch Ness monster*
Grant, Joan. *The monster that grew small*
Grindley, Sally. *Knock, knock! Who's there?*
Harshman, Terry Webb. *Porcupine's pajama party*
Hawkins, Colin. *Snap! Snap!*
  Take away monsters
Haywood, Carolyn. *The king's monster*
Heide, Florence Parry. *A monster is coming! A monster is coming!*
Hellard, Susan. *Eleanor and the babysitter*
Heller, Nicholas. *The monster in the cave*
Holleyman, Sonia. *Mona the vampire*

Hooks, William H. *Peach boy*
Howe, James. *There's a monster under my bed*
Hutchins, Pat. *The very worst monster*
Where's the baby?
Impey, Rose. *The flat man*
Scare yourself to sleep
Johnson, Jane. *Today I thought I'd run away*
Johnston, Tony. *Four scary stories*
Kahl, Virginia. *Giants, indeed!*
How do you hide a monster?
Kellogg, Steven (Stephen). *The island of the skog*
The mysterious tadpole
Kimura, Yasuko. *Fergus and the sea monster*
Koelling, Caryl. *Mad monsters mix and match*
Krahn, Fernando. *The mystery of the giant footprints*
Kunnas, Mauri. *One spooky night and other scary stories*
Lerner, Sharon. *Follow the monsters!*
Lifton, Betty Jean. *Goodnight orange monster*
Logue, Christopher. *The magic circus*
McKee, David. *Two monsters*
McQueen, John Troy. *A world full of monsters*
Marshall, Edward. *Four on the shore*
Marshall, James. *Three up a tree*
Mayer, Mercer. *Little Monster at home*
Little Monster at school
Little Monster at work
Little Monster's alphabet book
Little Monster's bedtime book
Little Monster's counting book
Little Monster's neighborhood
Liza Lou and the Yeller Belly Swamp
Mrs. Beggs and the wizard
Terrible troll
There's a nightmare in my closet
Meddaugh, Susan. *Beast*
Memling, Carl. *What's in the dark?*
Miller, Edward. *The curse of Claudia*
Minsberg, David. *The book monster*
Monster poems, ill. by Kay Chorao
Moore, Lilian. *See my lovely poison ivy, and other verses about witches, ghosts and things*
Mooser, Stephen. *Funnyman meets the monster from outer space*
Morris, Ann. *Eleanora Mousie in the dark*
Morris, Terry Nell. *Good night, dear monster!*
Mosel, Arlene. *The funny little woman*
Moss, Marissa. *After-school monster*
Mueller, Virginia. *A Halloween mask for Monster*
Monster and the baby
Monster can't sleep
Monster goes to school
Monster's birthday hiccups

A playhouse for Monster
Murphy, Shirley Rousseau. *Valentine for a dragon*
Myers, Amy. *I know a monster*
Namm, Diane. *Monsters!*
Newsham, Wendy. *The monster hunt*
Niland, Deborah. *ABC of monsters*
Nixon, Joan Lowery. *Bigfoot makes a movie*
O'Keefe, Susan Heyboer. *One hungry monster*
Paige, Rob. *Some of my best friends are monsters*
Parish, Peggy. *No more monsters for me!*
Zed and the monsters
Parker, Nancy Winslow. *Love from Aunt Betty*
Peet, Bill (William Bartlett). *Cyrus the unsinkable sea serpent*
Pinkwater, Daniel Manus. *The Frankenbagel monster*
I was a second grade werewolf
Polacco, Patricia. *Some birthday!*
Prelutsky, Jack. *The baby uggs are hatching*
Riddell, Chris. *The wish factory*
Robison, Nancy. *Ten tall soldiers*
Rockwell, Anne F. *Thump thump thump!*
Ross, David. *Gorp and the space pirates*
Space monster
Space Monster Gorp and the runaway computer
Ross, H. L. *Not counting monsters*
Ross, Tony. *I'm coming to get you!*
Towser and the terrible thing
Sabraw, John. *I wouldn't be scared*
Salter, Heidi. *Taddy McFinley and the great grey grimly*
Schroder, William. *Pea soup and serpents*
Seeger, Pete. *Abiyoyo*
Selsam, Millicent E. *Sea monsters of long ago*
Sendak, Maurice. *Seven little monsters*
Where the wild things are
Seymour, Peter. *What's at the beach?*
Sharmat, Marjorie Weinman. *The pizza monster*
Scarlet Monster lives here
Smith, Janice Lee. *The monster in the third dresser drawer and other stories about Adam Joshua*
Snow, Alan. *The monster book of ABC sounds*
Solotareff, Grégoire. *The ogre and the frog king*
Steig, William. *Rotten island*
Steptoe, John. *Daddy is a monster...sometimes*
Stern, Peter. *Max the dragon*
Stevens, Kathleen. *The beast in the bathtub*
Stevenson, James. *"Could be worse!"*
Taylor, Judy. *Dudley and the monster*
Turkle, Brinton. *Do not open*
Ungerer, Tomi. *The beast of Monsieur Racine*

Zeralda's ogre
Viorst, Judith. *My mama says there aren't any zombies, ghosts, vampires, creatures, demons, monsters, fiends, goblins, or things*
Wagner, Jenny. *Amy's monster*
  The bunyip of Berkeley's Creek
Wahl, Jan. *Dracula's cat*
  Dracula's cat and Frankenstein's dog
  Frankenstein's dog
Watson, Pauline. *Wriggles, the little wishing pig*
Whitlock, Susan Love. *Donovan scares the monsters*
Willis, Jeanne. *The monster bed*
Willoughby, Elaine Macmann. *Boris and the monsters*
Winthrop, Elizabeth. *Maggie and the monster*
Young, Ed (Edward). *The terrible Nung Gwama*
Zemach, Harve. *The judge*

Months of the year see Days of the week, months of the year

Moon

Alexander, Martha G. *Maggie's moon*
Asch, Frank. *Happy birthday, moon!*
  Moon bear
  Mooncake
  Moongame
Asimov, Isaac. *The moon*
Balet, Jan B. *Amos and the moon*
Balzola, Asun. *Munia and the moon*
Baum, Louis. *I want to see the moon*
Baylor, Byrd. *Moon song*
Berenstain, Stan. *The Berenstain bears on the moon*
Berger, Barbara Helen. *Grandfather Twilight*
Bess, Clayton. *The truth about the moon*
Branley, Franklyn M. *The moon seems to change*
  What the moon is like
Brown, Margaret Wise. *Goodnight moon*
  Wait till the moon is full
Buchanan, Heather S. *George and Matilda Mouse and the moon rocket*
Carle, Eric. *Papa, please get the moon for me*
Carlstrom, Nancy White. *Who gets the sun out of bed?*
Cazet, Denys. *Christmas moon*
Coats, Laura Jane. *Marcella and the moon*
Come out to play, ill. by Jeanette Winter
Dayrell, Elphinstone. *Why the sun and the moon live in the sky*
De Gerez, Toni. *Louhi, witch of North Farm*
De Paola, Tomie (Thomas Anthony). *The Prince of the Dolomites*
De Regniers, Beatrice Schenk. *Willy O'Dwyer jumped in the fire*

Duncan, Lois. *Birthday moon*
Ehlert, Lois. *Moon rope: Un lazo a la luna*
Freeman, Mae. *The sun, the moon and the stars*
  You will go to the moon
Fuchs, Erich. *Journey to the moon*
Gantschev, Ivan. *The moon lake*
Garelick, May. *Look at the moon*
Gay, Marie-Louise. *Moonbeam on a cat's ear*
Griffith, Helen V. *Alex remembers*
Heckman, Philip. *The moon is following me*
Hillert, Margaret. *Up, up and away*
Hillman, Elizabeth. *Min-Yo and the moon dragon*
Hines, Anna Grossnickle. *Moon's wish*
Hodges, Margaret. *Buried moon*
Iwamura, Kazuo. *The fourteen forest mice and the harvest moon watch*
Janosch. *Joshua and the magic fiddle*
King, Christopher. *The boy who ate the moon*
Lankford, Mary D. *Is it dark? Is it light?*
Levitin, Sonia. *Who owns the moon?*
Lewis, Claudia Louise. *When I go to the moon*
Lewis, J. Patrick. *The moonbow of Mr. B. Bones*
Lifton, Betty Jean. *The rice-cake rabbit*
Lussert, Anneliese. *The farmer and the moon*
McDermott, Gerald. *Anansi the spider*
  Papagayo, the mischief maker
Macsolis. *Baile de luna: Dance moon*
Manushkin, Fran. *Moon dragon*
Marton, Jirina. *Midnight visit at Molly's house*
Matura, Mustapha. *Moon jump*
Merrill, Jean. *Emily Emerson's moon*
Mitra, Annie. *Penguin moon*
Moche, Dinah L. *The astronauts*
Nicoll, Helen. *Meg on the moon*
Oakley, Graham. *The church mice and the moon*
Olsen, Ib Spang. *The boy in the moon*
Oxenbury, Helen. *Tom and Pippo see the moon*
Preston, Edna Mitchell. *Squawk to the moon, little goose*
Rosenberg, Liz. *Window, mirror, moon*
Salter, Mary Jo. *The moon comes home*
Schertle, Alice. *Witch Hazel*
Schweninger, Ann. *The man in the moon as he sails the sky and other moon verse*
Skofield, James. *Crow moon, worm moon*
Sleator, William. *The angry moon*
Stevens, Cat. *Teaser and the firecat*
Stevenson, Robert Louis. *The moon*
Thaler, Mike. *Moonkey*
Thurber, James. *Many moons,* ill. by Marc Simont
  Many moons, ill. by Louis Slobodkin

Turner, Charles. *The turtle and the moon*
Turska, Krystyna. *The magician of Cracow*
Udry, Janice May. *The moon jumpers*
Ungerer, Tomi. *Moon man*
Vaughn, Jenny. *On the moon*
Ver Dorn, Bethea. *Moon glows*
Wahl, Jan. *Cabbage moon*
Ward, Helen. *The moonrat and the white turtle*
Watson, Clyde. *Midnight moon*
Wildsmith, Brian. *What the moon saw*
Willard, Nancy. *The nightgown of the sullen moon*
Winter, Jeanette. *The girl and the moon man*
Wood, Audrey. *Moonflute*
Wynne-Jones, Tim. *Builder of the moon*
Yamaguchi, Tohr. *Two crabs and the moonlight*
Young, James. *Everyone loves the moon*
Ziefert, Harriet. *Who can boo the loudest?*
Ziegler, Ursina. *Squaps the moonling*
Zolotow, Charlotte (Shapiro). *The moon was the best*

Moose *see* Animals – moose

Mopeds *see* Motorcycles

Morning

Anglund, Joan Walsh. *Morning is a little child*
Barbato, Juli. *From bed to bus*
Beach, Stewart. *Good morning, sun's up!*
Brown, Margaret Wise. *A child's good morning book*
  The quiet noisy book
Caldwell, Mary. *Morning, rabbit, morning*
Carlstrom, Nancy White. *Who gets the sun out of bed?*
Chorao, Kay. *The baby's good morning book*
Christiansen, C. B. *Mara in the morning*
Craig, M. Jean. *Spring is like the morning*
  What did you dream?
Dennis, Lynne. *Raymond Rabbit's early morning*
Dennis, Wesley. *Flip and the morning*
Dragonwagon, Crescent. *Katie in the morning*
Dryden, Emma. *Good morning—good night*
Funakoshi, Canna. *One morning*
Harrison, David Lee. *Wake up, sun!*
Hellard, Susan. *Time to get up*
Henkes, Kevin. *Shhhh*
Hill, Eric. *Good morning, baby bear*
Himler, Ronald. *Wake up, Jeremiah*
Hudson, Cheryl Willis. *Good morning baby*
Johnston, Deborah. *Mathew Michael's beastly day*
Kandoian, Ellen. *Under the sun*
Lapp, Eleanor. *In the morning mist*

McNulty, Faith. *When a boy wakes up in the morning*
Mann, Peggy. *King Laurence, the alarm clock*
Ormerod, Jan. *Sunshine*
Oxenbury, Helen. *Good night, good morning*
Polushkin, Maria. *Morning*
Ray, Deborah Kogan. *Fog drift morning*
Rogers, Paul (Patrick). *Somebody's awake*
Shulevitz, Uri. *Dawn*
Tafuri, Nancy. *Early morning in the barn*
Tresselt, Alvin R. *Wake up, city!*
  Wake up, farm! ill. by author
  Wake up, farm! ill. by Carolyn Ewing
Tworkov, Jack. *The camel who took a walk*
Westcott, Nadine Bernard. *Getting up*
Yabuki, Seiji. *I love the morning*
Ziefert, Harriet. *Good morning, sun!*
  Say good night!
Zolotow, Charlotte (Shapiro). *Something is going to happen*
  Wake up and good night

Mosquitoes *see* Insects – mosquitoes

Mother Goose *see* Nursery rhymes

Mothers *see* Family life – mothers

Mother's Day *see* Holidays – Mother's Day

Moths *see* Insects – moths

Motorcycles

Cave, Ron. *Motorcycles*
Cleary, Beverly. *Lucky Chuck*
Dickens, Frank. *Boffo*
McPhail, David. *Captain Toad and the motorbike*
Zimnik, Reiner. *The bear on the motorcycle*

Mountain climbing *see* Sports – mountain climbing

Mouths *see* Anatomy – mouths

Moving

Adshead, Gladys L. *Brownies—they're moving*
Aliki. *We are best friends*
Asch, Frank. *Goodbye house*
Barbour, Karen. *Nancy*
Becker, Edna. *Nine hundred buckets of paint*
Berenstain, Stan. *The Berenstain bears' moving day*
Berg, Jean Horton. *The O'Learys and friends*
Bond, Felicia. *Poinsettia and her family*
Bottner, Barbara. *Horrible Hannah*

Carlstrom, Nancy White. *I'm not moving, mama!*

Carter, Anne. *Molly in danger*

Cassedy, Sylvia. *The best cat suit of all*

Clymer, Eleanor Lowenton. *A yard for John*

Cohen, Barbara. *Gooseberries to oranges*

DeLage, Ida. *The old witch finds a new house*

Dowling, Paul. *Meg and Jack are moving*
Meg and Jack's new friends

Felt, Sue. *Hello-goodbye*

Fiday, Beverly. *Time to go*

Finsand, Mary Jane. *The town that moved*

Fisher, Aileen Lucia. *Best little house*

Giffard, Hannah. *Red Fox on the move*

Graham, Bob. *First there was Frances*

Gretz, Susanna. *Teddy bears' moving day*

Hendry, Diana. *Not anywhere house*

Hest, Amy. *Best-ever good-bye party*

Hickman, Martha Whitmore. *My friend William moved away*

Hoff, Syd. *Who will be my friends?*

Hughes, Shirley. *Moving Molly*

Ilsley, Velma. *M is for moving*

Isadora, Rachel. *The Potters' kitchen*

Jennings, Michael. *The bears who came to breakfix*

Johnson, Angela. *The leaving morning*

Johnston, Tony. *The quilt story*

Jones, Penelope. *I'm not moving!*

Keats, Ezra Jack. *The trip*

Keyworth, C. L. *New day*

Koller, Jackie French. *Mole and shrew*

Komaiko, Leah. *Annie Bananie*

Lexau, Joan M. *The rooftop mystery*

Lobel, Arnold. *Ming Lo moves the mountain*

Lystad, Mary H. *That new boy*

McLerran, Alice. *I want to go home*

McNaughton, Colin. *Guess who's just moved in next door?*

Malone, Nola Langner. *A home*

Marshak, Samuel. *In the van*

Maschler, Fay. *T. G. and Moonie move out of town*

Milord, Sue. *Maggie and the goodbye gift*

Moore, Inga. *Little dog lost*

Morris, Jill. *The boy who painted the sun*

Obrist, Jürg. *Fluffy*

O'Donnell, Elizabeth Lee. *Maggie doesn't want to move*

O'Kelley, Mattie Lou. *Moving to town*

Patz, Nancy. *To Annabella Pelican from Thomas Hippopotamus*

Pedersen, Judy. *Out in the country*

Provensen, Alice. *Shaker Lane*

Pryor, Bonnie. *The beaver boys*

Rabe, Berniece. *A smooth move*

Rogers, Fred. *Moving*

Ross, Lillian Hammer. *Buba Leah and her paper children*

Schlein, Miriam. *My house*

Schulman, Janet. *The big hello*

Sharmat, Marjorie Weinman. *Gila monsters meet you at the airport*
Mitchell is moving
Scarlet Monster lives here

Shecter, Ben. *Grandma remembers*

Shefelman, Janice. *Victoria House*

Sherrow, Victoria. *There goes the ghost*

Singer, Marilyn. *Archer Armadillo's secret room*

Snape, Juliet. *Frog odyssey*

Steel, Danielle. *Martha's new school*

Stevenson, James. *No friends*

Strathdee, Jean. *The house that grew*

Teague, Mark. *The trouble with the Johnsons*

Tobias, Tobi. *Moving day*

Tsutsui, Yoriko. *Anna's secret friend*

Turner, Ann Warren. *Stars for Sarah*

Van Leeuwen, Jean. *Going west*

Waber, Bernard. *Ira says goodbye*

Watson, Jane Werner. *Sometimes a family has to move*

Watson, Wendy. *Moving*

Wilhelm, Hans. *A new home, a new friend*

Woodruff, Elvira. *The wing shop*

Ziefert, Harriet. *A new house for Mole and Mouse*

Zolotow, Charlotte (Shapiro). *Janey*

Mules *see* Animals – mules

Multi-ethnic *see* Ethnic groups in the U.S.

Multiple birth children *see* Triplets; Twins

Muppets *see* Puppets

Museums

Alexander, Liza. *A visit to the Sesame Street Museum*

Aliki. *My visit to the dinosaurs*

Berenstain, Stan. *The Berenstain bears and the missing dinosaur bone*

Binnamin, Vivian. *The case of the snoring stegosaurus*

Blance, Ellen. *Monster goes to the museum*

Brown, Laurie Krasny. *Visiting the art museum*

The Christmas story

Cohen, Miriam. *Lost in the museum*

De Paola, Tomie (Thomas Anthony). *Bill and Pete go down the Nile*

Everett, Gwen. *Li'l Sis and Uncle Willie*

Fradon, Dana. *Sir Dana—a knight*

Freeman, Don. *Norman the doorman*

Gramatky, Hardie. *Hercules*

Kellogg, Steven (Stephen). *Prehistoric Pinkerton*

Krementz, Jill. *A visit to Washington, D.C.*

Lionni, Leo. *Matthew's dream*
Mayers, Florence Cassen. *Egyptian art from the Brooklyn Museum: ABC*
The Museum of Fine Arts, Boston: ABC
The Museum of Modern Art, New York: ABC
The National Air and Space Museum: ABC
Mayhew, James. *Katie and the dinosaurs*
Munro, Roxie. *The inside-outside book of Washington, D.C.*
Papajani, Janet. *Museums*
Simmonds, Posy. *Lulu and the flying babies*
Thayer, Jane. *Gus and the baby ghost*
Vincent, Gabrielle. *Where are you, Ernest and Celestine?*
Weil, Lisl. *Let's go to the museum*

Music

Abisch, Roz. *Sweet Betsy from Pike*
'Twas in the moon of wintertime
Alexander, Cecil Frances. *All things bright and beautiful*
Alexander, Lloyd. *The truthful harp*
Alger, Leclaire Gowans. *Always room for one more*
Kellyburn Braes
Ambrus, Victor G. *Mishka*
The seven skinny goats
Arkin, Alan. *Black and white*
Ash, Jutta. *Wedding birds*
Atene, Ann (Anna). *The golden guitar*
Azarian, Mary. *The tale of John Barleycorn or, From barley to beer*
Bach, Othello. *Lilly, Willy and the mail-order witch*
Baer, Gene. *Thump thump rat-a-tat-tat*
Baker, Laura Nelson. *The friendly beasts*
O children of the wind and pines
Bascom, Joe. *Malcolm's job*
Behn, Harry. *What a beautiful noise*
Bianco, Margery Williams. *The hurdy-gurdy man*
Birchman, David F. *Brother Billy Bronto's bygone blues band*
Boesel, Ann Sterling. *Sing and sing again*
Singing with Peter and Patsy
Bolliger, Max. *The most beautiful song*
Bonne, Rose. *I know an old lady*, ill. by Abner Graboff
Bottner, Barbara. *Zoo song*
Botwin, Esther. *A treasury of songs for little children*
Bowles, Brad. *Grandma's band*
Bowman, Peter. *The Christmas songbook*
Boynton, Sandra. *Good night, good night*
Bratton, John. *The teddy bears' picnic*, ill. by Renate Kozikowski
Bring a torch, Jeannette, Isabella, ill. by Adrienne Adams
Brott, Ardyth. *Jeremy's decision*

Brown, Marc Tolon. *Play rhymes*
Brown, Margaret Wise. *The little brass band*
Bruna, Dick. *The orchestra*
Bryan, Ashley. *All night, all day: a child's first book of African-American spirituals*
Buffett, Jimmy. *The jolly mon*
Bunting, Eve (Anne Evelyn). *The traveling men of Ballycoo*
Burningham, John. *Jangle twang*
Trubloff
Carle, Eric. *I see a song*
Carryl, Charles Edward. *A capital ship: or, The walloping window-blind*, ill. by Paul Galdone
Caseley, Judith. *Ada potato*
Cathon, Laura E. *Tot Botot and his little flute*
Causley, Charles. *Early in the morning*
Chanover, Hyman. *Happy Hanukah everybody*
Children go where I send thee
Clement, Claude. *The voice of the wood*
Coco, Eugene Bradley. *The fiddler's son*
Colette. *The boy and the magic*
Conover, Chris. *Six little ducks*
Count me in
Craver, Mike. *Beaver ball at the bug club*
Crespi, Francesca. *Little Bear and the oompah-pah*
Cummings, W. T. (Walter Thies). *The kid*
Dallas-Smith, Peter. *Trumpets in Grumpetland*
Dalton, Alene. *My new picture book of songs*
Day, Betsy. *Stefan and Olga*
Delacre, Lulu. *Arroz con leche*
Las Navidades
Dillon, Eilis. *The cats' opera*
Domanska, Janina. *Busy Monday morning*
Duncan, Lois. *Songs from dreamland*
Durell, Ann. *The Diane Goode book of American folk tales and songs*
Engvick, William. *Lullabies and night songs*
The farmer in the dell. The farmer in the dell, ill. by Kathy Parkinson
The farmer in the dell, ill. by Mary Maki Rae
The farmer in the dell, ill. by Diane Stanley
Flack, Marjorie. *The restless robin*
Flanders, Michael. *The hippopotamus song*
Fleischman, Paul. *Rondo in C*
Freeman, Lydia. *Pet of the Met*
The friendly beasts, ill. by Sarah Chamberlain
The friendly beasts and A partridge in a pear tree, ill. by Virginia Pearsons
A frog he would a-wooing go (folk-song). *Froggie went a-courting*, ill. by Chris Conover
Wendy Watson's frog went a-courting

Gilbert, Yvonne. *Baby's book of lullabies and cradle songs*

Go tell Aunt Rhody. *Go tell Aunt Rhody*, ill. by Robert M. Quackenbush

Goffstein, M. B. (Marilyn Brooke). *A little Schubert*

Gomi, Taro. *Toot!*

Greene, Carol. *A computer went a-courting*
Hinny Winny Bunco
The thirteen days of Halloween
The world's biggest birthday cake

Greenfield, Eloise. *I make music*

Grifalconi, Ann. *The toy trumpet*

Griffith, Helen V. *Georgia music*

Guthrie, Woody. *Woody's twenty grow big songs*

Hague, Kathleen. *Jingle bells*

Hale, Sarah Josepha. *Mary had a little lamb*, ill. by Tomie de Paola
Mary had a little lamb, photos. by Bruce Millan

Haseley, Dennis. *The old banjo*

Hayes, Ann. *Meet the orchestra*

Hoban, Russell. *Emmet Otter's jug-band Christmas*

Horvath, Betty F. *Jasper makes music*

Hot cross buns, and other old street cries

Howe, Caroline Walton. *Teddy Bear's bird and beast band*

Hurd, Thacher. *Mama don't allow*
The pea patch jig

Hush little baby. *Hush little baby*, ill. by Aliki
Hush little baby, ill. by Jeanette Winter
Hush little baby, ill. by Margot Zemach

I sing a song of the saints of God, ill. by Judith Gwyn Brown

Ipcar, Dahlov. *The cat came back*
"The song of the day birds" and "The song of the night birds"

Isadora, Rachel. *Ben's trumpet*

Isele, Elizabeth. *Pooks*

Ivimey, John William. *The complete story of the three blind mice*, ill. by Paul Galdone
The complete version of ye three blind mice, ill. by Walton Corbould
Three blind mice, ill. by Lorinda Bryan Cauley
Three blind mice, ill. by Victoria Chess

Janosch. *Joshua and the magic fiddle*
Tonight at nine

Johnston, Tony. *Pages of music*

Jones, Carol. *This old man*

Kahl, Virginia. *Droopsi*

Kapp, Paul. *Cock-a-doodle-doo! Cock-a-doodle-dandy!*

Keats, Ezra Jack. *Apartment 3*
The little drummer boy

Kepes, Juliet. *The seed that peacock planted*

Kherdian, David. *The cat's midsummer jamboree*

Kimmel, Eric A. *Why worry?*

King, Bob. *Sitting on the farm*

Kingsland, Robin. *Bus stop bop*

Komaiko, Leah. *I like the music*

Koontz, Robin Michal. *This old man*

Kovalski, Maryann. *Jingle bells*
The wheels on the bus

Krull, Kathleen. *Songs of praise*

Langstaff, John M. *Oh, a-hunting we will go*
Ol' Dan Tucker
On Christmas day in the morning
Soldier, soldier, won't you marry me?
The swapping boy
The two magicians

Lasker, David. *The boy who loved music*

Lear, Edward. *Edward Lear's nonsense book*, ill. by Tony Palazzo
The pelican chorus, ill. by Harold Berson
The pelican chorus and the quangle wangle's hat, ill. by Kevin W. Maddison

Lenski, Lois. *At our house*
Davy and his dog
Davy goes places
Debbie and her grandma
A dog came to school
I like winter
I went for a walk

Lionni, Leo. *Frederick*
Geraldine, the music mouse

Lobel, Anita. *The troll music*

Löfgren, Ulf. *The flying orchestra*

McAllister, Angela. *The enchanted flute*

McCarthy, Bobette. *Buffalo girls*

McCloskey, Robert. *Lentil*

McCurdy, Michael. *The old man and the fiddle*

McKee, David. *The sad story of Veronica who played the violin*

McMillan, Bruce. *The alphabet symphony*

McNally, Darcie. *In a cabin in a wood*

Maiorano, Robert. *A little interlude*

Malcolmson, Anne. *The song of Robin Hood*

Maril, Lee. *Mr. Bunny paints the eggs*

Maxner, Joyce. *Nicholas Cricket*

Mayer, Mercer. *The queen always wanted to dance*

Medearis, Angela Shelf. *The zebra-riding cowboy*

Micucci, Charles. *A little night music*

Mills, Alan. *The hungry goat*

Modesitt, Jeanne. *Songs of Chanukah*

Mother Goose. *Hey diddle diddle*, ill. by Marilyn Janovitz
The Mother Goose songbook, ill. by Jacqueline Sinclair
Mother Goose's rhymes and melodies, ill. by J. L. Webb
Pat-a-cake, ill. by Marilyn Janovitz

Sing hey diddle diddle, ill. by Frank
    Francis and Bernard Cheese
Thirty old-time nursery songs, ill. by Paul
    Woodroffe
Neale, J. M. (John Mason). *Good King*
    Wenceslas
Nelson, Esther L. *The funny songbook*
  Holiday·singing and dancing games
  The silly songbook
Newbolt, Henry John, Sir. *Rilloby-rill*
Newland, Mary Reed. *Good King Wenceslas*
Nichol, B. P. *Once: a lullaby*
Niland, Kilmeny. *A bellbird in a flame tree*
Nussbaumer, Mares. *Away in a manger*
Old MacDonald had a farm. *Old*
    MacDonald had a farm, ill. by Lorinda
    Bryan Cauley
  Old MacDonald had a farm, ill. by Mel
    Crawford
  Old MacDonald had a farm, ill. by David
    Frankland
  Old MacDonald had a farm, ill. by Abner
    Graboff
  Old MacDonald had a farm, ill. by Nancy
    Hellen
  Old MacDonald had a farm, ill. by Carol
    Jones
  Old MacDonald had a farm, ill. by
    Tracey Campbell Pearson
  Old MacDonald had a farm, ill. by Robert
    M. Quackenbush
  Old MacDonald had a farm, ill. by Glen
    Rounds
  Old MacDonald had a farm, ill. by
    William Stobbs
  Old MacDonald had a farm, ill. by Prue
    Theobalds
On the little hearth, ill. by Gabriel Lisowski
Patterson, Geoffrey. *The lion and the gypsy*
Peek, Merle. *The balancing act*
Perrault, Charles. *Cinderella*, ill. by
    Emanuele Luzzati
Pillar, Marjorie. *Join the band!*
Pinkwater, Daniel Manus. *Doodle flute*
Poole, Valerie. *Obadiah Coffee and the music*
    contest
Poston, Elizabeth. *Baby's song book*
Poulin, Stéphane. *Benjamin and the pillow*
    saga
Price, Leontyne. *Aïda*
Prokofiev, Sergei Sergeievitch. *Peter and*
    the wolf, ill. by Warren Chappell
  Peter and the wolf, ill. by Barbara
    Cooney
  Peter and the wolf, ill. by Frans Haacken
  Peter and the wolf, ill. by Alan Howard
  Peter and the wolf, ill. by Charles
    Mikolaycak
  Peter and the wolf, ill. by Jörg Müller
  Peter and the wolf, ill. by Josef Paleček
  Peter and the wolf, ill. by Kozo Shimizu

Peter and the wolf, ill. by Erna Voigt
Quackenbush, Robert M. *Clementine*
  The man on the flying trapeze
  Pop! goes the weasel and Yankee Doodle
  She'll be comin' 'round the mountain
  Skip to my Lou
  There'll be a hot time in the old town
    tonight
Raffi. *Baby beluga*
  Down by the bay
  Everything grows
  One light, one sun
  Shake my sillies out
  Wheels on the bus
Raposo, Joe. *The Sesame Street song book*
Raschka, Chris. *Charlie Parker played be bop*
Rehnman, Mats. *The clay flute*
Rey, H. A. (Hans Augusto). *Humpty*
    Dumpty and other Mother Goose songs
Richardson, Jean. *Stephen's feast*
Robbins, Ruth. *Baboushka and the three*
    kings
Rodgers, Richard. *A real nice clambake*
Root, Phyllis. *Soup for supper*
Ross, Tony. *This old man*
Rounds, Glen. *The boll weevil*
  Casey Jones
  The strawberry roan
  Sweet Betsy from Pike
Sage, James. *The little band*
Schaaf, Peter. *The violin close up*
Schackburg, Richard. *Yankee Doodle*
Schick, Eleanor. *One summer night*
  A piano for Julie
Scholey, Arthur. *Baboushka*
Seeger, Pete. *The foolish frog*
Sendak, Maurice. *Maurice Sendak's Really*
    Rosie
Singer, Marilyn. *Will you take me to town on*
    strawberry day?
Slobodkin, Louis. *Wide-awake owl*
Spier, Peter. *The Erie Canal*
Stadler, John. *Hector, the accordion-nosed dog*
Staines, Bill. *All God's critters got a place in*
    the choir
Stapler, Sarah. *Trilby's trumpet*
Stecher, Miriam B. *Max, the music-maker*
Steig, William. *Roland, the minstrel pig*
Stern, Elsie-Jean. *Wee Robin's Christmas song*
Stevens, Bryna. *Handel and the famous*
    sword swallower of Halle
Stevenson, James. *Clams can't sing*
Sweet, Melissa. *Fiddle-i-fee*
Taylor, Mark. *The bold fisherman*
  Old Blue, you good dog you
Thomas, Ianthe. *Willie blows a mean horn*
Titus, Eve. *Anatole and the piano*
  Anatole and the Pied Piper
Tudor, Tasha. *Junior's tune*
Tusa, Tricia. *Miranda*

The twelve days of Christmas. English folk song. *Brian Wildsmith's The twelve days of Christmas*
Jack Kent's twelve days of Christmas
The twelve days of Christmas, ill. by Jan Brett
The twelve days of Christmas, ill. by Ilonka Karasz
The twelve days of Christmas, ill. by Ilse Plume
The twelve days of Christmas, ill. by Erika Schneider
The twelve days of Christmas, ill. by Sophie Windham
Uttley, Alison. *Sam Pig and the hurdy-gurdy man*
Vaughan, Marcia K. *Wombat stew*
Vincent, Gabrielle. *Bravo, Ernest and Celestine!*
Waddell, Martin. *The happy hedgehog band*
Wallner, John. *Old MacDonald had a farm*
Walter, Mildred Pitts. *Ty's one-man band*
Watson, Clyde. *Father Fox's feast of songs*
Fisherman lullabies
Weil, Lisl. *The magic of music*
Weiss, Nicki. *If you're happy and you know it*
Wenning, Elisabeth. *The Christmas mouse*
Westcott, Nadine Bernard. *Skip to my Lou*
There's a hole in the bucket
What a morning! ill. by Ashley Bryan
Wheeler, Opal. *Sing in praise*
Sing Mother Goose
Whittington, Mary K. *Carmina, come dance!*
Widdecombe Fair, ill. by Christine Price
Williams, Vera B. *Music, music for everyone*
Winter, Jeanette. *The girl and the moon man*
Wolkstein, Diane. *The banza*
Yeoman, John. *Old Mother Hubbard's dog learns to play*
Yolen, Jane. *The lap-time song and play book*
The lullaby songbook
Yulya. *Bears are sleeping*
Zelinsky, Paul O. *The wheels on the bus*
Zemach, Harve. *Mommy, buy me a China doll*
Zimelman, Nathan. *To sing a song as big as Ireland*

Musical instruments *see* Music

Musicians *see* Careers – musicians

Muskrats *see* Animals – muskrats

Mysteries *see* Problem solving

Mythical creatures

Ahlberg, Janet. *Jeremiah in the dark wood*
Arabian Nights. *The tale of Aladdin and the wonderful lamp*, ill. by Ju-Hong Chen
Aruego, José. *The king and his friends*

Asbjørnsen, P. C. (Peter Christen). *The three billy goats Gruff*, ill. by Marcia Brown
Three billy goats Gruff, ill. by Tom Dunnington
The three billy goats Gruff, ill. by Paul Galdone
The three billy goats Gruff, ill. by Janet Stevens
The three billy goats Gruff, ill. by William Stobbs
Aulaire, Ingri Mortenson d'. *The terrible troll-bird*
Carroll, Lewis. *Jabberwocky*, ill. by Graeme Base
Jabberwocky, ill. from Disney archives
Jabberwocky, ill. by Jane Breskin Zalben
Cole, Babette. *Cupid*
Cooper, Susan. *The Selkie girl*
Coville, Bruce. *Sarah and the dragon*
Dallas-Smith, Peter. *Trumpets in Grumpetland*
Decker, Dorothy W. *Stripe and the merbear*
Dunrea, Olivier. *Ravena*
Elzbieta. *Dikou the little troon who walks at night*
Fisher, Leonard Everett. *Cyclops*
Theseus and the minotaur
Foreman, Michael. *Panda and the bushfire*
Gilleo, Alma. *Learning about monsters*
Gramatky, Hardie. *Nikos and the sea god*
Hillert, Margaret. *The three goats*
Keeshan, Robert. *She loves me, she loves me not*
Lorenz, Lee. *The feathered ogre*
Mayer, Mercer. *Terrible troll*
Oram, Hiawyn. *Jenna and the troublemaker*
Peet, Bill (William Bartlett). *Cyrus the unsinkable sea serpent*
Jethro and Joel were a troll
No such things
The pinkish, purplish, bluish egg
Robb, Brian. *My grandmother's djinn*
Rockwell, Anne F. *Buster and the bogeyman*
Schroder, William. *Pea soup and serpents*
Small, David. *Paper John*
Solotareff, Grégoire. *Never trust an ogre*
Todaro, John. *Phillip the flower-eating phoenix*
Wagner, Jenny. *The bunyip of Berkeley's Creek*
Willis, Val. *The mystery in the bottle*
Yolen, Jane. *Greyling*
Wings

Mythical creatures – mermaids

Andersen, H. C. (Hans Christian). *The little mermaid*, ill. by Edward Frascino
The little mermaid, ill. by Chihiro Iwasaki
The little mermaid, ill. by Dorothy Pulis Lathrop

The little mermaid, ill. by Josef Paleček
The little mermaid, ill. by Daniel San Souci
The little mermaid, ill. by Katie Thamer Treherne
Binnamin, Vivian. *The case of the mysterious mermaid*
Noble, Trinka Hakes. *Hansy's mermaid*
San Souci, Robert D. *Sukey and the mermaid*
Spang, Günter. *Clelia and the little mermaid*

Mythical creatures – unicorns

Birrer, Cynthia. *The lady and the unicorn*
Coville, Bruce. *Sarah's unicorn*
Freeman, Jean Todd. *Cynthia and the unicorn*
Hague, Michael. *Michael Hague's world of unicorns*
Ipcar, Dahlov. *Sir Addlepate and the unicorn*
Mayer, Marianna. *The unicorn and the lake*
Moeri, Louise. *The unicorn and the plow*
Munthe, Adam John. *I believe in unicorns*
Preussler, Otfried. *The tale of the unicorn*

Nagging *see* Behavior – nagging

Name calling *see* Behavior – name calling

Names

Ackerman, Karen. *Flannery Row*
Alexander, Martha G. *Sabrina*
Bayer, Jane. *A my name is Alice*
Beim, Jerrold. *The smallest boy in the class*
Benton, Robert. *Little brother, no more*
Browner, Richard. *Everyone has a name*
Bryan, Ashley. *Turtle knows your name*
Cross, Diana Harding. *Some birds have funny names*
Some plants have funny names
Davis, Gibbs. *The other Emily*
De Paola, Tomie (Thomas Anthony). *Andy (that's my name)*
Dragonwagon, Crescent. *Wind Rose*
Engel, Diana. *Josephina hates her name*
Goffstein, M. B. (Marilyn Brooke). *School of names*
Henkes, Kevin. *Chrysanthemum*
Hoban, Julia. *Quick chick*
Hogan, Inez. *About Nono, the baby elephant*
Lester, Helen. *A porcupine named Fluffy*
Low, Joseph. *Adam's book of odd creatures*
McKee, David. *Two can toucan*

MacLachlan, Patricia. *Three names*
Mosel, Arlene. *Tikki Tikki Tembo*
Most, Bernard. *A dinosaur named after me*
Norman, Howard. *Who-Paddled-Backward-With-Trout*
Parish, Peggy. *Little Indian*
Peterson, Scott K. *What's your name?*
Raskin, Ellen. *A & The: or, William T. C. Baumgarten comes to town*
Rice, Eve. *Ebbie*
Tom Tit Tot. *Tom Tit Tot*, ill. by Evaline Ness
Vreeken, Elizabeth. *The boy who would not say his name*
Waber, Bernard. *But names will never hurt me*
Williams, Jay. *I wish I had another name*
Williams, Suzannne. *Mommy doesn't know my name*
Wold, Jo Anne. *Tell them my name is Amanda*
Wolf, Janet. *Adelaide to Zeke*

Napping *see* Sleep

Native Americans *see* Eskimos; Indians of North America; Indians of South America

Nature

Alexander, Martha G. *Where does the sky end, Grandpa?*
Allen, Marjorie N. *Changes*
Aragon, Jane Chelsea. *Salt hands*
Arnosky, Jim. *Come out, muskrats*
Crinkleroot's guide to knowing the trees
Crinkleroot's guide to walking in wild places
Ayres, Pam. *When dad cuts down the chestnut tree*
When dad fills in the garden pond
Baker, Alan. *Two tiny mice*
Banks, Merry. *Animals of the night*
Bash, Barbara. *Urban roosts*
Bastin, Marjolein. *Vera's special hobbies*
Baylor, Byrd. *I'm in charge of celebrations*
The other way to listen
Berenstain, Stan. *The Berenstain bears and the wild, wild honey*
Blake, Robert J. *The perfect spot*
Bliss, Corinne Demas. *Matthew's meadow*
Blyler, Allison. *Finding foxes*
Bowen, Betsy. *Antler, bear, canoe*
Brenner, Barbara A. *Two orphan cubs*
Burton, Jane. *Animals at home*
Animals at night
Animals at rest
Animals at work
Animals eating
Animals fighting
Animals keeping clean

Animals keeping cool
Animals keeping safe
Animals keeping warm
Animals learning
Animals talking
Campbell, Rod. *Buster's afternoon*
Carlstrom, Nancy White. *Northern lullaby*
Carter, Anne. *Molly in danger*
  Scurry's treasure
Chall, Marsha Wilson. *Up north at the cabin*
Cherry, Lynne. *A river ran wild*
Clay, Pat. *Ants*
Dunbar, Joyce. *Why is the sky up?*
Feldman, Judy. *The alphabet in nature*
  Shapes in nature
Fife, Dale. *Empty lot*
Fleming, Denise. *In the tall, tall grass*
Florian, Douglas. *Nature walk*
Gackenbach, Dick. *Mighty tree*
George, William T. *Beaver at Long Pond*
  Box turtle at Long Pond
Geraghty, Paul. *Over the steamy swamp*
Graham, Bob. *The wild*
Greeley, Valerie. *White is the moon*
Greenaway, Shirley. *Burrows*
  Forests
  Jungles
  Water
Greene, Carol. *I can be a forest ranger*
Griffith, Helen V. *Georgia music*
Guiberson, Brenda Z. *Spoonbill swamp*
Hands, Hargrave. *Bunny sees*
Hirschi, Ron. *Loon lake*
  Summer
Hoopes, Lyn Littlefield. *Mommy, daddy, me*
  My own home
Hurd, Edith Thacher. *Look for a bird*
Jordan, Helene J. (Helene Jamieson). *How a seed grows*
Koch, Michelle. *Hoot, howl, hiss*
Krull, Kathleen. *It's my earth too*
Lavies, Bianca. *Lily pad pond*
  Tree trunk traffic
Leach, Michael. *Rabbits*
Lewis, Naomi. *Swan*
Lionni, Leo. *A busy year*
Locker, Thomas. *The land of gray wolf*
Lyon, George-Ella. *The outside inn*
Michels, Tilde. *Rabbit spring*
Miller, Edna. *Patches finds a new home*
  Scamper: a gray tree squirrel
Norman, Charles. *The hornbean tree and other poems*
Oliver, Stephen. *Nature*
Peters, Lisa Westberg. *The sun, the wind and the rain*
  Water's way
Pets
Powzyk, Joyce. *Tasmania*
Radin, Ruth Yaffe. *High in the mountains*
Royston, Angela. *Small animals*

Russell, Naomi. *The stream*
  The tree
Ryder, Joanne. *Catching the wind*
  Chipmunk song
  Dancers in the garden
  Hello, tree!
  Lizard in the sun
  Mockingbird morning
  Step into the night
  Under your feet
  Where butterflies grow
  White bear, ice bear
  Winter whale
Sarton, May. *A walk through the woods*
Schoenherr, John. *Bear*
Schulz, Charles M. *Snoopy's facts and fun book about nature*
Seymour, Peter. *What's at the beach?*
Siebert, Diane. *Sierra*
Simon, Seymour. *Icebergs and glaciers*
Singer, Marilyn. *Turtle in July*
Skofield, James. *Crow moon, worm moon*
The song of the Three Holy Children, ill. by Pauline Baynes
Taylor, Kim. *Too fast to see*
  Too small to see
Tejima, Keizaburo. *Owl lake*
  Woodpecker forest
Thornhill, Jan. *Wildlife ABC*
  The wildlife 1-2-3
Tucker, Sian. *Going out*
Ward, Leila. *I am eyes, ni macho*
Watts, Barrie. *Apple tree*
Wells, Rosemary. *Forest of dreams*
Wildsmith, Brian. *Seasons*
Williams, David. *Walking to the creek*
Willington, Monica. *Seasons of swans*
Wilson, Ron. *Mice*
Wood, Jenny. *The animal kingdom*
Wyler, Rose. *Puddles and ponds*
Yoshida, Toshi. *Rhinoceros mother*
Ziefert, Harriet. *Sarah's questions*
Zolotow, Charlotte (Shapiro). *Say it!*
  The song
Zoo animals, Macmillan 1991
Zweifel, Frances. *Animal baby-sitters*

Needing someone *see* Behavior – needing someone

Neighborhoods *see* Communities, neighborhoods

Nepal *see* Foreign lands – Nepal

New Guinea *see* Foreign lands – New Guinea

New Year's *see* Holidays – New Year's

Nicaragua *see* Foreign lands – Nicaragu

Nigeria *see* Foreign lands – Nigeria

Night

Ackerman, Karen. *The banshee*
Adoff, Arnold. *Make a circle, keep us in*
Ahlberg, Allan. *Mystery tour*
Ahlberg, Janet. *Funnybones*
Alexander, Anne (Anna Barbara Cooke).
   Noise in the night
Alexander, Martha G. *Maggie's moon*
   We're in big trouble, Blackboard Bear
Aliki. *Overnight at Mary Bloom's*
Anrooy, Frans van. *The sea horse*
Aragon, Jane Chelsea. *Salt hands*
   Winter harvest
Ardizzone, Aingelda. *The night ride*
Armitage, Ronda. *One moonlit night*
Arnosky, Jim. *Raccoons and ripe corn*
Artis, Vicki Kimmel. *Pajama walking*
Asch, Frank. *Moon bear*
Axworthy, Anni. *Ben's Wednesday*
Aylesworth, Jim. *Tonight's the night*
   Two terrible frights
Babbitt, Natalie. *The something*
Balzola, Asun. *Munia and the moon*
Banks, Merry. *Animals of the night*
Bannon, Laura. *Little people of the night*
Baumgart, Klaus. *The little green dragon
   steps out*
Bennett, Rainey. *After the sun goes down*
Berends, Polly Berrien. *Ladybug and dog
   and the night walk*
Berenstain, Stan. *Bears in the night*
   The Berenstain bears in the dark
Berg, Jean Horton. *The wee little man*
Bilezikian, Gary. *While I slept*
Blocksma, Mary. *Did you hear that?*
Bolliger, Max. *The fireflies*
Bond, Felicia. *Poinsettia and the firefighters*
Bonsall, Crosby Newell. *Who's afraid of the
   dark?*
Bourgeois, Paulette. *Franklin in the dark*
Boyd, Lizi. *Sweet dreams, Willy*
Bradbury, Ray. *Switch on the night*
Brandenberg, Franz. *A robber! A robber!*
Brown, Margaret Wise. *A child's good night
   book*
   Night and day
   Wait till the moon is full
Brown, Myra Berry. *Pip camps out*
Buckley, Paul. *Amy Belligera and the fireflies*
Budney, Blossom. *After dark*
Bunting, Eve (Anne Evelyn). *Ghost's hour,
   spook's hour*
Burningham, John. *The blanket*
Burton, Jane. *Animals at night*
Butterworth, Nick. *One snowy night*
Callen, Larry. *Dashiel and the night*
Cass, Joan E. *The cat thief*
Cazet, Denys. *Mother night*
Chapouton, Anne-Marie. *Billy the brave*

Cole, Joanna. *Large as life nighttime animals*
Coles, Alison. *Michael in the dark*
Conford, Ellen. *Eugene the brave*
Cosgrove, Stephen (Edward). *Sleepy time
   bunny*
Credle, Ellis. *Big fraid, little fraid*
Crowe, Robert L. *Clyde monster*
DeLage, Ida. *The old witch and the crows*
Delton, Judy. *A walk on a snowy night*
Denslow, Sharon Phillips. *Night owls*
Denton, Kady MacDonald. *Granny is a
   darling*
Dinardo, Jeffrey. *Timothy and the night
   noises*
Donaldson, Lois. *Karl's wooden horse*
Dragonwagon, Crescent. *Half a moon and
   one whole star*
   When light turns into night
Dryden, Emma. *Good morning—good night*
Duncan, Lois. *Horses of dreamland*
Dupasquier, Philippe. *I can't sleep*
Duvoisin, Roger Antoine. *The missing
   milkman*
Edwards, Frank B. *Melody Mooner stayed up
   all night*
Emberley, Barbara. *Night's nice*
Erickson, Karen. *It's dark*
Erskine, Jim. *Bedtime story*
Farber, Werner. *Night lion*
Fenner, Carol. *Tigers in the cellar*
Fisher, Aileen Lucia. *In the middle of the
   night*
Fox, Mem. *Night noises*
Freeman, Don. *The night the lights went out*
Funakoshi, Canna. *One evening*
Garelick, May. *Sounds of a summer night*
Gay, Michel. *Night ride*
George, William T. *Beaver at Long Pond*
Ginsburg, Mirra. *Asleep, asleep*
   The sun's asleep behind the hill
   Where does the sun go at night?
Goode, Diane. *I hear a noise*
Goodenow, Earle. *The owl who hated the
   dark*
Greenfield, Eloise. *Night on Neighborhood
   Street*
Gretz, Susanna. *Hide-and-seek*
   Too dark!
Grifalconi, Ann. *Darkness and the butterfly*
Grossman, Patricia. *The night ones*
Hague, Kathleen. *Out of the nursery, into
   the night*
Hamilton, Morse. *Who's afraid of the dark?*
Haseley, Dennis. *The thieves' market*
Hasler, Eveline. *Winter magic*
Hawes, Judy. *Fireflies in the night*
Hawkins, Colin. *Snap! Snap!*
Hayes, Sarah. *This is the bear and the scary
   night*
Hazen, Barbara Shook. *The knight who was
   afraid of the dark*

Ver Dorn, Bethea. *Moon glows*
Vevers, Gwynne. *Animals of the dark*
Waddell, Martin. *Can't you sleep, Little Bear?*
  The park in the dark
Wahl, Jan. *The sleepytime book*
Wallace, Daisy. *Ghost poems*
Weir, Alison. *Peter, good night*
Weisner, David. *Tuesday*
Weiss, Nicki. *Where does the brown bear go?*
Westcott, Nadine Bernard. *Going to bed*
Willard, Nancy. *Night story*
  The nightgown of the sullen moon
  The well-mannered balloon
Winthrop, Elizabeth. *Potbellied possums*
Wittington, Mary K. *Troll games*
Wolff, Ashley. *Only the cat saw*
Wood, Audrey. *Moonflute*
Wouters, Anne. *This book is for us*
Wynne-Jones, Tim. *The hour of the frog*
Yeomans, Thomas. *For every child a star*
Yolen, Jane. *Owl moon*
Zalben, Jane Breskin. *Norton's nighttime*
Ziefert, Harriet. *Hurry up, Jessie!*
  Say good night!
Zolotow, Charlotte (Shapiro). *I have a horse of my own*
  Wake up and good night
  When the wind stops
  The white marble

Nightingales *see* Birds – nightingales

Nightmares *see* Bedtime; Goblins; Monsters; Night; Sleep

No text *see* Wordless

Noah *see* Religion – Noah

Noise, sounds

Alexander, Anne (Anna Barbara Cooke). *Noise in the night*
Alexander, Martha G. *Pigs say oink*
Allard, Harry. *Bumps in the night*
Allen, Pamela. *Bertie and the bear*
Aylesworth, Jim. *Country crossing*
  Hush up!
  Siren in the night
Bassett, Preston R. *Raindrop stories*
Behn, Harry. *What a beautiful noise*
Benjamin, Alan. *Rat-a-tat, pitter pat*
Bennett, David. *One cow moo moo*
Bennett, Jill. *Noisy poems*
Berenstain, Stan. *Bears in the night*
Berg, Jean Horton. *The noisy clock shop*
  The wee little man
Bilezikian, Gary. *While I slept*
Blanchard, Arlene. *Sounds my feet make*
Blocksma, Mary. *Did you hear that?*
Bond, Felicia. *Poinsettia and the firefighters*

Borten, Helen. *Do you hear what I hear?*
Boynton, Sandra. *Moo, baa, lalala*
Brandenberg, Franz. *Cock-a-doodle-doo*
  A robber! A robber!
Branley, Franklyn M. *High sounds, low sounds*
Bright, Robert. *Georgie and the noisy ghost*
  Gregory, the noisiest and strongest boy in Grangers Grove
Brodmann, Aliana. *Such a noise!*
Brown, Jane Clark. *Whonk, and whonk again*
Brown, Margaret Wise. *The country noisy book*
  Five little firemen
  The indoor noisy book
  Noisy book
  The quiet noisy book
  The seashore noisy book
  SHHhhh . . . Bang
  The summer noisy book
  The winter noisy book
Burningham, John. *Cluck baa*
  Jangle twang
  Skip trip
  Slam bang
  Sniff shout
  Wobble pop
Burton, Jane. *Animals talking*
Carle, Eric. *My very first book of sounds*
  The very quiet cricket
Causley, Charles. *"Quack!" said the billy-goat*
Christiansen, C. B. *Mara in the morning*
Chukovsky, Korney. *Good morning, chick*
Cleary, Beverly. *The hullabaloo ABC*
Cole, Joanna. *It's too noisy*
Cousins, Lucy. *What can rabbit hear?*
Crowe, Robert L. *Tyler Toad and the thunder*
Dinardo, Jeffrey. *Timothy and the night noises*
Dodds, Dayle Ann. *Do bunnies talk?*
Domanska, Janina. *Why so much noise?*
Dubov, Christine Salac. *Ding dong! and other sounds*
  Knock! and other sounds
  Oink! and other sounds
Duvoisin, Roger Antoine. *Petunia and the song*
Elizabeth Winthrop. *A very noisy girl*
Emberley, Ed (Edward Randolph). *Sounds*
Emberley, Rebecca. *City sounds*
  Jungle sounds
Evans, Mel. *The tiniest sound*
Farber, Norma. *There once was a woman who married a man*
Forrester, Victoria. *The magnificent moo*
Fowler, Richard. *Mr. Little's noisy car*
  Mr. Little's noisy truck
Fox, Mem. *Night noises*

Gaeddert, Lou Ann Bigge. *Noisy Nancy Nora*

Gannett, Ruth S. *Katie and the sad noise*

Garelick, May. *Sounds of a summer night*

Graham, John. *A crowd of cows*

Green, Suzanne. *The little choo-choo*

Hancock, Joy Elizabeth. *The loudest little lion*

Hindley, Judy. *Soft and noisy*

Horvath, Betty F. *The cheerful quiet*

Hughes, Shirley. *Noisy*

Hutchins, H. J. (Hazel J.). *Katie's babbling brother*

Hutchins, Pat. *Good night owl*

Isadora, Rachel. *I hear*

Jaquith, Priscilla. *Bo Rabbit smart for true*

Kauffman, Lois. *What's that noise?*

Kelley, True. *Look, baby! Listen, baby! Do, baby!*

Kilroy, Sally. *Animal noises*
Noisy homes

Kline, Suzy. *Shhhh!*

Koch, Michelle. *Hoot, howl, hiss*

Koenner, Alfred. *Be quite quiet beside the lake*

Kuskin, Karla. *All sizes of noises*
Roar and more

Leister, Mary. *The silent concert*

Lemieux, Michèle. *What's that noise?*

Leonard, Marcia. *Noisy neighbors*

Lillie, Patricia. *When the rooster crowed*

McCloskey, Robert. *Lentil*

McDonald, Amy. *Let's make a noise*

McDonald, Megan. *Whoo-oo is it?*

McGee, Marni. *The quiet farmer*

McGovern, Ann. *Too much noise*

McNulty, Faith. *When a boy wakes up in the morning*

Madden, Don. *Lemonade serenade or the thing in the garden*

Martin, Bill (William Ivan). *Polar bear, polar bear, what do you hear?*
Sounds around the clock
Sounds I remember
Sounds of home
Sounds of laughter
Sounds of numbers

Massie, Diane Redfield. *The baby beebee bird*

Meyer, Louis A. *The clean air and peaceful contentment dirigible airline*

Miles, Miska. *Noisy gander*

Miller, Jane. *Farm noises*

Morris, Winifred. *Just listen*

Morrison, Sean. *Is that a happy hippopotamus?*

Most, Bernard. *The cow that went oink*

Munsch, Robert N. *Mortimer*

Murphy, Jill. *Peace at last*

Myller, Rolf. *A very noisy day*

Ogle, Lucille. *I hear*

Owen, Annie. *Bumper to bumper*

Oxenbury, Helen. *I hear*

Panek, Dennis. *Detective Whoo*

Pearson, Tracey Campbell. *The howling dog*

Pickett, Carla. *Calvin Crocodile and the terrible noise*

Pizer, Abigail. *It's a perfect day*

Polushkin, Maria. *Who said meow?* ill. by Giulio Maestro
Who said meow? ill. by Ellen Weiss

Raskin, Ellen. *Who, said Sue, said whoo?*

Reddix, Valerie. *Millie and the mud hole*

Richter, Mischa. *Quack?*

Rockwell, Anne F. *Root-a-toot-toot*

Runcie, Jill. *Cock-a-doodle-doo*

Saltzberg, Barney. *It must have been the wind*

Scharer, Niko. *Emily's house*

Scheffler, Ursel. *Stop your crowing, Kasimir!*

Serfozo, Mary. *Rain talk*

Seuss, Dr. *Mr. Brown can moo! Can you?*

Shapiro, Arnold L. *Who says that?*

Showers, Paul. *The listening walk*

Sicotte, Virginia. *A riot of quiet*

Simms, Laura. *The squeaky door*

Skaar, Grace Marion. *What do the animals say?*

Slobodkin, Louis. *Colette and the princess*

Snow, Alan. *The monster book of ABC sounds*

Spier, Peter. *Crash! bang! boom!*
Gobble, growl, grunt

Stafford, William. *The animal that drank up sound*

Stanley, Diane. *The conversation club*

Stapler, Sarah. *Trilby's trumpet*

Steiner, Charlotte. *Listen to my seashell*

Stevenson, James. *Clams can't sing*

Strand, Mark. *The planet of lost things*

Tafuri, Nancy. *Do not disturb*

Thayer, Jane. *Quiet on account of dinosaur*

Thomas, Patricia. *The one and only, super-duper, golly-whopper, jim-dandy, really-handy clock-tock-stopper*

Titus, Eve. *The kitten who couldn't purr*

Tresselt, Alvin R. *Wake up, farm!* ill. by author
Wake up, farm! ill. by Carolyn Ewing

Voake, Charlotte. *Tom's cat*

Waddell, Martin. *Squeak-a-lot*

Webb, Angela. *Sound*

Wheeler, Cindy. *Marmalade's nap*

Whybrow, Ian. *Quacky quack-quack!*

Wildsmith, Brian. *Goat's trail*

Wynne-Jones, Tim. *The hour of the frog*

Zalben, Jane Breskin. *Norton's nighttime*

Ziefert, Harriet. *Listen! Piggety Pig*
On our way to the barn
On our way to the forest
On our way to the water
On our way to the zoo

Zolotow, Charlotte (Shapiro). *The poodle who barked at the wind*
The quiet mother and the noisy little boy

Norway *see* Foreign lands – Norway

Noses *see* Anatomy – noses; Senses – smelling

Numbers *see* Counting, numbers

Nuns *see* Careers – nuns

Nursery rhymes

Ahlberg, Janet. *The jolly Christmas postman*
Allison, Diane Worfolk. *This is the key to the kingdom*
Arnold, Tedd. *Mother Goose's words of wit and wisdom: a book of months*
Aylesworth, Jim. *The completed hickory dickory dock*
B. B. Blacksheep and Company
Barchilon, Jacques. *The authentic Mother Goose fairy tales and nursery rhymes*
Bartlett, Robert Merrill. *Jack Horner and song of sixpence*
Baum, L. Frank (Lyman Frank). *Mother Goose in prose*
Bayley, Nicola. *Nicola Bayley's book of nursery rhymes*
Blake, Pamela. *Peep-show*
Blake, Quentin. *Quentin Blake's nursery rhyme book*
Blegvad, Lenore. *Hark! Hark! The dogs do bark, and other poems about dogs*
Mittens for kittens and other rhymes about cats
This little pig-a-wig and other rhymes about pigs
Bodecker, N. M. (Nils Mogens). *"It's raining," said John Twaining*
Briggs, Raymond. *Fee fi fo fum*
Ring-a-ring o' roses
The white land
Brooke, L. Leslie (Leonard Leslie). *Oranges and lemons*
Brown, Marc Tolon. *Can you jump like a frog?*
One, two buckle my shoe
Play rhymes
Brown, Marcia. *Peter Piper's alphabet*
Brown, Ruth. *Ladybug, ladybug*
Butterworth, Nick. *Nick Butterworth's book of nursery rhymes*
Cakes and custard, ill. by Helen Oxenbury
Caldecott, Randolph. *Panjandrum picture book*
The Queen of Hearts
Randolph Caldecott's favorite nursery rhymes

Randolph Caldecott's John Gilpin and other stories
Randolph Caldecott's picture book, no. 1
Randolph Caldecott's picture book, no. 2
The three jovial huntsmen
Cassedy, Sylvia. *Moon-uncle, moon-uncle*
Cauley, Lorinda Bryan. *Pease porridge hot*
Causley, Charles. *Early in the morning*
Chorao, Kay. *The baby's bedtime book*
Clark, Leonard. *Drums and trumpets*
Cock Robin. *The courtship, merry marriage, and feast of Cock Robin and Jenny Wren*, ill. by Barbara Cooney
Who killed Cock Robin? ill. by William Stobbs
Come out to play, ill. by Jeanette Winter
Cope, Dawn. *Humpty Dumpty's favorite nursery rhymes*
Cremins, Robert. *My animal Mother Goose*
Crowther, Robert. *Pop goes the weasel!*
Dabcovich, Lydia. *The keys to my kingdom*
Dame Wiggins of Lee and her seven wonderful cats, ill. by Robert Broomfield
De Angeli, Marguerite. *The book of nursery and Mother Goose rhymes*
DeForest, Charlotte B. *The prancing pony*
Delessert, Etienne. *A long long song*
Demi. *Dragon kites and dragonflies*
Denslow, W. W. *Denslow's picture book treasury*
De Paola, Tomie (Thomas Anthony). *Favorite nursery tales*
Tomie de Paola's Mother Goose
De Regniers, Beatrice Schenk. *Catch a little fox*
Willy O'Dwyer jumped in the fire
Domanska, Janina. *A was an angler*
I saw a ship a-sailing
If all the seas were one sea
Emberley, Barbara. *Simon's song*
Emerson, Sally. *The nursery treasury*
Evans, Mari. *Singing black*
Fish, Helen Dean. *Four and twenty blackbirds*
Frankenberg, Lloyd. *Wings of rhyme*
From King Boggen's hall to nothing-at-all, ill. by Blair Lent
Galdone, Paul. *Cat goes fiddle-i-fee*
Little Bo-Peep
Gipson, Morrell. *Favorite nursery tales*
Greeley, Valerie. *Where's my share?*
Hale, Sarah Josepha. *Mary had a little lamb*, ill. by Tomie de Paola
Mary had a little lamb, photos. by Bruce Millan
Hannant, Judith Stuller. *Doorknob collection of nursery rhymes*
Hawkins, Colin. *Hey diddle diddle*
Humpty Dumpty
Hayes, Sarah. *Bad egg*
The Helen Oxenbury nursery rhyme book

Hellard, Susan. *This little piggy*

Hennessy, B. G. *The missing tarts*

Hopkins, Lee Bennett. *Animals from Mother Goose*

People from Mother Goose

The house that Jack built. *The house that Jack built*, ill. by Randolph Caldecott

The house that Jack built, ill. by Seymour Chwast

The house that Jack built, ill. by Antonio Frasconi

The house that Jack built, ill. by Rodney Peppé

The house that Jack built, ill. by Janet Stevens

The house that Jack built, ill. by Jenny Stow

The house that Jack built, ill. by Nadine Bernard Westcott

This is the house that Jack built, ill. by Liz Underhill

Humpty Dumpty and other first rhymes, ill. by Betty Youngs

Ivimey, John William. *The complete story of the three blind mice*, ill. by Paul Galdone

The complete version of ye three blind mice, ill. by Walton Corbould

Three blind mice, ill. by Lorinda Bryan Cauley

Three blind mice, ill. by Victoria Chess

Jack Sprat. *The life of Jack Sprat, his wife and his cat*, ill. by Paul Galdone

Kepes, Juliet. *Lady bird, quickly*

Kessler, Leonard P. *The silly Mother Goose*

Knapp, John II. *A pillar of pepper and other Bible nursery rhymes*

Koontz, Robin Michal. *Pussycat ate the dumplings*

Krensky, Stephen. *The missing Mother Goose*

Ladybug, ladybug, and other nursery rhymes, ill. by Eloise Wilkin

Lawson, Carol. *Teddy bear, teddy bear*

Lee, Dennis. *Alligator pie*

Levy, Sara G. *Mother Goose rhymes for Jewish children*

Little Tommy Tucker. *The history of Little Tom Tucker*, ill. by Paul Galdone

Livermore, Elaine. *Three little kittens lost their mittens*

Marshak, Samuel. *The merry starlings*

Martin, Bill (William Ivan). *Sounds I remember*

Martin, Sarah Catherine. *The comic adventures of Old Mother Hubbard and her dog*, ill. by Arnold Lobel

Old Mother Hubbard, ill. by Colin Hawkins

Old Mother Hubbard and her dog, ill. by Lisa Amoroso

Old Mother Hubbard and her dog, ill. by Paul Galdone

Old Mother Hubbard and her dog, ill. by Evaline Ness

Old Mother Hubbard and her wonderful dog, ill. by James Marshall

Marzollo, Jean. *The rebus treasury*

Mendoza, George. *Silly sheep and other sheepish rhymes*

Montgomerie, Norah. *This little pig went to market*

Mother Goose. *ABC rhymes*, ill. by Lulu Delarce

The annotated Mother Goose

As I was going up and down, ill. by Nicola Bayley

Baa, baa, black sheep, ill. by Moira Kemp

Baa baa black sheep, ill. by Sue Porter

Baa baa black sheep, ill. by Ferelith Eccles Williams

The baby's lap book, ill. by Kay Chorao

Blessed Mother Goose

Brian Wildsmith's Mother Goose

Carolyn Wells' edition of Mother Goose

Cats by Mother Goose, ill. by Carol Newsom

The Charles Addams Mother Goose

A child's book of old nursery rhymes, ill. by Joan Walsh Anglund

The Chinese Mother Goose rhymes, ill. by Ed Young

The city and country Mother Goose, ill. by Hilda Hoffmann

Frank Baber's Mother Goose

The gay Mother Goose, ill. by Françoise Seignobosc

The glorious Mother Goose, sel. by Cooper Edens

Grafa' Grig had a pig, ill. by Wallace Tripp

Gray goose and gander and other Mother Goose rhymes, ill. by Anne F. Rockwell

Gregory Griggs and other nursery rhyme people, ill. by Arnold Lobel

Hey diddle diddle, ill. by Marilyn Janovitz

Hey diddle diddle, ill. by Moira Kemp

Hey diddle diddle, ill. by Nita Sowter

Hey diddle diddle, ill. by Eleanor Wasmuth

Hey diddle diddle, and Baby bunting, ill. by Randolph Caldecott

Hey diddle diddle picture book, ill. by Randolph Caldecott

Hickory dickory dock, ill. by Moira Kemp

Hickory dickory dock and other nursery rhymes, ill. by Carol Jones

Humpty Dumpty, ill. by Colin and Jacqui Hawkins

Hurrah, we're outward bound! ill. by Peter Spier

Hush-a-bye baby, ill. by Nicola Bayley

In a pumpkin shell, ill. by Joan Walsh Anglund

Jack and Jill, ill. by Eleanor Wasmuth

Jack Kent's merry Mother Goose

James Marshall's Mother Goose

Kate Greenaway's Mother Goose

Kitten rhymes, ill. by Lulu Delarce

The Larousse book of nursery rhymes

Lavender's blue, ill. by Harold Jones

Little boy blue, ill. by Nita Sowter

The little Mother Goose, ill. by Jessie Willcox Smith

London Bridge is falling down, ill. by Ed Emberley

London Bridge is falling down, ill. by Peter Spier

Michael Foreman's Mother Goose

Mother Goose, ill. by Roger Antoine Duvoisin

Mother Goose, ill. by Miss Elliott

Mother Goose, ill. by C. B. Falls

Mother Goose, ill. by Gyo Fujikawa

Mother Goose, ill. by Vernon Grant

Mother Goose, ill. by Kate Greenaway

Mother Goose, ill. by Michael Hague

Mother Goose, ill. by Violet La Mont

Mother Goose, ill. by Arthur Rackham

Mother Goose, ill. by Frederick Richardson, 1915

Mother Goose, ill. by Frederick Richardson, 1976

Mother Goose, ill. by Gustaf Tenggren

Mother Goose, ill. by Tasha Tudor

Mother Goose and nursery rhymes, ill. by Philip Reed

A Mother Goose book, ill. by Joan Walsh Anglund

The Mother Goose book, ill. by Alice and Martin Provensen

The Mother Goose book, ill. by Sonia Roetter

Mother Goose house, ill. by Kate Klimo

Mother Goose in French, ill. by Barbara Cooney

Mother Goose in hieroglyphics, ill. by George S. Appleton

Mother Goose in Spanish, ill. by Barbara Cooney

Mother Goose melodies, facsimile of c.1833 Muroe and Francis edition

Mother Goose nursery rhymes, ill. by Arthur Rackham, 1969

Mother Goose nursery rhymes, ill. by Arthur Rackham, 1975

Mother Goose rhymes, ill. by Eulalie M. Banks and Lois Lenski

The Mother Goose songbook, ill. by Jacqueline Sinclair

The Mother Goose treasury, ill. by Raymond Briggs

Mother Goose's melodies, ill. by William A. Wheeler

Mother Goose's melody, facsimile of John Newbery's 1794 printing

Mother Goose's nursery rhymes, ill. by Allen Atkinson

Mother Goose's rhymes and melodies, ill. by J. L. Webb

Nursery rhyme book, ill. by L. Leslie Brooke

Nursery rhymes, ill. by Douglas Gorsline

Nursery rhymes, ill. by Eloise Wilkin

Nursery rhymes from Mother Goose in signed English

The old woman in a shoe, ill. by Eleanor Wasmuth

One I love, two I love, and other loving Mother Goose rhymes, ill. by Nonny Hogrogian

One misty moisty morning, ill. by Mitchell Miller

The only true Mother Goose melodies

Over the moon, ill. by Charlotte Voake

Pat-a-cake, ill. by Marilyn Janovitz

The piper's son, ill. by Emily N. Barto

A pocket full of posies, ill. by Marguerite De Angeli

Pussy cat, pussy cat, ill. by Ferelith Eccles Williams

The rainbow Mother Goose, ill. by Lili Cassel-Wronker

The real Mother Goose, ill. by Blanche Fisher Wright

The real Mother Goose clock book, ill. by Jane Chambless

Richard Scarry's best Mother Goose ever

Richard Scarry's favorite Mother Goose rhymes

Rimes de la Mere Oie, ill. by Seymour Chwast, Milton Glaser, and Barry Zaid

Ring o' roses, ill. by Leslie Brooke

The Sesame Street players present Mother Goose

Sing a song of Mother Goose, ill. by Barbara Reid

Sing a song of sixpence, ill. by Randolph Caldecott; Barron's, 1988

Sing a song of sixpence, ill. by Randolph Caldecott; Hart, 1977

Sing a song of sixpence, ill. by Margaret Chamberlain

Sing a song of sixpence, ill. by Leonard Lubin

Sing a song of sixpence, ill. by Ray Marshall and Korky Paul

Sing a song of sixpence, ill. by Ferelith Eccles Williams

Sing hey diddle diddle, ill. by Frank Francis and Bernard Cheese

Songs for Mother Goose, ill. by Maginel Wright Enright Barney
The tall Mother Goose, ill. by Feodor Rojankovsky
Thirty old-time nursery songs, ill. by Paul Woodroffe
This little pig, ill. by Leonard Lubin
This little pig, ill. by Eleanor Wasmuth
This little pig went to market, ill. by L. Leslie Brooke
This little pig went to market, ill. by Ferelith Eccles Williams
This little piggy, ill. by Moira Kemp
The three jovial huntsmen, ill. by Susan Jeffers
The three little kittens, ill. by Lorinda Bryan Cauley
The three little kittens, ill. by Paul Galdone
The three little kittens, ill. by Dorothy Stott
The three little kittens, ill. by Shelley Thornton
To market! To market! ill. by Emma Lillian Brock
To market! To market! ill. by Peter Spier
Tom, Tom the piper's son, ill. by Paul Galdone
Twenty nursery rhymes, ill. by Philip Van Aver
Wendy Watson's Mother Goose
Willy Pogany's Mother Goose
The moving adventures of Old Dame Trot and her comical cat, ill. by Paul Galdone
Namm, Diane. *Favorite nursery rhymes*
Nursery rhymes, ill. by Gertrude Elliott
One, two, buckle my shoe, ill. by Rowan Barnes-Murphy
One, two, buckle my shoe, ill. by Gail E. Haley
Over in the meadow, ill. by Paul Galdone
Palazzo, Tony (Anthony D.). *Animals 'round the mulberry bush*
Patterson, Pat. *Hickory dickory duck*
Pearson, Tracey Campbell. *Sing a song of sixpence*
Peppé, Rodney. *Cat and mouse*
Hey riddle diddle
Petersham, Maud. *The rooster crows*
Potter, Beatrix. *Appley Dapply's nursery rhymes*
Beatrix Potter's nursery rhyme book
Cecily Parsley's nursery rhymes
The pudgy book of Mother Goose, ill. by Richard Walz
Rey, H. A. (Hans Augusto). *Humpty Dumpty and other Mother Goose songs*
Robbins, Ruth. *The harlequin and Mother Goose*
Scarry, Richard. *Richard Scarry's animal nursery tales*

Sendak, Maurice. *Hector Protector, and As I went over the water*
Sieveking, Anthea. *Mary had a little lamb and other animal rhymes*
Polly put the kettle on and other play rhymes
Rub-a-dub-dub and other splashy rhymes
Twinkle, twinkle, little star and other bedtime rhymes
Simple Simon. *The adventures of Simple Simon*, ill. by Chris Conover
Simple Simon, ill. by Rodney Peppé
The story of Simple Simon, ill. by Paul Galdone
Stobbs, William. *This little piggy*
Tarrant, Margaret. *The Margaret Tarrant nursery rhyme book*
Thomson, Pat. *Rhymes around the day*
Tucker, Nicholas. *Mother Goose abroad*
Watson, Wendy. *Thanksgiving at our house*
Weil, Lisl. *Mother Goose picture riddles*
What do you feed your donkey on? ill. by Jenny Rodwell
Wheeler, Opal. *Sing Mother Goose*
Williams, Jenny. *Here's a ball for baby*
One, two, buckle my shoe
Ride a cockhorse
Ring around a rosy
Williams, Sarah. *Ride a cock-horse*
Yolen, Jane. *The lap-time song and play book*

Nursery school *see* School

Nurses *see* Careers – nurses

Oceans *see* Sea and seashore

Octopuses

Barrett, John M. *Oscar the selfish octopus*
Brandenberg, Franz. *Otto is different*
Carrick, Carol. *Octopus*
Drdek, Richard E. *Horace the friendly octopus*
Heller, Ruth. *How to hide an octopus*
Kraus, Robert. *Herman the helper*
Lauber, Patricia. *An octopus is amazing*
Most, Bernard. *My very own octopus*
Shaw, Evelyn S. *Octopus*
Spohn, Kate. *Ruth's bake shop*
Ungerer, Tomi. *Emile*
Waber, Bernard. *I was all thumbs*

Oil

Freeman, Don. *The seal and the slick*
Ungerer, Tomi. *The Mellops strike oil*

Old age

Ackerman, Karen. *Just like Max*
Allard, Harry. *It's so nice to have a wolf around the house*
Anderson, Lena Castell. *Stina's visit*
Ardizzone, Edward. *Lucy Brown and Mr. Grimes*
Armitage, Ronda. *The lighthouse keeper's rescue*
Bergman, Donna. *City fox*
Briggs, Raymond. *Jim and the beanstalk*
Carlstrom, Nancy White. *Blow me a kiss, Miss Lilly*
Coats, Laura Jane. *Mr. Jordan in the park*
Delton, Judy. *My grandma's in a nursing home*
Dugan, Barbara. *Loop the loop*
Edelman, Elaine. *Boom-de-boom*
Farber, Norma. *How does it feel to be old?*
Fassler, Joan. *My grandpa died today*
Fender, Kay. *Odette!*
Fink, Dale Borman. *Mr. Silver and Mrs. Gold*
Fox, Mem. *Wilfrid Gordon McDonald Partridge*
Gammell, Stephen. *Git along, old Scudder*
Goffstein, M. B. (Marilyn Brooke). *Fish for supper*
Graham, Bob. *Rose meets Mr. Wintergarten*
Greene, Carol. *The old ladies who liked cats*
Griffith, Helen V. *Georgia music*
Grimm, Jacob. *The Bremen town musicians*, ill. by Donna Diamond
The Bremen town musicians, ill. by Janina Domanska
The Bremen town musicians, ill. by Paul Galdone
Bremen town musicians, ill. by Josef Paleček
The Bremen town musicians, ill. by Ilse Plume
The Bremen town musicians, ill. by Bernadette Watts
The horse, the fox, and the lion, ill. by Paul Galdone
The musicians of Bremen, ill. by Svend Otto S.
The musicians of Bremen, ill. by Martin Ursell
The traveling musicians of Bremen, ill. by Kady MacDonald Denton
Guthrie, Donna. *Grandpa doesn't know it's me*
Hamm, Diane Johnston. *Grandma drives a motor bed*

Hazen, Barbara Shook. *Why did Grandpa die?*
Herriot, James. *Blossom comes home*
Hest, Amy. *The midnight eaters*
Hewett, Joan. *Rosalie*
Hindley, Judy. *The little train*
Hoff, Syd. *Barkley*
Holder, Heidi. *Carmine the crow*
Hughes, Shirley. *The snow lady*
Johnson, Angela. *When I am old with you*
Johnston, Tony. *Grandpa's song*
Kahl, Virginia. *Maxie*
Karkowsky, Nancy. *Grandma's soup*
Keeping, Charles. *Molly o' the moors*
Ketner, Mary Grace. *Ganzy remembers*
Kibbey, Marsha. *My grammy*
Klein, Leonore. *Old, older, oldest*
Knox-Wagner, Elaine. *My grandpa retired today*
Kunhardt, Dorothy. *Billy the barber*
Lasky, Kathryn. *Sea swan*
Leonard, Marcia. *Gregory and Mr. Grump*
Lewis, J. Patrick. *The Tsar and the amazing cow*
Littledale, Freya. *The snow child*
Nelson, Vaunda Micheaux. *Always Gramma*
Peet, Bill (William Bartlett). *Smokey*
Peters, Lisa Westberg. *Good morning, river!*
Pomerantz, Charlotte. *Buffy and Albert*
Rawlins, Donna. *Digging to China*
Ross, Lillian Hammer. *The little old man and his dreams*
Sakai, Kimiko. *Sachiko means happiness*
Schwartz, David M. *Supergrandpa*
Seligson, Susan. *Amos: the story of an old dog and his couch*
Skorpen, Liesel Moak. *Old Arthur*
Slobodkina, Esphyr. *Billy, the condominium cat*
Smith, Barry. *Minnie and Ginger*
Snow, Pegeen. *Mrs. Periwinkle's groceries*
Sonneborn, Ruth A. *I love Gram*
Taber, Anthony. *Cats' eyes*
Taylor, Mark. *Old Blue, you good dog you*
Tejima, Keizaburo. *Ho-limlim*
Tusa, Tricia. *Maebelle's suitcase*
Uchida, Yoshiko. *Sumi's special happening*
Waggoner, Karen. *The lemonade babysitter*
Wittman, Sally. *A special trade*
Zolotow, Charlotte (Shapiro). *I know a lady*

Olympics *see* Sports – Olympics

Only child *see* Family life – only child

Opossums *see* Animals – possums

Opposites *see* Concepts – opposites

Optical illusions

Anno, Mitsumasa. *Anno's alphabet*
  Anno's counting book
  Anno's counting house
  Anno's flea market
  Anno's Italy
  Anno's journey
  Anno's magical ABC
  Dr. Anno's magical midnight circus
  Topsy turvies: more pictures to stretch the imagination
  Topsy turvies: pictures to stretch the imagination
  Upside-downers
Baum, Arline. *Opt*
Doty, Roy. *Eye fooled you*
Gardner, Beau. *The look again...and again, and again, and again book*
  The turn about, think about, look about book
Noll, Sally. *Watch where you go*

Optimism *see* Character traits – optimism

Orphans

Ardizzone, Edward. *Lucy Brown and Mr. Grimes*
The babes in the woods. *The old ballad of the babes in the woods*, ill. by Edward Ardizzone
Bemelmans, Ludwig. *Madeline*
  Madeline [pop-up book]
  Madeline and the bad hat
  Madeline and the gypsies
  Madeline in London
  Madeline's Christmas
  Madeline's rescue
Bulla, Clyde Robert. *Poor boy, rich boy*
Gabel, Susan L. *Where the sun kisses the sea*
Mahy, Margaret. *Sailor Jack and the twenty orphans*
Moore, Inga. *The vegetable thieves*
Thomas, Kathy. *The angel's quest*
Ungerer, Tomi. *The three robbers*
Yorinks, Arthur. *Oh, brother*

Ostracism *see* Character traits – being different

Ostriches *see* Birds – ostriches

Otters *see* Animals – otters

Out and in *see* Concepts – in and out

Owls *see* Birds – owls

Oxen *see* Animals – oxen

Pack rats *see* Animals – pack rats

Painters *see* Activities – painting; Careers – artists

Painting *see* Activities – painting

Pakistan *see* Foreign lands – Pakistan

Panama *see* Foreign lands – Panama

Pandas *see* Animals – pandas

Panthers *see* Animals – leopards

Pants *see* Clothing – pants

Paper

Gibbons, Gail. *Deadline!*
  Paper, paper everywhere
Huff, Vivian. *Let's make paper dolls*
Lohf, Sabine. *Things I can make with paper*
Mitgutsch, Ali. *From wood to paper*
Small, David. *Paper John*
Tagore, Rabindranath. *Paper boats*
Testa, Fulvio. *The paper airplane*

Parades

Anderson, C. W. (Clarence Williams). *The rumble seat pony*
Baer, Gene. *Thump thump rat-a-tat-tat*
Brenner, Barbara A. *The snow parade*
Butler, Dorothy. *Higgledy, piggledy, hobbledy hoy*
Chalmers, Mary. *Easter parade*
Chwast, Seymour. *Alphabet parade*
Crews, Donald. *Parade*
Emberley, Ed (Edward Randolph). *The parade book*
Ets, Marie Hall. *Another day*
  In the forest
Feczko, Kathy. *Umbrella parade*
Flack, Marjorie. *Wait for William*
Janice. *Little Bear marches in the St. Patrick's Day parade*
Joosse, Barbara M. *Fourth of July*
Kroll, Steven. *The goat parade*
  Mary McLean and the St. Patrick's Day parade
Lasky, Kathryn. *Fourth of July bear*
Richter, Mischa. *Eric and Matilda*

Roth, Susan L. *We'll ride elephants through Brooklyn*
Slobodkina, Esphyr. *Pezzo the peddler and the circus elephant*
Spier, Peter. *Crash! bang! boom!*
Ziner, Feenie. *Counting carnival*

Parakeets *see* Birds – parakeets, parrots

Park rangers *see* Careers – park rangers

Parrots *see* Birds – parakeets, parrots

Participation

Agostinelli, Maria Enrica. *I know something you don't know*
Barrett, Judi. *What's left?*
Bauman, A. F. *Guess where you're going, guess what you'll do*
Bendick, Jeanne. *Why can't I?*
Bester, Roger. *Guess what?*
Black, Irma Simonton. *Is this my dinner?*
Blake, Quentin. *All join in*
Booth, Eugene. *At the circus*
  At the fair
  In the air
  In the garden
  In the jungle
  Under the ocean
Brown, Marc Tolon. *Finger rhymes*
Brown, Margaret Wise. *The country noisy book*
  The indoor noisy book
  Noisy book
  The quiet noisy book
  The seashore noisy book
  The summer noisy book
  The winter noisy book
Cameron, Polly. *"I can't," said the ant*
Carroll, Ruth. *Where's the bunny?*
Charlip, Remy. *Fortunately*
Cole, William. *Frances face-maker*
Corbett, Grahame. *Guess who?*
  What number now?
  Who is hiding?
  Who is inside?
  Who is next?
Craig, M. Jean. *Boxes*
Crume, Marion W. *Let me see you try*
  Listen!
  What do you say?
De Regniers, Beatrice Schenk. *It does not say meow!*
Elting, Mary. *Q is for duck*
Emberley, Ed (Edward Randolph). *Ed Emberley's amazing look through book*
  Klippity klop
Ets, Marie Hall. *Just me*
  Talking without words
French, Fiona. *Hunt the thimble*
Garten, Jan. *The alphabet tale*

Heilbroner, Joan. *This is the house where Jack lives*
Hewett, Anita. *The tale of the turnip*
Hoban, Tana. *Look again*
  Where is it?
The house that Jack built. *The house that Jack built*, ill. by Seymour Chwast
  The house that Jack built, ill. by Nadine Bernard Westcott
Hutchins, Pat. *Good night owl*
Ipcar, Dahlov. *Lost and found*
Jaynes, Ruth M. *Benny's four hats*
Johnson, Ryerson. *Let's walk up the wall*
Kepes, Juliet. *Run little monkeys, run, run, run*
Kunhardt, Edith. *Which one would you choose?*
  Which pig would you choose?
Kuskin, Karla. *Roar and more*
Löfgren, Ulf. *One-two-three*
MacGregor, Ellen. *Theodor Turtle*
Martin, Bill (William Ivan). *Brave little Indian*
Montgomerie, Norah. *This little pig went to market*
Ogle, Lucille. *I hear*
Paterson, Diane. *If I were a toad*
Rosen, Michael J. *We're going on a bear hunt*
Seignobosc, Françoise. *The things I like*
Seuss, Dr. *Mr. Brown can moo! Can you?*
  Wacky Wednesday
Shaw, Charles Green. *It looked like spilt milk*
Siewert, Margaret. *Bear hunt*
Simon, Norma. *What do I say?*
Sivulich, Sandra Stroner. *I'm going on a bear hunt*
Skaar, Grace Marion. *What do the animals say?*
Skorpen, Liesel Moak. *All the Lassies*
Slobodkina, Esphyr. *Caps for sale*
  Pezzo the peddler and the circus elephant
  Pezzo the peddler and the thirteen silly thieves
Spier, Peter. *Crash! bang! boom!*
  Gobble, growl, grunt
Steiner, Charlotte. *Five little finger playmates*
Sutton, Eve. *My cat likes to hide in boxes*
Ueno, Noriko. *Elephant buttons*
Watanabe, Shigeo. *How do I put it on?*
Weil, Lisl. *Owl and other scrambles*
Yudell, Lynn Deena. *Make a face*

Parties

Adams, Adrienne. *The Christmas party*
  A Halloween happening
Allard, Harry. *The Stupids have a ball*
  There's a party at Mona's tonight

Passover *see* Holidays – Passover

Patience *see* Character traits – patience

Peacocks, peahens *see* Birds – peacocks, peahens

Peddlers *see* Careers – peddlers

Pelicans *see* Birds – pelicans

Pen pals

Calmenson, Stephanie. *Wanted: warm, furry friend*
Caple, Kathy. *Harry's smile*

Penguins *see* Birds – penguins

Perseverance *see* Character traits – perseverance

Perseverance *see* Character traits – perseverance

Persia *see* Foreign lands – Persia

Persistence *see* Character traits – persistence

Perspective *see* Concepts – perspective

Peru *see* Foreign lands – Peru

Petroleum *see* Oil

Pets

Abercrombie, Barbara. *Charlie Anderson*
Ahlberg, Allan. *The pet shop*
Aiken, Joan. *Arabel and Mortimer*
Alexander, Martha G. *No ducks in our bathtub*
Allard, Harry. *It's so nice to have a wolf around the house*
Allen, Jonathan. *My cat*
My dog
Allen, Marjorie N. *One, two, three - ah-choo!*
Allen, Pamela. *My cat Maisie*
Ardizzone, Edward. *Diana and her rhinoceros*
Asch, Frank. *The last puppy*
Atwood, Margaret. *Anna's pet*
Baldner, Gaby. *Joba and the wild boar*
Balian, Lorna. *Amelia's nine lives*
Barasch, Marc Ian. *No plain pets!*
Bare, Colleen Stanley. *Guinea pigs don't read books*
To love a cat
To love a dog
Barton, Byron. *Jack and Fred*
Bastin, Marjolein. *A little dog for Vera*
Baylor, Byrd. *Amigo*

Beatty, Hetty Burlingame. *Moorland pony*
Belpré, Pura. *Santiago*
Benchley, Peter. *Jonathan visits the White House*
Berenstain, Stan. *The Berenstain bears' trouble with pets*
Bishop, Claire Huchet. *The truffle pig*
Blackwood, Gladys Rourke. *Whistle for Cindy*
Blance, Ellen. *Monster buys a pet*
Blegvad, Lenore. *The great hamster hunt*
Bliss, Corinne Demas. *That dog Melly!*
Boegehold, Betty. *Pawpaw's run*
Brenner, Barbara A. *The five pennies*
Brett, Jan. *Annie and the wild animals*
The first dog
Brice, Tony. *The bashful goldfish*
Brock, Emma Lillian. *A pet for Barbie*
Bröger, Achim. *Bruno takes a trip*
Francie's paper puppy
Brothers, Aileen. *Jiffy, Miss Boo and Mr. Roo*
Brown, Marc Tolon. *Arthur's pet business*
Brown, Ruth. *Our puppy's vacation*
Brunhoff, Laurent de. *Babar and the Wully-Wully*
Bryant, Donna. *My rabbit Roberta*
Burns, Theresa. *You're not my cat*
Calder, S. J. *If you were a cat*
Calders, Pere. *Brush*
Calhoun, Mary. *High-wire Henry*
Carlson, Natalie Savage. *Spooky night*
Carlstrom, Nancy White. *Who gets the sun out of bed?*
Carrick, Carol. *The accident*
A clearing in the forest
The foundling
Carroll, Ruth. *Pet tale*
Carter, Noelle. *My pet*
Chalmers, Mary. *Six dogs, twenty-three cats, forty-five mice, and one hundred sixteen spiders*
Chapouton, Anne-Marie. *Ben finds a friend*
Chenery, Janet. *Pickles and Jake*
Childress, Mark. *Joshua and Bigtooth*
Chittum, Ida. *The cat's pajamas*
Christian, Mary Blount. *Devin and Goliath*
Coerr, Eleanor. *The Josefina story quilt*
Coffelt, Nancy. *Good night, Sigmund*
Cohen, Miriam. *Jim's dog Muffins*
Cole, Babette. *Princess Smartypants*
Collington, Peter. *My darling kitten*
Collins, Pat Lowery. *Tumble, tumble, tumbleweed*
Cooney, Nancy Evans. *Go away monsters, lickety split!*
Cooper, Elizabeth K. *The fish from Japan*
Corrin, Ruth. *Mister cat*
Cousins, Lucy. *Pet animals*
Crane, Donn. *Flippy and Skippy*
Crowell, Maryalicia. *A horse in the house*

Reiser, Lynn. *Any kind of dog*
Remkiewicz, Frank. *The last time I saw Harris*
Ridlon, Marcia. *Kittens and more kittens*
Rockwell, Anne F. *I love my pets*
Roffey, Maureen. *Here, kitty kitty! Quick, catch Dan!*
Rogers, Fred. *When a pet dies*
Rosen, Winifred. *Henrietta and the day of the iguana*
Ross, George Maxim. *When Lucy went away*
Ross, Tony. *I want a cat*
Rylant, Cynthia. *Henry and Mudge*
   Henry and Mudge in puddle trouble
   Henry and Mudge in the green time
   Henry and Mudge under the yellow moon
Sandberg, Inger. *Nicholas' favorite pet*
Schaffer, Marion. *I love my cat!*
Schick, Alice. *Just this once*
Schlein, Miriam. *That's not Goldie!*
Schmeltz, Susan Alton. *Pets I wouldn't pick*
Schwartz, Henry. *Albert goes Hollywood*
   How I captured a dinosaur
Scruton, Clive. *Mary's pets*
Seabrooke, Brenda. *The best burglar alarm*
Seignobosc, Françoise. *The story of Colette*
Sendak, Maurice. *Some swell pup*
Sharmat, Marjorie Weinman. *I'm the best Nate the Great and the fishy prize*
Simon, Norma. *Cats do, dogs don't*
   Mama cat's year
   Oh, that cat!
Skorpen, Liesel Moak. *All the Lassies*
Smath, Jerry. *But no elephants*
Smith, Lane. *The big pets*
Smyth, Gwenda. *A pet for Mrs. Arbuckle*
Sneed, Brad. *Lucky Russell*
Snow, Pegeen. *A pet for Pat*
Spier, Peter. *The pet store*
Steiner, Charlotte. *Polka Dot*
Stevenson, James. *Mr. Hacker*
   Will you please feed our cat?
Stevenson, Suçie. *Jessica the blue streak*
Stoddard, Sandol. *My very own special particular private and personal cat*
Szilagyi, Mary. *Thunderstorm*
Tabler, Judith. *The new puppy*
Tallon, Robert. *Latouse my moose*
Thaler, Mike. *My puppy*
Tusa, Tricia. *Chicken*
Udry, Janice May. *"Oh no, cat!"*
   What Mary Jo wanted
Vaës, Alain. *The wild hamster*
Varga, Judy. *Miss Lollipop's lion*
Viorst, Judith. *The tenth good thing about Barney*
Vreeken, Elizabeth. *Henry*
Wahl, Jan. *Dracula's cat and Frankenstein's dog*
Wahl, Mats. *Grandfather's laika*
Ward, Lynd. *The biggest bear*

Wayland, April Halprin. *To Rabbittown*
Wilhelm, Hans. *I'll always love you*
Wirth, Beverly. *Margie and me*
Wisbeski, Dorothy Gross. *Pícaro, a pet otter*
Wolski, Slawomir. *Tiger cat*
Wong, Herbert H. *My goldfish*
Wright, Dare. *The lonely doll learns a lesson*
Zimelman, Nathan. *Positively no pets allowed*
Zinnemann-Hope, Pam. *Find your coat, Ned*
Zolotow, Charlotte (Shapiro). *The poodle who barked at the wind*
Zweifel, Frances. *Bony*

Philippines *see* Foreign lands – Philippines

Phoenix *see* Mythical creatures

Photography *see* Activities – photographing

Physical handicaps *see* Handicaps – physical

Physicians *see* Careers – doctors

Picnics *see* Activities – picnicking

Pigeons *see* Birds – pigeons

Pigs *see* Animals – pigs

Pilots *see* Careers – airplane pilots

Pirates
Allen, Pamela. *I wish I had a pirate suit*
Baum, Louis. *JuJu and the pirate*
Burningham, John. *Come away from the water, Shirley*
Carryl, Charles Edward. *A capital ship: or, The walloping window-blind*, ill. by Paul Galdone
   The walloping window blind, ill. by Ted Rand
Cole, Babette. *The trouble with Uncle*
Collington, Peter. *The angel and the soldier boy*
Devlin, Harry. *The walloping window blind*
Dewey, Ariane. *Laffite, the pirate*
Dyke, John. *Pigwig and the pirates*
Faulkner, Matt. *The amazing voyage of Jackie Grace*
Ginsburg, Mirra. *Four brave sailors*
Graham, Mary Stuart Campbell. *The pirates' bridge*
Haseley, Dennis. *The pirate who tried to capture the moon*
Hayes, Geoffrey. *The mystery of the pirate ghost*
Hutchins, Pat. *One-eyed Jake*

Isadora, Rachel. *The pirates of Bedford Street*

Joslin, Sesyle. *Señor Baby Elephant, the pirate*

Keats, Ezra Jack. *Maggie and the pirate*

Kessler, Leonard P. *The pirates' adventure on Spooky Island*

Kroll, Steven. *Are you pirates?*

Lloyd, David. *Grandma and the pirate*

Löfgren, Ulf. *Alvin the pirate*

Mahy, Margaret. *The horrendous hullabaloo*
The man whose mother was a pirate
Sailor Jack and the twenty orphans

Nash, Ogden. *Custard the dragon*, ill. by Linell Nash

Peppé, Rodney. *The kettleship pirates*

Perkins, Al. *Tubby and the lantern*

Roberts, Thom. *Pirates in the park*

Ross, David. *Gorp and the space pirates*

Ross, Tony. *Treasure of Cozy Cove*

Thompson, Brenda. *Pirates*

Walker, Barbara K. (Barbara Kerlin). *Pigs and pirates*

Ward, Helen. *The moonrat and the white turtle*

Weiss, Ellen. *The pirates of Tarnoonga*

Woychuk, Denis. *Pirates*

Young, James. *Penelope and the pirates*

Pixies *see* Elves and little people; Fairies

Planes *see* Airplanes, airports

Plants

Adelson, Leone. *Please pass the grass*

Aliki. *Corn is maize*

Ayer, Jacqueline. *The paper-flower tree*

Back, Christine. *Bean and plant*

Baker, Jeffrey J. W. *Patterns of nature*

Bash, Barbara. *Desert giant*

Berenstain, Stan. *The Berenstain bears and the prize pumpkin*

Berson, Harold. *Pop! goes the turnip*

Bishop, Gavin. *Mrs. McGinty and the bizarre plant*

Blackmore, Vivien. *Why corn is golden*

Brown, Marc Tolon. *Your first garden book*

Bulla, Clyde Robert. *A tree is a plant*

Busch, Phyllis S. *Cactus in the desert*
Lions in the grass

Carle, Eric. *The tiny seed*

Chapman, Carol. *Barney Bipple's magic dandelions*

Cole, Joanna. *Evolution*
Plants in winter

Craig, M. Jean. *Spring is like the morning*

Credle, Ellis. *Down, down the mountain*

Cristini, Ermanno. *In the pond*

Cross, Diana Harding. *Some plants have funny names*

Cross, Genevieve. *A trip to the yard*

Darby, Gene. *What is a plant?*

Domanska, Janina. *The turnip*

Ellentuck, Shan. *A sunflower as big as the sun*

Euvremer, Teryl. *The thieves of Peck's pocket*

Fisher, Aileen Lucia. *And a sunflower grew*
As the leaves fall down
Mysteries in the garden
Now that spring is here
Plant magic
Prize performance
Seeds on the go
Swords and daggers
We went looking

Gage, Wilson. *Anna's garden songs*
Anna's summer songs

Gibbons, Gail. *From seed to plant*

Ginsburg, Mirra. *Mushroom in the rain*
The green grass grows all around, ill. by Hilde Hoffmann

Greenberg, Polly. *Oh, Lord, I wish I was a buzzard*

Guiberson, Brenda Z. *Cactus hotel*

Heller, Ruth. *Plants that never ever bloom*

Hewett, Anita. *The tale of the turnip*

Hillert, Margaret. *The magic beans*

Hogan, Paula Z. *The dandelion*

Holmes, Anita. *The 100-year-old cactus*

Hutchins, Pat. *Titch*

Ipcar, Dahlov. *Hard scrabble harvest*

Jack and the beanstalk. *The history of Mother Twaddle and the marvelous achievements of her son Jack*, ill. by Paul Galdone

Jordan, Helene J. (Helene Jamieson). *Seeds of wind and water*

Kepes, Juliet. *The seed that peacock planted*

Kirkpatrick, Rena K. *Look at leaves*
Look at seeds and weeds

Krauss, Ruth. *The carrot seed*

Krings, Antoon. *Oliver's strawberry patch*

Kuchalla, Susan. *All about seeds*

Le Tord, Bijou. *Picking and weaving*

Lewis, Naomi. *Leaves*

Little, Lessie Jones. *I can do it by myself*

The little red hen. *The cock, the mouse and the little red hen*, ill. by Graham Percy
The little red hen, ill. by Janina Domanska
The little red hen, ill. by Paul Galdone
The little red hen, ill. by Mel Pekarsky
The little red hen, ill. by William Stobbs
The little red hen, ill. by Margot Zemach

Littledale, Freya. *The magic plum tree*

McDonald, Megan. *The great pumpkin switch*

Maestro, Giulio. *The remarkable plant in apartment 4*

Mahy, Margaret. *The pumpkin man and the crafty creeper*

Milhous, Katherine. *The turnip*

Miller, Judith Ransom. *Nabob and the geranium*
Nash, Ogden. *The animal garden*, ill. by Hilary Knight
Oleson, Claire. *For Pipita, an orange tree*
Petie, Haris. *The seed the squirrel dropped*
Pouyanne, Rési. *What I see hidden by the pond*
Pulver, Robin. *Nobody's mother is in second grade*
Ray, Mary Lyn. *Pumpkins*
Rey, H. A. (Hans Augusto). *Elizabite, adventures of a carnivorous plant*
Ring, Elizabeth. *Tiger lilies and other beastly plants*
Ringi, Kjell (Arne Sorensen). *The sun and the cloud*
Rockwell, Harlow. *The compost heap*
Rudolph, Marguerita. *How a shirt grew in the field*
Schertle, Alice. *Witch Hazel*
Selberg, Ingrid. *Nature's hidden world*
Selsam, Millicent E. *A first look at the world of plants*
  More potatoes!
  Seeds and more seeds
Shecter, Ben. *Partouche plants a seed*
Sugita, Yutaka. *The flower family*
Tolstoĭ, Alekseĭ Nikolaevich. *The great big enormous turnip*
Watts, Barrie. *Dandelion*
  Mushrooms
  Tomato
Wexler, Jerome (LeRoy). *Flowers, fruits, seeds*
  Wonderful pussy willows
Williams, Barbara. *Hello, dandelions!*
Wondriska, William. *The tomato patch*
Wong, Herbert H. *My plant*
Zion, Gene. *The plant sitter*
Zolotow, Charlotte (Shapiro). *In my garden*

Playing *see* Activities – playing

Plays *see* Theater

Poetry, rhyme

Aardema, Verna. *Bringing the rain to Kapiti Plain*
  The riddle of the drum
Abrons, Mary. *For Alice a palace*
Ackerman, Karen. *The banshee*
  Flannery Row
Adams, Richard (Richard Newbold). *The tyger voyage*
Adelborg, Ottilia. *Clean Peter and the children of Grubbylea*
Adelson, Leone. *Please pass the grass*
Adler, David A. *You think it's fun to be a clown!*

Adoff, Arnold. *Big sister tells me that I'm black*
  Birds
  Black is brown is tan
  The cabbages are chasing the rabbits
  Greens
  Hard to be six
  In for winter, out for spring
  Make a circle, keep us in
  Tornado!
  Where wild Willie?
Adorjan, Carol. *I can! Can you?*
Æsop. *Androcles and the lion*, ill. by Robert Rayevsky
  Once in a wood, ill. by Eve Rice
Ahlberg, Allan. *Cops and robbers*
Ahlberg, Janet. *Each peach pear plum*
  The jolly Christmas postman
  Peek-a-boo!
Aiken, Conrad Potter. *Tom, Sue and the clock*
Alborough, Jez. *Bare bear*
  Where's my teddy?
Alderson, Sue Ann. *Bonnie McSmithers is at it again!*
Aldis, Dorothy. *All together*
  Before things happen
  Hello day
  Quick as a wink
Alexander, Anne (Anna Barbara Cooke). *ABC of cars and trucks*
  I want to whistle
  My daddy and I
Alger, Leclaire Gowans. *All in the morning early*
  Kellyburn Braes
Allen, Jonathan. *A bad case of animal nonsense*
Allen, Marjorie N. *Changes*
Allen, Pamela. *Who sank the boat?*
Allison, Diane Worfolk. *In window eight, the moon is late*
Ambler, Christopher Gifford. *Ten little foxhounds*
Anastasio, Dina. *Pass the peas, please*
Andre, Evelyn M. *Places I like to be*
Anglund, Joan Walsh. *Love is a baby*
  Morning is a little child
Anholt, Catherine. *What I like*
Aragon, Jane Chelsea. *Salt hands*
  Winter harvest
Archambault, John. *Counting sheep*
Armour, Richard Willard. *The adventures of Egbert the Easter egg*
  Animals on the ceiling
  Have you ever wished you were something else?
  Sea full of whales
  The year Santa went modern
Arnold, Tedd. *Ollie forgot*
Asch, Frank. *Baby in the box*

City sandwich
Country pie
Ashley, Jill. *Riddles about Christmas*
Ashton, Elizabeth Allen. *An old-fashioned ABC book*
An old-fashioned one two three book
Attenberger, Walburga. *The little man in winter*
Who knows the little man?
Atwood, Ann. *The little circle*
Auerbach, Julie Jaslow. *Everything's changing—It's pesach!*
Aylesworth, Jim. *The folks in the valley*
Mary's mirror
Mr. McGill goes to town
Old Black Fly
One crow
Ayres, Pam. *Guess what?*
Guess who?
When dad cuts down the chestnut tree
When dad fills in the garden pond
Azarian, Mary. *The tale of John Barleycorn or, From barley to beer*
The babes in the woods. *The old ballad of the babes in the woods*, ill. by Edward Ardizzone
Babson, Jane F. *Babson's bestiary*
Bach, Othello. *Lilly, Willy and the mail-order witch*
Baer, Edith. *This is the way we go to school*
Words are like faces
Baker, Keith. *Hide and snake*
Who is the beast?
Baker, Sanna Anderson. *Who's a friend of the water-spurting whale*
Bang, Molly. *Ten, nine, eight*
Baningan, Sharon Stearns. *Circus magic*
Barasch, Marc Ian. *No plain pets!*
Barker, Cicely Mary. *Berry flower fairies*
Blossom flower fairies
Flower fairies of the garden
Flower fairies of the seasons
Flower fairies of the spring
Flower fairies of the summer
Flower fairies of the trees
Flower fairies postcard book
Spring flower fairies
Summer flower fairies
Barracca, Debra. *Maxi, the hero*
Barracca, Sal. *The adventures of taxi dog*
Barrett, Judi. *Pickles have pimples*
Barry, Katharina. *A bug to hug*
A is for anything
Barry, Robert E. *Animals around the world*
Mr. Willowby's Christmas tree
Barto, Emily N. *Chubby bear*
Baruch, Dorothy. *I would like to be a pony and other wishes*
Base, Graeme. *My grandma lived in Gooligulch*
Baskin, Leonard. *Hosie's zoo*

Baylor, Byrd. *Amigo*
The desert is theirs
Desert voices
Everybody needs a rock
The other way to listen
Behn, Harry. *Crickets and bullfrogs and whispers of thunder*
Trees
Beisner, Monika. *Catch that cat!*
Topsy turvy
Belloc, Hilaire. *The bad child's book of beasts, and more beasts for worse children*
The bad child's pop-up book of beasts
Matilda who told lies and was burned to death
More beasts for worse children
Belting, Natalia Maree. *Christmas folk*
Summer's coming in
Bemelmans, Ludwig. *Madeline*
Madeline and the bad hat
Madeline and the gypsies
Madeline in London
Madeline's Christmas
Madeline's rescue
Welcome home
Benét, William Rose. *Angels*
Benjamin, Alan. *A change of plans*
Rat-a-tat, pitter pat
Ribtickle Town
Bennett, Jill. *Animal fair*
A cup of starshine
Days are where we live and other poems
Machine poems
Noisy poems
People poems
Roger was a razor fish and other poems
Spooky poems
Tiny Tim
Bennett, Rainey. *The secret hiding place*
Bennett, Rowena. *The day is dancing and other poems*
Songs from around a toadstool table
Berenstain, Stan. *The bear detectives: the case of the missing pumpkin*
The Berenstain bears and the missing dinosaur bone
The Berenstain bears and the spooky old tree
The Berenstain bears' Christmas tree
He bear, she bear
Berg, Jean Horton. *The wee little man*
Berger, Judith. *Butterflies and rainbows*
Beskow, Elsa Maartman. *Children of the forest*
Peter in Blueberry Land
Peter's adventures in Blueberry land
Betz, Betty. *Manners for moppets*
Billy Boy, ill. by Glen Rounds
Birchman, David F. *Brother Billy Bronto's bygone blues band*
Bird, E. J. *How do bears sleep?*

Black, Irma Simonton. *Is this my dinner?*
Blackwood, Mary. *Derek the knitting dinosaur*
Blake, Quentin. *All join in*
Mister Magnolia
Quentin Blake's ABC
Blegvad, Erik. *Burnie's hill*
Blegvad, Lenore. *One is for the sun*
The parrot in the garret and other rhymes about dwellings
Blocksma, Mary. *Where's that duck?*
Bloom, Suzanne. *We keep a pig in the parlor*
Blos, Joan W. *Old Henry*
A seed, a flower, a minute, an hour
Blumenthal, Nancy. *Count-a-saurus*
Blyler, Allison. *Finding foxes*
Bodecker, N. M. (Nils Mogens). *"Let's marry" said the cherry, and other nonsense poems*
Snowman Sniffles and other verse
Bodwell, Gaile. *The long day of the giants*
Boegehold, Betty. *Pawpaw's run*
Boesky, Amy. *Planet Was*
Borchers, Elisabeth. *There comes a time*
Bornstein, Ruth Lercher. *The seedling child*
Borten, Helen. *Do you go where I go?*
Do you hear what I hear?
Do you know what I know?
Bottner, Barbara. *There was nobody there*
Bouton, Josephine. *Favorite poems for the children's hour*
A boy went out to gather pears
Boynton, Sandra. *But not the hippopotamus*
The going to bed book
Good night, good night
Hippos go berserk
Moo, baa, lalala
Bradman, Tony. *The bad babies' counting book*
This little baby
Braun, Kathy. *Kangaroo and kangaroo*
Brecht, Bertolt. *Uncle Eddie's moustache*
Brenner, Barbara A. *The color wizard*
Brent, Isabelle. *Cameo cats*
Bridgman, Elizabeth. *All the little bunnies*
Bright, Robert. *My hopping bunny*
Brooke, L. Leslie (Leonard Leslie). *Johnny Crow's garden*
Johnny Crow's new garden
Brooks, Gwendolyn. *Bronzeville boys and girls*
Brown, Beatrice Curtis. *Jonathan Bing*, ill. by Judith Gwyn Brown
Jonathan Bing, ill. by Pelagie Doane
Brown, Judith Gwyn. *Alphabet dreams*
Brown, Marc Tolon. *Finger rhymes*
Hand rhymes
Pickle things
The silly tail book
There's no place like home
Wings on things

Witches four
Brown, Margaret Wise. *Big red barn*, ill. by Felicia Bond
Big red barn, ill. by Rosella Hartman
Four fur feet
Nibble nibble
Sleepy ABC
Two little trains
Where have you been?
Whistle for the train
The wonderful story book
Brown, Myra Berry. *Best friends*
Browner, Richard. *Everyone has a name*
Browning, Robert. *The pied piper of Hamelin*, ill. by Patricia and Robin DeWitt
The pied piper of Hamelin, ill. by Kate Greenaway
The pied piper of Hamelin, ill. by Anatoly Ivanov
The pied piper of Hamelin, ill. by Errol Le Cain
Bruce, Sheilah B. *The radish day jubilee*
Bruchac, Joseph. *Thirteen moons on turtle's back*
Bruna, Dick. *Christmas*
The fish
Kitten Nell
Little bird tweet
The orchestra
Poppy Pig goes to market
Tilly and Tess
Bryan, Ashley. *Beat the story-drum, pum-pum*
The cat's purr
Buckley, Helen Elizabeth. *Josie and the snow*
Josie's Buttercup
Buckley, Kate. *Love notes*
Buckley, Richard. *The foolish tortoise*
The greedy python
Bucknall, Caroline. *One bear all alone*
One bear in the hospital
One bear in the picture
Budney, Blossom. *A kiss is round*
Buell, Ellen Lewis. *Read me a poem*
Buff, Mary. *Hurry, Skurry and Flurry*
Buller, Jon. *Toad on the road*
Bullock, Kathleen. *It chanced to rain*
Bunting, Eve (Anne Evelyn). *Happy birthday, dear duck*
Scary, scary Halloween
Burdekin, Harold. *A child's grace*
Burgess, Gelett. *The little father*
Burgunder, Rose. *From summer to summer*
Burnstein, John. *Slim Goodbody*
Burroway, Janet. *The truck on the track*
Bush, John. *The cross-with-us rhinoceros*
The fish who could wish
Butler, Dorothy. *Higgledy, piggledy, hobbledy hoy*

Cahill, Chris. *Bear magic*
Bunny magic
Calmenson, Stephanie. *Dinner at the Panda Palace*
Never take a pig to lunch and other funny poems about animals
Where will the animals stay?
Cameron, John. *If mice could fly*
Cameron, Polly. *A child's book of nonsense*
"I can't," said the ant
Carlson, Nancy. *Take time to relax*
Carlstrom, Nancy White. *Better not get wet, Jesse Bear*
Goodbye geese
Graham cracker animals 1-2-3
It's about time, Jesse Bear
Kiss your sister, Rose Marie
The moon came too
No nap for Benjamin Badger
Northern lullaby
Wild wild sunflower child Anna
Carroll, Kathleen Sullivan. *One red rooster*
Carroll, Lewis. *Jabberwocky*, ill. by Graeme Base
Jabberwocky, ill. from Disney archives
Jabberwocky, ill. by Jane Breskin Zalben
The walrus and the carpenter, ill. by Julian Doyle
The walrus and the carpenter, ill. by Jane Breskin Zalben
Carryl, Charles Edward. *The walloping window blind*, ill. by Ted Rand
Carter, Noelle. *My house*
My pet
Carton, Lonnie Caming. *Mommies*
Cassedy, Sylvia. *Red dragonfly on my shoulder*
Cassidy, Dianne. *Circus animals*
Circus people
Cate, Rikki. *A cat's tale*
Caudill, Rebecca. *Wind, sand and sky*
Cauley, Lorinda Bryan. *Clap your hands*
Causley, Charles. *"Quack!" said the billy-goat*
Cave, Kathryn. *Out for the count*
Cendrars, Blaise. *Shadow*
Chardiet, Bernice. *C is for circus*
Charles, Donald. *Calico Cat meets bookworm*
Calico cat's year
Shaggy dog's animal alphabet
Time to rhyme with Calico Cat
Charles, R. H. (Robert Henry). *The roundabout turn*
Cherry, Lynne. *Who's sick today?*
Chönz, Selina. *A bell for Ursli*
Florina and the wild bird
The snowstorm
Chorao, Kay. *The baby's bedtime book*
The baby's good morning book
Christelow, Eileen. *Five little monkeys jumping on the bed*
Five little monkeys sitting in a tree

Christmas in the stable, ill. by Beverly K. Duncan
Chukovsky, Korney. *The telephone*
Ciardi, John. *John J. Plenty and Fiddler Dan*
The monster den: or, Look what happened at my house—and to it
Clark, Leonard. *Drums and trumpets*
Clifford, Eth. *Red is never a mouse*
Clifton, Lucille. *Everett Anderson's Christmas coming*
Everett Anderson's friend
Everett Anderson's goodbye
Everett Anderson's nine months long
Everett Anderson's 1-2-3
Everett Anderson's year
Some of the days of Everett Anderson
Clithero, Sally. *Beginning-to-read poetry*
Coats, Laura Jane. *Ten little animals*
Coatsworth, Elizabeth. *The children come running*
The giant golden book of cat stories
A peaceable kingdom, and other poems
Cohen, Caron Lee. *Whiffle Squeek*
Cole, Babette. *Silly book*
Cole, Joanna. *Animal sleepyheads*
Golly Gump swallowed a fly
Cole, William. *Frances face-maker*
I went to the animal fair
That pest Jonathan
What's good for a four-year-old?
What's good for a six-year-old?
What's good for a three-year-old?
Coleridge, Sara. *January brings the snow*
Coletta, Irene. *From A to Z*
Conover, Chris. *Six little ducks*
Cooney, Barbara. *A garland of games and other diversions*
Copp, James (Andrew James). *Martha Matilda O'Toole*
Count me in
Counting rhymes, ill. by Corinne Malvern
Couture, Susan Arkin. *The block book*
Craft, Ruth. *The day of the rainbow*
The winter bear
Crowley, Arthur. *Bonzo Beaver*
The wagon man
Cummings, E. E. (Edward Estlin). *Hist whist*
In just-spring
Little tree
Cummings, Pat. *Clean your room, Harvey Moon!*
Jimmy Lee did it
Cummings, Phil. *Goodness gracious!*
Cushman, Doug. *Giants*
Once upon a pig
Dahl, Roald. *Dirty beasts*
Dalmais, Anne-Marie. *In my garden*
Dayton, Laura. *LeRoy's birthday circus*
Degen, Bruce. *Jamberry*
Teddy bear towers

De Gerez, Toni. *My song is a piece of jade*
Delacre, Lulu. *Arroz con leche*
  Las Navidades
Delaunay, Sonia. *Sonia Delaunay's alphabet*
Demi. *Demi's count the animals 1-2-3*
Demuth, Patricia Brennan. *Max, the bad-talking parrot*
Dennis, Suzanne E. *Answer me that*
De Paola, Tomie (Thomas Anthony).
  Songs of the fog maiden
De Regniers, Beatrice Schenk. *A bunch of poems and verses*
  Cats cats cats
  It does not say meow!
  May I bring a friend?
  Red Riding Hood
  Sam and the impossible thing
  So many cats!
  Something special
  Was it a good trade?
Dodd, Lynley. *Hairy Maclary from Donaldson's dairy*
  Hairy Maclary Scattercat
  Hairy Maclary's bone
  The nickle nackle tree
Dodds, Dayle Ann. *Do bunnies talk?*
  Wheel away!
Dodge, Mary Mapes. *Mary Anne*
  The dog writes on the window with his nose, and other poems
Domanska, Janina. *What do you see?*
Don't tell the scarecrow
Doolittle, Eileen. *World of wonders*
Dowers, Patrick. *One day scene through a leaf*
Dragonwagon, Crescent. *Half a moon and one whole star*
  The itch book
  Jemima remembers
  This is the bread I baked for Ned
Driz, Ovsei. *The boy and the tree*
Dubanevich, Arlene. *Tom's tail*
Duke, Kate. *Seven froggies went to school*
Duncan, Lois. *Birthday moon*
  Songs from dreamland
Eastwick, Ivy O. *Cherry stones! Garden swings!*
  Rainbow over all
Eberstadt, Isabel. *What is for my birthday?*
Edelman, Elaine. *Boom-de-boom*
Eichenberg, Fritz. *Dancing in the moon*
Elborn, Andrew. *Bird Adalbert*
Eliot, T. S. (Thomas Stearns). *Mr. Mistoffelees with Mungojerrie and Rumpelteazer*
Elkin, Benjamin. *The king who could not sleep*
Elliot, David. *An alphabet of rotten kids!*
Elves, fairies and gnomes, ill. by Rosekrans Hoffman
Emberley, Barbara. *Drummer Hoff*

Night's nice
One wide river to cross
Esbensen, Barbara Juster. *Ladder to the sky*
  The star maiden
  Who shrank my grandmother's house?
Ets, Marie Hall. *Beasts and nonsense*
Euvremer, Teryl. *After dark*
Evans, Katie. *Hunky Dory ate it*
Evans, Mel. *The tiniest sound*
Fairy poems for the very young, ill. by Beverlie Manson
Farber, Norma. *As I was crossing Boston Common*
  How the hibernators came to Bethlehem
  How the left-behind beasts built Ararat
  How to ride a tiger
  Never say ugh to a bug
  Small wonders
  There goes feathertop!
  There once was a woman who married a man
  Up the down elevator
  Where's Gomer?
Farjeon, Eleanor. *Around the seasons*
  Cats sleep anywhere.
  Mrs. Malone
Feder, Harriet K. *Not yet, Elijah!*
Fehlner, Paul. *Dog and cat*
Field, Eugene. *Wynken, Blynken and Nod*, ill. by Barbara Cooney
Field, Rachel Lyman. *General store*, ill. by Giles Laroche
  General store, ill. by Nancy Winslow Parker
  A road might lead to anywhere
Finfer, Celentha. *Grandmother dear*
First graces, ill. by Tasha Tudor
First prayers, ill. by Anna Maria Magagna
First prayers, ill. by Tasha Tudor
Fisher, Aileen Lucia. *And a sunflower grew*
  Anybody home?
  Best little house
  Do bears have mothers too?
  Going barefoot
  The house of a mouse
  I like weather
  I wonder how, I wonder why
  In one door and out the other
  In the middle of the night
  Like nothing at all
  Listen, rabbit
  My first Hanukkah book
  My mother and I
  Mysteries in the garden
  Now that spring is here
  Petals yellow and petals red
  Plant magic
  Prize performance
  Rabbits, rabbits
  Seeds on the go
  Sing, little mouse

Skip around the year
Swords and daggers
We went looking
When it comes to bugs
Where does everyone go?
Fisher, Leonard Everett. *Boxes! Boxes!*
Flanders, Michael. *Creatures great and small*
Fleischman, Paul. *Rondo in C*
Florian, Douglas. *A potter*
Fontane, Theodor. *Nick Ribbeck of Ribbeck of Havelland*
Sir Ribbeck of Ribbeck of Havelland
Foord, Jo. *The book of babies*
Forrester, Victoria. *Words to keep against the night*
Fowler, Richard. *Cat's story*
Fox, Dorothea Warren. *Follow me the leader*
Fox, Mem. *Shoes from grandpa*
Fox, Siv Cedering. *The blue horse and other night poems*
Frank, Josette. *More poems to read to the very young*
Poems to read to the very young
Frankenberg, Lloyd. *Wings of rhyme*
Frasconi, Antonio. *The snow and the sun, la nieve y el sol*
Frasier, Debra. *On the day you were born*
Freeman, Don. *The day is waiting*
Mop Top
Freeman, Jean Todd. *Cynthia and the unicorn*
Freschet, Berniece. *The ants go marching*
Frith, Michael K. *I'll teach my dog 100 words*
From morn to midnight, ill. by Satomi Ichikawa
Frost, Robert. *Stopping by woods on a snowy evening*
Fyleman, Rose. *A fairy went a-marketing*
Gág, Wanda. *ABC bunny*
Gage, Wilson. *Anna's garden songs*
Anna's summer songs
Down in the boondocks
Galdone, Joanna. *Gertrude, the goose who forgot*
The tailypo
García Lorca, Federico. *The Lieutenant Colonel and the gypsy*
Gardner, Beau. *Whooo's a fright on Halloween night?*
Gardner, Martin. *Never make fun of a turtle, my son*
Garelick, May. *Look at the moon*
Where does the butterfly go when it rains?
Garten, Jan. *The alphabet tale*
Gay, Marie-Louise. *Moonbeam on a cat's ear*
Gay, Marie-Louise. *Rainy day magic*
Gay, Zhenya. *Look!*
Gelbard, Jane. *My bye-bye bottle book*
My dressing book
My eating book

My sharing book
Gelman, Rita Golden. *Hey, kid*
Geraghty, Paul. *The cow is mooing anyhow*
Gerrard, Roy. *The Favershams*
Mik's mammoth
Rosie and the rustlers
Sir Cedric rides again
Sir Francis Drake
Gerstein, Mordicai. *Roll over!*
Gewing, Lisa. *Mama, daddy, baby and me*
Ghigna, Charles. *Good cats / Bad cats*
Good dogs / Bad dogs
Gibson, Myra Tomback. *What is your favorite thing to touch?*
Gilchrist, Theo E. *Halfway up the mountain*
The gingerbread boy. The gingerbread boy, ill. by Paul Galdone
Whiff, sniff, nibble and chew, ill. by Monica Incisa
Ginsburg, Mirra. *Four brave sailors*
Kitten from one to ten
The sun's asleep behind the hill
Giovanni, Nikki. *Spin a soft black song*
Goldblatt, Eli. *Leo loves round*
Goldstein, Bobbye S. *Bear in mind*
Poems on poetry
What's on the menu?
Gomi, Taro. *Toot!*
Goodspeed, Peter. *A rhinoceros wakes me up in the morning*
Gordon, Jeffie Ross. *Two badd babies*
Graham, Lorenz B. *Song of the boat*
Greaves, Margaret. *The mice of Nibbling Village*
Greeley, Valerie. *White is the moon*
The green grass grows all around, ill. by Hilde Hoffmann
Greenaway, Kate. *Marigold garden*
Under the window
Greenberg, Dan. *The bed who ran away from home*
Greenberg, David. *Slugs*
Greene, Carol. *The world's biggest birthday cake*
Greenfield, Eloise. *Big friend, little friend*
Daddy and I
Daydreamers
I make music
My doll, Keshia
Night on Neighborhood Street
Under the Sunday tree
Greenwood, Ann. *A pack of dreams*
Gregorich, Barbara. *My friend goes left*
Grimm, Jacob. *The traveling musicians of Bremen*, ill. by Kady MacDonald Denton
Grossman, Bill. *Donna O'Neeshuck was chased by some cows*
The guy who was five minutes late
Tommy at the grocery store
Grossman, Virginia. *Ten little rabbits*
Guarino, Deborah. *Is your mama a llama?*

Gundersheimer, Karen. *Happy winter*
Gunning, Monica. *The two Georges*
Haas, Irene. *The Maggie B*
Hague, Kathleen. *Alphabears*
 Bear huggs
 Out of the nursery, into the night
Hall, Pam. *On the edge of the eastern ocean*
Hallinan, P. K. (Patrick K.). *Just open a
 book*
 That's what a friend is
Hample, Stoo. *Yet another big fat funny silly
 book*
Hamsa, Bobbie. *Polly wants a cracker*
Harrison, David Lee. *The case of Og, the
 missing frog*
Harrison, Sarah. *In granny's garden*
Hawkes, Kevin. *Then the troll heard the
 squeak*
Hawkins, Colin. *Boo! Who?*
 Jen the hen
 Mig the pig
 Snap! Snap!
 Take away monsters
 Tog the dog
Hayes, Sarah. *Clap your hands*
 The grumpalump
 Nine ducks nine
 This is the bear
 This is the bear and the picnic lunch
 This is the bear and the scary night
Hazen, Barbara Shook. *Where do bears
 sleep?*
Heiligman, Deborah. *Into the night*
Heine, Helme. *Mollywoop*
Hellard, Susan. *Time to get up*
Heller, Ruth. *A cache of jewels and other
 collective nouns*
 How to hide a butterfly
 How to hide a polar bear
 How to hide an octopus
 Kites sail high
 The reason for a flower
Hennessy, B. G. *A, B, C, D, tummy, toes,
 hands, knee*
 Jake baked the cake
 The missing tarts
 School days
 When you were just a little girl
Henrietta. *A mouse in the house*
Herford, Oliver. *The most timid in the land*
Herson, Kathleen. *The copycat*
Highwater, Jamake. *Moonsong lullaby*
Hill, Susan. *Can it be true?*
Hillert, Margaret. *What is it?*
Hillman, Priscilla. *A Merry-Mouse book of
 favorite poems*
 A Merry-Mouse book of months
Hindley, Judy. *Uncle Harold and the green
 hat*
Hines, Anna Grossnickle. *It's just me, Emily*
Hoban, Russell. *Goodnight*

Hoban, Tana. *One little kitten*
 Where is it?
Hoberman, Mary Ann. *The cozy book*
 Fathers, mothers, sisters, brothers
 A fine fat pig other animal poems
 A house is a house for me
 I like old clothes
 Nuts to you and nuts to me
Hoffman, Phyllis. *We play*
Hofstrand, Mary. *Albion pig*
 By the sea
Holder, Heidi. *Crows*
Holl, Adelaide. *Mrs. McGarrity's peppermint
 sweater*
 Sir Kevin of Devon
Hood, Thomas. *Before I go to sleep*
Hooper, Patricia. *A bundle of beasts*
Hoopes, Lyn Littlefield. *Mommy, daddy, me*
 Wing-a-ding
Hopkins, Lee Bennett. *And God bless me*
 Best friends
 Circus! Circus!
 A dog's life
 Easter buds are springing
 Go to bed!
 Good books, good times
 I think I saw a snail
 Merrily comes our harvest in
 On the farm
 Ring out, wild bells
 The sea is calling me
 The sky is full of song
 Still as a star
 To the zoo
Hot cross buns, and other old street cries
Houston, John A. *The bright yellow rope*
Howells, Mildred. *The woman who lived in
 Holland*
Hudson, Cheryl Willis. *Bright eyes, brown
 skin*
 Good morning baby
 Good night baby
Hughes, Shirley. *All shapes and sizes*
 Bathwater's hot
 Colors
 Noisy
 Out and about
 Two shoes, new shoes
 When we went to the park
Hulme, Joy. *Sea squares*
Hurd, Edith Thacher. *Caboose*
 Come and have fun
Hutchins, Pat. *The tale of Thomas Mead*
 Which witch is which?
 The wind blew
Hymes, Lucia. *Oodles of noodles and other
 rhymes*
If dragon flies made honey
Ilsley, Velma. *A busy day for Chris*
 The pink hat
Ipcar, Dahlov. *Black and white*

The owl and the pussycat, ill. by Lori Farbanish

The owl and the pussy-cat, ill. by Gwen Fulton

The owl and the pussycat, ill. by Paul Galdone

The owl and the pussy-cat, ill. by Elaine Muis

The owl and the pussycat, ill. by Erica Rutherford

The owl and the pussycat, ill. by Janet Stevens

The owl and the pussycat, ill. by Louise Voce

The owl and the pussycat, ill. by Colin West

The owl and the pussy-cat, ill. by Owen Wood

The pelican chorus, ill. by Harold Berson

The pelican chorus and the quangle wangle's hat, ill. by Kevin W. Maddison

The pobble who has no toes, ill. by Emma Crosby

The pobble who has no toes, ill. by Kevin W. Maddison

The quangle wangle's hat, ill. by Emma Crosby

The quangle wangle's hat, ill. by Helen Oxenbury

The quangle wangle's hat, ill. by Janet Stevens

Two laughable lyrics, ill. by Paul Galdone

Whizz! ill. by Janina Domanska

Lee, Dennis. *Alligator pie*

Leedy, Loreen. *The dragon Halloween party*

The dragon Thanksgiving feast

A number of dragons

Leemis, Ralph. *Mister Momboo's hat*

Leichman, Seymour. *Shaggy dogs and spotty dogs and shaggy and spotty dogs*

The wicked wizard and the wicked witch

Leigh, Oretta. *The merry-go-round*

Lenski, Lois. *I like winter*

The life I live

Now it's fall

On a summer day

Sing a song of people

Spring is here

Susie Mariar

Leonard, Marcia. *Birthday in a bathtub*

Lerner, Marguerite Rush. *Dear little mumps child*

Lerner, Sharon. *Follow the monsters!*

Lessac, Frané. *Caribbean canvas*

Lester, Alison. *Magic beach*

Let's count and count out, ill. by Deborah Derr McClintock

Levens, George. *Kippy the koala*

Levine, Abby. *You push, I ride*

Lewin, Betsy. *Animal snackers*

Cat count

Lewis, J. Patrick. *A hippopotamusn't*

Two-legged, four-legged, no-legged rhymes

Lewis, Naomi. *The butterfly collector*

Once upon a rainbow

Lewis, Richard. *In a spring garden*

In the night, still dark

Lewison, Wendy C. *Going to sleep on the farm*

Lexau, Joan M. *More beautiful than flowers*

Lindbergh, Reeve. *Benjamin's barn*

Johnny Appleseed

Linden, Madelaine Gill. *Under the blanket*

Lindgren, Barbro. *The wild baby*

Lipkind, William. *Sleepyhead*

Little, Lessie Jones. *Children of long ago*

Livingston, Myra Cohn. *Birthday poems*

Cat poems

Celebrations

Dog poems

Higgledy-Piggledy

Poems for brothers, poems for sisters

Poems for fathers

Poems for mothers

Valentine poems

Lloyd, Megan. *Chicken tricks*

Lobe, Mira. *Valerie and the good-night swing*

Lobel, Arnold. *Martha, the movie mouse*

On Market Street

On the day Peter Stuyvesant sailed into town

The rose in my garden

Whiskers and rhymes

Lodge, Bernard. *Rhyming Nell*

Longfellow, Henry Wadsworth. *Hiawatha*, ill. by Susan Jeffers

Hiawatha's childhood

Paul Revere's ride, ill. by Paul Galdone

Paul Revere's ride, ill. by Nancy Winslow Parker

Loomans, Diane. *The lovables in the kingdom of self-esteem*

Lopshire, Robert. *I want to be somebody new!*

Put me in the zoo

Lord, Beman. *The days of the week*

Lord, John Vernon. *Mr. Mead and his garden*

Low, Alice. *Witch's holiday*

Low, Joseph. *Adam's book of odd creatures*

Lund, Doris Herold. *The paint-box sea*

Lunn, Carolyn. *A buzz is part of a bee*

Lüton, Mildred. *Little chicks' mothers and all the others*

Lyon, George-Ella. *The outside inn*

Together

MacBeth, George. *Noah's journey*

McCarthy, Bobette. *Ten little hippos*

McClintock, Marshall. *What have I got?*

McCord, David. *Every time I climb a tree*

The star in the pail

McCurdy, Michael. *The old man and the fiddle*

McDonald, Amy. *Rachel Fister's blister*

MacDonald, Elizabeth. *Miss Poppy and the honey cake*

McGinley, Phyllis. *All around the town*
How Mrs. Santa Claus saved Christmas
Lucy McLockett
Wonderful time

McGough, Roger. *Counting by numbers*

McGovern, Ann. *Eggs on your nose*
Feeling mad, feeling sad, feeling bad, feeling glad

McKié, Roy. *Snow*

McKissack, Patricia C. *Messy Bessey's closet*

McMillan, Bruce. *One sun*
Play day

Mado, Michio. *The animals*

Maestro, Betsy. *Fat polka-dot cat and other haiku*

Maguire, Gregory. *Lucas Fishbone*

Mahy, Margaret. *17 kings and 42 elephants*

Manning, Linda. *Animal hours*

Marcin, Marietta. *A zoo in her bed*

Margolis, Richard J. *Secrets of a small brother*

Marks, Marcia Bliss. *Swing me, swing tree*

Marshak, Samuel. *Hail to mail*
In the van
The merry starlings
The Month-Brothers
The pup grew up!
The tale of a hero nobody knows

Martin, Bill (William Ivan). *Barn dance!*
Brown bear, brown bear, what do you see?
The happy hippopotami
Listen to the rain
The magic pumpkin
Polar bear, polar bear, what do you hear?
Sounds around the clock
Sounds of home
Sounds of laughter
Sounds of numbers

Martin, Jerome. *Carrot—parrot*
Mitten—kitten

Marzollo, Jean. *Close your eyes*
Pretend you're a cat
The teddy bear book
Uproar on Hollercat Hill

Massie, Diane Redfield. *Cockle stew and other rhymes*
Tiny pin

Mathews, Louise. *Bunches and bunches of bunnies*

Maxner, Joyce. *Lady Bugatti*
Nicholas Cricket

Mayer, Mercer. *Little Monster's bedtime book*

Mayper, Monica. *Oh snow*

Medearis, Angela Shelf. *Dancing with the Indians*

Medina, Nina. *Have you ever noticed that rabbits don't sing?*

Meggendorfer, Lothar. *The genius of Lothar Meggendorfer*

Meigs, Mildred Plew. *Moon song*

Mellings, Joan. *It's fun to go to school*

Mendoza, George. *The hunter I might have been*
The scribbler

Merriam, Eve. *The birthday cow*
Blackberry ink
Halloween ABC
A poem for a pickle: funnybone verses
Train leaves the station

Messenger, Jannat. *Lullabies and baby songs*

Michels, Tilde. *Who's that knocking at my door?*

Miles, Betty. *Around and around... love*

Miles, Miska. *Apricot ABC*

Milios, Rita. *Sneaky Pete*

Miller, Edna. *Mousekin's ABC*

Miller, Moira. *The proverbial mouse*

Mitchell, Cynthia. *Halloweena Hecatee*
Here a little child I stand
Playtime
Under the cherry tree

Mizumura, Kazue. *If I were a cricket...*

Moncure, Jane Belk. *Happy healthkins*
The healthkin food train
Healthkins exercise!
Healthkins help

Monster poems, ill. by Kay Chorao

Montgomery, Michael. *'Night, America*

The moon's the north wind's cooky, ill. by Susan Russo

Moore, Clement C. *The night before Christmas*, ill. by Tomie de Paola
The night before Christmas, ill. by Michael Foreman
The night before Christmas, ill. by Gyo Fujikawa
The night before Christmas, ill. by Scott Gustafson
The night before Christmas, ill. by Cheryl Harness
The night before Christmas, ill. by Anita Lobel
The night before Christmas, ill. by James Marshall
The night before Christmas, ill. by Jacqueline Rogers
The night before Christmas, ill. by Robin Spowart
The night before Christmas, ill. by Gustaf Tenggren
The night before Christmas, ill. by Tasha Tudor
The night before Christmas, ill. by Wendy Watson
The night before Christmas, ill. by Jody Wheeler

A visit from St. Nicholas, ill. by Paul
  Galdone
Moore, Lilian. *I feel the same way*
*See my lovely poison ivy, and other verses
  about witches, ghosts and things*
Mora, Emma. *Gideon, the little bear cub*
Morgenstern, Constance. *Good night, feet*
Morice, Dave. *Dot town*
A visit from St. Alphabet
Morrison, Bill. *Squeeze a sneeze*
Morrison, Sean. *Is that a happy
  hippopotamus?*
Morse, Samuel French. *Sea sums*
Moss, Jeffrey. *The songs of Sesame Street in
  poems and pictures*
Mullins, Edward S. *Animal limericks*
Muntean, Michaela. *Bicycle bear*
Murphy, Elspeth Campbell. *Do you see me
  God?*
Namm, Diane. *Little bear*
Nash, Ogden. *The adventures of Isabel*, ill.
  by Walter Lorraine
The adventures of Isabel, ill. by James
  Marshall
The animal garden, ill. by Hilary Knight
A boy is a boy
Custard and Company
Custard the dragon and the wicked knight
Nave, Yolanda. *Goosebumps and butterflies*
Neitzel, Shirley. *The jacket I wear in the
  snow*
Nerlove, Miriam. *Christmas*
Halloween
Hanukkah
I made a mistake
I meant to clean my room today
If all the world were paper
Just one tooth
Passover
Thanksgiving
Newberry, Clare Turlay. *The kittens' ABC*
Nightingale, Sandy. *A giraffe on the moon*
Nims, Bonnie Larkin. *Where is the bear?*
Where is the bear at school?
Nolan, Dennis. *Wizard McBean and his
  flying machine*
Noll, Sally. *Off and counting*
Norman, Charles. *The hornbean tree and
  other poems*
Noyes, Alfred. *The highwayman*, ill. by Neil
  Waldman
O'Donnell, Elizabeth Lee. *The twelve days
  of summer*
O Huigin, Sean. *King of the birds*
O'Keefe, Susan Heyboer. *One hungry
  monster*
Olsen, Ib Spang. *The grown-up trap*
O'Neill, Mary. *Big red hen*
Oppenheim, Joanne. *Donkey's tale*
Have you seen roads?
Have you seen trees?

The story book prince
You can't catch me!
Orbach, Ruth. *Apple pigs*
Orgel, Doris. *Merry merry FIBruary*
Osborne, Valerie. *One big yo to go*
Otto, Carolyn. *Dinosaur chase*
Ducks, ducks, ducks
Over in the meadow, ill. by Ezra Jack Keats
Owens, Mary Beth. *A caribou alphabet*
Oxenbury, Helen. *Pig tale*
Pack, Robert. *How to catch a crocodile*
Then what did you do?
Packard, Mary. *The kite*
Pacovska, Kveta. *One, five, many*
Paré, Roger. *Animal capers*
Circus days
Play time
Summer days
Parr, Letitia. *A man and his hat*
Partch, Virgil Franklin. *The Christmas
  cookie sprinkle snitcher*
Paterson, A. B. (Andrew Barton). *The man
  from Ironbark*
Mulga Bill's bicycle
Patz, Nancy. *Moses supposes his toeses are
  roses and 7 other silly old rhymes*
Sarah Bear and Sweet Sidney
Pavey, Peter. *One dragon's dream*
Paxton, Tom. *Jennifer's rabbit*
Peaceable kingdom, ill. by Alice and Martin
  Provensen
Pearson, Tracey Campbell. *A apple pie*
Peck, Robert Newton. *Hamilton*
Peek, Merle. *The balancing act*
Peet, Bill (William Bartlett). *Ella*
Hubert's hair-raising adventures
Huge Harold
Kermit the hermit
The kweeks of Kookatumdee
The luckiest one of all
No such things
The pinkish, purplish, bluish egg
Randy's dandy lions
Smokey
Zella, Zack, and Zodiac
Pelham, David. *Sam's sandwich*
Peppé, Rodney. *Cat and mouse*
Hey riddle diddle
Perkins, Al. *The digging-est dog*
The ear book
Hand, hand, fingers, thumb
The nose book
Petie, Haris. *Billions of bugs*
The seed the squirrel dropped
Peyo. *What do smurfs do all day?*
Pfister, Marcus. *I see the moon*
Phillips, Joan. *Peek-a-boo! I see you!*
Phillips, Louis. *The upside down riddle book*
Piatti, Celestino. *Celestino Piatti's animal
  ABC*
Pike, Carol. *The nutty queen*

Pilkey, Dav. *'Twas the night before Thanksgiving*
Plath, Sylvia. *The bed book*
Plotz, Helen. *A week of lullabies*
Pomerantz, Charlotte. *All asleep*
  The ballad of the long-tailed rat
  Flap your wings and try
  How many trucks can a tow truck tow?
  If I had a Paka
  The piggy in the puddle
  The tamarindo puppy and other poems
Poskanzer, Susan Cornell. *Riddles about Hannukah*
Prater, John. *"No!" said Joe*
Prelutsky, Jack. *The baby uggs are hatching*
  Beneath a blue umbrella
  Circus
  The mean old mean hyena
  The pack rat's day and other poems
  The queen of Eene
  Rainy rainy Saturday
  The Random House book of poetry for children
  Read-aloud rhymes for the very young
  Ride a purple pelican
  The snopp on the sidewalk and other poems
  The terrible tiger
  Tyrannosaurus was a beast
Preston, Edna Mitchell. *Pop Corn and Ma Goodness*
Prince, Pamela. *The secret world of teddy bears*
Provensen, Alice. *Karen's opposites*
Puner, Helen Walker. *Daddys, what they do all day*
  The sitter who didn't sit
Puppies and kittens
Quackenbush, Robert M. *Pop! goes the weasel and Yankee Doodle*
Ra, Carol F. *Trot, trot to Boston*
Raphael, Elaine. *Turnabout*
Raskin, Ellen. *Ghost in a four-room apartment*
  Who, said Sue, said whoo?
Reddix, Valerie. *Millie and the mud hole*
Reeves, James. *Ragged Robin: poems from A to Z*
Reeves, Mona Rabun. *I had a cat*
  The spooky eerie night noise
Rey, H. A. (Hans Augusto). *Elizabite, adventures of a carnivorous plant*
  Feed the animals
  See the circus
  Where's my baby?
Rice, Eve. *City night*
Rice, James. *Gaston goes to Texas*
Rigby, Rodney. *There's a building on Sixth Avenue*
Riley, James Whitcomb. *Little Orphant Annie*

Robbins, Ruth. *Baboushka and the three kings*
Roberts, Cliff. *Start with a dot*
Robertson, Joanne. *Sea witches*
Roche, P. K. (Patrick K.). *Jump all the morning*
Rogers, Paul (Patrick). *From me to you*
  Sheepchase
  What will the weather be like today?
Roscoe, William. *The butterfly's ball*
Rose, Anne. *How does a czar eat potatoes?*
Rose, Deborah Lee. *Meredith's mother takes the train*
Rosen, Michael J. *How the animals got their colors*
  Smelly jelly smelly fish
  Under the bed
  You can't catch me!
Rosenberg, Liz. *Window, mirror, moon*
Rossetti, Christina Georgina. *Color*
  Fly away, fly away over the sea
  What is pink?
Russell, Sandra Joanne. *A farmer's dozen*
Russo, Susan. *The ice cream ocean and other delectable poems of the sea*
Ryder, Joanne. *Chipmunk song*
  Hello, tree!
  Mockingbird morning
  Step into the night
  Under your feet
Sage, Angie. *Monkeys in the jungle*
Sage, Michael. *Dippy dos and don'ts*
Saleh, Harold J. *Even tiny ants must sleep*
Samton, Sheila White. *Beside the bay*
  The world from my window
Sarton, May. *A walk through the woods*
Sazer, Nina. *What do you think I saw?*
Scharer, Niko. *Emily's house*
Schick, Eleanor. *City green*
Schmeltz, Susan Alton. *Pets I wouldn't pick*
Schwartz, Delmore. *"I am Cherry Alive," the little girl sang*
Schweninger, Ann. *The man in the moon as he sails the sky and other moon verse*
Scruton, Clive. *Mary's pets*
Sellers, Ronnie. *My first day at school*
Sendak, Maurice. *Pierre*
  Seven little monsters
Serfozo, Mary. *Dirty Kurt*
  Who wants one?
Serraillier, Ian. *Suppose you met a witch*
Seuss, Dr. *And to think that I saw it on Mulberry Street*
  The butter battle book
  The cat in the hat
  The cat in the hat comes back!
  The cat's quizzer
  Come over to my house
  Did I ever tell you how lucky you are?

Dr. Seuss's ABC
Dr. Seuss's sleep book
The eye book
The foot book
Fox in sox
A great day for up
Green eggs and ham
Happy birthday to you!
Hooper Humperdink...? Not him!
Hop on Pop
Horton hatches the egg
Horton hears a Who!
How the Grinch stole Christmas
Hunches in bunches
I am not going to get up today!
I can lick 30 tigers today and other stories
I can read with my eyes shut
I can write!
I had trouble getting to Solla Sollew
I wish that I had duck feet
If I ran the circus
If I ran the zoo
In a people house
The king's stilts
The Lorax
McElligot's pool
Marvin K. Mooney, will you please go now!
Mr. Brown can moo! Can you?
Oh say can you say?
Oh, the thinks you can think!
On beyond zebra
One fish, two fish, red fish, blue fish
Please try to remember the first of Octember!
Scrambled eggs super!
The shape of me and other stuff
The Sneetches, and other stories
There's a wocket in my pocket
Thidwick, the big-hearted moose
The tooth book
Wacky Wednesday
Sewall, Marcia. *Ridin' that strawberry roan*
Sexton, Gwain. *There once was a king*
Shannon, George. *Dancing the breeze*
Oh, I love!
Shapiro, Arnold L. *Who says that?*
Shaw, Nancy. *Sheep in a jeep*
Sheep in a shop
Sheep on a ship
Shea, Pegi Deitz. *Bungalow fungalow*
Sherman, Ivan. *Walking talking words*
Sherman, Nancy. *Gwendolyn and the weathercock*
Gwendolyn the miracle hen
Shortall, Leonard W. *One way*
Shulevitz, Uri. *Rain rain rivers*
Sicotte, Virginia. *A riot of quiet*
Siebert, Diane. *Heartland*
Mojave
Sierra

Train song
Truck song
Silverstein, Shel. *A giraffe and a half*
The giving tree
Simon, Mina Lewiton. *Is anyone here?*
Singer, Marilyn. *Turtle in July*
Will you take me to town on strawberry day?
Singh, Jacquelin. *Fat Gopal*
Skofield, James. *Crow moon, worm moon*
Slate, Joseph. *The star rocker*
Who is coming to our house?
Slepian, Jan. *The hungry thing returns*
Slobodkin, Louis. *Clear the track*
Friendly animals
Millions and millions and millions
One is good, but two are better
The seaweed hat
Up high and down low
Small, Terry. *The legend of William Tell*
Smaridge, Norah. *You know better than that*
Smart, Christopher. *For I will consider my cat Jeoffry*
Smith, Mavis. *Fred, is that you?*
Smith, William Jay. *Birds and beasts*
Puptents and pebbles
Smith-Moore, J. J. *Sally Small*
Snow, Alan. *The monster book of ABC sounds*
Snow, Pegeen. *A pet for Pat*
Snyder, Zilpha Keatley. *Come on, Patsy*
Southey, Robert. *The cataract of Lodore*
Sowden, Henry. *The grand old Duke of York*
Spier, Peter. *Noah's ark*
Spilka, Arnold. *A lion I can do without*
Little birds don't cry
A rumbudgin of nonsense
Stadler, John. *Cat is back at bat*
Starbird, Kaye. *The covered bridge house and other poems*
Steig, Jeanne. *Consider the lemming*
Steig, William. *An eye for elephants*
Stephenson, Dorothy. *The night it rained toys*
Stevens, Janet. *Animal fair*
Stevenson, Drew. *The ballad of Penelope Lou...and me*
Stevenson, Robert Louis. *Block city*, ill. by Ashley Wolff
A child's garden of verses, ill. by Erik Blegvad
A child's garden of verses, ill. by Pelagie Doane
A child's garden of verses, ill. by Toni Frissell
A child's garden of verses, ill. by Joan Hassall
The moon
Stobbs, William. *This little piggy*
Stoddard, Sandol. *Bedtime for bear*
Bedtime mouse

My very own special particular private and personal cat

Stone, Rosetta. *Because a little bug went ka-choo!*

Stover, Jo Ann. *If everybody did*

Sundgaard, Arnold. *Jethro's difficult dinosaur*

Supraner, Robyn. *Would you rather be a tiger?*

Sutton, Eve. *My cat likes to hide in boxes*

Svendsen, Carol. *Hulda*

Swann, Brian. *A basket full of white eggs*

Tagore, Rabindranath. *Paper boats*

Taylor, Scott. *Dinosaur James*

Tether, Graham. *The hair book*

Thayer, Ernest L. *Casey at the bat*, ill. by Patricia Polacco

Thomas, Patricia. *The one and only, super-duper, golly-whopper, jim-dandy, really-handy clock-tock-stopper*

"Stand back," said the elephant, "I'm going to sneeze!"

"There are rocks in my socks!" said the ox to the fox

Thompson, Carol. *Baby days*

Thomson, Ruth. *My bear: I can...can you?*

My bear: I like...do you?

The three little pigs. *The three little pigs*, ill. by Erik Blegvad

The three little pigs, ill. by Caroline Bucknall

The three little pigs, ill. by William Pène Du Bois

The three little pigs and the big bad wolf, retold and ill. by Glen Rounds

Tippett, James Sterling. *Counting the days*

Trent, Robbie. *The first Christmas*

Tresselt, Alvin R. *Follow the wind*

Tripp, Valerie. *Happy, happy Mother's Day*

Sillyhen's big surprise

Tryon, Leslie. *Albert's play*

Tudor, Tasha. *Around the year*

Turner, Ann Warren. *Tickle a pickle*

Turner, Ethel. *Walking to school*

Tyrrell, Anne. *Elizabeth Jane gets dressed*

Mary Ann always can

Udry, Janice May. *A tree is nice*

Vance, Eleanor Graham. *Jonathan*

Van der Beek, Deborah. *Superbabe!*

Van Laan, Nancy. *A mouse in my house*

People, people, everywhere

Possum come a-knocking

This is the hat

Van Vorst, M. L. *A Norse lullaby*

Ver Dorn, Bethea. *Moon glows*

Voake, Charlotte. *First things first*

Vogel, Ilse-Margaret. *The don't be scared book*

Waddell, Martin. *My great grandpa*

The park in the dark

Wadsworth, Olive A. *Over in the meadow*

Wahl, Jan. *Follow me cried Bee*

Rabbits on roller skates!

The sleepytime book

Wakefield, Joyce. *Ask a silly question*

From where you are

Wallace, Daisy. *Fairy poems*

Ghost poems

Giant poems

Wallner, Alexandra. *Munch*

Watson, Clyde. *Applebet*

Catch me and kiss me and say it again

Father Fox's feast of songs

Hickory stick rag

Watson, Wendy. *Hurray for the Fourth of July*

A Valentine for you

Weiss, Nicki. *Sun sand sea sail*

Welber, Robert. *Goodbye, hello*

Wells, Rosemary. *Don't spill it again, James*

Noisy Nora

Shy Charles

Wersba, Barbara. *Do tigers ever bite kings?*

West, Colin. *The king's toothache*

A moment in rhyme

Westcott, Nadine Bernard. *The lady with the alligator purse*

Peanut butter and jelly

Skip to my Lou

What do you feed your donkey on? ill. by Jenny Rodwell

Wheeling, Lynn. *When you fly*

Whybrow, Ian. *Quacky quack-quack!*

Wild, Robin. *Little Pig and the big bad wolf*

Wildsmith, Brian. *Animal tricks*

Willard, Nancy. *Night story*

Pish posh, said Hieronymous Bosch

A visit to William Blake's inn

The voyage of the Ludgate Hill

Williams, Barbara. *Donna Jean's disaster*

Williams, Garth. *The chicken book*

Williams, Jay. *I wish I had another name*

Williams, Sue. *I went walking*

Williams, Terry Tempest. *Between cattails*

Willis, Jeanne. *The monster bed*

Wilner, Isabel. *A garden alphabet*

Wilson, Sarah. *June is a tune that jumps on a stair*

Winthrop, Elizabeth. *Shoes*

Sledding

Wiseman, Bernard. *Little new kangaroo*

Witch poems, ill. by Trina Schart Hyman

Wittels, Harriet. *Things I hate!*

Wolf, Sallie. *Peter's trucks*

Wood, Audrey. *The napping house*

Silly Sally

Wood, Jakki. *One bear with bees in his hair*

Woolaver, Lance. *Christmas with the rural mail*

From Ben Loman to the sea

Wright, Josephine Lord. *Cotton Cat and Martha Mouse*

Yektai, Niki. *Bears in pairs*
 Hi bears, bye bears
Yeoman, John. *Old Mother Hubbard's dog*
 dresses up
 Old Mother Hubbard's dog learns to play
 Old Mother Hubbard's dog needs a doctor
 Old Mother Hubbard's dog takes up sport
 Our village
Yolen, Jane. *An invitation to the butterfly ball*
 Ring of earth
 The three bears rhyme book
Yoshi. *Who's hiding here?*
Young, James. *Everyone loves the moon*
 A million chameleons
Young, Ruth. *Golden Bear*
Zemach, Harve. *The judge*
Ziefert, Harriet. *On our way to the barn*
 On our way to the forest
 On our way to the water
 On our way to the zoo
Ziner, Feenie. *Counting carnival*
Zolotow, Charlotte (Shapiro). *River winding*
 Some things go together
 Summer is...

Poland *see* Foreign lands – Poland

Polar bears *see* Animals – polar bears

Police officers *see* Careers – police
 officers

Poltergeists *see* Ghosts

Poor *see* Homeless; Poverty

Pop-up books *see* Format, unusual – toy
 and moveable books

Porcupines *see* Animals – porcupines

Porpoise *see* Animals – dolphins

Portugal *see* Foreign lands – Portugal

Possums *see* Animals – possums

Potty training *see* Toilet training

Poverty

Alexander, Lloyd. *The king's fountain*
Ambrus, Victor G. *The three poor tailors*
Andersen, H. C. (Hans Christian). *The
 little match girl*, ill. by Rachel Isadora
The little match girl, ill. by Blair Lent
Balet, Jan B. *The fence*
Bettina (Bettina Ehrlich). *Pantaloni*
Brand, Oscar. *When I first came to this land*
Carey, Valerie Scho. *Maggie Mab and the
 bogey beast*

De Paola, Tomie (Thomas Anthony).
 Helga's dowry
Deveaux, Alexis. *Na-ni*
Goodman, Louise. *Ida's doll*
Greene, Jacqueline Dembar. *What his
 father did*
Hazen, Barbara Shook. *Tight times*
Hoban, Lillian. *Stick-in-the-mud turtle*
Keeping, Charles. *Joseph's yard*
Levine, Abby. *Too much mush!*
Lindgren, Astrid. *My nightingale is singing*
McCrea, James. *The king's procession*
Maiorano, Robert. *Francisco*
Miles, Lauren. *The rag coat*
Nolan, Madeena Spray. *My daddy don't go
 to work*
Provensen, Alice. *Shaker Lane*
Rose, Anne. *How does a czar eat potatoes?*
Sawyer, Ruth. *Journey cake, ho!*
Schermbrucker, Reviva. *Charlie's house*
Sonneborn, Ruth A. *Friday night is papa
 night*
 Seven in a bed
Steptoe, John. *Uptown*

Power failure

Baisch, Cris. *When the lights went out*
Freeman, Don. *The night the lights went out*
Rockwell, Anne F. *Blackout*

Practicality *see* Character traits –
 practicality

Prairie dogs *see* Animals – prairie dogs

Praying mantis *see* Insects – praying
 mantis

Prejudice

Anders, Rebecca. *A look at prejudice and
 understanding*
Carlson, Nancy. *Loudmouth George and the
 new neighbors*
Escudie, René. *Paul and Sebastian*
Glen, Maggie. *Ruby*

Pride *see* Character traits – pride

Princes *see* Royalty – princes

Princesses *see* Royalty – princesses

Printers *see* Careers – printers

Prisons

DuPasquier, Philippe. *The great escape*
Hickman, Martha Whitmore. *When can
 daddy come home?*
McKee, David. *123456789 Benn*

Solotareff, Grégoire. *Don't call me little bunny*

Problem solving

Adler, David A. *The children of Chelm*
Alexander, Martha G. *I'll protect you from the jungle beasts*
Move over, Twerp
Out! Out! Out!
We never get to do anything
We're in big trouble, Blackboard Bear
Alexander, Sue. *World famous Muriel*
World famous Muriel and the magic mystery
Allen, Laura Jean. *Rollo and Tweedy and the case of the missing cheese*
Where is Freddy?
Allington, Richard L. *Thinking*
Ames, Mildred. *The wonderful box*
Armitage, Ronda. *Ice creams for Rosie*
The lighthouse keeper's catastrophe
The lighthouse keeper's lunch
Arnosky, Jim. *Mud time and more*
Ashley, Bernard. *Dinner ladies don't count*
Bakken, Harold. *The special string*
Balet, Jan B. *The fence*
Barklem, Jill. *The secret staircase*
Barrett, Judi. *What's left?*
Barry, Katharina. *A bug to hug*
Beim, Lorraine. *Two is a team*
Benarde, Anita. *The pumpkin smasher*
Berenstain, Stan. *The bear detectives: the case of the missing pumpkin*
The Berenstain bears and the messy room
The Berenstain bears and the missing honey
The Berenstain bears and the missing dinosaur bone
Berg, Jean Horton. *The O'Learys and friends*
Bester, Roger. *Guess what?*
Binnamin, Vivian. *The case of the anteater's missing lunch*
The case of the planetarium puzzle
The case of the snoring stegosaurus
Blaine, Marge (Margery Kay). *The terrible thing that happened at our house*
Booth, Eugene. *At the circus*
At the fair
In the air
In the garden
In the jungle
Under the ocean
Bradford, Ann. *The mystery at Misty Falls*
The mystery of the blind writer
The mystery of the midget clown
The mystery of the missing dogs
The mystery of the square footsteps
The mystery of the tree house
Brillhart, Julie. *Story hour—starring Megan!*
Brodmann, Aliana. *Such a noise!*

Bröger, Achim. *Little Harry*
Brown, Jeff. *Flat Stanley*
Brown, Margaret Wise. *They all saw it*
Browne, Anthony. *Bear hunt*
Buchanan, Heather S. *George and Matilda Mouse and the floating school*
George Mouse's first summer
Bulette, Sara. *The splendid belt of Mr. Big*
Bunting, Eve (Anne Evelyn). *Jane Martin, dog detective*
Burton, Marilee Robin. *Tail toes eyes ears nose*
Calhoun, Mary. *Audubon cat*
Carlson, Nancy. *Harriet and the garden*
Carrick, Carol. *Ben and the porcupine*
Chaffin, Lillie D. *Tommy's big problem*
Chapman, Carol. *Herbie's troubles*
Christelow, Eileen. *Gertrude, the bulldog detective*
Christensen, Gardell Dano. *Mrs. Mouse needs a house*
Christian, Mary Blount. *The doggone mystery*
Cleary, Beverly. *The real hole*
Clymer, Ted. *The horse and the bad morning*
Cole, Babette. *Princess Smartypants*
Cole, Joanna. *It's too noisy*
Cooney, Nancy Evans. *The blanket that had to go*
Donald says thumbs down
Cooper, Jacqueline. *Angus and the Mona Lisa*
Corbalis, Judy. *The cuckoo bird*
Cressey, James. *Fourteen rats and a rat-catcher*
Cummings, Pat. *Jimmy Lee did it*
Darling, Kathy (Mary Kathleen). *The mystery in Santa's toyshop*
Deedy, Carmen Agra. *Agatha's feather bed*
Demarest, Chris L. *Kitman and Willy at sea*
De Paola, Tomie (Thomas Anthony). *Charlie needs a cloak*
Dewey, Ariane. *The fish Peri*
Dickinson, Mary. *Alex's bed*
Domanska, Janina. *The turnip*
Economakis, Olga. *Oasis of the stars*
Elkin, Benjamin. *Such is the way of the world*
Emberley, Ed (Edward Randolph). *Rosebud*
Farber, Norma. *How the left-behind beasts built Ararat*
Fassler, Joan. *Boy with a problem*
Feder, Paula Kurzband. *Where does the teacher live?*
Fowler, Richard. *Inspector Smart gets the message!*
Freschet, Berniece. *Bernard of Scotland Yard*
Gibbons, Gail. *The missing maple syrup sap mystery*
Gordon, Margaret. *The supermarket mice*

Greene, Carol. *The golden locket*
Hancock, Sibyl. *Freaky Francie*
Harber, Frances. *My king has donkey ears*
Hare, Norma Q. *Mystery at mouse house*
Harrison, David Lee. *Detective Bob and the great ape escape*
Heitler, Susan M. *David decides about thumbsucking*
Henwood, Simon. *The troubled village*
Hines, Anna Grossnickle. *Maybe a band-aid will help*
Hoban, Lillian. *Arthur's funny money*
The case of the two masked robbers
Horvath, Betty F. *The cheerful quiet*
Houston, John A. *The bright yellow rope*
A mouse in my house
Hughes, Shirley. *An evening at Alfie's*
Hulse, Gillian. *Morris, where are you?*
Ives, Penny. *Mrs. Santa Claus*
Jonas, Ann. *Holes and peeks*
The thirteenth clue
Keats, Ezra Jack. *Goggles*
Whistle for Willie
Keenen, George. *The preposterous week*
Kellogg, Steven (Stephen). *The mystery of the missing red mitten*
The mystery of the stolen blue paint
Klimowicz, Barbara. *The strawberry thumb*
Krahn, Fernando. *Arthur's adventure in the abandoned house*
Kraus, Robert. *The detective of London*
Kroll, Steven. *Looking for Daniela*
Leonard, Marcia. *Birthday in a bathtub*
Little owl leaves the nest
Levitin, Sonia. *Who owns the moon?*
Lewis, Thomas P. *Call for Mr. Sniff*
Mr. Sniff and the motel mystery
Lexau, Joan M. *Benjie*
Benjie on his own
The dog food caper
Lobel, Arnold. *On the day Peter Stuyvesant sailed into town*
Low, Joseph. *What if...?*
Lyon, David. *The brave little computer*
McCloskey, Robert. *Lentil*
McDonald, Megan. *The great pumpkin switch*
McKee, David. *123456789 Benn*
Maestro, Betsy. *The guessing game*
Maiorano, Robert. *Francisco*
Marie, Geraldine. *The magic box*
Maris, Ron. *Hold tight, bear!*
Marshall, James. *Four little troubles*
Marshall, Margaret. *Mike*
Martinez, Ruth. *Mrs. McDockerty's knitting*
Mason, Christopher. *The marvellous blue mouse*
Mayer, Mercer. *What do you do with a kangaroo?*
Merriam, Eve. *The birthday door*
Milhous, Katherine. *The turnip*

Miller, Edna. *Mousekin's mystery*
Mooser, Stephen. *Funnyman and the penny dodo*
Funnyman's first case
Munsch, Robert N. *Jonathan cleaned up— then he heard a sound*
Musicant, Elke. *The night vegetable eater*
Myers, Walter Dean. *The golden serpent*
Myrick, Jean Lockwood. *Ninety-nine pockets*
Ness, Evaline. *Do you have the time, Lydia?*
Nixon, Joan Lowery. *The Thanksgiving mystery*
The Valentine mystery
Oakley, Graham. *The church mice in action*
Obrist, Jürg. *They do things right in Albern*
Panek, Dennis. *Detective Whoo*
Pape, D. L. (Donna Lugg). *Snoino mystery*
Partridge, Jenny. *Hopfellow*
Mr. Squint
Peterkin Pollensnuff
Payne, Emmy. *Katy no-pocket*
Rice, Eve. *Peter's pockets*
Robb, Brian. *My grandmother's djinn*
Robison, Deborah. *Bye-bye, old buddy*
No elephants allowed
Schermer, Judith. *Mouse in house*
Schurr, Cathleen. *The long and the short of it*
Segal, Lore. *The story of old Mrs. Brubeck and how she looked for trouble and where she found him*
Seuss, Dr. *Did I ever tell you how lucky you are?*
Hunches in bunches
Sharmat, Marjorie Weinman. *Nate the Great and the fishy prize*
Nate the Great and the lost list
Nate the Great goes undercover
The pizza monster
Smith, Donald. *Who's wearing my baseball cap?*
Who's wearing my bow tie?
Who's wearing my sneakers?
Who's wearing my sunglasses?
Smith, Jim. *The frog band and the onion seller*
Sondheimer, Ilse. *The magic of Pomme*
Steel, Danielle. *Max and the baby sitter*
Stevenson, James. *Quick! Turn the page!*
Talbot, John. *Pins and needles*
Taylor, Mark. *The case of the missing kittens*
Thayer, Jane. *What's a ghost going to do?*
Thomas, Patricia. *"There are rocks in my socks!" said the ox to the fox*
Thompson, Vivian Laubach. *Camp-in-the-yard*
Thomson, Ruth. *Peabody all at sea*
Peabody's first case
Titus, Eve. *Anatole and the cat*
Anatole and the Pied Piper
Anatole and the poodle

Anatole and the robot
Anatole and the thirty thieves
Anatole and the toyshop
Anatole in Italy
Tolstoĭ, Alekseĭ Nikolaevich. *The great big enormous turnip*
Türk, Hanne. *Max versus the cube*
A surprise for Max
Tusa, Tricia. *Camilla's new hairdo*
Van Horn, William. *Twitchtoe, the beastfinder*
Winthrop, Elizabeth. *Maggie and the monster*
Wiseman, Bernard. *Doctor Duck and Nurse Swan*
Wold, Jo Anne. *Tell them my name is Amanda*
Wynne-Jones, Tim. *Builder of the moon*
Wyse, Lois. *Two guppies, a turtle and Aunt Edna*
Yagelski, Robert. *The day the lifting bridge stuck*
Yektai, Niki. *What's missing?*
Yolen, Jane. *Piggins*
Yorinks, Arthur. *Bravo, Minski*
Zemach, Margot. *It could always be worse*

Progress

Barton, Byron. *Wheels*
Burton, Virginia Lee. *The little house*
Duvoisin, Roger Antoine. *Lonely Veronica*
Fife, Dale. *Empty lot*
The little park
Goodall, John S. *The story of an English village*
Greene, Graham. *The little fire engine*
Harrison, David Lee. *Little turtle's big adventure*
Heine, Helme. *Prince Bear*
Hoban, Russell. *Arthur's new power*
Ipcar, Dahlov. *One horse farm*
MacGill-Callahan, Sheila. *And still the turtle watched*
Murschetz, Luis. *Mister Mole*
Peet, Bill (William Bartlett). *Countdown to Christmas*
Farewell to Shady Glade
The wump world
Ray, Mary Lyn. *Pumpkins*
Shecter, Ben. *Emily, girl witch of New York*
Steiner, Jörg. *The bear who wanted to be a bear*
Tusa, Tricia. *Sherman and Pearl*

Puerto Rican-Americans *see* Ethnic groups in the U.S. – Hispanic-Americans; Ethnic groups in the U.S. – Puerto Rican-Americans

Puerto Rico *see* Foreign lands – Puerto Rico

Puffins *see* Birds – puffins

Pumas *see* Animals – cougars

Puppets

Atene, Ann (Anna). *The golden guitar*
Blau, Judith. *Bunny Mitten's book*
Brandenberg, Franz. *Aunt Nina's visit*
Brennan, Joseph Killorin. *Gobo and the river*
Bruce, Sheilah B. *The radish day jubilee*
Cahill, Chris. *Bear magic*
Bunny magic
Spider magic
Turtle magic
Chernoff, Goldie Taub. *Puppet party*
Children's Television Workshop. *Muppets in my neighborhood*
Cleaver, Elizabeth. *The enchanted caribou*
Collodi, Carlo. *The adventures of Pinocchio*, ill. by Diane Goode
Eaton, Su. *Punch and Judy in the rain*
Elliott, Dan. *Ernie's little lie*
A visit to the Sesame Street firehouse
Freeman, Don. *The paper party*
Gikow, Louise. *Boober Fraggle's ghosts*
Follow that Fraggle!
Sprocket's Christmas tale
Gilmour, H. B. *Why Wembley Fraggle couldn't sleep*
Hautzig, Deborah. *It's not fair!*
A visit to the Sesame Street hospital
Heymans, Margriet. *Pippin and Robber Grumblecroak's big baby*
Howe, James. *The case of the missing mother*
Keats, Ezra Jack. *Louie*
Klimowicz, Barbara. *The strawberry thumb*
Lerner, Sharon. *Big Bird's copycat day*
Follow the monsters!
Lewis, Sheri. *Baby Lamb Chop loves animals*
Baby Lamb Chop loves numbers
Baby Lamb Chop loves nursery school
Baby Lamb Chop loves the beach
Baby Lamb Chop loves words
Little, Mary E. *Ricardo and the puppets*
Masks and puppets
Moss, Jeffrey. *The Sesame Street ABC storybook*
The songs of Sesame Street in poems and pictures
Mother Goose. *The Sesame Street players present Mother Goose*
Muntean, Michaela. *Mokey and the festival of the bells*
Muppet babies through the year
The Muppet Show book
One rubber duckie
Parsons, Virginia. *Pinocchio and Gepetto*
Pinocchio and the money tree

Pinocchio goes on the stage
Pinocchio plays truant
Peters, Sharon. *Puppet show*
Provensen, Alice. *Punch in New York*
Roberts, Sarah. *Bert and the missing mop
mix-up*
Ernie's big mess
I want to go home!
Ross, Anna. *I did it!*
I have to go
Naptime
Say the magic word, please
Sesame Street. *Ernie and Bert can...can
you?*
Sesame Street sign language fun
Sesame Street word book
Steiner, Charlotte. *Pete's puppets*
Stevenson, Jocelyn. *Jim Henson's Muppets at
sea*
Red and the pumpkins
Stiles, Norman. *I'll miss you, Mr. Hooper*
Stone, Jon. *Big Bird in China*
Tettelbaum, Michael. *The cave of the lost
Fraggle*
Tornborg, Pat. *The Sesame Street cookbook*
Weiss, Ellen. *Mokey's birthday present*
Pigs in space
You are the star of a Muppet adventure
Young, Ed (Edward). *The rooster's horns*

Purim *see* Holidays – Purim

Puzzles *see* Rebuses; Riddles

Queens *see* Royalty – queens

Questioning *see* Character traits –
questioning

Quicksand *see* Sand

Quilts
Brenner, Barbara A. *The flying patchwork
quilt*
Chorao, Kay. *Kate's quilt*
Coerr, Eleanor. *The Josefina story quilt*
Cole, Barbara Hancock. *Texas star*
Ernst, Lisa Campbell. *Sam Johnson and the
blue ribbon quilt*
Fleisher, Robbin. *Quilts in the attic*
Flournoy, Valerie. *The patchwork quilt*
Johnston, Tony. *The quilt story*
Jonas, Ann. *The quilt*

Martin, Jacqueline Briggs. *Bizzy Bones and
the lost quilt*
Ringgold, Faith. *Tar Beach*
Steiner, Charlotte. *The sleepy quilt*
Vincent, Gabrielle. *Ernest and Celestine's
patchwork quilt*
Whittington, Mary K. *The patchwork lady*
Willard, Nancy. *The mountains of quilt*
Zagwyn, Deborah Turney. *Pumpkin blanket*
Ziefert, Harriet. *Before I was born*

Rabbits *see* Animals – rabbits

Raccoons *see* Animals – raccoons

Race car drivers *see* Careers – race car
drivers

Racing *see* Sports – racing

Railroad engineers *see* Careers – railroad
engineers

Railroads *see* Trains

Rain *see* Weather – rain

Rainbows *see* Weather – rainbows

Rangers *see* Careers – park rangers

Rats *see* Animals – rats

Ravens *see* Birds – ravens

Reading *see* Activities – reading

Rebuses
Adler, David A. *Bunny rabbit rebus*
Coletta, Irene. *From A to Z*
Dodds, Siobhan. *Words and pictures*
Doolittle, Eileen. *The ark in the attic*
Downie, Jill. *Alphabet puzzle*
Heuck, Sigrid. *Pony and Bear are friends*
Who stole the apples?
Marzollo, Jean. *The rebus treasury*
Morris, Ann. *The Little Red Riding Hood
rebus book*
Mother Goose. *Mother Goose in
hieroglyphics*, ill. by George S. Appleton
Partch, Virgil Franklin. *The Christmas
cookie sprinkle snitcher*
Pizer, Abigail. *It's a perfect day*
Reit, Seymour. *Rebus bears*

Weil, Lisl. *Mother Goose picture riddles*
Wyllie, Stephen. *The great race*

Reindeer *see* Animals – reindeer

Religion

Adler, David A. *A picture book of Hanukkah*
A picture book of Israel
Æsop. *Androcles and the lion*, ill. by Janet Stevens
Androcles and the lion, ill. by Janusz Grabianski
Aichinger, Helga. *The shepherd*
Aleichem, Sholem. *Hanukah money*
Alexander, Cecil Frances. *All things bright and beautiful*
Aliki. *Mummies made in Egypt*
Anglund, Joan Walsh. *A book of good tidings from the Bible*
Aoki, Hisako. *Santa's favorite story*
Araten, Harry. *Two by two*
Baker, Betty. *And me, coyote!*
Baker, Sanna Anderson. *Who's a friend of the water-spurting whale*
Balet, Jan B. *The gift*
Barker, Peggy. *What happened when grandma died*
Baumann, Kurt. *The story of Jonah*
Bawden, Nina. *St. Francis of Assisi*
Bayar, Steven. *Rachel and Mischa*
Baylor, Byrd. *The way to start a day*
Baynes, Pauline. *Let there be light*
Thanks be to God
Behrens, June. *Hanukkah*
Passover
Berger, Barbara Helen. *The donkey's dream*
Bible. *Best-loved Bible verses for children*, ill. by Anna Maria Magagna
Bible. New Testament. *The Lord's prayer*, Catholic version, ill. by Ingri and Edgar Parin d'Aulaire
The Lord's prayer, Protestant version, ill. by Ingri and Edgar Parin d'Aulaire
The Lord's prayer, ill. by George Kraus
Bible. New Testament. Gospels. *Christmas*, ill. by Jan Pieńkowski
The first Christmas, ill. by Barbara Neustadt
The Nativity, ill. by Julie Vivas
The story of Christmas, ill. by Jane Ray
Bible. Old Testament. Daniel. *Daniel in the lions' den*, ill. by Leon Baxter
Shadrach, Meshack and Abednego, ill. by Paul Galdone
Bible. Old Testament. David. *David and Goliath*, ill. by Leon Baxter
Bible. Old Testament. Jonah. *The Book of Jonah*, ill. by Peter Spier
Jonah, ill. by Kurt Mitchell
Jonah and the great fish, ill. by Leon Baxter

Bible. Old Testament. Psalms. *The Lord is my shepherd*, ill. by George Kraus
The Lord is my shepherd, ill. by Tasha Tudor
Brin, Ruth F. *David and Goliath*
The story of Esther
Briscoe, Jill. *The innkeeper's daughter*
Brown, Margaret Wise. *On Christmas eve*
Bruna, Dick. *Christmas*
Bryan, Ashley. *All night, all day: a child's first book of African-American spirituals*
Bulla, Clyde Robert. *Jonah and the great fish*
Burdekin, Harold. *A child's grace*
Caswell, Helen. *Parable of the good Samaritan*
Chaikin, Miriam. *Exodus*
Chanover, Hyman. *Happy Hanukah everybody*
Chapman, Jean. *Moon-Eyes*
Chase, Catherine. *The miracles at Cana*
Children go where I send thee
Children's prayers from around the world
A child's book of prayers, ill. by Michael Hague
Christmas in the stable, ill. by Beverly K. Duncan
The Christmas story
Cohen, Barbara. *The donkey's story*
Cooney, Barbara. *A little prayer*
Dellinger, Annetta. *You are special to Jesus*
De Paola, Tomie (Thomas Anthony). *The clown of God*
The Lady of Guadalupe
The legend of Old Befana
My first Chanukah
The parables of Jesus
Patrick: patron saint of Ireland
The story of the three wise kings
De Regniers, Beatrice Schenk. *David and Goliath*
Din dan don, it's Christmas
Douglas, Robert W. *John Paul II*
Drucker, Malka. *Grandma's latkes*
A Jewish holiday ABC
Ehrlich, Amy. *The story of Hannukkah*
Eisenberg, Ann. *Bible heroes I can be*
I can celebrate
Farber, Norma. *How the hibernators came to Bethlehem*
Fass, David E. *The shofar that lost its voice*
Feder, Harriet K. *Not yet, Elijah!*
Field, Rachel Lyman. *Prayer for a child*
First graces, ill. by Tasha Tudor
First prayers, ill. by Anna Maria Magagna
First prayers, ill. by Tasha Tudor
Fisher, Leonard Everett. *The seven days of creation*
Fitch, Florence Mary. *A book about God*
Forrester, Victoria. *Poor Gabriella*
Fraser, James Howard. *Los Posadas*

The friendly beasts, ill. by Sarah
    Chamberlain
*The friendly beasts and A partridge in a pear
    tree,* ill. by Virginia Pearsons
Galdone, Paul. *The first seven days*
Goddard, Carrie Lou. *Isn't it a wonder!*
Goldin, Barbara Diamond. *Cakes and
    miracles*
Graham, Lorenz B. *David he no fear*
  Every man heart lay down
  Hongry catch the foolish boy
  A road down in the sea
Gramatky, Hardie. *Nikos and the sea god*
Groner, Judyth. *All about Hanukkah*
Haas, Dorothy. *My first communion*
Haiz, Danah. *Jonah's journey*
Hamil, Thomas Arthur. *Brother Alonzo*
Harmer, Juliet. *Prayers for children*
Hayward, Linda. *Baby Moses*
Heck, Elisabeth. *The black sheep*
Heine, Helme. *One day in paradise*
Hillman, Priscilla. *The Merry-Mouse book of
    prayers and graces*
Hirsh, Marilyn. *I love Passover*
  Joseph who loved the Sabbath
  Potato pancakes all around
Hodges, Margaret. *St. Jerome and the lion*
Hoffmann, Felix. *The story of Christmas*
Hopkins, Lee Bennett. *And God bless me*
Houselander, Caryll. *Petook*
Hughes, Shirley. *Lucy and Tom's Christmas*
Hunt Angela Elwell. *The tale of three trees*
Hutton, Warwick. *Adam and Eve*
  Jonah and the great fish
  Moses in the bulrushes
I sing a song of the saints of God, ill. by
    Judith Gwyn Brown
Ife, Elaine. *The childhood of Jesus*
  Moses in the bulrushes
  Stories Jesus told
Jones, Jessie Mae Orton. *A little child*
  Small rain
Jüchen, Aurel von. *The Holy Night*
Kahn, Katherine Janus. *The Shofar calls to
    us*
Karlinsky, Ruth Schild. *My first book of
    Mitzvos*
Keats, Ezra Jack. *God is in the mountain*
  The little drummer boy
Kimmel, Eric A. *The Chanukkah guest*
  Hershel and the Hanukkah goblins
Kipling, Rudyard. *The miracle of the
    mountain,* ill. by Willi Baum
Knapp, John II. *A pillar of pepper and other
    Bible nursery rhymes*
Koralek, Jenny. *Hanukkah: the festival of
    lights*
Krull, Kathleen. *Songs of praise*
Kuskin, Karla. *Jerusalem, shining still*
Lattimore, Deborah Nourse. *The sailor who
    captured the sea*

Laurence, Margaret. *The Christmas birthday
    story*
Leeton, Will C. *The Tower of Babel*
Levine, Arthur. *All the lights in the night*
Lexau, Joan M. *More beautiful than flowers*
Lindgren, Astrid. *Christmas in the stable*
Lines, Kathleen. *Once in royal David's city*
Little, Emily. *David and the giant*
MacBeth, George. *Jonah and the Lord*
McDermott, Beverly Brodsky. *Jonah*
McDermott, Gerald. *The voyage of Osiris*
McKissack, Patricia C. *My Bible ABC book*
Manushkin, Fran. *Latkes and applesause*
Marshall, Lyn. *Yoga for your children*
Michael, Emory H. *Androcles and the lion*
Mitchell, Cynthia. *Here a little child I stand*
Miyoshi, Sekiya. *Singing David*
Modesitt, Jeanne. *Songs of Chanukah*
Murphy, Elspeth Campbell. *Do you see me
    God?*
Nerlove, Miriam. *Hanukkah*
  Passover
Nussbaumer, Mares. *Away in a manger*
Patterson, Geoffrey. *Jonah and the whale*
Pieńkowski, Jan. *Easter*
Polacco, Patricia. *Chicken Sunday*
Price, Christine. *One is God*
Reed, Allison. *Genesis: the story of creation*
Rosenblum, Richard. *The old synagogue*
Sabuda, Robert James. *St. Valentine*
Sahagun, Bernardino de. *Spirit child*
Schanzer, Roz. *In the synagogue*
Scholey, Arthur. *Baboushka*
Schotter, Roni. *Hanukkah!*
Schwartz, Amy. *Mrs. Moskowitz and the
    Sabbath candlesticks*
Schwartz, Lynne Sharon. *The four questions*
Seignobosc, Françoise. *The thank-you book*
Shulevitz, Uri. *The magician*
Singer, Marilyn. *Minnie's Yom Kippur
    birthday*
Slate, Joseph. *Who is coming to our house?*
The song of the Three Holy Children, ill. by
    Pauline Baynes
Springer, Sally. *Let's make latkes*
Stan-Padilla, Viento. *Dream Feather*
Taylor, Mark. *"Lamb," said the lion, "I am
    here."*
Thomas, Kathy. *The angel's quest*
Thorne, Jenny. *Adam and Eve*
  Jonah and the whale
  The walls of Jericho
Titherington, Jeanne. *A child's prayer*
Tolstoĭ, Alekseĭ Nikolaevich. *Shoemaker
    Martin*
Trent, Robbie. *The first Christmas*
Tudor, Tasha. *More prayers*
Van der Meer, Ron. *Oh Lord!*
Vasiliu, Mircea. *Everything is somewhere*
Volkmer, Jane Anne. *Song of Chirimia: La
    Musica de la Chirimia*

What a morning! ill. by Ashley Bryan
Wheeler, Opal. *Sing in praise*
Wiesner, William. *The Tower of Babel*
Wijngaard, Juan. *The nativity*
Wildsmith, Brian. *The true cross*
Wilkoń, Józef. *Lullaby for a newborn king*
Williams, Marcia. *The first Christmas*
   Jonah and the whale
   Joseph and his magnificent coat of many
   colors
Winthrop, Elizabeth. *A child is born*
   He is risen
Wohl, Lauren L. *Matzoh mouse*
Wood, Douglas. *Old Turtle*
Zalben, Jane Breskin. *Happy Passover, Rosie*
   Leo and Blossom's Sukkah

Religion – Noah

Baynes, Pauline. *Noah and the ark*
Bible. Old Testament. *Noah and the ark*, ill.
   by Pauline Baynes
Bolliger, Max. *Noah and the rainbow*
Brent, Isabelle. *Noah's ark*
Chase, Catherine. *Noah's ark*
Delessert, Etienne. *The endless party*
De Paola, Tomie (Thomas Anthony). *Noah*
   and the ark
Duvoisin, Roger Antoine. *A for the ark*
Elborn, Andrew. *Noah and the ark and the*
   animals
Farber, Norma. *How the left-behind beasts*
   built Ararat
   Where's Gomer?
Fischetto, Laura. *Inside Noah's ark*
French, Fiona. *Rise and shine*
Fussenegger, Gertrud. *Noah's ark*
Geisert, Arthur. *The ark*
Goffstein, M. B. (Marilyn Brooke). *My*
   Noah's ark
Graham, Lorenz B. *God wash the world and*
   start again
Haubensak-Tellenbach, Margrit. *The story*
   of Noah's ark
Hewitt, Kathryn. *Two by two*
Hogrogian, Nonny. *Noah's ark*
Hutton, Warwick. *Noah and the great flood*
Ife, Elaine. *Noah and the ark*
Jonas, Ann. *Aardvarks, disembark!*
Kuskin, Karla. *The animals and the ark*
Lenski, Lois. *Mr. and Mrs. Noah*
Ludwig, Warren. *Old Noah's elephants*
MacBeth, George. *Noah's journey*
McCaughrean, Geraldine. *The story of*
   Noah and the ark
McKié, Roy. *Noah's ark*
Martin, Charles E. *Noah's ark*
Matias. *Mr. Noah and the animals*
Mee, Charles L. *Noah*
Olson, Arielle North. *Noah's cats and the*
   devil's fire
Palazzo, Tony (Anthony D.). *Noah's ark*

Rose, Gerald. *Trouble in the ark*
Rounds, Glen. *Washday on Noah's ark*
Singer, Isaac Bashevis. *Why Noah chose the*
   dove
Smith, Elmer Boyd. *The story of Noah's ark*
Smith, Roger. *How the animals saved the ark*
   and put two and two together
Spier, Peter. *Noah's ark*
Thorne, Jenny. *Noah's ark*
Webb, Clifford. *The story of Noah*
Wiesner, William. *Noah's ark*
Windham, Sophie. *Noah's ark*

Repetitive stories *see* Cumulative tales

Reptiles

Barrett, Judi. *Snake is totally tail*
Colby, C. B. (Carroll Burleigh). *Who went*
   there?
Cortesi, Wendy W. *Explore a spooky swamp*
Cristini, Ermanno. *In the pond*
Harris, Susan. *Reptiles*
Kuchalla, Susan. *What is a reptile?*
Pluckrose, Henry Arthur. *Reptiles*
Vyner, Sue. *The stolen egg*

Reptiles – alligators, crocodiles

Aliki. *Keep your mouth closed, dear*
   Use your head, dear
Aruego, José. *A crocodile's tale*
Balzola, Asun. *Munia and the orange*
   crocodile
Bare, Colleen Stanley. *Never kiss an*
   alligator
Bradman, Tony. *See you later, alligator*
Brown, Ruth. *Crazy Charlie*
Campbell, M. Rudolph. *The talking*
   crocodile
Carrick, Carol. *The crocodiles still wait*
Cazet, Denys. *The duck with squeaky feet*
Childress, Mark. *Joshua and Bigtooth*
Christelow, Eileen. *Five little monkeys sitting*
   in a tree
   Jerome the babysitter
Cushman, Doug. *Nasty Kyle the crocodile*
Dahl, Roald. *The enormous crocodile*
De Groat, Diane. *Alligator's toothache*
De Paola, Tomie (Thomas Anthony). *Bill*
   and Pete
   Bill and Pete go down the Nile
Dorros, Arthur. *Alligator shoes*
Dragonwagon, Crescent. *Alligator arrived*
   with apples
Dumbleton, Mike. *Dial-a-croc*
Duvoisin, Roger Antoine. *The crocodile in*
   the tree
   Crocus
Eastman, P. D. (Philip D.). *Flap your wings*
Engel, Diana. *Josephina hates her name*
Galdone, Paul. *The monkey and the crocodile*

Gantos, Jack (John, Jr.). *Swampy alligator*
Gross, Ruth Belov. *Alligators and other crocodilians*
Guiberson, Brenda Z. *Spoonbill swamp*
Guy, Rosa. *Mother crocodile*
Hartelius, Margaret A. *The chicken's child*
Hill, Eric. *Spot's baby sister*
Hirschi, Ron. *Who lives in... Alligator Swamp?*
Hoban, Russell. *Arthur's new power*
Dinner at Alberta's
Hodeir, André. *Warwick's three bottles*
Holland, Isabelle. *Kevin's hat*
Hurd, Thacher. *Mama don't allow*
Keven, Elisa. *Ernest*
Kinnell, Galway. *How the alligator missed breakfast*
Kirn, Ann. *The tale of a crocodile*
Knuppel, Helga. *The adventures of Christabel Crocodile*
Kunhardt, Edith. *Danny and the Easter egg*
Danny's Christmas star
Danny's mystery Valentine
Trick or treat, Danny!
Lexau, Joan M. *Crocodile and hen*
Lionni, Leo. *Cornelius*
McPhail, David. *Alligators are awful (and they have terrible manners, too)*
Mayer, Marianna. *Alley oop!*
Mayer, Mercer. *There's an alligator under my bed*
Minarik, Else Holmelund. *No fighting, no biting!*
Muntean, Michaela. *Alligator's garden*
Pack, Robert. *How to catch a crocodile*
Parker, Nancy Winslow. *The crocodile under Louis Finneberg's bed*
Peterson, Esther Allen. *Frederick's alligator*
Pickett, Carla. *Calvin Crocodile and the terrible noise*
Rice, James. *Gaston goes to Texas*
Rubel, Nicole. *It came from the swamp*
Schubert, Ingrid. *There's a crocodile under my bed!*
Sendak, Maurice. *Alligators all around*
Shaw, Evelyn S. *Alligator*
Stapler, Sarah. *Cordellia, dance!*
Stevenson, James. *Monty*
No need for Monty
Stone, Kazuko G. *Goodnight Twinklegator*
Velthuijs, Max. *Crocodile's masterpiece*
Venable, Alan. *The checker players*
Waber, Bernard. *Funny, funny Lyle*
Lovable Lyle
Lyle and the birthday party
Lyle finds his mother
Lyle, Lyle Crocodile
Wasmuth, Eleanor. *An alligator day*
The picnic basket
Watts, Marjorie-Ann. *Crocodile medicine*
Crocodile plaster

Weiss, Ellen. *Millicent Maybe*
West, Colin. *Have you seen the crocodile?*

Reptiles - crocodiles *see* Reptiles – alligators, crocodiles

Reptiles – iguanas

Newfield, Marcia. *Iggy*
Rosen, Winifred. *Henrietta and the day of the iguana*

Reptiles – lizards

Anderson, Lonzo. *Izzard*
Carle, Eric. *The mixed-up chameleon*
Conklin, Gladys. *I caught a lizard*
Himmelman, John. *Talester the lizard*
Lionni, Leo. *A color of his own*
Lopshire, Robert. *I am better than you*
McNeely, Jeannette. *Where's Izzy?*
Ryder, Joanne. *Lizard in the sun*
Shannon, George. *Lizard's song*

Reptiles – monitor lizards

Kennaway, Adrienne. *Bushbaby*

Reptiles – snakes

Aardema, Verna. *What's so funny, Ketu?*
Allard, Harry. *The cactus flower bakery*
Appleby, Leonard. *Snakes*
Baker, Keith. *Hide and snake*
Banchek, Linda. *Snake in, snake out*
Berson, Harold. *Joseph and the snake*
Bodsworth, Nan. *A nice walk in the jungle*
Buckley, Richard. *The greedy python*
Carlson, Natalie Savage. *Marie Louise and Christophe at the carnival*
Creighton, Jill. *One day there was nothing to do*
Demi. *The hallowed horse*
Forrester, Victoria. *Oddward*
Freschet, Berniece. *The watersnake*
Hoff, Syd. *Slithers*
Johnston, Tony. *Slither McCreep and his brother, Joe*
Kudrna, C. Imbior. *To bathe a boa*
Lauber, Patricia. *Snakes are hunters*
Le Guin, Ursula K. *Solomon Leviathan's nine hundred and thirty-first trip around the world*
Lemerise, Bruce. *Sheldon's lunch*
Lesikin, Joan. *Down the road*
Lionni, Leo. *In the rabbitgarden*
Newton, Patricia Montgomery. *The frog who drank the waters of the world*
Noble, Trinka Hakes. *The day Jimmy's boa ate the wash*
Jimmy's boa and the big splash birthday bash
Jimmy's boa bounces back

Oppenheim, Joanne. *Mrs. Peloki's snake*
Parsons, Alexandra. *Amazing snakes*
Prather, Ray. *The ostrich girl*
Reinl, Edda. *The little snake*
Smith, Mavis. *A snake mistake*
Ungerer, Tomi. *Crictor*
Waber, Bernard. *The snake*
Walsh, Ellen Stoll. *Mouse count*
Wildsmith, Brian. *Python's party*

Reptiles – turtles, tortoises

Abisch, Roz. *The clever turtle*
Æsop. *The hare and the tortoise*, ill. by Paul
    Galdone
    The hare and the tortoise, ill. by Gerald
    Rose
    The hare and the tortoise, ill. by Peter
    Weevers
    The tortoise and the hare, ill. by Janet
    Stevens
Asch, Frank. *Turtle tale*
Augarde, Steve (Stephen). *Barnaby Shrew,
    Black Dan and...the mighty wedgwood
    Barnaby Shrew goes to sea*
Baumann, Hans. *The hare's race*
Bourgeois, Paulette. *Franklin in the dark*
Bryan, Ashley. *Turtle knows your name*
Buckley, Richard. *The foolish tortoise*
Cahill, Chris. *Turtle magic*
Christian, Mary Blount. *Devin and Goliath*
Collins, Pat Lowery. *Tomorrow, up and
    away!*
Craig, Janet. *Turtles*
Creighton, Jill. *One day there was nothing to
    do*
Cromie, William J. *Steven and the green
    turtle*
Cummings, Betty Sue. *Turtle*
Darby, Gene. *What is a turtle?*
Davis, Alice Vaught. *Timothy Turtle*
Dodd, Lynley. *The smallest turtle*
Domanska, Janina. *Look, there is a turtle
    flying*
    The tortoise and the tree
Du Bois, William Pène. *The hare and the
    tortoise and the tortoise and the hare*
Elks, Wendy. *Charles B. Wombat and the
    very strange thing*
Emberley, Ed (Edward Randolph). *Rosebud*
Florian, Douglas. *Turtle day*
Freeman, Don. *The turtle and the dove*
Freschet, Berniece. *Turtle pond*
George, William T. *Box turtle at Long Pond*
Goldsmith, Howard. *Toto the timid turtle*
Graham, Al. *Timothy Turtle*
Harris, Dorothy Joan. *Four seasons for Toby*
Harrison, David Lee. *Little turtle's big
    adventure*
Hoban, Lillian. *Stick-in-the-mud turtle*
    Turtle spring
Jeffery, Graham. *Thomas the tortoise*

Joyce, William. *Bently and egg*
Kimmel, Eric A. *Anansi goes fishing*
La Fontaine, Jean de. *The hare and the
    tortoise*
Lesikin, Joan. *Down the road*
Lubell, Winifred. *Rosalie, the bird market
    turtle*
MacGill-Callahan, Sheila. *And still the turtle
    watched*
MacGregor, Ellen. *Theodor Turtle*
McGuire-Turcotte, Casey A. *How Honu the
    turtle got his shell*
McLenighan, Valjean. *Turtle and rabbit*
Maestro, Giulio. *The tortoise's tug of war*
Maris, Ron. *I wish I could fly*
Marshall, James. *Yummers too: the second
    course*
Matsutani, Miyoko. *The fisherman under the
    sea*
O'Donnell, Elizabeth Lee. *I can't get my
    turtle to move*
Parry, Marian. *King of the fish*
St. Pierre, Wendy. *Henry finds a home*
Shearer, Marilyn J. *The crown of fools*
Thayer, Jane. *Mr. Turtle's magic glasses*
Thayer, Mike. *In the middle of the puddle*
Troughton, Joanna. *Tortoise's dream*
Turner, Charles. *The turtle and the moon*
The turtle, ill. by Charlotte Knox
Van Woerkom, Dorothy. *Harry and
    Shelburt*
Ward, Helen. *The moonrat and the white
    turtle*
Wiese, Kurt. *The cunning turtle*
Williams, Barbara. *Albert's toothache*
Wilson, Barbara Ker. *The turtle and the
    island*
Wolf, Ann. *The rabbit and the turtle*
Wyse, Lois. *Two guppies, a turtle and Aunt
    Edna*
Yashima, Tarō. *Seashore story*
Ziefert, Harriet. *Where's the turtle?*

Rest *see* Sleep

Rhinoceros *see* Animals – rhinoceros

Rhyming text *see* Poetry, rhyme

Riddles

Aardema, Verna. *Ji-nongo-nongo means
    riddles*
Adler, David A. *The carsick zebra and other
    riddles*
Anno, Mitsumasa. *Anno's math games*
    Anno's math games II
    Anno's math games III
Ashley, Jill. *Riddles about Christmas*
Beisner, Monika. *Catch that cat!*
    Monika Beisner's book of riddles
Bell, Anthea. *The wise queen*

Bernstein, Joanne E. *Creepy crawly critter riddles*
What was the wicked witch's real name?
The big Peter Rabbit book
Bishop, Ann. *Chicken riddle*
 The Ella Fannie elephant riddle book
 Hey riddle riddle
 Merry-go-riddle
 Noah riddle?
 Oh, riddlesticks!
 The riddle ages
 Riddle-iculous rid-alphabet book
 Wild Bill Hiccup's riddle book
Brown, Marc Tolon. *Spooky riddles*
 What do you call a dumb bunny? and other rabbit riddles, games, jokes and cartoons
Burns, Diane L. *Elephants never forget!*
Burton, Marilee Robin. *Tail toes eyes ears nose*
Calmenson, Stephanie. *What am I?*
Cerf, Bennett Alfred. *Bennett Cerf's book of animal riddles*
 Bennett Cerf's book of laughs
 Bennett Cerf's book of riddles
 More riddles
Cole, Joanna. *The Clown-Arounds go on vacation*
 Get well, Clown-Arounds!
Crowley, Arthur. *The wagon man*
Daniels, Guy. *The Tsar's riddles*
Degen, Bruce. *The little witch and the riddle*
Delaney, M. C. (Michael Clark). *The marigold monster*
Demi. *Where is it?*
De Regniers, Beatrice Schenk. *It does not say meow!*
Doolittle, Eileen. *The ark in the attic*
Downie, Jill. *Alphabet puzzle*
Duncan, Riana. *A nutcracker in a tree*
Elkin, Benjamin. *The wisest man in the world*
Emberley, Ed (Edward Randolph). *Ed Emberley's amazing look through book*
Fleischman, Sid. *Kate's secret riddle*
Fletcher, Elizabeth. *What am I?*
Gackenbach, Dick. *Supposes*
Goundaud, Karen Jo. *A very mice joke book*
Gregorich, Barbara. *My friend goes left*
Grimm, Jacob. *Rumpelstiltskin*, ill. by Jacqueline Ayer
 Rumpelstiltskin, ill. by Donna Diamond
 Rumpelstiltskin, ill. by Paul Galdone
 Rumpelstiltskin, ill. by Jonathan Langley
 Rumpelstiltskin, ill. by Gennady Spirin
 Rumpelstiltskin, ill. by John Wallner
 Rumpelstiltskin, ill. by Paul O. Zelinsky
Hall, Malcolm. *CariCATures*
Hample, Stoo. *Stoo Hample's silly joke book*
 Yet another big fat funny silly book
 High on a hill

Jensen, Virginia Allen. *Red thread riddles*
Keller, Charles. *School daze*
Koontz, Robin Michal. *I see something you don't see*
Lewis, Naomi. *The butterfly collector*
Low, Joseph. *Five men under one umbrella*
 A mad wet hen and other riddles
Lyfick, Warren. *Animal tales*
 The little book of fowl jokes
McKié, Roy. *The riddle book*
Maestro, Giulio. *Halloween howls*
 A raft of riddles
 Riddle romp
Modell, Frank. *Look out, it's April Fools' Day*
Moncure, Jane Belk. *Riddle me a riddle*
Mooser, Stephen. *Funnyman's first case*
Most, Bernard. *Pets in trumpets and other word-play riddles*
 Zoodles
Peppé, Rodney. *Hey riddle diddle*
Peterson, Scott K. *What's your name?*
Phillips, Louis. *The upside down riddle book*
Poskanzer, Susan Cornell. *Riddles about Hannukah*
Potter, Beatrix. *The tale of Squirrel Nutkin*
Romanoli, Robert. *What's so funny?!!*
Roop, Peter. *Going buggy!*
 Let's celebrate!
 Stick out your tongue!
Rosenbloom, Joseph. *The funniest joke book ever!*
Selberg, Ingrid. *Nature's hidden world*
Seuss, Dr. *The cat's quizzer*
Swann, Brian. *A basket full of white eggs*
Thaler, Mike. *The yellow brick toad*
Türk, Hanne. *Max versus the cube*
Wakefield, Joyce. *Ask a silly question*
Walton, Rick. *Dumb clucks!*
 Something's fishy!
Zwetchkenbaum, G. *The Peanuts shape circus puzzle book*
 The Peanuts sleepy time puzzle book
 The Snoopy farm puzzle book
 Snoopy safari puzzle book

Right and left see Concepts – left and right

Rivers

Biro, Val. *The wind in the willows: the river bank*
Brennan, Joseph Killorin. *Gobo and the river*
Brook, Judy. *Tim mouse goes down the stream*
Bushey, Jerry. *The barge book*
Carrick, Carol. *The brook*
Cherry, Lynne. *A river ran wild*
Dabcovich, Lydia. *Follow the river*
Day, Alexandra. *River parade*
Flack, Marjorie. *The boats on the river*

Gramatky, Hardie. *Little Toot on the Mississippi*
Grasshopper to the rescue, ill. by Tasha Tudor
Grifalconi, Ann. *Flyaway girl*
Hadithi, Mwenye. *Hot hippo*
Holling, Holling C. (Holling Clancy). *Paddle-to-the-sea*
Keeping, Charles. *Alfie finds the other side of the world*
Locker, Thomas. *Where the river begins*
Michl, Reinhard. *A day on the river*
Murphy, Shirley Rousseau. *Tattie's river journey*
Oakley, Graham. *The church mice adrift*
Peters, Lisa Westberg. *Good morning, river!*
Reynolds, Jan. *Amazon*
Russell, Naomi. *The stream*
Schmid, Eleonore. *The water's journey*

Roads

Bate, Norman. *Who built the highway?*
Field, Rachel Lyman. *A road might lead to anywhere*
Goodall, John S. *The story of a main street*
Kehoe, Michael. *Road closed*
Lyon, George-Ella. *Who came down that road?*
Pringle, Laurence. *Jesse builds a road*
Roennfeldt, Robert. *A day on the avenue*
Royston, Angela. *Monster road builders*
Tusa, Tricia. *Sherman and Pearl*

Robbers *see* Crime

Robins *see* Birds – robins

Robots

Bradford, Ann. *The mystery of the square footsteps*
Bunting, Eve (Anne Evelyn). *The robot birthday*
Cole, Babette. *The trouble with dad*
Dupasquier, Philippe. *A robot named chip*
Greene, Carol. *Robots*
Hoban, Lillian. *The laziest robot in zone one*
Krahn, Fernando. *Robot-bot-bot*
Kroll, Steven. *Otto*
Lauber, Patricia. *Get ready for robots!*
Marshall, Edward. *Space case*
Marzollo, Jean. *Jed and the space bandits*
Jed's junior space patrol
Paul, Sherry. *2-B and the rock 'n roll band*
2-B and the space visitor
Titus, Eve. *Anatole and the robot*

Rockets *see* Space and space ships

Rocking chairs *see* Furniture – chairs

Rocking horses *see* Toys – rocking horses

Rocks

Baylor, Byrd. *Everybody needs a rock*
Chetwin, Grace. *Mr. Meredith and the truly remarkable stone*
Gans, Roma. *Rock collecting*
Harshman, Marc. *Rocks in my pocket*
Kehoe, Michael. *The rock quarry book*
Lee, Jeanne M. *Legend of the Li River*
Lionni, Leo. *On my beach there are many pebbles*
McKee, David. *The hill and the rock*
Parnall, Peter. *The rock*
Selsam, Millicent E. *A first look at rocks*
Walker, Alice. *Finding the green stone*

Roller skating *see* Sports – roller skating

Romania *see* Foreign lands – Romania

Roosters *see* Chickens – hens

Rosh Hashanah *see* Holidays – Rosh Hashanah

Royalty

Aardema, Verna. *The riddle of the drum*
Abrons, Mary. *For Alice a palace*
Aitken, Amy. *Ruby, the red knight*
Allen, Pamela. *Bertie and the bear*
A lion in the night
Andersen, H. C. (Hans Christian). *The swineherd*, ill. by Dorothée Duntze
Anderson, Lonzo. *Two hundred rabbits*
Asher, Sandy. *Princess Bee and the royal good-night story*
Babbitt, Samuel F. *The forty-ninth magician*
Bang, Betsy. *Tuntuni the tailor bird*
Bang, Molly. *Tye May and the magic brush*
Baring, Maurice. *The blue rose*
Basile, Giambattista. *Petrosinella*
Berenzy, Alix. *A frog prince*
Beresford, Elisabeth. *Jack and the magic stove*
Berson, Harold. *The thief who hugged a moonbeam*
Bohdal, Susi. *The magic honey jar*
Bolliger, Max. *The most beautiful song*
Bond, Michael. *Paddington at the palace*
Bowden, Joan Chase. *A new home for Snow Ball*
Brierley, Louise. *King Lion and his cooks*
Browne, Caroline. *Mrs. Christie's farmhouse*
Burningham, John. *Time to get out of the bath, Shirley*
Chapman, Gaynor. *The luck child*
Climo, Shirley. *The Egyptian Cinderella*
King of the birds

Company González, Mercè. *Killian and the dragons*

Coombs, Patricia. *Tilabel*

Cooney, Barbara. *Little brother and little sister*

Cretien, Paul D. *Sir Henry and the dragon*

Day, David. *The swan children*

De La Mare, Walter (Walter John). *Molly Whuppie*

De Regniers, Beatrice Schenk. *May I bring a friend?*

Dewey, Ariane. *Dorin and the dragon*

Domanska, Janina. *Look, there is a turtle flying*

Dos Santos, Joyce Audy. *The diviner*

Duke, Kate. *Aunt Isabel tells a good one*

Elkin, Benjamin. *Gillespie and the guards*
The wisest man in the world

Espenscheid, Gertrude E. *The oh ball*

Fisher, Leonard Everett. *Theseus and the minotaur*

Fleischman, Sid. *Longbeard the wizard*

Foreman, Michael. *War and peas*

Freeman, Don. *Forever laughter*

Galdone, Paul. *The amazing pig*
The monster and the tailor

Gay, Michel. *Bibi's birthday surprise*

Gianni, Peg. *Alex, the amazing juggler*

Glass, Andrew. *Chickpea and the talking cow*

The golden goose, ill. by William Stobbs

Grimm, Jacob. *The earth gnome*, ill. by Margot Tomes
The goose girl, ill. by Sabine Bruntjen
King Grisly-Beard, ill. by Maurice Sendak
Rumpelstiltskin, ill. by Jacqueline Ayer
Rumpelstiltskin, ill. by Donna Diamond
Rumpelstiltskin, ill. by Paul Galdone
Rumpelstiltskin, ill. by Jonathan Langley
Rumpelstiltskin, ill. by Gennady Spirin
Rumpelstiltskin, ill. by John Wallner
Rumpelstiltskin, ill. by Paul O. Zelinsky

Hayes, Sarah. *Bad egg*

Heine, Helme. *The most wonderful egg in the world*

Hilton, Nette. *Prince Lachlan*

Hoffmann, E. T. A. *The nutcracker*, ill. by Francesca Crespi
The nutcracker, ill. by Lisbeth Zwerger

Kahl, Virginia. *The Baron's booty*
The Duchess bakes a cake
Plum pudding for Christmas

Kennedy, Richard. *The lost kingdom of Karnica*

Kroll, Steven. *Fat magic*

Langner, Nola. *By the light of the silvery moon*

Langton, Jane. *The hedgehog boy*

Lasker, David. *The boy who loved music*

Laskowski, Jerzy. *Master of the royal cats*

Lee, Jeanne M. *Toad is the uncle of heaven*

Littledale, Freya. *The magic plum tree*

Lobel, Anita. *Sven's bridge*

Locker, Thomas. *The young artist*

Lorenz, Lee. *The feathered ogre*

McCrea, James. *The magic tree*

McDermott, Gerald. *The voyage of Osiris*

McLenighan, Valjean. *What you see is what you get*
You are what you are

McNaughton, Colin. *The rat race*

Mahood, Kenneth. *The laughing dragon*

Matsutani, Miyoko. *The fisherman under the sea*

Mayer, Marianna. *The black horse*
The spirit of the blue light

Miller, M. L. *Dizzy from fools*

Montresor, Beni. *The witches of Venice*

Mother Goose. *The golden goose book*, ill. by L. Leslie Brooke
Sing a song of sixpence, ill. by Leonard Lubin

Moxley, Susan. *Abdul's treasure*

Muller, Robin. *The sorcerer's apprentice*, ill. by Robin Muller

Myers, Walter Dean. *The golden serpent*

Myller, Rolf. *Rolling round*

Nesbit, Edith. *The last of the dragons*

Nishikawa, Osamu. *Alexander and the blue ghost*

Oram, Hiawyn. *Skittlewonder and the wizard*

Pittman, Helena Clare. *A grain of rice*

Price, Leontyne. *Aïda*

Richter, Mischa. *To bed, to bed!*

Rogasky, Barbara. *The water of life*

Rose, Anne. *How does a czar eat potatoes?*

Rose, Gerald. *The bird garden*

Ross, Tony. *Towser and the terrible thing*

Saddler, Allen. *The Archery contest*

San Souci, Robert D. *The white cat*

Schiller, Barbara. *The white rat's tale*

Scholey, Arthur. *Baboushka*

Schwartz, Amy. *Her Majesty, Aunt Essie*

Scott, Sally. *The magic horse*

Seuss, Dr. *Bartholomew and the Oobleck*

Shulevitz, Uri. *One Monday morning*

Steig, William. *Roland, the minstrel pig*

Stephenson, Dorothy. *The night it rained toys*

Tompert, Ann. *The Tzar's bird*

Torre, Betty L. *The luminous pearl*

Trez, Denise. *Maila and the flying carpet*
The royal hiccups

Vernon, Adele. *The riddle*

Wahl, Jan. *Cabbage moon*

Wiesner, David. *The loathsome dragon*

Williams, Jay. *School for sillies*

Winthrop, Elizabeth. *Vasilissa the beautiful*

Wisniewski, David. *The warrior and the wise man*

Yen, Clara. *Why rat comes first*

Yolen, Jane. *The seeing stick*

Young, Miriam Burt. *The sugar mouse cake*

Zemach, Harve. *The tricks of Master Dabble*

Royalty – emperors

Andersen, H. C. (Hans Christian). *The emperor's new clothes*, ill. by Erik Blegvad
The emperor's new clothes, ill. by Virginia Lee Burton
The emperor's new clothes, ill. by Robert Byrd
The emperor's new clothes, ill. by Jack and Irene Delano
The emperor's new clothes, ill. by Hélène Desputeaux
The emperor's new clothes, ill. by Birte Dietz
The emperor's new clothes, ill. by Dorothée Duntze
The emperor's new clothes, ill. by Pamela Baldwin Ford
The emperor's new clothes, ill. by Jack Kent
The emperor's new clothes, ill. by Monika Laimgruber
The emperor's new clothes, ill. by Anne F. Rockwell
The emperor's new clothes, ill. by Janet Stevens
The emperor's new clothes, ill. by Nadine Bernard Westcott
The emperor's nightingale, ill. from the Disney arcives
The emperor's nightingale, ill. by Georges Lemoine
The nightingale, ill. by Harold Berson
The nightingale, ill. by Nancy Ekholm Burkert
The nightingale, ill. by Demi
The nightingale, ill. by Beni Montresor
The nightingale, ill. by Lisbeth Zwerger
Hughes, Peter. *The emperor's oblong pancake*
Johnson, Crockett. *The emperor's gift*
Morris, Winifred. *The future of Yen-Tzu*
Nikly, Michelle. *The emperor's plum tree*
Yacowitz, Caryn. *The jade stone*
Yolen, Jane. *The emperor and the kite*
The emperor and the kite [Rev. ed.]

Royalty – kings

Alexander, Lloyd. *The king's fountain*
Aliki. *The king's day*
Anno, Mitsumasa. *The king's flower*
Aruego, José. *The king and his friends*
Auerbach, Marjorie. *King Lavra and the barber*
Balet, Jan B. *The king and the broom maker*
Birch, David. *The king's chessboard*
Boswell, Stephen. *King Gorboduc's fabulous zoo*
Brunhoff, Jean de. *Babar the king*
Babar the king, facsimile ed

Brunhoff, Laurent de. *Babar's visit to Bird Island*
Buffett, Jimmy. *The jolly mon*
Cole, Babette. *King Change-A-Lot*
Cole, Brock. *The king at the door*
Crabtree, Judith. *The sparrow's story at the king's command*
Cunliffe, John. *The king's birthday cake*
Degen, Bruce. *Teddy bear towers*
Domanska, Janina. *King Krakus and the dragon*
Elkin, Benjamin. *The king who could not sleep*
The king's wish and other stories
Fern, Eugene. *The king who was too busy*
Gackenbach, Dick. *Harvey, the foolish pig*
King Wacky
Gregory, Valiska. *Through the mickle woods*
Harber, Frances. *My king has donkey ears*
Haywood, Carolyn. *The king's monster*
Heine, Helme. *King Bounce the 1st*
Hewitt, Kathryn. *King Midas and the golden touch*
Hughes, Peter. *The king who loved candy*
Hutchins, Pat. *King Henry's palace*
Karlin, Nurit. *A train for the king*
Kessler, Leonard P. *Soup for the king*
Kraus, Robert. *The king's trousers*
McCrea, James. *The king's procession*
McKee, David. *King Rollo and the birthday*
King Rollo and the bread
King Rollo and the new shoes
McKissack, Patricia C. *King Midas and his gold*
The king's new clothes
McMullen, Eunice. *Dragon for breakfast*
Mahy, Margaret. *17 kings and 42 elephants*
Manson, Christopher. *A gift for the king*
Martin, C. L. G. *The dragon nanny*
Mayer, Marianna. *Marcel the pastry chef*
Milton, Nancy. *The giraffe that walked to Paris*
Myller, Rolf. *How big is a foot?*
Noble, Trinka Hakes. *The king's tea*
Noyes, Alfred. *The highwayman*, ill. by Neil Waldman
Peet, Bill (William Bartlett). *How Droofus the dragon lost his head*
Perkins, Al. *King Midas and the golden touch*
Perrault, Charles. *Puss in boots*, ill. by Marcia Brown
Puss in boots, ill. by Lorinda Bryan Cauley
Puss in boots, ill. by Jean Claverie
Puss in boots, ill. by Hans Fischer
Puss in boots, ill. by Paul Galdone
Puss in boots, retold and ill. by John S. Goodall
Puss in boots, retold and ill. by Gail E. Haley

Puss in boots, ill. by Julia Noonan
Puss in boots, ill. by Tony Ross
Puss in boots, ill. by William Stobbs
Puss in boots, ill. by Alain Vaes
Puss in boots, ill. by Barry Wilkinson
Pevear, Richard. *Our king has horns!*
Postgate, Oliver. *Noggin and the whale*
  Noggin the king
Reit, Seymour. *The king who learned to smile*
Robison, Nancy. *Ten tall soldiers*
Saddler, Allen. *The king gets fit*
Seuss, Dr. *The king's stilts*
Sexton, Gwain. *There once was a king*
Siekkinen, Raija. *Mister King*
Skipper, Mervyn. *The fooling of King Alexander*
Steptoe, John. *Mufaro's beautiful daughters*
Storr, Catherine (Cole). *King Midas*
Thomson, Peggy. *The king has horse's ears*
Va, Leong. *A letter to the king*
Van Laan, Nancy. *The legend of El Dorado*
Wersba, Barbara. *Do tigers ever bite kings?*
West, Colin. *The king of Kennelwick castle*
  The king's toothache
Wilkes, Larry. *The king's egg dance*
Wood, Audrey. *King Bidgood's in the bathtub*

Royalty – princes

Baum, Arline. *Opt*
Baumann, Kurt. *The prince and the lute*
Birrer, Cynthia. *The lady and the unicorn*
Boesky, Amy. *Planet Was*
Brenner, Barbara A. *The prince and the pink blanket*
Canfield, Jane White. *The frog prince*
Cole, Babette. *King Change-A-Lot*
  Prince Cinders
Damjan, Mischa. *The little prince and the tiger cat*
Dasent, George W. *East o' the sun, west o' the moon*
The firebird, ill. by Moira Kemp
The firebird, ill. by Kris Waldherr
The firebird, ill. by Boris Zvorykin
Grimm, Jacob. *Cinderella*, ill. by Nonny Hogrogian
  Cinderella, ill. by Svend Otto S.
  The donkey prince, ill. by Barbara Cooney
  The frog prince, ill. by Binette Schroeder
  Rapunzel, ill. by Jutta Ash
  Rapunzel, ill. by Bert Dodson
  Rapunzel, ill. by Trina Schart Hyman
  Rapunzel, ill. by Kris Waldherr
  Rapunzel, ill. by Bernadette Watts
Hastings, Selina. *The singing ringing tree*
Haugaard, Erik Christian. *Prince Boghole*
Heine, Helme. *Prince Bear*
Helldorfer, M. C. (Mary Claire). *The mapmaker's daughter*
Hilton, Nette. *Prince Lachlan*
Ikeda, Daisaku. *The snow country prince*

Jacobs, Joseph. *Tattercoats*, ill. by Margot Tomes
Johnson, Crockett. *The frowning prince*
Karlin, Barbara. *Cinderella*
Knight, Hilary. *Hilary Knight's Cinderella*
Lattimore, Deborah Nourse. *The prince and the golden ax*
Lobel, Arnold. *Prince Bertram the bad*
MacDonald, George. *Little Daylight*
McKissack, Patricia C. *Cinderella*
Manson, Christopher. *The crab prince*
Milne, A. A. (Alan Alexander). *Prince Rabbit*
Nones, Eric Jon. *Canary prince*
Oppenheim, Joanne. *The story book prince*
Patz, Nancy. *Gina Farina and the Prince of Mintz*
Perrault, Charles. *Cinderella*, ill. by Sheilah Beckett
Cinderella, ill. by Marcia Brown
Cinderella, ill. by Paul Galdone
Cinderella, ill. by Diane Goode
Cinderella, ill. by Susan Jeffers
Cinderella, ill. by Emanuele Luzzati
Cinderella, ill. by James Marshall
Cinderella, ill. by Phil Smith
The prince who knew his fate, ill. by Lise Manniche
Rogers, Paul (Patrick). *Tumbledown*
Sanderson, Ruth. *The enchanted wood*
Scieszka, Jon. *The frog prince, continued*
Sherman, Josepha. *Vassilisa the wise*
Wells, Rosemary. *The little lame prince*
Yolen, Jane. *Wings*

Royalty – princesses

Afanas'ev, Aleksandr N. *Salt*
Allen, Linda. *The mouse bride*
Andersen, H. C. (Hans Christian). *The princess and the pea*, ill. by Dorothée Duntze
The princess and the pea, ill. by Dick Gackenbach
The princess and the pea, ill. by Paul Galdone
The princess and the pea, ill. by Janet Stevens
The princess and the pea, ill. by Eve Tharlet
Bawden, Nina. *Princess Alice*
Cole, Babette. *Princess Smartypants*
Cooper, Susan. *Tam Lin*
Costa, Nicoletta. *The mischievous princess*
DeChristopher, Marlowe. *Greencoat and the swanboy*
Flot, Jeannette B. *Princess Kalina and the hedgehog*
Gekiere, Madeleine. *The frilly lily and the princess*
Grimm, Jacob. *The frog prince*, ill. by Binette Schroeder

The golden goose, ill. by Dorothée Duntze
The golden goose, ill. by Isadore Seltzer
The golden goose, ill. by Martin Ursell
The princess and the frog, retold and ill. by Rachel Isadora
The twelve dancing princesses, ill. by Kinuko Y. Craft
The twelve dancing princesses, ill. by Anne Dalton
The twelve dancing princesses, ill. by Dennis Hockerman
The twelve dancing princesses, ill. by Errol Le Cain
The twelve dancing princesses, ill. by Gerald McDermott
The twelve dancing princesses, ill. by Uri Shulevitz
Gwynne, Fred. *Pondlarker*
Hastings, Selina. *The singing ringing tree*
Haugaard, Erik Christian. *Princess Horrid*
Heine, Helme. *Prince Bear*
Huck, Charlotte. *Princess Furball*
Isele, Elizabeth. *The frog princess*
Kroll, Steven. *Princess Abigail and the wonderful hat*
Laroche, Michel. *The snow rose*
Lobel, Anita. *A birthday for the princess*
MacDonald, George. *The light princess*, ill. by Katie Thamer Treherne
Little Daylight
Martin, Claire. *Boots and the glass mountain*
The race of the golden apples
Miller, M. L. *Dizzy from fools*
Nesbit, Edith. *Melisande*
Ness, Evaline. *Pavo and the princess*
Nikly, Michelle. *The princess on the nut*
Nones, Eric Jon. *Canary prince*
Reesink, Marijke. *The princess who always ran away*
Scieszka, Jon. *The frog prince, continued*
Shearer, Marilyn J. *The Nubian princess*
Slobodkin, Louis. *Colette and the princess*
Thurber, James. *Many moons*, ill. by Marc Simont
Many moons, ill. by Louis Slobodkin
Turnbull, Ann. *The tapestry cats*
Vesey, A. *The princess and the frog*
Waddell, Martin. *The tough princess*
Williams, Jay. *The practical princess*
Zakhoder, Boris Vladimirovich. *The good stepmother*

Royalty – queens

Bell, Anthea. *The wise queen*
Bowden, Joan Chase. *A hat for the queen*
Garrett, Jennifer. *The queen who stole the sky*
Lobato, Arcadio. *The greatest treasure*
Mahy, Margaret. *The queen's goat*
Mayer, Mercer. *The queen always wanted to dance*

Myers, Bernice. *The flying shoes*
Oxenbury, Helen. *The queen and Rosie Randall*
Paxton, Tom. *Engelbert the elephant*
Pike, Carol. *The nutty queen*
Silverman, Maida. *The magic well*
Turnbull, Ann. *The tapestry cats*
Van Woerkom, Dorothy. *The queen who couldn't bake gingerbread*

Royalty – sultans

Ambrus, Victor G. *The Sultan's bath*

Running *see* Sports – racing

Running away *see* Behavior – running away

Russia *see* Foreign lands – Russia

Sadness *see* Emotions – sadness

Safety

Arnold, Caroline. *Who keeps us safe?*
Bahr, Amy C. *It's ok to say no*
Sometimes it's ok to tell secrets
What should you do when...?
Your body is your own
Baker, Eugene. *Bicycles*
Fire
Home
Outdoors
School
Water
Berenstain, Stan. *The Berenstain bears learn about strangers*
Brown, Marc Tolon. *Dinosaurs, beware!*
Brown, Margaret Wise. *Red light, green light*
Chlad, Dorothy. *Bicycles are fun to ride*
Matches, lighters, and firecrackers are not toys
Poisons make you sick
Cleary, Beverly. *Lucky Chuck*
Emecheta, Buchi. *Nowhere to play*
Girard, Linda Walvoord. *My body is private*
Joyce, Irma. *Never talk to strangers*
Leaf, Munro. *Safety can be fun*
Lindgren, Barbro. *Sam's lamp*
McKissack, Patricia C. *Who is coming?*
McLeod, Emilie Warren. *The bear's bicycle*
Maestro, Betsy. *Bike trip*
Meyer, Linda D. *Safety zone*

Moss, Elaine. *Polar*
Myller, Lois. *No! No!*
Petty, Kate. *Being careful with strangers*
Russell, Pamela. *Do you have a secret?*
Shortall, Leonard W. *One way*
Smaridge, Norah. *Watch out!*
Viorst, Judith. *Try it again, Sam*
Vogel, Carole Garbuny. *The dangers of strangers*
Yamashita, Haruo. *Mice at the beach*
Ziefert, Harriet. *No, no, Nicky!*

Sahara Desert *see* Foreign lands – Sahara Desert

Sailors *see* Careers – military

St. Patrick's Day *see* Holidays – St. Patrick's Day

Saint Patrick's Day *see* Holidays – St. Patrick's Day

Salamanders *see* Animals – salamanders

Sand

Bason, Lillian. *Castles and mirrors and cities of sand*
Jones, Rebecca C. *Down at the bottom of the deep dark sea*
Krementz, Jill. *Jack goes to the beach*
Lloyd, David. *Grandma and the pirate*
Nolan, Dennis. *The castle builder*
Ormondroyd, Edward. *Johnny Castleseed*
Roach, Marilynne K. *Dune fox*
Robbins, Ken. *Beach days*
Turnbull, Ann. *The sand horse*
Vasiliu, Mircea. *A day at the beach*
Watanabe, Shigeo. *I'm the king of the castle!*
Webb, Angela. *Sand*

Sandcastles *see* Sand

Sandman

Shepperson, Rob. *The sandman*
Strahl, Rudi. *Sandman in the lighthouse*
Twining, Edith. *Sandman*

Sandpipers *see* Birds – sandpipers

Saving things *see* Behavior – saving things

Scarecrows

Bolliger, Max. *The wooden man*
Farber, Norma. *There goes feathertop!*
Fleischman, Sid. *The scarebird*
Gordon, Sharon. *Sam the scarecrow*
Hart, Jeanne McGahey. *Scareboy*
Lewis, Robin Baird. *Hello, Mr. Scarecrow*

Lifton, Betty Jean. *Joji and the Amanojaku*
Joji and the dragon
Joji and the fog
Martin, Bill (William Ivan). *Barn dance!*
Miller, Edna. *Pebbles, a pack rat*
Oana, Kay D. *Robbie and the raggedy scarecrow*
Schertle, Alice. *Witch Hazel*
Tripp, Paul. *The strawman who smiled by mistake*
Watts, Bernadette. *Tattercoats*
Williams, Linda. *The little old lady who was not afraid of anything*

School

Adelson, Leone. *All ready for school*
Ahlberg, Allan. *The Cinderella show*
Ahlberg, Janet. *Starting school*
Alexander, Martha G. *Move over, Twerp*
Sabrina
Allard, Harry. *Miss Nelson has a field day*
Miss Nelson is back
Miss Nelson is missing!
Annett, Cora. *The dog who thought he was a boy*
Arnold, Caroline. *Where do you go to school?*
Arnold, Katrin. *Anna joins in*
Aseltine, Lorraine. *First grade can wait*
Ashley, Bernard. *Dinner ladies don't count*
Aulaire, Ingri Mortenson d'. *Children of the northlights*
Nils
Babbitt, Lorraine. *Pink like the geranium*
Baehr, Patricia. *School isn't fair*
Baer, Edith. *This is the way we go to school*
Baird, Anne. *The guppies of Hilly Dale House*
Baker, Eugene. *School*
Bare, Colleen Stanley. *Critter, the class cat*
Barkan, Joanne. *Whiskerville school*
Behrens, June. *Who am I?*
Beim, Jerrold. *The taming of Toby*
Bemelmans, Ludwig. *Madeline*
Berenstain, Stan. *The Berenstain bears go to school*
The Berenstain bears' trouble at school
Berquist, Grace. *Speckles goes to school*
Binnamin, Vivian. *The case of the anteater's missing lunch*
The case of the mysterious mermaid
Blance, Ellen. *Monster at school*
Monster goes to school
Blue, Rose. *How many blocks is the world?*
I am here: Yo estoy aqui
Bond, Felicia. *The Halloween performance*
Boon, Emilie. *1 2 3 how many animals can you see?*
Boreman, Jean. *Bantie and her chicks*
Bourgeois, Paulette. *Too many chickens*

Boyd, Selma. *I met a polar bear*
Bradman, Tony. *It came from outer space*
  Michael
Bram, Elizabeth. *I don't want to go to school*
Brandenberg, Franz. *No school today!*
  Six new students
Breinburg, Petronella. *Shawn goes to school*
Brillhart, Julie. *Anna's goodbye apron*
Brooks, Ron. *Timothy and Gramps*
Brown, Kathryn. *Muledred*
Brown, Marc Tolon. *Arthur's teacher trouble*
  Arthur's Valentine
  The true Francine
Brown, Tricia. *Hello, amigos!*
Bruna, Dick. *Miffy goes to school*
  The school
Buchanan, Heather S. *George and Matilda*
  Mouse and the floating school
Buchheimer, Naomi. *Let's go to a school*
Buckley, Kate. *Love notes*
Budney, Blossom. *N is for nursery school*
Burningham, John. *John Patrick Norman*
  McHennessy—the boy who was always late
Butler, Dorothy. *My brown bear Barney*
Butterworth, Nick. *The Nativity play*
Calmenson, Stephanie. *The kindergarten*
  book
Caple, Kathy. *The biggest nose*
Carlson, Nancy. *Arnie and the new kid*
  Louanne Pig in making the team
Carrick, Carol. *Left behind*
Caseley, Judith. *Ada potato*
  Molly Pink
Caudill, Rebecca. *A pocketful of cricket*
Cazet, Denys. *Are there any questions?*
  Daydreams
  A fish in his pocket
  Frosted glass
  Never spit on your shoes
Chapouton, Anne-Marie. *Sebastian is*
  always late
Charles, Donald. *Calico Cat at school*
Charmatz, Bill. *The Troy St. bus*
Chorao, Kay. *Molly's lies*
Clarke, Gus. *Eddie and Teddy*
Clewes, Dorothy. *Happiest day*
Clifton, Lucille. *All us come cross the water*
Cohen, Miriam. *Bee my Valentine!*
  Best friends
  Don't eat too much turkey!
  First grade takes a test
  It's George!
  Jim meets the thing
  Liar, liar, pants on fire!
  Lost in the museum
  The new teacher
  No good in art
  The real-skin rubber monster mask
  See you in second grade!
  See you tomorrow
  So what?

  Starring first grade
  Tough Jim
  When will I read?
  Will I have a friend?
Coker, Gylbert. *Naptime*
Cole, Babette. *The trouble with mom*
Cole, Joanna. *Norma Jean, jumping bean*
Coles, Alison. *Michael's first day*
Cooney, Nancy Evans. *The blanket that had*
  to go
Coontz, Otto. *A real class clown*
Copp, James (Andrew James). *Martha*
  Matilda O'Toole
Corrigan, Kathy. *Emily Umily*
Crews, Donald. *School bus*
Curious George goes to school
Cuyler, Margery. *Baby Dot: a dinosaur story*
Davies, Andrew. *Poonam's pets*
De Hamel, Joan. *Hemi's pet*
Delaney, Ned. *Rufus the doofus*
Delton, Judy. *My mom made me go to school*
  The new girl at school
  Rabbit goes to night school
Denton, Terry. *The school for laughter*
De Paola, Tomie (Thomas Anthony). *The*
  art lesson
  Bill and Pete
  Bill and Pete go down the Nile
Dinan, Carolyn. *Say cheese!*
Dorsky, Blanche. *Harry, a true story*
Dreifus, Miriam W. *Brave Betsy*
Duke, Kate. *Seven froggies went to school*
Ehrlich, Amy. *Leo, Zack and Emmie*
  Leo, Zack, and Emmie together again
Ets, Marie Hall. *Bad boy, good boy*
Fanshawe, Elizabeth. *Rachel*
Feder, Paula Kurzband. *Where does the*
  teacher live?
Fleischman, Paul. *Time train*
Gantos, Jack (John, Jr.). *Rotten Ralph's show*
  and tell
Garland, Sarah. *Billy and Belle*
Giff, Patricia Reilly. *The beast in Ms.*
  Rooney's room
  Happy birthday, Ronald Morgan!
  Next year I'll be special
  Today was a terrible day
  Watch out, Ronald Morgan!
Glen, Maggie. *Ruby to the rescue*
Goffstein, M. B. (Marilyn Brooke). *School*
  of names
Goodall, John S. *Naughty Nancy goes to*
  school
Grindley, Sally. *I don't want to!*
Gross, Alan. *What if the teacher calls on me?*
Hader, Berta Hoerner. *The mighty hunter*
Hale, Sarah Josepha. *Mary had a little*
  lamb, ill. by Tomie de Paola
  Mary had a little lamb, photos. by Bruce
  Millan

Hamilton-Merritt, Jane. *My first days of school*
Hathorn, Libby. *Freya's fantastic surprise*
Henkes, Kevin. *Chrysanthemum*
Jessica
Hennessy, B. G. *School days*
Hill, Donna. *Ms. Glee was waiting*
Hill, Eric. *Spot goes to school*
Hillman, Priscilla. *The Merry-Mouse schoolhouse*
Hoban, Russell. *Bread and jam for Frances*
Hoffman, Mary. *Amazing Grace*
Hoffman, Phyllis. *Meatball*
Steffie and me
We play
Holabird, Katharine. *Angelina and Alice*
Howe, James. *The day the teacher went bananas*
When you go to kindergarten
Ingoglia, Gina. *The art class*
Isadora, Rachel. *Willaby*
Jaynes, Ruth M. *Friends! friends! friends!*
Three baby chicks
Jenkin-Pearce, Susie. *Bad Boris goes to school*
Jenny, Anne. *The fantastic story of King Brioche the First*
Johnson, Dolores. *The best bug to be*
Johnson, Jean. *Teachers A to Z*
Johnston, Deborah. *Mathew Michael's beastly day*
Kantrowitz, Mildred. *Willy Bear*
Kaufman, Curt. *Rajesh*
Keller, Holly. *The new boy*
Keller, Irene. *Benjamin Rabbit and the stranger danger*
Kerr, Phyllis Forbes. *I tricked you*
Khdir, Kate. *Little ghost*
Krementz, Jill. *Katherine goes to nursery school*
Kuklin, Susan. *Going to my nursery school*
Kunhardt, Edith. *Red day, green day*
Lasker, Joe. *Nick joins in*
Lawlor, Laurie. *Second-grade dog*
Leaf, Munro. *Robert Francis Weatherbee*
Leedy, Loreen. *Messages in the mailbox*
Lenski, Lois. *Debbie goes to nursery school*
A dog came to school
Leonard, Marcia. *Hannah the hamster hunter*
Levy, Elizabeth. *Nice little girls*
Lewis, Sheri. *Baby Lamb Chop loves nursery school*
Lindgren, Astrid. *I want to go to school too*
McAllister, Angela. *Nesta, the little witch*
McCully, Emily Arnold. *School*
MacDonald, Maryann. *Little Hippo starts school*
MacLachlan, Patricia. *Three names*
McLenighan, Valjean. *I know you cheated*
McNaughton, Colin. *At playschool*

Maestro, Betsy. *Harriet at school*
Magorian, Michelle. *Who's going to take care of me?*
Malloy, Judy. *Bad Thad*
Marokvia, Merelle. *A French school for Paul*
Marshall, Edward. *Fox at school*
Marshall, James. *The Cut-Ups crack up*
The Cut-Ups cut loose
Martin, Charles E. *For rent*
Matthias, Catherine. *Out the door*
Mayer, Mercer. *Little Monster at school*
Mayne, William. *Barnabas walks*
Mellings, Joan. *It's fun to go to school*
Meshover, Leonard. *The guinea pigs that went to school*
The monkey that went to school
Miles, Miska. *Show and tell...*
Moremen, Grace E. *No, no, Natalie*
Morrison, Bill. *Louis James hates school*
Moss, Marissa. *But not Kate*
Regina's big mistake
Mueller, Virginia. *Monster goes to school*
Munsch, Robert N. *Show-and-tell*
Nichols, Paul. *Big Paul's school bus*
Nims, Bonnie Larkin. *Where is the bear at school?*
Noble, Trinka Hakes. *The day Jimmy's boa ate the wash*
O'Brien, Anne Sibley. *Come play with us*
Oppenheim, Joanne. *Mrs. Peloki's class play*
Mrs. Peloki's snake
Mrs. Peloki's substitute
Ormsby, Virginia H. *Twenty-one children plus ten*
Oxenbury, Helen. *First day of school*
Paek, Min. *Aekyung's dream*
Panek, Dennis. *Ba ba sheep wouldn't go to sleep*
Parish, Peggy. *Jumper goes to school*
Payne, Sherry Neuwirth. *A contest*
Pearson, Susan. *Everybody knows that!*
Phillips, Tamara. *Day care ABC*
Pillar, Marjorie. *Join the band!*
Polisar, Barry Louis. *The trouble with Ben*
Porte, Barbara Ann. *Harry's mom*
Poulin, Stéphane. *Can you catch Josephine?*
Powers, Mary E. *Our teacher's in a wheelchair*
Price, Michelle. *Mean Melissa*
Pulver, Robin. *Mrs. Toggle and the dinosaur*
Mrs. Toggle's zipper
Nobody's mother is in second grade
Quackenbush, Robert M. *First grade jitters*
Rabe, Berniece. *The balancing girl*
Rayner, Mary. *Crocodarling*
Rockwell, Anne F. *When Hugo went to school*
Rockwell, Harlow. *My nursery school*
Rogers, Fred. *Going to day care*
Rosenberg, Maxine B. *My friend Leslie*
Ross, Pat. *Molly and the slow teeth*

Roth, Harold. *Nursery school*
Rowe, Jeanne A. *A trip through a school*
Rubel, Nicole. *Goldie's nap*
Ryder, Eileen. *Winklet goes to school*
Sadler, Marilyn. *Alistair's time machine*
Schertle, Alice. *Jeremy Bean's St. Patrick's Day*
Schick, Eleanor. *The little school at Cottonwood Corners*
Schwartz, Amy. *Annabelle Swift, kindergartner*
Schweninger, Ann. *Off to school!*
Sellers, Ronnie. *My first day at school*
Selsam, Millicent E. *More potatoes!*
Sharmat, Mitchell. *Sherman is a slowpoke*
Simon, Norma. *I'm busy, too*
What do I do?
What do I say?
Smath, Jerry. *Elephant goes to school*
Solomon, Chuck. *Moving up*
Spier, Peter. *My school*
Spurr, Elizabeth. *Mrs. Minetta's car pool*
Stanley, Diane. *The good-luck pencil*
Staunton, Ted. *Taking care of Crumley*
Steel, Danielle. *Martha's new school*
Stein, Sara Bonnett. *A child goes to school*
Steptoe, John. *Jeffrey Bear cleans up his act*
Stevens, Carla. *Pig and the blue flag*
Stevenson, James. *That dreadful day*
Sundvall, Viveca. *Mimi and the biscuit factory*
Surat, Michele Maria. *Angel child, dragon child*
Thayer, Jane. *Gus was a real dumb ghost*
Tompert, Ann. *Will you come back for me?*
Tryon, Leslie. *Albert's alphabet*
Turner, Ethel. *Walking to school*
Turner, Gwenda. *Playbook*
Tyler, Linda Wagner. *Waiting for mom*
Udry, Janice May. *What Mary Jo shared*
Valens, Amy. *Jesse's day care*
Vigna, Judith. *Anyhow, I'm glad I tried*
Warren, Cathy. *Fred's first day*
Watson, Clyde. *Hickory stick rag*
Watts, Marjorie-Ann. *Zebra goes to school*
Weiss, Leatie. *My teacher sleeps in school*
Weiss, Nicki. *Barney is big*
Welber, Robert. *Goodbye, hello*
Wells, Rosemary. *Timothy goes to school*
White, Florence Meiman. *How to lose your lunch money*
White, Paul. *Janet at school*
Whitney, Alma Marshak. *Just awful*
Williams, Barbara. *Donna Jean's disaster*
Willis, Jeanne. *The long blue blazer*
Willis, Val. *The mystery in the bottle*
The secret in the matchbox
Winthrop, Elizabeth. *Tough Eddie*
Wiseman, Bernard. *Tails are not for painting*

Wittman, Sally. *The boy who hated Valentine's Day*
The wonderful Mrs. Trumbly
Wolde, Gunilla. *Betsy's first day at nursery school*
Wolf, Bernard. *Adam Smith goes to school*
Woodruff, Elvira. *Show and tell*
Yashima, Tarō. *Crow boy*

Science

Abisch, Roz. *Let's find out about butterflies*
Adler, David A. *Redwoods are the tallest trees in the world*
Aliki. *Corn is maize*
Digging up dinosaurs
Dinosaurs are different
Fossils tell of long ago
The long lost coelacanth and other living fossils
My feet
My hands
My visit to the dinosaurs
A weed is a flower
Wild and woolly mammoths
Allen, Gertrude E. *Everyday animals*
Allen, Martha Dickson. *Real life monsters*
Allen, Pamela. *Mr. Archimedes' bath*
Who sank the boat?
Allington, Richard L. *Science*
Talking
Anderson, Lucia Z. *The smallest life around us*
Andry, Andrew C. *How babies are made*
Annixter, Jane. *Brown rats, black rats*
Applebaum, Stan. *Going my way?*
Appleby, Leonard. *Snakes*
Ariane. *Small Cloud*
Arnold, Caroline. *The biggest living thing*
Five nests
Sun fun
Aruego, José. *Symbiosis*
Arvetis, Chris. *Why does it fly?*
Why is it dark?
Asimov, Isaac. *The best new things*
The moon
Back, Christine. *Bean and plant*
Chicken and egg
Spider's web
Tadpole and frog
Baker, Gayle. *Special delivery*
Baker, Jeannie. *One hungry spider*
Baker, Jeffrey J. W. *Patterns of nature*
Balestrino, Philip. *Hot as an ice cube*
The skeleton inside you
Balian, Lorna. *Where in the world is Henry?*
Baran, Tancy. *Bees*
Barner, Bob. *Elephant facts*
Bartlett, Margaret Farrington. *The clean brook*
Down the mountain
Where the brook begins

Bason, Lillian. *Castles and mirrors and cities of sand*
Batherman, Muriel. *Animals live here*
Baylor, Byrd. *If you are a hunter of fossils*
Behrens, June. *Whales of the world*
  Whalewatch!
Bendick, Jeanne. *All around you*
  What made you you?
  Why can't I?
Berenstain, Stan. *The Berenstain bears' science fair*
Berger, Melvin. *Early humans*
  Germs make me sick!
  Switch on, switch off
Boegehold, Betty. *Bear underground*
Boreman, Jean. *Bantie and her chicks*
Brady, Irene. *Wild mouse*
Branley, Franklyn M. *Air is all around you*
  Comets
  Earthquakes
  Eclipse: darkness in daytime
  Flash, crash, rumble, and roll
  Floating and sinking
  Gravity is a mystery
  High sounds, low sounds
  Hurricane watch
  Is there life in outer space?
  Journey into a black hole
  Light and darkness
  The moon seems to change
  North, south, east and west
  The planets in our solar system
  Rain and hail
  The sky is full of stars
  Snow is falling
  The sun, our nearest star
  Sunshine makes the seasons
  Tornado alert
  Volcanoes
  What makes day and night
  What the moon is like
Brasch, Kate. *Prehistoric monsters*
Brighton, Catherine. *Five secrets in a box*
Brooks, Robert B. *So that's how I was born*
Brouillette, Jeanne S. *Moths*
Budbill, David. *Christmas tree farm*
Burt, Olive. *Let's find out about bread*
Burton, Jane. *Chick*
Busch, Phyllis S. *Cactus in the desert*
  City lots
  Lions in the grass
  Once there was a tree
  Puddles and ponds
Carrick, Carol. *The blue lobster*
  The crocodiles still wait
  Octopus
  Patrick's dinosaurs
  Two coyotes
Challoner, Jack. *The science book of numbers*
Charosh, Mannis. *The ellipse*
Chenery, Janet. *The toad hunt*

Christenson, Larry. *The wonderful way that babies are made*
Clark, Harry. *The first story of the whale*
Clay, Pat. *Ants*
  Beetles
Cobb, Vicki. *Lots of rot*
Colby, C. B. (Carroll Burleigh). *Who lives there?*
  Who went there?
Coldrey, Jennifer. *The world of chickens*
  The world of crabs
  The world of frogs
  The world of rabbits
  The world of squirrels
Cole, Joanna. *A calf is born*
  A chick hatches
  Evolution
  Find the hidden insect
  A fish hatches
  How you were born
  Hungry, hungry sharks
  My puppy is born
  Plants in winter
Conklin, Gladys. *Cheetahs, the swift hunters*
  I caught a lizard
  I like beetles
  I like butterflies
  I like caterpillars
  I watch flies
  If I were a bird
  Journey of the gray whales
  Little apes
  Lucky ladybugs
  Praying mantis
  We like bugs
  When insects are babies
Cooke, Ann. *Giraffes at home*
Cosgrove, Margaret. *Wintertime for animals*
Craig, Janet. *Turtles*
Craig, M. Jean. *Dinosaurs and more dinosaurs*
Cromie, William J. *Steven and the green turtle*
Cutts, David. *Look...a butterfly*
Dabcovich, Lydia. *Busy beavers*
Daly, Kathleen N. *Today's biggest animals*
  Unusual animals
Daniel, Doris Temple. *Pauline and the peacock*
Darby, Gene. *What is a bird?*
  What is a butterfly?
  What is a fish?
  What is a plant?
  What is a turtle?
David, Eugene. *Crystal magic*
Davies, Kay. *My balloon*
  My mirror
DeLuise, Dom. *Charlie the caterpillar*
Dodd, Lynley. *The smallest turtle*
Dorros, Arthur. *Ant cities*
  Follow the water from brook to ocean

Eastman, David. *What is a fish?*
Eastman, Patricia. *Sometimes things change*
Engdahl, Sylvia. *Our world is earth*
Engelbrektson, Sune. *Gravity at work and play*
The sun is a star
Fischer, Vera Kistiakowsky. *One way is down*
Fischer-Nagel, Heiderose. *A kitten is born*
A puppy is born
Fisher, Aileen Lucia. *And a sunflower grew*
As the leaves fall down
Like nothing at all
Mysteries in the garden
Now that spring is here
Petals yellow and petals red
Plant magic
Prize performance
Seeds on the go
Swords and daggers
Florian, Douglas. *A bird can fly*
Flower, Phyllis. *Barn owl*
Fowler, Allan. *Cubs and colts and calves and kittens*
Freedman, Russell. *Hanging on*
Tooth and claw
When winter comes
Freeman, Mae. *The sun, the moon and the stars*
Freschet, Berniece. *Bear mouse*
The little woodcock
Moose baby
Wood duck baby
Friskey, Margaret (Margaret Richards). *Birds we know*
Frith, Michael K. *Some of us walk, some fly, some swim*
Gans, Roma. *Rock collecting*
When birds change their feathers
Garelick, May. *The tremendous tree book*
Gelman, Rita Golden. *A koala grows up*
George, Jean Craighead. *All upon a stone*
Gibbons, Gail. *From seed to plant*
Prehistoric animals
Sharks
Sun up, sun down
Girard, Linda Walvoord. *You were born on your very first birthday*
Goldin, Augusta. *Ducks don't get wet*
Salt
The shape of water
Spider silk
Straight hair, curly hair
Where does your garden grow?
Gore, Sheila. *My shadow*
Gross, Ruth Belov. *Alligators and other crocodilians*
Grosvenor, Donna. *Pandas*
Haines, Gail Kay. *Fire*
Hamberger, John. *The day the sun disappeared*

Harris, Louise Dyer. *Flash, the life of a firefly*
Harris, Susan. *Creatures that look alike*
Reptiles
Hawes, Judy. *Fireflies in the night*
Ladybug, ladybug, fly away home
Shrimps
Spring peepers
Watch honeybees with me
Why frogs are wet
Hawkinson, Lucy. *Birds in the sky*
Heller, Ruth. *Chickens aren't the only ones*
Hirschi, Ron. *What is a bird?*
Where do birds live?
Who lives in... Alligator Swamp?
Hirst, Robin. *My place in space*
Hoffman, Mary. *Animals in the wild: elephant*
Animals in the wild: monkey
Animals in the wild: panda
Animals in the wild: tiger
Hogan, Paula Z. *The black swan*
The butterfly
The dandelion
The frog
The honeybee
The oak tree
The penguin
The salmon
Holmes, Anita. *The 100-year-old cactus*
House mouse, ill. by David Thompson
Howell, Ruth. *Splash and flow*
Hurd, Edith Thacher. *Look for a bird*
The mother kangaroo
Sandpipers
Starfish
Isenbart, Hans-Heinrich. *A duckling is born*
Jackson, Jacqueline. *Chicken ten thousand*
Johnston, Johanna. *Penguin's way*
Whale's way
Jolliffe, Anne. *From pots to plastics*
Water, wind and wheels
Jones, Brian. *Space*
Jordan, Helene J. (Helene Jamieson). *How a seed grows*
Justice, Jennifer. *The tiger*
Kalas, Sybille. *The beaver family book*
Kane, Henry B. *Wings, legs, or fins*
Kaufmann, John. *Birds are flying*
Flying giants of long ago
Kirkpatrick, Rena K. *Look at flowers*
Look at leaves
Look at magnets
Look at pond life
Look at rainbow colors
Look at seeds and weeds
Look at trees
Look at weather
Knight, David C. *Dinosaur days*
Komori, Atsushi. *Animal mothers*
Krupp, E. C. *The comet and you*

Kuchalla, Susan. *All about seeds*
Kumin, Maxine. *Eggs of things*
Landshoff, Ursula. *Cats are good company*
Lane, Margaret. *The frog*
  The squirrel
Lauber, Patricia. *How we learned the earth is round*
  Snakes are hunters
  What's hatching out of that egg?
Leach, Michael. *Rabbits*
Leutscher, Alfred. *Earth*
  Water
Lewis, Naomi. *Swan*
Lilly, Kenneth. *Animal builders*
  Animal climbers
  Animal jumpers
  Animal runners
  Animal swimmers
Lloyd, David. *Air*
Mabey, Richard. *Oak and company*
McCauley, Jane. *Baby birds and how they grow*
McClung, Robert. *How animals hide*
  Sphinx
McKeever, Katherine. *A family for Minerva*
McMillan, Bruce. *Counting wildflowers*
McNulty, Faith. *Woodchuck*
Maestro, Betsy. *How do apples grow?*
Mainwaring, Jane. *My feather*
May, Charles Paul. *High-noon rocket*
Meshover, Leonard. *The guinea pigs that went to school*
  The monkey that went to school
Meyers, Susan. *The truth about gorillas*
Michels, Tilde. *At the frog pond*
Milgrom, Harry. *Egg-ventures*
Miller, Edna. *Jumping bean*
Miller, Judith Ransom. *Nabob and the geranium*
Millhouse, Nicholas. *Blue-footed booby*
Mitgutsch, Ali. *From gold to money*
  From graphite to pencil
  From sea to salt
  From swamp to coal
Moche, Dinah L. *The astronauts*
Moseley, Keith. *Dinosaurs*
Newton, James R. *A forest is reborn*
  Forest log
Oleson, Jens. *Snail*
Oxford Scientific Films. *Grey squirrel*
  The spider's web
Palazzo, Janet. *Our friend the sun*
Parish, Peggy. *Dinosaur time*
Parker, Nancy Winslow. *Bugs*
Parsons, Alexandra. *Amazing birds*
  Amazing mammals
  Amazing snakes
  Amazing spiders
Penner, Lucille Recht. *Dinosaur babies*
Peters, Lisa Westberg. *The sun, the wind and the rain*

  Water's way
Pluckrose, Henry Arthur. *Ants*
  Bears
  Bees and wasps
  Butterflies and moths
  Elephants
  Floating and sinking
  Horses
  Hot and cold
  Reptiles
  Whales
Polacco, Patricia. *Meteor!*
Pouyanne, Rési. *What I see hidden by the pond*
Powzyk, Joyce. *Tasmania*
Pursell, Margaret Sanford. *A look at birth*
  Polly the guinea pig
  Shelley the sea gull
  Sprig the tree frog
Rabinowitz, Sandy. *What's happening to Daisy?*
Richard, Jane. *A horse grows up*
Russell, Solveig Paulson. *What good is a tail?*
Ryder, Joanne. *Fireflies*
  Snail in the woods
  The spiders dance
  Where butterflies grow
Sadler, Marilyn. *Alistair's time machine*
Schilling, Betty. *Two kittens are born*
Schlein, Miriam. *Lucky porcupine!*
  What's wrong with being a skunk?
Schmid, Eleonore. *The water's journey*
Schneider, Herman. *Follow the sunset*
Schoberle, Ceile. *Beyond the Milky Way*
Schulz, Charles M. *Snoopy's facts and fun book about nature*
Selberg, Ingrid. *Nature's hidden world*
Selsam, Millicent E. *All kinds of babies*
  Egg to chick
  A first look at bird nests
  A first look at caterpillars
  A first look at cats
  A first look at flowers
  A first look at kangaroos, koalas and other animals with pouches
  A first look at monkeys
  A first look at owls, eagles and other hunters of the sky
  A first look at rocks
  A first look at seashells
  A first look at sharks
  A first look at spiders
  A first look at the world of plants
  A first look at whales
  How kittens grow
  How puppies grow
  Is this a baby dinosaur?
  More potatoes!
  Seeds and more seeds
  Where do they go? Insects in winter

Seymour, Peter. *How the weather works*
  What's in the deep blue sea?
  What's in the prehistoric forest?
Shapp, Martha. *Let's find out about babies*
Shaw, Evelyn S. *Alligator*
  Fish out of school
  Nest of wood ducks
  Octopus
  Sea otters
Sheehan, Angela. *The beaver*
  The duck
  The otter
  The penguin
Sheffield, Margaret. *Before you were born*
  Where do babies come from?
Showers, Paul. *Before you were a baby*
  A drop of blood
  Ears are for hearing
  No measles, no mumps for me
  *You can't make a move without your
    muscles*
Silverman, Maida. *Dinosaur babies*
Simon, Seymour. *Beneath your feet*
  Icebergs and glaciers
Stecher, Miriam B. *Max, the music-maker*
Stein, Sara Bonnett. *Cat*
  Mouse
Strange, Florence. *Rock-a-bye whale*
Sugita, Yutaka. *The flower family*
Thompson, Susan L. *Diary of a monarch
  butterfly*
Townsend, Anita. *The kangaroo*
Tresselt, Alvin R. *How far is far?*
  Rain drop splash
Van Woerkom, Dorothy. *Hidden messages*
Vasiliu, Mircea. *A day at the beach*
Vyner, Sue. *The stolen egg*
Wandelmaier, Roy. *Stars*
Watts, Barrie. *Apple tree*
  Bird's nest
  Butterfly and caterpillar
  Dandelion
  Hamster
  Ladybug
  Mushrooms
  Rabbit
  Tomato
Webb, Angela. *Air*
  Light
  Reflections
  Sand
  Soil
  Sound
  Water
Wexler, Jerome (LeRoy). *Flowers, fruits,
  seeds*
  Wonderful pussy willows
Williams, Gweneira Maureen. *Timid
  Timothy, the kitten who learned to be brave*
Wilson, Ron. *Mice*
Wong, Herbert H. *My goldfish*

My ladybug
My plant
Our caterpillars
Our earthworms
Our tree
Wyler, Rose. *Puddles and ponds*
  Raindrops and rainbows
  The starry sky
Yabuuchi, Masayuki. *Animals sleeping*
Zallinger, Peter. *Dinosaurs*
Ziefert, Harriet. *Getting ready for new baby*
Zoll, Max Alfred. *A flamingo is born*

Scotland *see* Foreign lands – Scotland

Scuba diving *see* Sports – skin diving

Sea and seashore
Agell, Charlotte. *The sailor's book*
Albert, Burton. *Where does the trail lead?*
Alexander, Sally Hobart. *Sarah's surprise*
Allen, Laura Jean. *Ottie and the star*
Allen, Pamela. *Hidden treasure*
Amoss, Berthe. *Old Hannibal and the
  hurricane*
Anderson, Lena Castell. *Stina*
Andrews, Jan. *Very last first time*
Anrooy, Frans van. *The sea horse*
Ardizzone, Edward. *Little Tim and the
  brave sea captain*
  Peter the wanderer
  Ship's cook Ginger
  Tim all alone
  Tim and Charlotte
  Tim and Ginger
  Tim and Lucy go to sea
  Tim in danger
  Tim to the rescue
  Tim's friend Towser
  Tim's last voyage
Asch, Frank. *Sand cake*
  Starbaby
Bang, Molly. *Yellow ball*
Barber, Antonia. *The mousehole cat*
Bare, Colleen Stanley. *Elephants on the
  beach*
Barklem, Jill. *Sea story*
Bate, Norman. *What a wonderful machine is
  a submarine*
Baum, Susan. *The beach*
Bennett, Rainey. *The secret hiding place*
Bentley, Anne. *The Groggs have a wonderful
  summer*
Blance, Ellen. *Monster goes to the beach*
Bond, Michael. *Paddington at the seaside*
Bonsall, Crosby Newell. *Mine's the best*
Booth, Eugene. *Under the ocean*
Bornstein, Ruth Lercher. *A beautiful
  seashell*
Bright, Robert. *Georgie and the noisy ghost*
Brown, Marc Tolon. *D. W. all wet*

Brown, Margaret Wise. *The seashore noisy book*

Bruna, Dick. *Miffy at the beach*
Miffy at the seaside

Buchanan, Heather S. *Emily Mouse's beach house*
George Mouse's covered wagon

Burningham, John. *Come away from the water, Shirley*

Carle, Eric. *A house for Hermit Crab*

Carrick, Carol. *Beach bird*

Carter, Debby L. *Clipper*

Cohen, Caron Lee. *Whiffle Squeek*

Cohen, Miriam. *See you in second grade!*

Cole, Babette. *The trouble with Uncle*

Cole, Sheila. *When the tide is low*

Coles, Alison. *Michael and the sea*

Cooney, Barbara. *Hattie and the wild waves*

Corney, Estelle. *Pa's top hat*

Craig, Janet. *What's under the ocean?*

Crane, Alan. *Pepita bonita*

Damjan, Mischa. *The little sea horse*

Davidson, Amanda. *Teddy at the seashore*

Decker, Dorothy W. *Stripe and the merbear*

Denton, Terry. *Home is the sailor*

De Paola, Tomie (Thomas Anthony). *Katie and Kit at the beach*

DeSaix, Frank. *The girl who danced with dolphins*

Dickens, Lucy. *At the beach*

Dodd, Lynley. *The smallest turtle*

Domanska, Janina. *If all the seas were one sea*

Donnelly, Liza. *Dinosaur beach*

Dos Santos, Joyce Audy. *Sand dollar, sand dollar*

Doubilet, Anne. *Under the sea from A to Z*

Dupasquier, Philippe. *Dear Daddy...*
Jack at sea

Dyke, John. *Pigwig and the pirates*

Faulkner, Keith. *Sam at the seaside*

Field, Eugene. *Wynken, Blynken and Nod*, ill. by Barbara Cooney

Florian, Douglas. *Beach day*

Foreman, Michael. *Jack's fantastic voyage*

Freeman, Don. *Come again, pelican*

Garelick, May. *Down to the beach*

Gay, Michel. *Little auto*

Gebert, Warren. *The old ball and the sea*

Gedin, Birgitta. *The little house from the sea*

George, Jean Craighead. *The wentletrap trap*

Gerrard, Jean. *Matilda Jane*

Gerrard, Roy. *Sir Francis Drake*

Ginsburg, Mirra. *Four brave sailors*

Goodall, John S. *Paddy under water*

Gordon, Sharon. *Dolphins and porpoises*

Goudey, Alice E. *Houses from the sea*

Graham, Bob. *Greetings from Sandy Beach*

Greenaway, Shirley. *Water*

Greenberg, Melanie Hope. *At the beach*

Gretz, Susanna. *Teddy bears at the seaside*

Haas, Irene. *The Maggie B*

Hellen, Nancy. *Creatures of the ocean*

Heller, Nicholas. *An adventure at sea*

Henley, Claire. *In the ocean*

Heyduck-Huth, Hilde. *The starfish*

Hill, Eric. *Spot goes to the beach*

Hirschi, Ron. *Ocean*

Hoff, Syd. *Albert the albatross*

Hofstrand, Mary. *By the sea*

Hopkins, Lee Bennett. *The sea is calling me*

Hulme, Joy. *Sea squares*

Hurd, Edith Thacher. *Starfish*

Imoto, Yoko. *Skipper at the beach*

Iwasaki, Chihiro. *What's fun without a friend?*

James, Simon. *Sally and the limpet*

Johnson, Jane. *Bertie on the beach*

Johnson, Pamela. *A mouse's tale*

Jones, Rebecca C. *Down at the bottom of the deep dark sea*

Joslin, Sesyle. *Baby elephant goes to China*

Kimura, Yasuko. *Fergus and the sea monster*

Kipling, Rudyard. *The crab that played with the sea*, ill. by Michael Foreman

Kitamura, Satoshi. *Captain Toby*

Koch, Dorothy Clarke. *I play at the beach*

Koch, Michelle. *By the sea*

Kraus, Robert. *Herman the helper*

Krementz, Jill. *Jack goes to the beach*

Kumin, Maxine. *The beach before breakfast*

Kuskin, Karla. *Sand and snow*

Leonard, Marcia. *Swimming in the sand*

Lester, Alison. *Magic beach*

Le Tord, Bijou. *Joseph and Nellie*

Levine, Evan. *Not the piano, Mrs. Medley!*

Lewis, Sheri. *Baby Lamb Chop loves the beach*

Lilly, Kenneth. *Animals of the ocean*

Lionni, Leo. *On my beach there are many pebbles*
Swimmy

Lloyd, David. *Grandma and the pirate*

Lobato, Arcadio. *The greatest treasure*

Lobel, Arnold. *Uncle Elephant*

Lund, Doris Herold. *The paint-box sea*

McAfee, Annalena. *The visitors who came to stay*

McCloskey, Robert. *Bert Dow, deep-water man*
One morning in Maine
Time of wonder

McDonald, Megan. *Is this a house for Hermit Crab?*

McKee, David. *The day the tide went out and out and out*

McMillan, Bruce. *One sun*

Maddern, Eric. *Curious clownfish*

Mahy, Margaret. *The man whose mother was a pirate*
Sailor Jack and the twenty orphans

Matsutani, Miyoko. *The fisherman under the sea*
Mendoza, George. *The scribbler*
Mogensen, Jan. *Teddy in the undersea kingdom*
Morgan, Allen. *Nicole's boat*
Morse, Samuel French. *Sea sums*
Munsch, Robert N. *A promise is a promise*
Nakatani, Chiyoko. *Fumio and the dolphins*
Nakawatari, Harutaka. *The sea and I*
Napoli, Guillier. *Adventure at Mont-Saint-Michel*
Nicoll, Helen. *Meg at sea*
Nolan, Dennis. *The castle builder*
O'Donnell, Elizabeth Lee. *The twelve days of summer*
Olujic, Grozdana. *Rose of Mother-of-Pearl*
Orgel, Doris. *On the sand dune*
Ormondroyd, Edward. *Johnny Castleseed*
Oxenbury, Helen. *Beach day*
Tom and Pippo on the beach
Pallotta, Jerry. *Going lobstering*
Patkau, Karen. *In the sea*
Peet, Bill (William Bartlett). *Cyrus the unsinkable sea serpent*
Kermit the hermit
Peters, Lisa Westberg. *The sun, the wind and the rain*
Pirani, Felix. *Abigail at the beach*
Poulin, Stéphane. *Travels for two*
Prater, John. *The perfect day*
Quinlan, Patricia. *Emma's sea journey*
Ray, Deborah Kogan. *Fog drift morning*
Richardson, Judith Benet. *The way home*
Robbins, Ken. *Beach days*
Roberts, Sarah. *I want to go home!*
Rockwell, Anne F. *At the beach*
Rodgers, Richard. *A real nice clambake*
Roffey, Maureen. *I spy on vacation*
Round, Graham. *Hangdog*
Royston, Angela. *Shells*
Russ, Lavinia. *Alec's sand castle*
Russo, Susan. *The ice cream ocean and other delectable poems of the sea*
Ryder, Joanne. *Beach party*
A wet and sandy day
Samton, Sheila White. *Beside the bay*
Schlein, Miriam. *The sun, the wind, the sea and the rain*
Schulz, Charles M. *Snoopy's facts and fun book about seashores*
Schumacher, Claire. *Alto and Tango*
The Sea World alphabet book
Selsam, Millicent E. *A first look at seashells*
Sea monsters of long ago
Seymour, Peter. *What lives in the sea?*
What's at the beach?
What's in the deep blue sea?
Sharratt, Nick. *Look what I found!*
Shaw, Evelyn S. *Fish out of school*
Octopus

Shea, Pegi Deitz. *Bungalow fungalow*
Simon, Mina Lewiton. *Is anyone here?*
Sis, Peter. *Beach ball*
Slobodkin, Louis. *The seaweed hat*
Smith, Raymond Kenneth. *The long dive*
Smith, Theresa Kalab. *The fog is secret*
Steiner, Barbara (Annette). *The whale brother*
Steiner, Charlotte. *Listen to my seashell*
Stevenson, James. *Clams can't sing*
July
Which one is Whitney?
Stevenson, Jocelyn. *Jim Henson's Muppets at sea*
Stock, Catherine. *Sophie's bucket*
Strahl, Rudi. *Sandman in the lighthouse*
Straker, Joan Ann. *Animals that live in the sea*
Tate, Suzanne. *Crabby's water wish*
Taylor, Mark. *The bold fisherman*
Thompson, Brenda. *The winds that blow*
Thompson, Richard. *Gurgle, bubble, splash*
Titherington, Jeanne. *Baby's boat*
Tobias, Tobi. *At the beach*
Tokuda, Wendy. *Humphrey the lost whale*
Tresselt, Alvin R. *Hide and seek fog*
I saw the sea come in
Turkle, Brinton. *Do not open*
Obadiah the Bold
The sky dog
Turnbull, Ann. *The sand horse*
Ungerer, Tomi. *The Mellops go diving for treasure*
Vasiliu, Mircea. *A day at the beach*
Vernon, Tannis. *Little Pig and the blue-green sea*
Vinson, Pauline. *Willie goes to the seashore*
Waber, Bernard. *I was all thumbs*
Waddell, Martin. *Sailor Bear*
Wahl, Jan. *The adventures of Underwater Dog*
Waters, Tony. *Sailor's bride*
Watson, Nancy Dingman. *When is tomorrow?*
The weekend, ill. by Roser Capdevila
Wegen, Ron. *Sand castle*
Weiss, Nicki. *Sun sand sea sail*
Weller, Frances Ward. *Riptide*
Willard, Nancy. *The voyage of the Ludgate Hill*
Wood, John Norris. *Oceans*
Woolaver, Lance. *From Ben Loman to the sea*
Yamashita, Haruo. *Mice at the beach*
Yashima, Tarō. *Seashore story*
Young, Ruth. *Daisy's taxi*
Ziefert, Harriet. *A dozen dogs*
Good night, Jessie!
Keeping daddy awake on the way home from the beach

Zolotow, Charlotte (Shapiro). *The seashore book*

Sea gulls *see* Birds – sea gulls

Sea lions *see* Animals – sea lions

Sea serpents *see* Monsters; Mythical creatures

Seahorses *see* Crustacea

Seals *see* Animals – seals

Seamstresses *see* Careers – seamstresses

Seashore *see* Sea and seashore

Seasons

Adoff, Arnold. *In for winter, out for spring*
Arnosky, Jim. *Outdoors on foot*
Barker, Cicely Mary. *Flower fairies of the seasons*
Beskow, Elsa Maartman. *Children of the forest*
Blegvad, Erik. *Burnie's hill*
Blocksma, Mary. *Apple tree! Apple tree!*
Borden, Louise. *Caps, hats, socks and mittens*
  The watching game
Bowen, Betsy. *Antler, bear, canoe*
Branley, Franklyn M. *Sunshine makes the seasons*
Brown, Margaret Wise. *The little island*
Bruchac, Joseph. *Thirteen moons on turtle's back*
Burningham, John. *Seasons*
Carle, Eric. *The tiny seed*
Carrick, Carol. *The old barn*
Charles, Donald. *Calico cat's year*
Clifton, Lucille. *Everett Anderson's year*
Coleridge, Sara. *January brings the snow*
Curti, Anna. *Seasons*
De Paola, Tomie (Thomas Anthony). *Four stories for four seasons*
Don't tell the scarecrow
Dow, Katharine. *My time of year*
Dragonwagon, Crescent. *Jemima remembers*
DuPasquier, Philippe. *Our house on the hill*
Duvoisin, Roger Antoine. *The house of four seasons*
Ehlert, Lois. *Red leaf, yellow leaf*
Farjeon, Eleanor. *Around the seasons*
Fisher, Aileen Lucia. *As the leaves fall down*
  Going barefoot
  Like nothing at all
Florian, Douglas. *A year in the country*
Foster, Doris Van Liew. *A pocketful of seasons*
Fowler, Susi Gregg. *When summer ends*
Fox, Charles Philip. *Mr. Stripes the gopher*

Gackenbach, Dick. *Ida Fanfanny*
Gibbons, Gail. *Farming*
  The seasons of Arnold's apple tree
Goennel, Heidi. *Seasons*
Gomi, Taro. *Spring is here*
Greydanus, Rose. *Changing seasons*
Haley, Gail E. *Go away, stay away*
  The green man
Hall, Donald. *The ox-cart man*
Hall, Fergus. *Groundsel*
Harris, Dorothy Joan. *Four seasons for Toby*
Heyduck-Huth, Hilde. *The strawflower*
Hopkins, Lee Bennett. *Ring out, wild bells*
Horton, Barbara Savadge. *What comes in spring?*
Howell, Ruth. *Everything changes*
Hurd, Edith Thacher. *The day the sun danced*
Ichikawa, Satomi. *A child's book of seasons*
Johnston, Tony. *Yonder*
Kandoian, Ellen. *Molly's seasons*
King-Smith, Dick. *Cuckoobush farm*
Krull, Kathleen. *Songs of praise*
Kwitz, Mary DeBall. *Mouse at home*
Lewis, Naomi. *Leaves*
Lionni, Leo. *A busy year*
  Mouse days
  When?
Littlewood, Valerie. *The season clock*
Llewelyn, Claire. *My first book of time*
Lobel, Arnold. *Frog and Toad all year*
McDermott, Gerald. *Daughter of earth*
Maestro, Betsy. *Through the year with Harriet*
Mangin, Marie-France. *Suzette and Nicholas and the seasons clock*
Manushkin, Fran. *The best toy of all*
Marshak, Samuel. *The Month-Brothers*
Miller, Edna. *Mousekin's fables*
Miller, Jane. *Seasons on the farm*
Miller, Moira. *The search for spring*
Mora, Emma. *Gideon, the little bear cub*
Muntean, Michaela. *Muppet babies through the year*
Oliver, Stephen. *Seasons*
Oppenheim, Joanne. *Have you seen trees?*
Pearson, Susan. *My favorite time of year*
Peters, Lisa Westberg. *Good morning, river!*
Pizer, Abigail. *Charlie the puppy*
  Hattie the goat
  Penelope pig
  Percy the duck
Provensen, Alice. *A book of seasons*
  The year at Maple Hill Farm
Roach, Marilynne K. *Dune fox*
Rockwell, Anne F. *First comes spring*
Ryder, Joanne. *Under your feet*
Schulz, Charles M. *Snoopy's facts and fun book about seasons*
Silverman, Erica. *Warm in winter*
Simon, Norma. *Mama cat's year*

Spohn, David. *Nate's treasure*
Stewart, Sarah. *The money tree*
Tresselt, Alvin R. *It's time now!*
  Johnny Maple-Leaf
Tudor, Tasha. *Around the year*
Udry, Janice May. *A tree is nice*
Watts, Bernadette. *Tattercoats*
Weiss, Nicki. *On a hot, hot day*
Welber, Robert. *Song of the seasons*
Wellington, Anne. *Apple pie*
Wildsmith, Brian. *Seasons*
Wolff, Ashley. *A year of birds*
Wood, Joyce. *Grandmother Lucy in her garden*
Yolen, Jane. *Ring of earth*
Ziefert, Harriet. *Bear all year*
Zimmermann, H. Werner (Heinz Werner). *Alphonse knows...twelve months make a year*
Zolotow, Charlotte (Shapiro). *In my garden*
  The song

Seasons - autumn *see* Seasons – fall

Seasons – fall

Adelson, Leone. *All ready for school*
Allington, Richard L. *Autumn*
Barklem, Jill. *Autumn story*
Blades, Ann. *Fall*
Bliss, Corinne Demas. *Matthew's meadow*
Cavagnaro, David. *The pumpkin people*
Cohen, Peter Zachary. *Authorized autumn charts of the Upper Red Canoe River country*
Denslow, Sharon Phillips. *At Taylor's place*
Dutton, Sandra. *The cinnamon hen's autumn day*
Fregosi, Claudia. *The happy horse*
Freschet, Berniece. *Owl in the garden*
Griffith, Helen V. *Alex remembers*
Hirschi, Ron. *Fall*
Hoban, Julia. *Amy loves the wind*
Hopkins, Lee Bennett. *Merrily comes our harvest in*
Iwamura, Kazuo. *The fourteen forest mice and the harvest moon watch*
Kumin, Maxine. *Follow the fall*
Lapp, Eleanor. *The mice came in early this year*
Lenski, Lois. *Now it's fall*
McNaughton, Colin. *Autumn*
Moncure, Jane Belk. *Word Bird's fall words*
Ott, John. *Peter Pumpkin*
Potter, Beatrix. *The tale of Squirrel Nutkin*
Roth, Harold. *Autumn days*
Rylant, Cynthia. *Henry and Mudge under the yellow moon*
Schweninger, Ann. *Autumn days*
Taylor, Mark. *Henry explores the mountains*
Tejima, Keizaburo. *The bears' autumn*
Tresselt, Alvin R. *Autumn harvest*
  Johnny Maple-Leaf

Udry, Janice May. *Emily's autumn*
Updike, David. *An autumn tale*
Van Allsburg, Chris. *The stranger*
Wheeler, Cindy. *Marmalade's yellow leaf*
Zagwyn, Deborah Turney. *Pumpkin blanket*
Zolotow, Charlotte (Shapiro). *Say it!*

Seasons – spring

Alexander, Sue. *There's more...much more*
Allington, Richard L. *Spring*
Anglund, Joan Walsh. *Spring is a new beginning*
Barker, Cicely Mary. *Flower fairies of the spring*
Barklem, Jill. *Spring story*
Barrett, John M. *The Easter bear*
Baum, Arline. *One bright Monday morning*
Beer, Kathleen Costello. *What happens in the spring*
Belting, Natalia Maree. *Summer's coming in*
Blades, Ann. *Spring*
Boon, Emilie. *It's spring, Peterkin*
Chönz, Selina. *A bell for Ursli*
Clifton, Lucille. *The boy who didn't believe in spring*
Cohen, Carol L. *Wake up, groundhog!*
Craig, M. Jean. *Spring is like the morning*
Cummings, E. E. (Edward Estlin). *In just-spring*
Dabcovich, Lydia. *Sleepy bear*
Delton, Judy. *Three friends find spring*
De Posadas Mane, Carmen. *Mister North Wind*
Dodd, Lynley. *Wake up, bear*
Fish, Helen Dean. *When the root children wake up*, published by Green Tiger Pr., 1988
  When the root children wake up, published by Lippincott, 1930
Fisher, Aileen Lucia. *My mother and I*
  Now that spring is here
Forrester, Victoria. *The touch said hello*
Hirschi, Ron. *Spring*
Hoban, Lillian. *The sugar snow spring*
  Turtle spring
Hopkins, Lee Bennett. *Easter buds are springing*
Hurd, Edith Thacher. *The day the sun danced*
Hurd, Thacher. *Blackberry ramble*
Ichikawa, Satomi. *Sun through small leaves*
Iwamura, Kazuo. *The fourteen forest mice and the spring meadow picnic*
Janice. *Little Bear's pancake party*
Johnson, Crockett. *Time for spring*
  Will spring be early?
Kesselman, Wendy. *Time for Jody*
Kraus, Robert. *The first robin*
Krauss, Ruth. *The happy day*
Kroll, Steven. *I love spring!*
Lenski, Lois. *Spring is here*

Lerner, Carol. *Flowers of a woodland spring*
Levens, George. *Kippy the koala*
McNaughton, Colin. *Spring*
Martin, Charles E. *Island rescue*
Miller, Edna. *Mouskin's Easter basket*
Minarik, Else Holmelund. *It's spring!*
Moncure, Jane Belk. *Word Bird's spring words*
Nordqvist, Sven. *Festus and Mercury: ruckus in the garden*
Patz, Nancy. *Sarah Bear and Sweet Sidney*
Pfister, Marcus. *Hopper*
Rockwell, Anne F. *My spring robin*
Rylant, Cynthia. *Henry and Mudge in puddle trouble*
Schlein, Miriam. *Little Red Nose*
Seignobosc, Françoise. *Springtime for Jeanne-Marie*
Selkowe, Valrie M. *Spring green*
Skofield, James. *Crow moon, worm moon*
Stafford, William. *The animal that drank up sound*
Taylor, Judy. *Dudley and the monster*
Taylor, Mark. *Henry the castaway*
Tresselt, Alvin R. *Hi, Mister Robin*
Warren, Cathy. *Springtime bears*
Waterton, Betty. *Pettranella*
Wells, Rosemary. *Forest of dreams*
   Max's chocolate chicken
Wilde, Oscar. *Fairy tales of Oscar Wilde: The selfish giant, and The star child*, adapt. and ill. by P. Craig Russell
   The selfish giant, ill. by Dom Mansell
   The selfish giant, ill. by Lisbeth Zwerger
Wolkstein, Diane. *The magic wings*
Wood, Joyce. *Grandmother Lucy in her garden*
Woolaver, Lance. *From Ben Loman to the sea*
Worth, Bonnie. *Peter Cottontail's surprise*
Zimmermann, H. Werner (Heinz Werner). *Alphonse knows...the colour of spring*
Zion, Gene. *Really spring*

Seasons – summer

Adelson, Leone. *All ready for summer*
Allington, Richard L. *Summer*
Barker, Cicely Mary. *Flower fairies of the summer*
Barklem, Jill. *Summer story*
Beim, Jerrold. *The swimming hole*
Belting, Natalia Maree. *Summer's coming in*
Bentley, Anne. *The Groggs have a wonderful summer*
Berenstain, Stan. *The Berenstain bears go to camp*
Blades, Ann. *Summer*
Bowden, Joan Chase. *Emilio's summer day*
Brown, Margaret Wise. *The summer noisy book*

Buchanan, Heather S. *George Mouse's first summer*
Burgunder, Rose. *From summer to summer*
Burn, Doris. *The summerfolk*
Cavagnaro, David. *The pumpkin people*
Chönz, Selina. *Florina and the wild bird*
Chwast, Seymour. *Still another children's book*
Craft, Ruth. *The day of the rainbow*
Denslow, Sharon Phillips. *Night owls*
Dragonwagon, Crescent. *The itch book*
Factor, Jane. *Summer*
Farjeon, Eleanor. *Mr. Garden*
Gage, Wilson. *Anna's summer songs*
Gans, Roma. *Hummingbirds in the garden*
Garelick, May. *Down to the beach*
Gerstein, Mordicai. *The seal mother*
Goodall, John S. *An Edwardian summer*
Griffith, Helen V. *Georgia music*
Haywood, Carolyn. *Hello, star*
Hedderwick, Mairi. *P. D. Pebbles' summer or winter book*
Henkes, Kevin. *Grandpa and Bo*
Hirschi, Ron. *Summer*
Iwamura, Kazuo. *The fourteen forest mice and the summer laundry day*
Knotts, Howard. *The summer cat*
Komoda, Beverly. *The too hot day*
Kuskin, Karla. *Sand and snow*
Lenski, Lois. *On a summer day*
Lund, Doris Herold. *The paint-box sea*
McCloskey, Robert. *Time of wonder*
McNaughton, Colin. *Summer*
Martin, Charles E. *For rent*
   Sam saves the day
Moncure, Jane Belk. *Word Bird's summer words*
Moore, Elaine. *Grandma's house*
O'Donnell, Elizabeth Lee. *The twelve days of summer*
Robins, Joan. *Addie runs away*
Rylant, Cynthia. *Henry and Mudge in the green time*
Schick, Eleanor. *One summer night*
Stevenson, James. *July*
Stobbs, William. *There's a hole in my bucket*
Taylor, Mark. *Henry explores the jungle*
Thomas, Ianthe. *Lordy, Aunt Hattie*
Wagner, Jenny. *Amy's monster*
Yashima, Tarō. *The village tree*
Yolen, Jane. *Milkweed days*
Zion, Gene. *The summer snowman*
Zolotow, Charlotte (Shapiro). *Summer is...*

Seasons – winter

Adelson, Leone. *All ready for winter*
Allington, Richard L. *Winter*
Aragon, Jane Chelsea. *Winter harvest*
Asch, Frank. *Mooncake*
Attenberger, Walburga. *The little man in winter*

Aulaire, Ingri Mortenson d'. *Children of the northlights*
Barklem, Jill. *The secret staircase*
Winter story
Barnhart, Peter. *The wounded duck*
Bartoli, Jennifer. *In a meadow, two hares hide*
Snow on bear's nose
Bassett, Lisa. *Beany and Scamp*
Bauer, Caroline Feller. *Midnight snowman*
Blades, Ann. *Winter*
Brown, Margaret Wise. *The winter noisy book*
Bruna, Dick. *Miffy in the snow*
Buckley, Helen Elizabeth. *Josie and the snow*
Bunting, Eve (Anne Evelyn). *Winter's coming*
Burton, Virginia Lee. *Katy and the big snow*
Carlson, Natalie Savage. *Surprise in the mountains*
Carlstrom, Nancy White. *Goodbye geese*
The snow speaks
Carrick, Carol. *Two coyotes*
Cartwright, Ann. *The winter hedgehog*
Chaffin, Lillie D. *We be warm till springtime comes*
Chönz, Selina. *The snowstorm*
Christiana, David. *White nineteens*
Cole, Joanna. *Plants in winter*
Cosgrove, Margaret. *Wintertime for animals*
Coutant, Helen. *First snow*
Coxe, Molly. *Whose footprints?*
Craft, Ruth. *The winter bear*
Dabcovich, Lydia. *Sleepy bear*
Delton, Judy. *My mom hates me in January*
Three friends find spring
Dionetti, Michelle. *The day Eli went looking for bear*
Dobson, Clive. *Fred's TV*
Fisher, Aileen Lucia. *Where does everyone go?*
Flack, Marjorie. *Angus lost*
Freedman, Russell. *When winter comes*
Freeman, Don. *The night the lights went out*
Frost, Robert. *Stopping by woods on a snowy evening*
Fujikawa, Gyo. *That's not fair!*
Funakoshi, Canna. *One evening*
Gundersheimer, Karen. *Happy winter*
Hartley, Deborah. *Up north in the winter*
Hasler, Eveline. *Winter magic*
Hedderwick, Mairi. *P. D. Pebbles' summer or winter book*
Hertz, Ole. *Tobias goes ice fishing*
Hirschi, Ron. *Winter*
Hoban, Russell. *Some snow said hello*
Hoff, Syd. *When will it snow?*
Hol, Coby. *Lisa and the snowman*
Hoopes, Lyn Littlefield. *When I was little*

Iwamura, Kazuo. *The fourteen forest mice and the winter sledding day*
Janosch. *Dear snowman*
Johnston, Tony. *Mole and Troll trim the tree*
Keats, Ezra Jack. *The snowy day*
Kinsey-Warnock, Natalie. *The wild horses of Sweetbriar*
Knotts, Howard. *The winter cat*
Komoda, Beerly. *The winter day*
Kovalski, Maryann. *Jingle bells*
Krauss, Ruth. *The happy day*
Kumin, Maxine. *A winter friend*
Kuskin, Karla. *In the flaky frosty morning*
Sand and snow
Lapp, Eleanor. *The mice came in early this year*
Lathrop, Dorothy Pulis. *Who goes there?*
Lenski, Lois. *I like winter*
Linch, Elizabeth Johanna. *Samson*
Lindgren, Astrid. *The tomten*
The tomten and the fox
Littledale, Freya. *The snow child*
McCully, Emily Arnold. *First snow*
McLaughlin, Lissa. *Why won't winter go?*
McNaughton, Colin. *Winter*
Mamin-Sibiryak, D. N. *Grey Neck*
Martchenko, Michael. *Bird feeder banquet*
Martin, Charles E. *Island winter*
Michels, Tilde. *Who's that knocking at my door?*
Miller, Edna. *Mousekin's golden house*
Moncure, Jane Belk. *Word Bird's winter words*
Moore, Elaine. *Grandma's promise*
Odoyevsky, Vladimir. *Old Father Frost*
Parnall, Peter. *Alfalfa Hill*
Winter barn
Patz, Nancy. *Sarah Bear and Sweet Sidney*
Pfister, Marcus. *Hopper*
Prusski, Jeffrey. *Bring back the deer*
Quinlan, Patricia. *Anna's red sled*
Radin, Ruth Yaffe. *A winter place*
Retan, Walter. *The snowplow that tried to go south*
Roberts, Bethany. *Waiting for spring stories*
Rockwell, Anne F. *The first snowfall*
Roth, Harold. *Winter days*
Ryder, Joanne. *Winter whale*
Schick, Eleanor. *City in the winter*
Schindler, Regina. *The bear's cave*
Schlein, Miriam. *Deer in the snow*
Go with the sun
Schweninger, Ann. *Wintertime*
Selsam, Millicent E. *Keep looking!*
Where do they go? Insects in winter
Silverman, Erica. *Warm in winter*
Spohn, David. *Winter wood*
Stafford, William. *The animal that drank up sound*
Steig, William. *Brave Irene*
Stevenson, James. *Brr!*

Taylor, Mark. *Henry the explorer*
Tejima, Keizaburo. *Fox's dream*
Tudor, Tasha. *Snow before Christmas*
Turkle, Brinton. *Thy friend, Obadiah*
Udry, Janice May. *Mary Jo's grandmother*
Van Vorst, M. L. *A Norse lullaby*
Vigna, Judith. *Boot weather*
Wabbes, Marie. *It's snowing, Little Rabbit*
Ward, Andrew. *Baby bear and the long sleep*
Watanabe, Shigeo. *Ice cream is falling!*
Watson, Wendy. *Has winter come?*
  Tales for a winter's eve
Weiss, Ellen. *Clara the fortune-telling chicken*
Wells, Rosemary. *Forest of dreams*
Winch, Madeleine. *Come by chance*

Secret codes

Balian, Lorna. *Humbug potion*

Secrets *see* Behavior – secrets

Seeds

Back, Christine. *Bean and plant*
Carle, Eric. *The tiny seed*
Gibbons, Gail. *From seed to plant*
Jordan, Helene J. (Helene Jamieson). *How a seed grows*
Kuchalla, Susan. *All about seeds*
Petie, Haris. *The seed the squirrel dropped*
Selsam, Millicent E. *Seeds and more seeds*
Shecter, Ben. *Partouche plants a seed*
Takihara, Koji. *Rolli*

Seeing *see* Anatomy – eyes; Handicaps – blindness; Senses – seeing

Seeking better things *see* Behavior – seeking better things

Self-concept

Alborough, Jez. *Beaky*
Anderson, Wayne. *Dragon*
Appell, Clara. *Now I have a daddy haircut*
Bach, Alice. *Warren Weasel's worse than measles*
Bahr, Amy C. *It's ok to say no*
  Sometimes it's ok to tell secrets
  What should you do when...?
  Your body is your own
Behrens, June. *Who am I?*
Bentley, Nancy. *I've got your nose!*
Berger, Terry. *I have feelings*
Berliner, Franz. *Miserable Marabou*
Bertrand, Cecile. *Mr. and Mrs. Smith have only one child, but what a child!*
Blume, Judy. *The one in the middle is a green kangaroo*
Bolliger, Max. *The rabbit with the sky blue ears*
Brown, Ruth. *Crazy Charlie*

Browne, Anthony. *Willy the wimp*
Caple, Kathy. *Harry's smile*
Carle, Eric. *The mixed-up chameleon*
Carlson, Nancy. *I like me*
Charlip, Remy. *Hooray for me!*
Charlot, Martin. *Felisa and the magic tikling bird*
Cohen, Miriam. *No good in art*
  So what?
DeLage, Ida. *Am I a bunny?*
De Regniers, Beatrice Schenk. *Everyone is good for something*
De Veaux, Alexis. *An enchanted hair tale*
Fitzhugh, Louise. *I am five*
  I am three
Girard, Linda Walvoord. *My body is private*
Glen, Maggie. *Ruby to the rescue*
Goldin, Barbara Diamond. *Cakes and miracles*
Gordon, Gaelyn. *Duckat*
Gwynne, Fred. *Pondlarker*
Hallinan, P. K. (Patrick K.). *I'm glad to be me*
  Where's Michael?
Harsh, Fred. *Alfie*
Hines, Anna Grossnickle. *All by myself*
Hoffman, Mary. *Amazing Grace*
Karlin, Nurit. *Little big moose*
  A train for the king
Keats, Ezra Jack. *Peter's chair*
  Whistle for Willie
Keller, Holly. *Horace*
Krauss, Ruth. *The carrot seed*
Kuskin, Karla. *What did you bring me?*
Lane, Megan Halsey. *Something to crow about*
Leaf, Munro. *Noodle*
Lionni, Leo. *Pezzettino*
Lipkind, William. *The little tiny rooster*
Loomans, Diane. *The lovables in the kingdom of self-esteem*
McAllister, Angela. *The enchanted flute*
Milios, Rita. *Yo soy—I am*
Moss, Marissa. *But not Kate*
  Regina's big mistake
Murphy, Jill. *A piece of cake*
Palmer, Mary Babcock. *No-sort-of-animal*
Pearson, Susan. *Lenore's big break*
Peet, Bill (William Bartlett). *Pamela Camel*
Polisar, Barry Louis. *The trouble with Ben*
Purdy, Carol. *Least of all*
Richardson, Jean. *Tall inside*
Roe, Eileen. *All I am*
Sadler, Marilyn. *It's not easy being a bunny*
Seuss, Dr. *Oh, the places you'll go!*
Sharmat, Marjorie Weinman. *I'm terrific*
  Taking care of Melvin
  The 329th friend
Shott, Stephen. *Look at me*
Simon, Norma. *Why am I different?*
Skulavik, Mary Alys. *Bert*

Slobodkin, Louis. *Magic Michael*
Stren, Patti. *Mountain Rose*
Supraner, Robyn. *Would you rather be a tiger?*
Talbott, Hudson. *Going Hollywood! A dinosaur's dream*
Titherington, Jeanne. *Big world, small world*
Tobias, Tobi. *Jane wishing*
Turnage, Sheila. *Trout the magnificent*
Tusa, Tricia. *Chicken*
 Libby's new glasses
Udry, Janice May. *How I faded away*
Waber, Bernard. *"You look ridiculous," said the rhinoceros to the hippopotamus*
Wagner, Karen. *Silly Fred*
Weiner, Beth Lee. *Benjamin's perfect solution*
Wold, Jo Anne. *Tell them my name is Amanda*
Wondriska, William. *Puff*
Zola, Meguido. *The dream of promise*

Self-esteem *see* Self-concept

Self-image *see* Self-concept

Selfishness *see* Character traits – selfishness

Senses

Crossley-Holland, Kevin. *Sleeping Nanna*
Fallwell, Cathryn. *Nicky loves daddy*

Senses – hearing

Aliki. *My five senses*
Allington, Richard L. *Hearing*
Ancona, George. *Handtalk zoo*
Arthur, Catherine. *My sister's silent world*
Aseltine, Lorraine. *I'm deaf and it's okay*
Baker, Pamela J. *My first book of sign*
Borten, Helen. *Do you hear what I hear?*
 Do you know what I know?
Bove, Linda. *Sign language ABC with Linda Bove*
Brenner, Barbara A. *Faces, faces, faces*
Chaplin, Susan Gibbons. *I can sign my ABCs*
Charlip, Remy. *Handtalk*
 Handtalk birthday
Cousins, Lucy. *What can rabbit hear?*
Fowler, Allan. *Hearing things*
Greenberg, Judith E. *What is the sign for friend?*
Hindley, Judy. *Soft and noisy*
Isadora, Rachel. *I hear*
Jaynes, Ruth M. *Melinda's Christmas stocking*
Lionni, Leo. *What?*
Litchfield, Ada B. *A button in her ear*
Moncure, Jane Belk. *Sounds all around*
Morris, Winifred. *Just listen*

Ogle, Lucille. *I hear*
Oxenbury, Helen. *I hear*
Pace, Elizabeth. *Chris gets ear tubes*
Perkins, Al. *The ear book*
Pluckrose, Henry Arthur. *Things we hear*
 Think about hearing
Showers, Paul. *Ears are for hearing*
 The listening walk
Wahl, Jan. *Jamie's tiger*
Wolf, Bernard. *Anna's silent world*

Senses – seeing

Aliki. *My five senses*
Allington, Richard L. *Looking*
Borten, Helen. *Do you know what I know?*
 Do you see what I see?
Bram, Elizabeth. *One day I closed my eyes and the world disappeared*
Brenner, Barbara A. *Faces, faces, faces*
Brighton, Catherine. *My hands, my world*
Brown, Marc Tolon. *Arthur's eyes*
Brown, Marcia. *Walk with your eyes*
Chapman, Elizabeth. *Suzy*
Cohen, Miriam. *See you tomorrow*
Cousins, Lucy. *What can rabbit see?*
DeArmond, Dale. *The seal oil lamp*
Fowler, Allan. *Seeing things*
Giff, Patricia Reilly. *Watch out, Ronald Morgan!*
Goodsell, Jane. *Katie's magic glasses*
Hay, Dean. *I see a lot of things*
Herman, Bill. *Jenny's magic wand*
Hoban, Tana. *Look again*
Isadora, Rachel. *I see*
Jaynes, Ruth M. *Melinda's Christmas stocking*
Jensen, Virginia Allen. *Catching*
 Red thread riddles
 What's that?
Johnson, Donna Kay. *Brighteyes*
Keats, Ezra Jack. *Apartment 3*
Keller, Holly. *Cromwell's glasses*
Kessler, Leonard P. *Mr. Pine's mixed-up signs*
Lasson, Robert. *Orange Oliver*
Lionni, Leo. *What?*
Litchfield, Ada B. *A cane in her hand*
MacDonald, Maryann. *Little Hippo gets glasses*
Martin, Bill (William Ivan). *Knots on a counting rope*
Matthiesen, Thomas. *Things to see*
Moncure, Jane Belk. *The look book*
Newth, Philip. *Roly goes exploring*
Ogle, Lucille. *I spy with my little eye*
Oxenbury, Helen. *I see*
Pluckrose, Henry Arthur. *Things we see*
 Think about seeing
Quigley, Lillian Fox. *The blind men and the elephant*
Raskin, Ellen. *Spectacles*

Reuter, Margaret. *My mother is blind*
Sargent, Susan. *My favorite place*
Saxe, John Godfrey. *The blind men and the elephant*
Shecter, Ben. *The stocking child*
Showers, Paul. *Look at your eyes*
Smith, Lane. *Glasses...who needs 'em?*
Thayer, Jane. *Mr. Turtle's magic glasses*
Thomson, Ruth. *Eyes*
Tusa, Tricia. *Libby's new glasses*
Yolen, Jane. *The seeing stick*
Young, Ed (Edward). *Seven blind mice*

Senses – smelling

Aliki. *My five senses*
Allen, Jonathan. *Mucky moose*
Allington, Richard L. *Smelling*
Borten, Helen. *Do you know what I know?*
Brenner, Barbara A. *Faces, faces, faces*
Doughtie, Charles. *Gabriel Wrinkles, the bloodhound who couldn't smell*
Fowler, Allan. *Smelling things*
Jaynes, Ruth M. *Melinda's Christmas stocking*
Lionni, Leo. *What?*
Moncure, Jane Belk. *What your nose knows!*
Perkins, Al. *The nose book*
Pluckrose, Henry Arthur. *Think about smelling*
Rose, Gerald. *Scruff*
Saunders, Susan. *A sniff in time*

Senses – tasting

Aliki. *My five senses*
Allington, Richard L. *Tasting*
Borten, Helen. *Do you know what I know?*
Brenner, Barbara A. *Faces, faces, faces*
Fowler, Allan. *Tasting things*
Jaynes, Ruth M. *Melinda's Christmas stocking*
Lionni, Leo. *What?*
Moncure, Jane Belk. *A tasting party*
Pluckrose, Henry Arthur. *Think about tasting*

Senses – touching

Aliki. *My five senses*
Allington, Richard L. *Touching*
Borten, Helen. *Do you know what I know?*
Brenner, Barbara A. *Faces, faces, faces*
Brown, Marcia. *Touch will tell*
Carle, Eric. *My very first book of touch*
Fowler, Allan. *Feeling things*
Gibson, Myra Tomback. *What is your favorite thing to touch?*
Isadora, Rachel. *I touch*
Jaynes, Ruth M. *Melinda's Christmas stocking*
Lionni, Leo. *What?*
Moncure, Jane Belk. *The touch book*
Oliver, Stephen. *Touch*
Oxenbury, Helen. *I touch*
Pluckrose, Henry Arthur. *Things we touch*

Think about touching

Sewing *see* Activities – sewing

Shadows

Anno, Mitsumasa. *In shadowland*
Asch, Frank. *Bear shadow*
Bond, Felicia. *Wake up, Vladimir*
Cendrars, Blaise. *Shadow*
Christelow, Eileen. *Henry and the dragon*
De Regniers, Beatrice Schenk. *The shadow book*
Dorros, Arthur. *Me and my shadow*
Gackenbach, Dick. *Mr. Wink and his shadow, Ned*
Goor, Ron. *Shadows: here, there and everywhere*
Gore, Sheila. *My shadow*
Haseley, Dennis. *Ghost catcher*
Hoban, Tana. *Shadows and reflections*
McHargue, Georgess. *Private zoo*
Mahy, Margaret. *The boy with two shadows*
Marol, Jean-Claude. *Vagabul and his shadow*
Michaels, William. *Clare and her shadow*
Narahashi, Keiko. *I have a friend*
Robison, Nancy. *Ten tall soldiers*
Severn, Jeffrey. *George and his giant shadow*
Simon, Seymour. *Shadow magic*
Tompert, Ann. *Nothing sticks like a shadow*
Zemke, Deborah. *The shadow of Matilda Hunt*

Shakespeare

Freeman, Don. *Will's quill*

Shape *see* Concepts – shape

Shaped books *see* Format, unusual

Sharing *see* Behavior – sharing

Sheep *see* Animals – sheep

Shepherds *see* Careers – shepherds

Ships *see* Boats, ships

Shirts *see* Clothing – shirts

Shoemakers *see* Careers – shoemakers

Shopping

Allard, Harry. *I will not go to market today*
Anholt, Catherine. *Truffles in trouble*
Ardizzone, Edward. *The little girl and the tiny doll*
Arnold, Caroline. *What will we buy?*
Baugh, Dolores M. *Supermarket*
Black, Irma Simonton. *The little old man who could not read*

Bond, Michael. *Paddington's lucky day*
Bradman, Tony. *Dilly speaks up*
  Wait and see
Brenner, Barbara A. *Somebody's slippers, somebody's shoes*
Butterworth, Nick. *Just like Jasper*
Calmenson, Stephanie. *The birthday hat*
Cass, Joan E. *The cats go to market*
Chase, Catherine. *Baby mouse goes shopping*
Chorao, Kay. *Molly's Moe*
Claverie, Jean. *Shopping*
Daly, Niki. *Mama, papa and baby Joe*
  Not so fast Songololo
Edwards, Linda Strauss. *The downtown day*
Faulkner, Keith. *Sam helps out*
Fyleman, Rose. *A fairy went a-marketing*
Garland, Sarah. *Going shopping*
Gretz, Susanna. *Teddy bears go shopping*
Greydanus, Rose. *Susie goes shopping*
Grossman, Bill. *Tommy at the grocery store*
Guzzo, Sandra E. *Fox and Heggie*
Hamm, Diane Johnston. *Laney's lost momma*
Hastings, Evelyn Beilhart. *The department store*
Hines, Anna Grossnickle. *Don't worry, I'll find you*
Hutchins, Pat. *Don't forget the bacon!*
Ichikawa, Satomi. *Suzanne and Nicholas at the market*
Kilroy, Sally. *Market day*
Leonard, Marcia. *Shopping for snowflakes*
Lobel, Arnold. *On Market Street*
McPhail, David. *The cereal box*
Maschler, Fay. *T. G. and Moonie go shopping*
Mother Goose. *To market! To market!* ill. by Emma Lillian Brock
Munsch, Robert N. *Something good*
Oliver, Stephen. *Shopping*
Oxenbury, Helen. *The shopping trip*
  Tom and Pippo go shopping
Patz, Nancy. *Pumpernickel tickle and mean green cheese*
Potter, Beatrix. *The tale of Little Pig Robinson*
Prater, John. *"No!" said Joe*
Rice, Eve. *New blue shoes*
Rockwell, Anne F. *The supermarket*
Rubel, Nicole. *Goldie*
Russell, Betty. *Big store, funny door*
Shaw, Nancy. *Sheep in a shop*
Shopping, ill. by Roser Capdevila
Smith, Barry. *Tom and Annie go shopping*
Solomon, Joan. *A present for Mum*
Spier, Peter. *Food market*
Winn, Chris. *My day*
Ziefert, Harriet. *Bear goes shopping*
Zinnemann-Hope, Pam. *Let's go shopping, Ned*

Shops *see* Stores

Shows *see* Theater

Shrews *see* Animals – shrews

Shyness *see* Character traits – shyness

Siam *see* Foreign lands – Thailand

Sibling rivalry

Adoff, Arnold. *Hard to be six*
Aitken, Amy. *Wanda's circus*
Alexander, Martha G. *I'll be the horse if you'll play with me*
  Marty McGee's space lab, no girls allowed
  Nobody asked me if I wanted a baby sister
  When the new baby comes, I'm moving out
Allen, Pamela. *Hidden treasure*
Amoss, Berthe. *It's not your birthday*
  Tom in the middle
Anholt, Catherine. *Aren't you lucky!*
Armitage, Ronda. *The bossing of Josie*
Arnstein, Helene S. *Billy and our new baby*
Bach, Alice. *The smartest bear and his brother Oliver*
Baker, Betty. *My sister says*
Baker, Charlotte. *Little brother*
Bassett, Lisa. *Koala Christmas*
Beecroft, John. *What? Another cat!*
Benson, Ellen. *Philip's little sister*
Berenstain, Stan. *The Berenstain bears and the double dare*
  The Berenstain bears get in a fight
Bider, Djemma. *A drop of honey*
Blume, Judy. *The Pain and The Great One*
Bond, Felicia. *Poinsettia and her family*
Bottner, Barbara. *Big boss! Little boss!*
  Jungle day: or, How I learned to love my nosey little brother
Boyd, Lizi. *Sam is my half brother*
Bradman, Tony. *Dilly speaks up*
  Brothers and sisters are like that!
Brown, Marc Tolon. *D. W. all wet*
Buchanan, Heather S. *Emily Mouse's garden*
Bulla, Clyde Robert. *Keep running, Allen!*
Bullock, Kathleen. *A surprise for Mitzi Mouse*
Byrne, David. *Stay up late*
Caines, Jeannette. *Abby*
Carlson, Nancy. *Harriet and Walt*
  The perfect family
Carlstrom, Nancy White. *Kiss your sister, Rose Marie*
Caseley, Judith. *Silly baby*
Castiglia, Julie. *Jill the pill*
Chalmers, Audrey. *Fancy be good*
Chenery, Janet. *Wolfie*
Chorao, Kay. *George told Kate*
Clarke, Gus. *Along came Eric*
Cleary, Beverly. *Janet's thingamajigs*
Clifton, Lucille. *My brother fine with me*
Climo, Shirley. *The Egyptian Cinderella*

Cole, Joanna. *The new baby at your house*
Conaway, Judith. *I'll get even*
Corey, Dorothy. *Will there be a lap for me?*
Crowley, Arthur. *Bonzo Beaver*
Daly, Niki. *Look at me!*
De Hamel, Joan. *Hemi's pet*
Delaney, Molly. *My sister*
De Lynam, Alicia Garcia. *It's mine!*
Dragonwagon, Crescent. *I hate my brother Harry*
I hate my sister Maggie
Drescher, Joan. *The marvelous mess*
Dubanevich, Arlene. *Pig William*
Dubois, Claude K. *He's my jumbo!*
Duncan, Lois. *Giving away Suzanne*
Edelman, Elaine. *I love my baby sister (most of the time)*
Ehrlich, Amy. *Bunnies at Christmastime*
Bunnies on their own
Engel, Diana. *Josephina, the great collector*
Etherington, Frank. *The spaghetti word race*
Fair, Sylvia. *The bedspread*
Fife, Dale. *Rosa's special garden*
Fisher, Iris L. *Katie-Bo*
Franklin, Jonathan. *Don't wake the baby*
Freudberg, Judy. *Susan and Gordon adopt a baby*
Galbraith, Kathryn Osebold. *Katie did!*
Roommates
Gauch, Patricia Lee. *Christina Katerina and the time she quit the family*
Gewing, Lisa. *Mama, daddy, baby and me*
Gili, Phillida. *Fanny and Charles*
Ginsburg, Mirra. *Two greedy bears*
Graham, Richard. *Jack and the monster*
Greene, Carol. *Hinny Winny Bunco*
Greenfield, Eloise. *She come bringing me that little baby girl*
Grimm, Jacob. *Cinderella*, ill. by Nonny Hogrogian
Cinderella, ill. by Svend Otto S.
Hamilton, Morse. *Big sisters are bad witches*
Little sister for sale
My name is Emily
Harper, Anita. *It's not fair!*
Hazen, Barbara Shook. *If it weren't for Benjamin (I'd always get to lick the icing spoon)*
Why couldn't I be an only kid like you, Wigger?
Hedderwick, Mairi. *Katie Morag and the tiresome Ted*
Heller, Nicholas. *An adventure at sea*
Helmering, Doris Wild. *We're going to have a baby*
Henkes, Kevin. *Julius, the baby of the world*
Henriod, Lorraine. *Grandma's wheelchair*
Hines, Anna Grossnickle. *They really like me!*
Hoban, Lillian. *Arthur's pen pal*
Hoban, Russell. *A baby sister for Frances*

The battle of Zormla
The great gum drop robbery
Some snow said hello
They came from Aargh!
Holabird, Katharine. *Angelina's baby sister*
Hooker, Ruth. *Sara loves her big brother*
Hoopes, Lyn Littlefield. *When I was little*
Hutchins, H. J. (Hazel J.). *Katie's babbling brother*
Hutchins, Pat. *The very worst monster*
Johnston, Tony. *I'm gonna tell mama I want an iguana*
Slither McCreep and his brother, Joe
Karlin, Barbara. *Cinderella*
Keller, Holly. *Too big*
Knight, Hilary. *Hilary Knight's Cinderella*
Knox-Wagner, Elaine. *The oldest kid*
Kroll, Steven. *The squirrels' Thanksgiving*
Lakin, Patricia. *Don't touch my room*
Oh, brother!
Lasky, Kathryn. *A baby for Max*
Leech, Jay. *Bright Fawn and me*
LeRoy, Gen. *Billy's shoes*
Lucky stiff!
Levinson, Riki. *Me baby!*
Lexau, Joan M. *The homework caper*
Lindgren, Astrid. *I want a brother or sister*
I want to go to school too
Lloyd, David. *The stopwatch*
Low, Alice. *The witch who was afraid of witches*
McCully, Emily Arnold. *New baby*
McDaniel, Becky Bring. *Katie did it*
McKissack, Patricia C. *Cinderella*
McPhail, David. *Sisters*
Mallett, Anne. *Here comes Tagalong*
Manushkin, Fran. *Little rabbit's baby brother*
Margolis, Richard J. *Secrets of a small brother*
Marron, Carol A. *No trouble for Grandpa*
Marshall, Edward. *Four on the shore*
Mayers, Patrick. *Just one more block*
Milgram, Mary. *Brothers are all the same*
Mills, Claudia. *A visit to Amy-Claire*
Moers, Hermann. *Hugo's baby brother*
Moss, Marissa. *Want to play?*
Noll, Sally. *That bothered Kate*
Ormerod, Jan. *101 things to do with a baby*
Ormondroyd, Edward. *Theodore's rival*
Paterson, Diane. *Hey, cowboy!*
Perrault, Charles. *Cinderella*, ill. by Sheilah Beckett
Cinderella, ill. by Marcia Brown
Cinderella, ill. by Paul Galdone
Cinderella, ill. by Diane Goode
Cinderella, ill. by Susan Jeffers
Cinderella, ill. by Emanuele Luzzati
Cinderella, ill. by James Marshall
Cinderella, ill. by Phil Smith
Politi, Leo. *Rosa*
Polushkin, Maria. *Baby brother blues*

Postma, Lidia. *The stolen mirror*
Pryor, Bonnie. *Amanda and April*
  The porcupine mouse
Ray, Deborah Kogan. *Sunday morning we went to the zoo*
Reesink, Marijke. *The princess who always ran away*
Riordan, James. *The three magic gifts*
Robins, Joan. *My brother, Will*
Roche, P. K. (Patrick K.). *Good-bye, Arnold!*
Rogasky, Barbara. *The water of life*
Rogers, Fred. *The new baby*
Root, Phyllis. *Moon tiger*
Rosen, Winifred. *Henrietta and the gong from Hong Kong*
Russo, Marisabina. *Only six more days*
Ruthstrom, Dorotha. *The big kite contest*
Sage, Chris. *The trouble with babies*
Samuels, Barbara. *Faye and Dolores*
  What's so great about Cindy Snappleby?
Sarnoff, Jane. *That's not fair*
Schick, Eleanor. *Peggy's new brother*
Schlein, Miriam. *Laurie's new brother*
Schwartz, Amy. *Annabelle Swift, kindergartner*
Scott, Ann Herbert. *On mother's lap*
Seuling, Barbara. *What kind of family is this?*
Sewell, Helen Moore. *Jimmy and Jemima*
Skorpen, Liesel Moak. *His mother's dog*
Smith, Lucia B. *A special kind of sister*
Smith, Peter. *Jenny's baby brother*
Smith, Wendy. *Twice mice*
Stanek, Muriel. *My little foster sister*
Stapler, Sarah. *Trilby's trumpet*
Steel, Danielle. *Max's new baby*
Steptoe, John. *Baby says*
Stevenson, James. *That's exactly the way it wasn't*
  Winston, Newton, Elton, and Ed
  Worse than Willy!
Stevenson, Suçie. *Christmas eve*
  Do I have to take Violet?
Stine, Jovial Bob. *Pork and beans: play date*
Thomas, Iolette. *Janine and the new baby*
Tierney, Hanne. *Where's your baby brother, Becky Bunting?*
Tudor, Tasha. *Junior's tune*
Turkle, Brinton. *Rachel and Obadiah*
Tyrrell, Anne. *Mary Ann always can*
Udry, Janice May. *Thump and Plunk*
Van der Beek, Deborah. *Superbabe!*
Vigna, Judith. *Daddy's new baby*
Viorst, Judith. *I'll fix Anthony*
Von Königslöw, Andrea Wayne. *That's my baby?*
Wahl, Jan. *Peter and the troll baby*
Weiss, Nicki. *Princess Pearl*
Wells, Rosemary. *Good night, Fred*
  Max's bedtime
  Max's breakfast
  Max's chocolate chicken
  Peabody
  Stanley and Rhoda
Williams, Barbara. *Donna Jean's disaster*
Winthrop, Elizabeth. *I think he likes me*
  That's mine
Wolde, Gunilla. *Betsy and the chicken pox*
Yorinks, Arthur. *Ugh*
Young, Ruth. *The new baby*
Zalben, Jane Breskin. *Buster gets braces*
Ziefert, Harriet. *Getting ready for new baby*
Zolotow, Charlotte (Shapiro). *If it weren't for you*
  Timothy too!

Sickness *see* Health; Illness

Sight *see* Anatomy – eyes; Handicaps – blindness; Senses – seeing

Singing *see* Activities – singing

Sisters *see* Family life; Family life – sisters; Sibling rivalry

Size *see* Concepts – size

Skating *see* Sports – ice skating

Skeletons *see* Anatomy – skeletons

Skiing *see* Sports – skiing

Skin diving *see* Sports – skin diving

Skunks *see* Animals – skunks

Sky

Asch, Frank. *Starbaby*
Belting, Natalia Maree. *The sun is a golden earring*
Birdseye, Tom. *A song of stars*
Branley, Franklyn M. *Comets*
  The sky is full of stars
Dayrell, Elphinstone. *Why the sun and the moon live in the sky*
Dayton, Mona. *Earth and sky*
Dee, Ruby. *Tower to heaven*
Gerson, Mary-Joan. *Why the sky is far away*
Ichikawa, Satomi. *Nora's stars*
Otto, Carolyn. *That sky, that rain*
Oughton, Jerrie. *How the stars fell into the sky*
Schoberle, Ceile. *Beyond the Milky Way*
Shaw, Charles Green. *It looked like spilt milk*
Spier, Peter. *Dreams*
Standiford, Natalie. *Dollhouse mouse*
Stone, Kazuko G. *Goodnight Twinklegator*
Wyler, Rose. *The starry sky*

Sledding *see* Sports – sledding

Sleep

Alexander, Martha G. *I'll protect you from the jungle beasts*

Andersen, H. C. (Hans Christian). *The princess and the pea*, ill. by Dorothée Duntze
The princess and the pea, ill. by Paul Galdone
The princess and the pea, ill. by Eve Tharlet

Asher, Sandy. *Princess Bee and the royal good-night story*

Aylesworth, Jim. *The bad dream*
Tonight's the night

Bach, Alice. *The smartest bear and his brother Oliver*

Baum, Louis. *I want to see the moon*

Beckman, Kaj. *Lisa cannot sleep*

Bilezikian, Gary. *While I slept*

Bottner, Barbara. *There was nobody there*

Brande, Marlie. *Sleepy Nicholas*

Bright, Robert. *Me and the bears*

Brown, Margaret Wise. *A child's good night book*
Sleepy ABC
The sleepy little lion

Brown, Myra Berry. *First night away from home*

Bunting, Eve (Anne Evelyn). *No nap*

Burstein, Fred. *Rebecca's nap*

Burton, Jane. *Animals at rest*

Calhoun, Mary. *While I sleep*

Carlstrom, Nancy White. *No nap for Benjamin Badger*

Cazet, Denys. *I'm not sleepy*
Mother night

Chalmers, Mary. *Take a nap, Harry*

Chislett, Gail. *Whump*

Chorao, Kay. *Lester's overnight*

Ciardi, John. *Scrappy the pup*

Coker, Gylbert. *Naptime*

Collington, Peter. *Little pickle*

Crossley-Holland, Kevin. *Sleeping Nanna*

De Paola, Tomie (Thomas Anthony). *Fight the night*
When everyone was fast asleep

Dodd, Lynley. *Wake up, bear*

Dupasquier, Philippe. *I can't sleep*

Edwards, Patricia Kier. *Chester and Uncle Willoughby*

Edwards, Roberta. *Anna Bear's first winter*

Elkin, Benjamin. *The king who could not sleep*

Evans, Eva Knox. *Sleepy time*

Farber, Werner. *Night lion*

Feldman, Eve B. *Animals don't wear pajamas*

Field, Eugene. *Wynken, Blynken and Nod*, ill. by Barbara Cooney

Fox, Mem. *Night noises*

Gilmour, H. B. *Why Wembley Fraggle couldn't sleep*

Gretz, Susanna. *I'm not sleepy*

Harshman, Terry Webb. *Porcupine's pajama party*

Haseley, Dennis. *The cave of snores*

Hazen, Barbara Shook. *Where do bears sleep?*

Heine, Helme. *King Bounce the 1st*
The marvelous journey through the night

Henkes, Kevin. *Shhhh*

Hindley, Judy. *The sleepy book*

Hopkins, Lee Bennett. *Still as a star*

Howard, Jane R. *When I'm sleepy*

Hutchins, Pat. *Good night owl*

Inkpen, Mick. *Kipper*

Irving, Washington. *Rip Van Winkle*, ill. by John Howe
Rip Van Winkle, ill. by Thomas Locker
Rip Van Winkle, ill. by Peter Wingham

James, Betsy. *The dream stair*

Jeffers, Susan. *All the pretty horses*

Kantrowitz, Mildred. *Willy Bear*

Karlin, Nurit. *The dream factory*

Keats, Ezra Jack. *Dreams*

Khalsa, Dayal Kaur. *Sleepers*

Kotzwinkle, William. *The nap master*

Krahn, Fernando. *Sleep tight, Alex Pumpernickel*

Kraus, Robert. *Good night little one*
Good night Richard Rabbit
Milton the early riser

Lewison, Wendy C. *Going to sleep on the farm*

Lucas, Barbara. *Sleeping over*

McCauley, Jane. *The way animals sleep*

McMullan, Kate. *The noisy giant's tea party*

McPhail, David. *The dream child*

Marino, Dorothy. *Edward and the boxes*

Massie, Diane Redfield. *The baby beebee bird*

Merriam, Eve. *Goodnight to Annie*

Mueller, Virginia. *Monster can't sleep*

Murphy, Jill. *Peace at last*

Mwalimu. *Awful aardvark*

Nichol, B. P. *Once: a lullaby*

Nolan, Dennis. *Dinosaur dream*

Novak, Matt. *While the shepherd slept*

O'Brien, Mary. *Counting sheep to sleep*

Oppenheim, Joanne. *The story book prince*

Ormerod, Jan. *Moonlight*
Sleeping

Oxenbury, Helen. *Say goodnight*

Panek, Dennis. *Ba ba sheep wouldn't go to sleep*

Pfister, Marcus. *The sleepy owl*

Plath, Sylvia. *The bed book*

Polushkin, Maria. *Mother, Mother, I want another*
Preston, Edna Mitchell. *Monkey in the jungle*
Reidel, Marlene. *Jacob and the robbers*
Riddell, Chris. *The wish factory*
Riggio, Anita. *Wake up, William!*
Rosenberg, Liz. *Adelaide and the night train*
Ross, Anna. *Naptime*
Rowand, Phyllis. *It is night*
Rubel, Nicole. *Goldie's nap*
Sage, Chris. *Sleepy baby*
Sage, James. *To sleep*
Saleh, Harold J. *Even tiny ants must sleep*
Schneider, Nina. *While Susie sleeps*
Seuss, Dr. *Dr. Seuss's sleep book*
  I am not going to get up today!
Shepperson, Rob. *The sandman*
Simon, Norma. *Where does my cat sleep?*
Slobodkin, Louis. *Wide-awake owl*
Sonneborn, Ruth A. *Seven in a bed*
Stanley, Diane. *Birdsong lullaby*
Stevenson, James. *We can't sleep*
Sugita, Yutaka. *Good night 1, 2, 3*
Szekeres, Cyndy. *Good night, Sammy*
Tafuri, Nancy. *Where we sleep*
Tobias, Tobi. *Chasing the goblins away*
Trez, Denise. *Good night, Veronica*
Twining, Edith. *Sandman*
Van Vorst, M. L. *A Norse lullaby*
Waber, Bernard. *Ira sleeps over*
Waddell, Martin. *Can't you sleep, Little Bear?*
Wahl, Jan. *The sleepytime book*
  Sylvester Bear overslept
  The toy circus
Weir, Alison. *Peter, good night*
Weisgard, Leonard. *Who dreams of cheese?*
Weiss, Nicki. *Where does the brown bear go?*
Wersba, Barbara. *Amanda dreaming*
Wheeler, Cindy. *Marmalade's nap*
Whiteside, Karen. *Lullaby of the wind*
Wolcott, Patty. *Eeeeeek!*
Wood, Audrey. *Moonflute*
  The napping house
Woolf, Virginia. *Nurse Lugton's curtain*
Yabuuchi, Masayuki. *Animals sleeping*
Yolen, Jane. *Dragon night and other lullabies*
Yulya. *Bears are sleeping*
Zagone, Theresa. *No nap for me*
Ziefert, Harriet. *Good night everyone!*
  I want to sleep in your bed!
  Say good night!
  Sleepy dog
Zolotow, Charlotte (Shapiro). *Sleepy book*
  The sleepy book

Slight-of-hand *see* Magic

Sloths *see* Animals – sloths

Smallness *see* Character traits – smallness

Smelling *see* Anatomy – noses; Senses – smelling

Snails *see* Animals – snails

Snakes *see* Reptiles – snakes

Snow *see* Weather – snow

Snowmen

Bauer, Caroline Feller. *Midnight snowman*
Briggs, Raymond. *Building the snowman*
  Dressing up
  The party
  The snowman
  Walking in the air
Chorao, Kay. *Kate's snowman*
Erskine, Jim. *The snowman*
Goffstein, M. B. (Marilyn Brooke). *Our snowman*
Gordon, Sharon. *Friendly snowman*
Hoban, Julia. *Amy loves the snow*
Hol, Coby. *Lisa and the snowman*
Holl, Adelaide. *The runaway giant*
Hughes, Shirley. *The snow lady*
Janosch. *Dear snowman*
Johnson, Crockett. *Time for spring*
Joos, Francoise. *The golden snowflake*
Kellogg, Steven (Stephen). *The mystery of the missing red mitten*
Komoda, Beerly. *The winter day*
Kuskin, Karla. *In the flaky frosty morning*
Lobe, Mira. *The snowman who went for a walk*
Loretan, Sylvia. *Bob the snowman*
Mack, Gail. *Yesterday's snowman*
McKee, David. *Snow woman*
Miller, Edna. *Mouskin's frosty friend*
Zion, Gene. *The summer snowman*

Snowplows *see* Machines

Soccer *see* Sports – soccer

Society Islands *see* Foreign lands – South Sea Islands

Socks *see* Clothing – socks

Sofas *see* Furniture – couches, sofas

Soldiers *see* Careers – military

Soldiers, toy *see* Toys – soldiers

Solitude *see* Behavior – solitude

Songs

Abisch, Roz. *Sweet Betsy from Pike*

Adams, Pam. *There was an old lady who swallowed a fly*
This old man

Alexander, Cecil Frances. *All things bright and beautiful*

Alger, Leclaire Gowans. *All in the morning early*
Kellyburn Braes

Arkin, Alan. *Black and white*

Ash, Jutta. *Wedding birds*

Bangs, Edward. *Yankee Doodle*

Billy Boy, ill. by Glen Rounds

Boesel, Ann Sterling. *Sing and sing again*
Singing with Peter and Patsy

Bonne, Rose. *I know an old lady*, ill. by Abner Graboff
I know an old lady who swallowed a fly, ill. by William Stobbs

Botwin, Esther. *A treasury of songs for little children*

Bowman, Peter. *The Christmas songbook*

Boynton, Sandra. *Good night, good night*

Brand, Oscar. *When I first came to this land*

Bratton, John. *The teddy bears' picnic*, ill. by Renate Kozikowski

Briggs, Raymond. *The white land*

Bring a torch, Jeannette, Isabella, ill. by Adrienne Adams

Brown, Marc Tolon. *Play rhymes*

Bryan, Ashley. *All night, all day: a child's first book of African-American spirituals*
I'm going to sing
Lion and the ostrich chicks

Buffett, Jimmy. *The jolly mon*

Byrne, David. *Stay up late*

Carryl, Charles Edward. *A capital ship: or, The walloping window-blind*, ill. by Paul Galdone

Caseley, Judith. *Molly Pink*

Child, Lydia Maria. *Over the river and through the wood*

Conover, Chris. *Six little ducks*

Count me in

Craver, Mike. *Beaver ball at the bug club*

Cutler, Ivor. *Doris*

Dalton, Alene. *My new picture book of songs*

Delacre, Lulu. *Arroz con leche*
Las Navidades

Delaney, A. *The gunnywolf*

Delessert, Etienne. *A long long song*

Denslow, W. W. *Denslow's picture book treasury*

Denver, John. *The children and the flowers*

De Regniers, Beatrice Schenk. *Was it a good trade?*

Devlin, Harry. *The walloping window blind*

Din dan don, it's Christmas

Domanska, Janina. *Busy Monday morning*

Duncan, Lois. *Songs from dreamland*

Durell, Ann. *The Diane Goode book of American folk tales and songs*

Duvoisin, Roger Antoine. *Petunia and the song*

Emberley, Barbara. *One wide river to cross*
Simon's song

The farmer in the dell. *The farmer in the dell*, ill. by Kathy Parkinson
The farmer in the dell, ill. by Mary Maki Rae
The farmer in the dell, ill. by Diane Stanley

Fern, Eugene. *Birthday presents*

Flanders, Michael. *The hippopotamus song*

The fox went out on a chilly night, ill. by Peter Spier

French, Fiona. *Rise and shine*

The friendly beasts and A partridge in a pear tree, ill. by Virginia Pearsons

A frog he would a-wooing go (folk-song). *Frog went a-courtin'*, ill. by Feodor Rojankovsky
Froggie went a-courting, ill. by Chris Conover
Wendy Watson's frog went a-courting

Gilbert, Yvonne. *Baby's book of lullabies and cradle songs*

Go tell Aunt Rhody. *Go tell Aunt Rhody*, ill. by Aliki
Go tell Aunt Rhody, ill. by Robert M. Quackenbush

The green grass grows all around, ill. by Hilde Hoffmann

Greene, Carol. *A computer went a-courting*
Hinny Winny Bunco
The thirteen days of Halloween

Guthrie, Woody. *Woody's twenty grow big songs*

Hague, Kathleen. *Jingle bells*

Harris, Leon A. *The great diamond robbery*

Hirsh, Marilyn. *One little goat*

Hoban, Brom. *Skunk Lane*

Hoban, Lillian. *Harry's song*

Hobzek, Mildred. *We came a-marching...1, 2, 3*

Hogrogian, Nonny. *The cat who loved to sing*

Homme, Bob. *The friendly giant's birthday*

Hot cross buns, and other old street cries

Houston, John A. *The bright yellow rope*
A mouse in my house
A room full of animals
I sing a song of the saints of God, ill. by Judith Gwyn Brown

Ipcar, Dahlov. *The cat came back*
"The song of the day birds" and "The song of the night birds"

Ivimey, John William. *The complete story of the three blind mice*, ill. by Paul Galdone
The complete version of ye three blind mice, ill. by Walton Corbould

Three blind mice, ill. by Lorinda Bryan Cauley

Three blind mice, ill. by Victoria Chess

Johnston, Mary Anne. *Sing me a song*

Johnston, Tony. *Grandpa's song*

Jones, Carol. *This old man*

Kapp, Paul. *Cock-a-doodle-doo! Cock-a-doodle-dandy!*

Keats, Ezra Jack. *The little drummer boy*

Kennedy, Jimmy. *The teddy bears' picnic*, ill. by Michael Hague

Key, Francis Scott. *The Star-Spangled Banner*, ill. by Paul Galdone

The Star-Spangled Banner, ill. by Peter Spier

Kimmel, Eric A. *Why worry?*

King, Bob. *Sitting on the farm*

Koontz, Robin Michal. *This old man*

Kovalski, Maryann. *Jingle bells*

The wheels on the bus

Krull, Kathleen. *Songs of praise*

Langstaff, John M. *Oh, a-hunting we will go*

Ol' Dan Tucker

On Christmas day in the morning

Over in the meadow

Soldier, soldier, won't you marry me?

The swapping boy

The two magicians

Lear, Edward. *The pelican chorus*, ill. by Harold Berson

The pelican chorus and the quangle wangle's hat, ill. by Kevin W. Maddison

Lenski, Lois. *At our house*

Davy and his dog

Davy goes places

Debbie and her grandma

A dog came to school

I like winter

I went for a walk

The life I live

Lord, Beman. *The days of the week*

Lubach, Peter. *Harry and the singing fish*

McCarthy, Bobette. *Buffalo girls*

Mack, Stanley (Stan). *Ten bears in my bed*

McLerran, Alice. *Dreamsong*

McNally, Darcie. *In a cabin in a wood*

Maril, Lee. *Mr. Bunny paints the eggs*

Medearis, Angela Shelf. *The zebra-riding cowboy*

Mills, Alan. *The hungry goat*

Modesitt, Jeanne. *Songs of Chanukah*

Mohr, Joseph. *Silent night*

Moon, Dolly M. *My very first book of cowboy songs*

Moss, Jeffrey. *The songs of Sesame Street in poems and pictures*

Moss, Marissa. *Knick knack paddywack*

Mother Goose. *London Bridge is falling down*, ill. by Ed Emberley

London Bridge is falling down, ill. by Peter Spier

The Mother Goose songbook, ill. by Jacqueline Sinclair

Mother Goose's melodies, ill. by William A. Wheeler

Thirty old-time nursery songs, ill. by Paul Woodroffe

Munsch, Robert N. *Mortimer*

Neale, J. M. (John Mason). *Good King Wenceslas*

Nelson, Esther L. *The funny songbook*

Holiday singing and dancing games

The silly songbook

Newbolt, Henry John, Sir. *Rilloby-rill*

Newland, Mary Reed. *Good King Wenceslas*

Niland, Kilmeny. *A bellbird in a flame tree*

Old MacDonald had a farm. *Old MacDonald had a farm*, ill. by Lorinda Bryan Cauley

Old MacDonald had a farm, ill. by Mel Crawford

Old MacDonald had a farm, ill. by David Frankland

Old MacDonald had a farm, ill. by Abner Graboff

Old MacDonald had a farm, ill. by Nancy Hellen

Old MacDonald had a farm, ill. by Carol Jones

Old MacDonald had a farm, ill. by Tracey Campbell Pearson

Old MacDonald had a farm, ill. by Robert M. Quackenbush

Old MacDonald had a farm, ill. by Glen Rounds

Old MacDonald had a farm, ill. by William Stobbs

Old MacDonald had a farm, ill. by Prue Theobalds

On the little hearth, ill. by Gabriel Lisowski

Oppenheim, Joanne. *The eency weency spider*

Over in the meadow, ill. by Ezra Jack Keats

A paper of pins, ill. by Margaret Gordon

Paterson, A. B. (Andrew Barton). *Waltzing Matilda*

Peek, Merle. *The balancing act*

Mary wore her red dress and Henry wore his green sneakers

Pfister, Marcus. *I see the moon*

Poston, Elizabeth. *Baby's song book*

Preston, Edna Mitchell. *Pop Corn and Ma Goodness*

Price, Christine. *One is God*

Quackenbush, Robert M. *Clementine*

The man on the flying trapeze

Pop! goes the weasel and Yankee Doodle

She'll be comin' 'round the mountain

Skip to my Lou

There'll be a hot time in the old town tonight
Raebeck, Lois. *Who am I?*
Raffi. *Baby beluga*
  Down by the bay
  Everything grows
  One light, one sun
  Shake my sillies out
  Wheels on the bus
Raposo, Joe. *The Sesame Street song book*
Rey, H. A. (Hans Augusto). *Humpty Dumpty and other Mother Goose songs*
Richardson, Jean. *Stephen's feast*
Robbins, Ruth. *Baboushka and the three kings*
Rodgers, Richard. *A real nice clambake*
Roll over! ill. by Merle Peek
Root, Phyllis. *Soup for supper*
Ross, Tony. *This old man*
Rounds, Glen. *The boll weevil*
  Casey Jones
  The strawberry roan
  Sweet Betsy from Pike
Schackburg, Richard. *Yankee Doodle*
Seeger, Pete. *The foolish frog*
Sewall, Marcia. *Animal song*
Shannon, George. *Lizard's song*
  Oh, I love!
Simon, Paul. *At the zoo*
Singer, Marilyn. *Will you take me to town on strawberry day?*
Slobodkin, Louis. *Wide-awake owl*
The song of the Three Holy Children, ill. by Pauline Baynes
Spier, Peter. *The Erie Canal*
Staines, Bill. *All God's critters got a place in the choir*
Stern, Elsie-Jean. *Wee Robin's Christmas song*
Stobbs, William. *There's a hole in my bucket*
Sweet, Melissa. *Fiddle-i-fee*
Taylor, Mark. *The bold fisherman*
  Old Blue, you good dog you
Trivas, Irene. *Emma's Christmas*
The twelve days of Christmas. English folk song. *Brian Wildsmith's The twelve days of Christmas*
  Jack Kent's twelve days of Christmas
  The twelve days of Christmas, ill. by Jan Brett
  The twelve days of Christmas, ill. by Ilonka Karasz
  The twelve days of Christmas, ill. by Ilse Plume
  The twelve days of Christmas, ill. by Erika Schneider
  The twelve days of Christmas, ill. by Sophie Windham
Vaughan, Marcia K. *Wombat stew*
Wallner, John. *Old MacDonald had a farm*
We wish you a merry Christmas, ill. by Tracey Campbell Pearson

Weiss, Nicki. *If you're happy and you know it*
Wenning, Elisabeth. *The Christmas mouse*
Westcott, Nadine Bernard. *Skip to my Lou*
  There's a hole in the bucket
What a morning! ill. by Ashley Bryan
Wheeler, Opal. *Sing in praise*
  Sing Mother Goose
Widdecombe Fair, ill. by Christine Price
Wolff, Ashley. *The bells of London*
Yolen, Jane. *The lap-time song and play book*
Yulya. *Bears are sleeping*
Zelinsky, Paul O. *The wheels on the bus*
Zemach, Harve. *Mommy, buy me a China doll*
Zolotow, Charlotte (Shapiro). *The song*

Sounds *see* Noise, sounds

South Africa *see* Foreign lands – South Africa

South America *see* Foreign lands – South America

South Sea Islands *see* Foreign lands – South Sea Islands

Space and space ships
Alexander, Martha G. *Marty McGee's space lab, no girls allowed*
Asimov, Isaac. *The best new things*
Barden, Rosalind. *TV monster*
Barton, Byron. *I want to be an astronaut*
Behrens, June. *I can be an astronaut*
Berenstain, Stan. *The Berenstain bears on the moon*
Blocksma, Mary. *Easy-to-make spaceships that really fly*
Bradman, Tony. *It came from outer space Michael*
Branley, Franklyn M. *Is there life in outer space?*
  Journey into a black hole
  The planets in our solar system
Brewster, Patience. *Ellsworth and the cats from Mars*
Brunhoff, Laurent de. *Babar visits another planet*
Carey, Valerie Scho. *Harriet and William and the terrible creature*
Cole, Babette. *The trouble with Gran*
Counsel, June. *But Martin!*
Delaney, Ned. *Cosmic chickens*
Eco, Umberto. *The three astronauts*
Freeman, Don. *Space witch*
Freeman, Mae. *You will go to the moon*
Fuchs, Erich. *Journey to the moon*
Glass, Andrew. *My brother tries to make me laugh*
Hillert, Margaret. *Up, up and away*
Hirst, Robin. *My place in space*

Johnson, Crockett. *Harold's trip to the sky*
Jones, Brian. *Space*
Keats, Ezra Jack. *Regards to the man in the moon*
Kroll, Steven. *The magic rocket*
Kuskin, Karla. *A space story*
Lorenz, Lee. *Hugo and the spacedog*
MacDonald, Suse. *Space spinners*
Marshall, Edward. *Space case*
Marshall, James. *Merry Christmas, space case*
Marzollo, Jean. *Jed and the space bandits*
  Jed's junior space patrol
May, Charles Paul. *High-noon rocket*
Mayer, Mercer. *Astronaut critter*
Mayers, Florence Cassen. *The National Air and Space Museum: ABC*
Moche, Dinah L. *The astronauts*
Mooser, Stephen. *Funnyman meets the monster from outer space*
Moss, Marissa. *Knick knack paddywack*
Murphy, Jill. *What next, baby bear!*
Oxenbury, Helen. *Tom and Pippo see the moon*
Paul, Sherry. *2-B and the space visitor*
Peet, Bill (William Bartlett). *The wump world*
Pinkwater, Daniel Manus. *Guys from space*
Podendorf, Illa. *Space*
Pryor, Bonnie. *Mr. Munday and the space creatures*
Rey, H. A. (Hans Augusto). *Curious George gets a medal*
Robison, Nancy. *UFO kidnap*
Ross, David. *Gorp and the space pirates*
  Space monster
  Space Monster Gorp and the runaway computer
Ross, Tony. *I'm coming to get you!*
Sadler, Marilyn. *Alistair in outer space*
  Alistair's time machine
Schoberle, Ceile. *Beyond the Milky Way*
Steadman, Ralph. *The little red computer*
Thompson, Richard. *Sky full of babies*
Ungerer, Tomi. *Moon man*
Vaughn, Jenny. *On the moon*
Weiss, Ellen. *Pigs in space*
Wildsmith, Brian. *Professor Noah's spaceship*
Willis, Jeanne. *Earth mobiles as explained by Professor Xargle*
  Earth tigerlets as explained by Professor Xargle
  Earthlets as explained by Professor Xargle
  The long blue blazer
Wynne-Jones, Tim. *Builder of the moon*
Yorinks, Arthur. *Company's coming*
Young, Ruth. *A trip to Mars*
Zaffo, George J. *The giant book of things in space*
Ziegler, Ursina. *Squaps the moonling*

Spain see Foreign lands – Spain

Sparrows see Birds – sparrows

Spectacles see Glasses

Speech see Language

Speed see Concepts – speed

Spelunking see Caves

Spiders

Aardema, Verna. *The vingananee and the tree toad*
Adelson, Leone. *Please pass the grass*
Back, Christine. *Spider's web*
Baker, Jeannie. *One hungry spider*
Brandenberg, Franz. *Fresh cider and apple pie*
Cahill, Chris. *Spider magic*
Carle, Eric. *The very busy spider*
Chenery, Janet. *Wolfie*
Climo, Shirley. *The cobweb Christmas*
Conklin, Gladys. *I caught a lizard*
Crothers, Samuel McChord. *Miss Muffet's Christmas party*
Fisher, Aileen Lucia. *When it comes to bugs*
Freschet, Berniece. *The web in the grass*
Galdone, Joanna. *Honeybee's party*
George, Jean Craighead. *All upon a stone*
Goldin, Augusta. *Spider silk*
Graham, Margaret Bloy. *Be nice to spiders*
Hawes, Judy. *My daddy longlegs*
Hawkins, Colin. *Incy wincy spider*
Joosse, Barbara M. *Spiders in the fruit cellar*
Kimmel, Eric A. *Anansi and the moss-covered rock*
  Anansi goes fishing
Kraus, Robert. *How spider saved Valentine's Day*
  The trouble with spider
McDermott, Gerald. *Anansi the spider*
MacDonald, Suse. *Space spinners*
McNulty, Faith. *The lady and the spider*
Oppenheim, Joanne. *The eency weency spider*
Oxford Scientific Films. *The spider's web*
Parsons, Alexandra. *Amazing spiders*
Rose, Anne. *Spider in the sky*
Ryder, Joanne. *The spiders dance*
Selsam, Millicent E. *A first look at spiders*
Wagner, Jenny. *Aranea*
Yolen, Jane. *Spider Jane*

Split page books see Format, unusual

Spooks see Ghosts; Goblins

Spoonbills see Birds – spoonbills

Sports

Berenstain, Stan. *The Berenstain bears go out for the team*
Blaustein, Muriel. *Play ball, Zachary!*
Carlson, Nancy. *Bunnies and their sports*
Carrick, Carol. *The climb*
Caseley, Judith. *Molly Pink goes hiking*
Hoberman, Mary Ann. *Mr. and Mrs. Muddle*
Martin, Bill (William Ivan). *White Dynamite and Curly Kidd*
Ormerod, Jan. *Bend and stretch*
Peterson, Esther Allen. *Penelope gets wheels*
Rayner, Mary. *Marathon and Steve*
Riddle, Tohby. *Careful with that ball, Eugene!*
Saddler, Allen. *The Archery contest*
Tinkelman, Murray. *Cowgirl*
Yeoman, John. *Old Mother Hubbard's dog takes up sport*

Sports – baseball

Christian, Mary Blount. *The sand lot*
Downing, Joan. *Baseball is our game*
Giff, Patricia Reilly. *Ronald Morgan goes to bat*
Gordon, Sharon. *Play ball, Kate!*
Greene, Carol. *I can be a baseball player*
Hillert, Margaret. *Play ball*
Hoff, Syd. *The littlest leaguer*
  Slugger Sal's slump
Isadora, Rachel. *Max*
Lexau, Joan M. *I'll tell on you*
McConnachie, Brian. *Elmer and the chickens vs. the big league*
Motomora, Mitchell. *Specs*
Perkins, Al. *Don and Donna go to bat*
Rubin, Jeff. *Baseball brothers*
Sachs, Marilyn. *Fleet-footed Florence*
  Matt's mitt
Schulman, Janet. *Camp Kee Wee's secret weapon*
Stadler, John. *Hooray for snail!*
Thayer, Ernest L. *Casey at the bat*, ill. by Patricia Polacco

Sports – basketball

Porte, Barbara Ann. *Harry's visit*

Sports – bicycling

Andersen, Karen Born. *What's the matter, Sylvie, can't you ride?*
Baker, Eugene. *Bicycles*
Bang, Molly. *Delphine*
Barbot, Daniel. *A bicycle for Rosaura*
Baugh, Dolores M. *Bikes*
Bentley, Anne. *The Groggs' day out*
Blake, Quentin. *Mrs. Armitage on wheels*

Blance, Ellen. *Monster, Lady Monster and the bike ride*
Breinburg, Petronella. *Shawn's red bike*
Bruna, Dick. *Miffy's bicycle*
Bunting, Eve (Anne Evelyn). *Summer wheels*
Chlad, Dorothy. *Bicycles are fun to ride*
Dowling, Paul. *You can do it, Rabbit*
Heine, Helme. *Friends*
Holabird, Katharine. *Angelina's birthday surprise*
Hughes, Shirley. *Wheels*
Krings, Antoon. *Oliver's bicycle*
McLeod, Emilie Warren. *The bear's bicycle*
Maestro, Betsy. *Bike trip*
Muntean, Michaela. *Bicycle bear*
Myers, Bernice. *Herman and the bears and the giants*
Paterson, A. B. (Andrew Barton). *Mulga Bill's bicycle*
Rey, H. A. (Hans Augusto). *Curious George rides a bike*
Rockwell, Anne F. *Bikes*
Say, Allen. *The bicycle man*
Schwartz, David M. *Sugargrandpa*
Stott, Dorothy. *Little Duck's bicycle ride*
Strub, Susanne. *Lulu on her bike*
Sueyoshi, Akiko. *Ladybird on a bicycle*
Thomas, Jane Resh. *Wheels*
Yorinks, Arthur. *Ugh*

Sports - camping *see* Camps, camping

Sports – fishing

Aldridge, Josephine Haskell. *Fisherman's luck*
  A peony and a periwinkle
Alexander, Sally Hobart. *Maggie's whopper*
Anderson, Lena Castell. *Bunny fun*
Bettina (Bettina Ehrlich). *Pantaloni*
Cook, Bernadine. *The little fish that got away*
Delacre, Lulu. *Nathan's fishing trip*
Delton, Judy. *Duck goes fishing*
Demarest, Chris L. *Orville's odyssey*
Elkin, Benjamin. *Six foolish fishermen*
George, William T. *Fishing at Long Pond*
Gibbons, Gail. *Surrounded by sea*
Goffstein, M. B. (Marilyn Brooke). *Fish for supper*
Gray, Catherine. *Tammy and the gigantic fish*
Griffith, Helen V. *Grandaddy's place*
Hall, Bill. *Fish tale*
Hann, Jacquie. *Up day, down day*
Hertz, Ole. *Tobias catches trout*
  Tobias goes ice fishing
Ipcar, Dahlov. *The biggest fish in the sea*
Kidd, Nina. *June Mountain secret*
Koller, Jackie French. *Fish fry tonight*
Lapp, Eleanor. *In the morning mist*

Long, Earlene. *Gone fishing*
Luenn, Nancy. *Nessa's fish*
McKissack, Patricia C. *A million fish...more or less*
Marzollo, Jean. *Amy goes fishing*
Mayer, Mercer. *A boy, a dog, a frog and a friend*
A boy, a dog and a frog
Miles, Miska. *No, no, Rosina*
Ness, Evaline. *Sam, Bangs, and moonshine*
Parker, Dorothy D. *Liam's catch*
Potter, Beatrix. *The tale of Mr. Jeremy Fisher*, ill. by David Jorgensen
The tale of Mr. Jeremy Fisher
Rey, Margřet (Margřet Elisabeth Waldstein). *Curious George flies a kite*
Say, Allen. *A river dream*
Stevenson, Robert Louis. *The moon*
Surany, Anico. *Ride the cold wind*
Taylor, Mark. *The bold fisherman*
Thorne, Jenny. *My uncle*
Wahl, Jan. *The fishermen*
Ward, Sally G. *Punky goes fishing*
Waterton, Betty. *A salmon for Simon*
Watson, Nancy Dingman. *Tommy's mommy's fish*
Wildsmith, Brian. *Pelican*
Wilson, Bob. *Stanley Bagshaw and the twenty-two ton whale*

Sports – football

Carlson, Nancy. *Louanne Pig in making the team*
Kuskin, Karla. *The Dallas Titans get ready for bed*
Myers, Bernice. *Sidney Rella and the glass sneaker*
Stadler, John. *Snail saves the day*

Sports – gymnastics

Brown, Marc Tolon. *D. W. flips!*
Kuklin, Susan. *Going to my gymnastics class*
Stevens, Carla. *Pig and the blue flag*
Wood, Tim. *Gymnastics*

Sports – hiking

Curious George goes hiking

Sports – hockey

Kidd, Bruce. *Hockey showdown*

Sports – hunting

Baker, Betty. *Sonny-Boy Sim*
Bemelmans, Ludwig. *Parsley*
Browne, Anthony. *Bear hunt*
Burch, Robert. *The hunting trip*
Burningham, John. *Harquin: the fox who went down to the valley*

Calhoun, Mary. *Houn' dog*
Carrick, Donald. *The deer in the pasture*
Harold and the great stag
De Paola, Tomie (Thomas Anthony). *The hunter and the animals*
De Regniers, Beatrice Schenk. *Catch a little fox*
Dionetti, Michelle. *The day Eli went looking for bear*
Duvoisin, Roger Antoine. *The happy hunter*
Gage, Wilson. *Cully Cully and the bear*
Hader, Berta Hoerner. *The mighty hunter*
Hertz, Ole. *Tobias goes seal hunting*
Hoban, Russell. *The dancing tigers*
Jones, Maurice. *I'm going on a dragon hunt*
Kahl, Virginia. *How do you hide a monster?*
Kamen, Gloria. *The ringdoves*
Kellogg, Steven (Stephen). *Tallyho, Pinkerton!*
Kilroy, Sally. *The baron's hunting party*
Krause, Ute. *Nora and the great bear*
Kroll, Steven. *One tough turkey*
Langstaff, John M. *Oh, a-hunting we will go*
Livermore, Elaine. *Looking for Henry*
Mari, Iela. *Eat and be eaten*
Mendoza, George. *The hunter I might have been*
Michels, Tilde. *Who's that knocking at my door?*
Parish, Peggy. *Good hunting, Blue Sky*
Ootah's lucky day
Peet, Bill (William Bartlett). *Buford the little bighorn*
The gnats of knotty pine
Prusski, Jeffrey. *Bring back the deer*
Rohmer, Harriet. *The invisible hunters*
Rosen, Michael J. *We're going on a bear hunt*
Steiner, Charlotte. *Pete and Peter*
Turnbull, Ann. *Rob goes a-hunting*
Wahl, Jan. *Tiger watch*
Wildsmith, Brian. *Hunter and his dog*
Withers, Carl. *The wild ducks and the goose*
Wolcott, Patty. *Eeeeeek!*

Sports – ice skating

DiVito, Anna. *Elephants on ice*
Hoban, Lillian. *Mr. Pig and Sonny too*
Lindman, Maj. *Snipp, Snapp, Snurr and the yellow sled*
Radin, Ruth Yaffe. *A winter place*
Van Stockum, Hilda. *A day on skates*
Weiss, Nicki. *Dog boy cap skate*

Sports – mountain climbing

Haswell, Peter. *Pog climbs Mount Everest*

Sports – Olympics

Schulz, Charles M. *You're the greatest, Charlie Brown*

Sports – racing

Aarle, Thomas Van. *Don't put your cart before the horse race*
Adams, Adrienne. *The great Valentine's Day balloon race*
Æsop. *The hare and the tortoise*, ill. by Paul Galdone
  The hare and the tortoise, ill. by Gerald Rose
  The hare and the tortoise, ill. by Peter Weevers
  The tortoise and the hare, ill. by Janet Stevens
Alborough, Jez. *Running Bear*
Baumann, Hans. *The hare's race*
Baynton, Martin. *Fifty and the great race*
Benchley, Nathaniel. *Walter the homing pigeon*
Berenstain, Stan. *The Berenstain bears and the big road race*
Calloway, Northern J. *Northern J. Calloway presents Super-vroomer!*
Dickens, Frank. *Boffo*
Hall, Derek. *Tiger runs*
Heine, Helme. *Three little friends: the racing cart*
Hurd, Edith Thacher. *Last one home is a green pig*
Isenberg, Barbara. *The adventures of Albert, the running bear*
  Albert the running bear gets the jitters
Kessler, Leonard P. *The big mile race*
La Fontaine, Jean de. *The hare and the tortoise*
McLenighan, Valjean. *Turtle and rabbit*
McNaughton, Colin. *The rat race*
Marshall, Edward. *Fox on wheels*
Moore, John. *Granny Stickleback*
Neuhaus, David. *His finest hour*
Otsuka, Yuzo. *Suho and the white horse*
Reimold, Mary Gallagher. *My mom is a runner*
Schwartz, David M. *Sugargrandpa*
Shearer, Marilyn J. *The crown of fools*
Van Woerkom, Dorothy. *Harry and Shelburt*
Wilkinson, Sylvia. *I can be a race car driver*
Wood, Tim. *Motor racing*
  Motorcycling
Wyllie, Stephen. *The great race*

Sports – roller skating

Crary, Elizabeth. *I'm frustrated*
Johnson, Mildred D. *Wait, skates!*
Wahl, Jan. *Rabbits on roller skates!*

Sports – skiing

Calhoun, Mary. *Cross-country cat*
Freeman, Don. *Ski pup*
Hutchins, H. J. (Hazel J.). *Ben's snow song*
Lindman, Maj. *Snipp, Snapp, Snurr and the red shoes*
Marol, Jean-Claude. *Vagabul goes skiing*
Peet, Bill (William Bartlett). *Buford the little bighorn*

Sports – skin diving

Carrick, Carol. *Dark and full of secrets*
Ungerer, Tomi. *The Mellops go diving for treasure*

Sports – sledding

Curious George goes sledding
Iwamura, Kazuo. *The fourteen forest mice and the winter sledding day*
Winthrop, Elizabeth. *Sledding*

Sports – soccer

Catalanotto, Peter. *Dylan's day out*

Sports – surfing

Ormondroyd, Edward. *Broderick*

Sports – swimming

Alexander, Martha G. *We never get to do anything*
Anderson, Lena Castell. *Bunny fun*
Beatty, Hetty Burlingame. *Droopy*
Beim, Jerrold. *The swimming hole*
Berridge, Celia. *Going swimming*
Brown, M. K. *Let's go swimming with Mr. Sillypants*
Cohn, Norma. *Brother and sister*
Coles, Alison. *Michael and the sea*
Cousins, Lucy. *Masy goes swimming*
Day, Alexandra. *River parade*
George, Lindsay Barrett. *William and Boomer*
Ginsburg, Mirra. *The chick and the duckling*
Hall, Derek. *Otter swims*
Krings, Antoon. *Oliver's pool*
Lasky, Kathryn. *Sea swan*
Moore, Inga. *Aktil's big swim*
Shortall, Leonard W. *Tony's first dive*
Stevens, Carla. *Hooray for pig!*
Stott, Dorothy. *Too much*
Strub, Susanne. *Lulu goes swimming*
Van Leeuwen, Jean. *Too hot for ice cream*
Watanabe, Shigeo. *Let's go swimming*

Sports – T-ball

Gemme, Leila Boyle. *T-ball is our game*

Sports – wrestling
Stren, Patti. *Mountain Rose*

Spring *see* Seasons – spring

Squirrels *see* Animals – squirrels

Stage *see* Theater

Stars
Allen, Laura Jean. *Ottie and the star*
Asch, Frank. *Starbaby*
Birdseye, Tom. *A song of stars*
Boon, Emilie. *Peterkin meets a star*
Branley, Franklyn M. *Journey into a black hole*
  The sky is full of stars
Coatsworth, Elizabeth. *Good night*
Elzbieta. *Dikou and the baby star*
Freeman, Mae. *The sun, the moon and the stars*
Hillman, Elizabeth. *Min-Yo and the moon dragon*
Hort, Lenny. *How many stars in the sky*
Ichikawa, Satomi. *Nora's stars*
Kuskin, Karla. *A space story*
Lee, Jeanne M. *The legend of the milky way*
Mobley, Jane. *The star husband*
Modesitt, Jeanne. *The night call*
Oughton, Jerrie. *How the stars fell into the sky*
Radley, Gail. *The night Stella hid the stars*
Ray, Deborah Kogan. *Stargazing sky*
Slate, Joseph. *The star rocker*
Stone, Kazuko G. *Goodnight Twinklegator*
Tibo, Gilles. *Simon and the snowflakes*
Wandelmaier, Roy. *Stars*
Widman, Christine. *The star grazers*
Winter, Jeanette. *Follow the drinking gourd*
Wyler, Rose. *The starry sky*
Yeomans, Thomas. *For every child a star*

Stealing *see* Behavior – stealing

Steam shovels *see* Machines

Steamrollers *see* Machines

Step families *see* Divorce; Family life – step families

Stepchildren *see* Divorce; Family life – Step families

Stepparents *see* Divorce; Family life – step families

Stones *see* Rocks

Storekeepers *see* Careers – storekeepers

Stores
Alexander, Liza. *Ernie gets lost*
Anholt, Catherine. *Truffles in trouble*
Baugh, Dolores M. *Let's go Supermarket*
Bograd, Larry. *Lost in the store*
Carlstrom, Nancy White. *Baby-O*
Cooper, Letice Ulpha. *The bear who was too big*
Field, Rachel Lyman. *General store*, ill. by Giles Laroche
  General store, ill. by Nancy Winslow Parker
Freeman, Don. *Corduroy*
Gibbons, Gail. *Department store*
Gordon, Margaret. *The supermarket mice*
Graham, Amanda. *Who wants Arthur?*
Grossman, Bill. *Tommy at the grocery store*
Hale, Kathleen. *Orlando the frisky housewife*
Hamm, Diane Johnston. *Laney's lost momma*
Harris, Leon A. *The great diamond robbery*
Haseley, Dennis. *The thieves' market*
Hastings, Evelyn Beilhart. *The department store*
Hoff, Syd. *Merry Christmas, Henrietta!*
Lippman, Peter. *The Know-It-Alls mind the store*
Lobel, Arnold. *On Market Street*
McNaughton, Colin. *At the stores*
Maschler, Fay. *T. G. and Moonie go shopping*
Meddaugh, Susan. *The witches' supermarket*
Miller, Alice P. *The little store on the corner*
Munsch, Robert N. *Something good*
Oliver, Stephen. *Shopping*
Pearson, Tracey Campbell. *The storekeeper*
Potter, Beatrix. *Ginger and Pickles*
Rockwell, Anne F. *The supermarket*
Rubel, Nicole. *Goldie*
Sawyer, Jean. *Our village shop*
Scarry, Richard. *Richard Scarry's great big mystery book*
Shelby, Anne. *We keep a store*
Solomon, Joan. *A present for Mum*
Spier, Peter. *Food market*
  The pet store
  The toy shop
Steiner, Jörg. *The bear who wanted to be a bear*
Wells, Rosemary. *Max's dragon shirt*
Williams, Barbara. *I know a salesperson*

Storks *see* Birds – storks

Storms *see* Weather – storms

Streams *see* Rivers

Streets *see* Roads

String

Bakken, Harold. *The special string*
Calhoun, Mary. *The traveling ball of string*

Stubbornness *see* Character traits –
stubbornness

Sukkot *see* Holidays – Sukkot

Sullivan Islands *see* Foreign lands –
South Sea Islands

Sultans *see* Royalty – sultans

Summer *see* Seasons – summer

Sun

Anno, Mitsumasa. *In shadowland*
Arnold, Caroline. *Sun fun*
Baylor, Byrd. *The way to start a day*
Bernstein, Margery. *How the sun made a
promise and kept it*
Branley, Franklyn M. *Eclipse: darkness in
daytime*
The planets in our solar system
The sun, our nearest star
Sunshine makes the seasons
Carlstrom, Nancy White. *Who gets the sun
out of bed?*
Dayrell, Elphinstone. *Why the sun and the
moon live in the sky*
De Gerez, Toni. *Louhi, witch of North Farm*
De Regniers, Beatrice Schenk. *Who likes
the sun?*
Elkin, Benjamin. *Why the sun was late*
Engelbrektson, Sune. *The sun is a star*
Euvremer, Teryl. *Sun's up*
Freeman, Mae. *The sun, the moon and the
stars*
Gerstein, Mordicai. *The sun's day*
Gibbons, Gail. *Sun up, sun down*
Ginsburg, Mirra. *How the sun was brought
back to the sky*
Where does the sun go at night?
Goudey, Alice E. *The day we saw the sun
come up*
Greene, Carol. *Shine, sun!*
Hamberger, John. *The day the sun
disappeared*
Harrison, David Lee. *Wake up, sun!*
Hurd, Edith Thacher. *The day the sun
danced*
Ivory, Lesley Anne. *Cats in the sun*
Kandoian, Ellen. *Under the sun*
Kinney, Jean. *What does the sun do?*
La Fontaine, Jean de. *The north wind and
the sun*
Mollel, Tolowa M. *A promise to the sun*
Novak, Matt. *Claude and Sun*
Obrist, Jürg. *The miser who wanted the sun*

Ormerod, Jan. *Sunshine*
Palazzo, Janet. *Our friend the sun*
Peet, Bill (William Bartlett). *Cock-a-doodle
Dudley*
Ringi, Kjell (Arne Sorensen). *The sun and
the cloud*
Roth, Susan L. *The story of light*
Schlein, Miriam. *The sun looks down*
The sun, the wind, the sea and the rain
Schneider, Herman. *Follow the sunset*
Shulevitz, Uri. *Dawn*
Tresselt, Alvin R. *Sun up*, ill. by author
Sun up, ill. by Henri Sorensen
Troughton, Joanna. *Who will be the sun?*
Wildsmith, Brian. *What the moon saw*

Surfing *see* Sports – surfing

Swallows *see* Birds – swallows

Swans *see* Birds – swans

Sweaters *see* Clothing – sweaters

Sweden *see* Foreign lands – Sweden

Swimming *see* Sports – swimming

Swinging *see* Activities – swinging

Switzerland *see* Foreign lands –
Switzerland

Tables *see* Furniture – tables

Tailors *see* Careers – tailors

Taiwain *see* Foreign lands – Taiwain

Talking to strangers *see* Behavior –
talking to strangers

Tapirs *see* Animals – tapirs

Tardiness *see* Behavior – tardiness

Tasting *see* Senses – tasting

Taxi drivers *see* Careers – taxi drivers

Taxis

Barracca, Sal. *The adventures of taxi dog*
Maestro, Betsy. *Taxi*
Moore, Lilian. *Papa Albert*

Ross, Jessica. *Ms. Klondike*

T-ball *see* Sports – T-ball

Teachers *see* Careers – teachers

Teddy bears *see* Toys – teddy bears

Teeth

Balzola, Asun. *Munia and the orange crocodile*
Barnett, Naomi. *I know a dentist*
Bate, Lucy. *Little rabbit's loose tooth*
Birdseye, Tom. *Airmail to the moon*
Brown, Marc Tolon. *Arthur's tooth*
Brown, Ruth. *Crazy Charlie*
Carson, Jo. *Pulling my leg*
Catalanotto, Peter. *Christmas always*
Cooney, Nancy Evans. *The wobbly tooth*
Curious George goes to the dentist
De Groat, Diane. *Alligator's toothache*
Dinan, Carolyn. *Say cheese!*
Duvoisin, Roger Antoine. *Crocus*
Eriksson, Eva. *The tooth trip*
Gunther, Louise. *A tooth for the tooth fairy*
Heller, Nicholas. *The tooth tree*
Jenkin-Pearce, Susie. *Boris's big ache*
Kaye, Marilyn. *The real tooth fairy*
Kroll, Steven. *Loose tooth*
McCloskey, Robert. *One morning in Maine*
MacDonald, Maryann. *Rosie's baby tooth*
McGinley, Phyllis. *Lucy McLockett*
McPhail, David. *The bear's toothache*
Mitra, Annie. *Tusk! Tusk!*
Nerlove, Miriam. *Just one tooth*
Pomerantz, Charlotte. *The mango tooth*
Quin-Harkin, Janet. *Helpful Hattie*
Richter, Alice Numeroff. *You can't put braces on spaces*
Ricketts, Michael. *Teeth*
Rockwell, Harlow. *My dentist*
Ross, Pat. *Molly and the slow teeth*
Seuss, Dr. *The tooth book*
Silverman, Martin. *My tooth is loose*
Stamper, Judith. *What's it like to be a dentist?*
Sundvall, Viveca. *Mimi and the biscuit factory*
West, Colin. *The king's toothache*
Williams, Barbara. *Albert's toothache*
Wolf, Bernard. *Michael and the dentist*
Zalben, Jane Breskin. *Buster gets braces*

Telephone

Allen, Jeffrey. *Mary Alice, operator number 9*
Mary Alice returns
King, Bob. *Sitting on the farm*
Telephones
Weiss, Ellen. *Telephone time*

Wyse, Lois. *Two guppies, a turtle and Aunt Edna*

Telephone operators *see* Careers – telephone operators

Television

Barden, Rosalind. *TV monster*
Berenstain, Stan. *The Berenstain bears and too much TV*
Brown, Marc Tolon. *The bionic bunny show*
Dobson, Clive. *Fred's TV*
Heilbroner, Joan. *Tom the TV cat*
McCully, Emily Arnold. *Zaza's big break*
McPhail, David. *Fix-it*

Telling time *see* Clocks, watches; Time

Temper tantrums *see* Emotions – anger

Textless *see* Wordless

Thailand *see* Foreign lands – Thailand

Thanksgiving *see* Holidays – Thanksgiving

Theater

Ahlberg, Allan. *The Cinderella show*
Alexander, Sue. *Seymour the prince*
Small plays for special days
Small plays for you and a friend
Behrens, June. *Christmas-magic wagon*
The feast of Thanksgiving
Berenstain, Stan. *The Berenstain bears get stage fright*
Brighton, Catherine. *Hope's gift*
Brown, Marc Tolon. *Arthur's Thanksgiving*
Butterworth, Nick. *The Nativity play*
Carlson, Nancy. *The talent show*
Cazet, Denys. *The duck with squeaky feet*
Cohen, Miriam. *Starring first grade*
De Paola, Tomie (Thomas Anthony). *The Christmas pageant*
Sing, Pierrot, sing
De Regniers, Beatrice Schenk. *Picture book theater*
Ernst, Lisa Campbell. *When Bluebell sang*
Ets, Marie Hall. *Another day*
Freeman, Don. *Hattie the backstage bat*
Will's quill
Freeman, Lydia. *Pet of the Met*
Frye, Dean. *Days of sunshine, days of rain*
Giff, Patricia Reilly. *The almost awful play*
Goffstein, M. B. (Marilyn Brooke). *An actor*
Goodall, John S. *Paddy's evening out*
Grimm, Jacob. *King Grisly-Beard*, ill. by Maurice Sendak
Hoffman, Mary. *Amazing Grace*

Hoffmann, E. T. A. *The nutcracker,* ill. by Maurice Sendak
Holabird, Katharine. *Angelina on stage*
Hughes, Shirley. *Angel Mae*
Isadora, Rachel. *Jesse and Abe*
Opening night
Johnson, Dolores. *The best bug to be*
Layton, Aviva. *The squeakers*
Leedy, Loreen. *The bunny play*
Lobel, Arnold. *Martha, the movie mouse*
Lubach, Peter. *Harry and the singing fish*
McCully, Emily Arnold. *The evil spell*
Speak up, Blanche!
Zaza's big break
Maiorano, Robert. *Backstage*
Martin, Judith. *The tree angel*
Novak, Matt. *While the shepherd slept*
Oppenheim, Joanne. *Mrs. Peloki's class play*
Patz, Nancy. *Gina Farina and the Prince of Mintz*
Pearson, Susan. *Lenore's big break*
Rose, Mitchell. *Norman*
Sage, James. *The boy and the dove*
Schwartz, Henry. *Albert goes Hollywood*
Sendak, Maurice. *Maurice Sendak's Really Rosie*
Steiner, Charlotte. *Kiki is an actress*
Tryon, Leslie. *Albert's play*
Wharton, Thomas. *Hildegard sings*
Yeoman, John. *The young performing horse*

Thumbsucking

Cooney, Nancy Evans. *Donald says thumbs down*
Heitler, Susan M. *David decides about thumbsucking*
Klimowicz, Barbara. *The strawberry thumb*

Thunder *see* Weather – storms; Weather – thunder

Tibet *see* Foreign lands – Tibet

Tigers *see* Animals – tigers

Time

Aiken, Conrad Potter. *Tom, Sue and the clock*
Aldag, Kurt. *Some things never change*
Allen, Jeffrey. *Mary Alice, operator number 9*
Allington, Richard L. *Time*
Ancona, George. *Handtalk zoo*
Aylesworth, Jim. *The completed hickory dickory dock*
Bodwell, Gaile. *The long day of the giants*
Bragdon, Lillian J. *Tell me the time, please*
Carle, Eric. *The grouchy ladybug*
Colman, Hila. *Watch that watch*
Fleischman, Paul. *Time train*

Gerstein, Mordicai. *The sun's day*
Gibbons, Gail. *Clocks and how they go*
Gordon, Sharon. *Tick tock clock*
Handford, Martin. *Find Waldo now*
Hawkins, Colin. *What time is it, Mr. Wolf?*
Hay, Dean. *Now I can count*
Hoff, Syd. *Henrietta, the early bird*
Hutchins, Pat. *Clocks and more clocks*
Katz, Bobbi. *Tick-tock, let's read the clock*
Killingback, Julia. *What time is it, Mrs. Bear?*
Krasilovsky, Phyllis. *The man who tried to save time*
Krensky, Stephen. *The big time bears*
Littlewood, Valerie. *The season clock*
Llewelyn, Claire. *My first book of time*
Lyon, George-Ella. *Father Time and the day boxes*
McGinley, Phyllis. *Wonderful time*
McMillan, Bruce. *Time to...*
Maestro, Betsy. *Around the clock with Harriet*
Manning, Linda. *Animal hours*
May, Charles Paul. *High-noon rocket*
Merriam, Eve. *Train leaves the station*
Mother Goose. *The real Mother Goose clock book,* ill. by Jane Chambless
Mueller, Virginia. *Monster goes to school*
Ness, Evaline. *Do you have the time, Lydia?*
Nobens, C. A. *Montgomery's time zone*
Pieńkowski, Jan. *Time*
Pluckrose, Henry Arthur. *Time*
Rockwell, Anne F. *Bear Child's book of hours*
Sadler, Marilyn. *Alistair's time machine*
Schlein, Miriam. *It's about time*
Seignobosc, Françoise. *What time is it, Jeanne-Marie?*
Singer, Marilyn. *Nine o'clock lullaby*
Skutina, Vladimir. *Nobody has time for me*
Slobodkin, Louis. *The late cuckoo*
Steinmetz, Leon. *Clocks in the woods*
Thompson, Carol. *Time*
Turner, Gwenda. *Once upon a time*
Watson, Nancy Dingman. *When is tomorrow?*
Ziner, Feenie. *The true book of time*
Zolotow, Charlotte (Shapiro). *Over and over*

Tin soldiers *see* Toys – soldiers

Toads *see* Frogs and toads

Toes *see* Anatomy – toes

Toilet training

Allison, Alida. *The toddler's potty book*
Caseley, Judith. *Annie's potty*
Civardi, Anne. *Potty time*
Cole, Joanna. *Your new potty*

Lindgren, Barbro. *Sam's potty*
Miller, Virginia. *On your potty!*
Reichmeier, Betty. *Potty time!*
Rogers, Fred. *Going to the potty*
Ross, Tony. *I want my potty*
Young, Ruth. *My potty chair*

Tongue twisters

Bodecker, N. M. (Nils Mogens). *Snowman Sniffles and other verse*
Brown, Marcia. *Peter Piper's alphabet*
Gordon, Jeffie Ross. *Six sleepy sheep*
Johnson, Odette. *One prickly porcupine*
Keller, Charles. *Tongue twisters*
Monster poems, ill. by Kay Chorao
Obligado, Lilian. *Faint frogs feeling feverish and other terrifically tantalizing tongue twisters*
Patz, Nancy. *Pumpernickel tickle and mean green cheese*
Pomerantz, Charlotte. *The piggy in the puddle*
Smith, Robert Paul. *Jack Mack*

Tools

Beim, Jerrold. *Tim and the tool chest*
Carle, Eric. *My very first book of tools*
DeSantis, Kenny. *A doctor's tools*
Gibbons, Gail. *Tool book*
Kesselman, Judi R. *I can use tools*
Lerner, Marguerite Rush. *Doctors' tools*
Miller, Margaret. *Who uses this?*
Pluckrose, Henry Arthur. *Things we cut*
Rockwell, Anne F. *The toolbox*
Zaffo, George J. *The giant nursery book of things that work*

Tortoises see Reptiles – turtles, tortoises

Toucans see Birds – toucans

Touching see Senses – touching

Towns see City

Toy and movable books see Format, unusual – toy and movable books.

Toys

Abolafia, Yossi. *Yanosh's Island*
Alexander, Martha G. *The story grandmother told*
Anderson, Lena Castell. *Bunny box*
Ardizzone, Aingelda. *The night ride*
Asch, Frank. *Baby in the box*
Ayer, Jacqueline. *Nu Dang and his kite*
Bailey, Debbie. *Toys*
Bambi, ill. by Christa Stephan
Beckman, Kaj. *Lisa cannot sleep*

Bianco, Margery Williams. *The velveteen rabbit*, ill. by Allen Atkinson
The velveteen rabbit, ill. by Michael Green
The velveteen rabbit, ill. by Michael Hague
The velveteen rabbit, ill. by David Jorgensen
The velveteen rabbit, ill. by William Nicholson
The velveteen rabbit, ill. by Ilse Plume
The velveteen rabbit, ill. by S. D. Schindler
The velveteen rabbit, ill. by Tien
Billam, Rosemary. *Fuzzy rabbit*
Binzen, Bill. *Alfred goes house hunting*
Bishop, Roma. *Toys*
Boegehold, Betty. *Hurray for Pippa!*
Bohdal, Susi. *Harry the hare*
Bornstein, Ruth Lercher. *Annabelle*
Brandenberg, Franz. *Aunt Nina and her nephews and nieces*
Breese, Gillian. *The amazing adventures of Teddy Tum Tum*
Brown, Ruth. *I don't like it!*
Browne, Anthony. *Gorilla*
Bryant, Dean. *See the bear*
Buchanan, Heather S. *George and Matilda Mouse and the floating school*
Burdick, Margaret. *Bobby Otter and the blue boat*
Burns, Maurice. *Go ducks, go!*
Butterworth, Nick. *Just like Jasper*
Campbell, Rod. *Buster's morning*
Chorao, Kay. *Kate's car*
Molly's Moe
Conrad, Pam. *The tub people*
Coombs, Patricia. *The lost playground*
Corbett, Grahame. *Guess who?*
Who is hiding?
Who is inside?
Who is next?
Couture, Susan Arkin. *The block book*
Craig, M. Jean. *Boxes*
Dale, Penny. *You can't*
Daly, Niki. *Vim, the rag mouse*
De Lynam, Alicia Garcia. *It's mine!*
Demi. *The magic boat*
DiFiori, Lawrence. *My toys*
Dobrin, Arnold Jack. *Josephine's 'magination*
Dowling, Paul. *Meg and Jack's new friends*
Drummond, Violet H. *Phewtus the squirrel*
Dugan, Barbara. *Loop the loop*
Dunbar, Joyce. *Lollopy*
Ernst, Lisa Campbell. *The rescue of Aunt Pansy*
Farber, Werner. *Night lion*
Francis, Anna B. *Pleasant dreams*
Frankel, Ben. *Tertius and Pliny*
Freeman, Don. *Corduroy's party*
Gackenbach, Dick. *Poppy the panda*

Galbraith, Kathryn Osebold. *Laura Charlotte*
Gay, Michel. *Bibi's birthday surprise*
Ginsburg, Mirra. *Four brave sailors*
Gomi, Taro. *Guess who?*
Greenleaf, Ann. *No room for Sarah*
Grifalconi, Ann. *The toy trumpet*
Gundersheimer, Karen. *Shapes to show*
Hale, Irina. *Chocolate mouse and sugar pig*
  The lost toys
Haus, Felice. *Beep! Beep! I'm a jeep*
Hayashi, Akiko. *Aki and the fox*
Hill, Eric. *Spot's toy box*
Hillert, Margaret. *The birthday car*
Hissey, Jane. *Jolly snow*
  Jolly Tall
  Little Bear lost
  Old Bear
Hoban, Russell. *La corona and the tin frog*
Hollyn, Lynn. *Lynn Hollyn's Christmas toyland*
Hoopes, Lyn Littlefield. *Wing-a-ding*
Howell, Lynn. *Winifred's new bed*
Hughes, Richard. *Gertrude's child*
Hughes, Shirley. *David and dog*
  Dogger
Hutchins, Pat. *Tidy Titch*
Ichikawa, Satomi. *Nora's castle*
  Nora's stars
Inkpen, Mick. *Kipper's toybox*
Johnson, Crockett. *The blue ribbon puppies*
  Ellen's lion
Johnson, Jane. *Sybil and the blue rabbit*
Jonas, Ann. *Now we can go*
Jones, Harold. *There and back again*
Kahn, Joan. *Seesaw*
Kent, Jack. *Piggy Bank Gonzalez*
Kerr, Judith. *Mog and bunny*
Kraus, Robert. *The tree that stayed up until next Christmas*
Kroll, Steven. *The magic rocket*
Leonard, Alain. *Barnaby and the big gorilla*
Leslie, Amanda. *Hidden toys*
Linden, Madelaine Gill. *Under the blanket*
Lindgren, Barbro. *Sam's car*
  Sam's wagon
  The wild baby goes to sea
Lionni, Leo. *Alexander and the wind-up mouse*
Low, Joseph. *Don't drag your feet...*
Lynn, Sara. *Toys*
Lyon, David. *The runaway duck*
McCue, Lisa. *Corduroy's toys*
McCully, Emily Arnold. *The Christmas gift*
McPhail, David. *Mistletoe*
  The party
Manushkin, Fran. *The best toy of all*
Marcin, Marietta. *A zoo in her bed*
Maris, Ron. *Are you there, bear?*
Marshall, James. *The Cut-Ups*

Meggendorfer, Lothar. *The genius of Lothar Meggendorfer*
Miller, Moira. *The proverbial mouse*
Modesitt, Jeanne. *The night call*
Moss, Marissa. *Want to play?*
Murrow, Liza Ketchum. *Good-bye, Sammy*
Newton, Laura P. *William the vehicle king*
Noll, Sally. *Off and counting*
Oliver, Stephen. *Things that go*
Ormerod, Jan. *Messy baby*
Oxenbury, Helen. *Pippo gets lost*
  Playing
  Tom and Pippo and the dog
  Tom and Pippo go shopping
  Tom and Pippo in the garden
  Tom and Pippo on the beach
  Tom and Pippo see the moon
  Tom and Pippo's day
Paterson, Bettina. *My toys*
Peppé, Rodney. *Little circus*
  Little dolls
  Little games
  Little numbers
  Little wheels
Petrie, Catherine. *Joshua James likes trucks*
Pollock, Penny. *Emily's tiger*
Potter, Beatrix. *The tale of two bad mice*
Price, Mathew. *Have you seen my sister?*
The pudgy book of toys, ill. by Julie Durrell
Quinlan, Patricia. *Anna's red sled*
Rabe, Berniece. *Where's Chimpy?*
Raney, Ken. *Stick horse*
Rayner, Mary. *Crocodarling*
Reiser, Lynn. *Any kind of dog*
Roche, P. K. (Patrick K.). *Plaid bear and the rude rabbit gang*
Royston, Angela. *Toys*
Sachar, Louis. *Monkey soup*
Sandburg, Carl (Charles August). *The wedding procession of the rag doll and the broom handle and who was in it*, ill. by Harriet Pincus
Sawicki, Norma Jean. *The little red house*
Schertle, Alice. *Goodnight, Hattie, my dearie, my dove*
Scholey, Arthur. *Baboushka*
Schreier, Joshua. *Luigi's all-night parking lot*
Seuss, Dr. *The king's stilts*
Sherrow, Victoria. *Wilbur waits*
Simons, Traute. *Paulino*
Smith, Raymond Kenneth. *The long dive*
  The long slide
Snoopy on wheels
Spier, Peter. *The toy shop*
Steger, Hans-Ulrich. *Traveling to Tripiti*
Stephenson, Dorothy. *The night it rained toys*
Stevenson, Robert Louis. *Block city*, ill. by Ashley Wolff
Stinson, Kathy. *Teddy Rabbit*
Tabler, Judith. *The new puppy*

Tafuri, Nancy. *In a red house*
Tagore, Rabindranath. *Paper boats*
Thelen, Gerda. *The toy maker*
Titus, Eve. *Anatole and the toyshop*
Tucker, Sian. *My toys*
Tudor, Bethany. *Samuel's tree house*
Tyrrell, Anne. *Elizabeth Jane gets dressed*
Vincent, Gabrielle. *Ernest and Celestine*
Von Königslöw, Andrea Wayne. *That's my baby?*
Wabbes, Marie. *Rose's bath*
Waddell, Martin. *The park in the dark*
Wahl, Jan. *Button eye's orange*
  Jamie's tiger
  The toy circus
Ward, Nick. *Giant*
Weiss, Nicki. *Where does the brown bear go?*
Wells, Rosemary. *Max's bedtime*
  Max's birthday
  Max's toys
Westcott, Nadine Bernard. *Going to bed*
Wild, Margaret. *Let the celebrations begin!*
Williams, Karen Lynn. *Galimoto*
Ziefert, Harriet. *Baby Ben's go-go book*
  Come out, Jessie!
  Good night everyone!

Toys – balloons

Baker, Alan. *Benjamin's balloon*
Barrows, Marjorie Wescott. *Muggins' big balloon*
Bonsall, Crosby Newell. *Mine's the best*
Boon, Emilie. *Belinda's balloon*
Bright, Robert. *Georgie and the runaway balloon*
Brock, Emma Lillian. *Surprise balloon*
Bullock, Kathleen. *Rabbits are coming*
Carrick, Carol. *The highest balloon on the common*
Chase, Catherine. *My balloon*
Coxe, Molly. *Louella and the yellow balloon*
Davies, Kay. *My balloon*
Fenton, Edward. *The big yellow balloon*
Glennon, Karen M. *Miss Eva and the red balloon*
Goodsell, Jane. *Toby's toe*
Gray, Nigel. *A balloon for grandad*
Inkpen, Mick. *The blue balloon*
Mari, Iela. *The magic balloon*
Matthias, Catherine. *Demasidados globos: Too many balloons*
  Too many balloons
Sharmat, Marjorie Weinman. *I don't care*
Watanabe, Yuichi. *Wally the whale who loved balloons*
Willard, Nancy. *The well-mannered balloon*

Toys – balls

Bang, Molly. *Yellow ball*
Espenscheid, Gertrude E. *The oh ball*

Hamberger, John. *The lazy dog*
Holl, Adelaide. *The remarkable egg*
Hooks, William H. *Where's Lulu?*
Kellogg, Steven (Stephen). *The mystery of the magic green ball*
Krahn, Fernando. *The biggest Christmas tree on earth*
Lindgren, Barbro. *Sam's ball*
McClintock, Marshall. *Stop that ball*
McMillan, Bruce. *Beach ball—left, right*
Maley, Anne. *Have you seen my mother?*
Tafuri, Nancy. *The ball bounced*
Yardley, Joanna. *The red ball*

Toys - bears *see* Toys – teddy bears

Toys – blocks

Hutchins, Pat. *Changes, changes*
Mayers, Patrick. *Just one more block*
Winthrop, Elizabeth. *That's mine*
Wynne-Jones, Tim. *Builder of the moon*

Toys – dolls

Ackerman, Karen. *Moveable Mabeline*
Ainsworth, Ruth. *The mysterious Baba and her magic caravan*
Ardizzone, Aingelda. *The night ride*
Ardizzone, Edward. *The little girl and the tiny doll*
Ayer, Jacqueline. *Little Silk*
Ayres, Becky Hickox. *Matreshka*
Bannon, Laura. *Manuela's birthday*
Barber, Antonia. *Satchelmouse and the doll's house*
Bernhard, Josephine Butkowska. *Nine cry-baby dolls*
Blegvad, Lenore. *Rainy day Kate*
Bonners, Susan. *The wooden doll*
Bright, Robert. *The travels of Ching*
Brown, Margaret Wise. *Dr. Squash the doll doctor*
Brown, Ruth. *I don't like it!*
Buffett, Jimmy. *Trouble dolls*
Dodge, Mary Mapes. *Mary Anne*
Dreifus, Miriam W. *Brave Betsy*
Francis, Frank. *Natasha's new doll*
Garelick, May. *Just my size*
Goffstein, M. B. (Marilyn Brooke). *Me and my captain*
  Our prairie home
Goodman, Louise. *Ida's doll*
Greenfield, Eloise. *My doll, Keshia*
Hines, Anna Grossnickle. *Don't worry, I'll find you*
  Keep your old hat
  Maybe a band-aid will help
Hoban, Russell. *The stone doll of Sister Brute*
Huff, Vivian. *Let's make paper dolls*
Jaques, Faith. *Tilly's house*

Tilly's rescue
Jennings, Linda M. *Coppelia*
Johnston, Johanna. *Sugarplum*
Keller, Holly. *Geraldine's blanket*
Kroll, Steven. *The hand-me-down doll*
Kunhardt, Dorothy. *Kitty's new doll*
Lamm, C. Drew. *Anniranni and Mollymishi, the wild-haired doll*
Lenski, Lois. *Debbie and her dolls*
Let's play house
Lexau, Joan M. *The rooftop mystery*
McGinley, Phyllis. *The most wonderful doll in the world*
McKissack, Patricia C. *Nettie Jo's friends*
McMillan, Bruce. *Ghost doll*
Mariana. *The journey of Bangwell Putt*
Maris, Ron. *Hold tight, bear!*
Ormerod, Jan. *Making friends*
Pellowski, Anne. *The nine crying dolls*
Pincus, Harriet. *Minna and Pippin*
Polacco, Patricia. *Babushka's doll*
Politi, Leo. *Rosa*
Pomerantz, Charlotte. *The chalk doll*
Pryor, Ainslie. *The baby blue cat and the smiley worm doll*
The baby blue cat and the whole batch of cookies
Rosenberg, Liz. *The scrap doll*
Sandburg, Carl (Charles August). *The wedding procession of the rag doll and the broom handle and who was in it*, ill. by Harriet Pincus
Schulman, Janet. *The big hello*
The great big dummy
Shecter, Ben. *The stocking child*
Skorpen, Liesel Moak. *Elizabeth*
Smith, Maggie (Margaret C.). *Noly Poly Rabbit Tail and me*
Steig, William. *Yellow and pink*
Tudor, Tasha. *The doll's Christmas*
Udry, Janice May. *Emily's autumn*
Waddell, Martin. *The hidden house*
Wahl, Jan. *The Muffletumps*
The Muffletumps' Christmas party
The Muffletumps' Halloween scare
Wells, Rosemary. *Peabody*
Wilson, Julia. *Becky*
Winthrop, Elizabeth. *Katharine's doll*
Vasilissa the beautiful
Wiseman, Bernard. *Oscar is a mama*
Wright, Dare. *The doll and the kitten*
Edith and Midnight
Edith and Mr. Bear
Edith and the duckling
The lonely doll
The lonely doll learns a lesson
Zemach, Harve. *Mommy, buy me a China doll*
Zolotow, Charlotte (Shapiro). *William's doll*

Toys - hobby horses *see* Toys – rocking horses

Toys - pandas *see* Toys – teddy bears

Toys – rocking horses

Donaldson, Lois. *Karl's wooden horse*
Lindman, Maj. *Snipp, Snapp, Snurr and the magic horse*
Roberts, Thom. *Pirates in the park*
Robertson, Lilian. *Runaway rocking horse*

Toys – soldiers

Andersen, H. C. (Hans Christian). *The steadfast tin soldier*, ill. by Thomas Di Grazia
The steadfast tin soldier, ill. by Paul Galdone
The steadfast tin soldier, ill. by David Jorgensen
The steadfast tin soldier, ill. by Monika Laimgruber
The steadfast tin soldier, ill. by P. J. Lynch
The steadfast tin soldier, ill. by Fred Marcellino
The steadfast tin soldier, ill. by Alain Vaës
Brown, Margaret Wise. *Dr. Squash the doll doctor*
Collington, Peter. *The angel and the soldier boy*
Nicholson, William, Sir. *Clever Bill*
Sowden, Henry. *The grand old Duke of York*

Toys – teddy bears

Alborough, Jez. *Where's my teddy?*
Alexander, Martha G. *I'll protect you from the jungle beasts*
Appiah, Sonia. *Amoko and Efua Bear*
Ardizzone, Aingelda. *The night ride*
Barker, Inga-Lil. *Why teddy bears are brown*
Behrens, June. *The manners book*
Bohdal, Susi. *Bobby the bear*
Boyle, Constance. *The story of little owl*
Breese, Gillian. *The amazing adventures of Teddy Tum Tum*
Brown, Myra Berry. *First night away from home*
Bucknall, Caroline. *One bear all alone*
One bear in the hospital
One bear in the picture
Butler, Dorothy. *My brown bear Barney*
Clarke, Gus. *Eddie and Teddy*
Cooper, Letice Ulpha. *The bear who was too big*
Craft, Ruth. *The winter bear*
Darling, Abigail. *Teddy bears' picnic cookbook*
Davidson, Amanda. *Teddy at the seashore*
Teddy goes outside
Teddy in the garden
Teddy's birthday

Teddy's first Christmas
Davis, Douglas F. *There's an elephant in the garage*
Decker, Dorothy W. *Stripe and the merbear*
Stripe visits New York
Degen, Bruce. *Teddy bear towers*
Douglas, Barbara. *Good as new!*
Douglass, Barbara. *Good as new*
Flora, James. *Sherwood walks home*
The fox went out on a chilly night, ill. by Peter Spier
Freeman, Don. *Beady Bear*
Corduroy
Corduroy's busy street and Corduroy goes to the doctor
Corduroy's party
A pocket for Corduroy
Freeman, Lydia. *Corduroy's day*
Galbraith, Richard. *Reuben runs away*
Gauch, Patricia Lee. *Bravo, Tanya*
Dance, Tanya
Glen, Maggie. *Ruby*
Gretz, Susanna. *Hide-and-seek*
I'm not sleepy
Teddy bears ABC
Teddy bears at the seaside
Teddy bears cure a cold
Teddy bears go shopping
Teddy bears' moving day
Teddy bears 1 - 10
Teddy bears stay indoors
Teddy bears take the train
Teddybears cookbook
Too dark!
Grindley, Sally. *Knock, knock! Who's there?*
Hague, Kathleen. *Alphabears*
Bear huggs
Numbears
Out of the nursery, into the night
Hale, Irina. *Brown bear in a brown chair*
How I found a friend
Hawkins, Colin. *Dip, dip, dip*
One finger, one thumb
Oops-a-Daisy
Where's bear?
Hayes, Geoffrey. *Bear by himself*
Hayes, Sarah. *This is the bear*
This is the bear and the picnic lunch
This is the bear and the scary night
Hines, Anna Grossnickle. *I'll tell you what they say*
Hissey, Jane. *Jolly snow*
Jolly Tall
Little Bear lost
Little Bear's trousers
Old Bear
Hoban, Lillian. *Arthur's honey bear*
Howe, Caroline Walton. *Teddy Bear's bird and beast band*
Ingpen, Robert. *The idle bear*
Inkpen, Mick. *One bear at bedtime*

Threadbear
Joerns, Consuelo. *The forgotten bear*
Kantrowitz, Mildred. *Willy Bear*
Keller, Holly. *A bear for Christmas*
Kelley, True. *Day-care teddy bear*
Kennedy, Jimmy. *The teddy bears' picnic,* ill. by Alexandra Day
The teddy bears' picnic, ill. by Michael Hague
The teddy bears' picnic, ill. by Prue Theobalds
Kočí, Marta. *Sarah's bear*
Lawson, Carol. *Teddy bear, teddy bear*
Le-Tan, Pierre. *Visit to the North Pole*
Lewis, Naomi. *Once upon a rainbow*
Lindgren, Barbro. *Sam's teddy bear*
Lindsay, Elizabeth. *A letter for Maria*
Little, Jean. *Jess was the brave one*
Lundell, Margo. *Teddy bear's birthday*
McCue, Lisa. *Corduroy's party*
Corduroy's toys
MacDonald, Maryann. *Sam's worries*
McLeod, Emilie Warren. *The bear's bicycle*
McPhail, David. *The dream child*
First flight
Mansell, Dom. *My old teddy*
Marcus, Susan. *The missing button adventure*
Maris, Ron. *Are you there, bear?*
Marzollo, Jean. *Jed's junior space patrol*
The teddy bear book
Milne, A. A. (Alan Alexander). *House at Pooh corner [a pop-up book]*
Pooh and some bees
Pooh goes visiting
Pooh's alphabet book
Pooh's counting book
Pooh's quiz book
Winnie-the-Pooh
Mogensen, Jan. *Teddy and the Chinese dragon*
Teddy in the undersea kingdom
Teddy's Christmas gift
When Teddy woke early
Moss, Elaine. *Polar*
Nims, Bonnie Larkin. *Where is the bear?*
Where is the bear at school?
O'Donnell, Peter. *Moonlit journey*
Ormondroyd, Edward. *Theodore*
Theodore's rival
Pearson, Susan. *Baby and the bear*
Phillips, Joan. *Lucky bear*
Pike, Carol. *The nutty queen*
Prince, Pamela. *The secret world of teddy bears*
Ratnett, Michael. *Jenny's bear*
Romanek, Enid Warner. *Teddy*
Siewert, Margaret. *Bear hunt*
Skorpen, Liesel Moak. *Charles*
Steger, Hans-Ulrich. *Traveling to Tripiti*
Thomson, Ruth. *My bear: I can...can you?*
My bear: I like...do you?

Tobias, Tobi. *Moving day*
Waber, Bernard. *Ira sleeps over*
Waddell, Martin. *Sailor Bear*
Wahl, Jan. *Humphrey's bear*
Weston, Martha. *Bea's four bears*
Wilhelm, Hans. *A cool kid—like me!*
Worthington, Phoebe. *Teddy bear baker*
  Teddy bear coalman
  Teddy bear farmer
Wright, Dare. *The doll and the kitten*
  Edith and Midnight
  Edith and Mr. Bear
  Edith and the duckling
  The lonely doll
  The lonely doll learns a lesson
Yektai, Niki. *Hi bears, bye bears*
Young, Ruth. *Golden Bear*
Zalben, Jane Breskin. *A perfect nose for Ralph*

Toys - tin soldiers *see* Toys – soldiers

Toys – trains

Green, Suzanne. *The little choo-choo*
Hindley, Judy. *The little train*
Kroll, Steven. *Toot! Toot!*
McPhail, David. *The train*
Merriam, Eve. *Train leaves the station*

Tractors

Baynton, Martin. *Fifty and the fox*
  Fifty and the great race
  Fifty gets the picture
  Fifty saves his friend
Israel, Marion Louise. *The tractor on the farm*
Laird, Elizabeth. *The day Patch stood guard*
  The day Sidney ran off
  The day the ducks went skating
  The day Veronica was nosy
Rickard, Graham. *Let's look at tractors*
Young, Miriam Burt. *If I drove a tractor*

Trading *see* Activities – trading

Traffic, traffic signs

Arnold, Tedd. *The signmaker's assistant*
Bank Street College of Education. *Green light, go*
Baugh, Dolores M. *Bikes*
Brown, Margaret Wise. *Red light, green light*
Krahn, Fernando. *Mr. Top*
Maestro, Betsy. *Traffic*
Shortall, Leonard W. *One way*
Thayer, Jane. *Andy and the runaway horse*
Yagelski, Robert. *The day the lifting bridge stuck*

Train engineers *see* Careers – railroad engineers

Trains

Ardizzone, Edward. *Nicholas and the fast-moving diesel*
Ayars, James Sterling. *Caboose on the roof*
Aylesworth, Jim. *Country crossing*
Ayres, Pam. *Piggo has a train ride*
Barkan, Joanne. *Boxcar*
  Caboose
  Locomotive
  Passenger car
Barton, Byron. *Trains*
Beim, Jerrold. *Country train*
Bemelmans, Ludwig. *Quito express*
Bontemps, Arna Wendell. *The fast sooner hound*
Brandenberg, Franz. *Everyone ready?*
Broekel, Ray. *Trains*
Bröger, Achim. *Bruno takes a trip*
Brown, Margaret Wise. *Two little trains*
  Whistle for the train
Bunce, William. *Freight trains*
Burningham, John. *Hey! Get off our train*
Burton, Virginia Lee. *Choo choo*
Corney, Estelle. *Pa's top hat*
Crews, Donald. *Freight train*
Cushman, Jerome. *Marvella's hobby*
Ehrlich, Amy. *The everyday train*
Emmett, Fredrick Rowland. *New world for Nellie*
Fleischman, Paul. *Time train*
Gantschev, Ivan. *The Christmas train*
  The train to Grandma's
Gibbons, Gail. *Trains*
Goble, Paul. *Death of the iron horse*
Gramatky, Hardie. *Homer and the circus train*
Greene, Graham. *The little train*
Gretz, Susanna. *Teddy bears take the train*
Hayashi, Akiko. *Aki and the fox*
Hines, Gary. *A ride in the crummy*
Hurd, Edith Thacher. *Caboose*
  Engine, engine number 9
Hurd, Thacher. *Hobo dog*
Kirby, David. *Cows are going to Paris*
Koscielniak, Bruce. *Hector and Prudence—all aboard!*
Kroll, Steven. *Toot! Toot!*
Lenski, Lois. *The little train*
Lyon, George-Ella. *A regular rolling Noah*
McPhail, David. *The train*
Maestro, Betsy. *All aboard overnight*
Magee, Doug. *All aboard ABC*
Marshak, Samuel. *The pup grew up!*
Marshall, Ray. *The train*
Martin, Bill (William Ivan). *Smoky Poky*
Meeks, Esther K. *One is the engine*, ill. by Ernie King
  One is the engine, ill. by Joe Rogers

Munsch, Robert N. *Jonathan cleaned up—then he heard a sound*
Nickl, Peter. *Ra ta ta tam*
Peet, Bill (William Bartlett). *The caboose who got loose*
  Smokey
Pierce, Jack. *The freight train book*
Piper, Watty. *The little engine that could*
Rockwell, Anne F. *Trains*
Rodgers, Frank. *Who's afraid of the ghost train?*
Rosenberg, Liz. *Adelaide and the night train*
Ross, Diana. *The story of the little red engine*
Rounds, Glen. *Casey Jones*
Sasaki, Isao. *Snow*
Sattler, Helen Roney. *Train whistles*
Scarry, Huck. *Huck Scarry's steam train journey*
Shine, Deborah. *The little engine that could pudgy word book*
Siebert, Diane. *Train song*
Slobodkin, Louis. *Clear the track*
Stinson, Kathy. *Teddy Rabbit*
Thayer, Jane. *I like trains*
Thompson, Richard. *Jesse on the night train*
Van Allsburg, Chris. *The polar express*
Weelen, Guy. *The little red train*
Wells, Rosemary. *Don't spill it again, James*
Wetterer, Margaret. *Kate Shelley and the midnight express*
Wondriska, William. *Puff*
Young, Miriam Burt. *If I drove a train*

Trains, toy *see* Toys – trains

Transportation

Ardizzone, Edward. *Nicholas and the fast-moving diesel*
Arnold, Caroline. *How do we travel?*
Baer, Edith. *This is the way we go to school*
Bagwell, Richard. *This is an airport*
Barkan, Joanne. *Boxcar*
  Caboose
  Locomotive
  Passenger car
Barner, Bob. *Elevator escalator book*
Barton, Byron. *Airport*
Baugh, Dolores M. *Trucks and cars to ride*
Billout, Guy. *By camel or by car*
Broekel, Ray. *Trains*
  Trucks
Brown, Richard Eric. *One hundred words about transportation*
Burton, Virginia Lee. *Maybelle, the cable car*
Calmenson, Stephanie. *Zip, whiz, zoom!*
Campbell, Rod. *Look inside! Land, sea, air*
Cars and trucks, ill. by Daisuke Yokoi
Cave, Ron. *Airplanes*
  Automobiles
  Motorcycles

Cleary, Beverly. *Lucky Chuck*
Crews, Donald. *School bus*
  Truck
Emberley, Ed (Edward Randolph). *Cars, boats, and planes*
Gay, Michel. *Little truck*
Gibbons, Gail. *New road!*
Gomi, Taro. *Bus stop*
Gramatky, Hardie. *Sparky*
Hellen, Nancy. *Bus stop*
Hoberman, Mary Ann. *How do I go?*
Ingoglia, Gina. *The big book of real airplanes*
Kimmel, Eric A. *Charlie drives the stage*
Koren, Edward. *Behind the wheel*
Lenski, Lois. *Davy goes places*
  Lois Lenski's big book of Mr. Small
Levinson, Riki. *I go with my family to Grandma's*
McNaught, Harry. *The truck book*
Marston, Hope Irvin. *Big rigs*
Morris, Ann. *On the go*
Munari, Bruno. *The birthday present*
Oliver, Stephen. *Things that go*
Olschewski, Alfred. *The wheel rolls over*
100 words about transportation, ill. by Richard Eric Brown
Oppenheim, Joanne. *Have you seen roads?*
Rey, H. A. (Hans Augusto). *How do you get there?*
Rockwell, Anne F. *Planes*
  Things that go
  Trains
Scarry, Richard. *Richard Scarry's hop aboard! Here we go!*
Stevenson, James. *No need for Monty*
Thayer, Jane. *I like trains*
  Trucks
Willis, Jeanne. *Earth mobiles as explained by Professor Xargle*
Young, Miriam Burt. *If I drove a bus*
  If I drove a car
  If I drove a train
  If I drove a truck
  If I flew a plane
Zaffo, George J. *The big book of real airplanes*
  The giant nursery book of things that go
  The giant nursery book of things that work

Traveling *see* Activities – traveling

Trees

Adler, David A. *Redwoods are the tallest trees in the world*
Adoff, Arnold. *Flamboyan*
Aliki. *Christmas tree memories*
  The story of Johnny Appleseed
Andersen, H. C. (Hans Christian). *The fir tree*, ill. by Stephanie Britt

Ryder, Joanne. *Hello, tree!*
Sato, Satoru. *I wish I had a big, big tree*
Schertle, Alice. *In my treehouse*
Stemp, Robin. *Guy and the flowering plum tree*
Stewart, Sarah. *The money tree*
Thelen, Gerda. *The toy maker*
Thornhill, Jan. *A tree in a forest*
Tresselt, Alvin R. *The dead tree*
 The gift of the tree
 Johnny Maple-Leaf
Tudor, Bethany. *Samuel's tree house*
Udry, Janice May. *A tree is nice*
Watts, Barrie. *Apple tree*
Wong, Herbert H. *Our tree*
Yashima, Tarō. *The village tree*
Young, Ed (Edward). *Up a tree*
Zolotow, Charlotte (Shapiro). *The beautiful Christmas tree*

Trickery *see* Behavior – trickery

Tricks *see* Magic

Trinidad *see* Foreign lands – Trinidad

Triplets

Abolafia, Yossi. *My three uncles*
Brunhoff, Jean de. *Babar and his children*
Lindman, Maj. *Flicka, Ricka, Dicka and a little dog*
 Flicka, Ricka, Dicka and the big red hen
 Flicka, Ricka, Dicka and the new dotted dress
 Flicka, Ricka, Dicka and the three kittens
 Flicka, Ricka, Dicka bake a cake
 Snipp, Snapp, Snurr and the buttered bread
 Snipp, Snapp, Snurr and the magic horse
 Snipp, Snapp, Snurr and the red shoes
 Snipp, Snapp, Snurr and the reindeer
 Snipp, Snapp, Snurr and the seven dogs
 Snipp, Snapp, Snurr and the yellow sled
Pirani, Felix. *Triplets*
Seuling, Barbara. *The triplets*

Trolleys *see* Cable cars, trolleys

Trolls

Aardema, Verna. *Bimwili and the Zimwi*
Asbjørnsen, P. C. (Peter Christen). *The three billy goats Gruff*, ill. by Marcia Brown
 Three billy goats Gruff, ill. by Tom Dunnington
 The three billy goats Gruff, ill. by Paul Galdone
 The three billy goats Gruff, ill. by Janet Stevens
 The three billy goats Gruff, ill. by William Stobbs
Aulaire, Ingri Mortenson d'. *The terrible troll-bird*
Berenstain, Michael. *The troll book*
De Paola, Tomie (Thomas Anthony). *The cat on the Dovrefell*
 Helga's dowry
Hawkes, Kevin. *Then the troll heard the squeak*
Heller, Nicholas. *A troll story*
Hillert, Margaret. *The three goats*
Johnston, Tony. *Mole and Troll trim the tree*
Lagerlöf, Selma. *The changeling*
Le Guin, Ursula K. *A ride on the red mare's back*
Leedy, Loreen. *The potato party and other troll tales*
Lindgren, Astrid. *The tomten*
 The tomten and the fox
Lobel, Anita. *The troll music*
Marshall, Edward. *Troll country*
Martin, Claire. *Boots and the glass mountain*
Mayer, Mercer. *Terrible troll*
Peet, Bill (William Bartlett). *Jethro and Joel were a troll*
Schertle, Alice. *Hob Goblin and the skeleton*
Svendsen, Carol. *Hulda*
Torgersen, Don Arthur. *The girl who tricked the troll*
 The troll who lived in the lake
Tudor, Tasha. *Corgiville fair*
Wahl, Jan. *Peter and the troll baby*
Wittington, Mary K. *Troll games*

Truck drivers *see* Careers – truck drivers

Trucks

Adkins, Jan. *Heavy equipment*
Alexander, Anne (Anna Barbara Cooke). *ABC of cars and trucks*
Barr, Jene. *Fire snorkel number 7*
Barton, Byron. *Trucks*
Baugh, Dolores M. *Trucks and cars to ride*
Broekel, Ray. *Trucks*
Burroway, Janet. *The truck on the track*
Bushey, Jerry. *Building a fire truck*
Cars and trucks, ill. by Daisuke Yokoi
Cartlidge, Michelle. *Teddy trucks*
Crews, Donald. *Truck*
Curious George and the dump truck
Fast rolling fire trucks, ill. by Carolyn Bracken
Fast rolling work trucks, ill. by Alan Singer
Fisher, Leonard Everett. *Pumpers, boilers, hooks and ladders*
Fowler, Richard. *Mr. Little's noisy truck*
Gay, Michel. *Little truck*
Gibbons, Gail. *Trucks*
Gramatky, Hardie. *Hercules*
Greydanus, Rose. *Big red fire engine*

Herman, Gail. *Make way for trucks*
Holl, Adelaide. *The ABC of cars, trucks and machines*
Homme, Bob. *The friendly giant's book of fire engines*
Horenstein, Henry. *Sam goes trucking*
Lyon, David. *The biggest truck*
McNaught, Harry. *The truck book*
McPhail, David. *Ed and me*
Magee, Doug. *Trucks you can count on*
Marston, Hope Irvin. *Big rigs*
Fire trucks
Newton, Laura P. *William the vehicle king*
Peppé, Rodney. *Little wheels*
Petrie, Catherine. *Joshua James likes trucks*
Pomerantz, Charlotte. *How many trucks can a tow truck tow?*
Potter, Tony. *See how it works: trucks*
Quackenbush, Robert M. *City trucks*
Robbins, Ken. *Trucks of every sort*
Rockwell, Anne F. *Fire engines*
Trucks
Royston, Angela. *Diggers and dump trucks*
Scarry, Richard. *The great big car and truck book*
Schulz, Charles M. *Snoopy's facts and fun book about trucks*
Selzer, Meyer. *Here comes the recycling truck!*
Seymour, Peter. *The pop-up book of big trucks*
Siebert, Diane. *Truck song*
Trucks
Trucks, ill. by Art Seiden
Wolf, Sallie. *Peter's trucks*
Wolfe, Robert L. *The truck book*
Young, Miriam Burt. *If I drove a truck*
Zaffo, George J. *The giant nursery book of things that go*
Ziefert, Harriet. *Where's mommy's truck?*

Turkey *see* Foreign lands – Turkey

Turkeys *see* Birds – turkeys

Turtles *see* Reptiles – turtles, tortoises

TV *see* Television

Twilight

Berger, Barbara Helen. *Grandfather Twilight*
Major, Beverly. *Playing sardines*
Udry, Janice May. *The moon jumpers*

Twins

Aliki. *Jack and Jake*
Anholt, Catherine. *Twins, two by two*
Balet, Jan B. *Ned and Ed and the lion*
Brennan, Jan. *Born two-gether*
Brown, Marc Tolon. *Arthur babysits*

Bruna, Dick. *Tilly and Tess*
Cleary, Beverly. *The growing-up feet*
The real hole
Two dog biscuits
Gliori, Debi. *New big sister*
Gordon, Jeffie Ross. *Two badd babies*
Greenberg, Dan. *The bed who ran away from home*
Hoban, Lillian. *Here come raccoons*
Hutchins, Pat. *Which witch is which?*
Impey, Rose. *My mom and our dad*
King-Smith, Dick. *Cuckoobush farm*
Kismaric, Carole. *The rumor of Pavel and Paali*
Lawrence, James. *Binky Brothers and the fearless four*
Binky Brothers, detectives
Leonard, Marcia. *The kitten twins*
McDermott, Gerald. *The magic tree*
McKissack, Patricia C. *Who is who?*
Moore, Lilian. *Little Raccoon and no trouble at all*
Neasi, Barbara J. *Just like me*
Obrist, Jürg. *Bear business*
Perkins, Al. *Don and Donna go to bat*
Rubel, Nicole. *Sam and Violet are twins*
Sam and Violet go camping
Simon, Norma. *How do I feel?*
Steel, Danielle. *Max's new baby*
Stewart, Elizabeth Laing. *The lion twins*
Thompson, Vivian Laubach. *Camp-in-the-yard*
Wagner, Jenny. *Amy's monster*
Wagner, Karen. *Chocolate chip cookies*
Wisniewski, David. *The warrior and the wise man*
Yeoman, John. *The young performing horse*
Yorinks, Arthur. *Oh, brother*

Tyrol *see* Foreign lands – Tyrol

Ukraine *see* Foreign lands – Ukraine

Umbrellas

Biro, Val. *Miranda's umbrella*
Blance, Ellen. *Monster and the magic umbrella*
Bright, Robert. *My red umbrella*
Chesworth, Michael. *Rainy day dream*
Ching. *The baboon's umbrella*
Cole, William. *Aunt Bella's umbrella*
Drescher, Henrik. *The yellow umbrella*
Feczko, Kathy. *Umbrella parade*
Levine, Rhoda. *Harrison loved his umbrella*

Lipkind, William. *Professor Bull's umbrella*
Pinkwater, Daniel Manus. *Roger's umbrella*
Smath, Jerry. *Mr. Digby's bad day*
Yashima, Tarō. *Umbrella*

Uncles *see* Family life – aunts, uncles

Unhappiness *see* Emotions – happiness;
Emotions – sadness

UNICEF

Coatsworth, Elizabeth. *The children come
running*

Unicorns *see* Mythical creatures –
unicorns

Unnoticed *see* Behavior – unnoticed,
unseen

Unseen *see* Behavior – unnoticed, unseen

Unusual format *see* Format, unusual

Up and down *see* Concepts – up and
down

U.S. history

Abisch, Roz. *The Pumpkin Heads*
  Sweet Betsy from Pike
Accorsi, William. *My name is Pocahontas*
Ackerman, Karen. *Araminta's paint box*
  The tin heart
Adler, David A. *A picture book of Abraham
  Lincoln*
  A picture book of Benjamin Franklin
  A picture book of Eleanor Roosevelt
  A picture book of George Washington
  A picture book of John F. Kennedy
  A picture book of Martin Luther King, Jr.
  A picture book of Thomas Jefferson
Aliki. *George and the cherry tree*
  The many lives of Benjamin Franklin
  The story of Johnny Appleseed
  The story of William Penn
  A weed is a flower
Andersen, H. C. (Hans Christian). *The
  tinderbox*, ill. by Barry Moser
Aulaire, Ingri Mortenson d'. *Abraham
  Lincoln*
  Pocahontas
Bangs, Edward. *Yankee Doodle*
Belting, Natalia Maree. *Verity Mullens and
  the Indian*
Benchley, Peter. *Jonathan visits the White
  House*
Bethell, Jean. *Three cheers for Mother Jones!*
Brandt, Betty. *Special delivery*
Bulla, Clyde Robert. *Washington's birthday*
Chenault, Nell. *Parsifal the Poddley*

Cherry, Lynne. *A river ran wild*
Cohen, Caron Lee. *Bronco dogs*
Dalgliesh, Alice. *The Thanksgiving story*
DeLage, Ida. *Pilgrim children on the
  Mayflower*
De Paola, Tomie (Thomas Anthony). *An
  early American Christmas*
Dewey, Ariane. *Laffite, the pirate*
Everett, Gwen. *Li'l Sis and Uncle Willie*
Fischetto, Laura. *All pigs on deck*
Gorsline, Marie. *North American Indians*
Haley, Gail E. *Jack Jouett's ride*
Harvey, Brett. *My prairie year*
Haskins, Jim. *The Statue of Liberty:
  America's proud lady*
Hiser, Berniece T. *The adventure of Charlie
  and his wheat-straw hat*
Holbrook, Stewart. *America's Ethan Allen*
Jakes, John. *Susanna of the Alamo*
Jones, Rebecca C. *The biggest (and best) flag
  that ever flew*
Kellogg, Steven (Stephen). *Johnny Appleseed*
  Pecos Bill
Key, Francis Scott. *The Star-Spangled
  Banner*, ill. by Paul Galdone
  The Star-Spangled Banner, ill. by Peter
  Spier
Kimmel, Eric A. *Charlie drives the stage*
Lawson, Robert. *They were strong and good*
Levinson, Riki. *Watch the stars come out*
Lindbergh, Reeve. *Johnny Appleseed*
Lobel, Arnold. *On the day Peter Stuyvesant
  sailed into town*
Longfellow, Henry Wadsworth. *Paul
  Revere's ride*, ill. by Paul Galdone
  Paul Revere's ride, ill. by Nancy Winslow
  Parker
Lowitz, Sadyebeth. *The pilgrims' party*
Lowrey, Janette Sebring. *Six silver spoons*
Lyndon, Kerry Raines. *A birthday for Blue*
Lyon, George-Ella. *Cecil's story*
McPhail, David. *Farm boy's year*
Maestro, Betsy. *The story of the Statue of
  Liberty*
Maxfield, Christine. *Christmas in Water
  Village*
Monjo, F. N. *The drinking gourd*
  Indian summer
  The one bad thing about father
  Poor Richard in France
Morrow, Barbara. *Edward's portrait*
Moskin, Marietta D. *Lysbet and the fire
  kittens*
Nixon, Joan Lowery. *If you say so, Claude*
  That's the spirit, Claude
  You bet your britches, Claude
Ortiz, Simon. *The people shall continue*
Petersham, Maud. *An American ABC*
Precek, Katharine Wilson. *Penny in the
  road*
Pryor, Bonnie. *The house on Maple Street*

Quackenbush, Robert M. *Clementine*
Pop! goes the weasel and Yankee Doodle
There'll be a hot time in the old town
    tonight
Schackburg, Richard. *Yankee Doodle*
Showers, Paul. *Columbus Day*
Siebert, Diane. *Heartland*
Smith, Barry. *The first voyage of Christopher*
    Columbus
Spier, Peter. *The Erie Canal*
The legend of New Amsterdam
We the people
Szekeres, Cyndy. *Long ago*
Turkle, Brinton. *The adventures of Obadiah*
Obadiah the Bold
Thy friend, Obadiah
Turner, Ann Warren. *Dakota dugout*
Van Leeuwen, Jean. *Going west*
Van Woerkom, Dorothy. *Becky and the bear*
Vaughn, Jenny. *On the moon*
Wetterer, Margaret. *Kate Shelley and the*
    midnight express
Whittier, John Greenleaf. *Barbara Frietchie*
Winter, Jeanette. *Follow the drinking gourd*
Yolen, Jane. *Letting Swift River go*

Vacationing *see* Activities – vacationing

Vacuum cleaners *see* Machines

Valentine's Day *see* Holidays – Valentine's
Day

Values

Mahy, Margaret. *Pillycock's shop*
Schlein, Miriam. *The pile of junk*

Vampires *see* Monsters

Vanity *see* Character traits – vanity

Vatican City *see* Foreign lands – Vatican
City

Venezuela *see* Foreign lands – Venezuela

Veterinarians *see* Careers – veterinarians

Vietnam *see* Foreign lands – Vietnam

Vietnamese-Americans *see* Ethnic groups
in the U.S. – Asian-Americans; Ethnic
groups in the U.S. – Vietnamese-
Americans

Violence, anti-violence

Charters, Janet. *The general*
Duvoisin, Roger Antoine. *The happy hunter*
Fitzhugh, Louise. *Bang, bang, you're dead*
Foreman, Michael. *Moose*
Hader, Berta Hoerner. *Mister Billy's gun*
Leaf, Munro. *The story of Ferdinand the bull*
Lobel, Anita. *Potatoes, potatoes*
Peet, Bill (William Bartlett). *The pinkish,*
    purplish, bluish egg
Sharmat, Marjorie Weinman. *Walter the*
    wolf
Wiesner, William. *Tops*
Wondriska, William. *The tomato patch*

Volcanoes

Branley, Franklyn M. *Volcanoes*
Grifalconi, Ann. *The village of round and*
    square houses
Lewis, Thomas P. *Hill of fire*

Vultures *see* Birds – vultures

Waiters *see* Careers – waiters, waitresses

Waitresses *see* Careers – waiters,
waitresses

Walking *see* Activities – walking

Walruses *see* Animals – walruses

War

Ackerman, Karen. *The tin heart*
When mama retires
Adler, David A. *The number on my*
    grandfather's arm
Ambrus, Victor G. *Brave soldier Janosch*
Aulaire, Ingri Mortenson d'. *Wings for Per*
Baumann, Kurt. *The prince and the lute*
Brunhoff, Laurent de. *Babar's battle*
De Paola, Tomie (Thomas Anthony). *The*
    mysterious giant of Barletta
Dupasquier, Philippe. *Jack at sea*
Eco, Umberto. *The bomb and the general*
Fitzhugh, Louise. *Bang, bang, you're dead*
Foreman, Michael. *War and peas*
Gauch, Patricia Lee. *Once upon a*
    Dinkelsbühl
Goble, Paul. *Death of the iron horse*
Grimm, Wilhelm. *Dear Mili*, ill. by
    Maurice Sendak
Hest, Amy. *The ring and the window seat*

Holbrook, Stewart. *America's Ethan Allen*
Hughes, Peter. *The king who loved candy*
Ikeda, Daisaku. *The cherry tree*
Jones, Rebecca C. *The biggest (and best) flag that ever flew*
Lyon, George-Ella. *Cecil's story*
McAllister, Angela. *The battle of Sir Cob and Sir Filbert*
Mattingley, Christobel. *The angel with a mouth-organ*
Miller, Edward. *Frederick Ferdinand Fox*
Morimoto, Junko. *My Hiroshima*
Norman, Philip Ross. *The carrot war*
Oppenheim, Shulamith Levey. *The lily cupboard*
Phillips, Louis. *The brothers Wrong and Wrong Again*
Rupprecht, Siegfried P. *The tale of the vanishing rainbow*
Seuss, Dr. *The butter battle book*
Stone, Bernard. *The charge of the mouse brigade*
Vigna, Judith. *Nobody wants a nuclear war*
Whittier, John Greenleaf. *Barbara Frietchie*
Wild, Margaret. *Let the celebrations begin!*
Yolen, Jane. *All those secrets of the world*
Ziefert, Harriet. *A new coat for Anna*

Warthogs *see* Animals – warthogs

Washington's Birthday *see* Holidays – Washington's Birthday

Wasps *see* Insects – wasps

Watches *see* Clocks, watches

Water

Dorros, Arthur. *Follow the water from brook to ocean*
Jolliffe, Anne. *Water, wind and wheels*
Koch, Michelle. *World water watch*
Leutscher, Alfred. *Water*
Peters, Lisa Westberg. *Water's way*
Pollock, Penny. *Water is wet*
Russell, Naomi. *The stream*
Schmid, Eleonore. *The water's journey*
Southey, Robert. *The cataract of Lodore*
Wyler, Rose. *Puddles and ponds*
Yolen, Jane. *Letting Swift River go*

Water buffaloes *see* Animals – water buffaloes

Weapons

Bolliger, Max. *The wooden man*
Duvoisin, Roger Antoine. *The happy hunter*
Emberley, Barbara. *Drummer Hoff*
Fitzhugh, Louise. *Bang, bang, you're dead*
Hader, Berta Hoerner. *Mister Billy's gun*

Wondriska, William. *The tomato patch*

Weasels *see* Animals – weasels

Weather

Allington, Richard L. *Autumn*
  Spring
  Summer
  Winter
Ardizzone, Edward. *Tim to the rescue*
Asch, Frank. *Country pie*
Barrett, Judi. *Cloudy with a chance of meatballs*
Baum, Arline. *One bright Monday morning*
Bell, Norman. *Linda's airmail letter*
Bolliger, Max. *The wooden man*
Branley, Franklyn M. *Rain and hail*
Brenner, Barbara A. *The snow parade*
Brown, Margaret Wise. *The little island*
Burgert, Hans-Joachim. *Samulo and the giant*
Davidson, Amanda. *Teddy goes outside*
Dewey, Ariane. *Febold Feboldson*
DeWitt, Lyndia. *What will the weather be?*
Fisher, Aileen Lucia. *I like weather*
Fowler, Allan. *What's the weather today?*
Frye, Dean. *Days of sunshine, days of rain*
Gackenbach, Dick. *Ida Fanfanny*
Gibbons, Gail. *Weather words and what they mean*
Ginsburg, Mirra. *Four brave sailors*
Gould, Deborah. *Camping in the Temple of the Sun*
Greenberg, Barbara. *The bravest babysitter*
Havill, Juanita. *Treasure nap*
Hayden, Lea. *Sunny day—rainy day*
Hill, Eric. *Spot looks at the weather*
A January fog will freeze a hog
Jaynes, Ruth M. *Benny's four hats*
Kirkpatrick, Rena K. *Look at weather*
Lewin, Betsy. *Hip, hippo, hooray!*
McCloskey, Robert. *Time of wonder*
Maestro, Betsy. *Temperature and you*
  Through the year with Harriet
Marshak, Samuel. *The Month-Brothers*
Mollel, Tolowa M. *A promise to the sun*
Palazzo, Janet. *What makes the weather*
Peters, Lisa Westberg. *The sun, the wind and the rain*
  Water's way
Pieńkowski, Jan. *Weather*
Rockwell, Anne F. *Blackout*
Rogers, Paul (Patrick). *What will the weather be like today?*
Schlein, Miriam. *The sun, the wind, the sea and the rain*
Seymour, Peter. *How the weather works*
Sherrow, Victoria. *Wilbur waits*
Tresselt, Alvin R. *Sun up*
  Sun up, ill. by Henri Sorensen
Vance, Eleanor Graham. *Jonathan*

Van Leeuwen, Jean. *Too hot for ice cream*
Vigna, Judith. *Boot weather*
Watts, Bernadette. *Tattercoats*
Zolotow, Charlotte (Shapiro). *The storm book*

Weather – clouds

Ariane. *Small Cloud*
Cummings, Pat. *C.L.O.U.D.S.*
De Paola, Tomie (Thomas Anthony). *The cloud book*
Greene, Carol. *Hi, clouds*
McFall, Gardner. *Jonathan's cloud*
Manushkin, Fran. *Swinging and swinging*
Marol, Jean-Claude. *Vagabul in the clouds*
Ray, Deborah Kogan. *The cloud*
Rayner, Mary. *The rain cloud*
Renberg, Dalia Hardof. *Hello, clouds!*
Ringi, Kjell (Arne Sorensen). *The sun and the cloud*
Shaw, Charles Green. *It looked like spilt milk*
Spier, Peter. *Dreams*
Turkle, Brinton. *The sky dog*
Wandelmaier, Roy. *Clouds*
Wegen, Ron. *Sky dragon*
Williams, Leslie. *A bear in the air*

Weather – cold

Hoban, Lillian. *The sugar snow spring*

Weather – droughts

Aardema, Verna. *Bringing the rain to Kapiti Plain*
Frascino, Edward. *Nanny Noony and the dust queen*
Hamilton, Virginia. *Drylongso*

Weather – floods

Alexander, Ellen. *Llama and the great flood*
Cartwright, Ann. *Norah's ark*
Ipcar, Dahlov. *A flood of creatures*
Lyon, George-Ella. *Come a tide*
McKié, Roy. *Noah's ark*
Morpurgo, Michael. *Jo-Jo the melon donkey*
Tapio, Pat Decker. *The lady who saw the good side of everything*

Weather – fog

Bacheller, Irving. *Lost in the fog*
Fry, Christopher. *The boat that mooed*
Keeping, Charles. *Alfie finds the other side of the world*
Lifton, Betty Jean. *Joji and the fog*
May, Robert Lewis. *Rudolph the red-nosed reindeer*
Morse, Samuel French. *Sea sums*
Munari, Bruno. *The circus in the mist*
Ryder, Joanne. *Fog in the meadow*

Schroder, William. *Pea soup and serpents*
Smith, Theresa Kalab. *The fog is secret*
Tresselt, Alvin R. *Hide and seek fog*

Weather – mist *see* Weather – fog

Weather – rain

Aardema, Verna. *Bringing the rain to Kapiti Plain*
Ariane. *Small Cloud*
Baker, Jill. *Basil of Bywater Hollow*
Bassett, Preston R. *Raindrop stories*
Bergere, Thea. *Paris in the rain with Jean and Jacqueline*
Blegvad, Lenore. *Rainy day Kate*
Bonnici, Peter. *The first rains*
Boon, Emilie. *Peterkin's wet walk*
Bourgeois, Paulette. *Big Sarah's little boots*
Branley, Franklyn M. *Rain and hail*
Bright, Robert. *My red umbrella*
Bullock, Kathleen. *It chanced to rain*
Burningham, John. *Mr. Gumpy's motor car*
Calhoun, Mary. *Euphonia and the flood*
Carlson, Nancy. *What if it never stops raining?*
Carrick, Carol. *Sleep out*
  The washout
Cartwright, Ann. *Norah's ark*
Cazet, Denys. *You make the angels cry*
Charlip, Remy. *Where is everybody?*
Claverie, Jean. *The picnic*
Cole, Sheila. *When the rain stops*
Cole, William. *Aunt Bella's umbrella*
Crary, Elizabeth. *I'm mad*
De Paola, Tomie (Thomas Anthony). *Katie and Kit at the beach*
Dragonwagon, Crescent. *Rainy day together*
Dubanevich, Arlene. *Pig William*
Ferro, Beatriz. *Caught in the rain*
Freeman, Don. *Dandelion*
Garelick, May. *Where does the butterfly go when it rains?*
Gay, Marie-Louise. *Rainy day magic*
Ginsburg, Mirra. *Mushroom in the rain*
Goudey, Alice E. *The good rain*
Greene, Carol. *Rain! Rain!*
Greenfield, Karen R. *Sister Yessa's story*
Hayden, Lea. *Sunny day—rainy day*
Hines, Anna Grossnickle. *Taste the raindrops*
Hoban, Julia. *Amy loves the rain*
Hoban, Russell. *The rain door*
Holl, Adelaide. *The rain puddle*
Hurd, Edith Thacher. *Johnny Lion's rubber boots*
Iwasaki, Chihiro. *Staying home alone on a rainy day*
Kalan, Robert. *Rain*
Keats, Ezra Jack. *A letter to Amy*
Keith, Eros. *Nancy's backyard*
Keller, Holly. *Will it rain?*

Kishida, Eriko. *The hippo boat*
Knutson, Kimberley. *Muddigush*
Krings, Antoon. *Oliver's bicycle*
Kuskin, Karla. *James and the rain*
Kwitz, Mary DeBall. *When it rains*
Lee, Jeanne M. *Toad is the uncle of heaven*
Lloyd, David. *Hello, goodbye*
Lukešová, Milena. *The little girl and the rain*
Marino, Dorothy. *Good-bye thunderstorm*
Martin, Bill (William Ivan). *Listen to the rain*
Murphy, Shirley Rousseau. *Tattie's river journey*
Nakabayashi, Ei. *The rainy day puddle*
Otto, Carolyn. *That sky, that rain*
Prelutsky, Jack. *Rainy rainy Saturday*
Preston, Edna Mitchell. *Pop Corn and Ma Goodness*
Raskin, Ellen. *And it rained*
Ricketts, Michael. *Rain*
Robbins, Ruth. *How the first rainbow was made*
Ryder, Joanne. *A wet and sandy day*
Scheer, Julian. *Rain makes applesauce*
Scheffler, Ursel. *A walk in the rain*
Schlein, Miriam. *The sun, the wind, the sea and the rain*
Seignobosc, Françoise. *The big rain*
Serfozo, Mary. *Rain talk*
Sherman, Nancy. *Gwendolyn and the weathercock*
Shulevitz, Uri. *Rain rain rivers*
Simon, Norma. *The wet world*
Skofield, James. *All wet! All wet!*
Smath, Jerry. *Mr. Digby's bad day*
Soya, Kiyoshi. *A house of leaves*
Spier, Peter. *Peter Spier's rain*
Stanley, Sanna. *The rains are coming*
Tapio, Pat Decker. *The lady who saw the good side of everything*
Taylor, Mark. *Henry the castaway*
Thayer, Mike. *In the middle of the puddle*
Tresselt, Alvin R. *Rain drop splash*
Türk, Hanne. *Rainy day Max*
Velthuijs, Max. *Little Man finds a home*
Vincent, Gabrielle. *Ernest and Celestine's picnic*
Wagner, Jenny. *Aranea*
Wahl, Jan. *Follow me cried Bee*
Wandelmaier, Roy. *Clouds*
Wells, Rosemary. *Don't spill it again, James*
Wyler, Rose. *Raindrops and rainbows*
Yashima, Tarō. *Umbrella*
Zinnemann-Hope, Pam. *Find your coat, Ned*
Zolotow, Charlotte (Shapiro). *The quarreling book*
The storm book

Weather – rainbows

Asch, Frank. *Skyfire*
Craft, Ruth. *The day of the rainbow*
Freeman, Don. *A rainbow of my own*
Haynes, Max. *Sparky's rainbow repair*
Kirkpatrick, Rena K. *Look at rainbow colors*
Kunhardt, Edith. *Red day, green day*
Kwitz, Mary DeBall. *When it rains*
Marino, Dorothy. *Buzzy Bear and the rainbow*
Rupprecht, Siegfried P. *The tale of the vanishing rainbow*
Weston, Martha. *Peony's rainbow*
Williams, Leslie. *A bear in the air*
Wyler, Rose. *Raindrops and rainbows*
Zolotow, Charlotte (Shapiro). *The storm book*

Weather – snow

Bahr, Robert. *Blizzard at the zoo*
Barklem, Jill. *Winter story*
Bartoli, Jennifer. *Snow on bear's nose*
Bauer, Caroline Feller. *Midnight snowman*
Branley, Franklyn M. *Snow is falling*
Brown, Margaret Wise. *The winter noisy book*
Bruna, Dick. *Another story to tell*
Miffy in the snow
Buckley, Helen Elizabeth. *Josie and the snow*
Burningham, John. *Trubloff*
Burton, Virginia Lee. *Katy and the big snow*
Butterworth, Nick. *One snowy night*
Carlson, Nancy. *Take time to relax*
Carlstrom, Nancy White. *The snow speaks*
Chönz, Selina. *The snowstorm*
Claverie, Jean. *Working*
Croll, Carolyn. *The little snowgirl*
Delaney, A. *Monster tracks?*
Delton, Judy. *Brimhall turns detective*
A walk on a snowy night
Dorian, Marguerite. *When the snow is blue*
Funakoshi, Canna. *One evening*
Greene, Carol. *Snow Joe*
Gunther, Louise. *Anna's snow day*
Hader, Berta Hoerner. *The big snow*
Harshman, Marc. *Snow company*
Hidaka, Masako. *Girl from the snow country*
Himmelman, John. *The day-off machine*
Hissey, Jane. *Jolly snow*
Hoban, Julia. *Amy loves the snow*
Hoban, Lillian. *The sugar snow spring*
Hoban, Russell. *Some snow said hello*
Hoff, Syd. *When will it snow?*
Hughes, Shirley. *The snow lady*
Hutchins, H. J. (Hazel J.). *Ben's snow song*
Hutchins, Hazel J. *Norman's snowball*
Iwasaki, Chihiro. *The birthday wish*
Janosch. *Dear snowman*
Joos, Francoise. *The golden snowflake*

Keats, Ezra Jack. *The snowy day*
Keller, Holly. *Geraldine's big snow*
Kovalski, Maryann. *Jingle bells*
Krauss, Ruth. *The happy day*
Kuskin, Karla. *In the flaky frosty morning*
Loretan, Sylvia. *Bob the snowman*
Ludwig, Warren. *Good morning, Granny Rose*
McCully, Emily Arnold. *First snow*
McKié, Roy. *Snow*
McPhail, David. *Snow lion*
Mayper, Monica. *Oh snow*
Parnall, Peter. *Alfalfa Hill*
Raphael, Elaine. *Donkey, it's snowing*
Retan, Walter. *The snowplow that tried to go south*
Rockwell, Anne F. *The first snowfall*
Sasaki, Isao. *Snow*
Sauer, Julia Lina. *Mike's house*
Saunders, Dave. *Snowtime*
Schick, Eleanor. *City in the winter*
Schlein, Miriam. *Deer in the snow*
Schmid, Eleonore. *The water's journey*
Schroeder, Binette. *Tuffa and the snow*
Simmonds, Posy. *Lulu and the flying babies*
Skofield, James. *Snow country*
Steig, William. *Brave Irene*
Tibo, Gilles. *Simon and the snowflakes*
Todd, Kathleen. *Snow*
Tresselt, Alvin R. *White snow, bright snow*
Tudor, Tasha. *Snow before Christmas*
Udry, Janice May. *Mary Jo's grandmother*
Updike, David. *A winter's journey*
Wabbes, Marie. *It's snowing, Little Rabbit*
Watanabe, Shigeo. *Ice cream is falling!*
Watson, Nancy Dingman. *Sugar on snow*
Wheeler, Cindy. *Marmalade's snowy day*
Zion, Gene. *The summer snowman*
Zolotow, Charlotte (Shapiro). *Hold my hand*
Something is going to happen

Weather – storms

Adoff, Arnold. *Make a circle, keep us in Tornado!*
Aldridge, Josephine Haskell. *Fisherman's luck*
Amoss, Berthe. *Old Hannibal and the hurricane*
Anderson, Lena Castell. *Stina*
Anderson, Lonzo. *The day the hurricane happened*
Arvetis, Chris. *Why does it thunder and lightning?*
Bahr, Robert. *Blizzard at the zoo*
Barber, Antonia. *The mousehole cat*
Branley, Franklyn M. *Hurricane watch*
Tornado alert
Burstein, Fred. *Anna's rain*
Butterworth, Nick. *One blowy night*
Chesworth, Michael. *Rainy day dream*
Chönz, Selina. *The snowstorm*

Delamare, David. *The Christmas secret*
Delton, Judy. *A walk on a snowy night*
Dennis, Morgan. *The sea dog*
Faulkner, Matt. *The amazing voyage of Jackie Grace*
Foreman, Michael. *Jack's fantastic voyage*
Gedin, Birgitta. *The little house from the sea*
Harshman, Marc. *Snow company*
Harvey, Brett. *My prairie Christmas*
Keats, Ezra Jack. *Clementina's cactus*
Keller, Holly. *Will it rain?*
Kitamura, Satoshi. *Captain Toby*
Lee, Jeanne M. *Ba-Nam*
Marino, Dorothy. *Good-bye thunderstorm*
Noble, Trinka Hakes. *Apple tree Christmas*
Olson, Arielle North. *The lighthouse keeper's daughter*
Polacco, Patricia. *Thunder cake*
Rettich, Margret. *The voyage of the jolly boat*
Steig, William. *Brave Irene*
Stolz, Mary Slattery. *Storm in the night*
Szilagyi, Mary. *Thunderstorm*
Taylor, Judy. *Sophie and Jack help out*
Van Allsburg, Chris. *The wreck of the Zephyr*
Weisner, David. *Hurricane*
Willard, Nancy. *The voyage of the Ludgate Hill*
Wilson, Sarah. *Beware the dragons!*

Weather – thunder

Arvetis, Chris. *Why does it thunder and lightning?*
Branley, Franklyn M. *Flash, crash, rumble, and roll*
Crowe, Robert L. *Tyler Toad and the thunder*
Marino, Dorothy. *Good-bye thunderstorm*
Novak, Matt. *Rolling*
Polacco, Patricia. *Thunder cake*
Sussman, Susan. *Hippo thunder*
Szilagyi, Mary. *Thunderstorm*

Weather – wind

Ardizzone, Edward. *Tim's last voyage*
Brown, Margaret Wise. *When the wind blew*
Burgess, Thornton. *Old Mother West Wind*
Butterworth, Nick. *One blowy night*
Calhoun, Mary. *Jack and the whoopee wind*
Cartwright, Ann. *The winter hedgehog*
Climo, Shirley. *The match between the winds*
De Posadas Mane, Carmen. *Mister North Wind*
Dorros, Arthur. *Feel the wind*
Ets, Marie Hall. *Gilberto and the wind*
Garrison, Christian. *Little pieces of the west wind*
Greene, Carol. *Please, wind?*
Hamilton, Virginia. *Drylongso*
Hoban, Julia. *Amy loves the wind*

Hutchins, Pat. *The wind blew*
Keats, Ezra Jack. *A letter to Amy*
La Fontaine, Jean de. *The north wind and the sun*
Leemis, Ralph. *Mister Momboo's hat*
Lexau, Joan M. *Who took the farmer's hat?*
Littledale, Freya. *Peter and the north wind*
Lobel, Arnold. *The turnaround wind*
MacDonald, Elizabeth. *The very windy day*
McKay, Louise. *Marny's ride with the wind*
Munsch, Robert N. *Millicent and the wind*
Purdy, Carol. *Iva Dunnit and the big wind*
Rice, Inez. *The March wind*
Saltzberg, Barney. *It must have been the wind*
Schick, Eleanor. *City in the winter*
Schlein, Miriam. *The sun, the wind, the sea and the rain*
Thompson, Brenda. *The winds that blow*
Tresselt, Alvin R. *Follow the wind*
The wind and Peter
Ungerer, Tomi. *The hat*
Uttley, Alison. *Sam Pig and the wind*
Vaughan, Marcia K. *The Sea-Breeze Hotel*
Whiteside, Karen. *Lullaby of the wind*
Widman, Christine. *Housekeeper of the wind*
Yolen, Jane. *The girl who loved the wind*
Zolotow, Charlotte (Shapiro). *When the wind stops*

Weaving *see* Activities – weaving

Weddings

Ambrus, Victor G. *Country wedding*
Ash, Jutta. *Wedding birds*
Balian, Lorna. *A sweetheart for Valentine*
Barklem, Jill. *Summer story*
Beck, Martine. *The wedding of Brown Bear and White Bear*
Caseley, Judith. *My sister Celia*
Claret, Maria. *Melissa Mouse*
Cock Robin. *The courtship, merry marriage, and feast of Cock Robin and Jenny Wren*, ill. by Barbara Cooney
Coombs, Patricia. *Mouse Café*
De Paola, Tomie (Thomas Anthony). *Helga's dowry*
Drescher, Joan. *My mother's getting married*
A frog he would a-wooing go (folk-song). *Froggie went a-courting*, ill. by Chris Conover
Wendy Watson's frog went a-courting
Ganly, Helen. *Jyoti's journey*
Goodall, John S. *Naughty Nancy*
Grimm, Jacob. *The goose girl*, ill. by Sabine Bruntjen
Mrs. Fox's wedding, ill. by Errol Le Cain
Rumpelstiltskin, ill. by Jacqueline Ayer
Rumpelstiltskin, ill. by Donna Diamond
Rumpelstiltskin, ill. by Paul Galdone
Rumpelstiltskin, ill. by Jonathan Langley

Rumpelstiltskin, ill. by Gennady Spirin
Rumpelstiltskin, ill. by John Wallner
Rumpelstiltskin, ill. by Paul O. Zelinsky
Snow White and Rose Red, ill. by Adrienne Adams
Snow White and Rose Red, ill. by John Wallner
Gross, Ruth Belov. *The girl who wouldn't get married*
Heine, Helme. *The pigs' wedding*
Hennessy, B. G. *Jake baked the cake*
Hoban, Lillian. *Mr. Pig and Sonny too*
Hogrogian, Nonny. *Carrot cake*
Hürlimann, Ruth. *The mouse with the daisy hat*
Kimmel, Eric A. *The greatest of all*
Langton, Jane. *The hedgehog boy*
Lewin, Hugh. *Jafta and the wedding*
Mayer, Marianna. *Marcel the pastry chef*
Patterson, José. *Mazal-Tov*
Quin-Harkin, Janet. *Peter Penny's dance*
Ross, Lillian Hammer. *The little old man and his dreams*
Samuels, Vyanne. *Carry go bring come*
Sandburg, Carl (Charles August). *The wedding procession of the rag doll and the broom handle and who was in it*, ill. by Harriet Pincus
Seguin-Fontes, Marthe. *A wedding book*
Simmonds, Posy. *The chocolate wedding*
Smith, Barry. *Minnie and Ginger*
The squire's bride, ill. by Marcia Sewall
Suhl, Yuri. *Simon Boom gives a wedding*
Trivas, Irene. *Emma's Christmas*
Varga, Judy. *Janko's wish*
West, Colin. *I brought my love a tabby cat*
Williams, Barbara. *Whatever happened to Beverly Bigler's birthday?*
Williams, Garth. *The rabbits' wedding*
Wittman, Sally. *The wonderful Mrs. Trumbly*
Young, James. *Everyone loves the moon*

Weekdays *see* Days of the week, months of the year

Weight *see* Concepts – weight

Welders *see* Careers – welders

Werewolves *see* Monsters

Whales *see* Animals – whales

Wheels

Barton, Byron. *Wheels*
Berenstain, Stan. *Bears on wheels*
Myller, Rolf. *Rolling round*
Olschewski, Alfred. *The wheel rolls over*
Snoopy on wheels

Whistling *see* Activities – whistling

Wildebeests *see* Animals – wildebeests

Willfulness *see* Character traits – willfulness

Wind *see* Weather – wind

Windmills
Yeoman, John. *Mouse trouble*

Window cleaners *see* Careers – window cleaners

Winter *see* Seasons – winter

Wishing *see* Behavior – wishing

Witches
Adams, Adrienne. *A Halloween happening*
   A woggle of witches
Adler, David A. *I know I'm a witch*
Alexander, Martha G. *The magic box*
Alexander, Sue. *More Witch, Goblin, and Ghost stories*
   Witch, Goblin and Ghost are back
   Witch, Goblin, and Ghost in the haunted woods
   Witch, Goblin and sometimes Ghost
Andersen, H. C. (Hans Christian). *The tinderbox*, ill. by Warwick Hutton
   The tinderbox, ill. by Barry Moser
Anderson, Robin. *Sinabouda Lily*
Anglund, Joan Walsh. *Nibble nibble mousekin*
Armitage, Ronda. *The bossing of Josie*
Ayres, Becky Hickox. *Matreshka*
Bach, Othello. *Hector McSnector and the mail-order Christmas witch*
   Lilly, Willy and the mail-order witch
Baden, Robert. *And Sunday makes seven*
Balian, Lorna. *Humbug potion*
   Humbug witch
Basile, Giambattista. *Petrosinella*
Benarde, Anita. *The pumpkin smasher*
Bentley, Nancy. *I've got your nose!*
Berridge, Celia. *Grandmother's tales*
Berson, Harold. *Charles and Claudine*
Biro, Val. *Miranda's umbrella*
Bridwell, Norman. *The witch grows up*
   The witch next door
Brown, Marc Tolon. *Spooky riddles*
   Witches four
Buckley, Paul. *Amy Belligera and the fireflies*
Burch, Robert. *The jolly witch*
Calhoun, Mary. *The witch of Hissing Hill*
   The witch who lost her shadow
   The witch's pig
   Wobble the witch cat
Carlson, Nancy. *Witch lady*

Carlson, Natalie Savage. *Spooky and the bad luck raven*
   Spooky and the witch's goat
   Spooky and the wizard's bats
   Spooky night
Christelow, Eileen. *Glenda Feathers casts a spell*
Cole, Babette. *The trouble with mom*
Cole, Joanna. *Bony-legs*
Cooney, Barbara. *Little brother and little sister*
Coville, Bruce. *Sarah and the dragon*
   Sarah's unicorn
Cretien, Paul D. *Sir Henry and the dragon*
Dasent, George W. *East o' the sun, west o' the moon*
Davis, Maggie S. *Rickety witch*
Degen, Bruce. *The little witch and the riddle*
De Gerez, Toni. *Louhi, witch of North Farm*
DeLage, Ida. *Beware! Beware! A witch won't share*
   The old witch and her magic basket
   The old witch and the crows
   The old witch and the dragon
   The old witch and the ghost parade
   The old witch finds a new house
De Paola, Tomie (Thomas Anthony). *Merry Christmas, Strega Nona*
   Strega Nona
   Strega Nona's magic lessons
De Regniers, Beatrice Schenk. *Willy O'Dwyer jumped in the fire*
Devlin, Wende. *Old Black Witch*
   Old Witch and the polka-dot ribbon
   Old Witch rescues Halloween
Embry, Margaret. *The blue-nosed witch*
Flora, James. *Grandpa's ghost stories*
Fox, Mem. *Guess what?*
Francis, Frank. *Natasha's new doll*
Frascino, Edward. *Nanny Noony and the dust queen*
   Nanny Noony and the magic spell
Freeman, Don. *Space witch*
   Tilly Witch
Giannini, Enzo. *Little Parsley*
Ginsburg, Mirra. *Pampalche of the silver teeth*
Gordon, Sharon. *Three little witches*
Greene, Carol. *The thirteen days of Halloween*
Greeson, Janet. *The stingy baker*
Grimm, Jacob. *Hansel and Gretel*, ill. by Adrienne Adams
   Hansel and Gretel, ill. by Anthony Browne
   Hansel and Gretel, ill. by Susan Jeffers
   Hansel and Gretel, ill. by Winslow P. Pels
   Hansel and Gretel, ill. by Conxita Rodriguez
   Hansel and Gretel, ill. by John Wallner

Hansel and Gretel, ill. by Paul O. Zelinsky
Hansel and Gretel, ill. by Lisbeth Zwerger
Jorinda and Joringel, ill. by Adrienne Adams
Jorinda and Joringel, ill. by Jutta Ash
Jorinda and Joringel, ill. by Margot Tomes
Rapunzel, ill. by Jutta Ash
Rapunzel, ill. by Bert Dodson
Rapunzel, ill. by Trina Schart Hyman
Rapunzel, ill. by Kris Waldherr
Rapunzel, ill. by Bernadette Watts
Snow White, ill. by Trina Schart Hyman
Snow White, ill. by Bernadette Watts
Snow White and the seven dwarves, ill. by Chihiro Iwasaki
Guthrie, Donna. *The witch who lives down the hall*
Hamilton, Morse. *Big sisters are bad witches*
Harrison, David Lee. *Little boy soup*
Haugaard, Erik Christian. *Princess Horrid*
Hayes, Geoffrey. *Elroy and the witch's child*
Helldorfer, M. C. (Mary Claire). *The mapmaker's daughter*
Himmelman, John. *Amanda and the magic garden*
Amanda and the witch switch
Hirsh, Marilyn. *The Rabbi and the twenty-nine witches*
Howe, James. *Scared silly*
Hurd, Edith Thacher. *The so-so cat*
Hutton, Warwick. *The nose tree*
Isele, Elizabeth. *The frog princess*
Jeschke, Susan. *Rima and Zeppo*
Johnston, Tony. *The vanishing pumpkin*
The witch's hat
Karlin, Nurit. *The tooth witch*
Keith, Eros. *Bedita's bad day*
Kellogg, Steven (Stephen). *The Christmas witch*
Kimmel, Eric A. *Baba Yaga*
Bearhead
Kroll, Steven. *The candy witch*
Kuskin, Karla. *What did you bring me?*
Langstaff, John M. *The two magicians*
Leichman, Seymour. *The wicked wizard and the wicked witch*
Lexau, Joan M. *The dog food caper*
Lobato, Arcadio. *The greatest treasure*
Lobel, Arnold. *Prince Bertram the bad*
Lodge, Bernard. *Rhyming Nell*
Low, Alice. *The witch who was afraid of witches*
Witch's holiday
McAllister, Angela. *Nesta, the little witch*
MacDonald, George. *The light princess*, ill. by Katie Thamer Treherne
MacLachlan, Patricia. *Moon, stars, frogs and friends*
McLenighan, Valjean. *You can go jump*

Mahy, Margaret. *The boy who was followed home*
The boy with two shadows
Manson, Christopher. *The crab prince*
Manushkin, Fran. *Hocus and Pocus at the circus*
Marshall, James. *Hansel and Gretel*
Massey, Jeanne. *The littlest witch*
Matsutani, Miyoko. *The witch's magic cloth*
Meddaugh, Susan. *The witches' supermarket*
Montresor, Beni. *The witches of Venice*
Moore, Lilian. *See my lovely poison ivy, and other verses about witches, ghosts and things*
Nash, Ogden. *The adventures of Isabel*, ill. by Walter Lorraine
The adventures of Isabel, ill. by James Marshall
Nicoll, Helen. *Meg and Mog*
Meg at sea
Meg on the moon
Meg's eggs
Mog's box
Nolan, Dennis. *Witch Bazooza*
Oram, Hiawyn. *Skittlewonder and the wizard*
Peet, Bill (William Bartlett). *Big bad Bruce*
The Whingdingdilly
Prather, Ray. *The ostrich girl*
Rehnman, Mats. *The clay flute*
Robertson, Joanne. *Sea witches*
Rosner, Ruth. *Nattie witch*
Ross, Tony. *The enchanted pig*
Hansel and Gretel
Schubert, Ingrid. *Little big feet*
Scieszka, Jon. *The frog prince, continued*
Serraillier, Ian. *Suppose you met a witch*
Shaw, Richard. *The kitten in the pumpkin patch*
Shecter, Ben. *The big stew*
Emily, girl witch of New York
Slate, Joseph. *The mean, clean, giant canoe machine*
Smith, Maggie (Margaret C.). *There's a witch under the stairs*
Springstubb, Tricia. *The magic guinea pig*
Steig, William. *Caleb and Kate*
Stevenson, James. *Emma*
Fried feathers for Thanksgiving
Happy Valentine's Day, Emma!
Yuck!
Thompson, Harwood. *The witch's cat*
Utton, Peter. *The witch's hand*
Walker, Barbara K. (Barbara Kerlin). *Teeny-Tiny and the witch-woman*
Walt Disney Productions. *Walt Disney's Snow White and the seven dwarfs*
Watson, Jane Werner. *Which is the witch?*
Weil, Lisl. *The candy egg bunny*
Williams, Jay. *The city witch and the country witch*
Winthrop, Elizabeth. *Vasilissa the beautiful*
Witch poems, ill. by Trina Schart Hyman

Wood, Audrey. *Heckedy Peg*
Zimmer, Dirk. *The trick-or-treat trap*

Wizards

Barber, Antonia. *The enchanter's daughter*
Bradfield, Roger (Jolly Roger). *Giants come in different sizes*
Brenner, Barbara A. *The color wizard*
Carlson, Natalie Savage. *Spooky and the wizard's bats*
De Regniers, Beatrice Schenk. *Picture book theater*
Dines, Glen. *Pitadoe, the color maker*
Fleischman, Sid. *Longbeard the wizard*
Grimm, Jacob. *The donkey prince*, ill. by Barbara Cooney
Haseley, Dennis. *The cave of snores*
Kimmel, Margaret Mary. *Magic in the mist*
Leichman, Seymour. *The wicked wizard and the wicked witch*
Lester, Helen. *The wizard, the fairy and the magic chicken*
Lobel, Arnold. *The great blueness and other predicaments*
McCrea, James. *The story of Olaf*
Madden, Don. *The Wartville wizard*
Mayer, Mercer. *Mrs. Beggs and the wizard*
Nolan, Dennis. *Wizard McBean and his flying machine*
Oksner, Robert M. *The incompetent wizard*
Oram, Hiawyn. *Skittlewonder and the wizard*
Saunders, Susan. *A sniff in time*
Scott, Sally. *The magic horse*
Service, Pamela F. *The wizard of wind and rock*
Snyder, Zilpha Keatley. *The changing maze*
Zijlstra, Tjerk. *Benny and his geese*
Zimmermann, H. Werner (Heinz Werner). *Alphonse knows...a circle is not a Valentine*
Alphonse knows...the colour of spring
Alphonse knows...twelve months make a year
Alphonse knows...zero is not enough

Wolves *see* Animals – wolves

Wombats *see* Animals – wombats

Woodchucks *see* Animals – groundhogs

Woodpeckers *see* Birds – woodpeckers

Woods *see* Forest, woods

Word games *see* Language

Wordless

Alexander, Martha G. *Bobo's dream*
The magic box
The magic hat

The magic picture
Out! Out! Out!
3 magic flip books: The magic hat; The magic box; The magic picture
Anderson, Lena Castell. *Bunny bath*
Bunny box
Bunny fun
Bunny party
Bunny story
Bunny surprise
Anno, Mitsumasa. *Anno's animals*
Anno's Britain
Anno's counting house
Anno's flea market
Anno's Italy
Anno's journey
Anno's peekaboo
Anno's U.S.A.
Dr. Anno's magical midnight circus
Topsy turvies: more pictures to stretch the imagination
Topsy turvies: pictures to stretch the imagination
Arnosky, Jim. *Mouse numbers and letters*
Mouse writing
Mud time and more
Asch, George. *Linda*
Baker, Jeannie. *Window*
Bakken, Harold. *The special string*
Bambi, ill. by Christa Stephan
Banchek, Linda. *Snake in, snake out*
Bang, Molly. *The grey lady and the strawberry snatcher*
Barton, Byron. *Where's Al?*
Baum, Willi. *Birds of a feather*
Blades, Ann. *Fall*
Spring
Summer
Winter
Bonners, Susan. *Just in passing*
Briggs, Raymond. *Building the snowman*
Dressing up
Father Christmas
Father Christmas goes on holiday
The party
The snowman
Walking in the air
Brown, Craig McFarland. *Patchwork farmer*
Bruna, Dick. *Another story to tell*
Bullock, Kathleen. *Rabbits are coming*
Burlson, Joe. *Space colony*
Burton, Marilee Robin. *The elephant's nest*
Butterworth, Nick. *Amanda's butterfly*
Campbell, Rod. *Look inside! All kinds of places*
Look inside! Land, sea, air
Carle, Eric. *Do you want to be my friend?*
I see a song
Carroll, Ruth. *What Whiskers did*
Where's the bunny?
Charlot, Martin. *Sunnyside up*

Chesworth, Michael. *Rainy day dream*
Chwast, Seymour. *Alphabet parade*
Still another alphabet book
City, ill. by Roser Capdevila
Collington, Peter. *The angel and the soldier
boy*
Little pickle
Cousins, Lucy. *Flower in the garden*
Hen on the farm
Kite in the park
Teddy in the house
Crews, Donald. *Truck*
Cristini, Ermanno. *In my garden*
In the woods
Daughtry, Duanne. *What's inside?*
Degen, Bruce. *Aunt Possum and the
pumpkin man*
De Groat, Diane. *Alligator's toothache*
Demarest, Chris L. *Orville's odyssey*
De Paola, Tomie (Thomas Anthony).
Country farm
Flicks
The hunter and the animals
Pancakes for breakfast
Sing, Pierrot, sing
Domestic animals
Drescher, Henrik. *The yellow umbrella*
Dubois, Claude K. *He's my jumbo!*
DuPasquier, Philippe. *The great escape*
I can't sleep
Our house on the hill
Emberley, Ed (Edward Randolph). *Ed
Emberley's big green drawing book*
Euvremer, Teryl. *Sun's up*
Feldman, Barbara. *Stephens' frog*
Feldman, Judy. *The alphabet in nature*
Shapes in nature
Felix, Monique. *The further adventures of
the little mouse trapped in a book*
*The story of a little mouse trapped in a
book*
Florian, Douglas. *The city*
Freeman, Don. *Forever laughter*
Fromm, Lilo. *Muffel and Plums*
Fuchs, Erich. *Journey to the moon*
Fujikawa, Gyo. *Millie's secret*
My favorite thing
Goodall, John S. *The adventures of Paddy
Pork*
The ballooning adventures of Paddy Pork
Creepy castle
An Edwardian Christmas
An Edwardian summer
Jacko
*The midnight adventures of Kelly, Dot and
Esmeralda*
Naughty Nancy
Naughty Nancy goes to school
Paddy goes traveling
Paddy Pork: odd jobs
Paddy Pork's holiday

Paddy to the rescue
Paddy under water
Paddy's evening out
Paddy's new hat
Shrewbettina's birthday
The story of a castle
The story of a farm
The story of a main street
The story of an English village
The surprise picnic
Gorey, Edward (St. John). *The tunnel
calamity*
Greeley, Valerie. *Farm animals*
Field animals
Pets
Zoo animals
Grimm, Jacob. *Hansel and Gretel*, ill. by
Conxita Rodriguez
Little Red Riding Hood, ill. by John S.
Goodall
Sleeping Beauty, ill. by Fina Rifa
The ugly duckling, ill. by Maria Ruis
Hamberger, John. *The lazy dog*
Hartelius, Margaret A. *The chicken's child*
Hauptmann, Tatjana. *A day in the life of
Petronella Pig*
Heller, Linda. *Lily at the table*
Hill, Eric. *At home*
The park
Up there
Hoban, Tana. *Big ones, little ones*
Circles, triangles, and squares
Dig, drill, dump, fill
Is it larger? Is it smaller?
Is it red? Is it yellow? Is it blue?
Is it rough? Is it smooth? Is it shiny?
Look again
Look! Look! Look!
1, 2, 3
Shadows and reflections
Shapes and things
Shapes, shapes, shapes
Take another look
What is it?
Hughes, Shirley. *Up and up*
Hutchins, Pat. *Changes, changes*
Hyman, Trina Schart. *The enchanted forest*
Imershein, Betsy. *Finding red, finding
yellow*
Keats, Ezra Jack. *Clementina's cactus*
Kitten for a day
Psst, doggie
Skates
Kent, Jack. *The egg book*
Kilroy, Sally. *Animal noises*
Kitchen, Bert. *Animal alphabet*
Koontz, Robin Michal. *Dinosaur dream*
Krahn, Fernando. *Amanda and the
mysterious carpet*
April fools
Arthur's adventure in the abandoned house

The biggest Christmas tree on earth
Catch that cat!
The creepy thing
A funny friend from heaven
The great ape
Here comes Alex Pumpernickel!
How Santa Claus had a long and difficult
journey delivering his presents
Little love story
The mystery of the giant footprints
Robot-bot-bot
Sebastian and the mushroom
The secret in the dungeon
Sleep tight, Alex Pumpernickel
Who's seen the scissors?
Lemke, Horst. *Places and faces*
Lewis, Stephen. *Zoo city*
Lilly, Kenneth. *Animals in the country*
Lionni, Leo. *What?*
When?
Where?
Who?
Lisker, Sonia O. *Lost*
Lubach, Peter. *Harry and the singing fish*
McCue, Lisa. *Corduroy's party*
Corduroy's toys
McCully, Emily Arnold. *The Christmas gift*
First snow
New baby
Picnic
School
MacGregor, Marilyn. *Baby takes a trip*
On top
Mari, Iela. *Eat and be eaten*
The magic balloon
Maris, Ron. *Hold tight, bear!*
Marol, Jean-Claude. *Vagabul and his shadow*
Vagabul escapes
Vagabul goes skiing
Vagabul in the clouds
Mayer, Mercer. *Ah-choo*
A boy, a dog, a frog and a friend
A boy, a dog and a frog
Bubble bubble
Frog goes to dinner
Frog on his own
Frog, where are you?
The great cat chase
Hiccup
One frog too many
Oops
Two moral tales
Mogensen, Jan. *The forty-six little men*
My body, ill. by Sue Porter
Nygren, Tord. *The red thread*
Oakley, Graham. *Graham Oakley's magical*
changes
Ogle, Lucille. *I spy with my little eye*
Ormerod, Jan. *Moonlight*
Sunshine
Oxenbury, Helen. *Beach day*

Good night, good morning
Monkey see, monkey do
Mother's helper
The shopping trip
Panek, Dennis. *Catastrophe Cat at the zoo*
Perrault, Charles. *Puss in boots*, retold and
ill. by John S. Goodall
Pitcher, Caroline. *Animals*
Cars and boats
Ponti, Claude. *Adele's album*
Prater, John. *The gift*
Raney, Ken. *Stick horse*
Rappus, Gerhard. *When the sun was shining*
Ringi, Kjell (Arne Sorensen). *The winner*
Roennfeldt, Robert. *A day on the avenue*
Rojankovsky, Feodor. *Animals on the farm*
Saltzberg, Barney. *The yawn*
Sara. *Across town*
The rabbit, the fox, and the wolf
Sasaki, Isao. *Snow*
Schick, Eleanor. *The little school at*
Cottonwood Corners
Making friends
Schories, Pat. *Mouse around*
Schubert, Dieter. *Where's my monkey?*
Selig, Sylvie. *Kangaroo*
Shimin, Symeon. *A special birthday*
Shopping, ill. by Roser Capdevila
Smith, Lane. *Flying Jake*
Spier, Peter. *Dreams*
Noah's ark
Peter Spier's rain
Stobbs, William. *Animal pictures*
Struppi
Sugita, Yutaka. *My friend Little John and me*
Tafuri, Nancy. *Do not disturb*
Junglewalk
Rabbit's morning
Türk, Hanne. *Goodnight Max*
Happy birthday Max
Max packs
Max the artlover
Max versus the cube
Merry Christmas Max
Rainy day Max
Raking leaves with Max
The rope skips Max
Snapshot Max
A surprise for Max
Turkle, Brinton. *Deep in the forest*
Ueno, Noriko. *Elephant buttons*
Ungerer, Tomi. *One, two, where's my shoe?*
Snail, where are you?
Vincent, Gabrielle. *Breakfast time, Ernest*
and Celestine
Ernest and Celestine's patchwork quilt
A visit to a pond
Ward, Lynd. *The silver pony*
Wegen, Ron. *The balloon trip*
Wezel, Peter. *The good bird*
The naughty bird

Wiesner, David. *Free fall*
Winter, Paula. *The bear and the fly*
  Sir Andrew
Wood, A. J. *Look! The ultimate spot-the-difference book*
Wouters, Anne. *This book is for us*
  This book is too small
Young animals in the zoo
Young domestic animals
Young, Ed (Edward). *Up a tree*
Zoo animals, Imported Pubs. 1983

Words *see* Language

Working *see* Activities – working

World

Anno, Mitsumasa. *All in a day*
Bendick, Jeanne. *All around you*
Branley, Franklyn M. *The planets in our solar system*
Brann, Esther. *'Round the world*
Brown, Margaret Wise. *Four fur feet*
Delessert, Etienne. *How the mouse was hit on the head by a stone and so discovered the world*
Domanska, Janina. *What do you see?*
Douglas, Michael. *Round, round world*
Ekker, Ernest A. *What is beyond the hill?*
Goffstein, M. B. (Marilyn Brooke). *School of names*
Johnson, Crockett. *Upside down*
Nesbit, Edith. *The ice dragon*
Peet, Bill (William Bartlett). *Chester the worldly pig*
Quin-Harkin, Janet. *Peter Penny's dance*
Schlein, Miriam. *Herman McGregor's world*
Schneider, Herman. *Follow the sunset*
Snow, Alan. *My first atlas*
Spier, Peter. *People*

Worms *see* Animals – worms

Worrying *see* Behavior – worrying

Wrecking machines *see* Machines

Wrens *see* Birds – wrens

Wrestling *see* Sports – wrestling

Writers *see* Careers – writers

Writing *see* Activities – writing

Writing letters *see* Letters

Yaks *see* Animals – yaks

Yom Kippur *see* Holidays – Yom Kippur

Zaire *see* Foreign lands – Zaire

Zanzibar *see* Foreign lands – Zanzibar

Zebras *see* Animals – zebras

Zodiac

Fisher, Leonard Everett. *Star signs*
Van Woerkom, Dorothy. *The rat, the ox and the zodiac*
Yen, Clara. *Why rat comes first*

Zookeepers *see* Careers – zookeepers

Zoos

Aitken, Amy. *Kate and Mona in the jungle*
Allen, Robert. *The zoo book*
Amery, H. *At the zoo*
  The zoo picture book
Ancona, George. *Handtalk zoo*
Argent, Kerry. *Animal capers*
Arthur, Catherine. *My sister's silent world*
Ashabranner, Brent. *I'm in the zoo, too*
Bahr, Robert. *Blizzard at the zoo*
Barry, Robert E. *Next please*
Baskin, Leonard. *Hosie's zoo*
Bauer, Helen. *Good times in the park*
Belloc, Hilaire. *Jim, who ran away from his nurse, and was eaten by a lion*
Bishop, Bonnie. *Ralph rides away*
Blance, Ellen. *Monster goes to the zoo*
Blue, Rose. *Black, black, beautiful black*
Blumberg, Rhoda. *Jumbo*
Bodsworth, Nan. *Monkey business*
Bolliger, Max. *Sandy at the children's zoo*
Bond, Michael. *Paddington at the zoo*
Boswell, Stephen. *King Gorboduc's fabulous zoo*
Bottner, Barbara. *Zoo song*
Brennan, John. *Zoo day*
Bridges, William. *Lion Island*

Bright, Robert. *Me and the bears*
Brown, Margaret Wise. *The big fur secret*
  Don't frighten the lion
Bruna, Dick. *Miffy at the zoo*
Calmenson, Stephanie. *Where will the animals stay?*
Campbell, Rod. *Dear zoo*
Canning, Kate. *A painted tale*
Carle, Eric. *1, 2, 3 to the zoo*
Carrick, Carol. *Patrick's dinosaurs*
Chalmers, Audrey. *Hundreds and hundreds of pancakes*
Charles, Donald. *Calico Cat at the zoo*
Clark, Emma Chichester. *The story of Horrible Hilda and Henry*
Cohen, Caron Lee. *Pigeon, pigeon*
Colonius, Lillian. *At the zoo*
Curious George visits the zoo
Cutler, Ivor. *The animal house*
Cuyler, Margery. *That's good! That's bad!*
DeLage, Ida. *ABC triplets at the zoo*
Drescher, Henrik. *The yellow umbrella*
Fatio, Louise. *The happy lion*
  The happy lion and the bear
  The happy lion in Africa
  The happy lion roars
  The happy lion's rabbits
  The happy lion's treasure
  Hector and Christina
  The three happy lions
Fay, Hermann. *My zoo*
Flora, James. *Leopold, the see-through crumbpicker*
Florian, Douglas. *At the zoo*
Gibbons, Gail. *Zoo*
Gordon, Shirley. *Grandma zoo*
Graham, Margaret Bloy. *Be nice to spiders*
Greeley, Valerie. *Zoo animals*
Greydanus, Rose. *Animals at the zoo*
Groening, Maggie. *Maggie Simpson's book of animals*
Grosvenor, Donna. *Zoo babies*
Hader, Berta Hoerner. *Lost in the zoo*
Hanlon, Emily. *What if a lion eats me and I fall into a hippopotamus' mud hole?*
Hanna, Jack. *The petting zoo*
Harrison, David Lee. *Detective Bob and the great ape escape*
Hellen, Nancy. *A visit to the zoo*
Henley, Claire. *At the zoo*
Hoban, Tana. *A children's zoo*
Hoff, Syd. *Sammy the seal*
Hopkins, Lee Bennett. *To the zoo*
Howe, James. *The day the teacher went bananas*
Irvine, Georgeanne. *Bo the orangutan*
  Elmer the elephant
  Georgie the giraffe
  Lindi the leopard
  The nursery babies
  Sasha the cheetah

Sydney the koala
Tully the tree kangaroo
Isenberg, Barbara. *The adventures of Albert, the running bear*
Jeram, Anita. *Bill's belly button*
Johnson, Louise. *Malunda*
Kilroy, Sally. *Babies' zoo*
Kishida, Eriko. *The hippo boat*
Knight, Hilary. *Where's Wallace?*
Lewis, Stephen. *Zoo city*
Lilly, Kenneth. *Animals at the zoo*
Lippman, Peter. *New at the zoo*
Lisker, Sonia O. *Lost*
Lobel, Arnold. *A holiday for Mister Muster*
  A zoo for Mister Muster
Löfgren, Ulf. *Alvin the zookeeper*
Loof, Jan. *Uncle Louie's fantastic sea voyage*
McCarthy, Ruth. *Katie and the smallest bear*
McGovern, Ann. *Zoo, where are you?*
Machotka, Hana. *What do you do at a petting zoo?*
Marshall, Janet Perry. *My camera: at the zoo*
Martin, Bill (William Ivan). *Polar bear, polar bear, what do you hear?*
Matthias, Catherine. *Too many balloons*
Meeks, Esther K. *Something new at the zoo*
Miklowitz, Gloria D. *The zoo that moved*
Munari, Bruno. *Bruno Munari's zoo*
Ormerod, Jan. *When we went to the zoo*
Oxenbury, Helen. *Monkey see, monkey do*
Panek, Dennis. *Catastrophe Cat at the zoo*
Parker, Nancy Winslow. *Working frog*
Pieńkowski, Jan. *Zoo*
Propp, James. *Tuscanini*
Ray, Deborah Kogan. *Sunday morning we went to the zoo*
Reitveld, Jane Klatt. *Monkey island*
Rey, H. A. (Hans Augusto). *Curious George takes a job*
  Feed the animals
Rice, Eve. *Sam who never forgets*
Roffey, Maureen. *I spy at the zoo*
Rojankovsky, Feodor. *Animals in the zoo*
Roosevelt, Michelle Chopin. *Zoo animals*
Ross, Christine. *Lily and the bears*
Rowan, James P. *I can be a zoo keeper*
San Diego Zoological Society. *Families*
  A visit to the zoo
Schumacher, Claire. *King of the zoo*
Seuss, Dr. *If I ran the zoo*
Simon, Paul. *At the zoo*
Snyder, Dick. *One day at the zoo*
  Talk to me tiger
Tensen, Ruth M. *Come to the zoo!*
Tester, Sylvia Root. *A visit to the zoo*
Unwin, Pippa. *The great zoo hunt!*
Woodruff, Elvira. *Mrs. McCloskey's monkeys*
Ylla. *Look who's talking*
Young, Miriam Burt. *Please don't feed Horace*
Ziefert, Harriet. *On our way to the zoo*

Bibliographic Guide

Arranged alphabetically by author's name in boldface (or by title, if author is unknown), each entry includes title, illustrator, publisher, publication date, and subjects. Joint authors and their titles appear as short entries, with the main author name (in parentheses after the title) citing where the complete entry will be found. Where only an author and title are given, complete information is listed under the *title* as the main entry. ISBNs are included for entries new to the third and fourth editions.

A is for alphabet by Cathy, Marly and Wendy; ill. by George Suyeoka. Scott, 1968. Subj: ABC books.

Aardema, Verna. *Bimwili and the Zimwi* ill. by Susan Meddaugh. Dial Pr., 1985. ISBN 0-8037-0213-2 Subj: Folk and fairy tales. Foreign lands – Africa. Foreign lands – Zanzibar. Trolls.

Borreguita and the coyote ill. by Petra Mathers. Knopf, 1991. ISBN 0-679-90921-4 Subj: Animals – coyotes. Animals – sheep. Behavior – trickery. Folk and fairy tales. Foreign lands – Mexico.

Bringing the rain to Kapiti Plain: a Nandi tale ill. by Beatriz A. Vidal. Dial, 1981. Subj: Cumulative tales. Folk and fairy tales. Foreign lands – Africa. Poetry, rhyme. Weather – droughts. Weather – rain.

Half-a-ball-of-kenki: an Ashanti tale retold by Verna Aardema; ill. by Diane Stanley. Warne, 1979. Subj: Animals – leopards. Folk and fairy tales. Foreign lands – Africa. Insects – flies.

Ji-nongo-nongo means riddles ill. by Jerry Pinkney. Four Winds Pr., 1978. Subj: Folk and fairy tales. Foreign lands – Africa. Riddles.

Oh, Kojo! How could you! an Ashanti tale ill. by Marc Brown. Dial, 1984. Subj: Folk and fairy tales. Foreign lands – Africa. Humor.

Pedro and the padre ill. by Friso Henstra. Dial, 1991. ISBN 0-8037-0523-9 Subj: Character traits – honesty. Folk and fairy tales. Foreign lands – Mexico.

Princess Gorilla and a new kind of water ill. by Victoria Chess. Dial Pr., 1988. ISBN 0-8037-0413-5 Subj: Animals. Animals – gorillas. Folk and fairy tales. Foreign lands – Africa.

Rabbit makes a monkey of lion ill. by Jerry Pinkney. Dial Pr., 1988. ISBN 0-8037-0297-3 Subj: Animals. Behavior – trickery. Foreign lands – Africa. Jungle.

The riddle of the drum: a tale from Tizapan, Mexico ill. by Tony Chen. Four Winds Pr., 1978. Subj: Cumulative tales. Folk and fairy tales. Foreign lands – Mexico. Poetry, rhyme. Royalty.

Traveling to Tondo ill. by Will Hillenbrand. Knopf, 1988. ISBN 0-679-90081-0 Subj: Activities – traveling. Animals. Folk and fairy tales. Foreign lands – Zaire.

The vingananee and the tree toad: a Liberian tale ill. by Ellen Weiss. Warne, 1983. Subj: Animals. Folk and fairy tales. Foreign lands – Africa. Spiders.

What's so funny, Ketu? a Nuer tale ill. by Marc Brown. Dial, 1982. Subj: Animals. Behavior – secrets. Humor. Reptiles – snakes.

Who's in Rabbit's house? ill. by Leo and Diane Dillon. Dial Pr., 1977. Subj: Animals. Folk and fairy tales. Foreign lands – Africa. Humor. Insects – butterflies, caterpillars.

Why mosquitoes buzz in people's ears: a West African tale ill. by Leo and Diane Dillon. Dial Pr., 1975. Subj: Animals. Caldecott award book. Folk and fairy tales. Foreign lands – Africa. Insects – mosquitoes.

Aarle, Thomas Van. *Don't put your cart before the horse race* ill. by Bob Barner. Houghton, 1980. Subj: Animals – horses. Sports – racing.

ABCDEF... *in English and Spanish* ill. by Robert Tallon. Lion Pr., 1969. Subj: ABC books. Foreign languages.

Abel, Ray. *The new sitter* (Abel, Ruth)

Abel, Ruth. *The new sitter* by Ruth and Ray Abel; ill. by Ray Abel. Oxford Univ. Pr., 1950. Subj: Activities – baby-sitting.

Abercrombie, Barbara. *Charlie Anderson* ill. by Mark Graham. Macmillan, 1990. ISBN 0-689-50486-1 Subj: Animals – cats. Family life. Pets.

Abisch, Roslyn Kroop *see* Abisch, Roz

Abisch, Roz. *The clever turtle* ill. by Boche Kaplan. Prentice-Hall, 1969. Subj: Animals. Folk and fairy tales. Foreign lands – Africa. Reptiles – turtles, tortoises.

Let's find out about butterflies ill. by Boche Kaplan. Subj: Insects – butterflies, caterpillars. Science.

Mai-Ling and the mirror: a Chinese folktale ill. by Boche Kaplan. Prentice-Hall, 1969. Subj: Emotions – envy, jealousy. Folk and fairy tales. Foreign lands – China.

Open your eyes ill. by Boche Kaplan. Parents, 1964. Subj: Concepts – color. Imagination.

The Pumpkin Heads ill. by Boche Kaplan. Prentice-Hall, 1968. Based on an anecdote from general history of Connecticut, by Reverend Samuel Peters Subj: Hair. U.S. history.

Sweet Betsy from Pike by Roz Abisch and Boche Kaplan; ill. by Boche Kaplan. McCall's, 1970. Subj: Character traits – perseverance. Folk and fairy tales. Music. Songs. U.S. history.

'Twas in the moon of wintertime: the first American Christmas carol adapt. by Roz Abisch; ill. by Boche Kaplan. Prentice-Hall, 1969. Subj: Indians of North America. Music.

Abolafia, Yossi. *A fish for Mrs. Gardenia* ill. by author. Greenwillow, 1988. ISBN 0-688-07468-5 Subj: Activities – cooking. Behavior – losing things.

Fox tale ill. by author. Greenwillow, 1991. ISBN 0-688-09542-9 Subj: Animals. Animals – foxes. Behavior – trickery.

My three uncles ill. by author. Greenwillow, 1984. ISBN 0-688-04025-X Subj: Character traits – individuality. Family life – aunts, uncles. Triplets.

Yanosh's Island ill. by author. Greenwillow, 1987. ISBN 0-688-06817-0 Subj: Activities – flying. Behavior – seeking better things. Islands. Toys.

Abrons, Mary. *For Alice a palace* ill. by Gertrude Barrer-Russell. W. R. Scott, 1966. Subj: ABC books. Birthdays. Poetry, rhyme. Royalty.

Accorsi, William. *My name is Pocahontas* ill. by author. Holiday, 1992. ISBN 0-8234-0932-5 Subj: Indians of North America. U.S. history.

Short short short stories ill. by author. Greenwillow, 1991. ISBN 0-688-10181-X Subj: Activities. Humor.

Ackerman, Karen. *Araminta's paint box* ill. by Betsy Lewin. Macmillan, 1990. ISBN 0-689-31462-0 Subj: Behavior – losing things. U.S. history.

The banshee ill. by David Ray. Putnam, 1990. ISBN 0-399-21924-2 Subj: Night. Poetry, rhyme.

Flannery Row ill. by Karen Ann Weinhaus. Little, 1986. ISBN 0-87113-054-8 Subj: ABC books. Names. Poetry, rhyme.

I know a place ill. by Deborah Kogan Ray. Houghton, 1992. ISBN 0-395-53932-3 Subj: Family life. Houses.

Just like Max ill. by George Schmidt. Knopf, 1990. ISBN 0-394-90176-2 Subj: Careers – tailors. Family life. Old age.

Moveable Mabeline ill. by Linda Allen. Putnam, 1990. ISBN 0-399-21580-8 Subj: Family life – sisters. Toys – dolls.

Song and dance man ill. by Stephen Gammell. Knopf, 1988. ISBN 0-394-89330-1 Subj: Activities – dancing. Caldecott award book. Family life – grandfathers.

The tin heart ill. by Michael Hays. Macmillan, 1990. ISBN 0-689-31461-2 Subj: U.S. history. War.

When mama retires ill. by Alexa Grace. Knopf, 1992. ISBN 0-679-90289-9 Subj: Activities – working. Family life – mothers. War.

Ackley, Edith Flack. *Please* ill. by Telka Ackley. Stokes, 1941. Subj: Etiquette.

Thank you ill. by Telka Ackley. Stokes, 1942. Subj: Etiquette.

Ada, Alma F. *The gold coin* ill. by Neil Waldman. Macmillan, 1991. ISBN 0-689-31633-X Subj: Behavior – stealing. Circular tales. Crime. Cumulative tales. Foreign lands – Central America.

Adam, Barbara. *The big big box* ill. by author. Doubleday, 1960. Subj: Activities – playing. Animals – cats. Imagination.

Adams, Adrienne. *The Christmas party* ill. by author. Scribner's, 1978. Subj: Animals – rabbits. Holidays – Christmas. Parties.

The Easter egg artists ill. by author. Scribner's, 1976. Subj: Activities – painting. Activities – vacationing. Animals – rabbits. Holidays – Easter.

The great Valentine's Day balloon race ill. by author. Scribner's, 1980. Subj: Activities – ballooning. Animals – rabbits. Careers – artists. Holidays – Valentine's Day. Sports – racing.

A Halloween happening ill. by author. Scribner's, 1981. Subj: Holidays – Halloween. Parties. Witches.

Two hundred rabbits (Anderson, Lonzo)

A woggle of witches ill. by author. Scribner's, 1971. Subj: Holidays – Halloween. Witches.

Adams, Pam. *There was an old lady who swallowed a fly* ill. by author. Child's Play-International, 1990. ISBN 0-85953-021-3 Subj: Cumulative tales. Folk and fairy tales. Foreign lands – Canada. Format, unusual. Humor. Songs.

This old man ill. by author. Child's Play-International, 1990. ISBN 0-85953-026-4 Subj: Counting, numbers. Elves and little people. Farms. Format, unusual. Songs.

Adams, Richard (Richard Newbold). *The tyger voyage* ill. by Nicola Bayley. Knopf, 1976. Subj: Animals – tigers. Humor. Poetry, rhyme.

Adamson, Gareth. *Old man up a tree* ill. by author. Abelard-Schuman, 1963. Subj: Character traits – curiosity. Crime. Humor.

Adamson, Joy. *Elsa* photos. by author. Pantheon, 1961. Subj: Animals – lions. Foreign lands – Africa.

Elsa and her cubs photos. by author. Harcourt, 1965. Subj: Animals – lions. Foreign lands – Africa.

Pippa the cheetah and her cubs photos. by author. Harcourt, 1971. Subj: Animals – cheetahs. Foreign lands – Africa.

Addy, Sharon Hart. *A visit with great-grandma* ill. by author. Albert Whitman, 1988. ISBN 0-8075-8497-5 Subj: Family life – grandmothers.

Adelberg, Doris *see* Orgel, Doris

Adelborg, Ottilia. *Clean Peter and the children of Grubbylea* tr. by Ada Wallas; ill. by author. Platt, 1968. Subj: Character traits – cleanliness. Poetry, rhyme.

Adelson, Leone. *All ready for school* ill. by Kathleen Elgin. McKay, 1957. Subj: School. Seasons – fall.

All ready for summer ill. by Kathleen Elgin. McKay, 1955. Subj: Seasons – summer.

All ready for winter ill. by Kathleen Elgin. McKay, 1952. Subj: Seasons – winter.

Please pass the grass ill. by Roger Antoine Duvoisin. McKay, 1960. Subj: Insects. Plants. Poetry, rhyme. Spiders.

Who blew that whistle? ill. by Oscar Fabrès. W. R. Scott, 1946. Subj: Careers – police officers. Character traits – helpfulness.

Adkins, Jan. *Heavy equipment* ill. by author. Scribner's, 1980. Subj: Machines. Trucks.

Adler, David A. *Base five* ill. by Larry Ross. Crowell, 1975. Subj: Counting, numbers.

Bunny rabbit rebus ill. by Madelaine Gill Linden. Crowell, 1983. Subj: Animals – rabbits. Food. Rebuses.

The carsick zebra and other riddles ill. by Tomie de Paola. Holiday, 1983. Subj: Animals. Riddles.

The children of Chelm ill. by Arthur Friedman. Bonium Books, 1980. Subj: Foreign lands – Poland. Humor. Jewish culture. Problem solving.

The children's book of Jewish holidays ill. by David Sears. Mesorah, 1987. ISBN 0-89906-810-3 Subj: Holidays. Jewish culture.

The house on the roof: a Sukkot story ill. by Marilyn Hirsh. Bonim, 1976. Subj: Houses. Jewish culture.

I know I'm a witch ill. by Suçie Stevenson. Holt, 1988. ISBN 0-8050-0427-0 Subj: Imagination. Witches.

A little at a time ill. by author. Random House, 1976. Subj: Character traits – questioning. Family life – grandfathers.

The number on my grandfather's arm ill. by Rose Eichenbaum. U A H C, 1987. ISBN 0-8074-0328-8 Subj: Jewish culture. War.

A picture book of Abraham Lincoln ill. by John and Alexandra Wallner. Holiday, 1989. ISBN 0-8234-0731-4 Subj: U.S. history.

A picture book of Benjamin Franklin ill. by John and Alexandra Wallner. Holiday, 1990. ISBN 0-8234-0792-6 Subj: U.S. history.

A picture book of Eleanor Roosevelt ill. by Robert Casilla. Holiday, 1991. ISBN 0-8234-0856-6 Subj: U.S. history.

A picture book of George Washington ill. by John and Alexandra Wallner. Holiday. 1989. ISBN 0-8234-0732-2 Subj: U.S. history.

A picture book of Hanukkah ill. by Linda Heller. Holiday, 1982. Subj: Holidays – Hanukkah. Jewish culture. Religion.

A picture book of Helen Keller ill. by John and Alexandra Wallner. Holiday, 1990. ISBN 0-8234-0818-3 Subj: Character traits – persistence. Handicaps.

A picture book of Israel ill. with photos. Holiday, 1984. Subj: Foreign lands – Israel. Jewish culture. Religion.

A picture book of Jewish holidays ill. by Linda Heller. Holiday, 1981. Subj: Holidays. Holidays – Hanukkah. Holidays – Passover. Jewish culture.

A picture book of John F. Kennedy ill. by Robert Casilla. Holiday, 1991. ISBN 0-8234-0884-1 Subj: U.S. history.

A picture book of Martin Luther King, Jr. ill. by Robert Casilla. Holiday, 1989. ISBN 0-8234-0770-5 Subj: Ethnic groups in the U.S. – Afro-Americans. U.S. history.

A picture book of Passover ill. by Linda Heller. Holiday, 1982. Subj: Holidays – Passover. Jewish culture.

A picture book of Thomas Jefferson ill. by John and Alexandra Wallner. Holiday, 1990. ISBN 0-8234-0791-8 Subj: U.S. history.

Redwoods are the tallest trees in the world ill. by Kazue Mizumura. Crowell, 1978. Subj: Forest, woods. Science. Trees.

3D, 2D, 1D ill. by Harvey Weiss. Crowell, 1975. Subj: Concepts – measurement. Concepts – perspective. Concepts – shape.

You think it's fun to be a clown! ill. by Ray Cruz. Doubleday, 1980. Subj: Circus. Clowns, jesters. Poetry, rhyme.

Adler, Irene *see* Storr, Catherine (Cole)

Adoff, Arnold. *Big sister tells me that I'm black* ill. by Lorenzo Lynch. Holt, 1976. Subj: Ethnic groups in the U.S. – Afro-Americans. Family life. Poetry, rhyme.

Birds ill. by Troy Howell. Lippincott, 1982. Subj: Birds. Poetry, rhyme.

Black is brown is tan ill. by Emily Arnold Mc-Cully. Harper, 1973. Subj: Family life. Marriage, interracial. Poetry, rhyme.

The cabbages are chasing the rabbits ill. by Janet Stevens. Harcourt, 1985. ISBN 0-15-213875-7 Subj: Cumulative tales. Poetry, rhyme.

Flamboyan ill. by Karen Barbour. Harcourt, 1988. ISBN 0-15-228404-4 Subj: Activities – flying. Dreams. Islands. Trees.

Greens ill. by Betsy Lewin. Lothrop, 1988. ISBN 0-688-04277-5 Subj: Concepts – color. Poetry, rhyme.

Hard to be six ill. by Cheryl Hanna. Lothrop, 1990. ISBN 0-688-09579-8 Subj: Family life – sisters. Poetry, rhyme. Sibling rivalry.

In for winter, out for spring ill. by Jerry Pinkney. Harcourt, 1991. ISBN 0-15-238637-8 Subj: Ethnic groups in the U.S. – Afro-Americans. Family life. Poetry, rhyme. Seasons.

Ma nDa La ill. by Emily Arnold McCully. Harper, 1971. Subj: Family life. Foreign lands – Africa.

Make a circle, keep us in: poems for a good day ill. by Ronald Himler. Delacorte Pr., 1975. Subj: Family life. Night. Poetry, rhyme. Weather – storms.

Tornado! poems ill. by Ronald Himler. Delacorte Pr., 1977. Subj: Poetry, rhyme. Weather – storms.

Where wild Willie? ill. by Emily Arnold McCully. Harper, 1978. Subj: Behavior – running away. City. Ethnic groups in the U.S. – Afro-Americans. Poetry, rhyme.

Adorjan, Carol. *I can! Can you?* ill. by Miriam Nerlove. Rev. ed. Albert Whitman, 1990. Orignal title: Someone I know ISBN 0-8075-3491-9 Subj: Activities – playing. Family life – sisters. Poetry, rhyme.

Adshead, Gladys L. *Brownies—hush!* ill. by Elizabeth Orton Jones. Oxford Univ. Pr., 1938. Subj: Character traits – helpfulness. Elves and little people. Folk and fairy tales.

Brownies—it's Christmas ill. by Velma Ilsley. Oxford Univ. Pr., 1955. Subj: Elves and little people. Holidays – Christmas.

Brownies—they're moving ill. by Richard Lebenson. Walck, 1970. Subj: Character traits – helpfulness. Elves and little people. Moving.

Æsop. *Æsop's fables* sel. and ill. by Gaynor Chapman. Atheneum, 1972. Subj: Folk and fairy tales.

Æsop's fables: a pull-the-tab-pop-up-book ill. by Claire Littlejohn. Dial Pr., 1988. ISBN 0-8037-0487-9 Subj: Folk and fairy tales. Format, unusual – toy and movable books.

Æsop's fables retold by Carol Watson; ill. by Nick Price. Usborne, 1982. Subj: Folk and fairy tales.

Æsop's fables ill. by Lisbeth Zwerger. Picture Book Studio, 1991. ISBN 0-88708-108-8 Subj: Folk and fairy tales.

Androcles and the lion adapt. and ill. by Janet Stevens. Holiday, 1989. ISBN 0-8234-0768-3 Subj: Animals – lions. Character traits – helpfulness. Character traits – kindness to animals. Folk and fairy tales. Foreign lands – Italy. Religion.

Androcles and the lion ill. by Janusz Grabianski. Watts, 1970. Subj: Animals – lions. Character traits – helpfulness. Character traits – kindness to animals. Folk and fairy tales. Foreign lands – Italy. Religion.

Androcles and the lion: and other Æsop fables adapted by Tom Paxton; ill. by Robert Rayevsky. Morrow, 1991. ISBN 0-688-09683-2 Subj: Folk and fairy tales. Foreign lands – Italy. Poetry, rhyme.

Anno's Æsop (Anno, Mitsumasa)

The ant and the dove retold by Mary Lewis Wang; ill. by Ching. Children's Pr., 1989. ISBN 0-516-02367-5 Subj: Birds – doves. Character traits – helpfulness. Folk and fairy tales. Friendship. Insects – ants.

Belling the cat and other Æsop fables (Paxton, Tom)

The best of Æsop's fables retold by Margaret Clark; ill. by Charlotte Voake. Little, 1990. ISBN 0-316-14499-1 Subj: Folk and fairy tales.

The country mouse and the city mouse ill. by Laura Lydecker. Knopf, 1987. ISBN 0-394-99027-7 Subj: Animals – mice. Folk and fairy tales.

Doctor Coyote (Bierhorst, John)

The donkey ride (Showalter, Jean B.)

The fables of Æsop ed. by Ruth Spriggs; ill. by Frank Baber. Rand McNally, 1975. Subj: Folk and fairy tales.

The hare and the frogs adapt. and ill. by William Stobbs. Merrimack, 1979. Subj: Animals – rabbits. Folk and fairy tales. Frogs and toads.

The hare and the tortoise ill. by Paul Galdone. Whittlesey House, 1962. Subj: Animals – rabbits. Folk and fairy tales. Reptiles – turtles, tortoises. Sports – racing.

The hare and the tortoise adapt. and ill. by Gerald Rose. Macmillan, 1988. ISBN 0-689-71197-2 Subj: Animals – rabbits. Folk and fairy tales. Reptiles – turtles, tortoises. Sports – racing.

The hare and the tortoise adapt. by Caroline Castle; ill. by Peter Weevers. Dial Pr., 1985. ISBN 0-8037-0138-1 Subj: Animals – rabbits. Folk and fairy tales. Reptiles – turtles, tortoises. Sports – racing.

The lion and the mouse adapt. and ill. by Gerald Rose. Macmillan, 1988. ISBN 0-689-71196-4 Subj: Animals – lions. Animals – mice. Character traits – helpfulness. Folk and fairy tales.

The lion and the mouse: an Æsop fable ill. by Ed Young. Doubleday, 1980. Subj: Animals – lions. Animals – mice. Character traits – helpfulness. Folk and fairy tales.

The miller, his son and their donkey ill. by Roger Antoine Duvoisin. McGraw-Hill, 1962. Subj: Animals – donkeys. Character traits – perseverance. Humor. Folk and fairy tales.

The miller, his son and their donkey ill. by Eugen Sopko. Holt, 1985. ISBN 0-8050-0475-0 Subj: Animals – donkeys. Character traits – perseverance. Folk and fairy tales.

Once in a wood: ten tales from Æsop adapt. and ill. by Eve Rice. Greenwillow, 1980. Subj: Folk and fairy tales. Poetry, rhyme.

The raven and the fox adapt. and ill. by Gerald Rose. Macmillan, 1988. ISBN 0-689-71194-8 Subj: Animals – foxes. Birds – ravens. Folk and fairy tales.

Seven fables from Æsop retold and ill. by Robert W. Alley. Dodd, 1986. ISBN 0-396-08820-1 Subj: Animals. Folk and fairy tales.

Tales from Æsop retold and ill. by Harold Jones. Watts, 1982. Subj: Folk and fairy tales.

Three fox fables ill. by Paul Galdone. Seabury Pr., 1971. Subj: Animals – foxes. Behavior – trickery. Character traits – flattery. Folk and fairy tales.

The tortoise and the hare: an Æsop fable adapt. and ill. by Janet Stevens. Holiday, 1984. ISBN 0-8234-0510-9 Subj: Animals – rabbits. Folk and fairy tales. Reptiles – turtles, tortoises. Sports – racing.

The town mouse and the country mouse ill. by Paul Galdone. McGraw-Hill, 1971. Subj: Animals – mice. Folk and fairy tales.

The town mouse and the country mouse adapt. and ill. by Janet Stevens. Holiday, 1987. ISBN 0-8234-0633-4 Subj: Animals – mice. Folk and fairy tales.

The town mouse and the country mouse ill. by Lorinda Bryan Cauley. Putnam's, 1984. Subj: Animals – mice. Folk and fairy tales.

The town mouse and the country mouse ill. by Tom Garcia. Troll Assoc., 1979. Subj: Animals – mice. Folk and fairy tales.

Twelve tales from Æsop (Carle, Eric)

Wolf! Wolf! adapt. and ill. by Gerald Rose. Macmillan, 1988. ISBN 0-689-71195-6 Subj: Behavior – lying. Behavior – trickery. Folk and fairy tales.

Afanas'ev, Aleksandr N. *Russian folk tales* tr. by Robert Chandler; ill. by Ivan I. Bilibin. Random House, 1980. Subj: Folk and fairy tales. Foreign lands – Russia.

Salt adapt. by Jane Langton; tr. by Alice Plume; ill. by Ilse Plume. Walt Disney, 1992. ISBN 1-56282-179-2 Subj: Behavior – greed. Family life – brothers. Folk and fairy tales. Foreign lands – Russia. Royalty – princesses.

Agard, John. *Dig away two-hole Tim* ill. by Jennifer Northway. Bodley Head, 1982. Subj: Behavior – misbehavior. Foreign lands – Guyana.

Agee, Joel. *The crow in the snow and other bedtime stories* (Moser, Erwin)

Agee, Jon. *Ellsworth* ill. by author. Pantheon, 1983. Subj: Activities – playing. Animals – dogs. Imagination.

The incredible painting of Felix Clousseau ill. by author. Farrar, 1988. ISBN 0-374-33633-4 Subj: Activities – painting. Art. Imagination.

Agell, Charlotte. *The sailor's book* ill. by author. Firefly, 1991. ISBN 0-920668-90-9 Subj: Boats, ships. Dragons. Sea and seashore.

Agostinelli, Maria Enrica. *I know something you don't know* ill. by author. Watts, 1970. Translation of Ich weiss etwas, was du nicht weisst Subj: Games. Participation.

On wings of love: the United Nations declaration of the rights of the child ill. by author. Collins-World, 1979. Subj: Birds – doves. Emotions – love.

Ahlberg, Allan. *The baby's catalogue* (Ahlberg, Janet)

The black cat ill. by Andre Amstutz. Greenwillow, 1990. ISBN 0-688-09904-1 Subj: Anatomy – skeletons. Animals – cats.

Burglar Bill (Ahlberg, Janet)

The Cinderella show by Allan and Janet Ahlberg; ill. by authors. Viking, 1987. ISBN 0-670-81037-1 Subj: Folk and fairy tales. Holidays – Christmas. School. Theater.

Cops and robbers ill. by Janet Ahlberg. Greenwillow, 1979. Subj: Careers – police officers. Crime. Foreign lands – England. Holidays – Christmas. Poetry, rhyme.

Dinosaur dreams ill. by Andre Amstutz. Greenwillow, 1991. ISBN 0-688-09956-4 Subj: Anatomy – skeletons. Dinosaurs. Dreams.

Each peach pear plum (Ahlberg, Janet)

Funnybones (Ahlberg, Janet)

Jeremiah in the dark wood (Ahlberg, Janet)

The jolly Christmas postman (Ahlberg, Janet)

The jolly postman (Ahlberg, Janet)

The little worm book (Ahlberg, Janet)

Mystery tour ill. by Andre Amstutz. Greenwillow, 1991. ISBN 0-688-09958-0 Subj: Anatomy – skeletons. Behavior – losing things. Humor. Night.

Peek-a-boo! (Ahlberg, Janet)

The pet shop ill. by Andre Amstutz. Greenwillow, 1990. ISBN 0-688-09906-8 Subj: Anatomy – skeletons. Pets.

Starting school (Ahlberg, Janet)

Ahlberg, Janet. *The baby's catalogue* by Janet and Allan Ahlberg; ill. by authors. Little, 1983. Subj: Babies. Family life.

Burglar Bill by Janet and Allan Ahlberg; ill. by authors. Greenwillow, 1977. Subj: Crime.

The Cinderella show (Ahlberg, Allan)

Each peach pear plum: an "I spy" story by Janet and Allan Ahlberg; ill. by authors. Viking, 1978. Subj: Games. Poetry, rhyme.

Funnybones by Janet and Allan Ahlberg; ill. by authors. Greenwillow, 1981. Subj: Activities – playing. Ghosts. Night.

Jeremiah in the dark wood by Janet and Allan Ahlberg; ill. by Janet Ahlberg. Viking, 1987. ISBN 0-670-40637-6 Subj: Behavior – stealing. Forest, woods. Mythical creatures.

The jolly Christmas postman by Janet and Allan Ahlberg; ill. by authors. Little, 1991. ISBN 0-316-02033-8 Subj: Careers – mail carriers. Format, unusual. Holidays – Christmas. Nursery rhymes. Poetry, rhyme.

The jolly postman by Janet and Allan Ahlberg; ill. by authors. Little, 1986. ISBN 0-316-02036-2 Subj: Careers – mail carriers.

The little worm book by Janet and Allan Ahlberg; ill. by authors. Viking, 1980. Subj: Animals – worms. Humor.

Peek-a-boo! by Janet and Allan Ahlberg; ill. by authors. Viking, 1981. Subj: Babies. Family life. Format, unusual. Games. Poetry, rhyme.

Starting school by Janet and Allan Ahlberg; ill. by authors. Viking, 1988. ISBN 0-670-82175-6 Subj: School.

Aichinger, Helga. *The shepherd* ill. by author. Crowell, 1967. Subj: Holidays – Christmas. Religion.

Aiello, Susan. *A hat like that* (Johnson, B. J.)

My blanket Burt (Johnson, B. J.)

Aiken, Conrad Potter. *Tom, Sue and the clock* ill. by Julie Maas. Macmillan, 1966. Subj: Clocks, watches. Poetry, rhyme. Time.

Aiken, Joan. *Arabel and Mortimer* ill. by Quentin Blake. Doubleday, 1981. Subj: Birds – ravens. Imagination. Pets.

Ainsworth, Ruth. *The mysterious Baba and her magic caravan* ill. by Joan Hickson. Deutsch, dist. by Elsevier-Dutton, 1980. Subj: Character traits – generosity. Toys – dolls.

Aitken, Amy. *Kate and Mona in the jungle* ill. by author. Bradbury Pr., 1981. Subj: Animals. Imagination. Jungle. Zoos.

Ruby! ill. by author. Bradbury Pr., 1979. Subj: Careers. Imagination.

Ruby, the red knight ill. by author. Bradbury Pr., 1983. Subj: Character traits – bravery. Imagination. Royalty.

Wanda's circus ill. by author. Bradbury Pr., 1985. ISBN 0-02-700370-1 Subj: Animals. Circus. Family life. Sibling rivalry.

Akens, Floyd *see* Baum, L. Frank (Lyman Frank)

Akers, Floyd *see* Baum, L. Frank (Lyman Frank)

Aksakov, Sergei. *The scarlet flower* tr. by Isadora Levin; ill. by Boris Diodorov. Harcourt, 1989. ISBN 0-15-270487-6 Subj: Activities – traveling. Family life – fathers. Flowers. Foreign lands – Russia.

Alan, Sandy. *The plaid peacock* ill. by Kelly Oechsli. Pantheon, 1965. Subj: Birds – peacocks, peahens. Foreign lands – India.

Albert, Burton. *Mine, yours, ours* ill. by Lois Axeman. Albert Whitman, 1977. Subj: Behavior – sharing. Concepts.

Where does the trail lead? ill. by J. Brian Pinkney. Simon & Schuster, 1991. ISBN 0-671-73409-1 Subj: Islands. Sea and seashore.

Alborough, Jez. *Bare bear* ill. by author. Knopf, 1984. Subj: Activities – bathing. Animals – polar bears. Humor. Poetry, rhyme.

Beaky ill. by author. Houghton, 1990. ISBN 0-395-53348-1 Subj: Animals. Birds. Self-concept.

The grass is always greener ill. by author. Dial Pr., 1987. ISBN 0-8037-0468-2 Subj: Animals – sheep. Behavior – seeking better things. Farms.

Running Bear ill. by author. Knopf, 1985. Subj: Animals – polar bears. Behavior – bad day. Sports – racing.

Where's my teddy? ill. by author. Candlewick Pr., 1992. ISBN 1-56402-048-7 Subj: Animals – bears. Forest, woods. Poetry, rhyme. Toys – teddy bears.

Alda, Arlene. *Arlene Alda's ABC* photos. by author. Celestial Arts, 1981. Subj: ABC books.

Matthew and his dad photos. by author. Simon and Schuster, 1983. Subj: Clothing. Family life – fathers.

Sonya's mommy works photos. by author. Messner, 1982. Subj: Activities – working. Family life – mothers.

Aldag, Kurt. *Some things never change* ill. by Ken Rush. Macmillan, 1992. ISBN 0-02-700205-5 Subj: Automobiles. Careers – mechanics. Time.

Alden, Laura. *Saying I'm sorry* ill. by Dan Siculan. Child's World, 1983. ISBN 0-89565-247-1 Subj: Etiquette.

When? ill. by Lois Axeman. Childrens Pr., 1983. Subj: Character traits – curiosity. Character traits – questioning.

Alderson, Sue Ann. *Bonnie McSmithers is at it again!* ill. by Fiona Garrick. Tree Frog Pr., 1980. Subj: Activities. Character traits – individuality. Poetry, rhyme.

Ida and the wool smugglers ill. by Ann Blades. Macmillan, 1987. ISBN 0-689-50440-3 Subj: Character traits – cleverness. Crime. Islands.

Aldis, Dorothy. *All together: a child's treasury of verse* ill. by Helen D. Jameson, Marjorie Flack and Margaret Freeman. Putnam's, 1952. Subj: Poetry, rhyme.

Before things happen ill. by Margaret Freeman. Putnam's, 1939. Subj: Poetry, rhyme.

Hello day ill. by Susan Elson. Putnam's, 1959. Subj: Poetry, rhyme.

Quick as a wink ill. by Peggy Westphal. Putnam's, 1960. Subj: Insects. Poetry, rhyme.

Aldridge, Josephine Haskell. *The best of friends* ill. by Betty Peterson. Parnassus, 1963. Subj: Animals. Friendship.

Fisherman's luck ill. by Ruth Robbins. Parnassus, 1966. Subj: Careers – fishermen. Character traits – luck. Sports – fishing. Weather – storms.

A peony and a periwinkle ill. by Ruth Robbins. Parnassus, 1961. Subj: Sports – fishing.

Aleichem, Sholem. *Hanukah money* ill. by Uri Shulevitz. Greenwillow, 1978. Subj: Folk and fairy tales. Foreign lands. Holidays – Hanukkah. Jewish culture. Religion.

Alexander, Anne (Anna Barbara Cooke). *ABC of cars and trucks* ill. by Ninon. Doubleday, 1956. Subj: ABC books. Automobiles. Poetry, rhyme. Trucks.

Boats and ships from A to Z ill. by Will Huntington. Rand McNally, 1961. Subj: Boats, ships.

I want to whistle ill. by Abner Graboff. Abelard-Schuman, 1958. Subj: Activities – whistling. Poetry, rhyme.

My daddy and I ill. by Cyril Satorsky. Abelard-Schuman, 1961. Subj: Counting, numbers. Poetry, rhyme. Family life – fathers.

Noise in the night ill. by Abner Graboff. Rand McNally, 1960. Subj: Emotions – fear. Night. Noise, sounds.

Alexander, Cecil Frances. *All things bright and beautiful: a hymn* ill. by Leo Politi. Scribner's, 1962. Subj: Music. Religion. Songs.

Alexander, Ellen. *Llama and the great flood* ill. by author. HarperCollins, 1989. ISBN 0-690-04729-0 Subj: Animals – llamas. Folk and fairy tales. Foreign lands – Peru. Weather – floods.

Alexander, Liza. *Ernie gets lost* ill. by Tom Cooke. Childrens Pr., 1985. ISBN 0-307-62115-4 Subj: Behavior – lost. Stores.

A visit to the Sesame Street Museum ill. by Joe Mathiew. Random House, 1987. ISBN 0-394-98715-2 Subj: Museums.

Alexander, Lloyd. *Fortune tellers* ill. by Trina Schart Hyman. Dutton, 1992. ISBN 0-525-44849-7 Subj: Careers – fortune tellers. Cumulative tales. Foreign lands – Africa.

The king's fountain ill. by Ezra Jack Keats. Dutton, 1971. Subj: Folk and fairy tales. Poverty. Royalty – kings.

The truthful harp ill. by Evaline Ness. Holt, 1967. Subj: Character traits – honesty. Folk and fairy tales. Music.

Alexander, Martha G. *And my mean old mother will be sorry, Blackboard Bear* ill. by author. Dial Pr., 1972. Subj: Animals – bears. Behavior – running away. Emotions – anger. Imagination – imaginary friends.

Blackboard Bear ill. by author. Dial Pr., 1969. Subj: Animals – bears. Imagination – imaginary friends.

Bobo's dream ill. by author. Dial Pr., 1970. Subj: Animals – dogs. Dreams. Ethnic groups in the U.S. – Afro-Americans. Imagination. Wordless.

Even that moose won't listen to me ill. by author. Dial Pr., 1988. ISBN 0-8037-0188-8 Subj: Animals – moose. Behavior – disbelief. Family life.

How my library grew by Dinah ill. by author. H. W. Wilson, 1982. Subj: Libraries.

I sure am glad to see you, Blackboard Bear ill. by author. Dial Pr., 1976. Subj: Animals – bears. Behavior – bullying. Imagination – imaginary friends.

I'll be the horse if you'll play with me ill. by author. Dial Pr., 1975. Subj: Activities – playing. Behavior – fighting, arguing. Sibling rivalry. Family life.

I'll protect you from the jungle beasts ill. by author. Dial Pr., 1973. Subj: Emotions – fear. Imagination – imaginary friends. Problem solving. Sleep. Toys – teddy bears.

Maggie's moon ill. by author. Dial Pr., 1982. Subj: Animals – dogs. Moon. Night.

The magic box ill. by author. Dial Pr., 1984. ISBN 0-8037-0051-2 Subj: Format, unusual. Magic. Monsters. Witches. Wordless.

The magic hat ill. by author. Dial Pr., 1984. ISBN 0-8037-0051-2 Subj: Animals – rabbits. Birds – doves. Format, unusual. Magic. Wordless.

The magic picture ill. by author. Dial Pr., 1984. ISBN 0-8037-0051-2 Subj: Animals – dogs. Format, unusual. Wordless.

Marty McGee's space lab, no girls allowed ill. by author. Dial Pr., 1981. Subj: Family life. Imagination. Sibling rivalry. Space and space ships.

Maybe a monster ill. by author. Dial Pr., 1968. Subj: Emotions – fear. Monsters.

Move over, Twerp ill. by author. Dial Pr., 1981. Subj: Behavior – bullying. Character traits – perseverance. Humor. Problem solving. School.

My outrageous friend Charlie ill. by author. Dial, 1989. ISBN 0-8037-0588-3 Subj: Character traits – confidence. Friendship. Magic.

No ducks in our bathtub ill. by author. Dial Pr., 1973. Subj: Frogs and toads. Pets.

Nobody asked me if I wanted a baby sister ill. by author. Dial Pr., 1971. Subj: Babies. Emotions – envy, jealousy. Sibling rivalry.

Out! Out! Out! ill. by author. Dial Pr., 1968. Subj: Birds. Problem solving. Wordless.

Pigs say oink: a first book of sounds ill. by author. Random House, 1978. Subj: Animals. Noise, sounds.

Sabrina ill. by author. Dial Pr., 1971. Subj: Emotions – embarrassment. Names. School.

The story grandmother told ill. by author. Dial Pr., 1969. Subj: Ethnic groups in the U.S. – Afro-Americans. Family life – grandmothers. Toys.

3 magic flip books: The magic hat; The magic box; The magic picture ill. by author. Dial Pr., 1984. Subj: Format, unusual – toy and movable books. Magic. Wordless.

We never get to do anything ill. by author. Dial Pr., 1970. Subj: Behavior – boredom. Character traits – perseverance. Games. Problem solving. Sports – swimming.

We're in big trouble, Blackboard Bear ill. by author. Dial Pr., 1980. Subj: Animals – bears. Behavior – misbehavior. Imagination – imaginary friends. Night. Problem solving.

When the new baby comes, I'm moving out ill. by author. Dial Pr., 1979. Subj: Babies. Emotions – envy, jealousy. Sibling rivalry.

Where does the sky end, Grandpa? ill. by author. Harcourt, 1992. ISBN 0-15-295603-4 Subj: Activities – walking. Character traits – questioning. Family life – grandfathers. Nature.

Alexander, Sally Hobart. *Maggie's whopper* ill. by Deborah Kogan Ray. Macmillan, 1992. ISBN 0-02-700201-2 Subj: Animals – bears. Family life – aunts, uncles. Sports – fishing.

Sarah's surprise ill. by Jill Kastner. Macmillan, 1990. ISBN 0-02-700391-4 Subj: Emotions – fear. Sea and seashore.

Alexander, Sue. *Dear Phoebe* ill. by Eileen Christelow. Little, 1984. Subj: Animals – mice. Behavior – growing up. Emotions – loneliness. Emotions – love. Family life.

Marc the Magnificent ill. by Tomie de Paola. Pantheon, 1978. Subj: Character traits – optimism. Magic.

More Witch, Goblin, and Ghost stories ill. by Jeanette Winter. Pantheon, 1978. Subj: Ghosts. Goblins. Witches.

Nadia the willful ill. by Lloyd Bloom. Pantheon, 1983. Subj: Character traits – willfulness. Emotions – love. Emotions – sadness. Family life. Foreign lands – Arabia.

Seymour the prince ill. by Lillian Hoban. Pantheon, 1979. Subj: Clubs, gangs. Theater.

Small plays for special days ill. by Tom Huffman. Seabury Pr., 1977. Subj: Holidays. Theater.

Small plays for you and a friend ill. by Olivia Cole. Houghton, 1974. Subj: Friendship. Theater.

There's more...much more ill. by Patience Brewster. Harcourt, 1987. ISBN 0-15-200605-2 Subj: Animals – squirrels. Seasons – spring.

Witch, Goblin and Ghost are back ill. by Jeanette Winter. Pantheon, 1985. ISBN 0-394-96296-6 Subj: Ghosts. Goblins. Witches.

Witch, Goblin, and Ghost in the haunted woods ill. by Jeanette Winter. Pantheon, 1981. Subj: Ghosts. Goblins. Witches.

Witch, Goblin and sometimes Ghost ill. by Jeanette Winter. Pantheon, 1976. Subj: Behavior – forgetfulness. Emotions – fear. Friendship. Ghosts. Goblins. Witches.

World famous Muriel ill. by Chris L. Demarest. Little, 1984. Subj: Birthdays. Humor. Problem solving.

World famous Muriel and the magic mystery ill. by Marla Frazee. HarperCollins, 1990. ISBN 0-690-04789-4 Subj: Libraries. Magic. Problem solving.

Alger, Leclaire Gowans. *All in the morning early* ill. by Evaline Ness. Holt, 1963. Subj: Caldecott award honor book. Folk and fairy tales. Foreign lands – Scotland. Poetry, rhyme. Songs.

Always room for one more ill. by Nonny Hogrogian. Holt, 1965. Children's story based on the Scottish ballad of the same title Subj: Caldecott award book. Cumulative tales. Folk and fairy tales. Foreign lands – Scotland. Houses. Music.

Kellyburn Braes ill. by Evaline Ness. Harcourt, 1968. Subj: Devil. Foreign lands – Scotland. Foreign languages. Music. Poetry, rhyme. Songs.

Aliki. *At Mary Bloom's* ill. by author. Greenwillow, 1976. Subj: Animals – mice. Babies.

Christmas tree memories ill. by author. HarperCollins, 1991. ISBN 0-06-020008-1 Subj: Family life. Holidays – Christmas. Trees.

Corn is maize: the gift of the Indians ill. by author. Crowell, 1976. Subj: Gardens, gardening. Indians of North America. Plants. Science.

Digging up dinosaurs ill. by author. Rev. ed. Crowell, 1988. ISBN 0-690-04716-9 Subj: Activities – digging. Dinosaurs. Humor. Science.

Dinosaur bones ill. by author. Harper, 1988. ISBN 0-690-04550-6 Subj: Dinosaurs.

Dinosaurs are different ill. by author. Crowell, 1985. ISBN 0-690-04458-5 Subj: Dinosaurs. Science.

Diogenes: the story of the Greek philosopher ill. by author. Prentice-Hall, 1969. Subj: Character traits – honesty. Folk and fairy tales. Foreign lands – Greece.

The eggs: a Greek folk tale ill. by adapt. Pantheon, 1969. Subj: Behavior – greed. Character traits – cleverness. Folk and fairy tales. Foreign lands – Greece. Humor.

Feelings ill. by author. Greenwillow, 1984. ISBN 0-688-03832-8 Subj: Emotions. Friendship.

Fossils tell of long ago ill. by author. Rev. ed. HarperCollins, 1990. Subj: Dinosaurs. Science.

George and the cherry tree ill. by author. Dial Pr., 1964. Subj: Character traits – bravery. Folk and fairy tales. U.S. history.

How a book is made ill. by author. Harper, 1986. ISBN 0-690-04498-4 Subj: Activities – reading. Libraries.

I wish I was sick, too! ill. by author. Greenwillow, 1976. Subj: Behavior – wishing. Illness.

I'm growing! ill. by author. HarperCollins, 1992. ISBN 0-06-020245-9 Subj: Behavior – growing up.

Jack and Jake ill. by author. Greenwillow, 1986. ISBN 0-688-06100-1 Subj: Behavior – mistakes. Character traits – individuality. Family life. Twins.

June 7! ill. by author. Macmillan, 1972. Subj: Birthdays. Cumulative tales. Family life.

Keep your mouth closed, dear ill. by author. Dial Pr., 1966. Subj: Behavior – carelessness. Family life. Reptiles – alligators, crocodiles.

The king's day ill. by author. HarperCollins, 1989. ISBN 0-690-04590-5 Subj: Foreign lands – France. Royalty – kings.

The long lost coelacanth and other living fossils ill. by author. Crowell, 1973. Subj: Fish. Science.

Manners ill. by author. Greenwillow, 1990. ISBN 0-688-09199-7 Subj: Etiquette.

The many lives of Benjamin Franklin ill. by author. Simon & Schuster, 1988. ISBN 0-671-66119-1 Subj: U.S. history.

Mummies made in Egypt ill. by author. Crowell, 1979. Subj: Death. Foreign lands – Egypt. Religion.

My feet ill. by author. HarperCollins, 1990. ISBN 0-690-04815-7 Subj: Anatomy – feet. Science.

My five senses ill. by author. Crowell, 1962. Subj: Senses – hearing. Senses – seeing. Senses – smelling. Senses – tasting. Senses – touching.

My hands ill. by author. Rev. ed. HarperCollins, 1990. ISBN 0-690-04880-7 Subj: Anatomy – hands. Science.

My visit to the dinosaurs ill. by author. Rev. ed. Crowell, 1985. ISBN 0-690-04423-2 Subj: Dinosaurs. Museums. Science.

Overnight at Mary Bloom's ill. by author. Greenwillow, 1987. ISBN 0-688-06765-4 Subj: Activities. Activities – playing. Friendship. Night.

The story of Johnny Appleseed ill. by author. Prentice-Hall, 1963. Subj: Character traits – generosity. Folk and fairy tales. Gardens, gardening. Trees. U.S. history.

The story of William Penn ill. by author. Prentice-Hall, 1964. Subj: Character traits – kindness. U.S. history.

Three gold pieces: a Greek folk tale ill. by author. Pantheon, 1967. Subj: Character traits – luck. Folk and fairy tales. Foreign lands – Greece.

The twelve months: a Greek folktale ill. by adapt. Greenwillow, 1978. Subj: Behavior – dissatisfaction. Character traits – optimism. Folk and fairy tales. Foreign lands – Greece.

The two of them ill. by author. Greenwillow, 1979. Subj: Character traits – helpfulness. Character traits – loyalty. Family life – grandfathers.

Use your head, dear ill. by author. Greenwillow, 1983. Subj: Behavior – forgetfulness. Birthdays. Reptiles – alligators, crocodiles.

We are best friends ill. by author. Greenwillow, 1982. Subj: Emotions – anger. Emotions – loneliness. Friendship. Moving.

A weed is a flower: the life of George Washington Carver ill. by author. Prentice-Hall, 1965. Subj: Character traits – perseverance. Ethnic groups in the U.S. – Afro-Americans. Science. U.S. history.

Welcome, little baby ill. by author. Greenwillow, 1987. ISBN 0-688-06811-1 Subj: Babies. Family life.

Wild and woolly mammoths ill. by author. Crowell, 1977. Subj: Animals. Science.

The wish workers ill. by author. Dial Pr., 1962. Subj: Behavior – dissatisfaction. Behavior – wishing. Birds. Magic.

The all-amazing ha ha book Oxford Univ. Pr. 1987. ISBN 0-19-554581-8 Subj: Folk and fairy tales. Foreign lands – Australia. Humor. Language.

Allamand, Pascale. *The animals who changed their colors* ill. by Elizabeth Watson Taylor. Morrow, 1979. Subj: Animals. Behavior – imitation. Character traits – individuality. Concepts – color. Humor.

Cocoa beans and daisies: how Swiss chocolate is made photos. by author. Warne, 1978. Subj: Food. Foreign lands – Switzerland.

The little goat in the mountains tr. by Michael Bullock; ill. by author. Warne, 1978. Subj: Animals – goats.

Allan, Nicholas. *The thing that ate Aunt Julia* ill. by author. Dial, 1991. ISBN 0-8037-0872-6 Subj: Family life – aunts, uncles. Imagination.

Allard, Harry. *Bumps in the night* ill. by James Marshall. Doubleday, 1979. Subj: Animals. Ghosts. Noise, sounds.

The cactus flower bakery ill. by Ned Delaney. HarperCollins, 1991. ISBN 0-06-020047-2 Subj: Animals – armadillos. Careers – bakers. Food. Friendship. Reptiles – snakes.

I will not go to market today ill. by James Marshall. Dial Pr., 1979. Subj: Birds – chickens. Shopping.

It's so nice to have a wolf around the house ill. by James Marshall. Doubleday, 1977. Subj: Crime. Old age. Pets.

May I stay? ill. by F. A. Fitzgerald. Prentice-Hall, 1977. Subj: Character traits – questioning. Folk and fairy tales. Foreign lands – Germany. Foreign lands – Norway.

Miss Nelson has a field day ill. by James Marshall. Houghton, 1985. Subj: Behavior – secrets. Humor. School.

Miss Nelson is back by Harry Allard and James Marshall; ill. by James Marshall. Houghton, 1982. Subj: Behavior – misbehavior. Careers – teachers. School.

Miss Nelson is missing! by Harry Allard and James Marshall; ill. by James Marshall. Houghton, 1977. Subj: Behavior – misbehavior. Careers – teachers. School.

The Stupids die ill. by James Marshall. Houghton, 1981. Subj: Behavior – misunderstanding. Humor.

The Stupids have a ball by Harry Allard and James Marshall; ill. by James Marshall. Houghton, 1978. Subj: Humor. Parties.

The Stupids step out ill. by James Marshall. Houghton, 1974. Subj: Humor.

The Stupids take off by Harry Allard and James Marshall; ill. by James Marshall. Houghton, 1989. ISBN 0-395-50068-0 Subj: Activities – flying. Humor.

There's a party at Mona's tonight ill. by James Marshall. Doubleday, 1981. Subj: Animals – pigs. Behavior – trickery. Humor. Parties.

Three is company (Waechter, Friedrich Karl)

Allbright, Viv. *Ten go hopping* ill. by author. Faber, 1985. ISBN 0-571-13473-4 Subj: Counting, numbers. Cumulative tales.

Allen, Allyn *see* Eberle, Irmengarde

Allen, Frances Charlotte. *Little hippo* ill. by Laura Jean Allen. Putnam's, 1971. Subj: Animals – hippopotami. Emotions – sadness.

Allen, Gertrude E. *Everyday animals* ill. by author. Houghton, 1961. Subj: Animals. Forest, woods. Science.

Allen, Jeffrey. *Bonzini! the tattooed man* ill. by James Marshall. Little, 1976. Subj: Circus. Clowns, jesters.

Mary Alice, operator number 9 ill. by James Marshall. Little, 1975. Subj: Activities – working. Animals. Birds – ducks. Careers – telephone operators. Telephone. Time.

Mary Alice returns ill. by James Marshall. Little, 1986. ISBN 0-316-03429-0 Subj: Birds – ducks. Careers – telephone operators. Telephone.

Nosey Mrs. Rat ill. by James Marshall. Viking, 1985. ISBN 0-670-80880-6 Subj: Animals. Behavior – gossip. Character traits – curiosity.

The secret life of Mr. Weird ill. by Ned Delaney. Little, 1982. Subj: Animals – dogs. Behavior – dissatisfaction. Behavior – seeking better things. Games. Imagination.

Allen, Jonathan. *A bad case of animal nonsense* ill. by author. Godine, 1981. Subj: Animals. Humor. Poetry, rhyme.

Mucky moose ill. by author. Macmillan, 1991. ISBN 0-02-700251-9 Subj: Animals – moose. Animals – wolves. Character traits – cleanliness. Senses – smelling.

My cat ill. by author. Dial Pr., 1986. ISBN 0-8037-0292-2 Subj: Animals – cats. Pets.

My dog ill. by author. Gareth Stevens, 1989. ISBN 0-8368-0095-8 Subj: Animals – dogs. Pets.

Allen, Laura Jean. *Ottie and the star* ill. by author. Harper, 1979. Subj: Animals – otters. Family life. Sea and seashore. Stars.

Rollo and Tweedy and the case of the missing cheese ill. by author. Harper, 1983. Subj: Animals – mice. Food. Foreign lands – France. Problem solving.

Where is Freddy? ill. by author. Harper, 1986. ISBN 0-06-020099-5 Subj: Activities – flying. Behavior – lost. Careers – detectives. Problem solving.

Allen, Linda. *The giant who had no heart* ill. by author. Philomel, 1988. ISBN 0-399-21446-1 Subj: Folk and fairy tales. Foreign lands – Norway. Giants.

Mr. Simkin's grandma ill. by Loretta Lustig. Morrow, 1979. Subj: Family life – grandmothers. Family life – grandparents. Humor.

The mouse bride ill. by author. Putnam, 1992. ISBN 0-399-22136-0 Subj: Animals – mice. Folk and fairy tales. Foreign lands – Finland. Royalty – princesses.

Mrs. Simkin's bed ill. by Loretta Lustig. Morrow, 1980. Subj: Animals. Humor. Furniture – beds.

Allen, Marjorie N. *Changes* by Marjorie N. Allen and Shelley Rotner; photos by Shelley Rotner. Macmillan, 1991. ISBN 0-02-700252-7 Subj: Nature. Poetry, rhyme.

One, two, three - ah-choo! ill. by Dick Gackenbach. Coward, 1980. Subj: Animals. Humor. Pets.

Allen, Martha Dickson. *Real life monsters* ill. by author. Prentice-Hall, 1979. Subj: Animals. Monsters. Science.

Allen, Pamela. *Bertie and the bear* ill. by author. Coward, 1984. Subj: Activities – dancing. Animals – bears. Animals – dogs. Noise, sounds. Royalty.

Fancy that! ill. by author. Orchard, 1988. ISBN 0-531-08363-2 Subj: Birds – chickens. Farms.

Hidden treasure ill. by author. Putnam's, 1987. Orig. published as Herbert and Harry ISBN 0-399-21427-5 Subj: Behavior – greed. Behavior – hiding things. Sea and seashore. Sibling rivalry.

I wish I had a pirate suit ill. by author. Viking, 1990. ISBN 0-670-82475-5 Subj: Activities – playing. Behavior – wishing. Imagination. Pirates.

A lion in the night ill. by author. Putnam's, 1986. ISBN 0-399-21203-5 Subj: Animals – lions. Babies. Behavior – wishing. Imagination. Royalty.

Mr. Archimedes' bath ill. by author. Lothrop, 1980. Subj: Activities – bathing. Animals. Humor. Science.

My cat Maisie ill. by author. Viking, 1991. ISBN 0-670-83251-0 Subj: Animals – cats. Friendship. Pets.

Who sank the boat? ill. by author. Coward, 1983. Subj: Animals. Boats, ships. Poetry, rhyme. Science.

Allen, Robert. *Numbers: a first counting book* ill. by Mottke Weissman. Platt, 1968. Subj: Counting, numbers.

Round and square ill. by Philippe Thomas. Platt, 1965. Subj: Concepts – shape.

Ten little babies count by Janet Martin [pseud.]; photos. by Michael Watson. St. Martin's, 1986. ISBN 0-312-79112-7 Subj: Babies. Clothing. Counting, numbers. Format, unusual – board books.

Ten little babies dress by Janet Martin [pseud.]; photos. by Michael Watson. St. Martin's, 1986. ISBN 0-312-79113-5 Subj: Babies. Clothing. Counting, numbers. Format, unusual – board books.

Ten little babies eat by Janet Martin [pseud.]; photos. by Michael Watson. St. Martin's, 1986. ISBN 0-312-79114-3 Subj: Babies. Counting, numbers. Food. Format, unusual – board books.

Ten little babies play: a book of colors by Janet Martin [pseud.]; photos. by Michael Watson. St. Martin's, 1986. ISBN 0-312-79115-1 Subj: Activities – playing. Babies. Concepts – color. Counting, numbers. Format, unusual – board books.

The zoo book: a child's world of animals photos. by Peter Sahula. Platt, 1968. Subj: Animals. Zoos.

Allen, Thomas B. *On grandaddy's farm* ill. by author. Knopf, 1989. ISBN 0-394-99613-5 Subj: Family life. Farms.

Where children live ill. by author. Prentice-Hall, 1980. Subj: Foreign lands.

Alley, Robert W. *Seven fables from Æsop* (Æsop)

Allington, Richard L. *Autumn* by Richard L. Allington and Kathleen Krull; ill. by Bruce Bond. Raintree, 1985. Subj: Seasons – fall. Weather.

Colors ill. by Noel Spangler. Raintree, 1985. ISBN 0-8172-1280-9 Subj: Concepts – color.

Feelings by Richard L. Allington and Kathleen Cowles; ill. by Brian Cody. Raintree, 1985. Subj: Activities. Emotions.

Hearing by Richard L. Allington and Kathleen Cowles; ill. by Wayne Dober. Raintree, 1985. Subj: Activities. Senses – hearing.

Letters ill. by Tom Garcia. Raintree, 1985. ISBN 0-8172-1384-8 Subj: ABC books. Games. Language.

Looking by Richard L. Allington and Kathleen Cowles; ill. by Bill Bober. Raintree, 1981. Subj: Activities. Senses – seeing.

Measuring by Richard L. Allington and Kathleen Krull; ill. by Noel Spangler. Raintree, 1985. ISBN 0-8172-1389-9 Subj: Concepts – measurement.

Numbers ill. by Tom Garcia. Raintree, 1985. ISBN 0-8172-1278-7 Subj: Counting, numbers.

Opposites ill. by Eulala Conner. Raintree, 1985. ISBN 0-8172-1279-5 Subj: Concepts – opposites.

Reading by Richard L. Allington and Kathleen Krull; ill. by Joel Naprstek. Raintree, 1985. ISBN 0-8172-1322-8 Subj: Activities – reading.

Science by Richard L. Allington and Kathleen Krull; ill. by James Teason. Raintree, 1985. ISBN 0-8172-1387-2 Subj: Science.

Shapes ill. by Lois Ehlert. Raintree, 1985. ISBN 0-8172-1277-9 Subj: Concepts – shape. Concepts – size.

Smelling by Richard L. Allington and Kathleen Cowles; ill. by Rick Thrun. Raintree, 1981. Subj: Activities. Senses – smelling.

Spring by Richard L. Allington and Kathleen Krull; ill. by Lynn Uhde. Raintree, 1981. Subj: Seasons – spring. Weather.

Summer by Richard L. Allington and Kathleen Krull; ill. by Dennis Hockerman. Raintree, 1985. Subj: Seasons – summer. Weather.

Talking by Richard L. Allington and Kathleen Krull; ill. by Rick Thrun. Raintree, 1985. ISBN 0-8172-2492-0 Subj: Communication. Language. Science.

Tasting by Richard L. Allington and Kathleen Cowles; ill. by Noel Spangler. Raintree, 1985. Subj: Activities. Senses – tasting.

Thinking by Richard L. Allington and Kathleen Krull; ill. by Tom Garcia. Raintree, 1985. ISBN 0-8172-1319-8 Subj: Problem solving.

Time by Richard L. Allington and Kathleen Krull; ill. by Yoshi Miyake. Raintree, 1985. ISBN 0-8172-1388-0 Subj: Time.

Touching by Richard L. Allington and Kathleen Cowles; ill. by Yoshi Miyake. Raintree, 1985. Subj: Activities. Senses – touching.

Winter by Richard L. Allington and Kathleen Krull; ill. by John Wallner. Raintree, 1985. Subj: Seasons – winter. Weather.

Words by Richard L. Allington and Kathleen Krull; ill. by Ray Cruz. Raintree, 1982. ISBN 0-8172-1385-6 Subj: Communication. Language.

Writing by Richard L. Allington and Kathleen Krull; ill. by Yoshi Miyake. Raintree, 1985. ISBN 0-8175-1321-X Subj: Activities – writing.

Allinson, Beverley. *Effie* ill. by Barbara Reid. Scholastic, 1991. ISBN 0-590-44045-4 Subj: Animals – elephants. Character traits – being different. Friendship. Insects – ants.

Allison, Alida. *The toddler's potty book* by Alida Allison and Paula Sapphire. Price Stern Sloan, 1981, 1979. Subj: Behavior – growing up. Toilet training.

Allison, Diane Worfolk. *In window eight, the moon is late* ill. by author. Little, 1988. ISBN 0-316-03435-5 Subj: Bedtime. Dreams. Poetry, rhyme.

This is the key to the kingdom ill. by reteller. Little, 1992. ISBN 0-316-03432-0 Subj: Ethnic groups in the U.S. – Afro-Americans. Flowers. Nursery rhymes.

Allred, Mary. *Grandmother Poppy and the children's tea party* ill. by Paul Behrens. Broadman Pr., 1984. ISBN 0-8054-4292-8 Subj: Family life – grandmothers. Parties.

Grandmother Poppy and the funny-looking bird ill. by Paul Behrens. Broadman Pr., 1981. Subj: Birds. Character traits – kindness to animals. Family life – grandmothers.

Althea. *Castle life* ill. by Maureen Galvani. Merrimack, 1980. Subj: Middle ages.

Jeremy Mouse and cat ill. by author. Merrimack, 1980. Subj: Animals – cats. Animals – mice. Behavior – trickery.

Ambler, Christopher Gifford. *Ten little foxhounds* Children's Pr., 1968. Subj: Animals – dogs. Counting, numbers. Foreign lands – England. Poetry, rhyme.

Ambrus, Gyozo Laszlo *see* Ambrus, Victor G.

Ambrus, Victor G. *Brave soldier Janosch* ill. by author. Harcourt, 1967. Subj: Careers – military. Foreign lands – Hungary. War.

Country wedding ill. by author. Addison-Wesley, 1975. Subj: Animals – foxes. Animals – wolves. Food. Weddings.

Grandma, Felix, and Mustapha Biscuit ill. by author. W. Morrow, 1982. Subj: Animals – cats. Animals – hamsters. Family life – grandmothers. Humor.

The little cockerel ill. by author. Harcourt, 1968. Subj: Birds – chickens. Character traits – perseverance. Folk and fairy tales.

Mishka ill. by author. Warne, 1978. Subj: Animals – elephants. Character traits – perseverance. Circus. Music.

Santa Claus takes off ill. by Glenys Ambrus. Oxford Univ. Pr., 1991. ISBN 0-19-279878-2 Subj: Holidays – Christmas.

The seven skinny goats ill. by author. Harcourt, 1969. Subj: Activities – dancing. Animals – goats. Folk and fairy tales. Humor. Music.

The Sultan's bath ill. by author. Oxford Univ. Pr., 1971. Subj: Activities – bathing. Folk and fairy tales. Foreign lands – India. Royalty – sultans.

The three poor tailors ill. by author. Harcourt, 1966. Subj: Activities – whistling. Animals – goats. Careers – tailors. Folk and fairy tales. Foreign lands – Hungary. Poverty.

Amery, H. *At the zoo* ill. by author. Educational Development Corp., 1984. ISBN 0-86020-854-0 Subj: Animals. Zoos.

The farm picture book ill. by author. Educational Development Corp., 1988. ISBN 0-7460-0128-2 Subj: Animals. Farms.

Going to the fair ill. by author. Educational Development Corp., 1987. ISBN 0-88110-262-8 Subj: Fairs.

Goldilocks and the three bears (The three bears)

The zoo picture book ill. by author. Educational Development Corp., 1988. ISBN 0-7460-0127-4 Subj: Animals. Format, unusual. Zoos.

Ames, Mildred. *The wonderful box* ill. by Richard Cuffari. Dutton, 1978. Subj: Character traits – curiosity. Problem solving.

Ames, Rose *see* Wyler, Rose

Amoit, Pierre. *Bijou the little bear* Coward, 1950. Subj: Animals – bears. Circus. Clowns, jesters.

Amoss, Berthe. *It's not your birthday* ill. by author. Harper, 1966. Subj: Birthdays. Sibling rivalry.

Old Hannibal and the hurricane ill. by author. Walt Disney, 1991. ISBN 1-56282-098-2 Subj: Boats, ships. Sea and seashore. Weather – storms.

Tom in the middle ill. by author. Harper, 1968. Subj: Family life. Sibling rivalry.

What did you lose, Santa? ill. by author. HarperCollins, 1987. ISBN 0-694-00197-X Subj: Behavior – losing things. Holidays – Christmas.

Anastasio, Dina. *Pass the peas, please: a book of manners* ill. by Katy Keck Arnsteen. Warner Brothers, 1988. ISBN 1-55782-021-X Subj: Etiquette. Poetry, rhyme.

Anchondo, Mary. *How we came to the fifth world* (Rohmer, Harriet)

Ancona, George. *Dancing is* ill. by author. Dutton, 1981. Subj: Activities – dancing.

Handtalk (Charlip, Remy)

Handtalk zoo by George and Mary Beth Ancona; photos. by George Ancona. Macmillan, 1989. ISBN 0-02-700801-0 Subj: Animals. Communication. Handicaps – deafness. Language. Senses – hearing. Time. Zoos.

Helping out photos. by author. Clarion, 1985. ISBN 0-89919-278-5 Subj: Character traits – helpfulness.

It's a baby! ill. by author. Dutton, 1979. Subj: Babies.

Ancona, Mary Beth. *Handtalk* (Charlip, Remy)

Handtalk zoo (Ancona, George)

Anders, Rebecca. *A look at death* photos. by Maria S. Forrai; foreword by Robert C. Slater. Lerner, 1978. Subj: Death.

A look at prejudice and understanding ill. by Maria S. Forrai. Lerner, 1976. Subj: Prejudice.

Andersen, H. C. (Hans Christian). *The emperor and the nightingale* ill. by James Watling. Troll Assoc., 1979. Subj: Birds – nightingales. Character traits – freedom. Folk and fairy tales. Foreign lands – China.

The emperor's new clothes ill. by Erik Blegvad. Harcourt, 1959. Translation of Kejserens nye klæder by Erik Blegvad Subj: Character traits – pride. Clothing. Folk and fairy tales. Humor. Imagination. Royalty – emperors.

The emperor's new clothes ill. by Virginia Lee Burton. Houghton, 1949. Translation of Kejserens nye klæder Subj: Character traits – pride. Clothing. Folk and fairy tales. Humor. Imagination. Royalty – emperors.

The emperor's new clothes retold by Riki Levinson; ill. by Robert Byrd. Dutton, 1991. ISBN 0-525-44611-7 Subj: Animals. Character traits – pride. Clothing. Folk and fairy tales. Humor. Imagination. Royalty – emperors.

The emperor's new clothes ill. by Jack and Irene Delano. Random House, 1971. Translation of Kejserens nye klæder Text adapted from Hans Christian Andersen and other sources by Jean Van Leeuwen Subj: Character traits – pride. Clothing. Folk and fairy tales. Humor. Imagination. Royalty – emperors.

The emperor's new clothes ill. by Hélène Desputeaux. Gallery Books, 1984. ISBN 0-8317-2736-5 Subj: Character traits – pride. Clothing. Folk and fairy tales. Humor. Imagination. Royalty – emperors.

The emperor's new clothes ill. by Birte Dietz; tr. by M. R. James; adapt. by Jean Van Leeuwen. Van Nostrand, 1972. Translation of Kejserens nye klæder Subj: Character traits – pride. Clothing. Folk and fairy tales. Humor. Imagination. Royalty – emperors.

The emperor's new clothes adapt. by Anthea Bell; ill. by Dorothée Duntze. Holt, 1986. ISBN 0-8050-0010-0 Subj: Character traits – pride. Clothing. Folk and fairy tales. Humor. Imagination. Royalty – emperors.

The emperor's new clothes ill. by Pamela Baldwin Ford. Troll Assoc., 1979. Translation of Kejserens nye klæder Subj: Character traits – pride. Clothing. Folk and fairy tales. Humor. Imagination. Royalty – emperors.

The emperor's new clothes ill. by Jack Kent. Four Winds Pr., 1977. Adaptation of Kejserens nye klæder by Ruth Belov Gross Subj: Character traits – pride. Clothing. Folk and fairy tales. Humor. Imagination. Royalty – emperors.

The emperor's new clothes ill. by Monika Laimgruber. Addison-Wesley, 1973. Translation of Kejserens nye klæder Subj: Character traits – pride. Clothing. Folk and fairy tales. Humor. Imagination. Royalty – emperors.

The emperor's new clothes ill. by Anne F. Rockwell. Crowell, 1982. Translation of Kejserens nye klæder by H. W. Dulcken Subj: Character traits – pride. Clothing. Folk and fairy tales. Humor. Imagination. Royalty – emperors.

The emperor's new clothes adapt. and ill. by Janet Stevens. Holiday, 1985. ISBN 0-8234-0566-4 Subj: Character traits – pride. Clothing. Folk and fairy tales. Humor. Imagination. Royalty – emperors.

The emperor's new clothes ill. by Nadine Bernard Westcott. Little, 1984. Subj: Character traits – pride. Clothing. Folk and fairy tales. Humor. Imagination. Royalty – emperors.

The emperor's nightingale retold by Teddy Slater; ill. from the Disney archives. Walt Disney, 1992. ISBN 1-56282-134-2 Subj: Birds – nightingales. Character traits – freedom. Folk and fairy tales. Foreign lands – China. Royalty – emperors.

The emperor's nightingale tr. by Erik Haugaard; ill. by Georges Lemoine. Schocken, 1981. Subj: Birds – nightingales. Character traits – freedom. Folk and fairy tales. Foreign lands – China. Royalty – emperors.

The fir tree ill. by Stephanie Britt. Ideals, 1989. ISBN 0-8249-8389-0 Subj: Folk and fairy tales. Holidays – Christmas. Trees.

The fir tree ill. by Nancy Ekholm Burkert. Harper, 1970. Translation of Grantræet by H. W. Dulcken Subj: Folk and fairy tales. Holidays – Christmas. Trees.

The fir tree adapt. and ill. by Diane Goode. Random House, 1988. ISBN 0-394-81941-1 Subj: Folk and fairy tales. Holidays – Christmas. Trees.

The fir tree adapt. by Marcel Imsand; ill. by Rita Marshall. Creative Education, 1983. ISBN 0-87191-949-4 Subj: Folk and fairy tales. Holidays – Christmas. Trees.

The fir tree adapt. and ill. by Bernadette Watts. North-South, 1990. ISBN 1-55858-093-X Subj: Folk and fairy tales. Holidays – Christmas. Trees.

It's perfectly true! adapt. and ill. by Janet Stevens. Holiday, 1987. ISBN 0-8234-0672-5 Subj: Behavior – gossip. Character traits – vanity. Death. Folk and fairy tales.

Little Ida's flowers ill. by Linda Allen. Putnam, 1990. ISBN 0-399-21571-9 Subj: Flowers. Folk and fairy tales.

The little match girl ill. by Rachel Isadora. Putnam's, 1987. Translation of Den lille pige med svovlstikkerne ISBN 0-399-21336-8 Subj: Folk and fairy tales. Holidays – New Year's. Poverty.

The little match girl ill. by Blair Lent. Houghton, 1968. Translation of Den lille pige med svovlstikkerne Subj: Folk and fairy tales. Holidays – New Year's. Poverty.

The little mermaid tr. by Eva Le Gallienne; ill. by Edward Frascino. Harper, 1971. Subj: Folk and fairy tales. Mythical creatures – mermaids.

The little mermaid adapt. by Anthea Bell; ill. by ChihiroIwasaki. Alphabet Pr., 1984. Adaptation of Den lille havfrue ISBN 0-907234-59-3 Subj: Folk and fairy tales. Mythical creatures – mermaids.

The little mermaid ill. by Dorothy Pulis Lathrop. Macmillan, 1939. Subj: Folk and fairy tales. Mythical creatures – mermaids.

The little mermaid ill. by Josef Paleček. Faber, 1981. Translation of Den lille havfrue by M. R. James Subj: Folk and fairy tales. Mythical creatures – mermaids.

The little mermaid adapt. by Freya Littledale; ill. by Daniel San Souci. Scholastic, 1986. ISBN 0-590-33590-1 Subj: Folk and fairy tales. Mythical creatures – mermaids.

The little mermaid retold and ill. by Katie Thamer Treherne. Harcourt, 1989. ISBN 0-15-246320-8 Subj: Folk and fairy tales. Mythical creatures – mermaids.

The nightingale ill. by Harold Berson. Lippincott, 1962. Subj: Birds – nightingales. Character traits – freedom. Folk and fairy tales. Foreign lands – China. Royalty – emperors.

The nightingale tr. by Eva Le Gallienne; ill. by Nancy Ekholm Burkert. Harper, 1965. Subj: Birds – nightingales. Character traits – freedom. Folk and fairy tales. Foreign lands – China. Royalty – emperors.

The nightingale adapt. by Anna Bier; ill. by Demi. Harcourt, 1985. Adaptation of Nattergalen ISBN 0-15-257427-1 Subj: Birds – nightingales. Character traits – freedom. Folk and fairy tales. Foreign lands – China. Royalty – emperors.

The nightingale ill. by Alison Claire Darke. Doubleday, 1989. ISBN 0-385-26082-2 Subj: Birds – nightingales. Character traits – freedom. Folk and fairy tales. Foreign lands – China.

The nightingale adapt. by Alan Benjamin; ill. by Beni Montresor. Crown, 1985. Adaptation of Nattergalen ISBN 0-517-55211-6 Subj: Birds – nightingales. Character traits – freedom. Folk and fairy tales. Foreign lands – China. Royalty – emperors.

The nightingale tr. by Naomi Lewis; ill. by Josef Paleček. North-South, 1990. ISBN 1-55858-090-5 Subj: Birds – nightingales. Character traits – freedom. Folk and fairy tales. Foreign lands – China.

The nightingale retold by Michael Bedard; ill. by Regolo Ricci. Houghton, 1992. ISBN 0-395-60735-3 Subj: Birds – nightingales. Character traits – freedom. Folk and fairy tales. Foreign lands – China.

The nightingale ill. by Lisbeth Zwerger; tr. from the Danish by Anthea Bell. Alphabet Pr., 1984. Adaptation of Nattergalen ISBN 0-907234-57-7 Subj: Birds – nightingales. Character traits – freedom. Folk and fairy tales. Foreign lands – China. Royalty – emperors.

The old man is always right ill. by Feodor Rojankovsky. Harper, 1940. Subj: Activities – trading. Folk and fairy tales. Humor.

The princess and the pea ill. by Dorothée Duntze. Holt, 1985. ISBN 0-8050-0170-0 Subj: Folk and fairy tales. Royalty – princesses. Sleep.

The princess and the pea ill. by Dick Gackenbach. Macmillan, 1983. Subj: Folk and fairy tales. Royalty – princesses.

The princess and the pea ill. by Paul Galdone. Seabury Pr., 1978. Translation of Den prindsessen paa aerten Subj: Folk and fairy tales. Royalty – princesses. Sleep.

The princess and the pea adapt. and ill. by Janet Stevens. Holiday, 1982. Subj: Folk and fairy tales. Royalty – princesses.

The princess and the pea tr. by Anthea Bell; ill. by Eve Tharlet. Picture Book Studio, 1987. ISBN 0-88708-052-9 Subj: Folk and fairy tales. Royalty – princesses. Sleep.

The red shoes tr. from Danish by Anthea Bell; ill. by Chihiro Iwasaki. Alphabet Pr., 1983. Subj: Activities – dancing. Angels. Character traits – pride. Clothing – shoes.

The snow queen tr. by Naomi Lewis; ill. by Angela Barrett. Holt, 1988. ISBN 0-8050-00830-6 Subj: Character traits – bravery. Emotions – love. Folk and fairy tales.

The snow queen ill. by Toma Bogdanovic. Scroll Pr., n.d. An adapt. by Naomi Lewis of Sneedrenningen Subj: Character traits – bravery. Emotions – love. Folk and fairy tales. Foreign lands – Denmark.

The snow queen ill. by June Atkin Corwin. Atheneum, 1968. Subj: Character traits – bravery. Emotions – love. Folk and fairy tales.

The snow queen sel. and ed. by Neil Philip; ill. by Sally Holmes. Lothrop, 1989. ISBN 0-688-09048-6 Subj: Character traits – bravery. Emotions – love. Folk and fairy tales.

The snow queen adapt. by Amy Ehrlich; ill. by Susan Jeffers. Dial Pr., 1982. Subj: Character traits – bravery. Emotions – love. Folk and fairy tales.

The snow queen adapt. by Naomi Lewis; ill. by Errol Le Cain. Viking, 1979. Subj: Character traits – bravery. Emotions – love. Folk and fairy tales.

The snow queen: a fairy tale adapt. by Anthea Bell; ill. by Bernadette Watts. Holt, 1987. First pub. in Sweden under the title Die Schneekönigin ISBN 0-8050-0485-8 Subj: Character traits – bravery. Emotions. Folk and fairy tales.

The snow queen tr. by Eva Le Galliene; ill. by Arieh Zeldich. Harper, 1985. ISBN 0-06-023695-7 Subj: Character traits – bravery. Emotions – love. Folk and fairy tales.

The snow queen and other stories from Hans Andersen ill. by Edmund Dulac. Doubleday, 1976. Subj: Folk and fairy tales.

The steadfast tin soldier ill. by Thomas Di Grazia. Prentice-Hall, 1981. Subj: Folk and fairy tales. Toys – soldiers.

The steadfast tin soldier ill. by Paul Galdone. Houghton, 1979. Translation of Den standhaftige tinsoldat Subj: Folk and fairy tales. Toys – soldiers.

The steadfast tin soldier adapt. by Joel Tuber; ill. by David Jorgensen. Knopf, 1986. ISBN 0-394-88402-7 Subj: Folk and fairy tales. Toys – soldiers.

The steadfast tin soldier ill. by Monika Laimgruber. Atheneum, 1971. Translation of Den standhaftige tinsoldat Subj: Folk and fairy tales. Toys – soldiers.

The steadfast tin soldier tr. from Danish by Naomi Lewis; ill. by P. J. Lynch. Harcourt, 1992. ISBN 0-15-200599-4 Subj: Folk and fairy tales. Toys – soldiers.

The steadfast tin soldier retold by Tor Seidler; ill. by Fred Marcellino. HarperCollins, 1992. ISBN 0-06-205001-X Subj: Folk and fairy tales. Toys – soldiers.

The steadfast tin soldier ill. by Alain Vaës. Little, 1983. Translation of Den standhaftige tinsoldat Subj: Folk and fairy tales. Toys – soldiers.

The swineherd ill. by Erik Blegvad. Harcourt, 1958. Translation of Den svinedrengen by Erik Blegvad Subj: Character traits – cleverness. Character traits – selfishness. Folk and fairy tales.

The swineherd ill. by Dorothée Duntze. Holt, 1987. Translation of Den svinedrengen by Naomi Lewis ISBN 0-8050-0232-4 Subj: Character traits – cleverness. Character traits – selfishness. Folk and fairy tales. Royalty.

The swineherd adapt. and ill. by Deborah Hahn. Lothrop. 1991. ISBN 0-688-10053-8 Subj: Character traits – cleverness. Character traits – selfishness. Folk and fairy tales.

The swineherd ill. by Lisbeth Zwerger. Morrow, 1982. Translation of Den svinedrengen by Anthea Bell Subj: Character traits – cleverness. Character traits – selfishness. Folk and fairy tales.

Thumbelina ill. by Adrienne Adams. Scribner's, 1961. Translation of Tommelise by R. P. Keigwin Subj: Character traits – smallness. Folk and fairy tales.

Thumbelina retold by James Riordan; ill. by Wayne Anderson. Putnam, 1991. ISBN 0-399-21756-8 Subj: Character traits – smallness. Folk and fairy tales.

Thumbelina ill. by Alison Claire Darke. Doubleday, 1991. ISBN 0-385-41404-8 Subj: Character traits – smallness. Folk and fairy tales.

Thumbelina ill. by Demi. Putnam, 1987. ISBN 0-396-09241-1 Subj: Character traits – smallness. Folk and fairy tales.

Thumbelina ill. by Susan Jeffers; retold by Amy Ehrlich. Dial Pr., 1979. Translation of Tommelise Subj: Character traits – smallness. Folk and fairy tales.

Thumbelina retold by Deborah Hautzig; ill. by Kaarina Kaila. Knopf, 1990. ISBN 0-679-90667-3 Subj: Character traits – smallness. Folk and fairy tales.

Thumbelina ill. by Christine Willis Nigognossian. Troll Assoc., 1979. Translation of Tommelise Subj: Character traits – smallness. Folk and fairy tales.

Thumbelina ill. by Gustaf Tenggren. Simon and Schuster, 1953. Translation of Tommelise Subj: Character traits – smallness. Folk and fairy tales.

Thumbelina ill. by Lisbeth Zwerger. Morrow, 1980. Translation of Tommelise by Richard and Clara Winston Subj: Character traits – smallness. Folk and fairy tales.

Thumbeline tr. by Anthea Bell; ill. by Lisbeth Zwerger. Picture Book Studio, 1985. ISBN 0-88708-006-5 Subj: Character traits – smallness. Folk and fairy tales.

The tinderbox ill. by Warwick Hutton. Macmillan, 1988. ISBN 0-689-50458-6 Subj: Folk and fairy tales. Magic. Witches.

The tinderbox ill. by Barry Moser. Little, 1990. ISBN 0-316-03938-1 Subj: Folk and fairy tales. Magic. U.S. history. Witches.

The ugly duckling ill. by Adrienne Adams. Scribner's, 1965. Translation of Den grimme ælling by R. P. Keigwin Subj: Birds – ducks. Birds – swans. Character traits – appearance. Character traits – being different. Folk and fairy tales.

The ugly duckling ill. by Lorinda Bryan Cauley. Harcourt, 1979. Subj: Birds – ducks. Birds – swans. Character traits – appearance. Character traits – being different. Folk and fairy tales.

The ugly duckling retold and ill. by Troy Howell. Putnam, 1990. ISBN 0-399-22158-1 Subj: Birds – ducks. Birds – swans. Character traits – appearance. Character traits – being different. Folk and fairy tales.

The ugly duckling ill. by Tadasu Izawa and Shigemi Hijikata. Grosset, 1971. Translation of Den grimme ælling by Phyllis Paleček Subj: Birds

– ducks. Birds – swans. Character traits – appearance. Character traits – being different. Folk and fairy tales.

The ugly duckling tr. by Anne Stewart; ill. by Monika Laimgruber. Greenwillow, 1985. ISBN 0-688-04951-6 Subj: Birds – ducks. Birds – swans. Character traits – appearance. Character traits – being different. Folk and fairy tales.

The ugly duckling ill. by Johannes Larsen. Ward, 1956. Translation of Den grimme ælling by R. P. Keigwin Subj: Birds – ducks. Birds – swans. Character traits – appearance. Character traits – being different. Folk and fairy tales.

The ugly duckling adapt. by Marianna Mayer; ill. by Thomas Locker. Macmillan, 1987. ISBN 0-02-765130-4 Subj: Birds – ducks. Birds – swans. Character traits – appearance. Character traits – being different. Folk and fairy tales.

The ugly duckling tr. by Anthea Bell; ill. by Alan Marks. Picture Book Studio, 1990. ISBN 0-88708-116-9 Subj: Birds – ducks. Birds – swans. Character traits – appearance. Character traits – being different. Folk and fairy tales.

The ugly duckling adapt. by Phyllis Hoffman; ill. by Josef Paleček. Abelard-Schuman, 1972. Subj: Birds – ducks. Birds – swans. Character traits – appearance. Character traits – being different. Folk and fairy tales.

The ugly duckling adapt. by Lilian Moore; ill. by Daniel San Souci. Scholastic, 1987. ISBN 0-590-40957-3 Subj: Birds – ducks. Birds – swans. Character traits – appearance. Character traits – being different. Folk and fairy tales.

The ugly duckling adapt. by Joel Tuber and Clara Stites; ill. by Robert Van Nutt. Knopf, 1986. ISBN 0-394-88403-5 Subj: Birds – ducks. Birds – swans. Character traits – appearance. Character traits – being different. Folk and fairy tales.

The ugly little duck adapt. by Patricia C. and Fredrick McKissack; ill. by Peggy Perry Anderson. Childrens Pr., 1986. Prepared under the direction of Robert Hillerick ISBN 0-516-03982-2 Subj: Birds – ducks. Birds – swans. Character traits – appearance. Character traits – being different. Folk and fairy tales.

The wild swans tr. from Danish by Naomi Lewis; ill. by Angela Barrett. Harper, 1984. Subj: Birds – swans. Folk and fairy tales. Magic.

The wild swans retold by Amy Ehrlich; ill. by Susan Jeffers. Dial Pr., 1981. Subj: Birds – swans. Folk and fairy tales. Magic.

The woman with the eggs adapt. by Jan Wahl; ill. by Ray Cruz. Crown, 1974. An adaptation of a poem by H. C. Andersen pub. in Den danske bondeven, 1836 Subj: Behavior – greed. Eggs. Folk and fairy tales.

Andersen, Karen Born. *What's the matter, Sylvie, can't you ride?* ill. by author. Dial Pr., 1981. Subj: Emotions. Sports – bicycling.

Anderson, Adrienne Adams *see* Adams, Adrienne

Anderson, C. W. (Clarence Williams). *Billy and Blaze* ill. by author. Macmillan, 1936. Subj: Animals – horses. Birthdays. Family life.

Blaze and the forest fire ill. by author. Macmillan, 1938. Subj: Animals – horses. Fire.

Blaze and the gray spotted pony ill. by author. Macmillan, 1968. Subj: Animals – horses.

Blaze and the gypsies ill. by author. Macmillan, 1937. Subj: Animals – horses. Crime. Gypsies.

Blaze and the Indian cave ill. by author. Macmillan, 1964. Subj: Animals – horses. Cowboys.

Blaze and the lost quarry ill. by author. Macmillan, 1966. Subj: Animals – horses. Cowboys.

Blaze and the mountain lion ill. by author. Macmillan, 1959. Subj: Animals – cougars. Animals – horses. Cowboys.

Blaze and Thunderbolt ill. by author. Macmillan, 1955. Subj: Animals – horses. Cowboys.

Blaze finds forgotten roads ill. by author. Macmillan, 1970. Subj: Animals – horses. Behavior – lost. Cowboys.

Blaze finds the trail ill. by author. Macmillan, 1950. Subj: Animals – horses. Behavior – lost. Cowboys.

Blaze shows the way ill. by author. Macmillan, 1969. Subj: Animals – horses.

The crooked colt ill. by author. Macmillan, 1954. Subj: Animals – horses.

Linda and the Indians ill. by author. Macmillan, 1952. Subj: Animals – horses. Indians of North America. Imagination.

Lonesome little colt ill. by author. Macmillan, 1961. Subj: Animals – horses. Character traits – kindness to animals.

A pony for Linda ill. by author. Macmillan, 1951. Subj: Animals – horses.

A pony for three ill. by author. Macmillan, 1958. Subj: Animals – horses.

The rumble seat pony ill. by author. Macmillan, 1971. Subj: Animals – horses. Character traits – kindness to animals. Parades.

Anderson, Douglas. *Let's draw a story* ill. by author. Sterling, 1959. Subj: Animals – cats. Animals – dogs. Art. Family life. Games.

Anderson, Joan. *Harry's helicopter* ill. by George Ancona. Morrow, 1990. ISBN 0-688-09187-3 Subj: Activities – flying. Helicopters. Imagination.

Anderson, John L. *see* Anderson, Lonzo

Anderson, Lena Castell. *Bunny bath* ill. by author. Farrar, 1991. ISBN 91-29-59652-1 Subj: Activities – bathing. Animals – rabbits. Format, unusual – board books. Wordless.

Bunny box ill. by author. Farrar, 1991. ISBN 91-29-59858-3 Subj: Animals – rabbits. Bedtime. Family life – mothers. Format, unusual – board books. Toys. Wordless.

Bunny fun ill. by author. Farrar, 1991. ISBN 91-29-59860-5 Subj: Animals – rabbits. Format, unusual – board books. Sports – fishing. Sports – swimming. Wordless.

Bunny party ill. by author. Farrar, 1991. ISBN 91-29-59134-1 Subj: Animals – rabbits. Format, unusual – board books. Parties. Wordless.

Bunny story ill. by author. Farrar, 1991. ISBN 91-29-59132-5 Subj: Animals. Animals – rabbits. Bedtime. Format, unusual – board books. Wordless.

Bunny surprise ill. by author. Farrar, 1991. ISBN 91-29-59654-8 Subj: Animals – rabbits. Format, unusual – board books. Wordless.

Stina ill. by author. Greenwillow, 1989. ISBN 0-688-08881-3 Subj: Family life – grandfathers. Sea and seashore. Weather – storms.

Stina's visit ill. by author. Greenwillow, 1991. ISBN 0-688-09666-2 Subj: Birthdays. Family life – grandfathers. Friendship. Old age.

Anderson, Leone Castell. *The wonderful shrinking shirt* ill. by Irene Trivas. Albert Whitman, 1983. Subj: Clothing – shirts. Humor.

Anderson, Lonzo. *Arion and the dolphins* ill. by Adrienne Adams. Scribner's, 1978. Based on an ancient Greek legend Subj: Animals – dolphins. Boats, ships. Folk and fairy tales. Foreign lands – Greece.

The day the hurricane happened ill. by Ann Grifalconi. Scribner's, 1974. Subj: Family life. Foreign lands – Caribbean Islands. Weather – storms.

The Halloween party ill. by Adrienne Adams. Scribner's, 1974. Subj: Holidays – Halloween. Parties.

Izzard ill. by Adrienne Adams. Scribner's, 1973. Subj: Foreign lands – Caribbean Islands. Reptiles – lizards.

Mr. Biddle and the birds ill. by Adrienne Adams. Scribner's, 1971. Subj: Activities – flying. Birds.

Two hundred rabbits by Lonzo Anderson and Adrienne Adams; ill. by Adrienne Adams. Viking, 1968. Subj: Animals – rabbits. Fairies. Magic. Royalty.

Anderson, Lucia Z. *The smallest life around us* ill. by Leigh Grant. Crown, 1978. Subj: Science.

Anderson, Neil *see* Beim, Jerrold

Anderson, Paul S. *Red fox and the hungry tiger* ill. by Robert Kraus. Addison-Wesley, 1962. Subj: Animals – foxes. Animals – tigers. Character traits – cleverness. Friendship.

Anderson, Peggy Perry. *Time for bed, the babysitter said* ill. by author. Houghton, 1987. ISBN 0-395-41851-8 Subj: Activities – baby-sitting. Bedtime. Frogs and toads.

Anderson, Robin. *Sinabouda Lily: a folk tale from Papua New Guinea* ill. by Jennifer Allen. Oxford Univ. Pr., 1979. Subj: Activities – swinging. Folk and fairy tales. Foreign lands – New Guinea. Magic. Witches.

Anderson, Wayne. *Dragon* ill. by author. Simon & Schuster, 1992. ISBN 0-671-78397-1 Subj: Dragons. Imagination. Self-concept.

Andre, Evelyn M. *Places I like to be* photos. by author. Abingdon Pr., 1980. Subj: Activities. Poetry, rhyme.

Andrews, F. Emerson (Frank Emerson). *Nobody comes to dinner* ill. by Lydia Dabcovich. Little, 1977. Subj: Behavior – bad day. Emotions – anger. Imagination – imaginary friends.

Andrews, Jan. *The auction* ill. by Karen Reczuch. Macmillan, 1991. ISBN 0-02-705535-3 Subj: Emotions – anger. Emotions – sadness. Family life – grandfathers. Farms.

Very last first time ill. by Ian Wallace. Atheneum, 1986. ISBN 0-689-50388-1 Subj: Eskimos. Food. Foreign lands – Canada. Sea and seashore.

Andrews, Wayne. *Snow White and Rose Red* (Grimm, Jacob)

Andry, Andrew C. *Hi, new baby: a book to help your child learn about the new baby* by Andrew C. Andry and Suzanne C. Kratka; ill. by Thomas Di Grazia. Simon and Schuster, 1979, c1968. Subj: Babies. Birth.

How babies are made by Andrew C. Andry and Steven Schepp; ill. by Blake Hampton Rev. ed. Time-Life, 1979. Subj: Babies. Birth. Science.

Angeli, Marguerite De *see* De Angeli, Marguerite

Angelis, Nancy de *see* Angelo, Nancy Carolyn Harrison

Angelo, Nancy Carolyn Harrison. *Camembert* ill. by author. Houghton, 1958. Subj: Animals – mice. Art. Careers – artists. Foreign lands – France.

Angelo, Valenti. *The acorn tree* ill. by author. Viking, 1958. Subj: Animals – chipmunks. Animals – squirrels. Birds – bluejays. Character traits – selfishness. Trees.

The candy basket ill. by author. Viking, 1960. Subj: Animals – mice. Behavior – greed.

Anglund, Joan Walsh. *A is for always: an ABC book* ill. by author. Harcourt, 1968. Subj: ABC books.

A book of good tidings from the Bible ill. by author. Harcourt, 1965. Subj: Religion.

The brave cowboy ill. by author. Harcourt, 1959. Subj: Character traits – bravery. Cowboys. Games.

Christmas is a time of giving ill. by author. Harcourt, 1961. Subj: Character traits – generosity. Holidays – Christmas.

Cowboy and his friend ill. by author. Harcourt, 1961. Subj: Animals – bears. Cowboys. Friendship. Imagination – imaginary friends.

The cowboy's Christmas ill. by author. Atheneum, 1972. Subj: Animals – bears. Cowboys. Holidays – Christmas. Imagination – imaginary friends.

Cowboy's secret life ill. by author. Harcourt, 1963. Subj: Cowboys. Games. Imagination.

A friend is someone who likes you ill. by author. Harcourt, 1958. Subj: Friendship.

Look out the window ill. by author. Random, 1978. Subj: Character traits – individuality.

Love is a baby ill. by author. Harcourt, 1992. ISBN 0-15-200517-X Subj: Babies. Emotions – love. Poetry, rhyme.

Love is a special way of feeling ill. by author. Harcourt, 1960. Subj: Emotions – love.

Love one another ill. by author. Determined Prod., 1981. Subj: Foreign lands. Foreign languages.

Morning is a little child: poems ill. by author. Harcourt, 1969. Subj: Morning. Poetry, rhyme.

Nibble nibble mousekin: a tale of Hansel and Gretel ill. by author. Harcourt, 1962. Subj: Folk and fairy tales. Forest, woods. Witches.

Spring is a new beginning ill. by author. Harcourt, 1963. Subj: Seasons – spring.

Anholt, Catherine. *All about you* by Catherine and Laurence Anholt; ill. by authors. Viking, 1992. ISBN 0-670-84488-8 Subj: Character traits – questioning. Language.

Aren't you lucky! ill. by author. Little, 1991. ISBN 0-316-04264-1 Subj: Babies. Family life – sisters. Sibling rivalry.

Chaos at Cold Custard Farm ill. by author. Oxford Univ. Pr., 1988. ISBN 0-19-520645-2 Subj: Animals. Farms.

Good days, bad days ill. by author. Putnam, 1991. ISBN 0-399-22283-9 Subj: Concepts – opposites. Family life.

Snow fairy and the spaceman ill. by author. Delacorte Pr., 1991. ISBN 0-385-30422-6 Subj: Birthdays. Friendship. Parties.

Tom's rainbow walk ill. by author. Little, 1990. ISBN 0-316-04261-7 Subj: Activities – knitting. Concepts – color. Family life – grandmothers.

Truffles in trouble ill. by author. Little, 1987. ISBN 0-316-04260-9 Subj: Animals – pigs. Shopping. Stores.

Truffles is sick ill. by author. Little, 1987. ISBN 0-316-04259-5 Subj: Animals – pigs. Illness.

Twins, two by two by Catherine and Laurence Anholt; ill. by authors. Candlewick Pr., 1992. ISBN 1-56402-041-X Subj: Animals. Bedtime. Twins.

What I like by Catherine and Laurence Anholt; ill. by Catherine Anholt. Putnam, 1991. ISBN 0-399-21863-7 Subj: Character traits – individuality. Emotions. Poetry, rhyme.

When I was a baby ill. by author. Little, 1989. ISBN 0-316-04262-5 Subj: Babies. Behavior – growing up. Family life.

Anholt, Laurence. *All about you* (Anholt, Catherine)

The forgotten forest ill. by author. Sierra Club 1992. ISBN 0-87156-569-2 Subj: Ecology. Forest, woods.

Twins, two by two (Anholt, Catherine)

What I like (Anholt, Catherine)

Annett, Cora. *The dog who thought he was a boy* ill. by Walter Lorraine. Houghton, 1965. Subj: Animals – dogs. Birthdays. School.

When the porcupine moved in ill. by Peter Parnall. Watts, 1971. Subj: Animals – porcupines. Animals – rabbits. Behavior – trickery.

Annixter, Jane. *Brown rats, black rats* by Jane and Paul Annixter; ill. by Gilbert Riswold. Prentice-Hall, 1977. Subj: Animals – rats. Science.

Annixter, Paul. *Brown rats, black rats* (Annixter, Jane)

Anno, Masaichiro. *Anno's magical ABC* (Anno, Mitsumasa)

Anno, Mitsumasa. *All in a day* by Mitsumasa Anno and others; ill. by Mitsumasa Anno. Putnam's, 1986. ISBN 0-399-21311-2 Subj: Activities. Foreign lands. World.

Anno's Æsop: a book of fables by Æsop and Mr. Fox adapt. and ill. by author. Watts, 1989. ISBN 0-531-08374-8 Subj: Animals – foxes. Folk and fairy tales.

Anno's alphabet: an adventure in imagination ill. by author. Crowell, 1975. Subj: ABC books. Imagination. Optical illusions.

Anno's animals ill. by author. Collins-World, 1979. Subj: Animals. Games. Imagination. Wordless.

Anno's Britain ill. by author. Philomel, 1982. Subj: Foreign lands – England. Games. Humor. Imagination. Wordless.

Anno's counting book ill. by author. Crowell, 1975. Subj: Counting, numbers. Imagination. Optical illusions.

Anno's counting house ill. by author. Philomel, 1982. Translation of 10-nin no yukai na hikkoshi Subj: Counting, numbers. Games. Humor. Imagination. Optical illusions. Wordless.

Anno's faces ill. by author. Putnam, 1989. ISBN 0-399-21711-8 Subj: Anatomy – faces. Concepts – shape. Format, unusual.

Anno's flea market ill. by author. Philomel, 1984. Translation of Nomi no ichi Subj: Games. Humor. Imagination. Optical illusions. Wordless.

Anno's hat tricks ill. by author. Putnam, 1985. ISBN 0-399-21212-4 Subj: Counting, numbers. Magic.

Anno's Italy ill. by author. Collins-World, 1980. Japanese ed. entitled My journey II, a translation of Tabi no ehon, II Subj: Foreign lands – Italy. Games. Humor. Imagination. Optical illusions. Wordless.

Anno's journey ill. by author. Putnam, 1981. Pub. in 1977 under title: My journey, a translation of Tabi no ehon Subj: Games. Humor. Imagination. Optical illusions. Wordless.

Anno's magical ABC: an anamorphic alphabet by Mitsumasa and Masaichiro Anno; ill. by authors. Putnam's, 1981. Subj: ABC books. Format, unusual – toy and movable books. Games. Imagination. Optical illusions.

Anno's math games ill. by author. Philomel, 1987. ISBN 0-399-21151-9 Subj: Concepts. Counting, numbers. Riddles.

Anno's math games II ill. by author. Putnam, 1989. ISBN 0-399-21615-4 Subj: Concepts. Counting, numbers. Riddles.

Anno's math games III ill. by author. Putnam, 1991. ISBN 0-399-22274-X Subj: Concepts. Counting, numbers. Riddles.

Anno's peekaboo ill. by author. Putnam's, 1988. ISBN 0-399-21520-4 Subj: Format, unusual. Wordless.

Anno's U.S.A. ill. by author. Philomel, 1983. Translation of Tabi no ehon, IV Subj: Games. Humor. Imagination. Wordless.

Dr. Anno's magical midnight circus ill. by author. Weatherhill, 1972. Subj: Circus. Clowns, jesters. Imagination. Optical illusions. Wordless.

In shadowland ill. by author. Watts, 1988. ISBN 0-531-08341-1 Subj: Folk and fairy tales. Shadows. Sun.

The king's flower ill. by author. Collins-World, 1979. Subj: Concepts – size. Flowers. Imagination. Royalty – kings.

Topsy turvies: more pictures to stretch the imagination ill. by author. Putnam, 1989. ISBN 0-399-21557-3 Subj: Games. Humor. Imagination. Optical illusions. Wordless.

Topsy turvies: pictures to stretch the imagination ill. by author. Weatherhill, 1970. Subj: Games. Humor. Imagination. Optical illusions. Wordless.

Upside-downers: more pictures to stretch the imagination adapt. into English by Meredith Weatherby and Susan Trumbull; ill. by author. Weatherhill, 1971. Subj: Games. Humor. Imagination. Optical illusions.

Anrooy, Frans van. *The sea horse* ill. by Jaap Tol. Harcourt, 1968. Originally pub. in Holland under the title of Het Zeepaardje Subj: Dreams. Emotions – fear. Night. Sea and seashore.

Aoki, Hisako. *Santa's favorite story* by Hisako Aoki and Ivan Gantschev; ill. by authors. Neugebauer, 1982. Subj: Holidays – Christmas. Religion.

Appelbaum, Neil. *Is there a hole in your head?* ill. by author. Ivan Obolensky, 1963. Subj: Animals – whales. Games.

Appell, Clara. *Now I have a daddy haircut* by Clara and Morey Appell; photos. by authors. Dodd, 1960. Subj: Behavior – growing up. Careers – barbers. Hair. Self-concept.

Appell, Morey. *Now I have a daddy haircut* (Appell, Clara)

Appiah, Sonia. *Amoko and Efua Bear* ill. by Carol Easmon. Macmillan, 1989. ISBN 0-02-705591-4 Subj: Foreign lands – Ghana. Toys – teddy bears.

Apple, Margot. *Blanket* ill. by author. Houghton, 1990. ISBN 0-395-51522-X Subj: Animals. Bedtime. Clothing.

Applebaum, Stan. *Going my way?* by Stan Applebaum and Victoria Cox; ill. by Leonard W. Shortall. Harcourt, 1976. Subj: Animals. Science.

Appleby, Leonard. *Snakes* photos. by author. A & C Black, 1983. Subj: Reptiles – snakes. Science.

Arabian Nights. *Arabian Nights entertainments: the first book of tales of ancient Araby* comp. by Charles Mozley. Watts, 1960. Subj: Folk and fairy tales. Foreign lands – Arabia.

The flying carpet ill. by Marcia Brown. Scribner's, 1956. Subj: Activities – flying. Folk and fairy tales. Magic.

The magic horse (Scott, Sally)

The tale of Aladdin and the wonderful lamp: a story from the Arabian Nights adapt. by Eric A. Kimmel; ill. by Ju-Hong Chen. Holiday, 1992. ISBN 08234-0938-4 Subj: Folk and fairy tales. Magic. Mythical creatures.

Aragon, Jane Chelsea. *Lullaby* ill. by Kandy Radzinski. Chronicle Books, 1989. ISBN 0-87701-576-7 Subj: Lullabies.

Salt hands ill. by Ted Rand. Dutton, 1989. ISBN 0-525-44489-0 Subj: Animals – deer. Nature. Night. Poetry, rhyme.

Winter harvest ill. by Leslie A. Baker. Little, 1989. ISBN 0-316-04937-9 Subj: Poetry, rhyme. Animals – deer. Character traits – kindness to animals. Night. Seasons – winter.

Araten, Harry. *Two by two* ill. by author. Kar-Ben Copies, 1991. ISBN 0-929371-53-4 Subj: Religion.

Arbeit, Eleanor Werner. *Mrs. Cat hides something* ill. by author. Gibbs M. Smith, 1985. ISBN 0-87905-205-8 Subj: Animals – cats. Babies. Family life.

Archambault, John. *Counting sheep* ill. by John Rombola. Holt, 1989. ISBN 0-8050-1135-8 Subj: Animals. Bedtime. Counting, numbers. Poetry, rhyme.

Here are my hands (Martin, Bill (William Ivan))

Knots on a counting rope (Martin, Bill (William Ivan))

Listen to the rain (Martin, Bill (William Ivan))

The magic pumpkin (Martin, Bill (William Ivan))

Up and down on the merry-go-round (Martin, Bill (William Ivan))

White Dynamite and Curly Kidd (Martin, Bill (William Ivan))

Ardizzone, Aingelda. *The night ride* ill. by Edward Ardizzone. Windmill, 1975. Subj: Holidays – Christmas. Night. Toys. Toys – dolls. Toys – teddy bears.

Ardizzone, Edward. *Diana and her rhinoceros* ill. by author. Walck, 1964. Subj: Animals – rhinoceros. Pets.

Johnny the clockmaker ill. by author. Walck, 1960. Subj: Careers – clockmakers. Clocks, watches.

The little girl and the tiny doll ill. by author. Delacorte Pr., 1967. Subj: Behavior – losing things. Shopping. Toys – dolls.

Little Tim and the brave sea captain ill. by author. Walck, 1955. Subj: Boats, ships. Character traits – bravery. Sea and seashore.

Lucy Brown and Mr. Grimes ill. by author. Walck, 1970. A new version of a story published in 1937 Subj: Emotions – loneliness. Foreign lands – England. Old age. Orphans.

Nicholas and the fast-moving diesel ill. by author. Eyre & Spottiswoode, 1980. Subj: Trains. Transportation.

Paul, the hero of the fire ill. by author. Walck, 1963. A new version of a story published in 1949 Subj: Activities – working. Behavior – growing up. Character traits – bravery. Merry-go-rounds.

Peter the wanderer ill. by author. Walck, 1963. Subj: Character traits – bravery. Character traits – cleverness. Character traits – honesty. Sea and seashore.

Ship's cook Ginger ill. by author. Macmillan, 1978. First published in London by Bodley Head, 1977 Subj: Boats, ships. Sea and seashore.

Tim all alone ill. by author. Oxford Univ. Pr., 1957. Subj: Boats, ships. Sea and seashore.

Tim and Charlotte ill. by author. Oxford Univ. Pr., 1979. Subj: Boats, ships. Character traits – bravery. Sea and seashore.

Tim and Ginger ill. by author. Walck, 1965. Subj: Boats, ships. Sea and seashore.

Tim and Lucy go to sea ill. by author. Walck, 1958. Subj: Boats, ships. Friendship. Sea and seashore.

Tim in danger ill. by author. Walck, 1953. Subj: Boats, ships. Sea and seashore.

Tim to the rescue ill. by author. Walck, 1949. Subj: Boats, ships. Character traits – bravery. Character traits – loyalty. Sea and seashore. Weather.

Tim's friend Towser ill. by author. Walck, 1962. Subj: Animals – dogs. Boats, ships. Sea and seashore.

Tim's last voyage ill. by author. Walck, 1972. Subj: Boats, ships. Sea and seashore. Weather – wind.

Argent, Kerry. *Animal capers* ill. by author. Dial, 1990. ISBN 0-8037-0752-5 Subj: ABC books. Animals. Foreign lands – Australia. Zoos.

Happy birthday, Wombat! ill. by author. Little, 1991. ISBN 0-316-05097-0 Subj: Animals – wombats. Birthdays. Format, unusual – toy and movable books.

One woolly wombat (Trinca, Rod)

Wombat and Bandicoot: best friends ill. by author. Little, 1990. ISBN 0-316-05096-2 Subj: Animals – bandicoots. Animals – wombats. Foreign lands – Australia. Friendship.

Argueta, Manlio. *The magic dogs of the volcanoes* tr. from Spanish by Stacey Ross; ill. by Elly Simmons. Children's Book Pr., 1990. ISBN 0-89239-064-6 Subj: Animals – dogs. Foreign lands – El Salvador. Magic.

Ariane. *Animal stories* ill. by Feodor Rojankovsky. Western Pub., 1944. Subj: Animals.

Small Cloud ill. by Annie Gusman. Dutton, 1984. ISBN 0-525-44085-2 Subj: Folk and fairy tales. Science. Weather – clouds. Weather – rain.

Arkin, Alan. *Black and white* music by Earl Robinson; ill. by author. Golden Pr., 1966. Subj: Foreign lands – Africa. Music. Songs.

Tony's hard work day ill. by James Stevenson. Harper, 1972. Subj: Activities – working. Family life. Houses.

Armalyte, Olimpija. *How the cock wrecked the manor* (Tempest, P.)

Armer, Laura Adams. *The forest pool* ill. by author. Longman, 1938. Subj: Caldecott award honor book. Forest, woods.

Armitage, David. *Ice creams for Rosie* (Armitage, Ronda)

The lighthouse keeper's catastrophe (Armitage, Ronda)

One moonlit night (Armitage, Ronda)

Armitage, Marcia. *Lupatelli's favorite nursery tales* ill. by Anthony Lupatelli. Grosset, 1977. Subj: Folk and fairy tales.

Armitage, Ronda. *The bossing of Josie* ill. by David Armitage. Elsevier-Dutton, 1980. Subj: Birthdays. Family life. Magic. Sibling rivalry. Witches.

Don't forget, Matilda ill. by David Armitage. Elsevier-Dutton, 1979. Subj: Family life. Foreign lands – England.

Ice creams for Rosie by Ronda and David Armitage; ill. by David Armitage. Elsevier-Dutton, 1981. Subj: Food. Islands. Problem solving.

The lighthouse keeper's catastrophe by Ronda and David Armitage; ill. by David Armitage. Dutton, 1986. ISBN 0-233-97891-7 Subj: Animals – cats. Behavior – losing things. Lighthouses. Problem solving.

The lighthouse keeper's lunch ill. by David Armitage. Elsevier-Dutton, 1979. Subj: Birds – sea gulls. Food. Lighthouses. Problem solving.

The lighthouse keeper's rescue ill. by David Armitage. Dutton, 1989. ISBN 0-233-98428-3 Subj: Animals – whales. Lighthouses. Old age.

One moonlit night by Ronda and David Armitage; ill. by David Armitage. Dutton, 1983. Subj: Family life. Night. Camps, camping.

Armour, Richard Willard. *The adventures of Egbert the Easter egg* ill. by Paul Galdone. McGraw-Hill, 1965. Subj: Holidays – Easter. Poetry, rhyme.

Animals on the ceiling ill. by Paul Galdone. McGraw-Hill, 1966. Subj: Animals. Humor. Imagination. Poetry, rhyme.

Have you ever wished you were something else? ill. by Scott Gustafson. Children's Pr., 1983. Subj: Animals. Poetry, rhyme.

Sea full of whales ill. by Paul Galdone. McGraw-Hill, 1974. Subj: Animals – whales. Poetry, rhyme.

The year Santa went modern ill. by Paul Galdone. McGraw-Hill, 1964. Subj: Holidays – Christmas. Poetry, rhyme.

Arneson, D. J. *Secret places* ill. by Peter Arnold. Holt, 1971. Subj: Ecology. Forest, woods.

Arnold, Caroline. *The biggest living thing* ill. by author. Carolrhoda Bks., 1983. Subj: Science. Trees.

Everybody has a birthday ill. by Anthony Accardo. Watts, 1987. ISBN 0-531-10094-4 Subj: Birthdays.

Five nests ill. by Ruth Sanderson. Dutton, 1980. Includes index Subj: Animals. Birds. Science.

How do we communicate? ill. by Ginger Giles. Watts, 1983. Subj: Communication.

How do we have fun? photos. by Ginger Giles. Watts, 1983. Subj: Activities. Activities – playing.

How do we travel? photos. by Ginger Giles. Watts, 1983. Subj: Activities – traveling. Transportation.

Sun fun ill. by author. Watts, 1981. Subj: Science. Sun.

The terrible Hodag ill. by Lambert Davis. Harcourt, 1989. ISBN 0-15-284750-2 Subj: Behavior – greed. Folk and fairy tales. Forest, woods. Monsters.

What is a community? ill. by Carole Bertole. Watts, 1982. Subj: Careers. Communities, neighborhoods.

What we do when someone dies ill. by Helen K. Davie. Watts, 1987. ISBN 0-531-10095-2 Subj: Death.

What will we buy? photos. by Ginger Giles. Watts, 1983. Subj: Money. Shopping.

Where do you go to school? ill. by Carole Bertole. Watts, 1982. Includes index Subj: Careers – teachers. Communities, neighborhoods. School.

Who keeps us healthy? ill. by Carole Bertole. Watts, 1982. Subj: Careers – doctors. Careers – nurses.

Who keeps us safe? photos. by Carole Bertole. Watts, 1983. Subj: Careers. Safety.

Who works here? ill. by Carole Bertole. Watts, 1982. Subj: Careers. Communities, neighborhoods.

Arnold, Katrin. *Anna joins in* ill. by Renate Seelig. Abingdon Pr., 1983. Subj: Handicaps. Illness. School.

Arnold, Tedd. *Mother Goose's words of wit and wisdom: a book of months* ill. by author. Dial, 1990. ISBN 0-8037-0826-2 Subj: Behavior. Days of the week, months of the year. Nursery rhymes.

No jumping on the bed! ill. by author. Dial Pr., 1987. ISBN 0-8037-0039-3 Subj: Bedtime. Behavior – misbehavior. Dreams. Furniture – beds. Imagination.

Ollie forgot ill. by author. Dial Pr., 1988. ISBN 0-8037-0488-7 Subj: Behavior – forgetfulness. Circular tales. Middle ages. Poetry, rhyme.

The signmaker's assistant ill. by author. Dial, 1992. ISBN 0-8037-1011-9 Subj: Behavior – misbehavior. Traffic, traffic signs.

The simple people ill. by Andrew Shachat. Dial, 1992. ISBN 0-8037-1013-5 Subj: Activities – making things. Communities, neighborhoods.

Arnosky, Jim. *Come out, muskrats* ill. by author. Lothrop, 1989. ISBN 0-688-05458-7 Subj: Animals – muskrats. Nature.

Crinkleroot's guide to knowing the trees ill. by author. Macmillan, 1992. ISBN 0-02-705855-7 Subj: Forest, woods. Nature. Trees.

Crinkleroot's guide to walking in wild places ill. by author. Bradbury Pr., 1990. ISBN 0-02-705842-5 Subj: Activities – walking. Nature.

Deer at the brook ill. by author. Lothrop, 1986. ISBN 0-688-04100-0 Subj: Animals – deer.

Mouse numbers and letters ill. by author. Harcourt, 1982. Subj: ABC books. Animals – mice. Counting, numbers. Wordless.

Mouse writing ill. by author. Harcourt, 1983. Subj: ABC books. Activities – writing. Animals – mice. Birds. Wordless.

Mud time and more: Nathaniel stories ill. by author. Addison-Wesley, 1979. Subj: Problem solving. Wordless.

Outdoors on foot ill. by author. Coward, 1978. Subj: Activities – walking. Humor. Seasons.

Raccoons and ripe corn ill. by author. Lothrop, 1987. ISBN 0-688-05456-0 Subj: Animals – raccoons. Farms. Food. Night.

Watching foxes ill. by author. Lothrop, 1985. ISBN 0-688-04260-0 Subj: Activities – playing. Animals – foxes.

Arnott, Kathleen. *Spiders, crabs and creepy crawlers: two African folktales* ill. by Bette Davis. Garrard, 1978. Subj: Folk and fairy tales. Foreign lands – Africa.

Arnstein, Helene S. *Billy and our new baby* ill. by M. Jane Smyth. Human Sciences Pr., 1973. Subj: Babies. Family life. Sibling rivalry.

Aronin, Ben. *The secret of the Sabbath fish* ill. by Shay Rieger. Jewish Pub. Soc., 1979. Subj: Folk and fairy tales. Food. Format, unusual – board books. Jewish culture.

Arquette, Lois S. *see* Duncan, Lois

Arthur, Catherine. *My sister's silent world* ill. by Nathan Talbot. Children's Pr., 1979. Subj: Birthdays. Handicaps – deafness. Family life. Senses – hearing. Zoos.

Artis, Vicki Kimmel. *Pajama walking* ill. by Emily Arnold McCully. Houghton, 1981. Subj: Activities – playing. Friendship. Night.

Artzybasheff, Boris. *Seven Simeons* ill. by author. Viking, 1937. Subj: Caldecott award honor book.

Aruego, Ariane *see* Dewey, Ariane

Aruego, José. *A crocodile's tale: a Philippine folk story* by José Aruego and Ariane Dewey; ill. by authors. Scribner's, 1972. Subj: Folk and fairy tales. Foreign lands – Philippines. Reptiles – alligators, crocodiles.

The king and his friends ill. by author. Scribner's, 1969. Subj: Dragons. Friendship. Mythical creatures. Royalty – kings.

Look what I can do ill. by author. Scribner's, 1971. Subj: Animals. Behavior – imitation. Folk and fairy tales. Foreign lands – Philippines. Games.

Pilyo the piranha ill. by author. Macmillan, 1971. Subj: Fish. Foreign lands – South America.

Symbiosis: a book of unusual friendships ill. by author. Scribner's, 1970. Subj: Science.

We hide, you seek by José Aruego and Ariane Dewey; ill. by authors. Greenwillow, 1979. Subj: Animals. Behavior – hiding. Foreign lands – Africa. Games.

Arundel, Anne *see* Arundel, Jocelyn

Arundel, Jocelyn. *Shoes for Punch* ill. by Wesley Dennis. McGraw-Hill, 1964. Subj: Animals – horses.

Arvetis, Chris. *Why does it fly?* by Chris Arvetis and Carole Palmer; ill. by James Buckley. Rand McNally, 1984. ISBN 0-528-82074-5 Subj: Activities – flying. Animals. Science.

Why does it thunder and lightning? by Chris Arvetis and Carole Palmer; ill. by James Buckley. Macmillan, 1985. ISBN 0-528-82671-9 Subj: Weather – storms. Weather – thunder.

Why is it dark? by Chris Arvetis and Carole Palmer; ill. by James Buckley. Rand McNally, 1984. ISBN 0-528-82075-3 Subj: Animals. Concepts. Science.

Asare, Meshack. *Cat... in search of a friend* ill. by author. Kane/Miller, 1986. ISBN 0-916291-07-3 Subj: Animals – cats. Behavior – needing someone. Friendship.

Asbjørnsen, P. C. (Peter Christian). *The man who kept house* by P. C. Asbjørnsen and J. E. Moe; ill. by Svend Otto S. Macmillan, 1992. ISBN 0-689-50560-4 Subj: Animals. Family life. Folk and fairy tales. Foreign lands – Norway.

The three billy goats Gruff ill. by Marcia Brown. Harcourt, 1957. Subj: Animals – goats. Character traits – cleverness. Cumulative tales. Folk and fairy tales. Mythical creatures. Trolls.

Three billy goats Gruff adapt. by Patricia C. and Fredrick McKissack; ill. by Tom Dunnington. Childrens Pr., 1987. ISBN 0-516-02366-7 Subj: Animals – goats. Character traits – cleverness. Cumulative tales. Folk and fairy tales. Mythical creatures. Trolls.

The three billy goats Gruff ill. by Paul Galdone. Seabury Pr., 1973. Translation of De tre bukkene Bruse Subj: Animals – goats. Character traits – cleverness. Cumulative tales. Folk and fairy tales. Mythical creatures. Trolls.

The three billy goats Gruff adapt. and ill. by Janet Stevens. Harcourt, 1987. ISBN 0-15-286396-6 Subj: Animals – goats. Character traits – cleverness. Cumulative tales. Folk and fairy tales. Mythical creatures. Trolls.

The three billy goats Gruff ill. by William Stobbs. McGraw-Hill, 1967. Subj: Animals – goats. Character traits – cleverness. Cumulative tales. Folk and fairy tales. Mythical creatures. Trolls.

Asch, Frank. *Baby in the box* ill. by author. Holiday, 1989. ISBN 0-8234-0725-X Subj: Babies. Poetry, rhyme. Toys.

Bear shadow ill. by author. Prentice-Hall, 1985. ISBN 0-13-071580-8 Subj: Animals – bears. Shadows.

Bear's bargain ill. by author. Prentice-Hall, 1985. ISBN 0-13-071606-5 Subj: Animals – bears. Birds. Emotions – envy, jealousy.

Bread and honey ill. by author. Parents, 1981. Adapted from the author's Monkey face Subj: Activities – painting. Animals. Animals – bears. Family life – mothers.

City sandwich ill. by author. Greenwillow, 1978. Subj: City. Imagination. Poetry, rhyme.

Country pie ill. by author. Greenwillow, 1979. Subj: Country. Poetry, rhyme. Weather.

Good lemonade ill. by author. Watts, 1976. Subj: Activities – working. Food.

Goodbye house ill. by author. Prentice-Hall, 1986. ISBN 0-13-360272-9 Subj: Animals – bears. Family life. Moving.

Goodnight horsey ill. by author. Prentice-Hall, 1981. Subj: Animals – horses. Bedtime. Family life – fathers. Games. Imagination.

Happy birthday, moon! ill. by author. Simon & Schuster, 1985. Subj: Animals – bears. Birthdays. Moon.

Here comes the cat! (Vagin, Vladimir)

Just like daddy ill. by author. Prentice-Hall, 1981. Subj: Animals – bears. Behavior – imitation. Family life – fathers.

The last puppy ill. by author. Prentice-Hall, 1980. Subj: Animals – dogs. Pets.

Little Devil's ABC ill. by author. Scribner's, 1979. Subj: ABC books. Devil.

Little Devil's 123 ill. by author. Scribner's, 1979. Subj: Counting, numbers. Devil.

MacGooses's grocery ill. by James Marshall. Dial Pr., 1978. Subj: Birds – geese. Eggs.

Moon bear ill. by author. Scribner's, 1978. Subj: Animals – bears. Birds. Food. Moon. Night.

Mooncake ill. by author. Prentice-Hall, 1983. Subj: Animals – bears. Birds. Moon. Seasons – winter.

Moongame ill. by author. Prentice-Hall, 1984. ISBN 0-13-3600503-9 Subj: Activities – dancing. Animals – bears. Behavior – hiding. Moon.

Oats and wild apples ill. by author. Holiday House, 1988. ISBN 0-8234-0677-6 Subj: Animals – bulls, cows. Animals – deer. Friendship.

Pearl's promise ill. by author. Delacorte Pr., 1984. ISBN 0-385-29321-6 Subj: Animals – mice.

Popcorn ill. by author. Parents, 1979. Subj: Animals – bears. Food. Holidays – Halloween. Parties.

Rebecka ill. by author. Harper, 1972. Subj: Activities – playing. Animals – dogs. Imagination.

Sand cake ill. by author. Parents, 1979. Subj: Activities – picnicking. Animals – bears. Humor. Sea and seashore.

Skyfire ill. by author. Simon & Schuster, 1988. Subj: Animals – bears. Weather – rainbows.

Starbaby ill. by author. Scribner's, 1980. Subj: Babies. Sea and seashore. Sky. Stars.

Turtle tale ill. by author. Dial Pr., 1978. Subj: Humor. Reptiles – turtles, tortoises.

Yellow, yellow ill. by Mark Alan Stamaty. McGraw-Hill, 1971. Subj: Clothing. Concepts – color.

Asch, George. *Linda* ill. by author. McGraw-Hill, 1969. Subj: City. Emotions – happiness. Wordless.

Aseltine, Lorraine. *First grade can wait* ill. by Virginia Wright-Frierson. Albert Whitman, 1988. ISBN 0-8075-2451-4 Subj: Behavior – growing up. School.

I'm deaf and it's okay by Lorrine Aseltine, Evelyn Mueller and Nancy Tait; ill. by Helen Cogancherry. Albert Whitman, 1986. ISBN 0-8075-3472-2 Subj: Emotions – anger. Emotions – fear. Handicaps – deafness. Senses – hearing.

I'm deaf and it's okay (Aseltine, Lorraine)

Ash, Jutta. *Rapunzel* (Grimm, Jacob)

Wedding birds ill. by author. Little, 1987. ISBN 0-87113-122-6 Subj: Birds. Music. Songs. Weddings.

Ashabranner, Brent. *I'm in the zoo, too* ill. by Janet Stevens. Dutton, 1989. ISBN 0-525-65002-4 Subj: Animals. Animals – squirrels. Zoos.

Asher, Sandy. *Princess Bee and the royal goodnight story* ill. by Cat Bowman Smith. Albert Whitman, 1989. ISBN 0-8075-6624-1 Subj: Bedtime. Behavior – needing someone. Family life. Royalty. Sleep.

Ashey, Bella *see* Breinburg, Petronella

Ashley, Bernard. *Dinner ladies don't count* ill. by Janet Duchesne. Watts, 1981. Subj: Behavior – misbehavior. Birthdays. Problem solving. School.

Ashley, Jill. *Riddles about Christmas* ill. by photos. by Rob Gray. Silver Pr., 1990. ISBN 0-671-70552-0 Subj: Holidays – Christmas. Poetry, rhyme. Riddles.

Ashton, Elizabeth Allen. *An old-fashioned ABC book* ill. by Jessie Willcox Smith. Viking, 1990. ISBN 0-670-83048-8 Subj: ABC books. Poetry, rhyme.

An old-fashioned one two three book ill. by Jessie Willcox Smith. Viking, 1991. ISBN 0-670-83499-8 Subj: Counting, numbers. Poetry, rhyme.

Asimov, Isaac. *Animals of the Bible* ill. by Howard Berelson. Doubleday, 1978. ISBN 0-385-07215-5 Subj: Animals.

The best new things ill. by Symeon Shimin. Collins-World, 1971. Subj: Earth. Science. Space and space ships.

The moon ill. by Alex Ebel. Follett, 1967. Subj: Moon. Science.

Astley, Judy. *When one cat woke up* ill. by author. Dial, 1990. ISBN 0-8037-0782-7 Subj: Animals – cats. Counting, numbers.

At the farm ill. by Roser Capdevila. Firefly Pr., 1985. ISBN 0-920303-08-0 Subj: Farms. Format, unusual – board books.

Ata, Te. *Baby rattlesnake* adapt. by Lynn Moroney; ill. by Veg Reisberg. Children's Book Pr. 1989. ISBN 0-89239-049-2 Subj: Folk and fairy tales. Indians of North America.

Atene, Ann (Anna). *The golden guitar* ill. by author. Little, 1967. Subj: Foreign lands – Italy. Music. Puppets.

Attenberger, Walburga. *The little man in winter* ill. by author. Random House, 1972. Translation of Het mannetje in de winter Subj: Foreign lands – Germany. Poetry, rhyme. Seasons – winter.

Who knows the little man? ill. by author. Random House, 1972. Translation of Wie kent dat kleine mannetje? Subj: Foreign lands – Germany. Poetry, rhyme.

Attenborough, Elizabeth. *Walk rabbit walk* (McNaughton, Colin)

Atwood, Ann. *The little circle* ill. by author. Scribner's, 1967. Subj: Concepts – shape. Poetry, rhyme.

Atwood, Margaret. *Anna's pet* by Margaret Atwood and Joyce Barkhouse; ill. by Ann Blades. Lorimer, 1980. Subj: Animals. Character traits – optimism. Country. Pets.

Auch, Mary Jane. *The Easter egg farm* ill. by author. Holiday, 1992. ISBN 0-8234-0917-1 Subj: Birds – chickens. Eggs. Holidays – Easter.

Auer, Martin. *Now, now Markus* by Martin Auer and Simone Klages; ill. by authors. Greenwillow, 1989. ISBN 0-688-08975-5 Subj: Behavior – misbehavior. Birds – swans. Giants.

Auerbach, Julie Jaslow. *Everything's changing—It's pesach!* ill. by Chari Radin. Kar-Ben Copies, 1986. ISBN 0-930494-53-9 Subj: Holidays – Passover. Jewish culture. Poetry, rhyme.

Auerbach, Marjorie. *King Lavra and the barber* ill. by author. Knopf, 1964. Subj: Behavior – secrets. Careers – barbers. Folk and fairy tales. Royalty – kings.

Augarde, Steve (Stephen). *Barnaby Shrew, Black Dan and...the mighty wedgwood* ill. by author. Elsevier-Dutton, 1980. Subj: Animals – mice. Animals – rats. Animals – shrews. Behavior – boasting. Birds – parakeets, parrots. Reptiles – turtles, tortoises.

Barnaby Shrew goes to sea ill. by author. Elsevier-Dutton, 1979. Subj: Animals – rats. Animals – shrews. Boats, ships. Reptiles – turtles, tortoises.

Pig ill. by author. Bradbury Pr., 1977. Subj: Animals – pigs. Farms. Fire.

Aulaire, Edgar Parin d'. *Abraham Lincoln* (Aulaire, Ingri Mortenson d'.)

Animals everywhere (Aulaire, Ingri Mortenson d'.)

Children of the northlights (Aulaire, Ingri Mortenson d'.)

Don't count your chicks (Aulaire, Ingri Mortenson d'.)

East of the sun and west of the moon (Aulaire, Ingri Mortenson d'.)

Foxie, the singing dog (Aulaire, Ingri Mortenson d'.)

Nils (Aulaire, Ingri Mortenson d'.)

Ola (Aulaire, Ingri Mortenson d'.)

Pocahontas (Aulaire, Ingri Mortenson d'.)

The terrible troll-bird (Aulaire, Ingri Mortenson d'.)

Too big (Aulaire, Ingri Mortenson d'.)

The two cars (Aulaire, Ingri Mortenson d'.)

Wings for Per (Aulaire, Ingri Mortenson d'.)

Aulaire, Ingri Mortenson d'. *Abraham Lincoln* by Ingri and Edgar Parin d'Aulaire; ill. by authors. Doubleday, 1939, 1957. Subj: Caldecott award book. U.S. history.

Animals everywhere by Ingri and Edgar Parin d'Aulaire; ill. by authors. Doubleday, 1940. Subj: Animals.

Children of the northlights by Ingri and Edgar Parin d'Aulaire; ill. by authors. Viking, 1962. Subj: Activities – bathing. Activities – playing. Animals. Family life. Folk and fairy tales. Foreign lands – Lapland. School. Seasons – winter.

Don't count your chicks by Ingri and Edgar Parin d'Aulaire; ill. by authors. Doubleday, 1943. Subj: Behavior – greed. Birds – chickens. Folk and fairy tales. Humor.

East of the sun and west of the moon ed. by Ingri and Edgar Parin d'Aulaire; ill. by eds. Doubleday, 1969. Subj: Folk and fairy tales.

Foxie, the singing dog by Ingri and Edgar Parin d'Aulaire; ill. by authors. Doubleday, 1949. Subj: Animals – cats. Animals – dogs. Birds – chickens.

Nils by Ingri and Edgar Parin d'Aulaire; ill. by authors. Doubleday, 1948. Subj: Character traits – being different. Cowboys. Family life. School.

Ola by Ingri and Edgar Parin d'Aulaire; ill. by authors. Doubleday, 1932. Subj: Foreign lands – Norway.

Pocahontas by Ingri and Edgar Parin d'Aulaire; ill. by authors. Doubleday, 1946. Subj: Indians of North America. U.S. history.

The terrible troll-bird by Ingri and Edgar Parin d'Aulaire; ill. by authors. Doubleday, 1976. Subj: Foreign lands – Norway. Mythical creatures. Trolls.

Too big by Ingri and Edgar Parin d'Aulaire; ill. by authors. Doubleday, 1945. Subj: Behavior – growing up. Concepts – size.

The two cars by Ingri and Edgar Parin d'Aulaire; ill. by authors. Doubleday, 1955. Subj: Automobiles.

Wings for Per by Ingri and Edgar Parin d'Aulaire; ill. by authors. Doubleday, 1944. Subj: Activities – flying. Character traits – bravery. Farms. War.

Austin, Margot. *Barney's adventure* ill. by author. Dutton, 1941. Subj: Circus. Clowns, jesters.

Averill, Esther. *The fire cat* ill. by author. Harper, 1960. Subj: Animals – cats. Careers – firefighters.

Axworthy, Anni. *Ben's Wednesday* ill. by author. David & Charles, 1986. ISBN 0-340-33289-1 Subj: Dreams. Monsters. Night.

Ayal, Ora. *The adventures of Chester the chest* by Ora Ayal and Naomi Löw Nakao; ill. by Ora Ayal. Harper, 1982. Subj: Activities – flying. Behavior – boredom. Imagination.

Ugbu tr. by Naomi Löw Nakao; ill. by author. Harper, 1979. Subj: Activities – playing. Imagination.

Ayars, James Sterling. *Caboose on the roof* ill. by Bob Hodgell. Abelard-Schuman, 1956. Subj: Houses. Humor. Trains.

Contrary Jenkins (Caudill, Rebecca)

Ayer, Jacqueline. *Little Silk* ill. by author. Harcourt, 1970. Subj: Behavior – lost. Toys – dolls.

Nu Dang and his kite ill. by author. Harcourt, 1959. Subj: Behavior – losing things. Foreign lands – Thailand. Kites. Toys.

The paper-flower tree: a tale from Thailand ill. by author. Harcourt, 1962. Subj: Character traits – optimism. Foreign lands – Thailand. Plants.

A wish for little sister ill. by author. Harcourt, 1962. Subj: Behavior – wishing. Birds. Birthdays. Family life. Foreign lands – Thailand.

Aylesworth, Jim. *The bad dream* ill. by Judith Friedman. Albert Whitman, 1985. ISBN 0-8075-0506-4 Subj: Animals – dogs. Dreams. Family life. Sleep.

The completed hickory dickory dock ill. by Eileen Christelow. Macmillan, 1990. ISBN 0-689-31606-2 Subj: Animals – mice. Clocks, watches. Counting, numbers. Nursery rhymes. Time.

Country crossing ill. by Ted Rand. Macmillan, 1991. ISBN 0-689-31580-5 Subj: Noise, sounds. Trains.

The folks in the valley ill. by Stefano Vitale. HarperCollins, 1992. ISBN 0-06-021929-7 Subj: ABC books. Poetry, rhyme.

Hanna's hog ill. by Glen Rounds. Atheneum, 1988. ISBN 0-689-31367-5 Subj: Animals – pigs. Behavior – stealing. Behavior – trickery.

Hush up! ill. by Glen Rounds. Holt, 1980. Subj: Character traits – laziness. Humor. Noise, sounds.

Mary's mirror ill. by Richard Egielski. Holt, 1982. Subj: Behavior – greed. Emotions – envy, jealousy. Poetry, rhyme.

Mr. McGill goes to town ill. by Thomas Graham. Holt, 1989. ISBN 0-8050-0772-5 Subj: Character traits – helpfulness. Cumulative tales. Friendship. Poetry, rhyme.

Mother Halverson's new cat ill. by Toni Goffe. Macmillan, 1989. ISBN 0-689-31465-5 Subj: Animals – cats. Character traits – practicality.

Old Black Fly ill. by Stephen Gammell. Holt, 1992. ISBN 0-8050-1401-2 Subj: ABC books. Insects – flies. Poetry, rhyme.

One crow: a counting rhyme ill. by Ruth Young. Harper, 1988. ISBN 0-397-32175-9 Subj: Animals. Counting, numbers. Farms. Poetry, rhyme.

Shenandoah Noah ill. by Glen Rounds. Holt, 1985. ISBN 0-03-003749-2 Subj: Activities – working. Emotions – embarrassment. Humor.

Siren in the night ill. by Tom Centola. Albert Whitman, 1983. Subj: Activities – walking. Emotions – fear. Family life. Noise, sounds.

Tonight's the night ill. by John Wallner. Albert Whitman, 1981. Subj: Bedtime. Dreams. Night. Sleep.

Two terrible frights ill. by Eileen Christelow. Atheneum, 1987. ISBN 0-689-31327-6 Subj: Animals – mice. Emotions – fear. Night.

Ayres, Becky Hickox. *Matreshka* ill. by Alexi Natchev. Doubleday, 1992. ISBN 0-385-30657-1 Subj: Folk and fairy tales. Foreign lands – Russia. Toys – dolls. Witches.

Victoria flies high ill. by Robin Michal Koontz. Dutton, 1990. ISBN 0-525-65014-8 Subj: Activities – flying. Animals – pigs. Magic.

Ayres, Pam. *Guess what?* ill. by Julie Lacome. Knopf, 1988. ISBN 0-394-99287-3 Subj: Poetry, rhyme.

Guess who? ill. by Julie Lacome. Knopf, 1988. ISBN 0-394-99288-1 Subj: Poetry, rhyme.

Piggo and the nosebag ill. by Andy Ellis. Parkwest, 1991. ISBN 0-563-20922-4 Subj: Animals – pigs.

Piggo has a train ride ill. by Andy Ellis. Parkwest, 1992. ISBN 0-563-20921-6 Subj: Animals – pigs. Trains.

When dad cuts down the chestnut tree ill. by Percy Graham. Knopf, 1988. ISBN 0-394-90435-4 Subj: Family life – fathers. Nature. Poetry, rhyme. Trees.

When dad fills in the garden pond ill. by Percy Graham. Knopf, 1988. ISBN 0-394-90441-4 Subj: Activities – digging. Family life – fathers. Nature. Poetry, rhyme.

Azaad, Meyer. *Half for you* ill. by Nāhīd Ḥaqīqāt. Carolrhoda, 1971. Subj: Behavior – sharing. Birds. Careers. Clothing.

Azarian, Mary. *A farmer's alphabet* ill. by author. Godine, 1981. Subj: ABC books. Activities. Farms.

The tale of John Barleycorn or, From barley to beer: a traditional English ballad ill. by author. Godine, 1983. Subj: Folk and fairy tales. Food. Foreign lands – England. Middle ages. Music. Poetry, rhyme.

B. B. Blacksheep and Company: *a collection of favorite nursery rhymes* ill. by Nick Butterworth. Grosset, 1982. Subj: Animals. Nursery rhymes.

Baba, Noboru. *Eleven cats and a pig* ill. by author. Carolrhoda Books, 1988. ISBN 0-87614-338-9 Subj: Animals – cats. Behavior – misbehavior. Character traits – selfishness.

Eleven cats and albatrosses ill. by author. Carolrhoda Books, 1988. ISBN 0-87614-335-4 Subj: Animals – cats. Behavior – misbehavior. Character traits – selfishness.

Eleven cats in a bag ill. by author. Carolrhoda Books, 1988. ISBN 0-87614-336-2 Subj: Animals – cats. Behavior – misbehavior. Character traits – selfishness.

Eleven hungry cats ill. by author. Carolrhoda Books, 1988. ISBN 0-87614-337-0 Subj: Animals – cats. Behavior – misbehavior. Character traits – selfishness.

Babbitt, Lorraine. *Pink like the geranium* ill. by author. Children's Pr., 1973. Subj: Behavior. Clothing. Family life. School.

Babbitt, Natalie. *Nellie, a cat on her own* ill. by author. Farrar, 1989. ISBN 0-374-35506-1 Subj: Activities – dancing. Animals – cats. Character traits – freedom.

The something ill. by author. Farrar, 1970. Subj: Emotions – fear. Monsters. Night.

Babbitt, Samuel F. *The forty-ninth magician* ill. by Natalie Babbitt. Pantheon, 1966. Subj: Magic. Royalty.

The babes in the woods. *The old ballad of the babes in the woods* ed. by Kathleen Lines; ill. by Edward Ardizzone. Walck, 1972. Derived from a Chapbook ed. published in 1640 Subj: Folk and fairy tales. Orphans. Poetry, rhyme.

Babson, Jane F. *Babson's bestiary* ill. by author. Winstead Pr., 1991. ISBN 0-940787-02-4 Subj: ABC books. Animals. Poetry, rhyme.

Baby's first book of colors ill. by Nina Barbaresi. Platt, 1986. ISBN 0-448-10827-5 Subj: Animals – rabbits. Concepts – color. Format, unusual – board books.

Baby's words photos. sel. by Debby Slier. Macmillan, 1988. ISBN 0-02-688751-7 Subj: Babies. Format, unusual – board books. Language.

Bach, Alice. *The day after Christmas* ill. by Mary Chalmers. Harper, 1975. Subj: Emotions. Holidays – Christmas.

Millicent the magnificent ill. by Steven Kellogg. Harper, 1978. Subj: Animals – bears. Circus. Emotions – envy, jealousy. Family life.

The smartest bear and his brother Oliver ill. by Steven Kellogg. Harper, 1975. ISBN 0-06-020335-8 Subj: Animals – bears. Family life. Food. Sibling rivalry. Sleep.

Warren Weasel's worse than measles ill. by Hilary Knight. Harper, 1980. Subj: Animals – bears. Animals – weasels. Self-concept.

Bach, Othello. *Hector McSnector and the mail-order Christmas witch* ill. by Timothy Hildebrandt. Caedmon, 1984. ISBN 0-89845-342-9 Subj: Holidays – Christmas. Magic. Witches.

Lilly, Willy and the mail-order witch ill. by Timothy Hildebrandt. Caedmon, 1983. Subj: Activities – working. Imagination. Magic. Music. Poetry, rhyme. Witches.

Bacheller, Irving. *Lost in the fog* adapt. and ill. by Loretta Krupinski. Little, 1990. ISBN 0-316-07462-4 Subj: Behavior – lost. Birds – geese. Weather – fog.

Back, Christine. *Bean and plant* photos. by Barrie Watts. Silver Burdett, 1986. ISBN 0-382-09286-4 Subj: Plants. Science. Seeds.

Chicken and egg photos. by Bo Jarner. Silver Burdett, 1986. ISBN 0-382-09284-8 Subj: Birds – chickens. Eggs. Science.

Spider's web photos. by Barrie Watts. Silver Burdett, 1986. ISBN 0-382-09288-8 Subj: Science. Spiders.

Tadpole and frog photos. by Barrie Watts. Silver Burdett, 1986. ISBN 0-382-09285-6 Subj: Frogs and toads. Science.

Bacon, Joan Chase *see* Bowden, Joan Chase

Baden, Robert. *And Sunday makes seven* ill. by Michelle Edwards. Albert Whitman, 1990. ISBN 0-8075-0356-8 Subj: Days of the week, months of the year. Folk and fairy tales. Foreign lands – Costa Rica. Foreign languages. Witches.

Baehr, Patricia. *School isn't fair* ill. by Robert W. Alley. Macmillan, 1989. ISBN 0-02-708130-3 Subj: School.

Baer, Edith. *This is the way we go to school* ill. by Steve Bjorkman. Scholastic, 1990. ISBN 0-590-43161-7 Subj: Poetry, rhyme. School. Transportation.

Words are like faces ill. by Karen Gundersheimer. Pantheon, 1980. Subj: Language. Poetry, rhyme.

Baer, Gene. *Thump thump rat-a-tat-tat* ill. by Lois Ehlert. HarperCollins, 1989. ISBN 0-06-020362-5 Subj: Music. Parades.

Bagwell, Elizabeth. *This is an airport* (Bagwell, Richard)

Bagwell, Richard. *This is an airport* by Richard and Elizabeth Bagwell; photos. by Lee Balterman. Follett, 1967. Subj: Airplanes, airports. Transportation.

Bahr, Amy C. *It's ok to say no: a book for parents and children to read together* ill. by Frederick Bennett Green. Grosset, 1986. ISBN 0-448-15328-9 Subj: Behavior – talking to strangers. Safety. Self-concept.

Sometimes it's ok to tell secrets: a book for parents and children to read together ill. by Frederick Bennett Green. Grosset, 1986. ISBN 0-448-15325-4 Subj: Behavior – secrets. Safety. Self-concept.

What should you do when...? a book for parents and children to read together ill. by Frederick Bennett Green. Grosset, 1986. ISBN 0-448-15327-0 Subj: Safety. Self-concept.

Your body is your own: a book for parents and children to read together ill. by Frederick Bennett Green. Grosset, 1986. ISBN 0-448-15326-2 Subj: Safety. Self-concept.

Bahr, Robert. *Blizzard at the zoo* ill. by Consuelo Joerns. Lothrop, 1982. Subj: Animals. Weather – snow. Weather – storms. Zoos.

Bailey, Debbie. *Clothes* photos. by Susan Huszar. Firefly, 1991. ISBN 1-55037-167-3 Subj: Clothing. Format, unusual – board books.

Hats photos. by Susan Huszar. Firefly, 1991. ISBN 1-55037-159-2 Subj: Clothing – hats. Format, unusual – board books.

My dad photos. by Susan Huszar. Firefly, 1991. ISBN 1-55037-164-9 Subj: Family life – fathers. Format, unusual – board books.

My mom photos. by Susan Huszar. Firefly, 1991. ISBN 1-55037-163-0 Subj: Family life – mothers. Format, unusual – board books.

Shoes photos. by Susan Huszar. Firefly, 1991. ISBN 1-55037-161-4 Subj: Clothing – shoes. Format, unusual – board books.

Toys photos. by Susan Huszar. Firefly, 1991. ISBN 1-55037-165-7 Subj: Format, unusual – board books. Toys.

Bailey, Jill. *Eyes* photos. by Jim Bailey. Putnam's, 1984. Subj: Anatomy – eyes. Animals. Birds. Format, unusual – board books.

Feet photos. by Jim Bailey. Putnam's, 1984. Subj: Anatomy – feet. Animals. Birds. Format, unusual – board books.

Mouths photos. by Jim Bailey. Putnam's, 1984. Subj: Anatomy – mouths. Animals. Birds. Format, unusual – board books.

Noses photos. by Jim Bailey. Putnam's, 1984. Subj: Anatomy – noses. Animals. Format, unusual – board books.

Baillie, Allan. *Drac and the gremlin* ill. by Jane Tanner. Dial, 1989. ISBN 0-8037-0628-6 Subj: Activities – playing. Games. Imagination.

Bains, Rae. *Hiccups, hiccups* ill. by Otto Coontz. Troll Assoc., 1981. Subj: Illness.

Baird, Anne. *Baby socks* ill. by author. Morrow, 1984. ISBN 0-688-02436-X Subj: Babies. Clothing – socks. Format, unusual – board books.

The Christmas lamb ill. by author. Morrow, 1989. ISBN 0-688-07775-7 Subj: Animals – sheep. Holidays – Christmas.

The guppies of Hilly Dale House ill. by Mary Morgan. Simon & Schuster, 1991. ISBN 0-671-69201-1 Subj: Activities. School.

Kiss, kiss ill. by author. Morrow, 1984. ISBN 0-688-02493-9 Subj: Babies. Family life. Format, unusual – board books.

Little tree ill. by author. Morrow, 1984. ISBN 0-688-02421-9 Subj: Format, unusual – board books. Trees.

No sheep ill. by author. Morrow, 1984. ISBN 0-688-02377-0 Subj: Bedtime. Format, unusual – board books.

Baisch, Cris. *When the lights went out* ill. by Ulises Wensell. Putnam's, 1987. ISBN 0-399-21415-1 Subj: Family life. Lights. Power failure.

Baker, Alan. *Benjamin and the box* ill. by author. Lippincott, 1978. Subj: Animals – hamsters. Friendship.

Benjamin bounces back ill. by author. Lippincott, 1978. Subj: Animals – hamsters. Humor. Imagination.

Benjamin's balloon ill. by author. Lothrop, 1990. ISBN 0-688-09744-8 Subj: Animals – hamsters. Toys – balloons.

Benjamin's book ill. by author. Lothrop, 1983. Subj: Animals – hamsters. Behavior – misbehavior. Humor.

Benjamin's dreadful dream ill. by author. Lippincott, 1980. Subj: Animals – hamsters. Behavior – misbehavior. Humor.

Benjamin's portrait ill. by author. Lothrop, 1987. ISBN 0-688-06878-2 Subj: Activities – painting. Animals – hamsters. Behavior – bad day. Careers – artists. Concepts – color. Humor.

Two tiny mice ill. by author. Dial, 1991. ISBN 0-8037-0973-0 Subj: Animals. Animals – mice. Nature.

Baker, Barbara. *Digby and Kate* ill. by Marsha Winborn. Dutton, 1988. ISBN 0-525-44370-3 Subj: Animals – cats. Animals – dogs. Friendship.

Digby and Kate again ill. by Marsha Winborn. Dutton, 1989. ISBN 0-525-44477-7 Subj: Animals – cats. Animals – dogs. Friendship.

Baker, Betty. *And me, coyote!* ill. by Maria Horvath. Macmillan, 1982. Subj: Animals – coyotes. Character traits – cleverness. Indians of North America. Folk and fairy tales. Religion.

My sister says ill. by Tricia Taggart. Macmillan, 1984. Subj: Behavior – wishing. Boats, ships. Family life – fathers. Imagination. Sibling rivalry.

Partners ill. by Emily Arnold McCully. Greenwillow, 1978. Subj: Animals – badgers. Animals – coyotes. Character traits – cleverness. Character traits – helpfulness. Character traits – laziness. Farms. Friendship.

Rat is dead and ant is sad: based on a Pueblo Indian tale ill. by Mamoru Funai. Harper, 1981. Subj: Cumulative tales. Death. Emotions – sadness. Indians of North America. Folk and fairy tales.

Sonny-Boy Sim ill. by Susanne Suba. Rand McNally, 1948. Subj: Animals. Family life. Humor. Sports – hunting.

Three fools and a horse ill. by Glen Rounds. Macmillan, 1975. Subj: Animals – horses. Indians of North America. Humor.

Worthington Botts and the steam machine ill. by Sal Murdocca. Macmillan, 1981. Subj: Activities – reading. Humor. Machines.

Baker, Bonnie Jeanne. *A pear by itself* ill. by author. Children's Pr., 1982. Subj: Counting, numbers.

Baker, Charlotte. *Little brother* ill. by author. McKay, 1959. Subj: Animals – dogs. Babies. Emotions – envy, jealousy. Family life. Sibling rivalry.

Baker, Donna. *I want to be a librarian* ill. by Richard Wahl. Children's Pr., 1978. Subj: Careers – librarians. Libraries.

I want to be a pilot ill. by Richard Wahl. Children's Pr., 1978. Subj: Careers – airplane pilots. Airplanes, airports.

I want to be a police officer ill. by Richard Wahl. Children's Pr., 1978. Subj: Careers – police officers.

Baker, Eugene. *Bicycles* ill. by Tom Dunnington. Creative Ed., 1980. Subj: Animals. Safety. Sports – bicycling.

Fire ill. by Tom Dunnington. Creative Ed., 1980. Subj: Animals. Fire. Safety.

Home ill. by Tom Dunnington. Creative Ed., 1980. Subj: Animals. Safety.

I want to be a computer operator ill. by Tom Dunnington. Children's Pr., 1973. Subj: Careers. Computers.

Outdoors ill. by Tom Dunnington. Creative Ed., 1980. Subj: Animals. Safety.

School ill. by Tom Dunnington. Creative Ed., 1980. Subj: Animals. Safety. School.

Water ill. by Tom Dunnington. Creative Ed., 1980. Subj: Animals. Safety.

Baker, Gayle. *Special delivery: a book for kids about cesarean and vaginal birth* ill. by Debra Hillyer. Chas. Franklin Pr., 1981. Subj: Babies. Birth. Family life – mothers. Hospitals. Science.

Baker, Jeannie. *Grandmother* ill. by author. Elsevier-Dutton, 1979. Subj: Art. Family life – grandmothers.

Home in the sky ill. by author. Greenwillow, 1984. Subj: Animals – dogs. Birds – pigeons. Character traits – kindness to animals. City.

Millicent ill. by author. Elsevier-Dutton, 1980. Subj: Birds – pigeons. Character traits – individuality. City.

One hungry spider ill. by author. Elsevier-Dutton, 1983. Subj: Counting, numbers. Science. Spiders.

Where the forest meets the sea ill. by author. Greenwillow, 1988. ISBN 0-688-06364-0 Subj: Ecology. Foreign lands – Australia. Forest, woods.

Window ill. by author. Greenwillow, 1991. ISBN 0-688-08918-6 Subj: Ecology. Foreign lands – Australia. Wordless.

Baker, Jeffrey J. W. *Patterns of nature* photos. by Jaroslav Salek. Doubleday, 1967. Subj: Animals. Birds. Flowers. Plants. Science. Trees.

Baker, Jill. *Basil of Bywater Hollow* ill. by Lynn Bywaters Ferris. Holt, 1987. ISBN 0-8050-0268-5 Subj: Animals – bears. Fairs. Weather – rain.

Baker, Keith. *The dove's letter* ill. by author. Harcourt, 1988. ISBN 0-15-224133-7 Subj: Birds – doves. Emotions – love. Letters.

Hide and snake ill. by author. Harcourt, 1991. ISBN 0-15-233986-8 Subj: Games. Poetry, rhyme. Reptiles – snakes.

The magic fan ill. by author. Harcourt, 1989. ISBN 0-15-250750-7 Subj: Careers – carpenters. Foreign lands – Japan. Imagination.

Who is the beast? ill. by author. Harcourt, 1990. ISBN 0-15-296057-0 Subj: Animals – tigers. Poetry, rhyme.

Baker, Laura Nelson. *The friendly beasts* ill. by Nicolas Sidjakov. Parnassus, 1958. Adapt. from an old English Christmas carol of the same title Subj: Animals. Holidays – Christmas. Music.

O children of the wind and pines ill. by Inez Storer. Lippincott, 1967. Subj: Indians of North America. Holidays – Christmas. Music.

Baker, Leslie A. *The antique store cat* ill. by author. Little, 1992. ISBN 0-316-07837-9 Subj: Animals – cats. Behavior – running away.

The third-story cat ill. by author. Little, 1987. ISBN 0-316-07832-8 Subj: Animals – cats. Behavior – running away.

Baker, Margaret. *A puppy called Spinach* by Margaret and Mary Baker; ill. by Mary Baker. Dodd, 1939. Subj: Animals – dogs. Behavior – misbehavior.

Baker, Mary. *A puppy called Spinach* (Baker, Margaret)

Baker, Olaf. *Where the buffaloes begin* ill. by Stephen Gammell. Warne, 1981. Subj: Animals – buffaloes. Caldecott award honor book. Indians of North America. Folk and fairy tales.

Baker, Pamela J. *My first book of sign* ill. by Patricia Bellan Gillen. Gallaudet Univ. Pr., 1986. ISBN 0-930323-20-3 Subj: Handicaps – deafness. Language. Senses – hearing.

Baker, Sanna Anderson. *Who's a friend of the water-spurting whale* handlettered and ill. by Tomie de Paola. David C. Cook, 1987. ISBN 0-89191-587-7 Subj: Poetry, rhyme. Religion.

Bakken, Harold. *The special string* ill. by Mischa Richter. Prentice-Hall, 1981. Subj: Character traits – helpfulness. Humor. Problem solving. String. Wordless.

Baldner, Gaby. *Joba and the wild boar: Joba und das wildschwein* ill. by Gerhard Oberländer. Hastings, 1961. Text in English and German Subj: Animals – pigs. Character traits – bravery. Foreign languages. Pets.

Balestrino, Philip. *Fat and skinny* ill. by Pam Makie. Crowell, 1975. Subj: Character traits – appearance.

Hot as an ice cube ill. by Tomie de Paola. Crowell, 1971. Subj: Concepts. Science.

The skeleton inside you ill. by True Kelley Rev. ed. HarperCollins, 1989. ISBN 0-690-04733-9 Subj: Anatomy – skeletons. Science.

Balet, Jan B. *Amos and the moon* ill. by author. Oxford Univ. Pr., 1948. Subj: Moon.

The fence: a Mexican tale ill. by author. Delacorte Pr., 1969. Translation of Der Zaun Subj: Family life. Folk and fairy tales. Foreign lands – Mexico. Poverty. Problem solving.

Five Rollatinis ill. by author. Lippincott, 1959. Subj: Animals – horses. Circus. Family life.

The gift: a Portuguese Christmas tale ill. by author. Delacorte, 1967. Subj: Foreign lands – Portugal. Holidays – Christmas. Religion.

Joanjo: a Portuguese tale ill. by author. Delacorte Pr., 1967. Subj: Character traits – ambition. Dreams. Fish. Foreign lands – Portugal.

The king and the broom maker ill. by author. Delacorte, 1968. Translation of König und der Besenbinder Subj: Behavior – dissatisfaction. Royalty – kings.

Ned and Ed and the lion ill. by author. Oxford Univ. Pr., 1949. Subj: Animals – lions. Imagination. Twins.

Balian, Lorna. *Amelia's nine lives* ill. by author. Abingdon Pr., 1986. ISBN 0-687-01250-3 Subj: Animals – cats. Behavior – lost. Pets.

Bah! Humbug? ill. by author. Abingdon, 1977. Subj: Holidays – Christmas.

A garden for a groundhog ill. by author. Abingdon Pr., 1985. ISBN 0-687-14009-9 Subj: Animals – groundhogs. Farms. Gardens, gardening. Holidays – Groundhog Day.

Humbug potion: an A B Cipher ill. by author. Abingdon, 1984. Subj: ABC books. Magic. Secret codes. Witches.

Humbug rabbit ill. by author. Abingdon, 1974. Subj: Animals – rabbits. Family life – grandmothers. Holidays – Easter.

Humbug witch ill. by author. Abingdon, 1965. Subj: Holidays – Halloween. Witches.

Leprechauns never lie ill. by author. Abingdon, 1980. Subj: Animals – cats. Elves and little people. Folk and fairy tales. Foreign lands – Ireland. Humor.

Sometimes it's turkey ill. by author. Abingdon, 1973. Subj: Birds – turkeys. Holidays – Thanksgiving.

A sweetheart for Valentine ill. by author. Abingdon, 1987. Subj: Giants. Holidays – Valentine's Day. Weddings.

Where in the world is Henry? ill. by author. Bradbury Pr., 1972. Subj: Concepts – size. Science.

Wilbur's space machine ill. by author. Holiday, 1990. ISBN 0-8234-0836-1 Subj: Activities – flying. Ecology. Friendship.

Ball, Duncan. *Jeremy's tail* ill. by Donna Rawlins. Orchard, 1991. ISBN 0-531-08551-1 Subj: Activities – traveling. Games.

Ballard, Robin. *Cat and Alex and the magic flying carpet* ill. by author. HarperCollins, 1991. ISBN 0-06-020390-0 Subj: Animals – cats. Magic.

Granny and me ill. by author. Greenwillow, 1992. ISBN 0-688-10549-1 Subj: Family life. Family life – grandmothers.

Balterman, Lee. *Girders and cranes* photos. by author. Albert Whitman, 1990. ISBN 0-8075-2923-0 Subj: Activities – making things. Buildings. Machines.

Balzano, Jeanne. *The wee moose* ill. by Enrico Arno. Parents, 1964. Subj: Animals – mice. Farms.

Balzola, Asun. *Munia and the day things went wrong* ill. by author. Cambridge Univ. Pr., 1988. ISBN 0-521-35643-1 Subj: Behavior – bad day. Family life.

Munia and the moon ill. by author. Cambridge Univ. Pr., 1989. ISBN 0-521-37143-0 Subj: Moon. Night.

Munia and the orange crocodile ill. by author. Cambridge Univ. Pr., 1988. ISBN 0-521-35642-3 Subj: Dreams. Reptiles – alligators, crocodiles. Teeth.

Munia and the red shoes ill. by author. Cambridge Univ. Pr., 1989. ISBN 0-521-37142-2 Subj: Behavior – growing up. Clothing – shoes.

Bambi ill. by Christa Stephan. Imported Pubs., 1983. Subj: Format, unusual – board books. Toys. Wordless.

Banbery, Fred. *Paddington at the circus* (Bond, Michael)

Banchek, Linda. *Snake in, snake out* ill. by Elaine Arnold. Crowell, 1978. Subj: Birds – parakeets, parrots. Concepts – in and out. Concepts – opposites. Reptiles – snakes. Wordless.

Bancroft, Laura *see* Baum, L. Frank (Lyman Frank)

Bang, Betsy. *The cucumber stem* ill. by Tony Chen. Greenwillow, 1980. Adapt. from a Bengali folk tale Subj: Character traits – smallness. Folk and fairy tales. Foreign lands – India.

The old woman and the red pumpkin ill. by Molly Bang. Macmillan, 1975. Adapt. and tr. from a Bengali folk tale by Betsy Bang Subj: Animals. Character traits – cleverness. Folk and fairy tales. Foreign lands – India.

The old woman and the rice thief ill. by Molly Bang. Greenwillow, 1978. Adapt. and tr. from a Bengali folk tale by Betsy Bang Subj: Animals. Character traits – cleverness. Folk and fairy tales. Foreign lands – India.

Tuntuni the tailor bird ill. by Molly Bang. Greenwillow, 1978. Adapt. and tr. from a Bengali folk tale by Betsy Bang Subj: Birds. Folk and fairy tales. Foreign lands – India. Royalty.

Bang, Molly. *Dawn* ill. by author. Morrow, 1983. An adaptation of the Japanese folk tale: Tsuru Nyōbō Also known as The Crane Wife Subj: Activities – weaving. Behavior – secrets. Birds –

cranes. Character traits – curiosity. Folk and fairy tales. Foreign lands – Japan.

Delphine ill. by author. Morrow, 1988. ISBN 0-688-05637-7 Subj: Animals. Sports – bicycling.

The goblins giggle and other stories ill. by author. Peter Smith, 1988. ISBN 0-8446-6360-3 Subj: Goblins.

The grey lady and the strawberry snatcher ill. by author. Four Winds Pr., 1980. Subj: Caldecott award honor book. Imagination. Wordless.

The paper crane ill. by author. Greenwillow, 1985. ISBN 0-688-04109-4 Subj: Birds – cranes. Character traits – kindness. Folk and fairy tales.

Ten, nine, eight ill. by author. Greenwillow, 1983. ISBN 0-688-00907-7 Subj: Bedtime. Caldecott award honor book. Counting, numbers. Ethnic groups in the U.S. – Afro-Americans. Poetry, rhyme.

Tye May and the magic brush ill. by author. Greenwillow, 1981. ISBN 0-688-84290-9 Subj: Activities – painting. Royalty.

Wiley and the hairy man: adapted from an American folk tale ill. by author. Macmillan, 1976. Subj: Bedtime. Character traits – cleverness. Ethnic groups in the U.S. – Afro-Americans. Folk and fairy tales. Monsters.

Yellow ball ill. by author. Morrow, 1991. ISBN 0-688-06315-2 Subj: Activities – playing. Sea and seashore. Toys – balls.

Bangs, Edward. *Yankee Doodle* ill. by Steven Kellogg. Parents, 1976. Subj: Songs. U.S. history.

Baningan, Sharon Stearns. *Circus magic* ill. by Katharina Maillard. Dutton, 1958. Subj: Circus. Magic. Poetry, rhyme.

Banish, Roslyn. *A forever family* photos. by author. HarperCollins, 1992. ISBN 0-06-021674-3 Subj: Adoption. Ethnic groups in the U.S. Family life.

I want to tell you about my baby Wingbow Pr., 1982. Subj: Babies. Family life.

Let me tell you about my baby photos. by author. Harper, 1988. ISBN 0-06-020383-8 Subj: Babies. Family life.

Bank Street College of Education. *Around the city* ill. by Aurelius Battaglia and others Rev. ed. Macmillan, 1972. Subj: City.

Green light, go ill. by Jack Endewelt and others Rev. ed. Subj: City. Traffic, traffic signs.

In the city ill. by Dan Dickas Rev. ed. Macmillan, 1972. Subj: City.

My city ill. by Ron Becker and others. Macmillan, 1965. Subj: City.

People read ill. by Dan Dickas Rev. ed. Macmillan, 1972. Subj: Activities – reading. Careers.

Uptown, downtown ill. by Ron Becker and others. Macmillan, 1965. Subj: City.

Banks, Kate. *Alphabet soup* ill. by Peter Sis. Knopf, 1988. ISBN 0-394-99151-6 Subj: Family life. Food. Imagination.

Banks, Merry. *Animals of the night* ill. by Ronald Himler. Macmillan, 1990. ISBN 0-684-19093-1 Subj: Animals. Nature. Night.

Bannerman, Helen. *Sambo and the twins* ill. by author. Lippincott, 1937. Subj: Folk and fairy tales. Foreign lands – India.

The story of little black Sambo ill. by author. Lippincott, 1943. Subj: Animals – tigers. Character traits – cleverness. Foreign lands – India.

The story of the teasing monkey ill. by author. Lippincott, 1907. Subj: Animals – lions. Animals – monkeys.

Bannon, Laura. *The best house in the world* ill. by author. Houghton, 1952. Subj: Animals. Houses. Imagination.

Hat for a hero: a Tarasean boy of Mexico ill. by author. Albert Whitman, 1954. Subj: Character traits – bravery. Clothing – hats. Foreign lands – Mexico.

Little people of the night ill. by author. Houghton, 1963. Subj: Animals. Emotions – fear. Night.

Manuela's birthday ill. by author. Albert Whitman, 1972. Orig. pub. in 1939 Subj: Birthdays. Foreign lands – Mexico. Toys – dolls.

Red mittens ill. by author. Houghton, 1946. Subj: Animals. Behavior – losing things. Clothing – gloves.

The scary thing ill. by author. Houghton, 1956. Subj: Animals. Emotions – fear.

Baran, Tancy. *Bees* ill. by author. Grosset, 1971. Subj: Insects – bees. Science.

Barasch, Lynne. *Rodney's inside story* ill. by author. Watts, 1992. ISBN 0-531-08593-7 Subj: Activities – reading. Animals – rabbits. Bedtime. Food.

Barasch, Marc Ian. *No plain pets!* ill. by Henrik Drescher. HarperCollins, 1991. ISBN 0-06-022473-8 Subj: Animals. Pets. Poetry, rhyme.

Barbaresi, Nina. *Firemouse* ill. by author. Crown, 1987. ISBN 0-517-56337-1 Subj: Animals – cats. Animals – mice. Careers – firefighters.

Barbato, Juli. *From bed to bus* ill. by Brian Schatell. Macmillan, 1985. ISBN 0-02-708380-2 Subj: Family life. Morning.

Mom's night out ill. by Brian Schatell. Macmillan, 1985. ISBN 0-02-708480-9 Subj: Family life – fathers. Food.

Barber, Antonia. *The enchanter's daughter* ill. by Errol Le Cain. Farrar, 1988. ISBN 0-374-32170-1 Subj: Birds. Magic. Wizards.

The mousehole cat ill. by Nicola Bayley. Macmillan, 1990. ISBN 0-02-708331-4 Subj: Animals – cats. Foreign lands – England. Sea and seashore. Weather – storms.

Satchelmouse and the dinosaurs ill. by Claudio Muñoz. Barron's, 1988. ISBN 0-8120-5872-0 Subj: Dinosaurs. Imagination. Magic.

Satchelmouse and the doll's house ill. by Claudio Muñoz. Barron's, 1988. ISBN 0-8120-5873-9 Subj: Character traits – kindness. Toys – dolls.

Barbot, Daniel. *A bicycle for Rosaura* ill. by Morella Fuenmayor. Kane/Miller, 1991. ISBN 0-916291-34-0 Subj: Animals. Birds – chickens. Birthdays. Foreign lands – Venezuela. Sports – bicycling.

Barbour, Karen. *Little Nino's pizzeria* ill. by author. Harcourt, 1987. ISBN 0-15-247650-4 Subj: Family life. Food.

Mr. Bow Tie ill. by author. Harcourt, 1991. ISBN 0-15-256165-X Subj: Character traits – kindness. Family life. Homeless.

Nancy ill. by author. Harcourt, 1989. ISBN 0-15-256675-9 Subj: Friendship. Moving. Parties.

Barchilon, Jacques. *The authentic Mother Goose fairy tales and nursery rhymes* Alan Swallow, 1960. Subj: Nursery rhymes.

Barden, Rosalind. *TV monster* ill. by author. Crown, 1989. ISBN 0-517-56934-5 Subj: Monsters. Space and space ships. Television.

Bare, Colleen Stanley. *Busy, busy squirrels* photos. by author. Dutton, 1991. ISBN 0-525-65063-6 Subj: Animals – squirrels.

Critter, the class cat photos. by author. Putnam, 1989. ISBN 0-399-21710-X Subj: Animals – cats. School.

Elephants on the beach photos. by author. Dutton, 1990. ISBN 0-525-65018-0 Subj: Animals – elephant seals. Sea and seashore.

Guinea pigs don't read books photos. by author. Dodd, 1985. ISBN 0-396-08538-5 Subj: Animals – guinea pigs. Pets.

Never kiss an alligator photos. by author. Dutton, 1989. ISBN 0-525-65003-2 Subj: Reptiles – alligators, crocodiles.

To love a cat photos. by author. Dodd, 1986. ISBN 0-396-08834-1 Subj: Animals – cats. Pets.

To love a dog photos. by author. Dodd, 1987. ISBN 0-396-09057-5 Subj: Animals – dogs. Pets.

Tree squirrels photos. by author. Putnam 1983. ISBN 0-396-08208-4 Subj: Animals – squirrels.

Who comes to the water hole? photos. by author. Dutton, 1991. ISBN 0-525-65073-3 Subj: Animals. Foreign lands – Africa. Jungle.

Baring, Maurice. *The blue rose* ill. by Anne Dalton. Heinemann, 1987. ISBN 0-7182-2100-1 Subj: Folk and fairy tales. Royalty.

Barkan, Joanne. *Boxcar* ill. by Richard Walz. Macmillan, 1992. ISBN 0-689-71573-0 Subj: Format, unusual – board books. Trains. Transportation.

Caboose ill. by Richard Walz. Macmillan, 1992. ISBN 0-689-71574-9 Subj: Format, unusual – board books. Trains. Transportation.

Locomotive ill. by Richard Walz. Macmillan, 1992. ISBN 0-689-71576-5 Subj: Format, unusual – board books. Trains. Transportation.

Passenger car ill. by Richard Walz. Macmillan, 1992. ISBN 0-689-71575-7 Subj: Format, unusual – board books. Trains. Transportation.

Whiskerville bake shop ill. by Karen Lee Schmidt. Putnam, 1990. ISBN 0-448-19467-8 Subj: Animals – mice. Buildings. Careers – bakers. Format, unusual – board books.

Whiskerville firehouse ill. by Karen Lee Schmidt. Putnam, 1990. ISBN 0-448-19468-6 Subj: Animals – mice. Buildings. Careers – firefighters. Format, unusual – board books.

Whiskerville post office ill. by Karen Lee Schmidt. Putnam, 1990. ISBN 0-448-19466-X Subj: Animals – mice. Buildings. Careers – mail carriers. Format, unusual – board books.

Whiskerville school ill. by Karen Lee Schmidt. Putnam, 1990. ISBN 0-448-19465-1 Subj: Animals – mice. Buildings. Careers – teachers. Format, unusual – board books. School.

Barker, Carol. *Achilles and Diana* (Bates, H. E. (Herbert Ernest))

Achilles the donkey (Bates, H. E. (Herbert Ernest))

Barker, Cicely Mary. *Berry flower fairies* ill. by author. Putnam's, 1981. Subj: Fairies. Flowers. Poetry, rhyme.

Blossom flower fairies ill. by author. Putnam's, 1981. Subj: Fairies. Flowers. Poetry, rhyme.

Flower fairies of the garden ill. by author. Viking, 1991. ISBN 0-7232-3758-1 Subj: Fairies. Flowers. Gardens, gardening. Poetry, rhyme.

Flower fairies of the seasons ill. by author. Harper, 1984. First published in 1923 Subj: Fairies. Flowers. Poetry, rhyme. Seasons. Trees.

Flower fairies of the spring ill. by author. Warne, 1991. ISBN 0-7232-3753-0 Subj: Fairies. Flowers. Poetry, rhyme. Seasons – spring.

Flower fairies of the summer ill. by author. Warne, 1991. ISBN 0-7232-3754-9 Subj: Fairies. Flowers. Poetry, rhyme. Seasons – summer.

Flower fairies of the trees ill. by author. Viking, 1991. ISBN 0-7232-3760-3 Subj: Fairies. Flowers. Poetry, rhyme. Trees.

Flower fairies postcard book ill. by author. Warne, 1991. ISBN 0-7232-3710-7 Subj: Fairies. Flowers. Poetry, rhyme.

Spring flower fairies ill. by author. Putnam's, 1981. Subj: Fairies. Flowers. Poetry, rhyme.

Summer flower fairies ill. by author. Putnam's, 1981. Subj: Fairies. Flowers. Poetry, rhyme.

Barker, George. *Why teddy bears are brown* (Barker, Inga-Lil)

Barker, Inga-Lil. *Why teddy bears are brown* by Inga-Lil and George Barker; ill. by authors. Crowell, 1946. Subj: Behavior – greed. Toys – teddy bears.

Barker, Melvern J. *Country fair* Oxford Univ. Pr., 1955. Subj: Animals – bulls, cows. Fairs.

Little island star Oxford Univ. Pr., 1954. Subj: Lighthouses.

Barker, Peggy. *What happened when grandma died* ill. by Patricia Mattozzi. Concordia, 1984. Subj: Death. Family life – grandmothers. Religion.

Barkhouse, Joyce. *Anna's pet* (Atwood, Margaret)

Barklem, Jill. *Autumn story* ill. by author. Putnam's, 1980. Subj: Animals – mice. Behavior – lost. Seasons – fall.

The big book of Brambly Hedge ill. by author. Putnam's, 1981. Subj: Animals – mice. Country.

The high hills ill. by author. Philomel, 1986. ISBN 0-399-21361-9 Subj: Activities – traveling. Animals – mice.

Sea story ill. by author. Putnam, 1991. ISBN 0-399-21844-0 Subj: Sea and seashore.

The secret staircase ill. by author. Putnam's, 1983. Subj: Animals – mice. Behavior – secrets. Food. Problem solving. Seasons – winter.

Spring story ill. by author. Putnam's, 1980. Subj: Animals – mice. Birthdays. Seasons – spring.

Summer story ill. by author. Putnam's, 1980. Subj: Animals – mice. Seasons – summer. Weddings.

Winter story ill. by author. Putnam's, 1980. Subj: Animals – mice. Seasons – winter. Weather – snow.

Barner, Bob. *Elephant facts* ill. by author. Dutton, 1979. Subj: Animals – elephants. Science.

Elevator escalator book ill. by author. Doubleday, 1990. ISBN 0-385-26667-7 Subj: Animals – dogs. Elevators, escalators. Transportation.

Barnett, Naomi. *I know a dentist* ill. by Linda Boehm. Putnam's, 1977. Subj: Careers – dentists. Teeth.

Barnhart, Peter. *The wounded duck* ill. by Adrienne Adams. Scribner's, 1979. Subj: Birds – ducks. Character traits – kindness to animals. Death. Seasons – winter.

Barr, Cathrine. *A horse for Sherry* ill. by author. Walck, 1963. Subj: Animals – horses. Farms.

Hound dog's bone ill. by author. Walck, 1961. Subj: Animals – dogs. Animals – foxes. Behavior – stealing. Humor.

Little Ben ill. by author. Walck, 1960. Subj: Animals – beavers. Character traits – bravery.

Sammy seal ov the sircus ill. by author [1st initial teaching alphabet ed.] Walck, 1955, 1964. Subj: Animals – seals. Circus. Clowns, jesters.

Barr, Jene. *Fire snorkel number 7* ill. by Joe Rogers. Albert Whitman, 1965. Subj: Careers – firefighters. Fire. Trucks.

Barracca, Debra. *The adventures of taxi dog* (Barracca, Sal)

Maxi, the hero ill. by Mark Buehner. Dial, 1991. ISBN 0-8037-0940-4 Subj: Animals – dogs. City. Crime. Poetry, rhyme.

Barracca, Sal. *The adventures of taxi dog* by Sal and Debra Barracca; ill. by Mark Buehner. Dial, 1990. ISBN 0-8037-0672-3 Subj: Animals – dogs. City. Poetry, rhyme. Taxis.

Maxi, the hero (Barracca, Debra)

Barrett, John M. *The bear who slept through Christmas* Ideals, 1980. Subj: Animals – bears. Hibernation. Holidays – Christmas. Humor.

The Easter bear Children's Pr., 1981. Subj: Animals – bears. Animals – rabbits. Holidays – Easter. Seasons – spring.

Oscar the selfish octopus ill. by Joe Servello. Human Sciences Pr., 1978. Subj: Character traits – selfishness. Octopuses.

Barrett, Joyce Durham. *Willie's not the hugging kind* ill. by Pat Cummings. HarperCollins, 1989. ISBN 0-06-020417-6 Subj: Character traits – confidence. Emotions – love. Ethnic groups in the U.S. Family life. Friendship.

Barrett, Judi. *Animals should definitely not act like people* ill. by Ron Barrett. Atheneum, 1980. Subj: Animals. Behavior – imitation.

Animals should definitely not wear clothing ill. by Ron Barrett. Atheneum, 1974. Subj: Animals. Behavior – imitation. Clothing.

An apple a day ill. by Tim Lewis. Atheneum, 1973. Subj: Food. Illness.

Benjamin's 365 birthdays ill. by Ron Barrett. Atheneum, 1974. Subj: Birthdays.

Cloudy with a chance of meatballs ill. by Ron Barrett. Atheneum, 1978. Subj: Family life – grandfathers. Food. Imagination. Weather.

I hate to go to bed ill. by Ray Cruz. Four Winds Pr., 1977. Subj: Bedtime. Imagination.

I hate to take a bath ill. by Charles B. Slackman. Atheneum, 1981. Subj: Behavior – growing up. Concepts – size.

I'm too small, you're too big ill. by David S. Rose. Atheneum, 1981. Subj: Behavior – growing up. Concepts – opposites. Family life – fathers.

Old MacDonald had an apartment house ill. by Ron Barrett. Atheneum, 1969. Subj: City. Farms. Gardens, gardening.

Peter's pocket ill. by Julia Noonan. Atheneum, 1974. Subj: Clothing.

Pickles have pimples ill. by Lonni Sue Johnson. Atheneum, 1986. ISBN 0-689-31187-7 Subj: Poetry, rhyme.

Snake is totally tail ill. by L. S. Johnson. Atheneum, 1983. Subj: Animals. Insects. Reptiles.

What's left? ill. by author. Atheneum, 1983. Subj: Participation. Problem solving.

Barrett, Lawrence Louis. *Twinkle, the baby colt* Knopf, 1945. Subj: Animals – horses. Behavior – running away.

Barrie, J. M. (James M.). *Peter Pan* ill. by Diane Goode. Random House, 1983. Subj: Elves and little people. Folk and fairy tales.

Barrows, Marjorie Wescott. *The book of favorite Muggins Mouse stories* ill. by Anne Sellers Leaf. Rand McNally, 1965. Subj: Animals – mice.

Fraidy cat ill. by Barbara Maynard. Rand McNally, 1942. Subj: Animals – cats. Character traits – bravery. Format, unusual.

The funny hat ill. by Norv Mink. Rand McNally, 1943. Subj: Behavior – losing things. Clothing – hats. Format, unusual.

Muggins' big balloon ill. by Anne Sellers Leaf. Rand McNally, 1967. Subj: Animals – mice. Toys – balloons.

Muggins Mouse ill. by Anne Sellers Leaf. Rand McNally, 1965. Subj: Animals – mice.

Muggins takes off ill. by Anne Sellers Leaf. Rand McNally, 1964. Subj: Animals – mice.

Timothy Tiger ill. by Keith Ward. Rand McNally, 1943. Subj: Animals – tigers.

Barry, Katharina. *A bug to hug* ill. by author. Harcourt, 1964. Subj: Imagination. Poetry, rhyme. Problem solving.

A is for anything ill. by author. Harcourt, 1961. Subj: ABC books. Poetry, rhyme.

Barry, Robert E. *Animals around the world* ill. by author. McGraw-Hill, 1967. Subj: ABC books. Animals. Poetry, rhyme.

Mr. Willowby's Christmas tree ill. by Paul Galdone. McGraw-Hill, 1963. Subj: Holidays – Christmas. Poetry, rhyme. Trees.

Next please ill. by author. Houghton, 1961. Subj: Careers – barbers. Zoos.

Barthelme, Donald. *The slightly irregular fire engine: or, The hithering thithering djinn* ill. by author. Farrar, 1971. Collage ill. made from nineteenth-century engravings Subj: Imagination.

Bartlett, Margaret Farrington. *The clean brook* ill. by Aldren Auld Watson. McGraw-Hill, 1960. Subj: Science.

Down the mountain: a book about the ever-changing soil ill. by Rhys Caparn. Addison-Wesley, 1963. Subj: Science.

Raindrop stories (Bassett, Preston R.)

Where the brook begins ill. by Aldren Auld Watson. Crowell, 1961. Subj: Science.

Bartlett, Robert Merrill. *Jack Horner and song of sixpence* ill. by Emily N. Barto. Longman, 1943. Subj: Nursery rhymes.

Bartlett, Susan. *A book to begin on libraries* ill. by Gioia Fiammenghi. Holt, 1964. Subj: Libraries.

Barto, Emily N. *Chubby bear* ill. by author. Longman, 1941. Subj: Animals – bears. Poetry, rhyme.

Bartoli, Jennifer. *In a meadow, two hares hide* ill. by Takeo Ishida; ed. by Kathy Pacini. Albert Whitman, 1978. Subj: Animals – rabbits. Seasons – winter.

Nonna ill. by Joan Drescher. Harvey House, 1975. Subj: Death. Emotions – sadness. Family life. Family life – grandmothers.

Snow on bear's nose: a story of a Japanese moon bear cub ed. by Caroline Rubin; ill. by Takeo Ishida. Albert Whitman, 1972. Subj: Animals – bears. Behavior – lost. Foreign lands – Japan. Hibernation. Seasons – winter. Weather – snow.

Barton, Byron. *Airplanes* ill. by author. Crowell, 1986. ISBN 0-690-04532-8 Subj: Airplanes, airports.

Airport ill. by author. Crowell, 1982. Subj: Airplanes, airports. Careers – airplane pilots. Transportation.

Boats ill. by author. Crowell, 1986. ISBN 0-690-04563-0 Subj: Boats, ships.

Bones, bones, dinosaur bones ill. by author. HarperCollins, 1990. ISBN 0-690-04827-0 Subj: Dinosaurs.

Building a house ill. by author. Greenwillow, 1981. Subj: Houses.

Buzz, buzz, buzz ill. by author. Macmillan, 1973. Subj: Cumulative tales. Insects – bees.

Dinosaurs, dinosaurs ill. by author. HarperCollins, 1989. ISBN 0-690-04768-1 Subj: Dinosaurs.

Harry is a scaredy-cat ill. by author. Macmillan, 1974. Subj: Circus. Emotions – fear.

I want to be an astronaut ill. by author. Crowell, 1988. ISBN 0-690-04744-4 Subj: Careers – astronauts. Character traits – ambition. Space and space ships.

Jack and Fred ill. by author. Macmillan, 1974. Subj: Animals – dogs. Animals – rabbits. Pets.

Machines at work ill. by author. Harper, 1987. ISBN 0-690-04573-5 Subj: Activities – working. Machines.

The three bears (The three bears)

Trains ill. by author. Crowell, 1986. ISBN 0-690-04534-4 Subj: Trains.

Trucks ill. by author. Crowell, 1986. ISBN 0-690-04530-1 Subj: Trucks.

Wheels ill. by author. Crowell, 1979. Subj: Progress. Wheels.

Where's Al? ill. by author. Seabury Pr., 1972. Subj: Animals – dogs. Behavior – lost. Wordless.

Barton, Julia. *Are you asleep, rabbit?* (Campbell, Alison)

Barton, Pat. *A week is a long time* ill. by Jutta Ash. Academy Chicago Ltd., 1980. Subj: Country. Clothing.

Bartos-Hoppner, Barbara. *The Pied Piper of Hamelin* tr. by Anthea Bell; ill. by Annegert Fuchshuber. Lippincott, 1987. Adapt. of the poem The pied piper of Hamelin by Robert Browning ISBN 0-397-32240-2 Subj: Animals – rats. Behavior – trickery. Folk and fairy tales. Foreign lands – Germany.

Baruch, Dorothy. *I would like to be a pony and other wishes* ill. by Mary Chalmers. Harper, 1959. Subj: Behavior – wishing. Poetry, rhyme.

Kappa's tug-of-war with the big brown horse: the story of a Japanese water imp ill. by Sanryo Sakai. Tuttle, 1962. Subj: Animals. Elves and little people. Farms. Folk and fairy tales. Foreign lands – Japan.

Bascom, Joe. *Malcolm Softpaws* ill. by author. Lippincott, 1958. Subj: Animals – cats. Behavior – greed. Character traits – selfishness.

Malcolm's job ill. by author. Lippincott, 1959. Subj: Animals – cats. Family life. Music.

Base, Graeme. *Animalia* ill. by author. Abrams, 1987. ISBN 0-8109-1868-4 Subj: ABC books. Animals.

My grandma lived in Gooligulch ill. by author. Australian Book Serv., 1988, 1983. ISBN 0-944176-01-1 Subj: Animals. Family life – grandmothers. Foreign lands – Australia. Poetry, rhyme.

Bash, Barbara. *Desert giant: the world of the Saguaro cactus* ill. by author. Little, 1988. ISBN 0-316-08301-1 Subj: Desert. Plants.

Urban roosts ill. by author. Little, 1990. ISBN 0-316-08306-2 Subj: Birds. City. Nature.

Bashevis, Isaac *see* Singer, Isaac Bashevis

Basile, Giambattista. *Petrosinella: a Neapolitan Rapunzel* adapt. by John Edward Taylor; ill. by

Diane Stanley. Warne, 1981. Subj: Folk and fairy tales. Foreign lands – Italy. Royalty. Witches.

Baskin, Leonard. *Hosie's alphabet* ill. by author; words by Hosea, Tobias and Lisa Baskin. Viking, 1972. Subj: ABC books. Caldecott award honor book. Children as authors.

Hosie's aviary ill. by author; words mostly by Tobias Baskin and others. Viking, 1979. Subj: Birds. Children as authors.

Hosie's zoo ill. by author; words by Tobias Baskin and others. Viking, 1981. Subj: Animals. Poetry, rhyme. Zoos.

Baskin, Tobias. *Hosie's aviary* (Baskin, Leonard)

Hosie's zoo (Baskin, Leonard)

Bason, Lillian. *Castles and mirrors and cities of sand* ill. by Allan Eitzen. Lothrop, 1968. Subj: Animals. Sand. Science.

Pick a raincoat, pick a whistle ill. by Allan Eitzen. Lothrop, 1966. Subj: Activities – whistling. Trees.

Those foolish Molboes! ill. by Margot Tomes. Coward, 1977. Subj: Behavior – hiding things. Character traits – cleverness. Character traits – foolishness. Folk and fairy tales. Foreign lands – Denmark.

Bassett, Lisa. *Beany and Scamp* ill. by Jeni Bassett. Dodd, 1987. ISBN 0-396-08822-8 Subj: Animals – bears. Animals – squirrels. Behavior – losing things. Behavior – lost. Seasons – winter.

Beany wakes up for Christmas ill. by Jeni Bassett. Putnam, 1988. ISBN 0-399-21668-5 Subj: Animals – bears. Animals – squirrels. Friendship. Hibernation. Holidays – Christmas.

A clock for Beany ill. by Jeni Bassett. Dodd, 1985. ISBN 0-396-08484-2 Subj: Animals. Animals – bears. Birthdays. Clocks, watches.

Koala Christmas ill. by Jeni Bassett. Dutton, 1991. ISBN 0-525-65065-2 Subj: Animals – koala bears. Foreign lands – Australia. Holidays – Christmas. Sibling rivalry.

Bassett, Preston R. *Raindrop stories* by Preston R. Bassett and Margaret Farrington Bartlett; ill. by Jim Arnosky. Four Winds Pr., 1981. Subj: Noise, sounds. Weather – rain.

Basso, Bill. *The top of the pizzas* ill. by author. Dodd, 1977. Subj: Activities – working. Food. Monsters.

Bastin, Marjolein. *A little dog for Vera* ill. by author. Stewart, Tabori & Chang, 1991. ISBN 0-55670-208-6 Subj: Animals – dogs. Animals – mice. Pets.

My name is Vera ill. by author. Barron's, 1985. ISBN 0-8120-5690-6 Subj: Animals – mice. Friendship.

Vera and her friends ill. by author. Barron's, 1985. ISBN 0-8120-5689-2 Subj: Animals – mice. Friendship.

Vera dresses up ill. by author. Barron's, 1985. ISBN 0-8120-5691-4 Subj: Animals – mice. Clothing.

Vera in the kitchen ill. by author. Barron's, 1988. ISBN 0-8120-6087-3 Subj: Activities – cooking. Animals – mice.

Vera the mouse ill. by author. Barron's, 1986. ISBN 0-8120-7391-6 Subj: Animals – mice.

Vera's special hobbies ill. by author. Barron's, 1985. ISBN 0-8120-5692-2 Subj: Animals – mice. Nature.

Bate, Lucy. *How Georgina drove the car very carefully from Boston to New York* ill. by Tamar Taylor. Crown, 1989. ISBN 0-517-57142-0 Subj: Activities – traveling. Family life – grandparents. Imagination.

Little rabbit's loose tooth ill. by Diane de Groat. Crown, 1975. Subj: Animals – rabbits. Fairies. Teeth.

Bate, Norman. *Vulcan* ill. by author. Scribner's, 1961. Subj: Machines.

What a wonderful machine is a submarine ill. by author. Scribner's, 1961. Subj: Boats, ships. Sea and seashore.

Who built the bridge? ill. by author. Crown, 1975. Subj: Machines.

Who built the highway? ill. by author. Scribner's, 1953. Subj: Machines. Roads.

Bates, H. E. (Herbert Ernest). *Achilles and Diana* by H. E. Bates and Carol Barker; ill. by Carol Barker. Dobson, 1963. Subj: Animals – donkeys.

Achilles the donkey by H. E. Bates and Carol Barker; ill. by Carol Barker. Watts, 1963. Subj: Animals – donkeys. Behavior – running away.

Batherman, Muriel. *Animals live here* ill. by author. Greenwillow, 1979. Subj: Animals. Science.

Some things you should know about my dog ill. by author. Prentice-Hall, 1976. Subj: Animals – dogs.

Battles, Edith. *One to teeter-totter* ill. by Rosalind Fry. Albert Whitman, 1973. Subj: Emotions – loneliness. Family life. Friendship. Games.

The terrible terrier ill. by Tom Funk. Addison-Wesley, 1972. Subj: Animals – dogs. Behavior – greed.

The terrible trick or treat ill. by Tom Funk. Addison-Wesley, 1970. Subj: Behavior – greed. Holidays – Halloween.

What does the rooster say, Yoshio? ill. by Toni Hormann. Albert Whitman, 1978. Subj: Animals. Foreign lands – Japan. Language.

Bauer, Caroline Feller. *Midnight snowman* ill. by Catherine Stock. Atheneum, 1987. ISBN 0-689-31294-6 Subj: Seasons – winter. Snowmen. Weather – snow.

My mom travels a lot ill. by Nancy Winslow Parker. Warne, 1981. Subj: Careers. Family life – mothers.

Too many books! ill. by Diane Paterson. Viking, 1986. ISBN 0-670-81130-0 Subj: Activities – reading. Behavior – collecting things. Libraries.

Bauer, Helen. *Good times in the park* photos. by Hubert A. Lowman. Melmont, 1954. Subj: Activities – playing. Birthdays. Zoos.

Baugh, Dolores M. *Bikes* by Dolores M. Baugh and Marjorie P. Pulsifer; ill. by Eve Hoffmann Rev. ed. Chandler, 1965. Subj: Sports – bicycling. Traffic, traffic signs.

Let's go by Dolores M. Baugh and Marjorie P. Pulsifer; ill. by Eve Hoffmann. Noble, 1970. Subj: Stores.

Let's see the animals by Dolores M. Baugh and Marjorie P. Pulsifer; ill. by Eve Hoffmann. Chandler, 1965. Subj: Animals.

Let's take a trip by Dolores M. Baugh and Marjorie P. Pulsifer; ill. by Richard Szumski and others. Chandler, 1965. Subj: Libraries. Machines.

Slides by Dolores M. Baugh and Marjorie P. Pulsifer; ill. by Eve Hoffmann. Noble, 1970. Subj: Activities – playing.

Supermarket by Dolores M. Baugh and Marjorie P. Pulsifer; ill. by Eve Hoffmann. Noble, 1970. Subj: Food. Shopping. Stores.

Swings by Dolores M. Baugh and Marjorie P. Pulsifer; ill. by Eve Hoffmann. Noble, 1970. Subj: Activities – playing. Activities – swinging.

Trucks and cars to ride by Dolores M. Baugh and Marjorie P. Pulsifer; ill. by Eve Hoffmann. Noble, 1970. Subj: Automobiles. Trucks. Transportation.

Baum, Arline. *One bright Monday morning* by Arline and Joseph Baum; ill. by Joseph Baum. Random House, 1962. Subj: Counting, numbers. Seasons – spring. Weather.

Opt: an illusionary tale by Arline and Joseph Baum; ill. by authors. Viking, 1987. ISBN 0-670-80870-9 Subj: Birthdays. Optical illusions. Royalty – princes.

Baum, Joseph. *One bright Monday morning* (Baum, Arline)

Opt (Baum, Arline)

Baum, L. Frank (Lyman Frank). *Mother Goose in prose* ill. by Maxfield Parrish. Bounty Books, 1901. Subj: Nursery rhymes.

Baum, Louis. *After dark* ill. by Susan Varley. Overlook Pr., 1990. ISBN 0-87951-382-9 Subj: Family life – mothers.

I want to see the moon ill. by Niki Daly. Overlook Pr., 1989. ISBN 0-87951-367-5 Subj: Bedtime. Moon. Sleep.

JuJu and the pirate ill. by Philippe Matter. Harper, 1984. Subj: Activities – traveling. Birds – parakeets, parrots. Pirates.

One more time ill. by Paddy Bouma. Morrow, 1986. ISBN 0-688-06587-2 Subj: Divorce. Family life – fathers.

Baum, Susan. *The beach* ill. by author. HarperCollins, 1991. ISBN 0-06-107416-0 Subj: Sea and seashore.

Baum, Willi. *Birds of a feather* ill. by author. Addison-Wesley, 1969. Subj: Birds. Wordless.

Bauman, A. F. *Guess where you're going, guess what you'll do* ill. by True Kelley. Houghton, 1989. ISBN 0-395-50211-X Subj: Concepts. Games. Participation.

Baumann, Hans. *Chip has many brothers* ill. by Eric Carle. Philomel, 1985. ISBN 0-399-21283-3 Subj: Animals. Character traits – kindness to animals. Folk and fairy tales. Magic.

The hare's race ill. by Antoni Boratynski; tr. from the German by Elizabeth D. Crawford. Morrow, 1976. Subj: Animals – rabbits. Folk and fairy tales. Reptiles – turtles, tortoises. Sports – racing.

Mischa and his brothers tr. from German by Peter Neumeyer; ill. by Reinhard Michl. Green Tiger Pr., 1985. ISBN 0-88138-051-2 Subj: Character traits – being different. Family life – brothers. Forest, woods.

Baumann, Kurt. *The paper airplane* ill. by Fulvio Testa. Little, 1982. Subj: Airplanes, airports. Imagination.

Piro and the fire brigade ill. by Jiri Bernard. Faber, 1981. Translation of: Piro und die Feuerwehr Subj: Animals – dogs. Careers – firefighters. Character traits – bravery. Fire. Foreign lands – Switzerland.

The prince and the lute ill. by Jean Claverie. North-South, 1986. First pub. in Switzerland under the title Der Prinz und die Laute ISBN 0-03-008018-5 Subj: Character traits – kindness. Folk and fairy tales. Royalty – princes. War.

Puss in boots (Perrault, Charles)

The story of Jonah tr. from German by Jock J. Curle; ill. by Allison Reed. Holt, 1987. ISBN 0-8050-233-2 Subj: Animals – whales. Behavior – misbehavior. Religion.

Baumgart, Klaus. *Anna and the little green dragon* ill. by author. Walt Disney, 1992. ISBN 1-56282-167-9 Subj: Behavior – misbehavior. Dragons.

The little green dragon steps out ill. by author. Hyperion, 1992. ISBN 1-56282-255-1 Subj: Activities – reading. Dragons. Dreams. Night.

Bawden, Juliet. *One year old* photos. by Helen Pask. Holt, 1990. ISBN 0-8050-1257-5 Subj: Counting, numbers.

Bawden, Nina. *Princess Alice* ill. by Phillida Gili. Dutton, 1986. ISBN 0-233-97746-5 Subj: Adoption. Family life. Royalty – princesses.

St. Francis of Assisi ill. by Pascale Allamand. Lothrop, 1983. Subj: Character traits – generosity. Religion.

William Tell ill. by Pascale Allamand. Lothrop, 1981. Subj: Character traits – bravery. Folk and fairy tales. Foreign lands – Switzerland.

Bax, Martin. *Edmond went far away* ill. by Michael Foreman. Harcourt, 1989. ISBN 0-15-225105-7 Subj: Activities – walking. Animals. Farms.

Bayar, Ilene. *Rachel and Mischa* (Bayar, Steven)

Bayar, Steven. *Rachel and Mischa* by Steven and Ilene Bayar; ill. by Marlene Lobell Ruthen; photos. by Joanne Strauss. Kar-Ben Copies, 1988. ISBN 0-930-49477-6 Subj: Character traits – freedom. Jewish culture. Religion.

Bayer, Jane. *A my name is Alice* ill. by Steven Kellogg. Dial Pr., 1984. Subj: ABC books. Animals. Names.

Bayley, Nicola. *Crab cat* ill. by author. Knopf, 1984. Subj: Animals – cats. Imagination.

Elephant cat ill. by author. Knopf, 1984. Subj: Animals – cats. Imagination.

Nicola Bayley's book of nursery rhymes ill. by author. Knopf, 1975. Subj: Nursery rhymes.

One old Oxford ox ill. by author. Atheneum, 1977. Subj: Animals. Counting, numbers.

Parrot cat ill. by author. Knopf, 1984. Subj: Animals – cats. Imagination.

Polar bear cat ill. by author. Knopf, 1984. Subj: Animals – cats. Imagination.

Spider cat ill. by author. Knopf, 1984. Subj: Animals – cats. Imagination.

Baylor, Byrd. *Amigo* ill. by Garth Williams. Macmillan, 1963. Subj: Animals – prairie dogs. Pets. Poetry, rhyme.

The best town in the world ill. by Ronald Himler. Scribner's, 1983. Subj: City.

Coyote cry ill. by Symeon Shimin. Lothrop, 1972. Subj: Animals – coyotes. Animals – dogs.

The desert is theirs ill. by Peter Parnall. Scribner's, 1975. Subj: Caldecott award honor book. Desert. Ecology. Indians of North America. Folk and fairy tales. Poetry, rhyme.

Desert voices ill. by Peter Parnall. Scribner's, 1981. Subj: Animals. Desert. Poetry, rhyme.

Everybody needs a rock ill. by Peter Parnall. Scribner's, 1974. Subj: Poetry, rhyme. Rocks.

A God on every mountain top: stories of southwest Indian sacred mountains ill. by Carol Brown. Scribner's, 1981. Subj: Indians of North America. Folk and fairy tales.

Guess who my favorite person is ill. by Robert Andrew Parker. Scribner's, 1977. Subj: Friendship. Games.

Hawk, I'm your brother ill. by Peter Parnall. Scribner's, 1976. Subj: Birds – hawks. Caldecott award honor book. Character traits – freedom. Indians of North America.

If you are a hunter of fossils ill. by Peter Parnall. Macmillan, 1980. ISBN 0-684-16419-1 Subj: Indians of North America. Science.

I'm in charge of celebrations ill. by Peter Parnall. Scribner's, 1986. ISBN 0-684-18579-2 Subj: Desert. Nature.

Moon song ill. by Ronald Himler. Scribner's, 1982. Subj: Animals – coyotes. Indians of North America. Folk and fairy tales. Moon.

The other way to listen ill. by Peter Parnall. Scribner's, 1978. Subj: Nature. Poetry, rhyme.

The way to start a day ill. by Peter Parnall. Scribner's, 1978. Subj: Caldecott award honor book. Folk and fairy tales. Foreign lands. Religion. Sun.

We walk in sandy places ill. by Marilyn Schweitzer. Scribner's, 1976. Subj: Animals. Desert.

When clay sings ill. by Tom Bahti. Scribner's, 1972. Subj: Art. Caldecott award honor book. Indians of North America.

Your own best secret place ill. by Peter Parnall. Scribner's, 1979. Subj: Behavior – hiding things. Behavior – secrets.

Baynes, Pauline. *How dog began* ill. by author. Holt, 1987. ISBN 0-8050-0011-9 Subj: Animals – dogs. Animals – wolves. Caves.

Let there be light ill. by author. Macmillan, 1991. ISBN 0-02-708542-2 Subj: Religion.

Noah and the ark ill. by author. Holt, 1988. ISBN 0-8050-0886-1 Subj: Boats, ships. Religion – Noah.

Thanks be to God ill. by author. Macmillan, 1990. ISBN 0-02-708541-4 Subj: Religion.

Baynton, Martin. *Fifty and the fox* ill. by author. Crown, 1986. ISBN 0-517-56069-0 Subj: Animals – foxes. Farms. Tractors.

Fifty and the great race ill. by author. Crown, 1987. ISBN 0-517-56354-1 Subj: Fairs. Farms. Tractors. Sports – racing.

Fifty gets the picture ill. by author. Crown, 1987. ISBN 0-517-56355-X Subj: Activities – digging. Careers – artists. Farms. Tractors.

Fifty saves his friend ill. by author. Crown, 1986. ISBN 0-517-56022-4 Subj: Animals – rats. Farms. Friendship. Tractors.

Why do you love me? ill. by author. Greenwillow, 1990. ISBN 0-688-09157-1 Subj: Character traits – questioning. Emotions – love. Family life – fathers.

Beach, Stewart. *Good morning, sun's up!* ill. by Yutaka Sugita. Scroll Pr., 1970. German ed. has title: Guten Morgen, liebe Sonne! Subj: Animals. Games. Morning.

Beatty, Hetty Burlingame. *Bucking horse* ill. by author. Houghton, 1957. Subj: Animals – horses. Cowboys.

Droopy ill. by author. Houghton, 1954. Subj: Animals – mules. Character traits – stubbornness. Sports – swimming.

Little Owl Indian ill. by author. Houghton, 1951. Subj: Animals – horses. Indians of North America. Fire.

Moorland pony ill. by author. Houghton, 1961. Subj: Activities – traveling. Animals – horses. Character traits – kindness to animals. Family life. Foreign lands – England. Pets.

Bechstein, Ludwig. *The rabbit catcher and other fairy tales* tr. and intro. by Randall Jarrell; ill. by Ugo Fontana. Macmillan, 1962. Subj: Folk and fairy tales. Foreign lands – Germany.

Beck, Martine. *Rescue of Brown Bear and White Bear* ill. by Marie H. Henry. Little, 1991. ISBN 0-316-08654-1 Subj: Animals – bears.

The wedding of Brown Bear and White Bear tr. from French by Aliyah Morgenstern; ill. by Marie H. Henry. Little, 1990. ISBN 0-316-08652-5 Subj: Animals – bears. Weddings.

Becker, Edna. *Nine hundred buckets of paint* ill. by Margaret Bradfield. Abingdon Pr., 1945. Subj: Activities – painting. Houses. Moving.

Becker, John Leonard. *Seven little rabbits* ill. by Barbara Cooney. Walker, 1973. Subj: Animals – rabbits. Counting, numbers.

Becker, May Lamberton. *The rainbow Mother Goose* (Mother Goose)

Beckett, Hilary. *The rooster's horns* (Young, Ed (Edward))

Beckman, Beatrice. *I can be a teacher* ill. with photos. Childrens Pr., 1985. ISBN 0-516-01843-4 Subj: Careers – teachers.

Beckman, Kaj. *Lisa cannot sleep* ill. by Per Beckman. Watts, 1970. Subj: Bedtime. Family life. Sleep. Toys.

Bedard, Michael. *The nightingale* (Andersen, H. C. (Hans Christian))

Bedford, A. N. (Annie North) *see* Watson, Jane Werner

The bedtime book : *a collection of fairy tales* ill. by Daniel San Souci. Messner, 1985. ISBN 0-671-60505-4 Subj: Folk and fairy tales.

Beech, Caroline. *Peas again for lunch* ill. by Gina Calleja. Annick Pr., 1981. Subj: Behavior – misbehavior. Imagination.

Beecroft, John. *What? Another cat!* ill. by Kurt Wiese. Dodd, 1960. Subj: Animals – cats. Sibling rivalry.

Beer, Kathleen Costello. *What happens in the spring* National Geographic Soc., 1977. Subj: Seasons – spring.

Behn, Harry. *Crickets and bullfrogs and whispers of thunder* sel. by Lee Bennett Hopkins; ill. by author. Harcourt, 1984. Subj: Poetry, rhyme.

Trees ill. by James R. Endicott. Holt, 1992. ISBN 0-8050-1926-X Subj: Poetry, rhyme. Trees.

What a beautiful noise ill. by Harold Berson. Collins-World, 1970. Subj: Humor. Music. Noise, sounds.

Behrens, June. *Can you walk the plank?* ill. by Michele and Tom Grimm. Childrens Pr., 1976. Subj: Activities. Games. Imagination.

Christmas-magic wagon ill. by Marjorie Burgeson. Children's Pr., 1975. ISBN 0-516-08880-7 Subj: Holidays – Christmas. Magic. Theater.

The feast of Thanksgiving ill. by Anne Siberell. Children's Pr. 1974. ISBN 0-516-08725-8 Subj: Holidays – Thanksgiving. Theater.

Fiesta! ill. by Scott Taylor. Childrens Pr., 1978. Subj: Ethnic groups in the U.S. – Mexican-Americans. Holidays – Cinco de Mayo.

Hanukkah ill. by Terry Behrens. Children's Pr. 1983. ISBN 0-516-02386-1 Subj: Holidays – Hanukkah. Jewish culture. Religion.

I can be a nurse ill. with photos. Childrens Pr., 1986. ISBN 0-516-01893-0 Subj: Careers – nurses.

I can be a pilot ill. with photos. Childrens Pr., 1985. ISBN 0-516-01888-4 Subj: Careers – airplane pilots.

I can be a truck driver ill. with photos. Childrens Pr., 1985. ISBN 0-516-01848-5 Subj: Careers – truck drivers.

I can be an astronaut ill. with photos. Children's Pr. 1984. ISBN 0-516-01837-X Subj: Careers – astronauts. Space and space ships.

The manners book: what's right, Ned? ill. by Michele and Tom Grimm. Childrens Pr., 1980. Subj: Etiquette. Toys – teddy bears.

Passover photos. by Terry Behrens. Childrens Pr., 1987. ISBN 0-516-02389-6 Subj: Holidays – Passover. Jewish culture. Religion.

Powwow Childrens Pr., 1983. ISBN 0-516-02387-X Subj: Indians of North America.

Soo Ling finds a way ill. by Tarō Yashima. Children's Pr., 1965. Subj: Ethnic groups in the U.S. – Chinese-Americans. Family life – grandfathers. Foreign lands – China. Laundry.

Whales of the world Childrens Pr., 1987. ISBN 0-516-08877-7 Subj: Animals – whales. Science.

Whalewatch! ill. by John Olguin. Childrens Pr., 1978. Photographs collected by John Olguin Subj: Animals – whales. Science.

Who am I? ill. by Ray Ambraziunas. Elk Grove Pr., 1968. Subj: School. Self-concept.

Beim, Jerrold. *Country mailman* ill. by Leonard W. Shortall. Morrow, 1958. Subj: Careers – mail carriers. Character traits – helpfulness. Emotions – envy, jealousy.

Country train ill. by Leonard W. Shortall. Morrow, 1950. Subj: Character traits – individuality. Trains.

Eric on the desert ill. by Louis Darling. Morrow, 1953. Subj: Animals. Character traits – bravery. Desert.

Freckle face ill. by Barbara Cooney. Crowell, 1957. Subj: Character traits – appearance. Character traits – being different. Character traits – individuality.

Jay's big job ill. by Tracy Sugarman. Morrow, 1957. Subj: Activities – painting. Activities – working. Family life.

The little igloo (Beim, Lorraine)

Lucky Pierre (Beim, Lorraine)

Sasha and the samovar (Beim, Lorraine)

Sir Halloween ill. by Tracy Sugarman. Morrow, 1959. Subj: Holidays – Halloween.

The smallest boy in the class ill. by Meg Wohlberg. Morrow, 1949. Subj: Behavior – sharing. Character traits – smallness. Names.

The swimming hole ill. by Louis Darling. Morrow, 1950. Subj: Behavior. Ethnic groups in the U.S. – Afro-Americans. Friendship. Seasons – summer. Sports – swimming.

The taming of Toby ill. by Tracy Sugarman. Morrow, 1953. Subj: Behavior – misbehavior. Imagination. School.

Tim and the tool chest ill. by Tracy Sugarman. Morrow, 1951. Subj: Tools.

Two is a team (Beim, Lorraine)

With dad alone ill. by Don Sibley. Harcourt, 1954. Subj: Death. Family life – fathers.

Beim, Lorraine. *The little igloo* by Lorraine and Jerrold Beim; ill. by Howard Simon. Harcourt, 1941. Subj: Animals – dogs. Eskimos.

Lucky Pierre by Lorraine and Jerrold Beim; ill. by Howard Simon. Harcourt, 1940. Subj: Behavior – collecting things. Careers – fishermen. Character traits – luck. Family life.

Sasha and the samovar by Lorraine and Jerrold Beim; ill. by Rafaello Busoni. Harcourt, 1944. Subj: Fairies. Foreign lands – Russia.

Two is a team by Lorraine and Jerrold Beim; ill. by Ernest Crichlow. Harcourt, 1945. Subj: Behav-

ior – fighting, arguing. Ethnic groups in the U.S. – Afro-Americans. Friendship. Problem solving.

Beisert, Heide Helene. *Poor fish* tr. from German by Marion Koenig; ill. by author. Harper, 1982. Subj: Birds. Ecology. Fish.

Beisner, Monika. *Catch that cat!* ill. by author. Farrar, 1990. ISBN 0-374-31226-5 Subj: Animals – cats. Poetry, rhyme. Riddles.

Monika Beisner's book of riddles ill. by author. Farrar, 1983. ISBN 0-374-30866-7 Subj: Riddles.

Secret spells and curious charms ill. by author. Farrar, 1986. ISBN 0-374-36692-6 Subj: Behavior – secrets. Magic.

Topsy turvy: the world of upside down ill. by author. Farrar, 1987. ISBN 0-374-37679-4 Subj: Concepts. Poetry, rhyme.

Bell, Anthea. *Billy the brave* (Chapouton, Anne-Marie)

The brave little tailor (Grimm, Jacob)

Bremen town musicians (Grimm, Jacob)

The Bremen town musicians (Grimm, Jacob)

The emperor's new clothes (Andersen, H. C. (Hans Christian))

The farmer and the moon (Lussert, Anneliese)

The fisherman and his wife (Grimm, Jacob)

Frog in love (Velthuijs, Max)

The golden goose (Grimm, Jacob)

Goodbye little bird (Damjan, Mischa)

The goose girl (Grimm, Jacob)

Grimm Tom Thumb (Tom Thumb)

The little mermaid (Andersen, H. C. (Hans Christian))

The magic honey jar (Bohdal, Susi)

Mumble bear (Ruck-Pauquèt, Gina)

Nick Ribbeck of Ribbeck of Havelland (Fontane, Theodor)

The nightingale (Andersen, H. C. (Hans Christian))

Noah's ark (Fussenegger, Gertrud)

The nutcracker (Hoffmann, E. T. A.)

The Pied Piper of Hamelin (Bartos-Hoppner, Barbara)

The princess and the pea (Andersen, H. C. (Hans Christian))

The proud white cat (Hürlimann, Ruth)

The red shoes (Andersen, H. C. (Hans Christian))

Sandman in the lighthouse (Strahl, Rudi)

The snow queen (Andersen, H. C. (Hans Christian))

Snow White and the seven dwarves (Grimm, Jacob)

The strange child (Hoffmann, E. T. A.)

Swan Lake: a traditional folktale ill. by Chihiro Iwasaki. Picture Book Studio, 1986. Adaptation of Tchaikovsky's Lebedinoe ozero ISBN 0-88708-028-6 Subj: Activities – dancing. Birds – swans. Folk and fairy tales. Magic.

The swineherd (Andersen, H. C. (Hans Christian))

Thumbeline (Andersen, H. C. (Hans Christian))

The trip to Panama (Janosch)

The ugly duckling (Andersen, H. C. (Hans Christian))

The wise queen ill. by Chihiro Iwasaki. Picture Book Studio, 1986. ISBN 0-88708-014-6 Subj: Character traits – cleverness. Folk and fairy tales. Riddles. Royalty – queens.

The wishing table (Grimm, Jacob)

Bell, Gina *see* Balzano, Jeanne

Bell, Janet *see* Clymer, Eleanor Lowenton

Bell, Norman. *Linda's airmail letter* ill. by Patricia Villemain. Follett, 1964. Subj: Birthdays. Friendship. Letters. Weather.

Bellamy, David. *How green are you?* ill. by Penny Dann. Crown, 1991. ISBN 0-517-58447-6 Subj: Animals – whales. Ecology.

The roadside ill. by Jill Dow. Crown, 1988. ISBN 0-517-56976-0 Subj: Ecology.

The rock pool ill. by Jill Dow. Crown, 1988. ISBN 0-517-56977-9 Subj: Ecology.

Beller, Janet. *A-B-C-ing: an action alphabet* Crown, 1984. Subj: ABC books. Activities.

Belling the cat and other stories retold by Leland B. Jacobs; ill. by Harold Berson. Golden Pr., 1960. Subj: Animals. Folk and fairy tales.

Belloc, Hilaire. *The bad child's book of beasts* ill. by Basil T. Blackwood [B.A.T.] Knopf, 1965. Originally published in 1896 Subj: Animals. Behavior. Humor.

The bad child's book of beasts, and more beasts for worse children ill. by Harold Berson. Grosset, 1966. Subj: Animals. Poetry, rhyme.

The bad child's pop-up book of beasts ill. by Wallace Tripp. Putnam's, 1987. ISBN 0-399-21431-3 Subj: Animals. Format, unusual – toy and movable books. Poetry, rhyme.

Jim, who ran away from his nurse, and was eaten by a lion ill. by Victoria Chess. Little, 1987. ISBN 0-316-13815-0 Subj: Animals – lions. Behavior – misbehavior. Behavior – running away. Zoos.

Matilda who told lies and was burned to death ill. by Steven Kellogg. Dial Pr., 1970. Subj: Behavior – lying. Behavior – misbehavior. Fire. Poetry, rhyme.

More beasts for worse children ill. by Basil T. Blackwood [B.A.T.] Knopf, 1966. Subj: Animals. Poetry, rhyme.

Bellows, Cathy. *Four fat rats* ill. by author. Macmillan, 1987. ISBN 0-02-708830-8 Subj: Animals – rats. Behavior – greed. Character traits – meanness.

The Grizzly sisters ill. by author. Macmillan, 1991. ISBN 0-02-709032-9 Subj: Animals – bears. Behavior – misbehavior.

The royal raccoon ill. by author. Macmillan, 1989. ISBN 0-02-709031-0 Subj: Animals – raccoons. Character traits – conceit.

Bellville, Cheryl Walsh. *Large animal veterinarians* (Bellville, Rod)

Bellville, Rod. *Large animal veterinarians* by Rod and Cheryl Walsh Bellville; photos. by authors. Carolrhoda Books, 1983. Subj: Animals. Careers – veterinarians.

Bell-Zano, Gina *see* Balzano, Jeanne

Belpré, Pura. *Dance of the animals: a Puerto Rican folk tale* ill. by Paul Galdone. Warne, 1972. Subj: Animals. Folk and fairy tales. Foreign lands – Puerto Rico.

Perez and Martina: a Portorican folk tale ill. by Carlos Sanchez Rev. ed. Warne, 1961. Originally pub. in 1960 Subj: Animals – mice. Folk and fairy tales. Foreign lands – Puerto Rico. Insects.

Santiago ill. by Symeon Shimin. Warne, 1969. Subj: Birds – chickens. Ethnic groups in the U.S. Ethnic groups in the U.S. – Puerto Rican-Americans. Pets.

Belting, Natalia Maree. *Christmas folk* ill. by Barbara Cooney. Holt, 1969. Subj: Foreign lands – England. Holidays – Christmas. Poetry, rhyme.

Summer's coming in ill. by Adrienne Adams. Holt, 1970. Subj: Foreign lands – England. Holidays. Poetry, rhyme. Seasons – spring. Seasons – summer.

The sun is a golden earring ill. by Bernarda Bryson. Holt, 1962. Subj: Caldecott award honor book. Folk and fairy tales. Sky.

Verity Mullens and the Indian ill. by Leonard Everett Fisher. Holt, 1960. Subj: Animals – dogs. Behavior – lost. Indians of North America. U.S. history.

Bemelmans, Ludwig. *Hansi* ill. by author. Viking, 1934. Subj: Activities – vacationing. Foreign lands – Tyrol. Holidays – Christmas.

Madeline ill. by author. Viking, 1939. Subj: Caldecott award honor book. Foreign lands – France. Hospitals. Orphans. Poetry, rhyme. School.

Madeline [pop-up book] ill. by author. Viking, 1987. ISBN 0-670-81667-1 Subj: Format, unusual – toy and movable books. Foreign lands – France. Hospitals. Orphans.

Madeline and the bad hat ill. by author. Viking, 1956. Subj: Behavior – animals, dislike of. Behavior – misbehavior. Foreign lands – France. Orphans. Poetry, rhyme.

Madeline and the gypsies ill. by author. Viking, 1959. Subj: Behavior – lost. Foreign lands – France. Gypsies. Orphans. Poetry, rhyme.

Madeline in London ill. by author. Viking, 1961. Subj: Animals – horses. Birthdays. Foreign lands – England. Orphans. Poetry, rhyme.

Madeline's Christmas ill. by author. Viking, 1985. ISBN 0-670-80666-8 Subj: Foreign lands – France. Holidays – Christmas. Illness. Magic. Orphans. Poetry, rhyme.

Madeline's rescue ill. by author. Viking, 1953. Subj: Animals – dogs. Caldecott award book. Foreign lands – France. Orphans. Poetry, rhyme.

Parsley ill. by author. Harper, 1955. Subj: Animals – deer. Sports – hunting. Trees.

Quito express ill. by author. Viking, 1938. Subj: Activities – traveling. Family life. Foreign lands – Ecuador. Trains.

Rosebud ill. by author. Random House, 1942. Subj: Animals. Character traits – pride. Folk and fairy tales. Foreign lands – Africa. Humor.

Sunshine ill. by author. Simon and Schuster, 1950. Subj: City. Family life. Houses. Humor.

Welcome home ill. by author. Harper, 1970. Based on a poem by Beverley Bogert Subj: Animals – foxes. Character traits – cleverness. Poetry, rhyme.

Benarde, Anita. *The pumpkin smasher* ill. by author. Walker, 1972. Subj: Holidays – Halloween. Problem solving. Witches.

Benchley, Nathaniel. *The deep dives of Stanley Whale* ill. by Mischa Richter. Harper, 1973. Subj: Animals – whales. Character traits – bravery.

The flying lessons of Gerald Pelican ill. by Mamoru Funai. Harper, 1970. Subj: Activities – flying. Birds – pelicans.

Walter the homing pigeon ill. by Whitney Darrow, Jr. Harper, 1981. Subj: Birds – pigeons. Food. Humor. Sports – racing.

Benchley, Peter. *Jonathan visits the White House* ill. by Richard Bergere. McGraw-Hill, 1964. Subj: Animals – dogs. Birthdays. Pets. U.S. history.

Bendick, Jeanne. *All around you* foreword by Glenn O. Blough; ill. by author. McGraw-Hill, 1951. Subj: Science. World.

What made you you? ill. by author. McGraw-Hill, 1971. Subj: Babies. Science.

Why can't I? ill. by author. McGraw-Hill, 1969. Subj: Animals. Behavior – imitation. Participation. Science.

Benedek, Elissa P. *The secret worry* ill. by Patricia Rosamilia. Human Sciences Pr., 1984. ISBN 0-89885-133-5 Subj: Behavior – worrying. Emotions – fear.

Benedictus, Roger. *Fifty million sausages* ill. by Kenneth Mahood. Elsevier-Dutton, 1979. Subj: Food. Humor. Imagination. Machines.

Benét, William Rose. *Angels* ill. by Constantin Alajalov. Crowell, 1947. Subj: Activities – playing. Angels. Poetry, rhyme.

Mother Goose (Mother Goose)

Beni, Ruth. *Sir Baldergog the great* ill. by author. Dutton, 1985. ISBN 0-233-97628-0 Subj: Activities. Behavior – lost. Islands.

Benjamin, Alan. *Busy bunnies* ill. by Christopher Santoro. Simon & Schuster, 1988. ISBN 0-671-64807-1 Subj: Activities. Animals – rabbits.

A change of plans ill. by Steven Kellogg. Four Winds Pr., 1982. Subj: Activities – picnicking. Boats, ships. Family life. Poetry, rhyme.

The nightingale (Andersen, H. C. (Hans Christian))

1000 monsters ill. by Sal Murdocca. Four Winds Pr., 1979. Subj: Format, unusual – toy and movable books. Humor. Monsters.

Rat-a-tat, pitter pat ill. by Margaret Miller. Harper, 1987. ISBN 0-690-04611-1 Subj: Language. Noise, sounds. Poetry, rhyme.

Ribtickle Town ill. by Ann Schweninger. Four Winds Pr., 1983. Subj: Behavior – lost. Food. Giants. Imagination. Poetry, rhyme.

Bennett, David. *One cow moo moo* ill. by Andy Cooke. Holt, 1990. ISBN 0-8050-1416-0 Subj: Animals. Counting, numbers. Cumulative tales. Noise, sounds.

Bennett, Jill. *Animal fair* ill. by Susie Jenkin-Pearce. Viking, 1990. ISBN 0-670-82691-X Subj: Animals. Poetry, rhyme.

A cup of starshine ill. by Graham Percy. Harcourt, 1992. ISBN 0-15-220982-4 Subj: Poetry, rhyme.

Days are where we live and other poems ill. by Maureen Roffey. Lothrop, 1982. Subj: Activities. Poetry, rhyme.

Machine poems ill. by Nick Sharratt. Oxford Univ. Pr., 1991. ISBN 0-19-276094-7 Subj: Machines. Poetry, rhyme.

Noisy poems ill. by Nick Sharratt. Oxford Univ. Pr. 1990. ISBN 0-19-276063-7 Subj: Noise, sounds. Poetry, rhyme.

People poems ill. by Nick Sharratt. Oxford Univ. Pr. 1991. ISBN 0-19-276094-7 Subj: Poetry, rhyme.

Roger was a razor fish and other poems ill. by Maureen Roffey. Lothrop, 1981. Subj: Humor. Poetry, rhyme.

Spooky poems collected by Jill Bennett; ill. by Mary Rees. Little, 1989. ISBN 0-316-08987-7 Subj: Monsters. Poetry, rhyme.

Teeny tiny ill. by Tomie de Paola. Putnam's, 1986. ISBN 0-399-21293-0 Subj: Folk and fairy tales. Foreign lands – England. Ghosts.

Tiny Tim: verses for children ill. by Helen Oxenbury. Delacorte Pr., 1982. Subj: Humor. Poetry, rhyme.

Bennett, Olivia. *A Turkish afternoon* photos. by Christopher Cormack. David and Charles, 1984. Subj: Family life. Foreign lands – England. Foreign lands – Turkey.

Bennett, Rainey. *After the sun goes down* ill. by author. Collins-World, 1961. Subj: Birds – owls. Night.

The secret hiding place ill. by author. Collins-World, 1960. Subj: Animals – hippopotami. Behavior – solitude. Poetry, rhyme. Sea and seashore.

Bennett, Rowena. *The day is dancing and other poems* ill. by Rainey Bennett. Follett, 1968. Subj: Imagination. Poetry, rhyme.

Songs from around a toadstool table ill. by Betty Fraser. Follett, 1967. Subj: Imagination. Poetry, rhyme.

Benson, Ellen. *Philip's little sister* ill. by Rachael Davis. Childrens Pr., 1979. Subj: Family life. Sibling rivalry.

Benson, Patrick. *Little penguin* ill. by author. Putnam, 1991. ISBN 0-399-21757-6 Subj: Birds – penguins. Concepts – size. Foreign lands – Antarctic.

Bentley, Anne. *The Groggs' day out* ill. by Roy Bentley. Elsevier-Dutton, 1981. Subj: Foreign lands – England. Sports – bicycling.

The Groggs have a wonderful summer by Anne and Roy Bentley; ill. by Roy Bentley. Elsevier-Dutton, 1980. Subj: Foreign lands – England. Sea and seashore. Seasons – summer.

Bentley, Nancy. *I've got your nose!* ill. by Don Madden. Doubleday, 1991. ISBN 0-385-41296-7 Subj: Anatomy – noses. Behavior – dissatisfaction. Behavior – wishing. Magic. Self-concept. Witches.

Bentley, Roy. *The Groggs have a wonderful summer* (Bentley, Anne)

Benton, Robert. *Don't ever wish for a 7-foot bear* ill. by Sally Benton. Knopf, 1972. Subj: Animals – bears. Behavior – wishing. Humor.

Little brother, no more ill. by author. Knopf, 1960. Subj: Family life. Names.

Berends, Polly Berrien. *Ladybug and dog and the night walk* ill. by Cyndy Szekeres. Random House, 1980. Subj: Animals – dogs. Friendship. Insects – fireflies. Insects – ladybugs. Night.

Berenstain, Jan. *After the dinosaurs* (Berenstain, Stan)

The bear detectives: the case of the missing pumpkin (Berenstain, Stan)

Bears in the night (Berenstain, Stan)

Bears on wheels (Berenstain, Stan)

The Berenstain bears and mama's new job (Berenstain, Stan)

The Berenstain bears and the bad dream (Berenstain, Stan)

The Berenstain bears and the bad habit. (Berenstain, Stan)

The Berenstain bears and the big road race (Berenstain, Stan)

The Berenstain bears and the double dare (Berenstain, Stan)

The Berenstain bears and the ghost of the forest (Berenstain, Stan)

The Berenstain bears and the messy room (Berenstain, Stan)

The Berenstain bears and the missing dinosaur bone (Berenstain, Stan)

The Berenstain bears and the missing honey (Berenstain, Stan)

The Berenstain bears and the prize pumpkin (Berenstain, Stan)

The Berenstain bears and the sitter (Berenstain, Stan)

The Berenstain bears and the slumber party (Berenstain, Stan)

The Berenstain bears and the spooky old tree (Berenstain, Stan)

The Berenstain bears and the trouble with friends (Berenstain, Stan)

The Berenstain bears and the truth (Berenstain, Stan)

The Berenstain bears and the week at grandma's (Berenstain, Stan)

The Berenstain bears and the wild, wild honey (Berenstain, Stan)

The Berenstain bears and too much birthday (Berenstain, Stan)

The Berenstain bears and too much junk food (Berenstain, Stan)

The Berenstain bears and too much TV (Berenstain, Stan)

The Berenstain bears and too much vacation (Berenstain, Stan)

The Berenstain bears blaze a trail (Berenstain, Stan)

The Berenstain bears' Christmas tree (Berenstain, Stan)

The Berenstain bears' counting book (Berenstain, Stan)

The Berenstain bears don't pollute anymore (Berenstain, Stan)

The Berenstain bears forget their manners (Berenstain, Stan)

The Berenstain bears get in a fight (Berenstain, Stan)

The Berenstain bears get stage fright (Berenstain, Stan)

The Berenstain bears get the gimmies (Berenstain, Stan)

The Berenstain bears go out for the team (Berenstain, Stan)

The Berenstain bears go to camp (Berenstain, Stan)

The Berenstain bears go to school (Berenstain, Stan)

The Berenstain bears go to the doctor (Berenstain, Stan)

The Berenstain bears in the dark (Berenstain, Stan)

The Berenstain bears learn about strangers (Berenstain, Stan)

The Berenstain bears meet Santa Bear (Berenstain, Stan)

The Berenstain bears' moving day (Berenstain, Stan)

The Berenstain bears: No girls allowed (Berenstain, Stan)

The Berenstain bears on the moon (Berenstain, Stan)

The Berenstain bears ready, set, go! (Berenstain, Stan)

The Berenstain bears' science fair (Berenstain, Stan)

The Berenstain bears trick or treat (Berenstain, Stan)

The Berenstain bears' trouble at school (Berenstain, Stan)

The Berenstain bears' trouble with money (Berenstain, Stan)

The Berenstain bears' trouble with pets (Berenstain, Stan)

The Berenstain bears visit the dentist (Berenstain, Stan)

The Berenstains' B book (Berenstain, Stan)

The day of the dinosaur (Berenstain, Stan)

He bear, she bear (Berenstain, Stan)

Inside outside upside down (Berenstain, Stan)

Old hat, new hat (Berenstain, Stan)

Berenstain, Michael. *The dwarks: book 1* ill. by author. Bantam, 1983. Subj: Elves and little people. Family life.

Peat Moss and Ivy and the birthday present ill. by author. Random House, 1986. ISBN 0-394-97605-3 Subj: Animals – chipmunks. Birthdays.

Peat Moss and Ivy's backyard adventure ill. by author. Random House, 1986. ISBN 0-394-97604-5 Subj: Animals – chipmunks.

The ship book ill. by author. McKay, 1978. Subj: Boats, ships.

The troll book ill. by author. Random House, 1980. Subj: Folk and fairy tales. Trolls.

Berenstain, Stan. *After the dinosaurs* by Stan and Jan Berenstain; ill. by authors. Random House, 1988. ISBN 0-394-90518-0 Subj: Animals – bears. Dinosaurs.

The bear detectives: the case of the missing pumpkin by Stan and Jan Berenstain; ill. by authors. Random House, 1975. Subj: Animals – bears. Careers – detectives. Poetry, rhyme. Problem solving.

Bears in the night by Stan and Jan Berenstain; ill. by authors. Random House, 1971. Subj: Animals – bears. Bedtime. Night. Noise, sounds.

Bears on wheels by Stan and Jan Berenstain; ill. by authors. Random House, 1969. Subj: Animals – bears. Counting, numbers. Wheels.

The Berenstain bears and mama's new job by Stan and Jan Berenstain; ill. by authors. Random House, 1984. ISBN 0-394-96881-6 Subj: Animals – bears. Careers.

The Berenstain bears and the bad dream by Stan and Jan Berenstain; ill. by authors. Random House, 1988. ISBN 0-394-97341-0 Subj: Animals – bears. Dreams.

The Berenstain bears and the bad habit. by Stan and Jan Berenstain; ill. by authors. Random House, 1987. ISBN 0-394-97340-2 Subj: Animals – bears.

The Berenstain bears and the big road race by Stan and Jan Berenstain; ill. by authors. Random House, 1987. ISBN 0-394-99134-6 Subj: Animals – bears. Sports – racing.

The Berenstain bears and the double dare by Stan and Jan Berenstain; ill. by authors. Random House, 1988. ISBN 0-394-99748-4 Subj: Animals – bears. Sibling rivalry.

The Berenstain bears and the ghost of the forest by Stan and Jan Berenstain; ill. by authors. Random House, 1988. ISBN 0-394-90565-2 Subj: Animals – bears. Forest, woods. Ghosts.

The Berenstain bears and the messy room by Stan and Jan Berenstain; ill. by authors. Random House, 1983. Subj: Animals – bears. Problem solving.

The Berenstain bears and the missing honey by Stan and Jan Berenstain; ill. by authors. Random House, 1987. ISBN 0-394-99133-8 Subj: Animals – bears. Problem solving.

The Berenstain bears and the missing dinosaur bone by Stan aand Jan Berenstain; ill. by authors.

Random House, 1980. Subj: Animals – bears. Museums. Poetry, rhyme. Problem solving.

The Berenstain bears and the prize pumpkin by Stan and Jan Berenstain; ill. by authors. Random House, 1990. ISBN 0-679-90847-1 Subj: Animals – bears. Holidays – Thanksgiving. Plants.

The Berenstain bears and the sitter by Stan and Jan Berenstain; ill. by authors. Random House, 1981. Subj: Activities – baby-sitting. Animals – bears. Magic.

The Berenstain bears and the slumber party by Stan and Jan Berenstain; ill. by authors. McKay, 1990. ISBN 0-679-90419-0 Subj: Animals – bears. Bedtime. Parties.

The Berenstain bears and the spooky old tree by Stan and Jan Berenstain; ill. by authors. Random House, 1978. Subj: Animals – bears. Poetry, rhyme. Trees.

The Berenstain bears and the trouble with friends by Stan and Jan Berenstain; ill. by authors. Random House, 1987. ISBN 0-394-97339-9 Subj: Animals – bears. Friendship.

The Berenstain bears and the truth by Stan and Jan Berenstain; ill. by authors. Random House, 1983. Subj: Animals – bears. Behavior – lying. Behavior – misbehavior. Family life.

The Berenstain bears and the week at grandma's by Stan and Jan Berenstain; ill. by authors. Random House, 1986. ISBN 0-394-97335-6 Subj: Animals – bears. Family life – grandmothers.

The Berenstain bears and the wild, wild honey by Stan and Jan Berenstain; ill. by authors. Random House, 1983. ISBN 0-394-85924-3 Subj: Animals – bears. Nature.

The Berenstain bears and too much birthday by Stan and Jan Berenstain; ill. by authors. Random House, 1986. ISBN 0-394-97332-1 Subj: Animals – bears. Birthdays.

The Berenstain bears and too much junk food by Stan and Jan Berenstain; ill. by authors. Random House, 1985. ISBN 0-394-97217-1 Subj: Animals – bears. Food.

The Berenstain bears and too much TV by Stan and Jan Berenstain; ill. by authors. Random House, 1984. Subj: Animals – bears. Family life. Television.

The Berenstain bears and too much vacation by Stan and Jan Berenstain; ill. by authors. Random House, 1989. ISBN 0-394-93014-2 Subj: Activities – vacationing. Animals – bears.

The Berenstain bears blaze a trail by Stan and Jan Berenstain; ill. by authors. Random House, 1987. ISBN 0-394-99132-X Subj: Animals – bears.

The Berenstain bears' Christmas tree by Stan and Jan Berenstain; ill. by authors. Random House, 1980. Subj: Animals – bears. Family life. Holidays – Christmas. Poetry, rhyme. Trees.

The Berenstain bears' counting book by Stan and Jan Berenstain; ill. by authors. Random House, 1976. Subj: Animals – bears. Counting, numbers.

The Berenstain bears don't pollute anymore by Stan and Jan Berenstain; ill. by authors. Random House, 1991. ISBN 0-679-92351-9 Subj: Animals – bears. Ecology.

The Berenstain bears forget their manners by Stan and Jan Berenstain; ill. by authors. Random, 1985. ISBN 0-394-97333-X Subj: Animals – bears. Etiquette. Family life.

The Berenstain bears get in a fight by Stan and Jan Berenstain; ill. by authors. Random House, 1982. Subj: Animals – bears. Behavior – bad day. Sibling rivalry.

The Berenstain bears get stage fright by Stan and Jan Berenstain; ill. by authors. Random House, 1986. ISBN 0-394-97337-2 Subj: Animals – bears. Emotions – fear. Theater.

The Berenstain bears get the gimmies by Stan and Jan Berenstain; ill. by authors. Random House, 1988. ISBN 0-394-90566-0 Subj: Animals – bears. Behavior – greed.

The Berenstain bears go out for the team by Stan and Jan Berenstain; ill. by authors. Random House, 1987. ISBN 0-394-97338-0 Subj: Animals – bears. Sports.

The Berenstain bears go to camp by Stan and Jan Berenstain; ill. by authors. Random House, 1982. Subj: Animals – bears. Seasons – summer. Camps, camping.

The Berenstain bears go to school by Stan and Jan Berenstain; ill. by authors. Random House, 1978. Subj: Animals – bears. School.

The Berenstain bears go to the doctor by Stan and Jan Berenstain; ill. by authors. Random House, 1981. Subj: Animals – bears. Careers – doctors.

The Berenstain bears in the dark by Stan and Jan Berenstain; ill. by authors. Random House, 1982. Subj: Animals – bears. Family life. Imagination. Night.

The Berenstain bears learn about strangers by Stan and Jan Berenstain; ill. by authors. Random, 1985. ISBN 0-394-87334-3 Subj: Animals – bears. Behavior – talking to strangers. Emotions – fear. Family life. Safety.

The Berenstain bears meet Santa Bear by Stan and Jan Berenstain; ill. by authors. Random House, 1988. ISBN 0-394-89797-8 Subj: Animals – bears. Holidays – Christmas.

The Berenstain bears' moving day by Stan and Jan Berenstain; ill. by authors. Random House, 1981. Subj: Animals – bears. Family life. Friendship. Moving.

The Berenstain bears: No girls allowed by Stan and Jan Berenstain; ill. by authors. Random House, 1986. ISBN 0-394-97331-3 Subj: Animals – bears. Clubs, gangs. Family life – brothers. Family life – sisters.

The Berenstain bears on the moon by Stan and Jan Berenstain; ill. by authors. Random House, 1985. ISBN 0-394-97180-9 Subj: Animals – bears. Animals – dogs. Moon. Space and space ships.

The Berenstain bears ready, set, go! by Stan and Jan Berenstain; ill. by authors. Random House, 1988. ISBN 0-394-90564-4 Subj: Animals – bears.

The Berenstain bears' science fair by Stan and Jan Berenstain; ill. by authors. Random House, 1977. Subj: Animals – bears. Science.

The Berenstain bears trick or treat by Stan and Jan Berenstain; ill. by authors. Random House, 1989. ISBN 0-679-90091-8 Subj: Animals – bears. Holidays – Halloween.

The Berenstain bears' trouble at school by Stan and Jan Berenstain; ill. by authors. Random House, 1987. ISBN 0-394-97336-4 Subj: Animals – bears. Behavior. School.

The Berenstain bears' trouble with money by Stan and Jan Berenstain; ill. by authors. Random House, 1983. Subj: Animals – bears. Money.

The Berenstain bears' trouble with pets by Stan and Jan Berenstain; ill. by authors. Random House, 1990. ISBN 0-679-90848-X Subj: Animals – bears. Pets.

The Berenstain bears visit the dentist by Stan and Jan Berenstain; ill. by authors. Random House, 1981. Subj: Animals – bears. Careers – dentists.

The Berenstains' B book by Stan and Jan Berenstain; ill. by authors. Random House, 1971. Subj: ABC books. Animals – bears.

The day of the dinosaur ill. by by Stan and Jan Berenstain; ill. by Michael Berenstain. Random House, 1987. ISBN 0-394-99130-3 Subj: Dinosaurs.

He bear, she bear by Stan and Jan Berenstain; ill. by authors. Random House, 1974. Subj: Animals – bears. Poetry, rhyme.

Inside outside upside down by Stan and Jan Berenstain; ill. by authors. Random House, 1968. Subj: Animals – bears. Concepts.

Old hat, new hat by Stan and Jan Berenstain; ill. by authors. Random House, 1970. Subj: Animals – bears. Concepts – shape. Concepts – size. Humor.

Berenzy, Alix. *A frog prince* ill. by author. Holt, 1989. ISBN 0-8050-0426-2 Subj: Folk and fairy tales. Frogs and toads. Royalty.

Beresford, Elisabeth. *Jack and the magic stove* ill. by Rita van Bilsen. Hutchinson, 1984. Subj: Behavior – wishing. Folk and fairy tales. Royalty.

Snuffle to the rescue ill. by Gunvor Edwards. Penguin, 1975. Subj: Animals – dogs.

Berg, Jean Horton. *The little red hen* (The little red hen)

The noisy clock shop ill. by Art Seiden. Grosset, 1950. Subj: Clocks, watches. Noise, sounds.

The O'Learys and friends ill. by Mary Stevens. Follett, 1961. Subj: Animals – cats. Behavior – misunderstanding. Moving. Problem solving.

The wee little man ill. by Charles Geer. Follett, 1963. Subj: Animals – cats. Elves and little people. Night. Noise, sounds. Poetry, rhyme.

Berg, Leila. *Folk tales for reading and telling* ill. by George Him. Collins-World, 1966. Subj: Folk and fairy tales. Foreign lands.

Berger, Barbara Helen. *The donkey's dream* ill. by author. Philomel, 1986. ISBN 0-399-21233-7 Subj: Animals – donkeys. Dreams. Holidays – Christmas. Religion.

Grandfather Twilight ill. by author. Putnam, 1986. ISBN 0-399-20996-4 Subj: Folk and fairy tales. Moon. Twilight.

When the sun rose ill. by author. Philomel, 1986. ISBN 0-399-21360-0 Subj: Friendship. Imagination – imaginary friends.

Berger, Judith. *Butterflies and rainbows* by Judith Berger and Terry Landau; ill. by Carmen Lowhar. Bande House, 1982. Subj: Concepts – color. Poetry, rhyme.

Berger, Melvin. *Early humans: a pop-up book* ill. by Michael Welply. Putnam's, 1988. ISBN 0-399-21476-3 Subj: Format, unusual – toy and movable books. Science.

Germs make me sick! ill. by Marylin Hafner. Crowell, 1985. ISBN 0-690-04429-1 Subj: Illness. Science.

Ouch! a book about cuts, scratches and scrapes ill. by Pat Stewart. Dutton, 1991. ISBN 0-525-67323-7 Subj: Health. Illness.

Prehistoric mammals devised and designed by Keith Moseley; ill. by Robert Cremins. Putnam, 1986. ISBN 0-399-21312-0 Subj: Animals. Format, unusual – toy and movable books.

Switch on, switch off ill. by Carolyn Croll. HarperCollins, 1992. ISBN 0-690-04786-X Subj: Lights. Science.

Why I cough, sneeze, shiver, hiccup and yawn ill. by Holly Keller. Crowell, 1983. Subj: Health. Illness.

Berger, Terry. *Ben's ABC day* photos. by Alice Kandell. Lothrop, 1982. Subj: ABC books.

Friends photos. by Alice Kandell. Messner, 1981. Subj: Friendship.

How does it feel when your parents get divorced? photos. by Miriam Shapiro. Messner, 1977. Subj: Divorce. Emotions. Family life.

I have feelings ill. by Howard Spivak. Behavioral, 1971. Subj: Emotions. Self-concept.

I have feelings too photos. by Michael E. Ach. Human Sciences Pr., 1979. Subj: Emotions.

The turtles' picnic and other nonsense stories ill. by Erkki Alanen. Crown, 1977. Subj: Activities – picnicking. Animals.

Bergere, Thea. *Paris in the rain with Jean and Jacqueline* ill. by Richard Bergere. McGraw-Hill, 1963. Subj: City. Foreign lands – France. Weather – rain.

Bergman, Donna. *City fox* ill. by Peter E. Hanson. Atheneum, 1992. ISBN 0-689-31687-9 Subj: Animals – foxes. Character traits – kindness to animals. City. Friendship. Old age.

Bergstrom, Corinne. *Losing your best friend* ill. by Patricia Rosamilia. Human Sciences Pr., 1980. Subj: Friendship.

Bergström, Gunilla. *Is that a monster, Alfie Atkins?* ill. by Robert Swindells. Farrar, 1989. ISBN 9-12-959136-8 Subj: Animals – rabbits. Monsters.

Who's scaring Alfie Atkins? tr. by Joan Sandin; ill. by author. Farrar, 1987. ISBN 91-29-58318-7 Subj: Emotions – fear. Family life – fathers. Ghosts.

You have a girlfriend, Alfie Atkins? ill. by Joan Sandin. Farrar, 1988. ISBN 9-12-959062-0 Subj: Emotions – love.

Beris, Sandra. *The cat's surprise* (Seguin-Fontes, Marthe)

A wedding book (Seguin-Fontes, Marthe)

Berkley, Ethel S. *Ups and down: a first book of space* ill. by Kathleen Elgin. Addison-Wesley, 1951. Subj: Concepts. Concepts – up and down.

Berliner, Franz. *Miserable Marabou* ill. by Irene Hedlund. Gareth Stevens, 1989. ISBN 0-8368-0094-X Subj: Birds. Birds – storks. Self-concept.

Wildebeest ill. by Lilian Brogger. Ideals, 1991. ISBN 0-8249-8488-9 Subj: Animals – wildebeests. Behavior – sharing. Character traits – individuality.

Berman, Linda. *The goodbye painting* ill. by Mark Hannon. Human Sciences Pr., 1983. Subj: Activities – baby-sitting.

Bernadette *see* Watts, Bernadette

Bernhard, Josephine Butkowska. *Lullaby: why the pussy-cat washes himself so often; a folk-tale adapted from the Polish* ill. by Irena Lorentowicz. Roy Pubs., 1944. Subj: Animals – cats. Folk and fairy tales. Foreign lands – Poland. Lullabies.

Nine cry-baby dolls ill. by Irena Lorentowicz. Roy Pubs., 1945. Subj: Folk and fairy tales. Foreign lands – Poland. Toys – dolls.

Bernheim, Evelyne. *In Africa* (Bernheim, Marc)

A week in Aya's world (Bernheim, Marc)

Bernheim, Marc. *In Africa* by Marc and Evelyne Bernheim; photos. by authors. Atheneum, 1973. Subj: Family life. Foreign lands – Africa.

A week in Aya's world: the Ivory Coast by Marc and Evelyne Bernheim; photos. by authors. Macmillan, 1970. Subj: Foreign lands – Africa.

Bernstein, Alan. *Regal the golden eagle* (Klinting, Lars)

Bernstein, Joanne E. *Creepy crawly critter riddles* by Joanne E. Bernstein and Paul Cohen; ill. by Rosekrans Hoffman. Albert Whitman, 1986. ISBN 0-8075-1345-8 Subj: Animals. Insects. Riddles.

What was the wicked witch's real name? and other character riddles by Joanne E. Bernstein and Paul Cohen; ill. by Ann Iosa. Albert Whitman, 1986. ISBN 0-8075-8854-7 Subj: Riddles.

When people die by Joanne E. Bernstein and Steven V. Gullo; photos. by Rosmarie Hausherr. Dutton, 1977. Subj: Death.

Bernstein, Margery. *Coyote goes hunting for fire: a California Indian myth* by Margery Bernstein and Janet Kobrin; ill. by Ed Heffernan. Scribner's, 1974. Subj: Animals. Animals – coyotes. Indians of North America. Fire. Folk and fairy tales.

Earth namer: a California Indian myth by Margery Bernstein and Janet Kobrin; ill. by Ed Heffernan. Scribner's, 1974. Subj: Earth. Folk and fairy tales. Indians of North America.

The first morning: an African myth by Margery Bernstein and Janet Kobrin; ill. by Enid Warner Romanek. Scribner's, 1976. Subj: Animals. Folk and fairy tales. Foreign lands – Africa.

How the sun made a promise and kept it: a Canadian Indian myth retold by Margery Bernstein and Janet Kobrin; ill. by Ed Heffernan. Scribner's, 1974. Subj: Folk and fairy tales. Indians of North America. Sun.

Berquist, Grace. *The boy who couldn't roar* ill. by Ruth Van Sciver. Abingdon Pr., 1960. Subj: Behavior – bullying. Character traits – selfishness.

Speckles goes to school ill. by Kathleen Elgin. Abingdon Pr., 1952. Subj: Birds – chickens. School.

Berridge, Celia. *At my house* ill. by author. Random House, 1987. ISBN 0-394-99166-4 Subj: Family life. Houses.

Going swimming ill. by author. Random House, 1987. ISBN 0-394-99165-6 Subj: Sports – swimming.

Grandmother's tales ill. by author. Elsevier-Dutton, 1981. Subj: Bedtime. Family life – grandmothers. Witches.

On my street ill. by author. Random House, 1987. ISBN 0-394-88163-X Subj: Communities, neighborhoods.

Berry, Christine. *Mama went walking* ill. by Maria Christina Brusca. Holt, 1990. ISBN 0-8050-1261-3 Subj: Activities – walking. Emotions – fear. Family life – mothers. Imagination.

Berry, Joy Wilt. *Being destructive* ill. by John Costanza Rev. ed. Childrens Pr., 1984. Subj: Behavior – misbehavior.

Being selfish ill. by John Costanza Rev. ed. Childrens Pr., 1984. Subj: Behavior – misbehavior. Character traits – selfishness.

Disobeying ill. by John Costanza Rev. ed. Childrens Pr., 1984. Subj: Behavior – misbehavior.

Fighting ill. by John Costanza Rev. ed. Childrens Pr., 1984. Subj: Behavior – fighting, arguing. Behavior – misbehavior.

Throwing tantrums ill. by John Costanza Rev. ed. Childrens Pr., 1984. Subj: Behavior – misbehavior.

Whining ill. by John Costanza Rev. ed. Childrens Pr., 1984. Subj: Behavior – misbehavior.

Berson, Harold. *Balarin's goat* ill. by author. Crown, 1972. Subj: Animals – goats. Folk and fairy tales.

Barrels to the moon ill. by author. Coward, 1982. Subj: Folk and fairy tales. Foreign lands – France.

The boy, the baker, the miller and more ill. by author. Crown, 1974. "The story is based on a French folk tale called Un Morceau de pain." Subj: Cumulative tales. Folk and fairy tales.

Charles and Claudine ill. by adapt. Macmillan, 1980. Subj: Folk and fairy tales. Foreign lands – France. Frogs and toads. Magic. Witches.

Henry Possum ill. by author. Crown, 1973. Subj: Animals – foxes. Animals – possums. Behavior – lost.

How the devil got his due ill. by adapt. Crown, 1972. Subj: Character traits – cleverness. Devil. Folk and fairy tales. Foreign lands – France.

Joseph and the snake ill. by author. Macmillan, 1979. Subj: Animals – foxes. Character traits – cleverness. Character traits – kindness to animals. Folk and fairy tales. Foreign lands – France. Reptiles – snakes.

Kassim's shoes ill. by adapt. Crown, 1977. Subj: Behavior – misunderstanding. Folk and fairy tales. Foreign lands – Africa.

A moose is not a mouse ill. by author. Crown, 1975. Subj: Animals – mice. Language.

Pop! goes the turnip ill. by author. Grosset, 1966. Subj: Animals – rabbits. Food. Gardens, gardening. Plants.

Raminagrobis and the mice ill. by author. Seabury Pr., 1966. Subj: Animals – cats. Animals – mice. Folk and fairy tales.

The rats who lived in the delicatessen ill. by author. Crown, 1976. Subj: Animals – rats. Behavior – greed. Food.

The thief who hugged a moonbeam ill. by author. Seabury Pr., 1972. Subj: Behavior – gossip. Crime. Magic. Royalty.

Truffles for lunch ill. by author. Macmillan, 1980. Subj: Animals – pigs. Behavior – wishing.

Why the jackal won't speak to the hedgehog: a Tunisian folk tale ill. by adapt. Seabury Pr., 1970. Subj: Animals. Animals – hedgehogs. Character traits – cleverness. Folk and fairy tales. Foreign lands – Africa.

Bertrand, Cecile. *Mr. and Mrs. Smith have only one child, but what a child!* ill. and tr. from French by author. Lothrop, 1992. ISBN 0-688-11330-3 Subj: Behavior. Family life – only child. Self-concept.

Bertrand, Lynne. *One day, two dragons* ill. by Janet Street. Crown, 1992. ISBN 0-517-58413-1 Subj: Careers – doctors. Counting, numbers. Dragons.

Beskow, Elsa Maartman. *Children of the forest* adapt. from the Swedish by William Jay Smith; ill. by author. Delacorte Pr., 1969. Subj: Foreign lands – Sweden. Forest, woods. Poetry, rhyme. Seasons.

Pelle's new suit ill. by author. Harper, 1919. Subj: Animals – sheep. Clothing. Foreign lands – Sweden.

Peter in Blueberry Land ill. by author. Merrimack, 1984. A new ed. of a 100-year-old picture book Subj: Birthdays. Elves and little people. Food. Foreign lands – Sweden. Magic. Poetry, rhyme.

Peter's adventures in Blueberry land adapt. by Sheila La Farge; ill. by author. Delacorte Pr., 1975. Pub. in Sweden in 1901 Subj: Birthdays. Elves and little people. Food. Foreign lands – Sweden. Magic. Poetry, rhyme.

Bess, Clayton. *The truth about the moon* ill. by Rosekrans Hoffman. Houghton, 1983. Subj: Folk and fairy tales. Foreign lands – Africa. Moon.

Bester, Roger. *Fireman Jim* photos. by author. Crown, 1981. Subj: Careers – firefighters. Fire.

Guess what? photos. by author. Crown, 1980. Subj: Animals. Participation. Problem solving.

Bethell, Jean. *Bathtime* Holt, 1979. Subj: Activities – bathing. Animals.

Hooray for Henry ill. by Sergio Leone. Grosset, 1966. Subj: Character traits – perseverance. Food.

Playmates photos. by author. Holt, 1981. Subj: Activities – playing. Animals.

Three cheers for Mother Jones! ill. by Kathleen Garry-McCord. Holt, 1980. Subj: Activities – working. U.S. history.

Bettina (Bettina Ehrlich). *Cocolo comes to America* ill. by author. Harper, 1949. Subj: Animals – donkeys.

Cocolo's home ill. by author. Harper, 1950. Subj: Animals – donkeys.

Of uncles and aunts ill. by author. Norton, 1964. Subj: Family life – aunts, uncles.

Pantaloni ill. by author. Harper, 1957. Subj: Animals – dogs. Foreign lands – Italy. Poverty. Sports – fishing.

Piccolo ill. by author. Harper, 1954. Subj: Animals – donkeys.

Bettinger, Craig. *Follow me, everybody* ill. by Edward S. Hollander. Doubleday, 1968. Subj: Ethnic groups in the U.S.

Betz, Betty. *Manners for moppets* ill. by author. Grosset, 1962. Subj: Etiquette. Poetry, rhyme.

Bianchi, John. *Swine snafu* ill. by author. Firefly, 1988. ISBN 0-921285-14-0 Subj: Animals – pigs. Family life. Friendship.

Bianco, Margery Williams. *The hurdy-gurdy man* ill. by Robert Lawson. Gregg, 1980. Subj: Activities – dancing. Music.

The velveteen rabbit: or, How toys became real ill. by Allen Atkinson. Knopf, 1983. Subj: Animals – rabbits. Emotions – love. Folk and fairy tales. Magic. Toys.

The velveteen rabbit: or, How toys became real ill. by Michael Green. Running Pr., 1984. ISBN 0-89741-291-8 Subj: Animals – rabbits. Emotions – love. Folk and fairy tales. Magic. Toys.

The velveteen rabbit: or, How toys became real ill. by Michael Hague. Holt, 1983. Subj: Animals – rabbits. Emotions – love. Folk and fairy tales. Magic. Toys.

The velveteen rabbit ill. by David Jorgensen. Knopf, 1985. ISBN 0-394-87711-X Subj: Animals – rabbits. Emotions – love. Folk and fairy tales. Magic. Toys.

The velveteen rabbit: or, How toys became real ill. by William Nicholson. Doubleday, n.d. Subj: Animals – rabbits. Emotions – love. Folk and fairy tales. Magic. Toys.

The velveteen rabbit: or, How toys became real ill. by Ilse Plume. Godine, 1983. Subj: Animals – rabbits. Emotions – love. Folk and fairy tales. Magic. Toys.

The velveteen rabbit: or, How toys became real ed. by David Eastman; ill. by S. D. Schindler. Troll Assoc., 1987. ISBN 0-8167-1061-9 Subj: Animals – rabbits. Emotions – love. Folk and fairy tales. Magic. Toys.

The velveteen rabbit: or, How toys became real ill. by Tien. Simon and Schuster, 1983. Subj: Animals – rabbits. Emotions – love. Folk and fairy tales. Magic. Toys.

Bibb, Eric. *The dolphin journey* (Orstadius, Brita)

Bible. *Best-loved Bible verses for children* ill. by Anna Maria Magagna. Grosset, 1983. Subj: Religion.

Bible, Charles. *Hamdaani: a traditional tale from Zanzibar* ill. by adapt. Holt, 1977. Subj: Animals. Folk and fairy tales. Foreign lands – Africa.

Jennifer's new chair ill. by author. Holt, 1978. Subj: Birthdays. Family life. Family life – grandmothers. Fire. Furniture – chairs. Parties.

Bible. New Testament. *The Lord's prayer* ill. by Ingri and Edgar Parin d'Aulaire Catholic version. Doubleday, 1934. Subj: Religion.

The Lord's prayer ill. by Ingri and Edgar Parin d'Aulaire Protestant version. Doubleday, 1934. Subj: Religion.

The Lord's prayer ill. by George Kraus. Dutton, 1970. Subj: Religion.

Bible. New Testament. Gospels. *Christmas: the King James Version* ill. by Jan Pieńkowski. Knopf, 1984. ISBN 0-394-86923-0 Subj: Holidays – Christmas. Religion.

The first Christmas: from the Gospels according to Saint Luke and Saint Matthew ill. by Barbara Neustadt. Crowell, 1960. Subj: Religion.

The Nativity ill. by Julie Vivas. Harcourt, 1988. Text consists of excerpts from the authorized King James version of the Bible ISBN 0-15-200535-8 Subj: Holidays – Christmas. Religion.

The story of Christmas: words from the Gospels of Matthew and Luke ill. by Jane Ray. Dutton, 1991. ISBN 0-525-44768-7 Subj: Holidays – Christmas. Religion.

Bible. Old Testament. *David and the giant* (Little, Emily)

Noah and the ark ill. by Pauline Baynes. Holt, 1988. ISBN 0-8050-0886-1 Subj: Religion – Noah.

Bible. Old Testament. Daniel. *Daniel in the lions' den* adapt. by Belinda Hollyer; ill. by Leon Baxter. Silver Burdett, 1984. ISBN 0-382-067090-8 Subj: Animals – lions. Religion.

Shadrach, Meshack and Abednego ill. by Paul Galdone. McGraw-Hill, 1965. Subj: Religion.

Bible. Old Testament. David. *David and Goliath* adapt. by Belinda Hollyer; ill. by Leon Baxter. Silver Burdett, 1984. ISBN 0-382-06791-6 Subj: Religion.

Bible. Old Testament. Jonah. *The Book of Jonah* adapt. and ill. by Peter Spier. Doubleday, 1985. ISBN 0-385-19335-1 Subj: Animals – whales. Religion.

Jonah: the complete text of Jonah from the Holy Bible, New International version ill. by Kurt Mitchell. Crossway, 1981. Subj: Animals – mice. Animals – cats. Animals – whales. Religion.

Jonah and the great fish adapt. by Belinda Hollyer; ill. by Leon Baxter. Silver Burdett, 1984. ISBN 0-382-06792-4 Subj: Animals – whales. Religion.

Bible. Old Testament. Psalms. *The Lord is my shepherd* ill. by George Kraus. Dutton, 1971. Subj: Religion.

The Lord is my shepherd: the twenty-third Psalm ill. by Tasha Tudor. Putnam, 1980. Subj: Religion.

Bider, Djemma. *The buried treasure* ill. by Debby L. Carter. Dodd, 1982. Subj: Folk and fairy tales. Foreign lands – Russia.

A drop of honey ill. by Armen Kojoyian. Simon & Schuster, 1989. ISBN 0-671-66265-1 Subj: Dreams. Folk and fairy tales. Foreign lands – Armenia. Sibling rivalry.

Bienenfeld, Florence. *My mom and dad are getting a divorce* ill. by Art Scott. EMC, 1980. Subj: Divorce. Emotions.

Bier, Anna. *The nightingale* (Andersen, H. C. (Hans Christian))

Bierhorst, John. *Doctor Coyote: a Native American Æsop's fables* ill. by Wendy Watson. Macmillan, 1987. ISBN 0-02-709780-3 Subj: Animals. Animals – coyotes. Folk and fairy tales. Indians of North America.

The ring in the prairie: a Shawnee legend tr. by John Bierhorst; ill. by Leo and Diane Dillon. Dial Pr., 1970. Subj: Folk and fairy tales. Indians of North America.

Spirit child (Sahagun, Bernardino de)

The big Peter Rabbit book: *things to do, games to play, stories, presents to make* ill. by Beatrix Potter. Warne, 1986. ISBN 0-7232-3409-4 Subj: Activities – making things. Animals. Games. Riddles.

Bileck, Marvin. *Rain makes applesauce* (Scheer, Julian)

Bilezikian, Gary. *While I slept* ill. by author. Orchard, 1990. ISBN 0-531-08475-2 Subj: Night. Noise, sounds. Sleep.

Billam, Rosemary. *Fuzzy rabbit* ill. by Vanessa Julian-Ottie. Random House, 1984. Subj: Behavior – needing someone. Birthdays. Emotions – love. Toys.

Billington, Elizabeth T. *The Randolph Caldecott treasury* (Caldecott, Randolph)

Billout, Guy. *By camel or by car: a look at transportation* ill. by author. Prentice-Hall, 1979. Subj: Activities – traveling. Transportation.

Billy Boy verses sel. by Richard Chase; ill. by Glen Rounds. Children's Pr., 1966. Subj: Folk and fairy tales. Poetry, rhyme. Songs.

Bingham, Mindy. *Minou* ill. by Itoko Maeno. Advocacy Pr., 1987. ISBN 0-911655-36-0 Subj: Animals – cats. Behavior – needing someone. Foreign lands – France.

My way Sally by Mindy Bingham and Penelope Colville Paine; ill. by Itoko Maeno. Advocacy Pr., 1988. ISBN 0-911655-27-1 Subj: Animals – dogs. Animals – foxes. Behavior – trickery.

Binnamin, Vivian. *The case of the anteater's missing lunch* ill. by Jeffrey S. Nelsen. Silver Pr., 1990. ISBN 0-671-68816-2 Subj: Activities – picnicking. Animals – anteaters. Problem solving. School.

The case of the mysterious mermaid ill. by Jeffrey S. Nelsen. Silver Pr., 1990. ISBN 0-671-68817-0 Subj: Aquariums. Mythical creatures – mermaids. School.

The case of the planetarium puzzle ill. by Jeffrey S. Nelsen. Silver Pr., 1990. ISBN 0-671-68819-7 Subj: Problem solving.

The case of the snoring stegosaurus ill. by Jeffrey S. Nelsen. Silver Pr., 1990. ISBN 0-671-68818-9 Subj: Dinosaurs. Museums. Problem solving.

Binzen, Bill. *Alfred goes house hunting* ill. by author. Doubleday, 1974. Subj: Animals. Houses. Toys.

Carmen photos. by author. Coward, 1970. Subj: City. Friendship.

Birch, David. *The king's chessboard* ill. by Devis Grebu. Dial Pr., 1988. ISBN 0-8037-0367-8 Subj: Character traits – pride. Royalty – kings.

Birchman, David F. *Brother Billy Bronto's bygone blues band* ill. by John O'Brien. Lothrop, 1992. ISBN 0-688-10424-X Subj: Dinosaurs. Ghosts. Music. Poetry, rhyme.

Bird, E. J. *How do bears sleep?* ill. by author. Carolrhoda, 1989. ISBN 0-87614-384-2 Subj: Animals – bears. Character traits – curiosity. Character traits – questioning. Hibernation. Poetry, rhyme.

Birdseye, Tom. *Airmail to the moon* ill. by Stephen Gammell. Holiday, 1988. ISBN 0-8234-0683-0 Subj: Behavior – losing things. Character traits – persistence. Teeth.

A song of stars ill. by Ju-Hong Chen. Holiday, 1990. ISBN 0-8234-0790-X Subj: Emotions – love. Folk and fairy tales. Foreign lands – China. Sky. Stars.

Waiting for baby ill. by Loreen Leedy. Holiday, 1991. ISBN 0-8234-0892-2 Subj: Babies. Family life.

Birnbaum, Abe. *Green eyes* ill. by author. Western Pr., 1953. Subj: Caldecott award honor book.

Biro, B. S. *see* Biro, Val

Biro, Val. *Gumdrop, the adventures of a vintage car* ill. by author. Follett, 1966. Subj: Automobiles.

Miranda's umbrella ill. by author. Peter Bedrick Bks., 1990. ISBN 0-87226-429-7 Subj: Giants. Umbrellas. Witches.

The pied piper of Hamelin ill. by reteller. Silver Burdett, 1985. ISBN 0-382-09014-4 Subj: Animals – rats. Behavior – trickery. Folk and fairy tales. Foreign lands – Germany. Middle ages.

The three little pigs (The three little pigs)

The wind in the willows: home sweet home ill. by author. Simon & Schuster, 1985. Subj: Animals. Houses.

The wind in the willows: the open road ill. by author. Simon & Schuster, 1985. ISBN 0-671-63626-X Subj: Activities – traveling. Animals.

The wind in the willows: the river bank ill. by author. Simon & Schuster, 1985. Subj: Animals. Rivers.

The wind in the willows: the wild wood ill. by author. Simon & Schuster, 1985. Subj: Animals. Forest, woods.

Birrer, Cynthia. *The lady and the unicorn* by Cynthia and William Birrer; ill. by authors. Lothrop, 1987. ISBN 0-688-04038-1 Subj: Character traits – kindness to animals. Folk and fairy tales. Magic. Mythical creatures – unicorns. Royalty – princes.

Song to Demeter by Cynthia and William Birrer; ill. by authors. Lothrop, 1987. ISBN 0-688-04041-1 Subj: Folk and fairy tales. Foreign lands – Greece.

Birrer, William. *The lady and the unicorn* (Birrer, Cynthia)

Song to Demeter (Birrer, Cynthia)

Bishop, Adela. *The Christmas polar bear* ill. by Carole Czapla. DOT Garnet, 1991. ISBN 0-9625620-2-5 Subj: Animals – polar bears. Holidays – Christmas.

The Easter wolf ill. by Carole Czapla. DOT Garnet, 1991. ISBN 0-9625620-1-7 Subj: Animals – rabbits. Animals – wolves. Birds – chickens. Character traits – kindness. Holidays – Easter.

Bishop, Ann. *Chicken riddle* ill. by Jerry Warshaw. Albert Whitman, 1972. Subj: Birds – chickens. Humor. Riddles.

The Ella Fannie elephant riddle book ill. by Jerry Warshaw. Albert Whitman, 1974. Subj: Animals – elephants. Humor. Riddles.

Hey riddle riddle ill. by Jerry Warshaw. Albert Whitman, 1968. Subj: Humor. Riddles.

Merry-go-riddle ill. by Jerry Warshaw. Albert Whitman, 1973. Subj: Humor. Riddles.

Noah riddle? ill. by Jerry Warshaw. Albert Whitman, 1970. Subj: Humor. Riddles.

Oh, riddlesticks! ill. by Jerry Warshaw. Albert Whitman, 1976. Subj: Humor. Riddles.

The riddle ages ill. by Jerry Warshaw. Albert Whitman, 1977. Subj: Humor. Middle ages. Riddles.

Riddle-iculous rid-alphabet book ill. by Jerry Warshaw. Albert Whitman, 1971. Subj: ABC books. Humor. Riddles.

Wild Bill Hiccup's riddle book ed. by Caroline Rubin; ill. by Jerry Warshaw. Albert Whitman, 1969. Subj: Cowboys. Humor. Riddles.

Bishop, Bonnie. *No one noticed Ralph* ill. by Jack Kent. Doubleday, 1979. Subj: Behavior – unnoticed, unseen. Birds – parakeets, parrots.

Ralph rides away ill. by Jack Kent. Doubleday, 1979. Subj: Activities – picnicking. Birds – parakeets, parrots. Zoos.

Bishop, Claire Huchet. *The five Chinese brothers* by Claire Huchet Bishop and Kurt Wiese; ill. by Kurt Wiese. Coward, 1938. Subj: Character traits – cleverness. Family life. Folk and fairy tales. Foreign lands – China.

The man who lost his head ill. by Robert McCloskey. Viking, 1942. Subj: Anatomy – heads. Humor.

The truffle pig ill. by Kurt Wiese. Coward, 1971. Subj: Animals – pigs. Foreign lands – France. Pets.

Twenty-two bears ill. by Kurt Wiese. Viking, 1964. Subj: Animals – bears. Counting, numbers. Cumulative tales.

Bishop, Gavin. *Chicken Licken* (Chicken Little)

Mrs. McGinty and the bizarre plant ill. by author. Oxford Univ. Pr., 1983. Subj: Gardens, gardening. Plants.

The three little pigs (The three little pigs)

Bishop, Roma. *Animals* ill. by author. Simon & Schuster, 1991. ISBN 0-671-74833-5 Subj: Animals. Format, unusual – board books. Format, unusual – toy and movable books.

Numbers ill. by author. Simon & Schuster, 1991. ISBN 0-671-74832-7 Subj: Counting, numbers. Format, unusual – board books. Format, unusual – toy and movable books.

Shapes ill. by author. Simon & Schuster, 1991. ISBN 0-671-74830-0 Subj: Concepts – shape. Format, unusual – board books. Format, unusual – toy and movable books.

Toys ill. by author. Simon & Schuster, 1991. ISBN 0-671-74831-9 Subj: Format, unusual – board books. Format, unusual – toy and movable books. Toys.

Black, Algernon D. *The woman of the wood: a tale from old Russia* ill. by Evaline Ness. Holt, 1973. Subj: Folk and fairy tales. Foreign lands – Russia.

Black, Floyd. *Alphabet cat* ill. by Carol Nicklaus. Elsevier-Dutton, 1979. Subj: ABC books. Animals – cats. Animals – rats.

Black, Irma Simonton. *Big puppy and little puppy* ill. by Theresa Sherman. Holiday, 1960. Subj: Animals – dogs. Concepts – size.

Is this my dinner? ill. by Rosalind Fry. Albert Whitman, 1972. Subj: Food. Participation. Poetry, rhyme.

The little old man who could not read ill. by Seymour Fleishman. Albert Whitman, 1968. Subj: Activities – reading. Shopping.

Blacker, Terence. *Herbie Hamster, where are you?* ill. by Pippa Unwin. Random House, 1990. ISBN 0-679-80838-8 Subj: Animals – hamsters. Behavior – hiding. Games.

Blackmore, Vivien. *Why corn is golden: stories about plants* ill. by Susana Martínez-Ostos. Little, 1984. Subj: Folk and fairy tales. Foreign lands – Mexico. Plants.

Blackwood, Gladys Rourke. *Whistle for Cindy* ill. by author. Albert Whitman, 1952. Subj: Activities – whistling. Animals – dogs. Pets.

Blackwood, Mary. *Derek the knitting dinosaur* ill. by Kerry Argent. Carolrhoda, 1990. ISBN 0-87614-400-8 Subj: Activities – knitting. Dinosaurs. Poetry, rhyme.

Blades, Ann. *Fall* ill. by author. Lothrop, 1990. ISBN 0-688-09232-2 Subj: Format, unusual – board books. Seasons – fall. Wordless.

Mary of mile 18 ill. by author. Scribner's, 1976. Subj: Animals – wolves. Character traits – perseverance. Farms. Foreign lands – Canada.

Spring ill. by author. Lothrop, 1990. ISBN 0-688-09230-6 Subj: Format, unusual – board books. Seasons – spring. Wordless.

Summer ill. by author. Lothrop, 1990. ISBN 0-688-09231-4 Subj: Format, unusual – board books. Seasons – summer. Wordless.

Winter ill. by author. Lothrop, 1990. ISBN 0-688-09233-0 Subj: Format, unusual – board books. Seasons – winter. Wordless.

Blaine, Marge (Margery Kay). *The terrible thing that happened at our house* ill. by John Wallner. Parents, 1975. Subj: Family life. Family life – mothers. Problem solving.

Blake, Jon. *Wriggly Pig* ill. by Susie Jenkin-Pearce. Morrow, 1992. ISBN 0-688-11296-X Subj: Animals – pigs. Behavior. Family life.

Blake, Pamela. *Peep-show: a little book of rhymes* ill. by author. Macmillan, 1973. Subj: Nursery rhymes.

Blake, Quentin. *All join in* ill. by author. Little, 1991. ISBN 0-316-09934-1 Subj: Participation. Poetry, rhyme.

Custard and Company (Nash, Ogden)

Mister Magnolia ill. by author. Jonathan Cape, 1980. Subj: Humor. Poetry, rhyme.

Mrs. Armitage on wheels ill. by author. Knopf, 1988. ISBN 0-394-99498-1 Subj: Humor. Sports – bicycling.

Quentin Blake's ABC ill. by author. Knopf, 1989. ISBN 0-394-94149-7 Subj: ABC books. Poetry, rhyme.

Quentin Blake's nursery rhyme book ill. by author. Harper, 1984. Subj: Humor. Nursery rhymes.

Snuff ill. by author. Lippincott, 1973. Subj: Crime. Knights.

The story of the dancing frog ill. by author. Knopf, 1985. Subj: Folk and fairy tales.

Blake, Robert J. *The perfect spot* ill. by author. Putnam, 1992. ISBN 0-399-22132-8 Subj: Family life – fathers. Forest, woods. Nature.

Blakeley, Peggy. *Two little ducks* ill. by Kenzo Kobayashi. Alphabet Pr., 1984. Subj: Communities, neighborhoods.

What shall I be tomorrow? ill. by Helga Aichinger. Alphabet Pr., 1984. Subj: Behavior – imitation. Imagination.

Blance, Ellen. *Lady Monster has a plan* by Ellen Blance and Ann Cook; ill. by Quentin Blake. Bowmar, 1977. Subj: Monsters.

Lady Monster helps out by Ellen Blance and Ann Cook; ill. by Quentin Blake. Bowmar, 1977. Subj: Monsters.

Monster and the magic umbrella by Ellen Blance and Ann Cook; ill. by Quentin Blake. Bowmar, 1973. Subj: Magic. Monsters. Umbrellas.

Monster and the mural by Ellen Blance and Ann Cook; ill. by Quentin Blake. Bowmar, 1977. Subj: Monsters.

Monster and the surprise cookie by Ellen Blance and Ann Cook; ill. by Quentin Blake. Bowmar, 1977. Subj: Monsters.

Monster at school by Ellen Blance and Ann Cook; ill. by Quentin Blake. Bowmar, 1973. Subj: Monsters. School.

Monster buys a pet by Ellen Blance and Ann Cook; ill. by Quentin Blake. Bowmar, 1977. Subj: Monsters. Pets.

Monster cleans his house by Ellen Blance and Ann Cook; ill. by Quentin Blake. Bowmar, 1973. Subj: Monsters.

Monster comes to the city by Ellen Blance and Ann Cook; ill. by Quentin Blake. Bowmar, 1973. Subj: City. Monsters.

Monster gets a job by Ellen Blance and Ann Cook; ill. by Quentin Blake. Bowmar, 1977. Subj: Activities – working. Monsters.

Monster goes around the town by Ellen Blance and Ann Cook; ill. by Quentin Blake. Bowmar, 1977. Subj: Monsters.

Monster goes to school by Ellen Blance and Ann Cook; ill. by Quentin Blake. Bowmar, 1973. Subj: Monsters. School.

Monster goes to the beach by Ellen Blance and Ann Cook; ill. by Quentin Blake. Bowmar, 1977. Subj: Monsters. Sea and seashore.

Monster goes to the circus by Ellen Blance and Ann Cook; ill. by Quentin Blake. Bowmar, 1977. Subj: Circus. Monsters.

Monster goes to the hospital by Ellen Blance and Ann Cook; ill. by Quentin Blake. Bowmar, 1977. Subj: Hospitals. Monsters.

Monster goes to the museum by Ellen Blance and Ann Cook; ill. by Quentin Blake. Bowmar, 1973. Subj: Monsters. Museums.

Monster goes to the zoo by Ellen Blance and Ann Cook; ill. by Quentin Blake. Bowmar, 1973. Subj: Monsters. Zoos.

Monster has a party by Ellen Blance and Ann Cook; ill. by Quentin Blake. Bowmar, 1973. Subj: Monsters. Parties.

Monster, Lady Monster and the bike ride by Ellen Blance and Ann Cook; ill. by Quentin Blake. Bowmar, 1977. Subj: Monsters. Sports – bicycling.

Monster looks for a friend by Ellen Blance and Ann Cook; ill. by Quentin Blake. Bowmar, 1973. Subj: Friendship. Monsters.

Monster looks for a house by Ellen Blance and Ann Cook; ill. by Quentin Blake. Bowmar, 1973. Subj: Monsters.

Monster meets Lady Monster by Ellen Blance and Ann Cook; ill. by Quentin Blake. Bowmar, 1973. Subj: Monsters.

Monster on the bus by Ellen Blance and Ann Cook; ill. by Quentin Blake. Bowmar, 1973. Subj: Buses. Monsters.

Blanchard, Arlene. *The naughty lamb* ill. by Tony Wells. Dial, 1989. ISBN 0-8037-0605-7 Subj: Animals – sheep. Behavior – hiding. Farms. Games.

Sounds my feet make ill. by Vanessa Julian-Ottie. Random House, 1989. ISBN 0-394-89648-3 Subj: Anatomy – feet. Noise, sounds.

Blathwayt, Benedict. *Bear's adventure* ill. by author. Knopf, 1988. ISBN 0-394-90568-7 Subj: Animals – bears.

Tangle and the silver bird ill. by author. Knopf, 1989. ISBN 0-394-92780-X Subj: Activities – flying. Animals.

Blau, Judith. *Bunny Mitten's book* ill. by author. Random House, 1991. ISBN 0-679-81315-2 Subj: Animals – rabbits. Puppets.

Blaustein, Muriel. *Baby Mabu and Auntie Moose* ill. by author. Four Winds Pr., 1983. Subj: Activities – baby-sitting. Behavior – misbehavior. Character traits – freedom. Family life – aunts, uncles.

Bedtime, Zachary! ill. by author. Harper, 1987. ISBN 0-06-020537-7 Subj: Animals – tigers. Bedtime. Behavior – misbehavior. Family life.

Make friends, Zachary! ill. by author. HarperCollins, 1990. ISBN 0-06-020546-6 Subj: Animals – tigers. Friendship. Camps, camping.

Play ball, Zachary! ill. by author. Harper, 1988. ISBN 0-06-020544-X Subj: Family life – fathers. Sports.

Blech, Dietlind. *Hello Irina* ill. by author. Holt, 1971. Translation of Allo Irina by Yaak Karsunke Subj: Activities – traveling. Animals – horses.

Blegvad, Erik. *Burnie's hill: a traditional rhyme* ill. by author. Atheneum, 1977. Subj: Cumulative tales. Foreign lands – Scotland. Poetry, rhyme. Seasons.

The emperor's new clothes (Andersen, H. C. (Hans Christian))

One is for the sun (Blegvad, Lenore)

The swineherd (Andersen, H. C. (Hans Christian))

Blegvad, Lenore. *Anna Banana and me* ill. by Erik Blegvad. Atheneum, 1985. ISBN 0-689-50274-5 Subj: Character traits – bravery. Emotions – fear. Imagination.

The great hamster hunt ill. by Erik Blegvad. Harcourt, 1969. Subj: Animals – hamsters. Pets.

Hark! Hark! The dogs do bark, and other poems about dogs ill. by Erik Blegvad. Atheneum, 1975. Subj: Animals – dogs. Nursery rhymes.

Mr. Jensen and cat ill. by Erik Blegvad. Harcourt, 1965. Subj: Animals – cats. Emotions – loneliness. Foreign lands – Denmark.

Mittens for kittens and other rhymes about cats ill. by Erik Blegvad. Atheneum, 1974. Subj: Animals – cats. Nursery rhymes.

One is for the sun by Lenore and Erik Blegvad; ill. by Erik Blegvad. Harcourt, 1968. Subj: Counting, numbers. Poetry, rhyme.

The parrot in the garret and other rhymes about dwellings ill. by Erik Blegvad. Atheneum, 1982. Subj: Birds – parakeets, parrots. Houses. Poetry, rhyme.

Rainy day Kate ill. by Erik Blegvad. Macmillan, 1988. ISBN 0-689-50442-X Subj: Activities – playing. Imagination. Toys – dolls. Weather – rain.

This little pig-a-wig and other rhymes about pigs ill. by Erik Blegvad. Atheneum, 1978. Subj: Animals – pigs. Nursery rhymes.

Bliss, Austin. *That dog Melly!* (Bliss, Corinne Demas)

Bliss, Corinne Demas. *Matthew's meadow* ill. by Ted Lewin. Harcourt, 1992. ISBN 0-15-200759-8 Subj: Birds – hawks. Nature. Seasons – fall.

That dog Melly! by Corinne Demas Bliss with Austin Bliss; photos. by Corinne Demas Bliss and Jim Judkis. Hastings, 1981. Subj: Animals – dogs. Friendship. Pets.

Blizzard, Gladys S. *Come look with me: enjoying art with children* Thomasson-Grant, 1991. ISBN 0-934738-76-9 Subj: Art.

Blocksma, Dewey. *Easy-to-make spaceships that really fly* (Blocksma, Mary)

Blocksma, Mary. *Apple tree! Apple tree!* ill. by Sandra Cox Kalthoff. Childrens Pr., 1983. Subj: Seasons. Trees.

The best dressed bear ill. by Sandra Cox Kalthoff. Childrens Pr., 1984. ISBN 0-516-01585-0 Subj: Activities – dancing. Animals – bears. Clothing.

Did you hear that? ill. by Sandra Cox Kalthoff. Childrens Pr., 1983. Subj: Bedtime. Night. Noise, sounds.

Easy-to-make spaceships that really fly by Mary and Dewey Blocksma; ill. by Marisabina Russo. Prentice-Hall, 1983. Subj: Activities – making things. Space and space ships.

Grandma Dragon's birthday ill. by Sandra Cox Kalthoff. Childrens Pr., 1983. Subj: Birthdays.

The pup went up ill. by Sandra Cox Kalthoff. Childrens Pr., 1983. Subj: Animals – dogs. Imagination.

Rub-a-dub-dub: What's in the tub? ill. by Sandra Cox Kalthoff. Childrens Pr., 1984. ISBN 0-516-01586-9 Subj: Activities – bathing. Animals – dogs.

Where's that duck? ill. by Sandra Cox Kalthoff. Childrens Pr., 1985. ISBN 0-516-01587-7 Subj: Birds – ducks. Farms. Poetry, rhyme.

Blood, Charles L. *The goat in the rug* by Charles L. Blood and Martin A. Link; ill. by Nancy Winslow Parker. Parents, 1976. Subj: Activities – weaving. Animals – goats. Indians of North America.

Bloom, Suzanne. *A family for Jamie* ill. by author. Crown, 1991. ISBN 0-517-57493-4 Subj: Adoption. Family life.

We keep a pig in the parlor ill. by author. Potter, 1988. ISBN 0-517-56829-2 Subj: Animals – pigs. Farms. Poetry, rhyme.

Bloome, Enid. *The air we breathe!* ill. with photos. Doubleday, 1972. Subj: Ecology.

The water we drink! ill. with photos. Doubleday, 1971. Subj: Ecology.

Blos, Joan W. *The grandpa days* ill. by Emily Arnold McCully. Simon & Schuster, 1989. ISBN 0-671-64640-0 Subj: Activities – making things. Family life – grandfathers.

Martin's hats ill. by Marc Simont. Morrow, 1984. Subj: Clothing – hats. Imagination.

Old Henry ill. by Stephen Gammell. Morrow, 1987. ISBN 0-688-06400-0 Subj: Behavior – indifference. Character traits – being different. Houses. Poetry, rhyme.

A seed, a flower, a minute, an hour ill. by Hans Poppel. Simon & Schuster, 1992. ISBN 0-671-73214-5 Subj: Poetry, rhyme.

Blough, Glenn O. *Christmas trees and how they grow* ill. by Jeanne Bendick. McGraw-Hill, 1961. Subj: Holidays – Christmas. Trees.

Who lives in this meadow? ill. by Jeanne Bendick. McGraw-Hill, 1961. Subj: Animals.

Blue, Rose. *Black, black, beautiful black* ill. by Emmett Wigglesworth. Watts, 1969. Subj: Ethnic groups in the U.S. – Afro-Americans. Zoos.

How many blocks is the world? ill. by Harold James. Watts, 1970. Subj: City. Concepts – size. Ethnic groups in the U.S. – Afro-Americans. Family life. School.

I am here: Yo estoy aqui ill. by Moneta Barnett. Watts, 1971. Subj: Character traits – being different. Ethnic groups in the U.S. Ethnic groups in the U.S. – Puerto Rican-Americans. Foreign languages. School.

Blumberg, Rhoda. *Jumbo* ill. by Jonathan Hunt. Macmillan, 1992. ISBN 0-02-711683-2 Subj: Animals – elephants. Circus. Zoos.

Blume, Judy. *The one in the middle is a green kangaroo* ill. by Irene Trivas. Macmillan, 1991. ISBN 0-02-711055-9 Subj: Family life. Self-concept.

The Pain and The Great One ill. by Irene Trivas. Bradbury Pr., 1984. Orig. pub. in Free to be... you and me, McGraw-Hill, 1974 Subj: Family life. Sibling rivalry.

Blumenthal, Nancy. *Count-a-saurus* ill. by Robert Jay Kaufman. Macmillan, 1989. ISBN 0-02-749391-1 Subj: Counting, numbers. Dinosaurs. Poetry, rhyme.

Blundell, Tony. *Beware of boys* ill. by author. Greenwillow, 1992. ISBN 0-688-10925-X Subj: Activities – cooking. Animals – wolves. Behavior – trickery.

Joe on Sunday ill. by author. Dial Pr., 1987. ISBN 0-8037-0446-1 Subj: Behavior. Imagination.

Blutig, Eduard *see* Gorey, Edward (St. John)

Blyler, Allison. *Finding foxes* ill. by Robert J. Blake. Putnam, 1991. ISBN 0-399-22264-2 Subj: Animals – foxes. Nature. Poetry, rhyme.

Blyth, Alan. *Cinderella* (Perrault, Charles)

Bodecker, N. M. (Nils Mogens). *Good night little one* (Kraus, Robert)

Good night Richard Rabbit (Kraus, Robert)

"It's raining," said John Twaining: Danish nursery rhymes ill. by author. Atheneum, 1973. Subj: Foreign lands – Denmark. Humor. Nursery rhymes.

"Let's marry" said the cherry, and other nonsense poems ill. by author. Atheneum, 1974. Subj: Humor. Poetry, rhyme.

Snowman Sniffles and other verse ill. by author. Atheneum, 1983. Subj: Humor. Poetry, rhyme. Tongue twisters.

Bodger, Joan. *Belinda's ball* ill. by Mark Thurman. Atheneum, 1981. Subj: Concepts.

Bodsworth, Nan. *Monkey business* ill. by author. Dial Pr., 1987. ISBN 0-8037-0393-7 Subj: Animals. Behavior – wishing. Imagination. Zoos.

A nice walk in the jungle ill. by author. Viking, 1990. ISBN 0-670-82476-3 Subj: Activities – walking. Jungle. Reptiles – snakes.

Bodwell, Gaile. *The long day of the giants* ill. by Leon Steinmetz. McGraw-Hill, 1975. Subj: Giants. Poetry, rhyme. Time.

Boegehold, Betty. *Bear underground* ill. by Jim Arnosky. Doubleday, 1980. Subj: Animals – bears. Insects. Science.

Daddy doesn't live here anymore: a book about divorce ill. by Deborah Borgo. Childrens Pr., 1985. ISBN 0-307-62480-3 Subj: Divorce. Emotions – anger. Family life.

Here's Pippa again! ill. by Cyndy Szekeres. Knopf, 1975. Subj: Animals – mice.

Hurray for Pippa! ill. by Cyndy Szekeres. Knopf, 1980. Subj: Behavior – talking to strangers. Imagination. Toys.

In the castle of cats ill. by Jan Brett. Dutton, 1981. Subj: Animals – cats. Imagination.

Pawpaw's run ill. by Christine Price. Dutton, 1968. Subj: Animals – cats. Behavior – lost. Character traits – cleverness. Emotions – love. Pets. Poetry, rhyme.

Pippa Mouse ill. by Cyndy Szekeres. Knopf, 1973. Subj: Animals – mice.

Pippa pops out! ill. by Cyndy Szekeres. Knopf, 1979. Subj: Animals – mice.

Small Deer's magic tricks ill. by Jacqueline Chwast. Coward, 1977. Subj: Animals – deer. Behavior – trickery.

Three to get ready ill. by Mary Chalmers. Harper, 1965. Subj: Animals – cats. Behavior.

Boesel, Ann Sterling. *Sing and sing again* ill. by Louise Costello. Oxford Univ. Pr., 1938. Subj: Music. Songs.

Singing with Peter and Patsy ill. by Pelagie Doane. Oxford Univ. Pr., 1944. Subj: Music. Songs.

Boesky, Amy. *Planet Was* ill. by Nadine Bernard Westcott. Little, 1990. ISBN 0-316-10084-6 Subj: Poetry, rhyme. Royalty – princes.

Bogart, Jo Ellen. *Daniel's dog* ill. by Janet Wilson. Scholastic, 1990. ISBN 0-590-43402-0 Subj: Babies. Ethnic groups in the U.S. – Afro-Americans. Family life – brothers. Family life – sisters.

Bogot, Howard. *I'm growing* by Howard Bogot and Daniel B. Syme; ill. by Janet Compere. Union of American Hebrew Congregations, 1982. Subj: Behavior – growing up. Jewish culture.

Bograd, Larry. *Egon* ill. by Dirk Zimmer. Macmillan, 1980. Subj: Animals. Character traits – curiosity.

Felix in the attic ill. by Dirk Zimmer. Harvey House, 1978. Subj: Family life.

Lost in the store ill. by Victoria Chess. Macmillan, 1981. Subj: Behavior – lost. Stores.

Bohanon, Paul. *Golden Kate* ill. by Gertrude Howe. Oxford Univ. Pr., 1943. Subj: Character traits – generosity. Farms.

Bohdal, Susi. *Bobby the bear* ill. by author. Holt, 1986. ISBN 0-03-008028-2 Subj: Format, unusual – board books. Friendship. Toys – teddy bears.

Harry the hare ill. by author. Holt, 1986. ISBN 0-03-008029-0 Subj: Format, unusual – board books. Toys.

The magic honey jar tr. by Anthea Bell; ill. by author. North-South, 1987. ISBN 0-8050-0491-2 Subj: Behavior – greed. Dreams. Royalty.

Tom cat ill. by author. Doubleday, 1977. Subj: Animals. Animals – cats. Communication.

Bohman, Nils. *Jim, Jock and Jumbo* ill. by Einar Norelius. Dutton, 1946. Subj: Animals – elephants. Animals – hippopotami. Animals – lions. Humor.

Boholm-Olsson, Eva. *Tuan* tr. by Dianne Jonasson; ill. by Pham van Don. Farrar, 1988. ISBN 91-29-58766-2 Subj: Family life. Foreign lands – Vietnam.

Bois, Ivy Du *see* DuBois, Ivy

Bois, William Pène Du *see* Du Bois, William Pène

Bolliger, Max. *The fireflies* ill. by Jiři Trnka. Atheneum, 1970. Based on a Czechoslovakian story: Broučci, by Jan Karafiát, first published in 1875; translated by Roseanna Hoover Subj: Family life. Folk and fairy tales. Foreign lands – Czechoslovakia. Insects – fireflies. Night.

The giants' feast ill. by Monica Laimgruber. Addison-Wesley, 1976. Translation of Das Reisenfest; English version by Barbara Willard Subj: Food. Giants.

The golden apple ill. by Celestino Piatti. Atheneum, 1970. Translated by Roseanna Hoover Subj: Behavior – greed. Family life. Food.

The lonely prince ill. by Jurg Obrist. Atheneum, 1982. Subj: Emotions – loneliness. Friendship.

The magic bird ill. by Jan Lenica. David & Charles, 1988. ISBN 0-86264-146-2 Subj: Behavior – growing up. Character traits – kindness to animals. Elves and little people. Giants.

The most beautiful song ill. by Jindra Capek. Little, 1981. Subj: Music. Royalty.

Noah and the rainbow: an ancient story tr. by Clyde Robert Bulla; ill. by Helga Aichinger. Crowell, 1972. Subj: Religion – Noah.

The rabbit with the sky blue ears ill. by Jürg Obrist. David & Charles, 1989. ISBN 0-86241-204-8 Subj: Anatomy – ears. Animals – rabbits. Self-concept.

Sandy at the children's zoo tr. from German by Elisabeth Gemming; ill. by Klaus Brunner. Crowell, 1967. Subj: Behavior – lost. Zoos.

The wooden man ill. by Fred Bauer. Seabury Pr., 1974. Translation of Der Mann aus Holz Subj: Scarecrows. Weapons. Weather.

Bolognese, Don. *Donkey and Carlo* (Raphael, Elaine)

Donkey, it's snowing (Raphael, Elaine)

A new day ill. by author. Delacorte Pr., 1970. Subj: Activities – traveling. Babies. Ethnic groups in the U.S. – Mexican-Americans. Family life. Holidays – Christmas.

The sleepy watchdog (Bolognese, Elaine)

Turnabout (Raphael, Elaine)

Bolognese, Elaine. *The sleepy watchdog* by Elaine and Don Bolognese; ill. by Don Bolognese. Lothrop, 1964. Subj: Animals – dogs. Character traits – laziness.

Bolton, Evelyn *see* Bunting, Eve (Anne Evelyn)

Bond, Felicia. *Christmas in the chicken coop* ill. by author. Crowell, 1983. Subj: Birds – chickens. Holidays – Christmas. Trees.

Four Valentines in a rainstorm ill. by author. Crowell, 1983. Subj: Friendship. Holidays – Valentine's Day.

The Halloween performance ill. by author. Crowell, 1983. Subj: Animals – mice. Holidays – Halloween. School.

Mary Betty Lizzie McNutt's birthday ill. by author. Crowell, 1983. Subj: Animals – pigs. Birthdays.

Poinsettia and her family ill. by author. Harper, 1981. ISBN 0-690-04145-4 Subj: Animals – pigs. Behavior. Family life. Moving. Sibling rivalry.

Poinsettia and the firefighters ill. by author. Crowell, 1984. Subj: Animals – pigs. Bedtime. Night. Noise, sounds.

Wake up, Vladimir ill. by author. Crowell, 1987. ISBN 0-690-04453-4 Subj: Animals – groundhogs. Behavior – running away. Dreams. Shadows.

Bond, Jean Carey. *A is for Africa* ill. by author. Watts, 1969. Subj: ABC books. Foreign lands – Africa.

Bond, Michael. *Paddington and the knickerbocker rainbow* ill. by David McKee. Putnam's, 1985. ISBN 0-399-21202-7 Subj: Animals – bears. Food. Foreign lands – England. Language.

Paddington at the circus by Michael Bond and Fred Banbery; ill. by Fred Banbery. Random House, 1973. Subj: Animals – bears. Circus. Foreign lands – England.

Paddington at the fair ill. by David McKee. Putnam's, 1986. ISBN 0-399-21271-X Subj: Animals – bears. Fairs. Foreign lands – England.

Paddington at the palace ill. by David McKee. Putnam's, 1986. ISBN 0-399-21340-6 Subj: Animals – bears. Foreign lands – England. Royalty.

Paddington at the seaside ill. by Fred Banbery. Random House, 1975. Subj: Activities – vacationing. Animals – bears. Foreign lands – England. Sea and seashore.

Paddington at the tower ill. by Fred Banbery. Random House, 1975. Subj: Animals – bears. Foreign lands – England.

Paddington at the zoo ill. by David McKee. Putnam's, 1985. ISBN 0-399-21201-9 Subj: Animals – bears. Behavior – losing things. Foreign lands – England. Zoos.

Paddington bear ill. by John Lobban. HarperCollins, 1992. ISBN 0-694-00394-8 Subj: Animals – bears. Family life. Foreign lands – England.

Paddington cleans up ill. by David McKee. Putnam's, 1986. ISBN 0-399-21339-2 Subj: Activities – working. Animals – bears. Foreign lands – England.

Paddington's ABC ill. by John Lobban. Viking, 1991. ISBN 0-670-84104-8 Subj: Animals – bears. ABC books.

Paddington's art exhibit ill. by David McKee. Putnam's, 1986. ISBN 0-399-21270-1 Subj: Activities – painting. Animals – bears. Art. Foreign lands – England.

Paddington's colors ill. by John Lobban. Viking, 1991. ISBN 0-670-84102-1 Subj: Animals – bears. Concepts – color.

Paddington's garden ill. by Fred Banbery. Random House, 1973. ISBN 0-394-92643-9 Subj: Animals – bears. Family life. Foreign lands – England. Gardens, gardening.

Paddington's lucky day ill. by Fred Banbery. Random House, 1973. Subj: Animals – bears. Character traits – luck. Foreign lands – England. Shopping.

Paddington's 1 2 3 ill. by John Lobban. Viking, 1991. ISBN 0-670-84103-X Subj: Animals – bears. Counting, numbers.

Bond, Ruskin. *Cherry tree* ill. by Allan Eitzen. Boyds Mills Pr. 1991. ISBN 0-878093-21-5 Subj: Family life – grandfathers. Foreign lands – India. Trees.

Flames in the forest ill. by Valerie Littlewood. Watts, 1981. Subj: Fire. Foreign lands – India. Forest, woods.

Bonino, Louise. *The cozy little farm* ill. by Angelia. Random House, 1946. Subj: Animals. Farms.

Bonne, Rose. *I know an old lady* ill. by Abner Graboff. Rand McNally, 1961. Music by Alan Mills Subj: Cumulative tales. Folk and fairy tales. Foreign lands – Canada. Humor. Music. Songs.

I know an old lady who swallowed a fly ill. by William Stobbs. Oxford Univ. Pr., 1987. ISBN 0-19-279837-5 Subj: Cumulative tales. Folk and fairy tales. Foreign lands – Canada. Humor. Songs.

Bonners, Susan. *Just in passing* ill. by author. Lothrop, 1989. ISBN 0-688-07712-9 Subj: Circular tales. Wordless.

The wooden doll ill. by author. Lothrop, 1991. ISBN 0-688-08282-3 Subj: Family life – grandparents. Toys – dolls.

Bonnici, Peter. *The festival* ill. by Lisa Kopper. Carolrhoda Books, 1985. ISBN 0-87614-229-3 Subj: Behavior – growing up. Foreign lands – India. Holidays.

The first rains ill. by Lisa Kopper. Carolrhoda Books, 1985. ISBN 0-87614-228-5 Subj: Weather – rain.

Bonsall, Crosby Newell. *The amazing the incredible super dog* ill. by author. Harper, 1986. ISBN 0-06-020591-1 Subj: Animals – cats. Animals – dogs. Behavior – boasting.

And I mean it, Stanley ill. by author. Harper, 1974. Subj: Activities – playing. Animals – dogs.

The day I had to play with my sister ill. by author. Harper, 1972. Subj: Family life. Games.

I'll show you cats (Ylla)

It's mine! A greedy book ill. by author. Harper, 1964. Subj: Behavior – greed. Friendship.

Listen, listen! by Crosby Newell Bonsall and Ylla; photos. by Ylla. Harper, 1961. Subj: Animals – cats. Animals – dogs. Character traits – appearance.

Look who's talking (Ylla)

Mine's the best ill. by author. Harper, 1973. Subj: Behavior – boasting. Sea and seashore. Toys – balloons.

Polar bear brothers (Ylla)

Who's afraid of the dark? ill. by author. Harper, 1980. Subj: Animals – dogs. Emotions – fear. Night.

Bontemps, Arna Wendell. *The fast sooner hound* by Arna Wendell Bontemps and Jack Conroy; ill. by Virginia Lee Burton. Houghton, 1942. Subj: Animals – dogs. Trains.

Boon, Emilie. *Belinda's balloon* ill. by author. Knopf, 1985. ISBN 0-394-97342-9 Subj: Animals – bears. Family life. Toys – balloons.

It's spring, Peterkin ill. by author. Random, 1986. ISBN 0-394-87997-X Subj: Character traits – kindness to animals. Format, unusual – board books. Seasons – spring.

1 2 3 how many animals can you see? ill. by author. Random, 1987. ISBN 0-531-08301-2 Subj: Animals. Counting, numbers. School.

Peterkin meets a star ill. by author. Random House, 1984. Subj: Imagination. Stars.

Peterkin's very own garden ill. by author. Random, 1987. ISBN 0-394-88666-6 Subj: Animals. Format, unusual – board books. Gardens, gardening.

Peterkin's wet walk ill. by author. Random House, 1984. Subj: Animals. Imagination. Weather – rain.

Booth, Eugene. *At the circus* ill. by Derek Collard. Raintree, 1977. Subj: Circus. Concepts. Games. Participation. Problem solving.

At the fair ill. by Derek Collard. Raintree, 1977. Subj: Concepts. Fairs. Games. Participation. Problem solving.

In the air ill. by Derek Collard. Raintree, 1977. Subj: Concepts. Games. Participation. Problem solving.

In the garden ill. by Derek Collard. Raintree, 1977. Subj: Concepts. Games. Participation. Problem solving.

In the jungle ill. by Derek Collard. Raintree, 1977. Subj: Concepts. Games. Jungle. Participation. Problem solving.

Under the ocean ill. by Derek Collard. Raintree, 1977. Subj: Concepts. Games. Participation. Problem solving. Sea and seashore.

Borack, Barbara. *Grandpa* ill. by Ben Shecter. Harper, 1967. Subj: Family life – grandfathers.

Borchers, Elisabeth. *Dear Sarah* tr. and adapt. from German by Elizabeth Shub; ill. by Wilhelm Schlote. Greenwillow, 1980. Subj: Activities – traveling. Communication. Foreign lands.

There comes a time tr. by Babette Deutsch; ill. by Dietlind Blech. Doubleday, 1969. Subj: Days of the week, months of the year. Poetry, rhyme.

Borden, Beatrice Brown. *Wild animals of Africa* photos. by author. Random House, 1982. Subj: Animals. Birds. Foreign lands – Africa.

Borden, Louise. *Caps, hats, socks and mittens* ill. by Lillian Hoban. Scholastic, 1989. ISBN 0-590-41257-4 Subj: Clothing. Seasons.

The watching game ill. by Teri Weidner. Scholastic, 1991. ISBN 0-590-43600-7 Subj: Country. Family life – grandmothers. Seasons.

Boreman, Jean. *Bantie and her chicks* ill. by June Hendrickson. Melmont, 1959. Subj: Birds – chickens. School. Science.

Borg, Inga. *Plupp builds a house* ill. by author. Warne, 1961. Subj: Animals. Elves and little people. Foreign lands – Lapland. Houses.

Bornstein, Ruth Lercher. *Annabelle* ill. by author. Crowell, 1978. Subj: Behavior – lost. Toys.

A beautiful seashell ill. by author. HarperCollins, 1990. ISBN 0-06-020595-4 Subj: Family life – great-grandparents. Sea and seashore.

The dancing man ill. by author. Seabury Pr., 1978. Subj: Activities – dancing. Foreign lands – Europe.

I'll draw a meadow ill. by author. Harper, 1979. Subj: Activities – vacationing. Animals – dogs.

Indian bunny ill. by author. Childrens Pr., 1973. Subj: Animals – rabbits. Indians of North America.

Jim ill. by author. Seabury Pr., 1978. Subj: Animals – dogs. Behavior – lost. Character traits – bravery.

Of course a goat ill. by author. Harper, 1980. Subj: Animals – goats. Family life.

The seedling child ill. by author. Harcourt, 1987. ISBN 0-15-272459-1 Subj: Friendship. Imagination – imaginary friends. Poetry, rhyme.

Borten, Helen. *Do you go where I go?* ill. by author. Abelard-Schuman, 1972. Subj: Humor. Poetry, rhyme.

Do you hear what I hear? ill. by author. Abelard-Schuman, 1960. Subj: Noise, sounds. Poetry, rhyme. Senses – hearing.

Do you know what I know? ill. by author. Abelard-Schuman, 1970. Subj: Poetry, rhyme. Senses – hearing. Senses – seeing. Senses – smelling. Senses – tasting. Senses – touching.

Do you move as I do? ill. by author. Abelard-Schuman, 1963. Subj: Emotions. Health.

Do you see what I see? ill. by author. Abelard-Schuman, 1959. Subj: Art. Concepts. Senses – seeing.

Halloween ill. by author. Crowell, 1965. Subj: Holidays – Halloween.

A picture has a special look ill. by author. Abelard-Schuman, 1961. Subj: Art.

Bos, Burny. *Ollie the elephant* ill. by Hans de Beer. North-South, 1989. ISBN 1-55858-012-3 Subj: Animals – elephants. Behavior – wishing. Family life.

Prince Valentino ill. by Hans de Beer. North-South, 1990. ISBN 1-55858-089-1 Subj: Birds – storks. Friendship. Frogs and toads.

Bossom, Naomi. *A scale full of fish and other turnabouts* ill. by author. Greenwillow, 1979. Subj: Humor. Language.

Boston. Children's Hospital Medical Center. *Curious George goes to the hospital* (Rey, Margret (Margret Elisabeth Waldstein))

Boswell, Stephen. *King Gorboduc's fabulous zoo* ill. by Beverley Gooding. Dutton, 1986. Subj: Dragons. Royalty – kings. Zoos.

Bothwell, Jean. *Paddy and Sam* ill. by Margaret Ayer. Abelard-Schuman, 1952. Subj: Behavior – lost. Birds – ducks.

Bottner, Barbara. *Big boss! Little boss!* ill. by author. Pantheon, 1978. ISBN 0-394-93939-5 Subj: Behavior – losing things. Sibling rivalry.

Horrible Hannah ill. by Joan Drescher. Crown, 1980. Subj: Animals – dogs. Friendship. Moving.

Jungle day: or, How I learned to love my nosey little brother ill. by author. Delacorte Pr., 1978. Subj: Sibling rivalry.

Mean Maxine ill. by author. Pantheon, 1980. Subj: Character traits – meanness. Friendship. Imagination.

Messy ill. by author. Delacorte Pr., 1979. Subj: Activities – dancing. Behavior – carelessness.

Myra ill. by author. Macmillan, 1979. Subj: Activities – dancing. Imagination.

There was nobody there ill. by author. Macmillan, 1978. Subj: Bedtime. Imagination. Poetry, rhyme. Sleep.

Zoo song ill. by Lynn Munsinger. Scholastic, 1987. ISBN 0-590-41005-9 Subj: Animals. Music. Zoos.

Botwin, Esther. *A treasury of songs for little children* ill. by Evelyn Urbanowich. Hart, 1954. Subj: Music. Songs.

Bouhuys, Mies. *The lady of Stavoren: a story from Holland* ill. by Francien Van Westering. Penguin, 1979. Subj: Folk and fairy tales. Foreign lands – Holland.

Boujon, Claude. *The fairy with the long nose* ill. by author. Macmillan, 1987. ISBN 0-689-50424-1 Subj: Anatomy – noses. Fairies. Magic.

Bour, Danièle. *The house from morning to night* ill. by author. Kane, 1985. Subj: Houses.

Bourgeois, Paulette. *Big Sarah's little boots* ill. by Brenda Clark. Kids Can Pr., 1987. ISBN 0-921103-11-5 Subj: Behavior – growing up. Clothing – shoes. Family life. Weather – rain.

Franklin in the dark ill. by Brenda Clark. Kids Can Pr., 1986. ISBN 0-919964-93-1 Subj: Emotions – fear. Night. Reptiles – turtles, tortoises.

Too many chickens ill. by Bill Slavin. Little, 1991. ISBN 0-316-10358-6 Subj: Animals. Birds – chickens. School.

Bourke, Linda. *Ethel's exceptional egg* ill. by author. Harvey House, 1977. Subj: Birds – chickens. Eggs. Fairs.

Boutell, Clarence Burley. *The fat baron* ill. by Frank Lieberman. Houghton, 1946. Subj: Food. Imagination. Knights.

Bouton, Josephine. *Favorite poems for the children's hour* ill. by Bonnie and Bill Rutherford; foreword by Carolyn Sherwin Bailey. Platt, 1967. Subj: Poetry, rhyme.

Boutwell, Edna. *Red rooster* ill. by Bernard Garbutt. Atheneum, 1950. Subj: Birds – chickens. Cumulative tales. Folk and fairy tales.

Bove, Linda. *Sign language ABC with Linda Bove* ill. by Tom Cooke. Random, 1985. ISBN 0-394-97516-2 Subj: ABC books. Handicaps – deafness. Language. Senses – hearing.

Bowden, Joan Chase. *The bear's surprise party* ill. by Jerry Scott. Golden Pr., 1975. Subj: Animals – bears. Parties.

Boo and the flying flews ill. by Don Leake. Western, 1974. Subj: Animals – dogs. Circus.

Bouncy baby bunny finds his bed ill. by Christine Westerberg. Western, 1977. Subj: Animals – rabbits. Bedtime.

Emilio's summer day ill. by Ben Shecter. Harper, 1966. Subj: City. Ethnic groups in the U.S. – Puerto Rican-Americans. Seasons – summer.

The Ginghams and the backward picnic ill. by Joane Koenig. Western, 1979. Subj: Activities – picnicking.

A hat for the queen ill. by Olindo Giacomini. Golden Pr., 1974. Subj: Clothing – hats. Royalty – queens.

Little grey rabbit ill. by Lorinda Bryan Cauley. Western, 1979. Subj: Animals – rabbits.

A new home for Snow Ball ill. by Jan Pyk. Western, 1979. Subj: Animals – horses. Royalty.

Strong John ill. by Sal Murdocca. Macmillan, 1980. Subj: Behavior – trickery. Folk and fairy tales.

Who took the top hat trick? ill. by Jim Cummins. Golden Pr., 1974. Subj: Behavior – losing things. Magic.

Bowen, Betsy. *Antler, bear, canoe* ill. by author. Little, 1991. ISBN 0-316-10376-4 Subj: ABC books. Forest, woods. Nature. Seasons.

Bowen, Vernon. *The lazy beaver* ill. by Jim Davis. McKay, 1948. Subj: Animals – beavers. Character traits – laziness.

Bowers, Kathleen Rice. *At this very minute* ill. by Linda Shute. Little, 1983. Subj: Bedtime. Imagination.

Bowles, Brad. *Grandma's band* ill. by Anthony Chan. Stemmer House, 1989. ISBN 0-88045-112-2 Subj: Family life – grandmothers. Music.

Bowling, David Louis. *Dirty Dingy Daryl* ill. by Patricia Hendy Bowling. Inka Dinka Ink, 1981. Subj: Character traits – cleanliness.

Bowman, Peter. *The Christmas songbook* ill. by author. Putnam, 1990. ISBN 0-399-21918-8 Subj: Format, unusual – toy and movable books. Holidays – Christmas. Music. Songs.

Boxer, Deborah. *26 ways to be somebody else* ill. by author. Pantheon, 1960. Subj: ABC books. Careers.

A boy went out to gather pears : *an old verse* ill. by Felix Hoffmann. Harcourt, 1966. Subj: Cumulative tales. Poetry, rhyme.

Boyd, Lizi. *Bailey the big bully* ill. by author. Viking, 1989. ISBN 0-670-82719-3 Subj: Behavior – bullying.

Half wild and half child ill. by author. Viking, 1988. ISBN 0-670-82072-5 Subj: Behavior – misbehavior. Character traits – willfulness.

The not-so-wicked stepmother ill. by author. Viking, 1987. ISBN 0-670-81589-6 Subj: Activities. Behavior – misunderstanding. Birds – ducks. Family life – step families.

Sam is my half brother ill. by author. Viking, 1990. ISBN 0-670-83046-1 Subj: Babies. Family life. Family life – step families. Sibling rivalry.

Sweet dreams, Willy ill. by author. Viking, 1992. ISBN 0-670-84382-2 Subj: Bedtime. Dreams. Imagination. Night.

Willy and the cardboard boxes ill. by author. Viking, 1991. ISBN 0-670-83636-2 Subj: Activities – playing. Imagination.

Boyd, Pauline. *The how: making the best of a mistake* (Boyd, Selma)

I met a polar bear (Boyd, Selma)

Boyd, Selma. *The how: making the best of a mistake* by Selma and Pauline Boyd; ill. by Peggy Luks. Human Sciences Pr., 1981. Subj: Behavior – mistakes. Emotions – embarrassment. Friendship.

I met a polar bear by Selma and Pauline Boyd; ill. by 0Patience Brewster. Lothrop, 1983. Subj: Animals. Behavior – tardiness. Imagination. School.

Boyle, Constance. *Little Owl and the weed* ill. by author. Barron's, 1985. ISBN 0-8120-5639-6 Subj: Birds. Gardens, gardening.

The story of little owl ill. by author. Barron's, 1985. Subj: Behavior – losing things. Birds – owls. Toys – teddy bears.

Boyle, Vere. *Beauty and the beast* ill. by author. Barron's, 1988. ISBN 0-8120-5902-6 Subj: Character traits – loyalty. Emotions – love. Folk and fairy tales. Magic.

Boynton, Sandra. *A is for angry* ill. by author. Workman, 1983. Subj: ABC books. Animals.

But not the hippopotamus ill. by author. Simon and Schuster, 1982. Subj: Animals – hippopotami. Format, unusual – board books. Poetry, rhyme.

Chloë and Maude ill. by author. Little, 1985. ISBN 0-316-10492-2 Subj: Animals – cats. Friendship.

Doggies ill. by author. Simon & Schuster, 1984. ISBN 0-671-49318-3 Subj: Animals – dogs. Format, unusual – board books.

The going to bed book ill. by author. Simon and Schuster, 1982. Subj: Animals. Bedtime. Format, unusual – board books. Poetry, rhyme.

Good night, good night ill. by author. Random, 1985. ISBN 0-394-97285-6 Subj: Animals. Bedtime. Music. Poetry, rhyme. Songs.

Hester in the wild ill. by author. Harper, 1979. Subj: Animals – hippopotami. Animals – pigs. Camps, camping.

Hippos go berserk ill. by author. Little, 1979. Subj: Animals – hippopotami. Counting, numbers. Poetry, rhyme.

Horns to toes and in between ill. by author. Simon & Schuster, 1984. ISBN 0-671-49319-1 Subj: Anatomy. Format, unusual – board books.

If at first... ill. by author. Little, 1980. Subj: Animals – elephants. Animals – mice. Character traits – perseverance. Humor.

Moo, baa, lalala ill. by author. Simon and Schuster, 1982. Subj: Animals. Format, unusual – board books. Noise, sounds. Poetry, rhyme.

Opposites ill. by author. Simon and Schuster, 1982. Subj: Concepts – opposites. Format, unusual – board books.

Bozzo, Maxine Zohn. *Toby in the country, Toby in the city* ill. by Frank Modell. Greenwillow, 1982. Subj: City. Country.

Bradbury, Ray. *Switch on the night* ill. by Madeleine Gekiere. Pantheon, 1955. Subj: Night.

Bradfield, Roger (Jolly Roger). *The flying hockey stick* ill. by author. Rand McNally, 1966. Subj: Activities – flying. Humor. Machines.

Giants come in different sizes ill. by author. Rand McNally, 1966. Subj: Giants. Wizards.

A good night for dragons ill. by author. Addison-Wesley, 1967. Subj: Dragons. Knights.

Bradford, Ann. *The mystery at Misty Falls* by Ann Bradford and Kal Gezi; ill. by Mina Gow McLean. Children's Pr., 1980. Subj: Animals – raccoons. Clubs, gangs. Problem solving.

The mystery in the secret club house by Ann Bradford and Kal Gezi; ill. by Mina Gow McLean. Children's Pr., 1978. Subj: Clubs, gangs. Crime.

The mystery of the blind writer by Ann Bradford and Kal Gezi; ill. by Mina Gow McLean. Children's Pr., 1980. Subj: Animals – dogs. Clubs, gangs. Crime. Handicaps – blindness. Problem solving.

The mystery of the live ghosts by Ann Bradford and Kal Gezi; ill. by Mina Gow McLean. Children's Pr., 1978. Subj: Holidays – Halloween.

The mystery of the midget clown by Ann Bradford and Kal Gezi; ill. by Mina Gow McLean. Children's Pr., 1980. Subj: Clowns, jesters. Clubs, gangs. Problem solving.

The mystery of the missing dogs by Ann Bradford and Kal Gezi; ill. by Mina Gow McLean. Children's

Pr., 1980. Subj: Animals – dogs. Clubs, gangs. Handicaps. Problem solving.

The mystery of the missing raccoon by Ann Bradford and Kal Gezi; ill. by Mina Gow McLean. Children's Pr., 1978. Subj: Animals – raccoons. Character traits – freedom.

The mystery of the square footsteps by Ann Bradford and Kal Gezi; ill. by Mina Gow McLean. Children's Pr., 1980. Subj: Clubs, gangs. Problem solving. Robots.

The mystery of the tree house by Ann Bradford and Kal Gezi; ill. by Mina Gow McLean. Children's Pr., 1980. Subj: Birds – parakeets, parrots. Clubs, gangs. Crime. Problem solving.

Bradman, Tony. *The bad babies' book of colors* ill. by Deborah Van der Beek. Knopf, 1987. ISBN 0-394-99046-3 Subj: Behavior – misbehavior. Birthdays. Concepts – color.

The bad babies' counting book ill. by Deborah Van der Beek. Knopf, 1986. ISBN 0-394-98352-1 Subj: Behavior – misbehavior. Counting, numbers. Poetry, rhyme.

Dilly speaks up ill. by Susan Hellard. Viking, 1991. ISBN 0-670-83680-X Subj: Dinosaurs. Sibling rivalry. Shopping.

It came from outer space ill. by Carol Wright. Dial, 1992. ISBN 0-8037-1098-4 Subj: School. Space and space ships.

Look out, he's behind you ill. by Margaret Chamberlain. Putnam's, 1988. ISBN 0-399-21485-2 Subj: Animals – wolves. Behavior – talking to strangers. Forest, woods. Format, unusual – toy and movable books.

Michael ill. by Tony Ross. Macmillan, 1991. ISBN 0-02-711850-9 Subj: Behavior – misbehavior. Character traits – individuality. School. Space and space ships.

Not like this, like that ill. by Joanna Burroughes. Oxford Univ. Pr., 1988. ISBN 0-19-520712-2 Subj: Character traits – foolishness. Counting, numbers. Family life – fathers.

See you later, alligator ill. by Colin Hawkins. Dial Pr., 1986. ISBN 0-8037-0267-1 Subj: Animals. Format, unusual – toy and movable books. Reptiles – alligators, crocodiles.

This little baby ill. by Jenny Williams. Putnam, 1990. ISBN 0-399-22202-2 Subj: Babies. Poetry, rhyme.

Through my window ill. by Eileen Browne. Silver Burdett, 1986. ISBN 0-382-09258-9 Subj: Family life. Illness.

Wait and see ill. by Eileen Browne. Oxford Univ. Pr., 1988. ISBN 0-19-520644-4 Subj: Family life. Shopping.

Brady, Irene. *Wild mouse* ill. by author. Scribner's, 1976. Subj: Animals – mice. Science.

Brady, Susan. *Find my blanket* ill. by author. Harper, 1988. ISBN 0-397-32248-8 Subj: Animals – mice. Behavior – hiding things. Family life.

Bragdon, Lillian J. *Tell me the time, please* ill. by Frank and Margaret Phares. Lippincott, 1937. Subj: Clocks, watches. Time.

Bram, Elizabeth. *I don't want to go to school* ill. by author. Greenwillow, 1977. Subj: School.

One day I closed my eyes and the world disappeared ill. by author. Dial Pr., 1978. Subj: Senses – seeing.

Saturday morning lasts forever ill. by author. Dial Pr., 1978. Subj: Activities – playing.

There is someone standing on my head ill. by author. Dial Pr., 1979. Subj: Imagination – imaginary friends.

Woodruff and the clocks ill. by author. Dial Pr., 1980. Subj: Behavior – collecting things. Clocks, watches.

Brand, Millen. *This little pig named Curly* ill. by John Hamberger. Crown, 1968. Subj: Animals – pigs. Farms.

Brand, Oscar. *When I first came to this land* ill. by Doris Burn. Putnam's, 1974. Subj: Cumulative tales. Folk and fairy tales. Poverty. Songs.

Brande, Marlie. *Sleepy Nicholas* adapted by Noel Streatfield; ill. by author. Follett, 1970. Subj: Foreign lands – Denmark. Sleep.

Brandenberg, Aliki *see* Aliki

Brandenberg, Franz. *Aunt Nina and her nephews and nieces* ill. by Aliki. Greenwillow, 1983. Subj: Animals. Animals – cats. Babies. Birthdays. Family life – aunts, uncles. Toys.

Aunt Nina, good night ill. by Aliki. Greenwillow, 1989. ISBN 0-688-07464-2 Subj: Bedtime. Family life – aunts, uncles.

Aunt Nina's visit ill. by Aliki. Greenwillow, 1984. Subj: Animals – cats. Family life – aunts, uncles. Puppets.

Cock-a-doodle-doo ill. by Aliki. Greenwillow, 1986. ISBN 0-688-06104-4 Subj: Animals. Farms. Noise, sounds.

Everyone ready? ill. by Aliki. Greenwillow, 1979. Subj: Activities – traveling. Animals – mice. Family life. Trains.

Fresh cider and apple pie ill. by Aliki. Macmillan, 1973. Subj: Food. Insects – flies. Spiders.

A fun weekend ill. by Alexa Brandenberg. Greenwillow, 1991. ISBN 0-688-09721-9 Subj: Activities – vacationing. Animals – bears. Family life.

The hit of the party ill. by Aliki. Greenwillow, 1985. ISBN 0-688-04241-4 Subj: Animals – hamsters. Parties.

No school today! ill. by Aliki. Subj: Animals – cats. Behavior – mistakes. School.

Otto is different ill. by James Stevenson. Greenwillow, 1985. ISBN 0-688-04254-6 Subj: Activities. Character traits – being different. Octopuses.

A robber! A robber! ill. by Aliki. Greenwillow, 1975. Subj: Animals – cats. Crime. Night. Noise, sounds.

A secret for grandmother's birthday ill. by Aliki. Greenwillow, 1975. Subj: Behavior – secrets. Birthdays. Family life – grandmothers.

Six new students ill. by Aliki. Greenwillow, 1978. Subj: Animals – mice. School.

What's wrong with a van? ill. by Aliki. Greenwillow, 1987. ISBN 0-688-06775-1 Subj: Animals – cats. Automobiles. Behavior – seeking better things. Family life.

Brandt, Betty. *Special delivery* ill. by Kathy Haubrich. Carolrhoda Books, 1988. ISBN 0-87614-312-5 Subj: Careers – mail carriers. Letters. U.S. history.

Branley, Franklyn M. *Air is all around you* ill. by Holly Keller Rev. ed. Crowell, 1986. ISBN 0-690-04503-4 Subj: Science.

Comets ill. by Giulio Maestro. Crowell, 1984. Subj: Science. Sky.

Earthquakes ill. by Richard Rosenblum. HarperCollins, 1990. ISBN 0-690-04663-4 Subj: Earth. Science.

Eclipse: darkness in daytime ill. by Donald Crews Rev. ed. Harper, 1988. ISBN 0-690-04619-7 Subj: Science. Sun.

Flash, crash, rumble, and roll ill. by Barbara and Ed Emberley Rev. ed. Crowell, 1985. ISBN 0-690-04425-9 Subj: Science. Weather – thunder.

Floating and sinking ill. by Robert Galster. Crowell, 1967. Subj: Science.

Gravity is a mystery ill. by Don Madden Rev. ed. Crowell, 1986. ISBN 0-690-04527-1 Subj: Science.

High sounds, low sounds ill. by Paul Showers. Crowell, 1967. Subj: Noise, sounds. Science.

How little and how much: a book about scales ill. by Byron Barton. Crowell, 1976. Subj: Concepts – measurement.

Hurricane watch ill. by Giulio Maestro. Crowell, 1985. ISBN 0-690-04471-2 Subj: Science. Weather – storms.

Is there life in outer space? ill. by Don Madden. Crowell, 1984. ISBN 0-690-04375-9 Subj: Science. Space and space ships.

Journey into a black hole ill. by Marc Simont. Crowell, 1986. ISBN 0-690-04544-1 Subj: Science. Space and space ships. Stars.

Light and darkness ill. by Reynold Ruffins. Crowell, 1975. Subj: Science.

The moon seems to change ill. by Barbara and Ed Emberley. Crowell, 1987. ISBN 0-690-04585-9 Subj: Moon. Science.

North, south, east and west ill. by Robert Galster. Crowell, 1966. Subj: Science.

The planets in our solar system ill. by Don Madden. Crowell, 1981. Subj: Science. Space and space ships. Sun. World.

Rain and hail ill. by Harriett Barton Rev. ed. Crowell, 1983. Subj: Science. Weather. Weather – rain.

The sky is full of stars ill. by Felicia Bond. Crowell, 1981. Subj: Science. Sky. Stars.

Snow is falling ill. by Holly Keller Rev. ed. Crowell, 1986. ISBN 0-690-04548-4 Subj: Science. Weather – snow.

The sun, our nearest star ill. by Helen Borten. Crowell, 1961. Subj: Science. Sun.

Sunshine makes the seasons ill. by Giulio Maestro Rev. ed. Crowell, 1985. ISBN 0-690-04482-8 Subj: Science. Seasons. Sun.

Tornado alert ill. by Giulio Maestro. Crowell, 1988. ISBN 0-690-04688-X Subj: Science. Weather – storms.

Volcanoes ill. by Marc Simont. Crowell, 1985. ISBN 0-690-04431-3 Subj: Science. Volcanoes.

What makes day and night ill. by Arthur Dorros Rev. ed. Crowell, 1986. ISBN 0-690-04524-7 Subj: Earth. Science.

What the moon is like ill. by True Kelley Rev. ed. Crowell, 1986. ISBN 0-690-04512-3 Subj: Moon. Science.

Brann, Esther. *A book for baby* ill. by author. Macmillan, 1945. Subj: Activities. Babies. Family life.

'Round the world ill. by author. Macmillan, 1935. Subj: Activities – traveling. Foreign lands. World.

Brasch, Kate. *Prehistoric monsters* photos. by Jean-Philippe Varin. Merrimack, 1985. ISBN 0-88162-098-X Subj: Animals. Dinosaurs. Science.

Bratton, John. *The teddy bears' picnic* ill. by Renate Kozikowski. Macmillan, 1990. ISBN 0-690-04703-7 Subj: Activities – picnicking. Format, unusual. Music. Songs.

Braun, Kathy. *Kangaroo and kangaroo* ill. by Jim McMullan. Doubleday, 1965. Subj: Animals – kangaroos. Behavior – collecting things. Poetry, rhyme.

Breathed, Berkeley. *A wish for wings that work* ill. by author. Little, 1991. ISBN 0-316-10758-1 Subj: Activities – flying. Behavior – wishing. Birds – penguins. Holidays – Christmas.

Brecht, Bertolt. *Uncle Eddie's moustache* ill. by Ursula Kirchberg. Pantheon, 1974. Translation of Onkel Ede hat einen Schnurrbart by Muriel Rukeyser Subj: Family life – aunts, uncles. Humor. Poetry, rhyme.

Breckler, Rosemary K. *Hoang breaks the lucky teapot* ill. by Adrian Frankel. Houghton, 1992. ISBN 0-395-57031-X Subj: Character traits – luck. Ethnic groups in the U.S. – Vietnamese-Americans. Family life. Foreign languages.

Breda, Tjalmar *see* DeJong, David Cornel

Breese, Gillian. *The amazing adventures of Teddy Tum Tum* by Gillian Breese and Tony Langham; ill. by Patrick Lowry. Arcade, 1992. ISBN 1-55970-185-4 Subj: Toys. Toys – teddy bears.

Breinburg, Petronella. *Doctor Shawn* ill. by Errol Lloyd. Crowell, 1975. Subj: Activities – playing. Careers – doctors. Ethnic groups in the U.S. – Afro-Americans.

Shawn goes to school ill. by Errol Lloyd. Crowell, 1973. Subj: Ethnic groups in the U.S. – Afro-Americans. Friendship. School.

Shawn's red bike ill. by Errol Lloyd. Crowell, 1976. Subj: Ethnic groups in the U.S. – Afro-Americans. Sports – bicycling.

Brennan, Jan. *Born two-gether* photos. by Leo Brennan. J & L Books, 1984. ISBN 0-9613536-1-9 Subj: Family life. Twins.

Brennan, John. *Zoo day* by John Brennan and Leonie Keaney; ill. with photos. Carolrhoda, 1989. ISBN 0-87614-358-3 Subj: Animals. Zoos.

Brennan, Joseph Killorin. *Gobo and the river* ill. by Diane Dawson Hearn. Holt, 1985. ISBN 0-03-004552-5 Subj: Character traits – perseverance. Puppets. Rivers.

Brennan, Patricia D. *Hitchety hatchety up I go!* ill. by Robert Rayevsky. Macmillan, 1985. ISBN 0-02-712300-6 Subj: Behavior – stealing. Elves and little people. Folk and fairy tales.

Brenner, Anita. *I want to fly* ill. by Lucienne Bloch. Addison-Wesley, 1943. Subj: Airplanes, airports. Imagination.

Brenner, Barbara A. *The color wizard* ill. by Leo and Diane Dillon. Bantam, 1989. ISBN 0-553-05825-8 Subj: Concepts – color. Poetry, rhyme. Wizards.

A dog I know ill. by Fred Brenner. Harper, 1983. Subj: Animals – dogs. Humor.

Faces, faces, faces photos. by George Ancona. Dutton, 1970. Subj: Anatomy – faces. Emotions. Ethnic groups in the U.S. Senses – hearing. Senses – seeing. Senses – smelling. Senses – tasting. Senses – touching.

The five pennies ill. by Erik Blegvad. Knopf, 1964. Subj: Money. Pets.

The flying patchwork quilt ill. by Fred Brenner. Addison-Wesley, 1965. Subj: Activities – flying. Magic. Quilts.

Good news ill. by Kate Duke. Bantam, 1991. ISBN 0-553-07091-6 Subj: Behavior – gossip. Birds – geese. Cumulative tales.

Lion and lamb (Hooks, William H.)

Mr. Tall and Mr. Small ill. by Tomi Ungerer. Addison-Wesley, 1966. Subj: Animals – giraffes. Animals – mice. Character traits – conceit. Fire.

Ostrich feathers ill. by Vera B. Williams and Evelyn Armstrong. Parents, 1979. Subj: Animals. Behavior – greed.

The prince and the pink blanket ill. by Nola Langner. Four Winds Pr., 1980. Subj: Family life. Royalty – princes.

The snow parade ill. by Mary Tara O'Keefe. Crown, 1984. ISBN 0-571-55210-8 Subj: Counting, numbers. Parades. Weather.

Somebody's slippers, somebody's shoes ill. by Leslie Jacobs. Addison-Wesley, 1957. Subj: Clothing – shoes. Shopping.

The tremendous tree book (Garelick, May)

Two orphan cubs by Barbara Brenner and May Garelick; ill. by Erika Kors. Walker, 1989. ISBN 0-8027-6869-5 Subj: Animals – bears. Character traits – kindness to animals. Nature.

Brent, Isabelle. *Cameo cats* ill. by selector. Little, 1992. ISBN 0-316-10836-7 Subj: Animals – cats. Art. Poetry, rhyme.

Noah's ark ill. by author. Little, 1992. ISBN 0-316-10837-5 Subj: Boats, ships. Religion – Noah.

Brentano, Clemens. *Schoolmaster Whackwell's wonderful sons* ill. by Maurice Sendak. Random House, 1962. Subj: Behavior – growing up. Careers. Folk and fairy tales.

Brett, Jan. *Annie and the wild animals* ill. by author. Houghton, 1985. Subj: Animals. Animals – cats. Emotions – loneliness. Pets.

The first dog ill. by author. Harcourt, 1988. ISBN 0-15-227650-5 Subj: Animals – dogs. Animals – wolves. Art. Caves. Pets.

Fritz and the beautiful horses ill. by author. Houghton, 1981. Subj: Animals – horses. Behavior – wishing. Character traits – cleverness. Folk and fairy tales.

Goldilocks and the three bears (The three bears)

The mitten ill. by author. Putnam, 1990. ISBN 0-399-21920-X Subj: Behavior – losing things. Folk and fairy tales. Foreign lands – Ukraine.

The wild Christmas reindeer ill. by author. Putnam, 1990. ISBN 0-399-22192-1 Subj: Animals – reindeer. Holidays – Christmas.

Brewster, Benjamin *see* Elting, Mary

Brewster, Patience. *Ellsworth and the cats from Mars* ill. by author. Houghton, 1981. Subj: Animals – cats. Behavior – lost. Space and space ships.

Nobody ill. by author. Houghton, 1982. Subj: Behavior – dissatisfaction. Imagination – imaginary friends.

Rabbit Inn ill. by author. Little, 1991. ISBN 0-316-10747-6 Subj: Animals – rabbits. Hotels.

Brice, Tony. *Baby animals* ill. by author. Rand McNally, 1945. Subj: Animals. Babies.

The bashful goldfish ill. by author. Rand McNally, 1942. Subj: Character traits – shyness. Fish. Pets.

Bridges, William. *Lion Island* photos. by Emmy Haas and Sam Dunton. Morrow, 1965. Subj: Animals – lions. Zoos.

Ookie, the walrus who likes people photos. by Emmy Haas and Sam Dunton. Morrow, 1962. Subj: Animals – walruses.

Bridgman, Elizabeth. *All the little bunnies: a counting book* ill. by author. Atheneum, 1977. Subj: Counting, numbers. Poetry, rhyme.

How to travel with grownups ill. by Eleanor Hazard. Crowell, 1980. Subj: Activities – traveling. Foreign lands.

Nanny bear's cruise ill. by author. Harper, 1981. Subj: Activities – traveling. Animals – bears. Boats, ships.

A new dog next door ill. by author. Harper, 1978. Subj: Animals – dogs.

Bridle, Martin. *Punch and Judy in the rain* (Eaton, Su)

Bridwell, Norman. *Clifford goes to Hollywood* ill. by author. Scholastic, 1981. Subj: Animals – dogs. Character traits – loyalty.

Clifford's ABC ill. by author. Scholastic, 1984. ISBN 0-590-33154-X Subj: ABC books. Animals – dogs.

Clifford's good deeds ill. by author. Four Winds Pr., 1975. Subj: Animals – dogs. Automobiles. Behavior – mistakes. Careers – firefighters. Character traits – helpfulness.

Clifford's Halloween ill. by author. Four Winds Pr., 1967. Subj: Animals – dogs. Holidays – Halloween.

The witch grows up ill. by author. Scholastic, 1980. Subj: Humor. Magic. Witches.

The witch next door ill. by author. Four Winds Pr., 1966. Subj: Witches.

Brierley, Louise. *King Lion and his cooks* ill. by author. Holt, 1982. Subj: Animals. Food. Royalty.

Briggs, Raymond. *Building the snowman* ill. by author. Little, 1985. ISBN 0-316-10813-8 Subj: Snowmen. Wordless.

Dressing up ill. by author. Little, 1985. ISBN 0-316-10814-6 Subj: Clothing. Snowmen. Wordless.

Father Christmas ill. by author. Coward, 1973. Subj: Holidays – Christmas. Wordless.

Father Christmas goes on holiday ill. by author. Coward, 1975. Subj: Activities – vacationing. Holidays – Christmas. Wordless.

Fee fi fo fum ill. by author. Coward, 1964. Subj: Nursery rhymes.

Jim and the beanstalk ill. by author. Coward, 1970. Subj: Folk and fairy tales. Giants. Humor. Old age.

The party ill. by author. Little, 1985. ISBN 0-316-10816-2 Subj: Parties. Snowmen. Wordless.

Ring-a-ring o' roses ill. by author. Coward, 1962. Subj: Nursery rhymes.

The snowman ill. by author. Random House, 1978. Subj: Friendship. Snowmen. Wordless.

Walking in the air ill. by author. Little, 1985. ISBN 0-316-10815-4 Subj: Imagination. Snowmen. Wordless.

The white land: a picture book of traditional rhymes and verses ill. by compiler. Coward, 1963. Subj: Nursery rhymes. Songs.

Bright, Robert. *Georgie* ill. by author. Doubleday, 1944. Subj: Family life. Farms. Ghosts.

Georgie and the baby birds ill. by author. Doubleday, 1983. Subj: Birds. Character traits – helpfulness. Ghosts. Humor.

Georgie and the ball of yarn ill. by author. Doubleday, 1983. Subj: Character traits – helpfulness. Ghosts. Humor.

Georgie and the buried treasure ill. by author. Doubleday, 1979. Subj: Ghosts. Humor.

Georgie and the little dog ill. by author. Doubleday, 1983. Subj: Animals – dogs. Character traits – helpfulness. Ghosts. Humor.

Georgie and the magician ill. by author. Doubleday, 1966. Subj: Ghosts. Humor. Magic.

Georgie and the noisy ghost ill. by author. Doubleday, 1971. Subj: Activities – vacationing. Ghosts. Noise, sounds. Sea and seashore.

Georgie and the robbers ill. by author. Doubleday, 1963. Subj: Crime. Ghosts.

Georgie and the runaway balloon ill. by author. Doubleday, 1983. Subj: Animals – mice. Character traits – helpfulness. Ghosts. Humor. Toys – balloons.

Georgie goes west ill. by author. Doubleday, 1973. Subj: Cowboys. Ghosts.

Georgie to the rescue ill. by author. Doubleday, 1956. Subj: City. Ghosts.

Georgie's Christmas carol ill. by author. Doubleday, 1975. Subj: Ghosts. Holidays – Christmas.

Georgie's Halloween ill. by author. Doubleday, 1958. Subj: Ghosts. Holidays – Halloween.

Gregory, the noisiest and strongest boy in Grangers Grove ill. by author. Doubleday, 1969. Subj: Character traits – laziness. Food. Noise, sounds.

I like red ill. by author. Doubleday, 1955. Subj: Concepts – color. Hair.

Me and the bears ill. by author. Doubleday, 1951. Subj: Animals – bears. Behavior – wishing. Friendship. Sleep. Zoos.

Miss Pattie ill. by author. Doubleday, 1954. Subj: Animals – cats.

My hopping bunny ill. by author. Doubleday, 1971. Subj: Activities – jumping. Animals – rabbits. Poetry, rhyme.

My red umbrella ill. by author. Morrow, 1959. Subj: Counting, numbers. Umbrellas. Weather – rain.

The travels of Ching ill. by author. Addison-Wesley, 1943. Subj: Foreign lands – China. Toys – dolls.

Which is Willy? ill. by author. Doubleday, 1962. Subj: Birds – penguins. Character traits – individuality.

Brightman, Alan. *Like me* ill. by author. Little, 1976. Subj: Character traits – being different. Handicaps.

Brighton, Catherine. *Five secrets in a box* ill. by author. Dutton, 1987. ISBN 0-525-44318-5 Subj: Behavior – secrets. Foreign lands – Italy. Science.

Hope's gift ill. by author. Doubleday, 1988. ISBN 0-385-24598-X Subj: Character traits – kindness to animals. Theater.

Mozart ill. by author. Doubleday, 1990. ISBN 0-385-41538-9 Subj: Careers – composers. Careers – musicians.

My hands, my world ill. by author. Macmillan, 1984. Subj: Handicaps – blindness. Imagination – imaginary friends. Senses – seeing.

Nijinsky ill. by author. Doubleday, 1989. ISBN 0-385-24926-8 Subj: Activities – dancing. Foreign lands – Russia.

Brillhart, Julie. *Anna's goodbye apron* ill. by author. Albert Whitman, 1990. ISBN 0-8075-0375-4 Subj: Careers – teachers. School.

Story hour—starring Megan! ill. by author. Albert Whitman, 1992. ISBN 0-8075-7628-X Subj: Activities – reading. Careers – librarians. Family life – mothers. Libraries. Problem solving.

Brimner, Larry Dane. *Country Bear's good neighbor* ill. by Ruth Tietjen Councell. Watts, 1988. ISBN 0-531-08308-X Subj: Animals – bears. Food.

Country bear's surprise ill. by Ruth Tietjen Councell. Orchard, 1991. ISBN 0-531-08411-6 Subj: Animals – bears. Birthdays. Parties.

Brin, Ruth F. *David and Goliath* ill. by H. Hechtkopf. Lerner, 1977. Subj: Foreign lands – Israel. Religion.

The story of Esther ill. by H. Hechtkopf. Lerner, 1976. Subj: Foreign lands – Israel. Religion.

Brinckloe, Julie. *Fireflies!* ill. by author. Macmillan, 1985. ISBN 0-02-713310-9 Subj: Behavior – growing up. Insects – fireflies.

Gordon's house ill. by author. Doubleday, 1976. Subj: Animals – bears.

Playing marbles ill. by author. Morrow, 1988. ISBN 0-688-07144-9 Subj: Activities – playing. Games.

Bring a torch, Jeannette, Isabella ill. by Adrienne Adams. Scribner's, 1963. A provincial carol attributed to Nicholas Saboly, seventeenth century Subj: Foreign lands – France. Holidays – Christmas. Music. Songs.

Briscoe, Jill. *The innkeeper's daughter* ill. by Dennis Hockerman. Childrens Pr., 1984. ISBN 0-516-09484-X Subj: Handicaps. Religion.

Brisson, Pat. *Magic carpet* ill. by Amy Schwartz. Macmillan, 1991. ISBN 0-02-714340-6 Subj: Activities – traveling. Family life – aunts, uncles. Imagination.

Your best friend, Kate ill. by Rick Brown. Bradbury Pr., 1989. ISBN 0-02-714350-3 Subj: Activities – traveling. Activities – vacationing. Family life. Letters.

Brister, Hope. *The cunning fox and other tales* ill. by Henry C. Pitz. Knopf, 1943. Subj: Animals. Folk and fairy tales.

Bro, Marguerite H. *The animal friends of Peng-u* ill. by Seong Moy. Doubleday, 1965. Subj: Animals. Folk and fairy tales. Foreign lands – China.

Brock, Emma Lillian. *The birds' Christmas tree* ill. by author. Knopf, 1946. Subj: Birds. Character traits – kindness to animals. Holidays – Christmas.

Mr. Wren's house ill. by author. Knopf, 1944. Subj: Birds – wrens. Family life. Humor.

Nobody's mouse ill. by author. Knopf, 1938. Subj: Animals. City. Humor.

One little Indian boy ill. by author. Hale, 1932. Subj: Indians of North America.

A pet for Barbie ill. by author. Knopf, 1947. Subj: Family life. Pets.

Pig with a front porch ill. by author. Knopf, 1937. Subj: Animals – pigs. Behavior – dissatisfaction.

A present for Auntie ill. by author. Knopf, 1939. Subj: Family life – aunts, uncles.

Skipping Island ill. by author. Knopf, 1958. Subj: Humor. Islands.

Surprise balloon ill. by author. Knopf, 1949. Subj: Activities – flying. Animals. Toys – balloons.

Brodmann, Aliana. *Such a noise!* tr. from German by Aliana Brodmann and David Fillingham; ill. by Hans Poppel. Kane/Miller, 1989. Translation of: Ein Wunderlicher Rat ISBN 0-916291-25-1 Subj: Folk and fairy tales. Humor. Jewish culture. Noise, sounds. Problem solving.

Brodsky, Beverly *see* McDermott, Beverly Brodsky

Broekel, Ray. *Dangerous fish* ill. with photos. Childrens Pr., 1982. Subj: Fish.

I can be an author ill. by author. Childrens Pr., 1986. ISBN 0-516-01891-4 Subj: Careers – writers.

I can be an auto mechanic Childrens Pr., 1985. ISBN 0-516-01885-X Subj: Automobiles. Careers – mechanics.

Trains ill. with photos. Children's Pr., 1981. Subj: Trains. Transportation.

Trucks ill. with photos. Childrens Pr., 1983. Subj: Trucks. Transportation.

Brogan, Peggy. *Sounds around the clock* (Martin, Bill (William Ivan))

Sounds I remember (Martin, Bill (William Ivan))

Sounds of home (Martin, Bill (William Ivan))

Sounds of laughter (Martin, Bill (William Ivan))

Sounds of numbers (Martin, Bill (William Ivan))

Bröger, Achim. *Bruno takes a trip* tr. from German by Caroline Gueritz; ill. by Gisela Kalow. Morrow, 1978. Subj: Activities – traveling. Pets. Trains.

Francie's paper puppy ill. by Michele Sambin; tr. from German. Alphabet Pr., 1984. Subj: Animals – dogs. Art. Country. Emotions – loneliness. Imagination. Pets.

Little Harry tr. from German by Elizabeth D. Crawford; ill. by Judy Morgan. Morrow, 1979. Subj: Humor. Imagination. Problem solving.

The Santa Clauses ill. by Ute Krause. Dial Pr., 1986. ISBN 0-8037-0266-3 Subj: Holidays – Christmas. Humor.

Bromhall, Winifred. *Bridget's growing day* ill. by author. Knopf, 1957. Subj: Behavior – growing up. Character traits – smallness. Foreign lands – Ireland.

Johanna arrives ill. by author. Knopf, 1941. Subj: Activities – traveling. Foreign lands – Holland.

Mary Ann's first picture ill. by author. Knopf, 1947. Subj: Activities – painting. Art. Birthdays.

Middle Matilda ill. by author. Knopf, 1962. Subj: Behavior – losing things. Clothing.

Brook, Judy. *Hector and Harriet the night hamsters: two adventures* ill. by author. Dutton, 1985. ISBN 0-233-97625-6 Subj: Animals – hamsters.

Tim mouse goes down the stream ill. by author. Lothrop, 1975. Subj: Animals – hedgehogs. Animals – mice. Character traits – bravery. Rivers.

Tim mouse visits the farm ill. by author. Lothrop, 1977. Subj: Animals – hedgehogs. Animals – mice. Farms.

Brooke, L. Leslie (Leonard Leslie). *The golden goose book* (Mother Goose)

Johnny Crow's garden ill. by author. Warne, 1903. Subj: Animals. Humor. Poetry, rhyme.

Johnny Crow's new garden ill. by author. Warne, 1935. Subj: Animals. Humor. Poetry, rhyme.

Johnny Crow's party ill. by author. Warne, 1907. Subj: Animals. Humor. Parties.

Oranges and lemons ill. by author. Warne, 1913. Subj: Nursery rhymes.

This little pig went to market (Mother Goose)

Brooks, Andrea. *The guinea pigs' adventure* ill. by author. Little, 1980. Subj: Animals – guinea pigs.

Brooks, Ben. *Lemonade parade* ill. by Bill Slavin. Albert Whitman, 1992. ISBN 0-8075-4432-9 Subj: Activities – working. Family life – fathers. Money.

Brooks, Gregory. *Monroe's island* ill. by author. Bradbury Pr., 1979. Subj: Imagination.

Brooks, Gwendolyn. *Bronzeville boys and girls* ill. by Ronni Solbert. Harper, 1956. Subj: Poetry, rhyme.

Brooks, Robert B. *So that's how I was born* ill. by Susan Perl. Simon and Schuster, 1983. Subj: Babies. Birth. Family life. Science.

Brooks, Ron. *Timothy and Gramps* ill. by author. Bradbury Pr., 1978. Subj: Family life – grandfathers. School.

Broome, Errol. *The smallest koala* ill. by Gwen Mason. Australian Book Source, 1988. ISBN 0-949447-65-X Subj: Animals – koala bears. Character traits – curiosity. Food.

Brothers, Aileen. *Jiffy, Miss Boo and Mr. Roo* ill. by Audean Johnson. Follett, 1966. Subj: Birds – chickens. Pets.

Sad Mrs. Sam Sack ill. by Muriel and Jim Collins. Follett, 1963. Subj: Behavior – dissatisfaction. Family life. Humor.

Brothers and sisters are like that! ill. by Michael Hampshire. Crowell, 1971. Selected by The Child Study Association of America Subj: Family life. Sibling rivalry.

Brott, Ardyth. *Jeremy's decision* ill. by Michael Martchenko. Kane/Miller, 1990. ISBN 0-916291-31-6 Subj: Careers. Music.

Brouillette, Jeanne S. *Moths* ill. by Bill Barss. Follett, 1966. Subj: Insects. Science.

Brown, Abbie Farwell. *The Christmas angel* ill. by Reginald Birch. Houghton, 1910. Subj: Angels. Holidays – Christmas.

Brown, Beatrice Curtis. *Jonathan Bing* ill. by Judith Gwyn Brown. Lothrop, 1968. Subj: Poetry, rhyme.

Jonathan Bing ill. by Pelagie Doane. Oxford Univ. Pr., 1937. Subj: Poetry, rhyme.

Brown, Craig McFarland. *My barn* ill. by author. Greenwillow, 1991. ISBN 0-688-08786-8 Subj: Animals. Barns. Farms.

Patchwork farmer ill. by author. Greenwillow, 1989. ISBN 0-688-07736-6 Subj: Activities – sewing. Careers – farmers. Clothing. Farms. Wordless.

Brown, Daphne Faunce *see* Faunce-Brown, Daphne

Brown, David. *Someone always needs a policeman* ill. by author. Simon and Schuster, 1972. Subj: Careers – police officers.

Brown, Elinor. *The little story book* ill. by author. Oxford Univ. Pr., 1940. Subj: Activities.

Brown, Jane Clark. *Whonk, and whonk again* ill. by author. Houghton, 1989. ISBN 0-395-49211-4 Subj: Behavior – lost. Boats, ships. City. Noise, sounds.

Brown, Jeff. *Flat Stanley* ill. by Tomi Ungerer. Harper, 1961. Subj: Family life. Humor. Problem solving.

Brown, Judith Gwyn. *Alphabet dreams* ill. by author. Prentice-Hall, 1976. Subj: ABC books. Poetry, rhyme.

The happy voyage ill. by author. Macmillan, 1965. Subj: Boats, ships.

Max and the truffle pig ill. by author. Abingdon Pr., 1963. Subj: Animals – pigs. Behavior – lost. Food. Foreign lands – France.

Brown, Kathryn. *Muledred* ill. by author. Harcourt, 1990. ISBN 0-15-256265-6 Subj: Animals – mules. Clocks, watches. Family life – grandfathers. School.

Brown, Laurie Krasny. *The bionic bunny show* (Brown, Marc Tolon)

Dinosaurs alive and well by Laurie Krasny Brown and Marc Tolon Brown; ill. by authors. Little, 1990. ISBN 0-316-10998-3 Subj: Dinosaurs. Health.

Dinosaurs to the rescue by Laurie Krasny Brown and Marc Tolon Brown; ill. by Marc Tolon Brown. Little, 1992. ISBN 0-316-11087-6 Subj: Dinosaurs. Ecology.

Dinosaurs travel by Laurie Krasny Brown and Marc Brown; ill. by Marc Brown. Little, 1988. ISBN 0-316-11076-0 Subj: Activities – traveling. Dinosaurs.

Visiting the art museum by Laurene Krasny Brown and Marc Brown; ill. by authors. Dutton, 1986. ISBN 0-525-44233-2 Subj: Art. Museums.

Brown, M. K. *Let's go swimming with Mr. Sillypants* ill. by author. Crown, 1986. ISBN 0-517-56185-9 Subj: Dreams. Sports – swimming.

Brown, Marc Tolon. *Arthur babysits* ill. by author. Little, 1992. ISBN 0-316-11293-3 Subj: Activities – baby-sitting. Animals – aardvarks. Twins.

Arthur goes to camp ill. by author. Little, 1982. Subj: Animals. Camps, camping.

Arthur meets the president ill. by author. Little, 1991. ISBN 0-316-11265-8 Subj: Activities – traveling. Animals – aardvarks. Family life – sisters.

Arthur's April fool ill. by author. Little, 1983. Subj: Animals. Holidays – April Fools' Day.

Arthur's baby ill. by author. Little, 1987. ISBN 0-316-11123-6 Subj: Animals – aardvarks. Babies. Family life.

Arthur's birthday ill. by author. Little, 1989. ISBN 0-316-11073-6 Subj: Animals – aardvarks. Birthdays. Friendship. Parties.

Arthur's Christmas ill. by author. Little, 1984. Subj: Animals. Holidays – Christmas.

Arthur's eyes ill. by author. Little, 1979. Subj: Animals. Glasses. Senses – seeing.

Arthur's Halloween ill. by author. Little, 1982. Subj: Animals. Holidays – Halloween.

Arthur's pet business ill. by author. Little, 1990. ISBN 0-316-11262-3 Subj: Animals – aardvarks. Animals – dogs. Pets.

Arthur's teacher trouble ill. by author. Little, 1986. ISBN 0-87113-091-2 Subj: Animals. School.

Arthur's Thanksgiving ill. by author. Little, 1983. Subj: Animals. Holidays – Thanksgiving. Theater.

Arthur's tooth ill. by author. Little, 1985. ISBN 0-87113-006-8 Subj: Animals. Teeth.

Arthur's Valentine ill. by author. Little, 1980. Subj: Animals. Holidays – Valentine's Day. School.

The bionic bunny show by Marc Brown and Laurene Krasny Brown; ill. by Marc Brown. Little, 1984. Subj: Animals. Animals – rabbits. Television.

Can you jump like a frog? ill. by author. Dutton, 1989. ISBN 0-525-44463-7 Subj: Format, unusual – toy and movable books. Frogs and toads. Nursery rhymes.

The cloud over Clarence ill. by author. Dutton, 1979. Subj: Animals – cats. Behavior – carelessness. Friendship.

D. W. all wet ill. by author. Little, 1988. ISBN 0-316-11077-9 Subj: Animals – anteaters. Sea and seashore. Sibling rivalry.

D. W. flips! ill. by author. Little, 1987. ISBN 0-316-11239-9 Subj: Animals. Sports – gymnastics.

Dinosaurs alive and well (Brown, Laurie Krasny)

Dinosaurs, beware! a safety guide by Marc Brown and Stephen Krensky; ill. by authors. Little, 1982. Subj: Dinosaurs. Safety.

Dinosaurs to the rescue (Brown, Laurie Krasny)

Dinosaurs travel (Brown, Laurie Krasny)

Finger rhymes ill. by author. Dutton, 1980. Subj: Games. Participation. Poetry, rhyme.

Hand rhymes ill. by selector. Dutton, 1985. ISBN 0-525-44201-4 Subj: Games. Poetry, rhyme.

Lenny and Lola ill. by author. Dutton, 1978. Subj: Circus.

Marc Brown's full house ill. by author. Addison-Wesley, 1977. Subj: Monsters.

Moose and goose ill. by author. Dutton, 1978. Subj: Animals – moose. Birds – geese.

One, two buckle my shoe ill. by author. Dutton, 1989. ISBN 0-525-44462-9 Subj: Animals – rabbits. Format, unusual – toy and movable books. Games. Nursery rhymes.

Perfect pigs: an introduction to manners by Marc Brown and Stephen Krensky; ill. by authors. Little, 1983. Subj: Animals – pigs. Etiquette.

Pickle things ill. by author. Parents, 1980. Subj: Food. Poetry, rhyme.

Play rhymes ill. by author. Dutton, 1987. ISBN 0-525-44336-3 Subj: Games. Nursery rhymes. Music. Songs.

The silly tail book ill. by author. Parents, 1983. Subj: Animals. Poetry, rhyme.

Spooky riddles ill. by author. Random House, 1983. Subj: Ghosts. Humor. Monsters. Riddles. Witches.

There's no place like home ill. by author. Parents, 1984. ISBN 0-8193-1125-1 Subj: Houses. Poetry, rhyme.

The true Francine ill. by author. Little, 1981. Subj: Animals. Behavior – lying. School.

Visiting the art museum (Brown, Laurie Krasny)

What do you call a dumb bunny? and other rabbit riddles, games, jokes and cartoons ill. by author. Little, 1983. Subj: Animals – rabbits. Format, unusual – toy and movable books. Games. Humor. Riddles.

Wings on things ill. by author. Random House, 1982. Subj: Activities – flying. Poetry, rhyme.

Witches four ill. by author. Parents, 1980. Subj: Poetry, rhyme. Witches.

Your first garden book ill. by author. Little, 1981. Subj: Gardens, gardening. Plants.

Brown, Marcia. *All butterflies: an ABC* ill. by author. Scribner's, 1974. Subj: ABC books.

The blue jackal ill. by author. Scribner's, 1977. Subj: Animals. Behavior – trickery. Folk and fairy tales. Foreign lands – India.

The bun: a tale from Russia ill. by author. Harcourt, 1972. Subj: Animals. Behavior – greed. Character traits – cleverness. Cumulative tales. Folk and fairy tales.

Dick Whittington and his cat (Dick Whittington and his cat)

Felice ill. by author. Scribner's, 1958. Subj: Animals – cats. Foreign lands – Italy.

Henry fisherman ill. by author. Scribner's, 1949. Subj: Caldecott award honor book. Careers – fishermen.

How, hippo! ill. by author. Scribner's, 1969. Subj: Animals – hippopotami.

Listen to a shape photos. by author. Watts, 1979. Subj: Concepts – shape.

The little carousel ill. by author. Scribner's, 1946. Subj: City. Emotions – loneliness. Kites. Merry-go-rounds. Money.

The neighbors ill. by author. Scribner's, 1967. "Text adapted from Afanas'yev." Subj: Animals – foxes. Animals – rabbits. Cumulative tales. Foreign lands – Russia. Houses.

Once a mouse... adapt. and ill. by author. Scribner's, 1961. An adaption of Hitopadeśa, a tale from ancient India Subj: Animals. Caldecott award book. Character traits – vanity. Concepts – size. Folk and fairy tales. Foreign lands – India. Magic.

Once a mouse... (Brown, Marcia)

Peter Piper's alphabet ill. by author. Scribner's, 1959. Subj: ABC books. Nursery rhymes. Tongue twisters.

Skipper John's cook ill. by author. Scribner's, 1951. Subj: Activities – cooking. Boats, ships. Caldecott award honor book.

Stone soup ill. by author. Scribner's, 1947. Subj: Caldecott award honor book. Careers – military. Character traits – cleverness. Folk and fairy tales. Food. Foreign lands – Russia.

Tamarindo! ill. by author. Scribner's, 1960. Subj: Animals – donkeys. Behavior – lost. Foreign lands – Greece.

Touch will tell photos. by author. Watts, 1979. Subj: Concepts. Senses – touching.

Walk with your eyes photos. by author. Watts, 1979. Subj: Concepts. Senses – seeing.

Brown, Margaret Wise. *Afro-bets: book of colors* ill. by Culverson Blair. Just Us Books, 1991. ISBN 0-940975-29-7 Subj: Concepts – color.

Afro-bets: book of shapes ill. by Culverson Blair. Just Us Books, 1991. ISBN 0-940975-28-9 Subj: Concepts – shape.

Baby animals ill. by Mary Cameron. Random House, 1941. Subj: Animals.

Baby animals ill. by Susan Jeffers Rev. ed. Random House, 1989. ISBN 0-394-92040-6 Subj: Animals.

Big dog, little dog ill. by Leonard Weisgard. Doubleday, 1943. Subj: Animals – dogs. Concepts – size.

The big fur secret ill. by Robert de Veyrac. Harper, 1944. Subj: Animals. Communication. Zoos.

Big red barn ill. by Felicia Bond. HarperCollins, 1989. ISBN 0-06-020749-3 Subj: Animals. Barns. Farms. Poetry, rhyme.

Big red barn ill. by Rosella Hartman. Addison-Wesley, 1956. Subj: Animals. Barns. Farms. Poetry, rhyme.

Bumble bugs and elephants ill. by Clement Hurd. Addison-Wesley, 1941. Subj: Concepts – size.

A child's good morning book ill. by Jean Charlot. Addison-Wesley, 1952. Subj: Morning.

A child's good night book ill. by Jean Charlot. Addison-Wesley, 1950. Subj: Bedtime. Caldecott award honor book. Night. Sleep.

Christmas in the barn ill. by Barbara Cooney. Crowell, 1952. Subj: Holidays – Christmas.

The country noisy book ill. by Leonard Weisgard. Harper, 1940. Subj: Animals – dogs. Country. Noise, sounds. Participation.

The dead bird ill. by Remy Charlip. W. R. Scott, 1958. Subj: Death.

Dr. Squash the doll doctor ill. by J. P. Miller. Simon and Schuster, 1952. Subj: Character traits – kindness. Toys – dolls. Toys – soldiers.

Don't frighten the lion ill. by H. A. Rey. Harper, 1942. Subj: Animals. Animals – dogs. Character traits – cleverness. Zoos.

Dream book ill. by Richard Floethe. Random House, 1950. Subj: Dreams.

The duck photos. by Ylla. Harper, 1953. Subj: Animals. Birds – ducks. Character traits – vanity.

Five little firemen by Margaret Wise Brown and Edith Thacher Hurd ill. by Tibor Gergely. Simon and Schuster, 1959. Subj: Careers – firefighters. Noise, sounds.

Four fur feet ill. by Remy Charlip. W. R. Scott, 1961. Subj: Activities – walking. Poetry, rhyme. World.

Fox eyes ill. by Garth Williams. Pantheon, 1977, 1951. Subj: Animals. Animals – foxes.

The golden birthday book ill. by Leonard Weisgard. Western, 1989. ISBN 0-307-12096-1 Subj: Animals. Birthdays.

The golden egg book ill. by Leonard Weisgard. Simon and Schuster, 1947. Subj: Animals – rabbits. Birds – ducks. Eggs. Holidays – Easter.

Goodnight moon ill. by Clement Hurd. Harper, 1934. Subj: Animals – rabbits. Bedtime. Moon.

House of a hundred windows Cat and architecture by Robert de Veyrac; ill. by Henri Rousseau and others. Harper, 1945. Subj: Animals – cats. Houses.

The indoor noisy book ill. by Leonard Weisgard. Harper, 1942. Subj: Animals – dogs. Games. Noise, sounds. Participation.

The little brass band ill. by Clement Hurd. Harper, 1948. Subj: Cumulative tales. Music.

Little chicken ill. by Leonard Weisgard. Harper, 1943. Subj: Animals – rabbits. Birds – chickens.

The little farmer ill. by Esphyr Slobodkina. Addison-Wesley, 1948. Subj: Dreams. Farms.

The little fir tree ill. by Barbara Cooney. Crowell, 1954. Subj: Holidays – Christmas. Trees.

The little fireman ill. by Esphyr Slobodkina. Addison-Wesley, 1952. Subj: Careers – firefighters. Fire.

The little fisherman ill. by Dahlov Ipcar. Addison-Wesley, 1945. Subj: Careers – fishermen. Fish.

The little fur family ill. by Garth Williams. Harper, 1946. Subj: Activities. Animals. Format, unusual.

The little island ill. by Leonard Weisgard. Doubleday, 1946. Subj: Caldecott award book. Islands. Seasons. Weather.

Little lost lamb ill. by Leonard Weisgard. Doubleday, 1945. Subj: Animals – sheep. Behavior – lost. Caldecott award honor book.

Nibble nibble ill. by Leonard Weisgard. Addison-Wesley, 1959. Subj: Poetry, rhyme.

Night and day ill. by Leonard Weisgard. Harper, 1942. Subj: Animals – cats. Emotions – fear. Night.

Noisy book ill. by Leonard Weisgard. Harper, 1939. Subj: Noise, sounds. Participation.

On Christmas eve ill. by Beni Montresor. W. R. Scott, 1961. Subj: Holidays – Christmas. Religion.

Once upon a time in pigpen and three other stories ill. by Ann Strugnell. Addison-Wesley, 1980. Subj: Animals. Humor.

Pussycat's Christmas ill. by Helen Stone. Harper, 1949. Subj: Animals – cats. Holidays – Christmas.

The quiet noisy book ill. by Leonard Weisgard. Harper, 1950. Subj: Animals – dogs. Morning. Noise, sounds. Participation.

Red light, green light ill. by Leonard Weisgard. Doubleday, 1944. Subj: Concepts – color. Safety. Traffic, traffic signs.

The runaway bunny ill. by Clement Hurd. Harper, 1942. Subj: Animals – rabbits. Behavior – running away. Holidays – Easter.

The seashore noisy book ill. by Leonard Weisgard. Harper, 1941. Subj: Noise, sounds. Participation. Sea and seashore.

SHHhhh....Bang: a whispering book ill. by Robert De Veyrac. Harper, 1943. Subj: Noise, sounds.

Sleepy ABC ill. by Esphyr Slobodkina. Lothrop, 1953. Subj: ABC books. Poetry, rhyme. Sleep.

The sleepy little lion ill. by Ylla. Harper, 1947. Subj: Animals – lions. Sleep.

Sneakers ill. by Jean Charlot. Addison-Wesley, 1979, 1955. Reissue of 1955 ed. published by W. R. Scott under title Seven stories about a cat named Sneakers. Subj: Animals – cats. Behavior – misbehavior.

The steamroller: a fantasy ill. by Evaline Ness. Walker, 1974. Published in 1938 in the author's collection, The fish with the deep sea smile. Subj: Holidays – Christmas. Machines.

Streamlined pig ill. by Kurt Wiese. Harper, 1938. Subj: Activities – flying. Airplanes, airports. Animals. Character traits – bravery.

The summer noisy book ill. by Leonard Weisgard. Harper, 1951. Subj: Farms. Noise, sounds. Participation. Seasons – summer.

They all saw it photos. by Ylla. Harper, 1944. Subj: Animals. Problem solving.

Three little animals ill. by Garth Williams. Harper, 1956. Subj: Activities – traveling. Animals. Behavior – lost. City.

Two little miners ill. by Edith Thacher Hurd. Simon and Schuster, 1949. Subj: Careers – miners.

Two little trains ill. by Jean Charlot. Addison-Wesley, 1949. Subj: Poetry, rhyme. Trains.

Wait till the moon is full ill. by Garth Williams. Harper, 1948. Subj: Animals. Animals – raccoons. Character traits – questioning. Moon. Night.

Wheel on the chimney by Margaret Wise Brown and Tibor Gergely; ill. by Tibor Gergely. Lippincott, 1954. Subj: Birds – storks. Caldecott award honor book. Character traits – luck. Foreign lands – Hungary.

When the wind blew ill. by Geoffrey Hayes. Harper, 1977, 1937. Subj: Animals – cats. Illness. Weather – wind.

Where have you been? ill. by Barbara Cooney Reissue of Crowell, 1952 ed. Hastings House, 1981. Subj: Animals. Poetry, rhyme.

Whistle for the train ill. by Leonard Weisgard. Doubleday, 1956. Subj: Poetry, rhyme. Trains.

The winter noisy book ill. by Charles Green Shaw. Harper, 1947. Subj: Animals – dogs. Noise, sounds. Participation. Seasons – winter. Weather – snow.

The wonderful house ill. by J. P. Miller. Simon and Schuster, 1950. Subj: Houses.

The wonderful story book ill. by J. P. Miller. Simon and Schuster, 1948. Subj: Poetry, rhyme.

Young kangaroo ill. by Symeon Shimin. Addison-Wesley, 1955. Subj: Animals – kangaroos.

Brown, Myra Berry. *Benjy's blanket* ill. by Dorothy Marino. Watts, 1952. Subj: Animals – cats. Behavior – growing up.

Best friends ill. by Don Freeman. Golden Gate, 1967. Subj: Friendship. Poetry, rhyme.

Company's coming for dinner ill. by Dorothy Marino. Watts, 1960. Subj: Character traits – helpfulness. Etiquette. Parties.

First night away from home ill. by Dorothy Marino. Watts, 1960. Subj: Activities – playing. Friendship. Sleep. Toys – teddy bears.

Pip camps out ill. by Phyllis Graham. Golden Gate, 1966. Subj: Family life. Night. Camps, camping.

Brown, Palmer. *Something for Christmas* ill. by author. Harper, 1958. Subj: Animals – mice. Character traits – generosity. Emotions – love. Holidays – Christmas.

Brown, Richard Eric. *One hundred words about animals* ill. by author. Harcourt, 1987. ISBN 0-15-200550-1 Subj: Animals.

One hundred words about transportation ill. by author. Harcourt, 1987. ISBN 0-15-200551-X Subj: Transportation.

Brown, Ruth. *Alphabet times four* ill. by author. Dutton, 1991. ISBN 0-525-44831-4 Subj: ABC books. Foreign languages.

The big sneeze ill. by author. Lothrop, 1985. ISBN 0-688-04666-5 Subj: Farms. Humor.

Crazy Charlie ill. by author. Rourke, 1982. Subj: Reptiles – alligators, crocodiles. Self-concept. Teeth.

A dark, dark tale ill. by author. Dial Pr., 1981. Subj: Cumulative tales. Foreign lands – England.

I don't like it! ill. by author. Dutton, 1990. ISBN 0-525-44559-5 Subj: Animals – dogs. Emotions – envy, jealousy. Toys. Toys – dolls.

Ladybug, ladybug ill. by author. Dutton, 1988. ISBN 0-525-44423-8 Subj: Insects – ladybugs. Nursery rhymes.

Our cat Flossie ill. by author. Dutton, 1986. ISBN 0-525-44256-1 Subj: Activities. Animals – cats.

Our puppy's vacation ill. by author. Dutton, 1987. ISBN 0-525-44326-6 Subj: Activities – playing. Activities – vacationing. Animals – dogs. Pets.

The world that Jack built ill. by author. Dutton, 1991. ISBN 0-525-44635-4 Subj: Cumulative tales. Ecology.

Brown, Tricia. *Hello, amigos!* photos. by Fran Ortiz. Holt, 1986. ISBN 0-8050-0090-9 Subj: Birthdays. Ethnic groups in the U.S. – Mexican-Americans. Family life. School.

Someone special, just like you photos. by Fran Ortiz. Holt, 1984. Subj: Emotions. Handicaps.

Browne, Anthony. *Bear goes to town* ill. by author. Doubleday, 1989. ISBN 0-385-26524-7 Subj: Animals. Animals – bears. Art. Imagination.

Bear hunt ill. by author. Atheneum, 1980. Subj: Animals – bears. Art. Problem solving. Sports – hunting.

Changes ill. by author. Julia MacRae Books, 1991. ISBN 0-679-91029-8 Subj: Babies. Family life. Imagination.

Gorilla ill. by author. Knopf, 1985, 1983. ISBN 0-394-97525-1 Subj: Animals – gorillas. Birthdays. Family life – fathers. Imagination. Toys.

I like books ill. by author. Knopf, 1989. ISBN 0-394-84186-7 Subj: Activities – reading. Animals – chimpanzees.

The little bear book ill. by author. Doubleday, 1989. ISBN 0-385-26006-7 Subj: Animals. Animals – bears. Art. Imagination.

Look what I've got! ill. by author. Watts, 1980. Subj: Behavior – boasting. Imagination.

Piggybook ill. by author. Knopf, 1986. ISBN 0-394-98416-1 Subj: Animals – pigs. Family life – mothers.

Things I like ill. by author. Knopf, 1989. ISBN 0-394-94192-6 Subj: Activities – playing. Animals – chimpanzees.

Willy and Hugh ill. by author. Knopf, 1991. ISBN 0-679-91446-3 Subj: Animals – chimpanzees. Animals – gorillas. Friendship.

Willy the champ ill. by author. Knopf, 1986. ISBN 0-394-97907-9 Subj: Animals – chimpanzees. Animals – gorillas. Behavior – bullying.

Willy the wimp ill. by author. Knopf, 1985. Subj: Animals – chimpanzees. Animals – gorillas. Self-concept.

Browne, Caroline. *Mrs. Christie's farmhouse* ill. by author. Doubleday, 1977. Subj: Country. Farms. Gardens, gardening. Humor. Royalty.

Browne, Eileen. *Where's that bus?* ill. by author. Simon & Schuster, 1991. ISBN 0-671-73810-0 Subj: Activities – picnicking. Animals – moles. Animals – rabbits. Animals – squirrels. Buses. Friendship.

Browner, Richard. *Everyone has a name* ill. by Emma Landau. Walck, 1961. Subj: Animals. Names. Poetry, rhyme.

Look again! ill. by Emma Landau. Atheneum, 1962. Subj: Concepts.

Browning, Robert. *The Pied Piper of Hamelin* (Bartos-Hoppner, Barbara)

The Pied Piper of Hamelin (Mayer, Mercer)

The pied piper of Hamelin adapt. by Sharon Chmielarz; ill. by Patricia and Robin DeWitt. Stemmer House, 1990. ISBN 0-88045-115-7 Subj: Animals – rats. Behavior – trickery. Folk and fairy tales. Foreign lands – Germany. Poetry, rhyme.

The pied piper of Hamelin ill. by Kate Greenaway. Warne, n.d. Subj: Animals – rats. Behavior – trickery. Folk and fairy tales. Foreign lands – Germany. Poetry, rhyme.

The pied piper of Hamelin ill. by Anatoly Ivanov. Lothrop, 1986. ISBN 0-688-03810-1 Subj: Animals – rats. Behavior – trickery. Folk and fairy tales. Foreign lands – Germany. Poetry, rhyme.

The pied piper of Hamelin adapt. by Sara and Stephen Corrin; ill. by Errol Le Cain. Harcourt, 1989. ISBN 0-15-261596-2 Subj: Animals – rats. Behavior – trickery. Folk and fairy tales. Foreign lands – Germany. Poetry, rhyme.

Bruce, Sheilah B. *The radish day jubilee* ill. by Lawrence DiFiori. Holt, 1983. Subj: Imagination. Poetry, rhyme. Puppets.

Bruchac, Joseph. *Thirteen moons on turtle's back* by Joseph Bruchac and Jonathan London; ill. by Thomas Locker. Putnam, 1992. ISBN 0-399-22141-7 Subj: Folk and fairy tales. Indians of North America. Poetry, rhyme. Seasons.

Bruna, Dick. *Another story to tell* ill. by author. Methuen, 1978. Subj: Weather – snow. Wordless.

B is for bear: an A-B-C ill. by author. Methuen, 1971. Subj: ABC books.

Christmas ill. by author. Doubleday, 1969. Translation of Kerstmis. English verse by Eve Merriam Subj: Holidays – Christmas. Poetry, rhyme. Religion.

The Christmas book ill. by author. Methuen, 1964. Subj: Holidays – Christmas.

Farmer John ill. by author. Price Stern Sloan, 1984. Subj: Farms.

The fish ill. by author. Follett, 1963. English verse translated from the Dutch by Sandra Greifenstein Subj: Fish. Food. Poetry, rhyme.

I can dress myself ill. by author. Methuen, 1977. Subj: Behavior – growing up. Clothing.

I can read difficult words ill. by author. Methuen, 1978. Subj: Activities – reading.

I know more about numbers ill. by author. Methuen, 1981. Subj: Counting, numbers.

Kitten Nell ill. by author. Follett, 1963. Subj: Animals – cats. Humor. Poetry, rhyme.

Little bird tweet ill. by author. Follett, 1963. Subj: Birds. Farms. Poetry, rhyme.

Miffy ill. by author. Follett, 1970. Translation of Nijntje Subj: Animals – rabbits. Family life.

Miffy at the beach ill. by author. Methuen, 1980. Subj: Animals – rabbits. Sea and seashore.

Miffy at the playground ill. by author. Methuen, 1980. Subj: Activities – playing. Animals – rabbits.

Miffy at the seaside ill. by author. Follett, 1970. Translation of Nijntje aan zee Subj: Animals – rabbits. Sea and seashore.

Miffy at the zoo ill. by author. Follett, 1970. Translation of Nijntje in de dierentuin Subj: Animals – rabbits. Zoos.

Miffy goes to school ill. by author. Price Stern Sloan, 1984. Subj: Animals – rabbits. School.

Miffy in the hospital ill. by author. Methuen, 1978. Subj: Animals – rabbits. Hospitals. Illness.

Miffy in the snow ill. by author. Follett, 1970. Translation of Nijntje in de sneeuw Subj: Animals – rabbits. Seasons – winter. Weather – snow.

Miffy's bicycle ill. by author. Price Stern Sloan, 1984. Subj: Animals – rabbits. Sports – bicycling.

Miffy's dream ill. by author. Methuen, 1980. Subj: Activities – playing. Animals – rabbits. Dreams.

The orchestra ill. by author. Price Stern Sloan, 1984. Subj: Music. Poetry, rhyme.

Poppy Pig goes to market ill. by author. Methuen, 1981. Subj: Animals – pigs. Counting, numbers. Poetry, rhyme.

The sailor ill. by author. Methuen, 1980. Subj: Activities – traveling. Boats, ships.

The school ill. by author. Methuen, 1980. Subj: School.

Tilly and Tess ill. by author. Follett, 1963. Subj: Birthdays. Poetry, rhyme. Twins.

Brunhoff, Jean de. *Babar and Father Christmas* tr. by Merle Haas; ill. by author. Random House, 1940. Translation of Babar et le Père Nöel Subj: Animals – elephants. Holidays – Christmas.

Babar and his children tr. by Merle Haas; ill. by author. Random House, 1938. Subj: Animals – elephants. Triplets.

Babar and Zephir tr. from French by Merle Haas; ill. by author Reprint of 1937 ed. Random House, 1942. Subj: Animals – elephants. Animals – monkeys.

Babar the king tr. by Merle Haas; ill. by author. Random House, 1935. Subj: Animals – elephants. Royalty – kings.

Babar the king tr. by Merle Haas; ill. by author Facsimile ed. Random House, 1986. ISBN 0-394-88245-8 Subj: Animals – elephants. Royalty – kings.

The story of Babar, the little elephant tr. by Merle Haas; ill. by author. Random House, 1960. Subj: Animals – elephants. Behavior – running away. Foreign lands – France.

The travels of Babar tr. by Merle Haas; ill. by author. Random House, 1934, 1961. Subj: Activities – traveling. Animals – elephants.

Brunhoff, Laurent de. *Babar and the ghost* ill. by author. Random House, 1981. Subj: Animals – elephants. Ghosts.

Babar and the ghost ill. by author Easy-to-read ed. Random House, 1986. ISBN 0-394-97908-7 Subj: Animals – elephants. Ghosts.

Babar and the Wully-Wully ill. by author. Random House, 1975. Subj: Animals – elephants. Pets.

Babar comes to America tr. by M. Jean Craig; ill. by author. Random House, 1965. Translation of Babar en Amérique Subj: Animals – elephants.

Babar learns to cook ill. by author. Random House, 1979. Subj: Activities – cooking. Animals – elephants.

Babar the magician ill. by author. Random House, 1980. Subj: Animals – elephants. Animals – monkeys. Magic.

Babar visits another planet tr. by Merle Haas; ill. by author. Random House, 1972. Translation of Babar sur la planète molle Subj: Animals – elephants. Space and space ships.

Babar's ABC ill. by author. Random House, 1983. Subj: ABC books. Animals – elephants.

Babar's battle ill. by author. Random House, 1992. ISBN 0-679-91068-9 Subj: Animals – elephants. Animals – rhinoceros. War.

Babar's birthday surprise ill. by author. Random House, 1970. Translation of Anniversaire de Babar Subj: Animals – elephants. Birthdays.

Babar's book of color ill. by author. Random House, 1984. Subj: Animals – elephants. Concepts – color.

Babar's castle tr. by Merle Haas; ill. by author. Random House, 1962. Subj: Animals – elephants.

Babar's counting book ill. by author. Random House, 1986. ISBN 0-394-97517-0 Subj: Animals. Animals – elephants. Counting, numbers.

Babar's cousin, that rascal Arthur tr. by Merle Haas; ill. by author. Random House, 1948. Translation of Babar et ce coquin d'Arthur A continuation of the Babar stories of Jean de Brunhoff Subj: Activities – vacationing. Animals – elephants. Behavior – misbehavior.

Babar's fair will be opened next Sunday tr. by Merle Haas; ill. by author. Random House, 1954. Translation of La fête de Célesteville Subj: Animals – elephants. Fairs.

Babar's little circus star ill. by author. Random House, 1988. ISBN 0-394-98959-7 Subj: Animals. Animals – elephants. Circus.

Babar's little girl ill. by author. Random House, 1987. ISBN 0-394-98689-X Subj: Animals – elephants. Behavior – carelessness. Behavior – lost. Character traits – kindness to animals.

Babar's mystery ill. by author. Random House, 1978. Subj: Activities – vacationing. Animals – elephants. Crime.

Babar's picnic ill. by author. Random House, 1959. Subj: Activities – picnicking. Animals – elephants.

Babar's visit to Bird Island ill. by author. Random House, 1952. Subj: Animals – elephants. Birds. Islands. Royalty – kings.

Serafina the giraffe ill. by author. Collins-World, 1961. Subj: Animals – giraffes. Birthdays. Humor.

Brustlein, Janice Tworkov *see* Janice

Bryan, Ashley. *All night, all day: a child's first book of African-American spirituals* ill. by selector. Macmillan, 1991. ISBN 0-689-31662-3 Subj: Ethnic groups in the U.S. – Afro-Americans. Music. Religion. Songs.

Beat the story-drum, pum-pum ill. by adapt. Atheneum, 1980. Subj: Cumulative tales. Folk and fairy tales. Foreign lands – Africa. Poetry, rhyme.

The cat's purr ill. by author. Atheneum, 1985. ISBN 0-689-31086-2 Subj: Animals – cats. Animals – rats. Folk and fairy tales. Poetry, rhyme.

I'm going to sing: Black American spirituals, Vol. II ill. by author. Atheneum, 1982. ISBN 0-689-30915-5 Subj: Ethnic groups in the U.S. – Afro-Americans. Songs.

Lion and the ostrich chicks: and other African tales ill. by author. Atheneum, 1986. ISBN 0-689-31311-X Subj: Folk and fairy tales. Foreign lands – Africa. Songs.

Sh-ko and his eight wicked brothers ill. by Fumio Yoshimura. Atheneum, 1988. ISBN 0-689-31446-9 Subj: Character traits – kindness to animals. Folk and fairy tales. Foreign lands – Japan.

Turtle knows your name ill. by author. Macmillan, 1989. ISBN 0-689-31578-3 Subj: Family life – grandmothers. Folk and fairy tales. Names. Reptiles – turtles, tortoises.

Bryan, Dorothy. *Friendly little Jonathan* by Dorothy and Marguerite Bryan; ill. by Marguerite Bryan. Dodd, 1939. Subj: Animals – dogs. Friendship.

Just Tammie! by Dorothy and Marguerite Bryan; ill. by Marguerite Bryan. Dodd, 1951. Subj: Animals – dogs.

Bryan, Marguerite. *Friendly little Jonathan* (Bryan, Dorothy)

Just Tammie! (Bryan, Dorothy)

Bryant, Bernice. *Follow the leader* ill. by author. Houghton, 1950. Subj: Behavior – bullying. Behavior – growing up. Character traits – selfishness.

Bryant, Dean. *Here am I* ill. by author. Rand McNally, 1947. Subj: Activities.

See the bear ill. by author. Rand McNally, 1947. Subj: Toys.

Bryant, Donna. *My rabbit Roberta* ill. by Jakki Wood. Barron's, 1991. ISBN 0-8120-6210-8 Subj: Animals – rabbits. Pets.

Bryant, Sara Cone. *Epaminondas* (Merriam, Eve)

Epaminondas and his auntie ill. by Inez Hogan. Houghton, 1938. Subj: Behavior – misunderstanding. Family life – aunts, uncles. Folk and fairy tales. Humor.

Bryson, Bernarda. *The twenty miracles of Saint Nicolas* ill. by author. Atlantic Monthly Pr., 1960. Subj: Folk and fairy tales. Foreign lands. Holidays – Christmas.

Buchanan, Heather S. *Emily Mouse saves the day* ill. by author. Dial Pr., 1985. ISBN 0-8037-0175-6 Subj: Animals – mice. Character traits – helpfulness. Family life.

Emily Mouse's beach house ill. by author. Dial Pr., 1987. ISBN 0-8037-0263-9 Subj: Animals – mice. Sea and seashore.

Emily Mouse's first adventure ill. by author. Dial Pr., 1985. ISBN 0-8037-0174-8 Subj: Animals – mice. Character traits – kindness to animals.

Emily Mouse's garden ill. by author. Dial Pr., 1987. ISBN 0-8037-0261-2 Subj: Animals – mice. Gardens, gardening. Sibling rivalry.

George and Matilda Mouse and the floating school ill. by author. Simon & Schuster, 1990. ISBN 0-671-70613-6 Subj: Animals – mice. Problem solving. School. Toys.

George and Matilda Mouse and the moon rocket ill. by author. Simon & Schuster, 1992. ISBN 0-671-75864-0 Subj: Animals – mice. Holidays – Guy Fawkes Day. Moon.

George Mouse learns to fly ill. by author. Dial Pr., 1985. ISBN 0-8037-0172-1 Subj: Activities – flying. Airplanes, airports. Animals – mice.

George Mouse's covered wagon ill. by author. Dial Pr., 1987. ISBN 0-8037-0258-2 Subj: Activities – traveling. Activities – vacationing. Animals – mice. Sea and seashore.

George Mouse's first summer ill. by author. Dial Pr., 1985. ISBN 0-8037-0173-X Subj: Animals – mice. Character traits – cleverness. Problem solving. Seasons – summer.

George Mouse's riverboat band ill. by author. Dial Pr., 1987. ISBN 0-8037-0260-4 Subj: Animals – mice. Boats, ships.

Buchanan, Joan. *It's a good thing* ill. by Barbara Di Lella. Firefly Pr., 1984. Subj: Activities – walking. Behavior – carelessness. Humor.

Buchanan, Ken. *This house is made of mud* ill. by Libba Tracy. Northland, 1991. ISBN 0-87358-518-6 Subj: Desert. Houses.

Buchheimer, Naomi. *Let's go to a post office* ill. by Ruth Van Sciver. Putnam's, 1957. Subj: Careers – mail carriers. Communication.

Let's go to a school ill. by Ruth Van Sciver. Putnam's, 1957. Subj: School.

Buck, Frank. *Jungle animals* by Frank Buck; text by Ferrin Fraser; ill. by Roger Vernam. Random House, 1945. Subj: Animals.

Buck, Pearl S. (Pearl Sydenstricker). *The Chinese story teller* ill. by Regina Shekerjian. John Day, 1971. Subj: Animals – cats. Animals – dogs. Emotions – envy, jealousy. Folk and fairy tales. Foreign lands – China.

The little fox in the middle ill. by Robert Jones. Collier, 1966. Subj: Animals – foxes. Emotions – loneliness. Family life. Friendship.

Buckaway, C. M. *Alfred, the dragon who lost his flame* ill. by Sarie Jenkins. Firefly Pr., 1982. Subj: Dragons. Imagination. Magic.

Buckingham, Simon. *Alec and his flying bed* ill. by author. Lothrop, 1991. ISBN 0-688-10556-4 Subj: Activities – flying. Furniture – beds. Imagination.

Buckley, Helen Elizabeth. *Grandfather and I* ill. by Paul Galdone. Lothrop, 1959. Subj: Activities – walking. Family life – grandfathers.

Grandmother and I ill. by Paul Galdone. Lothrop, 1961. Subj: Emotions – love. Family life – grandmothers.

Josie and the snow ill. by Evaline Ness. Lothrop, 1964. Subj: Poetry, rhyme. Seasons – winter. Weather – snow.

Josie's Buttercup ill. by Evaline Ness. Lothrop, 1967. Subj: Animals – dogs. Poetry, rhyme.

Someday with my father ill. by Ellen Eagle. Harper, 1985. ISBN 0-06-020877-5 Subj: Dreams. Family life – fathers. Illness.

"Take care of things," Edward said ill. by Katherine Coville. Lothrop, 1991. ISBN 0-688-07732-3 Subj: Activities – playing. Family life – brothers.

Buckley, Kate. *Love notes* ill. by author. Albert Whitman, 1988. ISBN 0-8075-4780-8 Subj: Behavior – growing up. Holidays – Valentine's Day. Poetry, rhyme. School.

Buckley, Paul. *Amy Belligera and the fireflies* ill. by Kate Buckley. Albert Whitman, 1987. ISBN 0-8075-0324-X Subj: Insects – fireflies. Magic. Night. Witches.

Buckley, Richard. *The foolish tortoise* ill. by Eric Carle. Picture Book Studio, 1985. ISBN 0-88708-002-2 Subj: Behavior – seeking better things. Folk and fairy tales. Poetry, rhyme. Reptiles – turtles, tortoises.

The greedy python ill. by Eric Carle. Picture Book Studio, 1985. ISBN 0-88708-001-4 Subj: Behavior – greed. Folk and fairy tales. Poetry, rhyme. Reptiles – snakes.

Buckmaster, Henrietta. *Lucy and Loki* ill. by Barbara Cooney. Scribner's, 1958. Subj: Animals – cats. Animals – dogs. Behavior – imitation.

Bucknall, Caroline. *One bear all alone* ill. by author. Dial Pr., 1986. ISBN 0-8037-0238-8 Subj: Counting, numbers. Poetry, rhyme. Toys – teddy bears.

One bear in the hospital ill. by author. Dial, 1991. ISBN 0-8037-0847-5 Subj: Hospitals. Illness. Poetry, rhyme. Toys – teddy bears.

One bear in the picture ill. by author. Dial Pr., 1988. ISBN 0-8037-0463-1 Subj: Character traits – cleanliness. Poetry, rhyme. Toys – teddy bears.

The three little pigs (The three little pigs)

Budbill, David. *Christmas tree farm* ill. by Donald Carrick. Macmillan, 1974. Subj: Farms. Holidays – Christmas. Science. Trees.

Budd, Lillian. *The people on Long Ago Street* ill. by Marilyn Miller. Rand McNally, 1964. Subj: Family life – great-grandparents. Imagination.

The pie wagon ill. by Marilyn Miller. Lothrop, 1960. Subj: ABC books. Food.

Budney, Blossom. *After dark* ill. by Tony Chen. Lothrop, 1975. Subj: Night.

A kiss is round ill. by Vladimir Bobri. Lothrop, 1954. Subj: Concepts – shape. Poetry, rhyme.

N is for nursery school ill. by Vladimir Bobri. Lothrop, 1956. Subj: ABC books. School.

Buell, Ellen Lewis. *Read me a poem: children's favorite poetry* ill. by Anna Maria Magagna. Grosset, 1965. Subj: Poetry, rhyme.

Buff, Conrad. *Dash and Dart* (Buff, Mary)

Forest folk (Buff, Mary)

Hurry, Skurry and Flurry (Buff, Mary)

Buff, Mary. *Dash and Dart* by Mary and Conrad Buff; ill. by authors. Viking, 1942. Subj: Animals – deer. Caldecott award honor book. Forest, woods.

Forest folk by Mary and Conrad Buff; ill. by authors. Viking, 1962. Subj: Animals. Animals – deer. Forest, woods.

Hurry, Skurry and Flurry by Mary and Conrad Buff; ill. by authors. Viking, 1954. Subj: Animals – squirrels. Poetry, rhyme.

Buffett, Jimmy. *The jolly mon* by Jimmy and Savannah Jane Buffett; ill. by Lambert Davis. Harcourt, 1988. ISBN 0-15-240530-5 Subj: Activities – traveling. Foreign lands – Caribbean Islands. Music. Royalty – kings. Songs.

Trouble dolls by Jimmy Buffet and Savannah Jane Buffet; ill. by Lambert Davis. Harcourt, 1991. ISBN 0-15-290790-4 Subj: Behavior – lost. Magic. Toys – dolls.

Buffett, Savannah Jane. *The jolly mon* (Buffett, Jimmy)

Trouble dolls (Buffett, Jimmy)

Bulette, Sara. *The elf in the singing tree* ill. by Tom Dunnington. Follett, 1964. Reading consultant: Morton Botel Subj: Elves and little people. Imagination.

The splendid belt of Mr. Big ill. by Lou Myers. Follett, 1964. Reading consultant: Morton Botel Subj: Animals – monkeys. Clothing. Concepts – size. Problem solving.

Bulla, Clyde Robert. *Dandelion Hill* ill. by Bruce Degen. Dutton, 1982. Subj: Animals – bulls, cows. Behavior – growing up. Farms.

Daniel's duck ill. by Joan Sandin. Harper, 1979. Subj: Activities. Art. Emotions – embarrassment.

Jonah and the great fish ill. by Helga Aichinger. Crowell, 1970. Subj: Animals – whales. Religion.

Keep running, Allen! ill. by Satomi Ichikawa. Crowell, 1978. Subj: Behavior – solitude. Sibling rivalry.

Noah and the rainbow (Bolliger, Max)

Poor boy, rich boy ill. by Marcia Sewall. Harper, 1982. Subj: Orphans.

The stubborn old woman ill. by Anne F. Rockwell. Crowell, 1980. Subj: Behavior – needing someone. Character traits – persistence. Character traits – stubbornness.

A tree is a plant ill. by Lois Lignell. Crowell, 1960. Subj: Plants. Trees.

Valentine cat ill. by Leonard Weisgard. Crowell, 1959. Subj: Animals – cats. Holidays – Valentine's Day.

Washington's birthday ill. by Don Bolognese. Crowell, 1967. Subj: Holidays – Washington's Birthday. U.S. history.

Buller, Jon. *Toad on the road* by Jon Buller and Susan Schade; ill. by authors. Random House, 1992. ISBN 0-679-92689-5 Subj: Animals. Automobiles. Frogs and toads. Poetry, rhyme.

Bullock, Kathleen. *It chanced to rain* ill. by author. Simon & Schuster, 1992. ISBN 0-671-66005-5 Subj: Activities – walking. Animals. Poetry, rhyme. Weather – rain.

Rabbits are coming ill. by author. Simon & Schuster, 1991. ISBN 0-671-72963-2 Subj: Animals – rabbits. Toys – balloons. Wordless.

A surprise for Mitzi Mouse ill. by author. Simon & Schuster, 1989. ISBN 0-671-67331-9 Subj: Animals – mice. Emotions – envy, jealousy. Family life – sisters. Sibling rivalry.

Bunce, William. *Freight trains* ill. by Lemuel B. Line. Putnam's, 1954. Subj: Trains.

Bundt, Nancy. *The fire station book* text by Jeff Linzer; photos. by Nancy Bundt. Carolrhoda Books, 1981. Subj: Careers – firefighters.

Bunin, Catherine. *Is that your sister? a true story of adoption* by Catherine Bunin and Sherry Bunin; ill. with photos. Pantheon, 1976. Subj: Adoption. Family life.

Bunin, Sherry. *Is that your sister?* (Bunin, Catherine)

Buntain, Ruth Jaeger. *The birthday story* ill. by Eloise Wilkin. Holiday, 1953. Subj: Birthdays. Emotions – loneliness. Friendship.

Bunting, Eve (Anne Evelyn). *The big red barn* ill. by Howard Knotts. Harcourt, 1979. Subj: Death. Family life.

Clancy's coat ill. by Lorinda Bryan Cauley. Warne, 1984. Subj: Foreign lands – Ireland. Friendship.

Fly away home ill. by Ronald Himler. Houghton, 1991. ISBN 0-395-55962-6 Subj: Airplanes, airports. Family life – fathers. Homeless.

Ghost's hour, spook's hour ill. by author. Clarion, 1987. ISBN 0-89919-484-2 Subj: Animals – dogs. Emotions – fear. Family life. Night.

Goose dinner ill. by Howard Knotts. Harcourt, 1981. Subj: Birds – geese. Farms.

Happy birthday, dear duck ill. by Jan Brett. Clarion, 1988. ISBN 0-89919-541-5 Subj: Animals. Birds – ducks. Birthdays. Poetry, rhyme.

The happy funeral ill. by Vo-Dinh Mai. Harper, 1982. Subj: Death. Ethnic groups in the U.S. – Chinese-Americans. Family life – grandfathers.

How many days to America? a Thanksgiving story ill. by Beth Peck. Clarion, 1988. ISBN 0-89919-521-0 Subj: Character traits – freedom. Holidays – Thanksgiving.

In the haunted house ill. by Susan Meddaugh. Houghton, 1990. ISBN 0-395-51589-0 Subj: Ghosts. Holidays – Halloween. Houses.

Jane Martin, dog detective ill. by Amy Schwartz. Harcourt, 1984. ISBN 0-15-239586-5 Subj: Animals – dogs. Behavior – lost. Careers – detectives. Problem solving.

Magic and the night river ill. by Allen Say. Harper, 1978. Subj: Birds – cormorants. Careers – fishermen. Family life – grandfathers. Foreign lands – Japan.

The man who could call down owls ill. by Charles Mikolaycak. Macmillan, 1984. Subj: Behavior – greed. Birds – owls. Magic.

Monkey in the middle ill. by Lynn Munsinger. Harcourt, 1984. Subj: Animals – monkeys. Emotions – envy, jealousy. Friendship.

The Mother's Day mice ill. by Jan Brett. Clarion, 1986. ISBN 0-89919-387-0 Subj: Animals – mice. Holidays – Mother's Day.

Night tree ill. by Ted Rand. Harcourt, 1991. ISBN 0-15-257425-5 Subj: Animals. Character traits – kindness to animals. Family life. Holidays – Christmas. Trees.

No nap ill. by Susan Meddaugh. Houghton, 1989. ISBN 0-89919-813-9 Subj: Bedtime. Sleep.

A perfect Father's Day ill. by Susan Meddaugh. Houghton, 1991. ISBN 0-395-52590-X Subj: Family life – fathers. Holidays – Father's Day.

The robot birthday ill. by Marie DeJohn. Dutton, 1980. Subj: Birthdays. Robots.

St. Patrick's Day in the morning ill. by Jan Brett. Houghton, 1980. Subj: Holidays – St. Patrick's Day.

Scary, scary Halloween ill. by Jan Brett. Houghton, 1986. ISBN 0-89919-414-1 Subj: Goblins. Holidays – Halloween. Monsters. Poetry, rhyme.

Summer wheels ill. by Thomas B. Allen. Harcourt, 1992. ISBN 0-15-207000-1 Subj: Friendship. Sports – bicycling.

Terrible things ill. by Stephen Gammell. Harper, 1980. Subj: Animals. Emotions – fear.

The traveling men of Ballycoo ill. by Kaethe Zemach. Harcourt, 1983. Subj: Activities – traveling. Music.

A turkey for Thanksgiving ill. by Diane de Groat. Tichnor & Fields, 1991. ISBN 0-89919-793-0 Subj: Animals – moose. Birds – turkeys. Holidays – Thanksgiving.

The Valentine bears ill. by Jan Brett. Seabury Pr., 1983. Subj: Animals – bears. Holidays – Valentine's Day.

The Wednesday surprise ill. by Donald Garrick. Tichnor & Fields, 1989. ISBN 0-89919-721-3

Subj: Activities – reading. Birthdays. Family life. Family life – grandmothers.

Winter's coming ill. by Howard Knotts. Harcourt, 1977. Subj: Family life – grandparents. Farms. Seasons – winter.

Burch, Robert. *The hunting trip* ill. by Susanne Suba. Scribner's, 1971. Subj: Character traits – kindness to animals. Family life. Food. Sports – hunting.

Joey's cat ill. by Don Freeman. Viking, 1969. Subj: Animals – cats. Animals – possums. Ethnic groups in the U.S. – Afro-Americans. Family life.

The jolly witch ill. by Leigh Grant. Dutton, 1975. Subj: Character traits – cleanliness. Witches.

Burchard, Peter. *The Carol Moran* ill. by author. Macmillan, 1958. Subj: Boats, ships.

Burdekin, Harold. *A child's grace* by Harold Burdekin and Ernest Claxton; the grace by Mrs. E. Rutter Leatham; photos. by Harold Burdekin. Dutton, 1938. Subj: Activities. Poetry, rhyme. Religion.

Burdick, Margaret. *Bobby Otter and the blue boat* ill. by author. Little, 1987. ISBN 0-316-11616-5 Subj: Activities – trading. Animals. Animals – otters. Toys.

Sara Raccoon and the secret place ill. by author. Little, 1992. ISBN 0-316-11617-3 Subj: Animals. Animals – raccoons. Behavior – solitude. Friendship.

Burgert, Hans-Joachim. *Samulo and the giant* ill. by author. Holt, 1970. Subj: Character traits – bravery. Weather.

Burgess, Anthony. *The land where the ice cream grows* (Testa, Fulvio)

Burgess, Gelett. *The little father* ill. by Richard Egielski. Farrar, 1985. ISBN 0-374-34596-1 Subj: Character traits – smallness. Family life – fathers. Poetry, rhyme.

Burgess, Thornton. *Old Mother West Wind* ill. by Michael Hague. Holt, 1990. ISBN 0-8050-1005-X Subj: Animals. Weather – wind.

Burgunder, Rose. *From summer to summer* ill. by author. Viking, 1965. Subj: Poetry, rhyme. Seasons – summer.

Burland, Brian. *St. Nicholas and the tub* ill. by Joseph Low. Holiday, 1964. Subj: Folk and fairy tales. Holidays – Christmas.

Burlingham, Mary. *The climbing book* (Steiner, Charlotte)

Burlson, Joe. *Space colony* ill. by author. Putnam's, 1984. Subj: Format, unusual. Wordless.

Burn, Doris. *The summerfolk* ill. by author. Coward, 1968. Subj: Seasons – summer.

Burningham, Helen Oxenbury *see* Oxenbury, Helen

Burningham, John. *Aldo* ill. by author. Crown, 1992. ISBN 0-517-58699-1 Subj: Emotions – loneliness. Friendship. Imagination – imaginary friends.

Avocado baby ill. by author. Crowell, 1982. Subj: Babies. Family life. Food.

The blanket ill. by author. Crowell, 1976, 1975. Subj: Behavior – losing things. Night.

Borka: the adventures of a goose with no feathers ill. by author. Random House, 1963. Subj: Birds – geese. Character traits – being different. Character traits – meanness. Foreign lands – England.

Cannonball Simp ill. by author. Bobbs-Merrill, 1966. Subj: Animals – dogs. Circus. Clowns, jesters.

Cluck baa ill. by author. Viking, 1985. ISBN 0-670-22580-0 Subj: Animals. Noise, sounds.

Come away from the water, Shirley ill. by author. Crowell, 1977. Subj: Imagination. Pirates. Sea and seashore.

Count up: learning sets ill. by author. Viking, 1983. Subj: Counting, numbers. Format, unusual – board books.

The cupboard ill. by author. Crowell, 1977. Subj: Food.

The dog ill. by author. Crowell, 1975. Subj: Animals – dogs. Format, unusual – board books.

Five down: numbers as signs ill. by author. Viking, 1983. Subj: Counting, numbers. Format, unusual – board books.

The friend ill. by author. Crowell, 1975. Subj: Friendship.

Grandpa ill. by author. Crown, 1985. ISBN 0-517-55643-X Subj: Death. Family life – grandfathers.

Harquin: the fox who went down to the valley ill. by author. Bobbs-Merrill, 1968. Subj: Animals – foxes. Character traits – cleverness. Sports – hunting.

Hey! Get off our train ill. by author. Crown, 1990. ISBN 0-517-57643-0 Subj: Animals. Dreams. Trains.

Humbert, Mister Firkin and the Lord Mayor of London ill. by author. Bobbs-Merrill, 1967. Subj: Animals – horses. Character traits – pride. Emotions – envy, jealousy.

Jangle twang ill. by author. Viking, 1985. ISBN 0-670-40570-5 Subj: Music. Noise, sounds.

John Burningham's ABC ill. by author. Bobbs-Merrill, 1977. Subj: ABC books.

John Burningham's colors ill. by author. Crown, 1986. ISBN 0-517-55961-7 Subj: Concepts – color.

John Patrick Norman McHennessy—the boy who was always late ill. by author. Crown, 1988. ISBN 0-517-56805-5 Subj: Behavior – tardiness. Imagination. School.

Just cats: learning groups ill. by author. Viking, 1983. Subj: Counting, numbers. Format, unusual – board books.

Mr. Gumpy's motor car ill. by author. Macmillan, 1975, 1973. Subj: Automobiles. Weather – rain.

Mr. Gumpy's outing ill. by author. Macmillan, 1971. Subj: Animals. Behavior – fighting, arguing. Boats, ships. Cumulative tales.

Pigs plus: learning addition ill. by author. Viking, 1983. Subj: Counting, numbers. Format, unusual – board books.

Read one: numbers as words ill. by author. Viking, 1983. Subj: Counting, numbers. Format, unusual – board books.

Ride off: learning subtraction ill. by author. Viking, 1983. Subj: Counting, numbers. Format, unusual – board books.

Seasons ill. by author. Bobbs-Merrill, 1970. Subj: Seasons.

The shopping basket ill. by author. Crowell, 1980. Subj: Character traits – cleverness. Counting, numbers. Humor.

Skip trip ill. by author. Viking, 1984. Subj: Activities. Noise, sounds.

Slam bang ill. by author. Viking, 1985. ISBN 0-670-65076-5 Subj: Automobiles. Noise, sounds.

Sniff shout ill. by author. Viking, 1984. Subj: Activities. Noise, sounds.

Time to get out of the bath, Shirley ill. by author. Crowell, 1978. Subj: Activities – bathing. Imagination. Royalty.

Trubloff: the mouse who wanted to play the balalaika ill. by author. Random House, 1965. Subj: Animals – mice. Music. Weather – snow.

Where's Julius? ill. by author. Crown, 1986. ISBN 0-517-56511-0 Subj: Activities – playing. Family life. Food. Imagination.

Wobble pop ill. by author. Viking, 1984. Subj: Activities. Noise, sounds.

Would you rather... ill. by author. Crowell, 1978. Subj: Imagination.

Burns, Diane L. *Arbor Day* ill. by Kathy Rogers. Carolrhoda Books, 1988. ISBN 0-87614-346-X Subj: Trees.

Elephants never forget! ill. by Joan Hanson. Lerner, 1987. ISBN 0-8225-0992-X Subj: Animals – elephants. Riddles.

Burns, Maurice. *Go ducks, go!* ill. by Ron Brooks. Scholastic, 1988. ISBN 0-590-41544-1 Subj: Activities – playing. Country. Family life. Toys.

Burns, Theresa. *You're not my cat* ill. by author. HarperCollins, 1989. ISBN 0-397-32341-7 Subj: Animals – cats. Pets.

Burnstein, John. *Slim Goodbody: what can go wrong and how to be strong* ill. with photos. and drawings. McGraw-Hill, 1978. Subj: Health. Poetry, rhyme.

Burroway, Janet. *The truck on the track* ill. by John Vernon Lord. Bobbs-Merrill, 1970. Subj: Humor. Poetry, rhyme. Trucks.

Bursik, Rose. *Amelia's fantastic flight* ill. by author. Holt, 1992. ISBN 0-8050-1872-7 Subj: Activities – traveling. Airplanes, airports. Imagination.

Burstein, Chaya M. *Joseph and Anna's time capsule* ill. by Nancy Edwards Calder. Simon and Schuster, 1984. Subj: Jewish culture.

Burstein, Fred. *Anna's rain* ill. by Harvey Stevenson. Orchard, 1990. ISBN 0-531-08427-2 Subj: Birds. Family life – fathers. Weather – storms.

Rebecca's nap ill. by Helen Cogancherry. Bradbury Pr., 1988. ISBN 0-02-715620-6 Subj: Family life. Sleep.

Whispering in the park ill. by Helen Cogancherry. Macmillan, 1992. ISBN 0-02-715621-4 Subj: Activities – playing. Fish.

Burt, Olive. *Let's find out about bread* ill. by Mimi Korach. Watts, 1966. Subj: Food. Science.

Burton, Jane. *Animals at home* ill. with photos. Newington Pr., 1991. ISBN 1-878137-12-3 Subj: Animals. Nature.

Animals at night ill. with photos. Newington Pr., 1991. ISBN 1-878137-13-1 Subj: Animals. Nature. Night.

Animals at rest ill. with photos. Newington Pr., 1991. ISBN 1-878137-14-X Subj: Animals. Nature. Sleep.

Animals at work ill. with photos. Newington Pr., 1991. ISBN 1-878137-15-8 Subj: Animals. Nature.

Animals eating ill. with photos. Newington Pr., 1991. ISBN 1-878137-00-X Subj: Animals. Food. Nature.

Animals fighting ill. with photos. Newington Pr., 1991. ISBN 1-878137-03-4 Subj: Animals. Behavior – fighting, arguing. Nature.

Animals keeping clean ill. with photos. Random House, 1989. ISBN 0-394-92261-1 Subj: Animals. Nature.

Animals keeping cool ill. with photos. Random House, 1989. ISBN 0-394-92260-3 Subj: Animals. Nature.

Animals keeping safe ill. with photos. Random House, 1989. ISBN 0-394-92263-8 Subj: Animals. Nature.

Animals keeping warm ill. with photos. Random House, 1989. ISBN 0-394-92262-X Subj: Animals. Nature.

Animals learning ill. with photos. Newington Pr., 1991. ISBN 1-878137-01-8 Subj: Animals. Nature.

Animals talking ill. with photos. Newington Pr., 1991. ISBN 1-878137-02-6 Subj: Animals. Nature. Noise, sounds.

Buffy the barn owl photos. by Jane Burton and Kim Taylor. Gareth Stevens, 1989. ISBN 0-8368-0202-0 Subj: Birds – owls.

Chester the chick photos. by Jane Burton and Kim Taylor. Gareth Stevens, 1989. ISBN 0-8368-0204-7 Subj: Birds – chickens.

Chick [written and ed. by Angela Royston] ill. by Rowan Clifford; photos. by author. Dutton, 1992. ISBN 0-525-67355-5 Subj: Birds – chickens. Birth. Format, unusual. Science.

Dabble the duckling photos. by Jane Burton and Kim Taylor. Gareth Stevens, 1989. ISBN 0-8368-0205-5 Subj: Birds – ducks.

Dazy the guinea pig photos. by Jane Burton and Kim Taylor. Gareth Stevens, 1989. ISBN 0-8368-0206-3 Subj: Animals – guinea pigs.

Freckles the rabbit photos. by Jane Burton and Kim Taylor. Gareth Stevens, 1989. ISBN 0-8368-0208-X Subj: Animals – rabbits.

Kitten [written and ed. by Angela Royston] photos. by author. Dutton, 1991. ISBN 0-525-67343-1 Subj: Animals – cats. Birth. Format, unusual – board books.

Puppy [written and ed. by Angela Royston] photos. by author. Dutton, 1991. ISBN 0-525-67342-3 Subj: Animals – dogs. Birth. Format, unusual – board books.

Trill the fox cub photos. by Jane Burton and Kim Taylor. Gareth Stevens, 1989. ISBN 0-8368-0212-8 Subj: Animals – foxes.

Burton, Marilee Robin. *Aaron awoke: an alphabet story* ill. by author. Harper, 1982. Subj: ABC books. Farms.

The elephant's nest ill. by author. Harper, 1979. Subj: Animals. Humor. Wordless.

Oliver's birthday ill. by author. Harper, 1986. ISBN 0-06-020880-5 Subj: Birds – ostriches. Birthdays.

Tail toes eyes ears nose ill. by author. Harper, 1988. ISBN 0-06-020874-0 Subj: Animals. Problem solving. Riddles.

Burton, Virginia Lee. *Choo choo: the story of a little engine who ran away* ill. by author. Houghton, 1937. Subj: Behavior – running away. Trains.

Katy and the big snow ill. by author. Houghton, 1943. Subj: City. Cumulative tales. Machines. Seasons – winter. Weather – snow.

The little house ill. by author. Houghton, 1939. Subj: Caldecott award book. City. Country. Ecology. Houses. Progress.

Maybelle, the cable car ill. by author. Houghton, 1939. Subj: Cable cars, trolleys. City. Transportation.

Mike Mulligan and his steam shovel ill. by author. Houghton, 1939. Subj: Activities – working. Machines.

Busch, Phyllis S. *Cactus in the desert* ill. by Harriett Barton. Crowell, 1979. Subj: Desert. Plants. Science.

City lots: living things in vacant spots photos. by Arline Strong. Collins-World, 1970. Subj: City. Science.

Lions in the grass: the story of the dandelion, a green plant photos. by Arline Strong. Collins-World, 1968. Subj: Plants. Science.

Once there was a tree: the story of the tree, a changing home for plants and animals photos. by Arline Strong. Collins-World, 1968. Subj: Science. Trees.

Puddles and ponds: living things in watery places photos. by Arline Strong. Collins-World, 1969. Subj: Ecology. Science.

Bush, John. *The cross-with-us rhinoceros* ill. by Paul Geraghty. Dutton, 1988. ISBN 0-525-44411-4 Subj: Animals – rhinoceros. Behavior – misunderstanding. Poetry, rhyme.

The fish who could wish ill. by Korky Paul. Kane/Miller, 1991. ISBN 0-916291-35-9 Subj: Behavior – wishing. Fish. Poetry, rhyme.

Bushey, Jerry. *The barge book* photos. by author. Carolrhoda Books, 1984. Subj: Activities – trading. Boats, ships. Rivers.

Building a fire truck photos. by author. Carolrhoda Books, 1981. Subj: Careers – firefighters. Trucks.

Busy baby photos. sel. by Debby Slier. Macmillan, 1988. ISBN 0-02-688753-3 Subj: Babies. Format, unusual – board books.

Butcher, Julia. *The sheep and the rowan tree* ill. by author. Holt, 1984. Subj: Behavior – wishing. Trees.

Butler, Dorothy. *Another happy tale* ill. by John Hurford. Interlink, 1991. ISBN 0-940793-88-1 Subj: Character traits – luck. Family life. Farms.

A happy tale ill. by John Hurford. Interlink, 1990. ISBN 0-940793-61-X Subj: Activities – traveling. Airplanes, airports. Character traits – luck.

Higgledy, piggledy, hobbledy hoy ill. by Lyn Kriegerd. Greenwillow, 1991. ISBN 0-688-08661-6 Subj: Activities – picnicking. Animals. Parades. Poetry, rhyme.

My brown bear Barney ill. by Elizabeth Fuller. Greenwillow, 1989. ISBN 0-688-08568-7 Subj: School. Toys – teddy bears.

Butler, Stephen. *Henny Penny* (Chicken Little)

Butterfield-Campbell, Jill. *The queen and Rosie Randall* (Oxenbury, Helen)

Butterworth, Nick. *Amanda's butterfly* ill. by author. Delacorte Pr., 1991. ISBN 0-385-30434-X Subj: Character traits – kindness. Fairies. Wordless.

Just like Jasper ill. by Mick Inkpen. Little, 1989. ISBN 0-316-11917-2 Subj: Animals – cats. Shopping. Toys.

My dad is awesome ill. by author. Candlewick Pr., 1992. ISBN 1-56402-033-9 Subj: Behavior – boasting. Family life – fathers.

The Nativity play by Nick Butterworth and Mick Inkpen; ill. by authors. Little, 1985. ISBN 0-316-11903-2 Subj: Holidays – Christmas. School. Theater.

Nice or nasty by Nick Butterworth and Mick Inkpen; ill. by authors. Little, 1987. ISBN 0-316-11915-6 Subj: Concepts – opposites.

Nick Butterworth's book of nursery rhymes ill. by selector. Viking, 1991. ISBN 0-670-83551-X Subj: Nursery rhymes.

One blowy night ill. by author. Little, 1992. ISBN 0-316-11919-9 Subj: Animals. Character traits – kindness to animals. Character traits – optimism. Weather – storms. Weather – wind.

One snowy night ill. by author. Little, 1990. ISBN 0-316-11918-0 Subj: Animals. Character traits – kindness to animals. Night. Weather – snow.

Buxbaum, Susan Kovacs. *Splash! all about baths* by Susan Kovacs Buxbaum and Rita Golden Gelman; ill. by Maryann Cocca-Leffler. Little, 1987. ISBN 0-316-30726-2 Subj: Activities – bathing.

Byars, Betsy Cromer. *Go and hush the baby* ill. by Emily Arnold McCully. Viking, 1971. Subj: Babies. Family life. Games.

The groober ill. by author. Harper, 1967. Subj: Animals. Behavior – dissatisfaction.

Byers, Rinda M. *Mycca's baby* ill. by David Tamura. Orchard, 1990. ISBN 0-531-08428-0 Subj: Babies. Family life.

Byfield, Barbara Ninde. *The haunted churchbell* ill. by author. Doubleday, 1971. Subj: Character traits – cleverness. Emotions – fear. Humor.

Byrd, Robert. *Marcella was bored* ill. by author. Dutton, 1985. ISBN 0-525-44156-5 Subj: Animals – cats. Behavior – running away. Family life.

Byrne, David. *Stay up late* ill. by Maira Kalman. Viking, 1987. ISBN 0-670-81895-X Subj: Babies. Family life. Sibling rivalry. Songs.

Cahill, Chris. *Bear magic* ill. by Mitchell Rose and Ruth Young. Schneider Educational, 1990. ISBN 1-877779-00-8 Subj: Animals – bears. Format, unusual – board books. Poetry, rhyme. Puppets.

Bunny magic ill. by Mitchell Rose and Ruth Young. Schneider Educational, 1990. ISBN 1-877779-02-4 Subj: Animals – rabbits. Format, unusual – board books. Poetry, rhyme. Puppets.

Spider magic ill. by Mitchell Rose and Ruth Young. Schneider Educational, 1990. ISBN 1-877779-03-2 Subj: Format, unusual. Format, unusual – board books. Puppets. Spiders.

Turtle magic ill. by Mitchell Rose and Ruth Young. Schneider Educational, 1990. ISBN 1-877779-01-6 Subj: Format, unusual. Format, unusual – board books. Puppets. Reptiles – turtles, tortoises.

Caines, Jeannette. *Abby* ill. by Steven Kellogg. Harper, 1973. Subj: Adoption. Ethnic groups in the U.S. – Afro-Americans. Family life. Sibling rivalry.

Chilly stomach ill. by Pat Cummings. Harper, 1986. ISBN 0-06-020977-1 Subj: Child abuse. Emotions – fear. Family life.

Daddy ill. by Ronald Himler. Harper, 1977. Subj: Divorce. Ethnic groups in the U.S. – Afro-Americans. Family life – fathers.

I need a lunch box ill. by Pat Cummings. Harper, 1988. ISBN 0-06-020985-2 Subj: Emotions – envy, jealousy. Family life.

Just us women ill. by Pat Cummings. Harper, 1982. Subj: Activities – traveling. Automobiles. Ethnic groups in the U.S. – Afro-Americans.

Window wishing ill. by Kevin Brooks. Harper, 1980. Subj: Family life – grandmothers.

Cairo, Jasmine. *Our brother has Down's syndrome* (Cairo, Shelley)

Cairo, Shelley. *Our brother has Down's syndrome: an introduction for children* by Shelley, Jasmine and Tara Cairo; photos. by Irene McNeil; designed by Helmut W. Weyerstrahs. Firefly Pr., 1985. ISBN 0-920303-30-7 Subj: Family life. Handicaps.

Cairo, Tara. *Our brother has Down's syndrome* (Cairo, Shelley)

Cakes and custard : *children's rhymes* comp. by Brian W. Alderson; ill. by Helen Oxenbury. Morrow, 1975, 1974. Subj: Nursery rhymes.

Caldecott, Randolph. *Panjandrum picture book* ill. by author. Warne, 1885. Subj: Nursery rhymes.

The Queen of Hearts ill. by author. Warne, 1881. Subj: Nursery rhymes.

The Randolph Caldecott treasury sel. and ed. by Elizabeth T. Billington; ill. by author. Warne, 1978. Subj: Folk and fairy tales.

Randolph Caldecott's favorite nursery rhymes ill. by author. Castle Books, 1980. Subj: Nursery rhymes.

Randolph Caldecott's John Gilpin and other stories ill. by author. Warne, 1977. The diverting history of John Gilpin.—The house that Jack built.—The frog he would a-wooing go.—The milkmaid Subj: Nursery rhymes.

Randolph Caldecott's picture book, no. 2 ill. by author. Warne, 1879. Subj: Nursery rhymes.

Randolph Caldecott's picture book, no. 1 ill. by author. Warne, 1879. Subj: Nursery rhymes.

Sing a song of sixpence (Mother Goose)

The three jovial huntsmen ill. by author. Warne, 1880. Subj: Nursery rhymes.

Calder, Lyn. *Walt Disney's Alice's tea party* ill. by Jesse Clay. Walt Disney, 1992. ISBN 1-56282-199-7 Subj: Activities – making things. Parties.

Calder, S. J. *If you were a bird* ill. by Cornelius Van Wright. Silver Pr., 1989. ISBN 0-671-68595-3 Subj: Birds – robins.

If you were a cat ill. by Cornelius Van Wright. Silver Pr., 1989. ISBN 0-671-68598-8 Subj: Animals – cats. Pets.

If you were a fish ill. by Cornelius Van Wright. Silver Pr., 1989. ISBN 0-671-68596-1 Subj: Aquariums. Fish.

If you were an ant ill. by Cornelius Van Wright. Silver Pr., 1989. ISBN 0-671-68597-X Subj: Insects – ants.

Calders, Pere. *Brush* tr. from Spanish by Marguerite Feitlowitz; ill. by Carme Solé Vendrell. Kane/Miller, 1986. ISBN 0-916291-05-7 Subj: Crime. Family life. Imagination. Pets.

Caldwell, Mary. *Morning, rabbit, morning* ill. by Ann Schweninger. Harper, 1982. Subj: Animals – rabbits. Morning.

Calhoun, Mary. *Audubon cat* ill. by Susan Bonners. Morrow, 1981. Subj: Animals – cats. Food. Problem solving.

Cross-country cat ill. by Erick Ingraham. Morrow, 1979. Subj: Animals – cats. Character traits – cleverness. Sports – skiing.

Euphonia and the flood ill. by Simms Taback. Parents, 1976. Subj: Animals. Boats, ships. Character traits – helpfulness. Weather – rain.

The goblin under the stairs ill. by Janet McCaffery. Morrow, 1968. Subj: Behavior – misbehavior. Folk and fairy tales. Goblins.

High-wire Henry ill. by Erick Ingraham. Morrow, 1991. ISBN 0-688-08984-4 Subj: Animals – cats. Animals – dogs. Emotions – envy, jealousy. Pets.

Hot-air Henry ill. by Erick Ingraham. Morrow, 1981. Subj: Activities – ballooning. Animals – cats.

Houn' dog ill. by Roger Antoine Duvoisin. Morrow, 1959. Subj: Animals – dogs. Animals – foxes. Sports – hunting.

The hungry leprechaun ill. by Roger Antoine Duvoisin. Harber, 1962. Subj: Elves and little people. Food. Foreign lands – Ireland. Holidays – St. Patrick's Day.

Jack and the whoopee wind ill. by Dick Gackenbach. Morrow, 1987. ISBN 0-688-06138-9 Subj: Character traits – cleverness. Machines. Weather – wind.

Jack the wise and the Cornish cuckoos ill. by Tasha Tudor. Morrow, 1978. Subj: Character traits – helpfulness. Folk and fairy tales.

Mrs. Dog's own house ill. by Janet McCaffery. Morrow, 1972. Subj: Animals – dogs. Houses.

The nine lives of Homer C. Cat ill. by Roger Antoine Duvoisin. Morrow, 1961. Subj: Animals – cats. Behavior – imitation. Humor.

Old man Whickutt's donkey ill. by Tomie de Paola. Parents, 1975. Subj: Animals – donkeys. Character traits – perseverance. Folk and fairy tales. Humor.

The pixy and the lazy housewife ill. by Janet McCaffery. Morrow, 1969. Subj: Behavior – trickery. Elves and little people. Folk and fairy tales. Foreign lands – England.

The runaway brownie ill. by Janet McCaffery. Morrow, 1967. Subj: Character traits – pride. Elves and little people. Folk and fairy tales. Foreign lands – Scotland.

The thieving dwarfs ill. by Janet McCaffery. Morrow, 1967. Subj: Character traits – kindness. Elves and little people. Folk and fairy tales. Foreign lands – Germany.

The traveling ball of string ill. by Janet McCaffery. Morrow, 1969. Subj: Behavior – saving things. Humor. String.

While I sleep ill. by Ed Young. Morrow, 1992. ISBN 0-688-08201-7 Subj: Bedtime. Sleep.

The witch of Hissing Hill ill. by Janet McCaffery. Morrow, 1964. Subj: Animals – cats. Holidays – Halloween. Witches.

The witch who lost her shadow ill. by Trinka Hakes Noble. Harper, 1979. Subj: Animals – cats. Character traits – loyalty. Emotions. Friendship. Witches.

The witch's pig: a Cornish folktale ill. by Tasha Tudor. Morrow, 1977. Subj: Animals – pigs. Folk and fairy tales. Foreign lands – England. Witches.

Wobble the witch cat ill. by Roger Antoine Duvoisin. Morrow, 1958. Subj: Animals – cats. Holidays – Halloween. Witches.

Callan, Elizabeth Koda. *Good luck pony* ill. by author. Workman, 1990. ISBN 0-89480-859-1 Subj: Animals – horses. Character traits – confidence. Character traits – luck. Emotions – fear.

Callen, Larry. *Dashiel and the night* ill. by Leslie Holt Morrill. Dutton, 1981. Subj: Bedtime. Dreams. Imagination. Insects – fireflies. Night.

Calloway, Northern J. *Northern J. Calloway presents Super-vroomer!* ill. by Sammis McLean. Doubleday, 1978. Written by Carol Hall; conceived by Northern J. Calloway Subj: Ethnic groups in the U.S. – Afro-Americans. Sports – racing.

Calmenson, Stephanie. *All aboard the goodnight train* ill. by Normand Chartier. Grosset, 1984. ISBN 0-448-11226-4 Subj: Animals. Bedtime. Lullabies.

The birthday hat ill. by Susan Gantner. Grosset, 1983. Subj: Animals – hippopotami. Birthdays. Shopping.

Dinner at the Panda Palace ill. by Nadine Bernard Westcott. HarperCollins, 1991. ISBN 0-06-021011-7 Subj: Animals. Animals – pandas. Counting, numbers. Poetry, rhyme.

The kindergarten book ill. by Beth Lee Weiner. Grosset, 1983. Subj: Activities. Animals. School.

Never take a pig to lunch and other funny poems about animals ill. by Hilary Knight. Doubleday, 1982. Subj: Animals – pigs. Poetry, rhyme.

Wanted: warm, furry friend ill. by Amy Schwartz. Macmillan, 1990. ISBN 0-02-716390-3 Subj: Animals – rabbits. Friendship. Pen pals.

What am I? ill. by Karen Gundersheimer. HarperCollins, 1989. ISBN 0-06-020998-4 Subj: Riddles.

Where is Grandma Potamus? ill. by Susan Gantner. Grosset, 1983. Subj: Animals – hippopotami. Behavior – lost.

Where will the animals stay? ill. by Ellen Appleby. Parents, 1983. Subj: Animals. Houses. Poetry, rhyme. Zoos.

Zip, whiz, zoom! ill. by Dorothy Stott. Little, 1992. ISBN 0-316-12478-8 Subj: Activities – traveling. Birthdays. Family life – grandmothers. Transportation.

Calvert, Elinor H. *see* Lasell, Fen

Cameron, Ann. *Harry (the monster)* ill. by Jeanette Winter. Pantheon, 1980. Subj: Bedtime. Character traits – bravery. Emotions – fear. Monsters.

Cameron, John. *If mice could fly* ill. by author. Atheneum, 1979. Subj: Animals – cats. Animals – mice. Character traits – cleverness. Poetry, rhyme.

Cameron, Polly. *The cat who thought he was a tiger* ill. by author. Coward, 1956. Subj: Animals – cats. Circus.

A child's book of nonsense ill. by author. Coward, 1960. Subj: Humor. Poetry, rhyme.

"I can't," said the ant: a second book of nonsense ill. by author. Coward, 1961. Subj: Family life. Insects – ants. Participation. Poetry, rhyme.

Campbell, Alison. *Are you asleep, rabbit?* by Alison Campbell and Julia Barton; ill. by Gill Scriven. Lothrop, 1990. ISBN 0-688-09491-0 Subj: Animals – rabbits. Bedtime.

Campbell, Ann. *Let's find out about boats* ill. by author. Watts, 1967. Subj: Boats, ships.

Let's find out about color ill. by author. Watts, 1966. Subj: Concepts – color.

Campbell, M. Rudolph. *The talking crocodile* ill. by Judy Piussi-Campbell. Atheneum, 1968. Adapt. from Krokodil by Fyodor Dostoyevsky Subj: Foreign lands – Russia. Reptiles – alligators, crocodiles.

Campbell, Rod. *Buster's afternoon* ill. by author. Harper, 1984. ISBN 0-911745-74-2 Subj: Character traits – curiosity. Flowers. Format, unusual – toy and movable books. Nature.

Buster's morning ill. by author. Harper, 1984. ISBN 0-911745-73-4 Subj: Character traits – curiosity. Format, unusual – toy and movable books. Houses. Toys.

Dear zoo ill. by author. Four Winds Pr., 1984. ISBN 0-02-716440-3 Subj: Animals. Format, unusual – toy and movable books. Zoos.

Henry's busy day ill. by author. Viking, 1984. ISBN 0-670-80024-4 Subj: Animals – dogs. Behavior – misbehavior. Format, unusual.

It's mine ill. by author. Barron's, 1988. ISBN 0-8120-5921-2 Subj: Anatomy. Animals. Format, unusual – toy and movable books.

Look inside! All kinds of places ill. by author. Harper, 1983. Subj: Format, unusual – board books. Wordless.

Look inside! Land, sea, air ill. by author. Harper, 1983. Subj: Format, unusual – board books. Transportation. Wordless.

Misty's mischief ill. by author. Viking, 1985. ISBN 0-670-80149-6 Subj: Animals – cats. Behavior – misbehavior. Format, unusual.

Oh dear! ill. by author. Four Winds Pr., 1986. ISBN 0-590-07944-1 Subj: Eggs. Farms. Format, unusual – toy and movable books.

Campbell, Wayne. *What a catastrophe!* ill. by Eileen Christelow. Bradbury Pr., 1987. ISBN 0-02-716420-9 Subj: Family life. Frogs and toads.

Canfield, Jane White. *The frog prince: a true story* ill. by Winn Smith. Harper, 1970. Subj: Frogs and toads. Royalty – princes.

Swan cove ill. by Jo Polseno. Harper, 1978. Subj: Birds – swans.

Canning, Kate. *A painted tale* ill. by author. Barron's, 1979. Subj: Animals – tigers. Art. Behavior – imitation. Zoos.

Cantieni, Benita. *Little Elephant and Big Mouse* tr. by Oliver Gadsby; ill. by Fred Gächter. Alphabet Pr., 1981. Orig. title: Der Kleine Elefant und die Grosse Maus Subj: Animals – elephants. Animals – mice. Concepts – size.

Caple, Kathy. *The biggest nose* ill. by author. Houghton, 1985. ISBN 0-395-36894-4 Subj: Anat-

omy – noses. Animals – elephants. Character traits – being different. School.

The coolest place in town ill. by author. Houghton, 1990. ISBN 0-395-51523-8 Subj: Animals – hippopotami. Family life – brothers. Family life – sisters.

Fox and bear ill. by author. Houghton, 1992. ISBN 0-395-55634-1 Subj: Animals – bears. Animals – foxes. Friendship.

Harry's smile ill. by author. Houghton, 1987. ISBN 0-395-43417-3 Subj: Friendship. Pen pals. Self-concept.

Inspector Aardvark and the perfect cake ill. by author. Windmill, 1980. Subj: Animals – aardvarks. Careers – bakers.

The purse ill. by author. Houghton, 1986. ISBN 0-395-41852-6 Subj: Activities – working. Family life. Money.

Caprio, Annie De *see* DeCaprio, Annie

Caputo, Robert. *More than just pets: why people study animals* photos. by author. Coward, 1980. Subj: Anatomy. Ecology.

Cardoza, Lois S. *see* Duncan, Lois

Carey, Helen H. *Adopted* (Greenberg, Judith E.)

Carey, Mary. *The owl who loved sunshine* ill. by Joe Giordano. Golden Pr., 1977. Subj: Birds – owls. Character traits – individuality. Character traits – kindness to animals.

Carey, Valerie Scho. *The devil and mother Crump* ill. by Arnold Lobel. Harper, 1987. ISBN 0-06-020983-6 Subj: Behavior – trickery. Character traits – meanness. Devil. Folk and fairy tales.

Harriet and William and the terrible creature ill. by Lynne Cherry. Dutton, 1985. ISBN 0-525-44154-9 Subj: Animals – squirrels. Character traits – helpfulness. Monsters. Space and space ships.

Maggie Mab and the bogey beast ill. by Johanna Westerman. Arcade, 1992. ISBN 1-55970-155-2 Subj: Character traits – optimism. Folk and fairy tales. Poverty.

Carigiet, Alois. *Anton the goatherd* ill. by author. Walck, 1966. Subj: Animals – goats. Behavior – lost.

The pear tree, the birch tree and the barberry bush ill. by author. Walck, 1967. Subj: Foreign lands – Switzerland. Trees.

Carle, Eric. *Do you want to be my friend?* ill. by author. Crowell, 1971. Subj: Animals – mice. Friendship. Wordless.

The grouchy ladybug ill. by author. Crowell, 1977. English title: The bad-tempered ladybird Subj: Behavior. Insects – ladybugs. Time.

Have you seen my cat? ill. by author. Watts, 1973. Subj: Animals – cats. Behavior – lost.

A house for Hermit Crab ill. by author. Picture Book Studio, 1988. ISBN 0-88708-056-1 Subj: Crustacea. Sea and seashore.

I see a song ill. by author. Crowell, 1973. Subj: Music. Wordless.

The mixed-up chameleon ill. by author. Crowell, 1975; rev. ed. 1984. Subj: Character traits – being different. Concepts – color. Reptiles – lizards. Self-concept.

My very first book of colors ill. by author. HarperCollins, 1985. ISBN 0-694-00011-6 Subj: Concepts – color. Format, unusual.

My very first book of food ill. by author. Crowell, 1986. ISBN 0-694-00130-9 Subj: Food. Format, unusual – toy and movable books.

My very first book of growth ill. by author. Crowell, 1986. ISBN 0-694-00094-9 Subj: Behavior – growing up. Format, unusual.

My very first book of heads and tails ill. by author. Crowell, 1986. ISBN 0-694-00128-7 Subj: Anatomy. Format, unusual – toy and movable books.

My very first book of homes ill. by author. Crowell, 1986. ISBN 0-694-00092-2 Subj: Format, unusual. Houses.

My very first book of motion ill. by author. Crowell, 1986. ISBN 0-694-00093-0 Subj: Concepts. Format, unusual.

My very first book of numbers ill. by author. HarperCollins, 1985. ISBN 0-694-00012-4 Subj: Counting, numbers. Format, unusual.

My very first book of shapes ill. by author. HarperCollins, 1985. ISBN 0-694-00013-2 Subj: Concepts – shape. Format, unusual.

My very first book of sounds ill. by author. Crowell, 1986. ISBN 0-694-00131-7 Subj: Format, unusual – toy and movable books. Noise, sounds.

My very first book of tools ill. by author. Crowell, 1986. ISBN 0-694-00129-5 Subj: Format, unusual – toy and movable books. Tools.

My very first book of touch ill. by author. Crowell, 1986. ISBN 0-694-00095-7 Subj: Format, unusual. Senses – touching.

My very first book of words ill. by author. HarperCollins, 1985. ISBN 0-694-00014-0 Subj: Format, unusual. Language.

1, 2, 3 to the zoo ill. by author. Collins-World, 1969. Subj: Animals. Counting, numbers. Zoos.

Pancakes, pancakes ill. by author. Knopf, 1970. Subj: Cumulative tales. Food.

Papa, please get the moon for me ill. by author. Alphabet Pr., 1986. ISBN 0-88708-026-X Subj: Format, unusual – toy and movable books. Moon.

The rooster who set out to see the world ill. by author. Watts, 1972. Subj: Activities – traveling. Birds – chickens. Counting, numbers.

Rooster's off to see the world ill. by author. Picture Book Studio, 1987. ISBN 0-88708-042-1 Subj: Activities – traveling. Birds – chickens. Counting, numbers.

The secret birthday message ill. by author. Crowell, 1972. Subj: Birthdays. Format, unusual – toy and movable books.

The tiny seed ill. by author Rev. ed. Picture Book Studio, 1987. ISBN 0-88708-015-4 Subj: Plants. Seasons. Seeds.

Twelve tales from Æsop ill. by adapt. Putnam's, 1980. Subj: Folk and fairy tales.

The very busy spider ill. by author. Philomel, 1985. ISBN 0-399-21166-7 Subj: Animals. Spiders.

The very hungry caterpillar ill. by author. Collins-World, 1969. Subj: Days of the week, months of the year. Format, unusual. Insects – butterflies, caterpillars.

The very quiet cricket ill. by author. Putnam, 1990. ISBN 0-399-21885-8 Subj: Format, unusual. Insects – crickets. Noise, sounds.

Walter the baker: an old story ill. by author. Knopf, 1972. Subj: Activities – working. Careers – bakers. Food.

Watch out! A giant! ill. by author. Collins-World, 1978. Subj: Format, unusual – toy and movable books. Giants.

Carleton, Barbee Oliver. *Benny and the bear* ill. by Dagmar Wilson. Follett, 1960. Subj: Animals – bears. Character traits – bravery.

Carlisle, Clark *see* Holding, James

Carlisle, Madelyn. *Bridges* (Carlisle, Norman)

Carlisle, Norman. *Bridges* by Norman and Madelyn Carlisle; ill. with photos. Childrens Pr., 1983. Subj: Bridges.

Carlson, Maria. *Peter and the wolf* (Prokofiev, Sergei Sergeievitch)

Carlson, Nancy. *Arnie and the new kid* ill. by author. Viking, 1990. ISBN 0-670-82499-2 Subj: Animals. Friendship. Handicaps – physical. School.

Arnie and the stolen markers ill. by author. Puffin, 1989. ISBN 0-14-050707-8 Subj: Animals. Behavior – stealing. Crime.

Bunnies and their hobbies ill. by author. Carolrhoda Books, 1984. Subj: Activities. Animals – rabbits.

Bunnies and their sports ill. by author. Viking, 1987. ISBN 0-670-81109-2 Subj: Animals – rabbits. Sports.

Harriet and the garden ill. by author. Carolrhoda Books, 1982. Subj: Animals – dogs. Problem solving.

Harriet and the roller coaster ill. by author. Carolrhoda Books, 1982. Subj: Animals – dogs. Character traits – bravery.

Harriet and Walt ill. by author. Carolrhoda Books, 1982. Subj: Animals – dogs. Sibling rivalry.

Harriet's Halloween candy ill. by author. Carolrhoda Books, 1982. Subj: Animals – dogs. Behavior – greed.

Harriet's recital ill. by author. Carolrhoda Books, 1982. Subj: Animals – dogs. Emotions – fear.

I like me ill. by author. Viking, 1988. ISBN 0-670-82062-8 Subj: Character traits – individuality. Self-concept.

Louanne Pig in making the team ill. by author. Carolrhoda Books, 1985. ISBN 0-87614-281-1 Subj: Animals. Friendship. School. Sports – football.

Loudmouth George and the big race ill. by author. Carolrhoda Books, 1983. Subj: Animals – rabbits. Behavior – boasting. Emotions – embarrassment.

Loudmouth George and the cornet ill. by author. Carolrhoda Books, 1983. Subj: Animals – rabbits. Behavior – boasting.

Loudmouth George and the fishing trip ill. by author. Carolrhoda Books, 1983. Subj: Animals – rabbits. Behavior – boasting.

Loudmouth George and the new neighbors ill. by author. Carolrhoda Books, 1983. Subj: Animals – rabbits. Behavior – boasting. Prejudice.

Loudmouth George and the sixth-grade bully ill. by author. Carolrhoda Books, 1983. Subj: Animals – rabbits. Behavior – boasting. Behavior – bullying. Behavior – stealing.

The mysterious Valentine ill. by author. Carolrhoda Books, 1985. ISBN 0-87614-282-X Subj: Animals – pigs. Holidays – Valentine's Day.

The perfect family ill. by author. Carolrhoda Books, 1985. ISBN 0-87614-282-X Subj: Animals – pigs. Family life. Sibling rivalry.

Poor Carl ill. by author. Viking, 1989. ISBN 0-670-81774-0 Subj: Animals – dogs. Emotions – envy, jealousy.

Take time to relax ill. by author. Viking, 1991. ISBN 0-670-83287-1 Subj: Animals – beavers. Family life. Poetry, rhyme. Weather – snow.

The talent show ill. by author. Carolrhoda Books, 1985. ISBN 0-87614-284-6 Subj: Animals. Theater.

What if it never stops raining? ill. by author. Viking, 1992. ISBN 0-670-81775-9 Subj: Behavior – worrying. Weather – rain.

Witch lady ill. by author. Carolrhoda Books, 1985. ISBN 0-87614-283-8 Subj: Animals – pigs. Emotions – fear. Witches.

Carlson, Natalie Savage. *Marie Louise and Christophe at the carnival* ill. by José Aruego and Ariane Dewey. Scribner's, 1981. Subj: Animals – mongooses. Reptiles – snakes.

Marie Louise's heyday ill. by José Aruego and Ariane Dewey. Scribner's, 1975. Subj: Activities – baby-sitting. Animals – mongooses. Animals – possums.

Runaway Marie Louise ill. by José Aruego and Ariane Dewey. Scribner's, 1977. Subj: Animals – mongooses. Behavior – running away.

Spooky and the bad luck raven ill. by Andrew Glass. Lothrop, 1988. ISBN 0-688-07651-3 Subj: Animals – cats. Witches.

Spooky and the ghost cat ill. by Andrew Glass. Lothrop, 1985. ISBN 0-688-04317-8 Subj: Animals – cats. Holidays – Halloween. Magic.

Spooky and the witch's goat ill. by Andrew Glass. Lothrop, 1989. ISBN 0-688-08541-5 Subj: Animals – cats. Animals – goats. Magic. Witches.

Spooky and the wizard's bats ill. by Andrew Glass. Lothrop, 1986. ISBN 0-688-06281-4 Subj: Animals – bats. Animals – cats. Holidays – Halloween. Magic. Witches. Wizards.

Spooky night ill. by Andrew Glass. Lothrop, 1982. Subj: Animals – cats. Holidays – Halloween. Pets. Witches.

Surprise in the mountains ill. by Elise Primavera. Harper, 1983. Subj: Animals. Holidays – Christmas. Seasons – winter.

Time for the white egret ill. by Charles Robinson. Scribner's, 1978. Subj: Animals – bulls, cows. Birds – egrets. Farms.

Carlstrom, Nancy White. *Baby-O* ill. by Suçie Stevenson. Little, 1992. ISBN 0-316-12851-1 Subj: Cumulative tales. Family life. Foreign lands – Caribbean Islands. Stores.

Better not get wet, Jesse Bear ill. by Bruce Degen. Macmillan, 1988. ISBN 0-02-717280-5 Subj: Animals – bears. Poetry, rhyme.

Blow me a kiss, Miss Lilly ill. by Amy Schwartz. HarperCollins, 1990. ISBN 0-06-021013-3 Subj: Death. Friendship. Old age.

Goodbye geese ill. by Ed Young. Putnam, 1991. ISBN 0-399-21832-7 Subj: Character traits – questioning. Family life – fathers. Poetry, rhyme. Seasons – winter.

Graham cracker animals 1-2-3 ill. by John Sandford. Macmillan, 1989. ISBN 0-02-717270-8 Subj: Counting, numbers. Poetry, rhyme.

Grandpappy ill. by Laurel Molk. Little, 1990. ISBN 0-316-12855-4 Subj: Family life – grandfathers.

Heather hiding ill. by Dennis Nolan. Macmillan, 1990. ISBN 0-02-717370-4 Subj: Activities – playing. Family life.

I'm not moving, mama! ill. by Thor Wickstrom. Macmillan, 1990. ISBN 0-02-717286-4 Subj: Animals – mice. Moving.

It's about time, Jesse Bear ill. by Bruce Degen. Macmillan, 1990. ISBN 0-02-717351-8 Subj: Animals – bears. Poetry, rhyme.

Jesse Bear, what will you wear? ill. by Bruce Degen. Macmillan, 1986. ISBN 0-02-717350-X Subj: Animals – bears. Clothing. Family life.

Kiss your sister, Rose Marie ill. by Thor Wickstrom. Macmillan, 1992. ISBN 0-02-717271-6

Subj: Animals – rabbits. Babies. Family life – sisters. Poetry, rhyme. Sibling rivalry.

The moon came too ill. by Stella Ormai. Macmillan, 1987. ISBN 0-02-717380-1 Subj: Activities – vacationing. Behavior – collecting things. Family life – grandmothers. Poetry, rhyme.

Moose in the garden ill. by Lisa Desimini. HarperCollins, 1990. ISBN 0-06-021014-1 Subj: Animals – moose. Food. Gardens, gardening.

No nap for Benjamin Badger ill. by Dennis Nolan. Macmillan, 1991. ISBN 0-02-717285-6 Subj: Animals – badgers. Poetry, rhyme. Sleep.

Northern lullaby ill. by Leo and Diane Dillon. Putnam, 1992. ISBN 0-399-21806-8 Subj: Bedtime. Eskimos. Lullabies. Nature. Poetry, rhyme.

The snow speaks ill. by Jane Dyer. Little, 1992. ISBN 0-316-12861-9 Subj: Country. Seasons – winter. Weather – snow.

Who gets the sun out of bed? ill. by David McPhail. Little, 1992. ISBN 0-316-12862-7 Subj: Animals – rabbits. Moon. Morning. Pets. Sun.

Wild wild sunflower child Anna ill. by Jerry Pinkney. Macmillan, 1987. ISBN 0-02-717360-7 Subj: Ethnic groups in the U.S. – Afro-Americans. Poetry, rhyme.

Carmi, Giora. *And Shira imagined* ill. by author. Jewish Pub. Soc., 1988. ISBN 0-8276-0288-X Subj: Activities – traveling. Family life. Foreign lands – Israel. Imagination.

Carrick, Carol. *The accident* ill. by Donald Carrick. Seabury Pr., 1976. Subj: Animals – dogs. Death. Pets.

Beach bird by Carol and Donald Carrick; ill. by Donald Carrick. Dial Pr., 1973. Subj: Birds – sea gulls. Sea and seashore.

Ben and the porcupine ill. by Donald Carrick. Houghton, 1981. Subj: Animals – dogs. Animals – porcupines. Problem solving.

Big old bones: a dinosaur tale ill. by Donald Carrick. Houghton, 1992. ISBN 0-395-61582-8 Subj: Dinosaurs.

The blue lobster: a life cycle by Carol and Donald Carrick; ill. by Donald Carrick. Dial Pr., 1975. Subj: Crustacea. Science.

The brook by Carol and Donald Carrick; ill. by Donald Carrick. Macmillan, 1967. Subj: Rivers.

A clearing in the forest by Carol and Donald Carrick; ill. by Donald Carrick. Dial Pr., 1970. Subj: Ecology. Forest, woods. Pets.

The climb ill. by Donald Carrick. Houghton, 1980. Subj: Activities – baby-sitting. Sports.

The crocodiles still wait ill. by Donald Carrick. Houghton, 1980. Subj: Dinosaurs. Reptiles – alligators, crocodiles. Science.

Dark and full of secrets ill. by Donald Carrick. Houghton, 1984. Subj: Emotions – fear. Sports – skin diving.

The foundling ill. by Donald Carrick. Seabury Pr., 1977. Subj: Animals – dogs. Pets.

The highest balloon on the common by Carol and Donald Carrick; ill. by Donald Carrick. Greenwillow, 1977. Subj: Behavior – lost. Fairs. Toys – balloons.

In the moonlight, waiting ill. by Donald Carrick. Clarion, 1990. ISBN 0-89919-867-8 Subj: Animals. Birth. Farms.

Left behind ill. by Donald Carrick. Clarion, 1988. ISBN 0-89919-535-0 Subj: Behavior – lost. City. School.

Octopus ill. by Donald Carrick. Seabury Pr., 1978. Subj: Octopuses. Science.

The old barn ill. by Donald Carrick. Bobbs-Merrill, 1966. Subj: Barns. Seasons.

Old Mother Witch ill. by Donald Carrick. Seabury Pr., 1975. Subj: Behavior – misunderstanding. Character traits – meanness. Holidays – Halloween. Illness.

Patrick's dinosaurs ill. by Donald Carrick. Houghton, 1983. Subj: Animals. Dinosaurs. Imagination. Science. Zoos.

A rabbit for Easter ill. by Donald Carrick. Greenwillow, 1979. Subj: Animals – rabbits. Behavior – carelessness. Holidays – Easter.

Sleep out ill. by Donald Carrick. Seabury Pr., 1973. Subj: Behavior – solitude. Camps, camping. Weather – rain.

Two coyotes ill. by Donald Carrick. Houghton, 1982. Subj: Animals – coyotes. Science. Seasons – winter.

The washout ill. by Donald Carrick. Seabury Pr., 1978. Subj: Activities – vacationing. Boats, ships. Weather – rain.

What happened to Patrick's dinosaurs? ill. by Donald Carrick. Houghton, 1986. ISBN 0-89919-406-0 Subj: Dinosaurs. Imagination.

Carrick, Donald. *Beach bird* (Carrick, Carol)

The blue lobster (Carrick, Carol)

The brook (Carrick, Carol)

A clearing in the forest (Carrick, Carol)

The deer in the pasture ill. by author. Greenwillow, 1976. Subj: Animals – bulls, cows. Animals – deer. Farms. Sports – hunting.

Harold and the giant knight ill. by author. Houghton, 1982. Subj: Farms. Knights.

Harold and the great stag ill. by author. Clarion, 1988. ISBN 0-89919-514-8 Subj: Animals – deer. Foreign lands – England. Forest, woods. Middle ages. Sports – hunting.

The highest balloon on the common (Carrick, Carol)

Milk ill. by author. Greenwillow, 1985. ISBN 0-688-04823-4 Subj: Animals – bulls, cows. Farms. Food.

Morgan and the artist ill. by author. Clarion, 1985. ISBN 0-89919-300-5 Subj: Activities – painting. Art. Careers – artists.

Carrick, Malcolm. *The extraordinary hatmaker* ill. by author. Grosset, 1977. Subj: Clothing – hats.

I can squash elephants! a Masai tale about monsters ill. by author. Viking, 1978. Subj: Animals. Folk and fairy tales. Foreign lands – Africa. Insects – butterflies, caterpillars. Monsters.

Carrier, Lark. *A Christmas promise* ill. by author. Picture Book Studio, 1986. ISBN 0-88708-032-4 Subj: Animals. Friendship. Holidays – Christmas. Trees.

Scout and Cody ill. by author. Picture Book Studio, 1987. ISBN 0-88708-013-8 Subj: Activities – playing. Animals – dogs. Behavior – growing up. Imagination.

There was a hill... ill. by author. Picture Book Studio, 1985. ISBN 0-907234-70-4 Subj: Format, unusual. Imagination.

Carroll, Kathleen Sullivan. *One red rooster* ill. by Suzette Barbier. Houghton, 1992. ISBN 0-395-60195-9 Subj: Animals. Concepts – color. Counting, numbers. Poetry, rhyme.

Carroll, Latrobe. *Pet tale* (Carroll, Ruth)

Carroll, Lewis. *Jabberwocky* ill. by Graeme Base. Abrams, 1989. ISBN 0-8109-1150-7 Subj: Humor. Mythical creatures. Poetry, rhyme.

Jabberwocky ill. from Disney archives. Walt Disney, 1992. ISBN 1-56282-246-2 Subj: Humor. Mythical creatures. Poetry, rhyme.

Jabberwocky ill. by Jane Breskin Zalben. Warne, 1977. Subj: Humor. Mythical creatures. Poetry, rhyme.

The nursery "Alice" intro. by Martin Gardner; ill. by Sir John Tenniel. McGraw-Hill, 1966. A facsimile of the 2d ed. (1890) of Carroll's adapt. of Alice's Adventures in Wonderland Subj: Dreams. Imagination.

The walrus and the carpenter ill. by Julian Doyle. Merrimack, 1986. ISBN 0-88162-218-4 Subj: Humor. Poetry, rhyme.

The walrus and the carpenter ill. by Jane Breskin Zalben. Holt, 1986. ISBN 0-8050-0071-2 Subj: Humor. Poetry, rhyme.

Carroll, Ruth. *Old Mrs. Billups and the black cats* ill. by author. Walck, 1961. Subj: Animals – cats. Humor.

Pet tale by Ruth and Latrobe Carroll; ill. by Ruth Carroll. Oxford Univ. Pr., 1949. Subj: Pets.

What Whiskers did ill. by author. Walck, 1965. Subj: Animals – dogs. Animals – foxes. Animals – rabbits. Behavior – running away. Wordless.

Where's the bunny? ill. by author. Walck, 1950. Subj: Activities – playing. Animals – rabbits. Games. Participation. Wordless.

Carryl, Charles Edward. *A capital ship: or, The walloping window-blind* ill. by Paul Galdone. McGraw-Hill, 1963. Subj: Boats, ships. Music. Pirates. Songs.

The walloping window blind ill. by Ted Rand. Arcade, 1992. ISBN 1-55970-154-4 Subj: Boats, ships. Pirates. Poetry, rhyme.

Cars and trucks ill. by Daisuke Yokoi. Simon and Schuster, 1984. Subj: Automobiles. Format, unusual – board books. Transportation. Trucks.

Carson, Jo. *Pulling my leg* ill. by Julie Downing. Orchard, 1990. ISBN 0-531-08417-5 Subj: Family life – aunts, uncles. Teeth.

You hold me and I'll hold you ill. by Annie Cannon. Orchard, 1992. ISBN 0-531-08495-7 Subj: Death. Emotions – sadness. Family life.

Carter, Angela. *The sleeping beauty and other favourite fairy tales* ill. by Michael Foreman. Schocken, 1984. ISBN 0-8052-3921-9 Subj: Folk and fairy tales.

Carter, Anne. *Beauty and the beast* ill. by Binette Schroeder. Potter, 1986. A retelling of Belle et la bête by Madame Leprince de Beaumont ISBN 0-517-56173-5 Subj: Emotions – love. Folk and fairy tales. Magic.

Bella's secret garden ill. by John Butler. Crown, 1987. ISBN 0-517-56308-8 Subj: Animals – rabbits. Animals – cats. Behavior – greed. Character traits – kindness to animals.

The fisherwoman ill. by Louise Brierley. Lothrop, 1991. ISBN 0-688-09873-8 Subj: Behavior – seeking better things. Magic.

Molly in danger ill. by John Butler. Crown, 1987. ISBN 0-517-56534-X Subj: Animals – moles. Moving. Nature.

Ruff leaves home ill. by John Butler. Crown, 1986. ISBN 0-517-56068-2 Subj: Animals – foxes. Behavior – lost.

Scurry's treasure ill. by John Butler. Crown, 1987. ISBN 0-517-56535-8 Subj: Animals – squirrels. Nature.

The twelve dancing princesses (Grimm, Jacob)

Carter, David A. *How many bugs in a box?* ill. by author. Simon & Schuster, 1988. ISBN 0-671-64965-5 Subj: Format, unusual – toy and movable books. Insects.

I'm a little mouse (Carter, Noelle)

Carter, Debby L. *Clipper* ill. by author. Harper, 1981. Subj: Animals – dogs. Sea and seashore.

Carter, James *see* Mayne, William

Carter, Katharine. *Houses* ill. with photos. Childrens Pr., 1982. Subj: Houses.

Ships and seaports ill. with photos. Children's Pr., 1982. Subj: Boats, ships.

Carter, Noelle. *I'm a little mouse* by Noelle and David A. Carter; ill. by David A. Carter. Holt, 1991. ISBN 0-8050-1420-9 Subj: Animals. Animals – mice. Behavior – lost. Format, unusual.

My house ill. by author. Viking, 1991. ISBN 0-670-83922-1 Subj: Animals. Format, unusual – toy and movable books. Houses. Poetry, rhyme.

My pet ill. by author. Viking, 1991. ISBN 0-670-83923-X Subj: Animals. Format, unusual – toy and movable books. Pets. Poetry, rhyme.

Carter, Peter. *My old grandad* (Harranth, Wolf)

Carter, Phyllis Ann *see* Eberle, Irmengarde

Cartlidge, Michelle. *The bear's bazaar: a story/craft book* ill. by author. Lothrop, 1980. Subj: Activities. Animals – bears.

A mouse's diary ill. by author. Lothrop, 1982. Subj: Activities. Animals – mice.

Pippin and Pod ill. by author. Pantheon, 1978. Subj: Activities – playing. Animals – mice. Behavior – lost. Behavior – misbehavior.

Teddy trucks ill. by author. Lothrop, 1982. Subj: Animals – bears. Careers – truck drivers. Trucks.

Carton, Lonnie Caming. *Mommies* ill. by Leslie Jacobs. Random House, 1960. Subj: Activities. Family life – mothers. Poetry, rhyme.

Cartwright, Ann. *Norah's ark* ill. by Reg Cartwright. Simon & Schuster, 1984. ISBN 0-671-52540-9 Subj: Animals. Farms. Weather – floods. Weather – rain.

The winter hedgehog ill. by Reg Cartwright. Macmillan, 1990. ISBN 0-02-717775-0 Subj: Animals – hedgehogs. Helicopters. Seasons – winter. Weather – wind.

Caseley, Judith. *Ada potato* ill. by author. Greenwillow, 1988. ISBN 0-688-07843-9 Subj: Character traits – cleverness. Music. School.

Annie's potty ill. by author. Greenwillow, 1990. ISBN 0-688-09066-4 Subj: Behavior – growing up. Toilet training.

Apple pie and onions ill. by author. Greenwillow, 1987. ISBN 0-688-06763-8 Subj: Ethnic groups in the U.S. Family life – grandmothers.

Cousins ill. by author. Greenwillow, 1990. ISBN 0-688-08434-6 Subj: Character traits – individuality. Family life – cousins.

Dear Annie ill. by author. Greenwillow, 1991. ISBN 0-688-10011-2 Subj: Activities – writing. Emotions – love. Family life – grandfathers. Letters.

Grandpa's garden lunch ill. by author. Greenwillow, 1990. ISBN 0-688-08817-1 Subj: Family life – grandparents. Food. Gardens, gardening.

Harry and Willy and Carrothead ill. by author. Greenwillow, 1991. ISBN 0-688-09493-7 Subj: Character traits – confidence. Friendship. Handicaps – physical.

Molly Pink ill. by author. Greenwillow, 1985. ISBN 0-688-04005-5 Subj: Emotions – embarrassment. School. Songs.

Molly Pink goes hiking ill. by author. Greenwillow, 1985. ISBN 0-688-05700-4 Subj: Character traits – appearance. Sports.

My sister Celia ill. by author. Greenwillow, 1986. ISBN 0-688-06484-1 Subj: Family life – sisters. Weddings.

Silly baby ill. by author. Greenwillow, 1988. ISBN 0-688-07356-5 Subj: Babies. Family life. Sibling rivalry.

Three happy birthdays ill. by author. Greenwillow, 1989. ISBN 0-688-08180-0 Subj: Birthdays.

When Grandpa came to stay ill. by author. Greenwillow, 1986. ISBN 0-688-06129-X Subj: Death. Family life – grandfathers. Jewish culture.

Casey, Denise. *The friendly prairie dog* photos. by Tim W. Clark and others. Dodd, 1987. ISBN 0-396-08901-1 Subj: Animals – prairie dogs.

Casey, Patricia. *Quack quack* ill. by author. Lothrop, 1988. ISBN 0-688-07765-X Subj: Birds – chickens. Birds – ducks. Eggs.

Cass, Joan E. *The cat thief* ill. by William Stobbs. Abelard-Schuman, 1961. Subj: Animals – cats. Behavior – stealing. Crime. Night.

The cats go to market ill. by William Stobbs. Abelard-Schuman, 1969. Subj: Animals – cats. Shopping.

Cassedy, Sylvia. *The best cat suit of all* ill. by Rosekrans Hoffman. Dial, 1991. ISBN 0-8037-0517-4 Subj: Animals – cats. Friendship. Holidays – Halloween. Illness. Moving.

Moon-uncle, moon-uncle: rhymes from India sel. and tr. by Sylvia Cassedy and Parvathi Thampi; ill. by Susanne Suba. Doubleday, 1973. Subj: Foreign lands – India. Nursery rhymes.

Red dragonfly on my shoulder tr. by Sylvia Cassedy and Kunihiro Suetake; ill. by Molly Bang. HarperCollins, 1992. ISBN 0-06-022625-0 Subj: Animals. Foreign lands – Japan. Poetry, rhyme.

Cassidy, Dianne. *Circus animals* ill. by author. Little, 1985. ISBN 0-316-13241-1 Subj: Animals. Circus. Format, unusual – board books. Format, unusual – toy and movable books. Poetry, rhyme.

Circus people ill. by author. Little, 1985. ISBN 0-316-13243-8 Subj: Circus. Format, unusual – board books. Format, unusual – toy and movable books. Poetry, rhyme.

Castagnetta, Grace. *The song of Robin Hood* (Malcolmson, Anne)

Castiglia, Julie. *Jill the pill* ill. by Steven Kellogg. Atheneum, 1979. Subj: Family life. Sibling rivalry.

Castillo, Violetta. *Animal babies* (Zoll, Max Alfred)

Castle, Caroline. *The hare and the tortoise* (Æsop)

Herbert Binns and the flying tricycle ill. by Peter Weevers. Dial Pr., 1987. ISBN 0-8037-0041-5 Subj: Animals. Animals – mice. Character traits – cleverness. Emotions – envy, jealousy.

Castle, Sue. *Face talk, hand talk, body talk* ill. by Frances McLaughlin-Gill. Doubleday, 1977. Subj: Anatomy. Emotions.

Caswell, Helen. *Parable of the good Samaritan* ill. by author. Abingdon Pr., 1992. ISBN 0-687-30023-1 Subj: Character traits – kindness. Religion.

Catalanotto, Peter. *Christmas always* ill. by author. Orchard, 1991. ISBN 0-531-08546-5 Subj: Bedtime. Holidays – Christmas. Teeth.

Dylan's day out ill. by author. Orchard, 1989. ISBN 0-531-08429-9 Subj: Animals – dogs. Sports – soccer.

Mr. Mumble ill. by author. Orchard, 1990. ISBN 0-531-08480-9 Subj: Animals. Behavior – misunderstanding.

Catchpole, Clive. *Deserts* ill. by Brian McIntyre. Dial Pr., 1984. Subj: Animals. Desert.

Grasslands ill. by Peter Snowball. Dial Pr., 1984. Subj: Animals.

Jungles ill. by Denise Finney. Dial Pr., 1984. Subj: Animals. Jungle.

Mountains ill. by Brian McIntyre. Dial Pr., 1984. Subj: Animals.

Cate, Rikki. *A cat's tale* ill. by Shirley Hughes. Harcourt, 1982. Subj: Animals – cats. Behavior – stealing. Foreign lands – Scotland. Poetry, rhyme.

The caterpillar who turned into a butterfly Simon and Schuster, 1980. Subj: Format, unusual – board books. Insects – butterflies, caterpillars.

Cathon, Laura E. *Tot Botot and his little flute* ill. by Arnold Lobel. Macmillan, 1970. Subj: Animals. Caldecott award honor book. Foreign lands – India. Music.

Caudill, Rebecca. *Contrary Jenkins* by Rebecca Caudill and James Sterling Ayars; ill. by Glen Rounds. Holt, 1969. Subj: Behavior. Country. Humor.

A pocketful of cricket ill. by Evaline Ness. Holt, 1964. Subj: Behavior – sharing. Caldecott award honor book. Farms. Insects – crickets. School.

Wind, sand and sky ill. by Donald Carrick. Dutton, 1976. Subj: Desert. Poetry, rhyme.

Cauley, Lorinda Bryan. *The animal kids* ill. by author. Putnam's, 1979. Subj: Animals. Behavior – imitation.

The bake-off ill. by author. Putnam's, 1978. Subj: Activities – cooking. Animals.

Clap your hands ill. by author. Putnam, 1992. ISBN 0-399-22118-2 Subj: Activities. Activities – playing. Games. Poetry, rhyme.

The cock, the mouse and the little red hen ill. by adapt. Putnam's, 1982. Subj: Animals. Character traits – cleverness. Folk and fairy tales.

Goldilocks and the three bears (The three bears)

The goose and the golden coins ill. by adapt. Harcourt, 1981. Subj: Birds – geese. Folk and fairy tales. Foreign lands – Italy.

The pancake boy (The gingerbread boy)

Pease porridge hot: a Mother Goose cookbook ill. by author. Putnam's, 1977. Subj: Activities – cooking. Food. Nursery rhymes.

Puss in boots (Perrault, Charles)

The trouble with Tyrannosaurus Rex ill. by author. Harcourt, 1988. ISBN 0-15-290880-3 Subj: Behavior – bullying. Character traits – cleverness. Dinosaurs.

Causley, Charles. *Dick Whittington* (Dick Whittington and his cat)

Early in the morning ill. by Michael Foreman. Viking, 1987. ISBN 0-670-80810-5 Subj: Music. Nursery rhymes.

"Quack!" said the billy-goat ill. by Barbara Firth. Lippincott, 1986. ISBN 0-397-32192-9 Subj: Animals. Humor. Noise, sounds. Poetry, rhyme.

Cavagnaro, David. *The pumpkin people* by David Cavagnaro and Maggie Cavagnaro; ill. with photos. Scribner's, 1979. Subj: Gardens, gardening. Holidays – Halloween. Seasons – fall. Seasons – summer.

Cavagnaro, Maggie. *The pumpkin people* (Cavagnaro, David)

Cave, Joyce. *Airplanes* (Cave, Ron)

Automobiles (Cave, Ron)

Motorcycles (Cave, Ron)

Cave, Kathryn. *Out for the count* ill. by Chris Riddell. Simon & Schuster, 1992. ISBN 0-671-75591-9 Subj: Bedtime. Animals. Counting, numbers. Cumulative tales. Poetry, rhyme.

Cave, Ron. *Airplanes* by Ron and Joyce Cave; ill. by David West and others. Watts, 1982. Subj: Airplanes, airports. Transportation.

Automobiles by Ron and Joyce Cave; ill. by David West and others. Watts, 1982. Subj: Automobiles. Transportation.

Motorcycles by Ron and Joyce Cave; ill. by David West and others. Watts, 1982. Subj: Motorcycles. Transportation.

Cazet, Denys. *Are there any questions?* ill. by author. Orchard, 1992. ISBN 0-531-08601-1 Subj: Animals. Animals – cats. School.

Big shoe, little shoe ill. by author. Bradbury Pr., 1984. Subj: Activities – baby-sitting. Animals – rabbits. Family life – grandparents.

Christmas moon ill. by author. Bradbury Pr., 1984. Subj: Animals – rabbits. Holidays – Christmas. Moon.

Daydreams ill. by author. Orchard, 1990. ISBN 0-531-08481-7 Subj: Dreams. Imagination. School.

December 24th ill. by author. Bradbury Pr., 1986. ISBN 0-02-717950-8 Subj: Animals – rabbits. Birthdays. Family life – grandfathers. Holidays.

The duck with squeaky feet ill. by author. Bradbury Pr., 1980. Subj: Animals. Birds – ducks. Reptiles – alligators, crocodiles. Theater.

A fish in his pocket ill. by author. Watts, 1987. ISBN 0-531-08313-6 Subj: Birthdays. Character traits – kindness. Death. School.

Frosted glass ill. by author. Bradbury Pr., 1987. ISBN 0-02-717960-5 Subj: Animals. Animals – dogs. Art. School.

Good morning, Maxine! ill. by author. Bradbury Pr., 1989. ISBN 0-02-717940-0 Subj: Animals – cats.

Great-Uncle Felix ill. by author. Watts, 1988. ISBN 0-531-08350-0 Subj: Animals – rhinoceros. Emotions – embarrassment. Family life – aunts, uncles.

I'm not sleepy ill. by author. Orchard, 1992. ISBN 0-531-08498-1 Subj: Bedtime. Family life – fathers. Sleep.

Lucky me ill. by author. Bradbury Pr., 1983. Subj: Animals. Birds – chickens. Character traits – luck. Food.

Mother night ill. by author. Orchard, 1989. ISBN 0-531-08430-2 Subj: Animals. Bedtime. Night. Sleep.

Never spit on your shoes ill. by author. Orchard, 1990. ISBN 0-531-08447-7 Subj: Animals. Animals – cats. School.

Saturday ill. by author. Bradbury Pr., 1985. ISBN 0-02-717800-5 Subj: Animals – dogs. Family life – grandparents.

Sunday ill. by author. Bradbury Pr., 1988. ISBN 0-02-717970-2 Subj: Animals. Family life.

You make the angels cry ill. by author. Bradbury Pr., 1982. ISBN 0-02-717830-7 Subj: Animals – rabbits. Weather – rain.

Cazzola, Gus. *The bells of Santa Lucia* ill. by Pierr Morgan. Putnam, 1991. ISBN 0-399-21804-1 Subj: Animals – sheep. Death. Family life – grandmothers. Foreign lands – Italy.

Cech, John. *My grandmother's journey* ill. by Sharon McGinley-Nally. Macmillan, 1991. ISBN 0-02-718135-9 Subj: Activities – traveling. Family life – grandmothers. Friendship.

Cecil, Mirabel. *Lottie's cats* ill. by Francesca Martin. Crown, 1990. ISBN 0-517-57707-0 Subj: Animals – cats. Holidays – Halloween.

Cendrars, Blaise. *Shadow* tr. and ill. by Marcia Brown. Scribner's, 1982. Subj: Caldecott award book. Folk and fairy tales. Foreign lands – Africa. Poetry, rhyme. Shadows.

Cerf, Bennett Alfred. *Bennett Cerf's book of animal riddles* ill. by Roy McKié. Random House, 1964. Subj: Humor. Riddles.

Bennett Cerf's book of laughs ill. by Carl Rose. Random House, 1959. Subj: Humor. Riddles.

Bennett Cerf's book of riddles ill. by Roy McKié. Random House, 1960. Subj: Humor. Riddles.

More riddles ill. by Roy McKié. Random House, 1961. Subj: Humor. Riddles.

Chafetz, Henry. *The legend of Befana* ill. by Ronni Solbert. Houghton, 1958. Subj: Folk and fairy tales. Foreign lands – Italy. Holidays – Christmas.

Chaffin, Lillie D. *Tommy's big problem* ill. by Haris Petie. Lantern Pr., 1965. Subj: Babies. Behavior – growing up. Family life. Problem solving.

We be warm till springtime comes ill. by Lloyd Bloom. Macmillan, 1980. Subj: Character traits – bravery. Seasons – winter.

Chaikin, Miriam. *Esther* ill. by Vera Rosenberry. Jewish Pub. Soc., 1987. ISBN 0-8276-0272-3 Subj: Foreign lands – Persia. Holidays. Jewish culture.

Exodus ill. by Charles Mikolaycak. Holiday, 1987. ISBN 0-8234-0607-5 Subj: Jewish culture. Religion.

Hanukkah ill. by Ellen Weiss. Holiday, 1990. ISBN 0-8234-0816-7 Subj: Holidays – Hanukkah. Jewish culture.

Chall, Marsha Wilson. *Mattie* ill. by Barbara Lehman. Lothrop, 1992. ISBN 0-688-09730-8 Subj: Family life – brothers. Family life – sisters.

Up north at the cabin ill. by Steve Johnson. Lothrop, 1992. ISBN 0-688-09733-2 Subj: Activities – vacationing. Forest, woods. Nature.

Challoner, Jack. *The science book of numbers* ill. with photos. Harcourt, 1992. ISBN 0-15-200623-0 Subj: Counting, numbers. Science.

Chalmers, Audrey. *Fancy be good* ill. by author. Viking, 1941. Subj: Animals – cats. Behavior – misbehavior. Sibling rivalry.

Hector and Mr. Murfit ill. by author. Viking, 1953. Subj: Animals – dogs. Concepts – size.

Hundreds and hundreds of pancakes ill. by author. Viking, 1942. Subj: Animals. Food. Humor. Zoos.

Chalmers, Mary. *Be good, Harry* ill. by author. Harper, 1967. Subj: Activities – baby-sitting. Animals – cats.

Boots finds a house ill. by author. Harper, 1958. Subj: Animals – cats. Boats, ships.

The cat who liked to pretend ill. by author. Harper, 1959. Subj: Animals – cats. Imagination.

A Christmas story ill. by author Rev. ed. Harper, 1987, 1956. ISBN 0-06-021191-1 Subj: Animals. Holidays – Christmas. Trees.

Come for a walk with me ill. by author. Harper, 1955. Subj: Animals – rabbits.

Come to the doctor, Harry ill. by author. Harper, 1981. Subj: Animals – cats. Illness.

Easter parade ill. by author. Harper, 1988. ISBN 0-06-021233-0 Subj: Animals. Holidays – Easter. Parades.

George Appleton ill. by author. Harper, 1957. Subj: Animals – cats. Dragons.

A hat for Amy Jean ill. by author. Harper, 1956. Subj: Birthdays. Character traits – generosity. Clothing – hats.

Here comes the trolley ill. by author. Harper, 1955. Subj: Activities – picnicking. Activities – traveling. Cable cars, trolleys.

Kevin ill. by author. Harper, 1957. Subj: Animals – rabbits. City.

Merry Christmas, Harry ill. by author. Harper, 1977. Subj: Animals – cats. Holidays – Christmas.

Mr. Cat's wonderful surprise ill. by author. Harper, 1961. Subj: Activities – picnicking. Animals – cats. Family life.

Six dogs, twenty-three cats, forty-five mice, and one hundred sixteen spiders ill. by author. Harper, 1986. ISBN 0-06-021189-X Subj: Humor. Parties. Pets.

Take a nap, Harry ill. by author. Harper, 1964. Subj: Animals – cats. Family life. Sleep.

Throw a kiss, Harry ill. by author. HarperCollins, 1990. ISBN 0-06-021245-4 Subj: Animals – cats. Careers – firefighters.

Chambless, Jane. *Tucker and the bear* ill. by author. Simon & Schuster, 1989. ISBN 0-671-67357-2 Subj: Animals – bears. Friendship.

Chan, Chin-Yi. *Good luck horse* ill. by Plao Chan. Whittlesey House, 1943. Subj: Animals – horses. Caldecott award honor book.

Chandler, Edna Walker. *Cattle drive* ill. by Jack Merryweather. Benefic Pr., 1966. Subj: Cowboys.

Cowboy Andy ill. by Raymond Kinstler. Random House, 1959. Subj: Cowboys.

Pony rider ill. by Jack Merryweather. Benefic Pr., 1966. Subj: Animals – horses. Cowboys.

Secret tunnel ill. by Jack Merryweather. Benefic Pr., 1967. Subj: Cowboys.

Chandler, Robert. *Russian folk tales* (Afanas'ev, Aleksandr N.)

Chandoha, Walter. *A baby bunny for you* ill. by author. Collins, 1968. Subj: Animals – rabbits.

A baby goat for you ill. by author. Collins, 1968. Subj: Animals – goats.

A baby goose for you ill. by author. Collins, 1968. Subj: Birds – geese.

Chanover, Alice. *Happy Hanukah everybody* (Chanover, Hyman)

Chanover, Hyman. *Happy Hanukah everybody* by Hyman and Alice Chanover; ill. by Maurice Sendak. United Synagogue Books, n.d. ISBN 0-8381-0712-5 Subj: Holidays – Hanukkah. Jewish culture. Music. Religion.

Chapin, Cynthia. *Squad car 55* ill. by Dale Fleming. Albert Whitman, 1966. Educational consultant: Jene Barr Subj: Careers – police officers.

Chaplin, Susan Gibbons. *I can sign my ABCs* ill. by Laura McCaul. Gallaudet Univ. Pr., 1986. ISBN 0-930323-19-X Subj: ABC books. Handicaps – deafness. Language. Senses – hearing.

Chapman, Carol. *Barney Bipple's magic dandelions* ill. by Steven Kellogg. Dutton, 1988, 1977. ISBN 0-525-44449-1 Subj: Behavior – wishing. Flowers. Magic. Plants.

Herbie's troubles ill. by Kelly Oechsli. Dutton, 1981. Subj: Behavior – bullying. Behavior – misbehavior. Problem solving.

The tale of Meshka the Kvetch ill. by Arnold Lobel. Dutton, 1980. Subj: Behavior – dissatisfaction. Folk and fairy tales. Jewish culture.

Chapman, Elizabeth. *Suzy* ill. by Margery Gill. Salem House, 1987. ISBN 0-370-30375-X Subj: Character traits – being different. Handicaps – blindness. Senses – seeing.

Chapman, Gaynor. *The luck child* ill. by author. Atheneum, 1968. Based on a story of the Brothers Grimm Subj: Folk and fairy tales. Royalty.

Chapman, Jean. *Moon-Eyes* ill. by Astra Lacis. McGraw-Hill, 1980. Subj: Animals – cats. Folk and fairy tales. Foreign lands – Italy. Holidays – Christmas. Religion.

Chapman, Noralee. *The story of Barbara* ill. by Helen S. Hull. John Knox Pr., 1963. Subj: Adoption.

Chapouton, Anne-Marie. *Ben finds a friend* tr. by Andrea Mernan; ill. by Ulises Wensell. Putnam's, 1986. ISBN 0-399-21268-X Subj: City. Friendship. Pets.

Billy the brave tr. from French by Anthea Bell; ill. by Jean Claverie. Holt, 1986. ISBN 0-03-008019-3 Subj: Character traits – bravery. Monsters. Night.

Sebastian is always late ill. by Chantal van der Berghe. Holt, 1987. ISBN 0-8050-0487-4 Subj: Imagination. School.

Charbonnet, Gabrielle. *Boodil, my dog* (Lindenbaum, Pija)

Chardiet, Bernice. *C is for circus* ill. by Brinton Turkle. Walker, 1971. Subj: ABC books. Circus. Poetry, rhyme.

Charles, Donald. *Calico Cat at school* ill. by author. Children's Pr., 1981. Subj: Animals – cats. School.

Calico Cat at the zoo ill. by author. Children's Pr., 1981. Subj: Animals. Animals – cats. Zoos.

Calico Cat meets bookworm ill. by author. Children's Pr., 1978. Subj: Animals – cats. Libraries. Poetry, rhyme.

Calico Cat's exercise book ill. by author. Children's Pr., 1982. Subj: Animals – cats. Animals – mice.

Calico cat's year ill. by author. Childrens Pr., 1984. ISBN 0-516-03461-8 Subj: Animals – cats. Days of the week, months of the year. Poetry, rhyme. Seasons.

Chancay and the secret of fire ill. by author. Putnam, 1990. ISBN 0-399-22129-8 Subj: Fire. Folk and fairy tales. Foreign lands – Peru.

Shaggy dog's animal alphabet ill. by author. Children's Pr., 1979. Subj: ABC books. Animals. Poetry, rhyme.

Shaggy dog's birthday ill. by author. Childrens Pr., 1986. ISBN 0-516-03576-2 Subj: Animals – dogs. Birthdays. Etiquette.

Shaggy dog's Halloween ill. by author. Childrens Pr., 1984. ISBN 0-516-03575-4 Subj: Animals – dogs. Character traits – appearance. Holidays – Halloween.

Shaggy dog's tall tale ill. by author. Children's Pr., 1980. Subj: Animals – dogs.

Time to rhyme with Calico Cat ill. by author. Children's Pr., 1978. Subj: Animals – cats. Animals – dogs. Poetry, rhyme.

Charles, Nicholas *see* Kuskin, Karla

Charles, R. H. (Robert Henry). *The roundabout turn* ill. by L. Leslie Brooke. Warne, 1930. Subj: Frogs and toads. Merry-go-rounds. Poetry, rhyme.

Charlip, Remy. *Arm in arm* ill. by author. Parents, 1969. Subj: Games. Humor.

Fortunately ill. by author. Parents, 1964. Subj: Humor. Participation.

Handtalk: an ABC of finger spelling and sign language by Remy Charlip, Mary Beth and George Ancona; ill. by George Ancona. Parents, 1974. Subj: ABC books. Communication. Handicaps – deafness. Language. Senses – hearing.

Handtalk birthday: a number and story book in sign language photos. by George Ancona. Four Winds Pr., 1987. ISBN 0-02-718080-8 Subj: Birthdays. Handicaps – deafness. Language. Senses – hearing.

Harlequin and the gift of many colors by Remy Charlip and Burton Supree; ill. by Remy Charlip.

Parents, 1973. Subj: Concepts – color. Folk and fairy tales. Foreign lands – France.

Hooray for me! by Remy Charlip and Lilian Moore; ill. by Vera B. Williams. Parents, 1975. Subj: Character traits – individuality. Family life. Self-concept.

"Mother, mother I feel sick" by Remy Charlip and Burton Supree; ill. by Remy Charlip. Parents, 1966. Subj: Careers – doctors. Humor. Illness.

Thirteen by Remy Charlip and Jerry Joyner; ill. by Remy Charlip. Parents, 1975. Subj: Counting, numbers. Humor.

The tree angel (Martin, Judith)

Where is everybody? ill. by author. Addison-Wesley, 1957. Subj: Games. Weather – rain.

Charlot, Martin. *Felisa and the magic tikling bird* ill. by Martin Charlot from a story by Jodi Parry Belknap. Island Heritage, 1973. Subj: Activities – dancing. Folk and fairy tales. Foreign lands – Philippines. Handicaps. Self-concept.

Sunnyside up ill. by author. Weatherhill, 1972. Subj: Wordless.

Charlton, Elizabeth. *Jeremy and the ghost* ill. by Celia Reisman. Dandelion, 1979. Subj: Character traits – bravery. Ghosts. Holidays – Halloween.

Terrible tyrannosaurus ill. by Andrew Glass. Elsevier-Nelson, 1981. Subj: Behavior – bullying. Behavior – imitation. Dinosaurs.

Charmatz, Bill. *The Troy St. bus* ill. by author. Macmillan, 1977. Subj: Animals – horses. School.

Charosh, Mannis. *The ellipse* ill. by Leonard P. Kessler. Crowell, 1972. Subj: Concepts – shape. Science.

Number ideas through pictures ill. by Giulio Maestro. Crowell, 1975. Subj: Concepts. Counting, numbers.

Charters, Janet. *The general* by Janet Charters and Michael Foreman; ill. by Michael Foreman. Dutton, 1961. Subj: Violence, anti-violence.

Chase, Alice *see* McHargue, Georgess

Chase, Catherine. *An alphabet book* ill. by June Goldsborough. Dandelion, 1979. Subj: ABC books.

Baby mouse goes shopping ill. by Jill Elgin. Elsevier-Nelson, 1981. Subj: Animals – mice. Shopping.

Baby mouse learns his ABC's ill. by Jill Elgin. Dandelion, 1979. Subj: ABC books. Animals – mice.

Feet ill. by Susan Reiss. Dandelion, 1979. Subj: Anatomy – feet. Concepts – left and right.

Hot and cold ill. by Gail Gibbons. Dandelion, 1979. Subj: Concepts.

The miracles at Cana ill. by Wayne Atkinson. Dandelion, 1979. Subj: Religion.

The mouse in my house ill. by Gail Gibbons. Dandelion, 1979. Subj: Animals – mice. Houses.

My balloon ill. by Gail Gibbons. Dandelion, 1979. Subj: Toys – balloons.

The nightingale and the fool ill. by Judith Cheng. Dandelion, 1979. Subj: Birds – nightingales. Folk and fairy tales. Foreign lands – India.

Noah's ark ill. by Elliot Ivenbaum. Dandelion, 1979. Subj: Religion – Noah.

Pete, the wet pet ill. by Gail Gibbons. Elsevier-Nelson, 1981. Subj: Animals – dogs. Family life.

Chase, Richard. *Jack and the three sillies* ill. by Joshua Tolford. Houghton, 1950. Subj: Folk and fairy tales.

Chasek, Judith. *Have you seen Wilhelmina Krumpf?* ill. by Sal Murdocca. Lothrop, 1973. Subj: Foreign lands – Holland.

Chaucer, Geoffrey. *Chanticleer and the fox* adapt. and ill. by Barbara Cooney. Crowell, 1958. Adapt. of the "Nun's priest's tale" from the Canterbury tales Subj: Animals – foxes. Birds – chickens. Caldecott award book. Character traits – flattery. Farms. Folk and fairy tales.

Chen, Tony. *Animals showing off* ill. by author. National Geographic Soc., 1989. ISBN 0-87044-724-6 Subj: Animals. Format, unusual – toy and movable books.

Chenault, Nell. *Parsifal the Poddley* ill. by Vee Guthrie. Little, 1960. Subj: Elves and little people. Emotions – loneliness. U.S. history.

Chenery, Janet. *Pickles and Jake* ill. by Lilian Obligado. Viking, 1975. Subj: Animals – cats. Animals – dogs. Pets.

The toad hunt ill. by Ben Shecter. Harper, 1967. Subj: Frogs and toads. Science.

Wolfie ill. by Marc Simont. Harper, 1969. Subj: Sibling rivalry. Spiders.

Cheng, Hou-Tien. *The Chinese New Year* ill. by author. Holt, 1976. Subj: Foreign lands – China. Holidays – Chinese New Year.

Chermayeff, Ivan. *Tomato and other colors* ill. by author. Prentice-Hall, 1981. Subj: Concepts – color.

Chernoff, Goldie Taub. *Clay-dough, play-dough* ill. and photos. by Margaret A. Hartelius. Walker, 1974. Subj: Activities.

Just a box? ill. by Margaret A. Hartelius. Walker, 1973. Subj: Activities.

Pebbles and pods: a book of nature crafts ill. by Margaret A. Hartelius. Walker, 1973. Subj: Activities.

Puppet party ill. by Margaret A. Hartelius. Walker, 1972. Subj: Activities. Puppets.

Cherry, Lynne. *Archie, follow me* ill. by author. Dutton, 1990. ISBN 0-525-44647-8 Subj: Animals – cats. Forest, woods.

A river ran wild ill. by author. Harcourt, 1992. ISBN 0-15-200542-0 Subj: Ecology. Nature. Rivers. U.S. history.

Who's sick today? ill. by author. Dutton, 1988. ISBN 0-525-44380-0 Subj: Animals. Illness. Poetry, rhyme.

Chess, Victoria. *Alfred's alphabet walk* ill. by author. Greenwillow, 1979. Subj: ABC books. Behavior – misbehavior.

Poor Esmé ill. by author. Holiday, 1982. Subj: Babies. Behavior – wishing. Emotions – loneliness.

Chesworth, Michael. *Rainy day dream* ill. by author. Farrar, 1992. ISBN 0-374-36177-0 Subj: Dreams. Umbrellas. Weather – storms. Wordless.

Chetwin, Grace. *Box and Cox* ill. by David Small. Bradbury Pr., 1990. ISBN 0-02-718314-9 Subj: Careers – hatters. Careers – printers. Humor.

Mr. Meredith and the truly remarkable stone ill. by Catherine Stock. Bradbury Pr., 1989. ISBN 0-02-718313-0 Subj: Rocks.

Chevalier, Christa. *The little bear who forgot* ed. by Kathleen Tucker; ill. by author. Albert Whitman, 1984. Subj: Animals – bears. Family life.

Spence and the sleepytime monster ill. by author. Albert Whitman, 1984. Subj: Bedtime. Imagination. Monsters.

Spence is small ill. by author. Albert Whitman, 1987. ISBN 0-8075-7567-4 Subj: Character traits – helpfulness. Character traits – smallness.

Spence isn't Spence anymore ill. by author. Albert Whitman, 1985. ISBN 0-8075-7565-8 Subj: Character traits – appearance.

Spence makes circles ill. by author. Albert Whitman, 1982. Subj: Behavior – mistakes. Humor.

Chevalier, Joan. *Suzette and Nicholas and the seasons clock* (Mangin, Marie-France)

Chevance, Audrey. *Tutu* ill. by author. Dutton, 1991. ISBN 0-525-44769-5 Subj: Activities – dancing. Careers – seamstresses.

Chicken Little. *Chicken Licken* text by Kenneth McLeish; ill. by Jutta Ash. Bradbury Pr., 1973. Subj: Animals. Behavior – gossip. Behavior – trickery. Birds – chickens. Cumulative tales. Folk and fairy tales.

Chicken Licken adapt. and ill. by Gavin Bishop. Oxford Univ. Pr., 1985. ISBN 0-19-558108-3 Subj: Animals. Behavior – gossip. Behavior – trickery. Birds – chickens. Cumulative tales. Folk and fairy tales.

Henny Penny ill. by Stephen Butler. Morrow, 1991. ISBN 0-688-09922-X Subj: Animals. Behav ior – gossip. Behavior – trickery. Birds – chickens. Cumulative tales. Folk and fairy tales.

Henny Penny ill. by Paul Galdone. Seabury Pr., 1968. Subj: Animals. Behavior – gossip. Behavior – trickery. Birds – chickens. Cumulative tales. Folk and fairy tales.

Henny Penny ill. by William Stobbs. Follett, 1968. Subj: Animals. Behavior – gossip. Behavior – trickery. Birds – chickens. Cumulative tales. Folk and fairy tales.

The story of Chicken Licken adapt. and ill. by Jan Ormerod. Lothrop, 1986. ISBN 0-688-06058-7 Subj: Animals. Behavior – gossip. Behavior – trickery. Birds – chickens. Cumulative tales. Folk and fairy tales.

Chiefari, Janet. *Kids are baby goats* ill. with photos. Dodd, 1984. Subj: Animals – goats. Fairs.

Child, Lydia Maria. *Over the river and through the wood* ill. by Brinton Turkle. Coward, 1974. First published in 1844 as The boy's Thanksgiving Day in the 2d vol. of the author's Flowers for children Subj: Family life – grandparents. Farms. Holidays – Thanksgiving. Songs.

Children go where I send thee : *an American spiritual* ill. by Kathryn E. Shoemaker. Winston Pr., 1980. ISBN 0-03-056673-8 Subj: Ethnic groups in the U.S. – Afro-Americans. Music. Religion.

Children's prayers from around the world Sadlier, 1981. Subj: Children as authors. Religion.

Children's Television Workshop. *Muppets in my neighborhood* ill. by Harry McNaught. Random House, 1977. Subj: Format, unusual – board books. Puppets.

The Sesame Street book of opposites with Zero Mostel (Mendoza, George)

The Sesame Street players present Mother Goose (Mother Goose)

The Sesame Street song book (Raposo, Joe)

A visit to the Sesame Street firehouse (Elliott, Dan)

Childress, Mark. *Joshua and Bigtooth* ill. by Rick Meyerowitz. Little, 1992. ISBN 0-316-14011-2 Subj: Activities – dancing. Parties. Pets. Reptiles – alligators, crocodiles.

A child's book of prayers ill. by Michael Hague. Holt, 1985. ISBN 0-03-001412-3 Subj: Religion.

A child's picture English-Hebrew dictionary ill. by Ita Meshi. Adama, 1985. ISBN 0-915361-07-8 Subj: ABC books. Dictionaries. Foreign languages. Jewish culture.

Chimaera *see* Farjeon, Eleanor

Ching. *The baboon's umbrella* ill. by author. Children's Pr., 1991. ISBN 0-516-05131-8 Subj: Ani-mals – baboons. Folk and fairy tales. Foreign lands – Africa. Umbrellas.

Chislett, Gail. *Melinda's no's cold* ill. by Hélène Desputeaux. Firefly, 1991. ISBN 1-55037-196-7 Subj: Careers – doctors. Illness. Language.

The rude visitors ill. by Barbara Di Lella. Firefly Pr., 1984. Subj: Behavior – carelessness. Imagination.

Whump ill. by Vladyana Krykorka. Firefly, 1989. ISBN 1-55037-041-3 Subj: Bedtime Family life. Furniture – beds. Sleep.

Chittum, Ida. *The cat's pajamas* ill. by Art Cumings. Parents, 1980. ISBN 0-8193-1030-1 Subj: Animals – cats. Pets.

Chlad, Dorothy. *Bicycles are fun to ride* ill. by Lydia Halverson. Children's Pr., 1984. Subj: Safety. Sports – bicycling.

Matches, lighters, and firecrackers are not toys ill. by Lydia Halverson. Children's Pr., 1982. Subj: Safety.

Poisons make you sick ill. by Lydia Halverson. Children's Pr., 1984. Subj: Safety.

Strangers ill. by Lydia Halverson. Children's Pr., 1982. Subj: Behavior – talking to strangers.

Chmielarz, Sharon. *The pied piper of Hamelin* (Browning, Robert)

Chocolate, Deborah M. Newton. *Kwanzaa* ill. by Melodye Rosales. Children's Pr., 1990. ISBN 0-516-03991-1 Subj: Ethnic groups in the U.S. – Afro-Americans. Family life. Holidays – Kwanzaa.

Chönz, Selina. *A bell for Ursli* ill. by Alois Carigiet. Walck, 1950. Subj: Foreign lands – Switzerland. Poetry, rhyme. Seasons – spring.

Florina and the wild bird tr. by Anne and Ian Serraillier; ill. by Alois Carigiet. Walck, 1966. Translation of Flurina und das Wildvöglein Subj: Birds. Foreign lands – Switzerland. Poetry, rhyme. Seasons – summer.

The snowstorm ill. by Alois Carigiet. Walck, 1958. Translated from the German Subj: Foreign lands – Switzerland. Poetry, rhyme. Seasons – winter. Weather – snow. Weather – storms.

Chorao, Kay. *The baby's bedtime book* ill. by comp. Dutton, 1984. Subj: Nursery rhymes. Poetry, rhyme.

Baby's Christmas treasury ill. by author. Random House, 1991. ISBN 0-679-90198-1 Subj: Babies. Holidays – Christmas.

The baby's good morning book ill. by adapt. Dutton, 1986. ISBN 0-525-44257-X Subj: Babies. Morning. Poetry, rhyme.

Cathedral mouse ill. by author. Dutton, 1988. ISBN 0-525-44400-9 Subj: Animals – mice. Houses.

The cherry pie baby ill. by author. Dutton, 1989. ISBN 0-525-44435-1 Subj: Activities – trading. Animals – dogs. Babies.

The child's story book ill. by adapt. Dutton, 1987. ISBN 0-525-44328-2 Subj: Folk and fairy tales.

George told Kate ill. by author. Dutton, 1987. ISBN 0-525-44293-6 Subj: Animals – elephants. Sibling rivalry.

Ida and Betty and the secret eggs ill. by author. Houghton, 1991. ISBN 0-395-52591-8 Subj: Animals – cats. Country. Eggs. Friendship.

Kate's box ill. by author. Dutton, 1982. Subj: Animals – elephants. Behavior – hiding.

Kate's car ill. by author. Dutton, 1982. Subj: Animals – elephants. Toys.

Kate's quilt ill. by author. Dutton, 1982. Subj: Animals – elephants. Quilts.

Kate's snowman ill. by author. Dutton, 1982. Subj: Animals – elephants. Snowmen.

Lemon moon ill. by author. Holiday, 1983. Subj: Animals. Bedtime. Dreams. Family life – grandmothers.

Lester's overnight ill. by author. Dutton, 1977. Subj: Emotions – fear. Family life. Imagination. Sleep.

Molly's lies ill. by author. Seabury Pr., 1979. Subj: Behavior – losing things. Behavior – lying. Friendship. School.

Molly's Moe ill. by author. Seabury Pr., 1976. Subj: Behavior – losing things. Shopping. Toys.

Chouinard, Mariko. *The amazing animal alphabet book* (Chouinard, Roger)

One magic box (Chouinard, Roger)

Chouinard, Roger. *The amazing animal alphabet book* by Roger and Mariko Chouinard; ill. by Roger Chouinard. Doubleday, 1988. ISBN 0-385-24029-5 Subj: ABC books. Animals.

One magic box by Roger and Mariko Chouinard; ill. by authors. Doubleday, 1989. ISBN 0-385-26204-3 Subj: Animals. Counting, numbers. Magic.

Chow, Octavio. *The invisible hunters* (Rohmer, Harriet)

Christelow, Eileen. *Five little monkeys jumping on the bed* ill. by author. Houghton, 1991. ISBN 0-395-55701-1 Subj: Animals – monkeys. Bedtime. Behavior – misbehavior. Counting, numbers. Poetry, rhyme.

Five little monkeys sitting in a tree ill. by author. Houghton, 1991. ISBN 0-395-54434-3 Subj: Activities – picnicking. Animals – monkeys. Behavior – misbehavior. Counting, numbers. Poetry, rhyme. Reptiles – alligators, crocodiles.

Gertrude, the bulldog detective ill. by author. Houghton, 1992. ISBN 0-395-58701-8 Subj: Animals – dogs. Careers – detectives. Problem solving.

Glenda Feathers casts a spell ill. by author. Houghton, 1990. ISBN 0-395-51122-4 Subj: Animals. Witches.

Henry and the dragon ill. by author. Houghton, 1984. Subj: Animals – rabbits. Bedtime. Dragons. Shadows.

Henry and the red stripes ill. by author. Houghton, 1982. Subj: Animals – foxes. Animals – rabbits. Illness.

Jerome the babysitter ill. by author. Houghton, 1985. Subj: Activities – baby-sitting. Behavior – trickery. Character traits – cleverness. Reptiles – alligators, crocodiles.

Olive and the magic hat ill. by author. Clarion, 1987. ISBN 0-89919-513-X Subj: Animals. Behavior – trickery. Clothing – hats. Magic.

The robbery at the diamond dog diner ill. by author. Clarion, 1986. ISBN 0-89919-425-7 Subj: Animals. Behavior – secrets. Behavior – trickery. Birds. Crime.

Christensen, Gardell Dano. *Mrs. Mouse needs a house* ill. by author. Holt, 1958. Subj: Animals. Animals – mice. Houses. Problem solving.

Christensen, Jack. *The forgotten rainbow* by Jack and Lee Christensen; ill. by authors. Morrow, 1960. Subj: Behavior – wishing. Folk and fairy tales.

Christensen, Lee. *The forgotten rainbow* (Christensen, Jack)

Christenson, Larry. *The wonderful way that babies are made* ill. by Dwight Walles. Bethany House, 1982. Subj: Babies. Birth. Family life. Science.

Christian, Mary Blount. *April fool* ill. by Diane Dawson. Macmillan, 1982. Subj: Folk and fairy tales. Foreign lands – England. Holidays – April Fools' Day.

The devil take you, Barnabas Beane! ill. by Anne Burgess. Crowell, 1980. Subj: Behavior – greed. Character traits – generosity. Character traits – selfishness.

Devin and Goliath ill. by Normand Chartier. Addison-Wesley, 1974. Subj: Pets. Reptiles – turtles, tortoises.

The doggone mystery ill. by Irene Trivas. Albert Whitman, 1980. Subj: Behavior – stealing. Crime. Problem solving.

Go west, swamp monsters ill. by Marc Brown. Dial Pr., 1985. ISBN 0-8037-0144-6 Subj: Activities – picnicking. Behavior – misbehavior. Behavior – running away. Monsters.

No dogs allowed, Jonathan! ill. by Don Madden. Addison-Wesley, 1973. Subj: Animals – dogs.

Nothing much happened today ill. by Don Madden. Addison-Wesley, 1973. Subj: Cumulative tales. Humor.

The sand lot ill. by Dennis Kendrick. Harvey House, 1978. Subj: Activities – playing. Behavior – fighting, arguing. Sports – baseball.

Christiana, David. *White nineteens* ill. by author. Farrar, 1992. ISBN 0-374-38390-1 Subj: Animals. Fairies. Forest, woods. Seasons – winter.

Christiansen, C. B. *Mara in the morning* ill. by Catherine Stock. Macmillan, 1991. ISBN 0-689-31616-X Subj: Morning. Noise, sounds.

My mother's house, my father's house ill. by Irene Trivas. Macmillan, 1989. ISBN 0-689-31394-2 Subj: Divorce. Emotions. Family life.

A Christmas book tr. from Danish by Joan Tate; ill. by Svend Otto S. Larousse, 1982. Subj: Foreign lands – Denmark. Holidays – Christmas.

Christmas in the stable poems sel. and ill. by Beverly K. Duncan. Harcourt, 1990. ISBN 0-15-217758-2 Subj: Animals. Holidays – Christmas. Poetry, rhyme. Religion.

The Christmas story told through paintings from the Metropolitan Museum of Art with commentary by Richard Mühlberger. Harcourt, 1990. ISBN 0-15-200426-2 Subj: Art. Holidays – Christmas. Museums. Religion.

Chukovsky, Korney. *Good morning, chick* adapt. by Mirra Ginsburg; ill. by Byron Barton. Greenwillow, 1980. Subj: Birds – chickens. Noise, sounds.

The telephone adapt. from Russian by William Jay Smith in collaboration with Max Hayward; ill. by Blair Lent. Delacorte Pr., 1977. Subj: Communication. Humor. Poetry, rhyme.

Church, Kristine. *My brother John* ill. by Kilmeny Niland. Morrow, 1991. ISBN 0-688-10801-6 Subj: Character traits – bravery. Emotions – fear. Family life – brothers. Family life – sisters. Monsters.

Chute, Beatrice Joy. *Joy to Christmas* ill. by Erik Blegvad. Dutton, 1958. Subj: Character traits – generosity. Holidays – Christmas.

Chwast, Seymour. *Alphabet parade* ill. by author. Harcourt, 1991. ISBN 0-15-200351-7 Subj: ABC books. Parades. Wordless.

Still another alphabet book by Seymour Chwast and Martin Stephen Moskof; ill. by authors. McGraw-Hill, 1969. Subj: ABC books. Wordless.

Still another children's book by Seymour Chwast and Martin Stephen Moskof; ill. by authors. McGraw-Hill, 1972. Subj: Dreams. Seasons – summer.

Still another number book by Seymour Chwast and Martin Stephen Moskof; ill. by authors. McGraw-Hill, 1971. Subj: Counting, numbers.

Tall city, wide country: a book to read forward and backward ill. by author. Viking, 1983. Subj: Activities – traveling. City. Country. Format, unusual.

Ciardi, John. *John J. Plenty and Fiddler Dan: a new fable of the grasshopper and the ant* ill. by Madeleine Gekiere. Lippincott, 1963. Subj: Behavior – saving things. Insects – ants. Insects – grasshoppers. Poetry, rhyme.

The monster den: or, Look what happened at my house—and to it ill. by Edward Gorey. Lippincott, 1966. Subj: Monsters. Poetry, rhyme.

Scrappy the pup ill. by Jane Miller. Lippincott, 1960. Subj: Animals – dogs. Behavior – growing up. Sleep.

Ciliotta, Claire. *"Why am I going to the hospital?"* by Claire Ciliotta and Carole Livingston; ill. by Dick Wilson. Lyle Stuart, 1982. Subj: Hospitals. Illness.

City ill. by Roser Capdevila. Firefly Pr., 1986. ISBN 0-920303-45-5 Subj: City. Format, unusual – board books. Wordless.

Civardi, Anne. *Potty time* ill. by Jonathan Langley. Simon & Schuster, 1988. ISBN 0-671-65896-4 Subj: Behavior – growing up. Toilet training.

Things people do ill. by Stephen Cartwright; designed by Roger Priddy. Usborne Pub., 1985. ISBN 0-86020-864-8 Subj: Activities – working. Careers. Games. Islands.

Claret, Maria. *The chocolate rabbit* ill. by author. Barron's, 1985. ISBN 0-416-48260-0 Subj: Animals – rabbits. Behavior – carelessness. Eggs. Holidays – Easter.

Melissa Mouse ill. by author. Barron's, 1985. Subj: Animals – mice. Weddings.

Clark, Ann Nolan. *In my mother's house* ill. by Velino Herrera. Viking, 1941. Subj: Caldecott award honor book. Indians of North America. Family life.

The little Indian basket maker ill. by Harrison Begay. Melmont, 1955. Subj: Activities – working. Indians of North America.

The little Indian pottery maker ill. by Don Perceval. Melmont, 1955. Subj: Activities – working. Indians of North America.

Tia Maria's garden ill. by Ezra Jack Keats. Viking, 1963. Subj: Desert.

Clark, Emma Chichester. *Lunch with Aunt Augusta* ill. by author. Dial, 1992. ISBN 0-8037-1104-2 Subj: Animals – lemurs. Family life – aunts, uncles. Food. Jungle.

The story of Horrible Hilda and Henry ill. by author. Little, 1989. ISBN 0-316-14498-3 Subj: Animals – lions. Behavior – misbehavior. Zoos.

Clark, Harry. *The first story of the whale* ill. by author. Houghton, 1938. Subj: Animals – whales. Games. Science.

Clark, Leonard. *Drums and trumpets: poetry for the youngest* ill. by Heather Copley. Bodley Head, 1979. Subj: Nursery rhymes. Poetry, rhyme.

Clark, Margaret. *The best of Æsop's fables* (Æsop)

Clark, Roberta. *Why?* ill. by Lois Axeman. Children's Pr., 1983. Subj: Character traits – curiosity. Character traits – questioning.

Clarke, Gus. *Along came Eric* ill. by author. Lothrop, 1991. ISBN 0-688-10301-4 Subj: Babies. Family life – brothers. Sibling rivalry.

Eddie and Teddy ill. by author. Lothrop, 1991. ISBN 0-688-10039-2 Subj: Friendship. School. Toys – teddy bears.

Claude-Lafontaine, Pascale. *Monsieur Bussy, the celebrated hamster* ill. by Annick Delhumeau. McGraw-Hill, 1968. Delhumeau's name appeared first on the title page of the French ed. pub. under title: Bussy, le hamster doré Subj: Animals – hamsters. Character traits – ambition.

Claverie, Jean. *The party* ill. by author. Crown, 1986. ISBN 0-517-56026-7 Subj: Behavior – misbehavior. Parties.

The picnic ill. by author. Crown, 1986. ISBN 0-517-56025-9 Subj: Activities – picnicking. Weather – rain.

Shopping ill. by author. Crown, 1986. ISBN 0-517-56024-0 Subj: Family life. Shopping.

Working ill. by author. Crown, 1986. ISBN 0-517-56021-6 Subj: Activities – working. Family life – fathers. Weather – snow.

Claxton, Ernest. *A child's grace* (Burdekin, Harold)

Clay, Helen. *Ants* (Clay, Pat)

Beetles (Clay, Pat)

Clay, Pat. *Ants* by Pat and Helen Clay; ill. with photos. Global Lib. Mktg. Serv., 1984. ISBN 0-7136-2386-1 Subj: Insects – ants. Nature. Science.

Beetles by Pat and Helen Clay; photos. by authors. A & C Black, 1983. Subj: Science.

Cleary, Beverly. *The growing-up feet* ill. by DyAnne DiSalvo-Ryan. Morrow, 1987. ISBN 0-688-06620-8 Subj: Behavior – growing up. Family life. Twins.

The hullabaloo ABC ill. by Earl Thollander. Parnassus, 1960. Subj: ABC books. Farms. Noise, sounds.

Janet's thingamajigs ill. by DyAnne DiSalvo-Ryan. Morrow, 1987. ISBN 0-688-06618-6 Subj: Behavior – collecting things. Behavior – growing up. Family life. Sibling rivalry.

Lucky Chuck ill. by J. Winslow Higginbottom. Morrow, 1984. Subj: Behavior – carelessness. Motorcycles. Safety. Transportation.

The real hole ill. by DyAnne DiSalvo-Ryan. Morrow, 1986. ISBN 0-688-05851-5 Subj: Activities – digging. Problem solving. Trees. Twins.

Two dog biscuits ill. by DyAnne DiSalvo-Ryan. Morrow, 1986. ISBN 0-688-05848-5 Subj: Animals – cats. Animals – dogs. Twins.

Cleaver, Elizabeth. *ABC* ill. by author. Atheneum, 1985. Subj: ABC books.

The enchanted caribou ill. by author. Atheneum, 1985. ISBN 0-689-31170-2 Subj: Animals – reindeer. Folk and fairy tales. Indians of North America. Magic. Puppets.

Clement, Claude. *The painter and the wild swans* ill. by Frederic Clement. Dial Pr., 1986. ISBN 0-8037-0268-X Subj: Birds – swans. Folk and fairy tales.

The voice of the wood ill. by Frederic Clement. Dial Pr., 1989. ISBN 0-8037-0635-9 Subj: Music. Trees.

Clements, Andrew. *Little pig, big trouble* (Tharlet, Eve)

Santa's secret helper ill. by Debrah Santini. Picture Book Studio, 1990. ISBN 0-88708-136-3 Subj: Character traits – helpfulness. Holidays – Christmas.

Where is Mr. Mole? (Gantschev, Ivan)

Cleveland, David. *The April rabbits* ill. by Nurit Karlin. Coward, 1978. ISBN 0-698-20463-8 Subj: Animals – rabbits. Counting, numbers.

Clewes, Dorothy. *Happiest day* ill. by Sofia. Coward, 1959. Subj: Emotions – loneliness. School.

Henry Hare's boxing match ill. by Patricia W. Turner. Coward, 1950. Subj: Animals. Behavior – imitation.

Hide and seek ill. by Sofia. Coward, 1960. Subj: Farms.

The wild wood ill. by Irene Hawkins. Coward, 1948. Subj: Animals. Character traits – kindness to animals.

Clifford, David. *Your face is a picture* (Clifford, Eth)

Clifford, Eth. *A bear before breakfast* ill. by Kelly Oechsli. Putnam's, 1962. Subj: Communication. Language.

Red is never a mouse ill. by Bill Heckler. Bobbs-Merrill, 1960. Subj: Concepts – color. Poetry, rhyme.

Your face is a picture by Eth and David Clifford; photos. by David Clifford; ed. consultant: Leo Fay. E. C. Seale, 1963. Subj: Emotions. Ethnic groups in the U.S.

Clifton, Lucille. *All us come cross the water* ill. by John Steptoe. Holt, 1973. Subj: Character traits – pride. Ethnic groups in the U.S. – Afro-Americans. School.

Amifika ill. by Thomas Di Grazia. Dutton, 1977. Subj: Emotions – fear. Ethnic groups in the U.S. – Afro-Americans. Family life. Family life – fathers.

The boy who didn't believe in spring ill. by Brinton Turkle. Dutton, 1973. Subj: City. Ethnic groups in the U.S. – Afro-Americans. Seasons – spring.

Don't you remember? ill. by Evaline Ness. Dutton, 1973. Subj: Birthdays. Ethnic groups in the U.S. – Afro-Americans. Family life.

Everett Anderson's Christmas coming ill. by Evaline Ness. Holt, 1971. Subj: City. Ethnic groups in the U.S. – Afro-Americans. Holidays – Christmas. Poetry, rhyme.

Everett Anderson's friend ill. by Ann Grifalconi. Holt, 1976. Subj: Ethnic groups in the U.S. – Afro-Americans. Friendship. Poetry, rhyme.

Everett Anderson's goodbye ill. by Ann Grifalconi. Holt, 1988, 1983. ISBN 0-8050-0800-4 Subj: Death. Emotions. Emotions – love. Ethnic groups in the U.S. – Afro-Americans. Family life. Poetry, rhyme.

Everett Anderson's nine months long ill. by Ann Grifalconi. Holt, 1987, 1970. Subj: Babies. Ethnic groups in the U.S. – Afro-Americans.. Family life. Poetry, rhyme.

Everett Anderson's 1-2-3 ill. by Ann Grifalconi. Holt, 1977. Subj: Ethnic groups in the U.S. – Afro-Americans. Family life. Poetry, rhyme.

Everett Anderson's year ill. by Ann Grifalconi. Holt, 1974. Subj: Ethnic groups in the U.S. – Afro-Americans. Poetry, rhyme. Seasons.

My brother fine with me ill. by Moneta Barnett. Holt, 1975. Subj: Behavior – running away. Ethnic groups in the U.S. – Afro-Americans. Family life. Sibling rivalry.

My friend Jacob ill. by Thomas Di Grazia. Dutton, 1980. Subj: Character traits – helpfulness. Ethnic groups in the U.S. – Afro-Americans. Friendship. Handicaps.

Some of the days of Everett Anderson ill. by Evaline Ness. Holt, 1987, 1970. Subj: Days of the week, months of the year. Ethnic groups in the U.S. – Afro-Americans. Family life. Poetry, rhyme.

Three wishes ill. by Stephanie Douglas. Viking, 1976. Subj: Behavior – wishing. Ethnic groups in the U.S. – Afro-Americans. Friendship.

Three wishes ill. by Michael Hays. Doubleday, 1992. ISBN 0-385-30497-8 Subj: Behavior – wishing. Ethnic groups in the U.S. – Afro-Americans. Friendship.

Climo, Lindee. *Chester's barn* ill. by author. Tundra, 1982. Subj: Barns. Farms. Foreign lands – Canada.

Clyde ill. by author. Tundra, 1986. ISBN 0-88776-185-2 Subj: Animals – horses. Behavior – seeking better things. Machines.

Climo, Shirley. *The adventure of Walter* ill. by Ingrid Fetz. Atheneum, 1965. Subj: Animals – whales. Character traits – curiosity.

The cobweb Christmas ill. by Joe Lasker. Crowell, 1982. Subj: Animals. Holidays – Christmas. Magic. Spiders.

The Egyptian Cinderella ill. by Ruth Heller. HarperCollins, 1989. ISBN 0-690-04824-6 Subj: Folk and fairy tales. Foreign lands – Egypt. Royalty. Sibling rivalry.

King of the birds ill. by Ruth Heller. Harper, 1988. ISBN 0-690-04623-5 Subj: Birds. Character traits – cleverness. Royalty.

The match between the winds ill. by Roni Shepherd. Macmillan, 1991. ISBN 0-02-719035-8 Subj: Folk and fairy tales. Foreign lands – Borneo. Weather – wind.

Clinton, Susan. *I can be an architect* Childrens Pr., 1986. ISBN 0-516-01890-6 Subj: Careers – architects.

Clithero, Myrtle E. *see* Clithero, Sally

Clithero, Sally. *Beginning-to-read poetry* Follett, 1967. Subj: Poetry, rhyme.

Clymer, Eleanor Lowenton. *The tiny little house* ill. by Ingrid Fetz. Atheneum, 1964. Subj: Houses.

A yard for John ill. by Mildred Boyle. McBride, 1943. Subj: Moving.

Clymer, Ted. *The horse and the bad morning* by Ted Clymer and Miska Miles; ill. by Leslie Holt Morrill. Dutton, 1982. Subj: Animals. Behavior – dissatisfaction. Problem solving.

Coats, Laura Jane. *City cat* ill. by author. Macmillan, 1987. ISBN 0-02-719051-X Subj: Animals – cats. City.

Marcella and the moon ill. by author. Macmillan, 1986. ISBN 0-02-719050-1 Subj: Activities – painting. Birds – ducks. Moon.

Mr. Jordan in the park ill. by author. Macmillan, 1988. ISBN 0-02-719053-6 Subj: Behavior – growing up. Old age.

The oak tree ill. by author. Macmillan, 1987. ISBN 0-02-719052-8 Subj: Trees.

Ten little animals ill. by author. Macmillan, 1990. ISBN 0-02-719054-4 Subj: Animals. Counting, numbers. Poetry, rhyme.

Coatsworth, Elizabeth. *The children come running: UNICEF greeting cards* Golden Pr., 1961. Subj: Holidays – Christmas. Poetry, rhyme. UNICEF.

The giant golden book of cat stories ill. by Feodor Rojankovsky. Simon and Schuster, 1953. Subj: Animals – cats. Folk and fairy tales. Poetry, rhyme.

Good night ill. by José Aruego. Macmillan, 1972. Subj: Bedtime. Stars.

Lonely Maria ill. by Evaline Ness. Pantheon, 1960. Subj: Emotions – loneliness. Family life – grandfathers. Islands.

A peaceable kingdom, and other poems ill. by Fritz Eichenberg. Pantheon, 1958. Subj: Animals. Poetry, rhyme.

Pika and the roses ill. by Kurt Wiese. Pantheon, 1959. Subj: Animals – rabbits. Character traits – cleverness.

Under the green willow ill. by Janina Domanska. Macmillan, 1971. Subj: Birds. Fish. Food.

Cobb, Vicki. *Feeding yourself* ill. by Marylin Hafner. HarperCollins, 1989. ISBN 0-397-32325-5 Subj: Behavior – growing up.

Getting dressed ill. by Marylin Hafner. HarperCollins, 1989. ISBN 0-397-32143-0 Subj: Behavior – growing up. Clothing.

How the doctor knows you're fine ill. by Anthony Ravielli. Lippincott, 1973. Subj: Careers – doctors. Health.

Keeping clean ill. by Marylin Hafner. HarperCollins, 1989. ISBN 0-397-32313-1 Subj: Character traits – cleanliness.

Lots of rot ill. by Brian Schatell. Lippincott, 1981. Subj: Science.

Writing it down ill. by Marylin Hafner. HarperCollins, 1989. ISBN 0-397-32327-1 Subj: Activities – writing.

Cobbett, Richard *see* Pluckrose, Henry Arthur

Cober, Alan E. *Cober's choice* ill. by author. Dutton, 1979. Subj: Animals. Art.

Cocagnac, A. M. (Augustin Maurice). *The three trees of the Samurai* adapt. from a Japanese no play; ill. by Alain Le Foll. Dial Pr., 1970. Subj: Folk and fairy tales. Foreign lands – Japan.

Cock Robin. *The courtship, merry marriage, and feast of Cock Robin and Jenny Wren: to which is added the doleful death of Cock Robin* ill. by Barbara Cooney. Scribner's, 1965. Subj: Animals. Birds – robins. Birds – wrens. Death. Nursery rhymes. Weddings.

Who killed Cock Robin? ill. by William Stobbs. Oxford Univ. Pr., 1990. ISBN 0-19-279862-6 Subj: Animals. Birds – robins. Birds – wrens. Death. Format, unusual – board books. Nursery rhymes.

Coco, Eugene Bradley. *The fiddler's son* ill. by Robert James Sabuda. Green Tiger Pr., 1988. ISBN 0-88138-111-X Subj: Music.

The wishing well ill. by Robert James Sabuda. Green Tiger Pr., 1988. ISBN 0-88138-112-8 Subj: Behavior – greed. Behavior – wishing. Circular tales. Magic.

Coe, Lloyd. *Charcoal* ill. by author. Crowell, 1946. Subj: Animals – sheep.

Coerr, Eleanor. *The big balloon race* ill. by Carolyn Croll. Harper, 1981. Subj: Activities – ballooning.

Chang's paper pony ill. by Deborah Kogan Ray. Harper, 1988. ISBN 0-06-021329-9 Subj: Animals – horses. Ethnic groups in the U.S. – Chinese-Americans.

The Josefina story quilt ill. by Bruce Degen. Harper, 1986. ISBN 0-06-021349-3 Subj: Activities – traveling. Birds – chickens. Pets. Quilts.

Coffelt, Nancy. *Good night, Sigmund* ill. by author. Harcourt, 1992. ISBN 0-15-200464-5 Subj: Activities – playing. Animals – cats. Pets.

Cohen, Barbara. *The demon who would not die* ill. by Anatoly Ivanov. Atheneum, 1982. Subj: Folk and fairy tales. Foreign lands – Russia. Monsters.

The donkey's story ill. by Susan Jeanne Cohen. Lothrop, 1988. ISBN 0-688-04105-1 Subj: Animals – donkeys. Religion.

Even higher ill. by Anatoly Ivanov. Lothrop, 1987. ISBN 0-688-06453-1 Subj: Character traits – generosity. Holidays. Jewish culture.

Gooseberries to oranges ill. by Beverly Brodsky McDermott. Lothrop, 1982. Subj: Jewish culture. Moving.

Here come the Purim players! ill. by Beverly Brodsky McDermott. Lothrop, 1984. Subj: Folk and fairy tales. Holidays – Purim. Jewish culture. Middle ages.

Cohen, Burton. *Nelson makes a face* ill. by William Schroder. Lothrop, 1978. Subj: Character traits – appearance.

Cohen, Carol L. *The mud pony: a traditional Skidi Pawnee tale* ill. by Shonto Begay. Scholastic, 1988. ISBN 0-590-41525-5 Subj: Animals – horses. Folk and fairy tales. Indians of North America.

Wake up, groundhog! ill. by author. Crown, 1975. Subj: Animals – groundhogs. Clocks, watches. Hibernation. Holidays – Groundhog Day. Seasons – spring.

Cohen, Caron Lee. *Bronco dogs* ill. by Roni Shepherd. Dutton, 1991. ISBN 0-525-44721-0 Subj: Animals – dogs. Cowboys. Crime. Ghosts. U.S. history.

Pigeon, pigeon ill. by G. Brian Karas. Dutton, 1992. ISBN 0-525-44866-7 Subj: Animals. Concepts – perspective. Zoos.

Renata, Whizbrain and the ghost ill. by Blanche Sims. Atheneum, 1987. ISBN 0-689-31271-1 Subj: Character traits – cleverness. Folk and fairy tales. Ghosts.

Sally Ann Thunder Ann Whirlwind Crockett ill. by Ariane Dewey. Greenwillow, 1985. ISBN 0-688-04007-1 Subj: Behavior – trickery. Folk and fairy tales.

Three yellow dogs ill. by Peter Sis. Greenwillow, 1986. ISBN 0-688-06231-8 Subj: Animals – dogs. Language.

Whiffle Squeek ill. by Ted Rand. Dodd, 1987. ISBN 0-396-08999-2 Subj: Animals – cats. Monsters. Poetry, rhyme. Sea and seashore.

Cohen, Daniel. *America's very own monsters* ill. by Tom Huffman. Dodd, 1982. Subj: Monsters.

Dinosaurs ill. by Jean Zallinger. Doubleday, 1987. ISBN 0-385-23415-5 Subj: Dinosaurs.

Cohen, Miriam. *Bee my Valentine!* ill. by Lillian Hoban. Greenwillow, 1978. Subj: Holidays – Valentine's Day. School.

Best friends ill. by Lillian Hoban. Macmillan, 1971. Subj: Friendship. School.

Don't eat too much turkey! ill. by Lillian Hoban. Greenwillow, 1987. ISBN 0-688-07142-2 Subj: Behavior – sharing. School.

First grade takes a test ill. by Lillian Hoban. Greenwillow, 1980. Subj: Friendship. School.

It's George! ill. by Lillian Hoban. Greenwillow, 1988. ISBN 0-688-06813-8 Subj: Character traits – being different. School.

Jim meets the thing ill. by Lillian Hoban. Greenwillow, 1981. Subj: Behavior – growing up. Emotions – fear. Monsters. School.

Jim's dog Muffins ill. by Lillian Hoban. Greenwillow, 1984. Subj: Animals – dogs. Death. Emotions. Pets.

Liar, liar, pants on fire! ill. by Lillian Hoban. Greenwillow, 1985. ISBN 0-688-04245-7 Subj: Behavior – lying. Character traits – generosity. Friendship. School.

Lost in the museum ill. by Lillian Hoban. Greenwillow, 1979. Subj: Behavior – lost. Museums. School.

The new teacher ill. by Lillian Hoban. Macmillan, 1972. Subj: School.

No good in art ill. by Lillian Hoban. Greenwillow, 1980. Subj: Art. School. Self-concept.

The real-skin rubber monster mask ill. by Lillian Hoban. Greenwillow, 1990. ISBN 0-688-09123-7 Subj: Emotions – fear. Holidays – Halloween. School.

See you in second grade! ill. by Lillian Hoban. Greenwillow, 1989. ISBN 0-688-07139-2 Subj: Friendship. Sea and seashore. School.

See you tomorrow ill. by Lillian Hoban. Greenwillow, 1983. Subj: Handicaps – blindness. School. Senses – seeing.

So what? ill. by Lillian Hoban. Greenwillow, 1982. Subj: School. Self-concept.

Starring first grade ill. by Lillian Hoban. Greenwillow, 1985. ISBN 0-688-04030-6 Subj: Behavior – misbehavior. School. Theater.

Tough Jim ill. by Lillian Hoban. Macmillan, 1974. Subj: Behavior – bullying. Parties. School.

When will I read? ill. by Lillian Hoban. Greenwillow, 1977. Subj: Activities – reading. School.

Will I have a friend? ill. by Lillian Hoban. Macmillan, 1967. Subj: Ethnic groups in the U.S. Friendship. School.

Cohen, Paul. *Creepy crawly critter riddles* (Bernstein, Joanne E.)

What was the wicked witch's real name? (Bernstein, Joanne E.)

Cohen, Peter Zachary. *Authorized autumn charts of the Upper Red Canoe River country* ill. by Tomie de Paola. Atheneum, 1972. Subj: ABC books. Boats, ships. Games. Seasons – fall.

Olson's meat pies tr. by Richard E. Fisher, ill. by Olof Landström. Farrar, 1989. ISBN 9-129-59180-5 Subj: Behavior – mistakes. Food.

Cohn, Janice. *I had a friend named Peter: talking to children about the death of a friend* ill. by Gail Owens. Morrow, 1987. ISBN 0-688-06686-0 Subj: Death. Friendship.

Cohn, Norma. *Brother and sister* ill. by author. Oxford Univ. Pr., 1942. Subj: Animals – cats. Sports – swimming.

Coker, Gylbert. *Naptime* ill. by author. Delacorte, 1978. Subj: School. Sleep.

Colby, C. B. (Carroll Burleigh). *Who lives there?* ill. by author. Atheneum, 1953. Subj: Animals. Birds. Houses. Insects. Science.

Who went there? ill. by author. Atheneum, 1953. Subj: Animals. Birds. Reptiles. Science.

Coldrey, Jennifer. *Penguins* photos. by Douglas Allan and others. André Deutsch, 1983. Subj: Birds – penguins.

The world of chickens ill. with photos. Gareth Stevens, 1987. ISBN 1-55532-071-6 Subj: Birds – chickens. Science.

The world of crabs photos. by Oxford Scientific Films. Gareth Stevens, 1986. ISBN 1-55532-063-5 Subj: Crustacea. Science.

The world of frogs photos. by Oxford Scientific Films. Gareth Stevens, 1986. ISBN 1-55532-024-4 Subj: Frogs and toads. Science.

The world of rabbits photos. by Oxford Scientific Films. Gareth Stevens, 1986. ISBN 1-55532-064-3 Subj: Animals – rabbits. Science.

The world of squirrels photos. by Oxford Scientific Films. Gareth Stevens, 1986. ISBN 1-55532-065-1 Subj: Animals – squirrels. Science.

Cole, Babette. *Cupid* ill. by author. Putnam, 1990. ISBN 0-399-22215-4 Subj: Emotions – love. Mythical creatures.

Hurray for Ethelyn ill. by author. Little, 1991. ISBN 0-316-15189-0 Subj: Animals – rats. Behavior – bullying. Emotions – envy, jealousy.

King Change-A-Lot ill. by author. Putnam, 1989. ISBN 0-399-21670-7 Subj: Behavior – dissatisfaction. Royalty – kings. Royalty – princes.

Nungu and the elephant ill. by author. McGraw-Hill, 1980. Subj: Animals – elephants. Foreign lands – Africa. Magic.

Nungu and the hippopotamus ill. by author. McGraw-Hill, 1979. Subj: Animals – hippopotami. Foreign lands – Africa.

Prince Cinders ill. by author. Putnam's, 1988. ISBN 0-399-21502-6 Subj: Folk and fairy tales. Magic. Royalty – princes.

Princess Smartypants ill. by author. Putnam's, 1987. ISBN 0-399-21409-7 Subj: Pets. Problem solving. Royalty – princesses.

Silly book ill. by author. Doubleday, 1990. ISBN 0-385-41238-X Subj: Friendship. Poetry, rhyme.

The trouble with dad ill. by author. Putnam's, 1986. ISBN 0-399-21206-X Subj: Activities – working. Family life – fathers. Robots.

The trouble with Gran ill. by author. Putnam's, 1987. ISBN 0-399-21428-3 Subj: Family life – grandmothers. Space and space ships.

The trouble with mom ill. by author. Coward, 1984. Subj: Family life – mothers. School. Witches.

The trouble with Uncle ill. by author. Little, 1992. ISBN 0-316-15190-4 Subj: Family life – aunts, uncles. Imagination. Pirates. Sea and seashore.

Cole, Barbara Hancock. *Texas star* ill. by Barbara Minton. Orchard, 1990. ISBN 0-531-08420-5 Subj: Family life. Quilts.

Cole, Brock. *The giant's toe* ill. by author. Farrar, 1986. ISBN 0-374-32559-6 Subj: Anatomy. Folk and fairy tales. Giants.

The king at the door ill. by author. Doubleday, 1979. Subj: Behavior – disbelief. Character traits – kindness. Foreign lands – England. Royalty – kings.

Nothing but a pig ill. by author. Doubleday, 1981. Subj: Animals – pigs. Behavior – imitation. Behavior – seeking better things. Friendship.

Cole, Davis *see* Elting, Mary

Cole, Joanna. *Animal sleepyheads: one to ten* ill. by Jeni Bassett. Scholastic, 1988. ISBN 0-590-40919-0 Subj: Animals. Counting, numbers. Poetry, rhyme.

Aren't you forgetting something, Fiona? ill. by Ned Delaney. Parents, 1984. Subj: Animals – elephants. Behavior – forgetfulness.

Bony-legs ill. by Dirk Zimmer. Four Winds Pr., 1983. Subj: Folk and fairy tales. Foreign lands – Russia. Magic. Witches.

A calf is born photos. by Jerome Wexler. Morrow, 1975. Subj: Animals – bulls, cows. Babies. Birth. Science.

A chick hatches photos. by Jerome Wexler. Morrow, 1976. Subj: Birds – chickens. Science.

The Clown-Arounds go on vacation ill. by Jerry Smath. Parents, 1984. Subj: Activities – vacationing. Behavior – lost. Clowns, jesters. Humor. Riddles.

Doctor Change ill. by Donald Carrick. Morrow, 1986. ISBN 0-688-06136-2 Subj: Character traits – cleverness. Folk and fairy tales.

Don't call me names! Just right for 4's and 5's ill. by Lynn Munsinger. McKay, 1990. ISBN 0-679-90258-9 Subj: Behavior – bullying. Friendship. Frogs and toads.

Don't tell the whole world ill. by Kate Duke. HarperCollins, 1990. ISBN 0-690-04811-4 Subj: Behavior. Behavior – secrets. Folk and fairy tales. Money.

Evolution ill. by Aliki. Crowell, 1987. ISBN 0-690-04598-0 Subj: Animals. Plants. Science.

Find the hidden insect by Joanna Cole and Jerome Wexler; photos. by Jerome Wexler. Morrow, 1979. Subj: Insects. Science.

A fish hatches photos. by Jerome Wexler. Morrow, 1978. Subj: Fish. Science.

Get well, Clown-Arounds! ill. by Jerry Smath. Parents, 1983. Subj: Clowns, jesters. Humor. Illness. Riddles.

Golly Gump swallowed a fly ill. by Bari Weissman. Parents, 1982. Subj: Folk and fairy tales. Humor. Poetry, rhyme.

How you were born photos. by Hella Hammid and others. Morrow, 1984. Subj: Babies. Birth. Family life. Science.

Hungry, hungry sharks ill. by Patricia Wynne. Random, 1986. ISBN 0-394-97471-9 Subj: Fish. Science.

It's too noisy ill. by Kate Duke. HarperCollins, 1989. ISBN 0-690-04737-1 Subj: Animals. Folk and fairy tales. Humor. Jewish culture. Noise, sounds. Problem solving.

Large as life daytime animals ill. by Kenneth Lilly. Knopf, 1985. ISBN 0-394-97188-4 Subj: Animals.

Large as life nighttime animals ill. by Kenneth Lilly. Knopf, 1985. ISBN 0-394-97189-2 Subj: Animals. Night.

Monster manners ill. by Jared D. Lee. Scholastic, 1985. ISBN 0-590-33592-8 Subj: Etiquette. Monsters.

My puppy is born photos. by Margaret Miller. Morrow, 1991. ISBN 0-688-09771-5 Subj: Animals – dogs. Birth. Science.

The new baby at your house photos. by Hella Hammid. Morrow, 1985. ISBN 0-688-05807-8 Subj: Babies. Emotions – envy, jealousy. Family life. Sibling rivalry.

Norma Jean, jumping bean ill. by Lynn Munsinger. Random House, 1987. ISBN 0-394-98668-7 Subj: Activities – jumping. Animals – kangaroos. School.

Plants in winter ill. by Kazue Mizumura. Crowell, 1973. Subj: Plants. Science. Seasons – winter. Trees.

The secret box ill. by Joan Sandin. Morrow, 1971. Subj: Behavior – stealing.

Your new potty ill. by Margaret Miller. Morrow, 1989. ISBN 0-688-06106-0 Subj: Behavior – growing up. Toilet training.

Cole, Michael. *Head in the sand* ill. by Rowan Clifford. Carolrhoda, 1990. ISBN 0-87614-435-0 Subj: Animals. Behavior – hiding. Birds.

Cole, Sheila. *When the rain stops* ill. by Henri Sorensen. Lothrop, 1991. ISBN 0-688-07655-6 Subj: Country. Family life – fathers. Weather – rain.

When the tide is low ill. by Virginia Wright-Frierson. Lothrop, 1985. ISBN 0-688-04067-5 Subj: Animals. Sea and seashore.

Cole, William. *Aunt Bella's umbrella* ill. by Jacqueline Chwast. Doubleday, 1970. Subj: Character traits – helpfulness. Family life – aunts, uncles. Umbrellas. Weather – rain.

Frances face-maker ill. by Tomi Ungerer. Collins-World, 1963. Subj: Bedtime. Emotions. Family life. Participation. Poetry, rhyme.

I went to the animal fair ill. by Colette Rosselli. Collins-World, 1959. Subj: Animals. Poetry, rhyme.

That pest Jonathan ill. by Tomi Ungerer. Harper, 1970. Subj: Behavior – misbehavior. Family life. Poetry, rhyme.

What's good for a four-year-old? ill. by Tomi Ungerer. Holt, 1967. Subj: Activities – playing. Poetry, rhyme.

What's good for a six-year-old? ill. by Ingrid Fetz. Holt, 1965. Subj: Activities – playing. Poetry, rhyme.

What's good for a three-year-old? ill. by Lillian Hoban. Holt, 1974. Subj: Activities – baby-sitting. Birthdays. Poetry, rhyme.

Coleridge, Sara. *January brings the snow: a book of months* ill. by Jenni Oliver. Dial Pr., 1986. ISBN 0-8037-0314-7 Subj: Days of the week, months of the year. Poetry, rhyme. Seasons.

Coles, Alison. *Michael and the sea* ill. by Michael Charlton. EDC, 1985. ISBN 0-88110-268-7 Subj: Emotions – fear. Sea and seashore. Sports – swimming.

Michael in the dark ill. by Michael Charlton. EDC, 1985. ISBN 0-88110-267-9 Subj: Emotions – fear. Night.

Michael's first day ill. by Michael Charlton. EDC, 1985. ISBN 0-88110-266-0 Subj: Emotions – fear. School.

Coletta, Hallie. *From A to Z* (Coletta, Irene)

Coletta, Irene. *From A to Z* by Irene and Hallie Coletta; ill. by Hallie Coletta. Prentice-Hall, 1979. Subj: ABC books. Poetry, rhyme. Rebuses.

Colette. *The boy and the magic* tr. by Christopher Fry; ill. by Gerard Hoffnung. Putnam's, 1965. Subj: Behavior – misbehavior. Magic. Music.

Collier, Ethel. *I know a farm* ill. by Honoré Guilbeau. Addison-Wesley, 1960. Subj: Farms.

Who goes there in my garden? ill. by Honoré Guilbeau. Abelard-Schuman, 1963. Subj: Character traits – helpfulness. Gardens, gardening.

Collier, James Lincoln. *Danny goes to the hospital* ill. by Yale Joel. Norton, 1970. Subj: Hospitals.

Collington, Peter. *The angel and the soldier boy* ill. by author. Knopf, 1987. ISBN 0-394-98626-1 Subj: Angels. Behavior – stealing. Pirates. Toys – soldiers. Wordless.

Little pickle ill. by author. Dutton, 1986. ISBN 0-525-44230-8 Subj: Behavior – misbehavior. Dreams. Sleep. Wordless.

My darling kitten ill. by author. Knopf, 1988. ISBN 0-394-89924-5 Subj: Animals – cats. Pets.

Collins, Bonnie. *Rocks in my pocket* (Harshman, Marc)

Collins, Judith Graham. *Josh's scary dad* ill. by Diane Paterson. Abingdon Pr., 1983. Subj: Character traits – appearance. Humor.

Collins, Pat Lowery. *My friend Andrew* ill. by Howard Berelson. Prentice-Hall, 1981. Subj: Behavior – boasting. Imagination.

Taking care of Tucker ill. by Maxie Chambliss. Putnam's, 1989. ISBN 0-399-21586-7 Subj: Behavior – misbehavior. Behavior – needing someone. Family life.

Tomorrow, up and away! ill. by Lynn Munsinger. Houghton, 1990. ISBN 0-395-51524-6 Subj: Activities – flying. Animals. Animals – squirrels. Reptiles – turtles, tortoises.

Tumble, tumble, tumbleweed ill. by Charles Robinson. Albert Whitman, 1982. Subj: Friendship. Pets.

Waiting for baby Joe ill. by Joan Whinham Dunn. Albert Whitman, 1990. ISBN 0-8075-8625-0 Subj: Babies. Family life – brothers. Family life – sisters.

Collodi, Carlo. *The adventures of Pinocchio* adapt. by Stephanie Spinner; ill. by Diane Goode. Random House, 1983. Subj: Behavior – lying. Behavior – misbehavior. Character traits – loyalty. Folk and fairy tales. Puppets.

Colman, Hila. *Peter's brownstone house* ill. by Leonard Weisgard. Morrow, 1963. Subj: City. Houses.

Watch that watch ill. by Leonard Weisgard. Morrow, 1962. Subj: Animals. Clocks, watches. Time.

Colonius, Lillian. *At the zoo* by Lillian Colonius and Glen W. Schroeder; ill. by Glen W. Schroeder. Melmont, 1954. Subj: Zoos.

Coman, Carolyn. *Losing things at Mr. Mudd's* ill. by Lance Hidy. Farrar, 1992. ISBN 0-374-34657-7 Subj: Behavior – losing things.

Come out to play ill. by Jeanette Winter. Knopf, 1986. ISBN 0-394-97742-4 Subj: City. Moon. Nursery rhymes.

Come to the circus Simon and Schuster, 1980. Subj: Circus. Format, unusual – board books.

Company González, Mercè. *Killian and the dragons* adapt. by Paula Franklin; ill. by Agustí Asensio Sauri. Silver Burdett, 1986. ISBN 0-382-09180-9 Subj: Dragons. Emotions – fear. Royalty.

Compton, Joanne. *Little Rabbit's Easter surprise* ill. by Kenn Compton. Holiday, 1992. ISBN 0-8234-0920-1 Subj: Animals – rabbits. Holidays – Easter.

Compton, Kenn. *Happy Christmas to all!* ill. by author. Holiday, 1991. ISBN 0-8234-0890-6 Subj: Behavior – secrets. Elves and little people. Holidays – Christmas.

Conaway, Judith. *I'll get even* ill. by Mark Gubin. Raintree Pub., 1977. Subj: Emotions – loneliness. Sibling rivalry.

Conford, Ellen. *Eugene the brave* ill. by John M. Larrecq. Little, 1978. Subj: Animals – possums. Character traits – bravery. Emotions – fear. Night.

Impossible, possum ill. by Rosemary Wells. Little, 1971. Subj: Animals – possums. Character traits – individuality.

Just the thing for Geraldine ill. by John M. Larrecq. Little, 1974. Subj: Animals – possums. Character traits – perseverance.

Why can't I be William? ill. by Philip Wende. Little, 1972. Subj: Emotions – envy, jealousy. Family life. Family life – only child. Friendship.

Conger, Lesley. *Tops and bottoms* ill. by Imero Gobbato. Four Winds Pr., 1970. Subj: Folk and fairy tales. Foreign lands – England. Monsters.

Conger, Marion. *The chipmunk that went to church* ill. by author. Simon and Schuster, 1952. Subj: Animals – chipmunks. Emotions – loneliness.

The little golden holiday book ill. by author. Simon and Schuster, 1951. Subj: Holidays.

Conklin, Gladys. *Cheetahs, the swift hunters* ill. by Charles Robinson. Holiday, 1976. Subj: Animals – cheetahs. Science.

I caught a lizard ill. by Artur Marokvia. Holiday, 1967. Subj: Animals. Insects. Reptiles – lizards. Science. Spiders.

I like beetles ill. by Jean Zallinger. Holiday, 1975. Subj: Insects – beetles. Science.

I like butterflies ill. by Barbara Latham. Holiday, 1960. Subj: Insects – butterflies, caterpillars. Science.

I like caterpillars ill. by Barbara Latham. Holiday, 1958. Subj: Insects – butterflies, caterpillars. Science.

I watch flies ill. by Jean Zallinger. Holiday, 1977. Subj: Insects – flies. Science.

If I were a bird ill. by Artur Marokvia. Holiday, 1965. Subj: Birds. Science.

Journey of the gray whales ill. by Leonard Everett Fisher. Holiday, 1974. Subj: Animals – whales. Science.

Little apes ill. by Joseph Cellini. Holiday, 1970. Subj: Animals – gorillas. Science.

Lucky ladybugs ill. by Glen Rounds. Holiday, 1968. Subj: Insects – ladybugs. Science.

Praying mantis: the garden dinosaur ill. by Glen Rounds. Holiday, 1978. Subj: Insects – praying mantis. Science.

We like bugs ill. by Artur Marokvia. Holiday, 1962. Subj: Insects. Science.

When insects are babies ill. by Artur Marokvia. Holiday, 1969. Subj: Insects. Science.

Conover, Chris. *Froggie went a-courting* (A frog he would a-wooing go (folk-song))

Mother Goose and the sly fox ill. by author. Farrar, 1991. ISBN 0-374-35072-8 Subj: Animals – foxes. Behavior – talking to strangers. Birds – geese. Folk and fairy tales.

Six little ducks ill. by author. Crowell, 1976. Subj: Birds – ducks. Counting, numbers. Music. Poetry, rhyme. Songs.

Conrad, Pam. *The tub people* ill. by Richard Egielski. HarperCollins, 1989. ISBN 0-06-021341-8 Subj: Activities – bathing. Toys.

Conran, Sebastian. *My first ABC book* ill. by author. Macmillan, 1988. ISBN 0-689-71198-0 Subj: ABC books.

Conroy, Jack. *The fast sooner hound* (Bontemps, Arna Wendell)

Conta, Marcia Maher. *Feelings between brothers and sisters* ill. by Jules M. Rosenthal. Raintree Pub., 1974. Subj: Emotions. Family life.

Feelings between friends ill. by Jules M. Rosenthal. Raintree Pub., 1974. Subj: Emotions. Friendship.

Feelings between kids and grownups ill. by Jules M. Rosenthal. Raintree Pub., 1974. Subj: Emotions.

Feelings between kids and parents ill. by Jules M. Rosenthal. Raintree Pub., 1974. Subj: Emotions. Family life.

Contos, Alexander. *Tanya and the tobo man / Tanya y el hombre tobo* (Koplow, Lesley)

Cook, Ann. *Lady Monster has a plan* (Blance, Ellen)

Lady Monster helps out (Blance, Ellen)

Monster and the magic umbrella (Blance, Ellen)

Monster and the mural (Blance, Ellen)

Monster and the surprise cookie (Blance, Ellen)

Monster at school (Blance, Ellen)

Monster buys a pet (Blance, Ellen)

Monster cleans his house (Blance, Ellen)

Monster comes to the city (Blance, Ellen)

Monster gets a job (Blance, Ellen)

Monster goes around the town (Blance, Ellen)

Monster goes to school (Blance, Ellen)

Monster goes to the beach (Blance, Ellen)

Monster goes to the circus (Blance, Ellen)

Monster goes to the hospital (Blance, Ellen)

Monster goes to the museum (Blance, Ellen)

Monster goes to the zoo (Blance, Ellen)

Monster has a party (Blance, Ellen)

Monster, Lady Monster and the bike ride (Blance, Ellen)

Monster looks for a friend (Blance, Ellen)

Monster looks for a house (Blance, Ellen)

Monster meets Lady Monster (Blance, Ellen)

Monster on the bus (Blance, Ellen)

Cook, Bernadine. *The little fish that got away* ill. by Crockett Johnson. Addison-Wesley, 1956. Subj: Fish. Sports – fishing.

Looking for Susie ill. by Judith Shahn. Addison-Wesley, 1959. Subj: Animals – cats. Family life. Farms.

Cook, Marion B. *Waggles and the dog catcher* ill. by Louis Darling. Morrow, 1951. Subj: Animals – dogs.

Cook, Scott. *The gingerbread boy* (The gingerbread boy)

Cooke, Ann. *Giraffes at home* ill. by Robert M. Quackenbush. Harper, 1972. Subj: Animals – giraffes. Science.

Cooke, Barbara *see* Alexander, Anne (Anna Barbara Cooke)

Coombs, Patricia. *Lisa and the grompet* ill. by author. Lothrop, 1970. Subj: Behavior – running away. Fairies. Family life.

The lost playground ill. by author. Lothrop, 1963. Subj: Behavior – losing things. Character traits – being different. Toys.

The magic pot ill. by author. Lothrop, 1977. Subj: Devil. Folk and fairy tales. Foreign lands – Denmark. Magic.

The magician and McTree ill. by author. Lothrop, 1984. Subj: Animals – cats. Behavior – secrets. Magic. Middle ages.

Molly Mullett ill. by author. Lothrop, 1975. Subj: Character traits – bravery. Monsters.

Mouse Café ill. by author. Lothrop, 1972. Subj: Animals – mice. Character traits – selfishness. Weddings.

Tilabel ill. by author. Lothrop, 1978. Subj: Activities – weaving. Animals – groundhogs. Folk and fairy tales. Foreign lands – Germany. Royalty.

Cooney, Barbara. *Chanticleer and the fox* (Chaucer, Geoffrey)

A garland of games and other diversions: an alphabet book initial letters by Suzanne R. Morse; ill. by author. Holt, 1969. Subj: ABC books. Poetry, rhyme.

Hattie and the wild waves ill. by author. Viking, 1990. ISBN 0-670-83056-9 Subj: Family life. Sea and seashore.

Island boy ill. by author. Viking, 1988. ISBN 0-670-81749-X Subj: Death. Family life. Islands.

Little brother and little sister ill. by author. Doubleday, 1982. Subj: Character traits – loyalty. Folk and fairy tales. Foreign lands – Germany. Royalty. Witches.

The little juggler ill. by author. Hastings, 1982. Reprint of 1961 ed Subj: Holidays – Christmas.

A little prayer ill. by author. Hastings, 1967. Subj: Religion.

Miss Rumphius ill. by author. Viking, 1982. Subj: Activities – traveling. Flowers.

Snow-White and Rose-Red (Grimm, Jacob)

Cooney, Nancy Evans. *The blanket that had to go* ill. by Diane Dawson. Putnam's, 1981. Subj: Behavior – growing up. Problem solving. School.

Donald says thumbs down ill. by Maxie Chambliss. Putnam's, 1987. ISBN 0-399-21373-2 Subj: Behavior – growing up. Emotions – embarrassment. Problem solving. Thumbsucking.

Go away monsters, lickety split! ill. by Maxie Chambliss. Putnam, 1990. ISBN 0-399-21935-8 Subj: Emotions – fear. Monsters. Pets.

The wobbly tooth ill. by Marylin Hafner. Putnam's, 1978. Subj: Teeth.

Coontz, Otto. *The quiet house* ill. by author. Little, 1978. Subj: Animals – dogs. Eggs. Emotions – loneliness. Friendship.

A real class clown ill. by author. Little, 1979. Subj: Circus. Clowns, jesters. School.

Starring Rosa ill. by author. Little, 1980. Subj: Animals – pigs. Food. Humor.

Cooper, Elizabeth K. *The fish from Japan* ill. by Beth and Joe Krush. Harcourt, 1969. Subj: Fish. Imagination. Kites. Pets.

Cooper, Jacqueline. *Angus and the Mona Lisa* ill. by author. Lothrop, 1981. Subj: Animals – cats. Behavior – stealing. Problem solving.

Cooper, Letice Ulpha. *The bear who was too big* ill. by Ruth Ives. Follett, 1963. Subj: Stores. Toys – teddy bears.

Cooper, Paulette. *Let's find out about Halloween* ill. by Errol Le Cain. Watts, 1972. Subj: Holidays – Halloween.

Cooper, Susan. *Matthew's dragon* ill. by Joseph A. Smith. Macmillan, 1991. ISBN 0-689-50512-4 Subj: Animals. Dragons. Dreams.

The Selkie girl ill. by Warwick Hutton. McElderry Books, 1986. ISBN 0-689-50390-3 Subj: Animals – seals. Folk and fairy tales. Foreign lands – Ireland. Foreign lands – Scotland. Mythical creatures.

The silver cow: a Welsh tale ill. by Warwick Hutton. Atheneum, 1983. Subj: Behavior – greed. Character traits – smallness. Folk and fairy tales. Foreign lands – England.

Tam Lin ill. by Warwick Hutton. Macmillan , 1991. ISBN 0-689-50505-1 Subj: Elves and little people. Folk and fairy tales. Foreign lands – Scotland. Royalty – princesses.

Coopersmith, Jerome. *A Chanukah fable for Christmas* ill. by Syd Hoff. Putnam's, 1969. Subj: Behavior – wishing. Holidays – Hanukkah. Jewish culture.

Cope, Dawn. *Humpty Dumpty's favorite nursery rhymes* comp. by Dawn and Peter Cope; ill. by Jessie M. King, Randolph Caldecott and others. Holt, 1981. Subj: Nursery rhymes.

Cope, Peter. *Humpty Dumpty's favorite nursery rhymes* (Cope, Dawn)

Copeland, Helen. *Meet Miki Takino* ill. by Kurt Werth. Lothrop, 1963. Subj: Ethnic groups in the U.S. – Japanese-Americans. Family life – grandparents.

Copp, Andrew James *see* Copp, James (Andrew James)

Copp, James (Andrew James). *Martha Matilda O'Toole* ill. by Steven Kellogg. Bradbury Pr., 1969. Originally appeared as a song in the author's phonorecord: Jim Copp tales Subj: Behavior – forgetfulness. Humor. Poetry, rhyme. School.

Copp, Jim *see* Copp, James (Andrew James)

Corbalis, Judy. *The cuckoo bird* ill. by David Armitage. HarperCollins, 1991. ISBN 0-06-021698-0 Subj: Behavior – greed. Birds – cuckoos. Family life – grandmothers. Problem solving.

Porcellus, the flying pig ill. by Helen Craig. Dial Pr., 1988. ISBN 0-8037-0486-0 Subj: Activities – flying. Animals – pigs. Character traits – being different.

Corbett, Grahame. *Guess who?* ill. by author. Dial Pr., 1982. Subj: Format, unusual – board books. Participation. Toys.

What number now? ill. by author. Dial Pr., 1982. Subj: Counting, numbers. Format, unusual – board books. Participation.

Who is hiding? ill. by author. Dial Pr., 1982. Subj: Format, unusual – board books. Participation. Toys.

Who is inside? ill. by author. Dial Pr., 1982. Subj: Format, unusual – board books. Participation. Toys.

Who is next? ill. by author. Dial Pr., 1982. Subj: Format, unusual – board books. Participation. Toys.

Corcos, Lucille. *The city book* ill. by author. Golden Pr., 1972. Subj: City.

Corddry, Thomas I. *Kibby's big feat* ill. by Quentin Blake. Follett, 1971. Subj: Bedtime. Behavior – lost. Jungle.

Corey, Dorothy. *Everybody takes turns* ill. by Lois Axeman. Albert Whitman, 1979. Subj: Behavior – sharing.

A shot for baby bear ill. by Doug Cushman. Albert Whitman, 1988. ISBN 0-8075-7348-5 Subj: Animals. Careers – doctors.

Tomorrow you can ill. by Lois Axeman. Albert Whitman, 1977. Subj: Behavior – growing up.

We all share ill. by Rondi Colette. Albert Whitman, 1980. Subj: Behavior – sharing.

Will it ever be my birthday? ill. by Eileen Christelow. Albert Whitman, 1986. ISBN 0-8075-9106-8 Subj: Animals. Birthdays. Emotions – envy, jealousy. Holidays – Halloween. Parties.

Will there be a lap for me? ill. by Nancy Poydar. Albert Whitman, 1992. ISBN 0-8075-9109-2 Subj: Babies. Behavior – needing someone. Family life. Sibling rivalry.

Cormack, M. Grant. *Animal tales from Ireland* ill. by Vana Earle. John Day, 1955. First published in England, 1954 Subj: Animals. Folk and fairy tales. Foreign lands – Ireland.

Corney, Estelle. *Pa's top hat* ill. by Hilary Abrahams. Elsevier-Dutton, 1981. Subj: Sea and seashore. Trains.

Cornish, Sam. *Grandmother's pictures* ill. by Jeanne Johns. Bradbury Pr., 1974. Subj: Family life. Family life – grandmothers.

Corrigan, Kathy. *Emily Umily* ill. by Vlasta van Kampen. Firefly, 1984. ISBN 0-920236-96-0 Subj: Emotions – embarrassment. Handicaps. School.

Corrin, Ruth. *Mister cat* ill. by John Hurford. Interlink, 1991. ISBN 0-940793-89-X Subj: Animals – cats. Birth. Pets.

Corrin, Sara. *Mrs. Fox's wedding* (Grimm, Jacob)

The pied piper of Hamelin (Browning, Robert)

Corrin, Stephen. *Mrs. Fox's wedding* (Grimm, Jacob)

The pied piper of Hamelin (Browning, Robert)

Cortesi, Wendy W. *Explore a spooky swamp* ill. by Joseph H. Bailey. National Geographic Soc., 1979. Subj: Animals. Birds. Frogs and toads. Reptiles.

Cosgrove, Margaret. *Wintertime for animals* ill. by author. Dodd, 1975. Subj: Animals. Science. Seasons – winter.

Cosgrove, Stephen (Edward). *Sleepy time bunny* by Stephen Cosgrove and Charles Reasoner. Price Stern Sloan, 1984. Subj: Animals – rabbits. Bedtime. Format, unusual – board books. Night.

Cossi, Olga. *Gus the bus* ill. by Howie Schneider. Scholastic, 1989. ISBN 0-590-41616-2 Subj: Buses.

Costa, Nicoletta. *The birthday party* ill. by author. Grosset, 1984. Subj: Animals – cats. Birthdays. Format, unusual – board books.

Dressing up ill. by author. Grosset, 1984. Subj: Animals – cats. Format, unusual – board books.

A friend comes to play ill. by author. Grosset, 1984. Subj: Animals – cats. Format, unusual – board books. Friendship.

The mischievous princess ill. by author. Silver Burdett, 1986. ISBN 0-382-09179-5 Subj: Folk and fairy tales. Royalty – princesses.

The missing cat ill. by author. Grosset, 1984. Subj: Animals – cats. Format, unusual – board books.

The naughty puppy ill. by author. Macmillan, 1985. ISBN 0-02-724660-4 Subj: Animals – dogs. Behavior – misbehavior.

The new puppy ill. by author. Macmillan, 1985. ISBN 0-02-724650-7 Subj: Animals – dogs. Behavior – misbehavior.

Cotler, Joanna. *Sky above earth below* ill. by author. HarperCollins, 1990. ISBN 0-06-021366-3 Subj: Airplanes, airports.

Counsel, June. *But Martin!* ill. by Carolyn Dinan. Faber, 1984. ISBN 0-571-13349-5 Subj: Character traits – being different. Space and space ships.

Count me in : *44 songs and rhymes about numbers* Sterling, 1985. ISBN 0-7136-2622-4 Subj: Counting, numbers. Music. Poetry, rhyme. Songs.

Counting rhymes ill. by Corinne Malvern. Simon and Schuster, 1946. Subj: Counting, numbers. Poetry, rhyme.

Cousins, Lucy. *Country animals* ill. by author. Morrow, 1991. ISBN 0-688-10070-8 Subj: Animals. Country. Format, unusual – board books.

Farm animals ill. by author. Morrow, 1991. ISBN 0-688-10071-6 Subj: Animals. Farms. Format, unusual – board books.

Flower in the garden ill. by author. Candlewick Pr., 1992. ISBN 1-56402-029-0 Subj: Flowers. Format, unusual. Wordless.

Garden animals ill. by author. Morrow, 1991. ISBN 0-688-10072-4 Subj: Animals. Format, unusual – board books.

Hen on the farm ill. by author. Candlewick Pr., 1992. ISBN 1-56402-032-0 Subj: Birds – chickens. Farms. Format, unusual. Wordless.

Kite in the park ill. by author. Candlewick Pr., 1992. ISBN 1-56402-031-0 Subj: Kites. Format, unusual. Wordless.

Maisy goes to bed ill. by author. Little, 1990. ISBN 0-316-15832-1 Subj: Bedtime. Format, unusual – toy and movable books.

Masy goes swimming ill. by author. Little, 1990. ISBN 0-316-15834-8 Subj: Format, unusual – toy and movable books. Sports – swimming.

Pet animals ill. by author. Morrow, 1991. ISBN 0-688-10073-2 Subj: Animals. Format, unusual – board books. Pets.

Portly's hat ill. by author. Dutton, 1989. ISBN 0-525-44457-2 Subj: Birds. Birds – penguins. Clothing – hats.

Teddy in the house ill. by author. Candlewick Pr., 1992. ISBN 1-56402-030-4 Subj: Format, unusual. Wordless.

What can rabbit hear? ill. by author. Morrow, 1991. ISBN 0-688-10455-X Subj: Animals. Animals – rabbits. Format, unusual – toy and movable books. Noise, sounds. Senses – hearing.

What can rabbit see? ill. by author. Morrow, 1991. ISBN 0-688-10454-1 Subj: Animals. Animals – rabbits. Format, unusual – toy and movable books. Glasses. Senses – seeing.

Coutant, Helen. *First snow* ill. by Vo-Dinh Mai. Knopf, 1974. Subj: Death. Family life – grandmothers. Seasons – winter.

Couture, Susan Arkin. *The block book* ill. by Petra Mathers. HarperCollins, 1990. ISBN 0-06-020524-5 Subj: Behavior – collecting things. Poetry, rhyme. Toys.

Coville, Bruce. *The foolish giant* by Bruce and Katherine Coville; ill. by Katherine Coville. Lippincott, 1978. Subj: Character traits – bravery. Character traits – kindness. Friendship. Giants. Magic.

Sarah and the dragon ill. by Beth Peck. Lippincott, 1984. Subj: Character traits – kindness. Dragons. Folk and fairy tales. Magic. Mythical creatures. Witches.

Sarah's unicorn by Bruce and Katherine Coville; ill. by authors. Lippincott, 1979. Subj: Animals. Character traits – meanness. Mythical creatures – unicorns. Witches.

Coville, Katherine. *The foolish giant* (Coville, Bruce)

Sarah's unicorn (Coville, Bruce)

Cowcher, Helen. *Rain forest* ill. by author. Farrar, 1988. ISBN 0-374-36167-3 Subj: Animals. Foreign lands – South America. Forest, woods. Machines.

Tigress ill. by author. Farrar, 1991. ISBN 0-374-37567-4 Subj: Animals – endangered animals. Animals – tigers. Character traits – kindness to animals.

Cowles, Kathleen. *Feelings* (Allington, Richard L.)

Hearing (Allington, Richard L.)

Looking (Allington, Richard L.)

Smelling (Allington, Richard L.)

Tasting (Allington, Richard L.)

Touching (Allington, Richard L.)

Cox, David. *Ayu and the perfect moon* ill. by author. Subj: Activities – dancing. Foreign lands – Bali.

Bossyboots ill. by author. Crown, 1987. ISBN 0-517-56491-2 Subj: Character traits – willfulness. Crime. Foreign lands – Australia.

Tin Lizzie and Little Nell ill. by author. Merrimack, 1984. ISBN 0-370-30922-7 Subj: Animals – horses. Foreign lands – Australia. Machines.

Cox, Lynn. *Crazy alphabet* ill. by Rodney McRae. Orchard, 1992. ISBN 0-531-08566-X Subj: ABC books. Cumulative tales.

Cox, Palmer. *Another Brownie book* ill. by author. McGraw-Hill, 1967. Re-publication of the orig. 1890 ed Subj: Elves and little people.

The Brownies: their book ill. by author. McGraw-Hill, 1967. Re-publication of the orig. 1887 ed Subj: Elves and little people.

Cox, Victoria. *Going my way?* (Applebaum, Stan)

Coxe, Molly. *Louella and the yellow balloon* ill. by author. Crowell, 1988. ISBN 0-690-04748-7 Subj: Circus. Toys – balloons.

Whose footprints? ill. by author. HarperCollins, 1990. ISBN 0-690-04837-8 Subj: Animals. Family life. Farms. Seasons – winter.

Crabtree, Judith. *The sparrow's story at the king's command* ill. by author. Oxford Univ. Pr., 1983. Subj: Birds – sparrows. Royalty – kings.

Craft, Ruth. *Carrie Hepple's garden* ill. by Irene Haas. Atheneum, 1979. Subj: Animals – cats. Character traits – bravery. Gardens, gardening.

The day of the rainbow ill. by Niki Daly. Viking, 1989. ISBN 0-670-82456-9 Subj: City. Behavior – losing things. Emotions – anger. Poetry, rhyme. Seasons – summer. Weather – rainbows.

The winter bear ill. by Erik Blegvad. Atheneum, 1974. Subj: Poetry, rhyme. Seasons – winter. Toys – teddy bears.

Craig, Helen. *The night of the paper bag monsters* ill. by author. Knopf, 1985. ISBN 0-394-97307-0 Subj: Animals – pigs. Friendship. Monsters.

Susie and Alfred in the knight, the princess and the dragon ill. by author. Knopf, 1985. Subj: Animals – pigs. Art. Imagination.

A welcome for Annie ill. by author. Knopf, 1986. ISBN 0-394-97954-0 Subj: Animals – pigs. Behavior – misbehavior. Behavior – trickery. Friendship.

Craig, Janet. *Ballet dancer* ill. by Barbara Todd. Troll Assoc., 1988. ISBN 0-8167-1434-7 Subj: Activities – dancing.

Turtles ill. by Kathie Kelleher. Troll Assoc., 1982. Subj: Reptiles – turtles, tortoises. Science.

What's under the ocean? ill. by Paul Harvey. Troll Assoc., 1982. Subj: Sea and seashore.

Craig, M. Jean. *Babar comes to America* (Brunhoff, Laurent de)

Boxes ill. by Joe Lasker. Norton, 1964. Subj: Concepts – shape. Concepts – size. Games. Participation. Toys.

Dinosaurs and more dinosaurs ill. by George Solonevich. Four Winds Pr., 1968. Subj: Dinosaurs. Science.

The donkey prince (Grimm, Jacob)

The dragon in the clock box ill. by Kelly Oechsli. Norton, 1962. Subj: Dragons. Family life. Imagination.

The man whose name was not Thomas ill. by Diane Stanley. Doubleday, 1981. Subj: Careers – bakers. Humor.

Spring is like the morning ill. by Don Almquist. Putnam's, 1965. Subj: Animals. Morning. Plants. Seasons – spring.

What did you dream? ill. by Margery Gill. Abelard-Schuman, 1964. Subj: Dreams. Morning.

Crampton, Patricia. *The beaver family book* (Kalas, Sybille)

The dragon with red eyes (Lindgren, Astrid)

The goose family book (Kalas, Sybille)

My nightingale is singing (Lindgren, Astrid)

The penguin family book (Somme, Lauritz)

Peter and the wolf (Prokofiev, Sergei Sergeievitch)

Crane, Alan. *Pepita bonita* ill. by author. Nelson, 1942. Subj: Birds – pelicans. Foreign lands – Mexico. Sea and seashore.

Crane, Donn. *Flippy and Skippy* ill. by author. Winston, 1940. Subj: Animals – squirrels. Pets.

Crary, Elizabeth. *I'm frustrated* ill. by Jean Whitney. Parenting Pr., 1992. ISBN 0-943990-64-5 Subj: Emotions. Sports – roller skating.

I'm mad ill. by Jean Whitney. Parenting Pr., 1992. ISBN 0-943990-62-9 Subj: Emotions – anger. Weather – rain.

I'm proud ill. by Jean Whitney. Parenting Pr., 1992. ISBN 0-943990-66-1 Subj: Character traits – pride.

Craven, Carolyn. *What the mailman brought* ill. by Tomie de Paola. Putnam's, 1987. ISBN 0-399-21290-6 Subj: Activities – painting. Emotions – loneliness. Illness. Imagination.

Craver, Mike. *Beaver ball at the bug club* ill. by Joan Kaghan. Farrar, 1992. ISBN 0-374-30662-1 Subj: Animals. Music. Parties. Songs.

Crawford, Elizabeth D. *Baby animals on the farm* (Isenbart, Hans-Heinrich)

Blackie and Marie (Kočí, Marta)

Hansel and Gretel (Grimm, Jacob)

The hare's race (Baumann, Hans)

Little Harry (Bröger, Achim)

Little red cap (Grimm, Jacob)

The seven ravens (Grimm, Jacob)

The three little pigs (The three little pigs)

Tiger cat (Wolski, Slawomir)

Crawford, Phyllis. *The blot: little city cat* ill. by Holling C. Holling. Cape, 1930. Subj: Animals – cats.

Crayder, Teresa *see* Colman, Hila

Credle, Ellis. *Big fraid, little fraid: a folktale* ill. by author. Macmillan, 1964. Subj: Emotions – fear. Folk and fairy tales. Night.

Down, down the mountain ill. by author. Nelson, 1934, 1961. Subj: Clothing. Family life. Plants.

Creighton, Jill. *Maybe a monster* ill. by Ruth Ohi. Firefly, 1989. ISBN 1-55037-037-5 Subj: Activities – playing. Imagination.

One day there was nothing to do ill. by Ruth Ohi. Firefly, 1990. ISBN 1-55037-091-X Subj: Activities. Animals. Behavior – boredom. Imagination. Reptiles – snakes. Reptiles – turtles, tortoises.

Cremins, Robert. *My animal ABC* ill. by author. Crown, 1983. Subj: ABC books. Animals. Format, unusual – toy and movable books.

My animal Mother Goose ill. by author. Crown, 1983. Subj: Animals. Format, unusual – toy and movable books. Nursery rhymes.

Pop up baby brontosaurus ill. by author; paper engineering by Dick Dudley. Dial, 1989. ISBN 0-8037-0726-6 Subj: Dinosaurs. Format, unusual – toy and movable books.

Pop up baby coelophysis ill. by author; paper engineering by Dick Dudley. Dial, 1989. ISBN 0-8037-0735-5 Subj: Dinosaurs. Format, unusual – toy and movable books.

Pop up baby pteranodon ill. by author; paper engineering by Dick Dudley. Dial, 1989. ISBN 0-8037-0732-0 Subj: Dinosaurs. Format, unusual – toy and movable books.

Pop up baby stegosaurus ill. by author; paper engineering by Dick Dudley. Dial, 1989. ISBN 0-8037-0733-9 Subj: Dinosaurs. Format, unusual – toy and movable books.

Pop up baby triceratops ill. by author; paper engineering by Dick Dudley. Dial, 1989. ISBN 0-8037-0734-7 Subj: Dinosaurs. Format, unusual – toy and movable books.

Pop up baby tyrannosaurus rex ill. by author; paper engineering by Dick Dudley. Dial, 1989. ISBN 0-8037-0731-2 Subj: Dinosaurs. Format, unusual – toy and movable books.

Crespi, Francesca. *Little Bear and the oompah-pah* ill. by author. Dial Pr., 1987. ISBN 0-8037-0394-5 Subj: Animals – bears. Holidays. Music.

Santa Clause is coming! ill. by author. Holt, 1987. ISBN 0-8050-0472-6 Subj: Format, unusual – toy and movable books. Holidays – Christmas.

Silent Night ill. by author. Holt, 1987. ISBN 0-8050-0471-8 Subj: Format, unusual – toy and movable books. Holidays – Christmas.

Cressey, James. *The dragon and George* ill. by Tamasin Cole. Prentice-Hall, 1979. Subj: Dragons. Foreign lands – England. Knights. Middle ages.

Fourteen rats and a rat-catcher ill. by Tamasin Cole. Prentice-Hall, 1978. Subj: Animals – rats. Family life. Problem solving.

Max the mouse ill. by Tamasin Cole. Prentice-Hall, 1979. Subj: Animals – mice. Crime.

Pet parrot ill. by Tamasin Cole. Prentice-Hall, 1979. Subj: Birds – parakeets, parrots. Crime.

Cresswell, Helen. *Two hoots and the king* ill. by Martine Blanc. Crown, 1978. Subj: Birds – owls. Behavior – mistakes.

Two hoots in the snow ill. by Martine Blanc. Crown, 1978. Subj: Birds – owls. Behavior – mistakes.

Cretan, Gladys Yessayan. *Lobo and Brewster* ill. by Patricia Coombs. Lothrop, 1971. Subj: Animals – cats. Animals – dogs. Emotions – envy, jealousy.

Ten brothers with camels ill. by Piero Ventura. Golden Pr., 1975. Subj: Counting, numbers. Desert.

Cretien, Paul D. *Sir Henry and the dragon* ill. by author. Follett, 1958. Subj: Animals – horses. Dragons. Knights. Royalty. Witches.

Crews, Donald. *Carousel* ill. by author. Greenwillow, 1982. Subj: Merry-go-rounds.

Flying ill. by author. Greenwillow, 1986. ISBN 0-688-04319-4 Subj: Activities – flying. Airplanes, airports.

Freight train ill. by author. Greenwillow, 1978. Subj: Caldecott award honor book. Trains.

Harbor ill. by author. Greenwillow, 1982. Subj: Boats, ships.

Light ill. by author. Greenwillow, 1981. Subj: Concepts. Lights.

Parade ill. by author. Greenwillow, 1983. Subj: City. Parades.

School bus ill. by author. Greenwillow, 1984. ISBN 0-688-02808-X Subj: Buses. School. Transportation.

Ten black dots ill. by author Rev. ed. Greenwillow, 1986. ISBN 0-688-06068-4 Subj: Concepts – shape. Counting, numbers.

Truck ill. by author. Greenwillow, 1980. Subj: Caldecott award honor book. Transportation. Trucks. Wordless.

We read: A to Z ill. by author. Harper, 1967. Subj: ABC books. Concepts.

Crichton, Michael *see* Douglas, Michael

Cristini, Ermanno. *In my garden* by Ermanno Cristini and Luigi Puricelli; ill. by authors. Alphabet Pr., 1981. Orig title: Falter, Blumen, Tierre und Ich Subj: Gardens, gardening. Wordless.

In the pond by Ermanno Cristini and Luigi Puricelli; ill. by authors. Alphabet Pr., 1984. Subj: Animals. Insects. Plants. Reptiles.

In the woods by Ermanno Cristini and Luigi Puricelli; ill. by authors. Alphabet Pr., 1983. Subj: Animals. Birds. Forest, woods. Wordless.

Croll, Carolyn. *The little snowgirl* ill. by author. Putnam, 1989. ISBN 0-399-21691-X Subj: Folk and fairy tales. Foreign lands – Russia. Holidays – Christmas. Weather – snow.

The three brothers ill. by author. Putnam, 1991. ISBN 0-399-22195-6 Subj: Family life – brothers. Family life – fathers. Farms. Folk and fairy tales. Foreign lands – Germany.

Too many babas ill. by author. Harper, 1979. Subj: Behavior – sharing. Food.

Cromie, William J. *Steven and the green turtle* ill. by Tom Eaton. Harper, 1970. Subj: Animals – endangered animals. Reptiles – turtles, tortoises. Science.

Crompton, Anne Eliot. *The lifting stone* ill. by Marcia Sewall. Holiday, 1978. Subj: Folk and fairy tales. Character traits – cleverness.

The winter wife: an Abenaki folktale ill. by Robert Andrew Parker. Little, 1975. Subj: Character traits – loyalty. Indians of North America. Folk and fairy tales.

Crompton, Margaret. *The house where Jack lives* ill. by Margery Gill. Merrimack, 1980. Subj: Family life. Foreign lands – England. Houses.

Crosby-Jones, Michael. *Goodbye Rune* (Kaldhol, Marit)

Cross, Diana Harding. *Some birds have funny names* ill. by Jan Brett. Crown, 1981. Subj: Birds. Names.

Some plants have funny names ill. by Jan Brett. Crown, 1983. Subj: Names. Plants.

Cross, Genevieve. *My bunny book* ill. by Charles Clement. Doubleday, 1952. Subj: Animals – rabbits. Holidays – Easter.

A trip to the yard ill. by Marjorie Hartwell and Rachel Dixon. Doubleday, 1952. Subj: Animals. Birds. Plants.

Crossley-Holland, Kevin. *The green children* ill. by Margaret Gordon. Seabury Pr., 1968. Subj: Character traits – being different. Folk and fairy tales. Foreign lands – England.

The pedlar of Swaffham ill. by Margaret Gordon. Seabury Pr., 1971. Subj: Careers – peddlers. Folk and fairy tales.

Sleeping Nanna ill. by Peter Melnyczuk. Ideals, 1990. ISBN 0-8249-8458-7 Subj: Dreams. Islands. Senses. Sleep.

Croswell, Volney. *How to hide a hippopotamus* ill. by author. Dodd, 1958. Subj: Animals – hippopotami. Behavior – hiding things. Concepts – size.

Crothers, Samuel McChord. *Miss Muffet's Christmas party* ill. by Olive M. Long. Houghton, 1929. Subj: Parties. Spiders.

Crowe, Robert L. *Clyde monster* ill. by Kay Chorao. Dutton, 1976. Subj: Emotions – fear. Monsters. Night.

Tyler Toad and the thunder ill. by Kay Chorao. Dutton, 1980. Subj: Animals. Noise, sounds. Weather – thunder.

Crowell, Maryalicia. *A horse in the house* ill. by Leonard P. Kessler. Addison-Wesley, 1957. Subj: City. Pets.

Crowley, Arthur. *Bonzo Beaver* ill. by Annie Gusman. Houghton, 1980. Subj: Activities – babysitting. Animals – beavers. Poetry, rhyme. Sibling rivalry.

The boogey man ill. by Annie Gusman. Houghton, 1978. Subj: Behavior – dissatisfaction. Behavior – misbehavior. Family life. Monsters.

The ugly book ill. by Annie Gusman. Houghton, 1982. Subj: Character traits – appearance.

The wagon man ill. by Annie Gusman. Houghton, 1981. Subj: Dreams. Poetry, rhyme. Riddles.

Crowley, Michael. *The new kid on Spurwick Ave.* ill. by Abby Carter. Little, 1992. ISBN 0-316-16230-2 Subj: Activities – making things. Clubs, gangs. Communities, neighborhoods. Imagination.

New kid on Spurwick Ave. ill. by Abby Carter. Little, 1992. ISBN 0-316-16230-2 Subj: Activities – playing. Friendship. Imagination.

Crowther, Robert. *Hide and seek counting book* ill. by author. Viking, 1981. Subj: Counting, numbers. Format, unusual – toy and movable books.

The most amazing hide-and-seek alphabet book ill. by author. Viking, 1978. Subj: ABC books. Format, unusual – toy and movable books.

The most amazing hide-and-seek opposites book ill. by author. Viking, 1985. ISBN 0-670-80121-6 Subj: Concepts – opposites. Format, unusual – toy and movable books.

Pop goes the weasel! 25 pop-up nursery rhymes ill. by comp. Viking, 1987. ISBN 0-670-81815-1 Subj: Format, unusual – toy and movable books. Nursery rhymes.

Croxford, Vera. *All kinds of animals* ill. by author. Grosset, 1972. Orig. title: All sorts of animals (Hamlyn Pub. Group, 1968) Subj: Animals.

Crume, Marion W. *Let me see you try* ill. by Jacques Rupp. Bowmar, 1968. Subj: Activities. Participation.

Listen! ill. by Cliff Rowe and Judy Houston. Bowmar, 1968. Subj: Activities. Ethnic groups in the U.S. Participation.

What do you say? ill. by Harvey Mandlin. Bowmar, 1967. Subj: Activities. Participation.

Crump, Donald J. *Creatures small and furry* ill. with photos. National Geographic Soc., 1983. Subj: Animals.

Cummings, Betty Sue. *Turtle* ill. by Susan Dodge. Atheneum, 1981. Subj: Behavior – lost. Pets. Reptiles – turtles, tortoises.

Cummings, E. E. (Edward Estlin). *Fairy tales* ill. by John Eaton. Harcourt, 1965. Subj: Folk and fairy tales. Imagination.

Hist whist ill. by Deborah Kogan Ray. Crown, 1989. ISBN 0-517-57258-3 Subj: Holidays – Halloween. Poetry, rhyme.

In just-spring ill. by Heidi Goennel. Little, 1988. ISBN 0-316-16390-2 Subj: Poetry, rhyme. Seasons – spring.

Little tree ill. by Deborah Kogan Ray. Crown, 1987. ISBN 0-517-56598-6 Subj: Holidays – Christmas. Poetry, rhyme. Trees.

Cummings, Pat. *Clean your room, Harvey Moon!* ill. by author. Bradbury Pr., 1991. ISBN 0-02-725511-5 Subj: Character traits – cleanliness. Ethnic groups in the U.S. – Afro-Americans. Poetry, rhyme.

C.L.O.U.D.S. ill. by author. Lothrop, 1986. ISBN 0-688-04683-5 Subj: Weather – clouds.

Jimmy Lee did it ill. by author. Lothrop, 1985. ISBN 0-688-04633-9 Subj: Ethnic groups in the U.S. – Afro-Americans. Family life – brothers. Imagination – imaginary friends. Poetry, rhyme. Problem solving.

Cummings, Phil. *Goodness gracious!* ill. by Craig Smith. Watts, 1992. ISBN 0-531-08567-8 Subj: Anatomy. Poetry, rhyme.

Cummings, W. T. (Walter Thies). *The kid* ill. by author. McGraw-Hill, 1960. Subj: Animals – horses. Behavior – seeking better things. Emotions – loneliness. Music.

Miss Esta Maude's secret ill. by author. McGraw-Hill, 1961. Subj: Automobiles. Behavior – secrets. Careers – teachers.

Wickford of Beacon Hill ill. by author. Subj: Birds – cockatoos.

Cuneo, Mary Louise. *Inside a sandcastle and other secrets* ill. by Jan Brett. Houghton, 1979. Subj: Character traits – smallness.

Cunliffe, John. *The king's birthday cake* ill. by Faith Jaques. Elsevier-Dutton, 1979. Subj: Activities – cooking. Birthdays. Cumulative tales. Royalty – kings.

Sara's giant and the upside down house ill. by Hilary Abrahams. Elsevier-Dutton, 1980. Subj: Giants.

Cunningham, Julia. *A mouse called Junction* ill. by Michael Hague. Pantheon, 1980. Subj: Animals – mice. Animals – rats. Emotions. Emotions – fear. Friendship.

The vision of Francois the fox ill. by Nicholas Angelo. Pantheon, 1969. Subj: Animals – foxes.

Curious George and the dinosaur ed. by Margret Rey and Alan J. Shalleck. Houghton, 1989. ISBN 0-395-51941-1 Subj: Animals – monkeys. Dinosaurs.

Curious George and the dump truck Houghton, 1984. ISBN 0-395-36635-6 Subj: Animals – monkeys. Character traits – curiosity. Trucks.

Curious George and the pizza Houghton, 1985. ISBN 0-395-39039-7 Subj: Animals – monkeys. Character traits – curiosity. Food.

Curious George at the fire station Houghton, 1985. ISBN 0-395-39037-0 Subj: Animals – monkeys. Careers – firefighters. Character traits – curiosity.

Curious George goes hiking Houghton, 1985. ISBN 0-395-39038-9 Subj: Animals – monkeys. Character traits – curiosity. Sports – hiking.

Curious George goes sledding Houghton, 1984. ISBN 0-395-36637-2 Subj: Animals – monkeys. Character traits – curiosity. Sports – sledding.

Curious George goes to an ice cream shop ed. by Margret Rey and Alan J. Shalleck. Houghton, 1989. ISBN 0-395-51943-8 Subj: Animals – monkeys. Food.

Curious George goes to school ed. by Margret Rey and Alan J. Shalleck. Houghton, 1989. ISBN 0-395-51944-6 Subj: Animals – monkeys. School.

Curious George goes to the aquarium Houghton, 1984. ISBN 0-395-36634-8 Subj: Animals – monkeys. Aquariums. Character traits – curiosity. Fish.

Curious George goes to the circus Houghton, 1984. ISBN 0-395-36636-4 Subj: Animals – monkeys. Character traits – curiosity. Circus.

Curious George goes to the dentist ed. by Margret Rey and Alan J. Shalleck. Houghton, 1989. ISBN 0-395-51941-1 Subj: Animals – monkeys. Careers – dentists. Teeth.

Curious George visits the zoo Houghton, 1985. ISBN 0-395-39036-2 Subj: Animals – monkeys. Character traits – curiosity. Zoos.

Curle, Jock J. *The four good friends* ill. by Bernadette Watts. Holt, 1987. ISBN 0-8050-0231-6 Subj: Animals. Character traits – helpfulness. Character traits – kindness to animals.

Lucky Hans (Grimm, Jacob)

The sleepy owl (Pfister, Marcus)

The story of Jonah (Baumann, Kurt)

Curry, Jane Louise. *Little, little sister* ill. by Erik Blegvad. Macmillan, 1989. ISBN 0-689-50459-4 Subj: Character traits – smallness. Family life. Family life – sisters. Farms.

Curry, Nancy. *The littlest house* ill. by Jacques Rupp. Bowmar, 1968. Subj: Family life. Houses.

Curry, Peter. *Animals* ill. by author. Price Stern Sloan, 1984. Subj: Animals.

Curti, Anna. *At home* ill. by author. Little, 1991. ISBN 0-316-16538-7 Subj: Family life.

Seasons ill. by author. Little, 1991. ISBN 0-316-16539-5 Subj: Animals – wolves. Seasons.

Curtis, Gavin. *Grandma's baseball* ill. by author. Crown, 1990. ISBN 0-517-57390-3 Subj: Emotions. Ethnic groups in the U.S. – Afro-Americans. Family life – grandparents.

Curtis Brown, Beatrice *see* Brown, Beatrice Curtis

Cushman, Doug. *Giants* ill. by comp. Platt, 1980. Subj: Giants. Poetry, rhyme.

Nasty Kyle the crocodile ill. by author. Grosset, 1983. Subj: Behavior – dissatisfaction. Concepts. Reptiles – alligators, crocodiles.

Once upon a pig ill. by comp. Grosset, 1982. Subj: Animals – pigs. Poetry, rhyme.

Possum stew ill. by author. Dutton, 1990. ISBN 0-525-44566-8 Subj: Animals – possums. Behavior – trickery. Food.

Cushman, Jerome. *Marvella's hobby* ill. by Prue Theobalds. Abelard-Schuman, 1962. Subj: Animals – bulls, cows. Trains.

Cutler, Ebbitt. *Paulino* (Simons, Traute)

Cutler, Ivor. *The animal house* ill. by Helen Oxenbury. Morrow, 1977, 1976. Subj: Animals. Houses. Zoos.

Doris ill. by Claudio Muñoz. Morrow, 1992. ISBN 0-688-11939-5 Subj: Birds. Songs.

Herbert: five stories ill. by Patrick Benson. Lothrop, 1988. ISBN 0-688-08148-7 Subj: Animals. Imagination.

Cutts, David. *The gingerbread boy* (The gingerbread boy)

Look...a butterfly ill. by Eulala Conner. Troll Assoc., 1982. Subj: Insects – butterflies, caterpillars. Science.

More about dinosaurs ill. by Gregory C. Wenzel. Troll Assoc., 1982. Subj: Dinosaurs.

Cuyler, Margery. *Baby Dot: a dinosaur story* ill. by Ellen Weiss. Houghton, 1990. ISBN 0-395-51934-9 Subj: Dinosaurs. School.

Fat Santa ill. by Marsha Winborn. Holt, 1987. ISBN 0-8050-0423-8 Subj: Character traits – helpfulness. Dreams. Holidays – Christmas.

Freckles and Jane ill. by Leslie Holt Morrill. Holt, 1989. ISBN 0-8050-0643-5 Subj: Animals – dogs. Friendship. Pets.

Freckles and Willie ill. by Marsha Winborn. Holt, 1986. ISBN 0-03-003772-7 Subj: Animals – dogs. Friendship.

Shadow's baby ill. by Ellen Weiss. Houghton, 1989. ISBN 0-89919-831-7 Subj: Animals – dogs. Babies. Family life.

Sir William and the pumpkin monster ill. by Marsha Winborn. Holt, 1984. Subj: Ghosts. Holidays – Halloween.

That's good! That's bad! ill. by David Catrow. Holt, 1991. ISBN 0-8050-1535-3 Subj: Animals. Zoos.

Czernecki, Stefan. *Pancho's piñata* ill. by author. Walt Disney, 1992. ISBN 1-56282-278-0 Subj: Foreign lands – Mexico. Holidays – Christmas.

The sleeping bread by Stefan Czernecki and Timothy Rhodes; ill. by Stefan Czernecki. Walt Disney, 1992. ISBN 1-56282-207-1 Subj: Folk and fairy tales. Food. Foreign lands – Guatemala.

Dabcovich, Lydia. *Busy beavers* ill. by author. Dutton, 1988. ISBN 0-525-44384-3 Subj: Animals – beavers. Science.

Follow the river ill. by author. Dutton, 1980. Subj: Rivers.

The keys to my kingdom ill. by author. Lothrop, 1992. ISBN 0-688-09775-8 Subj: Foreign languages. Nursery rhymes.

Mrs. Huggins and her hen Hannah ill. by author. Dutton, 1985. ISBN 0-525-44203-0 Subj: Birds – chickens. Death. Emotions. Friendship.

Sleepy bear ill. by author. Dutton, 1982. Subj: Animals – bears. Seasons – spring. Seasons – winter.

Dahl, Roald. *Dirty beasts* ill. by Rosemary Fawcett. Farrar, 1983. Subj: Bedtime. Dreams. Monsters. Poetry, rhyme.

The enormous crocodile ill. by Quentin Blake. Knopf, 1978. Subj: Animals. Reptiles – alligators, crocodiles.

The giraffe and the pelly and me ill. by Quentin Blake. Farrar, 1985. ISBN 0-374-32602-9 Subj: Activities – working. Animals. Careers – window cleaners. Crime.

Dahl, Tessa. *Babies, babies, babies* ill. by Siobhan Dodds. Viking, 1991. ISBN 0-670-83921-3 Subj: Babies. Birth. Family life.

The same but different ill. by Arthur Robins. Viking, 1989. ISBN 0-670-82572-7 Subj: Activities. Family life.

Dale, Penny. *You can't* ill. by author. Harper, 1988. ISBN 0-397-32256-9 Subj: Ethnic groups in the U.S. – Afro-Americans. Games. Toys.

Dale, Ruth Bluestone. *Benjamin — and Sylvester also* ill. by J. B. Handelsman. McGraw-Hill, 1960. Subj: Animals – dogs. Behavior – dissatisfaction. Country.

Dalgliesh, Alice. *The little wooden farmer* ill. by Anita Lobel. Macmillan, 1988, 1930. ISBN 0-02-725590-5 Subj: Farms.

The Thanksgiving story ill. by Helen Moore Sewell. Scribner's, 1954. Subj: Caldecott award honor book. Holidays – Thanksgiving. U.S. history.

The turnip (Milhous, Katherine)

Dallas-Smith, Peter. *Trumpets in Grumpetland* ill. by Peter Cross. Random House, 1985. ISBN 0-394-97028-4 Subj: Music. Mythical creatures.

Dalmais, Anne-Marie. *The butterfly book of birds* ill. by Guy Michel. Two Continents, 1977. Subj: Birds.

In my garden: learning to count ill. by Genji. Two Continents, 1977. Subj: Counting, numbers. Poetry, rhyme.

Dalton, Alene. *My new picture book of songs* scores by Reah Allen; ill. by Gini Bunnell. Osmond Pub., 1979. Subj: Music. Songs.

Daly, Kathleen N. *Dinosaurs* ill. by Tim and Greg Hildebrandt. Golden Pr., 1977. Subj: Dinosaurs.

The Giant little Golden Book of dogs ill. by Tibor Gergely. Simon and Schuster, 1957. Subj: Animals – dogs.

The Macmillan picture wordbook ill. by John Wallner. Macmillan, 1982. Subj: Dictionaries.

The three bears (The three bears)

Today's biggest animals ill. by Tim and Greg Hildebrandt. Golden Pr., 1977. Subj: Animals. Science.

Unusual animals ill. by Tim and Greg Hildebrandt. Golden Pr., 1977. Subj: Animals. Science.

Daly, Maureen. *Patrick visits the library* ill. by Paul Lantz. Dodd, 1961. Subj: Animals – dogs. Birthdays. Libraries.

Daly, Niki. *Joseph's other red sock* ill. by author. Atheneum, 1982. Subj: Clothing – socks.

Just like Archie ill. by author. Viking, 1986. ISBN 0-670-81253-6 Subj: Pets.

Look at me! ill. by author. Viking, 1986. ISBN 0-670-81252-8 Subj: Sibling rivalry.

Mama, papa and baby Joe ill. by author. Viking, 1991. ISBN 0-670-84161-7 Subj: Shopping.

Not so fast Songololo ill. by author. Atheneum, 1986. ISBN 0-689-50367-9 Subj: City. Family life – grandmothers. Foreign lands – Africa. Foreign lands – South Africa. Shopping.

Somewhere in Africa (Mennen, Ingrid)

Thank you Henrietta ill. by author. Viking, 1986. ISBN 0-670-81254-4 Subj: Character traits – helpfulness.

Vim, the rag mouse ill. by author. Atheneum, 1979. Subj: Crime. Toys.

Dame Wiggins of Lee and her seven wonderful cats ed. by John Ruskin; ill. by Robert Broomfield. McGraw-Hill, 1963. Ascribed to Richard Scrafton Sharpe and Mrs. Pearson. Endpapers: reproduction of Kate Greenaway drawings Subj: Nursery rhymes.

Damjan, Mischa. *Atuk* ill. by Józef Wilkoń. North-South, 1989. ISBN 1-55858-091-3 Subj: Animals – dogs. Animals – wolves. Eskimos. Foreign lands – Arctic.

Goodbye little bird tr. from German by Anthea Bell; ill. by Dorothée Duntze. Faber, 1983. Subj: Birds. Friendship.

The little prince and the tiger cat ill. by Ralph Steadman. McGraw-Hill, 1967. Subj: Animals – cats. Foreign lands – Japan. Royalty – princes.

The little sea horse ill. by Riccardo Bellettati. Faber, 1983. Subj: Fish. Sea and seashore.

The wolf and the kid ill. by Max Velthuijs. McGraw-Hill, 1967. Subj: Animals – goats. Animals – wolves. Character traits – cleverness.

Damrell, Liz. *With the wind* ill. by Stephen Marchesi. Watts, 1991. ISBN 0-531-08482-5 Subj: Animals – horses. Handicaps – physical.

D'Andrea, Annette Cole see Steiner, Barbara (Annette)

Daniel, Anne see Steiner, Barbara (Annette)

Daniel, Doris Temple. *Pauline and the peacock* ill. by Barbara Brown Schoenewolf. E. C. Temple, 1980. Subj: Birds – peacocks, peahens. Family life. Farms. Science.

Daniels, Guy. *The Tsar's riddles: or, the wise little girl* ill. by Paul Galdone. McGraw-Hill, 1967. Subj: Character traits – cleverness. Folk and fairy tales. Foreign lands – Russia. Riddles.

Dantzer-Rosenthal, Marya. *Some things are different, some things are the same* ill. by Miriam Nerlove. Albert Whitman, 1986. ISBN 0-8075-7535-6 Subj: Concepts.

Darby, Gene. *What is a bird?* ill. by Lucy and John Hawkinson. Benefic Pr., 1959. Subj: Birds. Science.

What is a butterfly? ill. by Lucy and John Hawkinson. Benefic Pr., 1958. Subj: Insects – butterflies, caterpillars. Science.

What is a fish? ill. by Lucy and John Hawkinson. Benefic Pr., 1958. Subj: Fish. Science.

What is a plant? ill. by Lucy and John Hawkinson. Benefic Pr., 1959. Subj: Plants. Science.

What is a turtle? ill. by Lucy and John Hawkinson. Benefic Pr., 1959. Subj: Reptiles – turtles, tortoises. Science.

Da Rif, Andrea. *The blueberry cake that little fox baked* ill. by author. Atheneum, 1984. Subj: Activities – cooking. Birthdays.

Darling, Abigail. *Teddy bears' picnic cookbook* ill. by Alexandra Day. Viking, 1991. ISBN 0-670-82947-1 Subj: Activities – cooking. Activities – picnicking. Food. Toys – teddy bears.

Darling, Kathy (Mary Kathleen). *The Easter bunny's secret* ill. by Kelly Oechsli. Garrard, 1978. Subj: Animals – rabbits. Holidays – Easter.

The mystery in Santa's toyshop ill. by Lori Pierson. Garrard, 1978. Subj: Holidays – Christmas. Problem solving.

Darling, Mary Kathleen see Darling, Kathy (Mary Kathleen)

Dasent, George W. *The cat on the Dovrefell* (De Paola, Tomie (Thomas Anthony))

East o' the sun, west o' the moon tr. by George W. Dasent; ill. by Gillian Barlow. Putnam's, 1988. ISBN 0-399-21570-0 Subj: Animals – polar bears. Folk and fairy tales. Foreign lands – Norway. Royalty – princes. Witches.

Daudet, Alphonse. *The brave little goat of Monsieur Séguin: a picture story from Provence* ill. by Chiyoko Nakatani. Collins-World, 1968. Translation and adaptation of La chèvre de M. Séguin Subj: Animals – goats. Animals – wolves. Foreign lands – France.

Dauer, Rosamond. *Bullfrog builds a house* ill. by Byron Barton. Greenwillow, 1977. Subj: Friendship. Frogs and toads. Houses.

Bullfrog grows up ill. by Byron Barton. Greenwillow, 1976. Subj: Animals – mice. Behavior – growing up. Frogs and toads.

My friend, Jasper Jones ill. by Jerry Joyner. Parents, 1977. Subj: Behavior – misbehavior. Imagination – imaginary friends.

The 300 pound cat ill. by Skip Morrow. Holt, 1981. Subj: Animals – cats. Behavior – greed.

Daugherty, Charles Michael. *Wisher* ill. by James Henry Daugherty. Viking, 1960. Subj: Animals – cats. Behavior – wishing. Dreams.

Daugherty, James Henry. *Andy and the lion* ill. by author. Viking, 1938. Subj: Animals – lions. Caldecott award honor book. Character traits – kindness to animals. Humor. Libraries.

The picnic: a frolic in two colors and three parts ill. by author. Viking, 1958. Subj: Activities – picnicking. Animals – lions. Animals – mice.

Daugherty, Sonia. *Vanka's donkey* ill. by James Henry Daugherty. Stokes, 1940. Subj: Animals – donkeys. Folk and fairy tales. Foreign lands – Russia.

Daughtry, Duanne. *What's inside?* photos. by author. Knopf, 1984. Subj: Concepts – in and out. Wordless.

D'Aulaire, Edgar Parin see Aulaire, Edgar Parin d'

D'Aulaire, Ingri Mortenson see Aulaire, Ingri Mortenson d'

Dauphin, Francine Legrand. *A French A. B. C.* ill. by author. Coward, 1947. Subj: ABC books. Foreign lands – France. Foreign languages.

David, Eugene. *Crystal magic* ill. by Abner Graboff. Prentice-Hall, 1965. Subj: Science.

Davidson, Amanda. *Teddy at the seashore* ill. by author. Holt, 1984. Originally published under title: Teddy at the seaside Subj: Foreign lands – England. Sea and seashore. Toys – teddy bears.

Teddy goes outside ill. by author. Holt, 1985. ISBN 0-03-005004-9 Subj: Format, unusual – board books. Toys – teddy bears. Weather.

Teddy in the garden ill. by author. Holt, 1986. ISBN 0-03-008502-0 Subj: Behavior – losing things. Gardens, gardening. Toys – teddy bears.

Teddy's birthday ill. by author. Holt, 1985. ISBN 0-03-002887-6 Subj: Birthdays. Toys – teddy bears.

Teddy's first Christmas ill. by author. Holt, 1982. Subj: Holidays – Christmas. Toys – teddy bears.

Davidson, Jill A. *And that's what happened to little Lucy* ill. by Paul Meisel. Random House, 1989. ISBN 0-394-99945-2 Subj: Activities – trading. Activities – walking. Animals. Forest, woods.

Davies, Andrew. *Poonam's pets* ill. by Paul Dowling. Viking, 1990. ISBN 0-670-83321-5 Subj: Animals – lions. Pets. School.

Davies, Kay. *My balloon* by Kay Davies and Wendy Oldfield; photos. by Fiona Pragoff. Doubleday, 1990. ISBN 0-385-41199-5 Subj: Activities. Concepts – perspective. Science. Toys – balloons.

My mirror by Kay Davies and Wendy Oldfield; photos. by Fiona Pragoff. Doubleday, 1990. ISBN 0-385-41196-0 Subj: Activities. Concepts – perspective. Science.

Davies, Sumiko *see* Sumiko

Davis, Alice Vaught. *Timothy Turtle* ill. by Guy Brown Wiser. Harcourt, 1940. Subj: Character traits – helpfulness. Reptiles – turtles, tortoises.

Davis, Douglas F. *The lion's tail* ill. by Ronald Himler. Atheneum, 1980. Subj: Animals – lions. Folk and fairy tales. Foreign lands – Africa.

There's an elephant in the garage ill. by Steven Kellogg. Dutton, 1979. Subj: Animals. Animals – cats. Imagination. Toys – teddy bears.

Davis, Gibbs. *Katy's first haircut* ill. by Linda Shute. Houghton, 1985. ISBN 0-395-38942-9 Subj: Emotions – embarrassment. Hair.

The other Emily ill. by Linda Shute. Houghton, 1984. Subj: Behavior – sharing. Names.

Davis, Lavinia (Riker). *Roger and the fox* ill. by Hildegard Woodward. Doubleday, 1947. Subj: Animals – foxes. Caldecott award honor book.

The wild birthday cake ill. by Hildegard Woodward. Doubleday, 1949. Subj: Birthdays. Caldecott award honor book.

Davis, Maggie S. *The best way to Ripton* ill. by Stephen Gammell. Holiday, 1982. Subj: Activities – traveling. Humor.

Grandma's secret letter ill. by John Wallner. Holiday, 1982. Subj: Behavior – secrets. Character traits – kindness. Elves and little people.

Rickety witch ill. by Kay Chorao. Holiday, 1984. Subj: Holidays – Halloween. Witches.

Something magic ill. by Mary O'Keefe Young. Simon & Schuster, 1991. ISBN 0-671-69627-0 Subj: Family life.

Davis, Reda. *Martin's dinosaur* ill. by Louis Slobodkin. Crowell, 1959. Subj: Dragons. Foreign lands – England.

Dawson, Linda. *Phoebe and the hot water bottles* (Furchgott, Terry)

Day, Alexandra. *Frank and Ernest* ill. by author. Scholastic, 1988. ISBN 0-590-41557-3 Subj: Animals – bears. Animals – elephants. Character traits – helpfulness. Language.

Paddy's pay-day ill. by author. Viking, 1989. ISBN 0-670-82598-0 Subj: Animals – dogs. Circus. Country. Money.

River parade ill. by author. Viking, 1990. ISBN 0-670-82946-3 Subj: Boats, ships. Family life – fathers. Rivers. Sports – swimming.

Day, Betsy. *Stefan and Olga* ill. by author. Dial, 1991. ISBN 0-8037-0817-3 Subj: Birds – geese. Farms. Friendship. Music. Pets.

Day, David. *The swan children* retold by David Day; ill. by Richard Evans. Ideals, 1991. ISBN 0-8249-8461-7 Subj: Birds – swans. Folk and fairy tales. Foreign lands – Ireland. Royalty.

Day, Edward C. *John Tabor's ride* ill. by Dirk Zimmer. Knopf, 1989. ISBN 0-394-98577-X Subj: Activities – traveling. Animals – whales. Folk and fairy tales.

Day, Marie. *Dragon in the rocks* ill. by author. Firefly, 1992. ISBN 0-920775-76-4 Subj: Animals. Character traits – persistence. Dragons.

Day, Michael E. *Berry Ripe Moon* ill. by Carol Whitmore. Tide Grass Pr., 1977. Subj: Indians of North America.

Day, Shirley. *Ruthie's big tree* ill. by author. Firefly Pr., 1982. Subj: Character traits – perseverance. Trees.

Waldo's back yard ill. by author. Firefly Pr., 1984. Subj: Behavior – dissatisfaction. Character traits – helpfulness.

Dayrell, Elphinstone. *Why the sun and the moon live in the sky: an African folktale* ill. by Blair Lent. Houghton, 1968. First published in 1914 in the author's Folk stories from southern Nigeria,

West Africa Subj: Caldecott award honor book. Folk and fairy tales. Foreign lands – Africa. Moon. Sky. Sun.

Dayton, Laura. *LeRoy's birthday circus* ill. by Susan Huggins. Nelson, 1981. Subj: Birthdays. Circus. Counting, numbers. Poetry, rhyme.

Dayton, Mona. *Earth and sky* ill. by Roger Antoine Duvoisin. Harper, 1969. Subj: Behavior – fighting, arguing. Earth. Sky.

Dean, Leigh. *Two special cards* (Lisker, Sonia O.)

De Angeli, Marguerite. *The book of nursery and Mother Goose rhymes* ill. by compiler. Doubleday, 1954. Subj: Caldecott award honor book. Nursery rhymes.

Yonie Wondernose: for three little Wondernoses, Nina, David and Kiki ill. by author. Doubleday, 1944. Subj: Caldecott award honor book. Family life. Farms.

DeArmond, Dale. *The seal oil lamp* ill. by author. Little, 1988. ISBN 0-316-17786-5 Subj: Character traits – kindness. Death. Eskimos. Folk and fairy tales. Handicaps – blindness. Senses – seeing.

De Beer, Hans. *Ahoy there, little polar bear* ill. by author. Holt, 1988. ISBN 3-85539-006-1 Subj: Animals – polar bears.

Little polar bear ill. by author. Holt, 1987. ISBN 0-8050-0486-6 Subj: Animals – polar bears. Behavior – lost. Friendship.

Little polar bear finds a friend ill. by author. North-South, 1990. ISBN 1-55858-092-1 Subj: Animals – polar bears. Character traits – freedom. Foreign lands – Arctic. Friendship.

De Brunhoff, Jean *see* Brunhoff, Jean de

De Brunhoff, Laurent *see* Brunhoff, Laurent de

De Bruyn, Monica. *Lauren's secret ring* ill. by author. Albert Whitman, 1980. Subj: Friendship.

DeCaprio, Annie. *One, two* ill. by Seymour Nydorf. Grosset, 1965. Designed by David Krieger Subj: Counting, numbers.

DeChristopher, Marlowe. *Greencoat and the swanboy* ill. by reteller. Putnam, 1991. ISBN 0-399-22165-4 Subj: Birds – swans. Folk and fairy tales. Royalty – princesses.

Decker, Dorothy W. *Stripe and the merbear* ill. by author. Dillon, 1986. ISBN 0-87518-329-8 Subj: Mythical creatures. Sea and seashore. Toys – teddy bears.

Stripe visits New York ill. by author. Dillon, 1986. ISBN 0-87518-267-4 Subj: Activities – painting. Art. City. Toys – teddy bears.

Dee, Ruby. *Tower to heaven* ill. by Jennifer Bent. Holt, 1991. ISBN 0-8050-1460-8 Subj: Folk and fairy tales. Foreign lands – Ghana. Sky.

Two ways to count to ten: a Liberian folktale ill. by Susan Meddaugh. Holt, 1988. ISBN 0-8050-0407-6 Subj: Character traits – cleverness. Folk and fairy tales. Foreign lands – Africa.

Deedy, Carmen Agra. *Agatha's feather bed: not just another wild goose story* ill. by Laura L. Seeley. Peachtree, 1991. ISBN 1-56145-008-1 Subj: Birds – geese. Furniture – beds. Problem solving.

DeFelice, Cynthia C. *When Grampa kissed his elbow* ill. by Karl Swanson. Macmillan, 1992. ISBN 0-02-726455-6 Subj: Country. Family life – grandfathers.

DeForest, Charlotte B. *The prancing pony: nursery rhymes from Japan* adapted into English verse for children, with "Kusa-e"; ill. by Keiko Hida. Walker, 1968. Subj: Foreign lands – Japan. Nursery rhymes.

Degen, Bruce. *Aunt Possum and the pumpkin man* ill. by author. Harper, 1977. Subj: Animals – cats. Animals – possums. Family life – aunts, uncles. Holidays – Halloween. Wordless.

Jamberry ill. by author. Harper, 1983. Subj: Animals – bears. Food. Poetry, rhyme.

The little witch and the riddle ill. by author. Harper, 1980. Subj: Friendship. Magic. Riddles. Witches.

Teddy bear towers ill. by author. HarperCollins, 1991. ISBN 0-06-021430-9 Subj: Family life – brothers. Imagination. Poetry, rhyme. Royalty – kings. Toys – teddy bears.

De Gerez, Toni. *Louhi, witch of North Farm* ill. by Barbara Cooney. Viking, 1986. A story from Finlands's epic poem The Kalevala ISBN 0-670-80556-4 Subj: Behavior – stealing. Folk and fairy tales. Foreign lands – Finland. Moon. Sun. Witches.

My song is a piece of jade: poems of ancient Mexico in English and Spanish ill. by William Stark. Little, 1984. Subj: Foreign lands – Mexico. Foreign languages. Poetry, rhyme.

De Groat, Diane. *Alligator's toothache* ill. by author. Crown, 1977. Subj: Illness. Reptiles – alligators, crocodiles. Teeth. Wordless.

De Hamel, Joan. *Hemi's pet* ill. by Christine Ross. Houghton, 1987. ISBN 0-395-43665-6 Subj: Pets. School. Sibling rivalry.

DeJong, David Cornel. *Looking for Alexander* ill. by Harvey Weiss. Little, 1963. Subj: Animals – cats. Family life – grandmothers.

De Kay, Ormonde. *Rimes de la Mere Oie* (Mother Goose)

Delacre, Lulu. *Arroz con leche: popular songs and rhymes from Latin America* ill. by author. Scholastic, 1989. ISBN 0-590-42442-4 Subj: Foreign languages. Games. Music. Poetry, rhyme. Songs.

Las Navidades: popular Christmas songs from Latin America sel. by Lulu Delacre; tr. from Spanish by Elena Paz; arranged by Ana-Maria Rosado; ill. by selector. Scholastic, 1990. ISBN 0-590-43548-5 Subj: Foreign languages. Holidays – Christmas. Music. Poetry, rhyme. Songs.

Nathan and Nicholas Alexander ill. by author. Scholastic, 1986. ISBN 0-590-33956-7 Subj: Animals – elephants. Animals – mice. Behavior – sharing.

Nathan's balloon adventure ill. by author. Scholastic, 1991. ISBN 0-590-44976-1 Subj: Activities – ballooning. Animals – elephants. Animals – mice.

Nathan's fishing trip ill. by author. Scholastic, 1988. ISBN 0-590-41281-7 Subj: Animals – elephants. Animals – mice. Friendship. Sports – fishing.

Peter Cottontail's Easter book ill. by author. Scholastic, 1991. ISBN 0-590-43338-5 Subj: Animals – rabbits. Holidays – Easter.

De La Fontaine, Jean *see* La Fontaine, Jean de

DeLage, Ida. *ABC Easter bunny* ill. by Ellen Sloan. Garrard, 1979. Subj: ABC books. Animals – rabbits. Holidays – Easter.

ABC triplets at the zoo ill. by Lori Pierson. Garrard, 1980. Subj: ABC books. Animals. Zoos.

Am I a bunny? ill. by Ellen Sloan. Garrard, 1978. Subj: Animals – rabbits. Self-concept.

Beware! Beware! A witch won't share ill. by Ted Schroeder. Garrard, 1991. ISBN 0-7910-1473-8 Subj: Behavior – sharing. Witches.

The old witch and her magic basket ill. by Ellen Sloan. Garrard, 1978. Subj: Holidays – Halloween. Witches.

The old witch and the crows ill. by Marianne Smith. Garrard, 1983. Subj: Birds – crows. Birds – owls. Night. Witches.

The old witch and the dragon ill. by Unada. Garrard, 1979. Subj: Dragons. Witches.

The old witch and the ghost parade ill. by Jody Taylor. Garrard, 1978. Subj: Ghosts. Witches.

The old witch finds a new house ill. by Pat Paris. Garrard, 1979. Subj: Moving. Witches.

Pilgrim children on the Mayflower ill. by Bert Dodson. Garrard, 1980. Subj: Boats, ships. U.S. history.

The squirrel's tree party ill. by Tracy McVay. Garrard, 1978. Subj: Animals – squirrels. Parties. Trees.

Delamare, David. *The Christmas secret* ill. by author. Simon & Schuster, 1991. ISBN 0-671-74822-X Subj: Animals. Friendship. Holidays – Christmas. Weather – storms.

De La Mare, Walter (Walter John). *Molly Whuppie* ill. by Errol Le Cain. Farrar, 1983. Subj: Character traits – bravery. Character traits – cleverness. Giants. Royalty.

Delaney, A. *The butterfly* ill. by author. Crown, 1977. Subj: Cumulative tales. Insects – butterflies, caterpillars.

The gunnywolf ill. by author. Harper, 1988. ISBN 0-06-021595-X Subj: Animals – wolves. Behavior – misbehavior. Flowers. Foreign lands – Germany. Songs.

Monster tracks? ill. by author. Harper, 1981. Subj: Imagination. Weather – snow.

Delaney, M. C. (Michael Clark). *The marigold monster* ill. by Ned Delaney. Dutton, 1983. Subj: Humor. Monsters. Riddles.

Delaney, Molly. *My sister* ill. by author. Atheneum, 1989. ISBN 0-689-31460-4 Subj: Family life – sisters. Sibling rivalry.

Delaney, Ned. *Bad dog!* ill. by author. Morrow, 1987. ISBN 0-688-06596-1 Subj: Animals – dogs. Behavior – lost. Behavior – misbehavior.

Bert and Barney ill. by author. Houghton, 1979. Subj: Friendship.

Cosmic chickens ill. by author. Harper, 1988. ISBN 0-06-021584-4 Subj: Birds – chickens. Farms. Space and space ships.

One dragon to another ill. by author. Houghton, 1976. Subj: Character traits – individuality. Dragons. Games. Insects – butterflies, caterpillars.

Rufus the doofus ill. by author. Houghton, 1978. Subj: Behavior – misbehavior. School.

Terrible things could happen ill. by author. Lothrop, 1983. Subj: Activities – working. Humor.

Delaunay, Sonia. *Sonia Delaunay's alphabet* ill. by author. Crowell, 1972. Subj: ABC books. Poetry, rhyme.

Delessert, Etienne. *The endless party* tr. by Jeffrey Tabberner; ill. by author. Oxford Univ. Pr., 1981. Subj: Religion – Noah.

How the mouse was hit on the head by a stone and so discovered the world text and ill. by Etienne Delessert in collaboration with Odie Mosimann; foreword by Jean Piaget; tr. by C. Ross Smith. Doubleday, 1971. Subj: Animals – mice. World.

A long long song ill. by author. Farrar, 1988. ISBN 0-374-34638-0 Subj: Imagination. Nursery rhymes. Songs.

Dellinger, Annetta. *You are special to Jesus* ill. by Jan Brett. Concordia, 1984. Subj: Character traits – appearance. Character traits – individuality. Religion.

Delton, Judy. *Bear and Duck on the run* ill. by Lynn Munsinger. Albert Whitman, 1984. Subj: Animals – bears. Birds – ducks.

The best mom in the world ill. by John Faulkner. Albert Whitman, 1979. Subj: Behavior – growing up. Family life – mothers.

Brimhall comes to stay ill. by Cyndy Szekeres. Lothrop, 1978. Subj: Animals – bears. Family life.

Brimhall turns detective ill. by Cherie R. Wyman. Carolrhoda, 1983. Subj: Animals – bears. Animals – rabbits. Weather – snow.

Brimhall turns to magic ill. by Bruce Degen. Lothrop, 1979. Subj: Animals – bears. Animals – rabbits. Magic.

Duck goes fishing ill. by Lynn Munsinger. Albert Whitman, 1983. Subj: Animals – foxes. Birds – ducks. Birds – owls. Friendship. Sports – fishing.

The elephant in Duck's garden ill. by Lynn Munsinger. Albert Whitman, 1985. ISBN 0-8075-1959-6 Subj: Animals – bears. Animals – elephants. Behavior – worrying. Birds – ducks.

Groundhog's Day at the doctor ill. by Giulio Maestro. Parents, 1981. Subj: Animals – groundhogs. Holidays – Groundhog Day. Illness.

I never win! ill. by Cathy Gilchrist. Carolrhoda, 1981. Subj: Character traits – luck. Games.

I'll never love anything ever again ill. by Rodney Pate. Albert Whitman, 1985. ISBN 0-8075-3521-4 Subj: Animals – dogs. Emotions – sadness. Pets.

I'm telling you now ill. by Lillian Hoban. Dutton, 1983. Subj: Activities. Behavior. Character traits – individuality.

It happened on Thursday ill. by June Goldsborough. Albert Whitman, 1978. Subj: Character traits – luck. Family life. Illness.

My grandma's in a nursing home ill. by Charles Robinson. Albert Whitman, 1986. ISBN 0-8075-5333-6 Subj: Emotions – loneliness. Family life – grandmothers. Old age.

My mom hates me in January ill. by John Faulkner. Albert Whitman, 1977. Subj: Behavior – boredom. Seasons – winter.

My mom made me go to school ill. by Lisa McCue. Delacorte Pr., 1991. ISBN 0-385-30330-0 Subj: Family life – mothers. School.

My mother lost her job today ill. by Irene Trivas. Albert Whitman, 1980. Subj: Activities – working. Character traits – optimism. Family life – mothers.

My Uncle Nikos ill. by Marc Simont. Crowell, 1983. Subj: Family life – aunts, uncles. Foreign lands – Greece.

The new girl at school ill. by Lillian Hoban. Dutton, 1979. Subj: School.

On a picnic ill. by Mamoru Funai. Doubleday, 1979. ISBN 0-385-12945-9 Subj: Activities – picnicking. Animals – gorillas. Animals – lions. Behavior – worrying. Birds – geese.

Penny wise, fun foolish ill. by Giulio Maestro. Crown, 1977. Subj: Animals – elephants. Behavior – saving things. Birds – ostriches. Fairs.

A pet for Duck and Bear ill. by Lynn Munsinger. Albert Whitman, 1982. Subj: Animals – bears. Birds – ducks. Friendship. Pets.

Rabbit goes to night school ill. by Lynn Munsinger. Albert Whitman, 1986. ISBN 0-8075-6725-6 Subj: Animals – rabbits. Magic. School.

Three friends find spring ill. by Giulio Maestro. Crown, 1977. Subj: Animals – rabbits. Birds – ducks. Friendship. Seasons – spring. Seasons – winter.

A walk on a snowy night ill. by Ruth Rosner. Harper, 1982. Subj: Night. Weather – snow. Weather – storms.

DeLuise, Dom. *Charlie the caterpillar* ill. by Christopher Santoro. Simon & Schuster, 1990. ISBN 0-671-69358-1 Subj: Animals – monkeys. Behavior – growing up. Insects – butterflies, caterpillars. Science.

Del Vecchio, Ellen. *Big city port* (Maestro, Betsy)

De Lynam, Alicia Garcia. *It's mine!* ill. by author. Dial Pr., 1988. ISBN 0-8037-0509-3 Subj: Behavior – sharing. Sibling rivalry. Toys.

Demarest, Chris L. *Benedict finds a home* ill. by author. Lothrop, 1982. Subj: Behavior – seeking better things. Birds.

Clemens' kingdom ill. by author. Lothrop, 1983. Subj: Animals – lions. Character traits – curiosity. Libraries.

Kitman and Willy at sea ill. by author. Simon & Schuster, 1991. ISBN 0-671-65696-1 Subj: Animals. Animals – cats. Animals – mice. Problem solving.

Morton and Sidney ill. by author. Macmillan, 1987. ISBN 0-02-728450-6 Subj: Behavior – sharing. Monsters.

No peas for Nellie ill. by author. Macmillan, 1988. ISBN 0-02-728460-3 Subj: Food. Imagination.

Orville's odyssey ill. by author. Prentice-Hall, 1986. ISBN 0-13-642851-7 Subj: Imagination. Sports – fishing. Wordless.

De Marolles, Chantal. *The lonely wolf* ill. by Eleonore Schmid. Holt, 1986. ISBN 0-8050-0006-2 Subj: Animals – wolves. Character traits – kindness to animals. Foreign lands – Russia.

De Mejo, Oscar. *La Bella Magellona and the little cavalier* ill. by author. Putnam, 1992. ISBN 0-399-22138-7 Subj: Concepts – shape. Concepts – size. Emotions – love. Folk and fairy tales.

Oscar de Mejo's ABC ill. by author. HarperCollins, 1992. ISBN 0-06-020517-2 Subj: ABC books. Art.

Demi. *The adventures of Marco Polo* ill. by author. Holt, 1982. Subj: Activities – traveling. Foreign lands – China.

The artist and the architect ill. by author. Holt, 1991. ISBN 0-8050-1685-6 Subj: Careers – architects. Careers – artists. Emotions – envy, jealousy. Foreign lands – China. Folk and fairy tales.

Chen Ping and his magic axe ill. by author. Dodd, 1987. ISBN 0-396-08907-0 Subj: Character traits – honesty. Folk and fairy tales. Foreign lands – China. Magic.

A Chinese zoo: fables and proverbs ill. by adapt. Harcourt, 1987. ISBN 0-15-217510-5 Subj: Animals. Folk and fairy tales. Foreign lands – China.

Demi's count the animals 1-2-3 ill. by author. Grosset, 1986. ISBN 0-448-18980-1 Subj: Animals. Counting, numbers. Poetry, rhyme.

Demi's find the animals A B C: an alphabet-game book ill. by author. Grosset, 1985. ISBN 0-448-18970-4 Subj: ABC books. Animals. Behavior – hiding things.

Demi's opposites: an animal game book ill. by author. Grosset, 1987. ISBN 0-448-18995-X Subj: Animals. Concepts – opposites. Games.

Demi's reflective fables ill. by author. Grosset, 1988. ISBN 0-448-09281-6 Subj: Folk and fairy tales. Foreign lands – China.

Dragon kites and dragonflies: a collection of Chinese nursery rhymes ill. by adapt. Harcourt, 1986. ISBN 0-15-224199-X Subj: Dragons. Foreign lands – China. Nursery rhymes.

Fleecy bunny ill. by author. Grosset, 1987. ISBN 0-448-19151-2 Subj: Animals – rabbits. Format, unusual – board books.

Fleecy lamb ill. by author. Grosset, 1987. ISBN 0-448-19152-0 Subj: Animals – sheep. Format, unusual – board books.

The hallowed horse ill. by adapt. Dodd, 1987. ISBN 0-396-08908-9 Subj: Animals – horses. Folk and fairy tales. Foreign lands – India. Reptiles – snakes.

Liang and the magic paintbrush ill. by author. Holt, 1988. ISBN 0-8050-0801-2 Subj: Activities – painting. Magic.

Little baby lamb ill. by author. Putnam, 1993. ISBN 0-448-40580-6 Subj: Animals – sheep. Format, unusual – board books.

Little lucky ducky ill. by author. Putnam, 1993. ISBN 0-448-40581-4 Subj: Birds – ducks. Format, unusual – board books.

The magic boat ill. by author. Holt, 1990. ISBN 0-8050-1141-2 Subj: Boats, ships. Folk and fairy tales. Foreign lands – China. Magic. Toys.

Under the shade of the mulberry tree ill. by author. Prentice-Hall, 1979. Subj: Character traits – cleverness. Folk and fairy tales. Foreign lands – China.

Where is it? ill. by author. Doubleday, 1979. Subj: Riddles.

Demuth, Patricia Brennan. *Max, the bad-talking parrot* ill. by Bo Zaunders. Dodd, 1986. ISBN 0-396-08767-1 Subj: Behavior – misunderstanding. Birds – parakeets, parrots. Etiquette. Poetry, rhyme.

Ornery morning ill. by Craig McFarland Brown. Dutton, 1991. ISBN 0-525-44688-5 Subj: Animals. Behavior – bad day. Careers – farmers. Cumulative tales. Farms.

Denison, Carol. *A part-time dog for Nick* ill. by Jane Miller. Dodd, 1959. Subj: Animals – dogs. Family life.

Dennis, Lynne. *Raymond Rabbit's early morning* ill. by author. Dutton, 1987. ISBN 0-525-44316-9 Subj: Animals – rabbits. Family life. Morning.

Dennis, Morgan. *Burlap* ill. by author. Viking, 1945. Subj: Animals – bears. Animals – dogs.

The pup himself ill. by author. Viking, 1943. Subj: Animals – dogs.

The sea dog ill. by author. Viking, 1958. Subj: Animals – dogs. Boats, ships. Weather – storms.

Skit and Skat ill. by author. Viking, 1952. Subj: Animals – cats. Animals – dogs.

Dennis, Suzanne E. *Answer me that* ill. by Owen Wood. Bobbs-Merrill, 1969. Subj: Animals. Humor. Poetry, rhyme.

Dennis, Wesley. *Flip* ill. by author. Viking, 1941. Subj: Animals. Dreams. Farms.

Flip and the cows ill. by author. Viking, 1942. Subj: Animals – bulls, cows. Animals – horses. Farms.

Flip and the morning ill. by author. Viking, 1951. Subj: Animals – horses. Morning.

Tumble, the story of a mustang ill. by author. Hastings, 1966. Subj: Animals – horses. Character traits – freedom.

Denslow, Sharon Phillips. *At Taylor's place* ill. by Nancy Carpenter. Bradbury Pr., 1990. ISBN 0-02-728685-1 Subj: Careers – carpenters. Farms. Seasons – fall.

Hazel's circle ill. by Sharon McGinley-Nally. Four Winds Pr., 1992. ISBN 0-02-728683-5 Subj: Birds – chickens. Communities, neighborhoods.

Night owls ill. by Kastner, Jill. Bradbury Pr., 1990. ISBN 0-02-728681-9 Subj: Activities. Night. Seasons – summer.

Riding with Aunt Lucy ill. by Nancy Carpenter. Bradbury Pr., 1991. ISBN 0-02-728686-X Subj: Activities – traveling. Animals – pigs. Family life – aunts, uncles.

Denslow, W. W. *Denslow's picture book treasury* ill. by author. Arcade, 1990. ISBN 1-55970-071-8 Subj: Nursery rhymes. Songs.

Denton, Kady MacDonald. *Christmas boot* ill. by author. Little, 1990. ISBN 0-316-18091-2 Subj: Clothing – shoes. Holidays – Christmas.

Granny is a darling ill. by author. Macmillan, 1988. ISBN 0-689-50452-7 Subj: Bedtime. Family life – grandmothers. Monsters. Night.

The picnic ill. by author. Dutton, 1988. ISBN 0-525-44376-2 Subj: Activities – picnicking. Family life.

Denton, Terry. *Home is the sailor* ill. by author. Houghton, 1989. ISBN 0-395-51525-4 Subj: Activities – traveling. Animals. Boats, ships. Sea and seashore.

The school for laughter ill. by author. Houghton, 1990. ISBN 0-395-53353-8 Subj: Behavior – losing things. School.

Denver, John. *The children and the flowers* ill. by Randi Gullerud. Green Tiger Pr., 1979. Subj: Flowers. Songs.

De Paola, Paula. *Rosie and the yellow ribbon* ill. by Janet Wolf. Little, 1992. ISBN 0-316-18100-5 Subj: Birthdays. City. Concepts – color. Friendship.

De Paola, Tomie (Thomas Anthony). *An early American Christmas* ill. by author. Holiday, 1987. ISBN 0-8234-0617-2 Subj: Holidays – Christmas. U.S. history.

De Paola, Tomie (Thomas Anthony). *Andy (that's my name)* ill. by author. Prentice-Hall, 1973. Subj: Behavior – greed. Character traits – smallness. Friendship. Games. Names.

The art lesson ill. by author. Putnam's, 1989. ISBN 0-399-21688-X Subj: Art. Family life. School.

Baby's first Christmas ill. by author. Putnam's, 1988. ISBN 0-399-21591-3 Subj: Babies. Holidays – Christmas.

Big Anthony and the magic ring ill. by author. Harcourt, 1979. Subj: Character traits – appearance. Magic.

Bill and Pete ill. by author. Putnam's, 1978. Subj: Foreign lands – Africa. Humor. Reptiles – alligators, crocodiles. School.

Bill and Pete go down the Nile ill. by author. Putnam's, 1987. ISBN 0-399-21395-3 Subj: Behavior – stealing. Birds. Foreign lands – Egypt. Museums. Reptiles – alligators, crocodiles. School.

Bonjour, Mister Satie ill. by author. Putnam, 1991. ISBN 0-399-21782-7 Subj: Animals – cats. Art. Family life – aunts, uncles. Foreign lands – France.

The cat on the Dovrefell: a Christmas tale tr. by George W. Dasent; ill. by author. Putnam's, 1979. Subj: Holidays – Christmas. Trolls.

Charlie needs a cloak ill. by author. Prentice-Hall, 1973. Subj: Animals – mice. Animals – sheep. Clothing – coats. Problem solving.

The Christmas pageant ill. by author. Winston Pr., 1978. Subj: Holidays – Christmas. Theater.

The cloud book ill. by author. Holiday, 1975. Subj: Weather – clouds.

The clown of God: an old story ill. by author. Harcourt, 1978. Subj: Foreign lands – Italy. Holidays – Christmas. Religion.

Country farm ill. by author. Putnam's, 1984. Subj: Animals. Farms. Format, unusual. Wordless.

Criss-cross applesauce photos. by B. A. King; ill. by the B. A. King children. Addison-Wesley, 1979. Subj: Children as illustrators.

The family Christmas tree book ill. by author. Holiday, 1980. Subj: Family life. Holidays – Christmas. Trees.

Favorite nursery tales ill. by adapt. Putnam's, 1986. ISBN 0-399-21319-8 Subj: Folk and fairy tales. Nursery rhymes.

Fight the night ill. by author. Lippincott, 1968. Subj: Bedtime. Sleep.

Fin M'Coul: the giant of Knockmany Hill ill. by author. Holiday, 1981. Subj: Folk and fairy tales. Foreign lands – Ireland. Giants.

Flicks ill. by author. Harcourt, 1979. Subj: Humor. Wordless.

Four stories for four seasons ill. by author. Prentice-Hall, 1977. Subj: Boats, ships. Gardens, gardening. Hibernation. Seasons.

Haircuts for the Woolseys ill. by author. Putnam's, 1989. ISBN 0-399-21662-6 Subj: Animals – sheep. Family life – grandmothers.

Helga's dowry ill. by author. Harcourt, 1977. Subj: Emotions – love. Poverty. Trolls. Weddings.

The hunter and the animals ill. by author. Holiday, 1981. Subj: Animals. Sports – hunting. Wordless.

Jamie O'Rourke and the big potato ill. by author. Putnam, 1992. ISBN 0-399-22257-X Subj: Behavior – laziness. Elves and little people. Folk and fairy tales. Foreign lands – Ireland.

Katie and Kit at the beach ill. by author. Little, 1987. ISBN 0-671-61722-2 Subj: Format, unusual – board books. Sea and seashore. Weather – rain.

Katie, Kit and cousin Tom ill. by author. Little, 1987. ISBN 0-671-61724-9 Subj: Behavior – bullying. Family life. Format, unusual – board books.

Katie's good idea ill. by author. Little, 1987. ISBN 0-671-61725-7 Subj: Behavior – growing up. Format, unusual – board books.

The knight and the dragon ill. by author. Putnam's, 1980. Subj: Dragons. Knights. Libraries.

The Lady of Guadalupe ill. by author. Holiday, 1980. Subj: Foreign lands – Mexico. Religion.

The legend of Old Befana ill. by author. Harcourt, 1980. Subj: Folk and fairy tales. Foreign lands – Italy. Religion.

The legend of the bluebonnet ill. by author. Putnam's, 1983. Subj: Indians of North America. Flowers. Folk and fairy tales.

The legend of the Indian paintbrush ill. by author. Putnam's, 1987. ISBN 0-399-21534-4 Subj: Activities – painting. Folk and fairy tales. Flowers. Indians of North America.

Little Grunt and the big egg : a prehistoric fairy tale ill. by author. Holiday, 1990. ISBN 0-8234-0730-6 Subj: Dinosaurs. Folk and fairy tales. Pets.

Marianna May and Nursey ill. by author. Holiday, 1983. Subj: Character traits – cleanliness.

Merry Christmas, Strega Nona ill. by author. Harcourt, 1986. ISBN 0-15-253183-1 Subj: Foreign lands – Italy. Holidays – Christmas. Magic. Witches.

Michael Bird-Boy ill. by author. Prentice-Hall, 1975. Subj: Ecology.

My first Chanukah ill. by author. Putnam, 1989. ISBN 0-399-21780-0 Subj: Format, unusual – board books. Holidays – Hanukkah. Jewish culture. Religion.

The mysterious giant of Barletta: an Italian folktale ill. by author. Harcourt, 1984. Subj: Folk and fairy tales. Foreign lands – Italy. Giants. War.

Nana upstairs and Nana downstairs ill. by author. Putnam's, 1973. Subj: Death. Emotions – sadness. Family life – grandmothers.

Noah and the ark ill. by author. Winston, 1983. Subj: Religion – Noah.

Now one foot, now the other ill. by author. Putnam's 1981. Subj: Family life – grandfathers. Illness.

Oliver Button is a sissy ill. by author. Harcourt, 1979. Subj: Activities – dancing. Character traits – individuality.

Pajamas for Kit ill. by author. Little, 1987. ISBN 0-671-61723-0 Subj: Bedtime. Clothing. Family life – grandparents. Format, unusual – board books.

Pancakes for breakfast ill. by author. Harcourt, 1978. Subj: Activities – cooking. Food. Wordless.

The parables of Jesus ill. by author. Holiday, 1987. ISBN 0-8234-0636-9 Subj: Religion.

Patrick: patron saint of Ireland ill. by author. Holiday, 1992. ISBN 0-8234-0924-4 Subj: Foreign lands – Ireland.. Religion.

The popcorn book ill. by author. Holiday, 1978. Subj: Activities – cooking. Food.

The Prince of the Dolomites ill. by author. Harcourt, 1980. Subj: Elves and little people. Folk and fairy tales. Foreign lands – Italy. Moon.

The quicksand book ill. by author. Holiday, 1977. Subj: Behavior – carelessness.

Sing, Pierrot, sing: a picture book in mime ill. by author. Harcourt, 1983. Subj: Clowns, jesters. Theater. Wordless.

Songs of the fog maiden ill. by author. Holiday, 1979. Subj: Poetry, rhyme.

The story of the three wise kings ill. by author. Putnam's, 1983. Subj: Holidays – Christmas. Religion.

Strega Nona: an old tale ill. by author. Prentice-Hall, 1975. Subj: Behavior – forgetfulness. Caldecott award honor book. Humor. Magic. Witches.

Strega Nona's magic lessons ill. by author. Harcourt, 1982. Subj: Behavior – carelessness. Humor. Magic. Witches.

Things to make and do for Valentine's Day ill. by author. Watts, 1976. Subj: Activities – cooking. Activities – making things. Games. Holidays – Valentine's Day.

Tomie de Paola's Mother Goose ill. by selector. Putnam's, 1985. ISBN 0-399-21258-2 Subj: Nursery rhymes.

Tony's bread ill. by author. Putnam, 1989. ISBN 0-399-21693-6 Subj: Careers – bakers. Folk and fairy tales. Food. Foreign lands – Italy.

Too many Hopkins ill. by author. Putnam's, 1989. ISBN 0-399-21661-8 Subj: Animals – rabbits. Family life. Gardens, gardening.

When everyone was fast asleep ill. by author. Holiday, 1976. Subj: Sleep.

De Posadas Mane, Carmen. *Mister North Wind* adapt. by Joanne Fink; tr. from Spanish by Candido A. Valderrama; ill. by Alfonso Ruano. Silver Burdett, 1986. ISBN 0-382-09191-4 Subj: Animals. Character traits – bravery. Seasons – spring. Weather – wind.

De Regniers, Beatrice Schenk. *A bunch of poems and verses* ill. by Mary Jane Dunton. Seabury Pr., 1977. Subj: Poetry, rhyme.

Catch a little fox: variations on a folk rhyme ill. by Brinton Turkle. Seabury Pr., 1979. Subj: Character traits – cleverness. Nursery rhymes. Sports – hunting.

Cats cats cats ill. by Bill Sokol. Pantheon, 1958. Subj: Animals – cats. Poetry, rhyme.

Circus photos. by Al Giese. Viking, 1966. Subj: Circus.

David and Goliath ill. by Richard M. Powers. Viking, 1965. Subj: Religion.

Everyone is good for something ill. by Margot Tomes. Houghton, 1980. Subj: Animals – cats. Folk and fairy tales. Foreign lands – Russia. Self-concept.

The giant story ill. by Maurice Sendak. Harper, 1953. Subj: Family life. Giants.

Going for a walk ill. by author. Harper, 1982. Orig. title: The little book Subj: Activities – walking.

How Joe the bear and Sam the mouse got together ill. by Bernice Myers. Lothrop, 1990. ISBN 0-688-09080-X Subj: Animals – bears. Animals – mice. Friendship.

It does not say meow! ill. by Paul Galdone. Seabury Pr., 1972. Subj: Animals. Participation. Poetry, rhyme. Riddles.

Jack and the beanstalk (Jack and the beanstalk)

Jack the giant killer (Jack and the beanstalk)

Laura's story ill. by Jack Kent. Atheneum, 1979. Subj: Imagination.

A little house of your own ill. by Irene Haas. Harcourt, 1954. Subj: Family life. Houses. Imagination.

Little Sister and the Month Brothers ill. by Margot Tomes. Seabury Pr., 1976. Subj: Days of the week, months of the year. Folk and fairy tales. Foreign lands.

May I bring a friend? ill. by Beni Montresor. Atheneum, 1964. Subj: Animals. Caldecott award book. Friendship. Humor. Poetry, rhyme. Royalty.

Picture book theater: the mysterious stranger and the magic spell ill. by William Lahey Cummings. Seabury Pr., 1982. Subj: Animals – cats. Animals – mice. Theater. Wizards.

Red Riding Hood ill. by Edward Gorey. Atheneum, 1972. Retold in verse for boys and girls to read themselves Subj: Animals – wolves. Behavior – talking to strangers. Folk and fairy tales. Poetry, rhyme.

Sam and the impossible thing ill. by Brinton Turkle. Norton, 1967. Subj: Activities – cooking. Food. Monsters. Poetry, rhyme.

The shadow book ill. by Isabel Gordon. Harcourt, 1960. Subj: Shadows.

So many cats! ill. by Ellen Weiss. Clarion, 1985. ISBN 0-89919-322-6 Subj: Animals – cats. Counting, numbers. Poetry, rhyme.

Something special ill. by Irene Haas. Harcourt, 1958. Subj: Poetry, rhyme.

A special birthday party for someone very special ill. by Brinton Turkle. Norton, 1966. Subj: Animals – skunks. Birthdays.

Waiting for mama ill. by Victoria de Larrea. Clarion, 1984. Subj: Imagination.

Was it a good trade? ill. by Irene Haas. Harcourt, 1956. Subj: Activities – trading. Poetry, rhyme. Songs.

What can you do with a shoe? ill. by Maurice Sendak. Harper, 1955. Subj: Games. Imagination.

Who likes the sun? ill. by Leona Pierce. Harcourt, 1961. Subj: Sun.

Willy O'Dwyer jumped in the fire variations on a folk rhyme ill. by Beni Montresor. Atheneum, 1968. Subj: Fire. Moon. Nursery rhymes. Witches.

DeSaix, Frank. *The girl who danced with dolphins* ill. by Debbi Durland DeSaix. Farrar, 1991. ISBN 0-374-32626-6 Subj: Animals – dolphins. Dreams. Sea and seashore.

DeSantis, Kenny. *A doctor's tools* photos. by Patricia Agre. Dodd, 1985. ISBN 0-396-08516-4 Subj: Careers – doctors. Tools.

Desimini, Lisa. *I am running away today* ill. by author. Walt Disney, 1992. ISBN 1-56282-121-0 Subj: Animals – cats. Behavior – running away.

Deutsch, Babette. *There comes a time* (Borchers, Elisabeth)

De Veaux, Alexis. *An enchanted hair tale* ill. by Cheryl Hanna. HarperCollins, 1987. ISBN 0-06-021624-7 Subj: Character traits – being different. Ethnic groups in the U.S. – Afro-Americans. Hair. Imagination. Self-concept.

Na-ni ill. by author. Harper, 1973. Subj: Character traits – questioning. City. Emotions – sadness. Poverty.

Devlin, Harry. *Aunt Agatha, there's a lion under the couch!* (Devlin, Wende)

Cranberry Christmas (Devlin, Wende)

Cranberry Easter (Devlin, Wende)

Cranberry summer (Devlin, Wende)

Cranberry Thanksgiving (Devlin, Wende)

Cranberry Valentine (Devlin, Wende)

Old Black Witch (Devlin, Wende)

Old Witch and the polka-dot ribbon (Devlin, Wende)

Old Witch rescues Halloween (Devlin, Wende)

The walloping window blind: an old nautical tale ill. by author. Van Nostrand, 1968. Adapted from an old sea tune Subj: Boats, ships. Pirates. Songs.

Devlin, Wende. *Aunt Agatha, there's a lion under the couch!* by Wende and Harry Devlin; ill. by authors. Van Nostrand, 1968. Subj: Animals – lions. Emotions – fear. Family life – aunts, uncles. Furniture. Imagination.

Cranberry Christmas by Wende and Harry Devlin; ill. by authors. Parents, 1976. Subj: Behavior – sharing. Character traits – helpfulness. Holidays – Christmas.

Cranberry Easter by Wende and Harry Devlin; ill. by Harry Devlin. Four Winds Pr., 1990. ISBN 0-02-729935-X Subj: Behavior – worrying. Holidays – Easter.

Cranberry Halloween ill. by Harry Devlin. Four Winds Pr., 1982. Subj: Behavior – stealing. Holidays – Halloween.

Cranberry summer by Wende and Harry Devlin; ill. by Harry Devlin. Four Winds Pr., 1992. ISBN 0-02-729181-2 Subj: Animals – donkeys. Animals – kindness to animals. Holidays – Fourth of July.

Cranberry Thanksgiving by Wende and Harry Devlin; ill. by Harry Devlin. Parents, 1971. Subj: Holidays – Thanksgiving.

Cranberry Valentine by Wende and Harry Devlin; ill. by authors. Four Winds Pr., 1986. ISBN 0-02-729200-2 Subj: Character traits – shyness. Holidays – Valentine's Day.

Old Black Witch by Wende and Harry Devlin; ill. by Harry Devlin. Encyclopaedia Brit., 1963. Subj: Activities – cooking. Witches.

Old Witch and the polka-dot ribbon by Wende and Harry Devlin; ill. by Harry Devlin. Parents, 1970. Subj: Activities – cooking. Fairs. Food. Witches.

Old Witch rescues Halloween by Wende and Harry Devlin; ill. by Harry Devlin. Parents, 1972. Subj: Activities – cooking. Holidays – Halloween. Witches.

De Vries, Maggie. *Once upon a golden apple* (Little, Jean)

Dewey, Ariane. *A crocodile's tale* (Aruego, José)

Dorin and the dragon ill. by author. Greenwillow, 1982. Subj: Dragons. Dreams. Magic. Royalty.

Febold Feboldson ill. by author. Greenwillow, 1984. Subj: Farms. Folk and fairy tales. Weather.

The fish Peri ill. by author. Macmillan, 1979. Subj: Folk and fairy tales. Foreign lands – Turkey. Magic. Problem solving.

Laffite, the pirate ill. by author. Greenwillow, 1985. ISBN 0-688-04230-9 Subj: Folk and fairy tales. Pirates. U.S. history.

Pecos Bill ill. by author. Greenwillow, 1983. Subj: Cowboys. Folk and fairy tales.

The thunder god's son: a Peruvian folktale ill. by author. Greenwillow, 1981. Subj: Folk and fairy tales. Foreign lands – Peru. Magic.

We hide, you seek (Aruego, José)

DeWitt, Jamie. *Jamie's turn* ill. by Julie Brinckloe. Raintree, 1984. ISBN 0-940742-37-3 Subj: Farms. Illness.

DeWitt, Lyndia. *What will the weather be?* ill. by Carolyn Croll. HarperCollins, 1991. ISBN 0-06-021597-6 Subj: Weather.

Diamond, Donna. *The Bremen town musicians* (Grimm, Jacob)

Rumpelstiltskin (Grimm, Jacob)

Dick Whittington and his cat. *Dick Whittington* retold by Kathleen Lines; ill. by Edward Ardizzone. Walck, 1970. Subj: Activities – trading. Animals – cats. Folk and fairy tales. Foreign lands – England. Middle ages.

Dick Whittington and his cat retold and ill. by Marcia Brown. Scribner's, 1950. Subj: Activities – trading. Animals – cats. Caldecott award honor book. Folk and fairy tales. Foreign lands – England. Middle ages.

Dick Whittington: a story from England retold by Charles Causley; ill. by Antony Maitland. Penguin, 1979. Subj: Activities – trading. Animals – cats. Folk and fairy tales. Foreign lands – England. Middle ages.

Dick Whittington and his cat retold by Eva Moore; ill. by Kurt Werth. Seabury Pr., 1974. Subj: Activities – trading. Animals – cats. Folk and fairy tales. Foreign lands – England. Middle ages.

Dickens, Frank. *Boffo: the great motorcycle race* ill. by author. Parents, 1978. Subj: Character traits – cleverness. Motorcycles. Sports – racing.

Dickens, Lucy. *At the beach* ill. by author. Viking, 1991. ISBN 0-670-83927-2 Subj: Activities – playing. Family life. Format, unusual – board books. Sea and seashore.

Dirty Henry ill. by author. Viking, 1991. ISBN 0-670-83578-1 Subj: Activities – bathing. Animals – dogs.

Go fish ill. by author. Viking, 1991. ISBN 0-670-84164-1 Subj: Animals – polar bears. Emotions – fear.

Our day ill. by author. Viking, 1991. ISBN 0-670-83929-9 Subj: Activities – playing. Family life. Format, unusual – board books.

Outside ill. by author. Viking, 1991. ISBN 0-670-83928-0 Subj: Activities – playing. Family life. Format, unusual – board books.

Playtime ill. by author. Viking, 1991. ISBN 0-670-83926-4 Subj: Activities – playing. Family life. Format, unusual – board books.

Dickinson, Mary. *Alex and Roy* ill. by Charlotte Firmin. Elsevier-Dutton, 1981. Subj: Friendship. Imagination.

Alex's bed ill. by Charlotte Firmin. Elsevier-Dutton, 1980. Subj: Character traits – cleanliness. Furniture – beds. Problem solving.

Alex's outing ill. by Charlotte Firmin. Dutton, 1983. Subj: Activities – picnicking. Behavior – nagging. Country.

Dickinson, Mike. *My dad doesn't even notice* ill. by author. Elsevier-Dutton, 1982. Subj: Behavior – misunderstanding. Imagination.

DiFiori, Lawrence. *Baby animals* ill. by author. Macmillan, 1983. Subj: Animals. Format, unusual – board books.

The farm ill. by author. Macmillan, 1983. Subj: Farms. Format, unusual – board books.

If I had a little car ill. by author. Golden Pr., 1985. Subj: Automobiles. Format, unusual – board books. Imagination.

My first book ill. by author. Macmillan, 1983. Subj: Activities – reading. Format, unusual – board books.

My toys ill. by author. Macmillan, 1983. Subj: Format, unusual – board books. Toys.

D'Ignazio, Fred. *Katie and the computer* ill. by Stan Gilliam. Creative Computing, 1980. Subj: Computers. Imagination.

Dijs, Carla. *Are you my daddy?* ill. by author. Simon & Schuster, 1990. ISBN 0-671-70227-0 Subj: Animals. Format, unusual – toy and movable books.

Are you my mommy? ill. by author. Simon & Schuster, 1990. ISBN 0-671-70226-2 Subj: Animals. Format, unusual – toy and movable books.

Big and small ill. by author. Grosset, 1989. ISBN 0-448-09075-9 Subj: Concepts – opposites. Format, unusual – toy and movable books.

How many? ill. by author. Grosset, 1989. ISBN 0-448-09076-7 Subj: Counting, numbers. Format, unusual – toy and movable books.

Dillon, Barbara. *The beast in the bed* ill. by Chris Conover. Morrow, 1981. Subj: Furniture – beds. Imagination – imaginary friends. Monsters.

Dillon, Eilis. *The cats' opera* ill. by Kveta Vanecek. Bobbs-Merrill, 1963. Subj: Animals – cats. Music.

Din dan don, it's Christmas ill. by Janina Domanska. Greenwillow, 1975. Text is a rendition of an anonymous Polish Christmas carol Subj: Foreign lands – Poland. Holidays – Christmas. Religion. Songs.

Dinan, Carolyn. *The lunch box monster* ill. by author. Faber, 1983. Subj: Imagination – imaginary friends. Monsters.

Say cheese! ill. by author. Viking, 1986. ISBN 0-670-80954-3 Subj: Character traits – being different. School. Teeth.

Dinardo, Jeffrey. *Timothy and the night noises* ill. by author. Prentice-Hall, 1986. ISBN 0-13-922048-8 Subj: Emotions – fear. Frogs and toads. Night. Noise, sounds.

The wolf who cried boy ill. by author. Grosset, 1989. ISBN 0-448-09314-6 Subj: Animals – wolves. Behavior – lying. Behavior – trickery. Folk and fairy tales.

Dines, Glen. *Gilly and the wicharoo* ill. by author. Lothrop, 1968. Subj: Behavior – trickery. Character traits – cleverness. Foreign lands – England.

Pitadoe, the color maker ill. by author. Macmillan, 1959. Subj: Concepts – color. Wizards.

A tiger in the cherry tree ill. by author. Macmillan, 1958. Subj: Animals – tigers. Behavior – forgetfulness. Character traits – shyness. Foreign lands – Japan. Magic.

Dinosaurs and monsters ill. by Louise Nevett. Watts, 1984. Subj: Activities. Dinosaurs. Monsters.

Dionetti, Michelle. *Coal mine peaches* ill. by Anita Riggio. Watts, 1991. ISBN 0-531-08548-1 Subj: Character traits – optimism. Ethnic groups in the U.S. – Italian-Americans. Family life – grandfathers.

The day Eli went looking for bear ill. by Joyce Audy Dos Santos. Addison-Wesley, 1980. Subj: Animals. Family life – mothers. Seasons – winter. Sports – hunting.

Thalia Brown and the blue bug ill. by James Calvin. Addison-Wesley, 1979. Subj: Art. Character traits – pride. Ethnic groups in the U.S. – Afro-Americans.

Diot, Alain. *Better, best, bestest* ill. by Joel Naprstek. Dial Pr., 1977. Subj: Behavior – boasting. Family life – fathers.

Diska, Pat. *Andy says ... Bonjour!* ill. by Chris Jenkyns. Vanguard, 1954. Subj: Animals – cats. Foreign lands – France. Foreign languages.

DiVito, Anna. *Elephants on ice* ill. by author. Dial, 1991. ISBN 0-8037-0798-3 Subj: Animals – elephants. Sports – ice skating.

Dixon, Ann. *How raven brought light to people* ill. by James Watts. Macmillan, 1992. ISBN 0-689-50536-1 Subj: Birds – ravens. Folk and fairy tales. Indians of North America.

Dobbs, Rose. *More once-upon-a-time stories* ill. by Flavia Gág. Random House, 1961. Subj: Folk and fairy tales.

Once-upon-a-time story book ill. by Walter Hodges. Random House, 1958. Subj: Folk and fairy tales.

Dobrin, Arnold Jack. *Josephine's 'magination* ill. by author. Four Winds Pr., 1973. Subj: Foreign lands – Caribbean Islands. Imagination. Toys.

Dobson, Clive. *Fred's TV* ill. by author. Firefly, 1989. ISBN 0-920668-60-7 Subj: Birds. Character traits – kindness to animals. Seasons – winter. Television.

Dodd, Lynley. *Hairy Maclary from Donaldson's dairy* ill. by author. Gareth Stevens, 1985. Subj: Animals – cats. Animals – dogs. Cumulative tales. Emotions – fear. Poetry, rhyme.

Hairy Maclary Scattercat ill. by author. Gareth Stevens, Inc., 1988. ISBN 1-555-32-123-2 Subj: Animals – cats. Animals – dogs. Behavior – bullying. Poetry, rhyme.

Hairy Maclary's bone ill. by author. Gareth Stevens, 1985. ISBN 0-918331-06-7 Subj: Animals – dogs. Character traits – cleverness. Cumulative tales. Poetry, rhyme.

The nickle nackle tree ill. by author. Macmillan, 1976. Subj: Counting, numbers. Poetry, rhyme.

The smallest turtle ill. by author. Gareth Stevens, 1985. ISBN 0-918331-07-5 Subj: Reptiles – turtles, tortoises. Science. Sea and seashore.

Wake up, bear ill. by author. Gareth Stevens, Inc., 1988. ISBN 1-555-32-124-0 Subj: Animals. Animals – bears. Seasons – spring. Sleep.

Dodds, Dayle Ann. *The color box* ill. by Giles Laroche. Little, 1992. ISBN 0-316-18820-4 Subj: Animals – monkeys. Concepts – color. Format, unusual – toy and movable books.

Do bunnies talk? ill. by Arlene Dubanevich. HarperCollins, 1992. ISBN 0-06-020249-1 Subj: Animals. Animals – rabbits. Language. Noise, sounds. Poetry, rhyme.

Wheel away! ill. by Thacher Hurd. HarperCollins, 1991. ISBN 0-06-021689-1 Subj: Circular tales. Format, unusual. Poetry, rhyme.

Dodds, Siobhan. *Charles Tiger* ill. by author. Little, 1988. ISBN 0-316-18817-4 Subj: Animals. Animals – tigers. Behavior – losing things.

Elizabeth Hen ill. by author. Little, 1988. ISBN 0-316-18818-2 Subj: Animals. Birds – chickens. Counting, numbers. Eggs. Farms.

Words and pictures ill. by author. Candlewick Pr., 1992. ISBN 1-56402-042-8 Subj: Activities. Dictionaries. Rebuses.

Dodge, Mary Mapes. *Mary Anne* ill. by June Amos Grammer. Lothrop, 1983. Subj: Poetry, rhyme. Toys – dolls.

Dodgson, Charles Lutwidge *see* Carroll, Lewis

The dog writes on the window with his nose, and other poems collected by David Kherdian; ill. by Nonny Hogrogian. Four Winds Pr., 1977. Subj: Poetry, rhyme.

Doherty, Berlie. *Paddiwak and cozy* ill. by Teresa O'Brien. Dial Pr., 1989. ISBN 0-8037-0483-6 Subj: Animals – cats. Emotions – envy, jealousy.

Domanska, Janina. *A was an angler* ill. by author. Greenwillow, 1991. ISBN 0-688-06991-6 Subj: ABC books. Nursery rhymes.

The best of the bargain ill. by author. Greenwillow, 1977. Subj: Animals – foxes. Animals – hedgehogs. Behavior – trickery. Character traits – cleverness. Folk and fairy tales. Foreign lands – Poland. Gardens, gardening.

Busy Monday morning ill. by author. Greenwillow, 1985. Subj: Folk and fairy tales. Foreign lands – Poland. Music. Songs.

I saw a ship a-sailing ill. by author. Macmillan, 1972. Subj: Boats, ships. Holidays – Christmas. Nursery rhymes.

If all the seas were one sea ill. by author. Macmillan, 1971. Subj: Caldecott award honor book. Nursery rhymes. Sea and seashore.

King Krakus and the dragon ill. by author. Greenwillow, 1979. Subj: Character traits – cleverness. Dragons. Folk and fairy tales. Foreign lands – Poland. Royalty – kings.

Look, there is a turtle flying ill. by author. Macmillan, 1968. Subj: Folk and fairy tales. Foreign lands – Poland. Reptiles – turtles, tortoises. Royalty.

Marek, the little fool ill. by author. Greenwillow, 1982. Subj: Folk and fairy tales. Foreign lands.

Palmiero and the ogre ill. by author. Macmillan, 1967. Subj: Behavior – forgetfulness. Folk and fairy tales. Magic.

A scythe, a rooster and a cat ill. by author. Greenwillow, 1981. Subj: Folk and fairy tales. Foreign lands – Russia.

The tortoise and the tree ill. by author. Greenwillow, 1978. Subj: Folk and fairy tales. Foreign lands – Africa. Reptiles – turtles, tortoises.

The turnip ill. by author. Macmillan, 1969. Subj: Cumulative tales. Farms. Folk and fairy tales. Foreign lands – Russia. Plants. Problem solving.

What do you see? ill. by author. Macmillan, 1974. Subj: Animals. Poetry, rhyme. World.

What happens next? ill. by author. Greenwillow, 1983. Subj: Folk and fairy tales.

Why so much noise? ill. by author. Harper, 1965. "Adaptation of the tale entitled 'The elephant has a bet with the tiger,' [as recorded] by Walter William Skeat." Subj: Animals – elephants. Animals – tigers. Character traits – cleverness. Folk and fairy tales. Foreign lands – India. Noise, sounds.

Domestic animals ill. with photos. Imported Pubs., 1983. Subj: Animals. Format, unusual – board books. Wordless.

Dominguez, Angel. *Diary of a Victorian mouse* ill. by author. Arcade, 1991. ISBN 1-55970-121-8 Subj: Animals – mice. Foreign lands – England.

Donaldson, Lois. *Karl's wooden horse* ill. by Annie Bergmann. Albert Whitman, 1970. Subj: Dreams. Holidays – Christmas. Night. Toys – rocking horses.

Donnelly, Liza. *Dinosaur beach* ill. by author. Scholastic, 1991. ISBN 0-590-42176-X Subj: City. Dinosaurs. Sea and seashore.

Dinosaur garden ill. by author. Scholastic, 1991. ISBN 0-590-43172-2 Subj: City. Dinosaurs. Gardens, gardening.

Dinosaurs' Halloween ill. by author. Scholastic, 1987. ISBN 0-590-41025-3 Subj: City. Dinosaurs. Holidays – Halloween.

Don't tell the scarecrow: *and other Japanese poems* by Issa, Yayū, Kikaku and other Japanese poets; ill. by Tālivaldis Stubis. Four Winds Pr., 1970. Subj: Foreign lands – Japan. Poetry, rhyme. Seasons.

Dooley, Norah. *Everybody cooks rice* ill. by Peter J. Thornton. Carolrhoda, 1991. ISBN 0-87614-412-1 Subj: Ethnic groups in the U.S. Family life. Food.

Doolittle, Eileen. *The ark in the attic: an alphabet adventure* photos. by Starr Ockenga. Godine, 1987. ISBN 0-87923-648-1 Subj: ABC books. Rebuses. Riddles.

World of wonders: a trip through numbers photos. by Starr Ockenga; ill. by author. Houghton, 1988. ISBN 0-325-48726-9 Subj: Counting, numbers. Imagination. Poetry, rhyme.

Dorian, Marguerite. *When the snow is blue* ill. by author. Lothrop, 1960. Subj: Animals – bears. Imagination. Weather – snow.

Dorros, Arthur. *Abuela* ill. by Elisa Kleven. Dutton, 1991. ISBN 0-525-44750-4 Subj: Activities – flying. City. Ethnic groups in the U.S. Family life – grandmothers. Foreign languages.

Alligator shoes ill. by author. Dutton, 1982. Subj: Reptiles – alligators, crocodiles.

Ant cities ill. by author. Crowell, 1987. ISBN 0-690-04570-0 Subj: Insects – ants. Science.

Feel the wind ill. by author. HarperCollins, 1989. ISBN 0-690-04741-X Subj: Weather – wind.

Follow the water from brook to ocean ill. by author. HarperCollins, 1991. ISBN 0-06-021599-2 Subj: Science. Water.

Me and my shadow ill. by author. Scholastic, 1990. ISBN 0-590-42772-5 Subj: Shadows.

Pretzels ill. by author. Greenwillow, 1981. Subj: Boats, ships. Humor.

Tonight is carnaval ill. with photos. of arpilleras sewn by the Club de Madres Virgen del Carmen of Lima, Peru. Dutton, 1991. ISBN 0-525-44641-9 Subj: Fairs. Farms. Foreign lands – Peru.

Dorsky, Blanche. *Harry, a true story* ill. by Muriel Batherman. Prentice-Hall, 1977. Subj: Animals – rabbits. School.

Dos Santos, Joyce Audy. *The diviner* ill. by author. Lippincott, 1980. Subj: Character traits – cleverness. Folk and fairy tales. Foreign lands – Canada. Royalty.

Henri and the Loup-Garou ill. by author. Pantheon, 1982. Subj: Folk and fairy tales. Foreign lands – Canada. Monsters.

Sand dollar, sand dollar ill. by author. Lippincott, 1980. Subj: Sea and seashore.

Dostoyevsky, Fyodor. *The talking crocodile* (Campbell, M. Rudolph)

Doty, Roy. *Eye fooled you: the big book of optical illusions* ill. by author. Macmillan, 1983. Subj: Optical illusions.

Old-one-eye meets his match ill. by author. Lothrop, 1978. Subj: Animals – mice. Animals – rats.

Doubilet, Anne. *Under the sea from A to Z* photos. by David Doubilet. Crown, 1991. ISBN 0-517-57837-9 Subj: ABC books. Sea and seashore.

Doughtie, Charles. *Gabriel Wrinkles, the bloodhound who couldn't smell* ill. by Charles D. Saxon. Dodd, 1959. Subj: Animals – dogs. Senses – smelling.

High Henry...the cowboy who was too tall to ride a horse ill. by Don Gregg. Dodd, 1960. Subj: Animals – giraffes. Cowboys.

Douglas, Barbara. *Good as new!* ill. by Patience Brewster. Morrow, 1989. ISBN 0-688-08739-6 Subj: Family life – grandfathers. Toys – teddy bears.

Douglas, Michael. *Round, round world* ill. by author. Golden Pr., 1960. Subj: Animals – cats. Foreign lands. World.

Douglas, Richardo Keens. *The nutmeg princess* ill. by Annouchka Galouchko. Firefly, 1992. ISBN 1-55037-239-4 Subj: Character traits – bravery. Character traits – selfishness. Foreign lands – Caribbean Islands. Gardens, gardening.

Douglas, Robert W. *John Paul II: the Pilgrim Pope* ill., map and photos. Children's Pr., 1979. Subj: Religion.

Douglass, Barbara. *The chocolate chip cookie contest* ill. by Eric Jon Nones. Lothrop, 1985. ISBN 0-688-04044-6 Subj: Activities – cooking. Clowns, jesters.

Good as new ill. by Patiences Brewster. Lothrop, 1982. Subj: Behavior – misbehavior. Family life – grandfathers. Toys – teddy bears.

Dow, Katharine. *My time of year* ill. by Walter Erhard. Walck, 1961. Subj: Seasons.

Dowdy, Mrs. Regera see Gorey, Edward (St. John)

Dowers, Patrick. *One day scene through a leaf* ill. by author. Green Tiger Pr., 1981. Subj: Poetry, rhyme.

Dowling, Paul. *Happy birthday, Owl* ill. by author. Walt Disney, 1992. ISBN 1-56282-253-5 Subj: Animals. Birds – owls. Birthdays. Parties.

Meg and Jack are moving ill. by author. Houghton, 1990. ISBN 0-395-53514-X Subj: Family life. Moving.

Meg and Jack's new friends ill. by author. Houghton, 1990. ISBN 0-395-53513-1 Subj: Behavior – sharing. Friendship. Moving. Toys.

Splodger ill. by author. Houghton, 1991. ISBN 0-395-57443-9 Subj: Bedtime. Behavior – misbehavior. Imagination.

You can do it, Rabbit ill. by author. Walt Disney, 1992. ISBN 1-56282-252-7 Subj: Animals – rabbits. Character traits – helpfulness. Sports – bicycling.

Downie, Jill. *Alphabet puzzle* ill. by author. Lothrop, 1988. ISBN 0-688-08044-8 Subj: ABC books. Rebuses. Riddles.

Downing, Joan. *Baseball is our game* ill. by Tony Freeman. Children's Pr., 1982. Subj: Sports – baseball.

Doyle, Donovan see Boegehold, Betty

Dragonwagon, Crescent. *Alligator arrived with apples: a potluck alphabet feast* ill. by José Aruego and Ariane Dewey. Macmillan, 1987. ISBN 0-02-733090-7 Subj: ABC books. Animals. Holidays – Thanksgiving. Reptiles – alligators, crocodiles.

Always, always ill. by Arieh Zeldich. Macmillan, 1984. Subj: Divorce.

Coconut ill. by Nancy Tafuri. Harper, 1984. Subj: Behavior – wishing. Birds – parakeets, parrots.

Diana, maybe ill. by Deborah Kogan Ray. Macmillan, 1987. ISBN 0-02-733180-6 Subj: Behavior – wishing. Family life.

Half a moon and one whole star ill. by Jerry Pinkney. Macmillan, 1986. ISBN 0-02-733120-2 Subj: Dreams. Night. Poetry, rhyme.

Home place ill. by Jerry Pinkney. Macmillan, 1990. ISBN 0-02-733190-3 Subj: Ethnic groups in the U.S. – Afro-Americans. Family life. Houses.

I hate my brother Harry ill. by Dick Gackenbach. Harper, 1983. Subj: Sibling rivalry.

I hate my sister Maggie ill. by Leslie Holt Morrill. Macmillan, 1989. ISBN 0-02-733150-4 Subj: Sibling rivalry.

The itch book ill. by Joseph Mahler. Macmillan, 1990. ISBN 0-02-733121-0 Subj: Poetry, rhyme. Seasons – summer.

Jemima remembers ill. by Troy Howell. Macmillan, 1984. ISBN 0-02-733070-2 Subj: Farms. Poetry, rhyme. Seasons.

Katie in the morning ill. by Betsy Day. Harper, 1983. Subj: Behavior – solitude. Morning.

Rainy day together ill. by Lillian Hoban. Harper, 1971. Subj: Emotions. Family life. Family life – only child. Weather – rain.

This is the bread I baked for Ned ill. by Isadore Seltzer. Macmillan, 1989. ISBN 0-02-733220-9 Subj: Activities – cooking. Cumulative tales. Food. Poetry, rhyme.

When light turns into night ill. by Robert Andrew Parker. Harper, 1975. Subj: Behavior – solitude. Night.

Wind Rose ill. by Ronald Himler. Harper, 1976. Subj: Babies. Emotions – love. Names.

Drdek, Richard E. *Horace the friendly octopus* ill. by Joseph Veno. Allyn and Bacon, 1965. Reading consultants: William D. Sheldon and Mary C. Austin Subj: Friendship. Octopuses.

Dreamer, Sue. *Circus ABC* ill. by author. Little, 1985. ISBN 0-316-19196-5 Subj: ABC books. Circus. Format, unusual – board books.

Circus 1, 2, 3 ill. by author. Little, 1985. ISBN 0-316-19195-7 Subj: Circus. Counting, numbers. Format, unusual – board books.

Dreifus, Miriam W. *Brave Betsy* ill. by Sheila Greenwald. Putnam's, 1961. Subj: Character traits – bravery. School. Toys – dolls.

Drescher, Henrik. *Looking for Santa Claus* ill. by author. Lothrop, 1984. Subj: Animals – bulls, cows. Holidays – Christmas. Imagination.

Simon's book ill. by author. Lothrop, 1983. Subj: Dreams. Monsters.

The yellow umbrella ill. by author. Bradbury Pr., 1987. ISBN 0-02-733240-3 Subj: Animals – monkeys. Jungle. Umbrellas. Wordless. Zoos.

Drescher, Joan. *I'm in charge!* ill. by author. Little, 1981. Subj: Behavior – growing up. Family life.

The marvelous mess ill. by author. Houghton, 1980. Subj: Family life. Sibling rivalry.

My mother's getting married ill. by author. Dial Pr., 1986. ISBN 0-8037-0176-4 Subj: Emotions – envy, jealousy. Family life – mothers. Weddings.

Your family, my family ill. by author. Walker, 1980. Subj: Family life.

Drew, Patricia. *Spotter Puff* ill. by author. Merrimack Book Serv., 1979. Subj: Birds – puffins. Character traits – kindness to animals.

Driz, Ovsei. *The boy and the tree* tr. by Joachim Neugroschel; ill. by Victor Pivovarov. Prentice-Hall, 1978. Subj: Poetry, rhyme.

Drucker, Malka. *Grandma's latkes* ill. by Eve Chwast. Harcourt, 1992. ISBN 0-15-200468-8 Subj: Family life – grandmothers. Food. Holidays – Hanukkah. Jewish culture. Religion.

A Jewish holiday ABC ill. by Rita Pocock. Harcourt, 1992. ISBN 0-15-200482-3 Subj: ABC books. Holidays. Jewish culture. Religion.

Drummond, Violet H. *The flying postman* ill. by author. Walck, 1964. Subj: Careers – mail carriers. Foreign lands – England. Helicopters.

Phewtus the squirrel ill. by author. Lothrop, 1987. ISBN 0-688-07013-2 Subj: Animals – squirrels. Behavior – lost. Toys.

Dryden, Emma. *Good morning—good night* ill. by Richard M. Kolding. Random House, 1990. ISBN 0-679-80066-2 Subj: Animals. Format, unusual. Morning. Night.

Dubanevich, Arlene. *Pig William* ill. by author. Bradbury Pr., 1985. ISBN 0-02-733200-4 Subj: Activities – picnicking. Animals – pigs. Behavior – indifference. Sibling rivalry. Weather – rain.

The piggest show on earth ill. by author. Watts, 1989. ISBN 0-531-05789-5 Subj: Animals – pigs. Circus.

Pigs at Christmas ill. by author. Bradbury Pr., 1986. ISBN 0-02-733160-1 Subj: Animals – pigs. Character traits – being different. Holidays – Christmas.

Pigs in hiding ill. by author. Four Winds Pr., 1983. Subj: Animals – pigs. Behavior – hiding. Games.

Tom's tail ill. by author. Viking, 1990. ISBN 0-670-83021-6 Subj: Animals – cats. Animals – mice. Poetry, rhyme.

Dubois, Claude K. *He's my jumbo!* ill. by author. Viking, 1990. ISBN 0-670-83029-1 Subj: Animals – bears. Behavior – sharing. Sibling rivalry. Wordless.

Looking for Ginny ill. by author. Viking, 1990. ISBN 0-670-83030-5 Subj: Animals – bears. Family life – brothers. Family life – sisters. Pets.

DuBois, Ivy. *Baby Jumbo* ill. by Elsie Wrigley. Grosset, 1977. Subj: Animals – elephants.

Mother fox ill. by Elsie Wrigley. Grosset, 1977. Subj: Animals – foxes.

Du Bois, William Pène. *Bear circus* ill. by author. Viking, 1971. Subj: Animals. Animals – koala bears. Character traits – helpfulness. Circus. Insects – grasshoppers.

Bear party ill. by author. Viking, 1951. Subj: Animals. Animals – koala bears. Caldecott award honor book. Emotions – anger. Parties.

Elisabeth the cow ghost ill. by author. Viking, 1964. Subj: Animals – bulls, cows. Ghosts.

Giant Otto ill. by author. Viking, n.d. Subj: Animals – dogs. Giants.

The hare and the tortoise and the tortoise and the hare: La liebre y la tortuga and La tortuga y la liebre by William Pène Du Bois and Lee Po; ill. by William Pène Du Bois. Doubleday, 1972. Subj: Animals – rabbits. Folk and fairy tales. Foreign languages. Reptiles – turtles, tortoises.

Lazy Tommy pumpkinhead ill. by author. Harper, 1966. Subj: Character traits – laziness. Machines.

Lion ill. by author. Viking, 1957. Subj: Animals – lions. Caldecott award honor book.

Otto and the magic potatoes ill. by author. Viking, 1970. Subj: Activities – vacationing. Animals – dogs. Fire. Giants.

Otto at sea ill. by author. Viking, 1936. Subj: Animals – dogs. Boats, ships. Giants.

Otto in Africa ill. by author. Viking, 1961. Subj: Animals – dogs. Foreign lands – Africa. Giants.

Otto in Texas ill. by author. Viking, 1959. Subj: Animals – dogs. Giants.

Dubov, Christine Salac. *Aleksandra, where are your toes?* photos. by Josef Schneider. St. Martin's, 1986. ISBN 0-312-01717-0 Subj: Anatomy – toes. Format, unusual – board books.

Aleksandra, where is your nose? photos. by Josef Schneider. St. Martin's, 1986. ISBN 0-312-01719-7 Subj: Anatomy – noses. Format, unusual – board books.

Ding dong! and other sounds ill. by Elizabeth Hathon. Morrow, 1991. ISBN 0-688-10162-3 Subj: Format, unusual – board books. Noise, sounds.

Knock! and other sounds ill. by Elizabeth Hathon. Morrow, 1991. ISBN 0-688-10161-5 Subj: Format, unusual – board books. Noise, sounds.

Oink! and other sounds ill. by Elizabeth Hathon. Morrow, 1991. ISBN 0-688-10102-X Subj: Animals. Format, unusual – board books. Noise, sounds.

Duchess of York. *Budgie at Bendick's Point* ill. by John Richardson. Simon & Schuster, 1989. ISBN 0-671-67684-9 Subj: Airplanes, airports. Helicopters.

Budgie the little helicopter ill. by John Richardson. Simon & Schuster, 1989. ISBN 0-671-67683-0 Subj: Airplanes, airports. Helicopters.

Dudley, Dick. *Pop up baby brontosaurus* (Cremins, Robert)

Pop up baby coelophysis (Cremins, Robert)

Pop up baby pteranodon (Cremins, Robert)

Pop up baby stegosaurus (Cremins, Robert)

Pop up baby triceratops (Cremins, Robert)

Pop up baby tyrannosaurus rex (Cremins, Robert)

Duff, Maggie (Margaret K.). *Dancing turtle* ill. by Maria Horvath. Macmillan, 1981. Subj: Animals. Behavior – trickery. Folk and fairy tales.

The princess and the pumpkin: from a Majorcan tale ill. by Catherine Stock. Macmillan, 1980. Subj: Folk and fairy tales. Foreign lands – Spain. Illness.

Rum pum pum ill. by José Aruego. Macmillan, 1978. Subj: Birds – blackbirds. Folk and fairy tales. Foreign lands – India.

Duffy, Dee Dee (Deborah). *Barnyard tracks* ill. by Janet Perry Marshall. Boyds Mills Pr., 1992. ISBN 1-878093-66-5 Subj: Animals. Games.

Dugan, Barbara. *Loop the loop* ill. by James Stevenson. Greenwillow, 1992. ISBN 0-688-09648-4 Subj: Friendship. Illness. Old age. Toys.

Dukas, P. (Paul Abraham). *The sorcerer's apprentice* Adapt. by Makoto Oishi; tr. by Ann Brannen; ill. by Ryohei Yanagihara. Gakken, 1971. Subj: Folk and fairy tales. Magic.

Duke, Kate. *Aunt Isabel tells a good one* ill. by author. Dutton, 1992. ISBN 0-525-44835-7 Subj: Animals. Animals – mice. Bedtime. Family life – aunts, uncles. Royalty.

Bedtime ill. by author. Dutton, 1986. ISBN 0-525-44207-3 Subj: Animals – guinea pigs. Bedtime. Family life. Format, unusual – board books.

Clean-up day ill. by author. Dutton, 1986. ISBN 0-525-44208-1 Subj: Activities – working. Animals – guinea pigs. Family life. Format, unusual – board books.

The guinea pig ABC ill. by author. Dutton, 1983. Subj: ABC books. Animals – guinea pigs.

Guinea pigs far and near ill. by author. Dutton, 1984. Subj: Animals – guinea pigs. Concepts.

The playground ill. by author. Dutton, 1986. ISBN 0-525-44206-5 Subj: Activities – playing. Animals – guinea pigs. Family life. Format, unusual – board books.

Seven froggies went to school ill. by author. Dutton, 1985. ISBN 0-525-44160-3 Subj: Frogs and toads. Poetry, rhyme. School.

What bounces? ill. by author. Dutton, 1986. ISBN 0-525-44209-X Subj: Animals – guinea pigs. Concepts. Family life. Format, unusual – board books.

Dulcken, H. W. *The fir tree* (Andersen, H. C. (Hans Christian))

Dumas, Philippe. *Caesar, cock of the village* ill. by author. Prentice-Hall, 1979. Subj: Birds – chickens. Foreign lands – France.

Laura, Alice's new puppy ill. by author. David and Charles, 1979. Subj: Animals – dogs.

Laura and the bandits ill. by author. David and Charles, 1980. Subj: Animals – dogs. Crime.

Laura loses her head ill. by author. David and Charles, 1982. Subj: Animals – dogs. Family life – grandfathers. Foreign lands – France.

Laura on the road ill. by author. David and Charles, 1979. Subj: Animals – dogs.

Lucy, a tale of a donkey ill. by author. Prentice-Hall, 1980. Subj: Animals – donkeys. Behavior – running away.

The story of Edward ill. by author. Parents, 1977. Subj: Animals – donkeys. Foreign lands – France.

Dumbleton, Mike. *Dial-a-croc* ill. by Ann James. Watts, 1991. ISBN 0-531-08545-7 Subj: Activities – working. Foreign lands – Australia. Reptiles – alligators, crocodiles.

Dunbar, Fiona. *You'll never guess!* ill. by author. Dial, 1991. Subj: Concepts – shape. Games.

Dunbar, Joyce. *A cake for Barney* ill. by Emilie Boon. Watts, 1988. ISBN 0-531-08335-7 Subj: Animals – bears. Character traits – assertiveness.

Lollopy ill. by Susan Varley. Macmillan, 1992. ISBN 0-02-733195-4 Subj: Animals – rabbits. Toys.

Why is the sky up? ill. by James Dunbar. Houghton, 1991. ISBN 0-395-57580-X Subj: Character traits – questioning. Family life. Nature.

Duncan, Gregory *see* McClintock, Marshall

Duncan, Jane. *Janet Reachfar and Chickabird* ill. by Mairi Hedderwick. Seabury Pr., 1978. Subj: Behavior – bad day. Farms. Foreign lands – Scotland.

Duncan, Lois. *Birthday moon* ill. by Susan Davis. Viking, 1989. ISBN 0-670-82238-8 Subj: Birthdays. Moon. Poetry, rhyme.

Giving away Suzanne ill. by Leonard Weisgard. Dodd, 1964. Subj: Sibling rivalry.

Horses of dreamland ill. by Donna Diamond. Little, 1985. ISBN 0-316-19554-5 Subj: Animals – horses. Dreams. Night.

Songs from dreamland ill. by Kay Chorao. Knopf, 1989. ISBN 0-394-99904-5 Subj: Lullabies. Music. Poetry, rhyme. Songs.

Duncan, Riana. *A nutcracker in a tree: a book of riddles* ill. by author. Delacorte, 1981. Subj: Animals. Riddles.

When Emily woke up angry ill. by author. Barron's, 1989. ISBN 0-8120-5985-9 Subj: Animals. Emotions – anger.

Dunham, Meredith. *Colors: how do you say it?* ill. by author. Lothrop, 1987. ISBN 0-688-06949-5 Subj: Concepts – color. Foreign languages. Language.

Numbers: how do you say it? ill. by author. Lothrop, 1987. ISBN 0-688-06951-7 Subj: Counting, numbers. Foreign languages. Language.

Picnic: how do you say it? ill. by author. Lothrop, 1987. ISBN 0-688-07097-3 Subj: Activities – picnicking. Foreign languages. Language.

Shapes: how do you say it? ill. by author. Lothrop, 1987. ISBN 0-688-06953-3 Subj: Concepts – shape. Foreign languages. Language.

Dunn, Judy. *The animals of Buttercup Farm* photos. by Phoebe Dunn. Random House, 1981. Subj: Animals. Farms.

The little duck ill. by Phoebe Dunn. Random House, 1978. Subj: Birds – ducks.

The little goat ill. by Phoebe Dunn. Random House, 1978. Subj: Animals – goats. Pets.

The little lamb ill. by Phoebe Dunn. Random House, 1977. Subj: Animals – sheep. Character traits – kindness to animals. Farms.

The little puppy photos. by Phoebe Dunn. Random House, 1984. Subj: Animals – dogs. Pets.

The little rabbit photos. by Phoebe Dunn. Random House, 1980. Subj: Animals – rabbits. Holidays – Easter. Pets.

Dunn, Phoebe. *Baby's animal friends* photos. by author. Random House, 1988. ISBN 0-394-89583-5 Subj: Animals. Babies. Format, unusual – board books.

Busy, busy toddlers photos. by author. Random House, 1987. ISBN 0-394-88604-6 Subj: Activities. Babies. Format, unusual – board books.

I'm a baby! photos. by author. Random House, 1987. ISBN 0-394-88605-4 Subj: Babies. Format, unusual – board books.

Dunrea, Olivier. *Deep down underground* ill. by author. Macmillan, 1989. ISBN 0-02-732861-9 Subj: Animals. Counting, numbers. Cumulative tales.

Eddy B, pigboy ill. by author. Atheneum, 1983. Subj: Animals – pigs. Farms.

Fergus and Bridey ill. by author. Holiday, 1985. ISBN 0-8234-0554-0 Subj: Animals – dogs. Boats, ships. Friendship.

Ravena ill. by author. Dell, 1992. ISBN 0-440-40645-5 Subj: Mythical creatures.

Dupasquier, Philippe. *Dear Daddy...* ill. by author. Bradbury Pr., 1985. ISBN 0-02-733170-9 Subj: Boats, ships. Careers. Family life – fathers. Sea and seashore.

The great escape ill. by author. Houghton, 1988. ISBN 0-395-46806-X Subj: Behavior – running away. Prisons. Wordless.

I can't sleep ill. by author. Watts, 1989. ISBN 0-531-08474-4 Subj: Family life. Night. Sleep. Wordless.

Jack at sea ill. by author. Prentice-Hall, 1987. ISBN 0-13-509209-4 Subj: Boats, ships. Sea and seashore. War.

Our house on the hill ill. by author. Viking, 1988. ISBN 0-670-81971-9 Subj: Seasons. Wordless.

A robot named chip ill. by author. Viking, 1991. ISBN 0-670-83574-9 Subj: Robots.

Duplaix, Georges *see* Ariane

Dupré, Ramona Dorrel. *Too many dogs* ill. by Howard Baer. Follett, 1960. Subj: Animals – dogs.

Du Quette, Keith. *Rippening day for a picnic* ill. by author. Viking, 1990. ISBN 0-670-83311-8 Subj: Activities – picnicking. Animals. Food.

Duran, Bonté. *The adventures of Arthur and Edmund: a tale of two seals* ill. by Quentin Blake. Atheneum, 1984. Subj: Animals – seals.

Durell, Ann. *The Diane Goode book of American folk tales and songs* collected by Ann Durell; ill. by Diane Goode. Dutton, 1989. ISBN 0-525-44458-0 Subj: Folk and fairy tales. Music. Songs.

Durrell, Julie. *Mouse tails* ill. by author. Crown, 1985. Subj: Animals. Animals – mice.

Dutton, Sandra. *The cinnamon hen's autumn day* ill. by author. Atheneum, 1988. ISBN 0-689-31414-0 Subj: Animals – rabbits. Birds – chickens. Seasons – fall.

Duvoisin, Roger Antoine. *A for the ark* ill. by author. Lothrop, 1952. Subj: ABC books. Animals. Religion – Noah.

The Christmas whale ill. by author. Knopf, 1945. Subj: Animals – whales. Holidays – Christmas. Illness.

The crocodile in the tree ill. by author. Knopf, 1973. Subj: Animals. Farms. Friendship. Reptiles – alligators, crocodiles.

Crocus ill. by author. Knopf, 1977. Subj: Careers – dentists. Character traits – pride. Farms. Reptiles – alligators, crocodiles. Teeth.

Day and night ill. by author. Knopf, 1960. Subj: Animals – dogs. Birds – owls.

Donkey-donkey ill. by author. Parents, 1968. Subj: Animals – donkeys.

Easter treat ill. by author. Knopf, 1954. Subj: Holidays – Easter.

The happy hunter ill. by author. Lothrop, 1961. Subj: Character traits – kindness to animals. Ecology. Sports – hunting. Violence, anti-violence. Weapons.

The house of four seasons ill. by author. Lothrop, 1956. Subj: Activities – painting. Concepts – color. Seasons.

Jasmine ill. by author. Knopf, 1973. Subj: Animals. Character traits – individuality. Clothing. Farms.

Lonely Veronica ill. by author. Knopf, 1963. Subj: Animals – hippopotami. City. Progress.

The missing milkman ill. by author. Knopf, 1967. Subj: Behavior – running away. Dreams. Night.

One thousand Christmas beards ill. by author. Knopf, 1955. Subj: Holidays – Christmas.

Our Veronica goes to Petunia's farm ill. by author. Knopf, 1962. Subj: Animals. Animals – hippopotami. Character traits – being different. Farms.

Periwinkle ill. by author. Knopf, 1976. Subj: Animals – giraffes. Emotions – loneliness. Etiquette. Friendship. Frogs and toads.

Petunia ill. by author. Knopf, 1950. Subj: Activities – reading. Animals. Birds – geese. Character traits – pride. Farms. Friendship.

Petunia and the song ill. by author. Knopf, 1951. Subj: Animals. Birds – geese. Crime. Farms. Friendship. Noise, sounds. Songs.

Petunia, beware! ill. by author. Knopf, 1958. Subj: Animals. Behavior – dissatisfaction. Birds – geese. Farms.

Petunia, I love you ill. by author. Knopf, 1965. Subj: Animals – raccoons. Behavior – trickery. Birds – geese. Birds – vultures. Farms. Friendship.

Petunia takes a trip ill. by author. Knopf, 1953. Subj: Activities – flying. Activities – vacationing. Animals. Birds – geese.

Petunia, the silly goose: stories ill. by author. Knopf, 1987. ISBN 0-394-98292-4 Subj: Animals. Birds – geese. Farms.

Petunia's Christmas ill. by author. Knopf, 1952. Subj: Birds – geese. Holidays – Christmas. Humor.

Petunia's treasure ill. by author. Knopf, 1975. Subj: Animals. Birds – geese. Farms. Friendship.

See what I am ill. by author. Lothrop, 1974. Subj: Behavior – boasting. Concepts – color.

Snowy and Woody ill. by author. Knopf, 1979. ISBN 0-394-94241-8 Subj: Animals – bears. Animals – polar bears. Birds – sea gulls. Friendship.

Two lonely ducks ill. by author. Knopf, 1955. Subj: Birds – ducks. Counting, numbers. Farms.

Veronica ill. by author. Knopf, 1961. Subj: Animals – hippopotami. Character traits – being different. City. Farms.

Veronica and the birthday present ill. by author. Knopf, 1971. Subj: Animals – cats. Animals – hippopotami. Birthdays. Farms.

Veronica's smile ill. by author. Knopf, 1964. Subj: Animals – hippopotami. Behavior – boredom.

Dyke, John. *Pigwig* ill. by author. Methuen, 1978. Subj: Animals – pigs. Behavior – stealing. Character traits – bravery. Emotions – love.

Pigwig and the pirates ill. by author. Methuen, 1979. Subj: Animals – pigs. Pirates. Sea and seashore.

Dynely, James *see* Mayne, William

Dyssegaard, Elisabeth. *The little house from the sea* (Gedin, Birgitta)

Eagle, Ellen. *Gypsy's cleaning day* ill. by author. Morrow, 1990. ISBN 0-688-07392-1 Subj: Animals – dogs. Behavior – losing things. Character traits – cleanliness.

Earle, Olive L. *Squirrels in the garden* ill. by author. Morrow, 1963. Subj: Animals – squirrels.

Eastman, David. *The story of dinosaurs* ill. by Joel Snyder. Troll Assoc., 1982. Subj: Dinosaurs.

The velveteen rabbit (Bianco, Margery Williams)

What is a fish? ill. by Lynn Sweat. Troll Assoc., 1982. Subj: Fish. Science.

Eastman, P. D. (Philip D.). *Are you my mother?* ill. by author. Random House, 1960. Subj: Behavior – misbehavior. Birds. Family life – mothers.

The cat in the hat beginner book dictionary (Seuss, Dr.)

Flap your wings ill. by author. Random House, 1969. Subj: Birds. Eggs. Reptiles – alligators, crocodiles.

Go, dog, go! ill. by author. Random House, 1961. Subj: Animals – dogs.

Sam and the firefly ill. by author. Random House, 1958. Subj: Birds – owls. Insects – fireflies.

Snow (McKie, Roy)

Eastman, Patricia. *Sometimes things change* ill. by Seymour Fleishman. Children's Pr., 1983. Subj: Science.

Easton, Violet. *Elephants never jump* ill. by Carme Solé Vendrell. Little, 1986. ISBN 0-87113-049-1 Subj: Activities – jumping. Animals. Animals – elephants. Humor.

Eastwick, Ivy O. *Cherry stones! Garden swings! poems* ill. by Robert Jones. Abingdon Pr., 1962. Subj: Poetry, rhyme.

Rainbow over all ill. by Anne Siberell. McKay, 1970. Subj: Poetry, rhyme.

Eaton, Su. *Punch and Judy in the rain* by Su Eaton and Martin Bridle; ill. by authors. Hamish Hamilton, 1985. Subj: Puppets.

Eberle, Irmengarde. *Fawn in the woods* photos. by Lilo Hess. Crowell, 1962. Subj: Animals – deer.

Eberstadt, Frederick. *What is for my birthday?* (Eberstadt, Isabel)

Eberstadt, Isabel. *What is for my birthday?* by Isabel and Frederick Eberstadt; ill. by Leonard Weisgard. Little, 1961. Subj: Birthdays. Illness. Poetry, rhyme.

Eckert, Horst *see* Janosch

Eco, Umberto. *The bomb and the general* ill. by Eugenio Carmi. Harcourt, 1989. ISBN 0-15-209700-7 Subj: War.

The three astronauts ill. by Eugenio Carmi. Harcourt, 1989. ISBN 0-15-286383-4 Subj: Careers – astronauts. Character traits – appearance. Space and space ships.

Economakis, Olga. *Oasis of the stars* ill. by Blair Lent. Coward, 1965. Subj: Foreign lands – Africa. Problem solving.

Edelman, Elaine. *Boom-de-boom* ill. by Karen Gundersheimer. Pantheon, 1980. Subj: Activities – dancing. Old age. Poetry, rhyme.

I love my baby sister (most of the time) ill. by Wendy Watson. Lothrop, 1984. Subj: Sibling rivalry.

Edens, Cooper. *The glorious Mother Goose* (Mother Goose)

Edman, Polly. *Red thread riddles* (Jensen, Virginia Allen)

Edwards, Al *see* Nourse, Alan Edward

Edwards, Dorothy. *A wet Monday* by Dorothy Edwards and Jenny Williams; ill. by Jenny Williams. Morrow, 1975. Subj: Birds – chickens. Character traits – pride.

Edwards, Frank B. *Melody Mooner stayed up all night* ill. by John Bianchi. Firefly, 1991. ISBN 0-921285-03-5 Subj: Animals – pigs. Bedtime. Night.

Mortimer Mooner stopped taking a bath ill. by John Bianchi. Firefly, 1990. ISBN 0-921285-21-3 Subj: Activities – bathing. Animals – pigs. Character traits – cleanliness. Family life.

Edwards, Linda Strauss. *The downtown day* ill. by author. Pantheon, 1983. Subj: Shopping.

Edwards, Lisa. *Disney's Beauty and the beast, a book of manners* ill. Walt Disney, 1993. ISBN 1-56282-130-X Subj: Etiquette. Folk and fairy tales.

Edwards, Michelle. *Alef-bet: a Hebrew alphabet book* ill. by author. Lothrop, 1992. ISBN 0-688-09725-1 Subj: ABC books. Family life. Handicaps – physical. Jewish culture. Foreign languages.

A baker's portrait ill. by author. Lothrop, 1991. ISBN 0-688-09713-8 Subj: Careers – artists. Careers – bakers. Family life – aunts, uncles. Jewish culture.

Chicken man ill. by author. Lothrop, 1991. ISBN 0-688-09709-X Subj: Birds – chickens. Communities, neighborhoods. Foreign lands – Israel.

Edwards, Patricia Kier. *Chester and Uncle Willoughby* ill. by Diane Worfolk Allison. Little, 1987. ISBN 0-316-21173-7 Subj: Family life – aunts, uncles. Imagination. Sleep.

Edwards, Roberta. *Anna Bear's first winter* ill. by Laura Lydecker. Random House, 1986. ISBN 0-3294-88199-0 Subj: Animals – bears. Format, unusual – board books. Sleep.

Five silly fishermen ill. by Sylvie Wickstrom. Random House, 1989. ISBN 0-679-90092-6 Subj: Careers – fishermen. Counting, numbers. Folk and fairy tales.

Eggs ill. by Esmé Eve. Grosset, 1971. Subj: Eggs.

Ehlert, Lois. *Circus* ill. by author. HarperCollins, 1992. ISBN 0-06-020253-X Subj: Circus.

Color farm ill. by author. HarperCollins, 1990. ISBN 0-397-32441-3 Subj: Concepts – color. Concepts – shape. Format, unusual.

Color zoo ill. by author. HarperCollins, 1990. ISBN 0-397-32260-7 Subj: Caldecott award honor book. Concepts – color. Concepts – shape. Format, unusual.

Growing vegetable soup ill. by author. Harcourt, 1987. ISBN 0-15-232575-1 Subj: Food. Gardens, gardening.

Moon rope: Un lazo a la luna ill. by adaptor. Harcourt, 1992. ISBN 0-15-255343-6 Subj: Animals – foxes. Animals – moles. Folk and fairy tales. Foreign lands – Peru. Foreign languages. Moon.

Planting a rainbow ill. by author. Harcourt, 1988. ISBN 0-15-262609-3 Subj: Flowers. Gardens, gardening.

Red leaf, yellow leaf ill. by author. Harcourt, 1991. ISBN 0-15-266197-2 Subj: Seasons. Trees.

Ehrhardt, Reinhold. *Kikeri: or, The proud red rooster* ill. by Bernadette Watts. Collins, 1969. Subj: Birds – chickens. Character traits – pride.

Ehrlich, Amy. *Bunnies all day long* ill. by Marie H. Henry. Dial Pr., 1985. ISBN 0-8037-0185-3 Subj: Activities. Animals – rabbits.

Bunnies and their grandma ill. by Marie H. Henry. Dial Pr., 1985. ISBN 0-8037-0186-1 Subj: Animals – rabbits. Family life – grandmothers.

Bunnies at Christmastime ill. by Marie H. Henry. Dial Pr., 1986. ISBN 0-8037-0321-X Subj: Animals – rabbits. Family life. Holidays – Christmas. Parties. Sibling rivalry.

Bunnies on their own ill. by Marie H. Henry. Dial Pr., 1986. ISBN 0-8037-0256-6 Subj: Animals – rabbits. Family life. Sibling rivalry.

Cinderella (Perrault, Charles)

The everyday train ill. by Martha G. Alexander. Dial Pr., 1977. Subj: Behavior – solitude. Trains.

Leo, Zack and Emmie ill. by Steven Kellogg. Dial Pr., 1981. Subj: Friendship. School.

Leo, Zack, and Emmie together again ill. by Steven Kellogg. Dial Pr., 1987. ISBN 0-8037-0382-1 Subj: Friendship. School.

Lucy's winter tale ill. by Troy Howell. Dial, 1992. ISBN 0-8037-0661-8 Subj: Animals. Circus.

Pome and Peel ill. by László Gál. Dial, 1990. ISBN 0-8037-0288-4 Subj: Folk and fairy tales. Foreign lands – Italy. Magic.

Rapunzel (Grimm, Jacob)

The snow queen (Andersen, H. C. (Hans Christian))

The story of Hannukkah ill. by Ori Sherman. Dial, 1989. ISBN 0-8037-0616-2 Subj: Jewish culture. Religion.

Thumbelina (Andersen, H. C. (Hans Christian))

The wild swans (Andersen, H. C. (Hans Christian))

Zeek Silver Moon ill. by Robert Andrew Parker. Dial Pr., 1972. Subj: Indians of North America. Family life.

Ehrlich, Bettina Bauer *see* Bettina (Bettina Ehrlich)

Eichenberg, Fritz. *Ape in cape* ill. by author. Harcourt, 1952. Subj: ABC books. Caldecott award honor book.

Dancing in the moon ill. by author. Harcourt, 1955. Subj: Animals. Counting, numbers. Poetry, rhyme.

Eisen, Armand. *Goldilocks and the three bears* (The three bears)

Eisenberg, Ann. *Bible heroes I can be* ill. by Roz Schanzer. Kar-Ben Copies, 1990. ISBN 0-929371-09-7 Subj: Religion.

I can celebrate ill. by Roz Schanzer. Kar-Ben Copies, 1989. ISBN 0-930494-93-8 Subj: Format, unusual – board books. Holidays. Jewish culture. Religion.

Eisenberg, Phyllis Rose. *A mitzvah is something special* ill. by Susan Jeschke. Harper, 1978. Subj: Family life – grandmothers. Family life – grandparents. Jewish culture.

You're my Nikki ill. by Jill Kastner. Dial, 1992. ISBN 0-8037-1129-8 Subj: Activities – working. Emotions – love. Family life – mothers.

Eisler, Colin. *Cats know best* ill. by Lesley Anne Ivory. Dial Pr., 1988. ISBN 0-8037-0560-3 Subj: Animals – cats.

Eisman, Carol. *I wish I had a big, big tree* (Sato, Satoru)

Ekker, Ernest A. *What is beyond the hill?* ill. by Hilde Heyduck-Huth. Lippincott, 1986. ISBN 0-397-32167-8 Subj: Activities – traveling. Imagination. World.

Elborn, Andrew. *Bird Adalbert* ill. by Susi Bohdal. Alphabet Pr., 1983. Subj: Behavior – dissatisfaction. Birds. Character traits – appearance. Poetry, rhyme.

Noah and the ark and the animals ill. by Ivan Gantschev. Picture Book Studio, 1984. ISBN 0-907234-58-5 Subj: Animals. Animals – horses. Religion – Noah.

Eliot, T. S. (Thomas Stearns). *Mr. Mistoffelees with Mungojerrie and Rumpelteazer* ill. by Errol Le Cain. Harcourt, 1991. ISBN 0-15-256230-3 Subj: Animals – cats. Poetry, rhyme.

Elizabeth Winthrop. *A very noisy girl* ill. by Ellen Weiss. Holiday, 1991. ISBN 0-8234-0858-2 Subj: Family life – mothers. Imagination. Noise, sounds.

Elkin, Benjamin. *Gillespie and the guards* ill. by James Henry Daugherty. Viking, 1956. Subj: Anatomy. Behavior – trickery. Caldecott award honor book. Character traits – cleverness. Royalty.

The king who could not sleep ill. by Victoria Chess. Parents, 1975. Subj: Cumulative tales. Poetry, rhyme. Royalty – kings. Sleep.

The king's wish and other stories ill. by Leonard W. Shortall. Random House, 1960. Subj: Folk and fairy tales. Royalty – kings.

Lucky and the giant ill. by Katherine Evans. Children's Pr., 1962. Subj: Character traits – cleverness. Character traits – luck. Character traits – selfishness. Giants.

Six foolish fishermen ill. by Katherine Evans. Children's Pr., 1957. Based on a folktale in Ashton's Chap-Books of the 18th century Subj: Counting, numbers. Folk and fairy tales. Sports – fishing.

Such is the way of the world ill. by Yōko Mitsuhashi. Parents, 1968. Subj: Animals – monkeys. Cumulative tales. Folk and fairy tales. Foreign lands – Africa. Problem solving.

Why the sun was late ill. by James Snyder. Parents, 1966. Subj: Animals. Cumulative tales. Insects – flies. Sun.

The wisest man in the world: a legend of ancient Israel retold by Benjamin Elkin; ill. by Anita Lobel. Parents, 1968. Subj: Folk and fairy tales. Foreign lands – Israel. Riddles. Royalty.

Elks, Wendy. *Charles B. Wombat and the very strange thing* ill. by author. David & Charles, 1989. ISBN 0-09-168910-4 Subj: Animals – wombats. Circus. Reptiles – turtles, tortoises.

Ellen, Barbara. *Phillip the flower-eating phoenix* (Todaro, John)

Ellentuck, Shan. *Did you see what I said?* ill. by author. Doubleday, 1967. Subj: Humor. Language.

A sunflower as big as the sun ill. by author. Doubleday, 1968. Subj: Behavior – boasting. Flowers. Humor. Plants.

Elliot, David. *An alphabet of rotten kids!* ill. by Oscar de Mejo. Putnam, 1991. ISBN 0-399-22260-X Subj: ABC books. Behavior. Poetry, rhyme.

Elliott, Dan. *Ernie's little lie* ill. by Joseph Mathieu. Random House, 1983. Subj: Art. Behavior – lying. Puppets.

A visit to the Sesame Street firehouse: featuring Jim Henson's Sesame Street Muppets ill. by Joseph Mathieu. Random House, 1983. Subj: Careers – firefighters. Fire. Puppets.

Elliott, Ingrid Glatz. *Hospital roadmap: a book to help explain the hospital experience to young children* ill. by author. Resources for Children in Hospitals, 1982. Subj: Hospitals. Illness.

Elliott, Robert *see* Allen, Robert

Ellis, Anne Leo. *Dabble Duck* ill. by Sue Truesdell. Harper, 1984. Subj: Birds – ducks. City. Emotions – loneliness. Friendship.

Elting, Mary. *The big book of real boats and ships* ill. by George J. Zaffo. Grosset, 1951. Subj: Boats, ships.

The Hopi way ill. by Louis Mofsie. Lippincott, 1970. Subj: Indians of North America.

Q is for duck: an alphabet guessing game by Mary Elting and Michael Folsom; ill. by Jack Kent. Houghton, 1980. Subj: ABC books. Animals. Games. Participation.

Elves, fairies and gnomes: *poems* sel. by Lee Bennett Hopkins; ill. by Rosekrans Hoffman. Knopf, 1980. Subj: Elves and little people. Fairies. Poetry, rhyme.

Elwell, Peter. *The king of the pipers* ill. by author. Macmillan, 1984. Subj: Devil. Folk and fairy tales.

Elzbieta. *Brave Babette and sly Tom* ill. by author. Dial Pr., 1989. ISBN 0-8037-0633-2 Subj: Animals – cats. Animals – mice. Birds. Family life.

Dikou and the baby star ill. by author. Crowell, 1988. ISBN 0-690-04721-5 Subj: Character traits – kindness. Stars.

Dikou and the mysterious moon sheep ill. by author. Crowell, 1988. ISBN 0-690-04694-4 Subj: Behavior – running away. Dreams. Family life. Imagination.

Dikou the little troon who walks at night ill. by author. Barron's, 1985. ISBN 0-8120-5621-3 Subj: Behavior – lying. Character traits – kindness. Mythical creatures.

Emberley, Barbara. *Drummer Hoff* ill. by Ed Emberley. Prentice-Hall, 1967. Adapted from a folk verse Subj: Caldecott award book. Careers – military. Cumulative tales. Poetry, rhyme. Weapons.

Night's nice by Barbara and Ed Emberley; ill. by Ed Emberley. Doubleday, 1963. Subj: Night. Poetry, rhyme.

One wide river to cross ill. by Ed Emberley. Prentice-Hall, 1966. Includes unacc. melody Adaptation of the American folk song Subj: Animals. Caldecott award honor book. Folk and fairy tales. Poetry, rhyme. Songs.

Simon's song ill. by Ed Emberley. Prentice-Hall, 1969. Includes unacc. melody Adaptation of the folk song Simple Simon Subj: Nursery rhymes. Songs.

Emberley, Ed (Edward Randolph). *Animals* ill. by author. Little, 1987. ISBN 0-316-23428-1 Subj: Animals. Format, unusual – board books.

Cars, boats, and planes ill. by author. Little, 1987. ISBN 0-316-23430-3 Subj: Airplanes, airports. Automobiles. Boats, ships. Format, unusual – board books. Transportation.

Ed Emberley's ABC ill. by author. Little, 1978. Subj: ABC books.

Ed Emberley's amazing look through book ill. by author. Little, 1979. Subj: Concepts. Format, unusual. Participation. Riddles.

Ed Emberley's big green drawing book ill. by author. Little, 1979. Subj: Art. Wordless.

Ed Emberley's big orange drawing book ill. by author. Little, 1980. Subj: Art.

Ed Emberley's big purple drawing book ill. by author. Little, 1981. Subj: Art.

Ed Emberley's crazy mixed-up face game ill. by author. Little, 1981. Subj: Anatomy – faces. Art. Games.

Ed Emberley's drawing book: make a world ill. by author. Little, 1972. ISBN 0-316-23598-9 Subj: Art.

Green says go ill. by author. Little, 1968. Subj: Communication. Concepts – color.

Home ill. by author. Little, 1987. ISBN 0-316-23433-8 Subj: Format, unusual – board books. Houses.

Klippity klop ill. by author. Little, 1974. Subj: Dragons. Games. Knights. Participation.

Night's nice (Emberley, Barbara)

The parade book ill. by author. Little, 1962. Subj: Parades.

Rosebud ill. by author. Little, 1966. Subj: Character traits – being different. Problem solving. Reptiles – turtles, tortoises.

Sounds ill. by author. Little, 1987. ISBN 0-316-23431-1 Subj: Format, unusual – board books. Noise, sounds.

Emberley, Michael. *More dinosaurs! and other prehistoric beasts* ill. by author. Little, 1983. Subj: Art. Dinosaurs.

The present ill. by author. Little, 1991. ISBN 0-316-23411-7 Subj: Birthdays. Character traits – generosity.

Ruby ill. by author. Little, 1990. ISBN 0-316-23643-8 Subj: Animals – cats. Animals – mice. Behavior – talking to strangers. City.

Emberley, Rebecca. *City sounds* ill. by author. Little, 1989. ISBN 0-316-23635-7 Subj: City. Noise, sounds.

Drawing with numbers and letters ill. by author. Little, 1981. Subj: Art.

Jungle sounds ill. by author. Little, 1989. ISBN 0-316-23636-5 Subj: Jungle. Noise, sounds.

Embry, Margaret. *The blue-nosed witch* ill. by Carl Rose. Holiday, 1956. Subj: Holidays – Halloween. Witches.

Emecheta, Buchi. *Nowhere to play* ill. by Peter Archer. Schocken, 1981. Subj: Activities – playing. Foreign lands – England. Safety.

Emerson, Sally. *The nursery treasury* ill. by Moira and Colin Maclean. Doubleday, 1988. ISBN 0-385-24650-1 Subj: Nursery rhymes.

Emmett, Fredrick Rowland. *New world for Nellie* ill. by author. Harcourt, 1952. Subj: Trains.

Emmons, Ramona Ware. *Your world: let's visit the hospital* (Pope, Billy N.)

Empress Michiko of Japan. *The animals* (Mado, Michio)

Encking, Louise F. *The little gardeners* (Morgenstern, Elizabeth)

The toy maker (Thelen, Gerda)

Enderle, Judith A. *Good junk* ill. by Gail Gibbons. Elsevier-Nelson, 1981. Subj: Behavior – collecting things.

Engdahl, Sylvia. *Our world is earth* ill. by Don Sibley. Atheneum, 1979. Subj: Communication. Earth. Science.

Engel, Diana. *Gino Badino* ill. by author. Morrow, 1991. ISBN 0-688-09503-8 Subj: Animals – mice. Family life. Food.

Josephina hates her name ill. by author. Morrow, 1989. ISBN 0-688-07796-X Subj: Family life. Names. Reptiles – alligators, crocodiles.

Josephina, the great collector ill. by author. Morrow, 1988. ISBN 0-688-07543-6 Subj: Behavior – collecting things. Sibling rivalry.

The little lump of clay ill. by author. Morrow, 1989. ISBN 0-688-08407-9 Subj: Activities – making things.

Engelbrektson, Sune. *Gravity at work and play* ill. by Eric Carle. Holt, 1963. Subj: Science.

The sun is a star ill. by Eric Carle. Holt, 1963. Subj: Science. Sun.

Engle, Joanna. *Cap'n kid goes to the South Pole* ill. by Pat Paris. Random House, 1983. Subj: Animals – whales.

English, Jennifer. *My mommy's special* ill. with photos. Childrens Pr., 1985. ISBN 0-516-03861-3 Subj: Family life – mothers. Handicaps.

Engvick, William. *Lullabies and night songs* ed. by William Engvick; music by Alec Wilder; ill. by Maurice Sendak. Harper, 1965. Subj: Bedtime. Lullabies. Music.

Ephron, Delia. *Santa and Alex* ill. by Elise Primavera. Little, 1983. Subj: Holidays – Christmas.

Erdoes, Richard. *Policemen around the world* ill. by author. McGraw-Hill, 1968. Subj: Careers – police officers.

Erickson, Karen. *Do I have to go home?* ill. by Maureen Roffey. Viking, 1989. ISBN 0-670-82673-1 Subj: Behavior.

I like to help ill. by Maureen Roffey. Viking, 1989. ISBN 0-670-82675-8 Subj: Character traits – helpfulness.

I was so mad ill. by Maureen Roffey. Viking, 1987. ISBN 0-670-81573-X Subj: Emotions – anger.

I'll try ill. by Maureen Roffey. Viking, 1987. ISBN 0-670-81572-1 Subj: Character traits – perseverance.

It's dark ill. by Maureen Roffey. Viking, 1987. ISBN 0-670-81571-3 Subj: Emotions – fear. Night.

No one is perfect ill. by Maureen Roffey. Viking, 1987. ISBN 0-670-81570-5 Subj: Behavior – mistakes.

Waiting my turn ill. by Maureen Roffey. Viking, 1989. ISBN 0-670-82674-X Subj: Character traits – patience.

Erickson, Phoebe. *Just follow me* ill. by author. Follett, 1960. Subj: Animals – dogs. Behavior – lost. Houses.

Erickson, Russell E. *Warton and the traders* ill. by Lawrence DiFiori. Lothrop, 1979. Subj: Animals – rats. Character traits – cleverness. Character traits – generosity. Frogs and toads.

Warton's Christmas eve adventure ill. by Lawrence DiFiori. Lothrop, 1977. Subj: Animals. Frogs and toads. Holidays – Christmas.

Eriksson, Ake. *Joel, Jasper, and Julia* ill. by author. Carolrhoda, 1990. ISBN 0-87614-419-9 Subj: Animals – pigs. Farms.

Eriksson, Eva. *Hocus-pocus* ill. by author; tr. from Swedish by Barbro Eriksson Roehrdanz. Carolrhoda Books, 1985. ISBN 0-87614-235-8 Subj: Bedtime. Friendship.

Jealousy ill. by author; tr. from Swedish by Barbro Eriksson Roehrdanz. Carolrhoda Books, 1985. ISBN 0-87614-237-4 Subj: Emotions – envy, jealousy. Friendship. Illness.

Mimi and the biscuit factory (Sundvall, Viveca)

One short week ill. by author; tr. from Swedish by Barbro Eriksson Roehrdanz. Carolrhoda Books, 1985. ISBN 0-87614-234-X Subj: Behavior – boredom. Birthdays. Friendship.

The tooth trip ill. by author; tr. from Swedish by Barbro Eriksson Roehrdanz. Carolrhoda Books, 1985. ISBN 0-87614-236-6 Subj: Behavior – losing things. Friendship. Teeth.

Ernst, Lisa Campbell. *A colorful adventure of the bee who left home one Monday morning and what he found along the way* ill. by Lee Ernst. Lothrop, 1986. ISBN 0-688-05564-8 Subj: Concepts – color. Insects – bees.

Ginger jumps ill. by author. Bradbury Pr., 1990. ISBN 0-02-733565-8 Subj: Animals – dogs. Circus.

Hamilton's art show ill. by author. Lothrop, 1986. ISBN 0-688-04121-3 Subj: Activities – painting. Animals. Art. Gardens, gardening.

Miss Penny and Mr. Grubbs ill. by author. Bradbury Pr., 1991. ISBN 0-02-733563-1 Subj: Animals – rabbits. Emotions – envy, jealousy. Fairs. Gardens, gardening.

Nattie Parsons' good-luck lamb ill. by author. Viking, 1988. ISBN 0-670-81778-3 Subj: Activities – weaving. Animals – sheep.

The prize pig surprise ill. by author. Lothrop, 1984. Subj: Animals – pigs. Behavior – greed. Character traits – cleverness.

The rescue of Aunt Pansy ill. by author. Viking, 1987. ISBN 0-670-81716-3 Subj: Animals – cats. Animals – mice. Family life – aunts, uncles. Format, unusual. Friendship. Toys.

Sam Johnson and the blue ribbon quilt ill. by author. Lothrop, 1983. Subj: Activities. Quilts.

Up to ten and down again ill. by author. Lothrop, 1986. ISBN 0-688-04542-1 Subj: Activities – picnicking. Counting, numbers.

Walter's tail ill. by author. Bradbury Pr., 1992. ISBN 0-02-733564-X Subj: Animals – dogs. Pets.

When Bluebell sang ill. by author. Bradbury Pr., 1989. ISBN 0-02-733561-5 Subj: Animals – bulls, cows. Theater.

Zinnia and Dot ill. by author. Viking, 1992. ISBN 0-670-83091-7 Subj: Animals – weasels. Behavior – fighting, arguing. Birds – chickens. Eggs.

Erskine, Jim. *Bedtime story* ill. by Ann Schweninger. Crown, 1982. Subj: Bedtime. Dreams. Night.

Bert and Susie's messy tale ill. by author. Crown, 1979. Subj: Activities. Animals – pigs.

The snowman ill. by author. Crown, 1978. Subj: Snowmen.

Esbensen, Barbara Juster. *Ladder to the sky: how the gift of healing came to the Ojibway nation* ill. by Helen K. Davie. Little, 1989. ISBN 0-316-24952-1 Subj: Folk and fairy tales. Indians of North America. Poetry, rhyme.

The star maiden: an Ojibway tale ill. by Helen K. Davie. Little, 1988. ISBN 0-316-24951-3 Subj: Folk and fairy tales. Indians of North America. Poetry, rhyme.

Who shrank my grandmother's house? ill. by Eric Beddows. HarperCollins, 1992. ISBN 0-06-021828-2 Subj: Behavior – growing up. Poetry, rhyme.

Escudie, René. *Paul and Sebastian* tr. by Roderick Townley; ill. by Ulises Wensell. Kane/Miller, 1988. ISBN 0-916291-19-7 Subj: Character traits – being different. Family life. Friendship. Prejudice.

Espenscheid, Gertrude E. *The oh ball* ill. by author. Crown, 1966. Subj: Royalty. Toys – balls.

Esterl, Arnica. *The fine round cake* tr. from German by Pauline Hejl; ill. by Andrej Dugin and Olga Dugina. Four Winds Pr., 1991. An adaptation of Johnny cake by Joseph Jacobs ISBN 0-02-733568-2 Subj: Cumulative tales. Folk and fairy tales. Food. Foreign lands – England.

Etherington, Frank. *The spaghetti word race* ill. by Gina Calleja. Firefly Pr., 1982. Subj: Imagination. Sibling rivalry.

Ets, Marie Hall. *Another day* ill. by author. Viking, 1953. Subj: Animals. Forest, woods. Parades. Theater.

Bad boy, good boy ill. by author. Crowell, 1967. Subj: Behavior. Ethnic groups in the U.S. – Mexican-Americans. Family life. School.

Beasts and nonsense ill. by author. Viking, 1952. Subj: Animals. Humor. Poetry, rhyme.

The cow's party ill. by author. Viking, 1958. Subj: Animals – bulls, cows. Behavior – dissatisfaction. Behavior – sharing. Parties.

Elephant in a well ill. by author. Viking, 1972. Subj: Animals. Animals – elephants. Character traits – helpfulness. Cumulative tales.

Gilberto and the wind ill. by author. Viking, 1963. Subj: Ethnic groups in the U.S. – Mexican-Americans. Weather – wind.

In the forest ill. by author. Viking, 1944. Subj: Activities – picnicking. Animals. Caldecott award honor book. Forest, woods. Imagination. Parades.

Just me ill. by author. Viking, 1965. Subj: Animals. Caldecott award honor book. Participation.

Little old automobile ill. by author. Viking, 1948. Subj: Automobiles.

Mister Penny ill. by author. Viking, 1935. Subj: Animals. Caldecott award honor book. Farms. Humor.

Mister Penny's circus ill. by author. Viking, 1961. Subj: Animals. Circus.

Mr. Penny's race horse ill. by author. Viking, 1956. Subj: Animals – horses. Caldecott award honor book. Fairs. Farms.

Mr. T. W. Anthony Woo ill. by author. Viking, 1951. Subj: Animals – cats. Animals – dogs. Animals – mice. Caldecott award honor book.

Nine days to Christmas ill. by author. Viking, 1959. Subj: Caldecott award book. Ethnic groups in the U.S. – Mexican-Americans. Foreign lands – Mexico. Holidays – Christmas.

Play with me ill. by author. Viking, 1955. Subj: Activities – playing. Animals. Behavior. Caldecott award honor book.

Talking without words ill. by author. Viking, 1968. Subj: Participation.

Euvremer, Teryl. *After dark* ill. by author. Crown, 1989. ISBN 0-517-57104-8 Subj: Poetry, rhyme.

Sun's up ill. by author. Crown, 1987. ISBN 0-517-56432-7 Subj: Activities – working. Farms. Sun. Wordless.

The thieves of Peck's pocket ill. by author. Crown, 1990. ISBN 0-517-57538-8 Subj: Animals. Behavior – stealing. Crime. Plants.

Evans, Eva Knox. *Sleepy time* ill. by Reed Champion. Houghton, 1962. Subj: Animals. Cumulative tales. Hibernation. Sleep.

That lucky Mrs. Plucky ill. by Jo Ann Stover. McKay, 1961. Subj: Animals – cats. Behavior – collecting things.

Where do you live? ill. by Beatrice Darwin. Golden Pr., 1960. Subj: Animals.

Evans, Katherine. *The boy who cried wolf* ill. by author. Albert Whitman, 1960. Subj: Animals – wolves. Behavior – lying. Behavior – trickery. Folk and fairy tales.

A bundle of sticks ill. by author. Albert Whitman, 1962. A retelling of an Æsop fable Subj: Folk and fairy tales.

The maid and her pail of milk ill. by author. Albert Whitman, 1959. Subj: Behavior – greed. Folk and fairy tales. Humor.

The man, the boy and the donkey ill. by author. Albert Whitman, 1958. Subj: Animals – donkeys. Character traits – practicality. Folk and fairy tales. Humor.

Evans, Katie. *Hunky Dory ate it* ill. by Janet M. Stoeke. Dutton, 1992. ISBN 0-525-44847-0 Subj: Animals – dogs. Food. Poetry, rhyme.

Evans, Mari. *Singing black* ill. by Ramon Price. Third World Pr., 1978. Subj: Ethnic groups in the U.S. – Afro-Americans. Nursery rhymes.

Evans, Mel. *The tiniest sound* ill. by Ed Young. Doubleday, 1969. Subj: Noise, sounds. Poetry, rhyme.

Everett, Gwen. *Li'l Sis and Uncle Willie: a story based on the life and paintings of William H. Johnson* ill. with photos of paintings by William H. Johnson. Rizzoli, 1992. ISBN 0-8478-1462-9 Subj: Art. Careers – artists. Ethnic groups in the U.S. – Afro-Americans. Family life – aunts, uncles. Museums. U.S. history.

Eversole, Robyn Harbert. *The magic house* ill. by Peter Palagonia. Orchard, 1992. ISBN 0-531-08524-4 Subj: Activities – dancing. Family life – sisters. Imagination.

Everton, Macduff. *El circo magico modelo: Finding the magic circus* ill. by author. Carolrhoda Books, 1979. Subj: Activities – vacationing. Circus. Foreign lands – Mexico. Foreign languages.

Facklam, Margery. *But not like mine* ill. by Jeni Bassett. Harcourt, 1988. ISBN 015-200585-4 Subj: Anatomy. Animals. Format, unusual – toy and movable books.

So can I ill. by Jeni Bassett. Harcourt, 1988. ISBN 0-15-200419-X Subj: Activities. Animals. Format, unusual – toy and movable books.

Factor, Jane. *Summer* ill. by Alison Lester. Viking, 1988. ISBN 0-670-81157-2 Subj: Family life. Foreign lands – Australia. Holidays – Christmas. Seasons – summer.

Fain, James W. *Rodeos* ill. with photos. Children's Pr., 1983. Subj: Animals – horses. Cowboys.

Fair, Sylvia. *The bedspread* ill. by author. Morrow, 1982. Subj: Activities. Sibling rivalry.

Fairclough, Chris. *Take a trip to China* photos. by author. Watts, 1981. Subj: Activities – traveling. Foreign lands – China.

Take a trip to England photos. by author. Watts, 1982. Subj: Activities – traveling. Foreign lands – England.

Take a trip to Holland photos. by author. Watts, 1982. Subj: Activities – traveling. Foreign lands – Holland.

Take a trip to Israel photos. by author. Watts, 1981. Subj: Activities – traveling. Foreign lands – Israel.

Take a trip to Italy photos. by author. Watts, 1981. Subj: Activities – traveling. Foreign lands – Italy.

Take a trip to West Germany photos. by author. Watts, 1981. Subj: Activities – traveling. Foreign lands – Germany.

Fairy poems for the very young ill. by Beverlie Manson. Doubleday, 1982. Subj: Fairies. Poetry, rhyme.

Faison, Eleanora. *Becoming* ill. by Cecelia Ercin. Patterson Pr., 1981. Subj: Behavior – growing up.

Falls, C. B. (Charles Buckles). *ABC book* ill. by author. Doubleday, 1923. Subj: ABC books.

Fallwell, Cathryn. *Clowning around* ill. by author. Watts, 1991. ISBN 0-531-08552-X Subj: Circus. Concepts – shape. Language.

Nicky and Alex ill. by author. Houghton, 1992. ISBN 0-395-56915-X Subj: Activities – making things. Activities – playing. Babies. Family life – brothers. Format, unusual.

Nicky and grandpa ill. by author. Houghton, 1991. ISBN 0-395-56917-6 Subj: Activities – playing. Babies. Family life – grandfathers. Format, unusual.

Nicky loves daddy ill. by author. Houghton, 1992. ISBN 0-395-60820-1 Subj: Activities – walking. Babies. Family life – fathers. Format, unusual. Senses.

Nicky, 1-2-3 ill. by author. Houghton, 1991. ISBN 0-395-56913-3 Subj: Counting, numbers. Babies. Format, unusual.

Nicky's walk ill. by author. Houghton, 1991. ISBN 0-395-56914-1 Subj: Activities – walking. Babies. Concepts – color. Family life – mothers. Format, unusual.

Where's Nicky? ill. by author. Houghton, 1991. ISBN 0-395-56936-2 Subj: Activities – playing. Babies. Format, unusual. Games.

Fanshawe, Elizabeth. *Rachel* ill. by Michael Charlton. Dutton, 1975. Subj: Handicaps. School.

Farber, Norma. *As I was crossing Boston Common* ill. by Arnold Lobel. Dutton, 1975. Subj: ABC books. Animals. Poetry, rhyme.

How does it feel to be old? ill. by Trina Schart Hyman. Dutton, 1988, 1979. ISBN 0-525-44367-3 Subj: Family life – grandparents. Old age.

How the hibernators came to Bethlehem ill. by Barbara Cooney. Walker, 1980. Subj: Animals. Holidays – Christmas. Poetry, rhyme. Religion.

How the left-behind beasts built Ararat ill. by Antonio Frasconi. Walker, 1978. Subj: Animals. Poetry, rhyme. Problem solving. Religion – Noah.

How to ride a tiger ill. by Claire Schumacher. Houghton, 1983. Subj: Animals. Animals – tigers. Poetry, rhyme.

Never say ugh to a bug ill. by José Aruego. Greenwillow, 1979. Subj: Insects. Poetry, rhyme.

Small wonders ill. by Kazue Mizumura. Coward, 1979. Subj: Poetry, rhyme.

There goes feathertop! ill. by Marc Brown. Unicorn-Dutton, 1979. Subj: Behavior – imitation. Poetry, rhyme. Scarecrows.

There once was a woman who married a man ill. by Lydia Dabcovich. Addison-Wesley, 1978. Subj: Humor. Noise, sounds. Poetry, rhyme.

Up the down elevator ill. by Annie Gusman. Addison-Wesley, 1979. Subj: Counting, numbers. Elevators, escalators. Poetry, rhyme.

Where's Gomer? ill. by William Pène Du Bois. Dutton, 1974. Subj: Behavior – lost. Poetry, rhyme. Religion – Noah.

Farber, Werner. *Night lion* Tr. from German by Jane Fior; ill. by Barbara Mossman. Houghton, 1991. ISBN 0-395-57816-7 Subj: Emotions – fear. Night. Sleep. Toys.

Farge, Phyllis La *see* La Farge, Phyllis

Farge, Sheila La *see* La Farge, Sheila

Farjeon, Eleanor. *Around the seasons: poems* ill. by Jane Paton. Walck, 1969. Subj: Poetry, rhyme. Seasons.

Cats sleep anywhere. ill. by Mary Price Jenkins. Lippincott, 1990. ISBN 0-397-32464-2 Subj: Animals – cats. Poetry, rhyme.

Mr. Garden ill. by Jane Paton. Walck, 1966. Subj: Gardens, gardening. Seasons – summer.

Mrs. Malone ill. by Edward Ardizzone. Walck, 1962. Subj: Character traits – generosity. Poetry, rhyme.

Farley, Walter. *Black stallion: an easy-to-read adaptation* ill. by Sandy Rabinowitz. Random House, 1986. ISBN 0-394-96876-X Subj: Animals – horses. Islands.

Farm animals Macmillan, 1991. ISBN 0-689-71403-3 Subj: Animals. Farms.

Farm animals photos. sel. by Debby Slier. Macmillan, 1988. ISBN 0-02-688752-5 Subj: Animals. Format, unusual – board books.

Farm house ill. by Zokeisha; ed. by Kate Klimo. Simon and Schuster, 1983. Subj: Animals. Farms. Format, unusual – board books. Houses.

The farmer in the dell. *The farmer in the dell* ed. by Ann Fay; ill. by Kathy Parkinson. Albert Whitman, 1988. ISBN 0-8075-2271-6 Subj: Games. Music. Songs.

The farmer in the dell ill. by Mary Maki Rae. Viking, 1988. ISBN 0-670-81853-4 Subj: Games. Music. Songs.

The farmer in the dell ill. by Diane Stanley. Little, 1978. Subj: Games. Music. Songs.

Fass, David E. *The shofar that lost its voice* ill. by Marlene Lobell Ruthen. Union of American Hebrew Cong., 1982. Subj: Jewish culture. Religion.

Fassler, David. *What's a virus, anyway? The kids' book about aids* ill. by Kelly McQueen. Waterfront Bks., 1990. ISBN 0-914525-14-X Subj: Health. Illness.

Fassler, Joan. *All alone with daddy* ill by Dorothy Lake Gregory. Behavioral, 1969. Subj: Family life – fathers.

Boy with a problem ill. by Stuart [i.e. Stewart] Kranz. Behavioral, 1971. Subj: Friendship. Problem solving.

Don't worry dear ill. by Stuart [i.e. Stewart] Kranz. Behavioral, 1971. Subj: Behavior – growing up. Ethnic groups in the U.S. – Afro-Americans.

Howie helps himself ill. by Joe Lasker. Albert Whitman, 1975. Subj: Handicaps.

The man of the house ill. by Peter Landa. Behavioral, 1969. Subj: Behavior – growing up. Dragons. Family life – mothers. Monsters.

My grandpa died today ill. by Stuart [i.e. Stewart] Kranz. Behavioral, 1971. Subj: Death. Family life – grandfathers. Jewish culture. Old age.

One little girl ill. by M. Jane Smyth. Behavioral, 1969. Subj: Family life. Handicaps.

Fast rolling fire trucks ill. by Carolyn Bracken. Grosset, 1984. Subj: Careers – firefighters. Format, unusual – board books. Trucks.

Fast rolling work trucks ill. by Alan Singer. Grosset, 1984. Subj: Format, unusual – board books. Trucks.

The fat cat ill. by Jack Kent. Parents, 1971. Translated from the Danish by Jack Kent Subj: Animals – cats. Cumulative tales.

Fatio, Louise. *Anna, the horse* ill. by Roger Antoine Duvoisin. Atheneum, 1951. Subj: Animals – horses. Holidays – Christmas.

The happy lion ill. by Roger Antoine Duvoisin. McGraw-Hill, 1954. Subj: Animals – lions. Foreign lands – France. Friendship. Zoos.

The happy lion and the bear ill. by Roger Antoine Duvoisin. McGraw-Hill, 1964. Subj: Animals – bears. Animals – lions. Character traits – appearance. Foreign lands – France. Zoos.

The happy lion in Africa ill. by Roger Antoine Duvoisin. McGraw-Hill, 1955. Subj: Animals – lions. Foreign lands – Africa. Foreign lands – France. Zoos.

The happy lion roars ill. by Roger Antoine Duvoisin. McGraw-Hill, 1957. Subj: Animals – lions. Emotions – loneliness. Foreign lands – France. Zoos.

The happy lion's quest ill. by Roger Antoine Duvoisin. McGraw-Hill, 1961. Subj: Animals – lions. Foreign lands – France.

The happy lion's rabbits ill. by Roger Antoine Duvoisin. McGraw-Hill, 1974. Subj: Animals – lions. Animals – rabbits. Character traits – kindness. Foreign lands – France. Zoos.

The happy lion's treasure ill. by Roger Antoine Duvoisin. McGraw-Hill, 1970. Subj: Animals – lions. Emotions – love. Foreign lands – France. Zoos.

The happy lion's vacation ill. by Roger Antoine Duvoisin. McGraw-Hill, 1967. Subj: Activities – vacationing. Animals – lions.

Hector and Christina ill. by Roger Antoine Duvoisin. McGraw-Hill, 1977. Subj: Birds – penguins. Character traits – freedom. Friendship. Zoos.

Hector penguin ill. by Roger Antoine Duvoisin. McGraw-Hill, 1973. Subj: Birds – penguins. Character traits – individuality.

Marc and Pixie and the walls in Mrs. Jones's garden ill. by Roger Antoine Duvoisin. McGraw-Hill, 1975. Subj: Animals – cats. Gardens, gardening.

The red bantam ill. by Roger Antoine Duvoisin. McGraw-Hill, 1963. Subj: Animals – foxes. Birds – chickens. Character traits – bravery. Farms.

The three happy lions ill. by Roger Antoine Duvoisin. McGraw-Hill, 1959. Subj: Animals – lions. Foreign lands – France. Zoos.

Faulkner, Anne Irvin *see* Faulkner, Nancy

Faulkner, Keith. *Sam at the seaside* ill. by Jonathan Lambert. Macmillan, 1988. ISBN 0-689-71183-2 Subj: Format, unusual – toy and movable books. Sea and seashore.

Sam helps out ill. by Jonathan Lambert. Macmillan, 1988. ISBN 0-689-71182-4 Subj: Format, unusual – toy and movable books. Shopping.

Faulkner, Matt. *The amazing voyage of Jackie Grace* ill. by author. Scholastic, 1987. ISBN 0-590-40713-9 Subj: Activities – bathing. Boats, ships. Imagination. Pirates. Weather – storms.

Faulkner, Nancy. *Small clown* ill. by Paul Galdone. Doubleday, 1960. Subj: Clowns, jesters.

Faunce-Brown, Daphne. *Snuffles' house* ill. by Frances Thatcher. Children's Pr., 1983. Subj: Activities. Animals – cats.

Fay, Ann. *Boot weather* (Vigna, Judith)

The farmer in the dell (The farmer in the dell)

I wish my daddy didn't drink so much (Vigna, Judith)

Ooops! (Kline, Suzy)

Fay, Hermann. *My zoo* ill. by author. Hubbard Sci., 1972. Subj: Animals. Zoos.

Fayon, Lavinia *see* Russ, Lavina

Fechner, Amrei. *I am a little dog* tr. from German by Robert Kimber; ill. by author. Barron's, 1983. Subj: Animals – dogs. Format, unusual – board books.

I am a little elephant ill. by author. Barron's, 1983. Subj: Animals – elephants. Format, unusual – board books.

I am a little lion ill. by author. Barron's, 1983. Subj: Animals – lions. Format, unusual – board books.

Feczko, Kathy. *Halloween party* ill. by Blanche Sims. Troll Assoc., 1985. ISBN 0-8167-0354-X Subj: Holidays – Halloween. Parties.

Umbrella parade ill. by Deborah Borgo. Troll Assoc., 1985. ISBN 0-8167-0356-6 Subj: Animals. Parades. Umbrellas.

Feder, Harriet K. *Not yet, Elijah!* ill. by Joan Halpern. Kar-Ben Copies, 1989. ISBN 0-930494-95-4 Subj: Holidays – Passover. Jewish culture. Poetry, rhyme. Religion.

What can you do with a bagel? ill. by Sally Springer. Kar-Ben Copies, 1992. ISBN 0-929371-59-3 Subj: Activities – cooking. Food. Jewish culture.

Feder, Jane. *Beany* ill. by Karen Gundersheimer. Pantheon, 1979. Subj: Animals – cats.

Feder, Paula Kurzband. *Where does the teacher live?* ill. by Lillian Hoban. Dutton, 1979. Subj: Careers – teachers. Houses. Problem solving. School.

Feelings, Muriel. *Jambo means hello: Swahili alphabet book* ill. by Tom Feelings. Dial Pr., 1974. Subj: ABC books. Caldecott award honor book. Foreign lands – Africa. Foreign languages.

Menjo means one: Swahili counting book ill. by Tom Feelings. Dial Pr., 1972. Subj: Caldecott award honor book. Counting, numbers. Foreign lands – Africa. Foreign languages.

Feeney, Stephanie. *Hawaii is a rainbow* photos. by Jeff Reese. Kolowalu Books, 1985. ISBN 0-8248-1007-4 Subj: Concepts – color.

Fehlner, Paul. *Dog and cat* ill. by Maxie Chambliss. Children's Pr., 1990. ISBN 0-516-05353-1 Subj: Animals – cats. Animals – dogs. Poetry, rhyme.

Feilen, John *see* May, Julian

Feinberg, Harold S. *Snail in the woods* (Ryder, Joanne)

Feistel, Sally. *The guinea pigs that went to school* (Meshover, Leonard)

The monkey that went to school (Meshover, Leonard)

Feitlowitz, Marguerite. *Brush* (Calders, Pere)

Feldman, Barbara. *Going, going* ill. by author. Firefly, 1989. ISBN 1-55037-045-6 Subj: Activities – traveling. Automobiles. Family life – mothers.

Stephens' frog ill. by author. Firefly, 1991. ISBN 1-55037-201-7 ISBN 1-55037-200-6 Subj: Farms. Family life – grandparents. Frogs and toads. Pets. Wordless.

Feldman, Eve B. *Animals don't wear pajamas* ill. by Mary Beth Owens. Holt, 1992. ISBN 0-8050-1710-0 Subj: Animals. Bedtime. Ethnic groups in the U.S. Sleep.

Feldman, Judy. *The alphabet in nature* ill. with photos. Children's Pr., 1991. ISBN 0-516-05101-6 Subj: ABC books. Nature. Wordless.

Shapes in nature ill. with photos. Children's Pr., 1991. ISBN 0-516-05102-4 Subj: Concepts – shape. Nature. Wordless.

Felix, Monique. *The further adventures of the little mouse trapped in a book* ill. by author. Green Tiger Pr., 1984. ISBN 0-88138-009-1 Subj: Animals – mice. Imagination. Wordless.

The story of a little mouse trapped in a book ill. by author. Green Tiger Pr., 1980. Subj: Animals – mice. Imagination. Wordless.

Felt, Sue. *Hello-goodbye* ill. by author. Doubleday, 1960. Subj: Friendship. Moving.

Rosa-too-little ill. by author. Doubleday, 1950. Subj: Activities – writing. Behavior – growing up. Ethnic groups in the U.S. – Mexican-Americans. Family life. Libraries.

Felton, Harold W. *Pecos Bill and the mustang* ill. by Leonard W. Shortall. Prentice-Hall, 1965. Subj: Animals – horses. Cowboys. Folk and fairy tales.

Fender, Kay. *Odette! a bird in Paris* ill. by Philippe Dumas. Prentice-Hall, 1978. Subj: Birds. Foreign lands – France. Old age.

Fenner, Carol. *Christmas tree on the mountain* ill. by author. Harcourt, 1966. Subj: Holidays – Christmas. Trees.

Tigers in the cellar ill. by author. Harcourt, 1963. Subj: Animals – tigers. Imagination. Night.

Fenton, Edward. *The big yellow balloon* ill. by Ib Spang Olsen. Doubleday, 1967. Subj: Cumulative tales. Humor. Toys – balloons.

Fierce John ill. by William Pène Du Bois. Doubleday, 1959. Subj: Family life. Imagination.

Fenton, Stephen H. *Who will pick me up when I fall?* (Molnar, Dorothy E.)

Ferguson, Alane. *That new pet!* ill. by Catherine Stock. Lothrop, 1986. ISBN 0-688-05516-8 Subj: Babies. Emotions – envy, jealousy. Pets.

Fern, Eugene. *Birthday presents* ill. by author. Farrar, 1967. Includes the song Sing me (2 p.) Subj: Birthdays. Songs.

The king who was too busy ill. by author. Ariel, 1966. Subj: Royalty – kings.

The most frightened hero ill. by author. Coward, 1961. Subj: Character traits – bravery. Foreign lands – Scotland.

Pepito's story ill. by author. Ariel, 1960. Subj: Activities – dancing. Character traits – being different. Illness.

What's he been up to now? ill. by author. Dial Pr., 1961. Subj: Animals – elephants. Friendship.

Fernandes, Kim. *Visiting granny* photos by Pat Lacroix; ill. by author. Firefly, 1990. ISBN 1-55037-077-4 Subj: Family life – grandmothers. Food.

Ferns, Ronald. *Osbert and Lucy* ill. by author. HarperCollins, 1989. ISBN 0-06-021836-3 Subj: Animals – dogs. Animals – rabbits. Behavior – running away. Friendship.

Ferraro, Renato. *Alex, the amazing juggler* (Gianni, Peg)

Ferro, Beatriz. *Caught in the rain* ill. by Michele Sambin. Doubleday, 1980. Subj: Weather – rain.

Fiday, Beverly. *Time to go* by Beverly and David Fiday; ill. by Thomas B. Allen. Harcourt, 1990. ISBN 0-15-200608-7 Subj: Family life. Farms. Moving.

Fiday, David. *Time to go* (Fiday, Beverly)

Fiddle-i-fee : a traditional American chant ill. by Diane Stanley. Little, 1979. Subj: Animals. Cumulative tales. Folk and fairy tales.

Field, Eugene. *Wynken, Blynken and Nod* ill. by Barbara Cooney. Hastings, 1964. Subj: Poetry, rhyme. Sea and seashore. Sleep.

Field, Rachel Lyman. *General store* ill. by Giles Laroche. Little, 1988. ISBN 0-316-28163-8 Subj: Poetry, rhyme. Stores.

General store ill. by Nancy Winslow Parker. Greenwillow, 1988. ISBN 0-688-07354-9 Subj: Poetry, rhyme. Stores.

Prayer for a child ill. by Elizabeth Orton Jones. Macmillan, 1944. Subj: Caldecott award book. Religion.

A road might lead to anywhere ill. by Giles Laroche. Little, 1990. ISBN 0-316-28178-6 Subj: Activities – traveling. Animals – mice. Dreams. Poetry, rhyme. Roads.

Fields, Sadie. *Hidden numbers* (Holmes, Stephen)

Fife, Dale. *Adam's ABC* ill. by Don Robertson. Coward, 1971. Subj: ABC books. City. Ethnic groups in the U.S. – Afro-Americans.

Empty lot ill. by Jim Arnosky. Little, 1991. ISBN 0-316-28167-0 Subj: Nature. Progress.

The little park ill. by Janet LaSalle. Albert Whitman, 1973. Subj: Animals. Ecology. Progress.

Rosa's special garden ill. by Marie DeJohn. Albert Whitman, 1985. ISBN 0-8075-7115-6 Subj: Ethnic groups in the U.S. – Mexican-Americans. Gardens, gardening. Sibling rivalry.

Fifield, Flora. *Pictures for the palace* ill. by Nola Langner. Vanguard, 1957. Subj: Art. Foreign lands – Japan.

Fillingham, David. *Such a noise!* (Brodmann, Aliana)

Fine, Anne. *Poor Monty* ill. by Clara Vulliamy. Houghton, 1992. ISBN 0-395-60472-9 Subj: Behavior – needing someone. Careers – doctors. Family life – mothers. Illness.

Finfer, Celentha. *Grandmother dear* by Celentha Finfer, Esther Wasserberg and Florence Weinberg; ill. by Roy Mathews. Follett, 1966. Subj: Activities – baby-sitting. Family life – grandmothers. Poetry, rhyme.

Fink, Dale Borman. *Mr. Silver and Mrs. Gold* ill. by Shirley Chan. Human Sciences Pr., 1980. Subj: Friendship. Old age.

Fink, Joanne. *Mister North Wind* (De Posadas Mane, Carmen)

Finsand, Mary Jane. *The town that moved* ill. by Reg Sandland. Carolrhoda, 1983. Subj: City. Moving.

Finzel, Julia. *Large as life* ill. by author. Lothrop, 1991. ISBN 0-688-10653-6 Subj: Animals. Concepts – size. Games. Insects – ladybugs.

Fior, Jane. *Night lion* (Farber, Werner)

Fire ill. by Michael Ricketts. Grosset, 1972. Subj: Fire.

The firebird retold and ill. by Moira Kemp. Godine, 1984. Subj: Behavior – stealing. Folk and fairy tales. Foreign lands – Russia. Magic. Royalty – princes.

The firebird adapt. by Robert D. San Souci; ill. by Kris Waldherr. Dial, 1992. ISBN 0-8037-0800-9 Subj: Behavior – stealing. Folk and fairy tales. Foreign lands – Russia. Magic. Royalty – princes.

The firebird: *and other Russian fairy tales* ill. by Boris Zvorykin; ed. by Jacqueline Onassis. Viking, 1978. Subj: Behavior – stealing. Folk and fairy tales. Foreign lands – Russia. Magic. Royalty – princes.

Firehouse ed. by Kate Klimo; ill. by Zokeisha. Simon and Schuster, 1983. Subj: Careers – firefighters. Fire. Format, unusual – board books. Houses.

Firmin, Peter. *Basil Brush and the windmills* ill. by author. Prentice-Hall, 1980. Subj: Animals – foxes. Animals – moles. Ecology.

Chicken stew ill. by author. Merrimack, 1982. Subj: Animals – wolves. Birds – chickens. Gardens, gardening.

Noggin and the whale (Postgate, Oliver)

Noggin the king (Postgate, Oliver)

First graces ill. by Tasha Tudor. Walck, 1955. Subj: Poetry, rhyme. Religion.

First prayers ill. by Anna Maria Magagna. Macmillan, 1983. Subj: Poetry, rhyme. Religion.

First prayers ill. by Tasha Tudor. Oxford Univ. Pr., 1952. Subj: Poetry, rhyme. Religion.

Fischer, Hans. *The birthday* ill. by author. Harcourt, 1954. Subj: Animals. Birthdays.

Puss in boots (Perrault, Charles)

Fischer, Vera Kistiakowsky. *One way is down: a book about gravity* ill. by Ward Brackett. Little, 1967. Subj: Concepts – weight. Science.

Fischer-Nagel, Andreas. *A kitten is born* (Fischer-Nagel, Heiderose)

A puppy is born (Fischer-Nagel, Heiderose)

A puppy is born (Fischer-Nagel, Heiderose)

Fischer-Nagel, Heiderose. *A kitten is born* by Heiderose and Andreas Fischer-Nagel; tr. from German by Andrea Mernan; photos. by authors. Putnam's, 1983. Subj: Animals – cats. Birth. Science.

A puppy is born by Heiderose and Andreas Fischer-Nagel; tr. from German by Andrea Mernan; photos. by authors. Putnam's, 1985. ISBN 0-399-21234-5 Subj: Animals – dogs. Birth. Science.

Fischetto, Laura. *All pigs on deck: Christopher Columbus's second marvelous voyage* ill. by Letizia Galli. Delacorte Pr., 1991. ISBN 0-385-30440-4 Subj: Animals – pigs. Boats, ships. U.S. history.

Inside Noah's ark ill. by Letizia Galli. Viking, 1989. ISBN 0-670-83028-3 Subj: Animals. Religion – Noah.

The jungle is my home ill. by Letizia Galli. Viking, 1991. ISBN 0-670-83550-1 Subj: Animals. Ecology. Foreign lands – South America. Jungle.

Fischtrom, Harvey see Zemach, Harve

Fish, Hans. *Pitschi, the kitten who always wanted to do something else* ill. by author. Harcourt, 1953. Subj: Animals – cats. Behavior – dissatisfaction.

Fish, Helen Dean. *Four and twenty blackbirds* ill. by Robert Lawson. Stokes, 1937. Subj: Caldecott award honor book. Nursery rhymes.

When the root children wake up ill. by Sibylle Von Olfers. Green Tiger Pr., 1988. ISBN 0-88138-103-9 Subj: Elves and little people. Seasons – spring.

When the root children wake up ill. by Sibylle Von Olfers. Lippincott, 1930. Subj: Elves and little people. Seasons – spring.

Fisher, Aileen Lucia. *And a sunflower grew* ill. by Trina Schart Hyman; lettering by Paul Taylor. Noble, 1977. Subj: Flowers. Plants. Poetry, rhyme. Science.

Anybody home? ill. by Susan Bonners. Crowell, 1980. Subj: Character traits – curiosity. Poetry, rhyme.

Arbor day ill. by Nonny Hogrogian. Crowell, 1965. Subj: Holidays. Trees.

As the leaves fall down ill. by Barbara Smith. Noble, 1977. Subj: Plants. Science. Seasons. Trees.

Best little house ill. by Arnold Spilka. Crowell, 1966. Subj: Houses. Moving. Poetry, rhyme.

Do bears have mothers too? ill. by Eric Carle. Crowell, 1973. Subj: Animals. Family life – mothers. Poetry, rhyme.

Going barefoot ill. by Adrienne Adams. Crowell, 1960. Subj: Poetry, rhyme. Seasons.

The house of a mouse ill. by Joan Sandin. Harper, 1988. ISBN 0-06-021849-5 Subj: Animals – mice. Houses. Poetry, rhyme.

I like weather ill. by Janina Domanska. Crowell, 1963. Subj: Animals – dogs. Poetry, rhyme. Weather.

I wonder how, I wonder why ill. by Carol Barker. Abelard-Schuman, 1963. Subj: Poetry, rhyme.

In one door and out the other: a book of poems ill. by Lillian Hoban. Crowell, 1969. Subj: Family life. Poetry, rhyme.

In the middle of the night ill. by Adrienne Adams. Crowell, 1965. Subj: Night. Poetry, rhyme.

Like nothing at all ill. by Leonard Weisgard. Crowell, 1962. Subj: Poetry, rhyme. Science. Seasons.

Listen, rabbit ill. by Symeon Shimin. Crowell, 1964. Subj: Animals – rabbits. Poetry, rhyme.

My first Hanukkah book ill. by Priscilla Kiedrowski. Childrens, 1985. ISBN 0-516-42905-1 Subj: Holidays – Hanukkah. Jewish culture. Poetry, rhyme.

My mother and I ill. by Kazue Mizumura. Crowell, 1967. Subj: Family life – mothers. Poetry, rhyme. Seasons – spring.

Mysteries in the garden ill. by Ati Forberg; lettering by Paul Taylor. Noble, 1977. Subj: Gardens, gardening. Plants. Poetry, rhyme. Science.

Now that spring is here ill. by Symeon Shimin; lettering by Paul Taylor. Noble, 1977. Subj: Plants. Poetry, rhyme. Science. Seasons – spring.

Petals yellow and petals red ill. by Albert John Pucci; lettering by Paul Taylor. Noble, 1977. Subj: Flowers. Poetry, rhyme. Science.

Plant magic ill. by Barbara Cooney; lettering by Paul Taylor. Noble, 1977. Subj: Plants. Poetry, rhyme. Science.

Prize performance ill by Margot Tomes. Noble, 1977. Subj: Plants. Poetry, rhyme. Science.

Rabbits, rabbits ill. by Gail Niemann. Harper, 1983. Subj: Animals – rabbits. Poetry, rhyme.

Seeds on the go ill. by Hans Zander; lettering by Paul Taylor. Noble, 1977. Subj: Plants. Poetry, rhyme. Science.

Sing, little mouse ill. by Symeon Shimin. Crowell, 1969. Subj: Animals – mice. Poetry, rhyme.

Skip around the year ill. by Gioia Fiammenghi. Crowell, 1967. Subj: Holidays. Poetry, rhyme.

Swords and daggers ill. by James Higa; lettering by Paul Taylor. Noble, 1977. Subj: Plants. Poetry, rhyme. Science.

We went looking ill. by Marie Angel. Crowell, 1968. Subj: Animals. Birds. Insects – ladybugs. Plants. Poetry, rhyme.

When it comes to bugs ill. by Chris and Bruce Degen. Harper, 1986. ISBN 0-06-021822-3 Subj: Insects. Poetry, rhyme. Spiders.

Where does everyone go? ill. by Adrienne Adams. Crowell, 1961. Subj: Animals. Hibernation. Poetry, rhyme. Seasons – winter.

Fisher, Iris L. *Katie-Bo: an adoption story* ill. by Miriam Schaer. Watts, 1988. ISBN 0-915361-91-4 Subj: Adoption. Babies. Ethnic groups in the U.S. Sibling rivalry.

Fisher, Leonard Everett. *Boxes! Boxes!* ill. by author. Viking, 1984. Subj: Concepts. Concepts – color. Counting, numbers. Poetry, rhyme.

Cyclops ill. by author. Holiday, 1991. ISBN 0-8234-0891-4 Subj: Folk and fairy tales. Mythical creatures.

A head full of hats ill. by author. Dial Pr., 1962. Subj: Clothing – hats.

Look around! a book about shapes ill. by author. Viking, 1987. ISBN 0-670-80869-5 Subj: Concepts – shape. Games.

Pumpers, boilers, hooks and ladders: a book of fire engines ill. by author. Dial Pr., 1961. Subj: Careers – firefighters. Trucks.

The seven days of creation ill. by the author. Holiday, 1981. Adapted from the Bible Subj: Religion.

Star signs ill. by author. Holiday, 1983. Subj: Folk and fairy tales. Zodiac.

Theseus and the minotaur ill. by author. Holiday, 1988. ISBN 0-8234-0703-9 Subj: Folk and fairy tales. Mythical creatures. Royalty.

Fisher, Richard E. *The boy and the dog* (Widerberg, Siv)

Mrs. Pepperpot and the moose (Prøysen, Alf)

Shorty takes off (Lindgren, Barbro)

Fitch, Florence Mary. *A book about God* ill. by Leonard Weisgard. Lothrop, 1953. Subj: Religion.

Fitzhugh, Louise. *Bang, bang, you're dead* by Louise Fitzhugh and Sandra Scoppetone; ill. by Louise

Fitzhugh. Harper, 1969. Subj: Activities – playing. Cowboys. Violence, anti-violence. War. Weapons.

I am five ill. by author. Delacorte, 1978. Subj: Self-concept.

I am three ill. by Susanna Natti. Delacorte, 1982. Subj: Self-concept.

Fitzpatrick, Jean Grasso. *Animals of the forest* (Mora, Emma)

Gideon, the little bear cub (Mora, Emma)

Fitzsimons, Cecilia. *My first birds* ill. by author. Harper, 1985. Subj: Birds. Format, unusual – board books.

My first butterflies ill. by author. Harper, 1985. Subj: Format, unusual – board books. Insects – butterflies, caterpillars.

Flack, Marjorie. *Angus and the cat* ill. by author. Doubleday, 1931. Subj: Animals – cats. Animals – dogs. Character traits – completing things. Character traits – curiosity.

Angus and the ducks ill. by author. Doubleday, 1930. Subj: Animals – dogs. Birds – ducks. Character traits – conceit. Character traits – curiosity.

Angus lost ill. by author. Doubleday, 1932. Subj: Animals – dogs. Behavior – lost. Seasons – winter.

Ask Mr. Bear ill. by author. Macmillan, 1932. Subj: Animals. Animals – bears. Birthdays. Emotions – love. Family life – mothers.

The boats on the river ill. by author. Viking, 1946. Subj: Boats, ships. Caldecott award honor book. Rivers.

The restless robin ill. by author. Houghton, 1937. Subj: Birds – robins. Music.

The story about Ping ill. by Kurt Wiese. Viking, 1933. Subj: Behavior – misbehavior. Birds – ducks. Foreign lands – China.

Tim Tadpole and the great bullfrog ill. by author. Doubleday, 1934. Subj: Frogs and toads.

Wait for William ill. by Marjorie Flack and Richard A. Holberg. Houghton, 1934. Subj: Circus. Family life. Parades.

William and his kitten ill. by author. Houghton, 1938. Subj: Animals – cats.

Flanders, Michael. *Creatures great and small* ill. by Marcello Minale. Holt, 1965. Subj: Animals. Birds. Poetry, rhyme.

The hippopotamus song: a muddy love story ill. by Nadine Bernard Westcott; music by Donald Swann and Michael Flanders. Little, 1991. ISBN 0-316-28557-9 Subj: Animals – hippopotami. Emotions – love. Music. Songs.

Fleischman, Paul. *The animal hedge* ill. by Lydia Dabcovich. Dutton, 1983. Subj: Activities – working. Farms. Folk and fairy tales.

The birthday tree ill. by Marcia Sewall. Harper, 1979. Subj: Birthdays. Trees.

Rondo in C ill. by Janet Wentworth. Harper, 1988. ISBN 0-06-021857-6 Subj: Imagination. Music. Poetry, rhyme.

Time train ill. by Claire Ewart. HarperCollins, 1991. ISBN 0-06-021710-3 Subj: Dinosaurs. School. Time. Trains.

Fleischman, Sid. *Kate's secret riddle* ill. by Barbara Bottner. Watts, 1977. Subj: Illness. Riddles.

Longbeard the wizard ill. by Charles Bragg. Little, 1970. Subj: Royalty. Wizards.

The scarebird ill. by Peter Sis. Greenwillow, 1988. ISBN 0-688-07317-4 Subj: Character traits – kindness. Farms. Friendship. Scarecrows.

Fleisher, Robbin. *Quilts in the attic* ill. by Ati Forberg. Macmillan, 1978. Subj: Family life. Games. Quilts.

Fleishman, Seymour. *Too hot in Potzburg* ill. by author. Walker, 1981. Subj: Animals – bears. Machines.

Fleming, Denise. *Count!* ill. by author. Holt, 1992. ISBN 0-8050-1595-7 Subj: Animals. Counting, numbers.

In the tall, tall grass ill. by author. Holt, 1991. ISBN 0-8050-1635-X Subj: Insects – butterflies, caterpillars. Nature.

Fletcher, Elizabeth. *The little goat* ill. by Deborah and Kilmeny Niland. Grosset, 1977. Subj: Animals – goats. Behavior – lost.

What am I? ill. by Deborah and Kilmeny Niland. Grosset, 1977. Subj: Animals. Riddles.

Flint, Russ. *Let's build a house* ill. by author. Ideals, 1990. ISBN 0-8249-8432-3 Subj: Activities – making things. Houses.

Flora. *Feathers like a rainbow* ill. by author. HarperCollins, 1989. ISBN 0-06-021838-X Subj: Birds. Concepts – color. Folk and fairy tales. Foreign lands – South America. Indians of South America.

Flora, James. *The day the cow sneezed* ill. by author. Harcourt, 1957. Subj: Animals. Cumulative tales. Humor.

Fishing with dad ill. by author. Harcourt, 1967. Subj: Boats, ships. Careers – fishermen.

Grandpa's farm: 4 tall tales ill. by author. Harcourt, 1965. Subj: Family life – grandfathers. Farms. Humor.

Grandpa's ghost stories ill. by author. Atheneum. Subj: Family life – grandfathers. Ghosts. Witches.

Leopold, the see-through crumbpicker ill. by author. Harcourt, 1961. Subj: Monsters. Zoos.

My friend Charlie ill. by author. Harcourt, 1964. Subj: Humor.

Sherwood walks home ill. by author. Harcourt, 1966. Subj: Toys – teddy bears..

Florian, Douglas. *Airplane ride* ill. by author. Crowell, 1984. Subj: Activities – flying. Airplanes, airports.

At the zoo ill. by author. Greenwillow, 1992. ISBN 0-688-09629-8 Subj: Animals. Zoos.

An auto mechanic ill. by author. Greenwillow, 1991. ISBN 0-688-10636-6 Subj: Automobiles. Careers – mechanics.

Beach day ill. by author. Greenwillow, 1990. ISBN 0-688-09105-9 Subj: Sea and seashore.

A bird can fly ill. by author. Greenwillow, 1980. Subj: Animals. Science.

A carpenter ill. by author. Greenwillow, 1991. ISBN 0-688-09761-8 Subj: Careers – carpenters.

The city ill. by author. Crowell, 1982. Subj: City. Wordless.

City street ill. by author. Greenwillow, 1990. ISBN 0-688-09544-5 Subj: City.

Nature walk ill. by author. Greenwillow, 1989. ISBN 0-688-08269-6 Subj: Activities – walking. Nature.

People working ill. by author. Crowell, 1983. Subj: Activities – working. Careers.

A potter ill. by author. Greenwillow, 1991. ISBN 0-688-10101-1 Subj: Activities – making things. Activities – working. Art. Poetry, rhyme.

A summer day ill. by author. Greenwillow, 1988. ISBN 0-688-07565-7 Subj: Activities – vacationing. Counting, numbers. Family life.

Turtle day ill. by author. HarperCollins, 1989. ISBN 0-690-04745-2 Subj: Reptiles – turtles, tortoises.

Vegetable garden ill. by author. Harcourt, 1991. ISBN 0-15-293383-2 Subj: Gardens, gardening.

A year in the country ill. by author. Greenwillow, 1989. ISBN 0-688-08187-8 Subj: Country. Farms. Seasons.

Flory, Jane. *The bear on the doorstep* ill. by Carolyn Croll. Houghton, 1980. Subj: Animals – bears. Animals – rabbits. Houses.

The unexpected grandchild ill. by Carolyn Croll. Houghton, 1977. Subj: Behavior – sharing. Family life – grandparents.

We'll have a friend for lunch ill. by Carolyn Croll. Houghton, 1974. Subj: Animals – cats. Food. Friendship.

Flot, Jeannette B. *Princess Kalina and the hedgehog* adapt. by Frances Marshall; ill. by Dorothée Duntze. Faber, 1981. Subj: Animals – hedgehogs. Character traits – cleanliness. Folk and fairy tales. Magic. Royalty – princesses.

Flöthe, Louise Lee. *The Indian and his pueblo* ill. by Richard Floethe. Scribner's, 1960. Subj: Indians of North America.

Flournoy, Valerie. *The best time of day* ill. by George Ford. Random House, 1979. Subj: Activities. Ethnic groups in the U.S. – Afro-Americans. Family life.

The patchwork quilt ill. by Jerry Pinkney. Dial Pr., 1985. ISBN 0-8037-0098-9 Subj: Ethnic groups in the U.S. – Afro-Americans. Family life – grandmothers. Quilts.

Flower, Phyllis. *Barn owl* ill. by Cherryl Pape. Harper, 1978. Subj: Birds – owls. Science.

Floyd, Lucy. *Agatha's alphabet, with her very own dictionary* ill. by Dora Leder. Rand McNally, 1975. Subj: ABC books. Dictionaries.

Foley, Bernice Williams. *The gazelle and the hunter: a folk tale from Persia* ill. by Diana Magnuson. Children's Pr., 1980. Subj: Folk and fairy tales. Foreign lands – Persia.

A walk among clouds: a folk tale from China ill. by Mina Gow McLean. Children's Pr., 1980. Subj: Folk and fairy tales. Foreign lands – China.

Folsom, Marcia. *Easy as pie: a guessing game of sayings* by Marcia and Michael Folsom; ill. by Jack Kent. Houghton, 1985. Subj: Humor. Language.

Folsom, Michael. *Easy as pie* (Folsom, Marcia)

Q is for duck (Elting, Mary)

Fontaine, Jan. *The spaghetti tree* ill. by Anne Marshall Runyon. Talespinner, 1980. Subj: Food. Gardens, gardening. Imagination.

Fontaine, Jean de La see La Fontaine, Jean de

Fontane, Theodor. *Nick Ribbeck of Ribbeck of Havelland* tr. from German by Anthea Bell; ill. by Marta Koci. Picture Book Studio, 1990. ISBN 0-88708-149-5 Subj: Character traits – generosity. Poetry, rhyme.

Sir Ribbeck of Ribbeck of Havelland tr. from German by Elizabeth Shub; ill. by Nonny Hogrogian. Macmillan, 1969. Subj: Character traits – generosity. Poetry, rhyme.

Foord, Jo. *The book of babies* photos. by author. Random House, 1991. ISBN 0-679-90955-9 Subj: Activities. Babies. Poetry, rhyme.

Ford, Bernette G. *Bright eyes, brown skin* (Hudson, Cheryl Willis)

Ford, George. *Walk on!* (Williamson, Mel)

Ford, Lauren. *The ageless story* ill. by author. Dodd, 1940. Subj: Caldecott award honor book.

Foreman, Michael. *Ben's baby* ill. by author. Harper, 1988. ISBN 0-06-021844-4 Subj: Babies. Family life.

Cat and canary ill. by author. Dial Pr., 1985. Subj: Animals – cats. Birds – canaries.

The general (Charters, Janet)

Jack's fantastic voyage ill. by author. Harcourt, 1992. ISBN 0-15-239496-6 Subj: Boats, ships. Dreams. Family life – grandfathers. Sea and seashore. Weather – storms.

Land of dreams ill. by author. Holt, 1982. Subj: Dreams.

Moose ill. by author. Pantheon, 1972. Subj: Animals – bears. Animals – moose. Birds – eagles. Violence, anti-violence.

Panda and the bushfire ill. by author. Prentice-Hall, 1986. ISBN 0-13-648395-X Subj: Animals. Animals – pandas. Fire. Foreign lands – Australia. Mythical creatures.

The two giants ill. by author. Pantheon, 1967. Subj: Giants.

War and peas ill by author. Crowell, 1974. Subj: Royalty. War.

Forest, Charlotte B. De *see* DeForest, Charlotte B.

Forest, Heather. *The baker's dozen* ill. by Susan Graber. Harcourt, 1988. ISBN 0-15-200412-2 Subj: Careers – bakers. Folk and fairy tales.

The woman who flummoxed the fairies ill. by Susan Gaber. Harcourt, 1990. ISBN 0-15-299150-6 Subj: Fairies. Folk and fairy tales. Food. Foreign lands – Scotland.

Forrester, Victoria. *The magnificent moo* ill. by author. Atheneum, 1983. Subj: Animals – bulls, cows. Animals – cats. Noise, sounds.

Oddward ill. by author. Atheneum, 1982. Subj: Holidays. Reptiles – snakes.

Poor Gabriella: a Christmas story ill. by Susan Boulet. Atheneum, 1986. ISBN 0-689-31266-0 Subj: Holidays – Christmas. Religion.

The touch said hello ill. by author. Atheneum, 1982. Subj: Seasons – spring.

Words to keep against the night ill. by author. Atheneum, 1983. Subj: Poetry, rhyme.

Fort, Patrick. *Redbird* ill. by author. Watts, 1988. ISBN 0-531-05746-1 Subj: Activities – flying. Airplanes, airports. Format, unusual.

Foster, Doris Van Liew. *A pocketful of seasons* ill. by Tālivaldis Stubis. Lothrop, 1961. Subj: Behavior – saving things. Seasons.

Tell me, Mr. Owl ill. by Helen Stone. Lothrop, 1957. Subj: Birds – owls. Holidays – Halloween.

Foster, Marian Curtis *see* Mariana

Foster, Sally. *A pup grows up* photos. by author. Dodd, 1984. Subj: Animals – dogs. Pets.

Foulds, Elfrida Vipont. *The elephant and the bad baby* ill. by Raymond Briggs. Coward, 1986, 1969. ISBN 0-698-20039-X Subj: Animals – elephants. Babies. Behavior – stealing. Cumulative tales.

Fournier, Catharine. *The coconut thieves* ill. by Janina Domanska. Scribner's, 1964. Subj: Animals. Folk and fairy tales. Foreign lands – Africa.

Fowler, Allan. *Cubs and colts and calves and kittens* ill. with photos. Children's Pr., 1991. ISBN 0-516-04913-5 Subj: Animals. Science.

Feeling things ill. with photos. Children's Pr., 1991. ISBN 0-516-04908-9 Subj: Senses – touching.

Hearing things ill. with photos. Children's Pr., 1991. ISBN 0-516-04909-7 Subj: Senses – hearing.

It could still be a bird ill. with photos. Children's Pr., 1990. ISBN 0-516-04901-1 Subj: Birds.

Seeing things ill. with photos. Children's Pr., 1991. ISBN 0-516-04910-0 Subj: Senses – seeing.

Smelling things ill. photos. Children's Pr., 1991. ISBN 0-516-04912-7 Subj: Senses – smelling.

Tasting things ill. photos. ISBN 0-516-04911-9 Subj: Senses – tasting.

What's the weather today? ill. with photos. ISBN 0-516-04918-6 Subj: Weather.

Fowler, Richard. *Cat's story* ill. by author. Grosset, 1985. Subj: Animals – cats. Format, unusual – board books. Poetry, rhyme.

Inspector Smart gets the message! ill. by author. Little, 1983. Subj: Birthdays. Problem solving.

Mr. Little's noisy car ill. by author. Grosset, 1986. ISBN 0-448-18977-1 Subj: Animals. Automobiles. Format, unusual – toy and movable books. Noise, sounds.

Mr. Little's noisy truck ill. by author. Grosset, 1989. ISBN 0-448-19021-4 Subj: Animals. Format, unusual – toy and movable books. Noise, sounds. Trucks.

Fowler, Susi Gregg. *When summer ends* ill. by Marisabina Russo. Greenwillow, 1989. ISBN 0-688-07606-8 Subj: Seasons.

Fowles, John. *Cinderella* (Perrault, Charles)

Fox, Charles Philip. *Come to the circus* photos. by author. Reilly and Lee, 1960. Subj: Circus.

A fox in the house photos. by author. Reilly and Lee, 1960. Subj: Animals – foxes.

Mr. Stripes the gopher photos. by author. Reilly and Lee, 1962. Subj: Animals. Family life. Seasons.

Fox, Dorothea Warren. *Follow me the leader* ill. by author. Parents, 1968. Subj: Games. Poetry, rhyme.

Fox, Mem. *Guess what?* ill. by Vivienne Goodman. Harcourt, 1990. ISBN 0-15-200452-1 Subj: Witches.

Hattie and the fox ill. by Patricia Mullins. Bradbury Pr., 1987. ISBN 0-02-735470-9 Subj: Animals. Birds – chickens. Cumulative tales. Farms.

Koala Lou ill. by Pamela Lofts. Harcourt, 1989. ISBN 0-15-200502-1 Subj: Animals – koala bears. Emotions – love. Family life – mothers.

Night noises ill. by Terry Denton. Harcourt, 1989. ISBN 0-15-200543-9 Subj: Animals – dogs. Birthdays. Night. Noise, sounds. Sleep.

Possum magic ill. by Julie Vivas. Abingdon, 1987. ISBN 0-687-31732-0 Subj: Activities – traveling. Animals – possums. Behavior – wishing. Food. Foreign lands – Australia.

Shoes from grandpa ill. by Patricia Mullins. Watts, 1990. ISBN 0-531-08448-5 Subj: Behavior – growing up. Clothing. Cumulative tales. Family life – grandfathers. Poetry, rhyme.

Wilfrid Gordon McDonald Partridge ill. by Julie Vivas. Kane/Miller, 1985. ISBN 0-916291-04-9 Subj: Behavior – forgetfulness. Old age.

With love, at Christmas ill. by Gary Lippincott. Abingdon Pr., 1988. ISBN 0-687-45863-3 Subj: Character traits – generosity. Death. Holidays – Christmas.

Fox, Siv Cedering. *The blue horse and other night poems* ill. by Donald Carrick. Seabury Pr., 1979. Subj: Bedtime. Poetry, rhyme.

The fox went out on a chilly night ill. by Peter Spier. Doubleday, 1961. Subj: Animals – foxes. Caldecott award honor book. Folk and fairy tales. Songs. Toys – teddy bears.

Fradon, Dana. *Sir Dana—a knight: as told by his trusty armor* ill. by author. Dutton, 1988. ISBN 0-525-44424-6 Subj: Knights. Middle ages. Museums.

Franceschelli, Christopher. *The bear's cave* (Schindler, Regina)

Francis, Anna B. *Pleasant dreams* ill. by author. Holt, 1983. Subj: Dreams. Monsters. Toys.

Francis, Frank. *The magic wallpaper* ill. by author. Abelard-Schuman, 1970. Subj: Animals. Behavior – lost. Dreams. Imagination.

Natasha's new doll ill. by author. O'Hara, 1971. Subj: Folk and fairy tales. Foreign lands – Russia. Toys – dolls. Witches.

Françoise *see* Seignobosc, Françoise

Frank, Josette. *More poems to read to the very young* ill. by Dagmar Wilson. Random House, 1968. Subj: Poetry, rhyme.

Poems to read to the very young ill. by Dagmar Wilson. Random House, 1988. ISBN 0-394-99768-9 Subj: Poetry, rhyme.

Frankel, Ben. *Tertius and Pliny* ill. by Emma Chichester Clark. Harcourt, 1992. ISBN 0-15-200604-4 Subj: Friendship. Toys.

Frankel, Bernice. *Half-As-Big and the tiger* ill. by Leonard Weisgard. Watts, 1961. Subj: Animals – deer. Animals – tigers. Character traits – cleverness.

Frankenberg, Lloyd. *Wings of rhyme* ill. by Alan Benjamin. Funk & Wagnalls, 1967. Subj: Nursery rhymes. Poetry, rhyme.

Franklin, Jonathan. *Don't wake the baby* ill. by author. Farrar, 1991. ISBN 0-374-31826-3 Subj: Babies. Family life – brothers. Family life – sisters. Imagination. Sibling rivalry.

Franklin, Paula. *Killian and the dragons* (Company González, Mercè)

Franklin, Sheila. *Egyptian art from the Brooklyn Museum: ABC* (Mayers, Florence Cassen)

The Museum of Fine Arts, Boston: ABC (Mayers, Florence Cassen)

The Museum of Modern Art, New York: ABC (Mayers, Florence Cassen)

The National Air and Space Museum: ABC (Mayers, Florence Cassen)

Frascino, Edward. *My cousin the king* ill. by author. Prentice-Hall, 1985. ISBN 0-13-608423-0 Subj: Animals. Animals – cats. Character traits – cleverness. Character traits – vanity.

Nanny Noony and the dust queen ill. by author. Pippin Pr., 1990. ISBN 0-945912-09-9 Subj: Animals – cats. Farms. Magic. Weather – droughts. Witches.

Nanny Noony and the magic spell ill. by author. Pippin Pr., 1988. ISBN 0-945912-00-5 Subj: Animals – cats. Birds – crows. Farms. Magic. Witches.

Frasconi, Antonio. *See again, say again: a picture book in four languages* ill. by author. Harcourt, 1964. Subj: Foreign languages.

See and say: a picture book in four languages ill. by author. Harcourt, 1955. Subj: Foreign languages.

The snow and the sun, la nieve y el sol: a South American folk rhyme in two languages ill. by author. Harcourt, 1961. Subj: Folk and fairy tales. Foreign lands – South America. Foreign languages. Poetry, rhyme.

Fraser, Ferrin. *Jungle animals* (Buck, Frank)

Fraser, James Howard. *Los Posadas: a Christmas story* ill. by Nick De Grazia. Northland, 1963. Subj: Ethnic groups in the U.S. – Mexican-Americans. Foreign lands – Mexico. Holidays – Christmas. Religion.

Fraser, Kathleen. *Adam's world, San Francisco* ill. by Helen D. Hipshman. Albert Whitman, 1971. Subj: City. Ethnic groups in the U.S. – Afro-Americans. Family life.

Fraser, Phyllis Maurine. *Mother Goose* (Mother Goose)

Mother Goose (Mother Goose)

Frasier, Debra. *On the day you were born* ill. by author. Harcourt, 1991. ISBN 0-15-257995-8 Subj: Babies. Birth. Poetry, rhyme.

Freedman, Florence B. *Brothers: a Hebrew legend* ill. by Robert Andrew Parker. Harper, 1985. ISBN 0-06-021872-X Subj: Emotions – love. Family life – brothers. Folk and fairy tales. Jewish culture.

Freedman, Russell. *Farm babies* photos. by author. Holiday, 1981. Subj: Animals. Farms.

Hanging on: how animals carry their young ill. by author. Holiday, 1977. Subj: Animals. Science.

Tooth and claw: a look at animal weapons photos. by author. Holiday, 1980. Subj: Animals. Science.

When winter comes ill. by Pamela Johnson. Dutton, 1981. Subj: Animals. Science. Seasons – winter.

Freedman, Sally. *Devin's new bed* ill. by Robin Oz. Albert Whitman, 1986. ISBN 0-8075-1565-5 Subj: Bedtime. Behavior – growing up. Furniture – beds.

Monster birthday party ill. by Diane Dawson. Albert Whitman, 1983. Subj: Birthdays. Monsters. Parties.

Freeman, Don. *Add-a-line alphabet* ill. by author. Golden Gate, 1968. Subj: ABC books. Animals.

Beady Bear ill. by author. Viking, 1954. Subj: Behavior – running away. Toys – teddy bears.

Bearymore ill. by author. Viking, 1976. Subj: Animals – bears. Circus. Hibernation.

The chalk box story ill. by author. Lippincott, 1976. Subj: Activities – painting. Concepts – color.

Come again, pelican ill. by author. Viking, 1961. Subj: Birds – pelicans. Sea and seashore.

Corduroy ill. by author. Viking, 1968. Subj: Clothing. Emotions – love. Ethnic groups in the U.S. – Afro-Americans. Stores. Toys – teddy bears.

Corduroy's busy street and Corduroy goes to the doctor ill. by author. Live Oak Media, 1989. ISBN 0-87499-133-1 Subj: Careers – doctors. Communities, neighborhoods. Format, unusual – board books. Toys – teddy bears.

Corduroy's party ill. by Lisa McCue. Viking, 1985. ISBN 0-670-80520-3 Subj: Birthdays. Format, unusual – board books. Parties. Toys. Toys – teddy bears.

Cyrano the crow ill. by author. Viking, 1960. Subj: Birds – crows.

Dandelion ill. by author. Viking, 1964. Subj: Animals – lions. Character traits – appearance. Parties. Weather – rain.

The day is waiting ill. by author; words by Linda Z. Knab. Viking, 1980. ISBN 0-670-71820-3 Subj: Activities. Poetry, rhyme.

Fly high, fly low ill. by author. Viking, 1957. Subj: Birds. Caldecott award honor book. City.

Forever laughter ill. by author. Golden Gate, 1970. Subj: Clowns, jesters. Humor. Royalty. Wordless.

The guard mouse ill. by author. Viking, 1967. Subj: Animals – mice. Birthdays. City. Foreign lands – England.

Hattie the backstage bat ill. by author. Viking, 1970. Subj: Animals – bats. Theater.

Mop Top ill. by author. Viking, 1955. Subj: Birthdays. Careers – barbers. Hair. Poetry, rhyme.

The night the lights went out ill. by author. Viking, 1958. Subj: Careers. Night. Power failure. Seasons – winter.

Norman the doorman ill. by author. Viking, 1959. Subj: Animals – mice. Art. Museums.

The paper party ill. by author. Viking, 1974. Subj: Imagination. Parties. Puppets.

Pet of the Met (Freeman, Lydia)

A pocket for Corduroy ill. by author. Viking, 1978. Subj: Clothing. Ethnic groups in the U.S. – Afro-Americans. Laundry. Toys – teddy bears.

Quiet! There's a canary in the library ill. by author. Golden Gate, 1969. Subj: Birds – canaries. Emotions – embarrassment. Imagination. Libraries.

A rainbow of my own ill. by author. Viking, 1966. Subj: Concepts – color. Weather – rainbows.

The seal and the slick ill. by author. Viking, 1974. Subj: Animals – seals. Character traits – kindness to animals. Ecology. Oil.

Ski pup ill. by author. Viking, 1963. Subj: Animals – dogs. Foreign lands – Switzerland. Sports – skiing.

Space witch ill. by author. Viking, 1959. Subj: Holidays – Halloween. Space and space ships. Witches.

Tilly Witch ill. by author. Viking, 1969. Subj: Character traits – meanness. Holidays – Halloween. Witches.

The turtle and the dove ill. by author. Viking, 1964. Subj: Birds – doves. Reptiles – turtles, tortoises.

Will's quill ill. by author. Viking, 1975. Subj: Birds – geese. Foreign lands – England. Shakespeare. Theater.

Freeman, Ira. *The sun, the moon and the stars* (Freeman, Mae)

You will go to the moon (Freeman, Mae)

Freeman, Jean Todd. *Cynthia and the unicorn* ill. by Leonard Weisgard. Norton, 1967. Subj: Holi days – Christmas. Mythical creatures – unicorns. Poetry, rhyme.

Freeman, Lydia. *Corduroy's day* ill. by Lisa McCue. Viking, 1985. ISBN 0-670-80521-1 Subj: Counting, numbers. Format, unusual – board books. Toys – teddy bears.

Pet of the Met ill. by Don Freeman. Viking, 1953. Subj: Animals – mice. Music. Theater.

Freeman, Mae. *The sun, the moon and the stars* by Mae and Ira Freeman; ill. by René Martin Rev. ed. Random House, 1979. Subj: Moon. Science. Stars. Sun.

You will go to the moon ill. by Lee J. Ames Rev. ed. Random House, 1971. Subj: Moon. Space and space ships.

Fregosi, Claudia. *The happy horse* ill. by author. Greenwillow, 1977. Subj: Animals – horses. Seasons – fall.

The pumpkin sparrow: adapt. from a Korean folktale ill. by author. Morrow, 1977. Subj: Birds – sparrows. Folk and fairy tales. Foreign lands – Korea.

Snow maiden ill. by author. Prentice-Hall, 1979. Subj: Folk and fairy tales. Foreign lands – Russia.

French, Fiona. *Anancy and Mr. Dry-Bone* ill. by author. Little, 1991. ISBN 0-316-29298-2 Subj: Animals. Clothing. Folk and fairy tales.

The blue bird ill. by author. Walck, 1972. Subj: Birds.

Hunt the thimble ill. by author. Oxford Univ. Pr., 1978. Subj: Games. Participation.

Rise and shine ill. by adaptor. Little, 1989. ISBN 0-316-29299-0 Subj: Boats, ships. Religion – Noah. Songs.

Snow White in New York ill. by author. Oxford Univ. Pr., 1987. ISBN 0-19-279808-1 Subj: City. Crime. Family life – step families.

French, Paul see Asimov, Isaac

French, Vivian. *One ballerina two* ill. by Jan Ormerod. Lothrop, 1991. ISBN 0-688-10334-0 Subj: Activities – dancing. Counting, numbers.

Freschet, Berniece. *The ants go marching* ill. by Stefan Martin. Scribner's, 1973. Subj: Activities – picnicking. Counting, numbers. Insects – ants. Poetry, rhyme.

Bear mouse ill. by Donald Carrick. Scribner's, 1973. Subj: Animals – mice. Science.

Bernard of Scotland Yard ill. by Gina Freschet. Scribner's, 1978. Subj: Animals – mice. Foreign lands – England. Problem solving.

Elephant and friends ill. by Glen Rounds. Scribner's, 1978. Subj: Animals – elephants. Character traits – cleverness.

Five fat raccoons ill. by Irene Brady. Scribner's, 1980. Subj: Animals – raccoons.

Furlie Cat ill. by Betsy Lewin. Lothrop, 1986. ISBN 0-688-05918-X Subj: Animals – cats. Behavior – bullying. Emotions – fear.

The little woodcock ill. by Leonard Weisgard. Scribner's, 1967. Subj: Birds. Science.

Moose baby ill. by Jim Arnosky. Putnam's, 1979. Subj: Animals – moose. Science.

The old bullfrog ill. by Roger Antoine Duvoisin. Scribner's, 1968. Subj: Frogs and toads.

Owl in the garden ill. by Carol Newsom. Lothrop, 1985. ISBN 0-688-04048-9 Subj: Animals. Behavior – stealing. Birds. Birds – owls. Seasons – fall.

Possum baby ill. by Jim Arnosky. Putnam's, 1978. Subj: Animals – possums.

Turtle pond ill. by Donald Carrick. Scribner's, 1971. Subj: Reptiles – turtles, tortoises.

The watersnake ill. by Susanne Suba. Scribner's, 1979. Subj: Reptiles – snakes.

The web in the grass ill. by Roger Antoine Duvoisin. Scribner's, 1972. Subj: Spiders.

Where's Henrietta's hen? ill. by Lorinda Bryan Cauley. Putnam's, 1980. Subj: Animals. Birds – chickens. Counting, numbers. Farms.

Wood duck baby ill. by Jim Arnosky. Putnam's, 1983. Subj: Birds – ducks. Science.

Freudberg, Judy. *Some, more, most* ill. by Richard Hefter. Larousse, 1976. Subj: Concepts.

Susan and Gordon adopt a baby by Judy Freudberg and Tony Geiss; ill. by Joseph Mathieu. Random House, 1986. ISBN 0-394-98341-6 Subj: Adoption. Family life. Sibling rivalry.

Fribourg, Marjorie G. *Ching-Ting and the ducks* ill. by Artur Marokvia. Sterling, 1957. Subj: Behavior – growing up. Birds – ducks. Foreign lands – China.

Friedman, Ina R. *How my parents learned to eat* ill. by Allen Say. Houghton, 1984. Subj: Family life.

Friedrich, Otto. *The Easter bunny that overslept* (Friedrich, Priscilla)

The marshmallow ghosts (Friedrich, Priscilla)

The wishing well in the woods (Friedrich, Priscilla)

Friedrich, Priscilla. *The Easter bunny that overslept* by Priscilla and Otto Friedrich; ill. by Adrienne Adams. Lothrop, 1957. Subj: Holidays – Easter.

The marshmallow ghosts by Priscilla and Otto Friedrich; ill. by Louis Slobodkin. Lothrop, 1960. Subj: Ghosts. Holidays – Halloween.

The wishing well in the woods by Priscilla and Otto Friedrich; ill. by Roger Antoine Duvoisin.

Lothrop, 1961. Subj: Animals. Behavior – wishing.

The friendly beasts ill. by Sarah Chamberlain. Dutton, 1991. ISBN 0-525-44773-3 Subj: Animals. Holidays – Christmas. Music. Religion.

The friendly beasts and A partridge in a pear tree ill. by Virginia Parsons; calligraphy by Sheila Waters. Doubleday, 1977. Subj: Holidays – Christmas. Music. Religion. Songs.

Friskey, Margaret (Margaret Richards). *Birds we know* ill. with photos. Children's Pr., 1981. Subj: Birds. Science.

Chicken Little, count-to-ten ill. by Katherine Evans. Children's Pr., 1946. Subj: Counting, numbers.

Indian Two Feet and his eagle feather ill. by John and Lucy Hawkinson. Children's Pr., 1967. Subj: Indians of North America.

Indian Two Feet and his horse ill. by Katherine Evans. Children's Pr., 1959. Subj: Animals – horses. Indians of North America.

Indian Two Feet and the wolf cubs ill. by John Hawkinson. Children's Pr., 1971. Subj: Animals – wolves. Indians of North America.

Indian Two Feet rides alone ill. by John Hawkinson. Children's Pr., 1980. Subj: Character traits – pride. Indians of North America.

Mystery of the gate sign ill. by Katherine Evans. Children's Pr., 1958. Subj: Activities – reading. Animals – rabbits.

Seven diving ducks ill. by Jean Morey. Children's Pr., 1965. Subj: Birds – ducks. Counting, numbers.

Three sides and the round one ill. by Mary Gehr. Children's Pr., 1973. Subj: Concepts – shape.

Frith, Michael K. *I'll teach my dog 100 words* ill. by P. D. Eastman. Random House, 1973. Subj: Animals – dogs. Humor. Poetry, rhyme.

Some of us walk, some fly, some swim ill. by author. Random House, 1971. Subj: Animals. Science.

Fritz, Jean. *The good giants and the bad Pukwudgies* ill. by Tomie de Paola. Putnam's, 1982. Subj: Indians of North America. Folk and fairy tales. Giants.

A frog he would a-wooing go (folk-song). *Frog went a-courtin'* adapt. and ill. by Feodor Rojankovsky. Harcourt, 1955. Subj: Caldecott award book. Frogs and toads. Humor. Songs.

Froggie went a-courting retold and ill. by Chris Conover. Farrar, 1986. ISBN 0-374-32466-2 Subj: Animals. Frogs and toads. Music. Songs. Weddings.

Wendy Watson's frog went a-courting ill. by Wendy Watson. Lothrop, 1990. ISBN 0-688-06540-6 Subj: Animals. Frogs and toads. Music. Songs. Weddings.

Froissart, Bénédicte. *Uncle Henry's dinner guests* ill. by Pierre Pratt. Firefly, 1990. ISBN 1-55037-141-X Subj: Birds – chickens. Clothing. Family life – aunts, uncles.

From King Boggen's hall to nothing-at-all: *a collection of improbable houses and unusual places found in traditional rhymes and limericks* ill. by Blair Lent. Little, 1967. Subj: Animals. Nursery rhymes.

From morn to midnight sel. by Elaine Moss; ill. by Satomi Ichikawa. Crowell, 1977. ISBN 0-690-01394-9 Subj: Poetry, rhyme.

Froman, Robert. *Angles are easy as pie* ill. by Byron Barton. Crowell, 1976. Subj: Concepts.

A game of functions ill. by Enrico Arno. Crowell, 1975. Subj: Concepts.

Froment, Eugène. *The story of a round loaf* adapt. and ill. by Kathleen Rebek. Prentice-Hall, 1979. Subj: Behavior – misbehavior. Foreign lands – France.

Fromm, Lilo. *Muffel and Plums* ill. by author. Macmillan, 1972. Subj: Animals. Wordless.

Frost, Erica *see* Supraner, Robyn

Frost, Robert. *Stopping by woods on a snowy evening* ill. by Susan Jeffers. Dutton, 1978. Subj: Forest, woods. Poetry, rhyme. Seasons – winter.

Fry, Christopher. *The boat that mooed* ill. by Leonard Weisgard. Macmillan, 1965. Subj: Boats, ships. Weather – fog.

The boy and the magic (Colette)

Frye, Dean. *Days of sunshine, days of rain* ill. by Roger Antoine Duvoisin. McGraw-Hill, 1965. Subj: Theater. Weather.

Fuchs, Erich. *Journey to the moon* ill. by author. Delacorte Pr., 1969. Translation of Hier Apollo 11 Subj: Moon. Space and space ships. Wordless.

Fuchshuber, Annegert. *Giant story—Mouse tale: a half picture book* ill. by author. Carolrhoda Books, 1988. ISBN 0-87614-319-2 Subj: Animals – mice. Character traits – bravery. Format, unusual. Friendship. Giants.

The wishing hat ill. by author. Morrow, 1977. Translation of Korbinian mit dem Wunschhut by Elizabeth D. Crawford Subj: Behavior – wishing. Humor. Magic.

Fujikawa, Gyo. *Gyo Fujikawa's A to Z picture book* ill. by author. Grosset, 1974. Subj: ABC books.

Let's grow a garden ill. by author. Grosset, 1978. Subj: Format, unusual – board books. Gardens, gardening.

Millie's secret ill. by author. Grosset, 1978. Subj: Animals – dogs. Format, unusual – board books. Wordless.

My favorite thing ill. by author. Grosset, 1978. Subj: Activities. Format, unusual – board books. Wordless.

Sam's all-wrong day ill. by author. Grosset, 1982. Subj: Behavior – bad day.

Shags finds a kitten ill. by author. Grosset, 1983. Subj: Animals – cats. Animals – dogs. Emotions – loneliness.

Surprise! Surprise! ill. by author. Grosset, 1978. Subj: Activities. Format, unusual – board books.

That's not fair! ill. by author. Grosset, 1983. Subj: Activities – playing. Seasons – winter.

Fujita, Tamao. *The boy and the bird* tr. from Japanese by Kiyoko Tucker; ill. by Chiyo Ono. Harper, 1972. Subj: Birds. Character traits – freedom. Foreign lands – Japan. Pets.

Fuller, Ted. *Barney the bus* ill. by Pamela DeVito. Windswept House, 1989. ISBN 0-932433-49-9 Subj: Buses.

Funai, Mamoru. *Moke and Poki in the rain forest* ill. by author. Harper, 1972. Subj: Elves and little people. Hawaii.

Funakoshi, Canna. *One Christmas* ill. by Yohji Izawa. Picture Book Studio, 1990. ISBN 0-88708-140-1 Subj: Holidays – Christmas.

One evening tr. and ill. by Yohji Izawa. Picture Book Studio, 1988. ISBN 0-88708-063-4 Subj: Night. Seasons – winter. Weather – snow.

One morning ill. by Yohji Izawa. Picture Book Studio, 1986. ISBN 0-88707-033-2 Subj: Animals – cats. Morning.

Funazaki, Yasuko. *Baby owl* ill. by Shuji Tateishi. Methune, 1980. Subj: Birds – owls. Emotions – loneliness.

Funk, Tom (Thompson). *I read signs* ill. by author. Holiday, 1962. Subj: Activities – reading.

Furchgott, Terry. *Phoebe and the hot water bottles* by Terry Furchgott and Linda Dawson; ill. by Terry Furchgott. Elsevier-Dutton, 1979. Subj: Animals – dogs. Character traits – bravery. Pets.

Furtado, Jo. *Sorry, Miss Folio!* ill. by Frederic Joos. Kane/Miller, 1988. ISBN 0-916291-18-9 Subj: Activities – reading. Imagination. Libraries.

Fussenegger, Gertrud. *Noah's ark* ill. by Annegert Fuchshuber. Lippincott, 1987. Tr. of Die Arche Noah by Anthea Bell ISBN 0-397-32242-9 Subj: Animals. Boats, ships. Religion – Noah.

Futamata, Eigorō. *How not to catch a mouse* ill. by author. Weatherhill, 1972. Translation of Nezumi wa tsukamaru ka. Subj: Animals. Animals – mice.

Fyleman, Rose. *A fairy went a-marketing* ill. by Jamichael Henterly. Dutton, 1986. ISBN 0-525-44258-8 Subj: Character traits – kindness. Fairies. Poetry, rhyme. Shopping.

Gabel, Susan L. *Where the sun kisses the sea* ill. by Joanne Bowring. Perspectives Pr., 1989. ISBN 0-944934-00-5 Subj: Adoption. Ethnic groups in the U.S. – Asian-Americans. Orphans.

Gackenbach, Dick. *Alice's special room* ill. by author. Houghton, 1991. ISBN 0-395-54433-5 Subj: Family life – mothers.

Annie and the mud monster ill. by author. Lothrop, 1982. Subj: Parties.

Arabella and Mr. Crack ill. by author. Macmillan, 1982. A retelling of Joseph Jacob's Master of all masters. Subj: Behavior – misunderstanding. Folk and fairy tales.

A bag full of pups ill. by author. Houghton, 1981. Subj: Animals – dogs.

Binky gets a car ill. by author. Houghton, 1983. Subj: Behavior – carelessness. Birthdays.

Claude and Pepper ill. by author. Coward, 1976. Subj: Animals – dogs. Behavior – running away.

Claude the dog ill. by author. Seabury Pr., 1974. Subj: Animals – dogs. Behavior – sharing. Holidays – Christmas.

Crackle, Gluck and the sleeping toad ill. by author. Seabury Pr., 1979. Subj: Behavior – lying. Farms. Frogs and toads.

The dog and the deep dark woods ill. by author. Harper, 1984. Subj: Animals – dogs. Character traits – pride.

Dog for a day ill. by author. Clarion, 1987. ISBN 0-899-19452-4 Subj: Animals – dogs. Machines.

Harry and the terrible whatzit ill. by author. Seabury Pr., 1977. Subj: Emotions – fear. Imagination. Monsters.

Harvey, the foolish pig ill. by author. Clarion, 1988. ISBN 0-89919-540-7 Subj: Animals – pigs. Animals – wolves. Character traits – foolishness. Character traits – luck. Royalty – kings.

Hattie be quiet, Hattie be good ill. by author. Harper, 1977. Subj: Animals – rabbits. Behavior. Illness.

Hattie rabbit ill. by author. Harper, 1971. Subj: Animals – rabbits. Behavior – wishing.

Hurray for Hattie Rabbit! ill. by author. Harper, 1986. ISBN 0-06-021983-1 Subj: Animals – pigs. Animals – rabbits. Family life – mothers.

Ida Fanfanny ill. by author. Harper, 1978. Subj: Magic. Seasons. Weather.

King Wacky ill. by author. Crown, 1984. Subj: Behavior – misunderstanding. Royalty – kings.

Little bug ill. by author. Houghton, 1981. Subj: Behavior – seeking better things. Insects.

Mag the magnificent ill. by author. Clarion, 1985. ISBN 0-89919-339-0 Subj: Imagination. Monsters.

Mighty tree ill. by author. Harcourt, 1992. ISBN 0-15-200519-6 Subj: Nature. Trees.

Mr. Wink and his shadow, Ned ill. by author. Harper, 1983. Subj: Shadows.

Mother Rabbit's son Tom ill. by author. Harper, 1978. Subj: Animals – rabbits. Behavior – dissatisfaction. Food. Pets.

Pepper and all the legs ill. by author. Seabury Pr., 1978. Subj: Animals – dogs. Behavior – misbehavior.

The perfect mouse: a Japanese tale ill. by author. Macmillan, 1984. Subj: Animals – mice. Folk and fairy tales. Foreign lands – Japan.

The pig who saw everything ill. by author. Seabury Pr., 1978. Subj: Animals – pigs. Character traits – curiosity. Farms. Humor.

Poppy the panda ill. by author. Houghton, 1984. Subj: Bedtime. Clothing. Toys.

Supposes ill. by author. Harcourt, 1989. ISBN 0-15-200594-3 Subj: Animals. Imagination. Riddles.

What's Claude doing? ill. by author. Houghton, 1984. Subj: Animals – dogs. Illness.

With love from Gran ill. by author. Houghton, 1989. ISBN 0-89919-842-2 Subj: Activities – traveling. Family life – grandmothers.

Gadsby, Oliver. *Little Elephant and Big Mouse* (Cantieni, Benita)

Gaeddert, Lou Ann Bigge. *Noisy Nancy Nora* ill. by Gioia Fiammenghi. Doubleday, 1965. Subj: Behavior. Noise, sounds.

Gág, Flavia. *Chubby's first year* ill. by author. Holt, 1960. Subj: Animals – cats. Days of the week, months of the year.

Gág, Wanda. *ABC bunny* ill. by author; hand lettered by Howard Gág. Doubleday, 1965. Subj: ABC books. Animals – rabbits. Poetry, rhyme.

The earth gnome (Grimm, Jacob)

The funny thing ill. by author. Coward, 1929. Subj: Dragons. Food. Monsters.

Gone is gone ill. by author. Coward, 1935. Subj: Activities – working. Behavior – mistakes.

Jorinda and Joringel (Grimm, Jacob)

Millions of cats ill. by author. Coward, 1928. Subj: Animals – cats. Character traits – practicality. Cumulative tales.

Nothing at all ill. by author. Coward, 1941. Subj: Animals – dogs. Caldecott award honor book. Emotions – loneliness. Magic.

The six swans (Grimm, Jacob)

Snippy and Snappy ill. by author. Coward, 1931. Subj: Animals – mice.

The sorcerer's apprentice ill. by Margot Tomes. Coward, 1979. Subj: Behavior – misbehavior. Folk and fairy tales. Magic.

Gage, Wilson. *Anna's garden songs* ill. by Lena Castell Anderson. Greenwillow, 1989. ISBN 0-688-08218-1 Subj: Gardens, gardening. Plants. Poetry, rhyme.

Anna's summer songs ill. by Lena Castell Anderson. Greenwillow, 1988. ISBN 0-688-07181-3 Subj: Plants. Poetry, rhyme. Seasons – summer.

The crow and Mrs. Gaddy ill. by Marylin Hafner. Greenwillow, 1984. Subj: Behavior – trickery. Birds – crows.

Cully Cully and the bear ill. by James Stevenson. Greenwillow, 1983. Subj: Animals – bears. Sports – hunting.

Down in the boondocks ill. by Glen Rounds. Greenwillow, 1977. Subj: Crime. Handicaps – deafness. Poetry, rhyme.

Mrs. Gaddy and the fast-growing vine ill. by Marylin Hafner. Greenwillow, 1985. ISBN 0-688-04232-5 Subj: Animals – goats. Behavior – seeking better things. Gardens, gardening.

Mrs. Gaddy and the ghost ill. by Marylin Hafner. Greenwillow, 1979. Subj: Ghosts. Imagination.

Galbraith, Kathryn Osebold. *Katie did!* ill. by Ted Ramsey. Atheneum, 1982. Subj: Behavior – misbehavior. Family life. Sibling rivalry.

Laura Charlotte ill. by Floyd Cooper. Putnam, 1990. ISBN 0-399-21613-8 Subj: Family life – mothers. Toys.

Roommates ill. by Mark Graham. Macmillan, 1990. ISBN 0-689-50487-X Subj: Babies. Behavior – growing up. Family life – sisters. Sibling rivalry.

Spots are special ill. by Diane Dawson. Atheneum, 1976. Subj: Illness. Imagination.

Waiting for Jennifer ill. by Irene Trivas. Macmillan, 1987. ISBN 0-689-50430-6 Subj: Babies. Behavior – secrets. Family life.

Galbraith, Richard. *Reuben runs away* ill. by author. Watts, 1989. ISBN 0-531-08390-X Subj: Behavior – running away. Toys – teddy bears.

Galdone, Joanna. *Amber day* ill. by Paul Galdone. McGraw-Hill, 1978. Subj: Devil. Folk and fairy tales.

Gertrude, the goose who forgot ill. by Paul Galdone. Watts, 1975. Subj: Behavior – forgetfulness. Birds – geese. Poetry, rhyme.

Honeybee's party ill. by Paul Galdone. Watts, 1972. Subj: Insects – bees. Parties. Spiders.

The little girl and the big bear ill. by Paul Galdone. Houghton, 1980. Subj: Animals – bears. Folk and fairy tales.

The tailypo: a ghost story ill. by Paul Galdone. Seabury Pr., 1977. Subj: Ghosts. Poetry, rhyme.

Galdone, Paul. *The amazing pig: an old Hungarian tale* ill. by author. Houghton, 1981. Subj: Animals – pigs. Folk and fairy tales. Royalty.

Androcles and the lion ill. by author. McGraw-Hill, 1970. Subj: Animals – lions. Character traits – kindness to animals. Folk and fairy tales. Foreign lands – Italy.

Cat goes fiddle-i-fee ill. by adapt. Clarion Books, 1985. ISBN 0-89919-336-6 Subj: Animals. Cumulative tales. Nursery rhymes.

Counting carnival (Ziner, Feenie)

The first seven days ill. by author. Crowell, 1962. Subj: Religion.

The greedy old fat man: an American folk tale ill. by author. Houghton, 1983. Subj: Cumulative tales. Folk and fairy tales.

Hans in luck (Grimm, Jacob)

King of the cats: a ghost story by Joseph Jacobs; ill. by adapt. Houghton, 1980. Subj: Animals – cats. Folk and fairy tales. Ghosts.

The life of Jack Sprat, his wife and his cat (Jack Sprat)

Little Bo-Peep ill. by author. Ticknor & Fields, 1986. ISBN 0-89919-395-1 Subj: Animals – sheep. Nursery rhymes.

The magic porridge pot ill. by author. Seabury Pr., 1976. Subj: Behavior – forgetfulness. Behavior – sharing. Folk and fairy tales. Food. Magic.

The monkey and the crocodile: a Jataka tale from India ill. by author. Seabury Pr., 1969. Subj: Animals – monkeys. Character traits – cleverness. Folk and fairy tales. Reptiles – alligators, crocodiles.

The monster and the tailor: a ghost story ill. by author. Houghton, 1982. An adaptation of Joseph Jacobs' The sprightly tailor Subj: Careers – tailors. Ghosts. Monsters. Royalty.

Obedient Jack ill. by author. Watts, 1971. Subj: Behavior – mistakes. Family life. Folk and fairy tales.

Rumpelstiltskin (Grimm, Jacob)

A strange servant: a Russian folktale tr. by Blanche Ross; ill. by author. Knopf, 1977. Subj: Animals – rabbits. Behavior – trickery. Folk and fairy tales. Foreign lands – Russia.

The table, the donkey and the stick (Grimm, Jacob)

The teeny-tiny woman: a ghost story ill. by adapt. Clarion, 1984. ISBN 0-89919-270-X Subj: Emotions. Folk and fairy tales. Ghosts.

What's in fox's sack? ill. by author. Houghton, 1982. Subj: Character traits – cleverness. Folk and fairy tales.

Galinsky, Ellen. *The baby cardinal* photos. by author. Putnam's, 1977. Subj: Birds – cardinals.

Gallant, Kathryn. *The flute player of Beppu* ill. by Kurt Wiese. Coward, 1960. Subj: Character traits – honesty.

Gallaudet Pre-school Signed English Project. *Nursery rhymes from Mother Goose in signed English* (Mother Goose)

Gallo, Giovanni. *The lazy beaver* ill. by Ermanno Samsa; tr. from Italian by Jane Fior. Putnam's, 1983. Subj: Activities – working. Animals – beavers.

Gambill, Henrietta. *Self-control* ill. by Kathryn Hutton Rev. ed. Children's Pr., 1982. Subj: Behavior. Ethnic groups in the U.S. – Afro-Americans.

Gammell, Stephen. *Git along, old Scudder* ill. by author. Lothrop, 1983. Subj: Old age.

Once upon MacDonald's farm ill. by author. Four Winds Pr., 1981. Subj: Animals. Farms.

The story of Mr. and Mrs. Vinegar ill. by author. Lothrop, 1982. Subj: Character traits – foolishness. Folk and fairy tales.

Wake up, bear ... It's Christmas! ill. by author. Morrow, 1990. ISBN 0-688-09934-3 Subj: Animals – bears. Hibernation. Holidays – Christmas.

Ganly, Helen. *Jyoti's journey* ill. by author. Dutton, 1986. ISBN 0-233-97899-2 Subj: Family life. Foreign lands – England. Foreign lands – India. Weddings.

Gannett, Ruth S. *Katie and the sad noise* ill. by Ellie Simmons. Random House, 1961. Subj: Animals – dogs. Character traits – kindness. Holidays – Christmas. Noise, sounds.

Gans, Roma. *Hummingbirds in the garden* ill. by Grambs Miller. Crowell, 1969. Subj: Birds. Gardens, gardening. Seasons – summer.

Rock collecting ill. by Holly Keller. Crowell, 1984. Subj: Behavior – collecting things. Rocks. Science.

When birds change their feathers ill. by Felicia Bond. Crowell, 1980. Subj: Birds. Science.

Gant, Elizabeth. *Little Red Riding Hood* (Grimm, Jacob)

Gant, Katherine. *Little Red Riding Hood* (Grimm, Jacob)

Gantos, Jack (John, Jr.). *Aunt Bernice* ill. by Nicole Rubel. Houghton, 1978. Subj: Behavior – carelessness. Family life – aunts, uncles.

Greedy Greeny ill. by Nicole Rubel. Doubleday, 1979. Subj: Dreams. Monsters.

Happy birthday, Rotten Ralph ill. by Nicole Rubel. Houghton, 1990. ISBN 0-395-53766-5 Subj: Animals – cats. Behavior – misbehavior. Birthdays.

The perfect pal ill. by Nicole Rubel. Houghton, 1979. Subj: Animals. Pets.

Rotten Ralph ill. by Nicole Rubel. Houghton, 1976. Subj: Animals – cats. Behavior – misbehavior.

Rotten Ralph's rotten Christmas ill. by Nicole Rubel. Houghton, 1984. Subj: Animals – cats. Character traits – meanness. Emotions – envy, jealousy. Holidays – Christmas.

Rotten Ralph's show and tell ill. by Nicole Rubel. Houghton, 1989. ISBN 0-395-44312-1 Subj: Animals – cats. Character traits – meanness. School.

Rotten Ralph's trick or treat ill. by Nicole Rubel. Houghton, 1986. ISBN 0-395-38943-7 Subj: Animals – cats. Character traits – meanness. Holidays – Halloween.

Swampy alligator ill. by Nicole Rubel. Windmill, 1980. Subj: Birthdays. Character traits – cleanliness. Reptiles – alligators, crocodiles.

The werewolf family ill. by Nicole Rubel. Houghton, 1980. Subj: Monsters.

Worse than Rotten Ralph ill. by Nicole Rubel. Houghton, 1978. Subj: Animals – cats. Behavior – misbehavior. Character traits – meanness.

Gantschev, Ivan. *The Christmas train* ill. by author; tr. from German by Karen M. Klockner. Little, 1984. Subj: Character traits – bravery. Holidays – Christmas. Trains.

Journey of the storks ill. by author. Alphabet Pr., 1983. Subj: Birds – storks.

The moon lake tr. by Oliver Gadsby; ill. by author. Alphabet Pr., 1981. Subj: Moon.

Otto the bear tr. from German by Karen M. Klockner; ill. by author. Little, 1986. ISBN 0-316-30348-8 Subj: Animals – bears. Character traits – kindness to animals.

RumpRump ill. by author. Alphabet Pr., 1984. Subj: Animals – bears. Food. Friendship.

Santa's favorite story (Aoki, Hisako)

The train to Grandma's ill. by author. Picture Book Studio, 1987. ISBN 0-88708-053-7 Subj: Activities – traveling. Family life – grandparents. Format, unusual. Islands. Trains.

Where is Mr. Mole? adapt. by Andrew Clements; ill. by author. Picture Book Studio, 1989. ISBN 0-88708-109-6 Subj: Animals – moles. Behavior – seeking better things. Birds – owls. Format, unusual.

Gantz, David. *Captain Swifty counts to 50* ill. by author. Doubleday, 1982. Subj: Counting, numbers.

The genie bear with the light brown hair word book ill. by author. Doubleday, 1982. Subj: ABC books. Animals – bears. Animals – mice.

Ganz, Yaffa. *The story of Mimmy and Simmy* ill. by Harvey Klineman. Feldheim, 1985. ISBN 0-87306-385-6 Subj: Behavior – seeking better things. Emotions – envy, jealousy. Jewish culture.

Garaway, Margaret Kahn. *Ashkii and his grandfather* ill. by Harry Warren. Treasure Chest, 1989. ISBN 0-918080-41-X Subj: Careers – shepherds. Family life – grandfathers. Indians of North America.

Garbutt, Bernard. *Roger, the rosin back* ill. by author. Hastings, 1961. Subj: Animals – horses. Circus.

García Lorca, Federico. *The Lieutenant Colonel and the gypsy* tr. and ill. by Marc Simont. Doubleday, 1971. Subj: Foreign lands – Spain. Gypsies. Poetry, rhyme.

Gardam, Catharine. *The animals' Christmas* ill. by Gavin Rowe. Macmillan, 1990. ISBN 0-689-50502-7 Subj: Animals. Holidays – Christmas.

Gardner, Beau. *Can you imagine...? a counting book* ill. by author. Dodd, 1987. ISBN 0-396-09001-X Subj: Animals. Counting, numbers.

Guess what? ill. by author. Lothrop, 1985. ISBN 0-688-04983-4 Subj: Animals. Concepts – shape. Games.

Have you ever seen...? an ABC book ill. by author. Dodd, 1986. ISBN 0-396-08825-2 Subj: ABC books. Humor.

The look again...and again, and again, and again book ill. by author. Lothrop, 1984. Subj: Optical illusions.

The turn about, think about, look about book ill. by author. Lothrop, 1980. Subj: Optical illusions.

What is it? ill. by author. Putnam, 1989. ISBN 0-399-21664-2 Subj: Concepts – shape. Format, unusual – toy and movable books. Games.

Whooo's a fright on Halloween night? ill. by author. Putnam, 1990. ISBN 0-399-22212-X Subj: Format, unusual – toy and movable books. Holidays – Halloween. Poetry, rhyme.

Gardner, Martin. *Never make fun of a turtle, my son* ill. by John Alcorn. Simon & Schuster, 1969. ISBN 0-671-65033-5 Subj: Etiquette. Poetry, rhyme.

Gardner, Mercedes. *Scooter and the magic star* by Mercedes and Jean Shannon Smith; ill. by Bob Johnson. Atheneum, 1980. Subj: Fairies.

Garelick, May. *Down to the beach* ill. by Barbara Cooney. Four Winds Pr., 1973. Subj: Sea and seashore. Seasons – summer.

Just my size ill. by William Pene du Bois. HarperCollins, 1990. ISBN 0-06-022419-3 Subj: Behavior – growing up. Clothing – coats. Toys – dolls.

Look at the moon ill. by Leonard Weisgard. Addison-Wesley, 1969. Subj: Animals. Moon. Poetry, rhyme.

Sounds of a summer night ill. by Beni Montresor. Addison-Wesley, 1963. Subj: Night. Noise, sounds.

The tremendous tree book by May Garelick and Barbara Brenner; ill. by Fred Brenner. Four Winds Pr., 1979. Subj: Science. Trees.

Two orphan cubs (Brenner, Barbara A.)

Where does the butterfly go when it rains? ill. by Leonard Weisgard. Addison-Wesley, 1961. Subj: Insects – butterflies, caterpillars. Poetry, rhyme. Weather – rain.

Garfinkel, Bernard *see* Allen, Robert

Garland, Michael. *My cousin Katie* ill. by author. HarperColins, 1989. ISBN 0-690-04740-1 Subj: Family life. Farms.

Garland, Sarah. *All gone!* ill. by author. Viking, 1990. ISBN 0-670-83074-7 Subj: Babies. Concepts.

Billy and Belle ill. by author. Viking, 1992. ISBN 0-670-84396-2 Subj: Animals. Babies. Family life – sisters. Pets. School.

Going shopping ill. by author. Little, 1985. ISBN 0-87113-001-7 Subj: Family life. Shopping.

Having a picnic ill. by author. Little, 1985. ISBN 0-87113-002-5 Subj: Activities – picnicking. Birds – ducks. Family life.

Polly's puffin ill. by author. Greenwillow, 1989. ISBN 0-688-08749-3 Subj: Babies. Behavior – losing things. City.

Garrett, Jennifer. *The queen who stole the sky* ill. by Linda Hendry. North Winds Pr., 1986. ISBN 0-590-71524-0 Subj: Character traits – selfishness. Character traits – stubbornness. Royalty – queens.

Garrison, Christian. *The dream eater* ill. by Diane Goode. Dutton, 1978. Subj: Dragons. Dreams. Foreign lands – Japan.

Little pieces of the west wind ill. by Diane Goode. Dutton, 1975. Subj: Cumulative tales. Weather – wind.

Garten, Jan. *The alphabet tale* ill. by Muriel Batherman. Random House, 1964. Subj: ABC books. Animals. Participation. Poetry, rhyme.

Gascoigne, Bamber. *Why the rope went tight* ill. by Christina Gascoigne. Lothrop, 1981. Subj: Circus.

Gaston, Susan. *New boots for Salvador* ill. by Lydia Schwartz. Ritchie, 1972. Subj: Animals – horses.

Gauch, Patricia Lee. *Bravo, Tanya* ill. by Satomi Ichikawa. Putnam, 1992. ISBN 0-399-22145-X Subj: Activities – dancing. Toys – teddy bears.

Christina Katerina and the time she quit the family ill. by Elise Primavera. Putnam's, 1987. ISBN 0-399-21408-9 Subj: Behavior – needing someone. Family life. Sibling rivalry.

Dance, Tanya ill. by Satomi Ichikawa. Putnam, 1989. ISBN 0-399-21521-2 Subj: Activities – dancing. Behavior – imitation. Toys – teddy bears.

The little friar who flew ill. by Tomie de Paola. Putnam's, 1980. Subj: Folk and fairy tales.

On to Widecombe Fair ill. by Trina Schart Hyman. Putnam's, 1978. Subj: Fairs. Folk and fairy tales. Foreign lands – England.

Once upon a Dinkelsbühl ill. by Tomie de Paola. Putnam's, 1977. Subj: War.

Gauthier, Bertrand. *Circus days* (Paré, Roger)

Gay, Marie-Louise. *Moonbeam on a cat's ear* ill. by author. Silver Burdett, 1986. ISBN 0-385-09162-0 Subj: Animals – cats. Animals – mice. Bedtime. Dreams. Moon. Poetry, rhyme.

Rainy day magic ill. by author. Albert Whitman, 1989. ISBN 0-8075-6767-1 Subj: Imagination. Family life. Illness. Poetry, rhyme. Weather – rain.

Gay, Michel. *Bibi takes flight* ill. by author. Morrow, 1988. ISBN 0-688-06829-4 Subj: Activities – flying. Airplanes, airports. Birds – penguins.

Bibi's birthday surprise ill. by author. Morrow, 1987. ISBN 0-688-06978-9 Subj: Animals. Birds – penguins. Parties. Royalty. Toys.

The Christmas wolf ill. by author. Greenwillow, 1983. ISBN 0-688-02291-X Subj: Animals – wolves. Holidays – Christmas.

Little auto ill. by author. Macmillan, 1986. ISBN 0-02-737900-0 Subj: Automobiles. Sea and seashore.

Little boat ill. by author. Macmillan, 1985. Subj: Boats, ships.

Little helicopter ill. by author. Macmillan, 1986. ISBN 0-02-737920-5 Subj: Character traits – smallness. Helicopters.

Little plane ill. by author. Macmillan, 1985. Subj: Airplanes, airports.

Little shoe ill. by author. Macmillan, 1986. ISBN 0-02-737890-X Subj: Behavior – losing things. Clothing – shoes.

Little truck ill. by author. Macmillan, 1985. Subj: Trucks. Transportation.

Night ride ill. by author. Morrow, 1987. ISBN 0-688-07287-9 Subj: Activities – traveling. Animals. Circus. Family life – fathers. Night.

Rabbit express ill. by author. Morrow, 1985. ISBN 0-688-04648-7 Subj: Animals – cats. Animals – rabbits. Friendship.

Take me for a ride ill. by author. Morrow, 1985. Subj: Behavior – lost.

Gay, Tenner Ottley. *Dinosaurs and their relatives in action* ill. by Jean Cassels. Macmillan, 1990. ISBN 0-689-71434-3 Subj: Dinosaurs. Format, unusual – toy and movable books.

Sharks in action ill. by Jean Cassels. Macmillan, 1990. ISBN 0-689-71435-1 Subj: Fish – sharks. Format, unusual – toy and movable books.

Gay, Zhenya. *I'm tired of lions* ill. by author. Viking, 1961. Subj: Animals – lions. Behavior – dissatisfaction.

Look! ill. by author. Viking, 1952. Subj: Animals. Libraries. Poetry, rhyme.

Small one ill. by author. Viking, 1958. Subj: Animals – rabbits. Behavior – lost.

Who's afraid? ill. by author. Viking, 1965. Subj: Emotions – fear.

Gebert, Warren. *The old ball and the sea* ill. by author. Bradbury Pr., 1988. ISBN 0-02-735821-6 Subj: Activities – playing. Sea and seashore.

Gedin, Birgitta. *The little house from the sea* tr. by Elisabeth Dyssegaard; ill. by Petter Pettersson. Farrar, 1988. ISBN 91-29-58770-0 Subj: Boats, ships. Houses. Sea and seashore. Weather – storms.

Geisel, Theodor Seuss *see* Seuss, Dr.

Geisert, Arthur. *The ark* ill. by author. Houghton, 1988. ISBN 0-395-43078-X Subj: Religion – Noah.

Geiss, Tony. *Susan and Gordon adopt a baby* (Freudberg, Judy)

Gekiere, Madeleine. *The frilly lily and the princess* ill. by author. Lippincott, 1960. Subj: Behavior – fighting, arguing. Royalty – princesses.

Gelbard, Jane. *My bye-bye bottle book* by Jane Gelbard and Betsy Bober Polivy; photos. by Arthur Klonsky. Grosset, 1989. ISBN 0-448-21526-8 Subj: Babies. Behavior – growing up. Format, unusual – board books. Poetry, rhyme.

My dressing book ill. by Jane Gelbard and Betsy Bober Polivy; photos. by Arthur Klonsky. Grosset, 1989. ISBN 0-448-21527-6 Subj: Babies. Behavior – growing up. Clothing. Format, unusual – board books. Poetry, rhyme.

My eating book ill. by Jane Gelbard and Betsy Bober Polivy; photos. by Arthur Klonsky. Grosset, 1989. ISBN 0-448-21528-4 Subj: Babies. Behavior – growing up. Food. Format, unusual – board books. Poetry, rhyme.

My sharing book ill. by Jane Gelbard and Betsy Bober Polivy; photos. by Arthur Klonsky. Grosset, 1989. ISBN 0-448-21529-2 Subj: Babies. Behavior – growing up. Behavior – sharing. Format, unusual – board books. Poetry, rhyme.

Gellman, Ellie. *It's Chanukah!* ill. by Katherine Janus Kahn. Kar-Ben Copies, 1985. ISBN 0-930494-51-2 Subj: Format, unusual – board books. Holidays – Hanukkah. Jewish culture.

It's Rosh Hashanah! ill. by Katherine Janus Kahn. Kar-Ben Copies, 1985. ISBN 0-930494-50-4 Subj: Format, unusual – board books. Holidays – Rosh Hashanah. Jewish culture.

Shai's Shabbat walk ill. by Chari R. McLean. Kar-Ben Copies, 1985. ISBN 0-930494-49-0 Subj: Format, unusual – board books. Holidays. Jewish culture.

Gelman, Amy. *Little big feet* (Schubert, Ingrid)

Gelman, Rita Golden. *Hey, kid* ill. by Carol Nicklaus. Watts, 1977. Subj: Humor. Poetry, rhyme.

A koala grows up ill. by Gioia Fiammenghi. Scholastic, 1986. ISBN 0-590-30563-8 Subj: Animals – koala bears. Science.

Splash! (Buxbaum, Susan Kovacs)

Gemme, Leila Boyle. *T-ball is our game* photos. by Richard Marshall. Children's Pr., 1978. Subj: Sports – T-ball.

Gemming, Elisabeth. *Sandy at the children's zoo* (Bolliger, Max)

George, Jean Craighead. *All upon a stone* ill. by Don Bolognese. Crowell, 1971. Subj: Insects. Science. Spiders.

The grizzly bear with the golden ears ill. by Tom Catania. Harper, 1982. Subj: Animals – bears.

The wentletrap trap ill. by Symeon Shimin. Dutton, 1978. Subj: Ethnic groups in the U.S. – Afro-Americans. Foreign lands – Caribbean Islands. Sea and seashore.

George, Lindsay Barrett. *Beaver at Long Pond* (George, William T.)

William and Boomer ill. by author. Greenwillow, 1987. ISBN 0-688-06641-0 Subj: Birds – geese. Pets. Sports – swimming.

George, William T. *Beaver at Long Pond* by William T. and Lindsay Barrett George; ill. by Lindsay Barrett George. Greenwillow, 1988. ISBN 0-688-07107-4 Subj: Animals – beavers. Nature. Night.

Box turtle at Long Pond ill. by Lindsay Barrett George. Greenwillow, 1989. ISBN 0-688-08185-1 Subj: Nature. Reptiles – turtles, tortoises.

Fishing at Long Pond ill. by Lindsay Barrett George. Greenwillow, 1991. ISBN 0-688-09402-3 Subj: Animals. Family life – grandfathers. Sports – fishing.

Georgiady, Nicholas P. *Gertie the duck* ill. by Dagmar Wilson. Follett, 1959. Subj: Birds – ducks. Character traits – kindness to animals.

Geraghty, Paul. *The cow is mooing anyhow* ill. by author. HarperCollins, 1991. ISBN 0-06-021987-4 Subj: ABC books. Animals. Poetry, rhyme.

Look out, Patrick! ill. by 90. Macmillan, 1990. ISBN 0-02-735822-4 Subj: Animals – mice. Character traits – luck.

Over the steamy swamp ill. by author. Harcourt, 1989. ISBN 0-15-200561-7 Subj: Animals. Insects. Nature.

Slobcat ill. by author. Macmillan, 1991. ISBN 0-02-735825-9 Subj: Animals – cats. Character traits – laziness.

Gerez, Toni De *see* De Gerez, Toni

Gergely, Tibor. *Wheel on the chimney* (Brown, Margaret Wise)

Geringer, Laura. *Look out, look out, it's coming!* ill. by Sue Truesdell. HarperCollins, 1992. ISBN 0-06-021712-X Subj: Imagination – imaginary friends. Monsters.

Molly's new washing machine ill. by Petra Mathers. Harper, 1986. ISBN 0-06-022151-8 Subj: Activities – dancing. Animals – rabbits. Behavior – mistakes. Machines.

A three hat day ill. by Arnold Lobel. Harper, 1985. ISBN 0-06-021989-0 Subj: Behavior – collecting things. Clothing – hats.

Yours 'til the ice cracks: a book of Valentines ill. by Andrea Baruffi. HarperCollins, 1992. ISBN 0-06-020399-4 Subj: Holidays – Valentine's Day.

Gerrard, Jean. *Matilda Jane* ill. by Roy Gerrard. Farrar, 1983. Subj: Foreign lands – England. Sea and seashore.

Gerrard, Roy. *The Favershams* ill. by author. Farrar, 1983. Subj: Poetry, rhyme.

Mik's mammoth ill. by author. Farrar, 1990. ISBN 0-374-31891-3 Subj: Animals. Character traits – individuality. Poetry, rhyme.

Rosie and the rustlers ill. by author. Farrar, 1989. ISBN 0-374-36345-5 Subj: Cowboys. Crime. Poetry, rhyme.

Sir Cedric rides again ill. by author. Farrar, 1987. ISBN 0-374-36961-5 Subj: Knights. Middle ages. Poetry, rhyme.

Sir Francis Drake: his daring deeds ill. by author. Farrar, 1988. ISBN 0-374-36962-3 Subj: Boats, ships. Foreign lands. Poetry, rhyme. Sea and seashore.

Gershator, Phillis. *Honi and his magic circle* ill. by Shay Rieger. Jewish Publication Society of America, 1980. Subj: Jewish culture.

Gerson, Corinne. *Good dog, bad dog* ill. by Emily Arnold McCully. Atheneum, 1983. Subj: Animals – dogs. Behavior – misbehavior. Pets.

Gerson, Mary-Joan. *Why the sky is far away* ill. by Carla Golembe. Little, 1992. ISBN 0-316-30852-8 Subj: Behavior – greed. Folk and fairy tales. Foreign lands – Nigeria. Sky.

Gerstein, Mordicai. *Anytime Mapleson and the hungry bears* ill. by Susan Yard Harris. HarperCollins, 1990. ISBN 0-06-022415-0 Subj: Animals – bears.

Follow me! ill. by author. Morrow, 1983. Subj: Birds – ducks.

The gigantic baby ill. by Arnie Levin. HarperCollins, 1991. ISBN 0-06-022106-2 Subj: Babies. Concepts – shape. Concepts – size. Family life – brothers. Family life – sisters.

The mountains of Tibet ill. by author. Harper, 1987. ISBN 0-06-022149-6 Subj: Death. Kites.

The new creatures ill. by author. HarperCollins, 1991. ISBN 0-06-022167-4 Subj: Animals – cats. Animals – dogs. Family life – grandfathers.

Prince Sparrow ill. by author. Four Winds Pr., 1984. Subj: Birds – sparrows. Emotions – love.

Roll over! ill. by author. Crown, 1984. Subj: Counting, numbers. Poetry, rhyme.

The seal mother ill. by author. Dial Pr., 1986. ISBN 0-8037-0303-1 Subj: Animals – seals. Folk and fairy tales. Seasons – summer.

The sun's day ill. by author. HarperCollins, 1989. ISBN 0-06-022405-3 Subj: Sun. Time.

William, where are you? ill. by author. Crown, 1985. ISBN 0-517-55644-8 Subj: Animals. Bedtime. Behavior – hiding. Format, unusual – toy and movable books.

Getz, Arthur. *Humphrey, the dancing pig* ill. by author. Dial Pr., 1980. Subj: Activities – dancing. Animals – pigs. Behavior – dissatisfaction.

Gewing, Lisa. *Mama, daddy, baby and me* ill. by Donna Larimer. Spirit Pr., 1989. ISBN 0-944296-04-1 Subj: Babies. Family life. Poetry, rhyme. Sibling rivalry.

Gezi, Kal. *The mystery at Misty Falls* (Bradford, Ann)

The mystery in the secret club house (Bradford, Ann)

The mystery of the blind writer (Bradford, Ann)

The mystery of the live ghosts (Bradford, Ann)

The mystery of the midget clown (Bradford, Ann)

The mystery of the missing dogs (Bradford, Ann)

The mystery of the missing raccoon (Bradford, Ann)

The mystery of the square footsteps (Bradford, Ann)

The mystery of the tree house (Bradford, Ann)

Ghigna, Charles. *Good cats / Bad cats* ill. by David Catrow. Walt Disney, 1992. ISBN 1-56282-293-4 Subj: Animals – cats. Behavior – misbehavior. Format, unusual. Poetry, rhyme.

Good dogs / Bad dogs ill. by David Catrow. Walt Disney, 1992. ISBN 1-56282-291-8 Subj: Animals – dogs. Behavior – misbehavior. Format, unusual. Poetry, rhyme.

Gianni, Peg. *Alex, the amazing juggler* by Peg Gianni and Renato Ferraro; ill. by Peg Gianni. Holt, 1981. Subj: Behavior – running away. Royalty.

Giannini, Enzo. *Little Parsley* ill. by author. Simon & Schuster, 1990. ISBN 0-671-67197-9 Subj: Folk and fairy tales. Foreign lands – Italy. Witches.

Gibbon, David. *Kittens* ill. with photos. Crescent Books, 1979. ISBN 84-499-5052-X Subj: Animals – cats.

Gibbons, Gail. *Boat book* ill. by author. Holiday, 1983. Subj: Boats, ships.

Check it out! the book about libraries ill. by author. Harcourt, 1985. ISBN 0-15-216400-6 Subj: Libraries.

Clocks and how they go ill. by author. Crowell, 1979. Subj: Clocks, watches. Time.

Deadline! from news to newspaper ill. by author. Harper, 1987. ISBN 0-690-04602-2 Subj: Activities – working. Paper.

Department store ill. by author. Crowell, 1984. Subj: Stores.

Dinosaurs ill. by author. Holiday, 1987. ISBN 0-8234-0657-1 Subj: Dinosaurs.

Easter ill. by author. Holiday, 1989. ISBN 0-8234-0737-3 Subj: Holidays – Easter.

Farming ill. by author. Holiday House, 1988. ISBN 0-8234-0682-2 Subj: Careers. Farms. Seasons.

Fill it up! all about service stations ill. by author. Crowell, 1985. ISBN 0-690-04440-2 Subj: Automobiles. Careers.

Fire! Fire! ill. by author. Crowell, 1984. Subj: Careers – firefighters.

Flying ill. by author. Holiday, 1986. ISBN 0-8234-0599-0 Subj: Activities – ballooning. Activities – flying. Airplanes, airports.

From seed to plant ill. by author. Holiday, 1991. ISBN 0-8234-0872-8 Subj: Plants. Science. Seeds.

Halloween ill. by author. Holiday, 1984. Subj: Holidays – Halloween.

Happy birthday! ill. by author. Holiday, 1986. ISBN 0-8234-0614-8 Subj: Birthdays.

How a house is built ill. by author. Holiday, 1990. ISBN 0-8234-0841-8 Subj: Activities – making things. Houses.

The milk makers ill. by author. Macmillan, 1985. ISBN 0-02-736640-5 Subj: Farms. Food.

The missing maple syrup sap mystery: or, How maple syrup is made ill. by author. Warne, 1979. Subj: Activities. Food. Problem solving. Trees.

Monarch butterfly ill. by author. Holiday, 1989. ISBN 0-8234-0773-X Subj: Insects – butterflies, caterpillars.

New road! ill. by author. Crowell, 1983. Subj: Transportation.

Paper, paper everywhere ill. by author. Harcourt, 1983. Subj: Paper.

Playgrounds ill. by author. Holiday, 1985. ISBN 0-8234-0553-2 Subj: Activities – playing.

The post office book: mail and how it moves ill. by author. Crowell, 1982. Subj: Careers – mail carriers. Communication.

The pottery place ill. by author. Harcourt, 1987. ISBN 0-15-263265-4 Subj: Careers.

Prehistoric animals ill. by author. Holiday, 1988. ISBN 0-8234-0707-1 Subj: Animals. Science.

Recycle! ill. by author. Little, 1992. ISBN 0-316-30971-0 Subj: Ecology.

The seasons of Arnold's apple tree ill. by author. Harcourt, 1988. ISBN 0-15-271246-1 Subj: Food. Seasons. Trees.

Sharks ill. by author. Holiday, 1992. ISBN 0-8234-0960-0 Subj: Fish. Science.

Sun up, sun down ill. by author. Harcourt, 1983. Subj: Science. Sun.

Surrounded by sea ill. by author. Little, 1991. ISBN 0-316-30961-3 Subj: Careers – fishermen. Islands. Sports – fishing.

Thanksgiving Day ill. by author. Holiday, 1983. Subj: Holidays – Thanksgiving.

The too-great bread bake book ill. by author. Warne, 1980. Subj: Activities – cooking.

Tool book ill. by author. Holiday, 1982. Subj: Tools.

Trains ill. by author. Holiday, 1987. ISBN 0-8234-0640-7 Subj: Trains.

Trucks ill. by author. Crowell, 1981. Subj: Trucks.

Tunnels ill. by author. Holiday, 1984. ISBN 0-8234-0507-9 Subj: Activities – digging.

Up goes the skyscraper! ill. by author. Four Winds Pr., 1986. ISBN 0-02-736780-0 Subj: Buildings. City.

Valentine's Day ill. by author. Holiday, 1985. ISBN 0-8234-0572-9 Subj: Holidays – Valentine's Day.

Weather words and what they mean ill. by author. Holiday, 1990. ISBN 0-8234-0805-1 Subj: Language. Weather.

Whales ill. by author. Holiday, 1991. ISBN 0-8234-0900-7 Subj: Animals – whales.

Zoo ill. by author. Crowell, 1987. ISBN 0-690-04633-2 Subj: Activities – working. Animals. Zoos.

Gibson, Betty. *The story of Little Quack* ill. by Kady MacDonald Denton. Little, 1991. ISBN 0-316-30966-4 Subj: Birds – ducks. Farms. Pets.

Gibson, Josephine *see* Joslin, Sesyle

Gibson, Myra Tomback. *What is your favorite thing to touch?* ill. by author. Grosset, 1965. Subj: Poetry, rhyme. Senses – touching.

Giesen, Rosemary. *Famous planes* (Thompson, Brenda)

Pirates (Thompson, Brenda)

Giff, Patricia Reilly. *The almost awful play* ill. by Susanna Natti. Viking, 1984. Subj: Theater.

The beast in Ms. Rooney's room ill. by Blanche Sims. Dell, 1984. Subj: Activities – reading. School.

Happy birthday, Ronald Morgan! ill. by Susanna Natti. Viking, 1986. ISBN 0-670-80741-9 Subj: Birthdays. Friendship. School.

I love Saturday ill. by Frank Remkiewicz. Viking, 1991. ISBN 0-685-26817-9 Subj: City. Days of the week, months of the year.

Next year I'll be special ill. by Marylin Hafner. Dutton, 1980. Subj: Behavior – seeking better things. Dreams. School.

Ronald Morgan goes to bat ill. by Susanna Natti. Viking, 1988. ISBN 0-670-81457-1 Subj: Sports – baseball.

Today was a terrible day ill. by Susanna Natti. Viking, 1980. Subj: Behavior – bad day. School.

Watch out, Ronald Morgan! ill. by Susanna Natti. Viking, 1985. ISBN 0-670-80433-9 Subj: Glasses. School. Senses – seeing.

Giffard, Hannah. *Red Fox* ill. by author. Dial, 1991. ISBN 0-8037-0869-6 Subj: Animals – foxes. Food.

Red Fox on the move ill. by author. Dial, 1992. ISBN 0-8037-1057-7 Subj: Animals – foxes. Family life. Moving.

Giganti, Paul. *Each orange had eight slices* ill. by Donald Crews. Greenwillow, 1992. ISBN 0-688-10429-0 Subj: Counting, numbers.

How many snails? a counting book by Paul Giganti, Jr.; ill. by Donald Crews. Greenwillow, 1988. ISBN 0-688-06370-5 Subj: Counting, numbers.

Gikow, Louise. *Boober Fraggle's ghosts* ill. by Lawrence DiFiori. Holt, 1985. ISBN 0-03-004549-5 Subj: Emotions – fear. Ghosts. Puppets.

Follow that Fraggle! ill. by Barbara Lanza. Holt, 1985. ISBN 0-03-004558-4 Subj: Activities – traveling. Animals – dogs. Puppets.

Sprocket's Christmas tale ill. by Lisa McCue. Holt, 1984. Subj: Holidays – Christmas. Puppets.

Gilbert, Helen Earle. *Dr. Trotter and his big gold watch* ill. by Margaret Bradfield. Abingdon Pr., 1948. Subj: Careers – doctors. Clocks, watches.

Mr. Plum and the little green tree ill. by Margaret Bradfield. Abingdon Pr., 1946. Subj: Careers – shoemakers. Trees.

Gilbert, Yvonne. *Baby's book of lullabies and cradle songs* ill. by author. Dial, 1990. ISBN 0-8037-0795-9 Subj: Lullabies. Music. Songs.

Gilchrist, Theo E. *Halfway up the mountain* ill. by Glen Rounds. Lippincott, 1978. Subj: Behavior – fighting, arguing. Poetry, rhyme.

Gili, Phillida. *Fanny and Charles: a regency escapade or, The trick that went wrong* ill. by author. Viking, 1983. Subj: Activities – vacationing. Animals – mice. Sibling rivalry.

Gill, Bob. *A balloon for a blunderbuss* by Bob Gill and Alastair Reid; ill. by Bob Gill. Harper, 1961. Subj: Activities – trading.

Gill, Joan. *Hush, Jon!* ill. by Tracy Sugarman. Doubleday, 1968. Subj: Babies. Emotions – envy, jealousy. Ethnic groups in the U.S. – Afro-Americans. Family life.

Gilleo, Alma. *Learning about monsters* ill. by Joe Van Severen. Children's Pr., 1982. Subj: Folk and fairy tales. Monsters. Mythical creatures.

Gillham, Bill. *Can you see it?* photos. by Fiona Horne. Putnam's, 1986. ISBN 0-399-21323-6 Subj: Games.

The early words picture book photos. by Sam Grainger. Coward, 1983. Subj: Activities – reading.

Let's look for colors by Bill Gillham and Susan Hulme; photos. by Jan Siegieda. Putnam's, 1984. Subj: Concepts – color.

Let's look for numbers by Bill Gillham and Susan Hulme; photos. by Jan Siegieda. Putnam's, 1984. Subj: Counting, numbers.

Let's look for opposites by Bill Gillham and Susan Hulme; photos. by Jan Siegieda. Putnam's, 1984. Subj: Concepts – opposites.

Let's look for shapes by Bill Gillham and Susan Hulme; photos. by Jan Siegieda. Putnam's, 1984. Subj: Concepts – shape.

What can you do? photos. by Fiona Horne. Putnam's, 1986. ISBN 0-399-21324-4 Subj: Games. Imagination.

What's the difference? photos. by Fiona Horne. Putnam's, 1986. ISBN 0-399-21321-X Subj: Concepts – opposites. Games.

Where does it go? photos. by Fiona Horne. Putnam's, 1986. ISBN 0-399-21322-8 Subj: Concepts. Games.

Gilliland, Judith Heide. *The day of Ahmed's secret* (Heide, Florence Parry)

Gilmour, H. B. *Why Wembley Fraggle couldn't sleep* ill. by Barbara McClintock. Holt, 1985. ISBN 0-03-004557-6 Subj: Puppets. Sleep.

The gingerbread boy. *The gingerbread boy* retold and ill. by Scott Cook. Knopf, 1987. ISBN 0-394-98698-9 Subj: Behavior – running away. Cumulative tales. Folk and fairy tales.

The gingerbread boy ill. by Paul Galdone. Seabury Pr., 1975. Subj: Behavior – running away. Cumulative tales. Folk and fairy tales. Food. Poetry, rhyme.

The gingerbread boy retold by David Cutts; ill. by Joan Elizabeth Goodman. Troll Assoc., 1979. Subj: Behavior – running away. Cumulative tales. Folk and fairy tales. Food.

The gingerbread boy ill. by William Curtis Holdsworth. Farrar, 1968. Subj: Behavior – running away. Cumulative tales. Folk and fairy tales. Food.

The gingerbread man retold by Barbara Ireson; ill. by Gerald Rose. Norton, 1963. Subj: Behavior – running away. Cumulative tales. Folk and fairy tales. Food.

The pancake boy adapt. and ill. by Lorinda Bryan Cauley. Putnam's, 1988. ISBN 0-399-21505-0 Subj: Behavior – running away. Cumulative tales. Folk and fairy tales. Food.

Whiff, sniff, nibble and chew: The Gingerbread boy retold by Charlotte Pomerantz; ill. by Monica Incisa. Greenwillow, 1984. ISBN 0-688-02552-8 Subj: Behavior – running away. Cumulative tales. Folk and fairy tales. Poetry, rhyme.

Ginsburg, Mirra. *Across the stream* ill. by Nancy Tafuri. Greenwillow, 1982. Subj: Animals – foxes. Birds – chickens. Birds – ducks. Dreams.

Asleep, asleep ill. by Nancy Tafuri. Greenwillow, 1992. ISBN 0-688-09153-9 ISBN 0-688-09154-7 Subj: Bedtime. Lullabies. Night.

The chick and the duckling ill. by José Aruego and Ariane Dewey. Macmillan, 1972. Translation of Tsyplenok i utenok by Vladimir Grigorévich Suteyev Subj: Birds – chickens. Birds – ducks. Sports – swimming.

The Chinese mirror ill. by Margot Zemach. Harcourt, 1988. ISBN 0-15-200420-3 Subj: Character traits – appearance. Folk and fairy tales. Foreign lands – Korea.

The fisherman's son ill. by Tony Chen. Greenwillow, 1979. Subj: Character traits – cleverness. Folk and fairy tales. Foreign lands – Russia.

Four brave sailors ill. by Nancy Tafuri. Greenwillow, 1987. ISBN 0-688-06515-5 Subj: Animals. Animals – mice. Boats, ships. Dreams. Pirates. Poetry, rhyme. Sea and seashore. Toys. Weather.

The fox and the hare ill. by Victor Nolden. Crown, 1969. Subj: Animals. Animals – foxes. Animals – rabbits. Folk and fairy tales. Foreign lands – Russia. Friendship.

Good morning, chick (Chukovsky, Korney)

How the sun was brought back to the sky: adapted from a Slovenian folk tale ill. by José Aruego and Ariane Dewey. Macmillan, 1975. Subj: Folk and fairy tales. Foreign lands – Czechoslovakia. Sun.

Kitten from one to ten ill. by Giulio Maestro. Crown, 1980. Subj: Animals – cats. Counting, numbers. Poetry, rhyme.

Mushroom in the rain ill. by José Aruego and Ariane Dewey. Macmillan, 1988, 1974. Adapted from the Russian of Valdimir Grigorévich Suteyev ISBN 0-02-736241-8 Subj: Animals. Animals – foxes. Plants. Weather – rain.

Ookie-Spooky ill. by Emily Arnold McCully. Crown, 1979. Subj: Monsters.

Pampalche of the silver teeth ill. by Rocco Negri. Crown, 1976. Subj: Folk and fairy tales. Foreign lands – Russia. Witches.

Striding slippers: an Udmurt tale ill. by Sal Murdocca. Macmillan, 1978. Subj: Behavior – stealing. Folk and fairy tales. Magic.

The strongest one of all ill. by José Aruego and Ariane Dewey. Greenwillow, 1977. Subj: Animals – sheep. Character traits – bravery. Foreign lands – Russia.

The sun's asleep behind the hill ill. by Paul O. Zelinsky. Greenwillow, 1982. Subj: Night. Poetry, rhyme.

Two greedy bears ill. by José Aruego and Ariane Dewey. Macmillan, 1976. Subj: Animals – bears. Animals – foxes. Behavior – greed. Foreign lands – Hungary. Sibling rivalry.

Where does the sun go at night? ill. by José Aruego and Ariane Dewey. Greenwillow, 1980. Subj: Night. Sun.

Which is the best place? ill. by Roger Antoine Duvoisin. Macmillan, 1976. Tr. from Gde luchshe by Pyotr Dubochkin Subj: Bedtime. Foreign lands – Russia.

Giovanni, Nikki. *Spin a soft black song* ill. by George Martins Rev. ed. Hill & Wang, 1985. ISBN 0-8090-8796-0 Subj: Ethnic groups in the U.S. – Afro-Americans. Poetry, rhyme.

Gipson, Morrell. *Favorite nursery tales* ill. by S. D. Schindler. Doubleday, 1983. Subj: Nursery rhymes.

Hello, Peter ill. by Clement Hurd. Doubleday, 1948. Subj: Activities.

Girard, Linda Walvoord. *Adoption is for always* ill. by Judi Friedman. Albert Whitman, 1986. ISBN 0-8075-0185-9 Subj: Adoption. Family life.

At Daddy's on Saturdays ill. by Judith Friedman. Albert Whitman, 1987. ISBN 0-8075-0475-0 Subj: Divorce. Emotions – love. Family life.

Jeremy's first haircut ill. by Maryjane Begin. Albert Whitman, 1986. ISBN 0-8075-3805-1 Subj: Emotions – fear. Hair.

My body is private ill. by Rodney Pate. Albert Whitman, 1984. ISBN 0-8075-5320-4 Subj: Safety. Self-concept.

You were born on your very first birthday ill. by Christa Kieffer. Albert Whitman, 1983. Subj: Babies. Birth. Science.

Girion, Barbara. *The boy with the special face* ill. by Heidi Palmer. Abingdon, 1978. Subj: Character traits – appearance.

Givens, Janet Eaton. *Just two wings* ill. by Susan Dodge. Atheneum, 1984. Subj: Birds.

Something wonderful happened ill. by Susan Dodge. Atheneum, 1982. Subj: Flowers.

Glaser, Byron. *Action alphabet* (Neumeier, Marty)

Glaser, Linda. *Keep your socks on, Albert!* ill. by Sally G. Ward. Dutton, 1992. ISBN 0-525-44838-1 Subj: Animals – possums. Clothing – socks. Emotions – fear. Family life – sisters.

Glass, Andrew. *Chickpea and the talking cow* ill. by author. Lothrop, 1987. ISBN 0-688-06175-3 Subj: Animals – bulls, cows. Character traits – smallness. Emotions – love. Family life. Farms. Royalty.

My brother tries to make me laugh ill. by author. Lothrop, 1984. Subj: Imagination. Space and space ships.

Glass, Marvin. *What happened today, Freddy Groundhog?* ill. by author. Crown, 1989. ISBN 0-517-57140-4 Subj: Animals – groundhogs. Holidays – Groundhog Day.

Glazer, Lee. *Cookie Becker casts a spell* ill. by Margot Apple. Little, 1980. Subj: Character traits – meanness. Magic.

Glen, Maggie. *Ruby* ill. by author. Putnam, 1991. ISBN 0-399-22281-2 Subj: Prejudice. Toys – teddy bears.

Ruby to the rescue ill. by author. Putnam, 1992. ISBN 0-399-22149-2 Subj: School. Self-concept.

Glennon, Karen M. *Miss Eva and the red balloon* ill. by Hans Poppel. Simon & Schuster, 1990. ISBN 0-671-68854-5 Subj: Careers – teachers. Magic. Toys – balloons.

Gliori, Debi. *New big house* ill. by author. Candlewick Pr., 1992. ISBN 1-56402-036-3 Subj: Activities – making things. Family life. Houses.

New big sister ill. by author. Bradbury Pr., 1991. ISBN 0-02-735995-6 Subj: Babies. Birth. Family life. Twins.

Go tell Aunt Rhody. *Go tell Aunt Rhody* ill. by Aliki. Macmillan, 1974. Subj: Family life – aunts, uncles. Folk and fairy tales. Games. Songs.

Go tell Aunt Rhody ill. by Robert M. Quackenbush. Lippincott, 1973. Subj: Family life – aunts, uncles. Games. Music. Songs.

Gobhai, Mehlli. *Lakshmi, the water buffalo who wouldn't* ill. by author. Hawthorn, 1969. Subj: Animals – water buffaloes. Foreign lands – India.

Usha, the mouse-maiden ill. by author. Hawthorn, 1969. Subj: Family life. Folk and fairy tales. Foreign lands – India.

Goble, Paul. *Beyond the ridge* ill. by author. Bradbury Pr., 1988. ISBN 0-02-736581-6 Subj: Death. Indians of North America.

Buffalo woman ill. by author. Bradbury Pr., 1984. Subj: Indians of North America. Folk and fairy tales.

Crow chief: a Plains Indian story ill. by author. Orchard, 1992. ISBN 0-531-08547-3 Subj: Birds – crows. Folk and fairy tales. Indians of North America.

Death of the iron horse ill. by author. Bradbury Pr., 1987. ISBN 0-02-737830-6 Subj: Indians of North America. Trains. War.

The dream wolf ill. by author Rev. ed. of The Friendly Wolf. Bradbury Pr., 1990. ISBN 0-02-736585-9 Subj: Folk and fairy tales. Indians of North America.

The friendly wolf ill. by author. Dutton, 1974. Subj: Animals – wolves. Behavior – lost. Indians of North America.

The gift of the sacred dog ill. by author. Bradbury Pr., 1980. Subj: Animals – horses. Indians of North America. Folk and fairy tales.

The girl who loved wild horses ill. by author. Dutton, 1978. Subj: Animals – horses. Caldecott award book. Indians of North America.

The great race: of the birds and animals ill. by author. Bradbury Pr., 1991. ISBN 0-689-71452-1 Subj: Animals. Birds. Folk and fairy tales. Indians of North America.

Her seven brothers ill. by author. Bradbury Pr., 1988. ISBN 0-02-737960-4 Subj: Animals – buffaloes. Folk and fairy tales. Indians of North America.

Iktomi and the berries: a Plains Indian story ill. by author. Orchard, 1989. ISBN 0-531-08419-1 Subj: Folk and fairy tales. Indians of North America.

Iktomi and the boulder ed. by Richard Jackson; ill. by author. Watts, 1988. ISBN 0-531-08360-8 Subj: Birthdays. Character traits – conceit. Folk and fairy tales. Indians of North America.

Iktomi and the buffalo skull: a Plains Indian story ill. by author. Orchard, 1991. ISBN 0-531-08511-2 Subj: Behavior – trickery. Character traits – conceit. Folk and fairy tales. Indians of North America.

Iktomi and the ducks: a Plains Indian story ill. by author. Orchard, 1990. ISBN 0-531-08483-3 Subj: Behavior – trickery. Folk and fairy tales. Indians of North America.

Star boy ill. by author. Bradbury Pr., 1983. ISBN 0-02-722660-3 Subj: Activities – dancing. Character traits – appearance. Folk and fairy tales. Indians of North America.

Goddard, Carrie Lou. *Isn't it a wonder!* ill. by Leigh Grant. Abingdon Pr., 1976. Subj: Religion.

Goennel, Heidi. *The circus* ill. by author. Morrow, 1992. ISBN 0-688-10884-9 Subj: Circus.

Colors ill. by author. Little, 1990. ISBN 0-316-31843-4 Subj: Concepts – color.

If I were a penguin ... ill. by author. Little, 1989. ISBN 0-316-31841-8 Subj: Animals. Imagination.

My day ill. by author. Little, 1988. ISBN 0-316-31839-6 Subj: Activities.

My dog ill. by author. Orchard, 1989. ISBN 0-531-08434-5 Subj: Animals – dogs. Pets.

Seasons ill. by author. Little, 1986. ISBN 0-316-31836-1 Subj: Seasons.

Sometimes I like to be alone ill. by author. Little, 1989. ISBN 0-316-31842-6 Subj: Activities. Character traits – solitude.

When I grow up... ill. by author. Little, 1987. ISBN 0-316-31838-8 Subj: Behavior – growing up.

Goff, Beth. *Where's daddy?* ill. by Susan Perl. Beacon Pr., 1969. Subj: Divorce.

Goffe, Toni. *Toby's animal rescue service* ill. by author. David and Charles, 1982. Subj: Activities – ballooning. Animals.

Goffin, Josse. *Who is the boss?* ill. by author. Houghton, 1992. ISBN 0-395-61192-X Subj: Behavior – fighting, arguing.

Goffstein, M. B. (Marilyn Brooke). *Across the sea* ill. by author. Farrar, 1968. Subj: Foreign lands.

An actor ill. by author. Harper, 1987. ISBN 0-06-022169-0 Subj: Activities – working. Careers. Theater.

Artists' helpers enjoy the evening ill. by author. Harper, 1987. ISBN 0-06-022182-8 Subj: Art. Concepts – color. Foreign lands – France.

Family scrapbook ill. by author. Farrar, 1978. Subj: Family life.

Fish for supper ill. by author. Dial Pr., 1976. Subj: Caldecott award honor book. Family life – grandmothers. Old age. Sports – fishing.

A house, a home photos. by author. HarperCollins, 1989. ISBN 0-06-0022437-1 Subj: Houses.

Laughing latkes ill. by author. Farrar, 1981. Subj: Holidays – Hanukkah. Jewish culture.

A little Schubert ill. by author. Harper, 1972. Subj: Music.

Me and my captain ill. by author. Farrar, 1974. Subj: Toys – dolls.

My Noah's ark ill. by author. Harper, 1978. Subj: Religion – Noah.

Natural history ill. by author. Farrar, 1979. Subj: Animals. Character traits – kindness to animals.

Neighbors ill. by author. Harper, 1979. Subj: Character traits – shyness. Emotions – loneliness.

Our prairie home: a picture album ill. by author. Harper, 1988. ISBN 0-06-022291-3 Subj: Country. Toys – dolls. Family life.

Our snowman ill. by author. Harper, 1986. ISBN 0-06-022153-4 Subj: Activities – playing. Family life. Snowmen.

School of names ill. by author. Harper, 1986. ISBN 0-06-021985-8 Subj: Names. School. World.

Sleepy people ill. by author. Farrar, 1966. Subj: Bedtime.

A writer ill. by author. Harper, 1984. Subj: Activities – working. Careers – writers.

Goldblatt, Eli. *Leo loves round* ill. by Wendy Osterweil. Harbinger House, 1990. ISBN 0-943173-49-3 Subj: Concepts – shape. Poetry, rhyme.

The golden goose ill. by William Stobbs. McGraw-Hill, 1967. Subj: Birds – chickens. Cumulative tales. Folk and fairy tales. Humor. Royalty.

Golden tales from long ago: *Like Grandpa, Only birds, The three kittens* Delacorte, 1980. Anonymous stories published by Ernest Nister in London near the turn of the century Subj: Format, unusual.

Goldfrank, Helen Colodny Kay *see* Kay, Helen

Goldrey, Jennifer. *Danger colors* (Oxford Scientific Films)

Danger colors (Oxford Scientific Films)

Hide and seek (Oxford Scientific Films)

Goldin, Augusta. *Ducks don't get wet* ill. by Leonard P. Kessler. Crowell, 1965. Subj: Birds – ducks. Science.

Salt ill. by Robert Galster. Crowell, 1966. Subj: Science.

The shape of water ill. by Demi. Doubleday, 1979. Subj: Science.

Spider silk ill. by Joseph Low. Crowell, 1964. Subj: Science. Spiders.

Straight hair, curly hair ill. by Ed Emberley. Crowell, 1966. Subj: Hair. Science.

Where does your garden grow? ill. by Helen Borten. Crowell, 1967. Subj: Gardens, gardening. Science.

Goldin, Barbara Diamond. *Cakes and miracles: a Purim tale* ill. by Erika Weihs. Viking, 1991. ISBN 0-670-83047-X Subj: Activities – cooking. Food. Handicaps – blindness. Jewish culture. Religion. Self-concept.

Just enough is plenty: a Hannukkah tale ill. by Seymour Chwast. Viking, 1988. ISBN 0-670-81852-6 Subj: Behavior – sharing. Holidays – Hanukkah. Jewish culture.

World's birthday ill. by Jeanette Winter. Harcourt, 1990. ISBN 0-15-299648-6 Subj: Birthdays. Holidays – Rosh Hashanah. Jewish culture.

Goldman, Dara. *There's no such thing!* ill. by author. Putnam, 1990. ISBN 0-399-22193-X Subj: Animals – bears. Behavior – trickery. Character traits – cleverness.

Goldman, Susan. *Cousins are special* ill. by author. Albert Whitman, 1978. Subj: Family life.

Grandma is somebody special ed. by Caroline Rubin; ill. by author. Albert Whitman, 1976. Subj: Family life – grandmothers.

Goldner, Kathryn Allen. *The dangers of strangers* (Vogel, Carole Garbuny)

Goldsmith, Howard. *Little lost dog* ill. by Ulises Wensell. Santillana, 1983. ISBN 0-88272-179-8 Subj: Animals – dogs. Behavior – lost. Character traits – honesty. Friendship. Illness.

Toto the timid turtle ill. by Shirley Chan. Human Sciences Pr., 1981. Subj: Reptiles – turtles, tortoises.

Goldstein, Bobbye S. *Bear in mind: a book of bear poems* ill. by William Pène du Bois. Viking, 1989. ISBN 0-670-81907-7 Subj: Animals – bears. Poetry, rhyme.

Poems on poetry ill. by Jane Breskin Zalben. Boyds Mills Pr. 1992. ISBN 1-56397-040-6 Subj: Poetry, rhyme.

What's on the menu? ill. by Chris L. Demarest. Viking, 1992. ISBN 0-670-83031-3 Subj: Food. Poetry, rhyme.

Gomi, Taro. *The big book of boxes* ill. by author. Chronicle Books, 1991. ISBN 0-8118-0067-9 Subj: Concepts – shape.

Bus stop ill. by author. Chronicle, 1988. ISBN 0-87701-551-1 Subj: Activities – traveling. Buses. Transportation.

Coco can't wait! ill. by author. Morrow, 1984. Subj: Family life – grandmothers.

First comes Harry ill. by author. Morrow, 1987. ISBN 0-688-06732-8 Subj: Behavior – hurrying.

Guess who? ill. by author. Chronicle Books, 1991. ISBN 0-8118-0021-0 Subj: Animals. Format, unusual – board books. Games. Toys.

Hi, butterfly! ill. by author. Morrow, 1985. ISBN 0-688-04138-8 Subj: Format, unusual. Insects – butterflies, caterpillars.

My friends ill. by author. Chronicle Books, 1990. ISBN 0-87701-688-7 Subj: Activities. Animals.

Seeing, saying, doing, playing ill. by author. Chronicle Books, 1991. ISBN 0-87701-859-6 Subj: Activities. Language.

Spring is here ill. by author. Chronicle Books, 1989. ISBN 0-87701-626-7 Subj: Animals – bulls, cows. Seasons.

Toot! ill. by author. Morrow, 1986. ISBN 0-688-06421-3 Subj: Illness. Music. Poetry, rhyme.

Where's the fish? ill. by author. Morrow, 1986. ISBN 0-688-06242-3 Subj: Behavior – hiding. Fish.

Who ate it? ill. by author. Millbrook, 1991. ISBN 1-56294-010-4 Subj: Games.

Who hid it? ill. by author. Millbrook Pr., 1991. ISBN 1-56294-011-2 Subj: Games.

The good-hearted youngest brother : *an Hungarian folktale* tr. by Emöke de Papp Severo; ill. by Diane Goode. Bradbury Pr., 1981. Subj: Character traits – kindness to animals. Folk and fairy tales. Foreign lands – Hungary. Magic.

Goodall, Daphne Machin. *Zebras* ill. with photos. Raintree, 1978. Subj: Animals – zebras.

Goodall, John S. *The adventures of Paddy Pork* ill. by author. Harcourt, 1968. Subj: Animals – pigs. Behavior – running away. Circus. Format, unusual. Wordless.

The ballooning adventures of Paddy Pork ill. by author. Harcourt, 1969. Subj: Animals – pigs. Format, unusual. Wordless.

Creepy castle ill. by author. Atheneum, 1975. Subj: Animals – mice. Format, unusual. Knights. Monsters. Wordless.

An Edwardian Christmas ill. by author. Atheneum, 1978. Subj: Foreign lands – England. Format, unusual. Holidays – Christmas. Wordless.

An Edwardian summer ill. by author. Atheneum, 1976. Subj: Foreign lands – England. Format, unusual. Seasons – summer. Wordless.

Jacko ill. by author. Harcourt, 1971. Subj: Animals – monkeys. Boats, ships. Format, unusual. Wordless.

The midnight adventures of Kelly, Dot and Esmeralda ill. by author. Atheneum, 1972. Subj: Format, unusual. Wordless.

Naughty Nancy ill. by author. Atheneum, 1975. Subj: Behavior – misbehavior. Format, unusual. Weddings. Wordless.

Naughty Nancy goes to school ill. by author. Atheneum, 1985. ISBN 0-689-50329-6 Subj: Behavior – misbehavior. Format, unusual. School. Wordless.

Paddy goes traveling ill. by author. Atheneum, 1982. Subj: Activities – traveling. Animals – pigs. Format, unusual. Wordless.

Paddy Pork: odd jobs ill. by author. Atheneum, 1983. Subj: Activities – working. Animals – pigs. Format, unusual. Wordless.

Paddy Pork's holiday ill. by author. Atheneum, 1976. Subj: Activities – vacationing. Animals – pigs. Format, unusual. Wordless.

Paddy to the rescue ill. by author. Atheneum, 1986. ISBN 0-689-50330-X Subj: Animals – pigs. Behavior – stealing. Character traits – bravery. Crime. Wordless.

Paddy under water ill. by author. Atheneum, 1984. Subj: Animals – pigs. Format, unusual. Sea and seashore. Wordless.

Paddy's evening out ill. by author. Atheneum, 1973. Subj: Animals – pigs. Format, unusual. Theater. Wordless.

Paddy's new hat ill. by author. Atheneum, 1980. Subj: Animals – pigs. Careers – police officers. Format, unusual. Wordless.

Puss in boots (Perrault, Charles)

Shrewbettina's birthday ill. by author. Harcourt, 1970. Subj: Animals – shrews. Birthdays. Format, unusual. Wordless.

The story of a castle ill. by author. Macmillan, 1986. ISBN 0-689-50405-5 Subj: Foreign lands – England. Format, unusual. Wordless.

The story of a farm ill. by author. Macmillan, 1988. ISBN 0-689-50479-9 Subj: Farms. Foreign lands – England. Format, unusual. Wordless.

The story of a main street ill. by author. Macmillan, 1987. ISBN 0-233-98070-9 Subj: City. Format, unusual. Roads. Wordless.

The story of an English village ill. by author. Atheneum, 1979. Subj: City. Foreign lands – England. Format, unusual. Progress. Wordless.

The surprise picnic ill. by author. Atheneum, 1977. Subj: Activities – picnicking. Animals – cats. Food. Format, unusual. Wordless.

Goode, Diane. *Cinderella* (Perrault, Charles)

The fir tree (Andersen, H. C. (Hans Christian))

I hear a noise ill. by author. Dutton, 1988. ISBN 0-525-44353-3 Subj: Bedtime. Dragons. Emotions – fear. Monsters. Night.

Where's our mama? ill. by author. Dutton, 1991. ISBN 0-525-44770-9 Subj: Behavior – lost. Family life – mothers. Foreign lands – France.

Goodenow, Earle. *The last camel* ill. by author. Walck, 1968. Subj: Animals – camels. Foreign lands – Egypt.

The owl who hated the dark ill. by author. Walck, 1969. Subj: Birds – owls. Emotions – fear. Night.

Goodman, Louise. *Ida's doll* ill. by Debby L. Carter. HarperCollins, 1989. ISBN 0-06-022276-X Subj: Family life – grandmothers. Family life – sisters. Poverty. Toys – dolls.

Goodsell, Jane. *Katie's magic glasses* ill. by Barbara Cooney. Subj: Careers – doctors. Glasses. Senses – seeing.

Toby's toe ill. by Gioia Fiammenghi. Morrow, 1986. ISBN 0-688-06162-1 Subj: Character traits – kindness. Character traits – meanness. Toys – balloons.

Goodspeed, Peter. *Hugh and Fitzhugh* ill. by Carol Nicklaus. Platt, 1974. Subj: Animals – dogs. Language.

A rhinoceros wakes me up in the morning: a bedtime tale ill. by Dennis Panek. Bradbury Pr., 1982. Subj: Animals. Bedtime. Poetry, rhyme.

Goor, Nancy. *All kinds of feet* (Goor, Ron)

In the driver's seat (Goor, Ron)

Shadows: here, there and everywhere (Goor, Ron)

Signs (Goor, Ron)

Goor, Ron. *All kinds of feet* by Ron and Nancy Goor; photos. by authors. Crowell, 1984. Subj: Anatomy – feet. Animals.

In the driver's seat by Ron and Nancy Goor; photos. by authors. Crowell, 1982. Subj: Activities. Machines.

Shadows: here, there and everywhere by Ron and Nancy Goor; photos. by authors. Crowell, 1981. Subj: Shadows.

Signs by Ron and Nancy Goor; photos. by authors. Crowell, 1983. Subj: Activities – reading. Communication.

Gorbaty, Norman. *Get up and go, little dinosaur!* ill. by author. Random House, 1990. ISBN 0-679-80693-8 Subj: Dinosaurs. Format, unusual – board books.

Gordon, Gaelyn. *Duckat* ill. by Chris Gaskin. Scholastic, 1992. ISBN 0-590-45455-2 Subj: Animals – cats. Birds – ducks. Self-concept.

Gordon, Jeffie Ross. *Six sleepy sheep* ill. by John O'Brien. Boyds Mills Pr. 1991. ISBN 1-878093-06-1 Subj: Animals – sheep. Language. Tongue twisters.

Two badd babies ill. by Chris L. Demarest. Boyds Mills Pr. 1992. ISBN 1-878093-85-1 Subj: Bedtime. Poetry, rhyme. Twins.

Gordon, Margaret. *Frogs' holiday* ill. by author. Viking, 1987. ISBN 0-670-80854-7 Subj: Activities – baby-sitting. Frogs and toads.

The supermarket mice ill. by author. Dutton, 1984. Subj: Animals – cats. Animals – mice. Problem solving. Stores.

Wilberforce goes on a picnic ill. by author. Morrow, 1982. Subj: Activities – picnicking. Animals – bears.

Wilberforce goes to a party ill. by author. Viking, 1985. ISBN 0-670-80148-8 Subj: Animals – bears. Behavior – misbehavior. Birthdays. Etiquette. Parties.

Gordon, Sharon. *Christmas surprise* ill. by John Magine. Troll Assoc., 1980. Subj: Animals – bears. Holidays – Christmas.

Dinosaurs in trouble ill. by Paul Harvey. Troll Assoc., 1980. Subj: Dinosaurs.

Dolphins and porpoises ill. by June Goldsborough. Troll Assoc., 1985. ISBN 0-8167-0340-X Subj: Animals – dolphins. Sea and seashore.

Easter Bunny's lost egg ill. by John Magine. Troll Assoc., 1980. Subj: Animals – rabbits. Eggs. Holidays – Easter.

Friendly snowman ill. by John Magine. Troll Assoc., 1980. Subj: Snowmen.

Pete the parakeet ill. by Paul Harvey. Troll Assoc., 1980. Subj: Birds – parakeets, parrots.

Play ball, Kate! ill. by Don Page. Troll Assoc., 1981. Subj: Sports – baseball.

Sam the scarecrow ill. by Don Silverstein. Troll Assoc., 1980. Subj: Scarecrows.

Three little witches ill. by Deborah Sims. Troll Assoc., 1980. Subj: Witches.

Tick tock clock ill. by Don Page. Troll Assoc., 1982. Subj: Clocks, watches. Time.

Trees ill. by Irene Trivas. Troll Assoc., 1983. Subj: Trees.

What a dog! ill. by Deborah Sims. Troll Assoc., 1980. Subj: Animals – dogs.

Gordon, Shirley. *Grandma zoo* ill. by Whitney Darrow, Jr. Harper, 1978. Subj: Animals. Family life – grandmothers. Zoos.

Gore, Sheila. *My shadow* photos. by Fiona Pragoff. Doubleday, 1990. ISBN 0-385-41198-7 Subj: Activities. Concepts – perspective. Science. Shadows.

Gorey, Edward (St. John). *The tunnel calamity* ill. by author. Putnam's, 1984. Subj: Format, unusual. Monsters. Wordless.

Gorham, Michael *see* Elting, Mary

Gorsline, Douglas. *North American Indians* (Gorsline, Marie)

Gorsline, Marie. *North American Indians* by Marie and Douglas Gorsline; ill. by authors. Random House, 1978. Subj: Indians of North America. U.S. history.

Goudey, Alice E. *The day we saw the sun come up* ill. by Adrienne Adams. Scribner's, 1961. Subj: Caldecott award honor book. Family life. Sun.

The good rain ill. by Nora Spicer Unwin. Dutton, 1950. Subj: Weather – rain.

Houses from the sea ill. by Adrienne Adams. Scribner's, 1959. Subj: Caldecott award honor book. Sea and seashore.

Red legs ill. by Marie Nonnast. Scribner's, 1966. Subj: Insects.

Gould, Deborah. *Aaron's shirt* ill. by Cheryl Harness. Bradbury Pr., 1989. ISBN 0-02-736351-1 Subj: Behavior – growing up. Clothing – shirts.

Brendan's best-timed birthday ill. by Jacqueline Rogers. Bradbury Pr., 1988. ISBN 0-02-737390-8 Subj: Behavior – sharing. Birthdays. Clocks, watches. Parties.

Camping in the Temple of the Sun ill. by Diane Paterson. Bradbury Pr., 1992. ISBN 0-02-736355-4 Subj: Camps, camping. Family life. Weather.

Grandpa's slide show ill. by Cheryl Harness. Lothrop, 1987. ISBN 0-688-06973-8 Subj: Death. Dreams. Family life – grandparents.

Goundaud, Karen Jo. *A very mice joke book* ill. by Lynn Munsinger. Houghton, 1981. Subj: Animals – mice. Riddles.

Goyder, Alice. *Holiday in Catland* ill. by author. Crowell, 1979. Subj: Activities – vacationing. Animals – cats.

Party in Catland ill. by author. Crowell, 1979. Subj: Animals – cats. Parties.

Grabianski, Janusz. *Cats* ill. by author. Watts, 1966. Subj: Animals – cats.

Grabianski's wild animals ill. by author. Watts, 1969. Translation of Tiere der Wildnis Subj: Animals.

Horses ill. by author. Watts, 1966. Subj: Animals – horses.

Graham, Al. *Timothy Turtle* ill. by Tony Palazzo. Walck, 1946. Subj: Caldecott award honor book. Character traits – ambition. Character traits – helpfulness. Friendship. Reptiles – turtles, tortoises.

Graham, Amanda. *Picasso, the green tree frog* ill. by John Siow. Gareth Stevens, 1987. ISBN 1-55532-152-6 Subj: Concepts – color. Frogs and toads.

Who wants Arthur? ill. by Donna Gynell. Gareth Stevens, 1987. ISBN 1-55532-153-4 Subj: Animals – dogs. Behavior – imitation. Stores.

Graham, Bob. *Crusher is coming!* ill. by author. Viking, 1987. ISBN 0-670-82081-4 Subj: Babies. Friendship.

First there was Frances ill. by author. Bradbury Pr., 1986. ISBN 0-02-737030-5 Subj: Animals. Family life. Moving.

Greetings from Sandy Beach ill. by author. Kane/Miller, 1992. ISBN 0-916291-40-5 Subj: Activities – vacationing. Camps, camping. Family life. Sea and seashore.

Has anyone here seen William? ill. by author. Little, 1989. ISBN 0-316-32313-6 Subj: Behavior – misbehavior.

Libby, Oscar and me ill. by author. Harper, 1985. Subj: Animals – cats. Animals – dogs. Activities – picnicking.

Pete and Roland ill. by author. Viking, 1984. ISBN 0-670-54912-6 Subj: Birds – parakeets, parrots. Character traits – kindness to animals.

The red woolen blanket ill. by author. Little, 1988. ISBN 0-316-32310-1 Subj: Behavior – growing up. Concepts – color.

Rose meets Mr. Wintergarten ill. by author. Candlewick Pr., 1992. ISBN 1-56402-039-8 Subj: Friendship. Old age.

The wild ill. by author. Harper, 1987. ISBN 0-87226-139-5 Subj: Family life. Nature. Pets.

Graham, John. *A crowd of cows* ill. by Feodor Rojankovsky. Harcourt, 1968. Subj: Animals. Noise, sounds.

I love you, mouse ill. by Tomie de Paola. Harcourt, 1976. Subj: Animals. Animals – mice.

Graham, Lorenz B. *David he no fear* ill. by Ann Grifalconi. Crowell, 1971. Subj: Religion.

Every man heart lay down ill. by Colleen Browning. Crowell, 1970. Subj: Religion.

God wash the world and start again ill. by Clare Romano. Crowell, 1971. Subj: Religion – Noah.

Hongry catch the foolish boy ill. by James Brown, Jr. Crowell, 1973. Story first appeared in the author's How God fix Jonah, published in 1946 Subj: Religion.

A road down in the sea ill. by Gregorio Prestopino. Crowell, 1970. Subj: Religion.

Song of the boat ill. by Leo and Diane Dillon. Crowell, 1975. Subj: Foreign lands – Africa. Poetry, rhyme.

Graham, Margaret Bloy. *Be nice to spiders* ill. by author. Harper, 1967. Subj: Spiders. Zoos.

Benjy and his friend Fifi ill. by author. Harper, 1988. ISBN 0-06-022253-0 Subj: Animals – dogs. Character traits – helpfulness. Emotions – fear.

Benjy and the barking bird ill. by author. Harper, 1971. Subj: Animals – dogs. Birds – parakeets, parrots. Emotions – envy, jealousy.

Benjy's boat trip ill. by author. Harper, 1977. Subj: Animals – dogs. Boats, ships.

Benjy's dog house ill. by author. Harper, 1973. Subj: Animals – dogs.

Graham, Mary Stuart Campbell. *The pirates' bridge* ill. by Winifred Lubell. Lothrop, 1960. Subj: Pirates.

Graham, Richard. *Jack and the monster* ill. by Susan Varley. Houghton, 1989. ISBN 0-395-49680-2 Subj: Babies. Emotions – envy, jealousy. Family life. Sibling rivalry.

Graham, Thomas. *Mr. Bear's boat* ill. by author. Dutton, 1988. ISBN 0-525-44375-4 Subj: Activities – picnicking. Animals – bears. Boats, ships.

Mr. Bear's chair ill. by author. Dutton, 1987. ISBN 0-525-44300-2 Subj: Activities – making things. Animals – bears. Family life. Furniture – chairs.

Grahame, Kenneth. *The open road* ill. by Beverley Gooding. Scribner's, 1980. Subj: Activities – traveling. Animals.

Gramatky, Hardie. *Bolivar* ill. by author. Putnam's, 1961. Subj: Animals – donkeys. Foreign lands – South America.

Hercules ill. by author. Putnam's, 1940. Subj: Careers – firefighters. Fire. Museums. Trucks.

Homer and the circus train ill. by author. Putnam's, 1957. Subj: Circus. Trains.

Little Toot ill. by author. Putnam's, 1939. Subj: Boats, ships. Character traits – ambition.

Little Toot and the Loch Ness monster ill. by Hardie and Dorothea Cooke Gramatky. Putnam, 1989. ISBN 0-399-21684-7 Subj: Boats, ships. Foreign lands – Scotland. Monsters.

Little Toot on the Mississippi ill. by author. Putnam's, 1973. Subj: Boats, ships. Rivers.

Little Toot on the Thames ill. by author. Putnam's, 1964. Subj: Boats, ships. Foreign lands – England.

Little Toot through the Golden Gate ill. by author. Putnam's, 1975. Subj: Boats, ships. City. Character traits – individuality.

Loopy ill. by author. Putnam's, 1941. Subj: Activities – flying. Airplanes, airports.

Nikos and the sea god ill. by author. Putnam's, 1963. Subj: Careers – fishermen. Folk and fairy tales. Mythical creatures. Religion.

Sparky: the story of a little trolley car ill. by author. Putnam's, 1952. Subj: Cable cars, trolleys. Transportation.

Grant, Joan. *The monster that grew small* ill. by Jill K. Schwarz. Lothrop, 1987. ISBN 0-688-06809-X Subj: Character traits – bravery. Character traits – kindness to animals. Emotions – fear. Folk and fairy tales. Foreign lands – Egypt. Monsters.

Grant, Matthew G. see May, Julian

Grasshopper to the rescue : *a Georgian story* tr. from the Russian by Bonnie Carey; ill. by Tasha Tudor. Morrow, 1979. Subj: Character traits – bravery. Cumulative tales. Insects – grasshoppers. Rivers.

Graves, Helen. *The brave little kittens* (Wilkoń, Piotr)

Gray, Catherine. *Tammy and the gigantic fish* by Catherine and James Gray; ill. by William Joyce. Harper, 1983. Subj: Family life. Sports – fishing.

Gray, Genevieve. *How far, Felipe?* ill. by Ann Grifalconi. Harper, 1978. Subj: Activities – traveling. Animals – donkeys. Character traits – perseverance.

Send Wendell ill. by Symeon Shimin. McGraw-Hill, 1974. Subj: Character traits – helpfulness. Ethnic groups in the U.S. – Afro-Americans. Family life.

Gray, James. *Tammy and the gigantic fish* (Gray, Catherine)

Gray, Jenny *see* Gray, Genevieve

Gray, Nigel. *A balloon for grandad* ill. by Jane Ray. Watts, 1988. ISBN 0-531-08355-1 Subj: Family life – fathers. Family life – grandfathers. Toys – balloons.

A country far away ill. by Philippe Dupasquier. Watts, 1989. ISBN 0-531-08392-6 Subj: Family life. Foreign lands.

I'll take you to Mrs. Cole! ill. by Michael Foreman. Kane/Miler, 1992. ISBN 0-916291-39-1 Subj: Behavior – running away. Ethnic groups in the U.S. – Afro-Americans.

It'll all come out in the wash ill. by Edward Frascino. Harper, 1979. Subj: Family life.

Little pig's tale ill. by Mary Rees. Macmillan, 1990. ISBN 0-02-736942-0 Subj: Animals – pigs. Birthdays. Family life.

Greaves, Margaret. *Henry's wild morning* ill. by Teresa O'Brien. Dial, 1991. ISBN 0-8037-0907-2 Subj: Animals – cats. Character traits – ambition.

Little Bear and the Papagini circus ill. by Francesca Crespi. Dial Pr., 1986. ISBN 0-8037-0264-7 Subj: Animals – bears. Circus. Family life.

The mice of Nibbling Village ill. by Jane Pinkney. Dutton, 1986. ISBN 0-525-44277-4 Subj: Animals – mice. Poetry, rhyme.

Once there were no pandas ill. by Beverley Gooding. Dutton, 1985. ISBN 0-525-44211-1 Subj: Animals – pandas. Character traits – bravery.

Greeley, Valerie. *Farm animals* ill. by author. Harper, 1984. Subj: Animals. Farms. Format, unusual – board books. Wordless.

Field animals ill. by author. Harper, 1984. Subj: Animals. Format, unusual – board books. Wordless.

Pets ill. by author. Harper, 1984. Subj: Animals. Format, unusual – board books. Pets. Wordless.

Where's my share? ill. by author. Macmillan, 1990. ISBN 0-02-736761-4 Subj: Animals. Birds. Circular tales. Food. Nursery rhymes.

White is the moon ill. by author. Macmillan, 1991. ISBN 0-02-736915-3 Subj: Animals. Concepts – color. Nature. Poetry, rhyme.

Zoo animals ill. by author. Harper, 1984. Subj: Animals. Format, unusual – board books. Wordless. Zoos.

Green, Adam *see* Weisgard, Leonard

The green grass grows all around: *a traditional folk song* ill. by Hilde Hoffmann. Macmillan, 1968. Subj: Plants. Poetry, rhyme. Songs.

Green, Marion. *The magician who lived on the mountain* ill. by John Dyke. Children's Pr., 1978. Subj: Art. Magic.

Green, Mary McBurney. *Everybody has a house and everybody eats* ill. by Louis Klein. Abelard-Schuman, 1944. Subj: Farms. Houses.

Is it hard? Is it easy? ill. by Lucienne Bloch. Abelard-Schuman, 1948. Subj: Concepts.

Green, Melinda. *Bembelman's bakery* ill. by Barbara Seuling. Parents, 1978. Subj: Careers – bakers.

Green, Norma B. *The hole in the dike* ill. by Eric Carle. Crowell, 1974. Subj: Character traits – helpfulness. Foreign lands – Holland.

Green, Phyllis. *Bagdad ate it* ill. by Joel Schick. Watts, 1980. Subj: Animals – dogs. Behavior – greed.

Uncle Roland, the perfect guest ill. by Marybeth Farrell. Four Winds Pr., 1983. Subj: Family life – aunts, uncles.

Green, Suzanne. *The little choo-choo: sounds, sights and opposites* ill. by Miho Fujita. Doubleday, 1988. ISBN 0-385-24426-6 Subj: Concepts – opposites. Noise, sounds. Toys – trains.

Greenaway, Kate. *A apple pie* ill. by author. Warne, 1886. Subj: ABC books.

Marigold garden ill. by author. Warne, 1885. Subj: Poetry, rhyme.

Under the window ill. by author. Warne, 1879. Subj: Poetry, rhyme.

Greenaway, Shirley. *Burrows* ill. with photos. Newington Pr., 1991. ISBN 1-878137-11-5 Subj: Animals. Nature.

Forests ill. with photos. Newington Pr., 1991. ISBN 1-878137-08-5 Subj: Animals. Forest, woods. Nature.

Jungles ill. with photos. Newington Pr., 1991. ISBN 1-878137-09-3 Subj: Animals. Jungle. Nature.

Water ill. with photos. Newington Pr., 1991. ISBN 1-878137-10-7 Subj: Fish. Nature. Sea and seashore.

Greenberg, Barbara. *The bravest babysitter* ill. by Diane Paterson. Dial Pr., 1977. Subj: Activities – baby-sitting. Babies. Emotions – fear. Weather.

Greenberg, Dan. *The bed who ran away from home* ill. by John Wallner. HarperCollins, 1991. ISBN 0-06-022280-8 Subj: Behavior – running away. Furniture – beds. Poetry, rhyme. Twins.

Greenberg, David. *Slugs* ill. by Victoria Chess. Little, 1983. Subj: Poetry, rhyme.

Greenberg, Judith E. *Adopted* by Judith E. Greenberg and Helen H. Carey; photos. by Barbara Kirk. Watts, 1987. ISBN 0-531-10290-4 Subj: Adoption. Babies.

What is the sign for friend? photos. by Gayle Rothschild. Watts, 1985. ISBN 0-531-04939-6 Subj: Handicaps – deafness. Language. Senses – hearing.

Greenberg, Melanie Hope. *At the beach* ill. by author. Dutton, 1989. ISBN 0-525-44474-2 Subj: Sea and seashore.

My father's luncheonette ill. by author. Dutton, 1991. ISBN 0-525-44725-3 Subj: Activities – cooking. Careers. City. Family life – fathers.

Greenberg, Polly. *Oh, Lord, I wish I was a buzzard* ill. by Aliki. Macmillan, 1968. Subj: Behavior – wishing. Ethnic groups in the U.S. – Afro-Americans. Farms. Plants.

Greenblat, Rodney A. *Aunt Ippy's museum of junk* ill. by author. HarperCollins, 1991. ISBN 0-06-022512-2 Subj: Behavior – collecting things. Family life – aunts, uncles.

Uncle Wizzmo's new used car ill. by author. HarperCollins, 1990. ISBN 0-06-022098-8 Subj: Automobiles. Family life – aunts, uncles.

Greene, Carla. *Doctors and nurses: what do they do?* ill. by Leonard P. Kessler. Harper, 1963. Subj: Careers – doctors. Careers – nurses.

I want to be a carpenter ill. by Frances Eckart. Children's Pr., 1959. Subj: Careers – carpenters.

A motor holiday ill. by Harold L. Van Pelt. Melmont, 1956. Subj: Activities – traveling.

Greene, Carol. *A computer went a-courting: a love song for Valentine's Day* ill. by Tom Dunnington. Children's Pr., 1983. Subj: Animals – mice. Computers. Holidays – Valentine's Day. Music. Songs.

The golden locket ill. by Marcia Sewall. Harcourt, 1992. ISBN 0-15-231220-X Subj: Behavior – worrying. Emotions – love. Problem solving.

Hi, clouds ill. by Gene Sharp. Grosset, 1989. Subj: Weather – clouds.

Hinny Winny Bunco ill. by Jeanette Winter. Harper, 1982. Subj: Music. Sibling rivalry. Songs.

I can be a baseball player ill. with photos. Childrens Pr., 1985. ISBN 0-516-01845-0 Subj: Careers. Sports – baseball.

I can be a forest ranger ill. with photos. Children's Pr., 1989. ISBN 0-516-41924-2 Subj: Careers – park rangers. Forest, woods. Nature.

I can be a model Childrens Pr., 1985. ISBN 0-516-01887-6 Subj: Careers – models.

The insignificant elephant ill. by Susan Gantner. Harcourt, 1985. Subj: Animals – elephants. Animals – rabbits.

The old ladies who liked cats ill. by Loretta Krupinski. HarperCollins, 1991. ISBN 0-06-022105-4 Subj: Animals – cats. Ecology. Islands. Old age.

Please, wind? ill. by Gene Sharp. Children's Pr., 1982. Subj: Weather – wind.

Rain! Rain! ill. by Larry Frederick. Children's Pr., 1982. Subj: Weather – rain.

Robots ill. with photos. Children's Pr., 1983. Subj: Robots.

Shine, sun! ill. by Gene Sharp. Children's Pr., 1983. Subj: Sun.

Snow Joe ill. by Paul Sharp. Children's Pr., 1982. Subj: Weather – snow.

The thirteen days of Halloween ill. by Tom Dunnington. Children's Pr., 1983. Subj: Holidays – Halloween. Music. Songs. Witches.

The world's biggest birthday cake ill. by Tom Dunnington. Childrens Pr., 1985. ISBN 0-516-08233-7 Subj: Birthdays. Food. Music. Poetry, rhyme.

Greene, Ellin. *The legend of the Christmas rose* (Lagerlöf, Selma)

The pumpkin giant ill. by Trina Schart Hyman. Lothrop, 1970. Orig. story by Mary E. Wilkins Subj: Food. Giants. Holidays – Halloween.

Greene, Graham. *The little fire engine* ill. by Edward Ardizzone. Doubleday, 1973. Subj: Fire. Progress.

The little train ill. by Edward Ardizzone. Doubleday, 1973. Subj: Behavior – running away. Trains.

Greene, Jacqueline Dembar. *Butchers and bakers, rabbis and kings* ill. by Marilyn Hirsh. Kar-Ben Copies, 1984. Subj: Jewish culture.

What his father did ill. by John O'Brien. Houghton, 1992. ISBN 0-395-55042-4 Subj: Folk and fairy tales. Food. Jewish culture. Poverty.

Greene, Laura. *Change: getting to know about ebb and flow* ill. by Gretchen Will Mayo. Human Sciences Pr., 1981. Subj: Concepts.

Help: getting to know about needing and giving ill. by retchen Will Mayo. Human Sciences Pr., 1981. Subj: Character traits – helpfulness.

Greene, Roberta. *Two and me makes three* ill. by Paul Galdone. Coward, 1970. Subj: Ethnic groups in the U.S.

Greenfield, Eloise. *Africa dream* ill. by Carole M. Byard. John Day, 1977. Subj: Dreams. Foreign lands – Africa.

Big friend, little friend ill. by Jan Spivey Gilchrist. Black Butterfly, 1991. ISBN 0-86316-204-5 Subj: Activities – playing. Ethnic groups in the U.S. – Afro-Americans. Format, unusual – board books. Friendship. Poetry, rhyme.

Daddy and I ill. by Jan Spivey Gilchrist. Black Butterfly, 1991. ISBN 0-86316-206-1 Subj: Ethnic groups in the U.S. – Afro-Americans. Family life – fathers. Format, unusual – board books. Poetry, rhyme.

Daydreamers ill. by Tom Feelings. Dial Pr., 1981. Subj: Ethnic groups in the U.S. – Afro-Americans. Poetry, rhyme.

First pink light ill. by Moneta Barnett. Crowell, 1976. Subj: Ethnic groups in the U.S. – Afro-Americans. Family life – fathers.

Grandpa's face ill. by Floyd Cooper. Putnam's, 1988. ISBN 0-399-21525-5 Subj: Character traits – appearance. Family life – grandfathers.

I can do it by myself (Little, Lessie Jones)

I make music ill. by Jan Spivey Gilchrist. Black Butterfly, 1991. ISBN 0-86316-205-3 Subj: Ethnic groups in the U.S. – Afro-Americans. Family life. Format, unusual – board books. Music. Poetry, rhyme.

Me and Nessie ill. by Moneta Barnett. Crowell, 1975. Subj: Ethnic groups in the U.S. – Afro-Americans. Family life. Imagination – imaginary friends.

My doll, Keshia ill. by Jan Spivey Gilchrist. Black Butterfly, 1991. ISBN 0-86316-203-7 Subj: Activities – playing. Ethnic groups in the U.S. – Afro-Americans. Format, unusual – board books. Poetry, rhyme. Toys – dolls.

Night on Neighborhood Street ill. by Jan Spivey Gilchrist. Dial, 1991. ISBN 0-8037-0778-9 Subj: City. Communities, neighborhoods. Ethnic groups in the U.S. – Afro-Americans. Night. Poetry, rhyme.

She come bringing me that little baby girl ill. by John Steptoe. Lippincott, 1974. Subj: Babies. Emotions – envy, jealousy. Ethnic groups in the U.S. – Afro-Americans. Sibling rivalry.

Under the Sunday tree ill. by Amos Ferguson. Harper, 1988. ISBN 0-06-022254-9 Subj: Foreign lands – Caribbean Islands. Islands. Poetry, rhyme.

Greenfield, Karen R. *Sister Yessa's story* ill. by Claire Ewart. HarperCollins, 1992. ISBN 0-06-020279-3 Subj: Animals. Weather – rain.

Greenleaf, Ann. *No room for Sarah* ill. by author. Dodd, 1983. Subj: Bedtime. Toys.

Greenstein, Elaine. *Emily and the crows* ill. by author. Picture Book Studio, 1992. ISBN 0-88708-238-6 Subj: Animals – bulls, cows. Birds – crows. Imagination.

Greenwood, Ann. *A pack of dreams* ill. by Bernard Colonna and Mary Elizabeth Gordon. Prentice-Hall, 1979. Subj: Dreams. Poetry, rhyme.

Greeson, Janet. *The stingy baker* ill. by David La-Rochelle. Carolrhoda, 1989. ISBN 0-87614-378-8 Subj: Angels. Careers – bakers. Folk and fairy tales. Magic. Witches.

Gregor, Arthur S. *Animal babies* (Ylla)

The little elephant (Ylla)

One, two, three, four, five ill. by Robert Doisneau. Lippincott, 1956. Subj: Counting, numbers.

Gregorich, Barbara. *My friend goes left* ill. by Joyce John; ed. by Joan Hoffman. School Zone Pub., 1984. Subj: Poetry, rhyme. Riddles.

Gregory, Valiska. *Sunny side up* ill. by Jeni Bassett. Four Winds Pr., 1986. ISBN 0-02-738050-5 Subj: Animals – dogs. Character traits – optimism.

Terribly wonderful ill. by Jeni Bassett. Four Winds Pr., 1986. ISBN 0-02-738110-1 Subj: Animals – dogs. Character traits – optimism.

Through the mickle woods ill. by Barry Moser. Little, 1992. ISBN 0-316-32779-4 Subj: Animals – bears. Death. Folk and fairy tales. Forest, woods. Royalty – kings.

Greifenstein, Sandra. *The fish* (Bruna, Dick)

Greisman, Joan. *Things I hate!* (Wittels, Harriet)

Grejniec, Michael. *When I open my eyes* ill. by author. Holt, 1990. ISBN 0-8050-1417-9 Subj: Animals – sheep. Imagination.

Gretz, Susanna. *Duck takes off* ill. by author. Four Winds, 1991. ISBN 0-02-737472-6 Subj: Activities – playing. Animals. Birds – ducks. Friendship.

Frog, duck and rabbit ill. by author. Four Winds, 1992. ISBN 0-02-737327-4 Subj: Animals. Friendship.

Frog in the middle ill. by author. Four Winds, 1991. ISBN 0-02-737471-8 Subj: Animals. Behavior – secrets. Birthdays. Emotions – envy, jealousy. Friendship. Frogs and toads.

Hide-and-seek ill. by author. Macmillan, 1986. ISBN 0-02-737400-9 Subj: Bedtime. Behavior – hiding. Emotions – fear. Format, unusual – board books. Games. Night. Toys – teddy bears.

I'm not sleepy ill. by author. Macmillan, 1986. ISBN 0-02-737470-X Subj: Bedtime. Format, unusual – board books. Games. Sleep. Toys – teddy bears.

It's your turn, Roger ill. by author. Dial Pr., 1985. ISBN 0-8037-0198-5 Subj: Animals – pigs. Behavior – sharing. Food.

Rabbit rambles on ill. by author. Four Winds, 1992. ISBN 0-02-737325-8 Subj: Animals. Animals – rabbits. Behavior – boasting. Character traits – honesty. Friendship.

Ready for bed ill. by author. Macmillan, 1986. ISBN 0-02-737460-2 Subj: Bedtime. Format, unusual – board books.

Roger loses his marbles! ill. by author. Dial Pr., 1988. ISBN 0-8037-0565-4 Subj: Animals – pigs. Birthdays. Character traits – practicality.

Roger takes charge! ill. by author. Dial Pr., 1987. ISBN 0-8037-0121-7 Subj: Activities – babysitting. Animals – pigs. Behavior – bullying.

Teddy bears ABC ill. by author. Follett, 1975. Subj: ABC books. Counting, numbers. Toys – teddy bears.

Teddy bears at the seaside by Susanna Gretz and Alison Sage; ill. by Susanna Gretz. Four Winds, 1989. ISBN 0-02-738141-2 Subj: Sea and seashore. Toys – teddy bears.

Teddy bears cure a cold by Susanna Gretz and Alison Sage; ill. by Susanna Gretz. Four Winds Pr., 1985. ISBN 0-590-07949-2 Subj: Illness. Toys – teddy bears.

Teddy bears go shopping ill. by author. Four Winds Pr., 1982. Subj: Shopping. Toys – teddy bears.

Teddy bears' moving day ill. by author. Four Winds Pr., 1981. Subj: Moving. Toys – teddy bears.

Teddy bears 1 - 10 ill. by author. Four Winds Pr., 1986, 1969. ISBN 0-02-738140-4 Subj: Counting, numbers. Toys – teddy bears.

Teddy bears stay indoors ill. by author. Four Winds Pr., 1987. ISBN 0-02-738150-1 Subj: Toys – teddy bears.

Teddy bears take the train by Susanna Gretz and Alison Sage; ill. by Susanna Gretz. Four Winds Pr., 1987. ISBN 0-02-738170-6 Subj: Activities – traveling. Toys – teddy bears. Trains.

Teddybears cookbook by Susanna Gretz and Alison Sage; ill. by Susanna Gretz. Doubleday, 1978. Subj: Activities – cooking. Toys – teddy bears.

Too dark! ill. by author. Macmillan, 1986. ISBN 0-02-737410-6 Subj: Bedtime. Emotions – fear. Format, unusual – board books. Night. Toys – teddy bears.

Greve, Andreas. *Christopher's dream car* ill. by author. Firefly, 1991. ISBN 1-55037-169-X Subj: Automobiles. Family life – grandparents. Imagination.

Greydanus, Rose. *Animals at the zoo* ill. by Susan Hall. Troll Assoc., 1980. Subj: Animals. Zoos.

Big red fire engine ill. by Paul Harvey. Troll Assoc., 1980. Subj: Careers – firefighters. Trucks.

Changing seasons ill. by Susan Hall. Troll Assoc., 1983. Subj: Seasons.

Freddie the frog ill. by Tom Garcia. Troll Assoc., 1980. Subj: Frogs and toads.

Horses ill. by Joel Snyder. Troll Assoc., 1983. Subj: Animals – horses.

My secret hiding place ill. by Paul Harvey. Troll Assoc., 1980. Subj: Behavior – hiding.

Susie goes shopping ill. by Margot Apple. Troll Assoc., 1980. Subj: Shopping.

Tree house fun ill. by Chris L. Demarest. Troll Assoc., 1980. Subj: Houses. Trees.

Willie the slowpoke ill. by Andrea Eberbach. Troll Assoc., 1980. Subj: Behavior – hurrying.

Grieg, E. H. (Edvard Hagerup). *E. H. Grieg's Peer Gynt* ill. by Yoshiharu Suzuki. Gakkenk, 1971. Adapt. by Makoto Oishi; tr. by Ann Brannen Subj: Folk and fairy tales. Foreign lands – Norway.

Griest, Virginia. *In between* ill. by Monica Wellington. Dutton, 1989. ISBN 0-525-44521-8 Subj: Concepts.

Grifalconi, Ann. *City rhythms* ill. by author. Bobbs-Merrill, 1965. Subj: City. Ethnic groups in the U.S. – Afro-Americans.

Darkness and the butterfly ill. by author. Little, 1987. ISBN 0-316-32863-4 Subj: Emotions – fear. Foreign lands – Africa. Insects – butterflies, caterpillars. Night.

Flyaway girl ill. by author. Little, 1992. ISBN 0-316-32866-9 Subj: Behavior – growing up. Foreign lands – Africa. Rivers.

The toy trumpet ill. by author. Bobbs-Merrill, 1968. Subj: Foreign lands – Mexico. Music. Toys.

The village of round and square houses ill. by author. Little, 1986. ISBN 0-316-32862-6 Subj: Caldecott award honor book. Folk and fairy tales. Foreign lands – Africa. Volcanoes.

Griffen, Elizabeth. *A dog's book of bugs* ill. by Peter Parnall. Atheneum, 1967. Subj: Insects.

Griffith, Helen V. *Alex and the cat* ill. by Joseph Low. Greenwillow, 1982. Subj: Animals – cats. Animals – dogs.

Alex remembers ill. by Donald Carrick. Greenwillow, 1983. Subj: Animals – cats. Animals – dogs. Moon. Seasons – fall.

Georgia music ill. by James Stevenson. Greenwillow, 1986. ISBN 0-688-06072-2 Subj: Family life – grandfathers. Gardens, gardening. Music. Nature. Old age. Seasons – summer.

Grandaddy's place ill. by James Stevenson. Greenwillow, 1987. ISBN 0-688-06254-7 Subj: Animals. Country. Family life – grandfathers. Sports – fishing.

Mine will, said John ill. by Muriel Batherman. Greenwillow, 1980. Subj: Animals – dogs. Family life. Pets.

More Alex and the cat ill. by Donald Carrick. Greenwillow, 1983. Subj: Animals – cats. Animals – dogs.

Nata ill. by Nancy Tafuri. Greenwillow, 1985. ISBN 0-688-04977-X Subj: Behavior – bad day. Fairies.

Pluck's dreams ill. by Susan Condie Lamb. Greenwillow, 1990. ISBN 0-688-08813-9 Subj: Animals – dogs. Dreams.

Grimm, Jacob. *The bear and the kingbird* by Jacob and Wilhelm Grimm; tr. by Lore Segal; ill. by Chris Conover. Farrar, 1979. Subj: Animals – bears. Birds. Folk and fairy tales.

The bearskinner by Jacob and Wilhelm Grimm; ill. by Felix Hoffmann. Atheneum, 1978. Translation of Der Bärenhäuter Subj: Devil. Folk and fairy tales.

The brave little tailor by Jacob and Wilhelm Grimm; ill. by Mark Corcoran. Troll Assoc., 1979.

Subj: Careers – tailors. Character traits – bravery. Folk and fairy tales. Giants.

The brave little tailor by Jacob and Wilhelm Grimm; tr. by Anthea Bell; ill. by Svend Otto S. Larousse, 1979. Subj: Careers – tailors. Character traits – bravery. Folk and fairy tales. Giants.

The brave little tailor by Jacob and Wilhelm Grimm; adapt. by Robert D. San Souci; ill. by Daniel San Souci. Doubleday, 1982. Subj: Careers – tailors. Character traits – bravery. Folk and fairy tales. Giants.

The brave little tailor by Jacob and Wilhelm Grimm; tr. by Anthea Bell; ill. by Eve Tharlet. Picture Book Studio, 1989. ISBN 0-88708-091-X Subj: Careers – tailors. Character traits – bravery. Folk and fairy tales. Giants.

The brave little tailor by Jacob and Wilhelm Grimm; retold by Peggy Thomson; ill. by James Warhola. Simon & Schuster, 1992. ISBN 0-671-73736-8 Subj: Careers – tailors. Character traits – bravery. Folk and fairy tales. Giants.

The Bremen town musicians by Jacob and Wilhelm Grimm; retold and ill. by Donna Diamond. Delacorte Pr., 1981. Subj: Animals. Folk and fairy tales. Old age.

The Bremen town musicians by Jacob and Wilhelm Grimm; tr. by Elizabeth Shub; ill. by Janina Domanska. Greenwillow, 1980. Subj: Animals. Folk and fairy tales. Old age.

The Bremen town musicians by Jacob and Wilhelm Grimm; ill. by Paul Galdone. McGraw-Hill, 1968. Tr. of Der Bremer Stadtmusikanten Subj: Animals. Folk and fairy tales. Old age.

Bremen town musicians by Jacob and Wilhelm Grimm; tr. by Anthea Bell; ill. by Josef Paleček. Picture Book Studio, 1988. ISBN 0-88708-071-5 Subj: Animals. Folk and fairy tales. Old age.

The Bremen town musicians by Jacob and Wilhelm Grimm; retold and ill. by Ilse Plume. Doubleday, 1980. Subj: Animals. Caldecott award honor book. Folk and fairy tales. Old age.

The Bremen town musicians by Jacob and Wilhelm Grimm; tr. by Anthea Bell; ill. by Bernadette Watts. North-South, 1992. ISBN 1-55858-148-0 Subj: Animals. Folk and fairy tales. Old age.

Cinderella by Jacob and Wilhelm Grimm; retold and ill. by Nonny Hogrogian. Greenwillow, 1981. Subj: Folk and fairy tales. Royalty – princes. Sibling rivalry.

Cinderella by Jacob and Wilhelm Grimm; tr. by Anne Rogers; ill. by Svend Otto S. Larouse, 1978. Subj: Folk and fairy tales. Sibling rivalry. Royalty – princes.

Clever Kate by Jacob and Wilhelm Grimm; adapt. by Elizabeth Shub; ill. by Anita Lobel. Macmillan, 1973. Subj: Folk and fairy tales. Humor.

The devil with the green hairs by Jacob and Wilhelm Grimm; retold and ill. by Nonny Hogrogian. Knopf, 1983. Subj: Devil. Folk and fairy tales.

The donkey prince by Jacob and Wilhelm Grimm; adapt. by M. Jean Craig; ill. by Barbara Cooney. Doubleday, 1977. Subj: Animals – donkeys. Folk and fairy tales. Magic. Royalty – princes. Wizards.

The earth gnome by Jacob and Wilhelm Grimm; tr. by Wanda Gág; ill. by Margot Tomes. Coward, 1985. ISBN 0-698-20618-5 Subj: Elves and little people. Folk and fairy tales. Magic. Royalty.

The elves and the shoemaker by Jacob and Wilhelm Grimm; ill. by Paul Galdone. Clarion, 1984. Based on Lucy Crane's tr. from the German Adaption of Wichtelmänner Subj: Careers – shoemakers. Character traits – helpfulness. Elves and little people. Folk and fairy tales. Foreign lands – Germany.

The elves and the shoemaker by Jacob and Wilhelm Grimm; adapt. and ill. by Bernadette Watts. Holt, 1986. ISBN 0-03-008022-3 Subj: Careers – shoemakers. Character traits – helpfulness. Elves and little people. Folk and fairy tales. Foreign lands – Germany.

The falling stars by Jacob and Wilhelm Grimm; ill. by Eugen Sopko. Holt, 1985. ISBN 0-03-005742-6 Subj: Character traits — generosity. Clothing. Folk and fairy tales.

The fisherman and his wife by Jacob and Wilhelm Grimm; tr. by Elizabeth Shub; ill. by Monika Laimgruber. Greenwillow, 1979. Subj: Behavior – greed. Folk and fairy tales.

The fisherman and his wife by Jacob and Wilhelm Grimm; tr. from German by Anthea Bell; ill. by Alan Marks. Picture Book Studio 1989. ISBN 0-88708-072-3 Subj: Behavior – greed. Folk and fairy tales.

The fisherman and his wife by Jacob and Wilhelm Grimm; adapt. by John Warren Stewig; ill. by Margot Tomes. Holiday, 1988. ISBN 0-8234-0714-4 Subj: Behavior – greed. Folk and fairy tales.

The fisherman and his wife by Jacob and Wilhelm Grimm; tr. by Randall Jarrell; ill. by Margot Zemach. Farrar, 1980. Subj: Behavior – greed. Folk and fairy tales.

The four clever brothers by Jacob and Wilhelm Grimm; ill. by Felix Hoffmann. Harcourt, 1967. Subj: Character traits – cleverness. Dragons. Folk and fairy tales.

The frog prince: or Iron Henry tr. from German by Naomi Lewis; ill. by Binette Schroeder. North-South, 1989. ISBN 1-55858-015-8 Subj: Folk and fairy tales. Frogs and toads. Royalty – princes. Royalty – princesses.

The glass mountain by Jacob and Wilhelm Grimm; adapt. and ill. by Nonny Hogrogian. Knopf, 1985. Originally titled The raven ISBN 0-394-96724-0 Subj: Folk and fairy tales. Giants.

Godfather Cat and Mousie by Jacob and Wilhelm Grimm; adapt. by Doris Orgel; ill. by Ann Schweninger. Macmillan, 1986. ISBN 0-02-768690-6 Subj: Animals – cats. Animals – mice. Folk and fairy tales.

The golden bird: and other fairy tales by Jacob and Wilhelm Grimm; tr. by Randall Jarrell; ill. by Sandro Nardini. Macmillan, 1962. Subj: Folk and fairy tales.

The golden goose by Jacob and Wilhelm Grimm; tr. by Anthea Bell; ill. by Dorothée Duntze. Holt, 1988. ISBN 3-85539-004-5 Subj: Character traits – kindness. Folk and fairy tales. Humor. Royalty – princesses.

The golden goose by Jacob and Wilhelm Grimm; adapt. by Susan Saunders; ill. by Isadore Seltzer. Scholastic, 1988. ISBN 0-590-41544-1 Subj: Character traits – kindness. Folk and fairy tales. Humor. Royalty – princesses.

The golden goose by Jacob and Wilhelm Grimm; ill. by Martin Ursell; text by Linda M. Jennings. Silver Burdett, 1985. ISBN 0-382-09147-7 Subj: Character traits – kindness. Folk and fairy tales. Humor. Royalty – princesses.

The goose girl by Jacob and Wilhelm Grimm; tr. by Anthea Bell; ill. by Sabine Bruntjen. Holt, 1988. ISBN 3-85539-003-7 Subj: Folk and fairy tales. Royalty. Weddings.

Grimm Tom Thumb (Tom Thumb)

Hans in luck by Jacob and Wilhelm Grimm; retold and ill. by Paul Galdone. Parents, 1979. Translation of Hans in Glück Subj: Character traits – foolishness. Character traits – luck. Folk and fairy tales.

Hans in luck by Jacob and Wilhelm Grimm; ed. and ill. by Felix Hoffmann. Atheneum, 1975. Translation of Hans in Glück Subj: Character traits – foolishness. Character traits – luck. Folk and fairy tales.

Hansel and Gretel by Jacob and Wilhelm Grimm; tr. by Charles Scribner, Jr.; ill. by Adrienne Adams. Scribner's, 1975. Subj: Folk and fairy tales. Forest, woods. Witches.

Hansel and Gretel by Jacob and Wilhelm Grimm; ill. by Anthony Browne. Watts, 1982. Subj: Folk and fairy tales. Forest, woods. Witches.

Hansel and Gretel by Jacob and Wilhelm Grimm; ill. by Susan Jeffers. Dial Pr., 1980. Subj: Folk and fairy tales. Forest, woods. Witches.

Hansel and Gretel by Jacob and Wilhelm Grimm; ill. by Winslow P. Pels. Scholastic, 1988. ISBN 0-590-41793-2 Subj: Behavior – lost. Folk and fairy tales. Forest, woods. Witches.

Hansel and Gretel by Jacob and Wilhelm Grimm; tr. from Spanish by Leland Northam; adapt. by M. Eulalia Valeri; ill. by Conxita Rodriguez. Silver Burdett, 1985. ISBN 0-392-09072-1 Subj: Folk and fairy tales. Forest, woods. Witches. Wordless.

Hansel and Gretel by Jacob and Wilhelm Grimm; ill. by John Wallner. Prentice-Hall, 1985. ISBN 0-13-383654-1 Subj: Folk and fairy tales. Forest, woods. Witches.

Hansel and Gretel by Jacob and Wilhelm Grimm; retold by Rika Lesser; ill. by Paul O. Zelinsky. Dodd, 1984. Subj: Caldecott award honor book. Folk and fairy tales. Forest, woods. Witches.

Hansel and Gretel by Jacob and Wilhelm Grimm; tr. from the German by Elizabeth D. Crawford; ill. by Lisbeth Zwerger. Morrow, 1980. Subj: Folk and fairy tales. Forest, woods. Witches.

The horse, the fox, and the lion by Jacob and Wilhelm Grimm; ill. by Paul Galdone. Seabury Pr., 1968. Adapt. from The fox and the horse [De Fuchs und das Pferd] Subj: Animals – dogs. Animals – foxes. Animals – horses. Animals – lions. Behavior – trickery. Folk and fairy tales. Old age.

Jorinda and Joringel by Jacob and Wilhelm Grimm; tr. by Elizabeth Shub; ill. by Adrienne Adams. Scribner's, 1968. Subj: Folk and fairy tales. Witches.

Jorinda and Joringel by Jacob and Wilhelm Grimm; adapt. by Naomi Lewis; ill. by Jutta Ash. David & Charles, 1987. ISBN 0-86264-064-4 Subj: Folk and fairy tales. Witches.

Jorinda and Joringel by Jacob and Wilhelm Grimm; retold by Wanda Gág; ill. by Margot Tomes. Coward, 1978. Subj: Folk and fairy tales. Witches.

King Grisly-Beard by Jacob and Wilhelm Grimm; tr. by Edgar Taylor; ill. by Maurice Sendak. Farrar, 1973. 1823 translation. Subj: Character traits – conceit. Folk and fairy tales. Royalty. Theater.

Little red cap by Jacob and Wilhelm Grimm; tr. from German by Elizabeth D. Crawford; ill. by Lisbeth Zwerger. Morrow, 1983. Subj: Animals – wolves. Behavior – talking to strangers. Folk and fairy tales.

Little Red Riding Hood by Jacob and Wilhelm Grimm; adapt. by Elizabeth and Katherine Gant; ill. by Frank Aloise. Abingdon Pr., 1969. Adapt. and music based on retelling of Rotkäppchen Incl. melodies with texts, with piano acc. Subj: Animals – wolves. Behavior – talking to strangers. Folk and fairy tales.

Little Red Riding Hood by Jacob and Wilhelm Grimm; adapt. by Margaret Hillert; ill. by Gwen Connelly. Follett, 1982. Subj: Animals – wolves. Behavior – talking to strangers. Folk and fairy tales.

Little Red Riding Hood by Jacob and Wilhelm Grimm; ill. by Paul Galdone. McGraw-Hill, 1974. Adapt. from the retelling of Rotkäppchen. Subj: Animals – wolves. Behavior – talking to strangers. Folk and fairy tales.

Little Red Riding Hood by Jacob and Wilhelm Grimm; ill. by John S. Goodall. Macmillan, 1988. ISBN 0-689-50457-8 Subj: Animals. Animals – mice. Animals – wolves. Behavior – talking to strangers. Folk and fairy tales. Format, unusual. Wordless.

Little Red Riding Hood by Jacob and Wilhelm Grimm; retold and ill. by Trina Schart Hyman. Holiday, 1983. Subj: Animals – wolves. Behavior – talking to strangers. Caldecott award honor book. Folk and fairy tales.

Little Red Riding Hood by Jacob and Wilhelm Grimm; ill. by Bernadette Watts. Collins-World,

1969. Subj: Animals – wolves. Behavior – talking to strangers. Folk and fairy tales.

Lucky Hans by Jacob and Wilhelm Grimm; tr. by Jock J. Curle; ill. by Eugen Sopko. Holt, 1986. ISBN 0-8050-0009-7 Subj: Character traits – foolishness. Character traits – luck. Folk and fairy tales.

Mother Holly by Jacob and Wilhelm Grimm ill. by Bernadette Watts. Crowell, 1972. Based on the Grimm brothers' Frau Holle Subj: Behavior – greed. Character traits – helpfulness. Character traits – laziness. Folk and fairy tales.

Mrs. Fox's wedding by Jacob and Wilhelm Grimm; retold by Sara and Stephen Corrin; ill. by Errol Le Cain. Doubleday, 1980. Subj: Animals – foxes. Counting, numbers. Folk and fairy tales. Weddings.

The musicians of Bremen by Jacob and Wilhelm Grimm; tr. by Anne Rogers; ill. by Svend Otto S. Larousse, 1974. Subj: Animals. Folk and fairy tales. Old age.

The musicians of Bremen by Jacob and Wilhelm Grimm; ill. by Martin Ursell; text by Linda M. Jennings. Silver Burdett, 1985. ISBN 0-382-09155-8 Subj: Animals. Folk and fairy tales. Old age.

Nanny goat and the seven little kids retold by Eric A. Kimmel; ill. by Janet Stevens. Holiday, 1990. An adaptation of: The wolf and the seven little kids ISBN 0-8234-0789-6 Subj: Animals – goats. Animals – wolves. Folk and fairy tales.

The princess and the frog by Jacob and Wilhelm Grimm; retold and ill. by Rachel Isadora. Greenwillow, 1989. ISBN 0-688-06374-8 Subj: Character traits – willfulness. Folk and fairy tales. Frogs and toads. Royalty – princesses.

Rapunzel by Jacob and Wilhelm Grimm; retold and ill. by Jutta Ash. Holt, 1982. Subj: Folk and fairy tales. Hair. Royalty – princes. Witches.

Rapunzel by Jacob and Wilhelm Grimm; ill. by Bert Dodson. Troll Assoc., 1979. Subj: Folk and fairy tales. Hair. Royalty – princes. Witches.

Rapunzel by Jacob and Wilhelm Grimm; retold by Barbara Rogasky; ill. by Trina Schart Hyman. Holiday, 1982. Subj: Folk and fairy tales. Hair. Royalty – princes. Witches.

Rapunzel by Jacob and Wilhelm Grimm; retold by Amy Ehrlich; ill. by Kris Waldherr. Dial, 1989. ISBN 0-8037-0655-3 Subj: Folk and fairy tales. Hair. Royalty – princes. Witches.

Rapunzel by Jacob and Wilhelm Grimm; adapt. and ill. by Bernadette Watts. Harper, 1975. ISBN 0-690-00980-1 Subj: Folk and fairy tales. Hair. Royalty – princes. Witches.

Rumpelstiltskin by Jacob and Wilhelm Grimm; ill. by Jacqueline Ayer. Harcourt, 1967. Subj: Folk and fairy tales. Magic. Riddles. Royalty. Weddings.

Rumpelstiltskin by Jacob and Wilhelm Grimm; retold and ill. by Donna Diamond. Holiday, 1983. Subj: Folk and fairy tales. Magic. Riddles. Royalty. Weddings.

Rumpelstiltskin by Jacob and Wilhelm Grimm; adapt. and ill. by Paul Galdone. Houghton, 1985. ISBN 0-89919-266-1 Subj: Folk and fairy tales. Magic. Riddles. Royalty. Weddings.

Rumpelstiltskin by Jacob and Wilhelm Grimm; retold and ill. by Jonathan Langley. HarperCollins, 1992. ISBN 0-06-020199-1 Subj: Folk and fairy tales. Magic. Riddles. Royalty. Weddings.

Rumpelstiltskin by Jacob and Wilhelm Grimm; retold by Alison Sage; ill. by Gennady Spirin. Dial, 1991. ISBN 0-8037-0908-0 Subj: Folk and fairy tales. Magic. Riddles. Royalty. Weddings.

Rumpelstiltskin by Jacob and Wilhelm Grimm; ill. by John Wallner. Prentice-Hall, 1984. Subj: Folk and fairy tales. Magic. Riddles. Royalty. Weddings.

Rumpelstiltskin by Jacob and Wilhelm Grimm; adapt. and ill. by Paul O. Zelinsky. Dutton, 1986. ISBN 0-525-44265-0 Subj: Folk and fairy tales. Magic. Riddles. Royalty. Weddings.

The seven ravens by Jacob and Wilhelm Grimm; ill. by Felix Hoffmann. Harcourt, 1963. Subj: Birds – ravens. Folk and fairy tales. Magic.

The seven ravens by Jacob and Wilhelm Grimm; tr. from German by Elizabeth D. Crawford; ill. by Lisbeth Zwerger. Morrow, 1981. Subj: Birds – ravens. Folk and fairy tales. Magic.

The shoemaker and the elves by Jacob and Wilhelm Grimm; ill. by Adrienne Adams. Macmillan, 1972. ISBN 0-684-12982-5 Subj: Careers – shoemakers. Character traits – helpfulness. Elves and little people. Folk and fairy tales. Foreign lands – Germany.

The shoemaker and the elves by Jacob and Wilhelm Grimm; ill. by Cynthia and William Birrer. Lothrop, 1983. Adapt. of Wichtelmänner Subj: Careers – shoemakers. Character traits – helpfulness. Elves and little people. Folk and fairy tales. Foreign lands – Germany.

The shoemaker and the elves by Jacob and Wilhelm Grimm; retold and ill. by Ilse Plume. Harcourt, 1991. ISBN 0-15-274050-3 Subj: Careers – shoemakers. Character traits – helpfulness. Elves and little people. Folk and fairy tales. Foreign lands – Germany.

The six swans by Jacob and Wilhelm Grimm; retold by Robert D. San Souci; ill. by Daniel San Souci. Simon & Schuster, 1989. ISBN 0-671-65848-4 Subj: Birds – swans. Folk and fairy tales. Magic.

The six swans by Jacob and Wilhelm Grimm; retold by Wanda Gág; ill. by Margot Tomes. Coward, 1982. Subj: Birds – swans. Folk and fairy tales. Magic.

The sleeping beauty by Jacob and Wilhelm Grimm; retold and ill. by Warwick Hutton. Atheneum, 1979. Subj: Folk and fairy tales.

The sleeping beauty by Jacob and Wilhelm Grimm; retold and ill. by Trina Schart Hyman. Little, 1977. Subj: Folk and fairy tales.

The sleeping beauty by Jacob and Wilhelm Grimm; adapt. and ill. by Mercer Mayer. Macmillan, 1984. ISBN 0-02-765340-4 Subj: Folk and fairy tales.

Sleeping Beauty by Jacob and Wilhelm Grimm; tr. from Spanish by Leland Northam; adapt. by M. Eulalia Valeri; ill. by Fina Rifa. Silver Burdett, 1985. ISBN 0-382-09068-3 Subj: Folk and fairy tales. Wordless.

The sleeping beauty by Jacob and Wilhelm Grimm; adapt. by Jane Yolen; ill. by Ruth Sanderson. Knopf, 1986. ISBN 0-394-55431-0 Subj: Folk and fairy tales.

Sleeping Beauty by Jacob and Wilhelm Grimm; adapt. and ill. by John Wallner. Viking, 1987. ISBN 0-670-81708-2 Subj: Folk and fairy tales. Format, unusual – toy and movable books.

Snow White by Jacob and Wilhelm Grimm; tr. from German by Paul Heins; ill. by Trina Schart Hyman. Little, 1975. Subj: Elves and little people. Emotions – envy, jealousy. Folk and fairy tales. Magic. Witches.

Snow White by Jacob and Wilhelm Grimm; ill. by Bernadette Watts. Faber, 1983. Subj: Elves and little people. Emotions – envy, jealousy. Folk and fairy tales. Magic. Witches.

Snow White and Rose Red by Jacob and Wilhelm Grimm; tr. by Wayne Andrews; ill. by Adrienne Adams. Scribner's, 1964. Subj: Animals – bears. Elves and little people. Folk and fairy tales. Magic. Weddings.

Snow-White and Rose-Red adapt. and ill. by Barbara Cooney. Dial Pr., 1966. Subj: Animals – bears. Elves and little people. Folk and fairy tales.

Snow White and Rose Red by Jacob and Wilhelm Grimm; tr. by Andrew Lang; ill. by John Wallner. Prentice-Hall, 1984. Subj: Animals – bears. Elves and little people. Folk and fairy tales. Magic. Weddings.

Snow White and Rose Red by Jacob and Wilhelm Grimm; adapt. and ill. by Bernadette Watts. Holt, 1988. ISBN 0-8050-0738-5 Subj: Animals – bears. Elves and little people. Folk and fairy tales. Magic.

Snow White and the seven dwarfs by Jacob and Wilhelm Grimm; ill. by Wanda Gág. Coward, 1938. Subj: Caldecott award honor book. Folk and fairy tales.

Snow White and the seven dwarves by Jacob and Wilhelm Grimm; adapt. by Anthea Bell; ill. by Chihiro Iwasaki. Picture Book Studio, 1985. ISBN 0-88708-012-X Subj: Elves and little people. Emotions – envy, jealousy. Folk and fairy tales. Magic. Witches.

The table, the donkey and the stick adapt. and ill. by Paul Galdone. McGraw-Hill, 1976. Adapt. from a retelling of Das tapfere Schneiderlein Subj: Cumulative tales. Folk and fairy tales. Furniture – tables.

Three Grimms' fairy tales: The fox and the geese; The magic porridge pot; The silver pennies by Jacob and Wilhelm Grimm; ill. by Bernadette Watts. Little, 1981. Subj: Folk and fairy tales.

Tom Thumb (Tom Thumb)

The traveling musicians of Bremen by Jacob and Wilhelm Grimm; retold by P. K. Page; ill. by Kady MacDonald Denton. Little, 1992. ISBN 0-316-68836-3 Subj: Animals. Folk and fairy tales. Old age. Poetry, rhyme.

The twelve dancing princesses by Jacob and Wilhelm Grimm; retold by Marianna Mayer; ill. by Kinuko Y. Craft. Morrow, 1989. ISBN 0-688-02026-7 Subj: Activities – dancing. Folk and fairy tales. Royalty – princesses.

The twelve dancing princesses by Jacob and Wilhelm Grimm; retold by Anne Carter; ill. by Anne Dalton. HarperCollins, 1989. ISBN 0-397-32373-5 Subj: Activities – dancing. Folk and fairy tales. Royalty – princesses.

The twelve dancing princesses by Jacob and Wilhelm Grimm; ill. by Dennis Hockerman. Troll Assoc., 1979. Subj: Activities – dancing. Folk and fairy tales. Royalty – princesses.

The twelve dancing princesses by Jacob and Wilhelm Grimm; ill. by Errol Le Cain. Viking, 1978. Subj: Activities – dancing. Folk and fairy tales. Royalty – princesses.

The twelve dancing princesses by Jacob and Wilhelm Grimm; retold by Marianna Mayer; ill. by Gerald McDermott. Morrow, 1988. ISBN 0-688-02026-7 Subj: Activities – dancing. Folk and fairy tales. Royalty – princesses.

The twelve dancing princesses by Jacob and Wilhelm Grimm; tr. by Elizabeth Shub; ill. by Uri Shulevitz. Scribner's, 1966. Subj: Activities – dancing. Folk and fairy tales. Royalty – princesses.

The ugly duckling by Jacob and Wilhelm Grimm; tr. from Spanish by Leland Northam; adapt. by M. Eulalia Valeri; ill. by Maria Ruis. Silver Burdett, 1985. ISBN 0-382-09071-3 Subj: Birds – ducks. Birds – swans. Character traits – appearance. Character traits – being different. Folk and fairy tales. Wordless.

The valiant little tailor by Jacob and Wilhelm Grimm; ill. by Victor G. Ambrus. Oxford Univ. Pr., 1980. First pub. in 1971 Subj: Careers – tailors. Character traits – bravery. Folk and fairy tales. Giants.

Walt Disney's Snow White and the seven dwarfs (Walt Disney Productions)

The water of life (Rogasky, Barbara)

The wishing table by Jacob and Wilhelm Grimm; tr. by Anthea Bell; ill. by Eve Tharlet. Picture Book Studio, 1988. ISBN 0-88708-064-2 Subj: Cumulative tales. Folk and fairy tales. Furniture – tables.

The wolf and the seven kids by Jacob and Wilhelm Grimm; ill. by Kinuko Y. Craft. Troll Assoc., 1979. Subj: Animals – goats. Animals – wolves. Folk and fairy tales.

The wolf and the seven little kids by Jacob and Wilhelm Grimm; tr. by Anne Rogers; ill. by Svend Otto S. Larousse, 1977. Subj: Animals – goats. Animals – wolves. Folk and fairy tales.

The wolf and the seven little kids by Jacob and Wilhelm Grimm; adapt. by Linda M. Jennings; ill. by Martin Ursell. Silver Burdett, 1986. ISBN 0-382-09306-2 Subj: Animals – goats. Animals – wolves. Folk and fairy tales.

Grimm, Wilhelm. *The bear and the kingbird* (Grimm, Jacob)

The bearskinner (Grimm, Jacob)

The brave little tailor (Grimm, Jacob)

The Bremen town musicians (Grimm, Jacob)

Bremen town musicians (Grimm, Jacob)

Cinderella (Grimm, Jacob)

Clever Kate (Grimm, Jacob)

Dear Mili tr. by Ralph Manheim; ill. by Maurice Sendak. Farrar, 1988. ISBN 0-374-31762-3 Subj: Death. Folk and fairy tales. War.

The devil with the green hairs (Grimm, Jacob)

The donkey prince (Grimm, Jacob)

The elves and the shoemaker (Grimm, Jacob)

The falling stars (Grimm, Jacob)

The fisherman and his wife (Grimm, Jacob)

The four clever brothers (Grimm, Jacob)

The frog prince (Grimm, Jacob)

The glass mountain (Grimm, Jacob)

Godfather Cat and Mousie (Grimm, Jacob)

The golden bird (Grimm, Jacob)

The golden goose (Grimm, Jacob)

The goose girl (Grimm, Jacob)

Grimm Tom Thumb (Tom Thumb)

Hans in luck (Grimm, Jacob)

Hansel and Gretel (Grimm, Jacob)

The horse, the fox, and the lion (Grimm, Jacob)

Jorinda and Joringel (Grimm, Jacob)

King Grisly-Beard (Grimm, Jacob)

Little red cap (Grimm, Jacob)

Little Red Riding Hood (Grimm, Jacob)

Lucky Hans (Grimm, Jacob)

Mother Holly (Grimm, Jacob)

Mrs. Fox's wedding (Grimm, Jacob)

The musicians of Bremen (Grimm, Jacob)

The princess and the frog (Grimm, Jacob)

Rapunzel (Grimm, Jacob)

Rumpelstiltskin (Grimm, Jacob)

The seven ravens (Grimm, Jacob)

The shoemaker and the elves (Grimm, Jacob)

The sleeping beauty (Grimm, Jacob)

Sleeping Beauty (Grimm, Jacob)

Snow White (Grimm, Jacob)

Snow White and Rose Red (Grimm, Jacob)

Snow White and the seven dwarfs (Grimm, Jacob)

Snow White and the seven dwarves (Grimm, Jacob)

Snow-White and Rose-Red (Grimm, Jacob)

The table, the donkey and the stick (Grimm, Jacob)

Three Grimms' fairy tales (Grimm, Jacob)

Tom Thumb (Tom Thumb)

The traveling musicians of Bremen (Grimm, Jacob)

The twelve dancing princesses (Grimm, Jacob)

The ugly duckling (Grimm, Jacob)

The valiant little tailor (Grimm, Jacob)

Walt Disney's Snow White and the seven dwarfs (Walt Disney Productions)

The water of life (Rogasky, Barbara)

The wishing table (Grimm, Jacob)

The wolf and the seven kids (Grimm, Jacob)

The wolf and the seven little kids (Grimm, Jacob)

Grindley, Sally. *Four black puppies* ill. by Clive Scruton. Lothrop, 1987. ISBN 0-688-07266-6 Subj: Animals – dogs. Behavior – misbehavior.

I don't want to! ill. by Carol Thompson. Little, 1990. ISBN 0-316-32893-6 Subj: Behavior. School.

Knock, knock! Who's there? ill. by Anthony Browne. Knopf, 1986. ISBN 0-394-98400-5 Subj: Bedtime. Family life – fathers. Games. Monsters. Toys – teddy bears.

Shhh! ill. by Peter Utton. Little, 1992. ISBN 0-316-32899-5 Subj: Format, unusual. Giants.

Groat, Diane *see* De Groat, Diane

Grode, Redway *see* Gorey, Edward (St. John)

Groening, Maggie. *Maggie Simpson's alphabet book* (Groening, Matt)

Maggie Simpson's book of animals by Maggie and Matt Groening; ill. by Matt Groening. HarperCollins, 1991. ISBN 0-06-020237-8 Subj: Animals. Zoos.

Maggie Simpson's book of colors and shapes by Maggie and Matt Groening; ill. by Matt Groening. HarperCollins, 1991. ISBN 0-06-020235-1 Subj: Concepts – color. Concepts – shape.

Maggie Simpson's counting book (Groening, Matt)

Groening, Matt. *Maggie Simpson's alphabet book* by Matt and Maggie Groening. HarperCollins, 1991. ISBN 0-06-020236-X Subj: ABC books.

Maggie Simpson's book of animals (Groening, Maggie)

Maggie Simpson's book of colors and shapes (Groening, Maggie)

Maggie Simpson's counting book by Matt and Maggie Groening. HarperCollins, 1991. ISBN 0-06-020238-6 Subj: Counting, numbers.

Groner, Judyth. *All about Hanukkah* by Judyth Groner and Madeline Wikler; ill. by Rosalyn Schanzer. Kar-Ben Copies, 1988. ISBN 0-930494-81-4 Subj: Holidays – Hanukkah. Jewish culture. Religion.

Let's build a Sukkah (Wikler, Madeline)

My first seder (Wikler, Madeline)

My very own Jewish community by Judyth Groner and Madeline Wikler; photos. by Madeline Wikler. Kar-Ben Copies, 1984. ISBN 0-930494-32-6 Subj: Communities, neighborhoods. Jewish culture.

The Purim parade (Wikler, Madeline)

Where is the Afikomen? by Judyth Groner and Madeline Wikler; ill. by Chari R. McLean. Kar-Ben Copies, 1985. ISBN 0-930494-52-0 Subj: Format, unusual – board books. Holidays. Jewish culture.

Gross, Alan. *Sometimes I worry...* ill. by Mike Venezia. Children's Pr., 1978. Subj: Behavior – worrying.

What if the teacher calls on me? ill. by Mike Venezia. Children's Pr., 1980. Subj: Behavior – worrying. School.

Gross, Michael. *The fable of the fig tree* ill. by Mila Lazarevich. Walck, 1975. Subj: Folk and fairy tales. Jewish culture.

Gross, Ruth Belov. *Alligators and other crocodilians* ill. with photos. Four Winds Pr., 1978. Subj: Reptiles – alligators, crocodiles. Science.

A book about your skeleton ill. by Deborah Robison. Hastings, 1979. Subj: Anatomy – skeletons. Health.

The emperor's new clothes (Andersen, H. C. (Hans Christian))

The girl who wouldn't get married ill. by Jack Kent. Four Winds Pr., 1983. Subj: Animals – horses. Folk and fairy tales. Weddings.

What's on my plate? ill. by Isadore Seltzer. Macmillan, 1990. ISBN 0-02-737000-3 Subj: Food.

Grossbart, Francine. *A big city* ill. by author. Harper, 1966. Subj: ABC books. City.

Grossman, Bill. *Donna O'Neeshuck was chased by some cows* ill. by Sue Truesdell. Harper, 1988. ISBN 0-06-022159-3 Subj: Cumulative tales. Poetry, rhyme.

The guy who was five minutes late ill. by Judy Glasser. HarperCollins, 1990. ISBN 0-06-022269-7 Subj: Behavior – tardiness. Poetry, rhyme.

Tommy at the grocery store ill. by Victoria Chess. HarperCollins, 1989. ISBN 0-06-022409-6 Subj: Animals – pigs. Behavior – lost. Poetry, rhyme. Shopping. Stores.

Grossman, Patricia. *The night ones* ill. by Lydia Dabcovich. Harcourt, 1991. ISBN 0-15-257438-7 Subj: Activities – working. Careers. Night.

Grossman, Virginia. *Ten little rabbits* ill. by Sylvia Long. Chronicle Books, 1991. ISBN 0-87701-552-X Subj: Animals – rabbits. Counting, numbers. Indians of North America. Poetry, rhyme.

Grosvenor, Donna. *Pandas* photos. by author; ill. by George Founds. National Geographic Soc., 1973. ISBN 0-87044-143-4 Subj: Animals – pandas. Science.

Zoo babies ill. by author. National Geographical Soc., 1979. Subj: Animals. Zoos.

Grover, Eulalie Osgood. *Mother Goose* (Mother Goose)

Groves-Raines, Antony. *The tidy hen* ill. by author. Harcourt, 1961. Subj: Character traits – cleanliness.

Gruber, Ruth see Michaels, Ruth

Guarino, Deborah. *Is your mama a llama?* ill. by Steven Kellogg. Scholastic, 1989. ISBN 0-590-41387-2 Subj: Animals. Animals – llamas. Poetry, rhyme.

Guiberson, Brenda Z. *Cactus hotel* ill. by Megan Lloyd. Holt, 1991. ISBN 0-8050-1333-4 Subj: Desert. Ecology. Plants.

Spoonbill swamp ill. by Megan Lloyd. Holt, 1992. ISBN 0-8050-1583-3 Subj: Birds – spoonbills. Nature. Reptiles – alligators, crocodiles.

Guilfoile, Elizabeth. *Have you seen my brother?* ill. by Mary Stevens. Follett, 1962. Subj: Behavior – lost. Careers – police officers. City.

Nobody listens to Andrew ill. by Mary Stevens. Follett, 1957. Subj: Animals – bears. Behavior – needing someone.

Valentine's Day ill. by Gordon Laite. Garrard, 1965. Subj: Holidays – Valentine's Day.

Guitar, Jeremy. *Tidy pig* (McQueen, Lucinda)

Gullikson, Sandy. *Trouble for breakfast* ill. by author. Dial, 1990. ISBN 0-8037-0776-2 Subj: Animals. Behavior – misbehavior. Food. Illness.

Gullo, Stephen V. *When people die* (Bernstein, Joanne E.)

Gundersheimer, Karen. *A B C say with me* ill. by author. Harper, 1984. Subj: ABC books.

Colors to know ill. by author. Harper, 1986. ISBN 0-06-022196-8 Subj: Animals. Concepts – color.

Happy winter ill. by author. Harper, 1982. Subj: Poetry, rhyme. Seasons – winter.

1 2 3 play with me ill. by author. Harper, 1984. Subj: Animals – mice. Counting, numbers.

Shapes to show ill. by author. Harper, 1986. ISBN 0-06-022197-6 Subj: Animals – mice. Concepts – shape. Toys.

Gunning, Monica. *The two Georges: Los dos Jorges* ill. by Veronica Mary Miracle. Blaine-Ethridge, 1976. Subj: ABC books. Foreign languages. Poetry, rhyme.

Gunther, Louise. *Anna's snow day* ill. by Paul Frame. Garrard, 1979. Subj: Weather – snow.

A tooth for the tooth fairy ill. by Jim Cummins. Garrard, 1978. Subj: Fairies. Teeth.

Gunthrop, Karen. *Adam and the wolf* ill. by Attilio Cassinelli. Doubleday, 1967. Translation of Il pulcino e il lupo. Subj: Animals – wolves. Behavior – disbelief. Food.

Rina at the farm ill. by Attilio Cassinelli. Doubleday, 1968. Subj: Farms.

Guthrie, Donna. *Grandpa doesn't know it's me* ill. by Katy Keck Arnsteen. Human Sciences Pr., 1986. ISBN 0-89885-308-7 Subj: Behavior – forgetfulness. Behavior – losing things. Behavior – lost. Family life – grandfathers. Illness – Alzheimer's. Old age.

The witch who lives down the hall ill. by Amy Schwartz. Harcourt, 1985. ISBN 0-15-298610-3 Subj: Holidays – Halloween. Magic. Witches.

Guthrie, Woody. *Woody's twenty grow big songs* ill. by author. HarperCollins, 1992. ISBN 0-06-020283-1 Subj: Music. Songs.

Guy, Ginger Foglesong. *Black crow, black crow* ill. by Nancy Winslow Parker. Greenwillow, 1991. ISBN 0-688-08957-7 Subj: Birds – crows. Imagination.

Guy, Rosa. *Mother crocodile* ill. by John Steptoe. Delacorte, 1981. Subj: Animals – monkeys. Folk and fairy tales. Foreign lands – Africa. Reptiles – alligators, crocodiles.

Guzzo, Sandra E. *Fox and Heggie* ill. by Kathy Parkinson. Albert Whitman, 1983. Subj: Animals – foxes. Animals – hedgehogs. Shopping.

Gwynne, Fred. *A little pigeon toad* ill. by author. Simon & Schuster, 1988. ISBN 0-671-66659-2 Subj: Imagination. Language.

Pondlarker ill. by author. Simon & Schuster, 1992. ISBN 0-671-70846-5 Subj: Frogs and toads. Royalty – princesses. Self-concept.

Haas, Dorothy. *My first communion* photos. by William Franklin McMahon. Albert Whitman, 1987. ISBN 0-8075-5331-X Subj: Religion.

Haas, Irene. *The Maggie B* ill. by author. Atheneum, 1975. Subj: Behavior – wishing. Boats, ships. Poetry, rhyme. Sea and seashore.

Haas, Merle. *Babar and Father Christmas* (Brunhoff, Jean de)

Babar and his children (Brunhoff, Jean de)

Babar and Zephir (Brunhoff, Jean de)

Babar the king (Brunhoff, Jean de)

Babar visits another planet (Brunhoff, Laurent de)

Babar's castle (Brunhoff, Laurent de)

Babar's cousin, that rascal Arthur (Brunhoff, Laurent de)

Babar's fair will be opened next Sunday (Brunhoff, Laurent de)

The story of Babar, the little elephant (Brunhoff, Jean de)

The travels of Babar (Brunhoff, Jean de)

Haddon, Mark. *Gilbert's gobstopper* ill. by author. Dial Pr., 1988. ISBN 0-8037-0506-9 Subj: Behavior – losing things.

Toni and the tomato soup ill. by author. Harcourt, 1989. ISBN 0-15-200610-9 Subj: Behavior – wishing. Food.

Hader, Berta Hoerner. *The big snow* by Berta and Elmer Hader; ill. by authors. Macmillan, 1948. Subj: Caldecott award book. Weather – snow.

Cock-a-doodle doo: the story of a little red rooster by Berta and Elmer Hader; ill. by authors. Macmillan, 1939. Subj: Birds – chickens. Birds – ducks. Caldecott award honor book. Farms.

Lost in the zoo by Berta and Elmer Hader; ill. by authors. Macmillan, 1951. Subj: Behavior – lost. Zoos.

The mighty hunter by Berta and Elmer Hader; ill. by authors. Macmillan, 1943. Subj: Caldecott award honor book. Ecology. Indians of North America. School. Sports – hunting.

Mister Billy's gun by Berta and Elmer Hader; ill. by authors. Macmillan, 1960. Subj: Birds. Gardens, gardening. Character traits – kindness to animals. Violence, anti-violence. Weapons.

The story of Pancho and the bull with the crooked tail by Berta and Elmer Hader; ill. by authors. Oxford Univ. Pr., 1933. Subj: Animals – bulls, cows. Foreign lands – Mexico.

Hader, Elmer. *The big snow* (Hader, Berta Hoerner)

Cock-a-doodle doo (Hader, Berta Hoerner)

Lost in the zoo (Hader, Berta Hoerner)

The mighty hunter (Hader, Berta Hoerner)

Mister Billy's gun (Hader, Berta Hoerner)

The story of Pancho and the bull with the crooked tail (Hader, Berta Hoerner)

Hadithi, Mwenye. *Crafty chameleon* ill. by Adrienne Kennaway. Little, 1987. ISBN 0-316-33723-4 Subj: Animals. Behavior – bullying. Behavior – unnoticed, unseen.

Greedy zebra ill. by Adrienne Kennaway. Little, 1984. ISBN 0-316-33721-8 Subj: Animals – zebras. Behavior – greed. Clothing. Folk and fairy tales. Foreign lands – Africa.

Hot hippo ill. by Adrienne Kennaway. Little, 1986. ISBN 0-316-33722-6 Subj: Animals – hippopotami. Foreign lands – Africa. Rivers.

Lazy lion ill. by Adrienne Kennaway. Little, 1990. ISBN 0-316-33725-0 Subj: Animals. Animals – lions. Character traits – laziness.

Tricky tortoise ill. by Adrienne Kennaway. Little, 1988. ISBN 0-316-33724-2 Subj: Animals. Behavior – bullying. Jungle.

Hague, Kathleen. *Alphabears: an ABC book* ill. by Michael Hague. Holt, 1984. Subj: ABC books. Poetry, rhyme. Toys – teddy bears.

Bear huggs ill. by Michael Hague. Holt, 1989. ISBN 0-8050-0512-9 Subj: Poetry, rhyme. Toys – teddy bears.

Jingle bells ill. by Michael Hague. Holt, 1990. ISBN 0-8050-1413-6 Subj: Holidays – Christmas. Music. Songs.

The man who kept house by Kathleen and Michael Hague; ill. by Michael Hague. Harcourt, 1981. Subj: Family life. Folk and fairy tales. Foreign lands – Norway.

Numbears: a counting book ill. by Michael Hague. Holt, 1986. ISBN 0-03-007194-1 Subj: Counting, numbers. Toys – teddy bears.

Out of the nursery, into the night ill. by Michael Hague. Holt, 1986. ISBN 0-8050-0088-7 Subj: Dreams. Night. Poetry, rhyme. Toys – teddy bears.

Hague, Michael. *The man who kept house* (Hague, Kathleen)

Michael Hague's world of unicorns ill. by author. Holt, 1986. ISBN 0-8050-0070-4 Subj: Format, unusual. Mythical creatures – unicorns.

Mother Goose (Mother Goose)

Hahn, Deborah. *The swineherd* (Andersen, H. C. (Hans Christian))

Hahn, Hannelore. *Take a giant step* ill. by Margot Zemach. Little, 1960. Subj: Games.

Haidle, Elizabeth. *Elmer the grump* ill. by author. Landmark, 1989. ISBN 0-933849-20-6 Subj: Children as authors. Children as illustrators. Elves and little people. Friendship.

Haines, Gail Kay. *Fire* ill. by Jacqueline Chwast. Morrow, 1975. Subj: Fire. Science.

Hains, Harriet. *My baby brother* ill. by author. Dorling Kindersley, 1992. ISBN 1-879431-76-9 Subj: Babies. Family life – brothers. Family life – sisters.

My new puppy ill. by author. Dorling Kindersley, 1992. ISBN 1-879431-77-7 Subj: Animals – dogs. Pets.

Hair ill. by Christine Sharr. Wonder Books, 1971. Subj: Hair.

Haiz, Danah. *Jonah's journey* ill. by H. Hechtkopf. Lerner, 1973. Subj: Animals – whales. Religion.

Hale, Irina. *Brown bear in a brown chair* ill. by author. Atheneum, 1983. Subj: Character traits – appearance. Furniture – chairs. Toys – teddy bears.

Chocolate mouse and sugar pig ill. by author. Atheneum, 1979. Subj: Animals – mice. Animals – pigs. Behavior – running away. Food. Toys.

Donkey's dreadful day ill. by author. Atheneum, 1982. Subj: Animals – donkeys. Circus. Dreams.

How I found a friend ill. by author. Viking, 1992. ISBN 0-670-84286-9 Subj: Friendship. Toys – teddy bears.

The lost toys ill. by author. Atheneum, 1985. ISBN 0-689-50328-8 Subj: Activities – trading. Behavior – forgetfulness. Toys.

Small big bad boy ill. by author. Viking, 1991. ISBN 0-670-83818-7 Subj: Behavior – growing up. Behavior – wishing.

Hale, Kathleen. *Orlando and the water cats* ill. by author. Merrimack, 1979. Subj: Activities – vacationing. Animals – cats. Family life.

Orlando buys a farm ill. by author. Merrimack, 1980. Subj: Animals – cats. Farms.

Orlando the frisky housewife ill. by author. Merrimack, 1979. Subj: Animals – cats. Stores.

Hale, Linda. *The glorious Christmas soup party* ill. by author. Viking, 1962. Subj: Animals – mice. Food. Holidays – Christmas.

Hale, Lucretia. *The lady who put salt in her coffee* adapt. and ill. by Amy Schwartz. Harcourt, 1989. ISBN 0-15-243475-5 Subj: Family life. Humor.

Hale, Michael. *Shoemaker Martin* (Tolstoĭ, Alekseĭ Nikolaevich)

Hale, Sarah Josepha. *Mary had a little lamb* ill. by Tomie de Paola. Holiday, 1984. ISBN 0-8234-0509-5 Subj: Animals – sheep. Music. Nursery rhymes. School.

Mary had a little lamb photos. by Bruce Millan. Scholastic, 1990. ISBN 0-590-43773-9 Subj: Animals – sheep. Music. Nursery rhymes. School.

Haley, Gail E. *Go away, stay away* ill. by author. Scribner's, 1977. Subj: Goblins. Seasons.

The green man ill. by author. Scribner's, 1980. Subj: Knights. Seasons.

Jack and the bean tree ill. by author. Crown, 1986. ISBN 0-517-55717-7 Subj: Folk and fairy tales. Giants. Magic.

Jack and the fire dragon ill. by author. Crown, 1988. ISBN 0-517-56814-4 Subj: Character traits – bravery. Dragons. Folk and fairy tales.

Jack Jouett's ride ill. by author. Viking, 1973. Subj: U.S. history.

Noah's ark ill. by author. Atheneum, 1971. ISBN 0-689-20659-3 Subj: Animals. Ecology.

The post office cat ill. by author. Scribner's, 1976. Subj: Animals – cats. Careers – mail carriers. Foreign lands – England.

Puss in boots (Perrault, Charles)

A story, a story ill. by author. Atheneum, 1970. Subj: Caldecott award book. Folk and fairy tales. Foreign lands – Africa.

Haley, Patrick. *The little person* ill. by Jonna Kool. East Eagle Pr., 1981. Subj: Activities – traveling.

Hall, Amanda. *The gossipy wife* ill. by author. Harper, 1984. Subj: Folk and fairy tales. Foreign lands – Russia.

Hall, Bill. *Fish tale* ill. by John E. Johnson. Norton, 1967. Subj: Fish. Sports – fishing.

Hall, Carol. *Northern J. Calloway presents Supervroomer!* (Calloway, Northern J.)

Hall, Derek. *Elephant bathes* ill. by John Butler. Sierra Club, 1985. ISBN 0-394-96529-9 Subj: Activities – bathing. Animals – elephants. Behavior – growing up. Family life.

Gorilla builds ill. by John Butler. Sierra Club, 1985. ISBN 0-394-96530-2 Subj: Animals – gorillas. Behavior – growing up. Family life.

Otter swims ill. by John Butler. Sierra Club/Knopf, 1984. ISBN 0-394-96503-5 Subj: Animals – otters. Emotions – fear. Sports – swimming.

Panda climbs ill. by John Butler. Sierra Club/Knopf, 1984. ISBN 0-394-96502-7 Subj: Animals – pandas. Emotions – fear. Trees.

Polar bear leaps ill. by John Butler. Sierra Club, 1985. ISBN 0-394-96531-0 Subj: Animals – polar bears. Behavior – growing up. Family life.

Tiger runs ill. by John Butler. Sierra Club/Knopf, 1984. ISBN 0-394-96504-3 Subj: Animals – tigers. Emotions – fear. Sports – racing.

Hall, Donald. *Andrew the lion farmer* ill. by Jane Miller. Watts, 1959. Subj: Humor.

The man who lived alone ill. by Mary Azarian. Godine, 1984. ISBN 0-87923-538-1 Subj: Behavior – solitude.

The ox-cart man ill. by Barbara Cooney. Viking, 1979. Subj: Activities – working. Caldecott award book. Farms. Seasons.

Hall, Fergus. *Groundsel* ill. by author. Merrimack, 1983. Subj: Gardens, gardening. Seasons.

Hall, Katy. *Skeletons! Skeletons! All about bones* ill. by Paige Billin-Frye. Grosset, 1991. ISBN 0-448-40108-8 Subj: Anatomy – skeletons.

Hall, Malcolm. *And then the mouse...* ill. by Stephen Gammell. Four Winds Pr., 1980. Subj: Animals – mice. Folk and fairy tales.

CariCATures ill. by Bruce Degen. Coward, 1978. Subj: Animals. Riddles.

The friends of Charlie Ant Bear ill. by Alexandra Wallner. Coward, 1980. Subj: Animals – anteaters. Character traits – optimism.

Hall, Pam. *On the edge of the eastern ocean* ill. by author. Silver Burdett, 1982. Subj: Birds – puffins. Poetry, rhyme.

Hall, Richard. *Humphrey the lost whale* (Tokuda, Wendy)

Haller, Danita Ross. *Not just any ring* ill. by Deborah Kogan Ray. Knopf, 1982. Subj: Magic.

Hallinan, P. K. (Patrick K.). *I'm glad to be me* ill. by author. Children's Pr., 1977. Subj: Activities. Family life – only child. Self-concept.

I'm thankful each day! ill. by author. Children's Pr., 1981. Subj: Folk and fairy tales.

Just being alone ill. by author. Children's Pr., 1976. Subj: Activities. Behavior – solitude. Family life – only child.

Just open a book ill. by author. Children's Pr., 1981. Subj: Activities – reading. Poetry, rhyme.

That's what a friend is ill. by author. Children's Pr., 1977. Subj: Friendship. Poetry, rhyme.

Where's Michael? ill. by author. Children's Pr., 1978. Subj: Behavior – imitation. Self-concept.

Halsey, William D. *The magic world of words: a very first dictionary* ed. by William D. Halsey and Christopher G. Morris. Macmillan, 1977. Subj: Dictionaries.

Hamberger, John. *The day the sun disappeared* ill. by author. Norton, 1964. Subj: Animals. Ecology. Science. Sun.

Hazel was an only pet ill. by author. Norton, 1968. Subj: Animals – dogs. Family life – only child. Pets.

The lazy dog ill. by author. Four Winds Pr., 1971. Subj: Animals – dogs. Toys – balls. Wordless.

The peacock who lost his tail ill. by author. Norton, 1967. Subj: Birds – peacocks, peahens. Character traits – pride.

This is the day ill. by author. Grosset, 1971. Subj: Animals – groundhogs. Holidays – Groundhog Day.

Hamil, Thomas Arthur. *Brother Alonzo* ill. by author. Macmillan, 1957. Subj: Religion.

Hamilton, Emily. *My name is Emily* (Hamilton, Morse)

Hamilton, Morse. *Big sisters are bad witches* ill. by Marylin Hafner. Greenwillow, 1981. Subj: Sibling rivalry. Witches.

How do you do, Mr. Birdsteps? ill. by Patience Brewster. Avon, 1983. Subj: Character traits – shyness.

Little sister for sale ill. by Gioia Fiammenghi. Dutton, 1992. ISBN 0-525-65078-4 Subj: Family life – sisters. Sibling rivalry.

My name is Emily by Morse and Emily Hamilton; ill. by Jenni Oliver. Greenwillow, 1979. Subj: Behavior – running away. Sibling rivalry.

Who's afraid of the dark? ill. by Patience Brewster. Avon, 1983. Subj: Emotions – fear. Night.

Hamilton, Virginia. *Drylongso* ill. by Jerry Pinkney. Harcourt, 1992. ISBN 0-15-224241-4 Subj: Ecology. Ethnic groups in the U.S. – Afro-Americans. Farms. Weather – droughts. Weather – wind.

Hamilton-Merritt, Jane. *My first days of school* photos. by author. Simon and Schuster, 1982. Subj: School.

Our new baby photos. by author. Simon and Schuster, 1982. Subj: Babies. Family life.

Hamley, Dennis. *Tigger and friends* ill. by Meg Rutherford. Lothrop, 1989. ISBN 0-688-08605-5 Subj: Animals – cats. Pets.

Hamm, Diane Johnston. *Grandma drives a motor bed* ill. by Charles Robinson. Albert Whitman, 1987. ISBN 0-8075-3025-5 Subj: Family life – grandmothers. Family life – grandparents. Furniture – beds. Handicaps. Illness. Old age.

How many feet in the bed? ill. by Kate Salley Palmer. Simon & Schuster, 1991. ISBN 0-671-72638-2 Subj: Anatomy – feet. Bedtime. Counting, numbers. Family life.

Laney's lost momma ill. by Sally G. Ward. Albert Whitman, 1991. ISBN 0-8075-4340-3 Subj: Behavior – lost. Family life – mothers. Shopping. Stores.

Hammarberg, Dyan. *Jessie the chicken* (Pursell, Margaret Sanford)

Polly the guinea pig (Pursell, Margaret Sanford)

Rusty the Irish setter (Overbeck, Cynthia)

Shelley the sea gull (Pursell, Margaret Sanford)

Sprig the tree frog (Pursell, Margaret Sanford)

Hammerstein, Oscar. *A real nice clambake* (Rodgers, Richard)

Hample, Stoo. *Stoo Hample's silly joke book* ill. by author. Delacorte, 1978. Subj: Humor. Riddles.

Yet another big fat funny silly book ill. by author. Delacorte, 1980. Subj: Poetry, rhyme. Riddles.

Hamsa, Bobbie. *Dirty Larry* ill. by Paul Sharp. Children's Pr., 1983. Subj: Character traits – cleanliness.

Polly wants a cracker ill. by Jerry Warshaw. Childrens, 1986. ISBN 0-516-02071-4 Subj: Birds – parakeets, parrots. Counting, numbers. Poetry, rhyme.

Your pet bear ill. by Tom Dunnington. Children's Pr., 1980. Subj: Animals – bears. Imagination.

Your pet beaver ill. by Tom Dunnington. Children's Pr., 1980. Subj: Animals – beavers. Imagination.

Your pet camel ill. by Tom Dunnington. Children's Pr., 1980. Subj: Animals – camels. Imagination.

Your pet elephant ill. by Tom Dunnington. Children's Pr., 1980. Subj: Animals – elephants. Imagination.

Your pet giraffe ill. by Tom Dunnington. Children's Pr., 1982. Subj: Animals – giraffes. Imagination.

Your pet kangaroo ill. by Tom Dunnington. Children's Pr., 1980. Subj: Animals – kangaroos. Imagination.

Your pet penguin ill. by Tom Dunnington. Children's Pr., 1980. Subj: Birds – penguins. Imagination.

Your pet sea lion ill. by Tom Dunnington. Children's Pr., 1982. Subj: Animals – sea lions. Imagination.

Hancock, Joy Elizabeth. *The loudest little lion* ill. by Eileen Christelow. Albert Whitman, 1988. ISBN 0-8075-4773-5 Subj: Animals – lions. Bedtime. Noise, sounds.

Hancock, Sibyl. *Esteban and the ghost* ill. by Dirk Zimmer. Dial Pr., 1983. Adapted from The tinker and the ghost by Ralph Steele Boggs and Mary Gould Davis Subj: Ghosts.

Freaky Francie ill. by Leonard W. Shortall. Prentice-Hall, 1979. Subj: Problem solving.

Old Blue ill. by Erick Ingraham. Putnam's, 1980. Subj: Animals – bulls, cows. Cowboys.

Handford, Martin. *Find Waldo now* ill. by author. Little, 1988. ISBN 0-316-34292-0 Subj: Activities – traveling. Games. Time.

The great Waldo search ill. by author. Little, 1989. ISBN 0-316-34282-3 Subj: Activities – traveling. Games.

Where's Waldo? ill. by author. Little, 1987. ISBN 0-316-34293-9 Subj: Activities – traveling. Behavior – losing things. Foreign lands. Games.

Handforth, Thomas. *Mei Li* ill. by author. Doubleday, 1938. Subj: Caldecott award book. Foreign lands – China. Holidays – Chinese New Year.

Hands, Hargrave. *Bunny sees* ill. by author. Grosset, 1985. ISBN 0-488-10577-2 Subj: Animals – rabbits. Format, unusual – board books. Nature.

Duckling sees ill. by author. Grosset, 1985. ISBN 0-448-10579-9 Subj: Animals. Format, unusual – board books.

Little lamb sees ill. by author. Grosset, 1985. ISBN 0-448-10576-4 Subj: Animals. Format, unusual – board books.

Hanhart, Brigitte. *Shoemaker Martin* (Tolstoĭ, Alekseĭ Nikolaevich)

Hanklin, Rebecca. *I can be a doctor* ill. with photos. Childrens Pr., 1985. ISBN 0-516-01846-9 Subj: Careers – doctors.

I can be a fire fighter ill. with photos. Childrens Pr., 1985. ISBN 0-516-01847-7 Subj: Careers – firefighters.

Hanlon, Emily. *What if a lion eats me and I fall into a hippopotamus' mud hole?* ill. by Leigh Grant. Delacorte Pr., 1975. Subj: Emotions – fear. Imagination. Zoos.

Hann, Jacquie. *Crybaby* ill. by author. Four Winds Pr., 1979. Subj: Emotions.

Follow the leader ill. by author. Crown, 1982. Subj: Activities – playing. Games.

Up day, down day ill. by author. Four Winds Pr., 1978. Subj: Character traits – luck. Sports – fishing.

Hanna, Jack. *The petting zoo* ill. by Neil Brennan. Doubleday, 1992. ISBN 0-385-41694-6 Subj: Animals. Format, unusual – toy and movable books. Zoos.

Hannan, Peter. *Sillyville or bust* ill. by author. Knopf, 1991. ISBN 0-679-90285-6 Subj: Activities – traveling. Automobiles. Behavior – boredom. Humor.

Hannant, Judith Stuller. *Doorknob collection of nursery rhymes* ill. by author. Little, 1991. ISBN 0-316-34343-9 Subj: Format, unusual. Format, unusual – board books. Nursery rhymes.

Hansen, Carla. *Barnaby Bear builds a boat* by Carla and Vilhelm Hansen; ill. by authors. Random House, 1979. Subj: Animals – bears. Boats, ships.

Barnaby Bear visits the farm by Carla and Vilhelm Hansen; ill. by authors. Random House, 1979. Subj: Animals – bears. Farms.

Hansen, Jeff. *Being a fire fighter isn't just squirtin' water* ill. by author. Vantage Pr., 1978. Subj: Careers – firefighters.

Hansen, Vilhelm. *Barnaby Bear builds a boat* (Hansen, Carla)

Barnaby Bear visits the farm (Hansen, Carla)

Hanson, Joan. *I don't like Timmy* ill. by author. Carolrhoda Books, 1972. Subj: Babies. Friendship.

I won't be afraid ill. by author. Carolrhoda Books, 1974. Subj: Behavior – growing up. Emotions – fear.

I'm going to run away ill. by author. Platt, 1978. Subj: Behavior – running away.

Hapgood, Miranda. *Martha's mad day* ill. by Emily Arnold McCully. Crown, 1977. Subj: Emotions – anger.

Harada, Joyce. *It's the ABC book* ill. by author. Heian Intl., 1982. Subj: ABC books.

It's the 0-1-2-3 book ill. by author. Heian, 1985. ISBN 0-89346-252-7 Subj: Counting, numbers.

Harber, Frances. *My king has donkey ears* ill. by Maryann Kovalski. North Winds Pr., 1986. ISBN 0-590-71522-4 Subj: Folk and fairy tales. Problem solving. Royalty – kings.

Hare, Lorraine. *Who needs her?* ill. by author. Atheneum, 1983. Subj: Character traits – cleanliness.

Hare, Norma Q. *Mystery at mouse house* ill. by Stella Ormai. Garrard, 1980. Subj: Behavior – stealing. Problem solving.

Hariton, Anca. *Egg story* ill. by author. Dutton, 1992. ISBN 0-525-44861-6 Subj: Birds – chickens. Birth. Eggs.

Harlow, Joan Hiatt. *Shadow bear* ill. by Jim Arnosky. Doubleday, 1981. Subj: Animals – polar bears. Emotions – fear. Eskimos.

Harmer, Juliet. *Prayers for children* ill. by author. Viking., 1990. ISBN 0-670-83348-7 Subj: Days of the week, months of the year. Religion.

Harms, D. *The merry starlings* (Marshak, Samuel)

Harper, Anita. *How we live* ill. by Christine Roche. Harper, 1977. Subj: Houses.

How we work ill. by Christine Roche. Harper, 1977. Subj: Activities – working. Careers.

It's not fair! ill. by Susan Hellard. Putnam's, 1986. ISBN 0-399-21365-1 Subj: Animals – kangaroos. Babies. Family life. Sibling rivalry.

Harper, Wilhelmina. *The gunniwolf* ill. by William Wiesner. Dutton, 1967. Subj: Animals – wolves. Behavior – misbehavior. Flowers. Foreign lands – Germany.

Harranth, Wolf. *My old grandad* tr. from German by Peter Carter; ill. by Christina Oppermann-Dimow. Merrimack, 1984. ISBN 0-19-279787-5 Subj: Death. Emotions – loneliness. Family life – grandfathers. Farms.

Harriott, Ted. *Coming home: a dog's true story* ill. by Lisa Kopper. David & Charles, 1985. ISBN 0-575-03583-8 Subj: Animals – dogs. Character traits – kindness to animals. Death.

Harris, Dorothy Joan. *Four seasons for Toby* ill. by Vlasta van Kampen. North Winds Pr., 1987. ISBN 0-590-71677-8 Subj: Reptiles – turtles, tortoises. Seasons.

Goodnight Jeffrey ill. by Nancy Hannans. Warne, 1983. Subj: Bedtime.

Harris, Joel Chandler. *Jump! the adventures of Brer Rabbit* adapt. by Van Dyke Parks and Malcolm Jones; ill. by Barry Moser. Harcourt, 1986. ISBN 0-15-241350-2 Subj: Animals. Folk and fairy tales.

Jump again! more adventures of Brer Rabbit adapt. by Van Dyke Parks; ill. by Barry Moser. Harcourt, 1987. ISBN 0-15-241352-9 Subj: Animals. Folk and fairy tales.

Harris, Leon A. *The great diamond robbery* ill. by Joseph Schindelman. Atheneum, 1985. ISBN 0-689-31188-5 Subj: Animals – mice. Character traits – bravery. Crime. Songs. Stores.

The great picture robbery ill. by Joseph Schindelman. Atheneum, 1963. Subj: Animals – mice. Art. Crime. Foreign lands – France.

Harris, Louise Dyer. *Flash, the life of a firefly* by Louise Dyer Harris and Norman Dyer Harris; ill. by Henry B. Kane. Little, 1966. Subj: Insects – fireflies. Science.

Harris, Norman Dyer. *Flash, the life of a firefly* (Harris, Louise Dyer)

Harris, Robie H. *Don't forget to come back* ill. by Tony DeLuna. Atheneum, 1963. Subj: Activities – baby-sitting. Behavior. Family life.

Hot Henry ill. by Nicole Hollander. St. Martin's, 1987. ISBN 0-312-01041-9 Subj: Clothing. Family life.

I hate kisses ill. by Diane Paterson. Knopf, 1981. Subj: Behavior – growing up.

Messy Jessie ill. by Nicole Hollander. St. Martin's, 1987. ISBN 0-312-01067-2 Subj: Behavior – carelessness. Family life.

Harris, Steven Michael. *This is my trunk* ill. by Norma Welliver. Atheneum, 1985. ISBN 0-689-31128-1 Subj: Careers. Circus. Clowns, jesters.

Harris, Susan. *Creatures that look alike* ill. by Don Forrest. Watts, 1980. Subj: Animals. Science.

Reptiles ill. by Jim Robins. Watts, 1978. Subj: Reptiles. Science.

Harrison, David Lee. *The case of Og, the missing frog* ill. by Jerry Warshaw. Rand McNally, 1972. Subj: Frogs and toads. Poetry, rhyme.

Detective Bob and the great ape escape ill. by Ned Delaney. Parents, 1980. Subj: Animals – gorillas. Problem solving. Zoos.

Little boy soup ill. by Toni Goffe. Ladybird, 1990. ISBN 0-7214-5267-1 Subj: Character traits – cleverness. Witches.

Little turtle's big adventure ill. by J. P. Miller. Random House, 1969. Subj: Character traits – kindness to animals. Progress. Reptiles – turtles, tortoises.

Wake up, sun! ill. by Hans Wilhelm. Random House, 1986. ISBN 0-394-88256-8 Subj: Animals. Morning. Sun.

Harrison, Sarah. *In granny's garden* ill. by Mike Wilks. Holt, 1980. Subj: Animals. Dinosaurs. Poetry, rhyme.

Harrison, Ted. *A northern alphabet: A is for arctic* ill. by author. Tundra Books, 1982. Subj: ABC books.

Harrop, Beatrice. *Sing hey diddle diddle* (Mother Goose)

Harsh, Fred. *Alfie* ill. by author. Ideals, 1991. ISBN 0-685-48862-4 Subj: Animals – dogs. Birds – crows. Self-concept.

Harshman, Marc. *Rocks in my pocket* by Marc Harshman and Bonnie Collins; ill. by Toni Goffe. Dutton, 1991. ISBN 0-525-65055-5 Subj: Folk and fairy tales. Rocks.

Snow company ill. by Leslie W. Bowman. Dutton, 1990. ISBN 0-525-65029-6 Subj: Weather – snow. Weather – storms.

Harshman, Terry Webb. *Porcupine's pajama party* ill. by Doug Cushman. Harper, 1988. ISBN 0-06-022249-2 Subj: Animals – otters. Animals – porcupines. Bedtime. Birds – owls. Parties. Monsters. Sleep.

Hart, Jeanne McGahey. *Scareboy* ill. by Gerhardt Hurt. Parnassus, 1957. Subj: Humor. Scarecrows.

Hartelius, Margaret A. *The chicken's child* ill. by author. Doubleday, 1975. Subj: Birds – chickens. Reptiles – alligators, crocodiles. Wordless.

Hartley, Deborah. *Up north in the winter* ill. by Lydia Dabcovich. Dutton, 1986. ISBN 0-525-

44268-5 Subj: Animals – foxes. Family life – grandfathers. Seasons – winter.

Hartman, Gail. *As the crow flies* ill. by Harvey Stevenson. Bradbury Pr., 1991. ISBN 0-02-743005-7 Subj: Animals. Maps.

For strawberry jam or fireflies ill. by Ellen Weiss. Bradbury Pr., 1989. ISBN 0-02-742990-3 Subj: Concepts. Language.

Harvey, Brett. *Immigrant girl: Becky of Eldridge Street* ill. by Deborah Kogan Ray. Holiday, 1987. ISBN 0-8234-0638-5 Subj: City. Family life. Jewish culture.

My prairie Christmas ill. by Deborah Kogan Ray. Holiday, 1990. ISBN 0-8234-0827-2 Subj: Holidays – Christmas. Weather – storms.

My prairie year: based on the diary of Elenore Plaisted ill. by Deborah Kogan Ray. Holiday, 1986. ISBN 0-8234-0604-0 Subj: Activities – working. Farms. U.S. history.

Haseley, Dennis. *The cave of snores* ill. by Eric Beddows. Harper, 1987. ISBN 0-06-022215-8 Subj: Animals. Folk and fairy tales. Magic. Sleep. Wizards.

Ghost catcher ill. by Lloyd Bloom. HarperCollins, 1991. ISBN 0-06-022247-6 Subj: Death. Emotions – love. Ghosts. Shadows.

Kite flier ill. by David Wiesner. Four Winds, 1986. ISBN 0-02-743110-X Subj: Family life – fathers. Kites.

The old banjo ill. by Stephen Gammell. Macmillan, 1983. Subj: Farms. Music.

The pirate who tried to capture the moon ill. by Sue Truesdell. Harper, 1983. Subj: Pirates.

The soap bandit ill. by Jane Chambless. Warne, 1984. Subj: Character traits – cleanliness.

The thieves' market ill. by Lisa Desimini. HarperCollins, 1991. ISBN 0-06-022493-2 Subj: Crime. Imagination. Night. Stores.

Haskins, Francine. *I remember "one hundred twenty-one"* ill. by author. Children's Book Pr., 1991. ISBN 0-89239-100-6 Subj: Communities, neighborhoods. Ethnic groups in the U.S. – Afro-Americans. Family life.

Haskins, Ilma. *Color seems* ill. by author. Vanguard, 1973. Subj: Concepts – color.

Haskins, Jim. *Count your way through China* ill. by Dennis Hockerman. Carolrhoda Books, 1987. ISBN 0-87614-302-8 Subj: Counting, numbers. Foreign lands – China.

Count your way through Japan ill. by Martin Skoro. Carolrhoda Books, 1987. ISBN 0-87614-301-X Subj: Counting, numbers. Foreign lands – Japan.

Count your way through Russia ill. by Vera Mednikov. Carolrhoda Books, 1987. ISBN 0-87614-303-6 Subj: Counting, numbers. Foreign lands – Russia.

Count your way through the Arab world ill. by Dana Gustafson. Carolrhoda Books, 1987. ISBN 0-87616-304-4 Subj: Counting, numbers. Foreign lands – Arabia.

The Statue of Liberty: America's proud lady ill. with photos. Lerner, 1986. ISBN 0-8225-1706-X Subj: Art. U.S. history.

Hasler, Eveline. *Martin is our friend* ill. by Dorothea Desmarowitz. Abingdon Pr., 1981. Subj: Animals – horses. Character traits – kindness. Handicaps.

Winter magic ill. by Michèle Lemieux. Morrow, 1985. ISBN 0-688-05258-4 Subj: Animals – cats. Night. Seasons – winter.

Hastings, Evelyn Beilhart. *The department store* ill. by Lewis A. Ogan. Melmont, 1956. Subj: Shopping. Stores.

Hastings, Selina. *The man who wanted to live forever* ill. by Reg Cartwright. Holt, 1988. ISBN 0-8050-0572-2 Subj: Death. Folk and fairy tales.

Peter and the wolf (Prokofiev, Sergei Sergeievitch)

The singing ringing tree ill. by Louise Brierley. Holt, 1988. ISBN 0-8050-0573-0 Subj: Character traits – kindness. Elves and little people. Folk and fairy tales. Magic. Royalty – princes. Royalty – princesses.

Haswell, Peter. *Pog* ill. by author. Watts, 1989. ISBN 0-531-08443-4 Subj: Animals – pigs. Character traits – questioning.

Pog climbs Mount Everest ill. by author. Watts, 1990. ISBN 0-531-08473-6 Subj: Animals – pigs. Sports – mountain climbing.

Hatcher, Charles. *What shape is it?* ill. by Gareth Adamson. Duell, 1966. Subj: Concepts – shape.

Hathorn, Libby. *Freya's fantastic surprise* ill. by Sharon Thompson. Scholastic, 1989. ISBN 0-86896-381-X Subj: Emotions – envy, jealousy. School.

Haubensak-Tellenbach, Margrit. *The story of Noah's ark* ill. by Erna Emhardt. Crown, 1983. Subj: Religion – Noah.

Haugaard, Erik Christian. *The emperor's nightingale* (Andersen, H. C. (Hans Christian))

Prince Boghole ill. by Julie Downing. Macmillan, 1987. ISBN 0-02-743440-0 Subj: Folk and fairy tales. Foreign lands – Ireland. Royalty – princes.

Princess Horrid ill. by Diane Dawson Hearn. Macmillan, 1990. ISBN 0-02-743445-1 Subj: Behavior. Folk and fairy tales. Royalty – princesses. Witches.

Hauptmann, Tatjana. *A day in the life of Petronella Pig* ill. by author. Holt, 1982. Subj: Animals – pigs. Format, unusual. Wordless.

Haus, Felice. *Beep! Beep! I'm a jeep: a toddler's book of "let's pretend"* ill. by Norman Gorbaty. Random, 1986. ISBN 0-394-88000-5 Subj: Activities – playing. Format, unusual – board books. Imagination. Toys.

Hausherr, Rosmarie. *My first kitten* photos. by author. Four Winds, 1985. ISBN 0-02-743420-6 Subj: Animals – cats. Pets.

My first puppy photos. by author. Four Winds, 1986. ISBN 0-02-743410-9 Subj: Animals – dogs. Pets.

Hautzig, Deborah. *Get well, Granny Bird* ill. by Joseph Mathieu. Random House, 1989. ISBN 0-394-92247-6 Subj: Birds. Family life – grandmothers. Illness.

It's not fair! ill. by Tom Leigh. Random House, 1986. ISBN 0-394-98151-0 Subj: Activities – working. Behavior – dissatisfaction. Puppets.

Thumbelina (Andersen, H. C. (Hans Christian))

A visit to the Sesame Street hospital ill. by Joseph Mathieu. Random House, 1985. ISBN 0-394-87062-X Subj: Hospitals. Puppets.

Why are you so mean to me? ill. by Tom Cooke. Random House, 1986. ISBN 0-394-98060-3 Subj: Emotions – anger.

Hautzig, Esther (Rudomin). *At home: a visit in four languages* ill. by Aliki. Macmillan, 1969. Subj: Family life. Foreign lands – France. Foreign lands – Russia. Foreign lands – Spain. Foreign languages.

In the park: an excursion in four languages ill. by Ezra Jack Keats. Macmillan, 1968. Subj: Foreign lands – France. Foreign lands – Russia. Foreign lands – Spain. Foreign languages.

Haviland, Virginia. *The talking pot* ill. by Melissa Sweet. Little, 1990. ISBN 0-316-35060-5 Subj: Folk and fairy tales. Foreign lands – Denmark.

Havill, Juanita. *Jamaica Tag-Along* ill. by Anne Sibley O'Brien. Houghton, 1989. ISBN 0-395-49602-0 Subj: Activities – playing. Ethnic groups in the U.S. – Afro-Americans. Family life – brothers. Family life – sisters. Friendship.

Jamaica's find ill. by Anne Sibley O'Brien. Houghton, 1986. ISBN 0-395-39376-0 Subj: Behavior – losing things. Character traits – honesty. Ethnic groups in the U.S. – Afro-Americans.

Magic fort ill. by Linda Shute. Houghton, 1991. ISBN 0-395-50067-2 Subj: Behavior – misbehavior. Family life – brothers. Trees.

Treasure nap ill. by Elivia Savadier. Houghton, 1992. ISBN 0-395-57817-5 Subj: Ethnic groups in the U.S. – Mexican-Americans. Family life. Weather.

Hawes, Judy. *Fireflies in the night* ill. by Ellen Alexander. HarperCollins, 1991. ISBN 0-06-022484-3 Subj: Family life – grandparents. Farms. Insects – fireflies. Night. Science.

Ladybug, ladybug, fly away home ill. by Ed Emberley. Crowell, 1968. Subj: Insects – ladybugs. Science.

My daddy longlegs ill. by Walter Lorraine. Crowell, 1972. ISBN 0-690-56656-5 Subj: Spiders.

Shrimps ill. by Joseph Low. Crowell, 1967. Subj: Fish. Science.

Spring peepers ill. by Graham Booth. Crowell, 1975. Subj: Frogs and toads. Science.

Watch honeybees with me ill. by Helen Stone. Crowell, 1964. Subj: Insects – bees. Science.

Why frogs are wet ill. by Don Madden. Crowell, 1968. Subj: Frogs and toads. Science.

Hawkes, Kevin. *Then the troll heard the squeak* ill. by author. Lothrop, 1991. ISBN 0-688-09757-X Subj: Behavior – misbehavior. Poetry, rhyme. Trolls.

Hawkesworth, Jenny. *The lonely skyscraper* ill. by Emanuel Schongut. Doubleday, 1980. Subj: City. Country.

Hawkins, Colin. *Boo! Who?* by Colin and Jacqui Hawkins; ill. by authors. Holt, 1984. Subj: Poetry, rhyme.

Busy ABC by Colin and Jacqui Hawkins; ill. by authors. Viking, 1987. ISBN 0-670-81153-X Subj: ABC books. Activities.

Dip, dip, dip ill. by author. Little, 1986. ISBN 0-87113-087-4 Subj: Activities – playing. Animals – bears. Bedtime. Toys – teddy bears.

The elephant by Colin and Jacqui Hawkins; ill. by authors. Viking, 1986. ISBN 0-670-80314-6 Subj: Animals – elephants. Format, unusual – toy and movable books.

Hey diddle diddle by Colin and Jacqui Hawkins; ill. by authors. Candlewick Pr., 1992. ISBN 1-56402-014-2 Subj: Format, unusual – board books. Nursery rhymes.

I'm not sleepy! by Colin and Jacqui Hawkins; ill. by authors. Crown, 1986. ISBN 0-517-55973-0 Subj: Animals – bears. Bedtime.

Incy wincy spider by Colin and Jacqui Hawkins; ill. by authors. Viking, 1986. ISBN 0-670-80317-0 Subj: Format, unusual – toy and movable books. Games. Spiders.

Jen the hen by Colin and Jacqui Hawkins; ill. by Colin Hawkins. Putnam's, 1985. ISBN 0-399-21207-8 Subj: Birthdays. Format, unusual. Poetry, rhyme.

Max and the magic word by Colin and Jacqui Hawkins; ill. by authors. Viking, 1986. ISBN 0-670-80853-9 Subj: Animals. Etiquette.

Mig the pig by Colin and Jacqui Hawkins; ill. by Colin Hawkins. Putnam's, 1984. Subj: Animals – pigs. Poetry, rhyme.

Old Mother Hubbard (Martin, Sarah Catherine)

One finger, one thumb ill. by author. Little, 1986. ISBN 0-87113-088-2 Subj: Activities – playing. Animals – bears. Bedtime. Toys – teddy bears.

Oops-a-Daisy ill. by author. Little, 1986. ISBN 0-87113-086-6 Subj: Activities – playing. Animals – bears. Bedtime. Toys – teddy bears.

Pat the cat by Colin and Jacqui Hawkins; ill. by Colin Hawkins. Putnam's, 1983. Subj: Animals – cats.

Round the garden by Colin and Jacqui Hawkins; ill. by authors. Viking, 1986. ISBN 0-670-80315-4 Subj: Format, unusual – toy and movable books. Games. Gardens, gardening.

Snap! Snap! by Colin and Jacqui Hawkins; ill. by Colin Hawkins. Putnam's, 1984. ISBN 0-399-21163-2 Subj: Emotions – fear. Monsters. Night. Poetry, rhyme.

Take away monsters ill. by author. Putnam's, 1984. ISBN 0-399-20962-X Subj: Counting, numbers. Format, unusual – toy and movable books. Monsters. Poetry, rhyme.

This little pig by Colin and Jacqui Hawkins; ill. by authors. Viking, 1986. ISBN 0-670-80316-2 Subj: Anatomy – toes. Animals – pigs. Format, unusual – toy and movable books. Games.

Tog the dog by Colin and Jacqui Hawkins; ill. by authors. Putnam's, 1986. ISBN 0-399-21338-4 Subj: Animals – dogs. Behavior – lost. Format, unusual. Language. Poetry, rhyme.

What time is it, Mr. Wolf? ill. by author. Putnam's, 1983. Subj: Animals – wolves. Format, unusual – toy and movable books. Time.

Where's bear? ill. by author. Little, 1986. ISBN 0-87113-090-4 Subj: Activities – playing. Animals – bears. Bedtime. Toys – teddy bears.

Where's my mommy? by Colin and Jacqui Hawkins; ill. by authors. Crown, 1986. ISBN 0-517-55974-9 Subj: Animals. Behavior – needing someone. Family life – mothers.

Hawkins, Jacqui. *Boo! Who?* (Hawkins, Colin)

Busy ABC (Hawkins, Colin)

The elephant (Hawkins, Colin)

Hey diddle diddle (Hawkins, Colin)

Humpty Dumpty (Hawkins, Colin)

I'm not sleepy! (Hawkins, Colin)

Incy wincy spider (Hawkins, Colin)

Jen the hen (Hawkins, Colin)

Max and the magic word (Hawkins, Colin)

Mig the pig (Hawkins, Colin)

Old Mother Hubbard (Martin, Sarah Catherine)

Pat the cat (Hawkins, Colin)

Round the garden (Hawkins, Colin)

Snap! Snap! (Hawkins, Colin)

This little pig (Hawkins, Colin)

Tog the dog (Hawkins, Colin)

Where's my mommy? (Hawkins, Colin)

Hawkins, Mark. *A lion under her bed* ill. by Jean Vallario. Holt, 1978. Subj: Animals – lions. Bedtime. Furniture – beds.

Hawkinson, John. *Birds in the sky* (Hawkinson, Lucy)

The old stump ill. by author. Albert Whitman, 1965. Subj: Animals – mice. Trees.

Robins and rabbits by John and Lucy Hawkinson; ill. by John Hawkinson. Albert Whitman, 1960. Subj: Animals. Birds – robins.

Where the wild apples grow ill. by author. Albert Whitman, 1967. Subj: Animals – horses. Character traits – freedom.

Hawkinson, Lucy. *Birds in the sky* by Lucy and John Hawkinson; ill. by authors. Children's Pr., 1966. Subj: Birds. Science.

Dance, dance, Amy-Chan! ill. by author. Albert Whitman, 1964. Subj: Ethnic groups in the U.S. – Japanese-Americans.

Robins and rabbits (Hawkinson, John)

Hawthorne, Nathaniel. *King Midas and the golden touch* (Hewitt, Kathryn)

Hay, Dean. *I see a lot of things* ill. by author. Lion, 1966. Subj: Senses – seeing.

Now I can count ill. by author. Lion, 1968. Subj: Counting, numbers. Time.

Hay, Timothy see Brown, Margaret Wise

Hayashi, Akiko. *Aki and the fox* ill. by author. Doubleday, 1991. ISBN 0-385-41948-1 Subj: Activities – traveling. Family life – grandmothers. Toys. Trains.

Hayden, Lea. *Sunny day—rainy day* ill. by Joe Ewers. Random House, 1990. ISBN 0-679-80068-9 Subj: Format, unusual. Weather. Weather – rain.

Hayes, Ann. *Meet the orchestra* ill. by Karmen Thompson. Harcourt, 1991. ISBN 0-15-200526-9 Subj: Animals. Music.

Hayes, Geoffrey. *Bear by himself* ill. by author. Harper, 1976. Subj: Behavior – solitude. Toys – teddy bears.

Elroy and the witch's child ill. by author. Harper, 1982. Subj: Animals – cats. Witches.

The mystery of the pirate ghost ill. by author. Random House, 1985. ISBN 0-394-97220-1 Subj: Ghosts. Pirates.

Patrick and his grandpa ill. by author. Random, 1986. ISBN 0-394-87287-8 Subj: Animals – bears. Family life – grandfathers. Format, unusual – board books.

Patrick and Ted ill. by author. Four Winds Pr., 1984. Subj: Animals – bears. Behavior – growing up.

The secret inside ill. by author. Harper, 1980. Subj: Animals – bears. Dreams.

Hayes, Sarah. *Bad egg: the true story of Humpty Dumpty* ill. by Charlotte Voake. Little, 1987. ISBN 0-316-35184-9 Subj: Behavior – misbehavior. Nursery rhymes. Royalty.

The cats of Tiffany Street ill. by author. Candlewick Pr., 1992. ISBN 1-56402-094-0 Subj: Animals – cats.

Clap your hands: finger rhymes ill. by Toni Goffe. Lothrop, 1988. ISBN 0-688-07693-9 Subj: Games. Poetry, rhyme.

Eat up, Gemma ill. by Jan Ormerod. Lothrop, 1988. ISBN 0-688-08149-5 Subj: Babies. Ethnic groups in the U.S. – Afro-Americans. Food.

The grumpalump ill. by Barbara Firth. Clarion, 1991. ISBN 0-89919-871-6 Subj: Activities – ballooning. Animals. Poetry, rhyme.

Happy Christmas, Gemma ill. by Jan Ormerod. Lothrop, 1986. ISBN 0-688-06508-2 Subj: Ethnic groups in the U.S. – Afro-Americans. Family life. Family life – grandmothers. Holidays – Christmas.

Mary Mary ill. by Helen Craig. Macmillan, 1990. ISBN 0-689-50514-0 Subj: Behavior – needing someone. Character traits – being different. Giants.

Nine ducks nine ill. by author. Lothrop, 1990. ISBN 0-688-09535-6 Subj: Animals – foxes. Birds – ducks. Character traits – cleverness. Poetry, rhyme.

This is the bear ill. by Helen Craig. Lippincott, 1986. ISBN 0-397-32171-6 Subj: Behavior – lost. Behavior – secrets. Poetry, rhyme. Toys – teddy bears.

This is the bear and the picnic lunch ill. by Helen Craig. Little, 1989. ISBN 0-316-35248-9 Subj: Activities – picnicking. Animals – dogs. Poetry, rhyme. Toys – teddy bears.

This is the bear and the scary night ill. by Helen Craig. Little, 1992. ISBN 0-316-35250-0 Subj: Character traits – bravery. Night. Poetry, rhyme. Toys – teddy bears.

Haynes, Max. *Dinosaur island* ill. by author. Lothrop, 1991. ISBN 0-688-10330-8 Subj: Dinosaurs. Islands.

Sparky's rainbow repair photos. and ill. by author. Lothrop, 1992. ISBN 0-688-11194-7 Subj: Games. Weather – rainbows.

Haynes, Robert. *The elephant that ga-lumphed* (Ward, Nanda Weedon)

Hays, Daniel. *Charley sang a song* (Hays, Hoffman Reynolds)

Hays, Hoffman Reynolds. *Charley sang a song* by Hoffman and Daniel Hays; ill. by Uri Shulevitz. Harper, 1964. Subj: Activities – flying.

Hays, Wilma Pitchford. *Little Yellow Fur* ill. by Richard Cuffari. Coward, 1973. Subj: Indians of North America.

Hayward, Linda. *All stuck up* ill. by Normand Chartier. McKay, 1990. ISBN 0-379-90216-3 Subj: Behavior – trickery. Animals – foxes. Animals – rabbits. Folk and fairy tales.

Baby Moses ill. by Barb Henry. Random House, 1989. ISBN 0-394-99410-8 Subj: Babies. Foreign lands – Egypt. Religion.

Hayward, Max. *The telephone* (Chukovsky, Korney)

Haywood, Carolyn. *A Christmas fantasy* ill. by Glenys and Victor G. Ambrus. Morrow, 1972. Subj: Holidays – Christmas.

Hello, star ill. by Julie Durrell. Morrow, 1987. ISBN 0-688-06651-8 Subj: Animals. Family life – grandparents. Farms. Seasons – summer.

How the reindeer saved Santa ill. by Victor G. Ambrus. Morrow, 1986. ISBN 0-688-05904-X Subj: Animals – reindeer. Character traits – loyalty. Holidays – Christmas.

The king's monster ill. by Victor G. Ambrus. Morrow, 1980. Subj: Monsters. Royalty – kings.

Santa Claus forever! ill. by Glenys and Victor G. Ambrus. Morrow, 1983. ISBN 0-688-02345-2 Subj: Behavior – bad day. Holidays – Christmas.

Hazelton, Elizabeth Baldwin. *Sammy, the crow who remembered* ill. by Ann Atwood. Scribner's, 1969. Subj: Birds – crows. Family life.

Hazen, Barbara Shook. *Even if I did something awful* ill. by Nancy Kincade. Atheneum, 1981. Subj: Emotions – love. Family life.

Fang ill. by Leslie Holt Morrill. Atheneum, 1987. ISBN 0-689-31307-1 Subj: Animals – dogs. Character traits – bravery. Emotions – fear.

The Fat Cats, Cousin Scraggs and the monster mice ill. by Lonni Sue Johnson. Atheneum, 1985. ISBN 0-689-31092-7 Subj: Animals – cats. Animals – mice. Behavior – dissatisfaction. Character traits – cleverness.

The gorilla did it! ill. by Ray Cruz. Atheneum, 1974. Subj: Animals – gorillas. Imagination – imaginary friends.

Gorilla wants to be the baby ill. by Jacqueline Bardner Smith. Atheneum, 1978. Subj: Animals – gorillas. Imagination – imaginary friends.

Happy, sad, silly, mad: a beginning book about emotions ill. by Elizabeth Dauber; ed. consultant: Mary Elting. Grosset, 1971. Subj: Emotions.

If it weren't for Benjamin (I'd always get to lick the icing spoon) ill. by Laura Hartman. Human Sciences Pr., 1979. Subj: Sibling rivalry.

The knight who was afraid of the dark ill. by Tony Ross. Dial Pr., 1988. ISBN 0-8037-0668-5 Subj: Emotions – fear. Knights. Middle ages. Night.

The me I see ill. by Ati Forberg. Abingdon, 1978. Subj: Activities – bathing. Anatomy.

Mommy's office ill. by David Soman. Atheneum, 1992. ISBN 0-689-31601-1 Subj: Activities – working. Careers. Family life – mothers.

The sorcerer's apprentice ill. by Tomi Ungerer. Lancelot Pr., 1969. Subj: Folk and fairy tales. Magic.

Stay, Fang ill. by Leslie Holt Morrill. Atheneum, 1990. ISBN 0-689-31599-6 Subj: Animals – dogs. Pets.

Tight times ill. by Trina Schart Hyman. Viking, 1979. Subj: Animals – cats. Family life. Family life – only child. Poverty.

Two homes to live in ill. by Peggy Luks. Human Sciences Pr., 1978. Subj: Divorce. Emotions.

Wally the worry-warthog ill. by Janet Stevens. Houghton, 1990. ISBN 0-89919-896-1 Subj: Animals – warthogs. Behavior – worrying. Emotions – fear.

Where do bears sleep? ill. by Ian E. Staunton. Addison-Wesley, 1970. Subj: Animals. Poetry, rhyme. Sleep.

Why couldn't I be an only kid like you, Wigger? ill. by Leigh Grant. Atheneum, 1975. Subj: Babies. Emotions – envy, jealousy. Family life – only child. Sibling rivalry.

Why did Grandpa die? a book about death ill. by Pat Schories. Childrens Pr., 1985. ISBN 0-307-62484-6 Subj: Death. Family life – grandfathers. Old age.

Hearn, Michael Patrick. *The porcelain cat* ill. by Leo and Diane Dillon. Little, 1985. ISBN 0-316-35330-2 Subj: Animals – cats. Animals – rats. Cumulative tales. Folk and fairy tales. Magic.

Heath, Amy. *Sofie's role* ill. by Sheila Hamanaka. Four Winds, 1992. ISBN 0-02-743505-9 Subj: Activities – cooking. Careers – bakers. Family life. Holidays – Christmas.

Heck, Elisabeth. *The black sheep* tr. by Karen M. Klockner; ill. by Sita Jucker. Little, 1986. ISBN 0-316-35402-3 Subj: Animals – sheep. Behavior – running away. Holidays – Christmas. Religion.

Heckman, Philip. *The moon is following me* ill. by Mary O'Keefe Young. Atheneum, 1991. ISBN 0-689-31565-1 Subj: Activities – traveling. Moon.

Hedderwick, Mairi. *Katie Morag and the big boy cousins* ill. by author. Little, 1987. ISBN 0-316-35403-1 Subj: Behavior – misbehavior. Family life. Family life – grandmothers. Foreign lands – Scotland. Islands.

Katie Morag and the tiresome Ted ill. by author. Little, 1986. ISBN 0-316-35401-5 Subj: Babies. Behavior – misbehavior. Emotions – envy, jealousy. Foreign lands – Scotland. Islands. Sibling rivalry.

Katie Morag and the two grandmothers ill. by author. Little, 1986. ISBN 0-316-35400-7 Subj: Activities – bathing. Animals – sheep. Fairs. Family life – grandmothers. Foreign lands – Scotland. Islands.

Katie Morag delivers the mail ill. by author. Little, 1987, 1984. ISBN 0-316-35405-8 Subj: Behavior – misbehavior. Careers – mail carriers. Family life – grandmothers. Foreign lands – Scotland. Islands.

P. D. Pebbles' summer or winter book ill. by author. Little, 1989. ISBN 0-316-35406-6 Subj: Family life. Format, unusual. Seasons – summer. Seasons – winter.

Hefter, Richard. *The strawberry book of shapes* ill. by author. Larousse, 1976. Subj: Concepts – shape.

Heide, Florence Parry. *The day of Ahmed's secret* by Florence Parry Heide and Judith Heide Gilliland; ill. by Ted Lewin. Lothrop, 1990. ISBN 0-688-08895-3 Subj: Activities – writing. Activities – working. Behavior – secrets. Foreign lands – Egypt.

A monster is coming! A monster is coming! by Florence Parry Heide and Roxanne Heide; ill. by Rachi Farrow. Watts, 1980. Subj: Monsters.

Heide, Roxanne. *A monster is coming! A monster is coming!* (Heide, Florence Parry)

Heilbroner, Joan. *Robert the rose horse* ill. by Philip Eastman. Random House, 1962. Subj: Animals – horses. Flowers. Humor.

This is the house where Jack lives ill. by Aliki. Harper, 1962. Subj: Cumulative tales. Participation.

Tom the TV cat ill. by Sal Murdocca. Random House, 1984. ISBN 0-394-96708-9 Subj: Animals – cats. Behavior – seeking better things. Television.

Heiligman, Deborah. *Into the night* ill. by Melissa Sweet. HarperCollins, 1990. ISBN 0-06-026382-2 Subj: Bedtime. Poetry, rhyme.

Heine, Helme. *Friends* ill. by author. Atheneum, 1982. Subj: Animals. Friendship. Sports – bicycling.

King Bounce the 1st ill. by author. Alphabet Pr., 1982. Subj: Royalty – kings. Sleep.

The marvelous journey through the night tr. by Ralph Manheim; ill. by author. Farrar, 1990. ISBN 0-374-38478-9 Subj: Dreams. Night. Sleep.

Merry-go-round ill. by author. Barron's, 1980. Subj: Activities – working.

Mr. Miller the dog ill. by author. Atheneum, 1980. Subj: Animals – dogs. Behavior – imitation.

Mollywoop tr. by Ralph Manheim; ill. by author. Farrar, 1991. ISBN 0-374-35001-9 Subj: Animals. Birds – chickens. Friendship. Poetry, rhyme.

The most wonderful egg in the world ill. by author. Atheneum, 1983. Subj: Birds – chickens. Character traits – appearance. Royalty.

One day in paradise ill. by adapt. Atheneum, 1986. ISBN 0-689-50394-6 Subj: Religion.

The pigs' wedding ill. by author. Atheneum, 1979. Subj: Animals – pigs. Weddings.

Prince Bear ill. by author. Macmillan, 1989. ISBN 0-689-50484-5 Subj: Animals – bears. Progress. Royalty – princes. Royalty – princesses.

Superhare ill. by author. Barron's, 1979. Subj: Animals – rabbits. Character traits – being different.

Three little friends: the alarm clock ill. by author. Atheneum, 1985. ISBN 0-689-71043-7 Subj: Animals. Birds – chickens. Friendship. Night.

Three little friends: the racing cart ill. by author. Atheneum, 1985. ISBN 0-689-71045-3 Subj: Animals. Birds – chickens. Friendship. Sports – racing.

Three little friends: the visitor ill. by author. Atheneum, 1985. ISBN 0-689-71044-5 Subj: Animals. Birds – chickens. Friendship.

Heins, Paul. *Snow White* (Grimm, Jacob)

Heinst, Marie. *My first number book* photos. by author. Dorling Kindersley, 1992. ISBN 1-879431-74-2 Subj: Concepts – shape. Counting, numbers. Ethnic groups in the U.S. Games.

Heitler, Susan M. *David decides about thumbsucking* photos. by Paula Singer. Reading Matters, 1985. ISBN 0-9614780-12 Subj: Behavior – growing up. Problem solving. Thumbsucking.

Hejl, Pauline. *The fine round cake* (Esterl, Arnica)

The Helen Oxenbury nursery rhyme book chosen by Brian W. Alderson; ill. by Helen Oxenbury. Morrow, 1987. ISBN 0-688-06899-5 Subj: Nursery rhymes.

Helena, Ann. *The lie* ill. by Ellen Pizer. Raintree, 1977. Subj: Behavior – lying. Emotions. Friendship.

Hellard, Susan. *Eleanor and the babysitter* ill. by author. Little, 1991. ISBN 0-316-35459-7 Subj: Activities – baby-sitting. Animals – anteaters. Animals – koala bears. Monsters.

Froggie goes a-courting ill. by adapt. Putnam's, 1988. ISBN 0-399-21508-5 Subj: Frogs and toads. Humor.

This little piggy ill. by author. Putnam, 1989. ISBN 0-399-21625-1 Subj: Animals – pigs. Format, unusual. Nursery rhymes.

Time to get up ill. by author. Putnam, 1990. ISBN 0-399-21948-X Subj: Format, unusual. Morning. Poetry, rhyme.

Helldorfer, M. C. (Mary Claire). *Daniel's gift* ill. by Julie Downing. Bradbury Pr., 1987. ISBN 0-02-743511-3 Subj: Animals – sheep. Holidays – Christmas.

The mapmaker's daughter ill. by Jonathan Hunt. Bradbury Pr., 1991. ISBN 0-02-743515-6 Subj: Character traits – bravery. Magic. Maps. Royalty – princes. Witches.

Sailing to the sea ill. by Loretta Krupinski. Viking, 1991. ISBN 0-670-83520-X Subj: Boats, ships. Family life – aunts, uncles.

Hellen, Nancy. *Animals of the jungle* ill. by author. Peter Bedrick Books (dist. by Harper), 1991. ISBN 0-87226-458-0 Subj: Animals. Jungle.

Bus stop ill. by author. Watts, 1988. ISBN 0-531-05765-8 Subj: Buses. Character traits – patience. Format, unusual. Transportation.

Creatures of the ocean ill. by author. Peter Bedrick Books (dist. by Harper), 1991. ISBN 0-87226-457-2 Subj: Sea and seashore.

A visit to the farm ill. by author. Peter Bedrick Books (dist. by Harper), 1990. ISBN 0-87226-432-7 Subj: Animals. Format, unusual – toy and movable books. Farms.

A visit to the zoo ill. by author. Peter Bedrick Books (dist. by Harper), 1990. ISBN 0-87226-431-9 Subj: Animals. Format, unusual – toy and movable books. Zoos.

Heller, George. *Hiroshi's wonderful kite* ill. by Kyuzo Tsugami. Silver Burdett, 1968. Subj: Crime. Foreign lands – Japan. Kites.

Heller, Linda. *Alexis and the golden ring* ill. by author. Macmillan, 1980. Subj: Folk and fairy tales. Foreign lands – Russia. Magic.

The castle on Hester Street ill. by author. Jewish Pub. Soc., 1982. Subj: Family life – grandparents.

Lily at the table ill. by author. Macmillan, 1979. Subj: Family life. Food. Furniture – tables. Wordless.

Heller, Nicholas. *An adventure at sea* ill. by author. Greenwillow, 1988. ISBN 0-688-07847-8 Subj: Imagination. Sea and seashore. Sibling rivalry.

The front hall carpet ill. by author. Greenwillow, 1990. ISBN 0-688-05273-8 Subj: Imagination.

Happy birthday, Moe dog ill. by author. Greenwillow, 1988. ISBN 0-688-07671-8 Subj: Animals – dogs. Birthdays.

Mathilda the dream bear ill. by author. Greenwillow, 1989. ISBN 0-688-08239-4 Subj: Animals. Animals – bears. Dreams.

The monster in the cave ill. by author. Greenwillow, 1987. ISBN 0-688-07314-X Subj: Family life. Holidays – Christmas. Monsters. Parties.

The tooth tree ill. by author. Greenwillow, 1991. ISBN 0-688-09393-0 Subj: Fairies. Teeth. Trees.

A troll story ill. by author. Greenwillow, 1990. ISBN 0-688-08971-2 Subj: Imagination. Trolls.

Heller, Ruth. *Animals born alive and well* ill. by author. Grosset, 1982. Subj: Animals.

A cache of jewels and other collective nouns ill. by author. Grosset, 1989. ISBN 0-448-19211-X Subj: Language. Poetry, rhyme.

Chickens aren't the only ones ill. by author. Grosset, 1981. Subj: Eggs. Science.

How to hide a butterfly: and other insects ill. by author. Grosset, 1985. ISBN 0-488-10478-4 Subj: Behavior – hiding. Insects. Insects – butterflies, caterpillars. Poetry, rhyme.

How to hide a polar bear: and other mammals ill. by author. Grosset, 1985. ISBN 0-488-10477-6 Subj: Animals. Animals – polar bears. Behavior – hiding. Poetry, rhyme.

How to hide an octopus: and other sea creatures ill. by author. Grosset, 1985. ISBN 0-488-10476-8 Subj: Animals. Crustacea. Octopuses. Poetry, rhyme.

Kites sail high: a book about verbs ill. by author. Grosset, 1988. ISBN 0-448-10480-6 Subj: Language. Poetry, rhyme.

Plants that never ever bloom ill. by author. Grosset, 1984. Subj: Plants.

The reason for a flower ill. by author. Grosset, 1983. Subj: Flowers. Poetry, rhyme.

Heller, Wendy. *Clementine and the cage* ill. by Rex J. Irvine. Kalimát, 1980. Subj: Behavior – running away. Birds – canaries.

Hello, baby photos. sel. by Debby Slier. Macmillan, 1988. ISBN 0-02-688750-9 Subj: Babies. Format, unusual – board books.

Hellsing, Lennart. *The wonderful pumpkin* ill. by Svend Otto S. Atheneum, 1976, 1975. Translation of Der underbara pumpan Subj: Animals – bears. Food. Holidays – Halloween.

Helmering, Doris Wild. *I have two families* ill. by Heidi Palmer. Abingdon Pr., 1981. Subj: Family life – step families.

We're going to have a baby by Doris and John William Helmering; ill. by Robert H. Cassell. Abingdon Pr., 1978. Subj: Babies. Family life. Sibling rivalry.

Helmering, John William. *We're going to have a baby* (Helmering, Doris Wild)

Helweg, Hans. *Farm animals* ill. by author. Random House, 1978. ISBN 0-394-93733-3 Subj: Animals. Birds. Farms.

Hendershot, Judith. *In coal country* ill. by Thomas B. Allen. Knopf, 1987. ISBN 0-394-98190-1 Subj: Family life. Family life – fathers.

Henderson, Kathy. *The baby's book of babies* photos. by Anthea Sieveking. Dial Pr., 1989. ISBN 0-837-0634-0 Subj: Babies.

I can be a farmer ill. with photos. Children's, 1989. ISBN 0-516-01923-6 Subj: Careers – farmers. Farms.

In the middle of the night ill. by Jennifer Eachus. Macmillan, 1992. ISBN 0-02-743545-8 Subj: Activities – working. City. Night.

Hendrickson, Karen. *Baby and I can play* ill. by Marina Megale. Parenting Pr., 1986. ISBN 0-943990-13-0 Subj: Activities – playing. Babies. Family life.

Fun with toddlers ill. by Marina Megale. Parenting Pr., 1986. ISBN 0-943990-14-9 Subj: Activities – playing. Babies. Family life.

Hendry, Diana. *Not anywhere house* ill. by Thor Wickstrom. Lothrop, 1991. ISBN 0-688-10194-1 Subj: Family life. Moving.

Henkes, Kevin. *All alone* ill. by author. Greenwillow, 1981. Subj: Behavior – solitude.

Bailey goes camping ill. by author. Greenwillow, 1985. ISBN 0-688-05702-0 Subj: Animals – rabbits. Family life. Camps, camping.

Chester's way ill. by author. Greenwillow, 1988. ISBN 0-688-07608-4 Subj: Animals – mice. Behavior – bullying.

Chrysanthemum ill. by author. Greenwillow, 1991. ISBN 0-688-09700-6 Subj: Animals. Names. School.

Clean enough ill. by author. Greenwillow, 1982. Subj: Activities – bathing.

Grandpa and Bo ill. by author. Greenwillow, 1986. ISBN 0-688-04957-5 Subj: Family life – grandfathers. Seasons – summer.

Jessica ill. by author. Greenwillow, 1989. ISBN 0-688-07830-3 Subj: Friendship. Imagination – imaginary friends. School.

Julius, the baby of the world ill. by author. Greenwillow, 1990. ISBN 0-688-08944-5 Subj: Family life. Sibling rivalry.

Once around the block ill. by Victoria Chess. Greenwillow, 1987. ISBN 0-688-04955-9 Subj: Behavior – boredom. Communities, neighborhoods.

Sheila Rae, the brave ill. by author. Greenwillow, 1987. ISBN 0-688-07156-2 Subj: Animals – mice. Behavior – lost. Character traits – bravery. Family life – sisters.

Shhhh ill. by author. Greenwillow, 1989. ISBN 0-688-07986-5 Subj: Family life. Morning. Sleep.

A weekend with Wendell ill. by author. Greenwillow, 1986. ISBN 0-688-06326-8 Subj: Activities – playing. Animals – mice. Behavior – misbehavior. Character traits – selfishness.

Henkle, Henrietta *see* Buckmaster, Henrietta

Henley, Claire. *At the zoo* ill. by author. Walt Disney, 1992. ISBN 1-56282-152-0 Subj: Activities. Animals. Zoos.

Farm day ill. by author. Dial, 1991. ISBN 0-8037-0954-4 Subj: Animals. Careers – farmers. Farms.

In the ocean ill. by author. Walt Disney, 1992. ISBN 1-56282-154-7 Subj: Animals. Fish. Sea and seashore.

Jungle day ill. by author. Dial, 1991. ISBN 0-8037-0959-5 Subj: Animals. Jungle.

Henley, Karyn. *Hatch!* ill. by Susan Kennedy. Carolrhoda Books, 1980. Subj: Animals.

Hennessy, B. G. *A, B, C, D, tummy, toes, hands, knee* ill. by Wendy Watson. Viking, 1989. ISBN 0-670-81703-1 Subj: Concepts. Family life. Poetry, rhyme.

The dinosaur who lived in my backyard ill. by Susan Davis. Viking, 1988. ISBN 0-670-81685-X Subj: Dinosaurs. Imagination.

Jake baked the cake ill. by Mary Morgan. Viking, 1990. ISBN 0-670-82237-X Subj: Food. Poetry, rhyme. Weddings.

The missing tarts ill. by Tracey Campbell Pearson. Viking, 1989. ISBN 0-670-82039-3 Subj: Behavior – stealing. Nursery rhymes. Poetry, rhyme.

School days ill. by Tracey Campbell Pearson. Viking, 1990. ISBN 0-670-83025-9 Subj: Poetry, rhyme. School.

When you were just a little girl ill. by Jeanne Arnold. Viking, 1991. ISBN 0-670-83998-6 Subj: Family life – grandmothers. Poetry, rhyme.

Henri, Adrian. *The postman's palace* ill. by Simon Henwood. Atheneum, 1990. ISBN 0-689-31667-4 Subj: Buildings. Careers – mail carriers. Dreams.

Henrietta. *A mouse in the house* ill. with photos. Dorling Kindersley, 1991. ISBN 1-879431-26-2 Subj: Animals – mice. Birthdays. Games. Poetry, rhyme.

Henriod, Lorraine. *Grandma's wheelchair* ill. by Christa Chevalier. Albert Whitman, 1982. Subj: Family life – grandmothers. Handicaps. Sibling rivalry.

Henry, O. *The gift of the Magi* ill. by Lisbeth Zwerger. Picture Book Studio, 1982. ISBN 0-907234-17-8 Subj: Character traits – generosity. Holidays – Christmas.

Henstra, Friso. *Wait and see* ill. by author. Addison-Wesley, 1978. Subj: Machines.

Henwood, Simon. *The troubled village* ill. by author. Farrar, 1991. ISBN 0-374-37780-4 Subj: Communities, neighborhoods. Problem solving.

The view (Yoaker, Harry)

Hepworth, Cathi. *ANTicks! an alphabetical anthology* ill. by author. Putnam, 1992. ISBN 0-399-21862-9 Subj: ABC books. Insects – ants.

Herford, Oliver. *The most timid in the land* ill. by Sylvia Long. Chronicle, 1992. ISBN 0-87701-862-6 Subj: Animals – rabbits. Middle ages. Poetry, rhyme.

Herman, Bill. *Jenny's magic wand* by Bill and Helen Herman; photos. by Don Perdue. Watts, 1988. ISBN 0-531-10292-0 Subj: Handicaps – blindness. Senses – seeing.

Herman, Charlotte. *My mother didn't kiss me goodnight* ill. by Bruce Degen. Dutton, 1980. Subj: Behavior – worrying.

Herman, Emily. *Hubknuckles* ill. by Deborah Kogan Ray. Crown, 1985. ISBN 0-517-55646-4 Subj: Ghosts. Holidays – Halloween.

Herman, Gail. *Make way for trucks: big machines on wheels* ill. by Christopher Santoro. McKay, 1990. ISBN 0-679-90110-8 Subj: Trucks.

Herman, Helen. *Jenny's magic wand* (Herman, Bill)

Herold, Ann Bixby. *The helping day* ill. by Victoria de Larrea. Coward, 1980. Subj: Character traits – helpfulness.

Herring, Ann. *Peter and the wolf* (Prokofiev, Sergei Sergeievitch)

Suho and the white horse (Otsuka, Yuzo)

Herriot, James. *Blossom comes home* ill. by Ruth Brown. St. Martin's, 1988. ISBN 0-312-02169-0 Subj: Animals – bulls, cows. Behavior – needing someone. Farms. Old age.

Bonny's big day ill. by Ruth Brown. St. Martin's, 1987. ISBN 0-312-01000-1 Subj: Animals – horses. Fairs. Farms.

Christmas Day kitten ill. by Ruth Brown. St. Martin's, 1986. ISBN 0-312-13407-X Subj: Animals – cats. Character traits – kindness to animals. Holidays – Christmas.

Moses the kitten ill. by Peter Barrett. St. Martin's, 1984. Subj: Animals – cats. Careers – veterinarians.

Only one woof ill. by Peter Barrett. St. Martin's, 1985. ISBN 0-312-58583-7 Subj: Animals. Animals – dogs. Careers – veterinarians.

Herrmann, Dagmar. *My father always embarrasses me* (Shalev, Meir)

Nobody has time for me (Skutina, Vladimir)

Herrmann, Frank. *The giant Alexander* ill. by George Him. McGraw-Hill, 1965. Subj: Foreign lands – England. Giants.

The giant Alexander and the circus ill. by George Him. McGraw-Hill, 1966. Subj: Circus. Foreign lands – England. Giants.

Herson, Kathleen. *The copycat* by Kathleen and Donald Herson; ill. by Catherine Stock. Atheneum, 1989. ISBN 0-689-31448-5 Subj: Animals. Behavior – imitation. Poetry, rhyme.

Herter, Jonina. *Eighty-eight kisses* ill. with photos. Boss Books, 1978. Subj: Babies. Family life – great-grandparents.

Hertz, Ole. *Tobias catches trout* tr. from Danish by Tobi Tobias; ill. by author. Carolrhoda Books, 1984. Subj: Foreign lands – Greenland. Sports – fishing.

Tobias goes ice fishing tr. from Danish by Tobi Tobias; ill. by author. Carolrhoda Books, 1984. Subj: Foreign lands – Greenland. Seasons – winter. Sports – fishing.

Tobias goes seal hunting tr. from Danish by Tobi Tobias; ill. by author. Carolrhoda Books, 1984. Subj: Foreign lands – Greenland. Sports – hunting.

Tobias has a birthday tr. from Danish by Tobi Tobias; ill. by author. Carolrhoda Books, 1984. Subj: Birthdays. Foreign lands – Greenland.

Hess, Edith. *Peter and Susie find a family* tr. from German by Miriam Moore; ill. by Jacqueline Blass. Abingdon Pr., 1985. ISBN 0-687-30848-8 Subj: Adoption. Family life.

Hessell, Jenny. *Staying at Sam's* ill. by Jenny Williams. Harper/Lippincott, 1990. ISBN 0-397-32433-2 Subj: Family life.

Hest, Amy. *Best-ever good-bye party* ill. by DyAnne DiSalvo-Ryan. Morrow, 1989. ISBN 0-688-07326-3 Subj: Friendship. Moving.

The crack-of-dawn walkers ill. by Amy Schwartz. Macmillan, 1984. Subj: Family life – grandfathers.

The go-between ill. by DyAnne DiSalvo-Ryan. Four Winds, 1992. ISBN 0-02-743632-2 Subj: Emotions – love. Family life – grandparents. Friendship.

The midnight eaters ill. by Karen Gundersheimer. Four Winds, 1989. ISBN 0-02-743630-6 Subj: Family life – grandmothers. Night. Old age.

The mommy exchange ill. by DyAnne DiSalvo-Ryan. Four Winds, 1988. ISBN 0-02-743650-0 Subj: Behavior – dissatisfaction. Family life – mothers.

The purple coat ill. by Amy Schwartz. Four Winds Pr., 1986. ISBN 0-02-743640-3 Subj: Careers – tailors. Clothing – coats. Concepts – color. Family life. Family life – grandfathers.

The ring and the window seat ill. by Deborah Haeffele. Scholastic, 1990. ISBN 0-590-41350-3 Subj: Careers – carpenters. Family life. War.

A sort-of sailor ill. by Lizzy Rockwell. Four Winds, 1990. ISBN 0-02-743641-1 Subj: Boats, ships. Emotions – fear.

Heuck, Sigrid. *Pony and Bear are friends* ill. by author. Knopf, 1990. ISBN 0-394-92311-1 Subj: Animals – bears. Animals – horses. Friendship. Rebuses.

Who stole the apples? ill. by author. Knopf, 1986. ISBN 0-394-98371-8 Subj: Activities – traveling. Animals. Behavior – sharing. Rebuses.

Hewett, Anita. *The tale of the turnip* ill. by Margery Gill. McGraw-Hill, 1961. Subj: Cumulative tales. Participation. Plants.

Hewett, Joan. *Fly away free* photos. by Richard Hewett. Walker, 1981. Subj: Birds – pelicans. Careers – veterinarians. Illness.

The mouse and the elephant photos. by Richard Hewett. Little, 1977. Subj: Animals – elephants. Animals – mice.

Rosalie ill. by Donald Carrick. Lothrop, 1987. ISBN 0-688-06229-6 Subj: Animals – dogs. Character traits – kindness to animals. Old age.

Hewitt, Kathryn. *King Midas and the golden touch* by Nathaniel Hawthorne; adapt. and ill. by Kathryn Hewitt. Harcourt, 1987. ISBN 0-15-242800-3 Subj: Behavior – greed. Folk and fairy tales. Royalty – kings.

The three sillies ill. by adapt. Harcourt, 1986. ISBN 0-15-286855-0 Subj: Animals. Animals – pigs. Character traits – foolishness. Folk and fairy tales.

Two by two: the untold story ill. by author. Harcourt, 1984. Subj: Religion – Noah.

Heyduck-Huth, Hilde. *The starfish: a treasure chest story* ill. by author. Macmillan, 1987. ISBN 0-689-50434-9 Subj: Behavior – collecting things. Crustacea. Sea and seashore.

The strawflower: a treasure chest story ill. by author. Macmillan, 1987. ISBN 0-689-50435-7 Subj: Behavior – collecting things. Flowers. Seasons.

Heyer, Marilee. *The weaving of a dream* ill. by author. Puffin, 1989. ISBN 0-14-050528-8 Subj: Folk and fairy tales. Foreign lands – China.

Heymans, Margriet. *Pippin and Robber Grumblecroak's big baby* ill. by author. Addison-Wesley, 1973. Subj: Crime. Puppets.

Heyward, Du Bose. *The country bunny and the little gold shoes* ill. by Marjorie Flack. Houghton, 1939. Subj: Animals – rabbits. Character traits – kindness. Holidays – Easter.

Hickman, Martha Whitmore. *Eeps creeps, it's my room!* ill. by Mary Alice Baer. Abingdon Pr., 1984. Subj: Character traits – cleanliness.

My friend William moved away ill. by Bill Myers. Abingdon Pr., 1979. Subj: Friendship. Moving.

When can daddy come home? ill. by Francis Livingston. Abingdon Pr., 1983. Subj: Crime. Family life. Prisons.

Hicks, Eleanor B. see Coerr, Eleanor

Hidaka, Masako. *Girl from the snow country* tr. from Japanese by Amanda Mayer Stinchecum; ill. by author. Kane/Miller, 1986. ISBN 0-916291-06-5

Subj: Flowers. Folk and fairy tales. Foreign lands – Japan. Weather – snow.

High on a hill : *a book of Chinese riddles* sel. and ill. by Ed Young. Collins-World, 1980. Subj: Folk and fairy tales. Foreign lands – China. Riddles.

Higham, Jon Atlas. *Aardvark's picnic* ill. by author. Little, 1987. ISBN 0-333-42822-6 Subj: Activities – picnicking. Animals. Animals – aardvarks.

Highwater, Jamake. *Moonsong lullaby* photos. by Marcia Keegan. Lothrop, 1981. Subj: Lullabies. Night. Poetry, rhyme.

Hill, Donna. *Ms. Glee was waiting* ill. by Diane Dawson. Atheneum, 1978. Subj: School.

Hill, Elizabeth Starr. *Evan's corner* ill. by Sandra Speidel Rev. ed. Viking, 1991. ISBN 0-670-82830-0 Subj: Character traits – helpfulness. Ethnic groups in the U.S. – Afro-Americans. Family life.

Hill, Eric. *At home* ill. by author. Random House, 1983. Subj: Animals – bears. Family life. Wordless.

Baby Bear's bedtime ill. by author. Random House, 1984. ISBN 0-394-96572-8 Subj: Animals – bears. Bedtime.

Good morning, baby bear ill. by author. Random House, 1984. Subj: Animals – bears. Morning.

My pets ill. by author. Random House, 1983. Subj: Animals – bears. Pets.

The park ill. by author. Random House, 1983. Subj: Activities – walking. Wordless.

Spot at home ill. by author. Putnam, 1991. ISBN 0-399-21774-6 Subj: Animals – dogs. Format, unusual – board books.

Spot at play ill. by author. Putnam's, 1985. ISBN 0-399-21228-0 Subj: Activities – playing. Animals. Animals – dogs.

Spot at the fair ill. by author. Putnam's, 1985. ISBN 0-399-21229-9 Subj: Animals. Animals – dogs. Fairs. Format, unusual – board books.

Spot counts from 1 to 10 ill. by author. Putnam, 1989. ISBN 0-399-21672-3 Subj: Animals. Animals – dogs. Counting, numbers. Format, unusual – board books.

Spot goes to school ill. by author. Putnam's, 1984. Subj: Animals – dogs. Format, unusual – toy and movable books. School.

Spot goes to the beach ill. by author. Putnam's, 1985. ISBN 0-399-21247-7 Subj: Activities – playing. Animals – dogs. Family life. Format, unusual – toy and movable books. Sea and seashore.

Spot goes to the circus ill. by author. Putnam's, 1986. ISBN 0-399-21317-1 Subj: Animals – dogs. Circus. Format, unusual – board books.

Spot goes to the farm ill. by author. Putnam's, 1987. ISBN 0-399-21434-8 Subj: Animals. Animals – dogs. Farms. Format, unusual – board books. Machines.

Spot in the garden ill. by author. Putnam, 1991. ISBN 0-399-21772-X Subj: Animals – dogs. Format, unusual – board books. Gardens, gardening.

Spot looks at colors ill. by author. Putnam's, 1986. ISBN 0-399-21349-X Subj: Animals – dogs. Concepts – color. Format, unusual – board books.

Spot looks at opposites ill. by author. Putnam, 1989. ISBN 0-399-21681-2 Subj: Animals – dogs. Concepts – opposites. Format, unusual – board books.

Spot looks at shapes ill. by author. Putnam's, 1986. ISBN 0-399-21350-3 Subj: Animals – dogs. Concepts – shape. Format, unusual – board books.

Spot looks at the weather ill. by author. Putnam, 1989. ISBN 0-399-21673-1 Subj: Animals – dogs. Format, unusual – board books. Weather.

Spot on the farm ill. by author. Putnam's, 1985. ISBN 0-399-21230-2 Subj: Animals. Animals – dogs. Farms. Format, unusual – board books.

Spot sleeps over ill. by author. Putnam, 1990. ISBN 0-399-21815-7 Subj: Activities – playing. Animals – dogs. Format, unusual – toy and movable books. Friendship.

Spot visits the hospital ill. by author. Putnam's, 1987. ISBN 0-399-21397-X Subj: Animals – dogs. Behavior – misbehavior. Hospitals.

Spot's baby sister ill. by author. Putnam, 1989. ISBN 0-399-21640-5 Subj: Animals – dogs. Animals – hippopotami. Format, unusual – toy and movable books. Reptiles – alligators, crocodiles.

Spot's big book of words; El libro grande de las palabras de Spot ill. by author Rev. ed. Putnam's, 1989. ISBN 0-399-21689-8 Subj: Animals – dogs. Foreign languages. Language.

Spot's birthday party ill. by author. Putnam's, 1982. Subj: Birthdays. Folk and fairy tales. Format, unusual – toy and movable books.

Spot's first Christmas ill. by author. Putnam's, 1983. ISBN 0-399-20963-8 Subj: Animals – dogs. Format, unusual – toy and movable books. Holidays – Christmas.

Spot's first Easter ill. by author. Putnam's, 1988. ISBN 0-399-21435-6 Subj: Animals – dogs. Eggs. Format, unusual – toy and movable books. Holidays – Easter.

Spot's first picnic ill. by author. Putnam's, 1987. ISBN 0-399-21398-8 Subj: Activities – picnicking. Animals – dogs. Behavior – misbehavior.

Spot's first walk ill. by author. Putnam's, 1981. Subj: Activities – walking. Animals – dogs. Format, unusual – toy and movable books.

Spot's first words ill. by author. Putnam's, 1986. ISBN 0-399-21348-1 Subj: Animals – dogs. Format, unusual – board books. Language.

Spot's toy box ill. by author. Putnam, 1991. ISBN 0-399-21773-8 Subj: Animals – dogs. Format, unusual – board books. Toys.

Up there ill. by author. Random House, 1983. Subj: Activities – flying. Animals – bears. Wordless.

Where's Spot? ill. by author. Putnam's, 1980. Subj: Behavior – lost. Folk and fairy tales. Format, unusual – toy and movable books.

Hill, Mary Lou. *My dad's a park ranger* ill. by Tom De Hart. Children's Pr., 1978. Subj: Careers – park rangers.

My dad's a smokejumper ill. by Don Hendricks. Children's Pr., 1978. Subj: Careers – firefighters. Forest, woods.

Hill, Monica *see* Watson, Jane Werner

Hill, Susan. *Can it be true?* ill. by Angela Barrett. Viking, 1988. ISBN 0-670-82517-4 Subj: Holidays – Christmas. Poetry, rhyme.

Go away, bad dreams! ill. by Vanessa Julian-Ottie. Random House, 1985. ISBN 0-394-97222-8 Subj: Dreams. Emotions – fear. Family life. Night.

Hille-Brandts, Lene. *The little black hen* tr. and adapt. by Marion Koenig; ill. by Sigrid Heuck. Children's Pr., 1968. Translation of Die Henne Gudula Subj: Behavior – dissatisfaction. Birds – chickens.

Hiller, Catherine. *Abracatabby* ill. by Victoria De Larrea. Coward, 1981. Subj: Animals – cats. Magic.

Argentaybee and the boonie ill. by Cyndy Szekeres. Coward, 1979. Subj: Behavior – misbehavior. Imagination – imaginary friends.

Hillert, Margaret. *The birthday car* ill. by Kelly Oechsli. Follett, 1966. Subj: Birthdays. Toys.

The funny baby ill. by Hertha Depper. Follett, 1966. The tale of The Ugly Duckling by H. C. Andersen Subj: Birds – ducks. Birds – swans. Character traits – appearance. Character traits – being different. Folk and fairy tales.

Happy birthday, dear dragon ill. by Carl Kock. Follett, 1977. Subj: Birthdays. Dragons.

The little cowboy and the big cowboy ill. by Dan Siculan. Follett, 1980. Subj: Cowboys. Family life – fathers.

Little Red Riding Hood (Grimm, Jacob)

The little runaway ill. by Irv Anderson. Follett, 1966. Subj: Animals – cats. Behavior – running away.

The magic beans ill. by Mel Pekarsky. Follett, 1966. The tale of Jack and the beanstalk Subj: Folk and fairy tales. Giants. Plants.

Merry Christmas, dear dragon ill. by Carl Kock. Follett, 1980. Subj: Dragons. Holidays – Christmas.

Play ball ill. by Dick Martin. Follett, 1978. Subj: Activities – playing. Games. Sports – baseball.

The three bears ill. by Irma Wilde. Follett, 1963. Subj: Animals – bears. Folk and fairy tales.

The three goats ill. by Mel Pekarsky. Follett, 1963. The tale of The three billy goats Gruff Subj: Animals – goats. Character traits – cleverness. Cumulative tales. Folk and fairy tales. Mythical creatures. Trolls.

The three little pigs (The three little pigs)

Tom Thumb (Tom Thumb)

Up, up and away ill. by Robert Masheris. Modern Curriculum, 1981. ISBN 0-8136-5096-8 Subj: Moon. Space and space ships.

What is it? ill. by Kinuko Y. Craft. Follett, 1978. ISBN 0-695-40882-8 Subj: Activities – playing. Animals – dogs. Imagination. Poetry, rhyme.

The yellow boat ill. by Ed Young. Follett, 1966. Subj: Boats, ships.

Hillman, Elizabeth. *Min-Yo and the moon dragon* ill. by John Wallner. Harcourt, 1992. ISBN 0-15-254230-2 Subj: Dragons. Folk and fairy tales. Foreign lands – China. Moon. Stars.

Hillman, Priscilla. *A Merry-Mouse book of favorite poems* ill. by author. Doubleday, 1981. Subj: Animals – mice. Poetry, rhyme.

A Merry-Mouse book of months ill. by author. Doubleday, 1980. Subj: Animals – mice. Days of the week, months of the year. Poetry, rhyme.

The Merry-Mouse book of prayers and graces ill. by author. Doubleday, 1983. Subj: Religion.

A Merry-Mouse Christmas A B C ill. by author. Doubleday, 1980. Subj: ABC books. Animals – mice. Holidays – Christmas.

The Merry-Mouse schoolhouse ill. by author. Doubleday, 1982. Subj: Animals – mice. School.

Hilton, Nette. *Dirty Dave* ill. by Roland Harvey. Watts, 1990. ISBN 0-531-08461-2 Subj: Careers – tailors. Clothing. Crime. Foreign lands – Australia.

The long red scarf ill. by Margaret Power. Carolrhoda, 1990. ISBN 0-87614-399-0 Subj: Activities – knitting. Clothing. Family life – grandfathers.

Prince Lachlan ill. by Ann James. Watts, 1990. ISBN 0-531-08463-9 Subj: Behavior – misbehavior. Royalty. Royalty – princes.

A proper little lady ill. by Cathy Wilcox. Watts, 1990. ISBN 0-531-08460-4 Subj: Clothing.

Himler, Ronald. *The girl on the yellow giraffe* ill. by author. Harper, 1976. Subj: City. Imagination.

Wake up, Jeremiah ill. by author. Harper, 1979. Subj: Morning.

Himmelman, John. *Amanda and the magic garden* ill. by author. Viking, 1987. ISBN 0-670-80823-7 Subj: Animals. Gardens, gardening. Magic. Witches.

Amanda and the witch switch ill. by author. Viking, 1985. ISBN 0-670-11531-2 Subj: Behavior – misbehavior. Behavior – wishing. Character traits – meanness. Frogs and toads. Witches.

The day-off machine ill. by author. Silver Pr., 1990. ISBN 0-671-69635-1 Subj: Activities – making things. Animals – beavers. Weather – snow.

Ellen and the goldfish ill. by author. HarperCollins, 1990. ISBN 0-06-022417-7 Subj: Activities – painting. Fish. Friendship.

The great leaf blast-off ill. by author. Silver Pr., 1990. ISBN 0-671-69634-3 Subj: Activities – making things. Animals – beavers. Family life. Trees.

A guest is a guest ill. by author. Dutton, 1991. ISBN 0-525-44720-2 Subj: Animals. Etiquette. Farms.

Montigue on the high seas ill. by author. Viking, 1988. ISBN 0-670-81861-5 Subj: Animals. Animals – mice. Animals – moles.

Talester the lizard ill. by author. Dial Pr., 1982. Subj: Reptiles – lizards.

The talking tree: or Don't believe everything you hear ill. by author. Viking, 1986. ISBN 0-670-80775-3 Subj: Animals – dogs. Trees.

Hindley, Judy. *The little train* ill. by Robert Kendall. Watts, 1990. ISBN 0-531-08450-7 Subj: Activities – making things. Old age. Toys – trains.

Maybe it's a pirate ill. by Selina Young. Thomasson-Grant, 1992. ISBN 1-56566-016-1 Subj: Bedtime. Emotions – fear. Imagination.

Mrs. Mary Malarky's seven cats ill. by Denise Teasdale. Watts, 1990. ISBN 0-531-084221 Subj: Activities – baby-sitting. Animals – cats.

The sleepy book ill. by Patrice Aggs. Watts, 1992. ISBN 0-531-08571-6 Subj: Bedtime. Night. Sleep.

Soft and noisy ill. by Patrice Aggs. Walt Disney, 1992. ISBN 1-56282-225-X Subj: Noise, sounds. Senses – hearing.

Uncle Harold and the green hat ill. by Peter Utton. Farrar, 1991. ISBN 0-374-38030-9 Subj: Clothing – hats. Family life – aunts, uncles. Magic. Poetry, rhyme.

Hine, Sesyle Joslin *see* Joslin, Sesyle

Hines, Anna Grossnickle. *All by myself* ill. by author. Clarion, 1985. ISBN 0-89919-293-9 Subj: Behavior – growing up. Self-concept.

Bethany for real ill. by author. Greenwillow, 1985. ISBN 0-688-04009-8 Subj: Activities – playing. Imagination.

Big like me ill. by author. Greenwillow, 1989. ISBN 0-688-08355-2 Subj: Babies. Behavior – growing up. Family life.

Come to the meadow ill. by author. Houghton, 1984. Subj: Activities – picnicking. Family life – grandmothers.

Daddy makes the best spaghetti ill. by author. Clarion, 1986. ISBN 0-89919-388-9 Subj: Family life. Family life – fathers.

Don't worry, I'll find you ill. by author. Dutton, 1986. ISBN 0-525-44228-6 Subj: Behavior – lost. Shopping. Toys – dolls.

Grandma gets grumpy ill. by author. Clarion, 1988. ISBN 0-89919-529-6 Subj: Activities – baby-sitting. Family life – grandmothers.

I'll tell you what they say ill. by author. Greenwillow, 1987. ISBN 0-688-06487-6 Subj: Animals. Animals – dogs. Farms. Toys – teddy bears.

It's just me, Emily ill. by author. Clarion, 1987. ISBN 0-89919-487-7 Subj: Activities – playing. Family life – mothers. Poetry, rhyme.

Jackie's lunch box ill. by author. Greenwillow, 1991. ISBN 0-688-09694-8 Subj: Family life – sisters.

Keep your old hat ill. by author. Dutton, 1987. ISBN 0-525-44299-5 Subj: Activities – playing. Toys – dolls.

Maybe a band-aid will help ill. by author. Dutton, 1984. ISBN 0-525-44115-8 Subj: Family life – mothers. Problem solving. Toys – dolls.

Moon's wish ill. by author. Houghton, 1992. ISBN 0-395-58114-1 Subj: Behavior – wishing. Family life. Moon.

Remember the butterflies ill. by author. Dutton, 1991. ISBN 0-525-44679-6 Subj: Death. Family life – grandfathers. Insects – butterflies, caterpillars.

The secret keeper ill. by author. Greenwillow, 1990. ISBN 0-688-08946-1 Subj: Behavior – secrets. Family life. Holidays – Christmas.

Taste the raindrops ill. by author. Greenwillow, 1983. Subj: Weather – rain.

They really like me! ill. by author. Greenwillow, 1989. ISBN 0-688-07734-X Subj: Activities – playing. Family life. Sibling rivalry.

Hines, Gary. *A ride in the crummy* ill. by Anna Grossnickle Hines. Greenwillow, 1991. ISBN 0-688-09692-1 Subj: Family life – grandfathers. Trains.

Hippel, Ursula Von *see* Von Hippel, Ursula

The hippo ill. by Caroline Binch. Rourke, 1983. Subj: Animals – hippopotami.

Hippopotamus, Eugene H. *see* Kraus, Robert

Hirano, Cathy. *The fox's egg* (Isami, Ikuyo)

Hirschberg, J. Cotter. *My friend the babysitter* (Watson, Jane Werner)

My friend the dentist (Watson, Jane Werner)

My friend the doctor (Watson, Jane Werner)

Sometimes a family has to move (Watson, Jane Werner)

Sometimes a family has to split up (Watson, Jane Werner)

Sometimes I get angry (Watson, Jane Werner)

Sometimes I'm afraid (Watson, Jane Werner)

Sometimes I'm jealous (Watson, Jane Werner)

Hirschi, Ron. *Fall* photos. by Thomas D. Mangelsen. Dutton, 1991. ISBN 0-525-65053-9 Subj: Animals. Seasons – fall.

Forest ill. by Barbara Bash. Bantam, 1991. ISBN 0-553-07469-5 Subj: Animals. Ecology. Forest, woods.

Loon lake photos. by Daniel J. Cox. Dutton, 1991. ISBN 0-525-65046-6 Subj: Animals. Birds – loons. Nature.

Ocean ill. by Barbara Bash. Bantam, 1991. ISBN 0-553-07470-9 Subj: Animals. Fish. Sea and seashore.

Seya's song ill. by Constance R. Bergum. Sasquatch, 1992. ISBN 0-912365-62-5 Subj: Indians of North America. Language.

Spring photos. by Thomas D. Mangelsen. Dutton, 1990. ISBN 0-525-65037-7 Subj: Animals. Seasons – spring.

Summer photos. by Thomas D. Mangelsen. Dutton, 1991. ISBN 0-525-65054-7 Subj: Animals. Nature. Seasons – summer.

What is a bird? photos. by Galen Burrell. Walker, 1987. ISBN 0-8027-6721-4 Subj: Birds. Science.

What is a horse? photos. by Linda Quartman Yonker and author. Walker, 1989. ISBN 0-8027-6877-6 Subj: Animals – horses.

Where do birds live? photos. by Galen Burrell. Walker, 1987. ISBN 0-8027-6723-0 Subj: Birds. Science.

Where do horses live? photos. by Linda Quartman Yonker and author. Walker, 1989. ISBN 0-8027-6879-2 Subj: Animals – horses.

Who lives in... Alligator Swamp? photos. by Galen Burrell. Dodd, 1987. ISBN 0-396-09123-7 Subj: Animals. Forest, woods. Reptiles – alligators, crocodiles. Science.

Who lives in... the forest? photos. by Galen Burrell. Dodd, 1987. ISBN 0-396-09121-0 Subj: Animals. Birds. Forest, woods.

Winter photos. by Thomas D. Mangelsen. Dutton, 1990. ISBN 0-525-65026-1 Subj: Animals. Seasons – winter.

Hirschmann, Linda. *In a lick of a flick of a tongue* ill. by Jeni Bassett. Dodd, 1980. Subj: Anatomy. Animals.

Hirsh, Marilyn. *Captain Jiri and Rabbi Jacob: from a Jewish folktale* ill. by author. Holiday, 1976. Subj: Folk and fairy tales. Jewish culture.

Could anything be worse? a Yiddish tale ill. by author. Holiday, 1974. Subj: Humor. Jewish culture.

Deborah the dybbuk: a ghost story ill. by author. Holiday, 1978. ISBN 0-8234-0315-7 Subj: Behavior – misbehavior. Character traits – kindness to animals. Ghosts.

I love Hanukkah ill. by author. Holiday, 1984. ISBN 0-8234-0525-7 Subj: Holidays – Hanukkah. Jewish culture.

I love Passover ill. by author. Holiday, 1985. ISBN 0-8234-0549-4 Subj: Holidays – Passover. Jewish culture. Religion.

Joseph who loved the Sabbath ill. by Devis Grebu. Viking, 1986. ISBN 0-670-81194-7 Subj: Folk and fairy tales. Jewish culture. Religion.

Leela and the watermelon by Marilyn Hirsh and Maya Narayan; ill. by Marilyn Hirsh. Crown, 1971. Subj: Babies. Food. Foreign lands – India.

One little goat: a Passover song ill. by author. Holiday, 1979. Subj: Folk and fairy tales. Jewish culture. Holidays – Passover. Songs.

The pink suit ill. by author. Crown, 1970. Subj: Activities – trading. Emotions – embarrassment. Family life. Jewish culture.

Potato pancakes all around: a Hanukkah tale ill. by author. Bonim Books, 1978. ISBN 0-88482-762-3 Subj: Food. Holidays – Hanukkah. Jewish culture. Religion.

The Rabbi and the twenty-nine witches ill. by author. Holiday, 1976. Subj: Character traits – cleverness. Jewish culture. Witches.

Where is Yonkela? ill. by author. Crown, 1969. Subj: Babies. Behavior – lost. Jewish culture.

Hirst, Robin. *My place in space* by Robin and Sally Hirst; ill. by Roland Harvey and Joe Levine. Watts, 1990. ISBN 0-531-08459-0 Subj: Astronomy. Buses. Science. Space and space ships.

Hirst, Sally. *My place in space* (Hirst, Robin)

Hiser, Berniece T. *The adventure of Charlie and his wheat-straw hat* ill. by Mary Szilagyi. Dodd, 1986. ISBN 0-396-08772-8 Subj: Character traits – bravery. Clothing – hats. Family life – grandmothers. U.S. history.

Hissey, Jane. *Jolly snow* ill. by author. Putnam, 1991. ISBN 0-399-22131-X Subj: Activities – playing. Toys. Toys – teddy bears. Weather – snow.

Jolly Tall ill. by author. Putnam, 1990. ISBN 0-399-21827-0 Subj: Activities – knitting. Toys. Toys – teddy bears.

Little Bear lost ill. by author. Putnam, 1989. ISBN 0-399-21743-6 Subj: Behavior – losing things. Games. Toys. Toys – teddy bears.

Little Bear's trousers: an Old Bear story ill. by author. Putnam, 1990. ISBN 0-399-22016-X Subj: Clothing – pants. Toys – teddy bears.

Old Bear ill. by author. Philomel, 1986. ISBN 0-399-21401-1 Subj: Friendship. Toys. Toys – teddy bears.

Hoban, Brom. *Skunk Lane* ill. by author. Harper, 1983. Subj: Animals – skunks. Behavior – growing up. Songs.

Hoban, Julia. *Amy loves the rain* ill. by Lillian Hoban. HarperCollins, 1989. ISBN 0-06-022358-8 Subj: Family life. Weather – rain.

Amy loves the snow ill. by Lillian Hoban. HarperCollins, 1989. ISBN 0-06-022395-2 Subj: Family life. Snowmen. Weather – snow.

Amy loves the sun ill. by Lillian Hoban. Harper, 1988. ISBN 0-06-022397-9 Subj: Family life. Flowers.

Amy loves the wind ill. by Lillian Hoban. Harper, 1988. ISBN 0-06-022403-7 Subj: Seasons – fall. Weather – wind.

Quick chick ill. by Lillian Hoban. Dutton, 1989. ISBN 0-525-44490-4 Subj: Animals. Birds – chickens. Farms. Names.

Hoban, Lillian. *Arthur's Christmas cookies* ill. by author. Harper, 1972. Subj: Activities – cooking. Animals – monkeys. Holidays – Christmas.

Arthur's funny money ill. by author. Harper, 1981. Subj: Animals – monkeys. Money. Problem solving.

Arthur's great big Valentine ill. by author. Harper, 1989. ISBN 0-06-022407-X Subj: Emotions – anger. Friendship. Holidays – Valentine's Day.

Arthur's honey bear ill. by author. Harper, 1973. Subj: Animals – monkeys. Toys – teddy bears.

Arthur's pen pal ill. by author. Harper, 1976. Subj: Activities – writing. Animals – monkeys. Sibling rivalry.

Arthur's prize reader ill. by author. Harper, 1978. Subj: Activities – reading. Animals – monkeys. Family life.

The case of the two masked robbers ill. by author. Harper, 1986. ISBN 0-06-022299-9 Subj: Animals. Animals – raccoons. Eggs. Problem solving.

Harry's song ill. by author. Greenwillow, 1980. Subj: Animals – rabbits. Songs.

Here come raccoons ill. by author. Holt, 1977. Subj: Animals – raccoons. Twins.

It's really Christmas ill. by author. Greenwillow, 1982. Subj: Animals – mice. Behavior – wishing. Holidays – Christmas.

The laziest robot in zone one by Lillian and Phoebe Hoban; ill. by Lillian Hoban. Harper, 1983. Subj: Animals – dogs. Behavior – lost. Robots.

Mr. Pig and family ill. by author. Harper, 1980. Subj: Animals – pigs. Family life.

Mr. Pig and Sonny too ill. by author. Harper, 1977. Subj: Animals – pigs. Sports – ice skating. Weddings.

Silly Tilly and the Easter bunny ill. by author. Harper, 1987. ISBN 0-06-022693-6 Subj: Animals – moles. Holidays – Easter. Humor.

Stick-in-the-mud turtle ill. by author. Greenwillow, 1977. Subj: Behavior – dissatisfaction. Poverty. Reptiles – turtles, tortoises.

The sugar snow spring ill. by author. Harper, 1973. Subj: Animals – mice. Seasons – spring. Weather – cold. Weather – snow.

Turtle spring ill. by author. Greenwillow, 1978. Subj: Reptiles – turtles, tortoises. Seasons – spring.

Hoban, Phoebe. *The laziest robot in zone one* (Hoban, Lillian)

Hoban, Russell. *Ace Dragon Ltd.* ill. by Quentin Blake. Merrimack, 1981. Subj: Activities – flying. Dragons.

Arthur's new power ill. by Byron Barton. Crowell, 1978. Subj: Progress. Reptiles – alligators, crocodiles.

A baby sister for Frances ill. by Lillian Hoban. Harper, 1964. Subj: Animals – badgers. Behavior – running away. Emotions – envy, jealousy. Family life. Sibling rivalry.

A bargain for Frances ill. by Lillian Hoban. Harper, 1970. Subj: Animals – badgers. Friendship.

The battle of Zormla ill. by Colin McNaughton. Putnam's, 1982. Subj: Sibling rivalry.

Bedtime for Frances ill. by Garth Williams. Harper, 1960. Subj: Animals – badgers. Bedtime.

Best friends for Frances ill. by Lillian Hoban. Harper, 1969. Subj: Animals – badgers. Friendship.

Big John Turkle ill. by Martin Baynton. Holt, 1984. Subj: Character traits – meanness.

A birthday for Frances ill. by Lillian Hoban. Harper, 1968. Subj: Animals – badgers. Birthdays. Emotions – envy, jealousy.

Bread and jam for Frances ill. by Lillian Hoban. Harper, 1964. Subj: Animals – badgers. Food. School.

Charlie Meadows ill. by Martin Baynton. Holt, 1984. ISBN 0-03-069502-3 Subj: Activities – dancing. Animals – mice. Birds – owls.

Charlie the tramp ill. by Lillian Hoban. Four Winds Pr., 1967. Subj: Activities – working. Animals – beavers.

La corona and the tin frog ill. by Nicola Bayley. Merrimack, 1981. Subj: Emotions. Toys.

The dancing tigers ill. by David Gentleman. Merrimack, 1981. Subj: Activities – dancing. Animals – tigers. Sports – hunting.

Dinner at Alberta's ill. by James Marshall. Crowell, 1975. Subj: Behavior. Etiquette. Food. Reptiles – alligators, crocodiles.

Emmet Otter's jug-band Christmas ill. by Lillian Hoban. Parents, 1971. Subj: Animals – otters. Character traits – generosity. Holidays – Christmas. Music.

Flat cat ill. by Clive Scruton. Putnam's, 1980. Subj: Animals – cats. Animals – mice. Animals – rats.

The flight of Bembel Rudzuk ill. by Colin McNaughton. Putnam's, 1982. Subj: Imagination.

Goodnight ill. by Lillian Hoban. Norton, 1966. Subj: Bedtime. Emotions – fear. Imagination. Poetry, rhyme.

The great gum drop robbery ill. by Colin McNaughton. Putnam's, 1982. Subj: Imagination. Sibling rivalry.

Harvey's hideout ill. by Lillian Hoban. Parents, 1969. Subj: Animals – muskrats. Behavior – fighting, arguing. Family life.

How Tom beat Captain Najork and his hired sportsmen ill. by Quentin Blake. Atheneum, 1974. Subj: Behavior – misbehavior. Games.

Jim Frog ill. by Martin Baynton. Holt, 1984. Subj: Frogs and toads. Insects – beetles.

Lavina bat ill. by Martin Baynton. Holt, 1984. Subj: Animals – bats.

The little Brute family ill. by Lillian Hoban. Macmillan, 1966. Subj: Character traits – meanness. Etiquette.

The mole family's Christmas ill. by Lillian Hoban. Parents, 1969. Subj: Animals – moles. Character traits – generosity. Holidays – Christmas.

A near thing for Captain Najork ill. by Quentin Blake. Atheneum, 1976. Subj: Humor.

Nothing to do ill. by Lillian Hoban. Harper, 1964. Subj: Animals – possums. Behavior – boredom.

The rain door ill. by Quentin Blake. Crowell, 1987. ISBN 0-690-04577-8 Subj: Animals – horses. Animals – lions. Imagination. Weather – rain.

Some snow said hello ill. by Lillian Hoban. Harper, 1963. Subj: Seasons – winter. Sibling rivalry. Weather – snow.

The sorely trying day ill. by Lillian Hoban. Harper, 1964. Subj: Behavior – bad day. Behavior – fighting, arguing.

The stone doll of Sister Brute ill. by Lillian Hoban. Macmillan, 1968. Subj: Animals – dogs. Emotions. Toys – dolls.

Ten what? a mystery counting book by Russell Hoban and Sylvie Selig; ill. by authors. Scribner's, 1974. Subj: Counting, numbers.

They came from Aargh! ill. by Colin McNaughton. Putnam's, 1981. Subj: Family life. Sibling rivalry.

Tom and the two handles ill. by Lillian Hoban. Harper, 1965. Subj: Behavior – fighting, arguing.

Hoban, Tana. *A B See!* photos. by author. Greenwillow, 1982. Subj: ABC books.

All about where photos. by author. Greenwillow, 1991. ISBN 0-688-09698-0 Subj: Concepts. Language.

Big ones, little ones ill. by author. Greenwillow, 1976. Subj: Animals. Concepts – size. Wordless.

A children's zoo photos. by author. Greenwillow, 1985. ISBN 0-688-05204-5 Subj: Animals. Birds. Zoos.

Circles, triangles, and squares ill. by author. Macmillan, 1974. Subj: Concepts – shape. Wordless.

Count and see ill. by author. Macmillan, 1972. Subj: Counting, numbers.

Dig, drill, dump, fill ill. by author. Greenwillow, 1975. Subj: Machines. Wordless.

Dots, spots, speckles, and stripes photos. by author. Greenwillow, 1987. ISBN 0-688-06863-4 Subj: Concepts. Concepts – color. Concepts – shape.

I read signs photos. by author. Greenwillow, 1983. Subj: Activities – reading. Communication.

I read symbols photos. by author. Greenwillow, 1983. Subj: Activities – reading. Communication.

I walk and read photos. by author. Greenwillow, 1984. Subj: Activities – reading. Activities – walking.

Is it larger? Is it smaller? photos. by author. Greenwillow, 1985. ISBN 0-688-04028-4 Subj: Concepts – size. Wordless.

Is it red? Is it yellow? Is it blue? photos. by author. Greenwillow, 1978. Subj: City. Concepts – color. Concepts – shape. Concepts – size. Wordless.

Is it rough? Is it smooth? Is it shiny? photos. by author. Greenwillow, 1984. Subj: Concepts. Wordless.

Look again photos. by author. Macmillan, 1971. Subj: Participation. Senses – seeing. Wordless.

Look! Look! Look! photos. by author. Greenwillow, 1988. ISBN 0-688-07240-2 Subj: Concepts. Format, unusual. Wordless.

Look up, look down photos. by author. Greenwillow, 1992. ISBN 0-688-10578-5 Subj: Concepts – up and down.

More than one photos. by author. Greenwillow, 1981. Subj: Language.

Of colors and things photos. by author. Greenwillow, 1989. ISBN 0-688-07535-5 Subj: Concepts – color.

One little kitten photos. by author. Greenwillow, 1979. Subj: Animals – cats. Poetry, rhyme.

1, 2, 3 photos. by author. Greenwillow, 1985. Subj: Counting, numbers. Format, unusual – board books. Wordless.

Panda, panda ill. by author. Greenwillow, 1986. ISBN 0-688-06564-3 Subj: Animals – pandas. Format, unusual – board books.

Push-pull, empty-full ill. by author. Macmillan, 1972. Subj: Concepts – opposites.

Red, blue, yellow shoe photos. by author. Greenwillow, 1986. ISBN 0-688-06563-5 Subj: Concepts – color. Format, unusual – board books.

Round and round and round photos. by author. Greenwillow, 1983. Subj: Concepts – shape.

Shadows and reflections photos. by author. Greenwillow, 1990. ISBN 0-688-07090-6 Subj: Shadows. Wordless.

Shapes and things ill. by author. Macmillan, 1970. Subj: Concepts – shape. Wordless.

Shapes, shapes, shapes photos. by author. Greenwillow, 1985. ISBN 0-688-05833-7 Subj: Concepts – shape. Wordless.

Take another look photos. by author. Greenwillow, 1981. Subj: Concepts. Wordless.

26 letters and 99 cents photos. by author. Greenwillow, 1987. ISBN 0-688-06362-4 Subj: ABC books. Counting, numbers. Format, unusual.

What is it? photos. by author. Greenwillow, 1985. Subj: Format, unusual – board books. Wordless.

Where is it? ill. by author. Macmillan, 1974. Subj: Animals – rabbits. Participation. Poetry, rhyme.

Hoberman, Mary Ann. *The cozy book* ill. by Tony Chen. Viking, 1982. Subj: Poetry, rhyme.

Fathers, mothers, sisters, brothers ill. by Marylin Hafner. Little, 1991. ISBN 0-316-36736-2 Subj: Family life. Poetry, rhyme.

A fine fat pig other animal poems ill. by Malcah Zeldis. HarperCollins, 1991. ISBN 0-06-022426-6 Subj: Animals. Poetry, rhyme.

A house is a house for me ill. by Betty Fraser. Viking, 1978. Subj: Houses. Poetry, rhyme.

How do I go? by Mary Ann and Norman Hoberman; ill. by authors. Little, 1958. Subj: Transportation.

I like old clothes ill. by Jacqueline Chwast. Knopf, 1976. Subj: Clothing. Poetry, rhyme.

Mr. and Mrs. Muddle ill. by Catharine O'Neill. Little, 1988. ISBN 0-316-36735-4 Subj: Animals – horses. Sports.

Nuts to you and nuts to me: an alphabet of poems ill. by Ronni Solbert. Knopf, 1974. Subj: ABC books. Poetry, rhyme.

Hoberman, Norman. *How do I go?* (Hoberman, Mary Ann)

Hobson, Bruce *see* Hadithi, Mwenye

Hobson, Laura Z. *"I'm going to have a baby!"* ill. by May Kirkham. John Day, 1967. Subj: Babies. Birth. Family life.

Hobzek, Mildred. *We came a-marching...1, 2, 3* ill. by William Pène Du Bois. Parents, 1978. Subj: Folk and fairy tales. Songs.

Hodeir, André. *Warwick's three bottles* by André Hodeir and Tomi Ungerer; ill. by Tomi Ungerer. Grove Pr., 1966. Subj: Behavior – misbehavior. Country. Reptiles – alligators, crocodiles.

Hodges, Margaret. *Buried moon* ill. by Jamichael Henterly. Little, 1990. ISBN 0-316-36793-1 Subj: Folk and fairy tales. Forest, woods. Moon.

The fire bringer: a Paiute Indian legend ill. by Peter Parnall. Little, 1972. ISBN 0-316-36783-4 Subj: Folk and fairy tales. Indians of North America.

The kitchen knight ill. by Trina Schart Hyman. Holiday, 1990. ISBN 0-8234-0787-X Subj: Behavior – fighting, arguing. Emotions – love. Folk and fairy tales. Knights. Middle ages.

Saint George and the dragon ill. by Trina Schart Hyman. Little, 1984. Subj: Caldecott award book. Folk and fairy tales.

St. Jerome and the lion ill. by Barry Moser. Orchard, 1991. ISBN 0-531-08538-4 Subj: Animals – lions. Character traits – kindness to animals. Folk and fairy tales. Religion.

The wave ill. by Blair Lent. Houghton, 1964. Subj: Caldecott award honor book.

Hodgetts, Blake Christopher. *Dream of the dinosaurs* ill. by Victoria Hodgetts. Doubleday, 1978. Subj: Dinosaurs. Dreams.

Hoff, Carol. *The four friends* ill. by Jim Ponter. Follett, 1958. Subj: Animals. Animals – mice.

Hoff, Syd. *Albert the albatross* ill. by author. Harper, 1961. Subj: Birds – albatrosses. Sea and seashore.

Barkley ill. by author. Harper, 1975. Subj: Animals – dogs. Circus. Old age.

Chester ill. by author. Harper, 1961. Subj: Animals – horses.

Grizzwold ill. by author. Harper, 1963. Subj: Animals – bears. Ecology.

Happy birthday, Henrietta! ill. by author. Garrard, 1983. Subj: Animals – pigs. Animals – goats. Birds – chickens. Birthdays.

Henrietta, circus star ill. by author. Garrard, 1978. Subj: Birds – chickens. Circus.

Henrietta goes to the fair ill. by author. Garrard, 1979. Subj: Birds – chickens. Fairs.

Henrietta, the early bird ill. by author. Garrard, 1978. Subj: Behavior – mistakes. Birds – chickens. Time.

Henrietta's Halloween ill. by author. Garrard, 1980. Subj: Birds – chickens. Holidays – Halloween. Parties.

The horse in Harry's room ill. by author. Harper, 1970. Subj: Animals – horses. Imagination – imaginary friends.

Julius ill. by author. Harper, 1959. Subj: Animals – gorillas.

Lengthy ill. by author. Putnam's, 1964. Subj: Animals – dogs.

The littlest leaguer ill. by author. Dutton, 1976. Subj: Character traits – smallness. Games. Sports – baseball.

Merry Christmas, Henrietta! ill. by author. Garrard, 1980. Subj: Birds – chickens. Holidays – Christmas. Stores.

Mrs. Brice's mice ill. by author. Harper, 1988. ISBN 0-06-022452-5 Subj: Animals – mice. Character traits – being different. Pets.

My Aunt Rosie ill. by author. Harper, 1972. Subj: Family life – aunts, uncles.

Oliver ill. by author. Harper, 1960. Subj: Animals – elephants. Character traits – optimism. Circus.

Sammy the seal ill. by author. Harper, 1959. Subj: Animals – seals. Zoos.

Santa's moose ill. by author. Harper, 1988, 1979. ISBN 0-06-022506-8 Subj: Animals – moose. Holidays – Christmas.

Slithers ill. by author. Putnam's, 1968. Subj: Reptiles – snakes.

Slugger Sal's slump ill. by author. Dutton, 1979. Subj: Character traits – perseverance. Sports – baseball.

Stanley ill. by author. Harper, 1962. Subj: Cavemen. Houses.

A walk past Ellen's house ill. by author. McGraw-Hill, 1973. ISBN 0-07-029176-4 Subj: Emotions – embarrassment.

Walpole ill. by author. Harper, 1977. Subj: Animals – walruses.

When will it snow? ill. by Mary Chalmers. Harper, 1971. Subj: Seasons – winter. Weather – snow.

Where's Prancer? ill. by author. Harper, 1960. Subj: Animals – reindeer. Holidays – Christmas.

Who will be my friends? ill. by author. Harper, 1960. Subj: Friendship. Moving.

Hoffman, Joan. *My friend goes left* (Gregorich, Barbara)

Hoffman, Mary. *Amazing Grace* ill. by Caroline Binch. Dial, 1991. ISBN 0-8037-1040-2 Subj: Ethnic groups in the U.S. – Afro-Americans. School. Self-concept. Theater.

Animals in the wild: elephant ill. by author. Random House, 1984. Subj: Animals – elephants. Science.

Animals in the wild: monkey ill. by author. Random House, 1984. Subj: Animals – monkeys. Science.

Animals in the wild: panda ill. by author. Random House, 1984. Subj: Animals – pandas. Science.

Animals in the wild: tiger ill. by author. Random House, 1984. Subj: Animals – tigers. Science.

Hoffman, Phyllis. *Baby's first year* ill. by Sarah Wilson. Harper, 1988. ISBN 0-06-022552-1 Subj: Babies. Behavior – growing up.

Meatball ill. by Emily Arnold McCully. HarperCollins, 1991. ISBN 0-06-022564-5 Subj: Ethnic groups in the U.S. Friendship. School.

Steffie and me ill. by Emily Arnold McCully. Harper, 1970. Subj: Ethnic groups in the U.S. – Afro-Americans. Family life. Friendship. School.

The ugly duckling (Andersen, H. C. (Hans Christian))

We play ill. by Sarah Wilson. HarperCollins, 1990. ISBN 0-06-022558-0 Subj: Activities – playing. Poetry, rhyme. School.

Hoffman, Rosekrans. *Sister Sweet Ella* ill. by author. Morrow, 1981. Subj: Babies. Family life. Magic.

Hoffmann, E. T. A. *The nutcracker* retold by Jean Richardson; ill. by Francesca Crespi. Arcade, 1990. ISBN 1-55970-105-6 Subj: Activities – dancing. Animals – mice. Folk and fairy tales. Holidays – Christmas. Imagination. Royalty.

The nutcracker retold and ill. by Rachel Isadora. Macmillan, 1981. Adapt. of Nussknacker und Mausekönig ISBN 0-02-747470-4 Subj: Activities – dancing. Animals – mice. Fairies. Folk and fairy tales. Holidays – Christmas. Imagination.

The nutcracker tr. by Ralph Manheim; ill. by Maurice Sendak. Crown, 1984. Subj: Activities – dancing. Animals – mice. Fairies. Folk and fairy tales. Holidays – Christmas. Imagination. Theater.

The nutcracker retold by Anthea Bell; ill. by Lisbeth Zwerger. Picture Book Studio, 1987. ISBN 0-88708-051-0 Subj: Animals – mice. Folk and fairy tales. Holidays – Christmas. Imagination. Royalty.

The strange child tr. and adapt. by Anthea Bell; ill. by Lisbeth Zwerger. Picture Book Studio, 1984. Adapt. of Das fremde Kind ISBN 0-907234-60-7 Subj: Death. Family life. Folk and fairy tales. Magic.

Hoffmann, Felix. *Hans in luck* (Grimm, Jacob)

The story of Christmas ill. by author. Atheneum, 1975. Subj: Holidays – Christmas. Religion.

Hofsepian, Sylvia A. *Why not?* ill. by Friso Henstra. Four Winds, 1991. ISBN 0-02-743980 Subj: Animals – cats. Emotions – loneliness.

Hofstrand, Mary. *Albion pig* ill. by author. Knopf, 1984. Subj: Animals – pigs. Poetry, rhyme.

By the sea ill. by author. Atheneum, 1989. ISBN 0-689-31421-3 Subj: Animals – pigs. Family life. Poetry, rhyme. Sea and seashore.

Hogan, Bernice. *My grandmother died but I won't forget her* ill. by Nancy Munger. Abingdon, 1983. Subj: Death. Family life – grandmothers.

Hogan, Inez. *About Nono, the baby elephant* ill. by author. Dutton, 1947. Subj: Animals – elephants. Behavior – misbehavior. Names.

Hogan, Kirk. *The hospital scares me* (Hogan, Paula Z.)

Hogan, Paula Z. *The black swan* ill. by Kinuko Y. Craft. Raintree, 1979. Subj: Birds – swans. Science.

The butterfly ill. by Geri K. Strigenz. Raintree, 1979. Subj: Insects – butterflies, caterpillars. Science.

The dandelion ill. by Yoshi Miyake. Raintree, 1979. Subj: Plants. Science.

The frog ill. by Geri K. Strigenz. Raintree, 1979. Subj: Frogs and toads. Science.

The honeybee ill. by Geri K. Strigenz. Raintree, 1979. Subj: Insects – bees. Science.

The hospital scares me by Paula Z. Hogan and Kirk Hogan; ill. by Mary Thelen. Raintree, 1980. ISBN 0-8172-1351-1 Subj: Ethnic groups in the U.S. Ethnic groups in the U.S. – Afro-Americans. Hospitals. Illness.

The oak tree ill. by Kinuko Y. Craft. Raintree, 1979. Subj: Science. Trees.

The penguin ill. by Geri K. Strigenz. Raintree, 1979. Subj: Birds – penguins. Science.

The salmon ill. by Yoshi Miyake. Raintree, 1979. Subj: Fish. Science.

Högner, Franz. *From blueprint to house* ill. by author. Carolrhoda Books, 1986. ISBN 0-87614-295-1 Subj: Houses.

Hogrogian, Nonny. *Carrot cake* ill. by author. Greenwillow, 1977. Subj: Animals – rabbits. Behavior. Character traits – compromising. Character traits – shyness. Weddings.

The cat who loved to sing ill. by author. Knopf, 1988. ISBN 0-394-99004-8 Subj: Animals – cats. Cumulative tales. Folk and fairy tales. Songs.

Cinderella (Grimm, Jacob)

The contest ill. by author. Greenwillow, 1976. Subj: Caldecott award honor book. Crime. Folk and fairy tales. Foreign lands – Armenia.

The devil with the green hairs (Grimm, Jacob)

The hermit and Harry and me ill. by author. Subj: Behavior – indifference. Friendship.

Noah's ark ill. by author. Knopf, 1986. ISBN 0-394-98191-X Subj: Boats, ships. Religion – Noah.

One fine day ill. by Nonny Hogrogian. Macmillan, 1971. Subj: Animals – foxes. Caldecott award book. Cumulative tales.

Rooster brother ill. by author. Macmillan, 1974. ISBN 0-02-743990-9 Subj: Behavior – stealing. Character traits – cleverness. Crime. Folk and fairy tales.

Hoguet, Susan Ramsay. *I unpacked my grandmother's trunk: a picture book game* ill. by author. Dutton, 1983. Subj: ABC books. Cumulative tales. Games.

Hoke, Helen L. *The biggest family in the town* ill. by Vance Locke. McKay, 1947. Subj: Family life.

Hol, Coby. *Henrietta saves the show* ill. by author. North-South, 1991. ISBN 1-55858-102-2 Subj: Animals – horses. Circus.

Lisa and the snowman ill. by author. North-South, 1989. ISBN 1-55858-022-0 Subj: Seasons – winter. Snowmen.

Tippy Bear and little Sam tr. from German; ill. by author. North-South, 1992. ISBN 1-55858-149-9 Subj: Animals – bears. Babies. Family life.

Tippy Bear goes to a party ill. by author. North-South, 1991. ISBN 1-55858-129-4 Subj: Animals – bears. Parties.

Tippy Bear hunts for honey ill. by author. North-South, 1991. ISBN 1-55858-128-6 Subj: Animals – bears. Character traits – helpfulness.

Holabird, Katharine. *Alexander and the dragon* ill. by Helen Craig. Potter, 1988. ISBN 0-517-56996-5 Subj: Bedtime. Behavior – fighting, arguing. Dragons. Friendship.

Alexander and the magic boat ill. by Helen Craig. Crown, 1990. ISBN 0-517-58149-3 Subj: Activities – traveling. Boats, ships. Family life. Imagination.

Angelina and Alice ill. by Helen Craig. Potter, 1987. ISBN 0-517-56074-7 Subj: Animals – mice. Friendship. School.

Angelina and the princess ill. by Helen Craig. Crown, 1984. Subj: Activities – dancing. Animals – mice.

Angelina at the fair ill. by Helen Craig. Crown, 1985. ISBN 0-517-55744-4 Subj: Animals – mice. Fairs.

Angelina ballerina ill. by Helen Craig. Crown, 1983. Subj: Activities – dancing. Animals – mice.

Angelina on stage ill. by Helen Craig. Crown, 1986. ISBN 0-517-56073-9 Subj: Activities – dancing. Animals – mice. Theater.

Angelina's baby sister ill. by Helen Craig. Crown, 1991. ISBN 0-517-58600-2 Subj: Animals – mice. Babies. Family life – sisters. Sibling rivalry.

Angelina's birthday surprise ill. by Helen Craig. Crown, 1989. ISBN 0-517-57325-3 Subj: Animals – mice. Birthdays. Sports – bicycling.

The little mouse ABC ill. by Helen Craig. Simon and Schuster, 1983. Subj: ABC books. Animals – mice.

Holbrook, Stewart. *America's Ethan Allen* ill. by Lynd Ward. Houghton, 1949. Subj: Caldecott award honor book. U.S. history. War.

Holcomb, Nan. *Patrick and Emma Lou* ill. by Dot Yoder. Jason & Nordic, 1989. ISBN 0-944727-03-4 Subj: Family life – brothers. Family life – sisters. Handicaps – physical.

Holden, Edith. *The hedgehog feast* ill. by Edith Holden; words by Rowena Stott. Dutton, 1978. Subj: Animals – hedgehogs. Food.

Holder, Heidi. *Carmine the crow* ill. by author. Farrar, 1992. ISBN 0-374-31119-6 Subj: Animals. Behavior – sharing. Birds – crows. Forest, woods. Old age.

Crows: an old rhyme ill. by author. Farrar, 1987. ISBN 0-374-31660-0 Subj: Animals – minks. Animals – weasels. Birds – crows. Counting, numbers. Poetry, rhyme.

Holding, James. *The lazy little Zulu* ill. by Aliki. Morrow, 1962. Subj: Character traits – laziness. Foreign lands – Africa.

Holl, Adelaide. *The ABC of cars, trucks and machines* ill. by William Dugan. American Heritage, 1970. Subj: ABC books. Automobiles. Machines. Trucks.

Most-of-the-time Maxie ill. by Hilary Knight. Xerox Family Education Services, 1974. ISBN 0-88375-202-6 Subj: Activities – reading. Imagination.

A mouse story: Minnikin, Midgie and Moppet ill. by Priscilla Hillman. Golden Pr., 1977. Subj: Animals – mice. City. Country.

Mrs. McGarrity's peppermint sweater ill. by Abner Graboff. Lothrop, 1966. Subj: Activities – knitting. Circus. Poetry, rhyme.

My father and I (Ringi, Kjell (Arne Sorensen))

The rain puddle ill. by Roger Antoine Duvoisin. Lothrop, 1965. Subj: Animals. Weather – rain.

The remarkable egg ill. by Roger Antoine Duvoisin. Lothrop, 1968. Subj: Toys – balls.

The runaway giant ill. by Mamoru Funai. Lothrop, 1967. Subj: Behavior – gossip. Snowmen.

Sir Kevin of Devon ill. by Leonard Weisgard. Lothrop, 1963. Subj: Character traits – bravery. Knights. Poetry, rhyme.

Small Bear builds a playhouse ill. by Cyndy Szekeres. Garrard, 1978. Subj: Animals. Animals – bears. Houses.

Small Bear solves a mystery ill. by Lorinda Bryan Cauley. Garrard, 1979. Subj: Animals – bears. Food. Illness.

Holland, Isabelle. *Kevin's hat* ill. by Leonard B. Lubin. Lothrop, 1984. Subj: Clothing – hats. Reptiles – alligators, crocodiles.

Holland, Janice. *You never can tell* ill. by adapt. Scribner's, 1963. Adapted from the tr. by Arthur W. Hummel from the book of Huai-nan tzu, written before 122 B.C Subj: Character traits – luck. Folk and fairy tales. Foreign lands – China.

Holland, Kevin Crossley *see* Crossley-Holland, Kevin

Holland, Viki. *We are having a baby* ill. by author. Scribner's, 1972. Subj: Babies. Family life.

Holleyman, Sonia. *Mona the vampire* ill. by author. Delacorte Pr., 1991. ISBN 0-385-30299-1 Subj: Activities – reading. Imagination. Monsters.

Holling, Holling C. (Holling Clancy). *Paddle-to-the-sea* ill. by author. Houghton, 1941. Subj: Caldecott award honor book. Foreign lands – Canada. Rivers.

Hollyer, Belinda. *Daniel in the lions' den* (Bible Old Testament. $k Daniel.)

David and Goliath (Bible Old Testament. David.)

Jonah and the great fish (Bible Old Testament. Jonah.)

Hollyn, Lynn. *Lynn Hollyn's Christmas toyland* ill. by Lori Anzalone. Knopf, 1985. ISBN 0-394-97631-2 Subj: Fairies. Holidays – Christmas. Toys.

Holm, Mayling Mack. *A forest Christmas* ill. by author. Harper, 1977. Subj: Animals. Holidays – Christmas.

Holman, Felice. *Victoria's castle* ill. by Lillian Hoban. Norton, 1966. Subj: Birds – parakeets, parrots. Humor. Imagination.

Holmes, Anita. *The 100-year-old cactus* ill. by Carol Lerner. Four Winds Pr., 1983. Subj: Desert. Plants. Science.

Holmes, Efner Tudor. *Amy's goose* ill. by Tasha Tudor. Crowell, 1977. Subj: Birds – geese. Character traits – helpfulness. Character traits – kindness to animals.

Carrie's gift ill. by Tasha Tudor. Collins-World, 1978. Subj: Animals – dogs. Character traits – kindness to animals.

The Christmas cat ill. by Tasha Tudor. Crowell, 1976. Subj: Animals – cats. Holidays – Christmas.

Holmes, Olivia. *The saint and the circus* (Piumini, Roberto)

Holmes, Stephen. *Hidden numbers* text by Sadie Fields. Harcourt, 1990. ISBN 0-15-200469-6 Subj: Counting, numbers. Format, unusual – toy and movable books. Games.

Holzenthaler, Jean. *My feet do* ill. by George Ancona. Dutton, 1979. Subj: Activities. Anatomy – feet.

My hands can ill. by Nancy Tafuri. Dutton, 1978. Subj: Activities. Anatomy – hands.

Homel, David. *Animal capers* (Paré, Roger)

Circus days (Paré, Roger)

A friend like you (Paré, Roger)

Play time (Paré, Roger)

Summer days (Paré, Roger)

Homme, Bob. *The friendly giant's birthday* ill. by Kim La Fave and Carol Snelling. CBC Merchandising, 1982. Subj: Birthdays. Giants. Songs.

The friendly giant's book of fire engines ill. by Kim La Fave and Carol Snelling. CBC Merchandising, 1981. Subj: Careers – firefighters. Giants. Trucks.

Hong, Lily Toy. *How the ox star fell from heaven* ill. by author. Albert Whitman, 1990. ISBN 0-8075-3428-5 Subj: Animals – oxen. Folk and fairy tales. Food. Foreign lands – China.

Hood, Thomas. *Before I go to sleep* ill. by Maryjane Begin-Callanan. Putnam, 1990. ISBN 0-399-21638-3 Subj: Animals. Bedtime. Imagination. Poetry, rhyme.

Hooker, Ruth. *At Grandma and Grandpa's house* ill. by Ruth Rosner. Albert Whitman, 1986. ISBN 0-8075-0477-7 Subj: Family life. Family life – grandparents.

Matthew the cowboy ill. by Cat Bowman Smith. Albert Whitman, 1990. ISBN 0-8075-4999-1 Subj: Cowboys. Imagination.

Sara loves her big brother ill. by Margot Apple. Albert Whitman, 1987. ISBN 0-8075-7244-6 Subj: Behavior – sharing. Family life. Sibling rivalry.

Hooks, William H. *Lion and lamb* by William H. Hooks and Barbara A. Brenner; ill. by Bruce Degen. Bantam, 1989. ISBN 0-553-05829-0 Subj: Animals – lions. Animals – sheep. Friendship.

Moss gown ill. by Donald Carrick. Clarion, 1987. ISBN 0-89919-460-5 Subj: Family life – fathers. Folk and fairy tales. Magic.

Peach boy ill. by June Otani. Bantam, 1992. ISBN 0-553-07621-3 Subj: Behavior – fighting, arguing. Character traits – bravery. Folk and fairy tales. Foreign lands – Japan. Monsters.

The three little pigs and the fox (The three little pigs)

Three rounds with rabbit ill. by Lissa McLaughlin. Lothrop, 1984. Subj: Animals – rabbits. Character traits – cleverness.

Where's Lulu? ill. by Robert W. Alley. Bantam, 1991. ISBN 0-553-07093-2 Subj: Animals – dogs. Ethnic groups in the U.S. – Afro-Americans. Toys – balls.

Hooper, Meredith. *Seven eggs* ill. by Terry McKenna. Harper, 1985. ISBN 0-06-022586-6 Subj: Counting, numbers. Cumulative tales. Days of the week, months of the year. Eggs. Format, unusual.

Hooper, Patricia. *A bundle of beasts* ill. by Mark Steele. Houghton, 1987. ISBN 0-395-44259-1 Subj: ABC books. Animals. Poetry, rhyme.

Hoopes, Lyn Littlefield. *Daddy's coming home* ill. by Bruce Degen. Harper, 1984. ISBN 0-06-022569-6 Subj: Family life.

Mommy, daddy, me ill. by Ruth Lercher Bornstein. Harper, 1988. ISBN 0-06-022550-5 Subj: Family life. Islands. Nature. Poetry, rhyme.

My own home ill. by Ruth Richardson. HarperCollins, 1991. ISBN 0-06-022571-8 Subj: Animals. Birds – owls. Nature.

Nana ill. by Arieh Zeldich. Harper, 1981. ISBN 0-06-022575-0 Subj: Death. Family life – grandmothers.

When I was little ill. by Marcia Sewall. Dutton, 1983. Subj: Emotions – love. Seasons – winter. Sibling rivalry.

Wing-a-ding ill. by Stephen Gammell. Little, 1990. ISBN 0-316-37237-4 Subj: Cumulative tales. Poetry, rhyme. Toys. Trees.

Hoover, Roseanna. *The golden apple* (Bolliger, Max)

Hopkins, Lee Bennett. *And God bless me: prayers, lullabies and dream-poems* ill. by Patricia Henderson Lincoln. Knopf, 1982. Subj: Lullabies. Poetry, rhyme. Religion.

Animals from Mother Goose: a question book ill. by Kathryn Hewitt. Harcourt, 1989. ISBN 0-15-200406-8 Subj: Animals. Character traits – questioning. Nursery rhymes.

Best friends ill. by James Watts. Harper, 1986. ISBN 0-06-022562-9 Subj: Friendship. Poetry, rhyme.

Circus! Circus! ill. by John O'Brien. Knopf, 1982. Subj: Circus. Poetry, rhyme.

Crickets and bullfrogs and whispers of thunder (Behn, Harry)

A dog's life ill. by Linda Rochester Richards. Harcourt, 1983. Subj: Animals – dogs. Poetry, rhyme.

Easter buds are springing ill. by Tomie de Paola. Harcourt, 1979. Subj: Holidays – Easter. Poetry, rhyme. Seasons – spring.

Go to bed! a book of bedtime poems ill. by Rosekrans Hoffman. Knopf, 1979. Subj: Bedtime. Poetry, rhyme.

Good books, good times ill. by Harvey Stevenson. HarperCollins, 1990. ISBN 0-06-022528-9 Subj: Activities – reading. Poetry, rhyme.

I loved Rose Ann ill. by Ingrid Fetz. Knopf, 1976. Subj: Behavior – misunderstanding. Emotions.

I think I saw a snail: young poems for city seasons ill. by Harold James. Crown, 1969. Subj: City. Ethnic groups in the U.S. – Afro-Americans. Poetry, rhyme.

Merrily comes our harvest in: poems for Thanksgiving ill. by Ben Shecter. Harcourt, 1978. Subj: Holidays – Thanksgiving. Poetry, rhyme. Seasons – fall.

On the farm ill. by Laurel Molk. Little, 1991. ISBN 0-316-37274-9 Subj: Farms. Poetry, rhyme.

People from Mother Goose: a question book ill. by Kathryn Hewitt. Harcourt, 1989. ISBN 0-15-200558-7 Subj: Character traits – questioning. Nursery rhymes.

Ring out, wild bells ill. by Karen Baumann. Harcourt, 1992. ISBN 0-15-267100-5 Subj: Holidays. Poetry, rhyme. Seasons.

The sea is calling me ill. by Walter Gaffney-Kessell. Harcourt, 1986. ISBN 0-15-271155-4 Subj: Poetry, rhyme. Sea and seashore.

The sky is full of song ill. by Dirk Zimmer. Harper, 1983. Subj: Poetry, rhyme.

Still as a star ill. by Karen Milone. Little, 1989. ISBN 0-316-37272-2 Subj: Poetry, rhyme. Sleep.

To the zoo ill. by John Wallner. Little, 1992. ISBN 0-316-37273-0 Subj: Animals. Poetry, rhyme. Zoos.

Hopkins, Margaret. *Sleepytime for baby mouse* ill. by Karen Lee Schmidt. Platt, 1985. ISBN 0-448-49875-9 Subj: Animals – mice. Bedtime. Family life. Format, unusual – board books.

Hopkins, Marjorie. *Three visitors* ill. by Anne F. Rockwell. Parents, 1967. Subj: Eskimos.

Hoppe, Matthias. *Mouse and elephant* ill. by Jan Lenica. Little, 1991. ISBN 0-316-37284-6 Subj: Animals. Animals – elephants. Animals – mice. Friendship.

Horenstein, Henry. *Sam goes trucking* photos. by author. Houghton, 1989. ISBN 0-395-44313-X Subj: Careers – truck drivers. Family life – fathers. Trucks.

Horio, Seishi. *The monkey and the crab* by Saru Kani; retold by Seishi Horio; tr. by D. T. Ooka; ill. by Tsutomu Murakami. Heian Int., 1985. ISBN 0-89346-246-2 Subj: Animals – monkeys. Crustacea. Death.

Horner, Althea J. *Little big girl* ill. by Patricia Rosamilia. Human Sciences Pr., 1983. Subj: Behavior – growing up.

Horowitz, Ruth. *Bat time* ill. by Susan Avishai. Four Winds, 1991. ISBN 0-02-744541-0 Subj: Animals – bats. Bedtime. Family life – fathers.

Hort, Lenny. *The boy who held back the sea* ill. by Thomas Locker. Dial Pr., 1987. Adapt. of Hans Brinker, or The Silver Skates by Mary Mapes Dodge ISBN 0-8037-0407-0 Subj: Behavior – misbehavior. Character traits – bravery. Folk and fairy tales.

How many stars in the sky ill. by James E. Ransome. Morrow, 1991. ISBN 0-688-10104-6 Subj: Ethnic groups in the U.S. – Afro-Americans. Family life – fathers. Night. Stars.

The tale of the unicorn (Preussler, Otfried)

Horton, Barbara Savadge. *What comes in spring?* ill. by Ed Young. Knopf, 1992. ISBN 0-679-90268-6 Subj: Babies. Birth. Family life. Seasons.

Horvath, Betty F. *Be nice to Josephine* ill. by Pat Grant Porter. Watts, 1970. Subj: Behavior. Family life.

The cheerful quiet ill. by Jo Ann Stover. Watts, 1969. Subj: Noise, sounds. Problem solving.

Hooray for Jasper ill. by Fermin Rocker. Watts, 1966. Subj: Character traits – smallness. Ethnic groups in the U.S. – Afro-Americans.

Jasper and the hero business ill. by Don Bolognese. Watts, 1977. Subj: Character traits – bravery. Ethnic groups in the U.S. – Afro-Americans.

Jasper makes music ill. by Fermin Rocker. Watts, 1967. Subj: Activities – working. Ethnic groups in the U.S. – Afro-Americans. Music.

Will the real Tommy Wilson please stand up? ill. by Charles Robinson. Watts, 1969. Subj: Character traits – individuality. Emotions. Friendship.

Horwitz, Elinor Lander. *Sometimes it happens* ill. by Susan Jeschke. Harper, 1981. Subj: Character traits – ambition. Imagination.

When the sky is like lace ill. by Barbara Cooney. Lippincott, 1975. Subj: Night.

Hot cross buns, and other old street cries sel. by John M. Langstaff; ill. by Nancy Winslow Parker. Atheneum, 1978. Subj: Music. Poetry, rhyme. Songs.

Houghton, Eric. *The backwards watch* ill. by Simone Abel. Orchard, 1992. ISBN 0-531-08568-6 Subj: Activities – playing. Family life – grandfathers.

Walter's magic wand ill. by Denise Teasdale. Watts, 1990. ISBN 0-531-08451-5 Subj: Libraries. Magic.

House mouse photos. by David Thompson. Putnam's, 1978. Subj: Animals – mice. Science.

The house that Jack built. *The house that Jack built* ill. by Randolph Caldecott. Avenel Books, n.d. Subj: Cumulative tales. Nursery rhymes.

The house that Jack built ill. by Seymour Chwast. Random House, 1973. Subj: Cumulative tales. Format, unusual – toy and movable books. Nursery rhymes. Participation.

The house that Jack built: la maison que Jacques a batie ill. by Antonio Frasconi. Harcourt, 1958. Subj: Caldecott award honor book. Cumulative tales. Foreign languages. Nursery rhymes.

The house that Jack built ill. by Rodney Peppé. Delacorte Pr., 1970. Subj: Cumulative tales. Nursery rhymes.

The house that Jack built: a Mother Goose nursery rhyme ill. by Janet Stevens. Holiday, 1985. ISBN 0-8234-0548-6 Subj: Circus. Cumulative tales. Nursery rhymes.

The house that Jack built ill. by Jenny Stow. Dial, 1992. ISBN 0-8037-1090-9 Subj: Cumulative tales. Nursery rhymes.

The house that Jack built ill. by Nadine Bernard Westcott. Little, 1991. ISBN 0-316-93138-1 Subj: Cumulative tales. Format, unusual – toy and movable books. Nursery rhymes. Participation.

This is the house that Jack built ill. by Liz Underhill. Holt, 1987. ISBN 0-8050-0339-8 Subj: Cumulative tales. Nursery rhymes.

Houselander, Caryll. *Petook: an Easter story* ill. by Tomie de Paola. Holiday, 1988. ISBN 0-8234-0681-4 Subj: Birds – chickens. Holidays – Easter. Religion.

Houston, Gloria. *My Great-Aunt Arizona* ill. by Susan Condie Lamb. HarperCollins, 1992. ISBN 0-06-022607-2 Subj: Careers – teachers. Family life – aunts, uncles.

The year of the perfect Christmas tree: an Appalachian story ill. by Barbara Cooney. Dial Pr., 1988. ISBN 0-8037-0300-7 Subj: Family life. Holidays – Christmas. Trees.

Houston, James. *Kiviok's magic journey: an Eskimo legend* ill. by author. Atheneum, 1973. Subj: Birds – geese. Eskimos. Folk and fairy tales.

Houston, John A. *The bright yellow rope* ill. by Winnie Fitch. Addison-Wesley, 1973. Subj: Behavior – sharing. Character traits – generosity. Character traits – helpfulness. Poetry, rhyme. Problem solving. Songs.

A mouse in my house ill. by Winnie Fitch. Addison-Wesley, 1973. Subj: Animals – mice. Cumulative tales. Problem solving. Songs.

A room full of animals ill. by Winnie Fitch. Addison-Wesley, 1973. Subj: Animals. Songs.

Howard, Elizabeth Fitzgerald. *Aunt Flossie's hats (and crab cakes later)* ill. by James E. Ransome. Houghton, 1991. ISBN 0-395-54682-6 Subj: Clothing – hats. Ethnic groups in the U.S. – Afro-Americans. Family life – aunts, uncles.

Chita's Christmas tree ill. by Floyd Cooper. Bradbury Pr., 1989. ISBN 0-02-744621-2 Subj: Ethnic groups in the U.S. – Afro-Americans. Holidays – Christmas.

The train to Lulu's ill. by Robert Casilla. Bradbury Pr., 1988. ISBN 0-02-744620-4 Subj: Activities – traveling. Family life – sisters.

Howard, Jane R. *When I'm sleepy* ill. by Lynne Cherry. Dutton, 1985. ISBN 0-525-44204-9 Subj: Imagination. Sleep.

Howard, Jean G. *Of mice and mice* ill. by author. Tidal Pr., 1978. Subj: Animals – mice.

Howard, Katherine. *Do you know color?* (Miller, J. P. (John Parr))

I can count to 100... can you? ill. by Michael Smollin. Random House, 1979. ISBN 0-394-84090-9 Subj: Counting, numbers.

My first picture dictionary ill. by Huck Scarry. Random House, 1978. Subj: Dictionaries.

Howard-Gibbon, Amelia Frances. *An illustrated comic alphabet* ill. by author. Walck, 1967. Subj: ABC books.

Howe, Caroline Walton. *Counting penguins* ill. by author. Harper, 1983. Subj: Birds – penguins. Counting, numbers.

Teddy Bear's bird and beast band ill. by author. Windmill, 1980. Subj: Music. Toys – teddy bears.

Howe, James. *The case of the missing mother* ill. by William Cleaver. Random House, 1983. Subj: Holidays – Mother's Day. Puppets.

Creepy-crawly birthday ill. by Leslie Holt Morrill. Morrow, 1991. ISBN 0-688-09688-3 Subj: Animals – cats. Animals – dogs. Birthdays. Pets.

The day the teacher went bananas ill. by Lillian Hoban. Dutton, 1984. Subj: Animals – gorillas. School. Zoos.

Hot fudge ill. by Leslie Holt Morrill. Morrow, 1990. ISBN 0-688-09701-4 Subj: Animals. Food.

I wish I were a butterfly ill. by Ed Young. Harcourt, 1987. ISBN 0-15-200470-X Subj: Behavior – wishing. Emotions – envy, jealousy.

Scared silly ill. by Leslie Holt Morrill. Morrow, 1989. ISBN 0-688-07667-X Subj: Animals – cats. Animals – dogs. Animals – rabbits. Holidays – Halloween. Witches.

There's a monster under my bed ill. by David S. Rose. Atheneum, 1986. ISBN 0-689-31178-8 Subj: Emotions – fear. Furniture – beds. Monsters. Night.

When you go to kindergarten photos. by Betsy Imershein. Knopf, 1986. ISBN 0-394-87303-3 Subj: School.

Howe, John. *Rip Van Winkle* (Irving, Washington)

Howell, Lynn. *Winifred's new bed* by Lynn and Richard Howell; ill. by authors. Knopf, 1985. ISBN 0-394-87772-1 Subj: Animals – cats. Days of the week, months of the year. Format, unusual. Furniture – beds. Toys.

Howell, Richard. *Winifred's new bed* (Howell, Lynn)

Howell, Ruth. *Everything changes* photos. by Arline Strong. Atheneum, 1968. Subj: Seasons.

Splash and flow photos. by Arline Strong. Atheneum, 1973. Subj: Science.

Howell, Troy. *The ugly duckling* (Andersen, H. C. (Hans Christian))

Howells, Mildred. *The woman who lived in Holland* ill. by William Curtis Holdsworth. Farrar,

1973. Text originally published in 1898 in St. Nicholas magazine under title: Going too far Subj: Character traits – cleanliness. Foreign lands – Holland. Poetry, rhyme.

Hubbard, Woodleigh. *Two is for dancing* ill. by author. Chronicle Books, 1991. ISBN 0-87701-895-2 Subj: Animals. Birds. Counting, numbers.

Huck, Charlotte. *Princess Furball* ill. by Anita Lobel. Greenwillow, 1989. ISBN 0-688-07838-9 Subj: Character traits – cleverness. Folk and fairy tales. Royalty – princesses.

Hudson, Cheryl Willis. *Bright eyes, brown skin* by Cheryl Willis Hudson and Bernette G. Ford; ill. by George Ford. Just Us Books, 1990. ISBN 0-940975-10-6 Subj: Ethnic groups in the U.S. – Afro-Americans. Poetry, rhyme.

Good morning baby ill. by George Ford. Scholastic, 1992. ISBN 0-590-45760-8 Subj: Babies. Ethnic groups in the U.S. – Afro-Americans. Format, unusual – board books. Morning. Poetry, rhyme.

Good night baby ill. by George Ford. Scholastic, 1992. ISBN 0-590-45760-8 Subj: Babies. Ethnic groups in the U.S. – Afro-Americans. Format, unusual – board books. Night. Poetry, rhyme.

Hudson, Eleanor. *A whale of a rescue* ill. by Pat Paris. Random House, 1983. Subj: Animals – whales.

Huff, Barbara A. *Once inside the library* ill. by Iris Van Rynbach. Little, 1990. ISBN 0-316-37967-0 Subj: Activities – reading. Libraries.

Huff, Vivian. *Let's make paper dolls* photos. by author. Harper, 1978. Subj: Activities – making things. Paper. Toys – dolls.

Hughes, Peter. *The emperor's oblong pancake* ill. by Gerald Rose. Abelard-Schuman, 1961. Subj: Concepts – shape. Food. Royalty – emperors.

The king who loved candy ill. by Gerald Rose. Abelard-Schuman, 1964. Subj: Food. Royalty – kings. War.

Hughes, Richard. *Gertrude's child* ill. by Rick Schreiter. Crown, 1966. Subj: Behavior – needing someone. Behavior – running away. Toys.

Hughes, Shirley. *Alfie gets in first* ill. by author. Lothrop, 1982. Subj: Cumulative tales. Houses.

Alfie gives a hand ill. by author. Lothrop, 1984. Subj: Behavior – needing someone. Birthdays. Parties.

Alfie's feet ill. by author. Lothrop, 1983. Subj: Activities – playing.

All shapes and sizes ill. by author. Lothrop, 1986. ISBN 0-688-04205-8 Subj: Concepts – shape. Concepts – size. Poetry, rhyme.

Angel Mae ill. by author. Lothrop, 1989. ISBN 0-688-08539-3 Subj: Babies. Family life. Holidays – Christmas. Theater.

Bathwater's hot ill. by author. Lothrop, 1985. ISBN 0-688-04202-3 Subj: Activities – bathing. Concepts – opposites. Family life. Foreign lands – England. Poetry, rhyme.

The big concrete lorry ill. by author. Lothrop, 1990. ISBN 0-688-08535-0 Subj: Activities – making things. City. Ethnic groups in the U.S. Houses.

Bouncing ill. by author. Candlewick Pr., 1993. ISBN 1-56402-128-9 Subj: Activities.

Colors ill. by author. Lothrop, 1986. ISBN 0-688-04206-6 Subj: Concepts – color. Poetry, rhyme.

David and dog ill. by author. Prentice-Hall, 1978. Edition of 1977 published under title: Dogger Subj: Activities – trading. Family life. Toys.

Dogger ill. by author. Lothrop, 1988, 1977. 1978 Prentice-Hall edition published under title David and dog ISBN 0-688-07981-4 Subj: Activities – trading. Family life. Toys.

An evening at Alfie's ill. by author. Lothrop, 1985. ISBN 0-688-04123-X Subj: Activities – babysitting. Family life. Problem solving.

George the babysitter ill. by author. Prentice-Hall, 1978. Subj: Activities – baby-sitting.

Lucy and Tom's A.B.C. ill. by author. Viking, 1986. ISBN 0-670-81256-0 Subj: ABC books. Family life. Foreign lands – England.

Lucy and Tom's Christmas ill. by author. Viking, 1986. ISBN 0-670-81255-2 Subj: Family life. Foreign lands – England. Holidays – Christmas. Religion.

Lucy and Tom's 1, 2, 3 ill. by author. Viking, 1987. ISBN 0-670-81763-5 Subj: Concepts. Counting, numbers. Family life.

Moving Molly ill. by author. Prentice-Hall, 1979. ISBN 0-13-604587-1 Subj: Emotions – loneliness. Family life. Friendship. Moving.

Noisy ill. by author. Lothrop, 1985. ISBN 0-688-04203-1 Subj: Family life. Foreign lands – England. Noise, sounds. Poetry, rhyme.

Out and about ill. by author. Lothrop, 1988. ISBN 0-688-07691-2 Subj: Family life. Foreign lands – England. Poetry, rhyme.

Sally's secret ill. by author. Merrimack, 1980. Subj: Behavior – secrets. Houses.

The snow lady ill. by author. Lothrop, 1990. ISBN 0-688-09875-4 Subj: Behavior – misbehavior. Foreign lands – England. Old age. Snowmen. Weather – snow.

Two shoes, new shoes ill. by author. Lothrop, 1986. ISBN 0-688-04207-4 Subj: Clothing – shoes. Poetry, rhyme.

Up and up ill. by author. Lothrop, 1986. First published by Prentice-Hall, 1979 ISBN 0-688-06261-X Subj: Activities – flying. Imagination. Wordless.

Wheels ill. by author. Lothrop, 1991. ISBN 0-688-09880-0 Subj: Birthdays. Friendship. Sports – bicycling.

When we went to the park ill. by author. Lothrop, 1985. ISBN 0-688-04204-X Subj: Counting, numbers. Family life. Family life – grandfathers. Foreign lands – England. Poetry, rhyme.

Hulbert, Jay. *Armando asked "Why?"* by Jay Hulbert and Sid Kantor; ill. by Pat Hoggan. Raintree, 1990. ISBN 0-8172-3576-0 Subj: Character traits – questioning. Ethnic groups in the U.S. – Afro-Americans. Libraries.

Hulme, Joy. *Sea squares* ill. by Carol Schwartz. Walt Disney, 1991. ISBN 1-56282-080-X Subj: Counting, numbers. Poetry, rhyme. Sea and seashore.

Hulme, Susan. *Let's look for colors* (Gillham, Bill)

Let's look for numbers (Gillham, Bill)

Let's look for opposites (Gillham, Bill)

Let's look for shapes (Gillham, Bill)

Hulse, Gillian. *Morris, where are you?* ill. by author. Oxford Univ. Pr., 1988. ISBN 0-19-520646-0 Subj: Animals – cats. Behavior – hiding. Problem solving.

Humpty Dumpty and other first rhymes ill. by Betty Youngs. Bodley Head, 1980. Subj: Nursery rhymes.

Hunt Angela Elwell. *The tale of three trees* ill. by Tim Jonke. Lion, 1989. ISBN 0-7459-1743-7 Subj: Folk and fairy tales. Religion. Trees.

Hunt, Bernice Kohn. *Your ant is a which* ill. by Jan Pyk. Harcourt, 1975. ISBN 0-15-299880-2 Subj: Language.

Hunt, Joyce. *A first look at bird nests* (Selsam, Millicent E.)

A first look at caterpillars (Selsam, Millicent E.)

A first look at cats (Selsam, Millicent E.)

A first look at dinosaurs (Selsam, Millicent E.)

A first look at dogs (Selsam, Millicent E.)

A first look at flowers (Selsam, Millicent E.)

A first look at kangaroos, koalas and other animals with pouches (Selsam, Millicent E.)

A first look at monkeys (Selsam, Millicent E.)

A first look at owls, eagles and other hunters of the sky (Selsam, Millicent E.)

A first look at rocks (Selsam, Millicent E.)

A first look at seashells (Selsam, Millicent E.)

A first look at sharks (Selsam, Millicent E.)

A first look at spiders (Selsam, Millicent E.)

A first look at the world of plants (Selsam, Millicent E.)

A first look at whales (Selsam, Millicent E.)

Keep looking! (Selsam, Millicent E.)

Hunt, Nan. *Families are funny* ill. by Deborah Niland. Orchard, 1992. ISBN 0-531-08569-4 Subj: Family life.

Hunter, C. W. *The green gourd* ill. by Tony Griego. Putnam, 1992. ISBN 0-399-22278-2 Subj: Folk and fairy tales.

Hunter, Norman. *Professor Branestawn's building bust-up* ill. by Gerald Rose. Merrimack, 1982. Subj: Houses. Humor. Machines.

Hurd, Edith Thacher. *The black dog who went into the woods* ill. by Emily Arnold McCully. Harper, 1980. Subj: Animals – dogs. Death. Pets.

Caboose ill. by Clement Hurd. Lothrop, 1950. Subj: Poetry, rhyme. Trains.

Christmas eve ill. by Clement Hurd. Harper, 1962. Subj: Animals. Holidays – Christmas.

Come and have fun ill. by Clement Hurd. Harper, 1962. Subj: Animals – cats. Animals – mice. Poetry, rhyme.

The day the sun danced ill. by Clement Hurd. Harper, 1965. Subj: Seasons. Seasons – spring. Sun.

Dinosaur, my darling ill. by Don Freeman. Harper, 1978. Subj: Dinosaurs.

Engine, engine number 9 ill. by Clement Hurd. Lothrop, 1940. Subj: Trains.

Five little firemen (Brown, Margaret Wise)

Hurry, hurry! ill. by Clement Hurd. Harper, 1960. Subj: Activities – baby-sitting. Behavior – hurrying.

I dance in my red pajamas ill. by Emily Arnold McCully. Harper, 1982. Subj: Activities – dancing. Family life – grandparents.

Johnny Lion's bad day ill. by Clement Hurd. Harper, 1970. Subj: Animals – lions. Illness.

Johnny Lion's book ill. by Clement Hurd. Harper, 1965. Subj: Activities – reading. Animals – lions.

Johnny Lion's rubber boots ill. by Clement Hurd. Harper, 1972. Subj: Animals – lions. Weather – rain.

Last one home is a green pig ill. by Clement Hurd. Harper, 1959. Subj: Animals – monkeys. Birds – ducks. Games. Sports – racing.

Little dog, dreaming by Edith Thacher Hurd and Thacher Hurd; ill. by Clement Hurd. Harper, 1967. Subj: Animals – dogs. Dreams.

Look for a bird ill. by Clement Hurd. Harper, 1977. ISBN 0-06-022720-6 Subj: Birds. Nature. Science.

The mother chimpanzee ill. by Clement Hurd. Little, 1978. Subj: Animals – chimpanzees. Family life – mothers.

The mother kangaroo ill. by Clement Hurd. Little, 1976. Subj: Animals – kangaroos. Family life. Science.

No funny business ill. by Clement Hurd. Harper, 1962. Subj: Activities – picnicking. Animals – cats.

Sandpipers ill. by Lucienne Bloch. Crowell, 1961. Subj: Birds – sandpipers. Science.

The so-so cat ill. by Clement Hurd. Harper, 1964. Subj: Animals – cats. Holidays – Halloween. Witches.

Starfish ill. by Lucienne Bloch. Crowell, 1962. Subj: Sea and seashore. Science.

Stop, stop ill. by Clement Hurd. Harper, 1961. Subj: Activities – baby-sitting. Character traits – cleanliness.

Under the lemon tree ill. by Clement Hurd. Little, 1980. Subj: Animals – donkeys. Animals – foxes. Character traits – loyalty. Farms.

What whale? Where? ill. by Clement Hurd. Harper, 1966. Subj: Animals – whales. Boats, ships.

The white horse ill. by Tony Chen. Harper, 1970. Subj: Imagination.

Wilson's world ill. by Clement Hurd. Harper, 1971. Subj: Art. Ecology.

Hurd, Thacher. *Axle the freeway cat* ill. by author. HarperCollins, 1988. ISBN 0-06-443173-8 Subj: Animals – cats. Friendship.

Blackberry ramble ill. by author. Crown, 1989. ISBN 0-517-57105-6 Subj: Animals – mice. Farms. Seasons – spring.

Hobo dog ill. by author. Scholastic, 1980. Subj: Activities – traveling. Animals – dogs. Trains.

Little dog, dreaming (Hurd, Edith Thacher)

Little Mouse's big Valentine ill. by author. HarperCollins, 1990. ISBN 0-06-026193-5 Subj: Animals – mice. Holidays – Valentine's Day.

Little Mouse's birthday cake ill. by author. HarperCollins, 1992. ISBN 0-06-020216-5 Subj: Animals – mice. Birthdays.

Mama don't allow ill. by author. Harper, 1984. Subj: Animals – possums. Music. Reptiles – alligators, crocodiles.

Mystery on the docks ill. by author. Harper, 1983. Subj: Animals – rats. Behavior – bad day.

A night in the swamp: a movable book ill. by author. Harper, 1987. ISBN 0-694-00177-5 Subj: Animals. Format, unusual – toy and movable books. Night.

The pea patch jig ill. by author. Crown, 1986. ISBN 0-517-56307-X Subj: Animals – mice. Gardens, gardening. Music.

The quiet evening ill. by author. Greenwillow, 1978. Subj: Night.

Tomato soup ill. by author. Crown, 1992. ISBN 0-517-58238-4 Subj: Animals – cats. Animals – mice. Farms. Illness.

Hurford, John. *The dormouse* ill. by author. Associated Booksellers, 1986. ISBN 0-907349-25-0 Subj: Animals. Animals – mice.

Huriet, Genevieve. *Dandelion's vanishing vegetable garden* ill. by Loic Jouannigot. Gareth Stevens, 1991. ISBN 0-8368-0526-7 Subj: Animals – rabbits. Gardens, gardening.

Hürlimann, Bettina. *Barry: the story of a brave St. Bernard* ill. by Paul Nussbaumer; tr. by Elizabeth D. Crawford. Harcourt, 1968. Subj: Animals – dogs. Character traits – bravery. Character traits – helpfulness.

Hürlimann, Ruth. *The mouse with the daisy hat* ill. by author. White, 1971. Subj: Animals – mice. Clothing – hats. Weddings.

The proud white cat tr. by Anthea Bell; ill. by author. Morrow, 1977. Translation of Der stolze weisse Kater Subj: Animals – cats. Character traits – pride. Folk and fairy tales. Foreign lands – Germany.

Hush little baby. *Hush little baby: a folk lullaby* ill. by Aliki. Prentice-Hall, 1968. Subj: Babies. Character traits – generosity. Cumulative tales. Lullabies. Music.

Hush little baby ill. by Jeanette Winter. Pantheon, 1984. Subj: Babies. Character traits – generosity. Cumulative tales. Folk and fairy tales. Lullabies. Music.

Hush little baby ill. by Margot Zemach. Dutton, 1976. Subj: Babies. Character traits – generosity. Cumulative tales. Lullabies. Music.

Hutchings, Tony. *Things that go word book* ill. by author. Rand McNally, 1977. Subj: Machines.

Hutchins, H. J. (Hazel J.). *Ben's snow song* ill. by Lisa Smith. Firefly, 1987. ISBN 0-920303-91-9 Subj: Sports – skiing. Weather – snow.

Katie's babbling brother ill. by Ruth Ohi. Firefly, 1991. ISBN 1-55037-153-3 Subj: Family life. Noise, sounds. Sibling rivalry.

Leanna builds a genie trap ill. by Catharine O'Neill. Firefly, 1986. ISBN 0-920303-54-4 Subj: Behavior – losing things. Furniture.

Nicholas at the library ill. by Ruth Ohi. Firefly, 1990. ISBN 1-55037-134-7 Subj: Activities – reading. Imagination. Libraries.

Hutchins, Hazel J. *Norman's snowball* ill. by Ruth Ohi. Firefly, 1989. ISBN 1-55037-053-7 Subj: Activities – playing. Behavior – losing things. Family life. Weather – snow.

Hutchins, Pat. *Changes, changes* ill. by author. Macmillan, 1971. Subj: Toys – blocks. Wordless.

Clocks and more clocks ill. by author. Macmillan, 1970. Subj: Clocks, watches. Humor. Time.

Don't forget the bacon! ill. by author. Greenwillow, 1975. Subj: Behavior – forgetfulness. Cumulative tales. Food. Humor. Shopping.

The doorbell rang ill. by author. Greenwillow, 1986. ISBN 0-688-05252-5 Subj: Behavior – sharing. Family life. Friendship.

Good night owl ill. by author. Macmillan, 1972. Subj: Birds – owls. Cumulative tales. Noise, sounds. Participation. Sleep.

Happy birthday, Sam ill. by author. Greenwillow, 1978. Subj: Birthdays. Family life – grandfathers.

King Henry's palace ill. by author. Greenwillow, 1983. Subj: Birthdays. Holidays – Christmas. Royalty – kings.

My best friend ill. by author. Greenwillow, 1993. ISBN 0-688-11486-5 Subj: Friendship.

One-eyed Jake ill. by author. Greenwillow, 1979. Subj: Pirates.

1 hunter ill. by author. Greenwillow, 1982. Subj: Animals. Counting, numbers.

Rosie's walk ill. by author. Macmillan, 1968. Subj: Animals – foxes. Birds – chickens. Farms. Humor.

The silver Christmas tree ill. by author. Macmillan, 1974. Subj: Animals. Holidays – Christmas. Trees.

The surprise party ill. by author. Macmillan, 1986, 1969. ISBN 0-02-745930-6 Subj: Animals. Behavior – gossip. Parties.

The tale of Thomas Mead ill. by author. Greenwillow, 1980. ISBN 0-688-84282-8 Subj: Activities – reading. Poetry, rhyme.

Tidy Titch ill. by author. Greenwillow, 1991. ISBN 0-688-09964-5 Subj: Behavior. Family life. Toys.

Titch ill. by author. Macmillan, 1971. Subj: Concepts – size. Cumulative tales. Family life. Plants.

The very worst monster ill. by author. Greenwillow, 1985. ISBN 0-688-04011-X Subj: Monsters. Sibling rivalry.

What game shall we play? ill. by author. Greenwillow, 1990. ISBN 0-688-09197-0 Subj: Animals. Games.

Where's the baby? ill. by author. Greenwillow, 1988. ISBN 0-688-05934-1 Subj: Babies. Behavior – lost. Behavior – misbehavior. Character traits – cleanliness. Monsters.

Which witch is which? ill. by author. Greenwillow, 1989. ISBN 0-688-06358-6 Subj: Games. Holidays – Halloween. Parties. Poetry, rhyme. Twins.

The wind blew ill. by author. Macmillan, 1974. Subj: Poetry, rhyme. Weather – wind.

You'll soon grow into them, Titch ill. by author. Greenwillow, 1983. Subj: Clothing. Family life.

Hutton, Warwick. *Adam and Eve: the Bible story* ill. by adapt. Macmillan, 1987. ISBN 0-689-50433-0 Subj: Religion.

Beauty and the beast retold and ill. by Warwick Hutton. Atheneum, 1985. Subj: Character traits – loyalty. Folk and fairy tales. Magic.

Jonah and the great fish ill. by adapt. Atheneum, 1984. Subj: Animals – whales. Religion.

Moses in the bulrushes ill. by adapt. Atheneum, 1986. ISBN 0-689-50393-8 Subj: Babies. Foreign lands – Egypt. Jewish culture. Religion.

Noah and the great flood ill. by author. Atheneum, 1977. Subj: Religion – Noah.

The nose tree ill. by adapt. Atheneum, 1981. Subj: Anatomy – noses. Character traits – cleverness. Friendship. Folk and fairy tales. Witches.

The sleeping beauty (Grimm, Jacob)

Hyatt, Christine. *Erik has a squirrel* (Peterson, Hans)

Hyman, Inge. *Casper and the rainbow bird* (Hyman, Robin)

Hyman, Robin. *Casper and the rainbow bird* by Robin and Inge Hyman; ill. by Yutaka Sugita. Barron's, 1979. Subj: Behavior – running away. Birds – crows. Birds – parakeets, parrots.

Hyman, Trina Schart. *The enchanted forest* ill. by author. Putnam's, 1984. Subj: Forest, woods. Format, unusual. Wordless.

A little alphabet ill. by author. Little, 1980. Subj: ABC books.

Little Red Riding Hood (Grimm, Jacob)

The sleeping beauty (Grimm, Jacob)

Hymes, James L. *Oodles of noodles and other rhymes* (Hymes, Lucia)

Hymes, Lucia. *Oodles of noodles and other rhymes* by Lucia and James L. Hymes, Jr.; ill. by authors. Addison-Wesley, 1964. Subj: Poetry, rhyme.

Hynard, Julia. *Percival's party* ill. by Frances Thatcher. Children's Pr., 1983. Subj: Activities. Parties.

Hynard, Stephen. *Snowy the rabbit* ill. by Frances Thatcher. Children's Pr., 1983. Subj: Activities. Animals – rabbits.

I sing a song of the saints of God ill. by Judith Gwyn Brown. Seabury Pr., 1981. An ill. version of Lesbia Scott's hymn, "I sing a song of the saints of God" written in 1929 Subj: Music. Religion. Songs.

Iannone, Jeanne Koppel *see* Balzano, Jeanne

Ichikawa, Satomi. *A child's book of seasons* ill. by author. Parents, 1976. Subj: Folk and fairy tales. Seasons.

Let's play ill. by author. Philomel, 1981. ISBN 0-399-61186-X Subj: Activities – playing.

Nora's castle ill. by author. Philomel, 1986. ISBN 0-399-21302-3 Subj: Animals. Houses. Parties. Toys.

Nora's duck ill. by author. Putman, 1991. ISBN 0-399-21805-X Subj: Animals. Birds – ducks. Character traits – kindness to animals.

Nora's stars ill. by author. Putnam, 1989. ISBN 0-399-21616-2 Subj: Family life – grandmothers. Sky. Stars. Toys.

Sun through small leaves: poems of spring ill. by comp. Collins-World, 1980. Subj: Folk and fairy tales. Seasons – spring.

Suzanne and Nicholas at the market ill. by author. Watts, 1977. Translation by Denise Sheldon of Suzette et Nicolas au marché ISBN 0-85166-669-8 Subj: Family life. Foreign lands – France. Shopping.

Suzanne and Nicholas in the garden tr. by Denise Sheldon; ill. by author. Watts, 1976. Translation of Suzette et Nicolas dans leur jardin Subj: Ecology. Foreign lands – France. Gardens, gardening.

Suzanne and Nicholas in the garden ill. by author. St. Martin's, 1978. Translation by Denise Sheldon of Suzette et Nicolas dans leur jardin ISBN 0-312-77982-8 Subj: Activities – playing. Family life. Flowers. Gardens, gardening.

If dragon flies made honey: *poems* col. by David Kherdian; ill. by José Aruego and Ariane Dewey. Greenwillow, 1977. Subj: Poetry, rhyme.

Ife, Elaine. *The childhood of Jesus* ill. by Eric Rowe. Rourke, 1983. Subj: Religion.

Moses in the bulrushes ill. by Eric Rowe. Rourke, 1983. Subj: Religion.

Noah and the ark ill. by Russell Lee. Rourke, 1983. Subj: Religion – Noah.

Stories Jesus told ill. by Russell Lee. Rourke, 1983. Subj: Religion.

Ignatowicz, Nina. *At the frog pond* (Michels, Tilde)

Leo the lion (Wagener, Gerda)

Iké, Jane Hori. *A Japanese fairy tale* by Jane Hori Iké and Baruch Zimmerman; ill. by Jane Hori Iké. Warne, 1982. Subj: Character traits – appearance. Folk and fairy tales. Foreign lands – Japan.

Ikeda, Daisaku. *The cherry tree* tr. from Japanese by Geraldine McCaughrean; ill. by Brian Wildsmith. Knopf, 1992. ISBN 0-679-92669-0 Subj: Foreign lands – Japan. Hope. Trees. War.

The snow country prince tr. from Japanese by Geraldine McCaughrean; ill. by Brian Wildsmith. Knopf, 1991. ISBN 0-679-91965-1 Subj: Character traits – kindness to animals. Folk and fairy tales. Foreign lands – Japan. Royalty – princes.

Illyés, Gyula. *Matt the gooseherd: a story from Hungary* ill. by Károly Reich. Penguin, 1979. Subj: Birds – geese. Folk and fairy tales. Foreign lands – Hungary.

Ilsley, Velma. *A busy day for Chris* ill. by author. Lippincott, 1957. Subj: ABC books. Poetry, rhyme.

M is for moving ill. by author. Walck, 1966. Subj: ABC books. Moving.

The pink hat ill. by author. Lippincott, 1956. Subj: Behavior – carelessness. Poetry, rhyme.

Imershein, Betsy. *Finding red, finding yellow* photos. by author. Harcourt, 1989. ISBN 0-15-200453-X Subj: Concepts – color. Format, unusual. Wordless.

Imoto, Yoko. *Skipper at the beach* ill. by author. Grosset, 1989. ISBN 0-448-09293-X Subj: Animals – cats. Family life. Sea and seashore.

Skipper is the daddy ill. by author. Grosset, 1989. ISBN 0-448-09294-8 Subj: Animals – cats. Family life.

Impey, Rose. *The flat man* ill. by Moira Kemp. Barron's, 1988. ISBN 0-8120-5975-1 Subj: Bedtime. Emotions – fear. Goblins. Monsters. Night.

Joe's café ill. by Sue Porter. Little, 1991. ISBN 0-316-41777-7 Subj: Activities – baby-sitting. Activities – playing. Family life – brothers. Family life – sisters.

My mom and our dad ill. by Maureen Galvani. Viking, 1991. ISBN 0-670-83663-X Subj: Family life – mothers. Family life – fathers. Twins.

Scare yourself to sleep ill. by Moira Kemp. Barron's, 1988. ISBN 0-8120-5974-3 Subj: Bedtime. Emotions – fear. Goblins. Monsters. Night.

Imsand, Marcel. *The fir tree* (Andersen, H. C. (Hans Christian))

Ingle, Annie. *The big city book* ill. by Tim and Greg Hildebrandt. Platt, 1976. Subj: City.

Ingoglia, Gina. *The art class* ill. by Ed Rodriguez. Walt Disney, 1992. ISBN 1-56282-227-6 Subj: Art. Character traits – assertiveness. School.

The big book of real airplanes ill. by George Guzzi. Putnam's, 1987. ISBN 0-448-19179-2 Subj: Airplanes, airports. Helicopters. Transportation.

Ingpen, Robert. *The idle bear* ill. by author. Harper, 1987. ISBN 0-87226-159-X Subj: Toys – teddy bears.

Inkiow, Dimiter. *Me and Clara and Baldwin the pony* tr. from German by Paula McGuire; ill. by Traudl and Walter Reiner. Pantheon, 1980. Subj: Animals – horses. Behavior – misbehavior.

Me and Clara and Casimir the cat tr. from German by Paula McGuire; ill. by Traudl and Walter Reiner. Pantheon, 1979. Subj: Animals – cats.

Me and Clara and Snuffy the dog tr. from German by Paula McGuire; ill. by Traudl and Walter Reiner. Pantheon, 1980. Subj: Animals – dogs. Behavior – misbehavior.

Me and my sister Clara tr. from German by Paula McGuire; ill. by Traudl and Walter Reiner. Pantheon, 1979. Subj: Behavior – misbehavior.

Inkpen, Mick. *Billy's beetle* ill. by author. Harcourt, 1992. ISBN 0-15-200427-0 Subj: Animals. Behavior – losing things. Cumulative tales. Insects – beetles.

The blue balloon ill. by author. Little, 1990. ISBN 0-316-41886-2 Subj: Format, unusual. Imagination. Toys – balloons.

If I had a pig ill. by author. Little, 1988. ISBN 0-316-41887-0 Subj: Animals – pigs. Friendship. Imagination.

If I had a sheep ill. by author. Little, 1988. ISBN 0-316-41888-9 Subj: Animals – sheep. Friendship. Imagination.

Kipper ill. by author. Little, 1992. ISBN 0-316-41883-8 Subj: Animals – dogs. Behavior – imitation. Sleep.

Kipper's toybox ill. by author. Harcourt, 1992. ISBN 0-15-200501-3 Subj: Animals – dogs. Animals – mice. Counting, numbers. Toys.

The Nativity play (Butterworth, Nick)

Nice or nasty (Butterworth, Nick)

One bear at bedtime ill. by author. Little, 1988. ISBN 0-316-41889-7 Subj: Animals. Bedtime. Counting, numbers. Imagination. Toys – teddy bears.

Threadbear ill. by author. Little, 1991. ISBN 0-316-41884-6 Subj: Format, unusual. Toys – teddy bears.

Ipcar, Dahlov. *Animal hide and seek* ill. by author. Addison-Wesley, 1947. Subj: Animals.

The biggest fish in the sea ill. by author. Viking, 1972. Subj: Concepts – size. Fish. Sports – fishing.

Black and white ill. by author. Knopf, 1963. Subj: Animals – dogs. Poetry, rhyme.

Bright barnyard ill. by author. Knopf, 1966. Subj: Animals. Birds. Farms.

Brown cow farm ill. by author. Doubleday, 1959. Subj: Animals. Counting, numbers. Farms.

Bug city ill. by author. Holiday, 1975. Subj: Insects.

The calico jungle ill. by author. Knopf, 1965. Subj: Animals. Bedtime.

The cat at night ill. by author. Doubleday, 1969. Subj: Animals – cats. Night.

The cat came back ill. by author. Knopf, 1971. Subj: Animals – cats. Music. Poetry, rhyme. Songs.

A flood of creatures ill. by author. Holiday, 1973. Subj: Animals. Weather – floods.

Hard scrabble harvest ill. by author. Doubleday, 1976. Subj: Farms. Holidays – Thanksgiving. Plants. Poetry, rhyme.

I like animals ill. by author. Knopf, 1960. Subj: Animals.

I love my anteater with an A ill. by author. Knopf, 1964. Subj: ABC books. Animals.

The land of flowers ill. by author. Viking, 1974. Subj: Animals – sheep. Concepts – size. Flowers. Gardens, gardening.

Lost and found: a hidden animal book ill. by author. Doubleday, 1981. Subj: Animals. Participation.

One horse farm ill. by author. Doubleday, 1950. Subj: Animals – horses. Farms. Machines. Progress.

Sir Addlepate and the unicorn ill. by author. Doubleday, 1971. Subj: Knights. Mythical creatures – unicorns.

"The song of the day birds" and "The song of the night birds" ill. by author. Doubleday, 1967. Subj: Birds. Music. Night. Songs.

Stripes and spots ill. by author. Doubleday, 1953. Subj: Animals – leopards. Animals – tigers.

Ten big farms ill. by author. Knopf, 1958. Subj: Counting, numbers. Farms.

Wild and tame animals ill. by author. Doubleday, 1962. Subj: Animals.

World full of horses ill. by author. Doubleday, 1955. Subj: Animals – horses.

Ireson, Barbara. *The gingerbread man* (The gingerbread boy)

Irvine, Georgeanne. *Bo the orangutan* photos. by Ron Garrison. Children's Pr., 1983. Subj: Animals – monkeys. Zoos.

Elmer the elephant photos. by Ron Garrison. Children's Pr., 1983. Subj: Animals – elephants. Zoos.

Georgie the giraffe photos. by Ron Garrison. Children's Pr., 1983. Subj: Animals – giraffes. Zoos.

Lindi the leopard photos. by Ron Garrison. Children's Pr., 1983. Subj: Animals – leopards. Zoos.

The nursery babies photos. by Ron Garrison. Children's Pr., 1983. Subj: Animals. Zoos.

Sasha the cheetah photos. by Ron Garrison. Children's Pr., 1982. Subj: Animals – cheetahs. Zoos.

Sydney the koala photos. by Ron Garrison. Childrens Pr., 1982. ISBN 0-516-09304-5 Subj: Animals – koala bears. Zoos.

Tully the tree kangaroo photos. by Ron Garrison. Children's Pr., 1983. Subj: Animals. Zoos.

Irving, Washington. *The legend of Sleepy Hollow* (Wolkstein, Diane)

The legend of Sleepy Hollow adapt. by Robert D. San Souci; ill. by Daniel San Souci. Doubleday,

1986. ISBN 0-385-23397-3 Subj: Folk and fairy tales. Holidays – Halloween.

Rip Van Winkle adapt. and ill. by John Howe. Little, 1988. ISBN 0-316-37578-0 Subj: Behavior – lost. Elves and little people. Folk and fairy tales. Sleep.

Rip Van Winkle adapt. and ill. by Thomas Locker. Little, 1988. ISBN 0-8037-0521-2 Subj: Behavior – lost. Elves and little people. Folk and fairy tales. Sleep.

Rip Van Winkle adapt. by Catherine Storr; ill. by Peter Wingham. Raintree, 1984. ISBN 0-8172-2108-5 Subj: Behavior – lost. Elves and little people. Folk and fairy tales. Sleep.

Isadora, Rachel. *At the crossroads* ill. by author. Greenwillow, 1991. ISBN 0-688-05271-1 Subj: Emotions. Family life. Foreign lands – South Africa.

Babies ill. by author. Greenwillow, 1990. ISBN 0-688-08032-4 Subj: Activities. Babies.

Ben's trumpet ill. by author. Greenwillow, 1979. Subj: Caldecott award honor book. Ethnic groups in the U.S. – Afro-Americans. Music.

City seen from A to Z ill. by author. Greenwillow, 1983. Subj: ABC books. City.

Friends ill. by author. Greenwillow., 1990. ISBN 0-688-08265-3 Subj: Activities. Friendship.

I hear ill. by author. Greenwillow, 1985. ISBN 0-688-04062-4 Subj: Babies. Family life. Noise, sounds. Senses – hearing.

I see ill. by author. Greenwillow, 1985. ISBN 0-688-04060-8 Subj: Babies. Family life. Senses – seeing.

I touch ill. by author. Greenwillow, 1985. ISBN 0-688-04256-2 Subj: Senses – touching.

Jesse and Abe ill. by author. Greenwillow, 1981. Subj: Family life – grandfathers. Theater.

Max ill. by author. Macmillan, 1976. Subj: Activities – dancing. Sports – baseball.

My ballet class ill. by author. Greenwillow, 1980. Subj: Activities – dancing.

No, Agatha! ill. by author. Greenwillow, 1980. Subj: Activities – traveling. Boats, ships.

The nutcracker (Hoffmann, E. T. A.)

Opening night ill. by author. Greenwillow, 1984. Subj: Activities – dancing. Theater.

Over the green hills ill. by author. Greenwillow, 1992. ISBN 0-688-10510-6 Subj: Activities – traveling. Communities, neighborhoods. Family life – grandmothers. Foreign lands – South Africa.

The pirates of Bedford Street ill. by author. Greenwillow, 1988. ISBN 0-688-05208-8 Subj: Imagination. Pirates.

The Potters' kitchen ill. by author. Greenwillow, 1977. Subj: Moving.

The princess and the frog (Grimm, Jacob)

Willaby ill. by author. Macmillan, 1977. Subj: School.

Isami, Ikuyo. *The fox's egg* tr. from Japanese by Cathy Hirano; ill. by author. Carolrhoda, 1989. ISBN 0-87614-339-7 Subj: Animals – foxes. Birds – chickens. Eggs.

Isele, Elizabeth. *The frog princess: a Russian tale retold* ill. by Michael Hague. Harper, 1984. ISBN 0-690-04218-3 Subj: Folk and fairy tales. Foreign lands – Russia. Frogs and toads. Magic. Royalty – princesses. Witches.

Pooks ill. by Chris L. Demarest. Lippincott, 1983. Subj: Activities – traveling. Animals – dogs. Music.

Isenbart, Hans-Heinrich. *Baby animals on the farm* tr. from German by Elizabeth D. Crawford; photos by Ruth Rau. Putnam's, 1984. Subj: Animals. Farms.

A duckling is born tr. by Catherine Edwards Sadler; photos. by Othmar Baumli. Putnam's, 1981. Subj: Birds – ducks. Birth. Science.

Isenberg, Barbara. *The adventures of Albert, the running bear* by Barbara Isenberg and Susan Wolf; ill. by Dick Gackenbach. Houghton, 1982. Subj: Animals – bears. Behavior – running away. Sports – racing. Zoos.

Albert the running bear gets the jitters by Barbara Isenberg and Susan Wolf; ill. by Diane de Groat. Clarion, 1987. ISBN 0-89919-532-6 Subj: Animals – bears. Behavior – bullying. Behavior – trickery. Sports – racing.

Albert the running bear's exercise book by Barbara Isenberg and Marjorie Jaffe; ill. by Diane de Groat. Houghton, 1984. Subj: Animals – bears. Health.

Ishii, Momoko. *The tongue-cut sparrow* tr. from the Japanese by Katherine Paterson; ill. by Suekichi Akaba. Lodestar, 1987. Tr. of Sita-kiri suzume ISBN 0-525-67199-4 Subj: Behavior – greed. Birds – sparrows. Character traits – kindness to animals. Folk and fairy tales. Foreign lands – Japan.

Israel, Marion Louise. *The tractor on the farm* ill. by Robert Dranko. Melmont, 1958. Subj: Farms. Tractors.

Ivanov, Anatoly. *Ol' Jake's lucky day* ill. by author. Lothrop, 1984. ISBN 0-688-02867-5 Subj: Behavior – seeking better things. Character traits – luck. Folk and fairy tales. Foreign lands – Russia. Imagination.

Iverson, Genie. *I want to be big* ill. by David McPhail. Dutton, 1979. Subj: Behavior – growing up.

Ives, Penny. *Mrs. Santa Claus* ill. by author. Delacorte Pr., 1991. ISBN 0-385-30302-5 Subj: Holidays – Christmas. Illness. Problem solving.

Ivimey, John William. *The complete story of the three blind mice* ill. by Paul Galdone. Clarion, 1987. ISBN 0-89919-481-8 Subj: Animals – mice. Music. Nursery rhymes. Songs.

The complete version of ye three blind mice ill. by Walton Corbould. Warne, 1909. Subj: Animals – mice. Music. Nursery rhymes. Songs.

Three blind mice ill. by Lorinda Bryan Cauley. Putnam, 1991. ISBN 0-399-21775-4 Subj: Animals – mice. Music. Nursery rhymes. Songs.

Three blind mice ill. by Victoria Chess. Little, 1990. ISBN 0-316-13867-3 Subj: Animals – mice. Music. Nursery rhymes. Songs.

Ivory, Lesley Anne. *Cats in the sun* ill. by author. Dial, 1991. ISBN 0-8037-0955-2 Subj: Animals – cats. Sun.

A day in London ill. by author. Burke, 1982. Subj: City. Foreign lands – England.

A day in New York ill. by author. Burke, 1982. Subj: City.

Iwamatsu, Jun *see* Yashima, Tarō

Iwamura, Kazuo. *The fourteen forest mice and the harvest moon watch* ill. by author. Gareth Stevens, 1991. ISBN 0-8368-0497-X Subj: Animals – mice. Forest, woods. Moon. Seasons – fall.

The fourteen forest mice and the spring meadow picnic ill. by author. Gareth Stevens, 1991. ISBN 0-8368-0498-8 Subj: Activities – picnicking. Animals – mice. Forest, woods. Seasons – spring.

The fourteen forest mice and the summer laundry day ill. by author. Gareth Stevens, 1991. ISBN 0-8368-0576-3 Subj: Animals – mice. Forest, woods. Laundry. Seasons – summer.

The fourteen forest mice and the winter sledding day ill. by author. Gareth Stevens, 1991. ISBN 0-8368-0499-6 Subj: Animals – mice. Forest, woods. Seasons – winter. Sports – sledding.

Tan Tan's hat ill. by author. Bradbury, 1983. Subj: Animals – monkeys. Clothing – hats.

Tan Tan's suspenders ill. by author. Bradbury, 1983. Subj: Animals – monkeys. Clothing.

Ton and Pon: big and little ill. by author. Bradbury, 1984. Subj: Animals – dogs. Concepts – size. Friendship.

Ton and Pon: two good friends ill. by author. Bradbury, 1984. Subj: Animals – dogs. Friendship.

Iwasaki, Chihiro. *The birthday wish* ill. by author. McGraw-Hill, 1974, 1972. Subj: Behavior – wishing. Birthdays. Weather – snow.

Staying home alone on a rainy day ill. by author. McGraw-Hill, 1968. Subj: Family life. Family life – only child. Weather – rain.

What's fun without a friend? ill. by author. McGraw-Hill, 1972. Subj: Animals – dogs. Sea and seashore.

Will you be my friend? ill. by author. McGraw-Hill, 1970. Subj: Friendship.

Izawa, Yohji. *One evening* (Funakoshi, Canna)

Jabar, Cynthia. *Bored blue? Think what you can do!* ill. by author. Little, 1991. ISBN 0-316-43458-2 Subj: Activities. Poetry, rhyme.

Party day! ill. by author. Little, 1987. ISBN 0-316-43456-6 Subj: Animals – rabbits. Birthdays. Counting, numbers.

Shimmy shake earthquake: don't forget to dance poems ed. and ill. by Cynthia Jaber. Little, 1992. ISBN 0-316-43459-0 Subj: Activities – dancing. Poetry, rhyme.

Jack and the beanstalk. *The history of Mother Twaddle and the marvelous achievements of her son Jack* ill. by Paul Galdone. Seabury Pr., 1974. A verse version of Jack and the beanstalk, written by Basil T. Blackwood [B.A.T.] and pub. in 1807 by J. Harris, London Subj: Folk and fairy tales. Giants. Plants. Poetry, rhyme.

Jack and the beanstalk retold and ill. by Val Biro. Oxford Univ. Pr, 1990. ISBN 0-19-278008-5 Subj: Folk and fairy tales. Giants.

Jack and the beanstalk adapt. and ill. by Lorinda Bryan Cauley. Putnam's, 1983. Subj: Folk and fairy tales. Giants.

Jack and the beanstalk ill. by Ed Parker. Troll Assoc., 1979. Subj: Folk and fairy tales. Giants.

Jack and the beanstalk adapt. and ill. by Tony Ross. Delacorte, 1981. Subj: Folk and fairy tales. Giants.

Jack and the beanstalk ill. by William Stobbs. Dial Pr., 1966. Subj: Folk and fairy tales. Giants.

Jack and the beanstalk retold by Susan Pearson; ill. by James Warhola. Simon and Schuster, 1989. ISBN 0-671-67196-0 Subj: Folk and fairy tales. Giants.

Jack and the beanstalk retold by Beatrice Schenk De Regniers; ill. by Anne Wilsdorf. Atheneum, 1985. ISBN 0-689-31174-5 Subj: Folk and fairy tales. Giants. Poetry, rhyme.

Jack the giant killer: Jack's first and finest adventure retold in verse as well as other useful information about giants including how to shake hands with a giant retold by Beatrice Schenk De Regniers; ill. by Anne Wilsdorf. Atheneum, 1987. ISBN 0-689-31218-0 Subj: Folk and fairy tales. Giants. Poetry, rhyme.

Jack the giantkiller adapt. and ill. by Tony Ross. David & Charles, 1987. ISBN 0-862-64060-1 Subj: Folk and fairy tales. Giants.

Jack Sprat. *The life of Jack Sprat, his wife and his cat* retold and ill. by Paul Galdone. McGraw-Hill, 1969. Subj: Animals – cats. Family life. Food. Nursery rhymes.

Jacka, Martin. *Waiting for Billy* ill. by author. Watts, 1991. ISBN 0-531-08533-3 Subj: Animals – dogs. Animals – dolphins. Animals – horses. Foreign lands – Australia.

Jackson, Ellen B. *Ants can't dance* ill. by Frank Remkiewicz. Macmillan, 1991. ISBN 0-02-747661-8 Subj: Behavior – disbelief.

The bear in the bathtub ill. by Margot Apple. Addison-Wesley, 1981. Subj: Activities – bathing. Animals – bears. Character traits – cleanliness.

Jackson, Jacqueline. *Chicken ten thousand* ill. by Barbara Morrow. Little, 1968. Subj: Birds – chickens. Science.

Jackson, Richard. *Iktomi and the boulder* (Goble, Paul)

Jacobs, Daniel. *What does it do? Inventions then and now* ill. with photos. Raintree, 1990. ISBN 0-817293586-8 Subj: Machines.

Jacobs, Joseph. *The crock of gold: being "The pedlar of Swaffham"* ill. by William Stobbs. Follett, 1971. Subj: Careers – peddlers. Dreams. Folk and fairy tales. Foreign lands – England.

Hereafterthis ill. by Paul Galdone. McGraw-Hill, 1973. Subj: Animals. Behavior – mistakes. Crime. Farms. Folk and fairy tales.

Hudden and Dudden and Donald O'Neary ill. by Doris Burn. Coward, 1968. Subj: Behavior – greed. Folk and fairy tales. Foreign lands – Ireland.

Johnny-cake ill. by Emma Lillian Brock. Putnam's, 1967. Subj: Cumulative tales. Folk and fairy tales. Food.

Johnny-cake ill. by William Stobbs. Viking, 1972, 1967. Subj: Cumulative tales. Folk and fairy tales. Food.

Lazy Jack ill. by Barry Wilkinson. World, 1969. Subj: Character traits – foolishness. Character traits – laziness. Folk and fairy tales.

Master of all masters ill. by Anne F. Rockwell. Grosset, 1972. Subj: Folk and fairy tales.

Old Mother Wiggle-Waggle ill. by William Stobbs. Bodley Head, 1980. Subj: Folk and fairy tales.

Tattercoats ill. by Margot Tomes. Putnam, 1989. ISBN 0-399-21584-0 Subj: Emotions – love. Family life – grandfathers. Folk and fairy tales. Foreign lands – England. Royalty – princes.

The three sillies ill. by Paul Galdone. Houghton, 1981. Subj: Folk and fairy tales.

Jacobs, Leland B. *Is somewhere always far away?* ill. by John E. Johnson. Holt, 1967. Subj: Character traits – questioning. Poetry, rhyme.

Jaffe, Marjorie. *Albert the running bear's exercise book* (Isenberg, Barbara)

Jaffe, Rona. *Last of the wizards* ill. by Erik Blegvad. Simon and Schuster, 1961. Subj: Behavior – wishing. Character traits – cleverness.

Jagendorf, Moritz A. *Kwi-na the eagle and other Indian tales* ill. by Jack Endewelt; consultant: Carolyn W. Field. Silver Burdett, 1968. Subj: Indians of North America. Folk and fairy tales.

Jakes, John. *Susanna of the Alamo* ill. by Paul Bacon. Harcourt, 1990. ISBN 0-15-200595-1 Subj: Character traits – bravery. U.S. history.

Jam, Teddy. *Night cars* ill. by Eric Beddows. Watts, 1989. ISBN 0-531-08393-4 Subj: Babies. City. Family life – fathers. Night. Poetry, rhyme.

James, Betsy. *The dream stair* ill. by Richard Jesse Watson. HarperCollins, 1990. ISBN 0-06-022788-5 Subj: Dreams. Ethnic groups in the U.S. Family life – grandmothers. Sleep.

He wakes me ill. by Helen K. Davie. Watts, 1991. ISBN 0-531-08554-6 Subj: Animals – cats. Pets.

James, Shirley Kerby. *Going to a horse farm* ill. by Laura Jacques. Charlesbridge, 1992. ISBN 0-88106-477-7 Subj: Animals – horses. Farms.

James, Simon. *Dear Mr. Blueberry* ill. by author. Macmillan, 1991. ISBN 0-689-50529-9 Subj: Animals – whales. Careers – teachers. Imagination. Letters.

My friend whale ill. by author. Bantam, 1991. ISBN 0-553-07065-7 Subj: Animals – whales.

Sally and the limpet ill. by author. Macmillan, 1991. ISBN 0-689-50528-0 Subj: Crustacea. Ecology. Sea and seashore.

Jameson, Cynthia. *The house of five bears* ill. by Lorinda Bryan Cauley. Putnam's, 1978. Subj: Character traits – cleverness. Folk and fairy tales. Foreign lands – Russia.

Janice. *Angélique* ill. by Roger Antoine Duvoisin. McGraw-Hill, 1960. Subj: Animals – dogs. Behavior – bullying. Birds – ducks.

Little Bear marches in the St. Patrick's Day parade ill. by Mariana. Subj: Animals – bears. Holidays – St. Patrick's Day. Parades.

Little Bear's Christmas ill. by Mariana. Lothrop, 1964. Subj: Animals – bears. Character traits – generosity. Hibernation. Holidays – Christmas.

Little Bear's New Year's party ill. by Mariana. Lothrop, 1973. Subj: Animals – bears. Holidays – New Year's. Parties.

Little Bear's pancake party ill. by Mariana. Lothrop, 1960. Subj: Animals – bears. Food. Parties. Seasons – spring.

Little Bear's Sunday breakfast ill. by Mariana. Lothrop, 1958. Subj: Animals – bears. Food.

Little Bear's Thanksgiving ill. by Mariana. Lothrop, 1967. Subj: Animals – bears. Holidays – Thanksgiving.

Minette ill. by Alain. McGraw-Hill, 1959. Subj: Animals – cats.

Mr. and Mrs. Button's wonderful watchdogs ill. by Roger Antoine Duvoisin. Lothrop, 1978. Subj: Animals – dogs. Crime.

Janosch. *Dear snowman* ill. by author. Collins, 1969. Subj: Seasons – winter. Snowmen. Weather – snow.

Hey Presto! You're a bear! tr. by Klauss Flugge; ill. by author. Little, 1980. Subj: Imagination.

Joshua and the magic fiddle ill. by author. Collins, 1967. Subj: Magic. Moon. Music.

Just one apple tr. by Refna Wilkin; ill. by author. Walck, 1965. Subj: Behavior – wishing. Dragons.

The magic auto ill. by author. Crown, 1971. Translation of Das Regenauto Subj: Automobiles. Magic.

Tonight at nine ill. by author. Walck, 1967. Translation of Heute um neune hinter der Scheune Subj: Animals. Music. Poetry, rhyme.

The trip to Panama tr. by Anthea Bell; ill. by author. Little, 1978. Translation of Oh, wie schon ist Panama Subj: Activities – traveling. Foreign lands – Panama.

A January fog will freeze a hog : *and other weather folklore* comp. and ed. by Hubert Davis; ill. by John Wallner. Crown, 1977. Subj: Folk and fairy tales. Weather.

Jaques, Faith. *Tilly's house* ill. by author. Atheneum, 1979. Subj: Houses. Toys – dolls.

Tilly's rescue ill. by author. Atheneum, 1981. ISBN 0-689-50175-7 Subj: Behavior – lost. Character traits – bravery. Friendship. Holidays – Christmas. Toys – dolls.

Jaquith, Priscilla. *Bo Rabbit smart for true: folktales from the Gullah* ill. by Ed Young. Putnam's, 1981. Subj: Animals – rabbits. Folk and fairy tales. Noise, sounds.

Jarrell, Mary. *The knee baby* ill. by Symeon Shimin. Farrar, 1973. Subj: Babies. Family life. Family life – grandmothers.

Jarrell, Randall. *A bat is born* ill. by John Schoenherr. Doubleday, 1978. Subj: Animals – bats. Birth. Poetry, rhyme.

The fisherman and his wife (Grimm, Jacob)

The golden bird (Grimm, Jacob)

The rabbit catcher and other fairy tales (Bechstein, Ludwig)

Jaynes, Ruth M. *Benny's four hats* ill. by Harvey Mandlin. Bowmar, 1967. Subj: Clothing – hats. Ethnic groups in the U.S. Participation. Weather.

The biggest house ill. by Jacques Rupp. Bowmar, 1968. Subj: Houses.

Friends! friends! friends! ill. by Harvey Mandlin. Bowmar, 1967. Subj: Ethnic groups in the U.S. Friendship. School.

Melinda's Christmas stocking ill. by Richard George. Bowmar, 1968. Subj: Ethnic groups in the U.S. – Mexican-Americans. Holidays – Christmas. Senses – hearing. Senses – seeing. Senses – smelling. Senses – tasting. Senses – touching.

Tell me please! What's that? ill. by Harvey Mandlin. Bowmar, 1968. Subj: Animals. Ethnic groups in the U.S. Ethnic groups in the U.S. – Mexican-Americans. Foreign languages.

That's what it is! ill. by Harvey Mandlin. Bowmar, 1968. Subj: Ethnic groups in the U.S. Ethnic groups in the U.S. – Mexican-Americans. Insects.

Three baby chicks ill. by Harvey Mandlin. Bowmar, 1967. Subj: Birds – chickens. School.

What is a birthday child? ill. by Harvey Mandlin. Bowmar, 1967. Subj: Birthdays. Character traits – individuality. Ethnic groups in the U.S. Ethnic groups in the U.S. – Mexican-Americans.

Jeake, Samuel *see* Aiken, Conrad Potter

Jefferds, Vincent. *Disney's elegant ABC book* Simon and Schuster, 1983. Subj: ABC books.

Disney's elegant book of manners Simon & Schuster, 1985. ISBN 0-671-60507-0 Subj: Etiquette. Poetry, rhyme.

Jeffers, Susan. *All the pretty horses* ill. by author. Macmillan, 1974. Subj: Animals – horses. Bedtime. Sleep.

Forest of dreams (Wells, Rosemary)

The three jovial huntsmen (Mother Goose)

Wild Robin ill. by author. Dutton, 1976. Based on a tale in Little Prudy's fairy book by R. S. Clarke Subj: Behavior – misbehavior. Foreign lands – Scotland.

Jeffery, Graham. *Thomas the tortoise* ill. by author. Crown, 1988. ISBN 0-517-57043-2 Subj: Character traits – individuality. Character traits – kindness to animals. Reptiles – turtles, tortoises.

Jenkin-Pearce, Susie. *Bad Boris and the new kitten* ill. by author. Macmillan, 1987. ISBN 0-02-747620-0 Subj: Animals – cats. Animals – elephants. Emotions – envy, jealousy.

Bad Boris goes to school ill. by author. Macmillan, 1989. ISBN 0-02-747621-9 Subj: Animals. School.

Boris's big ache ill. by author. Dial, 1989. ISBN 0-8037-0551-4 Subj: Animals – elephants. Behavior – growing up. Teeth.

The enchanted garden ill. by author. Oxford Univ. Pr., 1989. ISBN 0-19-279845-6 Subj: Gardens, gardening. Imagination.

Percy Short and Cuthbert ill. by author. Viking, 1991. ISBN 0-670-82803-3 Subj: Animals – hippopotami. Birds – pelicans. Behavior – dissatisfaction. Friendship.

Jenkins, Christopher N. H. *The little weaver of Thái-Yên Village* (Trân-Khánh-Tuyêt)

Jenkins, Jessica. *Thinking about colors* ill. by author. Dutton, 1992. ISBN 0-525-44908-6 Subj: Concepts – color. Emotions. Ethnic groups in the U.S.

Jenkins, Jordan. *Learning about love* ill. by Gene Ruggles. Children's Pr., 1979. Subj: Emotions – love. Family life – mothers. Illness.

Jennings, Linda M. *Coppelia* ill. by Krystyna Turska. Silver Burdett, 1984. ISBN 0-382-09241-4 Subj: Activities – dancing. Folk and fairy tales. Toys – dolls.

Crispin and the dancing piglet ill. by Krystyna Turska. Silver Burdett, 1986. ISBN 0-382-09242-2 Subj: Activities – dancing. Animals – pigs. Behavior – seeking better things.

The golden goose (Grimm, Jacob)

The musicians of Bremen (Grimm, Jacob)

The sleeping beauty: the story of the ballet ill. by Francesca Crespi. David & Charles, 1987. ISBN 0-340-33518-1 Subj: Activities – dancing. Folk and fairy tales.

The wolf and the seven little kids (Grimm, Jacob)

Jennings, Michael. *The bears who came to breakfix* ill. by Tom Dunnington. Children's Pr., 1977. Subj: Animals – bears. Dreams. Family life – mothers. Moving.

Robin Goodfellow and the giant dwarf ill. by Tomie de Paola. McGraw-Hill, 1981. Subj: Behavior – trickery. Giants.

Jennings, Sharon. *When Jeremiah found Mrs. Ming* ill. by Mireille Levert. Firefly, 1992. ISBN 1-55037-237-8 Subj: Activities. Behavior – boredom.

Jenny, Anne. *The fantastic story of King Brioche the First* ill. by Joycelyne Pache. Lothrop, 1970. Translation by Catherine Barton from La fantastique histoire d roi Brioche Ier Subj: Activities – flying. School.

Jensen, Helen Zane. *When Panda came to our house* ill. by author. Dial Pr., 1985. ISBN 0-8037-0236-1 Subj: Activities. Animals – pandas. Foreign lands – China.

Jensen, Patricia. *The mess* ill. by Molly Delaney. Children's Pr., 1990. ISBN 0-516-05357-4 Subj: Activities – playing. Behavior – messy. Poetry, rhyme.

Jensen, Virginia Allen. *Cat alley* (Olsen, Ib Spang)

Catching: a book for blind and sighted children with pictures to feel as well as to see ill. by author. Putnam's, 1984. Subj: Concepts – shape. Format, unusual. Handicaps – blindness. Senses – seeing.

Red thread riddles by Virginia Allen Jensen and Polly Edman; ill. by authors. Putnam's, 1980. Subj: Handicaps – blindness. Riddles. Senses – seeing.

Sara and the door ill. by Ann Strugnell. Addison-Wesley, 1977. Subj: Character traits – perseverance. Clothing. Ethnic groups in the U.S. – Afro-Americans.

What's that? ill. by Dorcas Woodbury Haller. Collins-World, 1979. Subj: Concepts. Handicaps – blindness. Senses – seeing.

Jeram, Anita. *Bill's belly button* ill. by author. Little, 1991. ISBN 0-316-46114-8 Subj: Anatomy. Animals – elephants. Behavior – losing things. Zoos.

It was Jake ill. by author. Little, 1991. ISBN 0-316-46120-2 Subj: Animals – dogs. Behavior – lying. Behavior – misbehavior. Pets.

Jerome, Judson. *I never saw...* ill. by Helga Aichinger. Albert Whitman, 1974. Subj: Poetry, rhyme.

Jeschke, Susan. *Angela and Bear* ill. by author. Holt, 1979. Subj: Animals – bears. Imagination – imaginary friends. Magic.

The devil did it ill. by author. Holt, 1979. Subj: Animals – bears. Imagination – imaginary friends.

Firerose ill. by author. Holt, 1974. Subj: Careers – fortune tellers. Dragons. Humor. Magic.

Lucky's choice ill. by author. Scholastic, 1987. ISBN 0-590-40520-9 Subj: Animals – cats. Behavior – needing someone. Behavior – running away. Friendship.

Mia, Grandma and the genie ill. by author. Holt, 1978. Subj: Fairies. Family life – grandmothers. Magic.

Perfect the pig ill. by author. Holt, 1981. Subj: Activities – flying. Animals – pigs.

Rima and Zeppo ill. by author. Dutton, 1976. Subj: Magic. Witches.

Tamar and the tiger ill. by author. Holt, 1980. Subj: Imagination.

Jessell, Camilla. *The kitten book* ill. by author. Candlewick Pr., 1992. ISBN 1-56402-020-7 Subj: Animals – cats. Birth.

The puppy book ill. by author. Candlewick Pr., 1992. ISBN 1-56402-021-5 Subj: Animals – dogs. Birth.

Jewell, Nancy. *ABC cat* ill. by Ann Schweninger. Harper, 1983. Subj: ABC books. Animals – cats. Poetry, rhyme.

Bus ride ill. by Ronald Himler. Harper, 1978. Subj: Buses.

The snuggle bunny ill. by Mary Chalmers. Harper, 1972. Subj: Animals – rabbits. Emotions – love.

Time for Uncle Joe ill. by Joan Sandin. Harper, 1981. Subj: Death. Emotions. Family life – aunts, uncles.

Try and catch me ill. by Leonard Weisgard. Harper, 1972. Subj: Activities – playing. Ecology. Friendship. Imagination.

Jijii, Hanasaka. *The old man who made the trees bloom* (Shibano, Tamizo)

Jitodai, Hitomi. *I wish I had a big, big tree* (Sato, Satoru)

Joerns, Consuelo. *The foggy rescue* ill. by author. Four Winds Pr., 1980. Subj: Animals – mice. Boats, ships. Behavior – lost.

The forgotten bear ill. by author. Four Winds Pr., 1978. Subj: Behavior – lost. Toys – teddy bears.

The lost and found house ill. by author. Four Winds Pr., 1979. Subj: Animals – mice. Houses.

Oliver's escape ill. by author. Four Winds Pr., 1981. Subj: Animals. Animals – dogs. Behavior – running away. Friendship.

John, Naomi. *Roadrunner* ill. by Peter and Virginia Parnall. Dutton, 1980. Subj: Birds. Desert.

Johnson, Angela. *Do like Kyla* ill. by James E. Ransome. Watts, 1990. ISBN 0-531-08452-3 Subj: Ethnic groups in the U.S. – Afro-Americans. Family life – brothers. Family life – sisters.

The leaving morning ill. by David Soman. Watts, 1992. ISBN 0-531-08592-9 Subj: Emotions. Ethnic groups in the U.S. – Afro-Americans. Family life. Moving.

One of three ill. by David Soman. Watts, 1991. ISBN 0-531-08555-4 Subj: Ethnic groups in the U.S. – Afro-Americans. Family life – sisters.

Tell me a story, mama ill. by David Soman. Watts, 1989. ISBN 0-531-05794-1 Subj: Family life – mothers.

When I am old with you ill. by David Soman. Watts, 1990. ISBN 0-531-08484-1 Subj: Ethnic groups in the U.S. – Afro-Americans. Family life – grandfathers. Old age.

Johnson, B. J. *A hat like that* by B. J. Johnson and Susan Aiello; ill. by authors. St. Martin's, 1986. ISBN 0-312-36416-4 Subj: Clothing – hats. Format, unusual – toy and movable books. Poetry, rhyme.

My blanket Burt by B. J. Johnson and Susan Aiello; ill. by authors. St. Martin's, 1986. ISBN 0-312-55600-4 Subj: Behavior – losing things. Format, unusual – toy and movable books. Poetry, rhyme.

Johnson, Bruce H. *Apples, alligators, and also alphabets* (Johnson, Odette)

Johnson, Crockett. *The blue ribbon puppies* ill. by author. Harper, 1958. Subj: Animals – dogs. Imagination. Toys.

Ellen's lion ill. by author. Harper, 1959. Subj: Imagination. Toys.

The emperor's gift ill. by author. Holt, 1965. Subj: Character traits. Character traits – generosity. Royalty – emperors.

The frowning prince ill. by author. Harper, 1959. Subj: Royalty – princes.

Harold and the purple crayon ill. by author. Harper, 1955. Subj: Art. Humor. Imagination.

Harold at the North Pole ill. by author. Harper, 1957. Subj: Holidays – Christmas. Imagination.

Harold's ABC: another purple crayon adventure ill. by author. Harper, 1963. Subj: ABC books. Imagination.

Harold's circus ill. by author. Harper, 1959. Subj: Circus. Humor. Imagination.

Harold's fairy tale: further adventures with the purple crayon ill. by author. Harper, 1956. Subj: Folk and fairy tales. Imagination.

Harold's trip to the sky ill. by author. Harper, 1957. Subj: Imagination. Space and space ships.

A picture for Harold's room ill. by author. Harper, 1960. Subj: Art. Imagination.

Terrible terrifying Toby ill. by author. Harper, 1957. Subj: Animals – dogs.

Time for spring ill. by author. Harper, 1957. Subj: Seasons – spring. Snowmen.

Upside down ill. by author. Albert Whitman, 1969. Subj: Animals – kangaroos. Concepts – up and down. Humor. World.

We wonder what will Walter be? When he grows up ill. by author. Holt, 1964. Subj: Animals. Behavior – growing up.

Will spring be early? ill. by author. Crowell, 1959. Subj: Animals – groundhogs. Holidays – Groundhog Day. Seasons – spring.

Johnson, Dolores. *The best bug to be* ill. by author. Macmillan, 1992. ISBN 0-02-747842-4 Subj: Ethnic groups in the U.S. – Afro-Americans. School. Theater.

What kind of baby-sitter is this? ill. by author. Macmillan, 1991. ISBN 0-02-747846-7 Subj: Activities – baby-sitting. Ethnic groups in the U.S. – Afro-Americans.

What will mommy do when I'm at school? ill. by author. Macmillan, 1990. ISBN 0-02-747845-9 Subj: Ethnic groups in the U.S. – Afro-Americans. Family life – mothers.

Johnson, Donna Kay. *Brighteyes* ill. by author. Holt, 1978. Subj: Animals – raccoons. Handicaps – blindness. Senses – seeing.

Johnson, Elizabeth. *All in free but Janey* ill. by Trina Schart Hyman. Little, 1968. Subj: Games. Imagination.

Johnson, Evelyne. *The cow in the kitchen: a folk tale* ill. by Anthony Rao. Simon and Schuster, 1983. Subj: Behavior – dissatisfaction. Character traits – foolishness.

Johnson, Jane. *Bertie on the beach* ill. by author. Four Winds Pr., 1981. Subj: Circus. Dreams. Sea and seashore.

Sybil and the blue rabbit ill. by author. Doubleday, 1980. Subj: Imagination. Toys.

Today I thought I'd run away ill. by author. Dutton, 1986. ISBN 0-525-44193-X Subj: Bedtime. Behavior – running away. Monsters.

Johnson, Jean. *Teachers A to Z* photos. by author. Walker, 1987. ISBN 0-8027-6677-3 Subj: ABC books. Careers – teachers. School.

Johnson, John E. *My first book of things* ill. by author. Random House, 1979. Subj: Format, unusual – board books.

Johnson, Louise. *Malunda* ill. by Edward Durose. Carolrhoda, 1982. Subj: Animals – rhinoceros. Illness. Zoos.

Johnson, Mildred D. *Wait, skates!* ill. by Tom Dunnington. Children's Pr., 1983. Subj: Activities – playing. Sports – roller skating.

Johnson, Neil. *Fire and silk: flying in a hot air balloon* photos. by author. Little, 1991. ISBN 0-316-46959-9 Subj: Activities – ballooning. Activities – flying.

Johnson, Odette. *Apples, alligators, and also alphabets* by Odette and Bruce H. Johnson; ill. by authors. Oxford Univ. Pr., 1991. ISBN 0-19-540757-1 Subj: ABC books.

One prickly porcupine Odette and Bruce H. Johnson; ill. by authors. Oxford Univ. Pr., 1992. ISBN 0-19-540834-9 Subj: Birthdays. Counting, numbers. Giants. Tongue twisters.

Johnson, Pamela. *A mouse's tale* ill. by author. Harcourt, 1991. ISBN 0-15-256032-7 Subj: Animals – mice. Behavior – collecting things. Boats, ships. Sea and seashore.

Johnson, Russell. *Trouble at Christmas* ill. by Bernadette Watts. North-South, 1991. ISBN 1-55858-116-2 Subj: Animals. Holidays – Christmas.

Johnson, Ryerson. *Let's walk up the wall* ill. by Eva Cellini. Holiday, 1967. Subj: Participation.

Upstairs and downstairs ill. by Lisl Weil. Crowell, 1962. Subj: Concepts.

Johnson, Walter Ryerson *see* Johnson, Ryerson

Johnston, Deborah. *Mathew Michael's beastly day* ill. by Seymour Chwast. Harcourt, 1992. ISBN 0-15-200521-8 Subj: Animals. Behavior – bad day. Family life. Imagination. Morning. School.

Johnston, Johanna. *Penguin's way* ill. by Leonard Weisgard. Doubleday, 1962. Subj: Birds – penguins. Science.

Sugarplum ill. by Marvin Bileck. Knopf, 1955. Subj: Character traits – smallness. Toys – dolls.

Whale's way ill. by Leonard Weisgard. Doubleday, 1965. Subj: Animals – whales. Science.

Johnston, Mary Anne. *Sing me a song* ill. by John Magine. Children's Pr., 1977. Subj: Animals – rabbits. Songs.

Johnston, Tony. *The badger and the magic fan* ill. by Tomie de Paola. Putnam, 1990. ISBN 0-399-21945-5 Subj: Animals – noses. Animals – badgers. Behavior – trickery. Folk and fairy tales. Foreign lands – Japan. Magic.

Farmer Mack measures his pig ill. by Megan Lloyd. Harper, 1986. ISBN 0-06-023018-5 Subj: Animals – pigs. Behavior – boasting. Farms.

Four scary stories ill. by Tomie de Paola. Putnam's, 1978. Subj: Ghosts. Goblins. Monsters.

Grandpa's song ill. by Brad Sneed. Dial, 1991. ISBN 0-8037-0802-5 Subj: Family life – grandfathers. Old age. Songs.

I'm gonna tell mama I want an iguana ill. by Lillian Hoban. Putnam, 1990. ISBN 0-399-21931-X Subj: Family life. Poetry, rhyme. Sibling rivalry.

Lorenzo the naughty parrot ill. by Leo Politi. Harcourt, 1992. ISBN 0-15-249350-6 Subj: Behavior – misbehavior. Birds – parakeets, parrots. Foreign lands – Mexico. Holidays – Christmas. Parties.

Mole and Troll trim the tree ill. by Wallace Tripp. Putnam's, 1974. ISBN 0-399-60909-1 Subj: Animals – moles. Behavior – sharing. Holidays – Christmas. Seasons – winter. Trees. Trolls.

Pages of music ill. by Tomie de Paola. Putnam's, 1988. ISBN 0-399-21436-4 Subj: Activities – painting. Islands. Music.

The quilt story ill. by Tomie de Paola. Putnam's, 1984. ISBN 0-399-21009-1 Subj: Family life. Moving. Quilts.

Slither McCreep and his brother, Joe ill. by Victoria Chess. Harcourt, 1992. ISBN 0-15-276100-4 Subj: Family life – brothers. Reptiles – snakes. Sibling rivalry.

Soup bone ill. by Margot Tomes. Harcourt, 1990. ISBN 0-15-277255-3 Subj: Anatomy – skeletons. Friendship. Holidays – Halloween.

The vanishing pumpkin ill. by Tomie de Paola. Putnam's, 1983. Subj: Holidays – Halloween. Witches.

Whale song ill. by Ed Young. Putnam's, 1987. ISBN 0-399-21402-X Subj: Animals – whales. Counting, numbers.

The witch's hat ill. by Margot Tomes. Putnam's, 1984. Subj: Clothing – hats. Magic. Witches.

Yonder ill. by Lloyd Bloom. Dial Pr., 1988. ISBN 0-8037-0278-7 Subj: Cumulative tales. Seasons.

Jolliffe, Anne. *From pots to plastics* ill. by author. Hawthorn, 1965. Subj: Science.

Water, wind and wheels ill. by author. Hawthorn, 1965. Subj: Science. Water.

Joly-Berbesson, Fanny. *Marceau Bonappetit* ill. by Agnes Mathieu. Carolrhoda, 1989. ISBN 0-87614-369-9 Subj: Animals – mice. Behavior – seeking better things. Food.

Jonas, Ann. *Aardvarks, disembark!* ill. by author. Greenwillow, 1990. ISBN 0-688-07207-0 Subj: ABC books. Animals. Animals – endangered animals. Religion – Noah.

Holes and peeks ill. by author. Greenwillow, 1984. Subj: Caldecott award honor book. Emotions – fear. Problem solving.

Now we can go ill. by author. Greenwillow, 1986. ISBN 0-688-04803-X Subj: Toys.

The quilt ill. by author. Greenwillow, 1984. Subj: Bedtime. Dreams. Quilts.

Reflections ill. by author. Greenwillow, 1987. ISBN 0-688-06141-9 Subj: Concepts. Format, unusual.

Round trip ill. by author. Greenwillow, 1983. ISBN 0-688-01781-9 Subj: Activities – traveling. City.

The thirteenth clue ill. by author. Greenwillow, 1992. ISBN 0-688-09742-1 Subj: Format, unusual. Problem solving.

The trek ill. by author. Greenwillow, 1985. ISBN 0-688-04799-8 Subj: Activities – walking. Animals. Games. Imagination.

Two bear cubs ill. by author. Greenwillow, 1982. Subj: Animals – bears. Behavior – lost. Family life – mothers.

When you were a baby ill. by author. Greenwillow, 1982. Subj: Activities. Behavior – growing up.

Where can it be? ill. by author. Greenwillow, 1986. ISBN 0-688-05246-0 Subj: Behavior – losing things. Format, unusual – toy and movable books.

Jonasson, Dianne. *Tuan* (Boholm-Olsson, Eva)

Jones, Brian. *Space: a three-dimensional journey* ill. by Richard Clifton-Day. Dial, 1991. ISBN 0-8037-0759-2 Subj: Astronomy. Science. Space and space ships.

Jones, Carol. *This old man* ill. by author. Houghton, 1990. ISBN 0-395-54699-0 Subj: Counting, numbers. Elves and little people. Farms. Format, unusual. Music. Songs.

Jones, Chuck. *William the backwards skunk* ill. by author. Crown, 1987. ISBN 0-517-56063-1 Subj: Animals – skunks. Behavior – imitation. Forest, woods.

Jones, Harold. *Tales from Æsop* (Æsop)

There and back again ill. by author. Atheneum, 1977. Subj: Toys.

Jones, Hettie. *The trees stand shining: poetry of the North American Indians* ill. by Robert Andrew Parker. Dial Pr., 1971. Subj: Indians of North America. Poetry, rhyme.

Jones, Jessie Mae Orton. *A little child: the Christmas miracle told in Bible verses* ill. by Elizabeth Orton Jones. Viking, 1946. Subj: Holidays – Christmas. Religion.

Small rain: verses from the Bible ill. by Elizabeth Orton Jones. Viking, 1943. Subj: Caldecott award honor book. Poetry, rhyme. Religion.

Jones, Malcolm. *Jump!* (Harris, Joel Chandler)

Jones, Maurice. *I'm going on a dragon hunt* ill. by Charlotte Firmin. Four Winds Pr., 1987. ISBN 0-02-748000-3 Subj: Dragons. Sports – hunting.

Jones, Penelope. *I didn't want to be nice* ill. by Rosalie Orlando. Bradbury Pr., 1977. Subj: Animals – squirrels. Birthdays. Parties.

I'm not moving! ill. by Amy Aitken. Bradbury Pr., 1980. Subj: Family life. Moving.

Jones, Rebecca C. *The biggest (and best) flag that ever flew* ill. by Charles Geer. Cornell Maritime Pr., 1988. ISBN 0-317-67910-4 Subj: U.S. history. War.

The biggest, meanest, ugliest dog in the whole wide world ill. by Wendy Watson. Macmillan, 1982. Subj: Animals – dogs. Character traits – meanness. Friendship.

Down at the bottom of the deep dark sea ill. by Virginia Wright-Frierson. Bradbury Pr., 1991. ISBN 0-02-747901-3 Subj: Emotions – fear. Sand. Sea and seashore.

Matthew and Tilly ill. by Beth Peck. Dutton, 1991. ISBN 0-525-44684-2 Subj: City. Ethnic groups in the U.S. – Afro-Americans. Friendship.

Jong, David Cornel De *see* DeJong, David Cornel

Jonhnson, Bruce H. *One prickly porcupine* (Johnson, Odette)

Joos, Francoise. *The golden snowflake* ill. by author. Little, 1991. ISBN 0-316-47328-6 Subj: Snowmen. Weather – snow.

Joosse, Barbara M. *Better with two* ill. by Catherine Stock. Harper, 1988. ISBN 0-06-023077-0 Subj: Animals – dogs. Death. Pets.

Dinah's mad, bad wishes ill. by Emily Arnold Mc-Cully. HarperCollins, 1989. ISBN 0-06-023099-1 Subj: Emotions – anger. Family life – mothers.

Fourth of July ill. by Emily Arnold McCully. Knopf, 1985. ISBN 0-394-95195-6 Subj: Behavior – growing up. Holidays – Fourth of July. Parades.

Jam day ill. by Emily Arnold McCully. Harper, 1987. ISBN 0-06-023097-5 Subj: Family life. Family life – grandparents.

Mama, do you love me? ill. by Barbara Lavallee. Chronicle Books, 1991. ISBN 0-87701-759-X Subj: Emotions – love. Eskimos. Family life – mothers.

Spiders in the fruit cellar ill. by Kay Chorao. Knopf, 1983. Subj: Emotions – fear. Spiders.

The thinking place ill. by Kay Chorao. Knopf, 1982. Subj: Behavior – misbehavior. Imagination – imaginary friends.

Jordan, Helene J. (Helene Jamieson). *How a seed grows* ill. by Loretta Krupinski Rev. ed. HarperCollins, 1992. ISBN 0-06-020185-1 Subj: Gardens, gardening. Nature. Science. Seeds.

Seeds of wind and water ill. by Nils Hogner. Crowell, 1962. Subj: Plants.

Jordan, June. *Kimako's story* ill. by Kay Burford. Houghton, 1981. ISBN 0-395-31604-9 Subj: Animals – dogs. City. Family life. Pets.

Jorgensen, Gail. *Crocodile Beat* ill. by Patricia Mullins. Bradbury Pr., 1989. ISBN 0-02-748010-0 Subj: Animals. Poetry, rhyme.

Joseph, Lynn. *Coconut kind of day* ill. by Sandra Speidel. Lothrop, 1992. ISBN 0-688-09120-2 Subj: Foreign lands – Trinidad. Islands. Poetry, rhyme.

Joslin, Sesyle. *Baby elephant and the secret wishes* ill. by Leonard Weisgard. Harcourt, 1962. Subj: Animals – elephants. Holidays – Christmas.

Baby elephant goes to China ill. by Leonard Weisgard. Harcourt, 1963. Subj: Animals – elephants. Foreign languages. Sea and seashore.

Baby elephant's trunk ill. by Leonard Weisgard. Harcourt, 1961. Subj: Animals – elephants. Foreign lands – France. Foreign languages.

Brave Baby Elephant ill. by Leonard Weisgard. Harcourt, 1960. Subj: Animals – elephants. Bedtime.

Dear dragon: and other useful letter forms for young ladies and gentlemen engaged in everyday correspondence ill. by Irene Haas. Harcourt, 1962. Subj: Activities – writing. Communication. Dragons. Etiquette. Humor.

Señor Baby Elephant, the pirate ill. by Leonard Weisgard. Harcourt, 1962. Subj: Animals – elephants. Foreign languages. Pirates.

What do you do, dear? ill. by Maurice Sendak. Addison-Wesley, 1961. Subj: Etiquette. Humor.

What do you say, dear? ill. by Maurice Sendak. Addison-Wesley, 1958. Subj: Caldecott award honor book. Etiquette. Humor.

Joyce, Irma. *Never talk to strangers* ill. by George Buckett. Golden Pr., 1967. Subj: Behavior – talking to strangers. Humor. Safety.

Joyce, James. *The cat and the devil* ill. by Richard Erdoes. Dodd, 1965. Subj: Behavior – trickery. Devil.

Joyce, William. *Bently and egg* ill. by author. HarperCollins, 1992. ISBN 0-06-020386-2 Subj: Birds – ducks. Character traits – helpfulness. Eggs. Reptiles – turtles, tortoises.

A day with Wilbur Robinson ill. by author. HarperCollins, 1990. ISBN 0-06-022968-3 Subj: Family life.

Dinosaur Bob: and his adventures with the family Lazardo ill. by author. Harper, 1988. ISBN 0-06-023047-9 Subj: Dinosaurs. Pets.

George shrinks ill. by author. Harper, 1985. ISBN 0-06-023071-1 Subj: Activities – baby-sitting. Concepts – size. Family life.

Joyner, Jerry. *Thirteen* (Charlip, Remy)

Jüchen, Aurel von. *The Holy Night: the story of the first Christmas* tr. from German by Cornelia Schaeffer; ill. by Celestino Piatti. Atheneum, 1968. Subj: Holidays – Christmas. Religion.

Justice, Jennifer. *The tiger* ill. by Graham Allen. Watts, 1979. Subj: Animals – tigers. Science.

Kahl, Virginia. *Away went Wolfgang* ill. by author. Scribner's, 1954. Subj: Animals – dogs. Foreign lands – Austria.

The Baron's booty ill. by author. Scribner's, 1963. Subj: Middle ages. Poetry, rhyme. Royalty.

Droopsi ill. by author. Scribner's, 1958. Subj: Foreign lands – Germany. Music.

The Duchess bakes a cake ill. by author. Scribner's, 1955. Subj: Activities – cooking. Food. Middle ages. Poetry, rhyme. Royalty.

Giants, indeed! ill. by author. Scribner's, 1974. Subj: Giants. Monsters.

How do you hide a monster? ill. by author. Scribner's, 1971. Subj: Monsters. Poetry, rhyme. Sports – hunting.

Maxie ill. by author. Scribner's, 1956. Subj: Animals – dogs. Character traits – perseverance. Foreign lands – Germany. Old age.

The perfect pancake ill. by author. Scribner's, 1960. Subj: Character traits – selfishness. Food. Poetry, rhyme.

Plum pudding for Christmas ill. by author. Scribner's, 1956. Subj: Food. Holidays – Christmas. Poetry, rhyme. Royalty.

Whose cat is that? ill. by author. Scribner's, 1979. Subj: Animals – cats. Cumulative tales.

Kahn, Joan. *Hi, Jock, run around the block* ill. by Whitney Darrow, Jr. Harper, 1978. Subj: City. Poetry, rhyme.

Seesaw ill. by Crosby Newell Bonsall. Harper, 1964. Subj: Games. Toys.

Kahn, Katherine Janus. *The Shofar calls to us* ill. by author. Kar-Ben Copies, 1992. ISBN 0-929371-61-5 Subj: Format, unusual – board books. Holidays – Rosh Hashanah. Jewish culture. Religion.

Kahn, Michèle. *My everyday Spanish word book* tr. from French by Michael Mahler and Gwen Marsh; ill. by Benvenuti. Barron's, 1982. Subj: Foreign languages.

Kahn, Rosemary. *Grandma's hat* ill. by Terry Milne. Viking, 1991. ISBN 0-670-84023-8 Subj: Clothing – hats. Family life – grandmothers. Foreign lands – South Africa.

Kahng, Kim. *The loathsome dragon* (Wiesner, David)

Kaizuki, Kiyonori. *A calf is born* ill. by author. Watts, 1990. ISBN 0-531-08462-0 Subj: Animals – bulls, cows. Birth.

Kalan, Robert. *Blue sea* ill. by Donald Crews. Greenwillow, 1979. Subj: Concepts – size. Fish.

Jump, frog, jump! ill. by Byron Barton. Greenwillow, 1981. Subj: Cumulative tales. Frogs and toads.

Rain ill. by Donald Crews. Greenwillow, 1978. Subj: Weather – rain.

Kalas, Klaus. *The beaver family book* (Kalas, Sybille)

Kalas, Sybille. *The beaver family book* by Sybille and Klaus Kalas; photos. by Sybille Kalas; tr. by Patricia Crampton. Picture Book Studio, 1987. ISBN 0-88708-050-2 Subj: Animals – beavers. Science.

The goose family book tr. by Patricia Crampton; preface by Konrad Lorenz; ill. with photos. Picture Book Studio, 1986. Tr. of Das gänse-kinderbuch ISBN 0-88708-019-7 Subj: Birds – geese.

The penguin family book (Somme, Lauritz)

Kaldhol, Marit. *Goodbye Rune* tr. by Michael Crosby-Jones; adapt. by Catherine Maggs; ill. by Wenche Øyen. Kane/Miller, 1987. Tr. of Farvel, Rune ISBN 0-916291-11-1 Subj: Death. Emotions – sadness. Friendship.

Kalman, Benjamin. *Animals in danger: poems from no man's valley* ill. by Cécile Curtis and Michael Jupp. Random House, 1982. Subj: Animals – endangered animals. Ecology. Poetry, rhyme.

Kalman, Maira. *Hey Willy, see the pyramids!* ill. by author. Viking, 1988. ISBN 0-670-82163-2 Subj: Bedtime. Family life – sisters. Imagination.

Sayonara, Mrs. Kackleman ill. by author. Viking, 1989. ISBN 0-670-82945-5 Subj: Activities – traveling. Foreign lands – Japan.

Kamal, Aleph. *The bird who was an elephant* ill. by Frané Lessac. Lippincott, 1990. ISBN 0-397-32446-4 Subj: Birds. Foreign lands – India.

Kamen, Gloria. *"Paddle," said the swan* ill. by author. Atheneum, 1989. ISBN 0-689-31330-6 Subj: Animals. Poetry, rhyme.

The ringdoves: from the fables of Bidpai ill. by adapt. Atheneum, 1988. ISBN 0-689-31312-8 Subj: Animals. Friendship. Sports – hunting.

Second-hand cat ill. by author. Atheneum, 1992. ISBN 0-689-31631-3 Subj: Animals – cats.

Kanagy, Ruth A. *The park bench* (Takeshita, Fumiko)

Kanao, Keiko. *Kitten up a tree* ill. by author. Knopf, 1987. ISBN 0-394-88817-0 Subj: Animals – cats. Character traits – curiosity. Family life – mothers.

Kandell, Alice. *Max, the music-maker* (Stecher, Miriam B.)

Kandoian, Ellen. *Is anybody up?* ill. by author. Putnam, 1989. ISBN 0-399-21749-5 Subj: Etiquette. Food.

Maybe she forgot ill. by author. Cutton, 1990. ISBN 0-525-65031-8 Subj: Behavior – growing up. Family life – mothers.

Molly's seasons ill. by author. Dutton, 1992. ISBN 0-525-65076-8 Subj: Seasons.

Under the sun ill. by author. Dodd, 1987. ISBN 0-396-09059-1 Subj: Morning. Night. Sun.

Kane, Henry B. *Wings, legs, or fins* photos. and ill. by author. Knopf, 1966. Subj: Animals. Science.

Kangas, Juli. *Fluffy Bunny's friend* ill. by author. Putnam, 1992. ISBN 0-448-40140-1 Subj: Animals – rabbits. Format, unusual – board books. Friendship.

Ginger Kitten's surprise ill. by author. Putnam, 1992. ISBN 0-448-40139-8 Subj: Animals – cats. Format, unusual – board books. Friendship.

Hello, Honey Bear ill. by author. Putnam, 1992. ISBN 0-0448-40141-X Subj: Animals – bears. Format, unusual – board books. Friendship.

Kani, Saru. *The monkey and the crab* (Horio, Seishi)

Kantor, MacKinlay. *The preposterous week* ill. by Kurt Wiese. Putnam's, 1942. Subj: Food. Humor.

Kantor, Sid. *Armando asked "Why?"* (Hulbert, Jay)

Kantrowitz, Mildred. *I wonder if Herbie's home yet* ill. by Tony DeLuna. Parents, 1971. Subj: Friendship.

When Violet died ill. by Emily Arnold McCully. Parents, 1973. Subj: Birds. Death.

Willy Bear ill. by Nancy Winslow Parker. Parents, 1976. Subj: School. Sleep. Toys – teddy bears.

Kaplan, Boche. *Sweet Betsy from Pike* (Abisch, Roz)

Kapp, Paul. *Cock-a-doodle-doo! Cock-a-doodle-dandy!* ill. by Anita Lobel. Harper, 1966. Subj: Music. Songs.

Kark, Nina Mary *see* Bawden, Nina

Karkowsky, Nancy. *Grandma's soup* ill. by Shelly O. Haas. Kar-Ben Copies, 1989. ISBN 0-930494-98-9 Subj: Family life – grandmothers. Illness – Alzheimer's. Jewish culture. Old age.

Karlin, Barbara. *Cinderella* ill. by James Marshall. Little, 1989. ISBN 0-316-54654-2 Subj: Folk and fairy tales. Royalty – princes. Sibling rivalry.

Cinderella (Perrault, Charles)

Karlin, Nurit. *The blue frog* ill. by author. Coward, 1983. Subj: Character traits – being different. Frogs and toads.

The dream factory ill. by author. Lippincott, 1988. ISBN 0-397-32212-7 Subj: Dreams. Sleep.

Little big moose ill. by author. HarperCollins, 1991. ISBN 0-06-021608-5 Subj: Animals – mice. Concepts – size. Self-concept.

The tooth witch ill. by author. Lippincott, 1985. ISBN 0-397-32120-1 Subj: Character traits – kindness. Fairies. Witches.

A train for the king ill. by author. Coward, 1983. Subj: Royalty – kings. Self-concept.

Karlinsky, Ruth Schild. *My first book of Mitzvos* photos. by Isaiah Karlinsky. Feldheim, 1986. ISBN 0-87306-388-0 Subj: Jewish culture. Religion.

Karn, George. *Circus big and small* ill. by author. Little, 1986. ISBN 0-316-30342-9 Subj: Circus. Concepts – opposites. Format, unusual – board books.

Circus colors ill. by author. Little, 1986. ISBN 0-316-30343-7 Subj: Circus. Concepts – color. Format, unusual – board books.

Karsunke, Yaak. *Hello Irina* (Blech, Dietlind)

Kasza, Keiko. *A mother for Choco* ill. by author. Putnam, 1992. ISBN 0-399-21841-6 Subj: Animals. Birds. Emotions – love. Family life – mothers.

The pigs' picnic ill. by author. Putnam's, 1988. ISBN 0-399-21543-3 Subj: Activities – picnicking. Animals – pigs. Character traits – appearance.

When the elephant walks ill. by author. Putnam, 1990. ISBN 0-399-21755-X Subj: Animals. Cumulative tales. Emotions – fear.

The wolf's chicken stew ill. by author. Putnam's, 1987. ISBN 0-399-21400-3 Subj: Animals – wolves. Birds – chickens. Character traits – generosity. Food.

Katz, Bobbi. *The creepy crawly book* ill. by S. D. Schindler. Random House, 1989. ISBN 0-394-82709-0 Subj: Animals. Insects.

Tick-tock, let's read the clock ill. by Carol Nicklaus. Random, 1988. ISBN 0-394-89399-9 Subj: Clocks, watches. Poetry, rhyme. Time.

Katz, Michael Jay. *Ten potatoes in a pot and other counting rhymes* ill. by June Otani. HarperCollins, 1990. ISBN 0-06-023107-6 Subj: Counting, numbers. Poetry, rhyme.

Kauffman, Lois. *What's that noise?* ill. by Allan Eitzen. Lothrop, 1965. Subj: Family life – fathers. Night. Noise, sounds.

Kaufman, Curt. *Hotel boy* by Curt and Gita Kaufman; photos. by Curt Kaufman. Atheneum, 1987. ISBN 0-689-31287-3 Subj: Activities. City. Ethnic groups in the U.S. – Afro-Americans. Family life.

Rajesh by Curt and Gita Kaufman; photos. by Curt Kaufman. Atheneum, 1985. ISBN 0-689-31074-9 Subj: Handicaps. School.

Kaufman, Gita. *Hotel boy* (Kaufman, Curt)

Rajesh (Kaufman, Curt)

Kaufmann, John. *Birds are flying* ill. by author. Crowell, 1979. Subj: Birds. Science.

Flying giants of long ago ill. by author. Crowell, 1984. Subj: Activities – flying. Animals. Birds. Insects. Science.

Kaune, Merriman B. *My own little house* ill. by author. Follett, 1957. Subj: Houses.

Kavanaugh, James J. *The crooked angel* ill. by Elaine Havelock. Nash, 1970. Subj: Angels. Poetry, rhyme.

Kay, Helen. *An egg is for wishing* ill. by Yaroslava. Abelard-Schuman, 1966. Subj: Behavior – animals, dislike of. Behavior – wishing. Eggs. Foreign lands – Ukraine. Holidays – Easter.

One mitten Lewis ill. by Kurt Werth. Lothrop, 1955. Subj: Behavior – losing things. Clothing – gloves.

A stocking for a kitten ill. by Yaroslava. Abelard-Schuman, 1965. Subj: Animals – cats. Family life – grandmothers.

Kay, Ormonde De *see* De Kay, Ormonde

Kaye, Geraldine. *The sea monkey: a picture story from Malaysia* ill. by Gay Galsworthy. Collins-World, 1968. Subj: Animals – monkeys. Foreign lands – Malaysia.

Kaye, Marilyn. *The real tooth fairy* ill. by Helen Cogancherry. Harcourt, 1990. ISBN 0-15-265780-0 Subj: Fairies. Teeth.

Keaney, Leonie. *Zoo day* (Brennan, John)

Keats, Ezra Jack. *Apartment 3* ill. by author. Macmillan, 1971. Subj: City. Ethnic groups in the U.S. – Afro-Americans. Family life. Handicaps – blindness. Music. Senses – seeing.

Clementina's cactus ill. by author. Viking, 1983. Subj: Desert. Weather – storms. Wordless.

Dreams ill. by author. Macmillan, 1974. Subj: Dreams. Ethnic groups in the U.S. – Afro-Americans. Imagination. Night. Sleep.

God is in the mountain ill. by author. Holt, 1966. Subj: Religion.

Goggles ill. by author. Macmillan, 1969. Subj: Behavior – bullying. Caldecott award honor book. City. Ethnic groups in the U.S. – Afro-Americans. Problem solving.

Hi, cat! ill. by author. Macmillan, 1970. Subj: Animals – cats. City. Ethnic groups in the U.S. – Afro-Americans.

Jennie's hat ill. by author. Harper, 1966. Subj: Behavior – dissatisfaction. Character traits – kindness to animals. Clothing – hats.

John Henry ill. by author. Harper, 1965. Subj: Character traits – perseverance. Character traits – pride. Ethnic groups in the U.S. – Afro-Americans. Folk and fairy tales.

Kitten for a day ill. by author. Watts, 1974. Subj: Animals – cats. Animals – dogs. Wordless.

A letter to Amy ill. by author. Harper, 1968. Subj: Ethnic groups in the U.S. – Afro-Americans. Friendship. Letters. Parties. Weather – rain. Weather – wind.

The little drummer boy ill. by author. Macmillan, 1968. Words and music by Katherine Davis, Henry Onorati and Harry Simeonne Subj: Holidays – Christmas. Music. Religion. Songs.

Louie ill. by author. Greenwillow, 1975. Subj: Character traits – shyness. Ethnic groups in the U.S. – Afro-Americans. Puppets.

Louie's search ill. by author. Four Winds Pr., 1980. Subj: Behavior – needing someone. Family life.

Maggie and the pirate ill. by author. Four Winds Pr., 1979. Subj: Death. Pets. Pirates.

My dog is lost! ill. by Ezra Jack Keats. Crowell, 1960. Subj: Animals – dogs. Behavior – lost. Careers – police officers. Ethnic groups in the U.S. Ethnic groups in the U.S. – Puerto Rican-Americans. Foreign languages.

Pet show! ill. by author. Macmillan, 1972. Subj: Animals. Ethnic groups in the U.S. – Afro-Americans. Pets.

Peter's chair ill. by author. Harper, 1967. Subj: Babies. Behavior – sharing. Ethnic groups in the U.S. – Afro-Americans. Family life. Friendship. Furniture – chairs. Self-concept.

Psst, doggie ill. by author. Watts, 1973. Subj: Animals – cats. Animals – dogs. Wordless.

Regards to the man in the moon ill. by author. Four Winds Pr., 1981. Subj: Imagination. Space and space ships.

Skates ill. by author. Watts, 1972. Subj: Activities – playing. Animals – dogs. Ethnic groups in the U.S. – Afro-Americans. Humor. Wordless.

The snowy day ill. by author. Viking, 1962. Subj: Activities – playing. Caldecott award book. Ethnic groups in the U.S. – Afro-Americans. Seasons – winter. Weather – snow.

The trip ill. by author. Greenwillow, 1978. Subj: Emotions – loneliness. Ethnic groups in the U.S. – Afro-Americans. Holidays – Halloween. Imagination. Moving.

Whistle for Willie ill. by author. Viking, 1964. Subj: Activities – whistling. Animals – dogs. Ethnic groups in the U.S. – Afro-Americans. Problem solving. Self-concept.

Keenan, Martha. *The mannerly adventures of Little Mouse* ill. by Meri Shardin. Crown, 1977. Subj: Animals – mice. Etiquette.

Keenen, George. *The preposterous week* ill. by Stanley Mack. Dial Pr., 1971. ISBN 0-8037-7072-3 Subj: Behavior – losing things. Character traits – foolishness. Days of the week, months of the year. Humor. Problem solving.

Keeping, Charles. *Alfie finds the other side of the world* ill. by author. Watts, 1968. Subj: City. Foreign lands – England. Rivers. Weather – fog.

Joseph's yard ill. by author. Watts, 1969. Subj: Gardens, gardening. Poverty.

Molly o' the moors: the story of a pony ill. by author. Collins, 1966. Subj: Animals – horses. Old age.

Through the window ill. by author. Watts, 1970. Subj: City. Foreign lands – England.

Willie's fire-engine ill. by author. Oxford Univ. Pr., 1980. Subj: Activities – playing. Careers – firefighters. Imagination.

Keeshan, Robert. *She loves me, she loves me not* ill. by Maurice Sendak. Harper, 1963. Subj: Games. Holidays – Valentine's Day. Mythical creatures.

Kehoe, Michael. *Road closed* photos. by author. Carolrhoda, 1982. Subj: Roads.

The rock quarry book photos. by author. Carolrhoda, 1981. Subj: Rocks.

Keigwin, R. P. *Thumbelina* (Andersen, H. C. (Hans Christian))

The ugly duckling (Andersen, H. C. (Hans Christian))

Keith, Eros. *Bedita's bad day* ill. by author. Harper, 1973. Subj: Behavior – bad day. Witches.

Nancy's backyard ill. by author. Harper, 1973. Subj: Dreams. Weather – rain.

Rrra-ah ill. by author. Bradbury Pr., 1969. Subj: Frogs and toads. Pets.

Keller, Beverly. *Fiona's bee* ill. by Diane Paterson. Coward, 1975. Subj: Character traits – shyness. Insects – bees.

Pimm's place ill. by Jacqueline Chwast. Coward, 1978. Subj: Behavior – solitude. Character traits – bravery. Emotions – fear.

When mother got the flu ill. by Maxie Chambliss. Coward, 1984. Subj: Behavior – misbehavior. Family life – mothers. Illness.

Keller, Charles. *School daze* ill. by Sam Q. Weissman. Prentice-Hall, 1979. Subj: Humor. Riddles.

Tongue twisters ill. by Ron Fritz. Simon & Schuster, 1989. ISBN 0-671-67123-5 Subj: Poetry, rhyme. Tongue twisters.

Keller, Holly. *A bear for Christmas* ill. by author. Greenwillow, 1986. ISBN 0-688-05989-9 Subj: Behavior – misbehavior. Family life. Holidays – Christmas. Toys – teddy bears.

The best present ill. by author. Greenwillow, 1989. ISBN 0-688-07320-4 Subj: Family life – grandmothers. Hospitals.

Cromwell's glasses ill. by author. Greenwillow, 1982. Subj: Animals – rabbits. Family life. Glasses. Senses – seeing.

Geraldine's big snow ill. by author. Greenwillow, 1988. ISBN 0-688-07514-2 Subj: Animals – pigs. Weather – snow.

Geraldine's blanket ill. by author. Greenwillow, 1984. ISBN 0-688-02540-4 Subj: Animals – pigs. Family life. Toys – dolls.

Goodbye, Max ill. by author. Greenwillow, 1987. ISBN 0-688-06562-7 Subj: Animals – dogs. Death. Pets.

Henry's Fourth of July ill. by author. Greenwillow, 1985. ISBN 0-688-04013-6 Subj: Activities – picnicking. Animals – possums. Holidays – Fourth of July.

Henry's happy birthday ill. by author. Greenwillow, 1990. ISBN 0-688-09451-1 Subj: Birthdays. Parties.

Horace ill. by author. Greenwillow, 1991. ISBN 0-688-09832-0 Subj: Adoption. Animals – leopards. Character traits – being different. Self-concept.

Lizzie's invitation ill. by author. Greenwillow, 1987. ISBN 0-688-06125-7 Subj: Birthdays. Emotions. Friendship.

The new boy ill. by author. Greenwillow, 1991. ISBN 0-688-09828-2 Subj: Animals – mice. Behavior. School.

Ten sleepy sheep ill. by author. Greenwillow, 1983. Subj: Bedtime.

Too big ill. by author. Greenwillow, 1983. Subj: Animals. Sibling rivalry.

What Alvin wanted ill. by author. Greenwillow, 1990. ISBN 0-688-08934-8 Subj: Activities – babysitting. Babies. Family life – brothers. Family life – sisters.

When Francie was sick ill. by author. Greenwillow, 1985. ISBN 0-688-05434-X Subj: Family life – mothers. Illness.

Will it rain? ill. by author. Greenwillow, 1984. Subj: Animals. Weather – rain. Weather – storms.

Keller, Irene. *Benjamin Rabbit and the stranger danger* ill. by Dick Keller. Dodd, 1985. ISBN 0-396-08655-1 Subj: Animals – rabbits. Behavior – talking to strangers. School.

The Thingumajig book of manners ill. by Dick Keller. Children's Pr., 1981. Subj: Character traits – appearance. Etiquette.

Keller, John G. *Krispin's fair* ill. by Ed Emberley. Little, 1976. Subj: Etiquette. Friendship.

Kelley, Anne. *Daisy's discovery* ill. by Metin Salih. Barron's, 1985. ISBN 0-8120-5676-0 Subj: Animals – dogs. Behavior – losing things. Birthdays. Family life.

Kelley, True. *Day-care teddy bear* ill. by author. Random House, 1990. ISBN 0-394-94305-8 Subj: Emotions – fear. Toys – teddy bears.

Let's eat ill. by author. Dutton, 1989. ISBN 0-525-44482-3 Subj: Food.

Look, baby! Listen, baby! Do, baby! ill. by author. Dutton, 1987. ISBN 0-525-44320-7 Subj: Activities. Babies. Noise, sounds.

A Valentine for Fuzzboom ill. by author. Houghton, 1981. Subj: Animals – rabbits. Holidays – Valentine's Day.

Kellogg, Steven (Stephen). *Aster Aardvark's alphabet adventures* ill. by author. Morrow, 1987. ISBN 0-688-07257-7 Subj: ABC books. Animals. Animals – aardvarks. Birds.

Best friends ill. by author. Dial Pr., 1986. ISBN 0-8037-0101-2 Subj: Animals – dogs. Emotions – envy, jealousy. Friendship.

Can I keep him? ill. by author. Dial Pr., 1971. Subj: Family life. Pets.

Chicken Little ill. by author. Morrow, 1985. ISBN 0-688-05691-1 Subj: Animals. Behavior – trickery. Birds – chickens. Folk and fairy tales.

The Christmas witch ill. by author. Dial, 1992. ISBN 0-8037-1269-3 Subj: Holidays – Christmas. Witches.

The island of the skog ill. by author. Dial Pr., 1973. Subj: Animals – mice. Boats, ships. Islands. Monsters.

Johnny Appleseed: a tall tale ill. by author. Morrow, 1988. ISBN 0-688-06417-5 Subj: Activities – traveling. Folk and fairy tales. Trees. U.S. history.

The mysterious tadpole ill. by author. Dial Pr., 1977. Subj: Frogs and toads. Monsters. Pets.

The mystery of the flying orange pumpkin ill. by author. Dial Pr., 1980. Subj: Holidays – Halloween.

The mystery of the magic green ball ill. by author. Dial Pr., 1978. Subj: Behavior – losing things. Gypsies. Toys – balls.

The mystery of the missing red mitten ill. by author. Dial Pr., 1974. Subj: Behavior – losing things. Problem solving. Snowmen.

The mystery of the stolen blue paint ill. by author. Dial Pr., 1982. Subj: Problem solving.

Pecos Bill ill. by adapt. Morrow, 1986. ISBN 0-688-05872-8 Subj: Cowboys. Folk and fairy tales. U.S. history.

Pinkerton, behave! ill. by author. Dial Pr., 1979. Subj: Animals – dogs.

Prehistoric Pinkerton ill. by author. Dial Pr., 1987. ISBN 0-8037-0323-6 Subj: Animals – dogs. Behavior – misbehavior. Dinosaurs. Museums.

Ralph's secret weapon ill. by author. Dial Pr., 1983. Subj: Activities – vacationing. Imagination.

A rose for Pinkerton ill. by author. Dial Pr., 1981. Subj: Animals – cats. Animals – dogs. Behavior – imitation.

Tallyho, Pinkerton! ill. by author. Dial Pr., 1982. Subj: Animals – cats. Animals – dogs. Sports – hunting.

Kemp, Anthea. *Mr. Percy's magic greenhouse* ill. by Penny Metcalfe. David & Charles, 1988. ISBN 0-575-03870-5 Subj: Animals. Gardens, gardening. Jungle. Magic.

Kennaway, Adrienne. *Awful aardvark* (Mwalimu)

Bushbaby ill. by author. Little, 1991. ISBN 0-316-48890-9 Subj: Animals – bushbabies. Food. Foreign lands – Africa. Reptiles – monitor lizards.

Little elephant's walk ill. by author. HarperCollins, 1992. ISBN 0-06-020378-1 Subj: Animals. Animals – elephants. Foreign lands – Africa.

Kennedy, Jimmy. *The teddy bears' picnic* ill. by Alexandra Day. Green Tiger Pr., 1983. Subj: Activities – picnicking. Toys – teddy bears.

The teddy bears' picnic ill. by Michael Hague. Holt, 1992. ISBN 0-8050-1008-4 Subj: Activities – picnicking. Poetry, rhyme. Songs. Toys – teddy bears.

The teddy bears' picnic ill. by Prue Theobalds. Harper, 1987. ISBN 0-87226-153-0 Subj: Activities – picnicking. Poetry, rhyme. Toys – teddy bears.

Kennedy, Richard. *The contests at Cowlick* ill. by Marc Simont. Little, 1975. Subj: Character traits – cleverness. Cowboys. Humor.

The leprechaun's story ill. by Marcia Sewall. Dutton, 1979. Subj: Elves and little people. Foreign lands – Ireland.

The lost kingdom of Karnica ill. by Uri Shulevitz. Sierra Club, 1979. ISBN 0-684-16164-8 Subj: Behavior – greed. Royalty.

The porcelain man ill. by Marcia Sewall. Little, 1976. Subj: Magic.

Kent, Jack. *The caterpillar and the polliwog* ill. by author. Prentice-Hall, 1982. Subj: Frogs and toads. Insects – butterflies, caterpillars.

The Christmas piñata ill. by author. Parents, 1975. Subj: Foreign lands – Mexico. Holidays – Christmas.

Clotilda ill. by author. Random House, 1978. Subj: Character traits – kindness. Fairies.

The egg book ill. by author. Macmillan, 1975. Subj: Eggs. Wordless.

Hoddy doddy ill. by author. Greenwillow, 1979. Subj: Foreign lands – Denmark. Humor.

Jack Kent's happy-ever-after book ill. by author. Random House, 1976. Subj: Folk and fairy tales.

Jack Kent's hokus pokus bedtime book ill. by author. Random House, 1979. Subj: Folk and fairy tales.

Joey ill. by author. Prentice-Hall, 1984. Subj: Activities – playing. Animals – kangaroos. Family life – mothers.

Joey runs away ill. by author. Prentice-Hall, 1985. ISBN 0-13-510462-9 Subj: Animals. Animals – kangaroos. Behavior – running away. Behavior – seeking better things. Family life.

Knee-high Nina ill. by author. Doubleday, 1981. Subj: Behavior – wishing.

Little Peep ill. by author. Prentice-Hall, 1981. Subj: Animals. Birds – chickens. Farms.

The once-upon-a-time dragon ill. by author. Harcourt, 1982. Subj: Bedtime. Behavior – imitation. Dragons.

Piggy Bank Gonzalez ill. by author. Parents, 1979. Subj: Animals – pigs. Money. Toys.

Round Robin ill. by author. Prentice-Hall, 1982. Subj: Birds – robins.

The scribble monster ill. by author. Harcourt, 1981. Subj: Behavior – misbehavior.

Silly goose ill. by author. Prentice-Hall, 1983. Subj: Animals – foxes. Birds – geese.

Socks for supper ill. by author. Parents, 1978. Subj: Friendship.

There's no such thing as a dragon ill. by author. Golden Pr., 1975. Subj: Behavior – needing someone. Dragons.

Kent, Lorna. *No, no, Charlie Rascal!* ill. by author. Viking, 1989. ISBN 0-670-82512-3 Subj: Animals – cats. Behavior – misbehavior. Format, unusual.

Kepes, Juliet. *Cock-a-doodle-doo* ill. by author. Pantheon, 1978. Subj: Animals – tigers. Birds – chickens.

Five little monkeys ill. by author. Houghton, 1952. Subj: Animals. Animals – monkeys. Caldecott award honor book.

Frogs, merry ill. by author. Pantheon, 1961. Subj: Frogs and toads. Hibernation.

Lady bird, quickly ill. by author. Little, 1964. Subj: Insects – ladybugs. Nursery rhymes.

Run little monkeys, run, run, run ill. by author. Pantheon, 1974. Subj: Animals – leopards. Animals – monkeys. Participation.

The seed that peacock planted ill. by author. Little, 1967. Subj: Birds – peacocks, peahens. Magic. Music. Plants.

The story of a bragging duck ill. by author. Houghton, 1983. Subj: Behavior – boasting. Birds – ducks. Character traits – vanity.

Kerr, Judith. *Mog and bunny* ill. by author. Knopf, 1989. ISBN 0-394-82249-8 Subj: Animals – cats. Family life. Pets. Toys.

Mog's Christmas ill. by author. Collins-World, 1976. Subj: Animals – cats. Holidays – Christmas.

Kerr, Phyllis Forbes. *I tricked you* ill. by author. Simon & Schuster, 1990. ISBN 0-671-69408-1 Subj: Animals – mice. Behavior. School.

Kerrigan, Anthony. *Mother Goose in Spanish* (Mother Goose)

Kerry, Lois *see* Duncan, Lois

Ker Wilson, Barbara *see* Wilson, Barbara Ker

Kesselman, Judi R. *I can use tools* by Judi R. Kesselman and Franklynn Peterson; ill. by Tomás Gonzales. Elsevier/Nelson, 1981. Subj: Tools.

Kesselman, Wendy. *Angelita* ill. by Norma Holt. Hill and Wang, 1970. Subj: City. Emotions – loneliness. Ethnic groups in the U.S. Ethnic groups in the U.S. – Puerto Rican-Americans.

Emma ill. by Barbara Cooney. Doubleday, 1980. Subj: Art. Emotions – loneliness.

There's a train going by my window ill. by Tony Chen. Doubleday, 1982. Subj: Activities – traveling.

Time for Jody ill. by Gerald Dumas. Harper, 1975. Subj: Animals – groundhogs. Hibernation. Holidays – Groundhog Day. Seasons – spring.

Kessler, Ethel. *Are there hippos on the farm?* by Ethel and Len Kessler; ill. by authors. Simon & Schuster, 1987. ISBN 0-671-62066-5 Subj: Animals. Farms. Format, unusual – board books.

Do baby bears sit in chairs? by Ethel and Leonard P. Kessler; ill. by authors. Doubleday, 1961. Subj: Animals. Furniture – chairs. Poetry, rhyme.

Is there an elephant in your kitchen? by Ethel and Len Kessler; ill. by authors. Simon & Schuster, 1987. ISBN 0-671-62065-7 Subj: Animals. Format, unusual – board books. Houses.

Two, four, six, eight: a book about legs by Ethel and Leonard P. Kessler; ill. by Leonard P. Kessler. Dodd, 1980. Subj: Counting, numbers.

Kessler, Jascha. *Rose of Mother-of-Pearl* (Olujic, Grozdana)

Kessler, Leonard P. *Are there hippos on the farm?* (Kessler, Ethel)

Are we lost, daddy? ill. by author. Grosset, 1967. Subj: Activities – vacationing. Behavior – lost. Family life. Family life – fathers.

The big mile race ill. by author. Greenwillow, 1983. Subj: Animals. Sports – racing.

Do baby bears sit in chairs? (Kessler, Ethel)

Do you have any carrots? ill. by Lori Pierson. Garrard, 1979. Subj: Animals. Food.

Is there an elephant in your kitchen? (Kessler, Ethel)

Mr. Pine's mixed-up signs ill. by author. Grosset, 1961. Subj: Glasses. Senses – seeing.

Mr. Pine's purple house ill. by author. Grosset, 1965. Subj: Activities – painting. Concepts – color.

Mrs. Pine takes a trip ill. by author. Grosset, 1966. Subj: Activities – traveling.

The pirates' adventure on Spooky Island ill. by author. Garrard, 1979. Subj: Islands. Pirates.

The silly Mother Goose ill. by author. Garrard, 1980. Subj: Nursery rhymes.

Soup for the king ill. by author. Grosset, 1969. Subj: Careers – bakers. Food. Royalty – kings.

Two, four, six, eight (Kessler, Ethel)

Ketner, Mary Grace. *Ganzy remembers* ill. by Barbara Sparks. Atheneum, 1991. ISBN 0-689-31610-0 Subj: Family life – grandmothers. Family life – great-grandparents. Hospitals. Old age.

Ketteman, Helen. *Not yet, Yvette* ill. by Irene Trivas. Albert Whitman, 1992. ISBN 0-8075-5771-4 Subj: Birthdays. Character traits – patience. Family life – fathers. Family life – mothers. Ethnic groups in the U.S. – Afro-Americans.

Kettner, Christine. *An ordinary cat* ill. by author. HarperCollins, 1991. ISBN 0-06-023173-4 Subj: Animals – cats. Behavior. Pets.

Keven, Elisa. *Ernest* ill. by author. Dutton, 1989. ISBN 0-525-44515-3 Subj: Character traits – questioning. Reptiles – alligators, crocodiles.

Key, Francis Scott. *The Star-Spangled Banner* ill. by Paul Galdone. Crowell, 1966. Subj: Songs. U.S. history.

The Star-Spangled Banner ill. by Peter Spier. Doubleday, 1973. Subj: Songs. U.S. history.

Keyser, Marcia. *Roger on his own* ill. by Diane Dawson. Crown, 1982. Subj: Animals – dogs. Behavior – solitude.

Keyworth, C. L. *New day* ill. by Carolyn Bracken. Morrow, 1986. ISBN 0-688-05922-8 Subj: Moving.

Khalsa, Dayal Kaur. *How pizza came to our town* ill. by author. Tundra, 1989. ISBN 0-88776-231-X Subj: Emotions – loneliness. Food.

I want a dog ill. by author. Crown, 1987. ISBN 0-517-56532-3 Subj: Animals – dogs. Behavior – growing up. Family life.

My family vacation ill. by author. Potter, 1988. ISBN 0-517-56697-4 Subj: Activities – vacationing. Family life.

Sleepers ill. by author. Crown, 1988. ISBN 0-517-56917-5 Subj: Bedtime. Sleep.

Tales of a gambling grandma ill. by author. Crown, 1986. ISBN 0-517-56137-9 Subj: Family life – grandmothers. Games.

Khdir, Kate. *Little ghost* ill. by Caroline Church. Barron's, 1991. ISBN 0-8120-6203-5 Subj: Ghosts. Holidays – Halloween. School.

Kherdian, David. *The animal* ill. by Nonny Hogrogian. Knopf, 1984. Subj: Animals.

The cat's midsummer jamboree ill. by Nonny Hogrogian. Putnam, 1990. ISBN 0-399-22222-7 Subj: Animals. Animals – cats. Music.

Country cat, city cat ill. by Nonny Hogrogian. Four Winds Pr., 1978. Subj: Animals – cats. Poetry, rhyme.

Right now ill. by Nonny Hogrogian. Knopf, 1983. Subj: Emotions.

Kibbey, Marsha. *My grammy* ill. by Karen Ritz. Carolrhoda Books, 1988. ISBN 0-87614-328-1 Subj: Character traits – patience. Family life – grandmothers. Illness. Old age.

Kidd, Bruce. *Hockey showdown* ill. by Leung O'Young. Lorimer, 1980. Subj: Character traits – meanness. Sports – hockey.

Kidd, Nina. *June Mountain secret* ill. by author. HarperCollins, 1991. ISBN 0-06-023168-8 Subj: Family life – fathers. Sports – fishing.

Kightley, Rosalinda. *ABC* ill. by author. Little, 1986. ISBN 0-316-49930-7 Subj: ABC books.

The farmer ill. by author. Macmillan, 1988. ISBN 0-02-750290-2 Subj: Careers – farmers. Farms.

Opposites ill. by author. Little, 1986. ISBN 0-316-49931-5 Subj: Concepts – opposites.

The postman ill. by author. Macmillan, 1988. ISBN 0-02-750270-8 Subj: City. Careers – mail carriers.

Shapes ill. by author. Little, 1986. ISBN 0-316-54005-6 Subj: Concepts – shape.

Kilburn, Greta. *The Christmas carp* (Tornqvist, Rita)

Killingback, Julia. *Busy Bears at the fire station* ill. by author. Oxford Univ. Pr., 1988. ISBN 0-19-520653-3 Subj: Animals – bears. Careers – firefighters.

Busy Bears' picnic ill. by author. Oxford Univ. Pr., 1988. ISBN 0-19-520654-1 Subj: Activities – picnicking. Animals – bears.

Monday is washing day ill. by author. Morrow, 1985. ISBN 0-688-04077-2 Subj: Activities – working. Animals – bears. Family life.

What time is it, Mrs. Bear? ill. by author. Morrow, 1985. ISBN 0-688-04076-4 Subj: Animals – bears. Family life. Time.

Kilreon, Beth *see* Walker, Barbara K. (Barbara Kerlin)

Kilroy, Sally. *Animal noises* ill. by author. Four Winds Pr., 1983. Subj: Animals. Format, unusual – board books. Noise, sounds. Wordless.

Babies' bodies ill. by author. Scholastic, 1983. Subj: Anatomy. Babies. Format, unusual – board books.

Babies' homes ill. by author. Scholastic, 1984. ISBN 0-590-07945-X Subj: Format, unusual – board books. Houses.

Babies' outings ill. by author. Scholastic, 1984. ISBN 0-590-07946-8 Subj: Format, unusual – board books.

Babies' zoo ill. by author. Scholastic, 1984. ISBN 0-590-07947-6 Subj: Animals. Format, unusual – board books. Zoos.

Baby colors ill. by author. Scholastic, 1983. Subj: Babies. Concepts – color. Format, unusual – board books.

The baron's hunting party ill. by author. Viking, 1988. ISBN 0-317-69208-9 Subj: Sports – hunting.

Busy babies ill. by author. Scholastic, 1984. ISBN 0-590-07948-4 Subj: Activities. Babies. Format, unusual – board books.

Copycat drawing book ill. by author. Dial Pr., 1981. Subj: Art.

Grandpa's garden ill. by author. Viking, 1986. ISBN 0-670-80338-3 Subj: Family life – grandparents. Gardens, gardening.

Market day ill. by author. Viking, 1986. ISBN 0-670-80339-1 Subj: Family life – fathers. Shopping.

Noisy homes ill. by author. Scholastic, 1983. Subj: Format, unusual – board books. Noise, sounds.

On the road ill. by author. Viking, 1986. ISBN 0-670-80337-5 Subj: Activities – traveling. Buses. Family life – mothers.

What a week! ill. by author. Viking, 1986. ISBN 0-670-80336-7 Subj: Family life.

Kimber, Robert. *I am a little cat* (Spanner, Helmut)

Kimmel, Eric A. *Anansi and the moss-covered rock* ill. by Janet Stevens. Holiday, 1990. ISBN 0-8234-0689-X Subj: Animals. Behavior – trickery. Folk and fairy tales. Spiders.

Anansi goes fishing ill. by Janet Stevens. Holiday, 1992. ISBN 0-8234-0918-X Subj: Behavior – trickery. Folk and fairy tales. Foreign lands – Africa. Reptiles – turtles, tortoises. Spiders.

Baba Yaga ill. by Megan Lloyd. Holiday, 1991. ISBN 0-8234-0854-X Subj: Behavior – trickery. Folk and fairy tales. Foreign lands – Russia. Witches.

Bearhead ill. by Charles Mikolaycak. Holiday, 1991. ISBN 0-8234-0902-3 Subj: Animals – bears. Folk and fairy tales. Foreign lands – Russia. Witches.

Boots and his brothers ill. by Kimberly Bulcken Root. Holiday, 1992. ISBN 0-8234-0886-8 Subj: Folk and fairy tales. Foreign lands – Norway. Magic.

The Chanukkah guest ill. by Giora Carmi. Holiday, 1990. ISBN 0-8234-0788-8 Subj: Holidays – Hanukkah. Jewish culture. Religion.

Charlie drives the stage ill. by Glen Rounds. Holiday, 1989. ISBN 0-8234-0738-1 Subj: Transportation. U.S. history.

The greatest of all ill. by Giora Carmi. Holiday, 1991. ISBN 0-8234-0885-X Subj: Animals – mice. Folk and fairy tales. Foreign lands – Japan. Weddings.

Hershel and the Hanukkah goblins ill. by Trina Schart Hyman. Holiday, 1989. ISBN 0-8234-0769-1 Subj: Caldecott award honor book. Goblins. Holidays – Hanukkah. Jewish culture. Religion.

I took my frog to the library ill. by Blanche Sims. Viking, 1990. ISBN 0-670-82418-6 Subj: Animals. Libraries. Pets.

Nanny goat and the seven little kids (Grimm, Jacob)

The tale of Aladdin and the wonderful lamp (Arabian Nights)

Why worry? ill. by Beth Cannon. Pantheon, 1979. Subj: Insects – crickets. Insects – grasshoppers. Music. Songs.

Kimmel, Margaret Mary. *Magic in the mist* ill. by Trina Schart Hyman. Atheneum, 1975. Subj: Dragons. Magic. Wizards.

Kimmelman, Leslie. *Frannie's fruits* ill. by Petra Mathers. HarperCollins, 1989. ISBN 0-06-023143-2 Subj: Animals – dogs. Careers – storekeepers. Family life.

Me and Nana ill. by Marilee Robin Burton. HarperCollins, 1990. ISBN 0-06-023163-7 Subj: Family life – grandmothers. Friendship.

Kimura, Yasuko. *Fergus and the sea monster* ill. by author. McGraw-Hill, 1978. Subj: Animals – dogs. Friendship. Monsters. Sea and seashore.

Kines, Pat Decker *see* Tapio, Pat Decker

King, B. A. *The very best Christmas tree* ill. by Michael McCurdy. Godine, 1984. ISBN 0-87923-539-X Subj: Holidays – Christmas. Trees.

King, Bob. *Sitting on the farm* ill. by Bill Slavin. Orchard, 1992. ISBN 0-531-08585-6 Subj: Activities – picnicking. Animals. Cumulative tales. Music. Songs. Telephone.

King, Christopher. *The boy who ate the moon* ill. by John Wallner. Putnam's, 1988. ISBN 0-399-21459-3 Subj: Activities – flying. Moon.

King, Deborah. *Cloudy* ill. by author. Putnam, 1990. ISBN 0-399-22242-1 Subj: Animals – cats.

Custer: the true story of a horse ill. by author. Putnam, 1992. ISBN 0-399-2247-6 Subj: Animals – horses. Friendship.

Sirius and Saba ill. by author. David and Charles, 1982. Subj: Animals – dogs. Islands.

King, Elizabeth. *Pumpkin patch* photos. by author. Dutton, 1990. ISBN 0-525-44640-0 Subj: Gardens, gardening. Holidays – Halloween.

King, Larry L. *Because of Lozo Brown* ill. by Amy Schwartz. Viking, 1988. ISBN 0-670-81031-2 Subj: Friendship. Imagination. Poetry, rhyme.

King, Patricia. *Mable the whale* ill. by Katherine Evans. Follett, 1958. Subj: Animals – whales.

King-Smith, Dick. *Cuckoobush farm* ill. by Kazuko. Greenwillow, 1988. ISBN 0-688-07681-5 Subj: Farms. Seasons. Twins.

Farmer Bungle forgets ill. by Martin Honeysett. Atheneum, 1987. ISBN 0-689-31370-5 Subj: Behavior – forgetfulness. Farms. Humor.

Kingman, Lee. *Catch the baby!* ill. Susanna Natti. Viking, 1989. ISBN 0-670-81751-1 Subj: Family life. Poetry, rhyme.

Peter's long walk ill. by Barbara Cooney. Doubleday, 1953. Subj: Activities – walking. Animals. Country. Friendship.

Pierre Pigeon ill. by Arnold E. Bare. Houghton, 1943. Subj: Birds – pigeons. Caldecott award honor book.

Kingsland, Robin. *Bus stop bop* ill. by Alex Ayliffe. Viking, 1991. ISBN 0-670-83919-1 Subj: Activities – dancing. Buses. Music.

King-Smith, Dick. *All pigs are beautiful* ill. by Anita Jeram. Candlewick Pr., 1993. ISBN 1-56402-148-3 Subj: Animals – pigs.

Kinnell, Galway. *How the alligator missed breakfast* ill. by Lynn Munsinger. Houghton, 1982. Subj: Reptiles – alligators, crocodiles.

Kinney, Jean. *What does the sun do?* ill. by Cle Kinney. W. R. Scott, 1967. Subj: Sun.

Kinsey, Elizabeth *see* Clymer, Eleanor Lowenton

Kinsey-Warnock, Natalie. *The wild horses of Sweetbriar* ill. by Ted Rand. Dutton, 1990. ISBN 0-525-65015-6 Subj: Animals – horses. Islands. Seasons – winter.

Kipling, Rudyard. *The beginning of the armadilloes* ill. by Charles Keeping. Harper, 1983. Subj: Animals – armadillos.

The beginning of the armadillos ill. by Lorinda Bryan Cauley. Harcourt, 1985. ISBN 0-15-206380-3 Subj: Animals – armadillos.

The crab that played with the sea ill. by Michael Foreman. Harper, 1983. Subj: Crustacea. Sea and seashore.

The elephant's child ill. by Louise Brierley. Harper, 1985. ISBN 0-87226-030-5 Subj: Animals. Animals – elephants. Character traits – curiosity. Foreign lands – Africa.

The elephant's child ill. by Lorinda Bryan Cauley. Harcourt, 1983. Subj: Animals. Animals – elephants. Character traits – curiosity. Foreign lands – Africa.

The elephant's child ill. by Tim Raglin. Knopf, 1986. ISBN 0-394-88401-9 Subj: Animals. Animals – elephants. Character traits – curiosity. Foreign lands – Africa.

How the camel got his hump ill. by Quentin Blake. Harper, 1985. ISBN 0-87226-029-1 Subj: Animals. Animals – camels. Foreign lands – Africa.

How the camel got his hump ill. by Tim Raglin. Picture Book Studio, 1989. Cassette narrated by Jack Nicholson ISBN 0-88708-097-9 Subj: Animals. Animals – camels. Foreign lands – Africa.

How the leopard got his spots ill. by Caroline Ebborn. Harper, 1986. ISBN 0-87226-072-0 Subj: Animals – leopards.

How the leopard got his spots ill. by Lori Loestoeter. Picture Book Studio, 1989. ISBN 0-88708-112-6 Subj: Animals – leopards.

How the rhinoceros got his skin ill. by Leonard Weisgard. Walker, 1974. Subj: Animals – rhinoceros.

The miracle of the mountain ill. by Willi Baum. Addison-Wesley, 1969. Adapted by Aroline Arnett Beecher Leach from The Miracle of Purun Bhagat, by Rudyard Kipling Subj: Animals. Foreign lands – India. Religion.

The sing-song of old man kangaroo ill. by Michael C. Taylor. Harper, 1986. ISBN 0-87226-073-9 Subj: Animals – kangaroos. Foreign lands – Australia.

Kirby, David. *Cows are going to Paris* by David Kirby and Allen Woodman; ill. by Chris L. Demarest. Boyds Mills Pr., 1991. ISBN 0-878093-11-8 Subj: Animals – bulls, cows. Foreign lands – France. Trains.

Kirk, Barbara. *Grandpa, me and our house in the tree* ill. by author. Macmillan, 1978. Subj: Family life – grandfathers. Houses. Trees.

Kirkpatrick, Rena K. *Look at flowers* ill. by Annabel Milne and Peter Stebbing. Raintree, 1978. Subj: Flowers. Science.

Look at leaves ill. by Annabel Milne and Peter Stebbing. Raintree, 1978. Subj: Plants. Science.

Look at magnets ill. by Ann Knight. Raintree, 1978. Subj: Science.

Look at pond life ill. by Annabel Milne and Peter Stebbing. Raintree, 1978. Subj: Science.

Look at rainbow colors ill. by Anna Barnard. Raintree, 1978. Subj: Concepts – color. Science. Weather – rainbows.

Look at seeds and weeds ill. by Debbie King. Raintree, 1978. Subj: Plants. Science.

Look at trees ill. by Jo Worth and Ann Knight. Raintree, 1978. Subj: Science. Trees.

Look at weather ill. by Janetta Lewin. Raintree, 1978. Subj: Science. Weather.

Kirn, Ann. *Beeswax catches a thief: from a Congo folktale* ill. by author. Norton, 1968. Subj: Animals. Ethnic groups in the U.S. – Afro-Americans.

I spy ill. by author. Norton, 1965. Subj: Birds – owls. Crime.

The tale of a crocodile: from a Congo folktale ill. by author. Norton, 1968. Subj: Animals – rabbits. Fire. Folk and fairy tales. Foreign lands – Africa. Reptiles – alligators, crocodiles.

Kirstein, Lincoln. *Puss in boots* (Perrault, Charles)

Kirtland, G. B. *see* Joslin, Sesyle

Kiser, SuAnn. *The birthday thing* by SuAnn and Kevin Kiser; ill. by Yossi Abolafia. Greenwillow, 1989. ISBN 0-688-07773-0 Subj: Activities – making things. Birthdays. Family life.

Kishida, Eriko. *The hippo boat* ill. by Chiyoko Nakatani. Collins, 1964. Subj: Animals – hippopotami. Weather – rain. Zoos.

The lion and the bird's nest ill. by Chiyoko Nakatani. Crowell, 1972. Subj: Animals – lions. Birds. Character traits – helpfulness. Friendship.

Kismaric, Carole. *A gift from Saint Nicholas* (Timmermans, Felix)

The rumor of Pavel and Paali: a Ukrainian folktale ill. by Charles Mikolaycak. Harper, 1988. ISBN 0-06-023278-1 Subj: Behavior – greed. Character traits – meanness. Folk and fairy tales. Twins.

Kitamura, Satoshi. *Captain Toby* ill. by author. Dutton, 1988. ISBN 0-525-44414-9 Subj: Animals – cats. Family life – grandparents. Sea and seashore. Weather – storms.

From acorn to zoo and everything in between in alphabetical order ill. by author. Farrar, 1992. ISBN 0-374-32470-0 Subj: ABC books.

Lily takes a walk ill. by author. Dutton, 1987. ISBN 0-525-44333-9 Subj: Animals – dogs. Emotions – fear. Imagination.

What's inside? ill. by author. Farrar, 1985. ISBN 0-374-38306-5 Subj: ABC books.

When sheep cannot sleep ill. by author. Farrar, 1986. ISBN 0-374-38311-1 Subj: Animals – sheep. Bedtime. Counting, numbers.

Kitchen, Bert. *Animal alphabet* ill. by author. Dial Pr., 1984. Subj: ABC books. Animals. Wordless.

Animal numbers ill. by author. Dial Pr., 1987. ISBN 0-8037-0459-3 Subj: Animals. Counting, numbers.

Pig in a barrow ill. by author. Dial, 1991. ISBN 0-8037-0943-9 Subj: Animals. Poetry, rhyme.

Tenrec's twigs ill. by author. Putnam, 1989. ISBN 0-399-21720-7 Subj: Animals. Foreign lands – Africa. Jungle.

Klages, Simone. *Now, now Markus* (Auer, Martin)

Klein, Arthur Luce. *Puss in boots* (Perrault, Charles)

Klein, Leonore. *Henri's walk to Paris* ill. by Saul Bass. Addison-Wesley, 1962. Subj: Activities – walking. Foreign lands – France.

Just like you ill. by Audrey Walters. Harvey House, 1968. Subj: Ethnic groups in the U.S.

Old, older, oldest ill. by Leonard P. Kessler. Hastings, 1983. Subj: Old age.

Klein, Norma. *Girls can be anything* ill. by Roy Doty. Dutton, 1973. Subj: Careers.

Visiting Pamela ill. by Kay Chorao. Dial Pr., 1979. Subj: Behavior – sharing. Friendship.

Klein, Robin. *Thing* ill. by Alison Lester. Oxford Univ. Pr., 1983. Subj: Dinosaurs. Pets.

Klein, Suzanne. *An elephant in my bed* ill. by Sharleen Pederson. Follett, 1974. Subj: Animals – elephants. Furniture – beds.

Kleven, Elisa. *The lion and the little red bird* ill. by author. Dutton, 1992. ISBN 0-525-44898-5 Subj: Animals – lions. Birds. Careers – artists. Concepts – color.

Klimo, Kate. *Mother Goose house* (Mother Goose)

Sing a song of sixpence (Mother Goose)

Klimowicz, Barbara. *The strawberry thumb* ill. by Gloria Kamen. Abingdon Pr., 1968. Subj: Poetry, rhyme. Problem solving. Puppets. Thumbsucking.

Kline, Suzy. *Don't touch!* ill. by Dora Leder. Albert Whitman, 1985. ISBN 0-8075-1707-0 Subj: Activities – playing. Behavior – misbehavior.

Ooops! ed. by Ann Fay; ill. by Dora Leder. Albert Whitman, 1988. ISBN 0-8075-6122-3 Subj: Behavior – bad day. Behavior – carelessness.

Shhhh! ill. by Dora Leder. Albert Whitman, 1984. ISBN 0-8075-7321-3 Subj: Noise, sounds.

Klinting, Lars. *Regal the golden eagle* tr. by Alan Bernstein; ill. by author. Farrar, 1988. ISBN 91-2958774-3 Subj: Behavior – growing up. Birds – eagles. Emotions – fear.

Klockner, Karen M. *The black sheep* (Heck, Elisabeth)

The Christmas train (Gantschev, Ivan)

Otto the bear (Gantschev, Ivan)

Klyce, Katherine P. *Kenya, jambo!* (McLean, Virginia O.)

Knab, Linda Z. *The day is waiting* (Freeman, Don)

Knaff, Jean Christian. *Manhattan* ill. by author. Knopf, 1989. ISBN 0-571-14653-8 Subj: Emotions – loneliness. Friendship. Imagination.

Knapp, John II. *A pillar of pepper and other Bible nursery rhymes* ill. by Dianne Turner Deckert. Cook, 1982. Subj: Nursery rhymes. Religion.

Knight, David C. *Dinosaur days* ill. by Joel Schick. McGraw-Hill, 1977. Subj: Dinosaurs. Science.

Knight, Hilary. *Angels and berries and candy canes* ill. by author. Harper, 1963. Subj: Angels. Holidays – Christmas.

A firefly in a fir tree ill. by author. Harper, 1963. Subj: Insects – fireflies.

Hilary Knight's Cinderella ill. by author. Random House, 1978. ISBN 0-394-93759-7 Subj: Folk and fairy tales. Royalty – princes. Sibling rivalry.

Hilary Knight's the owl and the pussy-cat ill. by author. Macmillan, 1983. Based on The owl and the pussy-cat by Edward Lear Subj: Imagination. Magic. Poetry, rhyme.

Sylvia the sloth ill. by author. Harper, 1969. Subj: Animals – sloths. Concepts – up and down.

Where's Wallace? ill. by author. Harper, 1964. Subj: Animals – monkeys. Behavior – running away. Zoos.

Knight, Joan. *Tickle-toe rhymes* ill. by John Wallner. Watts, 1988. ISBN 0-531-08373-X Subj: Games. Poetry, rhyme.

Knight, Margy Burns. *Talking walls* ill. by Anne Sibley O'Brien. Tilbury House, 1992. ISBN 0-88448-102-6 Subj: Foreign lands.

Knotts, Howard. *Great-grandfather, the baby and me* ill. by author. Atheneum, 1978. Subj: Family life – great-grandparents.

The lost Christmas ill. by author. Harcourt, 1978. Subj: Dreams. Holidays – Christmas. Illness.

The summer cat ill. by author. Harper, 1981. Subj: Animals – cats. Seasons – summer.

The winter cat ill. by author. Harper, 1972. Subj: Animals – cats. Seasons – winter.

Knox-Wagner, Elaine. *The best mom in the world* (Delton, Judy)

My grandpa retired today ill. by Charles Robinson. Albert Whitman, 1982. Subj: Emotions. Family life – grandfathers. Old age.

The oldest kid ill. by Gail Owens. Albert Whitman, 1981. Subj: Activities – picnicking. Sibling rivalry.

Knuppel, Helga. *The adventures of Christabel Crocodile* ill. by author. Interlink, 1991. ISBN 0-940793-74-1 Subj: Animals. Behavior – lost. Reptiles – alligators, crocodiles.

Knutson, Barbara. *How the guinea fowl got her spots: a Swahili tale of friendship* ill. by adapt. Carolrhoda, 1990. ISBN 0-87614-416-4 Subj: Animals. Birds – guinea fowl. Folk and fairy tales. Friendship.

Why the crab has no head: an African tale ill. by author. Carolrhoda Books, 1987. ISBN 0-87614-322-2 Subj: Behavior – boasting. Crustacea. Folk and fairy tales. Foreign lands – Africa. Foreign lands – Zaire.

Knutson, Kimberley. *Muddigush* ill. by author. Macmillan, 1992. ISBN 0-02-750843-9 Subj: Activities – playing. Poetry, rhyme. Weather – rain.

Kobayashi, Masako Matsuno *see* Matsuno, Masako

Kobayashi, Robert. *Maria Mazaretti loves spaghetti* ill. by author. Knopf, 1991. ISBN 0-679-91659-8 Subj: Animals. Careers – butchers. Food. Magic.

Kobayashi, Yuji. *Miss Josephine's secret walk* ill. by author. Green Tiger Pr., 1991. ISBN 0-88138-096-2 Subj: Activities – playing. Animals.

Kobrin, Janet. *Coyote goes hunting for fire* (Bernstein, Margery)

Earth namer (Bernstein, Margery)

The first morning (Bernstein, Margery)

How the sun made a promise and kept it (Bernstein, Margery)

Koch, Dorothy Clarke. *Gone is my goose* ill. by Doris Lee. Holiday, 1956. Subj: Birds – geese.

I play at the beach ill. by Feodor Rojankovsky. Random House, 1955. Subj: Family life. Games. Sea and seashore.

When the cows got out ill. by Paul Lantz. Holiday, 1958. Subj: Animals – bulls, cows. Farms.

Koch, Michelle. *By the sea* ill. by author. Greenwillow, 1991. ISBN 0-688-09550-X Subj: Concepts – opposites. Language. Sea and seashore.

Hoot, howl, hiss ill. by author. Greenwillow, 1991. ISBN 0-688-09652-2 Subj: Animals. Nature. Noise, sounds.

Just one more ill. by author. Greenwillow, 1989. ISBN 0-688-08128-2 Subj: Counting, numbers. Language.

World water watch ill. by author. Greenwillow, 1993. ISBN 0-688-11465-2 Subj: Ecology. Water.

Koči, Marta. *Blackie and Marie* tr. from German by Elizabeth D. Crawford; ill. by author. Morrow, 1981. Subj: Animals – dogs. Friendship.

Katie's kitten ill. by author. Alphabet Pr., 1982. Subj: Animals – cats. Behavior – lost.

Sarah's bear ill. by author. Picture Book Studio, 1987. ISBN 0-88708-038-3 Subj: Emotions – love. Toys – teddy bears.

Koehler, Phoebe. *The day we met you* ill. by author. Bradbury Pr., 1990. ISBN 0-02-750901-X Subj: Adoption. Babies. Family life.

Koelling, Caryl. *Animal mix and match* ill. by Roger Beerworth. Delacorte, 1980. Subj: Animals. Format, unusual – board books.

Mad monsters mix and match ill. by Linda Griffith. Delacorte, 1980. Subj: Format, unusual – board books. Monsters.

Silly stories mix and match ill. by Carroll Andrus. Delacorte, 1980. Subj: Format, unusual – board books. Humor.

Koenig, Marion. *The little black hen* (Hille-Brandts, Lene)

Poor fish (Beisert, Heide Helene)

The tale of fancy Nancy: a Spanish folktale ill. by Klaus Ensikat. Merrimack, 1979. Subj: Animals – cats. Animals – mice. Folk and fairy tales.

The wonderful world of night ill. by David Parry. Grosset, 1969. Subj: Animals – cats. Behavior – misbehavior. Night.

Koenner, Alfred. *Be quite quiet beside the lake* tr. from German by Georgia Peet; ill. by Karl-Heinz Appelmann. Imported Pub., 1981. Subj: Format, unusual – board books. Noise, sounds.

High flies the ball by Alfred Koenner and Siegfried Linke; tr. from German by Georgia Peet; ill. by Siegfried Linke. Imported Pub., 1983. Subj: Format, unusual – board books. Poetry, rhyme.

Koffler, Camilla *see* Ylla

Koide, Tan. *May we sleep here tonight?* ill. by Yasuko Koide. Atheneum, 1983. Subj: Animals. Bedtime.

Koike, Kay. *Left or right?* (Rehm, Karl)

Kojima, Naomi. *The flying grandmother* ill. by author. Crowell, 1981. Subj: Activities – flying. Behavior – wishing. Family life – grandmothers. Imagination.

Koller, Jackie French. *Fish fry tonight* ill. by Catharine O'Neill. Crown, 1992. ISBN 0-517-57815-8 Subj: Animals. Animals – mice. Food. Friendship. Poetry, rhyme. Sports – fishing.

Mole and shrew ill. by Stella Ormai. Atheneum, 1991. ISBN 0-689-31611-9 Subj: Animals – moles. Animals – shrews. Friendship. Houses. Moving.

Komaiko, Leah. *Annie Bananie* ill. by Laura Cornell. Harper, 1987. ISBN 0-06-023261-7 Subj: Friendship. Moving. Poetry, rhyme.

Earl's too cool for me ill. by Laura Cornell. Harper, 1988. ISBN 0-06-023282-X Subj: Behavior – misunderstanding. Friendship. Poetry, rhyme.

I like the music ill. by Barbara Westman. Harper, 1987. ISBN 0-06-023272-2 Subj: Music. Poetry, rhyme.

Lenora O'Grady ill. by Laura Cornell. HarperCollins, 1992. ISBN 0-06-021767-7 Subj: Homeless. Poetry, rhyme.

My perfect neighborhood ill. by Barbara Westman. HarperCollins, 1990. ISBN 0-06-023288-9 Subj: Communities, neighborhoods. Poetry, rhyme.

Komoda, Beerly. *The winter day* ill. by author. HarperCollins, 1991. ISBN 0-06-023302-8 Subj: Animals – rabbits. Illness. Snowmen. Seasons – winter.

Komoda, Beverly. *Simon's soup* ill. by author. Parents, 1978. Subj: Animals – cats. Animals – monkeys. Food.

The too hot day ill. by author. HarperCollins, 1991. ISBN 0-06-021612-3 Subj: Animals – rabbits. Family life. Seasons – summer.

Komori, Atsushi. *Animal mothers* ill. by Masayuki Yabuuchi. Putnam's, 1983. ISBN 0-399-20980-8 Subj: Animals. Science.

Konigsburg, E. L. (Elaine Lobl). *Samuel Todd's book of great colors* ill. by author. Atheneum, 1990. ISBN 0-689-31593-7 Subj: Concepts – color.

Samuel Todd's book of great inventions ill. by author. Atheneum, 1991. ISBN 0-689-31680-1 Subj: Family life.

Koontz, Robin Michal. *Dinosaur dream* ill. by author. Putnam's, 1988. ISBN 0-399-21669-3 Subj: Dinosaurs. Dreams. Wordless.

I see something you don't see ill. by author. Dutton, 1992. ISBN 0-525-65077-6 Subj: Riddles.

Pussycat ate the dumplings: cat rhymes from Mother Goose ill. by author. Dodd, 1987. ISBN 0-396-08899-6 Subj: Animals – cats. Nursery rhymes.

This old man: the counting song ill. by author. Putnam's, 1988. ISBN 0-396-09120-2 Subj: Counting, numbers. Elves and little people. Farms. Music. Songs.

Koopmans, Loek. *The woodcutter's mitten* ill. by author. Interlink, 1990. ISBN 0-940793-67-9 Subj: Animals. Clothing.

Kopczynski, Anna. *Jerry and Ami* ill. by author. Scribner's, 1963. Subj: Animals – dogs. Friendship.

Koplow, Lesley. *Tanya and the tobo man / Tanya y el hombre tobo* Tr. into Spanish by Alexander Contos; ill. by Eric Velasquez. Magination Pr., 1991. ISBN 0-945354-34-7 Subj: Ethnic groups in the U.S. – Afro-Americans. Foreign languages. Illness.

Kopper, Lisa. *An elephant came to swim* (Lewin, Hugh)

Ten little babies ill. by author. Dutton, 1990. ISBN 0-525-44643-5 Subj: Babies. Counting, numbers. Poetry, rhyme.

Koralek, Jenny. *The friendly fox* ill. by Beverley Gooding. Little, 1988. ISBN 0-316-50179-4 Subj: Animals. Animals – foxes. Farms. Friendship.

Hanukkah: the festival of lights ill. by Juan Wijngaard. Lothrop, 1990. ISBN 0-688-09329-9 Subj: Holidays – Hanukkah. Jewish culture. Religion.

Koren, Edward. *Behind the wheel* ill. by author. Holt, 1972. Subj: Transportation.

Korth-Sander, Irmtraut. *Will you be my friend?* tr. from German by Rosemary Lanning; ill. by author. Holt, 1986. ISBN 0-8050-0039-9 Subj: Animals – pigs. Friendship.

Koscielniak, Bruce. *Euclid Bunny delivers the mail* ill. by author. Knopf, 1991. ISBN 0-679-91069-7 Subj: Animals. Animals – rabbits. Behavior – carelessness. Careers – mail carriers.

Hector and Prudence ill. by author. Knopf, 1990. ISBN 0-394-94514-X Subj: Animals – pigs. Family life.

Hector and Prudence—all aboard! ill. by author. Knopf, 1990. ISBN 0-679-90486-7 Subj: Animals – pigs. Holidays – Christmas. Trains.

Kotzwinkle, William. *The day the gang got rich* ill. by Joe Servello. Viking, 1970. Subj: Clubs, gangs. Friendship.

The nap master ill. by Joe Servello. Harcourt, 1979. Subj: Bedtime. Dreams. Sleep.

Up the alley with Jack and Joe ill. by Joe Servello. Macmillan, 1974. Subj: Friendship.

Kouts, Anne. *Kenny's rat* ill. by Betty Fraser. Viking, 1970. Subj: Animals – rats. Pets.

Kovalski, Maryann. *Jingle bells* ill. by adapter. Little, 1988. Originally published in 1859 as "Jingle bells or the one horse open sleigh, song and chorus," by J. Pierpont ISBN 0-316-50258-8 Subj: City. Holidays – Christmas. Music. Seasons – winter. Songs. Weather – snow.

Pizza for breakfast ill. by author. Kids Can Pr., 1991. ISBN 0-688-10410-X Subj: Behavior – wishing. Food.

The wheels on the bus ill. by author. Little, 1987. ISBN 0-316-50256-1 Subj: Buses. Family life – grandmothers. Music. Songs.

Krahn, Fernando. *Amanda and the mysterious carpet* ill. by author. Clarion, 1985. ISBN 0-89919-258-0 Subj: Imagination. Magic. Wordless.

April fools ill. by author. Dutton, 1974. Subj: Holidays – April Fools' Day. Humor. Wordless.

Arthur's adventure in the abandoned house ill. by author. Dutton, 1981. ISBN 0-525-25945-7 Subj: Problem solving. Wordless.

The biggest Christmas tree on earth ill. by author. Little, 1978. Subj: Animals. Holidays – Christmas. Toys – balls. Trees. Wordless.

Catch that cat! ill. by author. Dutton, 1978. Subj: Animals – cats. Wordless.

The creepy thing ill. by author. Houghton, 1982. Subj: Imagination – imaginary friends. Wordless.

A funny friend from heaven ill. by author. Lippincott, 1977. Subj: Angels. Clowns, jesters. Wordless.

The great ape: being the true version of the famous saga of adventure and friendship newly discovered ill. by author. Viking, 1978. Subj: Animals – gorillas. Friendship. Islands. Wordless.

Here comes Alex Pumpernickel! ill. by author. Little, 1981. Subj: Behavior – bad day. Wordless.

How Santa Claus had a long and difficult journey delivering his presents ill. by author. Delacorte Pr., 1970. Holidays - Christmas Subj: Wordless.

Little love story ill. by author. Lippincott, 1976. Subj: Holidays – Valentine's Day. Wordless.

Mr. Top ill. by author. Morrow, 1983. ISBN 0-688-02369-X Subj: Crime. Traffic, traffic signs.

The mystery of the giant footprints ill. by author. Dutton, 1977. Subj: Cumulative tales. Monsters. Wordless.

Robot-bot-bot ill. by author. Dutton, 1979. Subj: Activities – playing. Activities – working. Robots. Wordless.

Sebastian and the mushroom ill. by author. Delacorte Pr., 1976. Subj: Dreams. Wordless.

The secret in the dungeon ill. by author. Houghton, 1983. Subj: Behavior – secrets. Dragons. Wordless.

Sleep tight, Alex Pumpernickel ill. by author. Little, 1982. Subj: Bedtime. Sleep. Wordless.

Who's seen the scissors? ill. by author. Dutton, 1975. Subj: Wordless.

Kramer, Anthony Penta. *Numbers on parade: 0 to 10* ill. by author. Lothrop, 1987. ISBN 0-688-05555-9 Subj: Animals. Counting, numbers.

Krasilovsky, Phyllis. *The cow who fell in the canal* ill. by Peter Spier. Doubleday, 1953. Subj: Animals – bulls, cows. Cumulative tales. Foreign lands – Holland.

The girl who was a cowboy ill. by Cyndy Szekeres. Doubleday, 1965. Subj: Clothing. Cowboys.

The man who did not wash his dishes ill. by Barbara Cooney. Doubleday, 1950. Subj: Character traits – cleanliness. Character traits – laziness.

The man who entered a contest ill. by Yuri Salzman. Doubleday, 1980. Subj: Activities – cooking. Behavior – misbehavior.

The man who tried to save time ill. by Marcia Sewall. Doubleday, 1979. ISBN 0-385-12999-8 Subj: Character traits – laziness. Time.

The man who was too lazy to fix things ill. by John Emil Cymerman. Morrow, 1992. ISBN 0-688-10395-2 Subj: Character traits – laziness.

Scaredy cat ill. by Ninon. Macmillan, 1959. Subj: Animals – cats.

The shy little girl ill. by Trina Schart Hyman. Houghton, 1970. Subj: Character traits – shyness. Friendship.

The very little boy ill. by Ninon. Doubleday, 1962. Subj: Babies. Behavior – growing up. Family life.

The very little girl ill. by Ninon. Doubleday, 1953. Subj: Babies. Behavior – growing up. Family life.

The very tall little girl ill. by Olivia Cole. Doubleday, 1969. Subj: Character traits – being different. Family life.

Kratka, Suzanne C. *Hi, new baby* (Andry, Andrew C.)

Kratky, Lada Josefa. *Arriba y abajo: Over and under* (Matthias, Catherine)

Demasiados globos: Too many balloons (Matthias, Catherine)

Sal y entra: Out the door (Matthias, Catherine)

Kraus, Bruce. *The detective of London* (Kraus, Robert)

Kraus, Robert. *Another mouse to feed* ill. by José Aruego and Ariane Dewey. Windmill, 1980. Subj: Animals – mice. Family life.

Big brother ill. by author. Parents, 1973. Subj: Animals – rabbits. Babies. Family life.

Boris bad enough ill. by José Aruego and Ariane Dewey. Dutton, 1976. Subj: Animals – elephants.

Come out and play, little mouse ill. by José Aruego and Ariane Dewey. Greenwillow, 1987. ISBN 0-688-05838-8 Subj: Activities – playing. Animals – cats. Animals – mice. Behavior – trickery.

Daddy Long Ears ill. by author. Simon and Schuster, 1970. Subj: Animals – rabbits. Holidays – Easter.

The detective of London by Robert and Bruce Kraus; ill. by Robert Byrd. Windmill-Dutton, 1978. Subj: Animals – dogs. Crime. Problem solving.

The first robin ill. by author. Windmill, 1965. ISBN 0-671-44565-0 Subj: Birds – robins. Character traits – kindness. Illness. Seasons – spring.

Good night little one by Robert Kraus and N. M. Bodecker; ill. by N. M. Bodecker. Dutton, 1972. Subj: Bedtime. Counting, numbers. Night. Sleep.

Good night Richard Rabbit by Robert Kraus and N. M. Bodecker; ill. by N. M. Bodecker. Dutton, 1972. Subj: Animals – rabbits. Bedtime. Counting, numbers. Night. Sleep.

Herman the helper ill. by José Aruego and Ariane Dewey. Dutton, 1974. Subj: Character traits – helpfulness. Octopuses. Sea and seashore.

How spider saved Valentine's Day ill. by author. Scholastic, 1986. ISBN 0-590-33743-2 Subj: Friendship. Holidays – Valentine's Day. Insects. Spiders.

I, Mouse ill. by author. Harper, 1958. Subj: Animals – mice.

The king's trousers ill. by Fred Gwynne. Windmill, 1981. ISBN 0-671-42259-6 Subj: Behavior – trickery. Clothing – pants. Royalty – kings.

Ladybug, ladybug! ill. by author. Harper, 1957. Subj: Behavior – misunderstanding. Friendship. Insects – ladybugs.

Leo the late bloomer ill. by José Aruego. Dutton, 1971. Subj: Animals – tigers. Behavior – growing up.

The little giant ill. by author. Harper, 1967. Subj: Concepts – size. Giants.

The littlest rabbit ill. by author. Harper, 1961. Subj: Animals – rabbits. Character traits – smallness.

Mert the blurt ill. by José Aruego and Ariane Dewey. Windmill, 1981. Subj: Behavior – gossip. Frogs and toads.

Milton the early riser ill. by José Aruego and Ariane Dewey. Dutton, 1972. Subj: Animals – bears. Sleep.

Noel the coward ill. by José Aruego and Ariane Dewey. Dutton, 1977. Subj: Emotions – fear.

Owliver ill. by José Aruego and Ariane Dewey. Prentice-Hall, 1987, 1974. ISBN 0-13-647538-8 Subj: Birds – owls. Careers. Character traits – individuality.

Phil the ventriloquist ill. by author. Greenwillow, 1989. ISBN 0-688-07988-1 Subj: Animals – rabbits. Family life.

Rebecca Hatpin ill. by Robert Byrd. Dutton, 1974. Subj: Careers – nurses. Character traits – helpfulness. Character traits – selfishness. Family life – grandmothers.

Springfellow ill. by Sam Savitt. Dutton, 1978. Subj: Animals – horses.

The three friends ill. by José Aruego and Ariane Dewey. Dutton, 1975. Subj: Friendship.

The tree that stayed up until next Christmas ill. by Edna Eicke. Dutton, 1972. ISBN 0-525-61001-4 Subj: Holidays – Christmas. Toys. Trees.

The trouble with spider ill. by author. Harper, 1962. Subj: Friendship. Insects – flies. Spiders.

Where are you going, little mouse? ill. by José Aruego and Arianne Dewey. Greenwillow, 1986. ISBN 0-688-04295-3 Subj: Animals – mice. Behavior – running away. Behavior – seeking better things.

Whose mouse are you? ill. by José Aruego. Macmillan, 1970. Subj: Animals – mice.

Krause, Ute. *Nora and the great bear* ill. by author. Dial, 1989. ISBN 0-8037-0685-5 Subj: Animals – bears. Behavior – lost. Sports – hunting.

Pig surprise ill. by author. Dial, 1989. ISBN 0-8037-0714-2 Subj: Animals – pigs. Behavior – misbehavior. Behavior – misunderstanding. Pets.

Krauss, Ruth. *The backward day* ill. by Marc Simont. Harper, 1950. Subj: Family life.

Bears ill. by Phyllis Rowand. Harper, 1948. Subj: Animals – bears. Poetry, rhyme.

Big and little ill. by Mary Szilagyi. Scholastic, 1988. ISBN 0-590-41707-X Subj: Concepts – size. Emotions – love.

A bouquet of littles ill. by Jane Flora. Harper, 1963. Subj: Concepts – size. Poetry, rhyme.

The bundle book ill. by Helen Stone. Harper, 1951. Subj: Bedtime. Emotions. Family life – mothers. Games.

The carrot seed ill. by Crockett Johnson. Harper, 1945. Subj: Character traits – optimism. Gardens, gardening. Plants. Self-concept.

Charlotte and the white horse ill. by Maurice Sendak. Harper, 1955. Subj: Animals – horses.

Everything under a mushroom ill. by Margot Tomes. Four Winds Pr., 1974. Subj: Elves and little people. Poetry, rhyme.

Eyes, nose, fingers, toes ill. by Elizabeth Schneider. Harper, 1964. Subj: Anatomy.

A good man and his good wife ill. by Marc Simont. Harper, 1962. Subj: Behavior – boredom. Friendship.

The happy day ill. by Marc Simont. Harper, 1949. Subj: Caldecott award honor book. Hibernation. Seasons – spring. Seasons – winter. Weather – snow.

The happy egg ill. by Crockett Johnson. O'Hara, 1967. Subj: Birds. Eggs.

A hole is to dig: a first book of first definitions ill. by Maurice Sendak. Harper, 1952. ISBN 0-06-023406-7 Subj: Language.

I write it ill. by Mary Chalmers. Harper, 1970. Subj: Activities – writing.

I'll be you and you be me ill. by Maurice Sendak. Harper, 1954. Subj: Friendship. Humor.

Mama, I wish I was snow. Child, you'd be very cold ill. by Ellen Raskin. Atheneum, 1962. Subj: Behavior – wishing. Games.

A moon or a button ill. by Remy Charlip. Harper, 1959. Subj: Imagination.

Open house for butterflies ill. by Maurice Sendak. Harper, 1960. Subj: Imagination.

Somebody else's nut tree, and other tales from children ill. by Maurice Sendak. Harper, 1958. Subj: Children as authors. Imagination.

This thumbprint ill. by author. Harper, 1967. Subj: Humor. Imagination.

A very special house ill. by Maurice Sendak. Harper, 1953. Subj: Caldecott award honor book. Houses. Imagination.

Krauze, Andrzej. *What's so special about today?* ill. by author. Lothrop, 1984. Subj: Animals. Birthdays. Character traits – questioning.

Krementz, Jill. *Benjy goes to a restaurant* photos. by author. Crown, 1986. ISBN 0-517-56166-2 Subj: Careers – waiters, waitresses. Family life. Format, unusual – board books.

Jack goes to the beach photos. by author. Random House, 1986. ISBN 0-394-88001-3 Subj: Family life. Format, unusual – board books. Sand. Sea and seashore.

Jamie goes on an airplane photos. by author. Random House, 1986. ISBN 0-394-88196-6 Subj: Activities – traveling. Airplanes, airports. Careers – airplane pilots. Format, unusual – board books.

Katherine goes to nursery school photos. by author. Random House, 1986. ISBN 0-394-88195-8 Subj: Activities. Format, unusual – board books. School.

Lily goes to the playground photos. by author. Random House, 1986. ISBN 0-394-87999-6 Subj: Activities – playing. Family life. Format, unusual – board books.

Taryn goes to the dentist photos. by author. Crown, 1986. ISBN 0-517-56168-9 Subj: Careers – dentists. Family life. Format, unusual – board books.

A very young gardener photos. by author. Dial, 1991. ISBN 0-8037-0875-0 Subj: Gardens, gardening.

A visit to Washington, D.C. photos. by author. Scholastic, 1987. ISBN 0-500-40582-9 Subj: Activities – traveling. City. Museums.

Krensky, Stephen. *The big time bears* ill. by Mary-ann Cocca-Leffler. Little, 1989. ISBN 0-316-50375-4 Subj: Animals – bears. Time.

Dinosaurs, beware! (Brown, Marc Tolon)

The lion upstairs ill. by Leigh Grant. Atheneum, 1983. Subj: Imagination – imaginary friends.

The missing Mother Goose ill. by Chris L. Demarest. Doubleday, 1991. ISBN 0-385-26273-6 Subj: Nursery rhymes.

My first dictionary ill. by George Ulrich. Houghton, 1980. Subj: Dictionaries.

Perfect pigs (Brown, Marc Tolon)

Kreye, Walter. *The giant from the little island* ill. by Tomek Bogacki. North-South, 1990. ISBN 1-55858-085-9 Subj: Activities – making things. Behavior – wishing. Friendship. Giants.

Krings, Antoon. *Oliver's bicycle* ill. by author. Walt Disney, 1992. ISBN 1-56282-161-X Subj: Animals – koala bears. Sports – bicycling. Weather – rain.

Oliver's pool ill. by author. Walt Disney, 1992. ISBN 1-56282-163-6 Subj: Animals – koala bears. Sports – swimming.

Oliver's strawberry patch ill. by author. Walt Disney, 1992. ISBN 1-56282-163-6 Subj: Animals – koala bears. Food. Gardens, gardening. Plants.

Kroll, Steven. *Amanda and the giggling ghost* ill. by Dick Gackenbach. Holiday, 1980. Subj: Behavior – stealing. Ghosts.

Are you pirates? ill. by Marylin Hafner. Pantheon, 1982. Subj: Imagination. Pirates.

The big bunny and the Easter eggs ill. by Janet Stevens. Holiday, 1982. Subj: Animals – rabbits. Holidays – Easter. Illness.

The big bunny and the magic show ill. by Janet Stevens. Holiday, 1986. ISBN 0-8234-0589-3 Subj: Animals – rabbits. Holidays – Easter. Magic.

Big Jeremy ill. by Donald Carrick. Holiday, 1989. ISBN 0-8234-0759-4 Subj: Friendship. Giants.

Branigan's cat and the Halloween ghost ill. by Carolyn Ewing. Holiday, 1990. ISBN 0-8234-0822-1 Subj: Animals – cats. Ghosts. Holidays – Halloween.

The candy witch ill. by Marylin Hafner. Holiday, 1979. Subj: Behavior – unnoticed, unseen. Holidays – Halloween. Magic. Witches.

Don't get me in trouble ill. by Marvin Glass. Crown, 1988. ISBN 0-517-56724-5 Subj: Animals – dogs. Friendship.

Fat magic ill. by Tomie de Paola. Holiday, 1978. Subj: Magic. Royalty.

The goat parade ill. by Tim Kirk. Parents, 1983. Subj: Animals – goats. Parades.

The hand-me-down doll ill. by Evaline Ness. Holiday, 1983. Subj: Toys – dolls.

Happy Father's Day ill. by Marylin Hafner. Holiday, 1987. ISBN 0-5234-0671-7 Subj: Family life – fathers. Holidays – Father's Day.

Happy Mother's Day ill. by Marylin Hafner. Holiday, 1985. ISBN 0-8234-0504-4 Subj: Family life. Holidays – Mother's Day.

The Hokey-Pokey man ill. by Deborah Kogan Ray. Holiday, 1989. ISBN 0-8234-0728-4 Subj: Food.

Howard and Gracie's luncheonette ill. by Michael Sours. Holt, 1991. ISBN 0-8050-1305-9 Subj: Activities – working. Careers.

I love spring! ill. by Kathryn E. Shoemaker. Holiday, 1987. ISBN 0-8234-0634-2 Subj: Seasons – spring.

If I could be my grandmother ill. by Tasha Tudor. Pantheon, 1977. Subj: Family life – grandmothers.

It's April Fools' Day! ill. by Jeni Bassett. Holiday, 1990. ISBN 0-8234-0747-0 Subj: Animals – cats. Behavior – bullying. Holidays – April Fools' Day.

It's Groundhog Day! ill. by Jeni Bassett. Holiday, 1987. ISBN 0-8234-0643-1 Subj: Activities – picnicking. Animals. Holidays – Groundhog Day.

Looking for Daniela ill. by Anita Lobel. Holiday, 1988. ISBN 0-8234-0695-4 Subj: Crime. Foreign lands – Italy. Problem solving.

Loose tooth ill. by Tricia Tusa. Holiday, 1984. Subj: Fairies. Teeth.

The magic rocket ill. by Will Hillenbrand. Holiday, 1992. ISBN 0-8234-0916-3 Subj: Animals – dogs. Imagination. Space and space ships. Toys.

Mary McLean and the St. Patrick's Day parade ill. by Michael Dooling. Scholastic, 1991. ISBN 0-590-43701-1 Subj: City. Ethnic groups in the U.S. – Irish-Americans. Holidays – St. Patrick's Day. Parades.

One tough turkey: a Thanksgiving story ill. by John Wallner. Holiday, 1982. Subj: Birds – turkeys. Holidays – Thanksgiving. Sports – hunting.

Otto ill. by Ned Delaney. Parents, 1983. Subj: Behavior – misbehavior. Robots.

Pigs in the house ill. by Tim Kirk. Parents, 1983. Subj: Animals – pigs. Behavior – misbehavior. Houses. Poetry, rhyme.

Princess Abigail and the wonderful hat ill. by Patience Brewster. Holiday, 1991. ISBN 0-8234-0853-1 Subj: Clothing – hats. Folk and fairy tales. Royalty – princesses.

Santa's crash-bang Christmas ill. by Tomie de Paola. Holiday, 1977. Subj: Holidays – Christmas.

The squirrels' Thanksgiving ill. by Jeni Bassett. Holiday, 1991. ISBN 0-8234-0823-X Subj: Animals – squirrels. Family life. Holidays – Thanksgiving. Sibling rivalry.

Toot! Toot! ill. by Anne F. Rockwell. Holiday, 1983. Subj: Family life – grandparents. Imagination. Toys – trains. Trains.

The tyrannosaurus game ill. by Tomie de Paola. Holiday, 1976. Subj: Cumulative tales. Dinosaurs. Games. Imagination.

Woof, woof! ill. by Nicole Rubel. Dial Pr., 1983. Subj: Animals – dogs. Crime.

Kroll, Virginia L. *Helen the fish* ill. by Teri Weidner. Albert Whitman, 1992. ISBN 0-8075-3194-4 Subj: Death. Family life – brothers. Fish. Pets.

Krull, Kathleen. *Autumn* (Allington, Richard L.)

It's my earth too ill. by Melanie Hope Greenberg. Doubleday, 1992. ISBN 0-385-42088-9 Subj: Ecology. Nature.

Measuring (Allington, Richard L.)

Reading (Allington, Richard L.)

Science (Allington, Richard L.)

Songs of praise ill. by Kathryn Hewitt. Harcourt, 1989. ISBN 0-15-277108-5 Subj: Music. Religion. Songs. Seasons.

Spring (Allington, Richard L.)

Summer (Allington, Richard L.)

Talking (Allington, Richard L.)

Thinking (Allington, Richard L.)

Time (Allington, Richard L.)

Winter (Allington, Richard L.)

Words (Allington, Richard L.)

Writing (Allington, Richard L.)

Krum, Charlotte. *The four riders* ill. by Katherine Evans. Follett, 1953. Subj: Animals – horses.

Krupinski, Loretta. *Lost in the fog* (Bacheller, Irving)

Krupp, E. C. *The comet and you* ill. by Robin Rector Krupp. Macmillan, 1985. ISBN 0-02-751250-9 Subj: Science.

Krupp, Robin Rector. *Get set to wreck!* ill. by author. Macmillan, 1988. ISBN 0-02-751140-5 Subj: Activities – playing. Imagination. Language.

Krush, Beth. *The fish from Japan* (Cooper, Elizabeth K.)

Krüss, James. *Johnny Longnose* by James Krüss and Naomi Lewis; ill. by Stasys Eidrigevicius. North-South, 1990. ISBN 1-55858-023-9 Subj: Anatomy – noses. Poetry, rhyme.

3 X 3: Three by three ill. by Eva Johanna Rubin; English text by Geoffrey Strachan. Macmillan, 1963. Subj: Animals. Counting, numbers. Poetry, rhyme.

Kubler, Susanne. *The three friends* ill. by author. Macmillan, 1985. ISBN 0-02-751150-2 Subj: Animals. Friendship.

Kübler-Ross, Elisabeth. *Remember the secret* ill. by Heather Preston. Celestial Arts, 1982. Subj: Death.

Kuchalla, Susan. *All about seeds* ill. by Jane McBee. Troll Assoc., 1982. Subj: Plants. Science. Seeds.

Baby animals ill. by Joel Snyder. Troll Assoc., 1982. Subj: Animals.

Bears ill. by Kathie Kelleher. Troll Assoc., 1982. Subj: Animals – bears.

Birds ill. by Gary Britt. Troll Assoc., 1982. Subj: Birds.

What is a reptile? ill. by Paul Harvey. Troll Assoc., 1982. Subj: Reptiles.

Kudrna, C. Imbior. *To bathe a boa* ill. by author. Carolrhoda Books, 1986. ISBN 0-87614-306-0 Subj: Activities – bathing. Behavior – hiding. Poetry, rhyme. Reptiles – snakes.

Kuklin, Susan. *Going to my ballet class* photos. by author. Bradbury Pr., 1989. ISBN 0-02-751235-5 Subj: Activities – dancing.

Going to my gymnastics class photos. by author. Bradbury Pr., 1991. ISBN 0-02-751236-3 Subj: Sports – gymnastics.

Going to my nursery school photos. by author. Bradbury Pr., 1990. ISBN 0-02-751237-1 Subj: School.

How my family lives in America photos. by author. Bradbury Pr., 1992. ISBN 0-02-751239-8 Subj: Ethnic groups in the U.S. Family life.

Taking my dog to the vet photos. by author. Bradbury Pr., 1988. ISBN 0-02-751234-7 Subj: Animals. Careers – veterinarians. Pets.

Thinking big: the story of a young dwarf photos. by author. Lothrop, 1986. ISBN 0-688-05827-2 Subj: Character traits – being different. Handicaps.

When I see my dentist photos. by author. Bradbury Pr., 1988. ISBN 0-02-751231-2 Subj: Careers – dentists. Health.

When I see my doctor photos. by author. Bradbury Pr., 1988. ISBN 0-02-751232-0 Subj: Careers – doctors.

Kumin, Maxine. *The beach before breakfast* ill. by Leonard Weisgard. Putnam's, 1964. Subj: Sea and seashore.

Eggs of things ill. by Leonard W. Shortall. Putnam's, 1963. Subj: Eggs. Frogs and toads. Humor. Science.

Follow the fall ill. by Artur Marokvia. Putnam's, 1961. Subj: Holidays. Imagination. Poetry, rhyme. Seasons – fall.

Joey and the birthday present by Maxine Kumin and Anne Sexton; ill. by Evaline Ness. McGraw-Hill, 1971. Subj: Animals – mice. Birthdays.

Mittens in May ill. by Eliott Gilbert. Putnam's, 1962. Subj: Birds. Character traits – kindness to animals. Clothing – gloves.

Sebastian and the dragon ill. by William D. Hayes. Putnam's, 1960. Subj: Character traits – smallness. Dragons. Poetry, rhyme.

Speedy digs downside up ill. by Ezra Jack Keats. Putnam's, 1964. Subj: Activities – digging. Character traits – ambition. Humor. Poetry, rhyme.

What color is Caesar? ill. by Evaline Ness. McGraw-Hill, 1978. Subj: Animals – dogs. Concepts – color.

A winter friend ill. by Artur Marokvia. Putnam's, 1961. Subj: Poetry, rhyme. Seasons – winter.

Kunhardt, Dorothy. *Billy the barber* ill. by William Pène Du Bois. Harper, 1961. Subj: Careers – barbers. Hair. Old age.

Kitty's new doll ill. by Lucinda McQueen. Golden Pr., 1984. Subj: Animals – cats. Toys – dolls.

Kunhardt, Edith. *Danny and the Easter egg* ill. by author. Greenwillow, 1989. ISBN 0-688-08036-7 Subj: Holidays – Easter. Reptiles – alligators, crocodiles.

Danny's Christmas star ill. by author. Greenwillow, 1989. ISBN 0-688-07906-7 Subj: Activities – making things. Holidays – Christmas. Reptiles – alligators, crocodiles.

Danny's mystery Valentine ill. by author. Greenwillow, 1987. ISBN 0-688-06854-5 Subj: Family life – grandmothers. Holidays – Valentine's Day. Reptiles – alligators, crocodiles.

I want to be a farmer photos. by author. Grosset, 1989. ISBN 0-448-09068-6 Subj: Careers – farmers. Farms.

I want to be a fire fighter photos. by author. Grosset, 1989. ISBN 0-448-09069-4 Subj: Careers – firefighters.

Pat the cat ill. by author. Golden Pr., 1984. Subj: Animals – cats. Format, unusual – toy and movable books. Pets.

Red day, green day ill. by Marylin Hafner. Greenwillow, 1992. ISBN 0-688-09400-7 Subj: Concepts – color. School. Weather – rainbows.

Trick or treat, Danny! ill. by author. Greenwillow, 1988. ISBN 0-688-07311-5 Subj: Holidays – Halloween. Illness. Reptiles – alligators, crocodiles.

Where's Peter? ill. by author. Greenwillow, 1988. ISBN 0-688-07205-4 Subj: Babies. Family life. Games.

Which one would you choose? ill. by author. Greenwillow, 1989. ISBN 0-688-07908-3 Subj: Activities. Participation.

Which pig would you choose? ill. by author. Greenwillow, 1990. ISBN 0-688-08982-8 Subj: Activities. Farms. Participation.

Kunnas, Mauri. *The nighttime book* by Mauri Kunnas with Tarja Kunnas; tr. from the Finnish by

Tim Steffa; ill. by author. Crown, 1985. ISBN 0-517-55819-X Subj: Activities. Night.

One spooky night and other scary stories by Mauri Kunnas with Tarja Kunnas; tr. by Tim Steffa; ill. by author. Crown, 1986. ISBN 0-517-56253-7 Subj: Ghosts. Holidays – Halloween. Monsters.

Santa Claus and his elves by Mauri Kunnas; assisted by Tarja Kunnas; ill. by authors. Harmony, 1982. Translation of Joulupukki Subj: Elves and little people. Holidays – Christmas.

Twelve gifts for Santa Claus by Mauri and Tarja Kunnas; tr. by Tim Steffa; ill. by authors. Crown, 1988. ISBN 0-517-56631-1 Subj: Character traits – generosity. Elves and little people. Holidays – Christmas.

Kunnas, Tarja. *The nighttime book* (Kunnas, Mauri)

One spooky night and other scary stories (Kunnas, Mauri)

Santa Claus and his elves (Kunnas, Mauri)

Twelve gifts for Santa Claus (Kunnas, Mauri)

Kuratomi, Chizuko. *Mr. Bear and the robbers* ill. by Kozo Kakimoto. Dial Pr., 1970. Subj: Animals – bears. Animals – rabbits.

Kuskin, Karla. *ABCDEFGHIJKLMNOPQRSTU-VWXYZ* ill. by author. Harper, 1963. Subj: ABC books.

All sizes of noises ill. by author. Harper, 1962. Subj: Concepts. Noise, sounds. Poetry, rhyme.

The animals and the ark ill. by author. Harper, 1958. Subj: Animals. Boats, ships. Poetry, rhyme. Religion – Noah.

A boy had a mother who bought him a hat ill. by author. Houghton, 1976. Subj: Cumulative tales. Poetry, rhyme.

The Dallas Titans get ready for bed ill. by Marc Simont. Harper, 1986. ISBN 0-06-023563-2 Subj: Bedtime. Clothing. Sports – football.

Herbert hated being small ill. by author. Houghton, 1979. Subj: Character traits – smallness. Concepts – size. Poetry, rhyme.

In the flaky frosty morning ill. by author. Harper, 1969. Subj: Poetry, rhyme. Seasons – winter. Snowmen. Weather – snow.

James and the rain ill. by author. Harper, 1957. Subj: Animals. Poetry, rhyme. Weather – rain.

Jerusalem, shining still ill. by David Frampton. Harper, 1987. ISBN 0-06-023549-7 Subj: City. Foreign lands – Israel. Religion.

Just like everyone else ill. by author. Harper, 1959. Subj: Activities – flying.

Night again ill. by author. Little, 1981. Subj: Bedtime.

The Philharmonic gets dressed ill. by Marc Simont. Harper, 1982. Subj: Clothing.

Roar and more ill. by author. Harper, 1956. Subj: Animals. Noise, sounds. Participation. Poetry, rhyme.

Sand and snow ill. by author. Harper, 1965. Subj: Poetry, rhyme. Sea and seashore. Seasons – summer. Seasons – winter.

Something sleeping in the hall ill. by author. Harper, 1985. ISBN 0-06-023634-5 Subj: Animals. Pets. Poetry, rhyme.

A space story ill. by Marc Simont. Harper, 1978. Subj: Bedtime. Space and space ships. Stars.

Watson, the smartest dog in the U.S.A. ill. by author. Harper, 1968. Subj: Activities – reading. Animals – dogs.

What did you bring me? ill. by author. Harper, 1973. Subj: Animals – mice. Behavior – greed. Self-concept. Witches.

Which horse is William? ill. by author. Harper, 1959. Subj: Character traits – individuality. Imagination.

Kusugak, Michael. *A promise is a promise* (Munsch, Robert N.)

Kwitz, Mary DeBall. *Little chick's breakfast* ill. by Bruce Degen. Harper, 1983. Subj: Birds – chickens. Farms. Food.

Little chick's story ill. by Cyndy Szekeres. Harper, 1978. Subj: Birds – chickens. Eggs.

Mouse at home ill. by author. Harper, 1966. Subj: Animals – mice. Seasons.

Rabbits' search for a little house ill. by Lorinda Bryan Cauley. Crown, 1977. Subj: Animals – rabbits. Houses.

When it rains ill. by author. Follett, 1974. Subj: Animals. Poetry, rhyme. Weather – rain. Weather – rainbows.

Kyte, Dennis. *Mattie and Cataragus* ill. by author. Doubleday, 1988. ISBN 0-385-24404-5 Subj: Animals – cats. Friendship.

Lacome, Julie. *Funny business* ill. by author. Morrow, 1991. ISBN 0-688-10159-3 Subj: Animals – dogs. Circus. Clowns, jesters. Concepts – color. Concepts – shape. Format, unusual – toy and movable books.

Hocus pocus ill. by author. Morrow, 1991. ISBN 0-688-10158-5 Subj: Animals – rabbits. Format, unusual – toy and movable books. Magic.

Lady Eden's School. *Just how stories* ill. by Derek Steele. Merrimack, 1981. Subj: Animals. Children as authors.

Ladybug, ladybug, and other nursery rhymes ill. by Eloise Wilkin. Random House, 1979. Subj: Format, unusual. Nursery rhymes.

La Farge, Phyllis. *Joanna runs away* ill. by Trina Schart Hyman. Holt, 1973. Subj: Animals – horses. Behavior – running away.

La Farge, Sheila. *The boy who ate more than the giant and other Swedish folktales* (Löfgren, Ulf)

Peter's adventures in Blueberry land (Beskow, Elsa Maartman)

La Fontaine, Jean de. *The hare and the tortoise* ill. by Brian Wildsmith. Watts, 1963. Subj: Animals – rabbits. Folk and fairy tales. Reptiles – turtles, tortoises. Sports – racing.

The lion and the rat ill. by Brian Wildsmith. Watts, 1963. Subj: Animals – lions. Animals – rats. Character traits – helpfulness. Folk and fairy tales.

The miller, the boy and the donkey adapt. and ill. by Brian Wildsmith. Watts, 1969. "Based on a fable by La Fontaine." Subj: Animals – donkeys. Character traits – practicality. Folk and fairy tales. Humor.

The north wind and the sun ill. by Brian Wildsmith. Watts, 1964. Subj: Folk and fairy tales. Sun. Weather – wind.

The turtle and the two ducks (Plante, Patricia)

The turtle and the two ducks (Plante, Patricia)

The turtle and the two ducks (Plante, Patricia)

Lafontaine, Pascale Claude *see* Claude-Lafontaine, Pascale

Lage, Ida De *see* DeLage, Ida

Lager, Claude. *A tale of two rats* ill. by Nicole Rutten. Stewart, Tabori & Chang, 1991. ISBN 1-55670-228-0 Subj: Animals – rats. Careers – artists. Foreign lands – Italy. Friendship.

Lagercrantz, Rose. *Brave little Pete of Geranium Street* by Rose and Samuel Lagercrantz; tr. by Jack Prelutsky; ill. by Eva Eriksson. Greenwillow, 1986. ISBN 0-688-06181-8 Subj: Behavior – bullying. Character traits – bravery. Poetry, rhyme.

Lagercrantz, Samuel. *Brave little Pete of Geranium Street* (Lagercrantz, Rose)

Lagerlöf, Selma. *The changeling* tr. from Swedish by Susanna Stevens; ill. by Jeanette Winter. Knopf, 1992. ISBN 0-679-91035-2 Subj: Babies. Emotions – love. Fairies. Format, unusual – toy and movable books. Trolls.

The legend of the Christmas rose retold by Ellin Greene; ill. by Charles Mikolaycak. Holiday, 1990. ISBN 0-8234-8021-3 Subj: Flowers. Folk and fairy tales. Holidays – Christmas.

Laird, Donivee Martin. *The three little Hawaiian pigs and the magic shark* ill. by Carol Jossem. Bess Pr., 1981. Subj: Animals – pigs. Fish. Hawaii.

Laird, Elizabeth. *The day Patch stood guard* ill. by Colin Reeder. Morrow, 1991. ISBN 0-688-10240-9 Subj: Animals – dogs. Farms. Foreign lands – England. Tractors.

The day Sidney ran off ill. by Colin Reeder. Morrow, 1991. ISBN 0-688-10242-5 Subj: Animals – pigs. Farms. Foreign lands – England. Tractors.

The day the ducks went skating ill. by Colin Reeder. Morrow, 1991. ISBN 0-688-10247-6 Subj: Animals. Birds – ducks. Careers – farmers. Character traits – kindness to animals. Farms. Tractors.

The day Veronica was nosy ill. by Colin Reeder. Morrow, 1991. ISBN 0-688-10249-2 Subj: Animals. Careers – farmers. Farms. Insects – hornets. Tractors.

Lakin, Patricia. *Don't touch my room* ill. by Patience Brewster. Little, 1985. ISBN 0-316-51230-3 Subj: Babies. Behavior – sharing. Emotions – fear. Family life. Sibling rivalry.

Oh, brother! ill. by Patience Brewster. Little, 1987. ISBN 0-316-51231-1 Subj: Family life. Sibling rivalry. Trees.

Lalicki, Barbara. *If there were dreams to sell* ill. by Margot Tomes. Lothrop, 1984. Subj: ABC books. Poetry, rhyme.

Lalli, Judy. *Feelings alphabet: an album of emotions from A to Z* photos. by Douglas L. Mason-Fry. Jalmar Pr., 1984. Subj: ABC books. Emotions.

La Mare, Walter De *see* De La Mare, Walter (Walter John)

Lamm, C. Drew. *Anniranni and Mollymishi, the wild-haired doll* ill. by Ruth Ohi. Firefly, 1990. ISBN 1-55037-105-3 Subj: Animals – dogs. Toys – dolls.

Lamont, Priscilla. *The troublesome pig* (The old woman and her pig)

Lampert, Emily. *A little touch of monster* ill. by Victoria Chess. Atlantic Monthly Pr., 1986. ISBN 0-87113-022-X Subj: Character traits – individuality. Family life.

Landa, Norbert. *Rabbit and chicken find a box* ill. by Hanne Turk. Morrow, 1992. ISBN 0-688-09968-8 Subj: Animals – rabbits. Birds – chickens. Character traits – helpfulness. Format, unusual – board books. Friendship.

Rabbit and chicken play hide and seek ill. by Hanne Turk. Morrow, 1992. ISBN 0-688-09970-X Subj: Activities – playing. Animals – rabbits. Birds – chickens. Friendship. Games.

Landau, Terry. *Butterflies and rainbows* (Berger, Judith)

Landshoff, Ursula. *Cats are good company* ill. by author. Harper, 1983. Subj: Animals – cats. Pets. Science.

Lane, Margaret. *The frog* ill. by Grahame Corbett. Dial Pr., 1981. Subj: Frogs and toads. Science.

The squirrel ill. by Kenneth Lilly. Dial Pr., 1981. Subj: Animals – squirrels. Science.

Lane, Megan Halsey. *Something to crow about* ill. by author. Dial, 1990. ISBN 0-8037-0698-7 Subj: Birds – chickens. Self-concept.

Lang, Andrew. *Nursery rhyme book* (Mother Goose)

Snow White and Rose Red (Grimm, Jacob)

Langham, Tony. *The amazing adventures of Teddy Tum Tum* (Breese, Gillian)

Langner, Nola. *By the light of the silvery moon* ill. by author. Lothrop, 1983. Subj: Behavior – running away. Imagination – imaginary friends. Royalty.

Freddy my grandfather ill. by author. Four Winds Pr., 1979. Subj: Family life – grandfathers.

Langstaff, Feodor. *Frog went a-courtin'* (A frog he would a-wooing go (folk-song))

Langstaff, John M. *Oh, a-hunting we will go* ill. by Nancy Winslow Parker. Atheneum, 1974. Subj: Folk and fairy tales. Music. Songs. Sports – hunting.

Ol' Dan Tucker ill. by Joe Krush. Harcourt, 1963. Subj: Folk and fairy tales. Music. Songs.

On Christmas day in the morning ill. by Antony Groves-Raines. Harcourt, 1959. Piano settings by Marshall Woodbridge Subj: Folk and fairy tales. Holidays – Christmas. Music. Songs.

Over in the meadow ill. by Feodor Rojankovsky. Harcourt, 1957. Includes Over in the meadow (for voice and piano) by Marshall Woodbridge Subj: Animals. Counting, numbers. Folk and fairy tales. Songs.

Soldier, soldier, won't you marry me? ill. by Anita Lobel. Doubleday, 1972. Subj: Careers – military. Folk and fairy tales. Music. Songs.

The swapping boy ill. by Beth and Joe Krush. Harcourt, 1960. Subj: Activities – trading. Folk and fairy tales. Music. Songs.

The two magicians ill. by Fritz Eichenberg. Atheneum, 1973. Adapt. by John Langstaff from an ancient ballad Subj: Folk and fairy tales. Magic. Music. Songs. Witches.

Langstaff, Nancy. *A tiny baby for you* ill. by Suzanne Szasz. Harcourt, 1955. Subj: Babies.

Langston, Jane. *Salt* (Afanas'ev, Aleksandr N.)

Langton, Jane. *The hedgehog boy: a Latvian folktale* ill. by Ilse Plume. Harper, 1985. ISBN 0-06-023697-3 Subj: Character traits – honesty. Folk and fairy tales. Foreign lands – Latvia. Royalty. Weddings.

Lankford, Mary D. *Is it dark? Is it light?* ill. by Stacey Schuett. Knopf, 1991. ISBN 0-679-91579-6 Subj: Concepts – opposites. Moon.

Lanning, Rosemary. *Camomile heads for home* (Moers, Hermann)

Can we help you, Saint Nicholas? (Scheidl, Gerda Marie)

Jonathan Mouse (Ostheeren, Ingrid)

Jonathan Mouse and the baby bird (Ostheeren, Ingrid)

Lullaby for a newborn king (Wilkoń, Józef)

Will you be my friend? (Korth-Sander, Irmtraut)

Lansdown, Brenda. *Galumpf* ill. by Ernest Crichlow. Houghton, 1963. Subj: Animals – cats. Ethnic groups in the U.S. Ethnic groups in the U.S. – Afro-Americans. Pets.

Lanton, Sandy. *Daddy's chair* ill. by Shelly O. Haas. Kar-Ben Copies, 1991. ISBN 0-929371-51-8 Subj: Death. Emotions. Family life – fathers. Furniture – chairs.

Lapp, Carolyn. *The dentists' tools* ill. by George Overlie. Lerner, 1961. Subj: Careers – dentists.

Lapp, Eleanor. *The blueberry bears* ill. by Margot Apple. Albert Whitman, 1983. Subj: Animals – bears. Food.

In the morning mist ill. by David Cunningham. Albert Whitman, 1978. Subj: Family life – grandfathers. Morning. Sports – fishing.

The mice came in early this year ill. by David Cunningham. Albert Whitman, 1976. Subj: Animals. Farms. Seasons – fall. Seasons – winter.

Lapsley, Susan. *I am adopted* ill. by Michael Charlton. Bradbury Pr., 1974. Subj: Adoption. Family life.

Laroche, Michel. *The snow rose* ill. by Sandra Laroche. Holiday, 1986. ISBN 0-8234-0594-X Subj: Character traits – cleverness. Folk and fairy tales. Royalty – princesses.

La Rochelle, David. *A Christmas guest* ill. by Martin Skoro. Carolrhoda Books, 1988. ISBN 0-87614-325-7 Subj: Character traits – kindness. Holidays – Christmas. Poetry, rhyme.

Larrick, Nancy. *Cats are cats* ill. by Ed Young. Putnam's, 1988. ISBN 0-399-21517-4 Subj: Animals – cats. Poetry, rhyme.

When the dark comes dancing: a bedtime poetry book ill. by John Wallner. Putnam's, 1983. Subj: Bedtime. Night. Poetry, rhyme.

Larsen, Hanne. *Don't forget Tom* ill. with photos. Crowell, 1978. Subj: Handicaps.

Lasell, Fen. *Fly away goose* ill. by author. Houghton, 1965. Subj: Birds – geese. Eggs. Imagination.

Michael grows a wish ill. by author. Houghton, 1974. Subj: Animals – horses. Behavior – wishing. Birthdays.

Lasher, Faith B. *Hubert Hippo's world* ill. by Leonard Lee Rue, III. Children's Pr., 1971. Subj: Animals – hippopotami.

Lasker, David. *The boy who loved music* ill. by Joe Lasker. Viking, 1979. Subj: Music. Royalty.

Lasker, Joe. *The do-something day* ill. by author. Viking, 1982. Subj: Behavior – running away.

He's my brother ill. by author. Albert Whitman, 1974. Subj: Character traits – loyalty. Family life. Handicaps.

Lentil soup ill. by author. Albert Whitman, 1977. Subj: Activities – cooking. Counting, numbers. Days of the week, months of the year. Food.

Mothers can do anything ill. by author. Albert Whitman, 1972. Subj: Activities – working. Careers. Family life – mothers.

Nick joins in ill. by author. Albert Whitman, 1980. Subj: Handicaps. School.

A tournament of knights ill. by author. Crowell, 1986. ISBN 0-690-04542-5 Subj: Behavior – fighting, arguing. Knights.

Laskin, Pamela L. *Wish upon a star a story for children with a parent who is mentally ill* by Pamela L. Laskin and Addie Alexander Moskowitz; ill. by Margo Lemieux. Magination Pr., 1991. ISBN 0-945354-30-4 Subj: Emotions. Family life. Illness.

Laskowski, Janina Domanska *see* Domanska, Janina

Laskowski, Jerzy. *Master of the royal cats* ill. by Janina Domanska. Seabury Pr., 1965. Subj: Animals – cats. Animals – dogs. Foreign lands – Africa. Foreign lands – Egypt. Royalty.

Lasky, Kathryn. *Agatha's alphabet, with her very own dictionary* (Floyd, Lucy)

A baby for Max photos. by Christopher G. Knight. Scribner's, 1984. Subj: Babies. Sibling rivalry.

Fourth of July bear ill. by Helen Cogancherry. Morrow, 1991. ISBN 0-688-08288-2 Subj: Animals – bears. Friendship. Holidays – Fourth of July. Parades.

I have four names for my grandfather ill. by Christopher G. Knight. Little, 1976. Subj: Emotions – love. Family life – grandfathers.

My island grandma ill. by Emily Arnold McCully. Warne, 1979. Subj: Family life – grandmothers. Islands.

Sea swan ill. by Catherine Stock. Macmillan, 1988. ISBN 0-02-751700-4 Subj: Behavior – seeking better things. Old age. Sports – swimming.

Lasson, Robert. *Orange Oliver: the kitten who wore glasses* ill. by Chuck Hayden. McKay, 1957. Subj: Animals – cats. Farms. Glasses. Senses – seeing.

Latham, Hugh. *Mother Goose in French* (Mother Goose)

Lathrop, Dorothy Pulis. *An angel in the woods* ill. by author. Macmillan, 1947. Subj: Angels. Holidays – Christmas.

Puppies for keeps ill. by author. Macmillan, 1943. Subj: Animals – dogs. Pets.

Who goes there? ill. by author. Macmillan, 1935. Subj: Activities – picnicking. Animals. Character traits – kindness to animals. Seasons – winter.

Latimer, Jim. *Going the moose way home* ill. by Donald Carrick. Scribner's, 1988. ISBN 0-684-18890-2 Subj: Animals – moose. Forest, woods. Friendship.

James Bear's pie ill. by Betsy Franco-Feeney. Scribners, 1992. ISBN 0-684-19226-8 Subj: Activities – cooking. Animals – bears. Animals – skunks. Birds – crows.

Lattimore, Deborah Nourse. *The dragon's robe* ill. by author. HarperCollins, 1990. ISBN 0-06-023723-6 Subj: Activities – weaving. Character traits – generosity. Character traits – selfishness. Dragons. Folk and fairy tales. Foreign lands – China.

The prince and the golden ax: a Minoan tale ill. by author. Harper, 1988. ISBN 0-06-023716-3 Subj: Character traits – willfulness. Folk and fairy tales. Royalty – princes.

The sailor who captured the sea: a story of the Book of Kells ill. by author. HarperCollins, 1991. ISBN 0-06-023711-2 Subj: Activities – reading. Activities – writing. Character traits – persistence. Foreign lands – Ireland. Religion.

Lattin, Anne. *Peter's policeman* ill. by Gertrude E. Espenscheid. Follett, 1958. Subj: Careers – police officers.

Lauber, Patricia. *Get ready for robots!* ill. by True Kelley. Harper, 1987. ISBN 0-690-04578-6 Subj: Robots.

How we learned the earth is round ill. by Megan Lloyd. Crowell,, 1990. ISBN 0-690-04863-3 Subj: Earth. Science.

An octopus is amazing ill. by Holly Keller. Crowell, 1990. ISBN 0-690-04862-9 Subj: Octopuses.

Snakes are hunters ill. by Holly Keller. Harper, 1988. ISBN 0-690-04630-8 Subj: Reptiles – snakes. Science.

What's hatching out of that egg? ill. with photos. Crown, 1979. Subj: Eggs. Science.

Laurence, Margaret. *The Christmas birthday story* ill. by Helen Lucas. Knopf, 1980. Subj: Birthdays. Holidays – Christmas. Religion.

Laurencin, Geneviève. *I wish I were* tr. from German by Andrea Mernan; ill. by Ulises Wensell. Putnam's, 1987. ISBN 0-399-21416-X Subj: Animals. Behavior – bullying. Behavior – wishing.

Laurin, Anne. *Little things* ill. by Marcia Sewall. Atheneum, 1978. Subj: Activities – knitting. Character traits – patience. Humor.

Perfect crane ill. by Charles Mikolaycak. Harper, 1981. Subj: Birds – cranes. Foreign lands – Japan. Magic.

Lauture, Denize. *Father and son* ill. by Jonathan Green. Putnam, 1993. ISBN 0-399-21867-X Subj: Family life – fathers.

Lavies, Bianca. *Lily pad pond* photos. by author. Dutton, 1989. ISBN 0-525-44483-1 Subj: Animals. Nature. Trees.

Tree trunk traffic photos. by author. Dutton, 1989. ISBN 0-525-44495-5 Subj: Animals. Insects. Nature. Trees.

Lawlor, Laurie. *Second-grade dog* ill. by Gioia Fiammenghi. Albert Whitman, 1990. ISBN 0-8075-7280-2 Subj: Animals – dogs. Behavior – boredom. School.

Lawrence, James. *Binky Brothers and the fearless four* ill. by Leonard P. Kessler. Harper, 1970. Subj: Careers – detectives. Twins.

Binky Brothers, detectives ill. by Leonard P. Kessler. Harper, 1968. Subj: Careers – detectives. Twins.

Lawrence, John. *The giant of Grabbist* ill. by author. White, 1969. Subj: Foreign lands – England. Giants.

Pope Leo's elephant ill. by author. Collins-World, 1970, 1969. Subj: Animals – elephants. Fire. Foreign lands – Vatican City.

Rabbit and pork: rhyming talk ill. by author. Crowell, 1976. Subj: Animals – cats. Animals – pigs. Animals – rabbits. Poetry, rhyme.

Lawson, Annetta. *The lucky yak* ill. by Allen Say. Houghton, 1980. Subj: Activities – baby-sitting. Animals – yaks. Birds – puffins.

Lawson, Carol. *Teddy bear, teddy bear* ill. by author. Dial, 1991. ISBN 0-8037-0970-6 Subj: Activities. Nursery rhymes. Toys – teddy bears.

Lawson, Robert. *They were strong and good* ill. by author. Viking, 1940. Subj: Caldecott award book. Family life. U.S. history.

Layton, Aviva. *The squeakers* ill. by Louise Scott. Mosaic Pr., 1982. Subj: Animals – mice. Family life. Theater.

Lazard, Naomi. *What Amanda saw* ill. by Paul O. Zelinsky. Greenwillow, 1981. Subj: Activities – vacationing. Animals. Parties.

Lazy Jack. *Lazy Jack* ill. by Bert Dodson. Troll Assoc., 1979. Subj: Character traits – laziness. Cumulative tales. Folk and fairy tales.

Lazy Jack ill. by Tony Ross. Dial Pr., 1986. ISBN 0-8037-0275-2 Subj: Character traits – laziness. Cumulative tales. Folk and fairy tales.

Lazy Jack ill. by Kurt Werth. Viking, 1970. Subj: Character traits – laziness. Cumulative tales. Folk and fairy tales.

Le Guin, Ursula K. *A ride on the red mare's back* ill. by Julie Downing. Watts, 1992. ISBN 0-531-08591-0 Subj: Animals – horses. Character traits – bravery. Family life – brothers. Family life – sisters. Folk and fairy tales. Trolls.

Leach, Aroline Arnett Beecher. *The miracle of the mountain* (Kipling, Rudyard)

Leach, Michael. *Rabbits* ill. with photos. Global Lib. Mktg. Serv., 1984. ISBN 0-7136-2387-X Subj: Animals – rabbits. Nature. Science.

Leaf, Margaret. *Eyes of the dragon* ill. by Ed Young. Lothrop, 1987. ISBN 0-688-06156-7 Subj: Activities – painting. Careers – artists. Character traits – stubbornness. Dragons. Foreign lands – China.

Leaf, Munro. *Boo, who used to be scared of the dark* ill. by author. Random House, 1948. Subj: Bedtime. Emotions – fear. Night.

A flock of watchbirds ill. by author. Lippincott, 1946. Subj: Behavior – misbehavior. Etiquette.

Gordon, the goat ill. by author. Lippincott, 1944. Subj: Animals – goats.

Grammar can be fun ill. by author. Lippincott, 1934. Subj: Language.

Health can be fun ill. by author. Stokes, 1943. Subj: Health.

How to behave and why ill. by author. Lippincott, 1946. Subj: Etiquette.

Manners can be fun ill. by author Rev. ed. Lippincott, 1958. Subj: Etiquette.

Noodle ill. by author. Four Winds Pr., 1965. Subj: Animals – dogs. Self-concept.

Robert Francis Weatherbee ill. by author. Lippincott, 1935. Subj: School.

Safety can be fun ill. by author New, rev. ed. Lippincott, 1961. Subj: Safety.

The story of Ferdinand the bull ill. by Robert Lawson. Viking, 1936. Subj: Animals – bulls, cows. Character traits – individuality. Foreign lands – Spain. Violence, anti-violence.

Wee Gillis ill. by Robert Lawson. Viking, 1938. Subj: Caldecott award honor book. Foreign lands – Scotland.

Leander, Ed. *Q is for crazy* ill. by Józef Sumichrast. Dial-Delacorte, 1977. Subj: ABC books.

Lear, Edward. *A was once an apple pie* ill. by Julie Lacome. Candlewick Pr., 1992. ISBN 1-56402-000-2 Subj: ABC books. Poetry, rhyme.

ABC ill. by author. McGraw-Hill, 1965. Subj: ABC books. Poetry, rhyme.

A book of nonsense ill. by author. Metropolitan Museum of Art-Viking, 1980. Subj: Poetry, rhyme.

The dong with the luminous nose ill. by Edward Gorey. Addison-Wesley, 1969. Subj: Humor. Poetry, rhyme.

An Edward Lear alphabet ill. by Carol Newsom. Lothrop, 1983. Subj: ABC books.

Edward Lear's ABC: alphabet rhymes for children ill. by Carol Pike. Merrimack, 1986. ISBN 0-88162-219-2 Subj: ABC books. Poetry, rhyme.

Edward Lear's nonsense book ill. by Tony Palazzo. Doubleday, 1956. Subj: Humor. Music. Poetry, rhyme.

Hilary Knight's the owl and the pussy-cat (Knight, Hilary)

The jumblies ill. by Emma Crosby. Merrimack, 1986. ISBN 0-88162-185-4 Subj: Poetry, rhyme.

The jumblies ill. by Ted Rand. Putnam, 1989. ISBN 0-399-21632-4 Subj: Poetry, rhyme.

A Learical lexicon sel. by Myra Cohn Livingston; ill. by Joseph Low. Atheneum, 1985. Subj: Humor. Poetry, rhyme.

Lear's nonsense verses ill. by Tomi Ungerer. Grosset, 1967. Subj: Humor. Poetry, rhyme.

Limericks by Lear ill. by Lois Ehlert. Collins-World, 1965. Subj: Poetry, rhyme.

Nonsense alphabets ill. by Richard Scarry. Doubleday, 1962. Subj: ABC books. Poetry, rhyme.

The nutcrackers and the sugar-tongs ill. by Marcia Sewall. Little, 1978. Subj: Humor. Poetry, rhyme.

The owl and the pussycat ill. by Jan Brett. Putnam, 1991. ISBN 0-399-21925-0 Subj: Animals – cats. Birds – owls. Poetry, rhyme.

The owl and the pussy-cat ill. by Lorinda Bryan Cauley. Putnam's, 1986. ISBN 0-399-21254-X Subj: Animals – cats. Birds – owls. Poetry, rhyme.

The owl and the pussy-cat ill. by Barbara Cooney. Little, 1969. First pub. in 1961 Subj: Animals – cats. Birds – owls. Poetry, rhyme.

The owl and the pussycat ill. by Emma Crosby. Merrimack, 1986. ISBN 0-88162-183-8 Subj: Animals – cats. Birds – owls. Poetry, rhyme.

The owl and the pussy-cat ill. by William Pène Du Bois. Doubleday, 1961. Subj: Animals – cats. Birds – owls. Poetry, rhyme.

The owl and the pussycat ill. by Lori Farbanish. Putnam's, 1988. ISBN 0-448-10229-3 Subj: Animals – cats. Birds – owls. Poetry, rhyme.

The owl and the pussy-cat ill. by Gwen Fulton. Atheneum, 1977. Subj: Animals – cats. Birds – owls. Poetry, rhyme.

The owl and the pussycat ill. by Paul Galdone. Houghton, 1987. ISBN 0-89919-505-9 Subj: Animals – cats. Birds – owls. Poetry, rhyme.

The owl and the pussy-cat ill. by Elaine Muis. Grosset, 1977. Subj: Animals – cats. Birds – owls. Poetry, rhyme.

The owl and the pussycat ill. by Erica Rutherford. Tundra, 1986. ISBN 0-88776-181-X Subj: Animals – cats. Birds – owls. Poetry, rhyme.

The owl and the pussycat ill. by Janet Stevens. Holiday, 1983. ISBN 0-8231-0474-9 Subj: Animals – cats. Birds – owls. Poetry, rhyme.

The owl and the pussycat ill. by Louise Voce. Lothrop, 1991. ISBN 0-688-09537-2 Subj: Animals – cats. Birds – owls. Poetry, rhyme.

The owl and the pussycat ill. by Colin West. Warne, 1988. ISBN 0-7232-3541-4 Subj: Animals – cats. Birds – owls. Poetry, rhyme.

The owl and the pussy-cat and other nonsense ill. by Owen Wood. Viking, 1979. Subj: Animals – cats. Birds – owls. Poetry, rhyme.

The pelican chorus ill. by Harold Berson. Parents, 1967. Subj: Birds – pelicans. Humor. Music. Poetry, rhyme. Songs.

The pelican chorus and the quangle wangle's hat ill. by Kevin W. Maddison. Viking, 1981. Subj: Birds – pelicans. Humor. Music. Poetry, rhyme. Songs.

The pobble who has no toes ill. by Emma Crosby. Merrimack, 1986. ISBN 0-88162-184-6 Subj: Humor. Poetry, rhyme.

The pobble who has no toes ill. by Kevin W. Maddison. Viking, 1977. Subj: Humor. Poetry, rhyme.

The quangle wangle's hat ill. by Emma Crosby. Merrimack, 1986. ISBN 0-88162-182-X Subj: Clothing – hats. Humor. Poetry, rhyme.

The quangle wangle's hat ill. by Helen Oxenbury. Watts, 1969. Subj: Clothing – hats. Humor. Poetry, rhyme.

The quangle wangle's hat ill. by Janet Stevens. Harcourt, 1988. ISBN 0-15-264450-4 Subj: Clothing – hats. Humor. Poetry, rhyme.

Two laughable lyrics: The pobble who has no toes, [and] The quangle wangle's hat ill. by Paul Galdone. Putnam's, 1966. Subj: Clothing – hats. Humor. Poetry, rhyme.

Whizz! ill. by Janina Domanska. Macmillan, 1973. Completed by Ogden Nash Subj: Cumulative tales. Humor. Poetry, rhyme.

Lecourt, Nancy. *Abracadabra to zigzag* ill. by Barbara Lehman. Lothrop, 1991. ISBN 0-688-09481-3 Subj: ABC books.

Lee, Dennis. *Alligator pie* ill. by Frank Newfeld. Houghton, 1975. Subj: Nursery rhymes. Poetry, rhyme.

Lee, Jeanne M. *Ba-Nam* ill. by author. Holt, 1987. ISBN 0-8050-0169-7 Subj: Character traits – kindness. Foreign lands – Vietnam. Weather – storms.

Legend of the Li River: an ancient Chinese tale ill. by author. Holt, 1983. ISBN 0-03-063523-3 Subj: Folk and fairy tales. Foreign lands – China. Rocks.

The legend of the milky way ill. by author. Holt, 1982. Subj: Folk and fairy tales. Foreign lands – China. Stars.

Silent lotus ill. by author. Farrar, 1991. ISBN 0-374-36911-9 Subj: Activities – dancing. Foreign lands – Cambodia. Handicaps – deafness. Handicaps – physical.

Toad is the uncle of heaven: a Vietnamese folk tale ill. by reteller. Holt, 1985. ISBN 0-03-004652-1 Subj: Animals. Folk and fairy tales. Frogs and toads. Royalty. Weather – rain.

Leech, Jay. *Bright Fawn and me* by Jay Leech and Zane Spencer; ill. by Glo Coalson. Crowell, 1979. Subj: Indians of North America. Fairs. Sibling rivalry.

Leedy, Loreen. *The bunny play* ill. by author. Holiday House, 1988. ISBN 0-8234-0679-2 Subj: Animals – rabbits. Theater.

A dragon Christmas: things to make and do ill. by author. Holiday, 1988. ISBN 0-8234-0716-0 Subj: Activities. Activities – making things. Dragons. Holidays – Christmas.

The dragon Halloween party ill. by author. Holiday, 1986. ISBN 0-8234-0611-3 Subj: Dragons. Holidays – Halloween. Parties. Poetry, rhyme.

The dragon Thanksgiving feast ill. by author. Holiday, 1990. ISBN 0-8234-0828-0 Subj: Dragons. Food. Holidays – Thanksgiving. Poetry, rhyme.

The Furry News ill. by author. Holiday, 1990. ISBN 0-8234-0793-4 Subj: Activities – writing. Animals. Careers – journalists. Communication. Communities, neighborhoods.

The great trash bash ill. by author. Holiday, 1991. ISBN 0-8234-0869-8 Subj: Animals. Ecology.

Messages in the mailbox ill. by author. Holiday, 1991. ISBN 0-8234-0889-2 Subj: Activities – writing. Letters. School.

A number of dragons ill. by author. Holiday, 1985. ISBN 0-8234-0568-0 Subj: Counting, numbers. Dragons. Poetry, rhyme.

Pingo the plaid panda ill. by author. Holiday, 1989. ISBN 0-8234-0727-6 Subj: Animals – pandas. Character traits – being different. Friendship.

The potato party and other troll tales ill. by author. Holiday, 1989. ISBN 0-8234-0761-6 Subj: Trolls.

Leemis, Ralph. *Mister Momboo's hat* ill. by Jeni Bassett. Dutton, 1991. ISBN 0-525-65045-8 Subj: Animals – hippopotami. Circular tales. Clothing – hats. Poetry, rhyme. Weather – wind.

Leeton, Will C. *The Tower of Babel* ill. by Jeffrey K. Lindberg. Dandelion, 1979. Subj: Language. Religion.

Le Galliene, Eva. *The snow queen* (Andersen, H. C. (Hans Christian))

Le Gallienne, Eva. *The little mermaid* (Andersen, H. C. (Hans Christian))

The nightingale (Andersen, H. C. (Hans Christian))

Le Guin, Ursula K. *Solomon Leviathan's nine hundred and thirty-first trip around the world* ill. by Alicia Austin. Putnam's, 1988. ISBN 0-399-21491-7 Subj: Animals – giraffes. Animals – whales. Behavior – seeking better things. Reptiles – snakes.

A visit from Dr. Katz ill. by Ann Barrow. Atheneum, 1988. ISBN 0-689-31332-2 Subj: Animals – cats. Illness.

Lehan, Daniel. *This is not a book about dodos* ill. by author. Dutton, 1992. ISBN 0-525-44878-0 Subj: Art. Birds – dodos. Careers – artists.

Leichman, Seymour. *Shaggy dogs and spotty dogs and shaggy and spotty dogs* ill. by author. Harcourt, 1973. Subj: Animals – dogs. Poetry, rhyme.

The wicked wizard and the wicked witch ill. by author. Harcourt, 1972. Subj: Magic. Poetry, rhyme. Witches. Wizards.

Leigh, Oretta. *The merry-go-round* ill. by Kathryn E. Shoemaker. Holiday, 1985. ISBN 0-8234-0544-3 Subj: Animals. Merry-go-rounds. Poetry, rhyme.

Leiner, Katherine. *Both my parents work* photos. by Steve Sax. Watts, 1986. ISBN 0-531-10101-0 Subj: Activities – working. Family life.

Leisk, David Johnson *see* Johnson, Crockett

Leister, Mary. *The silent concert* ill. by Yōko Mitsuhashi. Bobbs-Merrill, 1970. Subj: Forest, woods. Noise, sounds.

Lemerise, Bruce. *Sheldon's lunch* ill. by author. Parents, 1980. Subj: Activities – cooking. Food. Reptiles – snakes.

Lemieux, Michèle. *What's that noise?* ill. by author. Morrow, 1985. ISBN 0-688-04140-X Subj: Animals – bears. Noise, sounds.

Lemke, Horst. *Places and faces* ill. by author. Scroll Pr., 1971. Translation of Vielerlei aus Stadt und Land Subj: Wordless.

Lenski, Lois. *Animals for me* ill. by author. Walck, 1941. Subj: Animals.

At our house ill. by author. Walck, 1959. Music by Clyde Robert Bulla Subj: Family life. Music. Songs.

Big little Davy ill. by author. Walck, 1956. Subj: Animals.

Cowboy Small ill. by author. Oxford Univ. Pr., 1949. Subj: Cowboys.

Davy and his dog ill. by author. Walck, 1957. Subj: Animals – dogs. Music. Songs.

Davy goes places ill. by author. Walck, 1961. Subj: Activities – traveling. Music. Songs. Transportation.

Debbie and her dolls ill. by author. Walck, 1970. Subj: Animals – dogs. Toys – dolls.

Debbie and her family ill. by author. Walck, 1969. Subj: Family life.

Debbie and her grandma ill. by author. Walck, 1967. Subj: Family life – grandmothers. Music. Songs.

Debbie goes to nursery school ill. by author. Walck, 1970. Subj: School.

A dog came to school ill. by author. Oxford Univ. Pr., 1955. Subj: Animals – dogs. Music. School. Songs.

I like winter ill. by author. Walck, 1950. Subj: Music. Poetry, rhyme. Seasons – winter. Songs.

I went for a walk ill. by author. Walck, 1958. Subj: Activities – walking. Music. Songs.

Let's play house ill. by author. Walck, 1944. Subj: Activities – playing. Toys – dolls.

The life I live: collected poems ill. by author. Walck, 1966. Subj: Poetry, rhyme. Songs.

The little airplane ill. by author. Walck, 1938. Subj: Airplanes, airports.

The little auto ill. by author. Oxford Univ. Pr., 1934. Subj: Automobiles.

The little family ill. by author. Doubleday, 1932. Subj: Family life.

The little farm ill. by author. Walck, 1942. Subj: Farms.

The little fire engine ill. by author. Oxford Univ. Pr., 1946. Subj: Careers – firefighters.

The little train ill. by author. Oxford Univ. Pr., 1940. Subj: Careers – railroad engineers. Trains.

Lois Lenski's big book of Mr. Small ill. by author. Walck, 1979. Subj: Careers. Transportation.

Mr. and Mrs. Noah ill. by author. Crowell, 1948. Subj: Boats, ships. Religion – Noah.

Now it's fall ill. by author. Walck, 1948. Subj: Poetry, rhyme. Seasons – fall.

On a summer day ill. by author. Oxford Univ. Pr., 1953. Subj: Poetry, rhyme. Seasons – summer.

Papa Small ill. by author. Walck, 1951. Subj: Family life. Family life – fathers.

Policeman Small ill. by author. Walck, 1962. Subj: Careers – police officers. City.

Sing a song of people ill. by Giles Laroche. Little, 1987. ISBN 0-316-52074-8 Subj: City. Format, unusual. Poetry, rhyme.

Spring is here ill. by author. Walck, 1945. Subj: Poetry, rhyme. Seasons – spring.

A surprise for Davy ill. by author. Walck, 1947. Subj: Birthdays. Parties.

Susie Mariar ill. by author. Walck, 1967. First pub. in 1939 Subj: Cumulative tales. Folk and fairy tales. Poetry, rhyme.

Lent, Blair. *Bayberry Bluff* ill. by author. Houghton, 1987. ISBN 0-395-35384-X Subj: City. Islands.

John Tabor's ride ill. by author. Little, 1966. Subj: Animals – whales. Folk and fairy tales. Humor.

Pistachio ill. by author. Little, 1964. Subj: Animals – bulls, cows. Circus. Clowns, jesters.

Leodhas, Sorche Nic *see* Alger, Leclaire Gowans

Leonard, Alain. *Barnaby and the big gorilla* ill. by author. Morrow, 1992. ISBN 0-688-11292-7 Subj: Animals – rabbits. Character traits – bravery. Toys.

Leonard, Marcia. *Birthday in a bathtub* ill. by John Wallner. Silver Pr., 1989. ISBN 0-671-08588-0 Subj: Animals – pigs. Birthdays. Poetry, rhyme. Problem solving.

Goldilocks and the three bears (The three bears)

Gregory and Mr. Grump ill. by Maxie Chambliss. Silver Pr., 1990. ISBN 0-671-70402-8 Subj: Gardens, gardening. Old age.

Hannah the hamster hunter ill. by Maxie Chambliss. Silver Pr., 1990. ISBN 0-671-70399-4 Subj: Animals – hamsters. School.

Jeffrey Lee, future fireman ill. by Ann Iosa. Silver Pr., 1990. ISBN 0-671-70403-6 Subj: Careers – firefighters.

The kitten twins ill. by Maryann Cocca-Leffler. Troll, 1990. ISBN 0-8167-1724-9 Subj: Animals – cats. Concepts – opposites. Twins.

Laura Jean the yard sale queen ill. by Ann Iosa. Silver Pr., 1990. ISBN 0-671-70401-X Subj: Animals – dogs.

Little owl leaves the nest ill. by Carol Newsom. Bantam, 1984. Subj: Birds – owls. Problem solving.

Noisy neighbors ill. by Bari Weissman. Troll, 1990. ISBN 0-8167-1726-5 Subj: Animals. Noise, sounds.

Rainboots for breakfast ill. by John Himmelman. Silver Pr., 1989. ISBN 0-671-68587-2 Subj: Food. Frogs and toads.

Shopping for snowflakes ill. by John Himmelman. Silver Pr., 1989. ISBN 0-671-68590-2 Subj: Animals – rabbits. Shopping.

Swimming in the sand ill. by John Wallner. Silver Pr., 1989. ISBN 0-671-68589-9 Subj: Animals – hippopotami. Sea and seashore.

Lerner, Carol. *Flowers of a woodland spring* ill. by author. Morrow, 1979. Subj: Flowers. Forest, woods. Seasons – spring.

Lerner, Marguerite Rush. *Dear little mumps child* ill. by George Overlie. Lerner, 1959. Subj: Illness. Poetry, rhyme.

Doctors' tools ill. by George Overlie Rev. 2nd ed. Lerner, 1960. Subj: Careers – doctors. Tools.

Lefty, the story of left-handedness ill. by Rov André. Lerner, 1960. Subj: Character traits – being different. Left-handedness.

Michael gets the measles ill. by George Overlie. Lerner, 1959. Subj: Illness.

Peter gets the chickenpox ill. by George Overlie. Lerner, 1959. Subj: Illness.

Lerner, Sharon. *Big Bird's copycat day* featuring Jim Henson's Sesame Street Muppets; ill. by Jean-Pierre Jacquet. Random House, 1984. Subj: Puppets.

Follow the monsters! ill. by Tom Cooke. Random House, 1985. ISBN 0-394-97126-4 Subj: Monsters. Poetry, rhyme. Puppets.

LeRoy, Gen. *Billy's shoes* ill. by J. Winslow Higginbottom. McGraw-Hill, 1981. Subj: Clothing – shoes. Sibling rivalry.

Lucky stiff! ill. by J. Winslow Higginbottom. McGraw-Hill, 1981. Subj: Humor. Sibling rivalry.

LeSieg, Theo *see* Seuss, Dr.

Lesikin, Joan. *Down the road* ill. by author. Prentice-Hall, 1978. Subj: Behavior – sharing. Reptiles – snakes. Reptiles – turtles, tortoises.

Leslie, Amanda. *Hidden toys* ill. by author. Dial, 1989. ISBN 0-8037-0568-9 Subj: Games. Toys.

Lessac, Frané. *Caribbean canvas* ill. by author. Lippincott, 1989. ISBN 0-397-32368-9 Subj: Art. Foreign lands – Caribbean Islands. Poetry, rhyme.

My little island ill. by author. Lippincott, 1985. ISBN 0-397-32115-5 Subj: Foreign lands – Caribbean Islands. Islands.

Lesser, Carolyn. *The goodnight circle* ill. by Lorinda Bryan Cauley. Harcourt, 1984. Subj: Animals. Bedtime. Night.

Lesser, Rika. *Hansel and Gretel* (Grimm, Jacob)

Lester, Alison. *Clive eats alligators* ill. by author. Houghton, 1986. ISBN 0-395-40775-3 Subj: Activities. Character traits – individuality.

Imagine ill. by author. Houghton, 1990. ISBN 0-395-53753-3 Subj: Animals.

The journey home ill. by author. Houghton, 1991. ISBN 0-395-53355-4 Subj: Activities – traveling. Family life – brothers. Family life – sisters.

Magic beach ill. by author. Little, 1992. ISBN 0-316-52177-9 Subj: Family life. Imagination. Poetry, rhyme. Sea and seashore.

Rosie sips spiders ill. by author. Houghton, 1989. ISBN 0-395-5126-2 Subj: Family life. Foreign lands – Australia.

Ruby ill. by author. Houghton, 1988. ISBN 0-395-46477-3 Subj: Bedtime. Dreams.

Tessa snaps snakes ill. by author. Houghton, 1991. ISBN 0-395-59505-3 Subj: Activities. Character traits – individuality.

Lester, Helen. *It wasn't my fault* ill. by Lynn Munsinger. Houghton, 1985. ISBN 0-395-35629-6 Subj: Animals. Cumulative tales.

Pookins gets her way ill. by Lynn Munsinger. Houghton, 1987. ISBN 0-395-42636-7 Subj: Character traits – willfulness. Elves and little people.

A porcupine named Fluffy ill. by Lynn Munsinger. Houghton, 1986. ISBN 0-395-36895-2 Subj: Animals – porcupines. Names.

The revenge of the magic chicken ill. by Lynn Munsinger. Houghton, 1990. ISBN 0-395-50929-7 Subj: Birds – chickens. Magic.

Tacky the penguin ill. by Lynn Munsinger. Houghton, 1988. ISBN 0-395-45536-7 Subj: Animals – wolves. Birds – penguins. Character traits – individuality.

The wizard, the fairy and the magic chicken ill. by Lynn Munsinger. Houghton, 1983. Subj: Behavior – sharing. Birds – chickens. Fairies. Friendship. Wizards.

Lester, Julius. *The knee-high man and other tales* ill. by Ralph Pinto. Dial Pr., 1972. ISBN 0-8037-4593-1 Subj: Ethnic groups in the U.S. – Afro-Americans. Folk and fairy tales.

Le-Tan, Pierre. *The afternoon cat* ill. by author. Pantheon, 1977. Subj: Activities. Animals – cats.

Timothy's dream book ill. by author. Farrar, 1978. Subj: Careers. Imagination.

Visit to the North Pole ill. by author. Crown, 1983. Subj: Dreams. Imagination. Toys – teddy bears.

Le Tord, Bijou. *A brown cow* ill. by author. Little, 1989. ISBN 0-316-52166-3 Subj: Animals – bulls, cows.

Good wood bear ill. by author. Bradbury Pr., 1985. ISBN 0-02-756440-1 Subj: Animals – bears. Birds – geese. Houses.

Joseph and Nellie ill. by author. Bradbury Pr., 1986. ISBN 0-02-756450-9 Subj: Careers – fishermen. Sea and seashore.

My Grandma Leonie ill. by author. Bradbury Pr., 1987. ISBN 0-02-756490-8 Subj: Death. Family life – grandmothers.

Picking and weaving ill. by author. Four Winds Pr., 1980. Subj: Activities – weaving. Plants.

Rabbit seeds ill. by author. Four Winds Pr., 1984. Subj: Animals – rabbits. Gardens, gardening.

Let's count and count out comp. by Marion F. Grayson; ill. by Deborah Derr McClintock. Luce, 1975. Subj: Counting, numbers. Games. Poetry, rhyme.

Leupold, Nancy S. *Little ghost Godfry* (Sandberg, Inger)

Leutscher, Alfred. *Earth* ill. by John Butler. Dial Pr., 1983. Subj: Earth. Science.

Water ill. by Nick Hardcastle. Dial Pr., 1983. Subj: Ecology. Science. Water.

Levens, George. *Kippy the koala* ill. by Crosby Newell Bonsall. Harper, 1960. Subj: Animals – koala bears. Poetry, rhyme. Seasons – spring.

Leverich, Kathleen. *The hungry fox and the foxy duck* ill. by Paul Galdone. Parents, 1979. Subj: Animals – foxes. Birds – ducks. Character traits – cleverness.

Levin, Isadora. *The scarlet flower* (Aksakov, Sergei)

Levine, Abby. *Sometimes I wish I were Mindy* by Abby and Sarah Levine; ill. by Blanche Sims. Albert Whitman, 1986. ISBN 0-8075-7542-9 Subj: Emotions – envy, jealousy.

Too much mush! ill. by Kathy Parkinson. Albert Whitman, 1989. ISBN 0-8075-8025-2 Subj: Folk and fairy tales. Food. Magic. Poverty.

What did mommy do before you? ill. by DyAnne DiSalvo-Ryan. Albert Whitman, 1988. ISBN 0-8075-8819-9 Subj: Babies. Behavior – growing up. Family life – mothers.

You push, I ride ill. by Margot Apple. Albert Whitman, 1989. ISBN 0-8075-9444-X Subj: Animals – pigs. Family life. Poetry, rhyme.

Levine, Arthur. *All the lights in the night* ill. by James E. Ransome. Morrow, 1991. ISBN 0-688-10108-9 Subj: Family life – brothers. Foreign lands – Russia. Holidays – Hanukkah. Jewish culture. Religion.

Levine, Ellen. *I hate English!* ill. by Steve Bjorman. Scholastic, 1989. ISBN 0-590-42305-3 Subj: Ethnic groups in the U.S. – Chinese-Americans. Language.

Levine, Evan. *Not the piano, Mrs. Medley!* ill. by S. D. Schindler. Watts, 1991. ISBN 0-531-08556-2 Subj: Family life – grandmothers. Sea and seashore.

Levine, Joan. *A bedtime story* ill. by Gail Owens. Dutton, 1975. Subj: Bedtime.

Levine, Rhoda. *Harrison loved his umbrella* ill. by Karla Kuskin. Atheneum, 1964. Subj: Character traits – being different. Character traits – individuality. Umbrellas.

Levine, Sarah. *Sometimes I wish I were Mindy* (Levine, Abby)

Levinson, Nancy Smiler. *Clara and the bookwagon* ill. by Carolyn Croll. Harper, 1988. ISBN 0-06-023838-0 Subj: Activities – reading. Libraries.

Levinson, Riki. *The emperor's new clothes* (Andersen, H. C. (Hans Christian))

I go with my family to Grandma's ill. by Diane Goode. Dutton, 1990. ISBN 0-525-44261-8 Subj: Activities – photographing. Family life. Family life – grandmothers. Transportation.

Me baby! ill. by Marylin Hafner. Dutton, 1991. ISBN 0-525-44693-1 Subj: Babies. Behavior – unnoticed, unseen. Family life. Sibling rivalry.

Our home is the sea ill. by Dennis Luzak. Dutton, 1988. ISBN 0-525-44406-8 Subj: City. Family life. Foreign lands – China.

Touch! Touch! ill. by True Kelley. Dutton, 1987. ISBN 0-525-44309-6 Subj: Behavior – misbehavior. Family life.

Watch the stars come out ill. by Diane Goode. Dutton, 1985. ISBN 0-525-44205-7 Subj: Family life. Family life – grandmothers. U.S. history.

Levitin, Sonia. *All the cats in the world* ill. by Charles Robinson. Harcourt, 1982. Subj: Animals – cats. Character traits – kindness to animals.

The man who kept his heart in a bucket ill. by Jerry Pinkney. Dial, 1991. ISBN 0-8037-1030-5 Subj: Emotions – love.

Nobody stole the pie ill. by Fernando Krahn. Harcourt, 1980. Subj: Activities – cooking. Crime. Food.

A single speckled egg ill. by John M. Larrecq. Parnassus Pr., 1976. Subj: Behavior – worrying. Eggs. Farms.

Who owns the moon? ill. by John M. Larrecq. Parnassus, 1973. ISBN 0-395-27656-X Subj: Behavior – fighting, arguing. Moon. Problem solving.

Levoy, Myron. *The Hanukkah of Great-Uncle Otto* ill. by Donna Ruff. Jewish Pub. Soc., 1984. ISBN 0-8276-0242-1 Subj: Family life – aunts, uncles. Holidays – Hanukkah. Jewish culture.

Levy, Elizabeth. *Nice little girls* ill. by Mordicai Gerstein. Delacorte Pr., 1974. Subj: School.

Levy, Miriam F. *Adam's world, San Francisco* (Fraser, Kathleen)

Levy, Sara G. *Mother Goose rhymes for Jewish children* ill. by Jessie B. Robinson. Bloch, 1945. Subj: Jewish culture. Nursery rhymes.

Lewin, Betsy. *Animal snackers* ill. by author. Dodd, 1980. Subj: Animals. Food. Poetry, rhyme.

Cat count ill. by author. Dodd, 1981. Subj: Animals – cats. Counting, numbers. Poetry, rhyme.

Hip, hippo, hooray! ill. by author. Dodd, 1982. Subj: Animals – hippopotami. Counting, numbers. Illness. Weather.

Lewin, Hugh. *An elephant came to swim* by Hugh Lewin and Lisa Kopper; ill. by authors. David & Charles, 1986. ISBN 0-241-11432-2 Subj: Animals – elephants. Foreign lands – Africa.

Jafta ill. by Lisa Kopper. Carolrhoda, 1983. Subj: Emotions. Family life. Foreign lands – Africa.

Jafta and the wedding ill. by Lisa Kopper. Carolrhoda, 1983. Subj: Family life. Foreign lands – Africa. Weddings.

Jafta—the journey ill. by Lisa Kopper. Carolrhoda, 1984. Subj: Activities – traveling. Emotions. Foreign lands – Africa.

Jafta—the town ill. by Lisa Kopper. Carolrhoda, 1984. Subj: City. Emotions. Foreign lands – Africa.

Jafta's father ill. by Lisa Kopper. Carolrhoda, 1983. Subj: Family life – fathers. Foreign lands – Africa.

Jafta's mother ill. by Lisa Kopper. Carolrhoda, 1983. Subj: Family life – mothers. Foreign lands – Africa.

Lewis, Bobby. *Home before midnight: a traditional verse;* retold and ill. by Bobby Lewis. Lothrop, 1984. Subj: Animals – pigs. Cumulative tales.

Lewis, Claudia Louise. *When I go to the moon* ill. by Leonard Weisgard. Macmillan, 1961. Subj: Earth. Moon.

Lewis, Eils Moorhouse. *The snug little house* ill. by Elise Primavera. Atheneum, 1981. ISBN 0-689-50177-3 Subj: Character traits – helpfulness. Houses.

Lewis, J. Patrick. *A hippopotamusn't* ill. by Victoria Chess. Dial, 1990. ISBN 0-8037-0519-0 Subj: Animals. Poetry, rhyme.

The moonbow of Mr. B. Bones ill. by Dirk Zimmer. Knopf, 1992. ISBN 0-394-95365-7 Subj: Careers – peddlers. Magic. Moon.

The Tsar and the amazing cow ill. by Friso Henstra. Dial Pr., 1988. ISBN 0-8037-0411-9 Subj: Behavior – greed. Folk and fairy tales. Old age.

Two-legged, four-legged, no-legged rhymes ill. by Pamela Paparone. Knopf, 1991. ISBN 0-679-90771-8 Subj: Animals. Poetry, rhyme.

Lewis, Kim. *Emma's lamb* ill. by author. Four Winds, 1991. ISBN 0-02-758821-1 Subj: Animals – sheep. Behavior – needing someone. Farms.

Floss ill. by author. Candlewick Pr., 1992. ISBN 1-56402-010-X Subj: Activities – playing. Activities – working. Animals – dogs.

The shepherd boy ill. by author. Four Winds, 1990. ISBN 0-02-758581-6 Subj: Animals – sheep. Careers – shepherds.

Lewis, Lucia Z. *see* Anderson, Lucia Z.

Lewis, Naomi. *The butterfly collector* ill. by Fulvio Testa. Prentice-Hall, 1979. Subj: Behavior – collecting things. Insects – butterflies, caterpillars. Poetry, rhyme. Riddles.

The frog prince (Grimm, Jacob)

Hare and badger go to town ill. by Tony Ross. David & Charles, 1987. ISBN 0-905478-94-0 Subj: Animals. Ecology.

Johnny Longnose (Krüss, James)

Jorinda and Joringel (Grimm, Jacob)

Leaves ill. by Fulvio Testa. Harper, 1983. Subj: Plants. Seasons. Trees.

The nightingale (Andersen, H. C. (Hans Christian))

Once upon a rainbow ill. by Gabriele Eichenauer. Jonathan Cape, 1982. Subj: Concepts – color. Poetry, rhyme. Toys – teddy bears.

Puffin ill. by Deborah King. Lothrop, 1984. Subj: Birds – puffins. Foreign lands – Scotland.

The snow queen (Andersen, H. C. (Hans Christian))

The steadfast tin soldier (Andersen, H. C. (Hans Christian))

The stepsister ill. by Allison Reed. Dial Pr., 1987. ISBN 0-8037-0430-5 Subj: Animals – cats. Family life – step families.

Swan ill. by Deborah King. Lothrop, 1986. ISBN 0-688-05535-4 Subj: Birds – swans. Nature. Science.

The tale of the vanishing rainbow (Rupprecht, Siegfried P.)

The wild swans (Andersen, H. C. (Hans Christian))

Lewis, Richard. *In a spring garden* ill. by Ezra Jack Keats. Dial Pr., 1965. A collection of haiku Subj: Poetry, rhyme.

In the night, still dark ill. by Ed Young. Atheneum, 1988. ISBN 0-689-31310-1 Subj: Hawaii. Poetry, rhyme.

Lewis, Robin Baird. *Aunt Armadillo* ill. by author. Firefly Pr., 1985. ISBN 0-920303-38-2 Subj: Animals – armadillos. Family life – aunts, uncles. Libraries.

Friska, the sheep that was too small ill. by author. Farrar, 1988. ISBN 0-374-32461-1 Subj: Animals – sheep. Animals – wolves. Character traits – bravery.

Hello, Mr. Scarecrow ill. by author. Farrar, 1987. ISBN 0-374-32947-8 Subj: Days of the week, months of the year. Scarecrows.

Lewis, Sharon. *Orca! the killer whale* ill. by Linda Roberts. HarperCollins, 1990. ISBN 0-694-00295-X Subj: Animals – whales.

Tiger! ill. by Linda Roberts. HarperCollins, 1990. ISBN 0-694-00296-8 Subj: Animals – tigers.

Lewis, Sheri. *Baby Lamb Chop loves animals* ill. by Cathy Beylon. Random House, 1991. ISBN 0-679-81723-9 Subj: Animals. Format, unusual – board books. Puppets.

Baby Lamb Chop loves numbers ill. by Cathy Beylon. Random House, 1991. ISBN 0-679-81724-7 Subj: Counting, numbers. Format, unusual – board books. Puppets.

Baby Lamb Chop loves nursery school ill. by Cathy Beylon. Random House, 1991. ISBN 0-679-81725-5 Subj: Format, unusual – board books. Puppets. School.

Baby Lamb Chop loves the beach ill. by Cathy Beylon. Random House, 1991. ISBN 0-679-81726-3 Subj: Format, unusual – board books. Puppets. Sea and seashore.

Baby Lamb Chop loves words ill. by Cathy Beylon. Random House, 1991. ISBN 0-679-81722-0 Subj: Format, unusual – board books. Language. Puppets.

Lewis, Stephen. *Zoo city* ill. by author. Greenwillow, 1976. Subj: Animals. City. Format, unusual. Imagination. Wordless. Zoos.

Lewis, Thomas P. *Call for Mr. Sniff* ill. by Beth Lee Weiner. Harper, 1981. Subj: Animals – dogs. Birthdays. Problem solving.

Clipper ship ill. by Joan Sandin. Harper, 1978. ISBN 0-06-023809-7 Subj: Activities – traveling. Boats, ships.

Hill of fire ill. by Joan Sandin. Harper, 1971. Subj: Foreign lands – Mexico. Volcanoes.

Mr. Sniff and the motel mystery ill. by Beth Lee Weiner. Harper, 1984. ISBN 0-06-023825-9 Subj: Animals – dogs. Problem solving.

Lewison, Wendy C. *Going to sleep on the farm* ill. by Juan Wijngaard. Dial, 1992. ISBN 0-8037-1097-6 Subj: Animals. Cumulative tales. Farms. Poetry, rhyme. Sleep.

Where is Sammy's smile? ill. by Katy Bratun. Grosset, 1989. ISBN 0-448-40150-9 Subj: Animals – raccoons. Format, unusual.

Lewiton, Mina *see* Simon, Mina Lewiton

Lexau, Joan M. *Benjie* ill. by Don Bolognese. Dial Pr., 1964. Subj: Character traits – shyness. Ethnic groups in the U.S. – Afro-Americans. Family life. Family life – grandmothers. Problem solving.

Benjie on his own ill. by Don Bolognese. Dial Pr., 1970. Subj: City. Ethnic groups in the U.S. – Afro-Americans. Family life – grandmothers. Illness. Problem solving.

Cathy is company ill. by Aliki. Dial Pr., 1961. Subj: Etiquette. Friendship.

Come here, cat ill. by Steven Kellogg. Harper, 1973. Subj: Animals – cats. City.

Crocodile and hen ill. by Joan Sandin. Harper, 1969. Adaptation of Why the crocodile does not eat the hen, from Notes on the folklore of the Fjort (French Congo), by R. E. Dennett Subj: Birds – chickens. Cumulative tales. Folk and fairy tales. Foreign lands – Africa. Reptiles – alligators, crocodiles.

The dog food caper ill. by Marylin Hafner. Dial Pr., 1985. ISBN 0-8037-0108-X Subj: Animals – dogs. Animals – mice. Problem solving. Witches.

Every day a dragon ill. by Ben Shecter. Harper, 1967. Subj: Family life. Family life – fathers. Games.

Finders keepers, losers weepers ill. by Tomie de Paola. Lippincott, 1967. Subj: Babies. Behavior – losing things. Behavior – lying. Family life.

Go away, dog ill. by Crosby Newell Bonsall. Harper, 1963. Subj: Animals – dogs. Birthdays.

The homework caper ill. by Syd Hoff. Harper, 1966. Subj: Sibling rivalry.

A house so big ill. by Syd Hoff. Harper, 1968. Subj: Character traits – generosity. Emotions – love. Family life – mothers. Imagination.

I hate red rover ill. by Gail Owens. Dutton, 1979. Subj: Behavior – growing up. Games.

I should have stayed in bed ill. by Syd Hoff. Harper, 1965. Subj: Behavior – bad day. Emotions – embarrassment. Ethnic groups in the U.S. – Afro-Americans.

I'll tell on you ill. by Gail Owens. Dutton, 1981. ISBN 0-525-32542-5 Subj: Animals – dogs. Behavior – misbehavior. Sports – baseball.

It all began with a drip, drip, drip ill. by Joan Sandin. McCall, 1970. Subj: Behavior – mistakes. Character traits – bravery. Folk and fairy tales. Foreign lands – India.

Me day ill. by Robert Weaver. Dial Pr., 1971. Subj: Birthdays. City. Divorce. Ethnic groups in the U.S. – Afro-Americans. Family life. Family life – fathers.

Millicent's ghost ill. by Ben Shecter. Dial Pr., 1962. Subj: Ghosts. Night.

More beautiful than flowers ill. by Don Bolognese. Lippincott, 1966. Subj: Poetry, rhyme. Religion.

Olaf reads ill. by Harvey Weiss. Dial Pr., 1961. Subj: Activities – reading.

The rooftop mystery ill. by Syd Hoff. Harper, 1968. Subj: Ethnic groups in the U.S. – Afro-Americans. Moving. Toys – dolls.

Who took the farmer's hat? ill. by Fritz Siebel. Harper, 1963. Subj: Clothing – hats. Farms. Weather – wind.

Lifton, Betty Jean. *Goodnight orange monster* ill. by Cyndy Szekeres. Atheneum, 1972. Subj: Bedtime. Emotions – fear. Monsters. Night.

Joji and the Amanojaku ill. by Eiichi Mitsui. Norton, 1965. Subj: Birds. Foreign lands – Japan. Goblins. Scarecrows.

Joji and the dragon ill. by Eiichi Mitsui. Morrow, 1957. Subj: Birds. Dragons. Foreign lands – Japan. Scarecrows.

Joji and the fog ill. by Eiichi Mitsui. Morrow, 1959. Subj: Birds. Scarecrows. Weather – fog.

The many lives of Chio and Goro ill. by Yasuo Segawa. Norton, 1968. Subj: Animals – foxes. Birds – chickens. Foreign lands – Japan.

The rice-cake rabbit ill. by Eiichi Mitsui. Norton, 1966. Subj: Animals – rabbits. Foreign lands – Japan. Moon.

The secret seller ill. by Etienne Delessert and Norma Holt. Norton, 1967. Subj: Behavior – secrets. Imagination.

Lillegard, Dee. *I can be a baker* ill. with photos. Childrens Pr., 1986. ISBN 0-516-01892-2 Subj: Careers – bakers.

I can be a carpenter ill. with photos. Childrens Pr., 1986. ISBN 0-516-01884-1 Subj: Careers – carpenters.

I can be a welder by Dee Lillegard and Wayne Stoker. Childrens Pr., 1986. ISBN 0-516-01895-7 Subj: Careers – welders.

I can be an electrician ill. with photos. Childrens Pr., 1986. ISBN 0-516-01896-5 Subj: Careers – electricians.

Sitting in my box ill. by Jon Agee. Dutton, 1989. ISBN 0-525-44528-5 Subj: Activities – reading. Animals. Cumulative tales.

Lillie, Patricia. *Jake and Rosie* ill. by author. Greenwillow, 1989. ISBN 0-688-07625-4 Subj: Animals – cats. Ethnic groups in the U.S. – Afro-Americans. Friendship.

One very, very quiet afternoon ill. by author. Greenwillow, 1986. ISBN 0-688-04323-2 Subj: ABC books. Behavior – misbehavior. Parties.

When the rooster crowed ill. by Nancy Winslow Parker. Greenwillow, 1991. ISBN 0-688-09379-5 Subj: Animals. Cumulative tales. Farms. Noise, sounds.

Lilly, Kenneth. *Animal builders* ill. by author. Random House, 1984. Subj: Activities. Animals. Format, unusual – board books. Science.

Animal climbers ill. by author. Random House, 1984. Subj: Activities. Animals. Format, unusual – board books. Science.

Animal jumpers ill. by author. Random House, 1984. Subj: Activities. Animals. Format, unusual – board books. Science.

Animal runners ill. by author. Random House, 1984. Subj: Activities. Animals. Format, unusual – board books. Science.

Animal swimmers ill. by author. Random House, 1984. Subj: Activities. Animals. Format, unusual – board books. Science.

Animals at the zoo ill. by author. Simon and Schuster, 1982. Subj: Animals. Format, unusual – board books. Zoos.

Animals in the country ill. by author. Simon and Schuster, 1982. Subj: Animals. Format, unusual – board books. Wordless.

Animals in the jungle ill. by author. Simon and Schuster, 1982. Subj: Animals. Format, unusual – board books. Jungle.

Animals of the ocean ill. by author. Simon and Schuster, 1982. Subj: Animals – polar bears. Animals – dolphins. Animals – seals. Animals – whales. Birds – penguins. Format, unusual – board books. Sea and seashore.

Animals on the farm ill. by author. Simon and Schuster, 1982. Subj: Animals. Farms. Format, unusual – board books.

Linch, Elizabeth Johanna. *Samson* ill. by author. Harper, 1964. Subj: Animals – mice. Holidays – Christmas. Seasons – winter.

Lindberg, Reeve. *Midnight farm* ill. by Susan Jeffers. Dial Pr., 1987. ISBN 0-8037-0333-3 Subj: Animals. Counting, numbers. Farms. Night.

Lindbergh, Anne. *Tidy lady* ill. by Susan Ramsay Hoguet. Harcourt, 1989. ISBN 0-15-287150-0 Subj: Character traits – cleanliness. Cumulative tales.

Lindbergh, Reeve. *Benjamin's barn* ill. by Susan Jeffers. Dial, 1990. ISBN 0-8037-0614-6 Subj: Animals. Barns. Farms. Imagination. Poetry, rhyme.

The day the goose got loose ill. by Steven Kellogg. Dial, 1990. ISBN 0-8037-0409-7 Subj: Animals. Behavior – misbehavior. Birds – geese. Farms.

Johnny Appleseed ill. by Kathy Jakobsen. Little, 1990. ISBN 0-316-52618-5 Subj: Activities – traveling. Folk and fairy tales. Poetry, rhyme. Trees. U.S. history.

Lindbloom, Steven. *Let's give kitty a bath!* ill. by True Kelley. Addison-Wesley, 1982. Subj: Activities – bathing. Animals – cats.

Linden, Ann Marie. *One smiling grandma* ill. by Lynne Russell. Dial, 1992. ISBN 0-8037-1132-8 Subj: Counting, numbers. Family life – grandmothers. Foreign lands – Caribbean Islands.

Linden, Madelaine Gill. *Under the blanket* ill. by author. Little, 1987. ISBN 0-316-52626-6 Subj: Poetry, rhyme. Toys.

Lindenbaum, Pija. *Boodil, my dog* retold by Gabrielle Charbonnet; ill. by author. Green Tiger,

1992. ISBN 0-8050-2444-1 Subj: Animals – dogs. Character traits – appearance.

Else-Marie and her seven little daddies ill. by author. Holt, 1991. ISBN 0-8050-1752-6 Subj: Behavior – worrying. Family life – fathers.

Lindgren, Astrid. *A calf for Christmas* tr. from Swedish by Barbara Lucas; ill. by Marit Tornqvist. Farrar, 1991. ISBN 91-29-59920-2 Subj: Animals – bulls, cows. Foreign lands – Sweden. Holidays – Christmas.

Christmas in noisy village by Astrid Lindgren and Ilon Wikland. Tr. by Florence Lamborn; ill. by Ilon Wikland. Viking, 1964. Subj: Foreign lands – Sweden. Holidays – Christmas.

Christmas in the stable ill. by Harald Wiberg. Coward, 1962. Subj: Foreign lands – Sweden. Holidays – Christmas. Religion.

The dragon with red eyes ill. by Ilon Wikland; tr. by Patricia Crampton. Viking, 1987. ISBN 0-670-81620-5 Subj: Dragons. Farms.

The ghost of Skinny Jack ill. by Ilon Wikland. Viking, 1988. ISBN 0-670-81913-1 Subj: Emotions – fear. Family life – grandmothers. Folk and fairy tales. Ghosts.

I want a brother or sister tr. from Swedish by Barbara Lucas; ill. by Ilon Wikland. Harcourt, 1981. Subj: Babies. Emotions – envy, jealousy. Sibling rivalry.

I want to go to school too tr. by Barbara Lucas; ill. by Ilon Wikland. Farrar, 1987. ISBN 91-29-58328-4 Subj: School. Sibling rivalry.

Lotta's Christmas surprise ill. by Ilon Wikland. Farrar, 1990. ISBN 91-29-59782-X Subj: Foreign lands – Sweden. Holidays – Christmas. Trees.

My nightingale is singing ill. by Svend Otto; tr. by Patricia Crampton. Viking, 1986. ISBN 0-670-80997-7 Subj: Behavior – seeking better things. Emotions – sadness. Poverty.

Of course Polly can do almost everything ill. by Ilon Wikland. Follett, 1978. Subj: Character traits – optimism. Character traits – perseverance. Holidays – Christmas. Trees.

The tomten ill. by Harald Wiberg. Coward, 1961. Adapt. from a poem by Victor Rydberg Subj: Farms. Foreign lands – Sweden. Seasons – winter. Trolls.

The tomten and the fox adapt. from a poem by Karl-Erik Forsslund; ill. by Harald Wiberg. Coward, 1965. Subj: Animals – foxes. Foreign lands – Sweden. Seasons – winter. Trolls.

Lindgren, Barbro. *Sam's ball* ill. by Eva Eriksson. Morrow, 1983. Subj: Animals – cats. Toys – balls.

Sam's bath ill. by Eva Eriksson. Morrow, 1983. Subj: Activities – bathing. Animals – dogs.

Sam's car ill. by Eva Eriksson. Morrow, 1982. Subj: Behavior – sharing. Toys.

Sam's cookie ill. by Eva Eriksson. Morrow, 1982. Subj: Behavior – sharing. Pets.

Sam's lamp ill. by Eva Eriksson. Morrow, 1983. Subj: Safety.

Sam's potty ill. by Eva Eriksson. Morrow, 1986. ISBN 0-688-06603-8 Subj: Behavior – growing up. Toilet training.

Sam's teddy bear ill. by Eva Eriksson. Morrow, 1982. Subj: Toys – teddy bears.

Sam's wagon ill. by Eva Eriksson. Morrow, 1986. ISBN 0-688-05803-5 Subj: Animals – dogs. Toys.

Shorty takes off tr. by Richard E. Fisher; ill. by Olof Landström. Farrar, 1990. ISBN 91-29-59770-6 Subj: Activities – flying. Character traits – smallness.

The wild baby adapt. from Swedish by Jack Prelutsky; ill. by Eva Eriksson. Greenwillow, 1981. Subj: Behavior – misbehavior. Family life – mothers. Poetry, rhyme.

The wild baby goes to sea adapt. from Swedish by Jack Prelutsky; ill. by Eva Eriksson. Greenwillow, 1983. Subj: Activities – playing. Family life – mothers. Imagination. Toys.

A worm's tale ill. by Cecilia Torudd. Farrar, 1988. ISBN 91-29-59068-X Subj: Animals – worms. Friendship.

Lindman, Maj. *Flicka, Ricka, Dicka and a little dog* ill. by author. Albert Whitman, 1946. Subj: Animals – dogs. Family life. Foreign lands – Sweden. Triplets.

Flicka, Ricka, Dicka and the big red hen ill. by author. Albert Whitman, 1960. Subj: Birds – chickens. Family life. Triplets.

Flicka, Ricka, Dicka and the new dotted dress ill. by author. Albert Whitman, 1939. Subj: Character traits – helpfulness. Family life. Foreign lands – Sweden. Triplets.

Flicka, Ricka, Dicka and the three kittens ill. by author. Albert Whitman, 1941. Subj: Animals – cats. Family life. Triplets.

Flicka, Ricka, Dicka bake a cake ill. by author. Albert Whitman, 1955. Subj: Activities – cooking. Birthdays. Family life. Foreign lands – Sweden. Triplets.

Sailboat time ill. by author. Albert Whitman, 1951. Subj: Boats, ships. Foreign lands – Sweden.

Snipp, Snapp, Snurr and the buttered bread ill. by author. Albert Whitman, 1934. Subj: Cumulative tales. Family life. Farms. Foreign lands – Sweden. Triplets.

Snipp, Snapp, Snurr and the magic horse ill. by author. Albert Whitman, 1935. Subj: Family life. Foreign lands – Sweden. Magic. Toys – rocking horses. Triplets.

Snipp, Snapp, Snurr and the red shoes ill. by author. Albert Whitman, 1932. Subj: Activities – vacationing. Birthdays. Character traits – generosity. Character traits – helpfulness. Family life. Foreign lands – Lapland. Sports – skiing. Triplets.

Snipp, Snapp, Snurr and the reindeer ill. by author. Albert Whitman, 1957. Subj: Animals – deer. Family life. Foreign lands – Sweden. Triplets.

Snipp, Snapp, Snurr and the seven dogs ill. by author. Albert Whitman, 1959. Subj: Animals – dogs. Family life. Foreign lands – Sweden. Triplets.

Snipp, Snapp, Snurr and the yellow sled ill. by author. Albert Whitman, 1936. Subj: Animals – dogs. Family life. Foreign lands – Sweden. Sports – ice skating. Triplets.

Lindsay, Elizabeth. *A letter for Maria* ill. by Alex de Wolf. Watts, 1988. ISBN 0-531-08375-6 Subj: Activities – painting. Toys – teddy bears.

Lindsey, Treska. *When Batistine made bread* ill. by author. Macmillan, 1985. Subj: Activities – cooking. Activities – working. Food.

Lines, Kathleen. *Dick Whittington* (Dick Whittington and his cat)

Lavender's blue (Mother Goose)

The old ballad of the babes in the woods (The babes in the woods)

Once in royal David's city: a picture book of the Nativity, retold from the Gospels ill. by Harold Jones. Watts, 1956. Subj: Holidays – Christmas. Religion.

Link, Martin A. *The goat in the rug* (Blood, Charles L.)

Linn, Margot. *A trip to the dentist* ill. by Catherine Siracusa. Harper, 1988. ISBN 0-06-025834-9 Subj: Careers – dentists.

A trip to the doctor ill. by Catherine Siracusa. Harper, 1988. ISBN 0-06-025843-8 Subj: Careers – doctors.

Linscott, Jody. *Once upon A to Z* ill. by Claudia Porges Holland. Doubleday, 1991. ISBN 0-385-41907-4 Subj: ABC books. Careers – musicians.

Linzer, Jeff. *The fire station book* (Bundt, Nancy)

Lionni, Leo. *Alexander and the wind-up mouse* ill. by author. Pantheon, 1969. Subj: Animals – mice. Caldecott award honor book. Emotions – envy, jealousy. Friendship. Toys.

The biggest house in the world ill. by author. Pantheon, 1968. Subj: Animals. Behavior – greed.

A busy year ill. by author. Knopf, 1992. ISBN 0-679-92464-7 Subj: Animals – mice. Nature. Seasons. Trees.

A color of his own ill. by author. Pantheon, 1975. Subj: Character traits – individuality. Concepts – color. Reptiles – lizards.

Colors to talk about ill. by author. Pantheon, 1985. ISBN 0-394-870034 Subj: Animals – mice. Concepts – color. Format, unusual – board books.

Cornelius ill. by author. Pantheon, 1983. Subj: Character traits – being different. Reptiles – alligators, crocodiles.

Fish is fish ill. by author. Pantheon, 1970. Subj: Behavior – misunderstanding. Fish. Friendship. Frogs and toads.

Frederick ill. by author. Pantheon, 1967. Subj: Animals – mice. Caldecott award honor book. Music.

Frederick's fables ill. by author. Pantheon, 1985. ISBN 0-394-87710-1 Subj: Animals.

Geraldine, the music mouse ill. by author. Pantheon, 1979. Subj: Animals – mice. Music.

The greentail mouse ill. by author. Pantheon, 1973. Subj: Animals – mice. Mardi Gras.

In the rabbitgarden ill. by author. Pantheon, 1975. Subj: Animals – foxes. Animals – mice. Reptiles – snakes.

Inch by inch ill. by author. Astor-Honor, 1960. Subj: Birds. Caldecott award honor book. Concepts – measurement. Insects.

It's mine!: a fable ill. by author. Knopf, 1986. ISBN 0-394-97000-X Subj: Behavior – fighting, arguing. Frogs and toads.

Let's make rabbits ill. by author. Pantheon, 1982. Subj: Activities. Animals – rabbits. Art. Imagination.

Letters to talk about ill. by author. Pantheon, 1985. ISBN 0-394-87001-8 Subj: ABC books. Animals – mice. Format, unusual – board books.

Little blue and little yellow ill. by author. Astor-Honor, 1959. Subj: Concepts – color. Friendship.

Matthew's dream ill. by author. Knopf, 1991. ISBN 0-679-91075-1 Subj: Animals – mice. Careers – artists. Museums.

Mouse days ill. by author. Pantheon, 1981. Subj: Animals – mice. Seasons.

Nicholas, where have you been? ill. by author. Knopf, 1987. ISBN 0-394-98370-X Subj: Animals – mice. Friendship.

Numbers to talk about ill. by author. Pantheon, 1985. ISBN 0-394-87002-6 Subj: Animals – mice. Counting, numbers. Format, unusual – board books.

On my beach there are many pebbles ill. by author. Astor-Honor, 1961. Subj: Rocks. Sea and seashore.

Pezzettino ill. by author. Pantheon, 1975. Subj: Character traits – individuality. Concepts – shape. Self-concept.

Six crows ill. by author. Knopf, 1988. ISBN 0-394-99572-4 Subj: Birds – crows. Birds – owls. Farms.

Swimmy ill. by author. Pantheon, 1963. Subj: Caldecott award honor book. Fish. Sea and seashore.

Theodore and the talking mushroom ill. by author. Pantheon, 1971. Subj: Animals – mice. Character traits – optimism.

Tico and the golden wings ill. by author. Pantheon, 1964. Subj: Birds. Character traits – generosity. Character traits – individuality. Character traits – questioning.

Tillie and the wall ill. by author. Knopf, 1989. ISBN 0-394-82155-6 Subj: Animals – mice. Behavior – seeking better things.

What? pictures to talk about ill. by author. Pantheon, 1983. Subj: Animals – mice. Format, unusual – board books. Senses – hearing. Senses – seeing. Senses – smelling. Senses – tasting. Senses – touching. Wordless.

When? ill. by author. Pantheon, 1983. Subj: Animals – mice. Format, unusual – board books. Night. Seasons. Wordless.

Where? pictures to talk about ill. by author. Pantheon, 1983. Subj: Animals – mice. Format, unusual – board books. Humor. Wordless.

Who? pictures to talk about ill. by author. Pantheon Books, 1983. Subj: Animals – mice. Format, unusual – board books. Wordless.

Words to talk about ill. by author. Pantheon, 1985. ISBN 0-394-87004-2 Subj: Animals – mice. Format, unusual – board books. Language.

Lipkind, William. *Billy the kid* by William Lipkind and Nicolas Mordvinoff; ill. by Nicolas Mordvinoff. Harcourt, 1964. Subj: Animals – goats.

The boy and the forest by William Lipkind and Nicolas Mordvinoff; ill. by Nicolas Mordvinoff. Harcourt, 1964. Subj: Animals. Character traits – kindness to animals. Forest, woods. Magic.

Chaga by William Lipkind and Nicolas Mordvinoff; ill. by Nicolas Mordvinoff. Harcourt, 1955. Subj: Animals – elephants. Concepts – size.

The Christmas bunny by William Lipkind and Nicolas Mordvinoff; ill. by Nicolas Mordvinoff. Harcourt, 1953. Subj: Animals – foxes. Animals – rabbits. Holidays – Christmas. Parties.

Circus rucus by William Lipkind and Nicolas Mordvinoff; ill. by Nicolas Mordvinoff. Harcourt, 1954. Subj: Circus.

Even Steven by William Lipkind and Nicolas Mordvinoff; ill. by Nicolas Mordvinoff. Harcourt, 1952. Subj: Animals – dogs. Character traits – selfishness.

Finders keepers by William Lipkind and Nicolas Mordvinoff; ill. by Nicolas Mordvinoff. Harcourt, 1951. Subj: Animals – dogs. Caldecott award book. Character traits – selfishness.

Four-leaf clover by William Lipkind and Nicolas Mordvinoff; ill. by Nicolas Mordvinoff. Harcourt, 1959. Subj: Ethnic groups in the U.S. – Afro-Americans.

The little tiny rooster by William Lipkind and Nicolas Mordvinoff; ill. by Nicolas Mordvinoff. Harcourt, 1960. Subj: Animals – foxes. Birds – chickens. Character traits – smallness. Self-concept.

The magic feather duster by William Lipkind and Nicolas Mordvinoff; ill. by Nicolas Mordvinoff. Harcourt, 1958. Subj: Character traits – kindness. Folk and fairy tales. Magic.

Nubber bear ill. by Roger Antoine Duvoisin. Harcourt, 1966. Subj: Animals – bears. Behavior – misbehavior.

Professor Bull's umbrella by William Lipkind and Georges Schreiber; ill. by Georges Schreiber. Viking, 1954. Subj: Umbrellas.

Russet and the two reds by William Lipkind and Nicolas Mordvinoff; ill. by Nicolas Mordvinoff. Harcourt, 1962. Subj: Animals – cats.

Sleepyhead by William Lipkind and Nicolas Mordvinoff; ill. by Nicolas Mordvinoff. Harcourt, 1957. Subj: Activities – playing. Games. Poetry, rhyme.

The two reds by William Lipkind and Nicolas Mordvinoff; ill. by Nicolas Mordvinoff. Harcourt, 1950. Subj: Animals – cats. Caldecott award honor book. Friendship.

Lipniacka, Ewa. *To bed...or else!* ill. by Basia Bogdanowicz. Interlink, 1992. ISBN 0-940793-85-7 Subj: Bedtime. Friendship. Night.

Lippman, Peter. *The Know-It-Alls go to sea* ill. by author. Doubleday, 1982. Subj: Behavior – misbehavior. Boats, ships.

The Know-It-Alls help out ill. by author. Doubleday, 1982. Subj: Behavior – misbehavior. Houses.

The Know-It-Alls mind the store ill. by author. Doubleday, 1982. Subj: Behavior – misbehavior. Stores.

The Know-It-Alls take a winter vacation ill. by author. Doubleday, 1982. Subj: Activities – vacationing. Behavior – misbehavior.

New at the zoo ill. by author. Harper, 1969. Subj: Animals. Bedtime. Zoos.

Peter Lippman's numbers ill. by author. Grosset, 1988. ISBN 0-448-19105-9 Subj: Counting, numbers. Format, unusual – toy and movable books.

Peter Lippman's opposites ill. by author. Grosset, 1988. ISBN 0-448-19106-7 Subj: Concepts – opposites. Format, unusual – toy and movable books.

Lisker, Sonia O. *Lost* ill. by author. Harcourt, 1975. Subj: Behavior – lost. Wordless. Zoos.

Two special cards by Sonia O. Lisker and Leigh Dean; ill. by Sonia O. Lisker. Harcourt, 1976. Subj: Divorce. Family life.

Lisowski, Gabriel. *How Tevye became a milkman* ill. by author. Holt, 1976. Subj: Foreign lands – Ukraine. Jewish culture.

Roncalli's magnificent circus ill. by author. Doubleday, 1980. Subj: Animals – bears. Behavior – running away. Circus.

Litchfield, Ada B. *A button in her ear* ill. by Eleanor Mill. Albert Whitman, 1976. Subj: Handicaps – deafness. Senses – hearing.

A cane in her hand ill. by Eleanor Mill. Albert Whitman, 1977. Subj: Handicaps – blindness. Senses – seeing.

A little ABC book Simon and Schuster, 1980. Subj: ABC books. Format, unusual – board books.

A little book of colors Simon and Schuster, 1982. Subj: Concepts – color. Format, unusual – board books.

A little book of numbers Simon and Schuster, 1980. Subj: Counting, numbers. Format, unusual – board books.

Little, Debbie. *The potluck adventures of Mrs. Marmalade* (Swendson, Patsy)

Little, Emily. *David and the giant* ill. by Hans Wilhelm. . Random House, 1987. ISBN 0-394-98867-1 Subj: Behavior – bullying. Giants. Religion.

Little, Jean. *Jess was the brave one* ill. by Janet Wilson. Viking, 1992. ISBN 0-670-83495-5 Subj: Behavior – bullying. Character traits – bravery. Emotions – fear. Family life – sisters. Toys – teddy bears.

Once upon a golden apple by Jean Little and Maggie De Vries; ill. by Phoebe Gilman. Viking, 1991. ISBN 0-670-82963-3 Subj: Activities – picnicking. Activities – reading. Folk and fairy tales.

Little, Lessie Jones. *Children of long ago* ill. by Jan Spivey Gilchrist. Putnam's, 1988. ISBN 0-399-21473-9 Subj: Ethnic groups in the U.S. – Afro-Americans. Poetry, rhyme.

I can do it by myself by Lessie Jones Little and Eloise Greenfield; ill. by Carole M. Byard. Crowell, 1978. Subj: Birthdays. Character traits – bravery. Plants.

Little, Mary E. *ABC for the library* ill. by author. Atheneum, 1975. Subj: ABC books. Libraries.

Ricardo and the puppets ill. by author. Scribner's, 1958. Subj: Animals – mice. Libraries. Puppets.

The little red hen. *The cock, the mouse and the little red hen* ill. by Graham Percy. Candlewick Pr., 1992. ISBN 1-56402-008-8 Subj: Animals. Birds – chickens. Character traits – laziness. Cumulative tales. Farms. Folk and fairy tales. Plants.

The little red hen ill. by Janina Domanska. Macmillan, 1973. Subj: Animals. Birds – chickens. Character traits – laziness. Cumulative tales. Farms. Folk and fairy tales. Plants.

The little red hen ill. by Paul Galdone. Seabury Pr., 1973. Subj: Animals. Birds – chickens. Character traits – laziness. Cumulative tales. Farms. Folk and fairy tales. Plants.

The little red hen retold by Jean Horton Berg; reading consultant: Morton Betel; ill. by Mel Pekarsky. Follett, 1963. Subj: Animals. Birds – chickens. Character traits – laziness. Cumulative tales. Farms. Folk and fairy tales. Plants.

The little red hen adapt. and ill. by William Stobbs. Oxford Univ. Pr., 1985. ISBN 0-19-279807-3 Subj: Animals. Birds – chickens. Character traits – laziness. Cumulative tales. Farms. Folk and fairy tales. Plants.

The little red hen: an old story retold and ill. by Margot Zemach. Farrar, 1983. Subj: Animals. Birds – chickens. Character traits – laziness. Cumulative tales. Farms. Folk and fairy tales. Plants.

Little Red Riding Hood. *Little red cap* (Grimm, Jacob)

Little Red Riding Hood (Grimm, Jacob)

Red Riding Hood (De Regniers, Beatrice Schenk)

Little Tommy Tucker. *The history of Little Tom Tucker* ill. by Paul Galdone. McGraw-Hill, 1970. This version was published by J. Kendrew, York, England, ca. 1820 Subj: Nursery rhymes.

Little Tuppen: *an old tale* ill. by Paul Galdone. Seabury Pr., 1967. Subj: Birds – chickens. Cumulative tales. Folk and fairy tales.

Littledale, Freya. *The farmer in the soup* ill. by Molly Delaney. Scholastic, 1987. ISBN 0-590-40194-7 Subj: Behavior – sharing. Farms. Folk and fairy tales.

The little mermaid (Andersen, H. C. (Hans Christian))

The magic plum tree ill. by Enrico Arno. Crown, 1981. Subj: Character traits – individuality. Plants. Royalty.

Peter and the north wind ill. by Troy Howell. Scholastic, 1988. ISBN 0-590-40756-2 Subj: Folk and fairy tales. Weather – wind.

The snow child ill. by Leon Steinmetz. Scholastic, 1978. Subj: Behavior – wishing. Old age. Seasons – winter.

Littlefield, William. *The whiskers of Ho Ho* ill. by Vladimir Bobri. Lothrop, 1958. Subj: Animals – rabbits. Birds – chickens. Folk and fairy tales. Foreign lands – China. Holidays – Easter.

Littlewood, Valerie. *The season clock* ill. by author. Viking, 1987. ISBN 0-670-81433-4 Subj: Behavior – misbehavior. Character traits – bravery. Seasons. Time.

Livermore, Elaine. *Find the cat* ill. by author. Houghton, 1973. Subj: Animals – cats. Games.

Follow the fox ill. by author. Houghton, 1981. Subj: Animals – foxes. Behavior – lost. Behavior – needing someone.

Looking for Henry ill. by author. Houghton, 1988. ISBN 0-395-44240-0 Subj: Animals – leopards. Behavior – hiding. Sports – hunting.

Lost and found ill. by author. Houghton, 1975. Subj: Behavior – losing things. Games.

One to ten, count again ill. by author. Houghton, 1973. Subj: Counting, numbers. Games.

Three little kittens lost their mittens ill. by author. Houghton, 1979. Subj: Animals – cats. Behavior – losing things. Games. Nursery rhymes.

Livingston, Carole. *"Why am I going to the hospital?"* (Ciliotta, Claire)

"Why was I adopted?" ill. by Arthur Robins; designed by Paul Walter. Lyle Stuart, 1978. Subj: Adoption. Family life.

Livingston, Myra Cohn. *Birthday poems* ill. by Margot Tomes. Holiday, 1989. ISBN 0-8234-0783-7 Subj: Birthdays. Poetry, rhyme.

Cat poems ill. by Trina Schart Hyman. Holiday, 1987. ISBN 0-8234-0631-8 Subj: Animals – cats. Poetry, rhyme.

Celebrations Leonard Everett Fisher. Holiday, 1985. ISBN 0-8234-0550-8 Subj: Holidays. Poetry, rhyme.

Dog poems ill. by Leslie Holt Morrill. Holiday, 1990. ISBN 0-8234-0776-4 Subj: Animals – dogs. Poetry, rhyme.

Higgledy-Piggledy: verses and pictures by Myra Cohn Livingston and Peter Sis; ill. by Peter Sis. Macmillan, 1986. ISBN 0-689-50407-1 Subj: Behavior. Poetry, rhyme.

A Learical lexicon (Lear, Edward)

Poems for brothers, poems for sisters ill. by Jean Zallinger. Holiday, 1991. ISBN 0-8234-0861-2 Subj: Family life – brothers. Family life – sisters. Poetry, rhyme.

Poems for fathers ill. by Robert Casilla. Holiday, 1989. ISBN 0-5234-0729-2 Subj: Family life – fathers. Holidays – Father's Day. Poetry, rhyme.

Poems for mothers ill. by Deborah Kogan Ray. Holiday, 1988. ISBN 0-8234-0678-4 Subj: Holidays – Mother's Day. Poetry, rhyme.

Valentine poems ill. by Patience Brewster. Holiday, 1987. ISBN 0-8234-0587-7 Subj: Animals. Holidays – Valentine's Day. Poetry, rhyme.

Llewelyn, Claire. *My first book of time* ill. by Julie Carpenter; photos. by Paul Bricknell. Dorling Kindersley, 1992. ISBN 1-879431-78-5 Subj: Clocks, watches. Days of the week, months of the year. Format, unusual – toy and movable books. Seasons. Time.

Lloyd, David. *Air* ill. by Peter Visscher. Dial Pr., 1982. Subj: Science.

Cat and dog ill. by Clive Scruton. Lothrop, 1987. ISBN 0-688-07268-2 Subj: Animals – cats. Animals – dogs.

Duck ill. by Charlotte Voake. Lippincott, 1988. ISBN 0-397-32275-5 Subj: Animals. Birds – ducks. Family life – grandmothers.

Grandma and the pirate ill. by Gill Tomblin. Crown, 1986. ISBN 0-517-56023-2 Subj: Family life – grandmothers. Imagination. Pirates. Sand. Sea and seashore.

Hello, goodbye ill. by Louise Voce. Lothrop, 1988. ISBN 0-688-07699-8 Subj: Animals. Trees. Weather – rain.

The ridiculous story of Gammer Gurton's needle ill. by Charlotte Voake. Potter, 1987. ISBN 0-517-56513-7 Subj: Behavior – lying. Folk and fairy tales. Humor.

The stopwatch ill. by Penny Dale. Lippincott, 1986. ISBN 0-397-32193-7 Subj: Clocks, watches. Family life – grandmothers. Sibling rivalry.

Lloyd, Errol. *Nandy's bedtime* ill. by author. Merrimack, 1983. Subj: Bedtime. Night.

Nini at carnival ill. by author. Crowell, 1979. Subj: Character traits – helpfulness. Clothing.

Lloyd, Megan. *Chicken tricks* ill. by author. Harper, 1983. Subj: Birds – chickens. Eggs. Humor. Poetry, rhyme.

Lobato, Arcadio. *The greatest treasure* ill. by author. Picture Book Studio, 1991. Originally published in Spanish ISBN 0-88708-093-6 Subj: Animals – whales. Friendship. Royalty – queens. Sea and seashore. Witches.

Lobe, Mira. *The snowman who went for a walk* tr. from German by Peter Carter; ill. by Winfried Opgenoorth. Morrow, 1984. Subj: Activities – walking. Snowmen.

Valerie and the good-night swing tr. from German by Peter Carter; ill. by Winfried Opgenoorth. Oxford Univ. Pr., 1983. Subj: Bedtime. Poetry, rhyme.

Lobel, Anita. *Alison's zinnia* ill. by author. Greenwillow, 1990. ISBN 0-688-08866-X Subj: ABC books. Flowers.

A birthday for the princess ill. by author. Harper, 1973. Subj: Behavior – needing someone. Birthdays. Royalty – princesses.

The dwarf giant ill. by author. Holiday, 1991. ISBN 0-8234-0852-3 Subj: Elves and little people. Folk and fairy tales. Giants.

King Rooster, Queen Hen ill. by author. Greenwillow, 1975. Subj: Animals. Birds – chickens. Foreign lands – Denmark.

The pancake ill. by author. Greenwillow, 1978. Subj: Cumulative tales. Food.

Potatoes, potatoes ill. by author. Greenwillow, 1967. Subj: Violence, anti-violence.

The straw maid ill. by author. Greenwillow, 1983. Subj: Character traits – cleverness. Crime.

Sven's bridge ill. by author. Harper, 1965. Subj: Bridges. Royalty.

The troll music ill. by author. Harper, 1966. Subj: Magic. Music. Trolls.

Lobel, Arnold. *Days with Frog and Toad* ill. by author. Harper, 1979. Subj: Friendship. Frogs and toads.

Fables ill. by author. Harper, 1980. Subj: Animals. Caldecott award book.

Frog and Toad all year ill. by author. Harper, 1976. Subj: Friendship. Frogs and toads. Seasons.

Frog and Toad are friends ill. by author. Harper, 1970. Subj: Caldecott award honor book. Friendship. Frogs and toads.

The frog and toad pop-up book ill. by author. Harper, 1986. ISBN 0-06-023986-7 Subj: Format, unusual – toy and movable books. Frogs and toads.

Frog and Toad together ill. by author. Harper, 1971. Subj: Friendship. Frogs and toads.

Giant John ill. by author. Harper, 1964. Subj: Giants.

Grasshopper on the road ill. by author. Harper, 1978. Subj: Insects. Insects – grasshoppers.

The great blueness and other predicaments ill. by author. Harper, 1968. Subj: Concepts – color. Wizards.

A holiday for Mister Muster ill. by author. Harper, 1963. Subj: Animals. Illness. Zoos.

How the rooster saved the day ill. by Anita Lobel. Greenwillow, 1977. Subj: Birds – chickens. Character traits – cleverness. Crime.

Lucille ill. by author. Harper, 1964. Subj: Animals – horses. Humor.

The man who took the indoors out ill. by author. Harper, 1974. Subj: Behavior – running away.

Martha, the movie mouse ill. by author. Harper, 1966. Subj: Animals – mice. Poetry, rhyme. Theater.

Ming Lo moves the mountain ill. by author. Greenwillow, 1982. Subj: Foreign lands – China. Moving.

Mouse soup ill. by author. Harper, 1977. Subj: Animals – mice. Animals – weasels. Character traits – cleverness.

Mouse tales ill. by author. Harper, 1972. Subj: Animals – mice. Humor.

On Market Street ill. by Anita Lobel. Greenwillow, 1981. Subj: ABC books. Caldecott award honor book. Poetry, rhyme. Shopping. Stores.

On the day Peter Stuyvesant sailed into town ill. by author. Harper, 1971. Subj: Poetry, rhyme. Problem solving. U.S. history.

Owl at home ill. by author. Harper, 1975. Subj: Birds – owls.

Prince Bertram the bad ill. by author. Harper, 1963. Subj: Behavior – misbehavior. Dragons. Royalty – princes. Witches.

The rose in my garden ill. by Anita Lobel. Greenwillow, 1984. Subj: Animals – cats. Animals – mice. Cumulative tales. Flowers. Gardens, gardening. Insects – bees. Poetry, rhyme.

Small pig ill. by author. Harper, 1969. Subj: Animals – pigs. Behavior – running away. Farms.

A treeful of pigs ill. by Anita Lobel. Greenwillow, 1979. Subj: Animals – pigs. Character traits – laziness. Farms. Humor.

The turnaround wind ill. by author. Harper, 1988. ISBN 0-06-023988-3 Subj: Weather – wind.

Uncle Elephant ill. by author. Harper, 1981. Subj: Animals – elephants. Behavior – lost. Family life – aunts, uncles. Sea and seashore.

Whiskers and rhymes ill. by author. Greenwillow, 1985. ISBN 0-688-03836-0 Subj: Animals – cats. Poetry, rhyme.

A zoo for Mister Muster ill. by author. Harper, 1962. Subj: Animals. Zoos.

Locker, Thomas. *Family farm* ill. by author. Dial Pr., 1988. ISBN 0-8037-0490-9 Subj: Farms.

The land of gray wolf ill. by author. Dial, 1991. ISBN 0-8037-0937-4 Subj: Ecology. Indians of North America. Nature.

The mare on the hill ill. by author. Dial Pr., 1985. ISBN 0-8037-0208-6 Subj: Animals – horses. Family life – grandfathers. Farms.

Rip Van Winkle (Irving, Washington)

Sailing with the wind ill. by author. Dial Pr., 1986. ISBN 0-8037-0312-0 Subj: Activities – traveling. Boats, ships.

Where the river begins ill. by author. Dial Pr., 1984. Subj: Family life – grandfathers. Rivers.

The young artist ill. by author. Dial, 1989. ISBN 0-8037-0627-8 Subj: Careers – artists. Royalty.

Lockwood, Primrose. *Cat boy!* ill. by Clara Vulliamy. Houghton 1991. ISBN 0-395-55208-7 Subj: Animals – cats.

Cissy Lavender ill. by Emma Chichester Clark. Little, 1989. ISBN 0-316-14497-5 Subj: Activities – working. Activities – writing.

One winter's night ill. by Elaine Mills. Macmillan, 1991. ISBN 0-02-759235-9 Subj: Animals – dogs. Pets.

Lodge, Bernard. *Door to door* ill. by Maureen Roffey. Lothrop, 1980. Subj: Foreign lands – England. Format, unusual.

Rhyming Nell ill. by Maureen Roffey. Lothrop, 1979. Subj: Format, unusual. Poetry, rhyme. Witches.

Löfgren, Ulf. *Alvin the pirate* ill. by author. Carolrhoda, 1990. ISBN 0-87614-402-4 Subj: Imagination. Pirates.

Alvin the zookeeper ill. by author. Carolrhoda, 1991. ISBN 0-87614-689-2 Subj: Animals. Careers – zookeepers. Zoos.

The boy who ate more than the giant and other Swedish folktales tr. from Swedish by Sheila La Farge; ill. by author. Collins-World, 1978. Subj: Folk and fairy tales. Giants. Humor.

The color trumpet ill. by author. Addison-Wesley, 1973. English text by Alison Winn; adapt. by Ray Broekel Subj: Concepts – color.

The flying orchestra ill. by author. Addison-Wesley, 1973. English text by Alison Winn; adapt. by Ray Broekel Subj: Music.

One-two-three ill. by author. Addison-Wesley, 1973. English text by Alison Winn; adapt. by Ray Brockel Subj: Animals. Counting, numbers. Participation.

The traffic stopper that became a grandmother visitor ill. by author. Addison-Wesley, 1973. English text by Alison Winn; adapt. by Ray Broekel Subj: Animals – elephants. Automobiles. Machines.

The wonderful tree ill. by author. Delacorte Pr., 1969. Subj: Imagination. Trees.

Logue, Christopher. *The magic circus* ill. by Wayne Anderson. Viking, 1979. Subj: Character traits – cleverness. Circus. Monsters.

Lohf, Sabine. *Things I can make with buttons* ill. by author. Chronicle Books, 1990. ISBN 0-87701-687-9 Subj: Activities – making things.

Things I can make with cloth ill. by author. Chronicle Books, 1989. ISBN 0-87701-666-6 Subj: Activities – making things.

Things I can make with cork ill. by author. Chronicle Books, 1990. ISBN 0-87701-726-3 Subj: Activities – making things.

Things I can make with paper ill. by author. Chronicle Books, 1989. ISBN 0-87701-671-2 Subj: Activities – making things. Paper.

London, Jonathan. *The lion who had asthma* ill. by Nadine Bernard Westcott. Albert Whitman, 1992. ISBN 0-8075-4559-7 Subj: Imagination. Illness.

Thirteen moons on turtle's back (Bruchac, Joseph)

Long, Claudia. *Albert's story* ill. by Judy Glasser. Delacorte Pr., 1978. ISBN 0-440-00080-7 Subj: Dragons. Imagination.

Long, Earlene. *Gone fishing* ill. by Richard Eric Brown. Houghton, 1984. Subj: Concepts – size. Family life – fathers. Sports – fishing.

Johnny's egg photos. by Neal Slavin and Charles Mikolaycak. Addison-Wesley, 1980. Subj: Activities – cooking. Eggs.

Longfellow, Henry Wadsworth. *Hiawatha* ill. by Susan Jeffers. Dial Pr., 1983. Subj: Indians of North America. Poetry, rhyme.

Hiawatha's childhood ill. by Errol Le Cain. Farrar, 1984. Subj: Indians of North America. Poetry, rhyme.

Paul Revere's ride ill. by Paul Galdone. Crowell, 1963. ISBN 0-688-04015-2 Subj: Poetry, rhyme. U.S. history.

Paul Revere's ride ill. by Nancy Winslow Parker. Greenwillow, 1985. Subj: Poetry, rhyme. U.S. history.

Loof, Jan. *Uncle Louie's fantastic sea voyage* ill. by author. Random House, 1978. Subj: Activities – traveling. Boats, ships. Family life – aunts, uncles. Zoos.

Loomans, Diane. *The lovables in the kingdom of self-esteem* ill. *by Kim Howard* Starseed Pr., 1991. ISBN 0-915811-25-1 Subj: Animals. Self-concept. Poetry, rhyme.

Loomis, Christine. *My new baby-sitter* photos. by George Ancona. Morrow, 1991. ISBN 0-688-09626-3 Subj: Activities – baby-sitting.

Lopshire, Robert. *The biggest, smallest, fastest, tallest things you've ever heard of* ill. by author. Crowell, 1980. Subj: Concepts.

How to make snop snappers and other fine things ill. by author. Greenwillow, 1977. Subj: Activities – making things. Games.

I am better than you ill. by author. Harper, 1968. Subj: Behavior – boasting. Reptiles – lizards.

I want to be somebody new! ill. by author. Random House, 1986. ISBN 0-394-97616-9 Subj: Behavior – seeking better things. Character traits – individuality. Poetry, rhyme.

It's magic ill. by author. Macmillan, 1969. Subj: Magic.

Put me in the zoo ill. by author. Random House, 1960. Subj: Animals – dogs. Circus. Concepts – color. Poetry, rhyme.

Lorca, Federico García *see* García Lorca, Federico

Lord, Beman. *The days of the week* ill. by Walter Erhard. Walck, 1968. Subj: Days of the week, months of the year. Poetry, rhyme. Songs.

Lord, John Vernon. *Mr. Mead and his garden* ill. by author. Houghton, 1975. Subj: Animals – snails. Gardens, gardening. Poetry, rhyme.

Lord, Nancy *see* Titus, Eve

Lorenz, Konrad. *The goose family book* (Kalas, Sybille)

Lorenz, Lee. *Big Gus and Little Gus* ill. by author. Prentice-Hall, 1982. Subj: Character traits – laziness. Cumulative tales. Folk and fairy tales.

Dinah's egg ill. by author. Simon & Schuster, 1990. ISBN 0-671-68685-2 Subj: Dinosaurs. Eggs.

The feathered ogre ill. by author. Prentice-Hall, 1983. ISBN 0-13-308296-2 Subj: Character traits – cleverness. Folk and fairy tales. Magic. Mythical creatures. Royalty.

Hugo and the spacedog ill. by author. Prentice-Hall, 1983. ISBN 0-13-444497-3 Subj: Animals. Animals – dogs. Farms. Space and space ships.

Pinchpenny John ill. by author. Prentice-Hall, 1981. Subj: Behavior – greed. Folk and fairy tales.

Scornful Simkin ill. by author. Prentice-Hall, 1980. Subj: Folk and fairy tales.

A weekend in the city ill. by author. Pippin Pr., 1991. ISBN 0-945912-15-3 Subj: Animals. City. Country.

A weekend in the country ill. by author. Prentice-Hall, 1984. Subj: Animals – pigs. Birds – ducks. Country.

Lorenzini, Carlo *see* Collodi, Carlo

Loretan, Sylvia. *Bob the snowman* ill. by Jan Lenica. Viking, 1991. ISBN 0-670-83677-X Subj: Snowmen. Weather – snow.

Lorian, Nicole. *A birthday present for Mama* ill. by J. P. Miller. Random House, 1984. ISBN 0-394-96755-0 Subj: Animals. Animals – rabbits. Birthdays.

Lorimer, Janet. *The biggest bubble in the world* ill. by Diane Paterson. Watts, 1982. Subj: Behavior – misbehavior.

Lorimer, Lawrence T. *Noah's ark* (Martin, Charles E.)

Loriot. *Peter and the wolf* (Prokofiev, Sergei Sergeievitch)

Louie, Al-Ling. *Yeh Shen: A Cinderella story from China* ill. by Ed Young. Putnam, 1990. ISBN 0-399-20900-X Subj: Folk and fairy tales. Foreign lands – China.

Lourie, Helen *see* Storr, Catherine (Cole)

Loverseed, Amanda. *The thunder king* ill. by author. Bedrick, 1991. ISBN 0-87226-450-5 Subj: Folk and fairy tales. Foreign lands – Peru.

Tikkatoo's journey ill. by author. Bedrick, 1990. ISBN 0-87226-420-3 Subj: Eskimos. Folk and fairy tales.

Low, Alice. *The charge of the mouse brigade* (Stone, Bernard)

David's windows ill. by Tomie de Paola. Putnam's, 1974. Subj: Animals – horses. City. Family life – grandmothers.

Taro and the bamboo shoot (Matsuno, Masako)

The witch who was afraid of witches ill. by Karen Gundersheimer. Pantheon, 1978. Subj: Holidays – Halloween. Sibling rivalry. Witches.

Witch's holiday ill. by Tony Walton. Pantheon, 1971. Subj: Holidays – Halloween. Poetry, rhyme. Witches.

Low, Joseph. *Adam's book of odd creatures* ill. by author. Atheneum, 1962. Subj: ABC books. Animals. Names. Poetry, rhyme.

Benny rabbit and the owl ill. by author. Greenwillow, 1978. Subj: Birds – geese. Character traits – bravery. Emotions – fear. Farms.

Boo to a goose ill. by author. Atheneum, 1975. Subj: Birds – geese. Character traits – bravery. Emotions – fear. Farms.

The Christmas grump ill. by author. Atheneum, 1977. Subj: Animals – mice. Emotions – happiness. Emotions – sadness. Holidays – Christmas.

Don't drag your feet... ill. by author. Atheneum, 1983. Subj: Behavior. Dreams. Toys.

Five men under one umbrella ill. by author. Macmillan, 1975. Subj: Riddles.

A mad wet hen and other riddles ill. by author. Greenwillow, 1977. Subj: Riddles.

Mice twice ill. by author. Atheneum, 1980. Subj: Animals – mice. Caldecott award honor book.

My dog, your dog ill. by author. Macmillan, 1978. ISBN 0-02-761400-X Subj: Animals – dogs. Behavior.

What if...? fourteen encounters - some frightful, some frivolous - that might happen to anyone ill. by author. Atheneum, 1976. Subj: Problem solving.

Lowitz, Anson. *The pilgrims' party* (Lowitz, Sadyebeth)

Lowitz, Sadyebeth. *The pilgrims' party* by Sadyebeth and Anson Lowitz; ill. by Anson Lowitz. Lerner, 1931. Subj: Holidays – Thanksgiving. U.S. history.

Lowrey, Janette Sebring. *Six silver spoons* ill. by Robert M. Quackenbush. Harper, 1971. Subj: Birthdays. U.S. history.

Lubach, Peter. *Harry and the singing fish* ill. by author. Walt Disney, 1992. ISBN 1-56282-159-8 Subj: Fish. Songs. Theater. Wordless.

Lubell, Cicil. *Rosalie, the bird market turtle* (Lubell, Winifred)

Lubell, Winifred. *Here comes daddy: a book for twos and threes* ill. by author. Addison-Wesley, 1944. Subj: Family life – fathers.

I wish I had another name (Williams, Jay)

Rosalie, the bird market turtle by Winifred and Cicil Lubell; ill. by Winifred Lubell. Rand McNally, 1962. Subj: Behavior – lost. Birds. Foreign lands – France. Reptiles – turtles, tortoises.

Lubin, Leonard B. *Christmas gift-bringers* ill. by author. Lothrop, 1989. ISBN 0-688-07020-5 Subj: Animals – mice. Holidays – Christmas.

Lucas, Barbara. *A calf for Christmas* (Lindgren, Astrid)

Cats by Mother Goose (Mother Goose)

I want a brother or sister (Lindgren, Astrid)

I want to go to school too (Lindgren, Astrid)

Sleeping over ill. by Stella Ormai. Macmillan, 1986. ISBN 0-02-761360-7 Subj: Animals – bears. Frogs and toads. Sleep.

Ludwig, Warren. *Good morning, Granny Rose: an Arkansas folktale* ill. by reteller. Putnam, 1990.

ISBN 0-399-21950-1 Subj: Animals – bears. Animals – dogs. Folk and fairy tales. Hibernation. Weather – snow.

Old Noah's elephants ill. by adaptor. Putnam, 1991. ISBN 0-399-22256-1 Subj: Animals – elephants. Boats, ships. Folk and fairy tales. Religion – Noah.

Luenn, Nancy. *The dragon kite* ill. by Michael Hague. Harcourt, 1982. Subj: Folk and fairy tales. Foreign lands – Japan. Kites.

Mother earth ill. by Neil Waldman. Atheneum, 1992. ISBN 0-689-31668-2 Subj: Earth. Ecology.

Nessa's fish ill. by Neil Waldman. Atheneum, 1990. ISBN 0-689-31477-9 Subj: Eskimos. Family life – grandmothers. Indians of North America. Sports – fishing.

Lukešová, Milena. *Julian in the autumn woods* ill. by Jan Kudláček. Holt, 1977. Subj: Forest, woods.

The little girl and the rain ill. by Jan Kudláček. Holt, 1978. Subj: Emotions – loneliness. Weather – rain.

Lumley, Katheryn Wentzel. *I can be an animal doctor* Childrens Pr., 1985. ISBN 0-516-01836-1 Subj: Careers – veterinarians.

Lund, Doris Herold. *The paint-box sea* ill. by Symeon Shimin. McGraw-Hill, 1971. Subj: Poetry, rhyme. Sea and seashore. Seasons – summer.

You ought to see Herbert's house ill. by Steven Kellogg. McGraw-Hill, 1973. Subj: Behavior – boasting. Friendship.

Lundell, Margo. *Teddy bear's birthday* ill. by Dee deRosa. Platt, 1985. ISBN 0-448-40876-7 Subj: Birthdays. Format, unusual – board books. Toys – teddy bears.

Lunn, Carolyn. *A buzz is part of a bee* ill. by Tom Dunnington. Children's Pr., 1990. ISBN 0-516-02062-5 Subj: Poetry, rhyme.

Lunn, Janet. *Amos's sweater* ill. by Kim LaFave. Firefly Books, 1991. ISBN 0-88899-074-X Subj: Animals – sheep. Clothing – sweaters.

Duck cakes for sale ill. by Kim LaFave. Firefly Books, 1991. ISBN 0-88899-094-4 Subj: Birds – ducks.

Lurie, Morris. *The story of Imelda, who was small* ill. by Terry Denton. Houghton, 1988. ISBN 0-395-48863-7 Subj: Character traits – smallness. Food.

Lussert, Anneliese. *The farmer and the moon* tr. by Anthea Bell; ill. by Jozef Wilkon. Holt, 1987. ISBN 0-8050-0281-2 Subj: Behavior – greed. Magic. Moon.

Lüton, Mildred. *Little chicks' mothers and all the others* ill. by Mary Maki Rae. Viking, 1983. Subj: Animals. Farms. Poetry, rhyme.

Luttrell, Ida. *Lonesome Lester* ill. by Megan Lloyd. Harper, 1984. Subj: Animals – prairie dogs. Behavior – solitude. Emotions – loneliness.

Mattie and the chicken thief ill. by Thacher Hurd. Putnam's, 1988. ISBN 0-396-09126-1 Subj: Animals. Behavior – misbehavior. Birds – chickens.

Ottie Slockett ill. by Ute Krause. Dial, 1990. ISBN 0-8037-0711-8 Subj: Behavior. Friendship.

Three good blankets ill. by Michael McDermott. Atheneum, 1990. ISBN 0-689-31586-4 Subj: Animals. Behavior – sharing.

Lyfick, Warren. *Animal tales* ill. by Joe Kohl. Harvey House, 1980. Subj: Animals. Riddles.

The little book of fowl jokes ill. by Chris Cummings. Harvey House, 1980. Subj: Birds. Riddles.

Lynch, Marietta. *Mommy and daddy are divorced* (Perry, Patricia)

Lyndon, Kerry Raines. *A birthday for Blue* ill. by Michael Hays. Albert Whitman, 1989. ISBN 0-8075-0774-1 Subj: Activities – traveling. Birthdays. Family life. U.S. history.

Lynn, Patricia see Watts, Mabel (Pizzey)

Lynn, Sara. *Big animals* ill. by author. Aladdin, 1987. ISBN 0-689-71098-4 Subj: Animals. Format, unusual – board books.

Clothes ill. by author. Macmillan, 1986. ISBN 0-689-71095-X Subj: Clothing. Format, unusual – board books.

Colors ill. by author. Little, 1986. ISBN 0-316-54002-1 Subj: Clowns, jesters. Concepts – color.

Farm animals ill. by author. Aladdin, 1987. ISBN 0-689-71100-X Subj: Animals. Format, unusual – board books.

Food ill. by author. Macmillan, 1986. ISBN 0-689-71094-1 Subj: Food. Format, unusual – board books.

Garden animals ill. by author. Aladdin, 1987. ISBN 0-689-71101-8 Subj: Animals. Format, unusual – board books. Gardens, gardening.

Home ill. by author. Macmillan, 1986. ISBN 0-689-71097-6 Subj: Format, unusual – board books. Houses.

1 2 3 ill. by author. Little, 1986. ISBN 0-316-54004-8 Subj: Animals. Counting, numbers.

Small animals ill. by author. Aladdin, 1987. ISBN 0-689-71099-2 Subj: Animals. Format, unusual – board books.

Toys ill. by author. Macmillan, 1986. ISBN 0-689-71096-8 Subj: Format, unusual – board books. Toys.

Lyon, David. *The biggest truck* ill. by author. Lothrop, 1988. ISBN 0-688-05514-1 Subj: Activities – working. Night. Trucks.

The brave little computer ill. by Robert W. Alley. Simon & Schuster, 1984. ISBN 0-671-52455-0 Subj: Computers. Problem solving.

The runaway duck ill. by author. Lothrop, 1985. ISBN 0-688-04002-0 Subj: Toys.

Lyon, George-Ella. *A B Cedar: an alphabet of trees* designed and ill. by Tom Parker. Watts, 1989. ISBN 0-531-08395-0 Subj: ABC books. Trees.

Basket ill. by Mary Szilagyi. Watts, 1990. ISBN 0-531-08486-8 Subj: Behavior – losing things. Family life – grandfathers.

Cecil's story ill. by Peter Catalanotto. Watts, 1991. ISBN 0-531-08512-0 Subj: Emotions – fear. Family life. Illness. U.S. history. War.

Come a tide ill. by Stephen Gammell. Watts, 1990. ISBN 0-531-08454-X Subj: Family life. Weather – floods.

Father Time and the day boxes ill. by Robert Andrew Parker. Bradbury Pr., 1985. ISBN 0-02-761370-4 Subj: Time.

The outside inn ill. by Vera Rosenberry. Watts,, 1991. ISBN 0-531-08536-8 Subj: Food. Nature. Poetry, rhyme.

A regular rolling Noah ill. by Stephen Gammell. Bradbury Pr., 1986. ISBN 0-02-761330-5 Subj: Activities – traveling. Animals. Trains.

Together ill. by Vera Rosenberry. Watts, 1989. ISBN 0-531-08431-0 Subj: Friendship. Poetry, rhyme.

Who came down that road? ill. by Peter Catalanotto. Watts, 1992. ISBN 0-531-08587-2 Subj: Character traits – questioning. Family life. Roads.

Lystad, Mary H. *That new boy* ill. by Emily Arnold McCully. Crown, 1973. Subj: Character traits – individuality. Friendship. Moving.

Mabey, Richard. *Oak and company* ill. by Clare Roberts. Greenwillow, 1983. Subj: Ecology. Science. Trees.

McAfee, Annalena. *The visitors who came to stay* ill. by Anthony Browne. Viking, 1985. ISBN 0-670-74714-9 Subj: Behavior – trickery. Family life – fathers. Sea and seashore.

McAllister, Angela. *The battle of Sir Cob and Sir Filbert* ill. by author. Crown, 1992. ISBN 0-517-58730-0 Subj: Behavior – sharing. Emotions – envy, jealousy. Middle ages. War.

The enchanted flute ill. by Margaret Chamberlain. Delacorte Pr., 1991. ISBN 0-385-30327-0 Subj: Birthdays. Magic. Music. Self-concept.

Matepo ill. by Jill Newton. Dial, 1991. ISBN 0-8037-0838-6 Subj: Activities – trading. Animals. Animals – monkeys. Circular tales. Jungle.

Nesta, the little witch ill. by Susie Jenkin-Pearce. Viking, 1990. ISBN 0-670-83376-2 Subj: School. Witches.

Snail's birthday problem ill. by Susie Jenkin-Pearce. Viking, 1989. ISBN 0-670-82991-9 Subj: Animals – snails. Birthdays. Parties.

MacArthur-Onslow, Annette Rosemary. *Minnie* ill. by author. Rand McNally, 1971. Subj: Animals – cats.

Macaulay, David. *Castle* ill. by author. Houghton, 1977. Subj: Caldecott award honor book.

Cathedral ill. by author. Houghton, 1973. Subj: Caldecott award honor book.

Why the chicken crossed the road ill. by author. Houghton, 1987. ISBN 0-395-44241-9 Subj: Humor.

MacBean, Dilla Wittemore. *Picture book dictionary* ill. by Pauline B. Adams. Children's Pr., 1962. Subj: Dictionaries.

MacBeth, George. *Jonah and the Lord* ill. by Margaret Gordon. Holt, 1970. Subj: Folk and fairy tales. Religion.

Noah's journey ill. by Margaret Gordon. Viking, 1966. Subj: Poetry, rhyme. Religion – Noah.

McCarthy, Bobette. *Buffalo girls* ill. by author. Crown, 1987. ISBN 0-517-65568-4 Subj: Animals – buffaloes. Music. Songs.

Ten little hippos ill. by author. Bradbury Pr., 1992. ISBN 0-02-765445-1 Subj: Animals – hippopotami. Counting, numbers. Poetry, rhyme.

MacCarthy, Patricia. *Herds of words* ill. by author. Dial, 1991. ISBN 0-8037-0892-0 Subj: Language.

McCarthy, Ruth. *Katie and the smallest bear* ill. by Emilie Boon. Knopf, 1986. ISBN 0-394-97855-2 Subj: Activities – playing. Animals – bears. Zoos.

McCaughrean, Geraldine. *The cherry tree* (Ikeda, Daisaku)

Saint George and the dragon ill. by Nicki Palin. Doubleday, 1989. ISBN 0-385-26529-8 Subj: Dragons. Folk and fairy tales.

The snow country prince (Ikeda, Daisaku)

The story of Noah and the ark ill. by Helen Ward. Ideals, 1989. ISBN 0-8249-8403-X Subj: Boats, ships. Religion – Noah.

McCauley, Jane. *Baby birds and how they grow* ill. with photos. National Geographic Soc., 1983. Subj: Birds. Science.

The way animals sleep ill. with photos. National Geographic Soc., 1983. Subj: Animals. Sleep.

McClenathan, Louise. *The Easter pig* ill. by Rosekrans Hoffman. Morrow, 1982. Subj: Animals – pigs. Character traits – generosity. Holidays – Easter.

My mother sends her wisdom ill. by Rosekrans Hoffman. Morrow, 1979. Subj: Behavior – greed. Character traits – cleverness.

McClintock, Marshall. *A fly went by* ill. by Fritz Siebel. Random House, 1958. Subj: Behavior – misunderstanding. Cumulative tales. Insects – flies.

Stop that ball ill. by Fritz Siebel. Random House, 1959. Subj: Toys – balls.

What have I got? ill. by Leonard P. Kessler. Harper, 1961. Subj: Clothing. Imagination. Poetry, rhyme.

McClintock, Mike *see* McClintock, Marshall

McCloskey, Kevin. *Mrs. Fitz's flamingos* ill. by author. Lothrop, 1992. ISBN 0-688-10474-6 Subj: Birds – flamingos. City. Emotions – love.

McCloskey, Robert. *Bert Dow, deep-water man: a tale of the sea in the classic tradition* ill. by author. Viking, 1963. Subj: Animals – whales. Boats, ships. Sea and seashore.

Blueberries for Sal ill. by author. Viking, 1948. Subj: Animals – bears. Behavior – lost. Caldecott award honor book. Family life. Food.

Lentil ill. by author. Viking, 1940. Subj: Music. Noise, sounds. Problem solving.

Make way for ducklings ill. by author. Viking, 1941. Subj: Birds – ducks. Caldecott award book. Careers – police officers. City.

One morning in Maine ill. by author. Viking, 1952. Subj: Caldecott award honor book. Family life. Sea and seashore. Teeth.

Time of wonder ill. by author. Viking, 1957. Subj: Caldecott award book. Islands. Sea and seashore. Seasons – summer. Weather.

McClung, Robert. *How animals hide* ill. with photos. National Geographic Soc., 1973. ISBN 0-87044-144-2 Subj: Animals. Behavior – hiding. Science.

Sphinx: the story of a caterpillar ill. by Carol Lerner Rev. ed. Morrow, 1981. Subj: Insects – butterflies, caterpillars. Science.

McClure, Gillian. *Fly home McDoo* ill. by author. Dutton, 1980. Subj: Behavior – running away. Birds – pigeons.

Prickly pig ill. by author. Elsevier-Dutton, 1980. Subj: Animals – hedgehogs. Hibernation.

What's the time, Rory Wolf? ill. by author. Dutton, 1982. Subj: Animals – wolves. Emotions – loneliness. Friendship.

McConnachie, Brian. *Elmer and the chickens vs. the big league* ill. by Harvey Stevenson. Crown, 1992. ISBN 0-517-57617-1 Subj: Birds – chickens. Farms. Imagination. Sports – baseball.

Flying boy ill. by Jack Ziegler. Crown, 1988. ISBN 0-517-55980-3 Subj: Activities – flying. Character traits – helpfulness. Character traits – individuality.

Lily of the forest ill. by Jack Ziegler. Crown, 1987. ISBN 0-517-56595-1 Subj: Animals. Behavior – boredom. Behavior – running away. Family life. Forest, woods.

McCord, David. *Every time I climb a tree* ill. by Marc Simont. Little, 1967. ISBN 0-316-55514-2 Subj: Activities – playing. Poetry, rhyme. Trees.

The star in the pail ill. by Marc Simont. Little, 1976. Subj: Poetry, rhyme.

McCormack, John E. *Rabbit tales* ill. by Jenni Oliver. Dutton, 1980. Subj: Animals – rabbits. Character traits – cleverness. Character traits – individuality. Character traits – vanity. Friendship. Imagination.

Rabbit travels ill. by Lynne Cherry. Dutton, 1984. Subj: Activities – traveling. Animals – rabbits. Friendship.

McCrea, James. *The king's procession* by James and Ruth McCrea; ill. by authors. Atheneum, 1963. Subj: Animals – donkeys. Character traits – loyalty. Poverty. Royalty – kings.

The magic tree by James and Ruth McCrea; ill. by authors. Atheneum, 1965. Subj: Character traits – meanness. Emotions. Emotions – happiness. Royalty.

The story of Olaf by James and Ruth McCrea; ill. by authors. Atheneum, 1964. Subj: Dragons. Knights. Wizards.

McCrea, Lilian. *Mother hen* ill. by Edda Reinl. Picture Book Studio, 1987. ISBN 0-88708-037-5 Subj: Animals. Birds – chickens. Counting, numbers. Eggs. Farms.

McCrea, Ruth. *The king's procession* (McCrea, James)

The magic tree (McCrea, James)

The story of Olaf (McCrea, James)

McCready, Lady *see* Tudor, Tasha

McCready, Tasha Tudor *see* Tudor, Tasha

McCue, Lisa. *Corduroy's party* ill. by author. Viking, 1985. Subj: Birthdays. Format, unusual – board books. Toys – teddy bears. Wordless.

Corduroy's toys ill. by author. Viking, 1985. Subj: Format, unusual – board books. Toys. Toys – teddy bears. Wordless.

The little chick ill. by author. Random House, 1986. ISBN 0-394-88017-X Subj: Birds – chickens. Farms. Format, unusual – board books.

McCully, Emily Arnold. *The Christmas gift* ill. by author. Harper, 1988. ISBN 0-06-024212-4 Subj: Animals – mice. Family life – grandfathers. Holidays – Christmas. Toys. Wordless.

The evil spell ill. by author. HarperCollins, 1992. ISBN 0-06-024154-3 Subj: Animals – bears. Emotions – fear. Theater.

First snow ill. by author. Harper, 1985. ISBN 0-06-024129-2 Subj: Activities – playing. Animals – mice. Seasons – winter. Weather – snow. Wordless.

The grandma mix-up ill. by author. Harper, 1988. ISBN 0-06-024202-7 Subj: Activities – babysitting. Family life – grandmothers.

New baby ill. by author. Harper, 1988. ISBN 0-06-024131-4 Subj: Animals – mice. Sibling rivalry. Wordless.

Picnic ill. by author. Harper, 1984. Subj: Activities – picnicking. Animals – mice. Behavior – lost. Wordless.

School ill. by author. Harper, 1987. ISBN 0-06-024133-0 Subj: Animals – mice. School. Wordless.

Speak up, Blanche! ill. by author. HarperCollins, 1991. ISBN 0-06-024228-0 Subj: Animals – bears. Animals – sheep. Character traits – shyness. Theater.

Zaza's big break ill. by author. HarperCollins, 1989. ISBN 0-06-024224-8 Subj: Animals – bears. Careers – actors. Television. Theater.

McCunn, Ruthanne L. *Pie-Biter* ill. by You-Shah Tang. Design Ent., 1983. ISBN 0-932538-09-6 Subj: Activities – working. Behavior – seeking better things. Ethnic groups in the U.S. – Chinese-Americans.

McCurdy, Michael. *The devils who learned to be good* ill. by author. Little, 1987. ISBN 0-316-55527-4 Subj: Character traits – cleverness. Devil. Folk and fairy tales.

The old man and the fiddle ill. by author. Putnam, 1992. ISBN 0-399-21812-2 Subj: Music. Poetry, rhyme.

McDaniel, Becky Bring. *Katie did it* ill. by Lois Axeman. Children's Pr., 1983. Subj: Sibling rivalry.

McDermott, Beverly Brodsky. *The crystal apple: a Russian tale* ill. by author. Viking, 1974. Subj: Folk and fairy tales. Foreign lands – Russia. Imagination.

The Golem: a Jewish legend ill. by author. Lippincott, 1976. Subj: Caldecott award honor book. Folk and fairy tales. Jewish culture.

Jonah: an Old Testament story ill. by author. Lippincott, 1977. Subj: Religion.

McDermott, Gerald. *Anansi the spider: a tale from the Ashanti* ill. by author. Holt, 1972. Subj: Caldecott award honor book. Folk and fairy tales. Foreign lands – Africa. Moon. Spiders.

Arrow to the sun: a Pueblo Indian tale ill. by author. Viking, 1974. Subj: Caldecott award book. Folk and fairy tales. Indians of North America.

Daniel O'Rourke: an Irish tale ill. by author. Viking, 1986. ISBN 0-670-80924-1 Subj: Dreams. Elves and little people. Folk and fairy tales. Foreign lands – Ireland.

Daughter of earth: a Roman myth ill. by author. Delacorte, 1984. Subj: Folk and fairy tales. Seasons.

The magic tree: a tale from the Congo ill. by author. Holt, 1973. Subj: Character traits – appearance. Magic. Twins.

Papagayo, the mischief maker ill. by author. Windmill, 1980. Subj: Birds – parakeets, parrots. Moon.

The stonecutter: a Japanese folk tale ill. by author. Viking, 1975. Subj: Behavior – dissatisfaction. Folk and fairy tales. Foreign lands – Japan.

Tim O'Toole and the wee folk ill. by author. Viking, 1990. ISBN 0-670-80393-6 Subj: Behavior – trickery. Folk and fairy tales. Magic.

The voyage of Osiris: a myth of ancient Egypt ill. by author. Windmill Books, 1977. Subj: Folk and fairy tales. Foreign lands – Egypt. Religion. Royalty.

Zomo the rabbit ill. by author. Harcourt, 1992. ISBN 0-15-299967-1 Subj: Animals – rabbits. Behavior – trickery. Foreign lands – Africa.

McDonald, Amy. *Let's do it* ill. by Maureen Roffey. Candlewick Pr., 1992. ISBN 1-56402-024-X Subj: Activities. Format, unusual – board books. Games.

Let's make a noise ill. by Maureen Roffey. Candlewick Pr., 1992. ISBN 1-56402-025-8 Subj: Format, unusual – board books. Noise, sounds.

Let's try ill. by Maureen Roffey. Candlewick Pr., 1992. ISBN 1-56402-022-3 Subj: Activities. Format, unusual – board books.

Rachel Fister's blister ill. by Marjorie Priceman. Houghton, 1990. ISBN 0-395-52152-1 Subj: Illness. Poetry, rhyme.

MacDonald, Elizabeth. *John's picture* ill. by David McTaggart. Viking, 1991. ISBN 0-670-83579-X Subj: Art.

Mike's kite ill. by Robert Kendall. Watts, 1990. ISBN 0-531-08476-0 Subj: Counting, numbers. Cumulative tales. Kites.

Miss Poppy and the honey cake ill. by Claire Smith. Dial, 1989. ISBN 0-8037-0578-6 Subj: Activities – cooking. Animals – pigs. Poetry, rhyme.

Mr. Badger's birthday pie ill. by Claire Smith. Dial, 1989. ISBN 0-8037-0579-4 Subj: Activities – cooking. Animals – badgers. Birthdays.

My aunt and the animals by Elizabeth MacDonald and Annie Owen; ill. by Annie Owen. Barron's, 1985. ISBN 0-8120-5641-8 Subj: Animals. Counting, numbers. Days of the week, months of the year. Family life – aunts, uncles.

The very windy day ill. by Lesley Summers. Morrow, 1992. ISBN 0-688-11045-2 Subj: Circular tales. Weather – wind.

MacDonald, George. *The light princess* ill. by Maurice Sendak. Farrar, 1969. Subj: Folk·and fairy tales.

The light princess adapt. by Robin McKinley; ill. by Katie Thamer Treherne. Harcourt, 1987. ISBN 0-15-245300-8 Subj: Concepts – weight. Folk and fairy tales. Royalty – princesses. Witches.

Little Daylight ill. by Dorothée Duntze. Holt, 1987. ISBN 0-8050-0493-9 Subj: Fairies. Folk and fairy tales. Magic. Royalty – princes. Royalty – princesses.

MacDonald, Golden *see* Brown, Margaret Wise

MacDonald, Greville *see* MacDonald, George

MacDonald, Maryann. *Little Hippo gets glasses* ill. by Anna King. Dial, 1992. ISBN 0-8037-0964-1 Subj: Animals – hippopotami. Glasses. Senses – seeing.

Little Hippo starts school ill. by Anna King. Dial, 1990. ISBN 0-8037-0720-7 Subj: Animals – hippopotami. School.

Rabbit's birthday kite ill. by Lynn Munsinger. Bantam, 1991. ISBN 0-553-05876-2 Subj: Animals – hedgehogs. Animals – rabbits. Birthdays. Kites.

Rosie runs away ill. by Melissa Sweet. Atheneum, 1990. ISBN 0-689-31625-9 Subj: Animals – rabbits. Behavior – running away. Family life.

Rosie's baby tooth ill. by Melissa Sweet. Atheneum, 1991. ISBN 0-689-31626-7 Subj: Animals – rabbits. Fairies. Teeth.

Sam's worries ill. by Judith Riches. Walt Disney, 1991. ISBN 1-56282-082-6 Subj: Behavior – worrying. Toys – teddy bears.

McDonald, Megan. *The great pumpkin switch* ill. by Ted Lewin. Watts, 1992. ISBN 0-531-08600-3 Subj: Family life – grandfathers. Plants. Problem solving.

Is this a house for Hermit Crab? ill. by S. D. Schindler. Watts, 1990. ISBN 0-531-08455-8 Subj: Crustacea. Sea and seashore.

The potato man ill. by Ted Lewin. Watts, 1991. ISBN 0-531-08514-7 Subj: Careers – peddlers. Family life – grandfathers.

Whoo-oo is it? ill. by S. D. Schindler. Watts, 1992. ISBN 0-531-08574-0 Subj: Birds – owls. Night. Noise, sounds.

MacDonald, Suse. *Alphabatics* ill. by author. Bradbury Pr., 1986. ISBN 0-02-761520-0 Subj: ABC books. Caldecott award honor book.

Numblers by Suse MacDonald and Bill Oakes; ill. by authors. Dial Pr., 1988. ISBN 0-8037-0548-4 Subj: Counting, numbers.

Once upon another by Suse MacDonald and Bill Oakes; ill. by authors. Dial, 1990. ISBN 0-8037-0787-8 Subj: Folk and fairy tales. Format, unusual.

Space spinners ill. by author. Dial, 1991. ISBN 0-8037-1009-7 Subj: Space and space ships. Spiders.

McFall, Gardner. *Jonathan's cloud* ill. by Steven Guarnaccia. Harper, 1986. ISBN 0-06-024124-1 Subj: Weather – clouds.

MacFarland, Cynthia. *Cows in the parlor* photos. by author. Atheneum, 1990. ISBN 0-689-31584-8 Subj: Animals – bulls, cows. Farms.

McFarland, John. *The exploding frog and other fables from Æsop* retold by John McFarland; ill. by James Marshall. Little, 1981. Subj: Folk and fairy tales.

McGee, Barbara. *Counting sheep* ill. by author. Firefly, 1991. ISBN 1-55037-157-6 Subj: Animals – sheep. Counting, numbers.

McGee, Marni. *The quiet farmer* ill. by Lynne Dennis. Atheneum, 1991. ISBN 0-689-31678-X Subj: Animals. Farms. Noise, sounds.

MacGill-Callahan, Sheila. *And still the turtle watched* ill. by Barry Moser. Dial, 1991. ISBN 0-8037-0932-3 Subj: Art. Folk and fairy tales. Indians of North America. Progress. Reptiles – turtles, tortoises.

McGinley, Phyllis. *All around the town* ill. by Helen Stone. Lippincott, 1948. Subj: ABC books. Caldecott award honor book. City. Poetry, rhyme.

The horse who lived upstairs ill. by Helen Stone. Lippincott, 1944. Subj: Animals – horses. Behavior – dissatisfaction.

How Mrs. Santa Claus saved Christmas ill. by Kurt Werth. Lippincott, 1963. Subj: Holidays – Christmas. Poetry, rhyme.

Lucy McLockett ill. by Helen Stone. Lippincott, 1958. Subj: Behavior – losing things. Family life. Poetry, rhyme. Teeth.

The most wonderful doll in the world ill. by Helen Stone. Lippincott, 1950. Subj: Caldecott award honor book. Toys – dolls.

Wonderful time ill. by John Alcorn. Lippincott, 1966. Subj: Clocks, watches. Poetry, rhyme. Time.

McGough, Roger. *Counting by numbers* ill. by Marketa Prachaticka. Viking, 1990. ISBN 0-670-82671-5 Subj: Counting, numbers. Poetry, rhyme.

McGovern, Ann. *Black is beautiful* photos. by Hope Wurmfeld. Four Winds Pr., 1969. Subj: Ethnic groups in the U.S. – Afro-Americans.

Eggs on your nose ill. by Maxie Chambliss. Macmillan, 1987. ISBN 0-02-765750-7 Subj: Eggs. Food. Poetry, rhyme.

Feeling mad, feeling sad, feeling bad, feeling glad photos. by Hope Wurmfeld. Walker, 1977. Subj: Emotions. Poetry, rhyme.

Mr. Skinner's skinny house ill. by Mort Gerberg. Four Winds Pr., 1980. Subj: Character traits – being different. Emotions – loneliness. Houses.

Nicholas Bentley Stoningpot III ill. by Tomie de Paola. Holiday, 1982. Subj: Behavior – boredom. Boats, ships. Emotions – loneliness. Islands.

Too much noise ill. by Simms Taback. Houghton, 1967. Subj: Humor. Noise, sounds.

Zoo, where are you? ill. by Ezra Jack Keats. Harper, 1965. Subj: Zoos.

McGowan, Alan. *Sailing ships* by Alan McGowan and Ron van der Meer; ill. by Borje Svensson. Viking, 1984. Subj: Boats, ships. Format, unusual – toy and movable books.

McGowen, Tom (Thomas). *The only glupmaker in the U.S. Navy* ill. by author. Albert Whitman, 1966. Subj: Activities – working. Careers – military.

MacGregor, Ellen. *Mr. Pingle and Mr. Buttonhouse* ill. by Paul Galdone. McGraw-Hill, 1957. Subj: Friendship.

Theodor Turtle ill. by Paul Galdone. McGraw-Hill, 1955. Subj: Behavior – forgetfulness. Participation. Reptiles – turtles, tortoises.

MacGregor, Marilyn. *Baby takes a trip* ill. by author. Macmillan, 1985. ISBN 0-02-761940-0 Subj: Babies. Character traits – curiosity. Wordless.

Helen the hungry bear ill. by author. Four Winds Pr., 1987. ISBN 0-02-761950-8 Subj: Activities – picnicking. Animals – bears. Family life. Food.

On top ill. by author. Morrow, 1988. ISBN 0-688-07491-X Subj: Animals – sheep. Character traits – individuality. Wordless.

McGuire, Leslie. *Baby night owl* ill. by Mary Szilagyi. Random House, 1989. ISBN 0-394-99986-X Subj: Bedtime. Birds – owls.

Who will play with Little Dinosaur? ill. by Norman Gorbaty. Random House, 1989. ISBN 0-394-82129-7 Subj: Dinosaurs.

McGuire, Paula. *Me and Clara and Baldwin the pony* (Inkiow, Dimiter)

Me and Clara and Casimir the cat (Inkiow, Dimiter)

Me and Clara and Snuffy the dog (Inkiow, Dimiter)

Me and my sister Clara (Inkiow, Dimiter)

McGuire, Richard. *The orange book* ill. by author. Rizzoli/Children's Universe, 1992. ISBN 0-8478-1465-3 Subj: Counting, numbers. Food.

McGuire-Turcotte, Casey A. *How Honu the turtle got his shell* ill. by Dick Sakahara. Raintree, 1991.

ISBN 0-8172-2783-0 Subj: Folk and fairy tales. Hawaii. Reptiles – turtles, tortoises.

McGurn, Patty. *Me and Marie* ill. by author. Crown, 1989. ISBN 0-517-57218-4 Subj: Animals – cats. Pets.

McHale, Ethel Kharasch. *Son of thunder: an old Lapp tale* ill. by Ruth Lercher Bornstein. Children's Pr., 1974. Subj: Folk and fairy tales. Foreign lands – Lapland.

McHargue, Georgess. *Private zoo* ill. by Michael Foreman. Viking, 1975. Subj: Imagination. Shadows.

Machetanz, Fred. *A puppy named Gia* (Machetanz, Sara)

Machetanz, Sara. *A puppy named Gia* by Sara and Fred Machetanz; ill. by Fred Machetanz. Scribner's, 1957. Subj: Animals – dogs. Eskimos.

Machotka, Hana. *Breathtaking noses* photos. by author. Morrow, 1992. ISBN 0-688-09527-5 Subj: Anatomy – noses. Animals. Games.

What do you do at a petting zoo? photos. by author. Morrow, 1990. ISBN 0-688-08738-8 Subj: Animals. Zoos.

What neat feet! photos. by author. Morrow, 1990. ISBN 0-688-09475-9 Subj: Anatomy – feet. Animals. Games.

McIntire, Alta. *Follett beginning to read picture dictionary* ill. by Janet La Salle. Follett, 1959. Subj: Dictionaries.

Mack, Gail. *Yesterday's snowman* ill. by Erik Blegvad. Pantheon, 1979. ISBN 0-394-93662-0 Subj: Family life. Snowmen.

Mack, Stanley (Stan). *Ten bears in my bed: a goodnight countdown* ill. by author. Pantheon, 1974. Subj: Animals – bears. Bedtime. Counting, numbers. Songs.

McKay, George. *Marny's ride with the wind* (McKay, Louise)

MacKay, Jed. *The big secret* ill. by Heather Collins. Firefly Pr., 1984. ISBN 0-920236-88-X Subj: Adoption. Family life. Parties.

McKay, Louise. *Marny's ride with the wind* by Louise and George McKay; ill. by Margaret Smetana. New Harbinger, 1979. Subj: Friendship. Weather – wind.

McKee, David. *The day the tide went out and out and out* ill. by author. Abelard-Schuman, 1975. Subj: Animals – camels. Desert. Sea and seashore.

The hill and the rock ill. by author. Ticknor & Fields, 1985. ISBN 0-89919-341-2 Subj: Behavior – seeking better things. Rocks.

King Rollo and the birthday ill. by author. Little, 1979. Subj: Birthdays. Royalty – kings.

King Rollo and the bread ill. by author. Little, 1979. Subj: Food. Royalty – kings.

King Rollo and the new shoes ill. by author. Little, 1979. Subj: Clothing – shoes. Royalty – kings.

The man who was going to mind the house: a Norwegian folk-tale ill. by author. Abelard-Schuman, 1973. Subj: Folk and fairy tales.

123456789 Benn ill. by author. McGraw-Hill, 1970. Subj: Crime. Prisons. Problem solving.

The sad story of Veronica who played the violin ill. by author. Kane/Miller, 1991. ISBN 0-916291-37-5 Subj: Animals. Careers – musicians. Music.

Snow woman ill. by author. Lothrop, 1988. ISBN 0-688-07675-0 Subj: Family life. Snowmen.

Tusk tusk ill. by author. Barron's, 1979. Subj: Animals – elephants. Behavior – fighting, arguing.

Two can toucan ill. by author. Abelard-Schuman, 1964. Subj: Birds – toucans. Names.

Two monsters ill. by author. Bradbury Pr., 1986. ISBN 0-02-765760-4 Subj: Behavior – fighting, arguing. Monsters.

McKee, Douglas. *Good night, Veronica* (Trez, Denise)

Good night, Veronica (Trez, Denise)

Maila and the flying carpet (Trez, Denise)

The royal hiccups (Trez, Denise)

MacKeen, Leslie Ann. *Who can fix it?* ill. by author. Landmark Editions, 1989. ISBN 0-933849-19-2 Subj: Animals. Automobiles. Children as authors. Children as illustrators.

McKeever, Katherine. *A family for Minerva* photos. by author. Greey De Pencier Books, 1981. Subj: Birds – owls. Science.

McKelvey, David. *Bobby the mostly silky* ill. by author. Corona, 1984. Subj: Birds – chickens. Character traits – being different.

McKié, Roy. *Noah's ark* ill. by author. Random House, 1984. ISBN 0-394-96584-1 Subj: Religion – Noah. Weather – floods.

The riddle book ill. by author. Random House, 1978. Subj: Humor. Riddles.

Snow by Roy McKié and P. D. Eastman; ill. by P. D. Eastman. Random House, 1962. Subj: Activities. Poetry, rhyme. Weather – snow.

McKinley, Robin. *The light princess* (MacDonald, George)

My father is in the Navy ill. by Martine Gourbault. Greenwillow, 1992. ISBN 0-688-10640-4 Subj: Careers – military. Family life – fathers.

MacKinnon, Debbie. *What shape?* photos. by Anthea Sieveking. Dial, 1992. ISBN 0-8037-1244-8 Subj: Concepts – shape. Concepts – size.

McKissack, Fredrick. *Ada, la desordenada : Messy Bessy* (McKissack, Patricia C.)

Big bug book of counting (McKissack, Patricia C.)

Big bug book of opposites (McKissack, Patricia C.)

Big bug book of places to go (McKissack, Patricia C.)

Big bug book of the alphabet (McKissack, Patricia C.)

Cinderella (McKissack, Patricia C.)

Country mouse and city mouse (McKissack, Patricia C.)

King Midas and his gold (McKissack, Patricia C.)

The king's new clothes (McKissack, Patricia C.)

The little red hen (McKissack, Patricia C.)

Messy Bessey's closet (McKissack, Patricia C.)

My Bible ABC book (McKissack, Patricia C.)

Who is coming? (McKissack, Patricia C.)

McKissack, Patricia C. *Ada, la desordenada: Messy Bessy* by Patricia C. and Fredrick McKissack; ill. by Richard Hackney. Children's Pr., 1988. ISBN 0-516-32083-1 Subj: Behavior – messy. Character traits – cleanliness. Ethnic groups in the U.S. – Afro-Americans. Foreign languages.

Big bug book of counting by Patricia C. and Fredrick McKissack; ill. by Bartholomew. Milliken, 1987. ISBN 0-88335-762-3 Subj: Counting, numbers. Insects.

Big bug book of opposites by Patricia C. and Fredrick McKissack; ill. by Bartholomew. Milliken, 1987. ISBN 0-88335-763-1 Subj: Concepts – opposites. Insects.

Big bug book of places to go by Patricia C. and Fredrick McKissack; ill. by Bartholomew. Milliken, 1987. ISBN 0-88335-765-8 Subj: Activities – traveling. Insects.

Big bug book of the alphabet by Patricia C. and Fredrick McKissack; ill. by Bartholomew. Milliken, 1987. ISBN 0-88335-764-X Subj: ABC books. Insects.

Cinderella by Patricia C. and Fredrick McKissack; ill. by Tom Dunnington. Childrens Pr., 1985. ISBN 0-516-02361-6 Subj: Folk and fairy tales. Royalty – princes. Sibling rivalry.

Country mouse and city mouse by Patricia C. and Fredrick McKissack; ill. by Anne Sikorski. Childrens Pr., 1985. ISBN 0-516-02362-4 Subj: Animals – mice. City. Country.

Flossie and the fox ill. by Rachel Isadora. Dial Pr., 1986. ISBN 0-8037-0251-5 Subj: Animals – foxes. Ethnic groups in the U.S. – Afro-Americans.

King Midas and his gold by Patricia C. and Fredrick McKissack; ill. by Tom Dunnington. Chil-

684 • Bibliographic Guide

drens Pr., 1986. ISBN 0-516-03984-9 Subj: Behavior – greed. Behavior – wishing. Royalty – kings.

The king's new clothes by Patricia C. and Fredrick McKissack; ill. by Gwen Connelly. Childrens Pr., 1987. ISBN 0-516-02365-9 Subj: Character traits – pride. Clothing. Humor. Imagination. Royalty – kings.

The little red hen by Patricia C. and Fredrick McKissack; ill. by Dennis Hockerman. Childrens Pr., 1985. ISBN 0-516-02363-2 Subj: Animals. Birds – chickens. Character traits – laziness. Cumulative tales. Farms.

Messy Bessey's closet by Patricia C. and Fredrick McKissack; ill. by Richard Hackney. Children's Pr., 1989. ISBN 0-516-02091-9 Subj: Behavior – messy. Ethnic groups in the U.S. – Afro-Americans. Poetry, rhyme.

A million fish...more or less ill. by Dena Schutzer. Knopf, 1992. ISBN 0-679-90692-4 Subj: Folk and fairy tales. Sports – fishing.

Mirandy and brother wind ill. by Jerry Pinkney. Knopf, 1988. ISBN 0-394-88765-4 Subj: Activities – dancing. Caldecott award honor book. Ethnic groups in the U.S. – Afro-Americans. Folk and fairy tales.

My Bible ABC book by Patricia C. and Fredrick McKissack; ill. by Reed Merrill. Augsburg, 1987. ISBN 0-8066-2271-7 Subj: ABC books. Religion.

Nettie Jo's friends ill. by Scott Cook. Knopf, 1989. ISBN 0-394-89158-9 Subj: Clothing. Family life. Toys – dolls.

Three billy goats Gruff (Asbjørnsen, P. C. (Peter Christen))

Three billy goats Gruff (Asbjørnsen, P. C. (Peter Christen))

The ugly little duck (Andersen, H. C. (Hans Christian))

The ugly little duck (Andersen, H. C. (Hans Christian))

Who is coming? by Patricia C. and Fredrick McKissack; ill. by Clovis Martin. Childrens Pr., 1986. Prepared under the direction of Robert Hillerick ISBN 0-516-02073-0 Subj: Animals – monkeys. Behavior – running away. Foreign lands – Africa. Safety.

Who is who? ill. by Elizabeth M. Allen. Children's Pr., 1983. Subj: Twins.

MacLachlan, Patricia. *Mama one, Mama two* ill. by Ruth Lercher Bornstein. Harper, 1982. Subj: Family life – mothers. Illness.

Moon, stars, frogs and friends ill. by Tomie de Paola. Pantheon, 1980. Subj: Friendship. Frogs and toads. Witches.

Three names ill. by Alexander Pertzoff. HarperCollins, 1991. ISBN 0-06-024036-9 Subj: Animals – dogs. Family life – great-grandparents. Names. School.

McLaughlin, Lissa. *Why won't winter go?* ill. by author. Lothrop, 1983. Subj: Behavior – boredom. Seasons – winter.

McLean, Virginia O. *Kenya, jambo!* by Virginia O. McLean and Katherine P. Klyce; ill. with photos. and black and white drawings. Redbird Pr., 1989. Accompanying cassette by Regina and Evans Okuth ISBN 0-9606046-4-2 Subj: Foreign lands – Kenya.

McLeish, Kenneth. *Chicken Licken* (Chicken Little)

McLenighan, Valjean. *I know you cheated* photos. by Brent Jones. Raintree, 1977. ISBN 0-8172-0962-X Subj: Character traits – honesty. School.

One whole doughnut, one doughnut hole ill. by Steven Roger Cole. Childrens Pr., 1982. Subj: Activities – reading.

Stop-go, fast-slow ill. by Margrit Fiddle. Children's Pr., 1982. Subj: Concepts – opposites.

Three strikes and you're out ill. by Laurie Hamilton. Follett, 1980. Subj: Behavior – greed. Magic.

Turtle and rabbit ill. by Vernon McKissack. Follett, 1980. Subj: Animals – rabbits. Folk and fairy tales. Reptiles – turtles, tortoises. Sports – racing.

What you see is what you get ill. by Dev Appleyard. Four Winds Pr., 1980. Subj: Character traits – pride. Clothing. Folk and fairy tales. Humor. Imagination. Royalty.

You are what you are ill. by Jack Reilly. Follett, 1977. Subj: Folk and fairy tales. Frogs and toads. Royalty.

You can go jump ill. by Jared D. Lee. Follett, 1977. Subj: Elves and little people. Emotions – envy, jealousy. Folk and fairy tales. Magic. Witches.

McLeod, Emilie Warren. *The bear's bicycle* ill. by David McPhail. Little, 1975. Subj: Safety. Sports – bicycling. Toys – teddy bears.

One snail and me: a book of numbers and animals and a bathtub ill. by Walter Lorraine. Little, 1961. Subj: Activities – bathing. Animals. Counting, numbers. Imagination.

McLerran, Alice. *Dreamsong* ill. by Valery Vasiliev. Morrow, 1992. ISBN 0-688-10106-2 Subj: Dreams. Songs.

I want to go home ill. by Jill Kastner. Morrow, 1992. ISBN 0-688-10145-3 Subj: Animals – cats. Moving.

The mountain that loved a bird ill. by Eric Carle. Alphabet Pr., 1985. ISBN 0-88708-000-6 Subj: Behavior – needing someone. Birds. Character traits – loyalty. Emotions – sadness.

Roxaboxen ill. by Barbara Cooney. Lothrop, 1991. ISBN 0-688-07593-2 Subj: Activities – playing. Desert. Imagination.

McMillan, Bruce. *The alphabet symphony: an ABC book* photos. by author. Greenwillow, 1977. Subj: ABC books. Music.

Beach ball—left, right photos. by author. Holiday, 1992. ISBN 0-8234-0946-5 Subj: Concepts – left and right. Toys – balls.

Becca backward, Becca forward photos. by author. Lothrop, 1986. ISBN 0-688-06283-0 Subj: Concepts. Concepts – opposites.

Counting wildflowers ill. by author. Lothrop, 1986. ISBN 0-688-02860-8 Subj: Counting, numbers. Flowers. Science.

Dry or wet? photos. by author. Lothrop, 1988. ISBN 0-688-07101-5 Subj: Concepts.

Eating fractions photos. by author. Scholastic, 1991. ISBN 0-590-43770-4 Subj: Counting, numbers.

Fire engine shapes photos. by author. Lothrop, 1988. ISBN 0-688-07843-5 Subj: Concepts – shape.

Ghost doll ill. by author. Houghton, 1983. ISBN 0-395-33073-4 Subj: Ghosts. Toys – dolls.

Growing colors photos. by author. Lothrop, 1988. ISBN 0-688-07845-1 Subj: Concepts – color.

Here a chick, there a chick photos. by author. Lothrop, 1983. Subj: Concepts – opposites.

Kitten can... photos. by author. Lothrop, 1984. Subj: Animals – cats.

One sun: a book of terse verse photos. by author. Holiday, 1990. ISBN 0-8234-0810-8 Subj: Language. Poetry, rhyme. Sea and seashore.

One, two, one pair! photos. by author. Scholastic, 1991. ISBN 0-590-43767-4 Subj: Concepts. Counting, numbers.

Play day: a book of terse verse photos. by author. Holiday, 1991. ISBN 0-8234-0894-9 Subj: Activities – playing. Language. Poetry, rhyme.

Step by step photos. by author. Lothrop, 1987. ISBN 0-688-07234-8 Subj: Activities. Babies.

Super, super, superwords photos. by author. Lothrop, 1989. ISBN 0-688-08099-5 Subj: Language.

Time to... photos. by author. Lothrop, 1989. ISBN 0-688-08856-2 Subj: Clocks, watches. Time.

McMullan, Kate. *The noisy giant's tea party* ill. by Jim McMullan. HarperCollins, 1992. ISBN 0-06-205018-4 Subj: Dreams. Imagination. Sleep.

McMullen, Eunice. *Dragon for breakfast* by Eunice and Nigel McMullen; ill. by authors. Carolrhoda, 1990. ISBN 0-87614-650-7 Subj: Dragons. Royalty – kings.

McMullen, Nigel. *Dragon for breakfast* (McMullen, Eunice)

McNally, Darcie. *In a cabin in a wood* ill. by Robin Michal Koontz. Dutton, 1991. ISBN 0-525-65035-0 Subj: Animals. Character traits – kindness to animals. Music. Songs.

McNaught, Harry. *Baby animals* ill. by author. Random House, 1976. ISBN 0-394-83241-8 Subj: Animals. Format, unusual – board books.

The truck book ill. by author. Random House, 1978. Subj: Transportation. Trucks.

Words to grow on ill. by author. Random House, 1984. ISBN 0-394-96103-X Subj: Language.

McNaughton, Colin. *At home* ill. by author. Putnam's, 1982. Subj: Concepts – opposites. Format, unusual – board books.

At playschool ill. by author. Putnam's, 1982. Subj: Concepts – opposites. Format, unusual – board books. School.

At the park ill. by author. Putnam's, 1982. Subj: Concepts – opposites. Format, unusual – board books.

At the party ill. by author. Putnam's, 1982. Subj: Concepts – opposites. Format, unusual – board books. Parties.

At the stores ill. by author. Putnam's, 1982. Subj: Concepts – opposites. Format, unusual – board books. Stores.

Autumn ill. by author. Dutton, 1983. Subj: Activities. Format, unusual – board books. Seasons – fall.

Guess who's just moved in next door? ill. by author. Random House, 1991. ISBN 0-679-81802-2 Subj: Family life. Folk and fairy tales. Format, unusual. Moving.

The rat race: the amazing adventures of Anton B. Stanton ill. by author. Doubleday, 1978. Subj: Animals – rats. Royalty. Sports – racing.

Spring ill. by author. Dial Pr., 1984. Subj: Format, unusual – board books. Seasons – spring.

Summer ill. by author. Dial Pr., 1984. Subj: Format, unusual – board books. Seasons – summer.

Walk rabbit walk by Colin McNaughton and Elizabeth Attenborough; ill. by Colin McNaughton. Viking, 1977. Subj: Activities – walking. Animals – rabbits.

Winter ill. by author. Dutton, 1983. Subj: Activities. Format, unusual – board books. Seasons – winter.

McNeely, Jeannette. *Where's Izzy?* ill. by Bill Morrison. Follett, 1972. Subj: Behavior – losing things. Pets. Reptiles – lizards.

McNeer, May Yonge. *Little Baptiste* ill. by Lynd Ward. Houghton, 1954. Subj: Animals. Farms.

My friend Mac: the story of Little Baptiste and the moose ill. by Lynd Ward. Houghton, 1960. Subj: Animals – moose. Emotions – loneliness.

McNeill, Janet. *The giant's birthday* ill. by Walter Erhard. Walck, 1964. Subj: Birthdays. Giants.

McNulty, Faith. *The lady and the spider* ill. by Bob Marstall. Harper, 1986. ISBN 0-06-024192-6 Subj: Character traits – kindness to animals. Spiders.

Mouse and Tim ill. by Marc Simont. Harper, 1978. Subj: Animals – mice. Character traits – kindness to animals. Pets.

When a boy wakes up in the morning ill. by Leonard Weisgard. Knopf, 1962. Subj: Activities – playing. Morning. Noise, sounds.

Woodchuck ill. by Joan Sandin. Harper, 1974. Subj: Animals – groundhogs. Science.

McPhail, David. *Adam's smile* ill. by author. Dutton, 1987. ISBN 0-525-44327-4 Subj: Dreams. Illness. Night.

Alligators are awful (and they have terrible manners, too) ill. by author. Doubleday, 1980. Subj: Humor. Reptiles – alligators, crocodiles.

Andrew's bath ill. by author. Little, 1984. Subj: Activities – bathing. Animals. Behavior – misbehavior.

Animals A to Z ill. by author. Scholastic, 1988. ISBN 0-590-40715-5 Subj: ABC books. Animals.

Annie and Co. ill. by author. Holt, 1991. ISBN 0-8050-1686-4 Subj: Activities – working.

The bear's toothache ill. by author. Little, 1972. Subj: Animals – bears. Character traits – kindness to animals. Illness. Teeth.

Captain Toad and the motorbike ill. by author. Atheneum, 1978. Subj: Frogs and toads. Motorcycles.

The cereal box ill. by author. Little, 1974. Subj: Family life. Humor. Imagination. Shopping.

The dream child ill. by author. Dutton, 1985. ISBN 0-525-44109-3 Subj: Bedtime. Dreams. Night. Sleep. Toys – teddy bears.

Ed and me ill. by author. Harcourt, 1990. ISBN 0-15-224888-9 Subj: Country. Family life – fathers. Trucks.

Emma's pet ill. by author. Dutton, 1987. ISBN 0-525-44210-3 Subj: Activities – vacationing. Animals – bears. Behavior – needing someone. Family life. Pets.

Emma's vacation ill. by author. Dutton, 1987. ISBN 0-525-44315-0 Subj: Activities – vacationing. Animals – bears. Family life.

Farm boy's year ill. by author. Atheneum, 1992. ISBN 0-689-31679-8 Subj: Farms. U.S. history.

Farm morning ill. by author. Harcourt, 1985. ISBN 0-15-227299-2 Subj: Animals. Birds. Farms.

First flight ill. by author. Little, 1987. ISBN 0-316-56323-4 Subj: Activities – flying. Airplanes, airports. Toys – teddy bears.

Fix-it ill. by author. Dutton, 1984. Subj: Activities – reading. Television.

Great cat ill. by author. Dutton, 1982. Subj: Animals – cats. Behavior – needing someone. Islands.

Henry Bear's park ill. by author. Little, 1976. Subj: Animals – bears.

Lorenzo ill. by author. Doubleday, 1984. ISBN 0-385-15591-3 Subj: Activities – painting. Animals. Houses.

Lost ill. by author. Little, 1990. ISBN 0-316-56329-3 Subj: Animals – bears. Behavior – lost.

The magical drawings of Moony B. Finch ill. by author. Doubleday, 1978. Subj: Art. Magic.

Mistletoe ill. by author. Dutton, 1978. Subj: Dreams. Holidays – Christmas. Imagination. Toys.

The party ill. by author. Little, 1990. ISBN 0-316-56330-7 Subj: Animals. Family life – fathers. Parties. Toys.

Pig Pig and the magic photo album ill. by author. Dutton, 1986. ISBN 0-525-44238-3 Subj: Activities – photographing. Animals – pigs. Imagination.

Pig Pig gets a job ill. by author. Dutton, 1990. ISBN 0-525-44619-2 Subj: Activities – working. Animals – pigs. Careers.

Pig Pig goes to camp ill. by author. Dutton, 1983. Subj: Animals – pigs. Camps, camping.

Pig Pig grows up ill. by author. Dutton, 1980. Subj: Animals – pigs. Behavior – growing up.

Pig Pig rides ill. by author. Dutton, 1982. Subj: Activities – playing. Animals – pigs. Imagination.

Sisters ill. by author. Harcourt, 1984. Subj: Emotions – love. Sibling rivalry.

Snow lion ill. by author. Parents, 1983. Subj: Weather – snow.

Something special ill. by author. Little, 1988. ISBN 0-316-56324-2 Subj: Activities – painting. Animals – raccoons.

Stanley: Henry Bear's friend ill. by author. Little, 1979. Subj: Animals – bears. Animals – raccoons. Behavior – running away. Crime.

The train ill. by author. Little, 1977. Subj: Dreams. Imagination. Toys – trains. Trains.

Where can an elephant hide? ill. by author. Doubleday, 1979. ISBN 0-385-12941-6 Subj: Animals. Animals – elephants. Behavior – hiding.

A wolf story ill. by author. Scribner, 1981. Subj: Animals – wolves. Character traits – freedom. Character traits – kindness to animals.

McQueen, John Troy. *A world full of monsters* ill. by Marc Brown. Crowell, 1986. ISBN 0-690-04546-8 Subj: Family life – grandmothers. Monsters. Night.

McQueen, Lucinda. *Tidy pig* by Lucinda McQueen and Jeremy Guitar; ill. by authors. Random House, 1989. ISBN 0-394-90573-3 Subj: Animals – pigs. Character traits – cleanliness.

Macsolis. *Baile de luna: Dance moon* ill. by author. Donars Spanish Books, 1991. ISBN 84-261-2583-2 Subj: Animals – cats. Foreign languages. Moon.

McToots, Rudi. *The kid's book of games for cars, trains and planes* ill. by author. Bantam, 1980. Subj: Activities – traveling. Games.

Madden, Don. *Lemonade serenade or the thing in the garden* ill. by author. Albert Whitman, 1966. Subj: Elves and little people. Noise, sounds.

The Wartville wizard ill. by author. Macmillan, 1986. ISBN 0-02-762100-6 Subj: Character traits – cleanliness. Wizards.

Maddern, Eric. *Curious clownfish* ill. by Adrienne Kennaway. Little, 1990. ISBN 0-316-48894-1 Subj: Fish. Sea and seashore.

Madenski, Melissa. *Some of the pieces* ill. by Deborah Kogan Ray. Little, 1991. ISBN 0-316-54324-1 Subj: Death. Emotions – sadness. Family life – fathers.

Mado, Michio. *The animals* tr. by The Empress Michiko of Japan; ill. by Mitsumasa Anno. Macmillan, 1992. ISBN 0-689-50574-4 Subj: Animals. Poetry, rhyme.

Maestro, Betsy. *All aboard overnight* ill. by Giulio Maestro. Houghton, 1992. ISBN 0-395-51120-8 Subj: Language. Trains.

Around the clock with Harriet: a book about telling time ill. by Giulio Maestro. Crown, 1984. Subj: Animals – elephants. Clocks, watches. Time.

Big city port by Betsy Maestro and Ellen Del Vecchio; ill. by Giulio Maestro. Four Winds Pr., 1983. Subj: Boats, ships. City.

Bike trip ill. by Giulio Maestro. HarperCollins, 1992. ISBN 0-06-022732-X Subj: Family life. Safety. Sports – bicycling.

Busy day: a book of action words by Betsy and Giulio Maestro; ill. by Giulio Maestro. Crown, 1978. Subj: Activities. Circus.

Camping out: a book of action words by Betsy and Giulio Maestro; ill. by authors. Crown, 1985. ISBN 0-517-55119-5 Subj: Language. Camps, camping.

Delivery van ill. by Giulio Maestro. Houghton, 1990. ISBN 0-395-51119-4 Subj: City. Country. Language.

Dollars and cents for Harriet ill. by Giulio Maestro. Crown, 1988. ISBN 0-517-56958-2 Subj: Counting, numbers. Money.

Fat polka-dot cat and other haiku ill. by Giulio Maestro. Dutton, 1976. Subj: Poetry, rhyme.

Ferryboat by Betsy and Giulio Maestro; ill. by authors. Crowell, 1986. ISBN 0-690-04520-4 Subj: Activities – traveling. Boats, ships.

The guessing game ill. by Giulio Maestro. Grosset, 1983. Subj: Animals – pigs. Problem solving.

Harriet at home ill. by Giulio Maestro. Crown, 1984. Subj: Animals – elephants. Format, unusual – board books. Houses.

Harriet at play ill. by Giulio Maestro. Crown, 1984. Subj: Activities – playing. Animals – elephants. Format, unusual – board books.

Harriet at school ill. by Giulio Maestro. Crown, 1984. Subj: Animals – elephants. Format, unusual – board books. School.

Harriet at work ill. by Giulio Maestro. Crown, 1984. Subj: Activities – working. Animals – elephants. Format, unusual – board books.

Harriet goes to the circus by Betsy and Giulio Maestro; ill. by Giulio Maestro. Crown, 1977. Subj: Animals – elephants. Circus. Counting, numbers.

Harriet reads signs and more signs ill. by Giulio Maestro. Crown, 1981. Subj: Activities – reading. Animals – elephants.

How do apples grow? ill. by Giulio Maestro. HarperCollins, 1992. ISBN 0-06-020056-1 Subj: Food. Science. Trees.

On the go: a book of adjectives by Betsy and Giulio Maestro; ill. by authors. Crown, 1979. Subj: Animals – elephants. Language.

On the town: a book of clothing words by Betsy and Giulio Maestro; ill. by authors. Crown, 1983. Subj: Animals – elephants. Character traits – appearance. Clothing.

The pandas take a vacation ill. by Giulio Maestro. Western, 1986. ISBN 0-307-10258-0 Subj: Activities – vacationing. Animals – pandas.

The perfect picnic ill. by Giulio Maestro. Western, 1986. ISBN 0-307-10266-1 Subj: Activities – picnicking.

The story of the Statue of Liberty by Betsy and Giulio Maestro; ill. by Giulio Maestro. Lothrop, 1986. ISBN 0-688-05773-X Subj: Art. U.S. history.

Taxi ill. by Giulio Maestro. Clarion, 1989. ISBN 0-89919-528-8 Subj: City. Language. Taxis.

Temperature and you ill. by Giulio Maestro. Dutton, 1990. ISBN 0-525-67271-0 Subj: Concepts. Weather.

Through the year with Harriet by Betsy and Giulio Maestro; ill. by authors. Crown, 1985. ISBN 0-517-55613-8 Subj: Animals – elephants. Days of the week, months of the year. Seasons. Weather.

Traffic: a book of opposites by Betsy and Giulio Maestro; ill. by authors. Crown, 1981. ISBN 0-517-54427-X Subj: Concepts – opposites. Traffic, traffic signs.

Where is my friend? ill. by Giulio Maestro. Crown, 1976. Subj: Animals – elephants. Concepts.

Maestro, Giulio. *Busy day* (Maestro, Betsy)

Camping out (Maestro, Betsy)

Ferryboat (Maestro, Betsy)

Halloween howls: riddles that are a scream ill. by author. Dutton, 1983. Subj: Holidays – Halloween. Riddles.

Harriet goes to the circus (Maestro, Betsy)

Just enough Rosie ill. by author. Grosset, 1983. Subj: Animals – rhinoceros. Humor.

Leopard is sick ill. by author. Greenwillow, 1978. Subj: Animals. Animals – leopards. Friendship. Illness.

On the go (Maestro, Betsy)

On the town (Maestro, Betsy)

One more and one less ill. by author. Crown, 1974. Subj: Animals. Counting, numbers.

A raft of riddles ill. by author. Dutton, 1982. Subj: Humor. Riddles.

The remarkable plant in apartment 4 ill. by author. Bradbury Pr., 1973. Subj: City. Humor. Plants.

Riddle romp ill. by author. Houghton, 1983. Subj: Riddles.

The story of the Statue of Liberty (Maestro, Betsy)

Through the year with Harriet (Maestro, Betsy)

The tortoise's tug of war ill. by author. Bradbury Pr., 1971. Subj: Animals – tapirs. Animals – whales. Folk and fairy tales. Foreign lands – South America. Games. Reptiles – turtles, tortoises.

Traffic (Maestro, Betsy)

Magee, Doug. *All aboard ABC* by Doug Magee and Robert Newman; photos. by authors. Dutton, 1990. ISBN 0-525-65036-9 Subj: ABC books. Trains.

Trucks you can count on photos. by author. Dodd, 1985. ISBN 0-396-08507-5 Subj: Counting, numbers. Trucks.

Magnus, Erica. *Around me* ill. by author. Lothrop, 1992. ISBN 0-688-09753-7 Subj: Concepts. Format, unusual.

The boy and the devil ill. by author. Carolrhoda Books, 1986. ISBN 0-87614-305-2 Subj: Behavior – trickery. Devil. Folk and fairy tales. Foreign lands – Norway.

Old Lars ill. by author. Carolrhoda, 1984. Subj: Folk and fairy tales. Foreign lands – Norway.

Magorian, Michelle. *Who's going to take care of me?* ill. by James Graham Hale. HarperCollins, 1990. ISBN 0-06-024106-3 Subj: Behavior – worrying. Family life – brothers. Family life – sisters. School.

Maguire, Gregory. *Lucas Fishbone* ill. by Frank Gargiulo. HarperCollins, 1990. ISBN 0-06-024090-3 Subj: Death. Family life – grandmothers. Gardens, gardening. Poetry, rhyme.

Mahiri, Jabari. *The day they stole the letter J* ill. by Dorothy Carter. Third World Pr., 1981. Subj: Behavior – misbehavior. Careers – barbers. Magic.

Mählqvist, Stefan. *I'll take care of the crocodiles* ill. by Tord Nygren. Atheneum, 1979. Subj: Bedtime. Dreams.

Mahony, Elizabeth Winthrop *see* Winthrop, Elizabeth

Mahood, Kenneth. *The laughing dragon* ill. by author. Scribner's, 1970. Subj: Dragons. Fire. Humor. Royalty.

Why are there more questions than answers, Grandad? ill. by author. Bradbury Pr., 1974. Subj: Character traits – questioning. Family life – grandfathers.

Mahy, Margaret. *The boy who was followed home* ill. by Steven Kellogg. Watts, 1975. Subj: Animals – hippopotami. Humor. Witches.

The boy with two shadows ill. by Jenny Williams. Lippincott, 1988, 1971. ISBN 0-397-32271-2 Subj: Behavior – misbehavior. Character traits – meanness. Shadows. Witches.

The dragon of an ordinary family ill. by Helen Oxenbury. Watts, 1969. Subj: Dragons.

The great white man-eating shark ill. by Jonathan Allen. Dial, 1990. ISBN 0-8037-0749-5 Subj: Behavior – trickery. Fish – sharks.

The horrendous hullabaloo ill. by Patricia MacCarthy. Viking, 1992. ISBN 0-670-84547-7 Subj: Birds – parakeets, parrots. Family life – aunts, uncles. Pirates.

Jam: a true story ill. by Helen Craig. Atlantic Monthly Pr., 1986. ISBN 0-87113-048-3 Subj: Family life. Food.

Keeping house ill. by Wendy Smith. Macmillan, 1991. ISBN 0-689-50515-9 Subj: Character traits – cleanliness.

A lion in the meadow ill. by Jenny Williams. Watts, 1969. Subj: Animals – lions. Dragons.

Making friends ill. by Wendy Smith. Macmillan, 1990. ISBN 0-689-50498-5 Subj: Animals – dogs. Friendship.

The man whose mother was a pirate ill. by Margaret Chamberlain. Viking, 1986. ISBN 0-670-81070-3 Subj: Behavior – seeking better things. Pirates. Sea and seashore.

Mrs. Discombobulous ill. by Jan Brychta. Watts, 1969. Subj: Behavior – nagging. Family life. Gypsies.

Pillycock's shop ill. by Carol Baker. Watts, 1969. Subj: Fairies. Values.

The pumpkin man and the crafty creeper ill. by Helen Craig. Lothrop, 1991. ISBN 0-688-10347-2 Subj: Gardens, gardening. Plants.

The queen's goat ill. by Emma Chichester Clark. Dial, 1991. ISBN 0-8037-0938-2 Subj: Animals – goats. Pets. Royalty – queens.

Rooms for rent ill. by Jenny Williams. Watts, 1974. Subj: Behavior – greed. Hotels.

Sailor Jack and the twenty orphans ill. by Robert Bartelt. Watts, 1970. Subj: Boats, ships. Careers – military. Orphans. Pirates. Sea and seashore.

The seven Chinese brothers ill. by Jean and Mousien Tseng. Scholastic, 1990. ISBN 0-590-42055-0 Subj: Character traits – cleverness. Family life. Folk and fairy tales. Foreign lands – China.

17 kings and 42 elephants ill. by Patricia MacCarthy. Dial Pr., 1987. ISBN 0-8037-0458-5 Subj: Animals. Jungle. Poetry, rhyme. Royalty – kings.

Mainwaring, Jane. *My feather* photos. by Fiona Pragoff. Doubleday, 1990. ISBN 0-385-41197-9 Subj: Activities. Concepts – perspective. Science.

Maiorano, Robert. *Backstage* ill. by Rachel Isadora. Greenwillow, 1978. Subj: Theater.

Francisco ill. by Rachel Isadora. Macmillan, 1978. Subj: Foreign lands – South America. Poverty. Problem solving.

A little interlude ill. by Rachel Isadora. Coward, 1980. Subj: Activities – dancing. Behavior – sharing. Music.

Maitland, Antony. *Idle Jack* ill. by author. Farrar, 1979. Subj: Character traits – foolishness. Folk and fairy tales.

Majewski, Joe. *A friend for Oscar Mouse* ill. by Maria Majewska. Dial Pr., 1988. ISBN 0-8037-0348-1 Subj: Animals – mice. Friendship.

Major, Beverly. *Playing sardines* ill. by Andrew Glass. Scholastic, 1988. ISBN 0-590-41153-5 Subj: Activities – playing. Behavior – hiding. Games. Twilight.

Makower, Sylvia. *Samson's breakfast* ill. by author. Watts, 1961. Subj: Animals – lions.

Malcolmson, Anne. *The song of Robin Hood* sel. and ed. by Anne Malcolmson; music arranged by Grace Castagnetta; ill. by Virginia Lee Burton. Houghton, 1947. Subj: Caldecott award honor book. Folk and fairy tales. Music.

Malecki, Maryann. *Mom and dad and I are having a baby!* ill. by author. Pennypress, 1982. Subj: Babies. Family life.

Maley, Anne. *Have you seen my mother?* ill. by Yutaka Sugita. Subj: Circus. Family life – mothers. Toys – balls.

Mallett, Anne. *Here comes Tagalong* ill. by Steven Kellogg. Parents, 1971. Subj: Family life. Friendship. Sibling rivalry.

Malloy, Judy. *Bad Thad* ill. by Martha G. Alexander. Dutton, 1980. ISBN 0-525-26148-6 Subj: Behavior – misbehavior. Family life. School.

Malone, Nola Langner. *A home* ill. by author. Bradbury Pr., 1988. ISBN 0-02-751440-4 Subj: Friendship. Houses. Moving.

Mamin-Sibiryak, D. N. *Grey Neck* adapt. and tr. from the Russian by Marguerita Rudolph; ill. by Leslie Shuman Kronz. Stemmer House, 1988.

ISBN 0-88045-068-1 Subj: Birds – ducks. Character traits – kindness to animals. Folk and fairy tales. Seasons – winter.

Mandry, Kathy. *The cat and the mouse and the mouse and the cat* ill. by Joe Toto. Pantheon, 1972. Subj: Animals – cats. Animals – mice. Friendship.

Manes, Esther. *The bananas move to the ceiling* by Esther and Stephen Manes; ill. by Barbara Samuels. Watts, 1983. Subj: Family life. Humor.

Manes, Stephen. *The bananas move to the ceiling* (Manes, Esther)

Life is no fair! ill. by Warren Miller. Dutton, 1985. ISBN 0-525-44192-1 Subj: Humor.

Mangas, Brian. *A nice surprise for Father Rabbit* ill. by Sidney Levitt. Simon & Schuster, 1989. ISBN 0-671-67194-4 Subj: Animals – rabbits. Emotions – love. Family life – fathers.

Mangin, Marie-France. *Suzette and Nicholas and the seasons clock* tr. from French by Joan Chevalier; ill. by Satomi Ichikawa. Putnam's, 1982. Subj: Activities. Seasons.

Manheim, Ralph. *Dear Mili* (Grimm, Wilhelm)

The marvelous journey through the night (Heine, Helme)

Mollywoop (Heine, Helme)

The nutcracker (Hoffmann, E. T. A.)

Mann, Peggy. *King Laurence, the alarm clock* ill. by Ray Cruz. Doubleday, 1976. Subj: Animals. Animals – lions. Illness. Morning.

Manning, Linda. *Animal hours* ill. by Vlasta van Kampen. Oxford Univ. Pr., 1991. ISBN 0-19-540771-7 Subj: Animals. Cumulative tales. Poetry, rhyme. Time.

Mansell, Dom. *If dinosaurs came to town* ill. by author. Little, 1991. ISBN 0-316-54584-8 Subj: Dinosaurs. Imagination.

My old teddy ill. by author. Candlewick Pr., 1992. ISBN 1-56402-035-5 Subj: Toys – teddy bears.

Manson, Beverlie. *The fairies' alphabet book* ill. by author. Doubleday, 1982. Subj: ABC books. Fairies.

Manson, Christopher. *The crab prince* ill. by reteller. Holt, 1991. ISBN 0-8050-1215-X Subj: Crustacea. Folk and fairy tales. Foreign lands – Italy. Royalty – princes. Witches.

A gift for the king ill. by author. Holt, 1989. ISBN 0-8050-0951-5 Subj: Folk and fairy tales. Foreign lands – Persia. Royalty – kings.

Two travelers ill. by author. Holt, 1990. ISBN 0-8050-1214-1 Subj: Activities – traveling. Animals – elephants. Friendship.

Mantegazza, Giovanna. *The cat* ill. by Cristina Mesturini. Boyds Mills Pr., 1992. ISBN 1-56397-032-5 Subj: Animals – cats. Format, unusual – board books.

The hippopotamus ill. by Cristina Mesturini. Boyds Mills Pr., 1992. ISBN 1-56397-033-3 Subj: Animals – hippopotami. Format, unusual – board books. Foreign lands – Africa.

Mantinband, Gerda. *Blabbermouths* ill. by Paul Borovsky. Greenwillow, 1992. ISBN 0-688-10602-1 Subj: Behavior – gossip. Folk and fairy tales. Money.

Three clever mice ill. by Martine Gourbault. Greenwillow, 1993. ISBN 0-688-11370-2 Subj: Animals – mice. Character traits – cleverness.

Manushkin, Fran. *Baby* ill. by Ronald Himler. Harper, 1972. ISBN 0-06-024064-4 Subj: Babies. Family life.

Baby, come out! ill. by Ronald Himler. Harper, 1972. Orig. entitled Baby Subj: Babies. Birth.

Be brave, baby rabbit ill. by Diane de Groat. Crown, 1990. ISBN 0-517-57574-4 Subj: Family life – brothers. Family life – sisters. Holidays – Halloween.

The best toy of all ill. by Robin Ballard. Dutton, 1992. ISBN 0-525-44897-7 Subj: Activities – playing. Family life. Seasons. Toys.

Bubblebath! ill. by Ronald Himler. Harper, 1974. Subj: Activities – bathing. Family life.

Hocus and Pocus at the circus ill. by Geoffrey Hayes. Harper, 1983. Subj: Character traits – meanness. Holidays – Halloween. Witches.

Latkes and applesause ill. by Robin Spowart. Scholastic, 1990. ISBN 0-590-42261-8 Subj: Holidays – Hanukkah. Jewish culture. Religion.

Little rabbit's baby brother ill. by Diane de Groat. Crown, 1986. ISBN 0-517-56251-0 Subj: Animals – rabbits. Babies. Emotions – envy, jealousy. Family life. Sibling rivalry.

Moon dragon ill. by Geoffrey Hayes. Macmillan, 1982. Subj: Animals – mice. Dragons. Food. Moon.

The perfect Christmas picture ill. by Karen Ann Weinhaus. Harper, 1980. Subj: Activities – photographing. Family life. Holidays – Christmas.

Shirleybird ill. by Carl Stuart. Harper, 1975. ISBN 0-06-024064-4 Subj: Character traits – individuality.

Swinging and swinging ill. by Thomas Di Grazia. Harper, 1976. ISBN 0-06-024067-9 Subj: Activities – playing. Activities – swinging. Weather – clouds.

Walt Disney's one hundred one dalmations ill. by Russell Hicks. Walt Disney, 1991. ISBN 1-56282-032-X Subj: Animals – dogs. Counting, numbers.

Marceau, Marcel. *The Marcel Marceau counting book* (Mendoza, George)

The story of Bip ill. by author. Harper, 1976. Subj: Clowns, jesters. Imagination.

Marcin, Marietta. *A zoo in her bed* ill. by Sofia. Coward, 1963. Subj: Bedtime. Poetry, rhyme. Toys.

Marcus, Susan. *Casey visits the doctor* ill. by Deborah Drew-Brook. CBC Merchandising, 1982. Subj: Careers – doctors. Health.

The missing button adventure ill. by Hajime Sawada. CBC Merchandising, 1981. Subj: Behavior – losing things. Character traits – helpfulness. Toys – teddy bears.

Mare, Walter De La see De La Mare, Walter (Walter John)

Margalit, Avishai. *The Hebrew alphabet book: Me-Alef'ad Tav* ill. by author. Funk and Wagnalls, 1968. Subj: ABC books. Jewish culture.

Margolis, Matthew. *Some swell pup* (Sendak, Maurice)

Margolis, Richard J. *Big bear, spare that tree* ill. by Jack Kent. Greenwillow, 1980. Subj: Animals – bears. Birds – bluejays. Ecology. Trees.

Secrets of a small brother ill. by Donald Carrick. Macmillan, 1984. Subj: Poetry, rhyme. Sibling rivalry.

Mari, Iela. *Eat and be eaten* ill. by author. Barron's 1980. Subj: Animals. Format, unusual. Sports – hunting. Wordless.

The magic balloon ill. by author. S. G. Phillips, 1970. Subj: Toys – balloons. Wordless.

Mariana. *Doki, the lonely papoose* ill. by author. Lothrop, 1955. Subj: Indians of North America.

The journey of Bangwell Putt ill. by author. Lothrop, 1965. Subj: Holidays – Christmas. Toys – dolls.

Marie. *Nursery rhymes* (Mother Goose)

Marie, Geraldine. *The magic box* ill. by Michele Chessare. Elsevier-Nelson, 1981. Subj: Animals – dogs. Birthdays. Magic. Problem solving.

Maril, Lee. *Mr. Bunny paints the eggs* ill. by Irena Lorentowicz. Roy Pub., 1945. Subj: Animals – rabbits. Concepts – color. Holidays – Easter. Music. Songs.

Marino, Barbara Pavis. *Eric needs stitches* photos. by Richard Rudinski. Addison-Wesley, 1979. Subj: Hospitals.

Marino, Dorothy. *Buzzy Bear and the rainbow* ill. by author. Watts, 1962. Subj: Animals – bears. Weather – rainbows.

Buzzy Bear goes camping ill. by author. Watts, 1964. Subj: Animals – bears. Camps, camping.

Buzzy Bear in the garden ill. by author. Watts, 1963, 1961. Subj: Animals – bears. Gardens, gardening.

Buzzy Bear's busy day ill. by author. Watts, 1965. Subj: Animals – bears.

Edward and the boxes ill. by author. Lippincott, 1957. Subj: Activities – playing. Sleep.

Good-bye thunderstorm ill. by author. Lippincott, 1958. Subj: Weather – rain. Weather – storms. Weather – thunder.

Mariotti, Mario. *Hands off!* photos. by Roberto Marchiori. Kane/Miller, 1990. ISBN 0-916291-29-4 Subj: Imagination.

Hanimations photos. by Roberto Marchiori. Kane/Miller, 1989. Original title: Rimani ISBN 0-916291-22-7 Subj: Imagination.

Maris, Ron. *Are you there, bear?* ill. by author. Greenwillow, 1984. ISBN 0-688-03998-7 Subj: Behavior – lost. Toys. Toys – teddy bears.

Better move on, frog! ill. by author. Watts, 1982. Subj: Frogs and toads. Houses.

Hold tight, bear! ill. by author. Delacorte Pr., 1989. ISBN 0-440-50152-0 Subj: Animals – bears. Animals – donkeys. Forest, woods. Problem solving. Toys – dolls. Wordless.

I wish I could fly ill. by author. Greenwillow, 1986. ISBN 0-688-06655-0 Subj: Animals. Behavior – wishing. Reptiles – turtles, tortoises.

In my garden ill. by author. Greenwillow, 1988. ISBN 0-688-07631-9 Subj: Activities – picnicking. Animals. Counting, numbers. Flowers. Gardens, gardening.

Is anyone home? ill. by author. Greenwillow, 1985. ISBN 0-688-05899-X Subj: Family life – grandparents. Farms. Format, unusual – toy and movable books.

My book ill. by author. Watts, 1983. Subj: Animals – cats. Bedtime.

Markle, Sandra. *Outside and inside you* ill. by Susan Kuklin. Bradbury Pr., 1991. ISBN 0-02-762311-4 Subj: Anatomy.

Marks, Alan. *Nowhere to be found* ill. by author. Picture Book Studio, 1988. ISBN 0-88708-062-6 Subj: Behavior – lost. Behavior – losing things. Language.

Marks, Burton. *Animals* ill. by Paul Harvey. Troll, 1991. ISBN 0-8167-2415-6 Subj: Animals.

Colors and numbers ill. by Paul Harvey. Troll, 1991. ISBN 0-8167-2411-3 Subj: Concepts – color. Counting, numbers.

Marks, Marcia Bliss. *Swing me, swing tree* ill. by David Berger. Little, 1959. Subj: Activities – swinging. Poetry, rhyme.

Marokvia, Merelle. *A French school for Paul* ill. by Artur Marokvia. Lippincott, 1963. Subj: Circus. Foreign lands – France. School.

Marol, Jean-Claude. *Vagabul and his shadow* ill. by author. Creative Education, 1983. Subj: Shadows. Wordless.

Vagabul escapes ill. by author. Creative Education, 1983. Subj: Behavior – running away. Wordless.

Vagabul goes skiing ill. by author. Creative Education, 1983. Subj: Sports – skiing. Wordless.

Vagabul in the clouds ill. by author. Creative Education, 1983. Subj: Weather – clouds. Wordless.

Marron, Carol A. *Gretchen's grandma* (Root, Phyllis)

No trouble for Grandpa ill. by Chaya M. Burstein. Raintree, 1983. ISBN 0-940742-27-6 Subj: Family life – grandfathers. Handicaps. Sibling rivalry.

Marsh, Jeri. *Hurrah for Alexander* ill. by Joan Hanson. Carolrhoda Books, 1977. Subj: Humor.

Marshak, Samuel. *Hail to mail* tr. from Russian by Richard Pevear; ill. by Vladimir Radunsky. Holt, 1990. ISBN 0-8050-1132-3 Subj: Careers – mail carriers. Poetry, rhyme.

In the van tr. from Russian by Margaret Wettlin; ill. by V. Lebedev. Imported Pub., 1983. Subj: Animals – dogs. Moving. Poetry, rhyme.

The merry starlings by Samuel Marshak with D. Harms; tr. from Russian by Dorian Rottenberg; ill. by Arieh Zeldich. Harper, 1983. Subj: Birds. Nursery rhymes. Poetry, rhyme.

The Month-Brothers: a Slavic tale tr. from Russian by Thomas P. Whitney; ill. by Diane Stanley. Morrow, 1983. Subj: Foreign lands – Czechoslovakia. Poetry, rhyme. Seasons. Weather.

The pup grew up! tr. by Richard Pevear; ill. by Vladimir Radunsky. Holt, 1989. ISBN 0-8050-0952-3 Subj: Activities – traveling. Animals – dogs. Behavior – growing up. Behavior – losing things. Poetry, rhyme. Trains.

The tale of a hero nobody knows tr. from Russian by Peter Tempest; ill. by Vassili Shulzhenko. Imported Pub., 1983. Subj: Character traits – bravery. Foreign lands – Russia. Poetry, rhyme.

Marshall, Douglas *see* McClintock, Marshall

Marshall, Edward. *Four on the shore* ill. by James Marshall. Dial Pr., 1985. Subj: Monsters. Sibling rivalry.

Fox all week ill. by James Marshall. Dial Pr., 1984. ISBN 0-8037-0066-0 Subj: Animals. Animals – foxes. Friendship.

Fox and his friends ill. by James Marshall. Dial Pr., 1982. Subj: Animals – foxes. Behavior – misbehavior.

Fox at school ill. by James Marshall. Dial Pr., 1983. Subj: Animals – foxes. Humor. School.

Fox in love ill. by James Marshall. Dial Pr., 1982. Subj: Animals – foxes. Emotions – love.

Fox on wheels ill. by James Marshall. Dial Pr., 1983. Subj: Animals – foxes. Behavior – misbehavior. Sports – racing.

Space case ill. by James Marshall. Dial Pr., 1980. Subj: Holidays – Halloween. Robots. Space and space ships.

Three by the sea ill. by James Marshall. Dial Pr., 1981. Subj: Activities – picnicking. Friendship.

Troll country ill. by James Marshall. Dial Pr., 1980. Subj: Forest, woods. Trolls.

Marshall, Frances. *Princess Kalina and the hedgehog* (Flot, Jeannette B.)

Marshall, James. *The Cut-Ups* ill. by author. Viking, 1984. Subj: Behavior – misbehavior. Toys.

The Cut-Ups at Camp Custer ill. by author. Viking, 1989. ISBN 0-670-82051-2 Subj: Behavior – misbehavior. Camps, camping.

The Cut-Ups carry on ill. by author. Viking, 1990. ISBN 0-670-82051-2 Subj: Activities – dancing. Contests. Humor.

The Cut-Ups crack up ill. by author. Viking, 1992. ISBN 0-670-84486-1 Subj: Automobiles. Behavior – misbehavior. School.

The Cut-Ups cut loose ill. by author. Viking, 1987. ISBN 0-670-80740-0 Subj: Behavior – misbehavior. Friendship. School.

Four little troubles ill. by author. Houghton, 1975. Subj: Animals. Problem solving.

Fox on the job ill. by author. Dial Pr., 1988. ISBN 0-8037-0351-1 Subj: Activities – working. Animals – foxes. Behavior – misbehavior.

George and Martha ill. by author. Houghton, 1972. Subj: Animals – hippopotami. Friendship.

George and Martha back in town ill. by author. Houghton, 1984. Subj: Animals – hippopotami. Behavior – misbehavior. Friendship.

George and Martha encore ill. by author. Houghton, 1973. Subj: Activities – dancing. Animals – hippopotami. Friendship.

George and Martha one fine day ill. by author. Houghton, 1978. Subj: Animals – hippopotami. Friendship.

George and Martha rise and shine ill. by author. Houghton, 1976. Subj: Animals – hippopotami. Friendship.

George and Martha round and round ill. by author. Houghton, 1988. ISBN 0-395-46763-2 Subj: Activities – vacationing. Animals – hippopotami. Friendship. Imagination.

George and Martha, tons of fun ill. by author. Houghton, 1980. Subj: Animals – hippopotami. Character traits – vanity.

Goldilocks and the three bears (The three bears)

The guest ill. by author. Houghton, 1975. Subj: Animals – moose. Animals – snails. Friendship.

Hansel and Gretel ill. by reteller. Dial, 1990. ISBN 0-8037-0828-9 Subj: Folk and fairy tales. Forest, woods. Witches.

Merry Christmas, space case ill. by author. Dial Pr., 1986. ISBN 0-8037-0216-7 Subj: Holidays – Christmas. Space and space ships.

Miss Dog's Christmas ill. by author. Houghton, 1973. Subj: Animals – dogs. Food. Holidays – Christmas.

Miss Nelson is back (Allard, Harry)

Miss Nelson is missing! (Allard, Harry)

Portly McSwine ill. by author. Houghton, 1979. Subj: Animals – pigs. Behavior – worrying.

Rapscallion Jones ill. by author. Viking, 1983. ISBN 0-670-58965-9 Subj: Animals – foxes. Behavior – seeking better things.

Red Riding Hood ill. by adapt. Dial Pr., 1987. ISBN 0-8037-0345-7 Subj: Animals – wolves. Behavior – talking to strangers. Folk and fairy tales.

Speedboat ill. by author. Houghton, 1976. Subj: Animals – dogs. Boats, ships. Friendship.

The Stupids have a ball (Allard, Harry)

The Stupids take off (Allard, Harry)

The three little pigs (The three little pigs)

Three up a tree ill. by author. Dutton, 1986. ISBN 0-8037-0329-5 Subj: Activities – playing. Imagination. Monsters. Trees.

What's the matter with Carruthers? ill. by author. Houghton, 1972. Subj: Animals – bears. Bedtime. Character traits – helpfulness. Friendship. Hibernation.

Willis ill. by author. Houghton, 1974. Subj: Animals. Friendship.

Wings: a tale of two chickens ill. by author. Viking, 1986. ISBN 0-670-80961-6 Subj: Activities – reading. Animals – foxes. Birds – chickens.

Yummers! ill. by author. Houghton, 1973. Subj: Animals – pigs. Food. Illness.

Yummers too: the second course ill. by author. Houghton, 1986. ISBN 0-395-38990-9 Subj: Animals – pigs. Behavior – greed. Food. Reptiles – turtles, tortoises.

Marshall, Janet Perry. *My camera: at the zoo* ill. by author. Little, 1989. ISBN 0-316-54687-9 Subj: Activities – photographing. Animals. Games. Zoos.

Marshall, Lyn. *Yoga for your children* ill. with photos. Schocken, 1979. Subj: Health. Religion.

Marshall, Margaret. *Mike* ill. by Lorraine Spiro. Merrimack, 1983. Subj: Bedtime. Problem solving.

Marshall, Ray. *Pop-up numbers #1* by Ray Marshall and Korky Paul; ill. by authors. Dutton,

1984. Subj: Counting, numbers. Format, unusual – toy and movable books.

Pop-up numbers #2 by Ray Marshall and Korky Paul; ill. by authors. Dutton, 1984. Subj: Counting, numbers. Format, unusual – toy and movable books.

Pop-up numbers #3 by Ray Marshall and Korky Paul; ill. by authors. Dutton, 1984. Subj: Counting, numbers. Format, unusual – toy and movable books.

Pop-up numbers #4 by Ray Marshall and Korky Paul; ill. by authors. Dutton, 1984. Subj: Counting, numbers. Format, unusual – toy and movable books.

The train: watch it work by operating the moving diagrams! ill. by John Bradley. Viking, 1986. ISBN 0-670-81134-3 Subj: Format, unusual – toy and movable books. Trains.

Marston, Hope Irvin. *Big rigs* ill. with photos. Dodd, 1979. Subj: Transportation. Trucks.

Fire trucks ill. with photos. Dodd, 1984. Subj: Careers – firefighters. Trucks.

Martchenko, Michael. *Bird feeder banquet* ill. by author. Firefly, 1990. ISBN 1-55037-147-9 Subj: Birds. Character traits – assertiveness. Character traits – kindness to animals. Food. Seasons – winter.

Martel, Cruz. *Yagua days* ill. by Jerry Pinkney. Dial Pr., 1976. Subj: Family life. Foreign lands – Puerto Rico.

Martin, Bernard H. *Brave little Indian* (Martin, Bill (William Ivan))

Smoky Poky (Martin, Bill (William Ivan))

Martin, Bill (William Ivan). *Barn dance!* ill. by Ted Rand. Holt, 1986. ISBN 0-8050-0089-5 Subj: Activities – dancing. Barns. Country. Dreams. Night. Poetry, rhyme. Scarecrows.

Brave little Indian by Bill Martin, Jr. and Bernard H. Martin; ill. by Bernard H. Martin. Tell-Well Pr., 1951. Subj: Indians of North America. Participation.

Brown bear, brown bear, what do you see? ill. by Eric Carle. Holt, 1983. Subj: Animals – bears. Concepts – color. Cumulative tales. Poetry, rhyme.

The happy hippopotami ill. by Betsy Everitt. Harcourt, 1991. ISBN 0-15-233380-0 Subj: Animals – hippopotami. Poetry, rhyme.

Here are my hands by Bill Martin, Jr. and John Archambault; ill. by Ted Rand. Holt, 1987. ISBN 0-8050-0328-2 Subj: Anatomy.

Knots on a counting rope by Bill Martin, Jr. and John Archambault; ill. by Ted Rand. Holt, 1987. ISBN 0-8050-0571-4 Subj: Character traits – bravery. Emotions – love. Family life – grandfathers. Handicaps – blindness. Indians of North America. Senses – seeing.

Listen to the rain by Bill Martin, Jr. and John Archambault; ill. by James R. Endicott. Holt, 1988. ISBN 0-8050-0682-6 Subj: Poetry, rhyme. Weather – rain.

The magic pumpkin by Bill Martin, Jr. and John Archambault; ill. by Robert J. Lee. Holt, 1989. ISBN 0-8050-1134-X Subj: Holidays – Halloween. Magic. Poetry, rhyme.

My days are made of butterflies adapted by William Ivan Martin, Jr.; written by Sano M. Galea'i Fa'apouli; ill. by Vic Herman. Holt, 1970. Subj: Foreign lands – Mexico.

Polar bear, polar bear, what do you hear? ill. by Eric Carle. Holt, 1991. ISBN 0-8050-1759-3 Subj: Animals. Noise, sounds. Poetry, rhyme. Zoos.

Smoky Poky by Bill Martin, Jr. and Bernard H. Martin; ill. by Bernard H. Martin. Tell-Well Pr., 1947. Subj: Animals – elephants. Trains.

Sounds around the clock comp. by Bill Martin, Jr. in collaboration with Peggy Brogan. Holt, 1966. Subj: Noise, sounds. Poetry, rhyme.

Sounds I remember comp. by Bill Martin, Jr. in collaboration with Peggy Brogan. Holt, 1974. Subj: Counting, numbers. Noise, sounds. Nursery rhymes.

Sounds of home comp. by Bill Martin, Jr. in collaboration with Peggy Brogan. Holt, 1972. Subj: Noise, sounds. Poetry, rhyme.

Sounds of laughter comp. by Bill Martin, Jr. in collaboration with Peggy Brogan. Holt, 1972. Subj: Folk and fairy tales. Humor. Noise, sounds. Poetry, rhyme.

Sounds of numbers comp. by Bill Martin, Jr. in collaboration with Peggy Brogan. Holt, 1972. Subj: Counting, numbers. Noise, sounds. Poetry, rhyme.

Up and down on the merry-go-round by Bill Martin, Jr. and John Archambault; ill. by Ted Rand. Holt, 1988. ISBN 0-8050-0681-8 Subj: Merry-go-rounds.

White Dynamite and Curly Kidd by Bill Martin, Jr. and John Archambault; ill. by Ted Rand. Holt, 1986. ISBN 0-03-008399-0 Subj: Animals – bulls, cows. Family life. Sports.

Martin, C. L. G. *The dragon nanny* ill. by Robert Rayevsky. Macmillan, 1988. ISBN 0-02-762440-4 Subj: Activities – baby-sitting. Dragons. Royalty – kings.

Three brave women ill. by Peter Elwell. Macmillan, 1991. ISBN 0-02-762445-5 Subj: Emotions – fear. Family life – grandmothers. Family life – mothers.

Martin, Charles E. *Dunkel takes a walk* ill. by author. Greenwillow, 1983. Subj: Animals – dogs. Character traits – cleverness.

For rent ill. by author. Greenwillow, 1986. ISBN 0-688-05717-9 Subj: Activities – painting. Islands. School. Seasons – summer.

Island rescue ill. by author. Greenwillow, 1985. ISBN 0-688-04258-9 Subj: Hospitals. Islands. Seasons – spring.

Island winter ill. by author. Greenwillow, 1984. Subj: Islands. Seasons – winter.

Noah's ark retold by Lawrence T. Lorimer; ill. by Charles E. Martin. Random House, 1978. Subj: Religion – Noah.

Sam saves the day ill. by author. Greenwillow, 1987. ISBN 0-688-06815-4 Subj: Activities – traveling. Activities – vacationing. Seasons – summer.

Martin, Claire. *Boots and the glass mountain* ill. by Gennady Spirin. Dial, 1992. ISBN 0-8037-1111-5 Subj: Folk and fairy tales. Foreign lands – Norway. Royalty – princesses. Trolls.

The finest horse in town ill. by Susan Gaber. HarperCollins, 1992. ISBN 0-06-024152-7 Subj: Animals – horses.

The race of the golden apples ill. by Leo and Diane Dillon. Dial, 1991. ISBN 0-8037-0249-3 Subj: Animals – bears. Folk and fairy tales. Royalty – princesses.

Martin, Diane. *Mister Mole* (Murschetz, Luis)

Martin, Jacqueline Briggs. *Bizzy Bones and Moosemouse* ill. by Stella Ormai. Lothrop, 1986. ISBN 0-688-05746-2 Subj: Animals – mice. Behavior – lost. Friendship.

Bizzy Bones and the lost quilt ill. by Stella Ormai. Lothrop, 1988. ISBN 0-688-07408-1 Subj: Animals – mice. Behavior – losing things. Friendship. Quilts.

Bizzy Bones and Uncle Ezra ill. by Stella Ormai. Lothrop, 1984. Subj: Animals – mice. Emotions – fear. Family life – aunts, uncles.

Good times on Grandfather Mountain ill. by Susan Gaber. Watts, 1992. ISBN 0-531-08577-5 Subj: Activities – making things. Character traits – optimism.

Martin, Janet *see* Allen, Robert

Martin, Jerome. *Carrot - parrot* ill. by author. Simon & Schuster, 1991. ISBN 0-671-69555-X Subj: Format, unusual. Language. Poetry, rhyme.

Mitten - kitten ill. by author. Simon & Schuster, 1991. ISBN 0-671-69556-8 Subj: Format, unusual. Language. Poetry, rhyme.

Martin, Judith. *The tree angel* by Judith Martin and Remy Charlip; ill. by Remy Charlip. Knopf, 1962. Subj: Angels. Holidays – Christmas. Theater.

Martin, Patricia Miles *see* Miles, Miska

Friend of Miguel ill. by Genia. Rand McNally, 1967. Subj: Animals – horses. Foreign lands – Mexico.

Martin, Rafe. *Foolish rabbit's big mistake* ill. by Ed Young. Putnam's, 1985. ISBN 0-399-21178-0 Subj: Animals – rabbits. Behavior – mistakes. Folk and fairy tales.

The hungry tigress: and other traditional Asian tales ill. by Richard Wehrman. Shambhala, 1984. Subj: Folk and fairy tales.

The rough-face girl ill. by David Shannon. Putnam, 1992. ISBN 0-399-21859-9 Subj: Family life – sisters. Folk and fairy tales. Indians of North America.

Will's mammoth ill. by Stephen Grammell. Putnam, 1989. ISBN 0-399-21627-8 Subj: Animals. Imagination.

Martin, Sarah Catherine. *The comic adventures of Old Mother Hubbard and her dog* ill. by Arnold Lobel. Bradbury Pr., 1968. Subj: Animals – dogs. Nursery rhymes.

Old Mother Hubbard adapt. by Colin and Jacqui Hawkins; ill. by Colin Hawkins. Putnam's, 1985. ISBN 0-399-21162-4 Subj: Animals – dogs. Format, unusual – toy and movable books. Nursery rhymes.

Old Mother Hubbard and her dog ill. by Lisa Amoroso. Knopf, 1987. ISBN 0-394-98922-8 Subj: Animals – dogs. Nursery rhymes.

Old Mother Hubbard and her dog ill. by Paul Galdone. McGraw-Hill, 1960. Subj: Animals – dogs. Nursery rhymes.

Old Mother Hubbard and her dog ill. by Evaline Ness. Holt, 1972. Subj: Animals – dogs. Nursery rhymes.

Old Mother Hubbard and her wonderful dog ill. by James Marshall. Farrar, 1991. ISBN 0-374-35621-1 Subj: Animals – dogs. Nursery rhymes.

Martinez, Ruth. *Mrs. McDockerty's knitting* ill. by Catherine O'Neill. Houghton, 1990. ISBN 0-395-51591-2 Subj: Activities – knitting. Animals – cats. Animals – dogs. Animals – pigs. Cumulative tales. Problem solving.

Marton, Jirina. *Flowers for mom* ill. by author. Firefly, 1991. ISBN 1-55037-155-X Subj: Behavior – bullying. Character traits – generosity. Flowers.

I'll do it myself ill. by author. Firefly, 1989. ISBN 1-55037-063-4 Subj: Dreams. Family life – mothers. Hair.

Midnight visit at Molly's house ill. by author. Firefly, 1988. ISBN 0-920303-99-4 Subj: Dreams. Moon. Night.

Marzollo, Claudio. *Jed and the space bandits* (Marzollo, Jean)

Jed's junior space patrol (Marzollo, Jean)

Marzollo, Jean. *Amy goes fishing* ill. by Ann Schweninger. Dial Pr., 1980. Subj: Family life – fathers. Sports – fishing.

Close your eyes ill. by Susan Jeffers. Dial Pr., 1978. Subj: Bedtime. Family life – fathers. Poetry, rhyme.

Jed and the space bandits by Jean and Claudio Marzollo; ill. by Peter Sis. Dial Pr., 1987. ISBN 0-8037-0136-5 Subj: Crime. Pets. Robots. Space and space ships.

Jed's junior space patrol by Jean and Claudio Marzollo; ill. by David S. Rose. Dial Pr., 1982. Subj: Robots. Space and space ships. Toys – teddy bears.

Pretend you're a cat ill. by Jerry Pinkney. Dial, 1990. ISBN 0-8037-0774-6 Subj: Animals. Behavior – imitation. Imagination. Poetry, rhyme.

The rebus treasury ill. by Carol D. Carson. Dial Pr., 1986. ISBN 0-8037-0255-8 Subj: Nursery rhymes. Rebuses.

The silver bear il. by Susan Meddaugh. Dial Pr., 1987. ISBN 0-8037-0369-4 Subj: Imagination.

The teddy bear book ill. by Ann Schweninger. Dial, 1989. ISBN 0-8037-0632-4 Subj: Poetry, rhyme. Toys – teddy bears.

The three little kittens (Mother Goose)

Uproar on Hollercat Hill ill. by Steven Kellogg. Dial Pr., 1980. Subj: Animals – cats. Behavior – misbehavior. Poetry, rhyme.

Maschler, Fay. *T. G. and Moonie go shopping* ill. by Sylvie Selig. Doubleday, 1978. Subj: Animals – cats. Birds – owls. Shopping. Stores.

T. G. and Moonie have a baby ill. by Sylvie Selig. Doubleday, 1979. Subj: Animals – cats. Birds – owls. Family life.

T. G. and Moonie move out of town ill. by Sylvia Selig. Doubleday, 1978. Subj: Animals – cats. Birds – owls. Moving.

Masks and puppets ill. by Louise Nevett. Watts, 1984. Subj: Activities. Puppets.

Mason, Ann Maree. *The weird things in Nanna's house* ill. by Cathy Wilcox. Watts, 1992. ISBN 0-531-08570-8 Subj: Family life – grandmothers. Houses.

Mason, Christopher. *The marvellous blue mouse* ill. by author. Holt, 1992. ISBN 0-8050-1622-8 Subj: Animals – mice. Behavior – trickery. Middle ages. Problem solving.

Mason, Lura. *A book of boxes* ill. by author. Simon & Schuster, 1989. ISBN 0-671-67801-9 Subj: Format, unusual – toy and movable books. Holidays.

Massey, Jeanne. *The littlest witch* ill. by Adrienne Adams. Knopf, 1959. Subj: Holidays – Halloween. Witches.

Massie, Diane Redfield. *The baby beebee bird* ill. by author. Harper, 1963. Subj: Animals. Birds. Noise, sounds. Sleep.

Cockle stew and other rhymes ill. by author. Atheneum, 1967. Subj: Poetry, rhyme.

Tiny pin ill. by author. Harper, 1964. Subj: Animals – porcupines. Behavior – growing up. Poetry, rhyme.

Walter was a frog ill. by author. Simon and Schuster, 1970. Subj: Behavior – dissatisfaction. Frogs and toads.

Mathers, Petra. *Maria Theresa* ill. by author. HarperCollins, 1992. ISBN 0-06-443282-3 Subj: Birds – chickens. City.

Sophie and Lou ill. by author. HarperCollins, 1991. ISBN 0-06-024072-5 Subj: Activities – dancing. Animals – mice. Character traits – shyness.

Theodor and Mr. Balbini ill. by author. Harper, 1988. ISBN 0-06-024144-6 Subj: Animals – dogs. Pets.

Mathews, Judith. *And Sunday makes seven* (Baden, Robert)

Mathews, Louise. *Bunches and bunches of bunnies* ill. by Jeni Bassett. Dodd, 1978. Subj: Animals – rabbits. Counting, numbers. Poetry, rhyme.

Cluck one ill. by Jeni Bassett. Dodd, 1982. Subj: Animals – weasels. Birds – chickens. Counting, numbers. Eggs.

The great take-away ill. by Jeni Bassett. Dodd, 1980. Subj: Animals – pigs. Character traits – laziness. Counting, numbers. Crime.

Mathiesen, Egon. *Oswald, the monkey* adapt. from Danish by Nancy and Edward Maze; ill. by author. Astor-Honor, 1959. Subj: Animals – monkeys.

Matias. *Mr. Noah and the animals: Monsieur Noe et les animaux* ill. by author. Walck, 1960. Subj: Religion – Noah.

Matsui, Susan. *The bears' autumn* (Tejima, Keizaburo)

The sea and I (Nakawatari, Harutaka)

Matsuno, Masako. *A pair of red clogs* ill. by Kazue Mizumura. Collins, 1960. Subj: Character traits – honesty. Clothing – shoes. Foreign lands – Japan.

Taro and the bamboo shoot: a Japanese tale ill. by Yasuo Segawa. Pantheon, 1964. Adapted from the Japanese by Alice Low Subj: Folk and fairy tales. Foreign lands – Japan.

Taro and the Tofu ill. by Kazue Mizumura. Collins-World, 1962. Subj: Character traits – honesty. Foreign lands – Japan.

Matsutani, Miyoko. *The fisherman under the sea* English version by Alvin Tresselt; ill. by Chihiro Iwasaki. Parents, 1969. Translation of Urashima Tarō Subj: Careers – fishermen. Folk and fairy tales. Foreign lands – Japan. Reptiles – turtles, tortoises. Royalty. Sea and seashore.

How the withered trees blossomed ill. by Yasuo Segawa. Lippincott, 1969. Subj: Behavior – greed. Foreign lands – Japan. Foreign languages.

The witch's magic cloth English version by Alvin Tresselt; ill. by Yasuo Segawa. Parents, 1969. Subj: Character traits – bravery. Folk and fairy tales. Foreign lands – Japan. Witches.

Matthias, Catherine. *Arriba y abajo: Over and under* tr. from English by Lada Josefa Kratky; ill. by Gene Sharp. Children's Pr., 1989. ISBN 0-516-32048-3 Subj: Concepts. Foreign languages.

Demasiados globos: Too many balloons tr. from English by Lada Josefa Kratky; ill. by Gene Sharp. Children's Pr., 1989. ISBN 0-516-33633-9 Subj: Foreign languages. Toys – balloons.

I can be a computer operator ill. with photos. Childrens Pr., 1985. ISBN 0-516-01838-8 Subj: Careers. Computers.

I love cats ill. by Tom Dunnington. Children's Pr., 1983. Subj: Animals – cats.

Out the door ill. by Eileen Mueller Neill. Children's Pr., 1982. Subj: Buses. School.

Over-under ill. by Gene Sharp. Children's Pr., 1984. Subj: Concepts – opposites.

Sal y entra: Out the door tr. from English by Lada Josefa Kratky; ill. by Eileen Mueller Neill. Children's Pr., 1989. ISBN 0-516-33560-X Subj: Concepts – in and out. Concepts – up and down. Foreign languages.

Too many balloons ill. by Gene Sharp. Childrens Pr., 1982. ISBN 0-516-03633-5 Subj: Counting, numbers. Toys – balloons. Zoos.

Matthiesen, Thomas. *Things to see: a child's world of familiar objects* photos. by author. Platt, 1968. ISBN 0-448-41051-6 Subj: Concepts. Senses – seeing.

Mattingley, Christobel. *The angel with a mouth-organ* ill. by Astra Lacis. Holiday, 1984. ISBN 0-8234-0593-1 Subj: Death. Holidays – Christmas. War.

Matura, Mustapha. *Moon jump* ill. by Jane Gifford. Knopf, 1988. ISBN 0-394-91976-9 Subj: Bedtime. Imagination. Moon.

Matus, Greta. *Where are you, Jason?* ill. by author. Lothrop, 1974. Subj: Behavior – hiding. Imagination. Night.

Maury, Inez. *My mother the mail carrier: Mi mama la cartera* tr. by Norah E. Alemany; ill. by Tasha Tudor. Feminist Pr., 1976. Subj: Careers – mail carriers. Foreign languages.

Mauver, Judy A. *Dusty wants to help* (Sandberg, Inger)

Maxfield, Christine. *Christmas in Water Village* ill. by Jean Colquhoun. Prima Design, 1989. ISBN 0-9621029-0-3 Subj: Holidays – Christmas. U.S. history.

Maxner, Joyce. *Lady Bugatti* ill. by Kevin Hawkes. Lothrop, 1991. ISBN 0-688-10341-3 Subj: Insects. Poetry, rhyme. Parties.

Nicholas Cricket ill. by William Joyce. HarperCollins, 1989. ISBN 0-06-024222-1 Subj: Animals. Insects – crickets. Music. Poetry, rhyme.

May, Charles Paul. *High-noon rocket* ill. by Brinton Turkle. Holiday, 1966. Subj: Activities – traveling. Science. Space and space ships. Time.

May, Julian. *Why people are different colors* ill. by Symeon Shimin. Holiday, 1971. Subj: Ethnic groups in the U.S.

May, Robert Lewis. *Rudolph the red-nosed reindeer* ill. by Diana Magnuson. Four Winds Pr., 1980. Subj: Animals – reindeer. Elves and little people. Holidays – Christmas. Weather – fog.

Mayer, Marianna. *Alley oop!* ill. by Gerald McDermott. Holt, 1985. Subj: Animals – mice. Counting, numbers. Reptiles – alligators, crocodiles.

Beauty and the beast ill. by Mercer Mayer. Four Winds Pr., 1978. Subj: Animals. Character traits – appearance. Emotions – love. Folk and fairy tales.

The black horse ill. by Katie Thamer. Dial Pr., 1984. ISBN 0-8037-0076-8 Subj: Animals – horses. Behavior – trickery. Folk and fairy tales. Magic. Royalty.

The Brambleberrys animal alphabet ill. by Gerald McDermott. Boyds Mills, 1991. ISBN 1-878093-78-9 Subj: ABC books. Animals.

The Brambleberrys animal book of big and small shapes ill. by Gerald McDermott. Boyds Mills, 1991. ISBN 1-878093-77-0 Subj: Animals. Concepts – shape. Concepts – size.

The Brambleberrys animal book of counting ill. by Gerald McDermott. Boyds Mills, 1991. ISBN 1-878093-75-4 Subj: Animals. Counting, numbers.

The little jewel box ill. by Margot Tomes. Dial Pr., 1986. ISBN 0-8037-0149-7 Subj: Animals. Birds. Character traits – kindness. Character traits – luck. Elves and little people. Folk and fairy tales. Magic.

Marcel the pastry chef ill. by Gerald McDermott. Bantam, 1991. ISBN 0-553-05192-X Subj: Activities – cooking. Animals – hippopotami. Careers – bakers. Royalty – kings. Weddings.

Mine! (Mayer, Mercer)

My first book of nursery tales: five favorite bedtime tales ill. by William Joyce. Random House, 1983. Subj: Folk and fairy tales.

One frog too many (Mayer, Mercer)

The spirit of the blue light ill. by Gerald McDermott. Macmillan, 1990. ISBN 0-02-765350-1 Subj: Behavior – wishing. Folk and fairy tales. Foreign lands – Germany. Magic. Royalty.

The twelve dancing princesses (Grimm, Jacob)

The ugly duckling (Andersen, H. C. (Hans Christian))

The unicorn and the lake ill. by Michael Hague. Dial Pr., 1982. Subj: Character traits – bravery. Mythical creatures – unicorns.

Mayer, Mercer. *Ah-choo* ill. by author. Dial Pr., 1976. Subj: Animals – elephants. Illness. Wordless.

Appelard and Liverwurst ill. by Steven Kellogg. Four Winds Pr., 1978. Subj: Animals. Behavior – misbehavior. Farms.

Astronaut critter ill. by author. Simon & Schuster, 1986. ISBN 0-671-61142-9 Subj: Format, unusual – board books. Space and space ships.

A boy, a dog, a frog and a friend ill. by author. Dial Pr., 1971. Subj: Friendship. Frogs and toads. Sports – fishing. Wordless.

A boy, a dog and a frog ill. by author. Dial Pr., 1967. Subj: Friendship. Frogs and toads. Sports – fishing. Wordless.

Bubble bubble ill. by author. Parents, 1973. Subj: Imagination. Wordless.

Cowboy critter ill. by author. Simon & Schuster, 1986. ISBN 0-671-61141-0 Subj: Cowboys. Format, unusual – board books.

Fireman critter ill. by author. Simon & Schuster, 1986. ISBN 0-671-61143-7 Subj: Careers – firefighters. Format, unusual – board books.

Frog goes to dinner ill. by author. Dial Pr., 1974. Subj: Food. Frogs and toads. Wordless.

Frog on his own ill. by author. Dial Pr., 1973. Subj: Frogs and toads. Wordless.

Frog, where are you? ill. by author. Dial Pr., 1969. Subj: Friendship. Frogs and toads. Wordless.

The great cat chase ill. by author. Four Winds Pr., 1974. Subj: Animals – cats. Wordless.

Hiccup ill. by author. Dial Pr., 1976. Subj: Animals – hippopotami. Illness. Wordless.

How the trollusk got his hat ill. by author. Golden Pr., 1979. Subj: Character traits – appearance. Character traits – honesty.

I am a hunter ill. by author. Dial Pr., 1969. Subj: Imagination.

Just for you ill. by author. Golden Pr., 1975. Subj: Character traits – helpfulness. Emotions – love. Family life – mothers.

Just me and my dad ill. by author. Golden Pr., 1977. Subj: Family life – fathers. Camps, camping.

Little Monster at home ill. by author. Golden Pr., 1978. Subj: Houses. Monsters.

Little Monster at school ill. by author. Golden Pr., 1978. Subj: Monsters. School.

Little Monster at work ill. by author. Golden Pr., 1978. Subj: Careers. Family life – grandfathers. Monsters.

Little Monster's alphabet book ill. by author. Golden Pr., 1978. Subj: ABC books. Monsters.

Little Monster's bedtime book ill. by author. Golden Pr., 1978. Subj: Bedtime. Monsters. Poetry, rhyme.

Little Monster's counting book ill. by author. Golden Pr., 1978. Subj: Counting, numbers. Monsters.

Little Monster's neighborhood ill. by author. Golden Pr., 1978. Subj: City. Monsters.

Liverwurst is missing ill. by Steven Kellogg. Four Winds Pr., 1981. Subj: Character traits – bravery. Circus. Crime.

Liza Lou and the Yeller Belly Swamp ill. by author. Parents, 1976. Subj: Character traits – bravery. Ethnic groups in the U.S. – Afro-Americans. Monsters.

Mine! by Mercer and Marianna Mayer; ill. by Mercer Mayer. Simon and Schuster, 1970. Subj: Concepts. Emotions.

Mrs. Beggs and the wizard ill. by author. Parents, 1973. Subj: Magic. Monsters. Wizards.

One frog too many by Mercer and Marianna Mayer; ill. by Mercer Mayer. Dial Pr., 1975. Subj: Emotions – envy, jealousy. Frogs and toads. Wordless.

Oops ill. by author. Dial Pr., 1977. Subj: Animals – hippopotami. Behavior – carelessness. Wordless.

The Pied Piper of Hamelin adapt and ill. by Mercer Mayer. Macmillan, 1987. Adapt. of the poem The pied piper of Hamelin by Robert Browning ISBN 0-02-765361-7 Subj: Animals – rats. Behavior – trickery. Folk and fairy tales. Foreign lands – Germany.

Policeman critter ill. by author. Simon & Schuster, 1986. ISBN 0-671-61140-2 Subj: Careers – police officers. Format, unusual – board books.

The queen always wanted to dance ill. by author. Simon and Schuster, 1971. Subj: Activities – dancing. Humor. Music. Royalty – queens.

The sleeping beauty (Grimm, Jacob)

A special trick ill. by author. Dial Pr., 1976. ISBN 0-8037-8103-2 Subj: Magic.

Terrible troll ill. by author. Dial Pr., 1968. Subj: Imagination. Knights. Monsters. Mythical creatures. Trolls.

There's a nightmare in my closet ill. by author. Dial Pr., 1968. Subj: Bedtime. Emotions – fear. Monsters.

There's an alligator under my bed ill. by author. Dial Pr., 1987. ISBN 0-8037-0375-9 Subj: Bedtime. Emotions – fear. Reptiles – alligators, crocodiles.

There's something in my attic ill. by author. Dial Pr., 1988. ISBN 0-8037-0415-1 Subj: Dreams. Emotions – fear. Night.

Two moral tales ill. by author. Four Winds Pr., 1974. Bear's new clothes.—Bird's new hat Subj: Animals – bears. Birds. Clothing. Clothing – hats. Wordless.

What do you do with a kangaroo? ill. by author. Four Winds Pr., 1973. Subj: Animals. Humor. Problem solving.

Whinnie the lovesick dragon ill. by Diane Dawson Hearn. Macmillan, 1986. ISBN 0-02-765180-0 Subj: Behavior – needing someone. Dragons. Emotions – love. Magic. Middle ages.

You're the scaredy cat ill. by author. Parents, 1974. Subj: Emotions – fear. Night. Camps, camping.

Mayers, Florence Cassen. *Egyptian art from the Brooklyn Museum: ABC* designed by Florence Cassen Mayers; ed. by Sheila Franklin. Abrams, 1988. ISBN 0-8109-1888-3 Subj: ABC books. Art. Foreign lands – Egypt. Museums.

The Museum of Fine Arts, Boston: ABC designed by Florence Cassen Mayers; ed. by Sheila Franklin. Abrams, 1986. ISBN 0-8109-1847-1 Subj: ABC books. Art. Museums.

The Museum of Modern Art, New York: ABC designed by Florence Cassen Mayers; ed. by Sheila Franklin. Abrams, 1986. ISBN 0-8109-1849-8 Subj: ABC books. Art. Museums.

The National Air and Space Museum: ABC designed by Florence Cassen Mayers; ed. by Sheila Franklin. Abrams, 1988. ISBN 0-8109-1859-5 Subj: ABC books. Museums. Space and space ships.

Mayers, Patrick. *Just one more block* ill. by Lucy Hawkinson. Albert Whitman, 1970. Subj: Activities – playing. Emotions. Sibling rivalry. Toys – blocks.

Mayhew, James. *Katie and the dinosaurs* ill. by author. Bantam, 1992. ISBN 0-553-08129-2 Subj: Dinosaurs. Museums.

Mayle, Peter. *Divorce can happen to the nicest people* ill. by Arthur Robins. Macmillan, 1980. Subj: Divorce. Family life.

Why are we getting a divorce? ill. by Arthur Robins. Crown, 1988. ISBN 0-517-56527-7 Subj: Divorce. Family life.

Maynard, Joyce. *Camp-out* ill. by Steve Bethel. Harcourt, 1985. ISBN 0-15-214077-8 Subj: Family life. Camps, camping.

New house ill. by Steve Bethel. Harcourt, 1987. ISBN 0-15-257042-X Subj: Activities – working. Houses. Trees.

Mayne, William. *Barnabas walks* ill. by Barbara Firth. Prentice-Hall, 1987. ISBN 0-13-057001-X Subj: Animals – guinea pigs. School.

The blue book of hob stories ill. by Patrick Benson. Putnam's, 1984. Subj: Character traits – helpfulness. Elves and little people.

Come, come to my corner ill. by Kenneth Lilly. Prentice-Hall, 1987. ISBN 0-13-152497-6 Subj: Animals. Animals – rabbits.

The green book of Hob stories ill. by Patrick Benore. Putnam's, 1984. ISBN 0-399-21039-3 Subj: Character traits – helpfulness. Elves and little people. Fairies.

A house in town ill. by Sarah Fox-Davis. Prentice-Hall, 1988. ISBN 0-13-395880-9 Subj: Animals – foxes.

Mousewing ill. by Martin Baynton. Prentice-Hall, 1988. ISBN 0-13-604240-6 Subj: Animals – mice.

The patchwork cat ill. by Nicola Bayley. Knopf, 1981. Subj: Animals – cats. Behavior – saving things. Emotions – love.

The red book of Hob stories ill. by Patrick Benson. Putnam's, 1984. ISBN 0-399-21047-4 Subj: Character traits – helpfulness. Elves and little people. Fairies.

Tibber ill. by Jonathan Heale. Prentice-Hall, 1987. ISBN 0-13-921214-0 Subj: Animals – cats. Farms.

The yellow book of Hob stories ill. by Patrick Benson. Putnam's, 1984. ISBN 0-399-21050-4 Subj: Character traits – helpfulness. Elves and little people. Fairies.

Mayper, Monica. *After good-night* ill. by Peter Sis. Harper, 1987. ISBN 0-06-024121-7 Subj: Bedtime. Dreams. Family life.

Oh snow ill. by June Otani. HarperCollins, 1991. ISBN 0-06-024204-3 Subj: Activities – playing. Poetry, rhyme. Weather – snow.

Maze, Edward. *Oswald, the monkey* (Mathiesen, Egon)

Maze, Nancy. *Oswald, the monkey* (Mathiesen, Egon)

Mazer, Anne. *The salamander room* ill. by Steve Johnson. Knopf, 1991. ISBN 0-394-92945-4 Subj: Animals – salamanders. Ecology. Imagination. Pets.

Watch me ill. by Stacey Schuett. Knopf, 1990. ISBN 0-394-92946-2 Subj: Activities. Family life.

The yellow button ill. by Judy Pedersen. Knopf, 1990. ISBN 0-394-92935-7 Subj: Concepts.

M'Bane, Phumla *see* Phumla

McGillicuddy, Mr. *see* Abisch, Roz

Meddaugh, Susan. *Beast* ill. by author. Houghton, 1981. ISBN 0-395-30349-4 Subj: Character traits – kindness. Monsters.

Maude and Claude go abroad ill. by author. Houghton, 1980. Subj: Activities – traveling. Animals – foxes. Boats, ships. Foreign lands – France.

Too short Fred ill. by author. Houghton, 1978. Subj: Animals – cats. Character traits – smallness.

Tree of birds ill. by author. Houghton, 1990. ISBN 0-395-53147-0 Subj: Birds. Character traits – kindness to animals.

The witches' supermarket ill. by author. Houghton, 1991. ISBN 0-395-57034-4 Subj: Animals – dogs. Holidays – Halloween. Stores. Witches.

Medearis, Angela Shelf. *Dancing with the Indians* ill. by Samuel Byrd. Holiday, 1991. ISBN 0-8234-0893-0 Subj: Activities – dancing. Ethnic groups in the U.S. – Afro-Americans. Indians of North America. Poetry, rhyme.

The zebra-riding cowboy ill. by Maria Christina Brusca. Holt, 1992. ISBN 0-8050-1712-7 Subj: Animals – horses. Cowboys. Ethnic groups in the U.S. Music. Songs.

Medina, Nina. *Have you ever noticed that rabbits don't sing?* ill. by author. Harpswell Pr., 1989. ISBN 0-88448-061-5 Subj: Activities – dancing. Animals – rabbits. Poetry, rhyme.

Mee, Charles L. *Noah* by Charles L. Mee, Jr.; ill. by Ken Munowitz. Harper, 1978. Subj: Religion – Noah.

Meeks, Esther K. *The curious cow* ill. by Mel Pekarsky. Follett, 1960. Also published in German as "Die neugierige Kuh"; in French as "La vache curieuse"; and in Spanish as "La Vaca curiosa." Subj: Animals – bulls, cows. Character traits – curiosity.

Friendly farm animals Follett, 1965. Subj: Animals. Farms.

The hill that grew ill. by Lazlo Roth. Follett, 1959. Subj: Activities – playing.

One is the engine ill. by Ernie King. Follett, 1956. Subj: Counting, numbers. Trains.

One is the engine: a counting book ill. by Joe Rogers. Follett, 1947, 1972. Subj: Counting, numbers. Trains.

Playland pony ill. by Mary Miller Salem. Follett, 1951. Subj: Animals – horses.

Something new at the zoo ill. by Hazel Hoecker. Follett, 1957. Subj: Animals. Zoos.

Meggendorfer, Lothar. *The genius of Lothar Meggendorfer* ill. by Jim Deesing. Random House, 1985. ISBN 0-394-54690-3 Subj: Format, unusual – toy and movable books. Poetry, rhyme. Toys.

Meigs, Mildred Plew. *Moon song* ill. by Chris Conover. Morrow, 1990. ISBN 0-688-08707-8 Subj: Lullabies. Poetry, rhyme.

Mellings, Joan. *It's fun to go to school* ill. by Sandra Laroche. Lippincott, 1986. ISBN 0-694-00125-2 Subj: Poetry, rhyme. School.

Melville, Herman. *Catskill eagle* ill. by Thomas Locker. Putnam, 1991. ISBN 0-399-21857-2 Subj: Birds – eagles.

Memling, Carl. *What's in the dark?* ill. by John E. Johnson. Parent's, 1971. Subj: Monsters. Night.

Mendelson, S. T. *Stupid Emilien* ill. by author. Stewart, Tabori & Chang, 1991. ISBN 1-55670-213-2 Subj: Animals – rabbits. Folk and fairy tales. Foreign lands – Russia.

Mendoza, George. *The alphabet boat: a seagoing alphabet book* ill. by author. American Heritage, 1972. Subj: ABC books. Boats, ships.

Alphabet sheep ill. by Kathleen Reidy. Grosset, 1982. Subj: ABC books. Animals – sheep. Behavior – lost.

The gillygoofang ill. by Mercer Mayer. Dial Pr., 1982. ISBN 0-8037-2875-1 Subj: Fish.

Henri Mouse ill. by Joelle Boucher. Viking, 1985. Subj: Animals – mice. Art.

Henri Mouse, the juggler ill. by Joelle Boucher. Viking, 1986. ISBN 0-670-80945-4 Subj: Animals – mice. Foreign lands – France. Magic.

The hunter I might have been photos. by De Wayne Dalrymple. Astor-Honor, 1968. Subj: Death. Emotions. Poetry, rhyme. Sports – hunting.

The Marcel Marceau counting book photos. by Milton H. Greene. Doubleday, 1971. Subj: Clowns, jesters.

Need a house? Call Ms. Mouse ill. by Doris Susan Smith. Grosset, 1981. Subj: Animals. Animals – mice. Houses.

Norman Rockwell's American ABC ill. by Norman Rockwell. Abrams, 1975. Subj: ABC books.

The scribbler ill. by Robert M. Quackenbush. Holt, 1971. Subj: Birds – sandpipers. Poetry, rhyme. Sea and seashore.

The Sesame Street book of opposites with Zero Mostel photos. by Sheldon Secunda; book design by Nicole Sekora-Mendoza. Platt, 1974. Subj: Concepts – opposites.

Silly sheep and other sheepish rhymes ill. by Kathleen Reidy. Grosset, 1982. Subj: Animals – sheep. Nursery rhymes.

Mennen, Ingrid. *Somewhere in Africa* by Ingrid Mennen and Niki Daly; ill. by Nicholaas Maritz. Dutton, 1992. ISBN 0-525-44848-9 Subj: City. Foreign lands – South Africa.

Menter, Ian. *The Albany Road mural* photos. by Will Guy. David and Charles, 1984. Subj: Activities – painting. Art.

Carnival photos. by Will Guy. David and Charles, 1983. Subj: Foreign lands – England. Holidays.

Meredith, Lucy. *The princess on the nut* (Nikly, Michelle)

Mernan, Andrea. *Ben finds a friend* (Chapouton, Anne-Marie)

I wish I were (Laurencin, Geneviève)

A walk in the rain (Scheffler, Ursel)

Meroux, Felix. *The prince of the rabbits* ill. by Cooper Edens. Green Tiger Pr., 1985. ISBN 0-88138-030-X Subj: Animals – rabbits. Behavior – boredom.

Merriam, Eve. *The birthday cow* ill. by Guy Michel. Knopf, 1978. ISBN 0-394-93808-9 Subj: Animals. Humor. Poetry, rhyme.

The birthday door ill. by Peter J. Thornton. Morrow, 1986. ISBN 0-688-06194-X Subj: Animals – cats. Birthdays. Houses. Problem solving.

Blackberry ink ill. by Hans Wilhelm. Morrow, 1985. ISBN 0-688-04151-5 Subj: Poetry, rhyme.

Boys and girls, girls and boys ill. by Harriet Sherman. Holt, 1972. Subj: Activities – playing. Ethnic groups in the U.S.

Christmas (Bruna, Dick)

The Christmas box ill. by David Small. Morrow, 1985. ISBN 0-688-05256-8 Subj: Family life. Holidays – Christmas.

Epaminondas ill. by Trina Schart Hyman. Follett, 1968. Originally published in 1938 as "Epaminondas and his Aunty" by Sara Cone Bryant Subj: Ethnic groups in the U.S. – Afro-Americans. Family life – aunts, uncles. Folk and fairy tales.

Fighting words ill. by David Small. Morrow, 1992. ISBN 0-688-09677-8 Subj: Behavior – fighting, arguing. Behavior – name calling. City. Country.

Good night to Annie ill. by John Wallner. Four Winds Pr., 1980. Subj: ABC books. Bedtime.

Goodnight to Annie ill. by Carol Schwartz. Four Winds, 1992. ISBN 1-56282-206-3 Subj: ABC books. Animals. Bedtime. Lullabies. Sleep.

Halloween ABC ill. by Lane Smith. Macmillan, 1987. ISBN 0-02-766870-3 Subj: ABC books. Holidays – Halloween. Poetry, rhyme.

Mommies at work ill. by Eugenie Fernandes. Simon & Schuster, 1989. Subj: Activities – working. Careers. Family life – mothers.

A poem for a pickle: funnybone verses ill. by Sheila Hamanaka. Morrow, 1989. ISBN 0-688-08138-X Subj: Poetry, rhyme.

Train leaves the station ill. by Dale Gottlieb. Holt, 1992. ISBN 0-8050-1934-0 Subj: Counting, numbers. Poetry, rhyme. Time. Toys – trains.

Where is everybody? ill. by Diane de Groat. Simon & Schuster, 1989. ISBN 0-671-64964-7 Subj: ABC books. Animals.

Merrill, Jean. *Emily Emerson's moon* by Jean Merrill and Ronni Solbert; ill. by Ronni Solbert. Little, 1960. Subj: Family life. Moon.

How many kids are hiding on my block? by Jean Merrill and Frances Gruse Scott; ill. by Frances Gruse Scott. Albert Whitman, 1970. Subj: Counting, numbers. Ethnic groups in the U.S. Games.

Tell about the cowbarn, Daddy ill. by Lili Cassel-Wronker. Addison-Wesley, 1963. Subj: Animals – bulls, cows. Barns. Farms.

Merritt, Jane Hamilton *see* Hamilton-Merritt, Jane

Meryl, Debra. *Baby's peek-a-boo album* ill. by True Kelley. Putnam, 1989. ISBN 0-448-15375-0 Subj: Activities – playing. Format, unusual – toy and movable books. Games.

Meshover, Leonard. *The guinea pigs that went to school* by Leonard Meshover and Sally Feistel; photos. by Eve Hoffmann. Follett, 1968. Subj: Animals – guinea pigs. School. Science.

The monkey that went to school by Leonard Meshover and Sally Feistel; photos. by Eve Hoffmann. Follett, 1978. Subj: Animals – monkeys. School. Science.

Messenger, Jannat. *Lullabies and baby songs* ill. by author. Dial Pr., 1988. ISBN 0-8037-0491-7 Subj: Lullabies. Poetry, rhyme.

Meyer, Elizabeth C. *The blue china pitcher* ill. by author. Abingdon Pr., 1974. Subj: Holidays. Parties.

Meyer, June *see* Jordan, June

Meyer, Linda D. *Safety zone* ill. by Marina Megale. Chas. Franklin Pr., 1984. Subj: Behavior – talking to strangers. Safety.

Meyer, Louis A. *The clean air and peaceful contentment dirigible airline* ill. by author. Little, 1972. Subj: Ecology. Humor. Noise, sounds.

Meyers, Susan. *The truth about gorillas* ill. by John Hamberger. Dutton, 1980. Subj: Animals – gorillas. Science.

Michael, Emory H. *Androcles and the lion* ill. by Mia Hatchem. Winston-Derek, 1988. ISBN 1-55523-132-2 Subj: Animals – lions. Character traits – helpfulness. Character traits – kindness to animals. Folk and fairy tales. Foreign lands – Italy. Religion.

Michaels, Ruth. *The family that grew* (Rondell, Florence)

Michaels, William. *Clare and her shadow* ill. by author. Linnet Books, 1991. ISBN 0-208-02301-1 Subj: Family life – grandfathers. Shadows.

Michel, Anna. *Little wild lion cub* ill. by Tony Chen. Pantheon, 1981. Subj: Animals – lions.

Michels, Tilde. *At the frog pond* tr. by Nina Ignatowicz; ill. by Reinhard Michl. Lippincott, 1989. ISBN 0-397-32315-8 Subj: Ecology. Frogs and toads. Science.

Rabbit spring ill. by Käthi Bhend. Harcourt, 1989. ISBN 0-15-200568-4 Subj: Animals – rabbits. Nature.

Who's that knocking at my door? ill. by Reinhard Michl. Barron's, 1986. ISBN 0-8120-5732-5 Subj: Poetry, rhyme. Seasons – winter. Sports – hunting.

Michl, Reinhard. *A day on the river* ill. by author. Barron's, 1986. ISBN 0-8120-5715-5 Subj: Rivers.

Micucci, Charles. *A little night music* ill. by author. Morrow, 1989. ISBN 0-688-07901-6 Subj: Animals – cats. Music. Night.

Miklowitz, Gloria D. *Bearfoot boy* ill. by Jim Collins. Follett, 1964. Subj: Birthdays. Clothing.

Save that raccoon! ill. by St. Tamara. Harcourt, 1978. Subj: Animals – raccoons. Character traits – kindness to animals. Fire. Forest, woods.

The zoo that moved ill. by Don Madden. Follett, 1968. Subj: Animals. Zoos.

Miles, Betty. *Around and around... love* ill. with photos. Knopf, 1975. Subj: Emotions – love. Poetry, rhyme.

Having a friend ill. by Erik Blegvad. Knopf, 1958. Subj: Friendship.

A house for everyone ill. by Jo Lowery. Knopf, 1958. Subj: Houses.

Miles, Lauren. *The rag coat* ill. by author. Little, 1991. ISBN 0-316-57407-4 Subj: Behavior – sharing. Clothing. Friendship. Poverty.

Miles, Miska. *Apricot ABC* ill. by Peter Parnall. Little, 1969. Subj: ABC books. Poetry, rhyme. Trees.

Chicken forgets ill. by Jim Arnosky. Little, 1976. Subj: Behavior – forgetfulness. Birds – chickens. Humor.

The fox and the fire ill. by John Schoenherr. Little, 1966. Subj: Animals – foxes. Fire. Forest, woods.

The horse and the bad morning (Clymer, Ted)

Jump frog jump ill. by Earl Thollander. Putnam's, 1965. Subj: Fairs. Frogs and toads.

Mouse six and the happy birthday ill. by Leslie Holt Morrill. Dutton, 1978. Subj: Animals – mice. Birthdays. Family life – mothers.

No, no, Rosina ill. by Earl Thollander. Putnam's, 1964. Subj: Boats, ships. Careers – fishermen. Character traits – smallness. City. Sports – fishing.

Noisy gander ill. by Leslie Holt Morrill. Dutton, 1978. Subj: Animals. Birds – ducks. Farms. Noise, sounds.

The pointed brush... ill. by Roger Antoine Duvoisin. Lothrop, 1959. Subj: Activities – writing. Foreign lands – China.

Rabbit garden ill. by John Schoenherr. Little, 1967. Subj: Animals – rabbits. Ecology. Gardens, gardening.

The raccoon and Mrs. McGinnis ill. by Leonard Weisgard. Putnam's, 1961. Subj: Animals – raccoons. Barns. Crime.

The rice bowl pet ill. by Ezra Jack Keats. Crowell, 1962. Subj: Pets.

Rolling the cheese ill. by Alton Raible. Atheneum, 1966. Subj: City. Games.

Show and tell... ill. by Thomas Arthur Hamil. Putnam's, 1962. Subj: Animals – dogs. School.

Small rabbit ill. by Jim Arnosky. Little, 1977. Subj: Animals – rabbits.

Somebody's dog ill. by John Schoenherr. Little, 1973. Subj: Animals – dogs. Pets.

Sylvester Jones and the voice in the forest ill. by Leonard Weisgard. Lothrop, 1958. Subj: Animals. Forest, woods.

This little pig ill. by Leslie Holt Morrill. Dutton, 1980. Subj: Animals – pigs. Behavior – lost. Behavior – running away. Farms.

Wharf rat ill. by John Schoenherr. Little, 1972. Subj: Animals – rats.

Miles, Sally. *Alfi and the dark* ill. by Errol Le Cain. Chronicle, 1988. ISBN 0-87701-527-9 Subj: Bedtime. Friendship. Night.

Milgram, Mary. *Brothers are all the same* ill. by Rosmarie Hausherr. Dutton, 1978. Subj: Adoption. Family life. Sibling rivalry.

Milgrom, Harry. *Egg-ventures: first science experiments* ill. by Giulio Maestro. Dutton, 1974. Subj: Eggs. Science.

Milhous, Katherine. *The egg tree* ill. by author. Scribner's, 1950. Subj: Caldecott award book. Holidays – Easter.

The turnip by Katherine Milhouse and Alice Dalgliesh; ill. by Pierr Morgan. Putnam, 1990. From : Once on a time by Katherine Milhouse and Alice Dalgliesh (1938) ISBN 0-399-22229-4 Subj: Cumulative tales. Farms. Folk and fairy tales. Foreign lands – Russia. Plants. Problem solving.

Milios, Rita. *Sneaky Pete* ill. by Clovis Martin. Children's Pr., 1989. ISBN 0-516-02092-7 Subj: Behavior – hiding. Poetry, rhyme.

Yo soy—I am ill. by Clovis Martin. Children's Pr., 1990. ISBN 0-516-32081-5 Subj: Activities. Concepts – opposites. Foreign languages. Self-concept.

Milius, Winifred *see* Lubell, Winifred

Miller, Albert *see* Mills, Alan

Miller, Alice P. *The little store on the corner* ill. by John Lawrence. Abelard-Schuman, 1961. Subj: Stores.

The mouse family's blueberry pie ill. by Carol Bloch. Elsevier-Nelson, 1981. Subj: Activities – cooking. Animals – mice.

Miller, Edna. *Jumping bean* ill. by author. Prentice-Hall, 1980. Subj: Science.

Mousekin finds a friend ill. by author. Prentice-Hall, 1967. Subj: Animals – mice. Friendship.

Mousekin's ABC ill. by author. Prentice-Hall, 1972. Subj: ABC books. Animals – mice. Forest, woods. Poetry, rhyme.

Mousekin's Christmas eve ill. by author. Prentice-Hall, 1965. Subj: Animals – mice. Holidays – Christmas.

Mousekin's close call ill. by author. Prentice-Hall, 1978. Subj: Animals – mice. Forest, woods.

Mousekin's fables ill. by author. Prentice-Hall, 1982. Subj: Animals – mice. Folk and fairy tales. Seasons.

Mousekin's family ill. by author. Prentice-Hall, 1969. Subj: Animals – mice. Family life.

Mousekin's golden house ill. by author. Prentice-Hall, 1964. Subj: Animals – mice. Hibernation. Holidays – Halloween. Seasons – winter.

Mousekin's lost woodland ill. by author. Simon & Schuster, 1992. ISBN 0-671-74938-2 Subj: Animals – mice. Ecology. Forest, woods.

Mousekin's mystery ill. by author. Prentice-Hall, 1983. Subj: Animals – mice. Problem solving.

Mouskin takes a trip ill. by author. Prentice-Hall, 1976. ISBN 0-13-604363-1 Subj: Activities – traveling. Animals – mice.

Mouskin's Easter basket ill. by author. Prentice-Hall, 1987. ISBN 0-13-604141-8 Subj: Animals – mice. Holidays – Easter. Seasons – spring.

Mouskin's frosty friend ill. by author. Simon & Schuster, 1990. ISBN 0-671-70445-1 Subj: Animals – mice. Character traits – kindness to animals. Food. Snowmen.

Mouskin's Thanksgiving ill. by author. Prentice-Hall, 1985. ISBN 0-13-604299-6 Subj: Animals. Animals – mice. Forest, woods. Holidays – Thanksgiving.

Patches finds a new home ill. by author. Simon & Schuster, 1989. ISBN 0-671-66266-X Subj: Animals – cats. Nature.

Pebbles, a pack rat ill. by author. Prentice-Hall, 1976. Subj: Animals – pack rats. Scarecrows.

Scamper: a gray tree squirrel ill. by author. Pippin Pr., 1991. ISBN 0-915912-12-9 Subj: Animals – squirrels. Nature.

Miller, Edward. *The curse of Claudia* ill. by author. Crown, 1989. ISBN 0-517-57409-8 Subj: Character traits – cleanliness. Emotions – happiness. Monsters.

Frederick Ferdinand Fox ill. by author. Crown, 1987. ISBN 0-517-56356-8 Subj: Animals – foxes. War.

Miller, J. P. (John Parr). *Do you know color?* by J. P. Miller and Katherine Howard; ill. by J. P. Miller. Random House, 1979. Subj: Concepts – color.

Farmer John's animals ill. by author. Random House, 1979. ISBN 0-394-84270-7 Subj: Animals. Farms.

Good night, Little Rabbit ill. by author. Random House, 1986. ISBN 0-394-87992-9 Subj: Animals – rabbits. Bedtime. Family life. Format, unusual – board books.

Learn about colors with Little Rabbit ill. by author. Random House, 1984. Subj: Concepts – color.

Learn to count with Little Rabbit ill. by author. Random House, 1984. ISBN 0-394-96149-8 Subj: Animals – rabbits. Counting, numbers.

Miller, Jane. *Farm alphabet book* photos. by author. Prentice-Hall, 1984. Subj: ABC books. Farms.

Farm counting book photos. by author. Prentice-Hall, 1983. Subj: Counting, numbers. Farms.

Farm noises photos. by author. Simon & Schuster, 1989. ISBN 0-671-67450-1 Subj: Animals. Farms. Noise, sounds.

Seasons on the farm ill. by author. Prentice-Hall, 1986. ISBN 0-13-797275-X Subj: Animals. Farms. Seasons.

Miller, Judith Ransom. *Nabob and the geranium* ill. by Marilyn Neuhart. Golden Gate, 1967. Subj: Plants. Science.

Miller, M. L. *Dizzy from fools* ill. by Eve Tharlet. Alphabet Pr., 1985. ISBN 0-88708-004-9 Subj: Character traits – questioning. Clowns, jesters. Royalty. Royalty – princesses.

Miller, Margaret. *At my house* ill. by author. Crowell, 1989. ISBN 0-694-00276-3 Subj: Babies. Family life. Format, unusual – board books.

Every day photos. by author. HarperCollins, 1991. ISBN 0-694-00304-2 Subj: Activities. Format, unusual – board books. Language.

In my room ill. by author. Crowell, 1989. ISBN 0-694-00271-2 Subj: Babies. Family life. Format, unusual – board books.

Me and my clothes ill. by author. Crowell, 1989. ISBN 0-694-00272-0 Subj: Babies. Clothing. Family life. Format, unusual – board books.

My birthday photos. by author. HarperCollins, 1991. ISBN 0-694-00302-6 Subj: Birthdays. Format, unusual – board books. Language. Parties.

On my street photos. by author. HarperCollins, 1991. ISBN 0-694-00303-4 Subj: Communities, neighborhoods. Format, unusual – board books. Language.

Playtime photos. by author. HarperCollins, 1991. ISBN 0-694-00301-8 Subj: Activities – playing. Concepts – opposites. Format, unusual – board books. Language.

Time to eat ill. by author. Crowell, 1989. ISBN 0-694-00274-X Subj: Babies. Family life. Food. Format, unusual – board books.

Who uses this? photos. by author. Greenwillow, 1990. ISBN 0-688-08279-3 Subj: Careers. Tools.

Whose hat? photos. by author. Greenwillow, 1988. ISBN 0-688-06907-X Subj: Careers. Clothing – hats.

Whose shoe? photos. by author. Greenwillow, 1991. ISBN 0-688-10009-0 Subj: Clothing – shoes. Games.

Miller, Moira. *The moon dragon* ill. by Ian Deuchar. Dial, 1989. ISBN 0-8037-0566-2 Subj: Behavior – boasting. Folk and fairy tales. Foreign lands – China. Kites.

Oscar Mouse finds a home ill. by Maria Majewska. Dial Pr., 1985. ISBN 0-8037-0229-9 Subj: Animals – mice. Behavior – seeking better things.

The proverbial mouse ill. by Ian Deuchar. Dial Pr., 1987. ISBN 0-8037-0195-0 Subj: Animals – mice. Poetry, rhyme. Toys.

The search for spring ill. by Ian Deuchar. Dial Pr., 1988. ISBN 0-8037-0445-3 Subj: Seasons.

Miller, Virginia. *On your potty!* ill. by author. Greenwillow, 1991. ISBN 0-688-10618-8 Subj: Animals – bears. Behavior – growing up. Etiquette. Toilet training.

Miller, Warren. *The goings on at Little Wishful* ill. by Edward Sorel. Little, 1959. Subj: Behavior – boasting. Emotions – envy, jealousy.

Pablo paints a picture ill. by Edward Sorel. Little, 1959. Subj: Activities – painting. Careers – artists.

Millhouse, Nicholas. *Blue-footed booby: bird of the Galápagos* ill. by Margret Bowman. Walker, 1986. ISBN 0-8027-6629-3 Subj: Animals. Birds. Islands. Science.

Mills, Alan. *The hungry goat* ill. by Abner Graboff. Rand McNally, 1964. Subj: Animals – goats. Humor. Music. Songs.

Mills, Claudia. *A visit to Amy-Claire* ill. by Sheila Hamanaka. Macmillan, 1992. ISBN 0-02-766991-2 Subj: Emotions – envy, jealousy. Family life. Family life – sisters. Sibling rivalry.

Millward, David Wynn. *Jenny and Bob* ill. by Kady MacDonald Denton. Delacorte, 1991. ISBN 0-385-30431-5 Subj: Emotions. Family life.

Milne, A. A. (Alan Alexander). *House at Pooh corner [a pop-up book]* Dutton, 1986. ISBN 0-525-44245-6 Subj: Format, unusual – toy and movable books. Houses. Toys – teddy bears.

Pooh and some bees ill. by Robert Cremins. Dutton, 1987. ISBN 0-525-44339-8 Subj: Format, unusual – toy and movable books. Insects. Toys – teddy bears.

Pooh goes visiting ill. by Robert Cremins. Dutton, 1987. ISBN 0-525-44337-1 Subj: Format, unusual – toy and movable books. Toys – teddy bears.

Pooh's alphabet book ill. by E. H. Shepard. Dutton, 1976. Subj: ABC books. Toys – teddy bears.

Pooh's counting book ill. by E. H. Shepard. Dutton, 1982. Subj: Counting, numbers. Toys – teddy bears.

Pooh's quiz book ill. by E. H. Shepard. Dutton, 1977. Subj: Games. Humor. Toys – teddy bears.

Prince Rabbit: and, The princess who could not laugh ill. by Mary Shepard. Dutton, 1967. Subj: Animals – rabbits. Folk and fairy tales. Royalty – princes.

Winnie-the-Pooh: a pop-up book ill. by Chuck Murphy; engineering by Keith Moseley. Dutton, 1984. ISBN 0-525-44119-0 Subj: Character traits – bravery. Format, unusual – toy and movable books. Toys – teddy bears.

Milord, Jerry. *Maggie and the goodbye gift* (Milord, Sue)

Milord, Sue. *Maggie and the goodbye gift* by Sue and Jerry Milord; ill. by authors. Lothrop, 1979. Subj: Family life. Moving.

Milton, Joyce. *Dinosaur days* ill. by Richard Roe. Random House, 1985. ISBN 0-394-97023-3 Subj: Dinosaurs.

Milton, Nancy. *The giraffe that walked to Paris* ill. by Roger Roth. Crown, 1992. ISBN 0-517-58133-7 Subj: Activities – traveling. Animals – giraffes. Foreign lands – France. Royalty – kings.

Minarik, Else Holmelund. *Cat and dog* ill. by Fritz Siebel. Harper, 1960. Subj: Animals – cats. Animals – dogs.

Father Bear comes home ill. by Maurice Sendak. Harper, 1959. Subj: Animals – bears. Family life – fathers.

It's spring! ill. by Margaret Bloy Graham. Greenwillow, 1989. ISBN 0-688-07620-3 Subj: Animals – cats. Seasons – spring.

A kiss for Little Bear ill. by Maurice Sendak. Harper, 1959. Subj: Animals – bears.

Little Bear ill. by Maurice Sendak. Harper, 1957. Subj: Animals – bears. Birthdays.

Little Bear's friend ill. by Maurice Sendak. Harper, 1960. Subj: Animals – bears. Friendship.

Little Bear's visit ill. by Maurice Sendak. Harper, 1961. Subj: Animals – bears. Caldecott award honor book. Family life – grandparents.

The little giant girl and the elf boys ill. by Garth Williams. Harper, 1963. Subj: Elves and little people. Giants.

The little girl and the dragon ill. by Martine Gourlault. Greenwillow, 1991. ISBN 0-688-09914-9 Subj: Animals. Behavior – bullying. Character traits – stubbornness. Dragons.

No fighting, no biting! ill. by Maurice Sendak. Harper, 1958. Subj: Behavior – fighting, arguing. Reptiles – alligators, crocodiles.

Percy and the five houses ill. by James Stevenson. Greenwillow, 1989. ISBN 0-688-08105-3 Subj: Animals – beavers. Houses.

Minsberg, David. *The book monster* ill. by Shelley Matheis. Littlebee Pr., 1982. Subj: Activities – reading. Monsters.

Mintzberg, Yvette. *Sally, where are you?* ill. by author. David & Charles, 1988. ISBN 0-434-95158-7 Subj: Behavior – hiding. Family life.

Mintzer, Jo. *Con mi hermano - With my brother* (Roe, Eileen)

Miranda, Anne. *Baby talk* ill. by Dorothy Stott. Dutton, 1987. ISBN 0-525-44319-3 Subj: Babies. Family life. Format, unusual – toy and movable books.

Baby walk ill. by Dorothy Stott. Dutton, 1988. ISBN 0-525-44421-1 Subj: Activities – playing. Babies. Format, unusual.

Baby-sit ill. by Dorothy Stott. Little, 1990. ISBN 0-316-57454-6 Subj: Activities – baby-sitting. Family life – mothers. Format, unusual – toy and movable books.

Mirkovic, Irene. *The greedy shopkeeper* ill. by Harold Berson. Harcourt, 1980. Translated and adapt. from a Serbian folk tale Subj: Behavior – trickery. Careers – judges. Folk and fairy tales.

Mitchell, Adrian. *Our mammoth* ill. by Priscilla Lamont. Harcourt, 1987. ISBN 0-15-258838-8 Subj: Animals. Humor.

Mitchell, Cynthia. *Halloweena Hecatee* ill. by Eileen Browne. Crowell, 1979. Subj: Activities – playing. Games. Poetry, rhyme.

Here a little child I stand: poems of prayer and praise for children ill. by Satomi Ichikawa. Putnam's, 1985. ISBN 0-399-21244-2 Subj: Foreign lands. Poetry, rhyme. Religion.

Playtime ill. by Satomi Ichikawa. Collins-World, 1978. Subj: Activities – playing. Emotions. Poetry, rhyme.

Under the cherry tree ill. by Satomi Ichikawa. Collins-World, 1979. Subj: Poetry, rhyme.

Mitchell, Joyce Slayton. *My mommy makes money* ill. by True Kelley. Little, 1984. Subj: Activities – working. Careers. Family life – mothers.

Mitgutsch, Ali. *From gold to money* ill. by author. Carolrhoda Books, 1985. ISBN 0-87614-230-7 Subj: Science.

From graphite to pencil ill. by author. Carolrhoda Books, 1985. ISBN 0-87614-231-5 Subj: Science.

From lemon to lemonade ill. by author. Carolrhoda Books, 1986. ISBN 0-87614-298-6 Subj: Food.

From rubber tree to tire ill. by author. Carolrhoda Books, 1986. ISBN 0-87614-297-8 Subj: Automobiles.

From sea to salt ill. by author. Carolrhoda Books, 1985. ISBN 0-87614-232-3 Subj: Science.

From swamp to coal ill. by author. Carolrhoda Books, 1985. ISBN 0-87614-233-1 Subj: Science.

From wood to paper ill. by author. Carolrhoda Books, 1986. ISBN 0-87614-296-X Subj: Paper.

Mitra, Annie. *Penguin moon* ill. by author. Holiday, 1989. ISBN 0-8234-0749-7 Subj: Behavior – wishing. Birds – penguins. Moon.

Tusk! Tusk! ill. by author. Holiday, 1990. ISBN 0-8234-0819-1 Subj: Animals – elephants. Careers – dentists. Teeth.

Miyoshi, Sekiya. *Singing David* ill. by author. Watts, 1969. Subj: Religion.

Mizumura, Kazue. *If I built a village* ill. by author. Crowell, 1971. Subj: Character traits – kindness. City. Ecology. Houses.

If I were a cricket... ill. by author. Crowell, 1973. Subj: Animals. Emotions – love. Insects – crickets. Poetry, rhyme.

If I were a mother ill. by author. Crowell, 1967. Subj: Family life – mothers.

Moak, Allan. *A big city ABC* ill. by author. Tundra (dist. by Scribner's), 1984. Subj: ABC books. City. Foreign lands – Canada.

Mobley, Jane. *The star husband* ill. by Anna Vojtech. Doubleday, 1979. Subj: Folk and fairy tales. Indians of North America. Stars.

Moche, Dinah L. *The astronauts* ill. with photos. from NASA. Random House, 1979. Subj: Moon. Science. Space and space ships.

Modell, Frank. *Goodbye old year, hello new year* ill. by author. Greenwillow, 1984. Subj: Holidays – New Year's.

Ice cream soup ill. by author. Greenwillow, 1988. ISBN 0-688-07771-4 Subj: Birthdays. Parties.

Look out, it's April Fools' Day ill. by author. Greenwillow, 1985. ISBN 0-688-04017-9 Subj: Holidays – April Fools' Day. Riddles.

One zillion Valentines ill. by author. Greenwillow, 1981. Subj: Character traits – practicality. Holidays – Valentine's Day.

Seen any cats? ill. by author. Greenwillow, 1979. Subj: Animals – cats. Circus.

Skeeter and the computer ill. by author. Greenwillow, 1988. ISBN 0-688-03706-2 Subj: Animals – dogs. Computers.

Tooley! Tooley! ill. by author. Greenwillow, 1979. Subj: Animals – dogs. Behavior – lost. Humor.

Modesitt, Jeanne. *The night call* ill. by Robin Spowart. Viking, 1989. ISBN 0-670-82500-X Subj: Animals. Night. Stars. Toys.

Songs of Chanukah ill. by Robin Spowart; music arranged by Uri Ophir. Little, 1992. ISBN 0-316-57739-1 Subj: Holidays – Hanukkah. Jewish culture. Music. Religion. Songs.

The story of Z ill. by Lonni Sue Johnson. Picture Book Studio, 1990. ISBN 0-88708-105-3 Subj: Emotions.

Moe, J. E. *The man who kept house* (Asbjørnsen, P. C. (Peter Christian))

Moeri, Louise. *Star Mother's youngest child* ill. by Trina Schart Hyman. Houghton, 1975. ISBN 0-395-21406-8 Subj: Folk and fairy tales. Holidays – Christmas.

The unicorn and the plow ill. by Diane Goode. Dutton, 1982. Subj: Character traits – luck. Farms. Mythical creatures – unicorns.

Moers, Hermann. *Camomile heads for home* tr. by Rosemary Lanning; ill. by Marcus Pfister. Holt, 1987. ISBN 0-8050-0280-4 Subj: Animals – bulls, cows. Behavior – growing up.

Hugo's baby brother ill. by Józef Wilkoń. North-South, 1991. ISBN 1-55858-146-4 Subj: Animals – lions. Family life. Sibling rivalry.

Lullaby for a newborn king (Wilkoń, Józef)

Moffett, Martha A. *A flower pot is not a hat* ill. by Susan Perl. Dutton, 1972. Subj: Humor.

Mogensen, Jan. *The forty-six little men* ill. by author. Greenwillow, 1991. ISBN 0-688-09284-5 Subj: Elves and little people. Imagination. Wordless.

Teddy and the Chinese dragon ill. by author. Gareth Stevens, 1985. ISBN 1-55532-002-3 Subj: Dragons. Toys – teddy bears.

Teddy in the undersea kingdom ill. by author. Gareth Stevens, 1985. ISBN 1-55532-000-7 Subj: Crustacea. Sea and seashore. Toys – teddy bears.

Teddy's Christmas gift ill. by author. Gareth Stevens, 1985. ISBN 1-55532-004-X Subj: Character traits – kindness to animals. Holidays – Christmas. Toys – teddy bears.

The tiger's breakfast ill. by author. Interlink, 1991. ISBN 0-940793-83-0 Subj: Animals – elephants. Animals – mice. Behavior – trickery. Character traits – cleverness.

When Teddy woke early ill. by author. Gareth Stevens, 1985. ISBN 1-55532-006-6 Subj: Behavior – lost. Toys – teddy bears.

Mohr, Joseph. *Silent night* verses by Joseph Mohr; ill. by Susan Jeffers. Dutton, 1984. Orig. title: Stille Nacht, heilige Nacht Subj: Holidays – Christmas. Songs.

Mollel, Tolowa M. *Orphan boy* ill. by Paul Morin. Clarion, 1991. ISBN 0-89919-985-2 Subj: Folk and fairy tales. Foreign lands – Kenya.

A promise to the sun ill. by Beatriz A. Vidal. Little, 1992. ISBN 0-316-57813-4 Subj: Animals – bats. Birds. Foreign lands – Kenya. Sun. Weather.

Rhinos for lunch and elephants for supper ill. by Barbara Spurll. Houghton, 1992. ISBN 0-395-60734-5 Subj: Animals. Cumulative tales. Emotions – fear. Foreign lands – Kenya.

Molnar, Dorothy E. *Who will pick me up when I fall?* by Dorothy E. Molnar and Stephan H. Fen-ton; ill. by Irene Trivas. Albert Whitman, 1991. ISBN 0-8075-9072-X Subj: Days of the week, months of the year. Family life.

Molnar, Joe. *Graciela: a Mexican-American child tells her story* photos. by author. Watts, 1972. Subj: Ethnic groups in the U.S. – Mexican-Americans.

Moncure, Jane Belk. *Happy healthkins* ill. by Lois Axeman. Children's Pr., 1982. Subj: Elves and little people. Health. Poetry, rhyme.

The healthkin food train ill. by Lois Axeman. Children's Pr., 1982. Subj: Elves and little people. Health. Poetry, rhyme.

Healthkins exercise! ill. by Lois Axeman. Children's Pr., 1982. Subj: Elves and little people. Health. Poetry, rhyme.

Healthkins help ill. by Lois Axeman. Children's Pr., 1982. Subj: Elves and little people. Health. Poetry, rhyme.

The look book ill. by Lois Axeman. Children's Pr., 1982. Subj: Senses – seeing.

Now I am five! ill. by Helen Endes. Childrens Pr., 1984. ISBN 0-516-01879-5 Subj: Activities. Behavior – growing up.

Now I am four! ill. by Kathryn Hutton. Childrens Pr., 1984. ISBN 0-516-01878-7 Subj: Activities. Behavior – growing up.

Now I am three! ill. by Linda Hohag. Childrens Pr., 1984. ISBN 0-516-01877-9 Subj: Activities. Behavior – growing up.

Riddle me a riddle ill. by Marc Belenchia. Children's Pr., 1977. Subj: Animals. Magic. Riddles.

Sounds all around ill. by Lois Axeman. Children's Pr., 1982. Subj: Senses – hearing.

The talking tabby cat: a folk tale from France ill. by Helen Endres. Children's Pr., 1980. Subj: Animals – cats. Folk and fairy tales.

A tasting party ill. by Lois Axeman. Children's Pr., 1982. Subj: Senses – tasting.

The touch book ill. by Lois Axeman. Children's Pr., 1982. Subj: Senses – touching.

What your nose knows! ill. by Lois Axeman. Children's Pr., 1982. Subj: Anatomy – noses. Senses – smelling.

Where? ill. by Lois Axeman. Children's Pr., 1983. Subj: Character traits – curiosity. Character traits – questioning.

Word Bird's fall words ill. by Linda Hohag. Childrens Pr., 1985. ISBN 0-89565-308-7 Subj: Language. Seasons – fall.

Word Bird's spring words ill. by Vera Gohman. Childrens Pr., 1985. ISBN 0-89565-310-9 Subj: Language. Seasons – spring.

Word Bird's summer words ill. by Linda Hohag. Childrens Pr., 1985. ISBN 0-89565-311-7 Subj: Language. Seasons – summer.

Word Bird's winter words ill. by Vera Gohman. Childrens Pr., 1985. ISBN 0-89565-309-5 Subj: Language. Seasons – winter.

Monfried, Lucia. *Baby's world* ill. by Stephen Shott. Dutton, 1990. ISBN 0-525-44617-6 Subj: Babies. Format, unusual. Language.

Monjo, F. N. *The drinking gourd* ill. by Fred Brenner. Harper, 1970. Subj: Ethnic groups in the U.S. – Afro-Americans. Indians of North America. U.S. history.

Indian summer ill. by Anita Lobel. Harper, 1968. Subj: Indians of North America. U.S. history.

The one bad thing about father ill. by Rocco Negri. Harper, 1970. Subj: Family life – fathers. U.S. history.

Poor Richard in France ill. by Brinton Turkle. Holt, 1973. Subj: U.S. history.

Rudi and the distelfink ill. by George Kraus. Windmill, 1972. Subj: Family life.

Monsell, Helen Albee. *Paddy's Christmas* ill. by Kurt Wiese. Knopf, 1942. Subj: Animals – bears. Holidays – Christmas.

Monsell, Mary Elise. *Armadillo* ill. by Sylvie Wickstrom. Macmillan, 1991. ISBN 0-689-31676-3 Subj: Animals – armadillos. Friendship.

Underwear! ill. by Lynn Munsinger. Albert Whitman, 1988. ISBN 0-8075-8308-1 Subj: Animals. Clothing. Humor.

Monster poems ed. by Daisy Wallace; ill. by Kay Chorao. Holiday House, 1976. Subj: Monsters. Poetry, rhyme. Tongue twisters.

Montenegro, Laura Nyman. *One stuck drawer* ill. by author. Houghton, 1991. ISBN 0-395-57319-X Subj: Furniture – dressers.

Montgomerie, Norah. *This little pig went to market: play rhymes* ill. by Margery Gill. Watts, 1967. Subj: Games. Nursery rhymes. Participation.

Montgomery, Michael. *'Night, America* ill. by author. Contemporary Books, 1989. ISBN 0-8092-4397-0 Subj: Bedtime. Night. Poetry, rhyme.

Montresor, Beni. *A for angel: Beni Montresor's ABC picture-stories* ill. by author. Knopf, 1969. Subj: ABC books.

Bedtime! ill. by author. Harper, 1978. Subj: Bedtime. Dreams.

The witches of Venice ill. by author. Doubleday, 1989. ISBN 0-385-26355-4 Subj: Dreams. Flowers. Royalty. Witches.

Moon, Carl. *One little Indian* (Moon, Grace Purdie)

Moon, Cliff. *Pigs on the farm* ill. by Anna Jupp. Watts, 1983. ISBN 0-531-04696-6 Subj: Animals – pigs. Farms.

Moon, Dolly M. *My very first book of cowboy songs: 21 favorite songs in easy piano arrangements* ill. by Frederic Remington. Dover, 1982. Subj: Cowboys. Folk and fairy tales. Songs.

Moon, Grace Purdie. *One little Indian* by Grace and Carl Moon; ill. by Carl Moon. Albert Whitman, 1950. Subj: Birthdays. Indians of North America.

The moon's the north wind's cooky : *night poems* comp. and ill. by Susan Russo. Lothrop, 1979. Subj: Bedtime. Night. Poetry, rhyme.

Moorat, Joseph. *Thirty old-time nursery songs* (Mother Goose)

Moore, Clement C. *The night before Christmas* ill. by Tomie de Paola. Holiday, 1980. Subj: Holidays – Christmas. Poetry, rhyme.

The night before Christmas ill. by Michael Foreman. Viking, 1988. ISBN 0-670-82388-0 Subj: Holidays – Christmas. Poetry, rhyme.

The night before Christmas ill. by Gyo Fujikawa. Grosset, 1961. Subj: Holidays – Christmas. Poetry, rhyme.

The night before Christmas ill. by Scott Gustafson. Knopf, 1985. ISBN 0-394-54809-4 Subj: Holidays – Christmas. Poetry, rhyme.

The night before Christmas ill. by Cheryl Harness. Random House, 1990. ISBN 0-394-92698-6 Subj: Holidays – Christmas. Poetry, rhyme.

The night before Christmas ill. by Anita Lobel. Knopf, 1984. Subj: Holidays – Christmas. Poetry, rhyme.

The night before Christmas ill. by James Marshall. Scholastic, 1989. ISBN 0-590-33805-6 Subj: Holidays – Christmas. Poetry, rhyme.

The night before Christmas ill. by Jacqueline Rogers. Platt, 1988. ISBN 0-448-19097-4 Subj: Holidays – Christmas. Poetry, rhyme.

The night before Christmas ill. by Robin Spowart. Dodd, 1986. ISBN 0-396-08798-1 Subj: Holidays – Christmas. Poetry, rhyme.

The night before Christmas ill. by Gustaf Tenggren. Simon and Schuster, 1951. Subj: Holidays – Christmas. Poetry, rhyme.

The night before Christmas ill. by Tasha Tudor. Rand McNally, 1975. Subj: Holidays – Christmas. Poetry, rhyme.

The night before Christmas ill. by Wendy Watson. Houghton, 1990. ISBN 0-395-53624-3 Subj: Holidays – Christmas. Poetry, rhyme.

The night before Christmas ill. by Jody Wheeler. Ideals, 1988. ISBN 0-8249-8279-7 Subj: Holidays – Christmas. Poetry, rhyme.

A visit from St. Nicholas: 'Twas the night before Christmas ill. by Paul Galdone. McGraw-Hill, 1968. Subj: Holidays – Christmas. Poetry, rhyme.

Moore, Elaine. *Grandma's house* ill. by Elise Primavera. Lothrop, 1985. ISBN 0-688-04116-7 Subj: Animals. Country. Family life – grandmothers. Seasons – summer.

Grandma's promise ill. by Elise Primavera. Lothrop, 1988. ISBN 0-688-06741-7 Subj: Country. Family life – grandmothers. Seasons – winter.

Moore, Eva. *Dick Whittington and his cat* (Dick Whittington and his cat)

Moore, Inga. *Aktil's big swim* ill. by author. Oxford Univ. Pr., 1981. Subj: Animals – rats. Sports – swimming.

Fifty red night-caps ill. by Linda Moore. Chronicle, 1988. ISBN 0-87701-520-1 Subj: Animals – monkeys. Behavior – imitation. Behavior – stealing. Clothing – hats. Forest, woods.

Little dog lost ill. by author. Macmillan, 1991. ISBN 0-02-767648-X Subj: Animals – dogs. Behavior – running away. Country. Friendship. Moving.

Oh, little Jack ill. by author. Candlewick Pr., 1992. ISBN 1-56402-028-2 Subj: Animals – rabbits. Character traits – smallness. Family life.

Six dinner Sid ill. by author. Simon & Schuster, 1991. ISBN 0-671-73199-8 Subj: Animals – cats. Pets.

The sorcerer's apprentice ill. by author. Macmillan, 1989. ISBN 0-02-767645-5 Subj: Folk and fairy tales. Magic.

The truffle hunter ill. by author. Kane/Miller, 1987. ISBN 0-91629-09-X Subj: Animals – pigs. Behavior – seeking better things. Country. Foreign lands – France.

The vegetable thieves ill. by author. Viking, 1984. Subj: Animals – mice. Gardens, gardening. Orphans.

Moore, John. *Granny Stickleback* by John Moore and Martin Wright; ill. by authors. Hamish Hamilton, 1982. Subj: Animals. Crime. Sports – racing.

Moore, Lilian. *Hooray for me!* (Charlip, Remy)

I feel the same way ill. by Robert M. Quackenbush. Atheneum, 1967. Subj: Poetry, rhyme.

Little Raccoon and no trouble at all ill. by Gioia Fiammenghi. McGraw-Hill, 1972. Subj: Activities – baby-sitting. Animals – chipmunks. Animals – raccoons. Twins.

Little Raccoon and the outside world ill. by Gioia Fiammenghi. McGraw-Hill, 1965. Subj: Animals – raccoons.

Little Raccoon and the thing in the pool ill. by Gioia Fiammenghi. McGraw-Hill, 1963. Subj: Animals – raccoons. Emotions – fear.

Papa Albert ill. by Gioia Fiammenghi. Atheneum, 1964. Subj: Careers – taxi drivers. Family life. Foreign lands – France. Foreign languages. Taxis.

See my lovely poison ivy, and other verses about witches, ghosts and things ill. by Diane Dawson. Atheneum, 1975. Subj: Animals – cats. Monsters. Poetry, rhyme. Witches.

The ugly duckling (Andersen, H. C. (Hans Christian))

Moore, Miriam. *Peter and Susie find a family* (Hess, Edith)

Moore, Sheila. *Samson Svenson's baby* ill. by Karen Ann Weinhaus. Harper, 1983. Subj: Birds – ducks. Character traits – appearance. Character traits – kindness to animals.

Mooser, Stephen. *The fat cat* by Stephen Mooser and Lin Oliver; ill. by Susan Day. Warner, 1988. ISBN 1-55782-022-8 Subj: Animals – cats.

Funnyman and the penny dodo ill. by Tomie De Paola. Watts, 1984. ISBN 0-531-04393-2 Subj: Crime. Humor. Problem solving.

Funnyman meets the monster from outer space ill. by Maxie Chambliss. Scholastic, 1987. ISBN 0-590-33959-1 Subj: Monsters. Space and space ships.

Funnyman's first case ill. by Tomie de Paola. Watts, 1981. ISBN 0-531-04300-2 Subj: Careers – waiters, waitresses. Problem solving. Riddles.

The ghost with the Halloween hiccups ill. by Tomie de Paola. Watts, 1977. Subj: Ghosts. Holidays – Halloween.

Mora, Emma. *Animals of the forest* tr. from Italian by Jean Grasso Fitzpatrick; ill. by Kennedy. Barron's, 1986. ISBN 0-8120-5722-8 Subj: Animals. Forest, woods.

Gideon, the little bear cub tr. from Italian by Jean Grasso Fitzpatrick; ill. by Kennedy. Barron's, 1986. ISBN 0-8120-5728-7 Subj: Forest, woods. Poetry, rhyme. Seasons.

Mordvinoff, Nicolas. *Billy the kid* (Lipkind, William)

The boy and the forest (Lipkind, William)

Chaga (Lipkind, William)

The Christmas bunny (Lipkind, William)

Circus rucus (Lipkind, William)

Coral Island ill. by author. Doubleday, 1957. Subj: Behavior – growing up. Foreign lands – South Sea Islands. Islands.

Even Steven (Lipkind, William)

Finders keepers (Lipkind, William)

Four-leaf clover (Lipkind, William)

The little tiny rooster (Lipkind, William)

The magic feather duster (Lipkind, William)

Russet and the two reds (Lipkind, William)

Sleepyhead (Lipkind, William)

The two reds (Lipkind, William)

Morel, Eve. *Fairy tales* ill. by Gyo Fujikawa. Grosset, 1980. Subj: Folk and fairy tales.

Fairy tales and fables ill. by Gyo Fujikawa. Grosset, 1970. Subj: Folk and fairy tales.

Moremen, Grace E. *No, no, Natalie* photos. by Geoffrey P. Fulton. Children's Pr., 1973. Subj: Animals – rabbits. Behavior – misbehavior. School.

Morgan, Allen. *Matthew and the midnight money van* ill. by Michael Martchenko. Firefly Pr., 1987. ISBN 0-920303-75-7 Subj: Behavior – losing things. Holidays – Mother's Day.

Molly and Mr. Maloney ill. by Maryann Kovalski. Kids Can Pr., 1982. Subj: Animals – raccoons. Behavior – misbehavior. Pets.

Nicole's boat ill. by Jirina Marton. Firefly Pr., 1986. ISBN 0-920303-60-9 Subj: Bedtime. Boats, ships. Dreams. Family life – fathers. Sea and seashore.

Morgan, Michaela. *Dinostory* ill. by Prue Kelley. Dutton, 1991. ISBN 0-525-44726-1 Subj: Dinosaurs.

Edward gets a pet ill. by Sue Porter. Dutton, 1987. ISBN 0-525-44349-5 Subj: Animals. Imagination. Pets.

Visitors for Edward ill. by Sue Porter. Dutton, 1988. ISBN 0-525-44354-1 Subj: Family life – grandparents. Imagination.

Morgenstern, Aliyah. *The wedding of Brown Bear and White Bear* (Beck, Martine)

Morgenstern, Constance. *Good night, feet* ill. by Cat Bowman Smith. Holt, 1991. ISBN 0-8050-1453-5 Subj: Anatomy – feet. Bedtime. Poetry, rhyme.

Morgenstern, Elizabeth. *The little gardeners* tr. from German by Elizabeth Morgenstern; retold by Louise F. Encking; ill. by Marigard Bantzer. Albert Whitman, 1933. Subj: Foreign lands – Germany. Gardens, gardening.

Morice, Dave. *Dot town* ill. by author. Toothpaste Pr., 1982. Subj: Poetry, rhyme.

The happy birthday handbook ill. by author. Coffee House Pr., 1982. Subj: Birthdays.

A visit from St. Alphabet ill. by author. Coffee House Pr., 1980. Subj: ABC books. Poetry, rhyme.

Morimoto, Junko. *The inch boy* ill. by author. Viking, 1986. ISBN 0-670-80955-1 Subj: Elves and little people. Family life. Folk and fairy tales.

Mouse's marriage ill. by author. Viking, 1986. ISBN 0-670-81071-1 Subj: Animals – mice. Folk and fairy tales.

My Hiroshima ill. by author. Viking, 1990. ISBN 0-670-83181-6 Subj: War.

Moroney, Lynn. *Baby rattlesnake* (Ata, Te)

Morozumi, Atsuko. *One gorilla* ill. by author. Farrar, 1990. ISBN 0-374-35644-0 Subj: Animals. Animals – gorillas. Counting, numbers.

Morpurgo, Michael. *Jo-Jo the melon donkey* ill. by Chris Molan. Prentice-Hall, 1988. ISBN 0-13-510009-7 Subj: Animals – donkeys. Foreign lands – Italy. Weather – floods.

Morris, Ann. *Bread, bread, bread* photos. by Ken Heyman. Lothrop, 1989. ISBN 0-688-06335-7 Subj: Food.

Cuddle up ill. by Maureen Roffey. Harper, 1986. ISBN 0-694-00072-8 Subj: Bedtime. Family life – mothers. Night.

Eleanora Mousie catches a cold ill. by Ruth Young. Macmillan, 1987. ISBN 0-02-767500-9 Subj: Animals – mice. Illness.

Eleanora Mousie in the dark ill. by Ruth Young. Macmillan, 1987. ISBN 0-02-767530-0 Subj: Animals – mice. Monsters. Night.

Eleanora Mousie makes a mess ill. by Ruth Young. Macmillan, 1987. ISBN 0-02-767520-3 Subj: Animals – mice. Character traits – cleanliness.

Eleanora Mousie's gray day ill. by Ruth Young. Macmillan, 1987. ISBN 0-02-767510-6 Subj: Animals – mice. Behavior – bad day. Friendship.

Hats, hats, hats photos by Ken Heyman. Lothrop, 1989. ISBN 0-688-06339-X Subj: Clothing – hats.

Kiss time ill. by Maureen Roffey. Harper, 1986. ISBN 0-694-00073-6 Subj: Bedtime. Night.

The Little Red Riding Hood rebus book ill. by Ljiljana Rylands. Orchard, 1987. ISBN 0-531-08330-6 Subj: Animals – wolves. Behavior – talking to strangers. Folk and fairy tales. Rebuses.

Loving photos. by Ken Heyman. Lothrop, 1990. ISBN 0-688-06341-1 Subj: Emotions – love. Family life. Foreign lands.

Night counting ill. by Maureen Roffey. Harper, 1986. ISBN 0-694-00074-4 Subj: Bedtime. Counting, numbers. Night.

On the go photos. by Ken Heyman. Lothrop, 1990. ISBN 0-688-06337-3 Subj: Foreign lands. Transportation.

Sleepy, sleepy ill. by Maureen Roffey. Harper, 1986. ISBN 0-694-00075-2 Subj: Bedtime. Night.

Morris, Christopher G. *The magic world of words* (Halsey, William D.)

Morris, Jill. *The boy who painted the sun* ill. by Geoff Hocking. Viking, 1984. Subj: Activities – painting. Behavior – solitude. City. Moving.

Monkey creates havoc in heaven (Pen Cai Ying)

Morris, Linda Lowe. *Morning milking* ill. by David DeRan. Picture Book Studio, 1991. ISBN 0-88708-173-8 Subj: Animals. Animals – bulls, cows. Farms.

Morris, Neil. *Find the canary* by Neil Morris and Ting; ill. by Anna Clarke. Little, 1983. Subj: Games.

Hide and seek by Neil Morris and Ting; ill. by Anna Clarke. Little, 1983. Subj: Games.

Search for Sam by Neil Morris and Ting; ill. by Anna Clarke. Little, 1983. Subj: Games.

Where's my hat? by Neil Morris and Ting; ill. by Anna Clarke. Little, 1983. Subj: Clothing – hats. Games.

Morris, Terry Nell. *Good night, dear monster!* ill. by author. Knopf, 1980. Subj: Bedtime. Imagination – imaginary friends. Monsters.

Lucky puppy! Lucky boy! ill. by author. Knopf, 1980. Subj: Animals – dogs. Behavior – needing someone.

Morris, Winifred. *The future of Yen-Tzu* ill. by Friso Henstra. Atheneum, 1992. ISBN 0-689-31501-5 Subj: Folk and fairy tales. Foreign lands – China. Royalty – emperors.

Just listen ill. by Patricia Cullen-Clark. Atheneum, 1990. ISBN 0-689-31588-0 Subj: Family life – grandmothers. Noise, sounds. Senses – hearing.

The magic leaf ill. by Ju-Hong Chen. Atheneum, 1987. ISBN 0-689-31358-6 Subj: Folk and fairy tales. Foreign lands – China.

What if the shark wears tennis shoes? ill. by Betsy Lewin. Atheneum, 1990. ISBN 0-689-31587-2 Subj: Bedtime. Emotions – fear. Imagination.

Morrison, Bill. *Louis James hates school* ill. by author. Houghton, 1978. Subj: Careers. School.

Squeeze a sneeze ill. by author. Houghton, 1977. Subj: Poetry, rhyme.

Morrison, Sean. *Is that a happy hippopotamus?* ill. by Aliki. Crowell, 1966. Subj: Animals. Humor. Noise, sounds. Poetry, rhyme.

Morrow, Barbara. *Edward's portrait* ill. by author. Macmillan, 1991. ISBN 0-02-767591-2 Subj: Activities – photographing. Family life. U.S. history.

Morrow, Elizabeth Cutter. *The painted pig* ill. by René D'Harnoncourt. Knopf, 1930. Subj: Foreign lands – Mexico.

Morrow, Suzanne Stark. *Inatuck's friend* ill. by Ellen Raskin. Little, 1968. Subj: Eskimos. Friendship.

Morse, Samuel French. *All in a suitcase* ill. by Barbara Cooney. Little, 1966. Subj: ABC books. Animals.

Sea sums ill. by Fuku Akino. Little, 1970. Subj: Counting, numbers. Poetry, rhyme. Sea and seashore. Weather – fog.

Mosel, Arlene. *The funny little woman* ill. by Blair Lent. Dutton, 1972. Based on The old woman and her dumpling by Lafcadio Hearn Subj: Caldecott award book. Foreign lands – Japan. Monsters.

Tikki Tikki Tembo ill. by Blair Lent. Holt, 1968. Subj: Folk and fairy tales. Foreign lands – China. Names.

Moseley, Keith. *Big creatures from the past* (Watson, Claire)

Dinosaurs: a lost world ill. by Robert Cremins. Putnam's, 1984. ISBN 0-399-21063-6 Subj: Dinosaurs. Format, unusual – toy and movable books. Science.

Prehistoric mammals (Berger, Melvin)

Moser, Erwin. *The crow in the snow and other bedtime stories* tr. from German by Joel Agee; ill. by author. Adama, 1986. ISBN 0-915361-49-3 Subj: Animals. Imagination.

Wilma the elephant ill. by author. Adama, 1986. ISBN 0-915361-45-0 Subj: Animals – elephants. Behavior – lost. Behavior – needing someone.

Mosimann, Odie. *How the mouse was hit on the head by a stone and so discovered the world* (Delessert, Etienne)

Moskin, Marietta D. *Lysbet and the fire kittens* ill. by Margot Tomes. Coward, 1973. Subj: Animals – cats. Behavior – carelessness. Fire. U.S. history.

Moskof, Martin Stephen. *Still another alphabet book* (Chwast, Seymour)

Still another children's book (Chwast, Seymour)

Still another number book (Chwast, Seymour)

Moskowitz, Addie Alexander. *Wish upon a star* (Laskin, Pamela L.)

Mosley, Francis. *The dinosaur eggs* ill. by author. Barron's, 1988. ISBN 0-8120-5910-7 Subj: Dinosaurs. Family life.

Moss, Elaine. *Polar* ill. by Jeannie Baker. Elsevier-Dutton, 1979. Subj: Activities – playing. Illness. Safety. Toys – teddy bears.

Moss, Jeffrey. *The Sesame Street ABC storybook* featuring Jim Henson's Muppets; by Jeffrey Moss, Norman Stiles and Daniel Wilcox; ill. by Peter Cross and others. Random House, 1974. Subj: ABC books. Puppets.

The songs of Sesame Street in poems and pictures by Jeffrey Moss and others; ill. by Normand Chartier. Random House, 1983. Subj: Poetry, rhyme. Puppets. Songs.

Moss, Marissa. *After-school monster* ill. by author. Lothrop, 1991. ISBN 0-688-10117-8 Subj: Character traits – assertiveness. Character traits – bravery. Emotions – fear. Ethnic groups in the U.S. Monsters.

But not Kate ill. by author. Lothrop, 1992. ISBN 0-688-10601-3 Subj: Animals – mice. Character traits – individuality. Magic. School. Self-concept.

Knick knack paddywack ill. by author. Houghton, 1992. ISBN 0-395-54701-6 Subj: Activities – making things. Animals – dogs. Counting, numbers. Cumulative tales. Songs. Space and space ships.

Regina's big mistake ill. by author. Houghton, 1990. ISBN 0-395-55330-X Subj: Activities – drawing. Careers – artists. School. Self-concept.

Want to play? ill. by author. Houghton, 1990. ISBN 0-395-52022-3 Subj: Activities – playing. Sibling rivalry. Toys.

Who was it? ill. by author. Houghton, 1989. ISBN 0-395-49699-3 Subj: Behavior – misbehavior. Character traits – honesty. Family life – mothers.

Most, Bernard. *The cow that went oink* ill. by author. Harcourt, 1990. ISBN 0-15-220195-5 Subj: Animals. Noise, sounds.

Dinosaur cousins? ill. by author. Harcourt, 1990. ISBN 0-15-223498-5 Subj: Animals. Dinosaurs.

A dinosaur named after me ill. by author. Harcourt, 1991. ISBN 0-15-223494-2 Subj: Dinosaurs. Names.

Happy holidaysaurus! ill. by author. Harcourt, 1992. ISBN 0-15-233386-X Subj: Dinosaurs. Holidays.

If the dinosaurs came back ill. by author. Harcourt, 1978. Subj: Dinosaurs. Imagination.

The littlest dinosaurs ill. by author. Harcourt, 1989. ISBN 0-15-248125-7 Subj: Dinosaurs.

My very own octopus ill. by author. Harcourt, 1980. Subj: Octopuses. Pets.

Pets in trumpets and other word-play riddles ill. by author. Harcourt, 1991. ISBN 0-15-261210-6 Subj: Language. Pets. Riddles.

There's an ant in Anthony ill. by author. Morrow, 1980. Subj: Activities – reading.

There's an ape behind the drape ill. by author. Morrow, 1981. ISBN 0-688-00381-8 Subj: Animals – gorillas. Games. Language.

Whatever happened to the dinosaurs? ill. by author. Harcourt, 1984. ISBN 0-15-295295-0 Subj: Dinosaurs.

Zoodles ill. by author. Harcourt, 1992. ISBN 0-15-299969-8 Subj: Animals. Birds. Riddles.

Mostel, Zero. *The Sesame Street book of opposites with Zero Mostel* (Mendoza, George)

Mother Goose. *ABC rhymes* ill. by Lulu Delarce. Simon & Schuster, 1984. ISBN 0-671-49685-9 Subj: ABC books. Format, unusual – board books. Nursery rhymes.

Animals from Mother Goose (Hopkins, Lee Bennett)

The annotated Mother Goose: nursery rhymes old and new arranged and explained by William S. and Ceil Baring-Gould; chapter decorations by E. M. Simon; ill. by Walter Crane and others. Potter, 1962. Subj: Nursery rhymes.

As I was going up and down: and other nonsense rhymes ill. by Nicola Bayley. Lothrop, 1986. ISBN 0-02-708590-2 Subj: Nursery rhymes.

The authentic Mother Goose fairy tales and nursery rhymes (Barchilon, Jacques)

Baa, baa, black sheep ill. by Moira Kemp. Dutton, 1991. ISBN 0-525-67331-8 Subj: Format, unusual – board books. Nursery rhymes.

Baa baa black sheep ill. by Sue Porter. Peter Bedrick Books (dist. by Harper), 1984. Subj: Format, unusual – board books. Nursery rhymes.

Baa baa black sheep ill. by Ferelith Eccles Williams. David & Charles, 1985. ISBN 0-437-86003-5 Subj: Format, unusual – board books. Nursery rhymes.

The baby's lap book ill. by Kay Chorao. Dutton, 1977. Subj: Nursery rhymes.

Blessed Mother Goose: favorite nursery rhymes for today's children ill. by Kaye Luke. House-Warven, 1951. Subj: Nursery rhymes.

Brian Wildsmith's Mother Goose ill. by Brian Wildsmith. Watts, 1964. Subj: Nursery rhymes.

Carolyn Wells' edition of Mother Goose ill. by Margeria Cooper and others. Doubleday, 1946. Subj: Nursery rhymes.

Cats by Mother Goose sel. by Barbara Lucas; ill. by Carol Newsom. Lothrop, 1986. ISBN 0-688-04635-5 Subj: Animals – cats. Nursery rhymes.

The Charles Addams Mother Goose ill. by Charles Addams. Harper, 1967. Subj: Nursery rhymes.

A child's book of old nursery rhymes ill. by Joan Walsh Anglund. Atheneum, 1973. Subj: Nursery rhymes.

The Chinese Mother Goose rhymes sel. and ed. by Robert Wyndham; ill. by Ed Young. Putnam's, 1982. Orig. pub. by World, 1968 Subj: Nursery rhymes.

The city and country Mother Goose ill. by Hilda Hoffmann. American Heritage, 1969. Subj: Nursery rhymes.

The comic adventures of Old Mother Hubbard and her dog (Martin, Sarah Catherine)

Frank Baber's Mother Goose Sel. by Ruth Spriggs; ill. by Frank Baber. Crown, 1976. Subj: Nursery rhymes.

The gay Mother Goose ill. by Françoise Seignobosc. Scribner's, 1938. Subj: Nursery rhymes.

The glorious Mother Goose sel. by Cooper Edens. Atheneum, 1988. ISBN 0-689-31434-5 Subj: Nursery rhymes.

The golden goose book ill. by L. Leslie Brooke. Warne, 1977, 1905. ISBN 0-7232-1979-6 Subj: Birds – geese. Folk and fairy tales. Humor. Royalty.

Grafa' Grig had a pig, and other rhymes without reason from Mother Goose ill. by Wallace Tripp. Little, 1976. Subj: Nursery rhymes.

Gray goose and gander and other Mother Goose rhymes ill. by Anne F. Rockwell. Crowell, 1980. Subj: Nursery rhymes.

Gregory Griggs and other nursery rhyme people sel. and ill. by Arnold Lobel. Greenwillow, 1978. Subj: Nursery rhymes.

Here's a ball for baby (Williams, Jenny)

Hey diddle diddle adapt. and ill. by Marilyn Janovitz. Walt Disney, 1992. ISBN 1-56282-169-5 Subj: Animals. Music. Nursery rhymes.

Hey diddle diddle ill. by Moira Kemp. Dutton, 1991. ISBN 0-525-67329-6 Subj: Format, unusual – board books. Nursery rhymes.

Hey diddle diddle ill. by Nita Sowter. Peter Bedrick Books (dist. by Harper), 1984. Subj: Format, unusual – board books. Nursery rhymes.

Hey diddle diddle ill. by Eleanor Wasmuth. Simon & Schuster, 1986. ISBN 0-671-61726-5 Subj: Format, unusual – board books. Nursery rhymes.

Hey diddle diddle, and Baby bunting ill. by Randolph Caldecott. Warne, 1882. Subj: Nursery rhymes.

Hey diddle diddle picture book ill. by Randolph Caldecott. Warne, 1883. Subj: Nursery rhymes.

Hickory dickory dock ill. by Moira Kemp. Dutton, 1991. ISBN 0-525-67328-8 Subj: Format, unusual – board books. Nursery rhymes.

Hickory dickory dock and other nursery rhymes ill. by Carol Jones. Houghton, 1992. ISBN 0-395-60834-1 Subj: Format, unusual. Nursery rhymes.

Humpty Dumpty ill. by Colin and Jacqui Hawkins. Candlewick Pr., 1992. ISBN 1-56402-015-0 Subj: Format, unusual – board books. Nursery rhymes.

Hurrah, we're outward bound! ill. by Peter Spier. Doubleday, 1968. Subj: Nursery rhymes.

Hush-a-bye baby: and other bedtime rhymes ill. by Nicola Bayley. Lothrop, 1986. ISBN 0-02-708610-0 Subj: Bedtime. Nursery rhymes.

In a pumpkin shell ill. by Joan Walsh Anglund. Harcourt, 1960. Subj: ABC books. Nursery rhymes.

Jack and Jill ill. by Eleanor Wasmuth. Simon & Schuster, 1986. ISBN 0-671-61729-X Subj: Format, unusual – board books. Nursery rhymes.

Jack Kent's merry Mother Goose ill. by Jack Kent. Golden Pr., 1977. Subj: Nursery rhymes.

James Marshall's Mother Goose ill. by James Marshall. Farrar, 1979. Subj: Nursery rhymes.

Kate Greenaway's Mother Goose ill. by Kate Greenaway. Dial Pr., 1988. ISBN 0-8037-0479-8 Subj: Format, unusual – board books. Nursery rhymes.

Kitten rhymes ill. by Lulu Delarce. Simon & Schuster, 1984. ISBN 0-671-49687-5 Subj: Animals – cats. Format, unusual – board books. Nursery rhymes.

The Larousse book of nursery rhymes ed. by Robert Owen; ill. with photos. Larousse, 1984. Ill. are full color photos. of tile pictures, painted during the late 19th and early 20th cents., created by the Royal Doulton Co., designed by Margaret Thompson, William Rowe and John H. McLennan Subj: Nursery rhymes.

Lavender's blue: a book of nursery rhymes comp. by Kathleen Lines; ill. by Harold Jones. Oxford Univ. Pr., 1982. Subj: Nursery rhymes.

Little boy blue ill. by Nita Sowter. Peter Bedrick Books (dist. by Harper), 1984. Subj: Format, unusual – board books. Nursery rhymes.

The little Mother Goose ill. by Jessie Willcox Smith. Dodd, 1918. Subj: Nursery rhymes.

London Bridge is falling down ill. by Ed Emberley. Little, 1967. Subj: Folk and fairy tales. Foreign lands – England. Games. Nursery rhymes. Songs.

London Bridge is falling down ill. by Peter Spier. Doubleday, 1967. Subj: Folk and fairy tales. Foreign lands – England. Games. Nursery rhymes. Songs.

The Margaret Tarrant nursery rhyme book (Tarrant, Margaret)

Michael Foreman's Mother Goose ill. by Michael Foreman. Harcourt, 1991. ISBN 0-15-255820-9 Subj: Nursery rhymes.

Mother Goose: a comprehensive collection of the rhymes comp. by William Rose Benét; ill. by Roger Antoine Duvoisin. Heritage Pr., 1943. Subj: Nursery rhymes.

Mother Goose sel. by Phyllis Maurine Fraser; ill. by Miss Elliott. Simon and Schuster, 1942. Subj: Nursery rhymes.

Mother Goose ill. by C. B. Falls. Doubleday, 1924. Subj: Nursery rhymes.

Mother Goose ill. by Gyo Fujikawa. Grosset, 1967. Subj: Nursery rhymes.

Mother Goose as told by Kellogg's singing lady ill. by Vernon Grant. Kellogg Co., 1933. Subj: Nursery rhymes.

Mother Goose: or, the old nursery rhymes sel. by Phyllis Maurine Fraser; ill. by Kate Greenaway. Routledge, 1881. Illustrated as originally engraved and printed by Edmund Evans Subj: Nursery rhymes.

Mother Goose: a collection of classic nursery rhymes sel. and ill. by Michael Hague. Holt, 1984. Subj: Nursery rhymes.

Mother Goose: sixty-seven favorite rhymes ill. by Violet La Mont. Simon and Schuster, 1957. Subj: Nursery rhymes.

Mother Goose: the old nursery rhymes ill. by Arthur Rackham. Century, 1913. Subj: Nursery rhymes.

Mother Goose arranged and ed. by Eulalie Osgood Grover; ill. by Frederick Richardson The Volland ed. Volland, 1915. Subj: Nursery rhymes.

Mother Goose re-arranged and edited in this form by Eulalie Osgood Grover; ill. by Frederick Richardson The classic Volland ed. Rand McNally, 1976. Reprint of the 1971 ed. published by Hubbard Press, Northbrook, Ill Subj: Nursery rhymes.

Mother Goose ill. by Gustaf Tenggren. Little, 1940. Subj: Nursery rhymes.

Mother Goose: seventy-seven verses ill. by Tasha Tudor. Walck, 1944. Subj: Caldecott award honor book. Nursery rhymes.

Mother Goose abroad (Tucker, Nicholas)

Mother Goose and nursery rhymes ill. by Philip Reed. Atheneum, 1963. Subj: Caldecott award honor book. Nursery rhymes.

A Mother Goose book ill. by Joan Walsh Anglund. Harcourt, 1991. ISBN 0-15-200529-3 Subj: Nursery rhymes.

The Mother Goose book ill. by Alice and Martin Provensen. Random House, 1976. Subj: Nursery rhymes.

The Mother Goose book gathered from many sources; ill. by Sonia Roetter. Peter Pauper Pr., 1946. Subj: Nursery rhymes.

Mother Goose house ill. by Zokeisha; ed. by Kate Klimo. Simon and Schuster, 1983. Subj: Format, unusual – board books. Houses. Nursery rhymes.

Mother Goose in French: Poesies de la vraie Mere Oie tr. by Hugh Latham; ill. by Barbara Cooney. Crowell, 1964. Subj: Foreign languages. Nursery rhymes.

Mother Goose in hieroglyphics ill. by George S. Appleton. Houghton, 1962. Reproduction of the 1st ed. published in 1849 Subj: Games. Hieroglyphics. Nursery rhymes. Rebuses.

Mother Goose in prose (Baum, L. Frank (Lyman Frank))

Mother Goose in Spanish: Poesias de la Madre Oca tr. by Alastair Reid and Anthony Kerrigan; ill. by Barbara Cooney. Crowell, 1968. Subj: Foreign languages. Nursery rhymes.

Mother Goose melodies intro. and bib. note by E. F. Bleiler; ill. with engravings Facsimile ed. of the Munroe and Francis c.1833 version. Dover, 1970. Subj: Nursery rhymes.

Mother Goose nursery rhymes ill. by Arthur Rackham. Viking, 1975. Subj: Nursery rhymes.

Mother Goose nursery rhymes ill. by Arthur Rackham. Watts, 1969. Reprint of the 1913 ed Subj: Nursery rhymes.

Mother Goose rhymes ed. by Watty Piper; ill. by Eulalie M. Banks and Lois Lenski. Platt, 1947, 1956. Subj: Nursery rhymes.

The Mother Goose songbook ill. by Jacqueline Sinclair. David & Charles, 1985. ISBN 0-434-92841-0 Subj: Music. Nursery rhymes. Songs.

The Mother Goose treasury ill. by Raymond Briggs. Coward, 1966. Subj: Nursery rhymes.

Mother Goose's melodies: or, songs for the nursery ed. by William A. Wheeler. Houghton, 189? Subj: Nursery rhymes. Songs.

Mother Goose's melody: or, sonnets for the cradle Facsimile of John Newbery's collection of Mother Goose rhymes, reproduced from the earliest known perfect copy of the 1794 printing. Frederic G. Melcher, 1945. Subj: Nursery rhymes.

Mother Goose's nursery rhymes ill. by Allen Atkinson. Knopf, 1984. ISBN 0-394-53699-1 Subj: Nursery rhymes.

Mother Goose's rhymes and melodies ill. by J. L. Webb; music and melodies by E. I. Lane. Cassell, 1888. Subj: Music. Nursery rhymes.

Nursery rhyme book ed. by Andrew Lang; ill. by L. Leslie Brooke. Warne, 1897. Subj: Nursery rhymes.

Nursery rhymes sel. by Marie; ill. by Douglas Gorsline. Random House, 1977. Subj: Nursery rhymes.

Nursery rhymes ill. by Eloise Wilkin. Random House, 1979. Subj: Nursery rhymes.

Nursery rhymes from Mother Goose in signed English Prepared under the supervision of the staff of the Pre-School Signed English Project: Barbara M. Kanapell and others. Gallaudet College Pr., 1972. Subj: Handicaps – deafness. Nursery rhymes.

Old Mother Hubbard and her dog (Martin, Sarah Catherine)

The old woman in a shoe ill. by Eleanor Wasmuth. Simon & Schuster, 1986. ISBN 0-671-61728-1 Subj: Format, unusual – board books. Nursery rhymes.

One I love, two I love, and other loving Mother Goose rhymes ill. by Nonny Hogrogian. Dutton, 1972. Subj: Nursery rhymes.

One misty moisty morning: rhymes from Mother Goose ill. by Mitchell Miller. Farrar, 1971. Subj: Nursery rhymes.

One, two, buckle my shoe (Williams, Jenny)

The only true Mother Goose melodies intro. by Edward Everett Hale. Lothrop, 1905. An exact and full-size reproduction of the original edition published and copyrighted in Boston in the year 1833 by Munroe and Francis Subj: Nursery rhymes.

Over the moon: a book of nursery rhymes ill. by Charlotte Voake. Crown, 1985. ISBN 0-517-55873-4 Subj: Nursery rhymes.

Pat-a-cake adapt. and ill. by Marilyn Janovitz. Walt Disney, 1992. ISBN 1-56282-171-7 Subj: Animals. Birthdays. Music. Nursery rhymes.

People from Mother Goose (Hopkins, Lee Bennett)

The piper's son ill. by Emily N. Barto. Longmans, 1942. Subj: Nursery rhymes.

A pocket full of posies ill. by Marguerite De Angeli. Doubleday, 1961. First pub. in 1954 Subj: Nursery rhymes.

Pussy cat, pussy cat ill. by Ferelith Eccles Williams. David & Charles, 1985. ISBN 0-437-86009-4 Subj: Format, unusual – board books. Nursery rhymes.

Pussycat ate the dumplings (Koontz, Robin Michal)

The rainbow Mother Goose ed. with an intro. by May Lamberton Becker; ill. by Lili Cassel-Wronker. Collins-World, 1947. Subj: Nursery rhymes.

The real Mother Goose ill. by Blanche Fisher Wright. Rand McNally, 1916. Subj: Nursery rhymes.

The real Mother Goose clock book ill. by Jane Chambless. Rand McNally, 1984. ISBN 0-528-82329-9 Subj: Clocks, watches. Nursery rhymes. Time.

Richard Scarry's best Mother Goose ever ill. by Richard Scarry. Golden Pr., 1964. Subj: Nursery rhymes.

Richard Scarry's favorite Mother Goose rhymes ill. by Richard Scarry. Golden Pr., 1976. Subj: Nursery rhymes.

Ride a cock-horse (Williams, Sarah)

Ride a cockhorse (Williams, Jenny)

Rimes de la Mere Oie: Mother Goose rhymes rendered into French by Ormonde De Kay, Jr.; ill. by Seymour Chwast, Milton Glaser, and Barry Zaid. Little, 1971. Subj: Foreign languages. Nursery rhymes.

Ring around a rosy (Williams, Jenny)

Ring o' roses ill. by L. Leslie Brooke. Warne, 1923. Subj: Nursery rhymes.

The Sesame Street players present Mother Goose: featuring Jim Henson's Sesame Street Muppets ill. by Michael Smollin Q. Random House-Children's Television Workshop, 1982. Subj: Nursery rhymes. Puppets.

Sing a song of Mother Goose ill. by Barbara Reid. North Winds Pr., 1987. ISBN 0-590-71781-2 Subj: Nursery rhymes.

Sing a song of sixpence ill. by Randolph Caldecott New ed. Hart, 1977. Reprint of orig. Warne pub. between 1876 and 1886 Subj: Nursery rhymes.

Sing a song of sixpence comp. and ill. by Randolph Caldecott. Barron's, 1988. Reprint of 1888 ed ISBN 0-8120-5900-X Subj: Nursery rhymes.

Sing a song of sixpence ill. by Margaret Chamberlain. Peter Bedrick Books (dist. by Harper), 1984. Subj: Format, unusual – board books. Nursery rhymes.

Sing a song of sixpence ill. by Leonard B. Lubin. Lothrop, 1987. ISBN 0-688-00545-4 Subj: Nursery rhymes. Royalty.

Sing a song of sixpence ed. by Kate Klimo; ill. by Ray Marshall and Korky Paul. Simon & Schuster, 1983. ISBN 0-671-46237-7 Subj: Format, unusual – toy and movable books. Nursery rhymes.

Sing a song of sixpence ill. by Ferelith Eccles Williams. David & Charles, 1985. ISBN 0-437-86002-7 Subj: Format, unusual – board books. Nursery rhymes.

Sing hey diddle diddle: 66 nursery rhymes with their traditional tunes comp. by Beatrice Harrop; ill. by Frank Francis and Bernard Cheese. Sterling, 1983. Subj: Music. Nursery rhymes.

Songs for Mother Goose ill. by Maginel Wright Enright Barney; set to music by Sidney Homer. Macmillan, 1920. Subj: Nursery rhymes.

The tall Mother Goose ill. by Feodor Rojankovsky. Harper, 1942. Subj: Nursery rhymes.

Thirty old-time nursery songs ed. by Joseph Moorat; ill. by Paul Woodroffe. Norton, 1980. Orig. pub. in 1912 Subj: Music. Nursery rhymes. Songs.

This little pig: a Mother Goose favorite ill. by Leonard B. Lubin. Lothrop, 1985. ISBN 0-688-04089-6 Subj: Animals – pigs. Nursery rhymes.

This little pig ill. by Eleanor Wasmuth. Simon & Schuster, 1986. ISBN 0-671-61727-3 Subj: Format, unusual – board books. Nursery rhymes.

This little pig went to market ill. by L. Leslie Brooke. Warne, 1922. Subj: Animals – pigs. Nursery rhymes.

This little pig went to market ill. by Ferelith Eccles Williams. David & Charles, 1985. ISBN 0-437-86004-3 Subj: Format, unusual – board books. Games. Nursery rhymes.

This little piggy ill. by Moira Kemp. Dutton, 1991. ISBN 0-525-67326-1 Subj: Format, unusual – board books. Nursery rhymes.

The three jovial huntsmen ill. by Susan Jeffers. Bradbury Pr., 1973. Subj: Caldecott award honor book. Nursery rhymes.

The three little kittens ill. by Lorinda Bryan Cauley. Putnam's, 1982. Subj: Animals – cats. Behavior – losing things. Games. Nursery rhymes.

The three little kittens ill. by Paul Galdone. Clarion, 1986. ISBN 0-89919-426-5 Subj: Animals – cats. Behavior – losing things. Nursery rhymes.

The three little kittens ill. by Dorothy Stott. Putnam's, 1984. ISBN 0-448-10216-1 Subj: Animals – cats. Behavior – losing things. Format, unusual – board books. Nursery rhymes.

The three little kittens adapt. by Jean Marzollo; ill. by Shelley Thornton. Scholastic, 1986. ISBN 0-590-33370-4 Subj: Animals – cats. Behavior – losing things. Games. Nursery rhymes.

To market! To market! ill. by Emma Lillian Brock. Knopf, 1930. Subj: Nursery rhymes. Shopping.

To market! To market! ill. by Peter Spier. Doubleday, 1967. Subj: Nursery rhymes.

Tom, Tom the piper's son ill. by Paul Galdone. McGraw-Hill, 1964. Subj: Nursery rhymes.

Tomie de Paola's Mother Goose (De Paola, Tomie (Thomas Anthony))

Twenty nursery rhymes ill. by Philip Van Aver. Grabhorn-Hoyem, 1970. Subj: Nursery rhymes.

Wendy Watson's Mother Goose ill. by Wendy Watson. Lothrop, 1989. ISBN 0-688-05708-X Subj: Nursery rhymes.

Willy Pogany's Mother Goose ill. by Willy Pogany. Nelson, 1928. Subj: Nursery rhymes.

Motomora, Mitchell. *Specs: the true story of baseball player George Toporcer* ill. by Nina Barbaresi. Raintree, 1990. ISBN 0-8172-3585-X Subj: Glasses. Sports – baseball.

Motyka, Sally Mitchell. *An ordinary day* ill. by Donna Ayers. Simon & Schuster, 1989. ISBN 0-67167118-9 Subj: Activities. Family life.

Mouse house ed. by Kate Klimo; ill. by Zokeisha. Simon and Schuster, 1983. Subj: Animals – mice. Format, unusual – board books. Houses.

The moving adventures of Old Dame Trot and her comical cat ill. by Paul Galdone. McGraw-Hill, 1973. Subj: Animals – cats. Nursery rhymes.

Mower, Nancy. *I visit my Tūtū and Grandma* ill. by Patricia A. Wozniak. Press Pacifica, 1984. ISBN 0-9166390-41-2 Subj: Family life – grandmothers. Hawaii.

Moxley, Susan. *Abdul's treasure* ill. by author. David & Charles, 1988. ISBN 0-340-38918-4 Subj: Careers – fishermen. Folk and fairy tales. Royalty.

Mozley, Charles. *Arabian Nights entertainments* (Arabian Nights)

Mude, O. *see* Gorey, Edward (St. John)

Mueller, Evelyn. *I'm deaf and it's okay* (Aseltine, Lorraine)

Mueller, Virginia. *A Halloween mask for Monster* ill. by Lynn Munsinger. Albert Whitman, 1986. ISBN 0-8075-3134-0 Subj: Holidays – Halloween. Monsters.

Monster and the baby ill. by Lynn Munsinger. Albert Whitman, 1985. ISBN 0-8075-5253-4 Subj: Activities – baby-sitting. Babies. Monsters.

Monster can't sleep ill. by Lynn Munsinger. Albert Whitman, 1986. ISBN 0-8075-5261-5 Subj: Bedtime. Monsters. Sleep.

Monster goes to school ill. by Lynn Munsinger. Albert Whitman, 1991. ISBN 0-8075-5264-X Subj: Clocks, watches. Monsters. School. Time.

Monster's birthday hiccups ill. by Lynn Munsinger. Albert Whitman, 1991. ISBN 0-8075-5267-4 Subj: Birthdays. Illness. Monsters. Parties.

A playhouse for Monster ill. by Lynn Munsinger. Albert Whitman, 1985. ISBN 0-8075-6541-5 Subj: Activities – playing. Monsters.

Muller, Gerda. *The garden in the city* ill. by author. Dutton, 1992. ISBN 0-525-44697-4 Subj: City. Gardens, gardening.

Muller, Robin. *The lucky old woman* Kids Can Pr., 1987. ISBN 0-921103-07-7 Subj: Folk and fairy tales.

The sorcerer's apprentice ill. by author. Silver Burdett, 1986. ISBN 0-382-09382-8 Subj: Folk and fairy tales. Magic. Royalty.

Mullins, Edward S. *Animal limericks* ill. by author. Follett, 1966. Subj: Animals. Poetry, rhyme.

Mullins, Patricia. *The Sea-Breeze Hotel* (Vaughan, Marcia K.)

Munari, Bruno. *ABC* ill. by author. Collins-World, 1960. Subj: ABC books.

Animals for sale ill. by author. Collins-World, 1957. Subj: Animals.

The birthday present ill. by author. Collins-World, 1959. Subj: Birthdays. Games. Transportation.

Bruno Munari's zoo ill. by author. Collins-World, 1963. Subj: Animals. Birds. Zoos.

The circus in the mist ill. by author. Collins, 1968. Subj: Circus. Format, unusual. Weather – fog.

The elephant's wish ill. by author. Collins, 1959. First pub. in 1945 Subj: Animals. Behavior – wishing. Format, unusual – toy and movable books.

Jimmy has lost his cap ill. by author. Collins, 1959. Subj: Behavior – losing things. Format, unusual – toy and movable books.

Tic, Tac and Toc ill. by author. Collins-World, 1957. Subj: Birds. Format, unusual – toy and movable books.

Who's there? Open the door tr. by Maria Cimino; ill. by author. Collins-World, 1957. Subj: Animals. Format, unusual – toy and movable books.

Munro, Roxie. *Christmastime in New York City* ill. by author. Dodd, 1987. ISBN 0-396-08909-7 Subj: City. Holidays – Christmas.

The inside-outside book of London ill. by author. Dutton, 1989. ISBN 0-525-44522-6 Subj: City. Foreign lands – England.

The inside-outside book of New York City ill. by author. Dodd, 1985. ISBN 0-396-08513-X Subj: City.

The inside-outside book of Paris ill. by author. Dutton, 1992. ISBN 0-525-44863-2 Subj: City. Foreign lands – France.

The inside-outside book of Washington, D.C. ill. by author. Dutton, 1987. ISBN 0-525-44298-7 Subj: Activities – traveling. City. Museums.

Munsch, Robert N. *Angela's airplane* ill. by Michael Martchenko. Firefly, 1988. ISBN 1-55037-027-8 Subj: Activities – flying. Airplanes, airports. Behavior – misbehavior.

David's father ill. by Michael Martchenko. Firefly Pr., 1983. Subj: Character traits – kindness. Giants.

The fire station ill. by Michael Martchenko. Firefly, 1991. ISBN 1-55037-170-3 Subj: Careers – firefighters.

I have to go! ill. by Michael Martchenko. Firefly Pr., 1987. ISBN 0-920303-77-3 Subj: Behavior – growing up. Family life.

Jonathan cleaned up—then he heard a sound: or, blackberry subway jam ill. by Michael Martchenko. Firefly Pr., 1981. Subj: Machines. Problem solving. Trains.

Millicent and the wind ill. by Suzanne Duranceau. Firefly Pr., 1984. ISBN 0-920236-98-7 Subj: Behavior – needing someone. Behavior – wishing. Friendship. Weather – wind.

Moira's birthday ill. by Michael Martchenko. Firefly, 1987. ISBN 0-920303-85-4 Subj: Behavior – misbehavior. Birthdays. Parties.

Mortimer ill. by Michael Martchenko. Firefly, 1985. ISBN 0-920303-12-9 Subj: Bedtime. Noise, sounds. Songs.

The paper bag princess ill. by Michael Martchenko. Firefly, 1980. ISBN 0-920236-82-0 Subj: Character traits – appearance. Dragons.

Pigs ill. by Michael Martchenko. Firefly, 1989. ISBN 1-550370-39-1 Subj: Animals – pigs.

A promise is a promise by Robert N. Munsch and Michael Kusugak; ill. by Vladyana Krykorka. Firefly, 1988. ISBN 1-55037-009-X Subj: Eskimos. Foreign lands – Canada. Folk and fairy tales. Sea and seashore.

Show-and-tell ill. by Michael Martchenko. Firefly, 1991. ISBN 1-55037-195-9 Subj: School.

Something good ill. by Michael Martchenko. Firefly, 1990. ISBN 1-55037-099-5 Subj: Family life – fathers. Shopping. Stores.

Muntean, Michaela. *Alligator's garden* ill. by Nicole Rubel. Dial Pr., 1984. Subj: Gardens, gardening. Reptiles – alligators, crocodiles.

Bicycle bear ill. by Doug Cushman. Parents, 1983. Subj: Animals – bears. Poetry, rhyme. Sports – bicycling.

The house that bear built ill. by Nicole Rubel. Dial Pr., 1984. Subj: Animals – bears. Houses.

Mokey and the festival of the bells ill. by Michael Adams. Holt, 1985. ISBN 0-03-004553-3 Subj: Character traits – generosity. Puppets.

Muppet babies through the year ill. by Bruce McNally. Random House, 1984. Subj: Puppets. Seasons.

Munthe, Adam John. *I believe in unicorns* ill. by Elizabeth Falconer. Merrimack, 1980. Subj: Emotions – loneliness. Mythical creatures – unicorns.

The Muppet Show book ill. by Tudor Banus. Abrams, 1978. Subj: Puppets.

Murdocca, Sal. *Christmas bear* ill. by author. Simon & Schuster, 1990. ISBN 0-671-64565-X Subj: Animals – bears. Holidays – Christmas.

Murphey, Sara. *The animal hat shop* reading consultant: Morton Botel; ill. by Mel Pekarsky. Follett, 1964. Subj: Animals – cats. Birds – chickens. Clothing – hats.

The roly poly cookie reading consultant: Morton Botel; ill. by Leonard W. Shortall. Follett, 1963. Subj: Cumulative tales. Food.

Murphy, Elspeth Campbell. *Do you see me God? prayers for young children* ill. by Bill Duca. David C. Cook, 1989. ISBN 1-55513-457-2 Subj: Poetry, rhyme. Religion.

Murphy, Jill. *All in one piece* ill. by author. Putnam's, 1987. ISBN 0-399-21433-X Subj: Animals – elephants. Behavior – misbehavior. Family life.

Five minutes' peace ill. by author. Putnam's, 1986. ISBN 0-399-21354-6 Subj: Animals – elephants. Family life.

Peace at last ill. by author. Dial Pr., 1980. Subj: Animals – bears. Noise, sounds. Sleep.

A piece of cake ill. by author. Putnam, 1989. ISBN 0-399-21590-5 Subj: Animals – elephants. Food. Self-concept.

What next, baby bear! ill. by author. Dial Pr., 1984. Subj: Animals – bears. Bedtime. Imagination. Night. Space and space ships.

Murphy, Jim. *The call of the wolves* ill. by Mark Alan Weatherby. Scholastic, 1989. ISBN 0-590-41941-2 Subj: Animals – wolves.

Dinosaur for a day ill. by Mark Alan Weatherby. Scholastic, 1992. ISBN 0-590-42866-7 Subj: Dinosaurs.

Murphy, Shirley Rousseau. *Tattie's river journey* ill. by Tomie de Paola. Dial Pr., 1983. Subj: Houses. Rivers. Weather – rain.

Valentine for a dragon ill. by Kay Chorao. Atheneum, 1984. Subj: Dragons. Emotions – loneliness. Holidays – Valentine's Day. Monsters.

Murrow, Liza Ketchum. *Good-bye, Sammy* ill. by Gail Owens. Holiday, 1989. ISBN 0-8234-0726-8 Subj: Behavior – losing things. Toys.

Murschetz, Luis. *Mister Mole* tr. by Diane Martin; ill. by author. Prentice-Hall, 1976. Translation of Der Maulwurf Grabowski Subj: Animals – moles. Ecology. Progress.

Musgrove, Margaret. *Ashanti to Zulu* Dial Pr., 1976. Subj: ABC books. Caldecott award book. Foreign lands – Africa.

Musicant, Elke. *The night vegetable eater* by Elke and Ted Musicant; ill. by Jeni Bassett. Dodd, 1981. ISBN 0-396-07923-7 Subj: Animals. Gardens, gardening. Problem solving.

Musicant, Ted. *The night vegetable eater* (Musicant, Elke)

Mwalimu. *Awful aardvark* by Mwalimu and Adrienne Kennaway; ill. by Adrienne Kennaway. Little, 1989. ISBN 0-316-59218-8 Subj: Animals – aardvarks. Animals – mongooses. Folk and fairy tales. Foreign lands – Africa. Night. Sleep.

My body ill. by Sue Porter. Harper, 1985. Subj: Anatomy. Format, unusual – board books. Wordless.

My first book of baby animals ill. by Karen Lee Schmidt. Platt, 1986. ISBN 0-448-10826-7 Subj: Animals. Format, unusual – board books.

Myers, Amy. *I know a monster* ill. by author. Addison-Wesley, 1979. Subj: Character traits – appearance. Games. Monsters.

Myers, Arthur. *Kids do amazing things* ill. by Anthony Rao. Random House, 1980. Subj: Activities.

Myers, Bernice. *Charlie's birthday present* ill. by author. Scholastic, 1981. Subj: Birthdays. Trees.

The flying shoes ill. by author. Lothrop, 1992. ISBN 0-688-10696-X Subj: Activities – flying. Animals. Clothing – shoes. Magic. Royalty – queens.

The gold watch ill. by author. Lothrop, 1991. ISBN 0-688-09889-4 Subj: Careers. Clocks, watches. Family life – fathers.

Herman and the bears and the giants ill. by author. Scholastic, 1978. Subj: Animals – bears. Circus. Sports – bicycling.

It happens to everyone ill. by author. Lothrop, 1990. ISBN 0-688-09082-6 Subj: Behavior – hurrying. Careers – teachers.

The millionth egg ill. by author. Lothrop, 1991. ISBN 0-688-09886-X Subj: Birds – chickens. Eggs.

Sidney Rella and the glass sneaker ill. by author. Macmillan, 1985. ISBN 0-02-767790-7 Subj: Behavior – wishing. Fairies. Sports – football.

Myers, Walter Dean. *The golden serpent* ill. by Alice and Martin Provensen. Viking, 1980. ISBN 0-670-34445-1 Subj: Folk and fairy tales. Foreign lands – India. Problem solving. Royalty.

Myller, Lois. *No! No!* ill. by Cyndy Szekeres. Simon and Schuster, 1971. Subj: Animals – hedgehogs. Behavior. Behavior – misbehavior. Etiquette. Family life. Safety.

Myller, Rolf. *How big is a foot?* ill. by author. Atheneum, 1962. Subj: Birthdays. Concepts – measurement. Humor. Royalty – kings.

Rolling round ill. by author. Atheneum, 1963. Subj: Royalty. Wheels.

A very noisy day ill. by author. Atheneum, 1981. ISBN 0-689-30853-1 Subj: Animals – dogs. Crime. Noise, sounds.

Myrick, Jean Lockwood. *Ninety-nine pockets* ill. by Haris Petie. Lantern Pr., 1966. Subj: Birthdays. Clothing. Problem solving.

Nagel, Andreas Fischer *see* Fischer-Nagel, Andreas

Nagel, Heiderose Fischer *see* Fischer-Nagel, Heiderose

Nakabayashi, Ei. *The rainy day puddle* ill. by author. Random House, 1989. ISBN 0-394-82095-9 Subj: Animals. Concepts – size. Weather – rain.

Nakano, Hirotaka. *Elephant blue* tr. by Fukuinkan Shoten; ill. by author. Bobbs-Merrill, 1970. Subj: Animals. Animals – elephants. Character traits – helpfulness.

Nakao, Naomi Löw. *The adventures of Chester the chest* (Ayal, Ora)

Ugbu (Ayal, Ora)

Nakatani, Chiyoko. *The day Chiro was lost* ill. by author. Collins-World, 1969. Subj: Animals – dogs. Behavior – lost.

Fumio and the dolphins ill. by author. Addison-Wesley, 1970. First published in Japan by Fukuinkan-Shoten, Tokyo, 1969 Subj: Animals – dolphins. Character traits – kindness to animals. Foreign lands – Japan. Sea and seashore.

My day on the farm ill. by author. Crowell, 1976. Subj: Farms.

The zoo in my garden ill. by author. Crowell, 1973. Translation of Boku no uchi no dōbutsuen Subj: Animals.

Nakawatari, Harutaka. *The sea and I* tr. by Susan Matsui; ill. by author. Farrar, 1992. ISBN 0-374-36428-1 Subj: Boats, ships. Careers – fishermen. Sea and seashore.

Namm, Diane. *Favorite nursery rhymes* comp. by Diane Namm; ill. by Delana Bettoli. Little, 1986. ISBN 0-671-60264-0 Subj: Nursery rhymes.

Little bear ill. by Lisa McCue. Children's Pr., 1990. ISBN 0-516-05356-6 Subj: Animals – bears. Poetry, rhyme.

Monsters! ill. by Maxie Chambliss. Children's Pr., 1990. ISBN 0-516-05358-2 Subj: Counting, numbers. Monsters.

Napoli, Guillier. *Adventure at Mont-Saint-Michel* ill. by author. McGraw-Hill, 1966. Subj: Careers – fishermen. Character traits – curiosity. Foreign lands – France. Sea and seashore.

Narahashi, Keiko. *I have a friend* ill. by author. McElderry, 1987. ISBN 0-689-50432-2 Subj: Shadows.

Narayan, Maya. *Leela and the watermelon* (Hirsh, Marilyn)

Nash, Ogden. *The adventures of Isabel* ill. by Walter Lorraine. Little, 1963. Subj: Animals – bears. Character traits – bravery. Emotions – fear. Giants. Poetry, rhyme. Witches.

The adventures of Isabel ill. by James Marshall. Little, 1991. ISBN 0-316-59874-7 Subj: Animals – bears. Character traits – bravery. Emotions – fear. Giants. Poetry, rhyme. Witches.

The animal garden ill. by Hilary Knight. Lippincott, 1963. Subj: Humor. Plants. Poetry, rhyme.

A boy is a boy ill. by Arthur Shilstone. Watts, 1960. Subj: Humor. Poetry, rhyme.

Custard and Company sel. and ill. by Quentin Blake. Little, 1980. Subj: Dragons. Humor. Poetry, rhyme.

Custard the dragon ill. by Linell Nash. Little, 1961. ISBN 0-316-59841-0 Subj: Animals. Character traits – bravery. Dragons. Pirates.

Custard the dragon and the wicked knight ill. by Linell Nash. Little, 1959. Subj: Dragons. Poetry, rhyme.

Nave, Yolanda. *Goosebumps and butterflies* ill. by author. Watts, 1990. ISBN 0-531-08504-X Subj: Emotions. Poetry, rhyme.

Naxt, Elsa Ruth *see* Watson, Jane Werner

Naylor, Phyllis Reynolds. *The baby, the bed, and the rose* ill. by Mary Szilagyi. Clarion, 1987. ISBN 0-899-19459-1 Subj: Babies. Emotions – love. Family life.

King of the playground ill. by Nola Langner Malone. Atheneum, 1991. ISBN 0-689-31558-9 Subj: Activities – playing. Behavior – bullying. Friendship.

Old Sadie and the Christmas bear ill. by Patricia Montgomery Newton. Atheneum, 1984. Subj: Animals – bears. Holidays – Christmas.

Neale, J. M. (John Mason). *Good King Wenceslas* ill. by Jamichael Henterly. Dutton, 1988. ISBN 0-525-44420-3 Subj: Folk and fairy tales. Holidays – Christmas. Music. Songs.

Neasi, Barbara J. *Just like me* ill. by Lois Axeman. Children's Pr., 1984. Subj: Twins.

Listen to me ill. by Gene Sharp. Childrens Pr., 1986. ISBN 0-516-02072-2 Subj: Family life – grandmothers.

Neitzel, Shirley. *The jacket I wear in the snow* ill. by Nancy Winslow Parker. Greenwillow, 1989. ISBN 0-688-08030-8 Subj: Clothing. Cumulative tales. Poetry, rhyme.

Nelson, Brenda. *Mud fore sale* ill. by Richard Eric Brown. Houghton, 1984. Subj: Activities. Friendship.

Nelson, Esther L. *The funny songbook* ill. by Joyce Behr. Sterling, 1984. Subj: Music. Songs.

Holiday singing and dancing games photos. by Shirley Zeiberg. Sterling, 1980. Subj: Activities – dancing. Games. Music. Songs.

The silly songbook ill. by Joyce Behr. Sterling, 1982. Subj: Music. Songs.

Nelson, Vaunda Micheaux. *Always Gramma* ill. by Kimanne Uhler. Putnam's, 1988. ISBN 0-399-21542-5 Subj: Family life. Family life – grandmothers. Illness – Alzheimer's. Old age.

Nerlove, Miriam. *Christmas* ill. by author. Albert Whitman, 1990. ISBN 0-8075-1148-X Subj: Holidays – Christmas. Poetry, rhyme.

Halloween ill. by author. Albert Whitman, 1989. ISBN 0-8075-3131-6 Subj: Holidays – Halloween. Poetry, rhyme.

Hanukkah ill. by author. Albert Whitman, 1989. ISBN 0-8075-3143-X Subj: Holidays – Hanukkah. Jewish culture. Poetry, rhyme. Religion.

I made a mistake ill. by author. Atheneum, 1985. ISBN 0-689-50327-X Subj: Animals. Poetry, rhyme.

I meant to clean my room today ill. by author. Macmillan, 1988. ISBN 0-689-50438-1 Subj: Character traits – cleanliness. Imagination. Poetry, rhyme.

If all the world were paper ill. by author. Albert Whitman, 1990. ISBN 0-8075-3535-4 Subj: Activities – painting. Imagination. Poetry, rhyme.

Just one tooth ill. by author. Macmillan, 1989. ISBN 0-689-50465-9 Subj: Poetry, rhyme. Teeth.

Passover ill. by author. Albert Whitman, 1989. ISBN 0-8075-6360-9 Subj: Jewish culture. Poetry, rhyme. Religion.

Thanksgiving ill. by author. Albert Whitman, 1990. ISBN 0-8075-7818-5 Subj: Holidays – Thanksgiving. Poetry, rhyme.

Nesbit, Edith. *Beauty and the beast* ill. by Julia Christie. Warne, 1988. ISBN 0-7232-3540-6 Subj: Character traits – appearance. Character traits – loyalty. Emotions – love. Folk and fairy tales.

Cockatoucan ill. by Elory Hughes. Dial Pr., 1988. ISBN 0-8037-0474-7 Subj: Birds. Imagination.

The ice dragon ill. by Carole Gray. Dial Pr., 1988. ISBN 0-8037-0475-5 Subj: World.

The last of the dragons ill. by Peter Firmin. McGraw-Hill, 1980. ISBN 0-07-046285-2 Subj: Character traits – kindness. Dragons. Folk and fairy tales. Royalty.

Melisande ill. by P. J. Lynch. Harcourt, 1989. ISBN 0-15-253164-5 Subj: Fairies. Folk and fairy tales. Hair. Magic. Royalty – princesses.

Ness, Evaline. *Do you have the time, Lydia?* ill. by author. Dutton, 1971. Subj: Birds – sea gulls. Character traits – completing things. Problem solving. Time.

Exactly alike ill. by author. Scribner's, 1964. Subj: Family life.

Fierce: the lion ill. by author. Holiday, 1980. Subj: Animals – lions. Circus.

The girl and the goatherd: or, this and that and thus and so ill. by author. Dutton, 1970. Subj: Character traits – appearance. Folk and fairy tales.

Josefina February ill. by author. Scribner's, 1963. Subj: Animals – donkeys. Birthdays. Character traits – generosity. Foreign lands – Caribbean Islands.

Pavo and the princess ill. by author. Scribner's, 1964. Subj: Birds. Character traits – helpfulness. Emotions. Royalty – princesses.

Sam, Bangs, and moonshine ill. by author. Holt, 1966. Subj: Caldecott award book. Imagination. Sports – fishing.

Neugroschel, Joachim. *The boy and the tree* (Driz, Ovsei)

Neuhaus, David. *His finest hour* ill. by author. Viking, 1984. Subj: Friendship. Sports – racing.

Neumeier, Marty. *Action alphabet* by Marty Neumeier and Byron Glaser; ill. by authors. Greenwillow, 1985. ISBN 0-688-05704-7 Subj: ABC books. Activities.

Neumeyer, Peter. *Mischa and his brothers* (Baumann, Hans)

Neville, Emily Cheney. *The bridge* ill. by Ronald Himler. Harper, 1988. ISBN 0-06-024386-4 Subj: Bridges. Family life. Machines.

Newberry, Clare Turlay. *April's kittens* ill. by author. Harper, 1940. Subj: Animals – cats. Caldecott award honor book. Pets.

Barkis ill. by author. Harper, 1938. Subj: Animals – dogs. Caldecott award honor book. Pets.

Cousin Toby ill. by author. Harper, 1939. Subj: Babies.

Herbert the lion ill. by author. Harper, 1956. First pub. in 1931 Subj: Animals – lions. Pets.

The kittens' ABC verse and pictures by Clare Turlay Newberry New and rev. ed.; completely redrawn. Harper, 1965. Subj: ABC books. Animals – cats. Poetry, rhyme.

Marshmallow ill. by author. Harper, 1942. Subj: Animals – cats. Animals – rabbits. Caldecott award honor book. Friendship.

Pandora ill. by author. Harper, 1944. Subj: Animals – cats.

Percy, Polly and Pete ill. by author. Harper, 1952. Subj: Animals – cats. Behavior – growing up. Character traits – kindness to animals. Pets.

Smudge ill. by author. Harper, 1948. Subj: Animals – cats.

T-Bone, the baby-sitter story and pictures by author. Harper, 1950. Subj: Activities – baby-sitting. Animals – cats. Babies. Caldecott award honor book.

Widget ill. by author. Harper, 1958. Subj: Animals – cats.

Newbolt, Henry John, Sir. *Rilloby-rill* ill. by Susanna Gretz. O'Hara, 1973. Subj: Insects – grasshoppers. Fairies. Music. Songs.

Newell, Crosby *see* Bonsall, Crosby Newell

Newell, Peter. *Topsys and turvys* ill. by author. Dover, 1965. Subj: Format, unusual. Humor.

Newfield, Marcia. *Iggy* ill. by Jacqueline Chwast. Houghton, 1972. Subj: Pets. Reptiles – iguanas.

Newland, Mary Reed. *Good King Wenceslas: a legend in music and pictures* ill. by author. Seabury Pr., 1980. Subj: Holidays – Christmas. Music. Songs.

Newman, Robert. *All aboard ABC* (Magee, Doug)

Newman, Shirlee. *Tell me, grandma; tell me, grandpa* ill. by Joan Drescher. Houghton, 1979. Subj: Family life – grandparents.

Newsham, Ian. *The monster hunt* (Newsham, Wendy)

Newsham, Wendy. *The monster hunt* by Wendy and Ian Newsham; ill. by authors. Hamish Hamilton, 1983. Subj: Monsters.

Newth, Philip. *Roly goes exploring: a book for blind and sighted children, in Braille and standard type, with pictures to feel as well as see* Putnam's, 1981. Subj: Concepts – shape. Format, unusual. Handicaps – blindness. Senses – seeing.

Newton, James R. *A forest is reborn* ill. by Susan Bonners. Crowell, 1982. Subj: Fire. Forest, woods. Science.

Forest log ill. by Irene Brady. Crowell, 1980. Subj: Ecology. Forest, woods. Science. Trees.

Newton, Laura P. *Me and my aunts* ill. by Robin Oz. Albert Whitman, 1986. ISBN 0-8075-5029-9 Subj: Emotions – love. Family life – aunts, uncles.

William the vehicle king ill. by Jacqueline Rogers. Bradbury Pr., 1987. ISBN 0-02-768230-7 Subj: Automobiles. Imagination. Toys. Trucks.

Newton, Pam. *The stonecutter* ill. by reteller. Putnam, 1990. ISBN 0-399-22187-5 Subj: Folk and fairy tales. Foreign lands – India.

Newton, Patricia Montgomery. *The five sparrows* ill. by author. Atheneum, 1982. Subj: Character traits – kindness. Folk and fairy tales. Foreign lands – Japan.

The frog who drank the waters of the world ill. by author. Atheneum, 1983. ISBN 0-689-30993-7 Subj: Animals. Birds – bluejays. Frogs and toads. Reptiles – snakes.

Vacation surprise ill. by author. Atheneum, 1986. ISBN 0-689-31264-4 Subj: Activities – vacationing. Animals – pigs.

Nic Leodhas, Sorche *see* Alger, Leclaire Gowans

Nichol, B. P. *Once: a lullaby* ill. by Anita Lobel. Greenwillow, 1986. ISBN 0-688-04285-6 Subj: Animals. Bedtime. Lullabies. Music. Night. Sleep.

Nichols, Cathy. *Tuxedo Sam: a penguin of a different color* ill. by Haruo Takahashi. Random House, 1983. Subj: Birds – penguins. City.

Nichols, Paul. *Big Paul's school bus* ill. by William Marshall. Prentice-Hall, 1981. Subj: Buses. Careers. School.

Nicholson, Jack. *How the camel got his hump* (Kipling, Rudyard)

Nicholson, William, Sir. *Clever Bill* ill. by author. Farrar, 1977. Subj: Toys – soldiers.

Nickl, Peter. *Ra ta ta tam* by Peter Nickl and Binette Schroeder; ill. by authors. Merrimack, 1984. Subj: Character traits – meanness. Format, unusual – board books. Trains.

Nicolas *see* Mordvinoff, Nicolas

Nicoll, Helen. *Meg and Mog* by Helen Nicoll and Jan Pieńkowski; ill. by Jan Pieńkowski. Atheneum, 1972. Subj: Animals – cats. Holidays – Halloween. Magic. Witches.

Meg at sea by Helen Nicoll and Jan Pieńkowski; ill. by Jan Pieńkowski. Harvey House, 1974. Subj: Animals – cats. Birds – owls. Magic. Sea and seashore. Witches.

Meg on the moon by Helen Nicoll and Jan Pieńkowski; ill. by Jan Pieńkowski. Harvey House, 1974. Subj: Animals – cats. Magic. Moon. Witches.

Meg's eggs by Helen Nicoll and Jan Pieńkowski; ill. by Jan Pieńkowski. Atheneum, 1972. Subj: Animals – cats. Birds – owls. Dinosaurs. Eggs. Magic. Witches.

Mog's box ill. by Jan Pieńkowski. David & Charles, 1987. ISBN 0-434-95658-9 Subj: Animals – cats. Magic. Witches.

Nightingale, Sandy. *A giraffe on the moon* ill. by author. Harcourt, 1992. ISBN 0-15-230950-0 Subj: Dreams. Poetry, rhyme.

Pink pigs aplenty ill. by author. Harcourt, 1992. ISBN 0-15-261882-1 Subj: Animals – pigs. Circus. Counting, numbers.

Nikly, Michelle. *The emperor's plum tree* tr. from French by Elizabeth Shub; ill. by author. Greenwillow, 1982. Subj: Friendship. Royalty – emperors. Trees.

The princess on the nut: or, the curious courtship of the son of the princess on the pea tr. by Lucy Meredith; ill. by Jean Claverie. Faber, 1981. Subj: Folk and fairy tales. Royalty – princesses.

Nikola-Lisa, W. *Night is coming* ill. by Jamichael Henterly. Dutton, 1991. ISBN 0-525-44687-7 Subj: Country. Family life – grandfathers. Night.

One, two, three Thanksgiving! ill. by Robin Kramer. Albert Whitman, 1991. ISBN 0-8075-6109-6 Subj: Counting, numbers. Family life. Holidays – Thanksgiving.

Niland, Deborah. *ABC of monsters* ill. by author. McGraw-Hill, 1978. Subj: ABC books. Monsters.

Niland, Kilmeny. *A bellbird in a flame tree* ill. by author. Morrow, 1991. ISBN 0-688-10798-2 Subj: Foreign lands – Australia. Holidays – Christmas. Music. Songs.

Nilsson, Ulf. *Little sister rabbit* ill. by Eva Eriksson. Little, 1985. ISBN 0-87113-009-2 Subj: Activities – baby-sitting. Animals – rabbits. Family life.

Nims, Bonnie Larkin. *Where is the bear?* ill. by John Wallner. Albert Whitman, 1988. ISBN 0-8075-8933-0 Subj: Behavior – lost. Poetry, rhyme. Toys – teddy bears.

Where is the bear at school? ill. by Madelaine Gill. Albert Whitman, 1989. ISBN 0-8075-8935-7 Subj: Games. Poetry, rhyme. School. Toys – teddy bears.

Nishikawa, Osamu. *Alexander and the blue ghost* ill. by author. Morrow, 1986. ISBN 0-688-06267-9 Subj: Character traits – bravery. Ghosts. Royalty.

Nister, Ernest. *Little tales from long ago: Cat's cradle, The tale of a dog, Three friends, Three little maids* ill. by author. Delacorte Pr., 1979. Subj: Folk and fairy tales.

Nixon, Joan Lowery. *Beats me, Claude* ill. by Tracey Campbell Pearson. Viking, 1986. ISBN 0-670-80781-8 Subj: Activities – cooking. Humor.

Bigfoot makes a movie ill. by Syd Hoff. Putnam's, 1979. ISBN 0-399-20684-1 Subj: Behavior – misunderstanding. Folk and fairy tales. Monsters.

Fat chance, Claude ill. by Tracey Campbell Pearson. Viking, 1987. ISBN 0-670-81459-8 Subj: Careers – miners.

If you say so, Claude ill. by Lorinda Bryan Cauley. Warne, 1980. ISBN 0-7232-6183-0 Subj: Activities – traveling. Behavior – seeking better things. U.S. history.

If you were a writer ill. by Bruce Degen. Four Winds Pr., 1988. ISBN 0-02-768210-2 Subj: Activities – writing.

The Thanksgiving mystery ill. by Jim Cummins. Albert Whitman, 1980. Subj: Ghosts. Holidays – Thanksgiving. Problem solving.

That's the spirit, Claude ill. by Tracey Campbell Pearson. Viking, 1992. ISBN 0-670-83434-3 Subj: Holidays – Christmas. Humor. U.S. history.

The Valentine mystery ill. by Jim Cummins. Albert Whitman, 1979. Subj: Holidays – Valentine's Day. Problem solving.

You bet your britches, Claude ill. by Tracey Campbell Pearson. Viking, 1989. ISBN 0-670-82310-4 Subj: Adoption. Family life. Humor. U.S. history.

Nobens, C. A. *Montgomery's time zone* ill. by author. Carolrhoda, 1990. ISBN 0-87614-398-2 Subj: Dreams. Time.

Noble, June. *Two homes for Lynn* ill. by Yuri Salzman. Holt, 1979. Subj: Behavior – sharing. Divorce. Family life. Imagination – imaginary friends.

Noble, Trinka Hakes. *Apple tree Christmas* ill. by author. Dial Pr., 1984. Subj: Holidays – Christmas. Trees. Weather – storms.

The day Jimmy's boa ate the wash ill. by Steven Kellogg. Dial Pr., 1980. Subj: Activities. Reptiles – snakes. School.

Hansy's mermaid ill. by author. Dial Pr., 1983. Subj: Character traits – kindness. Mythical creatures – mermaids.

Jimmy's boa and the big splash birthday bash ill. by Steven Kellogg. Dial, 1989. ISBN 0-8037-0540-9 Subj: Birthdays. Pets. Reptiles – snakes.

Jimmy's boa bounces back ill. by Steven Kellogg. Dial Pr., 1984. Subj: Humor. Reptiles – snakes.

The king's tea ill. by author. Dial Pr., 1979. Subj: Cumulative tales. Royalty – kings.

Meanwhile back at the ranch ill. by Tony Ross. Dial Pr., 1987. ISBN 0-8037-0354-6 Subj: Behavior – boredom. Humor.

Nodset, Joan L. *see* Lexau, Joan M.

Noguere, Suzanne. *Little raccoon* ill. by Tony Chen. Holt, 1981. Subj: Animals – raccoons.

Nolan, Dennis. *The castle builder* ill. by author. Macmillan, 1987. ISBN 0-02-768240-4 Subj: Dragons. Imagination. Knights. Sand. Sea and seashore.

Dinosaur dream ill. by author. Macmillan, 1990. ISBN 0-02-768145-9 Subj: Dreams. Dinosaurs. Sleep.

Witch Bazooza ill. by author. Prentice-Hall, 1979. Subj: Holidays – Halloween. Houses. Witches.

Wizard McBean and his flying machine ill. by author. Prentice-Hall, 1977. Subj: Airplanes, airports. Cumulative tales. Magic. Poetry, rhyme. Wizards.

Nolan, Madeena Spray. *My daddy don't go to work* ill. by Jim LaMarche. Carolrhoda Books, 1978. Subj: Ethnic groups in the U.S. – Afro-Americans. Family life. Family life – fathers. Poverty.

Noll, Sally. *Jiggle wiggle prance* ill. by author. Greenwillow, 1987. ISBN 0-688-06761-1 Subj: Activities. Animals.

Off and counting ill. by author. Greenwillow, 1984. Subj: Counting, numbers. Frogs and toads. Poetry, rhyme. Toys.

That bothered Kate ill. by author. Greenwillow, 1991. ISBN 0-688-10096-1 Subj: Behavior – growing up. Behavior – imitation. Family life – sisters. Sibling rivalry.

Watch where you go ill. by author. Greenwillow, 1990. ISBN 0-688-08499-0 Subj: Animals – mice. Optical illusions.

Nomura, Takaaki. *Grandpa's town* tr. from Japanese by Amanda Mayer Stinchecum; ill. by author. Kane/Miller, 1991. ISBN 0-916291-36-7 Subj: Family life – grandfathers. Foreign lands – Japan. Foreign languages.

Nones, Eric Jon. *Canary prince* ill. by author. Farrar, 1991. ISBN 0-374-31029-7 Subj: Birds – canaries. Folk and fairy tales. Foreign lands – Italy. Magic. Royalty – princes. Royalty – princesses.

Wendell ill. by author. Farrar, 1989. ISBN 0-374-38266-2 Subj: Animals – cats. Behavior – misbehavior. Elves and little people. Family life.

Norby, Lisa. *The Herself the elf storybook* Scholastic, 1983. Subj: Elves and little people. Magic.

Nordlicht, Lillian. *I love to laugh* ill. by Allen Davis. Raintree, 1980. ISBN 0-8172-1364-3 Subj: Behavior – growing up. Character traits – being different.

Nordqvist, Sven. *Festus and Mercury: ruckus in the garden* ill. by author. Carolrhoda, 1991. ISBN 0-87614-678-7 Subj: Animals – cats. Gardens, gardening. Seasons – spring.

The fox hunt ill. by author. Morrow, 1988. ISBN 0-688-06882-0 Subj: Animals – cats. Animals – foxes. Behavior – trickery. Careers – farmers.

Pancake pie ill. by author. Morrow, 1985. Subj: Animals – cats. Food.

Porker finds a chair ill. by author. Carolrhoda, 1989. ISBN 0-87614-367-2 Subj: Animals – bears. Behavior – misunderstanding. Furniture – chairs.

Willie in the big world: adventures with numbers ill. by author. Morrow, 1986. ISBN 0-688-06143-5 Subj: Activities – traveling. Counting, numbers.

Norman, Charles. *The hornbean tree and other poems* ill. by Ted Rand. Holt, 1988. ISBN 0-8050-0417-3 Subj: Animals. Birds. Nature. Poetry, rhyme.

Norman, Howard. *The owl-scatterer* ill. by Michael McCurdy. Atlantic Monthly Pr., 1986. ISBN

0-87113-058-0 Subj: Behavior – disbelief. Birds – owls. Foreign lands – Canada.

Who-Paddled-Backward-With-Trout ill. by Ed Young. Little, 1987. ISBN 0-316-61182-4 Subj: Folk and fairy tales. Indians of North America. Names.

Norman, Philip Ross. *The carrot war* ill. by author. Little, 1992. ISBN 0-316-61200-6 Subj: Animals – rabbits. Food. War.

Norris, Lori P. *D is for divorce* ill. by author. Health Communications, 1991. ISBN 1-55874-140-2 Subj: Divorce.

North, George Captain *see* Stevenson, Robert Louis

Northam, Leland. *Hansel and Gretel* (Grimm, Jacob)

Sleeping Beauty (Grimm, Jacob)

The ugly duckling (Grimm, Jacob)

Northrup, Mili. *The watch cat* ill. by Adrina Zanazanian; designed by Kent Salisbury. Bobbs-Merrill, 1968. Subj: Animals – cats. Foreign lands – Thailand.

Norton, Natalie. *A little old man* ill. by Will Huntington. Rand McNally, 1959. Subj: Emotions – loneliness.

Nourse, Alan Edward. *Lumps, bumps and rashes: a look at kids' diseases* Watts, 1976. Subj: Illness.

Novak, Matt. *Claude and Sun* ill. by author. Bradbury, 1987. ISBN 0-02-768151-3 Subj: Friendship. Sun.

Mr. Floop's lunch ill. by author. Watts, 1990. ISBN 0-531-08426-4 Subj: Animals. Behavior – sharing. Character traits – kindness to animals.

Rolling ill. by author. Bradbury Pr., 1986. ISBN 0-02-768150-5 Subj: Weather – thunder.

While the shepherd slept ill. by author. Watts, 1991. ISBN 0-531-08515-5 Subj: Animals – sheep. Sleep. Theater.

Noyes, Alfred. *The highwayman* ill. by Neil Waldman. Harcourt, 1990. ISBN 0-15-234340-7 Subj: Crime. Emotions – love. Poetry, rhyme. Royalty – kings.

Numeroff, Laura Joffe. *Amy for short* ill. by author. Macmillan, 1976. Subj: Character traits – appearance. Friendship.

Emily's bunch by Laura Joffe Numeroff and Alice Numeroff Richter; ill. by Laura Joffe Numeroff. Macmillan, 1978. Subj: Holidays – Halloween.

If you gave a moose a muffin ill. by Felicia Bond. HarperCollins, 1991. ISBN 0-06-024406-2 Subj: Animals – moose. Character traits – kindness to animals. Circular tales.

If you give a mouse a cookie ill. by Felicia Bond. Harper, 1985. ISBN 0-06-024587-5 Subj: Animals

– mice. Behavior – imitation. Character traits – kindness to animals. Circular tales.

Phoebe Dexter has Harriet Peterson's sniffles ill. by author. Greenwillow, 1977. Subj: Illness.

You can't put braces on spaces (Richter, Alice Numeroff)

Nunes, Susan. *Tiddalick the frog* ill. by Ju-Hong chen. Atheneum, 1989. ISBN 0-689-31502-3 Subj: Folk and fairy tales. Foreign lands – Australia. Frogs and toads.

Nursery rhymes ill. by Gertrude Elliott. Simon and Schuster, 1948. Subj: Nursery rhymes.

Nussbaumer, Mares. *Away in a manger: a story of the Nativity* by Mares and Paul Nussbaumer; ill. by Paul Nussbaumer. Harcourt, 1965. Translation of Ihr Kinderlein kommet Subj: Holidays – Christmas. Music. Religion.

Nussbaumer, Paul. *Away in a manger* (Nussbaumer, Mares)

Nygren, Tord. *The red thread* ill. by author. Farrar, 1988. ISBN 91-29-59005-1 Subj: Imagination. Wordless.

Oakes, Bill. *Numblers* (MacDonald, Suse)

Once upon another (MacDonald, Suse)

Oakley, Graham. *The church cat abroad* ill. by author. Atheneum, 1973. Subj: Animals – cats. Animals – mice. Foreign lands – England.

The church mice adrift ill. by author. Atheneum, 1976. Subj: Animals – mice. Animals – rats. Rivers.

The church mice and the moon ill. by author. Atheneum, 1974. Subj: Animals – cats. Animals – mice. Foreign lands – England. Moon.

The church mice at bay ill. by author. Atheneum, 1978. Subj: Animals – cats. Animals – mice. Foreign lands – England.

The church mice at Christmas ill. by author. Atheneum, 1980. Subj: Animals – mice. Holidays – Christmas.

The church mice in action ill. by author. Atheneum, 1983. Subj: Animals – mice. Problem solving.

The church mice spread their wings ill. by author. Atheneum, 1975. Subj: Animals – cats. Animals – mice. Foreign lands – England.

The church mouse ill. by author. Atheneum, 1972. Subj: Animals – cats. Animals – mice. Foreign lands – England.

The diary of a church mouse ill. by author. Atheneum, 1987. ISBN 0-689-31334-9 Subj: Activities – writing. Animals – cats. Animals – mice.

Graham Oakley's magical changes ill. by author. Atheneum, 1980. Subj: Format, unusual – toy and movable books. Imagination. Wordless.

Hetty and Harriet ill. by author. Atheneum, 1982. Subj: Behavior – running away. Birds – chickens.

Oana, Kay D. *Robbie and the raggedy scarecrow* ill. by Jackie Stephens. Oddo, 1978. Subj: Birds. Scarecrows. Trees.

Shasta and the shebang machine ill. by Jackie Stephens. Oddo, 1978. Subj: Animals – cats. Behavior – misbehavior.

Obligado, Lilian. *Faint frogs feeling feverish and other terrifically tantalizing tongue twisters* ill. by author. Viking, 1983. Subj: ABC books. Animals. Tongue twisters.

O'Brien, Anne Sibley. *Come play with us* ill. by author. Holt, 1985. ISBN 0-03-005008-1 Subj: Activities. Format, unusual – board books. School.

I want that! ill. by author. Holt, 1985. ISBN 0-03-005012-X Subj: Behavior – sharing. Format, unusual – board books.

I'm not tired ill. by author. Holt, 1985. ISBN 0-03-005009-X Subj: Character traits – stubbornness. Format, unusual – board books.

Where's my truck? ill. by author. Holt, 1985. ISBN 0-03-005013-8 Subj: Behavior – losing things. Format, unusual – board books.

O'Brien, Mary. *Counting sheep to sleep* ill. by Bobette McCarthy. Little, 1992. ISBN 0-316-62206-0 Subj: Animals – sheep. Bedtime. Counting, numbers. Farms. Sleep.

Obrist, Jürg. *Bear business* ill. by author. Atheneum, 1986. ISBN 0-689-31149-4 Subj: Animals – bears. Behavior – misbehavior. Twins.

Fluffy: the story of a cat ill. by author. Atheneum, 1981. Subj: Animals – cats. Moving.

The miser who wanted the sun ill. by author. Atheneum, 1984. Subj: Behavior – greed. Character traits – cleverness. Sun.

They do things right in Albern ill. by author. Atheneum, 1978. Subj: Animals – moles. Problem solving.

O'Callahan, Jay. *Tulips* ill. by Debrah Santini. Picture Book Studio, 1992. ISBN 0-88708-223-8 Subj: Behavior – trickery. Family life – grandmothers. Foreign lands – France. Flowers. Gardens, gardening.

O'Connor, Jane. *The teeny tiny woman* ill. by Robert W. Alley. Random House, 1986. ISBN 0-394-98320-3 Subj: Folk and fairy tales. Ghosts.

O'Cuilleanain, Eilis Dillon *see* Dillon, Eilis

O'Donnell, Elizabeth Lee. *I can't get my turtle to move* ill. by Maxie Chambliss. Morrow, 1989. ISBN 0-688-07324-7 Subj: Counting, numbers. Pets. Reptiles – turtles, tortoises.

Maggie doesn't want to move ill. by Amy Schwartz. Four Winds Pr., 1987. ISBN 0-02-768830-5 Subj: Behavior – dissatisfaction. Behavior – running away. Emotions. Family life. Moving.

The twelve days of summer ill. by Karen Lee Schmidt. Morrow, 1991. ISBN 0-688-08203-3 Subj: Counting, numbers. Poetry, rhyme. Sea and seashore. Seasons – summer.

O'Donnell, Peter. *Moonlit journey* ill. by author. Scholastic, 1991. ISBN 0-590-44655-X Subj: Animals. Emotions – fear. Forest, woods. Night. Toys – teddy bears.

Odoyevsky, Vladimir. *Old Father Frost* tr. from Russian by James Riordan; ill. by Vassili Shulzhenko. Imported Pubs., 1983. Subj: Folk and fairy tales. Foreign lands – Russia. Seasons – winter.

Oechsli, Helen. *Fly away!* by Helen and Kelly Oechsli; ill. by Kelly Oechsli. Macmillan, 1992. ISBN 0-02-768520-9 Subj: Activities – traveling. Airplanes, airports. Family life – grandparents.

In my garden: a child's gardening book by Helen and Kelly Oechsli; ill. by Kelly Oechsli. Macmillan, 1985. ISBN 0-02-768510-1 Subj: Gardens, gardening.

Oechsli, Kelly. *Fly away!* (Oechsli, Helen)

In my garden (Oechsli, Helen)

Offen, Hilda. *Nice work, little wolf!* ill. by author. Dutton, 1992. ISBN 0-525-44880-2 Subj: Animals – pigs. Animals – wolves.

Ogle, Lucille. *A B See* by Lucille Ogle and Tina Thoburn; ill. by Ralph Stobart. McGraw-Hill, 1973. Subj: ABC books.

I hear by Lucille Ogle and Tina Thoburn; ill. by Eloise Wilkin. American Heritage, 1971. Subj: Noise, sounds. Participation. Senses – hearing.

I spy with my little eye ill. by Joe Kaufman. McGraw-Hill, 1970. Subj: Senses – seeing. Wordless.

O'Hagan, Caroline. *It's easy to have a caterpillar visit you* ill. by Judith Allan. Lothrop, 1980. Subj: Insects – butterflies, caterpillars. Pets.

It's easy to have a snail visit you ill. by Judith Allan. Lothrop, 1980. Subj: Animals – snails. Pets.

It's easy to have a worm visit you ill. by Judith Allan. Lothrop, 1980. Subj: Animals – worms. Pets.

O Huigin, Sean. *King of the birds* ill. by Tim Dixon. Firefly, 1991. ISBN 0-88753-168-7 Subj: Birds. Folk and fairy tales. Giants. Poetry, rhyme.

Oishi, Makoto. *E. H. Grieg's Peer Gynt* (Grieg, E. H. (Edvard Hagerup))

O'Keefe, Susan Heyboer. *One hungry monster* ill. by Lynn Munsinger. Little, 1989. ISBN 0-316-63385-2 Subj: Counting, numbers. Food. Monsters. Poetry, rhyme.

O'Kelley, Mattie Lou. *Circus!* ill. by author. Atlantic Monthly Pr., 1986. ISBN 0-87113-094-7 Subj: Behavior – misbehavior. Circus. Family life. Farms.

Moving to town ill. by author. Little, 1991. ISBN 0-316-63805-6 Subj: Activities – traveling. City. Moving.

Okimoto, Jean Davies. *Blumpoe the grumpoe meets Arnold the cat* ill. by Howie Schneider. Little, 1990. ISBN 0-316-62811-0 Subj: Animals – cats.

Oksner, Robert M. *The incompetent wizard* ill. by Janet McCaffery. Morrow, 1965. Subj: Dragons. Magic. Wizards.

Old MacDonald had a farm. *Old MacDonald had a farm* ill. by Lorinda Bryan Cauley. Putnam, 1989. ISBN 0-399-21628-6 Subj: Animals. Cumulative tales. Farms. Music. Songs.

Old MacDonald had a farm ill. by Mel Crawford. Golden Pr., 1967. Subj: Animals. Cumulative tales. Farms. Music. Songs.

Old MacDonald had a farm ill. by David Frankland. Merrill, 1980. Subj: Animals. Cumulative tales. Farms. Music. Songs.

Old MacDonald had a farm ill. by Abner Graboff. Four Winds Pr., 1970. Subj: Animals. Cumulative tales. Farms. Music. Songs.

Old MacDonald had a farm ill. by Nancy Hellen. Watts, 1990. ISBN 0-531-05872-7 Subj: Animals. Cumulative tales. Farms. Music. Songs.

Old MacDonald had a farm ill. by Carol Jones. Houghton, 1989. ISBN 0-395-49212-2 Subj: Animals. Cumulative tales. Farms. Format, unusual. Music. Songs.

Old MacDonald had a farm ill. by Tracey Campbell Pearson. Dial Pr., 1984. Subj: Animals. Cumulative tales. Farms. Music. Songs.

Old MacDonald had a farm ill. by Robert M. Quackenbush. Lippincott, 1972. Subj: Animals. Cumulative tales. Farms. Music. Songs.

Old MacDonald had a farm ill. by Glen Rounds. Holiday, 1989. ISBN 0-8234-0739-X Subj: Animals. Cumulative tales. Farms. Music. Songs.

Old MacDonald had a farm ill. by William Stobbs. Oxford Univ. Pr., 1986. ISBN 0-19-279817-0 Subj: Animals. Cumulative tales. Farms. Music. Songs.

Old MacDonald had a farm ill. by Prue Theobalds. Bedrick, 1991. ISBN 0-87226-452-1 Subj: Animals. Cumulative tales. Farms. Music. Songs.

The old woman and her pig. *The old woman and her pig* ill. by Paul Galdone. McGraw-Hill, 1960. Subj: Cumulative tales. Folk and fairy tales.

The troublesome pig retold and ill. by Priscilla Lamont. Crown, 1985. ISBN 0-517-55546-8 Subj: Cumulative tales. Folk and fairy tales.

The old-fashioned children's storybook Wanderer, 1980. Subj: Folk and fairy tales.

Oldfield, Pamela. *Melanie Brown climbs a tree* ill. by Carolyn Dinan. Faber, 1980. Subj: Behavior – misbehavior. Foreign lands – England.

Oldfield, Wendy. *My balloon* (Davies, Kay)

My mirror (Davies, Kay)

Olds, Elizabeth. *Feather mountain* ill. by author. Houghton, 1951. Subj: Birds. Caldecott award honor book.

Little Una ill. by author. Scribner's, 1963. Subj: City.

Plop plop ploppie ill. by author. Scribner's, 1962. Subj: Animals – sea lions. Clowns, jesters.

Olds, Helen Diehl. *Miss Hattie and the monkey* ill. by Dorothy Marino. Follett, 1958. Subj: Animals – monkeys. Careers – seamstresses.

Oleson, Claire. *For Pipita, an orange tree* ill. by Margot Tomes. Doubleday, 1967. Subj: Foreign lands – Spain. Plants.

Oleson, Jens. *Snail* photos. by Bo Jarner. Silver Burdett, 1986. ISBN 0-382-09289-9 Subj: Animals – snails. Science.

Oliver, Dexter. *I want to be...* by Dexter and Patricia Oliver; photos. by Dexter Oliver. Third World Pr., 1974. Subj: ABC books. Careers.

Oliver, Lin. *The fat cat* (Mooser, Stephen)

Oliver, Patricia. *I want to be...* (Oliver, Dexter)

Oliver, Stephen. *Clothes* photos. by Steve Gorton. Random House, 1991. ISBN 0-679-81806-5 Subj: Clothing.

My first look at colors photos. by author. McKay, 1990. ISBN 0-679-80535-4 Subj: Concepts – color.

My first look at numbers photos. by author. McKay, 1990. ISBN 0-679-80533-8 Subj: Counting, numbers.

My first look at shapes photos. by author. McKay, 1990. ISBN 0-679-80534-6 Subj: Concepts – shape.

My first look at sizes photos. by author. McKay, 1990. ISBN 0-679-80532-X Subj: Concepts – size.

Nature photos. by Steve Gorton. Random House, 1991. ISBN 0-679-81805-7 Subj: Nature.

Opposites photos. by author. Random House, 1990. ISBN 0-679-80620-2 Subj: Concepts – opposites.

Seasons photos. by author. Random House, 1990. ISBN 0-679-80621-0 Subj: Seasons.

Shopping photos. by Steve Gorton. Random House, 1991. ISBN 0-679-81803-0 Subj: Shopping. Stores.

Things that go photos. by Steve Gorton. Random House, 1991. ISBN 0-679-81804-9 Subj: Toys. Transportation.

Touch photos. by author. Random House, 1990. ISBN 0-679-80623-7 Subj: Senses – touching.

Olney, Ross R. *Construction giants* ill. with photos. Atheneum, 1984. Subj: Machines.

Farm giants ill. with photos. Atheneum, 1982. Subj: Farms. Machines.

Olschewski, Alfred. *We fly* ill. by author. Little, 1967. Subj: Airplanes, airports.

The wheel rolls over ill. by author. Little, 1962. Subj: Transportation. Wheels.

Olsen, Ib Spang. *The boy in the moon* ill. by author. Parents, 1977. Tr. of Dregen i manen from the Danish by Virginia Allen Jensen ISBN 0-8193-0734-3 Subj: Moon.

Cat alley tr. by Virginia Allen Jensen; ill. by author. Coward, 1971. Translation of Kattehuset Subj: Behavior – lost. City.

The grown-up trap ill. by author. Thomasson-Grant, 1992. ISBN 0-934738-96-3 Subj: Behavior – needing someone. Emotions – loneliness. Family life. Imagination. Poetry, rhyme.

Olson, Arielle North. *Hurry home, Grandma!* ill. by Lydia Dabcovich. Dutton, 1984. ISBN 0-525-44113-1 Subj: Family life – grandmothers. Holidays – Christmas.

The lighthouse keeper's daughter ill. by Elaine Wentworth. Little, 1987. ISBN 0-316-65053-6 Subj: Character traits – bravery. Flowers. Islands. Lighthouses. Weather – storms.

Noah's cats and the devil's fire ill. by Barry Moser. Watts, 1992. ISBN 0-531-08584-8 Subj: Animals – cats. Animals – mice. Boats, ships. Devil. Folk and fairy tales. Foreign lands – Romania. Religion – Noah.

Olson, Helen Kronberg. *The strange thing that happened to Oliver Wendell Iscovitch* ill. by Betsy Lewin. Dodd, 1983. Subj: Behavior – misbehavior. Ghosts. Humor.

Olujic, Grozdana. *Rose of Mother-of-Pearl* tr. from Serbo-Croatian by Grozdana Olujic and Jascha Kessler; ill. by Kathy Jacobi. Toothpaste Pr., 1983. Subj: Behavior – dissatisfaction. Sea and seashore.

On the little hearth tr. by Miriam Chaikin; ill. by Gabriel Lisowski; score by Mark Warshawski. Holt, 1978. Subj: Foreign languages. Jewish culture. Music. Songs.

100 words about transportation ill. by Richard Eric Brown. Harcourt, 1987. ISBN 0-15-200551-X Subj: Language. Transportation.

100 words about working ill. by Richard Eric Brown. Harcourt, 1988. ISBN 0-15-200553-6 Subj: Activities – working. Careers. Language.

One rubber duckie: *a Sesame Street counting book* photos. by John E. Barrett. Random House, 1982. Subj: Counting, numbers. Puppets.

One, two, buckle my shoe: *a book of counting rhymes* comp. and ill. by Rowan Barnes-Murphy. Simon & Schuster, 1988. ISBN 0-671-63791-6 Subj: Counting, numbers. Nursery rhymes.

One, two, buckle my shoe ill. by Gail E. Haley. Doubleday, 1964. Subj: Counting, numbers. Nursery rhymes.

O'Neill, Catharine. *Mrs. Dunphy's dog* ill. by author. Viking, 1987. ISBN 0-670-81135-1 Subj: Activities – reading. Animals – dogs.

O'Neill, Mary. *Big red hen* ill. by Judy Piussi-Campbell. Doubleday, 1971. Subj: Birds – chickens. Eggs. Poetry, rhyme.

Ooka, D. T. *The monkey and the crab* (Horio, Seishi)

The old man who made the trees bloom (Shibano, Tamizo)

Ophir, Uri. *Songs of Chanukah* (Modesitt, Jeanne)

Oppenheim, Joanne. *Donkey's tale* ill. by Chris L. Demarest. Bantam, 1991. ISBN 0-553-07090-8 Subj: Animals – donkeys. Character traits – practicality. Folk and fairy tales. Humor. Poetry, rhyme.

The eency weency spider ill. by S. D. Schindler. Bantam, 1991. ISBN 0-553-07316-8 Subj: Games. Songs. Spiders.

Have you seen birds? ill. by Barbara Reid. Scholastic, 1986. ISBN 0-590-40585-3 Subj: Birds.

Have you seen roads? ill. by Gerard Nook. Addison-Wesley, 1969. Subj: Poetry, rhyme. Transportation.

Have you seen trees? ill. by Irwin Rosenhouse. Addison-Wesley, 1967. Subj: Poetry, rhyme. Seasons. Trees.

James will never die ill. by True Kelley. Dodd, 1982. Subj: Activities – playing.

Left and right ill. by Rosanne Litzinger. Harcourt, 1989. ISBN 0-15-200505-6 Subj: Careers – shoemakers. Concepts – left and right. Family life – brothers.

Mrs. Peloki's class play ill. by Joyce Audy dos Santos. Dodd, 1984. Subj: School. Theater.

Mrs. Peloki's snake ill. by Joyce Audy dos Santos. Dodd, 1980. Subj: Reptiles – snakes. School.

Mrs. Peloki's substitute ill. by Joyce Audy Zarins. Dodd, 1987. ISBN 0-396-08918-6 Subj: Behavior – trickery. School.

"Not now!" said the cow ill. by Chris L. Demarest. Bantam, 1989. ISBN 0-553-34691-1 Subj: Animals. Birds – crows. Character traits – laziness. Cumulative tales. Farms.

On the other side of the river ill. by Aliki. Watts, 1972. Subj: Behavior – needing someone. Bridges. Careers.

Rooter remembers ill. by Lynn Munsinger. Viking, 1991. ISBN 0-670-82865-3 Subj: Family life.

The story book prince ill. by Rosanne Litzinger. Harcourt, 1987. ISBN 0-15-200590-0 Subj: Bedtime. Poetry, rhyme. Royalty – princes. Sleep.

Waiting for Noah ill. by Lillian Hoban. HarperCollins, 1990. ISBN 0-06-024634-0 Subj: Birth. Family life – grandparents.

You can't catch me! ill. by Andrew Shachat. Houghton, 1986. ISBN 0-395-41452-0 Subj: Animals. Behavior – boasting. Cumulative tales. Insects – flies. Poetry, rhyme.

Oppenheim, Shulamith Levey. *The lily cupboard* ill. by Ronald Himler. HarperCollins, 1992. ISBN 0-06-024670-7 Subj: Behavior – hiding. Character traits – bravery. Emotions – fear. War.

Oram, Hiawyn. *A boy wants a dinosaur* ill. by Satoshi Kitamura. Farrar, 1991. ISBN 0-374-30939-6 Subj: Dinosaurs. Dreams. Family life – grandfathers. Pets.

In the attic ill. by Satoshi Kitamura. Holt, 1985. Subj: Activities – playing. Behavior – boredom. Imagination.

Jenna and the troublemaker ill. by Tony Ross. Holt, 1986. ISBN 0-8050-0025-9 Subj: Behavior – dissatisfaction. Mythical creatures.

Mine! ill. by Mary Rees. Barron's, 1992. ISBN 0-8120-6303-1 Subj: Behavior – sharing. Friendship.

Ned and the Joybaloo ill. by Satoshi Kitamura. David & Charles, 1988. ISBN 0-86264-048-2 Subj: Behavior – misbehavior. Character traits – individuality. Imagination – imaginary friends.

Reckless Ruby ill. by Tony Ross. Crown, 1992. ISBN 0-517-58744-0 Subj: Behavior – carelessness. Family life.

Skittlewonder and the wizard ill. by Jenny Rodwell. Dial Pr., 1980. Subj: Folk and fairy tales. Games. Gypsies. Royalty. Witches. Wizards.

Orbach, Ruth. *Apple pigs* ill. by author. Collins-World, 1977. Subj: Food. Poetry, rhyme. Trees.

Please send a panda ill. by author. Collins-World, 1978. Subj: Behavior – wishing. Family life – grandmothers. Pets.

O'Reilly, Edward. *Brown pelican at the pond* ill. by Florence Strange. Manzanita, 1979. Subj: Birds – pelicans. Children as authors.

Orgel, Doris. *Godfather Cat and Mousie* (Grimm, Jacob)

Little John by Theodor Storm; retold from the German by Doris Orgel; ill. by Anita Lobel. Farrar, 1972. Subj: Bedtime. Dreams.

Merry merry FIBruary ill. by Arnold Lobel. Parents, 1978. Subj: Poetry, rhyme.

On the sand dune ill. by Leonard Weisgard. Harper, 1968. Subj: Character traits – smallness. Sea and seashore.

Ormerod, Jan. *Bend and stretch* ill. by author. Lothrop, 1987. ISBN 0-688-07272-0 Subj: Babies. Family life – mothers. Sports.

Come back, kittens ill. by author. Lothrop, 1992. ISBN 0-688-09134-2 Subj: Animals – cats. Counting, numbers. Format, unusual.

Come back, puppies ill. by author. Lothrop, 1992. ISBN 0-688-09135-0 Subj: Animals – dogs. Counting, numbers. Format, unusual.

Dad's back ill. by author. Lothrop, 1985. ISBN 0-688-04126-4 Subj: Babies. Clothing. Family life – fathers.

Just like me ill. by author. Lothrop, 1986. ISBN 0-688-04211-2 Subj: Babies. Character traits – appearance.

Kitten day ill. by author. Lothrop, 1989. ISBN 0-688-08537-7 Subj: Animals – cats. Pets.

Making friends ill. by author. Lothrop, 1987. ISBN 0-688-07270-4 Subj: Babies. Family life – mothers. Toys – dolls.

Messy baby ill. by author. Lothrop, 1985. ISBN 0-688-04128-0 Subj: Babies. Family life – fathers. Toys.

Mom's home ill. by author. Lothrop, 1987. ISBN 0-688-07274-7 Subj: Babies. Family life – mothers.

Moonlight ill. by author. Lothrop, 1982. Subj: Bedtime. Family life. Sleep. Wordless.

101 things to do with a baby ill. by author. Lothrop, 1984. Subj: Babies. Behavior – sharing. Sibling rivalry.

Our Ollie ill. by author. Lothrop, 1986. ISBN 0-688-04208-2 Subj: Babies. Character traits – appearance.

Reading ill. by author. Lothrop, 1985. Subj: Activities – reading. Family life – fathers.

The saucepan game ill. by author. Lothrop, 1989. ISBN 0-688-08519-9 Subj: Activities – playing. Animals – cats. Babies. Imagination.

Silly goose ill. by author. Lothrop, 1986. ISBN 0-688-04209-0 Subj: Babies. Character traits – appearance.

Sleeping ill. by author. Lothrop, 1985. ISBN 0-688-04129-9 Subj: Babies. Family life – fathers. Sleep.

The story of Chicken Licken (Chicken Little)

Sunshine ill. by author. Lothrop, 1981. Subj: Morning. Sun. Wordless.

This little nose ill. by author. Lothrop, 1987. ISBN 0-688-07276-3 Subj: Anatomy – noses. Babies. Family life – mothers. Illness.

When we went to the zoo ill. by author. Lothrop, 1991. ISBN 0-688-09879-7 Subj: Animals. Zoos.

Young Joe ill. by author. Lothrop, 1986. ISBN 0-688-04210-4 Subj: Babies. Counting, numbers.

Ormondroyd, Edward. *Broderick* ill. by John M. Larrecq. Parnassus, 1969. Subj: Activities – reading. Animals – mice. Sports – surfing.

Johnny Castleseed ill. by Diana Thewlis. Houghton, 1985. ISBN 0-395-38355-2 Subj: Sand. Sea and seashore.

Theodore ill. by John M. Larrecq. Parnassus, 1966. Subj: Character traits – appearance. Character traits – kindness. Laundry. Toys – teddy bears.

Theodore's rival ill. by John M. Larrecq. Parnassus, 1971. Subj: Emotions – envy, jealousy. Sibling rivalry. Toys – teddy bears.

Ormsby, Virginia H. *Twenty-one children plus ten* ill. by author. Lippincott, 1971. Subj: Ethnic groups in the U.S. – Mexican-Americans. School.

Orstadius, Brita. *The dolphin journey* tr. from Swedish by Eric Bibb; ill. by Lennart Didoff. Farrar, 1989. ISBN 9-12-959138-4 Subj: Animals – dolphins. Character traits – kindness to animals. Foreign lands.

Ortiz, Simon. *The people shall continue* ill. by Sharol Graves. Childrens Book Pr., 1988. ISBN 0-89239-041-7 Subj: Indians of North America. U.S. history.

Osborne, Mary Pope. *Moonhorse* ill. by S. M. Saelig. Knopf, 1991. ISBN 0-394-98960-0 Subj: Activities – flying. Animals – horses. Behavior – wishing. Night.

Osborne, Valerie. *One big yo to go* ill. by Jiri Tibor Novak. Oxford Univ. Pr., 1981. Subj: Poetry, rhyme.

Osborne, Victor. *Rex, the most special car in the world* ill. by Scoular Anderson. Carolrhoda, 1989. ISBN 0-87614-357-5 Subj: Automobiles.

O'Shell, Marcia. *Alphabet Annie announces an all-American album* by Marcia O'Shell and Susan Purviance; ill. by Ruth Brunner-Strosser. Houghton, 1988. ISBN 0-395-48070-1 Subj: ABC books. City.

Osofsky, Audrey. *Dreamcatcher* ill. by Ed Young. Watts, 1992. ISBN 0-531-08588-0 Subj: Dreams. Family life. Folk and fairy tales. Indians of North America.

Ostheeren, Ingrid. *Jonathan Mouse* ill. by Agnès Mathieu; tr. by Rosemary Lanning. Holt, 1986. ISBN 0-03-005848-1 Subj: Animals – mice. Concepts – color. Magic.

Jonathan Mouse and the baby bird tr. from German by Rosemary Lanning; ill. by Agnes Mathieu. North-South, 1991. ISBN 1-55858-108-1 Subj: Animals – mice. Birds – sparrows. Farms.

Jonathan Mouse and the magic box tr. by Rosemary Lanning; ill. by Agnes Mathieu. North-South, 1990. ISBN 1-55858-087-5 Subj: Animals – mice. Magic.

Ostrovsky, Vivian. *Mumps!* ill. by Rose Ostrovsky. Holt, 1978. Subj: Illness.

Otey, Mimi. *Daddy has a pair of striped shorts* ill. by author. Farrar, 1990. ISBN 0-374-31675-9 Subj: Clothing. Family life – fathers.

Otsuka, Yuzo. *Suho and the white horse: a legend of Mongolia* tr. by Ann Herring; ill. by Suekichi Akaba. Viking, 1981. Subj: Animals – horses. Emotions – love. Sports – racing.

Ott, John. *Peter Pumpkin* originated by Peter Coley; ill. by Ivan Chermayeff. Doubleday, 1963. Subj: Holidays – Halloween. Holidays – Thanksgiving. Seasons – fall.

Otto, Carolyn. *Dinosaur chase* ill. by Thacher Hurd. HarperCollins, 1991. ISBN 0-06-021614-X Subj: Bedtime. Dinosaurs. Poetry, rhyme.

Ducks, ducks, ducks ill. by Molly Coxe. HarperCollins, 1991. ISBN 0-06-024639-1 Subj: Birds – ducks. City. Poetry, rhyme.

That sky, that rain ill. by Megan Lloyd. HarperCollins, 1990. ISBN 0-690-04765-7 Subj: Family life – grandfathers. Farms. Sky. Weather – rain.

Otto, Margaret Glover. *The little brown horse* ill. by Barbara Cooney. Knopf, 1959. Subj: Animals – cats. Animals – horses. Birds – chickens.

Otto, Svend. *The giant fish and other stories* by Svend Otto S.; tr. from Danish by Joan Tate; ill. by author. Larousse, 1982. Subj: Behavior – growing up. Foreign lands.

Taxi dog by Svend Otto S.; ill. by author. Parents, 1978. Subj: Animals – dogs. Behavior – running away. Careers – taxi drivers.

Oughton, Jerrie. *How the stars fell into the sky* ill. by Lisa Desimini. Houghton, 1992. ISBN 0-395-58798-0 Subj: Folk and fairy tales. Indians of North America. Sky. Stars.

Our house ill. by Roser Capdevila. Firefly Pr., 1985. ISBN 0-920303-10-2 Subj: City. Format, unusual – board books. Houses.

Over in the meadow: *an old nursery counting rhyme* adapt. and ill. by Paul Galdone. Prentice-Hall, 1986. ISBN 0-13-646654-0 Subj: Animals. Counting, numbers. Nursery rhymes.

Over in the meadow ill. by Ezra Jack Keats. Four Winds Pr., 1971. Subj: Animals. Counting, numbers. Folk and fairy tales. Poetry, rhyme. Songs.

Overbeck, Cynthia. *Rusty the Irish setter* rev. English text by Cynthia Overbeck; original French text by Anne Marie Pajot; tr. by Dyan Hammarberg; photos. by Antoinette Barrère; ill. by L'Enc Matte. Carolrhoda Books, 1977. Original ed. published under title: Jimmy, le grand chien Subj: Animals – dogs.

The winds that blow (Thompson, Brenda)

Owen, Annie. *Bumper to bumper* ill. by author. Knopf, 1991. ISBN 0-679-91448-X Subj: Activities – traveling. Automobiles. Birthdays. Noise, sounds.

My aunt and the animals (MacDonald, Elizabeth)

Owens, Mary Beth. *A caribou alphabet* ill. by Mark McCollough. Farrar, 1990. ISBN 0-374-41043-7 Subj: ABC books. Animals – reindeer. Poetry, rhyme.

Oxenbury, Helen. *All fall down* ill. by author. Macmillan, 1987. ISBN 0-02-769040-7 Subj: Activities – playing. Babies. Format, unusual – board books. Games.

Beach day ill. by author. Dial Pr., 1982. Subj: Family life. Format, unusual – board books. Sea and seashore. Wordless.

The birthday party ill. by author. Dial Pr., 1983. Subj: Birthdays.

The car trip ill. by author. Dial Pr., 1983. Subj: Automobiles. Behavior – bad day. Behavior – misbehavior.

The checkup ill. by author. Dial Pr., 1983. Subj: Careers – doctors. Health.

Clap hands ill. by author. Macmillan, 1987. ISBN 0-02-769030-X Subj: Activities – playing. Babies. Format, unusual – board books.

The dancing class ill. by author. Dial Pr., 1983. Subj: Activities – dancing.

Dressing ill. by author. Simon & Schuster, 1981. ISBN 0-671-42113-1 Subj: Clothing. Format, unusual – board books.

Eating out ill. by author. Dial Pr., 1983. Subj: Food.

Family ill. by author. Simon and Schuster, 1981. Subj: Family life. Format, unusual – board books.

First day of school ill. by author. Dial Pr., 1983. Subj: Friendship. School.

Friends ill. by author. Simon and Schuster, 1981. Subj: Animals. Format, unusual – board books. Friendship.

Good night, good morning ill. by author. Dial Pr., 1982. Subj: Bedtime. Morning. Wordless.

Grandma and Grandpa ill. by author. Dial Pr., 1984. ISBN 0-8037-0128-4 Subj: Activities – playing. Family life – grandparents.

Helen Oxenbury's ABC of things ill. by author. Watts, 1971. Subj: ABC books.

I can ill. by author. Random House, 1985. ISBN 0-394-87482-X Subj: Activities. Babies. Format, unusual – board books.

I hear ill. by author. Random House, 1985. ISBN 0-394-87481-1 Subj: Babies. Format, unusual – board books. Noise, sounds. Senses – hearing.

I see ill. by author. Random House, 1985. ISBN 0-394-87479-X Subj: Babies. Format, unusual – board books. Senses – seeing.

I touch ill. by author. Random House, 1985. ISBN 0-394-87480-3 Subj: Babies. Format, unusual – board books. Senses – touching.

The important visitor ill. by author. Dial Pr., 1984. ISBN 0-8037-0125-X Subj: Behavior – misbehavior.

Monkey see, monkey do ill. by author. Dial Pr., 1982. Subj: Animals. Wordless. Zoos.

Mother's helper ill. by author. Dial Pr., 1982. Subj: Character traits – helpfulness. Family life – mothers. Wordless.

Numbers of things ill. by author. Watts, 1968. Subj: Counting, numbers.

Our dog ill. by author. Dial Pr., 1984. ISBN 0-8037-0127-6 Subj: Activities – walking. Animals – dogs. Family life. Pets.

Pig tale ill. by author. Morrow, 1974. Subj: Animals – pigs. Poetry, rhyme.

Pippo gets lost ill. by author. Macmillan, 1989. ISBN 0-689-71336-3 Subj: Animals. Behavior – losing things. Toys.

Playing ill. by author. Wanderer Books, 1981. Subj: Activities – playing. Babies. Format, unusual – board books. Toys.

The queen and Rosie Randall by Helen Oxenbury from an idea by Jill Butterfield-Campbell; ill. by author. Morrow, 1979. Subj: Foreign lands – England. Games. Parties. Royalty – queens.

Say goodnight ill. by author. Macmillan, 1987. ISBN 0-02-769010-5 Subj: Activities – playing. Babies. Format, unusual – board books. Sleep.

729 curious creatures ill. by author. Harper, 1980. Subj: Animals. Format, unusual – board books. Imagination.

729 merry mix-ups ill. by author. Harper, 1980. Subj: Animals. Format, unusual – board books. Imagination.

729 puzzle people ill. by author. Harper, 1980. Subj: Format, unusual – board books. Imagination.

The shopping trip ill. by author. Dial Pr., 1982. Subj: Format, unusual – board books. Shopping. Wordless.

Tickle, tickle ill. by author. Macmillan, 1987. ISBN 0-02-769020-2 Subj: Activities – playing. Babies. Format, unusual – board books.

Tom and Pippo and the dog ill. by author. Macmillan, 1989. ISBN 0-689-71338-X Subj: Activities – playing. Animals – dogs. Animals – monkeys. Friendship. Toys.

Tom and Pippo go shopping ill. by author. Macmillan, 1989. ISBN 0-689-71278-2 Subj: Animals – monkeys. Shopping. Toys.

Tom and Pippo in the garden ill. by author. Macmillan, 1989. ISBN 0-689-71275-8 Subj: Animals – monkeys. Gardens, gardening. Toys.

Tom and Pippo on the beach ill. by author. Candlewick Pr., 1993. ISBN 1-56402-181-5 Subj: Animals – monkeys. Sea and seashore. Toys.

Tom and Pippo see the moon ill. by author. Macmillan, 1989. ISBN 0-689-71277-4 Subj: Animals – monkeys. Moon. Space and space ships. Toys.

Tom and Pippo's day ill. by author. Macmillan, 1989. ISBN 0-689-71276-6 Subj: Activities. Animals – monkeys. Toys.

Oxford Scientific Films. *Danger colors* ed. by Jennifer Coldrey and Karen Goldie-Morrison. Putnam's, 1986. ISBN 0-399-21341-4 Subj: Behavior – hiding. Concepts – color.

Grey squirrel photos. by George Bernard and John Paling. Putnam's, 1982. Subj: Animals – squirrels. Science.

Hide and seek ed. by Jennifer Coldrey and Karen Goldie-Morrison. Putnam's, 1986. ISBN 0-399-21342-2 Subj: Behavior – hiding. Concepts – color.

The spider's web photos. by John Cooke. Putnam's, 1978. Subj: Spiders. Science.

Pace, Elizabeth. *Chris gets ear tubes* ill. by Kathryn Hutton. Gallaudet Univ. Pr., 1987. ISBN 0-930323-36-X Subj: Handicaps – deafness. Hospitals. Illness. Senses – hearing.

Pacheco, Miguel Angel. *Kangaroo* (Sanchez, Jose Louis Garcia)

Pack, Robert. *How to catch a crocodile* ill. by Nola Langner. Knopf, 1964. Subj: Character traits – laziness. Imagination. Poetry, rhyme. Reptiles – alligators, crocodiles.

Then what did you do? ill. by Nola Langner. Macmillan, 1961. Subj: Animals. Cumulative tales. Humor. Poetry, rhyme.

Packard, Mary. *The kite* ill. by Benrei Huang. Children's Pr., 1990. ISBN 0-516-05355-8 Subj: Kites. Poetry, rhyme.

Where is Jake? ill. by Carolyn Ewing. Children's Pr., 1990. ISBN 0-516-05361-2 Subj: Activities – playing. Games.

Pacovska, Kveta. *One, five, many* ill. by author. Houghton, 1990. ISBN 0-395-54997-3 Subj: Counting, numbers. Format, unusual. Poetry, rhyme.

Paek, Min. *Aekyung's dream* ill. by author. Childrens Book Pr., 1989. ISBN 0-89239-042-5 Subj: Character traits – being different. Ethnic groups in the U.S. School.

Page, Eleanor *see* Coerr, Eleanor

Page, P. K. (Patricia Kathleen). *The traveling musicians of Bremen* (Grimm, Jacob)

Paige, Rob. *Some of my best friends are monsters* ill. by Paul Yalowitz. Bradbury Pr., 1988. ISBN 0-02-769640-5 Subj: Monsters.

Paine, Penelope Colville. *My way Sally* (Bingham, Mindy)

Pajot, Anne Marie. *Rusty the Irish setter* (Overbeck, Cynthia)

Palacios, Argentina. *This can lick a lollipop* (Rothman, Joel)

Paladino, Catherine. *Our vanishing farm animals* ill. with photos. Little, 1992. ISBN 0-316-68891-6 Subj: Animals – endangered animals. Farms.

Palazzo, Janet. *Our friend the sun* ill. by Susan Hall. Troll Assoc., 1982. Subj: Science. Sun.

What makes the weather ill. by Paul Harvey. Troll Assoc., 1982. Subj: Weather.

Palazzo, Tony (Anthony D.). *Animal babies* ill. by author. Doubleday, 1960. Subj: Animals.

Animals 'round the mulberry bush ill. by author. Doubleday, 1958. Subj: Animals. Nursery rhymes.

Noah's ark ill. by author. Doubleday, 1955. Subj: Religion – Noah.

Waldo the woodchuck ill. by author. Duell, 1964. Subj: Animals – groundhogs. Holidays – Groundhog Day.

Paleček, Phyllis. *The ugly duckling* (Andersen, H. C. (Hans Christian))

Pallotta, Jerry. *Going lobstering* ill. by Rob Bolster. Charlesbridge, 1990. ISBN 0-88106-475-0 Subj: Careers – fishermen. Sea and seashore.

Palmer, Carole. *Why does it fly?* (Arvetis, Chris)

Why does it thunder and lightning? (Arvetis, Chris)

Why is it dark? (Arvetis, Chris)

Palmer, Mary Babcock. *No-sort-of-animal* ill. by Abner Graboff. Houghton, 1964. Subj: Animals. Behavior – dissatisfaction. Self-concept.

Palmisciano, Diane. *Garden partners* ill. by author. Atheneum, 1989. ISBN 0-689-31415-9 Subj: Family life – grandmothers. Gardens, gardening.

Panek, Dennis. *Ba ba sheep wouldn't go to sleep* ill. by author. Watts, 1988. ISBN 0-531-08376-4 Subj: School. Sleep.

Catastrophe Cat ill. by author. Bradbury Pr., 1978. Subj: Animals – cats. Behavior – carelessness.

Catastrophe Cat at the zoo ill. by author. Bradbury Pr., 1979. Subj: Animals – cats. Wordless. Zoos.

Detective Whoo ill. by author. Bradbury Pr., 1981. ISBN 0-87888-183-2 Subj: Birds – owls. Careers – detectives. Circus. Noise, sounds. Problem solving.

Matilda Hippo has a big mouth ill. by author. Bradbury Pr., 1980. Subj: Animals – hippopotami. Behavior.

Paola, Tomi (Thomas Anthony) de *see* De Paola, Tomi (Thomas Anthony)

Papajani, Janet. *Museums* ill. with photos. Children's Pr., 1983. Subj: Museums.

Papas, William. *Taresh the tea planter* ill. by author. Collins-World, 1968. Subj: Character traits – laziness. Foreign lands – India.

Pape, D. L. (Donna Lugg). *Doghouse for sale* ill. by Tom Eaton. Garrard, 1979. Subj: Animals – dogs. Houses.

Snoino mystery ill. by William Hutchinson. Garrard, 1980. Subj: Problem solving.

Where is my little Joey? ill. by Tom Eaton. Garrard, 1978. Subj: Animals – kangaroos.

A paper of pins ill. by Margaret Gordon. Seabury Pr., 1975. Subj: Folk and fairy tales. Money. Songs.

Paré, Roger. *Animal capers* by Roger Paré with Bertrand Gauthier; tr. by David Homel; ill. by Roger Paré. Firefly, 1992. ISBN 1-55037-243-2 Subj: Animals. Poetry, rhyme.

Circus days by Roger Paré with Bertrand Gauthier; tr. by David Homel; ill. by Roger Paré. Firefly, 1988. ISBN 1-55037-021-9 Subj: Animals. Circus. Poetry, rhyme.

A friend like you tr. by David Homel; ill. by author. Firefly, 1984. ISBN 0-920303-04-8 Subj: Animals – cats. Friendship.

Play time by Roger Paré with Bertrand Gauthier; tr. by David Homel; ill. by Roger Paré. Firefly, 1990. ISBN 1-55037-087-1 Subj: Animals. Poetry, rhyme.

Summer days by Roger Paré with Bertrand Gauthier; tr. by David Homel; ill. by Roger Paré. Firefly, 1989. ISBN 1-55037-043-X Subj: Activities – playing. Animals. Poetry, rhyme.

Parenteau, Shirley. *I'll bet you thought I was lost* ill. by Lorna Tomei. Lothrop, 1981. Subj: Behavior – lost.

Paris, Lena. *Mom is single* ill. by Mark Christianson. Childrens Pr., 1980. ISBN 0-516-01477-3 Subj: Divorce. Family life – fathers. Family life – mothers.

Parish, Peggy. *Be ready at eight* ill. by Leonard P. Kessler. Macmillan, 1979. Subj: Behavior – forgetfulness. Birthdays.

The cat's burglar ill. by Lynn Sweat. Greenwillow, 1983. Subj: Animals – cats. Crime.

Dinosaur time ill. by Arnold Lobel. Harper, 1974. Subj: Dinosaurs. Science.

Good hunting, Blue Sky ill. by James Watts. Harper, 1988. ISBN 0-06-024662-6 Subj: Indians of North America. Sports – hunting.

Good hunting, Little Indian ill. by Leonard Weisgard. Addison-Wesley, 1962. Subj: Indians of North America.

Granny and the desperadoes ill. by Steven Kellogg. Macmillan, 1970. Subj: Crime. Family life – grandmothers. Humor.

Granny and the Indians ill. by Brinton Turkle. Macmillan, 1969. Subj: Family life – grandmothers. Humor. Indians of North America.

Granny, the baby and the big gray thing ill. by Lynn Sweat. Macmillan, 1972. Subj: Animals – wolves. Babies. Family life – grandmothers. Humor. Indians of North America.

I can—can you? ill. by Marylin Hafner. Greenwillow, 1984. Set of 4 books: levels 1-4 Subj: Activities. Behavior – growing up. Format, unusual – board books.

Jumper goes to school ill. by Cyndy Szekeres. Simon and Schuster, 1969. Subj: Animals – monkeys. School.

Little Indian ill. by John E. Johnson. Simon and Schuster, 1968. Subj: Indians of North America. Names.

Mind your manners ill. by Marylin Hafner. Greenwillow, 1978. Subj: Etiquette.

No more monsters for me! ill. by Marc Simont. Harper, 1981. Subj: Monsters. Pets.

Ootah's lucky day ill. by Mamoru Funai. Harper, 1970. Subj: Eskimos. Sports – hunting.

Scruffy ill. by Kelly Oechsli. Harper, 1988. ISBN 0-06-024660-X Subj: Animals – cats. Birthdays. Pets.

Snapping turtle's all wrong day ill. by John E. Johnson. Simon and Schuster, 1970. Subj: Birthdays. Indians of North America.

Too many rabbits ill. by Leonard P. Kessler. Macmillan, 1974. Subj: Animals – rabbits.

Zed and the monsters ill. by Paul Galdone. Doubleday, 1979. Subj: Character traits – cleverness. Monsters.

Park, Ruth. *When the wind changed* ill. by Deborah Niland. Coward, 1981. Subj: Character traits – appearance.

Park, W. B. *Bakery business* ill. by author. Little, 1983. Subj: Animals. Birthdays.

The costume party ill. by author. Little, 1983. Subj: Animals. Emotions – loneliness. Parties.

Parke, Margaret B. *Young reader's color-picture dictionary* ill. by Cynthia and Alvin Koehler. Grosset, 1958. Subj: Dictionaries.

Parker, Dorothy D. *Liam's catch* ill. by Robert Andrew Parker. Viking, 1972. Subj: Careers – fishermen. Foreign lands – Ireland. Sports – fishing.

Parker, Kristy. *My dad the magnificent* ill. by Lillian Hoban. Dutton, 1987. ISBN 0-525-44314-2 Subj: Behavior – boasting. Family life – fathers.

Parker, Nancy Winslow. *Bugs* by Nancy Winslow Parker and Joan Richards Wright; ill. by Nancy Winslow Parker. Greenwillow, 1987. ISBN 0-688-06624-0 Subj: Insects. Science.

The Christmas camel ill. by author. Dodd, 1983. Subj: Animals – camels. Holidays – Christmas.

Cooper, the McNallys' big black dog ill. by author. Dodd, 1981. Subj: Animals – dogs. Behavior – misbehavior. Character traits – helpfulness.

The crocodile under Louis Finneberg's bed ill. by author. Dodd, 1978. Subj: Behavior – running away. Behavior – trickery. Furniture – beds. Reptiles – alligators, crocodiles.

Love from Aunt Betty ill. by author. Dodd, 1983. Subj: Activities – cooking. Family life – aunts, uncles. Monsters.

Love from Uncle Clyde ill. by author. Dodd, 1977. Subj: Animals – hippopotami. Birthdays. Family life – aunts, uncles.

Poofy loves company ill. by author. Dodd, 1980. Subj: Animals – dogs. Behavior – misbehavior.

Puddums, the Cathcarts' orange cat ill. by author. Atheneum, 1980. Subj: Animals – cats. Behavior.

Working frog ill. by author. Greenwillow, 1992. ISBN 0-688-09919-X Subj: Animals. Frogs and toads. Zoos.

Parkin, Rex. *The red carpet* ill. by author. Macmillan, 1988, 1948. ISBN 0-02-770010-0 Subj: Hotels. Humor.

Parkinson, Kathy. *The enormous turnip* ill. by adapt. Albert Whitman, 1985. ISBN 0-8075-2062-4 Subj: Behavior – sharing. Cumulative tales. Folk and fairy tales.

Parks, Van Dyke. *Jump!* (Harris, Joel Chandler)

Jump again! (Harris, Joel Chandler)

Parnall, Peter. *Alfalfa Hill* ill. by author. Doubleday, 1975. Subj: Animals. Birds. Seasons – winter. Weather – snow.

The great fish ill. by author. Doubleday, 1973. Subj: Ecology. Indians of North America. Fish. Folk and fairy tales.

The rock ill. by author. Macmillan, 1991. ISBN 0-02-770181-6 Subj: Ecology. Forest, woods. Rocks.

Winter barn ill. by author. Macmillan, 1986. ISBN 0-02-770170-0 Subj: Animals. Barns. Seasons – winter.

Parr, Letitia. *A man and his hat* ill. by Paul Terrett; photos. by Bob Peters. Putnam, 1991. ISBN 0-399-22255-3 Subj: Behavior – losing things. Clothing – hats. Poetry, rhyme.

Parry, Marian. *King of the fish* ill. by author. Macmillan, 1977. Subj: Animals – rabbits. Character traits – cleverness. Fish. Folk and fairy tales. Foreign lands – Korea. Reptiles – turtles, tortoises.

Parsons, Alexandra. *Amazing birds* photos. by Jerry Young. Knopf, 1990. ISBN 0-679-90223-6 Subj: Birds. Science.

Amazing mammals photos. by Jerry Young. Knopf, 1990. ISBN 0-679-90224-4 Subj: Animals. Science.

Amazing snakes photos. by Jerry Young. Knopf, 1990. ISBN 0-679-90225-2 Subj: Reptiles – snakes. Science.

Amazing spiders photos. by Jerry Young. Knopf, 1990. ISBN 0-679-90226-0 Subj: Science. Spiders.

Parsons, Virginia. *Pinocchio and Gepetto* ill. by adapt. McGraw-Hill, 1979. Subj: Folk and fairy tales. Puppets.

Pinocchio and the money tree ill. by adapt. McGraw-Hill, 1979. Subj: Folk and fairy tales. Puppets.

Pinocchio goes on the stage ill. by adapt. McGraw-Hill, 1979. Subj: Folk and fairy tales. Puppets.

Pinocchio plays truant ill. by adapt. McGraw-Hill, 1979. Subj: Folk and fairy tales. Puppets.

Partch, Virgil Franklin. *The Christmas cookie sprinkle snitcher* ill. by author. Windmill Books, 1969. Subj: Crime. Holidays – Christmas. Poetry, rhyme. Rebuses.

Partridge, Jenny. *Colonel Grunt* ill. by author. Holt, 1982. Subj: Animals.

Grandma Snuffles ill. by author. Holt, 1983. Subj: Animals. Clothing.

Hopfellow ill. by author. Holt, 1982. Subj: Animals. Boats, ships. Frogs and toads. Problem solving.

Mr. Squint ill. by author. Holt, 1982. Subj: Animals. Problem solving.

Peterkin Pollensnuff ill. by author. Holt, 1982. Subj: Animals. Character traits – helpfulness. Problem solving.

Parvathi, Thampi. *Moon-uncle, moon-uncle* (Cassedy, Sylvia)

Passen, Lisa. *Fat, fat Rose Marie* ill. by author. Holt, 1991. ISBN 0-8050-1653-8 Subj: Behavior – bullying. Character traits – being different. Friendship.

Grammy and Sammy ill. by author. Holt, 1990. ISBN 0-8050-1415-2 Subj: Animals – cats. Family life – grandmothers.

Patent, Dorothy Hinshaw. *Babies!* photos. by author. Holiday House, 1988. ISBN 0-8234-0685-7 Subj: Babies.

Maggie, a sheep dog photos. by William Muñoz. Dodd, 1986. ISBN 0-396-08617-9 Subj: Animals – dogs. Animals – sheep.

Paterson, A. B. (Andrew Barton). *The man from Ironbark* ill. by Quentin Hole. Collins-World, 1975. Subj: Character traits – cleverness. Poetry, rhyme.

Mulga Bill's bicycle ill. by Kilmeny and Deborah Niland. Parents, 1975. Subj: Animals – horses. Foreign lands – Australia. Poetry, rhyme. Sports – bicycling.

Waltzing Matilda ill. by Desmund Digby. Holt, 1970. Subj: Foreign lands – Australia. Songs.

Paterson, Bettina. *Bun and Mrs. Tubby* ill. by author. Watts, 1987. ISBN 0-531-08300-4 Subj: Activities – baby-sitting. Animals – elephants.

Bun's birthday ill. by author. Watts, 1988. ISBN 0-531-08336-5 Subj: Animals – elephants. Behavior – sharing. Birthdays. Parties.

In my house ill. by author. Holt, 1992. ISBN 0-8050-1882-4 Subj: Format, unusual – board books.

In my yard ill. by author. Holt, 1992. ISBN 0-8050-1881-6 Subj: Format, unusual – board books.

My clothes ill. by author. Holt, 1992. ISBN 0-8050-1884-0 Subj: Clothing. Format, unusual – board books.

My first wild animals ill. by author. HarperCollins, 1991. ISBN 0-690-04773-8 Subj: Animals.

My toys ill. by author. Holt, 1992. ISBN 0-8050-1883-2 Subj: Format, unusual – board books. Toys.

Paterson, Diane. *The bathtub ocean* ill. by author. Dial Pr., 1979. Subj: Activities – bathing. Imagination.

Eat ill. by author. Dial Pr., 1975. Subj: Food. Humor.

Hey, cowboy! ill. by author. Knopf, 1983. Subj: Family life – grandfathers. Sibling rivalry.

If I were a toad ill. by author. Dial Pr., 1977. Subj: Animals. Behavior – wishing. Participation.

Smile for auntie ill. by author. Dial Pr., 1976. Subj: Family life – aunts, uncles. Humor.

Soap and suds ill. by author. Knopf, 1984. Subj: Activities – working. Behavior – misbehavior.

Wretched Rachel ill. by author. Dial Pr., 1978. Subj: Behavior. Emotions – love. Family life.

Paterson, Katherine. *The crane wife* (Yagawa, Sumiko)

The tale of the Mandarin ducks ill. by Leo and Diane Dillon. Dutton, 1990. ISBN 0-525-67283-4 Subj: Birds – ducks. Folk and fairy tales. Foreign lands – Japan.

The tongue-cut sparrow (Ishii, Momoko)

Patkau, Karen. *In the sea* ill. by author. Firefly, 1989. ISBN 1-55037-067-7 Subj: Sea and seashore.

Paton Walsh, Jill see Walsh, Jill Paton

Patrick, Denice. *Look inside a house* tr. by Denice Patrick; ill. by Mario Gomboli. Putnam, 1989. ISBN 0-448-19351-5 Subj: Format, unusual – board books. Houses.

Look inside a house (Patrick, Denice)

Look inside a ship (Patrick, Denice)

Look inside a ship tr. by Denice Patrick; ill. by Mario Gomboli. Putnam, 1989. ISBN 0-448-19352-3 Subj: Boats, ships. Format, unusual – board books.

Patron, Susan. *Burgoo stew* ill. by Mike Shenon. Watts, 1991. ISBN 0-531-08516-3 Subj: Activities – cooking. Character traits – cleverness. Folk and fairy tales. Food. Foreign lands – France.

Patterson, Geoffrey. *Jonah and the whale* ill. by adaptor. Lothrop, 1992. ISBN 0-688-11238-2 Subj: Animals – whales. Religion.

The lion and the gypsy ill. by author. Doubleday, 1991. ISBN 0-385-41536-2 Subj: Animals. Gypsies. Music.

A pig's tale ill. by author. Dutton, 1983. ISBN 0-233-97477-6 Subj: Animals – pigs. Behavior – running away. Farms.

Patterson, José. *Mazal-Tov: a Jewish wedding* photos. by Liba Taylor. David & Charles, 1988. ISBN 0-241-12269-4 Subj: Jewish culture. Weddings.

Patterson, Pat. *Hickory dickory duck: a book of very funny rhymes and picture puzzles* by Pat Patterson and Joe Weissmann. Greey de Pencier Books, 1982. Subj: Games. Nursery rhymes.

Pattison, Darcy. *The river dragon* ill. by Jean and Mou-Sien Tseng. Lothrop, 1991. ISBN 0-688-10427-4 Subj: Dragons. Folk and fairy tales. Foreign lands – China.

Patz, Nancy. *Gina Farina and the Prince of Mintz* ill. by author. Harcourt, 1986. ISBN 0-15-230815-6 Subj: Activities – traveling. Character traits – meanness. Character traits – persistence. Royalty – princes. Theater.

Moses supposes his toeses are roses and 7 other silly old rhymes ill. by author. Harcourt, 1983. Subj: Poetry, rhyme.

No thumpin' no bumpin' no rumpus tonight! ill. by author. Atheneum, 1990. ISBN 0-689-31510-4 Subj: Animals – elephants. Birthdays. Family life – mothers. Food. Imagination – imaginary friends.

Pumpernickel tickle and mean green cheese ill. by author. Watts, 1978. Subj: Animals – elephants. Behavior – forgetfulness. Humor. Shopping. Tongue twisters.

Sarah Bear and Sweet Sidney ill. by author. Four Winds, 1989. ISBN 0-02-770270-7 Subj: Animals – bears. Hibernation. Poetry, rhyme. Seasons – spring. Seasons – winter.

To Annabella Pelican from Thomas Hippopotamus ill. by author. Four Winds, 1991. ISBN 0-02-770280-4 Subj: Animals – hippopotami. Birds – pelicans. Friendship. Moving.

Paul, Anthony. *The tiger who lost his stripes* ill. by Michael Foreman. Harcourt, 1982. Subj: Animals – tigers. Character traits – cleverness. Forest, woods.

Paul, Jan S. *Hortense* ill. by Madelaine Gill Linden. Harper, 1984. ISBN 0-690-04371-6 Subj: Animals. Behavior – lost. Farms.

Paul, Korky. *Pop-up numbers #1* (Marshall, Ray)

Pop-up numbers #2 (Marshall, Ray)

Pop-up numbers #3 (Marshall, Ray)

Pop-up numbers #4 (Marshall, Ray)

Paul, Sherry. *2-B and the rock 'n roll band* ill. by Bob Miller. Children's Pr., 1981. Subj: Character traits – helpfulness. Robots.

2-B and the space visitor ill. by Bob Miller. Children's Pr., 1981. Subj: Holidays – Halloween. Robots. Space and space ships.

Pavey, Peter. *I'm Taggarty Toad* ill. by author. Bradbury Pr., 1980. Subj: Behavior – boasting. Frogs and toads. Imagination.

One dragon's dream ill. by author. Bradbury Pr., 1979. Subj: Counting, numbers. Dragons. Dreams. Poetry, rhyme.

Paxton, Tom. *Androcles and the lion* (Æsop)

Belling the cat and other Æsop fables ill. by Robert Rayevsky. Morrow, 1990. ISBN 0-688-08159-2 Subj: Animals. Folk and fairy tales.

Engelbert the elephant ill. by Steven Kellogg. Morrow, 1990. ISBN 0-688-08936-4 Subj: Activities – dancing. Animals – elephants. Etiquette. Parties. Royalty – queens.

Jennifer's rabbit ill. by Donna Ayers. Morrow, 1988. ISBN 0-688-07432-4 Subj: Behavior – running away. Dreams. Poetry, rhyme.

Payne, Emmy. *Katy no-pocket* ill. by Hans Augusto Rey. Houghton, 1944. Subj: Animals – kangaroos. Clothing. Problem solving.

Payne, Joan Balfour. *The stable that stayed* ill. by author. Ariel, 1952. Subj: Animals. Careers – artists. Country.

Payne, Sherry Neuwirth. *A contest* ill. by Jeff Kyle. Carolrhoda, 1982. ISBN 0-87614-176-9 Subj: Character traits – being different. Handicaps. School.

Paz, Elena. *Las Navidades* (Delacre, Lulu)

Peaceable kingdom : *the Shaker abecedarius* ill. by Alice and Martin Provensen. Viking, 1978. Subj: ABC books. Animals. Poetry, rhyme.

Pearce, Philippa. *Emily's own elephant* ill. by John Lawrence. Greenwillow, 1988. ISBN 0-688-07679-3 Subj: Animals – elephants. Family life. Pets.

Pearce, Q. L. *In the African grasslands* by Q. L. and W. J. Pearce; ill. by Delana Bettoli. Silver Pr., 1990. ISBN 0-671-68827-8 Subj: Animals. Foreign lands – Africa.

In the African grasslands (Pearce, Q. L.)

In the desert by Q. L. and W. J. Pearce; ill. by Delana Bettoli. Silver Pr., 1990. ISBN 0-671-68825-1 Subj: Animals. Desert.

Pearce, W. J. *In the desert* (Pearce, Q. L.)

Pearson, Kit. *The singing basket* ill. by Ann Blades. Firefly, 1990. ISBN 0-88899-104-5 Subj: Behavior – lying. Folk and fairy tales. Foreign lands – Canada.

Pearson, Susan. *Baby and the bear* ill. by Nancy Carlson. Viking, 1987. ISBN 0-670-81299-4 Subj: Format, unusual – board books. Toys – teddy bears.

Everybody knows that! ill. by Diane Paterson. Dial Pr., 1978. Subj: Friendship. School.

Happy birthday, Grampie ill. by Ronald Himler. Dial Pr., 1987. ISBN 0-8037-3457-3 Subj: Birthdays. Family life – grandfathers.

Jack and the beanstalk (Jack and the beanstalk)

Karin's Christmas walk ill. by Trinka Hakes Noble. Dial Pr., 1980. Subj: Family life. Holidays – Christmas.

Lenore's big break ill. by Nancy Carlson. Viking, 1992. ISBN 0-670-83474-2 Subj: Birds. Self-concept. Theater.

My favorite time of year ill. by John Wallner. Harper, 1988. ISBN 0-06-024682-0 Subj: Seasons.

Saturday, I ran away ill. by Susan Jeschke. Harper, 1981. ISBN 0-397-31958-4 Subj: Behavior – running away. Family life.

That's enough for one day! ill. by Kay Chorao. Dial Pr., 1977. Subj: Activities – playing. Activities – reading.

Well, I never! ill. by James Warhola. Simon & Schuster, 1990. ISBN 0-671-69199-6 Subj: Farms.

When baby went to bed ill. by Nancy Carlson. Viking, 1987. ISBN 0-670-81300-1 Subj: Babies. Bedtime. Counting, numbers. Format, unusual – board books.

Pearson, Tracey Campbell. *A apple pie* ill. by author. Dial Pr., 1986. ISBN 0-8037-0252-3 Subj: ABC books. Format, unusual. Poetry, rhyme.

The howling dog ill. by author. Farrar, 1991. ISBN 0-374-33502-8 Subj: Animals – dogs. Behavior – misbehavior. Night. Noise, sounds.

Sing a song of sixpence ill. by author. Dial Pr., 1985. Subj: Behavior – misbehavior. Humor. Nursery rhymes.

The storekeeper ill. by author. Dial Pr., 1988. ISBN 0-8037-0370-8 Subj: Animals – cats. Careers – storekeepers. Stores.

The peasant's pea patch tr. by Guy Daniels; ill. by Robert M. Quackenbush. Delacorte Pr., 1971. Subj: Birds – cranes. Folk and fairy tales. Foreign lands – Russia.

Peavy, Linda. *Allison's grandfather* ill. by Ronald Himler. Scribner's, 1981. Subj: Death. Family life – grandfathers.

Peck, Robert Newton. *Hamilton* ill. by Laura Lydecker. Little, 1976. Subj: Animals – pigs. Animals – wolves. Farms. Poetry, rhyme.

Pedersen, Judy. *Out in the country* ill. by author. Knopf, 1991. ISBN 0-679-90630-4 Subj: Country. Family life. Houses. Moving.

The tiny patient ill. by author. Knopf, 1989. ISBN 0-394-80170-9 Subj: Birds. Character traits – kindness to animals. Illness.

Peek, Merle. *The balancing act: a counting book* ill. by author. Clarion, 1987. ISBN 0-89919-458-3 Subj: Animals. Animals – elephants. Counting, numbers. Music. Poetry, rhyme. Songs.

Mary wore her red dress and Henry wore his green sneakers ill. by adapt. Clarion, 1985. ISBN 0-89919-324-2 Subj: Animals. Animals – bears. Birthdays. Concepts – color. Songs.

Peet, Bill (William Bartlett). *The ant and the elephant* ill. by author. Little, 1972. Subj: Animals. Animals – elephants. Character traits – helpfulness. Character traits – selfishness. Cumulative tales. Insects – ants.

Big bad Bruce ill. by author. Houghton, 1977. Subj: Animals – bears. Behavior – bullying. Forest, woods. Humor. Witches.

Bill Peet: an autobiography ill. by author. Houghton, 1989. ISBN 0-395-50932-7 Subj: Caldecott award honor book.

Buford the little bighorn ill. by author. Houghton, 1967. Subj: Animals – sheep. Character traits – individuality. Humor. Sports – hunting. Sports – skiing.

The caboose who got loose ill. by author. Houghton, 1971. Subj: Behavior – dissatisfaction. Ecology. Trains.

Chester the worldly pig ill. by author. Houghton, 1965. Subj: Animals – pigs. Circus. Humor. World.

Cock-a-doodle Dudley ill. by author. Houghton, 1990. ISBN 0-395-55331-8 Subj: Animals. Birds – chickens. Farms. Sun.

Countdown to Christmas ill. by author. Houghton, 1972. Subj: Holidays – Christmas. Humor. Magic. Progress.

Cowardly Clyde ill. by author. Houghton, 1979. Subj: Animals – horses. Character traits – bravery. Humor. Knights.

Cyrus the unsinkable sea serpent ill. by author. Houghton, 1975. Subj: Character traits – helpfulness. Monsters. Mythical creatures. Sea and seashore.

Eli ill. by author. Houghton, 1978. Subj: Animals – lions. Birds – vultures. Friendship. Humor.

Ella ill. by author. Houghton, 1964. Subj: Animals – elephants. Behavior – lost. Character traits – conceit. Circus. Poetry, rhyme.

Encore for Eleanor ill. by author. Houghton, 1981. Subj: Animals – elephants. Art.

Farewell to Shady Glade ill. by author. Houghton, 1966. Subj: Animals. Ecology. Progress.

Fly, Homer, fly ill. by author. Houghton, 1969. Subj: Birds – pigeons. City. Ecology.

The gnats of knotty pine ill. by author. Houghton, 1975. Subj: Animals. Ecology. Insects – gnats. Sports – hunting.

How Droofus the dragon lost his head ill. by author. Houghton, 1971. Subj: Dragons. Knights. Royalty – kings.

Hubert's hair-raising adventures ill. by author. Houghton, 1959. Subj: Animals – lions. Careers – barbers. Humor. Poetry, rhyme.

Huge Harold ill. by author. Houghton, 1961. Subj: Animals – rabbits. Character traits – kindness to animals. Concepts – size. Humor. Poetry, rhyme.

Jennifer and Josephine ill. by author. Houghton, 1967. Subj: Animals – cats. Automobiles. Humor.

Jethro and Joel were a troll ill. by author. Houghton, 1987. ISBN 0-395-43081-X Subj: Humor. Magic. Mythical creatures. Trolls.

Kermit the hermit ill. by author. Houghton, 1965. Subj: Behavior – greed. Crustacea. Humor. Poetry, rhyme. Sea and seashore.

The kweeks of Kookatumdee ill. by author. Houghton, 1985. ISBN 0-395-37902-4 Subj: Activities – flying. Behavior – greed. Birds. Poetry, rhyme.

The luckiest one of all ill. by author. Houghton, 1982. Subj: Behavior – dissatisfaction. Emotions – envy, jealousy. Poetry, rhyme.

Merle the high flying squirrel ill. by author. Houghton, 1974. Subj: Activities – flying. Animals – squirrels. Humor. Kites. Trees.

No such things ill. by author. Houghton, 1983. ISBN 0-395-33888-3 Subj: Animals. Mythical creatures. Poetry, rhyme.

Pamela Camel ill. by author. Houghton, 1984. Subj: Animals – camels. Behavior – running away. Self-concept.

The pinkish, purplish, bluish egg ill. by author. Houghton, 1963. Subj: Birds. Birds – doves. Eggs. Mythical creatures. Poetry, rhyme. Violence, anti-violence.

Randy's dandy lions ill. by author. Houghton, 1964. Subj: Animals – lions. Circus. Humor. Poetry, rhyme.

Smokey ill. by author. Houghton, 1962. Subj: Old age. Poetry, rhyme. Trains.

The spooky tail of Prewitt Peacock ill. by author. Houghton, 1973. Subj: Birds – peacocks, peahens. Character traits – being different. Character traits – individuality.

The Whingdingdilly ill. by author. Houghton, 1970. Subj: Animals – dogs. Behavior – dissatisfaction. Character traits – optimism. Witches.

The wump world ill. by author. Houghton, 1970. Subj: Ecology. Progress. Space and space ships.

Zella, Zack, and Zodiac ill. by author. Houghton, 1986. ISBN 0-395-40567-5 Subj: Animals – zebras. Behavior – needing someone. Birds – ostriches. Poetry, rhyme.

Peet, Georgia. *Be quite quiet beside the lake* (Koenner, Alfred)

High flies the ball (Koenner, Alfred)

Pelham, David. *A is for animals* ill. by author. Simon & Schuster, 1991. ISBN 0-671-72495-9 Subj: ABC books. Animals. Format, unusual – toy and movable books.

Sam's sandwich ill. by author. Dutton, 1991. ISBN 0-525-44751-2 Subj: Family life – brothers. Family life – sisters. Food. Format, unusual. Poetry, rhyme.

Worms wiggle ill. by Michael Foreman. Simon & Schuster, 1989. ISBN 0-671-67218-5 Subj: Activities. Animals. Format, unusual – toy and movable books.

Pellegrini, Nina. *Families are different* ill. by author. Holiday, 1991. ISBN 0-8234-0887-6 Subj: Adoption. Ethnic groups in the U.S. Ethnic groups in the U.S. – Korean-American. Family life.

Pellowski, Anne. *The nine crying dolls: a story from Poland* ill. by Charles Mikolaycak. Philomel, 1980. ISBN 0-399-61162-2 Subj: Folk and fairy tales. Foreign lands – Poland. Toys – dolls.

Stairstep farm: Anna Rose's story ill. by Wendy Watson. Putnam's, 1981. Subj: Behavior – growing up. Family life. Farms.

Pellowski, Michael. *Clara joins the circus* ill. by True Kelley. Parents, 1981. Subj: Animals – bulls, cows. Circus. Clowns, jesters.

Pen Cai Ying. *Monkey creates havoc in heaven* tr. from Chinese by Ye Pin Kwei and Jill Morris; ill. by Xin Kuan Liang and others. Viking, 1989. ISBN 0-670-81805-4 Subj: Animals – monkeys. Folk and fairy tales. Foreign lands – China.

Pender, Lydia. *Barnaby and the horses* ill. by Alie Evers. Abelard-Schuman, 1961. Subj: Animals – horses. Behavior – carelessness. Country.

Pendery, Rosemary. *A home for Hopper* ill. by Robert M. Quackenbush. Morrow, 1971. Subj: Frogs and toads.

Pène Du Bois, William *see* Du Bois, William Pène

The penguin ill. by Norman Weaver. Rourke, 1983. Subj: Birds – penguins.

Penn, Ruth Bonn *see* Clifford, Eth

Penner, Lucille Recht. *Dinosaur babies* ill. by Peter Barrett. Random House, 1991. ISBN 0-679-91207-X Subj: Dinosaurs. Science.

Peppé, Rodney. *The alphabet book* ill. by author. Four Winds Pr., 1968. Subj: ABC books.

Cat and mouse: a book of rhymes : comp. and ill. by Rodney Peppé. Holt, 1973. Subj: Animals – cats. Animals – mice. Nursery rhymes. Poetry, rhyme.

Circus numbers: a counting book ill. by author. Delacorte Pr., 1969. Subj: Circus. Counting, numbers.

Hey riddle diddle ill. by author. Holt, 1971. Subj: Nursery rhymes. Poetry, rhyme. Riddles.

The kettleship pirates ill. by author. Lothrop, 1983. Subj: Animals – mice. Birthdays. Boats, ships. Imagination. Pirates.

Little circus ill. by author. Viking, 1984. Subj: Animals. Circus. Format, unusual – board books. Toys.

Little dolls ill. by author. Viking, 1984. Subj: Clothing. Format, unusual – board books. Toys.

Little games ill. by author. Viking, 1984. Subj: Format, unusual – board books. Games. Toys.

Little numbers ill. by author. Viking, 1984. Subj: Counting, numbers. Format, unusual – board books. Toys.

Little wheels ill. by author. Viking, 1984. Subj: Automobiles. Format, unusual – board books. Toys. Trucks.

The mice and the clockwork bus ill. by author. Lothrop, 1987. ISBN 0-688-06543-0 Subj: Animals – mice. Animals – rats. Buses.

The mice and the flying basket ill. by author. Lothrop, 1985. ISBN 0-688-04252-X Subj: Activities – ballooning. Animals – mice. Animals – rats. Behavior – greed.

The mice who lived in a shoe ill. by author. Lothrop, 1982. Subj: Animals – mice. Houses.

Odd one out ill. by author. Viking, 1974. Subj: Concepts. Games.

Rodney Peppé's puzzle book ill. by author. Viking, 1977. Subj: Concepts. Games.

Thumbprint circus ill. by author. Delacorte, 1989. ISBN 0-440-50154-7 Subj: Circus.

Perera, Lydia. *Frisky* ill. by Oscar Liebman. Random House, 1966. Subj: City. Merry-go-rounds.

Peretz, Isaac Loeb. *The magician* (Shulevitz, Uri)

Perez, Carla. *Your turn, doctor* (Robison, Deborah)

Perkins, Al. *The digging-est dog* ill. by Eric Gurney. Random House, 1967. Subj: Activities – digging. Animals – dogs. Poetry, rhyme.

Don and Donna go to bat ill. by Barney Tobey. Random House, 1968. Subj: Sports – baseball. Twins.

The ear book ill. by William O'Brian. Random House, 1968. Subj: Anatomy – ears. Poetry, rhyme. Senses – hearing.

Hand, hand, fingers, thumb ill. by Eric Gurney. Random House, 1969. Subj: Anatomy – hands. Poetry, rhyme.

King Midas and the golden touch ill. by Harold Berson. Random House, 1970. Subj: Behavior – greed. Behavior – wishing. Royalty – kings.

The nose book ill. by Roy McKié. Random House, 1970. Subj: Anatomy – noses. Poetry, rhyme. Senses – smelling.

Tubby and the lantern ill. by Rowland B. Wilson. Random House, 1971. Subj: Animals – elephants. Birthdays. Foreign lands – China. Pirates.

Tubby and the Poo-Bah ill. by Rowland B. Wilson. Random House, 1972. Subj: Animals – elephants. Boats, ships.

Perrault, Charles. *Cinderella* adapt. by John Fowles; ill. by Sheilah Beckett. Little, 1974. Adapt.

from Perrault's Cendrillon of 1697 Subj: Folk and fairy tales. Royalty – princes. Sibling rivalry.

Cinderella: or, the little glass slipper ill. by Marcia Brown. Scribner's, 1954. Subj: Caldecott award book. Folk and fairy tales. Royalty – princes. Sibling rivalry.

Cinderella ill. by Paul Galdone. McGraw-Hill, 1978. Subj: Folk and fairy tales. Royalty – princes. Sibling rivalry.

Cinderella tr. and ill. by Diane Goode. Knopf, 1988. ISBN 0-394-99603-8 Subj: Folk and fairy tales. Royalty – princes. Sibling rivalry.

Cinderella retold by Amy Ehrlich; ill. by Susan Jeffers. Dial Pr., 1985. ISBN 0-8037-0206-X Subj: Folk and fairy tales. Royalty – princes. Sibling rivalry.

Cinderella: the story of Rossini's opera adapt. by Alan Blyth; ill. by Emanuele Luzzati. Watts, 1982. Subj: Folk and fairy tales. Music. Royalty – princes. Sibling rivalry.

Cinderella retold by Barbara Karlin; ill. by James Marshall. Little, 1989. ISBN 0-316-54654-2 Subj: Folk and fairy tales. Royalty – princes. Sibling rivalry.

Cinderella ill. by Phil Smith. Troll Assoc., 1979. Subj: Folk and fairy tales. Royalty – princes. Sibling rivalry.

Puss in boots a free translation from the French; ill. by Marcia Brown. Scribner's, 1952. Subj: Animals – cats. Caldecott award honor book. Character traits – cleverness. Folk and fairy tales. Royalty – kings.

Puss in boots adapt. and ill. by Lorinda Bryan Cauley. Harcourt, 1986. ISBN 0-15-264227-7 Subj: Animals – cats. Character traits – cleverness. Folk and fairy tales. Royalty – kings.

Puss in boots retold by Kurt Baumann; ill. by Jean Claverie. Faber, 1982. Subj: Animals – cats. Character traits – cleverness. Folk and fairy tales. Royalty – kings.

Puss in boots adapt. and ill. by Hans Fischer. Harcourt, 1959. Subj: Animals – cats. Character traits – cleverness. Folk and fairy tales. Royalty – kings.

Puss in boots ill. by Paul Galdone. Seabury Pr., 1976. Subj: Animals – cats. Character traits – cleverness. Folk and fairy tales. Royalty – kings.

Puss in boots retold and ill. by John S. Goodall. Macmillan, 1990. ISBN 0-689-50521-3 Subj: Animals – cats. Character traits – cleverness. Folk and fairy tales. Royalty – kings. Wordless.

Puss in boots retold and ill. by Gail E. Haley. Dutton, 1991. ISBN 0-525-44740-7 Subj: Animals – cats. Character traits – cleverness. Folk and fairy tales. Royalty – kings.

Puss in boots adapt. by Arthur Luce Klein; ill. by Julia Noonan. Doubleday, 1970. Adaptation of Le Chat botté Subj: Animals – cats. Character traits – cleverness. Folk and fairy tales. Foreign lands – France. Royalty – kings.

Puss in boots: the story of a sneaky cat adapt. and ill. by Tony Ross. Delacorte Pr., 1981. Subj: Animals – cats. Character traits – cleverness. Folk and fairy tales. Royalty – kings.

Puss in boots ill. by William Stobbs. McGraw-Hill, 1975. A retelling of Maître Chat Subj: Animals – cats. Character traits – cleverness. Folk and fairy tales. Royalty – kings.

Puss in boots retold by Lincoln Kirstein; ill. by Alain Vaes. Little, 1992. ISBN 0-316-89506-7 Subj: Animals – cats. Character traits – cleverness. Folk and fairy tales. Royalty – kings.

Puss in boots ill. by Barry Wilkinson. Collins-World, 1969. Subj: Animals – cats. Character traits – cleverness. Folk and fairy tales. Royalty – kings.

The sleeping beauty tr. and ill. by David Walker. Crowell, 1977. Subj: Folk and fairy tales.

Tom Thumb (Tom Thumb)

Perrine, Mary. *Salt boy* ill. by Leonard Weisgard. Houghton, 1968. Subj: Indians of North America.

Perry, Patricia. *Mommy and daddy are divorced* by Patricia Perry and Marietta Lynch; ill. by authors. Dial Pr., 1978. Subj: Divorce.

Pershall, Mary K. *Hello, Barney!* ill. by Mark Wilson. Viking, 1989. ISBN 0-670-82406-2 Subj: Birds – cockatoos. Foreign lands – Australia. Pets.

Peters, Lisa Westberg. *Good morning, river!* ill. by Deborah Kogan Ray. Arcade, 1990. ISBN 1-55970-011-4 Subj: Old age. Rivers. Seasons.

The sun, the wind and the rain ill. by Ted Rand. Holt, 1988. ISBN 0-8050-0699-0 Subj: Nature. Science. Sea and seashore. Weather.

Water's way ill. by Ted Rand. Arcade, 1991. ISBN 1-55970-062-9 Subj: Nature. Science. Water. Weather.

Peters, Sharon. *Animals at night* ill. by Paul Harvey. Troll Assoc., 1983. Subj: Animals. Night.

Fun at camp ill. by Irene Trivas. Troll Assoc., 1980. Subj: Camps, camping.

Happy birthday ill. by Paul Harvey. Troll Assoc., 1980. Subj: Birthdays.

Happy Jack ill. by Paul Harvey. Troll Assoc., 1980. Subj: Careers – waiters, waitresses.

Messy Mark ill. by Bill Morrison. Troll Assoc., 1980. Subj: Character traits – cleanliness.

Puppet show ill. by Alana Lee. Troll Assoc., 1980. Subj: Puppets.

Ready, get set, go! ill. by Irene Trivas. Troll Assoc., 1980. Subj: Animals – rabbits.

Stop that rabbit ill. by Don Silverstein. Troll Assoc., 1980. Subj: Animals – rabbits.

Trick or treat Halloween ill. by Susan Hall. Troll Assoc., 1980. Subj: Holidays – Halloween.

Petersham, Maud. *An American ABC* by Maud and Miska Petersham; ill. by authors. Macmillan, 1941. Subj: ABC books. Caldecott award honor book. U.S. history.

The circus baby by Maud and Miska Petersham; ill. by authors. Macmillan, 1950. Subj: Animals – elephants. Circus. Clowns, jesters. Etiquette.

Off to bed by Maud and Miska Petersham; ill. by authors. Macmillan, 1954. Subj: Bedtime.

The rooster crows by Maud and Miska Petersham; ill. by authors. Macmillan, 1945. Subj: Caldecott award book. Nursery rhymes.

Petersham, Miska. *An American ABC* (Petersham, Maud)

The circus baby (Petersham, Maud)

Off to bed (Petersham, Maud)

The rooster crows (Petersham, Maud)

Peterson, Esther Allen. *Frederick's alligator* ill. by Susanna Natti. Crown, 1979. Subj: Animals. Behavior – boasting. Reptiles – alligators, crocodiles.

Penelope gets wheels ill. by Susanna Natti. Crown, 1982. ISBN 0-517-54467-9 Subj: Birthdays. Sports.

Peterson, Franklynn. *I can use tools* (Kesselman, Judi R.)

Peterson, Hans. *Erik and the Christmas horse* tr. from the Swedish by Christine Hyatt; ill. by Ilon Wikland. Lothrop, 1970. Translation of Magnus, Lindberg och hästen Mari Subj: Character traits – kindness. Foreign lands – Sweden. Holidays – Christmas.

Erik has a squirrel tr. from Swedish by Christine Hyatt; ill. by Ilon Wikland. Farrar, 1989. ISBN 9-12-959140-6 Subj: Animals – squirrels. Friendship.

Peterson, Jeanne Whitehouse. *Sometimes I dream horses* ill. by Eleanor Schick. Harper, 1987. ISBN 0-06-024713-4 Subj: Animals – horses. Family life – grandmothers.

That is that ill. by Deborah Kogan Ray. Harper, 1979. Subj: Divorce.

Peterson, Scott K. *What's your name? jokes about names* ill. by Joan Hanson. Lerner, 1987. ISBN 0-8225-0994-6 Subj: Names. Riddles.

Petie, Haris. *Billions of bugs* ill. by author. Prentice-Hall, 1975. Subj: Counting, numbers. Insects. Poetry, rhyme.

The seed the squirrel dropped ill. by author. Prentice-Hall, 1976. Subj: Activities – cooking. Cumulative tales. Food. Plants. Poetry, rhyme. Seeds. Trees.

Petrides, Heidrun. *Hans and Peter* ill. by author. Harcourt, 1962. Subj: Activities – working. Character traits – completing things.

Petrie, Catherine. *Hot Rod Harry* ill. by Paul Sharp. Children's Pr., 1982. Subj: Automobiles.

Joshua James likes trucks ill. by Jerry Warshaw. Childrens Pr., 1982. ISBN 0-516-43525-6 Subj: Toys. Trucks.

Pets ill. with photos. Macmillan, 1991. ISBN 0-689-71404-1 Subj: Nature. Pets.

Pettigrew, Eileen. *Night-time* ill. by William Kimber. Firefly, 1992. ISBN 1-55037-235-1 Subj: Family life – fathers. Night.

Petty, Kate. *Being careful with strangers* ill. by Lisa Kopper. Watts, 1988. ISBN 0-531-17107-8 Subj: Behavior – talking to strangers. Safety.

Dinosaurs ill. by Alan Baker. Watts, 1984. ISBN 0-531-04811-X Subj: Dinosaurs.

Gerbils photos. by George Thompson. Watts, 1989. ISBN 0-531-17158-2 Subj: Animals – gerbils. Pets.

Hamsters photos. by George Thompson. Watts, 1989. ISBN 0-531-17159-0 Subj: Animals – hamsters. Pets.

On a plane ill. by Aline Riquier. Watts, 1984. ISBN 0-531-04716-4 Subj: Activities – traveling. Airplanes, airports. Foreign lands – England.

Rabbits photos. by George Thompson. Watts, 1989. ISBN 0-531-17160-4 Subj: Animals – rabbits. Pets.

Petty, Roberta *see* Petie, Haris

Pevear, Richard. *Hail to mail* (Marshak, Samuel)

Mister Cat-and-a-Half ill. by Robert Rayevsky. Macmillan, 1986. ISBN 0-02-773910-4 Subj: Animals. Animals – cats. Animals – foxes. Folk and fairy tales.

Our king has horns! ill. by Robert Rayevsky. Macmillan, 1987. ISBN 0-02-773920-1 Subj: Behavior – secrets. Folk and fairy tales. Foreign lands – Russia. Royalty – kings.

The pup grew up! (Marshak, Samuel)

Peyo. *The Smurfs and their woodland friends* ill. by author. Random House, 1983. Subj: Animals. Forest, woods. Insects.

What do smurfs do all day? ill. by author. Random House, 1983. Subj: Activities. Poetry, rhyme.

Pfanner, Louise. *Louise builds a boat* ill. by author. Watts, 1990. ISBN 0-531-08488-4 Subj: Activities – making things. Boats, ships.

Louise builds a house ill. by author. Watts, 1989. ISBN 0-531-08396-9 Subj: Activities – making things. Houses. Imagination.

Pfister, Marcus. *Hopper* ill. by author. North-South, 1991. ISBN 1-55858-106-5 Subj: Animals – rabbits. Seasons – spring. Seasons – winter.

I see the moon ill. by author. North-South, 1991. ISBN 1-55858-119-7 Subj: Lullabies. Night. Poetry, rhyme. Songs.

The sleepy owl tr. from German by Jock J. Curle; ill. by author. Holt, 1986. ISBN 0-03-008023-1 Subj: Birds – owls. Friendship. Sleep.

Where is my friend? ill. by author. Holt, 1986. ISBN 0-03-008033-9 Subj: Animals – porcupines. Format, unusual – board books. Friendship.

Pfloog, Jan. *Kittens* ill. by author. Random House, 1977. Subj: Animals – cats. Format, unusual – board books.

Puppies ill. by author. Random House, 1979. Subj: Animals – dogs. Format, unusual – board books.

Phang, Ruth. *Patchwork tales* (Roth, Susan L.)

Philip, Neil. *The snow queen* (Andersen, H. C. (Hans Christian))

Phillips, Jack *see* Sandburg, Carl (Charles August)

Phillips, Joan. *Lucky bear* ill. by J. P. Miller. Random House, 1986. ISBN 0-394-97987-7 Subj: Toys – teddy bears.

My new boy ill. by Lynn Munsinger. Random House, 1986. ISBN 0-394-98277-0 Subj: Animals – dogs. Pets.

Peek-a-boo! I see you! ill. by Kathy Wilburn. Putnam's, 1983. ISBN 0-488-03092-6 Subj: Animals – bears. Format, unusual – board books. Poetry, rhyme.

Phillips, Louis. *The brothers Wrong and Wrong Again* ill. by J. Winslow Higginbottom. McGraw-Hill, 1979. Subj: Character traits – foolishness. Dragons. Middle ages. War.

The upside down riddle book ill. by Beau Gardner. Lothrop, 1982. Subj: Poetry, rhyme. Riddles.

Phillips, Mildred. *The sign in Mendel's window* ill. by Margot Zemach. Macmillan, 1985. ISBN 0-02-774600-3 Subj: Folk and fairy tales. Jewish culture.

Phillips, Tamara. *Day care ABC* ill. by Dora Leder. Albert Whitman, 1989. ISBN 0-8075-1483-7 Subj: ABC books. School.

Phumla. *Nomi and the magic fish: a story from Africa* ill. by Carole M. Byard. Doubleday, 1973. Subj: Children as authors. Folk and fairy tales. Foreign lands – Africa. Magic.

Piatti, Celestino. *Celestino Piatti's animal ABC* English text by Jon Reid; ill. by author. Atheneum, 1966. Subj: ABC books. Animals. Poetry, rhyme.

The happy owls ill. by author. Atheneum, 1964. Subj: Birds – owls. Character traits – optimism. Emotions – happiness.

Pickett, Carla. *Calvin Crocodile and the terrible noise* ill. by Carroll Dolezal. Steck-Vaughn, 1972. Subj: Noise, sounds. Reptiles – alligators, crocodiles.

Pieńkowski, Jan. *Colors* ill. by author. Harvey House, 1974. Subj: Concepts – color.

Easter ill. by author. Knopf, 1989. ISBN 0-394-82455-5 Subj: Holidays – Easter. Religion.

Faces ill. by author. Simon & Schuster, 1991. ISBN 0-671-72846-6 Subj: Anatomy – faces. Format, unusual – board books.

Farm ill. by author. David & Charles, 1985. ISBN 0-434-95651-1 Subj: Animals. Farms.

Food ill. by author. Simon & Schuster, 1991. ISBN 0-671-72845-8 Subj: Food. Format, unusual – board books.

Homes ill. by author. Messner, 1983. Subj: Animals. Houses.

Meg and Mog (Nicoll, Helen)

Meg at sea (Nicoll, Helen)

Meg on the moon (Nicoll, Helen)

Meg's eggs (Nicoll, Helen)

Numbers ill. by author. Harvey House, 1975. Subj: Counting, numbers.

Shapes ill. by author. Harvey House, 1975. Subj: Concepts – shape.

Sizes ill. by author. Messner, 1983. Orig. pub. by Harvey House, 1974 Subj: Concepts – size.

Time ill. by author. Messner, 1983. Subj: Clocks, watches. Time.

Weather ill. by author. Messner, 1983. Subj: Weather.

Zoo ill. by author. David & Charles, 1985. ISBN 0-434-95652-X Subj: Animals. Zoos.

Pierce, Jack. *The freight train book* photos. by author. Carolrhoda, 1980. Subj: Trains.

Piers, Helen. *Grasshopper and butterfly* ill. by Pauline Baynes. McGraw-Hill, 1975. Subj: Hibernation. Insects – butterflies, caterpillars. Insects – grasshoppers.

The mouse book photos. by author. Watts, 1968. Subj: Animals – mice.

Puppy's ABC photos. by author. Oxford Univ. Pr., 1987. ISBN 0-19-520606-1 Subj: ABC books. Animals – dogs.

Pike, Carol. *The nutty queen* ill. by author. Trafalgar Square, 1990. ISBN 0-09-173795-8 Subj: Poetry, rhyme. Royalty – queens. Toys – teddy bears.

Pike, Norman. *The peach tree* ill. by Robin and Patricia DeWitt. Stemmer House, 1983. Subj: Gardens, gardening. Trees.

Pilkey, Dav. *'Twas the night before Thanksgiving* ill. by author. Watts, 1990. ISBN 0-531-08505-8 Subj: Birds – turkeys. Holidays – Thanksgiving. Poetry, rhyme.

When cats dream ill. by author. Watts, 1992. ISBN 0-531-08597-X Subj: Animals – cats. Art. Dreams.

Pillar, Marjorie. *Join the band!* photos. by author. HarperCollins, 1992. ISBN 0-06-021829-0 Subj: Music. School.

Pizza man photos. by author. HarperCollins, 1990. ISBN 0-690-04836-X Subj: Careers – chefs. Food.

Pincus, Harriet. *Minna and Pippin* ill. by author. Farrar, 1972. Subj: Toys – dolls.

Pinkney, Gloria Jean. *Back home* ill. by Jerry Pinkney. Dial, 1992. ISBN 0-8037-1169-7 Subj: Ethnic groups in the U.S. – Afro-Americans. Family life. Farms.

Pinkwater, Daniel Manus. *Aunt Lulu* ill. by author. Macmillan, 1988. ISBN 0-02-774661-5 Subj: Animals – dogs. Careers – librarians. Family life – aunts, uncles.

The bear's picture ill. by author. Dutton, 1984. Subj: Animals – bears. Art. Careers – artists. Concepts – color.

The big orange splot ill. by author. Hastings, 1977. Subj: Activities – painting. Character traits – individuality. Concepts – color. Houses.

Devil in the drain ill. by author. Dutton, 1984. Subj: Character traits – curiosity. Devil.

Doodle flute ill. by author. Macmillan, 1991. ISBN 0-02-774635-6 Subj: Behavior – sharing. Friendship. Music.

The Frankenbagel monster ill. by author. Dutton, 1986. ISBN 0-525-44260-X Subj: Careers – bakers. Monsters.

Guys from space ill. by author. Macmillan, 1989. ISBN 0-02-774672-0 Subj: Space and space ships.

I was a second grade werewolf ill. by author. Dutton, 1983. Subj: Imagination. Monsters.

Pickle creature ill. by author. Four Winds Pr., 1979. Subj: Imagination – imaginary friends.

Roger's umbrella ill. by James Marshall. Dutton, 1982. Subj: Animals – cats. Umbrellas.

Tooth-gnasher superflash ill. by author. Four Winds Pr., 1981. Subj: Automobiles. Imagination.

Wempires ill. by author. Macmillan, 1991. ISBN 0-02-774411-6 Subj: Family life. Imagination.

Piper, Watty. *The little engine that could* ill. by George and Doris Hauman. Platt, 1961. Retold from The pony engine, by Mable C. Bragg. This version first pub. in 1955 Subj: Character traits – perseverance. Trains.

Mother Goose rhymes (Mother Goose)

Pirani, Felix. *Abigail at the beach* ill. by Christine Roche. Dial, 1989. ISBN 0-8037-0561-1 Subj: Activities – playing. Imagination. Sea and seashore.

Triplets ill. by Christine Roche. Viking, 1991. ISBN 0-670-83375-4 Subj: Triplets.

Pirotta, Saviour. *Little bird* ill. by Stephen Butler. Morrow, 1992. ISBN 0-688-11290-0 Subj: Activities. Activities – flying. Animals. Birds.

Pitcher, Caroline. *Animals* ill. by Louise Nevett. Watts, 1983. Subj: Activities. Animals. Wordless.

Cars and boats ill. by Louise Nevett. Watts, 1983. Subj: Activities. Automobiles. Boats, ships. Wordless.

Pittaway, Margaret. *The rainforest children* ill. by Heather Philpott. Oxford Univ. Pr., 1980. Subj: Behavior – running away. Behavior – seeking better things. Foreign lands – Australia.

Pittman, Helena Clare. *A dinosaur for Gerald* ill. by author. Carolrhoda, 1990. ISBN 0-87614-431-8 Subj: Birthdays. Dinosaurs. Pets.

The gift of the willows ill. by author. Carolrhoda Books, 1988. ISBN 0-87614-354-0 Subj: Folk and fairy tales. Foreign lands – Japan.

A grain of rice ill. by author. Hastings, 1986. ISBN 0-8038-9289-6 Subj: Character traits – cleverness. Folk and fairy tales. Foreign lands – China. Royalty.

Miss Hindy's cats ill. by author. Carolrhoda, 1990. ISBN 0-87614-368-0 Subj: ABC books. Animals – cats.

Once when I was scared ill. by Ted Rand. Dutton, 1988. ISBN 0-525-44407-6 Subj: Animals. Emotions – fear. Imagination. Night.

Piumini, Roberto. *The saint and the circus* tr. from Italian by Olivia Holmes; ill. by Barrett V. Root. Morrow, 1991. ISBN 0-688-10377-4 Subj: Circus.

Pizer, Abigail. *Charlie the puppy* ill. by author. Carolrhoda, 1989. ISBN 0-87614-363-X Subj: Animals – dogs. Farms. Seasons.

Harry's night out ill. by author. Dial, 1987. ISBN 0-8037-0055-5 Subj: Activities. Animals – cats. Night.

Hattie the goat ill. by author. Carolrhoda, 1989. ISBN 0-87614-364-8 Subj: Animals – goats. Farms. Seasons.

It's a perfect day ill. by author. HarperCollins, 1992. ISBN 0-06-443302-1 Subj: Animals. Farms. Noise, sounds. Rebuses.

Loppylugs ill. by author. Viking, 1990. ISBN 0-670-83209-X Subj: Animals – rabbits. Behavior – running away.

Nosey Gilbert ill. by author. Dial, 1987. ISBN 0-8037-0081-4 Subj: Animals – cats. Animals – dogs. Birds – geese. Emotions – fear. Insects – bees.

Penelope pig ill. by author. Carolrhoda, 1989. ISBN 0-87614-366-4 Subj: Animals – pigs. Farms. Seasons.

Percy the duck ill. by author. Carolrhoda, 1989. ISBN 0-87614-365-6 Subj: Birds – ducks. Farms. Seasons.

Planes ill. with photos. Dorling Kindersley, 1993. ISBN 1-56458-135-7 Subj: Airplanes, airports.

Plante, Patricia. *The turtle and the two ducks: animal fables* retold from La Fontaine by Patricia Plante and David Bergman; ill. by Anne F. Rockwell. Harper, 1981. ISBN 0-690-04147-0 Subj: Animals. Folk and fairy tales.

Plath, Sylvia. *The bed book* ill. by Emily Arnold McCully. Harper, 1976. Subj: Bedtime. Poetry, rhyme. Sleep.

Plotz, Helen. *A week of lullabies* comp. and ed. by Helen Plotz; ill. by Marisabina Russo. Greenwillow, 1988. ISBN 0-688-06653-4 Subj: Bedtime. Days of the week, months of the year. Lullabies. Poetry, rhyme.

Pluckrose, Henry Arthur. *Ants* ill. by Tony Swift and David Cook. Watts, 1981. Subj: Insects – ants. Science.

Bears ill. by Richard Orr. Watts, 1979. Subj: Animals – bears. Animals – pandas. Animals – polar bears. Science.

Bees and wasps ill. by Tony Swift and Norman Weaver. Watts, 1981. Subj: Insects – bees. Insects – wasps. Science.

Big and little photos. by Chris Fairclough. Watts, 1987. ISBN 0-531-10373-0 Subj: Concepts – size.

Butterflies and moths ill. by Norman Weaver and others. Watts, 1981. Subj: Insects – butterflies, caterpillars. Insects – moths. Science.

Counting photos. by Chris Fairclough. Watts, 1988. ISBN 0-531-10524-5 Subj: Counting, numbers.

Elephants ill. by Peter Barrett. Watts, 1979. Subj: Animals – elephants. Science.

Floating and sinking photos. by Chris Fairclough. Watts, 1987. ISBN 0-531-10294-7 Subj: Science.

Fur and feathers ill. with photos. Watts, 1989. ISBN 0-531-10720-5 Subj: Anatomy. Animals.

Horses ill. by Peter Barrett and Maurice Wilson. Watts, 1979. Subj: Animals – horses. Science.

Hot and cold photos. by Chris Fairclough. Watts, 1987. ISBN 0-531-10295-5 Subj: Science.

Join it! ill. with photos. Watts, 1989. ISBN 0-531-10730-2 Subj: Activities. Language.

Lions and tigers ill. by Eric Tenny and Maurice Wilson. Archon Pr., 1979. Subj: Animals – lions. Animals – tigers.

Numbers photos. by Chris Fairclough. Watts, 1988. ISBN 0-531-10453-2 Subj: Counting, numbers.

Paws and claws ill. with photos. Watts, 1989. ISBN 0-531-10721-3 Subj: Anatomy. Animals.

Reptiles ill. by Gary Hincks and others. Watts, 1981. Subj: Reptiles. Science.

Shape photos. by Chris Fairclough. Watts, 1987. ISBN 0-531-10374-9 Subj: Concepts – shape.

Skin, shell and scale ill. with photos. Watts, 1989. ISBN 0-531-10722-7 Subj: Anatomy. Animals.

Things we cut ill. by G. W. Hales. Watts, 1976. Subj: Tools.

Things we hear ill. by G. W. Hales. Watts, 1976. Subj: Senses – hearing.

Things we see ill. by G. W. Hales. Watts, 1976. Subj: Senses – seeing.

Things we touch ill. by G. W. Hales. Watts, 1976. Subj: Senses – touching.

Think about hearing photos. by Chris Fairclough. Watts, 1986. ISBN 0-531-10170-3 Subj: Senses – hearing.

Think about seeing photos. by Chris Fairclough. Watts, 1986. ISBN 0-531-10171-1 Subj: Senses – seeing.

Think about smelling photos. by Chris Fairclough. Watts, 1986. ISBN 0-531-10172-X Subj: Senses – smelling.

Think about tasting photos. by Chris Fairclough. Watts, 1986. ISBN 0-531-10173-8 Subj: Senses – tasting.

Think about touching photos. by Chris Fairclough. Watts, 1986. ISBN 0-531-10174-6 Subj: Senses – touching.

Time photos. by Chris Fairclough. Watts, 1988. ISBN 0-531-10452-4 Subj: Time.

Weight photos. by Chris Fairclough. Watts, 1988. ISBN 0-531-10525-3 Subj: Concepts – weight.

Whales ill. by Norman Weaver. Watts, 1979. Subj: Animals – whales. Science.

Plume, Alice. *Salt* (Afanas'ev, Aleksandr N.)

Plume, Ilse. *The Bremen town musicians* (Grimm, Jacob)

The story of Befana: an Italian Christmas tale ill. by adapt. Godine, 1981. Subj: Folk and fairy tales. Foreign lands – Italy. Holidays – Christmas.

Po, Lee. *The hare and the tortoise and the tortoise and the hare* (Du Bois, William Pène)

Pochocki, Ethel. *Rosebud and red flannel* ill. by Mary Beth Owens. Holt, 1991. ISBN 0-8050-1213-3 Subj: Clothing. Emotions – love.

Pocock, Rita. *Annabelle and the big slide* ill. by author. Harcourt, 1989. ISBN 0-15-200407-6 Subj: Activities – playing. Character traits – confidence.

Podendorf, Illa. *Color* ill. by Wayne Stuart. Children's Pr., 1971. Subj: Concepts – color.

Shapes, sides, curves and corners ill. by Frank Rakoncay. Children's Pr., 1970. Subj: Concepts – shape.

Space ill. with photos. Children's Pr., 1982. Subj: Space and space ships.

Polacco, Patricia. *Appelemando's dreams* ill. by author. Putnam, 1991. ISBN 0-399-21800-9 Subj: Dreams. Imagination.

Babushka's doll ill. by author. Simon & Schuster, 1990. ISBN 0-671-68343-8 Subj: Toys – dolls.

Chicken Sunday ill. by author. Putnam, 1992. ISBN 0-399-22133-6 Subj: Eggs. Ethnic groups in the U.S. – Afro-Americans. Family life – grandmothers. Friendship. Holidays – Easter. Religion.

Just plain Fancy ill. by author. Bantam, 1990. ISBN 0-553-07062-2 Subj: Birds – peacocks, peahens. Eggs. Farms.

Meteor! ill. by author. Dodd, 1987. ISBN 0-396-08910-0 Subj: Country. Science.

Rechenka's eggs ill. by author. Putnam's, 1988. ISBN 0-399-21501-8 Subj: Birds – geese. Eggs. Folk and fairy tales.

Some birthday! ill. by author. Simon & Schuster, 1991. ISBN 0-671-72750-8 Subj: Birthdays. Family life – fathers. Monsters. Parties.

Thunder cake ill. by author. Putnam, 1990. ISBN 0-399-22231-6 Subj: Emotions – fear. Family life – grandmothers. Weather – storms. Weather – thunder.

Polette, Nancy. *The little old woman and the hungry cat* ill. by Frank Modell. Greenwillow, 1989. ISBN 0-688-08315-3 Subj: Animals – cats. Cumulative tales.

Polhamus, Jean Burt. *Dinosaur do's and don'ts* ill. by Steve O'Neill. Prentice-Hall, 1975. Subj: Dinosaurs. Etiquette.

Doctor Dinosaur ill. by Steve O'Neill. Prentice-Hall, 1981. Subj: Careers – veterinarians. Dinosaurs. Illness.

Polisar, Barry Louis. *The trouble with Ben* ill. by David Clark. Rainbow Morning Music, 1992. ISBN 0-938663-13-5 Subj: Animals – bears. Character traits – being different. School. Self-concept.

Politi, Leo. *Emmet* ill. by author. Scribner's, 1971. Subj: Animals – dogs. Crime.

Juanita ill. by author. Scribner's, 1948. Subj: Caldecott award honor book. Ethnic groups in the U.S. – Mexican-Americans.

Lito and the clown ill. by author. Scribner's, 1964. Subj: Animals – cats. Clowns, jesters. Foreign lands – Mexico. Pets.

Little Leo ill. by author. Scribner's, 1951. Subj: Clothing. Family life. Foreign lands – Italy.

Moy Moy ill. by author. Scribner's, 1960. Subj: Ethnic groups in the U.S. – Chinese-Americans. Holidays – Chinese New Year.

The nicest gift ill. by author. Scribner's, 1973. Subj: Animals – dogs. Behavior – lost. Holidays – Christmas.

Pedro, the angel of Olvera Street ill. by author. Scribner's, 1946. Subj: Caldecott award honor book. Ethnic groups in the U.S. – Mexican-Americans. Holidays – Christmas.

Rosa ill. by author. Scribner's, 1963. Subj: Babies. Foreign lands – Mexico. Holidays – Christmas. Sibling rivalry. Toys – dolls.

Song of the swallows ill. by author. Scribner's, 1949. Subj: Birds – swallows. Caldecott award book. Ethnic groups in the U.S. – Mexican-Americans. Missions.

Polivy, Betsy Bober. *My bye-bye bottle book* (Gelbard, Jane)

My dressing book (Gelbard, Jane)

My eating book (Gelbard, Jane)

My sharing book (Gelbard, Jane)

Pollock, Penny. *Emily's tiger* ill. by author. Paulist Pr., 1985. Subj: Pets. Toys.

Water is wet photos. by Barbara Beirne. Putnam's, 1985. ISBN 0-399-21180-2 Subj: Activities – playing. Water.

Polushkin, Maria. *Baby brother blues* ill. by Ellen Weiss. Bradbury Pr., 1987. ISBN 0-02-774780-8 Subj: Babies. Family life. Sibling rivalry.

Bubba and Babba: based on a Russian folktale ill. by Diane de Groat. Crown, 1976. Subj: Animals – bears. Character traits – cleanliness. Folk and fairy tales.

Here's that kitten ill. by Betsy Lewin. Bradbury Pr., 1990. ISBN 0-02-774741-7 Subj: Animals – cats.

Kitten in trouble ill. by Betsy Lewin. Bradbury Pr., 1988. ISBN 0-02-774740-9 Subj: Animals – cats. Behavior – misbehavior.

The little hen and the giant ill. by Yuri Salzman. Harper, 1977. Subj: Birds – chickens. Character traits – bravery. Folk and fairy tales. Foreign lands – Russia. Giants.

Morning ill. by Bill Morrison. Four Winds Pr., 1983. Subj: Farms. Morning.

Mother, Mother, I want another ill. by Diane Dawson. Crown, 1978. Subj: Animals – mice. Behavior – misunderstanding. Family life – mothers. Sleep.

Who said meow? ill. by Giulio Maestro. Crown, 1975. An adaptation of Vladimir Grigor'evich Suteev's Kto skazal "Macm204;˜ ;i;au"? Subj: Animals – cats. Animals – dogs. Noise, sounds.

Who said meow? ill. by Ellen Weiss. Bradbury Pr., 1988. An adaptation of Vladimir Grigor'evich Suteev's Kto skazal "Macm204;˜ ;i;au"? ISBN 0-02-774770-0 Subj: Animals – cats. Animals – dogs. Noise, sounds.

Pomerantz, Charlotte. *All asleep* ill. by Nancy Tafuri. Greenwillow, 1984. Subj: Bedtime. Lullabies. Poetry, rhyme.

The ballad of the long-tailed rat ill. by Marian Parry. Macmillan, 1975. Subj: Animals – cats. Animals – rats. Character traits – pride. Poetry, rhyme.

Buffy and Albert ill. by Yossi Abolafia. Greenwillow, 1982. Subj: Animals – cats. Family life – grandfathers. Old age.

The chalk doll ill. by Frané Lessac. HarperCollins, 1989. ISBN 0-397-32319-0 Subj: Family life – mothers. Toys – dolls.

Flap your wings and try ill. by Nancy Tafuri. Greenwillow, 1989. ISBN 0-688-08020-0 Subj: Activities – flying. Birds. Poetry, rhyme.

The half-birthday party ill. by DyAnne DiSalvo-Ryan. Houghton, 1984. Subj: Birthdays.

How many trucks can a tow truck tow? ill. by Robert W. Alley. Random House, 1987. ISBN 0-394-88775-1 Subj: Poetry, rhyme. Trucks.

If I had a Paka: poems of eleven languages ill. by Nancy Tafuri. Greenwillow, 1982. Subj: Foreign languages. Poetry, rhyme.

The mango tooth ill. by Marylin Hafner. Greenwillow, 1977. Subj: Family life. Teeth.

One duck, another duck ill. by José Aruego and Ariane Dewey. Greenwillow, 1984. Subj: Birds – ducks. Counting, numbers.

The piggy in the puddle ill. by James Marshall. Macmillan, 1974. Subj: Animals – pigs. Poetry, rhyme. Tongue twisters.

Posy ill. by Catherine Stock. Greenwillow, 1983. Subj: Bedtime. Family life.

Serena Katz ill. by Robert W. Alley. Macmillan, 1992. ISBN 0-02-774901-0 Subj: Activities. Friendship.

The tamarindo puppy and other poems ill. by Byron Barton. Greenwillow, 1980. Subj: Foreign languages. Poetry, rhyme.

Timothy Tall Feather ill. by Catherine Stock. Greenwillow, 1986. ISBN 0-688-04247-3 Subj: Family life – grandfathers. Imagination. Indians of North America.

Where's the bear? ill. by Byron Barton. Greenwillow, 1984. ISBN 0-688-01753-3 Subj: Animals – bears.

Whiff, sniff, nibble and chew (The gingerbread boy)

Ponti, Claude. *Adele's album* ill. by author. Dutton, 1988. ISBN 0-525-44412-2 Subj: Imagination. Wordless.

Poole, Valerie. *Obadiah Coffee and the music contest* ill. by author. HarperCollins, 1991. ISBN 0-06-021620-4 Subj: Animals. Animals – rabbits. Careers – musicians. Music.

Pope, Billy N. *Your world: let's visit the hospital* by Billy N. Pope and Ramona Ware Emmons. Taylor, 1968. Subj: Hospitals.

Porazińska, Janina. *The enchanted book: a tale from Krakow* ill. by Jan Brett; tr. by Bożena Smith. Harcourt, 1987. ISBN 0-15-225950-3 Subj: Activities – reading. Family life – sisters. Folk and fairy tales. Foreign lands – Poland.

The porcupine ill. by Patrick Oxenham. Rourke, 1983. Subj: Animals – porcupines.

Porte, Barbara Ann. *Harry in trouble* ill. by Yossi Abolafia. Greenwillow, 1989. ISBN 0-688-07722-6 Subj: Careers – librarians. Character traits – helpfulness.

Harry's dog ill. by Yossi Abolafia. Greenwillow, 1983. ISBN 0-688-02556-0 Subj: Animals – dogs. Family life – fathers. Illness.

Harry's mom ill. by Yossi Abolafia. Greenwillow, 1985. ISBN 0-688-04818-8 Subj: Death. Family life. Family life – fathers. Family life – mothers. Family life – grandparents. School.

Harry's visit ill. by Yossi Abolafia. Greenwillow, 1983. Subj: Behavior – sharing. Sports – basketball.

Porter, David Lord. *Mine!* ill. by author. Houghton, 1981. Subj: Behavior – greed.

Porter, Sue. *Little Wolf and the giant* ill. by author. Simon & Schuster, 1990. ISBN 0-671-70363-3 Subj: Animals – wolves. Forest, woods. Giants.

One potato ill. by author. Bradbury Pr., 1989. ISBN 0-02-774910-X Subj: Animals. Food.

Porter-Gaylord, Laurel. *I love my daddy because...* ill. by Ashley Wolff. Dutton, 1991. ISBN 0-525-44624-9 Subj: Animals. Emotions – love. Family life – fathers.

I love my mommy because... ill. by Ashley Wolff. Dutton, 1991. ISBN 0-525-44625-7 Subj: Animals. Emotions – love. Family life – mothers.

Portnoy, Mindy Avra. *Ima on the Bima: my mommy is a Rabbi* ill. by Steffi Karen Rubin. Kar-Ben Copies, 1986. ISBN 0-930494-55-5 Subj: Careers. Family life – mothers. Jewish culture.

Mommy never went to Hebrew school ill. by Shelly O. Haas. Kar-Ben Copies, 1989. ISBN 0-930494-96-2 Subj: Family life. Jewish culture.

Poskanzer, Susan Cornell. *Riddles about Hannukah* photos. by Rob Gray. Silver Pr., 1990. ISBN 0-671-70553-9 Subj: Holidays – Hanukkah. Poetry, rhyme. Riddles.

Postgate, Oliver. *Noggin and the whale* by Oliver Postgate and Peter Firmin; ill. by Peter Firmin. White, 1967. Subj: Animals – whales. Humor. Royalty – kings.

Noggin the king by Oliver Postgate and Peter Firmin; ill. by Peter Firmin. White, 1965. Subj: Birds. Character traits – kindness. Humor. Royalty – kings.

Postma, Lidia. *The stolen mirror* ill. by author. McGraw-Hill, 1976. Translation of De gestolen Spiegel Subj: Imagination. Magic. Sibling rivalry.

Tom Thumb (Tom Thumb)

Poston, Elizabeth. *Baby's song book* ill. by William Stobbs. Crowell, 1971. Subj: Music. Songs.

Potter, Beatrix. *Appley Dapply's nursery rhymes* ill. by author. Warne, 1917. Subj: Animals. Nursery rhymes.

Beatrix Potter's nursery rhyme book ill. by author. Warne, 1984. ISBN 0-7232-3254-7 Subj: Animals. Nursery rhymes.

Cecily Parsley's nursery rhymes ill. by author. Warne, 1922. Subj: Animals. Nursery rhymes.

The complete adventures of Peter Rabbit ill. by author. Warne, 1982. Subj: Animals – rabbits. Behavior – misbehavior.

Ginger and Pickles ill. by author. Warne, 1937. First pub. in 1909 Subj: Animals. Stores.

More tales from Beatrix Potter ill. by author. Warne, 1987. ISBN 0-7232-3366-7 Subj: Animals.

Peter Rabbit's ABC ill. by author. Warne, 1987. ISBN 0-7232-3423-X Subj: ABC books. Animals.

Peter Rabbit's one two three ill. by author. Warne, 1988. ISBN 0-7232-3424-8 Subj: Animals – rabbits. Counting, numbers.

The pie and the patty-pan ill. by author. Warne, 1933. First pub. in 1905 Subj: Animals – cats. Animals – dogs. Behavior – trickery.

Rolly-polly pudding ill. by author. Warne, 1936. First pub. in 1908 Subj: Animals – cats.

The sly old cat ill. by author. Warne, 1971. Subj: Animals – cats. Animals – rats. Character traits – cleverness. Etiquette. Parties.

The story of fierce bad rabbit ill. by author. Warne, 1906. Subj: Animals – rabbits.

The story of Miss Moppet ill. by author. Warne, 1906. Subj: Animals – cats. Behavior – trickery.

The tailor of Gloucester ill. by author. Warne, 1931. Subj: Animals – mice. Careers – tailors. Character traits – helpfulness.

The tale of Benjamin Bunny ill. by author. Warne, 1904. Subj: Animals – rabbits. Behavior – misbehavior.

The tale of Jemima Puddle-Duck and other farmyard tales: The tale of Mr. Jeremy Fisher; The tale of Mrs. Tiggy-Winkle; The tale of Pigling Bland ill. by author Large format ed. Warne, 1987. ISBN 0-7232-3425-6 Subj: Animals. Birds.

The tale of Jemima Puddle-Duck ill. by author. Warne, 1936. First pub. in 1910 Subj: Birds – ducks. Eggs.

The tale of Johnny Town-Mouse ill. by author. Warne, 1918. Subj: Animals – mice.

The tale of Little Pig Robinson ill. by author. Warne, 1930. Subj: Animals – pigs. Behavior – talking to strangers. Boats, ships. Shopping.

The tale of Mr. Jeremy Fisher ill. by David Jorgensen. Picture Book Studio, 1989. ISBN 0-88708-094-4 Subj: Frogs and toads. Sports – fishing.

The tale of Mr. Jeremy Fisher ill. by author. Warne, 1934. Subj: Frogs and toads. Sports – fishing.

The tale of Mr. Tod ill. by author. Warne, 1939. First pub. in 1911 Subj: Animals – badgers. Animals – foxes. Animals – rabbits.

The tale of Mrs. Tiggy-Winkle ill. by author. Warne, 1905. Subj: Animals – hedgehogs. Clothing.

The tale of Mrs. Tittlemouse ill. by author. Warne, 1910. Subj: Animals – mice. Character traits – cleanliness.

The tale of Mrs. Tittlemouse and other mouse stories: The tale of Johnny Town-Mouse; The tale of two bad mice; The tailor of Gloucester ill. by author Large format ed. Warne, 1985. ISBN 0-7232-3324-1 Subj: Animals – mice.

The tale of Peter Rabbit ill. by Margot Apple. Troll Assoc., 1979. Subj: Animals – rabbits. Behavior – misbehavior.

The tale of Peter Rabbit ill. by author. Warne, 1902. Subj: Animals – rabbits. Behavior – misbehavior. Farms.

The tale of Peter Rabbit and other stories ill. by Allen Atkinson. Knopf, 1982. Subj: Animals.

The tale of Pigling Bland ill. by author. Warne, 1913, 1941. Subj: Animals – pigs.

The tale of Squirrel Nutkin ill. by author. Warne, 1903. Subj: Animals – squirrels. Birds – owls. Riddles. Seasons – fall.

The tale of the faithful dove ill. by Marie Angel. Warne, 1970. Subj: Birds – doves. Character traits – loyalty.

The tale of the Flopsy Bunnies ill. by author. Warne, 1909, 1937. Subj: Animals – rabbits. Character traits – cleverness.

The tale of Timmy Tiptoes ill. by author. Warne, 1911, 1939. Subj: Animals – squirrels.

The tale of Tom Kitten ill. by author. Warne, 1907. Subj: Animals – cats. Humor.

The tale of Tuppeny ill. by Marie Angel. Warne, 1971. Subj: Animals – guinea pigs.

The tale of two bad mice ill. by author. Warne, 1904, 1934. Subj: Animals – mice. Behavior – misbehavior. Toys.

A treasury of Peter Rabbit and other stories ill. by author. Watts, 1978. Subj: Animals.

The two bad mice: pop-up book ill. by author. Warne, 1986. ISBN 0-7232-3360-8 Subj: Animals – mice. Behavior – misbehavior. Format, unusual – toy and movable books.

Where's Peter Rabbit? ill. by Colin Twinn. Warne, 1988. ISBN 0-7232-3519-8 Subj: Animals – rabbits. Behavior – misbehavior. Format, unusual.

Yours affectionately, Peter Rabbit: miniature letters ill. by author. Warne, 1984. Subj: Animals. Communication.

Potter, Stephen. *Squawky, the adventures of a clasperchoice* ill. by George Him. Lippincott, 1964. Subj: Birds – parakeets, parrots.

Potter, Tony. *See how it works: cars* ill. by Robin Lawrie. Aladdin, 1989. ISBN 0-689-71303-7 Subj: Automobiles. Format, unusual.

See how it works: earth movers ill. by Robin Lawrie. Aladdin, 1989. ISBN 0-689-71302-9 Subj: Format, unusual. Machines.

See how it works: planes ill. by Robin Lawrie. Aladdin, 1989. ISBN 0-689-71304-5 Subj: Airplanes, airports. Format, unusual.

See how it works: trucks ill. by Robin Lawrie. Aladdin, 1989. ISBN 0-689-71301-0 Subj: Format, unusual. Trucks.

Poulin, Stéphane. *Benjamin and the pillow saga* ill. by author. Firefly, 1989. ISBN 1-55037-069-3 Subj: Magic. Music.

Can you catch Josephine? ill. by author. Tundra, 1987. ISBN 0-88776-198-4 Subj: Animals – cats. Behavior – misbehavior. Foreign lands – Canada. School.

Have you seen Josephine? ill. by author. Tundra, 1986. ISBN 0-88776-180-1 Subj: Animals – cats. Behavior – running away. Foreign lands – Canada.

My mother's loves: stories and lies from my childhood ill. by author. Firefly, 1990. ISBN 1-55037-149-5 Subj: Behavior – growing up. Family life.

Travels for two ill. by author. Firefly, 1991. ISBN 1-55037-205-X Subj: Activities – traveling. Family life. Islands. Sea and seashore.

Pouyanne, Rési. *What I see hidden by the pond* ill. by Gerda Muller. Two Continents, 1977. Subj: Animals. Plants. Science.

Power, Barbara. *I wish Laura's mommy was my mommy* ill. by Marylin Hafner. Lippincott, 1979. Subj: Behavior – growing up. Behavior – wishing. Family life – mothers.

Powers, Mary E. *Our teacher's in a wheelchair* photos. by author. Albert Whitman, 1986. ISBN 0-8075-6240-8 Subj: Careers – teachers. Handicaps. School.

Powzyk, Joyce. *Tasmania: a wildlife journey* ill. by author. Lothrop, 1987. ISBN 0-688-06460-4 Subj: Animals. Foreign lands – Australia. Nature. Science.

Prager, Annabelle. *The spooky Halloween party* ill. by Tomie de Paola. Pantheon, 1981. Subj: Holidays – Halloween. Parties.

The surprise party ill. by Tomie de Paola. Random House, 1988. ISBN 0-394-93235-8 Subj: Birthdays. Parties.

Pragoff, Fiona. *Odd one out* ill. by author. Doubleday, 1989. ISBN 0-385-26410-0 Subj: Concepts. Format, unusual – board books. Games.

Opposites ill. by author. Doubleday, 1989. ISBN 0-385-26409-7 Subj: Concepts – opposites. Format, unusual – board books.

Shapes ill. by author. Doubleday, 1989. ISBN 0-385-26408-9 Subj: Concepts – shape. Concepts – size. Format, unusual – board books.

Prall, Jo. *My sister's special* ill. with photos. Childrens Pr., 1985. ISBN 0-516-03862-1 Subj: Family life – sisters. Handicaps.

Prater, John. *Along came Tom* ill. by author. Trafalgar Square, 1992. ISBN 0-370-31411-5 Subj: Family life.

The gift ill. by author. Viking, 1986. ISBN 0-670-80952-7 Subj: Behavior – wishing. Wordless.

"No!" said Joe ill. by author. Candlewick, 1992. ISBN 1-56402-037-1 Subj: Behavior – misbehavior. Poetry, rhyme. Shopping.

On Friday something funny happened ill. by author. Random House, 1988. ISBN 0-370-30449-7 Subj: Behavior – misbehavior. Days of the week, months of the year.

The perfect day ill. by author. Dutton, 1987. ISBN 0-525-44282-0 Subj: Behavior – bad day. Sea and seashore.

You can't catch me! ill. by author. Salem House, 1986. ISBN 0-370-30594-9 Subj: Behavior – misbehavior. Behavior – running away.

Prather, Ray. *Double dog dare* ill. by author. Macmillan, 1975. Subj: Animals – dogs. Humor.

The ostrich girl ill. by author. Scribner's, 1978. Subj: Folk and fairy tales. Foreign lands – Africa. Forest, woods. Reptiles – snakes. Witches.

Precek, Katharine Wilson. *Penny in the road* ill. by Patricia Cullen-Clark. Macmillan, 1989. ISBN 0-02-774970-3 Subj: Behavior – losing things. U.S. history.

Preiss, Byron. *The first crazy word book: verbs* by Byron Preiss and Ralph Reese; ill. by Ralph Reese. Watts, 1982. Subj: Language.

Prelutsky, Jack. *The baby uggs are hatching* ill. by James Stevenson. Greenwillow, 1982. Subj: Humor. Imagination. Monsters. Poetry, rhyme.

Beneath a blue umbrella ill. by Garth Williams. Greenwillow, 1990. ISBN 0-688-06429-9 Subj: Animals. Poetry, rhyme.

Brave little Pete of Geranium Street (Lagercrantz, Rose)

Circus ill. by Arnold Lobel. Macmillan, 1974. Subj: Circus. Poetry, rhyme.

The mean old mean hyena ill. by Arnold Lobel. Greenwillow, 1978. Subj: Animals – hyenas. Character traits – meanness. Poetry, rhyme.

The pack rat's day and other poems ill. by Margaret Bloy Graham. Macmillan, 1974. Subj: Animals. Poetry, rhyme.

The queen of Eene ill. by Victoria Chess. Greenwillow, 1978. Subj: Humor. Poetry, rhyme.

Rainy rainy Saturday ill. by Marylin Hafner. Greenwillow, 1980. Subj: Poetry, rhyme. Weather – rain.

The Random House book of poetry for children ill. by Arnold Lobel. Random House, 1983. Subj: Humor. Poetry, rhyme.

Read-aloud rhymes for the very young ill. by Marc Brown. Knopf, 1986. ISBN 0-394-97218-X Subj: Poetry, rhyme.

Ride a purple pelican ill. by Garth Williams. Greenwillow, 1986. ISBN 0-688-04031-4 Subj: Imagination. Poetry, rhyme.

The snopp on the sidewalk and other poems ill. by Byron Barton. Greenwillow, 1977. ISBN 0-688-84084-1 Subj: Humor. Imagination. Poetry, rhyme.

The terrible tiger ill. by Arnold Lobel. Macmillan, 1970. Subj: Animals – tigers. Cumulative tales. Poetry, rhyme.

Tyrannosaurus was a beast ill. by Arnold Lobel. Greenwillow, 1988. ISBN 0-688-06443-4 Subj: Dinosaurs. Poetry, rhyme.

The wild baby (Lindgren, Barbro)

The wild baby goes to sea (Lindgren, Barbro)

Presencer, Alain. *Roaring lion tales* ill. by Ron Van der Meer. Harper, 1984. ISBN 0-216-91606-2 Subj: Animals – lions. Folk and fairy tales. Format, unusual – toy and movable books.

Preston, Edna Mitchell. *Horrible Hepzibah* ill. by Ray Cruz. Viking, 1971. Subj: Behavior – misbehavior. Humor.

Monkey in the jungle ill. by Clement Hurd. Viking, 1968. Subj: Animals – monkeys. Bedtime. Night. Sleep.

One dark night ill. by Kurt Werth. Viking, 1969. Subj: Cumulative tales. Holidays – Halloween.

Pop Corn and Ma Goodness ill. by Robert Andrew Parker. Viking, 1969. Subj: Caldecott award honor book. Humor. Poetry, rhyme. Songs. Weather – rain.

Squawk to the moon, little goose ill. by Barbara Cooney. Viking, 1974. Subj: Animals – foxes. Behavior – misbehavior. Birds – geese. Moon.

Preussler, Otfried. *The tale of the unicorn* tr. by Lenny Hort; ill. by Gennady Spirin. Dial, 1989. ISBN 0-8037-0583-2 Subj: Folk and fairy tales. Mythical creatures – unicorns.

Price, Christine. *One is God: two old counting songs* ill. by author. Warne, 1970. Subj: Counting, numbers. Religion. Songs.

Price, Dorothy E. *Speedy gets around* ill. by Betsy Warren. Steck-Vaughn, 1965. Subj: Animals – chipmunks. Camps, camping.

Price, Leontyne. *Aïda* ill. by Leo and Diane Dillon. Harcourt, 1990. Retells the story of Giuseppe Verdi's opera ISBN 0-15-200405-X Subj: Emotions – love. Foreign lands – Egypt. Music. Royalty.

Price, Mathew. *Do you see what I see?* ill. by Sue Porter. Harper, 1986. ISBN 0-694-00002-7 Subj: Animals. Behavior – losing things. Circus. Format, unusual.

Have you seen my sister? ill. by Errol Le Cain. Harcourt, 1992. ISBN 0-15-200467-X Subj: Family life – sisters. Format, unusual. Friendship. Imagination. Toys.

Peekaboo! ill. by Jean Claverie. Knopf, 1985. ISBN 0-394-87142-1 Subj: Family life. Format, unusual – toy and movable books.

Price, Michelle. *Mean Melissa* ill. by author. Bradbury Pr., 1977. Subj: Character traits – meanness. School.

Price, Roger. *The last little dragon* ill. by Mamoru Funai. Harper, 1969. Subj: Behavior – dissatisfaction. Dragons.

Priceman, Marjorie. *Friend or frog* ill. by author. Houghton, 1989. ISBN 0-395-44523-X Subj: Friendship. Frogs and toads.

Price-Thomas, Brian. *The magic ark* ill. by author. Crown, 1987. ISBN 0-517-56705-9 Subj: Animals. Imagination.

Primavera, Elise. *Basil and Maggie* ill. by author. Lippincott, 1983. Subj: Animals – horses. Character traits – appearance.

Prince, Pamela. *The secret world of teddy bears* photos. by Elaine Faris Keenan. Crown, 1983. Subj: Poetry, rhyme. Toys – teddy bears.

The prince who knew his fate : an ancient Egyptian tale tr. from hieroglyphs and ill. by Lise Manniche. Putnam's, 1982. Subj: Folk and fairy tales. Foreign lands – Egypt. Hieroglyphics. Magic. Royalty – princes.

Pringle, Laurence. *Jesse builds a road* ill. by Leslie Holt Morrill. Macmillan, 1989. ISBN 0-02-775311-5 Subj: Imagination. Machines. Roads.

Prokofiev, Sergei Sergeievitch. *Peter and the wolf* adapt. by Selina Hastings; ill. by Reg Cartwright. Holt, 1987. ISBN 0-8050-0408-4 Subj: Animals – wolves. Character traits – cleverness. Folk and fairy tales. Foreign lands – Russia.

Peter and the wolf ill. by Warren Chappell; foreword by Serge Koussevitsky; calligraphy by Hollis Holland. Knopf, 1940. Subj: Animals – wolves. Character traits – cleverness. Folk and fairy tales. Foreign lands – Russia. Music.

Peter and the wolf ill. by Barbara Cooney. Viking, 1986. ISBN 0-670-80849-0 Subj: Animals – wolves. Character traits – cleverness. Folk and fairy tales. Foreign lands – Russia. Format, unusual – toy and movable books. Music.

Peter and the wolf ill. by Frans Haacken. Watts, 1961. Subj: Animals – wolves. Character traits – cleverness. Folk and fairy tales. Foreign lands – Russia. Music.

Peter and the wolf ill. by Alan Howard. Transatlantic, 1954. Subj: Animals – wolves. Character traits – cleverness. Folk and fairy tales. Foreign lands – Russia. Music.

Peter and the wolf tr. by Maria Carlson; ill. by Charles Mikolaycak. Viking, 1982. Subj: Animals – wolves. Character traits – cleverness. Folk and fairy tales. Foreign lands – Russia. Music.

Peter and the wolf adapt. by Loriot; ill. by Jörg Müller. Knopf, 1986. Book-cassette included ISBN 0-394-88417-5 Subj: Animals – wolves. Character traits – cleverness. Folk and fairy tales. Foreign lands – Russia. Music.

Peter and the wolf tr. by Patricia Crampton; ill. by Josef Paleček. Picture Book Studio, 1987. ISBN 0-88708-049-9 Subj: Animals – wolves. Character traits – cleverness. Folk and fairy tales. Foreign lands – Russia. Music.

Peter and the wolf retold by Ann Herring; ill. by Kozo Shimizu; photos. by Yasugi Yajima. Gakken, 1971. Subj: Animals – wolves. Character traits – cleverness. Folk and fairy tales. Foreign lands – Russia. Music.

Peter and the wolf ill. by Erna Voigt. Godine, 1980. ISBN 0-87923-331-1 Subj: Animals – wolves. Character traits – cleverness. Folk and fairy tales. Foreign lands – Russia. Music.

Propp, James. *Tuscanini* ill. by Ellen Weiss. Bradbury Pr., 1992. ISBN 0-02-774911-8 Subj: Animals – elephants. Crime. Zoos.

Provensen, Alice. *A book of seasons* by Alice and Martin Provensen; ill. by authors. Random House, 1976. Subj: Seasons.

The glorious flight: across the channel with Louis Blériot by Alice and Martin Provensen; ill. by authors. Viking, 1983. Subj: Activities – flying. Airplanes, airports. Caldecott award book.

Karen's opposites by Alice and Martin Provensen; ill. by authors. Golden Pr., 1963. Subj: Concepts – opposites. Poetry, rhyme.

My little hen by Alice and Martin Provensen; ill. by authors. Random House, 1973. Subj: Birds – chickens.

Our animal friends by Alice and Martin Provensen; ill. by authors. Random House, 1974. Subj: Animals. Farms.

An owl and three pussycats by Alice and Martin Provensen; ill. by authors. Atheneum, 1981. Subj: Family life. Farms. Pets.

Punch in New York ill. by author. Viking, 1991. ISBN 0-670-82790-8 Subj: Behavior – misbehavior. Puppets.

Shaker Lane by Alice and Martin Provensen; ill. by authors. Viking, 1987. ISBN 0-670-81568-3 Subj: City. Moving. Poverty.

Town and country by Alice and Martin Provensen; ill. by authors. Crown, 1984. Subj: City. Country.

The year at Maple Hill Farm by Alice and Martin Provensen; ill. by authors. Atheneum, 1978. Subj: Animals. Days of the week, months of the year. Farms. Seasons.

Provensen, Martin. *A book of seasons* (Provensen, Alice)

The glorious flight (Provensen, Alice)

Karen's opposites (Provensen, Alice)

My little hen (Provensen, Alice)

Our animal friends (Provensen, Alice)

An owl and three pussycats (Provensen, Alice)

Shaker Lane (Provensen, Alice)

Town and country (Provensen, Alice)

The year at Maple Hill Farm (Provensen, Alice)

Prøysen, Alf. *Mrs. Pepperpot and the moose* tr. from Swedish by Richard E. Fisher; ill. by Björn Berg. Farrar, 1991. ISBN 91-29-59924-5 Subj: Animals – moose. Character traits – smallness. Concepts – size.

Prusski, Jeffrey. *Bring back the deer* ill. by Neil Waldman. Harcourt, 1988. ISBN 0-15-200418-1 Subj: Animals – deer. Animals – wolves. Family life. Forest, woods. Indians of North America. Seasons – winter. Sports – hunting.

Pryor, Ainslie. *The baby blue cat and the dirty dog brothers* ill. by author. Viking, 1987. ISBN 0-670-81781-3 Subj: Activities – bathing. Animals – cats. Animals – dogs.

The baby blue cat and the smiley worm doll ill. by author. Viking, 1990. ISBN 0-670-83531-5 Subj: Animals – cats. Behavior – losing things. Toys – dolls.

The baby blue cat and the whole batch of cookies ill. by author. Viking, 1989. ISBN 0-670-81782-1 Subj: Behavior – losing things. Toys – dolls.

The baby blue cat who said no ill. by author. Viking, 1988. ISBN 0-670-81780-5 Subj: Animals – cats. Bedtime.

Pryor, Bonnie. *Amanda and April* ill. by Diane de Groat. Morrow, 1986. ISBN 0-688-05870-1 Subj: Animals – pigs. Family life – sisters. Parties. Sibling rivalry.

The beaver boys ill. by Karen Lee Baker. Morrow, 1991. ISBN 0-688-08703-5 Subj: Animals – beavers. Houses. Moving.

Greenbrook farm ill. by Mark Graham. Simon & Schuster, 1991. ISBN 0-671-69205-4 Subj: Animals. Babies. Farms.

The house on Maple Street ill. by Beth Peck. Morrow, 1987. ISBN 0-688-06381-0 Subj: U.S. history.

Merry Christmas, Amanda and April ill. by Diane de Groat. Morrow, 1990. ISBN 0-688-07545-2 Subj: Animals – pigs. Family life – sisters. Holidays – Christmas.

Mr. Munday and the rustlers ill. by Wallop Manyum. Prentice-Hall, 1988. ISBN 0-13-604737-8 Subj: Crime. Farms.

Mr. Munday and the space creatures ill. by Lee Lorenz. Simon & Schuster, 1989. ISBN 0-671-67114-6 Subj: Careers – mail carriers. Space and space ships.

The porcupine mouse ill. by Maryjane Begin. Morrow, 1988. ISBN 0-688-07154-6 Subj: Animals – mice. Character traits – bravery. Emotions – fear. Sibling rivalry.

The pudgy book of babies ill. by Kathy Wilburn. Putnam's, 1984. ISBN 0-448-10207-2 Subj: Babies. Format, unusual – board books.

The pudgy book of farm animals ill. by Julie Durrell. Putnam's, 1984. ISBN 0-448-10211-0 Subj: Animals. Farms. Format, unusual – board books.

The pudgy book of here we go ill. by Beth Lee Weiner. Putnam's, 1984. ISBN 0-448-10208-0 Subj: Format, unusual – board books.

The pudgy book of make-believe ill. by Andrea Brooks. Putnam's, 1984. ISBN 0-448-10209-9 Subj: Format, unusual – board books. Imagination.

The pudgy book of Mother Goose ill. by Richard Walz. Putnam's, 1984. ISBN 0-448-10212-9 Subj: Format, unusual – board books. Nursery rhymes.

The pudgy book of toys ill. by Julie Durrell. Grosset, 1983. Subj: Format, unusual – board books. Toys.

The pudgy bunny book ill. by Ruth Sanderson. Putnam's, 1984. ISBN 0-448-10210-2 Subj: Animals – rabbits. Format, unusual – board books.

The pudgy fingers counting book ill. by Doug Cushman. Grosset, 1983. Subj: Counting, numbers. Format, unusual – board books.

The pudgy pals ill. by Kathy Wilburn. Grosset, 1983. Subj: Format, unusual – board books.

The pudgy pat-a-cake book ill. by Terri Super. Grosset, 1983. Subj: Format, unusual – board books. Games.

The pudgy peek-a-boo book ill. by Amye Rosenberg. Grosset, 1983. Subj: Format, unusual – board books. Games.

The pudgy rock-a-bye book ill. by Kathy Wilburn. Grosset, 1983. Subj: Format, unusual – board books.

Pulsifer, Marjorie P. *Bikes* (Baugh, Dolores M.)

Let's go (Baugh, Dolores M.)

Let's see the animals (Baugh, Dolores M.)

Let's take a trip (Baugh, Dolores M.)

Slides (Baugh, Dolores M.)

Supermarket (Baugh, Dolores M.)

Swings (Baugh, Dolores M.)

Trucks and cars to ride (Baugh, Dolores M.)

Pulver, Robin. *Mrs. Toggle and the dinosaur* ill. by Robert W. Alley. Four Winds, 1991. ISBN 0-02-775452-9 Subj: Dinosaurs. School.

Mrs. Toggle's zipper ill. by Robert W. Alley. Four Winds, 1990. ISBN 0-02-775451-0 Subj: Clothing – coats. Humor. School.

Nobody's mother is in second grade ill. by G. Brian Karas. Dial, 1992. ISBN 0-8037-1211-1 Subj: Family life – mothers. Plants. School.

Puner, Helen Walker. *Daddys, what they do all day* ill. by Roger Antoine Duvoisin. Lothrop, 1946. Subj: Activities – working. Careers. Family life – fathers. Poetry, rhyme.

The sitter who didn't sit ill. by Roger Antoine Duvoisin. Lothrop, 1949. Subj: Activities – babysitting. Humor. Poetry, rhyme.

Puppies and kittens photos. by Walter Chandoha. Platt, 1983. Subj: Animals – cats. Animals – dogs. Format, unusual – board books. Poetry, rhyme.

Purcell, John Wallace. *African animals* ill. with photos Rev. ed. Children's Pr., 1982. Subj: Animals. Foreign lands – Africa.

Purdy, Carol. *Iva Dunnit and the big wind* ill. by Steven Kellogg. Dial Pr., 1985. ISBN 0-8037-0184-5 Subj: Family life. Weather – wind.

Least of all ill. by Tim Arnold. Macmillan, 1987. ISBN 0-689-50404-7 Subj: Activities – reading. Activities – working. Family life. Self-concept.

Puricelli, Luigi. *In my garden* (Cristini, Ermanno)

In the pond (Cristini, Ermanno)

In the woods (Cristini, Ermanno)

Pursell, Margaret Sanford. *Jessie the chicken* orig. tr. by Dyan Hammarberg; photos. by Claudie Fayn-Rodriguez; ill. by L'Enc Matte. Based on Anne Marie Pajot's Picota la poule Subj: Birds – chickens. Eggs.

A look at birth ill. by Maria S. Forrai. Lerner, 1976. Subj: Babies. Birth. Science.

A look at divorce ill. by Maria S. Forrai. Lerner, 1976. Subj: Divorce. Emotions.

Polly the guinea pig orig. tr. by Dyan Hammarberg; photos. by Antoinette Barrére; ill. by L'enc Matte. Carolrhoda Books, 1977. Original ed. published under title: Amilcar le cochon d'Inde Subj: Animals – guinea pigs. Pets. Science.

Shelley the sea gull tr. by Dyan Hammarberg; photos. by Jean Christian David, Guy Dhuit and Claudie Fayn-Rodriguez. Carolrhoda Books, 1977. Original ed. published under title: Gwelan le goeland Subj: Birds – sea gulls. Pets. Science.

Sprig the tree frog tr. by Dyan Hammarberg; ill. by Yves Vial. Carolrhoda Books, 1977. Subj: Eggs. Frogs and toads. Science.

Purviance, Susan. *Alphabet Annie announces an all-American album* (O'Shell, Marcia)

Quackenbush, Robert M. *Chuck lends a paw* ill. by author. Clarion, 1986. ISBN 0-89919-363-3 Subj: Animals – mice. Character traits – helpfulness.

City trucks ill. by author. Albert Whitman, 1981. Subj: City. Trucks.

Clementine ill. by author. Lippincott, 1974. Subj: Folk and fairy tales. Music. Songs. U.S. history.

First grade jitters ill. by author. Lippincott, 1982. Subj: Animals – rabbits. School.

Funny bunnies ill. by author. Houghton, 1984. Subj: Animals – rabbits. Humor.

Henry babysits ill. by author. Parents, 1983. Subj: Activities – baby-sitting. Birds – ducks.

I don't want to go, I don't know how to act ill. by author. Lippincott, 1983. Subj: Animals – koala bears. Behavior. Etiquette. Family life.

The man on the flying trapeze: the circus life of Emmett Kelly, Sr., told with pictures and song! ill. by author. Lippincott, 1975. Subj: Circus. Clowns, jesters. Music. Songs.

Mouse feathers ill. by author. Clarion, 1988. ISBN 0-89919-527-X Subj: Behavior – misbehavior. Family life.

No mouse for me ill. by author. Watts, 1981. Subj: Cumulative tales. Pets.

Pete Pack Rat ill. by author. Lothrop, 1976. Subj: Animals. Animals – pack rats. Cowboys. Humor.

Pop! goes the weasel and Yankee Doodle: New York in 1776 and today ill. by author. Harper, 1988, 1976. ISBN 0-397-32265-8 Subj: Music. Poetry, rhyme. Songs. U.S. history.

She'll be comin' 'round the mountain ill. by author. Lippincott, 1973. Subj: Folk and fairy tales. Music. Songs.

Sheriff Sally Gopher and the Thanksgiving caper ill. by author. Lothrop, 1982. Subj: Holidays – Thanksgiving.

Skip to my Lou ill. by author. Lippincott, 1975. Subj: Folk and fairy tales. Music. Songs.

There'll be a hot time in the old town tonight: the great Chicago fire of 1871 ill. by author. Harper, 1988, 1974. ISBN 0-397-32267-4 Subj: Fire. Folk and fairy tales. Music. Songs. U.S. history.

Quigley, Lillian Fox. *The blind men and the elephant* ill. by Janice Holland. Scribner's, 1959. Subj: Animals – elephants. Folk and fairy tales. Foreign lands – India. Handicaps – blindness. Senses – seeing.

Quindlen, Anna. *The tree that came to stay* ill. by Nancy Carpenter. Crown, 1992. ISBN 0-517-58146-9 Subj: Family life. Holidays – Christmas. Trees.

Quin-Harkin, Janet. *Benjamin's balloon* ill. by Robert Censoni. Parents, 1979. Subj: Activities – ballooning. Character traits – willfulness.

Helpful Hattie ill. by Susanna Natti. Harcourt, 1983. Subj: Birthdays. Hair. Parties. Teeth.

Peter Penny's dance ill. by Anita Lobel. Dial Pr., 1976. Subj: Activities – dancing. Weddings. World.

Quinlan, Patricia. *Anna's red sled* ill. by Lindsay Grater. Firefly, 1989. ISBN 1-55037-073-1 Subj: Family life – mothers. Seasons – winter. Toys.

Emma's sea journey ill. by Jirina Marton. Firefly, 1991. ISBN 1-55037-179-7 Subj: Activities – playing. Sea and seashore.

My dad takes care of me ill. by Vlasta van Kampen. Firefly Pr., 1987. ISBN 0-920303-79-X Subj: Activities – working. Family life – fathers. Family life – mothers.

Quinsey, Mary Beth. *Why does that man have such a big nose?* photos. by Wilson Chan. Parenting Pr., 1986. ISBN 0-943990-25-4 Subj: Character traits – appearance. Character traits – being different.

Ra, Carol F. *Trot, trot to Boston: play rhymes for baby* ill. by Catherine Stock. Lothrop, 1987. ISBN 0-688-06191-5 Subj: Games. Poetry, rhyme.

Rabe, Berniece. *The balancing girl* ill. by Lillian Hoban. Dutton, 1981. ISBN 0-525-26160-5 Subj: Handicaps. School.

A smooth move ill. by Linda Shute. Albert Whitman, 1987. ISBN 0-8075-7486-4 Subj: Activities – traveling. Moving.

Where's Chimpy? photos. by Diane Schmidt. Albert Whitman, 1988. ISBN 0-8075-8928-4 Subj: Behavior – losing things. Family life – fathers. Handicaps. Toys.

Rabinowitz, Sandy. *A colt named mischief* ill. by author. Doubleday, 1979. Subj: Animals – horses. Behavior – misbehavior.

What's happening to Daisy? ill. by author. Harper, 1977. Subj: Animals – horses. Birth. Science.

Racioppo, Larry. *Halloween* photos. by author. Scribner's, 1980. Subj: Holidays – Halloween.

Radford, Derek. *Building machines and what they do* ill. by author. Candlewick Pr., 1992. ISBN 1-56402-006-1 Subj: Machines.

Cargo machines and what they do ill. by author. Candlewick Pr., 1992. ISBN 1-56402-005-3 Subj: Machines.

Harry builds a house ill. by author. Aladdin, 1990. ISBN 0-689-71439-4 Subj: Activities – making things. Houses.

Radin, Ruth Yaffe. *High in the mountains* ill. by Ed Young. Macmillan, 1989. ISBN 0-02-775650-5 Subj: Family life – grandfathers. Nature.

A winter place ill. by Mattie Lou O'Kelley. Little, 1982. Subj: Seasons – winter. Sports – ice skating.

Radlauer, Ruth Shaw. *Breakfast by Molly* ill. by Emily Arnold McCully. Prentice-Hall, 1988. ISBN 0-671-66165-5 Subj: Birthdays. Family life – mothers. Food.

Molly ill. by Emily Arnold McCully. Prentice-Hall, 1987. ISBN 0-13-599762-3 Subj: Activities – picnicking. Activities – walking.

Molly at the library ill. by Emily Arnold McCully. Prentice-Hall, 1988. ISBN 0-671-66166-3 Subj: Activities – reading. Family life – fathers. Libraries.

Molly goes hiking ill. by Emily Arnold McCully. Prentice-Hall, 1987. ISBN 0-13-599770-4 Subj: Activities – picnicking. Activities – walking.

Of course, you're a horse! ill. by Abner Graboff and Sheila Greenwald. Abelard-Schuman, 1959. Subj: Health. Imagination.

Radley, Gail. *The night Stella hid the stars* ill. by John Wallner. Crown, 1978. Subj: Imagination. Stars.

Raebeck, Lois. *Who am I?* ill. by June Goldsborough. Follett, 1970. Subj: Activities – playing. Games. Songs.

Rael, Rick. *Baseball brothers* (Rubin, Jeff)

Raffi. *Baby beluga* ill. by Ashley Wolff. Crown, 1990. ISBN 0-517-57840-9 Subj: Animals – endangered animals. Animals – whales. Foreign lands – Arctic. Music. Songs.

Down by the bay ill. by Nadine Bernard Westcott. Crown, 1987. ISBN 0-517-56644-3 Subj: Music. Songs.

Everything grows photos. by Bruce McMillan. Crown, 1989. ISBN 0-517-57275-3 Subj: Music. Songs.

One light, one sun ill. by Eugenie Fernandes. Crown, 1988. ISBN 0-517-56785-7 Subj: Family life. Music. Songs.

Shake my sillies out ill. by David Allender. Crown, 1987. ISBN 0-517-56646-X Subj: Music. Songs.

Wheels on the bus ill. by Sylvie Wickstrom. Crown, 1988. ISBN 0-517-56784-9 Subj: Foreign lands – France. Music. Songs.

Rahn, Joan Elma. *Holes* photos. by author. Houghton, 1984. Subj: Concepts.

Rand, Ann. *Little 1* ill. by Paul Rand. Harcourt, 1962. Subj: Counting, numbers.

Sparkle and spin: a book about words ill. by Paul Rand. Harcourt, 1957. Subj: Language.

Rand, Gloria. *Salty dog* ill. by Ted Rand. Holt, 1989. ISBN 0-8050-0837-3 Subj: Animals – dogs. Boats, ships. Careers – boat builders. Character traits – individuality.

Salty takes off ill. by Ted Rand. Holt, 1991. ISBN 0-8050-1159-5 Subj: Airplanes, airports. Alaska. Animals – dogs.

Rand McNally picturebook dictionary: *a thousand words to see and say* comp. by Robert L. Hillerich and others; ill. by Dan Siculan. Rand McNally, 1971. Subj: Dictionaries.

Raney, Ken. *Stick horse* ill. by author. Green Tiger, 1991. ISBN 0-9625261-4-2 Subj: Activities – playing. Activities – traveling. Toys. Wordless.

Ransome, Arthur. *The fool of the world and the flying ship* ill. by Uri Shulevitz. Farrar, 1968. Subj:

Activities – flying. Boats, ships. Caldecott award book. Character traits – cleverness.

Raphael, Elaine. *Donkey and Carlo* by Elaine Raphael and Don Bolognese; ill. by authors. Harper, 1978. Subj: Animals – donkeys. Farms. Friendship.

Donkey, it's snowing by Elaine Raphael and Don Bolognese; ill. by authors. Harper, 1981. Subj: Animals – donkeys. Farms. Weather – snow.

Turnabout by Elaine Raphael and Don Bolognese; ill. by authors. Viking, 1980. Subj: Animals – bears. Behavior – boasting. Family life. Folk and fairy tales. Poetry, rhyme.

Raposo, Joe. *The Sesame Street song book* words and music by Joe Raposo and Jeffrey Moss; arrangements by Sy Oliver; ill. by Loretta Trezzo. Simon and Schuster, 1971. "Published in conjunction with Children's Television Workshop." Subj: Music. Songs.

Rappaport, Doreen. *Journey of Meng* ill. by Yang Ming-Yi. Dial, 1991. ISBN 0-8037-0896-3 Subj: Death. Folk and fairy tales. Foreign lands – China.

Rappus, Gerhard. *When the sun was shining* ill. by author. Imported Pubs., 1983. Subj: Activities – picnicking. Animals – goats. Behavior – misbehavior. Wordless.

Raschka, Chris. *Charlie Parker played be bop* ill. by author. Watts, 1992. ISBN 0-531-08599-6 Subj: Careers – musicians. Ethnic groups in the U.S. – Afro-Americans. Music.

Raskin, Ellen. *A & The: or, William T. C. Baumgarten comes to town* ill. by author. Atheneum, 1970. Subj: Friendship. Names.

And it rained ill. by author. Atheneum, 1969. Subj: Animals. Weather – rain.

Franklin Stein ill. by author. Atheneum, 1972. Subj: City. Friendship. Humor. Imagination.

Ghost in a four-room apartment ill. by author. Atheneum, 1969. Subj: Cumulative tales. Family life. Ghosts. Poetry, rhyme.

Nothing ever happens on my block ill. by author. Atheneum, 1966. Subj: Behavior – boredom. City. Humor.

Spectacles ill. by author. Atheneum, 1968. Subj: Glasses. Imagination. Senses – seeing.

Who, said Sue, said whoo? ill. by author. Atheneum, 1973. Subj: Animals. Noise, sounds. Poetry, rhyme.

Ratnett, Michael. *Jenny's bear* ill. by June Goulding. Putnam, 1992. ISBN 0-399-22325-8 Subj: Animals – bears. Behavior – wishing. Imagination. Toys – teddy bears.

Marmaduke and the scary story ill. by June Goulding. Trafalgar Square, 1992. ISBN 0-09-174084-3 Subj: Animals – rabbits. Emotions – fear.

Ratz de Tagyos, Paul. *A coney tale* ill. by author. Houghton, 1992. ISBN 0-395-58834-0 Subj: Animals – rabbits. Communities, neighborhoods.

Rauch, Hans-Georg. *The lines are coming: a book about drawing* ill. by author. Scribner's, 1978. Subj: Art.

Ravilious, Robin. *The runaway chick* ill. by author. Macmillan, 1987. ISBN 0-02-775640-8 Subj: Behavior – running away. Birds – chickens. Character traits – curiosity.

Two in a pocket ill. by author. Little, 1991. ISBN 0-316-73449-7 Subj: Animals – mice. Birds – wrens. Friendship.

Rawlins, Donna. *Digging to China* ill. by author. Watts, 1989. ISBN 0-531-08414-0 Subj: Activities – digging. Old age.

Ray, Deborah Kogan. *The cloud* ill. by author. Harper, 1984. Subj: Activities – walking. Weather – clouds.

Fog drift morning ill. by author. Harper, 1983. Subj: Morning. Sea and seashore.

Stargazing sky ill. by author. Crown, 1991. ISBN 0-517-57838-7 Subj: Family life – mothers. Night. Stars.

Sunday morning we went to the zoo ill. by author. Harper, 1981. Subj: Family life. Sibling rivalry. Zoos.

Ray, Mary Lyn. *Pumpkins* ill. by Barry Root. Harcourt, 1992. ISBN 0-15-252252-2 Subj: Ecology. Gardens, gardening. Plants. Progress.

Rayevsky, Inna. *The talking tree* ill. by Robert Rayevsky. Putnam, 1990. ISBN 0-399-21631-6 Subj: Folk and fairy tales. Foreign lands – Italy. Trees.

Rayner, Mary. *Crocodarling* ill. by author. Bradbury Pr., 1986. ISBN 0-02-775770-6 Subj: Behavior – bullying. Behavior – needing someone. School. Toys.

Garth Pig and the ice cream lady ill. by author. Atheneum, 1977. Subj: Animals – pigs. Animals – wolves.

Marathon and Steve ill. by author. Dutton, 1989. ISBN 0-525-44456-4 Subj: Animals – dogs. Sports. Pets.

Mr. and Mrs. Pig's evening out ill. by author. Atheneum, 1976. Subj: Activities – baby-sitting. Animals – pigs. Animals – wolves.

Mrs. Pig gets cross and other stories ill. by author. Dutton, 1987. ISBN 0-525-44280-4 Subj: Animals – pigs. Family life.

Mrs. Pig's bulk buy ill. by author. Atheneum, 1981. Subj: Animals – pigs. Food.

The rain cloud ill. by author. Atheneum, 1980. Subj: Character traits – helpfulness. Weather – clouds.

Rayner, Shoo. *My first picture joke book* ill. by author. Viking, 1990. ISBN 0-670-82450-X Subj: Animals. Humor.

Raynor, Dorka. *Grandparents around the world* ed. by Caroline Rubin; photos. by author. Albert Whitman, 1977. Subj: Family life – grandparents.

Rea, Jesus Guerrero. *Atariba and Niguayona* (Rohmer, Harriet)

Reader, Dennis. *Butterfingers* ill. by author. Houghton, 1991. ISBN 0-395-57581-8 Subj: Babies. Behavior – carelessness. Family life – brothers. Family life – sisters.

I want one! ill. by author. Ideals, 1990. ISBN 0-8249-8442-0 Subj: Character traits – selfishness.

Reardon, Maureen. *Feelings between brothers and sisters* (Conta, Marcia Maher)

Feelings between friends (Conta, Marcia Maher)

Feelings between kids and grownups (Conta, Marcia Maher)

Feelings between kids and parents (Conta, Marcia Maher)

Reasoner, Charles. *Sleepy time bunny* (Cosgrove, Stephen (Edward))

Reavin, Sam. *Hurray for Captain Jane!* ill. by Emily Arnold McCully. Parents, 1971. Subj: Activities – bathing. Boats, ships. Imagination.

Reddix, Valerie. *Dragon kite of the autumn moon* ill. by Jean and Mou-sien Tseng. Lothrop, 1992. ISBN 0-688-11031-2 Subj: Dragons. Family life – grandfathers. Foreign lands – Taiwan. Kites.

Millie and the mud hole ill. by Thor Wickstrom. Lothrop, 1992. ISBN 0-688-10213-1 Subj: Animals. Animals – pigs. Farms. Noise, sounds. Poetry, rhyme.

Redies, Rainer. *The cats' party* ill. by Gerta Melle. Barron's, 1986. ISBN 0-8120-5720-1 Subj: Animals – cats. Character traits – individuality. Family life. Parties.

Reece, Colleen L. *What?* ill. by Lois Axeman. Children's Pr., 1983. Subj: Character traits – curiosity. Character traits – questioning.

Reed, Allison. *Genesis: the story of creation* ill. by author. Schocken, 1981. Subj: Religion.

Reed, Jonathan. *Do armadillos come in houses?* ill. by Carol Nicklaus. Atheneum, 1981. Subj: Emotions – fear.

Reed, Kit. *When we dream* ill. by Yutaka Sugita. Hawthorn, 1966. Subj: Behavior – wishing. Dreams.

Reed, Lillian Craig *see* Reed, Kit

Reed, Mary M. *Biddy and the ducks* (Sondergaard, Arensa)

Rees, Mary. *Ten in a bed* ill. by adapt. Little, 1988. ISBN 0-316-73708-9 Subj: Bedtime. Counting, numbers. Family life.

Reese, Ralph. *The first crazy word book: verbs* (Preiss, Byron)

Reesink, Marijke. *The golden treasure* ill. by Jaap Tol. Harcourt, 1968. Translation of Het vrouwtje van Stavoren Subj: Boats, ships. Character traits – selfishness. Folk and fairy tales. Foreign lands – Holland.

The princess who always ran away ill. by Françoise Trésy. McGraw-Hill, 1981. Subj: Behavior – solitude. Character traits – being different. Folk and fairy tales. Royalty – princesses. Sibling rivalry.

Reeves, James. *Ragged Robin: poems from A to Z* ill. by Emma Chichester Clark. Little, 1990. ISBN 0-316-73829-8 Subj: ABC books. Poetry, rhyme.

Reeves, Mona Rabun. *I had a cat* ill. by Julie Downing. Bradbury Pr., 1989. ISBN 0-02-775731-5 Subj: Animals. Poetry, rhyme.

The spooky eerie night noise ill. by Paul Yalowitz. Bradbury Pr., 1989. ISBN 0-02-775732-3 Subj: Animals – skunks. Emotions – fear. Night. Poetry, rhyme.

Regniers, Beatrice De *see* De Regniers, Beatrice Schenk

Rehm, Karl. *Left or right?* by Karl Rehm and Kay Koike; photos. by author. Houghton, 1991. ISBN 0-395-58080-3 Subj: Concepts – left and right.

Rehnman, Mats. *The clay flute* ill. by author. Farrar, 1989. ISBN 91-29-59184-8 Subj: Foreign lands. Magic. Music. Witches.

Reich, Hanns. *Animal babies* (Zoll, Max Alfred)

Reichmeier, Betty. *Potty time!* ill. by author. Random, 1988. ISBN 0-394-89403-0 Subj: Behavior – growing up. Toilet training.

Reid, Alastair. *A balloon for a blunderbuss* (Gill, Bob)

Mother Goose in Spanish (Mother Goose)

Supposing ill. by Abe Birnbaum. Little, 1960. Subj: Humor. Imagination.

Reid, Jon. *Celestino Piatti's animal ABC* (Piatti, Celestino)

Reidel, Marlene. *Jacob and the robbers* ill. by author. Atheneum, 1967. Subj: Crime. Night. Sleep.

Reimold, Mary Gallagher. *My mom is a runner* photos. by Sid Dorris. Abingdon Pr., 1987. ISBN 0-687-27545-8 Subj: Family life – mothers. Sports – racing.

Reinl, Edda. *The little snake* ill. by author. Alphabet Pr., 1982. Subj: Emotions – love. Reptiles – snakes.

Reiser, Lynn. *Any kind of dog* ill. by author. Greenwillow, 1992. ISBN 0-688-10915-2 Subj: Animals. Animals – dogs. Family life. Pets. Toys.

Bedtime cat ill. by author. Greenwillow, 1991. ISBN 0-688-10026-0 Subj: Animals – cats. Bedtime.

Dog and cat ill. by author. Greenwillow, 1991. ISBN 0-688-09893-2 Subj: Animals – cats. Animals – dogs.

Reiss, John J. *Colors* ill. by author. Bradbury Pr., 1969. Subj: Concepts – color.

Numbers ill. by author. Bradbury Pr., 1971. Subj: Counting, numbers.

Shapes ill. by author. Bradbury Pr., 1974. Subj: Concepts – shape.

Reit, Seymour. *The king who learned to smile* ill. by Gordon Laite. Golden Pr., 1960. Subj: Behavior – boredom. Royalty – kings.

Rebus bears ill. by Kenneth Smith. Bantam, 1989. ISBN 0-553-34689-X Subj: Animals – bears. Folk and fairy tales. Rebuses.

Round things everywhere photos. by Carol Basen. McGraw-Hill, 1969. Subj: Concepts – shape. Ethnic groups in the U.S.

Reitveld, Jane Klatt. *Monkey island* ill. by author. Viking, 1963. Subj: Animals – monkeys. Zoos.

Remkiewicz, Frank. *Greedyanna* ill. by author. Lothrop, 1992. ISBN 0-688-10295-6 Subj: Behavior. Character traits – selfishness. Family life.

The last time I saw Harris ill. by author. Lothrop, 1991. ISBN 0-688-10292-1 Subj: Behavior – lost. Birds – parakeets, parrots. Pets.

Renberg, Dalia Hardof. *Hello, clouds!* ill. by Alona Frankel. Harper, 1985. ISBN 0-06-024839-4 Subj: Imagination. Weather – clouds.

Ressner, Phil. *August explains* ill. by Crosby Newell Bonsall. Harper, 1963. Subj: Animals – bears.

Dudley Pippin ill. by Arnold Lobel. Harper, 1965. Subj: City. Imagination.

Retan, Walter. *The snowplow that tried to go south* by Walter Retan [i.e. George Walters]; ill. by John Resko. Atheneum, 1950. Subj: Machines. Seasons – winter. Weather – snow.

The steam shovel that wouldn't eat dirt ill. by Roger Antoine Duvoisin. Atheneum, 1948. Subj: Food. Machines.

Rettich, Margret. *The voyage of the jolly boat* tr. from German by Joy Backhouse; ill. by author. Methuen, 1981. Subj: Boats, ships. Careers – fishermen. Weather – storms.

Reuter, Margaret. *My mother is blind* ill. by Philip Lanier. Children's Pr., 1979. Subj: Family life – mothers. Handicaps – blindness. Senses – seeing.

Rey, H. A. (Hans Augusto). *Anybody at home?* ill. by author. Houghton, 1942. Subj: Format, unusual. Houses.

Billy's picture (Rey, Margřet (Margřet Elisabeth Waldstein))

Cecily G and the nine monkeys ill. by author. Houghton, 1942. Subj: Animals – giraffes. Animals – monkeys. Humor.

Curious George ill. by author. Houghton, 1941. Subj: Animals – monkeys. Careers – firefighters. Character traits – curiosity. Humor.

Curious George gets a medal ill. by author. Houghton, 1957. Subj: Animals – monkeys. Character traits – curiosity. Humor. Space and space ships.

Curious George goes to the hospital (Rey, Margřet (Margřet Elisabeth Waldstein))

Curious George learns the alphabet ill. by author. Houghton, 1963. Subj: ABC books. Animals – monkeys. Character traits – curiosity.

Curious George rides a bike ill. by author. Houghton, 1952. Subj: Animals – monkeys. Character traits – curiosity. Circus. Humor. Sports – bicycling.

Curious George takes a job ill. by author. Houghton, 1947. Subj: Animals – monkeys. Careers – window cleaners. Character traits – curiosity. Humor. Zoos.

Elizabite, adventures of a carnivorous plant ill. by author. Harper, 1942. Subj: Humor. Plants. Poetry, rhyme.

Feed the animals ill. by author. Houghton, 1944. Subj: Poetry, rhyme. Zoos.

How do you get there? ill. by author. Houghton, 1941. Subj: Format, unusual. Transportation.

Humpty Dumpty and other Mother Goose songs ill. by author. Harper, 1943. Subj: Music. Nursery rhymes. Songs.

Look for the letters ill. by author. Harper, 1942. Subj: ABC books.

See the circus ill. by author. Houghton, 1956. Subj: Circus. Format, unusual. Poetry, rhyme.

Tit for tat ill. by author. Harper, 1942. Subj: Animals. Humor.

Where's my baby? ill. by author. Houghton, 1943. Subj: Animals. Format, unusual. Poetry, rhyme.

Rey, Margřet (Margřet Elisabeth Waldstein). *Billy's picture* by Margřet and Hans Augusto Rey; ill. by Hans Augusto Rey. Harper, 1948. Subj: Animals. Art. Humor.

Curious George flies a kite ill. by Hans Augusto Rey. Houghton, 1958. Subj: Animals – monkeys. Character traits – curiosity. Humor. Kites. Sports – fishing.

Curious George goes to the hospital by Margřet and Hans Augusto Rey in collaboration with the Children's Hospital Medical Center, Boston; ill. by Hans Augusto Rey. Houghton, 1966. Subj: Animals – monkeys. Behavior – lost. Character traits – curiosity. Hospitals. Humor.

Pretzel ill. by Hans Augusto Rey. Harper, 1941. Subj: Animals – dogs.

Pretzel and the puppies ill. by Hans Augusto Rey. Harper, 1946. Subj: Animals – dogs.

Spotty ill. by Hans Augusto Rey. Harper, 1945. Subj: Animals – rabbits. Character traits – being different.

Reyher, Becky. *My mother is the most beautiful woman in the world* ill. by Ruth S. Gannett. Lothrop, 1945. Subj: Caldecott award honor book. Family life – mothers.

Reynolds, Jan. *Amazon* photos. by author. Harcourt, 1993. ISBN 0-15-202832-3 Subj: Foreign lands – South America. Indians of South America. Rivers.

Down under photos. by author. Harcourt, 1992. ISBN 0-15-224182-5 Subj: Foreign lands – Australia.

Far north photos. by author. Harcourt, 1992. ISBN 0-15-227178-3 Subj: Foreign lands – Arctic. Foreign lands – Norway. Foreign lands – Lapland.

Himalaya photos. by author. Harcourt, 1991. ISBN 0-15-234465-9 Subj: Foreign lands – Nepal.

Sahara photos. by author. Harcourt, 1991. ISBN 0-15-269959-7 Subj: Desert. Foreign lands – Sahara Desert.

Rhodes, Timothy. *The sleeping bread* (Czernecki, Stefan)

Rice, Eve. *Aren't you coming too?* ill. by Nancy Winslow Parker. Greenwillow, 1988. ISBN 0-688-06447-7 Subj: Activities. Family life – grandfathers.

At Grammy's house ill. by Nancy Winslow Parker. Greenwillow, 1990. ISBN 0-688-08875-9 Subj: Family life – grandparents.

Benny bakes a cake ill. by author. Greenwillow, 1981. Subj: Activities – cooking. Animals – dogs. Behavior – misbehavior. Birthdays.

City night ill. by Peter Sis. Greenwillow, 1987. ISBN 0-688-06857-X Subj: City. Family life. Night. Poetry, rhyme.

Ebbie ill. by author. Greenwillow, 1975. Subj: Family life. Names.

Goodnight, goodnight ill. by author. Greenwillow, 1980. Subj: Bedtime. Night.

New blue shoes ill. by author. Macmillan, 1975. Subj: Clothing – shoes. Family life – mothers. Shopping.

Papa's lemonade and other stories ill. by author. Greenwillow, 1976. Subj: Animals – dogs. Family life.

Peter's pockets ill. by Nancy Winslow Parker. Greenwillow, 1989. ISBN 0-688-07242-9 Subj: Clothing – pants. Problem solving.

Sam who never forgets ill. by author. Greenwillow, 1977. Subj: Animals. Food. Zoos.

What Sadie sang ill. by author. Greenwillow, 1976. Subj: Babies. Emotions – happiness.

Rice, Inez. *A long long time* ill. by Robert M. Quackenbush. Lothrop, 1964. Subj: Character traits – optimism. Imagination.

The March wind ill. by Vladimir Bobri. Lothrop, 1957. Subj: Clothing. Imagination. Weather – wind.

Rice, James. *Cajun alphabet* ill. by author. Pelican, 1991. ISBN 0-88289-822-1 Subj: ABC books.

Gaston goes to Texas ill. by author. Pelican, 1978. Subj: Poetry, rhyme. Reptiles – alligators, crocodiles.

Richard, Jane. *A horse grows up* ill. by Bert Hardy. Walker, 1972. Subj: Animals – horses. Science.

Richardson, Jack E. *Six in a mix* by Jack E. Richardson, Jr., and others; ill. by Carlos Alfonso and others. Benziger, 1971. Subj: Language.

Richardson, Jean. *Clara's dancing feet* ill. by Joanna Carey. Putnam's, 1987. ISBN 0-399-21388-0 Subj: Activities – dancing. Character traits – shyness.

The nutcracker (Hoffmann, E. T. A.)

The sleeping beauty: the story of Tchaikovsky's ballet ill. by Francesca Crespi. Arcade, 1991. ISBN 1-55970-142-0 Subj: Activities – dancing. Folk and fairy tales.

Stephen's feast ill. by Alice Englander. Little, 1991. ISBN 0-316-74435-2 Subj: Holidays – Christmas. Middle ages. Music. Songs.

Tall inside ill. by Alice Englander. Putnam's, 1988. ISBN 0-399-21486-0 Subj: Clowns, jesters. Self-concept.

Thomas's sitter ill. by Dawn Holmes. Four Winds, 1991. ISBN 0-02-776146-0 Subj: Activities – babysitting. Behavior – misbehavior.

Richardson, Judith Benet. *The way home* ill. by Salley Mavor. Macmillan, 1991. ISBN 0-02-776145-2 Subj: Animals – elephants. Sea and seashore.

Riches, Judith. *Giraffes have more fun* ill. by author. Morrow, 1992. ISBN 0-688-11043-6 Subj: Animals – giraffes. Imagination.

Richter, Alice Numeroff. *Emily's bunch* (Numeroff, Laura Joffe)

You can't put braces on spaces by Alice Numeroff Richter and Laura Joffe Numeroff; ill. by Laura Joffe Numeroff. Greenwillow, 1979. Subj: Careers – dentists. Teeth.

Richter, Mischa. *Eric and Matilda* ill. by author. Harper, 1967. Subj: Birds – ducks. Parades.

Quack? ill. by author. Harper, 1978. Subj: Animals. Birds – ducks. Noise, sounds.

To bed, to bed! ill. by author. Prentice-Hall, 1981. Subj: Bedtime. Royalty.

Rickard, Graham. *Let's look at tractors* ill. by Clifford Meadway. Watts, 1990. ISBN 0-531-18256-8 Subj: Tractors.

Ricketts, Michael. *Rain* ill. by author. Wonder Books, 1971. Subj: Weather – rain.

Teeth ill. by author. Grosset, 1971. Subj: Teeth.

Riddell, Chris. *The bear dance* ill. by author. Simon & Schuster, 1990. ISBN 0-671-70974-7 Subj: Activities – dancing. Animals – bears.

Ben and the bear ill. by author. Lippincott, 1986. ISBN 0-397-32194-5 Subj: Animals – bears. Behavior – sharing.

Bird's new shoes ill. by author. Holt, 1987. ISBN 0-8050-0326-6 Subj: Animals. Behavior – imitation. Character traits – being different. Clothing – shoes. Cumulative tales.

The trouble with elephants ill. by author. Lippincott, 1988. ISBN 0-397-32273-9 Subj: Animals – elephants.

The wish factory ill. by author. Ideals, 1990. ISBN 0-8249-8482-X Subj: Behavior – wishing. Dreams. Monsters. Sleep.

Riddell, Edwina. *One hundred first words* ill. by author. Barron's, 1988. ISBN 0-8120-5786-4 Subj: Language.

Riddle, Tohby. *Careful with that ball, Eugene!* ill. by author. Watts, 1991. ISBN 0-531-08517-1 Subj: Imagination. Sports.

Rider, Alex. *A la ferme. At the farm: learn-a-language book in French and English* ill. by Paul Davis. Doubleday, 1962. Subj: Farms. Foreign lands – France. Foreign languages.

Chez nous. At our house: learn-a-language book in French and English ill. by Isadore Seltzer. Doubleday, 1962. Subj: Family life. Foreign lands – France. Foreign languages.

Ridlon, Marcia. *Kittens and more kittens* ill. by Elizabeth Dauber. Follett, 1967. Subj: Animals – cats. Pets.

Riehecky, Janet. *Apatosaurus* ill. by Lydia Halverson. Child's World, 1988. ISBN 0-89565-423-7 Subj: Dinosaurs.

Rigby, Rodney. *Hello, this is your penguin speaking* ill. by author. Walt Disney, 1992. ISBN 1-56282-232-2 Subj: Activities – flying. Birds – penguins. Character traits – persistence.

There's a building on Sixth Avenue ill. by author. Walt Disney, 1992. ISBN 1-56282-156-3 Subj: Poetry, rhyme.

Rigby, Shirley Lincoln. *Smaller than most* ill. by Debby L. Carter. Harper, 1985. ISBN 0-06-025028-3 Subj: Animals – pandas. Babies. Character traits – smallness. Family life. Family life – grandfathers.

Riggio, Anita. *Wake up, William!* ill. by author. Atheneum, 1987. ISBN 0-689-31344-6 Subj: Family life. Sleep.

Rikys, Bodel. *Red bear* ill. by author. Dial, 1992. ISBN 0-8037-1048-8 Subj: Animals – bears. Concepts – color.

Riley, James Whitcomb. *Little Orphant Annie* ill. by Diane Stanley. Putnam's, 1983. Subj: Poetry, rhyme.

Ring, Elizabeth. *Tiger lilies and other beastly plants* ill. by Barbara Bash. Walker, 1985. Subj: Character traits – appearance. Plants.

Ringgold, Faith. *Tar Beach* ill. by author. Crown, 1991. ISBN 0-517-58031-4 Subj: Activities – flying. Caldecott award honor book. City. Dreams. Ethnic groups in the U.S. – Afro-Americans. Quilts.

Ringi, Kjell (Arne Sorensen). *My father and I* by Kjell Ringi and Adelaide Holl; ill. by Kjell Ringi. Watts, 1972. Subj: Character traits – ambition. Family life – fathers. Imagination.

The sun and the cloud ill. by author. Harper, 1971. Subj: Plants. Sun. Weather – clouds.

The winner ill. by author. Harper, 1969. Subj: Behavior. Wordless.

Riordan, James. *Old Father Frost* (Odoyevsky, Vladimir)

The three magic gifts ill. by Errol le Cain. Oxford Univ. Pr., 1980. Subj: Character traits – perseverance. Folk and fairy tales. Sibling rivalry.

Thumbelina (Andersen, H. C. (Hans Christian))

Ripley, Catherine. *Two dozen dinosaurs* ill. by Bo-Kim Louie. Firefly, 1992. ISBN 0-920775-55-1 Subj: Dinosaurs. Games.

Rippon, Penelope. *My day* ill. by author. Viking, 1990. ISBN 0-670-83459-9 Subj: Babies. Family life.

Rister, Claude see Marshall, James

Roach, Marilynne K. *Dune fox* ill. by author. Little, 1977. Subj: Animals – foxes. Ecology. Sand. Seasons.

Two Roman mice by Horace; ill. by author. Crowell, 1975. Based on a version of Æsop's fable about the country mouse and the city mouse as it appeared in Horace's Satirae II, 6 Subj: Animals – mice. City. Country.

Robart, Rose. *The cake that Mack ate* ill. by Maryann Kovalski. Little, 1987. ISBN 0-87113-121-8 Subj: Cumulative tales. Farms. Food.

Robb, Brian. *My grandmother's djinn* ill. by author. Parents, 1978. Subj: Family life. Foreign lands. Mythical creatures. Problem solving.

Robbins, Ken. *Beach days* photos. by author. Viking, 1987. ISBN 0-670-80138-0 Subj: Sand. Sea and seashore.

City/country: a car trip in photographs photos. by author. Viking, 1985. ISBN 0-670-80743-5 Subj: Activities – traveling. Automobiles.

Trucks of every sort photos. by author. Crown, 1981. Subj: Trucks.

Robbins, Ruth. *Baboushka and the three kings* ill. by Nicolas Sidjakov; verse by Edith R. Thomas; music by Mary Clement Sanks. Parnassus, 1960. Adapted from a Russian folk tale Subj: Caldecott award book. Folk and fairy tales. Foreign lands – Russia. Holidays – Christmas. Music. Poetry, rhyme. Songs.

The harlequin and Mother Goose: or, The magic stick ill. by Nicolas Sidjakov. Parnassus, 1965. Subj: Nursery rhymes.

How the first rainbow was made ill. by author. Houghton, 1980. Subj: Folk and fairy tales. Indians of North America. Weather – rain.

Roberts, Bethany. *Waiting-for-Papa stories* ill. by Sarah Stapler. HarperCollins, 1990. ISBN 0-06-025051-8 Subj: Animals – rabbits. Family life – fathers.

Waiting for spring stories ill. by William Joyce. Harper, 1984. Subj: Animals – rabbits. Seasons – winter.

Roberts, Cliff. *The dot* ill. by author. Watts, 1960. Subj: Concepts – shape.

Start with a dot ill. by author. Watts, 1960. Subj: Concepts – shape. Poetry, rhyme.

Roberts, Sarah. *Bert and the missing mop mix-up* ill. by Joseph Mathieu. Random House, 1983. Subj: Behavior – misunderstanding. Puppets.

Ernie's big mess ill. by Joseph Mathieu. Random House, 1981. ISBN 0-394-94847-5 Subj: Behavior – carelessness. Puppets.

I want to go home! ill. by Joseph Mathieu. Random House, 1985. ISBN 0-394-97027-6 Subj: Behavior – needing someone. Family life – grandmothers. Puppets. Sea and seashore.

Roberts, Thom. *Pirates in the park* ill. by Harold Berson. Crown, 1973. Subj: Imagination. Pirates. Toys – rocking horses.

Robertson, Joanne. *Sea witches* ill. by Laszlo Gal. Dial, 1991. ISBN 0-8037-1070-4 Subj: Family life – grandmothers. Folk and fairy tales. Foreign lands – Scotland. Poetry, rhyme. Witches.

Robertson, Lilian. *Picnic woods* ill. by author. Harcourt, 1949. Subj: Activities – picnicking.

Runaway rocking horse ill. by author. Harcourt, 1948. Subj: Toys – rocking horses.

Robertus, Polly M. *The dog who had kittens* ill. by Janet Stevens. Holiday, 1991. ISBN 0-8234-0860-4 Subj: Animals – cats. Animals – dogs.

Robins, Joan. *Addie meets Max* ill. by Sue Truesdell. Harper, 1985. Subj: Animals – dogs. Friendship.

Addie runs away ill. by Sue Truesdell. HarperCollins, 1989. ISBN 0-06-025081-X Subj: Behavior – running away. Camps, camping. Seasons – summer.

My brother, Will ill. by Marylin Hafner. Greenwillow, 1986. ISBN 0-688-05223-1 Subj: Babies. Family life – brothers. Sibling rivalry.

Robinson, Adjai. *Femi and old grandaddie* ill. by Jerry Pinkney. Coward, 1972. Subj: Folk and fairy tales. Foreign lands – Africa.

Robinson, Earl. *Black and white* (Arkin, Alan)

Robinson, Irene Bowen. *Picture book of animal babies* by Irene and W. W. Robinson; ill. by Irene Bowen Robinson. Macmillan, 1947. Subj: Animals.

Robinson, Nancy K. *Firefighters!* ill. with photos. Scholastic, 1979. Subj: Careers – firefighters.

Robinson, Thomas P. *Buttons* ill. by Peggy Bacon. Viking, 1938. Subj: Animals – cats.

Robinson, W. W. (William Wilcox). *On the farm* ill. by Irene Bowen Robinson. Macmillan, 1939. Subj: Animals. Farms.

Picture book of animal babies (Robinson, Irene Bowen)

Robison, Deborah. *Bye-bye, old buddy* ill. by author. Houghton, 1983. Subj: Problem solving.

No elephants allowed ill. by author. Houghton, 1981. Subj: Bedtime. Emotions – fear. Problem solving.

Your turn, doctor by Deborah Robison and Carla Perez; ill. by Deborah Robison. Dial Pr., 1982. Subj: Behavior – misbehavior. Careers – doctors.

Robison, Nancy. *Ten tall soldiers* ill. by Hilary Knight. Holt, 1991. ISBN 0-8050-0768-7 Subj: Monsters. Royalty – kings. Shadows.

UFO kidnap ill. by Edward Frascino. Lothrop, 1978. Subj: Space and space ships.

Roche, A. K. *see* Kaplan, Boche

Roche, A. K. *see* Abisch, Roz

Roche, P. K. (Patrick K.). *Good-bye, Arnold!* ill. by author. Dial Pr., 1979. Subj: Animals – mice. Family life. Sibling rivalry.

Jump all the morning: a child's day in verses ill. by author. Viking, 1984. Subj: Poetry, rhyme.

Plaid bear and the rude rabbit gang ill. by author. Dial Pr., 1982. Subj: Behavior – bullying. Toys.

Webster and Arnold go camping ill. by author. Viking, 1989. ISBN 0-670-81993-X Subj: Animals – mice. Camps, camping. Family life – brothers.

Rockwell, Anne F. *Apples and pumpkins* ill. by Lizzy Rockwell. Macmillan, 1989. ISBN 0-02-777270-5 Subj: Food. Holidays – Halloween.

At the beach ill. by Harlow Rockwell. Macmillan, 1987. ISBN 0-02-777940-8 Subj: Activities – playing. Sea and seashore.

Bafana: a Christmas story ill. by author. Atheneum, 1974. Subj: Folk and fairy tales. Holidays – Christmas.

A bear, a bobcat and three ghosts ill. by author. Macmillan, 1977. Subj: Animals – bears. Animals – bobcats. Careers – peddlers. Ghosts. Holidays – Halloween.

Bear Child's book of hours ill. by author. Crowell, 1987. ISBN 0-690-04551-4 Subj: Animals – bears. Time.

Big bad goat ill. by author. Dutton, 1982. ISBN 0-525-45100-5 Subj: Animals. Character traits – helpfulness. Insects – bees.

Big boss ill. by author. Macmillan, 1975. Subj: Animals – foxes. Animals – tigers. Character traits – cleverness. Frogs and toads.

Big wheels ill. by author. Dutton, 1986. ISBN 0-525-44226-X Subj: Machines.

Bikes ill. by author. Dutton, 1987. ISBN 0-525-44287-1 Subj: Sports – bicycling.

Blackout by Anne F. and Harlow Rockwell; ill. by authors. Macmillan, 1979. Subj: Family life. Power failure. Weather.

Boats ill. by author. Dutton, 1982. Subj: Animals – bears. Boats, ships.

The bump in the night ill. by author. Greenwillow, 1979. Subj: Character traits – cleverness. Character traits – helpfulness.

Buster and the bogeyman ill. by author. Four Winds Pr., 1978. Subj: Bedtime. Dreams. Mythical creatures.

Can I help? by Anne F. and Harlow Rockwell; ill. by authors. Macmillan, 1982. Subj: Character traits – helpfulness.

Cars ill. by author. Dutton, 1984. Subj: Automobiles.

Come to town ill. by author. Crowell, 1987. ISBN 0-690-04646-4 Subj: Animals – bears. City.

The emergency room by Anne and Harlow Rockwell; ill. by authors. Macmillan, 1985. ISBN 0-02-777300-0 Subj: Hospitals. Illness.

Fire engines ill. by author. Dutton, 1986. ISBN 0-525-44259-6 Subj: Animals – dogs. Careers – firefighters. Trucks.

First comes spring ill. by author. Crowell, 1985. ISBN 0-690-04455-0 Subj: Animals – bears. Seasons.

The first snowfall by Anne and Harlow Rockwell; ill. by authors. Macmillan, 1987. ISBN 0-02-777770-7 Subj: Seasons – winter. Weather – snow.

Gogo's pay day ill. by author. Doubleday, 1978. Subj: Character traits – generosity. Clowns, jesters. Money.

The gollywhopper egg ill. by author. Macmillan, 1974. Subj: Behavior – trickery. Eggs. Farms.

The good llama ill. by author. World, 1963. Subj: Animals. Animals – llamas. Foreign lands – South America.

Handy Hank will fix it ill. by author. Holt, 1988. ISBN 0-8050-0697-4 Subj: Careers – handyman. Character traits – helpfulness.

Happy birthday to me by Anne F. and Harlow Rockwell; ill. by authors. Macmillan, 1981. Subj: Birthdays.

Honk honk! ill. by author. Dutton, 1980. Subj: Animals. Behavior – misbehavior. Birds. Cumulative tales.

How my garden grew by Anne F. and Harlow Rockwell; ill. by authors. Macmillan, 1982. Subj: Gardens, gardening.

Hugo at the park ill. by author. Macmillan, 1990. ISBN 0-02-777301-9 Subj: Animals – dogs.

Hugo at the window ill. by author. Macmillan, 1988. ISBN 0-02-777330-2 Subj: Animals – dogs. Birthdays. City.

I like the library ill. by author. Dutton, 1977. Subj: Libraries.

I love my pets by Anne F. and Harlow Rockwell; ill. by authors. Macmillan, 1982. Subj: Pets.

I play in my room by Anne F. and Harlow Rockwell; ill. by authors. Macmillan, 1981. Subj: Activities – playing.

In our house ill. by author. Crowell, 1985. ISBN 0-690-04488-7 Subj: Activities. Animals – bears. Family life.

Machines by Anne F. and Harlow Rockwell; ill. by Harlow Rockwell. Macmillan, 1972. Subj: Machines.

The Mother Goose cookie-candy book ill. by author. Random House, 1983. Subj: Activities – cooking. Food.

My back yard by Anne F. and Harlow Rockwell; ill. by authors. Macmillan, 1984. Subj: Activities – playing.

My barber by Anne F. and Harlow Rockwell; ill. by authors. Macmillan, 1981. Subj: Careers – barbers. Hair.

My spring robin ill. by Harlow Rockwell and Lizzy Rockwell. Macmillan, 1989. ISBN 0-02-777611- Subj: Birds – robins. Flowers. Seasons – spring.

Nice and clean by Anne F. and Harlow Rockwell; ill. by authors. Macmillan, 1984. Subj: Character traits – cleanliness. Houses.

The night we slept outside by Anne F. and Harlow Rockwell; ill. by authors. Macmillan, 1983. Subj: Night. Camps, camping.

The old woman and her pig and 10 other stories ill. by adapt. Crowell, 1979. Subj: Folk and fairy tales.

On our vacation ill. by author. Dutton, 1989. ISBN 0-525-44487-7 Subj: Activities – vacationing. Animals – bears. Camps, camping. Islands.

Our garage sale ill. by Harlow Rockwell. Greenwillow, 1984. Subj: Garage sales.

Our yard is full of birds ill. by Lizzy Rockwell. Macmillan, 1992. ISBN 0-02-777273-X Subj: Birds.

Planes by Anne and Harlow Rockwell; ill. by authors. Dutton, 1985. ISBN 0-525-44159-X Subj: Airplanes, airports. Transportation.

Poor Goose: a French folktale ill. by author. Crowell, 1976. Subj: Animals. Birds – geese. Cumulative tales. Folk and fairy tales. Foreign lands – France.

Root-a-toot-toot ill. by author. Macmillan, 1991. ISBN 0-02-777272-1 Subj: Animals. Cumulative tales. Noise, sounds.

Sick in bed by Anne F. and Harlow Rockwell; ill. by authors. Macmillan, 1982. Subj: Illness.

The stolen necklace: a picture story from India ill. by author. Collins-World, 1968. "Based on a tale from the Jataka." Subj: Animals – monkeys. Character traits – cleverness. Foreign lands – India.

The story snail ill. by author. Macmillan, 1974. Subj: Animals – snails. Magic.

The supermarket by Anne F. and Harlow Rockwell; ill. by authors. Macmillan, 1979. Subj: Shopping. Stores.

Things that go ill. by author. Dutton, 1986. ISBN 0-525-44266-9 Subj: Transportation.

The three bears and 15 other stories ill. by author. Crown, 1975. Subj: Folk and fairy tales.

Thump thump thump! ill. by author. Dutton, 1981. Subj: Folk and fairy tales. Monsters.

Toad by Anne F. and Harlow Rockwell; ill. by authors. Doubleday, 1972. Subj: Frogs and toads.

The toolbox by Anne F. and Harlow Rockwell; ill. by Harlow Rockwell. Macmillan, 1971. Subj: Tools.

Trains ill. by author. Dutton, 1988. ISBN 0-525-44377-0 Subj: Trains. Transportation.

Trucks ill. by author. Dutton, 1984. Subj: Trucks.

When Hugo went to school ill. by author. Macmillan, 1991. ISBN 0-02-777305-1 Subj: Animals – dogs. School.

When I go visiting by Anne F. and Harlow Rockwell; ill. by authors. Macmillan, 1984. Subj: Family life – grandmothers. Family life – grandparents.

Willy can count ill. by author. Little, 1989. ISBN 1-55970-013-0 Subj: Activities – walking. Counting, numbers. Country. Family life – mothers.

Willy runs away ill. by author. Dutton, 1978. ISBN 0-525-42795-3 Subj: Animals – dogs. Behavior – running away.

The wolf who had a wonderful dream ill. by author. Crowell, 1973. Subj: Animals – wolves. Dreams. Folk and fairy tales. Food. Foreign lands – France.

The wonderful eggs of Furicchia: a picture story from Italy ill. by author. Collins-World, 1969. Subj: Birds – chickens. Eggs. Folk and fairy tales. Foreign lands – Italy. Magic.

Rockwell, Harlow. *Blackout* (Rockwell, Anne F.)

Can I help? (Rockwell, Anne F.)

The compost heap ill. by author. Doubleday, 1974. Subj: Gardens, gardening. Plants.

The emergency room (Rockwell, Anne F.)

The first snowfall (Rockwell, Anne F.)

Happy birthday to me (Rockwell, Anne F.)

How my garden grew (Rockwell, Anne F.)

I did it ill. by author. Macmillan, 1974. Subj: Activities.

I love my pets (Rockwell, Anne F.)

I play in my room (Rockwell, Anne F.)

Look at this ill. by author. Macmillan, 1978. Subj: Activities.

Machines (Rockwell, Anne F.)

My back yard (Rockwell, Anne F.)

My barber (Rockwell, Anne F.)

My dentist ill. by author. Greenwillow, 1975. Subj: Careers – dentists. Teeth.

My doctor ill. by author. Macmillan, 1973. Subj: Careers – doctors. Health.

My kitchen ill. by author. Greenwillow, 1980. Subj: Food.

My nursery school ill. by author. Greenwillow, 1976. Subj: School.

Nice and clean (Rockwell, Anne F.)

The night we slept outside (Rockwell, Anne F.)

Planes (Rockwell, Anne F.)

Sick in bed (Rockwell, Anne F.)

The supermarket (Rockwell, Anne F.)

Toad (Rockwell, Anne F.)

The toolbox (Rockwell, Anne F.)

When I go visiting (Rockwell, Anne F.)

Rockwell, Norman. *Norman Rockwell's counting book* sel. by Glorina Taborin; ill. by author. Harmony Books, 1977. Subj: Counting, numbers. Games. Holidays – April Fools' Day.

Rodanas, Kristina. *The dragonfly's tale* ill. by author. Houghton, 1992. ISBN 0-395-57003-4 Subj: Folk and fairy tales. Indians of North America. Insects – dragonflies.

The story of Wali Dâd ill. by author. Lothrop, 1988. ISBN 0-688-07363-1 Subj: Character traits – generosity. Foreign lands – India.

Roddie, Shen. *Animal stew* ill. by Patrick J. Gallagher. Houghton, 1992. ISBN 0-395-57582-6 Subj: Animals. Cumulative tales. Format, unusual. Giants.

Hatch, egg, hatch! ill. by Frances Cony. Little, 1991. ISBN 0-316-75345-9 Subj: Babies. Birds – chickens. Birth. Eggs. Format, unusual – toy and movable books.

Rodgers, Frank. *Who's afraid of the ghost train?* ill. by author. Harcourt, 1989. ISBN 0-15-200642-7 Subj: Emotions – fear. Family life – grandfathers. Ghosts. Imagination.. Trains.

Rodgers, Richard. *A real nice clambake* by Richard Rodgers and Oscar Hammerstein; ill. by Nadine Bernard Westcott. Little, 1992. ISBN 0-316-75422-6 Subj: Activities – picnicking. Music. Sea and seashore. Songs.

Roe, Eileen. *All I am* ill. by Helen Cogancherry. Bradbury Pr., 1990. ISBN 0-02-777372-8 Subj: Self-concept.

Con mi hermano—With my brother tr. to Spanish by Jo Mintzer; ill. by Robert Casilla. Bradbury Pr., 1991. ISBN 0-02-777373-6 Subj: Ethnic groups in the U.S. – Mexican-Americans. Family life – brothers. Foreign languages.

Staying with Grandma ill. by Jacqueline Rogers. Bradbury Pr., 1989. ISBN 0-02-777371-X Subj: Country. Family life – grandmothers.

Roe, Richard. *Animal ABC* ill. by author. Random House, 1984. ISBN 0-394-96864-6 Subj: ABC books. Animals.

Roehrdanz, Barbro Eriksson. *Hocus-pocus* (Eriksson, Eva)

Jealousy (Eriksson, Eva)

One short week (Eriksson, Eva)

The tooth trip (Eriksson, Eva)

Roennfeldt, Robert. *A day on the avenue* ill. by author. Viking, 1984. Subj: Roads. Wordless.

Roffey, Maureen. *Bathtime* ill. by author. Four Winds, 1989. ISBN 0-02-777161-X Subj: Activities – bathing. Family life.

Family scramble ill. by author. Dutton, 1987. ISBN 0-525-44290-1 Subj: Family life. Format, unusual.

Here, kitty kitty! ill. by author. Houghton, 1991. ISBN 0-395-5758-2 Subj: Animals – cats. Family life. Format, unusual. Pets.

Home sweet home ill. by author. Coward, 1983. Subj: Format, unusual – toy and movable books. Houses.

I spy at the zoo ill. by author. Four Winds Pr., 1988. ISBN 0-02-777150-4 Subj: Animals. Zoos.

I spy on vacation ill. by author. Four Winds Pr., 1988. ISBN 0-02-777160-1 Subj: Activities – vacationing. Sea and seashore.

Look, there's my hat! ill. by author. Putnam's, 1985. Subj: Behavior – greed. Format, unusual.

Meatime ill. by author. Four Winds, 1989. ISBN 0-02-777151-2 Subj: Activities – picnicking. Birthdays. Family life. Food.

Quick, catch Dan! ill. by author. Houghton, 1991. ISBN 0-395-5758 Subj: Animals – dogs. Family life. Format, unusual. Pets.

Rogasky, Barbara. *Rapunzel* (Grimm, Jacob)

The water of life ill. by. Trina Schart Hyman. Holiday, 1986. Adapt. of Das Wasser des Lebens by Jacob and Wilhelm Grimm ISBN 0-8234-0552-4 Subj: Character traits – pride. Folk and fairy tales. Magic. Royalty. Sibling rivalry.

Rogers, Anne. *Cinderella* (Grimm, Jacob)

The musicians of Bremen (Grimm, Jacob)

The wolf and the seven little kids (Grimm, Jacob)

Rogers, Edmund. *Elephants* ill. with photos. Raintree, 1978. Subj: Animals – elephants.

Rogers, Fred. *Going on an airplane* photos. by Jim Judkis. Putnam, 1989. ISBN 0-399-21635-9 Subj: Activities – traveling. Airplanes, airports.

Going to day care photos. by Jim Judkis. Putnam's, 1985. ISBN 0-399-21235-3 Subj: School.

Going to the doctor photos. by Jim Judkis. Putnam's, 1986. ISBN 0-399-21298-1 Subj: Careers – doctors.

Going to the hospital photos. by Jim Judkis. Putnam's, 1988. ISBN 0-399-21503-4 Subj: Hospitals. Illness.

Going to the potty photos. by Jim Judkis. Putnam's, 1986. ISBN 0-399-21296-5 Subj: Behavior – growing up. Toilet training.

If we were all the same ill. by Pat Sustendal. Random House, 1988. ISBN 0-394-98778-0 Subj: Character traits – individuality.

Making friends photos. by Jim Judkis. Putnam's, 1987. ISBN 0-399-21382-1 Subj: Activities – playing. Emotions. Friendship.

Moving photos. by Jim Judkis. Putnam's, 1987. ISBN 0-399-21383-X Subj: Communities, neighborhoods. Emotions. Family life. Friendship. Moving.

The new baby photos. by Jim Judkis. Putnam's, 1985. ISBN 0-399-21236-1 Subj: Babies. Sibling rivalry.

When a pet dies photos. by Jim Judkis. Putnam's, 1988. ISBN 0-399-21504-2 Subj: Death. Pets.

Rogers, Helen Spelman. *Morris and his brave lion* ill. by Glo Coalson. McGraw-Hill, 1975. Subj: Divorce.

Rogers, Jean. *Runaway mittens* ill. by Rie Munoz. Greenwillow, 1988. ISBN 0-688-07054-X Subj: Behavior – losing things. Clothing – gloves.

Rogers, Margaret. *Green is beautiful* by Margaret Rogers and Bernadette Watts; ill. by Bernadette Watts. State Mutual Books, 1982. Subj: Concepts – color. Folk and fairy tales.

Rogers, Paul (Patrick). *Don't blame me!* ill. by Robin Bell Corfield. Trafalgar Square, 1992. ISBN 0-370-31204-X Subj: Activities – painting. Circular tales. Foreign lands – England.

Forget-me-not ill. by Celia Berridge. Viking, 1984. Subj: Behavior – forgetfulness. Behavior – losing things.

From me to you ill. by Jane Johnson. Watts, 1988. ISBN 0-531-08332-2 Subj: Family life – grandmothers. Poetry, rhyme.

Lily's picnic ill. by John Prater. The Bodley Head Ltd., 1988. ISBN 0-370-31098-5 Subj: Activities – picnicking. Family life.

The shapes game ill. by Sian Tucker. Holt, 1990. ISBN 0-8050-1280-X Subj: Concepts – shape.

Sheepchase ill. by Celia Berridge. Viking, 1986. ISBN 0-670-80599-8 Subj: Animals – sheep. Behavior – running away. Poetry, rhyme.

Somebody's awake ill. by Robin Bell Corfield. Atheneum, 1988. ISBN 0-689-31490-6 Subj: Family life. Food. Morning.

Somebody's sleepy ill. by Robin Bell Corfield. Atheneum, 1988. ISBN 0-689-31491-4 Subj: Bedtime. Family life.

Tumbledown ill. by Robin Bell Corfield. Atheneum, 1988. ISBN 0-689-31392-6 Subj: City. Royalty – princes.

What will the weather be like today? ill. by Kazuko. Greenwillow, 1990. ISBN 0-688-08951-8 Subj: Poetry, rhyme. Weather.

Rogow, Zak. *Oranges* ill. by Mary Szilagyi. Watts, 1988. ISBN 0-531-08343-8 Subj: Food. Trees.

Rohmer, Harriet. *Atariba and Niguayona: a story from the Taino people of Puerto Rico* adapt. by Harriet Rohmer and Jesus Guerrero Rea; ill. by Consuelo Mendez. Childrens Book Pr., 1988. ISBN

0-89239-026-3 Subj: Character traits – kindness. Foreign lands – Puerto Rico. Illness.

How we came to the fifth world: a creation story from Ancient Mexico adapt. by Harriet Rohmer and Mary Anchondo; ill. by Graciela Carrillo. Childrens Book Pr., 1988. ISBN 0-89239-024-7 Subj: Folk and fairy tales. Foreign lands – Mexico.

The invisible hunters by Harriet Rohmer, Octavio Chow and Morris Vidaure; ill. by Joe Sam. Childrens Book Pr., 1987. ISBN 0-89239-031-X Subj: Behavior – greed. Folk and fairy tales. Foreign lands – Nicaragua. Sports – hunting.

Mother scorpion country by Harriet Rohmer and Dorminster Wilson; ill. by Virginia Stearns. Childrens Book Pr., 1987. ISBN 0-89239-032-8 Subj: Emotions – love. Folk and fairy tales. Foreign lands – Nicaragua.

Rojankovsky, Feodor. *ABC, an alphabet of many things* ill. by author. Golden Pr., 1970. Subj: ABC books.

Animals in the zoo ill. by author. Knopf, 1962. Subj: ABC books. Animals. Zoos.

Animals on the farm ill. by author. Knopf, 1962. Subj: Animals. Farms. Wordless.

The great big animal book ill. by author. Simon and Schuster, 1950. Subj: Animals. Farms.

The great big wild animal book ill. by author. Western, 1951. Subj: Animals.

Roll over! *a counting song* ill. by Merle Peek. Houghton, 1981. Subj: Counting, numbers. Songs.

Romanek, Enid Warner. *Teddy* ill. by author. Scribner's, 1978. Subj: Toys – teddy bears.

Romanoli, Robert. *What's so funny?!!* ill. by Jerry Zimmerman. Grosset, 1978. Subj: Riddles.

Ronay, Jadja. *Ginger* ill. by Anthony Accardo. Magnolia, 1981. Subj: Folk and fairy tales. Magic.

Rondell, Florence. *The family that grew* by Florence Rondell and Ruth Michaels. Crown, 1965. Subj: Adoption.

Roop, Connie. *Going buggy!* (Roop, Peter)

Let's celebrate! (Roop, Peter)

Stick out your tongue! (Roop, Peter)

Roop, Peter. *Going buggy!* by Peter and Connie Roop; ill. by Joan Hanson. Lerner, 1986. ISBN 0-8225-0988-1 Subj: Insects. Riddles.

Let's celebrate! jokes about holidays by Peter and Connie Roop; ill. by Joan Hanson. Lerner, 1986. ISBN 0-8225-0989-X Subj: Holidays. Riddles.

Stick out your tongue! by Peter and Connie Roop; ill. by Joan Hanson. Lerner, 1986. ISBN 0-8225-0990-3 Subj: Careers – doctors. Riddles.

Roosevelt, Michelle Chopin. *Zoo animals* ill. by author. Random House, 1983. Subj: Format, unusual – board books. Zoos.

Root, Phyllis. *Gretchen's grandma* by Phyllis Root and Carol A. Marron; ill. by Deborah Kogan Ray. Raintree, 1983. ISBN 0-940742-16-0 Subj: Birthdays. Family life – grandmothers. Language.

Moon tiger ill. by Ed Young. Holt, 1985. ISBN 0-03-000042-4 Subj: Animals. Animals – tigers. Imagination. Sibling rivalry.

The old red rocking chair ill. by John Sanford. Little, 1992. ISBN 1-55970-063-7 Subj: Circular tales. Furniture – chairs.

Soup for supper ill. by Sue Truesdell. Harper, 1986. ISBN 0-06-025071-2 Subj: Folk and fairy tales. Food. Friendship. Giants. Music. Songs.

Rosado, Ana-Maria. *Las Navidades* (Delacre, Lulu)

Rosales, Melodye. *Double Dutch and the voodoo shoes* ill. by author. Children's Pr., 1992. ISBN 0-516-05133-4 Subj: Ethnic groups in the U.S. – Afro-Americans. Games. Magic.

Rosario, Idalia. *Idalia's project ABC: an urban alphabet book in English and Spanish* ill. by author. Holt, 1981. Subj: ABC books. City. Foreign languages.

Roscoe, William. *The butterfly's ball* ill. by Don Bolognese. McGraw-Hill, 1967. Subj: Animals. Insects – butterflies, caterpillars. Poetry, rhyme.

Rose, Agatha. *Hide-and-seek in the yellow house* ill. by Kate Spohn. Viking, 1992. ISBN 0-670-84383-0 Subj: Animals – cats.

Rose, Anne. *Akimba and the magic cow: a folktale from Africa* ill. by Hope Meryman. Four Winds Pr., 1979. Subj: Folk and fairy tales. Foreign lands – Africa. Magic.

As right as right can be ill. by Arnold Lobel. Dial Pr., 1976. Subj: Behavior – seeking better things. Money.

How does a czar eat potatoes? ill. by Janosch. Lothrop, 1973. Subj: Poetry, rhyme. Poverty. Royalty.

Pot full of luck ill. by Margot Tomes. Lothrop, 1982. Subj: Folk and fairy tales. Foreign lands – Africa.

Spider in the sky ill. by Gail Owens. Harper, 1978. Based on the story How the Sun came from American Indian mythology by Alice Marriott and Carol K. Rachlin Subj: Animals. Folk and fairy tales. Indians of North America. Spiders.

The talking turnip ill. by Paul Galdone. Parents, 1979. ISBN 0-8193-1006-9 Subj: Cumulative tales. Folk and fairy tales.

The triumphs of Fuzzy Fogtop ill. by Tomie de Paola. Dial Pr., 1979. Subj: Folk and fairy tales.

Rose, David S. *It hardly seems like Halloween* ill. by author. Lothrop, 1983. Subj: Holidays – Halloween.

Rose, Deborah Lee. *Meredith's mother takes the train* ill. by Irene Trivas. Albert Whitman, 1990. ISBN 0-8075-5061-2 Subj: Activities – working. Family life – mothers. Poetry, rhyme.

Rose, Gerald. *The bird garden* ill. by author. Salem House, 1987. ISBN 0-370-30690-2 Subj: Birds. Language. Royalty.

The hare and the tortoise (Æsop)

The lion and the mouse (Æsop)

PB takes a holiday ill. by author. Bodley Head, 1981. Subj: Activities – traveling. Animals – polar bears.

The raven and the fox (Æsop)

Scruff ill. by author. Salem House, 1985. ISBN 0-370-30619-8 Subj: Animals – dogs. Senses – smelling.

The tiger-skin rug ill. by author. Prentice-Hall, 1979. Subj: Animals – tigers. Crime.

Trouble in the ark ill. by author. Merrimack, 1985. ISBN 0-370-30833-6 Subj: Animals. Behavior – fighting, arguing. Religion – Noah.

Rose, Mitchell. *Norman* ill. by author. Simon and Schuster, 1970. Subj: Animals – dogs. Theater.

Rosen, Anne. *A family Passover* by Anne Rosen and others; photos. by Laurence Salzmann. Jewish Pub. Soc., 1980. Subj: Holidays – Passover. Jewish culture.

Rosen, Michael J. *Elijah's angel* ill. by Aminah Brenda Lynn Robinson. Harcourt, 1992. ISBN 0-15-225394-7 Subj: Ethnic groups in the U.S. – Afro-Americans. Friendship. Holidays – Christmas. Holidays – Hanukkah. Jewish culture.

Home: a collaboration of thirty authors and illustrators to aid the homeless HarperCollins, 1992. ISBN 0-06-021789-8 Subj: Homeless.

How the animals got their colors: animal myths from around the world ill. by John Clementson. Harcourt, 1992. ISBN 0-15-236783-7 Subj: Animals. Concepts – color. Folk and fairy tales. Poetry, rhyme.

Little rabbit Foo Foo ill. by Arthur Robins. Simon & Schuster, 1990. ISBN 0-671-70968-2 Subj: Animals. Animals – rabbits.

Smelly jelly smelly fish ill. by Quentin Blake. Prentice-Hall, 1987. ISBN 0-13-814567-9 Subj: Humor. Poetry, rhyme.

Under the bed: the bedtime book ill. by Quentin Blake. Prentice-Hall, 1986. ISBN 0-13-935412-3 Subj: Bedtime. Furniture – beds. Poetry, rhyme.

We're going on a bear hunt ill. by Helen Oxenbury. Macmillan, 1989. ISBN 0-689-50476-4 Subj: Animals – bears. Games. Participation. Sports – hunting.

You can't catch me! ill. by Quentin Blake. Elsevier-Dutton, 1982. Subj: Humor. Poetry, rhyme.

Rosen, Winifred. *Dragons hate to be discreet* ill. by Edward Koren. Knopf, 1978. Subj: Dragons. Imagination.

Henrietta and the day of the iguana ill. by Kay Chorao. Four Winds Pr., 1978. Subj: Behavior – wishing. Pets. Reptiles – iguanas.

Henrietta and the gong from Hong Kong ill. by Kay Chorao. Four Winds Pr., 1981. Subj: Family life – grandparents. Sibling rivalry.

Rosenberg, David *see* Clifford, David

Rosenberg, Ethel *see* Clifford, Eth

Rosenberg, Liz. *Adelaide and the night train* ill. by Lisa Desimini. HarperCollins, 1989. ISBN 0-06-025103-4 Subj: Bedtime. Night. Sleep. Trains.

The scrap doll ill. by Robin Ballard. HarperCollins, 1991. ISBN 0-06-024865-3 Subj: Activities – making things. Toys – dolls.

Window, mirror, moon ill. by Ruth Richardson. HarperCollins, 1990. ISBN 0-06-025076-3 Subj: Babies. Circular tales. Moon. Night. Poetry, rhyme.

Rosenberg, Maxine B. *Being adopted* photos. by George Ancona. Lothrop, 1984. Subj: Adoption. Ethnic groups in the U.S. Family life.

Brothers and sisters photos. by George Ancona. Houghton, 1991. ISBN 0-395-51121-6 Subj: Family life – brothers. Family life – sisters.

My friend Leslie: the story of a handicapped child photos. by George Ancona. Lothrop, 1983. Subj: Handicaps. School.

Rosenberg, Nancy Sherman *see* Sherman, Nancy

Rosenbloom, Joseph. *Deputy Dan and the bank robbers* ill. by Tim Raglin. Random House, 1985. ISBN 0-394-97045-4 Subj: Crime.

The funniest joke book ever! ill. by Hans Wilhelm. Sterling, 1986. ISBN 0-8069-4724-1 Subj: Riddles.

Rosenblum, Richard. *The old synagogue* ill. by author. Jewish Pub. Soc., 1989. ISBN 0-8276-0322-3 Subj: City. Jewish culture. Religion.

Rosner, Ruth. *Arabba gah zee, Marissa and Me!* ill. by author. Albert Whitman, 1987. ISBN 0-8075-0442-4 Subj: Activities – playing. Friendship. Imagination.

Nattie witch ill. by author. HarperCollins, 1989. ISBN 0-06-025099-2 Subj: Witches.

Ross, Anna. *I did it!* ill. by Norman Gorbaty. Random House, 1990. ISBN 0-394-86019-5 Subj: Behavior – growing up. Character traits – pride. Puppets.

I have to go ill. by Norman Gorbaty. Random House, 1990. ISBN 0-394-86051-9 Subj: Behavior – growing up. Puppets.

Naptime ill. by Norman Gorbaty. Random House, 1990. ISBN 0-394-85828-X Subj: Puppets. Sleep.

Say the magic word, please ill. by Norman Gorbaty. Random House, 1990. ISBN 0-394-85857-3 Subj: Etiquette. Puppets.

Ross, Christine. *Lily and the bears* ill. by author. Houghton, 1991. ISBN 0-395-55332-6 Subj: Animals – bears. Behavior – imitation. Zoos.

Ross, David. *Gorp and the space pirates* ill. by author. Walker, 1983. Subj: Monsters. Pirates. Space and space ships.

More hugs! ill. by author. Crowell, 1984. ISBN 0-694-00147-3 Subj: Emotions.

Space monster ill. by author. Walker, 1981. Subj: Monsters. Space and space ships.

Space Monster Gorp and the runaway computer ill. by author. Walker, 1984. Subj: Computers. Monsters. Space and space ships.

Ross, Diana. *The story of the little red engine* ill. by Leslie Wood. Transatlantic, 1947. Subj: Foreign lands – England. Trains.

Ross, George Maxim. *When Lucy went away* ill. by Ingrid Fetz. Dutton, 1976. Subj: Animals – cats. Pets.

Ross, H. L. *Not counting monsters* ill. by Doug Cushman. Platt, 1978. Subj: Activities. Counting, numbers. Monsters.

Ross, Jessica. *Ms. Klondike* ill. by author. Viking, 1977. Subj: Activities – working. Careers – taxi drivers. Taxis.

Ross, Joel. *Your first airplane trip* (Ross, Pat)

Ross, Katharine. *When you were a baby* photos. by Phoebe Dunn. Random, 1988. ISBN 0-394-89897-4 Subj: Babies. Behavior – growing up. Family life.

Ross, Lillian Hammer. *Buba Leah and her paper children* ill. by Mary Morgan. Jewish Pub. Soc., 1991. ISBN 0-8276-0375-4 Subj: Jewish culture. Letters. Moving.

The little old man and his dreams ill. by Deborah Healy. HarperCollins, 1990. ISBN 0-06-025095-X Subj: Dreams. Jewish culture. Old age. Weddings.

Ross, Pat. *Meet M and M* ill. by Marylin Hafner. Pantheon, 1980. Subj: Friendship.

Molly and the slow teeth ill. by Jerry Milord. Lothrop, 1980. Subj: School. Teeth.

Your first airplane trip by Pat and Joel Ross; ill. by Lynn Wheeling. Lothrop, 1981. Subj: Activities – flying. Airplanes, airports. Emotions – fear.

Ross, Stacey. *The magic dogs of the volcanoes* (Argueta, Manlio)

Ross, Tony. *The boy who cried wolf* ill. by author. Dial, 1991. ISBN 0-8037-0193-4 Subj: Animals – wolves. Behavior – lying. Behavior – trickery. Folk and fairy tales.

The enchanted pig: an old Rumanian tale ill. by author. Harper, 1983. Subj: Animals – pigs. Folk and fairy tales. Magic. Witches.

A fairy tale ill. by author. Little, 1992. ISBN 0-316-75750-0 Subj: Fairies. Friendship.

The greedy little cobbler ill. by author. Barron's, 1980. Subj: Behavior – greed. Careers – shoemakers.

Hansel and Gretel ill. by author. Trafalgar Square, 1990. ISBN 0-86264-210-8 Subj: Folk and fairy tales. Forest, woods. Witches.

Happy blanket ill. by author. Farrar, 1990. ISBN 0-374-32843-9 Subj: Emotions – fear. Format, unusual.

Hugo and Oddsock ill. by author. Follett, 1978. Subj: Animals – mice. Imagination – imaginary friends.

Hugo and the bureau of holidays ill. by author. Follett, 1982. Subj: Animals – mice. Holidays.

Hugo and the man who stole colors ill. by author. Follett, 1982. Subj: Animals – mice. Behavior – stealing. Concepts – color.

I want a cat ill. by author. Farrar, 1989. ISBN 0-374-33621-0 Subj: Animals – cats. Character traits – persistence. Pets.

I want my potty ill. by author. Kane/Miller, 1986. ISBN 0-916291-08-1 Subj: Behavior – growing up. Toilet training.

I'm coming to get you! ill. by author. Dial Pr., 1984. ISBN 0-8037-0119-5 Subj: Emotions – fear. Monsters. Space and space ships.

Jack the giantkiller (Jack and the beanstalk)

Oscar got the blame ill. by author. Dial Pr., 1988. ISBN 0-8037-0499-2 Subj: Behavior – misbehavior.

The pied piper of Hamelin retold and ill. by Tony Ross. Lothrop, 1978. Subj: Animals – rats. Folk and fairy tales. Foreign lands – Germany.

Stone soup ill. by author. Dial Pr., 1987. ISBN 0-8037-0401-1 Subj: Animals – wolves. Birds – chickens. Character traits – cleverness. Folk and fairy tales.

This old man: a musical counting book ill. by author. Macmillan, 1990. ISBN 0-689-71386-X Subj: Animals – dogs. Counting, numbers. Format, unusual – toy and movable books. Music. Songs.

Towser and the terrible thing ill. by author. Pantheon, 1984. Subj: Animals – dogs. Monsters. Royalty.

Treasure of Cozy Cove ill. by author. Farrar, 1990. ISBN 0-374-37744-8 Subj: Activities. Animals – cats. Pirates.

Rossetti, Christina Georgina. *Color* ill. by Mary Teichman. HarperCollins, 1992. ISBN 0-06-022650-1 Subj: Concepts – color. Poetry, rhyme.

Fly away, fly away over the sea ill. by Bernadette Watts. North-South, 1991. ISBN 1-55858-101-4 Subj: Birds. Poetry, rhyme.

What is pink? ill. by José Aruego. Macmillan, 1971. Subj: Birds – flamingos. Concepts – color. Poetry, rhyme.

Rossner, Judith. *What kind of feet does a bear have?* ill. by Irwin Rosenhouse. Bobbs-Merrill, 1963. Subj: Humor.

Roth, Harold. *Autumn days* photos. by author. Grosset, 1986. ISBN 0-448-10680-9 Subj: Format, unusual – board books. Seasons – fall.

A checkup photos. by author. Grosset, 1986. ISBN 0-448-10683-3 Subj: Format, unusual – board books. Health.

Let's look all around the farm photos. by author. Putnam's, 1988. ISBN 0-448-10687-6 Subj: Farms. Format, unusual – toy and movable books.

Let's look all around the house photos. by author. Putnam's, 1988. ISBN 0-448-10685-X Subj: Format, unusual – toy and movable books. Houses.

Let's look all around the town photos. by author. Putnam's, 1988. ISBN 0-448-10684-1 Subj: City. Format, unusual – toy and movable books.

Let's look for surprises all around photos. by author. Putnam's, 1988. ISBN 0-448-10686-8 Subj: Format, unusual – toy and movable books.

Nursery school photos. by author. Grosset, 1986. ISBN 0-448-10682-5 Subj: Format, unusual – board books. School.

Winter days photos. by author. Grosset, 1986. ISBN 0-448-10681-7 Subj: Format, unusual – board books. Seasons – winter.

Roth, Susan L. *Fire came to the earth people: a Dahomean folktale* ill. by adapt. St. Martin's, 1988. ISBN 0-312-01723-5 Subj: Fire. Folk and fairy tales. Foreign lands – Africa.

Kanahena: a Cherokee story ill. by adapt. St. Martin's, 1988. ISBN 0-312-01722-7 Subj: Animals – wolves. Folk and fairy tales. Indians of North America.

Patchwork tales by Susan L. Roth and Ruth Phang; ill. by authors. Atheneum, 1984. Subj: Family life – grandmothers.

The story of light ill. by author. Morrow, 1990. ISBN 0-688-08677-2 Subj: Folk and fairy tales. Indians of North America. Sun.

We'll ride elephants through Brooklyn ill. by author. Farrar, 1990. ISBN 0-374-38258-1 Subj: Family life – grandfathers. Illness. Parades.

Rothman, Joel. *This can lick a lollipop: body riddles for kids; esto goza chupando un caramelo: las partes del cuerpo en adivinanzas infantiles* English by Joel Rothman, Spanish by Argentina Palacios; photos. by Patricia Ruben. Doubleday, 1979. ISBN 0-385-13072-4 Subj: Anatomy. Foreign languages.

Rotner, Shelley. *Changes* (Allen, Marjorie N.)

Rottenberg, Dorian. *The merry starlings* (Marshak, Samuel)

Roughsey, Dick. *The giant devil-dingo* ill. by author. Macmillan, 1973. Subj: Animals. Folk and fairy tales. Foreign lands – Australia.

Round, Graham. *Hangdog* ill. by author. Dial Pr., 1987. ISBN 0-8037-0448-8 Subj: Animals – dogs. Animals – tigers. Boats, ships. Friendship. Islands. Sea and seashore.

Rounds, Glen. *The boll weevil* Ill. by author. Golden Gate, 1967. Subj: Folk and fairy tales. Insects. Music. Songs.

Casey Jones: the story of a brave engineer ill. by author. Golden Gate, 1968. Subj: Folk and fairy tales. Music. Songs. Trains.

Cowboys ill. by author. Holiday, 1991. ISBN 0-8234-0867-1 Subj: Cowboys.

The day the circus came to Lone Tree ill. by author. Holiday, 1973. Subj: Circus. Humor.

Once we had a horse ill. by author. Holiday, 1971. Subj: Animals – horses.

The strawberry roan ill. by comp. Golden Gate, 1970. Subj: Animals – horses. Music. Songs.

Sweet Betsy from Pike ill. by comp. Children's Pr., 1973. Subj: Folk and fairy tales. Music. Songs.

Washday on Noah's ark ill. by author. Holiday, 1985. ISBN 0-8234-0555-9 Subj: Animals. Character traits – cleanliness. Religion – Noah.

Routh, Jonathan. *The Nuns go to Africa* ill. by author. Bobbs-Merrill, 1971. Subj: Careers – nuns. Foreign lands – Africa.

Rovetch, Lissa. *Trigwater did it* ill. by author. Morrow, 1989. ISBN 0-688-08058-8 Subj: Behavior – misbehavior. Imagination – imaginary friends.

Rowan, James P. *I can be a zoo keeper* Childrens Pr., 1985. ISBN 0-516-01889-2 Subj: Animals. Careers. Zoos.

Rowand, Phyllis. *Every day in the year* ill. by author. Little, 1959. Subj: Emotions – love. Holidays – Christmas.

George ill. by author. Little, 1956. Subj: Animals – dogs.

George goes to town ill. by author. Little, 1958. Subj: Animals – dogs.

It is night ill. by author. Harper, 1953. Subj: Night. Sleep.

Rowe, Cliff. *Listen!* (Crume, Marion W.)

Rowe, Jeanne A. *City workers* Watts, 1969. Subj: Careers. City.

A trip through a school Watts, 1969. Subj: School.

Roy, Ronald. *Breakfast with my father* ill. by Troy Howell. Houghton, 1980. Subj: Divorce. Family life.

A thousand pails of water ill. by Vo-Dinh Mai. Knopf, 1978. Subj: Animals – whales. Character traits – kindness to animals. Foreign lands – Japan.

Three ducks went wandering ill. by Paul Galdone. Seabury Pr., 1979. Subj: Behavior – indifference. Birds – ducks. Humor.

Whose hat is that? ill. by Rosmarie Hausherr. Clarion, 1987. ISBN 0-89919-446-X Subj: Clothing – hats.

Whose shoes are these? photos. by Rosmarie Hausherr. Clarion, 1988. ISBN 0-89919-445-1 Subj: Clothing – shoes.

Royston, Angela. *Cars* ill. by Jane Cradock-Watson and Dave Hopkins; photos. by Tim Ridley. Macmillan, 1991. ISBN 0-689-71517-X Subj: Automobiles. Format, unusual – board books.

Chick (Burton, Jane)

Cow ill. by Bob Bampton. Watts, 1990. ISBN 0-531-19077-3 Subj: Animals – bulls, cows. Farms.

Diggers and dump trucks ill. by Jane Cradock-Watson and Dave Hopkins; photos. by Tim Ridley. Macmillan, 1991. ISBN 0-689-71516-1 Subj: Machines. Trucks.

Dinosaurs ill. by Jane Cradock-Watson and Dave Hopkins; photos. by Colin Keates. Macmillan, 1991. ISBN 0-689-71518-8 Subj: Dinosaurs.

Duck (Watts, Barrie)

Frog (Taylor, Kim)

The goat ill. by Eric Robson. Watts, 1990. ISBN 0-531-19078-1 Subj: Animals – goats. Farms.

The hen ill. by Dave Cook. Watts, 1990. ISBN 0-531-19079-X Subj: Birds – chickens. Farms.

Jungle animals ill. by Martine Blaney and Dave Hopkins; photos. by Philip Dowell. Macmillan, 1991. ISBN 0-689-71519-6 Subj: Animals. Jungle.

Kitten (Burton, Jane)

Monster road builders ill. by Graham Thompson. Barron's, 1989. ISBN 0-8120-6126-8 Subj: Machines. Roads.

My body ill. by Richard Manning. Dorling Kindersley, 1991. ISBN 1-879431-22-X Subj: Anatomy.

The pig ill. by Jim Channel. Watts, 1990. ISBN 0-531-19080-3 Subj: Animals – pigs. Farms.

The pony ill. by Bob Bampton. Watts, 1990. ISBN 0-531-19081-1 Subj: Animals – horses. Farms.

Puppy (Burton, Jane)

Rabbit (Watts, Barrie)

The sheep ill. by Josephine Martin. Watts, 1990. ISBN 0-531-19082-X Subj: Animals – sheep. Farms.

Shells ill. by Richard Manning. Dorling Kindersley, 1991. ISBN 1-879431-25-4 Subj: Format, unusual. Sea and seashore.

Small animals ill. by Richard Manning. Dorling Kindersley, 1991. ISBN 1-879431-24-6 Subj: Animals. Format, unusual. Nature.

Toys $ ill. by Richard Manning Dorling Kindersley, 1991. ISBN 1-879431-23-8 Subj: Toys.

Rubel, Nicole. *Bruno Brontosaurus* ill. by author. Camelot, 1983. Subj: Dinosaurs.

The ghost family meets its match ill. by author. Dial, 1992. ISBN 0-8037-1094-1 Subj: Ghosts.

Goldie ill. by author. HarperCollins, 1989. ISBN 0-06-025097-6 Subj: Birds – chickens. Shopping. Stores.

Goldie's nap ill. by author. HarperCollins, 1991. ISBN 0-06-025107-7 Subj: Behavior – misbehavior. Birds – chickens. School. Sleep.

It came from the swamp ill. by author. Dial Pr., 1988. ISBN 0-8037-0515-8 Subj: Behavior – lost. Humor. Reptiles – alligators, crocodiles.

Me and my kitty ill. by author. Macmillan, 1983. Subj: Activities. Animals – cats.

Sam and Violet are twins ill. by author. Camelot, 1981. Subj: Animals – cats. Character traits – individuality. Twins.

Sam and Violet go camping ill. by author. Camelot, 1981. Subj: Animals – cats. Character traits – individuality. Camps, camping. Twins.

Uncle Henry and Aunt Henrietta's honeymoon ill. by author. Dial Pr., 1986. ISBN 0-8037-0247-7 Subj: Activities – baby-sitting. Boats, ships. Family life – aunts, uncles.

Ruben, Patricia. *Apples to zippers: an alphabet book* ill. by author. Doubleday, 1976. Subj: ABC books.

True or false? ill. by author. Lippincott, 1978. Subj: Concepts.

Rubin, Caroline. *Snow on bear's nose* (Bartoli, Jennifer)

Tell them my name is Amanda (Wold, Jo Anne)

Wild Bill Hiccup's riddle book (Bishop, Ann)

Rubin, Cynthia Elyce. *ABC Americana from the National Gallery of Art* Harcourt, 1989. ISBN 0-15-200660-5 Subj: ABC books. Art.

Rubin, Jeff. *Baseball brothers* by Jeff Rubin and Rick Rael; ill. by Sandy Kossin. Lothrop, 1976. Subj: Friendship. Sports – baseball.

Ruby-Spears Enterprises. *The puppy's new adventures: hide and seek* ill. by Ruby-Spears Enterprises. Antioch, 1983. Subj: Animals – dogs. Crime. Format, unusual – toy and movable books.

Ruck-Pauquèt, Gina. *Little hedgehog* ill. by Marianne Richter. Hastings, 1959. Subj: Animals – hedgehogs.

Mumble bear tr. by Anthea Bell; ill. by Erika Dietzsch-Capelle. Putnam's, 1980. Subj: Animals – bears. Character traits – individuality.

Oh, that koala! ill. by Anna Mossakowska. McGraw-Hill, 1979. Subj: Animals – koala bears. Behavior – misbehavior.

Rudolph, Marguerita. *The good stepmother* (Zakhoder, Boris Vladimirovich)

Grey Neck (Mamin-Sibiryak, D. N.)

How a piglet crashed the Christmas party (Zakhoder, Boris Vladimirovich)

How a shirt grew in the field adapt. from the Russian of K. Ushinsky; ill. by Yaroslava. McGraw-Hill, 1967. Subj: Clothing – shirts. Foreign lands – Ukraine. Plants.

Rosachok (Zakhoder, Boris Vladimirovich)

Rudomin, Esther *see* Hautzig, Esther (Rudomin)

Ruffins, Reynold. *My brother never feeds the cat* ill. by author. Scribner's, 1979. Subj: Family life.

Rukeyser, Muriel. *More night* ill. by Symeon Shimin. Harper, 1981. Subj: Activities. Night.

Uncle Eddie's moustache (Brecht, Bertolt)

Runcie, Jill. *Cock-a-doodle-doo* ill. by Lee Lorenz. Simon & Schuster, 1991. ISBN 0-671-72602-1 Subj: Animals. Circular tales. Farms. Noise, sounds.

Rupprecht, Siegfried P. *The tale of the vanishing rainbow* tr. by Naomi Lewis; ill. by Józef Wilkoń. North-South, 1989. ISBN 1-55858-001 Subj: Animals. War. Weather – rainbows.

Rusling, Albert. *The mouse and Mrs. Proudfoot* ill. by author. Prentice-Hall, 1985. Subj: Animals. Houses. Humor.

Russ, Lavinia. *Alec's sand castle* ill. by James Stevenson. Harper, 1972. Subj: Activities – playing. Imagination. Sea and seashore.

Russell, Betty. *Big store, funny door* ill. by Mary Gehr. Albert Whitman, 1955. Subj: Character traits – luck. Shopping.

Run sheep run ill. by Mary Gehr. Albert Whitman, 1952. Subj: Animals – sheep.

Russell, Naomi. *The stream* ill. by author. Dutton, 1991. ISBN 0-525-44729-6 Subj: Nature. Rivers. Water.

The tree ill. by author. Dutton, 1989. ISBN 0-525-44468-8 Subj: Format, unusual. Nature. Trees.

Russell, P. Craig. *Fairy tales of Oscar Wilde: The selfish giant, and The star child* (Wilde, Oscar)

Russell, Pamela. *Do you have a secret? How to get help for scary secrets* by Pamela Russell and Beth Stone; ill. by Mary McKee. CompCare, 1986. ISBN 0-89638-098-X Subj: Behavior – secrets. Safety.

Russell, Sandra Joanne. *A farmer's dozen* ill. by author. Harper, 1982. Subj: Farms. Poetry, rhyme.

Russell, Solveig Paulson. *What good is a tail?* ill. by Ezra Jack Keats. Bobbs-Merrill, 1962. Subj: Animals. Science.

Russo, Marisabina. *The line up book* ill. by author. Greenwillow, 1986. ISBN 0-688-06205-9 Subj: Activities – playing. Family life. Games.

Only six more days ill. by author. Greenwillow, 1988. ISBN 0-688-07072-8 Subj: Birthdays. Sibling rivalry.

A visit to Oma ill. by author. Greenwillow, 1991. ISBN 0-688-09624-7 Subj: Family life – great-grandparents.

Waiting for Hannah ill. by author. Greenwillow, 1989. ISBN 0-688-08016-2 Subj: Babies. Birth. Family life – mothers. Gardens, gardening.

Where is Ben? ill. by author. Greenwillow, 1990. ISBN 0-688-08013-8 Subj: Activities – playing. Games.

Why do grownups have all the fun? ill. by author. Greenwillow, 1987. ISBN 0-688-06626-7 Subj: Bedtime. Behavior – dissatisfaction. Family life. Imagination.

Russo, Susan. *The ice cream ocean and other delectable poems of the sea* ill. by author. Lothrop, 1984. Subj: Poetry, rhyme. Sea and seashore.

Ruthstrom, Dorotha. *The big kite contest* ill. by Lillian Hoban. Pantheon, 1980. Subj: Kites. Sibling rivalry.

Ryan, Cheli Durán. *Hildilid's night* ill. by Arnold Lobel. Macmillan, 1971. Subj: Caldecott award honor book. Night.

Ryden, Hope. *Wild animals of Africa ABC* photos. by author. Dutton, 1989. ISBN 0-525-67290-7 Subj: ABC books. Foreign lands – Africa.

Ryder, Eileen. *Winklet goes to school* ill. by Stephanie Lang. John Godon Burke, 1982. Subj: School.

Winston's new cap ill. by Stephanie Lang. John Godon Burke, 1982. Subj: Behavior – losing things. Clothing – hats.

Ryder, Joanne. *Beach party* ill. by Diane Stanley. Warne, 1982. Subj: Animals – sheep. Family life. Sea and seashore.

Catching the wind ill. by Michael Rothman. Morrow, 1989. ISBN 0-688-07171-6 Subj: Birds – geese. Nature.

Chipmunk song ill. by Lynne Cherry. Dutton, 1987. ISBN 0-525-67191-9 Subj: Animals – chipmunks. Nature. Poetry, rhyme.

Dancers in the garden ill. by Judith Lopez. Sierra Club, 1992. ISBN 0-87156-578-1 Subj: Birds – humming birds. Gardens, gardening. Nature.

Fireflies ill. by Don Bolognese. Harper, 1977. Subj: Insects – fireflies. Science.

Fog in the meadow ill. by Gail Owens. Harper, 1979. Subj: Animals. Weather – fog.

Hello, tree! ill. by Michael Hays. Dutton, 1991. ISBN 0-525-67310-5 Subj: Nature. Poetry, rhyme. Trees.

Lizard in the sun ill. by Michael Rothman. Morrow, 1990. ISBN 0-688-07173-2 Subj: Nature. Reptiles – lizards.

Mockingbird morning ill. by Dennis Nolan. Four Winds Pr., 1989. ISBN 0-02-777961-0 Subj: Birds – mockingbirds. Nature. Poetry, rhyme.

The night flight ill. by Amy Schwartz. Four Winds Pr., 1985. ISBN 0-02-778020-1 Subj: Animals. City. Dreams. Night.

Snail in the woods by Joanne Ryder with the assistance of Harold S. Feinberg; ill. by Jo Polseno. Harper, 1979. Subj: Animals – snails. Science.

The snail's spell ill. by Lynne Cherry. Warne, 1982. Subj: Animals – snails. Night.

The spiders dance ill. by Robert J. Blake. Harper, 1981. Subj: Science. Spiders.

Step into the night ill. by Dennis Nolan. Four Winds Pr., 1988. ISBN 0-02-777951-3 Subj: Nature. Night. Poetry, rhyme.

Under your feet ill. by Dennis Nolan. Macmillan, 1990. ISBN 0-02-777955-6 Subj: Nature. Poetry, rhyme. Seasons.

A wet and sandy day ill. by Donald Carrick. Harper, 1977. Subj: Sea and seashore. Weather – rain.

Where butterflies grow ill. by Lynne Cherry. Dutton, 1989. ISBN 0-525-67284-2 Subj: Insects – butterflies, caterpillars. Nature. Science.

White bear, ice bear ill. by Michael Rothman. Morrow, 1989. ISBN 0-688-07175-9 Subj: Animals – polar bears. Foreign lands – Arctic. Nature.

Winter whale ill. by Michael Rothman. Morrow, 1991. ISBN 0-688-07177-5 Subj: Animals – whales. Nature. Seasons – winter.

Rylant, Cynthia. *All I see* ill. by Peter Catalanotto. Watts, 1988. ISBN 0-531-08377-2 Subj: Activities – painting. Art. Friendship.

Appalacia: the voices of sleeping birds ill. by Barry Moser. Harcourt, 1991. ISBN 0-15-201605-8 Subj: Country.

Birthday presents ill. by Suçie Stevenson. Watts, 1987. ISBN 0-531-08305-5 Subj: Behavior – sharing. Birthdays. Family life.

Henry and Mudge ill. by Suçie Stevenson. Bradbury Pr., 1987. ISBN 0-02-778001-5 Subj: Animals – dogs. Behavior – lost. Pets.

Henry and Mudge in puddle trouble ill. by Suçie Stevenson. Bradbury Pr., 1987. ISBN 0-02-778002-3 Subj: Animals – cats. Animals – dogs. Character traits – kindness to animals. Pets. Seasons – spring.

Henry and Mudge in the green time ill. by Suçie Stevenson. Bradbury Pr., 1987. ISBN 0-02-778003-1 Subj: Animals – dogs. Pets. Seasons – summer.

Henry and Mudge in the sparkle days ill. by Suçie Stevenson. Bradbury Pr., 1988. ISBN 0-02-778005-8 Subj: Animals – dogs. Family life. Holidays – Christmas.

Henry and Mudge under the yellow moon ill. by Suçie Stevenson. Bradbury Pr., 1987. ISBN 0-02-778004-X Subj: Animals – dogs. Holidays – Halloween. Holidays – Thanksgiving. Pets. Seasons – fall.

Miss Maggie ill. by Thomas Di Grazia. Dutton, 1983. Subj: Character traits – curiosity. Friendship.

Mr. Griggs' work ill. by Julie Downing. Watts, 1989. ISBN 0-531-08369-1 Subj: Activities – working. Careers – mail carriers. Character traits – pride.

Night in the country ill. by Mary Szilagyi. Bradbury, 1986. ISBN 0-02-777210-1 Subj: Animals. Country. Night.

The relatives came ill. by Stephen Gammell. Bradbury Pr, 1985. ISBN 0-02-777220-9 Subj: Activities – traveling. Caldecott award honor book. Family life.

This year's garden ill. by Mary Szilagyi. Bradbury Pr., 1984. Subj: Gardens, gardening.

When I was young in the mountains ill. by Diane Goode. Dutton, 1982. Subj: Caldecott award honor book. Family life.

Sabraw, John. *I wouldn't be scared* ill. by author. Watts, 1989. ISBN 0-531-08418-3 Subj: Emotions – fear. Imagination. Monsters.

Sabuda, Robert James. *St. Valentine* ill. by author. Macmillan, 1993. ISBN 0-689-31762-X Subj: Holidays – Valentine's Day. Religion.

Sachar, Louis. *Monkey soup* ill. by Cat Bowman Smith. Knopf, 1992. ISBN 0-679-90297-X Subj: Family life – fathers. Illness. Toys.

Sachs, Marilyn. *Fleet-footed Florence* ill. by Charles Robinson. Doubleday, 1981. Subj: Behavior – wishing. Magic. Sports – baseball.

Matt's mitt ill. by Hilary Knight. Doubleday, 1975. Subj: Sports – baseball.

Sackett, Elisabeth. *Danger on the African grassland* ill. by Martin Camm. Little, 1991. ISBN 0-316-76596-1 Subj: Animals – endangered animals. Animals – rhinoceros. Foreign lands – Africa.

Danger on the Arctic ice ill. by Martin Camm. Little, 1991. ISBN 0-316-76598-8 Subj: Animals – endangered animals. Animals – seals. Foreign lands – Arctic.

Saddler, Allen. *The Archery contest* ill. by Joe Wright. Oxford Univ. Pr., 1983. Subj: Humor. Magic. Royalty. Sports.

The king gets fit ill. by Joe Wright. Oxford Univ. Pr., 1983. Subj: Humor. Royalty – kings.

Sadler, Catherine Edwards. *A duckling is born* (Isenbart, Hans-Heinrich)

A flamingo is born (Zoll, Max Alfred)

Sadler, Marilyn. *Alistair in outer space* ill. by Roger Bollen. Prentice-Hall, 1984. Subj: Libraries. Space and space ships.

Alistair's elephant ill. by Roger Bollen. Prentice-Hall, 1983. Subj: Animals – elephants. Behavior – misbehavior.

Alistair's time machine ill. by Roger Bollen. Prentice-Hall, 1986. ISBN 0-317-39621-8 Subj: Machines. School. Science. Space and space ships. Time.

It's not easy being a bunny ill. by Roger Bollen. Random House, 1983. Subj: Animals – rabbits. Behavior – dissatisfaction. Self-concept.

Sage, Alison. *Rumpelstiltskin* (Grimm, Jacob)

Teddy bears at the seaside (Gretz, Susanna)

Teddy bears cure a cold (Gretz, Susanna)

Teddy bears take the train (Gretz, Susanna)

Teddybears cookbook (Gretz, Susanna)

Sage, Angie. *Happy baby* (Sage, Chris)

Monkeys in the jungle ill. by author. Dutton, 1989. ISBN 0-525-44466-1 Subj: Animals. Jungle. Poetry, rhyme.

Sleepy baby (Sage, Chris)

Sage, Chris. *Happy baby* by Chris and Angie Sage; ill. by Angie Sage. Dial, 1990. ISBN 0-8037-0883-1 Subj: Babies. Format, unusual – board books.

Sleepy baby by Chris and Angie Sage; ill. by Angie Sage. Dial, 1990. ISBN 0-8037-0888-2 Subj: Babies. Format, unusual – board books. Sleep.

That's mine, that's yours ill. by Angie Sage. Viking, 1991. ISBN 0-670-83746-6 Subj: Activities. Behavior – sharing. Family life – sisters.

The trouble with babies ill. by Angie Sage. Viking, 1990. ISBN 0-670-82392-9 Subj: Babies. Sibling rivalry.

Sage, James. *The boy and the dove* photos. by Robert Doisneau. Workman, 1978. Subj: Birds – doves. Theater.

The little band ill. by Keiko Narahashi. Macmillan, 1991. ISBN 0-689-50516-7 Subj: Ethnic groups in the U.S. Music.

To sleep ill. by Warwick Hutton. Macmillan, 1990. ISBN 0-689-50497-7 Subj: Bedtime. Dreams. Sleep.

Sage, Juniper *see* Hurd, Edith Thacher

Sage, Juniper *see* Brown, Margaret Wise

Sage, Michael. *Dippy dos and don'ts* by Michael Sage and Arnold Spilka; ill. by Arnold Spilka. Viking, 1967. Subj: Humor. Poetry, rhyme.

If you talked to a boar ill. by Arnold Spilka. Lippincott, 1960. Subj: Humor. Language.

Sahagun, Bernardino de. *Spirit child: a story of the Nativity* tr. from the Aztec by John Bierhorst; ill. by Barbara Cooney. Morrow, 1984. Subj: Folk and fairy tales. Foreign lands – Mexico. Holidays – Christmas. Religion.

St. Germain, Sharon. *The terrible fight* ill. by Deborah Zemke. Houghton, 1990. ISBN 0-395-50069-9 Subj: Behavior – fighting, arguing. Friendship.

St. George, Judith. *The Halloween pumpkin smasher* ill. by Margot Tomes. Putnam's, 1978. Subj: Animals – raccoons. Holidays – Halloween. Imagination – imaginary friends.

St. Pierre, Wendy. *Henry finds a home* ill. by Barbara Eidlitz. Firefly Pr., 1981. Subj: Children as authors. Reptiles – turtles, tortoises.

Sakai, Kimiko. *Sachiko means happiness* ill. by Tomie Arai. Children's Book Pr., 1990. ISBN 0-89239-065-4 Subj: Ethnic groups in the U.S. – Japanese-Americans. Family life – grandmothers. Illness – Alzheimer's. Old age.

Salazar, Violet. *Squares are not bad* ill. by Harlow Rockwell. Golden Pr., 1967. Subj: Concepts – shape.

Saleh, Harold J. *Even tiny ants must sleep* ill. by Jerry Pinkney. McGraw-Hill, 1967. Subj: Animals. Poetry, rhyme. Sleep.

Salt, Jane. *See and say picture word book* ill. by Sarah Pooley. Random House, 1989. ISBN 0-679-90099-3 Subj: Language.

Salter, Heidi. *Taddy McFinley and the great grey grimly* ill. by author. Landmark Ed., 1989. ISBN

0-933849-21-4 Subj: Children as authors. Children as illustrators. Family life – grandfathers. Imagination. Monsters.

Salter, Mary Jo. *The moon comes home* ill. by Stacey Schuett. Knopf, 1989. ISBN 0-394-99983-5 Subj: Activities – traveling. Moon. Night.

Saltzberg, Barney. *Cromwell* ill. by author. Atheneum, 1986. ISBN 0-689-31282-2 Subj: Animals – dogs. Humor.

It must have been the wind ill. by author. Harper, 1982. Subj: Bedtime. Noise, sounds. Weather – wind.

The yawn ill. by author. Atheneum, 1985. ISBN 0-689-31073-0 Subj: Behavior – imitation. Wordless.

Salus, Naomi Panush. *My daddy's mustache* ill. by Tomie de Paola. Doubleday, 1979. Subj: Character traits – appearance.

Samton, Sheila White. *Amazing Aunt Agatha* ill. by Yvette Banek. Raintree, 1990. ISBN 0-8172-3575-2 Subj: ABC books. Ethnic groups in the U.S. – Afro-Americans.

Beside the bay ill. by author. Putnam's, 1987. ISBN 0-399-21420-8 Subj: Poetry, rhyme. Sea and seashore.

Jenny's journey ill. by author. Viking, 1991. ISBN 0-670-83490-4 Subj: Boats, ships. Friendship. Imagination.

Moon to sun ill. by author. Boyds Mills Pr., 1991. ISBN 1-878093-13-4 Subj: Counting, numbers.

On the river ill. by author. Boyds Mills Pr., 1991. ISBN 1-878093-14-2 Subj: Counting, numbers.

The world from my window ill. by author. Crown, 1985. ISBN 0-517-55645-6 Subj: Counting, numbers. Poetry, rhyme.

Samuels, Barbara. *Duncan and Dolores* ill. by author. Bradbury Pr., 1986. ISBN 0-02-778210-7 Subj: Activities. Animals – cats. Family life – sisters. Humor.

Faye and Dolores ill. by author. Bradbury Pr., 1985. Subj: Emotions – love. Sibling rivalry.

Happy birthday, Dolores ill. by author. Watts, 1989. ISBN 0-531-08391-8 Subj: Birthdays. Parties.

What's so great about Cindy Snappleby? ill. by author. Watts, 1992. ISBN 0-531-08579-1 Subj: Family life – sisters. Frogs and toads. Sibling rivalry.

Samuels, Vyanne. *Carry go bring come* ill. by Jennifer Northway. Macmillan, 1989. ISBN 0-02-778121-6 Subj: Ethnic groups in the U.S. – Afro-Americans. Family life. Weddings.

San Diego Zoological Society. *Families* photos. by Ron Garrison and F. D. Schmidt of the Zoological Society of San Diego; captions ed. by Georgeanne Irvine. Heian International, 1983. ISBN 0-89346-218-7 Subj: Animals. Zoos.

A visit to the zoo photos. by Ron Garrison and F. D. Schmidt of the Zoological Society of San Diego; captions ed. by Georgeanne Irvine. Heian International, 1983. ISBN 0-89346-219-5 Subj: Animals. Zoos.

Sanchez, Jose Louis Garcia. *Kangaroo* by Jose Louis Garcia Sanchez and Miguel Angel Pacheco; ill. by Nella Bosnia. H P Books, 1983. Subj: Animals – kangaroos.

Sandberg, Inger. *Come on out, Daddy!* by Inger and Lasse Sandberg; ill. by Lasse Sandberg. Delacorte Pr., 1971. Translation of Pappa, kom ut Subj: Activities – working. Careers. Family life – fathers.

Dusty wants to borrow everything ill. by Lasse Sandberg. Farrar, 1988. ISBN 91-29-58782-4 Subj: Character traits – curiosity. Family life – grandparents.

Dusty wants to help tr. from Swedish by Judy A. Mauver; ill. by Lasse Sandberg. Farrar, 1987. ISBN 91-29-58336-5 Subj: Behavior – misbehavior. Family life – grandfathers.

Little Anna saved by Inger and Lasse Sandberg; ill. by Lasse Sandberg. Lothrop, 1966. Subj: Games.

Little ghost Godfry by Inger and Lasse Sandberg; tr. by Nancy S. Leupold; ill. by Lasse Sandberg. Delacorte Pr., 1968. Subj: Ghosts.

Nicholas' favorite pet by Inger and Lasse Sandberg; ill. by Lasse Sandberg. Delacorte Pr., 1969. Translation of Niklas' önskedjur Subj: Animals. Animals – dogs. Birthdays. Pets.

Nicholas' red day by Inger and Lasse Sandberg; ill. by authors. Delacorte Pr., 1964. Subj: Behavior – misbehavior. Concepts – color. Illness.

Sandberg, Lasse. *Come on out, Daddy!* (Sandberg, Inger)

Little Anna saved (Sandberg, Inger)

Little ghost Godfry (Sandberg, Inger)

Nicholas' favorite pet (Sandberg, Inger)

Nicholas' red day (Sandberg, Inger)

Sandburg, Carl (Charles August). *The wedding procession of the rag doll and the broom handle and who was in it* ill. by Harriet Pincus. Harcourt, 1978, 1922. ISBN 0-15-294930-5 Subj: Toys. Toys – dolls. Weddings.

Sandburg, Helga. *Anna and the baby buzzard* ill. by Brinton Turkle. Dutton, 1970. Subj: Birds – buzzards. Character traits – kindness to animals.

Sanderson, Ruth. *The enchanted wood* ill. by author. Little, 1991. ISBN 0-316-77018-3 Subj: Folk and fairy tales. Royalty – princes.

Sandin, Joan. *Who's scaring Alfie Atkins?* (Bergström, Gunilla)

Sanford, Doris. *David has AIDS* ill. by Graci Evans. Multnomah, 1989. ISBN 0-88070-299-0 Subj: Death. Illness.

San Souci, Robert D. *The boy and the ghost* ill. by J. Brian Pinkney. Simon & Schuster, 1989. ISBN 0-671-67176-6 Subj: Ethnic groups in the U.S. – Afro-Americans. Ghosts. Houses.

The brave little tailor (Grimm, Jacob)

The brave little tailor (Grimm, Jacob)

The enchanted tapestry ill. by László Gál. Dial Pr., 1987. ISBN 0-8037-0306-6 Subj: Activities – weaving. Behavior – greed. Character traits – bravery. Family life – brothers. Folk and fairy tales. Foreign lands – China.

The legend of Scarface ill. by Daniel San Souci. Doubleday, 1987. ISBN 0-385-15874-2 Subj: Folk and fairy tales. Indians of North America.

The legend of Sleepy Hollow (Irving, Washington)

The six swans (Grimm, Jacob)

The six swans (Grimm, Jacob)

Song of Sedna ill. by Daniel San Souci. Doubleday, 1981. Subj: Eskimos. Folk and fairy tales.

Sukey and the mermaid ill. by J. Brian Pinkney. Four Winds, 1992. ISBN 0-02-778141-0 Subj: Ethnic groups in the U.S. – Afro-Americans. Folk and fairy tales. Mythical creatures – mermaids.

The talking eggs ill. by Jerry Pinkney. Dial, 1989. ISBN 0-8037-0619-7 Subj: Caldecott award honor book. Character traits – kindness. Eggs. Folk and fairy tales. Magic.

The white cat ill. by Gennady Spirin. Watts, 1990. ISBN 0-531-08409-4 Subj: Animals – cats. Folk and fairy tales. Magic. Royalty.

Sant, Laurent Sauveur. *Dinosaurs* ill. by author. Wonder Books, 1971. Subj: Dinosaurs.

Santoro, Christopher. *Book of shapes* ill. by author. Dutton, 1979. ISBN 0-525-69406-4 Subj: Concepts – shape.

Santos, Joyce Audy Dos *see* Dos Santos, Joyce Audy

Sapphire, Paula. *The toddler's potty book* (Allison, Alida)

Sara. *Across town* ill. by author. Watts, 1991. ISBN 0-531-08532-5 Subj: Animals – cats. City. Wordless.

The rabbit, the fox, and the wolf ill. by author. Watts, 1991. ISBN 0-531-08553-8 Subj: Animals – foxes. Animals – rabbits. Animals – wolves. Wordless.

Sargent, Susan. *My favorite place* by Susan Sargent and Donna Aaron Wirt; ill. by Allan Eitzen. Abingdon Pr., 1983. Subj: Handicaps – blindness. Senses – seeing.

Sarnoff, Jane. *That's not fair* ill. by Reynold Ruffins. Scribner's, 1980. Subj: Behavior – dissatisfaction. Family life. Sibling rivalry.

Sarrazin, Johan. *Tootle* ill. by Aislin. Tundra, 1984. ISBN 0-88776-168-2 Subj: Animals – dogs. Behavior – misbehavior.

Sarton, May. *Punch's secret* ill. by Howard Knotts. Harper, 1974. Subj: Emotions – loneliness. Friendship.

A walk through the woods ill. by Kazue Mizumura. Harper, 1976. ISBN 0-06-025190-5 Subj: Activities – walking. Nature. Poetry, rhyme.

Sasaki, Isao. *Snow* ill. by author. Viking, 1982. Subj: Trains. Weather – snow. Wordless.

Sato, Satoru. *I wish I had a big, big tree* tr. from Japanese by Hitomi Jitodai and Carol Eisman; ill. by Tsutomu Murakami. Lothrop, 1989. ISBN 0-688-07304-2 Subj: Activities – playing. Imagination. Trees.

Sattler, Helen Roney. *No place for a goat* ill. by Bari Weissman. Elsevier-Nelson, 1981. Subj: Animals – goats. Houses.

Train whistles ill. by Giulio Maestro Rev. ed. Lothrop, 1985. ISBN 0-688-03980-4 Subj: Language. Trains.

Sauer, Julia Lina. *Mike's house* ill. by Don Freeman. Viking, 1954. Subj: Behavior – lost. City. Libraries. Weather – snow.

Saul, Carol P. *Peter's song* ill. by Diane de Groat. Simon & Schuster, 1992. ISBN 0-671-73812-7 Subj: Activities – singing. Animals – pigs. Friendship. Frogs and toads.

Saunders, Dave. *Snowtime* by Dave and Julie Saunders; ill. by Dave Saunders. Bradbury Pr., 1991. ISBN 0-02-781075-5 Subj: Animals. Birds – ducks. Birds – geese. Weather – snow.

Saunders, Julie. *Snowtime* (Saunders, Dave)

Saunders, Susan. *Charles Rat's picnic* ill. by Robert Byrd. Dutton, 1983. Subj: Activities – picnicking. Animals – armadillos. Animals – rats. Friendship.

Fish fry ill. by S. D. Schindler. Viking, 1982. Subj: Activities – picnicking.

The golden goose (Grimm, Jacob)

A sniff in time ill. by Michael Mariano. Macmillan, 1982. ISBN 0-689-30890-6 Subj: Magic. Senses – smelling. Wizards.

Wales' tale ill. by Marilyn Hirsh. Viking, 1980. Subj: Animals – dogs.

Savage, Kathleen. *Bear hunt* (Siewert, Margaret)

Savage, Stephen. *Making tracks* ill. by author. Dutton, 1992. ISBN 0-525-67353-9 Subj: Animals. Format, unusual.

Saville, Lynn. *Horses in the circus ring* ill. by author. Dutton, 1989. ISBN 0-525-44417-3 Subj: Animals – horses. Circus.

Sawicki, Norma Jean. *The little red house* ill. by Toni Goffe. Lothrop, 1989. ISBN 0-688-07892-3 Subj: Concepts – color. Toys.

Something for mom ill. by Martha Weston. Lothrop, 1987. ISBN 0-688-05590-7 Subj: Birthdays. Family life – mothers.

Sawyer, Jean. *Our village shop* ill. by Faith Jaques. Putnam's, 1984. Subj: Stores.

Sawyer, Ruth. *The Christmas Anna angel* ill. by Kate Seredy. Viking, 1944. Subj: Angels. Caldecott award honor book. Holidays – Christmas.

Journey cake, ho! ill. by Robert McCloskey. Viking, 1953. Subj: Caldecott award honor book. Cumulative tales. Folk and fairy tales. Poverty.

Saxe, John Godfrey. *The blind men and the elephant* ill. by Paul Galdone. McGraw-Hill, 1963. Subj: Animals – elephants. Handicaps – blindness. Senses – seeing.

Saxon, Charles D. *Don't worry about Poopsie* ill. by author. Dodd, 1958. Subj: Animals – dogs. Behavior – lost.

Saxon, Gladys Relyea *see* Seyton, Marion

Say, Allen. *The bicycle man* ill. by author. Houghton, 1982. Subj: Foreign lands – Japan. Sports – bicycling.

Once under the cherry blossom tree: an old Japanese tale ill. by author. Harper, 1974. Subj: Folk and fairy tales. Foreign lands – Japan.

A river dream ill. by author. Houghton, 1988. ISBN 0-395-48294-1 Subj: Dreams. Family life. Illness. Sports – fishing.

Tree of cranes ill. by author. Houghton, 1991. ISBN 0-395-52024-X Subj: Family life – mothers. Foreign lands – Japan. Holidays – Christmas.

Sazer, Nina. *What do you think I saw? a nonsense number book* ill. by Lois Ehlert. Pantheon, 1976. Subj: Counting, numbers. Humor. Poetry, rhyme.

Scamell, Ragnhild. *Solo plus one* ill. by Elizabeth Martland. Little, 1992. ISBN 0-316-77242-9 Subj: Animals – cats. Birds – ducks. Eggs.

Scarry, Huck. *Huck Scarry's steam train journey* ill. by author. Collins-World, 1979. Subj: Trains.

Looking into the Middle Ages ill. by author. Harper, 1985. Subj: Format, unusual – toy and movable books. Knights. Middle ages.

On the road ill. by author. Putnam's, 1981. Subj: Automobiles.

Scarry, Richard. *Egg in the hole* ill. by author. Golden Pr., 1967. Subj: Birds – chickens. Eggs. Format, unusual.

The great big car and truck book ill. by author. Golden Pr., 1951. Subj: Automobiles. Trucks.

Is this the house of Mistress Mouse? ill. by author. Golden Pr., 1964. Subj: Animals. Houses.

Mr. Frumble's worst day ever ill. by author. Random House, 1992. ISBN 0-679-81616-X Subj: Animals – pigs. Behavior – bad day.

My first word book ill. by author. Random, 1986. ISBN 0-394-88016-1 Subj: Activities – picnicking. Format, unusual – board books.

Pig Will and Pig Won't: a book of manners ill. by author. Random House, 1984. ISBN 0-394-96585-X Subj: Animals – pigs. Behavior.

Pig Will/Pig Won't ill. by author. Random House, 1990. ISBN 0-679-80067-0 Subj: Animals – pigs. Behavior. Format, unusual.

Richard Scarry's ABC word book ill. by author. Random House, 1971. Subj: ABC books.

Richard Scarry's animal nursery tales ill. by author. Golden Pr., 1975. Subj: Animals. Folk and fairy tales. Nursery rhymes.

Richard Scarry's best Christmas book ever! ill. by author. Random House, 1981. Subj: Holidays – Christmas.

Richard Scarry's best counting book ever! ill. by author. Random House, 1975. Subj: Counting, numbers.

Richard Scarry's best first book ever! ill. by author. Random House, 1979. Subj: Concepts. Days of the week, months of the year.

Richard Scarry's biggest word book ever! ill. by author. Random House, 1985. ISBN 0-394-87374-2 Subj: Dictionaries. Format, unusual. Language.

Richard Scarry's busiest people ever ill. by author. Random House, 1976. Subj: Careers.

Richard Scarry's busy houses ill. by author. Random House, 1981. Subj: Animals – worms. Format, unusual – board books. Houses.

Richard Scarry's great big mystery book ill. by author. Random House, 1969. Subj: Animals. Crime. Stores.

Richard Scarry's hop aboard! Here we go! ill. by author. Golden Pr., 1972. Subj: Transportation.

Richard Scarry's Lowly Worm word book ill. by author. Random House, 1981. Subj: Format, unusual – board books.

Richard Scarry's mix or match storybook ill. by author. Random House, 1979. Subj: Animals. Format, unusual – toy and movable books.

Richard Scarry's Peasant Pig and the terrible dragon ill. by author. Random House, 1980. Subj: Animals – pigs. Character traits – bravery. Dragons. Middle ages.

Richard Scarry's please and thank you book ill. by author. Random House, 1973. Subj: Etiquette.

Richard Scarry's Postman Pig and his busy neighbors ill. by author. Random House, 1978. Subj: Animals. Careers. Careers – mail carriers. City.

Richard Scarry's storybook dictionary ill. by author. Golden Pr., 1966. Subj: Dictionaries.

Schaaf, Peter. *An apartment house close up* photos. by author. Four Winds Pr., 1980. Subj: Houses.

The violin close up photos. by author. Four Winds Pr., 1980. Subj: Music.

Schackburg, Richard. *Yankee Doodle* ill. by Ed Emberley. Prentice-Hall, 1965. Subj: Music. Songs. U.S. history.

Schade, Susan. *Toad on the road* (Buller, Jon)

Schaffer, Libor. *Arthur sets sail* ill. by Agnès Mathieu. Holt, 1987. ISBN 0-8050-0489-0 Subj: Animals – aardvarks. Animals – pigs. Boats, ships. Character traits – appearance.

Schaffer, Marion. *I love my cat!* ill. by Kathy Vanderlinden. Kids Can Pr., 1981. Subj: Animals – cats. Foreign languages. Pets.

Schanzer, Roz. *In the synagogue* ill. by author. Kar-Ben Copies, 1991. ISBN 0-929371-60-7 Subj: Format, unusual – board books. Jewish culture. Religion.

Schären, Beatrix. *Tillo* Translated by Gwen Marsh. Addison-Wesley, 1974. Subj: Birds – owls.

Scharer, Niko. *Emily's house* ill. by Joanne Fitzgerald. Firefly, 1991. ISBN 0-88899-111-8 Subj: Animals. Houses. Noise, sounds. Poetry, rhyme.

Schatell, Brian. *Farmer Goff and his turkey Sam* ill. by author. Lippincott, 1982. Subj: Behavior – misbehavior. Birds – turkeys. Fairs.

The McGoonys have a party ill. by author. Lippincott, 1985. ISBN 0-397-32134-4 Subj: Behavior – forgetfulness. Behavior – misunderstanding. Handicaps.

Midge and Fred ill. by author. Lippincott, 1983. Subj: Fish. Humor.

Sam's no dummy, Farmer Goff ill. by author. Lippincott, 1984. Subj: Birds – turkeys. Character traits – cleverness.

Schatz, Letta. *The extraordinary tug-of-war* ill. by John Burningham. Follett, 1968. Subj: Animals. Character traits – cleverness. Folk and fairy tales. Foreign lands – Africa.

Whiskers, my cat ill. by Paul Galdone. McGraw-Hill, 1967. Subj: Animals – cats.

Scheer, Julian. *Rain makes applesauce* by Julian Scheer and Marvin Bileck; ill. by Marvin Bileck. Holiday, 1964. Subj: Caldecott award honor book. Humor. Weather – rain.

Scheffler, Ursel. *Stop your crowing, Kasimir!* ill. by Silke Brix-Henker. Carolrhoda Books, 1988. ISBN

0-87614-323-0 Subj: Birds – chickens. Communities, neighborhoods. Country. Noise, sounds.

A walk in the rain tr. by Andrea Mernan; ill. by Ulises Wensell. Putnam's, 1986. ISBN 0-399-21267-1 Subj: Family life – grandmothers. Family life – grandparents. Weather – rain.

Scheffrin-Falk, Gladys. *Another celebrated dancing bear* ill. by Barbara Garrison. Scribners, 1991. ISBN 0-684-19164-4 Subj: Activities – dancing. Animals – bears. Circus. Friendship.

Scheidl, Gerda Marie. *Can we help you, Saint Nicholas?* tr. by Rosemary Lanning; ill. by Jean-Pierre Corderoc'h. North-South, 1992. ISBN 1-55858-155-3 Subj: Animals. Forest, woods. Holidays – Christmas.

Scheller, Melanie. *My grandfather's hat* ill. by Keiko Narahashi. Macmillan, 1992. ISBN 0-689-50540-X Subj: Clothing – hats. Death. Family life – grandfathers.

Schenk, Esther M. *Christmas time* ill. by Vera Stone Norman. Follett, 1931. Subj: Holidays – Christmas.

Schepp, Steven. *How babies are made* (Andry, Andrew C.)

Schermbrucker, Reviva. *Charlie's house* ill. by Niki Daly. Viking, 1991. ISBN 0-670-84024-6 Subj: Family life. Foreign lands – South Africa. Houses. Poverty.

Schermer, Judith. *Mouse in house* ill. by author. Houghton, 1979. Subj: Animals – mice. Family life. Problem solving.

Schertle, Alice. *Bill and the google-eyed goblins* ill. by Patricia Coombs. Lothrop, 1987. ISBN 0-688-06702-6 Subj: Activities – dancing. Goblins. Holidays – Halloween.

Goodnight, Hattie, my dearie, my dove ill. by Linda Strauss Edwards. Lothrop, 1985. ISBN 0-688-03934-0 Subj: Bedtime. Counting, numbers. Toys.

The gorilla in the hall ill. by Paul Galdone. Lothrop, 1977. Subj: Animals – gorillas. Character traits – bravery. Emotions – fear.

Hob Goblin and the skeleton ill. by Katherine Coville. Lothrop, 1982. Subj: Holidays – Halloween. Trolls.

In my treehouse ill. by Meredith Dunham. Lothrop, 1983. Subj: Behavior – solitude. Houses. Trees.

Jeremy Bean's St. Patrick's Day ill. by Linda Shute. Lothrop, 1987. ISBN 0-688-04814-5 Subj: Behavior – hiding. Character traits – being different. Holidays – St. Patrick's Day. Parties. School.

Little Frog's song ill. by Leonard Everett Fisher. HarperCollins, 1992. ISBN 0-06-020060-X Subj: Behavior – lost. Frogs and toads.

My two feet ill. by Meredith Dunham. Lothrop, 1985. ISBN 0-688-02677-X Subj: Anatomy – feet.

That Olive! ill. by Cindy Wheeler. Lothrop, 1986. ISBN 0-688-04091-8 Subj: Animals – cats. Behavior – hiding.

That's what I thought ill. by John Wallner. HarperCollins, 1990. ISBN 0-06-025205-7 Subj: Character traits – questioning. Family life.

Witch Hazel ill. by Margot Tomes. HarperCollins, 1991. ISBN 0-06-025141-7 Subj: Family life – brothers. Moon. Plants. Scarecrows.

Schick, Alice. *Just this once* by Alice and Joel Schick; ill. by Joel Schick. Lippincott, 1978. Subj: Animals – wolves. Pets.

Schick, Eleanor. *Art lessons* ill. by author. Greenwillow, 1987. ISBN 0-688-05121-9 Subj: Art.

City green ill. by author. Macmillan, 1974. Subj: City. Poetry, rhyme.

City in the winter ill. by author. Macmillan, 1970. Subj: City. Family life – only child. Seasons – winter. Weather – snow. Weather – wind.

I have another language: the language is dance ill. by author. Macmillan, 1992. ISBN 0-02-781209-X Subj: Activities – dancing.

The little school at Cottonwood Corners ill. by author. Harper, 1965. Subj: Caldecott award honor book. School. Wordless.

Making friends ill. by author. Macmillan, 1969. Subj: Friendship. Wordless.

One summer night ill. by author. Greenwillow, 1977. Subj: City. Music. Seasons – summer.

Peggy's new brother ill. by author. Macmillan, 1970. Subj: Babies. Emotions – envy, jealousy. Family life. Sibling rivalry.

Peter and Mr. Brandon ill. by Donald Carrick. Macmillan, 1973. Subj: Activities – baby-sitting. City.

A piano for Julie ill. by author. Greenwillow, 1984. Subj: Family life. Music.

A surprise in the forest ill. by author. Harper, 1964. Subj: Animals. Eggs. Forest, woods.

Schick, Joel. *Just this once* (Schick, Alice)

Schiller, Barbara. *The white rat's tale* ill. by Adrienne Adams. Holt, 1967. Subj: Animals – rats. Folk and fairy tales. Foreign lands – France. Royalty.

Schilling, Betty. *Two kittens are born: from birth to two months* photos. by author. Holt, 1980. Subj: Animals – cats. Birth. Science.

Schindel, John. *Who are you?* ill. by James Watts. Macmillan, 1991. ISBN 0-689-50523-X Subj: Animals – bears. Bedtime. Parties.

Schindler, Regina. *The bear's cave* tr. from German by Christopher Franceschelli; ill. by Sita Jucker.

Dutton, 1990. ISBN 0-525-44553-6 Subj: Animals. Behavior – boasting. Seasons – winter.

Schlein, Miriam. *The amazing Mr. Pelgrew* ill. by Harvey Weiss. Abelard-Schuman, 1957. Subj: Careers – police officers.

Big talk ill. by Joan Auclair Rev. ed. Bradbury Pr., 1990. ISBN 0-02-781231-6 Subj: Animals – kangaroos. Behavior – boasting.

Big talk ill. by Laura Lydecker. Albert Whitman, 1988. ISBN 0-8075-0729-6 Subj: Animals – kangaroos. Behavior – boasting.

Billy, the littlest one ill. by Lucy Hawkinson. Albert Whitman, 1966. Subj: Behavior – growing up. Character traits – smallness. Family life.

Deer in the snow ill. by Leonard P. Kessler. Abelard-Schuman, 1965. Subj: Animals – deer. Seasons – winter. Weather – snow.

Elephant herd ill. by Symeon Shimin. Addison-Wesley, 1954. Subj: Animals – elephants.

Fast is not a ladybug ill. by Leonard P. Kessler. Addison-Wesley, 1953. Subj: Concepts – speed. Insects – ladybugs.

The four little foxes ill. by Louis Quintanilla. Addison-Wesley, 1953. Subj: Animals – foxes.

Go with the sun ill. by Symeon Shimin. Addison-Wesley, 1952. Subj: Family life – grandfathers. Seasons – winter.

Heavy is a hippopotamus ill. by Leonard P. Kessler. Addison-Wesley, 1954. Subj: Concepts – weight.

Here comes night ill. by Harvey Weiss. Albert Whitman, 1957. Subj: Night.

Herman McGregor's world ill. by Harvey Weiss. Albert Whitman, 1959. Subj: Behavior – growing up. World.

Home, the tale of a mouse ill. by E. Harper Johnson. Abelard-Schuman, 1958. Subj: Animals – mice.

It's about time ill. by Leonard P. Kessler. Addison-Wesley, 1955. Subj: Time.

Laurie's new brother ill. by Elizabeth Donald. Abelard-Schuman, 1961. Subj: Babies. Family life. Sibling rivalry.

Little Rabbit, the high jumper ill. by Theresa Sherman. Addison-Wesley, 1957. Subj: Animals – rabbits.

Little Red Nose ill. by Roger Antoine Duvoisin. Abelard-Schuman, 1955. Subj: Seasons – spring.

Lucky porcupine! ill. by Martha Weston. Four Winds Pr., 1980. Subj: Animals – porcupines. Science.

My family ill. by Harvey Weiss. Abelard-Schuman, 1960. Subj: Family life.

My house ill. by Joe Lasker. Albert Whitman, 1971. Subj: Family life. Houses. Moving.

The pile of junk ill. by Harvey Weiss. Abelard-Schuman, 1962. Subj: Character traits – practicality. Values.

Shapes ill. by Sam Berman. Addison-Wesley, 1952. Subj: Concepts – shape.

Something for now, something for later ill. by Leonard Weisgard. Harper, 1956. Subj: Farms.

The sun looks down ill. by Abner Graboff. Abelard-Schuman, 1954. Subj: Sun.

The sun, the wind, the sea and the rain ill. by Joe Lasker. Abelard-Schuman, 1960. Subj: Sea and seashore. Sun. Weather. Weather – rain. Weather – wind.

That's not Goldie! ill. by Susan Gough Magurn. Simon & Schuster, 1990. ISBN 0-671-70005-7 Subj: Fish. Pets.

What's wrong with being a skunk? ill. by Ray Cruz. Four Winds Pr., 1974. Subj: Animals – skunks. Science.

When will the world be mine? The story of a snowshoe rabbit ill. by Jean Charlot. Addison-Wesley, 1953. Subj: Behavior – growing up. Caldecott award honor book.

Schmeltz, Susan Alton. *Pets I wouldn't pick* ill. by Ellen Appleby. Parents, 1982. Subj: Pets. Poetry, rhyme.

Schmid, Eleonore. *Farm animals* ill. by author. Holt, 1986. ISBN 0-03-008032-0 Subj: Animals. Farms. Format, unusual – board books.

The water's journey ill. by author. North-South, 1990. ISBN 1-55858-013-1 Subj: Rivers. Science. Water. Weather – snow.

Schmidt, Eric von. *The young man who wouldn't hoe corn* ill. by author. Houghton, 1964. Subj: Character traits – laziness. Farms. Humor.

Schneider, Elisa. *The merry-go-round dog* ill. by author. Knopf, 1988. ISBN 0-394-99069-2 Subj: Animals – dogs. Merry-go-rounds.

Schneider, Herman. *Follow the sunset* by Herman and Nina Schneider; ill. by Lucille Corcos. Doubleday, 1952. Subj: Science. Sun. World.

Schneider, Howie. *The amazing Amos and the greatest couch on earth* (Seligson, Susan)

Amos ahoy: a couch adventure on land and sea (Seligson, Susan)

Amos camps out: a couch adventure in the woods (Seligson, Susan)

Amos: the story of an old dog and his couch (Seligson, Susan)

Schneider, Nina. *Follow the sunset* (Schneider, Herman)

While Susie sleeps ill. by Dagmar Wilson. Addison-Wesley, 1948. Subj: Bedtime. Night. Sleep.

Schnitter, Jane. *William is my brother* ill. by Gerald Kruck. Perspectives Pr., 1991. ISBN 0-944934-03-X Subj: Adoption. Family life – brothers.

Schoberle, Ceile. *Beyond the Milky Way* ill. by author. Crown, 1986. ISBN 0-517-55716-9 Subj: Imagination. Science. Sky. Space and space ships.

Schoen, Mark. *Bellybuttons are navels* ill. by M. J. Quay. Focus International, 1990. ISBN 0-87975-585-7 Subj: Anatomy.

Schoenherr, John. *The barn* ill. by author. Little, 1968. Subj: Animals – mice. Animals – skunks. Barns. Birds – owls. Farms.

Bear ill. by author. Putnam, 1991. ISBN 0-399-22177-8 Subj: Alaska. Animals – bears. Nature.

Scholey, Arthur. *Baboushka* ill. by Ray Burrows. Good News, 1983. ISBN 0-89107-281-0 Subj: Music. Religion. Royalty. Toys.

Schongut, Emanuel. *Look kitten* ill. by author. Simon and Schuster, 1983. Subj: Animals.

Schories, Pat. *Mouse around* ill. by author. Farrar, 1991. ISBN 0-374-35080-9 Subj: Activities – traveling. Animals – mice. Circular tales. Wordless.

Schotter, Roni. *Bunny's night out* ill. by Margot Apple. Little, 1989. ISBN 0-316-77465-0 Subj: Animals – rabbits. Bedtime. Night.

Captain Snap and the children of Vinegar Lane ill. by Marcia Sewall. Watts, 1989. ISBN 0-531-08397-7 Subj: Character traits – being different. Character traits – generosity. Character traits – kindness.

Hanukkah! ill. by Marylin Hafner. Little, 1990. ISBN 0-316-77466-9 Subj: Holidays – Hanukkah. Jewish culture. Religion.

Schreiber, Georges. *Bambino goes home* ill. by author. Viking, 1959. Subj: Clowns, jesters. Friendship.

Bambino the clown ill. by author. Viking, 1947. Subj: Animals – sea lions. Caldecott award honor book. Clowns, jesters.

Professor Bull's umbrella (Lipkind, William)

Schreier, Joshua. *Luigi's all-night parking lot* ill. by author. Dutton, 1990. ISBN 0-525-44626-5 Subj: Bedtime. Imagination. Toys.

Schroder, William. *Pea soup and serpents* ill. by author. Lothrop, 1977. Subj: Monsters. Mythical creatures. Weather – fog.

Schroeder, Alan. *Ragtime Tumpie* ill. by Bernie Fuchs. Little, 1989. ISBN 0-316-77497-9 Subj: Activities – dancing. Ethnic groups in the U.S. – Afro-Americans.

Schroeder, Binette. *Ra ta ta tam* (Nickl, Peter)

Tuffa and her friends ill. by author. Dial Pr., 1983. Subj: Animals – dogs. Format, unusual – board books. Friendship.

Tuffa and the bone ill. by author. Dial Pr., 1983. Subj: Animals – dogs. Format, unusual – board books.

Tuffa and the ducks ill. by author. Dial Pr., 1983. Subj: Animals – dogs. Birds – ducks. Format, unusual – board books.

Tuffa and the picnic ill. by author. Dial Pr., 1983. ISBN 0-8037-9896-2 Subj: Activities – picnicking. Animals – dogs. Behavior – misbehavior. Format, unusual – board books.

Tuffa and the snow ill. by author. Dial Pr., 1983. Subj: Animals – dogs. Format, unusual – board books. Weather – snow.

Schroeder, Glen W. *At the zoo* (Colonius, Lillian)

Schubert, Dieter. *Little big feet* (Schubert, Ingrid)

There's a crocodile under my bed! (Schubert, Ingrid)

Where's my monkey? ill. by author. Dial Pr., 1987. ISBN 0-8037-0069-5 Subj: Animals – monkeys. Behavior – losing things. Behavior – needing someone. Wordless.

Schubert, Ingrid. *Little big feet* by Ingrid and Dieter Schubert; tr. from Dutch by Amy Gelman; ill. by authors. Carolrhoda, 1990. ISBN 0-87614-426-1 Subj: Anatomy – feet. Witches.

There's a crocodile under my bed! by Ingrid and Dieter Schubert; ill. by authors. McGraw-Hill, 1981. Subj: Bedtime. Furniture – beds. Reptiles – alligators, crocodiles.

Schuchman, Joan. *Two places to sleep* ill. by Jim LaMarche. Carolrhoda, 1979. Subj: Divorce. Family life.

Schulman, Janet. *The big hello* ill. by Lillian Hoban. Greenwillow, 1976. Subj: Friendship. Moving. Toys – dolls.

Camp Kee Wee's secret weapon ill. by Marylin Hafner. Greenwillow, 1979. Subj: Sports – baseball. Camps, camping.

The great big dummy ill. by Lillian Hoban. Greenwillow, 1979. ISBN 0-688-84208-9 Subj: Animals – dogs. Friendship. Toys – dolls.

Jungles (Wood, John Norris)

Schulz, Charles M. *Bon voyage, Charlie Brown (and don't come back!!)* ill. by author. Random House, 1980. Subj: Activities – traveling. Foreign lands.

The Charlie Brown dictionary based on the rainbow dictionary by Wendell W. Wright; asst. by Helene Laird; ill. by author. Random House, 1973. Subj: Dictionaries.

Life is a circus, Charlie Brown ill. by author. Random House, 1981. Subj: Circus.

Snoopy's facts and fun book about boats ill. by author. Random House, 1979. Subj: Animals – dogs. Boats, ships.

Snoopy's facts and fun book about farms ill. by author. Random House, 1980. Subj: Animals – dogs. Farms.

Snoopy's facts and fun book about houses ill. by author. Random House, 1979. Subj: Animals – dogs. Houses.

Snoopy's facts and fun book about nature ill. by author. Random House, 1979. Subj: Animals – dogs. Nature. Science.

Snoopy's facts and fun book about planes ill. by author. Random House, 1979. Subj: Animals – dogs. Airplanes, airports.

Snoopy's facts and fun book about seasons ill. by author. Random House, 1979. Subj: Animals – dogs. Seasons.

Snoopy's facts and fun book about seashores ill. by author. Random House, 1979. Subj: Animals – dogs. Sea and seashore.

Snoopy's facts and fun book about trucks ill. by author. Random House, 1979. Subj: Animals – dogs. Trucks.

You're the greatest, Charlie Brown ill. by author. Random House, 1979. Subj: Sports – Olympics.

Schumacher, Claire. *Alto and Tango* ill. by author. Morrow, 1984. ISBN 0-688-02740-7 Subj: Birds. Fish. Friendship. Sea and seashore.

Brave Lily ill. by author. Morrow, 1985. ISBN 0-688-04963-X Subj: Character traits – bravery. Family life. Frogs and toads.

King of the zoo ill. by author. Morrow, 1985. Subj: Animals. Behavior – misbehavior. Friendship. Zoos.

Nutty's birthday ill. by author. Morrow, 1986. ISBN 0-688-06496-5 Subj: Activities – flying. Animals. Animals – squirrels. Birthdays.

Nutty's Christmas ill. by author. Morrow, 1984. Subj: Animals – squirrels. Holidays – Christmas.

Tim and Jim ill. by author. Dodd, 1987. ISBN 0-396-09040-0 Subj: Animals. Behavior – lost. Friendship.

Tommy the winner ill. by author. HarperCollins, 1991. ISBN 0-06-026905-7 Subj: Animals – mice. Letters.

Schurr, Cathleen. *The long and the short of it* ill. by Dorothy Maas. Vanguard, 1950. Subj: Problem solving.

Schwalje, Marjory. *Mr. Angelo* ill. by Abner Graboff. Abelard-Schuman, 1960. Subj: Activities – cooking. Food. Humor.

Schwartz, Alvin. *All of our noses are here and other stories* ill. by Karen Ann Weinhaus. Harper, 1985. ISBN 0-06-025288-X Subj: Folk and fairy tales. Humor.

Schwartz, Amy. *Annabelle Swift, kindergartner* ill. by author. Orchard, 1988. ISBN 0-531-08337-3 Subj: Character traits – pride. School. Sibling rivalry.

Bea and Mr. Jones ill. by author. Bradbury Pr., 1982. Subj: Behavior – imitation. Family life – fathers.

Begin at the beginning ill. by author. Harper, 1983. Subj: Behavior – growing up.

Camper of the week ill. by author. Watts, 1991. ISBN 0-531-08542-2 Subj: Behavior – misbehavior. Camps, camping. Friendship.

Her Majesty, Aunt Essie ill. by author. Bradbury Pr., 1984. ISBN 0-02-781450-5 Subj: Behavior – boasting. Family life – aunts, uncles. Royalty.

The lady who put salt in her coffee (Hale, Lucretia)

Mrs. Moskowitz and the Sabbath candlesticks ill. by author. Jewish Pub. Soc., 1985. Subj: Jewish culture. Religion.

Oma and Bobo ill. by author. Bradbury Pr., 1987. ISBN 0-02-781500-5 Subj: Animals – dogs. Family life – grandmothers.

Yossel Zissel and the wisdom of Chelm ill. by author. Jewish Pub. Soc., 1988. ISBN 0-8276-0258-8 Subj: Character traits – foolishness. Folk and fairy tales. Jewish culture.

Schwartz, David M. *How much is a million?* ill. by Steven Kellogg. Lothrop, 1985. ISBN 0-688-04050-0 Subj: Concepts – size. Counting, numbers.

Sugargrandpa ill. by Bert Dodson. Lothrop, 1991. ISBN 0-688-09899-1 Subj: Family life – grandfathers. Foreign lands – Sweden. Old age. Sports – bicycling. Sports – racing.

Schwartz, Delmore. *"I am Cherry Alive," the little girl sang* ill. by Barbara Cooney. Harper, 1979. Subj: Poetry, rhyme.

Schwartz, Henry. *Albert goes Hollywood* ill. by Amy Schwartz. Watts, 1992. ISBN 0-531-08580-5 Subj: Dinosaurs. Pets. Theater.

How I captured a dinosaur ill. by Amy Schwartz. Watts, 1989. ISBN 0-531-08370-5 Subj: Dinosaurs. Pets. Camps, camping.

Schwartz, Lynne Sharon. *The four questions* ill. by Ori Sherman. Dial, 1989. ISBN 0-8037-0601-4 Subj: Holidays – Passover. Jewish culture. Religion.

Schwartz, Mary. *Spiffen: a tale of a tidy pig* ill. by Lynn Munsinger. Albert Whitman, 1988. ISBN 0-8075-7580-1 Subj: Animals – pigs. Character traits – cleanliness.

Schwartz, Roslyn. *Rose and Dorothy* ill. by author. Watts, 1991. ISBN 0-531-08518-X Subj: Animals – elephants. Animals – mice. Friendship.

Schweitzer, Iris. *Hilda's restful chair* ill. by author. Atheneum, 1982. Subj: Animals. Friendship. Furniture – chairs.

Schweninger, Ann. *Autumn days* ill. by author. Viking, 1991. ISBN 0-670-82758-4 Subj: Animals – dogs. Seasons – fall.

Birthday wishes ill. by author. Viking, 1986. ISBN 0-670-80742-7 Subj: Animals – rabbits. Behavior – wishing. Birthdays. Parties.

Christmas secrets ill. by author. Viking, 1984. Subj: Animals – rabbits. Holidays – Christmas.

Halloween surprises ill. by author. Viking, 1984. Subj: Animals – rabbits. Holidays – Halloween.

The hunt for rabbit's galosh ill. by Kay Chorao. Doubleday, 1976. Subj: Animals – rabbits. Behavior – forgetfulness. Holidays – Valentine's Day.

The man in the moon as he sails the sky and other moon verse ill. by author. Dodd, 1979. Subj: Moon. Poetry, rhyme.

Off to school! ill. by author. Viking, 1987. ISBN 0-670-81447-4 Subj: Animals – rabbits. School.

Valentine friends ill. by author. Viking, 1988. ISBN 0-670-81448-2 Subj: Animals – rabbits. Family life. Holidays – Valentine's Day.

Wintertime ill. by author. Viking, 1990. ISBN 0-670-83420-3 Subj: Animals – dogs. Seasons – winter.

Scieszka, Jon. *The frog prince, continued* ill. by Steve Johnson. Viking, 1991. ISBN 0-670-83421-1 Subj: Folk and fairy tales. Frogs and toads. Royalty – princes. Royalty – princesses. Witches.

The true story of the three little pigs by A. Wolf, as told to John ill. by Lane Smith. Viking, 1989. ISBN 0-670-82759-2 Subj: Animals – pigs. Animals – wolves. Folk and fairy tales.

Scoppetone, Sandra. *Bang, bang, you're dead* (Fitzhugh, Louise)

Scott, Ann Herbert. *Big Cowboy Western* ill. by Richard Lewis. Lothrop, 1965. Subj: Clothing. Cowboys. Ethnic groups in the U.S. – Afro-Americans. Imagination.

Grandmother's chair ill. by Meg Kelleher Aubrey. Houghton, 1990. ISBN 0-395-52001-0 Subj: Family life – grandmothers. Furniture – chairs.

Let's catch a monster ill. by H. Tom Hall. Lothrop, 1967. Subj: City. Ethnic groups in the U.S. – Afro-Americans. Holidays – Halloween.

On mother's lap ill. by Glo Coalson Rev. ed. Houghton, 1992. ISBN 0-395-58920-7 Subj: Behavior – needing someone. Emotions – love. Eskimos. Family life. Family life – mothers. Sibling rivalry.

One good horse ill. by Lynn Sweat. Greenwillow, 1990. ISBN 0-688-09147-4 Subj: Counting, numbers. Cowboys.

Sam ill. by Symeon Shimin. McGraw-Hill, 1967. Subj: Behavior – needing someone. Ethnic groups in the U.S. – Afro-Americans. Family life.

Someday rider ill. by Ronald Himler. Houghton, 1989. ISBN 0-89919-792-2 Subj: Animals – horses. Behavior – growing up. Cowboys.

Scott, Cora Annett *see* Annett, Cora

Scott, Frances Gruse. *How many kids are hiding on my block?* (Merrill, Jean)

Scott, Geoffrey. *Memorial Day* ill. by Peter E. Hanson. Carolrhoda Books, 1983. Subj: Holidays – Memorial Day.

Scott, Natalie (Anderson). *Firebrand, push your hair out of your eyes* ill. by Sandra Smith. Carolrhoda Books, 1969. Subj: Character traits – appearance. Hair.

Scott, Rochelle. *Colors, colors all around* ill. by Leonard P. Kessler. Grosset, 1965. Subj: Concepts – color.

Scott, Sally. *Little Wiener* ill. by Beth Krush. Harcourt, 1951. Subj: Animals – dogs.

The magic horse ill. by adapt. Greenwillow, 1985. Retold and adapted from "The Ebony Horse," a story from The Arabian Nights tr. by Sir Richard Burton ISBN 0-688-05898-1 Subj: Folk and fairy tales. Foreign lands. Magic. Royalty. Wizards.

There was Timmy! ill. by Beth Krush. Harcourt, 1957. Subj: Animals – dogs.

The three wonderful beggars ill. by author. Greenwillow, 1988. ISBN 0-688-06657-7 Subj: Folk and fairy tales.

Scott, William R. *This is the milk that Jack drank* adapt. from Mother Goose; ill. by Charles Green Shaw. Addison-Wesley, 1944. Subj: Cumulative tales.

Scribner, Charles. *The devil's bridge: a legend* retold by Charles Scribner, Jr.; ill. by Evaline Ness. Scribner's, 1978. Subj: Folk and fairy tales. Foreign lands – France. Devil.

Hansel and Gretel (Grimm, Jacob)

Scruton, Clive. *Bubble and squeak* ill. by author. Random House, 1985. ISBN 0-394-87101-4 Subj: Animals – mice. Birds – ducks. Friendship.

Circus cow ill. by author. Random House, 1985. Subj: Animals – bulls, cows. Character traits – foolishness.

Mary's pets ill. by author. Lothrop, 1989. ISBN 0-688-08520-2 Subj: Animals. Format, unusual. Games. Pets. Poetry, rhyme.

Pig in the air ill. by author. Random House, 1985. ISBN 0-394-87103-0 Subj: Activities – flying. Animals – pigs.

Scaredy cat ill. by author. Random House, 1985. ISBN 0-394-87014-X Subj: Animals – cats. Emotions – fear.

Scullard, Sue. *Miss Fanshawe and the great dragon adventure* ill. by author. St. Martin's, 1987. ISBN 0-312-00510-5 Subj: Dragons. Format, unusual.

The Sea World alphabet book concept by Sally and Alan Sloan. Sea World Pr., 1979. Subj: ABC books. Sea and seashore.

Seabrooke, Brenda. *The best burglar alarm* ill. by Loretta Lustig. Morrow, 1978. Subj: Crime. Pets.

The seal ill. by Charlotte Knox. Rourke, 1983. Subj: Animals – seals.

Sedges, John *see* Buck, Pearl S. (Pearl Sydenstricker)

Seed, Jenny. *Ntombi's song* ill. by Anno Berry. Beacon Pr., 1989. ISBN 0-8070-8318-6 Subj: Character traits – confidence. Foreign lands – South Africa.

Seeger, Charles. *The foolish frog* (Seeger, Pete)

Seeger, Pete. *Abiyoyo* ill. by Michael Hays. Macmillan, 1986. ISBN 0-02-781490-4 Subj: Folk and fairy tales. Magic. Monsters.

The foolish frog by Pete Seeger and Charles Seeger; ill. by Miloslav Jágr; adapted and designed from Firebird Film by Gene Deitch. Macmillan, 1973. Subj: Cumulative tales. Folk and fairy tales. Frogs and toads. Music. Songs.

Segal, Lore. *All the way home* ill. by James Marshall. Farrar, 1973. Subj: Cumulative tales.

The bear and the kingbird (Grimm, Jacob)

The story of old Mrs. Brubeck and how she looked for trouble and where she found him ill. by Marcia Sewall. Pantheon, 1981. Subj: Behavior – worrying. Problem solving.

Tell me a Mitzi ill. by Harriet Pincus. Farrar, 1970. Subj: Family life. Jewish culture.

Tell me a Trudy ill. by Rosemary Wells. Farrar, 1977. Subj: Family life. Jewish culture.

Segal, Sheila. *Joshua's dream* ill. by Jana Paiss. Union of American Hebrew Congregations, 1985. ISBN 0-8074-0272-9 Subj: Foreign lands – Israel. Jewish culture.

Seguin-Fontes, Marthe. *The cat's surprise* adapt. by Sandra Beris; ill. by author. Larousse, 1983. Subj: Animals – cats.

A wedding book adapt. by Sandra Beris; ill. by author. Larousse, 1983. Subj: Activities – photographing. Weddings.

Seidler, Rosalie. *Grumpus and the Venetian cat* ill. by author. Atheneum, 1964. Subj: Animals – cats. Animals – mice. Birds. Foreign lands – Italy.

Seidler, Tor. *The steadfast tin soldier* (Andersen, H. C. (Hans Christian))

Seignobosc, Françoise. *The big rain* ill. by author. Scribner's, 1961. Subj: Animals. Farms. Foreign lands – France. Weather – rain.

Biquette, the white goat ill. by author. Scribner's, 1953. Subj: Animals – goats. Foreign lands – France. Illness.

Chouchou ill. by author. Scribner's, 1958. Subj: Animals – donkeys. Foreign lands – France.

Jeanne-Marie at the fair ill. by author. Scribner's, 1959. Subj: Fairs. Foreign lands – France.

Jeanne-Marie counts her sheep ill. by author. Scribner's, 1951. Subj: Behavior – wishing. Counting, numbers. Foreign lands – France.

Jeanne-Marie in gay Paris ill. by author. Scribner's, 1956. Subj: Character traits. Foreign lands – France.

Minou ill. by author. Scribner's, 1962. Subj: Animals – cats. Behavior – lost. Foreign lands – France.

Noël for Jeanne-Marie ill. by author. Scribner's, 1953. Subj: Foreign lands – France. Holidays – Christmas.

Small-Trot ill. by author. Scribner's, 1952. Subj: Animals – mice. Circus.

Springtime for Jeanne-Marie ill. by author. Scribner's, 1955. Subj: Animals – goats. Behavior – lost. Birds – ducks. Foreign lands – France. Seasons – spring.

The story of Colette ill. by author. Hale, 1940. Subj: Animals. Emotions – loneliness. Pets.

The thank-you book ill. by author. Scribner's, 1947. Subj: Etiquette. Religion.

The things I like ill. by author. Scribner's, 1960. Subj: Participation.

What do you want to be? ill. by author. Scribner's, 1957. Subj: Careers. Character traits – ambition.

What time is it, Jeanne-Marie? ill. by author. Scribner's, 1963. Subj: Time.

Selberg, Ingrid. *Nature's hidden world* ill. by Andrew Miller. Putnam's, 1984. Subj: Animals. Format, unusual – toy and movable books. Plants. Riddles. Science.

Selden, George. *The mice, the monks and the Christmas tree* ill. by Jan Balet. Macmillan, 1963. Subj: Animals – mice. Holidays – Christmas.

Sparrow socks ill. by Peter Lippman. Harper, 1965. Subj: Birds – sparrows. Clothing – socks.

Selig, Sylvie. *Kangaroo* ill. by author. Merrimack, 1980. Subj: Animals – kangaroos. Wordless.

Ten what? (Hoban, Russell)

Seligman, Dorothy Halle. *Run away home* ill. by Christine Hoffmann. Golden Gate, 1969. Subj: Behavior – running away. Family life.

Seligson, Susan. *The amazing Amos and the greatest couch on earth* by Susan Seligson and Howie Schneider; ill. by Howie Schneider. Little, 1989. ISBN 0-316-78033-2 Subj: Animals – dogs. Circus. Furniture – couches, sofas. Humor. Imagination.

Amos ahoy: a couch adventure on land and sea by Susan Seligson and Howie Schneider; ill. by Howie Schneider. Little, 1990. ISBN 0-316-77403-0 Subj: Animals – dogs. Furniture – couches, sofas. Imagination.

Amos camps out: a couch adventure in the woods by Susan Seligson and Howie Schneider; ill. by Howie Schneider. Little, 1992. ISBN 0-316-77402-2 Subj: Animals – dogs. Camps, camping. Forest, woods. Furniture – couches, sofas.

Amos: the story of an old dog and his couch by Susan Seligson and Howie Schneider; ill. by Howie Schneider. Little, 1987. ISBN 0-316-77404-9 Subj: Animals – dogs. Furniture – couches, sofas. Humor. Imagination. Old age.

Selkowe, Valrie M. *Spring green* ill. by Jeni Bassett. Lothrop, 1985. ISBN 0-688-04056-X Subj: Animals. Concepts – color. Parties. Seasons – spring.

Sellers, Ronnie. *My first day at school* ill. by Patti Stren. Caedmon, 1985. ISBN 0-89845-373-9 Subj: Poetry, rhyme. School.

Selsam, Millicent E. *All kinds of babies* ill. by Symeon Shimin. Four Winds Pr., 1967. Subj: Animals. Science.

Egg to chick ill. by Barbara Wolff Rev. ed. Harper, 1970. Subj: Birds – chickens. Birth. Eggs. Science.

A first look at bird nests by Millicent E. Selsam and Joyce Hunt; ill. by Harriett Springer. Walker, 1985. ISBN 0-8027-6565-3 Subj: Birds. Science.

A first look at caterpillars by Millicent E. Selsam and Joyce Hunt; ill. by Harriett Springer. Walker, 1987. ISBN 0-8027-6702-8 Subj: Insects – butterflies, caterpillars. Science.

A first look at cats by Millicent E. Selsam and Joyce Hunt; ill. by Harriett Springer. Walker, 1981. ISBN 0-8027-6399-5 Subj: Animals – cats. Science.

A first look at dinosaurs by Millicent E. Selsam and Joyce Hunt; ill. by Harriett Springer. Walker, 1982. Subj: Dinosaurs.

A first look at dogs by Millicent E. Selsam and Joyce Hunt; ill. by Harriett Springer. Walker, 1981. Subj: Animals – dogs. Animals – foxes. Animals – wolves.

A first look at flowers by Millicent E. Selsam and Joyce Hunt; ill. by Harriett Springer. Walker, 1977. Subj: Flowers. Science.

A first look at kangaroos, koalas and other animals with pouches by Millicent E. Selsam and Joyce Hunt; ill. by Harriett Springer. Walker, 1985. ISBN 0-8027-6579-3 Subj: Animals. Science.

A first look at monkeys by Millicent E. Selsam and Joyce Hunt; ill. by Harriett Springer. Walker, 1979. Subj: Animals – gorillas. Animals – monkeys. Science.

A first look at owls, eagles and other hunters of the sky by Millicent E. Selsam and Joyce Hunt; ill. by Harriett Springer. Walker, 1986. ISBN 0-8027-6642-0 Subj: Birds. Science.

A first look at rocks by Millicent E. Selsam and Joyce Hunt; ill. by Harriett Springer. Walker, 1984. Subj: Rocks. Science.

A first look at seashells by Millicent E. Selsam and Joyce Hunt; ill. by Harriett Springer. Walker, 1983. Subj: Animals. Sea and seashore. Science.

A first look at sharks by Millicent E. Selsam and Joyce Hunt; ill. by Harriett Springer. Walker, 1979. Subj: Fish. Science.

A first look at spiders by Millicent E. Selsam and Joyce Hunt; ill. by Harriett Springer. Walker, 1983. Subj: Science. Spiders.

A first look at the world of plants by Millicent E. Selsam and Joyce Hunt; ill. by Harriett Springer. Walker, 1978. ISBN 0-8027-6299-9 Subj: Plants. Science.

A first look at whales by Millicent E. Selsam and Joyce Hunt; ill. by Harriett Springer. Walker, 1980. Subj: Animals – whales. Science.

Hidden animals ill. by David Shapiro. Harper, 1969. First pub. in 1947 Subj: Animals.

How kittens grow photos. by Esther Bubley. Four Winds Pr., 1975. Subj: Animals – cats. Science.

How puppies grow photos. by Esther Bubley. Four Winds Pr., 1971. Subj: Animals – dogs. Science.

Is this a baby dinosaur? and other science picture puzzles Harper, 1972. Subj: Games. Science.

Keep looking! by Millicent E. Selsam and Joyce Hunt; ill. by Normand Chartier. Macmillan, 1988. ISBN 0-02-781840-3 Subj: Animals. Farms. Seasons – winter.

More potatoes! ill. by Ben Shecter. Harper, 1972. Subj: Farms. Plants. School. Science.

Night animals ill. with photos. Four Winds Pr., 1980. Subj: Animals. Night.

Sea monsters of long ago ill. by John Hamberger. Four Winds Pr., 1978. Subj: Monsters. Sea and seashore.

Seeds and more seeds ill. by Tomi Ungerer. Harper, 1959. Subj: Plants. Science. Seeds.

Where do they go? Insects in winter ill. by Arabelle Wheatley. Scholastic, 1984. ISBN 0-02-778080-5 Subj: Insects. Science. Seasons – winter.

Selway, Martina. *Don't forget to write* ill. by author. Ideals, 1992. ISBN 0-8249-8543-5 Subj: Emotions. Family life – aunts, uncles. Family life – grandfathers. Farms. Letters.

Greedyguts ill. by author. Trafalgar Square, 1992. ISBN 0-09-174151-3 Subj: Behavior – greed. Giants.

Selzer, Meyer. *Here comes the recycling truck!* photos. by author. Albert Whitman, 1992. ISBN 0-8075-3235-5 Subj: Ecology. Trucks.

Sendak, Maurice. *Alligators all around: an alphabet* ill. by author. Harper, 1962. Subj: ABC books. Reptiles – alligators, crocodiles.

Chicken soup with rice ill. by author. Harper, 1962. Subj: Days of the week, months of the year.

Hector Protector, and As I went over the water: two nursery rhymes ill. by author. Harper, 1965. Subj: Nursery rhymes.

In the night kitchen ill. by author. Harper, 1970. Subj: Caldecott award honor book. Dreams. Imagination.

Maurice Sendak's Really Rosie: starring the Nutshell Kids ill. by author; music by Carole King; design by Jane Byers Bierhorst. Harper, 1976. Subj: Activities – playing. Music. Theater.

One was Johnny: a counting book ill. by author. Harper, 1962. Subj: Counting, numbers.

Outside over there ill. by author. Harper, 1981. Subj: Activities – baby-sitting. Babies. Caldecott award honor book. Goblins.

Pierre: a cautionary tale in five chapters and a prologue ill. by author. Harper, 1962. Subj: Behavior – indifference. Character traits – individuality. Humor. Poetry, rhyme.

Seven little monsters ill. by author. Harper, 1977. Subj: Counting, numbers. Monsters. Poetry, rhyme.

The sign on Rosie's door ill. by author. Harper, 1960. Subj: Activities – playing. Imagination.

Some swell pup: or Are you sure you want a dog? by Maurice Sendak and Matthew Margolis; ill. by Maurice Sendak. Farrar, 1976. ISBN 0-374-46963-6 Subj: Animals – dogs. Pets.

Very far away ill. by author. Harper, 1957. Subj: Animals. Behavior – needing someone. Behavior – running away.

Where the wild things are ill. by author. Harper, 1963. Subj: Behavior – misbehavior. Caldecott award book. Imagination. Monsters.

Serfozo, Mary. *Dirty Kurt* ill. by Nancy Poydar. Macmillan, 1992. ISBN 0-689-50537-X Subj: Behavior – carelessness. Character traits – cleanliness. Poetry, rhyme.

Rain talk ill. by Keiko Narahashi. Macmillan, 1990. ISBN 0-689-50496-9 Subj: Noise, sounds. Weather – rain.

Welcome Roberto! Bienvenido, Roberto! ill. by John Serfozo. Follett, 1969. Subj: Ethnic groups in the U.S. – Mexican-Americans. Foreign languages.

Who said red? ill. by Keiko Narahashi. Macmillan, 1988. ISBN 0-689-50455-1 Subj: Concepts – color.

Who wants one? ill. by Keiko Narahashi. Macmillan, 1989. ISBN 0-689-50474-8 Subj: Counting, numbers. Poetry, rhyme.

Serraillier, Anne. *Florina and the wild bird* (Chönz, Selina)

Serraillier, Ian. *Florina and the wild bird* (Chönz, Selina)

Suppose you met a witch ill. by Ed Emberley. Little, 1973. Subj: Poetry, rhyme. Witches.

Service, Pamela F. *The wizard of wind and rock* ill. by Laura Marshall. Macmillan, 1990. ISBN 0-689-31600-3 Subj: Folk and fairy tales. Foreign lands – England. Wizards.

Sesame Street. *Ernie and Bert can...can you?* ill. by Michael Smollin. Random House, 1982. Subj: Format, unusual – board books. Puppets.

Sesame Street sign language fun ill. with photos. Random House, 1980. Subj: Language. Puppets.

Sesame Street word book ill. by Tom Leigh. Golden Pr., 1983. Subj: Language. Puppets.

The Sesame Street book of letters created in cooperation with the Children's Television Workshop, producers of Sesame Street. Designed by Charles I. Miller and James J. Harvin. Preschool Pr.; distributed in assoc. with Time-Life Books, 1970. Subj: ABC books.

The Sesame Street book of numbers created in cooperation with the Children's Television Workshop, producers of Sesame Street. Designed by Charles I. Miller and James J. Harvin. Preschool Pr.; distributed in assoc. with Time-Life Books, 1970. Subj: Counting, numbers.

The Sesame Street book of people and things created in cooperation with the Children's Television Workshop, producers of Sesame Street. Designed by Charles I. Miller and James J. Harvin. Preschool Pr.; distributed in assoc. with Time-Life Books, 1970. Subj: Careers. Concepts. Emotions.

The Sesame Street book of shapes created in cooperation with the Children's Television Workshop, producers of Sesame Street. Designed by Charles I. Miller and James J. Harvin. Preschool Pr.; distributed in assoc. with Time-Life Books, 1970. Subj: Concepts – shape.

Seuling, Barbara. *The teeny tiny woman: an old English ghost tale* ill. by author. Viking, 1976. Subj: Folk and fairy tales. Foreign lands – England. Ghosts.

The triplets ill. by author. Houghton, 1980. Subj: Character traits – individuality. Triplets.

What kind of family is this? a book about step families ill. by Ellen Dolce. Childrens Pr., 1985. ISBN 0-307-62482-X Subj: Family life. Family life – step families. Sibling rivalry.

Seuss, Dr. *And to think that I saw it on Mulberry Street* ill. by author. Vanguard, 1937. Subj: Humor. Imagination. Poetry, rhyme.

Bartholomew and the Oobleck ill. by author. Random House, 1949. Subj: Caldecott award honor book. Humor. Royalty.

The butter battle book ill. by author. Random House, 1984. Subj: Poetry, rhyme. War.

The cat in the hat ill. by author. Random House, 1957. Subj: Animals – cats. Humor. Poetry, rhyme.

The cat in the hat beginner book dictionary: by the Cat himself and P. D. Eastman; ill. by Dr. Seuss. Random House, 1964. Subj: Dictionaries. Humor.

The cat in the hat comes back! ill. by author. Random House, 1958. Subj: Animals – cats. Humor. Poetry, rhyme.

The cat's quizzer ill. by author. Random House, 1976. Subj: Humor. Poetry, rhyme. Riddles.

Come over to my house by Theo. LeSeig; ill. by Richard Erdoes. Random House, 1966. ISBN 0-394-90044-8 Subj: Houses. Poetry, rhyme.

Did I ever tell you how lucky you are? ill. by Richard Erdoes. Random House, 1973. Subj: Character traits – luck. Humor. Poetry, rhyme. Problem solving.

Dr. Seuss's ABC ill. by author. Random House, 1963. Subj: ABC books. Humor. Poetry, rhyme.

Dr. Seuss's sleep book ill. by author. Random House, 1962. Subj: Humor. Poetry, rhyme. Sleep.

The eye book ill. by Roy McKié. Random House, 1968. Subj: Anatomy – eyes. Animals – rabbits. Poetry, rhyme.

The foot book ill. by author. Random House, 1968. Subj: Anatomy – feet. Humor. Poetry, rhyme.

Fox in sox ill. by author. Random House, 1965. Subj: Humor. Poetry, rhyme.

A great day for up ill. by Quentin Blake. Random House, 1974. Subj: Concepts – up and down. Humor. Poetry, rhyme.

Green eggs and ham ill. by author. Random House, 1960. Subj: Cumulative tales. Food. Humor. Poetry, rhyme.

Happy birthday to you! ill. by author. Random House, 1959. Subj: Birthdays. Humor. Poetry, rhyme.

Hooper Humperdink...? Not him! ill. by Charles E. Martin. Random House, 1976. Subj: ABC books. Birthdays. Humor. Poetry, rhyme.

Hop on Pop ill. by author. Random House, 1963. Subj: Humor. Poetry, rhyme.

Horton hatches the egg ill. by author. Random House, 1940. Subj: Animals – elephants. Birds. Character traits – helpfulness. Eggs. Humor. Poetry, rhyme.

Horton hears a Who! ill. by author. Random House, 1954. Subj: Animals – elephants. Character traits – kindness. Humor. Poetry, rhyme.

How the Grinch stole Christmas ill. by author. Random House, 1957. Subj: Character traits – meanness. Holidays – Christmas. Humor. Poetry, rhyme.

Hunches in bunches ill. by author. Random House, 1982. Subj: Poetry, rhyme. Problem solving.

I am not going to get up today! ill. by James Stevenson. Random House, 1987. ISBN 0-394-99217-2 Subj: Humor. Poetry, rhyme. Sleep.

I can draw it myself: by me, myself, with a little help from my friend Dr. Seuss ill. by author. Random House, 1987. ISBN 0-394-08009-7 Subj: Art. Character traits – individuality.

I can lick 30 tigers today and other stories ill. by author. Random House, 1969. Subj: Humor. Poetry, rhyme.

I can read with my eyes shut ill. by author. Random House, 1978. Subj: Activities – reading. Humor. Poetry, rhyme.

I can write! a book by me, myself, with a little help from Theo. LeSeig and Roy McKié ill. by Roy McKié. Random House, 1971. Subj: Activities – writing. Humor. Poetry, rhyme.

I had trouble getting to Solla Sollew ill. by author. Random House, 1965. Subj: Activities – traveling. Humor. Poetry, rhyme.

I wish that I had duck feet ill. by Barney Tobey. Random House, 1965. Subj: Behavior – wishing. Poetry, rhyme.

If I ran the circus ill. by author. Random House, 1956. Subj: Circus. Humor. Poetry, rhyme.

If I ran the zoo ill. by author. Random House, 1950. Subj: Caldecott award honor book. Humor. Poetry, rhyme. Zoos.

In a people house ill. by Roy McKié. Random House, 1972. Subj: Houses. Humor. Poetry, rhyme.

The king's stilts ill. by author. Random House, 1939. Subj: Humor. Poetry, rhyme. Royalty – kings. Toys.

The Lorax ill. by author. Random House, 1971. Subj: Ecology. Humor. Poetry, rhyme.

McElligot's pool ill. by author. Random House, 1947. Subj: Caldecott award honor book. Fish. Humor. Imagination. Poetry, rhyme.

Marvin K. Mooney, will you please go now! ill. by author. Random House, 1972. Subj: Humor. Poetry, rhyme.

Mr. Brown can moo! Can you? ill. by author. Random House, 1970. Subj: Animals. Humor. Noise, sounds. Participation. Poetry, rhyme.

Oh say can you say? ill. by author. Random House, 1979. Subj: Humor. Imagination. Poetry, rhyme.

Oh, the places you'll go! ill. by author. Random House, 1990. ISBN 0-679-90527-8 Subj: Self-concept.

Oh, the thinks you can think! ill. by author. Random House, 1975. Subj: Humor. Imagination. Poetry, rhyme.

On beyond zebra ill. by author. Random House, 1955. Subj: Humor. Letters. Poetry, rhyme.

One fish, two fish, red fish, blue fish ill. by author. Random House, 1960. Subj: Fish. Humor. Poetry, rhyme.

Please try to remember the first of Octember! ill. by author. Random House, 1977. Subj: Behavior – wishing. Humor. Poetry, rhyme.

Scrambled eggs super! ill. by author. Random House, 1953. Subj: Food. Humor. Poetry, rhyme.

The shape of me and other stuff ill. by author. Random House, 1973. Subj: Concepts – shape. Humor. Poetry, rhyme.

The Sneetches, and other stories ill. by author. Random House, 1961. Subj: Emotions – fear. Humor. Poetry, rhyme.

Ten apples up on top by Theo LeSieg; ill. by Roy McKié. Random House, 1961. ISBN 0-394-90019-7 Subj: Counting, numbers.

There's a wocket in my pocket ill. by author. Random House, 1974. Subj: Humor. Poetry, rhyme.

Thidwick, the big-hearted moose ill. by author. Random House, 1948. Subj: Animals – moose. Birds. Humor. Poetry, rhyme.

The tooth book ill. by Roy McKié. Random House, 1981. Subj: Health. Poetry, rhyme. Teeth.

Wacky Wednesday ill. by George Booth. Random House, 1974. Subj: Humor. Participation. Poetry, rhyme.

Would you rather be a bullfrog? ill. by Roy McKié. Random House, 1975. Subj: Animals. Character traits – optimism. Frogs and toads.

Severn, Jeffrey. *George and his giant shadow* ill. by author. Chronicle Books, 1990. ISBN 0-87701-634-8 Subj: Animals. Shadows.

Sewall, Marcia. *Animal song* ill. by author. Little, 1988. ISBN 0-316-78191-6 Subj: Animals. Folk and fairy tales. Songs.

The cobbler's song ill. by author. Dutton, 1982. Subj: Behavior – worrying.

The little wee tyke: an English folktale ill. by author. Atheneum, 1979. Subj: Animals – dogs. Folk and fairy tales. Foreign lands – England.

Ridin' that strawberry roan ill. by adapt. Viking, 1985. ISBN 0-670-80623-4 Subj: Animals – horses. Cowboys. Poetry, rhyme.

The wee, wee mannie and the big, big coo: a Scottish folk tale ill. by author. Little, 1977. Subj: Animals – bulls, cows. Folk and fairy tales. Foreign lands – Scotland.

Sewell, Helen Moore. *Birthdays for Robin* ill. by author. Macmillan, 1943. Subj: Animals – dogs. Birthdays.

Blue barns ill. by author. Macmillan, 1933. Subj: Barns. Birds – ducks. Birds – geese. Farms.

Jimmy and Jemima ill. by author. Macmillan, 1940. Subj: Character traits – bravery. Sibling rivalry.

Ming and Mehitable ill. by author. Macmillan, 1936. Subj: Animals – dogs.

Peggy and the pony ill. by author. Oxford Univ. Pr., 1936. Subj: Animals – horses. Behavior – wishing.

Sexton, Gwain. *There once was a king* ill. by author. Scribner's, 1959. Subj: Poetry, rhyme. Royalty – kings.

Seymour, Dorothy Z. *The tent* ill. by Nancé Holman. Grosset, 1965. Subj: Cumulative tales.

Seymour, Peter. *Animals in disguise* ill. by Jean Cassels Helmer. Macmillan, 1985. ISBN 0-02-782160-9 Subj: Animals. Format, unusual – toy and movable books.

How the weather works ill. by Sally Springer. Macmillan, 1985. Subj: Format, unusual – toy and movable books. Science. Weather.

Insects: a close-up look ill. by Jean Cassels Helmer. Macmillan, 1985. ISBN 0-02-782120-X Subj: Format, unusual – toy and movable books. Insects.

The pop-up book of big trucks ill. by Chuck Murphy. Little, 1989. ISBN 0-316-78197-5 Subj: Format, unusual – toy and movable books. Trucks.

What lives in the sea? ill. by Pamela Johnson. Macmillan, 1985. ISBN 0-02-782170-6 Subj: Format, unusual – toy and movable books. Sea and seashore.

What's at the beach? ill. by David A. Carter. Holt, 1985. Subj: Monsters. Nature. Sea and seashore.

What's in the deep blue sea? ill. by David A. Carter. Holt, 1990. ISBN 0-8050-1449-7 Subj: Format, unusual – toy and movable books. Science. Sea and seashore.

What's in the prehistoric forest? ill. by David A. Carter. Holt, 1990. ISBN 0-8050-1450-0 Subj: Forest, woods. Format, unusual – toy and movable books. Science.

Seyton, Marion. *The hole in the hill* ill. by Leonard W. Shortall. Follett, 1960. Subj: Cavemen. Family life.

Shalev, Meir. *My father always embarrasses me* tr. by Dagmar Herrmann; ill. by Yossi Abolafia. Wellington, 1990. ISBN 0-922984-02-6 Subj: Emotions – embarrassment. Family life – fathers.

Shannon, George. *Beanboy* ill. by Peter Sis. Greenwillow, 1984. Subj: City. Cumulative tales. Humor.

Dancing the breeze ill. by Jacqueline Rogers. Macmillan, 1991. ISBN 0-02-782190-0 Subj: Activities – dancing. Family life – fathers. Flowers. Poetry, rhyme.

Lizard's song ill. by José Aruego and Ariane Dewey. Greenwillow, 1981. Subj: Animals – bears. Reptiles – lizards. Songs.

Oh, I love! ill. by Cheryl Harness. Bradbury Pr., 1988. ISBN 0-02-782180-3 Subj: Cumulative tales. Folk and fairy tales. Poetry, rhyme. Songs.

The Piney Woods peddler ill. by Nancy Tafuri. Greenwillow, 1982. Subj: Activities – trading. Folk and fairy tales.

The surprise ill. by José Aruego and Ariane Dewey. Greenwillow, 1983. Subj: Animals – squirrels. Birthdays.

Shapiro, Arnold L. *Circle* ill. by Bari Weissman. Dial, 1992. ISBN 0-8037-1144-1 Subj: Concepts – shape. Format, unusual – toy and movable books.

Square ill. by Bari Weissman. Dial, 1992. ISBN 0-8037-1146-8 Subj: Activities – picnicking. Concepts – shape. Format, unusual – toy and movable books.

Triangles ill. by Bari Weissman. Dial, 1992. ISBN 0-8037-1147-6 Subj: Concepts – shape. Format, unusual – toy and movable books.

Who says that? ill. by Monica Wellington. Dutton, 1991. ISBN 0-525-44698-2 Subj: Animals. Noise, sounds. Poetry, rhyme.

Shapp, Charles. *Let's find out about babies* (Shapp, Martha)

Let's find out about houses (Shapp, Martha)

Let's find out what's big and what's small by Charles and Martha Shapp; ill. by Vana Earle. Watts, 1959. Subj: Concepts – size.

Shapp, Martha. *Let's find out about babies* by Martha and Charles Shapp and Sylvia Shepard; ill. by Jenny Williams. Watts, 1975. Subj: Babies. Science.

Let's find out about houses by Martha and Charles Shapp; ill. by Tomie de Paola. Watts, 1975. Subj: Houses.

Let's find out what's big and what's small (Shapp, Charles)

Sharmat, Andrew. *Smedge* ill. by Chris L. Demarest. Macmillan, 1989. ISBN 0-02-782261-3 Subj: Animals – dogs.

Sharmat, Marjorie Weinman. *Attila the angry* ill. by Lillian Hoban. Holiday, 1985. Subj: Animals – squirrels. Emotions – anger.

Bartholomew the bossy ill. by Normand Chartier. Macmillan, 1984. Subj: Animals. Behavior – growing up. Friendship.

The best Valentine in the world ill. by Lilian Obligado. Holiday, 1982. Subj: Animals – foxes. Holidays – Valentine's Day.

A big fat enormous lie ill. by David McPhail. Dutton, 1978. Subj: Behavior – lying.

Burton and Dudley ill. by Barbara Cooney. Holiday, 1975. Subj: Activities – walking. Character traits – laziness. Friendship.

Gila monsters meet you at the airport ill. by Byron Barton. Macmillan, 1980. Subj: Behavior – misunderstanding. Moving.

Gladys told me to meet her here ill. by Edward Frascino. Harper, 1970. Subj: Friendship.

Go to sleep, Nicholas Joe ill. by John Himmelman. Harper, 1988. ISBN 0-06-025504-8 Subj: Bedtime. Family life.

Goodnight, Andrew. Goodnight, Craig ill. by Mary Chalmers. Harper, 1969. Subj: Bedtime. Family life.

Grumley the grouch ill. by Kay Chorao. Holiday, 1980. Subj: Behavior – dissatisfaction.

Helga high-up ill. by David Neuhaus. Scholastic, 1988. ISBN 0-590-40692-2 Subj: Anatomy. Animals – giraffes. Character traits – being different.

Hooray for Father's Day! ill. by John Wallner. Holiday, 1987. ISBN 0-8234-0637-7 Subj: Animals – mules. Holidays – Father's Day.

Hooray for Mother's Day! ill. by John Wallner. Holiday, 1986. ISBN 0-8234-0588-5 Subj: Birds – chickens. Holidays – Mother's Day.

I don't care ill. by Lillian Hoban. Macmillan, 1977. Subj: Behavior – indifference. Emotions – sadness. Ethnic groups in the U.S. – Afro-Americans. Toys – balloons.

I want mama ill. by Emily Arnold McCully. Harper, 1974. Subj: Family life – only child. Illness.

I'm not Oscar's friend any more ill. by Tony DeLuna. Dutton, 1975. Subj: Behavior – fighting, arguing. Emotions – anger. Friendship.

I'm Santa Claus and I'm famous ill. by Marylin Hafner. Holiday, 1990. ISBN 0-8234-0826-4 Subj: Careers. Holidays – Christmas.

I'm terrific ill. by Kay Chorao. Holiday, 1977. Subj: Animals – bears. Character traits – conceit. Character traits – pride. Self-concept.

I'm the best ill. by Will Hillenbrand. Holiday, 1991. ISBN 0-8234-0859-0 Subj: Animals – dogs. Pets.

Lucretia the unbearable ill. by Janet Stevens. Holiday, 1981. ISBN 0-8234-0395-5 Subj: Animals – bears. Behavior – worrying. Health.

Mitchell is moving ill. by José Aruego and Ariane Dewey. Macmillan, 1978. Subj: Dinosaurs. Friendship. Moving.

Mooch the messy ill. by Ben Shecter. Harper, 1976. Subj: Animals – rats. Character traits – cleanliness.

My mother never listens to me ed. by Kathleen Tucker; ill. by Lynn Munsinger. Albert Whitman, 1984. ISBN 0-8075-5347-6 Subj: Activities – reading. Family life – mothers. Imagination.

Nate the Great ill. by Marc Simont. Coward, 1972. Subj: Careers – detectives. Food.

Nate the Great and the fishy prize ill. by Marc Simont. Coward, 1985. ISBN 0-698-30745-3 Subj: Animals – dogs. Pets. Problem solving.

Nate the Great and the lost list ill. by Marc Simont. Coward, 1975. Subj: Careers – detectives. Food. Problem solving.

Nate the Great and the phony clue ill. by Marc Simont. Coward, 1977. Subj: Careers – detectives. Food.

Nate the Great goes undercover ill. by Marc Simont. Coward, 1974. Subj: Careers – detectives. Food. Problem solving.

The pizza monster by Marjorie and Mitchell Sharmat; ill. by Denise Brunkus. Delacorte Pr., 1989. ISBN 0-385-29722-X Subj: Friendship. Monsters. Problem solving.

Rex ill. by Emily Arnold McCully. Harper, 1967. Subj: Behavior – running away.

Rollo and Juliet...forever! ill. by Marylin Hafner. Doubleday, 1981. Subj: Behavior – fighting, arguing. Emotions – anger. Friendship.

Sasha the silly ill. by Janet Stevens. Holiday, 1984. Subj: Animals – dogs. Character traits – vanity.

Scarlet Monster lives here ill. by Dennis Kendrick. Harper, 1979. Subj: Behavior. Friendship. Monsters. Moving.

Sometimes mama and papa fight ill. by Kay Chorao. Harper, 1980. Subj: Behavior – fighting, arguing. Family life.

Sophie and Gussie ill. by Lillian Hoban. Macmillan, 1973. Subj: Animals – squirrels. Friendship.

Taking care of Melvin ill. by Victoria Chess. Holiday, 1980. Subj: Animals. Friendship. Self-concept.

Thornton, the worrier ill. by Kay Chorao. Holiday, 1978. Subj: Animals – rabbits. Behavior – worrying.

The 329th friend ill. by Cyndy Szekeres. Four Winds, 1992. ISBN 0-02-782259-1 Subj: Animals. Animals – raccoons. Counting, numbers. Friendship. Self-concept.

The trip: and other Sophie and Gussie stories ill. by Lillian Hoban. Macmillan, 1976. Subj: Animals – squirrels. Behavior – losing things. Behavior – sharing. Clothing. Friendship.

Two ghosts on a bench ill. by Nola Langner. Harper, 1982. Subj: Ghosts.

Walter the wolf ill. by Kelly Oechsli. Holiday, 1975. Subj: Animals. Animals – wolves. Violence, anti-violence.

What are we going to do about Andrew? ill. by Ray Cruz. Macmillan, 1980. Subj: Character traits – individuality. Family life.

Sharmat, Mitchell. *Gregory, the terrible eater* ill. by José Aruego and Ariane Dewey. Four Winds Pr., 1980. Subj: Animals – goats. Food.

The pizza monster (Sharmat, Marjorie Weinman)

The seven sloppy days of Phineas Pig ill. by Sue Truesdell. Harcourt, 1983. Subj: Animals – pigs. Character traits – cleanliness.

Sherman is a slowpoke ill. by David Neuhaus. Scholastic, 1988. ISBN 0-590-40938-7 Subj: Animals – sloths. Character traits – individuality. School.

Sharon, Mary Bruce. *Scenes from childhood* ill. by author. Dutton, 1978. Subj: Art. Careers – artists.

Sharpe, Sara. *Gardener George goes to town* ill. by Susan Moxley. Harper, 1982. Subj: Gardens, gardening.

Sharr, Christine. *Homes* ill. by author. Wonder Books, 1971. Subj: Family life. Houses.

Sharratt, Nick. *I look like this* ill. by author. Candlewick Pr., 1992. ISBN 1-56402-016-9 Subj: Emotions. Format, unusual. Games.

Look what I found! ill. by author. Caldlewick Pr., 1992. ISBN 1-56402-017-7 Subj: Format, unusual. Sea and seashore.

Shaw, Charles Green. *The blue guess book* ill. by author. Addison-Wesley, 1942. Subj: Games.

The guess book ill. by author. Addison-Wesley, 1941. Subj: Games.

It looked like spilt milk ill. by author. Harper, 1947. Subj: Concepts – shape. Games. Imagination. Participation. Sky. Weather – clouds.

Shaw, Evelyn S. *Alligator* ill. by Frances Zweifel. Harper, 1972. Subj: Reptiles – alligators, crocodiles. Science.

Fish out of school ill. by Ralph Carpentier. Harper, 1970. Subj: Fish. Science. Sea and seashore.

Nest of wood ducks ill. by Cherryl Pape. Harper, 1976. Subj: Birds – ducks. Science.

Octopus ill. by Ralph Carpentier. Harper, 1971. Subj: Octopuses. Science. Sea and seashore.

Sea otters ill. by Cherryl Pape. Harper, 1980. Subj: Animals – otters. Science.

Shaw, Nancy. *Sheep in a jeep* ill. by Margot Apple. Houghton, 1986. ISBN 0-395-41105-X Subj: Animals – sheep. Poetry, rhyme.

Sheep in a shop ill. by Margot Apple. Houghton, 1991. ISBN 0-395-53681-2 Subj: Animals – sheep. Poetry, rhyme. Shopping.

Sheep on a ship ill. by Margot Apple. Houghton, 1989. ISBN 0-395-48160-0 Subj: Animals – sheep. Boats, ships. Poetry, rhyme.

Shaw, Richard. *The kitten in the pumpkin patch* ill. by Jacqueline Kahane. Warne, 1973. Subj: Animals – cats. Holidays – Halloween. Witches.

Shay, Arthur. *What happens when you go to the hospital* ill. by author. Reilly and Lee, 1969. Subj: Hospitals. Illness.

Shea, Pegi Deitz. *Bungalow fungalow* ill. by Elizabeth Sayles. Houghton, 1991. ISBN 0-395-55387-3 Subj: Activities – vacationing. Poetry, rhyme. Sea and seashore.

Shearer, Marilyn J. *The crown of fools: based on: The tortoise and the hare* ill. by author. Lauren Ashley & Joshua Storybooks, 1993. ISBN 1-879567-19-9 Subj: Character traits – perseverance. Folk and fairy tales. Reptiles – turtles, tortoises. Sports – racing.

I like to play ill. by Tom Roerts. Lauren Ashley & Joshua Storybooks, 1993. ISBN 0-685-30097-8 Subj: Activities – playing.

The Nubian princess ill. by Larry Walker. Lauren Ashley & Joshua Storybooks, 1993. ISBN 0-685-30091-9 Subj: Royalty – princesses.

The original three little pigs re-told (The three little pigs)

Shecter, Ben. *The big stew* ill. by author. HarperCollins, 1991. ISBN 0-06-025610-9 Subj: Activities – cooking. Food. Witches.

Conrad's castle ill. by author. Harper, 1967. Subj: Imagination.

The discontented mother ill. by author. Harcourt, 1980. Subj: Behavior – wishing.

Emily, girl witch of New York ill. by author. Dial Pr., 1963. Subj: City. Houses. Magic. Progress. Witches.

Grandma remembers ill. by author. HarperCollins, 1989. ISBN 0-06-025618-4 Subj: Family life – grandmothers. Moving.

Hester the jester ill. by author. Harper, 1977. Subj: Character traits – ambition. Clowns, jesters.

If I had a ship ill. by author. Doubleday, 1970. Subj: Boats, ships. Character traits – generosity. Emotions – love. Imagination.

Partouche plants a seed ill. by author. Harper, 1966. Subj: Animals – pigs. Foreign lands – France. Gardens, gardening. Plants. Seeds.

The stocking child ill. by author. Harper, 1976. Subj: Senses – seeing. Toys – dolls.

Sheehan, Angela. *The beaver* ill. by Graham Allen. Watts, 1979. Subj: Animals – beavers. Science.

The duck ill. by Maurice Pledger and Bernard Robinson. Warwick Pr., 1979. Subj: Birds – ducks. Science.

The otter ill. by Bernard Robinson. Warwick Pr., 1979. Subj: Animals – otters. Science.

The penguin ill. by Trevor Boyer. Watts, 1979. Subj: Birds – penguins. Science.

Shefelman, Janice. *Victoria House* ill. by Tom Shefelman. Harcourt, 1988. ISBN 0-15-200630-3 Subj: Houses. Moving.

Sheffield, Margaret. *Before you were born* ill. by Sheila Bewley. Knopf, 1984. Subj: Babies. Birth. Science.

Where do babies come from? ill. by Sheila Bewley. Knopf, 1973. Subj: Babies. Birth. Science.

Shelby, Anne. *Potluck* ill. by Irene Trivas. Watts, 1991. ISBN 0-531-08519-8 Subj: ABC books. Ethnic groups in the U.S. Food.

We keep a store ill. by John Ward. Watts, 1990. ISBN 0-531-08456-6 Subj: Careers – storekeepers. Ethnic groups in the U.S. – Afro-Americans. Family life. Stores.

Sheldon, Aure. *Of cobblers and kings* ill. by Don Leake. Parents, 1978. Subj: Careers – shoemakers. Character traits – cleverness.

Sheldon, Dyan. *The whales' song* ill. by Gary Blythe. Dial, 1991. ISBN 0-8037-0972-2 Subj: Animals – kindness to animals. Animals – whales. Family life – grandmothers.

Shepard, Steve. *Elvis Hornbill, international business bird* ill. by author. Holt, 1991. ISBN 0-8050-1617-1 Subj: Birds – hornbills. Careers. Family life – fathers. Foreign lands – Africa.

Shepard, Sylvia. *Let's find out about babies* (Shapp, Martha)

Sheppard, Jeff. *The right number of elephants* ill. by Felicia Bond. HarperCollins, 1990. ISBN 0-06-025616-8 Subj: Animals – elephants. Counting, numbers.

Shepperson, Rob. *The sandman* ill. by author. Farrar, 1990. ISBN 0-374-36405-2 Subj: Bedtime. Dreams. Sandman. Sleep.

Sherman, Eileen Bluestone. *The odd potato: a Chanukah story* ill. by Katherine Janus Kahn. Kar-Ben Copies, 1984. ISBN 0-930494-36-9 Subj: Family life. Holidays – Hanukkah. Jewish culture.

Sherman, Elizabeth *see* Friskey, Margaret (Margaret Richards)

Sherman, Ivan. *I am a giant* ill. by author. Harcourt, 1975. Subj: Giants. Imagination.

I do not like it when my friend comes to visit ill. by author. Harcourt, 1973. Subj: Behavior – sharing. Etiquette. Friendship.

Walking talking words ill. by author. Harcourt, 1980. Subj: Language. Poetry, rhyme.

Sherman, Josepha. *Vassilisa the wise: a tale of medieval Russia* ill. by Daniel San Souci. Harcourt, 1988. ISBN 0-15-293240-2 Subj: Folk and fairy tales. Foreign lands – Russia. Royalty – princes.

Sherman, Nancy. *Gwendolyn and the weathercock* ill. by Edward Sorel. Golden Pr., 1961. Subj: Birds – chickens. Farms. Poetry, rhyme. Weather – rain.

Gwendolyn the miracle hen ill. by Edward Sorel. Western Pub., 1961. Subj: Birds – chickens. Dragons. Poetry, rhyme.

Sherrow, Victoria. *There goes the ghost* ill. by Megan Lloyd. Harper, 1985. ISBN 0-06-025510-2 Subj: Behavior – misbehavior. Ghosts. Houses. Moving.

Wilbur waits ill. by James Watts. HarperCollins, 1990. ISBN 0-06-025484-X Subj: Birthdays. Friendship. Toys. Weather.

Shi, Zhang Xiu. *Monkey and the white bone demon* tr. by Ye Ping Kuei; rev. by Jill Morris; ill. by Lin Zheng and others. Viking, 1984. Adapted from the 16th century novel, The pilgrimage to the west, by Wu Cheng En Subj: Animals – monkeys. Folk and fairy tales. Foreign lands – China.

Shibano, Tamizo. *The old man who made the trees bloom* by Hanasaka Jijii; retold by Tamizo Shibano; tr. by D. T. Ooka; ill. by Bunshu Iguchi. Heian Int., 1985. ISBN 0-89346-247-0 Subj: Animals – dogs. Behavior – greed. Character traits – kindness. Character traits – meanness.

Shimin, Symeon. *I wish there were two of me* ill. by author. Warne, 1976. Subj: Behavior – wishing. Dreams. Imagination.

A special birthday ill. by author. McGraw-Hill, 1976. Subj: Birthdays. Wordless.

Shine, Deborah. *The little engine that could pudgy word book* ill. by Christina Ong. Putnam's, 1988. ISBN 0-448-19054-0 Subj: Character traits – perseverance. Format, unusual – board books. Trains.

Shipton, Jonathan. *Busy! Busy! Busy!* ill. by Michael Foreman. Delacorte Pr., 1991. ISBN 0-385-30306-8 Subj: Activities – working. Emotions – love. Family life – mothers.

In the night ill. by Gill Scriven. Little, 1992. ISBN 0-316-78586-5 Subj: Bedtime. Night.

Shire, Ellen. *The mystery at number seven, Rue Petite* ill. by author. Random House, 1978. Subj: Character traits – bravery. Crime.

Shles, Larry. *Moths and mothers, feathers and fathers: a story about a tiny owl named Squib* ill. by author. Houghton, 1984. ISBN 0-395-36695-X Subj: Birds – owls. Character traits – being different.

Shopping ill. by Roser Capdevila. Firefly Pr., 1986. ISBN 0-920303-43-9 Subj: Shopping. Format, unusual – toy and movable books. Wordless.

Short, Mayo. *Andy and the wild ducks* ill. by Paul M. Souza. Melmont, 1959. Subj: Animals. Ecology. Farms.

Shortall, Leonard W. *Andy, the dog walker* ill. by author. Morrow, 1968. Subj: Animals – dogs. Behavior – lost.

One way: a trip with traffic signs ill. by author. Prentice-Hall, 1975. Subj: Holidays – Fourth of July. Poetry, rhyme. Safety. Traffic, traffic signs.

Tod on the tugboat ill. by author. Morrow, 1971. Subj: Boats, ships.

Tony's first dive ill. by author. Morrow, 1972. Subj: Emotions – fear. Sports – swimming.

Shostak, Myra. *Rainbow candles: a Chanukah counting book* ill. by Katherine Janus Kahn. Kar-Ben Copies, 1986. ISBN 0-930494-59-8 Subj: Counting, numbers. Format, unusual – board books. Holidays – Hanukkah. Jewish culture.

Shoten, Fukuinkan. *Elephant blue* (Nakano, Hirotaka)

Shott, Stephen. *Bathtime* photos. by author. Dutton, 1991. ISBN 0-525-44754-7 Subj: Activities – bathing. Format, unusual – board books.

Look at me photos. by author. Dutton, 1991. ISBN 0-525-44755-5 Subj: Anatomy. Format, unusual – board books. Self-concept.

Mealtime photos. by author. Dutton, 1991. ISBN 0-525-44756-3 Subj: Food. Format, unusual – board books.

El mundo del bebe (Baby's World) photos. by author. Dutton, 1992. ISBN 0-525-44846-2 Subj: Foreign languages.

Playtime photos. by author. Dutton, 1991. ISBN 0-525-44757-1 Subj: Activities – playing. Format, unusual – board books.

Showalter, Jean B. *The donkey ride* ill. by Tomi Ungerer. Doubleday, 1967. Subj: Animals – donkeys. Folk and fairy tales. Humor.

Showers, Kay Sperry. *Before you were a baby* (Showers, Paul)

Showers, Paul. *Before you were a baby* by Paul Showers and Kay Sperry Showers; ill. by Ingrid Fetz. Crowell, 1968. Subj: Babies. Birth. Science.

Columbus Day ill. by Ed Emberley. Crowell, 1965. Subj: Holidays – Columbus Day. U.S. history.

A drop of blood ill. by Don Madden Rev. ed. HarperCollins, 1989. ISBN 0-690-04717-7 Subj: Anatomy. Science.

Ears are for hearing ill. by Holly Keller. HarperCollins, 1990. ISBN 0-690-04720-7 Subj: Anatomy – ears. Science. Senses – hearing.

How you talk ill. by Megan Lloyd Rev. ed. HarperCollins, 1992. ISBN 0-06-022768-0 Subj: Anatomy. Communication. Language.

The listening walk ill. by Aliki Rev. ed. HarperCollins, 1991. ISBN 0-06-021638-7 Subj: Activities – walking. Noise, sounds. Senses – hearing.

Look at your eyes ill. by Paul Galdone. Crowell, 1962. Subj: Anatomy – eyes. Ethnic groups in the U.S. – Afro-Americans. Senses – seeing.

No measles, no mumps for me ill. by Harriett Barton. Crowell, 1980. Subj: Illness. Science.

You can't make a move without your muscles ill. by Harriett Barton. Crowell, 1982. Subj: Anatomy. Science.

Your skin and mine ill. by Kathleen Kuchera Rev. ed. HarperCollins, 1991. ISBN 0-06-022523-8 Subj: Anatomy. Ethnic groups in the U.S. – Afro-Americans.

Shub, Elizabeth. *The Bremen town musicians* (Grimm, Jacob)

Clever Kate (Grimm, Jacob)

Dear Sarah (Borchers, Elisabeth)

Dragon Franz text by Josef Guggenmos; adapt. by Elizabeth Shub; ill. by Ursula Konopka. Greenwillow, 1976. Orig. pub. in German under the title Franz, der Drache Subj: Character traits – being different. Concepts – color. Dragons.

The emperor's plum tree (Nikly, Michelle)

The fisherman and his wife (Grimm, Jacob)

Jorinda and Joringel (Grimm, Jacob)

Seeing is believing ill. by Rachel Isadora. Greenwillow, 1979. Subj: Elves and little people. Folk and fairy tales.

Sir Ribbeck of Ribbeck of Havelland (Fontane, Theodor)

The twelve dancing princesses (Grimm, Jacob)

Why Noah chose the dove (Singer, Isaac Bashevis)

Shulevitz, Uri. *Dawn* ill. by author. Farrar, 1974. Subj: Family life – grandfathers. Morning. Camps, camping. Sun.

The magician adapt. from the Yiddish of Isaac Loeb Peretz by Uri Shulevitz; ill. by adapt. Macmillan, 1973. Subj: Jewish culture. Magic. Religion.

One Monday morning ill. by author. Scribner's, 1967. Subj: Days of the week, months of the year. Imagination. Royalty.

Rain rain rivers ill. by author. Farrar, 1969. Subj: Poetry, rhyme. Weather – rain.

The treasure ill. by author. Farrar, 1978. Subj: Caldecott award honor book. Dreams. Folk and fairy tales.

Shulman, Milton. *Prep, the little pigeon of Trafalgar Square* ill. by Dale Maxey. Random House, 1964. Subj: Birds – pigeons. Foreign lands – England.

Shute, Linda. *Clever Tom and the leprechaun* ill. by author. Lothrop, 1988. ISBN 0-688-07489-8 Subj: Elves and little people. Folk and fairy tales.

Momotaro, the peach boy ill. by author. Lothrop, 1986. ISBN 0-688-05864-7 Subj: Behavior – fighting, arguing. Character traits – bravery. Devil. Folk and fairy tales. Foreign lands – Japan.

Shuttlesworth, Dorothy E. *ABC of buses* ill. by Leonard W. Shortall. Doubleday, 1965. Subj: ABC books. Buses.

Shyer, Marlene Fanta. *Here I am, an only child* ill. by Donald Carrick. Scribner's, 1985. ISBN 0-684-18296-3 Subj: Family life – only child.

Stepdog ill. by Judith Schermer. Scribner's, 1983. Subj: Animals – dogs. Emotions – envy, jealousy. Family life.

Sibbick, John. *Creatures of long ago: dinosaurs* ill. by author. National Geographic Soc., 1989. ISBN 0-87044-723-8 Subj: Dinosaurs. Format, unusual – toy and movable books.

Siberell, Anne. *A journey to paradise* ill. by author. Holt, 1990. ISBN 0-8050-1212-5 Subj: Folk and fairy tales. Foreign lands – India.

Whale in the sky ill. by author. Dutton, 1982. Subj: Animals – whales. Folk and fairy tales. Indians of North America.

Sicotte, Virginia. *A riot of quiet* ill. by Edward Ardizzone. Holt, 1969. Subj: Imagination. Noise, sounds. Poetry, rhyme.

Siddiqui, Ashraf. *Bhombal Dass, the uncle of lion: a tale from Pakistan* ill. by Thomas Arthur Hamil. Macmillan, 1959. Subj: Animals – goats. Animals – lions. Character traits – cleverness. Folk and fairy tales. Foreign lands – Pakistan.

Siebert, Diane. *Heartland* ill. by Wendell Minor. HarperCollins, 1989. ISBN 0-690-04732-0 Subj: Poetry, rhyme. U.S. history.

Mojave ill. by Wendell Minor. Harper, 1988. ISBN 0-690-04569-7 Subj: Desert. Poetry, rhyme.

Sierra ill. by Wendell Minor. HarperCollins, 1991. ISBN 0-06-021640-9 Subj: Nature. Poetry, rhyme.

Train song ill. by Mike Wimmer. HarperCollins, 1990. ISBN 0-690-04728-2 Subj: Poetry, rhyme. Trains.

Truck song ill. by Byron Barton. Crowell, 1984. Subj: Poetry, rhyme. Trucks.

Siekkinen, Raija. *Mister King* tr. from Finnish by Tim Steffa; ill. by Hannu Taina. Carolrhoda Books, 1987. ISBN 0-87614-315-X Subj: Animals – cats. Emotions – loneliness. Royalty – kings.

Siepmann, Jane. *The lion on Scott Street* ill. by Clement Hurd. Oxford Univ. Pr., 1952. Subj: Animals – lions. Imagination.

Sieveking, Anthea. *Mary had a little lamb and other animal rhymes* photos. by author. Barron's, 1991. ISBN 0-8120-6217-5 Subj: Format, unusual – board books. Nursery rhymes.

Polly put the kettle on and other play rhymes photos. by author. Barron's, 1991. ISBN 0-8120-6218-3 Subj: Format, unusual – board books. Nursery rhymes.

Rub-a-dub-dub and other splashy rhymes photos. by author. Barron's, 1991. ISBN 0-8120-6219-1 Subj: Format, unusual – board books. Nursery rhymes.

Twinkle, twinkle, little star and other bedtime rhymes photos. by author. Barron's, 1991. ISBN 0-8120-6220-5 Subj: Format, unusual – board books. Nursery rhymes.

What color? photos. by author. Dial, 1991. ISBN 0-8037-0909-9 Subj: Concepts – color.

Siewert, Margaret. *Bear hunt* by Margaret Siewert and Kathleen Savage; ill. by Leonard W. Shortall. Prentice-Hall, 1976. Subj: Animals – bears. Games. Participation. Toys – teddy bears.

Silsbe, Brenda. *Just one more color* ill. by Shawn Steffler. Firefly, 1991. ISBN 1-55037-133-9 Subj: Activities – painting. Concepts – color. Houses.

Silver, Jody. *Isadora* ill. by author. Doubleday, 1981. Subj: Animals – donkeys. Clothing.

Silverman, Erica. *On Grandma's roof* ill. by Deborah Kogan Ray. Macmillan, 1990. ISBN 0-02-782681-3 Subj: City. Family life – grandmothers. Houses.

Warm in winter ill. by Michael J. Deraney. Macmillan, 1989. ISBN 0-02-782661-9 Subj: Animals – badgers. Animals – rabbits. Friendship. Seasons. Seasons – winter.

Silverman, Maida. *Bunny's ABC* ill. by Ellen Blonder. Grosset, 1986. ISBN 0-448-01464-5 Subj: ABC books. Animals – rabbits. Format, unusual – board books.

Dinosaur babies ill. by Carol Inouye. Simon & Schuster, 1988. ISBN 0-671-65897-2 Subj: Dinosaurs. Science.

Ladybug's color book ill. by Nancy Duell. Grosset, 1986. ISBN 0-448-01461-0 Subj: Concepts – color. Format, unusual – board books. Insects – ladybugs.

The magic well ill. by Manuel Boix. Simon & Schuster, 1989. ISBN 0-617-67885-X Subj: Emotions – love. Fairies. Family life – mothers. Magic. Royalty – queens.

Mouse's shape book ill. by Frederic Marvin. Grosset, 1986. ISBN 0-448-01463-7 Subj: Animals – mice. Concepts – shape. Format, unusual – board books.

Silverman, Martin. *My tooth is loose* ill. by Amy Aitken. Viking, 1992. ISBN 0-670-83862-4 Subj: Teeth.

Silverstein, Shel. *A giraffe and a half* ill. by author. Harper, 1964. Subj: Cumulative tales. Humor. Poetry, rhyme.

The giving tree ill. by author. Harper, 1964. Subj: Character traits – generosity. Poetry, rhyme.

The missing piece ill. by author. Harper, 1976. Subj: Character traits – individuality. Concepts – shape.

Simmonds, Posy. *The chocolate wedding* ill. by author. Knopf, 1991. ISBN 0-679-91447-1 Subj: Behavior – boasting. Behavior – misbehavior. Dreams. Weddings.

Fred ill. by author. Knopf, 1988. ISBN 0-394-98627-X Subj: Animals – cats. Death.

Lulu and the flying babies ill. by author. Knopf, 1988. ISBN 0-394-99597-X Subj: Family life – fathers. Imagination. Museums. Weather – snow.

Simms, Laura. *The squeaky door* ill. by Sylvie Wickstrom. Crown, 1991. ISBN 0-517-57584-1 Subj: Bedtime. Cumulative tales. Emotions – fear. Folk and fairy tales. Noise, sounds.

Simon, Carly. *Amy the dancing bear* ill. by Margot Datz. Doubleday, 1989. ISBN 0-385-26721-5 Subj: Activities – dancing. Animals – bears.

Simon, Howard. *If you were an eel, how would you feel?* (Simon, Mina Lewiton)

Simon, Mina Lewiton. *If you were an eel, how would you feel?* by Mina and Howard Simon; ill. by Howard Simon. Follett, 1963. Subj: Animals.

Is anyone here? ill. by Howard Simon. Atheneum, 1967. Subj: Poetry, rhyme. Sea and seashore.

Simon, Norma. *All kinds of families* ill. by Joe Lasker. Albert Whitman, 1976. Subj: Family life.

Cats do, dogs don't ill. by Dora Leder. Albert Whitman, 1986. ISBN 0-8075-1102-1 Subj: Animals – cats. Animals – dogs. Pets.

The daddy days ill. by Abner Graboff. Abelard-Schuman, 1958. Subj: Divorce. Family life – fathers.

How do I feel? ill. by Joe Lasker. Albert Whitman, 1970. Subj: Emotions. Family life. Twins.

I am not a crybaby! ill. by Helen Cogancherry. Albert Whitman, 1988. ISBN 0-8075-3447-1 Subj: Emotions. Ethnic groups in the U.S.

I know what I like ill. by Dora Leder. Albert Whitman, 1971. Subj: Character traits – individuality.

I was so mad! ill. by Dora Leder. Albert Whitman, 1974. Subj: Emotions – anger.

I wish I had my father ill. by Arieh Zeldich. Albert Whitman, 1983. ISBN 0-8075-3522-2 Subj: Behavior – wishing. Family life – fathers. Holidays – Father's Day.

I'm busy, too ill. by Dora Leder. Albert Whitman, 1980. ISBN 0-8075-3464-1 Subj: Activities. Activities – working. School.

Mama cat's year ill. by Dora Leder. Albert Whitman, 1991. ISBN 0-8075-4958-4 Subj: Animals – cats. Pets. Seasons.

Oh, that cat! ill. by Dora Leder. Albert Whitman, 1986. ISBN 0-8075-5919-9 Subj: Animals – cats. Family life. Pets.

The saddest time ill. by Jacqueline Rogers. Albert Whitman, 1986. ISBN 0-8075-7203-9 Subj: Death.

The wet world ill. by Jane Miller. Lippincott, 1954. Subj: Weather – rain.

What do I do? ill. by Joe Lasker. Albert Whitman, 1969. Subj: Activities. Character traits – helpfulness. City. Ethnic groups in the U.S. – Puerto Rican-Americans. School.

What do I say? ill. by Joe Lasker. Albert Whitman, 1967. Subj: Ethnic groups in the U.S. Ethnic groups in the U.S. – Puerto Rican-Americans. Family life. Foreign languages. Participation. School.

Where does my cat sleep? ill. by Dora Leder. Albert Whitman, 1982. Subj: Animals – cats. Sleep.

Why am I different? ill. by Dora Leder. Albert Whitman, 1976. Subj: Character traits – being different. Character traits – individuality. Self-concept.

Simon, Paul. *At the zoo* ill. by Valerie Michaut. Doubleday, 1991. ISBN 0-385-41906-6 Subj: Animals. Songs. Zoos.

Simon, Seymour. *Animal fact—animal fable* ill. by Diane de Groat. Crown, 1979. Subj: Animals.

Beneath your feet ill. by Daniel Nevins. Walker, 1977. Subj: Earth. Science.

Icebergs and glaciers ill. with photos. Morrow, 1987. ISBN 0-688-06187-7 Subj: Nature. Science.

The largest dinosaurs ill. by Pamela Carroll. Macmillan, 1986. ISBN 0-02-782910-3 Subj: Dinosaurs.

Shadow magic ill. by Stella Ormai. Lothrop, 1985. ISBN 0-688-02682-6 Subj: Shadows.

The smallest dinosaurs ill. by Anthony Rao. Crown, 1982. Subj: Dinosaurs.

Simon, Sidney B. *The armadillo who had no shell* ill. by Walter Lorraine. Norton, 1966. Subj: Animals – armadillos. Character traits – being different.

Henry, the uncatchable mouse ill. by Nola Langner. Norton, 1964. Subj: Animals – mice. Character traits – cleverness.

Simons, Traute. *Paulino* tr. by Ebbitt Cutler; ill. by Susi Bohdal. Tundra (dist. by Scribner's), 1978. Subj: Dreams. Toys.

Simont, Marc. *How come elephants?* ill. by author. Harper, 1965. Subj: Animals – elephants. Character traits – questioning.

Simple Simon. *The adventures of Simple Simon* ill. by Chris Conover. Farrar, 1987. ISBN 0-374-36921-6 Subj: Nursery rhymes.

Simple Simon ill. by Rodney Peppé. Holt, 1973. Subj: Nursery rhymes.

The story of Simple Simon ill. by Paul Galdone. McGraw-Hill, 1966. "The version used in this book was published in London in 1840 by A. Park." Subj: Nursery rhymes.

Simpson, Gretchen Dow. *Gretchen's ABC* ill. by author. HarperCollins, 1991. ISBN 0-06-025646-X Subj: ABC books. Art.

Singer, Isaac Bashevis. *Why Noah chose the dove* tr. by Elizabeth Shub; ill. by Eric Carle. Farrar, 1974. Subj: Animals. Birds – doves. Religion – Noah.

Singer, Marilyn. *Archer Armadillo's secret room* ill. by Beth Lee Weiner. Macmillan, 1985. Subj: Animals – armadillos. Behavior – running away. Moving.

The dog who insisted he wasn't ill. by Kelly Oechsli. Dutton, 1976. Subj: Animals – dogs. Character traits – individuality. Humor.

Minnie's Yom Kippur birthday ill. by Ruth Rosner. HarperCollins, 1989. ISBN 0-06-025847-0 Subj: Birthdays. Holidays – Yom Kippur. Jewish culture. Religion.

Nine o'clock lullaby ill. by Frané Lessac. HarperCollins, 1991. ISBN 0-06-025648-6 Subj: Foreign lands. Time.

Pickle plan ill. by Steven Kellogg. Dutton, 1978. Subj: Behavior – needing someone. Character traits – individuality.

Turtle in July ill. by Jerry Pinkney. Macmillan, 1989. ISBN 0-02-782881-6 Subj: Animals. Days of the week, months of the year. Nature. Poetry, rhyme.

Will you take me to town on strawberry day? ill. by Trinka Hakes Noble. Harper, 1981. Subj: Music. Poetry, rhyme. Songs.

Singh, Jacquelin. *Fat Gopal* ill. by Demi. Harcourt, 1984. Subj: Character traits – cleverness. Poetry, rhyme. Foreign lands – India.

Sipiera, Paul P. *I can be a geologist* ill. with photos. Childrens Pr., 1986. ISBN 0-516-01897-3 Subj: Careers – geologists.

Siracusa, Catherine. *No mail for Mitchell* ill. by author. McKay, 1990. ISBN 0-679-90476-X Subj: Animals. Careers – mail carriers. Illness. Letters.

Sirois, Allen. *Dinosaur dress up* ill. by Janet Street. Morrow, 1992. ISBN 0-688-10460-6 Subj: Clothing. Dinosaurs.

Sis, Peter. *Beach ball* ill. by author. Greenwillow, 1990. ISBN 0-688-09182-2 Subj: Concepts. Sea and seashore.

Going up! ill. by author. Greenwillow, 1989. ISBN 0-688-08125-8 Subj: Birthdays. Concepts – color. Counting, numbers. Elevators, escalators.

Higgledy-Piggledy (Livingston, Myra Cohn)

Rainbow Rhino ill. by author. Knopf, 1987. ISBN 0-394-99009-9 Subj: Animals – rhinoceros. Birds. Friendship.

Waving ill. by author. Greenwillow, 1988. ISBN 0-688-07160-0 Subj: Counting, numbers.

Sitomer, Harry. *How did numbers begin?* (Sitomer, Mindel)

Sitomer, Mindel. *How did numbers begin?* by Mindel and Harry Sitomer; ill. by Richard Cuffari. Crowell, 1976. Subj: Counting, numbers.

Sivulich, Sandra Stroner. *I'm going on a bear hunt* ill. by Glen Rounds. Dutton, 1973. Subj: Animals – bears. Games. Participation.

Skaar, Grace Marion. *Nothing but (cats) and all about (dogs)* ill. by author. Addison-Wesley, 1947. Subj: Animals – cats. Animals – dogs.

The very little dog: and, The smart little kitty by Grace Marion Skaar and Louise Phinney Woodcock; ill. by authors. Addison-Wesley, 1967. Subj: Animals – cats. Animals – dogs.

What do the animals say? ill. by author. Addison-Wesley, 1968. 1950 ed. published under title: What do they say! Subj: Animals. Noise, sounds. Participation.

Skipper, Mervyn. *The fooling of King Alexander* ill. by Gaynor Chapman. Atheneum, 1967. Originally published in The white man's garden, by Mervyn Skipper. London, Mathews, 1931 Subj: Foreign lands – China. Royalty – kings.

Skofield, James. *All wet! All wet!* ill. by Diane Stanley. Harper, 1984. Subj: Weather – rain.

Crow moon, worm moon ill. by Joyce Powzyk. Four Winds, 1990. ISBN 0-02-782915-4 Subj: Animals. Moon. Nature. Poetry, rhyme. Seasons – spring.

Snow country ill. by Laura Jean Allen. Harper, 1983. Subj: Family life – grandparents. Farms. Weather – snow.

Skorpen, Liesel Moak. *All the Lassies* ill. by Bruce Martin Scott. Dial Pr., 1970. Subj: Animals. Animals – dogs. Character traits – perseverance. Cumulative tales. Family life – only child. Participation. Pets.

Charles ill. by Martha G. Alexander. Harper, 1971. Subj: Behavior – needing someone. Toys – teddy bears.

Elizabeth ill. by Martha G. Alexander. Harper, 1970. Subj: Toys – dolls.

His mother's dog ill. by M. E. Mullin. Harper, 1978. Subj: Animals – dogs. Emotions – envy, jealousy. Family life. Sibling rivalry.

If I had a lion ill. by Ursula Landshoff. Harper, 1967. Subj: Animals – lions. Imagination.

Old Arthur ill. by Wallace Tripp. Harper, 1972. Subj: Animals – dogs. Old age.

Outside my window ill. by Mercer Mayer. Harper, 1968. Subj: Animals – bears. Bedtime.

Skulavik, Mary Alys. *Bert* ill. by Zofia Kostyrko. Walker, 1990. ISBN 0-8027-6963-2 Subj: Computers. Family life. Self-concept.

Skurzynski, Gloria. *Martin by himself* ill. by Lynn Munsinger. Houghton, 1979. Subj: Activities – working. Emotions – loneliness. Family life – mothers.

Skutina, Vladimir. *Nobody has time for me* tr. by Dagmar Herrmann; ill. by Marie-Jose Sacre. Wellington, 1991. ISBN 0-922984-07-7 Subj: Time.

Slate, Joseph. *Lonely Lula cat* ill. by Bruce Degen. Harper, 1985. Subj: Animals – cats. Emotions – loneliness. Friendship.

The mean, clean, giant canoe machine ill. by Lynn Munsinger. Crowell, 1983. Subj: Activities – bathing. Animals – pigs. Witches.

The star rocker ill. by Dirk Zimmer. Harper, 1982. Subj: Poetry, rhyme. Stars.

Who is coming to our house? ill. by Ashley Wolff. Putnam's, 1988. ISBN 0-399-21537-9 Subj: Animals. Animals – mice. Poetry, rhyme. Religion.

Slater, Teddy. *The cow that could tap dance* ill. by Sandra Forrest. Silver Pr., 1991. ISBN 0-671-70408-7 Subj: Behavior – boasting. Character traits – questioning.

The emperor's nightingale (Andersen, H. C. (Hans Christian))

The fabulous fish from Lake Wiggawalla ill. by Laura Rankin. Silver Pr., 1991. ISBN 0-671-70409-5 Subj: Activities – traveling. Behavior – boasting.

Jan and Dan and the super dads ill. by Sandra Forrest. Silver Pr., 1991. ISBN 0-671-70410-9 Subj: Family life – fathers.

Sleator, William. *The angry moon* ill. by Blair Lent. Little, 1970. Subj: Caldecott award honor book. Folk and fairy tales. Indians of North America. Moon.

That's silly ill. by Lawrence DiFiori. Dutton, 1981. ISBN 0-525-40981-5 Subj: Imagination. Magic.

Sleep, baby, sleep : *an old cradle song* ill. by Trudi Oberhänsli. Atheneum, 1967. Includes melody with words Subj: Lullabies.

Slepian, Jan. *The hungry thing returns* ill. by Richard E. Martin. Scholastic, 1990. ISBN 0-590-42890-X Subj: Food. Poetry, rhyme.

Sloan, Carolyn. *Carter is a painter's cat* ill. by Fritz Wegner. Simon and Schuster, 1971. Subj: Animals – cats. Careers – artists.

Sloat, Teri. *From letter to letter* ill. by author. Dutton, 1989. ISBN 0-525-44518-8 Subj: ABC books.

Slobodkin, Louis. *Clear the track* ill. by author. Macmillan, 1945. Subj: Family life. Imagination. Poetry, rhyme. Trains.

Colette and the princess ill. by author. Dutton, 1965. Subj: Animals – cats. Folk and fairy tales. Foreign lands – France. Noise, sounds. Royalty – princesses.

Dinny and Danny ill. by author. Macmillan, 1951. Subj: Cavemen. Character traits – helpfulness. Dinosaurs. Friendship.

Friendly animals ill. by author. Vanguard, 1944. Subj: Animals. Poetry, rhyme.

Hustle and bustle ill. by author. Macmillan, 1962. Subj: Animals – hippopotami. Behavior – fighting, arguing.

The late cuckoo ill. by author. Vanguard, 1962. Subj: Clocks, watches. Time.

Magic Michael ill. by author. Macmillan, 1944. Subj: Family life. Imagination. Magic. Self-concept.

Melvin, the moose child ill. by author. Macmillan, 1957. Subj: Animals. Animals – moose. Forest, woods.

Millions and millions and millions ill. by author. Vanguard, 1955. Subj: Character traits – individuality. Poetry, rhyme.

Moon Blossom and the golden penny ill. by author. Vanguard, 1963. Subj: Foreign lands – China. Money.

One is good, but two are better ill. by author. Vanguard, 1956. Subj: Poetry, rhyme.

Our friendly friends ill. by author. Vanguard, 1951. Subj: Animals.

The polka-dot goat ill. by author. Macmillan, 1964. Subj: Animals – goats. Foreign lands – India.

The seaweed hat ill. by author. Macmillan, 1947. Subj: Poetry, rhyme. Sea and seashore.

Thank you—you're welcome ill. by author. Vanguard, 1957. Subj: Etiquette.

Trick or treat ill. by author. Macmillan, 1959. Subj: Holidays – Halloween.

Up high and down low ill. by author. Macmillan, 1960. Subj: Animals – goats. Animals – sheep. Concepts – up and down. Poetry, rhyme.

Wide-awake owl ill. by author. Macmillan, 1958. Subj: Birds – owls. Music. Sleep. Songs.

Yasu and the strangers ill. by author. Macmillan, 1965. Subj: Behavior – lost. Foreign lands – Japan.

Slobodkina, Esphyr. *Billy, the condominium cat* ill. by author. Addison-Wesley, 1980. ISBN 0-201-09204-2 Subj: Animals – cats. Old age.

Boris and his balalaika ill. by Vladimir Bobri. Abelard-Schuman, 1964. Subj: Foreign lands – Russia.

Caps for sale ill. by author. Addison-Wesley, 1940. Subj: Animals – monkeys. Careers – peddlers. Clothing – hats. Humor. Participation.

Pezzo the peddler and the circus elephant ill. by author. Abelard-Schuman, 1967. Subj: Animals – elephants. Careers – peddlers. Circus. Clothing. Humor. Parades. Participation.

Pezzo the peddler and the thirteen silly thieves ill. by author. Abelard-Schuman, 1970. Subj: Careers – peddlers. Clothing. Crime. Humor. Participation.

Pinky and the petunias ill. by author. Abelard-Schuman, 1959. Based on a story by Tamara Schildkraut Subj: Animals – cats. Flowers.

The wonderful feast ill. by author. Lothrop, 1955. Subj: Animals. Animals – horses. Farms. Food.

Slocum, Rosalie. *Breakfast with the clowns* ill. by author. Viking, 1937. Subj: Circus. Clowns, jesters. Food.

Slote, Elizabeth. *Nelly's garden* ill. by author. Morrow, 1991. ISBN 0-688-10014-7 Subj: Dragons. Flowers. Gardens, gardening.

Slovenz-Low, Madeline. *Lion dancer: Ernie Wan's Chinese new year* (Waters, Kate)

Small, David. *Eulalie and the hopping head* ill. by author. Macmillan, 1982. Subj: Animals – foxes. Character traits – kindness. Frogs and toads.

Imogene's antlers ill. by author. Crown, 1985. Subj: Animals. Character traits – appearance.

Paper John ill. by author. Farrar, 1987. ISBN 0-374-35738-2 Subj: Behavior – misbehavior. Character traits – cleverness. Emotions – anger. Mythical creatures. Paper.

Ruby Mae has something to say ill. by author. Crown, 1992. ISBN 0-517-58249-X Subj: Handicaps. Language. Machines.

Small, Ernest see Lent, Blair

Small, Terry. *The legend of William Tell* ill. by author. Bantam, 1991. ISBN 0-553-07031-2 Subj: Character traits – bravery. Folk and fairy tales. Poetry, rhyme.

Smallman, Clare. *Outside in* ill. by Edwina Riddell. Barron's, 1986. ISBN 0-8120-5760-0 Subj: Anatomy. Format, unusual – toy and movable books.

Smalls-Hector, Irene. *Irene and the big, fine nickel* ill. by Tyrone Geter. Little, 1991. ISBN 0-316-79871-1 Subj: City. Communities, neighborhoods. Ethnic groups in the U.S. – Afro-Americans.

Jonathan and his mommy ill. by Michael Hays. Little, 1992. ISBN 0-316-79870-3 Subj: Activities – walking. City. Communities, neighborhoods. Ethnic groups in the U.S. – Afro-Americans. Family life – mothers.

Smaridge, Norah. *Peter's tent* ill. by Brinton Turkle. Viking, 1965. Subj: Friendship.

Watch out! ill. by Susan Perl. Abingdon Pr., 1965. Subj: Safety.

You know better than that ill. by Susan Perl. Abingdon Pr., 1973. Subj: Etiquette. Poetry, rhyme.

Smart, Christopher. *For I will consider my cat Jeoffry* ill. by Emily Arnold McCully. Atheneum, 1984. Subj: Animals – cats. Poetry, rhyme.

Smath, Jerry. *But no elephants* ill. by author. Parents, 1979. Subj: Animals – elephants. Pets.

Elephant goes to school ill. by author. Parents, 1984. ISBN 0-8193-1126-X Subj: Animals – elephants. School.

Mr. Digby's bad day by Jerry and Valerie Smath; ill. by authors. Simon & Schuster, 1989. ISBN 0-671-67802-7 Subj: Behavior – bad day. Umbrellas. Weather – rain.

Smath, Valerie. *Mr. Digby's bad day* (Smath, Jerry)

Smee, Nicola. *Finish the story, dad* ill. by author. Simon & Schuster, 1991. ISBN 0-671-74478-X Subj: Bedtime. Dreams. Family life – fathers.

Smith, Barry. *A child's guide to bad behavior* ill. by author. Houghton, 1991. ISBN 0-395-57435-8 Subj: Behavior – misbehavior. Etiquette. Family life.

Cumberland Road ill. by author. Houghton, 1989. ISBN 0-395-51739-7 Subj: Behavior – losing things. Communities, neighborhoods.

The first voyage of Christopher Columbus ill. by author. Viking, 1992. ISBN 0-670-84051-3 Subj: Activities – traveling. Boats, ships. U.S. history.

Minnie and Ginger ill. by author. Crown, 1991. ISBN 0-517-58253-8 Subj: Family life. Foreign lands – England. Old age. Weddings.

Tom and Annie go shopping ill. by author. Houghton, 1989. ISBN 0-395-51738-9 Subj: Shopping.

Smith, Bożena. *The enchanted book* (Porazińska, Janina)

Smith, Cara Lockhart. *Twenty-six rabbits run riot* ill. by author. Little, 1990. ISBN 0-316-80185-2 Subj: Animals – rabbits. Behavior – lost. Behavior – misbehavior.

Smith, Catriona Mary. *The long dive* (Smith, Raymond Kenneth)

The long slide (Smith, Raymond Kenneth)

Smith, Donald. *Farm numbers 1, 2, 3* ill. by author. Abingdon Pr., 1970. Subj: Counting, numbers. Farms.

Who's wearing my baseball cap? ill. by author. Dial Pr., 1987. ISBN 0-8037-0396-1 Subj: Animals. Clothing – hats. Format, unusual – board books. Problem solving.

Who's wearing my bow tie? ill. by author. Dial Pr., 1987. ISBN 0-8037-0395-3 Subj: Animals. Clothing. Format, unusual – board books. Problem solving.

Who's wearing my sneakers? ill. by author. Dial Pr., 1987. ISBN 0-8037-0398-8 Subj: Animals. Clothing – shoes. Format, unusual – board books. Problem solving.

Who's wearing my sunglasses? ill. by author. Dial Pr., 1987. ISBN 0-8037-0399-6 Subj: Animals. Format, unusual – board books. Glasses. Problem solving.

Smith, Elmer Boyd. *The story of Noah's ark* ill. by author. Houghton, 1904. Subj: Religion – Noah.

Smith, Henry Lee. *Frog fun* (Stratemeyer, Clara Georgeanna)

Pepper (Stratemeyer, Clara Georgeanna)

Tuggy (Stratemeyer, Clara Georgeanna)

Smith, Janice Lee. *The monster in the third dresser drawer and other stories about Adam Joshua* ill. by Dick Gackenbach. Harper, 1981. Subj: Behavior – misbehavior. Emotions – fear. Monsters.

Smith, Jean Shannon. *Scooter and the magic star* (Gardner, Mercedes)

Smith, Jim. *The frog band and Durrington Dormouse* ill. by author. Little, 1977. Subj: Animals – mice. Frogs and toads.

The frog band and the onion seller ill. by author. Little, 1976. Subj: Animals. Frogs and toads. Humor. Problem solving.

The frog band and the owlnapper ill. by author. Little, 1981. Subj: Animals. Birds – owls. Frogs and toads. Humor.

Nimbus the explorer ill. by author. Little, 1981. ISBN 0-316-80168-2 Subj: Animals. Dinosaurs. Imagination. Jungle.

Smith, Lane. *The big pets* ill. by author. Viking, 1991. ISBN 0-670-83378-9 Subj: Animals. Dreams. Pets.

Flying Jake ill. by author. Macmillan, 1988. ISBN 0-02-785830-8 Subj: Activities – flying. Birds. Wordless.

Glasses...who needs 'em? ill. by author. Viking, 1991. ISBN 0-670-84160-9 Subj: Glasses. Senses – seeing.

Smith, Lucia B. *A special kind of sister* ill. by Chuck Hall. Holt, 1979. Subj: Family life. Handicaps. Sibling rivalry.

Smith, Maggie (Margaret C.). *My grandma's chair* ill. by author. Lothrop, 1992. ISBN 0-688-10664-1 Subj: Family life – grandmothers. Furniture – chairs. Imagination.

Noly Poly Rabbit Tail and me ill. by author. Lothrop, 1990. ISBN 0-688-09571-2 Subj: Friendship. Toys – dolls.

There's a witch under the stairs ill. by author. Lothrop, 1991. ISBN 0-688-09885-1 Subj: Emotions – fear. Imagination. Witches.

Smith, Mary. *Long ago elf* by Mary and Robert Alan Smith; ill. by authors. Follett, 1968. Subj: Elves and little people.

Smith, Mavis. *Circles* ill. by author. Little, 1991. ISBN 1-55782-366-9 Subj: Concepts – shape. Concepts – size.

Fred, is that you? ill. by author. Little, 1992. ISBN 0-316-80241-7 Subj: Animals. Birds – ducks. Format, unusual – toy and movable books. Poetry, rhyme.

A snake mistake ill. by author. HarperCollins, 1991. ISBN 0-06-026909-X Subj: Behavior – trickery. Eggs. Farms. Reptiles – snakes.

Smith, Peter. *Jenny's baby brother* ill. by Bob Graham. Viking, 1984. ISBN 0-670-40636-8 Subj: Babies. Family life. Sibling rivalry.

Smith, Raymond Kenneth. *The long dive* by Raymond Kenneth and Catriona Mary Smith; ill. by authors. Atheneum, 1978. Subj: Sea and seashore. Toys.

The long slide by Raymond Kenneth and Catriona Mary Smith; ill. by authors. Atheneum, 1977. Subj: Toys.

Smith, Robert Alan. *Long ago elf* (Smith, Mary)

Smith, Robert Paul. *Jack Mack* ill. by Erik Blegvad. Coward, 1960. Subj: Humor. Tongue twisters.

Nothingatall, nothingatall, nothingatall ill. by Alan E. Cober. Harper, 1965. Subj: Bedtime.

When I am big ill. by Lillian Hoban. Harper, 1965. Subj: Behavior – growing up.

Smith, Roger. *The empty island* ill. by author. Interlink, 1991. ISBN 0-940793-69-5 Subj: Islands.

How the animals saved the ark and put two and two together ill. by author. Simon & Schuster, 1989. ISBN 0-671-66560-X Subj: Animals. Religion – Noah.

Smith, Theresa Kalab. *The fog is secret* ill. by author. Prentice-Hall, 1966. Subj: Sea and seashore. Weather – fog.

Smith, Wendy. *The lonely, only mouse* ill. by author. Viking, 1986. ISBN 0-670-81251-X Subj: Animals – mice. Behavior – sharing. Emotions – loneliness. Family life – only child.

Say hello, Tilly ill. by author. Bantam, 1991. ISBN 0-553-07160-2 Subj: Animals – bears. Behavior – shyness. Birthdays.

Twice mice ill. by author. Carolrhoda, 1989. ISBN 0-87614-371-0 Subj: Animals – mice. Emotions. Family life. Sibling rivalry.

Smith, William Jay. *Birds and beasts* ill. by Jacques Hnizdovsky. Godine, 1990. ISBN 0-87923-865-8 Subj: Animals. Birds. Poetry, rhyme.

Children of the forest (Beskow, Elsa Maartman)

Puptents and pebbles: nonsense ABC ill. by Juliet Kepes. Little, 1959. Subj: ABC books. Humor. Poetry, rhyme.

The telephone (Chukovsky, Korney)

Smith-Moore, J. J. *Sally Small* ill. by author. Price Stern Sloan, 1989. ISBN 0-8431-2360-5 Subj: Concepts – shape. Concepts – size. Dreams. Poetry, rhyme.

Smucker, Anna Egan. *No star nights* ill. by Steve Johnson. Knopf, 1989. ISBN 0-394-99925-8 Subj: City. Machines.

Smyth, Gwenda. *A pet for Mrs. Arbuckle* ill. by Ann James. Crown, 1981. ISBN 0-517-55434-8 Subj: Activities – traveling. Animals – cats. Pets.

Snape, Charles. *Frog odyssey* (Snape, Juliet)

Snape, Juliet. *Frog odyssey* by Juliet and Charles Snape; ill. by authors. Simon & Schuster, 1992. ISBN 0-671-74741-X Subj: Ecology. Frogs and toads. Moving.

Sneed, Brad. *Lucky Russell* ill. by author. Putnam's, 1992. ISBN 0-399-22329-0 Subj: Animals. Animals – cats. Farms. Pets.

Snell, Nigel. *A bird in hand...: a child's guide to sayings* ill. by author. David & Charles, 1987. ISBN 0-241-11815-8 Subj: Language.

Sniff, Mr. *see* Abisch, Roz

Snoopy on wheels ill. by Charles M. Schulz. Random House, 1983. Subj: Animals – dogs. Birds. Toys. Wheels.

Snow, Alan. *The monster book of ABC sounds* ill. by author. Dial, 1991. ISBN 0-8037-0935-8 Subj: ABC books. Animals – rats. Monsters. Noise, sounds. Poetry, rhyme.

My first atlas ill. by author. Troll, 1992. ISBN 0-8167-2517-9 Subj: World.

My first dictionary ill. by author. Troll, 1992. ISBN 0-8167-2515-2 Subj: Language.

Snow, Pegeen. *Mrs. Periwinkle's groceries* ill. by Jerry Warshaw. Children's Pr., 1981. Subj: Character traits – helpfulness. Cumulative tales. Old age.

A pet for Pat ill. by Tom Dunnington. Children's Pr., 1984. Subj: Pets. Poetry, rhyme.

Snyder, Anne. *The old man and the mule* ill. by Mila Lazarevich. Holt, 1978. Subj: Animals – mules. Character traits – meanness.

Snyder, Dianne. *The boy of the three-year nap* ill. by Allen Say. Houghton, 1988. ISBN 0-395-44090-4 Subj: Behavior – trickery. Caldecott award honor book. Character traits – laziness. Folk and fairy tales.

Snyder, Dick. *One day at the zoo* photos. by author. Scribner's, 1960. Subj: Animals. Animals – koala bears. Zoos.

Talk to me tiger photos. by author; foreword by George H. Pournelle. Golden Gate, 1965. Subj: Animals. Zoos.

Snyder, Zilpha Keatley. *The changing maze* ill. by Charles Mikolaycak. Macmillan, 1985. ISBN 0-02-785900-2 Subj: Animals – sheep. Folk and fairy tales. Magic. Wizards.

Come on, Patsy ill. by Margot Zemach. Atheneum, 1982. Subj: Activities – playing. Behavior – growing up. Poetry, rhyme.

Sobol, Harriet Langsam. *A book of vegetables* photos. by Patricia Agre. Dodd, 1984. ISBN 0-396-08450-8 Subj: Food. Gardens, gardening.

Clowns photos. by Patricia Agre. Coward, 1982. Subj: Clowns, jesters.

Jeff's hospital book photos. by Patricia Agre. Walck, 1975. Subj: Hospitals.

We don't look like our mom and dad photos. by Patricia Agre. Coward, 1984. Subj: Adoption. Ethnic groups in the U.S. Family life.

Solbert, Ronni (Romaine G.). *Emily Emerson's moon* (Merrill, Jean)

Solomon, Chuck. *Moving up* photos. by author. Crown, 1989. ISBN 0-517-57286-9 Subj: Behavior – growing up. School.

Solomon, Joan. *A present for Mum* photos. by Joan and Ryan Solomon. Hamish Hamilton, 1982. Subj: Foreign lands – England. Shopping. Stores.

Solotareff, Grégoire. *Don't call me little bunny* ill. by author. Farrar, 1988. ISBN 0-374-35012-4 Subj: Animals – rabbits. Behavior – misbehavior. Crime. Prisons.

Never trust an ogre ill. by author. Greenwillow, 1988. ISBN 0-688-07741-2 Subj: Animals. Behavior – greed. Mythical creatures.

The ogre and the frog king ill. by author. Greenwillow, 1988. ISBN 0-688-07079-5 Subj: Frogs and toads. Monsters.

Somme, Lauritz. *The penguin family book* by Lauritz Somme and Sybille Kalas; tr. by Patricia Crampton; ill. with photos. Picture Book Studio, 1988. ISBN 0-88708-057-X Subj: Birds – penguins.

Sommers, Tish. *Bert and the broken teapot* ill. by Diane Dawson Hearn. Childrens Pr., 1985. ISBN 0-307-62114-6 Subj: Behavior – carelessness. Friendship.

Sonberg, Lynn. *A horse named Paris* ill. by Ken Robbins. Bradbury Pr., 1986. ISBN 0-02-786260-7 Subj: Animals – horses.

Sondergaard, Arensa. *Biddy and the ducks* by Arensa Sondergaard and Mary M. Reed; ill. by Doris Henderson and Marion Henderson. Heath, 1941. Subj: Birds – chickens. Birds – ducks.

Sondheimer, Ilse. *The boy who could make his mother stop yelling* ill. by Dee deRosa. Rainbow Pr., 1982. Subj: Behavior – bad day. Family life – mothers.

The magic of Pomme ill. by Dee deRosa. Rainbow, 1990. ISBN 0-943156-02-5 Subj: Food. Magic. Problem solving.

The song of the Three Holy Children ill. by Pauline Baynes. Holt, 1986. The text of this edition is taken from The Book of Common Prayer, 1662 ISBN 0-8050-0134-4 Subj: Nature. Religion. Songs.

Sonneborn, Ruth A. *Friday night is papa night* ill. by Emily Arnold McCully. Viking, 1970. Subj: City. Ethnic groups in the U.S. – Puerto Rican-Americans. Family life – fathers. Poverty.

I love Gram ill. by Leo Carty. Viking, 1971. Subj: City. Family life – grandmothers. Hospitals. Illness. Old age.

Lollipop's party ill. by Brinton Turkle. Viking, 1967. Subj: City. Emotions – loneliness. Ethnic groups in the U.S. – Puerto Rican-Americans.

Seven in a bed ill. by Don Freeman. Viking, 1968. Subj: Ethnic groups in the U.S. – Puerto Rican-Americans. Family life. Poverty. Sleep.

Sonnenschein, Harriet. *Harold's runaway nose* ill. by Jürg Obrist. Simon & Schuster, 1989. ISBN 0-671-66912-5 Subj: Animals – rabbits. Behavior – losing things. Illness.

Sopko, Eugen. *Townsfolk and countryfolk* ill. by author. Faber, 1982. Subj: City. Country. Foreign lands – Europe.

Sorine, Stephanie Riva. *Our ballet class* photos. by Daniel S. Sorine. Knopf, 1981. Subj: Activities – dancing.

Southey, Robert. *The cataract of Lodore* ill. by Mordicai Gerstein. Dial, 1991. ISBN 0-8037-1026-7 Subj: Foreign lands – England. Poetry, rhyme. Water.

Sowden, Henry. *The grand old Duke of York* photos. by author. Trafalgar Square, 1989. ISBN 0-575-04081-5 Subj: Poetry, rhyme. Toys – soldiers.

Soya, Kiyoshi. *A house of leaves* ill. by Akiko Hayashi. Putnam's, 1987. ISBN 0-399-21422-4 Subj: Insects. Weather – rain.

Spagnoli, Cathy. *Judge Rabbit and the tree spirit* (Wall, Lina Mao)

Nine-in-one Grr! Grr! (Xiong, Blia)

Spang, Günter. *Clelia and the little mermaid* ill. by Pepperl Ott. Abelard-Schuman, 1967. Translation of Clelia und die kleine Wassernixe Subj: Emotions – loneliness. Foreign lands – Germany. Friendship. Mythical creatures – mermaids.

Spangenburg, Judith Dunn see Dunn, Judy

Spanner, Helmut. *I am a little cat* tr. from German by Robert Kimber; ill. by author. Barron's, 1983. Subj: Animals – cats. Format, unusual – board books.

Speare, Jean. *A candle for Christmas* ill. by Ann Blades. Macmillan, 1987. ISBN 0-689-50417-9 Subj: Foreign lands – Canada. Holidays – Christmas. Indians of North America.

Spencer, Zane. *Bright Fawn and me* (Leech, Jay)

Spiegel, Doris. *Danny and Company 92* ill. by author. Coward, 1945. Subj: Careers – firefighters. Fire.

Spier, Peter. *Bill's service station* ill. by author. Doubleday, 1981. Subj: Automobiles. Format, unusual – board books.

The Book of Jonah (Bible Old Testament. $k Jonah.)

Bored—nothing to do! ill. by author. Doubleday, 1978. Subj: Airplanes, airports. Behavior – boredom. Humor.

Crash! bang! boom! ill. by author. Doubleday, 1972. Subj: Noise, sounds. Parades. Participation.

Dreams ill. by author. Doubleday, 1986. ISBN 0-385-19336-X Subj: Dreams. Sky. Weather – clouds. Wordless.

The Erie Canal ill. by author. Doubleday, 1970. Subj: Folk and fairy tales. Music. Songs. U.S. history.

Fast-slow, high-low: a book of opposites ill. by author. Doubleday, 1972. Subj: Concepts – opposites. Concepts – speed.

Firehouse ill. by author. Doubleday, 1981. Subj: Careers – firefighters. Format, unusual – board books.

Food market ill. by author. Doubleday, 1981. Subj: Food. Format, unusual – board books. Shopping. Stores.

Gobble, growl, grunt ill. by author. Doubleday, 1971. Subj: Animals. Noise, sounds. Participation.

The legend of New Amsterdam ill. by author. Doubleday, 1979. Subj: Folk and fairy tales. U.S. history.

Little cats ill. by author. Doubleday, 1984. Subj: Animals – cats. Format, unusual – board books.

Little dogs ill. by author. Doubleday, 1984. Subj: Animals – dogs. Format, unusual – board books.

Little ducks ill. by author. Doubleday, 1984. Subj: Birds – ducks. Format, unusual – board books.

Little rabbits ill. by author. Doubleday, 1984. Subj: Animals – rabbits. Format, unusual – board books.

My school ill. by author. Doubleday, 1981. Subj: Format, unusual – board books. School.

Noah's ark ill. by author. Doubleday, 1977. Includes P. Spier's translation of The flood, by Jacobus Revius Subj: Boats, ships. Caldecott award book. Poetry, rhyme. Religion – Noah. Wordless.

Oh, were they ever happy! ill. by author. Double-day, 1978. Subj: Activities – painting. Concepts – color. Humor.

People ill. by author. Doubleday, 1980. Subj: World.

The pet store ill. by author. Doubleday, 1981. Subj: Animals. Format, unusual – board books. Pets. Stores.

Peter Spier's Christmas! ill. by author. Doubleday, 1983. Subj: Holidays – Christmas.

Peter Spier's rain ill. by author. Doubleday, 1982. Subj: Weather – rain. Wordless.

The toy shop ill. by author. Doubleday, 1981. Subj: Format, unusual – board books. Stores. Toys.

We the people: the Constitution of the United States of America ill. by author. Doubleday, 1987. ISBN 0-385-23789-8 Subj: U.S. history.

Spilka, Arnold. *Dippy dos and don'ts* (Sage, Michael)

A lion I can do without ill. by author. Walck, 1964. Subj: Humor. Poetry, rhyme.

Little birds don't cry ill. by author. Viking, 1965. Subj: Animals. Poetry, rhyme.

A rumbudgin of nonsense ill. by author. Scribner's, 1970. Subj: Humor. Poetry, rhyme.

Spinelli, Eileen. *Somebody loves you, Mr. Hatch* ill. by Paul Yalowitz. Bradbury Pr., 1992. ISBN 0-02-786015-9 Subj: Behavior – needing someone. Careers – mail carriers. Communities, neighborhoods. Holidays – Valentine's Day.

Thanksgiving at Tappletons' ill. by Maryann Cocca-Leffler. Addison-Wesley, 1982. Subj: Behavior – sharing. Family life. Holidays – Thanksgiving. Humor.

Spinner, Stephanie. *The adventures of Pinocchio* (Collodi, Carlo)

The pirates of Tarnoonga (Weiss, Ellen)

Spohn, David. *Nate's treasure* ill. by author. Lothrop, 1991. ISBN 0-688-10091-0 Subj: Anatomy – skeletons. Animals. Death. Seasons.

Winter wood ill. by author. Lothrop, 1991. ISBN 0-688-10094-5 Subj: Family life – fathers. Forest, woods. Seasons – winter.

Spohn, Kate. *Clementine's winter wardrobe* ill. by author. Watts, 1989. ISBN 0-531-08441-8 Subj: Animals – cats. Clothing.

Introducing Fanny. ill. by author. Watts, 1991. ISBN 0-531-08520-1 Subj: Food. Friendship.

Ruth's bake shop ill. by author. Watts, 1990. ISBN 0-531-08489-2 Subj: Activities – cooking. Octopuses.

Spriggs, Ruth. *The fables of Æsop* (Æsop)

Frank Baber's Mother Goose (Mother Goose)

Springer, Sally. *Let's make latkes* ill. by author. Kar-Ben Copies, 1991. ISBN 0-929371-58-5 Subj: Food. Format, unusual – board books. Jewish culture. Religion.

Springstubb, Tricia. *The magic guinea pig* ill. by Bari Weissman. Morrow, 1982. Subj: Behavior – mistakes. Witches.

Spurr, Elizabeth. *The biggest birthday cake in the world* ill. by Rosanne Litzinger. Harcourt, 1991. ISBN 0-15-207150-4 Subj: Behavior – sharing. Birthdays. Food. Parties.

Mrs. Minetta's car pool ill. by Blanche Sims. Atheneum, 1985. ISBN 0-689-31103-6 Subj: Activities – flying. Automobiles. School.

The squire's bride: *a Norwegian folk tale* orig. told by P. C. Asbjørnsen; ill. by Marcia Sewall. Atheneum, 1975. Subj: Folk and fairy tales. Foreign lands – Norway. Weddings.

S-Ringi, Kjell *see* Ringi, Kjell (Arne Sorensen)

Stadler, John. *Animal cafe* ill. by author. Bradbury Pr., 1980. Subj: Animals. Behavior – greed. Food.

The ballad of Wilbur and the moose ill. by author. Warner, 1990. ISBN 1-55782-047-3 Subj: Animals – pigs. Animals – moose. Cowboys.

Cat is back at bat ill. by author. Dutton, 1991. ISBN 0-525-44762-8 Subj: Animals. Poetry, rhyme.

Gorman and the treasure chest ill. by author. Bradbury Pr., 1984. Subj: Animals. Behavior – sharing.

Hector, the accordion-nosed dog ill. by author. Macmillan, 1987. ISBN 0-02-786680-7 Subj: Animals – dogs. Music.

Hooray for snail! ill. by author. Crowell, 1984. ISBN 0-06-443075-8 Subj: Animals – snails. Sports – baseball.

Snail saves the day ill. by author. Crowell, 1985. ISBN 0-690-04469-0 Subj: Animals – snails. Sports – football.

Three cheers for hippo! ill. by author. Crowell, 1987. ISBN 0-690-04670-7 Subj: Activities – flying. Animals – hippopotami.

Stafford, Kay. *Ling Tang and the lucky cricket* ill. by Louise Zibold. McGraw-Hill, 1944. Subj: Character traits – luck. Foreign lands – China.

Stafford, William. *The animal that drank up sound* ill. by Debra Frasier. Harcourt, 1992. ISBN 0-15-203563-X Subj: Animals. Insects – crickets. Noise, sounds. Seasons – spring. Seasons – winter.

Stage, Mads. *The greedy blackbird* ill. by author. John Godon Burke, 1981. Subj: Behavior – greed. Behavior – sharing. Birds.

The lonely squirrel ill. by author. John Godon Burke, 1980. Subj: Animals – squirrels. Emotions – loneliness.

Staines, Bill. *All God's critters got a place in the choir* ill. by Margot Zemach. Dutton, 1989. ISBN 0-525-44469-6 Subj: Animals. Farms. Music. Songs.

Stalder, Valerie. *Even the devil is afraid of a shrew: a folktale of Lapland* adapt. by Ray Brocket; ill. by Richard Eric Brown. Addison-Wesley, 1972. Subj: Behavior – nagging. Devil. Folk and fairy tales. Foreign lands – Lapland.

Stamaty, Mark Alan. *Minnie Maloney and Macaroni* ill. by author. Dial Pr., 1976. Subj: Food. Humor.

Stamper, Judith. *What's it like to be a dentist?* ill. by Dana Gustafson. Troll, 1989. ISBN 0-8167-1799-0 Subj: Careers – dentists. Teeth.

What's it like to be a veterinarian ill. by Marcy Dunn Ramsey. Troll, 1989. ISBN 0-8167-1817-2 Subj: Animals. Careers – veterinarians.

Standiford, Natalie. *Dollhouse mouse* ill. by Denise Fleming. Random House, 1989. ISBN 0-394-99935-5 Subj: Animals – mice. Sky.

Standon, Anna. *Little duck lost* by Anna and Edward Cyril Standon; ill. by Edward Cyril Standon. Delacorte Pr., 1965. Subj: Behavior – lost. Birds – ducks. Eggs. Family life – mothers.

The singing rhinoceros ill. by Edward Cyril Standon. Coward, 1963. Subj: Animals – rhinoceros.

Three little cats by Anna and Edward Cyril Standon; ill. by authors. Delacorte Pr., 1964. ISBN 0-87459-000-3 Subj: Activities – playing. Animals – cats. Behavior – misbehavior. Foreign languages.

Standon, Edward Cyril. *Little duck lost* (Standon, Anna)

Three little cats (Standon, Anna)

Stanek, Muriel. *All alone after school* ill. by Ruth Rosner. Albert Whitman, 1985. ISBN 0-8075-0278-2 Subj: Character traits – bravery. Emotions – loneliness. Family life – mothers.

Left, right, left, right! ill. by Lucy Hawkinson. Albert Whitman, 1969. Subj: Concepts – left and right. Emotions – embarrassment.

My little foster sister ill. by Judith Cheng. Albert Whitman, 1981. Subj: Adoption. Behavior – sharing. Sibling rivalry.

One, two, three for fun ill. by Seymour Fleishman. Albert Whitman, 1967. Subj: Counting, numbers. Ethnic groups in the U.S.

Stang, Judit *see* Varga, Judy

Stanley, Diane. *Birdsong lullaby* ill. by author. Morrow, 1985. ISBN 0-688-05805-1 Subj: Birds. Imagination. Lullabies. Night. Sleep.

Captain Whiz-Bang ill. by author. Morrow, 1987. ISBN 0-688-06227-X Subj: Animals – cats. Behavior – growing up.

The conversation club ill. by author. Macmillan, 1983. Subj: Animals – mice. Clubs, gangs. Communication. Noise, sounds.

A country tale ill. by author. Four Winds Pr., 1985. ISBN 0-02-786780-3 Subj: Animals – cats. Behavior – seeking better things. City. Country. Friendship.

The good-luck pencil ill. by Bruce Degen. Macmillan, 1986. ISBN 0-02-786800-1 Subj: Character traits – luck. Magic. School.

Siegfried ill. by John Sandford. Bantam, 1991. ISBN 0-553-07022-3 Subj: Animals – cats. Clocks, watches. Emotions – envy, jealousy.

Stanley, John. *It's nice to be little* ill. by Jean Tamburine. Rand McNally, 1965. Subj: Character traits – smallness.

Stanley, Sanna. *The rains are coming* ill. by author. Greenwillow, 1993. ISBN 0-688-10949-7 Subj: Weather – rain.

Stanovich, Betty Jo. *Big boy, little boy* ill. by Virginia Wright-Frierson. Lothrop, 1984. Subj: Family life – grandmothers.

Hedgehog adventures ill. by Chris L. Demarest. Lothrop, 1983. Subj: Animals – groundhogs. Animals – hedgehogs. Character traits – loyalty.

Stan-Padilla, Viento. *Dream Feather* ill. by author. Atheneum, 1980. Subj: Folk and fairy tales. Indians of North America. Religion.

Stansfield, Ian. *The legend of the whale* ill. by author. Godine, 1986. ISBN 0-87923-628-0 Subj: Animals – whales. Folk and fairy tales.

Stanton, Elizabeth. *Sometimes I like to cry* by Elizabeth and Henry Stanton; ill. by Richard Leyden. Albert Whitman, 1978. Subj: Emotions.

The very messy room by Elizabeth and Henry Stanton; ill. by Richard Leyden. Albert Whitman, 1978. Subj: Character traits – cleanliness. Family life.

Stanton, Henry. *Sometimes I like to cry* (Stanton, Elizabeth)

The very messy room (Stanton, Elizabeth)

Stapler, Sarah. *Cordellia, dance!* ill. by author. Dial, 1990. ISBN 0-8037-0793-2 Subj: Activities – dancing. Character traits – being different. Reptiles – alligators, crocodiles.

Spruce the moose cuts loose ill. by author. Putnam's, 1992. ISBN 0-399-21861-0 Subj: Animals – moose. Birthdays. Parties.

Trilby's trumpet ill. by author. Harper, 1988. ISBN 0-06-025827-6 Subj: Animals – bears. Format, unusual – toy and movable books. Music. Noise, sounds. Sibling rivalry.

Starbird, Kaye. *The covered bridge house and other poems* ill. by Jim Arnosky. Four Winds Pr., 1979. Subj: Poetry, rhyme.

Starret, William *see* McClintock, Marshall

Staunton, Ted. *Taking care of Crumley* ill. by Tina Holdcroft. Kids Can Pr., 1984. ISBN 0-919964-75-3 Subj: Behavior – bullying. School.

Steadman, Ralph. *The bridge* ill. by author. Subj: Behavior – fighting, arguing. Bridges. Friendship.

The little red computer ill. by author. McGraw-Hill, 1969. Subj: Computers. Space and space ships.

Stecher, Miriam B. *Daddy and Ben together* photos. by Alice Kandell. Lothrop, 1981. Subj: Family life – fathers.

Max, the music-maker by Miriam B. Stecher and Alice Kandell; photos. by Alice Kandell. Lothrop, 1980. Subj: Music. Science.

Steel, Barry. *Greek cities* ill. by Bernard Long. Watts, 1990. ISBN 0-531-18326-2 Subj: City. Foreign lands – Greece.

Steel, Danielle. *Martha's best friend* ill. by Jacqueline Rogers. Delacorte Pr., 1989. ISBN 0-385-29801-3 Subj: Friendship.

Martha's new daddy ill. by Jacqueline Rogers. Delacorte Pr., 1989. ISBN 0-385-29799-8 Subj: Divorce. Family life. Family life – step families.

Martha's new school ill. by Jacqueline Rogers. Delacorte Pr., 1989. ISBN 0-385-29800-5 Subj: Friendship. Moving. School.

Max and the baby sitter ill. by Jacqueline Rogers. Delacorte Pr., 1989. ISBN 0-385-29796-3 Subj: Activities – baby-sitting. Animals – cats. Emotions – fear. Family life. Problem solving.

Max's daddy goes to the hospital ill. by Jacqueline Rogers. Delacorte Pr., 1989. ISBN 0-385-29797-1 Subj: Careers – firefighters. Family life – fathers. Hospitals. Illness.

Max's new baby ill. by Jacqueline Rogers. Delacorte Pr., 1989. ISBN 0-385-29798-X Subj: Babies. Family life. Sibling rivalry. Twins.

Steele, Mary Quintard Govan *see* Gage, Wilson

Steffa, Tim. *Mister King* (Siekkinen, Raija)

The nighttime book (Kunnas, Mauri)

One spooky night and other scary stories (Kunnas, Mauri)

Twelve gifts for Santa Claus (Kunnas, Mauri)

Steger, Hans-Ulrich. *Traveling to Tripiti* tr. by Elizabeth D. Crawford; ill. by author. Harcourt, 1967. Subj: Activities – traveling. Cumulative tales. Toys. Toys – teddy bears.

Stehr, Frédéric. *Quack-quack* ill. by author. Farrar, 1987. ISBN 0-374-36161-4 Subj: Animals. Behavior – needing someone. Birds – ducks. Family life – mothers.

Steig, Jeanne. *Consider the lemming* ill. by William Steig. Farrar, 1988. ISBN 0-374-31536-1 Subj: Animals – lemmings. Poetry, rhyme.

Steig, William. *Abel's Island* ill. by author. Farrar, 1976. ISBN 0-374-30010-0 Subj: Animals – mice. Islands.

The amazing bone ill. by author. Farrar, 1976. Subj: Animals – pigs. Caldecott award honor book. Magic.

The bad speller ill. by author. Windmill Books, 1970. Subj: Games. Language.

Brave Irene ill. by author. Farrar, 1986. ISBN 0-374-30947-7 Subj: Character traits – bravery. Character traits – perseverance. Seasons – winter. Weather – snow. Weather – storms.

Caleb and Kate ill. by author. Farrar, 1977. Subj: Animals – dogs. Magic. Witches.

Doctor De Soto ill. by author. Farrar, 1982. Subj: Animals – foxes. Animals – mice. Character traits – cleverness.

Doctor De Soto goes to Africa ill. by author. HarperCollins, 1992. ISBN 0-06-205003-6 Subj: Animals – elephants. Animals – mice. Careers – dentists. Foreign lands – Africa.

An eye for elephants ill. by author. Windmill Books, 1970. Subj: Animals – elephants. Poetry, rhyme.

Farmer Palmer's wagon ride ill. by author. Farrar, 1974. Subj: Animals – donkeys. Animals – pigs. Humor.

Gorky rises ill. by author. Farrar, 1980. Subj: Frogs and toads. Magic.

Roland, the minstrel pig ill. by author. Windmill Books, 1968. Subj: Animals – foxes. Animals – pigs. Music. Royalty.

Rotten island ill. by author Rev. ed. of The bad island issued in 1969. Godine, 1984. Subj: Flowers. Islands. Monsters.

Solomon the rusty nail ill. by author. Farrar, 1985. ISBN 0-374-37131-8 Subj: Animals – cats. Animals – rabbits. Behavior – trickery. Magic.

Spinky sulks ill. by author. Farrar, 1988. ISBN 0-374-38321-9 Subj: Character traits – stubbornness. Emotions – happiness. Family life.

Sylvester and the magic pebble ill. by author. Windmill Books, 1969. Subj: Animals. Animals – donkeys. Caldecott award book. Family life. Magic.

Tiffky Doofky ill. by author. Farrar, 1987. ISBN 0-374-37542-9 Subj: Animals – dogs. Careers – garbage collectors. Emotions – love. Magic.

Yellow and pink ill. by author. Farrar, 1984. Subj: Toys – dolls.

The Zabajaba Jungle ill. by author. Farrar, 1987. ISBN 0-374-38790-7 Subj: Dreams. Jungle.

Stein, Sara Bonnett. *About dying: an open family book for parents and children together* by Sara

Bonnett Stein, in cooperation with Gilbert W. Kliman [et al.]; photos. by Dick Frank; graphic design by Michael Goldberg. Walker, 1974. Subj: Death.

About handicaps: an open family book for parents and children together by Sara Bonnett Stein, in cooperation with Gilbert W. Kliman [et al.]; photos. by Dick Frank; graphic design by Michael Goldberg. Walker, 1974. Subj: Handicaps.

The adopted one: an open family book for parents and children together Thomas R. Holman, consultant; photos. by Erika Stone. Walker, 1979. Subj: Adoption. Family life.

Cat ill. by Manuel Garcia. Harcourt, 1985. Subj: Animals – cats. Science.

A child goes to school photos. by Don Connors. Doubleday, 1978. Subj: School.

A hospital story: an open family book for parents and children together photos. by Doris Pinney; graphic design by Michel Goldberg. Walker, 1974. Subj: Careers – doctors. Careers – nurses. Hospitals. Illness.

Mouse ill. by Manuel Garcia. Harcourt, 1985. Subj: Animals – mice. Science.

On divorce: an open family book for parents and children together Thomas R. Holman, consultant; photos. by Erika Stone. Walker, 1979. Subj: Divorce. Family life.

That new baby: an open family book for parents and children together by Sara Bonnett Stein, in cooperation with Gilbert W. Kliman [et al.]; photos by Dick Frank; graphic design by Michael Goldberg. Walker, 1974. Subj: Babies. Family life.

Steiner, Barbara (Annette). *But not Stanleigh* photos. by George and Ruth Cloven. Children's Pr., 1980. Subj: Animals – raccoons.

The whale brother ill. by Gretchen Will Mayo. Walker, 1988. ISBN 0-8027-6805-9 Subj: Art. Animals – whales. Eskimos. Sea and seashore.

Steiner, Charlotte. *Birthdays are for everyone* ill. by author. Doubleday, 1964. Subj: Birthdays.

Charlotte Steiner's ABC ill. by author. Watts, 1946. Subj: ABC books.

The climbing book by Charlotte Steiner and Mary Burlingham; ill. by Charlotte Steiner. Vanguard, 1943. Subj: Format, unusual. Holidays – Christmas.

Daddy comes home ill. by author. Doubleday, 1944. Subj: Family life. Family life – fathers.

Five little finger playmates ill. by author. Grosset, 1951. Subj: Counting, numbers. Games. Participation.

A friend is "Amie" ill. by author. Knopf, 1956. Subj: Foreign languages. Friendship.

Kiki and Muffy ill. by author. Doubleday, 1943. Subj: Animals – cats. Family life – grandmothers.

Kiki is an actress ill. by author. Doubleday, 1958. Subj: Theater.

Kiki's play house ill. by author. Doubleday, 1962. Subj: Activities – playing.

Listen to my seashell ill. by author. Knopf, 1959. Subj: Noise, sounds. Sea and seashore.

Look what Tracy found ill. by author. Knopf, 1972. Subj: Activities – playing. Imagination.

Lulu ill. by author. Doubleday, 1939. Subj: Animals – dogs. Imagination – imaginary friends.

My bunny feels soft ill. by author. Knopf, 1958. Subj: Animals – rabbits.

My slippers are red ill. by author. Knopf, 1958. Subj: Concepts – color.

Pete and Peter ill. by author. Doubleday, 1941. Subj: Animals – dogs. Sports – hunting.

Pete's puppets ill. by author. Doubleday, 1952. Subj: Puppets.

Polka Dot ill. by author. Doubleday, 1947. Subj: Pets.

Red Ridinghood's little lamb ill. by author. Knopf, 1964. Subj: Animals – sheep. Elves and little people. Games.

The sleepy quilt ill. by author. Doubleday, 1947. Subj: Bedtime. Quilts.

What's the hurry, Harry? ill. by author. Lothrop, 1968. Subj: Behavior – hurrying. Character traits – patience.

Steiner, Jörg. *The bear who wanted to be a bear* from an idea by Frank Tashlin; ill. by Jörg Müller. Atheneum, 1977. Subj: Animals – bears. Progress. Stores.

Rabbit Island ill. by Jörg Müller. Harcourt, 1978. Subj: Animals – rabbits. Character traits – freedom.

Steinmetz, Leon. *Clocks in the woods* ill. by author. Harper, 1979. Subj: Animals. Clocks, watches. Time.

Stemp, Robin. *Guy and the flowering plum tree* ill. by Carolyn Dinan. Atheneum, 1981. Subj: Imagination. Trees.

Stemple, Adam. *The lap-time song and play book* (Yolen, Jane)

Stephens, Karen. *Jumping* ill. by George Wiggins. Grosset, 1965. Subj: Activities – jumping.

Stephenson, Dorothy. *How to scare a lion* ill. by John E. Johnson. Follett, 1965. Subj: Animals – lions. Illness.

The night it rained toys ill. by John E. Johnson. Follett, 1963. Subj: Holidays – Christmas. Poetry, rhyme. Royalty. Toys.

Stepto, Michele. *Snuggle Piggy and the magic blanket* ill. by John Himmelman. Dutton, 1987. ISBN 0-525-44308-8 Subj: Animals – pigs. Family life. Night.

Steptoe, John. *Baby says* ill. by author. Lothrop, 1988. ISBN 0-688-07424-3 Subj: Activities – playing. Babies. Sibling rivalry.

Birthday ill. by author. Holt, 1972. Subj: Birthdays. Ethnic groups in the U.S. – Afro-Americans.

Daddy is a monster...sometimes ill. by author. Lippincott, 1980. Subj: Family life – fathers. Monsters.

Jeffrey Bear cleans up his act ill. by author. Lothrop, 1983. Subj: Animals – bears. School.

Mufaro's beautiful daughters: an African tale ill. by author. Lothrop, 1987. ISBN 0-688-04046-2 Subj: Caldecott award honor book. Character traits – kindness. Character traits – meanness. Folk and fairy tales. Foreign lands – Africa. Royalty – kings.

My special best words ill. by author. Viking, 1974. Subj: Ethnic groups in the U.S. – Afro-Americans. Family life. Language.

Stevie ill. by author. Harper, 1969. Subj: Ethnic groups in the U.S. – Afro-Americans. Friendship.

The story of jumping mouse: a Native American legend ill. by author. Lothrop, 1984. Subj: Animals – mice. Caldecott award honor book. Folk and fairy tales. Frogs and toads. Magic.

Uptown ill. by author. Harper, 1970. Subj: City. Ethnic groups in the U.S. – Afro-Americans. Poverty.

Sterling, Helen *see* Hoke, Helen L.

Stern, Elsie-Jean. *Wee Robin's Christmas song* ill. by Elsie McKean. Nelson, 1945. Subj: Birds – robins. Holidays – Christmas. Music. Songs.

Stern, Mark. *It's a dog's life* ill. by author. Atheneum, 1978. Subj: Animals – dogs. Character traits – freedom.

Stern, Peter. *Floyd, a cat's story* ill. by author. Harper, 1982. Subj: Animals – cats.

Max the dragon ill. by author. Crown, 1990. ISBN 0-517-57588-4 Subj: Animals – mice. Dragons. Monsters.

Stern, Ronnie. *Pop's secret* (Townsend, Maryann)

Stern, Simon. *Mrs. Vinegar* ill. by author. Prentice-Hall, 1979. Subj: Houses.

Vasily and the dragon: an epic Russian fairy tale ill. by author. Merrimack, 1983. ISBN 0-7207-1331-5 Subj: Dragons. Folk and fairy tales. Foreign lands – Russia.

Stevens, Bryna. *Borrowed feathers and other fables* ill. by Freire Wright and Michael Foreman. Random House, 1978. Subj: Folk and fairy tales.

Handel and the famous sword swallower of Halle ill. by Ruth Tietjen Councell. Putnam, 1990. ISBN 0-399-21548-4 Subj: Family life – fathers. Music.

Stevens, Carla. *Hooray for pig!* ill. by Rainey Bennett. Seabury Pr., 1974. Subj: Animals. Animals – pigs. Sports – swimming.

Pig and the blue flag ill. by Rainey Bennett. Seabury Pr., 1977. Subj: Animals. Animals – pigs. School. Sports – gymnastics.

Stories from a snowy meadow ill. by Eve Rice. Seabury Pr., 1976. Subj: Animals. Character traits – kindness. Death. Friendship.

Stevens, Cat. *Teaser and the firecat* ill. by author. Four Winds, 1974. ISBN 0-590-07372-9 Subj: Animals – cats. Foreign languages. Imagination. Moon. Night.

Stevens, Harry. *Fat mouse* ill. by author. Viking, 1987. ISBN 0-670-80529-7 Subj: Animals. Animals – mice. Circular tales. Format, unusual – board books.

Parrot told snake ill. by author. Viking, 1987. ISBN 0-670-80530-0 Subj: Animals. Behavior – gossip. Format, unusual – board books.

Stevens, Janet. *Androcles and the lion* (Æsop)

Animal fair adapt. and ill. by Janet Stevens. Holiday, 1981. Subj: Animals. Dreams. Fairs. Poetry, rhyme.

The emperor's new clothes (Andersen, H. C. (Hans Christian))

Goldilocks and the three bears (The three bears)

It's perfectly true! (Andersen, H. C. (Hans Christian))

The princess and the pea (Andersen, H. C. (Hans Christian))

The three billy goats Gruff (Asbjørnsen, P. C. (Peter Christen))

The tortoise and the hare (Æsop)

The town mouse and the country mouse (Æsop)

Stevens, Kathleen. *The beast in the bathtub* ill. by Ray Bowler. Gareth Stevens, Inc., 1985. ISBN 0-918831-15-6 Subj: Activities – bathing. Bedtime. Monsters.

Stevens, Margaret (Dean). *When grandpa died* ill. by Kenneth Uland. Children's Pr., 1979. Subj: Death. Family life – grandfathers.

Stevens, Susanna. *The changeling* (Lagerlöf, Selma)

Stevenson, Drew. *The ballad of Penelope Lou...and me* ill. by Marcia Sewall. Crossing Pr., 1978. Subj: Character traits – bravery. Emotions – fear. Poetry, rhyme.

Stevenson, James. *Are we almost there?* ill. by author. Greenwillow, 1985. ISBN 0-688-04239-2 Subj: Activities – traveling. Animals – dogs. Behavior – fighting, arguing.

Brr! ill. by author. Greenwillow, 1991. ISBN 0-688-09211-X Subj: Family life – grandfathers. Seasons – winter.

Clams can't sing ill. by author. Greenwillow, 1980. Subj: Animals. Music. Noise, sounds. Sea and seashore.

"Could be worse!" ill. by author. Greenwillow, 1977. Subj: Family life. Family life – grandfathers. Farms. Monsters.

Emma ill. by author. Greenwillow, 1985. ISBN 0-688-04021-7 Subj: Behavior – trickery. Witches.

Fried feathers for Thanksgiving ill. by author. Greenwillow, 1986. ISBN 0-688-06676-3 Subj: Behavior – trickery. Character traits – meanness. Witches.

Grandpa's great city tour: an alphabet book ill. by author. Greenwillow, 1983. Subj: ABC books. Activities – flying. City. Family life – grandfathers.

Grandpa's too-good garden ill. by author. Greenwillow, 1989. ISBN 0-688-08486-9 Subj: Family life – grandfathers. Gardens, gardening.

The great big especially beautiful Easter egg ill. by author. Greenwillow, 1983. Subj: Eggs. Family life – grandfathers.

Happy Valentine's Day, Emma! ill. by author. Greenwillow, 1987. ISBN 0-688-07358-1 Subj: Animals. Character traits – meanness. Holidays – Valentine's Day. Humor. Witches.

Higher on the door ill. by author. Greenwillow, 1987. ISBN 0-688-06637-2 Subj: Behavior – growing up. Family life – grandparents.

Howard ill. by author. Greenwillow, 1980. Subj: Behavior – lost. Birds – ducks. Friendship.

July ill. by author. Greenwillow, 1990. ISBN 0-688-08823-6 Subj: Family life – grandparents. Sea and seashore. Seasons – summer.

Mr. Hacker ill. by author. Greenwillow, 1990. ISBN 0-688-09217-9 Subj: Animals. Emotions – loneliness. Pets.

Monty ill. by author. Greenwillow, 1992. ISBN 0-688-11241-2 Subj: Animals – rabbits. Birds – ducks. Frogs and toads. Reptiles – alligators, crocodiles.

National worm day ill. by author. Greenwillow, 1990. ISBN 0-688-08772-8 Subj: Animals. Friendship.

No friends ill. by author. Greenwillow, 1986. ISBN 0-688-06507-4 Subj: Family life – grandfathers. Friendship. Moving.

No need for Monty ill. by author. Greenwillow, 1987. ISBN 0-688-07084-1 Subj: Animals. Reptiles – alligators, crocodiles. Transportation.

Quick! Turn the page! ill. by author. Greenwillow, 1990. ISBN 0-688-09309-4 Subj: Problem solving.

Rolling Rose ill. by author. Greenwillow, 1992. ISBN 0-688-10675-7 Subj: Activities. Activities – walking. Babies.

The Sea View Hotel ill. by author. Greenwillow, 1978. Subj: Activities – vacationing. Animals – mice. Hotels.

The stowaway ill. by author. Greenwillow, 1990. ISBN 0-688-08620-9 Subj: Animals – mice. Boats, ships. Friendship.

That dreadful day ill. by author. Greenwillow, 1985. ISBN 0-688-04036-5 Subj: Family life – grandfathers. School.

That terrible Halloween night ill. by author. Greenwillow, 1980. Subj: Family life – grandfathers. Holidays – Halloween.

That's exactly the way it wasn't ill. by author. Greenwillow, 1991. ISBN 0-688-09869-X Subj: Family life – brothers. Family life – grandfathers. Sibling rivalry.

There's nothing to do! ill. by author. Greenwillow, 1986. ISBN 0-688-04699-1 Subj: Behavior – boredom. Family life – grandfathers.

We can't sleep ill. by author. Greenwillow, 1982. Subj: Animals. Bedtime. Family life – grandfathers. Sleep.

What's under my bed? ill. by author. Greenwillow, 1983. Subj: Bedtime. Furniture – beds. Emotions – fear. Family life – grandfathers.

When I was nine ill. by author. Greenwillow, 1986. ISBN 0-688-05943-0 Subj: Family life.

Which one is Whitney? ill. by author. Greenwillow, 1990. ISBN 0-688-09062-1 Subj: Animals. Fish. Sea and seashore.

Wilfred the rat ill. by author. Greenwillow, 1977. Subj: Animals – chipmunks. Animals – rats. Animals – squirrels. Friendship.

Will you please feed our cat? ill. by author. Greenwillow, 1987. ISBN 0-688-06848-0 Subj: Character traits – helpfulness. Family life – grandfathers. Pets.

Winston, Newton, Elton, and Ed ill. by author. Greenwillow, 1978. Subj: Animals – walruses. Birds – penguins. Sibling rivalry.

The wish card ran out! ill. by author. Greenwillow, 1981. Subj: Behavior – wishing.

Worse than Willy! ill. by author. Greenwillow, 1984. Subj: Babies. Family life. Family life – grandfathers. Imagination. Sibling rivalry.

The worst person in the world ill. by author. Greenwillow, 1978. Subj: Friendship.

The worst person in the world at Crab Beach ill. by author. Greenwillow, 1988. ISBN 0-688-07299-2 Subj: Friendship. Humor.

The worst person's Christmas ill. by author. Greenwillow, 1991. ISBN 0-688-10211-5 Subj: Character traits – meanness. Holidays – Christmas.

Yuck! ill. by author. Greenwillow, 1984. Subj: Magic. Witches.

Stevenson, Jocelyn. *Jim Henson's Muppets at sea* ill. by Graham Thompson. Random House, 1980. Subj: Boats, ships. Puppets. Sea and seashore.

Red and the pumpkins ill. by Kelly Oechsli. Holt, 1983. Subj: Food. Imagination. Puppets.

Stevenson, Robert Louis. *Block city* ill. by Ashley Wolff. Dutton, 1988. ISBN 0-525-44399-1 Subj: Poetry, rhyme. Toys.

A child's garden of verses ill. by Erik Blegvad. Random House, 1978. Subj: Poetry, rhyme.

A child's garden of verses ill. by Pelagie Doane. Doubleday, 1942. Subj: Poetry, rhyme.

A child's garden of verses ill. by Toni Frissell. U.S. Camera, 1944. Subj: Poetry, rhyme.

A child's garden of verses ill. by Joan Hassall. Harper, 1986. ISBN 0-87226-051-8 Subj: Poetry, rhyme.

The moon ill. by Denise Saldutti. Harper, 1984. Subj: Family life. Moon. Poetry, rhyme. Sports – fishing.

Stevenson, Suçie. *Christmas eve* ill. by author. Putnam's, 1988. ISBN 0-399-21667-7 Subj: Animals – rabbits. Holidays – Christmas. Sibling rivalry.

Do I have to take Violet? ill. by author. Dodd, 1987. ISBN 0-396-08921-6 Subj: Activities – playing. Animals – rabbits. Sibling rivalry.

I forgot ill. by author. Watts, 1988. ISBN 0-531-08344-6 Subj: Animals. Behavior – forgetfulness. Birthdays.

Jessica the blue streak ill. by author. Watts, 1989. ISBN 0-531-08398-5 Subj: Animals – dogs. Behavior – misbehavior. Family life – fathers. Pets.

Stewart, Anne. *The ugly duckling* (Andersen, H. C. (Hans Christian))

Stewart, Charles P. *Dinosaurs and other creatures of long ago* (Stewart, Frances Todd)

Stewart, Elizabeth Laing. *The lion twins* photos. by Marlin and Carol Morse Perkins. Atheneum, 1964. Subj: Animals – lions. Twins.

Stewart, Frances Todd. *Dinosaurs and other creatures of long ago* by Frances Todd Stewart and Charles P. Stewart, III; ill. by Forest Rogers and Kathy Borland. Harper, 1988. ISBN 0-694-00229-1 Subj: Dinosaurs.

Stewart, Robert S. *The daddy book* ill. by Don Madden. American Heritage, 1972. Subj: Careers. Family life – fathers.

Stewart, Sarah. *The money tree* ill. by David Small. Farrar, 1991. ISBN 0-374-35014-0 Subj: Money. Seasons. Trees.

Stewig, John Warren. *The fisherman and his wife* (Grimm, Jacob)

Stone soup ill. by Margot Tomes. Holiday, 1991. ISBN 0-8234-0863-9 Subj: Character traits – cleverness. Folk and fairy tales. Food.

Stickland, Paul. *A child's book of things* ill. by author. Watts, 1990. ISBN 0-531-08506-6 Subj: Activities. Family life.

Machines as big as monsters ill. by author. Random House, 1989. ISBN 0-394-93913-1 Subj: Concepts – size. Machines.

Stiles, Norman. *I'll miss you, Mr. Hooper* ill. by Joseph Mathieu. Random House, 1984. ISBN 0-394-96600-7 Subj: Death. Puppets.

The Sesame Street ABC storybook (Moss, Jeffrey)

Still, James. *Jack and the wonder beans* ill. by Margot Tomes. Putnam's, 1977. Subj: Folk and fairy tales. Giants.

Stilz, Carol Curtis. *Kirsty's kite* ill. by Gwen Harrison. Albatross, 1988. ISBN 0-86760-089-6 Subj: Death. Family life – mothers. Family life – grandfathers. Kites.

Stinchecum, Amanda Mayer. *Girl from the snow country* (Hidaka, Masako)

Grandpa's town (Nomura, Takaaki)

Stine, Jovial Bob. *Pork and beans: play date* ill. by José Aruego and Ariane Dewey. Scholastic, 1989. ISBN 0-590-41579-4 Subj: Activities – playing. Animals – pigs. Games. Sibling rivalry.

Stinson, Kathy. *The bare naked book* ill. by Heather Collins. Firefly Pr., 1986. ISBN 0-920303-52-8 Subj: Anatomy.

The dressed up book ill. by Heather Collins. Firefly, 1990. ISBN 1-55037-104-5 Subj: Activities – playing. Clothing. Imagination.

Mom and dad don't live together any more ill. by Nancy Lou Reynolds. Firefly Pr., 1984. ISBN 0-920236-92-8 Subj: Divorce.

Red is best ill. by Robin Baird Lewis. Firefly Pr., 1982. Subj: Concepts – color.

Teddy Rabbit ill. by Stéphane Poulin. Firefly, 1988. ISBN 1-55037-017-0 Subj: Toys. Trains.

Those green things ill. by Mary McLoughlin. Firefly Pr., 1985. ISBN 0-920303-40-4 Subj: Humor. Imagination.

Stites, Clara. *The ugly duckling* (Andersen, H. C. (Hans Christian))

Stobbs, Joanna. *One sun, two eyes, and a million stars* by Joanna and William Stobbs; ill. by authors. Merrimack, 1983. Subj: Counting, numbers.

Stobbs, William. *Animal pictures* ill. by author. Bodley Head, 1982. Subj: Animals. Wordless.

A car called beetle ill. by author. Merrimack, 1979. Bodley Head, 1979. Subj: Automobiles.

The hare and the frogs (Æsop)

The little red hen (The little red hen)

One sun, two eyes, and a million stars (Stobbs, Joanna)

There's a hole in my bucket ill. by author. Merrimack, 1983. Subj: Seasons – summer. Songs.

This little piggy ill. by author. Bodley Head, 1981. Subj: Animals – pigs. Counting, numbers. Nursery rhymes. Poetry, rhyme.

Stock, Catherine. *Alexander's midnight snack: a little elephant's ABC* ill. by author. Clarion, 1988. ISBN 0-89919-512-1 Subj: ABC books. Animals – elephants. Bedtime. Food.

The birthday present ill. by author. Bradbury Pr., 1991. ISBN 0-02-788401-5 Subj: Birthdays. Parties.

Christmas time ill. by author. Bradbury Pr., 1990. ISBN 0-02-788403-1 Subj: Family life – fathers. Holidays – Christmas.

Easter surprise ill. by author. Bradbury Pr., 1991. ISBN 0-02-788371-X Subj: Family life – mothers. Holidays – Easter.

Emma's dragon hunt ill. by author. Lothrop, 1984. ISBN 0-688-02698-2 Subj: Dragons. Family life – grandfathers.

Halloween monster ill. by author. Bradbury Pr., 1990. ISBN 0-02-788404-X Subj: Activities. Emotions – fear. Holidays – Halloween.

Sampson the Christmas cat ill. by author. Putnam's, 1984. Subj: Animals – cats. Holidays – Christmas.

Secret Valentine ill. by author. Bradbury Pr., 1991. ISBN 0-02-788372-8 Subj: Character traits – kindness. Holidays – Valentine's Day.

Sophie's bucket ill. by author. Lothrop, 1985. Subj: Family life. Sea and seashore.

Sophie's knapsack ill. by author. Lothrop, 1988. ISBN 0-688-06458-2 Subj: Family life. Camps, camping.

Thanksgiving treat ill. by author. Bradbury Pr., 1990. ISBN 0-02-788402-3 Subj: Family life – grandfathers. Holidays – Thanksgiving.

Stoddard, Sandol. *Bedtime for bear* ill. by Lynn Munsinger. Houghton, 1985. ISBN 0-395-38811-2 Subj: Animals – bears. Bedtime. Poetry, rhyme.

Bedtime mouse ill. by Lynn Munsinger. Houghton, 1981. ISBN 0-395-31609-X Subj: Animals. Animals – mice. Bedtime. Cumulative tales. Poetry, rhyme.

Curl up small ill. by Trina Schart Hyman. Houghton, 1964. Subj: Concepts – shape. Concepts – size. Family life. Imagination.

My very own special particular private and personal cat ill. by Remy Charlip. Houghton, 1963. Subj: Animals – cats. Pets. Poetry, rhyme.

The thinking book ill. by Ivan Chermayeff. Little, 1960. Subj: Family life. Imagination.

Stoeke, Janet Morgan. *Minerva Louise* ill. by author. Dutton, 1988. ISBN 0-525-44374-6 Subj: Behavior – misunderstanding. Birds – chickens.

Stoker, Wayne. *I can be a welder* (Lillegard, Dee)

Stolz, Mary Slattery. *Storm in the night* ill. by Pat Cummings. Harper, 1988. ISBN 0-06-025912-4 Subj: Ethnic groups in the U.S. – Afro-Americans. Family life – grandfathers. Night. Weather – storms.

Zekmet, the stone carver: a tale of Ancient Egypt ill. by Deborah Nourse Lattimore. Harcourt, 1988. ISBN 0-15-299961-2 Subj: Activities – working. Foreign lands – Egypt.

Stone, A. Harris. *The last free bird* ill. by Sheila Heins. Prentice-Hall, 1967. Subj: Birds. Ecology.

Stone, Bernard. *The charge of the mouse brigade* by Bernard Stone with Alice Low; ill. by Tony Ross. Pantheon, 1980. Subj: Animals – cats. Animals – mice. War.

Emergency mouse ill. by Ralph Steadman. Prentice-Hall, 1978. Subj: Animals – mice. Hospitals.

Stone, Beth. *Do you have a secret?* (Russell, Pamela)

Stone, Jon. *Big Bird in China* photos. by Victor DiNapoli. Random House, 1983. Subj: Foreign lands – China. Puppets.

Stone, Kazuko G. *Goodnight Twinklegator* ill. by author. Scholastic, 1990. ISBN 0-590-43183-8 Subj: Bedtime. Imagination. Night. Reptiles – alligators, crocodiles. Sky. Stars.

Stone, Rosetta. *Because a little bug went ka-choo!* ill. by Michael K. Frith. Random House, 1975. Subj: Cumulative tales. Humor. Insects. Poetry, rhyme.

Stonehouse, Bernard. *Kangaroos* ill. with photos. Raintree, 1978. Subj: Animals – kangaroos.

Storm, Theodor. *Little John* (Orgel, Doris)

Storr, Catherine (Cole). *Clever Polly and the stupid wolf* ill. by Marjorie-Ann Watts. Faber, 1979. Subj: Animals – wolves. Character traits – cleverness.

Hugo and his grandma ill. by Nita Sowter. Merrimack, 1980. Subj: Activities – knitting. Family life – grandmothers.

King Midas ill. by Mike Codd. Raintree, 1985. ISBN 0-8172-2112-3 Subj: Behavior – greed. Behavior – wishing. Royalty – kings.

Rip Van Winkle (Irving, Washington)

Robin Hood ill. by Chris Collingwood. Raintree, 1984. ISBN 0-8172-2109-3 Subj: Foreign lands – England. Forest, woods. Middle ages.

Stott, Dorothy. *Little Duck's bicycle ride* ill. by author. Dutton, 1991. ISBN 0-525-44728-8 Subj: Birds – ducks. Farms. Sports – bicycling.

Too much ill. by author. Dutton, 1990. ISBN 0-525-44569-2 Subj: Birds – ducks. Sports – swimming.

Stott, Rowena. *The hedgehog feast* ill. by Edith Holden. Dutton, 1978. Subj: Animals – hedgehogs. Hibernation. Parties.

Stover, Jo Ann. *If everybody did* ill. by author. McKay, 1960. Subj: Behavior. Etiquette. Poetry, rhyme.

Why? Because ill. by author. McKay, 1961. Subj: Character traits – questioning.

Strahl, Rudi. *Sandman in the lighthouse* tr. and adapt. by Anthea Bell; ill. by Eberhard Binder. Children's Pr., 1967, 1969. Subj: Bedtime. Lighthouses. Sandman. Sea and seashore.

Straker, Joan Ann. *Animals that live in the sea* National Geographical Soc., 1979. Subj: Sea and seashore.

Strand, Mark. *The night book* ill. by William Pène Du Bois. Crown, 1985. ISBN 0-517-55047-4 Subj: Emotions – fear. Night.

The planet of lost things ill. by William Pène du Bois. Crown, 1983. Subj: Bedtime. Dreams. Noise, sounds.

Strange, Florence. *Rock-a-bye whale: a story of the birth of a humpback whale* ill. by author. Manzanita Pr., 1977. ISBN 0-931644-08-3 Subj: Animals – whales. Science.

Stratemeyer, Clara Georgeanna. *Frog fun* by Clara G. Stratemeyer and Henry Lee Smith, Jr.; ill. by Lucy Hawkinson. Harper, 1963. Subj: Frogs and toads.

Pepper by Clara G. Stratemeyer and Henry Lee Smith, Jr. Benziger, 1971. Subj: Animals. Animals – cats.

Tuggy by Clara Georgeanna Stratemeyer and Henry Lee Smith, Jr. Harper, 1971. Subj: Animals – dogs. Frogs and toads.

Strathdee, Jean. *The house that grew* ill. by Jessica Wallace. Oxford Univ. Pr., 1980. Subj: Family life. Houses. Moving.

Strauss, Gwen. *The night shimmy* ill. by Anthony Browne. Knopf, 1992. ISBN 0-679-92384-5 Subj: Behavior – needing someone. Dreams. Friendship. Imagination – imaginary friends. Kites.

Streatfield, Noel. *Sleepy Nicholas* (Brande, Marlie)

Stren, Patti. *Hug me* ill. by author. Harper, 1977. Subj: Animals – porcupines. Emotions – loneliness.

Mountain Rose ill. by author. Dutton, 1982. Subj: Character traits – appearance. Self-concept. Sports – wrestling.

Strete, Craig Kee. *Big thunder magic* ill. by Craig McFarland Brown. Greenwillow, 1990. ISBN 0-688-08854-6 Subj: Animals – sheep. Friendship. Indians of North America.

Stroyer, Poul. *It's a deal* ill. by author. Astor-Honor, 1960. Subj: Activities – trading. Humor.

Strub, Susanne. *Lulu goes swimming* ill. by author. Viking, 1990. ISBN 0-670-83460-2 Subj: Behavior – growing up. Dreams. Sports – swimming.

Lulu on her bike ill. by author. Viking, 1990. ISBN 0-670-83461-0 Subj: Behavior – growing up. Dreams. Sports – bicycling.

Struppi ill. by Ingrid Graichen. Imported Pubs., 1983. Subj: Animals. Format, unusual – board books. Wordless.

Stuart, Mary see Graham, Mary Stuart Campbell

Stubbs, Joanna. *Happy Bear's day* ill. by author. Elsevier-Dutton, 1979. Subj: Animals – bears. Behavior – solitude.

With cat's eyes you'll never be scared of the dark ill. by author. Dutton, 1983. Subj: Emotions – fear. Magic. Night.

Sturgis, Matthew. *Tosca's surprise* ill. by Anne Mortimer. Dial, 1991. ISBN 0-8037-0946-3 Subj: Animals – cats.

Sturtzel, Howard A. see Annixter, Paul

Sturtzel, Jane Levington see Annixter, Jane

Suba, Susanne. *The monkeys and the pedlar* ill. by author. Viking, 1970. Subj: Animals – monkeys. Careers – peddlers. Humor.

Suben, Eric. *Pigeon takes a trip* ill. by Tiziana Zanetti; graphic design by Giorgio Vanetti. Golden Books, 1984. Subj: Activities – traveling. Birds – pigeons. Format, unusual – board books.

Suetake, Kunihiro. *Red dragonfly on my shoulder* (Cassedy, Sylvia)

Sueyoshi, Akiko. *Ladybird on a bicycle* ill. by Viv Allbright. Faber, 1983. Subj: Insects – ladybugs. Sports – bicycling.

Sugita, Yutaka. *The flower family* ill. by author. McGraw-Hill, 1975. Subj: Flowers. Plants. Science.

Good night 1, 2, 3 ill. by author. Scroll Pr., 1971. Subj: Bedtime. Counting, numbers. Sleep.

Helena the unhappy hippopotamus ill. by author. McGraw-Hill, 1972. Subj: Animals – hippopotami. Behavior – needing someone. Emotions – loneliness. Emotions – sadness. Friendship.

My friend Little John and me ill. by author. McGraw-Hill, 1972. Subj: Animals – dogs. Wordless.

Suhl, Yuri. *The Purim goat* ill. by Kaethe Zemach. Four Winds Pr., 1980. Subj: Animals – goats. Character traits – helpfulness. Holidays – Purim.

Simon Boom gives a wedding ill. by Margot Zemach. Four Winds Pr., 1972. Subj: Cumulative tales. Humor. Jewish culture. Weddings.

Sumiko. *Kittymouse* ill. by author. Harcourt, 1979. Subj: Animals – cats. Animals – mice.

Sundgaard, Arnold. *The bear who loved Puccini* ill. by Dominic Catalano. Putnam, 1992. ISBN 0-399-22135-2 Subj: Activities – singing. Animals – bears.

Jethro's difficult dinosaur ill. by Stanley Mack. Pantheon, 1977. Subj: Dinosaurs. Eggs. Humor. Poetry, rhyme.

The lamb and the butterfly ill. by Eric Carle. Watts, 1988. ISBN 0-531-08379-9 Subj: Animals – sheep. Character traits – freedom. Insects – butterflies, caterpillars.

Meet Jack Appleknocker ill. by Sheila White Samton. Putnam's, 1988. ISBN 0-399-21472-0 Subj: Imagination.

Sundvall, Viveca. *Mimi and the biscuit factory* tr. from Swedish by Eris Bibb; ill. by Eva Eriksson. Farrar, 1989. ISBN 9-12-959142-2 Subj: Careers – bakers. Foreign lands – Sweden. School. Teeth.

The Superman mix or match storybook ill. by Ross Andru and Joe Orlando. Random House, 1979. Subj: Format, unusual – toy and movable books.

Supraner, Robyn. *Giggly-wiggly, snickety-snick* ill. by Stan Tusan. Parents, 1978. Subj: Concepts.

Would you rather be a tiger? ill. by Barbara Cooney. Houghton, 1973. Subj: Behavior. Imagination. Poetry, rhyme. Self-concept.

Supree, Burton. *Harlequin and the gift of many colors* (Charlip, Remy)

"Mother, mother I feel sick" (Charlip, Remy)

Surany, Anico. *Kati and Kormos* ill. by Leonard Everett Fisher. Holiday, 1966. Subj: Animals – dogs. Emotions – loneliness. Foreign lands – Hungary.

Ride the cold wind ill. by Leonard Everett Fisher. Putnam's, 1964. Subj: Boats, ships. Foreign lands – South America. Sports – fishing.

Surat, Michele Maria. *Angel child, dragon child* ill. by Vo-Dinh Mai. Raintree, 1983. ISBN 0-940742-12-8 Subj: Ethnic groups in the U.S. – Vietnamese-Americans. School.

Sussman, Susan. *Hippo thunder* ill. by John C. Wallner. Albert Whitman, 1982. Subj: Bedtime. Emotions. Weather – thunder.

Sutherland, Harry A. *Dad's car wash* ill. by Maxie Chambliss. Atheneum, 1988. ISBN 0-689-31335-7 Subj: Activities – bathing. Bedtime. Imagination.

Sutton, Elizabeth Henning. *A pony for keeps* ill. by Mary Brant Gamma. Thomasson-Grant, 1991. ISBN 0-934738-77-7 Subj: Animals – horses. Birthdays.

Sutton, Eve. *My cat likes to hide in boxes* ill. by Lynley Dodd. Parents, 1973. Subj: Animals – cats. Cumulative tales. Participation. Poetry, rhyme.

Sutton, Jane. *What should a hippo wear?* ill. by Lynn Munsinger. Houghton, 1979. ISBN 0-395-27800-7 Subj: Activities – dancing. Animals. Animals – hippopotami. Clothing.

Svendsen, Carol. *Hulda* ill. by Julius Svendsen. Houghton, 1974. Subj: Behavior. Poetry, rhyme. Trolls.

Swados, Elizabeth. *Lullaby* ill. by Faith Hubley. Harper, 1980. Subj: Bedtime. Lullabies.

Swan, Donald. *The hippopotamus song* (Flanders, Michael)

Swann, Brian. *A basket full of white eggs: riddle-poems* ill. by Ponder Goembel. Watts, 1988. ISBN 0-531-08334-9 Subj: Poetry, rhyme. Riddles.

Sweet, Melissa. *Fiddle-i-fee* ill. by adaptor. Little, 1992. ISBN 0-316-82516-6 Subj: Animals. Cumulative tales. Farms. Music. Songs.

Swendson, Patsy. *The potluck adventures of Mrs. Marmalade* by Patsy Swendson and Debbie Little; ill. by authors. Eakin Pr., 1989. ISBN 0-89015-718-9 Subj: Activities – cooking. Animals. Animals – possums.

Swift, Hildegarde Hoyt. *The little red lighthouse and the great gray bridge* by Hildegarde H. Swift and Lynd Ward; ill. by Lynd Ward. Harcourt, 1942. Subj: Boats, ships. Bridges. Lighthouses.

Switzer, Robert E. *My friend the babysitter* (Watson, Jane Werner)

My friend the dentist (Watson, Jane Werner)

My friend the doctor (Watson, Jane Werner)

Sometimes a family has to move (Watson, Jane Werner)

Sometimes a family has to split up (Watson, Jane Werner)

Sometimes I get angry (Watson, Jane Werner)

Sometimes I'm afraid (Watson, Jane Werner)

Sometimes I'm jealous (Watson, Jane Werner)

Swope, Sam. *The Araboolies of Liberty Street* ill. by Barry Root. Crown, 1989. ISBN 0-517-57411-X Subj: Behavior. Communities, neighborhoods.

Syme, Daniel B. *I'm growing* (Bogot, Howard)

Szekeres, Cyndy. *Cyndy Szekeres' counting book, 1 to 10* ill. by author. Golden Pr., 1984. Subj: Animals – mice. Counting, numbers.

Good night, Sammy ill. by author. Western, 1991. ISBN 0-307-12238-7 Subj: Animals – foxes. Format, unusual – board books. Sleep.

Hide-and-seek duck ill. by author. Western, 1991. ISBN 0-307-12235-2 Subj: Animals – rabbits. Behavior – hiding. Birds – ducks. Format, unusual – board books.

Ladybug, ladybug, where are you? ill. by author. Western, 1991. ISBN 0-307-12340-5 Subj: Activities – picnicking. Animals – mice. Insects – ladybugs.

Long ago ill. by author. McGraw-Hill, 1977. Subj: Animals. U.S. history.

Nothing-to-do puppy ill. by author. Western, 1991. ISBN 0-307-12237-9 Subj: Animals – dogs. Format, unusual – board books.

Suppertime for Frieda Fuzzypaws ill. by author. Western, 1991. ISBN 0-307-12234-4 Subj: Animals – cats. Behavior – trickery. Food. Format, unusual – board books.

Szilagyi, Mary. *Thunderstorm* ill. by author. Bradbury Pr., 1985. ISBN 0-02-788580-1 Subj: Emotions – fear. Pets. Weather – storms. Weather – thunder.

Taback, Simms. *Joseph had a little overcoat* ill. by author. Random House, 1977. Subj: Clothing – coats. Format, unusual.

On our way to the barn (Ziefert, Harriet)

On our way to the forest (Ziefert, Harriet)

On our way to the water (Ziefert, Harriet)

On our way to the zoo (Ziefert, Harriet)

Tabberner, Jeffrey. *The endless party* (Delessert, Etienne)

Taber, Anthony. *Cats' eyes* ill. by author. Dutton, 1978. Subj: Animals – cats. Old age.

Tabler, Judith. *The new puppy* ill. by Pat Sustendal. Random House, 1986. ISBN 0-394-88038-2 Subj: Animals – dogs. Format, unusual – board books. Pets. Toys.

Taborin, Glorina. *Norman Rockwell's counting book* (Rockwell, Norman)

Tafuri, Nancy. *All year long* ill. by author. Greenwillow, 1983. Subj: Days of the week, months of the year.

The ball bounced ill. by author. Greenwillow, 1989. ISBN 0-688-07871-0 Subj: Babies. Toys – balls.

Do not disturb ill. by author. Greenwillow, 1987. ISBN 0-688-06542-2 Subj: Activities. Animals. Family life. Night. Noise, sounds. Camps, camping. Wordless.

Early morning in the barn ill. by author. Greenwillow, 1983. Subj: Farms. Morning.

Have you seen my duckling? ill. by author. Greenwillow, 1984. Subj: Birds – ducks. Caldecott award honor book. Character traits – individuality.

In a red house ill. by author. Greenwillow, 1987. ISBN 0-688-07185-6 Subj: Concepts – color. Format, unusual – board books. Toys.

Junglewalk ill. by author. Greenwillow, 1988. ISBN 0-688-07183-X Subj: Animals. Dreams. Imagination. Jungle. Wordless.

My friends ill. by author. Greenwillow, 1987. ISBN 0-688-07187-2 Subj: Animals. Babies. Format, unusual – board books. Friendship.

One wet jacket ill. by author. Greenwillow, 1988. ISBN 0-688-07465-0 Subj: Clothing – coats. Format, unusual – board books.

Rabbit's morning ill. by author. Greenwillow, 1985. ISBN 0-688-04064-0 Subj: Animals. Animals – rabbits. Wordless.

Two new sneakers ill. by author. Greenwillow, 1988. ISBN 0-688-07462-6 Subj: Clothing – shoes. Format, unusual – board books.

Where we sleep ill. by author. Greenwillow, 1987. ISBN 0-688-07189-9 Subj: Animals. Format, unusual – board books. Sleep.

Who's counting? ill. by author. Greenwillow, 1986. ISBN 0-688-06131-1 Subj: Animals. Animals – dogs. Counting, numbers. Farms.

Tagore, Rabindranath. *Paper boats* ill. by Grayce Bochak. Boyds Mills Pr., 1992. ISBN 1-878093-12-6 Subj: Boats, ships. Paper. Poetry, rhyme. Toys.

Taha, Karen T. *A gift for Tia Rose* ill. by Dee deRosa. Dillon Pr., 1986. ISBN 0-87518-306-9 Subj: Death. Ethnic groups in the U.S. – Mexican-Americans. Family life. Friendship.

Tait, Nancy. *I'm deaf and it's okay* (Aseltine, Lorraine)

Takeshita, Fumiko. *The park bench* tr. by Ruth A. Kanagy; ill. by Mamoru Suzuki. Kane/Miller, 1988. ISBN 0-916291-15-4 Subj: Activities. Foreign lands – Japan. Foreign languages.

Takihara, Koji. *Rolli* ill. by author. Picture Book Studio, 1988. ISBN 0-88708-058-8 Subj: Animals – moles. Seeds.

Talbot, John. *Pins and needles* ill. by author. Dial, 1992. ISBN 0-8037-0942-0 Subj: Animals – elephants. Animals – mice. Problem solving.

Talbott, Hudson. *Going Hollywood! A dinosaur's dream* ill. by author. Crown, 1989. ISBN 0-517-57309-1 Subj: Dinosaurs. Friendship. Self-concept.

Tallarico, Tony. *At home* ill. by author. Tuffy Books, 1984. Subj: Family life. Houses.

Tallon, Robert. *Latouse my moose* ill. by author. Knopf, 1983. Subj: Animals – dogs. Pets.

Talus, Taylor. *Animal hide-and-seek* (Tison, Annette)

Inside and outside (Tison, Annette)

Tamburine, Jean. *I think I will go to the hospital* ill. by author. Abingdon Pr., 1965. Subj: Hospitals.

Tan, Amy. *The moon lady* ill. by Gretchen Schields. Macmillan, 1992. ISBN 0-02-788830-4 Subj: Behavior – lost. Foreign lands – China. Holidays.

Tan, Pierre Le *see* Le-Tan, Pierre

Tanaka, Beatrice. *The chase: a Kutenai Indian tale* ill. by Michel Gay. Crown, 1991. ISBN 0-517-58624-X Subj: Animals. Cumulative tales. Folk and fairy tales. Indians of North America.

Tanaka, Hideyuki. *The happy dog* ill. by author. Atheneum, 1983. Subj: Animals – dogs.

Tangvald, Christine. *Mom and dad don't live together anymore* Cook, 1988. ISBN 1-55513-502-1 Subj: Divorce.

Taniuchi, Kota. *Trolley* ill. by author. Watts, 1969. Subj: Cable cars, trolleys. Imagination.

Tapio, Pat Decker. *The lady who saw the good side of everything* ill. by Paul Galdone. Seabury Pr., 1975. Subj: Activities – traveling. Animals – cats. Character traits – optimism. Emotions – happiness. Humor. Weather – floods. Weather – rain.

Tarrant, Graham. *Rabbits* ill. by Tonny King. Putnam's, 1984. Subj: Animals – rabbits. Format, unusual.

Tarrant, Margaret. *Fairy tales* ill. with photos. Crowell, 1978. Subj: Folk and fairy tales.

The Margaret Tarrant nursery rhyme book ill. by author. Merrimack, 1986. ISBN 0-00-183732-X Subj: Nursery rhymes.

Tate, Joan. *The giant fish and other stories* (Otto, Svend)

Tate, Suzanne. *Crabby's water wish* ill. by James Melvin. Nags Head Art, 1991. ISBN 1-878405-04-7 Subj: Ecology. Sea and seashore.

Tatham, Campbell *see* Elting, Mary

Tax, Meredith. *Families* ill. by Marylin Hafner. Little, 1981. Subj: Family life.

Taylor, Anelise. *Lights on, lights off* ill. by author. Oxford Univ. Pr., 1988. ISBN 0-19-279843-X Subj: Emotions – fear. Night.

Taylor, Edgar. *King Grisly-Beard* (Grimm, Jacob)

Taylor, John Edward. *Petrosinella* (Basile, Giambattista)

Taylor, Judy. *Dudley and the monster* ill. by Peter Cross. Putnam's, 1986. ISBN 0-399-21329-5 Subj: Animals – mice. Monsters. Seasons – spring.

Dudley and the strawberry shake ill. by Peter Cross. Putnam's, 1987. ISBN 0-399-21330-9 Subj: Animals – mice. Food.

Dudley goes flying ill. by Peter Cross. Putnam's, 1986. ISBN 0-399-21328-7 Subj: Activities – flying. Animals – mice.

Dudley in a jam ill. by Peter Cross. Putnam's, 1987. ISBN 0-399-21331-7 Subj: Animals – mice. Food.

Sophie and Jack ill. by Susan Gantner. Putnam's, 1983. Subj: Activities – picnicking. Animals – hippopotami. Family life.

Sophie and Jack help out ill. by Susan Gantner. Putnam's, 1984. Subj: Animals – hippopotami. Gardens, gardening. Weather – storms.

Taylor, Kim. *Frog* [written and ed. by Angela Royston] photos. by Kim Taylor and Jane Burton. Dutton, 1991. ISBN 0-525-67345-8 Subj: Birth. Format, unusual – board books. Frogs and toads.

Too fast to see photos. by author. Delacorte, 1991. ISBN 0-385-30219-3 Subj: Nature.

Too small to see photos. by author. Delacorte, 1991. ISBN 0-385-30221-5 Subj: Nature.

Taylor, Livingston. *Pajamas* by Livingston and Maggie Taylor; ill. by Tim Bowers. Harcourt, 1988. ISBN 0-15-200564-1 Subj: Bedtime. Lullabies.

Taylor, Maggie. *Pajamas* (Taylor, Livingston)

Taylor, Mark. *The bold fisherman* ill. by Graham Booth. Golden Gate, 1967. Subj: Folk and fairy tales. Music. Sea and seashore. Songs. Sports – fishing.

The case of the missing kittens ill. by Graham Booth. Atheneum, 1978. Subj: Animals – cats. Animals – dogs. Behavior – lost. Problem solving.

Henry explores the jungle ill. by Graham Booth. Atheneum, 1968. Subj: Animals – tigers. Character traits – bravery. Circus. Seasons – summer.

Henry explores the mountains ill. by Graham Booth. Atheneum, 1975. Subj: Character traits – bravery. Fire. Helicopters. Seasons – fall.

Henry the castaway ill. by Graham Booth. Atheneum, 1972. Subj: Behavior – lost. Boats, ships. Seasons – spring. Weather – rain.

Henry the explorer ill. by Graham Booth. Atheneum, 1966. Subj: Animals – bears. Behavior – lost. Character traits – bravery. Seasons – winter.

"Lamb," said the lion, "I am here." ill. by Anne Siberell. Golden Gate, 1971. Subj: Animals. Religion.

Old Blue, you good dog you ill. by Gene Holtan. Golden Gate, 1970. Subj: Animals – dogs. Animals – possums. Folk and fairy tales. Friendship. Games. Music. Songs. Old age.

Taylor, Scott. *Dinosaur James* ill. by author. Morrow, 1990. ISBN 0-688-08577-6 Subj: Behavior – bullying. Dinosaurs. Poetry, rhyme.

Taylor, Sydney. *The dog who came to dinner* ill. by John E. Johnson. Follett, 1966. Subj: Animals – dogs. Ethnic groups in the U.S. – Afro-Americans.

Mr. Barney's beard ill. by Charles Geer. Follett, 1961. Subj: Birds. Character traits – laziness.

Tazewell, Charles. *The littlest angel* ill. by Paul Micich. Ideals, 1991. ISBN 0-8249-8516-8 Subj: Angels. Holidays – Christmas.

Teague, Mark. *The trouble with the Johnsons* ill. by author. Scholastic, 1989. ISBN 0-590-42394-0 Subj: Animals – cats. Dinosaurs. Moving.

Tejima, Keizaburo. *The bears' autumn* tr. from the Japanese by Susan Matsui; ill. by author. Green Tiger Pr., 1986. ISBN 0-88138-080-6 Subj: Animals – bears. Seasons – fall.

Fox's dream ill. by author. Philomel, 1987. ISBN 0-399-21455-0 Subj: Animals – foxes. Dreams. Forest, woods. Seasons – winter.

Ho-limlim ill. by author. Putnam, 1990. ISBN 0-399-22156-5 Subj: Animals – rabbits. Foreign lands – Japan. Old age.

Owl lake ill. by author. Philomel, 1987. ISBN 0-399-21426-7 Subj: Birds – owls. Family life. Nature. Night.

Swan sky ill. by author. Putnam's, 1988. ISBN 0-399-21547-6 Subj: Birds – swans. Death.

Woodpecker forest ill. by author. Putnam, 1989. ISBN 0-399-21618-9 Subj: Birds – woodpeckers. Forest, woods. Nature.

Teleki, Geza. *Aerial apes: Gibbons of Asia* by Geza Teleki and others; ill. with photos. Coward, 1979. Subj: Animals – monkeys.

Telephones ill. by Christine Sharr. Wonder Books, 1971. Subj: Communication. Telephone.

Tellenbach, Margrit Haubensak *see* Haubensak-Tellenbach, Margrit

Tempest, P. *How the cock wrecked the manor* tr. from Lithuanian by Olimpija Armalyte; ill. by Albina Makūnaite. Imported Pub., 1982. Subj: Folk and fairy tales. Magic.

Tempest, Peter. *The tale of a hero nobody knows* (Marshak, Samuel)

Tennyson, Noel. *The lady's chair and the ottoman* ill. by author. Lothrop, 1987. ISBN 0-688-04098-5 Subj: Behavior – needing someone. Furniture – chairs.

Tensen, Ruth M. *Come to the zoo!* Reilly, 1948. Subj: Animals. Zoos.

Testa, Fulvio. *The ideal home* ill. by author. Harper, 1986. ISBN 0-87226-055-0 Subj: Houses.

If you look around ill. by author. Dial Pr., 1983. Subj: Concepts – shape.

If you take a paintbrush: a book of colors ill. by author. Dial Pr., 1983. Subj: Concepts – color.

If you take a pencil ill. by author. Dial Pr., 1982. Subj: Counting, numbers.

The land where the ice cream grows story and ill. by Fulvio Testa; told by Anthony Burgess. Doubleday, 1979. Subj: Food. Imagination.

Never satisfied ill. by author. North-South, 1988. ISBN 3-85539-009-6 Subj: Behavior – dissatisfaction.

The paper airplane ill. by author. Holt, 1988. ISBN 0-8050-0743-1 Subj: Activities – flying. Airplanes, airports. Paper.

Wolf's favor ill. by author. Dial Pr., 1986. ISBN 0-8037-0244-2 Subj: Animals. Character traits – generosity.

Tester, Sylvia Root. *Chase!* ill. by author. Children's Pr., 1980. Subj: Animals.

Never monkey with a monkey: a book of homographic homophones ill. by John Keely. Children's Pr., 1977. Subj: Language.

Parade! ill. by author. Children's Pr., 1980. Subj: Circus.

A visit to the zoo photos. by author. Childrens Pr., 1987. ISBN 0-516-01494-3 Subj: Animals. Zoos.

What did you say? a book of homophones ill. by John Keely. Children's Pr., 1977. Subj: Language.

Tether, Graham. *The hair book* ill. by Roy McKié. Random House, 1979. Subj: Hair. Poetry, rhyme.

Skunk and possum ill. by Lucinda McQueen. Houghton, 1979. Subj: Activities – picnicking. Animals – possums. Animals – skunks. Friendship.

Tettelbaum, Michael. *The cave of the lost Fraggle* ill. by Peter Elwell. Holt, 1985. ISBN 0-03-004554-1 Subj: Caves. Character traits – pride. Puppets.

Thacher, Edith *see* Hurd, Edith Thacher

Thaler, Mike. *Hippo lemonade* ill. by Maxie Chambliss. Harper, 1986. ISBN 0-06-026162-5 Subj: Animals. Animals – hippopotami. Behavior – wishing.

It's me, hippo! ill. by Maxie Chambliss. Harper, 1983. Subj: Animals. Animals – hippopotami. Friendship.

Madge's magic show ill. by Carol Nicklaus. Watts, 1978. Subj: Magic.

Moonkey ill. by Giulio Maestro. Harper, 1981. Subj: Animals – monkeys. Friendship. Moon.

My puppy ill. by Madeleine Fishman. Harper, 1980. Subj: Animals – dogs. Imagination – imaginary friends. Pets.

Owley ill. by David Wiesner. Harper, 1982. ISBN 0-06-026152-8 Subj: Birds – owls. Character traits – questioning. Family life – mothers.

Pack 109 ill. by Normand Chartier. Dutton, 1988. ISBN 0-525-44393-2 Subj: Animals. Clubs, gangs. Humor.

There's a hippopotamus under my bed ill. by Ray Cruz. Watts, 1977. Subj: Animals – hippopotami. Furniture – beds.

What could a hippopotamus be? ill. by Robert Grossman. Simon & Schuster, 1990. ISBN 0-671-70847-3 Subj: Animals – hippopotami. Careers.

The yellow brick toad: funny frog cartoons, riddles, and silly stories ill. by author. Doubleday, 1978. Subj: Humor. Riddles.

Tharlet, Eve. *Little pig, big trouble* tr. by Andrew Clements; ill. by author. Picture Book Studio, 1989. Translation of: Henri, le petit cochon bleu ISBN 0-88708-073-1 Subj: Animals – pigs. Behavior – misbehavior. Friendship.

Thayer, Ernest L. *Casey at the bat: a ballad of the Republic, sung in the year 1888* ill. by Patricia Polacco. Putnam's, 1988. ISBN 0-399-21585-9 Subj: Poetry, rhyme. Sports – baseball.

Thayer, Jane. *Andy and his fine friends* ill. by Meg Wohlberg. Morrow, 1960. Subj: Animals. Imagination – imaginary friends.

Andy and the runaway horse ill. by Meg Wohlberg. Morrow, 1963. Subj: Animals – horses. Traffic, traffic signs.

Andy and the wild worm ill. by Beatrice Darwin. Morrow, 1973, 1954. Subj: Animals – worms. Imagination.

The cat that joined the club ill. by Seymour Fleishman. Morrow, 1967. Subj: Animals – cats.

The clever raccoon ill. by Holly Keller. Morrow, 1981. Subj: Animals – raccoons. Behavior – trickery.

Gus and the baby ghost ill. by Seymour Fleishman. Morrow, 1972. Subj: Babies. Ghosts. Museums.

Gus loved his happy home ill. by Seymour Fleishman. Shoe String Pr., 1989. ISBN 0-208-02249-X Subj: Ghosts. Kites.

Gus was a friendly ghost ill. by Seymour Fleishman. Morrow, 1962. Subj: Friendship. Ghosts.

Gus was a gorgeous ghost ill. by Seymour Fleishman. Morrow, 1978. Subj: Clothing. Ghosts. Holidays – Halloween.

Gus was a real dumb ghost ill. by Joyce Audy dos Santos. Morrow, 1982. Subj: Ghosts. School.

The horse with the Easter bonnet ill. by Jay Hyde Barnum. Morrow, 1953. Subj: Animals – horses. Clothing – hats. Holidays – Easter.

I like trains ill. by George Fonseca. Harper, 1965. Subj: Trains. Transportation.

Mr. Turtle's magic glasses ill. by Mamoru Funai. Morrow, 1971. Subj: Behavior – boredom. Glasses. Magic. Reptiles – turtles, tortoises. Senses – seeing.

The popcorn dragon ill. by Jay Hyde Barnum. Morrow, 1953. Subj: Dragons. Food. Friendship.

The popcorn dragon ill. by Lisa McCue. Morrow, 1989. ISBN 0-688-08876-7 Subj: Dragons. Food. Friendship.

The puppy who wanted a boy ill. by Seymour Fleishman. Morrow, 1958. Subj: Animals – dogs. Holidays – Christmas.

The puppy who wanted a boy ill. by Lisa McCue. Morrow, 1986. ISBN 0-688-05945-7 Subj: Animals – dogs. Holidays – Christmas.

Quiet on account of dinosaur ill. by Seymour Fleishman. Morrow, 1964. Subj: Dinosaurs. Noise, sounds.

What's a ghost going to do? ill. by Seymour Fleishman. Morrow, 1966. Subj: Ghosts. Houses. Problem solving.

Thayer, Mike. *In the middle of the puddle* ill. by Bruce Degen. Harper, 1988. ISBN 0-06-026054-8 Subj: Frogs and toads. Reptiles – turtles, tortoises. Weather – rain.

The three bears. *The three bears* (Hillert, Margaret)

Thelen, Gerda. *The toy maker: how a tree becomes a toy village* retold by Louise F. Encking; ill. by Fritz Kukenthal. Albert Whitman, 1935. Subj: Activities – making things. Toys. Trees.

Thiele, Colin. *Farmer Schulz's ducks* ill. by Mary Milton. Harper, 1988. ISBN 0-06-026183-8 Subj: Birds – ducks. Farms. Foreign lands – Australia.

Thoburn, Tina. *A B See* (Ogle, Lucille)

I hear (Ogle, Lucille)

Thomas, Art. *Merry-go-rounds* ill. by George Overlie. Carolrhoda, 1981. Subj: Merry-go-rounds.

Thomas, Ianthe. *Lordy, Aunt Hattie* ill. by Thomas di Grazia. Harper, 1973. Subj: Ethnic groups in the U.S. – Afro-Americans. Family life – aunts, uncles. Seasons – summer.

Walk home tired, Billy Jenkins ill. by Thomas di Grazia. Harper, 1974. Subj: Activities – walking. City. Ethnic groups in the U.S. – Afro-Americans. Imagination.

Willie blows a mean horn ill. by Ann Toulmin-Rothe. Harper, 1981. Subj: Family life – fathers. Music.

Thomas, Iolette. *Janine and the new baby* ill. by Jennifer Northway. Dutton, 1987. ISBN 0-233-97916-6 Subj: Babies. Sibling rivalry.

Thomas, Jane Resh. *Saying good-bye to grandma* ill. by Marcia Sewall. Clarion, 1988. ISBN 0-89919-645-4 Subj: Death. Family life – grandmothers.

Wheels ill. by Emily Arnold McCully. Ticknor & Fields, 1986. ISBN 0-89919-410-9 Subj: Sports – bicycling.

Thomas, Karen. *The good thing...the bad thing* ill. by Yaroslava. Prentice-Hall, 1979. ISBN 0-13-360354-7 Subj: Behavior.

Thomas, Kathy. *The angel's quest* ill. by Jacqueline Seitz. Living Flame Pr., 1983. Subj: Angels. Character traits – perseverance. Orphans. Religion.

Thomas, Patricia. *The one and only, super-duper, golly-whopper, jim-dandy, really-handy clock-tock-stopper* ill. by John O'Brien. Lothrop, 1990. ISBN 0-688-09341-8 Subj: Animals – porcupines. Animals – rabbits. Clocks, watches. Noise, sounds. Poetry, rhyme.

"Stand back," said the elephant, "I'm going to sneeze!" ill. by Wallace Tripp. Lothrop, 1971. Subj: Animals. Humor. Poetry, rhyme.

"There are rocks in my socks!" said the ox to the fox ill. by Mordicai Gerstein. Lothrop, 1979. Subj: Animals – bulls, cows. Animals – foxes. Poetry, rhyme. Problem solving.

Thompson, Brenda. *Famous planes* by Brenda Thompson and Rosemary Giesen; ill. by Andrew Martin and Rosemary Giesen. Lerner, 1977. Subj: Airplanes, airports.

Pirates by Brenda Thompson and Rosemary Giesen; ill. by Simon Stern and Rosemary Giesen. Lerner, 1977. Subj: Pirates.

The winds that blow by Brenda Thompson and Cynthia Overbeck; ill. by Simon Stern and Rosemary Gieson. Lerner, 1977. Subj: Concepts – measurement. Sea and seashore. Weather – wind.

Thompson, Carol. *Baby days* ill. by author. Macmillan, 1991. ISBN 0-02-789325-1 Subj: Activities. Babies. Poetry, rhyme.

Time ill. by author. Delacorte Pr., 1989. ISBN 0-385-29765-3 Subj: Animals – bears. Clocks, watches. Time.

Thompson, Elizabeth. *The true book of time* (Ziner, Feenie)

Thompson, George Selden *see* Selden, George

Thompson, Harwood. *The witch's cat* ill. by Quentin Blake. Addison-Wesley, 1971. Subj: Animals – cats. Folk and fairy tales. Foreign lands – England. Witches.

Thompson, Richard. *Effie's bath* ill. by Eugenie Fernandes. Firefly, 1989. ISBN 1-55037-055-3 Subj: Activities – bathing. Friendship. Imagination.

Foo ill. by Eugenie Fernandes. Firefly, 1988. ISBN 1-55037-005-7 Subj: Emotions – love. Family life.

Gurgle, bubble, splash ill. by Eugenie Fernandes. Firefly, 1989. ISBN 1-55037-029-4 Subj: Family life. Imagination. Sea and seashore.

I have to see this ill. by Eugenie Fernandes. Firefly, 1988. ISBN 1-55037-015-4 Subj: Activities – walking. Family life – fathers. Night.

Jenny's Neighbours ill. by Kathryn E. Shoemaker. Firefly, 1987. ISBN 0-920303-73-0 Subj: Activities – playing. Friendship. Imagination.

Jesse on the night train ill. by Eugenie Fernandes. Firefly, 1990. ISBN 1-55037-093-6 Subj: Imagination. Night. Trains.

Sky full of babies ill. by Eugenie Fernandes. Firefly, 1987. ISBN 0-920303-93-5 Subj: Family life. Imagination. Space and space ships.

Thompson, Susan L. *Diary of a monarch butterfly* graphic design by Sas Colby; ill. by Judy LaMotte. Walker, 1976. Subj: Insects – butterflies, caterpillars. Science.

One more thing, dad ill. by Dora Leder. Albert Whitman, 1980. Subj: Counting, numbers.

Thompson, Vivian Laubach. *Camp-in-the-yard* ill. by Brinton Turkle. Holiday, 1961. Subj: Problem solving. Camps, camping. Twins.

The horse that liked sandwiches ill. by Aliki. Putnam's, 1962. Subj: Animals – horses. Food.

Thomson, Pat. *Beware of the aunts!* ill. by Emma Chichester Clark. Macmillan, 1992. ISBN 0-689-50538-8 Subj: Character traits – individuality. Family life – aunts, uncles.

Rhymes around the day ill. by Jan Ormerod. Lothrop, 1983. Subj: Family life. Nursery rhymes.

Thomson, Peggy. *The brave little tailor* (Grimm, Jacob)

The king has horse's ears ill. by David Small. Simon & Schuster, 1988. ISBN 0-671-64953-1 Subj: Behavior – secrets. Character traits – appearance. Royalty – kings.

Thomson, Ruth. *Eyes* ill. by Mike Galletly. Watts, 1988. ISBN 0-531-10549-0 Subj: Anatomy – eyes. Senses – seeing.

My bear: I can...can you? ill. by Ian Beck. Dial Pr., 1985. ISBN 0-8037-0110-1 Subj: Activities. Poetry, rhyme. Toys – teddy bears.

My bear: I like...do you? ill. by Ian Beck. Dial Pr., 1985. ISBN 0-8037-0105-5 Subj: Poetry, rhyme. Toys – teddy bears.

Peabody all at sea ill. by Ken Kirkwood. Lothrop, 1978. Subj: Activities – vacationing. Animals – dogs. Boats, ships. Careers – detectives. Crime. Problem solving.

Peabody's first case ill. by Ken Kirkwood. Lothrop, 1978. Subj: Animals – dogs. Careers – detectives. Crime. Problem solving.

Thoreau, Henry D. *What befell at Mrs. Brooks's* ill. by George Overlie. Lerner, 1974. ISBN 0-8225-0284-4 Subj: Behavior – hurrying.

Thorne, Ian *see* May, Julian

Thorne, Jenny. *Adam and Eve* ill. by author. Aladdin, 1989. ISBN 0-689-71305-3 Subj: Religion.

Jonah and the whale ill. by author. Aladdin, 1989. ISBN 0-689-71307-X Subj: Animals – whales. Religion.

My uncle ill. by author. Atheneum, 1982. Subj: Activities. Dreams. Family life – aunts, uncles. Sports – fishing.

Noah's ark ill. by author. Aladdin, 1989. ISBN 0-689-71306-1 Subj: Boats, ships. Religion – Noah.

The walls of Jericho ill. by author. Aladdin, 1989. ISBN 0-689-71308-8 Subj: Religion.

Thornhill, Jan. *A tree in a forest* ill. by author. Simon & Schuster, 1992. ISBN 0-671-75901-9 Subj: Ecology. Forest, woods. Trees.

Wildlife ABC ill. by author. Simon & Schuster, 1990. ISBN 0-671-67925-2 Subj: ABC books. Animals. Nature.

The wildlife 1-2-3 ill. by author. Simon & Schuster, 1989. ISBN 0-671-67926-0 Subj: Animals. Counting, numbers. Nature.

Threadgall, Colin. *Proud rooster and the fox* ill. by author. Morrow, 1992. ISBN 0-688-11124-6 Subj: Animals – foxes. Birds – chickens. Character traits – cleverness. Farms.

The three bears. *Goldilocks and the three bears* retold and ill. by H. Amery. E D C, 1988. ISBN 0-88110-318-7 Subj: Animals – bears. Folk and fairy tales.

Goldilocks and the three bears retold by Marcia Leonard; ill. by Yvette Banek. Silver Pr., 1990. ISBN 0-671-69346-8 Subj: Animals – bears. Folk and fairy tales.

Goldilocks and the three bears retold and ill. by Jan Brett. Dodd, 1987. ISBN 0-396-08925-9 Subj: Animals – bears. Folk and fairy tales.

Goldilocks and the three bears adapt. and ill. by Lorinda Bryan Cauley. Putnam's, 1981. Subj: Animals – bears. Folk and fairy tales.

Goldilocks and the three bears ill. by Jane Dyer. Grosset, 1984. ISBN 0-448-10213-7 Subj: Animals – bears. Folk and fairy tales. Format, unusual – board books.

Goldilocks and the three bears adapt. by Armand Eisen; ill. by Lynn Bywaters Ferris. Knopf, 1987. ISBN 0-394-55882-0 Subj: Animals – bears. Folk and fairy tales.

Goldilocks and the three bears adapt. and ill. by James Marshall. Dial Pr., 1988. ISBN 0-8037-0543-3 Subj: Animals – bears. Caldecott award honor book. Folk and fairy tales.

Goldilocks and the three bears retold and ill. by Janet Stevens. Holiday, 1985. ISBN 0-8234-0608-3 Subj: Animals – bears. Folk and fairy tales.

Goldilocks and the three bears adapt. and ill. by Bernadette Watts. Knopf, 1985. ISBN 0-03-005737-X Subj: Animals – bears. Folk and fairy tales.

The story of the three bears ill. by L. Leslie Brooke. Warne, 1934. Subj: Animals – bears. Folk and fairy tales.

The story of the three bears ill. by William Stobbs. McGraw-Hill, 1964. Subj: Animals – bears. Folk and fairy tales.

The three bears adapt. and ill. by Byron Barton. HarperCollins, 1991. ISBN 0-06-020424-9 Subj: Animals – bears. Folk and fairy tales.

The three bears ill. by Paul Galdone. Seabury Pr., 1972. Subj: Animals – bears. Folk and fairy tales.

The three bears adapted by Kathleen N. Daly; ill. by Feodor Rojankovsky. Golden Pr., 1967. Subj: Animals – bears. Folk and fairy tales.

The three bears ill. by Robin Spowart. Knopf, 1987. ISBN 0-394-98862-0 Subj: Animals – bears. Folk and fairy tales.

The three little pigs. *The original three little pigs re-told* adapt. by Marilyn J. Shearer; ill. by Jonathan Smith. Lauren Ashley & Joshua Storybooks, 1990. ISBN 0-685-33065-6 Subj: Animals – pigs. Animals – wolves. Character traits – cleverness. Folk and fairy tales.

The story of the three little pigs ill. by L. Leslie Brooke. Warne, 1934. Subj: Animals – pigs. Animals – wolves. Character traits – cleverness. Folk and fairy tales.

The story of the three little pigs ill. by William Stobbs. McGraw-Hill, 1965. Subj: Animals – pigs. Animals – wolves. Character traits – cleverness. Folk and fairy tales.

Three little pigs Facsimile ed. Bragdon, 1987. Reprint of 1924 ed ISBN 0-916410-38-2 Subj: Animals – pigs. Animals – wolves. Character traits – cleverness. Folk and fairy tales.

The three little pigs retold and ill. by Val Biro. Oxford Univ. Pr., 1991. ISBN 0-19-279880-4 Subj: Animals – pigs. Animals – wolves. Character traits – cleverness. Folk and fairy tales. Format, unusual – board books.

The three little pigs retold and ill. by Gavin Bishop. Scholastic, 1990. ISBN 0-590-43358-X Subj: Animals – pigs. Animals – wolves. Character traits – cleverness. Folk and fairy tales.

The three little pigs ill. by Erik Blegvad. Atheneum, 1980. Subj: Animals – pigs. Animals – wolves. Character traits – cleverness. Poetry, rhyme.

The three little pigs adapt. and ill. by Caroline Bucknall. Dial Pr., 1987. ISBN 0-8037-0100-4 Subj: Animals – pigs. Animals – wolves. Character traits – cleverness. Folk and fairy tales. Poetry, rhyme.

The three little pigs retold by H. Amery; ill. by Stephen Cartwright. E D C, 1987. ISBN 0-88110-293-8 Subj: Animals – pigs. Animals – wolves. Character traits – cleverness. Folk and fairy tales.

The three little pigs ill. by Lorinda Bryan Cauley. Putnam's, 1980. Subj: Animals – pigs. Animals – wolves. Character traits – cleverness. Folk and fairy tales.

The three little pigs tr. and adapt. by Elizabeth D. Crawford; ill. by Jean Claverie. North-South, 1989. ISBN 155858-004-2 Subj: Animals – pigs. Animals – wolves. Character traits – cleverness. Folk and fairy tales.

The three little pigs: in verse ill. by William Pène Du Bois. Viking, 1962. Subj: Animals – pigs. Animals – wolves. Character traits – cleverness. Folk and fairy tales. Poetry, rhyme.

The three little pigs ill. by Paul Galdone. Seabury Pr., 1970. Subj: Animals – pigs. Animals – wolves. Character traits – cleverness. Folk and fairy tales.

The three little pigs retold and ill. by James Marshall. Dial, 1989. ISBN 0-8037-0594-8 Subj: Animals – pigs. Animals – wolves. Character traits – cleverness. Folk and fairy tales.

The three little pigs ill. by Rodney Peppé. Lothrop, 1980. Subj: Animals – pigs. Animals – wolves. Character traits – cleverness. Folk and fairy tales.

The three little pigs ill. by Edda Reinl. Picture Book Studio, 1983. ISBN 0-907234-32-1 Subj: Animals – pigs. Animals – wolves. Character traits – cleverness. Folk and fairy tales.

The three little pigs ill. by John Wallner. Viking, 1987. ISBN 0-670-81707-4 Subj: Animals – pigs. Animals – wolves. Character traits – cleverness. Folk and fairy tales. Format, unusual – toy and movable books.

The three little pigs retold by Margaret Hillert; ill. by Irma Wilde. Follett, 1963. Subj: Animals – pigs. Animals – wolves. Character traits – cleverness. Folk and fairy tales.

The three little pigs: an old story ill. by Margot Zemach. Farrar, 1988. ISBN 0-374-37527-5 Subj: Animals – pigs. Animals – wolves. Character traits – cleverness. Folk and fairy tales.

The three little pigs and the big bad wolf retold and ill. by Glen Rounds. Holiday, 1992. ISBN 0-8234-0923-6 Subj: Animals – pigs. Animals – wolves. Character traits – cleverness. Folk and fairy tales. Poetry, rhyme.

The three little pigs and the fox adapt. by William H. Hooks; ill. by S. D. Schindler. Macmillan, 1989. ISBN 0-02-744431-7 Subj: Animals – pigs. Animals – foxes. Birds – chickens. Character traits – cleverness. Folk and fairy tales.

The three pigs ill. by Tony Ross. Pantheon, 1983. Subj: Animals – pigs. Animals – wolves. Character traits – cleverness. Folk and fairy tales.

Thurber, James. *Many moons* ill. by Marc Simont. Harcourt, 1990. ISBN 0-15-251872-X Subj: Clowns, jesters. Illness. Moon. Royalty – princesses.

Many moons ill. by Louis Slobodkin. Harcourt, 1943. Subj: Caldecott award book. Clowns, jesters. Illness. Moon. Royalty – princesses.

Thwaite, Ann. *The day with the Duke* ill. by George Him. World, 1969. Subj: Games.

Thwaites, Lyndsay. *Super Adam and Rosie Wonder* ill. by author. André Deutsch, 1983. ISBN 0-233-97532-2 Subj: Activities – playing. Family life.

Tibo, Gilles. *Simon and the snowflakes* ill. by author. Tundra, 1988. ISBN 0-88776-218-2 Subj: Friendship. Stars. Weather – snow.

Tierney, Hanne. *Where's your baby brother, Becky Bunting?* ill. by Paula Winter. Doubleday, 1979. Subj: Behavior – misbehavior. Family life. Sibling rivalry.

Timlock, Jason. *Basil, the loneliest boy* ill. by Brett Colquhoun. Viking, 1990. ISBN 0-670-83125-5 Subj: Emotions – loneliness.

Timmermans, Felix. *A gift from Saint Nicholas* adapt. by Carole Kismaric; ill. by Charles Mikolaycak. Holiday, 1988. ISBN 0-8234-0674-1 Subj: Character traits – generosity. Holidays – Christmas.

Ting. *Find the canary* (Morris, Neil)

Hide and seek (Morris, Neil)

Search for Sam (Morris, Neil)

Where's my hat? (Morris, Neil)

Tinkelman, Murray. *Cowgirl* ill. by author. Greenwillow, 1984. ISBN 0-688-02883-7 Subj: Animals – horses. Sports.

Tippett, James Sterling. *Counting the days* ill. by Elizabeth Tyler Wolcott. Harper, 1940. Subj: Holidays – Christmas. Poetry, rhyme.

Tison, Annette. *The adventures of the three colors* by Annette Tison and Talus Taylor. Collins-World, 1971. Subj: Concepts – color. Format, unusual.

Animal hide-and-seek by Annette Tison and Talus Taylor; ill. by authors. Collins-World, 1972. Subj: Activities – photographing. Animals. Format, unusual. Games. Insects.

Animals in color magic ill. by author. Merrill, 1980. Subj: Animals. Format, unusual.

Inside and outside by Annette Tison and Taylor Talus. Collins-World, 1972. Subj: Format, unusual. Houses.

Titherington, Jeanne. *Baby's boat* ill. by author. Greenwillow, 1992. ISBN 0-688-08556-3 Subj: Babies. Bedtime. Boats, ships. Lullabies. Sea and seashore.

Big world, small world ill. by author. Greenwillow, 1985. ISBN 0-688-04023-3 Subj: Concepts – perspective. Family life – mothers. Self-concept.

A child's prayer ill. by author. Greenwillow, 1989. ISBN 0-688-08318-8 Subj: Bedtime. Religion.

A place for Ben ill. by author. Greenwillow, 1987. ISBN 0-688-06494-9 Subj: Babies. Emotions – loneliness. Family life – brothers.

Pumpkin pumpkin ill. by author. Greenwillow, 1985. ISBN 0-688-50696-1 Subj: Gardens, gardening. Holidays – Halloween.

Where are you going, Emma? ill. by author. Greenwillow, 1988. ISBN 0-688-07082-5 Subj: Behavior – lost. Family life – grandfathers.

Titus, Eve. *Anatole* ill. by Paul Galdone. McGraw-Hill, 1957. Subj: Animals – mice. Caldecott award honor book. Foreign lands – France.

Anatole and the cat ill. by Paul Galdone. McGraw-Hill, 1957. Subj: Animals – cats. Animals – mice. Caldecott award honor book. Character traits – bravery. Foreign lands – France. Problem solving.

Anatole and the piano ill. by Paul Galdone. McGraw-Hill, 1966. Subj: Animals – mice. Foreign lands – France. Music.

Anatole and the Pied Piper ill. by Paul Galdone. McGraw-Hill, 1979. Subj: Animals – mice. Foreign lands – France. Music. Problem solving.

Anatole and the poodle ill. by Paul Galdone. McGraw-Hill, 1965. Subj: Animals – dogs. Animals – mice. Foreign lands – France. Problem solving.

Anatole and the robot ill. by Paul Galdone. McGraw-Hill, 1960. Subj: Animals – mice. Foreign lands – France. Problem solving. Robots.

Anatole and the thirty thieves ill. by Paul Galdone. McGraw-Hill, 1969. Subj: Animals – mice. Crime. Foreign lands – France. Problem solving.

Anatole and the toyshop ill. by Paul Galdone. McGraw-Hill, 1970. Subj: Animals – mice. Foreign lands – France. Problem solving. Toys.

Anatole in Italy ill. by Paul Galdone. McGraw-Hill, 1973. Subj: Animals – mice. Foreign lands – Italy. Problem solving.

Anatole over Paris ill. by Paul Galdone. McGraw-Hill, 1961. Subj: Activities – flying. Animals – mice. Foreign lands – France. Kites.

The kitten who couldn't purr ill. by Amrei Fechner. Morrow, 1991. ISBN 0-688-09364-7 Subj: Animals. Animals – cats. Noise, sounds.

Tobias, Tobi. *At the beach* ill. by Gloria Singer. McKay, 1978. Subj: Activities – vacationing. Family life. Sea and seashore.

Chasing the goblins away ill. by Victor G. Ambrus. Warne, 1977. Subj: Bedtime. Goblins. Night. Sleep.

The dawdlewalk ill. by Jeanette Swofford. Carolrhoda, 1983. Subj: Activities – walking.

A day off ill. by Ray Cruz. Putnam's, 1973. ISBN 0-399-60762-5 Subj: Family life. Illness.

Jane wishing ill. by Trina Schart Hyman. Viking, 1977. Subj: Behavior – wishing. Emotions – happiness. Family life. Humor. Self-concept.

Moving day ill. by William Pène du Bois. Knopf, 1976. Subj: Emotions. Moving. Toys – teddy bears.

Tobias catches trout (Hertz, Ole)

Tobias goes ice fishing (Hertz, Ole)

Tobias goes seal hunting (Hertz, Ole)

Tobias has a birthday (Hertz, Ole)

Todaro, John. *Phillip the flower-eating phoenix* by John Todaro and Barbara Ellen; ill. by John Todaro. Abelard-Schuman, 1961. Subj: Mythical creatures.

Todd, Kathleen. *Snow* ill. by author. Addison-Wesley, 1982. Subj: Activities – playing. Family life. Weather – snow.

Tokuda, Wendy. *Humphrey the lost whale: a true story* by Wendy Tokuda and Richard Hall; ill. by Hanako Wakiyama. Heian, 1986. ISBN 0-89346-270-5 Subj: Animals – whales. Behavior – lost. Behavior – needing someone. Sea and seashore.

Tolhurst, Marilyn. *Somebody and the three Blairs* ill. by Simone Abel. Watts, 1991. ISBN 0-531-08478-7 Subj: Animals – bears. Folk and fairy tales.

Tolkien, Baillie. *The Father Christmas letters* (Tolkien, J. R. R. (John Ronald Reuel))

Tolkien, J. R. R. (John Ronald Reuel). *The Father Christmas letters* ed. by Baillie Tolkien; ill. by author. Houghton, 1977. Subj: Communication. Holidays – Christmas.

Tolstoĭ, Alekseĭ Nikolaevich. *The great big enormous turnip* ill. by Helen Oxenbury. Watts, 1968. Subj: Cumulative tales. Farms. Folk and fairy tales. Foreign lands – Russia. Plants. Problem solving.

Shoemaker Martin tr. from Russian by Michael Hale; adapt. by Brigitte Hanhart; ill. by Bernadette Watts. Holt, 1986. ISBN 0-8050-0040-2 Subj: Character traits – generosity. Character traits – kindness. Religion.

Tom Thumb. *Grimm Tom Thumb* by Jacob and Wilhelm Grimm; tr. by Anthea Bell; ill. by Svend Otto S. Larousse, 1976. Translation of Tommeliden Subj: Elves and little people. Folk and fairy tales.

Tom Thumb ill. by L. Leslie Brooke. Warne, 1904. Subj: Elves and little people. Folk and fairy tales.

Tom Thumb adapt. by Margaret Hillert; ill. by Dennis Hockerman. Follett, 1982. Subj: Elves and little people. Folk and fairy tales.

Tom Thumb by the Brothers Grimm; ill. by Felix Hoffmann. Atheneum, 1973. Translation of Der Daumling Subj: Elves and little people. Folk and fairy tales.

Tom Thumb: a tale adapt. and ill. by Lidia Postma. Schocken, 1983. Based on a tale by Charles Perrault Subj: Elves and little people. Folk and fairy tales.

Tom Thumb adapt. and ill. by Richard Jesse Watson. Harcourt, 1989. ISBN 0-15-289280-X Subj: Elves and little people. Folk and fairy tales.

Tom Thumb ill. by William Wiesner. Walck, 1974. Subj: Elves and little people. Folk and fairy tales.

Tom Tit Tot. *Tom Tit Tot: an English folk tale* ill. by Evaline Ness. Scribner's, 1965. Subj: Caldecott award honor book. Folk and fairy tales. Magic. Names.

Tomchek, Ann Heinrichs. *I can be a chef* Childrens Pr., 1985. ISBN 0-516-01886-8 Subj: Activities – cooking. Careers – chefs.

Tomfool *see* Farjeon, Eleanor

Tomkins, Jasper. *The catalog* ill. by author. Green Tiger Pr., 1981. Subj: Animals. Humor.

Tompert, Ann. *Badger on his own* ill. by Diane de Groat. Crown, 1978. Subj: Animals – badgers. Birds – owls.

Charlotte and Charles ill. by John Wallner. Crown, 1979. Subj: Giants. Middle ages.

Grandfather Tang's story ill. by Robert Andrew Parker. Crown, 1990. ISBN 0-517-57272-9 Subj: Animals – foxes. Family life – grandfathers. Foreign lands – China.

Little Fox goes to the end of the world ill. by John Wallner. Crown, 1976. Subj: Animals – foxes. Imagination.

Little Otter remembers and other stories ill. by John Wallner. Crown, 1977. Subj: Animals – otters. Family life – mothers.

Nothing sticks like a shadow ill. by Lynn Munsinger. Houghton, 1984. Subj: Animals – groundhogs. Animals – rabbits. Shadows.

Savina, the gypsy dancer ill. by Dennis Nolan. Macmillan, 1991. ISBN 0-02-789205-0 Subj: Activities – dancing. Gypsies.

The silver whistle ill. by Beth Peck. Macmillan, 1988. ISBN 0-02-789160-7 Subj: Foreign lands – Mexico. Holidays – Christmas.

The Tzar's bird ill. by Robert Rayevsky. Macmillan, 1990. ISBN 0-02-789401-0 Subj: Emotions – fear. Foreign lands – Russia. Royalty.

Will you come back for me? ill. by Robin Kramer. Albert Whitman, 1988. ISBN 0-8075-9112-2 Subj: Behavior – needing someone. Dreams. Emotions – fear. School.

Tord, Bijou Le *see* Le Tord, Bijou

Torgersen, Don Arthur. *The girl who tricked the troll* ill. by Tom Dunnington. Children's Pr., 1978. Subj: Farms. Trolls.

The troll who lived in the lake ill. by Tom Dunnington. Children's Pr., 1978. Subj: Ecology. Trolls.

Tornborg, Pat. *The Sesame Street cookbook* ill. by Robert Dennis. Platt, 1978. Subj: Activities – cooking. Puppets.

Tornqvist, Rita. *The Christmas carp* tr. from Swedish by Greta Kilburn; ill. by Marit Tornqvist. Farrar, 1990. ISBN 91-29-59784-6 Subj: Behavior – wishing. Family life. Holidays – Christmas.

Torre, Betty L. *The luminous pearl* ill. by Carol Inouye. Watts, 1990. ISBN 0-531-08490-6 Subj: Character traits – honesty. Character traits – kindness. Dragons. Folk and fairy tales. Foreign lands – China. Royalty.

Towle, Faith M. *The magic cooking pot: a folktale of India* ill. by author. Houghton, 1975. Subj: Folk and fairy tales. Food. Foreign lands – India. Magic.

Townsend, Anita. *The kangaroo* ill. by Michael Atkinson. Watts, 1979. Subj: Animals – kangaroos. Science.

Townsend, Kenneth. *Felix, the bald-headed lion* ill. by author. Delacorte, 1967. Subj: Animals – lions. Clothing. Emotions – embarrassment. Hair.

Townsend, Maryann. *Pop's secret* by Maryann Townsend and Ronnie Stern; ill. with photos. Addison-Wesley, 1980. Subj: Death. Family life – grandfathers.

Townson, Hazel. *Terrible Tuesday* ill. by Tony Ross. Morrow, 1986. ISBN 0-688-06244-X Subj: Emotions – fear. Family life. Imagination.

What on earth...? ill. by Mary Rees. Little, 1991. ISBN 0-316-85138-8 Subj: Activities – playing. Imagination. Family life – fathers.

Toye, William. *Fire stealer* photos. by Elizabeth Cleaver. Oxford Univ. Pr., 1988. ISBN 0-19-540515-3 Subj: Folk and fairy tales. Indians of North America.

How summer came to Canada photos. by Elizabeth Cleaver. Oxford Univ. Pr., 1988. ISBN 0-19-540290-1 Subj: Folk and fairy tales. Indians of North America.

The loon's necklace photos. by Elizabeth Cleaver. Oxford Univ. Pr., 1988. ISBN 0-19-540278-2 Subj: Folk and fairy tales. Indians of North America.

The mountain goats of Temlaham photos. by Elizabeth Cleaver. Oxford Univ. Pr., 1988. ISBN 0-19-540320-7 Subj: Folk and fairy tales. Indians of North America.

Trân-Khánh-Tuyêt. *The little weaver of Thái-Yên Village* tr. from Vietnamese by Christopher N. H. Jenkins and author; ill. by Nancy Hom. Childrens Book Pr., 1987. ISBN 0-89239-030-1 Subj: Activities – weaving. Foreign lands – Vietnam. Language.

Tredez, Alain *see* Trez, Alain

Tredez, Denise *see* Trez, Denise

Treherne, Katie Thamer. *The little mermaid* (Andersen, H. C. (Hans Christian))

Trent, Robbie. *The first Christmas* ill. by Marc Simont. Harper, 1948. Subj: Holidays – Christmas. Poetry, rhyme. Religion.

Tresselt, Alvin R. *Autumn harvest* ill. by Roger Antoine Duvoisin. Lothrop, 1951. Subj: Holidays – Thanksgiving. Seasons – fall.

The beaver pond ill. by Roger Antoine Duvoisin. Lothrop, 1970. Subj: Animals – beavers. Ecology.

The dead tree ill. by Charles Robinson. Parents, 1972. Subj: Ecology. Trees.

The fisherman under the sea (Matsutani, Miyoko)

Follow the wind ill. by Roger Antoine Duvoisin. Lothrop, 1950. Subj: Poetry, rhyme. Weather – wind.

Frog in the well ill. by Roger Antoine Duvoisin. Lothrop, 1958. Subj: Frogs and toads.

The gift of the tree ill. by Henri Sorensen. Lothrop, 1992. Original title: The dead tree ISBN 0-688-10685-4 Subj: Ecology. Forest, woods. Trees.

Hi, Mister Robin ill. by Roger Antoine Duvoisin. Lothrop, 1950. ISBN 0-688-51168-6 Subj: Birds – robins. Family life. Seasons – spring.

Hide and seek fog ill. by Roger Antoine Duvoisin. Lothrop, 1965. Subj: Caldecott award honor book. Sea and seashore. Weather – fog.

How far is far? ill. by Ward Brackett. Parents, 1964. Subj: Concepts – distance. Science.

I saw the sea come in ill. by Roger Antoine Duvoisin. Lothrop, 1954. Subj: Behavior – solitude. Sea and seashore.

It's time now! ill. by Roger Antoine Duvoisin. Lothrop, 1969. Subj: City. Seasons.

Johnny Maple-Leaf ill. by Roger Antoine Duvoisin. Lothrop, 1948. Subj: Seasons. Seasons – fall. Trees.

The mitten: an old Ukrainian folktale ill. by Yaroslava. Lothrop, 1964. Adapted by Alvin Tresselt from the version by E. Rachev Subj: Animals. Folk and fairy tales. Foreign lands – Ukraine.

The rabbit story ill. by Carolyn Ewing. Lothrop, 1989. ISBN 0-688-08651-9 Subj: Animals – rabbits.

Rabbit story ill. by Leonard Weisgard. Lothrop, 1957. Subj: Animals – rabbits.

Rain drop splash ill. by Leonard Weisgard. Lothrop, 1946. Subj: Caldecott award honor book. Cumulative tales. Science. Weather – rain.

Smallest elephant in the world ill. by Milton Glaser. Knopf, 1959. Subj: Animals – elephants. Character traits – smallness. Circus.

Sun up ill. by Roger Antoine Duvoisin. Lothrop, 1949. Subj: Farms. Sun. Weather.

Sun up ill. by Henri Sorensen. Lothrop, 1991. ISBN 0-688-08657-8 Subj: Farms. Sun. Weather.

Wake up, city! ill. by Carolyn Ewing. Lothrop, 1989. ISBN 0-688-08653-5 Subj: City. Morning.

Wake up, farm! ill. by Roger Antoine Duvoisin. Lothrop, 1955. ISBN 0-688-51162-7 Subj: Animals. Farms. Morning. Noise, sounds.

Wake up, farm! ill. by Carolyn Ewing. Lothrop, 1991. ISBN 0-688-08655-1 Subj: Animals. Farms. Morning. Noise, sounds.

What did you leave behind? ill. by Roger Antoine Duvoisin. Lothrop, 1978. Subj: Emotions.

White snow, bright snow ill. by Roger Antoine Duvoisin. Lothrop, 1947. Subj: Caldecott award book. Weather – snow.

The wind and Peter ill. by Garry McKenzie. Oxford Univ. Pr., 1948. Subj: Weather – wind.

The witch's magic cloth (Matsutani, Miyoko)

The world in the candy egg ill. by Roger Antoine Duvoisin. Lothrop, 1967. Subj: Eggs. Holidays – Easter. Magic.

Trez, Alain. *The little knight's dragon* (Trez, Denise)

Rabbit country (Trez, Denise)

Trez, Denise. *Good night, Veronica* by Denise and Alain Trez; tr. by Douglas McKee; ill. by authors. Viking, 1968. Subj: Bedtime. Dreams. Sleep.

The little knight's dragon by Denise and Alain Trez; ill. by authors. Collins-World, 1963. Subj: Dragons. Knights.

Maila and the flying carpet by Denise and Alain Trez; tr. by Douglas McKee; ill. by authors. Viking, 1969. Subj: Activities – flying. Foreign lands – India. Magic. Royalty.

Rabbit country by Denise and Alain Trez; ill. by authors. Viking, 1966. Subj: Animals – rabbits.

The royal hiccups by Denise and Alain Trez; tr. by Douglas McKee; ill. by authors. Viking, 1965. Subj: Emotions – fear. Illness. Royalty.

Trimby, Elisa. *Mr. Plum's paradise* ill. by author. Lothrop, 1977. Subj: City. Gardens, gardening.

Trinca, Rod. *One woolly wombat* by Rod Trinca and Kerry Argent; ill. by Kerry Argent. Kane/Miller, 1985. ISBN 0-916291-00-6 Subj: Animals. Counting, numbers. Foreign lands – Australia.

Tripp, Paul. *The strawman who smiled by mistake* ill. by Wendy Watson. Doubleday, 1967. Subj: Emotions – happiness. Farms. Friendship. Scarecrows.

Tripp, Valerie. *Happy, happy Mother's Day* ill. by Sandra Kalthoff Martin. Children's Pr., 1989. ISBN 0-516-01521-4 Subj: Animals. Holidays – Mother's Day. Poetry, rhyme.

Sillyhen's big surprise ill. by Sandra Kalthoff Martin. Children's Pr., 1989. ISBN 0-516-01522-2 Subj: Birds – chickens. Poetry, rhyme.

Tripp, Wallace. *My Uncle Podger* ill. by author. Little, 1975. Based on a passage from Three men in a boat (to say nothing of the dog) by Jerome Klapka Jerome Subj: Animals – rabbits. Family life – aunts, uncles. Humor.

The tale of a pig: a caucasian folktale adapt. and ill. by Wallace Tripp. McGraw-Hill, 1968. Subj: Animals – pigs. Folk and fairy tales.

Trivas, Irene. *Annie...Anya: a month in Moscow* ill. by author. Watts, 1992. ISBN 0-531-08602-X Subj: Friendship. Foreign lands – Russia.

Emma's Christmas ill. by author. Watts, 1988. ISBN 0-531-08380-2 Subj: Holidays – Christmas. Songs. Weddings.

Troughton, Joanna. *How rabbit stole the fire* ill. by adapt. Harper, 1986. ISBN 0-87226-040-2 Subj: Animals – rabbits. Fire. Folk and fairy tales. Indians of North America.

How the birds changed their feathers: a South American Indian folk tale ill. by adapt. Harper, 1986. ISBN 0-87226-080-1 Subj: Birds. Concepts – color. Folk and fairy tales. Foreign lands – South America.

Make-believe tales ill. by reteller. Bedrick, 1991. ISBN 0-87226-451-3 Subj: Animals. Folk and fairy tales. Foreign lands – Burma.

Mouse-Deer's market ill. by adapt. Harper, 1984. ISBN 0-911745-63-7 Subj: Animals. Animals – deer. Character traits – cleverness.

The quail's egg ill. by author. Bedrick, 1988. ISBN 0-87226-185-9 Subj: Birds. Cumulative tales. Eggs.

Tortoise's dream: an African folk tale ill. by adapt. Harper, 1986. ISBN 0-87226-039-9 Subj: Dreams. Folk and fairy tales. Foreign lands – Africa. Reptiles – turtles, tortoises.

What made Tiddalik laugh: an Australian Aborigine folk tale ill. by adapt. Harper, 1986. ISBN 0-87226-081-X Subj: Folk and fairy tales. Foreign lands – Australia. Frogs and toads.

Who will be the sun? ill. by adapt. Harper, 1986. ISBN 0-87226-038-0 Subj: Folk and fairy tales. Indians of North America. Sun.

Trucks ill. with photos. Macmillan, 1991. ISBN 0-689-71405-X Subj: Transportation. Trucks.

Trucks ill. by Art Seiden. Platt, 1983. Subj: Trucks.

Tryon, Leslie. *Albert's alphabet* ill. by author. Atheneum, 1991. ISBN 0-689-31642-9 Subj: ABC books. Activities – making things. Birds – ducks. School.

Albert's play ill. by author. Atheneum, 1992. ISBN 0-689-31525-2 Subj: Animals. Poetry, rhyme. Theater.

Tsow, Ming. *A day with Ling* photos. by Christopher Cormack. Hamish Hamilton, 1983. Subj: Family life.

Tsultim, Yeshe. *The mouse king: a story from Tibet* ill. by Kusho Ralla. Penguin, 1979. Subj: Animals – mice. Folk and fairy tales. Foreign lands – Tibet.

Tsutsui, Yoriko. *Anna in charge* ill. by Akiko Hayashi. Viking, 1989. ISBN 0-670-81672-8 Subj: Activities – baby-sitting. Behavior – lost. Emotions – fear. Family life.

Anna's secret friend ill. by Akiko Hayashi. Viking, 1987. ISBN 0-670-81670-1 Subj: Family life. Friendship. Moving.

Before the picnic ill. by Akiko Hayashi. Putnam's, 1987. ISBN 0-399-21458-5 Subj: Activities – picnicking. Family life.

Tuber, Joel. *The steadfast tin soldier* (Andersen, H. C. (Hans Christian))

The ugly duckling (Andersen, H. C. (Hans Christian))

Tucker, Kathleen. *The little bear who forgot* (Chevalier, Christa)

My mother never listens to me (Sharmat, Marjorie Weinman)

Tucker, Nicholas. *Mother Goose abroad: nursery rhymes* ill. by Trevor Stubley. Crowell, 1974. Subj: Nursery rhymes.

Tucker, Sian. *At home* ill. by author. Simon & Schuster, 1991. ISBN 0-671-73399-0 Subj: Babies. Family life. Format, unusual – board books.

Going out ill. by author. Simon & Schuster, 1991. ISBN 0-671-73397-4 Subj: Babies. Nature. Format, unusual – board books.

My clothes ill. by author. Simon & Schuster, 1991. ISBN 0-671-73396-6 Subj: Babies. Clothing. Format, unusual – board books.

My toys ill. by author. Simon & Schuster, 1991. ISBN 0-671-73398-2 Subj: Babies. Format, unusual – board books. Toys.

Tudor, Bethany. *Samuel's tree house* ill. by author. Collins-World, 1979. Subj: Birds – ducks. Friendship. Houses. Toys. Trees.

Skiddycock Pond ill. by author. Lippincott, 1965. Subj: Birds – ducks. Boats, ships.

Tudor, Tasha. *Around the year* ill. by author. Walck, 1957. Subj: Days of the week, months of the year. Poetry, rhyme. Seasons.

Corgiville fair ill. by author. Crowell, 1971. Subj: Animals – goats. Fairs. Trolls.

The doll's Christmas ill. by author. Oxford Univ. Pr., 1950. Subj: Holidays – Christmas. Toys – dolls.

Junior's tune ill. by author. Holiday, 1980. Subj: Music. Sibling rivalry.

Mildred and the mummy ill. by author. Holiday, 1980. Subj: Libraries.

Miss Kiss and the nasty beast ill. by author. Holiday, 1979. Subj: Emotions – love.

More prayers ill. by author. McKay, 1967. ISBN 0-8098-1954-6 Subj: Religion.

1 is one ill. by author. Walck, 1956. Subj: Caldecott award honor book. Counting, numbers.

Snow before Christmas ill. by author. Oxford Univ. Pr., 1941. Subj: Holidays – Christmas. Seasons – winter. Weather – snow.

A tale for Easter ill. by author. McKay, 1972. ISBN 0-8098-1807-8 Subj: Dreams. Holidays – Easter.

Tulloch, Richard. *Danny in the toybox* ill. by Armin Greder. Morrow, 1991. ISBN 0-688-10502-5 Subj: Behavior – hiding. Emotions – anger. Family life.

Stories from our house ill. by Julie Vivas. Cambridge Univ. Pr., 1987. ISBN 0-521-33485-3 Subj: Family life. Humor.

Tune, Suelyn Ching. *How Maui slowed the sun* ill. by Robin Yoko Burningham. Univ. of Hawaii, 1988. ISBN 0-8248-1083-X Subj: Folk and fairy tales. Hawaii. Magic.

Türk, Hanne. *Goodnight Max* ill. by author. Firefly Pr., 1983. Subj: Animals – mice. Bedtime. Wordless.

Happy birthday Max ill. by author. Alphabet Pr., 1984. Subj: Animals – mice. Birthdays. Wordless.

Max packs ill. by author. Alphabet Pr., 1984. Subj: Activities – traveling. Animals – mice. Wordless.

Max the artlover ill. by author. Alphabet Pr., 1983. Subj: Animals – mice. Art. Wordless.

Max versus the cube ill. by author. Alphabet Pr., 1982. Subj: Animals – mice. Problem solving. Riddles. Wordless.

Merry Christmas Max ill. by author. Firefly Pr., 1983. Subj: Animals – mice. Holidays – Christmas. Wordless.

Rainy day Max ill. by author. Alphabet Pr., 1983. Subj: Activities – walking. Animals – mice. Weather – rain. Wordless.

Raking leaves with Max ill. by author. Firefly Pr., 1983. Subj: Activities – working. Animals – mice. Wordless.

The rope skips Max ill. by author. Alphabet Pr., 1982. Subj: Activities. Animals – mice. Wordless.

Snapshot Max ill. by author. Alphabet Pr., 1984. Subj: Activities – photographing. Animals – mice. Wordless.

A surprise for Max ill. by author. Alphabet Pr., 1982. Subj: Animals – mice. Problem solving. Wordless.

Turkle, Brinton. *The adventures of Obadiah* ill. by author. Viking, 1977. ISBN 0-670-10614-3 Subj: Behavior – lying. Character traits – honesty. U.S. history.

Deep in the forest ill. by author. Dutton, 1976. Subj: Animals – bears. Folk and fairy tales. Wordless.

Do not open ill. by author. Dutton, 1981. Subj: Animals – cats. Behavior – trickery. Behavior – wishing. Monsters. Sea and seashore.

The magic of Millicent Musgrave ill. by author. Viking, 1967. Subj: Magic.

Obadiah the Bold story and pictures by Brinton Turkle. Viking, 1965. Subj: Activities – playing. Behavior – growing up. Sea and seashore. U.S. history.

Rachel and Obadiah ill. by author. Dutton, 1978. Subj: Behavior – sharing. Money. Sibling rivalry.

The sky dog ill. by author. Viking, 1969. Subj: Animals – dogs. Imagination. Sea and seashore. Weather – clouds.

Thy friend, Obadiah ill. by author. Viking, 1969. Subj: Birds – sea gulls. Caldecott award honor book. Character traits – kindness to animals. Seasons – winter. U.S. history.

Turnage, Sheila. *Trout the magnificent* ill. by Janet Stevens. Harcourt, 1984. Subj: Behavior – dissatisfaction. Fish. Self-concept.

Turnbull, Ann. *Rob goes a-hunting* ill. by Denise Teasdale. Watts, 1990. ISBN 0-531-08477-9 Subj: Animals – dogs. Behavior – lost. Sports – hunting.

The sand horse ill. by Michael Foreman. Atheneum, 1989. ISBN 0-689-31581-3 Subj: Careers – artists. Sand. Sea and seashore.

The tapestry cats ill. by Carol Morley. Little, 1992. ISBN 0-316-85626-6 Subj: Animals – cats. Behavior – wishing. Birthdays. Fairies. Royalty – princesses. Royalty – queens.

Turner, Ann Warren. *Dakota dugout* ill. by Ronald Himler. Macmillan, 1985. ISBN 0-02-789700-1 Subj: Farms. U.S. history.

Hedgehog for breakfast ill. by Lisa McCue. Macmillan, 1989. ISBN 0-02-789241-7 Subj: Animals – foxes. Animals – hedgehogs. Behavior – misunderstanding.

Nettie's trip south ill. by Ronald Himler. Macmillan, 1987. ISBN 0-02-789240-9 Subj: Activities – traveling. Behavior – disbelief. Ethnic groups in the U.S. – Afro-Americans. Family life.

Stars for Sarah ill. by Mary Teichman. HarperCollins, 1991. ISBN 0-06-026187-0 Subj: Family life – mothers. Moving.

Through moon and stars and night skies ill. by James Graham Hale. HarperCollins, 1990. ISBN 0-06-026190-0 Subj: Adoption.

Tickle a pickle ill. by Karen Ann Weinhaus. Macmillan, 1986. ISBN 0-02-789280-8 Subj: Poetry, rhyme.

Turner, Charles. *The turtle and the moon* ill. by Melissa Bay Mathis. Dutton, 1991. ISBN 0-525-44659-1 Subj: Activities – playing. Moon. Reptiles – turtles, tortoises.

Turner, Ethel. *Walking to school* ill. by Peter Gouldthorpe. Watts, 1989. ISBN 0-531-08399-3 Subj: Activities – walking. Emotions. Foreign lands – Australia. Poetry, rhyme. School.

Turner, Gwenda. *Colors* ill. by author. Viking, 1990. ISBN 0-670-82552-2 Subj: Concepts – color.

Once upon a time ill. by author. Viking, 1990. ISBN 0-670-82551-4 Subj: Family life. Time.

Playbook ill. by author. Viking, 1986. ISBN 0-670-80660-9 Subj: School.

Shapes ill. by author. Viking, 1991. ISBN 0-670-83744-X Subj: Concepts – shape.

Turner, Josie *see* Crawford, Phyllis

Turska, Krystyna. *The magician of Cracow* ill. by author. Greenwillow, 1975. Subj: Character traits – ambition. Devil. Folk and fairy tales. Foreign lands – Poland. Magic. Moon.

The woodcutter's duck ill. by author. Macmillan, 1972. Subj: Birds – ducks. Character traits – kindness to animals. Folk and fairy tales. Foreign lands – Poland. Frogs and toads.

The turtle ill. by Charlotte Knox. Rourke, 1983. Subj: Reptiles – turtles, tortoises.

Tusa, Tricia. *Camilla's new hairdo* ill. by author. Farrar, 1991. ISBN 0-374-31021-1 Subj: Character traits – individuality. Hair. Imagination. Problem solving.

Chicken ill. by author. Macmillan, 1986. ISBN 0-02-789320-0 Subj: Behavior – misunderstanding. Birds – chickens. Pets. Self-concept.

Libby's new glasses ill. by author. Holiday, 1984. Subj: Glasses. Self-concept. Senses – seeing.

Maebelle's suitcase ill. by author. Macmillan, 1987. ISBN 0-02-789250-6 Subj: Birds. Clothing. Old age.

Miranda ill. by author. Macmillan, 1985. ISBN 0-02-789520-3 Subj: Character traits – stubbornness. Music.

Sherman and Pearl ill. by author. Macmillan, 1989. ISBN 0-02-789542-4 Subj: Progress. Roads.

Stay away from the junkyard! ill. by author. Macmillan, 1988. ISBN 0-02-789541-6 Subj: Art. Behavior – collecting things.

Tutt, Kay Cunningham. *And now we call him Santa Claus* ill. by author. Lothrop, 1963. Subj: Holidays – Christmas.

The twelve days of Christmas. English folk song.
Brian Wildsmith's The twelve days of Christmas ill. by Brian Wildsmith. Watts, 1972. Subj: Cumulative tales. Holidays – Christmas. Music. Songs.

Jack Kent's twelve days of Christmas ill. by Jack Kent. Parents, 1973. Subj: Cumulative tales. Holidays – Christmas. Humor. Music. Songs.

The twelve days of Christmas ill. by Jan Brett. Dodd, 1986. ISBN 0-396-08821-X Subj: Cumulative tales. Holidays – Christmas. Music. Songs.

The twelve days of Christmas ill. by Ilonka Karasz. Harper, 1949. Subj: Cumulative tales. Holidays – Christmas. Music. Songs.

The twelve days of Christmas ill. by Ilse Plume. HarperCollins, 1990. ISBN 0-06-024738-X Subj: Cumulative tales. Holidays – Christmas. Music. Songs.

The twelve days of Christmas ill. by Erika Schneider. Alphabet Pr., 1984. Subj: Cumulative tales. Format, unusual. Holidays – Christmas. Music. Songs.

The twelve days of Christmas ill. by Sophie Windham. Putnam's, 1986. ISBN 0-399-21327-9 Subj: Cumulative tales. Holidays – Christmas. Music. Songs.

Twining, Edith. *Sandman* ill. by author. Doubleday, 1991. ISBN 0-385-41259-2 Subj: Bedtime. Boats, ships. Dreams. Sandman. Sleep.

Tworkov, Jack. *The camel who took a walk* ill. by Roger Antoine Duvoisin. Aladdin Books, 1951. Subj: Activities – walking. Animals. Animals – camels. Animals – tigers. Cumulative tales. Morning.

Tyler, Linda Wagner. *After Christmas tree* ill. by Susan Davis. Viking, 1990. ISBN 0-670-83045-3 Subj: Character traits – kindness to animals. Holidays – Christmas.

The sick-in-bed birthday book ill. by Susan Davis. Viking, 1988. ISBN 0-670-81823-2 Subj: Animals – pigs. Birthdays. Illness.

Waiting for mom ill. by Susan Davis. Viking, 1987. ISBN 0-670-81408-3 Subj: Animals – hippopotami. Behavior – worrying. Family life – mothers. School.

When daddy comes home ill. by Susan Davis. Viking, 1986. ISBN 0-670-80301-4 Subj: Animals – hippopotami. Family life – fathers.

Tyrrell, Anne. *Elizabeth Jane gets dressed* ill. by Caroline Castle. Barron's, 1987. ISBN 0-8120-

5775-9 Subj: Clothing. Days of the week, months of the year. Poetry, rhyme. Toys.

Mary Ann always can ill. by Caroline Castle. Barron's, 1988. ISBN 0-8120-5939-5 Subj: Character traits – individuality. Poetry, rhyme. Sibling rivalry.

Uchida, Yoshiko. *Sumi's prize* ill. by Kazue Mizumura. Scribner's, 1964. Subj: Character traits – ambition. Foreign lands – Japan. Kites.

Sumi's special happening ill. by Kazue Mizumura. Scribner's, 1966. Subj: Birthdays. Foreign lands – Japan. Old age.

The two foolish cats ill. by Margot Zemach. Macmillan, 1987. ISBN 0-689-50397-0 Subj: Animals – cats. Folk and fairy tales. Food.

Udry, Janice May. *Alfred* ill. by Judith S. Roth. Albert Whitman, 1960. Subj: Animals – dogs. Behavior – animals, dislike of. Emotions – fear.

Emily's autumn ill. by Erik Blegvad. Albert Whitman, 1969. Subj: Farms. Seasons – fall. Toys – dolls.

How I faded away ill. by Monica De Bruyn. Albert Whitman, 1976. Subj: Behavior – unnoticed, unseen. Emotions – embarrassment. Self-concept.

Is Susan here? ill. by Peter Edwards. Abelard-Schuman, 1962. Subj: Animals. Character traits – helpfulness. Family life – mothers. Imagination.

Let's be enemies ill. by Maurice Sendak. Harper, 1961. Subj: Behavior – fighting, arguing. Emotions – hate. Friendship.

Mary Ann's mud day ill. by Martha G. Alexander. Harper, 1967. Subj: Activities – playing. Ethnic groups in the U.S. – Afro-Americans.

Mary Jo's grandmother ill. by Eleanor Mill. Albert Whitman, 1970. Subj: Ethnic groups in the U.S. – Afro-Americans. Family life – grandmothers. Illness. Seasons – winter. Weather – snow.

The mean mouse and other mean stories ill. by Ed Young. Harper, 1962. Subj: Character traits – meanness.

The moon jumpers ill. by Maurice Sendak. Harper, 1959. Subj: Caldecott award honor book. Moon. Twilight.

"Oh no, cat!" ill. by Mary Chalmers. Coward, 1976. Subj: Animals – cats. Pets.

Theodore's parents ill. by Adrienne Adams. Lothrop, 1958. Subj: Adoption. Family life.

Thump and Plunk ill. by Ann Schweninger. Harper, 1981. Subj: Animals – mice. Family life – mothers. Sibling rivalry.

A tree is nice ill. by Marc Simont. Harper, 1956. Subj: Caldecott award book. Poetry, rhyme. Seasons. Trees.

What Mary Jo shared ill. by Eleanor Mill. Albert Whitman, 1966. Subj: Character traits – shyness. Ethnic groups in the U.S. Ethnic groups in the U.S. – Afro-Americans. Family life – fathers. School.

What Mary Jo wanted ill. by Eleanor Mill. Albert Whitman, 1968. Subj: Animals – dogs. Ethnic groups in the U.S. – Afro-Americans. Family life. Pets.

Ueno, Noriko. *Elephant buttons* ill. by author. Harper, 1973. Subj: Animals. Concepts – in and out. Concepts – size. Circular tales. Games. Humor. Participation. Wordless.

Uncle Gus *see* Rey, H. A. (Hans Augusto)

Ungerer, Jean Thomas *see* Ungerer, Tomi

Ungerer, Tomi. *The beast of Monsieur Racine* ill. by author. Farrar, 1971. Subj: Behavior – trickery. Foreign lands – France. Humor. Monsters.

Christmas eve at the Mellops ill. by author. Harper, 1960. Subj: Animals – pigs. Holidays – Christmas.

Crictor ill. by author. Harper, 1958. Subj: Humor. Reptiles – snakes.

Emile ill. by author. Harper, 1960. Subj: Humor. Octopuses.

The hat ill. by author. Parents, 1970. Subj: Clothing – hats. Foreign lands – Italy. Magic. Weather – wind.

The Mellops go diving for treasure ill. by author. Harper, 1957. Subj: Animals – pigs. Sea and seashore. Sports – skin diving.

The Mellops go flying ill. by author. Harper, 1957. Subj: Activities – flying. Airplanes, airports. Animals – pigs.

The Mellops go spelunking ill. by author. Harper, 1963. Subj: Animals – pigs. Caves. Character traits – perseverance.

The Mellops strike oil ill. by author. Harper, 1958. Subj: Animals – pigs. Fire. Oil.

Moon man ill. by author. Harper, 1967. Subj: Moon. Space and space ships.

No kiss for mother ill. by author. Harper, 1973. Subj: Animals – cats. Family life – mothers.

One, two, where's my shoe? ill. by author. Harper, 1964. Subj: Games. Wordless.

Orlando, the brave vulture ill. by author. Harper, 1966. Subj: Birds – vultures. Desert. Foreign lands – Mexico.

Rufus ill. by author. Harper, 1961. Subj: Animals – bats.

Snail, where are you? ill. by author. Harper, 1962. Subj: Animals – snails. Games. Wordless.

The three robbers ill. by author. Atheneum, 1962. Subj: Crime. Orphans.

Warwick's three bottles (Hodeir, André)

Zeralda's ogre ill. by author. Harper, 1967. Subj: Activities – cooking. Character traits – kindness. Giants. Monsters.

Untermeyer, Louis. *The kitten who barked* ill. by Lilian Obligado. Golden Pr., 1962. Subj: Animals – cats. Animals – dogs.

Unwin, Pippa. *The great zoo hunt!* ill. by author. Doubleday, 1990. ISBN 0-385-41107-3 Subj: Animals. Behavior – hiding. Zoos.

Updike, David. *An autumn tale* ill. by Robert Andrew Parker. Pippin Pr., 1988. ISBN 0-945912-02-1 Subj: Imagination. Night. Seasons – fall.

A winter's journey ill. by Robert Andrew Parker. Prentice-Hall, 1985. ISBN 0-13-961566-0 Subj: Animals – dogs. Dreams. Family life. Weather – snow.

Upham, Elizabeth. *Little brown bear loses his clothes* ill. by Normand Chartier. Platt, 1978. Subj: Animals – bears. Behavior – losing things.

Upton, Pat. *Who does this job?* ill. by Matt Novak. Boyds Mills Pr., 1991. ISBN 1-878093-20-7 Subj: Careers.

Who lives in the woods? ill. by Karen Lee Schmidt. Boyds Mills Pr., 1991. ISBN 1-878093-19-3 Subj: Animals. Forest, woods.

Usher, Margo Scegge *see* McHargue, Georgess

Uttley, Alison. *The Christmas box* ill. by Graham Percy. Faber, 1989. ISBN 0-571-15264-7 Subj: Animals – pigs. Holidays – Christmas.

Sam Pig and the dragon ill. by Graham Percy. Faber, 1989. ISBN 0-571-15294-5 Subj: Animals – pigs. Dragons.

Sam Pig and the hurdy-gurdy man ill. by Graham Percy. Faber, 1989. ISBN 0-571-15076-4 Subj: Animals – pigs. Music.

Sam Pig and the wind ill. by Graham Percy. Faber, 1989. ISBN 0-571-15295-3 Subj: Animals – pigs. Clothing – pants. Weather – wind.

Utton, Peter. *The witch's hand* ill. by author. Farrar, 1989. ISBN 0-374-38463-0 Subj: Family life. Witches.

Uysal, Ahmet E. *New patches for old* (Walker, Barbara K. (Barbara Kerlin)

Va, Leong. *A letter to the king* tr. from Norwegian by James Anderson; ill. by author. HarperCollins, 1991. ISBN 0-06-020070-7 Subj: Character traits – bravery. Character traits – loyalty. Folk and fairy tales. Foreign lands – China. Foreign languages. Royalty – kings.

Vaës, Alain. *The porcelain pepper pot* ill. by author. Little, 1985. ISBN 0-14-050727-2 Subj: Activities – picnicking. Emotions – love. Farms.

The wild hamster ill. by author. Little, 1985. ISBN 0-316-89504-0 Subj: Animals – hamsters. Pets.

Vagin, Vladimir. *Here comes the cat!* by Vladimir Vagin and Frank Asch; ill. by authors. Scholastic, 1989. ISBN 0-590-41859-9 Subj: Animals – cats. Animals – mice. Foreign languages.

Valderrama, Candido A. *Mister North Wind* (De Posadas Mane, Carmen)

Valens, Amy. *Jesse's day care* ill. by Richard Eric Brown. Houghton, 1990. ISBN 0-395-53357-0 Subj: Activities – working. Family life – mothers. School.

Valens, Evans G. *Wingfin and Topple* ill. by Clement Hurd. Collins-World, 1962. Subj: Activities – flying. Fish.

Valentine, Johnny. *The duke who outlawed jelly beans and other stories* ill. by Lynette Schmidt. Alyson, 1991. ISBN 1-55583-199-0 Subj: Folk and fairy tales.

Valeri, M. Eulalia. *Hansel and Gretel* (Grimm, Jacob)

Sleeping Beauty (Grimm, Jacob)

The ugly duckling (Grimm, Jacob)

Van Allsburg, Chris. *The garden of Abdul Gasazi* ill. by author. Houghton, 1979. Subj: Animals – dogs. Behavior – misbehavior. Caldecott award honor book. Imagination. Magic.

Jumanji ill. by author. Houghton, 1981. Subj: Caldecott award book. Games. Imagination. Jungle.

The mysteries of Harris Burdick ill. by author. Houghton, 1984. Subj: Imagination.

The polar express ill. by author. Houghton, 1985. ISBN 0-395-38949-6 Subj: Caldecott award book. Holidays – Christmas. Imagination. Night. Trains.

The stranger ill. by author. Houghton, 1986. ISBN 0-395-42331-7 Subj: Behavior – forgetfulness. Country. Seasons – fall.

Two bad ants ill. by author. Houghton, 1988. ISBN 0-395-48668-8 Subj: Houses. Insects – ants.

The wreck of the Zephyr ill. by author. Houghton, 1983. Subj: Boats, ships. Weather – storms.

The Z was zapped ill. by author. Houghton, 1987. ISBN 0-395-44612-0 Subj: ABC books.

Van Caster, Nancy. *An alligator lives in Benjamin's house* ill. by Dale Gottlieb. Putnam, 1990. ISBN 0-399-21489-5 Subj: Animals. Behavior – imitation. Family life. Imagination.

Vance, Eleanor Graham. *Jonathan* ill. by Albert John Pucci. Follett, 1966. Subj: Character traits – questioning. Poetry, rhyme. Weather.

Van den Honert, Dorry. *Demi the baby sitter* ill. by Meg Wohlberg. Morrow, 1961. Subj: Activities – baby-sitting. Animals – dogs.

Van der Beek, Deborah. *Alice's blue cloth* ill. by author. Putnam's, 1989. ISBN 0-399-216227 Subj: Birthdays. Family life.

Superbabe! ill. by author. Putnam's, 1988. ISBN 0-399-21507-7 Subj: Babies. Family life. Poetry, rhyme. Sibling rivalry.

Van der Meer, Atie. *Oh Lord!* (Van der Meer, Ron)

Pigs at home (Van der Meer, Ron)

Van der Meer, Ron. *Oh Lord!* by Ron and Atie van der Meer; ill. by authors. Crown, 1980. Subj: Humor. Religion.

Pigs at home by Ron and Atie Van der Meer; ill. by authors. Atheneum, 1988. ISBN 0-689-71232-4 Subj: Animals – pigs. Format, unusual.

Sailing ships (McGowan, Alan)

Van Emst, Charlotte. *Little Rabbit's big day* ill. by author. Little, 1990. ISBN 0-316-89623-3 Subj: Animals – rabbits. Concepts – size.

Van Haeringen, Annemarie. *The cats' tale* ill. by author. Oxford Univ. Pr., 1989. ISBN 0-19-279819-7 Subj: Animals – cats. Family life – grandparents. Giants.

Van Horn, Grace. *Little red rooster* ill. by Sheila Perry. Abelard-Schuman, 1961. Subj: Birds – chickens. Farms.

Van Horn, William. *Harry Hoyle's giant jumping bean* ill. by author. Atheneum, 1978. Subj: Animals – cats. Animals – pack rats. Behavior – collecting things.

Twitchtoe, the beastfinder ill. by author. Atheneum, 1978. Subj: Problem solving.

Van Laan, Nancy. *The big fat worm* ill. by Marisabina Russo. Knopf, 1987. ISBN 0-394-98763-2 Subj: Animals. Birds. Circular tales.

The legend of El Dorado story and ill. by Beatriz A. Vidal; adapt. by Nancy Van Laan. Knopf, 1991. ISBN 0-679-90136-1 Subj: Folk and fairy tales.

Foreign lands – South America. Indians of South America. Royalty – kings.

A mouse in my house ill. by Marjorie Priceman. Knopf, 1990. ISBN 0-679-90043-8 Subj: Animals. Behavior. Poetry, rhyme.

People, people, everywhere ill. by Nadine Bernard Westcott. Knopf, 1992. ISBN 0-679-91063-8 Subj: Activities. City. Poetry, rhyme.

Possum come a-knocking ill. by George Booth. Knopf, 1990. ISBN 0-394-92206-9 Subj: Animals – possums. Cumulative tales. Family life. Poetry, rhyme.

Rainbow crow ill. by Beatriz A. Vidal. Knopf, 1989. ISBN 0-394-99577-5 Subj: Birds – crows. Concepts – color. Fire. Folk and fairy tales. Indians of North America.

This is the hat ill. by Holly Meade. Little, 1992. ISBN 0-316-89727-2 Subj: Animals. Clothing – hats. Circular tales. Poetry, rhyme.

Van Leeuwen, Jean. *The emperor's new clothes* (Andersen, H. C. (Hans Christian))

Going west ill. by Thomas B. Allen. Dial, 1992. ISBN 0-8037-1028-3 Subj: Family life. Moving. U.S. history.

More tales of Oliver Pig ill. by Arnold Lobel. Dial Pr., 1981. Subj: Animals – pigs. Family life.

Too hot for ice cream ill. by Martha G. Alexander. Dial Pr., 1974. ISBN 0-8037-6077-9 Subj: Behavior – bad day. Sports – swimming. Weather.

Van Liew Foster, Doris *see* Foster, Doris Van Liew

Van Pallandt, Nicholas. *The butterfly night of Old Brown Bear* ill. by author. Farrar, 1992. ISBN 0-374-31009-2 Subj: Animals – bears. Dreams. Insects – butterflies, caterpillars.

VanRynbach, Iris. *The soup stone* adapt. and ill. by Iris VanRynbach. Greenwillow, 1988. ISBN 0-688-07255-0 Subj: Careers – military. Character traits – cleverness. Folk and fairy tales. Food.

Van Stockum, Hilda. *A day on skates: the story of a Dutch picnic* ill. by author. Hale, 1934. Subj: Activities – picnicking. Foreign lands – Holland. Sports – ice skating.

Van Vorst, M. L. *A Norse lullaby* ill. by Margot Tomes. Lothrop, 1988. ISBN 0-688-05813-2 Subj: Animals. Lullabies. Poetry, rhyme. Seasons – winter. Sleep.

Van Woerkom, Dorothy. *Alexandra the rock-eater: an old Rumanian tale retold* ill. by Rosekrans Hoffman. Knopf, 1978. Subj: Dragons. Family life. Folk and fairy tales. Food. Foreign lands.

Becky and the bear ill. by Margot Tomes. Putnam's, 1975. Subj: Animals – bears. Character traits – bravery. U.S. history.

Donkey Ysabel ill. by Normand Chartier. Macmillan, 1978. Subj: Animals – donkeys. Humor.

Harry and Shelburt ill. by Erick Ingraham. Macmillan, 1977. Subj: Animals – rabbits. Friendship. Reptiles – turtles, tortoises. Sports – racing.

Hidden messages ill. by Lynne Cherry. Crown, 1980. Subj: Communication. Insects. Science.

The queen who couldn't bake gingerbread ill. by Paul Galdone. Knopf, 1975. Subj: Folk and fairy tales. Foreign lands – Germany. Humor. Royalty – queens.

The rat, the ox and the zodiac: a Chinese legend ill. by Errol Le Cain. Crown, 1976. Subj: Animals. Animals – rats. Character traits – cleverness. Folk and fairy tales. Foreign lands – China. Zodiac.

Sea frog, city frog ill. by José Aruego and Ariane Dewey. Macmillan, 1975. Subj: Folk and fairy tales. Foreign lands – Japan. Frogs and toads.

Something to crow about ill. by Paul Harvey. Albert Whitman, 1982. Subj: Birds – chickens. Family life – fathers.

Varekamp, Marjolein. *Little Sam takes a bath* ill. by author. Watts, 1991. ISBN 0-531-05944-8 Subj: Activities – bathing. Animals – pigs. Format, unusual – toy and movable books.

Varga, Judy. *Circus cannonball* ill. by author. Morrow, 1975. Subj: Circus.

Janko's wish ill. by author. Morrow, 1969. Subj: Behavior – wishing. Foreign lands – Hungary. Magic. Weddings.

The mare's egg ill. by author. Morrow, 1972. Subj: Animals – foxes. Behavior – trickery. Folk and fairy tales. Foreign lands – Russia.

Miss Lollipop's lion ill. by author. Morrow, 1963. Subj: Animals – lions. Circus. Pets.

The monster behind Black Rock ill. by author. Morrow, 1971. Subj: Animals. Behavior – gossip. Cumulative tales.

Varley, Dimitry. *The whirly bird* ill. by Feodor Rojankovsky. Knopf, 1961. Subj: Birds. Character traits – kindness to animals.

Varley, Susan. *Badger's parting gifts* ill. by author. Lothrop, 1984. Subj: Animals – badgers. Death. Friendship.

Vasiliu, Mircea. *A day at the beach* ill. by author. Random House, 1978. ISBN 0-394-93475-X Subj: Activities – playing. Family life. Sand. Science. Sea and seashore.

Everything is somewhere ill. by author. John Day, 1970. Subj: Religion.

What's happening? ill. by author. John Day, 1970. Subj: Activities. City.

Vaughan, Marcia K. *The Sea-Breeze Hotel* by Marcia Vaughn and Patricia Mullins; ill. by Patricia Mullins. HarperCollins, 1992. ISBN 0-06-020504-0 Subj: Hotels. Kites. Weather – wind.

Wombat stew ill. by Pamela Lofts. ISBN 0-382-09211-2 Subj: Animals. Foreign lands – Australia. Music. Songs.

Vaughn, Jenny. *On the moon* ed. by Jenny Vaughn; Angela Grunsell, consultant; ill. by Tessa Barwick and Elsa Godfrey. Watts, 1983. ISBN 0-531-04631-1 Subj: Moon. Space and space ships. U.S. history.

Velthuijs, Max. *Crocodile's masterpiece* ill. by author. Farrar, 1992. ISBN 0-374-31658-9 Subj: Animals – elephants. Careers – artists. Imagination. Reptiles – alligators, crocodiles.

Frog and the birdsong ill. by author. Farrar, 1991. ISBN 0-374-32467-0 Subj: Animals. Death. Frogs and toads.

Frog in love tr. from Dutch by Anthea Bell; ill. by author. Farrar, 1989. ISBN 0-374-32465-4 Subj: Birds – ducks. Emotions – love. Frogs and toads.

Little Man finds a home ill. by author. Holt, 1985. ISBN 0-03-005734-5 Subj: Elves and little people. Houses. Weather – rain.

Little Man to the rescue ill. by author. Holt, 1986. ISBN 0-8050-0036-4 Subj: Animals – rabbits. Character traits – kindness to animals. Elves and little people. Emotions – envy, jealousy. Frogs and toads.

Little Man's lucky day tr. from German by Rosemary Lanning; ill. by author. Holt, 1986. ISBN 0-03-005847-3 Subj: Character traits – luck. Elves and little people.

The painter and the bird tr. by Ray Broekel; ill. by author. Addison-Wesley, 1975. Translation of Der Maler und der Vogel Subj: Birds. Careers – artists. Imagination.

Venable, Alan. *The checker players* ill. by Byron Barton. Lippincott, 1973. Subj: Animals – bears. Behavior – fighting, arguing. Boats, ships. Friendship. Games. Reptiles – alligators, crocodiles.

Venino, Suzanne. *Animals helping people* ill. with photos. National Geographic Soc., 1983. Subj: Animals. Character traits – helpfulness.

Ventura, Marisa. *The painter's trick* (Ventura, Piero)

Ventura, Piero. *The painter's trick* by Piero and Marisa Ventura; ill. by Marisa Ventura. Random House, 1977. Subj: Careers – artists.

Venturo, Betty Lou Baker *see* Baker, Betty

Ver Dorn, Bethea. *Moon glows* ill. by Thomas Graham. Arcade, 1990. ISBN 1-55970-073-4 Subj: Animals. Moon. Night. Poetry, rhyme.

Verdi, Giuseppe. *Aïda* (Price, Leontyne)

Vernon, Adele. *The riddle* ill. by Robert Rayevsky and Vladimir Radunsky. Dodd, 1987. ISBN 0-396-08920-8 Subj: Folk and fairy tales. Foreign lands – Spain. Royalty.

Vernon, Tannis. *Little Pig and the blue-green sea* ill. by author. Crown, 1986. ISBN 0-517-56118-2 Subj: Animals – pigs. Behavior – running away. Boats, ships. Sea and seashore.

Vesey, A. *Merry Christmas, Thomas!* ill. by author. Little, 1986. ISBN 0-87113-096-3 Subj: Animals – cats. Family life. Holidays – Christmas.

The princess and the frog ill. by author. Little, 1985. ISBN 0-87113-038-6 Subj: Character traits – willfulness. Folk and fairy tales. Frogs and toads. Royalty – princesses.

Vessel, Matthew F. *My goldfish* (Wong, Herbert H.)

My ladybug (Wong, Herbert H.)

My plant (Wong, Herbert H.)

Our caterpillars (Wong, Herbert H.)

Our earthworms (Wong, Herbert H.)

Our tree (Wong, Herbert H.)

Vevers, Gwynne. *Animal homes* ill. by Wendy Bramall. Merrimack, 1982. Subj: Animals. Houses.

Animal parents ill. by Colin Threadgall. Merrimack, 1982. Subj: Animals. Family life.

Animals of the dark ill. by Wendy Bramall. Merrimack, 1982. Subj: Animals. Night.

Animals that store food ill. by Joyce Bee. Merrimack, 1982. Subj: Animals. Food.

Animals that travel ill. by Matthew Hillier. Merrimack, 1982. Subj: Activities – traveling. Animals.

Vidal, Beatriz A. *The legend of El Dorado* (Van Laan, Nancy)

Vidaure, Morris. *The invisible hunters* (Rohmer, Harriet)

Vigna, Judith. *Anyhow, I'm glad I tried* ill. by author. Albert Whitman, 1978. Subj: Behavior – misbehavior. Character traits – kindness. School.

Boot weather ed. by Ann Fay; ill. by author. Albert Whitman, 1988. ISBN 0-8075-0837-3 Subj: Activities – playing. Clothing – shoes. Imagination. Seasons – winter. Weather.

Couldn't we have a turtle instead? ill. by author. Albert Whitman, 1975. Subj: Animals. Babies. Emotions – envy, jealousy. Family life. Family life – mothers.

Daddy's new baby ill. by author. Albert Whitman, 1982. Subj: Divorce. Family life – fathers. Sibling rivalry.

Everyone goes as a pumpkin ill. by author. Albert Whitman, 1977. Subj: Family life – grandmothers. Holidays – Halloween.

Grandma without me ill. by author. Albert Whitman, 1984. Subj: Divorce. Family life – grandmothers.

The hiding house ill. by author. Albert Whitman, 1979. Subj: Behavior – hiding. Behavior – sharing. Friendship.

I wish my daddy didn't drink so much ed. by Ann Fay; ill. by author. Albert Whitman, 1988. ISBN 0-8075-3523-0 Subj: Behavior – wishing. Family life – fathers. Illness.

Mommy and me by ourselves again ill. by author. Albert Whitman, 1987. ISBN 0-8075-5232-1 Subj: Behavior – needing someone. Birthdays. Family life – mothers.

Nobody wants a nuclear war ill. by author. Albert Whitman, 1986. ISBN 0-8075-5739-0 Subj: Emotions – fear. Family life. War.

Saying goodbye to daddy ill. by author. Albert Whitman, 1990. ISBN 0-8075-7253-5 Subj: Death. Emotions. Family life – fathers.

She's not my real mother ill. by author. Albert Whitman, 1980. Subj: Behavior – misbehavior. Divorce. Family life.

Villarejo, Mary. *The art fair* ill. by author. Knopf, 1960. Subj: Art.

The tiger hunt ill. by author. Knopf, 1959. Subj: Activities – photographing. Animals. Animals – tigers. Foreign lands – India.

Vincent, Gabrielle. *Bravo, Ernest and Celestine!* ill. by author. Greenwillow, 1982. Subj: Animals – bears. Animals – mice. Behavior – sharing. Money. Music.

Breakfast time, Ernest and Celestine ill. by author. Greenwillow, 1985. ISBN 0-688-04555-3 Subj: Animals – bears. Animals – mice. Behavior – misbehavior. Friendship. Wordless.

Ernest and Celestine ill. by author. Greenwillow, 1982. Subj: Animals – bears. Animals – mice. Holidays – Christmas. Toys.

Ernest and Celestine at the circus ill. by author. Greenwillow, 1989. ISBN 0-688-08685-3 Subj: Animals – bears. Animals – mice. Circus.

Ernest and Celestine's patchwork quilt ill. by author. Greenwillow, 1985. ISBN 0-688-04577-X Subj: Animals – bears. Animals – mice. Behavior – sharing. Friendship. Quilts. Wordless.

Ernest and Celestine's picnic ill. by author. Morrow, 1988, 1982. ISBN 0-688-07809-5 Subj: Activities – picnicking. Animals – bears. Animals – mice. Weather – rain.

Merry Christmas, Ernest and Celestine ill. by author. Greenwillow, 1984. ISBN 0-688-02606-0 Subj: Animals – bears. Animals – mice. Friendship. Holidays – Christmas. Parties.

Smile, Ernest and Celestine ill. by author. Greenwillow, 1982. Subj: Activities – photographing. Animals – bears. Animals – mice.

Where are you, Ernest and Celestine? ill. by author. Greenwillow, 1986. ISBN 0-688-06235-0 Subj: Animals – bears. Animals – mice. Behavior – lost. Museums.

Vinson, Pauline. *Willie goes to the seashore* ill. by author. Macmillan, 1954. Subj: Animals – mice. Sea and seashore.

Viorst, Judith. *Alexander and the terrible, horrible, no good, very bad day* ill. by Ray Cruz. Atheneum, 1972. Subj: Behavior – bad day. Family life.

Alexander, who used to be rich last Sunday ill. by Ray Cruz. Atheneum, 1978. Subj: Money.

The good-bye book ill. by Kay Chorao. Atheneum, 1988. ISBN 0-689-31308-X Subj: Activities – babysitting. Activities – reading. Imagination.

I'll fix Anthony ill. by Arnold Lobel. Harper, 1969. Subj: Family life. Sibling rivalry.

My mama says there aren't any zombies, ghosts, vampires, creatures, demons, monsters, fiends, goblins, or things ill. by Kay Chorao. Atheneum, 1973. Subj: Bedtime. Emotions – fear. Family life – mothers. Imagination. Monsters.

Rosie and Michael ill. by Lorna Tomei. Atheneum, 1974. Subj: Friendship.

Sunday morning ill. by Hilary Knight. Harper, 1968. Subj: Activities – playing. Family life. Humor.

The tenth good thing about Barney ill. by Erik Blegvad. Atheneum, 1971. Subj: Animals – cats. Death. Careers – doctors. Pets.

Try it again, Sam: safety when you walk ill. by Paul Galdone. Lothrop, 1970. Subj: Activities – walking. Character traits – individuality. Safety.

Vipont, Charles *see* Foulds, Elfrida Vipont

Vipont, Elfrida *see* Foulds, Elfrida Vipont

A visit to a pond ill. with photos. Imported Pubs., 1983. Subj: Animals. Format, unusual – board books. Wordless.

Voake, Charlotte. *First things first: a baby's companion* ill. by author. Little, 1988. ISBN 0-316-90510-0 Subj: Activities. Poetry, rhyme.

Mrs. Goose's baby ill. by author. Little, 1989. ISBN 0-316-90511-9 Subj: Adoption. Birds – chickens. Birds – geese. Character traits – being different.

Tom's cat ill. by author. Lippincott, 1986. ISBN 0-397-32195-3 Subj: Animals – cats. Noise, sounds.

Vogel, Carole Garbuny. *The dangers of strangers* by Carole Garbuny Vogel and Kathryn Allen Goldner; ill. by Lynette Schmidt. Dillon, 1983. Subj: Behavior – talking to strangers. Safety.

Vogel, Ilse-Margaret. *The don't be scared book: scares, remedies and pictures* ill. by author. Atheneum, 1964. Subj: Emotions – fear. Imagination. Poetry, rhyme.

Volkmer, Jane Anne. *Song of Chirimia: La Musica de la Chirimia* tr. by Lori Ann Schatschneider; ill. by adaptor. Carolrhoda, 1990. ISBN 0-87614-423-7 Subj: Folk and fairy tales. Foreign lands – Mexico. Foreign languages. Indians of North America. Religion.

Von Hippel, Ursula. *The craziest Halloween* ill. by author. Coward, 1957. Subj: Holidays – Halloween.

Von Jüchen, Aurel *see* Jüchen, Aurel von

Von Königslöw, Andrea Wayne. *That's my baby?* ill. by author. Firefly, 1986. ISBN 0-920303-56-0 Subj: Babies. Family life. Sibling rivalry. Toys.

Von Storch, Anne B. *see* Malcolmson, Anne

Vreeken, Elizabeth. *The boy who would not say his name* ill. by Leonard W. Shortall. Follett, 1959. Subj: Behavior – lost. Careers – police officers. Imagination. Names.

Henry ill. by Polly Jackson. Follett, 1961. Subj: Animals – mice. Pets.

One day everything went wrong ill. by Leonard W. Shortall. Follett, 1966. Subj: Behavior – bad day.

Vyner, Sue. *The stolen egg* ill. by Tim Vyner. Viking, 1992. ISBN 0-670-84460-8 Subj: Birds. Circular tales. Eggs. Reptiles. Science.

Wabbes, Marie. *Good night, Little Rabbit* ill. by author. Little, 1987. ISBN 0-871-13127-7 Subj: Animals – rabbits. Bedtime.

Happy birthday, Little Rabbit ill. by author. Little, 1987. ISBN 0-87113-129-3 Subj: Animals – rabbits. Birthdays.

It's snowing, Little Rabbit ill. by author. Little, 1987. ISBN 0-87113-128-5 Subj: Animals – rabbits. Seasons – winter. Weather – snow.

Little Rabbit's garden ill. by author. Little, 1987. ISBN 0-871-13126-9 Subj: Animals – rabbits. Gardens, gardening.

Rose is hungry ill. by author. Messner, 1988. ISBN 0-671-66611-8 Subj: Animals – pigs. Food.

Rose is muddy ill. by author. Messner, 1988. ISBN 0-671-66610-X Subj: Animals – pigs. Character traits – cleanliness.

Rose's bath ill. by author. Messner, 1988. ISBN 0-671-66612-6 Subj: Activities – bathing. Animals – pigs. Toys.

Rose's picture ill. by author. Messner, 1988. ISBN 0-671-66611-8 Subj: Activities – painting. Art. Animals – pigs.

Waber, Bernard. *An anteater named Arthur* ill. by author. Houghton, 1967. Subj: ABC books. Animals – anteaters.

Bernard ill. by author. Houghton, 1982. Subj: Animals – dogs. Behavior – running away. Behavior – sharing.

But names will never hurt me ill. by author. Houghton, 1976. Subj: Behavior – name calling. Names.

Funny, funny Lyle ill. by author. Houghton, 1987. ISBN 0-395-43619-2 Subj: Behavior – misunderstanding. Family life. Reptiles – alligators, crocodiles.

How to go about laying an egg ill. by author. Houghton, 1963. Subj: Birds – chickens. Eggs. Humor.

I was all thumbs ill. by author. Houghton, 1975. Subj: Octopuses. Sea and seashore.

Ira says goodbye ill. by author. Houghton, 1988. ISBN 0-395-48315-8 Subj: Emotions. Friendship. Moving.

Ira sleeps over ill. by author. Houghton, 1972. Subj: Activities – playing. Bedtime. Friendship. Sleep. Toys – teddy bears.

Lorenzo ill. by author. Houghton, 1961. Subj: Character traits – curiosity. Fish.

Lovable Lyle ill. by author. Houghton, 1969. Subj: Friendship. Reptiles – alligators, crocodiles.

Lyle and the birthday party ill. by author. Houghton, 1966. Subj: Birthdays. Emotions – envy, jealousy. Reptiles – alligators, crocodiles.

Lyle finds his mother ill. by author. Houghton, 1974. Subj: Family life – mothers. Reptiles – alligators, crocodiles.

Lyle, Lyle Crocodile ill. by author. Houghton, 1965. Subj: Character traits – helpfulness. Reptiles – alligators, crocodiles.

Mice on my mind ill. by author. Houghton, 1977. Subj: Animals – cats. Animals – mice.

Nobody is perfick ill. by author. Houghton, 1971. Subj: Behavior – mistakes. Friendship. Humor.

Rich cat, poor cat ill. by author. Houghton, 1963. Subj: Animals – cats.

The snake: a very long story ill. by author. Houghton, 1978. Subj: Format, unusual. Reptiles – snakes.

"You look ridiculous," said the rhinoceros to the hippopotamus ill. by author. Houghton, 1979. ISBN 0-395-07156-9 Subj: Animals. Animals – hippopotami. Character traits – individuality. Self-concept.

You're a little kid with a big heart ill. by author. Houghton, 1980. Subj: Behavior – growing up. Behavior – wishing. Magic.

Waddell, Martin. *Alice the artist* ill. by Jonathan Langley. Dutton, 1988. ISBN 0-525-44385-1 Subj: Art. Careers – artists.

Amy said ill. by Charlotte Voake. Little, 1990. ISBN 0-316-91636-6 Subj: Behavior – misbehavior. Family life – grandmothers.

Can't you sleep, Little Bear? ill. by Barbara Firth. Candlewick Pr., 1992. ISBN 1-56402-007-X Subj: Animals – bears. Emotions – fear. Family life – fathers. Night. Sleep.

Farmer Duck ill. by Helen Oxenbury. Candlewick Pr., 1992. ISBN 1-56402-009-6 Subj: Animals. Birds – ducks. Careers – farmers. Character traits – helpfulness. Farms.

Grandma's Bill ill. by Jane Johnson. Watts, 1991. ISBN 0-531-08523-6 Subj: Family life – grandparents.

The happy hedgehog band ill. by Jill Barton. Candlewick Pr., 1992. ISBN 1-56402-011-8 Subj: Animals. Animals – hedgehogs. Music.

The hidden house ill. by Angela Barrett. Putnam, 1990. ISBN 0-399-22228-6 Subj: Emotions – loneliness. Toys – dolls.

Let's go home, Little Bear ill. by Barbara Firth. Candlewick Pr., 1993. ISBN 1-56402-131-9 Subj: Animals – bears. Family life – fathers.

My great grandpa ill. by Dom Mansell. Putnam, 1990. ISBN 0-399-22155-7 Subj: Family life – great-grandparents. Handicaps – physical. Poetry, rhyme.

Once there were giants ill. by Penny Dale. Delacorte Pr., 1989. ISBN 0-385-29806-4 Subj: Behavior – growing up. Family life.

The park in the dark ill. by Barbara Firth. Lothrop, 1989. ISBN 0-688-08517-2 Subj: Emotions – fear. Night. Poetry, rhyme. Toys.

Sailor Bear ill. by Virginia Austin. Candlewick Pr., 1992. ISBN 1-56402-040-1 Subj: Behavior – lost. Boats, ships. Sea and seashore. Toys – teddy bears.

Squeak-a-lot ill. by Virginia Miller. Greenwillow, 1991. ISBN 0-688-10245-X Subj: Activities – playing. Animals – mice. Noise, sounds.

The tough princess ill. by Patrick Benson. Putnam's, 1987. ISBN 0-399-21380-5 Subj: Fairies. Folk and fairy tales. Royalty – princesses.

We love them ill. by Barbara Firth. Lothrop, 1990. ISBN 0-688-09332-9 Subj: Animals – dogs. Animals – rabbits. Friendship.

Wade, Alan. *I'm flying!* ill. by Petra Mathers. Knopf, 1990. ISBN 0-394-94510-7 Subj: Activities – ballooning.

Wade, Anne. *A promise is for keeping* ill. by Jon Petersson. Children's Pr., 1979. Subj: Friendship.

Wade, Barrie. *Little monster* ill. by Katinka Kew. Lothrop, 1990. ISBN 0-688-09597-6 Subj: Behavior – misbehavior. Emotions – love. Family life.

Wadhams, Margaret. *Anna* ill. by Michael Charlton. Salem House, 1987. ISBN 0-370-30612-0 Subj: Character traits – being different. Illness.

Wadsworth, Olive A. *Over in the meadow: a counting-out rhyme* ill. by Mary Maki Rae. Viking, 1985. Subj: Counting, numbers. Poetry, rhyme.

Waechter, Friedrich Karl. *Three is company* tr. by Harry Allard; ill. by author. Doubleday, 1980. Subj: Animals – pigs. Birds. Fish. Friendship.

Wagener, Gerda. *Leo the lion* tr. from German by Nina Ignatowicz; ill. by Reinhard Michl. HarperCollins, 1991. ISBN 0-06-021657-3 Subj: Animals – lions. Emotions – loneliness.

Waggoner, Karen. *Dad Gummit and Ma Foot* ill. by Anita Riggio. Watts, 1990. ISBN 0-531-08491-4 Subj: Behavior – fighting, arguing. Family life.

The lemonade babysitter ill. by Dorothy Donohue. Little, 1992. ISBN 0-316-91711-7 Subj: Activities – baby-sitting. Behavior. Old age.

Wagner, Elaine Knox *see* Knox-Wagner, Elaine

Wagner, Jenny. *Amy's monster* ill. by Terry Denton. Viking, 1991. ISBN 0-670-82748-7 Subj: Behavior – bullying. Family life – cousins. Monsters. Seasons – summer. Twins.

Aranea: a story about a spider ill. by Ron Brooks. Bradbury Pr., 1978. Subj: Spiders. Weather – rain.

The bunyip of Berkeley's Creek ill. by Ron Brooks. Bradbury Pr., 1977. Subj: Foreign lands – Australia. Monsters. Mythical creatures.

John Brown, Rose and the midnight cat ill. by Ron Brooks. Bradbury Pr., 1978. Subj: Animals – cats. Animals – dogs.

Wagner, Karen. *Chocolate chip cookies* ill. by Leah Palmer Preiss. Holt, 1990. ISBN 0-8050-1268-0 Subj: Activities – cooking. Family life. Twins.

Silly Fred ill. by Normand Chartier. Macmillan, 1989. ISBN 0-02-792280-4 Subj: Animals. Animals – pigs. Self-concept.

Wahl, Jan. *The adventures of Underwater Dog* ill. by Tim Bowers. Putnam, 1989. ISBN 0-448-09313-8 Subj: Animals – dogs. Crime. Sea and seashore.

Button eye's orange ill. by Wendy Watson. Warne, 1980. Subj: Handicaps. Toys.

Cabbage moon ill. by Adrienne Adams. Holt, 1965. Subj: Humor. Moon. Royalty.

Carrot nose ill. by James Marshall. Farrar, 1978. Subj: Animals – rabbits.

Doctor Rabbit's foundling ill. by Cyndy Szekeres. Pantheon, 1977. Subj: Animals – rabbits. Careers – doctors. Frogs and toads.

Dracula's cat ill. by Kay Chorao. Prentice-Hall, 1978. Subj: Animals – cats. Monsters.

Dracula's cat and Frankenstein's dog ill. by Kay Chorao. Simon & Schuster, 1990. ISBN 0-671-70820-1 Subj: Animals – cats. Animals – dogs. Format, unusual. Monsters. Pets.

The fishermen ill. by Emily Arnold McCully. Norton, 1969. Subj: Family life – grandfathers. Sports – fishing.

The five in the forest ill. by Erik Blegvad. Follett, 1974. Subj: Animals – rabbits. Eggs. Forest, woods. Holidays – Easter.

Follow me cried Bee ill. by John Wallner. Crown, 1976. Subj: Cumulative tales. Insects – bees. Poetry, rhyme. Weather – rain.

Frankenstein's dog ill. by Kay Chorao. Prentice-Hall, 1977. Subj: Animals – dogs. Monsters.

Hello, elephant ill. by Edward Ardizzone. Holt, 1964. Subj: Animals – elephants.

Humphrey's bear ill. by William Joyce. Holt, 1987. ISBN 0-8050-0332-0 Subj: Bedtime. Dreams. Toys – teddy bears.

Jamie's tiger ill. by Tomie de Paola. Harcourt, 1978. Subj: Handicaps – deafness. Illness. Senses – hearing. Toys.

Little Eight John ill. by Wil Clay. Dutton, 1992. ISBN 0-525-67367-9 Subj: Behavior – misbehavior. Folk and fairy tales.

Mrs. Owl and Mr. Pig ill. by Eileen Christelow. Dutton, 1991. ISBN 0-525-67311-3 Subj: Animals – pigs. Behavior – sharing. Birds – owls. Character traits.

The Muffletumps ill. by Edward Ardizzone. Holt, 1966. Subj: Toys – dolls.

The Muffletumps' Christmas party ill. by Cyndy Szekeres. Follett, 1975. Subj: Holidays – Christmas. Toys – dolls.

The Muffletumps' Halloween scare ill. by Cyndy Szekeres. Follett, 1977. Subj: Toys – dolls.

Old Hippo's Easter egg ill. by Lorinda Bryan Cauley. Harcourt, 1980. Subj: Animals – hippopotami. Animals – mice. Birds – ducks. Emotions – love. Family life.

Peter and the troll baby ill. by Erik Blegvad. Golden Pr., 1984. Subj: Activities – baby-sitting. Sibling rivalry. Trolls.

Pleasant Fieldmouse ill. by Maurice Sendak. Harper, 1964. Subj: Animals. Animals – mice.

Pleasant Fieldmouse's Halloween party ill. by Wallace Tripp. Putnam, 1974. Subj: Animals. Animals – mice. Holidays – Halloween.

Push Kitty ill. by Garth Williams. Harper, 1968. Subj: Activities – playing. Animals – cats.

Rabbits on roller skates! ill. by David Allender. Crown, 1986. ISBN 0-517-55935-8 Subj: Animals – rabbits. Poetry, rhyme. Sports – roller skating.

The sleepytime book ill. by Arden Johnson. Morrow, 1992. ISBN 0-688-10276-X Subj: Animals. Babies. Bedtime. Night. Poetry, rhyme. Sleep.

Sylvester Bear overslept ill. by Lee Lorenz. Parents, 1979. Subj: Animals – bears. Circus. Family life. Sleep.

Tiger watch ill. by Charles Mikolaycak. Harcourt, 1982. Subj: Animals – tigers. Death. Foreign lands – India. Sports – hunting.

The toy circus ill. by Tim Bowers. Harcourt, 1986. ISBN 0-15-200609-5 Subj: Circus. Dreams. Sleep. Toys.

The woman with the eggs (Andersen, H. C. (Hans Christian))

Wahl, Mats. *Grandfather's laika* ill. by Tord Nygren. Carolrhoda, 1990. ISBN 0-87614-434-2 Subj: Animals – dogs. Death. Family life – grandfathers. Pets.

Wahl, Robert. *Pyxx* ill. by author. Price Stern Sloan, 1989. ISBN 0-8431-2347-8 Subj: Behavior. Imagination.

Wakefield, Joyce. *Ask a silly question* ill. by Mike Venezia. Children's Pr., 1979. Subj: Poetry, rhyme. Riddles.

From where you are ill. by Tom Dunnington. Children's Pr., 1978. Subj: Concepts – perspective. Poetry, rhyme.

Walbrecker, Dirk. *Benny's hat* ill. by Hans Poppel. Atomium, 1991. ISBN 1-56182-028-8 Subj: Clothing – hats.

Walker, Alice. *Finding the green stone* ill. by Catherine Deeter. Harcourt, 1991. ISBN 0-15-227538-X Subj: Behavior. Character traits. Ethnic groups in the U.S. – Afro-Americans. Rocks.

To hell with dying ill. by Catherine Deeter. Harcourt, 1987. ISBN 0-15-289075-0 Subj: Death. Ethnic groups in the U.S. – Afro-Americans. Friendship.

Walker, Barbara K. (Barbara Kerlin). *New patches for old: a Turkish folktale* retold by Barbara K. Walker and Ahmet E. Uysal; ill. by Harold Berson. Parents, 1974. Subj: Behavior – mistakes. Folk and fairy tales.

Pigs and pirates: a Greek tale ill. by Harold Berson. White, 1969. Subj: Animals – pigs. Foreign lands – Greece. Pirates.

Teeny-Tiny and the witch-woman ill. by Michael Foreman. Pantheon, 1975. Subj: Character traits – cleverness. Foreign lands – Turkey. Witches.

Wall, Lina Mao. *Judge Rabbit and the tree spirit* adapt. by Cathy Spagnoli; ill. by Nancy Hom. Children's Book Pr., 1991. ISBN 0-89239-071-9 Subj: Character traits – vanity. Folk and fairy tales. Foreign lands – Cambodia. Language.

Wallace, Barbara Brooks. *Argyle* ill. by John Sandford. Abingdon, 1987. ISBN 0-687-01724-6 Subj: Animals – sheep. Character traits – being different.

Wallace, Daisy. *Fairy poems* ill. by Trina Schart Hyman. Holiday, 1980. ISBN 0-8234-0371-8 Subj: Fairies. Poetry, rhyme.

Ghost poems ill. by Tomie de Paola. Holiday, 1979. Subj: Ghosts. Night. Poetry, rhyme.

Giant poems ill. by Margot Tomes. Holiday, 1978. ISBN 0-8234-0326-2 Subj: Giants. Poetry, rhyme.

Wallace, Ian. *Chin Chiang and the dragon's dance* ill. by author. Atheneum, 1984. Subj: Emotions – fear. Ethnic groups in the U.S. – Chinese-Americans. Family life – grandfathers. Holidays – Chinese New Year.

Morgan the magnificent ill. by author. Macmillan, 1988. ISBN 0-689-50441-1 Subj: Angels. Behavior – misbehavior. Circus.

The sparrow's song ill. by author. Viking, 1987. ISBN 0-670-81453-9 Subj: Behavior – misbehavior. Birds – sparrows. Character traits – kindness to animals. Death.

Wallas, Ada. *Clean Peter and the children of Grubbylea* (Adelborg, Ottilia)

Wallis, Diz. *Pip's adventure* ill. by author. Boyds Mills Pr., 1991. ISBN 1-878093-43-6 Subj: Activities – cooking. Animals – cats. Animals – mice.

Wallis, Lisa. *Island child* ill. by Deborah Haeffele. Dutton, 1992. ISBN 0-525-67324-5 Subj: Family life. Islands.

Wallner, Alexandra. *Munch* ill. by author. Crown, 1976. Subj: Food. Poetry, rhyme.

Wallner, John. *Look and find* ill. by author. Putnam's, 1988. ISBN 0-448-19068-0 Subj: Concepts.

Old MacDonald had a farm: a musical pop-up book ill. by author. Dutton, 1986. ISBN 0-525-44279-0 Subj: Animals. Cumulative tales. Farms. Format, unusual – toy and movable books. Music. Songs.

Sleeping Beauty (Grimm, Jacob)

Walsh, Ellen Stoll. *Mouse count* ill. by author. Harcourt, 1991. ISBN 0-15-256023-8 Subj: Animals – mice. Counting, numbers. Reptiles – snakes.

Mouse paint ill. by author. Harcourt, 1989. ISBN 0-15-256025-4 Subj: Activities – painting. Animals – mice. Behavior – hiding.

Two too much ill. by Pat Cummings. Bradbury Pr., 1990. ISBN 0-02-792290-1 Subj: Emotions. Ethnic groups in the U.S. – Afro-Americans. Family life – brothers. Family life – sisters.

You silly goose ill. by author. Harcourt, 1992. ISBN 0-15-299865-9 Subj: Animals – foxes. Animals – mice. Birds – geese.

Walsh, Grahame L. *Didane the koala* ill. by John Morrison. Univ. of Queensland Pr., 1986. ISBN 0-7022-1889-8 Subj: Animals – koala bears. Folk and fairy tales. Foreign lands – Australia.

The goori goori bird ill. by John Morrison. Univ. of Queensland Pr., 1986. ISBN 0-7022-1777-8 Subj: Birds. Folk and fairy tales. Foreign lands – Australia.

Walsh, Jill Paton. *Lost and found* ill. by Mary Rayner. Deutsch (dist. by Dutton), 1985. Subj: Behavior – losing things. Character traits – luck. Family life – grandfathers.

Walt Disney Productions. *Tod and Copper* Random House, 1981. Subj: Animals – dogs. Animals – foxes.

Tod and Vixey Random House, 1981. Subj: Animals – dogs. Animals – foxes.

Walt Disney's Snow White and the seven dwarfs Viking, 1979. Subj: Elves and little people. Emotions – envy, jealousy. Folk and fairy tales. Magic. Witches.

Walt Disney's The adventures of Mr. Toad Random House, 1981. Subj: Animals – moles. Animals – rats. Frogs and toads.

Walter, Mildred Pitts. *Brother to the wind* ill. by Leo and Diane Dillon. Lothrop, 1985. ISBN 0-688-03811-5 Subj: Activities – flying. Foreign lands – Africa.

My mama needs me ill. by Pat Cummings. Lothrop, 1983. Subj: Emotions – loneliness. Ethnic groups in the U.S. – Afro-Americans. Family life.

Ty's one-man band ill. by Margot Tomes. Four Winds Pr., 1980. ISBN 0-02-792300-2 Subj: Folk and fairy tales. Music.

Walter, Villiam Christian *see* Andersen, H. C. (Hans Christian)

Walters, Marguerite. *The city-country ABC: My alphabet walk in the country, and My alphabet ride in the city* ill. by Ib Spang Olsen. Doubleday, 1966. The two stories are bound dos-á-dos Subj: ABC books. City. Country. Format, unusual.

Walton, Ann. *Dumb clucks!* (Walton, Rick)

Something's fishy! (Walton, Rick)

Walton, Rick. *Dumb clucks! jokes about chickens* by Rick and Ann Walton; ill. by Joan Hanson. Lerner, 1987. ISBN 0-8225-0991-1 Subj: Birds – chickens. Riddles.

Something's fishy! jokes about sea creatures by Rick and Ann Walton; ill. by Joan Hanson. Lerner, 1987. ISBN 0-8225-0993-8 Subj: Fish. Riddles.

Wandelmaier, Roy. *Clouds* ill. by John Jones. Troll Assoc., 1985. ISBN 0-8167-0338-8 Subj: Weather – clouds. Weather – rain.

Stars ill. by Irene Trivas. Troll Assoc., 1985. ISBN 0-8167-0339-6 Subj: Science. Stars.

Wang, Mary Lewis. *The ant and the dove* (Æsop)

Wang, Rosalind C. *The fourth question* ill. by Ju-Hong Chen. Holiday, 1991. ISBN 0-8234-0855-8 Subj: Character traits – generosity. Folk and fairy tales. Foreign lands – China.

Warbler, J. M. *see* Cocagnac, A. M. (Augustin Maurice)

Warburton, Nick. *Mr. Tite's belongings* ill. by Alex Ayliffe. Viking, 1992. ISBN 0-670-84155-2 Subj: Character traits – selfishness.

Ward, Andrew. *Baby bear and the long sleep* ill. by John Walsh. Little, 1980. Subj: Animals – bears. Hibernation. Seasons – winter.

Ward, Cindy. *Cookie's week* ill. by Tomie de Paola. Putnam's, 1988. ISBN 0-399-21498-4 Subj: Animals – cats. Behavior – misbehavior. Days of the week, months of the year.

Ward, Helen. *The golden pear* ill. by author. Ideals, 1991. ISBN 0-8249-8471-4 Subj: Friendship. Folk and fairy tales.

The moonrat and the white turtle ill. by author. Ideals, 1990. ISBN 0-8249-8467-6 Subj: Character traits – selfishness. Moon. Pirates. Reptiles – turtles, tortoises.

Ward, Leila. *I am eyes, ni macho* ill. by Nonny Hogrogian. Greenwillow, 1978. Subj: Foreign lands – Africa. Nature.

Ward, Lynd. *The biggest bear* ill. by author. Houghton, 1952. Subj: Animals – bears. Caldecott award book. Character traits – kindness to animals. Foreign lands – Canada. Pets.

The little red lighthouse and the great gray bridge (Swift, Hildegarde Hoyt)

Nic of the woods ill. by author. Houghton, 1965. Subj: Animals. Animals – dogs. Foreign lands – Canada. Forest, woods.

The silver pony ill. by author. Houghton, 1973. Subj: Animals – horses. Dreams. Wordless.

Ward, May McNeer *see* McNeer, May Younge

Ward, Nanda Weedon. *The black sombrero* ill. by Lynd Ward. Ariel, 1952. Subj: Animals. Clothing – hats. Cowboys.

The elephant that ga-lumphed by Nanda Weedon Ward and Robert Haynes; ill. by Robert Haynes. Ariel, 1959. Subj: Animals. Animals – elephants. Foreign lands – India.

Ward, Nick. *Giant* Oxford Univ. Pr., 1983. Subj: Behavior – misbehavior. Giants. Toys.

Ward, Sally G. *Charlie and Grandma* ill. by author. Scholastic, 1986. ISBN 0-590-33954-0 Subj: Behavior – misbehavior. Family life – grandmothers.

Molly and Grandpa ill. by author. Scholastic, 1986. ISBN 0-590-33955-9 Subj: Character traits – persistence. Family life – grandfathers. Food.

Punky goes fishing ill. by author. Dutton, 1991. ISBN 0-525-44681-8 Subj: Family life – grandfathers. Sports – fishing.

What goes around comes around ill. by author. Doubleday, 1991. ISBN 0-385-41223-1 Subj: Character traits – generosity. Communities, neighborhoods. Family life – grandmothers.

Warren, Cathy. *Fred's first day* ill. by Pat Cummings. Lothrop, 1984. ISBN 0-688-03814-X Subj: Friendship. School.

Saturday belongs to Sara ill. by DyAnne DiSalvo-Ryan. Bradbury Pr., 1988. ISBN 0-02-792491-2 Subj: Character traits – kindness. Family life – mothers.

Springtime bears ill. by Pat Cummings. Lothrop, 1987. ISBN 0-688-05906-6 Subj: Animals – bears. Behavior – hiding. Seasons – spring.

The ten-alarm camp-out ill. by Steven Kellogg. Lothrop, 1983. Subj: Counting, numbers. Camps, camping.

Warren, Elizabeth *see* Supraner, Robyn

Warshofsky, Isaac *see* Singer, Isaac Bashevis

Wasmuth, Eleanor. *An alligator day* ill. by author. Grosset, 1983. Subj: Activities – playing. Reptiles – alligators, crocodiles.

The picnic basket ill. by author. Grosset, 1983. Subj: Activities – picnicking. Food. Reptiles – alligators, crocodiles.

Wasserberg, Esther. *Grandmother dear* (Finfer, Celentha)

Wasson, Valentina Pavlovna. *The chosen baby* ill. by Glo Coalson 3rd ed. Harper, 1977. ISBN 0-397-31738-7 Subj: Adoption.

Watanabe, Shigeo. *Daddy, play with me!* ill. by Yasuo Ohtomo. Putnam's, 1985. ISBN 0-399-21211-6 Subj: Activities – playing. Animals – bears. Family life – fathers.

How do I put it on? ill. by Yasuo Ohtomo. Putnam's, 1979. Subj: Animals – bears. Clothing. Participation.

I can build a house! ill. by Yasuo Ohtomo. Philomel, 1983. ISBN 0-399-20950-6 Subj: Activities – playing. Animals – bears. Character traits – perseverance. Houses.

I can ride it! ill. by Yasuo Ohtomo. Putnam's, 1982. Subj: Activities – playing. Animals – bears. Character traits – perseverance.

I can take a bath! ill. by Yasuo Ohtomo. Putnam's, 1987. ISBN 0-399-21362-7 Subj: Activities – bathing. Animals – bears. Family life – fathers.

I can take a walk! ill. by Yasuo Ohtomo. Putnam's, 1984. Subj: Activities – walking. Animals – bears.

Ice cream is falling! ill. by Yasuo Ohtomo. Putnam, 1989. ISBN 0-399-21550-6 Subj: Animals – bears. Seasons – winter. Weather – snow.

I'm the king of the castle! ill. by Yasuo Ohtomo. Putnam's, 1982. Subj: Activities – playing. Animals – bears. Sand.

It's my birthday ill. by Yasuo Ohtomo. Putnam's, 1988. ISBN 0-399-21492-5 Subj: Animals – bears. Birthdays. Family life – grandparents.

Let's go swimming ill. by Yasuo, Ohtomo. Putnam, 1990. ISBN 0-399-21896-3 Subj: Animals – bears. Family life – fathers. Sports – swimming.

What a good lunch! ill. by Yasuo Ohtomo. Collins-World, 1980. Subj: Animals – bears. Food. Humor.

Where's my daddy? ill. by Yasuo Ohtomo. Philomel, 1982. ISBN 0-399-20899-2 Subj: Animals – bears. Behavior – lost. Character traits – perseverance. Family life – fathers.

Watanabe, Yuichi. *Wally the whale who loved balloons* tr. from Japanese by D. T. Ooka; ill. by author. Heian, 1982. Subj: Animals – whales. Behavior – misbehavior. Toys – balloons.

Waters, Kate. *Lion dancer: Ernie Wan's Chinese new year* by Kate Waters and Madeline Slovenz-Low; photos by Martha Cooper. Scholastic, 1990. ISBN 0-590-43046-7 Subj: Activities – dancing. Ethnic groups in the U.S. – Chinese-Americans. Holidays – Chinese New Year.

Waters, Tony. *Sailor's bride* ill. by author. Doubleday, 1991. ISBN 0-385-41441-2 Subj: Animals – mice. Behavior – lost. Boats, ships. Sea and seashore.

Waterton, Betty. *Orff, 27 dragons (and a snarkel)* ill. by Karen Kulyk. Firefly, 1984. ISBN 0-920303-02-1 Subj: Activities – flying. Character traits – perseverance. Dragons. Dreams.

Pettranella ill. by Ann Blades. Vanguard, 1981. ISBN 0-8149-0844-6 Subj: Family life – grandmothers. Foreign lands – Canada. Seasons – spring.

A salmon for Simon ill. by Ann Blades. Atheneum, 1980. Subj: Character traits – kindness to animals. Sports – fishing.

Watson, Carol. *Opposites* ill. by David Higham. Usborne, 1983. Subj: Concepts – opposites.

Shapes ill. by David Higham. Usborne, 1983. Subj: Concepts – shape.

Sizes ill. by David Higham. Usborne, 1983. Subj: Concepts – size.

Æsop's fables (Æsop)

Watson, Claire. *Big creatures from the past* ill. by Robert Cremins; design and paper engineering by Keith Moseley. Putnam, 1990. ISBN 0-399-22159-X Subj: Dinosaurs. Format, unusual – toy and movable books.

Watson, Clyde. *Applebet: an ABC* ill. by Wendy Watson. Farrar, 1982. Subj: ABC books. Poetry, rhyme.

Catch me and kiss me and say it again ill. by Wendy Watson. Collins-World, 1978. Subj: Family life. Poetry, rhyme.

Father Fox's feast of songs ill. by Wendy Watson. Putnam's, 1983. Subj: Animals – foxes. Music. Poetry, rhyme.

Fisherman lullabies ed. and ill. by Wendy Watson; music by Clyde Watson. Collins-World, 1968. Subj: Bedtime. Lullabies. Music.

Hickory stick rag ill. by Wendy Watson. Crowell, 1976. Subj: Activities – picnicking. Humor. Poetry, rhyme. School.

How Brown Mouse kept Christmas ill. by Wendy Watson. Farrar, 1980. Subj: Animals – mice. Holidays – Christmas.

Midnight moon ill. by Susanna Natti. Collins-World, 1979. Subj: Activities – flying. Bedtime. Imagination. Moon.

Tom Fox and the apple pie ill. by Wendy Watson. Crowell, 1972. Subj: Animals – foxes. Behavior – sharing. Fairs. Food.

Valentine foxes ill. by Wendy Watson. Watts, 1988. ISBN 0-531-08400-0 Subj: Animals – foxes. Family life. Food. Holidays – Valentine's Day.

Watson, Jane Werner. *My friend the babysitter* by Jane Werner Watson, Robert E. Switzer and J. Cotter Hirschberg; ill. by Hilde Hoffmann. Golden Pr., 1971. Subj: Activities – baby-sitting.

My friend the dentist by Jane Werner Watson, Robert E. Switzer and J. Cotter Hirschberg; ill. by Cat Bowman Smith. Crown, 1987. ISBN 0-517-56485-X Subj: Careers – dentists. Health.

My friend the doctor by Jane Werner Watson, Robert E. Switzer and J. Cotter Hirschberg; ill. by Cat Bowman Smith. Crown, 1987. ISBN 0-517-56485-8 Subj: Careers – doctors. Health.

Sometimes a family has to move by Jane Werner Watson, Robert E. Switzer and J. Cotter Hirschberg; ill. by Cat Bowman Smith. Crown, 1988. ISBN 0-517-56593-5 Subj: Family life. Moving.

Sometimes a family has to split up by Jane Werner Watson, Robert E. Switzer and J. Cotter Hirschberg; ill. by Cat Bowman Smith. Crown, 1988. ISBN 0-517-56811-X Subj: Divorce. Family life.

Sometimes I get angry by Jane Werner Watson, Robert E. Switzer and J. Cotter Hirschberg; ill. by Hilde Hoffmann. Golden Pr., 1971. Subj: Emotions – anger.

Sometimes I'm afraid by Jane Werner Watson, Robert E. Switzer and J. Cotter Hirschberg; ill. by Hilde Hoffmann. Golden Pr., 1971. Subj: Emotions – fear.

Sometimes I'm jealous by Jane Werner Watson, Robert E. Switzer and J. Cotter Hirschberg; ill. by Irene Trivas. Crown, 1986. ISBN 0-517-56062-3 Subj: Emotions – envy, jealousy.

Which is the witch? ill. by Victoria Chess. Pantheon, 1979. Subj: Holidays – Halloween. Witches.

Watson, Nancy Dingman. *The birthday goat* ill. by Wendy Watson. Crowell, 1974. Subj: Animals – goats. Birthdays. Crime. Fairs.

Sugar on snow ill. by Aldren Auld Watson. Viking, 1964. Subj: Food. Weather – snow.

Tommy's mommy's fish ill. by Aldren Auld Watson. Viking, 1971. Subj: Birthdays. Family life – mothers. Sports – fishing.

What does A begin with? ill. by Aldren Auld Watson. Knopf, 1956. Subj: ABC books. Farms.

What is one? ill. by Aldren Auld Watson. Knopf, 1954. Subj: Counting, numbers. Farms.

When is tomorrow? ill. by Aldren Auld Watson. Knopf, 1955. Subj: Sea and seashore. Time.

Watson, Pauline. *Curley Cat baby-sits* ill. by Lorinda Bryan Cauley. Harcourt, 1977. Subj: Activities – baby-sitting. Animals – cats.

Days with Daddy ill. by Joanne Scribner. Prentice-Hall, 1977. Subj: Family life. Family life – fathers.

The walking coat ill. by Tomie de Paola. Walker, 1980. ISBN 0-8027-6351-0 Subj: Clothing – coats.

Wriggles, the little wishing pig ill. by Paul Galdone. Seabury Pr., 1978. Subj: Animals – pigs. Behavior – wishing. Monsters.

Watson, Richard Jesse. *Tom Thumb* (Tom Thumb)

Watson, Wendy. *The bunnies' Christmas eve* ill. by author. Putnam's, 1983. Subj: Animals – rabbits. Format, unusual. Holidays – Christmas.

Fisherman lullabies (Watson, Clyde)

Has winter come? ill. by author. Collins-World, 1978. Subj: Animals – groundhogs. Hibernation. Seasons – winter.

Hurray for the Fourth of July ill. by author. Houghton, 1992. ISBN 0-395-53627-8 Subj: Family life. Holidays – Fourth of July. Poetry, rhyme.

Lollipop ill. by author. Crowell, 1976. Subj: Animals – rabbits. Behavior – misbehavior.

Moving ill. by author. Crowell, 1978. Subj: Moving.

Tales for a winter's eve ill. by author. Farrar, 1988. ISBN 0-374-37373-6 Subj: Animals – foxes. Illness. Seasons – winter.

Thanksgiving at our house ill. by author. Houghton, 1991. ISBN 0-395-53626-X Subj: Family life. Holidays – Thanksgiving. Nursery rhymes.

A Valentine for you ill. by author. Houghton, 1991. ISBN 0-395-53625-1 Subj: Emotions – love. Holidays – Valentine's Day. Poetry, rhyme.

Wattenberg, Jane. *Mrs. Mustard's baby faces* photos. by author. Chronicle, 1989. ISBN 0-87701-659-3 Subj: Babies. Format, unusual.

Watts, Barrie. *Apple tree* photos. by author. Silver Burdett, 1987. ISBN 0-382-09436-0 Subj: Nature. Science. Trees.

Bird's nest photos. by author. Silver Burdett, 1987. ISBN 0-382-09439-5 Subj: Animals. Birds. Science.

Butterfly and caterpillar photos. by author. Silver Burdett, 1986. ISBN 0-382-09282-1 Subj: Insects – butterflies, caterpillars. Science.

Dandelion photos. by author. Silver Burdett, 1987. ISBN 0-382-09438-7 Subj: Plants. Science.

Duck [written and ed. by Angela Royston] photos. by author. Dutton, 1991. ISBN 0-525-67346-6 Subj: Birds – ducks. Birth. Format, unusual – board books.

Hamster photos. by author. Silver Burdett, 1986. ISBN 0-382-09281-3 Subj: Animals – hamsters. Science.

Kitten photos. by Jane Burton. Dutton, 1991. ISBN 0-525-67343-1 Subj: Animals – cats. Birth. Format, unusual – board books.

Ladybug photos. by author. Silver Burdett, 1987. ISBN 0-382-09437-9 Subj: Insects – ladybugs. Science.

Mushrooms photos. by author. Silver Burdett, 1986. ISBN 0-382-09287-2 Subj: Plants. Science.

Rabbit [written and ed. by Angela Royston] ill. by Rowan Clifford; photos. by author. Dutton, 1992. ISBN 0-525-67356-3 Subj: Animals – rabbits. Birth. Format, unusual. Science.

Tomato photos. and ill. by author. Silver Burdett, 1990. ISBN 0-382-24008-1 Subj: Gardens, gardening. Plants. Science.

Watts, Bernadette. *David's waiting day* ill. by author. Prentice-Hall, 1978. Subj: Babies. Family life.

The fir tree (Andersen, H. C. (Hans Christian))

Goldilocks and the three bears (The three bears)

Green is beautiful (Rogers, Margaret)

Rapunzel (Grimm, Jacob)

St. Francis and the proud crow ill. by author. Watts, 1988. ISBN 0-531-08358-6 Subj: Behavior – seeking better things. Folk and fairy tales.

Snow White and Rose Red (Grimm, Jacob)

Tattercoats ill. by author. North-South, 1989. ISBN 1-55858-002-6 Subj: Gardens, gardening. Scarecrows. Seasons. Weather.

Watts, Mabel (Pizzey). *The day it rained watermelons* ill. by Lee Albertson. Lantern Pr., 1964. Subj: Behavior – indifference.

Something for you, something for me ill. by Abner Graboff. Abelard-Schuman, 1960. Subj: Activities – trading. Behavior – sharing.

Weeks and weeks ill. by Abner Graboff. Abelard-Schuman, 1962. Subj: Activities – photographing.

Watts, Marjorie-Ann. *Crocodile medicine* ill. by author. Warne, 1978. Subj: Behavior – boredom. Hospitals. Illness. Reptiles – alligators, crocodiles.

Crocodile plaster ill. by author. Dutton, 1984. ISBN 0-233-96962-4 Subj: Hospitals. Illness. Reptiles – alligators, crocodiles.

Zebra goes to school ill. by author. Elsevier-Dutton, 1981. Subj: Imagination – imaginary friends. School.

Waxman, Stephanie. *What is a girl? What is a boy?* photos. by author. HarperCollins, 1989. ISBN 0-690-04711-8 Subj: Anatomy. Behavior – growing up. Character traits – individuality.

Wayland, April Halprin. *To Rabbittown* ill. by Robin Spowart. Scholastic, 1989. ISBN 0-590-40852-6 Subj: Animals – rabbits. Imagination. Pets.

We wish you a merry Christmas : *a traditional Christmas carol* ill. by Tracey Campbell Pearson. Dial Pr., 1983. ISBN 0-8037-9400-2 Subj: Behavior – misbehavior. Holidays – Christmas. Songs.

Weary, Ogdred *see* Gorey, Edward (St. John)

Weatherill, Stephen. *The very first Lucy Goose book* ill. by author. Prentice-Hall, 1987. ISBN 0-13-941410-X Subj: Birds. Birds – geese. Humor.

Webb, Angela. *Air* photos. by Chris Fairclough. Watts, 1987. ISBN 0-531-10369-2 Subj: Science.

Light photos. by Chris Fairclough. Watts, 1988. ISBN 0-531-10455-9 Subj: Concepts. Science.

Reflections photos. by Chris Fairclough. Watts, 1988. ISBN 0-531-10457-5 Subj: Concepts. Science.

Sand photos. by Chris Fairclough. Watts, 1987. ISBN 0-531-10370-6 Subj: Sand. Science.

Soil photos. by Chris Fairclough. Watts, 1987. ISBN 0-531-10371-4 Subj: Science.

Sound photos. by Chris Fairclough. Watts, 1988. ISBN 0-531-10456-7 Subj: Concepts. Noise, sounds. Science.

Water photos. by Chris Fairclough. Watts, 1987. ISBN 0-531-10372-2 Subj: Science.

Webb, Clifford. *The story of Noah* ill. by author. Warne, 1949. Subj: Religion – Noah.

Weber, Alfons. *Elizabeth gets well* ill. by Jacqueline Blass. Crowell, 1970. Translation of Elisabeth wird gesund Subj: Hospitals. Illness.

The weekend ill. by Roser Capdevila. Firefly Pr., 1986. ISBN 0-920303-44-7 Subj: Activities – picnicking. Country. Sea and seashore.

Weelen, Guy. *The little red train* ill. by Mamoru Funai. Lothrop, 1966. Subj: Foreign lands – France. Trains.

Wegen, Ron. *The balloon trip* ill. by author. Houghton, 1981. Subj: Activities – ballooning. Family life. Wordless.

Billy Gorilla ill. by author. Lothrop, 1983. Subj: Behavior – trickery. Holidays – April Fools' Day.

The Halloween costume party ill. by author. Houghton, 1983. Subj: Holidays – Halloween. Parties.

Sand castle ill. by author. Greenwillow, 1977. Subj: Sea and seashore.

Sky dragon ill. by author. Greenwillow, 1982. Subj: Weather – clouds.

Where can the animals go? ill. by author. Greenwillow, 1978. Subj: Animals. Ecology.

Weihs, Erika. *Count the cats* ill. by author. Doubleday, 1976. Subj: Animals – cats. Counting, numbers.

Weil, Ann. *Animal families* ill. by Roger Vernam. Children's Pr., 1956. Subj: Animals.

Weil, Lisl. *The candy egg bunny* ill. by author. Holiday, 1975. Subj: Animals – rabbits. Holidays – Easter. Witches.

Gertie and Gus ill. by author. Parents, 1977. Subj: Careers – fishermen. Family life.

Gillie and the flattering fox ill. by author. Atheneum, 1978. Subj: Animals – foxes. Birds – chickens. Friendship.

Let's go to the circus ill. by author. Holiday, 1988. ISBN 0-8234-0693-8 Subj: Circus.

Let's go to the library ill. by author. Holiday, 1990. ISBN 0-8234-0529-9 Subj: Libraries.

Let's go to the museum ill. by author. Holiday, 1989. ISBN 0-8234-0784-5 Subj: Museums.

The magic of music ill. by author. Holiday, 1989. ISBN 0-8234-0735-7 Subj: Music.

Mother Goose picture riddles: a book of rebuses ill. by author. Holiday, 1981. Subj: Nursery rhymes. Rebuses.

Owl and other scrambles ill. by author. Dutton, 1980. Subj: Games. Participation.

Pandora's box ill. by adapt. Atheneum, 1986. ISBN 0-689-31216-4 Subj: Character traits – curiosity. Folk and fairy tales.

Santa Claus around the world ill. by author. Holiday, 1987. ISBN 0-8234-0665-2 Subj: Holidays – Christmas.

To sail a ship of treasures ill. by author. Atheneum, 1984. Subj: Behavior – collecting things.

Weilerstein, Sadie Rose. *The best of K'tonton* ill. by Marilyn Hirsh. Jewish Pub. Soc., 1980. Subj: Jewish culture.

Weinberg, Florence. *Grandmother dear* (Finfer, Celentha)

Weinberg, Lawrence. *The Forgetful Bears* ill. by Paula Winter. Houghton, 1982. ISBN 0-89919-068-5 Subj: Animals – bears. Behavior – forgetfulness.

The Forgetful Bears meet Mr. Memory ill. by author. Scholastic, 1987. ISBN 0-590-40781-3 Subj: Animals – bears. Animals – elephants. Behavior – forgetfulness.

Weiner, Beth Lee. *Benjamin's perfect solution* ill. by author. Warner, 1979. Subj: Animals – porcupines. Animals – possums. Behavior – mistakes. Self-concept.

Weir, Alison. *Peter, good night* ill. by Deborah Kogan Ray. Dutton, 1989. ISBN 0-525-44464-5 Subj: Bedtime. Night. Sleep.

Weir, Bob. *Panther dream* by Bob and Wendy Weir; ill. by Wendy Weir. Walt Disney, 1991. ISBN 1-56282-075-3 Subj: Foreign lands – Africa. Forest, woods. Food.

Weir, Wendy. *Panther dream* (Weir, Bob)

Weisgard, Leonard. *The funny bunny factory* ill. by author. Grosset, 1950. Subj: Animals – rabbits. Holidays – Easter.

Mr. Peaceable paints ill. by author. Scribner's, 1956. Subj: Activities – painting. Careers – artists.

Silly Willy Nilly ill. by author. Scribner's, 1953. Subj: Animals – elephants. Behavior – forgetfulness.

Who dreams of cheese? ill. by author. Scribner's, 1950. Subj: Behavior – wishing. Dreams. Sleep.

Weisner, David. *Hurricane* ill. by author. Houghton, 1990. ISBN 0-395-54382-7 Subj: Family life – brothers. Family life – sisters. Imagination. Weather – storms.

Tuesday ill. by author. Houghton, 1991. ISBN 0-395-55113-7 Subj: Activities – flying. Caldecott award book. Frogs and toads. Magic. Night.

Weiss, Ellen. *Clara the fortune-telling chicken* ill. by author. Dutton, 1978. Subj: Animals – sheep. Birds – chickens. Careers – fortune tellers. Seasons – winter.

Millicent Maybe ill. by author. Watts, 1979. Subj: Reptiles – alligators, crocodiles.

Mokey's birthday present ill. by Elizabeth Miles. Holt, 1985. ISBN 0-03-004559-2 Subj: Birthdays. Friendship. Puppets.

Pigs in space ill. by Alastair Graham. Random House, 1983. Subj: Animals – pigs. Puppets. Space and space ships.

The pirates of Tarnoonga ed. by Stephanie Spinner; ill. by Bunny Carter. Random House, 1986. ISBN 0-394-87926-0 Subj: Pirates.

Telephone time: a first book of telephone do's and don'ts ill. by Hilary Knight. Random House, 1986. ISBN 0-394-98252-5 Subj: Etiquette. Telephone.

You are the star of a Muppet adventure ill. by Benjamin Alexander. Random House, 1983. Subj: Puppets.

Weiss, Harvey. *My closet full of hats* ill. by author. Abelard-Schuman, 1962. Subj: Clothing – hats.

The sooner hound: a tale from American folklore ill. by author. Putnam's, 1959. Subj: Animals – dogs. Careers – firefighters. Folk and fairy tales.

Weiss, Leatie. *Funny feet!* ill. by Ellen Weiss. Watts, 1978. Subj: Anatomy – feet. Birds – penguins. Clothing – shoes.

My teacher sleeps in school ill. by Ellen Weiss. Warne, 1984. ISBN 0-7232-6253-5 Subj: Animals – elephants. Careers – teachers. School.

Weiss, Miriam *see* Schlein, Miriam

Weiss, Monica. *Mmmm...cookies!* ill. by Rosemary Berlin. Troll, 1992. ISBN 0-8167-2486-6 Subj: Counting, numbers. Food. Frogs and toads.

Weiss, Nicki. *Barney is big* ill. by author. Greenwillow, 1988. ISBN 0-688-07587-8 Subj: Behavior – growing up. Family life. School.

Battle day at Camp Delmont ill. by author. Greenwillow, 1985. ISBN 0-688-04307-0 Subj: Friendship. Camps, camping.

Dog boy cap skate ill. by author. Greenwillow, 1989. ISBN 0-688-08276-9 Subj: Animals. Sports – ice skating.

A family story ill. by author. Greenwillow, 1987. ISBN 0-688-06505-8 Subj: Family life – sisters. Friendship.

If you're happy and you know it ill. by author. Greenwillow, 1987. ISBN 0-688-06444-2 Subj: Folk and fairy tales. Music. Songs.

Maude and Sally ill. by author. Greenwillow, 1983. Subj: Friendship.

On a hot, hot day ill. by author. Putnam, 1992. ISBN 0-399-22119-0 Subj: Activities. Ethnic groups in the U.S. – Hispanic-Americans. Family life – mothers. Seasons.

Princess Pearl ill. by author. Greenwillow, 1986. ISBN 0-688-05895-7 Subj: Family life – sisters. Sibling rivalry.

Sun sand sea sail ill. by author. Greenwillow, 1989. ISBN 0-688-08271-8 Subj: Family life. Poetry, rhyme. Sea and seashore.

Waiting ill. by author. Greenwillow, 1981. Subj: Character traits – patience.

Weekend at Muskrat Lake ill. by author. Greenwillow, 1984. Subj: Activities – vacationing. Family life.

Where does the brown bear go? ill. by author. Greenwillow, 1989. ISBN 0-688-07863-X Subj: Animals. Bedtime. Night. Sleep. Toys.

Weissmann, Joe. *Hickory dickory duck* (Patterson, Pat)

Welber, Robert. *Goodbye, hello* ill. by Cyndy Szekeres. Pantheon, 1974. Subj: Animals. Behavior – growing up. Poetry, rhyme. School.

Song of the seasons ill. by Deborah Kogan Ray. Pantheon, 1973. Subj: Seasons.

Welch, Martha McKeen. *Will that wake mother?* photos. by author. Dodd, 1982. Subj: Animals – cats.

Weller, Frances Ward. *The closet gorilla* ill. by Cat Bowman Smith. Macmillan, 1991. ISBN 0-02-

792531-5 Subj: Animals – gorillas. Family life – aunts, uncles. Holidays – Halloween.

Riptide ill. by Robert J. Blake. Putnam, 1990. ISBN 0-399-21675-8 Subj: Animals – dogs. Sea and seashore.

Wellington, Anne. *Apple pie* ill. by Nita Sowter. Prentice-Hall, 1978. Subj: Seasons.

Wellington, Monica. *All my little ducklings* ill. by author. Dutton, 1989. ISBN 0-525-44459-9 Subj: Activities. Birds – ducks.

The sheep follow ill. by author. Dutton, 1992. ISBN 0-525-44837-3 Subj: Animals – dogs. Animals – sheep. Careers – shepherds. Farms.

Wells, H. G. (Herbert George). *The adventures of Tommy* ill. by author. Knopf, 1967. Subj: Animals – elephants. Character traits – bravery. Character traits – kindness.

Wells, Rosemary. *Abdul* ill. by author. Dial Pr., 1986. ISBN 0-8037-4462-5 Subj: Animals – camels. Animals – horses. Character traits – being different.

Don't spill it again, James ill. by author. Dial, 1990. ISBN 0-8037-2118-8 Subj: Animals – foxes. Poetry, rhyme. Trains. Weather – rain.

Forest of dreams by Rosemary Wells and Susan Jeffers; ill. by Susan Jeffers. Dial Pr., 1988. ISBN 0-8037-0570-0 Subj: Nature. Seasons – spring. Seasons – winter.

Fritz and the mess fairy ill. by author. Dial, 1991. ISBN 0-8037-0983-8 Subj: Animals – skunks. Behavior – misbehavior. Character traits – cleanliness. Fairies.

Good night, Fred ill. by author. Dial Pr., 1981. Subj: Behavior – misbehavior. Imagination. Sibling rivalry.

Hazel's amazing mother ill. by author. Dial Pr., 1985. ISBN 0-8037-0210-8 Subj: Animals. Animals – badgers. Behavior – misbehavior. Family life – mothers.

Hooray for Max ill. by author. Dial Pr., 1986. ISBN 0-8037-0202-7 Subj: Animals – rabbits. Format, unusual – board books.

A lion for Lewis ill. by author. Dial Pr., 1982. Subj: Activities – playing. Imagination.

The little lame prince ill. by author. Dial, 1990. ISBN 0-8037-0789-4 Subj: Animals – pigs. Behavior – greed. Folk and fairy tales. Handicaps – physical. Royalty – princes.

Max's bath ill. by author. Dial Pr., 1985. ISBN 0-8037-0162-4 Subj: Activities – bathing. Animals – rabbits. Format, unusual – board books.

Max's bedtime ill. by author. Dial Pr., 1985. ISBN 0-8037-0160-8 Subj: Animals – rabbits. Bedtime. Format, unusual – board books. Sibling rivalry. Toys.

Max's birthday ill. by author. Dial Pr., 1985. ISBN 0-8037-0163-2 Subj: Animals – rabbits. Birthdays. Format, unusual – board books. Toys.

Max's breakfast ill. by author. Dial Pr., 1985. Subj: Animals – rabbits. Character traits – patience. Format, unusual – board books. Sibling rivalry.

Max's chocolate chicken ill. by author. Dial Pr., 1988. ISBN 0-8037-0585-9 Subj: Animals – rabbits. Holidays – Easter. Seasons – spring. Sibling rivalry.

Max's Christmas ill. by author. Dial Pr., 1986. ISBN 0-8037-0290-6 Subj: Animals – rabbits. Holidays – Christmas.

Max's dragon shirt ill. by author. Dial, 1991. ISBN 0-8037-0945-5 Subj: Activities – baby-sitting. Animals – rabbits. Behavior – lost. Clothing. Family life – brothers. Family life – sisters. Stores.

Max's first word ill. by author. Dial Pr., 1979. ISBN 0-8037-6066-3 Subj: Animals – rabbits. Format, unusual – board books. Language.

Max's new suit ill. by author. Dial Pr., 1979. Subj: Animals – rabbits. Clothing. Format, unusual – board books.

Max's ride ill. by author. Dial Pr., 1979. ISBN 0-8037-6069-8 Subj: Animals – rabbits. Format, unusual – board books. Language.

Max's toys: a counting book ill. by author. Dial Pr., 1979. ISBN 0-8037-6068-X Subj: Animals – rabbits. Counting, numbers. Format, unusual – board books. Toys.

Noisy Nora ill. by author. Dial Pr., 1973. Subj: Animals – mice. Behavior – needing someone. Poetry, rhyme.

Peabody ill. by author. Dial Pr., 1983. Subj: Sibling rivalry. Toys – dolls.

Shy Charles ill. by author. Dial Pr., 1988. ISBN 0-8037-0564-6 Subj: Activities – baby-sitting. Animals – mice. Character traits – individuality. Family life. Poetry, rhyme.

Stanley and Rhoda ill. by author. Dial Pr., 1978. Subj: Activities – baby-sitting. Animals – mice. Sibling rivalry.

Timothy goes to school ill. by author. Dial Pr., 1981. Subj: Animals – raccoons. Behavior – growing up. School.

Unfortunately Harriet ill. by author. Dial Pr., 1972. Subj: Behavior – bad day.

Wells, Tony. *Allsorts* ill. by author. Macmillan, 1988. ISBN 0-689-71185-9 Subj: Concepts – color. Concepts – shape. Games.

Puzzle doubles ill. by author. Macmillan, 1988. ISBN 0-689-71186-7 Subj: Concepts – color. Concepts – size. Games.

Wende, Philip. *Bird boy* ill. by author. Cowles, 1970. Subj: Activities – flying. Dreams.

Wenning, Elisabeth. *The Christmas mouse* ill. by Barbara Remington. Holt, 1959. Subj: Animals – mice. Holidays – Christmas. Music. Songs.

Werner, Jane *see* Watson, Jane Werner

Wersba, Barbara. *Amanda dreaming* ill. by Mercer Mayer. Atheneum, 1973. Subj: Dreams. Sleep.

Do tigers ever bite kings? ill. by Mario Rivoli. Atheneum, 1966. Subj: Animals – tigers. Character traits – kindness to animals. Poetry, rhyme. Royalty – kings.

West, Colin. *Go tell it to the toucan* ill. by author. Bantam, 1990. ISBN 0-553-05889-4 Subj: Animals. Birthdays. Cumulative tales. Parties.

Have you seen the crocodile? ill. by author. Lippincott, 1986. ISBN 0-397-32172-4 Subj: Birds. Cumulative tales. Reptiles – alligators, crocodiles.

I brought my love a tabby cat ill. by Caroline Anstey. Chronicle, 1988. ISBN 0-87701-518-X Subj: Animals. Careers – tailors. Clothing. Weddings.

The king of Kennelwick castle ill. by Anne Dalton. Lippincott, 1987. ISBN 0-397-32197-X Subj: Cumulative tales. Royalty – kings.

The king's toothache ill. by Anne Dalton. Lippincott, 1988. ISBN 0-397-32252-6 Subj: Cumulative tales. Illness. Poetry, rhyme. Royalty – kings. Teeth.

A moment in rhyme ill. by Julie Banyard. Dial Pr., 1987. ISBN 0-8037-0259-0 Subj: Poetry, rhyme.

"Pardon?" said the giraffe ill. by author. Lippincott, 1986. ISBN 0-397-32173-2 Subj: Animals. Character traits – persistence. Frogs and toads.

West, Emily *see* Payne, Emmy

West, Ian. *Silas, the first pig to fly* ill. by author. Grosset, 1977. Subj: Activities – flying. Animals – pigs.

West, James *see* Withers, Carl

West, Keith. *Little Pig's special day* ill. by author. Putnam, 1991. ISBN 0-399-22209-X Subj: Animals – pigs. Babies. Family life.

Westcott, Nadine Bernard. *Getting up* ill. by author. Little, 1987. ISBN 0-316-93131-4 Subj: Family life. Morning.

The giant vegetable garden ill. by author. Little, 1981. Subj: Activities – picnicking. Gardens, gardening.

Going to bed ill. by author. Little, 1987. ISBN 0-316-93132-2 Subj: Bedtime. Family life. Night. Toys.

The lady with the alligator purse ill. by author. Little, 1988. ISBN 0-316-93135-7 Subj: Games. Humor. Poetry, rhyme.

Peanut butter and jelly: a play rhyme ill. by author. Dutton, 1987. ISBN 0-525-44317-7 Subj: Animals – elephants. Careers – bakers. Family life. Food. Poetry, rhyme.

Skip to my Lou ill. by adaptor. Little, 1989. ISBN 0-316-93137-3 Subj: Farms. Folk and fairy tales. Music. Poetry, rhyme. Songs.

There's a hole in the bucket ill. by adaptor. HarperCollins, 1990. ISBN 0-06-026423-3 Subj: Animals. Farms. Music. Songs.

Westell, Kerry. *Amanda's book* ill. by Ruth Ohi. Firefly, 1991. ISBN 1-55037-185-1 Subj: Animals – cats. Behavior – collecting things. Imagination.

Westerberg, Christine. *The cap that mother made* ill. by adapt. Prentice-Hall, 1977. Subj: Clothing – hats. Folk and fairy tales. Foreign lands – Sweden.

Westman, Barbara. *Dancing dogs: Charlotte and Emilio at the circus* ill. by author. HarperCollins, 1991. ISBN 0-06-022460-6 Subj: Activities – dancing. Animals – dogs. Circus.

The day before Christmas: A story of Charlotte and Emilio ill. by author. HarperCollins, 1990. ISBN 0-06-026429-2 Subj: Animals – dogs. Holidays – Christmas.

Weston, Martha. *Bea's four bears* ill. by author. Houghton, 1992. ISBN 0-395-57791-8 Subj: Activities – picnicking. Behavior – sharing. Counting, numbers. Toys – teddy bears.

Peony's rainbow ill. by author. Lothrop, 1981. Subj: Animals – pigs. Weather – rainbows.

Westwood, Jennifer. *Going to Squintum's: a foxy folktale* ill. by Fiona French. Dial Pr., 1985. ISBN 0-8037-0015-6 Subj: Animals – foxes. Character traits – cleverness. Folk and fairy tales.

Wetterer, Margaret. *Kate Shelley and the midnight express* ill. by Karen Ritz. Carolrhoda, 1990. ISBN 0-87614-425-3 Subj: Character traits – bravery. Trains. U.S. history.

Patrick and the fairy thief ill. by Enrico Arno. Atheneum, 1980. Subj: Character traits – cleverness. Fairies. Family life – mothers.

Wexler, Jerome (LeRoy). *Find the hidden insect* (Cole, Joanna)

Flowers, fruits, seeds photos. by author. Prentice-Hall, 1988. ISBN 0-13-322397-3 Subj: Plants. Science.

Wonderful pussy willows photos. by author. Dutton, 1992. ISBN 0-525-44867-5 Subj: Plants. Science.

Wezel, Peter. *The good bird* ill. by author. Harper, 1964. Subj: Behavior – sharing. Birds. Fish. Wordless.

The naughty bird ill. by author. Follett, 1967. Translation of Der freche Vogel Figaro Subj: Animals – cats. Birds. Wordless.

Wharton, Thomas. *Hildegard sings* ill. by author. Farrar, 1991. ISBN 0-374-33242-8 Subj: Animals – hippopotami. Emotions – fear. Theater.

What a morning! the Christmas story in Black spirituals sel. and ed. by John M. Langstaff; ill. by Ashley Bryan; musical arrangements by John Andrew Ross. McElderry, 1987. ISBN 0-689-50422-5 Subj: Holidays – Christmas. Music. Religion. Songs.

What do babies do? ill. with photos. Random House, 1985. ISBN 0-394-87279-7 Subj: Babies. Format, unusual – board books.

What do toddlers do? ill. with photos. Random House, 1985. ISBN 0-394-87280-0 Subj: Babies. Format, unusual – board books.

What do you feed your donkey on? Rhymes from a Belfast childhood col. by Colette O'Hare; ill. by Jenny Rodwell. Collins-World, 1978. Subj: Foreign lands – Ireland. Nursery rhymes. Poetry, rhyme.

What we do ill. by Roser Capdevila. Firefly Pr., 1986. ISBN 0-920303-46-3 Subj: Activities.

Wheeler, Cindy. *Marmalade's Christmas present* ill. by author. Knopf, 1984. ISBN 0-394-96794-1 Subj: Animals – cats. Holidays – Christmas.

Marmalade's nap ill. by author. Knopf, 1983. Subj: Animals – cats. Noise, sounds. Sleep.

Marmalade's picnic ill. by author. Knopf, 1983. Subj: Activities – picnicking. Animals – cats.

Marmalade's snowy day ill. by author. Knopf, 1982. Subj: Animals – cats. Weather – snow.

Marmalade's yellow leaf ill. by author. Knopf, 1982. Subj: Animals – cats. Seasons – fall.

Rose ill. by author. Knopf, 1985. ISBN 0-394-96233-8 Subj: Animals – pigs. Farms.

Wheeler, M. J. (Mary Jane). *First came the Indians* ill. by James Houston. Atheneum, 1983. Subj: Indians of North America.

Wheeler, Opal. *Sing in praise: a collection of the best loved hymns* ill. by Marjorie Torrey. Dutton, 1946. Subj: Caldecott award honor book. Music. Religion. Songs.

Sing Mother Goose ill. by Marjorie Torrey; music by Opal Wheeler. Dutton, 1945. Subj: Caldecott award honor book. Music. Nursery rhymes. Songs.

Wheeler, William A. *Mother Goose's melodies* (Mother Goose)

Wheeling, Lynn. *When you fly* ill. by author. Little, 1967. Subj: Activities – flying. Airplanes, airports. Poetry, rhyme.

Whelan, Gloria. *A week of raccoons* ill. by Lynn Munsinger. Knopf, 1988. ISBN 0-394-88396-9 Subj: Animals – raccoons.

White, Florence Meiman. *How to lose your lunch money* ill. by Chris Jenkyns. Ritchie, 1970. Subj: Behavior – losing things. Behavior – misbehavior. School.

White, Paul. *Janet at school* photos. by Jeremy Finlay. Crowell, 1978. Subj: Handicaps. School.

Whiteside, Karen. *Lullaby of the wind* ill. by Kazue Mizumura. Harper, 1984. ISBN 0-06-026412-8 Subj: Bedtime. Lullabies. Sleep. Weather – wind.

Whitlock, Susan Love. *Donovan scares the monsters* ill. by Yossi Abolafia. Greenwillow, 1987. ISBN 0-688-06439-6 Subj: Family life – grandmothers. Monsters.

Whitmore, Adam. *Max in America* ill. by Janice Poltrick Donato. Silver Burdett, 1986. ISBN 0-382-09244-9 Subj: Animals – cats. Character traits – being different.

Max in Australia ill. by Janice Poltrick Donato. Silver Burdett, 1986. ISBN 0-382-09246-5 Subj: Animals – cats. Character traits – being different. Foreign lands – Australia.

Max in India ill. by Janice Poltrick Donato. Silver Burdett, 1986. ISBN 0-382-09245-7 Subj: Animals – cats. Character traits – being different. Foreign lands – India.

Max leaves home ill. by Janice Poltrick Donato. Silver Burdett, 1986. ISBN 0-382-09243-0 Subj: Animals – cats. Behavior – running away. Character traits – being different.

Whitney, Alex. *Once a bright red tiger* ill. by Charles Robinson. Walck, 1973. Subj: Animals – tigers. Character traits – pride.

Whitney, Alma Marshak. *Just awful* ill. by Lillian Hoban. Addison-Wesley, 1971. Subj: Careers – nurses. Illness. School.

Leave Herbert alone ill. by David McPhail. Addison-Wesley, 1972. Subj: Animals – cats. Character traits – kindness to animals.

Whitney, Dorothy B. *Creatures of an exceptional kind* ill. by author. Humanics, 1989. ISBN 0-89334-127-4 Subj: Animals. Character traits – individuality. Handicaps.

Whittier, John Greenleaf. *Barbara Frietchie* ill. by Paul Galdone. Crowell, 1965. ISBN 0-690-11532-6 Subj: Character traits – loyalty. U.S. history. War.

Whittington, Mary K. *Carmina, come dance!* ill. by Michael McDermott. Macmillan, 1989. ISBN 0-689-31554-6 Subj: Activities – dancing. Family life – great-grandparents. Imagination. Music.

The patchwork lady ill. by Jane Dyer. Harcourt, 1991. ISBN 0-15-259580-5 Subj: Birthdays. Quilts.

Whybrow, Ian. *Quacky quack-quack!* ill. by Russell Ayto. Four Winds, 1991. ISBN 0-02-792741-5 Subj: Animals. Circular tales. Noise, sounds. Poetry, rhyme.

Wickstrom, Sylvie (Sylvie Kantrovitz). *Mothers can't get sick* ill. by author. Crown, 1989. ISBN 0-517-57181-1 Subj: Birthdays. Family life. Family life – mothers. Illness.

Turkey on the loose! ill. by author. Dial, 1990. ISBN 0-8037-0820-3 Subj: Birds – turkeys.

**Widdecombe Fair : ** *an old English folk song* ill. by Christine Price. Warne, 1968. Subj: Fairs. Folk and fairy tales. Foreign lands – England. Music. Songs.

Widerberg, Siv. *The boy and the dog* tr. from Swedish by Richard E. Fisher; ill. by Jens Ahlbom. Farrar, 1991. ISBN 91-29-59926-1 Subj: Animals – dogs. Emotions – fear.

Widman, Christine. *Housekeeper of the wind* ill. by Lisa Desimini. HarperCollins, 1990. ISBN 0-06-026468-3 Subj: Behavior – fighting, arguing. Careers – housekeepers. Emotions – anger. Weather – wind.

The star grazers ill. by Robin Spowart. HarperCollins, 1989. ISBN 0-06-026473-X Subj: Animals – sheep. Stars.

Wiese, Kurt. *The cunning turtle* ill. by author. Viking, 1956. Subj: Reptiles – turtles, tortoises.

The dog, the fox and the fleas ill. by author. McKay, 1953. Subj: Animals – dogs. Animals – foxes. Insects – fleas.

Fish in the air ill. by author. Viking, 1948. Subj: Caldecott award honor book. Foreign lands – China. Humor. Kites.

The five Chinese brothers (Bishop, Claire Huchet)

Happy Easter ill. by author. Viking, 1952. Subj: Animals – rabbits. Holidays – Easter.

The story about Ping (Flack, Marjorie)

You can write Chinese ill. by author. Viking, 1945. Subj: Caldecott award honor book. Foreign languages.

Wiesner, David. *Free fall* ill. by author. Lothrop, 1988. ISBN 0-688-05584-2 Subj: Activities – reading. Bedtime. Caldecott award honor book. Dragons. Dreams. Wordless.

The loathsome dragon by David Wiesner and Kim Kahng; ill. by David Wiesner. Putnam's, 1987. ISBN 0-399-21407-0 Subj: Dragons. Folk and fairy tales. Magic. Royalty.

Wiesner, William. *Happy-Go-Lucky: a Norwegian tale* ill. by author. Seabury Pr., 1970. Subj: Character traits – optimism. Cumulative tales. Farms. Foreign lands – Norway. Humor.

Noah's ark ill. by author. Dutton, 1966. Subj: Religion – Noah.

Tops ill. by author. Viking, 1969. Subj: Friendship. Giants. Violence, anti-violence.

The Tower of Babel ill. by author. Viking, 1968. "Based on the book of Genesis and on commentaries ... in the book Hebrew myths by Robert Graves and Raphael Patai." Subj: Language. Religion.

Turnabout: a Norwegian tale ill. by author. Seabury Pr., 1972. "This text has been adapted from the version of Edouard Laboulaye." Subj: Behavior – dissatisfaction. Foreign lands – Norway. Humor.

Wijngaard, Juan. *Bear* ill. by author. Crown, 1991. ISBN 0-517-58201-5 Subj: Animals – bears. Format, unusual – board books.

Cat ill. by author. Crown, 1991. ISBN 0-517-58202-3 Subj: Animals – cats. Format, unusual – board books.

Dog ill. by author. Crown, 1991. ISBN 0-517-58203-1 Subj: Animals – dogs. Format, unusual – board books.

Duck ill. by author. Crown, 1991. ISBN 0-517-58204-X Subj: Birds – ducks. Format, unusual – board books.

The nativity ill. by author. Lothrop, 1990. ISBN 0-7445-1260-3 Subj: Holidays – Christmas. Religion.

Wikland, Ilon. *Christmas in noisy village* (Lindgren, Astrid)

Wikler, Madeline. *All about Hanukkah* (Groner, Judyth)

Let's build a Sukkah by Madeline Wikler and Judyth Groner; ill. by Katherine Janus Kahn. Kar-Ben Copies, 1986. ISBN 0-930494-58-X Subj: Format, unusual – board books. Holidays. Jewish culture.

My first seder by Madeline Wikler and Judyth Groner; ill. by Katherine Janus Kahn. Kar-Ben Copies, 1986. ISBN 0-930494-61-X Subj: Food. Format, unusual – board books. Holidays – Passover. Jewish culture.

My very own Jewish community (Groner, Judyth)

The Purim parade by Madeline Wikler and Judyth Groner; ill. by Katherine Janus Kahn. Kar-Ben Copies, 1986. ISBN 0-930494-60-1 Subj: Format, unusual – board books. Holidays – Purim. Jewish culture.

Where is the Afikomen? (Groner, Judyth)

Wilcox, Daniel. *The Sesame Street ABC storybook* (Moss, Jeffrey)

Wild, Jocelyn. *The bears' ABC book* (Wild, Robin)

The bears' counting book (Wild, Robin)

Florence and Eric take the cake ill. by author. Dial Pr., 1987. ISBN 0-8037-0305-8 Subj: Animals – sheep. Behavior – misunderstanding. Family life.

Little Pig and the big bad wolf (Wild, Robin)

Spot's dogs and the alley cats (Wild, Robin)

Wild, Margaret. *Let the celebrations begin!* ill. by Julie Vivas. Watts, 1991. ISBN 0-531-08537-6 Subj: Toys. War.

Mr. Nick's knitting ill. by Dee H. Huxley. Harcourt, 1989. ISBN 0-15-200518-8 Subj: Activities – knitting. Friendship. Hospitals. Illness.

The very best of friends ill. by Julie Vivas. Harcourt, 1990. ISBN 0-15-200625-7 Subj: Animals – cats. Death. Farms. Friendship.

Wild, Robin. *The bears' ABC book* by Robin and Jocelyn Wild; ill. by authors. Lippincott, 1978. Subj: ABC books. Animals – bears.

The bears' counting book by Robin and Jocelyn Wild; ill. by authors. Lippincott, 1978. Subj: Animals – bears. Counting, numbers.

Little Pig and the big bad wolf by Robin and Jocelyn Wild; ill. by authors. Coward, 1972. Subj: Animals – pigs. Animals – wolves. Character traits – cleverness. Holidays – Christmas. Poetry, rhyme.

Spot's dogs and the alley cats by Robin and Jocelyn Wild; ill. by authors. Lippincott, 1979. Subj: Animals – cats. Animals – dogs. Behavior – trickery.

Wilde, Oscar. *Fairy tales of Oscar Wilde: The selfish giant, and The star child* adapt. and ill. by P. Craig Russell. NBM, 1992. Vol. 1 ISBN 1-56163-056-X Subj: Character traits. Folk and fairy tales. Seasons – spring.

The selfish giant ill. by Dom Mansell. Prentice-Hall, 1986. ISBN 0-13-803586-5 Subj: Character traits – kindness. Character traits – selfishness. Seasons – spring.

The selfish giant ill. by Lisbeth Zwerger. Alphabet Pr., 1984. ISBN 0-907234-30-5 Subj: Character traits – kindness. Character traits – selfishness. Seasons – spring.

Wildsmith, Brian. *Animal games* ill. by author. Oxford Univ. Pr., 1980. Subj: Animals. Games.

Animal homes ill. by author. Oxford Univ. Pr., 1980. Subj: Animals. Houses.

Animal shapes ill. by author. Oxford Univ. Pr., 1980. Subj: Animals. Concepts – shape.

Animal tricks ill. by author. Oxford Univ. Pr., 1980. Subj: Animals. Poetry, rhyme.

Bear's adventure ill. by author. Pantheon, 1982. Subj: Activities – ballooning. Animals – bears.

Brian Wildsmith's birds ill. by author. Watts, 1967. Subj: Birds.

Brian Wildsmith's circus ill. by author. Watts, 1970. Subj: Circus.

Brian Wildsmith's fishes ill. by author. Watts, 1968. Subj: Fish.

Brian Wildsmith's puzzles ill. by author. Watts, 1970. Subj: Games.

Brian Wildsmith's wild animals ill. by author. Watts, 1967. Subj: Animals.

Carousel ill. by author. Knopf, 1988. ISBN 0-394-91937-8 Subj: Dreams. Fairs. Illness. Merry-go-rounds.

Give a dog a bone ill. by author. Pantheon, 1985. ISBN 0-394-97709-2 Subj: Animals – dogs. Format, unusual.

Goat's trail ill. by author. Knopf, 1986. ISBN 0-394-98276-2 Subj: Animals. Animals – goats. Cumulative tales. Format, unusual. Noise, sounds.

Hunter and his dog ill. by author. Oxford Univ. Pr., 1979. Subj: Animals – dogs. Character traits – kindness to animals. Sports – hunting.

The lazy bear ill. by author. Watts, 1974. Subj: Animals – bears. Character traits – laziness. Friendship.

The little wood duck ill. by author. Watts, 1972. Subj: Birds – ducks.

The miller, the boy and the donkey (La Fontaine, Jean de)

The owl and the woodpecker ill. by author. Watts, 1971. Subj: Birds – owls. Birds – woodpeckers. Character traits – compromising.

Pelican ill. by author. Pantheon, 1983. Subj: Birds – pelicans. Format, unusual. Sports – fishing.

Professor Noah's spaceship ill. by author. Oxford Univ. Pr., 1980. ISBN 0-19-279741-7 Subj: Space and space ships.

Python's party ill. by author. Watts, 1975. Subj: Animals. Behavior – trickery. Reptiles – snakes.

Seasons ill. by author. Oxford Univ. Pr., 1980. Subj: Nature. Seasons.

The true cross ill. by author. Oxford Univ. Pr., 1985, 1977. ISBN 0-19-279718-2 Subj: Folk and fairy tales. Religion.

What the moon saw ill. by author. Oxford Univ. Pr., 1978. Subj: Animals. Concepts – opposites. Language. Moon. Sun.

Wilhelm, Hans. *Bunny trouble* ill. by author. Scholastic, 1991. ISBN 0-590-63153-5 Subj: Animals – rabbits.

A cool kid—like me! ill. by author. Crown, 1990. ISBN 0-517-57822-0 Subj: Character traits – confidence. Family life – grandmothers. Toys – teddy bears.

I'll always love you ill. by author. Crown, 1985. ISBN 0-517-55648-0 Subj: Animals – dogs. Death. Pets.

Let's be friends again! ill. by author. ISBN 0-517-56252-9 Subj: Emotions – anger. Family life – sisters. Friendship.

More bunny trouble ill. by author. Scholastic, 1989. ISBN 0-590-41589-1 Subj: Animals – foxes. Animals – rabbits. Eggs. Holidays – Easter.

A new home, a new friend ill. by author. Random House, 1985. Subj: Animals – dogs. Family life. Friendship. Moving.

Oh, what a mess ill. by author. Crown, 1988. ISBN 0-517-56909-4 Subj: Animals – pigs. Character traits – cleanliness.

Schnitzel's first Christmas ill. by author. Simon & Schuster, 1991. ISBN 0-671-74494-1 Subj: Animals – dogs. Behavior – needing someone. Holidays – Christmas.

Tyrone the horrible ill. by author. Scholastic, 1988. ISBN 0-590-41471-2 Subj: Behavior – bullying. Dinosaurs.

Wilkes, Angela. *My first word book* ill. by author. Dorling Kindersley., 1991. ISBN 0-879431-36-X Subj: Dictionaries. Language.

Wilkes, Larry. *The king's egg dance* ill. by author. Carolrhoda, 1990. ISBN 0-87614-446-6 Subj: Activities – dancing. Eggs. Royalty – kings.

Wilkins, Mary Huiskamp Calhoun *see* Calhoun, Mary

Wilkinson, Sylvia. *Automobiles* ill. with photos. Children's Pr., 1982. Subj: Automobiles.

I can be a race car driver ill. with photos. Childrens Pr., 1986. ISBN 0-516-01898-1 Subj: Automobiles. Careers – race car drivers. Sports – racing.

Wilkoń, Piotr. *The brave little kittens* tr. by Helen Graves; ill. by Józef Wilkoń. North-South, 1991. ISBN 1-55858-103-0 Subj: Animals – cats. Character traits – bravery.

Wilkoń, Józef. *Lullaby for a newborn king* by Józef Wilkoń and Hermann Moers; tr. from German by Rosemary Lanning; ill. by Józef Wilkoń. North-South, 1991. ISBN 1-55858-123-5 Subj: Holidays – Christmas. Lullabies. Religion.

Wilkoń, Piotr. *Rosie the cool cat* ill. by Józef Wilkoń. Viking, 1991. ISBN 0-670-83707-5 Subj: Animals – cats. Behavior – running away. Character traits – being different.

Will *see* Lipkind, William

Willard, Barbara. *To London! To London!* ill. by Antony Maitland. Weybright and Talley, 1968. Subj: Foreign lands – England.

Willard, Nancy. *The high rise glorious skittle skat roarious sky pie angel food cake* ill. by Richard Jesse Watson. Harcourt, 1990. ISBN 0-15-234332-6 Subj: Activities – cooking. Angels. Birthdays. Family life – mothers.

The marzipan moon ill. by Marcia Sewell. Harcourt, 1981. ISBN 0-15-252962-4 Subj: Behavior – wishing. Birthdays. Food. Magic.

The mountains of quilt ill. by Tomie de Paola. Harcourt, 1987. ISBN 0-15-256010-6 Subj: Dreams. Family life – grandmothers. Magic. Quilts.

Night story ill. by Ilse Plume. Harcourt, 1986. ISBN 0-15-257348-8 Subj: Dreams. Night. Poetry, rhyme.

The nightgown of the sullen moon ill. by David McPhail. Harcourt, 1983. Subj: Moon. Night.

Pish posh, said Hieronymous Bosch ill. by Leo and Diane Dillon. Harcourt, 1991. ISBN 0-15-262210-1 Subj: Careers – artists. Poetry, rhyme.

Simple pictures are best ill. by Tomie de Paola. Harcourt, 1977. Subj: Activities – photographing. Humor.

A visit to William Blake's inn: poems for innocent and experienced travelers ill. by Alice and Martin Provensen. Harcourt, 1981. Subj: Caldecott award honor book. Imagination. Poetry, rhyme.

The voyage of the Ludgate Hill: travels with Robert Louis Stevenson ill. by Alice and Martin Provensen. Harcourt, 1987. ISBN 0-15-294464-8 Subj: Activities – traveling. Animals. Boats, ships. Poetry, rhyme. Sea and seashore. Weather – storms.

The well-mannered balloon ill. by Haig and Regina Shekerjian. Harcourt, 1991. ISBN 0-15-294986-0 Subj: Behavior – misbehavior. Night. Toys – balloons.

Willhoite, Michael. *Daddy's roomate* ill. by author. Alyson, 1990. ISBN 1-55583-178-8 Subj: Divorce. Family life – fathers. Homosexuality.

Williams, Barbara. *Albert's toothache* ill. by Kay Chorao. Dutton, 1974. Subj: Illness. Reptiles – turtles, tortoises. Teeth.

Chester Chipmunk's Thanksgiving ill. by Kay Chorao. Dutton, 1974. Subj: Animals – chipmunks. Holidays – Thanksgiving.

Donna Jean's disaster ill. by Margot Apple. Albert Whitman, 1986. ISBN 0-8075-1682-1 Subj: Family life. Poetry, rhyme. School. Sibling rivalry.

Hello, dandelions! photos. by author. Holt, 1979. Subj: Flowers. Plants.

I know a salesperson ill. by Frank Aloise. Putnam's, 1978. Subj: Careers. Stores.

If he's my brother ill. by Tomie de Paola. Harvey House, 1976. Subj: Character traits – questioning. Family life.

Jeremy isn't hungry ill. by Martha G. Alexander. Dutton, 1978. Subj: Activities – baby-sitting. Babies. Humor.

Kevin's grandma ill. by Kay Chorao. Dutton, 1975. Subj: Family life – grandmothers. Friendship.

So what if I'm a sore loser? ill. by Linda Strauss Edwards. Harcourt, 1981. Subj: Character traits – conceit. Family life.

Someday, said Mitchell ill. by Kay Chorao. Dutton, 1976. Subj: Behavior – wishing. Character traits – helpfulness. Character traits – smallness. Emotions – happiness.

Whatever happened to Beverly Bigler's birthday? ill. by Emily Arnold McCully. Harcourt, 1979. Subj: Behavior – misbehavior. Birthdays. Weddings.

Williams, Charles *see* Collier, James Lincoln

Williams, David. *Walking to the creek* ill. by Thomas B. Allen. Knopf, 1990. ISBN 0-394-90598-9 Subj: Activities – walking. Country. Nature.

Williams, Garth. *The big golden animal ABC* ill. by author. Simon and Schuster, 1957. First published under the title: The golden animal A.B.C Subj: ABC books. Animals.

The chicken book ill. by author. Delacorte Pr., 1970. Subj: Birds – chickens. Counting, numbers. Poetry, rhyme.

The rabbits' wedding ill. by author. Harper, 1958. Subj: Animals – rabbits. Weddings.

Williams, Gweneira Maureen. *Timid Timothy, the kitten who learned to be brave* ill. by Leonard Weisgard. Addison-Wesley, 1944. Subj: Food. Science. Emotions – fear.

Williams, Jay. *The city witch and the country witch* ill. by Ed Renfro. Macmillan, 1979. Subj: Activities – vacationing. City. Country. Witches.

Everyone knows what a dragon looks like ill. by Mercer Mayer. Four Winds Pr., 1976. Subj: Dragons. Foreign lands – China.

I wish I had another name by Jay Williams and Winifred Lubell; ill. by authors. Atheneum, 1962. Subj: Names. Poetry, rhyme.

The practical princess ill. by Friso Henstra. Parents, 1969. Subj: Folk and fairy tales. Royalty – princesses.

School for sillies ill. by Friso Henstra. Parents, 1969. Subj: Character traits – cleverness. Humor. Royalty.

The surprising things Maui did ill. by Charles Mikolaycak. Four Winds Pr., 1980. Subj: Folk and fairy tales. Hawaii.

Williams, Jenny. *Here's a ball for baby: finger rhymes for young children* ill. by author. Dial Pr., 1987. ISBN 0-8037-0388-0 Subj: Nursery rhymes.

One, two, buckle my shoe: counting rhymes for young children ill. by author. Dial Pr., 1987. ISBN 0-8037-0390-2 Subj: Counting, numbers. Nursery rhymes.

Ride a cockhorse: animal rhymes for young children ill. by author. Dial Pr., 1987. ISBN 0-8037-0389-9 Subj: Animals. Nursery rhymes.

Ring around a rosy: action rhymes for young children ill. by author. Dial Pr., 1987. ISBN 0-8037-0391-0 Subj: Games. Nursery rhymes.

A wet Monday (Edwards, Dorothy)

Williams, Julie Stewart. *And the birds appeared* ill. by Robin Yoko Burningham. Univ. of Hawaii Pr., 1988. ISBN 0-8248-1194-1 Subj: Birds. Folk and fairy tales. Hawaii.

Williams, Karen Lynn. *Galimoto* ill. by Catherine Stock. Lothrop, 1990. ISBN 0-688-08790-6 Subj: Foreign lands – Africa. Toys.

When Africa was home ill. by Floyd Cooper. Watts, 1991. ISBN 0-531-08525-2 Subj: Family life. Foreign lands – Africa. Friendship.

Williams, Leslie. *A bear in the air* ill. by Carme Solé Vendrell. Stemmer House, 1980. Subj: Animals – bears. Weather – clouds. Weather – rainbows.

Williams, Linda. *The little old lady who was not afraid of anything* ill. by Megan Lloyd. Crowell, 1986. ISBN 0-690-04586-7 Subj: Cumulative tales. Emotions – fear. Scarecrows.

Williams, Marcia. *The first Christmas* ill. by author. Random House, 1988. ISBN 0-394-80434-1 Subj: Holidays – Christmas. Religion.

Jonah and the whale ill. by author. Random House, 1989. ISBN 0-394-92345-6 Subj: Animals – whales. Religion.

Joseph and his magnificent coat of many colors ill. by author. Candlewick Pr., 1992. ISBN 1-56402-019-3 Subj: Clothing – coats. Religion.

Not a worry in the world ill. by author. Crown, 1991. ISBN 0-517-58156-6 Subj: Behavior – worrying. Family life.

Williams, Margery *see* Bianco, Margery Williams

Williams, Sarah. *Ride a cock-horse* ill. by Ian Beck. Oxford Univ. Pr., 1987. ISBN 0-19-279831-6 Subj: Nursery rhymes.

Williams, Sherley Anne. *Working cotton* ill. by Carole M. Byard. Harcourt, 1992. ISBN 0-15-299624-9 Subj: Activities – working. Ethnic groups in the U.S. – Afro-Americans. Family life.

Williams, Sue. *I went walking* ill. by Julie Vivas. Harcourt, 1990. ISBN 0-15-200471-8 Subj: Activities – walking. Animals. Concepts – color. Poetry, rhyme.

Williams, Susan. *Poppy's first year* ill. by author. Macmillan, 1989. ISBN 0-02-793031-9 Subj: Babies. Family life – brothers. Family life – sisters.

Williams, Suzannne. *Mommy doesn't know my name* ill. by Andrew Shachat. Houghton, 1990. ISBN 0-395-54228-6 Subj: Family life – mothers. Names.

Williams, Terry Tempest. *Between cattails* ill. by Peter Parnall. Scribner's, 1985. ISBN 0-684-18309-9 Subj: Ecology. Poetry, rhyme.

Williams, Vera B. *A chair for my mother* ill. by author. Greenwillow, 1982. Subj: Behavior – seeking better things. Caldecott award honor book. Family life. Furniture – chairs.

Cherries and cherry pits ill. by author. Greenwillow, 1986. ISBN 0-688-05146-4 Subj: Art. Ethnic groups in the U.S. – Afro-Americans. Imagination.

"More more more," said the baby ill. by author. Greenwillow, 1991. ISBN 0-688-09174-1 Subj: Babies. Caldecott award honor book. Ethnic groups in the U.S. Family life.

Music, music for everyone ill. by author. Greenwillow, 1984. Subj: Family life. Family life – grandmothers. Illness. Music.

Something special for me ill. by author. Greenwillow, 1983. Subj: Birthdays. Family life.

Three days on a river in a red canoe ill. by author. Greenwillow, 1981. Subj: Boats, ships. Camps, camping.

Williamson, Hamilton. *Little elephant* ill. by Berta and Elmer Hader. Doubleday, 1930. Subj: Animals – elephants.

Monkey tale ill. by Berta and Elmer Hader. Doubleday, 1929. Subj: Animals – monkeys.

Williamson, Mel. *Walk on!* by Mel Williamson and George Ford; ill. by authors. Third Pr., 1972. Subj: City. Ethnic groups in the U.S. – Afro-Americans.

Williamson, Stan. *The no-bark dog* ill. by Tom O'Sullivan. Follett, 1962. Subj: Animals – dogs. Ethnic groups in the U.S. – Afro-Americans.

Willington, Monica. *Seasons of swans* ill. by author. Dutton, 1990. ISBN 0-525-44621-4 Subj: Birds – swans. Birth. Nature.

Willis, Jeanne. *Earth mobiles as explained by Professor Xargle* ill. by Tony Ross. Dutton, 1992. ISBN 0-525-44892-6 Subj: Activities – traveling. Space and space ships. Transportation.

Earth tigerlets as explained by Professor Xargle ill. by Tony Ross. Dutton, 1991. ISBN 0-525-44732-6 Subj: Animals – cats. Space and space ships.

Earthlets as explained by Professor Xargle ill. by Tony Ross. Dutton, 1989. ISBN 0-525-44465-3 Subj: Babies. Space and space ships.

The long blue blazer ill. by Susan Varley. Dutton, 1988. ISBN 0-525-44381-9 Subj: Character traits – being different. School. Space and space ships.

The monster bed ill. by Susan Varley. Lothrop, 1987. ISBN 0-688-06805-7 Subj: Bedtime. Furniture – beds. Emotions – fear. Monsters. Poetry, rhyme.

The tale of Georgie Grub ill. by Margaret Chamberlain. Holt, 1982. Subj: Activities – bathing. Character traits – cleanliness.

Willis, Val. *The mystery in the bottle* ill. by John Shelley. Farrar, 1991. ISBN 0-374-35194-5 Subj: Format, unusual – board books. Mythical creatures. School.

The secret in the matchbox ill. by John Shelley. Farrar, 1988. ISBN 0-374-36603-9 Subj: Behavior – secrets. Dragons. School.

Silly little chick ill. by Judy Brook. Dutton, 1989. ISBN 0-233-98307-4 Subj: Behavior – growing up. Birds – chickens. Farms.

Willoughby, Elaine Macmann. *Boris and the monsters* ill. by Lynn Munsinger. Houghton, 1980. Subj: Animals – dogs. Monsters.

Wilner, Isabel. *A garden alphabet* ill. by Ashley Wolff. Dutton, 1991. ISBN 0-525-44731-8 Subj: ABC books. Animals. Gardens, gardening. Poetry, rhyme.

Wilson, Barbara Ker. *ABC et/and 123* ill. by Gisèle Daigle. Fitzhenry and Whiteside, 1981. Subj: ABC books. Counting, numbers. Foreign languages.

The turtle and the island ill. by Frané Lessac. Lippincott, 1990. ISBN 0-397-32439-1 Subj: Folk and fairy tales. Foreign lands – New Guinea. Islands. Reptiles – turtles, tortoises.

Wilson, Beth P. *Jenny* ill. by Dolores Johnson. Macmillan, 1990. ISBN 0-02-793120-X Subj: Ethnic groups in the U.S. – Afro-Americans. Family life – grandmothers.

Wilson, Bob. *Stanley Bagshaw and the twenty-two ton whale* ill. by author. David & Charles, 1984. ISBN 0-241-10812-8 Subj: Animals – whales. Sports – fishing.

Wilson, Christopher Bernard. *Hobnob* ill. by William Wiesner. Viking, 1968. Subj: Behavior – sharing.

Wilson, Dorminster. *Mother scorpion country* (Rohmer, Harriet)

Wilson, Joyce Lancaster. *Tobi* ill. by Anne Thiess. Funk and Wagnalls, 1968. Subj: Animals – cats.

Wilson, Julia. *Becky* ill. by John Wilson. Crowell, 1966. Subj: Character traits – honesty. Ethnic groups in the U.S. – Afro-Americans. Toys – dolls.

Wilson, Lynn. *Baby whale* ill. by author. Putnam, 1991. ISBN 0-448-40073-1 Subj: Animals – whales.

Wilson, Robina Beckles. *Merry Christmas! children at Christmastime around the world* ill. by Satomi Ichikawa. Putnam's, 1983. ISBN 0-399-20921-2 Subj: Holidays – Christmas.

Wilson, Ron. *Mice* ill. with photos. Global Lib. Mktg. Serv., 1984. ISBN 0-7136-2388-8 Subj: Animals – mice. Nature. Science.

Wilson, Sarah. *Beware the dragons!* ill. by author. Harper, 1985. ISBN 0-06-026509-4 Subj: Dragons. Folk and fairy tales. Weather – storms.

The day that Henry cleaned his room ill. by author. Simon & Schuster, 1990. ISBN 0-671-69202-X Subj: Character traits – cleanliness.

June is a tune that jumps on a stair ill. by author. Simon & Schuster, 1992. ISBN 0-671-73919-0 Subj: Poetry, rhyme.

Muskrat, muskrat, eat your peas! ill. by author. Simon & Schuster, 1989. ISBN 0-671-67515-X Subj: Animals – muskrats. Family life. Food.

Uncle Albert's flying birthday ill. by author. Simon & Schuster, 1991. ISBN 0-671-72793-1 Subj: Activities – bathing. Birthdays. Parties.

Wilson-Kelly, Becky. *Mother Grumpy's dog biscuits* ill. by author. Holt, 1990. ISBN 0-8050-1287-7 Subj: Activities – cooking. Animals – dogs. Character traits. Food.

Winch, Madeleine. *Come by chance* ill. by author. Crown, 1990. ISBN 0-517-57667-8 Subj: Animals. Houses. Seasons – winter.

Windham, Sophie. *Noah's ark* ill. by author. Putnam's, 1989. ISBN 0-399-21564-6 Subj: Animals. Food. Format, unusual. Religion – Noah.

Winn, Chris. *Archie's acrobats* ill. by author. Trafalgar Square, 1990. ISBN 0-575-04481-0 Subj: Activities. Circus.

Helping ill. by author. Holt, 1986. ISBN 0-8050-0064-X Subj: Activities. Format, unusual – board books.

Holiday ill. by author. Holt, 1986. ISBN 0-8050-0067-4 Subj: Holidays. Format, unusual – board books.

My day ill. by author. Holt, 1986. ISBN 0-8050-0066-6 Subj: Family life. Format, unusual – board books. Shopping.

Playing ill. by author. Holt, 1986. ISBN 0-8050-0065-8 Subj: Activities – playing. Format, unusual – board books.

Winston, Clara. *Thumbelina* (Andersen, H. C. (Hans Christian))

Winston, Richard. *Thumbelina* (Andersen, H. C. (Hans Christian))

Winter, Jeanette. *Follow the drinking gourd* ill. by author. Knopf, 1988. ISBN 0-394-89694-7 Subj: Ethnic groups in the U.S. – Afro-Americans. Stars. U.S. history.

The girl and the moon man: a Siberian folktale ill. by author. Pantheon, 1984. Subj: Animals. Folk and fairy tales. Foreign lands – Russia. Moon. Music.

Winter, Jonah. *Diego* ill. by Jeanette Winter. Knopf, 1991. ISBN 0-679-91987-2 Subj: Art. Careers – artists. Foreign languages.

Winter, Paula. *The bear and the fly* ill. by author. Crown, 1976. Subj: Animals – bears. Insects – flies. Wordless.

Sir Andrew ill. by author. Crown, 1980. Subj: Animals – donkeys. Character traits – vanity. Wordless.

Winteringham, Victoria. *Penguin day* ill. by author. Harper, 1982. Subj: Activities. Birds – penguins.

Winthrop, Elizabeth. *Bear and Mrs. Duck* ill. by Patience Brewster. Holiday, 1988. ISBN 0-8234-0687-3 Subj: Activities – baby-sitting. Animals – bears. Birds – ducks.

Bear's Christmas surprise ill. by Patience Brewster. Holiday, 1991. ISBN 0-8234-0888-4 Subj: Activities – baby-sitting. Animals – bears. Birds – ducks. Holidays – Christmas.

The Best Friends Club ill. by Martha Weston. Lothrop, 1989. ISBN 0-688-07583-5 Subj: Character traits – selfishness. Clubs, gangs. Friendship.

Bunk beds ill. by Ronald Himler. Harper, 1972. ISBN 0-06-026532-9 Subj: Activities – playing. Bedtime. Furniture – beds. Family life. Imagination.

A child is born: the Christmas story adapt. from the New Testament; ill. by Charles Mikolaycak. Holiday, 1983. Subj: Holidays – Christmas. Religion.

He is risen: the Easter story ill. by Charles Mikolaycak. Holiday, 1985. ISBN 0-8234-0547-8 Subj: Holidays – Easter. Religion.

I think he likes me ill. by Denise Saldutti. Harper, 1980. Subj: Family life. Sibling rivalry.

Katharine's doll ill. by Marylin Hafner. Dutton, 1983. ISBN 0-525-44061-5 Subj: Friendship. Toys – dolls.

Lizzie and Harold ill. by Martha Weston. Lothrop, 1986. ISBN 0-688-02712-1 Subj: Friendship.

Maggie and the monster ill. by Tomie de Paola. Holiday, 1987. ISBN 0-8234-0639-2 Subj: Bedtime. Monsters. Problem solving.

Potbellied possums ill. by Barbara McClintock. Holiday, 1977. ISBN 0-8234-0289-4 Subj: Animals – possums. Emotions – fear. Food. Night.

Shoes ill. by William Joyce. Harper, 1986. ISBN 0-06-026592-2 Subj: Clothing – shoes. Poetry, rhyme.

Sledding ill. by Sarah Wilson. HarperCollins, 1989. ISBN 0-06-026566-3 Subj: Poetry, rhyme. Sports – sledding.

Sloppy kisses ill. by Anne Burgess. Macmillan, 1980. Subj: Animals – pigs. Friendship.

That's mine ill. by Emily Arnold McCully. Holiday House, 1977. Subj: Activities – playing. Behavior – fighting, arguing. Behavior – greed. Behavior – sharing. Sibling rivalry. Toys – blocks.

Tough Eddie ill. by Lillian Hoban. Dutton, 1985. Subj: Character traits – pride. School.

Vasilissa the beautiful ill. by Alexander Koshkin. HarperCollins, 1991. ISBN 0-06-021663-8 Subj: Folk and fairy tales. Foreign lands – Russia. Royalty. Toys – dolls. Witches.

Wirt, Donna Aaron. *My favorite place* (Sargent, Susan)

Wirth, Beverly. *Margie and me* ill. by Karen Ann Weinhaus. Four Winds Pr., 1983. Subj: Animals – dogs. Pets.

Wisbeski, Dorothy Gross. *Pícaro, a pet otter* ill. by Edna Miller. Hawthorn, 1971. Subj: Animals – otters. Pets.

Wiseman, Bernard. *Christmas with Morris and Borris* ill. by author. Scholastic, 1991. ISBN 0-590-42434-3 Subj: Animals – bears. Animals – moose. Holidays – Christmas.

Doctor Duck and Nurse Swan ill. by author. Dutton, 1984. Subj: Animals. Problem solving.

Don't make fun! ill. by author. Houghton, 1982. Subj: Animals – pigs. Behavior – misbehavior.

Little new kangaroo ill. by Robert Lopshire. Macmillan, 1973. Subj: Animals. Animals – kangaroos. Foreign lands – Russia. Poetry, rhyme.

Morris and Boris at the circus ill. by author. Harper, 1988. ISBN 0-06-026478-0 Subj: Animals – bears. Animals – moose. Circus.

Morris has a birthday party! ill. by author. Little, 1983. Subj: Animals – bears. Animals – moose. Behavior – misunderstanding. Parties.

Morris the moose ill. by author Rev. ed. HarperCollins, 1989. ISBN 0-06-026476-4 Subj: Animals – bulls, cows. Animals – moose. Behavior – misunderstanding.

Oscar is a mama ill. by author. Garrard, 1980. Subj: Animals – bulls, cows. Toys – dolls.

Tails are not for painting ill. by author. Garrard, 1980. Subj: Animals. Behavior – mistakes. Humor. School.

Wishinsky, Frieda. *Oonga boonga* ill. by Suçie Stevenson. Little, 1990. ISBN 0-316-94872-1 Subj: Babies. Family life – brothers. Family life – sisters.

Wisniewski, David. *Elfwyn's saga* ill. by author. Lothrop, 1990. ISBN 0-688-09590-9 Subj: Folk and fairy tales. Foreign lands – Iceland. Handicaps – blindness. Magic.

Rain player ill. by author. Houghton, 1991. ISBN 0-395-55112-9 Subj: Foreign lands – Central America. Foreign lands – Mexico. Games. Indians of North America.

The warrior and the wise man ill. by author. Lothrop, 1989. ISBN 0-688-07890-7 Subj: Folk and fairy tales. Foreign lands – Japan. Royalty. Twins.

Witch poems ed. by Daisy Wallace; ill. by Trina Schart Hyman. Holiday, 1976. ISBN 0-8234-0281-9 Subj: Poetry, rhyme. Witches.

Withers, Carl. *The tale of a black cat* ill. by Alan E. Cober. Holt, 1966. Subj: Animals – cats. Games.

The wild ducks and the goose ill. by Alan E. Cober. Holt, 1968. Subj: Birds – ducks. Games. Sports – hunting.

Wittels, Harriet. *Things I hate!* by Harriet Wittels and Joan Greisman; ill. by Jerry McConnel. Behavioral Pub., 1973. Subj: Behavior. Emotions. Poetry, rhyme.

Wittington, Mary K. *Troll games* ill. by Betsy Day. Macmillan, 1991. ISBN 0-689-31630-5 Subj: Games. Night. Trolls.

Wittman, Sally. *The boy who hated Valentine's Day* ill. by Chaya M. Burstein. Harper, 1987. ISBN 0-06-026594-9 Subj: Character traits – kindness. Friendship. Holidays – Valentine's Day. School.

Pelly and Peak ill. by author. Harper, 1978. ISBN 0-06-026560-4 Subj: Birds – peacocks, peahens. Birds – pelicans. Friendship.

Plenty of Pelly and Peak ill. by author. Harper, 1980. Subj: Birds – peacocks, peahens. Birds – pelicans. Friendship.

A special trade ill. by Karen Gundersheimer. Harper, 1978. Subj: Behavior – growing up. Friendship. Old age.

The wonderful Mrs. Trumbly ill. by Margot Apple. Harper, 1982. Subj: Friendship. School. Weddings.

Wodge, Dreary *see* Gorey, Edward (St. John)

Wohl, Lauren L. *Matzoh mouse* ill. by Pamela Keavney. HarperCollins, 1991. ISBN 0-06-026581-7 Subj: Family life. Holidays – Passover. Jewish culture. Religion.

Wolcott, Patty. *Double-decker, double-decker, double-decker bus* ill. by Bob Barner. Addison-Wesley, 1980. Subj: Buses. Friendship.

Eeeeeek! ill. by Ned Delaney. Random, 1991. ISBN 0-679-91929-5 Subj: Animals. Sleep. Sports – hunting.

Wold, Jo Anne. *Tell them my name is Amanda* ed. by Caroline Rubin; ill. by Dennis Hockerman. Albert Whitman, 1977. Subj: Character traits – shyness. Names. Problem solving. Self-concept.

Well! Why didn't you say so? ill. by Unada. Albert Whitman, 1975. Subj: Animals – dogs. Behavior – lost. Behavior – misunderstanding. City.

Wolde, Gunilla. *Betsy and Peter are different* ill. by author. Random House, 1979. Translation of Annorlunda Emma och Per Subj: Family life. Friendship.

Betsy and the chicken pox ill. by author. Random House, 1976. Translation of Emmas lillebror ar sjuk ISBN 0-394-83328-7 Subj: Behavior – needing someone. Illness. Sibling rivalry.

Betsy and the doctor ill. by author. Random House, 1978. Translation of Emma hos doktorn ISBN 0-394-95382-7 Subj: Careers – doctors. Hospitals. Illness.

Betsy and the vacuum cleaner ill. by author. Random House, 1979. Subj: Family life. Machines.

Betsy's first day at nursery school ill. by author. Random House, 1976. Translation of Emmas första dag på dagis ISBN 0-394-95381-9 Subj: School.

Betsy's fixing day ill. by author. Random House, 1978. Subj: Character traits – helpfulness. Family life.

This is Betsy ill. by author. Random House, 1975. Translation of Emma tvärtimot ISBN 0-394-93161-0 Subj: Emotions. Family life.

Wolf, Ann. *The rabbit and the turtle* ill. by author. Wonder Books, 1965. Subj: Animals – rabbits. Folk and fairy tales. Reptiles – turtles, tortoises.

Wolf, Bernard. *Adam Smith goes to school* photos. by author. Lippincott, 1978. Subj: School.

Anna's silent world photos. by author. Lippincott, 1977. Subj: Handicaps – deafness. Senses – hearing.

Don't feel sorry for Paul photos. by author. Lippincott, 1974. Subj: Handicaps.

Michael and the dentist photos. by author. Four Winds Pr., 1980. Subj: Careers – dentists. Emotions – fear. Teeth.

Wolf, Janet. *Adelaide to Zeke* ill. by author. Harper, 1987. ISBN 0-06-026598-1 Subj: ABC books. Names.

The best present is me ill. by author. Harper, 1984. Subj: Art. Family life – grandmothers.

The rosy fat magenta radish ill. by author. Little, 1990. ISBN 0-316-95045-9 Subj: Gardens, gardening.

Wolf, Sallie. *Peter's trucks* ill. by Cat Bowman Smith. Albert Whitman, 1992. ISBN 0-8075-6519-9 Subj: Circular tales. Poetry, rhyme. Trucks.

Wolf, Susan. *The adventures of Albert, the running bear* (Isenberg, Barbara)

Albert the running bear gets the jitters (Isenberg, Barbara)

Wolf, Winfried. *The Easter bunny* ill. by Agnès Mathieu. Dial Pr., 1986. ISBN 0-8037-0239-6 Subj: Animals – rabbits. Holidays – Easter.

Wolfe, Robert L. *The truck book* photos. by author. Carolrhoda, 1981. Subj: Trucks.

Wolff, Ashley. *The bells of London* ill. by author. Dodd, 1985. Subj: Birds – doves. Emotions – sadness. Foreign lands – England. Songs.

Only the cat saw ill. by author. Dodd, 1985. ISBN 0-396-08727-2 Subj: Animals – cats. Family life. Night.

A year of beasts ill. by author. Dutton, 1986. ISBN 0-525-44240-5 Subj: Animals. Days of the week, months of the year. Farms.

A year of birds ill. by author. Dodd, 1984. Subj: Birds. Days of the week, months of the year. Seasons.

Wolff, Ferida. *The woodcutter's coat* ill. by Anne Wilsdorf. Little, 1992. ISBN 0-316-95048-3 Subj: Clothing – coats. Circular tales. Crime.

Wolff, Robert Jay. *Feeling blue* ill. by author. Scribner's, 1968. Subj: Concepts – color.

Hello, yellow! ill. by author. Scribner's, 1968. Subj: Concepts – color.

Seeing red ill. by author. Scribner's, 1968. Subj: Concepts – color.

Wolkstein, Diane. *The banza: a Haitian story* ill. by Marc Brown. Dial Pr., 1981. Subj: Animals – goats. Animals – tigers. Character traits – bravery. Folk and fairy tales. Music.

The cool ride in the sky ill. by Paul Galdone. Knopf, 1973. Subj: Activities – flying. Animals – monkeys. Birds – buzzards. Birds – vultures. Character traits – cleverness. Folk and fairy tales.

The legend of Sleepy Hollow ill. by Robert W. Alley. Morrow, 1987. Based on the story by Washington Irving ISBN 0-688-06533-3 Subj: Ghosts. Folk and fairy tales. Holidays – Halloween. Humor.

Little Mouse's painting ill. by Maryjane Begin. Morrow, 1992. ISBN 0-688-07610-6 Subj: Animals. Animals – mice. Careers – artists. Friendship.

The magic wings: a tale from China ill. by Robert Andrew Parker. Dutton, 1983. Subj: Activities – flying. Behavior – wishing. Cumulative tales. Folk and fairy tales. Foreign lands – China. Seasons – spring.

Oom razoom; or, Go I know not where, Bring back I know not what ill. by Dennis McDermott. Morrow, 1991. ISBN 0-688-09417-1 Subj: Folk and fairy tales. Foreign lands – Russia. Magic.

White wave: a Chinese tale ill. by Ed Young. Crowell, 1979. Subj: Folk and fairy tales. Foreign lands – China.

Wolski, Slawomir. *Tiger cat* tr. by Elizabeth D. Crawford; ill. by Józef Wilkoń. Holt, 1988. ISBN 0-8050-0741-5 Subj: Animals – tigers. Pets.

Wondriska, William. *Mr. Brown and Mr. Gray* ill. by author. Holt, 1968. Subj: Animals – pigs. Emotions – happiness. Money.

Puff ill. by author. Pantheon, 1960. Subj: Self-concept. Trains.

The stop ill. by author. Holt, 1972. Subj: Animals – horses. Character traits – kindness to animals. Desert. Emotions – fear. Indians of North America.

The tomato patch ill. by author. Holt, 1964. Subj: Plants. Violence, anti-violence. Weapons.

Wong, Herbert H. *My goldfish* by Herbert H. Wong and Matthew F. Vessel; ill. by Arvis L. Stewart. Addison-Wesley, 1969. Subj: Fish. Pets. Science.

My ladybug by Herbert H. Wong and Matthew F. Vessel; ill. by Marie Nonast Bohlen. Addison-Wesley, 1969. Subj: Insects – ladybugs. Science.

My plant by Herbert H. Wong and Matthew F. Vessel; ill. by Richard Cuffari. Addison-Wesley, 1976. Subj: Plants. Science.

Our caterpillars by Herbert H. Wong and Matthew F. Vessel; ill. by Arvis L. Stewart. Addison-Wesley, 1977. Subj: Insects – butterflies, caterpillars. Science.

Our earthworms by Herbert H. Wong and Matthew F. Vessel; ill. by Bill Davis. Addison-Wesley, 1977. Subj: Animals – worms. Science.

Our tree by Herbert H. Wong and Matthew F. Vessel; ill. by Kenneth Longtemps. Addison-Wesley, 1969. Subj: Science. Trees.

Wood, A. J. *Amazing animals* ill. by Helen Ward. Boyds Mills Pr., 1991. ISBN 1-878093-46-0 Subj: Animals.

Beautiful birds ill. by Helen Ward. Boyds Mills Pr., 1991. ISBN 1-878093-47-9 Subj: Birds.

Look! The ultimate spot-the-difference book ill. by April Wilson. Dial, 1990. ISBN 0-8037-0925-0 Subj: Concepts. Games. Wordless.

Wood, Audrey. *Elbert's bad word* ill. by author. Harcourt, 1988. ISBN 0-15-225320-3 Subj: Behavior – misbehavior. Family life. Language.

Heckedy Peg ill. by Don Wood. Harcourt, 1987. ISBN 0-15-233678-8 Subj: Behavior – talking to strangers. Character traits – cleverness. Days of the week, months of the year. Folk and fairy tales. Food. Witches.

King Bidgood's in the bathtub ill. by Don Wood. Harcourt, 1985. ISBN 0-15-242730-9 Subj: Activities. Activities – bathing. Caldecott award honor book. Humor. Royalty – kings.

Little Penguin's tale ill. by author. Harcourt, 1989. ISBN 0-15-246475-1 Subj: Activities – dancing. Animals. Animals – whales. Birds. Birds – penguins. Foreign lands – Antarctic.

Moonflute ill. by Don Wood. Harcourt, 1986. ISBN 0-15-255337-1 Subj: Bedtime. Moon. Night. Sleep.

The napping house ill. by Don Wood. Harcourt, 1984. ISBN 0-15-256708-9 Subj: Animals. Cumulative tales. Family life – grandmothers. Poetry, rhyme. Sleep.

Oh my baby bear! ill. by author. Harcourt, 1990. ISBN 0-15-257698-3 Subj: Animals – bears. Bedtime. Behavior – growing up.

Piggies (Wood, David)

Silly Sally ill. by author. Harcourt, 1992. ISBN 0-15-274428-2 Subj: Activities – traveling. Animals. Cumulative tales. Poetry, rhyme.

Weird parents ill. by author. Dial, 1990. ISBN 0-8037-0649-9 Subj: Character traits – being different. Emotions – embarrassment. Family life.

Wood, David. *Happy birthday, Mouse!* ill. by Richard Fowler. Grosset, 1990. ISBN 0-448-19023-0 Subj: Animals – mice. Birthdays. Counting, numbers. Format, unusual. Parties.

Piggies by Don and Audrey Wood; ill. by Don Wood. Harcourt, 1991. ISBN 0-15-256341-5 Subj: Animals – pigs. Games.

Wood, Douglas. *Old Turtle* ill. by Cheng-Khee Chee. Pfeifer-Hamilton, 1991. ISBN 0-938586-48-3 Subj: Animals. Ecology. Religion.

Wood, Jakki. *Dads are such fun* ill. by Rog Bonner. Simon & Schuster, 1992. ISBN 0-671-75342-8 Subj: Activities – playing. Animals. Family life – fathers.

Moo moo, brown cow ill. by Rog Bonner. Harcourt, 1992. ISBN 0-15-200533-1 Subj: Animals. Animals – cats. Concepts – color. Counting, numbers. Farms.

One bear with bees in his hair ill. by author. Dutton, 1991. ISBN 0-525-44695-8 Subj: Animals – bears. Counting, numbers. Poetry, rhyme.

Wood, Jenny. *The animal kingdom* ill. by Andrew Bale. Macmillan, 1992. ISBN 0-02-793395-4 Subj: Animals. Nature.

Wood, John Norris. *Jungles* ed. by Janet Schulman; ill. by Kevin Dean. Knopf, 1987. ISBN 0-394-87802-7 Subj: Animals. Behavior – hiding. Format, unusual. Jungle.

Oceans ill. by Mark Harrison. Knopf, 1985. ISBN 0-394-87583-4 Subj: Behavior – hiding. Fish. Format, unusual. Sea and seashore.

Wood, Joyce. *Grandmother Lucy goes on a picnic* ill. by Frank Francis. Collins-World, 1976. Subj: Activities – picnicking. Activities – walking. Family life – grandmothers.

Grandmother Lucy in her garden ill. by Frank Francis. Collins-World, 1975. Subj: Family life – grandmothers. Foreign lands – England. Seasons. Seasons – spring.

Wood, Leslie. *A dog called Mischief* ill. by author. Oxford Univ. Pr., 1984. ISBN 0-19-272155-0 Subj: Animals – dogs. Behavior – hiding things. Food.

Wood, Nancy C. *Little wrangler* ill. by Myron Wood. Doubleday, 1966. Subj: Cowboys.

Wood, Tim. *Gymnastics* photos. by Chris Fairclough. Watts, 1989. ISBN 0-531-10826-0 Subj: Sports – gymnastics.

Motor racing ill. by Chris Fairclough. Watts, 1989. ISBN 0-531-10828-7 Subj: Automobiles. Sports – racing.

Motorcycling ill. by Chris Fairclough. Watts, 1989. ISBN 0-531-10827-9 Subj: Sports – racing.

Woodcock, Louise Phinney. *The very little dog* (Skaar, Grace Marion)

Wooding, Sharon L. *Arthur's Christmas wish* ill. by author. Atheneum, 1986. ISBN 0-689-31211-3 Subj: Animals – mice. Behavior – wishing. Holidays – Christmas.

Woodman, Allen. *Cows are going to Paris* (Kirby, David)

Woodruff, Elvira. *Mrs. McCloskey's monkeys* ill. by Jill Kastner. Scholastic, 1991. ISBN 0-590-41233-7 Subj: Animals – monkeys. Behavior – misbehavior. Family life – brothers. Zoos.

Show and tell ill. by Denise Brunkus. Holiday, 1991. ISBN 0-8234-0883-3 Subj: Magic. School.

Tubtime ill. by Suçie Stevenson. Holiday, 1990. ISBN 0-8234-0777-2 Subj: Activities – bathing. Family life – brothers. Family life – sisters. Imagination.

The wing shop ill. by Stephen Gammell. Holiday, 1991. ISBN 0-8234-0825-6 Subj: Activities – flying. Moving.

Woolaver, Lance. *Christmas with the rural mail* ill. by Maud Lewis. Nimbus Pub., 1981. Subj: Foreign lands – Canada. Holidays – Christmas. Poetry, rhyme.

From Ben Loman to the sea ill. by Maud Lewis. Nimbus Pub., 1981. Subj: Behavior – running away. Poetry, rhyme. Sea and seashore. Seasons – spring.

Woolf, Virginia. *Nurse Lugton's curtain* ill. by Julie Vivas. Harcourt, 1982. ISBN 0-15-200545-5 Subj: Activities – sewing. Animals. Careers – nurses. Imagination. Sleep.

Woolley, Catherine see Thayer, Jane

Worley, Daryl. *Billy and the attic adventure* ill. by John Daab. Tyke Corp., 1989. ISBN 0-924067-00-4 Subj: Family life – fathers. Houses.

Worth, Bonnie. *Peter Cottontail's surprise* ill. by Greg Hildebrandt. Unicorn Publishing House, 1985. ISBN 0-88101-015-4 Subj: Animals – rabbits. Birthdays. Parties. Seasons – spring.

Worthington, Joan. *Teddy bear farmer* (Worthington, Phoebe)

Worthington, Phoebe. *Teddy bear baker* by Phoebe and Selby Worthington; ill. by authors. Warne,

1980. Subj: Careers – bakers. Foreign lands – England. Toys – teddy bears.

Teddy bear coalman: a story for the very young by Phoebe and Selby Worthington; ill. by authors. Warne, 1980. Subj: Foreign lands – England. Toys – teddy bears.

Teddy bear farmer by Phoebe and Joan Worthington; ill. by authors. Viking, 1985. ISBN 0-670-80342-1 Subj: Animals. Farms. Toys – teddy bears.

Worthington, Selby. *Teddy bear baker* (Worthington, Phoebe)

Teddy bear coalman (Worthington, Phoebe)

Worthy, Judith. *Eyes* ill. by Beba Hall. Doubleday, 1989. ISBN 0-385-24966-7 Subj: Anatomy – eyes. Animals.

Wouters, Anne. *This book is for us* ill. by author. Dutton, 1992. ISBN 0-525-44882-9 Subj: Animals – moles. Animals – polar bears. Night. Wordless.

This book is too small ill. by author. Dutton, 1992. ISBN 0-525-4481-0 Subj: Animals – moles. Animals – polar bears. Wordless.

Woychuk, Denis. *The other side of the wall* ill. by Kim Howard. Lothrop, 1991. ISBN 0-688-09895-9 Subj: Animals – hippopotami. Animals – mice. Emotions – love. Middle ages.

Pirates ill. by Kim Howard. Lothrop, 1992. ISBN 0-688-10337-5 Subj: Animals – hippopotami. Animals – mice. Pirates.

Wright, Betty Ren. *The cat next door* ill. by Gail Owens. Holiday, 1991. ISBN 0-8234-0896-5 Subj: Animals – cats. Death. Family life – grandmothers.

Wright, Dare. *The doll and the kitten* photos. by author. Doubleday, 1960. Subj: Animals – cats. Toys – dolls. Toys – teddy bears.

Edith and Midnight photos. by author. Doubleday, 1978. Subj: Toys – dolls. Toys – teddy bears.

Edith and Mr. Bear photos. by author. Random House, 1964. Subj: Behavior – running away. Toys – dolls. Toys – teddy bears.

Edith and the duckling photos. by author. Doubleday, 1981. Subj: Birds – ducks. Eggs. Toys – dolls. Toys – teddy bears.

The lonely doll photos. by author. Doubleday, 1957. Subj: Toys – dolls. Toys – teddy bears.

The lonely doll learns a lesson photos. by author. Random House, 1961. Subj: Animals – cats. Pets. Toys – dolls. Toys – teddy bears.

Look at a calf photos. by author. Random House, 1974. Subj: Animals – bulls, cows. Farms.

Look at a colt photos. by author. Random House, 1969. Subj: Animals – horses. Farms.

Look at a kitten photos. by author. Random House, 1975. Subj: Animals – cats.

Wright, Freire. *Beauty and the beast* ill. by adapt. David & Charles, 1985. ISBN 0-7182-6091-0 Subj: Character traits – loyalty. Folk and fairy tales. Magic.

Wright, Jill. *The old woman and the jar of ums* ill. by Glen Rounds. Putnam, 1990. ISBN 0-399-21736-3 Subj: Behavior – misbehavior. Magic.

The old woman and the Willy Nilly Man ill. by Glen Rounds. Putnam's, 1987. ISBN 0-399-21355-4 Subj: Activities – dancing. Behavior – trickery. Clothing. Folk and fairy tales. Humor.

Wright, Joan Richards. *Bugs* (Parker, Nancy Winslow)

Wright, Josephine Lord. *Cotton Cat and Martha Mouse* ill. by John E. Johnson. Dutton, 1966. Subj: Animals – cats. Animals – mice. Behavior – sharing. Poetry, rhyme.

Wright, Martin. *Granny Stickleback* (Moore, John)

Wyler, Rose. *Puddles and ponds* ill. by Steven James Petruccio. Messner, 1990. ISBN 0-671-66348-8 Subj: Animals. Nature. Science. Water.

Raindrops and rainbows ill. by Steven James Petruccio. Messner, 1989. ISBN 0-671-66346-1 Subj: Science. Weather – rain. Weather – rainbows.

The starry sky ill. by Steven James Petruccio. Messner, 1989. ISBN 0-671-66345-3 Subj: Earth. Science. Sky. Stars.

Wyllie, Stephen. *Dinner with fox* ill. by Korky Paul. Dial, 1990. ISBN 0-8037-0796-7 Subj: Animals – foxes. Animals – wolves. Food. Format, unusual – toy and movable books.

The great race ill. by Anni Axworthy. HarperCollins, 1987. ISBN 0-694-00126-0 Subj: Animals. Format, unusual. Rebuses. Sports – racing.

Snappity snap ill. by Maureen Roffey. HarperCollins, 1989. ISBN 0-06-026630-9 Subj: Activities – photographing. Animals. Counting, numbers. Format, unusual – toy and movable books.

White Rabbit builds a dream house ill. by Anni Axworthy. Ideals, 1990. ISBN 0-8249-8363-7 Subj: Animals – rabbits. Animals – rabbits. Format, unusual. Houses.

Wyndham, Robert. *The Chinese Mother Goose rhymes* (Mother Goose)

Wynne-Jones, Tim. *Builder of the moon* ill. by Ian Wallace. Macmillan, 1989. ISBN 0-689-50472-1 Subj: Moon. Problem solving. Space and space ships. Toys – blocks.

The hour of the frog ill. by Catharine O'Neill. Little, 1990. ISBN 0-316-96309-7 Subj: Frogs and toads. Night. Noise, sounds.

Wynot, Jillian. *The Mother's Day sandwich* ill. by Maxie Chambliss. Watts, 1990. ISBN 0-531-08457-4 Subj: Family life – mothers. Food. Holidays – Mother's Day.

Wyse, Lois. *Two guppies, a turtle and Aunt Edna* ill. by Roger Coast. Collins-World, 1966. Subj: Family life – aunts, uncles. Fish. Problem solving. Reptiles – turtles, tortoises. Telephone.

Xiong, Blia. *Nine-in-one Grr! Grr!* adapt. by Cathy Spagnoli; ill. by Nancy Hom. Children's Book Pr., 1989. ISBN 0-89239-048-4 Subj: Animals – tigers. Folk and fairy tales. Foreign lands – Laos.

Yabuki, Seiji. *I love the morning* ill. by author. Collins-World, 1969. Subj: Emotions – happiness. Morning.

Yabuuchi, Masayuki. *Animals sleeping* ill. by author. Putnam's, 1983. ISBN 0-399-20983-2 Subj: Animals. Sleep. Science.

Whose baby? ill. by author. Putnam's, 1985. ISBN 0-399-21210-8 Subj: Animals.

Whose footprints? ill. by author. Putnam's, 1985. ISBN 0-399-21209-4 Subj: Animals.

Yacowitz, Caryn. *The jade stone* ill. by Ju-Hong Chen. Holiday, 1992. ISBN 0-8234-0919-8 Subj: Careers – artists. Folk and fairy tales. Foreign lands – China. Royalty – emperors.

Yaffe, Alan. *The magic meatballs* ill. by Karen Born Andersen. Dial Pr., 1979. Subj: Behavior – dissatisfaction. Family life. Magic.

Yagawa, Sumiko. *The crane wife* tr. from Japanese by Katherine Paterson; ill. by Suekichi Akaba. Morrow, 1982. ISBN 0-688-00496-2 Subj: Activities – weaving. Birds – cranes. Character traits – kindness to animals. Folk and fairy tales. Foreign lands – Japan.

Yagelski, Robert. *The day the lifting bridge stuck* ill. by Jennifer Beck Harris. Bradbury Pr., 1992. ISBN 0-02-793595-7 Subj: Bridges. Machines. Problem solving. Traffic, traffic signs.

Yamaguchi, Tohr. *Two crabs and the moonlight* ill. by Marianne Yamaguchi. Holt, 1965. Subj: Crustacea. Moon.

Yamashita, Haruo. *Mice at the beach* ill. by Kazuo Iwamura. Morrow, 1987. ISBN 0-688-07064-7 Subj: Animals – mice. Family life. Safety. Sea and seashore.

Yardley, Joanna. *The red ball* ill. by author. Harcourt, 1991. ISBN 0-15-200894-2 Subj: Family life. Imagination. Toys – balls.

Yashima, Mitsu. *Momo's kitten* ill. by Tarō Yashima. Viking, 1961. Subj: Animals – cats. Ethnic groups in the U.S. – Japanese-Americans.

Plenty to watch ill. by Tarō Yashima. Viking, 1954. Subj: Foreign lands – Japan.

Yashima, Tarō. *Crow boy* ill. by author. Viking, 1955. ISBN 0-670-24931-9 Subj: Caldecott award honor book. Character traits – shyness. Emotions – loneliness. Foreign lands – Japan. School.

Momo's kitten (Yashima, Mitsu)

Seashore story ill. by author. Viking, 1967. Subj: Caldecott award honor book. Folk and fairy tales. Reptiles – turtles, tortoises. Sea and seashore.

Umbrella ill. by author. Viking, 1958. Subj: Birthdays. Caldecott award honor book. City. Ethnic groups in the U.S. – Japanese-Americans. Umbrellas. Weather – rain.

The village tree ill. by author. Viking, 1953. Subj: Foreign lands – Japan. Seasons – summer. Trees.

The youngest one ill. by author. Viking, 1962. Subj: Character traits – shyness. Ethnic groups in the U.S. – Japanese-Americans. Friendship.

Ye Pin Kwei. *Monkey creates havoc in heaven* (Pen Cai Ying)

Yee, Paul. *Roses sing on new snow* ill. by Harvey Chan. Macmillan, 1992. ISBN 0-02-793622-8 Subj: Activities – cooking. Ethnic groups in the U.S. – Chinese-Americans.

Yektai, Niki. *Bears in pairs* ill. by Diane de Groat. Bradbury Pr., 1987. ISBN 0-02-793691-0 Subj: Animals – bears. Concepts. Poetry, rhyme.

Hi bears, bye bears ill. by Diane de Groat. Watts, 1990. ISBN 0-531-08458-2 Subj: Poetry, rhyme. Toys – teddy bears.

What's missing? ill. by Susannah Ryan. Clarion, 1987. ISBN 0-89919-510-5 Subj: Games. Problem solving.

Yen, Clara. *Why rat comes first* ill. by Hideo C. Yoshida. Children's Book Pr., 1991. ISBN 0-89239-072-7 Subj: Animals. Royalty. Foreign lands – China. Zodiac.

Yeoman, John. *The bear's water picnic* ill. by Quentin Blake. Atheneum, 1987, 1970. ISBN 0-689-31386-1 Subj: Activities – picnicking. Animals – bears. Animals – hedgehogs. Animals – pigs. Animals – squirrels. Frogs and toads.

Mouse trouble ill. by Quentin Blake. Macmillan, 1972. Subj: Animals – cats. Animals – mice. Friendship. Windmills.

Old Mother Hubbard's dog dresses up ill. by Quentin Blake. Houghton, 1990. ISBN 0-394-53358-9 Subj: Animals – dogs. Clothing. Poetry, rhyme.

Old Mother Hubbard's dog learns to play ill. by Quentin Blake. Houghton, 1990. ISBN 0-395-53360-0 Subj: Animals – dogs. Music. Poetry, rhyme.

Old Mother Hubbard's dog needs a doctor ill. by Quentin Blake. Houghton, 1990. ISBN 0-395-53359-7 Subj: Animals – dogs. Poetry, rhyme.

Old Mother Hubbard's dog takes up sport ill. by Quentin Blake. Houghton, 1990. ISBN 0-395-53361-9 Subj: Animals – dogs. Poetry, rhyme. Sports.

Our village ill. by Quentin Blake. Atheneum, 1988. ISBN 0-689-31451-5 Subj: Communities, neighborhoods. Poetry, rhyme.

The wild washerwomen: a new folk tale ill. by Quentin Blake. Crown, 1986. ISBN 0-517-56255-3 Subj: Activities – working. Behavior – misbehavior. Folk and fairy tales.

The young performing horse ill. by Quentin Blake. Parents, 1979. Subj: Animals – horses. Theater. Twins.

Yeomans, Thomas. *For every child a star: a Christmas story* ill. by Tomie de Paola. Holiday, 1986. ISBN 0-8234-0526-5 Subj: Holidays – Christmas. Night. Stars.

Yezback, Steven A. *Pumpkinseeds* ill. by Mozelle Thompson. Bobbs-Merrill, 1969. Subj: Behavior – solitude. City. Ethnic groups in the U.S. – Afro-Americans.

Ylla. *Animal babies* by Ylla and Arthur S. Gregor; ill. by Ylla. Harper, 1959. Designed by Luc Bouchage Subj: Animals.

I'll show you cats by Ylla and Crosby Newell Bonsall; ill. by Ylla. Harper, 1964. Planned by Charles Rado; designed by Luc Bouchage Subj: Animals – cats.

Listen, listen! (Bonsall, Crosby Newell)

The little elephant by Ylla and Arthur S. Gregor; ill. by Ylla. Harper, 1956. Designed by Luc Bouchage Subj: Animals – elephants.

Look who's talking by Ylla and Crosby Newell Bonsall; ill. by Ylla. Harper, 1962. Planned by Charles Rado; designed by Luc Bouchage Subj: Birds – ostriches. Zoos.

Polar bear brothers by Ylla and Crosby Newell Bonsall; ill. by Ylla. Harper, 1960. Designed by Luc Bouchage Subj: Animals – polar bears.

Two little bears ill. by author. Harper, 1954. Subj: Animals – bears. Behavior – lost.

Yoaker, Harry. *The view* by Harry Yoaker and Simon Henwood; ill. by Simon Henwood. Dial, 1992. ISBN 0-8037-1105-0 Subj: Communities, neighborhoods. Houses.

Yolen, Jane. *All in the woodland early: an ABC book* ill. by Jane Breskin Zalben; music and lyrics by author. Collins-World, 1980. Subj: ABC books. Forest, woods.

All those secrets of the world ill. by Leslie A. Baker. Little, 1991. ISBN 0-316-96891-9 Subj: Concepts – perspective. Family life – fathers. War.

Baby Bear's bedtime book ill. by Jane Dyer. Harcourt, 1990. ISBN 0-15-205120-1 Subj: Activities – baby-sitting. Animals – bears. Bedtime.

Dragon night and other lullabies ill. by Demi. Methuen, 1980. Subj: Animals. Bedtime. Lullabies. Sleep.

Eeny, meeny, miney mole ill. by Kathryn Brown. Harcourt, 1992. ISBN 0-15-225350-5 Subj: Animals – moles. Character traits – curiosity.

Elfabet ill. by Lauren Mills. Little, 1989. ISBN 0-316-96900-1 Subj: ABC books. Activities. Elves and little people.

The emperor and the kite ill. by Ed Young. Collins-World, 1967. Subj: Caldecott award honor book. Character traits – smallness. Family life – fathers. Foreign lands – China. Kites. Royalty – emperors.

The emperor and the kite ill. by Ed Young Rev. ed. Putnam's, 1988. ISBN 0-399-21499-2 Subj: Character traits – smallness. Family life – fathers. Foreign lands – China. Kites. Royalty – emperors.

The giant's farm ill. by Tomie de Paola. Seabury Pr., 1977. Subj: Farms. Giants.

The giants go camping ill. by Tomie de Paola. Seabury Pr., 1979. Subj: Giants. Camps, camping.

The girl who loved the wind ill. by Ed Young. Crowell, 1972. Subj: Behavior – running away. Weather – wind.

Greyling ill. by David Ray. Putnam, 1991. ISBN 0-399-22262-6 Subj: Animals – seals. Careers – fishermen. Folk and fairy tales. Foreign lands – Scotland. Mythical creatures.

An invitation to the butterfly ball: a counting rhyme ill. by Jane Breskin Zalben. Parents, 1976. Subj: Animals. Counting, numbers. Poetry, rhyme.

The lap-time song and play book musical arrangements by Adam Stemple; ill. by Margot Tomes. Harcourt, 1989. ISBN 0-15-243588-3 Subj: Games. Music. Nursery rhymes. Songs.

Letting Swift River go ill. by Barbara Cooney. Little, 1992. ISBN 0-316-9689-4 Subj: Country. U.S. history. Water.

The lullaby songbook ill. by Charles Mikolaycak; scores by Adam Stemple. Harcourt, 1986. ISBN 0-15-249903-2 Subj: Bedtime. Lullabies. Music.

Milkweed days photos. by Gabriel Amadeus Cooney. Crowell, 1976. Subj: Seasons – summer.

No bath tonight ill. by Nancy Winslow Parker. Crowell, 1978. Subj: Activities – bathing. Days of the week, months of the year. Family life – grandmothers.

Owl moon ill. by John Schoenherr. Philomel, 1987. ISBN 0-399-21457-7 Subj: Birds – owls. Caldecott award book. Family life – fathers. Forest, woods. Night.

Picnic with Piggins ill. by Jane Dyer. Harcourt, 1988. ISBN 0-15-261534-2 Subj: Activities – picnicking. Animals. Animals – pigs. Birthdays.

Piggins ill. by Jane Dyer. Harcourt, 1987. ISBN 0-15-261685-3 Subj: Animals. Animals – pigs. Behavior – stealing. Parties. Problem solving.

Ring of earth: a child's book of seasons ill. by John Wallner. Harcourt, 1986. ISBN 0-15-267140-4 Subj: Poetry, rhyme. Seasons.

The seeing stick ill. by Remy Charlip and Demetra Maraslis. Crowell, 1977. Subj: Foreign lands – China. Handicaps – blindness. Royalty. Senses – seeing.

Sky dogs ill. by Barry Moser. Harcourt, 1990. ISBN 0-15-275480-6 Subj: Animals – horses. Folk and fairy tales. Indians of North America.

The sleeping beauty (Grimm, Jacob)

Spider Jane ill. by Stefen Bernath. Coward, 1978. Subj: Behavior – sharing. Birds. Insects – flies. Spiders.

Street rhymes around the world ill. by 17 international artists. Boyds Mills Pr., 1992. ISBN 1-878093-53-3 Subj: Counting, numbers. Foreign lands. Foreign languages. Games. Indians of North America.

The three bears rhyme book ill. by Jane Dyer. Harcourt, 1987. ISBN 0-15-286-386-9 Subj: Animals – bears. Folk and fairy tales. Poetry, rhyme.

Wings ill. by Dennis Nolan. Harcourt, 1992. ISBN 0-15-297850-X Subj: Activities – flying. Mythical creatures. Royalty – princes.

Yorinks, Arthur. *Bravo, Minski* ill. by Richard Egielski. Farrar, 1988. ISBN 0-374-30951-5 Subj: Behavior – seeking better things. Problem solving.

Christmas in July ill. by Richard Egielski. HarperCollins, 1991. ISBN 0-06-020257-2 Subj: Behavior – losing things. Clothing. Holidays – Christmas.

Company's coming ill. by David Small. Crown, 1988. ISBN 0-517-56751-2 Subj: Behavior – misunderstanding. Humor. Space and space ships.

Hey, Al ill. by Richard Egielski. Farrar, 1986. ISBN 0-374-33060-3 Subj: Animals – dogs. Behavior – running away. Caldecott award book. Dreams. Imagination.

Louis the fish ill. by Richard Egielski. Farrar, 1980. Subj: Careers – butchers. Fish. Imagination.

Oh, brother ill. by Richard Egielski. Farr, 1989. ISBN 0-374-35599-1 Subj: Behavior – fighting, arguing. Careers – tailors. Family life – brothers. Orphans. Twins.

Ugh ill. by Richard Egielski. Farrar, 1990. ISBN 0-374-38028-7 Subj: Family life – brothers. Sibling rivalry. Sports – bicycling.

Yoshi. *One, two, three* ill. by author. Picture Book Studio, 1991. ISBN 0-88708-159-2 Subj: Counting, numbers.

Who's hiding here? ill. by author. Picture Book Studio, 1987. ISBN 0-88708-041-3 Subj: Animals. Format, unusual – toy and movable books. Poetry, rhyme.

Yoshida, Toshi. *Elephant crossing* ill. by author. Putnam, 1989. ISBN 0-399-21745-2 Subj: Animals. Animals – elephants. Foreign lands – Africa.

Rhinoceros mother ill. by author. Putnam, 1991. Original title: Quarrel ISBN 0-399-22270-7 Subj: Animals. Animals – rhinoceros. Birds. Foreign lands – Africa. Nature.

Young lions ill. by author. Putnam, 1989. ISBN 0-399-21546-8 Subj: Animals – lions. Behavior – growing up. Foreign lands – Africa.

Youldon, Gillian. *Colors* ill. by author. Watts, 1979. Subj: Concepts – color. Format, unusual – toy and movable books.

Counting ill. by James Hodgson. Watts, 1980. Subj: Counting, numbers. Format, unusual.

Numbers ill. by author. Watts, 1979. Subj: Counting, numbers. Format, unusual – toy and movable books.

Shapes ill. by author. Watts, 1979. Subj: Concepts – shape. Format, unusual.

Sizes ill. by author. Watts, 1979. Subj: Concepts – size. Format, unusual.

Young animals in the zoo ill. with photos. Imported Pubs., 1983. Subj: Animals. Format, unusual – board books. Wordless.

Young domestic animals ill. with photos. Imported Pubs., 1983. Subj: Animals. Format, unusual – board books. Wordless.

Young, Ed (Edward). *Lon Po Po: a Red Riding Hood story from China* ill. by author. Putnam, 1989. ISBN 0-399-21619-7 Subj: Animals – wolves. Caldecott award book. Folk and fairy tales. Foreign lands – China.

The rooster's horns: a Chinese puppet play to make and perform by Ed Young and Hilary Beckett; ill. by Ed Young. Collins-World, 1978. Subj: Folk and fairy tales. Foreign lands – China. Puppets.

Seven blind mice ill. by author. Putnam, 1992. ISBN 0-399-22261-8 Subj: Animals – elephants. Animals – mice. Days of the week, months of the year. Foreign lands – India. Handicaps – blindness. Senses – seeing.

The terrible Nung Gwama: a Chinese folktale ill. by author. Collins-World, 1978. Subj: Character traits – cleverness. Folk and fairy tales. Foreign lands – China. Monsters.

Up a tree ill. by author. Harper, 1983. Subj: Animals – cats. Trees. Wordless.

Young, Evelyn. *The tale of Tai* ill. by author. Oxford Univ. Pr., 1940. Subj: Behavior – lost. Foreign lands – China. Holidays – Chinese New Year.

Wu and Lu and Li ill. by author. Oxford Univ. Pr., 1939. Subj: Family life. Foreign lands – China.

Young, Helen. *A throne for Sesame* ill. by Shirley Hughes. Elsevier-Dutton, 1979. Subj: Behavior – growing up.

Young, James. *Everyone loves the moon* ill. by author. Little, 1992. ISBN 0-316-97130-8 Subj: Animals – possums. Animals – raccoons. Moon. Poetry, rhyme. Weddings.

A million chameleons ill. by author. Little, 1990. ISBN 0-316-97129-4 Subj: Concepts – color. Poetry, rhyme.

Penelope and the pirates ill. by author. Arcade, 1990. ISBN 1-55970-074-2 Subj: Animals – cats. Boats, ships. Pirates.

Young, Miriam Burt. *If I drove a bus* ill. by Robert M. Quackenbush. Lothrop, 1973. Subj: Buses. Careers – bus drivers. Transportation.

If I drove a car ill. by Robert M. Quackenbush. Lothrop, 1971. Subj: Automobiles. Transportation.

If I drove a tractor ill. by Robert M. Quackenbush. Lothrop, 1973. Subj: Tractors.

If I drove a train ill. by Robert M. Quackenbush. Lothrop, 1972. Subj: Trains. Transportation.

If I drove a truck ill. by Robert M. Quackenbush. Lothrop, 1967. Subj: Careers – truck drivers. Transportation. Trucks.

If I flew a plane ill. by Robert M. Quackenbush. Lothrop, 1970. Subj: Activities – flying. Airplanes, airports. Careers – airplane pilots. Transportation.

If I rode a horse ill. by Robert M. Quackenbush. Lothrop, 1973. Subj: Animals – horses.

If I rode an elephant ill. by Robert M. Quackenbush. Lothrop, 1974. Subj: Animals – elephants.

If I sailed a boat ill. by Robert M. Quackenbush. Lothrop, 1971. Subj: Boats, ships.

Jellybeans for breakfast ill. by Beverly Komoda. Parents, 1968. Subj: Activities – playing. Imagination.

Miss Suzy's Easter surprise ill. by Arnold Lobel. Parents, 1972. Subj: Animals – squirrels. Holidays – Easter.

Please don't feed Horace ill. by Abner Graboff. Dial Pr., 1961. Subj: Animals – hippopotami. Zoos.

The sugar mouse cake ill. by Margaret Bloy Graham. Scribner's, 1964. Subj: Activities – cooking. Animals – mice. Careers – bakers. Food. Royalty.

Young, Ruth. *Daisy's taxi* ill. by Marcia Sewall. Watts, 1991. ISBN 0-531-08521-X Subj: Boats, ships. Concepts – opposites. Sea and seashore.

Golden Bear ill. by Rachel Isadora. Viking, 1992. ISBN 0-670-82577-8 Subj: Ethnic groups in the U.S. – Afro-Americans. Poetry, rhyme. Toys – teddy bears.

My baby-sitter ill. by author. Viking, 1987. ISBN 0-670-81305-2 Subj: Activities – baby-sitting.

My blanket ill. by author. Viking, 1987. ISBN 0-670-81306-0 Subj: Babies.

My potty chair ill. by author. Viking, 1987. ISBN 0-670-81307-9 Subj: Behavior – growing up. Toilet training.

The new baby ill. by author. Viking, 1987. ISBN 0-670-81304-4 Subj: Babies. Sibling rivalry.

A trip to Mars ill. by Maryann Cocca-Leffler. Watts, 1990. ISBN 0-531-08492-2 Subj: Imagination. Space and space ships.

Youngs, Betty. *One panda: an animal counting book* ill. by author. Merrimack, 1985. ISBN 0-370-30150-1 Subj: Animals. Counting, numbers.

Pink pigs in mud: a color book ill. by author. Merrimack, 1985. ISBN 0-370-30344-X Subj: Animals. Concepts – color.

Yudell, Lynn Deena. *Make a face* ill. by author. Little, 1970. Subj: Anatomy – faces. Emotions. Games. Participation.

Yulya. *Bears are sleeping* ill. by Nonny Hogrogian. Scribner's, 1967. Subj: Animals – bears. Hibernation. Music. Sleep. Songs.

Zacharias, Thomas. *But where is the green parrot?* by Thomas and Wanda Zacharias; ill. by Wanda Zacharias. Delacorte Pr., 1968. Translation of Und wo ist der grüne Papagei? Subj: Birds – parakeets, parrots. Concepts – color. Games.

Zacharias, Wanda. *But where is the green parrot?* (Zacharias, Thomas)

Zaffo, George J. *The big book of real airplanes* ill. by author. Grosset, 1951. Subj: Airplanes, airports. Helicopters. Transportation.

Big book of real fire engines text by Elizabeth Cameron; ill. by author. Grosset, 1950. Subj: Careers – firefighters.

The giant book of things in space ill. by author. Doubleday, 1969. Subj: Space and space ships.

The giant nursery book of things that work ill. by author. Doubleday, 1967. Subj: Machines. Tools. Transportation.

The giant nursery book of things that go: fire engines, trains, boats, trucks, airplanes ill. by author. Doubleday, 1959. Subj: Airplanes, airports. Boats, ships. Transportation. Trucks.

Zagone, Theresa. *No nap for me* ill. by Lillian Hoban. Dutton, 1978. Subj: Behavior – growing up. Sleep.

Zagwyn, Deborah Turney. *Pumpkin blanket* ill. by author. Celestial Arts, 1991. ISBN 0-89087-637-1 Subj: Behavior – growing up. Family life – fathers. Gardens, gardening. Quilts. Seasons – fall.

Zakhoder, Boris Vladimirovich. *The good stepmother* adapt. by Marguerita Rudolph; ill. by Darcy May. Simon & Schuster, 1992. ISBN 0-671-68270-9 Subj: Character traits – cleverness. Family life – step families. Foreign lands – Russia. Royalty – princesses.

How a piglet crashed the Christmas party tr. by Marguerita Rudolph; ill. by Kurt Werth. Lothrop, 1971. Subj: Animals – pigs. Holidays – Christmas.

Rosachok tr. by Marguerita Rudolph; ill. by Yaroslava. Lothrop, 1970. Translation of Rusachok Subj: Animals – rabbits. Behavior – dissatisfaction. Character traits – optimism. Frogs and toads.

Zalben, Jane Breskin. *Basil and Hillary* ill. by author. Macmillan, 1975. Subj: Animals. Animals – pigs. Farms.

Beni's first Chanukah ill. by author. Holt, 1988. ISBN 0-8050-0479-3 Subj: Animals – bears. Family life. Friendship. Holidays – Hanukkah. Jewish culture.

Buster gets braces ill. by author. Holt, 1992. ISBN 0-8050-1682-1 Subj: Careers – dentists. Dinosaurs. Family life – brothers. Family life – sisters. Sibling rivalry. Teeth.

Happy Passover, Rosie ill. by author. Holt, 1990. ISBN 0-8050-1221-4 Subj: Animals – bears. Family life. Holidays – Passover. Jewish culture. Religion.

Leo and Blossom's Sukkah ill. by author. Holt, 1990. ISBN 0-8050-1226-5 Subj: Animals – bears. Family life. Holidays – Sukkot. Jewish culture. Religion.

Norton's nighttime ill. by author. Collins-World, 1979. Subj: Animals. Bedtime. Forest, woods. Night. Noise, sounds.

Oliver and Alison's week ill. by Emily Arnold McCully. Farrar, 1980. Subj: Activities. Friendship.

A perfect nose for Ralph ill. by John Wallner. Putnam's, 1980. Subj: Emotions – love. Toys – teddy bears.

Zallinger, Peter. *Dinosaurs* ill. by author. Random House, 1977. Subj: Dinosaurs. Science.

Zander, Hans. *My blue chair* ill. by author. Firefly Pr., 1985. ISBN 0-920303-16-1 Subj: Behavior – losing things. Furniture – chairs.

Zaslavsky, Claudia. *Count on your fingers African style* ill. by Jerry Pinkney. Crowell, 1980. Subj: Counting, numbers. Foreign lands – Africa.

Zero! Is it something? Is it nothing? ill. by Jeni Bassett. Watts, 1989. ISBN 0-531-10693-4 Subj: Counting, numbers. Concepts.

Zelinsky, Paul O. *The lion and the stoat* ill. by author. Greenwillow, 1984. Subj: Animals – lions. Animals – weasels. Art. Friendship.

The maid and the mouse and the odd-shaped house ill. by author. Dodd, 1981. Subj: Animals – mice. Folk and fairy tales. Houses.

Rumpelstiltskin (Grimm, Jacob)

The wheels on the bus ill. by adaptor. Dutton, 1990. ISBN 0-525-44644-3 Subj: Buses. Family life – grandmothers. Format, unusual – toy and movable books. Music. Songs.

Zemach, Harve. *Duffy and the devil: a Cornish tale* ill. by Margot Zemach. Farrar, 1973. Subj: Caldecott award book. Devil. Folk and fairy tales. Foreign lands – England.

The judge: an untrue tale ill. by Margot Zemach. Farrar, 1969. Subj: Caldecott award honor book. Careers – judges. Monsters. Poetry, rhyme.

Mommy, buy me a China doll: adapted from an Ozark children's song ill. by Margot Zemach. Follett, 1966. Subj: Music. Songs. Toys – dolls.

Nail soup: a Swedish folk tale ill. by Margot Zemach. Follett, 1964. Subj: Character traits – cleverness. Folk and fairy tales. Foreign lands – Sweden.

The tricks of Master Dabble ill. by Margot Zemach. Holt, 1965. Subj: Behavior – trickery. Humor. Royalty.

Zemach, Kaethe. *The beautiful rat* ill. by author. Four Winds Pr., 1979. Subj: Animals – rats. Folk and fairy tales.

The funny dream ill. by author. Greenwillow, 1988. ISBN 0-688-07501-0 Subj: Dreams. Family life.

Zemach, Margot. *It could always be worse: a Yiddish folk tale* ill. by author. Farrar, 1976. Subj: Caldecott award honor book. Folk and fairy tales. Humor. Jewish culture. Problem solving.

Jake and Honeybunch go to heaven ill. by author. Farrar, 1982. ISBN 0-374-33652-0 Subj: Animals – mules. Behavior – misbehavior. Ethnic groups in the U.S. – Afro-Americans. Folk and fairy tales.

The little tiny woman ill. by author. Bobbs-Merrill, 1965. Subj: Folk and fairy tales. Ghosts.

The three wishes: an old story adapt. and ill. by Margot Zemach. Farrar, 1986. ISBN 0-374-37529-1 Subj: Behavior – wishing. Character traits – foolishness. Folk and fairy tales.

To Hilda for helping ill. by author. Farrar, 1977. Subj: Character traits – helpfulness. Emotions – envy, jealousy. Family life.

Zemke, Deborah. *The shadow of Matilda Hunt* ill. by author. Houghton, 1991. ISBN 0-395-55334-2 Subj: Behavior – misbehavior. Imagination – imaginary friends. Shadows.

The way it happened ill. by author. Houghton, 1988. ISBN 0-395-47984-3 Subj: Behavior – misunderstanding. Behavior – secrets.

Ziefert, Harriet. *All clean!* ill. by Henrik Drescher. Harper, 1986. ISBN 0-694-00100-7 Subj: Animals.

All gone! ill. by Henrik Drescher. Harper, 1986. ISBN 0-694-00098-1 Subj: Animals.

Baby Ben's bow-wow book ill. by Norman Gorbaty. Random House, 1984. ISBN 0-394-86821-8 Subj: Animals. Babies. Format, unusual – board books.

Baby Ben's busy book ill. by Norman Gorbaty. Random House, 1984. ISBN 0-394-86819-6 Subj: Activities. Babies. Format, unusual – board books.

Baby Ben's go-go book ill. by Norman Gorbaty. Random House, 1984. ISBN 0-394-86820-X Subj: Activities – playing. Babies. Format, unusual – board books. Toys.

Baby Ben's noisy book ill. by Norman Gorbaty. Random House, 1984. ISBN 0-394-86822-6 Subj: Activities. Babies. Format, unusual – board books.

Bear all year ill. by Arnold Lobel. Harper, 1986. ISBN 0-694-0087-6 Subj: Animals – bears. Format, unusual – toy and movable books. Games. Seasons.

Bear gets dressed ill. by Arnold Lobel. Harper, 1986. ISBN 0-694-0086-8 Subj: Animals – bears. Clothing. Format, unusual – toy and movable books. Games.

Bear goes shopping ill. by Arnold Lobel. Harper, 1986. ISBN 0-694-00085-X Subj: Animals – bears. Format, unusual – toy and movable books. Games. Shopping.

Bear's busy morning ill. by Arnold Lobel. Harper, 1986. ISBN 0-694-00084-1 Subj: Activities. Animals – bears. Format, unusual – toy and movable books. Games.

Before I was born ill. by Rufus Coes. Knopf, 1989. ISBN 0-394-95128-X Subj: Activities – making things. Babies. Family life. Quilts.

Breakfast time! ill. by author. Viking, 1988. ISBN 0-670-81579-9 Subj: Animals – rabbits. Babies. Food.

Bye-bye, daddy! ill. by author. Viking, 1988. ISBN 0-670-81581-0 Subj: Animals – rabbits. Babies.

A car trip for mole and mouse ill. by David Prebenna. Viking, 1991. ISBN 0-670-83858-6 Subj: Activities – traveling. Animals – mice. Animals – moles. Automobiles.

Chocolate mud cake ill. by Karen Gundersheimer. Harper, 1988. ISBN 0-06-026892-1 Subj: Family life – grandparents.

City shapes ill. by Susan Baum. HarperCollins, 1991. ISBN 0-06-107417-9 Subj: City. Concepts – shape.

A clean house for Mole and Mouse ill. by David Prebenna. Penguin, 1988. ISBN 0-670-82032-6 Subj: Animals – mice. Animals – moles. Character traits – cleanliness.

Cock-a-doodle-doo! ill. by Henrik Drescher. Harper, 1986. ISBN 0-694-00099-X Subj: Animals.

Come out, Jessie! ill. by Mavis Smith. HarperCollins, 1991. ISBN 0-06-107414-4 Subj: Activities – playing. Toys.

Dancing ill. by Laura Rader. HarperCollins, 1991. ISBN 0-06-107422-5 Subj: Activities – dancing.

A dozen dogs: a read-and-count story ill. by Carol Nicklaus. Random House, 1985. ISBN 0-394-96935-9 Subj: Animals – dogs. Counting, numbers. Sea and seashore.

Getting ready for new baby ill. by Laura Rader. HarperCollins, 1990. ISBN 0-06-026897-2 Subj: Babies. Emotions – envy, jealousy. Science. Sibling rivalry.

Good luck, bad luck ill. by Lillie James. Viking, 1992. ISBN 0-670-84275-3 Subj: Character traits – luck.

Good morning, sun! ill. by author. Viking, 1988. ISBN 0-670-81578-0 Subj: Animals – rabbits. Babies. Morning.

Good night everyone! ill. by author. Little, 1988. ISBN 0-316-98756-5 Subj: Bedtime. Sleep. Toys.

Good night, Jessie! ill. by Mavis Smith. Random House, 1987. ISBN 0-394-89193-7 Subj: Behavior – losing things. Family life. Sea and seashore.

Happy birthday, Grandpa! ill. by Sidney Levitt. Harper, 1988. ISBN 0-694-00242-9 Subj: Animals. Animals – rabbits. Birthdays. Family life – grandfathers.

Happy Easter, Grandma! ill. by Sidney Levitt. Harper, 1988. ISBN 0-694-00225-9 Subj: Animals – rabbits. Birds. Eggs. Holidays – Easter.

Harry takes a bath ill. by Mavis Smith. Viking, 1987. ISBN 0-670-81721-X Subj: Activities – bathing. Animals – hippopotami.

Hurry up, Jessie! ill. by Mavis Smith. Random House, 1987. ISBN 0-394-89194-5 Subj: Character traits – cleanliness. Night.

I want to sleep in your bed! ill. by Mavis Smith. HarperCollins, 1990. ISBN 0-06-026895-6 Subj: Bedtime. Family life. Sleep.

I won't go to bed! ill. by Andrea Baruffi. Little, 1987. ISBN 0-316-98768-9 Subj: Bedtime.

Jason's bus ride ill. by Simms Taback. Viking, 1987. ISBN 0-670-81718-X Subj: Buses.

Keeping daddy awake on the way home from the beach ill. by Seymour Chwast. Harper, 1986. ISBN 0-694-00080-9 Subj: Activities – traveling. Family life. Sea and seashore.

Let's get dressed! ill. by author. Viking, 1988. ISBN 0-670-81580-2 Subj: Animals – rabbits. Babies. Clothing.

Let's go! Piggety Pig ill. by David Prebenna. Little, 1986. ISBN 0-316-98760-3 Subj: Animals – mice. Animals – pigs. Concepts – opposites.

Lewis the fire fighter ill. by Carol Nicklaus. Random House, 1986. ISBN 0-394-97618-5 Subj: Activities – playing. Fire. Imagination.

Listen! Piggety Pig ill. by David Prebenna. Little, 1986. ISBN 0-316-98761-1 Subj: Animals. Noise, sounds.

Me, too! Me, too! ill. by Karen Gundersheimer. Harper, 1988. ISBN 0-06-026893-X Subj: Behavior – sharing.

Mike and Tony: best friends ill. by Catherine Siracusa. Viking, 1987. ISBN 0-670-81719-8 Subj: Friendship.

My getting-ready-for-school book ill. by Mavis Smith. Random House, 1989. ISBN 0-394-82248-X Subj: Concepts. Format, unusual – board books.

My sister says nothing ever happens when we go sailing ill. by Seymour Chwast. Harper, 1986. ISBN 0-694-00081-7 Subj: Boats, ships. Family life.

A new coat for Anna ill. by Anita Lobel. Knopf, 1988. ISBN 0-394-97426-3 Subj: Clothing – coats. Family life. War.

A new house for Mole and Mouse ill. by Mavis Smith. Viking, 1987. ISBN 0-670-81720-1 Subj: Animals – mice. Animals – moles. Houses. Moving.

Nicky upstairs and down ill. by Richard Eric Brown. Viking, 1987. ISBN 0-670-81717-1 Subj: Animals – cats.

Nicky's Christmas surprise ill. by Richard Eric Brown. Penguin, 1985. ISBN 0-14-050555-5 Subj: Animals – cats. Holidays – Christmas.

Nicky's friends ill. by Richard Eric Brown. Viking, 1986. ISBN 0-670-81298-6 Subj: Animals – cats. Friendship. Format, unusual – board books.

No more! Piggety Pig ill. by David Prebenna. Little, 1986. ISBN 0-316-98763-8 Subj: Animals – mice. Animals – pigs. Concepts – color.

No, no, Nicky! ill. by Richard Eric Brown. Viking, 1986. ISBN 0-670-81297-8 Subj: Animals – cats. Format, unusual – board books. Safety.

On our way to the barn by Harriet Ziefert and Simms Taback; ill. by Simms Taback. Harper, 1985. ISBN 0-06-026877-8 Subj: Animals. Farms. Format, unusual – board books. Noise, sounds. Poetry, rhyme.

On our way to the forest by Harriet Ziefert and Simms Taback; ill. by Simms Taback. Harper,

1985. ISBN 0-06-026878-6 Subj: Forest, woods. Format, unusual – board books. Noise, sounds. Poetry, rhyme.

On our way to the water by Harriet Ziefert and Simms Taback; ill. by Simms Taback. Harper, 1985. ISBN 0-06-026879-4 Subj: Format, unusual – board books. Noise, sounds. Poetry, rhyme.

On our way to the zoo by Harriet Ziefert and Simms Taback; ill. by Simms Taback. Harper, 1985. ISBN 0-06-026880-8 Subj: Animals. Format, unusual – board books. Noise, sounds. Poetry, rhyme. Zoos.

Piggety Pig from morn 'til night ill. by David Prebenna. Little, 1986. ISBN 0-316-98764-6 Subj: Activities. Animals – pigs.

Run! Run! ill. by Henrik Drescher. Harper, 1986. ISBN 0-694-00097-3 Subj: Animals.

Sam and Lucy ill. by Claire Schumacher. HarperCollins, 1992. ISBN 0-06-026974-X Subj: Animals – dogs. Behavior – running away.

Sarah's questions ill. by Susan Bonners. Lothrop, 1986. ISBN 0-688-05615-6 Subj: Character traits – questioning. Family life – mothers. Nature.

Say good night! ill. by Catherine Siracusa. Viking, 1987. ISBN 0-670-81722-8 Subj: Bedtime. Morning. Night. Sleep.

Sleepy dog ill. by Norman Gorbaty. Random House, 1984. Subj: Animals – dogs. Sleep.

Strike four! ill. by Mavis Smith. Viking, 1988. ISBN 0-670-82033-4 Subj: Activities – playing. Behavior – misbehavior. Family life.

Surprise! ill. by Mary Morgan. Viking, 1988. ISBN 0-670-82036-9 Subj: Birthdays. Family life – mothers. Food.

When daddy had the chicken pox ill. by Lionel Kalish. HarperCollins, 1991. ISBN 0-06-026907-3 Subj: Family life – fathers. Illness.

Where's daddy's car? ill. by Andrea Baruffi. HarperCollins, 1992. ISBN 0-694-00378-6 Subj: Automobiles. Format, unusual – toy and movable books.

Where's mommy's truck? ill. by Andrea Baruffi. HarperCollins, 1992. ISBN 0-694-00377-8 Subj: Format, unusual – toy and movable books. Trucks.

Where's the cat? ill. by Arnold Lobel. Harper, 1987. ISBN 0-694-00185-6 Subj: Animals – cats. Behavior – hiding. Format, unusual. Format, unusual – board books.

Where's the dog? ill. by Arnold Lobel. Harper, 1987. ISBN 0-694-00184-8 Subj: Animals – dogs. Behavior – hiding. Format, unusual. Format, unusual – board books.

Where's the guinea pig? ill. by Arnold Lobel. Harper, 1987. ISBN 0-694-00182-1 Subj: Animals – guinea pigs. Behavior – hiding. Format, unusual. Format, unusual – board books.

Where's the turtle? ill. by Arnold Lobel. Harper, 1987. ISBN 0-694-00183-X Subj: Behavior – hiding. Format, unusual. Format, unusual – board books. Reptiles – turtles, tortoises.

Who can boo the loudest? ill. by Claire Schumacher. HarperCollins, 1990. ISBN 0-06-026899-9 Subj: Ghosts. Moon.

With love from Grandma ill. by Deborah Kogan Ray. Viking, 1989. ISBN 0-670-83004-6 Subj: Activities – knitting. Emotions – love. Family life – grandmothers.

Ziegler, Sandra. *A visit to the bakery* photos. by author. Childrens Pr., 1987. ISBN 0-516-01495-1 Subj: Careers – bakers.

Ziegler, Ursina. *Squaps the moonling* tr. by Barbara Kowall Gollob; ill. by Sita Jucker. Atheneum, 1969. Translation of Squaps, der Mondling Subj: Moon. Space and space ships.

Zijlstra, Tjerk. *Benny and his geese* ill. by Ivo de Weerd. McGraw-Hill, 1975. Translation of Bennie en zijn ganzen Subj: Birds – geese. Folk and fairy tales. Wizards.

Zimelman, Nathan. *The great adventure of Wo Ti* ill. by Julie Downing. Macmillan, 1992. ISBN 0-02-793731-3 Subj: Animals – cats. Behavior – trickery. Fish. Foreign lands – China.

If I were strong enough... ill. by Diane Paterson. Abingdon Pr., 1982. Subj: Behavior – growing up. Family life.

Mean Murgatroyd and the ten cats ill. by Tony Auth. Dutton, 1984. Subj: Animals – cats. Animals – dogs. Character traits – meanness.

Once when I was five ill. by Carol Rogers. Steck-Vaughn, 1967. Subj: Birthdays. Imagination.

Positively no pets allowed ill. by Pamela Johnson. Dutton, 1980. Subj: Animals – gorillas. Pets.

The star of Melvin ill. by Olivier Dunrea. Macmillan, 1987. ISBN 0-02-793750-X Subj: Angels. Holidays – Christmas.

To sing a song as big as Ireland ill. by Joseph Low. Follett, 1967. Subj: Behavior – wishing. Foreign lands – Ireland. Elves and little people. Holidays – St. Patrick's Day. Music.

Treed by a pride of irate lions ill. by Toni Goffe. Little, 1990. ISBN 0-316-98802-2 Subj: Animals – lions. Family life – fathers. Foreign lands – Africa.

Walls are to be walked ill. by Donald Carrick. Dutton, 1977. ISBN 0-525-42175-0 Subj: Activities – playing.

Zimmer, Dirk. *The trick-or-treat trap* ill. by author. Harper, 1982. Subj: Holidays – Halloween. Parties. Witches.

Zimmerman, Andrea Griffing. *Yetta, the trickster* ill. by Harold Berson. Seabury Pr., 1978. Subj: Foreign lands – Russia. Humor.

Zimmerman, Baruch. *A Japanese fairy tale* (Iké, Jane Hori)

Zimmermann, H. Werner (Heinz Werner). *Alphonse knows...a circle is not a Valentine* ill. by author. Oxford Univ. Pr., 1991. ISBN 0-19-540744-X Subj: Concepts – shape. Holidays – Valentine's Day. Wizards.

Alphonse knows...the colour of spring ill. by author. Oxford Univ. Pr., 1991. ISBN 0-19-540743-1 Subj: Seasons – spring. Wizards.

Alphonse knows...twelve months make a year ill. by author. Oxford Univ. Pr., 1990. ISBN 0-19-540798-9 Subj: Animals – mice. Days of the week, months of the year. Seasons. Wizards.

Alphonse knows...zero is not enough ill. by author. Oxford Univ. Pr., 1990. ISBN 0-19-540797-0 Subj: Counting, numbers. Wizards.

Zimnik, Reiner. *The bear on the motorcycle* tr. by Cornelia Schaeffer; ill. by author. Atheneum, 1963. Translation of Der bär auf dem motorrad Subj: Animals – bears. Behavior – running away. Circus. Motorcycles.

The proud circus horse ill. by author. Pantheon, 1957. Subj: Animals – horses. Behavior – running away. Character traits – pride. Circus.

Zindel, Paul. *I love my mother* ill. by John Melo. Harper, 1975. Subj: Emotions – loneliness. Emotions – love. Family life – mothers.

Ziner, Feenie. *Counting carnival* by Feenie Ziner and Paul Galdone; ill. by Paul Galdone. Coward, 1962. Subj: Activities – playing. Counting, numbers. Cumulative tales. Ethnic groups in the U.S. – Afro-Americans. Parades. Poetry, rhyme.

The true book of time by Feenie Ziner and Elizabeth Thompson; ill. by Katherine Evans. Children's Pr., 1956. Subj: Time.

Zinnemann-Hope, Pam. *Find your coat, Ned* ill. by Kady MacDonald Denton. Macmillan, 1988. ISBN 0-689-50426-9 Subj: Behavior – losing things. Clothing – coats. Pets. Weather – rain.

Let's go shopping, Ned ill. by Kady MacDonald Denton. Macmillan, 1987. ISBN 0-689-50416-0 Subj: Shopping.

Let's play ball, Ned ill. by Kady MacDonald Denton. Macmillan, 1988. ISBN 0-689-50427-6 Subj: Activities – playing. Family life.

Time for bed, Ned ill. by Kady MacDonald Denton. Macmillan, 1987. ISBN 0-689-50415-2 Subj: Bedtime. Family life – mothers.

Zion, Gene. *All falling down* ill. by Margaret Bloy Graham. Harper, 1951. Subj: Caldecott award honor book. Concepts – up and down.

Dear garbage man ill. by Margaret Bloy Graham. Harper, 1957. Subj: Careers – garbage collectors. City.

Harry, the dirty dog ill. by Margaret Bloy Graham. Harper, 1956. Subj: Activities – bathing. Animals – dogs. Behavior – running away.

Hide and seek day ill. by Margaret Bloy Graham. Harper, 1954. Subj: Behavior – hiding. City. Games.

Jeffie's party ill. by Margaret Bloy Graham. Harper, 1957. Subj: Games. Parties.

The meanest squirrel I ever met ill. by Margaret Bloy Graham. Scribner's, 1962. Subj: Animals – squirrels. Character traits – meanness. Friendship. Holidays – Thanksgiving.

No roses for Harry ill. by Margaret Bloy Graham. Harper, 1958. Subj: Animals – dogs. Clothing.

The plant sitter ill. by Margaret Bloy Graham. Harper, 1959. Subj: Plants.

Really spring ill. by Margaret Bloy Graham. Harper, 1956. Subj: Seasons – spring.

The summer snowman ill. by Margaret Bloy Graham. Harper, 1955. Subj: Holidays – Fourth of July. Seasons – summer. Snowmen. Weather – snow.

Zirbes, Laura. *How many bears?* ill. by E. Harper Johnson. Putnam's, 1960. Subj: Animals – bears. Counting, numbers.

Zirkel, Lynn. *The shell dragon* ill. by Peter Bowman. Oxford Univ. Pr., 1989. ISBN 0-19-279838-3 Subj: Birds. Dragons.

Zola, Meguido. *The dream of promise: a folktale in Hebrew and English* ill. by Ruben Zellermayer. Kids Can Pr., 1981. Subj: Folk and fairy tales. Foreign languages. Jewish culture. Self-concept.

Only the best ill. by Valerie Littlewood. Watts, 1982. Subj: Emotions – love. Family life – fathers.

Zoll, Max Alfred. *Animal babies* tr. by Violetta Castillo; ed. by Hanns Reich; ill. by author. Hill and Wang, 1971. Translation of Tierkinder Subj: Animals.

A flamingo is born tr. by Catherine Edwards Sadler; photos. by Winifried Noack. Putnam's, 1978. Subj: Birds – flamingos. Science.

Zolotow, Charlotte (Shapiro). *The beautiful Christmas tree* ill. by Ruth Robbins. Parnassus Pr., 1972. Subj: Holidays – Christmas. Trees.

Big sister and little sister ill. by Martha G. Alexander. Harper, 1966. Subj: Behavior – running away. Family life.

The bunny who found Easter ill. by Betty Peterson. Parnassus Pr., 1959. Subj: Animals – rabbits. Holidays – Easter.

But not Billy ill. by Kay Chorao. Harper, 1983. Subj: Babies. Behavior – growing up.

Do you know what I'll do? ill. by Garth Williams. Harper, 1958. Subj: Babies. Emotions – love. Family life.

Flocks of birds ill. by Ruth Lercher Bornstein. Crowell, 1981. Subj: Bedtime. Birds.

The hating book ill. by Ben Shecter. Harper, 1969. Subj: Behavior – gossip. Emotions – hate. Friendship.

Hold my hand ill. by Thomas di Grazia. Harper, 1972. Subj: Friendship. Weather – snow.

I have a horse of my own ill. by Yoko Mitsuhashi. Crowell, 1980. Subj: Animals – horses. Dreams. Night.

I know a lady ill. by James Stevenson. Greenwillow, 1984. Subj: Character traits – kindness. Old age.

I like to be little ill. by Erik Blegvad. Harper, 1987. ISBN 0-690-04674-X Subj: Behavior – growing up. Family life – mothers.

If it weren't for you ill. by Ben Shecter. Harper, 1966. Subj: Family life. Sibling rivalry.

In my garden ill. by Roger Antoine Duvoisin. Lothrop, 1960. Subj: Plants. Seasons.

It's not fair ill. by William Pène Du Bois. Harper, 1976. Subj: Behavior – dissatisfaction. Emotions – envy, jealousy. Family life.

Janey ill. by Ronald Himler. Harper, 1973. Subj: Emotions – loneliness. Friendship. Moving.

May I visit? ill. by Erik Blegvad. Harper, 1976. Subj: Behavior – growing up. Emotions – love. Family life.

Mr. Rabbit and the lovely present ill. by Maurice Sendak. Harper, 1962. Subj: Animals – rabbits. Birthdays. Caldecott award honor book. Concepts – color. Family life – mothers. Holidays – Easter.

The moon was the best ill. by Tana Hoban. Greenwillow, 1993. ISBN 0-688-09941-6 Subj: Moon.

My friend John ill. by Ben Shecter. Harper, 1968. Subj: Friendship.

My grandson Lew ill. by William Pène Du Bois. Harper, 1974. Subj: Death. Family life. Family life – grandfathers.

The new friend ill. by Emily Arnold McCully. Crowell, 1981. Subj: Behavior – sharing. Friendship.

One step, two... ill. by Roger Antoine Duvoisin. Lothrop, 1955. Subj: Activities – walking. City. Counting, numbers.

Over and over ill. by Garth Williams. Harper, 1957. Subj: Holidays. Time.

The park book ill. by Hans Augusto Rey. Harper, 1944. Subj: Activities – playing. City.

The poodle who barked at the wind ill. by Roger Antoine Duvoisin. Lothrop, 1964. Subj: Animals – dogs. Noise, sounds. Pets.

The quarreling book ill. by Arnold Lobel. Harper, 1963. Subj: Behavior – fighting, arguing. Cumulative tales. Emotions – anger. Weather – rain.

The quiet mother and the noisy little boy ill. by Marc Simont. HarperCollins, 1989. ISBN 0-06-026979-0 Subj: Family life. Noise, sounds.

River winding ill. by Kazue Mizumura. Crowell, 1978. Subj: Poetry, rhyme.

A rose, a bridge, and a wild black horse ill. by Robin Spowart. Harper, 1987. ISBN 0-06-026939-1 Subj: Emotions – love. Family life.

Say it! ill. by James Stevenson. Greenwillow, 1980. Subj: Activities – walking. Emotions – love. Family life – mothers. Nature. Seasons – fall.

The seashore book ill. by Wendell Minor. HarperCollins, 1992. ISBN 0-06-020214-9 Subj: Family life – mothers. Imagination. Sea and seashore.

The sky was blue ill. by Garth Williams. Harper, 1963. Subj: Emotions – love. Family life.

Sleepy book ill. by Ilse Plume Rev. ed. Harper, 1988. ISBN 0-06-026968-5 Subj: Animals. Bedtime. Sleep.

The sleepy book ill. by Vladimir Bobri. Lothrop, 1958. Subj: Bedtime. Sleep.

Some things go together ill. by Karen Gundersheimer Rev. ed. Crowell, 1983. Subj: Family life – mothers. Poetry, rhyme.

Someday ill. by Arnold Lobel. Harper, 1965. Subj: Behavior – wishing. Dreams.

Someone new ill. by Erik Blegvad. Harper, 1978. ISBN 0-06-027018-7 Subj: Behavior – growing up. Family life.

Something is going to happen ill. by Catherine Stock. Harper, 1988. ISBN 0-06-027029-2 Subj: Morning. Weather – snow.

The song ill. by Nancy Tafuri. Greenwillow, 1982. Subj: Nature. Seasons. Songs.

The storm book ill. by Margaret Bloy Graham. Harper, 1952. Subj: Caldecott award honor book. Emotions – fear. Weather. Weather – rain. Weather – rainbows.

Summer is... ill. by Ruth Lercher Bornstein. Crowell, 1983. Subj: Poetry, rhyme. Seasons – summer.

The summer night ill. by Ben Shecter. Harper, 1974. Published in 1958 under the title The night when mother was away ISBN 0-06-026960-X Subj: Activities – walking. Bedtime. Family life. Family life – fathers.

This quiet lady ill. by Anita Lobel. Greenwillow, 1992. ISBN 0-688-09306-X Subj: Family life – mothers.

Three funny friends ill. by Mary Chalmers. Harper, 1961. Subj: Emotions – loneliness. Friendship. Imagination – imaginary friends.

A tiger called Thomas ill. by Catherine Stock. Lothrop, 1988. ISBN 0-688-06697-6 Subj: Character traits – shyness. Emotions – loneliness. Holidays – Halloween.

A tiger called Thomas ill. by Kurt Werth. Lothrop, 1963. Subj: Character traits – shyness. Emotions – loneliness. Holidays – Halloween.

Timothy too! ill. by Ruth Robbins. Houghton, 1986. ISBN 0-395-39378-7 Subj: Friendship. Sibling rivalry.

The unfriendly book ill. by William Pène Du Bois. Harper, 1975. ISBN 0-06-026931-6 Subj: Behavior – fighting, arguing. Friendship.

Wake up and good night ill. by Leonard Weisgard. Harper, 1971. Subj: Bedtime. Morning. Night.

When I have a son ill. by Hilary Knight. Harper, 1967. Subj: Behavior – growing up. Family life. Imagination.

When the wind stops ill. by Joe Lasker. Abelard-Schuman, 1962. Subj: Bedtime. Night. Weather – wind.

The white marble ill. by Lilian Obligado. Abelard-Schuman, 1963. Subj: Activities – playing. Friendship. Night.

William's doll ill. by William Pène Du Bois. Harper, 1972. Subj: Family life. Family life – grandmothers. Toys – dolls.

Zoo animals ill. with photos. and drawings. Macmillan, 1991. ISBN 0-689-71406-8 Subj: Animals. Nature.

Zoo animals ill. with photos. Imported Pubs., 1983. Subj: Animals. Format, unusual – board books. Wordless.

Zusman, Evelyn. *The Passover parrot* ill. by Katherine Janus Kahn. Kar-Ben Copies, 1984. Subj: Birds – parakeets, parrots. Family life. Holidays – Passover. Jewish culture.

Zweifel, Frances. *Animal baby-sitters* ill. by Irene Brady. Morrow, 1981. Subj: Activities – babysitting. Animals. Nature.

Bony ill. by Whitney Darrow, Jr. Harper, 1977. ISBN 0-06-027071-3 Subj: Animals – squirrels. Pets.

Zwetchkenbaum, G. *The Peanuts shape circus puzzle book* ill. by author. Scholastic, 1983. Subj: Riddles.

The Peanuts sleepy time puzzle book ill. by author. Scholastic, 1983. Subj: Riddles.

The Snoopy farm puzzle book ill. by author. Scholastic, 1983. Subj: Riddles.

Snoopy safari puzzle book ill. by author. Scholastic, 1983. Subj: Riddles.

Title Index

Titles appear in alphabetical sequence with the author's name in parentheses, followed by the page number of the Bibliographic Guide. For identical title listings, the illustrator's name is given to further identify the version. In the case of variant titles, both the original and differing titles are listed.

A

C

D

E

G

H

I

It looked like spilt milk (Shaw, Charles Green), 782

It must have been the wind (Saltzberg, Barney), 767

It was Jake (Jeram, Anita), 634

It wasn't my fault (Lester, Helen), 664

The itch book (Dragonwagon, Crescent), 547

It'll all come out in the wash (Gray, Nigel), 586

It's a baby! (Ancona, George), 437

It's a deal (Stroyer, Poul), 801

It's a dog's life (Stern, Mark), 797

It's a good thing (Buchanan, Joan), 496

It's a perfect day (Pizer, Abigail), 739

It's about time (Schlein, Miriam), 771

It's about time, Jesse Bear (Carlstrom, Nancy White), 506

It's April Fools' Day! (Kroll, Steven), 654

It's Chanukah! (Gellman, Ellie), 575

It's dark (Erickson, Karen), 555

It's easy to have a caterpillar visit you (O'Hagan, Caroline), 722

It's easy to have a snail visit you (O'Hagan, Caroline), 722

It's easy to have a worm visit you (O'Hagan, Caroline), 722

It's fun to go to school (Mellings, Joan), 699

It's George! (Cohen, Miriam), 521

It's Groundhog Day! (Kroll, Steven), 654

It's just me, Emily (Hines, Anna Grossnickle), 613

It's magic (Lopshire, Robert), 675

It's me, hippo! (Thaler, Mike), 806

It's mine (Campbell, Rod), 504

It's mine! (De Lynam, Alicia Garcia), 538

It's mine! (Lionni, Leo), 670

It's mine! A greedy book (Bonsall, Crosby Newell), 480

It's my birthday (Watanabe, Shigeo), 826

It's my earth too (Krull, Kathleen), 654

It's nice to be little (Stanley, John), 794

It's not easy being a bunny (Sadler, Marilyn), 766

It's not fair! (Harper, Anita), 601

It's not fair! (Hautzig, Deborah), 603

It's not fair (Zolotow, Charlotte (Shapiro)), 852

It's not your birthday (Amoss, Berthe), 436

It's ok to say no (Bahr, Amy C.), 451

It's perfectly true! ill. by Janet Stevens (Andersen, H. C. (Hans Christian)), 438

"It's raining," said John Twaining (Bodecker, N. M. (Nils Mogens)), 477

It's really Christmas (Hoban, Lillian), 615

It's Rosh Hashanah! (Gellman, Ellie), 575

It's snowing, Little Rabbit (Wabbes, Marie), 821

It's so nice to have a wolf around the house (Allard, Harry), 434

It's spring! (Minarik, Else Holmelund), 703

It's spring, Peterkin (Boon, Emilie), 480

It's the ABC book (Harada, Joyce), 600

It's the 0-1-2-3 book (Harada, Joyce), 600

It's time now! (Tresselt, Alvin R.), 812

It's too noisy (Cole, Joanna), 522

It's your turn, Roger (Gretz, Susanna), 588

Iva Dunnit and the big wind (Purdy, Carol), 747

I've got your nose! (Bentley, Nancy), 466

Izzard (Anderson, Lonzo), 441

J

Jabberwocky, ill. by Graeme Base (Carroll, Lewis), 508

Jabberwocky, ill. from Disney archives (Carroll, Lewis), 508

Jabberwocky, ill. by Jane Breskin Zalben (Carroll, Lewis), 508

Jack and Fred (Barton, Byron), 458

Jack and Jake (Aliki), 433

Jack and Jill, ill. by Eleanor Wasmuth (Mother Goose), 711

Jack and the bean tree (Haley, Gail E.), 598

Jack and the beanstalk, ill. by Paul Galdone (Jack and the beanstalk) *The history of Mother Twaddle and the marvelous achievements of her son Jack*, 631

Jack and the beanstalk, ill. by Val Biro, 631

Jack and the beanstalk, ill. by Lorinda Bryan Cauley, 631

Jack and the beanstalk, ill. by Ed Parker, 631

Jack and the beanstalk, ill. by Tony Ross, 631

Jack and the beanstalk, ill. by William Stobbs, 631

Jack and the beanstalk, ill. by James Warhola, 631

Jack and the beanstalk, ill. by Anne Wilsdorf, 631

Jack and the fire dragon (Haley, Gail E.), 598

Jack and the magic stove (Beresford, Elisabeth), 469

Jack and the monster (Graham, Richard), 585

Jack and the three sillies (Chase, Richard), 514

Jack and the whoopee wind (Calhoun, Mary), 503

Jack and the wonder beans (Still, James), 799

Jack at sea (Dupasquier, Philippe), 550

Jack goes to the beach (Krementz, Jill), 653

Jack Horner and song of sixpence (Bartlett, Robert Merrill), 458

Jack Jouett's ride (Haley, Gail E.), 598

Jack Kent's happy-ever-after book (Kent, Jack), 643

Jack Kent's hokus pokus bedtime book (Kent, Jack), 643

Jack Kent's merry Mother Goose (Mother Goose), 711

Jack Kent's twelve days of Christmas (The twelve days of Christmas. English folk song), 815

Jack Mack (Smith, Robert Paul), 790

Jack the giant killer, ill. by Anne Wilsdorf (Jack and the beanstalk), 631

Jack the giantkiller, ill. by Tony Ross (Jack and the beanstalk), 632

Jack the wise and the Cornish cuckoos (Calhoun, Mary), 503

The jacket I wear in the snow (Neitzel, Shirley), 717

Jackie's lunch box (Hines, Anna Grossnickle), 613

Jacko (Goodall, John S.), 582

Jack's fantastic voyage (Foreman, Michael), 565

Jacob and the robbers (Reidel, Marlene), 751

The jade stone (Yacowitz, Caryn), 844

Jafta (Lewin, Hugh), 666

L

M

P

Q

T

W

Z

Illustrator Index

Illustrators appear alphabetically in boldface followed by their titles. Names in parentheses are authors of the titles when different than the illustrator. Page numbers refer to the full listing in the Bibliographic Guide.

B

Cartwright, Stephen. *Things people do* (Civardi, Anne), 517

The three little pigs (The three little pigs), 809

Carty, Leo. *I love Gram* (Sonneborn, Ruth A.), 792

Caseley, Judith. *Ada potato*, 509

Annie's potty, 509

Apple pie and onions, 509

Cousins, 509

Dear Annie, 509

Grandpa's garden lunch, 509

Harry and Willy and Carrothead, 509

Molly Pink, 509

Molly Pink goes hiking, 509

My sister Celia, 509

Silly baby, 509

Three happy birthdays, 509

When Grandpa came to stay, 509

Casey, Patricia. *Quack quack*, 509

Casilla, Robert. *Con mi hermano - With my brother* (Roe, Eileen), 757

A picture book of Eleanor Roosevelt (Adler, David A.), 427

A picture book of John F. Kennedy (Adler, David A.), 427

A picture book of Martin Luther King, Jr. (Adler, David A.), 427

Poems for fathers (Livingston, Myra Cohn), 673

The train to Lulu's (Howard, Elizabeth Fitzgerald), 623

Cassel, Lilli *see* Cassel-Wronker, Lilli

Cassell, Robert H. *We're going to have a baby* (Helmering, Doris Wild), 608

Cassels, Jean. *Dinosaurs and their relatives in action* (Gay, Tenner Ottley), 575

Sharks in action (Gay, Tenner Ottley), 575

Cassel-Wronker, Lili. *The rainbow Mother Goose* (Mother Goose), 713

Tell about the cowbarn, Daddy (Merrill, Jean), 700

Cassidy, Dianne. *Circus animals*, 509

Circus people, 509

Cassinelli, Attilio. *Adam and the wolf* (Gunthrop, Karen), 596

Rina at the farm (Gunthrop, Karen), 596

Castle, Caroline. *Elizabeth Jane gets dressed* (Tyrrell, Anne), 815

Mary Ann always can (Tyrrell, Anne), 816

Caswell, Helen. *Parable of the good Samaritan*, 510

Catalano, Dominic. *The bear who loved Puccini* (Sundgaard, Arnold), 802

Catalanotto, Peter. *All I see* (Rylant, Cynthia), 765

Cecil's story (Lyon, George-Ella), 678

Christmas always, 510

Dylan's day out, 510

Mr. Mumble, 510

Who came down that road? (Lyon, George-Ella), 678

Catania, Tom. *The grizzly bear with the golden ears* (George, Jean Craighead), 575

Catrow, David. *Good cats / Bad cats* (Ghigna, Charles), 577

Good dogs / Bad dogs (Ghigna, Charles), 577

That's good! that's bad! (Cuyler, Margery), 532

Cauley, Lorinda Bryan. *The animal kids*, 510

The bake-off, 510

The beginning of the armadillos (Kipling, Rudyard), 647

Clancy's coat (Bunting, Eve (Anne Evelyn)), 497

Clap your hands, 510

The cock, the mouse and the little red hen, 510

Curley Cat baby-sits (Watson, Pauline), 827

The elephant's child (Kipling, Rudyard), 647

Goldilocks and the three bears (The three bears), 808

The goodnight circle (Lesser, Carolyn), 664

The goose and the golden coins, 510

The house of five bears (Jameson, Cynthia), 632

If you say so, Claude (Nixon, Joan Lowery), 719

Jack and the beanstalk (Jack and the beanstalk), 631

Little grey rabbit (Bowden, Joan Chase), 482

Old Hippo's Easter egg (Wahl, Jan), 823

Old MacDonald had a farm (Old MacDonald had a farm), 723

The owl and the pussycat (Lear, Edward), 661

The pancake boy (The gingerbread boy), 579

Pease porridge hot, 510

Puss in boots (Perrault, Charles), 735

Rabbits' search for a little house (Kwitz, Mary DeBall), 656

Small Bear solves a mystery (Holl, Adelaide), 620

Three blind mice (Ivimey, John William), 631

The three little kittens (Mother Goose), 713

The three little pigs (The three little pigs), 809

The town mouse and the country mouse (Æsop), 429

The trouble with Tyrannosaurus Rex, 510

The ugly duckling (Andersen, H. C. (Hans Christian)), 439

Where's Henrietta's hen? (Freschet, Berniece), 568

Cazet, Denys. *Are there any questions?* 510

Big shoe, little shoe, 511

Christmas moon, 511

Daydreams, 511

December 24th, 511

The duck with squeaky feet, 511

A fish in his pocket, 511

Frosted glass, 511

Good morning, Maxine! 511

Great-Uncle Felix, 511

I'm not sleepy, 511

Lucky me, 511

Mother night, 511

Never spit on your shoes, 511

Saturday, 511

Sunday, 511

You make the angels cry, 511

Cellini, Eva. *Let's walk up the wall* (Johnson, Ryerson), 636

Doubilet, David. *Under the sea from A to Z* (Doubilet, Anne), 546

Douglas, Michael. *Round, round world*, 546

Douglas, Stephanie. *Three wishes* (Clifton, Lucille), 519

Dow, Jill. *The roadside* (Bellamy, David), 464
The rock pool (Bellamy, David), 464

Dowdy, Mrs. Regera *see* Gorey, Edward (St. John)

Dowell, Philip. *Jungle animals* (Royston, Angela), 763

Dowers, Patrick. *One day scene through a leaf*, 546

Dowling, Paul. *Happy birthday, Owl*, 546
Meg and Jack are moving, 546
Meg and Jack's new friends, 546
Poonam's pets (Davies, Andrew), 535
Splodger, 546
You can do it, Rabbit, 546

Downie, Jill. *Alphabet puzzle*, 546

Downing, Julie. *Daniel's gift* (Helldorfer, M. C. (Mary Claire)), 607
The great adventure of Wo Ti (Zimelman, Nathan), 851
I had a cat (Reeves, Mona Rabun), 751
Mr. Griggs' work (Rylant, Cynthia), 765
Prince Boghole (Haugaard, Erik Christian), 602
Pulling my leg (Carson, Jo), 508
A ride on the red mare's back (Le Guin, Ursula K.), 660

Doyle, Julian. *The walrus and the carpenter* (Carroll, Lewis), 508

Dranko, Robert. *The tractor on the farm* (Israel, Marion Louise), 630

Dreamer, Sue. *Circus ABC*, 547
Circus 1, 2, 3, 547

Drescher, Henrik. *All clean!* (Ziefert, Harriet), 849
All gone! (Ziefert, Harriet), 849
Cock-a-doodle-doo! (Ziefert, Harriet), 849
Looking for Santa Claus, 547
No plain pets! (Barasch, Marc Ian), 455
Run! Run! (Ziefert, Harriet), 850
Simon's book, 547
The yellow umbrella, 547

Drescher, Joan. *Horrible Hannah* (Bottner, Barbara), 481
I'm in charge! 547
The marvelous mess, 547
My mother's getting married, 547
Nonna (Bartoli, Jennifer), 458
Tell me, grandma; tell me, grandpa (Newman, Shirlee), 718
Your family, my family, 547

Drew, Patricia. *Spotter Puff*, 547

Drew-Brook, Deborah. *Casey visits the doctor* (Marcus, Susan), 690

Drummond, Violet H. *The flying postman*, 547
Phewtus the squirrel, 547

Dubanevich, Arlene. *Do bunnies talk?* (Dodds, Dayle Ann), 544
Pig William, 547
The piggest show on earth, 547
Pigs at Christmas, 547
Pigs in hiding, 547

Tom's tail, 547

Dubois, Claude K. *He's my jumbo!* 547
Looking for Ginny, 547

Du Bois, William Pène. *Bear circus*, 548
Bear in mind (Goldstein, Bobbye S.), 582
Bear party, 548
Billy the barber (Kunhardt, Dorothy), 655
Elisabeth the cow ghost, 548
Fierce John (Fenton, Edward), 560
Giant Otto, 548
The hare and the tortoise and the tortoise and the hare, 548
It's not fair (Zolotow, Charlotte (Shapiro)), 852
Just my size (Garelick, May), 574
Lazy Tommy pumpkinhead, 548
Lion, 548
Moving day (Tobias, Tobi), 810
My grandson Lew (Zolotow, Charlotte (Shapiro)), 852
The night book (Strand, Mark), 801
Otto and the magic potatoes, 548
Otto at sea, 548
Otto in Africa, 548
Otto in Texas, 548
The owl and the pussy-cat (Lear, Edward), 661
The planet of lost things (Strand, Mark), 801
The three little pigs (The three little pigs), 809
The unfriendly book (Zolotow, Charlotte (Shapiro)), 853
We came a-marching...1, 2, 3 (Hobzek, Mildred), 617
Where's Gomer? (Farber, Norma), 558
William's doll (Zolotow, Charlotte (Shapiro)), 853

Duca, Bill. *Do you see me God?* (Murphy, Elspeth Campbell), 715

Duchesne, Janet. *Dinner ladies don't count* (Ashley, Bernard), 447

Duell, Nancy. *Ladybug's color book* (Silverman, Maida), 785

Dugan, William. *The ABC of cars, trucks and machines* (Holl, Adelaide), 620

Dugin, Andrej. *The fine round cake* (Esterl, Arnica), 556

Dugina, Olga. *The fine round cake* (Esterl, Arnica), 556

Duke, Kate. *Aunt Isabel tells a good one*, 548
Bedtime, 548
Clean-up day, 548
Don't tell the whole world (Cole, Joanna), 522
Good news (Brenner, Barbara A.), 485
The guinea pig ABC, 548
Guinea pigs far and near, 548
It's too noisy (Cole, Joanna), 522
The playground, 548
Seven froggies went to school, 548
What bounces? 548

Dulac, Edmund. *The snow queen and other stories from Hans Andersen* (Andersen, H. C. (Hans Christian)), 439

Dumas, Gerald. *Time for Jody* (Kesselman, Wendy), 644

Dumas, Philippe. *Caesar, cock of the village*, 549

E

Jaques, Faith. *The king's birthday cake* (Cunliffe, John), 531
Our village shop (Sawyer, Jean), 769
Tilly's house, 633
Tilly's rescue, 633
Jarner, Bo. *Chicken and egg* (Back, Christine), 450
Snail (Oleson, Jens), 723
Jeffers, Susan. *All the pretty horses*, 633
Baby animals (Brown, Margaret Wise), 491
Benjamin's barn (Lindbergh, Reeve), 668
Cinderella (Perrault, Charles), 735
Close your eyes (Marzollo, Jean), 695
Forest of dreams (Wells, Rosemary), 830
Hansel and Gretel (Grimm, Jacob), 591
Hiawatha (Longfellow, Henry Wadsworth), 675
Midnight farm (Lindberg, Reeve), 668
Silent night (Mohr, Joseph), 705
The snow queen (Andersen, H. C. (Hans Christian)), 438
Stopping by woods on a snowy evening (Frost, Robert), 569
The three jovial huntsmen (Mother Goose), 713
Thumbelina (Andersen, H. C. (Hans Christian)), 439
Wild Robin, 633
The wild swans (Andersen, H. C. (Hans Christian)), 440
Jeffery, Graham. *Thomas the tortoise*, 633
Jenkin-Pearce, Susie. *Animal fair* (Bennett, Jill), 465
Bad Boris and the new kitten, 633
Bad Boris goes to school, 633
Boris's big ache, 634
The enchanted garden, 634
Nesta, the little witch (McAllister, Angela), 678
Percy Short and Cuthbert, 634
Snail's birthday problem (McAllister, Angela), 678
Wriggly Pig (Blake, Jon), 475
Jenkins, Jessica. *Thinking about colors*, 634
Jenkins, Mary Price. *Cats sleep anywhere.* (Farjeon, Eleanor), 558
Jenkins, Sarie. *Alfred, the dragon who lost his flame* (Buckaway, C. M.), 496
Jenkyns, Chris. *Andy says ... Bonjour!* (Diska, Pat), 544
How to lose your lunch money (White, Florence Meiman), 833
Jensen, Helen Zane. *When Panda came to our house*, 634
Jensen, Virginia Allen. *Catching*, 634
Red thread riddles, 634
Jeram, Anita. *All pigs are beautiful* (King-Smith, Dick), 647
Bill's belly button, 634
It was Jake, 634
Jeschke, Susan. *Angela and Bear*, 634
The devil did it, 634
Firerose, 634
Lucky's choice, 634
Mia, Grandma and the genie, 634

A mitzvah is something special (Eisenberg, Phyllis Rose), 552
Perfect the pig, 634
Rima and Zeppo, 634
Saturday, I ran away (Pearson, Susan), 733
Sometimes it happens (Horwitz, Elinor Lander), 622
Tamar and the tiger, 634
Jessell, Camilla. *The kitten book*, 634
The puppy book, 634
Joel, Yale. *Danny goes to the hospital* (Collier, James Lincoln), 523
Joerns, Consuelo. *Blizzard at the zoo* (Bahr, Robert), 451
The foggy rescue, 635
The forgotten bear, 635
The lost and found house, 635
Oliver's escape, 635
John, Joyce. *My friend goes left* (Gregorich, Barbara), 588
John, Marie De see DeJohn Marie
Johns, Jeanne. *Grandmother's pictures* (Cornish, Sam), 526
Johnson, Arden. *The sleepytime book* (Wahl, Jan), 823
Johnson, Audean. *Jiffy, Miss Boo and Mr. Roo* (Brothers, Aileen), 489
Johnson, B. J. *A hat like that*, 635
My blanket Burt, 635
Johnson, Bob. *Scooter and the magic star* (Gardner, Mercedes), 573
Johnson, Bruce H. *Apples, alligators, and also alphabets* (Johnson, Odette), 636
One prickly porcupine (Johnson, Odette), 636
Johnson, Crockett. *The blue ribbon puppies*, 635
The carrot seed (Krauss, Ruth), 652
Ellen's lion, 635
The emperor's gift, 635
The frowning prince, 635
The happy egg (Krauss, Ruth), 652
Harold and the purple crayon, 635
Harold at the North Pole, 635
Harold's ABC, 635
Harold's circus, 635
Harold's fairy tale, 635
Harold's trip to the sky, 635
The little fish that got away (Cook, Bernadine), 525
A picture for Harold's room, 635
Terrible terrifying Toby, 635
Time for spring, 635
Upside down, 635
We wonder what will Walter be? When he grows up, 635
Will spring be early? 635
Johnson, Dolores. *The best bug to be*, 635
Jenny (Wilson, Beth P.), 838
What kind of baby-sitter is this? 635
What will mommy do when I'm at school? 635
Johnson, Donna Kay. *Brighteyes*, 636
Johnson, E. Harper (Eugene Harper). *Home, the tale of a mouse* (Schlein, Miriam), 771
How many bears? (Zirbes, Laura), 852
Johnson, Jane. *Bertie on the beach*, 636
From me to you (Rogers, Paul (Patrick)), 758
Grandma's Bill (Waddell, Martin), 822

Melnyczuk, Peter. *Sleeping Nanna* (Crossley-Holland, Kevin), 530

Melo, John. *I love my mother* (Zindel, Paul), 851

Melvin, James. *Crabby's water wish* (Tate, Suzanne), 804

Mendelson, S. T. *Stupid Emilien*, 699

Mendez, Consuelo. *Atariba and Niguayona* (Rohmer, Harriet), 758

Mendoza, George. *The alphabet boat*, 699

Merrill, Reed. *My Bible ABC book* (McKissack, Patricia C.), 684

Merritt, Jane Hamilton *see* Hamilton-Merritt, Jane

Merryweather, Jack. *Cattle drive* (Chandler, Edna Walker), 512

Pony rider (Chandler, Edna Walker), 512

Secret tunnel (Chandler, Edna Walker), 512

Meryman, Hope. *Akimba and the magic cow* (Rose, Anne), 759

Meshi, Ita. *A child's picture English-Hebrew dictionary*, 515

Messenger, Jannat. *Lullabies and baby songs*, 700

Mesturini, Cristina. *The cat* (Mantegazza, Giovanna), 690

The hippopotamus (Mantegazza, Giovanna), 690

Metcalfe, Penny. *Mr. Percy's magic greenhouse* (Kemp, Anthea), 643

Meyer, Elizabeth C. *The blue china pitcher*, 700

Meyer, Louis A. *The clean air and peaceful contentment dirigible airline*, 700

Meyerowitz, Rick. *Joshua and Bigtooth* (Childress, Mark), 515

Michaels, William. *Clare and her shadow*, 700

Michaut, Valerie. *At the zoo* (Simon, Paul), 786

Michel, Guy. *The birthday cow* (Merriam, Eve), 700

The butterfly book of birds (Dalmais, Anne-Marie), 533

Michl, Reinhard. *At the frog pond* (Michels, Tilde), 700

A day on the river, 701

Leo the lion (Wagener, Gerda), 823

Mischa and his brothers (Baumann, Hans), 460

Who's that knocking at my door? (Michels, Tilde), 700

Micich, Paul. *The littlest angel* (Tazewell, Charles), 805

Micucci, Charles. *A little night music*, 701

Mikolaycak, Charles. *Bearhead* (Kimmel, Eric A.), 646

The changing maze (Snyder, Zilpha Keatley), 791

A child is born (Winthrop, Elizabeth), 839

Exodus (Chaikin, Miriam), 511

A gift from Saint Nicholas (Timmermans, Felix), 809

He is risen (Winthrop, Elizabeth), 839

Johnny's egg (Long, Earlene), 675

The legend of the Christmas rose (Lagerlöf, Selma), 657

The lullaby songbook (Yolen, Jane), 845

The man who could call down owls (Bunting, Eve (Anne Evelyn)), 498

The nine crying dolls (Pellowski, Anne), 734

Perfect crane (Laurin, Anne), 660

Peter and the wolf (Prokofiev, Sergei Sergeievitch), 745

The rumor of Pavel and Paali (Kismaric, Carole), 648

The surprising things Maui did (Williams, Jay), 836

Tiger watch (Wahl, Jan), 823

Miles, Elizabeth. *Mokey's birthday present* (Weiss, Ellen), 829

Miles, Lauren. *The rag coat*, 701

Milhous, Katherine. *The egg tree*, 701

Milius, Winifred Lubell *see* Lubell, Winifred

Mill, Eleanor. *A button in her ear* (Litchfield, Ada B.), 671

A cane in her hand (Litchfield, Ada B.), 672

Mary Jo's grandmother (Udry, Janice May), 816

What Mary Jo shared (Udry, Janice May), 816

What Mary Jo wanted (Udry, Janice May), 816

Millan, Bruce. *Mary had a little lamb* (Hale, Sarah Josepha), 598

Miller, Andrew. *Nature's hidden world* (Selberg, Ingrid), 776

Miller, Bob. *2-B and the rock 'n roll band* (Paul, Sherry), 732

2-B and the space visitor (Paul, Sherry), 732

Miller, Edna. *Jumping bean*, 701

Mousekin finds a friend, 701

Mousekin's ABC, 701

Mousekin's Christmas eve, 702

Mousekin's close call, 702

Mousekin's fables, 702

Mousekin's family, 702

Mousekin's golden house, 702

Mousekin's lost woodland, 702

Mousekin's mystery, 702

Mouskin takes a trip, 702

Mouskin's Easter basket, 702

Mouskin's frosty friend, 702

Mouskin's Thanksgiving, 702

Patches finds a new home, 702

Pebbles, a pack rat, 702

Pícaro, a pet otter (Wisbeski, Dorothy Gross), 839

Scamper: a gray tree squirrel, 702

Miller, Edward. *The curse of Claudia*, 702

Frederick Ferdinand Fox, 702

Miller, Grambs. *Hummingbirds in the garden* (Gans, Roma), 572

Miller, J. P. (John Parr). *A birthday present for Mama* (Lorian, Nicole), 676

Do you know color? 702

Dr. Squash the doll doctor (Brown, Margaret Wise), 491

Farmer John's animals, 702

Good night, Little Rabbit, 702

Learn about colors with Little Rabbit, 702

Learn to count with Little Rabbit, 702

Little turtle's big adventure (Harrison, David Lee), 601

S